Handbook of Special Education

Special education is now an established part of public education in the United States—by law and by custom. However, it is still widely misunderstood and continues to be dogged by controversies related to such things as categorization, grouping, assessment, placement, funding, instruction, and a variety of legal issues. The purpose of this 13-part, 57-chapter handbook is to help profile and bring greater clarity to this sprawling and growing field. To ensure consistency across the volume, chapter authors review and integrate existing research, identify strengths and weaknesses, note gaps in the literature, and discuss implications for practice and future research. Key features include:

Comprehensive Coverage—Fifty-seven chapters cover all aspects of special education in the United States including cultural and international comparisons.

Issues & Trends—In addition to synthesizing empirical findings and providing a critical analysis of the status and direction of current research, chapter authors discuss issues related to practice and reflect on trends in thinking.

Categorical Chapters—In order to provide a comprehensive and comparative treatment of the twelve categorical chapters in section IV, chapter authors were asked to follow a consistent outline: Definition, Causal Factors, Identification, Behavioral Characteristics, Assessment, Educational Programming, and Trends and Issues.

Expertise—Edited by two of the most accomplished scholars in special education, chapter authors include a carefully chosen mixture of established and rising young stars in the field.

This book is an appropriate reference volume for anyone (researchers, scholars, graduate students, practitioners, policy makers, and parents) interested in the state of special education today: its research base, current issues and practices, and future trends. It is also appropriate as a textbook for graduate level courses in special education.

James M. Kauffman (Ed.D., University of Kansas) is Professor Emeritus of Education at the Curry School of Education at the University of Virginia. He was the William Clay Parrish Professor of Education from 1992–1994, the Charles S. Robb Professor of Education 1999–2003, and received the Outstanding Faculty Award from the Curry School of Education in 1997. He received the Research Award, Council for Exceptional Children in 1994 and the Outstanding Leadership Award, Council for Children with Behavioral Disorders in 2002. He is the author or co-author of many books, chapters, and articles in special education.

Daniel P. Hallahan (Ph.D., University of Michigan) is the Charles S. Robb Professor of Education at the University of Virginia's Curry School of Education, where he has been a faculty member since 1971. He was the inaugural editor of *Exceptionality* and serves on the editorial boards of *Learning Disabilities Research and Practice*, *Learning Disability Quarterly*, *The Journal of Special Education*, and *Exceptionality*. He is a past president of the Division of Learning Disabilities of CEC and in 2000 received the CEC Career Research Award. He is the author or co-author of many books, chapters, and articles in special education.

Handbook of Special Education

Edited by

James M. Kauffman

University of Virginia

Daniel P. Hallahan

University of Virginia

NEW YORK AND LONDON

First published 2011
by Routledge
711 Third Avenue, New York, NY 100176

Simultaneously published in the UK
by Routledge
2 Park Square, Milton Park, Abingdon, Oxon OX14 4RN

Routledge is an imprint of the Taylor & Francis Group, an informa business

Library of Congress Cataloging-in-Publication Data
Handbook of special education / edited by James M. Kauffman, Daniel P. Hallahan.
p. cm.
Includes bibliographical references and index.
1. Special education—United States—Handbooks, manuals, etc. I. Kauffman, James M. II. Hallahan, Daniel P., 1944–
LC3965.H262 2011
371.90973—dc22
2010037513

ISBN13: 978-0-415-80071-6 (hbk)
ISBN13: 978-0-415-80072-3 (pbk)
ISBN13: 978-0-203-83730-6 (ebk)

Typeset in Times by
EvS Communication Networx, Inc.

Printed and bound in the United States of America on acid-free paper by
Sheridan Books, Inc.

Contents

Preface

Special education is now a part of public education in the United States by custom and by law (the Individuals with Disabilities Education Improvement Act of 2004 and preceding federal mandates dating from 1975). However, special education is often misunderstood as a general project, and certain aspects of it—including problems related to particular categories of exceptionality, legal issues, grouping, assessment, placement, administration, funding, instruction, and so on—are matters of considerable controversy.

In spite of the many controversies regarding special education and its future, relatively little has been done to clarify what special education is as a general enterprise and to bring together information about various controversies and categories in a single reference volume. We have attempted to do that in this handbook. The last handbook of special education that we edited was published in 1981, and an updated reference work is clearly needed.

We asked our contributors to summarize what we know about the topic of their chapter. We also asked them to suggest what we need most to find out. Thus, the handbook is a convenient summary of research findings, best practices, and legal precedents to date and suggests, implicitly or explicitly, research programs for those working in the field.

This handbook may well find users in other nations, as many of the issues having to do with disabilities are not tied to the legislation, legal decisions, or traditions of any given nation. It is focused primarily on current issues in the United States, but it includes cultural and international comparisons and issues that are not tied to any particular nation or culture. Like other handbooks, it is intended to be a reference volume for students, instructors, researchers, and administrators in the USA and other nations.

We have organized the handbook into 13 sections, each of which addresses a critical aspect of the field of special education. Some of the critical and controversial issues in the field do not have a particular chapter devoted to them because they are covered in multiple chapters. One such issue is inclusion, which is addressed in many of the chapters. Another is the disproportional identification for and placement in restrictive special education environments of various groups, an issue dealt with in multiple chapters. Readers should not mistakenly assume that if an issue does not have a chapter title it is unimportant or that the handbook does not address it.

The first section is devoted to general issues that provide background for the others. The chapters explain the history of the field, contemporary issues, statistical realities, group research design, and teacher education. All of these are matters that serve as a backdrop for other aspects of special education.

The second section summarizes U. S. law as it stands at the end of the first decade of the 21st century. The law is particularly important, as it is one of the basic tools of advocacy for exceptional children. Interpretation of the law, particularly its requirements of appropriate education and least restrictive environment, are among the most controversial issues in early 21st century America. Consequently, understanding the details of the law, including not only the American federal statute but the rules and regulations and court findings related to it, is crucial to special education practices.

The third section addresses what has been a controversial issue for decades in many nations of the world—the relationship between general and special education. This has become an increasingly important issue as United States general education laws, such as the No Child Left Behind Act of the early 21st century, have become the focus of efforts to reform schools. Just where exceptional children fit into the general education effort to move toward response to intervention, standards-based reforms, and co-teaching remains an important matter.

The fourth section is devoted to the special problems encountered in the categories of disability and giftedness that are usually addressed in introductory courses in special education. In spite of efforts to move toward noncategorical special education, the differences among various groups of exceptional children remain critically important.

Section V deals with problems of assessing exceptional children, including issues such as high-stakes testing, academic progress monitoring, and response to intervention that have become hot topics in the context of educational reform and inclusion. Accurate and useful assessment is also the beginning point for identification and for writing individual education programs (IEPs) for children with disabilities or special gifts and talents.

The sixth section is about the issues that every administrator must confront, including problems related to money and personnel. Educational programs for exceptional children do not just magically appear; they are designed and controlled by administrators, who must be knowledgeable about the law and student exceptionality and must work within a framework of real-world constraints.

Effective instruction is surely central to appropriate education, and we have addressed instructional issues in the seventh and eighth sections, for students with high- and low-incidence cognitive disabilities respectively. Teaching is too often not given sufficient attention as the variable that makes special education special. The chapters in sections VII and VIII get down to the nitty-gritty of what special education needs to be.

Our ninth and tenth sections deal with transition for those with high- and low-incidence disabilities respectively. Federal law requires attention to transition, and special educators have too often given insufficient attention to what students will do next in their lives. The chapters in sections IX and X deal with the futures of students who are receiving special education.

Section XI is focused on parent and family issues, and Section XII addresses early identification and intervention. These are among the most important aspects of appropriate services for exceptional children. Federal special education law became a reality in 1975 primarily because of the concerns and action of parents. Exceptional children must be seen in the context of their families if special education is to serve them appropriately. Moreover, it is increasingly obvious that the earlier we can identify children as needing special services and provide appropriate intervention the more likely we are to be successful and prevent later problems.

Finally, the thirteenth section is devoted to cultural and international issues, topics of increasing importance as the population of the United States becomes more diverse and international communication becomes easier and quicker. Multicultural understanding, sensitivity to cultural differences, the disproportional identification for special programs of students in various groups, and international comparisons are all matters of critical importance in contemporary education, general and special.

We have attempted to consider all of the critical aspects of special education in the early 21st century, and it is tempting to assume that this book says it all. But there is always more to say, and if we have missed no issue that is important today then one is certain to appear soon. Our hope is that the foundation of information and wisdom found in the pages of this book will be of help in addressing problems we may have missed or that may become obvious in the future.

We thank our section editors and chapter authors for working with us on this project. Without their help and dedication, our efforts would have fallen far short. We thank them in particular for doing the work for this project without compensation of any kind. Because of their selfless work on this project, we are able to turn all of the royalty earnings of this book into a fund providing a yearly award for a researcher whose work has led to more effective education of exceptional children.

We are grateful to our able graduate assistants, Kristen Ashworth and Shelly Pearson Lovelace, for their help in completing many of the tasks we faced as general editors of the handbook. They helped us keep track of correspondence, convert our paper edits to electronic versions, keep a log the various drafts of chapters, and in many significant ways keep our endeavors organized.

Finally, we acknowledge the encouragement and support of our editor at Routledge, Lane Akers, who suggested this project to us, guided us to a conclusion, and supported our idea of using the royalty earnings of the book as the source of an annual award to a researcher in special education.

J. M. K.
D. P. H.

List of Contributors

Dimitris Anastasiou, University of Western Macedonia, Greece

Jean F. Andrews, Lamar University

Kristen E. Ashworth, University of Virginia

Donald B. Bailey, Jr., RTI International

Manju Banerjee, University of Connecticut

Barbara D. Bateman, Creswell, Oregon

Sheri Berkeley, George Mason University

Bonnie S. Billingsley, Virginia Polytechnic Institute and State University

Martin E. Block, University of Virginia

Mary Lynn Boscardin, University of Massachusetts Amherst

M. Renee Bradley, U.S. Department of Education

Catherine M. Brighton, University of Virginia

Fredda Brown, Queens College, City University of New York

William H. Brown, University of South Carolina

Susan M. Bruce, Boston College

Carolyn M. Callahan, University of Virginia

Deanna B. Cash, Lynchburg College

Paul T. Cirino, University of Houston

Maureen A. Conroy, University of Florida

Bryan G. Cook, University of Hawaii

Sara Cothren Cook, University of Hawaii

Martha J. Coutinho, East Tennessee State University

Jean B. Crockett, University of Florida

Maria K. Denney, University of Florida

Erik Drasgow, University of South Carolina

Carl J. Dunst, Orelena Hawks Puckett Institute

Stacy K. Dymond, University of Illinois, Urbana-Champaign

Laszlo A. Erdodi, Eastern Michigan University and London Health Science Centre

Brandy L. Ethridge, University of California, Santa Barbara

Jane M. Everson, Appalachian State University

Jack M. Fletcher, University of Houston

Douglas Fuchs, Vanderbilt University

Lynn S. Fuchs, Vanderbilt University

Nicholas Gage, University of Missouri–Columbia

J. Emmet Gardner, University of Oklahoma

Ralph Gardner, III, The Ohio State University

Michael M. Gerber, University of California, Santa Barbara

Russell Gersten, Instructional Research Group/ University of Oregon

Steve Graham, Vanderbilt University

Noel Gregg, University of Georgia

Philip L. Gunter, Valdosta State University

Zahra Hajiaghamohseni, University of South Carolina

Daniel P. Hallahan, University of Virginia

James Halle, University of Illinois

Carol L. Hamlett, Vanderbilt University

Jenifer Harr-Robins, American Institutes for Research, Washington, DC

Karen R. Harris, Vanderbilt University

Betsy P. Humphreys, University of North Carolina at Chapel Hill

Katherine J. Inge, Virginia Commonwealth University

Jane M. Jarvis, Flinders University

Antonis Katsiyannis, Clemson University

James M. Kauffman, University of Virginia

Clayton Keller, Qatar University

Luke E. Kelly, University of Virginia

Amanda Kloo, University of Pittsburgh

Herman Knopf, University of South Carolina

Renée Lajiness-O'Neill, Eastern Michigan University and Henry Ford Health System

Timothy J. Landrum, University of Louisville

Holly B. Lane, University of Florida

Jennifer H. Lindstrom, University of Georgia

John Wills Lloyd, University of Virginia

Gabriel Lomas, Western Connecticut State University

Filip T. Loncke, University of Virginia

Shelly P. Lovelace, University of Virginia

Joseph W. Madaus, University of Connecticut

Lisa Marshak, Fairfax County Public Schools, Fairfax, VA

Kathleen Marshall, University of South Carolina

Margo A. Mastropieri, George Mason University

Christine Maul, California State University, Fresno

John McDonnell, University of Utah

Kimberly A. McDuffie-Landrum, Bellarmine University

Tara W. McLaughlin, University of Florida

Deborah Merchant, Keene State College

Domna Michail, University of Western Macedonia, Greece

Jason Miller, University of Maryland

Sara Mills, George Mason University

Devery R. Mock, Appalachian State University

M. Sherril Moon University of Maryland

C. Michael Nelson, University of Kentucky

Marvalin A. Nelson, St. Lucia Schools, West Indies

Rebecca A. Newman-Gonchar, University of Oregon

Rollanda E. O'Connor, University of California at Riverside

Linda Oshita, University of Hawaii

Donald P. Oswald, Virginia Commonwealth University

Thomas Parrish, American Institutes for Research, Washington, DC

James R. Patton, University of Texas at Austin

Edward A. Polloway, Lynchburg College

Sarah R. Powell, Vanderbilt University

Paige C. Pullen, University of Virginia

Rachel F. Quenemoen, University of Minnesota

Marshall Raskind, Bainbridge Island, Washington

Melissa Raspa, RTI International

Adell Renzaglia, University of Illinois

Paul J. Riccomini, The Pennsylvania State University

Jay W. Rojewski, University of Georgia

Karen J. Rooney, Educational Enterprises, Inc., Richmond, VA

Michael Rozalski, State University of New York at Geneseo

Ann M. Sam, University of North Carolina at Chapel Hill

Victoria Sanchez, University of California at Riverside

Lana Santoro, Instructional Research Group/University of Oregon

David Scanlon, Boston College

Maureen A. Schloss, Lowndes County School District, Valdosta, GA

Thomas E. Scruggs, George Mason University

Pamela M. Seethaler, Vanderbilt University

Pamela C. Shaw, Charleston County School District, Charleston, SC

Karrie A. Shogren, University of Illinois, Urbana-Champaign

Richard L. Simpson, University of Kansas

George H. S. Singer, University of California, Santa Barbara

Patricia A. Snyder, University of Florida

Fred Spooner, University of North Carolina at Charlotte

Angie Stewart, State University of New York at Geneseo

Janine P. Stichter, University of Missouri–Columbia

Martha L. Thurlow, University of Minnesota

Meghan H. Trowbridge, University of South Carolina School of Medicine

Ann P. Turnbull, Beach Center on Disability, University of Kansas

H. Rutherford Turnbull, III, Beach Center on Disability, University of Kansas

Mian Wang, University of California, Santa Barbara

Michael L. Wehmeyer, University of Kansas

Cheryl A. Wissick, University of South Carolina

Mark Wolery, Vanderbilt University

Mitchell L. Yell, University of South Carolina

Kim T. Zebehazy, University of British Columbia

Naomi P. Zigmond, University of Pittsburgh

George J. Zimmerman, University of Pittsburgh

Section I

Historical and Contemporary Issues in Educating Exceptional Learners

Section Editor: James M. Kauffman
University of Virginia

Understanding any field of study requires knowing something about how it got started and being able to discuss important aspects of its current methods and controversies. This understanding includes not only foundational ideas themselves but where and how these concepts were formulated, the social forces that shaped the concepts, and the legal bases for the field's practices. The education of exceptional learners, usually known as special education, cannot be well understood aside from its history. Where it came from and how it has been shaped by the forces of history are logically connected to its current struggles and its trajectory.

Special education's contemporary issues grew out of its history, and they are also the foundation for its future. Becoming conversant with the major issues that the field of special education confronts in contemporary life is critical to understanding its practices. Many of the major issues are perpetual—never actually resolved, just revisited by each generation of special educators. The major issues of today are remarkably like those of the past, and they are no doubt much like the those of the future. In part, this is likely a function of the fact that they are both conceptual and social—intellectual challenges with important social ramifications.

An important aspect of any field of study is the source(s) of information it takes most seriously. No field of study can make much progress if it ignores important realities. Perhaps the most immovable of those realities is the mathematics on which the field depends for its legitimacy. Social judgments are realities that can and do change; mathematical realities are not likely to be altered by social judgments. Special education ignores statistical-mathematical realities only if it cares nothing about its demise.

One might ask of any field of study, on what kind of information does it base its concepts and practices? If the field of study purports to be research-based or evidence-based, we need to ask what kind of research or evidence it looks to for its advances. Thus, the way problems are studied is a critical feature of what is considered best practice. Research design says much about how we might judge the changes special educators hope to induce in individuals and groups.

In special education, we like to think that teachers are educated to put research into practice. The education of teachers to work with exceptional children is, indeed, a thorny contemporary issue. It is a matter of great importance because the way teachers are prepared determines in large measure what happens to exceptional children in school. Since teachers organized the Council for Exceptional Children about a century ago, the matter of what teachers should know or be able to do has been a bone of great contention.

Where did we come from? How did we get here? What are our biggest problems? What realities may we ignore only at our greatest peril? What should be the focus of our research? How should teachers be prepared? How do we know? This section of the handbook provides background for the sections that follow.

1
A History of Special Education

MICHAEL M. GERBER
University of California, Santa Barbara

Beyond events, actors, and artifacts, human history represents the evolution of human culture and the attitudes, beliefs, and ideas that evolve, are for some time shared, discarded and replaced with new attitudes, beliefs, and ideas. In some sense, the timeline of events, actors, and artifacts that most equate with history are themselves the products of the succession of attitudes, beliefs, and ideas that form the psychological and emotional backbone of communities and societies. Ideas animate people and the events they produce, and new ideas emanate from the efforts and inventions of those same people. The history of special education is no different, and this chapter will take that perspective.

There are now several excellent histories relevant to special education, some in scholarly articles (e.g., Dorn, Fuchs, & Fuchs, 1996; Hoffman, 1975; Smith, 1998) and some with book length treatments (e.g., Danforth, 2009; Osgood, 2005, 2008; Pritchard, 1963; Sarason & Doris, 1979; Winzer, 1993). Some are rather peripheral in that they focus on the social treatment of individuals with various disabilities and may only touch on issues of education (e.g., Deutsch, 1949; Kanner, 1964; Lane, 1979; Levine & Levine, 1992; Safford & Safford, 1996; Sears, 1975; Woodill, 1995). Those that discuss education often focus on the origins and development of educational treatments or treatment facilities for specific disabilities (e.g., Flaherty, 2003; Kauffman & Landrum, 2006; Hallahan & Mercer, 2002; Scheerenberger, 1987; Trent, 1994; Wiederholt, 1974). Still others attempt to sketch all of the many converging influences on modern special education but, like the present chapter, are forced to paint a portion of the whole picture and, then, only with broad strokes (Itkonen, 2009; Kauffman, 1981; Lane, 1979; Osgood, 1999; Yell, Rogers, & Rogers, 1998).

All of these authors have written broadly about education, particularly as it has occurred in the quasi-therapeutic contexts of hospitals, homes, charitable asylums, state and private schools. But what most characterizes these historical studies is the location of educational practice as a small, often non-specific, part of the sweeping vistas created by emergence and clash of large-scale social, philosophical, political, and sometimes scientific forces. This chapter will not—cannot—repeat or enhance these previous, scholarly treatments of the landmarks, milestones, and visionary champions of individuals with disabilities. Rather, this chapter, for reasons of economy of space, but also differing intellectual stance, will focus on the fact that, while it represents many and diverse influences from prior centuries, special education as we know it in America today is clearly a product of the 20th century. Moreover, although educational opportunities and innovations exist elsewhere, it is in and as part of public schooling, that modern special education has found its culminating expression.

Special Education and the 20th Century

The choice to focus attention on special education as education in public schools in the 20th century is not arbitrary. Indeed, the 20th century, particularly in the United States, marked a stark departure from prior social history in general and the social treatment of those with disabilities in particular. The century produced historically unprecedented levels and scales of scientific knowledge, manufacturing and agricultural expansion, transportation and communications technologies, economic growth and productivity, and urbanization—and as a function of these changes, the 20th century can be seen in stunning relief against the extremes of cultural and political differences and the rigid barriers of time and space. The time needed to exchange even simple information collapsed first into hours, minutes, and then seconds. The almost unbridgeable geography that divided nations and regions and communities from one another seem to have evaporated as miles melted into fewer and fewer degrees of personal separation.

The 20th century was like no other in creating a global, now virtually inescapable, sense of interconnectedness of personal, community, national, and even international well-being. If this characterization makes the century sound idyllic, as if there was no pain, no strife, no brutal struggle, nothing could be further from the truth. Indeed, the 20th century's high speed technological and social contraction of the planet was associated with pain, strife, and brutal struggle on a global scale as well. It was as if each dramatic reduction of time and resources needed to produce, move, communicate, and inform was perceived as a parallel surge in threat, menace, and risk.

It was a century of contradictions—ever broadening and deepening communities, but unparalleled hostility and lethal aggression. A tidal ebb in of age-old justifications for social devaluation of differences and exclusion was followed in cycles by a new flood of animosities and grievances. Heroic efforts to tear down walls were mirrored by desperate efforts to rebuild them.

Modern special education was a product of this century, and its history must be understood accordingly. In the United States, modern special education emerged at the convergence of extraordinary economic expansion that was accompanied by a heady mix of rapid industrialization, unstoppable urbanization, and massive—historically unprecedented—immigration. The cities were the crucible for all the change that followed. The cities not only were the locus of huge and rapidly growing congregations of humanity—people streaming from small towns and farms, a deluge of immigrants pouring from ships at every major port—but also a teeming laboratory of social, political, and economic experiment. How were people to move? Where would they live? How would they have heat, water, light? How were they to be safeguarded against others, against themselves? How would they be policed, guarded against fire, protected from disease? How would they be governed?

Looming large in every answer was the idea of public education. Growing from the older idea of a common school (Jefferson, 1779/1905; Main, 1907), public education was a different matter, in scale, in purpose, and in organization and management. Its success became fused with the success of democracy itself (Dewey, 1903).

Memories and Biographies

If the history of special education is "a collection of the memories and stories that serve as a foundation for the field" (Smith, 1998), then, like all histories, it begs a timeline, landmarks and milestones, as well as the biographies that crystallize important innovations or ideas. My perspective here is limited to the 20th century in America. The importance of the 20th century in the history of special education—by which I mean the public school enterprise of educating children with disabilities—derives of course from its recency and, therefore, its relevance to our current moment. Focus on America is not meant to diminish the important developments in special education that occurred elsewhere in the world, some of which predate the American experience by half a century or more. Rather, American special education is unique and could not have existed elsewhere, or in another century. Its birth was a unique confluence of time, place, and circumstance. That time was the year 1900—or the school year 1899–1900 to be precise, the very beginning of the 20th century. The circumstance was the convergence of astonishing industrial growth, massive immigration, and a progressive political philosophy in a comparatively young democracy that, in 1900, still had living memory of a great civil war. The place was not only a particular city, what was (and remains) one of the great cities of the world, New York, but on a particular street. Special education—the special education we see in our schools today, the special education that is part of a remarkable national policy, the special education that continues to focus attention on questions about the nature of individual differences, the proper role and organization of public education, the meaning of equality—*that* special education begins on Henry Street in the Lower East Side of Manhattan in the classroom of a single teacher, Elizabeth Farrell.

In this chapter, I try to show how special education developed from the imagination, convictions, and tireless efforts of this young woman who was aided and abetted by political and philosophical allies who supported her and by school administrators and politicians who either joined in her campaign or found it met their needs to not stand in her way. Even as Farrell was inventing modern special education, she was herself swept along in a tide of transformative ideas and events. I will describe how the components that described special education at its inception in Elizabeth Farrell's decades' long invention are precisely the ones that preoccupy us over a century later, and what that history may portend for special education's future.

Contemplating Art and the Artist

In the 1640s, about the same years that Descartes was laying down the principles of philosophy and what became the natural sciences, and Newton was actually inventing those sciences, Diego Rodríguez de Silva y Velázquez, a court painter for Phillip IV of Spain, produced a remarkable series of portraits depicting little people kept for the (mostly) benign amusement of the royal court. Whereas Descartes and Newton shared a common conviction that nature would yield to reason, Velázquez's paintings are compassionate and empathetic. He does not merely report what he observes; he clearly records his impressions, what he feels, as well. In these portraits, Velázquez presents the personality of these people first and their physical or mental impairments only as a sober, but not judgmental, nod to realism.

There is nothing ironic about these unusual portraits, nor is Velázquez making a political statement. Indeed, for a court painter, perhaps one of the most prolific portraitists of his age, one who was employed to portray wealthy and powerful persons, it is extraordinary that Velázquez chose to paint these people—Don Antonio el Ingles, Don Diego de Acedo el Primo, Don Juan Calabazas, Francisco Lezcano—at all. Nevertheless, whatever his thoughts on the matter may have been, there is no real parallel example of persons with disabilities being treated with such consideration and respect.

What do Velázquez and his portraits of those with disabilities tell us about the history of special education? The answer is: not very much, really. Rather, the appearance of both Velázquez and his paintings at a particular moment in time helps to illustrate the potential for confusing the art with the artist. Why did Velázquez paint these portraits? We do not know. What does the fact of these paintings tell us about societal attitudes and activities regarding those with disabilities? Velázquez's story probably tells us even less about that.

What Velázquez and his paintings tell us is that it was within the capacity of one person to envision a kind of equality for those with disabilities, and that an environment existed that, however limited it may have been, tolerated that person acting on his vision. And that *is* important to understanding the history of special education. Without the ability at least of some in society to regard children with disabilities with similar consideration and respect, and the reciprocal willingness of society—its citizens, institutions, power structures, and economy—to tolerate people acting on their impulse to promote equal dignity for those with disabilities, it is difficult to imagine how there could ever be something called "special" education at all. Without a succession of actors and tolerance, if not support, for their actions, there can be no history of special education.

However, in pursuit of a history of special education, a distinction might be usefully drawn between the evolving social and cultural regard for sometimes extreme differences in physical, mental, or behavioral characteristics of individuals, on one hand, and the nature of educational opportunity afforded, on the other. Similarly, scholarly study of human differences may entail some mention of *education* as a context that illustrates or clarifies the consequence of significant differences. For example, blindness necessitates adoption or adaptation of instructional methods that circumvent the problems of development and learning that blindness creates. On the other hand, study of *special education* seems to imply a focus not only on the adoptions and adaptations, but how they are organized, provided, sustained, or improved. Put differently, if one wishes to study disabilities, one must study individual differences in conditions of gestation, development, and experience and their consequences for functioning—i.e., the *what* of disabilities. But, if one wishes to study *special education*, one must study the *how*.

Similarly, this history of one is not necessarily the history of the other. To note, for example, that John Dix Fisher led a movement to establish a school for the blind in 1826 Boston, is an interesting historical fact, but one which alone tells us neither about blindness nor why Dr. Fisher was so motivated. That he inspired other like-minded, well-connected individuals—most notably Samuel Gridley Howe—to actually create the school (i.e., the famous Perkins Institution and Massachusetts Asylum for the Blind) also makes for an intriguing story, but not one that necessarily says much about the school or the nature of the education that occurred there. In fact, what often passes for *history* in special education tends to rely on the fascinating strands of strangely intersecting biographies. These are used by authors to mark or suggest broad social movements or innovations concerning education but, oddly, reveal little about the education itself.

To be sure, these are arresting stories, stories that persuade us that modern special education arises, progresses, and is sustained in the best humanist traditions of the Enlightenment. These stories are recounted, albeit in abbreviated form, in almost every introductory textbook on special education. But, as the biography of the painter is separable from an appreciation of the painting, a history of special education needs to dwell both on those persons or landmark events which, when artfully aligned, can seem to mark a straight path from a dark past to an enlightened future, and the history of the public education enterprise we recognize as "special education"—i.e., teachers and students in school classrooms engaged in the practical processes of education.

Women and Special Education

There is an unmistakable and influential feminine presence in the practical history of special education. Not only have there been many prominent female teachers or clinicians who wrote, lectured, and lobbied about teaching children with disabilities (e.g., women like Elizabeth Farrell, Marianne Frostig, and Evelyn Deno), but also some of the most prominent men in the field in the 20th century, names always included in our histories, worked in partnership with strong female teachers or clinicians. For example, special education history often mentions names like Samuel Orton (Anna Gillingham, Bessie Stillman, Marion Monroe), Alfred Strauss (Laura Lehtinen Rogan), Samuel Kirk (Marion Monroe, Winifred Kirk, Jeanne McRae McCarthy, Barbara Bateman, Janet Lerner), Helmer Myklebust (Doris Johnson), and William Cruickshank (Jane E. Dolphin). In each case, it seems that the women on these famous teams provided much of the insight into actual practice, what the instruction would look like, what specific techniques were to be use to reach desirable outcomes and, importantly, what would be the substance of training provided to other teachers and clinicians. While the men seem to be remembered for articulating links to medical, psychological, or educational theories, it was the women who knew how to translate research into practice.

If any of this is true, it would not be surprising or unusual. In the 20th century, most teachers have been female. However, it seems too that there is a *feminist*, not merely *feminine*, story to be told. In 1900, a woman who was unmarried, well-educated, wanted a profession, or was interested in being socially or politically engaged had few options. Becoming a teacher or a nurse were culturally acceptable types of publicly visible employment for such women. Their acceptability as pre-marital occupations probably has deep origins in male concepts of female capabilities, but after the Civil War and into the first decades of the 20th century, women cultivated their public involvement in community matters pertaining to family health and education. Men generally conceded that these were extensions of women's inherent responsibilities for the health and well-being of their families and, therefore, within the boundaries of women's legitimate role. However, there was broader, and probably not incidental, political content to women's advocacy for community health and education. Arising issues of community health and education gave women an acceptable way to gather for "clubs" and "societies" for overtly political purposes. Not having the right to vote, home meetings and gatherings of women also served as a platform from which nevertheless to offer opinions relevant to local, state, and national elections. Indeed, without the political opportunities health and education issues provided to them, the suffragette movement would have had little ability to reach and incite the vast majority of women in their homes.

Indeed, decades before women won the right to vote in the United States, a broad networked group of well-educated and committed women became the most powerful advocates for children's well-being, women like Lillian Wald, founder of the Henry Street Settlement House, Florence Kelly, anti-child labor activist, and Julia Lathrop, a veteran of Hull House (e.g., see Addams, 1908) in Chicago and first director of the Federal Children's Bureau. Lathrop captured these women's common sense of the connection between home, children's welfare and the quality of life in the larger American society in a speech to the National Education Association in 1919:

> We cannot help the world toward democracy if we despise democracy at home; and it is despised when mother or child die needlessly. It is despised in the person of every child who is left to grow up ignorant, weak, unskilled, unhappy, no matter what his race or color. (quoted in Bradbury, 1956, pp. 11–12)

They were allies and friends in dozens of parallel and converging causes that characterized the progressive movement of the early 20th century including, of course, women's suffrage, a goal that was consistent with, and not necessarily subordinate to, activism aimed at obtaining justice and opportunity for the least powerful members of the society. It is remarkable that, in the absence of political equality, these women leveraged the one role that had been conceded to them, guardians of family health and education of children. With skillful, patient, but unremitting, advocacy, they grew powerful as a political force, depending on each other, offering advice and assistance to each other, and working tirelessly to draw others to their causes.

Henry Street

The Henry Street Settlement House was located just down the street from Public School 1 in the Lower East Side of Manhattan in the early years of the 20th century. In 1901, Henry Street ran through one of the most squalid tenements in all of New York City. The multi-storied brick public school was large but inadequate for the demand even by turn-of-the-century standards. The young woman who established and steered the course of the Henry Street Settlement was Lillian Wald, who had originally trained as a nurse. The Settlement House began as a health education outreach, a new kind of public health nursing in which specially prepared nurses visited families in their overcrowded, unsanitary, and often structurally dangerous tenement buildings. But Henry Street soon became more, a hub of social activism, a showcase of cultural differences, and an incubator of progressive politics, made possible by the patronage Wald cultivated from big donors and powerful politicians. Although men were certainly involved, the Wald's Henry Street Settlement House really was a kind of commune for educated women from respectable families where they could freely engage in the exercise of their minds and social consciousness. Wald ultimately became a powerful advocate for the view that the world at large was just a more complex, multicultural neighborhood, where problems would yield to the same commitment, activism and volunteerism so strongly in evidence at the Henry Street Settlement House. She was both idealist and political pragmatist. Her life-long interest in the well-being of the poor, and children of the poor, was expressed as unyielding activism.

For example, in 1903, she and Florence Kelly, a leader in the National Consumers League, while having breakfast at the Settlement House, conceived of a federal "children's bureau." If the federal government could invest itself in the problems of agriculture, they reasoned, why not invest as well in the welfare of children. It was not a casual conversation over coffee. Both mobilized their considerable networks of influential people, quickly extending to the President, who signed on to the idea immediately. In 1909, Roosevelt convened the first White House conference on children (i.e., the White House Conference on the Care of Dependent Children). Establishment of a federal children's bureau was among the nine recommendations "concerning the use of institutional care for dependent and neglected children" proposed by the conference (Child Welfare League of America, 2009). Wald lobbied relentlessly, including testifying before Congress, for the next nine years and, on April 9, 1912, President Taft signed the law establishing the Federal Children's Bureau.

At the large public school nearby on Henry Street was another young woman, about the same age as Wald, who had about five years of experience as a teacher. This was Elizabeth Farrell, who did her first teaching in a one-room multi-grade school before moving to New York City and P. S. 1. Unlike Wald, Elizabeth was a child of immigrants, but her father had been a modest success and was able to send her to college where she studied to be a teacher. Teaching in a small one-room, rural school would seem not to be ideal preparation for teaching in the crowded classrooms of the Henry Street School. But such teaching required that Elizabeth learn to manage different grade-level curricula with students who, because of age differences, might have very different abilities. Because students at P. S. 1 represented different immigrant cultures and languages, varying degrees of impoverishment, and significant differences in their general health, she found that her graded class much more resembled her multi-graded rural classroom than one would think.

Both women were from rural parts of the state, but found themselves working in the center of the simultaneous collapse of urban life and its re-creation in New York City. Both were unusual in that they had received some college-level education, something few women, even those from modest middle-class homes could expect. Thus, the nursing and teaching professions became vehicles for expressing their intellectual gifts and moral energies. Both women were horrified by the poverty and degradation they saw in the urban slums and both women had gravitated to Henry Street with an unusual confidence that they could do something about it. Almost inevitably, perhaps, both women, working a short walk apart, met, encouraged one another, and became champions of each other's work. For Elizabeth Farrell, in particular, meeting Lillian Wald and participating in the activities of the settlement house encouraged her to act on her ideas in ways that she might not have otherwise. Lillian and her benefactors were politically as well as socially well-connected and they often helped boost the young teacher's visibility in the vast school system. But, perhaps, more importantly, Farrell probably found in Wald and the other women on Henry Street the firm conviction that public education could be improved to the benefit of students who, for whatever deficiencies, were likely to be left behind.

The problems faced and surmounted by Farrell was like a script for 20th century special education. Virtually every issue that now provokes national debate has a discernable origin in the 30 years during which Farrell had unprecedented influence over what became special education in the public schools.

Elizabeth Farrell in New York City

Dozens of doctors, sociologists, psychologists, and philosophers contributed to the intellectual architecture of special education. But the edifice was built by teachers. Today, after years of discussion in many fields, not just special education, about the "barriers" of translating research into practice, there is new recognition that applied research can—and perhaps should—grow not from abstract theory but from contemplation of practice itself. Being immersed in the many, layered tasks of instructing children in classrooms on a daily basis provides unique opportunity, if not the time nor resources that a typical teacher might need, to methodically develop her insights. That is, unless she has the confidence and convictions of an Elizabeth Farrell.

Farrell was 29 when she came to the school on Henry Street in 1899. She had already taught in a single-room school in Oneida Castle, New York, a small rural community. There she must have sharpened her teaching skills and struggled to meet the various educational needs of her small, but multi-age class. In is logical, therefore, that Farrell began experimenting with adapting the curriculum and instruction in her classroom at P. S. 1 from the start (Farrell, 1909).

Despite her being in a cultural, political, and professional environment that was many scales of magnitude larger and more complex than anything she had experienced in Oneida Castle, she seems to have had great confidence in herself and her professional thinking from the moment she began at P.S. 1. She was thoughtful, well educated and, apparently, well read, methodical in solving problems of classroom teaching practice, and worked with a sense of experimentation, slowly refining her ideas about how the curriculum could be adapted or, in modern terms, how instruction could be differentiated. She did not seem intimidated by her surroundings, but rather, like many modern young teachers who begin their careers in tough urban schools, she must have had great energy and commitment to her work.

Many young teachers with a difficult teaching assignment would have been satisfied to organize their own classrooms in a manner that satisfied them. Fewer would be so confident in what they were doing that they would think in terms of systems change. But, Elizabeth Farrell, while cautious, was not timid. She proceeded cautiously, not apparently because of any anxiety about where her experimentation would lead, but rather because she wanted to validate her ideas in practice before taking next steps.

Part of her boldness certainly was afforded by her personality and intellect. She viewed her work with children very seriously, and thought the larger enterprise of public education was of such critical importance that much of human advance in the 20th century depended on it. Nor did she seem inordinately sentimental or in any sense romantic about teaching. Her writing is sober, clear, strenuously argued, and always on the basis of empirical data.

A third reason that Farrell may have moved ahead so boldly was because she received substantial validation by the progressive political climate in New York City at that time, particularly on Henry Street. There were enormous problems to be solved. In 1908, the city boasted that its school system was "bigger than the biggest corporation in the United States" with property worth $100 million, $45 million in annual spending, 15,000 employees, and 600,000 students (*New York Times*, 1908). Nevertheless, despite the best enforced attendance laws in the country, the rapid increase in city population due to immigration would still leave over 50,000 children with only part-time instruction. Class size was considered generously small at 43 students per classroom in elementary school, whereas

Boston and Chicago had average class sizes over 46. But, public education in New York was ambitious. It included

> … special industrial training which prepares children for some useful vocation; instruction for mental and physical defectives, who in the eyes of the law are equally as much entitled to an education as a normal child; rescuing the truant and the incorrigible children whose lives are drifting toward criminality; playgrounds for the poor who … would otherwise be deprived of the benefits of play…. (*New York Times*, 1908)

The *Times* called educating children with "hereditary or acquired" disabilities ("defective children") "one of the most important and humanitarian activities of the Board of Education," giving these children "the benefits of free public education, to which they are entitled equally." In 1907, somewhat over 50% of the 1,417 children who were "examined" were "assigned to ungraded classes." Those who attended these special education classes were estimated to be about a fourth of the number of "feeble-minded" children in the city who were eligible (*New York Times*, 1908). On Broome Street, at P. S. 120, a "tough assortment of incorrigibles and habitual truants" were given one final chance. A new school prepared for 25 classes (one teacher per class) was about to open on E. 23rd Street to try to provide special education for children who were "physically defective" (e.g., deaf and mute) as the system had for students who were "mentally defective." In addition, plans were underway to open four classes in January of 1909 for students who were blind (*New York Times*, 1908)

The scale of the New York City Public School System and its unprecedented growth responded to a practical necessity caused by the collision of New York's strict compulsory attendance laws and thousands of new immigrants arriving monthly. But the ambitious programs for children with disabilities went further. Other school systems around the country had compulsory attendance laws; they just didn't enforced them, or enforced them selectively, a strategy that would end nationally only with the passage of the Education of All Handicapped Children's Act (EAHCA; Public Law 94-142) 66 years later.

Progressive political philosophy and policy permeated the burgeoning public school system as well as city government. Both projected the sense that the great problems of urban life—wage labor, poverty, cultural diversity, and immigration—could be seized and solved and that mankind would be better for it. Whether such attitudes might again characterize our current era remains to be seen, but a similar zeal for public life, service, and energetic effort to improve the lives of others may have occurred in the 1960s when public education was seen as the key to ending family poverty and the host of societal problems that grew from it.

The Great Society of Lyndon Johnson was an ideological grandchild of the progressive movement that characterized New York in 1900. President Johnson, after all, learned his politics during the progressive policy-making that led the national recovery from the Great Depression in the 1930s. The first time Franklin Roosevelt as a young man ever saw a tenement, he was being given a tour of a settlement house on the Lower East Side by a young woman volunteer from a well-to-do family, Eleanor Roosevelt. Eleanor Roosevelt, of course, went on to marry Franklin and to become his very visible public surrogate in matters related to poverty, civil rights, and education.

Lyndon Johnson's themes were much the same in 1965 when Congress passed first massive federal intervention in public education, the Elementary and Secondary Education Act (ESEA). The civil rights basis for this otherwise extra-constitutional excursion into public education was the foundation 10 years later for the EAHCA, the first substantial federal assumption of responsibility for special education. As this chapter is being written, Congress is about to take up the reauthorization of ESEA. Moreover, there appears to be strong interest in further reconciling ESEA with the legislative descendent of EAHCA, the Individuals with Disabilities Education Act of 1990 (IDEA). One substantial motive may be to reconcile the broad national goals for public education of high academic achievement with the historical goal, set by Elizabeth Farrell, to adapt the school to children with disabilities, and not they to it. Many people date the origin of modern special education to EAHCA, but really, it began on Henry Street in New York City in 1900.

Ungraded Classes and Modern Special Education

It is clear that Farrell was quickly aware of the Henry Street Settlement House soon after beginning her teaching assignment at P. S. 1. The Settlement House had been working in the neighborhood since 1893. In fact, Farrell must have felt a strong enough affinity for the women and men who lived and worked at the Settlement House that she moved in and still resided there in 1913 when the Settlement House celebrated its 20th anniversary (*New York Times*, 1923). A year earlier, Wald publicly defended Farrell's request for two additional doctors, two assistant supervisors, and a visiting teacher, noting that she had been "in a position to know something of the work for defective children and for the 'ungraded' classes in the public schools since their inception some twelve years ago" (Wald, 1912).

Wald was 32 years old when Elizabeth Farrell arrived to teach at the Henry Street School, only 3 years older than Farrell, but already with seven years of experience building the Settlement House. She had established the original "Nurses Settlement" project in her apartment building but then, with the help of benefactors moved to the old, but stately, house on Henry Street. In the seven years before she met Farrell, Wald, who was a gifted leader and administrator, had already proved her concept for public health nursing, built a thriving center of social activism, and secured a substantial following of wealthy and influential supporters. The Henry Street "house" was an enterprise of far-reaching impact in the city and beyond. By its 20th anniversary in 1913, the *New York Times* detailed Wald's success in a special celebratory article. By 1913, the "house" was seven houses, including two others not on Henry Street (one at 60th Street was for "colored" nurses). In addition the Henry Street Settlement House included three rented stores downtown that served as general stock rooms, milk dispensaries, and clinics (*New York Times*, 1913). The Henry Street Settlement House had 3,000 members that year. Although it administered 92 volunteer on-call nurses for Manhattan and the Bronx, who had made 200,000 home visits the year before, it was a fixture in New York City that also sponsored or organized a number of cultural and social activities that spread its reputation as an important intellectual and political center as well.

After garnering support from Lillian Wald, who facilitated the support of school administrators, additional ungraded classrooms were attempted in the city's schools in consultation with Farrell. In 1903, there were 10. The classrooms became a special department within the New York City Schools in 1906 and Farrell was appointed "inspector" of ungraded classes, responsible for organization, training, hiring and experimentation with both curriculum and instruction. By 1909, there were "nearly 100" classes in the city with over 1,700 students. Farrell estimated that there were probably 7,000 children in the city's schools who needed these special classes. She was zealous in her advocacy and bragged that in three years New York had been able to serve about a quarter of all its backward children, a feat that, she pointed out, took 46 years for the entire country of Germany (Farrell, 1909). Her reputation spread. She was invited to lecture about her work in other states, and her associates fiercely defended her and New York City as the originators of the ungraded class model (Moore, 1911). In another three years, enrollment had grown to 2,200 children in 142 ungraded classes (Kelley, 1912; Wald, 1912 put the number of classes at 144 and student enrollment significantly beyond the 2,200 a year earlier).

To put the energy and effectiveness of Farrell's advocacy in perspective, consider a comparison with Boston schools, the first in the country by almost 60 years to have a public education system. According to Osgood (1999), Boston began a special ungraded class in the same year that Farrell began experimenting with her own class in New York. By 1902, there were three classes in the Boston Schools. In 1911, Boston Schools had nine classes with 133 students. A year later, growth accelerated and there were 20 classes for 200 students, about a tenth of the New York's enrollment and well below the amount of resources (classes and personnel) that New York had devoted to the effort.

Although many large cities had begun to think of special, ungraded, classes at the same time that Farrell began her work, why was she so singularly successful then and in the years that followed? Why did Farrell's specific model of ungraded class become, with only scant refinements, the national model for special education for the next 75 years?

Whatever motivated her, she was astonishingly successful in changing not only the public schools in New York City, but schools across the country. What she created for "backward" and "feeble-minded" students, those we might classify as having mild to moderate disabilities today, became the institutional model for other special classes for other disabilities. Her ungraded class model would not only become the basis for modern special education, it was recognizably modern in 1906 when she was appointed director of all ungraded classes. The problems she faced, and the solutions she devised and for which she advocated in lecture, letter, report, and articles are as relevant now as they were innovative then.

Once the concept of special education—ungraded classes—was established, Farrell immediately realized the need to establish an examination (i.e., eligibility) process. There was a frighteningly large population of potentially eligible students in the city, partly because of immigration-driven growth, but partly because establishment of a class option encouraged referral. The public schools faced a parallel problem once EAHCA was implemented in the late 1970s. The identification of students as having a learning disability grew from Congress's low-ball estimate of 1% to over 5% in seven years.

Farrell knew that teachers needed to be involved in the process. She saw the special education provided, not as clinical treatment, but as a reasonable instructional and institutional accommodation to the difficult differences these children represented. What identified them, in modern parlance, was their unresponsiveness to normal instruction.

However, she also respected expertise and included medical judgments in her selection process, but with Farrell clearly in charge.

> So thoroughly co-ordinated is the work of Miss Farrell and her medical assistant, Dr. Isabelle Smart, that they know the individual idiosyncrasies and needs of almost every child in the ungraded classes. (*New York Times*, 1908)

When it was pressed later as a selection criterion by Henry Goddard, a famous research director of the Vineland Training School (New Jersey), she resisted mental testing as the sole criterion for identifying students for ungraded class placement. She also publicly, and ultimately successfully, challenged Goddard who had criticized special education in New York schools and recommended a state hospital-type (e.g., Vineland) orientation rather than the school-centered approach that Farrell had pioneered (Kode, 2002).

But soon, she yielded to the complexity of the problems that emerged in selecting students. She saw the need to differentiate the ungraded classes categorically by the similar needs of the students who attended them. In 1913, she incorporated all the available expertise in psychology, social services, medicine, and education (Kode, 2002) into a more elaborate scheme, not unlike our modern multidisciplinary assessment teams. Specifically, she designed a psycho-educational clinic model in which teacher referrals could be examined more systematically and comprehensively

Once placed in a special class, students were examined twice a year, and their homes visited once year, with reports sent to the superintendent. In anticipation of the modern concept, that program should be matched to determination of individual needs, those who had "no serious physical defect can be coached…in their weakest subjects until they are able to return to their classes for part or whole time" (*New York Times*, 1908).

The "detailed" reports constituted practical resources for teachers receiving these students so she would know "exactly what she may expect in a child, what traits and habits she must look for, and what kind of work she may exact" (*New York Times*, 1908).

Of course, the core concept of ungraded classes was that of differentiated curriculum and instruction—i.e., "special" education. Farrell vocally rejected the idea of special schools. She seemed to accept the commonly held belief that the most severely disabled children probably could not be accommodated, but clearly the New York schools were pushing the boundaries despite an onslaught of underserved children. Farrell saw special classes as segregation, to be sure, but not as we understand that term today. The purpose of the special class was to accomplish what demonstrably could not be accomplished in classes of 43 students, i.e., addressing the learning potential of individual students. Despite their special class placement, Farrell always was inclined to promote access to the general education curriculum: "The classes are conducted as far as it is possible in the same way as the regular grade work" (*New York Times*, 1908).

That is, students received "the three R's" each day. They were assigned homework, and their academic skills were tested. In a clear indication of what now might be called "inclusive practices," ungraded class students played with other children at recess and "…join in any games that they can understand" (*New York Times*, 1908). Farrell, the one-time one-room schoolteacher, saw that individual differences in ability within a class were natural and that the differences within the class were, from a teacher's perspective, more important that differences between classes.

But, of course, the purpose of the ungraded class primarily was to

> accentuate those things which the child can do and to ignore, so far as it is possible, those things which it cannot grasp. Except in the very worst cases almost every child can be trained to do something useful. (*New York Times*, 1908)

Farrell's ideas for adapting curriculum and differentiating instruction focused on building individual achievement by close attention to what was motivating at a particular time. She strongly believed in holistic and hands on strategies to motivate learning in students who had previously had little academic success.

> Instead of using books, examples, and copy books … and appeal is made to the constructive, the acquisitive, the initiative instincts in the child. The making of toys, playing games, working with things that are the self-appointed tasks… The whole child, his soul as well as his body, is appealed to. (*New York Times*, 1908)

For students thought by others to be hopelessly incapable, Farrell thought of the ungraded class program as a means to value such students and wanted to emphasize to outsiders what could be learned from a skilled and very patient teacher. The *New York Times* (1908) described the special class teachers this way:

> It is the duty of the special teacher to bring to light these capacities and make of them a specialty… It is exhausting work, because they must put all of their vitality, their energy, and their enthusiasm into work from which there are no returns save, perhaps the satisfaction of seeing these poor mites smiling and happy.

These were teachers of "peculiar natural gifts," the *New York Times* opined (1908). Although many special class teachers were sent for special training at state hospitals (Trent, 1994), Farrell took seriously her responsibilities to staff her classes and supervise the work that was done. Therefore, she promoted local training, what we consider programs of professional development. As an administrator, she was persistently vocal in her advocacy, not afraid of openly confronting the Board in letters—or having her influential friends write—to the *Times* when lobbying the Board for more—more classes, more teachers, more specialists (*New York Times*, 1921; Kode, 2002; Wald, 1912).

The rapid innovation and national acceptance of the ungraded class movement had always been part progressive thinking based on the optimism that urban society could cure its ills and shape its future through good government, scientific thinking, and compassion for the poor and disadvantaged. But an honest appraisal will show that support for special classes also reflected general fear of difference, including specifically those who were different because they were new immigrants and represented unfamiliar cultures and languages. Social policy of that era had this push-pull character to it, part optimism, and part fear. Fears were stoked further by intellectuals and scientists who offered pseudo-scientific analyses of heritability of deviance and, therefore, the moral, if not mortal, dangers that individuals with mental and physical deficiencies posed to society. Foreign-born, non-English speakers were lumped together with those with impairments by suggesting that non-White, non-northern European nationalities were already in decline because of the cumulative effects of inherited deficiency and disease which explained the large numbers of impoverished people who were coming to America and, thereby, threatening our society.

For the progressives, education was the cure. For the social-Darwinists, education was a waste of time and money. The very success of the ungraded class movement—as evidenced by its rapid spread throughout the nation—began to arouse alarm among those who believed that those with disabilities should be isolated where they would not threaten society. This same thinking gave rise to large state-sponsored hospitals and asylums a generation before. Now, the ungraded class movement was revealing that there were thousands of deficient children yet unserved. While Farrell and her allies argued strenuously for expansion of special education, others argued that more state institutions should be built for housing these "vicious" children.

In the end, beginning about 1912, the ideological road divided. Ungraded classes continued to develop and become integrated in local school systems while, at the same time, the eugenics movement with its shameful taints of bigotry, racism, forcible sterilization, and xenophobia also continued to proliferate and permeate American society. The special educators successfully defended their ground, in part, because of the energetic advocacy they and their allies could mount, but also because of the economics of the matter. The public schools were well established as the country's major instrument of socialization and education of "defective" children, at least until such time as they were adults and could be eligible for state care. Actually, it was simply economically impossible to expand state-sponsored hospitals sufficiently to handle these school-identified masses of individuals with disabilities. Mandatory attendance at schools kept these children off the street and controlled them, it was thought, so accepting expansion of special education probably seemed a practical necessity.

The Second Half of the Century

For a short while, Farrell accepted leadership of what had become a national movement. She published the journal *Ungraded* to promote special education and to encourage exchange of knowledge as practical experiments proliferated everywhere. In 1920, she began the Council for Exceptional Children, still the largest special education teachers' association in the world, to give voice and leverage to the growing numbers of teachers of special classes across the country. Within those two decades, the basic idea of ungraded classes had become the norm, universally accepted as special education in the public schools.

Of course, it would be over simplifying to say that the following decades saw only refinements of Farrell's ungraded class model, or New York City's unusual support of it. Even in the presence of some professional agreement about training standards, curriculum standards, or eligibility standards, different locales built their systems within the constraints of their politics and resources, including teachers of Farrell's talents and commitment. Women's suffrage was won. Those powerful women who had so successfully brought local and national attention to the cause of children and families continued their work as part of what had become established bureaucracies or large professional associations, or moved on to other issues. The Great Depression and World War II, in turns, elevated public concern for economic security and the need to protect the well-being of citizens.

But, public education emerged into a different world after World War II. America found itself in a leadership role regarding international economic and political affairs and in an aggressive competition with the Soviet Union, in particular, in investment in the kind of science and technology advances that now governed international economic stature and military power. Public education was generally seen more than before as a potentially potent instrument of national, rather than state and local, policy. Whereas national well-being was often evoked in discussions about public education, the federal government actually had played little, if any, direct role in the first part of the century. By tradition and law, the federal government really had no Constitutional role to play in public education. But, following World War II, the economic and military value of an educated populace was becoming clear, and by the end of the 1950s, the dominant progressive ideas that were the early impetus both for general and special education were overshadowed by heightened national concern for academic achievement, most particularly in science and mathematics. When Congress, during the Eisenhower administration, sought to increase and improve the flow of talented people into elementary and secondary teaching, national defense was the primary justification (i.e., National Defense Education Act of 1958).

In fact, the federal government already had acted assertively with regard to education in 1944 by passage of the Servicemen's Readjustment Act, popularly known as the G. I. Bill. Although the central purpose of the law was to demonstrate national gratitude towards and provide some compensation for sacrifices made by veterans, one of the powerful effects of the legislation was to break the historical connection between family wealth and educational opportunity for over 2 million returning servicemen. This new sense of the importance of educational opportunity was strongly reinforced not only by the needs of countries devastated by the war, but also the disparities in wealth and economic viability made apparent by former European colonies in Africa and Asia and American or European dominated economies in Latin and South America. Economic historians and international development economists argued that national investment in "human capital"—a large component of which was education—was a prerequisite for successful economic development. The development problems of what was called the "third world" echoed the debates over immigration in the first decades of the century. Progressives, aided by these new economic ideas, saw the potential of international improvement through education and assistance. A new generation of social-Darwinists saw ex-colonial people as fundamentally flawed and incapable of raising their nation states to the level of America and Western Europe. Education was beside the point. The tendency for underdeveloped countries to act in ways that were dangerous and threatening to American interests (e.g., to align with the Communist powers) had to be checked and controlled.

As these ideologies played out their differing worldviews on the international stage, a domestic version of international economic disparity was becoming impossible to avoid. In the United States, there were obvious economic disparities between racial or ethnic groups, between communities, and between regions of the country. Progressive thinkers predictably expressed their views in policy recommendations focused on equality of rights and pubic investment in education and social assistance programs (e.g., health care, employment opportunity, and community development). With the landmark *Brown v. Board of Education* decision in 1954, Congress took a large step toward creating a federal role in public education, not on the basis of moral imperative but rather based on an expanded view of the 14th Amendment to the Constitution and its guarantee of equal rights. Equality of educational opportunity was defined as equal access to (approximately equivalent) public education. Then, the shocking assassination of John F. Kennedy created the unexpected presidency of Lyndon Johnson, a New Deal Democrat whose governing philosophy drew not only on Roosevelt's social activism on behalf of the poor, but also from those same progressive ideas and policies that were so in evidence in the New York City of Lillian Wald and Elizabeth Farrell.

The foundational ideas of Johnson's Great Society concerned civil rights, and its centerpieces were the Civil Rights Act of 1964, to be sure, but also the Elementary and Secondary Education Act of 1965 (ESEA). Although ESEA was aiming specifically at "underachievement" as the indicator of unequal access, it wasn't long before the same civil rights logic was applied to the first national policy supporting special education, the Education of All Handicapped Children's Act of 1975. It was estimated that only one-fifth of all children with disabilities were receiving a public education. But what really had changed since Farrell's day was the large, organized, coalesced, and coordinated interest groups of middle-class, socially active, and vocal parents of children with disabilities that had formed since the 1930s (Itkonen, 2009; Yell, Rogers, & Rogers, 1998). The variable and sometimes arbitrary exclusion of children with disabilities from public schools across the United States became a highly charged grievance for these groups and elevated the problem to a national level. Government intervention was expected. When cast in terms of inequality of access to education (i.e., opportunity), special education became a national civil rights issue as well. States and local districts, realizing that judicial pressure was inevitable, joined with the parents in attempt to secure some off-setting funds from the federal government.

Whereas, New York City had invested relatively enormous resources in its commitment to special education in Farrell's day, the costs associated with modern schooling are many magnitudes larger in real terms. President Ford, in reluctantly signing EAHCA into law, was prescient in forecasting what would happen once the entitlement was implemented, what cost burdens it would create for local schools, how the floodgates would open to all the underachieving students whom schools did not, could not, or would not educate satisfactorily.

> Unfortunately, this bill promises more than the Federal Government can deliver, and its good intentions could be thwarted by the many unwise provisions it contains. Everyone can agree with the objective stated in the title of this bill—educating all handicapped children in our Nation. … Even the strongest supporters of this measure know as well as I that they are falsely raising the expectations of the groups affected by claiming authorization levels which are excessive and unrealistic. (President Ford's statement on signing the EAHCA, December 2, 1975)

Moreover, the logic of equal access as the hallmark of equal opportunity misses when it comes to children with disabilities. If understood only as "access" to a public school, the idea of "equal opportunity" for students with disabilities becomes very narrow, as Elizabeth Farrell and her allies recognized 75 years earlier when they established *within* a public school *differentiated* curricula and instruction based on assessment of students' individual differences. The equation of equal access and equal opportunity assumes that (a) different schools are tolerably similar in the opportunity to learn that they provide, and (b) if social discrimination barriers to access are removed, the sorting of achievement outcomes that then occurs is acceptably fair. This idea might work well for, say, ethnic minority students who historically have been barred from access to the same array of (acceptably adequate) schools solely because of their ethnicity. Removing the barrier presumably allows a natural distribution of abilities, and thus achievement outcomes, to emerge. However, if disabled students are defined exactly because of their departure from the same achievement expectations, equal access cannot possibly represent meaningful equality of opportunity.

In the years immediately following passage of EAHCA, the conundrum seems to have been recognized as local schools struggled to implement individualized education plans (IEPs), solidly in the Farrell ungraded class tradition. IEPs were to be tailored to individuals based on the consensus of a multidisciplinary assessment (also a descendent of Farrell's psycho-educational clinic—e.g., see Kode, 2002) and consideration of age-related curricular expectations.

In the early 1980s, however, some disaffection with EAHCA became apparent, chief of which were concerns about the cost burden on local schools. Under EAHCA, they operated under a strict mandate to find, identify, and educationally serve children with disabilities, but most of the costs incurred had to be covered by local resources. However, in the late 1970s, the majority of American homeowners who paid property taxes in support of local services, including schools, were no longer parents of school children. A movement swept across the nation that had the effect of restricting local schools' abilities to autonomously increase taxes to raise money to cover their costs. Special education, once supported by school administrators, now began to be viewed by them as somehow unfairly distorting expenditures of local resources. The real issue, of course, was that the federal government had mandated expenditures by mandating specific standards of special education and left it to states and locales to manage how they would secure the necessary resources. The great coalition that successfully lobbied passage of EAHCA disintegrated (Itkonen, 2009; Yell, 1998).

Two general strategies were adopted by those who now thought special education national policy had overreached. One was to question whether many identifications of disabilities, particularly identifications of *learning disability*, were legitimate. Students identified as having a learning disability had increased from an expectation of 1% of school enrollment to an actual classification of over 5% in the five years between 1977 and 1982. Also, as in Farrell's time, rising program costs and arguable methods of identification became contentious and raised opposition (Kode, 2002). A second strategy that emerged was to suggest that general education was shirking its responsibilities to educate *all* children. Policy, it was claimed, made it too easy for schools to shunt any student they viewed as problematic to special education which produced a kind of social apartheid; it also was costly. Although Farrell had argued convincingly that the "segregation" of ungraded classes was intended to benefit students with disabilities, the modern revolt casts *any* difference in treatment as *de facto* segregation.

Contemporary special education is 35 years old, but as described in this chapter, it is now over 100 years old—i.e., 100 years of institutional, legal, and technical experiment. In this time, virtually every aspect of public life has been transformed—communication, transportation, information extraction and exchange. The public schools, although "modern" in many senses, are fundamentally the same as P. S. 1 on Henry Street was in 1900. More disheartening, perhaps is the fact that special education, a declared *national* interest, with the same lofty ambitions, is still frustrated by many of the same problems that Farrell and her supporters faced.

It is easy to see that contemporary opposition to special education sometimes appears in the guise of a kind of advocacy expressed by "moral" arguments for its re-integration into the common experiences and academic expectations of everyday schooling. Although these arguments may sometimes be advanced cynically, they also represent a number of valid observations about social, economic, and political barriers to truly universal education. Beneath the debates about what is and what is not segregating, or when differences are real, or how schools can or should respond to difference, is a larger, more complex debate about whether we, as a nation, are still committed to Thomas Jefferson's notion of a common school—whether we are really *able* to commit to it, given the complex and expensive functions that modern schools are expected to perform. Imagine special education in its original meaning—a publicly supported education responsive to sometimes extreme individual differences. Imagine that a consensus can exist that this is what public schools in a democracy should be bound by law and moral conviction to do. Now imagine schools doing it as well as our understanding of human differences, teaching, and technology will allow. If we imagine all of that, it is likely that we are imagining schools that are quite different—organizationally sustainably, and technically—than are typical in the United States in 2011. These two ideas that seemed so compatible in 1900—national well-being through improvement of public education and access to individually responsive education as a key to equal opportunity—have resonated in the background of the special education movement throughout the 20th century. It remains to be seen if they can be reconciled in the 21st century.

References

Addams, J. (1908). The home and the special child. *Journal of Proceedings and Addresses of the National Education Association* (pp. 99–102), reprinted in J. B. Elshtain (2002), *The Jane Addams reader*. New York, NY: Basic Books.

Bradbury, D. E. (1956). *Four decades of action for children. A short history of the Children's Bureau.* Washington, DC: Children's Bureau, U. S. Department of Health, Education, and Welfare.

Child Welfare League of America. (2009). *History of White House conferences on children and youth*. Retrieved June 3, 2010, from http://www.cwla.org/advocacy/whitehouseconfhistory.pdf

Danforth, S. (2009). *The incomplete child: An intellectual history of learning disabilities*. New York, NY: Peter Lang.

Deutsch, A. (1949). *The mentally ill in America: A history of their care and treatment from colonial times.* New York, NY: Columbia University Press.

Dewey, J. (1903). Democracy in education. *The Elementary School Teacher, 4*(4), 193–204.

Dorn, S., Fuchs, D., & Fuchs, L. S. (1996). A historical perspective on special education reform. *Theory into Practice, 35*, 12–19.

Farrell, E. E. (Nov. 1, 1909). Atypical children (Letter to the Editor). *New York Times.* Retrieved from http://query.nytimes.com/search/

Flaherty, L. T. (2003). History of school-based mental health services in the United States. In M. D. Weist, S. W. Evans, & N. A Lever (Eds.), *Handbook of school mental health: Advancing practice and research* (pp. 11–22). New York, NY: Kluwer Academic/Plenum Publishers.

Ford, G. R. (1975, December 2). *Education for all Handicapped Children Act. Signing statement*. Ann Arbor, MI: Ford Library and Museum.

Hallahan, D. P., & Mercer, C. D. (2002). Learning disabilities: Historical perspectives. In R. Bradley, L. Danielson, & D. P. Hallahan (Eds.), *Identification of learning disabilities: Research to practice* (pp. 1–67). Mahwah, NJ: Erlbaum.

Hoffman, E. (1975). The American public school and the deviant child: The origins of their involvement. *Journal of Special Education, 9*, 415–423.

Itkonen, T. (2009). *The role of special education interests groups in national policy.* Amherst, NY: Cambria Press.

Jefferson, T. (1905). Bill for the more general diffusion of knowledge (chapter lxxix). *The works of Thomas Jefferson, Vol. 2.* (Federal Edition). New York, NY: G.P. Putnam's Sons. (Original work published 1779)

Kanner, L. (1964). *A history of the care and study of the mentally retarded.* Springfield, IL: Charles C. Thomas.

Kauffman, J. M. (1981). Introduction: Historical trends and contemporary issues in special education in the United States. In J. M. Kauffman & D. P. Hallahan (Eds.), *Handbook of special education* (pp. 3–23). Englewood Cliffs, NJ: Prentice-Hall.

Kauffman, J. M., & Landrum, T. J. (2006). *Children and youth with emotional and behavioral disorders: A history of their education.* Austin, TX: Pro-Ed.

Kelley, F. (Oct. 28, 1912). For defective children. (Letter to the Editor). *New York Times.* Retrieved from http://query.nytimes.com/search/

Kode, K. (2002). *Elizabeth Farrell and the history of special education.* Arlington, VA: Council for Exceptional Children.

Lane, H. (1979). *The wild boy of Aveyron.* Boston, MA: Harvard University Press.

Levine, M., & Levine, A. (1992). *Helping children: A social history.* New York, NY: Oxford University Press.

Main, J. H. T. (1907).The common school and the state. *The Elementary School Teacher, 7*(9), 497–509.

Moore, A. (Aug. 26, 1911). Training backward children. *New York Times.* Retrieved from http://query.nytimes.com/search/

New York Times. (September 13, 1908). The greatest system in the country. *New York Times.* Retrieved from http://query.nytimes.com/search/

New York Times. (July 17, 1921). 30 Psychologists wanted in schools. *New York Times.* Retrieved from http://query.nytimes.com/search/

New York Times. (June 1, 1923). The Henry St. Settlement celebrates its 20th anniversary. *New York Times.* Retrieved from http://query.nytimes.com/search/

Osgood, R. L. (1999). Becoming a special educator: Specialized professional training for teachers of children with disabilities in Boston, 1870–1930. *Teachers College Record, 101*, 82–105.

Osgood, R. L. (2005). *The history of inclusion in the United States.* Washington, DC: Gallaudet University Press.

Osgood, R. L. (2008). *The history of special education; a struggle for equality in American public schools* . Greenwich, CT: Greenwood.

Pritchard, D. G. (1963). *Education and the handicapped 1760–1960.* London: Routledge & Kegan Paul.

Safford, L., & Safford, E. J. (1996). *A history of childhood and disability.* New York, NY: Teachers' College Press.

Sarason, S. B., & Doris, J. (1979). *Educational handicap, public policy, and social history: a broadened perspective on mental retardation.* New York, NY: Free Press.

Scheerenberger, R. C. (1987). *A history of mental retardation.* Baltimore, MD: P. H. Brookes.

Sears, R. R. (1975). Your ancients revisited. In E. M. Hetherington (Ed.), *Review of child development research* (Vol. 5, pp. 1–73). Chicago: University of Chicago Press.

Smith, J. D. (1998). Histories of special education: Stories from our past, insights for our future. *Remedial and Special Education, 19*, 196–200.

Trent, J. W. (1994). *Inventing the feeble mind: A history of mental retardation in the United States.* Berkeley: University of California Press.

Wald, L. D. (1912, Oct. 5). The feeble-minded in the schools. (Letter to the Editor). *New York Times.* Retrieved from http://query.nytimes.com/search/

Wiederholt, J. L. (1974). Historical perspectives on the education of the learning disabled. In L. Mann & D. Sabatino (Eds.), *The second review of special education* (pp. 103–152). Philadelphia: JSE Press.

Winzer, M. A. (1993). *The history of special education from isolation to integration.* Washington, DC: Gallaudet University Press.

Woodill, G. (1995). From charity and exclusion to emerging independence: An introduction to the history of disabilities. *Journal on Developmental Disabilities, 4*, 1–11.

Yell, M. L., Rogers, D., & Rogers, E. L. (1998). The legal history of special education: What a long, strange trip it's been!" *Remedial and Special Education, 19*, 219–228.

2
Contemporary Issues

James M. Kauffman
University of Virginia

C. Michael Nelson
University of Kentucky

Richard L. Simpson
University of Kansas

Devery R. Mock
Appalachian State University

Most important issues in special education are both contemporary and perpetual. Never fully resolved, they must be revisited by every generation. The perpetual issues of *who*, *how*, and *where* (Bateman, 1994) suggest questions: Who should receive special education, and who should teach it? How should students be identified, and what and where should they be taught? These core questions have been pertinent since special education was invented and likely will always be important.

Basic issues are overlapping and perpetual. The conceptual underpinnings of special education clearly involve at least how and whom to teach and lead us to ask how we make decisions. Response to intervention (RtI) involves both whom to serve and how to do it. School-wide positive behavior support (SWPBS) involves how and who and where. (Our use of PBIS or positive behavioral interventions and support should not be confused with the faddish, anti-scientific rejection of all aversive consequences described by Mulick and Butter, 2005; our view is that punishment has a legitimate role in behavior management, albeit the emphasis should be overwhelmingly on positive support.) Disproportionality and cultural sensitivity are about who, how, and where. Inclusion involves more than where. Teacher education involves all perpetual issues. We discuss four issues: basic concepts, decision-making, inclusion, and teacher education.

Perpetual issues wax and wane, but they are seemingly permanent fixtures of our lives. They may appear in different guises in different eras, but their renaming or "reframing" is a mere change of costume, not a change of essence. Thus, at some level all of the issues of concept and practice that we address in this chapter are recycled—addressed anew and perhaps in new terminology. However, none is something that no one has ever thought of before.

Conceptual Underpinnings

Conceptual or philosophical issues are particularly controversial in contemporary special education. Basic philosophical issues are certainly not peculiar to special education, nor are the controversies about doubt, certainty, or the best bases for human dignity or social justice anything new (cf. Blackburn, 2005; Hecht, 2003; Neiman, 2008). Nevertheless, after a period of relative philosophical quiescence, during which a natural science approach was clearly dominant in special education, alternatives to Enlightenment thinking have been proposed with considerable vigor. This has occurred following a rise in interest in alternative ideas in philosophy and attempts to apply these ideas to the humanities and what have been called "social sciences" (Kauffman, Brigham, & Mock, 2004; Kauffman & Sasso, 2006a, 2006b; Sasso, 2001, 2007). Because Enlightenment science has been the dominant way of thinking about exceptionality, we first summarize our understanding of the role of science in special education.

The Role of Science in Special Education

For most of its history, special education has depended on rational analysis and the tenets of Enlightenment science. In many ways, what we know as special education was invented within a century of the Enlightenment era of discovery of science, and it has depended primarily on scientific thinking about cognitive, emotional, and physical development and learning (cf. Kauffman, 2011; Kauffman & Landrum, 2006; Mann, 1979).

This is not to say that special education policies and practices have always been based on scientific evidence. Indeed, some of special education's great advances in policy (e.g., mandatory federal legislation in the United States) were made in the absence of scientific evidence. Nevertheless, scientific evidence has played a major role in many advances in educational practices, such as behavioral intervention and direct instruction (DI; Alberto & Troutman, 2009, Crockett, 2001; Crockett, Gerber, & Landrum, 2007; Kerr & Nelson, 2010; Mostert, Kavale, & Kauffman, 2008).

Emphasis on evidence-based education is essentially an appeal to science (cf. Detrich, Keyworth, & States, 2008; Morris & Mather, 2008). The evidence to which "evidence-based" refers in most discussions of teaching is empirical and quantitative, depending on inquiry in the Enlightenment scientific tradition. It is not the idiosyncratic, subjective, personal beliefs to which some may appeal.

The Challenge of Postmodernism and Other Anti-Scientific Ideologies

Gallagher (1998, 2004) questioned the scientific foundations of special education, apparently assuming that ideological beliefs cannot be questioned by data because the idea of objective data is itself untenable. Proponents of nonscientific views think that others will eventually understand that their ideas are true regardless of any "so-called" objective evidence to the contrary ("so-called" because the proponents of these ideas believe that the existence of objective evidence is impossible or that such evidence is not as important as their philosophy). As Conquest (2000) notes, postmodernism and other anti-scientific ideologies require the acceptance of an Idea (an ideology, signified by the capital letter) that cannot be refuted by data. The Idea is an abandonment of knowledge and judgment in favor of the intrigue of the Idea. Under the guise of being intellectually intriguing, ideology is anti-intellectualism of the highest order. Conquest suggests that Ideologies inevitably bring catastrophe, usually in the form of authoritarianism but also because of their refusal to recognize the existence of objective data indicating success or failure that does not correspond to the Idea. In special education, some have asserted that faulty, anti-scientific notions could signal the decline, if not the demise, of special education (e.g., Anastasiou & Kauffman, 2010, 2011; Heward, 2003; Heward & Silvestri, 2005; Kauffman, 1999, 2011; Kauffman et al., 2004; Kauffman & Sasso, 2006a, 2006b; Mostert et al., 2008; Sasso, 2001, 2007).

From a scientific viewpoint, disability is objectifiable, although admittedly an arbitrary designation. A disability is assumed to be a measurable difference from normal or typical in an individual's ability to accomplish particular tasks. The extent of the measured difference from normal is arbitrary but is assumed to have an objective reality. Likewise, a student's performance is assumed to be a measurable, objective reality. Anti-scientific visions of disability and performance reject such assumptions of objective reality. They call into question, on basic philosophical or ideological grounds, all attempts to objectify and measure both disability and learning.

Complicating the matter of scientific underpinnings is the claim that postmodern views are, in fact, scientific, albeit not scientific in the Enlightenment tradition. Makers of this claim do not want to be excluded in discussions of science, although their views are not scientific in the usual sense. For example, Erickson and Gutierrez (2002) and St. Pierre (2002) complain that their perspectives were excluded by Shavelson and Towne (2002; see Towne, Wise, & Winters, 2005). Arguments that "alternative science" has been ignored complicate the discrimination of reliable scientific evidence from false claims. Perhaps it is wise to recognize what postmodernism is at a conceptual level:

> Drawing on a range of theoretical perspectives (critical theory, postcolonial theory, poststructuralism), postmodern scholars question the modern belief in the power of science to objectively determine the universal laws of human development…. Instead, science is viewed as a social construction, imbued with the values of its creators and therefore enacting a particular set of power relations in its application. (Ryan & Grieshaber, 2005, p. 35)

Ideologists make their ideas intellectually intriguing and ostensibly rational while rejecting rationality. Their ideology is actually the ultimate anti-intellectualism, for it is the subjugation of reason to belief (Neiman, 2008). Postmodern ideology makes frequent use of words like "social justice," "critical theory," "postcolonial," and "poststructural." It appears not to recognize that the revolutionary idea of Enlightenment science was and is liberating. Those who bash the Enlightenment seem determined to misinterpret its benefits in achieving social justice and equality. An important feature of Enlightenment science is its assumption of common (i.e., scientific) knowledge as opposed to idiosyncratic "knowledges" or ways of knowing that are alternatives to reason.

A particularly important challenge for special education of the 21st century is reaffirming its scientific and logical foundations and rejecting alternative conceptualizations of disability and progress in helping students with disabilities learn. This is not easy, as postmodernism has already made significant inroads in some of the other academic disciplines from which special education draws important concepts (e.g., psychology; see Kauffman, 2010b; Kauffman & Sasso, 2006a; Krueger, 2002; Ruscio, 2002). Moreover, special education must contend with the postmodern suggestion that science is just another ideology (e.g., Brantlinger, 1997). Such suggestions miss the point (see Blackburn, 2005; Kauffman, 2011; Neiman, 2008). Unlike ideological claims that dismiss as irrelevant any empirical evidence contrary to the Idea, Enlightenment science subjects itself to the same scrutiny it requires of all other claims.

Decision-Making Frameworks

The federal No Child Left Behind law (NCLB) and the Individuals with Disabilities Education Act (IDEIA, or simply IDEA) have focused attention on "evidence-based practices" with students at risk of failing or placement in special education. IDEA encourages schools to use RtI as a process for identifying students who require more intensive instruction or intervention. For example, it permits districts to "use a process that determines if the child responds to scientific, research-based intervention as a part of the evaluation procedures," to identify students with learning difficulties in lieu of a discrepancy between ability and achievement (PL 108-446 § 614[b][6][A]; § 614[b][2 & 3]). SWPBS also uses RtI logic as a basis for deciding what levels of support are needed and for determining whether adjustments in instruction or intervention are needed (Cheney, Flower, & Templeton, 2008; Fairbanks, Sugai, Guardino, & Lathrop, 2007). Although initially intended for academic instruction, RtI offers a basis for decisions about students' need for more intensive instruction *or* behavioral intervention, as well as for evaluating intervention effectiveness.

Characteristics of the RtI and SWPBS Logic

RtI is typically composed of at least the following: (a) a continuum of evidence-based services available to all students, from the universal to the highly intensive and individualized (Marston, Muyskens, Lau, & Canter, 2003); (b) points for deciding whether students are performing significantly below same-age peers academically or behaviorally (Vaughn, Linan-Thompson, & Hickman, 2003); (c) ongoing monitoring of progress (Gresham et al., 2005); (d) more intensive or different intervention when students do not improve; and (e) evaluation for special education services if students do not respond as expected (Fuchs, Mock, Morgan, & Young, 2003).

School safety, zero tolerance, use of exclusionary discipline (i.e., suspension, expulsion), and student retention and matriculation have prompted educators to consider a more preventative approach to student discipline (Mayer, 2006; Sugai & Horner, 2008). SWPBS, now being implemented in thousands of schools across the United States, focuses on preventing problem behavior through teaching and reinforcing appropriate student behaviors. Two major features of SWPBS are (a) conceptualizing schools as "host environments," and (b) a focus on improving the capacity of the host environment (school setting) to support the use of effective practices (Sugai & Horner, 2007). Strategies that promote positive behavior across the total school environment (e.g., SWPBS) reduce disciplinary referrals, improve school climate, and are associated with gains in academic performance (Horner et al., 2009; Sugai & Horner, 2008).

Why should a school-wide initiative that affects all students be considered a special education issue? A prime example of an ill-fated attempt by special educators to induce a change in general education was the regular education initiative (REI) of the 1990s (see Nelson & Kauffman, 2009). And like REI, SWPBS has been crafted by special educators; unlike REI, general education has the dominant role in implementation of SWPBS. Also, because it uses RtI decision-making and intervention processes, SWPBS functionally links assessment for intervention to assessment for special education identification.

RtI and SWPBS share several common features. Conceptually, both are based on a problem-solving model and emphasize the use of evidence-based practices based on a multitiered intervention process, in which progressively more-intensive interventions are provided to students who fail with less-concentrated interventions (Sandomierski, Kincaid, & Algozzine, 2007; Sailor, Doolittle, Bradley, & Danielson, 2009). Widely used in public health, this model has only recently been applied in other human service agencies, including education, mental health, social work, and crime prevention. Both RtI and SWPBS emerged, at least in part, as an alternative to waiting until a student's academic or behavioral failure has been obvious or protracted before initiating more powerful interventions (Sailor et al., 2009; Scheuermann & Lawrence, 2007). Both initiatives typically are facilitated by multidisciplinary teams (Sugai & Horner, 2008).

SWPBS and RtI have several common features in application. Interventions are organized in progressively more intensive tiers linked to a decision-making framework. The primary tier emphasizes prevention of academic failure or problem behavior through universal practices involving all staff and applied to all students. The secondary tier is for students who have not been successful with primary tier interventions or who are at higher risk. The tertiary tier is reserved for students who are not responsive to primary *or* secondary level interventions, or who demonstrate serious, chronic problems. At this level, the process of identifying students for special education eligibility may be initiated. Across all three tiers the emphasis is on team-based planning and use of an array of assessment information for effective decision-making (Sandomierski et al., 2007; Sailor et al., 2009; Sugai & Horner, 2008).

Federal legislation and the logic of RtI and SWPBS have placed increasing pressure on schools to select and use evidence-based practices for academic instruction and behavioral intervention. This raises several important questions: How are these practices identified? What is the evidence base for practices for students with or at risk of disabilities? Are they effectively used?

How Are Evidence-Based Practices Identified?

The term "evidence-based practices" and "research validated practices" are used interchangeably to designate educational practices that have been documented as effective through empirical research. Fixen, Naoom, Blasé,

Friedman, and Wallace (2005) make a further distinction between evidence-based *practices* and evidence-based *programs*. Programs are groups of practices that share a common rationale. Practices are specific components of programs—procedures that can be used by individuals.

The NCLB law defines "scientifically based research" as "research that involves the application of rigorous, systematic, and objective procedures to obtain reliable and valid knowledge relevant to education activities and programs" (NCLB, 20 U.S.C. § 7801 (37)). Efforts to establish standards for evidence-based practice and to identify strategies and programs that meet these standards are ongoing. Professional groups and government agencies have been engaged in evaluating and sorting the knowledge base of practices into categories variously labeled "best practice," "promising practice," "blueprint programs," "promising programs," "empirically supported," and "well established and probably efficacious" (e.g., American Federation of Teachers; Center for the Study and Prevention of Violence; Council for Exceptional Children; Division 12 Task Force of the American Psychological Association; Office of the Surgeon General; Safe, Disciplined, and Drug-Free Expert Panel; Substance Abuse and Mental Health Services Administration; Task Force on Evidence-Based Interventions in School Psychology; U.S. Department of Education's Institute of Education Sciences). These agencies and organizations have proposed an array of criteria for how the research literature should be examined to determine the level of experimental rigor and for the degree of confidence with which any statement about "evidence-based" effects can be claimed. Although these criteria vary, they contain several common elements: (a) use of a sound experimental or evaluation design and appropriate analytical procedures; (b) empirical validation of effects; (c) clear implementation procedures; (d) replication of outcomes across implementation sites; and (e) evidence of sustainability (Kerr & Nelson, 2010; Mayer, 2006). Sugai and Horner (2007) further suggest that any claim that a practice or procedure is evidence-based should be framed in the context of (a) explicit description of the procedure or practice, (b) clear definition of the settings and implementers who use the procedure/practice, (c) identification of the population of individuals who are expected to benefit, and (d) the specific outcomes expected.

The U.S. Department of Education's Institute of Education Sciences established the What Works Clearinghouse (WWC, 2008), which adopted a set of "evidence standards" to help educators and education policymakers incorporate scientifically-based research into their educational decisions. The WWC uses these standards to "identify research studies that provide the strongest evidence of effects: primarily, well-conducted randomized controlled trials and regression discontinuity studies, and secondarily quasi-experimental studies of especially strong design" (Available at: http://www.w-w-c.org/reviewprocess/standards.html). A summary of suggestions for defining evidence-based practices from quantitative (Gersten et al., 2005) and single subject (Horner et al., 2005) research methods were reviewed for educational literature in a special issue of *Exceptional Children* (Odom et al., 2005). Cook, Tankersley, and Landrum (2009) have led groups of researchers using the "quality indicators" (the features identified by the Gersten et al. and Horner et al. as present in high-quality group research and single-subject studies) to begin the process of developing guidelines for evidence-based practices in special education.

One consequence of multiple groups conducting independent reviews of practices is that the criteria used by different groups are not identical; thus, a practice that one group deems "effective" or "best" practice may not be designated as such by another. For example, DI is widely cited as an effective, research-based practice in the professional literature (Simonsen, Fairbanks, Briesch, Myers, & Sugai, 2008; Yell, 2009). Yet the WWC concluded from its review of DI research that no studies met eligibility standards. J. W. Lloyd (personal communication, May, 2007) observed that

> Part of the reason for these outcomes may be [the] work model that the WWC uses. The lead researchers conceptualize the question and lead the effort, but most of the actual analysis is conducted by early career research assistants who are to apply a set of procedures. They may faithfully apply those procedures without sufficient contextual knowledge to capture some of the nuance inherent in virtually any body of literature.

Another issue with respect to the rules used to identify research-validated practices is the insistence on research designs involving randomized controlled trials (RCTs) as the "gold standard." A key element of such designs is, of course, random assignment of subjects to comparison conditions—a requirement difficult to meet in schools, and one that is antithetical to addressing goals in the IEPs of students with disabilities. Another requirement of RCT research is having sufficiently large samples of subjects in both experimental and comparison groups to compensate for measurement errors and subject attrition. This requirement most assuredly is alien to the demographics of special education. An alternative is to use single-subject research designs, but the WWC is still developing evidence standards for single-case designs (WWC, December 2008). Cook et al. (2009) noted the dearth of group research relative to single subject designs in special education, and quoted Viadero and Huff's (2006) wry reference to the WWC as the "nothing works clearinghouse" (p. 8). In the meantime, Department of Education funding for research involving single subject designs has practically dried up, and single-subject research are not even mentioned in early 21st century publications regarding the science of education by the National Research Council (Shavelson & Towne, 2002; Towne, Wise, & Winters, 2005). It seems incongruous that research involving careful manipulation of independent variables, precise and continuous measurement of dependent variables, with resulting high levels of internal validity (Kennedy, 2005) can be given short shrift in a field that is essentially based on single case evaluation.

What Is the Evidence Base for Practices in Special Education?

The use of evidence-based practices in the context of RtI decision-making is not confined to special education. To the contrary, effective practices are important to ensuring the academic and behavioral success of *all* students. Despite the variance among professionals and organizations regarding the evidence base for practices used with students in special education, substantial research supports the use of instructional practices that increase academic engaged time, produce high rates of correct academic responding, and increase content covered (Yell, 2009). Strategies that produce such outcomes include brisk instructional pacing, reviewing students' work frequently, giving systematic and constructive corrective feedback, minimizing pupil errors and providing frequent praise for correct responding, offering guided practice, modeling new behaviors, providing transitions between lessons or concepts, and monitoring student performance (Darch & Kame'enui, 2004; Kame'enui, Carnine, Dixon, Simmons, & Coyne, 2002; Landrum, Tankersley, & Kauffman, 2003; Lewis, Hudson, Richter, & Johnson, 2004; Mercer & Mercer, 2005; Rosenshine, 1997, 2008). On the behavioral side, empirical support for strategies that support desired behavior and prevent or reduce undesired behavior is plentiful (Kerr & Nelson, 2010; Yell, Meadows, Drasgow, & Shriner, 2009). These include structuring the environment, clarifying expectations, providing active supervision, using contingent praise, giving precision requests, using precorrection and behavioral momentum, applying corrective feedback, providing direct instruction in social skills, and using group-oriented contingencies and response-contingent punishment procedures such as reprimands, response cost, and time out (Alberto & Troutman, 2009; Kerr & Nelson, 2010; Landrum & Kauffman, 2006; Landrum et al., 2003; Lewis et al., 2004; Simonsen et al., 2008; Yell et al., 2009). Fixen et al. (2005) identify a number of evidence-based "manualized practices" (i.e., those that are guided by specific steps or instructions), including cognitive mapping, cognitive behavior therapy, the good behavior game, systematic desensitization, and token economy systems. In spite of the availability of many effective practices, we must ask: To what extent are they used?

Do Educators use Evidence-Based Practices Effectively?

Teacher access to effective evidence-based practices depends on training and dissemination. Pre-service teachers are exposed to a variety of curricula to learn academic and behavioral strategies. However, professors are not required to prepare teachers to use evidence-based practices. Most general educators receive *little* or *no* instruction in practices proven to be effective in managing the behavior of diverse learners. This is particularly alarming because the majority of students with disabilities are educated in general education classrooms by general education teachers (U.S. Department of Education, 2006). Teachers may have access to information regarding evidence-based practices through professional development. Certification programs offer the same potential shortcomings as pre-service teacher preparation, and professional development activities are affected by logistical constraints and decisions by school district administrators or boards of education. The trend toward providing on-line pre- and in-service training is alarming because the effective development of fluency in instructional or intervention skills requires direct, hands-on instruction. Paper-and-pencil assessment of pedagogical skills defies explanation.

Teachers can access information *about* effective practices through the Internet and professional reading. The WWC web site offers detailed descriptions of practices that meet its standards of evidence. The Council for Exceptional Children's Division of Learning Disabilities and the Division for Research jointly publish periodic user-friendly summaries of research on specific practices, *Current Practice Alerts,* alerting readers to practices that are clearly effective ("Go for it") and those whose effectiveness is more doubtful ("Use caution"). Professional journals publish frequent research reports and reviews. Naturally, this begs the question, "If we build it, will they come?"

Concerning the application of evidence-based practices in clinical psychology, Kazdin (2008) observed that controlled research studies introduce such features as randomized selection of participants, standardized application of treatments and fixed content and length of treatment substantially different from the conditions under which they are used in the field. To what extent can we be sure that professionals in the field use practices with the same fidelity as when they were validated through research? Some practices, such as those used in the implementation of SWPBS, do include tools to assess fidelity of implementation (e.g., Sugai et al., 2005), but this is far from typical. So too, is the use of manualized treatments (Kauffman, 2010a; Mayer, 2006). Fixen et al. (2005) observed that, in medicine, the effort to eliminate errors, reduce variability, and improve consumer outcomes through reducing research findings and best practices to "clinical guidelines" has proven difficult as physicians' adherence to these guidelines often diminishes over time. On the other hand, intervention protocols that do not allow practitioners to adapt procedures to existing conditions are not likely to be accepted or effective. Cook et al. (2009) expressed their belief that evidence-based practices "should interface with the professional wisdom of teachers to maximize the outcomes of students with disabilities" (p. 380).

We have been careful to portray both RtI and SWPBS as decision models, not as practices, although SWPBS incorporates practices that do have an evidence base (Simonsen et al., 2008), and randomized controlled trials are underway to evaluate the relative effects of SWPBS (Horner et al., 2009). In this context, using RtI or SWPBS as a framework for making important educational decisions presents difficult questions. Even if data help us judge fidelity of implementation and outcomes, how can we verify that instruction or behavior intervention is so good that students can be identified by their lack of response to it? How much response to good practice is sufficient to conclude that the student is no longer at risk of failure? Under what specific conditions should a more intensive intervention be implemented? The answers to these questions are important because they will guide educators toward making decisions that are based on evidence, not on what is available or popular (Nelson & Kauffman, 2009).

Disproportionality and Cultural Sensitivity

Disproportionality

In special education, disproportionality refers to a difference between a given group's proportion of the child population and that group's proportion of children identified for a particular category of special education or for special education without reference to category. Disproportionality may involve any identifiable group and may be characterized by over-representation or under-representation. For example, if males comprise 50% of the child population but 80% of those identified as emotionally disturbed for special education purposes, then they are over-represented in the emotionally disturbed category. Categories may involve males combined with other identities (e.g., Hispanic males). Disproportionality of ethnic or color groups has received most attention. The facts of disproportionality are often in doubt or are poorly understood. Annual reports to Congress on implementation of federal special education law and other research clearly show that not all "children of color" (those not White) are overidentified for special education (see Donovan & Cross, 2002). However, the data also unequivocally show disproportional over-representation of African American students in some categories of special education, particularly emotional disturbance and mental retardation.

A common error in thinking about disproportionality is confusion of the percentage of a group in the general population of children and the percentage of that group comprising those identified for special education. For example, people may wrongly assume that if 25% of students receiving special education are from group X, then 25% of group X has been identified for special education. Actually, if 1% of children who comprise group X are identified for a given category of special education and 25% of the children receiving special education in that category are from group X, then 0.25% of the students in group X have been identified for that category. Still, if group X comprises 12.5% of the general population of children but 25% of those identified, then members of group X are disproportionately over-represented in that category by a factor of 2 (that is, they are twice as likely to be identified as would be expected based on their proportion of the general population of children).

In most societies, disproportional over-representation is seen as undesirable when the service following identification is disadvantageous, and under-representation is seen as undesirable when the service is advantageous (Kauffman & Landrum, 2009). The fact that special education in the early 21st century is seen by many to be ultimately more disadvantageous than advantageous is underscored by a statement from the U. S. Office of Education that states need not consider under-representation (Letter, 2008). Such appraisals of the consequences of identification for special education may be consistent with judgments that it is malicious and with predictions of its demise (Kauffman, 2009).

As of the early years of the 21st century, researchers have not found a reliable explanation of disproportionality in special education (Donovan & Cross, 2002; Kauffman & Landrum, 2009). Identification is subject to error, both false positive and false negative, and although the false positive must be risked more to achieve prevention, it is the error occasioning the most vociferous complaints about special education (see Kauffman, 2007; Kauffman, Mock, & Simpson, 2007; Kauffman, Simpson, & Mock, 2009).

Disproportionality in special education is most often assumed to be a matter of bias in evaluation and decision making. Alternatively, it may be a function of disproportionality in life circumstances outside of school, the assumption being that causal factors are disproportional across groups. Strict proportionality assumes that the causes of exceptionality are randomly distributed across all groups, which seems to us unlikely for many disabilities, particularly high incidence disorders (those occurring most frequently). We hope that future research will reveal why disproportionality occurs.

Cultural Sensitivity

Sensitivity to cultural differences among students and their families is required of all teachers. However, "cultural competence," "cultural sensitivity," "cultural responsiveness," and "cultural appropriateness" are often not defined so that a teacher is able to identify a practice that is multicultural or culturally responsive or a practice that is not. For example, the statement "*Culturally responsive teaching* refers to the extent to which educators use students' cultural contributions in transforming their lives and the lives of their families and communities by making education relevant and meaningful" (Shealey & Callins, 2007, p. 195) often leaves teachers uncertain about whether a particular teaching strategy is culturally responsive.

Constructivist views of education have become associated with cultural sensitivity (see Villegas & Lucas, 2007); in contrast, teacher-directed programs such as DI are assumed to be insensitive to cultural differences. Vavrus (2008) also defines "culturally responsive" teaching as "student-centered." Nevertheless, children do not seem to be differentially responsive to effective instruction depending on their color, national origin, gender, or religion. In fact, effective instruction seems not to depend on the cultural markers of ethnicity, socioeconomic level, gender, or religion. It seems virtually impossible for a teacher to be sensitive to individual children without being sensitive to their culture, although differentiating instruction on the basis of a presumptive cultural marker with the aim of being culturally sensitive could reduce sensitivity to individuals (see Kauffman, Conroy, Gardner, & Oswald, 2008).

Given the evidence regarding effective instruction and cultural diversity, our view is that cultural sensitivity is better approached as a part of effective instruction rather than as a separate objective (e.g., Carnine, Silbert, Kame'enui, & Tarver, 2005, 2010). To the extent that a teacher offers truly effective instruction, it will be culturally sensitive (Coyne, Kame'enui, & Carnine, 2006). That is, effective instruction is necessary and sufficient to insure cultural sensitivity; cultural sensitivity is necessary but not sufficient to insure effective instruction.

Inclusion in Theory and Practice

Our earlier observation that salient issues in the field of special education are perpetual and overlapping is well illustrated by the inclusion issue, which is unmatched. Countless authors have identified a wide array of placement options for students with disabilities, generally ranging from only general education (full inclusion) to highly restrictive and specialized settings such as residential and institutional programs. Disagreement about the desirability of various placement options is longstanding and strident. Beliefs about the extent to which students with disabilities should be integrated with non-disabled students also remain controversial. Moreover, perceptions of the most and least preferred placement options are likely to be little more than reflections of individuals' values and emotional judgments. Many or most of these placement preferences do not rest clearly on scientific fact. Indeed, even if stakeholders aspire to make inclusion decisions using empirically-based research, they encounter a paucity of scientific evidence linked to the types of settings best geared to provide the most appropriate instruction. Research does not clearly indicate that one type of placement is most apt to lead to maximum academic and social benefits (Fuchs & Fuchs, 1994; Kauffman, Mock, Tankersley, & Landrum, 2008; MacMillan, Gresham, & Forness, 1996; Simpson & Sasso, 1992; Zigmond, 2003).

Inclusion has long been a judgment based primarily on civil rights arguments (Kauffman & Landrum, 2009). Advocates have perceived inclusion as a matter of legislative and legal evenhandedness, impartial justice, human values, and emotionally-driven belief systems frequently unrelated to proven educational and behavioral benefit (see Simpson & Kauffman, 2007; Stainback & Stainback, 1991). Consider, for example, educational reformers of the 1980s and 1990s who argued for unfettered integration of students with disabilities and challenged the efficacy and appropriateness of separate classes. Without convincing empirical evidence, they argued that separate classes and resource rooms were ineffective, stigmatizing, and exclusionary (e.g., Blackman, 1992; Reynolds, Wang, & Walberg, 1987; Stainback & Stainback, 1991). They also argued, again without logical scientific evidence linking outcomes to settings, that all students with disabilities were best served in general education classrooms and that students with special needs were the shared responsibility of general and special educators (Wang, Reynolds, & Walberg, 1986). Ironically, there is remarkably little concern that inclusion has been the subject of so little objective, scientific investigation. This irony is compounded by movement of education toward a more scientific enterprise.

How and why inclusion has escaped the eye of educational science is unclear. Unfortunately, scant evidence indicates that inclusion arguments based on something other than science and reason will be abandoned in the foreseeable future. In part, this may be due to the fact that the most avid promoters of inclusion tend to be the most avid consumers of postmodern ideologies. However, philosophical differences related to inclusion are not the only explanations for the present quandary. Conflicting interpretations of law related to inclusion are also factors (Bateman, 2007; Crockett & Kauffman, 1999; Simpson, de Boer-Ott, & Myles, 2003). For example, there is no agreement about whether the term "inclusion" refers to both partial and full inclusion or whether all children and adolescents with disabilities—no exceptions—should be included in general education settings. To us, it is alarming that there is so little basic agreement about what constitutes the least restrictive environment. Inclusion has real-world consequences and meaning for students. Teachers, related service personnel, administrators, and parents regularly confront the challenge of when and how to integrate students with disabilities into general education programs most efficiently and effectively.

Flaws in the current system have created problems and exacerbated the challenges of providing a high quality education, particularly for children and youth who have learning and behavior difficulties (MacMillan et al., 1996). Careful, individualized planning based on use of empirically-based effective practices is a prerequisite for success. We think it is obvious that a possible explanation for the relatively poor outcomes for many students with disabilities who are educated in general education settings is that their inclusion-based education has been woefully lacking in methods that have been objectively vetted in a variety of typical general education classrooms. We recommend that students with disabilities who are placed in general education settings be the beneficiaries of empirically supported methods and strategies. We further recommend that the same level of attention historically devoted to inclusion philosophy and legislation be given to the development of procedures and strategies that ensure the success of learners with disabilities in a variety of settings. We recommend more concern for what students learn than for where they learn it (Kauffman & Hung, 2009).

A basic step toward making inclusion more thoughtful, objective, and utilitarian is support of research that addresses socially valid, inclusion-related outcomes and targets. This step requires that inclusion be a clearly identified and managed independent variable. Research should address such basic questions as: (a) Do learners with disabilities in inclusion programs make better academic gains than their peers who are in non-inclusion programs or who spend less time in general education contact? (b) Do learners with disabilities enrolled in inclusion programs demonstrate better social competence and more positive peer and adult relationships than their peers in more restrictive programs? (c) Do typically developing and achieving peers have more positive or less positive perceptions of students with disabilities as a consequence of the inclusion of students with disabilities in general education programs? (d) Are post-school outcomes such as employment, incarceration, social service, and mental health contacts improved by students' inclusion in general education?

Finally, we note that for far too many advocates inclusion is more about placement than about learning, much to the detriment of the purpose of placement. Warnock (2005) recommended that

> The idea of inclusion should be rethought insofar at least as it applies to education at school. If it is too much to hope that it will be demoted from its present position at the top of the list of educational values, then at least let it be redefined so that it allows children to pursue the common goals of education in the environment within which they can best be taught to learn. (p. 50)

Warnock suggests that inclusion has been supported and promoted by social philosophy and ideology. To us, it seems to be a well-intentioned idea rooted primarily in a misinterpretation of civil rights laws (Kauffman & Landrum, 2009) and magical thinking about disability and effective instruction. We agree with Warnock that "Inclusion should mean being involved in a common enterprise of learning, rather than being necessarily under the same roof" (p. 36).

Teacher Education

The preparation of teachers is another perpetual issue in special education. Here, we offer only a sketch of the problem, to which the following chapter in this section is devoted. To emphasize its contemporary aspects, we note the current policy context: "In the current policy context, much is at stake for teacher educators. We have been challenged to demonstrate the warrant of our work and to do so using the high standard of impact on student outcomes" (Sindelar, Bishop, Brownell, Rosenberg, & Connelly, 2005, p. 45).

The current policy context is best understood by first examining three precipitating events in the beginning of the 21st century. Reauthorization of the Elementary and Secondary Education Act (better known as NCLB) in 2001 mandated that states: (a) set measureable goals for student achievement; (b) implement instructional practices with scientific research bases; and (c) ensure that all students participate in and make adequate yearly progress on annual state assessments. States or schools failing to meet these standards faced fiscal sanctions and corrective actions. Rosenberg, Sindelar, and Hardman (2004) suggested that the era preceding NCLB was one of "high-stakes accountability" (p. 268). Indeed, by the close of the 20th century, 40 states had implemented, or were in the process of implementing, assessments that could potentially result in significant consequences for both schools and teachers (Thurlow, 2000).

Beyond its accountability requirements, NCLB also mandated that all teachers be *highly qualified* by 2006. To be highly qualified, teachers were to: (a) hold at least a bachelor's degree from a college or university; (b) achieve full state certification or licensure; and (c) demonstrate subject-matter competency in core academic subjects in which they teach. This law expanded federal involvement in an unprecedented way and marked the first time that the federal government defined what it means to be a highly qualified teacher. Noticeably absent from this definition was the importance of pedagogy in teacher training.

In 2002, Secretary of Education Rod Paige issued his report on teacher quality (U.S. Department of Education, 2002). He highlighted verbal ability and subject matter competence as the two teacher variables most closely related to student achievement. His report also contained strong criticism of traditional teacher preparation, suggesting that such programs and the institutions that house them produce unprepared teachers who are academically weaker and less likely to remain in the classroom than individuals who pursued alternative routes to licensure. Implicit in both NCLB and the Secretary's report was the assertion that *highly qualified teachers* are also *teachers of high quality* (Rosenberg et al., 2004), creating the expectation of producing highly qualified teachers with less training, not more.

The Individuals with Disabilities Education Improvement Act, like its predecessors, was intended to safeguard the educational rights of students with disabilities. It also sought to bring IDEA into alignment with NCLB (Yell, Shriner, & Katsiyannis, 2006). To this end, special educators were to be highly qualified teachers, students with disabilities were to be included in statewide assessments, and special education practices were to be based on peer-reviewed research.

Unfortunately, both NCLB and IDEA ignore pedagogical expertise and emphasize subject area knowledge. Researchers have cautioned that subject area knowledge alone does not ensure that teachers can and will offer effective instruction (Berliner, 2004; Bromley, 2005; Hamre & Pianta, 2005). We maintain that training and hiring teachers who are highly qualified under NCLB and IDEA may result in undesired consequences for special education: "Whereas our problem had been a shortage of fully certified teachers, it soon may become a shortage of adequately prepared teachers" (Rosenberg et al., 2004, p. 271).

In traditional teacher training programs, teacher candidates typically acquire proficiency in (a) knowledge of learners, (b) understanding of curriculum content and goals, and (c) understanding of and skills for teaching (Darling-Hammond & Baratz-Snowden, 2005). Candidates regularly earn teaching licensure in specific domains and then accept teaching positions at elementary, middle, and high schools across the United States. Despite this ready supply of licensed candidates, our educational system has difficulty hiring and retaining qualified teachers (Crutchfield, 1997; Hanushek, Kain, & Rivkin, 2001; Rossi & Grossman, 2002). For the past two decades, more teachers have left than entered the profession (Darling-Hammond, 2003). Attrition in the first few years of teaching is an especially grave problem. The Texas Center for Educational Research estimated that each beginning teacher who left in the first few years of employment cost the system $8,000 (2000; as cited in Darling-Hammond, 2003). Furthermore, evidence suggests that effectiveness increases sharply after the first few years of teaching (Kain & Singleton, 1996); thus, beginning-teacher attrition carries a significant instructional cost. Another group of individuals at high risk for attrition are teachers who enter classrooms lacking full certification (Henke, Chen, & Geis, 2000; Miller, Brownell, & Smith, 1999). Henke, Chen, and Geis reported that 29% of teachers who had not participated in a supervised student teaching experience before entering the classroom left the profession within the first five years. In comparison, only 15% of teachers completing student teaching left the classroom within the same period. Henke, Chen, Geis, and Knepper (2000) found that teachers who entered the classroom without specific training and supervision in pedagogy left the profession at nearly twice the rate of those who had completed such training.

In the current policy context, teacher educators have been called upon to demonstrate the warrant of their work. Specifically, they have been called to conduct rigorous research in impossible settings to account for the influence that teacher training has on student achievement. In a context that is to be ostensibly ordered by logic and science, it seems surprising to conceive of a less intensive form of teacher training that would actually yield more qualified teachers.

Future Directions

We could discuss many more specific contemporary issues. All have long roots, as Gerber's initial chapter in this volume suggests. For example, we might discuss how special education could be integrated with a variety of clinical services to children, making the school the center for a variety of services that could be "wrapped around" students and their families. Emphasis on the contemporary encourages the idea that this is a new idea and ignores the fact that this has been an often-described model for decades (e.g., Rothman & Berkowitz, 1967).

The direction special education will take is anyone's guess (Kauffman, 2008). Special education could collapse and become an invisible part of general education. This is particularly likely if general education is considered best for all students. Alternatively, special education may shrink to include only the most severe disabilities. This seems most likely if special education is thought to have become too large or to serve many students who do not actually need it. Still another possibility is that special education will come to be seen as a good idea that needs improvement, resulting in better teacher preparation and more specialized, effective instruction. That future might be realized if special education is considered to be primarily about instruction, not place, and if the success of special education is judged by what students achieve with it versus without it. What happens will be determined in large measure by societal attitudes toward children and public concepts of fairness.

References

Alberto, P. A., & Troutman, A. C. (2009). *Applied behavior analysis for teachers* (8th ed.). Upper Saddle River, NJ: Pearson Merrill Prentice Hall.

Anastasiou, D., & Kauffman, J. M. (2010). Disability as cultural difference: Implications for special education. *Remedial and Special Education.* OnlineFirst, doi:10.1177/0741932510383163

Anastasiou, D., & Kauffman, J. M. (2011). A social constructivist approach to disability: Implications for special education. *Exceptional Children, 77,* 367–384.

Bateman, B. D. (1994). Who, how, and where: Special education's issues in perpetuity. *Journal of Special Education, 27,* 509–520.

Bateman, B. D. (2007). Law and the conceptual foundations of special education practice. In J. B. Crockett, M. M. Gerber, & T. J. Landrum (Eds.), *Achieving the radical reform of special education: Essays in honor of James M. Kauffman* (pp. 95–114). Mahwah, NJ: Erlbaum.

Berliner, D. C. (2004). Describing the behavior and document the accomplishments of expert teachers. *Bulletin of Science, Technology & Society, 24*(3), 200–212.

Blackburn, S. (2005). *Truth: A guide.* New York: Oxford University Press.

Blackman, H. P. (1992). Surmounting the disability of isolation. *The School Administrator, 49*(2), 28–29.

Brantlinger, E. (1997). Using ideology: Cases of nonrecognition of the politics of research and practice in special education. *Review of Educational Research, 67,* 425–460.

Bromley, A. (2005, November 18). Good teachers: Testing won't determine them, Pianta says. *Inside UVA, 35*(20), 1–2.

Carnine, D.W., Silbert, J., & Kame'enui, E. J., & Tarver, S. G. (2005). *Teaching struggling and at-risk readers: A direct instruction approach.* Upper Saddle River, NJ: Merrill Prentice-Hall.

Carnine, D.W., Silbert, J., Kame'enui, E. J., & Tarver, S. G. (2010). *Direct instruction reading* (5th ed.). Upper Saddle River, NJ: Merrill Prentice-Hall.

Cheney, D., Flower, A., & Templeton, T. (2008). Applying response to intervention metrics in the social domain for students at risk of developing emotional or behavioral disorders. *The Journal of Special Education, 42,* 108–126.

Conquest, R. (2000). *Reflections on a ravaged century.* New York: Norton.

Cook, B. G., Tankersley, M., & Landrum. T. J. (2009). Determining evidence-based practices in special education. *Exceptional Children, 75,* 365–383.

Coyne, M. D., Kame'enui, E. J., & Carnine, D. W. (2006). *Effective teaching strategies that accommodate diverse learners* (3rd ed.). Upper Saddle River, NJ: Merrill Prentice Hall.

Crockett, J. B. (Ed.). (2001). The meaning of science and empirical rigor in the social sciences. *Behavioral Disorders, 27*(1) [special issue].

Crockett, J. B., Gerber, M. M., & Landrum, T. J. (Eds.). (2007). *Achieving the radical reform of special education: Essays in honor of James M. Kauffman.* Mahwah, NJ: Erlbaum.

Crockett, J. B., & Kauffman, J. M. (1999). *The least restrictive environment: Its origins and interpretation in special education.* Mahwah, NJ: Erlbaum.

Crutchfield, M. (1997). *Who's teaching our children with disabilities?* Washington, DC: National Information Center for Children and Youth with Disabilities. (ERIC Document Reproduction Service, No. ED 410 715).

Darch, C. B., & Kame'enui, E. J. (2004). *Instructional classroom management: A proactive approach to behavior management* (2nd ed.). Upper Saddle River, NJ: Pearson Merrill Prentice Hall.

Darling-Hammond, L. (2003). *Keeping good teachers: Why it matters, what leaders can do. Educational Leadership, 60*(8), 6–13.

Darling-Hammond, L., & Baratz-Snowden, J. (Eds.). (2005). *A good teacher in every classroom: Preparing the highly qualified teachers our children deserve.* San Francisco: Jossey-Bass.

Detrich, R., Keyworth, R., & States, J. (Eds.). (2008). *Advances in evidence-based education. Vol. I. A roadmap to evidence-based education.* Oakland, CA: Wing Institute.

Donovan, M. S., & Cross, C. T. (Eds.). (2002). *Minority students in special and gifted education.* Washington, DC: National Academy Press.

Erickson F., & Gutierrez, K. (2002). Culture, rigor, and science in educational research. *Educational Researcher, 31*(8), 21–24.

Fairbanks, S., Sugai, G., Guardino, D., & Lathrop, M. (2007). Response to intervention: Examining classroom behavior support in second grade. *Exceptional Children, 73*, 288–310.

Fixen, D. L., Naoom, S. F., Blasé, K. A., Friedman, R. M., & Wallace, F. (2005). *Implementation research: A synthesis of the literature.* Tampa: University of South Florida.

Fuchs, D., & Fuchs, L. S. (1994). Inclusive schools movement and the radicalization of special education reform. *Exceptional Children, 60*, 294–309.

Fuchs, D., Mock, D., Morgan, P. L., & Young, C. L. (2003). Responsiveness-to-intervention: Definitions, evidence, and implications for the learning disabilities construct. *Learning Disabilities Research & Practice, 18*, 157–171.

Gallagher, D.J. (1998). The scientific knowledge base of special education: Do we know what we think we know? *Exceptional Children, 64*, 493–502.

Gallagher, D. J. (Ed.). (2004). *Challenging orthodoxy in special education: Dissenting voices.* Denver, CO: Love.

Gersten, R., Fuchs, L. S., Compton, D., Coyne, M., Greenwood, C., & Innocenti, M. S. (2005), Quality indicators for group experimental and quasi-experimental research in special education. *Exceptional Children, 71*, 149–164.

Gresham, F. M., Reschly, D. J., Tilly, W. D., Fletcher, J., Burns, M., Prasse, D., et al. (2005). A response to intervention perspective. *The School Psychologist, 59*, 26–33.

Hamre, B. K., & Pianta, R. C. (2005). Can instructional and emotional support in the first-grade classroom make a difference for children at risk of school failure? *Child Development, 76*, 949–967.

Hanushek, E. A., Kain, J. F., & Rivkin, S. G. (2001). *Why public schools lose teachers.* Greensboro, NC: Smith Richardson Foundation, Inc. (ERIC Document Reproduction Service No. ED 482 901).

Hecht, J. M. (2003). *Doubt: A history.* San Francisco: Harper.

Henke, R., Chen, X., & Geis, S. (2000). *Progress through the teacher pipeline: 1992–93 college graduates and elementary/secondary school teaching as of 1997.* Washington, DC: U.S. Department of Education, National Center for Education Statistics.

Henke, R., Chen, X., Geis, S., & Knepper, P. (2000). Progress through the teacher pipeline: 1992–93 college graduates and elementary/secondary school teaching as of 1997. *Education Statistics Quaterly, 2*, 91–98.

Heward, W. L. (2003). Ten faulty notions about teaching and learning that hinder the effectiveness of special education. *The Journal of Special Education, 36*, 186–205.

Heward, W. L., & Silvestri, S. M. (2005). The neutralization of special education. In J. W. Jacobson, R. M. Foxx, & J. A. Mulick (Eds.), *Controversial therapies for developmental disabilities: Fad, fashion, and science in professional practice* (pp. 193–214). Mahwah, NJ: Erlbaum.

Horner, R. H., Carr, E. G., Halle, J., McGee, G., Odom, S., & Wolery, M. (2005). The use of single subject research to identify evidence-based practice in special education. *Exceptional Children, 71*, 165–179.

Horner, R., Sugai, G., Smolkowski, K., Eber, L., Todd, A., Nakasato, J., & Esperanza, J. (2009). A randomized, wait-list controlled effectiveness trial assessing school-wide positive behavior support in elementary schools. *Journal of Positive Behavior Interventions, 11*, 133–144.

Kain, J. F. & Singleton, K. (1996, May/June). Equality of educational opportunity revisited. *New England Economic Review,* 87–111.

Kame'enui, E. J., Carnine, E. W., Dixon R. C., Simmons, D. C., & Coyne, M. D. (2002). *Effective teaching strategies that accommodate diverse learners* (2nd ed.). Upper Saddle River, NJ: Pearson Merrill Prentice Hall.

Kauffman, J. M. (1999). Commentary: Today's special education and its messages for tomorrow. *The Journal of Special Education, 32*, 244–254.

Kauffman, J. M. (2007). Conceptual models and the future of special education. *Education and Treatment of Children, 30*, 241–258.

Kauffman, J. M. (2008). Special education. In T. L. Good (Ed.), *21st Century education: A reference handbook: Vol. 1* (pp. 405–413). Thousand Oaks, CA: Sage.

Kauffman, J. M. (2009). Attributions of malice to special education policy and practice. In T. E. Scruggs & M. A. Mastropieri (Eds.), *Advances in learning and behavioral disabilities: Vol. 22. Policy and practice* (pp. 33–66). Bingley, UK: Emerald.

Kauffman, J. M. (2010a, April). *Science and the education of teachers.* Paper presented at the Fifth Annual Summit on Evidence-Based Education, Wing Institute, Berkeley, CA.

Kauffman, J. M. (2010b). *The tragicomedy of public education: Laughing and crying, thinking and fixing.* Verona, WI: Attainment.

Kauffman, J. M. (2011). *Towards a science of education: The battle between rouge and real science.* Verona, WI: Attainment.

Kauffman, J. M., Brigham, F. J., & Mock, D. R. (2004). Historical to contemporary perspectives on the field of behavioral disorders. In R. B. Rutherford, M. M. Quinn, & S. R. Mathur (Eds.), *Handbook of research in emotional and behavioral disorders* (pp. 15–31). New York: Guilford.

Kauffman, J. M., Conroy, M., Gardner, R., & Oswald, D. (2008). Cultural sensitivity in the application of behavior principles to education. *Education and Treatment of Children, 31*, 239–262.

Kauffman, J. M., & Hung, L. Y. (2009). Special education for intellectual disability: Current trends and perspectives. *Current Opinion in Psychiatry, 22,* 452–456.

Kauffman, J. M., & Landrum, T. J. (2006). *Children and youth with emotional and behavioral disorders: A history of their education.* Austin, TX: Pro-Ed.

Kauffman, J. M., & Landrum, T. J. (2009). Politics, civil rights, and disproportional identification of students with emotional and behavioral disorders. *Exceptionality, 17*, 177–188.

Kauffman, J. M., Mock, D. R., & Simpson, R. L. (2007). Problems related to underservice of students with emotional or behavioral disorders. *Behavioral Disorders, 33*, 43–57.

Kauffman, J. M., Mock, D. R., Tankersley, M., & Landrum, T. J. (2008). Effective service delivery models. In R. J. Morris & N. Mather (Eds.), *Evidence-based interventions for students with learning and behavioral challenges.* (pp. 359–378). Mahwah, NJ: Erlbaum.

Kauffman, J. M., & Sasso, G. M. (2006a). Toward ending cultural and cognitive relativism in special education. *Exceptionality, 14,* 65–90.

Kauffman, J. M., & Sasso, G. M. (2006b). Certainty, doubt, and the reduction of uncertainty: A rejoinder. *Exceptionality, 14,* 109–120.

Kauffman, J. M., Simpson, R. L., & Mock, D. R. (2009). Problems related to underservice: A rejoinder. *Behavioral Disorders, 34,* 172–180.

Kazdin, A. E. (2008). *Behavior modification in applied settings* (6th ed.). Belmont, CA: Wadsworth.

Kennedy, C. H. (2005). *Single-case designs for educational research.* Upper Saddle River, NJ: Merrill/Prentice-Hall.

Kerr, M. M., & Nelson, C. M. (2010). *Strategies for addressing behavior problems in the classroom* (6th ed). Upper Saddle River, NJ: Pearson Merrill Prentice Hall.

Krueger, J. I. (2002). Postmodern parlor games. *American Psychologist, 57,* 461–462.

Landrum, T. J., & Kauffman, J. M. (2006). Behavioral approaches to classroom management. In C. M. Evertson & C. S. Weinstein (Eds.), *Handbook of classroom management: Research, practice, and contemporary issues* (pp. 47–71). Mahwah, NJ: Erlbaum.

Landrum, T. J., Tankersley, M., & Kauffman, J. M. (2003). What is special about special education for students with emotional or behavioral disorders? *The Journal of Special Education, 37,* 148–156.

Letter from Office of Special Education and Rehabilitative Services (2008, July 28) from William Knudsen, Acting Director of Office of Special Education Programs, to Chief State School Officers and State Directors of Special Education: *Coordinated Early Intervening Services (CEIS) Under Part B of the Individuals with Disabilities Education Act (IDEA).*

Lewis, T. J., Hudson, S., Richter, M., & Johnson, N. (2004). Scientifically supported practices in emotional and behavioral disorders: A proposed approach and brief review of current practices. *Behavioral Disorders, 29,* 247–259.

MacMillan, D. L., Gresham, F. M., & Forness, S. R. (1996). Full inclusion: An empirical perspective. *Behavioral Disorders, 21,* 145–159.

Mann, L. (1979). *On the trail of process: A historical perspective on cognitive processes and their training*. New York: Grune & Stratton.

Marston, D., Muyskens, P. L., Lau, M., & Canter, A. (2003). Problem-solving model for decision making with high-incidence disabilities: The Minneapolis experience. *Learning Disabilities Research & Practice, 18,* 187–200.

Mayer, M. J. (2006). The current state of methodological knowledge and emerging practice in evidence-based evaluation: Applications to school violence prevention research. In S. Jimerson & M. J. Furlong (Eds.), *Handbook of school violence and school safety: From research to practice* (pp. 171–190). Hillsdale, NJ: Erlbaum.

Mercer, C. D., & Mercer, A. R. (2005). *Teaching students with learning problems* (7th ed). Upper Saddle River, NJ: Pearson Merill Prentice Hall.

Miller, M. D., Brownell, M. T., & Smith, S. W. (1999). Factors that predict teachers staying in, leaving, or transferring from the special education classroom. *Exceptional Children, 65,* 201–218.

Morris, R. J., & Mather, N. (Eds.). (2008). *Evidence-based interventions for students with learning and behavioral challenges*. Mahwah, NJ: Erlbaum.

Mostert, M. P., Kavale, K. A., & Kauffman, J. M. (Eds.). (2008). *Challenging the refusal of reasoning in special education*. Denver, CO: Love.

Mulick, J. A., & Butter, E. M. (2005). Positive behavior support: A paternalistic utopian delusion. In J. W. Jacobson, R. M. Foxx, & J. A. Mulick (Eds.), *Controversial therapies for developmental disabilities: Fad, fashion, and science in professional practice* (pp. 385–404). Mahwah, NJ: Erlbaum.

Neiman, S. (2008). *Moral clarity: A guide for grown-up idealists*. New York: Harcourt.

Nelson, C. M., & Kauffman, J. M. (2009). The past is prologue: Suggestions for moving forward in emotional and behavioral disorders. *Beyond Behavior, 18*(2), 36–41.

Odom, S. L., Brantlinger, E., Gersten, R., Horner, R. H., Thompson, B., & Harris, K. R. (2005). Research in special education: Scientific methods and evidence-based practices. *Exceptional Children, 71,* 137–148.

Reynolds, M. C., Wang, M. C., & Walberg, H. J. (1987). The necessary restructuring of regular and special education. *Exceptional Children, 53,* 391–398.

Rosenberg, M. S., Sindelar, P. T. & Hardman, M. L. (2004). Preparing highly qualified teachers for students with emotional or behavioral disorders: The impact of NCLB and IDEA. *Behavioral Disorders, 29,* 266–278.

Rosenshine, B. (1997). Advances in research on instruction. In J. W. Lloyd, E. J. Kameenui, & D. Chard (Eds.), *Issues in educating students with disabilities* (pp. 197–220). Mahwah, NJ: Erlbaum.

Rosenshine, B. (2008). Systematic instruction. In T. L. Good (Ed.), *21st Century education: A reference handbook: Vol. 1* (pp. 235–243). Thousand Oaks, CA: Sage.

Rossi, R., & Grossman, K. (2002, July 8). Many teachers don't meet certification standards. *Chicago Sun Times,* A6.

Rothman, E. P., & Berkowitz, P. H. (1967). The clinical school—a paradigm. In P. H. Berkowitz & E. P. Rothman (Eds.), *Public education for disturbed children in New York City* (pp. 355–369). Springfield, IL: Thomas.

Ruscio, J. (2002). *Clear thinking with psychology: Separating sense from nonsense*. Pacific Grove, CA: Wadsworth.

Ryan, S., & Grieshaber, S. (2005). Shifting from developmental to postmodern practices in early childhood teacher education. *Journal of Teacher Education, 56,* 34–45.

Sailor, W., Doolittle, J. Bradley, R., & Danielson, L. (2009). Response to intervention and positive behavior support. In W. Sailor, G. Dunlap, G. Sugai, & R. Horner (Eds.), *Handbook of positive behavior support* (pp. 729–753). New York: Springer.

St. Pierre, E. A. (2002). "Science" rejects postmodernism. *Educational Researcher, 31*(8), 25–27.

Sandomierski, T., Kincaid, D., & Algozzine, B. (2007). Response to intervention and positive behavior support: Brothers from different mothers or sisters with different misters? Retrieved October 16, 2007, from http://www.pbis.org.

Sasso, G. M. (2001). The retreat from inquiry and knowledge in special education. *The Journal of Special Education, 34,* 178–193.

Sasso, G. M. (2007). Science and reason in special education: The legacy of Derrida and Foucault. In J. B. Crockett, M. M. Gerber, & T. J. Landrum (Eds.), *Achieving the radical reform of special education: Essays in honor of James M. Kauffman* (pp. 143–167). Mahwah, NJ Erlbaum.

Scheuermann, B., & Lawrence, C. (2007, October). *Response-to-intervention: Implications for students with learning and behavior problems.* Paper presented at the Forum for Change: School-Wide Positive Behavior Interventions & Support-Planning for Systems Change, Chicago, IL.

Shavelson, R. J., & Towne, L. (Eds.). (2002). *Scientific research in education.* Washington, DC: National Academies Press.

Shealey, M. W., & Callins, T. (2007). Creating culturally responsive literacy programs in inclusive classrooms. *Intervention in School and Clinic, 42,* 195–197.

Simonsen, B., Fairbanks, S., Briesch, A., Myers, D., & Sugai, G. (2008). Evidence-based practices in classroom management: Considerations for research to practice. *Education and Treatment of Children, 31,* 351–380.

Simpson, R. L., de Boer-Ott, S., & Myles, B. (2003). Inclusion of learners with autism spectrum disorders in general education settings. *Topics in Language Disorders, 23*(2), 116–133.

Simpson, R. L., & Kauffman, J. M. (2007). Inclusão de alunos deficientes em salas de aula regulares [Inclusion of students with disabilities in general education]. In J. M. Kauffman & J. A. Lopes (Eds.), *Pode a educação especial deixar de ser especial?* (pp. 167–190). Braga, Portugal: Psiquilíbrios Edições.

Simpson, R., & Sasso, G. (1992). Full inclusion of students with autism in general education settings: Values vs. science. *Focus on Autistic Behavior, 7*(3), 1–13.

Sindelar, P. T., Bishop, A. G., Brownell, M. T., Rosenberg, M. S., & Connelly, V. J. (2005). Lessons from special education research. *Teacher Education Quarterly, 32*(3), 35–48.

Stainback, W., & Stainback, S. (1991). A rationale for integration and restructuring: A synopsis. In J. W. Lloyd, N. N. Singh, & A. C. Repp (Eds.), *The Regular Education Initiative: Alternative perspectives on concepts, issues, and models* (pp. 226–239). Sycamore, IL: Sycamore.

Sugai, G., & Horner, R. H. (2007). Is school-wide positive behavior support an evidence-based practice? Retrieved November 6, 2007, from http://www.pbis.org

Sugai, G., & Horner, R. H. (2008). What we know and need to know about preventing problem behavior in schools. *Exceptionality, 16*, 67–77.

Sugai, G., Horner, R.H., Sailor, W., Dunlap, G., Eber, L., Lewis, … Nelson, M. (2005). *School-wide positive behavior support: Implementers' blueprint and self-assessment*. Eugene: University of Oregon.

Thurlow, M. L. (2000). Standards-based reform and students with disabilities: Reflections on a decade of change. *Focus on Exceptional Children, 33*(3), 1–15.

Towne, L., Wise, L. L., & Winters, T. M. (Eds.). (2005). *Advancing scientific research in education*. Washington, DC: National Academies Press.

U.S. Department of Education. (2002). *Meeting the highly qualified teachers challenge: The Secretary's annual report on teacher quality*. Washington, DC: Author.

U.S. Department of Education. (2006). *26th annual report to Congress on the implementation of the Individuals with Disability Education Act*. Washington, DC: Author.

Vaughn, S., Linan-Thompson, S., & Hickman, P. (2003). Response to instruction as a means of identifying students with reading /learning disabilities. *Exceptional Children, 69*, 391–409.

Vavrus, M. (2008). Culturally responsive teaching. In T. L. Good (Ed.), *21st Century education: A reference handbook: Vol. 2* (pp. 49–57). Thousand Oaks, CA: Sage.

Villegas, A. M., & Lucas, T. (2007). The culturally responsive teacher. *Educational Leadership, 64*(6), 28–33.

Wang, M. C., Reynolds, M. C., & Walberg, H. J. (1986). Rethinking special education. *Educational Leadership, 44*(1), 26–31.

Warnock, M. (2005). *Special educational needs: A new look. Impact No. 11*. London: Philosophy of Education Society of Great Britain.

What Works Clearinghouse (2008, December). WWC Procedures and Standards Handbook: Version 2.0. Retrieved March 1, 2009, from http://ies.ed.gov/ncee/wwc/references/idocviewer/Doc.aspx?docId=19&tocId=4

Yell, M. L. (2009). Teaching students with EBD I: Effective teaching. In M. L. Yell, N. B. Meadows, E. Drasgow, & J. G. Shriner (Eds.), *Evidence-based practices for educating students with emotional and behavioral disorders* (pp. 320–341). Upper Saddle River, NJ: Pearson Education.

Yell, M. L., Meadows, N. B., Drasgow, E., & Shriner, J. G. (2009). *Evidence-based practices for educating students with emotional and behavioral disorders*. Upper Saddle River, NJ: Pearson Education.

Yell, M. L., Shriner J. G., & Katsiyannis, A. (2006). Individuals with Disabilities Education Improvement Act of 2004 and IDEA Regulations of 2006: Implications for Educators, Administrators, and Teacher Trainers. *Focus on Exceptional Children, 39*(1), 1–24.

Zigmond, N. (2003). Where should students with disabilities receive special education services? Is one place better than another? *The Journal of Special Education, 37*, 193-199.

3

Statistics, Data, and Special Educational Decisions

Basic Links to Realities

James M. Kauffman and John Wills Lloyd
University of Virginia

Should we identify a specific student as eligible for special education? What could be the consequence for our students if we use some specific teaching method with all of them? How might adopting this method affect the achievement of students who are struggling and those who are not? What might happen to our highest performing students if we do employ a new method? To what extent are we willing to give up achievement gains in our high-performing students or our low-performing students for gains of average students? Do we have to choose between maximum improvement of the average test score and maximum gains in the highest or the lowest test scores? What should we anticipate if we adopt an effective prevention program? Answers to these and many other perplexing questions are not easy, and part of the reason that they are difficult is that educators too often ignore the mathematical and statistical aspects of them.

Not every important question can be fully understood as a mathematical equation, but all important questions have mathematical-statistical foundations. Thus, mathematics and statistics can help us reach better-informed conclusions. Controversies about classification, identification, effectiveness of services, and virtually all other issues reveal fundamental mathematical-statistical concepts that we need to understand better if we are to make better choices. In fact, in our judgment it is impossible to make morally defensible decisions without considering what we know about the mathematics or statistics involved.

Educators are not alone in failing to examine statistical realities. Tversky and Kahneman (1971) related an example in which specialists in mathematical psychology ignored problems with small sample sizes in making recommendations about experiments. Sometimes people overlook mathematical or statistical problems because we prefer stories to statistics (Kida, 2006). We may be more willing to accept and repeat a good yarn that fits our biases than to struggle with understanding and explaining mathematical or statistical ideas. Our judgments are usually based on intuitive understandings that are biased in well-known ways, especially when the situations we must judge are complicated and not transparent (Tversky & Kahneman, 1974).

Consider some examples. Most of us are more likely to discuss testing problems created by the No Child Left Behind Act (better known as NCLB) by telling stories than by explaining the statistical-mathematical realities involved in the law, even though the statistics of it might be nonsensical or absurd (Ho, 2008; Rothstein, Jacobsen, & Wilder, 2006). We would rather say how NCLB is absurd by comparing it to waving to Ray Charles than working through its statistical inadequacies (see Kauffman, 2005b). But the mathematical-statistical realities involved in education dog every decision and every policy with which we are concerned.

When states establish cut-off scores on tests for advancement, graduation, or other judgments of students' achievement, certain mathematical-statistical realities apply. When we make judgments about disabilities based on test scores or performance or response to intervention (RtI), these statistical-mathematical principles apply. When people are selected for various jobs—including the job of teaching—based on measures of their performance, these concepts must be considered (Gladwell, 2008). In the economic difficulties beginning in late 2008 in which someone had to decide which individuals or institutions to help (e.g., with refinancing of their home mortgages or with institutional problems of debit and credit), statistical realities applied.

In short, we simply cannot escape statistical-mathematical issues, regardless of the social, economic, psychological, or educational program involved. And although good stories are often helpful, the success or failure of our policies ultimately depends on the math behind those policies, not just on what people like or believe. The mathematics or statistics behind most policies are not terribly complicated. The realities we discuss are well within the grasp of most adults.

We explain how, no matter how much we might think we are making decisions that are not affected by mathematics, we educators are actually making decisions that have important mathematical or statistical components. It is important to recognize the realities that constrain us so that our decisions do not merely become the object of humor. In the popular vernacular, we need to reject the thinking—in our profession endeavors—associated with Garrison Keillor's entertaining tales of Lake Wobegon (Mr. Keillor's imaginary home town, of which he speaks on the show, *A Prairie Home Companion*). As most of us know, in Lake Wobegon *all* of the children are above average. Most people recognize that this is statistically impossible, so it is funny. We do not laugh, however, when our fellow educators contend that it is possible for every child to be at or above grade level or that all students will be high achievers, although these suggestions are equally as absurd as Keillor's description of Lake Wobegon. We will begin to address educational problems successfully when we see the tragicomedy in statements about education that ignore inconvenient statistical realities (Kauffman, 2010a, 2010b). To make the best decisions we can in the real world, we have to confront inconvenient truths, whether they are obvious to most people or not.

The reason we focus on the mathematics or statistics underlying measurement and measurement theory is that measurement and comparisons of individuals within statistical distributions are an important part of identification of individuals needing special education and of assessing their progress. Actually, the mathematical realities to which we refer apply to all statistical distributions of measurements, regardless of whether they are measures of educational phenomena or measures of something else.

Particular measurement devices are critical in considering statistical data. For example, a test or other instrument could, in fact, be found to have admirable statistical properties, yet be useless or worse in helping anyone make good decisions about the classification or education of students. However, in our discussion the particular instrument is not the issue. The mathematics of statistical distributions is the issue.

We begin with measurement theory because measurement and related statistics are the primary bases for most decisions and for many controversies in education. Subsequently, we discuss some examples of problems that we face in making sound decisions. These include problems in improving education overall, identifying students for special programs, and preventing undesirable characteristics.

Measurement and Measurement Theory

"Theory" in mathematics and statistics has a meaning quite different from its popular meaning. In popular language, theory is often assumed to mean speculation, a concept that scientists and mathematicians would probably refer to as hypothesis. However, theory in mathematics, as in all sciences, refers to a body of organized knowledge that is based on reliable observation and that allows accurate prediction. Thus, "number theory," "set theory," "probability theory," "measurement theory," and so on do not connote speculation about what might occur. Rather, they refer to well-established relationships and predictions that can be tested and confirmed or disconfirmed.

Measurement is required for any scientific endeavor. In fact, measurement at some level is required for any kind of evaluation, even if the evaluation is qualitative and the simple conclusion of the evaluation is that $a = b$ or that $a > b$ or $b > a$. Measurement is an inseparable part of accountability. Suggestions that measurement and accountability should be uncoupled are not coherent (cf. Kauffman & Konold, 2007). Granted, we may complain about particular measurement instruments, and unhappiness might be justified, but accountability requires measurement. Our discussion therefore assumes that the instrument used to measure is actually valid and reliable.

Most attempts to evaluate various individuals, groups, or programs involve more complex or sophisticated measurement than simply $a = b$ or $a \neq b$. As we learned in our fundamental courses, measurements may represent nominal, ordinal, interval, or ratio data.

1. Sometimes, the variables measured are *categorical* (female-male; qualified or not qualified; Asian, Black, or White). Even when the data are categorical or nominal, people often apply basic mathematical concepts. For example, they might say that event or condition A occurred more often than event or condition B.
2. Usually, however, educational measurement involves scores that statisticians consider at least *ordinal*. For example, the familiar categories primary, elementary, and secondary are aligned in an order. That is, they at least imply a rank order, like first, second, third, and so on.
3. Often, educational measures are assumed to be *interval* data, so that the steps between scores are assumed to be equal, as in the numbers 1, 2, 3, 4, and so on. In fact, most test scores are assumed to be interval data.
4. Only a few scores used by educators qualify as *ratio* data, a level of measurement in which the ratio of two scores is meaningful (for example, a change from 5 to 10 is equivalent to a change from 20 to 40). Some scores on curriculum-based measures, for example, qualify as ratio data.

Measurement theory helps us make sense of data. The organized body of knowledge that comprises the mathematics of statistical tests allows us to estimate with considerable precision the probability of obtaining various measurements and differences and to determine the confidence we should place in a given measurement. Measurement theory also tells us that all measurement contains error, that measurement with absolute precision (no error whatsoever) is not possible, and that measurement always produces a statistical distribution of values, including error.

"Error" in measurement does not mean "mistake." It is simply unexplained variation, differences in measurement that have not been attributed to known factors such as the conditions in effect when the measurements were made, differences in the measurement system, and so forth. When measures have a relatively low proportion of error, they are better (i.e., more trustworthy), but they can never be completely free from error.

Most measurements of educational performance produce a score distribution that lies atop a *continuous* statistical distribution of outcomes (Kauffman & Konold, 2007; Konold & Kauffman, 2009). Continuous distributions are those in which what is measured varies from a little to a lot with fine gradations or increments being possible (cf. Kauffman & Hallahan, 2005). There are no natural, inherent, or obvious breaks in a continuous distribution. Height and weight are examples of continuous distributions, as are speed and rate. In education, we usually consider such things as intelligence and academic achievement to be continuous distributions.

The reason we say a distribution of obtained scores "lies atop" rather than "is" the distribution is that measurement of human performance always produces a *discrete* statistical distribution—one with "saw teeth" rather than one that is completely smooth. That is, the distribution can also be represented by a bar graph or histogram, and the "curve" representing it is really the histogram smoothed out. Another way of stating this is that regardless of the degree of precision of measurement (e.g., tenths, hundredths, thousandths…), there is a break in the scale when moving from one measured point to another (a sort of "saw tooth" or bar on a graph). Often, however, the data resemble a continuous, *normal* distribution, in that a graph of the scores approximates the symmetry of a bell by modeling the underlying continuous scale that is inherent to the variable being measured (hence, "bell-shaped curve" or "bell curve"). Not all distributions or curves are normal; some are lopsided (i.e., skewed) and some are more peaked (leptokurtotic) or flatter (platykurtotic) than normal. Some distributions are different from normal in both skew and kurtosis. And some distributions of larger populations may have "lumps" or *subdistributions* consisting of smaller groups.

Normal distributions do not really exist in nature but are mathematically idealized concepts. However, "many concepts in mathematics and science that are never quite true give good practical results nevertheless, and so does the normal distribution" (Hays, 1963, p. 218). Good, practical results are what we are after, and the math underlying the idea of the normal curve and other approximations of nature are often highly useful in making sound decisions about people. Moreover, all continuous distributions, whether normal or not, have immutable properties known to statisticians as *moments*.

Measurement theory includes four statistical moments: *central tendency*, *variability*, *skew*, and *kurtosis*. These are well-established realities that apply to all groups—including all groups of averages for schools, districts, states, nations, and subgroups of students. Any criterion used to categorize individuals (e.g., a student did or did not meet a criterion used to sort students into those needing or not needing additional instruction) are actually derived from the measurement of continuous distributions.

These realities lead inevitably to the issue of a distribution's extremes and to the matter of marginalization. *Marginalizing* often means trivializing, isolating, or disenfranchising people. We do not mean to trivialize the serious issue of marginalizing people in the sense of disenfranchising or isolating them socially. Nevertheless, our topic here is the mathematical-statistical aspects of what might in some sense be called *statistical marginalization*. Whenever possible, we refer to this phenomenon with other terminology to avoid any possible confusion.

We use the term *extreme score* (EXT) to refer to a subset of the population relatively far from the central tendency in a statistical distribution. For example, a tested IQ of 35 is far below the mean IQ (100), so a score of 35 would be considered an EXT—far below average. Remember, too, that the scores we consider to indicate an *Intellectual Disability* (ID) is a relatively small group compared to those judged *not* to indicate ID and that ID may have its own distribution and its own EXTs, both those far above and far below whatever IQ is the mean for ID.

We use the term *close to criterion* (CTC) to refer to scores that are in close proximity to a cut point and are very close to (just below or just above) the cut point. Suppose that the cut point for what we call ID is an *intelligence quotient* (IQ) of 70. Then an IQ of 67 or 72, for example, would also be considered a CTC score. Or, we might say that gifted IQ starts at 135. But, then, a student with an IQ of 134 would be considered to have a score that is CTC too, as we use the term, and one with an IQ of 176 would have a score that is EXT. That is, a score that we consider a CTC is located in the proximity of a line of demarcation on a particular measure and an EXT is very clearly within the smaller subset defined by that cut point. In education, the criterion for whatever we measure may be either low or high in the distribution. That is, it could be in either *tail* (extreme high or extreme low) of the distribution. Obviously, in any given distribution we could have two criteria, one high and one low (we might refer to CTC+ or CTC– or to EXT+ or EXT–).

We might use another example of these concepts: those who are CTC financially or EXT on a measure of financial worth. Financial CTC– includes are those who are near but just below a criterion of low financial assets, and those with EXT– are clearly in a group we might consider "poor." Financial CTC+ includes those who are near but a little over a criterion of great financial assets, and those with EXT+ are clearly in a group we might consider "rich." So people could be considered poor if their net worth is $10,000 (if that is the cut point) or below, but those whose net worth is $10,500 would be considered CTC+ because they're very close to and just over the cut point for "poor," and a net worth of $5,000 would be way beyond the cut point (EXT–).

We might point out, too, that the designation of EXT and CTC are arbitrary but useful concepts. Although statistical moments may be well established and immutable phenomena, the designation of a distribution's tails, or EXTs, is a matter of choice, not a mathematical function. Moreover, CTC is also a matter of judgment. We do recognize the fact that the designation of *tail of the curve*, *EXT*, or *CTC* are arbitrary or judgmental, although the facts of a distribution and its moments are not. And although these are arbitrary designations, they are extremely useful in the sense that voting age, driving age, senior citizen, low birth weight, and many other arbitrary decisions about continuously distributed variables are useful, if not unavoidable, if social justice is to be realized.

Statistical Effects of Better Education for All Students

Better education (or better educational outcomes) for *all* students is in our judgment a good idea. We believe that we have a moral obligation to give every student the best education we can. At the same time, we realize that we may have to face the prospect of trade-offs in helping one group versus another. Moral and ethical decisions are not easy, and they are sometimes complicated by knowing more about the likely outcomes of our actions. Nevertheless, making decisions without considering available knowledge is not wise either, in our opinion.

To say that we seek better education for students begs the question, "Better than what?" The word "better" is a comparative, so there is a mathematical foundation for it. Something is better than something else. Although we do not have an absolute answer for what constitutes a better education, we think special education has specified the fundamental process for moving toward it: In concert with parents, identify the most important goals for education of students; implement with fidelity the most effective educational practices for achieving those goals; monitor students' progress toward meeting the goals; adjust instruction on the basis of students' progress.

Our efforts to educate *all* students to the best of our ability must be informed by mathematical-statistical realities or we will almost certainly fail to make the best decisions we can or even to know what we are doing. For example, we need to know whether giving equal effort to improving every student's performance is likely to increase or decrease population variance—the "spreadoutness" of scores. The issue is really whether equally improved education for all students will have the effect of increasing or decreasing the homogeneity of the population. We need to ask ourselves, "Given equal educational effort, will differences between high and low achievers be reduced or become greater?"

The effect of equalizing inputs may be small, but it is important, even if it is small. To the extent that the population becomes more homogeneous by even a little, the effect of better education for all students will be consistent with the desire to close the gap between high and low achievers. To the extent that the population becomes less homogeneous by even a little, the effect is inconsistent with the desire to close the gap or distance between high and low achievers.

We also need to consider what might happen to the distribution's skew and kurtosis if we improve education for all students equally. If the distribution has a negative skew (i.e., the left tail representing lower achievement is elongated), then more than half of the population will assuredly fall above the arithmetic average (mean); the opposite is true, too, so that if the distribution has a positive skew, then it is entirely predictable that less than half of the population will be above the mean (arithmetic average). For example, it is possible that, depending on how teacher effort is distributed across individuals, more low performers may advance toward the mean than high performers gain in distance from it, and the distribution of scores may become more leptokurtotic (the standard deviation may shrink). This seems a likely outcome based on measurement theory if we give disproportionate effort to increasing the low achievers' compared to high achievers' scores. Alternatively, it is possible that the distribution of teacher effort may result in gains for all students but that high performers may gain more in absolute performance than do low performers, thereby expanding the range of scores (i.e., the distribution may become more platykurtotic, having a larger standard deviation). This seems likely if we give equal effort to improving the achievement of students regardless of their current level of performance.

We may want to believe that no tradeoffs are required in education and that we need never give up one thing for another. However, this does not seem likely on the basis of a mathematical analysis of the problem. Gerber (2005) has shown how mathematical realities related to economic theory inevitably limit a teacher's distribution of effort when teaching more than a single student. He has shown how teachers must make choices about the dispersion of their efforts to achieve maximum mean achievement gains when teaching groups. The reality is that teachers cannot be all things to all students, even if they expend optimum effort. Mathematical realities dictate that in any given instructional circumstance they must give up achievement gains of one student when they seek to increase the achievement of another. If a teacher is disbursing 100 units of teaching effort and she or he needs to reallocate units to a struggling student or group, then the teacher must take units from some other student or group to allocate them to the student(s) to whom she or he delivers extra help. This is not because teachers are feckless, but simply because their efforts are constrained by the mathematical realities of finite capacity. Gerber's analysis does mean, however, that "differentiated instruction" offered in larger groups cannot include the concentrated teacher attention that can be given in smaller groups or in individual instruction.

Policy makers must remember these aspects of statistical distributions if they are to enact policies that achieve their intended effects. To the extent that the improvement of instruction for all children is the goal, such that each child's potential for learning reaches its maximum, population variance (difference among students) is likely to increase (see Kauffman, 2002, for discussion of the effects of differences in rate of learning). The late physicist Richard Feynman (1985) said, "For instance, in education you increase differences. If someone's good at something, you try to develop his ability, which results in differences, or inequalities" (p. 281). The basic mathematical-statistical reality is that if you help all students equally to get better at something and they already differ in their ability to do it—whether their differences are innate or due to experience such as exposure to or practice of what you are teaching them—then the differences among them become greater.

To the extent that all students reaching an established criterion of performance is the desired end, population variance (difference among students) is likely to decrease. Devoting units of educational effort to raise the scores of low achievers up to some specified standard is likely to come at the expense of devoting those units to promoting the performance of high achievers (see Kauffman & Konold, 2007; Konold & Kauffman, 2009). In any case, consideration of the effects of programs intended to improve educational progress overall should include the entire statistical distribution, not simply assess differences in means or gaps based on cut scores (Ho, 2008). Indeed, increasing what most students can do (the average, whether defined as mean or median) is desirable, but an important consideration is also whether this increases population variance and what happens at the extremes of the distribution (the outliers). Just as having a few wealthy software engineers move into a middle-class neighborhood would raise the average per-household income, boosting the scores of a few very high-achieving students would raise the average score for a local school.

These are problems involving social justice as well as statistics, but our judgments must be made in the light of what we can predict on the basis of measurement theory about effects on all parts of a statistical distribution of outcomes. Ho (2008) suggests that the old injunction to measure twice and cut once should be rephrased for thinking about cut points in education; cut once, measure everywhere, he advises.

Effects on Extreme Scores (EXT) and Scores Close to Criterion (CTC)

The effects of education on students whose scores are EXT or CTC (i.e., those under the tails of a distribution or close to a cut point) are important for at least two reasons. First, on tests of psychological and educational variables, the students whose scores are EXT or CTC are likely to be considered exceptional children, either because they are identified as having disabilities or because they are identified as gifted. Second, these students can contribute significantly to the disproportional representation of a given group in any activity for which performance is measured and either exceptionally high or exceptionally low performance is the selection criterion. Taking an example from athletics, it could be that different ethnic groups have about the same average running ability, but if, say, those who are EXT in ability to run very fast are predominantly from a particular ethnic group, then that ethnic group is going to be disproportionately represented among fast runners (see Gladwell, 1997). In education, small differences in students with EXT scores might result in serious disproportionality among those identified as exceptional in any given category even though the averages of the groups in question are not significantly different. Gladwell (1997) points out that many people misinterpret the meanings of the central tendency and other aspects of statistical distributions and, therefore, misinterpret the meanings of disproportionality in any area of performance. It is exceptionally important, therefore, that we better understand what happens when we establish cut points in statistical distributions for special education programs.

By definition, the tails of a distribution (or EXT scores) involve relatively low numbers and small percentages of a sample or population (see also Ho, 2008). Thus, if a given effort to improve education results in even small changes in EXT in a distribution, it can have substantial effects on the proportion of minority members included, whether the minority is defined by race, gender, ability, or any other specified characteristic that may be unrelated to the average (mean or median) of the variable being measured. Consequently, decisions that involve (or affect) either tail of a distribution without consideration of (or changing) the central tendency may have profound moral and practical implications. When educators should focus on the central tendency and when on the EXT or tails and when on both are matters of great importance, but confusing the meaning of typical and EXT certainly will lead to tragicomic decisions (see Kauffman, 2010b).

Unavoidability of Lines and Margins

Qualification of an individual for any special program requires establishing criteria for participation. Sometimes, the criteria themselves are categorical (e.g., male or female, is or is not a citizen of a particular state), but categories are often established based on arbitrary lines drawn in a continuous distribution (e.g., age of designation as "senior," voting age, financial assets required for a home loan, pecuniary assets excluding someone from an assistance program, test scores required for admission, height required for admission, and so on). Moreover, the line in a continuous distribution, regardless of where it is drawn, can be changed at will (i.e., it is arbitrary, although it may be defensible). So, for example, we could say that a discrepancy of 20% difference between a student's performance in reading and the local norm or expectation defines need for additional assistance in reading. But, what of 21%, or even 20.5%, or, say, 19%? We could, in fact, question any CTC as well as the criterion itself. There is no magic by which the possibility of error or a near miss disappears.

Being hesitant to categorize children or dichotomize groups or designate binary classifications is warranted, but those who are going to do something to help students have to face the mathematical realities of categories and line-drawing (Kauffman, 2009). That is, they have to make decisions about the qualification of particular individuals for particular programs. Not every individual can be included in every education program that is offered, nor is such universal, all-pervasive inclusion defensible on logical or moral grounds. So, what should be the criterion, regardless of how it is determined, and what do we do about the near misses (CTCs)? We have no ready answer. Our point is that we cannot avoid the question. Finding a new instrument never solves the basic problem.

Inevitably, lines drawn in continuous statistical distributions create margins—measurements that approach but do not quite reach the designated criterion and those that surpass it by only a little (CTC+ and CTC–). Neither drawing the line nor creating the margin can be avoided if a subset of the larger group is to be designated. The matter is just this simple—no line, no special program. And the matter of margins is equally simple—every line has margins, which include regions close to the line; one is close but does not quite reach the criterion, and the other is close but just a little beyond the line. The line's margins can be determined by a variety of mathematical computations, but those whose scores are CTC are always an arbitrarily designated and necessary subgroup.

Prevention

Kauffman (1999, 2004, 2005a, 2007, 2010a) and Kauffman and Landrum (2009) have described how drawing lines and dealing with the line's margins are part of the problem of early intervention and prevention. The line is the cut point established for deciding which students qualify and which students do not. The margins are the close calls either way, a little above or a little below the cut point (CTC+ or CTC–). Margins may also be thought of as regions of statistical error, the plus-or-minus distance from the score that statisticians call a standard error. The margins or close calls also tell us something about the kind of mistake we might make, a *false positive* or a *false negative*. A false positive means that we identified a student when we should not have. A false negative means that we should have identified a student but did not. Both are mistakes in identification. In a false positive, we got the wrong one; in a false negative, we failed to get the right one.

Consider an example involving special education. We could identify a student as eligible for special education due to an emotional or behavioral disorder when, actually, the student does not have this disorder. His identification was a mistake. He was falsely identified. His case would then be considered a false positive. Or we could miss identifying a student who we should have identified. We find out later that although he was not identified, he should have been. We made a mistake. In this case, our mistake was nonidentification. His case would then be considered a false negative.

Let us think about disabilities and false positives and false negatives further. Actually, false positives may be found at any location in the distribution that is designated as the smaller subset for which services *are* intended (that is, it is possible for a student to be tested and found to be extremely discrepant from the norm, yet to be falsely identified). The opposite kind of error, false negatives may be found at any location in the distribution designated as the larger subset for which services are *not* intended (that is, it is possible for a student to be tested and found to be typical or even superior in relation to the norm, yet be missed and remain unidentified). People do not make mistakes *only* about students who are close to a cut point (CTC). But when people make a mistake, they *usually* make it about a close call. To the extent that the measurement tool is valid and reliable for the variable in question, the false positives will be concentrated within the margin of the criterion further from the central tendency and the false negatives will be concentrated within the margin of the criterion closer to the median (or other measure of central tendency)—that is, the highest probability of error is in cases close to the cut point (CTC).

The reason that false positives and false negatives are related to prevention is that in prevention we are trying to keep something from happening—catch it *before* it happens and prevent it. So, we have to think about how we would identify cases *before* they get to a certain point, either before they occur at all (primary prevention) or before they get as bad as they are by the time we usually catch them (secondary or tertiary prevention). So, prevention requires that we think about the kind of mistake we might make (false positive or false negative) if we try to prevent something—unless we believe we can avoid mistakes altogether (not likely, being human).

The following comments apply to secondary and tertiary prevention only, not to primary prevention for which no identification of a subset of the population in question is necessary (see Kauffman, 1999, 2005a; Simeonsson, 1991, for discussion of differences among primary, secondary, and tertiary prevention). When we consider what is required for prevention and early intervention in the light of statistical distributions, it is obvious not only that more students must be identified as needing help but that the risk of false positive identification will increase, given the same means of identification. Prevention cannot occur without encountering greater risk of false positives because of the mathematics of distributions, not because of preferences for or aversions of certain risks or because of ideologies (Kauffman, 2010a). The reality is simply that as the criterion for identification is moved from more extreme or obvious to less extreme or obvious cases a greater number of cases will be included and more cases will be found at the margins of the cut point (i.e., more will be CTC+ or CTC–, depending on whether a lower or higher score is considered a sign of danger). This is true whether the distribution is for age of onset, duration of the problem before intervention, or intensity or degree of disability. For example, if we say that students qualify as having an emotional or behavioral disorder when their score is 2.0 standard deviations above the mean on a measure of misbehavior, then if we move the criterion to 1.75 standard deviations from the mean (i.e., we move it closer to the central tendency), we're going to have a greater number of students (the area designated under the curve is greater).

And, because more individuals will be identified as eligible for the program, the risk of making a mistake known as a false positive will be greater. The only exceptions to this reality require (a) a significantly improved means of identification *and* the finding that a smaller percentage of the population actually has the condition for which identification is necessary than was previously thought to be the case or (b) the finding, using current methods of identification, that the prevalence of the condition is, indeed, lower than believed.

Noting the mathematical realities involved in the risk of false positives does not discount the importance of early intervention and prevention in special education. In fact, given the realities and risks, we would argue *for* these efforts (e.g., Kauffman & Brigham, 2009; Lloyd & deBettencourt, 1986). However, it is important to acknowledge the mathematical realities that are involved—that there will by necessity be an increase in the number of students identified as needing or likely needing special services. Moreover, the same effects will be seen regardless of the scale used for assessment and regardless of whether the issue is prevention of school failure, prevention of child abuse, or prevention of any other undesirable phenomenon.

Effects of Kurtosis and Skew on Extreme Scores (EXT) and Those Near a Criterion (CTC)

Kurtosis and skewness alter the effects of decision rules, especially for values or scores near the cut point or criterion (CTC). Educators might make decisions on the basis of a cut score (e.g., all individuals with values below a given value are eligible for a program) or on the basis of a percentage (e.g., the lowest given percentage of values indicate eligibility for the program). Here, the statistics become somewhat more abstract, but think about what the shape of a distribution (lopsided one way or the other or more peaked or more flattened) would mean for who gets identified for a special program.

Greater kurtosis means that more of the variance in a distribution is due to infrequent and extreme deviations from the mean than from the more frequent and less extreme deviations in a normal distribution. Thus, the distribution is more peaked than normal (and the standard deviation is smaller). If a particular absolute value below or above the mean is chosen as a cut point (say, a score of 80 on a given test) and the distribution of scores remains constant in its skewness, mean, and standard deviation but the distribution becomes more leptokurtotic, then fewer people will have scores that are EXT or CTC according to our definition. However, given the same assumptions about the distribution but a percentage of the population (say, 20%) or a standard deviation (say, a standard deviation of −1.25) is chosen as the rule for eligibility (or another decision) and the distribution becomes more leptokurtotic, then the same percentage will have EXT or CTC scores by our definition.

Also, with respect to those on the end of the distribution below the central tendency, a negative skew is more likely to result in fewer individuals with scores at the margins than is a positive skew, given that the criterion for designating those with EXT or CTC scores is a fixed value on the measurement scale, not a percentage of the population. Of course, the opposite is also true under similar assumptions; a positive skew is more likely to result in fewer EXT and CTC scores on the positive end of the distribution than is a negative skew. And, if having an EXT score is defined as a percentage of the population (say, 15%) or a standard deviation (say, 2.0), then the number or percentage of individuals having an EXT score cannot change, regardless of skew or kurtosis (i.e., absolute value can change, but not value relative to the mean). If, for example, educators decide that 10% of all students will receive a service (say, eye glasses), then the shape of the distribution of needs-eye-glasses scores would be irrelevant; this is true no matter whether the cut point is 5% or 15% of students.

Alternative Measurements Used for Eligibility for Special Education

Ordinarily, a single line of demarcation is used to indicate eligibility for a special education program. For example, special education in any given categorical area is usually a matter of determining eligibility on the basis of a single criterion (although one that may, as in the case of learning disabilities [LD] defined as a discrepancy between ability and achievement, be based on multiple test scores). In fact, for a sample of students considered for eligibility for special education services as students with learning disabilities, there would be a set of discrepancies between ability and achievement. That set of scores will, of course, have statistical moments. Some discrepancies will be above the mean and others below it. If the distribution is roughly normal, about 50% will be above the mean. Moreover, the cut score on this distribution will be arbitrary and subject to all of the statistical phenomena we have discussed to this point.

Alternative procedures for identifying students as eligible for special education (e.g., response to intervention or RtI) face the same problems—continuous distributions (in the case of RtI, responsiveness to given instruction) and an arbitrary criterion for selection. That is, all of the following aspects of RtI are continuously distributed: (a) nature or quality of instruction, (b) length of time given instruction has been used, (c) responsiveness to instruction, (d) starting levels (i.e., intercepts), and (e) rates of progress. Thus, in no way does RtI overcome the statistical realities that apply to other measurements or methods of identification. The possible advantages of RtI may be found in (a) the benefits of employing primary prevention (i.e., using curricula and teaching methods for all students in general education that demonstrably yield lower failure rates) and (b) the validity and reliability of its measurement, not its avoidance of mathematical or statistical criteria related to the nature of distributions.

Other Statistical Issues and Problems

Other statistical matters that must be considered include error and subdistributions. Ordinarily, an error term (or standard error) is calculated for an entire distribution and assumed to apply to the extreme scores under a distribution as well as to scores near the central tendency. In some cases, however, it is extremely difficult and perhaps risky to assume that error is equally probable near the central tendency and several standard deviations from it.

Moreover, if a subdistribution (of LD, for example) is fully contained within the larger statistical distribution with a smooth tail that is characteristic of idealized or hypothetical curves, then all the effects we discuss apply to the larger distribution. However the subdistribution may also contribute a "hump" or "lump" to the tail of a larger distribution, such that the usual statistical assumptions or mathematical calculations must be altered somewhat or are indeterminate (we might call such a hump or lump a *perturbation* of the curve's tail). For example, there might be a "hump" in the lower end of the distribution of adaptive behavior. Moving away from the central tendency of the larger distribution, the left tail might go up before it goes down again toward the baseline. In that case, moving a cut point for prevention toward the central tendency of the larger distribution will still result in more cases being identified, although depending on just where the cut point is moved fewer cases than would be expected without the perturbation would be identified. A greater number of cases will be identified simply because moving a cut point toward the central tendency of a distribution *always, without fail, regardless of any perturbations*, includes more individuals—a larger area, a larger percentage of the sample represented by the distribution—regardless of the shape of the distribution. Given that the cut point is moved from within the perturbation's downward slope and toward the central tendency of the larger distribution's, the risk of false positives could decline and would rise again only if the cut point were moved up the slope of the larger distribution.

The fact is that for many variables, we are not certain just what the statistical distribution is. The "normal" distribution gives us only an idealized model. It may be a very useful model and may be the best guess we can make, but if we actually obtained the data and sketched a distribution of them, we may be surprised at what we find.

Discussion

Although we have described neither all of the statistical-mathematical realities that apply to the data of education or any other endeavor nor all of the problems or issues in education to which these might apply, we have examined some of the cornerstone statistics and some of the primary issues involved in education. Certainly, it is important to apply statistical-mathematical realities to the distributions of actual data, not only to hypothetical distributions or models. Nevertheless, we make two observations: (a) the principles we described apply to actual data as well as to hypothetical distributions and (b) sometimes a hypothetical distribution or an approximation of existing data is the only or the best model we can obtain.

As special educators, we are particularly concerned about EXT and CTC scores and the effects that particular interventions may have on the shapes of statistical distributions, especially students whose scores are EXT or CTC. What happens to the extremes or tails of distributions can have a profound effect on public perceptions as well as the individuals who fall far from the central tendency on any given measure. Although two publications of the National Research Council on science in research on education contain many important ideas, they include no discussion of topics important to research in special education—statistical distributions and EXT or CTC scores in them (Shavelson &Towne, 2002; Towne, Wise, & Winters, 2004). We are disappointed that these publications do not address scientific issues that are essential to special education (see also Kauffman, 2011).

We are also disappointed that an article by Gladwell (2008) includes neither discussion of statistical extremes in groups of students being taught nor cut points in statistical distributions of teaching finesse. Although Gladwell discusses the dramatic differences between success in college football and success in professional football, his discussion of education does not include differences between teaching children with disabilities and those without disabilities. As Kauffman (2010b) notes, we could make the assumption that no student is truly special for instructional purposes. Like award-winning general education teacher Esquith (2007), who makes no mention whatever of students with disabilities, we could assume that if the teacher teaches well, then children with disabilities are just like everyone else in the class, so no one needs to mention them or what is required to teach them. Our suspicion is that good teaching of modal students and those who are exceptional for instructional purposes may be substantially different.

One implication of our description of statistical and mathematical realities is that educators and those who make policy decisions about education should take these into account in discussions of the data they have and their descriptions of the data-based outcomes they desire. Although it is possible for anyone to propose programs or policies based on wishes that are not reality-based, as discussed by Kauffman and others (e.g., Kauffman, 2010b, 2011; Kauffman & Konold, 2007; Konold & Kauffman, 2009), such actions are, in our opinion, ill-advised.

If someone is serious about secondary or tertiary prevention of a difficulty (regardless of what it may be), then the statistical and mathematical certainties are that, given the identification procedures now practiced, (a) more individuals, not fewer, must be involved in the preventative intervention and (b) greater, not lesser, risk of false positive identification will be encountered. These certainties will apply unless (a) the accuracy of identification is improved over current methods *and* the actual prevalence of the condition is found to be lower than previously believed, (b) the actual prevalence of the condition is found to be lower, using the current method of identification, than previously believed, or (c) the distribution is found to have a perturbation and movement of the cut point is related to it in the way we have discussed. Thus, if someone argues that students are now often mistakenly identified for a service or intervention (say, LD) and that such misidentification should be reduced but that we need to practice prevention of LD, then it is incumbent upon that person to show how identification of LD can be made sufficiently more accurate by using alternative identification method B relative to identification using current method A *and* that the true prevalence LD is lower than previously thought—or, simply, that the prevalence of LD using current identification method A is considerably lower than previously thought. In the absence of such demonstration, one must assume that identification method A = identification method B in accuracy, that the true prevalence of EBD or LD is as presumed, and therefore that prevention requires risking more false positives. However, a perturbation in the distribution and movement of the cut point required for prevention could be demonstrated to occur as discussed above, resulting in a lowered risk of false positives until the cut point reached the region in which the perturbation gives way to the distribution for the larger population.

An important point here is *accuracy* of identification, such that both false positives and false negatives are reduced. That is, it might be possible to devise an alternative identification method B that reduces identification for special education, yet results in increases in false negatives. In that case, method B might *appear*, at least for a time, to result in prevention while reducing the number of students identified, but in the long run it will become obvious that nothing has been prevented, only that more students have gone without identification and treatment.

Another implication is that some current efforts to reform education are seriously misguided. For example, a major goal of the No Child Left Behind (NCLB) law is eliminating gaps between the mean test scores of students with and without disabilities. Besides recognizing the fact that this is logically impossible (cf. Ho, 2008; Kauffman, 2005b, 2010b; Kauffman & Konold, 2007; Konold & Kauffman, 2009; Rothstein et al., 2006), educators need to consider the consequences of differentially disbursing instructional resources on the nature of statistical distributions of outcomes (Gerber, 2005; Kauffman, 1990, 2002). Would the result of investing very heavily in raising the scores of those below the mean cause a distribution to change its shape in predictable and desirable ways? Or would the result be change in undesirable ways? For example, would most of the scores on the low side of the normal distribution simply be pushed up to the mean, or would the dedication of resources to students below the mean result in a concomitant reduction in resources, and an associated lowering of outcomes, for those who scored above the mean under previous conditions?

We argue that better thinking and more responsible educational reform are possible only when our thinking is constrained by the "box" of statistical and mathematical realities. Some outcomes that educational policies describe implicitly or explicitly as desirable (e.g., increasing mean achievement while reducing population variance in test scores; eliminating mean test score gaps between certain groups) may not be achievable in the real world. Recognizing the difference between the thinkable and the possible is something with which educators have struggled, but not always successfully. We emphasize our agreement with philosopher Susan Neiman, who stated, "This is important: Not everything that's thinkable is genuinely possible, and distinguishing between the two is what allows us to distinguish between demands for utopia and for responsible social change" (2008, p. 142).

In other words, as suggested by the title of Thomas Kida's (2006) book and a bumper sticker we have seen, "Don't believe everything you think." We advocate responsible social change, which gives more learning opportunities to individual students of every description. Ignoring statistical and mathematical realities in pursuing this goal is in our opinion inimical to achieving the responsible social change we desire.

References

Esquith, R. (2007). *Teach like your hair's on fire: The methods and madness inside room 56.* New York: Viking.

Feynman, R. P. (1985). *"Surely your joking, Mr. Feynman!" Adventures of a curious character.* New York: Norton.

Gerber, M. M. (2005). Teachers are still the test: Limitations of response to instruction strategies for identifying children with learning disabilities. *Journal of Learning Disabilities, 38,* 516–524.

Gladwell, M. (1997, May 19). The sports taboo: Why blacks are like boys and whites are like girls. *The New Yorker,* 50–55.

Gladwell, M. (2008, December 15). Annals of education: Most likely to succeed. *The New Yorker,* 36–42.

Hays, W. L. (1963). *Statistics.* New York: Holt, Rinehart, & Winston.

Ho, A. D. (2008). The problem with "proficiency": Limitations of statistics and policy under No Child Left Behind. *Educational Researcher, 37,* 351–360.

Kauffman, J. M. (1990, April). *What happens when special education works? The sociopolitical context of research in the 1990s.* Invited address, Special Education Special Interest Group, American Educational Research Association Meeting, Boston, MA.

Kauffman, J. M. (1999). How we prevent the prevention of emotional and behavioral disorders. *Exceptional Children, 65,* 448–468.

Kauffman, J. M. (2002). *Education deform: Bright people sometimes say stupid things about education.* Lanham, MD: Rowman & Littlefield Education.

Kauffman, J. M. (2004). The president's commission and the devaluation of special education. *Education and Treatment of Children, 27,* 307–324.

Kauffman, J. M. (2005a). How we prevent the prevention of emotional and behavioural difficulties in education. In P. Clough, P. Garner, J. T. Pardeck, & F. K. O. Yuen (Eds.), *Handbook of emotional and behavioural difficulties* (pp. 429–440). London: Sage.

Kauffman, J. M. (2005b). Waving to Ray Charles: Missing the meaning of disability. *Phi Delta Kappan, 86,* 520–521, 524.

Kauffman, J. M. (2007). Conceptual models and the future of special education. *Education and Treatment of Children, 30,* 241–258.

Kauffman, J. M. (2009). Attributions of malice to special education policy and practice. In T. E. Scruggs & M. A. Mastropieri (Eds.), *Advances in learning and behavioral disabilities: Vol. 22,* policy and practice (pp. 33–66). Bingley, UK: Emerald.

Kauffman, J. M. (2010a, April). *Science and the education of teachers.* Paper presented at the Fifth Annual Summit on Evidence-Based Education, Wing Institute, Berkeley, CA.

Kauffman, J. M. (2010b). *The tragicomedy of public education: Laughing, crying, thinking, fixing.* Verona, WI: Full Court Press.

Kauffman, J. M. (2011). *Towards a science of education: The battle between rogue and real science.* Verona, WI: Attainment.

Kauffman, J. M., & Brigham, F. J. (2009). *Working with troubled children.* Verona, WI: Full Court Press.

Kauffman, J. M., & Hallahan, D. P. (2005). *Special education: What it is and why we need it.* Boston: Allyn & Bacon.

Kauffman, J. M., & Konold, T. R. (2007). Making sense in education: Pretense (including NCLB) and realities in rhetoric and policy about schools and schooling. *Exceptionality, 15,* 75–96.

Kauffman, J. M., & Landrum, T. J. (2009). *Characteristics of emotional and behavioral disorders of children and youth* (9th ed.). Upper Saddle River, NJ: Merrill Prentice-Hall.

Kida, T. (2006). *Don't believe everything you think: The 6 basic mistakes we make in thinking.* Amherst, NY: Prometheus.

Konold, T. R., & Kauffman, J. M. (2009). The No Child Left Behind Act: Making decisions without data or other reality checks. In T. J. Kowalski & T. J. Lasley (Eds.), *Handbook of data-based decision making for education* (pp. 72–86). New York: Routledge.

Lloyd, J. W., & deBettencourt, L. J. (1986). Prevention of achievement deficits. In B. Edelstein & L. Michelson (Eds.), *Handbook of prevention* (pp. 117–132). New York: Plenum.

Neiman, S. (2008). *Moral clarity: A guide for grown-up idealists.* New York: Harcourt.

Rothstein, R., Jacobsen, R., & Wilder, T. (2006, November). *"Proficiency for all"—An oxymoron.* Paper presented at a symposium on "Examining America's commitment to closing achievement gaps: NCLB and its alternatives." Columbia University, Teachers College. New York.

Shavelson, R. J., & Towne, L. (Eds.). (2002). *Scientific research in education.* Washington, DC: National Academies Press.

Simeonsson, R. J. (1991). Primary, secondary, and tertiary prevention in early intervention. *Journal of Early Intervention, 15,* 124–134

Towne, L., Wise, L. L., & Winters, T. M. (Eds.). (2004). *Advancing scientific research in education.* Washington, DC: National Academies Press.

Tversky, A., & Kahneman, D. (1971). Belief in the law of small numbers. *Psychological Bulletin, 76,* 105–110.

Tversky, A., & Kahneman, D. (1974). Judgement under uncertainty: Heuristics and biases. *Science, 185,* 1124–1131.

4

Designing Rigorous Group Studies in Special Education

Common Understandings of Efficacy, Effectiveness, and Evidence Standards

Lana Santoro, Russell Gersten, and Rebecca A. Newman-Gonchar
Instructional Research Group/University of Oregon

This chapter explores the implications of the recent emphasis on rigorous scientific research in education. Our purpose is to provide guidance for special education researchers and professionals about conducting high-quality intervention and evaluation studies relying on the guidelines adopted by the What Works Clearinghouse (WWC) of the Institute of Education Sciences (IES). This type of research will help identify effective practices, programs, and policies that directly improve student learning and development.

The Role of Science in Determining Efficacy and Effectiveness in Special Education

Special education research has a history of employing different methodologies. Research methods in special education were originally derived from medicine. Many who studied individuals with disabilities, such as Itard, Sequin, Montessori, Fernald, and Goldstein, were also physicians (Odom et al., 2005). As psychology, sociology, and anthropology became disciplines, new methodologies were incorporated into special education research. For example, Blatt and Kaplan's *Christmas in Purgatory* (1966) drew from sociology and anthropology to document the quality of life for individuals with intellectual disabilities living in state institutions. Due to a rich and varied history of the use of science in education, a range of methodological approaches—including the use of sophisticated multivariate designs, qualitative research designs, discourse analysis, ethnographic research, and program evaluation—are available to researchers in special education (Duke & Mallette, 2004; Martella, Nelson, & Marcharnd-Martella, 1999).

The use of disparate methodologies raises the question of how science should guide practice in special education. With science, there are objective and systematic criteria to evaluate what works. Slavin noted:

> The reason education goes from fad to fad rather than making the steady generational progress characteristic of, for example, medicine or agriculture is that in education practice so often outruns (or ignores) the evidence supporting it. We see a crisis and mandate solutions on a massive scale long before the data are in. (1986, p. 170)

Special education and medicine share a central research question: Does the treatment work? Or, is the treatment or instructional intervention effective? Research can help us evaluate whether A is better than B. According to standards of researched-based evidence, we can determine what works and what doesn't work in improving student outcomes.

Efficacy data is needed to examine whether specific patterns of instructional outcomes do, in fact, occur in the real world of special education. Efficacy designs are typically randomized control trials (RCTs) conducted in real school settings that are reasonably conducive to the intervention. These studies explore the beneficial effects of a program under optimal or controlled conditions of delivery. If classrooms or schools are used as the unit of assignment, efficacy trials must be large (e.g., a minimum sample of 20 for an effect size of .20). Even though efficacy trials are defined by the use of optimal controls, larger samples often mean impacts are not measured in ideal or, more likely, receptive conditions.

Effectiveness research, on the other hand, typically focuses on the evaluation of interventions "taken to scale" (also known as "scale-up"). In other words, factors such as quality of implementation are examined under real-world conditions or in natural settings (Flay, 1986). Effectiveness studies may also establish for whom and under what conditions of delivery a practice or program is effective (Flay, 1986; Flay et al., 2005). Overall, effectiveness requires research designs that can establish causal effects. In other words, there should be confidence that a program or policy, rather than some other factor, is responsible for the observed impact (Flay et al., 2005). There is also a need for much larger samples and multiple sites. Specifically, effectiveness research cannot be based on secondary data analyses (e.g., a meta-analysis) or single subject experimental designs.

Overall, one benefit of implementing efficacy and effectiveness trials is a reduction in the gap between research and practice because significant effects will only be found for feasible interventions and approaches. Small scale, tightly controlled efficacy trials do not help us bridge the gap between research and practice. Large scale, less tightly controlled field experiments are likely to decrease the cynicism among professional educators about the value of research. Therefore, in order to bridge the research-to-practice gap, research must progress from efficacy to effectiveness with large-scale studies implemented under real conditions.

With terms such as "research-based" and "evidence-based" frequently becoming part of contemporary special education jargon, there is current interest in what practices, programs, or policies work. Despite their common use, what truly constitutes "research-based," "scientifically-based" or "evidence-based" practices has been ambiguous. The following section outlines how scientific research evolved in special education. Through that evolution, a new emphasis on rigorous scientific research emerges along with standards for evaluating the rigor and quality of the special education research that determines whether practices, programs, or polices are considered "research-based." In other words, a common understanding of evidence standards that define what works in special education is established.

A New Emphasis on Rigorous Scientific Research

Forty-five years ago, Campbell and Stanley (1966) wrote their seminal work, *Experimental and Quasi-Experimental Designs for Research*. In addition to providing a guide to common pitfalls in the design of field research in education, the Campbell and Stanley monograph presented a passionate argument for rigorous controlled research on significant topics in the real world of schools, classrooms, and other service settings. Campbell and Stanley (1966) urged that the social and educational programs that emerged during the Lyndon Johnson administration (1963–1968), such as Head Start and Title I required evaluation using rigorous research methodologies. By increasing awareness of the potential "threats to internal and external validity," and moving away from the weak "matching designs"[1] often used in educational research at that time, the authors tried to guide educational researchers away from doing highly controlled studies on topics of no particular interest to the real world of educational practice (i.e., studies of paired associative learning that were prevalent in special education at that time) towards studies of real educational interventions, even if the designs of such studies were imperfect.

Campbell and Stanley (1966) urged that researchers to conduct studies on significant topics in education even if it means forgoing some of the controls possible in laboratory research. In other words, researchers should consider conducting "quasi-experiments" (i.e., studies in which random assignment of students, teachers, or schools in treatment conditions is not possible). Quasi-experiments are studies where researchers "compare outcomes . . . between two groups that are similar except for the causal variable (e.g., the educational intervention)" (National Research Council, NRC, 2002, p. 113). However, several years later, Campbell had second thoughts about quasi-experiments and noted the numerous potential problems in a subsequent chapter (Campbell & Boruch, 1975). Campbell urged researchers to continue conducting rigorous research in field settings, but to use random assignment of participants to treatment, whenever possible.

In the same era, Baer, Wolf, and Risley (1968) wrote an article on designs for applied behavior analysis that initiated a prolific stream of rigorous applied research in special education. These designs (usually called single-subject designs despite the fact that there are usually three to four subjects) have been used across many disability categories (e.g., Lovitt, 1966).

The 1990s was, in general, a rather bleak decade for scientific research in special education. Gersten, Baker, and Lloyd (2000) also reported "the number of research studies investigating the effectiveness of special education instructional approaches [was] at one of its lowest levels in 30 years" (p. 2). In fact, there was a statistically significant decrease in the proportion of rigorous experimental studies funded by the Office of Special Education of the U. S. Department of Education from 1987–1988 (20.4%) to 1997–1998 (11.1%) (Gersten, Baker, Smith-Johnson, Flojo, & Hagan-Burke, 2004). Larry Cuban (1990) also described the profound cynicism that abounded in educational professions such as special education at the time. Although every field—from medicine to anthropology—is plagued with cynicism about research, the cynicism about the utility and validity of research in education was extraordinary when compared to other professions. Some questioned whether the paradigms underlying scientific research had become outdated in the postmodernist era (Heshusius, 1991).

In 2001, Congressman Michael Castle of Delaware declared:

> Education research is broken in this country...and Congress must work to make it more useful...Research needs to be conducted on a more scientific basis. Educators and policy makers need objective, reliable research. (NRC, 2002, p. 28)

Congress considered abolishing educational research due to the poor overall quality of the work and the fact that research findings rarely made their way into everyday practice. As a result, congress asked the NRC to explore ways for the field to improve the quality of its research. The panel concluded there was no reason why education could not be subject to the same scientific methods as other disciplines. Indeed, the NRC report concluded, "the guiding principles for scientific research in education are the same as those in *the social, physical and life sciences* [emphasis added]" (NRC, 2002, p. 80). Although the authors of the report observed that "each field has features that influence what questions are asked, how research is designed, how it is carried out, and how it is interpreted and generalized" (NRC, 2002, p. 80), they were clear that there was nothing about education that precluded rigorous research. The report specifically noted that RCTs can and should be conducted in education. Indeed, RCTs remain "the single best methodological route to ferreting out systematic relations between actions and outcomes" (Feuer, Towne, & Shavelson, 2002, p. 8). An elegant RCT by special education researchers Lynn and Douglas Fuchs (1998) was cited as an example for the entire field of education to follow.

The NRC emphasis on scientific research was also reflected in education policy and legislation. The Education Sciences Reform Act of 2002 formed the Institute of Education Sciences (IES) to make educational research more rigorous, objective, and scientific. IES was created as an independent institution rather than an agency within the U. S. Department of Education to curtail direct political interference in IES-supported research (similar to the National Institutes of Health model). IES's mission is to bring "rigorous and relevant research, evaluation and statistics to our nation's education system" (http://ies.ed.gov). Since 2004, the charge was expanded to include special education.

The special education and broader education research community is only beginning to develop the depth of knowledge necessary to conduct this type of rigorous research. There is still concern about the quality of research in the field of education and disagreement about the type of research information that is acceptable evidence of effectiveness (Odom et al., 2005; White & Smith, 2002).

Establishment of Standards for Evaluating the Quality and Rigor of Evidence by the Institute of Education Sciences

In 2002, the What Works Clearinghouse (WWC) was established as an IES initiative. The WWC's purpose is to assess the rigor of research evidence on the effectiveness of interventions (programs, products, practices, and policies); develop and implement standards for reviewing and synthesizing education research; producing user friendly practice guides for educators that address instructional challenges with research-based recommendations for schools and classrooms; and provide a public and easily accessible registry of education evaluation researchers to assist schools, school districts, and program developers with designing and carrying out rigorous evaluations (http://ies.ed.gov/ncee/wwc). To establish the WWC initiative, IES relied heavily on individuals with expertise in economics, sociology, public policy, and public health, which had a strong record of conducting rigorous randomized trials in topics such as employment training for individuals receiving welfare, mental health issues, and preventative research relating to substance abuse. These individuals were able to help the field of education develop guidelines for conducting rigorous research in applied settings, incorporating contemporary standards from health, medicine, and economics.

Many think of the WWC as a sort of Consumer's Guide that evaluates the quality of evidence supporting educational products, but it also plays another important role—establishing standards to guide educational research and evaluation efforts. It is that role that is most relevant for special education researchers. Specifically, the WWC established evidence-based standards to guide those conducting rigorous evaluation research in education. Because no such source previously existed, and this source is not well known to all in the special education research community, we explain some of the key principles. Many of these principles have not always been stressed in previous attempts to formulate guidelines for special education research (e.g., Gersten et al., 2000; Gersten et al., 2005). Important issues, however, were raised in earlier work to establish research guidelines. We believe a good deal of that earlier material remains relevant—particularly in terms of the study of program implementation.

Overall, the WWC considers three major aspects of a group design study to determine "the strength of the evidence that the study provides" (WWC, 2002, p. 1):

- the study design,
- level of attrition in both experimental and comparison groups, and
- equivalence of groups at baseline.

In other words, to provide rigorous evidence that an intervention is effective, the study must be an experimental or quasi-experimental group design and meet standards for attrition, and demonstrate baseline equivalence of groups. Figure 4.1 provides an overview of the questions to ask before determining whether a group design provides valid evidence of an intervention's effectiveness. Confounding is also of critical importance. In addition, research is evaluated, and if need be reanalyzed, to ensure that the authors use contemporary standards for determining whether an effect is statistically significant (i.e., whether the findings are possibly due to chance or are unlikely chance findings; see Figure 4.1).

Note that two other types of designs do provide causal evidence. These include single case designs and regression discontinuity. Standards for single case designs have just been recently developed and standards for regression discontinuity designs are being developed. Neither will be discussed in this chapter, however, which focuses on the mainstay of evaluation research—experimental and quasi-experimental group designs. The following sections describe the WWC standards for group design studies in more detail.

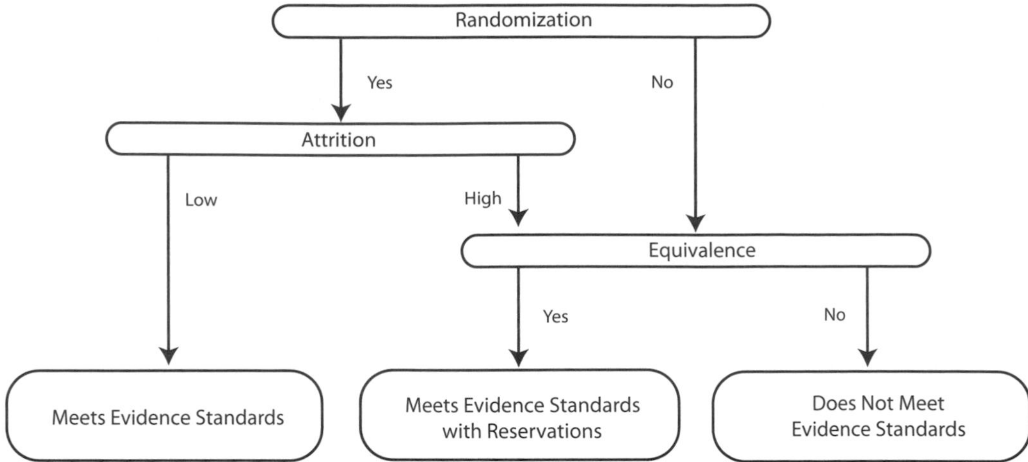

Figure 4.1 Evidence standards from WWC Version 2.0 handbook (2008).

Study Design and the Importance of Randomization

Randomized Controlled Trials

The NRC reported that to establish causal claims (i.e., to claim that an approach is an effective means to positively impact or accelerate the development of learners), the best method is via experiments that entail random assignment of participants to conditions (Mosteller & Boruch, 2002). Therefore, the RCT, in which study participants are randomly assigned to form experimental and control groups of study participants is considered the "gold standard," as it is in other fields such as medicine, public health, clinical psychology, and economics. When done correctly, randomization results in experimental and control groups that possess similar characteristics. "Random assignment removes the possibility that other factors influence student outcomes and enables researchers to make causal statements linking student outcomes to the intervention" (Dynarski, 2008–2009, p. 50). If results of an RCT indicate a difference in outcomes, the difference is likely due to the intervention itself and not the characteristics of the groups.

Quasi-Experimental Designs

As we mentioned earlier, quasi-experiments are studies in which groups "that are similar except for the causal variable (e.g., the educational intervention)" are compared (NRC, 2002, p. 113). The WWC standards require that quasi-experimental designs (QEDs) establish the baseline equivalence of the groups on pretest characteristics and/or demographic characteristics that are likely to affect the outcomes. Although a study author can establish equivalence on observed characteristics, we are never sure if the groups are equivalent on other unmeasured characteristics. Did one group perform better on an assessment because the assessment worked or because the groups were different in terms of some unobserved characteristic (e.g., the control group was more motivated or more interested in the topic)? Therefore, QEDs are always considered acceptable with reservations (i.e., not truly trustworthy). Criteria for pretest equivalence are very stringent. Experimental and control groups cannot differ by more than .05 standard deviation units on any relevant pretest variable.

Attrition, Differential Attrition, and Intent-to-Treat Analysis

Problems related to attrition and differential attrition in field research and evaluation studies were a major emphasis in the original guides to experiments and quasi-experiments developed by Campbell and Stanley (1966). However, issues of attrition and differential attrition have rarely been taken seriously in special education research or much of educational research until recently. Lessons learned from research in public health, counseling, and labor economics teach us that issues related to attrition and differential attrition are, indeed, serious. Through our work with IES and the WWC, we have also learned major lessons about how attrition and differential attrition impact study outcomes. International experts such as Larry Hedges, Thomas Cook, David Myers, and David Francis also acknowledge that an understanding of the implications resulting from attrition and differential attrition is essential.

A study can have overall attrition or differential attrition. Overall attrition means that there is a difference between the initial sample size and the sample for which data are available. Differential attrition occurs when there is a difference between those levels for the groups—experimental and control. High levels of differential attrition compromise the initial equivalence of the groups and introduce bias that can impact the effect estimates. For example, if high attrition was observed in a math intervention study, it would be difficult to directly attribute the study's outcome to the math intervention because students remaining in the intervention may all have similar qualities. What if high attrition was related to family poverty or seasonal migrant work, and only a "low risk" group of students remained in the intervention throughout the duration of the study? With high levels of attrition it is also possible that unobserved characteristics were involved in a decision to leave the study (e.g., students who left the study did not have time for the intervention or did not like the intervention).

A typical special education intervention research study will include data only on students who attended virtually all instructional sessions. In some cases, analysis will be limited to those who received an intervention developed and implemented with high fidelity. In cases of an evaluation of teacher professional development, the analysis sample may only include experimental group teachers who fully and actively participated in the professional development effort. Whereas in earlier research, we often excluded students who missed a good many sessions due to absence or students who dropped out before the intervention period ended or did not receive the intervention, we no longer do so. All students and all teachers randomly assigned to a treatment condition should remain in the final analysis. Thus, the experimental sample is often called an "intent to treat" sample. We now include participants who did not fully receive the intervention because we are most interested in understanding the effects on students (or in some cases, teachers) in general. For example, teachers or students who chose to drop out or teachers who choose not to implement a particular intervention are still representative of the sample of individuals who would participate in an intervention if a school principal chose that intervention for a school.

The key to evaluating an intervention, educational policy, or instructional strategy is the assessment of its impacts on the array of teachers and students who currently attend school. For example, knowing a method works only for teachers who are willing to work an extra five hours a day or only for special education students whose parents can help them with homework on a daily basis or only for students who persist despite experiencing frequent failure—is not, in the long haul, very useful to the field.

One reason, we believe, that there is such cynicism about research findings in special education is that many studies are limited in generalizability and usability to paid graduate assistants who teach according to scripts and are able to prepare lessons for an hour a day. As these findings are "translated" by commercial publishers into actual curricula for teachers to use, effects can dissipate. Ultimately, a key goal of special education research needs to be to assess impacts of actual interventions in a rigorous fashion, using real world conditions. To do so, analyses should include all participants assigned to the experimental treatment. If this is not possible, researchers need to document that those unavailable for post-testing were, in fact, similar on relevant pretest variables to the full sample and that rates of attrition were comparable for experimental and control groups. Only then can a result be considered credible.

Establishing Equivalence

A common misconception is that all RCTs are high quality studies without design flaws and imperfections. In fact, RCTs, too, are vulnerable to threats to internal validity (e.g., Greene, Caracelli, & Graham, 1989). Therefore RCTs with high attrition, as well as all QEDs, must present evidence that the groups are alike relative to observed characteristics at pretest. This reduces, but does fully eradicate, the bias that may be introduced with unobserved characteristics. The difference between the groups can be no greater than .25 of a standard deviation. If the difference is between .05 and .25 of a standard deviation, then the study must take the necessary steps to adjust for the baseline differences, such as using analysis of covariance.

Even when QEDs include very closely matched comparison group designs, the overall conclusions are likely to be correct in most cases, but the estimates of the size of the interventions' impact is often inaccurate (U.S. Department of Education, 2003). QEDs are considered worthy contributors, but only if they equate groups and control for pretest differences. RCTs can account for unobserved variables (e.g., motivation) with random assignment. QEDs, however, can never account for unobserved variables and require the exclusion of other potential explanations.

Confounding of Teacher/Interventionist or School with Experimental Method

A major contribution of the second author of this chapter to the WWC standards includes raising the issue of a serious flaw in experimental and quasi-experimental designs—the flaw of the intervention confounding with either a teacher/interventionist, a school, or a classroom. This problem has occasionally occurred in special education research, especially early special education research, and creates a situation where no valid inferences can be drawn from the study. If only Teacher A uses an intervention and only Teacher B teaches in the control condition, then we simply do not know whether the teacher or the intervention caused the impact. The same problem occurs if only School A uses the intervention and only School B is the control group. Studies with this problem—technically called total confounding of the independent variable—are simply uninterpretable. Yet, studies with intervention confounding have slipped into recent meta-analyses (e.g., Francis, Lesaux, & August, 2006), and the problem is rarely discussed in textbooks on field research.

Accurate, Non-Inflated Statistical Significance Levels

In the past, researchers often used classrooms or schools as the unit of assignment, yet analyzed data at the student level. This approach led to serious problems. Very often student performance is "clustered" in a class or school. For instance, students in that class tend to perform more closely to each other than a random sample of similar students. With hierarchic linear modeling (HLM), we can adjust for clustering and develop an accurate probability value (Bryk & Raudenbush, 1992). The National Research Council, for example, found that the percentage of experimental or quasi-experimental comparisons with significant differences between curricular approaches decreased when the appropriate unit of statistical analysis was employed (NRC, 2005). Until as late as 2001, many educational research studies failed to account for clustering or misaligned the unit of statistical analysis with the unit of assignment. When conducting reviews, the WWC will often recalculate an analysis from studies that do not use the appropriate statistical technique. There are current methods for obtaining a reasonable, more conservative, and accurate estimate of the true level of statistical significant (Hedges, 2005).

Another problem related to the reports of inflated statistical significance is the use of multiple comparisons or multiple outcome measures without adequate statistical adjustments. Recently IES has actively encouraged researchers to use the Benjamini-Hochberg correction for multiple comparisons, which is much more accurate, and much more conservative, than techniques frequently used in special education research.

As researchers begin to estimate the statistical power of proposed designs using contemporary techniques, they will almost invariably find that they will need a reasonably large sample to conduct an efficacy trial. The details will vary depending on the estimated impact (minimal detectable effect size), the reliability of the measures used, and the ability to control for initial pretest scores and demographics using analysis of covariance. However, it is not atypical for research to require a total of 60 or 80 classrooms or schools. In this sense, educational research is beginning to resemble research in public health.

The increased breadth of these studies greatly increases the generalizability of findings and the real world value of the studies. However, studies of this scope often will require collaboration among research institutes, university faculty/graduate students and colleagues at other institutions in different regions of the country. In the long haul, this is invaluable for the growth of the field. However, we predict profound changes in the culture of special education research with the shift to far more rigorous, far more ambitious studies that are much larger in scope. The benefit of all these changes is likely to be research findings that are much more credible, studies that no longer raise the type of cynicism that educators often now feel about so-called scientific research in education.

Field-based Complexities and Confounds

As discussed previously, the WWC focuses on using evidence standards to determine whether a practice is effective based on research employing RCT and QED designs. Within this context of rigorous, scientific research, there is still a realization that things work very differently in the real world of schools. The more rarified world of tightly controlled laboratory experiments, experimental medical trials, or training situations is quite different from the complexities associated with school schedules, varying levels of teacher experience, and classrooms of students with diverse learning needs. With such field-based complexities, many educational researchers grapple with the challenge of conducting RCTs in district, school, and classroom settings.

In his commentary on the National Academy of Sciences (NAS) report on scientific research in education, Berliner (2002) noted that the use of RCTs emphasized by IES and the U.S. Department of Education is based on hard sciences, such as physics, chemistry, and biology. He proposed that science in education is not a hard science but the "hardest-to-do science." Berliner stated:

> We [educational researchers] do our science under conditions that physical scientists find intolerable. We face particular problems and must deal with local conditions that limit generalization and theory building—problems that are different from those faced by the easier-to-do sciences [chemistry, biology, medicine]. (p. 18)

We challenge an aspect of Berliner's commentary. Randomized controlled trials have been successfully implemented in many areas of social science—most notably, public health, mental health, job training, welfare-to-work initiatives, and substance abuse. It is unclear that circumstances in education in general or special education in particular are any more difficult than those confronting researchers in areas such as drug abuse, mental illness, or the complex world of welfare-to-work programs. We can—and should—learn a good deal from these research efforts.

Berliner did legitimately note that special education research, because of its complexity, might be one of the hardest of the many hardest-to-do sciences (Odom et al., 2005). Complexity can contribute to confounds and confounds lead to an inability to establish a causal effect. As discussed previously, before making claims about the effectiveness of a particular special education practice, researchers must ensure that the practice, program, or intervention, not some other factor, is responsible for an observed, positive outcome. If claims of effectiveness are biased or untrue due to confounding variables or a complicated mix of factors, it is necessary to consider all of the competing explanations that could potentially lead to the expected outcome (Flay et al., 2005).

The variability of the participants adds to the complexity of special education research. Variability between participants is a major factor in what we call error in research design and statistics. We need to develop sophisticated means to statistically control for this variance, or it will lead to findings that are not reliable and not statistically significant. For example, the Individuals with Disabilities Education Act (IDEA) outlines 12 eligibility (or disability) categories in special education (Office of Special Education and Rehabilitation Services, OSERS, 1997). Within these categories are several different identifiable conditions. Increased variability also results from the greater ethnic and linguistic diversity that occurs in special education because of disproportionate representation of some minority groups (Donovan & Cross, 2002).

Finally, there is early prevention and intervention for targeted at-risk populations. "At-risk" is not homogeneous and can include students at schools serving rurally isolated or inner city populations, students who struggle with early reading or mathematics skills, or students with low vocabulary knowledge and/or speech and language differences. Of course, "at-risk" and "disability" also become more complicated depending on whether school- or researcher-based identification criteria are used. As Response to Intervention (RtI) research becomes more prevalent, there will be even more focus on the still ill-defined category of "at-risk."

Another aspect of complexity is educational context (Odom et al., 2005). Special education is a service, not a specific place or location. There is a wide range of variables related to potential intervention setting. Students with disabilities may participate in a combination of general education and special education classes or receive services in home-based settings or in an inclusive child care setting outside of a public school context (e.g., Head Start). Special education may take the form of community living programs, vocational preparation, or transition services from high school to the work place.

Overall, complexity in special education has several implications for research. Researchers cannot just address a simple question about whether a practice in special education is effective; they must specify clearly for whom the practice is effective and in what context (Guralnick, 1999). Even with randomization and stratification, participant heterogeneity raises significant challenges related to the establishment of group equivalence. For research with low incidence disability populations, establishing appropriate levels of power may be very difficult or not feasible. Specifically, there is tension between identifying populations with sufficient homogeneity and constituting groups large enough to provide adequate power for group comparisons. Too often, intervention studies in special education yield nonsignificant results because there are too few participants in each group (Gersten et al, 2000).

In addition, because IDEA ensures the right to a free appropriate public education, some research and policy questions (e.g., Are IEPs effective in promoting student progress?) may not be addressed through research methodologies that require random assignment to a "nontreatment" group or condition. In special education, students with disabilities are often "clustered" in classrooms, and in experimental group design, the classroom rather than the student becomes the unit on which researchers base random assignment, data analysis, and power estimates (e.g., Gersten et al., 2004). Finally, other challenges connected to scale-up include identifying large samples from small special populations, finding multiple sites, and the expense of providing materials for larger samples of teachers and students.

Implications for Special Education

While there has been increased emphasis on high quality research, researchers in special education are also grappling with challenges associated with rigorous design implementation. For example, studies with researcher-developed measures have been a mainstay of special education instructional research. In the areas of vocabulary and comprehension, researchers have relied on their own comprehension passages, retelling procedures, or word knowledge assessments. Assessments of reading comprehension that systematically tap into deeper levels of comprehension are also needed (Graesser, 2007). Overall, developing, validating, and scaling-up the use of standardized assessment measures is essential in special education research.

In addition to assessment, there is increased pressure to demonstrate that public and private dollars are spent on interventions that are effectively implemented with integrity. Understanding implementation is a serious issue. Program impact can be compromised if implementation lacks fidelity (Elliott & Mihalic, 2004; Greenberg, 2004). The procedural checklists traditionally used to document fidelity of implementation are no longer adequate for large-scale analyses.

As mentioned earlier, a challenge in special education research includes the design of studies targeting specific populations of students with disabilities. For example, many instructional challenges for deaf and hard of hearing students are specific and unique, yet it would be very difficult to design a large scale study given the relatively small sample size of this population. Therefore, the field of special education may need to consider the establishment of regional or national consortiums to help design large scale, multi-site studies as a way to increase sample size for low incidence populations.

The field also needs increased awareness of the new WWC standards for other research methodologies such as single case research, specifically in regards to the added strategies for data interpretation (e.g., visual inspection of data, agreement on an effect size index) and added strategies of application (e.g., a protocol for the inclusion of single subject research in meta-analyses) (Horner, Sugai, Swaminathan, Kratochwill, & Levin, 2007).

A Unique Role for Special Education in the Era of Scientific Research

The push for scientific research has begun, and will continue, to greatly impact special education. Interestingly, the emphasis on rigorous research in special education coincides with increased interest in prevention and Response to Intervention (RtI). Recent research on the RtI model emphasizes two critical components: (a) assessing the performance of a classroom of students to determine the overall student learning within the classroom and whether there are any students that differ significantly from their peers, and (b) determining the rate or actual progress in learning over time (Speece, Case, & Molloy, 2003). There is an intrinsic link between assessment and instruction, which has always been the goal of special education assessment and intervention (e.g. Gersten, Keating, & Irvin, 1995; Fuchs & Deno, 1991).

Given the current emphasis in both research and legislation (IDEA 2004) on responsiveness to instruction, as well as increased use of assessment to both inform and reflect instructional accountability, it is essential to consider evidence-based interventions. RtI model validity requires interventions with proven evidence-based instructional success for students with disabilities. A critical aspect of research methodology involves evaluating the instructional impact of interventions on student performance and providing workable answers to problems identified by practitioners, policymakers, and consumers. Rigorous experimental research incorporating randomized controlled trials are a prerequisite to being considered "an evidence-based instructional approach" per federal policy.

Special education research on various components of the RtI model has also contributed to what we currently know about identifying students in need of intervention and the use of evidence-based practices to promote achievement (Gersten et al., 2008). In the area of reading (K–2), the WWC RtI practice guide reported moderate levels of evidence in support of the recommendation to screen all students for potential reading probes at the beginning and middle of the year and to monitor regularly students who are at risk of developing reading disabilities (Gersten et al., 2008). Strong evidence was found in support of the recommendation to provide intensive, systematic instruction on up to three foundational reading skills in small groups of students who score below the benchmark on universal screening. Overall, 11 studies met WWC standards or met standards with reservations on the use of tier 2 interventions.

The RtI research provides several examples of needed research in the field of special education. For example, we know exceedingly little from rigorous studies of effective practices for improving expressive and receptive language outcomes for students with language/learning disabilities. Because children with language delays often use ineffective methods for representing language (Bishop, 2000), supplemental instruction focused on language—not just word learning and comprehension strategies—will need to continue to be explored for future tier 2 intervention research. Specifically, of the 11 tier 2 studies examined for the WWC RtI practice guide on multi-tier reading interventions, all included phonological awareness or decoding components. Only three included vocabulary in intervention instruction (Ehri, Dreyer, Flugman, & Gross, 2007; Mathes et al., 2005; Vaughn et al., 2006; Gersten et al., 2008). None explicitly addressed language. More research on language intervention is needed to identify effective practices for addressing complex syntax, vocabulary, receptive language and pragmatics, service delivery models, and optimal treatment dosage.

Despite over 50 years of research on special education and remedial instruction, major gaps persist in the knowledge of how to teach reading to the 3% to 5% of students with the most severe reading difficulties (tier 3). The research reveals little about students whose response to typical interventions is low. Although the WWC RtI practice guide identified five studies related to tier 3 interventions that met WWC standards or met standards with reservations, none of the studies reported statistically significant impacts on reading outcomes (Gersten et al., 2008).

Recommendations for Special Education Research

The use of rigorous research methods will enhance the quality of research in special education, improve our understanding of what works for whom and in what context, and improve the education we provide to students. While we encourage use of well-designed group studies, it is important to remember that no experimental design is perfect. There are always tradeoffs and considerations related to the alignment of research questions with appropriate methodologies. We conclude by reinforcing the importance of effectiveness. When determining the effectiveness of special education practices, it is better to get closer to causation than claim that benefits are actually due to other circumstances or competing explanations. Based on the standards established by the WWC and the rigor endorsed by the IES research goals and policy, we recommend 9 guidelines when designing future studies.

1. Always include more than one teacher or one school per condition. This is true even if students are the unit of assignment and the unit of analysis. Otherwise, it is unclear whether the teacher, the school, or the educational program leads to the effect.
2. Randomize whenever possible. Be creative and explain that so many of our methods in special education are chosen by tradition or by word of mouth. Science requires random assignment of classes, schools, or students to conditions. In our experience, school personnel are quite open to random assignment and do hear about the use of random assignment from television, the news media, Internet etc. Randomly assigning schools or classes is often less disruptive for individual students, especially with long-term projects.
3. If you can't randomize, or if randomization is compromised by movement or nonrandom placement, then collect baseline data on relevant pre-intervention measures. Provide evidence of equivalence and adjust for baseline differences if necessary.
4. Take steps to reduce attrition. If you have high attrition, be sure to provide evidence of baseline equivalence of groups.
5. Match your unit of analysis with your unit of assignment. Work with a statistician skilled in HLM.
6. If unit of analysis and unit of assignment are not matched, account for clustering.
7. Don't use too many outcome measures. Be more selective and use a wider array of measures in a pilot to see how the measures fit the type of students your work focuses on. If you do use several outcome measures,

make statistical adjustments to account for multiple measures.

8. Clearly describe the intervention and measures.
9. Build partnerships. Establish collaborations with other research institutions, state educational agencies, technical training and assistance programs, districts, schools, teachers, parents, and students. This is the only way you can conduct the type of large scale, rigorous studies that we need in the field.

In conclusion, our chapter discussed the history and resurgence of educational research in the context of current policy and legislation and identified sources of support for scientific methods in educational research. We also presented a framework of common understandings for how efficacy, effectiveness, and evidence standards can reduce the gap between research and practice. Specifically, scientific methods guide the development of practices in special education by allowing us to ask questions like "Does it work? Is the intervention or treatment effective? or Is A better than B?" To determine what works and what doesn't work, evaluation research with efficacy data and effectiveness trials are required. With the What Works Clearinghouse guidelines, there are current standards for evaluation research quality and acceptability. The WWC guidelines have potentially important implications for discerning whether a practice can ultimately be called evidence-based, research-based, or scientifically-based, and thus are critical for researchers to become familiar with. While the use of randomized control trials (RCTs) may move the field of special education closer to the goal of identifying specific evidence-based practices for special populations of students (Gersten et al., 2004), there still remain many complexities and confounds inherent in special education. Despite these challenges, high quality research in special education will serve a unique role in the current era of scientific research in areas such as RtI and instruction for students with the most significant reading and learning difficulties.

Notes

1. Matching designs entail after-the-fact matching of students in a class receiving an intervention with students in another class not receiving the intervention. A major problem with these designs is that we don't know if the class or students are really comparable because, for example, the teacher in the experimental class might be more motivated, students may have received a stronger reading or language program, etc.

References

Baer, D. M., Wolf, M. M., & Risley, T. R. (1968). Some current dimensions of applied behavior analysis. *Journal of Applied Behavior Analysis, 1*, 91–97.

Berliner, D. C. (2002). Educational research: The hardest science of all. *Educational Researchers, 31*(8), 18–20.

Bishop, D. V. M. (2000). How does the brain learn language? Insights from the study of children with and without language impairment. *Developmental Medicine and Child Neurology, 42,* 133–142.

Blatt, B., & Kaplan, F. (1966). *Christmas in purgatory: A photographic essay on mental retardation.* Boston: Allyn & Bacon.

Bryk, A. S., & Raudenbush, S. W. (1992). *Hierarchical linear models: Applications and data analysis methods.* Newbury Park, CA: Sage.

Campbell D. T., & Boruch R.F. (1975). Making the case for randomized assignment to treatments by considering the alternatives: Six ways in which quasi-experimental evaluations in compensatory education tend to underestimate effects. In C. A. Bennett & A. A. Lumsdaine (Eds.), *Central issues in program evaluation* (pp. 195–296). New York: Academic Press.

Campbell, D. T., & Stanley, J. C. (1996). *Experimental and quasi-experimental designs for research.* Boston: Houghton Mifflin.

Cuban, L. (1990). Reforming again, again, and again. *Educational Researcher, 19*(1), 3–13.

Donovan, M. S., & Cross, C. T. (Eds.). (2002). *Minority students in special education and gifted education.* Washington, DC: National Academy Press.

Duke, N. K., & Mallette, M. H. (2004). *Literacy research methodologies.* New York: Guilford.

Dynarski, M. (2008–2009). Researchers and educators: Allies in learning. *Educational Leadership, 66*(4), 48–53.

Education Sciences Reform Act of 2002 (Pub. L. No. 107-279). Retrieved March 17, 2010, from http://www2.ed.gov/about/offices/list/ies/index.html

Ehri, L. C., Dreyer, L. G., Flugman, B., & Gross, A. (2007). Reading rescue: An effective tutoring intervention model for language-minority students who are struggling readers in first grade. *American Educational Research Journal, 44*, 414–448.

Elliott, D. S., & Mihalic, S. (2004). Issues in disseminating and replicating effective prevention programs. *Prevention Science, 5*(1), 47–52.

Feuer, M. J., Towne, L., & Shavelson, R. J. (2002). Scientific culture and educational research. *Educational Researcher, 31*(8), 4–14.

Flay, B. R. (1986). Efficacy and effectiveness trials (and other phases of research) in the development of health promotion programs. *Preventative Medicine, 15*, 451–474.

Flay, B. R., Biglan, A., Boruch, R. F., Castro, F. G., Gottfredson, D., Kellam, S., et al. (2005). Standards of evidence: Criteria for efficacy, effectiveness and dissemination. *Prevention Science, 6*, 151–175.

Francis, D. J., Lesaux, N. K., & August, D. (2006). Language of instruction. In D. August & T. Shanahan (Eds.), *Developing literacy in second-language learners: Report of the national literacy panel on language-minority children and youth* (pp. 365–413). Mahwah, NJ: Erlbaum.

Fuchs, D., & Fuchs, L. S. (1998). Researchers and teachers working together to adapt instruction for diverse learners. *Learning Disabilities Research & Practice, 13*,126–137.

Fuchs, L. S., & Deno, S. L. (1991). Paradigmatic distinctions between instructionally relevant measurement models. *Exceptional Children, 57*, 488–500.

Gersten, R., Baker, S., & Lloyd, J. W. (2000). Designing high quality research in special education: Group experimental design. *Journal of Special Education, 34*, 2–18.

Gersten, R., Baker, S., Smith-Johnson, J., Flojo, J., & Hagan-Burke, S. (2004). A tale of two decades: trends in support for federally funded experimental research in special education. *Exceptional Children, 70*, 323–332.

Gersten, R., Compton, D., Connor, C.M., Dimino, J., Santoro, L., Linan-Thompson, S., and Tilly, W. D. (2008). *Assisting students struggling with reading: Response to Intervention and multi-tier intervention for reading in the primary grades. A practice guide.* (NCEE 2009-4045). Washington, DC: National Center for Education Evaluation and Regional Assistance, Institute of Education Sciences, U.S. Department of Education. Retrieved from http://ies.ed.gov/ncee/wwc/ publications/practiceguides/

Gersten, R., Fuchs, L. S., Compton, D., Coyne, M., Greenwood, C., & Innocenti, M. (2005). Quality indicators for group experimental and quasi-experimental research in special education. *Exceptional Children, 71*, 149–164.

Gersten, R., & Hitchcock, J. (2008). What is credible evidence in education: The role of What Works Clearinghouse in informing the process. In S. I. Donaldson, C. A. Christie, & M. M. Mark (Eds.), *What counts as credible evidence in applied research and evaluation practice?* (pp. 78–95). Thousand Oaks, CA: Sage.

Gersten, R., Keating, T. J. & Irvin, L. K. (1995). The burden of proof: Validity as improvement of instructional practice. *Exceptional Children, 61*, 510–519.

Gersten, R., Williams, J., Fuchs, L., Baker, S., Koppenhaver, D., Spadorica, S., & Harrison, M. (1998). *Improving reading comprehension for children with disabilities: A review of research.* Washington, DC: American Institutes for Research.

Graesser, A. (2007). *Assessments of reading at deeper levels of comprehension.* Presentation at the 2nd Annual Institute of Education Sciences Research Conference, Washington, DC.

Greenberg, M. T. (2004). Current and future challenges in school-based preventions: The researcher perspective. *Prevention Science, 5*(1), 5–13.

Greene, J. C., Caracelli, V. J., & Graham, W. F. (1989). Toward a conceptual framework for mixed-method evaluation designs. *Educational Evaluation and Policy Analysis, 11*, 255–274.

Guralnick, M. J. (1999). Second-generation research in the field of early intervention. In M. Guralnick (Ed.), *The effectiveness of early intervention* (pp. 3–22), Baltimore, MD: Paul Brookes.

Hedges, L. V. (2005). *Correcting a significance test for clustering.* Unpublished manuscript.

Heshusius, L. (1991). Curriculum-based assessment and direct instruction: Critical reflections on fundamental assumptions. *Exceptional Children, 57*, 315–328.

Horner, R., Sugai, G., Swaminathan, H., Kratochwill, & Levin, J. (2007). *Toward a comprehensive analysis of single-case designs*. Presentation at the 2nd Annual Institute of Education Sciences Research Conference, Washington, DC.

Institute of Education Sciences (IES). (2004). *Director's introduction.* Washington, DC: Author. Retrieved September 20, 2004, from http://www.ed.gov/about/offices/list/ies/director.html

Lovitt, T. C. (1966). Applied behavior analysis techniques and curriculum research: Implications for instruction. In N. G. Haring & R. L. Schiefelbusch (Eds.), *Teaching special children* (pp. 112–156). New York: McGraw-Hill.

Martella, R. C., Nelson, R., & Marchand-Martella, N. E. (1999). *Research methods: Learning to become a critical consumer*. Boston: Allyn & Bacon.

Mathes, P. G., Denton, C., Fletcher, J., Anthony, J., Francis, D., & Schatschneider, D. (2005). The effects of theoretically different instruction and student characteristics on the skills of struggling readers. *Reading Research Quarterly, 40*, 148–182.

Mosteller, F., & Boruch, R. (Eds.). (2002). *Evidence matters: Randomized trials in education research.* Washington, DC: Brookings.

National Research Council (NRC). (2005). *On evaluating curricular effectiveness: Judging the quality of K-12 mathematics evaluations.* Washington, DC: National Academy Press.

National Research Council (NRC). (2002). *Scientific research in education.* R. J. Shavelson & L. Towne, Eds., Committee on Scientific Principles for Educational Research. Washington, DC: National Academy Press.

Odom, S., Brantlinger, E., Gersten, R., Horner, R., Thompson, B., & Harris, K. (2005). Research in special education: Scientific methods and evidence-based practices. *Exceptional Children, 71*, 137–148.

Office of Special Education and Rehabilitation Services. (1997). *Individuals with Disabilities Education Act, 1997 Reauthorization.* Washington DC: Author. Retrieved October 22, 2003, from http://www.ed.gov/offices/OSERS/Policy/IDEA/the_law.html

Slavin, R. E. (1986). Best-evidence synthesis: An alternative to meta-analytic and traditional reviews. *Educational Researcher, 15*(9), 5–11.

Speece, D. L., Case, L. P., & Molloy, D. E. (2003). Responsiveness to general education instruction as the first gate to learning disabilities identification. *Learning Disabilities Research and Practice, 18*, 147–156.

U.S. Department of Education. (2003). *Proven methods: Questions and answers on No Child Left Behind.* Washington, DC: Author. Retrieved October 29, 2003, from http://www.ed.gov/nclb/methods/whatworks/doing.html

Vaughn, S., Mathes, P., Linan-Thompson, S., Cirino, P., Carlson, C., Pollard-Durodola, S., et al. (2006). Effectiveness of an English intervention for first-grade English language learners at risk for reading proglems. *Elementary School Journal, 107*, 153–180.

What Works Clearinghouse (WWC). (2008, December). *Procedures and standards handbook (version 2.0).* Retrieved January 2008, from http://ies.ed.gov/ncee/wwc/references/idocviewer/doc.aspx?docid=19&tocid=1

White, E., & Smith, C. S. (Eds.). (2002). Theme issue on scientific research in Education. *Educational Researcher, 31*(8), 3–29.

5
Special Education Teacher Preparation

Margo A. Mastropieri, Thomas E. Scruggs, and Sara Mills
George Mason University

Special education researchers over the past several decades have identified a number of highly effective treatments for students with mild disabilities in areas such as reading (Swanson, 1999), writing (Rogers & Graham, 2008), math (Kroesbergen & Van Luit, 2003), and content area learning (Scruggs, Mastropieri, Berkeley, & Graetz, 2010). Yet, these effective treatments, however well validated, are of little practical utility without a force of highly trained personnel, competent to carry them out. In this chapter, we discuss significant issues in the preparation of special education teachers, including supply and demand, the components of effective teacher licensure programs, essential knowledge and skills for beginning and expert special education teachers, and challenges for beginning special educators.

Special Education Teacher Supply and Demand

With the passage of Education for All Handicapped Children Act of 1975, which mandated services for children with special needs, there was an increased need for qualified special education teachers. Over 3.5 million children with special needs received services that inaugural year (Whorton, Siders, Fowler, & Naylor, 2000). Each subsequent reauthorization of the Individuals with Disabilities Education Act (IDEA) and Individuals with Disabilities Education Improvement Act (IDEIA, 2004; see Yell, Shriner, & Katsiyannis, 2006, for a review) required changes that ranged from minor to substantive. Some amendments added services for early childhood (birth to 6 years) and included new disability areas (e.g., autism and traumatic brain injury), additional parental roles and rights, changes to the IEP, provisions for access to the general education curriculum, use of evidence-based practices and response to intervention (RtI), and an increase in the qualifications needed for special education teachers to be considered "highly qualified."

Some IDEA changes were directly related to the 2001 passage of the No Child Left Behind Act (NCLB, 2002). NCLB was designed to improve academic performance of all students by reforming schools, increasing accountability, and challenging low student expectations. A major stipulation of NCLB required that all teachers be highly qualified by 2005–2006 and that schools use effective evidence-based practices. Although everyone would agree that schools should have highly qualified teachers and that teachers should possess adequate content knowledge and skills, these new requirements placed additional challenges for the preparation of highly qualified special education teachers. In order to meet the highly qualified standard, one now had to demonstrate content mastery in all subject areas he or she taught. For example, now a secondary math special education teacher had to demonstrate this mastery to meet highly qualified standards in teaching math as well as in special education. Each state developed its own High Objective Uniform State Standard of Evaluation (HOUSSE), which teachers had to meet (The White House Report on No Child Left Behind, n.d.). Moreover, provisionally licensed teachers were provided more stringent time lines to fulfill licensure requirements.

Although these amendments were intended to improve the quality of services for individuals with disabilities, they nonetheless created some unintended consequences. Special education is continually identified as having major teacher shortages in all areas. The need for qualified special education personnel not only persisted under the new law, but increased. The Council for Exceptional Children (CEC) studied the conditions of special education teaching and learning and reported that special education had reached a crisis with rising numbers of students with disabilities resulting in an ever increasing demand for qualified teachers (Kozleski, Mainzer, & Deshler, 2000). Boe, Sunderland, and Cook (2006) reported a need for 74,000 teachers.

Ninety-eight percent of the nation's schools reported special education teacher shortages (ERIC Clearinghouse on Disabilities and Gifted Education, 2001). Demand for new special education teachers may continue to exceed current estimates (Boe, 2006).

This increased demand for new special education teachers has created a new category of teachers, those with provisional or emergency licenses. These individuals, who are not fully credentialed, licensed, nor highly qualified, have been hired with the stipulation that state licensure requirements would be fulfilled within a pre-specified time period. In many cases, these individuals have no special or general education background and, as in the case of the Commonwealth of Virginia, may have only taken an Introduction to Special Education course. Boe and Cook (2006) reported that only 53% of first-year special education teachers were fully credentialed. Unfortunately, this category of under-prepared special education teachers is often assigned to the most challenging classroom positions, or positions that veteran teachers left. For example, in a recent conversation with a new special education teacher with a provisional license, we found that this teacher, who had taken only a single special education course, had been assigned a classroom of 15 middle school students with serious emotional and behavioral disabilities. This type of classroom teaching position is challenging even for the most seasoned special education teachers, but for someone with only an Introduction to Special Education class, it can be totally overwhelming—and far from optimal for enhancing student learning. It is not surprising that many unlicensed special education teachers may find their positions professionally unsatisfying.

The shortage of qualified special education teachers is due not only to a high need from school districts to fill new positions, but also to their need to fill positions vacated by qualified special educators. Billingsley (2005) reported that one-half of special education teachers either transfer to general education, or leave the profession within the first four years of teaching. The reasons for attrition are complex, but include lack of support, behavior management problems, excessive paperwork, insufficient time to collaborate, and other personal reasons (Gersten, Keating, Yovanoff, & Harniss, 2001). Beginning special education teachers reported they felt more isolated and lacked administrative support (e.g., Billingsley, 2002). These findings were corroborated by a survey of Florida teachers, which reported that lack of building administrator support and stress were among primary reasons for discontent among special education teachers (Miller, Brownell, & Smith, 1999). Furthermore, many beginning special education teachers report a mismatch between their preparation programs and their teaching positions, which creates tension, stress, and anxieties, and can lead to job dissatisfaction and decisions to leave the profession (e.g., Mastropieri, 2001; Carter & Scruggs, 2001). Providing additional supports during those first years of teaching may be most critical for socialization into the profession, including nurturing development of a healthy professional attitude. For many, the strongest influence on keeping their teaching positions appears to be job satisfaction, including having supportive administrators, positive school climates, and clear teaching role assignments (Singh & Billingsley, 1996). Although the reasons for leaving the profession are complex and multifaceted, excellent teacher preparation programs could help improve teacher competence.

What Do Effective Teacher Licensure Programs Look Like?

Every state has its own teacher credentialing process. Special education preparation traditionally involved attending a state approved college or university program that may have also been approved by an accrediting board such as National Council for Accreditation of Teacher Education (NCATE). The CEC provides 10 standards for special education preparation programs (CEC, 2009) which are frequently used by traditional preparation programs as guidelines. These standards include mastering knowledge of foundations of the field, characteristics of learners, and individual learning differences; instructional planning, strategies, and learning environments; assessment, communication and collaboration, and professional ethics (CEC). The standards provide a sound logical basis for professional development.

In traditional teacher preparation programs individuals obtain licensure in specific areas such as special education at the elementary level in learning disabilities and emotional behavioral disabilities; master content about teaching and pedagogy, characteristics of learners, and content areas; complete supervised student teaching; and then begin teaching (e.g., Darling-Hammond & Baratz-Snowden, 2005). However, with ever increasing teacher shortages, traditional programs have been unable to meet schools' needs. Therefore, there has been an increasing trend in the development of alternative certification routes for teacher preparation and certification (e.g., Rosenberg & Sindelar, 2005; Washburn-Moses & Rosenberg, 2008). Alternative certification (AC) programs have not only grown rapidly in number across the country, but also vary widely in scope, sequence, and requirements. Rosenberg, Boyer, Sindelar, and Misra (2007) reported that 39 states had allowed use of AC programs and that over 174 variation of AC options existed. Feistritzer (2007) reported that AC approaches are being used in all states and the District of Columbia to assist individuals in meeting the highly qualified teacher requirements. In 2005 it was reported that over 25,000 special education teachers were prepared annually via AC programs (e.g., Connelly, Sindelar, & Rosenberg, 2005). Most AC programs were found to be shorter in duration than traditional programs, require a bachelor's degree, and enroll emergency licensed teachers (e.g., Washburn-Moses & Rosenberg, 2008). Some major features of AC programs differ from traditional programs. For example, Washburn-Moses and Rosenberg reported that distance learning was employed in 68% of the AC programs and that 58% of the AC programs relied on school district staff development rather than university-based teaching. Rosenberg and Sindelar (2005) reviewed 10 existing AC studies, of which six were program evaluations and four were comparative studies. With such a small data base of four comparative studies, we actually know little about the effects of AC programs compared with traditional programs. One study, however, provided positive promising evidence for traditional university programs over AC and provisionally licensed special education teachers.

Nougaret, Scruggs, and Mastropieri (2005) conducted one of the few studies to examine the effectiveness of teachers who had been prepared in traditional university programs compared with teachers who had been given emergency provisional licensure. Two groups of first-year special education teachers were compared on their pedagogical skills. Forty first-year teachers participated in the study. Twenty participants had completed traditional teacher preparation programs associated with state approved programs in colleges or universities, and 20 had been given emergency provisional licensure and had completed no more than six credit hours toward graduation. The sample was diverse: 15 were currently teaching elementary school, 16 middle school, and 9 high school. The majority (36) of the sample were teaching students with learning and or emotional/behavioral disabilities. All teachers were observed by a retired administrator twice during instruction of primary content areas. The observer, unaware of the licensure status of the teachers, rated them using adapted measures from *The Framework of Professional Practice* (Danielson, 1996). The measure was divided into the three subscales of planning and preparation, classroom atmosphere, and instruction. The observer took notes and completed the observation measures, assigning a score of 1 = unsatisfactory, 2 = basic, 3 = proficient, 4 = distinguished, to each item. Teacher and student artifacts, including teachers' lesson plans, were also reviewed.

Findings revealed that traditionally prepared teachers at all grade levels taught significantly better on all subscales of the measure than provisionally licensed teachers. Obtained effect sizes were all large, ranging from 1.57 on classroom atmosphere, 1.60 on planning and preparation to 1.68 on instruction, indicating a substantial advantage for the traditionally prepared group. All teachers were also asked to rate their own teaching abilities, and somewhat surprisingly, there were no differences between traditionally prepared teachers and alternatively licensed teachers. Teachers who had not participated in traditional programs seemed to lack a self-awareness of their teaching shortcomings that were noted by an independent observer.

Findings such as these provide strong support for traditional teacher preparation programs. However, given the dramatic increase in AC programs, it is important to examine their content and approaches. The emphasis and substance of AC programs varies widely. Some existing AC programs created collaborations between universities and local school districts to help meet the needs for highly qualified special education teachers. Some of these collaborations resulted in the development of cohort programs.

Although various cohort organizations exist, cohort models share some common characteristics (e.g., Mastropieri, Morrison, Scruggs, Bowdey, & Werner, 2008). Students enroll in classes as a group, with group size ranging from small to large. The number of classes within cohorts varies from several classes to entire licensure or degree programs. Cohorts consist of open or closed enrollment, meaning some cohorts allow new members to join, others do not. Faculty assignments to cohorts can differ. Some cohorts have only "cohort" faculty while others may have any faculty member. The emphasis of cohort programs has also differed considerably from elementary to secondary to leadership to special education. Mastropieri et al. reviewed 24 studies examining aspects of cohort programs, seven of which examined cohort programs in special education teacher preparation. Both benefits and challenges were reported from special education cohort programs. The most frequently reported benefits included an increase in social emotional support, improved collaboration skills, academic support and growth, and developing a sense of community (e.g., Ross, Stafford, Church-Pupke, & Bondy, 2006). For example, Esposito and Lal (2005) described a cohort program that included courses and field experiences designed to prepare special education teachers to work in diverse urban settings. At exit interviews, students reported feeling prepared and qualified to teach in diverse urban settings. Some cohorts, however, identified challenges that affected both students and faculty negatively. For example, negative group dynamics were reported which developed in single classes and, unfortunately, spread throughout a cohort program (e.g., Sapon-Shevin & Chandler-Olcott, 2001). When negativity develops and spreads throughout a cohort, the unintended consequences can be detrimental to entire programs. Some of the participants in these cohorts, however, reported more positive outcomes.

One type of collaborative cohort program was established between George Mason University (GMU) and two large local school districts. Mastropieri et al. (in press) recently evaluated this alternative program. The cohort program was designed to include identical courses to the traditional program housed on campus. Students enrolled in the cohort program maintained the advantages of a university-based program, with face to face instruction with faculty and adjunct faculty, use of faculty advisors, and library and student support services. However, there were several major value-added features to assist transitioning of emergency-licensed individuals through program requirements more rapidly. A more flexible academic schedule that coincided with the district rather than the university calendar was provided. This allowed three "semesters" rather than two during the academic year and time offerings that were a better fit with district daily schedules. University classes were held in the districts to reduce teacher driving time and university parking fees. A more flexible tuition schedule based on cohort enrollment was established with districts, and tuition assistance was provided. Arrangements were made to allow cohort students to complete on-the-job internships. Finally, the curriculum was slightly adjusted to cover district-specific policies, such as using district adopted IEP forms, and covering district assessment procedures.

Researchers sent emails to all individuals (229) who had participated in one of 15 cohorts established between two districts and GMU requesting their participation in an electronic survey. Respondents (164) were all full-time, conditionally licensed special education teachers (91.5%) or full-time instructional assistants (8.5%). Individual follow-up interviews were completed with a representative sample of 29. At the time of the survey, half of the respondents had completed or were about to complete all licensure and cohort requirements. Respondents were an average of 41 years of age, predominantly female (132), White (81.7%), and had been teaching for an average of 3.3 years. Individuals had previously been employed in a variety of positions, including business, retail, marketing, and the military.

Reported teaching positions were evenly divided among elementary, middle and high school. The classroom settings included self-contained (42%); combinations of self-contained, resource, inclusion, and co-teaching (34%); and full-time inclusion and co-teaching (16%). Over 70% reported teaching students from more than two disability areas, including learning disabilities, emotional disabilities, developmental delays, other health impairments, autism, visual impairments, and hearing impairments. The wide range of disability areas was especially enlightening because the purpose of the licensure program was to prepare students to teach students with learning disabilities and emotional disabilities.

Results were overwhelmingly positive about the cohort program. Respondents reported benefits of social emotional, academic, and teaching support; improved teaching skills such as academic strategies; and logistical and financial supports. They also reported numerous challenges of being enrolled in a full-time graduate program while holding down a new special education teaching position and maintaining a family/personal life. The perceived benefits of this particular cohort alternative licensure program appear to support the notion that alternative licensure programs can result in positive attitudes about programs. What is unknown, however, is whether these improved attitudes result in better teaching competence, greater student achievement, and teacher retention. It may prove fruitful to examine what beginning teachers need to know in order to be successful teachers.

What Do Effective Beginning Special Educators Need to Know?

Given the condensed preparation that many new teachers face, it is critical to identify the knowledge and skills within these domains that are essential to ensure teacher success in the classroom. To identify this essential knowledge and skills, it is useful to look at what effective beginning special education teachers do in the classroom. Additionally, studies of more experienced, expert special educators mirror findings from beginning teacher studies, and can provide a more nuanced understanding of what practices distinguish effective teachers from their less successful peers.

Research suggests that effective teacher preparation programs include coursework that integrates knowledge of learning and learners, knowledge of content and curriculum, and knowledge of teaching (Brownell, Ross, Colón, & McCallum, 2005; Fueyo, Koorland, & Rasch, 2008; Imig & Imig, 2006). The CEC professional standards for teachers in the field of special education also identify professional ethics, assessment, and communication as separate standards and can be integrated within the overall program.

Knowledge of Learning and Learners

New special education teachers must understand the characteristics of diverse learners and how those characteristics influence student learning in the classroom (Brownell, Leko, Kamman, & Streeper-King, 2008; Fueyo et al., 2008). Several CEC professional standards (CEC, 2009) highlight the need for teachers to understand typical and atypical child development, as well as to recognize how learning differs as a result of exceptional conditions. This in-depth understanding of learning and learners provides the basis for special education teachers to identify individual learning needs of students so that instructional strategies may be selected to address each students' strengths and needs. Three of the CEC's standards highlight specific competencies in learners and learning for beginning special education teachers:

1. Foundations
2. Development and Characteristics of Learners
3. Individual Learning Differences

In their study of expert special education teachers, Stough and Palmer (2003) reported that teachers used their extensive knowledge of individual student's learning characteristics to make instructional decisions throughout lessons. Although teachers did not think of students in terms of their disability labels, they did use that as a "jumping off place" (p. 214) to understand their students' academic and behavior needs. This detailed knowledge about the individual learning needs and approaches of each student allowed the expert special education teachers to tailor their instruction to meet those needs. Without such in-depth, individualized knowledge of their students as learners, the teachers would not be able to provide the individualized instruction their students required.

Conners (2008) provided compelling evidence that expert special education teachers developed not only a deep knowledge of individual students' strengths and needs, but also a personal and almost intuitive sense of students' individual characteristics and needs, both academically and social-emotionally. A major component of her conceptualization of expert special educators included a focus on students, including an in-depth knowledge of disabilities and individual students.

Knowledge of Content and Curriculum

No Child Left Behind and IDEA define highly qualified teachers as those with subject-matter knowledge (Brownell et al., 2005; Rosenberg, Sindelar, & Harman, 2004). Special education teachers who are responsible for instructing students in core content areas must demonstrate that they have mastery of the subject matter they are teaching. Some research on effective teaching suggests that subject-matter knowledge (as measured by, for example, number of courses taken in a particular subject area, or academic major) affects student achievement in the areas of secondary math and science (Brownell et al., 2008). The link between subject-matter expertise and student achievement is less clear in language arts or at lower grade levels, however. Additionally, we know little about how subject-matter knowledge affects the effectiveness of special education teachers.

An emerging area of research suggests that simply majoring in mathematics or language arts may be insufficient to be effective in the classroom. Teachers must know subject matter content in specialized ways in order to be able to teach it to others. That is, they must have detailed knowledge of the subject they are teaching, along with *pedagogical* knowledge of the content that allows them to understand how students learn that particular subject matter (Phelps & Schilling, 2004). For example, a teacher working on decoding skills with a beginning reader may notice that her student is experiencing difficulties. A good reader would recognize that the student is having trouble but may lack subject-specific pedagogical knowledge to identify that the student is not recognizing long vowel patterns. Monk (1994) reported that, although background content knowledge in math and science, as measured by number of content specific courses taken, was important for teaching success, coursework in teaching methods also had a strong influence on effective teaching (see also Darling-Hammond & Youngs, 2002). Similarly, Critchfield (2001) assessed math teachers' knowledge of algebra and sought to determine whether relationships existed between teacher knowledge of algebra and student achievement in algebra. Because no relationships were found between student achievement and teacher knowledge of algebra, other factors such as pedagogical skills might be influencing student achievement gains.

In an effort to develop an instrument to measure teachers' "pedagogical content knowledge" (p. 31) in reading, Phelps and Schilling (2004) found that teachers' knowledge of reading comprehension was distinct from teachers' knowledge of how to *teach* reading comprehension. Simply being a good reader and knowing strategies to comprehend text was not the same as being able to teach students how to comprehend text. Teachers understand their subject matter in precise ways that allow them to analyze student work and select instructional strategies to develop students' understanding of the content. Subsequent research has referred to this type of knowledge as "engaged knowledge" (Carlisle, Phelps, Rowan, & Johnson, 2006, in Brownell et al., 2009).

Studies of exemplary teachers have found that teachers who are more engaging and effective demonstrate high levels of engaged knowledge (Rankin-Erickson & Pressley, 2000; Seo, Brownell, Bishop, & Dingle, 2008; Stough & Palmer, 2003). In one study, Seo et al. observed 14 beginning special education teachers and rated them on their ability to engage students in literacy instruction. A long-standing body of research indicates that the more students are engaged, the more they learn. One of the teachers in the study was identified as the most engaging beginning special education teacher. One characteristic that set this teacher apart from her less-engaging peers was her use of a variety of curricular materials to meet the needs of her struggling readers. The teacher was able to blend components of different programs to individualize instruction. She clearly had deep knowledge of reading development and effective literacy pedagogy to be able to select materials and methods to meet the needs of each student. She understood that there was not one program that could meet the needs of all of the students in her class. Low-engaging teachers, on the other hand, showed little subject-specific engaged knowledge. As a result, they were unable to differentiate their instruction to meet the needs of the diverse learners in their classrooms. In fact, low-engaging teachers often read to their students directly from the teacher's edition of the textbook.

Similarly, Stough and Palmer (2003) found that expert special education teachers used a wide range of instructional strategies to tailor instruction to meet individual student needs. In their study of 19 expert special education teachers, they found a pattern of instructional decision making that was consistent across the expert teachers. Based on their in-depth knowledge of individual students' learning patterns and needs, teachers made hypotheses about a student's thinking throughout instruction. Teachers then selected instructional strategies to meet that student's learning needs at that moment. This decision-making process was repeated throughout a lesson, with teachers making hypotheses and instructional modifications many times for individual students throughout one instructional session. The decision-making model outlined by Stough and Palmer illustrates engaged knowledge in practice—teachers understand the curriculum in detail, and understand the way students learn the material and the mistakes they make during the learning process. The instructional strategies teachers select to remediate these learning challenges are specific to the subject-matter they are teaching.

Rankin-Erickson and Pressley (2000) surveyed special education teachers nominated by their school districts as exemplary literacy instructors about their instructional practice. Exemplary teachers were found to have high levels of engaged knowledge. Specifically, these teachers had extensive knowledge about both subject-matter and subject-specific pedagogy. Furthermore, the researchers found that

> teachers who are effective at promoting literacy development have experiences with a variety of instructional approaches and have extensive background knowledge that helps them make decisions about what and how to integrate the "new" with what they successfully have used in the past. (p. 220)

Taken together, these studies indicate that engaged knowledge is critical for effective teaching. Special educators must have a detailed understanding of content and of how students learn that content in order to provide instruction targeted to students' learning needs. Therefore, special education preparation programs must emphasize subject-matter knowledge along with subject-specific pedagogical knowledge.

In fact, this training goes beyond pre-service teacher education programs. Support for the value of engaged knowledge of subject-matter can also be found in the literature on professional development. Several studies have found that professional development aimed at improving teachers' content-knowledge may be the most important method for improving teachers' practice and student achievement (Brownell et al., 2008). These studies indicate that content-focused, professional development delivered over time, rather than through one-time-only workshops, is effective in improving teachers' instructional practice and, in turn, increase student achievement.

Knowledge of Teaching

While the legislative definition of teacher quality focuses exclusively on subject-matter knowledge, research indicates that both content knowledge *and* general pedagogical skills have a significant impact on student achievement (Darling-Hammond & Youngs, 2002). Several CEC standards address knowledge of teaching, including instructional planning, strategies, creating learning environments, communication, and collaboration.

Brownell and her colleagues (2009) studied beginning special education teachers' knowledge of literacy and their related classroom practices. Participants included 34 beginning special education teachers from 9 school districts in 3 states. Brownell et al. used combination of measures of teacher content knowledge, classroom practice, and student achievement in word identification and fluency. The investigators were interested in learning how teacher content knowledge affected teacher practice in the classroom. Furthermore, they were interested in finding out how teacher classroom practice influenced student achievement. Results showed that teacher content knowledge did not have a significant impact on classroom practice. Rather, teachers' generic classroom practices contributed more to the variance in student achievement. Classroom management, in particular, affected achievement more than any other practice. Additionally, teachers who provided intensive, continuous instruction and were able to engage students had more of an influence on student achievement gains than their peers. This suggests that beginning teachers must have strong classroom management and general pedagogical skills, a finding in-line with previous research on effective special education teachers.

Educational researchers in the 1970s and 1980s were particularly interested in identifying explicit teacher behaviors that influenced student achievement. One of the major findings of this research was the importance of direct, active, and engaging instruction to improve student learning (Brownell et al., 2008; Mastropieri & Scruggs, 2010; Seo et al., 2008;). Teachers who were able to actively engage students demonstrated specific behaviors, including efficient use of class time, use of active instructional techniques, less time spent on seatwork, use of large- and small-group instruction, use of positive reinforcement rather than negative criticism, and consistent progress monitoring (Brownell et al.; Seo et al.). In studies conducted by Pressley and his colleagues (Pressley, Rankin, & Yokoi, 1996; Rankin-Erickson & Pressley, 2000), effective literacy teachers also highlighted the importance of creating supportive and motivating environments for learning.

In addition to these effective teacher behaviors identified in the general education literature, effective special education teachers must possess further pedagogical skills to address the needs of their diverse, struggling learners (Brownell et al., 2008; Fueyo et al., 2008; Rankin-Erickson & Pressley, 2000; Rosenberg et al., 2004; Seo et al., 2008). First, effective special education teachers spend more time on skill instruction than their general education peers. Second, effective special education teachers spend more class time engaged in teacher-directed instruction than their general education counterparts. Another pedagogical skill that distinguishes special education teachers is the use of explicit classroom management approaches. Finally, more so than their general education colleagues, special education teachers engage in consistent monitoring of student learning, provide extensive feedback to students, and use a variety of materials to meet individual student needs.

Research on effective beginning special education and expert special education teachers confirms the need for these pedagogical skills. In their survey of effective special education literacy teachers, Rankin-Erickson and Pressley (2000) found that special education literacy teachers spent more time than their general education colleagues teaching letter- and word-level skills. Additionally, they used more class time for drill-and-practice activities than general education teachers. Instruction in basic skills is critical for the academic growth of students in special education. Special education teachers, therefore, must have the knowledge and skills to provide such instruction to their students.

Expertise in behavior management is another critical skill for beginning special education teachers. As Brownell et al. (2009) reported, beginning special education teachers' behavior management skills had the biggest impact on student achievement in reading, even more so than subject matter knowledge. Qualitative studies of expert special education teachers have also noted the importance of behavior management skills. In Seo et al.'s (2008) study, the most engaging beginning literacy teachers all demonstrated strong behavior management skills. They addressed behavior issues immediately, using positive redirection. Additionally, they anticipated potential distractions and made environmental and instructional changes to keep students engaged. Low-engaging teachers' behavior management, on the other hand, seemed more focused on managing behavior than on promoting student learning.

Similar findings were reported by Stough and Palmer (2003). Like the beginning teachers in Seo et al.'s (2008) study, these more experienced teachers relied on effective behavior management to promote student learning. By communicating their expectations, teachers prevented problems that might occur. Additionally, seasoned teachers employed a range of behavioral strategies. They used their substantial knowledge of individual students to tailor these behavior strategies to individual student needs. The strategies the teachers used were generally positive. When behavior problems did occur, expert teachers tended to redirect students rather than call attention to behavior problems. They took prompt action to refocus students who were off-task.

Behavior management skills are especially important for teachers working with students with emotional and behavioral disorders. Rosenberg et al. (2004) highlight the need for teachers of these students to have strong behavior management skills and the ability to teach social skills. As they point out, a disproportionate number of novice teachers are given teaching assignments in high-demand classrooms, including classrooms with students with persistent behavior problems. (Imig & Imig, 2006; Rosenberg et al., 2004). Placing under-prepared teachers in such classrooms has been linked to high rates of teacher attrition. Therefore, it is essential that teacher preparation programs include a focus on behavior management skills.

Finally, Seo et al. (2008) and Stough and Palmer (2003) found that both engaging, beginning teachers and expert special education teachers monitored student learning, provided extensive feedback to students, and used a variety of materials to meet individual student needs. Expert special education teachers engaged in these actions as part of their instructional decision making process (Stough & Palmer). That is, teachers closely monitored student behavior to gauge their learning and selected instructional strategies and materials to meet those needs.

Seo et al.'s (2008) most engaging and, therefore, most effective beginning special education literacy teacher demonstrated all of these skills. She provided frequent feedback to students on their work, and gave them a variety of supports to accomplish tasks. She also quickly addressed errors in student work. As previously mentioned, the most engaging teacher was able to blend curricular materials to meet the individual needs of each student in her classroom, rather than using a one-size-fits-all approach.

Of relevance to content included in special education preparation is the recent government report on teacher preparation for general educators that highlighted knowledge and skills needed by general educators for teaching students with disabilities and English Language Learners (ELL; U.S. Government Accountability Office, 2009). This report, which was based on survey results from all 50 states, provides important information because students with disabilities and ELLs spend approximately 80% of their school day in general education classes. The general education preparation programs that were surveyed covered several relevant categories, e.g., of disabilities and legislation, differentiated instruction, positive behavioral supports, accommodations, universal design, assistive technology, data driven instruction, collaboration, IEPs, and Response to Intervention (U.S. Government Accountability Office). All of these topics would also need to be covered well for beginning special education teachers in their preparation programs.

What Do Expert Special Educators Know?

In depth studies of expert special educators can provide insights into designing more optimal teacher preparation, induction, and inservice programs. One recent study provided insights into the development of special education teachers from novice to expert teachers (Conners, 2008). Conners studied expert middle school special education teachers from a large school district containing 26 middle schools and over 22,000 students with disabilities using extensive observations, interviews, and artifact review. School district administrators and supervisors identified expert special educators who also first met the following criteria: had a minimum of five years special education teaching experience, held professional teaching licenses, and were teaching seventh- or eighth-grade students. From the initial pool of 33 identified special education teachers, 30 agreed to participate in her observational and interview study. All teachers were individually interviewed and observed teaching special education and co-taught classes when teachers also had co-teaching teaching assignments. Teachers had been teaching a mean number of 14.6 years (SD = 9.8) with a range of 5 to 36 years. All teachers, except four, held masters' degrees. Teachers held a variety of positions with a range of students with disabilities. Four teachers taught students with autism, two taught at a special middle school for students with emotional and behavioral disorders, and one teacher taught at an alternative middle school. The other teachers all taught a variety of students with high incidence disabilities. Some teachers taught in self-contained classes for students with disabilities (e.g., reading for students with disabilities). Others co-taught in inclusive classes and also taught in self-contained settings (e.g., math for students with disabilities and co-taught in inclusive math classes). One teacher only taught in co-taught math classes. Content areas instructed by teachers varied considerably. Three teachers taught reading, seven taught English, three taught science, seven taught math, and two taught social studies.

Conners' (2008) data sources included semi-structured interviews, teaching observations using a protocol to note numbers and types of students, classroom organization, lesson structure, content, specialized instructional procedures, teaching behaviors, and use of questioning and strategies, field notes, a teacher engagement scale, and artifacts including teacher lesson plans and student products. The teacher engagement rating scale included six items addressing teacher and student behaviors that could be rated 1 = low, 2 = average, or 3 = high (Mastropieri & Scruggs, 2008).

All of these nominated expert special educators exhibited common traits within and across special education settings, including high expectations for themselves and others and a deeper personal knowledge of their students. These teachers were structured and organized but also flexible with themselves and others, were responsive to individual needs, and emphasized self-regulation skills with students. Finally, teachers valued their profession and special education students.

All teachers also exhibited common classroom management skills, including evidence of structure and routines in their teaching. All exhibited excellent use of engaged time-on-task, and their students were always actively engaged in academic learning tasks. These teachers were excellent at redirecting students in a variety of ways to guide them to expected classroom behaviors. They were proactive in defusing situations to avoid any escalations in inappropriate behaviors. All teachers excelled at using positive reinforcement and recognizing student positive behaviors.

Conners (2008) developed a conceptual framework for expert special education middle school teachers based on her analyses. Her findings revealed that these highly skilled educators held expertise in three overlapping areas, including instructional practices, self-efficacy, and knowledge of students; which was based in part on their previous experiences in teacher preparation programs, inservice professional development activities, collaboration with colleagues, life experiences, and having had life and professional mentors who also recognized their abilities as teacher leaders early on in their careers. The superior knowledge of instructional practices included expert knowledge of pedagogy and content domain knowledge. Self-efficacy also included motivation and a belief system of self-confidence, resiliency, reflective practice and risk taking. Finally, these teachers were totally focused on students and possessed an in-depth knowledge of students with disabilities, in general, and their students, in particular.

Professional development models for beginning teachers could be examined more thoroughly. Earlier induction programs might facilitate the development of stronger instructional pedagogy, classroom management, and collaboration skills. Ongoing mentoring support might provide stronger self-efficacy and resiliency among developing teachers. Such efforts could lead to increased expertise among special education teachers.

Challenges for Beginning Special Educators

Numerous challenges exist for beginning special educators, including the overwhelming task of paper work. Mehrenberg (2009) recently completed a mixed methods study to examine the perceptions of beginning special education teachers toward their paperwork responsibilities and other beginning teacher issues. A national, random sample of beginning special education teachers with five or fewer years of experience were contacted and asked to complete a web-based survey and to participate in follow-up, one-on-one interviews. The survey consisted of four sections, including background demographic data, first-year teaching information, paperwork demands, and teaching and professional morale. Items included several formats such as multiple choice, Likert-scale, yes–no, and open-ended formats. Respondents identified the grade levels, settings, and types of disabilities of students taught during their first year of teaching.

The paperwork demands section asked about special education paperwork tasks, including writing IEPs and behavior plans, but explicitly not about paperwork associated with any teaching (e.g., lesson plans and grading student work). Participants were asked if they were provided a lighter teaching and paperwork load than more seasoned teachers and asked about administrators' support. The final section on morale addressed items around the three constructs of job satisfaction, job stress, and commitment to the profession of special education teaching. Individuals responded about whether they received a reduced teaching assignment during the first year and how a reduced assignment may have influenced their instructional practices. Questions focused on experiences from the first year of teaching. Individuals, who were selected for the follow-up interview based on their demographic data diversity, participated in one-on-one phone interviews, with items intended to obtain corroboration and elaboration of survey items. For example, one representative open-ended item was "What one factor has been the most valuable in helping you prepare for the paperwork demands of your job? Can you give an example of something beneficial that you learned or experienced in your pre-service training that helped prepare you for the bureaucratic duties of being a special education teacher?" (Mehrenberg, 2009, pp. 156–157).

Although no significant correlations were found between the amount of paperwork and any of the morale scales, respondents who had a reduced teaching assignment during year one estimated they might have as much as three additional hours they could spend on instructional activities. Moreover, those individuals who reported reduced teaching loads also reported that they received more assistance completing paper work and greater job satisfaction. Follow-up interviews corroborated this evidence by revealing not only some specific issues associated with paperwork, but also recommendations for assisting new special educators. Major recommendations were to support new teachers with reduced caseloads and to provide more optimal mentoring and induction support (Mehrenberg, 2009).

Morrison (2010) provided corroborating evidence and additional feedback on induction programs from beginning special education teachers. Morrison completed a mixed methods study on the perceptions of beginning special education teachers with respect to their school district induction programs for professional development activities and mentoring support and their influence on retention. She also sought to determine teachers' perceptions of supports provided at the local school level with respect to working conditions, administrative support and the local school culture. A national random sample of beginning special educators was asked to complete an online web-based survey and to participate in one-on-one follow-up interviews. The electronic survey consisted of six major sections. The introductory section contained the consent form for human subject review board and provided directions for the survey. The next section asked participants to describe their first teaching position and included grade levels, settings, academic content and/or social areas, types of students and disabilities, school climate, and other sources of support or concern. The next section contained items about mentoring and induction programs that were available during that beginning teaching experience. Respondents rated the effectiveness of such programs on a Likert scale. The fourth survey section addressed types of supports available within individuals' schools, including administrative and peer support and their respective effectiveness. Other items within this section addressed job satisfaction. The next survey section solicited participant demographic data and individuals' teacher preparation programs and intent to remain teaching. The final section contained open-ended items and allowed participants to volunteer to the follow-up interview. The semi-structured, follow-up interview consisted of items designed to solicit more information on participants' mentoring and induction programs, teacher preparation programs, collaboration with colleagues and overall reflections on their first year of teaching.

Morrison (2010) had a fairly equivalent distribution of elementary (43.4%) and secondary (56.6%) teachers who reported having one to six preparations daily (although 9% reported having seven or more preps a day). They taught all types of students with disabilities in all kinds of settings during their first year of teaching, including self-contained setting (43%), resource or consultation (36%), and co-teaching in general education classroom (32%). Participants indicated that professional development activities were the most frequently offered activity during induction programs in which they participated several times annually. The topics they ranked as most beneficial were transition issues and dealing with stress. Over 90% indicated they were not provided a reduced teaching load, which would have been beneficial in assisting them as new teachers with the demands of the position, including paperwork. In addition, only 62% were assigned mentors who were special education teachers. Twenty-four percent reported having a mentor who had daily contact with them, while 21% reported mentors contacted them five or fewer times (including never) throughout the entire first year of teaching. The highest effectiveness ratings for mentors were for assistance with IEPs, followed by scheduling assistance.

When asked what they liked best about their positions, responses were coded into three major themes of student learning and success, special education teaching, and personal fulfillment. They frequently reported statements such as "making a difference in the lives of students with disabilities." When asked about job satisfaction with their positions, major concerns were noted including excessive paperwork, inadequate planning time with colleagues and for themselves, designing lessons for students with varying ranges of skills, role conflicts, managing student behaviors, high case loads, and inadequate leadership and resources. Teachers also identified concerns with students that specifically addressed inclusion in general education, federal and state assessment requirements, and concerns about their students' learning. On open-ended and follow-up interviews, three areas were identified that could be improved for beginning special education teachers. These included job design, school leadership and culture, and mentoring. With respect to job design, the vast majority of respondents recommended reducing paperwork demands and caseloads, allocating more time for planning with colleagues, and more training on how to complete IEPs. School leadership and culture recommendations included having clearer role expectations and procedures, scheduling more regular sessions for feedback on instruction, hands-on professional development activities on behavior management, writing IEPs, co-teaching, and fostering a climate of inclusion throughout the school. Mentoring recommendations included assigning special education teachers' mentors located in the same building who taught similar contents and students, and providing opportunities to shadow mentors and other veteran teachers. Morrison's (2010) data clearly point to some recommendations that could facilitate the support and growth of beginning special educators at both elementary and secondary levels.

Reports from beginning teachers indicate that preparation programs and schools can do much to improve the perceptions and job satisfaction for beginning special educators, which could lead to more optimal teacher retention and the development of expert special educators. Some recommendations may be cost prohibitive, but it appears that many simple, less costly solutions exist that could be implemented to facilitate beginning teachers transition more smoothly and effectively into the profession and help facilitate their progress not only toward being effective teachers, but toward being expert teachers. These include examining ways to increase support, reduce the paperwork burdens, provide more effective mentors early on who can help beginning teachers learn and understand the school's IEP, assessment, and other school district specific systems. Examination of ways to reduce teaching loads of beginning teachers, to provide opportunities for shadowing expert teachers, and enhancing acculturation to the profession may do much to support and retain beginning special education teachers.

Summary

There continues to be a significant need for special education teachers because of increases in enrollment and traditional teacher preparation programs' inability to produce enough certified teachers annually. The serious teacher shortage has resulted in enormous numbers of emergency-licensed personnel who begin teaching with as few as one special education course, which has resulted in the development of numerous alternative certification (AC) programs across the country. It has been reported that many AC programs are shorter in duration, more likely to be delivered via distance education, and are staffed by district, rather than university instructors. Traditional and alternative certification programs are obligated to design programs to meet respective state licensure requirements, many of which also meet NCATE and CEC standards. However, many traditional and AC programs may not be required to meet NCATE or CEC standards. This inconsistency in meeting standards has the potential to result in less skilled special education teachers.

There is also growing evidence that beginning special education teachers could benefit from additional supports to help them become more successful teachers. Mentoring and induction programs do exist, but they could be strengthened to provide additional supports to assist beginning teachers with the transition from preparation programs to the profession of teaching. Teachers have reported that some mentors are supportive and excellent, whereas others are often unavailable to meet and may lack the specificity of knowledge that teachers want because they teach other content areas or age/grade levels. Reports from Mehrenberg (2009) and Morrison (2010) reveal that beginning teachers frequently feel overwhelmed with excess paper work and high caseloads, IEP demands, co-teaching, variety of roles and responsibilities, district-specific policies and procedures, and could benefit from additional administrator and peer support.

Research has also identified what individuals need to learn and master in their preparation programs, including: (a) learners and learning characteristics of children; (b) subject curriculum and content areas including reading, writing, math, science and social studies; (c) teaching and pedagogical skills, including effective teaching behaviors, classroom management, positive behavior support, response to intervention, and learning strategies; (d) school acculturation, including getting along within a school system and understanding the roles and responsibilities of the position; and (e) becoming a reflective teacher who is committed to providing exciting learning environments for students. Expert special education teachers develop their expertise from a variety of sources, including preparation programs, professional development in schools, but more important, from mentors and life experiences. Conners (2008) provided some guidelines for fostering the development of teachers into experts, including providing nurturing, supportive environments at critical early career stages.

It seems logical that if we want to assist the development of excellent special education teachers who will stay in the field and develop into expert teachers, then universities and school districts should become partners. Preparation programs can provide foundational knowledge, which will be augmented by field experiences with veteran teachers, but districts can provide more intensive mentoring and induction programs to help facilitate the acculturation process to the profession of teaching and provide the supports required to master district-specific requirements (e.g., district IEPs and policies). Schools could consider reducing caseloads for beginning teachers while they master some of these district specific procedures. Programs, traditional or alternative, must ensure that learners are provided supportive, nurturing environments to become reflective teachers who have mastered knowledge of learning, content areas, and the required pedagogical skills. Support from administrators, mentors, and induction programs can do much to help facilitate the novice teacher along the path to becoming a more seasoned and expert teacher.

References

Billingsley, B. S. (2002). *Beginning special educators: Characteristics, qualifications, and experiences*. Retrieved June 22, 2009, from http://ferdig.coe.ufl.edu/spense/policymaker5.pdf

Billingsley, B. S. (2005). *Cultivating and keeping committed special education teachers*. Thousand Oaks, CA: Corwin Press.

Boe, E. E. (2006). Long-term trends in the national demand, supply, and shortage of special education teachers. *The Journal of Special Education, 40*, 138–150.

Boe, E. E., & Cook, L. H. (2006). The chronic and increasing shortage of fully certified teachers in special and general education. *Exceptional Children, 72*, 443–460.

Boe, E. E., Cook, L. H., & Sunderland, R. J. (2006). *Attrition of beginning teachers: Does teacher preparation matter?* (Report No. 2006-TSDQ2). Philadelphia: University of Pennsylvania, Graduate School of Education, Center for Research and Evaluation in Social Policy.

Boe, E., Sunderland, B., & Cook, L. (2006, November). *Special education teachers: supply and demand*. Paper presented at the meeting of Teacher Education Division of the Council for Exceptional Children, San Diego, CA.

Brownell, M. T., Bishop, A. G., Gersten, R., Klingner, J. K., Penfield, R. D., Dimino, J., …Sindelar, P. T. (2009). The role of domain expertise in beginning special education teacher quality. *Exceptional Children, 75*, 391–411.

Brownell, M., Leko, M., Kamman, M. & Streeper-King, L. (2008). Defining and preparing high-quality teachers in special education: What do we know from the research? In T. E. Scruggs & M. A. Mastropieri (Eds.), *Personnel preparation: Advances in learning and behavioral disabilities* (Vol. 21, pp. 35–74). Oxford, UK: Emerald.

Brownell, M. T., Ross, D. D., Colón, E. P., & McCallum, C. L. (2005). Critical features of special education teacher preparation: A comparison with general teacher education. *The Journal of Special Education, 38*, 242–252.

Carter, K. B., & Scruggs, T. E. (2001). Thirty-one students. *Journal of Special Education, 35*, 100–104.

Connelly, V. J., Sindelar, P. T., & Rosenberg, M. S. (2005, February). Special education teachers who are prepared through alternative certification routes: What do we know about them? *Center on Personnel Studies in Special Education Research Preview.* Gainesville, FL: COPSSE.

Conners, N. (2008). *An in-depth study of expert middle school special educators.* Unpublished doctoral dissertation, George Mason University, Fairfax, VA.

Council for Exceptional Children (CEC). (2009). *What every special educator must know: Ethics, standards, and guidelines* (6th ed.). Author.

Critchfield, S. E. (2001) *The impact of middle school teachers' conceptions of functions on student achievement.* Unpublished doctoral dissertation, George Mason University, Fairfax, VA.

Danielson, C. (1996). *Enhancing professional practice: A framework for teaching.* Alexandria, VA: Association for Supervision and Curriculum Development.

Darling-Hammond, L., & Baratz-Snowden, J. (Eds.). (2005). *A good teacher in every classroom: Preparing the highly qualified teachers our children deserve.* San Francisco, CA: Jossey-Bass.

Darling-Hammond, L., & Youngs, P. (2002). Defining "highly qualified teachers": What does "scientifically-based research" actually tell us? *Educational Researcher, 31,* 13–25.

Education for All Handicapped Children Act. (1975). Public Law 94-142, 20. U.S.C. Sections 1400-1461.

ERIC Clearinghouse on Disabilities and Gifted Education. (2001). *Educating exceptional children: A statistical profile.* Arlington, VA: The Council for Exceptional Children.

Esposito, M. C., & Lal, S. (2005). Responding to special education teacher shortages in diverse urban settings: An accelerated alternative credential program. *Teacher Education and Special Education, 28,* 100–103.

Feistritzer, C. E. (2007, May). *Preparing teachers for the classroom: The role of the Higher Education Act and No Child Left Behind.* Testimony for the U.S. House of Representatives Committee on Education and Labor. Retrieved July 8, 2007, from http://edlabor.house.gov

Fueyo, V., Koorland, M., & Rasch, K. (2008). A conceptual framework for analyzing issues and dilemmas in the preparation of special education teachers. In T. E. Scruggs & M. A. Mastropieri (Eds.), *Personnel preparation: Advances in learning and behavioral disabilities* (Vol. 21, pp. 1–34). Oxford, UK: Emerald.

Gersten, R., Keating, T., Yovanoff, P., & Harniss, M. K. (2001). Working in special education: Factors that enhance special educators' intent to stay. *Exceptional Children, 67,* 549–567.

Imig, D., & Imig, S. (2006). What do beginning teachers need to know? An essay. *Journal of Teacher Education, 57,* 286–291.

Individuals with Disabilities Education Act Reauthorization. (2004). Retrieved July 3, 2009 from http://idea.ed.gov

Kozleski, E., Mainzer, R., & Deshler, D. (2000). *Bright futures for exceptional learners: An action agenda to achieve quality conditions for teaching and learning.* Reston, VA: Council for Exceptional Children.

Kroesbergen, E. H., & Van Luit, J. E. H. (2003). Mathematics interventions for children with special educational needs: A meta-analysis. *Remedial and Special Education, 24,* 97–114.

Mastropieri, M. (2001). Is the glass half full or half empty? Challenges encountered by first-year special education teachers. *The Journal of Special Education, 35,* 66–74.

Mastropieri, M. A., Conners, N., Kealy, M., Morrison, N., Scruggs, T. E., & Werner, T. (in press). Special education cohorts as partnerships between universities and public schools. In T. E. Scruggs & M. A. Mastropieri (Eds.), *Advances in learning and behavioral disabilities: Vol. 24. Assessment and intervention.* Bingley, UK: Emerald.

Mastropieri, M. A., Morrison, N., Scruggs, T. E., Bowdey, F. R., & Werner, T. (2008). The use of cohort programs in personnel preparation: Benefits and challenges. In T. E. Scruggs & M. A. Mastropieri (Eds.), *Personnel preparation: Advances in learning and behavioral disabilities* (Vol. 21, pp. 151–179). Oxford, UK: Emerald.

Mastropieri, M. A., & Scruggs, T. E. (2008). *The teacher engagement rating scale.* Unpublished measure, George Mason University, Fairfax, VA.

Mastropieri, M. A., & Scruggs, T. E. (2010). *The inclusive classroom: Strategies for effective instruction* (4th ed.). Upper Saddle River, NJ: Prentice Hall.

Mehrenberg, R. (2009). *An investigation of the effects of paperwork demands on the morale of first year teachers: Does "red tape" overwhelm green teachers?* Unpublished doctoral dissertation, George Mason University, Fairfax, VA.

Miller, M. D., Brownell, M. T., & Smith, S. W. (1999). Factors that predict teachers staying, leaving, or transferring from the special education classroom. *Exceptional Children, 65,* 201–210.

Monk, D. (1994). Subject area preparation of secondary mathematics and science teachers and student achievement. *Economics of Education Review, 13,* 125–145.

Morrison, N. (2010). *The effects of induction, mentoring, and local school culture on retention of beginning special education teachers.* Unpublished doctoral dissertation, George Mason University, Fairfax, VA.

No Child Left Behind Act of 2001. (2002). Retrieved June 28, 2009, from http://www.ed.gov/policy/elsec/leg/esea02/107-110.pdf

Nougaret, A. A., Scruggs, T. E., & Mastropieri, M. A. (2005). The impact of licensure status on the pedagogical competence of first year special education teachers. *Exceptional Children, 71,* 217–229.

Phelps, G., & Schilling, S. (2004). Developing measures of content knowledge for teaching reading. *Elementary School Journal, 105,* 31–48.

Pressley, M., Rankin, J., & Yokoi, L. (1996). A survey of instructional practices of primary-teachers nominated as effective in promoting literacy. *Elementary School Journal, 96,* 363–384.

Rankin-Erickson, J., & Pressley, M. (2000). A survey of instructional practices of special education teachers nominated as effective teachers of literacy. *Learning Disabilities Research & Practice, 15,* 206–225.

Rogers, L. A., & Graham, S. (2008). A meta-analysis of single subject design writing intervention research. *Journal of Educational Psychology, 100,* 879–906.

Rosenberg, M. S., Boyer, K. L., Sindelar, P. T., & Misra, S. (2007). Alternative route programs to certification in special education: What we know about program infrastructure, instructional delivery, and participant characteristics. *Exceptional Children, 73,* 224–241.

Rosenberg, M. S., & Sindelar, P. T. (2005). The proliferation of alternative routes to certification in special education: A critical review of the literature. *Journal of Special Education, 39,* 117–127.

Rosenberg, M. S., Sindelar, P., & Harman, M. (2004). Preparing highly qualified teachers for students with emotional or behavioral disorders: The impact of NCLB and IDEA. *Behavioral Disorders, 29,* 266–278.

Ross, D. D., Stafford, L., Church-Pupke, P., & Bondy, E. (2006). Practicing collaboration: What we learn from a cohort that functions well. *Teacher Education and Special Education, 29,* 32–43.

Sapon-Shevin, M., & Chandler-Olcott, K. (2001). Student cohorts: Communities of critique or dysfunctional families? *Journal of Teacher Education, 52,* 350–364.

Scruggs, T. E., Mastropieri, M. A., Berkeley, S., & Graetz, J. (2010). Do special education interventions improve learning of secondary content? A meta-analysis. *Remedial and Special Education , 31,* 437–449. doi: 10.1177/0741932508327465

Seo, S., Brownell, M., Bishop, A., & Dingle, M. (2008). Beginning special education teachers' classroom reading instruction: Practices that engage elementary students with learning disabilities. *Exceptional Children, 75,* 97–122.

Singh, K., & Billingsley, B. S. (1996). Intent to stay in teaching: Teachers of student with emotional disorders versus other special educators. *Remedial and Special Education, 17,* 37–47.

Stough, L. & Palmer, D. (2003). Special thinking in special settings: A qualitative study of expert special educators. *Journal of Special Education, 26,* 206–222.

Swanson, H. L. (1999). Reading research for students with LD: A meta-analysis of intervention outcomes. *Journal of Learning Disabilities, 32,* 504–532.

U.S. Government Accountability Office. (2009). *Teacher preparation: Multiple federal education offices support teacher preparation for instructing students with disabilities and English Language Learn-*

ers, but systematic department wide coordination could enhance this assistance.(GAO-09-573).

Washburn-Moses, L., & Rosenberg, M. S. (2008). Alternative route special education teacher preparation program guidelines. *Teacher Education and Special Education, 31,* 257–267.

White House report on no child left behind. (n.d.). Retrieved July 14, 2009, from http://www.whitehouse.gov/news/reports/no-child-left-behind.html#4

Whorton, J. E., Siders, J. A., Fowler, R. E., & Naylor, D. L. (2000). A two decade review of the number of students with disabilities receiving federal monies and the types of educational placements used. *Education, 121*, 287–297.

Yell, M. L., Shriner J. G., & Katsiyannis, A. (2006). Individuals with Disabilities Education Improvement Act of 2004 and IDEA Regulations of 2006: Implications for educators, administrators, and teacher trainers. *Focus on Exceptional Children, 39*(1), 1–24.

Section II

Legal Aspects of Special Education

Section Editor: Mitchell L. Yell
University of South Carolina

Federal laws mandating the provision of special education to students with disabilities have been in effect for more than 35 years. The Individuals with Disabilities Education Act (IDEA) is the most significant of these laws. To understand the field of special education, where it has been, where it is, and where it is going, it is necessary to have an understanding of this law and how it affects students with disabilities, their parents, and teachers. The IDEA grants eligible students with disabilities and their parents both procedural and substantive rights. These rights include (a) the right to publicly funded special education programs, (b) the right to an education that is specifically designed to address a student's educational needs and delivered in accordance with his or her individualized education program, (c) the right to be educated with nondisabled children to the maximum extent appropriate, and (d) the right to an education that confers meaningful educational benefit. The IDEA also places great responsibilities on general education teachers, special education teachers, administrators, and related service personnel (and those who prepare them for their jobs) by requiring that they develop and implement special education programs that are educationally appropriate and legally correct. Moreover, this important law has led to research, technical assistance centers, and personnel preparation programs that have improved the lives of students with disabilities

The IDEA has been reauthorized and amended many times since its original passage in 1975. Through this amendment process, the focus of the IDEA has evolved from a law to ensure access to public education for students with disabilities to a law that focuses on results and accountability. When the IDEA, then the Education for All Handicapped Children Act, was passed in 1975 the primary goal of the law was to open the doors of public education to students with disabilities. In this respect the law has been successful. Since the reauthorization of 1997, the emphasis of the IDEA has shifted to ensuring that special education programs confer *meaningful* educational benefit. It does this by requiring that school based teams (a) conduct meaningful and relevant assessments, (b) base students' IEPs on peer-reviewed research, (c) develop measurable annual goals for each area of student needs, and (d) monitor students' progress toward their goals by collecting and reacting to data. As written in the Congressional findings section of IDEA 2004, "improving educational results for children with disabilities in an essential element of our national policy of ensuring equality of opportunity, full participation, independent living, and economic self-sufficiency for individuals with disabilities" (20 U.S.C. § 1401(c)(1)). Thus, over its history the IDEA has evolved in ways that continue to guide the field of special education to improve its outcomes and have a positive impact on the lives of all students with disabilities.

6

The Individuals with Disabilities Education Act

The Evolution of Special Education Law

Mitchell L. Yell
University of South Carolina

Antonis Katsiyannis
Clemson University

M. Renee Bradley
U.S. Department of Education

On November 9, 2010, the Individuals with Disabilities Education Act (IDEA) had been law for 35 years. On November 9, 2000, the 25th anniversary of the signing into law of the IDEA (then the Education of All Handicapped Children Act), President Clinton made the following remarks:

> Today I join millions of Americans in celebrating the 25th anniversary of the Individuals with Disabilities Education Act (IDEA)—a landmark law that opens the doors to education and success for more than six million American children each year. As we recognize this milestone, we know that education is the key to our children's future, and it is the IDEA that ensures all children with disabilities have access to a free appropriate public education. We have seen tremendous progress over the past 25 years—students with disabilities are graduating from high school, completing college, and entering the competitive workforce in record numbers—and we must continue this progress over the next 25 years and beyond. (U.S. Department of Education)

President Clinton spoke about how successful the law had been in opening the doors in public education to students with disabilities and also how greatly the law, in its quarter of a century of existence, had improved educational opportunities for students with disabilities in the United States. Our purpose is to review the IDEA and how it has evolved since 1975. First, we examine the first 35 years of the IDEA, including the litigative and legislative developments that led to the passage of the law. Second, we examine the major principles of the IDEA. Third, we discuss some of the litigation that has interpreted the IDEA. Finally, we reflect on the evolution of the IDEA and what the law now means for educators.

The History of the Individuals with Disabilities Education Act

In the early 1970s only 20% of children with disabilities were educated in America's public schools. During these times students with disabilities were denied educational opportunities in two major ways. First, many students were completely excluded from public schools. Congressional findings in 1974 indicated that more than 1.75 million students with disabilities did not receive educational services. In fact, some states had laws that actually excluded certain categories of students with disabilities from receiving a public education (Office of Special Education Programs, 2000). Second, over 3 million students with disabilities who were admitted to school did not receive an education that was appropriate to their needs (Zettel & Ballard, 1982). In the words of Chief Justice Rehnquist, these children were often "left to fend for themselves in classrooms designed for education of their nonhandicapped peers" (*Board of Education v. Rowley,* p. 191). Because of the limited educational opportunities offered by the public schools, families were often forced to look elsewhere for appropriate services. Often such services could only be found at great distance from their homes and at their own expense. Prior to 1975, therefore, the education of students with disabilities was seen as a privilege, rather than a right (Huefner, 2000). The lack of educational programs and the haphazard nature of services for students with disabilities often led to parents and advocates to seek solutions to these problems through court actions. We begin our review of the history of the IDEA with an examination of court involvement in the education of students with disabilities.

Litigation and the Education of Students with Disabilities
The civil rights movement of the 1950s and 1960s was a catalyst to parents of children with disabilities and advocacy groups for the disabled to begin using the courts in an attempt to force states to provide a public education that was appropriate for their children's unique educational needs. In *Brown v. Board of Education*, the U.S. Supreme Court outlawed segregation by race in public education. The Supreme Court ruled that segregation denied equal educational opportunity, and thus, was a violation of the 14th Amendment to the U.S. Constitution. The high court held that when a state provides an education to some of its citizens, then they must do so for all its citizens on an equal basis. Basing their arguments on this decision, advocates for students with disabilities argued that if segregation by race was a denial of equal educational opportunity, then the exclusion of students with disabilities from schools was also a denial of equal educational opportunity (Winzer, 1993).

Beginning in the early 1970s, advocates for students with disabilities (e.g., parents, advocacy organizations) began to sue states, claiming that exclusion and inappropriate educational services violated students' rights to equal educational opportunity under the U.S. Constitution. In 1972, two landmark court cases, *Pennsylvania Association for Retarded Children v. Commonwealth of Pennsylvania* (hereafter PARC) and *Mills v. Board of Education* (hereafter Mills), began the nation-wide establishment of the right of students with disabilities to receive a public education. Both cases resulted in schools being required to provide educational services to students with disabilities.

In PARC, the Pennsylvania Association for Retarded Children sued the State of Pennsylvania to require the state to provide educational services for students with mental retardation. Many school districts in Pennsylvania routinely excluded children with mental disabilities from receiving an education because of their disability. The case resulted in a consent decree that prohibited the state from denying educational opportunity to these students.

The Mills case involved children with many kinds of disabilities, including problem behaviors. The students brought a class action suit against the board of education of the District of Columbia because they were routinely excluded from public schools through means such as expulsion, suspension, and reassignment. In Mills, as in PARC, the public school defendants were required to provide access to public school education for students with disabilities. Moreover, both cases resulted in the basic procedural rights of notice and hearing being extended to students with disabilities before they could be placed in special education programs.

Following the successful conclusions to the PARC and Mills cases, similar lawsuits were filed in many states across the country. Unfortunately, despite similar court rulings in 28 states and the enactment of laws in many states establishing these educational rights, many students with disabilities were still denied services. Additionally, a great variability of level and quality of educational services for students with disabilities existed across the states. Because of the variability in educational programming, many advocates, parents, and legislators believed that a federal standard was needed. In the next section we review federal involvement in the education of children and youth with disabilities.

Federal Legislation and the Education of Students with Disabilities

Given the challenges faced by students with disabilities in their efforts to access educational services, the U.S. Congress enacted legislation to assure the educational rights of students with disabilities. In the following section we review some of these laws.

The Elementary and Secondary Education Act
One of the earliest Congressional efforts to provide educational funding at the federal level occurred in the Elementary and Secondary Education Act (1965). This law, which was the first law in which the federal government offered direct aid to states for educational purposes, provided money to assist states in educating students whose families fell below the poverty line. Federal money was also available to improve the education of students with disabilities in state schools for the blind, deaf, and retarded. A 1966 amendment to the Elementary and Secondary Education Act created the bureau of Education for the Handicapped in the Department of Health, Education, and Welfare. This bureau later became the Office of Special Education Programs (OSEP). The first law that exclusively addressed students with disabilities, the Education of the Handicapped Act, was passed in 1970.

The Education of the Handicapped Act of 1970
The Education of the Handicapped Act (EHA) expanded the federal grant programs of the Elementary and Secondary Education Act. Grants were offered to institutions of higher education to develop programs to train teachers of students with disabilities. Regional resource centers to deliver technical assistance to state and local school districts were also funded. Following decisions in the PARC and Mills cases, the EHA was amended in 1974 to include a requirement that states that received federal funds adopt the goal of full educational opportunity for students with disabilities. A year later another amendment to the EHA, the Education for All Handicapped Children Act, became the first major federal effort to ensure a free and appropriate education for students with disabilities.

The Education for All Handicapped Children Act of 1975
On November 29, 1975, President Gerald Ford signed into law the most significant increase in the role of the federal government in special education to date, the *Education for All Handicapped Children Act* (EAHCA)[1]. The EAHCA, often called P.L. 94-142, was actually an amendment to the EHA. The EAHCA, which became Part B of the

EHA, combined an educational bill of rights with the promise of federal financial incentives to states that chose to accept EAHCA funds. The law offered grants to states that provided direct services to students with disabilities covered by the law.

The EAHCA was enacted to (a) ensure that children with disabilities received a free appropriate public education, (b) protect the rights of students and their parents, and (c) assist states and localities in their efforts to provide such services. Through this law, the federal government offered grants to states if they would provide appropriate educational programs for students with disabilities who were covered by the EAHCA. To receive funding under the EAHCA, states had to pass laws and prove that they were educating students with disabilities in accordance with law's principles. With the passage of the EAHCA, therefore, the federal government became a partner with states in educating students with disabilities.

To ensure that each student with a disability received an education that was individually designed to address his or her unique needs, Congress granted every student in special education the right to receive a free appropriate public education (FAPE). The law required that students with disabilities receive special education and related services that (a) are provided at public expense, (b) meet the standards of the State educational agency, (c) include an appropriate preschool, elementary, and secondary school education in the State involved; and (d) are provided in conformity with an individualized education program (IEP) designed for each student (IDEA, 20 U.S.C. §1401(8)).

Amendments to the EAHCA

Since the passage of the original EAHCA in 1975, there have been numerous changes to the law. Some of these changes have been minor (e.g., P.L. 100-630 in 1988 altered some of the statute's language and P.L. 102-119 in 1991 modified parts of the infants and toddlers program). Some of the amendments, however, have made important changes to the law. These changes have expanded the rights of students with disabilities under the EAHCA. We next review several of these amendments.

The Handicapped Children's Protection Act of 1986. In 1986 Congress amended the IDEA in the Handicapped Children's Protection Act (P.L. 99-372). This law granted courts the authority to award attorneys fees to parents or guardians if they prevailed in lawsuits in either due process hearings or court cases under the IDEA. This law nullified the U.S. Supreme Court's decision in *Smith v. Robinson* (1984), which prohibited courts from awarding attorneys fees in IDEA cases.

The Infants and Toddlers with Disabilities Act of 1986. That same year Congress also passed the Infants and Toddlers with Disabilities Act (P.L. 99-457). This amendment to the IDEA created incentives for states to educate infants, from birth through age 2, with disabilities or at-risk of developing disabilities. The amendments also extended coverage under the EAHCA to 3- to 5-year-olds.

The Individuals with Disabilities Education Act of 1990. The 1990 amendments to the EAHCA changed the name of the law to the Individuals with Disabilities Education Act (IDEA). Major changes included in IDEA were: (a) the language of the law was changed to emphasize the person first, including the renaming of the law to the Individuals with Disabilities Education Act (IDEA), as well as changing the terms handicapped student and handicapped child to child or student with a disability; (b) students with autism and traumatic brain injury were identified as a separate and distinct disability category entitled to the law's benefits; and (c) a plan for transition was required to be included on every student's IEP by the time he or she turned age sixteen. This law also nullified the U.S. Supreme Court's decision in *Delmuth v. Muth* (1989), which granted states immunity from lawsuits under the IDEA.

The Individuals with Disabilities Education Act Amendments of 1997. When Congress passed the EAHCA in 1975, the law opened the doors of public education for the nation's students with disabilities who needed special education and related services. Thus, the original law emphasized access to educational programs rather than any level of educational opportunity (Eyer, 1998). Although IDEA was dramatically successful in providing access for children with disabilities to public education, Congress determined that the promise of the IDEA had not yet been fulfilled for too many children with disabilities. The IDEA Amendments of 1997 (hereafter IDEA '07) were passed to reauthorize and make improvements to the IDEA. In passing the amendments, Congress noted that the IDEA had been very successful in ensuring access to a FAPE and improving educational results for students with disabilities. Nevertheless, the implementation of the IDEA had been impeded by an insufficient focus on translating research to practice and had placed too much emphasis on paperwork and legal requirements at the expense of teaching and learning. The changes that Congress made to the law were seen as the next step in providing special education and related services by ensuring that students with disabilities received a quality public education by emphasizing the improvement of student performance.

Congress included a number of changes in the IEP requirements to emphasize the necessity of improving educational outcomes. For example, the IDEA '07 required that each student's IEP contain *measurable* annual goals and an explanation of the methods by which a student's progress toward his or her goals would be measured. Furthermore, IEP teams were required to regularly inform parents of students in special education of their child's progress toward his or her annual goals and the extent to which this progress was sufficient to enable the child to achieve these goals. The IDEA also conveyed a clear requirement that if a student failed to make progress toward his or her annual goals, the IEP must be revised (Clark 1999). Last, but not least, special education services developed in the IEP planning process had to allow a student to *advance appropriately* toward attaining the annual goals.

As Eyer (1998) aptly stated:

> The IDEA can no longer be fairly perceived as a statute which merely affords children access to education. Today, the IDEA is designed to improve the effectiveness of special education and increase the benefits afforded to children with disabilities to the extent such benefits are necessary to achieve measurable progress. (p. 16)

IDEA '97 required that schools further the educational achievement of students with disabilities by developing an IEP that provides a special education program that confers measurable and meaningful educational progress.

Since the passage of the Education of All Handicapped Children Act in 1975, disciplining students with disabilities has been an extremely controversial and confusing issue. The IDEA created a detailed set of rules and guidelines to ensure the appropriate education of students who were eligible for special education programs. However, the law contained no federal requirements regarding discipline. Administrators and teachers, therefore, had little legislative guidance with respect to their rights and responsibilities when having to discipline students with disabilities. In IDEA '97, Congress addressed a number of issues related to discipline. Many questions regarding discipline were further clarified when the U.S. Department of Education released the final regulations to IDEA '97, which became effective on May 11, 1999.

The disciplinary provisions of IDEA '97 were based on the following assumptions: (a) all students, including students with disabilities, deserve safe, well-disciplined schools and orderly learning environments; (b) teachers and school administrators should have the tools they need to assist them in preventing misconduct and discipline problems and to address those problems, if they arise; (c) there must be a balanced approach to the issue of discipline of students with disabilities that reflects the need for orderly and safe schools and the need to protect the right of students with disabilities to a FAPE; and (d) students have the right to an appropriately developed IEP with well-designed behavior intervention strategies (Senate Report, 1997). By including the discipline provisions in the 1997 amendments, Congress sought to expand the authority of school officials to protect the safety of all children by maintaining an orderly, drug-free, and disciplined school environment, while ensuring that the essential rights and protections for students with disabilities were protected (*Letter to Anonymous*, 1999). Congress sought to help school officials and IEP teams to (a) respond appropriately when students with disabilities exhibit serious problem behavior, and (b) address problem behavior in the IEP process. IDEA '97 added a section on discipline to the procedural safeguards section of Part B. This section on discipline reflects Congress' intention to balance school official's obligation to ensure that schools are safe and orderly environments conducive to learning and the school's obligation to ensure that students with disabilities receive a FAPE. We will examine additional aspects of the discipline requirements of the IDEA later in this chapter.

The Individuals with Disabilities Education Act Amendments of 2004. On December 3, 2004, President Bush signed the Individuals with Disabilities Education Improvement Act (hereafter IDEA '04) into law. The law, also known as P.L. 108-446, was passed to reauthorize and amend the IDEA. Members of congress believed that the IDEA had successfully ensured access to educational services for millions of children and youth with disabilities. Nevertheless, the success of the IDEA had been impeded by low expectations and an insufficient focus on applying scientifically based research on proven methods of teaching children and youth with disabilities. The purpose of the 2004 reauthorization, therefore, was to increase the quality of special education programs for students in special education by increasing accountability for results.

The primary goal of IDEA 2004 was to improve outcomes for students with disabilities. Congress changed the IDEA through this reauthorization by (a) emphasizing the substantive requirements of the special education process; (b) aligning IDEA with provisions of the Elementary and Secondary Education Act (the law formerly known as the No Child Left Behind Act); (c) altering eligibility requirements; and (d) allowing, and sometimes requiring, school districts to use 15% of their IDEA funds on early intervening services. Additionally, Congress made important changes to the IEP, the disciplinary process, and the dispute resolution system.

Perhaps the most significant change for special education teachers in IDEA '04 was the requirement that their students' IEPs must include a statement of the special education and related services and supplementary aids and services, based on *peer-reviewed research* to the extent practicable. When an IEP team develops a student's special education program, therefore, the services that are provided should be based on reliable evidence that has been published in a peer-reviewed journal or approved by an independent panel of experts.

Another major area of change in IDEA '04 was in special education eligibility requirements. The law included three new requirements. First, a student's parents, the state educational agency (SEA), other state agency, or local education agency (LEA) could request an initial evaluation. Furthermore, eligibility determinations had to be made within 60 days of consent for evaluation, or, if the state has a timeframe for evaluation, within that timeframe. Second, a student could not be determined to have a disability under the IDEA if the fundamental problem of the student resulted from the lack of (a) scientifically-based instruction in reading, including in the essential components of reading instruction (e.g., phonemic awareness, phonics, vocabulary development, reading fluency, and reading comprehension strategies); (b) lack of appropriate teaching in math, or (c) limited English proficiency. This requirement meant that IEP teams had to examine the programming that a student had received in general education to ensure that poor programming was not the cause of the student's problems. Third, when determining whether a child has a specific learning disability, the SEA could no longer require that school districts use a discrepancy formula for determining whether a student has a learning disability (IDEA Regulations, 34 C.F.R. § 300.307(a)(1)). A discrepancy formula is a method for determining if there is a significant enough gap between a student's intellectual ability and academic achievement to make them eligible for special education services in programs for children and youth with learning disabilities.

According to a report issued by the President's Commission on Excellence in Special Education (President's Commission, 2001), when school district personnel rely on a traditional discrepancy model for determining eligibility for special education services in the category of learning disabilities, it essentially required IEP teams to adopt a wait-to-fail approach to meeting the needs of struggling learners. That is, students had to have failed to learn for a couple of years before they have a significant enough gap between ability and achievement to qualify under a discrepancy formula. The problem is that when waiting for a student to exhibit a severe enough discrepancy to qualify for services, precious time is lost in which the student's learning problems may have been remediated. Prior to IDEA '04 states and school districts were required by federal regulations and state laws or regulations to identify students with learning disabilities by using a discrepancy formula. In IDEA '04 Congress included the language which prohibited states from requiring that local school districts use a discrepancy model to identify students with learning disabilities: Instead SEAs must permit LEAs to use a process that determines if the child responds to scientific, research-based intervention as a part of the evaluation procedures (IDEA Regulations, 34 C.F.R. § 300.307(a)(2)). This type of model has been referred to as a response to intervention or RTI model. An RTI system is designed to identify students who are having academic problems when these problems first become apparent and then matching evidence-based instruction to their educational needs. Additionally, RTI models use progress-monitoring systems to track if students are responding to interventions, so that the intensity of the interventions can be increased when students fail to respond.

Because the use of discrepancy formulas to identify students with learning disabilities are clearly discouraged by the federal government and the response to intervention is strongly encouraged, states and school districts may develop new systems for identification. Thus, IDEA '04 changed the emphasis in identification of students with learning disabilities from a process that primarily was concerned with assessment to one that was primarily concerned with achievement and the quality of instruction and intervention. Moreover, if school officials chose to adopt or develop an RTI system, the model will need to include (a) procedures to determine that students were provided with appropriate scientific research-based instruction in general education (IDEA Regulations, 34 C.F.R. § 300.306 (b)(1)(i-ii) and IDEA Regulations, 34 C.F.R. § 300.309(b)(1)); (b) data-based progress monitoring system to continually track how students are responding to instruction (IDEA Regulations, 34 C.F.R. § 300.309(b)(2)); (c) scientific research-based interventions for addressing the needs of students who do not respond to instruction and are placed in special education (IDEA Regulations, 34 C.F.R. § 300.320(a)(3)); and (d) procedures for informing students' parents about the amount and nature of student performance data that is collected, information about general education services, and research-based strategies that will be used to increase a student's rate of learning (IDEA Regulations, 34 C.F.R. § 300.311(a)(7)(ii)(A & B)).

Another very significant change in the reauthorized IDEA is the addition of early intervening services (EIS) to the section in the IDEA regarding the ways that a LEA may spend their IDEA funds (IDEIA 20 U.S.C. § 613(a)(2)(C)). This section allows school districts to use up to 15% of the IDEA Part B funds that it receives from the federal government through the states each year. These Part B funds may be used in combination with other funds, such as funds from the Elementary and Secondary Education Act to develop and implement EIS for students in kindergarten through grade 12, with an emphasis on students in kindergarten through grade three, who have *not* been identified as needing special education or related services but who need additional academic and behavioral support to succeed in the general education environment (IDEIA 20 U.S.C. § 613(f)(1)). Furthermore, if a school district has "significant disproportionality" in its special education programs, the district *must* use 15% of their IDEA Part B funds to establish such services. Early intervening services consist of coordinated, structured, additional academic and behavioral supports that are provided to students who are in general education to enable them to succeed in that environment. The purpose of EIS is to identify young students who are at risk for developing academic and behavioral problems while they are still in general education settings, and then to address these problems by delivering interventions in a systematic manner by using research-based academic and behavioral interventions along with progress monitoring systems to assess the students progress. The law also requires that when school districts deliver EIS they should (a) provide school wide academic and behavioral assessments for all students; (b) implement school wide academic and behavioral services to students identified as needing additional services, including scientifically based reading instruction and positive behavior support systems; and (c) offer professional development activities to teachers and other school staff to enable them to deliver scientifically based academic and behavioral interventions.

When school districts use IDEA funds for EIS, the district officials must report the services that they are providing to general education students to their state educational agencies. Furthermore, the district officials must report on the number of students who are served in their EIS system and the number of students in the services who were eventually found eligible for special education services. The advantages of an EIS model is that school districts will (a) identify students early in their school careers using a risk model rather than a deficit model, (b) emphasize research-based practices in intervention, and (c) focus on student outcomes rather than services that student receive (Vaughn & Fuchs, 2003; Lane, Gresham, & O'Shaughnessy, 2002).

The Structure of the IDEA

Since its passage 35 years ago, the IDEA has been the most significant legislation for students with disabilities. The IDEA is a comprehensive law that provides funding to assist states in their efforts to educate students with disabilities, and governs how students with disabilities will be educated. According to the IDEA, eligible students with disabilities must be provided with a FAPE that consists of special education and related services. The term "special education" means specially designed instruction, at no cost to parents, to meet the unique needs of a child with a disability, including instruction conducted in the classroom, in the home, in hospitals and institutions, and in other settings, and instruction in physical education (IDEA, 20 U.S.C. §1401(25)). A student is eligible for the IDEA if he or she has at least one of 13 types of disability[2] specifically listed under the IDEA and who, by reason thereof, needs special education and related services.

The IDEA is divided into five provisions: Part A, B, C, D, and E. Part A contains the general provision of the act, including Congressional justification for the authorization of the IDEA and includes findings of fact regarding the education of students with disabilities that existed when the IDEA was passed. This section defines the meaning of terms used in the IDEA. Part B contains the explanation of the provisions of providing assistance for education of all children with disabilities, including state and local educational agency eligibility, individualized education programs and placements, procedural safeguards, and other IDEA administration procedures. Part B ensures that all students with disabilities aged 3 through 21 residing in a state that accepts funding under the IDEA have the right to a FAPE. The obligation to make FAPE available to each eligible child residing in the state begins no later than the child's third birthday. This is the section that special education teachers and administrators are most familiar. Part C covers infants and toddlers from birth through age 2. This part of the law was formerly Part H, but became Part C when the IDEA was amended in 1997. Part C provides funds to eligible states for early intervention services for infants and toddlers with disabilities or who would be at risk of experiencing a substantial developmental delay if early intervention services were not provided to the individual (IDEA, 20 U.S.C. §1432(1)). Part D of the IDEA contains provisions that are vitally important to the development of special education and related services through national activities to improve education of children with disabilities. The activities funded by Part D included a variety of program authorities to improve services and results for children with disabilities including technical assistance and dissemination activities, parent training and information, personnel development, and technology and media. Part E created the National Center for Special Education Research within the Department of Education's Institute of Education Sciences. The following sections examine Parts B, C, D, and E in detail.

Part B of the IDEA: Assistance for Education of All Children with Disabilities

In addition to setting forth the funding mechanisms by which the states receive federal IDEA funds, Part B also contains the principles that states must adhere to when educating children with disabilities. Part B is permanently funded, and therefore, does not require periodic Congressional reauthorization, although Congress may reconsider any portion of the IDEA when it considers any other Part of the IDEA. Thus, Congress may amend Part B whenever it decides that it is necessary, including the funding mechanisms and the major principles of Part B of the IDEA.

Funding mechanisms. Part B sets forth the criteria by which states can be eligible for federal funds. To qualify, states must demonstrate to the satisfaction of the U.S. Secretary of Education that the state has in effect policies and procedures to ensure that it meets the conditions set forth in Part B. These conditions include, but are not limited to, (a) the system for identifying, locating, and evaluating children and youth with disabilities known specifically as the child find provisions of the IDEA; (b) the programs that will be used to ensure that eligible students with disabilities receive special education and related services; and (c) the procedural safeguards that will ensure that appropriate programming is provided to eligible children with disabilities.

States that meet the IDEA requirements receive federal funding for the education of children with disabilities. The IDEA funds are received by the SEA for distribution to the LEAs. The federal funds do not cover the entire cost of special education, but rather are intended to provide financial assistance to the states. Congress originally intended to fund 40% of states' costs in providing special education and related services through the IDEA. The actual levels of funding to the states, however, usually amounted to approximately 8% to 10% of states' total special education expenditures. Recently, expenditures have reached approximately 17%. Thus, the IDEA has never been fully funded in accordance with the original Congressional intentions in 1975.

The federal money received by the states must not be used to supplant or substitute for state funds but must be used to supplement and increase funding of special education and related services. This requirement, often referred to as the nonsupplanting requirement of the IDEA, ensures that states will not use IDEA funds to relieve state- and local-level financial obligations, but instead that the funds will increase the level of state expenditures on special education and related services. Each state is ultimately responsible for ensuring the appropriate use of funds. States may use not more than 20% of the maximum amount it may retain for any fiscal year or $800,000, whichever is greater, for administrative costs. The remaining amount must be distributed to local educational agencies (e.g., school districts).

Principles of Part B. Some scholars have divided Part B into six major principles for discussion purposes (Huefner, 2000; Turnbull, Turnbull, Stowe, & Huerta, 2006; Yell, 2006). Neither the IDEA's statutory language nor OSEP in the U.S. Department of Education recognizes the division of the law into these six principles, nonetheless, this division does provide a useful structure for purposes of this discussion; therefore, we provide a brief overview of these major principles in this section.

Zero reject. According to the zero reject principle, all students with disabilities eligible for services under the IDEA are entitled to a FAPE. This principle applies regardless of the severity of the child's disability. According to the U.S. Court of Appeals for the First Circuit, special education is to be provided to all students with educational disabilities, unconditionally and without exception (*Timothy W. v Rochester, New Hampshire School District*). If, however, a student has received a legitimate high school diploma prior to the age of 21, his or her eligibility for services under the IDEA cease.

States must ensure that all students with disabilities, from age 3 to age 21, residing in the state who are in need of special education and related services, or are suspected of having disabilities and in need of special education, are identified, located, and evaluated (IDEA Regulations, 34 C.F.R. § 300.220). These requirements include children with disabilities attending private schools. This requirement is called the child find system. States are free to develop their own child find systems (IDEA, 20 U.S.C. § 1414(a)(1)(A)). The state plan must identify the agency that will coordinate the child find tasks, the activities that it will use, and resources needed to accomplish the child find. School districts are usually responsible for conducting child find activities within their jurisdiction. The child find requirement applies to all children and youth in the specified age range regardless of the severity of the disability. Furthermore, the child find requirement is an affirmative duty. Parents do not have to request that a school district identify and evaluate a student with disabilities, the school must locate all students with disabilities. In fact, parents' failure to notify a school district will not relieve the district of its obligation to identify their child if he or she has a disability. It is up to the school district, therefore, to find these students. When students are identified in the child find, the school district is required to determine whether they have a disability under the IDEA.

Protection in evaluation. Before a student can receive special education and related services for the first time, he or she must receive a full and individual evaluation administered by trained and knowledgeable personnel in accordance with any instructions provided by the producer of the tests. Tests and other evaluation materials used to assess a child must be selected and administered so as not to be discriminatory on a racial or cultural basis; and a variety of assessment tools and strategies must be used to gather relevant functional and developmental information about the child, including information provided by the parent, and information related to enabling the child to be involved in and progress in the general curriculum, among other evaluation requirements. A fair and accurate evaluation is extremely important to ensure proper placement and, therefore, an appropriate education.

Upon completing the administration of tests and other evaluation materials, a group of qualified professionals and the parents of the child must determine whether the child has a disability under the IDEA. Additionally, the team must determine whether, because of this disability, a child needs special education and related services. In other words, the disability must adversely affect a child's educational performance.

When an evaluation team has decided that a student qualifies for special education under the IDEA, a team is appointed to develop the student's education program. This program, called the IEP, is designed to meet the student's unique educational needs.

Free appropriate public education. Students who are determined eligible for special education and related services under the IDEA have the right to receive a FAPE. A FAPE consists of special education and related services that (a) are provided at public expense; (b) are under public supervision and direction, and without charge; (c) meet the standards of the SEA; (d) include preschool, elementary school, or secondary school education in the child's state; and (e) are provided in conformity with an IEP that meets the requirements of the IDEA.

Special education services are specially designed instruction, provided at no cost to parents, that meets the unique needs of a child with a disability (IDEA, 20 U.S.C. § 1401 (25)). Related services are supportive services that may be required to assist a student with a disability to benefit from special education services (IDEA, 20 U.S.C. § 1401 (22)). Related services may include, but are not limited to, developmental, corrective, and supportive services such as speech and language therapy, audiology programs, psychological services, physical and occupational therapy, social work services, and counseling services. Related services do not include medical services that can only be performed by a physician nor do they include surgically implanted devices, such as cochlear implants.

The key to providing a FAPE is individualized programming. To ensure that each student covered by the IDEA receives a FAPE, Congress required that school-based teams develop IEPs for all students with disabilities receiving special education services. The IEP is both a collaborative process between the parents and the school, in which each child's educational program is developed, and a written document that contains the essential components of a student's educational program (Norlin, 2009).

The written document, developed by a team of educators and a student's parents describes a student's educational needs and details the special education and related services that will be provided to the student. The IEP also contains a student's academic and functional goals and how his or her progress toward meeting these goals will be measured and evaluated. Students' IEPs must also address involvement and participation in the general education curriculum. The IDEA mandates the process and procedures for developing the IEP.

Least restrictive environment. The IDEA mandates that students with disabilities are educated with their peers without disabilities to the maximum extent appropriate. This mandate consists of two requirements. First, the IDEA requires that students with disabilities must be educated with students without disabilities to the maximum extent appropriate. This means that the law creates a presumption that students with disabilities be educated together with children who do not have disabilities in the general education classroom. This requirement ensures that students with disabilities are educated in the least restrictive environment (LRE) that is suitable for their individual needs. The second requirement is that students with disabilities cannot be removed from general education settings unless education in those settings cannot be achieved satisfactorily, but only after the use of supplementary aids and services were considered to mitigate the learning environment. This requirement means that even though school districts should educate students with and without disabilities together to the greatest degree possible, the school district may move a student to a more restrictive setting when the general education setting is not appropriate for the student.

The term "LRE" refers to the educational placement that is closest to the general education classroom in which a student can receive a FAPE. Moreover, students in special education can only be removed from the regular classroom to separate classes or schools when the nature or severity of the child's disability is such that the child cannot receive an appropriate education in a general education classroom with supplementary aids and services. When this happens, the student may be removed to a more specialized and restrictive setting that meets his or her needs. The LRE, therefore, will not necessarily be the general education classroom. Furthermore, the exact nature of the placement that is the LRE for a student can only be determined individually for each student after the team has decided what educational services are necessary for a student to receive a FAPE.

To ensure that students are educated in the LRE that is appropriate for their needs, school districts must ensure that a complete continuum of alternative placements is available. The continuum of services ranges from settings that are less restrictive and more typical to settings that are more restrictive and specialized. The most typical and least restrictive setting for most students is the (a) regular education classroom or (b) regular classroom and resource room or (c) itinerant instruction. Additional settings that must be available along the continuum include special classes, special schools, home instruction, and instruction in hospitals and institutions. The less a placement resembles the general education environment, the more restrictive it is considered (Norlin & Gorn, 2005). The hospital or institution is the most restrictive, therefore, because it is the setting that is least like the general education setting.

When determining the educational placement of a child with a disability, including a preschool child with a disability, each public agency shall ensure that the placement decision is made by a group of persons, including the parents and other persons knowledgeable about the child, the meaning of the evaluation data, and the placement options are made in conformity with the LRE provisions of the IDEA. The child's placement is determined at least annually and must be based on the child's IEP, and is as close as possible to the child's home. It is important to point out that unless the IEPs of students with disabilities require some other arrangement, students should be educated in the school that they would attend if they did not have a disability.

Procedural safeguards. Part B of the IDEA contains an extensive system of procedural safeguards to ensure that all eligible students with disabilities receive a FAPE. Schools must follow these procedures when developing special education programs for students with disabilities. The purpose of the procedures is to safeguard a student's right to a FAPE by ensuring that parents are meaningfully involved in the development of their child's IEP. These safeguards include (a) prior notice, (b) informed parental consent, (c) an opportunity to examine records, (d) the right to an independent educational evaluation at public expense, and (e) the right to request an impartial due process hearing (IDEA Regulations, 34 C.F.R. §§300.500-515).

The major purpose of the procedural safeguards requirements of the IDEA is to ensure that a student's parents are meaningfully involved in the special education programming for their child. Indeed, parental involvement is crucial to successful results for students and is one of the cornerstones of the IDEA.

When there is a disagreement between the school and the parents on any proposals to initiate or change the identification, evaluation, educational placement, or the provision of FAPE to the child, or if the school refuses to initiate or change any of these areas, parents may initiate an impartial due process hearing. School districts or the SEA may also request an impartial due process hearing under these same matters. The IDEA amendments of 1997 required that states offer parents the option of resolving their disputes through the mediation process prior to going to a due process hearing. The mediation process is voluntary and must not be used to deny or delay a parent's right to a due process hearing.

Any party in a due process hearing has the right to be accompanied and advised by counsel and by individuals with special knowledge or training with respect to the problems of children with disabilities. Moreover, any party may present evidence, compel the attendance of witnesses, examine and cross-examine witnesses, prohibit the introduction of evidence not introduced five days prior to the hearing, obtain a written or electronic verbatim record of the hearing, and be provided with the written or, at the option of the parents, electronic findings of fact and decisions by the hearing officer. The public agency shall ensure that no later than 45 days after the receipt of a request for a hearing a final decision is reached in the hearing and a copy of the decision is mailed to each of the parties. This decision is binding on both parties. Either party, however, may appeal the decision. In most states, the appeal is to the SEA. The SEA shall ensure that no later than 30 days after the receipt of a request for a review (e.g., appeal) a final decision is reached in the review, and a copy of the decision is mailed to each of the parties. The decision of the SEA can then be appealed to state or federal court as a civil action with respect to the complaint presented to the hearing officer and appealed to the state.

Parent participation. Since the early days of special education litigation, the parents of children with disabilities have played an extremely important role in helping schools meet the educational needs of their children. In fact, parents are coequal partners in the IEP process. Key provisions of the IDEA requiring parental participation are scattered throughout the law. Parents must be involved in initial evaluation, IEP meetings, and placement decisions. The IDEA Amendments of 1997 also required that schools regularly inform parents of their children's progress toward their goals, at least as often as parents of nondisabled children are informed of their progress. The goal of this principle is to have parents play a meaningful role in the education of their children and to maintain a partnership between schools and parents. Parental involvement is crucial to successful results for students and indeed this provision has been, and continues to be, one of the cornerstones of the IDEA.

Enforcement of the IDEA

The Office of Special Education and rehabilitative Services (OSERS) within the U.S. Department of Education is responsible for enforcing, monitoring, and implementing the IDEA. A division within the OSERS, OSEP writes the regulations that implement the IDEA. OSEP is the subdivision of OSERS that is responsible for monitoring and enforcing the IDEA. States are required to annually demonstrate adherence to the policies and procedures of the IDEA by submitting state plans to the Department of Education (IDEA, 20 U.S.C. § 1412 *et seq.*). OSEP monitors these plans to ensure that they are in compliance with the IDEA. Additionally OSEP conducts program audits of state educational agencies and local educational agencies (i.e., school districts) to ensure compliance with the law. The Department of Education has the authority to withhold IDEA funds from states that are not in compliance with IDEA's rules and regulations (IDEA, 20 U.S.C. § 1416 *et seq.*). Disputes regarding IDEA compliance are usually handled through a negotiation process; however, the Department of Education has used its authority to withhold IDEA funds.

Part C of the IDEA: Infants and Toddlers with Disabilities Congress recognized the importance of early intervention for young children when it passed the Education of the Handicapped Amendments in 1986. This law, which became a subchapter of the IDEA (Part H), made categorical grants to states contingent on their adhering to the provisions of law. The amendment required participating states to develop and implement statewide interagency programs of early intervention services for infants and toddlers with disabilities or at-risk of developmental delay and their parents. With the consolidation of the IDEA in the amendments of 1997, Part H became Part C.

For purposes of the law, infants and toddlers are defined as children from birth through age two who need early intervention services because they are experiencing developmental delays or have a diagnosed physical or mental condition that puts the child at-risk of developing developmental delays. Early intervention services are developmental services that are provided under public supervision, and are provided at no cost except where Federal or state law provides for a system of payments by families, including a schedule of sliding fees, and are designed to meet the developmental needs of an infant or toddler with a disability in any one or more of the following areas—physical, cognitive, communication, social or emotional, or adaptive. Early intervention services may include: family training, counseling, home visits, special instruction, speech-language pathology and audiology services, occupational therapy, physical therapy, psychological services, case management services, medical services (for diagnostic or evaluation purposes only); early identification, screening, and assessment services; health services; social work services; vision services; assistive technology devices and services; transportation, and related costs. To the maximum extent appropriate, these services must be provided in natural environments (e.g., home and community settings) in which children without disabilities participate.

The infants and toddlers program requires that state officials designate a state agency to become the lead agency that assumes responsibility and is referred to as the lead agency. The lead agency may be, but does not have to be, the SEA. State officials may designate the state welfare department, the health department, or any other unit of state government to be the lead agency. Many states provide Part C services through multiple state agencies. In these cases, an interagency coordinating council is the primary planning body that works out the agreements between the agencies regarding jurisdiction and funding.

Part D of the IDEA: National Activities to Improve the Education of Children with Disabilities

Perhaps the least known section of the IDEA to most people, including teachers and administrators, is Part D. This section, however, has made significant contributions to improve practices in special education. OSEP states that Part D programs account for less than 1% of the national expenditure to educate students with disabilities (OSEP, 2000); however, programs funded by the Part D national programs play a crucial role in identifying, implementing, evaluating, and disseminating information about effective practices in educating all children with disabilities. The Part D national programs also provide an infrastructure of practice improvement that supports the other 99% of our national expenditure to educate students with disabilities (OSEP, 2000). In the IDEA Amendments of 1997, seven Part D programs were reauthorized. These programs provide federal support for (a) funding research to improve educational programs for students with disabilities, (b) developing devices and strategies to make technology accessible and usable for children with disabilities, (c) training personnel to work with children with disabilities, (d) funding national programs that provide for technical assistance and dissemination, (e) supporting projects that train parents of children with disabilities, (f) evaluating progress in educating students with disabilities, and (g) funding state improvement grants that promote statewide reforms and improvements in the education of students with disabilities.

Part D national programs are often referred to as support programs because the primary purpose of these programs is to support the implementation of the IDEA and to assist states in improving the education of students with disabilities. The Part D national programs, even though they constitute a small amount of the total federal expenditure for the IDEA, help to ensure that the field of special education will continue to move forward by translating research to practice and improving the future of students with disabilities. Throughout the history of IDEA, the Part D investments have been responsible for pushing the envelope of what is possible for students with disabilities in areas such as early intervention, early childhood, assessment, assistive technology, academic achievement, and behavior.

Part E of the IDEA: National Center for Special Education Research

In IDEA '04, Congress established the National Center for Special Education Research (NCSER). The mission of the center, which is housed in the U.S. Department of Education's Institute of Education Sciences, is to sponsor research that expands the knowledge and understanding of infants, toddlers, children, and youth with disabilities in order to improve the development, education, and transition of these individuals. The center also seeks to (a) support the implementation of the IDEA, (b) improve services under the law, and (c) evaluates the implementation and effectiveness of the IDEA. The center also issues publications and holds periodic conferences on special education. The website of NCSER is http://ies.ed.gov/ncser/.

Evolution of the IDEA

The IDEA is an example of a federal law that has been very successful in meeting its original purpose: opening the doors of public education to students with disabilities. Today, the right to access to education for students with disabilities is ensured. In fact, according to the 22nd annual report to Congress (U.S. Department of Education, 2000), in the 1998–1999 school year over 6 million students with disabilities, aged 3 through 21, received special education services under the IDEA. Additionally, almost 50% of students with disabilities, aged 6 through 21, received educational services in the regular classroom for at least 80% of the school day. As former Secretary of Education, Richard Riley, stated on the 25th anniversary of the IDEA: "Twenty-five years ago, IDEA opened the doors to our schoolhouses for our students with disabilities. Today, millions of students with disabilities attend our public schools. We have made steady progress toward educating students with disabilities" (U.S. Department of Education, 2000). The IDEA Amendments of 1997 and 2004 made significant changes to the law. In fact, these amendments represented perhaps the most significant changes to the IDEA since its passage in 1975.

Issues

Despite the successes of the past 30 years, the IDEA has not been without its share of controversy. These controversies have resulted in numerous court decisions, including a number of cases heard by the U.S. Supreme Court. The decisions by the High Court that directly involved the IDEA and students in special education or their parents are listed in Table 6.1.

In the following sections, we examine the most significant of these legal controversies. Two areas that have proven to be very controversial, the free appropriate public education and least restrictive environment principles, are addressed in later chapters in this section and will not be examined here. Another contentious issue, which has led to many due process hearings and court cases, has been the discipline of students with disabilities.

TABLE 6.1
Selected Supreme Court Decisions

Case	Issue	Ruling
Board of Education of the Hendrick Hudson Central School District v. Rowley, 458 U.S. 176 (1982).	FAPE	FAPE is provided if the IEP, developed according to IDEA's procedures, is reasonably calculated to confer educational benefit.
Irving Independent School District v. Tatro, 468 U.S. 883 (1984).	Related services	Health care service must be performed by a nurse or other qualified person (services performed by a physician are excluded).
Burlington School Committee v. Massachusetts Department of Education, 471 U.S. 359 (1985)	Tuition Reimbursement	Prevailing parents who placed their child in a private school were entitled to tuition reimbursement and living expenses when a school failed to provide a FAPE
Honig v. Doe, 108 S. Ct. 592 (1988)	Discipline	Unilateral exclusions for misbehavior that is related to disability are prohibited; Exclusions over 10 consecutive days constitutes a change of placement and as such requires IEP team involvement; stay-put provision applies during administrative and judicial proceedings
Florence County School District v. Carter, 510 U.S. 114 (1993)	Tuition Reimbursement	Private schools do not need to meet state standards for prevailing parents to be reimburse tuition expenses
Zobrest v. Catalina Foothills school District, 509 U.S. 1 (1993)	Procedure	The First Amendment's Establishment Clause did not bar a public school district from providing an interpreter for a student who attended a sectarian school
Cedar Rapids Community School District v. Garrett F., 526 U.S 66 (1999)	Related Services	School districts must provide health care-related services if they are supportive services needed from a student to benefit from special education as long as the services can be provided by a non-physician
Schaffer v. Weast, 546 U.S. 49 (2005).	Procedure	The burden of persuasion for due process hearings is placed upon the party challenging the IEP
Arlington v. Murphy, 548 U.S. 291 (2006)	Procedure	Prevailing parents cannot use the IDEA to recover fees for expert witnesses
Winkelman v. Parma City School District, 550 U.S. 127 (2007).	Procedure	Parents have the right to represent their children in IDEA-related cases. Parental rights are not limited to procedural and reimbursement related matters, but also the entitlement to a FAPE for their child.
Forest Grove v. T.A., U.S. 129 S.Ct. 2484 (2009).	Tuition Reimbursement	A child's parents do not have to received special education services for the parents to receive tuition reimbursement

Disciplining Students with Disabilities

Although the IDEA and its implementing regulations have always been quite detailed, there were no specific federal guidelines regarding the discipline of students with disabilities until the passage of the IDEA Amendments of 1997. This lack of statutory or regulatory requirements resulted in uncertainty among school administrators and teachers regarding appropriate disciplinary procedures for children with disabilities. This uncertainty led to many due process hearings and court cases. We next briefly examine the IDEA and the discipline of students with disabilities.

Disciplinary procedures. School officials may discipline a student with a disability in the same manner as they discipline students without disabilities with a few notable exceptions. For example, school officials may suspend a student with disabilities from school for violating school rules, if a similar violation of school rules would result in the suspension of a nondisabled student. The IDEA Amendments, however, restrict the number of days that a student served under the IDEA can be removed from school without being provided educational services. Students with disabilities cannot be removed from schools in excess of 10 consecutive school days or 10 cumulative days if such removals constitute a change in a student's placement. In this situation, if school officials do not follow the IDEA's change of placement procedures (e.g., written notice to the student's parents, convening the IEP team), the suspension is a violation of the law. Additionally, if a student is removed for more than 10 cumulative days, his or her IEP team must be convened to conduct a functional behavioral assessment and write or revise the behavior intervention plan.

Manifestation Determination. Before using long-term disciplinary removals such as expulsion or long-term suspensions (e.g., in excess of 10 consecutive days), an IEP team must conduct a manifestation determination. In a manifestation hearing, the student's IEP team reviews the relationship between the student's misbehavior and his or her disability. There are two steps that IEP teams should follow when conducting the manifestation determination. First, the IEP team must gather all relevant information regarding the misbehavior, including assessment and diagnostic results, informal assessments, direct observations, interviews, and school records. It is important that this information is up to date. Additionally, the student's parents can supply any evaluation data they want to be considered by the team. The team's task is to use the data to determine if the student understood the consequences of his or her behavior and was capable of controlling it.

The second step of the process involves reviewing the evaluation data to determine if the misbehavior was related to the student's disability. This part of the manifestation determination has been referred to as the relationship test (Hartwig & Reusch, 2000; Kubick, Bard, & Perry, 2000; Yell et al., 2000). The relationship test is based on an individualized analysis of a student, his or her disability, and the student's misbehavior. The relationship test must not be categorically driven. This means that it is not appropriate to make the manifestation determination based on a student's disability or categorical label. Neither does the team base its decision on an analysis of whether the student knew right from wrong (*Doe v. Maher*, 1986). When conducting the relationship test, the team must answer two questions: (a) Was the conduct in question caused by, or did it have a direct and substantial relationship to the student's disability, and (b) was the conduct in question the direct result of the LEAs failure to implement the student's IEP? If the answer to either of these questions is yes, the manifestation determination ends and the misbehavior is considered related to, or a manifestation of, the student's disability. When the behavior is a manifestation of the student's disability, the IEP team must conduct a FBA and develop and implement a BIP. If a BIP was already in place, the IEP team must review the plan and modify it as necessary. Additionally, the student must be returned to the placement from where he or she was removed unless special circumstances exist (e.g., the student brought a weapon to school) or the student's parents and school personnel agree to a change in placement.

On the other hand, if the team determines there is no relationship between the misconduct and disability, the same disciplinary procedures as would be used with students who are not disabled may be imposed on a student with disabilities, including long-term suspension and expulsion. Educational services, however, must be continued. The IEP team, of course, is the proper forum in which to make decisions regarding a student's educational services.

Special disciplinary circumstances. If a student with disabilities (a) brings a weapon to school or a school function (e.g., school dance, school sponsored sporting event); (b) knowingly possesses, uses, or sells an illegal drug or controlled substance at school or a school function; or (c) commits an act that inflicts serious bodily harm on a person while at school, or on school premises, or at a school function the student may be placed in an interim alternative educational setting for up to 45 school days. In these situations a student with disabilities may be removed without regard to whether the misbehavior was a manifestation of a student's disability. However, following removal to an interim alternative educational setting (IAES) the school-based team should conduct a manifestation determination. If a student is a danger to him/herself or others, he or she may also be removed to an interim alternative educational setting for 45 days. However, only an impartial hearing officer, and not school officials, may remove the dangerous student.

Interim alternative educational settings. The situations presented above represent the only times in which school officials may unilaterally remove students with disabilities to an IAES. Students may also be removed to an IAES if an impartial due process hearing officer orders the placement or if a team that conducts the manifestation determination determines there is no relationship between a student's disability and his or her misbehavior. In that situation a student may be subjected to the same disciplinary standard as would a student without disabilities. Of course, educational services must continue for the student with disabilities. The location of the IEAS and the type of educational services provided to the student with disabilities in these situations is an important consideration. The IAES must provide education services that "enable the child to continue to participate in the general education curriculum (although in another setting)… and to progress toward meeting the goals set out in the child's IEP" (IDEA Regulations, 34 C.F.R. § 300.530(d)(1)(i)). The student's IEP team, therefore, should determine the location and the services provided in the IAES. To address a student's misbehavior, the team should conduct a functional behavioral assessment and development or revise the behavior intervention plan. These services should be designed to prevent future occurrences of the misbehavior (*Horry County School District v. P.F,* 1998).

Changing placement for disciplinary reasons. The question of how students with disabilities can be disciplined remains a complicated and confusing issue for many educational officials. Future hearings, court rulings, and legislation will provide answers to these confusing issues. However, when a student's IEP decides to change his or her placement for disciplinary reasons, the team must follow the procedural requirements of the IDEA. This means that the school must request that the child's IEP team convene to make these changes. In such a situation, a student's parents must be given notice to they can fully participate in the meeting. Minor changes in the student's educational program that do not involve a change in the general nature of the program are not a change in placement and do not require prior notification. Changes in the educational program that substantially or significantly affect the delivery of education to the student, however, do constitute a change in placement and are not permissible without full consideration by the IEP team.

Positive behavior support in the IEP. Perhaps the most important implications of the discipline provisions of IDEA '97 were the sections of the law that required IEP teams to take a proactive, problem-solving approach toward addressing the problem behaviors of students with disabilities. The 1997 amendments require that if a student with a disability has behavior problems (regardless of the student's disability category), the IEP team shall consider strategies, including positive behavioral interventions, strategies, and supports, to address these problems (IDEA, 20 U.S.C. § 1414(d)(3)(B)(i)). In such situations a proactive behavior management plan, based on a functional behavioral assessment, must be included in the student's IEP. This means that IEP teams must become competent in conducting appropriate assessments and evaluations (Yell, Rozalski, & Drasgow, 2001). Furthermore, the IEP team must design and deliver appropriate programming based on positive behavioral interventions and supports to meet the needs of students with disabilities who have behavior problems. School districts, therefore, will need to employ people who are competent in conducting functional behavioral assessments and developing positive behavior intervention plans to include in students' IEPs. Finally, IEP teams need to become proficient at developing data collection systems to determine each student's progress toward his or her behavioral goals. Moreover, instructional decisions should be based on the data collected.

Providing Judicial Relief

As we have noted in this chapter, the IDEA has been the subject of much litigation. This is because the statute allows parents or school districts to take their grievance to administrative hearings, and then to bring a civil action in state or federal court (IDEA, 20 U.S.C. § 1415(i)(2)(A)). The IDEA also empowers courts to grant such relief as the court determines is appropriate (IDEA, 20 U.S.C. § 1415(i)(2)(B)). Courts have fashioned many types of remedies for violations of the IDEA. Of these remedies, tuition reimbursement and compensatory education have been the most frequently used in recent years.

With respect to tuition reimbursement, three U.S. Supreme Court cases, *Burlington School Committee v. Massachusetts Department of Education, Florence County School District v. Carter,* and *Forest Grove v. TA* have held that if a local educational agency fails to provide a FAPE to a student, and the parent unilaterally places him or her in a private setting, the local educational agency will be liable for tuition reimbursement and other costs. For relief to be granted in such situations, the private placement must have provided an appropriate education, even if it was not on a state-approved list of private schools. In Forest Grove, the Supreme Court ruled that even if a student has never received special education services in a school district, the district may be responsible for tuition reimbursement if it failed to make a FAPE available to a student and the parents demonstrate that the private placement was appropriate. See Table 6.1 for a brief synopsis of these decisions.

Compensatory education extends a student's IDEA eligibility beyond the statutory age limits. This type of relief compensates parents for a school district's failure to provide a FAPE. The logic of providing compensatory services past the age where a student would no longer be eligible for services is that such services provides a remedy for parents who could not afford to remove their child from school and then seek tuition reimbursement, when their child was denied a FAPE (Huefner, 1999). Table 6.2 lists some of decisions in which the courts have ruled on the availability of compensatory education. As is the case with tuition reimbursement, an LEA must have failed to provide a FAPE and the parents must prove that the private placement was appropriate. Due process hearing officers may also order compensatory education (IDEA, 34 C.F.R. § 300.660).

As we can see by the amount of litigation, along with the successes of the IDEA, there has also been controversy. The issues of what constitutes the (a) correct application of disciplinary procedures and (b) appropriate ways to address problem behavior in students' IEPs are difficult issues for school district personnel. These issues have been the subject of numerous due process hearings and court cases, and no doubt will continue to be the subject of future legislation and litigation.

Response to Intervention

In IDEA'04, Congress prohibited states from using a discrepancy model to identify students with learning disabilities, instead preferring a system whereby students are identified as learning disabilities if they fail to respond to evidence-based instruction. This identification system, which has become known as RTI, has moved far beyond a method for improving the identification of students with learning disabilities to a schoolwide approach to

TABLE 6.2
Selected Cases on Compensatory Education (Appellate Courts)

Case	Ruling
Lester H. v. Gilhool, 916 F. 2d 865, 872-73 (3d Cir. 1990)	Failure to secure an appropriate residential placement by the district resulted in the award of two and a half years of compensatory education
Ridgewood Bd. of Educ. v. N.E., 30 IDELR 41 (3d Cir. 1999)	Compensatory education belongs to the child and "shouldn't depend on the parents to file an action in a timely fashion; The court allowed parents to pursue compensatory education for an alleged denial of FAPE that occurred eight years prior to the filing a due process hearing.
Reid v. District of Columbia, 401 F.3d 516 (D.C. Cir. 2005)	Compensatory education is an equitable remedy which must rely on fact specific, individually based considerations; the court rejected the argument that one hour of lost FAPE should equate to one hour of compensatory education.
Draper v. Atlanta Indep. Sch. Sys., 108 LRP 13764 (11th Cir. 2008).	The district had to pay up to $38,000 a year for the student's private placement because the of the use of an ineffective reading program for three years despite a student's failure to make progress

adapting instruction to meet the needs of students who are having problems learning in the general curriculum. Additionally, schools can now use 15% of the IDEA funds to implement RTI systems. The purpose of an RTI system, which combines evidence-based instruction, increasing intensity of academic and behavioral supports, and progress monitoring, is to increase the number of at risk students who needs are addressed so that they may learn successfully in general education before their problems become so severe that they need special education services. In many RTI models there are three levels or tiers of response. The purpose of the first level is to provide high quality instruction while monitoring student progress. During level two, students who are not responding to level one instruction are provided with more intensive evidence-based interventions while progress-monitoring continues. In level three, highly intensive evidence-based interventions, which will often include special education programming, are provided while progress monitoring continues.

Many school districts, and even states, have been developing RTI models. The move to RTI models will undoubtedly require dramatic alterations in the ways that school districts identify and intervene with students who are at risk of developing academic and behavior problems. That is because the focus of RTI is prevention, evidence-based practices, and progress monitoring rather than remediation. Yell and Walker (2010) provided the following recommendations to school districts that are developing or adopting an RTI model:

Recommendation #1: Provide professional development activities for administrators and teachers regarding their responsibilities under the IDEA 2004. The IDEA and the 2006 regulations have made the following two important changes to the assessment and eligibility process (a) states can no longer require that school districts use a discrepancy formula to determine eligibility of students with LD, (b) school districts are encouraged, and sometimes required, to implement EIS to identify and intervene with students who exhibit academic and behavior problems before they are placed in special education programs. These changes will present immense challenges to school district administrators and teachers. Therefore, extensive professional development will be needed to ensure that school district personnel are able to meet these challenges. For teachers and administrators who are currently working in education, inservice training must be conducted to acquaint them with these new requirements and how to best implement them. Additionally college and university instructors who teach assessment and special education courses must understand the new requirements so they can offer appropriate preservice training opportunities to their students.

Recommendation #2: Develop schoolwide early intervention models. In IDEA 2004 and the 2006 regulations, Congress and the U.S. Department of Education emphasized the importance of identifying students with academic and behavior problems early in their school careers so that educators can intervene using research based strategies and procedures before these students' need special education services. To ensure that school districts' develop early prevention and intervention models, Congress allowed them to use up to 15% of their IDEA funds to develop and implement such programs. School districts should adopt research based early intervention and intervention programs that can be used in general education settings. Moreover, the details of the program must be clearly specified (e.g., how long a student should remain at a particular tier or level, the progress monitoring system that will be used to monitor students' response to instruction).

Recommendation #3: Use instructional procedures grounded in scientifically-based research in general education classrooms. A student cannot be determined to have an IDEA-related disability, and thus be eligible for special education services, if his or her academic problems were due to a lack of appropriate instruction in reading or mathematics. The reasoning behind this section of the law is that when a student fails to learn because of inappropriate instruction, he or she does not have a disability; rather the student is an instructional casualty (President's Commission on Excellence in Special Education, 2001). The decision to determine if a student is truly disabled or failing to learn because of an inappropriate curriculum will fall on a school's multidisciplinary team (IDEA Regulations, § 300.306(b)(1)(i)). Thus, it will be important that team members have information on the effectiveness of the programming used in the general education classroom so that they decide if a student's academic problems were caused by inappropriate instruction. School districts, therefore, should ensure that schools use reading and mathematics programming that research has shown to be effective in the general education setting.

Recommendation #4: Adopt and use research-based progress monitoring systems to collect data on student performance. Early intervening systems that use an RTI process to identify and intervene with students who are failing to learn will need a system that assesses students' responses to scientific, research-based interventions. Therefore, schools using such models will need to frequently and systematically collect data on student progress in the regular education program, and (b) information on the instructional strategies used in regular education classrooms. This information can then be used by a school's multidisciplinary team determine if a student is responding to intervention in the general education. If a student is failing to respond to instruction then the team can use this data to determine the student's eligibility for special education services. School district personnel will need to make decision on the type of the progress monitoring data that they collect. Data collection systems must be reliable, valid, easily administered, inexpensive, and sensitive to changes in student performance.

Recommendation #5: Ensure that the Response to Intervention system does not interfere with a student's rights under the IDEA. If school district officials adopt or develop an RTI system, they must ensure that the system does not interfere with students' right under the IDEA. These rights will always trump school districts' RTI policies. Moreover, if the length of time that a student spends at various tiers is excessive, and a student is not making progress, the school district could be in violation of the IDEA. To ensure that school districts do not violate the run afoul of the IDEA we make the following recommendations. First, the RTI process should consist of no more than three or four tiers and that the top tier of intensive interventions for nonresponders either be special education or result in immediate referral to special education. It is much more likely that those school districts that have multiple tiers (e.g., 6 or 7) in their RTI systems and insist that all students go through all tiers before making a referral to special education will likely be in violation of the child find and evaluation requirements of the IDEA. Second, school districts should use data-based progress monitoring systems to frequently monitor the educational progress of students who have not responded to the first tier of instruction. Third, if a student's parents or teachers make a referral to special education, school districts should act on the referral and not use RTI as an excuse to delay evaluation.

Perspectives on 35 Years of the IDEA

Few parents, educators, advocates, and researchers would dispute the tremendous benefits that children and youth with disabilities and their families have received as a result of the IDEA. In 35 years, the IDEA has clearly met its original goal to open the doors of public education to students with disabilities. Today, this right is assured for virtually all eligible students with disabilities, including children with severe and profound disabilities. Additionally, many of the world's nations have adopted the principles of the IDEA for educating their own children and youth with disabilities.

A second related goal of the IDEA was to provide a process to ensure collaboration between educators and parents. The law achieved this goal largely through the procedural protections that it offered to parents of children with disabilities. Extending these protections to parents was an indication of the importance Congress placed of parental involvement in special education programs. Indeed, through these protections, the IDEA has succeeded in involving parents in the development of their children's educational programs in meaningful ways.

A third important goal of the IDEA was to increase federal support and involvement in improving the education of students with disabilities. In addition to funding state's programs, the U.S Department of Education also funds the training of special education teachers and higher education personnel to provide these training opportunities. Federal funds also support research and demonstration projects' efforts to improve the education of students with disabilities, as well as outreach efforts to ensure that the important findings of research make their way into the classroom. Furthermore, the IDEA also funds national studies, technical assistance, technology development, and parent education programs that support the implementation of the law.

The IDEA continues to put forth an extraordinary vision for improving the outcomes for children with disabilities and their families. No other group of children has experienced the educational improvements that children with disabilities have over the past 25 years. Moreover, this law has also had an important effect on general education. The achievements of this past quarter century are certainly a testament to this exceptional law and provide a strong foundation of experience and progress for future reauthorizations of the law and continued improvements in practice.

Authors Note

Renee Bradley participated in this manuscript as a former teacher, consultant, clinical professor, and professional colleague. Opinions expressed herein are those of the authors and do not necessarily reflect the position of the U.S. Department of Education, Office of Special Education Programs, and no official endorsement should be inferred.

Notes

1. The EAHCA and all subsequent amendments can be found listed in the United States Code as the Individuals with Disabilities Education Act, which is the current name of the law (see references).
2. The disability categories are: Autism, deaf-blind, deafness, emotional disturbance, hearing impairment, mental retardation, multiple disabilities, orthopedic impairments, other health impairment, specific learning disability, speech and language impairment, traumatic brain injury, and visual impairment including blindness.

References

Arlington v. Murphy, 548 U.S. 291 (2006).

Board of Education of the Hendrick Hudson Central School District v. Rowley, 458 U.S. 176 (1982).

Brown v. Board of Education, 347 U.S. 483 (1954).

Burlington School Committee v. Massachusetts Department of Ed*ucation*, 471 U.S. 359 (1985).

Cedar Rapids Community School District v. Garrett F., 526 U.S 66 (1999).

Clark, S. G. (1999). Assessing IEPs for IDEA compliance. *Education Law Report, 137*, 35–42.

Delmuth v. Muth, 491 U.S. 223 (1989).

Doe v. Maher, 793 F2d. 1470 (9th Cir. 1986).

Draper v. Atlanta Independent Sch. Sys., 108 LRP 13764 (11th Cir. 2008).

Elementary and Secondary Education Act, 20 U.S.C. 70 Section 6301 *et seq.*

Eyer, T.L. (1998). Greater expectations: How the 1997 IDEA Amendments raise the basic floor of opportunity for children with disabilities. *Education Law Report, 126*, 1–19.

Florence County School District v. Carter, 510 U.S. 114 (1993).

Forest Grove v. T.A., 129 S.Ct. 2484 (2009).

Hartwig, E. P., & Reusch, G. M. (2000). Disciplining students in special education. *Journal of Special Education, 33*, 240–247.

Honig v. Doe, 108 S. Ct. 592 (1988).

Horry County School District v. P.F. (29 IDELR 354, D.S.C., 1998).

Huefner, D. S. (1999). The legalization and federalization of special education. In J.W. Lloyd, E. J. Kameenui, & D. Chard, *Issues in educating students with disabilities* (pp. 343–362). Mahwah, NJ: Erlbaum.

Huefner, D. S. (2000). *Getting comfortable with special education law: A framework for working with children with disabilities*. Norwood, MA: Christopher-Gordon.

Individuals with Disabilities Education Act, 20 U.S.C. § 1400 et seq.

Individuals with Disabilities Education Act Regulations, 34 C.F R. § 300.1 et seq.

Irving Independent School District v. Tatro, 484 U.S. 883 (1984).

Kubick, R. J., Bard, E. M., & Perry, J. D. (2000). Manifestation determinations: discipline guidelines for children with disabilities. In C. Telzrow & M. Tankersley (Eds.), *IDEA Amendments of 1997: Practice guidelines for school-based teams* (pp. 199–240). Bethesda, MD: National Association of School Psychologists.

Lane, K. L., Gresham, F. M., & O'Shaughnessy, T. E. (2002). Serving students with or at-risk for emotional or behavior disorders: Future challenges. *Education and Treatment of Children, 25*, 507–521.

Lester H. v. Gilhool, 916 F. 2d 865 (3d Cir. 1990).

Letter to Anonymous, 30 IDELR 707 (OSEP 1999).

Mills v. Board of Education of the District of Columbia, 348 F. Supp. 866 (D.D.C. 1972).

Norlin, J. W. (2009). *What do I do when: The answer book on individualized education programs* (3rd ed.). Horsham, PA: LRP.

Norlin, J. W. & Gorn, S. (2005). *What do I do when: The answer book on special education law* (4th ed.). Horsham, PA: LRP.

Office of Special Education Programs (OSEP). (2000). IDEA 25th anniversary website. Available at http://www.ed.gov/offices/OSERS/IDEA 25th.html

Pennsylvania Association for Retarded Citizens (PARC) v. Commonwealth of Pennsylvania, 343 F. Supp. 279 (E.D. Pa. 1972).

President's Commission on Excellence in Special Education. (2001). *A new era: Revitalizing special education for children and their families*. Washington, DC: Education Publications Center, U.S. Department of Education.

Reid v. District of Columbia, 401 F.3d 516 (D.C. Cir. 2005).

Ridgewood Bd. of Educ. v. N.E., 30 IDELR 41 (3d Cir. 1999).

Schaffer v. Weast, 546 U.S. 49 (2005).

Senate report of the IDEA Amendments of 1997, No. 106-17, 105th Cong., 1st Sess. 28-29, 1997. Available at http://www.wais.access.gpo.gov

Smith v. Robinson, 468 U.S. 992 (1984).

Timothy W. v Rochester, New Hampshire School District, 875 F.2d 954 (1st Cir. 1989).

Turnbull, H.R., Turnbull, A.P., Stowe, M., & Huerta, N. (2006). *Free appropriate public education: The law and children with disabilities*. Denver, CO: Love Publishing.

U.S. Department of Education (2000, Nov. 29). Education department celebrates IDEA 25th anniversary; progress continues for students with disabilities. Available at http://www.ed.gov/PressReleases/11-2000/112900.html and http://docs.google.com/gview?a=v&q=cache:e7DNpxLvsTEJ:bulk.resource.org/gpo.gov/papers/2000/2000_vol3_2592.pdf+remarks+of+president+clinton+on+the+25th+anniversay+of+the+individuals+with+disabilities+education+act&hl=en&gl=us.

Vaughn, S., & Fuchs, L.S. (2003). Redefining learning disabilities as inadequate response to instruction: The promise and potential problems. *Learning Disabilities Research & Practice, 18*, 137–146.

Winkelman v. Parma City School District, 550 U.S. 127 (2007).

Winzer, M. A. (1993). *History of special education from isolation to integration*. Washington, D.C.: Gallaudet Press.

Yell, M. L. (2006). *The law and special education* (2nd ed.). Upper Saddle River, NJ: Pearson/Merrill Education.

Yell, M. L., Katsiyannis, A., Bradley, R., & Rozalski, M. (2000). Ensuring compliance with the disciplinary provisions of IDEA '97: Challenges and opportunities. *Journal of Special Education Leadership, 13*, 3–18.

Yell, M. L. & Rozalski, M.E., Drasgow, E. (2001). Disciplining students with disabilities. *Focus on Exceptional Children, 33*(9), 1–20.

Yell, M. L. & Walker, D. W. (2010). The legal basis of response to intervention: Analysis and implications. *Exceptionality, 18*, 124–136.

Zettel, J. J., & Ballard, J. (1982). The Education for All Handicapped Children Act of 1975 (P.L. 94-142): Its history, origins, and concepts. In J. Ballard, B. Ramirez, & F. Weintraub (Eds.), *Special education in America: Its legal and governmental foundations* (pp. 11–22). Reston, VA: Council for Exceptional Children.

Zobrest v. Catalina Foothills school District, 509 U.S. 1 (1993).

7

Free Appropriate Public Education

Mitchell L. Yell
University of South Carolina

Jean B. Crockett
University of Florida

Prior to the Education for All Handicapped Children Act[1] (EAHCA) becoming law in 1975, access to educational opportunities for students with disabilities was limited in two major ways (Yell, 2006; Yell, Drasgow, Bradley, & Justesen, 2004). First, many students with disabilities were completely excluded from public schools. In fact, according to Congressional estimates in the early 1970s only one in five children with disabilities was receiving an education in public schools in the United States (U.S. Department of Education, 2007). Second, over 3 million students with disabilities who were attending public schools did not receive an education that was appropriate to their needs (U.S. Department of Education, 2007). According to Chief Justice William Rehnquist, these students were often "left to fend for themselves in classrooms designed for education of their nonhandicapped peers" (*Board of Education of the Hendrick Hudson School District v. Rowley*, 1982, p. 191). Additionally, state laws protecting the rights of students with disabilities to a public education varied greatly. Some states had good laws; however, many other states had weak laws or no laws protecting the educational rights of these children and youth.

President Gerald Ford signed the EAHCA into law in 1975. The EAHCA provided federal financial assistance to states to aid in the development and improvement of educational programs for students who qualified for special education under the law. To qualify for assistance through the EAHCA, states were required to submit state plans that assured that all eligible students with disabilities would receive a free appropriate public education (FAPE). The law eventually required that a FAPE must be provided to all eligible students with disabilities between the ages of 3 and 21. This included students who have been suspended or expelled from school.

In the decades following the passage of the EAHCA, the question of what exactly constituted a free and appropriate public education has generated much discussion, controversy, and litigation. Our purpose is to review the FAPE requirement of the IDEA. First, we examine the definition of a FAPE in the IDEA and show how the meaning of FAPE has evolved. Second, we review cases that have examined the FAPE principle, including the first special education case heard by the U.S. Supreme Court, *Board of Education of the Hendrick Hudson School District v. Rowley* (1982). Third, we offer guidance to school districts to meet this most important principle of the IDEA.

The FAPE Mandate of the IDEA

After a student is determined eligible for special education services under the IDEA, an individualized education program (IEP) team develops his or her program of special education. This program, which provides the students with a FAPE, consists of specially designed instruction and services provided at public expense. The IDEA defines a FAPE as special education and related services that

(A) are provided at public expense, under public supervision and direction, and without charge,
(B) meet standards of the State educational agency,
(C) include an appropriate preschool, elementary, or secondary school education in the state involved, and
(D) are provided in conformity with the individualized education program. (IDEA, 20 U.S.C. § 1401(a)(18))

The key to providing a FAPE is for school personnel to develop and implement a program of specially designed instruction, based on a full and individualized assessment that is tailored to meet the unique needs of a student with a disability (Yell, 2006). Specially designed instruction refers to more than just academic instruction; it also may include social, emotional, behavioral, physical, and vocational needs (*County of San Diego v. California Special Education Hearing Office*, 1996).

Congressional writers of the IDEA understood that it would be impossible to define a FAPE in such a way that the actual substantive educational requirements were listed, so instead they defined a FAPE primarily in accordance with the procedures necessary to ensure that parents and school personnel would collaborate to develop a program of special education and related services that would meet the unique educational needs of individual students. The IDEA, therefore, was specific in setting forth the procedures by which parents and school personnel, working together, would create programs that would provide an appropriate education. Thus, the definition of a FAPE in the law is primarily procedural rather than substantive.

These procedural mechanisms included requiring school personnel to (a) provide notice to parents anytime their child's education program was discussed so they could participate in the discussions in a meaningful way, (b) invite parents to participate in meetings to develop their child's educational program, (c) secure parental consent prior to initiating evaluations of their child or placing their child in a special education program, (c) allow parents the opportunity to examine their child's educational records, and (d) permit parents to obtain an independent educational evaluation at public expense if the parents disagreed with the school's evaluation. Furthermore, if parents and school personnel cannot agree on a child's evaluation, programming, or placement, the parents can request mediation, an impartial due process hearing, and even file a suit in federal or state court to resolve (IDEA Regulations, 34 C.F.R. § 300.500–515). The purpose of these procedural safeguards is to ensure parental participation and consultation throughout the special education process. Congress believed that requiring meaningful collaboration between parents and school personnel and providing protections for parents when collaboration did not occur would help to ensure that a FAPE would be developed and implemented for all students in special education.

Components of a FAPE

Some of the components of a FAPE have proven to be more controversial that others. Nonetheless it is important that school personnel understand that these are all important elements, and they must be considered when developing students' special education programs.

Free Education

Any special education and related services that are part of a student's IEP must be provided at no charge to parents or guardians of the student. The IDEA does not allow school districts to refuse to provide special education services because of the cost of those services.

Although Congress specifically rejected limitations of federal funding as justification for denying a FAPE, IEP team members may consider cost when making decisions about a student's special education program. Cost considerations are only relevant, however, when an IEP team is choosing one of several options, all of which offer an appropriate education. When only one option is appropriate, the IEP team must choose this option, regardless of cost (*Clevenger v. Oak Ridge School Board*, 1984). For example, if school personnel had to choose between two assistive technology devices for a student, and both options were appropriate, the IEP team could choose the less expensive of the two options. The key would be that both devices had to be appropriate. According to the Office of Special Education Programs (OSEP) of the U.S. Department of Education it is important that school personnel do not make FAPE decisions solely on the basis of cost of services, but that they make decisions based on the individual needs of a student (*Letter to Greer,* 1992).

The regulations implementing the IDEA (IDEA Regulations, 34 C.F.R. § 300.301) clearly indicate that the free service provision of the law pertains only to the parents or guardians and does not relieve other governmental agencies, insurers, or third-party payers from valid obligations to pay for services. For example, Spaller and Thomas (1994) noted that schools can often use private insurance companies as a funding source for costs related to a student's special education. Additionally, school districts are not precluded from charging incidental fees, such as fees for art supplies or field trips, to the parents of students with disabilities. In such cases it is important that the fees are also charged to students without disabilities as part of their educational program (OSEP Policy Letter, 1992).

State Standards

The FAPE mandate of the IDEA includes the requirement that an appropriate education meet the standards of the state educational agency in the state where the student receives his or her education. This was the way that Congress acknowledged the fact that providing an education to the citizens of a state is the responsibility of the state rather than the federal government. As discussed in the previous chapter on IDEA, provisions of the IDEA require states to submit state special education plans that assure qualified students with disabilities the right to a FAPE. These plans, at a minimum, must meet the requirements set forth by the federal government in the special education law.

The state standards requirement also specifies that the education must meet any standards required by the state, including licensure and certification requirements for teachers (IDEA Regulations, 34 C.F.R. § 300.153). Any additional educational requirements enacted by state legislatures must also be followed. If a special education teacher wants to teach in a state, therefore, the teacher must meet the certification or licensure requirements in that state.

Appropriate Education

The *free* education and the *public* education components of a FAPE have rarely been disputed; what constitutes an *appropriate* education for any given student has frequently been the subject of debate and litigation (Wenkart, 2000). To ensure that each student covered by the IDEA receives an individualized FAPE, Congress required that an IEP be developed for all students receiving special education. Thus, a student's FAPE is realized through the development of an IEP.

The IEP formalizes and defines a student's FAPE (Bateman & Linden, 2006; Eyer, 1998; Huefner, 2000; Katsiyannis, Yell, & Bradley, 2002). The IEP is so crucial to a student's education that the failure to develop and implement an IEP properly may render a student's entire special education program invalid in the eyes of the courts (Horsnell & Kitch, 1996; Yell et al., 2004).

The chapter by Bateman (this volume) examines the IEP in great detail; therefore, we do not address IEP development. Nonetheless, we examine a few aspects of a FAPE that must be considered when developing and implementing IEPs. The IDEA sets forth very specific procedural requirements regarding the IEP process. *Procedural requirements* are the requirements that school-based teams must follow when developing students' IEPs. For example, participants in the meeting must include, at a minimum, a representative of the public agency, the student's teacher, and the student's parents. Other individuals may be included at the request of the parent or school district. It is the task of this team to formulate the student's special education program. The IEP must include (a) a statement of the student's present level of educational performance, (b) measurable annual goals, (c) a statement of the specific special education and related services required, (d) a statement of needed transition services, (e) the date the special education services will begin and the anticipated duration of these services, and (f) appropriate objective criteria and evaluation procedures. Adherence to these requirements is important because major procedural errors on the part of a school district may render an IEP inappropriate, and thus deny a student a FAPE, in the eyes of a hearing officer or court (Bateman & Linden, 2006; Yell, 2006). Serious procedural errors that could deprive students of their right to FAPE include those errors that (a) impede a student's right to a FAPE, (b) interfere with a student's parents' opportunity to participate in the special education decision-making process, or (c) cause a deprivation of educational benefits (IDEA 20 U.S.C. § 1415(f)(1)(B)(i)(3)(E)(ii)(I-III)). Procedural errors can be avoided when IEP team members know the requirements of the IDEA (Yell, Meadows, Drasgow, & Shriner, 2009).

Developing IEPs that meet the FAPE requirements of the IDEA, however, is not just about following procedures. To provide a FAPE, IEP teams must develop educationally beneficial special education programs. A procedurally correct IEP, however, will not meet FAPE standards unless the IEP also meets the substantive requirements of the law. Substantive requirements compel IEP teams to develop special education programs that confer meaningful educational benefit. This does not mean that a student's IEP guarantees that he or she will achieve a particular level of educational performance, nor does it hold teachers or administrators liable if a student does not meet specified goals. The IEP, however, does commit the school to providing the special education and related services listed in the IEP and to making good faith efforts to achieve the goals. We next examine components of the IEP that are particularly important in the provision of a FAPE.

Conducting meaningful and relevant assessments. A full and individualized assessment of a student must be conducted prior to providing special education services. The purpose of the assessment is (a) to determine a student's eligibility for special education services and (b) to determine the student's educational needs for planning a student's IEP program. With respect to the provision of FAPE, the second purpose is very important because the assessment forms the basis of a student's annual goals and special education services. The second aspect of the assessment, which is entered into the IEP as the present levels of academic achievement and functional performance (PLAAFP), describes the academic and nonacademic problems that interfere with the student's education so that (a) annual goals can be developed, (b) special educations services can be determined, and (c) a student's progress can be measured (Yell et al., 2009). In effect, the PLAAFP statements become baselines by which IEP teams develop and measure the success of a student's program of special education. If the assessment or the PLAAFP statements are deficient, these deficiencies could result in a denial of FAPE. For example, in *Pocatello School District* (1991), the Indiana state educational agency ruled that a school district had failed to provide a FAPE because the IEP was based on vague and subjective PLAAFP statements that "were not suitable as a baseline to measure future student progress" (Norlin, 2009, p. 4.4). Similarly a District Court in West Virginia ruled that a student's present levels of educational performance must be specified in the IEP so that annual goals can be developed and his or her progress be measured (*Kirby v. Cabell Board of Education*, 2006). Because the PLAAFP statements form the basis of the IEP, all components that follow in the IEP must be logically related to these statements.

Developing measurable annual goals. Every student's IEP must include measurable annual goals.[2] According to language in the IDEA, annual goals, which include academic and functional goals, must be designed to (a) meet the student's needs that result from the child's disability, (b) permit the student to be involved in and make progress in the general education curriculum, (c) enable the IEP team to develop strategies that will be most effective in meeting the goals, and (d) allow the IEP team to monitor a student's progress (IDEA Regulations, 34 C.F.R. § 300.320(a)(2)(i)).

The annual goals focus on remediating a student's academic or nonacademic problems that are detailed in his or her PLAAFP statements. Annual goals are projections the team makes regarding the progress of the student in one school year. Annual goals tell members of the IEP team if the anticipated outcomes for the student are being met, and whether the special education services and placement are effective (IDEA Regulations, 34 C.F.R., Appendix to Part 300-Notice of Interpretation, Question 38). Correctly written goals enable the teachers and parents to monitor a student's progress in a special education program and make educational adjustments to the program when a student is not making adequate progress (Deno, 1992). In fact, when Congress reauthorized the IDEA in 1997, it viewed the requirement of "measurable" annual goals "crucial to the success of the IEP" (Senate Report, 1997, p. 25). Thus, if the annual goals are to meet the substantive requirements of a FAPE it is important that the goals (a) address all the needs identified in the PLAAFP statements, (b) be ambitious enough that achieving the goals will result in a student receiving meaningful benefit from the goals, (c) be measurable and then actually be measured. According to Bateman and Linden (2006), if the annual goals are not measurable, this may result in an invalid IEP and the denial of a FAPE (see also *Susquentia School District v. Raelee,* 1996). Moreover, if goals are not measured this may also result in an invalid IEP and the denial of a FAPE (Bateman & Linden, 2006).

Determining special education services. The language in the IDEA requires that all IEPs must include:

> A statement of the special education and related services and supplementary aids and services, based on peer-reviewed research to the extent practicable, to be provided to the child, or on behalf of the child, and a statement of the program modifications or supports for school personnel that will be provided for the child to (1) progress toward the annual goals, (2) be involved in and make progress in the general curriculum and participate in extracurricular and other non-academic activities, and (3) be educated and participate with children with and without disabilities. (IDEA, 20 U.S.C. § 1414(d)(1)(A)(i)(IV))

These special education services include, if necessary, related services, supplementary aids and services, and program modifications that are needed to assist a student to benefit from his or her special education services and to be involved in the general education curriculum. The services represent the programming that the IEP team determines are required for a student to achieve his or her annual goals.

Basing special education services on peer-reviewed research. The reauthorization of the IDEA in 2004, titled the Individuals with Disabilities Education Improvement Act (hereafter IDEIA), added the important requirement that every IEP must now include "a statement of the special education and related services and supplementary aids and services, based on peer-reviewed research to the extent practicable" (IDEA, 20 U.S.C. § 1414(d)(1)(A)(i)(IV)). The peer-reviewed research (PRR) requirement applies to any academic (e.g., reading, mathematics) or nonacademic (behavioral interventions, assistive technology) services included in the IEP. According to the U.S. Department of Education, PRR refers to "research that is reviewed by qualified and independent reviewers to ensure that the quality of the information meets the standards of the field before the research is published" (*Analysis of Comments and Changes to 2006 IDEA Part B Regulations*, 71 Federal Register, 46664, 2006). When the IEP team proposes that a program or service is included in a student's IEP, therefore, there should be reliable evidence that the program or service is effective. This evidence should be based on research that is in the peer-reviewed literature or approved by a panel of independent experts through a rigorous, objective, and scientific review. The PRR requirements applies to the selection and provision of special education methodology (e.g., reading programming, speech & language services, behavioral interventions), related services (e.g., counseling services, physical therapy, psychological services), and supplementary aids, services, and supports, and program modifications provided in general education settings.

According to the U.S. Department of Education, the inclusion of the language "to the extent practicable" means that special education services and supplementary aids and supports should be based on PRR to the extent that PRR in an area is available (*Analysis of Comments and Changes to 2006 IDEA Part B Regulations*, 2006). For example, if an IEP team is determining special education services for a student in reading, there is large body of peer-reviewed research on teaching reading to students with disabilities. Thus, the IEP team would need to base the services in the IEP on this body of research. On the other hand, if an IEP team were considering services in an area in which there is little or no PRR, then clearly the team would not be able to base the services on PRR. Nevertheless, because PRR in special education is expanding so rapidly, it is important that IEP team members keep abreast of developments in PRR. Because of this requirement it is clearly important that IEP team members understand their responsibility regarding including PRR in students' IEPs. Zirkel (2008) asserted that the "most likely lever" (p. 409) for a judicially constructing elevated substantive for FAPE is the PRR requirement of the IDEIA. Whatever the effect of this provision on litigation may be, the effects on students in special education, if IEP teams include PRR in students' IEPs, will certainly be "stronger and more effective programs for students with disabilities" (Yell, Katsiyannis, & Hazelkorn, 2007, p. 9).

Providing access to the general education curriculum. A student's special education services must allow a student access to the general education curriculum; therefore, this should be a major focus of the IEP team. For example, the PLAAFP statements must include information of how a student's disability affects his or her involvement and progress in the general education curriculum (IDEA Regulations, 34 C.F.R. § 300.320(a)(1)(ii)). Additionally, the IEP must contain a description of how a student will be involved in and make progress in the general education curriculum in both the annual goals (IDEA Regulations, 34 C.F.R. § 300.320(a)(1)) and the special education services (IDEA, 20 U.S.C. § 1414(d)(1)(A)(i)(IV)). These requirements in the IDEA emphasize how (a) special education and general education must be integrated, and (b) IEP teams must focus on how students with disabilities must have access to general education curricula.

This requirement is often misunderstood. It does not mean that the IEP must include the general education curriculum; rather it means that the IEP must be directed to assisting special education students to access the general education curriculum. So, for example, if a student with an IEP cannot read, the IEP must include methods, strategies, and services to teach the student to read. If the student learns to read, he or she will be able to access the general curriculum. It would be a serious mistake to conclude that because the student is in a certain grade that the student's IEP must teach the student to read from the general education reading curriculum from that grade. Similarly, it is a mistake to conclude that state standards or the general education curriculum should be included in the IEP as annual goals or special education services if those standards or curricula are not appropriate given the student's needs. The specially designed instruction that must be provided to students with IEPs must include methodology and instruction that meets his or her unique educational needs. It would be inconsistent with the FAPE requirements of the IDEA to have all special education students being taught with the same curricula, methods, and materials, even if used in the general education setting. Moreover, because addressing the unique needs of a student may encompass more than just academic achievement issues, the IEP must include areas, such as behavior, social skills, self-care, and health needs, which may also be needed to allow the student to access the general education curriculum.

Adopting methods to monitor student progress. The 2006 regulations to the IDEA require that every IEP include a description of how a student's progress toward meeting his or her annual goals will be measured and requires that the team issues periodic reports on the student's progress (IDEA Regulations, 34 C.F.R. § 300.320(a)(2)). Although, the regulations do not mandate how these reports will be issued, it is suggested that this can be accomplished through quarterly or other periodic reports concurrent with the issuance of report cards.

It is absolutely essential that IEP teams determine how a student's progress toward meeting his or her annual goals will be measured for two primary reasons. First, an appropriate means of monitoring student progress will allow a teacher to determine if the instruction that is being provided is effective. If the data show that instruction is not effective, a teacher can make changes and continue to monitor a student's progress. When such data are not available to a teacher, he or she will be making instructional decisions based primarily on hunches regarding a student's progress or lack thereof. Thus when an IEP team collects and uses progress-monitoring data, it is much more likely that a student's special education will result in meaningful progress, which is a major reason for providing special education services. Second, the progress monitoring data is a key to proving that a student did make meaningful educational progress and received educational benefit, thus meeting the school district's obligation to provide a FAPE.

A number of hearings and court cases have found that school districts did not provide FAPE because the IEP team did not measure a student's progress toward meeting his or her goals. For example, in *Independent School District No. 371 v. J.T* (2006) a school district's IEP failed to provide a FAPE to a student with an emotional and behavior disorder and learning disability because the student's goals were so vague and immeasurable that there was "an absolute lack of evidence that any academic progress was made" (p. 96). Similarly, in *Kuszewski v. Chippewa Valley Schools* (2001) a school district's IEP did not provide FAPE because the IEP did not have sufficiently objective criteria to measure student progress.

It is important to note that neither passing nor failing grades in general education report cards are sufficient to establish that a district has either provided FAPE or failed to provide FAPE. The 2006 regulations to the IDEA compel states to "ensure that a FAPE is available to any individual child with a disability who needs special education and related services, even though the child has not failed or been retained in a course or grade, and is advancing from grade to grade" (IDEA Regulations, 34 C.F.R. § 300.101(c)(1)). Thus grades may serve as evidence of compliance with FAPE; however, they are not sufficient to prove compliance with the FAPE mandate of the IDEA or lack thereof.

Subjective data, such as teacher observation, will not constitute evidence that a student is making progress toward his or her goals (Bateman & Linden, 2006). As Bateman and Linden observed, "objective, real measurement of (student) progress is the only way to insure that the (special education) services are effective and resulting in increased performance levels" (p. 77). Progress monitoring data showing that a student is making progress toward meeting his or her goals is evidence that a school district has provided a FAPE. The corollary is also true, without such data, a district cannot show that they have provided a FAPE.

Related Services and FAPE

A FAPE sometimes requires that students with disabilities be provided with related services in addition to their special education services (Yell, 2006). Related services are defined in the IDEA as "supportive services … as may be required to assist a child with a disability to benefit from special education" (IDEA Regulations, 34 C.F.R. § 300.16(a)). The IDEA defines related services as:

> Transportation, and such developmental, corrective, and other supportive services (including speech-language pathology and audiology services, interpreting services, psychological services, physical and occupational therapy, recreation, including recreation, social work services, school nurse services designed to enable a child with a disability to receive a free appropriate public education as

described in the individualized education program of the child, counseling services, including rehabilitation counseling, orientation and mobility services, and medical services, except that such medical services shall be for diagnostic and evaluation purposes only) as may be required to assist a child with a disability to benefit from special education, and includes the early identification and assessment of disabling conditions in children The term *does not* include a medical device that is surgically implanted, or the replacement of such device (IDEA 20 U.S.C. § 1402(26)(A)).

The list of related services included in this definition is not exhaustive. With the exception of medical services (i.e., the services of a licensed physician) and medical devices (e.g., cochlear implants), there are no restrictions on IEP teams when they determine what, if any, related services a student needs. Additionally, with the passage of IDEIA, schools were not required to provide or maintain surgically implanted devices, such as cochlear implants.

When related services are provided to a student in special education, such services must be provided at no cost. Courts have ordered school districts to reimburse parents for the unilateral provision of related services when it has been determined that the service was necessary for educational benefit but was not provided by the school (*Max M. v. Illinois State Board of Education,* 1986; *Seals v. Loftis,* 1985).

Decisions regarding related services can only be made on an individual basis. The team that develops the IEP, therefore, is the proper forum to determine which services are required in order to provide a FAPE (Huefner, 2008; Yell, 2006). The IEP team, in addition to determining the types of related services to be provided, must include the amount of services provided. This is required so that the commitment of needed resources will be clear to the parents and other IEP team members (IDEA Regulations, Notice of Interpretation on IEPs, Question 51).

Related services can never be provided without an accompanying special education services (Pitasky, 2000). Some related services, for example, speech therapy, might also qualify as a special education service. Nonetheless, related services cannot be included in a student's IEP if no special education is being provided to the student. Additionally, medical services that are covered by the IDEA are only those services provided by a licensed physician for diagnostic or evaluation purposes; all other medical services provided by a licensed physician are excluded.

The most controversial of the related services has been complex health services provided to medically fragile students with disabilities. A particularly difficult challenge for school districts had been distinguishing school health services from medical services when determining what related services should be provided to a student. School health services, which are "provided by a qualified school nurse or other qualified person," are required under the IDEA (IDEA Regulations, 34 C.F.R. § 300.16). Moreover, the definition of school health services is extremely broad and may run the gamut from activities requiring almost no training (e.g., dispensing oral medication), to those requiring increased levels of training (e.g., catheterization), to those requiring extensive training and requiring a substantial amount of time (e.g., tracheotomy care and chest physiotherapy) (Lear, 1995).

When health care services must be provided by a physician, however, they are not required related services but are excluded medical services. School districts have often argued against the established legislative and regulatory language that differentiates medical from health services simply on the nature of who provides the service (i.e., physician or nonphysician) and contended that when the health services become extremely complex and burdensome to a school district, the health services become medical and, therefore, school did not have to provide these services (Katisyannis & Yell, 2000). This issue became moot with the U.S. Supreme Court's decision in *Cedar Rapids v. Garrett F* (1999).

This case involved very complex and expensive health procedures. Garrett Frey, the litigant, was paralyzed from a motorcycle accident when he was four. He was ventilator dependent and could only breathe by use of an electric ventilator or with someone manually pumping an air bag attached to his tracheotomy tube. In his early school years, Garrett's parents provided for his nursing care during the school day. Using funds from their insurance and proceeds from a settlement with the motorcycle company, a licensed practical nurse was hired to care for Garrett's physical needs. When Garrett was in middle school, his mother requested that the school district accept the financial responsibility for the physical care during the school day. School district officials refused the request arguing that they were not legally obligated to provide continuous nursing care. Garrett's mother requested a due process hearing. Following extensive testimony, Larry Bartlett, the administrative law judge (AJL), issued a ruling, which relied on a bright-line standard,[3] in which he ordered the school district to pay for the services. The AJL found that the distinction between health care services and medical services in the IDEA was that the former are provided by a qualified school nurse or other qualified person whereas the latter refers to services performed by a licensed physician (Yell, 2006). The school district eventually appealed to the U.S. Supreme Court. The high court agreed with the lower courts and the hearing officer that the requested services were related services because they did not require the services of a licensed physician and that Garrett could not attend school without the services. These complex health services, therefore, were not excluded medical services and must be provided by the school district.

According to language in the IDEA, medical services covered under the law are only those services provided by a licensed physician for diagnostic or evaluation purposes; all other medical services provided by a licensed physician are excluded. A school health service or the services of the school nurse, however, may be required if (a) the service is necessary to assist a child with disabilities in benefiting from special education, (b) the service must be performed during school hours, and (c) the service can be provided by a person other than a licensed physician, such as a school nurse or some other properly trained school employee (*Letter to Greer*, 1992).

Related services, therefore, are an important component of a FAPE for certain students in special education. When a related service is (a) necessary to assist a student with disabilities to benefit from their special education; (b) performed during school hours; and (c) provided by a person other than a licensed physician, then that service is a required to provide a FAPE. We next examine litigation that has examined the FAPE requirement of the IDEA.

Parental Participation and FAPE

The educational rights of children and youth with disabilities were gained largely through the efforts of parents and advocacy groups in the courts and legislatures of this country (Yell, Rogers, & Rogers, 2006). Certainly the advocacy of parents was an important factor in Congress requiring that parents be included on the IEP teams. In fact, Congress empowered parents to be key players and decision-makers in their children's education. Thus, the law requires that a student's parents are equal participants in determining a FAPE for their child.

The role of the parents is so important in the IEP process that school personnel actions that result in parents not being involved in the development of their child's IEP is one of the two reasons that hearing officers can rule that a procedural error had denied a child a FAPE (IDEA Regulations, 34 C.F.R § 300.5123(a)(2)). For example, in November 2009 the U.S. Court of Appeals for the Ninth Circuit in *Drobnicki by Drobnicki v. Poway Unified School District* ruled that school district personnel's lack of efforts to include a student's parents in an IEP meeting amounted to a denial of FAPE. The school-based team had scheduled a student's IEP meeting without consulting his parents. When the parents told the district personnel that they were unavailable on that date, there was no attempt made to reschedule the meeting. Rather, district personnel told the parents they could participate by speakerphone. According to the Court's opinion, the school district did not meet its affirmative duty to schedule the IEP meeting at a mutually agreeable time and place, thus depriving the parents the opportunity to participate in the IEP meeting, thereby denying the student a FAPE.

On May 21, 2007, the U.S. Supreme Court issued a ruling in the case *Winkelman v. Parma City School District*. Justice Kennedy wrote the opinion of the Court in the unanimous ruling. The case addressed the right of the parents of Joseph Winkleman to represent him in an IDEA case, even though they were not attorneys. According to Wright and Wright (2007), the importance of this decision goes far beyond the issue of whether parents can represent their child in special education cases. This is because the Supreme Court ruled that the IDEA grants parents independent, enforceable rights, which are not limited to procedural and reimbursement-related matters, but encompass the entitlement to a FAPE for their child. In essence the high court essentially expanded the definition of a FAPE by ruling that the IDEA mandates that (a) parents must be meaningfully involved in the development of their child's IEP, (b) parents have enforceable rights under the law, and (c) parental participation in the special education process is crucial to ensuring that children with disabilities receive a FAPE. The court also noted a central purpose of the parental protections under the IDEA is to facilitate the provision of a FAPE through parental involvement in the IEP process. According to the Supreme Court:

> We conclude IDEA grants independent, enforceable rights. These rights, which are not limited to certain procedural and reimbursement-related matters, encompass the entitlement to a free appropriate public education for the parents' child. (p. 2005)

Clearly, school districts must ensure that parents are involved in their children's special education identification, assessment, programming, and placement.

Litigation and FAPE

Board of Education of the Hendrick Hudson School District v. Rowley

In 1982, a case from the U.S. Court of Appeals for the Second Circuit became the first special education case to be heard by the U.S. Supreme Court. In *Board of Education of the Hendrick Hudson School District v. Rowley* (hereafter *Rowley*), the high court considered the meaning of a FAPE. The case involved the education of Amy Rowley, a student at the Furnace Woods School in the Hendrick Hudson Central School District. She was deaf and was eligible for special education services under the IDEA. Amy had minimal residual hearing and was an excellent lip-reader. The year prior to her attending Furnace Woods, a meeting was held between her parents and school officials to determine future placement and services. A decision was made to place Amy in the regular kindergarten class to determine what supplemental services she might need. Several school personnel learned sign language, and a teletype machine was placed in the school office to facilitate communication between Amy and her parents, who were also deaf. A sign language interpreter was also present in the classroom. Following a trial period in the kindergarten placement, a decision was made that Amy would remain in the class, with the school providing a hearing aid. Amy successfully completed her kindergarten year.

An IEP was prepared for Amy prior to her entry into first grade. Her IEP provided for (a) education in a general education classroom, (b) continued use of the hearing aid, (c) instruction from a tutor for deaf children for an hour daily, and (d) speech therapy three hours a week. The Rowleys requested a qualified sign language interpreter in all of Amy's academic classes. Because Amy's kindergarten interpreter believed that Amy did not need the services at that time, the school officials concluded, after consulting with the school district's Committee on the Handicapped, that the interpreter was not necessary. The Rowleys then requested a due process hearing. The hearing officer agreed with the school district that the interpreter was not required by the IDEA, and this decision was affirmed by the New York Commissioner of Education. The Rowleys brought an action in federal district court, claiming that the district's refusal to provide a sign language interpreter denied Amy a FAPE.

The district court found Amy to be a well-adjusted child who was doing better than the average child. Nevertheless, the court ruled that Amy was not learning as much as she could without her handicap. The disparity between Amy's actual achievement and her potential convinced the district court that Amy had been denied a FAPE, which the court defined as "an opportunity to achieve [her] full potential commensurate with the opportunity provided to other children" (*Rowley,* p. 534). Moreover, because the requirements of a FAPE were unclear, the court stated that the responsibility for determining a FAPE had been left to the federal courts.

The U.S. Court of Appeals for the Second Circuit, in a divided decision, affirmed the lower court's ruling. The U.S. Supreme Court granted certiorari to the Board of Education's appeal. The high court considered two questions: What is a FAPE, and what is the role of state and federal courts in reviewing special education decisions?

Justice Rehnquist wrote the majority opinion. According to the Court's decision a FAPE consisted of educational instruction designed to meet the unique needs of a student with disabilities, supported by such services as needed to permit the student to *benefit* from instruction. The Court also ruled that the IDEA required that special education services be provided at public expense, meet state standards, and comport with the student's IEP. Therefore, if individualized instruction allowed the child to benefit from educational services and met the other requirements of the law, the student was receiving a FAPE. Justice Rehnquist wrote that any substantive standard prescribing the level of education to be accorded students with disabilities was conspicuously missing from the language of the IDEA.

According to the Supreme Court, Congress's primary objective in passing the law was to make public education available to students with disabilities. "The intent of the Act was more to open the door of public education to handicapped children on appropriate terms than to guarantee any particular level of education once inside" (*Rowley,* p. 192). The Court disagreed with the Rowleys' contention that the goal of the IDEA was to provide each student with disabilities with an equal educational opportunity. The Court stated that

> the educational opportunities provided by our public school systems undoubtedly differ from student to student, depending upon a myriad of factors that might affect a particular student's ability to assimilate information presented in the classroom. The requirement that states provide "equal" educational opportunities would thus seem to present an entirely unworkable standard requiring impossible measurements and comparisons. Similarly, furnishing handicapped children with only such services as are available to nonhandicapped children would in all probability fall short of the statutory requirement of "free appropriate public education"; to require, on the other hand, the furnishing of every special service necessary to maximize each handicapped child's potential is, we think, further than Congress intended to go. (pp. 198–199)

The Court, however, held that the education to which the IDEA provided access had to be "sufficient to confer some educational benefit upon the handicapped child" (p. 200). Therefore, the purpose of FAPE was to provide students with disabilities a "basic floor of opportunity" consisting of access to specialized instruction and related services individually designed to confer "educational benefit." Moreover, the high court specifically rejected the argument that school districts were required to provide the best possible education to students with disabilities (Wenkart, 2000).

The Rowley Standard. The Supreme Court developed a two-part test to be used by courts in determining if a school has met its obligations under the IDEA to provide a FAPE. "First, has the [school] complied with the procedures of the Act? And second, is the individualized education program developed through the Act's procedures reasonably calculated to enable the child to receive educational benefits?" (*Rowley,* pp. 206–207). If these requirements were met, a school had complied with the requirements of a FAPE. The court cautioned the lower courts, however, that they were not establishing *any one test* for determining the adequacy of educational benefits.

Applying the two-part test to the *Rowley* case, the Supreme Court found that the school district had complied with the procedures of the IDEA, and Amy had received an appropriate education because she was performing better than many children in her class and was advancing easily from grade to grade. In a footnote, the high court noted that the decision was a narrow one and that it should not be read too broadly. The Court stated that the ruling should not be interpreted to mean that every student with a disability who was advancing from grade to grade in a regular school was automatically receiving a FAPE. Rather, the FAPE standard can only be arrived at through a multifactorial evaluation conducted on a case-by-case basis. The Court also noted that in this case the sign language interpreter was not required to provide a FAPE to Amy Rowley. The decisions of the district and circuit court were reversed.

The Supreme Court also addressed the rule of the courts in determining whether a school had provided a FAPE to a student. Regarding this role, Rehnquist wrote that

> courts must be careful to avoid imposing their view of preferable educational methods upon the states. The primary responsibility for formulating the education to be accorded

> a handicapped child, and for choosing the educational method most suitable to the child's needs, was left by the Act to state and local educational agencies in cooperation with the parents or guardian of the child. (*Rowley,* p. 207)

In special education cases involving FAPE, therefore, the courts' role are (a) to determine if the procedural requirements are being met, (b) to examine the substantive requirements of FAPE, and (c) to determine if the special education is providing educational benefit. In making this determination, courts should not substitute their judgments for the judgments of educators, because courts lack the "specialized knowledge and experience necessary to resolve persistent and difficult questions of educational policy" (*San Antonio ISD v. Rodriquez,* 1973, p. 42).

The Supreme Court ruled that students with disabilities do not have an enforceable right to the best possible education or an education that allows them to achieve their maximum potential. Rather, they are entitled to an education that is reasonably calculated to confer educational benefit.

Post-*Rowley* Litigation

The first principle of the *Rowley* test establishes the importance of adherence to the procedural aspects of a FAPE. Clearly, a court could rule that a school district has denied a FAPE if the district has not adhered to the procedural safeguards in the IDEA. The second principle of the *Rowley* test is substantive. The principle requires courts to determine whether the IEP developed by the school is reasonably calculated to enable the child to receive educational benefits.

A number of post-*Rowley* decisions have ruled that based on procedural violations alone, schools had denied a FAPE. In *W.G. v. Board of Trustees* (1992), the U.S. Court of Appeals for the Ninth Circuit ruled that a school that had failed to include the classroom teacher or representative of a private school in developing an IEP had denied a FAPE to a student with disabilities. The court also noted, however, that procedural violations do not automatically require a finding of a denial of a FAPE. In *Tice v. Botetourt County School Board* (1990), the U.S. Court of Appeals for the Fourth Circuit ruled that a school had denied a FAPE because of a 6-month delay in evaluating a child and developing an IEP. Two decisions by the U.S. Court of Appeals for the Fourth Circuit also ruled that schools had denied students with disabilities a FAPE because of procedural violations. In *Spielberg v. Henrico County Public Schools* (1988), the school's determination to change a student's placement prior to developing an IEP violated the parents' right to participate in the development of the IEP and, therefore, violated the IDEA. In *Hall v. Vance County Board of Education* (1985), a school was found to have denied a FAPE because of its repeated failure to notify parents of their rights under IDEA.

A number of post-*Rowley* rulings, however, have held that technical violations of the IDEA may not violate the FAPE requirement of the IDEA if they result in no harm to the student's education. For example, in *Doe v. Alabama Department of Education* (1990), the U.S. Court of Appeals for the Eleventh Circuit held that, because the parents had participated fully in the IEP process, a school's technical violation in failing to notify parents of their rights did not warrant relief. In *Doe v. Defendant 1* (1990), the U.S. Court of Appeals for the Sixth Circuit ruled that the failure of school officials to include a student's present level of educational performance and appropriate criteria for determining achievement of objectives did not invalidate the IEP when the parents were aware of this information. The school's procedural violations of inadequately notifying the parents of refusal to reimburse private tuition and failure to perform the 3-year evaluation in a timely manner were harmless errors because the parents had actual notice and their child's progress had not been harmed.

The IDEIA made it less likely that procedural violations made by a school district would result in a ruling that the district has violated a student's right to a FAPE. This is because the law directs hearing officers to rule primarily on substantive grounds. The only exception is when procedural violations have impeded a student's right to a free appropriate public education, significantly impeded the parent's participation in the decision making process, or deprived a student of educational benefits (IDEA 20 U.S.C.§615(f)(3)(E)). The crucial determinant in ruling a procedural violation a denial of FAPE is the degree of harm caused to the student's educational program. Procedural violations that have not caused significant difficulties in the delivery of a special education have not resulted in adverse court rulings in the past, and the language in IDEIA ensures that this trend will continue.

The second principle of the *Rowley* test—the determination of whether the IEP was reasonably calculated to enable a student to receive educational benefits—has proven to be a more difficult determination than the first principle. Early post-*Rowley* rulings appeared to indicate that if students received some educational benefit from their special education program, the IEP was appropriate (Osborne, 1992). In these early rulings, the courts seemingly regarded IEPs as appropriate if a school was able to show that the IEP was developed to provide some educational benefit, no matter how minimal it might be. Cases in which this line of judicial reasoning was followed include *Doe v. Lawson* (1984), *Karl v. Board of Education* (1984), and *Manual R. v. Ambach* (1986). Recent decisions, however, have indicated that minimal or trivial benefit may not be sufficient, and that special education services must confer meaningful benefit.

The U.S. Court of Appeals for the Fourth Circuit, in *Hall v. Vance County Board of Education* (1985), held that the *Rowley* decision required courts to examine the IEP to determine what substantive standards meet the second principle of the *Rowley* test. Additionally, the court cited *Rowley* as stating that this could only be accomplished on a case-by-case basis. The appeals court affirmed the district court's ruling that because the plaintiff, who had a learning disability, had made no educational progress in the public school, and because the IEP was inadequate, the school district had to reimburse the parents for private school tuition. The court noted that Congress did not intend that schools offer educational programs that produce only trivial academic advancement.

In *Carter v. Florence County School District Four* (1991), the U.S. Court of Appeals for the Fourth Circuit affirmed a district court's ruling that the school district's IEP had failed to satisfy the FAPE requirement of the IDEA. The IEP, which contained annual reading goals of 4 months' growth over a school year, did not, according to the district and circuit courts, represent meaningful growth, even if the goals were achieved. The case was later heard by the U.S. Supreme Court on a different issue. In *J.C. v. Central Regional School District* (1996) the U.S. Court of Appeals for the Third Circuit ruled that school districts must provide more than a *de minimus* or trivial education, and that districts are responsible for the adequacy of the IEP. In this case, the IEP developed for a student with severe disabilities failed to address important educational needs. Furthermore, the student had made little progress in the current program and had actually regressed in some areas.

The courts have not provided a precise definition to follow when determining whether the education offered is meaningful or trivial. This lack of precision is appropriate because what will constitute a meaningful education for a given student can only be determined on a case-by-case basis. There can be no bright line formula (i.e., no clear standard) that will apply to all students. It is clear that courts, when determining if the substantive requirements of a FAPE have been met, will look to the school's IEP to determine if a meaningful education designed to confer benefit has been provided.

Polk v. Central Susquehanna Intermediate Unit 16 (1988). The U.S. Court of Appeals for the Third Circuit in its decision in *Polk v. Central Susquehanna Intermediate Unit 16* (1988) noted that because *Rowley* involved a student who did very well in the general education class, the high court was able to avoid the substantive second principle of the *Rowley* test and concentrate on the procedural principle. In other words, because Amy Rowley was an excellent student, the Court really only had to examine the procedures the district followed; clearly, she must have been receiving an appropriate education if she was one of the top students in her class and had been advanced to the next grade. In Polk, however, the court had to address the substantive question of how much benefit was required to meet the "meaningful" standard in educating the plaintiff, Christopher Polk.

Christopher Polk was a 14-year-old with severe mental and physical disabilities. The severity of his disabilities necessitated physical therapy, but the school's IEP provided only consultative services of a physical therapist. Christopher's parents brought action under the IDEA (then the EAHCA), claiming that the school had failed to provide an appropriate education. A federal district court held for the school district, finding that the *Rowley* standard held that the conferral of any degree of educational benefit, no matter how small, could qualify as an appropriate education. The circuit court reversed the district court, declaring that just as

> Congress did not write a blank check, neither did it anticipate that states would engage in the idle gesture of providing special education designed to confer only trivial benefit. … Congress intended to afford children with special needs an education that would confer meaningful benefit. (*Polk,* p. 184)

The court also stated the type of education that constitutes a meaningful education can only be determined in the light of a student's potential. Courts in *Board of Education v. Diamond* (1986), *Doe v. Smith* (1988), and *Hall v. Vance County Board of Education* (1985) all reached similar conclusions.

Cypress-Fairbanks Independent School District v. Michael F. (1997). In this case the parents of Michael F. had requested an impartial due process hearing, claiming that the school had denied their son an appropriate education under the IDEA. The hearing officer ruled in favor of the parents. The school district appealed to Federal District Court. The district court reversed the decision of the hearing office and ruled in favor of the school district. The district court based its decision on a four-part test devised by an expert witness in the case. The four factors were:

1. Was the program individualized on the basis of the student's assessment and performance?
2. Was the program delivered in the least restrictive environment?
3. Were the services provided in a coordinated and collaborative manner by key stakeholders?
4. Were positive academic and nonacademic benefits demonstrated?

The parents appealed the decision to the U.S. Court of Appeals for the Fifth Circuit. The court, using the four factors, ruled that the school district had (a) conducted a thorough assessment of Michael F., (b) developed an appropriate program which was tailored to his individual needs, (c) implemented the IEP as written, (d) educated Michael in the least restrictive environment, and (e) developed a program that resulted in academic and nonacademic benefits. The court ruled, therefore, that Michael F. had received an appropriate education, thus affirming the decision of the lower court.

Houston Independent School District v. Bobby R. (2000). The U.S. Court of Appeals for the Fifth Circuit in *Houston Independent School District v. Bobby R.* (2000) ruled that a student with learning disabilities received an appropriate education because the school had data that the student had received academic and nonacademic benefit.

Moreover, the circuit adopted the four-part test used by the circuit court in the Cypress-Fairbanks case. To determine if academic benefits had been demonstrated, the court examined the school's testing data. Finding that Robbie's test scores had shown a good rate of improvement, even though it was not commensurate with his peers in general education, the court held that the student's progress should be measured in relation to his own degree of improvement rather than in relation to his nondisabled peers. The court ruled, therefore, that Robbie's IEP was reasonably calculated to provide him with meaningful educational benefit, thus meeting the requirements of the IDEA.

IDEA '97, IDEIA, and FAPE

When the EAHCA was passed in 1975, Congress intended that the law open the doors of public education for students with disabilities. Thus, the emphasis of the original law was on access to educational programs rather than any level of educational opportunity (Eyer, 1998, Yell & Drasgow, 2000). Although IDEA had been dramatically successful in including children with disabilities in public education, Congress believed that the promise of the law had not been fulfilled for too many children with disabilities (House Report, 1997). The underlying theme of IDEA '97 and IDEIA, therefore, was to improve the effectiveness of special education by requiring demonstrable improvements in the educational achievement of students with disabilities. Indeed, because a quality education for each student with disabilities became the new goal of IDEA in the reauthorizations of 1997 and 2004, some scholars believed that the *Rowley* standard was too low (Eyer, 1998; Johnson, 2003). Eyer wrote that:

> The IDEA can no longer be fairly perceived as a statute which merely affords children access to education. Today, the IDEA is designed to improve the effectiveness of special education and increase the benefits afforded to children with disabilities to the extent such benefits are necessary to achieve measurable progress. (p. 16)

Similarly, Johnson asserted that the reauthorization of the IDEA in 1997 would require that schools develop, implement, and evaluate IEPs, and these changes should influence how courts assess the FAPE requirement. Johnson also believed that the changes in the IDEA required a reexamination of *Rowley* and its some educational benefit standard. Reexamining the *Rowley* decision was no small undertaking, he wrote, because the standard set forth in the case had provided the framework for FAPE cases for the past 20 years. Nonetheless, Johnson argued that

> the 1997 Amendments to the IDEA make clear that the foundation underlying the reasoning in Rowley is no longer present. That is, the IDEA is no longer simply intended to provide students with access to educational services that provide some benefit. The IDEA is intended to go well beyond this… (p. 586)

The IDEA requires schools to further the educational achievement of students with disabilities by developing an IEP that provides a special education program that confers measurable and meaningful educational progress in the least restrictive environment. Moreover, school districts are also required to provide instruction that is grounded in peer-reviewed research. In fact, school districts may be vulnerable to special education lawsuits if they do not offer programs based on peer-reviewed research and if programs fail to show student progress. This is especially true of reading instruction.

Post-IDEA '97 and IDEIA Litigation

Since the passage of IDEA '97 and IDEIA, special education and legal scholars have argued that the IDEA now has a higher standard for a FAPE (Crockett & Yell, 2008; Eyer, 1998; Huefner, 2008; Johnson, 2003; Yell et al., 2007). A reading of documents from the U.S. Congress following passage of IDEA '97 and IDEIA would also seem to support such an interpretation. In fact, according to language in the law, the primary purpose of the IDEIA was to "ensure that educators and parents have the necessary tools to improve educational results for children with disabilities" (IDEA, 20 U.S.C. § 1401(d)(3)) and "to assess and ensure the effectiveness of efforts to educate children with disabilities" (IDEA, 20 U.S.C. § 1401(d)(4)). Additionally, the House Committee on the Reauthorization of IDEA 1997 reported that "the Committee believes that the critical issue now is to place greater emphasis on improving student performance and ensuring that children with disabilities receive a quality public education" (H.R.105-95 at 83-84, May 13, 1997). The committee further noted that the reauthorization of the IDEA was intended to move to the next step of providing special education and related services to children with disabilities to improve and increase their educational achievement. This would seem to indicate that Congress intended that the new standard was to provide a meaningful, measurable, and demonstrably effective program of special education for students with disabilities.

However, as Zirkel (2008) noted Congress did not change the statutory definition of a FAPE. Following the reauthorizations of the IDEA, courts were split in their interpretations of the meaningful benefit standard of a FAPE. Some courts relied on earlier rulings that meaningful benefit meant no more than adequate or some educational benefit, whereas others reasoned that the educational standard should be to produce significant learning (Huefner, 2008).

The U.S. Court of Appeals for the Third Circuit in *T.E. ex rel. N.R. v. Kingwood Township Board* (2000) and the U.S. Court of Appeals for the Sixth Circuit in *Deal v. Hamilton County Board of Education* (2004) required that a student's potential must be considered when determining the adequacy of educational benefit provided by an IEP. To meet such a standard it is critical that an IEP team measure student progress. A number of courts have held that student progress as shown by state-mandated standardized tests was sufficient to prove that a school district had provided meaningful benefit (*K.C. v. Fulton County School District*, 2006; *Bradley v. Arkansas Department of Education*, 2006; *Nack v. Orange County School District*, 2006).

Huefner (2008) noted that courts have different interpretations of FAPE. Some courts have seemingly paid little attention to IEP goals, requiring that students' IEPs produce, or be calculated to produce, measurable progress that is more than trivial; other courts, recognizing the *Rowley* precedent, have examined the goals on students' IEPs, requiring that measures show significant student progress. This split among lower courts regarding the FAPE standard used when judging school districts' special education programming may eventually result in the U.S. Supreme Court hearing another FAPE case. A number of scholars have suggested that courts, including the U.S. Supreme Court, should interpret FAPE, and update the *Rowley* decision, in light of the language in IDEA '07 and IDEIA requiring measurable goals, services based on peer-reviewed research, and progress monitoring (Eyer, 1998; Huefner, 2008; Johnson, 2003; Yell et al., 2007). Huefner asserted that The Supreme Court would be the most useful venue for updating the FAPE standard; however, in the case that such a decision is not forthcoming, lower courts need to understand the statutory progression over the years and express the increased educational expectations of the IDEA.

Guidelines for Providing FAPE

An analysis of the IDEA reauthorizations of 1997 and 2004, and related litigation, indicates that IDEA now extends beyond providing access to education, or merely affording students a basic floor of opportunity. The law now embraces peer reviewed research, progress monitoring, and significant learning outcomes for students with disabilities; however, the IEP requirements remain "the substantive heart of the FAPE" (Huefner, 2008, p. 378). To ensure that public schools fulfill their obligations to ensure an appropriate education under the IDEA, school-based teams must be able to develop and implement legally correct and educationally meaningful IEPs.

The following guidance, derived from recent IDEA reauthorizations and relevant case law, is offered as a means for restoring the promise of the IEP as the tool for demonstrating the effectiveness of specially designed instruction. The implementation of these guidelines relies on the knowledge and commitment of special education teachers and administrators (a) who understand the IEP requirements of the IDEA, as amended in 1997 and 2004; (b) who understand and use research-based procedures; and (c) who collect and use formative data to monitor student progress.

Guideline 1: Conduct meaningful and relevant assessments. A FAPE depends on assessments that provide information to teachers on a student's unique academic and functional needs and how best to address those needs. Assessments determine a student's eligibility for special education services. Most important to a FAPE, assessments inform the PLAAFP statement of an IEP by describing academic and non-academic problems that interfere with learning so that annual goals can be developed, services determined, and progress monitored.

Guideline 2: Develop measureable annual goals. A FAPE depends on measureable annual goals designed to (a) address a student's unique needs, (b) encourage participation and progress in the general curriculum, (c) confer educational benefit, and (d) monitor academic and functional progress over the school year. The IEP should include measureable annual goals that are designed to remediate a student's academic or nonacademic problems detailed in the PLAAFP statement.

Guideline 3: Determine special education services. A FAPE depends on programming that helps a student to achieve his or her annual goals. The IEP should emphasize special education, and when necessary, related services, supplementary aids and services, and program modifications needed for the student's individual benefit, and involvement in the general curriculum and school activities.

Guideline 4: Base special education services on peer reviewed research. A FAPE depends on the selection and provision of research validated academic and non-academic interventions. The IEP must include programs or services with reliable evidence of their effectiveness based on a rigorous, objective, and scientific review to the extent practicable. Thus, teachers must understand and properly implement educational practices based on the latest research.

Guideline 5: Provide access to the general education curriculum. A FAPE depends on assisting special education students to access the general curriculum. The IEP should not include the general curriculum. Instead, the PLAAFP statement must describe how the student's disability affects involvement in the general curriculum, and the annual goals and special education services must include instructional methods that facilitate access by meeting the student's individual needs, including behavior, social skills, self-care, and health needs.

Guideline 6: Adopt methods to monitor student progress. A FAPE depends on collecting data on a student's growth toward annual goals, and making instructional changes when necessary. The IEP must include a description of how a student's progress toward meeting the annual goals will be measured and how often that progress will be reported. Progress monitoring data that demonstrates a student's progress toward his or her annual goals provides evidence that the school district is providing a FAPE.

Guideline 7: Provide related services so that the student can benefit from his or her special

education. A FAPE depends on related services when they are (a) needed to help a student with disabilities benefit from special education, (b) performed during the school day, and (c) provided by a person other than a licensed physician. Related services are provided to students with disabilities at no cost to their parents. The IEP team must determine the types and the amount of required related services so that the school district can commit the necessary resources.

Guideline 8: Involve parents as full partners in the IEP process. A FAPE depends on ensuring that parents are meaningfully involved in their children's special education identification, assessment, programming, and placement. The IDEA grants parents an enforceable right to pursue a FAPE for their child with a disability, and as members of the IEP team, parents are considered equal partners with school personnel in determining the components of their child's appropriate education.

These guidelines are offered to restore the promise of the IEP to ensure a FAPE to students with disabilities by helping teams of parents and educators to be vigilant in meeting students' individual needs and diligent in using data and peer reviewed research to guide instruction. School personnel can ensure that programs deliver a FAPE by using educational practices that show evidence of producing meaningful outcomes. Given that special education programs are required to deliver meaningful benefit, it should be noted that without the use of effective instructional strategies this level of benefit is not likely to be realized. School personnel can also ensure that special education programs confer meaningful benefit by collecting data to determine if their interventions are working and their students are making progress toward meeting their measurable annual goals. Adjusting instruction in response to student performance makes it more likely that students will make progress that leads to increased academic achievement and functional performance.

Since 1982 the *Rowley* decision has provided the framework for courts to determine whether students were provided with a FAPE. The IDEA now embraces research, progress monitoring, and demonstrated results for students with disabilities. Clearly, this emphasis on accountability for student outcomes requires changes in the ways that teams of parents and educators develop IEPs, and may influence courts on the meaning and measurement of FAPE.

Notes

1. In the reauthorization of the Education for All Handicapped Children Act in 1990, the name of the law was changed to the Individuals with Disabilities Education Act. The act is codified as the IDEA, and not the EAHCA.
2. IEPs have required annual goals since its original passage in 1975. The IDEA Reauthorization Act in 1997 added the requirement that the goals be measurable.
3. A bright-line standard refers to a clear defined rule in the law that requires little or no interpretation. In this case, the bright-line standard was that the only related services excluded under the IDEA were medical services provided by a licensed physician.

References

Analysis of Comments and Changes to 2006 IDEA Part B Regulations, 71 Federal Register, 46565 and 46664, August 14, 2006.

Bateman, B. D., & Linden, M. A. (2006). *Better IEPs: How to develop legally correct and educationally useful programs* (4th ed.). Verona, WI: IEP Resources/Attainment.

Board of Education of the Hendrick Hudson School District v. Rowley, 458 U.S. 176 (1982).

Board of Education v. Diamond, 808 F.2d 987 (3rd Cir. 1986).

Bradley v. Arkansas Department of Education, 443 F.3d 965 (8th Cir. 2006).

Carter v. Florence County School District Four, 950 D.2d 156 (4th Cir. 1991).

Cedar Rapids Community School District v. Garrett F. (526 U.S.1999).

Clevenger v. Oak Ridge School Board, 744 F.2d 514 (6th Cir. 1984).

County of San Diego v. California Special Education Hearing Office, 24, IDELR 756 (9th Cir. 1996).

Crockett, J. B., & Yell, M. L. (2008). Without data all we have our assumptions: Revisiting the meaning of a free appropriate public education. *Journal of Law and Education*, *37*(3), 381–392.

Cypress-Fairbanks Independent School District v. Michael F. 118 F.3d 245 (5th Cir. 1997).

Deal v. Hamilton County Board of Education, 392 F.3d 840 (6th Cir. 2004).

Deno, S. L. (1992). The nature and development of curriculum-based measurement. *Preventing School Failure*, *36*, 5–11.

Doe v. Alabama Department of Education, 915 F.2d 651 (11th Cir. 1990).

Doe v. Defendant 1, 898 F.2d 1186 (6th Cir. 1990).

Doe v. Lawson, 579 F.Supp. 1314 (D. Mass. 1984), aff'd 745 F.2d 43 (1st Cir. 1984).

Doe v. Smith, EHLR 559:391 (N.D. Tenn. 1988).

Drobnicki by Drobnicki v. Poway Unified School District, WL 4912163, C.A. 9 (2009).

Eyer, T. L. (1998). Greater expectations: How the 1997 IDEA Amendments raise the basic floor of opportunity for children with disabilities. *Education Law Report, 126*, 1–19.

Hall v. Vance County Board of Education, 774 F.2d 629 (4th Cir. 1985).

Horsnell, M., & Kitch, J. (1996). Bullet-proofing the IEP. In *Proceedings of the 15th National Institute on Legal Issues in Educating Individuals with Disabilities*. Alexandria, VA: LRP Publications.

House Report105-95 at 83-84, May 13, 1997.

Houston Independent School District v. Bobby R., 200 F.3d 342 (5th Cir. 2000).

Huefner, D. S. (2000). The risks and opportunities of the IEP requirements of IDEA '97. *Journal of Special Education*, *33*, 195–204.

Huefner, D. S. (2008). Understanding the FAPE requirements under IDEA. *Journal of Law and Education*, *37*(3), 367–380.

Individuals with Disabilities Education Act, 20 U.S.C. § 1401 *et seq.*

Individuals with Disabilities Education Act Regulations, 34 C.F.R. § 300 *et seq.*

Independent School District No. 371 v. J.T, 45 IDELR 92 (D. MN. 2006).

J. C. v. Central Regional School District, 23 IDELR 1181 (3rd Cir. 1996).

Johnson, S. F. (2003). Reexamining Rowley: A new focus in special education law. *BYU Education and Law Journal*, *3*, 561–588.

K. C. v. Fulton County School District, U.S. Dist. Lexis 47652, N.D. GA 2006.

Karl v. Board of Education, 736 F.2d 873 (2nd Cir. 1984).

Katisyannis, A., & Yell, M. L. (2000). The Supreme Court and school health services: *Cedar Rapids v. Garrett F. Exceptional Children*, *66*, 317–326.

Katsiyannis, A., Yell, M. L., & Bradley, M. R. (2002). Reflections on the 25th anniversary of the *Individuals with Disabilities Education Act*. *Remedial and Special Education*, *22*, 324–334.

Kirby v. Cabell Board of Education, 46 IDELR 156, (D. W.VA. 2006).

Kuszewski v. Chippewa Valley Schools, 131 F.Supp2d 926 (E.D., MI, 2001).

Lear, R. (1995). The extent of public school's responsibility to provide health-related services. In *Proceedings of the 16th National Institute on Legal Issues in Educating Individuals with Disabilities*. Alexandria, VA: LRP.

Letter to Greer, 19 IDELR 348 (OSEP, 1992).

Manual R. v. Ambach, 635 F.Supp 791 (E.D.N.Y1986).

Max M. v. Illinois State Board of Education, 684 F.Supp. 514 (N.D. Ill. 1986).

Nack v. Orange County School District, 454 F.3d 604 (6th Cir. 2006).

Norlin, J (2009). *What do I do when: The answer book on special education law* (5th ed.). Horsham, PA: LRP.

Osborne, A. G. (1992). Legal standards for an appropriate education in the post-Rowley era. *Exceptional Children, 58*, 488–494.

OSEP Policy Letter, 18 IDELR 1303 (OSEP 1992).

Pitasky, V. M. (2000). *The complete OSEP handbook*. Horsham, PA: LRP.

Pocatello School District, 18 IDELR 83 (SEA 1991).

Polk v. Central Susquehanna Intermediate Unit 16, 853 F.2d 171 (3rd Cir. 1988).

San Antonio ISD v. Rodriquez, 411 U.S. 1 (1973).

Seals v. Loftis, 614 F.Supp. 302 (E.D. Tenn. 1985).

Senate Report on the Individuals with Disabilities Act Amendments of 1997. Retrieved March 11, 2008, from http://www2.ed.gov/policy/speced/leg/idea/idea.pdf

Spaller, K. D., &Thomas, S. B. (1994). A timely idea: Third party billing for related services. *Education Law Reporter, 86*, 581–592.

Spielberg v. Henrico County Public Schools, 853 F.2d 256 (4th Cir. 1988).

Susquentia School District v. Raelee, 96 F.3d 78 (3rd Cir 1996).

T. E. ex rel. N.R. v. Kingwood Township Board, 205 F.3d 577 (3rd Cir. 2000).

Tice v. Botetourt County School Board, 908 F.2d 1200 (4th Cir.1990).

U.S. Department of Education. (2007). Twenty-five years of progress in educating children with disabilities through IDEA. Retrieved March 11, 2008, from http://www2.ed.gov/policy/speced/leg/idea/history.html

Wenkart, R. D. (2000). *Appropriate education for students with disabilities: How courts determine compliance with the IDEA*. Horsham, PA: LRP.

W. G. v. Board of Trustees, 960 F.2d 1479 (9th Cir. 1992).

Winkelman v. Parma City School District, 550 U.S. 516 127 S. Ct. 1994, (2007).

Wright, W. D., & Wright, P. (2007). *Supreme Court rules: "Parents have independent enforceable rights."* Retrieved May 22, 2007, from http://www.wrightslaw.com

Yell, M. L. (2006). *The law and special education* (2nd ed.). Upper Saddle River, NJ: Pearson/Merrill Education.

Yell, M. L., & Drasgow, E. (2000). Litigating a free appropriate public education: The Lovaas hearings and cases. *Journal of Special Education, 33*, 206–215.

Yell, M. L., Drasgow, E., Bradley, M. R., & Justesen, T. (2004). Critical legal issues in special education. In A. McCray Sorrels, H. J. Reith, & P. T. Sindelar (Eds.), *Issues in special education* (pp. 16–37). Boston: Allyn and Bacon.

Yell, M. L., Katsiyannis, A., & Hazelkorn, M. (2007). Reflections on the 25th anniversary of the U.S. Supreme Court's decision in *Board of Education v. Rowley*. *Focus on Exceptional Children, 39*(9), 1–12.

Yell, M. L., Meadows, N. B., Drasgow, E., & Shriner, J. G. (2009). *Evidence-based practices for educating students with emotional and behavioral disorders*. Upper Saddle River, NJ: Pearson/Merrill Education.

Yell, M. L., Rogers, D., & Rogers, E. L. (2006). The history of the law and children with disabilities. In M. L. Yell (Ed.), *The law and special education* (2nd ed., pp. 61–81). Upper Saddle River, NJ: Pearson/Merrill Education.

Zirkel, P. A. (2008). Have the amendments to the *Individuals with Disabilities Education Act* razed Rowley and raised the substantive standard for "free sppropriate public rducation"? *Journal of the National Association of Administrative Law Judiciary, 28*, 396–418.

8

Individual Education Programs for Children with Disabilities

Barbara D. Bateman
Creswell, Oregon

Individual education programs (IEPs) are at the core of the Individuals with Disabilities Education Act of 2004 (IDEA), 20 U.S.C.§1400 *et seq.*, the purpose of which is to make a free, appropriate public education (FAPE) available to every child in special education. The responsibility to make FAPE available rests with the public school district in which the child resides and ultimately with the state. If a district fails to make FAPE available and the parents then obtain appropriate services such as a private school placement, the district may be required to reimburse the parents' expenses. In some circumstances, compensatory education may also be awarded. When a dispute arises, the determination of whether a program provides FAPE is first made by a hearing officer (HO) or an administrative law judge (ALJ) in a due process hearing. That decision may be appealed to a state review officer or panel (in two tier states) or to a federal district court (or state appellate court) and then to a federal circuit court and possibly to the U.S. Supreme Court.

The IEP is at the center of many, perhaps most, IDEA disputes, especially those over reimbursement for private school placements. The IEP is the primary evidence of the appropriateness of the child's educational program—its development, implementation and efficacy.

Basic Legal Requirements

Perhaps the most basic of all IDEA requirements related to IEPs is that the parents are full and equal participants with the district in IEP development. In theory, such a level playing field also exists between parents and the district in resolving disputes regarding IEPs and FAPE.

Since late 2005, two U.S. Supreme Court decisions have raised awareness of the level playing field issue. The first case was *Schaffer v. Weast* (2005) in which the Court determined that when parents challenge their child's IEP and its provision of FAPE, the parents bear the *burden of persuasion* (proof), i.e., parents must have more evidence on their side to win and they lose if the evidence is in exact equipoise. Many believe that the district should have that burden, as it has better access to pertinent information, more control over its witnesses and greater educational expertise than the parents. Furthermore, under IDEA, districts have an affirmative duty to provide FAPE.

In *Arlington v. Murphy* (2006) the U.S. Supreme Court held that even when parents win, they are not entitled to recover their expert witness fees. The majority held that *costs,* which are recoverable, do not generally include expert witness fees, but they acknowledged that Congress did intend that expert fees would be recoverable under IDEA. Most parents are unable, without experts, to match the firepower of the district's professionals. The result is far from the level playing field Congress intended.

Parents' recourse is to persuade Congress to pass legislation to restore their entitlement to reimbursement for experts' fees when they prevail and such an effort is underway. Districts also have far greater resources than most parents to appeal a case it loses all the way to the U.S. Supreme Court. Parents are more likely to go only as far as the hearing process. The decisions by state HOs and ALJs do not establish precedent, and thus one parents' hearing win is not necessarily helpful to another in a seemingly similar situation. When hearing decisions are cited in this chapter it is *only* for the purpose of illustrating the issues that arise around IEPs. Only courts and legislatures pronounce the law.

The importance of the IEP in IDEA cannot be over estimated. It is the centerpiece of the law (*Honig v. Doe*, 1988). An IEP is more than a mere public relations exercise, it is the basis of the disabled child's entitlement to FAPE (*GARC v. McDaniel*, 1983).

The FAPE Standard

Free in FAPE means at no cost to the parents. Public means the education must meet public school standards.

Education is broadly construed and includes social, emotional, vocational, academic, language, physical and independent living skills, and more. Appropriate, according to the U.S. Supreme Court (*Board of Education of Hendrick Hudson School District v. Rowley*, 1982) [hereinafter *Rowley*] requires a personalized education program which is (a) reasonably calculated to enable the child to receive educational benefit and (b) procedurally compliant with the procedures of IDEA.

Educational benefit. Cases following *Rowley* have struggled with the question of how much educational benefit is required to be appropriate. The federal circuit courts have established varying standards to describe the benefit required. The Eleventh Circuit Court is the least generous, as it held that some or any benefit will suffice for FAPE even if the skill or benefit is not generalized beyond the classroom (*J.S.K. v. Hendry*, 1991). Most circuits require some version of a meaningful benefit.

Whether the child's potential is to be considered in evaluating progress is also an issue. The Sixth Circuit Court has taken a very different view. It held in *Deal v. Hamilton County Board of Education* (2004) [hereinafter *Deal*] that an IEP must confer a meaningful educational benefit relative to the child's potential, and it must focus on a goal of self-sufficiency.

Fifteen years after *Rowley*, Congress amended IDEA, and now some courts and legal scholars believe that *Rowley* is no longer good law. A federal district court in Washington, DC addressed this squarely:

> Satisfied that the goal of 'access' had been reached, in 1997 Congress enacted the IDEA with the express purpose of addressing implementation problems resulting from 'low expectations, and an insufficient focus on applying replicable research on proven methods of teaching and learning for children with disabilities'. 20 U.S.C.§1400(c)(4). The statute clearly stated its commitment to 'our national policy of ensuring equality of opportunity, full participation, *independent living*, and *economic self-sufficiency* for individuals with disabilities'. (20 U.S.C.§1400(c)(1)) (emphasis added)
>
> This represented a significant shift in focus from the disability education system in place prior to 1997. In defining the applicable standard, the District and the ALJ place much reliance on the Supreme Court case of *Hendrick Hudson District Board of Education v. Rowley;* 458 U.S. 176 (1982), a case which interprets the Education of the Handicapped Act (EHA; the 1975 designation for IDEA). To the extent that the Supreme Court at that time was interpreting a statute which had no requirement (1) that programming for disabled students be designed to transition them to post-secondary or (2) that schools review IEPs to determine whether annual goals were being attained, the Court must consider that opinion [*Rowley*] superseded by later legislation, and the district's and ALJ's reliance on it misplaced.… [A]ny citation to pre-1997 case law on special education is suspect. (*J.L. v. Mercer Island School District*, 2006, pp.1186–1187)

Not everyone agrees that the 1997 IDEA changed the amount of educational benefit to which a child is entitled. Some HOs, ALJs, and courts still believe that FAPE is provided if the student receives more than minimal benefit or makes even trivial progress regardless of ability or expected level of performance. As said earlier, in the Eleventh Circuit Court, any benefit will suffice *(J.S.K. v. Hendry, 1991*). A Pennsylvania state court found that a student of average intelligence who made 2 months of progress in 20 months of reading instruction had received some educational benefit and that was sufficient for FAPE (*Delaware Valley School District v. Daniel G.,* 2002).

Generally, the IEP is accepted in legal proceedings as accurately depicting the child's program, absent evidence of implementation failures, and it is the primary basis for finding whether FAPE was delivered. At least one judge, however, believes "it is certainly appropriate for the Hearing Officer to decide whether experiences show the pretty picture painted in an individual education program is more an impressionistic than a realistic rendering of what actually happens in the classroom" *(Board of Education of the City of Chicago v. Illinois State Board of Education*, 2006, p. 963).

Procedural compliance. IDEA, case law, and agency rulings provide procedural guidance on the IEP components and on the process of IEP development. Hearing decisions bind the parties, but do not create precedent, as each is based on its own, presumably unique, facts. In this chapter, they merely illustrate specific issues that have arisen involving IEPs.

The IDEA mandates districts' compliance with requirements regarding (a) participants in IEP meetings, (b) procedures in developing IEPs, (c) content of IEPs, (d) implementation of IEPs, and (e) resolution of and remedies for IEP disputes. Even though districts are required to comply with IDEA's procedural requirements, procedural flaws do not automatically require a finding of a denial of a FAPE. IDEA 2004 requires that a decision that FAPE has been denied, i.e., that the IEP is legally deficient, must be made on *substantive* grounds:

> Before an IEP is set aside, there must be some rational basis to believe that procedural inadequacies compromised the pupil's right to an appropriate education, seriously hampered the parents' opportunity to participate in the formulation process, or caused a deprivation of educational benefits. *(Michael D.M. v. Pemi-Baker Regional School District,* 2004, p. 1133)

The parents' right to participate is the central issue in many significant cases. The *Rowley* court said:

> [W]e think that the importance Congress attached to these procedural safeguards cannot be gainsaid. It seems to us no exaggeration to say the Congress placed every bit as much emphasis upon compliance with procedures giving

> parents and guardians a large measure of participation at every stage of the administrative process as it did upon the measurement of the resulting IEP against a substantive standard. (*Rowley*, 1982, p. 205)

Evaluation and the IEP

If the IEP were a house, the evaluation of the student would be the foundation, the IEP itself the framing, and the placement decision the roof. The IEP must stand solidly and squarely on a foundation of current, accurate evaluations of the student's level of performance in academic and functional areas. The placement decision must follow completion of the IEP and be based on it. The relationships between evaluations and IEPs and between IEPs and placements are key to understanding the IEP process.

Evaluations of the student's performance reveal the unique educational needs to which the IEP must be addressed. To the extent that evaluations are incomplete, inaccurate or outdated, the IEP is inadequate. A district court judge put it directly:

> If the IEP fails to assess the 'child's present levels of academic achievement and functional performance' the IEP does not comply with §1414 [IDEA]. This deficiency goes to the heart of the IEP; the child's level of academic achievement and functional performance is the foundation on which the IEP must be built. Without a clear identification of [the child's] present levels, the IEP cannot set measurable goals, evaluate the child's progress and determine which educational and related services are needed. (*Kirby v. Cabell County Board of Education,* 2006, p. 694)

An Illinois hearing decision illustrates the failure of an IEP to address all the student's needs as identified in the evaluation, which included sleeping in class, crying, irrational outbursts, a lack of friends, and an inability to cope. The district's offer of only large mainstream classes with minimal social work and psychological services denied FAPE (*Evanston-Skokie School District No. 65*, 2007).

Another Illinois hearing decision dealt with a district's failure to address the needs of a child who has autism. His IEP had no goals to improve receptive or expressive language (except one related to greeting people), to address academic or pre-academic skills, to generalize, to address sensory issues, distractibility, self-care, written communication, self-regulation, or attention—all common issues for children with autism (*Elmhurst School District No. 205*, 2006).

Other cases on evaluation and the IEP often involve a school district's unwillingness to give full credence to the findings and recommendations of parents' independent evaluators. Another frequent problem arises when the evaluation shows unique needs, only some or none of which are academic. Most courts, but not all, recognize that needs other than academic often require special education.

Placement and the IEP

Placement decisions must be based on a completed IEP (IDEA Regulations, 34 C.F.R. §300.116(b)(2006)) and they may, but need not, appear on the IEP unless the state so requires. The placement decision is not technically part of the IEP process. However, the decision is almost always made by the IEP team and included in the IEP. This practice is fully acceptable because parents are participating members of both teams and most IEP teams also meet the placement team requirements, i.e., persons knowledgeable about the child, the meaning of the evaluation data and the placement options (IDEA Regulations, 34 C.F.R.§300.116(a)(1)(2006)). Hearing officers and courts usually treat placement as part of the IEP process (see, e.g., *Elmhurst School District No. 205*, 2006).

The IEP Process

The IEP meeting and the resulting written document are both part of the IEP process. IDEA requires that (a) IEP meetings be scheduled at a mutually agreeable time and place (b) the mandated team members participate in the process and (c) certain components be included in the IEP.

IEP Team Participants

IDEA requires that the IEP team include (a) the child's parents, (b) a regular education teacher if the child is or may be participating in regular education, (c) the child's special education teacher or provider, (d) a representative of the public agency, (e) someone who can interpret the instructional implications of evaluation results, (f) others the district or parent invite, and (g) the child as appropriate (IDEA Regulations, 34 C.F.R.§300.321(a)(2006)).

A team participant listed above in (b) through (e) need not attend the IEP meeting when that person's areas of curriculum or related services is not to be modified or discussed, if the parent and district so agree in writing. Even if his or her area of contribution is a topic for the meeting, excusal may still be granted by written agreement if that team member submits written input to the parent and district prior to the meeting (IDEA Regulations, 34 C.F.R.§300.321(e)(1,2)(2006)). However, best practice suggests a complete team is usually preferable.

Parent Participation

Parents' participation is of the utmost importance to the provision of FAPE, as the U.S. Supreme Court has emphasized from *Rowley* (1982) through *Forest Grove v. T.A.* (2009).

Full and equal participation. IDEA makes parental participation central in all decisions regarding the child's program and placement and when full and equal parent participation is abridged or denied, a denial of FAPE will most likely be found. Few, if any, of IDEA's procedural rights are more vigorously protected by courts. The Ninth Circuit Court has held that interference with parental participation in IEP development undermines the very essence of the IDEA (*Amanda J. v. Clark County School District,* 2001). The court explained that an IEP that truly addresses the unique needs of the child can be developed only if the people who know the child best are fully involved and informed.

A parent's right to participate in IEP development was violated when a district refused to discuss the qualifications of two aides who had not followed specified procedures for feeding her two children. The IEP meeting was terminated after 10 minutes by the district's attorney who said the aides' qualifications were a personnel matter (*Paradise (Cal.) Unified School District,* 2006). This is common, but ill-advised, when parents want to discuss staff qualifications, especially in light of recent attention to the importance of highly qualified teachers.

The IDEA regulatory provisions ensuring full and equal parental participation include: (a) providing adequate notice of the meetings; (b) scheduling the meeting at a mutually agreed upon time and place; (c) informing the parents of the purpose, time, and place of the meetings and who will attend by district request; and (d) informing the parents of their right to bring others of their choice to the meeting (IDEA Regulations, 34 C.F.R.§300.322)(2006).

An Alaska hearing officer found an IEP was not valid because the district failed to have a teacher and speech therapist at the triennial review meeting. Even though the parents were there, they could not fully participate due to lack of input from the missing members (*In re Student with a Disability*, 2006). Another way parents were denied full participation, while physically present, was by a district discounting or ignoring evaluations obtained by the parents. This caused substantive harm and denied FAPE (*West Lincoln-Broadwell Elementary School District*, 2004).

Parents' participation is so vital it is sometimes held to override other also arguably important factors. When parents agreed to a placement in which the student then failed, their earlier agreement was said to preclude any relief under IDEA (*Hinson v. Merritt Educational Center*, 2008). Similarly, parental participation and agreement to goals defeated their later claim for reimbursement (*B.B. v. Department of Education, Hawaii*, 2006). These rulings raise the question of what parents should do if they believe that a placement or program that seemed appropriate prospectively proved not to be so, or when goals that seemed reasonable are later found not to be appropriate.

When parents do not participate in IEP meetings. When parents remove themselves from the IEP process, HOs and courts tend to deny them any remedies and to hold any procedural violations the district may have committed to be *harmless error* (see, e.g., *System v. Academy School District No. 20, 2008; M. M. v. School District of Greenville County, 2002; Hjortness v. Neenah Joint School District,* 2007).

Hearing officers may find it difficult to determine whether parents refused to participate or were constructively excluded from the IEP process. It is clear that if parents are believed to have unreasonably refused to participate, then they have waived substantial rights. If a district cannot persuade the parents to attend or to participate by alternate means, it must keep a record of its attempts and must provide a copy of the IEP to the parents (IDEA Regulations, 34 C.F.R.§300.322(d)(f)(2006)).

After the annual meeting for the school year, parents and the district may agree to make changes to an IEP by written agreement rather than an actual meeting. Although it is never recommended for a first meeting or a difficult one, a routine IEP meeting may be held by telephone, video conference, etc. It is important this new statutory and regulatory flexibility not be confused with a failure to participate (IDEA Regulations, 34 C.F.R.§300.322(c)(d)(2006)).

Scheduling. IEP meetings must be scheduled at a "mutually agreeable time and place" (IDEA Regulations, 34 C.F.R.§300.322(a)(2)(2006)). Hearing officers and courts take this requirement more seriously than do some districts, which insist they be held at the school immediately before or after school, Monday through Friday.

If a district makes inadequate efforts to schedule an IEP meeting at a time and place agreeable to the parent as well as to the district, that failure may be a denial of FAPE. If so, the district may be responsible for private school tuition reimbursement and attorney's fees (see *Mr. & Mrs. "M" v. Ridgefield Board of Education,* 2007; *Rutherford County School,* 2006; *Department of Education, Hawaii*, 2005).

Parents told a district they were placing their daughter in a private school. The district later had an IEP meeting in which they developed an appropriate IEP without the parents present. The district then refused the parents' request to reschedule the IEP, thus denying FAPE (*K.M. v. Ridgefield Board of Education,* 2008).

Observation. Parents and their experts often need to observe a child in his or her classroom(s) or other school settings in order to be informed and able to participate meaningfully and equally in the IEP and/or hearing process. Districts often refuse parental requests to observe or strictly limit observations, and little recourse is available. Parents frequently accept the limitations without question, even though district personnel have virtually unlimited opportunity to observe the student. In a New York hearing, the district allowed the parent one 39-minute classroom observation during which a written test was given. The decision was that the limitation did not significantly impede the parents' opportunity to participate in IEP development (*Board of Education of the Carmel School District,* 2007). The opposite conclusion was reached by a California court when a district limited the parents' expert to one 20-minute observation. The court held FAPE was denied inasmuch as the parents' right to gather evidence regarding placement and to participate in IEP development was impermissibly abridged (*L.M. v. Capistrano Unified School District,* 2007). School districts denying an observation often cite "confidentiality" or "privacy."

Predetermination

A glaring example of the not-so-level playing field between districts and parents is called predetermination. Predetermination refers to allowing the parent to "participate" in an IEP meeting when the decision about program or placement has already been made by the district and the "participation" is a charade.

Predetermination often goes unchallenged. Parents may agree with the predetermined service or placement, may not know they can challenge it, or may want to challenge it but not have the resources to do so.

Cases of predetermination. The leading case on predetermination is *Spielberg v. Henrico County Public School* (1988). Early on in IDEA implementation, the district had placed a student in a residential setting and was paying for it. The district later developed its own program, and informed the parents that the student must return to the district, as the district would no longer pay for the residential placement. The court pointed out that every placement decision must be based on the IEP, but in this case the decision preceded IEP development.

In a similar case, the district developed an IEP to place the student in a predetermined, already ongoing program and did not consider other options. The court said the district had to conduct not just an IEP meeting, but a meaningful meeting (*W.G. v. Board of Target Range School District No. 23,* 1992).

One of the most blatant cases of predetermination is *Deal.* The Sixth Circuit Court found the school had an unofficial policy of refusing to provide one-on-one applied behavior analysis (ABA) programs, even when the parents shared ABA's impressive results with their son and district personnel openly admired the child's progress. The court believed the district was immovable, regardless of ABA's efficacy. A typical predetermination scenario appeared in a Hawaii case:

> [I]t is apparent that the DOE had predetermined the physical location of Kelii's placement. The parents were the only team members who knew Kelii. There was no team discussion about the physical location for Kelii's placement and no discussion about potential harmful effects.... Nor was there a consideration of alternatives.... Predetermination of a child's placement is a violation of IDEA because it deprives the parents of meaningful participation in the IEP process. (*Kelii H. v. Department of Education, Hawaii*, 2008, p. 411)

When courts fail to find predetermination, it is usually because the parents were believed to have participated in a meaningful way, the school personnel had open minds, or placement options were seriously discussed. District personnel can come to the meeting with suggestions and opinions, but they must be open to more than one course of action.

In an interesting variation on preventing meaningful parent participation, a district "promoted" a student with Down Syndrome to 12th grade, thereby excluding him from the alternative testing program which was available in 11th grade but not in 12th. The parents had requested the testing to provide a better basis for his IEP, especially for transition. The district did not notify the parents of the deletion of the alternative testing nor of their right to protest the decision, thus denying FAPE (*County School Board of York County, Virginia. v. A.L.,* 2006).

In a clear example of predetermination, a district special education director coerced the IEP staff into selecting services and placements only from a pre-printed list, based on budget and logistic concerns, regardless of what they believed the student actually needed. This procedure violated Section§504 Regulations (34 C.F.R.§100.35(c) (2006)) (*Ellenville New York Central School District*, 2004).

In a similar case, a chart called "District Responsibility" (for services to the child) had been prepared prior to the IEP meeting. The court found the district was not open-minded when it offered only what the chart indicated, and the offer preceded, selection of the final goals. Finally, even though the District proposed to drop 30–35 hours of in-home ABA per week, the district personnel refused to even deal with providing the services necessary to support that transition. This predetermination denied FAPE (*T.P. v. Mamaroneck Union Free School District,* 2007).

General Education Teachers

IDEA requires that a general education teacher participate in IEP development, review, and revision (IDEA Regulations, 34 C.F.R.§300.324 (b)(3)(2006)). A general education team member may be excused from a meeting with written consent of parent and district, but written input may be necessary.

If no general education teacher is on the team, the district is vulnerable to charges of pre-determining the placement. The only reason for not having a general education teacher on the IEP team is that the child is not and will not be in general education. This placement determination cannot properly be made until the IEP is complete, so a general education teacher should be on the team. An IEP that proposed some mainstreaming for a student was held to be *null and void* because no general education teacher was present at the meeting (*District of Columbia Public Schools*, 2007).

A 6-year-old student had autism, mental retardation, and macrocephaly. He had frequent temper tantrums, was non-verbal, had virtually no communication skills, was not toilet trained, and displayed aggressive behavior such as biting and pinching. His cognitive ability was in the 1st percentile. He was placed in an integrated kindergarten class with a series of full-time, one-on-one instructional assistants to work with him. Each one of them quit after only one day, even though he was allowed to listen to his favorite music all day. After five days, the district offered a new IEP and a self-contained special education placement. No general education teacher was present on the IEP team and the Ninth Circuit Court held that the omission denied

FAPE because a general education placement decision was possible and a general teacher's input might have affected the writing of the IEP (*M.L. v. Federal Way School District*, 2002). When a general education teacher participated in an IEP meeting by phone, but did not have a copy of the IEP in hand, IDEA was also violated (*Board of Education of Wappingers Central School District*, 2004). The HO believed that meaningful participation required the teacher have an IEP in hand.

A New York district argued unsuccessfully that a reading specialist was a valid substitute for the general education teacher on the IEP team for a learning disabled student who was primarily placed in general education (*Board of Education of the Arlington Central School District,* 2004).

Private School Personnel

The participation of private school personnel when the student is or may be attending the private school at public expense can be problematic. Some private schools do not encourage or do not even allow their personnel to attend district IEP meetings. If the parents and public school agree to written or telephone input, no problem is presented. However, if no district professionals know the child, it could be found crucial to have a private school person who does know the child present at the meeting.

A public school made no effort to include the child's private school teacher in an IEP meeting, even though the child had never attended the public school. Furthermore, no general education teacher was present, even though the prior notice to parents said one would be there and the child was in general education in the private school two-thirds of the time. Neither omission was harmless error—both interfered with parent participation, denied education opportunities, and impeded the student's right to FAPE. No district person knew the child beyond a few hours of assessment, and that was not sufficient for IEP development (*Chula Vista Elementary School District,* 2007).

Special Education Teachers

Parents and the special education teachers/providers who work with the child are often the team's experts on the child. The other participants seldom know the child as well. A denial of FAPE was found when an IEP meeting was held without a special education teacher present, and the IEP itself was flawed by its failure to provide services for identified social/emotional concerns and by vague goals and objectives with no criteria for measurement. The decision noted that if a special education teacher been present, those deficiencies might not have occurred (*Board of Education of the West Seneca Central School District,* 2004).

A preschool teacher provided input to an IEP meeting through questionnaires and interviews. However, the district thereby denied FAPE because, had she been physically present, she might have influenced the team to include needed behavioral and other provisions, which were omitted (*S.B. v. Pomona Unified School District,* 2008). According to the Ninth Circuit Court, IDEA (1997) 20 U.S.C.§1414 (d)(1)(B)(iii) requires a special education teacher on the team who has actually taught the student, but not necessarily the current teacher *(R.B. v. Napa Valley Unified School District*, 2007).

District Representative

The district representative (IDEA Regulations, 34 C.F.R.§300.321(a)(2006)) is one of the most problematic members of the IEP team, due to confusion over who may serve in that capacity. In 2007, the Office of Special Education and Rehabilitation Services (OSERS) reiterated its long held view that it may not be reasonable to excuse from attendance a district representative when that person may be needed to "ensure that decisions can be made at the meeting about *commitment of agency resources* [emphasis added] that are necessary to implement the child's IEP" (*Questions*, 2007, p. 779).

The requirement that decisions, even expensive ones, must be made at IEP meetings by the appropriate team has been a logistically difficult mandate for many districts. In clear violation of IDEA, some have even set up systems in which final decisions on IEP services and programs are made by special education administrators or board members who did not attend the IEP meeting. The notion that an IEP team, including the parents, must make the decision that a student will receive something very expensive (e.g., a $75,000 a year private placement or a 40 hour-a-week, in-home ABA program at $50 an hour) is difficult for some districts. Decisions with substantial financial impact have traditionally been made by school boards and/or high-level administration, without regard to the needs of one individual special education student. However, states and local districts do now receive substantial federal funds, although not what was originally promised, to implement IDEA. Furthermore, all 50 states voluntarily participate in IDEA and agree to comply with it to receive those funds.

Interpreter of Instructional Implications of Evaluations

Few cases have dealt with the requirement that a member of the IEP team be able to interpret the instructional implications of evaluation results. This is not due to its lack of importance. Arguably, the relationship between evaluation data and the needed instruction is paramount, but it is often downplayed or even ignored by IEP teams. Parents are often unaware of the importance of the expertise required to interpret evaluations, and they seldom make an issue of it. When the question does arise, the district typically indicates that someone present at the meeting is qualified and the matter rests. The reality is that the relationship between evaluation and instructional methodology too often remains unexplored by IEP teams, even though it may be absolutely essential in determining whether the services provided actually meet the child's needs and constitute FAPE. To successfully develop an IEP and provide FAPE, it is necessary to determine the child's unique needs, establish goals and objectives for each, and provide the services that will meet the needs and enable the child to reach the goals.

Content

Each IEP must be written, reviewed, and revised in an IEP meeting unless the district and parent have agreed to alternative forms of meeting. The required content is clearly delineated in IDEA Regulations: (a) present levels of academic achievement and functional performance; (b) measurable annual goals; (c) a description of how progress toward meeting goals will be measured; (d) a statement of the needed special education and related services and supplementary aids and services, based on peer-reviewed research to the extent practicable, and a statement of the program modifications or supports for school personnel; (e) an explanation of the extent, if any, to which the child will not participate with non-disabled children in the regular class and in [other] activities; (f) a statement of accommodations, if any, necessary in assessments and/or in assessment standards; and (g) the projected date, frequency, location and duration of services and modifications (IDEA Regulations, 34 C.F.R.§300.320(2006)).

Beginning with the first IEP in effect when the student turns 16 years old, a transition plan must also be included containing (a) measurable postsecondary goals based on age- appropriate transition assessments, (b) services needed to enable the student to reach the goals, and (c) a statement that IDEA rights transfer from parents to the student upon reaching the age of majority under state law (IDEA Regulations, 34 C.F.R.§300.320(b, c)(2006)).

The content of the IEP reveals that three questions lie at the heart of the IEP: (a) what are this student's unique educational needs, (b) what services are needed to address the needs, and (c) how will we determine the effectiveness of the services? These questions are addressed in the IEP's present levels of performance, services and measurable goals.

If a service or accommodation is needed, it must be written in the IEP. Some districts require that meeting minutes be kept and that parents' requests be written there rather than in the IEP itself. Disputes then arise as to whether such minutes are enforceable as part of the IEP. The better practice is to record each meeting and avoid the dispute. Unfortunately, what has been said at the meeting and what is written in the IEP may not be the same. One team agreed at the meeting to write "Orchestra" into the student's IEP, but later refused to do so based on administrative concerns, violating IDEA (*Houston Independent School District,* 2004).

When asked by parents, a district recommended a particular residential program for the student. The parents made the placement and paid for the recommended residential program, believing the district would reimburse them. However, the child's IEP said *day program.* The court held that generally its rulings must be limited to the written terms of the IEP itself, regardless of the understandings of the parties (*Avjian v. Weast*, 2007). This view is not widely held. However, without a recording, written or otherwise, it may be difficult to prove an understanding.

Present Levels of Performance and the Child's Unique Educational Needs

Every IEP must contain the child's present levels of academic and functional performance (PLOPs), as determined by a variety of objective and current assessments. PLOPs must contain accurate, objective baseline data—the starting points from which to measure progress for the IEP year—as well as parents' perceptions.

The student's needs and the PLOPs as shown in current evaluations are the foundation of the IEP. Although IDEA does not explicitly require the team to list the child's unique needs, a successful meeting begins with agreeing upon those needs and the PLOP in each.

If an IEP team agrees, e.g., that a child needs to control his anger, the next question is, what is his PLOP in anger management. If he averages five inappropriate outbursts daily, that is the PLOP from which progress is to be measured after intervention.

If a team finds a child needs more fluent and legible handwriting, the question is how the student currently performs in writing. Ideally, the teacher spent two minutes before the IEP meeting timing the entire class on writing the alphabet and copying words. Our student printed four legible letters per minute, far below the other students and below a functional rate. Her PLOP is four legible letters per minute, a clear starting point from which to measure future progress.

How current must PLOPs be? In one hearing, eight-month-old data were clearly not current (*Rio Rancho Public Schools*, 2003). Data more than a few weeks old are seldom likely to be considered PLOPs. Best practice would have PLOPs determined as close to the IEP meeting time as possible and seldom more than a month prior.

The relationship between the evaluation, the student's needs, and the PLOPs was emphasized by a state review officer who found FAPE was denied because the IEP did not accurately reflect the student's PLOPs, nor did it reflect evaluative data or information about the student's needs (*In re: Student with a Disability*, 2008).

March IEP meeting notes showed a district knew the student needed orientation, mobility, and assistive technology, but they were not added to the IEP until November. The parents were awarded reimbursement for the private placement they made when school began with no completed IEP (*Alfonso v. District of Columbia,* 2006).

Measurable Annual Goals and Objectives

Measurable annual goals are critical IEP components along with the PLOPs and the services, and yet only a fraction of IEPs contain measurable goals. Measurable goals begin with measured PLOPs. An Alaska HO succinctly observed that PLOPs are the starting point for determining goals and it is from them the student's progress is measured (*Anchorage School District,* 2008).

Measurable annual goals are fundamental to both the IEP and to FAPE. The New Mexico HO cited earlier explained that their purpose is to allow the team to assess progress toward the goal during the year and to revise the IEP accordingly. Thus they are critical to planning and implementing FAPE. She found that in this case:

> Student's annual goals and objectives in each IEP simply do not contain objective criteria which permit measurement of Student's progress.... A goal of 'increasing' reading comprehension skills or 'improving decoding skills' is not a measurable goal.... Even if [PLOPs] were clearly stated, an open-ended statement that Student will 'improve' does not meet the requirement ... for a 'measurable' goal. The addition of a percentage of accuracy is not helpful where the IEP fails to define a starting point, an ending point, the curriculum in which Student will achieve 80 to 85% accuracy, or a procedure for pre and post-testing of Student. (*Rio Rancho Public Schools*, 2003, p. 563)

As many have said, if we don't know where we're going, we probably won't get there. This was never more true than with IEP goals and the cycle of non-accountability, in which non-measurable goals are written and never measured, more non-measurable goals are written, etc.

This cycle of non-accountability has gone unchallenged largely because too few IEP members know how to write measurable goals and too few goal writers intend that anyone ever actually measure the progress the child has made. Additionally, IEPs and their goals are viewed by many as "mere" paperwork to be filed and forgotten, and are not seen as the daily guide to the child's education.

If a goal is not measurable—e.g., Lenny will improve his behavior 75% of the time; Tyler will navigate the world in school; Fred will develop behavioral, emotional, and social skills with 85% accuracy—it is clear that no one ever intended to measure it. Not knowing how to write a measurable goal plus not intending to try to assess progress toward it leave IEP goals meaningless and useless (Bateman, 2007).

A Pennsylvania review panel took a less generous view and awarded compensatory education to a student whose district repeatedly failed to include measurable reading and math goals and objectives in his IEP (*Philadelphia City School District,* 2006). In a similar case, the district failed to provide measurable math goals for a student whose learning disability was in math. This denial of FAPE resulted in an award of private school tuition and more (*D. H. v. Mannheim Township School District,* 2005). A New Jersey court held that an IEP that contained no goals or objectives nevertheless offered FAPE, as parents participated and there was no loss of educational opportunity (*G.N. v. Board of Education of the Township of Livingston*, 2007).

A Pennsylvania court noted that:

> [M]easuring annual goals in terms of grade equivalencies is inadequate. Goals such as '[C.F.] will complete the fourth grade curriculum in the areas of science, social studies and reading' and '[C.F.] will improve his organization skills so that he fulfills expected levels of achievement attached to short-term objectives' do not provide an objectively measurable basis for tracking C.F.'s progress. 'Completing' a curriculum is an extremely vague goal for a developmentally disabled child and does not provide sufficient guidance for providing a FAPE. (*Penn. Trafford School District v. C.F.,* 2006, p. 174)

IDEA requires measurable goals in all the child's areas of need related to the disability. Controversy has arisen over whether goals must be written in social skills or other deficit areas when academic achievement is not substantially deficient. This issue often arises with students who have Asperger's syndrome, whose academic performance is adequate or even superior, but whose social skills deficits require specially designed instruction. Cases have been decided both ways.

Short-term objectives. Prior to IDEA 2004, short-term objectives were required for each IEP goal. Now they are required only for the special education students who are assessed on state/district tests using alternate assessments and alternate standards. OSEP has said states may choose whether to include short-term IEP objectives in those years a student does not take assessments (*Letter to Kelly*, 2007). The requirements for goals and objectives are identical except for the length of time anticipated for accomplishment. Objectives may be progressive and sequential steps toward a goal, e.g., he will name 10 colors by Oct. 1, 15 by Nov. 1, etc. or the objectives may be *component parts* of a goal such as setting a formal dining table, where the order in which one learns placement of napkins, silverware, plates, or glassware is not critical.

The most essential requirement is that all annual goals and required short-term objectives must be objectively measurable and measured—requirements too seldom met.

Measuring and Reporting Progress

Each IEP must describe *how and when* progress toward goals will be measured (IDEA Regulations, 34 C.F.R.§300.320(a)(3)(i, ii)(2006)). A common practice is that a special education teacher subjectively indicates progress on each goal by a checkmark or a letter, e.g., N = no progress, P = progress or M = mastered. IDEA requires this reporting be done as often as parents of nondisabled children receive progress reports, usually every 6 or 9 weeks.

Assuming that Ns and Ps or similar indicators are reported regularly to parents, the real issue is whether these are meaningful measures of progress and whether the child is on track to meet the annual goal. If the child is not on track then something in the program must be changed, recognizing that time is of the essence in providing appropriate programs for IDEA students. In special education "early and intensive" is far better than "later and less."

A federal court in Ohio noted that standardized tests are

not required in measuring progress toward IEP goals (*Pierce v. Mason City School District Board of Education*, 2007).

While standardized testing can be valuable to show growth over a year, these tests are not appropriate for showing the short-term progress required by IDEA, typically every 6 or 9 weeks.

A better practice for reporting progress is to assess the child's performance on the goal activity itself. If the goal is to initiate three appropriate interactions with peers at recess for three consecutive days, then one should observe the student at recess on three consecutive days and count his initiations of peer interactions. The student's performance is described in absolute terms, not relative to other students'. Criterion-referenced measurement is highly appropriate for use with IEPs, as recognized in *Pierce v. Mason City Sch. Dist. Bd. of Ed.* (2007).

Importance of measured progress. How much progress has been made can be a factor in whether FAPE was provided. In early cases, attention focused on whether the IEP, as written, was reasonably calculated to enable the student to receive educational benefit, following *Rowley* (1982). More recent decisions frequently also examine the student's actual progress.

FAPE was denied in a case involving a student who made no academic gains, even though he made progress on social/emotional skills (*Cranston School District v. Q.D.*, 2008). In another case, measured achievement progress showed FAPE was not denied, even though the IEP was seriously flawed (*M.P. v. South Brunswick Board of Education*, 2008).

The Third Circuit Court found an IEP did not result in satisfactory education benefits when grades were based on effort rather than on achievement and did not reflect progress. Further, the IEP did not address the student's depression and suicidal tendencies, nor did it provide services significantly different from those proven ineffective for him in regular education (*Montgomery Township Board of Education v. S.C.*, 2005).

A student did not master any goals or objectives on his fourth-grade IEP, which was identical to his third-grade IEP. In response, the fifth-grade IEP team reduced his special education services. The next year, the sixth-grade team proposed an IEP identical to that of the fifth grade. The court found that his failure to meet the goals and objectives of the prior IEP meant the proposed IEP was not appropriate (*Taylor v. Sandusky*, 2005).

A district failed to base an IEP on timely and accurate assessment and continued to use the same ineffective reading program for 3 years. The student showed no progress, FAPE was denied, and a private placement was awarded for 4 years or until the student earned a regular high school diploma (*Draper v. Atlanta Independent School System*, 2007).

In an important case, the Sixth Circuit Court ruled in favor of the parent's request for private school reimbursement on the grounds that the district's IEP was not in place at the beginning of the school year, nor did it have objective criteria for measuring progress. Frequent, accurate, and objective progress measuring and reporting are essential for the required annual IEP review and revision (*Cleveland Heights-University Heights City School District v. Boss*, 1998).

Many IEPs have no measurable goals or objectives, but occasionally one will have measurable objectives. Arguably, demonstrated mastery of short-term objectives could show progress and partially compensate for inadequate goals. However, IDEA clearly requires both goals and objectives be measurable and measured.

Services

The services to which an eligible child with a disability is entitled include special education, related services, supplementary services, modifications, accommodations, and support for personnel. A child is only IDEA-eligible if special education is required as a result of the disability. Thus, IDEA's definition of special education is crucial—*specially designed instruction to meet the unique needs* of a child with a disability (IDEA Regulations, 34 C.F.R.§300.39(a) (2006)). Specially designed instruction means *adapting the content, methodology or delivery of instruction* (IDEA Regulations, 34 C.F.R.§300.39(b)(3)(2006)). These definitions are important in inclusion or mainstreaming. For example, if a child is on a "consultation" IEP, meaning only that the regular teacher "consults" with a special education teacher monthly, is that special education? If not, the child is not IDEA-eligible and may not be counted by the district for funding purposes. Does special education include an "integrated regular class" with 15 non-disabled students, 8 students who have disabilities, 2 paraprofessionals, and 1 general education teacher?

Related services include transportation and such developmental, corrective, and other supportive services as are required to assist a child to benefit from special education. Most related services, such as speech, occupational and physical therapy, are widely recognized. Others, such as therapeutic recreation and medical services for diagnostic or evaluation purposes, are seldom provided (IDEA Regulations, 34 C.F.R.§300.34(a)(2006)). The related services named in IDEA are illustrative, not exhaustive. A California hearing officer recognized this when ruling that IDEA was violated by a district's refusal to include football, swimming, and basketball on a 20-year-old's IEP when the sports were necessary for him to progress socially and vocationally (*San Diego School District*, 2005).

The difference between modifications and accommodations is important only in statewide or districtwide assessments in which accommodations are allowed (e.g., Braille) but modifications that affect the validity of the test (e.g., reading aloud a reading test to a student or administering only half the items) are not allowed. Personnel support services are not defined further but presumably include staff training and/or additional personnel. Supplementary aids and services are those provided to enable children with disabilities to be educated with nondisabled children to the maximum extent appropriate (IDEA Regulations, 34 C.F.R.§300.42(2006)).

Since IDEA 2004, services must be "based on peer-reviewed research to the extent practicable" (IDEA Regulations, 34 C.F.R.§300.320(a)(4)(2006)). The U.S. Department of Education (USDOE) has declined to define peer-reviewed research but has offered that *extent practicable* means *to the extent it is possible, given the availability of peer-reviewed research* (*USDOE Commentary*, 2008). It remains to be seen what impact this potentially revolutionary requirement will have.

Administrative and judicial decisions on IEP services. A district offered a kindergarten placement with limited adult supervision and 6 hours and 10 minutes per week of nursing services to a child who had a tracheostomy, gastronomy tube, and reactive airway disease. The child needed personnel able to assess and minister to his medical needs throughout the day, and the failure to provide that denied FAPE (*Department of Education, Hawaii*, 2007).

In a Texas case, a mother requested a designated aide to change her 7-year-old son's diapers. The court ordered more frequent diaper changes, but not a designated aide (*E.S. v. Skidmore Tynan School District,* 2007).

Parents often request a one-on-one aide to enable a child to be placed in a regular classroom when that placement would not otherwise be possible. Districts often acquiesce, believing that IDEA requires such a placement. In an instructive New York case, a one-on-one aide was characterized as a "crutch" or "palliative measure" when one of the student's most significant needs was for independence. FAPE was being denied by fostering "learned helplessness" (*A.C. v. Board of Education of Chappaqua Central School District,* 2007). In *J.L. v. Mercer Island School District* (2006), the court found that providing an aide to read to a 17-year-old student of average intelligence was at odds with IDEA's goals of self-sufficiency and independent living. The student met only three of seven IEP objectives in reading. In determining that FAPE had been denied by the public school, the court considered the progress the student later made in a private placement, as is allowed by the Ninth Circuit Court (*Ojai Unified School District v. Jackson*, 1993).

A Hawaii school denied FAPE by failing to provide a one-on-one aide "within arms reach" of the student to follow the prescribed emergency action when the child was injured. Neither the teacher nor the aide attended mandatory training regarding the child's medical condition (*Department of Education, Hawaii*, 2008).

A service dog for a student who had autism was deemed more restrictive than an aide and not necessary for FAPE, so it was not a related service (*Bakersfield City School District,* 2008).

Whether school personnel are required to administer prescription medicines is vigorously, if infrequently, contested. A student's IEP required that medication would be taken at school or the student could face exclusion. A federal court in Washington distinguished *Valerie J. v. Derry Cooperative School District* (1991) which said attendance could not be conditioned on medication without parental consent having been given. The court said that IDEA 20 U.S.C.§1412(a)(25)(A) does not apply because it prohibits the district from requiring a child to obtain a prescription. Here, the student had the medication already and the parents had consented to it because he took it at home (*S.J. v. Issaquah School District No. 411*, 2007).

In recent years, the numbers of children diagnosed with a disorder on the autism spectrum has increased geometrically, and more cases, proportionately, deal with autism than with other disabilities. In the early 1990s most of these dealt with appropriate methodology. The dispute was typically between applied behavior analysis (ABA) techniques and eclectic methods. Many cases were simply disposed of by holding that methodology was for the district to determine. Gradually, parents began to succeed in those cases by presenting substantial research on the effectiveness of ABA (see, e.g., *Deal).*

In a Colorado hearing, the student's IEP failed to address his difficulties with generalization across settings and with regression. The student, who has autism, was fully toilet trained in school, but not so outside of school. Many other behaviors were reportedly far more advanced in school than at home, church, or in public. The hearing officer agreed with the parents' experts that a residential setting was necessary to teach generalization and prevent regression and was to be at public expense because the school's IEP omissions denied FAPE (*Thompson School District R2-J,* 2005). This hearing ruling was in direct contrast to the Eleventh Circuit Court's holding in *J.S.K. v. Hendry County School Board* (1991) that generalization of skills across settings is *not* required for or relevant to FAPE.

Parents and districts frequently disagree as to what should be in the IEP. The general rule is that all of the student's needs related to the disability must be addressed (*Letter to Anonymous,* 2008). Additions to IEPs that may be required include (a) increased individualized tutoring in specific areas, (b) consultation among teachers and specialists, (c) expert-recommended therapies, (d) summer programs, or (e) on-going monitoring by an outside evaluator. Ongoing monitoring of IEP implementation by outsiders may be seen by a district as intrusive, but parents typically welcome it and some districts see the added expertise as helpful.

A child with severe autism was in a private full-day preschool pursuant to his IEP. He received 25 hours a week of instruction in a class of six students, a teacher, and two aides, one of whom worked exclusively with him. He received occupational, speech/language, and physical therapy. The IEP also provided for parent counseling. However, he made only minimal and limited progress, and the court found he had the opportunity only for trivial, not meaningful educational benefit. He was denied FAPE, and the court ordered 10 hours per week of in-home, one-on-one ABA instruction be added to his IEP (*D.F. v. Ramapo Central School District*, 2004).

Changes in their environment are difficult for many who have autism, and so transitions from one grade or school to another are often an issue. In at least two recent cases, FAPE was denied when the IEP failed to address transition into a new class for a child who had autism (*Maine School Administration District No. 61*, 2008; *T.P. v. Mamaroneck Union Free School District,* 2007).

In *Deal*, perhaps the best known case involving a child with autism, the Sixth Circuit Court resolved a hard fought contest between ABA and the Treatment and Education of Autistic and Related Communication-Handicapped Children method (TEACCH). TEACCH is often preferred by districts, as it was in this case, because it is less intensive, less structured, and less expensive than ABA and it was designed for classroom use. The school district argued that it had invested in the TEACCH program for students with autism and should be able to use it exclusively for all students with autism. The court noted that in determining what services are to be provided a district may consider costs, but not without fully considering the child's individual needs and characteristics, including any demonstrated response to particular educational programs. After citing cases in which districts were not required to provide such intensive and expensive educational programs as ABA, the court observed that allowing the district to choose the methodology may not be appropriate if the difference in outcomes between the methods is too great. Here the outcome research, and therefore the decision, conclusively favored ABA.

Program descriptions in IEPs should be understandable to parents and others. No undefined terms or abbreviations whose meaning is not readily apparent should be used, e.g., "consultation general education," "self-contained integrated," "SLP," SLD," or "230 minutes per quarter" (*see Inglewood Cal. Unified School District*, 2008).

Behavioral Intervention Plans

IDEA requires that the IEP team consider the use of positive behavioral interventions to address behavior that impedes the child's learning or that of others (IDEA Regulations, 34 C.F.R.§300.324(a)(2)(i)(2006)). In a disciplinary context, when a student's inappropriate conduct is found to be the result of, or substantially related to, the disability, a behavioral intervention plan (BIP) must be developed from a functional behavioral assessment (FBA). If a BIP already exists, it must be reviewed and modified (IDEA Regulations, 34 C.F.R.§300.530(f)(l)(2006)). IDEA makes no other references to BIPs and is silent as to whether a BIP is a part of the IEP. Logically, behavioral interventions are analogous to speech/language services or to any other special interventions.

Even though a BIP is to be developed by the IEP team and must, under some circumstances, be based on a FBA, there are no substantive criteria for a BIP (*Alex R. v. Forrestville Valley Community Unit School District No. 221*, 2004). The Eighth Circuit Court has held a BIP need not be written and that irregularities related to the BIP do not constitute a denial of FAPE (*School Board of Independent School District No. 11 v. Renollett*, 2006).

Transition Plans

One of the purposes of IDEA 2004 is to prepare students who have disabilities for "further education, employment and independent living" (20 U.S.C.§1400(d)(1)(A)(2004)).

The IEP in effect when a student reaches age 16 must contain a plan for providing transition services, defined in IDEA 2004 as:

> A coordinated set of activities for a child with a disability that: (a) is designed to be a results-oriented process, that is focused on improving the academic and functional achievement of the child with a disability to facilitate the child's movement from school to post-school activities, including post-secondary education, vocational education, integrated employment (including supported employment), continuing and adult education, adult services, independent living, or community participation; (b) is based on the individual child's needs, taking into account the child's strengths, preferences, and interests; and (c) includes instruction, related services, community experiences, the development of employment and other post-school adult living objectives, and, when appropriate, acquisition of daily living skills and functional vocational evaluation. (20 U.S.C.§1401 (34)(2006))

Transition plans must comply with IDEA procedural regulations and be reasonably calculated to enable the student to receive benefit. They must contain measurable postsecondary goals based on assessments related to training, education, employment and, when appropriate, independent living skills. The services needed to assist the student to reach the goals must also be included in the plan (IDEA Regulations 34 C.F.R.§300.320(b)(2006)).

Few transition cases have reached the courts. In one that did, a South Dakota school district believed providing transition was just communicating to the family about agencies that might be of future help and creating linkages to them. The court found that this was not an acceptable approach to the district's obligation (*Yankton School District v. Schramm*, 1995, 1996) *aff'd* 93 F.3d 1369 (8th Cir. 1996).

A student's IEP obligated the district to provide a 1-year, post-secondary college preparatory transition program. Instead, the district prepared a new IEP, without involving the parents, which called for that year to be in special education in the district. The court ordered the district to reimburse the parents for the college preparatory program for which they had paid (*Susquehanna Township School District v. Frances J.*, 2003).

Transition plans must be based on age-appropriate transition assessments. An Iowa district argued unsuccessfully that such assessments were to be done by adult service agencies, not by school districts. The ALJ noted that under IDEA, the responsibility for transition assessments was not on parents or other agencies, but solely on school districts. The ALJ also observed that the student's career interests were not related to his IEP goals, suggesting deficiencies in the evaluations. These assessment flaws provided the legal basis for preventing the district from graduating the student and thereby terminating his special education services (*Mason City Community School District*, 2006).

A federal district court in Washington described transition as preparing students to live as independent, productive adults to the greatest possible extent (*J.L. v. Mercer Island School District, 2006*). The following year, the federal district court in Hawaii espoused a very different and unique view of transition plans. Sixteen-year-old Rachael's entire transition plan consisted of graduating from high school, attending college, and being employed in the community. The court recognized this was not a "model" plan and not based on Rachael's individual needs, strengths, or interests. It was vague and incomplete and could apply to almost every high school student in the nation. The student's interests section was marked not applicable. Neither student nor parents participated in developing the plan. The court criticized the district for making no effort to complete the plan and pointed out that it did not comply with IDEA. However, such as it was, the plan was deemed mere harmless error and did not deny FAPE (*Virginia S. v. Department of Education, Hawaii,* 2007). Many school districts and some judges have found it difficult to accept IDEA's shifting of some responsibility for transition from parents to schools.

Developing IEPs

IDEA envisions that a team of people—parents and professionals—who know the child well and who have knowledge of and the authority to allocate district resources will develop the IEP. The crucial role of parents in this process has been discussed above.

Although it is not permissible for the district to complete an IEP prior to the meeting the district may prepare recommendations if it makes clear to the parents they are *only* recommendations. The team, and not any one member, is responsible for developing the goals and objectives (*Letter to Anonymous*, 2003a).

IDEA requires that in developing the IEP the team must consider the child's strengths, the concerns of the parents, and the most recent evaluations as well as the academic, developmental, and functional needs of the child. If the child's behavior impedes his or her learning or that of others, consideration must be given to addressing that behavior, including the use of positive behavioral interventions. If the child has limited English proficiency, those language needs must be considered. For children who are blind or severely visually impaired, there is a presumption that Braille instruction is appropriate, and if not, an explanation must be provided in the IEP. The communication needs of the child must be considered, and if the child is deaf or hard of hearing then the team must consider the child's needs, academic level, and opportunities for direct communication and direct instruction in the child's language/communication mode. Consideration must also be given, for all IDEA-eligible children, to needs for assistive technology (IDEA Regulations, 34 C.F.R.§300.324)(2006)).

An IEP must be completed and in place at the beginning of the school year. In a New Hampshire case, the parent, not the district was responsible for the IEP not being in place at beginning of school year, as they would neither approve the IEP nor say what was wrong with it (*Lessard v. Wilton-Lyndborough Cooperative School District*, 2007).

Every IEP must be reviewed at least annually to determine whether the annual goals are being reached and must be revised to address any lack of progress and/or reevaluation data or new information from parents (IDEA Regulations, 34 C.F.R.§300.324(b)(2006)).

The requirement that the IEP be reviewed every year and revised as needed is important and must be observed even though the stay-put provision has been triggered and a stay-put IEP is implemented while the dispute is pending *(Letter to Watson*, 2007). A Delaware state court found FAPE was denied by a failure to change the IEP when the student made no progress in decoding and very little in written expression (*Fisher v. Board of Education of Christina School District,* 2004). In a hearing involving a student who made no progress, the failure to revise both the IEP and the placement denied FAPE. Further, the IEPs were identical 2 years in a row, and the mother's signature appeared forged on the second one (*District of Columbia Public Schools (Backus Middle School)*, 2008).

In recent amendments to IDEA, provision was made for parents and districts to agree that after the annual IEP meeting, changes to the IEP may be made without a meeting (i.e., by a written document). Provision was also made for consolidation of IEP meetings (IDEA Regulations, 34 C.F.R.§300.324 (a)(4)(i)(4,5)(2006)) and for participation in meetings by alternative means such as video conference and conference calls (IDEA Regulations, 34 C.F.R.§300.328(2006)).

IDEA is silent regarding audio or video recording of IEP meetings. Agency rulings, however, are clear that a district may set the policy on recording, provided that parents who need to tape it to fully and meaningfully participate in the IEP process are allowed to do so. Parents may have language or learning differences or other conditions that require taping in order to participate fully. If the district records the meeting and keeps the record, it becomes an educational record under the Family Educational Privacy Rights Act (FERPA) (*Letter to Anonymous*, 2003b).

Multiple Errors in IEPs

Often, an IEP team that makes one error in developing an IEP makes multiple errors. The cumulative effect of multiple errors may be to deny FAPE, either by denying full and equal parent participation or by actually impeding the child's educational opportunities. Personal conversations with district IEP team members reveal several reasons for these errors. First, many members believe they are required to write "standards-based" IEPs in which goals are derived from state general education standards rather than from the child's unique educational needs. Next, many districts require the use of a specific software program and its IEP form. These programs and forms are far less conducive to true individualization than is a blank piece of paper or a very simple form, e.g., the "non-form" recommended by Bateman and Linden (2006). Third, many errors result from inadequate knowledge of what IDEA, state laws, and case law actually say. Often "knowledge" of the law is passed by word of mouth from one partially informed team member to another. Few IEP team members consult the federal or state regulations regularly and almost never do they have ready access to them in an IEP meeting. A fourth cause of IEP errors is a belief that district policy mandates or prohibits certain IEP content. For example, in *Deal*, the Sixth Circuit Court concluded:

> The facts of this case strongly suggest that the school system has an unofficial policy of refusing to provide one-on-one ABA programs.... This conclusion is bolstered by evidence that the school system steadfastly refused even to discuss the possibility of providing an ABA program, even in the face of impressive results.... The clear implication is that no matter how strong the evidence presented by the Deals, the school system still would have refused to provide the services. (*Deal*, 2004, p. 848)

An Illinois hearing illustrates common IEP errors and raises concerns about the use of computer-generated IEP programs:

> The proposed IEP did not specify whether therapies [occupational and physical] were to be performed in class or on a pull-put basis or whether they were to be individual or in a group.... In addition, the IEP has many errors, possibly due to the fact that it was computer generated that opens questions [*sic*] as to whether this document was specifically designed for [student] or whether it was one developed to be used for all the students in the ABC classroom.... [O]n page 11 of the IEP the name "Michael" [not the student's name] appears under present levels of performance and under the checked categories in relation to autism eligibility, categories are checked that do not even apply to [student]. (*Elmhurst School District No. 205*, 2006, p. 120)

A Texas district wanted to return one of its students from a residential placement to a day program in the district. However, the IEP they developed did not deal with major essential elements in the situation, including transition, transportation, reintegration, escalating aggression, and needed home services (*Beaumont Independent School District,* 2008).

A model hearing decision from New Mexico found the district made multiple errors including (a) 8-month-old data were not adequate for present levels of performance, (b) the lack of objective criteria in the goals and objectives made measurement impossible, (c) a special education teacher with regular education certification could not substitute for a regular education teacher at the IEP meeting, and (d) the transition plan was not updated annually.

The hearing officer noted that these deficiencies alone would normally deny FAPE, but here the even greater problem was that the parents' right to fully participate in the IEP development was denied by (a) no clear explanation of the student's PLOPS in reading, (b) no clear goals and objectives, (c) no regular rate-of-progress reports, (d) no regular education teacher at the high school IEP meeting, and (e) no prior written notice of a plan to change placement. Overall, the continued absence of clear PLOPs and the lack of objective evaluation of progress toward measurable goals made it next to impossible for an adequate IEP to be prepared (*Rio Rancho Public Schools*, 2003).

In another case a district court found (a) in spite of 22 disciplinary actions in 7 months there was no functional behavior analysis or behavior intervention plan (BIP) in the IEP, (b) there were no adequate PLOPs, and (c) no objective criteria against which achievement could be measured. These deficiencies denied FAPE (*Independent School District No.36, International Falls v. C.L.*, 2004).

FAPE was denied in an Alabama hearing when the IEP (a) lacked PLOPs in three important areas, (b) indicated no special education services, (c) contained goals that were not designed to provide any objective measurement of progress, and (4) had no FBA or BIP (*Mobile County Board of Education*, 2004). In an earlier Alabama case, FAPE was denied when an IEP contained no strategies for the full-time return to school of a student who had social phobia and anxiety disorders. There was no contemplation of the services necessary before she returned (*E.D. v. Enterprise City Board of E*ducation, 2003).

Another combination of IEP flaws that denied FAPE and provided the basis for awarding private school placement costs to the parents included: (a) no goals in the essential area of reading fluency; (b) vague goals and objectives that did not allow for specific measurement; (c) Insufficient, intensive multi-sensory reading instruction; (d) insufficient repetition was provided, given the student's working memory problems; (e) the IEP was unduly restrictive in that a one-on-one aide was required; and (f) The goals were the same as those 2 years earlier (*J. S. v. Springfield Township Board of Education,* 2007).

A year of compensatory education was awarded when a state review panel found an IEP to be acceptable although it lacked a standard for measuring progress, there were no goals in some areas of identified need, and the transition plan was not individualized (*Pennsbury School District*, 2007). These same deficiencies are found in too many IEPs.

A variety of IEP defects resulted in private school reimbursement to the parents. The IEP failed to offer (a) a plan to transition the student back into school, (b) specific recommended teacher training, (c) follow-up meetings with team as transition occurred, (d) family training and communication, (e) transportation, and (f) assistive technology. These omissions made regression likely and so denied FAPE (*Regional School District No.9 Board of Education v. Mr. & Mrs. P.,* 2009).

Thousands of decisions could be used to illustrate serious

IEP deficiencies. Prominent among the IEP flaws that most often deny FAPE and result in private placements and/or compensatory services awards and therefore are the most serious include: (a) inaccurate, dated, subjective, or absent present levels of performance; (b) annual goals that are not measurable; (c) inadequate or inappropriate description of how progress will be objectively measured; (d) services not tailored to meet all disability-related unique needs, not of sufficient intensity, or absent altogether; and (e) parents not allowed to participate fully, equally, and meaningfully in developing the IEP.

Implementation

Once an IEP has been properly developed by the team, the next step is to implement it. The question arises as to how perfect the implementation must be in order to comply with IDEA. In other words, how much leeway does the school have?

The Second Circuit Court has said IDEA requires *compliance*, distinguishing that as less than *substantial compliance* which is the standard a state must observe to receive federal IDEA funding (*D.D. v. N.Y. City Board of Education,* 2006). The Fifth Circuit Court's standard requires a failure to implement *substantial or significant provisions* of the IEP to find a violation (*Houston Independent School District v. Bobby R.*, 2000).

In the Eighth Circuit Court the standard is that IDEA is violated when the school fails to implement an essential provision of the IEP that was necessary for the child to receive an educational benefit. Applying this standard requires consideration of both the short-fall in services and the progress of the child (*Neosho R-V School District v. Clark*, 2003).

The Ninth Circuit Court adopted a materiality standard—more than a minor discrepancy between what was provided and what the IEP required. This standard does not require a showing of educational harm, but the child's progress or lack of it may be considered in determining the materiality of the failure (*Van Duyn v. Baker Sch. District 5J*, 2007). The dissent in this case argued vigorously that such a standard was unworkably vague and inconsistent with the language of IDEA, which says services must be provided "in conformity with" or "in accordance with" the IEP (20 U.S.C.§1401 (9)(D)(2004); 34 C.F.R.§300. 323 (c)(2)(2006). The dissent proposed a *per se* rule where *any* deviation in implementation of the IEP would violate IDEA.

The federal appellate courts that have addressed the question are in essential agreement that a school is to be granted some leeway in IEP implementation. But how much? If an IEP specifies 20 hours a week of special education and the student receives 19, is that sufficient? 15? 10? And so on. If the IEP calls for small group instruction in reading, is a group of 20 small? 10? 5?

Some understanding of how these lines are drawn can be gleaned from a sampling of actual implementation failures. In an easy case, the district offered only 1 hour per week of reading instruction to a student for whom 20 hours of intensive reading teaching per week had been recommended. Private services were awarded (*Grossmont Union High School Ass'n*, 2006).

A district denied FAPE when it failed from September to January to provide the 20 hours per week of special education required by the IEP, failed to give prior written notice of a proposed amendment to the IEP, and did not ensure the reading teacher attended the entire IEP amendment process (*Anchorage School District v. Parents of M.P.*, 2006).

FAPE was denied when daily "special education teacher support services" were provided on only 74 of 97 days (*New York City (N.Y.) Department of Education*, 2006) and when a student whose IEP said no time was to be in general education was placed there 32% of the time (*Termine v. William S. Hart Union High School District*, 2007). FAPE was also denied by a failure to provide: (a) specified instructional materials (*Poudre School District,* 2004); (b) Braille, mobility training, and progress reports (School Union No. 92, 2004); and (c) peer tutoring (*Clark County (Nevada) School District,* 2004).

The failure to implement behavior intervention plans (BIPs) is a common problem, and legal decisions are often based on the egregiousness of the failure and its behavioral consequences. When some teachers didn't know that a BIP existed and others were misinformed about its provisions, a violation was found (*Jefferson County (Kentucky) Public School*, 2004). Similarly, if misbehavior resulting from a failure to implement the BIP has serious consequences, such as severe injury, a violation will probably be found.

The district staff responsible for IEP implementation must be informed of their specific responsibilities, as well as the modification and supports required by the IEP. In a Minnesota hearing, the district did not have an appropriate plan for offering the concrete, positive reinforcers the student's IEP required. In a finding of interest to many schools, the general classroom rules did not meet this IEP's requirement for individualized, clearly defined behavioral limits (*Onamia Independent School District No. 480*, 2007).

Another issue in the implementation of BIPs is that frequently a BIP is implemented, if at all, by only one teacher and not by all the other adults in the student's daily life at school. In these situations it is often also true that the BIP was not drafted by a behavior specialist (see, e.g., *Guntersville City Board of Education,* 2006).

The frequent intertwining of IEP development and implementation issues was well illustrated in a case involving the provision of physical therapy and speech/language therapy. The district (a) did not monitor how much therapy was given to students with severe disabilities; (b) provided only "consultation" in lieu of actual therapy because of staffing shortages; and (c) provided only medically necessary physical therapy and ignored educational needs, due to a contract with an outside agency (*Konocti (California) United School District,* 2003).

A language arts teacher's failure to implement the test-retake provision in a student's IEP, when the teacher did not have a copy of the IEP and the wording in the IEP was unclear, constituted a denial of FAPE (*Hemlock (Michigan) Public School District,* 2008).

FAPE was also denied when an unqualified teacher who had no degree in education, no certification in any state, and no experience in special education, was unable to implement an IEP (*Damian J. v. School District of Philadelphia*, 2008).

A high school student, with the help and determination of his parents, made good grades in his college preparation courses in spite of the district's failure to implement his IEP in reading. The student made no gains in reading and remained at a second- or third-grade level, showing that FAPE had been denied (*Sanford School Department,* 2006).

A common problem is the failure to deliver all the services specified on the IEP, often due to related service personnel's absence or to scheduling problems. Other common problems occur when district personnel, some or all, simply fail to use the IEP to guide educational activities and services.

Conclusion

IEPs—the team participants, content, development and implementation—are the heart and soul of IDEA and of providing FAPE to children who have disabilities. After over 30 years of IDEA implementation, millions of children have been served, many very well and some not so well. This chapter has highlighted common difficulties school districts have had with IEPs in an effort to reduce their occurrence and improve services delivered to students.

Author's Note

The author thanks Pamela Anne Bahnsen for her extensive and invaluable assistance in converting my handwritten yellow tablet pages to a finished manuscript, using the obligatory and difficult mixture of APA and Blue Book styles.

References

A.C. v. Bd. of Educ. of Chappaqua Central Sch. Dist., 47 IDELR 294 (S.D. N.Y. 2007).
Alex R. v. Forrestville Valley Cmty. Unit Sch. Dist. No. 221, 375 F.3d 603 (7th Cir. 2004).
Alfonso v. District of Columbia, 45 IDELR 118 (D. D.C. 2006).
Amanda J. v. Clark County Sch. Dist., 260 F.3d 1106 (9th Cir. 2001).
Anchorage Sch. Dist. v. Parents of M. P., 45 IDELR 253 (Alaska Superior Court, 2006).
Anchorage Sch. Dist., 51 IDELR 230 (SEA Alaska 2008).
Arlington v. Murphy, 548 U.S. 291 (2006).
Avjian v. Weast, 48 IDELR 61 (4th Cir. 2007).
B.B. v. Dep't of Educ. Hawaii, 46 IDELR 213 (D. Haw. 2006).
Bakersfield City Sch. Dist., 51 IDELR 142 (SEA Cal. 2008).
Bateman, B. D. (2007). *From gobbledygook to clearly written IEP goals.* Verona, WI: Attainment.
Bateman, B. D., & Linden, M. A. (2006). *Better IEPs*. Verona, WI: Attainment.
Bd. of Educ. of Hendrick Hudson Sch. Dist. v. Rowley, 458 U.S. 176 (1982).
Bd. of Educ. of the Arlington Central Sch. Dist., 42 IDELR 226 (SEA N.Y. 2004).
Bd. of Educ. of the Carmel Sch. Dist., 48 IDELR 144 (SEA N.Y. 2007).
Bd. of Educ. of the City of Chicago v. Illinois St. Bd. of Educ., 46 IDELR 219 (N.D. Ill. 2006).
Bd. of Educ. of the West Seneca Central Sch. Dist., 41 IDELR 256 (SEA N.Y. 2004).
Bd. of Educ. of Wappingers Central Sch. Dist., 42 IDELR 131 (SEA N.Y. 2004).
Beaumont Indep. Sch. Dist., 50 IDELR 269 (SEA Tex. 2008).
Chula Vista Elem. Sch. Dist., 48 IDELR 113 (SEA Cal. 2007).
Clark County (Nev.) Sch. Dist., 42 IDELR 247 (OCR 2004).
Cleveland Heights-University Heights City Sch. Dist. v. Boss, 144 F.3d 391 (6th Cir. 1998).
Commentary. 49 IDELR 210 at 945 (USDOE, 2008).
County Sch. Bd. of York County, Va. v. A.L., 46 IDELR 94 (4th Cir. 2006).
Cranston Sch. Dist. v. Q. D., 51 IDELR 41 (D. R.I. 2008).
D.D. v. New York City Bd. of Educ., 46 IDELR 181 (2nd Cir. 2006).
D.F. v. Ramapo Cent. Sch. Dist., 43 IDELR 56 (S.D. N.Y. 2004).
D.H. v Mannheim Township Sch. Dist., 45 IDELR 38 (E. D. Pa. 2005).
Damian J. v. Sch. Dist. of Philadelphia, 49 IDELR 161 (E.D. Pa. 2008).
Deal v. Hamilton County Bd. of Educ., 392 F.3d 840 (6th Cir. 2004).
Delaware Valley Sch. Dist. v. Daniel G., 800 A.2d 989 (Pa. Comm. 2002).
Dep't of Educ., Hawaii, 45 IDELR 84 (SEA Haw. 2005).
Dep't of Educ., Hawaii, 47 IDELR 148 (SEA Haw. 2007).
Dep't of Educ. Hawaii, 50 IDELR 179 (SEA Haw. 2008).
District of Columbia Pub. Sch. (Backus Middle Sch.), 49 IDELR 267 (SEA D.C. 2008).
District of Columbia Pub. Sch., 49 IDELR 26 (SEA D.C. 2007).
Draper v. Atlanta Indep. Sch. System, 47 IDELR 260 (N.D. Ga. 2007).
E.D. v. Enterprise City Bd. of Ed., 273 F. Supp. 2d 1252 (D. Ala. 2003).
E.S. v. Skidmore Tynan Sch. Dist., 47 IDELR 40 (S.D. Tex. 2007).
Ellenville (N.Y.) Central Sch. Dist., 43 IDELR 145 (OCR 2004).
Elmhurst Sch. Dist. No. 205, 46 IDELR 25 (SEA Ill. 2006).
Evanston-Skokie Sch. Dist. No. 65, 40 IDELR 239 (SEA Ill. 2007).
Fisher v. Bd. of Educ. of Christina Sch. Dist., 856 A. 2d 552 (Del. 2004).
Forest Grove v. T.A., 557 U.S. ______ (2009)
G. N. v. Bd. of Educ. of the Township of Livingston, 48 IDELR 160 (D. N.J. 2007).
GARC v. McDaniel, 716 F.2d 1565 (11th Cir.1983).
Grossmont Union High Sch. Ass'n, 47 IDELR 144 (SEA Cal. 2006).
Guntersville City Bd. of Educ., 47 IDELR 84 (SEA Ala. 2006).
Hemlock (Mich.) Pub. Sch. Dist., 51 IDELR 170 (OCR 2008).
Hinson v. Merritt Educ. Ctr., 579 F. Supp. 2d. 89 (D. D. C. 2008).
Hjortness v. Neenah Joint Sch. Dist., 507 F.3d 1060 (7th Cir. 2007).
Honig v. Doe, 484 U.S. 305 (1988).
Houston Indep. Sch. Dist. v. Bobby R., 200 F.3d 341 (5th Cir. 2000).
Houston Indep. Sch. Dist., 42 IDELR 157 (SEA Tex. 2004).
In re Student with a Disability, 47 IDELR 119 (SEA Alaska 2006).
In re Student with a Disability, 50 IDELR 236 (SEA N.Y. 2008).
Indep. Sch. Dist. No. 36, International Falls v. C.L., 40 IDELR 231 (D. Minn. 2004).
Individuals with Disabilities Education Act (IDEA) of 2004, 20 U.S.C.§1401 *et seq.*
Individuals with Disabilities Education Act Regulations of 2006, 34 C.F.R.§300.1 *et seq.*
Inglewood (Cal.) Unified Sch. Dist., 51 IDELR 21 (OCR 2008).]
J. S. v. Springfield Township Bd. of Educ., 48 IDELR 102 (D. N.J. 2007).
J. L. v. Mercer Island Sch. Dist., 46 IDELR 273 (W.D. Wa. 2006).
J. L. v. Mercer Island Sch. Dist., No. C06-494P (W.D. Wa. 2006).
J. S. K. v. Hendry, 941 F.2d 1563 (11th Cir. 1991).
Jefferson County (Ky.) Pub. Sch., 43 IDELR 144 (OCR 2004).
K. M. v. Ridgefield Bd. of Educ., 50 IDELR 10 (D. Conn. 2008).
Kelii H. v. Dep't of Educ., Hawaii, 50 IDELR 94 (D. Haw. 2008).
Kirby v. Cabell County Bd. of Educ., 46 IDELR 156 (S.D. W.Va. 2006).
Konocti (Cal.) United Sch. Dist., 40 IDELR 49 (OCR 2003).

L. M. v. Capistrano Unified Sch. Dist., 48 IDELR 189 (C.D. Cal. 2007).
Lessard v. Wilton - Lyndborough Coop. Sch. Dist., 47 IDELR 299 (D. N.H. 2007).
Letter to Anonymous, 41 IDELR 11 (OSEP 2003a).
Letter to Anonymous, 40 IDELR 70 (OSEP 2003b).
Letter to Anonymous, 51 IDELR 251 (OSEP 2008).
Letter to Kelly, 49 IDELR 165 (OSEP 2007).
Letter to Watson, 48 IDELR 284 (OSEP 2007).
M. L. v. Federal Way Sch. Dist., 387 F.3d 1101 (9th Cir. 2002).
M. M. v. Sch. Dist. of Greenville County, 303 F.3d 523 (4th Cir. 2002).
M. P. v. South Brunswick Bd. of Educ., 51 IDELR 219 (D.N. J. 2008).
Maine Sch. Admin. Dist. No. 61, 49 IDELR 264 (SEA Me. 2008).
Mason City Community Sch. Dist., 46 IDELR 148 (SEA Iowa 2006).
Michael D.M. v. Pemi-Baker Regional Sch. Dist, 41 IDELR 267 (D. N.H. 2004).
Mobile County Bd. of Educ., 40 IDELR 226 (SEA Ala. 2004).
Montgomery Township Bd. of Educ.. v. S.C., 43 IDELR 186 (3rd Cir. 2005).
Mr. & Mrs. "M" v. Ridgefield Bd. of Educ. 47 IDELR 258 (D. Conn. 2007).
Neosho R-V Sch. Dist. v. Clark, 315 F.3d 1022 (8th Cir. 2003).
New York City (N.Y.) Dep't of Educ., 48 IDELR 112 (OCR 2006).
Ojai Unified Sch. Dist. v. Jackson, 4 F.3d 1467 (9th Cir. 1993).
Onamia Indep. Sch. Dist. No. 480, 48 IDELR 235 (SEA Minn. 2007).
Paradise (Cal.) Unified Sch. Dist., 47 IDELR 271 (OCR 2006).
Penn Trafford Sch. Dist. v. C.F., 45 IDELR 156 (W.D. Pa. 2006).
Pennsbury Sch. Dist., 48 IDELR 262 (SEA Pa. 2007).
Philadelphia City Sch. Dist., 46 IDELR 206 (SEA Pa. 2006).
Pierce v. Mason City Sch. Dist. Bd. of Educ., 48 IDELR 7 (S.D. Ohio 2007).
Poudre Sch. Dist., 43 §¶16 (SEA Colo. 2004).
Questions and answers on individual education programs, evaluations and reevaluations. 47 §¶166 (OSERS, 2007).
R. B. v. Napa Valley Unified. Sch. Dist., 496 F.3d 932 (9th Cir. 2007).
Regional Sch. Dist. No. 9 Bd. of Educ. v. Mr. & Mrs. P., 51 IDELR 241 (D. Conn. 2009).
Rio Rancho Pub. Sch., 40 IDELR 140 (SEA N.M. 2003).
Rutherford County Sch., 47 IDELR 279 (SEA Tenn. 2006).
S. B. v. Pomona Unified Sch. Dist., 50 IDELR 72 (C.D. Cal. 2008).
S. J. v. Issaquah Sch. Dist. No. 411, 48 IDELR 218 (W.D. Wa. 2007).
San Diego Sch. Dist., 42 IDELR 249 (SEA Cal. 2005).
Sanford Sch. Dep't, 47 IDELR 176 (SEA Me. 2006).
Sch. Bd. of Indep. Sch. Dist. No. 11 v. Renollett, 440 F.3d 1007 (8th Cir. 2006).
Sch. Union No. 92, 43 IDELR 93 (OCR 2004).
Schaffer v. Weast, 546 U.S. 49 (2005).
Spielberg v. Henrico County Pub. Sch., 853 F.2d 256 (4th Cir. 1988).
Susquehanna Township Sch. Dist. v. Frances J., 823 A. 2d 249 (Pa. Commw. Ct. 2003).
System v. Acad. Sch. Dist. No. 20, 50 IDELR 213 (11th Cir. 2008).
T. P. v. Mamaroneck Union Free Sch. Dist., 47 IDELR 287 (S.D. N.Y. 2007).
Taylor v. Sandusky, 43 IDELR 4 (D. Md. 2005).
Termine v. William S. Hart Union High Sch. Dist., 48 IDELR 272 (9th Cir. 2007).
Thompson Sch. Dist. R2-J, 43 IDELR 240 (SEA Colo. 2005).
Valerie J. v. Derry Coop. Sch. Dist., 771 F. Supp. 483 (D.N.H. 1991).).
Van Duyn v. Baker Sch. Dist. 5J, 481 F.3d 770 (9th Cir. 2007).
Virginia S. v. Dep't of Educ., Hawaii, 47 IDELR 42 (D. Haw. 2007).
W. G. v. Bd. of Target Range Sch. Dist. No. 23, 960 F.2d 1479 (9th Cir. 1992).
West Lincoln-Broadwell Elem. Sch. Dist., 41 IDELR 75 (SEA Ill. 2004).
Yankton Sch. Dist. v. Schramm, 900 F.2d 1182 (D.S.D. 1995) aff'd, 93 F.3d 1369 (8th Cir. 1996).

9
Least Restrictive Environment

Michael Rozalski
State University of New York at Geneseo

Jason Miller
University of Maryland

Angie Stewart
State University of New York at Geneseo

Students with disabilities have not always been educated in public schools. Prior to 1975, there was no federal law that entitled students with disabilities to a public education. However, with the passage of the Education of All Handicapped Children Act (EAHCA) in 1975, public schools were required to provide students with disabilities with a "free appropriate public education" (FAPE). The FAPE required that schools not only provide an education to students with disabilities but also do so in settings with students without disabilities "to the maximum extent possible." This principle is known as the least restrictive environment (LRE). The definition of the LRE would evolve over time because the EAHCA simply required that public schools must educate all students with disabilities in their LRE.

Since the LRE is not a specific placement, but varies according to a student's academic and behavioral needs, school personnel have struggled to consistently provide an appropriate FAPE to students with disabilities in the LRE. What constitutes the LRE for students with disabilities has been the subject of much debate (e.g., Bartlett, 1993; Osborne & DiMattia, 1994a; Osborne & DiMattia, 1994b; Palley, 2006). Some have argued that all students with disabilities should be instructed in the general education setting with students without disabilities (i.e., full inclusion), while others have disagreed based on both philosophical grounds (Kavale & Forness, 2005; Kauffman & Hallahan, 2005a; Kauffman, Lloyd, Baker, & Riedel, 2005; Mock & Kauffman, 2005a, 2005b), and on a lack of empirical evidence suggesting that full inclusion works (Kauffman, Bantz, & McCullough, 2005; MacMillan, Gresham, & Forness, 2005). According to the Individuals with Disabilities Education Act (IDEA; formerly the EAHCA until the re-authorization in 1990), the nature of some students' disabilities prevents them from being educated successfully in the general education setting without individualized services and supports. Some students, therefore, because of the severity of their disability, may actually require specialized placement entirely outside of the general education environment.

In this chapter, we: (a) discuss the concept of LRE and how it has evolved; (b) review legal influences, including federal legislation and court cases that have helped define the LRE; and (c) offer practical suggestions for schools attempting to determine the most appropriate and LRE for an individual student with a disability.

The Least Restrictive Environment

What is LRE?

The IDEA requires the local education agency to provide students with disabilities an education in the LRE. The definition of LRE in the law is:

> to the maximum extent appropriate, children with disabilities, including children in public or private institutions or other care facilities, are educated with children who are not disabled, and that special classes, separate schooling, or other removal of children with disabilities from the regular educational environment occurs only when the nature or severity of the disability is such that education in regular classes with the use of supplementary aids and services cannot be achieved satisfactorily (IDEA, 20 U.S.C. § 1412 (612)(a)(5)(A)).

The two elements of IDEA's LRE requirement sometimes create confusion. The first part, the "presumptive right" (Yell, 1995a), establishes the right of all students with disabilities to receive educational services with students without disabilities and requires schools to place and support students in the general education environment. However, when a student cannot be successful in the regular education classroom because of the severity of his or her disability, schools have an obligation to provide the appropriate education in a more restrictive setting. These elements have been referred to as the "rebuttable presumption" (Turnbull, Turnbull, Stowe, & Huerta, 2006) and place the responsibility on school officials to support students, with supplementary aids and services, in the general education environment before considering more restrictive settings.

How Is LRE Different from Inclusion?

The terms "LRE" and "inclusion" are not synonymous, although professionals and parents occasionally use them interchangeably. Inclusion, or full inclusion, is a general philosophical stance that schools sometimes adopt as practice. It is simply the idea that all students with disabilities will spend the majority of their time in the general educational environment. IDEA does not mandate full inclusion (Gorn, 1996). In fact, officials in the U.S. Department of Education, recognizing that the LRE is not a particular placement, required in the 1999 IDEA regulations that school districts ensure a continuum of alternative placements be available to provide the most appropriate education to students with disabilities (IDEA Regulations, 34 C.F.R. § 300.551(a)).

What Schools Must Offer the LRE?

Because all students with disabilities have a presumptive right to be educated with students without disabilities, schools must make considerable effort to place students and support their appropriate education in the LRE, regardless of whether these students are educated in public or private schools or other care facilities (e.g., residential treatment centers or correctional facilities).

Legal Influences

In this section, we (a) identify federal legislation that has mandated the LRE, (b) discuss case law that has further defined the LRE, and (c) offer a timeline that shows the progression of the LRE concept (Figure 9.1).

Federal Legislation

Education for All Handicapped Children Act

The EAHCA, also referred to as Public Law or PL 94-142 because it was the 142nd Act passed by the 94th Congress, was passed in 1975. The EAHCA followed enactment of the Rehabilitation Act of 1973, which first specified in section 504 that, "no otherwise qualified individual with handicaps ... shall solely by reason of her or his handicap, be excluded from the participation in, be denied benefits of, or be subject to discrimination under any program or activity receiving Federal financial assistance." In the EAHCA, Congress went beyond the Rehabilitation Act's effort to prohibit discrimination (Stafford, 1978) and provide federal money to states that chose to offer special education services for eligible children between the ages of 5–21 (Zirkel, 2000). All interested states were required to develop detailed plans that ensured students with disabilities would receive a FAPE in the LRE. Although one state (i.e., New Mexico) initially

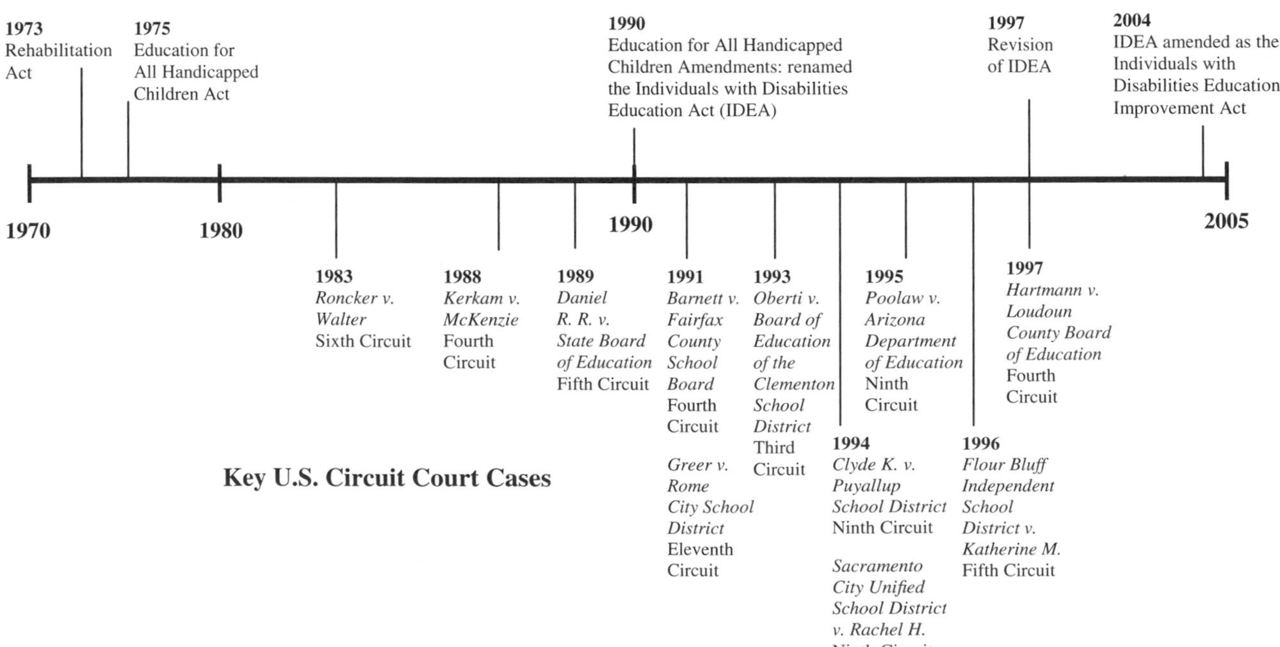

Figure 9.1 Timeline: The Evolution of the LRE.

refused the federal funds and others were slow to move forward, all states eventually developed the plans, which included specific details about evaluation, identification, classification and service delivery through the IEP.

IDEA and its Subsequent Amendments

In 1990, the EAHCA was reauthorized and renamed the IDEA (also referred to as PL 101-476). Seven years later, in 1997, IDEA was substantially amended and included extension provisions for mediation and discipline, expanded services for younger students, and provided additional support for technical assistance to parents and professionals. Although in 2004, IDEA was reauthorized and amended as the Individuals with Disabilities Education Improvement Act (IDEIA), the name of the law is still the IDEA. That revision, which aligned IDEA with the No Child Left Behind Act of 2001, did not change any of the specific language related to the LRE or how it is determined. Despite clear language in the "Additional Requirements" of LRE:

> A State funding mechanism shall not result in placements that violate the requirements of subparagraph (A), and a State shall not use a funding mechanism by which the State distributes funds on the basis of the type of setting in which a child is served that will result in the failure to provide a child with a disability a free appropriate public education according to the unique needs of the child as described in the child's IEP. (IDEA 20 U.S.C. § 1412 (612)(a)(5)(B)(i))

there exists the potential for conflict regarding the LRE, depending on how school officials implement several of IDEA's new provisions (e.g., changes in the IEP process and manifestation determination standards) and parents place students in private schools (IDEA, 20 U.S.C. § 1412 (612)(a)(10)(A)).

Case Law

At times, school personnel and parents disagree about what placement constitutes the LRE for an individual student with disabilities. If they cannot resolve their disagreements, either parents or school personnel may request an impartial due process hearing to resolve their differences. A decision by a hearing officer must be carried out unless, it is appealed and taken to court. If a case moves to court, it will initially be heard in the district court and a ruling from the district court will only apply to that particular case. If the losing party appeals the district court's decision and the case is then heard in a circuit court, the circuit court ruling will be the "case law" for that particular circuit; in this way, circuit court decisions are more meaningful than a district court decision. Courts in the United States are organized into circuits so some of the rulings discussed will only apply to a particular area of the country (see Table 9.1), although circuit courts sometimes follow the rulings and legal rationales delivered in other circuit court opinions. If either party appealed the circuit court decision, it may be heard by the United States Supreme Court. In this case, the ruling would apply throughout the U.S. (see Figure 9.2). To date, no LRE cases have been heard by the U.S. Supreme Court.

TABLE 9.1
U.S. Circuit Courts, Their Jurisdictions and Selected Cases Which Have Informed the Interpretation of FAPE and LRE

Circuit Court	States and Territories Included	Case Name and Date Decided
1	Maine, Massachusetts, New Hampshire, Puerto Rico, Rhode Island.	None
2	Connecticut, New York, Vermont	None
3	Delaware, New Jersey, Pennsylvania, U.S. Virgin Islands	*Oberti v. Board of Education of the Borough of Clementon School District* (May 28, 1993)
4	Maryland, North Carolina, South Carolina, Virginia, Washington DC, West Virginia	*Kerkam v. McKenzie* (December 9, 1988) *Barnett v. Fairfax* (January 28, 1991) *Hartmann v. Loudoun County* (July 8, 1997)
5	Louisiana, Mississippi, Texas	*Daniel R. R. v. State Board of Education* (June 12, 1989) *Flour Bluff Independent School District v. Katherine M.* (July 30, 1996)
6	Kentucky, Michigan, Ohio, Tennessee	*Roncker v. Walter* (February 23, 1983)
7	Illinois, Indiana, Wisconsin	*Lachman v. Illinois State Board of Education* (July 18, 1988)
8	Arkansas, Iowa, Minnesota, Missouri, Nebraska, North Dakota, South Dakota	*Schuldt v. Mankato* (July 5, 1991)
9	Alaska, Arizona, California, Hawaii, Idaho, Montana, Nevada, Oregon, Washington, Mariana Islands, Guam	*Sacramento City Unified School District Board of Education v. Rachel H.* (January 24, 1994) *Clyde K. v. Puyallup School District* (September 13, 1994) *Poolaw v. Bishop* (October 4, 1995)
10	Colorado, Kansas, New Mexico, Oklahoma, Utah, Wyoming	*Urban v. Jefferson County* (December 3, 1994)
11	Alabama, Georgia, Florida	*Greer v. Rome City School District* (December 26, 1991)

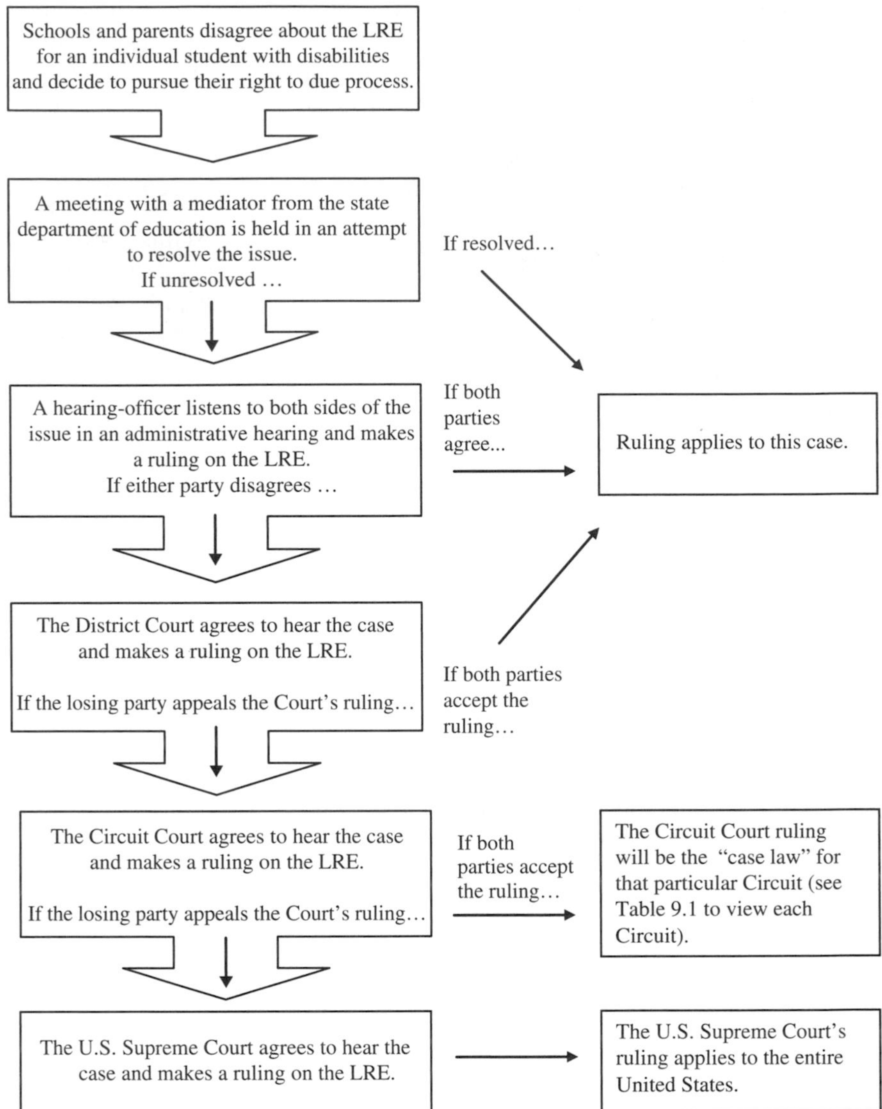

Schools and parents disagree about the LRE for an individual student with disabilities and decide to pursue their right to due process.
A meeting with a mediator from the state department of education is held in an attempt to resolve the issue.
If unresolved ...
If resolved...
A hearing-officer listens to both sides of the issue in an administrative hearing and makes a ruling on the LRE.
If either party disagrees ...
If both parties agree...
Ruling applies to this case.
The District Court agrees to hear the case and makes a ruling on the LRE.
If the losing party appeals the Court's ruling...
If both parties accept the ruling...
The Circuit Court agrees to hear the case and makes a ruling on the LRE.
If the losing party appeals the Court's ruling...
If both parties accept the ruling...
The Circuit Court ruling will be the "case law" for that particular Circuit (see Table 9.1 to view each Circuit).
The U.S. Supreme Court agrees to hear the case and makes a ruling on the LRE.
The U.S. Supreme Court's ruling applies to the entire United States.

Figure 9.2 Mediation, Due Process and the Role of U.S. Courts.

U.S. Circuit Court Cases

In this section, we have summarized individual cases chronologically from earliest to most recent to establish how the concepts of FAPE and LRE have evolved. Again, because these decisions have been made in U.S. Circuit Court, the decisions apply only to the states in each Court's jurisdiction.

Roncker v. Walter (1983). The parents of a student with severe mental retardation challenged the district's placement of the student and brought action against the district pursuant to the Education of All Handicapped Children Act (EAHCA; 20 U.S.C.S. §§ 1401 *et seq*). The student was evaluated, and it was believed that he would benefit from interaction with peers without disabilities; however, the school district placed him in a setting exclusively for children with mental retardation where there would be no such contact. When a district court found in favor of the school district, the parents appealed the decision. On appeal the United States Court of Appeals for the Sixth Circuit reversed the district court ruling, stating that the lower court "erred in reviewing the school district's placement under the deferential abuse of discretion standard" and that it did not give "due weight" to state administrative proceedings. In establishing what has become known as the *Roncker* portability test (Huefner, 1994), the court also stated that, "The act (PL 94-142) does not require mainstreaming in every case but its requirement that mainstreaming be provided to the maximum extent appropriate indicates a very strong congressional preference" (p. 1063). The questions that must be addressed by school officials when determining if the supports and services that make the more restrictive setting "appropriate" can be transferred to the less restrictive setting are outlined in Table 9.2.

Kerkam v. McKenzie (1988). The parents of a student with severe mental retardation placed him in a residential private school for children with disabilities at their own expense. After moving into the District of Columbia Public Schools (DCPS) system, an IEP was created and the DCPS decided to place him in a day program in the district rather than continue to have him educated at the private school

TABLE 9.2
The Evolution of the Questions: What the IEP Team Should Ask When Making the LRE Decision

Court Case and Year	Circuit	The "Test"	Specific Questions to Consider Based on Circuit Court Ruling
Roncker v. Walter (1983)	6	*Roncker* portability test	1) Was it determined that the student could not receive services in the general education setting before an alternative, more-restrictive setting was considered?
Daniel R. R. v. Board of Education (1989)	5	*Daniel* two-part test	1) If the school provides supplemental services, could the student be educated in the general education classroom? 2) If the appropriate placement for a student is an alternative setting, is the student included with students without disabilities to the maximum extent possible?
Greer v. Rome City School District (1991)	11		* *The 11th and 3rd Circuit adopted the 5th Circuit's Daniel two-part test when making their rulings.*
Oberti v. Board of Education (1993)	3		
Sacramento City Unified School District v. Rachel H. (1994)	9	*Rachel H.* four-factor test	1) Will placement in a general education or special education setting be most beneficial to the student's education? 2) Will placement in a general education setting with peers without disabilities provide social benefits to the student? 3) How may inclusion of the student in the general education classroom impact the educational experience of other students in the classroom? 4) Are the costs associated with providing the supplementary aids and services necessary for the student to be successful in the general education classroom excessive?
Clyde K. v. Puyallup School District (1994)	9	Progress test	1) Will the student make adequate progress and benefit academically from a placement in the general education classroom?
Poolaw v. Bishop (1995)	9	Proximity tests	1) Based on the student's needs, is a local inclusive setting more appropriate than a distant, more-restrictive specialized placement? 2) Is the student's educational placement located in the district that is closest to the student's home? 3) If not, could the student receive the services/support needed for an appropriate education in the district closest to home?
Flour Bluff School District v. Katherine M. (1996)	5		
Hartmann v. Loudoun County Board of Education (1997)	4	Hartmann three-part test	1) Does the student receive an educational benefit from the general education placement? 2) Does the student disrupt the educational experience for others in the general education classroom? 3) Do the benefits of the general education placement significantly outweigh those available in a separate instructional setting?

that his parents requested. A hearing officer found that the DCPS's placement was acceptable, however a district court found that the placement offered was inadequate and ordered the DCPS to reimburse the cost of the private school. The case went to United States Circuit Court of Appeals for the District of Columbia Circuit, which reversed and remanded the district court's decision noting that the EAHCA did not require education to maximize the potential of a student with disabilities but rather required a district to provide some form of specialized education. The Circuit Court noted that the District Court used an "impermissible standard in assessing the DCPS's proposed placement" (p. 3) by insisting that the specialized education had to maximize the potential of the student with a disability.

Lachman v. Illinois State Board of Education (1988). The parents of a 7-year-old student who was profoundly deaf brought action against the school district for failing to provide a "free appropriate public education" pursuant to the EAHCA. The district proposed that the student be placed for at least half a day in a special placement with other hearing-impaired children while the parents wanted him to remain in a regular classroom with a full time assistant. A district court determined that the issue under contention was an issue of educational methodology and dismissed the parents' claims. The parents appealed to the United States Court of Appeals for the Seventh Circuit, which held that the district complied with the Education for All Handicapped Children Act and the proposed education program for the student would have provided him with EAHCA's FAPE requirement. The Circuit Court further specified that the conditions of the EAHCA had been satisfied in terms of mainstreaming and it was up to state, not the courts, to determine issues concerning methodology.

Daniel R. R. v. State Board of Education (1989). The parents of a 6-year-old student with Down syndrome, brought action against the El Paso Independent School District for violating the EAHCA after the district decided that the student could no longer be mainstreamed in public kindergarten. The student was originally placed in a combined regular and special education program, and it was apparent that the student could not master any skills taught by the regular teacher even with use of a variety of supplements and modifications. The parents disagreed with the school fully placing the student in the special education program and wanted the student to remain in the regular classroom with his peers. The United States Court of Appeals for the Fifth Circuit affirmed the District Court's ruling in favor of the school district citing evidence that the regular classroom teacher did try a continuum of services before recommending special placement and the student was mainstreamed as much as possible by having lunch and recess with his peers without disabilities. The court developed a twofold test for determining if mainstreaming is appropriate (a) with the use of supplements and aids could the student achieve satisfactorily in the regular classroom and, (b) if not, is the student mainstreamed to the maximum extend appropriate relative to his or her needs? Additional details are summarized in Table 9.2.

Schuldt v. Mankato Independent School District (1990). The Mankato School District placed a 9-year-old student with spina bifida, who was paralyzed from the waist down, in an elementary school other than her neighborhood school because the school was not adequately accessible to students with Schuldt's limited physical mobility. Schuldt's parents brought this action to the District Court to request that the school district make modifications to make the neighborhood school accessible to their daughter. The District Court found that the school district was providing Schuldt with a free appropriate public education in the least restrictive environment available, thereby complying with the Education of All Handicapped Children Act. The Schuldts appealed the ruling of the District Court. The United States Court of Appeals for the Eighth Circuit affirmed the decision to dismiss the parents' request for the Mankato Independent School District to modify a neighborhood school to make it accessible to their disabled daughter. "By bussing Schuldt to one of several nearby schools, the school district is providing her with a fully integrated public education, thereby meeting its obligation under the Act" (p. 5). The court found that the phrase "as close as possible" did not require the district to modify a building to accommodate the student and interpreted section 34 C.F.R. § 300.552 to mean a district had to place the student in a setting where teachers could fully implement the student's program.

Greer v. Rome City School District (1991). Christy Greer, a 10-year-old girl with Down syndrome, brought action, through her father, against her local school district claiming that the IEP prepared by the school did not comply with the Education of All Handicapped Children Act (20 U.S.C. §§ 1400-1485) because it removed her from the regular class at her local school and placed her in a self-contained special education class at another school. Neither the minutes nor the transcripts taken during the placement committee meetings or the proposed IEP show that the district considered any other options for Christy other than the two presented by the parties (i.e., the district's proposal for instruction in the self-contained class and the parent's proposal for instruction supplemented by speech therapy at the local school). In deciding the case, the United States Court of Appeals for the Eleventh Circuit developed a two part test for determining compliance with the mainstreaming requirement asking (a) if satisfactory education can be achieved in the regular classroom with use of supplemental aids and services and, (b) if the child is to be instructed outside the regular classroom, has the school has mainstreamed the child to "the maximum extent appropriate?" The court ruled that the IEP created by the district was not in compliance with federal law because during the creation of the IEP, school officials did not share supplemental aid and service options with the parents that could have been used in the regular classroom and thus failed the first part of the test.

Barnett v. Fairfax County School Board (1991). The parents of a high school student with a profound hearing-impairment brought action against the Fairfax county school board claiming that its policy of placing students using a special speech program at one central location in the district violated the EAHCA. While the parents agreed that the program currently offered to the student was appropriate and of high quality, they objected to the fact that it was offered at a school which was five miles farther than his local school. The school offering the speech services was not a center for only students with hearing impairments or other students with disabilities and the student was mainstreamed, excelling in all academic classes with the assistance provided by his interpreters. The district court ruled that the student's needs were adequately considered and a district is not required to duplicate specialized services at each neighborhood school when the services were provided at another school. Additionally, because the student was not excluded from any program that was federally funded, the districts refusal to offer the speech program at the local school did not violate § 504 of the Rehabilitation Act (29 U.S.C.S. § 794). When appealed to the U.S. Circuit Court of Appeals for the Fourth Circuit, the Circuit Court affirmed the ruling by the district court.

Oberti v. Board of Education of the Clementon School District (1993). A student with Down syndrome was placed in a mainstreamed class for half a day and a special education placement for the second half of the day. The parents of the student did not agree with the IEP and the district's placement of the student but agreed to the placement on the condition that the district would look for ways to mainstream the student and place him in a regular classroom in the future. The district however, made no plans to mainstream the student citing the fact that the student experienced several behavioral incidences in the mainstream room that did not occur in the special education placement. The parents brought action against the district pursuant to the Individuals with Disabilities Education Act (IDEA), 20 U.S.C.S. § 1400-1485 to develop an inclusive plan for the student. After hearing expert testimony from both sides, the district court and then the United States

Court of Appeals for the Third Circuit concluded that the student could be successful in a mainstream classroom and that his behavior incidences were largely a result of the districts failure to provide appropriate supplemental aids and services to him. Therefore, the district had failed to mainstream the student to the maximum extent possible, did not create and IEP that adequately met the students needs, and failed to consider aids and services that would help the student be successful.

Sacramento City Unified School District v. Rachel H. (1994). The parents of a student who was moderately mentally retarded maintained that their daughter learned social and academic skills better in a regular classroom than a special education placement and requested that she be placed in a regular classroom. The district disagreed and instead proposed that the student be placed in a special education setting for academic subjects and in regular classes for specials (i.e., art, music, gym). The parents appealed to a state hearing officer who decided that the school had not made adequate effort to educate the student in a regular classroom according to the IDEA. The school district took the case to the United States District Court for the Eastern District of California which examined (a) the educational benefits received in a regular classroom with aides and supplements compared to those received in a special education classroom, (b) the social benefits of interaction with students without disabilities, (c) the effect of the student on the teacher and other children in the classroom and, (d) the cost of mainstreaming the student. After reviewing evidence to these factors, the court concluded that the district had not provided evidence that the student would be better suited for placement in a special education classroom. The district appealed, and the appealing court found that the district court did not err in using the factors to interpret IDEA's requirements (20 U.S.C.S. §1412 (612)(5)(b)) and that the student benefitted from and made progress toward the IEP goals in the regular education classroom. The four questions that should be considered by school officials are outlined in Table 9.2.

Clyde K. v. Puyallup School District (1994). A 15-year-old student with Tourette's Syndrome was receiving special education services and because of increasingly disruptive behavior, the parents and school district decided to temporarily remove the student from regular classes and place him in an off campus, self-contained program to receive instruction until reintegration into the mainstream became feasible. The parents later changed their mind and brought action against the district claiming that the program was not the least restrictive environment for the student and thus violated of the IDEA. The district court and then the United States Court of Appeals for the Ninth Circuit ruled in favor of the district saying that the temporary placement of the student in the self-contained program was not in violation of the act as evidence showed that (a) the student's disruptive behavior in the regular classroom prevented him from academic learning, (b) there was no evidence that he modeled his behavior on peers without disabilities and, (c) he was having a negative impact on his peers in the class. Although these three issues are significant, the court essentially asked a specific question, "Will the student make adequate progress and benefit academically from a placement in the general education classroom?" We refer to this query as the "Progress" test, which is discussed in detail below and outlined in Table 9.2.

Urban v. Jefferson County (1994). A student sought injunctive relief in order to be placed at his local school with community-based education and transitional services as well as injunctive relief to receive compensatory education after he turned 21 for the period of time in which he claims he was denied a "free an appropriate education" pursuant to the IDEA. The student stated that placement outside of the local school and community denied him the opportunity to make friends in his community and that the jobsite training obtained outside his community would not be transferable. The court concluded that the student did not meet the burden of proof that his IEP was inappropriate and that he was receiving a FAPE. Additionally, the student was not guaranteed the rights under IDEA, Rehabilitation Act, or Americans with Disabilities Act to receive education at his local school. The United States District Court for the District of Colorado did conclude that there was a procedural error with regards to the student's IEP, however because both the district and parents were aware of the relevant information the IEP was considered sufficient. When the case was heard on appeal by the U.S. Circuit Court of Appeals for the Tenth Circuit, the Circuit Court affirmed the ruling by the district court.

Poolaw v. Bishop (1995). The parents of a 13-year-old student who was profoundly deaf brought action against the school district challenging the decision to place the student in a school 280 miles from his home which they contended was not "as close as possible" as stated in the IDEA. Upon reviewing the IEP a district court determined that the student would not receive any educational benefit from being mainstreamed until he received intensive American Sign Language (ASL) instruction, which could not be provided at a school closer than the one recommended by the district. The parents appealed and the United States Court of Appeals for the Ninth Circuit upheld the decision made by the district court. It was decided that placing the student in the Arizona School for the Deaf and Blind which was 280 miles from his home was appropriate because mainstreaming the student would not benefit him educationally.

Flour Bluff Independent School District v. Katherine M. (1996). A student who was deaf was placed at a regional day school and the student's mother sought to have her transferred to the school she would have otherwise attended. The district court determined that the IEP was not based on the student's needs in that it failed to place the student close to home as stated in the IDEA. On appeal, the United States Court of Appeals for the Fifth Circuit found that "close to home" was only one of many factors determining the student's least restrictive environment and the lower court misinterpreted proximity as a controlling factor when the difference in distance between the schools was less than 10 miles. The district court incorrectly identified the student's local school as the best placement even though it lacked services that the student needed and therefore overturned the ruling and stated that the regional day school was the appropriate setting for the student.

Hartmann v. Loudoun County Board of Education (1997). The parents of a student with autism claimed that their son's new placement in a self-contained class for students with autism did not include their son with students without disabilities to the "maximum extent appropriate" under IDEA. The district maintained that a self-contained classroom was an appropriate setting for Hartmann, since he was making no academic progress in the regular classroom and was often disruptive to other students in the general education classroom. Hartmann's parents appealed to a state hearing officer who agreed with the school district that Hartmann received no academic benefit from being placed in the regular education classroom. The parents challenged the hearing officer's decision in the United States District Court, which ruled that the school district did not act appropriately to ensure that Hartmann was included in a regular class and reversed the hearing officer's decision. The school district took the case to the United States Court of Appeals for the Fourth Circuit, which ruled that Hartmann was not making adequate academic progress in the general education classroom despite modifications and accommodations. The Circuit Court reversed and remanded the District Court's ruling, concluding that Hartmann's placement in a self-contained class was appropriate given his current needs. The Circuit Court established what Yell (2006) has referred to as the Hartmann 3-part test, which again acknowledged the IDEA preference for placement in the general education environment balanced against the need for schools to offer a meaningful educational experience to both the student with disabilities and the peers who may be impacted by the student's disruptive behavior. Three specific questions (outlined in Table 9.2) can be derived from the court's ruling.

U.S. District Court Cases

In the following section, we summarize two cases heard in U.S. District Courts. Although the ruling only applied to the cases involved and not to a broader geographic, the findings have helped illuminate the definition of the LRE for students with disabilities.

MR v. Lincolnwood (1994). A 13-year-old student with an emotional disorder was placed by the district in a therapeutic day school after being unsuccessful in a self-contained behavior disorder classroom with some mainstream classes. The parents wanted him to have a mainstream placement and, after two hearing officers upheld the district's placement, the parents appealed to district court. The court found that efforts were made to mainstream the student as much as possible and that these attempts were unsuccessful as evidenced by the student's behavior that was disruptive to staff and other students. On appeal, the United States District Court, Northern District of Illinois found that the district did not err in its placement. Additionally, videotaped evidence of the student's behavior presented by the school was not in violation of the Family Educational Rights and Privacy Act as it was used for legitimate education interests and enforcement of federal legal requirements.

Hudson v. Bloomfield Hills School District (1995). The mother of a 14-year-old student classified as "trainable mentally impaired" wanted the student placed in regular education classes all day at her local middle school while the individualized education planning committee recommended that the student's day be split between a special education and general education program. Before the action was filed, a compromise was reached where the student would spend a half-day in the special education program and a half-day in the regular school setting. The student however, was found to be unsuccessful at developing any "independent living" skills and was not benefitting academically from a placement in regular education classes. In challenging the IEP, the mother had the burden of proving the school's recommended placement was inappropriate and the court failed to be presented with convincing evidence that this was the case. Therefore the United States District Court for the Eastern District of Michigan concluded that the school district was correct and did not violate the Individuals with Disabilities Act or any regulations in not placing the student in her local middle school for the entire day.

Determining Least Restrictive Environment

Despite the clear federal mandate to include students in the LRE and over 40 years of litigation in which the LRE has been interpreted, schools still struggle to provide the most appropriate LRE for some students with disabilities. Contradictory interpretations and case law that only applies in some areas of the country does not make the task easier for IEP teams. In this section we will (a) summarize the importance of using the general education classroom as the preferential placement, (b) discuss the need for collaborative relationships among the general education teacher, special education teacher and related service providers, (c) review the continuum of alternative placements, and (d) offer guidance for IEP teams making the LRE decision.

General Education Classroom as Preference

Students with disabilities have a presumptive right to be educated in the same settings as their peers without disabilities. The IDEA clearly specifies that "children with disabilities … are [to be] educated with children who are not disabled" (IDEA, 20 U.S.C. § 1412 (612)(5) (B)). Although there is a recognition that "special classes, separate schooling, or other removal of children with disabilities from the regular educational environment" can occur (IDEA, 20 U.S.C. § 1412 (612)(5)(B)), this exception occurs only when the nature or severity of the disability prevents that education from being offered in the general education environment. The courts have repeatedly supported this preference and expected that schools will make significant efforts to educate students with disabilities in inclusive settings.

Support for General Education Teacher

As the general education classroom is the preferred placement for students with disabilities, general education teachers must be adequately prepared to support students with disabilities in the classroom (Mock & Kauffmann, 2005a; Singer, 2005). Although students with disabilities are likely to receive at least partial education from a special education teacher, general education teachers will share the responsibility of ensuring that students with special needs are making adequate progress in the general education setting. It is extremely beneficial to the students' education for collaborative relationships to exist among the special education teacher, general education teacher, and related service providers. The importance of this collaborative relationship and the means to foster it must begin in pre-service teacher preparation programs, where future special educators learn what it is like to be a general education teacher first (Kauffman & Hallahan, 2005c). By establishing a system of open communication and sharing of expertise among colleagues, IEP teams can be confident that students with disabilities will receive an appropriate education if placed in the general education setting.

Continuum of Alternative Placements (CAP)

If the presumptive LRE for all students with disabilities is initially the general education environment, then we must acknowledge that other settings would be considered more restrictive. Nonetheless, the IDEA requires that districts offer IEP teams a variety of placement options when determining the most appropriate LRE for a student with disabilities. Some authors (e.g., Kauffman & Hallahan, 2005b) have argued that it is crucial to maintain this CAP. After the IEP team establishes the student's academic and behavioral needs and has determined that the education cannot occur successfully in the general education environment, then school officials may consider other placement options. According to the regulations from the Office of Special Education Programs:

a) Each [school district] shall ensure that a continuum of alternative placements is available to meet the needs of children with disabilities for special education and related services
b) The continuum required … must:
   (1) Include the alternative placements; and
   (2) Make provision for supplementary services to be provided in conjunction with regular class placement. (IDEA Regulations, 34 C.F.R. § 300.551).

These regulations also clearly establish the minimum alternatives that schools must provide (see Figure 9.3; IDEA Regulations, 34 C.F.R. § 300.551). Table 9.3 provides a brief description of each of those placement options.

Although schools occasionally contend that their limited resources prevent them from providing a full range of placements, the courts have consistently ruled that a school cannot refuse to place a child in the LRE because it does not have that specific placement option in its district (Tucker &

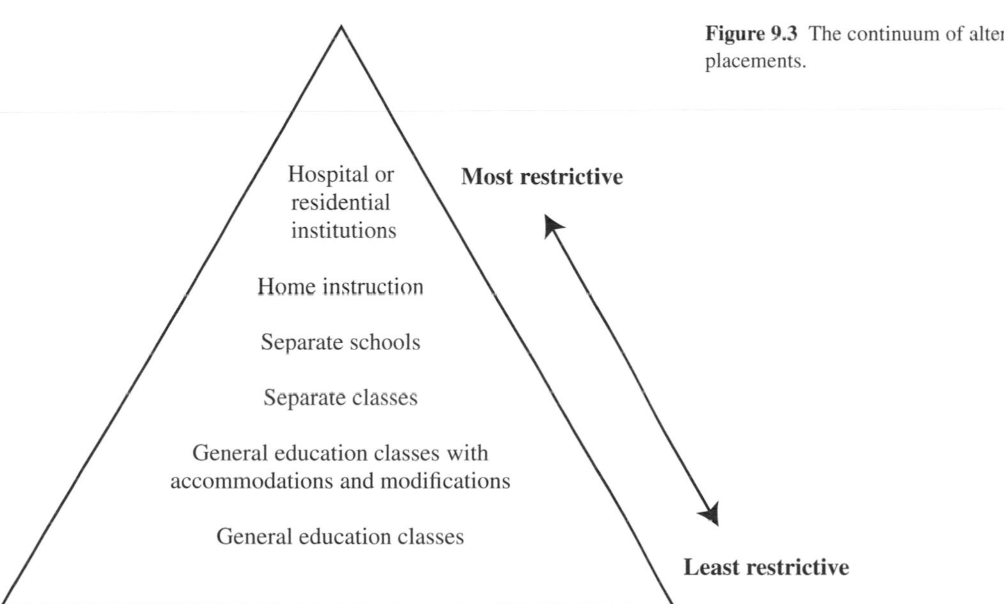

Figure 9.3 The continuum of alternative placements.

TABLE 9.3
The Continuum of Alternative Placements

Option	Description
General education class	The LRE is the general education classroom. The student is educated with his/her peers without disabilities and the general education teacher is responsible for the student's education program.
General education class with accommodations and modifications	The student is placed in the general education setting with appropriate accommodations and services. The general education teacher is responsible for altering instruction to meet the needs of the student. Supportive services may provide indirect support, or "push-in" and "pull out" students from the general education classroom to receive direct instruction from a special education teacher or related services professional.
Separate classes	The student's primary placement may be a self-contained special education classroom within the school building with peers without disabilities. The special education teacher is primarily responsible for the student's education program. The student may spend part of the day with peers without disabilities (such as lunch, recess, specials).
Separate schools	The student is educated in a separate school than that of their peers without disabilities. This placement may be a special day school or a residential school.
Home instruction	The student is taught by a teacher within his/her own home.
Hospital or residential institution	The student, due to very severe disabilities, may be placed in a hospital or institution. This placement is extremely restrictive and should only be used if the student cannot make adequate process in a less restrictive setting.

Goldstein, 1992). Case law has established that if a school cannot provide a placement option that would be less restrictive than the ones it maintains within its boundaries, then the school must pay for a student to attend a nearby public or private school to provide the placement most appropriate to meet the student's academic and behavioral needs.

Guidance for IEP Teams Making the LRE

Although the prevailing preference for schools to place students with disabilities in the general education environment and the need to maintain an appropriate CAP is clear, at times schools and parents still struggle to agree on the LRE for individuals with disabilities. In this next section, we offer guidance for IEP teams attempting to make the difficult LRE decision. We begin by (a) suggesting a single 3-part question that gives general guidance, (b) summarizing specific questions gleaned from case law, and then (c) offering a flow map that will help IEP teams systematically make the placement decision.

Questions to Consider

When IEP teams are determining the LRE for students with disabilities, they should initially ask the following 3-part question that is inferred from federal law and regulations, "Is the placement decision appropriate, supplemented and individualized?"

Appropriate? Schools are obligated to provide a FAPE for all students with disabilities. Although the preference is for the instruction to occur in the general education environment, the nature of the disability may make it impractical for some students with disabilities to be educated there. Some have argued that this makes it difficult to establish that the LRE can be anything but the general education classroom (Dubow, 1989) but others have clearly articulated ways that schools must provide FAPE first, LRE second (Champagne, 1993; McColl, 1992).

Supplemented? IEP teams are expected to carefully select the LRE. Before entertaining the possibility of a more restrictive setting, they should carefully consider whether supplementary supports, accommodations and modifications would allow a student with disabilities to succeed in the less restrictive placement option (Gorn, 1996; Huefner, 1994). Although it is unclear if schools are obligated to attempt or simply consider the placement with supplementary services (Yell, 1995a; Yell, 1994), IEP teams should fully document their deliberations on the matter.

Individualized? Although the LRE mandate requires that "to the maximum extent possible" students with disabilities be educated with their peers without disabilities, the Office of Special Education and Rehabilitative Services (OSERS) in 1991, clearly articulated that "The determination of whether to place a child with disabilities in an integrated setting must be made on a case-by-case basis" (*Stutler & McCoy,* 1991, p. 308). Unfortunately, OSERS did not provide specific guidelines to IEP teams on how to best make these case-by-case decisions. Although there is some guidance from case law, it is clear that schools should not develop comprehensive policies that systematically place students with a specific disability in a particular setting, even if that setting is the general education environment (Crockett & Kauffman, 2001; Lewis, Chard, & Scott, 1994; Osborne, 1993; Osborne & DiMattia, 1994a; Sharp & Pitasku, 2002; Yell, 1995b; Yell, 1994).

Specific Questions from Case Law

More specific guidance is available from the case law. Although the district court decisions discussed are limited to the specific cases to which they applied and the circuit court rulings are technically limited to the states for which the circuit covers, some consider it best practice when determining the LRE to consider the lessons learned from the collective case law. There has been numerous summaries of the Roncker portability test (Dubow, 1989; Huefner, 1994; McColl, 1992; Sharp & Pitasku, 2002), the Daniel 2-part test (Bartlett, 1993; Huefner, 1994; Lewis et al., 1994; McColl, 1992; Sharp & Pitasku, 2002, Yell, 1994), the Rachel H. four-factor test (Huefner, 1994; Lewis et al., 1994; Sharp & Pitasku, 2002; Yell 1995a), and the Hartmann 3-part test (Yell, 2006). Again, we have summarized these tests in Table 9.2, along with "Progress and Proximity Tests."

The "Progress" test is informed by *Clyde K. v. Puyallup School District* (1994) and specifically addresses the question of whether the student with a disability will succeed academically in the general education environment. The "Proximity" test asks a series of questions regarding how distant an alternative placement is from the student's "home" district or school. Although the courts have routinely held that schools could place students in the appropriate LRE whether it is a neighboring school that is five miles further than the "home" school (*Barnett v. Fairfax, 1991*), is a special school almost 300 miles away (*Poolaw v. Bishop, 1995*), or prevents the school from having to make significant building modifications (*Schuldt v. Mankato, 1991*), it is important to consider the "proximity" to appropriate services for students with disabilities (Osborne & Dimattia, 1994a). In *Flour Bluff School District v. Katherine M.* (1996), district officials were found to have made a bad placement decision when they kept a student in his home school despite not having the appropriate services, which were available in a neighboring district.

The LRE Flow Map

Although the general questions above will provide some guidance to the IEP team as they attempt to identify the appropriate LRE for each individual student, we have outlined a more detailed flow map (see Figure 9.4) that should provide the IEP team additional support. This flow map can be used after a student has been initially identified for service and the IEP team is placing the student with disabilities in the LRE, but it should also be used during annual IEP reviews and reevaluation meetings as well. It is crucial that IEP teams not consider the current placement to be the de facto placement for a student with a disability as the student may have gained the skills necessary to allow success in a less restrictive setting. Answering the questions and considering the flow map during all IEP team meetings will help ensure that the student is always placed in the least restrictive environment necessary to meet his or her current educational needs.

Summary

Prior to the passage of the EAHCA in 1975, schools were not federally mandated to provide a "free appropriate public education" to students with disabilities. Since the fundamental right to a publicly provided education was established, students with disabilities and their parents have often sought to receive that education with students without disabilities. The mandate for the LRE in the IDEA actually requires that, "to the maximum extent appropriate," students with disabilities be educated alongside their peers without disabilities. Acknowledging that some students with disabilities will still struggle to succeed in

After determining a student is eligible for services and identifying the services needed, the IEP team needs to decide a student's LRE by using the following steps:

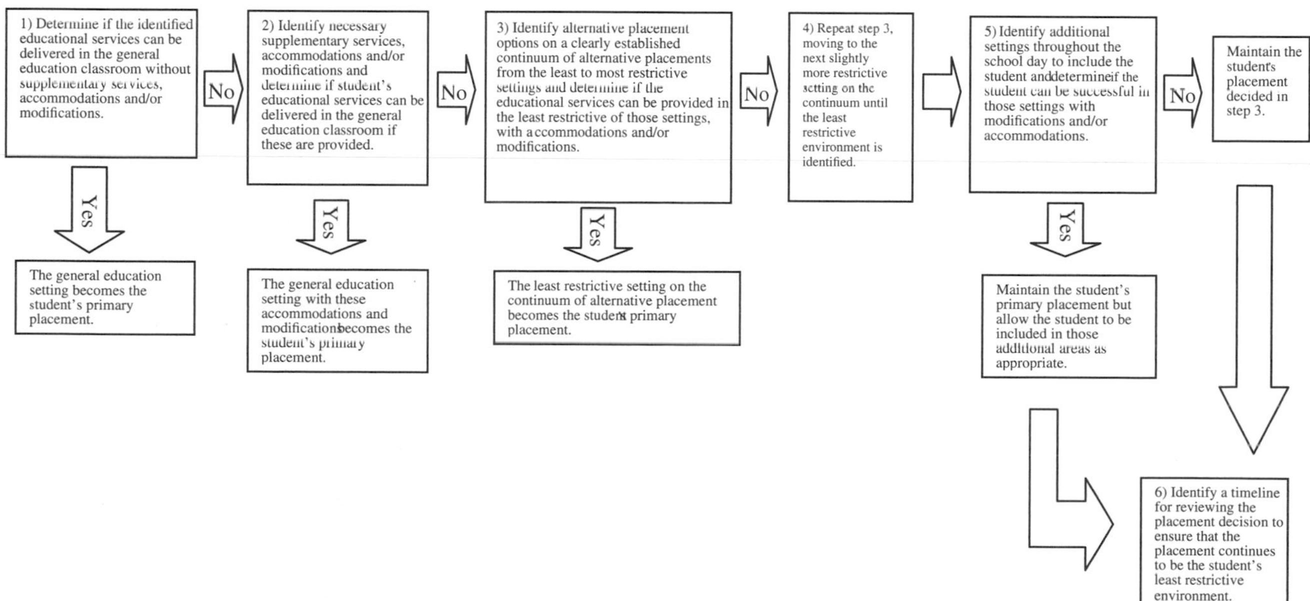

Figure 9.4 Flow map of the LRE decision making process.

the general education environment, even with significant accommodations and modifications, IDEA also requires schools to establish a continuum of alternative placements that vary in the degree to which a student is removed from general education. Nonetheless, if a student with a disability is to be removed from the general education setting because the severity of the disability prevents the student from receiving an appropriate education, the school bears the burden of carefully documenting that all supplementary services, accommodations and modifications have been seriously considered in an attempt to serve the student in the general education environment. This federal mandate and over 40 years of case law have clearly established that schools must systematically ensure that students with disabilities are educated in the least restrictive environment possible.

References

Americans with Disabilities Act of 1990, 42 U.S.C. 12101 *et seq.*

Barnett v. Fairfax, 17 EHLR 350 (4th Cir. 1991).

Bartlett, L. D. (1993). Mainstreaming: On the road to clarification. *Education Law Reporter, 76,* 17–25.

Champagne, J. F. (1993). Decisions in sequence: How to make placements in the least restrictive environment. *EdLaw Briefing Paper, 9 & 10,* 1–16.

Clyde K. v. Puyallup School District, 35 F.3d 1396 (9th Cir. 1994).

Crockett, J. B., & Kauffman, J. M. (2005). The concept of the least restrictive environment and learning disabilities: Least restrictive of what? In J. M. Kauffman & D. P. Hallahan (Eds.), *The illusion of full inclusion: A comprehensive critique of a current special education bandwagon* (2nd ed., pp. 97–119). Austin, TX: PRO-ED.

Daniel R. R. v. State Board of Education, 874 F.2d 1036 (5th Cir. 1989).

Dubow, S. (1989). Into the turbulent mainstream: A legal perspective on the weight to be given to the least restrictive environment in placement decisions for deaf children. *Journal of Law and Education, 18,* 215–228.

Education for All Handicapped Children Act of 1975, 20 U.S.C. § 1401 *et seq.*

Education of the Handicapped Amendments of 1974, Pub. L. No. 93–380, 88 Stat. 580.

Flour Bluff Independent School District v. Katherine M., 24 IDELR 673 (5th Cir. 1996).

Gorn, S. (1996). *What do I do when ... The answer book on special education law.* Horsham, PA: LRP Publications.

Greer v. Rome City School District, 950 F.2d 688 (11th Cir. 1991).

Hartmann v. Loudoun County Board of Education (4th Cir. 1997). Available at http://www.wrightslaw.com/law/caselaw/case_Hartmann4thCir.html

Hudson v. Bloomfield Hills School District, 23 IDELR 612 (E.D. Mich 1995).

Huefner, D. S. (1994). The mainstreaming cases: Tensions and trends for school administrators. *Educational Administration Quarterly, 30,* 27–55.

Individuals with Disabilities Education Act of 1990, 20 U.S.C. § 1401 *et seq.*

Individuals with Disabilities Education Act of Regulations, 34 C.F.R. § 300 *et seq.*

Kauffman, J. M., Bantz, J., & McCullough, J. (2005). Separate and better: A special public school class for students with emotional and behavioral disorders. In J. M. Kauffman & D. P. Hallahan (Eds.), *The illusion of full inclusion: A comprehensive critique of a current special education bandwagon* (2nd ed., pp. 393–424). Austin, TX: PRO-ED.

Kauffman, J. M., & Hallahan, D. P. (Eds.). (2005a). *The illusion of full inclusion: A comprehensive critique of a current special education bandwagon* (2nd ed.). Austin, TX: PRO-ED.

Kauffman, J. M., & Hallahan, D. P. (2005b). A diversity of restrictive environments: Placement as a problem of social ecology. In J. M. Kauffman & D. P. Hallahan (Eds.), *The illusion of full inclusion: A comprehensive critique of a current special education bandwagon* (2nd ed., pp. 185–205). Austin, TX: PRO-ED.

Kauffman, J. M., & Hallahan, D. P. (2005c). Toward a comprehensive delivery system for special education. In J. M. Kauffman & D. P. Hallahan (Eds.), *The illusion of full inclusion: A comprehensive critique of a current special education bandwagon* (2nd ed., pp. 149–184). Austin, TX: PRO-ED.

Kauffman, J. M., Lloyd, J. W., Baker, J., & Riedel, T. M. (2005). Inclusion of all students with emotional and behavioral disorders? Let's think again. In J. M. Kauffman & D. P. Hallahan (Eds.), *The illusion of full inclusion: A comprehensive critique of a current special education bandwagon* (2nd ed., pp. 381–392). Austin, TX: PRO-ED.

Kavale, K. A., & Forness, S. R. (2005). History, rhetoric, and reality: Analysis of the inclusion debate. In J. M. Kauffman & D. P. Hallahan (Eds.), *The illusion of full inclusion: A comprehensive critique of a current special education bandwagon* (2nd ed., pp. 235–278). Austin, TX: PRO-ED.

Kerkam v. McKenzie, 862 F.2d 884 (D.C. Cir. 1988).

Lachman v. Illinois Board of Education, 852 F.2d 290 (7th Cir. 1988).

Lewis, T. J., Chard, D., & Scott, T. M. (1994). Full inclusion and the education of children and youth with emotional and behavioral disorders. *Behavioral Disorders, 19,* 277–293.

MacMillan, D. L., Gresham, F. M., & Forness, S. R., (2005). Full inclusion: An empirical perspective. In J. M. Kauffman & D. P. Hallahan (Eds.), *The illusion of full inclusion: A comprehensive critique of a current special education bandwagon* (2nd ed., pp. 207–234). Austin, TX: PRO-ED.

McColl, A. (1992). Placement in the least restrictive environment for children with disabilities. *School Law Bulletin, 26,* 13–21.

Mock, D. R., & Kauffman, J. M. (2005a). Preparing teachers for full inclusion: Is it possible? In J. M. Kauffman & D. P. Hallahan (Eds.), *The illusion of full inclusion: A comprehensive critique of a current special education bandwagon* (2nd ed., pp. 279–294). Austin, TX: PRO-ED.

Mock, D. R. & Kauffman, J. M. (2005b). The delusion of full inclusion. In J. M. Kauffman & D. P. Hallahan (Eds.), *The illusion of full inclusion: A comprehensive critique of a current special education bandwagon* (2nd ed., pp. 295–316). Austin, TX: PRO-ED.

MR v. Lincolnwood Board of Education, 20 IDELR 1323 (N.D. Ill. 1994).

Oberti v. Board of Education of the Borough of Clementon School District, 995 F.2d 1204 (3rd Cir. 1993).

Osborne, A. G. (1993). The IDEA's least restrictive environment mandate: Implications for public policy. *Education Law Reporter, 74,* 369–380.

Osborne, A. G., & DiMattia, P. (1994a). The IDEA's least restrictive environment mandate: Legal implications. *Exceptional Children, 61,* 6–14.

Osborne, A. G., & DiMattia, P. (1994b). Counterpoint: IDEA's LRE mandate: Another look. *Exceptional Children, 61,* 582–584.

Palley, E. (2006). Challenges of rights-based law: Implementing the least restrictive environment mandate. *Journal of Disability Policy Studies, 16,* 229–235.

Poolaw v. Bishop, 23 IDELR 407 (9th Cir. 1995).

Roland M. v. Concord School Committee, 910 F.2d 983 (1st Cir. 1990).

Roncker v. Walter, 700 F.2d 1058 (6th Cir. 1983).

Sacramento City Unified School District Board of Education v. Holland, 786 F. Supp. 874 (E.D. Col. 1992).

Sacramento City Unified School District Board of Education v. Rachel H., 14 F.3d 1398 (9th Cir. 1994).

Schuldt v. Mankato ISD, 937 F.2d 1357 (8th Cir. 1991).

Section 504 Regulations, 34 C.F.R. § 104 *et seq.*

Sharp, K. G., & Pitasku, V. M. (2002). The current legal status of inclusion. Horsham, PA: LRP Publications.

Singer, J. D. (2005). Should special education merge with regular education? In Hallahan, D.H., & Kauffman, J.M. (Ed.), *The illusion of full inclusion: A comprehensive critique of a current special education bandwagon* (2nd ed., pp. 7–24). Austin, TX: PRO-ED.

Stafford, R. (1978). Education for the handicapped: A senator's perspective. *Vermont Law Review, 3,* 71–76.

Stutler and McCoy, Letter to, 18 IDELR 307 (OSERS 1991).

Tucker, B. P., & Goldstein, B. A. (1992). *Legal rights of persons with disabilities: An analysis of public law.* Horsham, PA: LRP Publications.

Turnbull, H. R., Turnbull, A. P., Stowe, M., & Huerta, N. (2006). *Free appropriate public education: The law and children with disabilities* (7th ed.). Denver, CO: Love Publishing.

Urban v. Jefferson County School District R-1, 21 IDELR 985 (D. Col. 1994).

Yell, M. L. (2006). *The law and special education.* Upper Saddle River, NJ: Merrill.

Yell, M. L. (1995a). Least restrictive environment, inclusion, and students with disabilities: Analysis and commentary. *Journal of Special Education, 28,* 389–404.

Yell, M. L. (1995b). *Clyde K. and Sheila K. v. Puyallup School District.* The courts, inclusion, and students with behavioral disorders. *Behavioral Disorders, 20,* 179–189.

Yell, M. L. (1994). The LRE cases: Judicial activism or judicial restraint? *Exceptional Children, 61,* 578–581.

Zirkel, P. (2000). *Section 504 and the schools.* Horsham, PA: LRP Publications.

Section III

The General Education Context of Special Education

Section Editor: Naomi P. Zigmond
University of Pittsburgh

> Context: the interrelated conditions in which something exists; the environment in which a 'business' operates; the parts … that surround a word and can throw light on its meaning. (Merriam-Webster Online Dictionary)

After the passage of PL 94-142, the Education of All Handicapped Children Act, in 1975 guaranteeing a free, appropriate public education for all students with disabilities, multiple reauthorizations of IDEA have refined, revised, and renewed the nation's moral and pedagogical commitment to providing well planned, public, inclusive, and appropriate education to all students with disabilities. Conflicting views of where that education should take place, what that education should consist of, and how that education should be delivered continue to plague the field of special education, but the commitment is unwavering.

In the 2004 reauthorization of federal special education legislation (the Individuals with Disabilities Educational Improvement Act), some of the conflicts appear to have been resolved. The reauthorization asserts that students with disabilities belong in general education classrooms and should be removed from those classrooms only if such removal, even for a short time, is fully justified. It asserts that all students with disabilities should have access not only to the general education curriculum but also to the accountability assessments that measure proficiency in that curriculum. It asserts that all students with disabilities should be taught alongside their non-disabled peers and held to the same high standards of achievement as their classmates. These assertions derive from the moral and ethical commitment made to students with disabilities in 1975, but are they grounded in any research evidence? Do they lead to service delivery systems that "work better" to increase the achievement of students with disabilities? Do they help to clarify the roles and responsibilities of the special educator, or muddy the waters? The chapters in this section of the handbook pose these, and other, questions and provide tentative answers. O'Connor and Sanchez explore the evidence that responsiveness to carefully designed and implemented intervention is the best way to determine eligibility for special education. They examine whether general education Responsiveness to Intervention (RtI) models that include progress monitoring and tiered instruction have succeeded in improving academic and behavioral outcomes of struggling learners, have reduced the incidence or severity of learning disabilities, or have identified students with LD more reliably that past practices. Cook, McDuffie, Oshita, and Cothren Cook review the empirical evidence for the effectiveness of co-teaching, the service delivery model of special education most often associated with inclusion programs that provide full access of students with disabilities to the general education curriculum and accountability assessments. Thurlow and Quenemoen consider the ways in which students with disabilities have been impacted by the standards based reform movement in general education, the barriers to standards based education for students with disabilities, and the consequences of their inclusion in standards-based educational systems. Zigmond and Kloo question the wisdom of merging general and special education programs either for students or for preparation of teachers, and find historical, legal, and educational underpinnings that make real and substantial differences between general and special education worth preserving.

At the end of the first decade of the 21st century, about 6 million students in the United States (out of about 55 million) qualified for special education and had Individualized Education Programs (IEPs). A little more than half of these students were in inclusive settings for 80% or more of each school day. A little less than half received some kinds of special services outside the general education classroom for at least some portion of their school day. All of these students (including those with the most severe cognitive disabilities) had be part of the increasingly rigorous accountability systems imposed by federal and state governments. All were required to have access to the general education curriculum taught by teachers expert in the content they were teaching, though perhaps not expert in the pedagogy required to reach these students effectively. Efforts to improve the capacity of all teachers to serve an increasingly diverse student body led to calls for unification of special and general education service delivery and teacher preparation.

Education is perhaps the single most important means for individuals to actualize their personal endowments, build capability levels, overcome constraints, and, in the process, enlarge their life opportunities and choices. Education is important for enabling the processes of acquisition, assimilation, and communication of information and knowledge. Education enhances a person's quality of life. Most importantly, education is a "critical invasive instrument"[1] for bringing about social, economic, and political inclusion and a durable integration of people, particularly those "excluded" from the mainstream of any society. The chapters in this section of the handbook examine the research evidence that should help shape that "critically invasive instrument" to maximally benefit students with disabilities.

Note

1. Tamil Nadu State Planning Commission, Tenth Five Year Plan, 2002–2007, Chapter 4, p. 105, accessed December 17, 2009. from http://www.tn.gov.in/spc/tenthplan/default.htm

10

Responsiveness to Intervention Models for Reducing Reading Difficulties and Identifying Learning Disability

Rollanda E. O'Connor and Victoria Sanchez
University of California at Riverside

With the reauthorization of the Individuals with Disabilities Educational Improvement Act (IDEIA) of 2004, states and districts have been encouraged to consider responsiveness to scientifically based instruction and intervention (RtI) as one of many markers of potential eligibility for special education under the category of learning disabilities (LD). The reasoning behind this change is that RtI models have potential for improving academic and behavioral outcomes of struggling learners. By monitoring student learning, we should be able to provide help to students who need academic or behavioral assistance beyond what is available typically in whole group instruction and before students are eligible formally for special education. By doing so, we might be able to improve long-term outcomes for struggling learners and identify students with LD earlier than when we relied on IQ-achievement discrepancy.

We argue that while improved general class instruction and early intervention clearly help many students to improve their academic skills, we know little about whether RtI reduces the incidence or severity of LD or whether it identifies students with LD more reliably than earlier practices. Most models of RtI have been researched with students in the early primary grades; however, students with LD have been identified most frequently in Grades 2 through 5, which is beyond the strongest of the research base for RtI. Few implementations of RtI systems have been of sufficient duration (i.e., into Grades 4–5) to determine whether RtI is a better approach to identification of LD or whether it might decrease the proportion of students eligible for special education.

To many special educators of students with LD, the RtI process sounds familiar, because advocates for students with LD have proposed prereferral interventions since the 1970s, whether interventions have been designed by "teacher assistance teams," "child study teams," "round-table reviews," or other similar groups of school personnel (e.g., Chalfont, 1987). But where prereferral interventions tended to be short in duration (e.g., 4 to 6 weeks) and focused on just one presenting problem (e.g., lack of attention, starting on assignments, aggressive behavior), RtI models focus on academic or behavioral interventions designed to close the gap between a low-skilled child and his or her peers.

Preventative multilayered or multitiered service delivery systems are not a new idea; they existed prior to the federal mandating of RtI in the IDEIA. RtI is a reconceptualization of the multitiered service delivery approach; it emphasizes not only early preventative intervention, but also individual response to intervention (Chard & Linan-Thompson, 2008; Fletcher & Vaughn, 2009; Fuchs & Fuchs, 2006). Researchers agree on most of the core principles of RtI, including high quality general class instruction, universal screening in academic and/or behavioral areas, research-based interventions for students who fall below an accepted criterion in the school context, continued monitoring of progress during these interventions, fidelity measures of implementation, and consideration for special education when students make insufficient growth during interventions (Bradley, Danielson, & Doolittle, 2005). Nevertheless the details of implementation—such as criteria for risk and for what constitutes growth in interventions, indicators for students being no longer at risk, and determinations for type and content of interventions—varies across system-designed and researcher-designed models of RtI, and among researchers.

The notion of RtI received substantial boosts from early intervention research in the 1990s and early 2000s. For example, by the late 1980s reading researchers were aware of the association between phonemic awareness (i.e., the ability to hear and manipulate the sounds in spoken words) and alphabet letters and sounds measured in kindergarten, and reading ability one or more years later (Juel, 1988; Perfetti, Beck, Bell, & Hughes, 1987; Share, Jorm, MacLean, & Matthews, 1984). The rationale behind most early intervention efforts in kindergarten and first grade was to encourage children to learn about sounds in words and features of print within the windows of time that these understandings develop for typically achieving children. In this view, if by the end of kindergarten all children could blend and segment spoken words (phonemic awareness) and link these speech sounds to letter sounds (the alphabetic principle), they would be prepared to learn to decode and recognize words in first grade. Likewise, if children learned to decode and recognize words in first grade alongside maintaining adequate vocabulary growth, they would be prepared for building reading fluency and comprehension in later grades.

Researchers tested these relationships by designing instructional studies that focused on phonemic awareness and letter knowledge to determine whether acquiring these skills might decrease the incidence or severity of reading disability (RD) (Ball & Blachman, 1991; Bus & Ijzendoorn, 1999; O'Connor, Jenkins, & Slocum, 1995; Torgesen, Morgan, & Davis, 1992; Vellutino et al., 1996). The collection of experiments suggested that phoneme awareness could be taught to children who did not acquire it naturally, and that doing so generated small but reliable effects on reading words.

By the late 1990s, researchers began experimenting with models of intervention that included general class teachers in the first layer of intervention (i.e., Tier 1). In these studies, improvements in classroom teaching were brought about by ongoing professional development for teachers with frequent measurement of students' reading progress (Blachman, Tangel, Ball, Black, & McGraw, 1999; O'Connor, 2000; O'Connor, Fulmer, Harty, & Bell, 2005; Vaughn, Linan-Thompson, & Hickman, 2003). The combination of professional development and additional intervention for students who remained at risk for reading difficulties yielded improved reading of words and improved reading comprehension.

Intervention research with children at risk for reading disability reports positive effects for children in kindergarten (Blachman, Ball, Black, & Tangel, 1994; O'Connor et al., 1995; O'Connor, Notari-Syverson, & Vadasy, 1996) and first grade (Blachman et al., 1994; Coyne, Kame'enui, Simmons, & Harn, 2004; Foorman, Francis, Fletcher, Schatschneider, & Mehta, 1998; O'Connor, 2000; Vellutino et al., 1996); however, few studies have followed students into second grade or beyond, as reading becomes more complicated. According to Wagner, Torgesen, and colleagues (1997), the practice of universal screening of phonemic awareness and letter knowledge to identify students who may develop reading difficulties is strongly supported by research from the last two decades. The studies above used a research design that included screening students for difficulties in phonemic awareness and letter knowledge, reading instruction that included specific activities to teach these skills, monitoring the progress students made in acquiring early reading skills, and intervening right away with students who made poor progress—in essence these studies provided the backbone for the current recommendation to implement RtI.

As we consider potential benefits of RtI models, it is important to keep in mind that most investigations of RtI's possibilities have been designed to improve reading performance of students *at risk* for LD (McMaster, Fuchs, Fuchs, & Compton, 2005; O'Connor et al., 2005; Simmons et al., 2007; Vellutino, Scanlon, Small, & Fanuele, 2006), many of whom were likely false positives in the selection for Tier 2 interventions. Thus, when the proportion of students who appeared to be at risk decreased following intervention, this decrease also included students who were not seriously at risk to begin with. Moreover, students with LD are a heterogeneous group. Many of them need better reading instruction, but very little is known about how RtI might be managed for students whose reading disability is due to language delays and poor comprehension (Catts, Adlof, & Weismer, 2006), let alone aspects of learning other than reading, such as for mathematics or written language. In addition, many students at risk for LD are learning English, and RtI for these students has received little attention (Klingner, Artiles, & Barletta, 2006; Linklater, O'Connor, & Palardy, 2009; Lovett et al., 2008).

If good instruction can be assured (instruction that helps most students in the class improve adequately in academic skills), then Tier 1 could reduce the number of inappropriate referrals for LD. As Haring and Bateman noted decades ago (1977), some students may be inappropriately referred to special education due to instructional failures, rather than disabilities. Combined with Tier 2, in which a few students receive more intensive instruction than most students receive (smaller groups, more focused content tailored to students' needs, more time, etc.), some students are likely to catch up with their peers and avoid the referral process altogether. Reducing referrals and placement of students in special education are important considerations here because regulations in IDEIA 2004 allow up to 15% of a district's special education budget to be spent on early intervening and professional development in general education. If RtI does not reduce referrals and placements, then teachers and families of students with special needs will be asked to do more with fewer resources.

Most of the RtI research to date has focused on reading and behavior with young children, although RtI models are being developed for mathematics and for older students, also. In this chapter, we will focus on reading primarily, because the research base is strongest in this area. We hope that by showing the strongest evidence to date that we will also be able to reveal the fragility of evidence for using RtI to identify LD.

Taken together, most studies of RtI have focused either on early intervention and its effects, or on the reliability and validity of identification of LD. In the sections that follow, we review studies that have taken either or both approaches.

Tier 1

Primary prevention, more commonly referred to as Tier 1, comprises the general education setting, where children receive research-principled instruction. Professional development to enhance primary prevention conditions often focuses on effective instructional strategies, differentiation, and intensity mechanisms typically achieved through grouping strategies, progress evaluations, time management, instructional focus, and lesson structure (Fletcher & Vaughn, 2009; Torgesen, 2009). In order to meet all of the requirements at Tier 1, Fletcher and Vaughn (2009) argue that a continuous supply of well-trained and committed professionals are needed to implement ongoing professional development regimens, which sadly are not always available. Progress of students is monitored at this stage using standardized, norm-referenced, and/or curriculum-based measurements (Compton, Fuchs, Fuchs, & Bryant, 2006; Fuchs, Fuchs, & Compton, 2004), and those who fall behind their peers or state or national norms are deemed at-risk and targeted for more intensive intervention.

The notion of responsiveness to good instruction as a marker for increasing instructional intensity and identification of LD is the hallmark of any RtI process. Therefore, it may seem surprising that Tier 1 instruction—the evidence-based teaching by the general educator—has received so little research attention. As Gersten and Dimino (2006) have pointed out, a child could be nonresponsive with an unskilled teacher or when instruction is implemented poorly. To demonstrate this problem, Al Otaiba and Fuchs (2006) conducted fidelity ratings of general class teachers in their study, and found that nonresponsive students were most often in classrooms with poor quality teaching in kindergarten and first grade. Additionally, these students exemplified greater levels of problem behavior. Researchers may need to think more deeply about this co-occurrence; problem behavior, poor reading, and lower fidelity of implementation are so tightly woven together that it is difficult to identify which came first. A recent investigation (O'Connor et al., 2009) also saw noted themes of lower fidelity, problem behavior, and poor progress in secondary or Tier 2 intervention.

Considerable research shows how poor teaching limits student academic growth. As examples, poor class management in schools serving students in low income communities has been linked to increased incidence of identification for disabilities, particularly in the judgmental categories of LD and emotional disturbance (Donovan & Cross, 2002).

Management and instruction are related to opportunities to learn. Brophy and Good (1986) noted decades ago that features of teacher instruction acted positively or negatively on academic learning in the classroom. In a structural equation model of the influence of teacher qualifications and classroom practices on student learning, Connor, Son, Hindman, and Morrison (2005) demonstrated a complex model of interactions. As others have found, home environment (including mother's education and socioeconomic level) exerts a strong influence on children's vocabulary and literacy development. Nevertheless, they also found that teacher warmth and responsiveness to students in first grade have a positive and significant effect on student vocabulary, and that time on academic tasks is also important. These teacher characteristics act to reduce risk and promote resilience among students from high-poverty homes.

Comparisons of reading programs for struggling readers (Hatcher, Hulme, & Ellis, 1994; Juel & Minden-Cupp, 2000) have found that the best approaches were those that combined features of effective instruction in a consistent package delivered with sufficient intensity and duration. Fostered by research that has identified "necessary but insufficient" instructional components for word reading in kindergarten and first grade, researchers have reached moderate consensus on what "evidence-based" means in the first year or two of formal reading instruction.

Despite this consensus among researchers, implementation of these practices is far from universal. In an introduction to a special issue of the *Journal of Learning Disabilities* on teacher knowledge of reading instruction, Moats (2009) cautions that many teachers feel unprepared to teach students with reading or language problems effectively. One of the reasons teachers feel unprepared is that many teacher educators lack sufficient knowledge of language structure and reading development to guide preservice teachers in the key skills that support reading acquisition, such as phonemic awareness and phonics (Joshi et al., 2009).

Inservice teachers may also lack this knowledge. Cunningham, Zibulsky, Stanovich, and Stanovich (2009) surveyed 121 first-grade teachers in general and special education across 37 schools to examine their knowledge of language elements important for teaching reading, along with their preferred use of instructional time for language arts. The National Reading Panel Report (2000) suggested that beginning reading instruction should include primarily letters and sounds, phonemic awareness, phonics, and vocabulary. Across the two-hour hypothetical block of time, on average teachers in Cunningham et al.'s study allocated 19% of the time on these core activities, which are necessary for teaching children to read words. In contrast, teachers preferred to allocate 31% of their time to writing and independent reading, which most first graders—who are just beginning to read words—cannot do very well. Assessment to guide the path of instruction was given less than 1% of the available time.

Following a year-long study for building this knowledge among first-grade teachers, Brady et al. (2009) suggested that although teachers gained knowledge overall, teacher attitudes prior to professional development (PD) in these areas exert a strong influence over the likelihood that teachers will learn language structure and apply it to their teaching. In particular, Brady and colleagues found that teachers who were disinclined at the outset to participate gained less from the PD and mentoring, as did teachers whose goal for participating was to gain service credits; conversely teachers who felt less prepared to teach reading (newer teachers) welcomed the PD and learned the most.

Taken together, these studies suggest that many teachers in the early grades are not using instruction that the research community would classify as evidence-based. Because the RtI models rely on an assumption that instruction in Tier

1 is generally effective, some have devoted considerable resources to ongoing professional development in effective instructional practices (McCutchen et al., 2002; O'Connor et al., 2005; Podhajski, Mather, Nathan, & Sammons, 2009). Other studies observed and measured fidelity of implementation of an evidence-based curriculum, but provided no training or mentoring in implementation where it was less than optimal (Abbott et al., 2008).

Some of the professional development (PD) models to improve general class instruction have been intensive. As examples, O'Connor (2000; O'Connor et al., 2005) met with teachers in small groups monthly over a two to four-year period. McCutchen et al. (2002) trained kindergarten teachers to implement explicit phonemic awareness and phonics instruction over a year-long period and found positive changes in teaching behavior and significant gains for students in their classes on letter-sound knowledge and decoding. Podhajski et al. (2009) trained first- and second-grade teachers through a 35-hour course that included 10 hours of in-class mentoring. McCutchen, Green, Abbott, and Sanders (2009) intervened with third-, fourth-, and fifth-grade teachers for 10 days of PD. In all four cases, observations of teachers revealed substantial changes in instructional targets, specificity of instructional language, and student groupings. The researchers found concurrent improvement for students in grades K–3 in some areas of student learning (e.g., phonemic awareness, reading fluency, and comprehension) but not in others (e.g., vocabulary), except for older students, who gained vocabulary and writing skill with improved Tier 1 instruction. Research has also focused on improving the knowledge and instructional skills of preservice reading teachers. For example, Spear-Swerling (2009) incorporated supervised reading tutoring in a language arts course for future special educators and improved the knowledge and skills of the teachers and the reading achievement of the tutored students.

The consensus on evidence-based instruction is less clear for instruction in second through fourth grade, as students are expected to master most features of independent reading. Despite this lack of clear agreement among researchers or teachers on what evidence-based instruction means after first grade, the term "evidence-based" defines the Tier 1 instruction to which students respond well, moderately, or poorly. The students who respond poorly to general class instruction are then offered additional, and more carefully designed instruction that might be delivered by the same classroom teacher to whom the student did not respond earlier, or by someone else.

As we consider responsiveness to intervention in Tier 1, it will now be clear that the instruction delivered as Tier 1 will show considerable variation in content and teaching effectiveness. Where teaching is less effective for any reason, we might expect the number of students identified for Tier 2 to increase. Moreover, this increase in poor response may have little, if anything, to do with disability or need for special education. If we combine the possibility of poor responsiveness to poorly delivered Tier 1 instruction with a Tier 2 protocol delivered by an individual with even less training than that of the Tier 1 teacher (e.g., an uncertified teaching assistant or specialist with little specific training in reading development or behavioral management), we set up the likelihood of continued poor response to intervention for children who may be responsive in improved situations.

Tier 2 Interventions

Even in the presence of the most effective classroom instruction, there can be as many as 20%–30% of students who continue to be at-risk for reading difficulties and who require sustained supports (Wanzek & Vaughn, 2007). To complicate matters further, during the most evidenced-based and sustained supports approximately 2%–5% of children fail to thrive and are termed "treatment resistors," "nonresponders," or poor responders (McMaster et al., 2005; O'Connor, Bocian, Beebe-Frankenberger, & Linklater, 2010; Torgesen, 2000). Al Otaiba and Fuchs (2006) suggest that "the percentage of nonresponders among children with learning disabilities may be as high as 50%" (p. 414), which ultimately begs the question, are all of these nonresponders students with LD?

Secondary prevention, often synonymous with Layer or Tier 2, is supplementary to general education instruction and involves an intervention that ranges in program and other instructional components (i.e., instructors, group-size, frequency, duration, intervention design, progress monitoring tools, and instructional fidelity). A review of RtI models across the United States indicated that a major difference across models is the development of the Tier 2 program (Berkeley, Bender, Peaster, & Saunders, 2009). For instance, states such as Iowa and Nebraska among others determine interventions through a problem-solving approach. In such an approach, a team develops a specific program based on the individual needs of the student. Other states, such as Florida, Oregon, and California, provide a list of research-based interventions for educators' selection for their Tier 2 intervention. These programs are designed to target challenging areas and allow for groupings of students that maximize resources. Currently, there is considerable disagreement around these issues, which we discuss later.

Core components of supplemental reading programs focus on critical literacy skills, such as phonemic awareness, alphabetic code, decoding skills, fluency, vocabulary, and comprehension. In an early exploration of the effect of increasingly intensive layers (or tiers) of instruction over time, O'Connor (2000) identified 59 of 189 kindergarten students from three schools as demonstrating risk for reading difficulties. The risk criteria were based on cut-points for measures of phonological awareness, letter knowledge, and rapid naming found to be predictive in a previous study (O'Connor & Jenkins, 1999). Reasoning that these high-poverty schools had a long history of poor reading outcomes, the first layer of intervention was to improve general class instruction through professional development. O'Connor continued to monitor student progress through the fall, and for students with poor gains (e.g., a slope criteria) designed short, focused, small-group sessions that mirrored the general class activities but provided more support and engagement. In first grade when measures of "real" reading could be administered, she used a normative cut-point criteria of scores below 86 on a standardized measure to select students for more intensive instruction.

Across the two years, improved kindergarten instruction decreased the proportion of high risk students from 40% to 30%. Layer 2 instruction for the last four months of kindergarten reduced the proportion of risk to 18%, which dropped to 14% by mid-first grade, and to 12% by the end of first grade. Throughout the interventions, strong response was defined as (a) a rate of growth that matched or exceeded that of typical readers in the same classes, and (b) standard scores above 85 on the Woodcock-Johnson reading subtest. In comparison to first graders in the year prior to the start of this study, RtI reduced risk from 40% to 12% over two years. Three problems noted in the conclusion have yet to be resolved in nearly a decade of RtI research that has followed: (a) although risk was reduced, RtI did not reduce the incidence of students eligible for special education in this study; (b) some students who appeared strong at one stage of reading development (e.g., at the end of kindergarten) demonstrated risk once again as reading became more complicated over time; and (c) many of the strong responders to more intensive interventions were students later identified for special education. Vaughn and colleagues (2003) raised this last point again a few years later. These problems raise a paradox around the notion that students with "real" disabilities will not respond well to good instruction.

O'Connor et al. (2005) replicated this study with a two-school sample (i.e., one high and one low SES school) that engaged in RtI practices from kindergarten through third grade. Their RtI model included four years of professional development for teachers in scientifically based reading instruction, ongoing measurement of reading progress, and additional small group or individual instruction for students whose progress was insufficient to maintain grade-level reading achievement. Although students in the more affluent community ended third grade with higher reading scores than those in the low SES school, the growth of students in the interventions across the schools did not differ. Specifically, students in the low SES school began kindergarten with uniformly lower scores; however, their gains during the interventions were as strong as their more affluent peers. By the end of third grade, overall reading achievement was significantly higher for students in the RtI years than for students in the historical control (i.e., the same schools and teachers in the year before RtI). A sub-analysis of third-grade outcomes for the students most at risk in kindergarten produced similar findings.

Al Otaiba and Fuchs (2006) implemented a peer-assisted intervention for at-risk readers in kindergarten and first grade. The intervention was implemented by classroom teachers and progressed from phonological awareness in kindergarten to decoding, sight word training, and reading connected text in first grade. The kindergarten intervention was conducted in 15–20 minute sessions, three times per week for 16 to 20 weeks. Grade 1 intervention occurred in 20 minute sessions, three times per week for 20 weeks. About half of the students in kindergarten demonstrated adequate pre-to-post growth in early literacy skills, while 13% of the students did not demonstrate adequate achievement in letter-sounds or segmentation through peer tutoring. Across both years of intervention, 57% of the students demonstrated adequate achievement in oral reading fluency, while 25% read fewer than 40 words per minute near the end of first grade. In contrast, 72% of the students in the control conditions were not performing adequately. Although the intervention raised reading achievement overall, the proportion of poor readers at the end of first grade was still substantial.

Several commonalities should be noted across these studies. First, the proportion of students in the high-risk category decreased with more intensive intervention. Also two of the studies identified transience of "catching up" for some students—a phenomenon that is difficult to detect in studies of just one or two years duration. As O'Connor et al. (2005) observed, "Other students—with assistance offered through Layer 2—were able to keep up with their peers when reading generally consisted of one-syllable words. Because they caught up, we released them from Layer 2, only to catch them up again as words became commonly multisyllabic…" (p. 452). The measures used in kindergarten caught nearly all of the students who were later identified for special education; however, the pretests could not discriminate which students would be good and poor responders, a phenomenon also found by O'Connor et al. (2010). They noted that students who were identified for special education were also students whose scores on reading measures dropped over the summer, while those not at risk tended to rise or maintain. Moreover, many of the good responders needed the additional support provided by Tier 2 instruction to maintain steady growth in reading.

A recent study by Vellutino, Scanlon, Zhang, and Schatschneider (2008) identified this summer slippage again for poor responders to Tier 2 and Tier 3 interventions. To test the long-term effect of Tier 2 intervention, they followed the reading progress of children who had received intensive Tier 2 interventions in kindergarten, first grade, or both. By the end of third grade, only 16% of the 117 at-risk students identified in kindergarten remained at risk, which suggests that interventions in kindergarten and first grade can have lasting effects. Even though (as Vellutino et al. admit) it is likely that the kindergarten measures selected more students than were actually at risk for reading problems, these lasting effects for early intervention are noteworthy.

To account for these lasting effects, Shaywitz, Gruen, and Shaywitz (2008) suggested a biological change in children as a response to intervention. In their study remedial, evidence-based, phonological reading interventions facilitated development of the neural systems that underlie skilled reading, especially the development of neural systems in the anterior and posterior regions of the brain. In essence, their evidence showed that intervention produces significant and durable changes in brain organization for atypical readers that resemble patterns of activation in good readers. With recent improvements in brain imaging techniques and increasing collaboration among medical and educational researchers, these possibilities will receive attention.

Nonresponsiveness to Tier 2 Interventions

Another controversial topic concerns the portion of students who do not improve with additional instruction. Research indicates that limited information is available regarding supplementary intervention for nonresponsive (NR) students (Al-Otaiba & Fuchs, 2006). In fact, many researchers are still untangling information about the characteristics of NR students.

Al Otaiba and Fuchs (2002), in their best-evidence synthesis, found seven categories to be associated with NR in the primary grades (K–3): (a) phonological awareness; (b) verbal memory; (c) rapid naming; (d) vocabulary, verbal ability, and IQ; (e) attention or behavior problems; (f) orthographic awareness; and (g) home background. Nelson, Benner, and Gonzales (2003) reviewed 30 studies that identified students as poor responders and determined student characteristics linked to poor responding. The two most influential student characteristics were rapid naming and phonological awareness, which were statistically equivalent predictors and have been reported for many years. Although only 7 of the studies assessed problem behavior, its effect was as strong as rapid naming and phonological awareness. Other significant characteristics were (in descending order of magnitude of effect) alphabetic principle (which combines letter knowledge with phonemic awareness), memory, and IQ. The studies were consistent in finding demographics related to poverty as the least likely indicator, and many of the predictors coincide with the characteristics of children with LD (see Berninger, 2008, for review).

Demographic characteristics also included special education eligibility in Nelson et al.'s (2003) study, which calls into question the notion of using responsiveness as an indicator of disability. It is possible that nonresponders are students with a constellation of literacy problems that may include dysgraphia, dyslexia, specific language impairment, and working memory. In effect, if we limit our study of responsiveness to failure to acquire phonemic awareness or letter knowledge, we may be moving backward from what we already know about students with LD. It seems likely that the etiological smorgasbord of potential reasons for reading difficulty are also at play among students who respond poorly to interventions.

Studies of the proportions of poor responders show similar variability. Burns, Appleton, and Stehouwer (2005) reviewed effects of four systemic RtI models (i.e., Heartland Agency in Iowa, Ohio's Intervention Based Assessment, Pennsylvania's Instructional Support Teams, and Minneapolis Public Schools' Problem-Solving Model) along with several researcher-designed RtI models. The average percentage of poor responders was 19.8% among those selected for Tier 2 interventions; however, criteria for Tier 2 was not addressed, and so it is difficult to determine what percent of the school population responded poorly in these models.

In Tier 3 interventions, the proportion of poor responders increases, as one might expect. Nevertheless, among 8- to 10-year-old students already identified as LD, Torgesen et al. (2001) found that 40% of the students with LD responded so well to the intensive, Tier-3-like reading instruction that they were no longer eligible for special education in the year following the treatment. Moreover, the gains made during treatments maintained two years later for the students returned full-time to general education. Although the remaining 60% also showed strong reading gains overall, particularly on word-level skills, their growth was insufficient for catching up to their nondisabled peers. Torgesen et al.'s study shows a paradox found in many studies of the responsiveness of students with LD to strong interventions: students with LD respond well to good instruction and intervention. So how should we consider responsiveness as a marker of LD?

There is currently no widely supported method of identifying students who respond poorly to instruction or intervention. Compton et al. (2006) compared several types of decision rules on measures collected in first grade to identify students labeled as poor readers at the end of second grade. They compared decisions based on first grade measures of (a) a multivariate screening battery of phonemic awareness, rapid digit naming, and oral vocabulary; (b) these measures plus word identification fluency (WIF) level and slope; and (c) a classification tree analysis of if/then statements based on cut-points across WIF level, sound matching, rapid digit naming, WIF slope, and oral vocabulary. The classification tree was the most accurate identifier of students who might benefit from additional instruction; however, it was also the most cumbersome process. Dexter and Hughes (2009) reviewed the literature for the varying ways of establishing nonresponders. Their search yielded 6 methods of establishing inadequate response—dual discrepancy, median split, final normalization, final benchmark, slope discrepancy, and exit groups. Barth et al. (2008) analyzed a large data set using several of these methods, but noted that agreement was generally poor and that different methods tended to identify different students as non-responders. They concluded that a cut-point was the most reliable determinant of responder status; however cut-points are arbitrary because they imply that students performing below the cut-point should receive secondary or tertiary interventions, while students above the cut-point are safe from reading failure. They also recommend adopting a "gold standard" for determining responsiveness, but note that researchers have not yet found one combination of measures that most accurately identifies students with chronic reading difficulties. So despite the national interest in using RtI to generate a more stable diagnosis of LD, our current methods appear to fall short of this aim.

Two troubling aspects followed these reviews. First, the research community lacks agreement on procedures for identification of responsiveness. Worse, the methods do not converge on identification of the same subset of individuals as unresponsive. Reynolds and Shaywitz (2009) sharply criticized RTI models for their inability to define the R in RTI. Although researchers are unable to offer reliable evidence regarding responsiveness, policy now suggests that school districts may identify LD by the use of RtI models. It is possible that future research will define a convergent model that has sufficient reliability for identifying students with LD, but that has not happened yet.

Moreover, research has identified some students with LD who do not have the phonological difficulties that RtI models currently use for identification for Tier 2 or 3 interventions and for responsiveness. These students may have what some researchers call "late identified" LD, or LD seated in reading comprehension, language, and writing areas (see Berninger 2008; Catts et al., 2006, O'Connor & Jenkins, 1999; Scarborough, 2005).

Instructional Features of Responsiveness

Our review of studies suggests considerable variability in the nature and content of interventions, the skills of the interventionist, and the language of the student and instruction. For students who fail in Tier 1, which kinds of Tier 2 instruction identify good and poor responders? In other words, what should be the nature and content of Tier 2? One way to think about these questions is whether we want a good intervention to be delivered, or for interventions to be adjusted or changed altogether when students do not respond as expected. Several researchers have suggested a "first response" package based on research regarding what students need to know and be able to do to read on grade level. Thus the content may change across grade levels, but be uniform within grade. As examples, Vadasy, Jenkins, Antil, Wayne, and O'Connor (1997) developed an effective scripted Tier 2 intervention for first graders that could be implemented by teaching assistants and parent volunteers. Kamps et al. (2008) developed a Tier 2 package with directed, explicit instruction for students in kindergarten and first grade that improved reading outcomes over the comparison group. Taking an alternative approach, O'Connor and colleagues (2005) designed the content of Tier 2 based on students' scores on progress monitoring tools, so that Tier 2 content not only changed across grades, but varied within grade based on students' progress across a range of reading skills. In between these approaches, Simmons et al. (2007) compared Tier 2 packages for kindergarteners that differed in their length (15 or 30 minutes) and degree of instructionally explicit design. They found that 15 minutes of carefully designed instruction was sufficient for learning phonological skills, but that 30 minutes was more effective for decoding and spelling. The longer package was especially beneficial to those who began kindergarten with the lowest prereading skills, which implied that effectiveness might be improved by taking child characteristics into account before selecting the Tier 2 content.

The notion of varying Tier 2 content in response to students' growth could be important—especially in eligibility decisions for special education. In a reading intervention study with third-, fourth-, and fifth-grade poor readers that used two Tier 2-like packages, students received daily half-hour supplemental lessons for 16 weeks using one of two packages (O'Connor et al., 2002). Both methods were effective, meaning that students greatly improved their rate of progress in reading and significantly outperformed students in the control group. Therefore, both treatments demonstrated strong evidence for effectiveness for most very poor readers in those grades. For the 7 poor responders, the researchers changed the type of intervention from one effective model to the other and continued another 8 weeks of intervention. Under the new conditions, 6 of the 7 formerly poor responders became good responders.

The point here is that no intervention is a silver bullet, and so schools should be wary of identifying poor responders based on just one evidence-based treatment. Moreover, this kind of one-size-fits-all intervention could be especially problematic for English Learner students. Fuchs and Fuchs (2006) have suggested that standard protocols lead to fewer false positives, or children who appear to be in need of special education, when actually they are not. This suggestion assumes that standard protocols are more intensive than instruction adjusted to student response; however, there is no evidence as of 2009 to support the claim. Clearly, these issues deserve experimental attention.

The packaged vs. targeted approaches to Tier 2 also have implications for the skills required of the people who implement Tier 2. Some RtI models use classroom teachers or reading specialists as interveners; other models use teaching assistants, college undergraduates, or other non-certified staff. When students have failed to respond good Tier 1 instruction delivered by a trained teacher, it may be necessary to enlist a teacher with even more training and more focused instructional knowledge for delivering Tier 2, although well-trained and closely monitored instructional assistants have also produced good response from students (e.g., Vadasy, Sanders, & Tudor, 2007). Responsiveness of students can be related to how the teacher responds to students during instruction, and changing or fine-tuning instruction is hallmark of good teaching across tiers. This fine-tuning brings its own headaches to designing an effective RtI system, because changing instruction can look like poor fidelity if the competing goal is adherence to a standard Tier 2 protocol. Moreover, it will be difficult to replicate these skilled revisions to an instructional package performed on behalf of particular students. So despite the encouragement to states and districts to implement RtI models, researchers disagree on selection of content for each Tier and the necessary instructional qualifications for implementing them.

RtI and Special Education

As we consider RtI and special education, we have many unanswered questions. Success stories of RtI models reducing incidence of disability comes largely from studies of early intervention in kindergarten and first grade, before many cases of LD are identified in "business as usual" environments. Moreover, several studies of RtI approaches report strong immediate gains in isolated skills such as phonemic awareness, letter-sound correspondences, and one-syllable decoding tasks; however, when researchers follow up on the children who made these early gains, the effects often dissipate by second grade. When children who make these gains in Tier 2 are returned to Tier 1, some will encounter the same difficulty keeping up with their peers as they experienced before as the skills that constitute reading become more complex and reliant on fast processing of print.

We also worry about the small percentage of children who exhibit less than optimal response to early intervention. Perhaps these children are those the early intervention net intended to capture—those with a high risk for developing disability. Or they may be children for whom the Tier 2 content was inappropriate. After first grade, we know less about just what that content should entail. By third or fourth grade, we have few validated Tier 2 instructional packages to consider for children who lag seriously behind their peers in reading, behavior, or mathematics. And by middle school, interventions that have been found effective with younger students may be ineffective and inappropriate (Denton, Wexler, Vaughn, & Bryan, 2008).

Moreover, researchers of long-term studies of RtI identify troubling in-and-out patterns for children who respond well with Tier 2 instruction by learning the foundation skills that are the targets of early intervention, but still fail to grow in reading ability when returned to Tier 1 with learning rates that keep them within the range of normal reading development. In the next screening cycle or the one after that, they again qualify for Tier 2. This problem differs from the notion of using responsiveness to identify LD, because the children responded well in Tier 2 (therefore not proceeding to Tier 3, or special education). For them, Tier 1 is insufficient; however, Tier 2 keeps them growing in skills appropriately. For these children, should we consider a formal evaluation for special education eligibility?

A recent update on the progress of states in RtI implementation (Berkeley et al., 2009) has shown that models of implementation vary widely. Data collected by the end of 2007 revealed that 15 states had adopted an RtI model, 22 states were in a developmental stage, 10 were providing assistance to districts to develop their models, and 3 had not formally begun implementation. Across states, models varied in the numbers of tiers, prescriptiveness of instructional content and delivery, group size, intervention intensity and duration, skill of interventionists, and whether the model was used just for early intervention, or for intervention and identification of disabilities. Moreover, some states were developing models for implementation of RtI in secondary schools, even though few studies suggest that it is feasible or effective past third grade.

Mellard, McKnight, and Woods (2009) administered a more fine-grained survey to 41 schools in 16 states that met their criteria as "implementers" based on having core components of an RtI model in place. An integral piece of RTI is universal screening and the monitoring of student response to instruction. Special emphasis is given to those tests that are quick to administer and have adequate sensitivity and specificity (Fletcher & Vaughn, 2009). More often than not progress monitoring comes in the form of curriculum-based measures, which have considerable evidence supporting their use for instruction adjustment and providing reliable and valid information. Yet this process is not without flaws; the time at which the screening is completed or progress is monitored need to be considered—tests may demonstrate floor effects which may lead to inadequate identification (Catts, Petscher, Schatschneider, Bridges, & Mendoza, 2009). Reynolds and Shaywitz (2009) highlight this particular problem, and Berninger (2008) cautions that with all the emphasis on phonological processing other forms of reading disability may be overlooked.

Mellard et al.'s (2009) intent was to describe screening and progress measures used in these schools and consider implications for equity of identifying students for intensive instruction or special education. Unfortunately, the schools that met their eligibility criteria for study were not representative of public schools nationally. Only 3% served a high proportion of students from low-income families, and nearly half had less than 1% of students classified as English Learners. A striking finding across the schools was the variety in measures, criteria for identifying risk, and proportions of students they considered in need of additional instructional intensity. Moreover, the difficulty of keeping and using records of student progress was a recurring theme across sites. Where multiple measures were administered, school personnel seemed uncertain about which were most important for instructional decisions. Given the similar range of variability in the models used in current research, the outcomes of implementation of RtI will be difficult to evaluate.

Reynolds and Shaywitz (2009) criticize RtI models place within the identification of LD. They suggest there is lack of evidence for the assumptions in the implementation process, lack of evidence for the full model efficiency, uncertainty regarding child characteristics of identified students and unsupported assumptions regarding the identification of children who have LD. They claim there is no evidence to date to suggest that RtI is a better method than cognitive assessment and that there is little evidence to suggest that RtI offers the promise of fixing the flatlined growth for many students, especially those in special education. They argue that identification of LD through an RtI model, assessment of low achievement, and exclusionary criteria "represents a fundamental alteration in the concept of disability and cuts out the very roots basic to the concept of LD as an unexpected difficulty in learning intrinsic to the child" (p.

46). Even Swanson (class presentation, May 28, 2009) suggests that less that 15% of the variance in reading outcome is related to instruction. Proponents of RtI will argue LD cannot be identified solely on the basis of responsiveness, but it should be an integral criteria for the consideration of LD among other criteria (Fletcher & Vaughn, 2009).

Given the current challenges, there are still "perks" of RtI. Many RtI models nationwide report an increase in overall academic achievement and a decrease in special education referrals (Torgesen, 2009). Reviewing RTI implementation in Florida's Reading First schools, Torgesen found a gradual reduction in the percentage of students who demonstrated serious academic performance problems and a reduction in the identification of students for special education service. More specifically, across their 318 schools for three years of intervention, rates of identification of students with LD dropped. From the end of the kindergarten year to three years later the LD identification rate was reduced 81%. There were also decreases in the percentage of students with reading difficulties although they were not as dramatic. Interestingly, Torgesen (2009) touches on the idea that perhaps fewer students are identified because schools feel more confident and comfortable with their ability to work with low performing students. Furthermore, he suggests also that perhaps schools are exploring more options before referring for special education. Either explanation could lead to an increase in special education referrals and placements in later grades. Until studies assess responsiveness and achievement in reading and other aspects of learning disability through the grades in which LD is usually identified, we cannot determine the extent to which the incidence of LD is decreased and the reliability of accurate identification of LD is enhanced through RtI.

Summary

We are unconvinced that responsiveness to carefully designed and implemented intervention is the best way to determine eligibility for disability. Children with disabilities can and do respond well to good interventions. Thus lack of responsiveness may not be hallmark for special education. Nevertheless, we have seen many children make substantial progress through early intervention. Some children who have received early intervention may also show less serious delays in key academic and behavioral areas. Moreover, the speed with which early interventions can be delivered as need becomes apparent far outstrips the pace of identification and service delivery in the special education system. Where these Tier 2 interventions are designed thoughtfully and delivered carefully and consistently over time to very small groups of children, the conditions may mirror what special education was designed to do. Clearly, some students may struggle with reading throughout their schooling and into adulthood—despite early identification, early intervention, and ongoing support.

As Kavale and Spaulding (2008) noted, RtI remains an experimental process and more research is necessary. RtI models were developed initially to identify learning difficulties early in a child's schooling, and to provide key strategic instruction that might help us to separate children who lacked preparatory skills (e.g., children in low socioeconomic communities, children with few preschool or enrichment experiences; children learning English) from children with disabilities. For children who lack phonological awareness or letter knowledge, early identification measures can help teachers to find them early and begin catch-up instruction. Although these early skills are useful in preparing children to read words, they are not the only difficulties children encounter with learning to read, particularly after first grade.

It is possible that some of our failures in identification and Tier 2 instruction could be attributed to comprehension-based reading problems, which our current measures and treatments were not designed to catch or improve. We do not suggest that RtI models will fail in respect to these problems, just that we have a long way to go in designing models that can perform the same functions for these children as the RtI models around phonological skills and decoding. In short, even if we can inoculate young children against failure in phonemic awareness, it will prove more difficult to inoculate them against failures in reading comprehension.

References

Abbott, M., Wills, H., Kamps, D., Greenwood, S. R., Dawson-Bannister, H., Kaufman, J., … Fillingin, D. (2008). The Kansas reading and behavior center's K-3 prevention model. In C. R. Greenwood, T. R. Kratochwill, & M. Clements (Eds.), *Schoolwide prevention models: Lessons learned in elementary schools* (pp. 215–265). New York: Guilford.

Al Otaiba, S., & Fuchs, D. (2002). Characteristics of children who are unresponsive to early literacy intervention: A review of the literature. *Remedial and Special Education, 23*(5), 300–316.

Al Otaiba, S., & Fuchs, D. (2006). Who are the young children for whom best practices in reading are ineffective? An experimental and longitudinal study. *Journal of Learning Disabilities, 39*(5), 414–431.

Ball, E. W., & Blachman, B. A. (1991). Does phoneme segmentation training in kindergarten make a difference in early word recognition and developmental spelling? *Reading Research Quarterly, 26,* 49–66.

Barth, A. E., Stuebing, K. K., Anthony, J. L., Denton, C. A., Fletcher, J. M., & Francis, D. J. (2008). Agreement among response to intervention criteria for identifying responder status. *Learning and Individual Differences, 18,* 296–307.

Berkeley, S., Bender, W. N., Peaster, L. G., & Saunders, L. (2009). Implementation of response to intervention: A snapshot of progress. *Journal of Learning Disabilities, 42,* 85–95.

Berninger, V. (2008). Defining and differentiating dysgraphia, dyslexia, and language learning disability within a working memory model. In M. Mody & E. Silliman (Eds.), *Brain, behavior, and learning in language and reading disorders* (pp. 103–134). New York: Guilford.

Blachman, B. A., Ball, E. W., Black, R. S., & Tangel, D. M. (1994). Kindergarten teachers develop phoneme awareness in low-income, inner-city classrooms. *Reading and Writing: An Interdisciplinary Journal, 6,* 1–18.

Blachman, B. A., Tangel, D. M., Ball, E. W., Black, R. S., & McGraw, C.

K. (1999). Developing phonological awareness and word recognition skills: A two-year intervention with low-income, inner-city children. *Reading and Writing: An Interdisciplinary Journal, 11*, 239–273.

Bradley, R., Danielson, L., & Doolittle, J. (2005). Response to intervention. *Journal of Learning Disabilities, 38*, 485–486.

Brady, S., Gillis, M., Smith, T., Lavaette, M., Liss-Bronstein, L., Lowe, E., … Wilder, T. D. (2009). First grade teachers' knowledge of phonological awareness and code concepts: Examining gains from an intensive form of professional development and corresponding teacher attitudes. *Reading & Writing Quarterly, 22*, 425–455.

Brophy, J. E., & Good, T. L. (1986). Teaching behavior and student achievement. In M.C. Wittrock (Ed.), *Handbook of research on teaching* (3rd ed., pp. 328–375). New York: Macmillan.

Burns, M. K., Appleton, J. J., & Stehouwer, J. D. (2005). Meta-analytic review of responsiveness-to-Intervention research: Examining field-based and research-implemented models. *Journal of Psychological Assessment, 23*, 381–394.

Bus, A. G., & Ijzendoorn, M. H. (1999). Phonological awareness and early reading: A meta-analysis of experimental training studies. *Journal of Educational Psychology, 91*, 403–414.

Catts, H., Adlof, S., & Weismer, S. (2006). Language deficits in poor comprehenders: A case for the simple view of reading. *Journal of Speech, Language, and Hearing Research, 49*, 278–293.

Catts, H., Petscher, Y., Schatschneider, C., Bridges, M. S., & Mendoza, K. (2009). Floor effects associated with universal screening and their impact on the early identification of reading disabilities. *Journal of Learning Disabilities, 42*, 163–176.

Chalfont, J. (1987). Providing services to all children with learning problems: Implications for policy and programs. In S. Vaughn & C. Bos (Eds.), *Research in learning disabilities: Issues and future directions* (pp. 239–251). Boston: Little, Brown.

Chard, D., & Linan-Thompson, S. (2008). Introduction to the special series on systemic, multitier instructional models: Emerging research on factors that support prevention of reading difficulties. *Journal of Learning Disabilities, 41*, 99–101.

Compton, D. L., Fuchs, D., Fuchs, L. S., & Bryant, J. D. (2006). Selecting at-risk readers in first grade for early intervention: A two-year longitudinal study of decision rules and procedures. *Journal of Educational Psychology, 98*, 394–409.

Connor, C. M., Son, S., Hindman, A. H., & Morrison, F. J. (2005). Teacher qualifications, classroom practices, family characteristics, and preschool experience: Complex effects on first graders' vocabulary and early reading outcomes. *Journal of School Psychology, 43*, 343–375.

Coyne, M. D., Kame'enui, E. J., Simmons, D. C., & Harn, B. A. (2004). Beginning reading as inoculation or insulin: First-grade reading performance of strong responders to kindergarten intervention. *Journal of Learning Disabilities, 37*, 90–104.

Cunningham, A. E., Zibulsky, J., Stanovich, K. E., & Stanovich, P. J. (2009). How teachers would spend their time teaching language arts. *Journal of Learning Disabilities, 42*, 418–430.

Denton, C. A., Wexler, J., Vaughn, S., & Bryan, D. (2008). Intervention provided to linguistically diverse middle school students with severe reading difficulties. *Learning Disabilities Research & Practice, 23*, 79–89.

Dexter, D. D., & Hughes, C. A. (2009, April). *Identification of nonresponders to Tier 2 interventions within an RTI model.* Poster presented at the meeting of the Council for Exceptional Children, Seattle, WA.

Donovan, M. S., & Cross, C. T. (2002). *Minority students in special and gifted education.* Washington, DC: National Academy Press.

Fletcher, J., & Vaughn, S. (2009). Response to intervention: Preventing and remediating academic difficulties. *Child Development Perspectives, 3*(1), 30–37.

Foorman, B. R., Francis, D. J., Fletcher, J. M., Schatschneider, C., & Mehta, P. (1998). The role of instruction in learning to read: Preventing reading failure in at-risk children. *Journal of Educational Psychology, 90*, 37–55.

Fuchs, D., & Fuchs, L. (2006). Introduction to response to intervention: What, why, and how valid is it? *Reading Research Quarterly, 41*, 93–99.

Fuchs, D., Fuchs, L. S., & Compton, D. L. (2004). Monitoring early reading development in first grade: Word identification fluency versus nonsense word fluency. *Exceptional Children, 71*, 7–21.

Gersten, R., & Dimino, J. A. (2006). RtI (Response to Intervention): Rethinking special education for students with reading difficulties (yet again). *Reading Research Quarterly, 41*, 99–107.

Haring, N. G., & Bateman, B. (1977). *Teaching the learning disabled child.* Englewood Cliffs, NJ: Prentice-Hall.

Hatcher, P., Hulme, C., & Ellis, A. (1994). Ameliorating early reading failure by integrating the teaching of reading and phonological skills: The phonological linkage hypothesis. *Child Development, 65*, 41–57.

Joshi, R. M., Binks, E., Hougen, M., Dahlgren, M. E., Ocker-Dean, E. & Smith, D. L. (2009). Why elementary teachers might be inadequately prepared to teach reading. *Journal of Learning Disabilities, 42*, 392–402.

Juel, C. (1988). Learning to read and write: A longitudinal study of 54 children from first through fourth grades. *Journal of Educational Psychology, 80*, 437–447.

Juel, C., & Minden-Cupp, C. (2000). Learning to read words: Linguistic units and instructional strategies *Reading Research Quarterly, 35*, 458–492.

Kamps, D., Abbott, M., Greenwood, C., Wills, H., Veerkamp, M., & Kaufman, J. (2008). Effects of small-group reading instruction and curriculum differences for students most at risk in kindergarten: Two-year results for secondary- and tertiary-level interventions. *Journal of Learning Disabilities, 41*, 101–114.

Kavale, K. A., & Spaulding, L. S. (2008). Is response to intervention good policy for specific learning disability? *Learning Disabilities Research and Practice, 23*, 169–179.

Klingner, J. K., Artiles, A. J., & Barletta, L. M. (2006). English language learners who struggle with reading: Language acquisition or learning disabilities? *Journal of Learning Disabilities, 39*, 108–128.

Linklater, D., O'Connor, R. E., & Palardy, G. P. (2009). Kindergarten Literacy Assessment of English Only and English Language Learner Students: Which Measures Are Most Predictive of Reading Skills? *Journal of School Psychology, 47*, 369–394.

Lovett, M. W., de Palma, M., Frijters, J., Steinbach, K., Temple, M., Benson, N., & Lacerenza, L. (2008). Interventions for reading difficulties: A comparison of response to intervention by ELL and EFL struggling readers. *Journal of Learning Disabilities, 41*, 333–352.

McCutchen, D., Abbott, R. D., Green, L. B., Beretvas, S. N., Cox, S., Potter, N. S., …Gray, A. L. (2002). Beginning literacy: Links among teacher knowledge, teacher practice, and student learning. *Journal of Learning Disabilities, 35*, 69–86.

McCutchen, D., Green, L., Abbott, R. D., & Sanders, E. A. (2009). Further evidence for teacher knowledge: Supporting struggling readers in grades three through five. *Reading & Writing Quarterly, 22*, 401–423.

McMaster, K. L., Fuchs, D., Fuchs, L. S., & Compton, D. L. (2005). Responding to nonresponders: An experimental field trial of identification and intervention methods. *Exceptional Children, 71*(4), 445–463.

Mellard, D. F., McKnight, M., & Woods, K. (2009). Response to intervention screening and progess-monitoring practices in 41 local schools. *Learning Disabilities Research & Practice, 24*, 186–195.

Moats, L. (2009). Still wanted: Teachers with knowledge of language. *Journal of Learning Disabilities, 42*, 387–391.

National Reading Panel. (2000). *Teaching children to read: An evidence-based assessment of the scientific research literature on reading and its implications for reading instruction.* Rockville, MD: NICHD Clearinghouse.

Nelson, J. J., Benner, G. J., & Gonzales, J. (2003). Learner characteristics that influencethe treatment effectiveness of early literacy interventions: A meta-analytic review. *Learning Disabilities Research & Practice, 18*, 255–267.

O'Connor, R. E. (2000). Increasing the Intensity of Intervention in Kindergarten and First Grade. *Learning Disabilities Research and Practice, 15*, 43–54.

O'Connor, R. E., Bell, K. M., Harty, K. R., Larkin, L. K., Sackor, S., & Zigmond, N. (2002). Teaching reading to poor readers in the intermediate grades: A comparison of text difficulty. *Journal of Educational Psychology, 94*, 474–485.

O'Connor, R. E., Bocian, K., Beebe-Frankenberger, M., & Linklater, D. (2010). Responsiveness of students with language difficulties to early intervention in reading. *Journal of Special Education, 43*, 220–235.

O'Connor, R. E., Bocian, K., Lewis, J., Nam, J., Sanchez, V., & Sun, J. (2009, April). *Responsiveness to intervention in grades K-2.* Paper presented at the annual conference of the Council for Exceptional Children, Seattle.

O'Connor, R. E., Fulmer, D., Harty, K., & Bell, K. (2005). Layers of reading intervention in kindergarten through third grade: Changes in teaching and child outcomes. *Journal of Learning Disabilities, 38*, 440–455.

O'Connor, R. E., & Jenkins, J. R. (1999). The prediction of reading disabilities in kindergarten and first grade. *Scientific Studies of Reading, 3,* 159–197.

O'Connor, R. E., Jenkins, J. R., & Slocum, T. A. (1995). Transfer among phonological tasks in kindergarten: Essential instructional content. *Journal of Educational Psychology, 2,* 202–217.

O'Connor, R. E., Notari-Syverson, N., & Vadasy, P. (1996). Ladders to literacy: The effects of teacher-led phonological activities for kindergarten children with and without disabilities. *Exceptional Children, 63*, 117–130.

Perfetti, C., Beck, I., Bell, L., & Hughes, C. (1987). Phonemic knowledge and learning to read are reciprocal: A longitudinal study of first grade children. *Merrill-Palmer Quarterly, 33*, 283–319.

Podhajski, B., Mather, N., Nathan, J., & Sammons, J. (2009). Professional development in scientifically based reading instruction: Teacher knowledge and reading outcomes. *Journal of Learning Disabilities, 42*, 403–417.

Reynolds, C. R., & Shaywitz, S. E. (2009). Response to intervention: Ready or not? Or, from wait-to-fail to watch-them-fail. *School Psychology Quarterly, 24*, 130–145.

Scarborough, H. (2005). Developmental relationships between language and reading: Reconciling a beautiful hypothesis with some ugly facts. In H. W. Catts & A. G. Kahmi (Eds.), *The connections between language and reading disabilities* (pp. 3–24). Mahwah, NJ: Erlbaum.

Share, D., Jorm, A., MacLean, R., & Matthews, R. (1984). Sources of individual differences in reading acquisition. *Journal of Educational Psychology, 76*, 1309–1324.

Shaywitz, S. E., Gruen, J. R., & Shaywitz, B. A. (2008) Dyslexia: A new look at neural substrates. In M. Mody & E. R. Silliman (Eds.), *Brain, behavior, and learning in language disorders* (pp. 209–239). New York: Guilford.

Simmons, D. C., Kame'enui, E. J., Harn, B., Coyne, M. D., Stoolmiller, M., Santoro, L. E., …Kaufman, N. K. (2007). Attributes of effective and efficient kindergarten reading intervention: An examination of instructional time and design specificity. *Journal of Learning Disabilities, 40*, 331–347.

Spear-Swerling, L. (2009). A literacy tutoring experience for prospective special educators and struggling second graders. *Journal of Learning Disabilities, 42*, 431–443.

Torgesen, J. K. (2000). Individual differences in response to early interventions in reading: The lingering problem of treatment resisters. *Learning Disabilities Research & Practice, 15*, 55–64.

Torgesen, J. K. (2009). The response to intervention instructional model: Some outcomes from a large-scale implementation in Reading First schools. *Child Development Perspectives, 3*(1), 38–40.

Torgesen, J. K., Alexander, A. W., Wagner, R. K., Rshotte, A. A., Voeller, K. K. S., & Conway, T. (2001). Intensive remedial instruction for children with severe reading disabilities: Immediate and long-term outcomes from two instructional approaches. *Journal of Learning Disabilities, 34*, 33–58, 78.

Torgesen, J., Morgan, S., & Davis, C. (1992). Effects of two types of phonological awareness training on word learning in Kindergarten children. *Journal of Educational Psychology, 84,* 364–370.

Vadasy, P. F., Jenkins, J. R., Antil, L. R., Wayne, S. K., & O'Connor, R. E. (1997). The effectiveness of one-to-one tutoring by community tutors for at-risk beginning readers. *Learning Disability Quarterly, 20*, 126–139.

Vadasy, P. F., Sanders, E.A., & Tudor, S. (2007). Effectiveness of paraeducator-supplemented individual instruction: Beyond basic decoding skills. *Journal of Learning Disabilities, 40*, 508–525.

Vaughn, S., Linan-Thompson, S., & Hickman, P. (2003). Response to instruction as a means of identifying students with reading/learning disabilities. *Exceptional Children, 69*, 391–409.

Vellutino, F. R., Scanlon, D. M., Sipay, E. R., Small, S. G., Pratt, A., Chen, R., & Denckla, M. B. (1996). Cognitive profiles of difficult-to-remediate and readily remediated poor readers: Early identification as a vehicle for distinguishing between cognitive and experiential deficits as basic causes of specific reading disability. *Journal of Educational Psychology, 88*, 601–638.

Vellutino, F. R., Scanlon, D. M., Small, S., & Fanuele, D. P. (2006). Response to intervention as a vehicle for distinguishing between children with and without reading disabilities: Evidence for the role of kindergarten and first-grade interventions. *Journal of Learning Disabilities, 39*, 157–169.

Vellutino, F. R., Scanlon, D. M., Zhang, H., & Schatschneider, C. (2008). Using response to kindergarten and first grade intervention to identify children at-risk for long-term reading difficulties. *Reading and Writing: An Interdisciplinary Journal, 21,* 437–480.

Wagner, R. K., Torgesen, J. K., Rashotte, C. A., Hecht, S. A., Barker, T. A., Burgess, … Garon, T. (1997). Changing causal relations between phonological processing abilities and word-level reading as children develop from beginning to fluent readers: A five-year longitudinal study. *Developmental Psychology, 33*, 468–479.

Wanzek, J., & Vaughn, S. (2007). Research-based implications from extensive early reading interventions. *School Psychology Review, 36*, 541–561.

11

Standards-Based Reform and Students with Disabilities

Martha L. Thurlow and Rachel F. Quenemoen
National Center on Educational Outcomes, University of Minnesota

In the last quarter of the 20th century, school reform ideas came and went with remarkable speed. One reform came and stayed. *Standards-based reform,* which grew out of the work of a bi-partisan group of governors in the mid-1980s (National Governors' Association, 1986), remains the dominant reform in place across the country today (Shepard, Hannaway, & Baker, 2009). Its staying power is related, in part, to the fact that it has been accompanied by federal laws and policies that require that all students—those with disabilities, poor students, and students of all ethnic groups—be included in the implementation of academic standards. Unlike most previous reform efforts, the emphasis was on measuring outcomes to improve the results of public education systems, rather than to sort students for promotion or placement (Goertz, 2007). This shift in accountability from the student to schools and school districts forced a rethinking of commonly held assumptions about what special education was meant to do.

The Education for All Handicapped Children Act of 1975 (PL 94-142) required local public schools to provide an "appropriate public education" to all students identified as eligible for special educations services. Congress imposed detailed due process procedures on local educators and gave parents of the children legal rights to appeal, first administratively, then in court, educational plans with which they disagreed. Predictably, legal hearings became common (Neal & Kirp, 1986), and federal courts became the principal forum for defining an "appropriate public education" (Melnick, 1995). In contrast, with the advent of standards-based reform, each state publicly articulated academic standards that defined the expected outcomes of a public education. Federal funding requirements held public schools accountable for the learning of all students—including those with disabilities—as articulated in these standards. These standards now define an "appropriate public education" for all students.

We examine standards-based reform and its implications for students with disabilities. We describe the legal and policy frameworks for standards-based reform, and then address the critical components of standards-based reform. We explore the ways in which students with disabilities are included in standards-based systems, the barriers to standards-based education reform for students with disabilities, and evidence of the consequences of their inclusion in standards-based educational systems. We review and integrate relevant literature and discuss implications for practice, policy, and future research.

Legal and Policy Frameworks

In the 1960s and 70s, the civil rights era resulted in substantial federal requirements to ensure that students who were disadvantaged by poverty or ethnic status received an equitable public education. By the end of the 1970s, federal policy (in the form of PL 94-142) guaranteed that students with disabilities also had access to public schools. These federal laws funding both special education and education for the disadvantaged were reshaped by the standards-based reform agenda in the 1990s. These reauthorized laws defined the right of students with disabilities to the same goals and standards as all other students, and also required the full inclusion of every student in assessments designed to provide data on how well all students were being taught the standards-based curriculum.

Title I of the Elementary and Secondary Education Act (ESEA) as reauthorized in 2001 (No Child Left Behind Act) is the primary federal driver of educational reform today. For students with disabilities, the reauthorizations of the Individuals with Disabilities Education Act in 1997 and 2004 introduced and then reinforced the inclusion of all students—including those with disabilities—in a common definition of educational standards. The reauthorization of IDEA in 1997 specifically addressed the 1970s notion of "access" by requiring that students with disabilities should not only have access to the school building, but also to the general curriculum offered there. Further, students with disabilities were expected to make progress in that curriculum. In the 2004 reauthorization, these requirements were clarified, referencing the same goals and standards that apply to all students under ESEA. Although the focus in IDEA is on individual accountability and the focus in ESEA is on systems accountability, the laws systematically work together with the goal of raising academic achievement through high expectations and high-quality education programs (Cortiella, 2006).

Even though these federal laws increased the impetus for full inclusion of all students in standards-based reform, decisions about what every student should know and be able to do in a standards-based system are made at the state and local levels and not at the federal level. Since the late 1990s, policymakers and citizens in every state have grappled with the fundamental question of "What is a well-prepared student?" Each state, and some districts, answered by defining content standards (what) and achievement standards (how well) that identify essential skills and knowledge for students to master at each grade level. Cumulatively, these standards define what a high school graduate is expected to know and be able to do.

Still, federal funding is the extra incentive in federal law. States receiving federal funding under either IDEA or Title I must ensure that these standards apply to all students receiving educational services tied to public school funding. The state-developed content and achievement standards are the foundation on which states build assessment systems that inform a standards-based accountability system that assures common standards for all students. Title I of ESEA requires states to assess all students once annually in grades 3–8 and at least once in grades 10–12 in mathematics and reading, and once annually in each of three grade bands in science. IDEA clarifies that students who receive special education services are to have access to and make progress in the general curriculum based on these same standards, and reinforces the requirement of full inclusion of all students with disabilities in the ESEA-required assessments (as well as in all other assessments administered by the schools). IDEA further specifies that states and districts must provide appropriate options for all students with disabilities to participate in these assessments, including requirements for universal design of assessments, accommodations, and alternate assessments.

Critical Components of Standards-Based Reform

Current standards-based educational reform is grounded in five critical components: content standards, achievement standards, teaching/instruction, testing, and accountability. Understanding of these components has changed some over time, and several of the components have been surrounded by confusion by educators and the public. Definitions of the components inform our discussion of standards-based reform and students with disabilities.

Content Standards

State academic content and achievement standards are central to ensuring that all students have access to and make progress in the general curriculum. Content standards define what students should know and be able to do. They define the learning targets for all students. The Council of Chief State School Officers (CCSSO, 2003) indicated that content standards are "statements of subject-specific knowledge and skills that schools are expected to teach students, indicating what students should know and be able to do" (p. 10).

Content standards are not the curriculum, but they do define the target skills and knowledge that the curriculum should encompass. Considerable effort has been devoted to clarifying the distinctions among the various levels of content standards (e.g., content domain, strand, goals or benchmarks, and objectives/performance indicators) (Bolt & Roach, 2009). Methods for "unpacking" the standards and defining effective practices for the attainment of standards have been replete in the literature (e.g., McREL, 2009).

Achievement Standards

Academic achievement standards define how well students must perform on the academic content to be considered proficient. They are generally defined in terms of proficiency levels—basic, proficient, and advanced, for example. Proficiency levels are defined by states for the assessments required under standards-based reform accountability provisions. Achievement standards are generally referred to as "performance standards" in the field of educational measurement, but the language used by Congress in ESEA in 2001 referred to them as "achievement standards" in the context of standards-based accountability testing requirements. CCSSO (2003) defined performance standards broadly as "indices of qualities that specify how adept or competent a student demonstration must be" (p. 10), and included four components (levels that provide descriptive labels; descriptions of what students must demonstrate at each level; examples of the range of student work within each level; and cut scores clearly separating each level). Because states define their achievement standards, they differ from state to state, just as content standards differ. The process of defining achievement standards requires involvement of experts and practitioners, and should reflect deep understanding of how students build knowledge and skills over time. There are various approaches to standard-setting, varying understanding of the nature of good standard-setting processes, and variability in the resulting achievement standards across states (Haertel, 2008; Perie, 2008)

Teaching/Instruction in Relation to Standards

Teachers use a variety of curriculum materials and instructional strategies to ensure that students reach the grade-level targets defined in the content standards. For all students, but particularly for students with disabilities, teachers tailor the curriculum and their instructional strategies to meet individual learning needs. In that process, discussions inevitably arise about what the "general curriculum" really means in IDEA, and what individualized education program (IEP) teams can do to ensure that each student has the services, supports, and specialized instruction needed to achieve proficiency on the goals and standards defined by the state for all students.

Testing in Relation to Standards

Content and achievement standards drive decisions about what an assessment will cover and the nature of the assessment (multiple choice, performance based, etc.). Downing (2006) described the test development process as a series of 12 steps, with the first step being definition of the content. Following this is the development of test specifications (or blueprints), which provide operational definitions for the test developer to use.

Martineau, Paek, Keene, and Hirsch (2007) proposed that test blueprints should "either representatively sample or comprehensively measure the assessable content standards in the same proportions as they appear in the complete set of content standards" (p. 30), indicating as well that they should reflect the breadth of topics and the depth of knowledge in the standards. They also clarified that the "accessibility" of the content is determined by whether some content is better assessed through assessments other than large-scale state tests (such as classroom assessments). In standards-based assessments, states must obtain external, independent reviews of the degree to which their assessments cover the full range of their academic content standards, and allow students to demonstrate their skills and knowledge across the full range of their achievement standards.

Accountability in Relation to Standards

Accountability within a standards-based framework focuses on results—the outcomes of education. Although accountability was a part of standards-based reform from the beginning, it has become increasingly important over time. In part, this reflected the increasing requirements that accompanied ESEA 2001. Because of this, some authors began to change the term from standards-based reform to standards-based accountability (Hamilton et al., 2007).

The law provided for public reporting and a tiered set of consequences for schools, from developing an improvement plan after one year of failing to show adequate yearly progress, to offering school choice after two years, to offering supplemental educational services as well as school choice after three years. By the time a school had failed to show adequate yearly progress for four consecutive years, the consequences entailed not only offering school choice and supplemental services, but also taking corrective actions such as instituting a new curriculum, bringing in an outside expert, extending the school day or year, or even closing the building and reassigning students. These consequences were substantial, increased the stakes for schools and districts, and spurred action and controversy. Prior to ESEA 2001, there were few consequences for poor performance over time, other than the implications of public reporting itself.

IDEA requirements reflected a different approach to accountability. Special education accountability historically has reflected a compliance focus, targeted on monitoring the extent to which states and districts have adhered to the requirements of IDEA. McLaughlin and Thurlow (2003) described the two major ways that special education accountability has differed from standards-based accountability: (a) a focus on system compliance with legal procedures, and (b) an individualized focus that is based on individualized goals and an IEP review process rather than on public standards, public testing, and public reporting. Following recommendations by a National Research Council panel (McDonnell, McLaughlin, & Morison, 1997), the notion of access to the general curriculum emerged as a cornerstone of IDEA 1997. The preamble to that law stated: "Almost 20 years of research and experience has demonstrated that the education of children with disabilities can be made more effective by high expectations for such children and ensuring their access to the general education curriculum in the regular classroom, to the maximum extent possible…." (p. 5). Still, when the law was reauthorized in 2004, the same words appeared, except that 20 years was replaced by 30 years. Despite the incorporation of requirements to report state assessment participation and performance of students with disabilities via Annual Performance Reports that states submit to the U.S. Department of Education (see Altman, Rogers, Bremer, & Thurlow, 2009), there remains a tension between the compliance focus of special education and a standards-based accountability focus.

Avenues to the Inclusion of Students with Disabilities in Standards-Based Systems

The goal of including *all* students in standards-based educational systems has been slow in its realization. McDonnell et al. (1997) described special education as historically built on assumptions about "valued post-school outcomes, curricula, and instruction that reflect the diversity of students with disabilities and their educational needs" (p. 113) rather than the content and performance standards that drive standards-based education systems. This shift in focus has led to important discussions and progress toward the inclusion of students with disabilities in standards-based reform. These discussions and progress have been realized by considering students with disabilities when defining academic standards and by considering content standards when developing students' IEPs, by determining ways to identify and implement accommodations, and by ensuring that assessments and accountability systems are appropriate for all students.

Development of Academic Standards

All students should be considered from the very beginning in development of academic standards. The purpose of this involvement is not to reduce the rigor of the standards, but rather to address whether proposed language for content standards may create artificial barriers for students with some disabilities. Examples of these types of artificial barriers as implemented in assessments include students who are deaf being required to match sounds of words, students who are blind being required to select objects of the same color, and students who are dyslexic being required to decode a passage even though the intent is to measure understanding of the text (Thurlow, Johnstone, Thompson, & Case, 2008).

Standards should be developed with all students in mind. This means that students who are blind and use Braille or assistive technology (such as text readers) to access written materials should be able to demonstrate their comprehension skills without having to decode printed text and their modeling of physical objects with geometric shapes using alternate formats. Students who are deaf should not be precluded from demonstrating their "listening skills" by the way the standard is written. And, students who have physical disabilities that prohibit movement of arms and hands should not be precluded by the way the standard is written from demonstrating with assistive technology their use of tools for constructing shapes, for example.

There are many instances of state standards in which the challenges of specific disabilities have been overlooked. For example, for writing or for application to real life situations, it is important to ensure that nothing is included that would preclude the use of a scribe, computer, or speech-to-text technology. Attending to the interpretation of standards that will occur when assessments are developed is an essential part of developing content standards.

It has been hypothesized that the narrower the standard statement, the greater the possibility that some students will have barriers in accessing the standards because of the nature of their disabilities. Broader standard statements, in fact, might allow for more ways to get to the content represented in the standard, and for varied avenues for assessing that content.

Academic Standards and IEPs

Until the 1997 reauthorization of IDEA, IEPs documented special education services and an individualized curriculum that was not always the same as general education services and curriculum provided to students who did not have disabilities (Ahearn, 2006). The 1997 and 2004 IDEA reauthorizations reinforced the new focus for IDEA of the same goals and standards applying to all students. Based on interviews with representatives from 18 states after the 2004 reauthorization, Ahearn found confusion in the field about just what the standards are, and great variation in how states were interpreting the relationship of standards and the IEP process. All states seemed to build on the required determination of a student's present level of performance, but then they diverged. Some required that goals focus on the skills a student needs to build skills and knowledge for content standards that have not yet been mastered. Others more generally required consideration of broadly construed content standards and not necessarily any reference to specific grade-level expectations or achievement levels. Although Ahearn did not study the implications of these divergent approaches, Karvonen (2009) concluded, based on review of research of the shifts in IEP focus, that consideration of the content and achievement standards for the student's grade level can make the planning process focus on educational goals, grounded in a clear understanding of student needs.

McLaughlin and colleagues (McLaughlin, Henderson, & Morando-Rhim, 1998; McLaughlin, Nolet, Rhim, & Henderson, 1999) addressed questions about access to the general education curriculum and whether it really involved just paperwork and procedure changes, or actually reinventing special education. They cited a survey of both general and special educators that found that many teachers did not understand the meaning of "curriculum," with many speculating that curriculum meant lesson plans, units, or textbooks. Teachers also reported that scope and sequence of the curriculum typically was not considered in IEP planning. They reported that the subject matter in standards and curricular frameworks were very challenging in terms of numbers of skills and concepts, and in complexity. Teachers commented on competing priorities, specifying concerns about (a) whether to move forward on content or remediate past content not yet mastered, (b) how to set priorities on some content over other content, and (c) concerns about how decisions in one school year affect opportunities in the future.

McLaughlin and colleagues (1998; 1999) also noted complicating factors, such as the professional orientations that teachers reported being in conflict; some were concerned about functional skills instruction instead of teaching academics. Developmental perspectives seemed to emerge as well, with a sense that students needed to be ready to move up a sequence, and instruction in higher content was precluded if lower skills were not in place. Teachers also reported that finding time for learning strategy instruction and supports while the student was progressing in the general curriculum was a challenge, as was accommodating learning in more challenging content when students were still building basic skills.

The solutions that McLaughlin and her colleagues (1998; 1999) identified to ensure that special education practices reflect true standards-based reform instead of paperwork included: (a) more collaboration of general and special education; (b) time and resources to build joint understanding of what the general curriculum is and an understanding that not all skills and knowledge are equal in implementation; and (c) training on instructional accommodations and differentiated instruction so that students can move forward in the content while receiving intensive instruction on targeted prerequisite skills. They proposed what they considered to be a four-step best-practice collaborative planning process, involving parents, students, and teacher: (a) define critical knowledge and performance expectations in the general curriculum; (b) identify aids, supports, and services necessary; (c) reflect a longitudinal view of learning; and (d) integrate and align content and instruction.

Quenemoen (2009a) developed a tool for schools and decision makers based on the steps proposed by McLaughlin and colleagues. The planning tool includes two columns for action—the first column defines the role of the school and district in providing key information and resources. The second column defines the role of the IEP team in identifying the services, supports, and specialized instruction needed for the student to be successful. In the standards-based planning process, each IEP team must count on the full support and participation of someone representing the school/district in ways that guarantee system resources will be in place to support the student's success. A key consideration in the Quenemoen tool is the realization that although the IEP team plans for success for one student at a time, success for any student cannot be achieved in isolation from the fully inclusive, standards-based system at the school and district level. That is, if the opportunities at the school and district level (e.g., highly skilled teachers instructing in the content areas, regardless of instructional setting) are not matched to the student's strengths and needs, then the IEP team has limited capacity to intervene successfully. Components of this tool are featured later in this chapter in a table that includes research on successful schools.

Accommodations

Accommodations are changes to materials or procedures that provide students access to instruction and assessments. This definition is broad, allowing for both changes for instructional purposes and changes for assessments. Considerable care has been taken to clarify what assessment accommodations are, in contrast to assessment modifications. Appropriate assessment accommodations, as now defined, are changes in test materials or procedures that *do not* alter the content being measured (Lazarus, Thurlow, Lail, & Christensen, 2009). Assessment modifications, in contrast, are changes in test materials or procedures that *do alter* the content being measured. Instructional accommodations and modifications generally have been less carefully defined, allowing occasionally for the use of changes (such as scaffolding and similar supports) that may alter the concepts being taught in some way (Elliott & Thurlow, 2006). Still, in a standards-based context, careful consideration must be given to whether a change in materials or procedures changes the content target or the expectation of achievement; although both curricular and instructional strategies can change to meet needs, the standards cannot.

Considerable research now has been conducted to examine the effects of accommodations on assessment results (Zenisky & Sireci, 2007). This research has changed over time, with an increasing focus on whether an accommodation changes the construct being measured, and whether a differential boost is created for students with disabilities compared to students without disabilities (Laitusis, 2007; Sireci, Scarpati, & Li, 2005). Nevertheless, the research does not provide easy answers for those developing state policies about accommodations.

All 50 states in the United States, and many of the other educational entities that receive U.S. special education funding, have policies and guidelines that define which accommodations may be used during their state assessments (Christensen, Lazarus, Crone, & Thurlow, 2008). Still, the field has realized that the appropriate provision of accommodations depends on much more than policy (Crawford, 2007). IEP teams must understand the nature of the content, the assessment, student characteristics and needs, and accommodation policies to be able to make good accommodation decisions for individual students (Elliott & Thurlow, 2006; Thurlow, Lazarus, & Christensen, 2008). Further, states and districts need to invest in monitoring procedures as well as training programs to ensure that what should happen is what actually happens when it comes to the provision of accommodations to students with disabilities to ensure access to the curriculum and to assessments (Christensen, Thurlow, & Wang, 2009).

Assessments

State large-scale assessment systems include not only the regular assessment that most students take (including most students with disabilities), but also several alternate assessments available only to students with IEPs. The alternate assessment based on alternate achievement standards (AA-AAS) is intended for students with the most significant cognitive disabilities (Schafer & Lissitz, 2009); all states have at least one AA-AAS. This assessment became known as the 1% assessment because, for ESEA accountability, only the number of students with disabilities up to 1% of the total student population could have proficient scores from an AA-AAS count toward the adequately yearly progress (AYP) indicator.

The alternate assessment based on modified achievement standards (AA-MAS) was first allowed for ESEA accountability in April 2007; it is an assessment that is optional for states. When developed, it is to be designed for students with disabilities whose progress to date, in response to appropriate instruction, is such that the student is unlikely to meet grade-level proficiency within the year covered by the student's IEP (Thurlow, 2008). This assessment became known as the 2% assessment because, for ESEA accountability, only the number of students with disabilities up to 2% of the total student population could have proficient scores from an AA-MAS count toward AYP.

The alternate assessment based on grade-level achievement standards (AA-GLAS) is an assessment option for students with disabilities that is designed to allow them an alternative way to demonstrate their grade-level knowledge and skills. This type of alternate assessment has not been developed by many states (Wiener, 2005).

Accountability
Accountability emerged in the early 1990s as the balance for flexibility given to states, districts, and schools to set their own content standards, develop their own assessments, and determine their own proficiency levels. Elmore and Rothman (1999) presented the standards-based reform model as one that depended on four major components—standards, assessments, flexibility, and accountability. Accountability was to focus on student learning improvements, not on the rules and procedures that had been the focus of accountability in the past.

Despite the rhetoric of exchanging flexibility for results, accountability has become a much more complex concept as IDEA 1997 and 2004 and ESEA 2001 were implemented. The poor performance of some states, schools, and districts led to increased attention to the federal accountability system. In addition, some states had their own accountability systems, which they either retained or they dropped. Adding special education requirements to ESEA accountability and, for some states, a state accountability system, resulted in the requirements becoming increasingly complex and sometimes contradictory.

Barriers to Standards-Based Reforms for Students with Disabilities

The inclusion of students with disabilities in standards-based reforms has been a bumpy road. There are several reasons for this, grounded in the history of special education and general education. We address three barriers that seem to have created particular challenges for including students with disabilities in standards-based reform.

General Misunderstandings about Who Students with Disabilities Are
The perceptions of the public, policymakers, and even some educators have made it difficult for many to embrace standards-based reform for students with disabilities. These misperceptions range from believing that the majority of students with disabilities have intellectual impairments to believing that special education eligibility is an excuse to expect less from a child. Recent investigations of low performing students (e.g., Hess, McDivitt, & Fincher, 2008) have shown that about half of the lowest performing students were students *without* disabilities, and that the demographic characteristics (e.g., ethnicity, socioeconomic status) of the students were very similar for the two groups. In many locations, the assessment and accountability provisions of ESEA have helped shed light on the problem of low expectations for students with disabilities.

In addition to the misperceptions are the challenges that the diversity of students with disabilities creates. McDonnell et al. (1997) referred to the unreliability of the diagnosis of a disability, with overlapping characteristics across disability category labels and classification criteria varying within and among states. Add to this the inadequate quality of measures used to diagnose specific disabilities, and the likelihood for confusion increases. The issue was considered such a challenge to the field, particularly with respect to students with learning disabilities that the President's Commission of Excellence in Special Education (2002) recommended that identification and eligibility determinations be simplified, and that a response to intervention approach be used.

Difficulty in identifying the specific characteristics of students with specific difficulties has repercussions for instructional and assessment decision making. Although it would be easiest for educators and IEP teams to simply select from an array of instructional supports and accommodations, for example, based on a category of disability, this simply does not work. Educators and IEP decision makers must identify each student's needs and characteristics and determine from those the most appropriate instructional and assessment accommodations and approaches, a much more difficult task. Considerable evidence suggests that the field has not yet figured out how to do this well and continues to need professional development around these topics (Ketterlin-Geller, Alonzo, Braun-Monegan, & Tindal, 2007; Thurlow, Lazarus, et al., 2008).

Expectations for Students with Disabilities
In a standards-based system, when some students or groups of students are not achieving to the levels expected for all students, the expectations do not change. Instead, the services, supports, and specialized instruction that ensure all students achieve the standards should change. This is not currently the universal response to low student achievement. IDEA and ESEA jointly support this shift, but much work needs to be done to overcome decades of low expectations and deeply engrained beliefs among some stakeholders that nothing can be done to improve the achievement of students who have disabilities. The literature on teacher expectations on student achievement is deep and strong: what teachers expect is typically what students do (e.g., Jussim, Madon, & Chatman, 1994).

For many educators, special education labels have become code words that say "this child can't learn." McGrew and Evans (2004) looked at the academic achievement of students of varying measured IQs, a common measurement used for eligibility for the special education category of mental retardation, and concluded that "intelligence tests are fallible predictors of academic achievement" (p. 10). They also noted that "Stereotyping students with disabilities (often on the basis of a disability label or test scores) as a group that should be excluded from general education standards and assessments is not supported by the best evidence from current science in the field of psychological and educational measurement" (p. 10).

Lack of Universal Design in Instruction and Assessment
Concerns about access issues for students with disabilities in both instruction and assessment have been voiced since federal laws supported accountability for all students. The research of McLaughlin et al. (1998; 1999) and

others (Acrey, Johnstone, & Milligan, 2005; Rose, Meyer, & Hitchcock, 2005) confirm that access to the general education curriculum remains an issue nearly a decade after IDEA first identified it as a primary goal. Similar concerns have been voiced about the design of assessment systems. Citing the lack of attention to all students, Thompson, Thurlow, and Malouf (2004) called for the application of the principles of universal design to assessments. The elements identified by Thompson et al. are shown in Table 11.1. These beginning concepts were expanded for states and test developers considering the application of universal design to the test development process (Johnstone, Thompson, Miller, & Thurlow, 2008). Dolan and colleagues (2009) identified a set of guidelines for application to computer-based testing.

Research on the Inclusion of Students with Disabilities in Standards-based Education

There has been relatively little research on the effects of standards-based reform, in general, and even less focused on the inclusion of students with disabilities. Still, some research has addressed the extent to which reforms have shifted expectations and access for students with disabilities. Furney, Hasazi, Clark/Keefe, and Hartnett (2003) found sustainability of positive outcomes of early reform efforts (e.g., increased use of educational support systems and teams), but increases in referrals to special education and more restrictive special education placements, where presumably students have less access to the general curriculum rather than more. Similarly, survey research in 34 large school districts found that students with disabilities were not considered in the same way as other students in the context of reforms (Gagnon, McLaughlin, Rhim, & Davis, 2002).

Nolet and McLaughlin (2005) noted that many special educators did not understand the meaning of "curriculum" and saw state content standards and curricular frameworks as too challenging for their students. Many teachers reported that it was more important to use instructional time for functional skills than academics; they showed limited understanding of alternative strategies to meet instructional needs within academically challenging content. Continued emphasis on a separate curriculum that prioritizes functional or adaptive skills as most important and that is inconsistent with the intent of standards-based policy continues to emerge in research (Dymond, Renzaglia, Gilson, & Slagor, 2007; Mayrowetz, 2009). Increasing numbers of studies indicate that instructional and curricular deficits are a common factor in the low performance of students with disabilities (Perie, 2009; Thurlow, 2008).

Perhaps nowhere have the positive consequences (and some negative consequences) of standards-based reform been so evident as they have for students with significant cognitive disabilities who participate in alternate assessments based on alternate achievement standards and for the assessments in which they participate (Quenemoen, 2009b). We now have a better sense of who the students are who have "significant cognitive disabilities" (Kearns, Towles-Reeves, Kleinert, Kleinert, & Thomas, in press). Educators generally have risen to the challenge of figuring out how content standards apply to their students (Browder & Spooner, 2006; Browder, Wakeman, Flowers, Rickelman, Pugalee, & Karvonen, 2007). University professionals have generated new approaches and techniques to improve the validity of results from the AA-AAS (e.g., Flowers, Wakeman, Browder, & Karvonen, 2009).

Despite the challenges of including students with disabilities in standards-based reform efforts, progress is occurring. This progress is evident from several sources, including a large qualitative study in Massachusetts (Donahue Institute, 2004), analyses and interviews conducted by the National Center for Learning Disabilities (Cortiella & Burnette, 2008), and findings from both national and state assessments, and accountability results.

Donahue Institute Study of Urban Schools

The Donahue Institute (2004) examined educational practices that supported the state test achievement of

TABLE 11.1
Elements of Universally Designed Assessments

Element	Explanation
Inclusive Assessment Population	Tests designed for state, district, or school accountability must include every student … and this is reflected in assessment design and field testing procedures.
Precisely Defined Constructs	The specific constructs tested must be clearly defined so that all construct irrelevant cognitive, sensory, emotional, and physical barriers can be removed.
Accessible, Non-Biased Items	Accessibility is built into items from the beginning, and bias review procedures ensure that quality is retained in all items.
Amenable to Accommodations	The test design facilitates the use of needed accommodations (e.g., all items can be Brailled).
Simple, Clear, and Intuitive Instructions and Procedures	All instructions and procedures are simple, clear, and presented in understandable language.
Maximum Readability and Comprehensibility	A variety of readability and plain language guidelines are followed (e.g., sentence length and number of difficult words are kept to a minimum) to produce readable and comprehensible text.
Maximum Legibility	Characteristics that ensure easy decipherability are applied to text, to tables, figures, and illustrations, and to response formats/

From Thompson and Thurlow (2002); reprinted with permission.

students with special needs who were in urban public schools. Institute researchers first identified schools in which students with disabilities performed better than expected; these became case study schools. A qualitative approach was used in the case study schools to glean information about the practices considered essential to the achievement of special needs students. More than 140 school personnel were interviewed in 5 schools; 10 schools were visited during the study to gather information. Eleven practices were identified by the researchers as ones that advance the achievement of special needs students in urban districts: (a) A pervasive emphasis on curriculum alignment with the [state] frameworks; (b) Effective systems to support curriculum alignment; (c) Emphasis on inclusion and access to the curriculum; (d) Culture and practices that support high standards and student achievement; (e) A well disciplined academic and social environment; (f) Use of student assessment data to inform decision making; (g) Unified practice supported by targeted professional development; (h) Access to resources to support key initiatives; (i) effective staff recruitment, retention, and deployment; (j) Flexible leaders and staff that work effectively in a dynamic environment; and (k) Effective leadership is essential to success. Similar practices and principles have been identified in other research (e.g., Education Trust, 2005; Herman et al., 2008), but those studies were not specifically focused on students with disabilities.

Challenging Change Findings

Cortiella and Burnette (2008) examined two schools and three districts to determine what they were doing to increase the academic success of students receiving special education services. This effort was a follow-up to an earlier report (National Center for Learning Disabilities, 2007), which examined how special education students were faring under NCLB. Cortiella and Burnette found that a variety of approaches were being used to improve the learning and performance of students with disabilities. Each of the approaches resulted from "[taking] a hard look at their instructional approach and expectations for students with disabilities, [recognizing] the need for improvement, and [taking] action" (Cortiella & Burnette, 2008, p. 3). Cortiella and Burnette recommended five approaches, all of which were evident in the schools and districts that they studied, "regardless of the school or district's size, student characteristics, resources or philosophy" (p. 24): (a) raising expectations for students with disabilities; (b) collaboration between general and special education; (c) inclusive practices; (d) data-based decision making; and (e) consumer satisfaction. These approaches, although fewer in number, are consistent with those identified by the Donahue Institute (2004) and by other studies not focused on students with disabilities.

Assessment Findings

The National Assessment of Educational Progress (NAEP) recently has become thought of as the gold standard for determining how students are performing under educational reform, in part because of concerns about the variability in state standards and assessments (McLaughlin et al., 2008). Although there continue to be issues surrounding the full inclusion of students with disabilities (Thurlow, 2009), the NAEP data for students with disabilities overwhelmingly demonstrate that these students are making progress within the standards-based context (National Center for Learning Disabilities, 2007). Figure 11.1 provides an example of the progress of students with disabilities on NAEP from 1998 through 2005.

Similar findings have been obtained from analyses of state assessment data across time. Despite changes in some states' standards and assessments, there has been improvement over time in the participation and performance

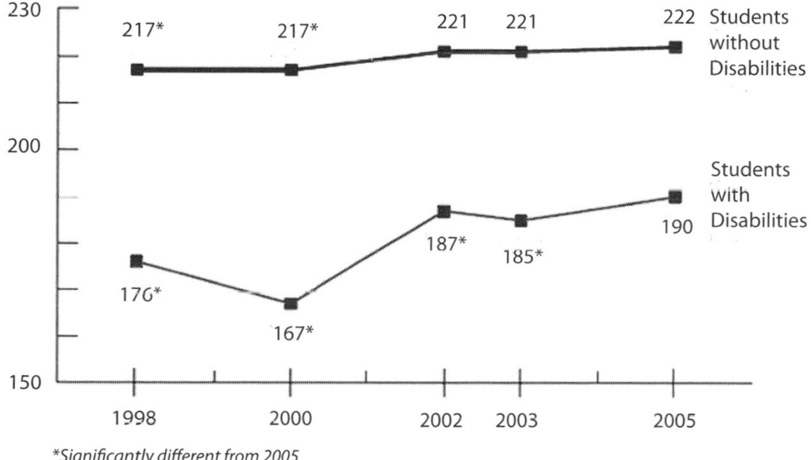

Figure 11.1 Performance of Students with Disabilities over Time on NAEP. Source: National Center for Learning Disabilities, 2007.

of students with disabilities on regular assessments (Altman, Thurlow, & Quenemoen, 2008; Thurlow, Quenemoen, Altman, & Cuthbert, 2008). Not enough data are available to check similar changes over time for students participating in the AA-AAS.

Accountability Findings

Accountability systems in which there are requirements for disaggregated public reporting of the performance of students with disabilities and separate accountability for those students raise concerns among schools, districts, and states held responsible for the performance results. This ESEA requirement ultimately resulted in educators suggesting that students with disabilities disproportionately were the reason that their schools and districts were not meeting AYP goals. Despite lack of evidence to support this hypothesis (Elledge, LeFloch, Taylor, & Anderson, 2009), Simpson, Gong, and Marion (2006) examined whether, in fact, some of the flexibility provisions of ESEA (e.g., minimum cell size before inclusion in accountability, confidence intervals around scores) actually obscured the information that we have about the performance of students with disabilities and their contribution to AYP results. As a result of their simulations, Simpson et al. concluded:

> Confidence intervals will not help the special education subgroup pass when they should really not pass (i.e., they are far below the AMO), but can help the state leaders make this decision [with] more reliability. On the other hand, minimum-*n* approaches do little to improve the reliability of subgroup decisions (at least within the range of minimum-*n* levels being used by most states), but can have severe negative consequences for subgroups excluded and, by extension, threaten the validity of the accountability system. (p. 16)

Thus, at the same time that there was good news in terms of increasing scores for students with disabilities (Thurlow, Quenemoen, Altman, et al.,, 2008), there continued to be concern that either too many students with disabilities were not included in accountability calculations because their numbers did not reach the minimum-n (as demonstrated by Simpson et al., 2006) and that the inclusion of students with disabilities in accountability was causing the schools to look bad.

Implications for Practice and Future Research

Standards-based reform has had remarkable staying power, and the federal commitment to it has continued through presidential administrations and Congresses on both sides of the aisle. Although policymakers may disagree on some of the details, they have achieved remarkable consensus on the importance of (a) identifying standards of what students should know and be able to do, (b) defining how well students must perform, (c) implementing curricula and instructional strategies to ensure that students reach the targets defined for their grade level, (d) checking on the performance of students using large-scale assessments, and (e) holding schools accountable for the progress of their students.

Despite the general agreement on the part of policymakers that standards-based reform is a critical mechanism for improving the outcomes of education for all students, the implementation and progress of standards-based reform has been uneven. Part of the challenge has been the commitment to including all students in standards-based reform, particularly students with disabilities. These students have been surrounded by a history of low expectations and the challenge of how best to instruct them and how to assess their knowledge and skills without confounding the results with the effects of their disabilities.

The challenges associated with including all students in standards-based reform, particularly those students with disabilities, suggest that there is still work to be done both in practice and in research. We suggest several avenues to be pursued in the continued implementation of and research on standards-based reform and students with disabilities.

Implementation of Standards-Based Reform and Students with Disabilities

Continued attention to what "access to the general curriculum" means for the practice of teaching and making decisions for individual students with disabilities is essential for students with disabilities to benefit as intended from standards-based reform. These benefits will not be realized if we continue to approach the problem "one student at a time."

Quenemoen (2009a) identified specific responsibilities for districts and schools to implement standards-based reform and ensure access to the general education curriculum. These responsibilities align with results of the Donahue Institute's 2004 study of successful school characteristics. Thus, district and school leaders can use the Donahue characteristics as the basis for a self-assessment tool to uncover areas that need work. Insights from the self-assessment then can be compared to the requirements for an IEP team to be successful when focusing on one student at a time. Districts and schools can identify where they have strengths and where they have gaps so that they can build on their strengths and address those gaps that get in the way of successful students.

Table 11.2 shows a tool that districts and schools can use to assess their strengths and uncover their weaknesses. It includes the Donahue Institute (2004) characteristics of successful schools for students with disabilities. Side-by-side with these characteristics are related questions posed by Quenemoen (2009a) to address (a) how the school supports IEP teams, and (b) how the IEP team supports each student, one student at a time. By working through this side-by-side table, districts and schools can identify where they need to go to implement standards-based reform and be successful with their students with disabilities.

TABLE 11.2
Tool to Assess Strengths and Uncover Weaknesses

Donahue Institute Successful School Characteristics by Cluster[a]	How School Supports IEP Teams (Answer these questions)[b]	How the IEP Team Supports One Student at a Time (Answer these questions)[b]
CURRICULAR FOCUS A pervasive emphasis on curriculum alignment with the [state] frameworks Effective systems to support curriculum alignment Emphasis on inclusion and access to the curriculum	What is the required content in the next grade level? Where and when during the school year is the required content taught in Math? ELA? Science? Social Studies? Other? How is it taught? What instructional and curricular options are currently available in this school to allow all students to achieve proficiency in the goals and standards set for all students? What is the curricular map into the future, what are essential understandings every student needs to achieve this year?	What are the student's current strengths and needs in the academic content areas? What data do we have to make that determination? What accelerated or remedial services and supports are necessary to ensure success in the content for the next grade level? What adaptations and accommodations can the student use to access the grade level content regardless of specific deficit basic skills in reading or mathematics or English language? What data do we have to support these choices? How will we determine if their use is effective or needs changing? What specific instructional strategies work well for this student? What types of curricular materials work well for this student?
CULTURE Culture and practices that support high standards and student achievement A well disciplined academic and social environment Use of student assessment data to inform decision making	What array of services does the school provide to meet the students' other needs?	How can we set priorities to ensure the essential understandings are mastered by this student, but still allow the TIME the school and the student needs to address all needs.
INFRASTRUCTURE OF SUPPORTS Use of student assessment data to inform decision making Unified practice supported by targeted professional development Access to resources to support key initiatives Effective staff recruitment, retention, and deployment	How does all this go together, with professional development, support, continuous improvement, community linkages … so that ALL children are successful?	If the needs of this student and the options available don't align well, what aids, services, supports, and instruction does the student need to be successful in spite of gaps? How can the current options be changed? What specific nonacademic needs does this student have? What goals and objectives will address those needs? How do these relate to the student's academic success?
LEADERSHIP Flexible leaders and staff that work effectively in a dynamic environment Effective leadership is essential to success	How does all this go together, with professional development, support, continuous improvement, community linkages … so that ALL children are successful?	How do we align curriculum, instruction, supports, services, and needs so that THIS child is successful at grade level?

[a] Based on Donahue Institute (2004) findings.
[b] Based on Quenemoen (2009a).

Districts and schools can take advantage of a substantial literature base on evidence-based strategies to ensure that all students are taught well, including students with disabilities. There are numerous technical assistance organizations now available to states and districts on evidence-based strategies and tools to assist in making the shifts that support standards-based education and access to the general education curriculum for students with disabilities. Many of the resources available have emerged from special education, including instructional approaches and strategies (www.k8accesscenter.org/index.php), effective school-wide disciplinary practices (http://www.pbis.org), and dropout prevention interventions (www.dropoutprevention.org/ndpcdefault.htm; www.ndpc-sd.org). The Institute of Education Sciences has identified evidence-based practices for specific content areas, including reading (Gersten et al., 2008) and mathematics (Gersten et al., 2009), and for using data to make instructional decisions (Hamilton et al., 2009). Some states have partnered with school administrators and other educators to develop resources to guide reform efforts (e.g., Ohio Department of Education, 2004). All of these resources and more are available to support the realization of standards-based reform in schools and districts.

Research on Standards-Based Reform and Students with Disabilities

The critical components of standards-based reform are areas ripe for further research. For example, one area that continues to benefit from research and that is in need of additional research are those assessments used to document student achievement and growth (see Thurlow, Quenemoen, Lazarus, et al., 2008). Examining ways to increase the appropriate application of universal design principles to assessments is a new and increasingly important area of research. One example of a recent effort in this area is the work of three projects devoted to developing and researching accessible reading assessments. These three projects (Designing Accessible Reading Assessments —DARA, www.ets.org/dara; Partnership for Accessible Reading Assessment—PARA, www.readingassessment.info; Technology Assisted Reading Assessment—TARA, www.naraptara.info), joined together as the National Accessible Reading Assessment Projects (www.narap.info) to develop a set of accessibility principles, pulling together the results of the projects' studies as well as other evidence and support in the field (www.narap.info/publications/NARAPprinciples.pdf). The variety of assessment options that are available to students with disabilities will continue to prompt researchers to document current practice and its effects. There will also be a need to explore the ways in which the validity of results from these assessments can be maximized, including the exploration of standard-setting techniques, the relation of the assessments to instruction, and the use of alternate assessments to document the growth of students across school years.

Related areas that continue to be a challenge for the nation, states, districts, and schools are alternate assessments and accommodations. The National Alternate Assessment Center (NAAC, www.naacpartners.org) has been a hub for research on alternate assessments, and continues to provide needed resources on instruction and assessment of students with the most significant cognitive disabilities. There is a need for continued research on the effects of accommodations, as well as on the variables that affect appropriate implementation of instructional and assessment accommodations. The National Center on Educational Outcomes (NCEO) hosts an online accommodations bibliography, a searchable data base of peer-reviewed research on accommodations practices (www2.nceo.info/accommodations). In addition, research on the decision-making process and on the variables that affect appropriate implementation of instructional and assessment accommodations decisions is needed.

References

Acrey, C., Johnstone, C., & Milligan, C. (2005). Using universal design to unlock the potential for academic achievement of at-risk learners. *Teaching Exceptional Children, 38*(2), 32–38.

Ahearn, E. (2006). *Standards-based IEPs: Implementation in selected states*. Alexandria: Project Forum, National Association of State Directors of Special Education (NASDE). Retrieved October 9, 2009, from http://www.projectforum.org/docs/Standards-BasedIEPs-ImplementationinSelectedStates.pdf

Altman, J., Rogers, C., Bremer, C., & Thurlow, M. (2009). *States challenged to meet special education targets for assessment indicator* (Technical Report). Minneapolis: University of Minnesota, National Center on Educational Outcomes.

Altman, J., Thurlow, M., & Quenemoen, R. (2008). *NCEO brief: Trends in the participation and performance of students with disabilities.* Minneapolis: University of Minnesota, National Center on Educational Outcomes.

Bolt, S. E., & Roach, A.T. (2009). *Inclusive assessment and accountability: A guide to accommodations for students with diverse needs.* New York: Guilford.

Browder, D. M., & Spooner, F. (Eds.). (2006). *Teaching language arts, math, & science to students with significant cognitive disabilities.* Baltimore: Paul H. Brookes.

Browder, D. M., Wakeman, S. Y., Flowers, C., Rickelman, R. J., Pugalee, D., & Karvonen, D. (2007). Creating access to the general curriculum with links to grade level content for students with significant cognitive disabilities: An explication of the concept. *Journal of Special Education, 41,* 2–16.

Christensen, L. L., Lazarus, S. S., Crone, M., & Thurlow, M. L. (2008). *2007 state policies on assessment participation and accommodations for students with disabilities* (Synthesis Report 69). Minneapolis: University of Minnesota, National Center on Educational Outcomes.

Christensen, L. L., Thurlow, M. L., & Wang, T. (2009). *Improving accommodations outcomes: Monitoring assessment accommodations for students with disabilities.* Minneapolis: National Center on Educational Outcomes with Council of Chief State School Officers.

Cortiella, C. (2006). *NCLB and IDEA: What parents of students with disabilities need to know and do.* Minneapolis: University of Minnesota, National Center on Educational Outcomes.

Cortiella, C., & Burnette, J. (2008). *Challenging change: How schools and districts are improving the performance of special education students.* New York: National Center for Learning Disabilities.

Council of Chief State School Officers. (2003). *Glossary of assessment terms and acronyms.* Washington, DC: Author.

Crawford, L. (2007). *State testing accommodations: A look at their value and validity.* New York: National Center for Learning Disabilities.

Dolan, R. P., Burling, K. S., Harms, M., Beck, R., Hanna, E., Jude, J., … & Way, W. (2009). *Universal design for computer-based testing guidelines.* Iowa City, IA: Pearson.

Donahue Institute. (2004). *A study of MCAS achievement and promising practices in urban special education: Data analysis and site selection methodology.* Amherst: University of Massachusetts.

Downing, S. M. (2006). Twelve steps for effective test development. In S. M. Downing & T. M. Haladyna (Eds.), *Handbook of test development* (pp. 225–258). Mahwah, NJ: Erlbaum.

Dymond, S., Renzaglia, A. Gilson, C., & Slagor, M. (2007). Defining access to the general curriculum for high school students with significant cognitive disabilities. *Research and Practice for Persons with Severe Disabilities, 32*(1), 1–15.

Education Trust. (2005). *Gaining traction, gaining ground: How some high schools accelerate learning for struggling students.* Washington, DC: Education Trust. Available at http://www2.edtrust.org/NR/rdonlyres/6226B581-83C3-4447-9CE7-31C5694B9EF6/0/GainingTractionGainingGround.pdf

Elledge, A., LeFloch, K. C., Taylor, J., & Anderson, L. (2009). *State and local implementation of the No Child Left Behind Act* (Volume V – Implementation of the 1 percent rule and 2 percent interim policy options). Washington, DC: American Institutes for Research. Retrieved September 30, 2009, from http://www.ed.gov/rschstat/eval/disadv/nclb-disab/nclb-disab.pdf

Elliott, J. L., & Thurlow, M. L. (2006). *Improving test performance of students with disabilities on district and state assessments* (2nd ed.). Thousand Oaks, CA: Corwin.

Elmore, R. F., & Rothman, R. (Eds.). (1999). *Testing, teaching, and learning: A guide for states and school districts.* Washington, DC: National Academy Press.

Flowers, C., Wakeman, S., Browder, D., & Karvonen, M. (2009). An alignment protocol for alternate assessments based on alternate achievement standards. *Educational Measurement: Issues and Practice, 28*(1), 25–37.

Furney, K. S., Hasazi, S. B., Clark/Keefe, K., & Hartnett, J. (2003). A longitudinal analysis of shifting policy landscapes in special and general education reform. *Exceptional Children, 70*(1), 81–94.

Gagnon, J. C., McLaughlin, M. J., Rhim, L. M., & Davis, G. A. (2002). Standards-driven reform policies at the local level: Report on a survey of local special education directors in large districts. *Journal of Special Education Leadership, 15*(1), 3–9.

Gersten, R., Beckmann, S., Clarke, B., Foegen, A., Marsh, L., Star, J. R., & Witzel, B. (2009). *Assisting students struggling with mathematics: Response to Intervention (RtI) for elementary and middle schools* (NCEE 2009-4060). Washington, DC: U.S. Department of Education, Institute of Education Sciences. Retrieved October 5, 2009, from http://ies.ed.gov/ncee/wwc/publications/practiceguides

Gersten, R., Compton, D., Connor, C. M., Dimino, J., Santoro, L., Linan-Thompson, S., & Tilly, W. D. (2008). *Assisting students struggling with reading: Response to Intervention and multi-tier intervention for reading in the primary grades. A practice guide* (NCEE 2009-4045). Washington, DC: National Center for Education Evaluation and Regional Assistance, Institute of Education Sciences, U.S. Department of Education. Retrieved from http://ies.ed.gov/ncee/wwc/publications/practiceguides

Goertz, M. (2007). *Standards-based reform: Lessons from the past, directions for the future.* Paper presented at the Conference on the Uses of History to Inform and Improve Education Policy, Brown University, Providence, RI. Retrieved September 30, 2009 from http://www7.nationalacademies.org/cfe/Goertz%20Paper.pdf

Haertel, E. H. (2008). Standard setting. In K. E. Ryan, & Shepard, L. A. (Eds.), *The future of test-based educational accountability.* New York: Routledge.

Hamilton, L., Halverson, R., Jackson, S., Mandinach, E., Supovitz, J., & Wayman, J. (2009). *Using student achievement data to support instructional decision making* (NCEE 2009-4067). Washington, DC: U.S. Department of Education, Institute of Education Sciences. Retrieved October 5, 2009, from http://ies.ed.gov/ncee/wwc/publications/practiceguides/

Hamilton, L. S., Stecher, B. M., Marsh, J. A., McCombs, J. S., Robyn, A., Russell, J. L., ... & Barney, H. (2007). *Standards-based accountability under No Child Left Behind: Experiences of teachers and administrators in three states.* Santa Monica, CA: RAND Corporation.

Herman, R., Dawson, P., Dee, T., Greene, J., Maynard, R., Redding, S., & Darwin, M. (2008). *Turning around chronically low-performing schools: A practice guide* (NCEE #2008-4020). Washington, DC: U.S. Department of Education, Institute of Education Sciences.

Hess, K., McDivitt, P., & Fincher, M. (2008). *Who are the 2% students and how do we design items that provide greater access for them? Results from a pilot study with Georgia students.* Paper presented at the CCSSO National Conference on Student Assessment, Orlando, FL. Retrieved from http://www.nciea.org/publications/CCSSO_KHPMMF08.pdf

Individuals With Disabilities Education Act (IDEA) of 1997, 20 U.S.C. 1412 et seq. (1997).

Individuals With Disabilities Education Act (IDEA) of 2004, 20 U.S.C. 1415 et seq. (2004).

Johnstone, C. J., Thompson, S. J., Miller, N. A., & Thurlow, M. L. (2008). Universal design and multi-method approaches to item review. *Educational Measurement: Issues and Practice, 27*(1), 25–36.

Jussim, L. J., Madon, S., & Chatman, C. (1994). Teacher expectations and student achievement: Self-fulfilling prophecies, biases, and accuracy. In L. Heath, & R. S. Tindale (Eds.), *Applications of heuristics and biases to social issues* (pp. 303 334). New York: Plenum.

Karvonen, M. (2009). Developing standards-based IEPs that promote effective instruction. In M. Perie (Ed.), *Considerations for the alternate assessment based on modified achievement standards (AA-MAS): Understanding the eligible population and applying that knowledge to their instruction and assessment* (pp. 51–89). Retrieved December 12, 2009, from www.nceo.info/AAMAS/AAMASwhitePaper.pdf

Kearns, J., Towles-Reeves, E., Kleinert, H., Kleinert, J., & Thomas, M. (in press). Student population in alternate assessments based on alternate achievement standards. *Journal of Special Education.*

Ketterlin-Geller, L. R., Alonzo, J., Braun-Monegan, J., & Tindal, G. (2007). Recommendations for accommodations: Implications for (in)consistency. *Remedial and Special Education, 28*(4), 194–206.

Laitusis, C. C. (2007). Research designs and analysis for studying accommodations on assessments. In C. C. Laitusis & L. L. Cook (Eds.), *Large-scale assessment and accommodations: What works?* Arlington, VA: Council for Exceptional Children.

Lazarus, S. S., Thurlow, M. L., Lail, K. E., & Christensen, L. (2009). A longitudinal analysis of state accommodations policies: Twelve years of change 1993–2005. *Journal of Special Education, 43*(2), 67–80.

Martineau, J., Paek, P., Keene, J., & Hirsch, T. (2007). Integrated, comprehensive alignment as a foundation for measuring student progress. *Educational Measurement: Issues and Practice, 26*(1), 28–35.

Mayrowetz, D. (2009). Instructional practice in the context of converging policies: Teaching mathematics in inclusive elementary classrooms in the standards reform era. *Educational Policy, 23*(4), 554–588.

McDonnell, L. M., McLaughlin, M. J., & Morison, P. (Eds.). (1997). *Educating one & all: Students with disabilities and standards-based reform.* Washington, DC: National Academy Press.

McGrew, K. S., & Evans, J. (2004). *Expectations for students with cognitive disabilities: Is the cup half empty or half full? Can the cup flow over?* (Synthesis Report 55). Minneapolis: University of Minnesota, National Center on Educational Outcomes.

McLaughlin, D. H., Bandeira de Mello, V., Blankenship, C., Chaney, K., Esra, P., Hikawa, H., ... Wolman, M. (2008). *Comparison between NAEP and state reading assessment results: 2003* (NCES 2008-474). Washington, DC: U.S. Department of Education, National Center for Education Statistics. Available at http://nces.ed.gov/pubs2008/2008474_1.pdf

McLaughlin, M. J., Henderson, K., & Morando-Rhim, L. (1998). The inclusion of students with disabilities in school reform: An analysis of five local school districts. In S. Vitello & D. Mithaug (Eds.), *Inclusive schooling: National and international perspectives* (pp. 54–75). Hillsdale, NJ: Erlbaum.

McLaughlin, M. J., Nolet, V., Rhim, L. M., & Henderson, K. (1999). Integrating standards: Including all students. *Teaching Exceptional Children, 31*, 66–71.

McLaughlin, M. J., & Thurlow, M. (2003). Educational accountability and students with disabilities: Issues and challenges. *Educational Policy, 17*(4), 431–451.

McREL. (2009). *Content knowledge: A compendium of content standards and benchmarks for K-12 education* (4th ed.). Retrieved September 30, 2009, from http://www.mcrel.org/standards-benchmarks/index.asp

Melnick, R. S. (1995). Separation of powers and the strategy of rights: The expansion of special education. In M. Landy & M. Levin (Eds.), *The new politics of public policy* (pp. 23–46). Baltimore: Johns Hopkins Press.

National Center for Learning Disabilities. (2007). *Rewards & roadblocks: How special education students are faring under No Child Left Behind.* New York: Author.

National Governors' Association. (1986). *Time for results: The governors' 1991 report.* Washington, DC: Author.

Neal, D., & Kirp, D. L. (1986). The allure of legalization reconsidered: The case of special education. In D. L. Kirp & D. Jensen (Eds.), *School days, rule days: The legalization and regulation of education* (pp. 343–365). New York: Falmer Press.

Nolet, V., & McLaughlin, M.J. (2005). *Accessing the general curriculum: Including students with disabilities in standards-based reform* (2nd ed). Thousand Oaks, CA: Corwin Press.

Ohio Department of Education. (2004). *Standards-based instruction for all learners: A treasure chest for principal-led building teams in improving results for learners most at-risk.* Columbus, OH: Author. Retrieved October 9, 2009, from http://education.ohio.gov/GD/Templates/Pages/ODE/ODEDetail.aspx?page=3&TopicRelationID=981&ContentID=7874&Content=75200

Perie, M. (2008). A guide to understanding and developing performance level descriptors. *Educational Measurement: Issues and Practice, 27*(4), 15–29.

Perie, M. (Ed.). (2009). *Considerations for the alternate assessment based on modified achievement Standards (AA-MAS): Understanding the eligible population and applying that knowledge to their instruction and assessment.* Washington, DC: U.S. Department of Education.

President's Commission on Excellence in Special Education. (2002). *A new era: Revitalizing special education for children and their families.* Washington, DC: U.S. Department of Education.

Quenemoen, R. F. (2009a). *Success one student at a time: What the IEP team does.* Minneapolis: University of Minnesota, National Center on Educational Outcomes. Retrieved April 20, 2009, from www.nceo.info/Tools/StandardsIEPtool.pdf

Quenemoen, R. F. (2009b). The long and winding road of alternate assessments: Where we started, where we are now, and the road ahead. In W. D. Schafer & R. W. Lissitz (Eds.), *Alternate assessments based on alternate achievement standards: Policy, practice, and potential* (pp. 127–153). Baltimore: Paul H. Brookes.

Rose, D. H., Meyer, A., & Hitchcock, C. (2005). *The universally designed classroom: Accessible curriculum and digital technologies.* Cambridge, MA: Harvard Education Press.

Schafer, W. D., & Lissitz, R. W. (2009). *Alternate assessments based on alternate achievement standards: Policy, practice, and potential.* Baltimore: Paul H. Brookes.

Shepard, L., Hannaway, J., & Baker, E. (2009). *Standards, assessments, and accountability* (Education Policy White Paper). Washington, DC: National Academy of Education. Retrieved September 25, 2009, from http://www.naeducation.org/Standards_Assessments_Accountability_White_Paper.pdf

Simpson, M., Gong, B., & Marion, S. (2006). *Effect of minimum cell sizes and confidence interval sizes for special education subgroups on school-level AYP determinations* (Synthesis Report 61). Minneapolis: University of Minnesota, National Center on Educational Outcomes.

Sireci, S. G., Scarpati, S. E., & Li, S. (2005). Test accommodations for students with disabilities: An analysis of the interaction hypothesis. *Review of Educational Research, 75*(4), 457–490.

Thompson, S., & Thurlow, M. (2002). *Universally designed assessments: Better tests for everyone!* (Policy Directions No. 14). Minneapolis: University of Minnesota, National Center on Educational Outcomes.

Thompson, S. J., Thurlow, M. L., & Malouf, D. (2004). Creating better tests for everyone through universally designed assessments. *Journal of Applied Testing Technology, 10*(2). Available at http:// www.testpublishers.org/atp.journal.htm

Thurlow, M. L. (2008). Assessment and instructional implications of the alternate assessment based on modified academic achievement standards (AA-MAS). *Journal of Disability Policy Studies, 19*(3), 132–139.

Thurlow, M. L. (2009). *Back to the future for NAEP: NAEP and students with disabilities and English language learners.* Paper presented at the National Assessment Governing Board 20th Anniversary, Washington, DC. Retrieved September 25, 2009, from www.nagb.org/who-we-are/board-anniv.htm

Thurlow, M. L., Johnstone, C., Thompson, S. J., & Case, B. J. (2008). Using universal design research and perspectives to increase the validity of scores on large-scale assessments. In R. C. Johnson & R. E. Mitchell (Eds.), *Testing deaf students in an age of accountability* (pp. 63–75). Washington, DC: Gallaudet University Press.

Thurlow, M. L., Lazarus, S. S., & Christensen, L.L. (2008). Role of assessment accommodations in accountability. *Perspectives on Language and Learning, 34*(4), 17–20.

Thurlow, M., Quenemoen, R., Altman, J., & Cuthbert, M. (2008). *Trends in the participation and performance of students with disabilities* (Technical Report 50). Minneapolis: University of Minnesota, National Center on Educational Outcomes.

Thurlow, M. L., Quenemoen, R. F., Lazarus, S. S., Moen, R. E., Johnstone, C. J., Liu, K. K., ... & Altman, J. (2008). *A principled approach to accountability assessments for students with disabilities* (Synthesis Report 70). Minneapolis: University of Minnesota, National Center on Educational Outcomes.

Wiener, D. (2005). *One state's story: Access and alignment to the GRADE-LEVEL content for students with significant cognitive disabilities* (Synthesis Report 57). Minneapolis: University of Minnesota, National Center on Educational Outcomes.

Zenisky, A. L., & Sireci, S. G. (2007). *A summary of the research on the effects of test accommodations: 2005–2006* (Technical Report 47). Minneapolis: University of Minnesota, National Center on Educational Outcomes.

12

Co-Teaching for Students with Disabilities

A Critical Analysis of the Empirical Literature

Bryan G. Cook
University of Hawaii

Kimberly A. McDuffie-Landrum
Bellarmine University

Linda Oshita and Sara Cothren Cook
University of Hawaii

Co-teaching involves two professionals, often a special education teacher and a general education teacher, delivering instruction to students with and without disabilities in a single physical space (Cook & Friend, 1995). Co-teaching has been described generally as the blending of two pedagogical experts, one (the general educator) with expertise in understanding, structuring, and pacing of the curriculum; and one (the special educator) an expert in identifying students' unique learning needs and adapting the curriculum and instruction accordingly (e.g., Kloo & Zigmond, 2008; McDuffie, Landrum, & Gelman, 2008). In theory, co-teachers collaboratively plan, instruct, manage behavior, and assess (Friend, Reising, & Cook, 1993).

A number of co-teaching models have been described in the literature (Friend & Cook, 2003; McDuffie et al., 2008) including (a) one teach, one assist, (b) station teaching, (c) parallel teaching, (d) alternative teaching, and (e) team teaching. In *one teach, one assist*, one teacher assumes the instructional lead (often, but not necessarily, the general education teacher) while the other teacher monitors student learning and provides assistance to struggling students (often, but not necessarily, the special education teacher). In *station teaching*, typically three independent work-stations are created, two that involve teacher-directed instruction and one that is an independent activity, with three groups of students rotating through each station. In *parallel teaching*, the class is divided into two groups and each group is simultaneously taught the same content by one of the co-teachers. *Alternative teaching* is similar to parallel teaching except that students are grouped based on their individual needs so that specialized instruction can occur. In *team teaching*, co-teachers lead instructional activities together.

Co-teaching has been for some time the most frequently used model for delivering special education in inclusive classrooms (National Center on Educational Restructuring and Inclusion, 1995) and its popularity continues to increase (Kloo & Zigmond, 2008). The popularity of co-teaching no doubt has been spurred by federal and state mandates promoting inclusive instruction, access to the general education curriculum for students with disabilities (SWDs), and highly qualified teachers (HQTs; Quigney, 2009; Scruggs, Mastropieri, & McDuffie, 2007; Simmons & Magiera, 2007). Specifically, recent reauthorizations of the Individuals with Disabilities Education Act (IDEA; 1997, 2004) require that SWDs are (a) educated in the least restrictive environment and (b) involved and progress in the general education curriculum. Further, IDEA 2004 and the No Child Left Behind Act of 2001 stress that SWDs receive instruction from HQTs. In secondary schools, teachers must be experts in the content areas they teach to be considered highly qualified (unless they teach students who take alternate state assessments). This can be problematic for special educators who often teach a number of content areas and typically are not trained as content area experts. Thus, assuming that the general education co-teacher is highly qualified, co-teaching allows schools to provide SWDs access to the general curriculum in an inclusive setting with instruction delivered by a HQT.

In addition to addressing policy mandates, co-teaching's popularity also stems from its strong intuitive appeal (e.g., two heads are better than one). Putting two teachers' heads together to collaboratively deliver instruction in an inclusive environment has been hypothesized to benefit student learning for a number of reasons, including: (a) reduced student:teacher ratio and increased responsiveness to students, (b) improved quality of instruction due to combining the skill sets of general and special education teachers, (c) modeling of collaboration and teamwork, and (d) elimination of the stigma associated with segregated education (e.g., Villa, Thousand, & Nevin, 2008). Indeed, it seems that co-teaching could, potentially, provide SWDs the best of both general and special education—instruction that is (a) based in the general curriculum and delivered in an inclusive environment by a content expert, yet also (b) adapted and modified for students' individual learning needs by a special educator.

Yet despite its instinctive appeal and growing popularity, scholars have suggested that co-teaching should not be considered an effective or evidence-based practice based on the research literature (e.g., Murawski & Swanson, 2001; Weiss & Brigham, 2000). For example, in their meta-analysis, Murawski and Swanson identified only six quantitative studies on co-teaching that met their inclusion criteria—three of which were ERIC documents and none of which explicitly measured treatment integrity. Thus, it is not surprising that Zigmond and Magiera (2001) recommended that co-teaching be *used with caution* due to limited empirical support. Accordingly, Weiss (2004) suggested that the popularity of co-teaching is due to advocacy efforts having outpaced the empirical evidence.

In contrast to inclusion, which has been advanced as an ethical imperative (e.g., Lipsky & Gartner, 1996), co-teaching cannot be justified by claiming a moral high ground. Having two teachers in the same class is inherently no more just than only one teacher. Therefore, the crux of the argument for supporting co-teaching, it seems, lies in its efficacy. Thus, in this chapter, we examine the extant research base regarding the impact of co-teaching on student outcomes. Our review builds on the meta-analysis conducted by Murawski and Swanson (2001) by (a) updating it and (b) applying the standards for evidence-based practices in special education proposed by Gersten et al. (2005) and Horner et al. (2005). Additionally, we critically examine research on co-teaching that has used other research designs (i.e., explanatory, quantitative descriptive, and qualitative) to more fully investigate the empirical support that exists for co-teaching. We conclude the chapter by discussing a theory-based explanation of research findings, challenges and issues to consider when examining the effectiveness of co-teaching, and the implications of research findings for policy and practice.

A Review of Empirical Literature on Co-teaching for SWDs

Previous reviews of the literature can be interpreted as offering some level of support for the effectiveness of co-teaching. For example, Murawski and Swanson's (2001) meta-analysis of quantitative studies on co-teaching yielded an average effect size of 0.40. Although Murawski and Swanson noted that the low number (n = 6) of studies reviewed warrants considerable caution in interpreting their findings, readers may have interpreted the positive effect size to indicate that co-teaching is a research-based, effective practice. We critically analyze the studies examined by Murawski and Swanson and expand upon their review by reviewing (a) experimental and explanatory studies conducted subsequent to their review and (b) non-experimental explanatory (i.e., correlational) and descriptive (i.e., quantitative observational, qualitative) studies to broadly survey the research base on co-teaching and examine whether educators can conclude meaningfully that co-teaching works for SWDs.

Proposed standards for evidence-based practices in special education have been developed for research designs that exhibit experimental control (i.e., group experimental and single-subject research) (Gersten et al., 2005; Horner et al., 2005). Although other research designs contribute to understanding various aspects of special education, they cannot be used to determine reliably whether practices *cause* changes in student outcomes (Cook, Tankersley, Cook, & Landrum, 2008). Accordingly, we review group experiments—both true experiments and quasi-experiments, as well as single-subject research studies on co-teaching and apply standards for determining whether it is an evidence-based practice in special education.

Experimental Research on Co-Teaching for SWDs

Gersten et al. (2005) proposed that for a practice to be considered evidence-based in special education on the basis of group experimental studies (i.e., true experiments and group quasi-experimental designs), it must be supported by two high quality or four acceptable quality group experimental studies and meet minimum thresholds for weighted effect sizes. Practices may also be identified as evidence-based in special education on the basis of single-subject research studies (Horner et al., 2005); however, we located no single-subject research that examined the effects of co-teaching on the outcomes of SWDs.

None of the studies reviewed by Murawski and Swanson (2001) are true group experimental studies in which participants are randomly assigned to groups and researchers actively introduce the intervention. However, we identified two group experiments on co-teaching conducted subsequent to Murawski and Swanson's meta-analysis. Fontana (2005) examined the effect of co-teaching on the English and math grades of students with learning disabilities (LD). Students with LD randomly assigned to the control group (n = 16) were taught in English and math classes with one teacher. Students with LD randomly assigned to the target group (n = 17) were placed in co-taught English and math classes taught by three general education teachers who volunteered to co-teach. Students with LD in both the control and target groups received one period of resource room support. The only comparisons between the outcomes of the two groups involved English and math grades. Grades (calculated from objective measures such as unit tests and quizzes) of target students increased significantly from the end of the previous school year to the end of the co-taught year, whereas no significant improvement was reported for control students with LD. From the data reported by Fontana (2005), we calculated effect sizes (*d*) of 0.81 for English grades and 0.40 for math grades in favor of co-teaching. Findings from this study are difficult to interpret because (a) students in both groups received resource support; (b) no specific approach to co-teaching was described and "teachers used a variety of co-teaching methods throughout the investigation" (p. 20); (c) teacher grades, rather than psychometrically sound assessments, were used as outcome measures; and (d) the limited number of essential quality indicators addressed in the study (see Table 12.1) represent several important threats to the validity of findings.

Murawski (2006) studied the relation of co-teaching to a variety of student outcomes for 110 9th graders (38 of whom were identified as LD) in six English classes in one urban high school. The four conditions consisted of non-inclusive general education class (with no included SWDs), two solo-taught inclusive classes, two co-taught inclusive classes, and one special education class. Three general educators were randomly assigned to general education, solo-taught inclusion, and co-taught inclusion classes. Students with LD were assigned to an inclusive or special education class based on student ability and family preference. However, students with LD selected for an inclusive class were randomly assigned to the co-taught (n = 12) or solo-taught class (n = 8). Covarying for pre-test and ability scores, 2-level hierarchical analyses examining treatment within teacher indicated no significant main effects for condition for standardized tests of spelling, math, vocabulary, reading comprehension, or writing after the 10-week intervention. Specific comparisons of students with LD in the co-taught versus non-co-taught classes were not conducted. However, from the data reported by Murawski (2006), we computed effect sizes for co-teaching (in comparison to solo-teaching) on standardized test results for students with LD in spelling ($d = 1.15$), math ($d = -0.49$), vocabulary ($d = -0.51$), spontaneous writing ($d = -0.95$), and reading comprehension ($d = 0.62$) (mean effect size = –0.04). These effects should be interpreted cautiously due to (a) the low number of participants and (b) multiple threats to validity represented in the quality indicators not met in the study (see Table 12.1).

In quasi-experimental study, researchers do not randomly assign participants to groups for ethical and practical reasons; this increases the likelihood that groups differ meaningfully and warrants caution when interpreting the results of these studies (Cook, Cook, Landrum, & Tankersley, 2008; Creswell, 2009). Nonetheless, quasi-experiments of high or acceptable quality can be used to meet the standards for an evidence-based practice in special education (Gersten et al., 2005). Murawski and Swanson

TABLE 12.1
Presence of Essential Quality Indicators among Group Experimental Studies on Co-teaching

	Rosman, 1994	Fontana, 2005	Murawski, 2006
Describing Participants			
1.1 Was sufficient information provided to determine/confirm whether the participants demonstrated the disability(ies) or difficulties presented?	No	Yes	No
1.2 Were appropriate procedures used to increase the likelihood that relevant characteristics of participants in the sample were comparable across conditions?	Yes	Yes	Yes
1.3 Was sufficient information given characterizing the interventionists or teachers provided? Did it indicate whether they were comparable across conditions?	No	No	No
Implementation of Intervention and Description of Comparison Conditions			
2.1 Was the intervention clearly described and specified?	No	No	No
2.2 Was the fidelity of implementation described and assessed?	No	No	Yes
2.3 Was the nature of services provided in comparison conditions described?	No	No	No
Outcome Measures			
3.1 Were multiple measures used to provide an appropriate balance between measures closely aligned with the intervention and measures of generalized performance?	Yes	Yes	Yes
3.2 Were outcomes for capturing the intervention's effect measured at the appropriate time?	Yes	Yes	Yes
Data Analysis			
4.1 Were the data analysis techniques appropriately linked to key research questions and hypotheses? Were they appropriately linked to the unit of analysis in the study?	Yes	No	Yes
4.2 Did the research report include not only inferential statistics but also effect size calculations?	No*	No*	No*

*Although effect sizes were not reported, data from which effect sizes could be calculated were reported.

(2001) reviewed one quasi-experimental study in their meta-analysis on co-teaching, reporting an average effect size of 0.24 for Rosman's (1994) examination of student outcomes in four "Basics of Algebra" classes at one high school. In this study, one general educator taught the control class, without any involvement of the special educator, as well as a period of "in room assistance" in which the special educator assisted individual students but did not co-plan or deliver large group instruction. A second general educator co-taught two periods of the class with the special educator. The intervention lasted for three weeks, the time it took to cover one chapter in the textbook. After controlling for scores on the previous unit, unit scores for all students were significantly higher in one of the co-teaching classes, but not the other, in comparison to control and in room assistance classes. Analyses conducted specifically on SWDs were not significant, although the largest mean gains in math performance for SWDs occurred for children in the two co-taught classes ($n = 6$). These findings are difficult to interpret due to (a) the low number of participating SWDs; (b) the use of unit scores rather than psychometrically sound assessments as outcome measures; (c) different teachers used for the comparison and intervention conditions; and (d) the low number of essential quality indicators met (see Table 12.1), indicating a number of threats to the validity of findings.

Applying standards for evidence-based practice. To be considered an evidence-based practice in special education on the basis of group experimental research, an intervention must be supported by at least two high (i.e., meeting all but one of 10 essential quality indicators and at least four desirable quality indicators) or four acceptable (i.e., meeting all but one of 10 essential quality indicators and at least one desirable quality indicator) quality studies (Gersten et al., 2005). Two authors independently reviewed each group experimental study for the presence of essential quality indicators. Inter-rater agreement rate across the three studies reviewed was 86.7%. The two reviewers discussed disagreements until they reached consensus. None of the studies met the initial criterion for being an acceptable or high quality study (i.e., addressing all but one of the essential quality indicators). Co-teaching cannot, then, be considered an evidence-based practice in special education according to Gersten et al.'s proposed standards based on the extant literature. None of the studies reviewed sufficiently (a) characterized the interventionists/teachers and indicated that they were comparable across conditions, (b) described and specified the intervention, (c) described the nature of services in the comparison condition, or (d) reported effect sizes (although they all reported data from which effect sizes could be calculated). Moreover, only Murawski addressed fidelity of implementation. These studies did exhibit some methodological strengths. For example, all studies met criteria related to outcome measures and used appropriate procedures to show that participants were comparable across conditions.

Non-experimental, Explanatory Research on Co-teaching for SWDs

Non-experimental, explanatory research designs, which include research that is often referred to as correlational and causal-comparative (Johnson, 2001), examine the relationship between two or more variables. However, because explanatory research may not involve actively introducing an intervention or a comparison group, causality should not be inferred (Cook & Cook, 2008; Creswell, 2009). For example, a researcher may examine student outcomes in one school that had been co-teaching for 3 years and in one that had not used co-teaching. Even if students in the co-teaching school achieved at a higher level, because the researchers did not actively introduce the intervention, it is not clear whether co-teaching caused higher student achievement, high student achievement led to co-teaching, or another variable(s) caused both co-teaching and high achievement. In explanatory studies that examine outcomes among a single group of students before and after co-teaching, one cannot infer causality because without a control group it is impossible to determine whether outcome changes would have occurred in the absence of co-teaching or were caused by variables other than co-teaching.

Although the results of Murawski and Swanson's (2001) meta-analysis have been interpreted as supporting the efficacy of co-teaching (e.g., Morocco & Aguilar, 2002; Wilson & Michaels, 2006), we consider five of the six studies reviewed to be explanatory. Indeed, the largest average effect size (0.95) reported by Murawski and Swanson was for Self, Benning, Marston, and Magnusson's (1991) explanatory study on the effects of placing at-risk students in the Cooperative Teaching Program (CTP), which involved 25 minutes of daily, small group instruction in reading from a special education co-teacher. In the first year of the program, the rates of improvement in words read correctly per minute for nine low achieving students rose from an average of 0.8 words per week before being placed in CTP after to an average of 2.9 words CTP placement—a non-significant difference. In the second year of the program, the improvement rate of 28 referred students increased from 0.6 words per minute each week before CTP placement to 1.8 afterward—a statistically significant difference. However, without a comparison group, it is impossible to know whether reading rates would have accelerated in the absence of the intervention or whether a variable other than the 25 minutes of daily co-teaching caused increased reading rates. Moreover, CTP appears to be a pre-referral program and Self et al. make no mention of SWDs participating in the study.

Lundeen and Lundeen (1993) reported that 49% of all students earned higher grades (whereas 24% earned lower grades) after one semester in a co-teaching program than they had after one semester in the previous year, which was a significantly different proportion than expected by chance. However, at end of school year, 39% of all students had improved grades, whereas 34% had poorer grades, compared to the year before—which was not significantly different from chance. The modestly positive average effect size of 0.25 reported by Murawski and Swanson (2001) is difficult to interpret because (a) of the absence of a meaningful comparison group; (b) analyses were not disaggregated for student with disabilities; and (c) grades, for which "instructors established their own evaluation criteria" (p. 5), rather than scores from psychometrically sound assessments of achievement were used as outcome measures.

Walsh and Snyder (1993) examined student outcomes in 15 co-taught and 15 solo-taught ninth-grade academic classrooms. Across subject areas, no significant differences were found between the absences, referrals, or course grades for the co-taught ($n = 343$) and solo-taught ($n = 363$) participants. However, a significantly higher proportion of co-taught students passed minimum competency tests (67%) than those in solo-taught classes (53%)—resulting in an average effect size of 0.41 (Murawski & Swanson, 2001). However, a number of important threats to validity exist regarding the study's findings, including: (a) researchers did not actively implement the intervention, making it impossible to determine the direction of the relationship between improved student outcomes and co-teaching; (b) severe attrition for the competency test analysis; (c) no data were provided indicating that the groups were equivalent; (d) no information was provided regarding SWDs (e.g., number of students, types of disabilities); and (e) results were not disaggregated for SWDs (indeed, it is not clear whether SWDs were present in solo taught classes).

Vaughn, Elbaum, Schumm, and Hughes (1998) conducted the only study that investigated the relation between co-teaching and social outcomes reviewed by Murawski and Swanson (2001), indicating a negligible average effect size (0.08). The only statistically significant findings favored students who attended a school that used a consultation/collaboration model ($n = 114$), in which a special education teacher was present in inclusive classes for 1 to 2 hours a day. These students improved significantly more in the course of a school year on measures of peer acceptance and friendship quality than did students attending a school that implemented co-teaching ($n = 71$). The authors noted that student group (LD, low/average achiever, high achiever) did not significantly affect findings, and specific comparisons just for students with LD were not conducted. Because the researchers did not actively implement the intervention, readers cannot conclude confidently that consultative/collaborative approaches cause significantly better peer acceptance and quality of friendships than co-teaching.

Klingner, Vaughn, Hughes, Schumm, and Elbaum's (1998) study of co-teaching at an elementary school that implemented a model of "responsible" inclusion that included co-teaching did not involve a comparison group. The improvement of 25 students with LD from fall to spring in co-taught classes was not statistically significant in math computation or application, but it was in reading performance. However, the magnitude of change in reading performance for students with LD was small. Indeed, despite extensive professional development focused on improving student reading performance and an average effect size of 0.50 reported by Murawski and Swanson (2001), Klingner et al. concluded that, "very poor readers … as a group made no progress" (p. 159). Findings from this study are limited further in their generalizability because only those students with LD who were considered likely to benefit from inclusion were placed in the co-taught classes.

Subsequent to the publication of Murawski and Swanson's (2001) meta-analysis, we identified two additional explanatory studies related to co-teaching. Rea, McLaughlin, and Walther-Thomas (2002) compared outcomes of students with LD from a middle school that practiced inclusive co-teaching ($n = 22$) to those of students attending a school that used a pullout model ($n = 36$). Significant findings favoring co-taught students with LD were reported for grades, scores on the Iowa Test of Basic Skills (ITBS) in language and math, and attendance. No significant differences existed between groups on proficiency test scores in reading, writing, or math; on ITBS scores in reading, science, and social studies; and on school suspensions. However, because researchers did not actively introduce the intervention it is difficult to discern the nature of the relationship between co-teaching and student outcomes.

McDuffie, Mastropieri, and Scruggs (2009) examined the differential effects of a peer tutoring intervention in seventh grade co-taught and non co-taught science classes. Participants included 203 seventh-grade students, 62 of whom received special education services. Results indicated statistically significant main effects for co-teaching on both unit tests and cumulative posttest. Effect sizes for SWDs were 0.35 for unit tests and 0.29 for the cumulative test. Limitations to the study include (a) the outcome measures were researcher developed rather than psychometrically sound assessments and (b) researchers did not actively manipulate co-teaching, thereby obfuscating the nature of the relationship between co-teaching and student performance.

Despite a moderate average effect size of 0.40 reported by Murawski and Swanson (2001), five of the six studies reviewed in their meta-analysis used explanatory designs and therefore do not provide strong evidence that co-teaching caused any observed changes in student outcomes. Moreover, the explanatory literature on co-teaching in relation to student outcomes contains mixed findings and many studies are limited by important methodological shortcomings (e.g., co-teaching defined incompletely, no information on treatment fidelity, findings not disaggregated for SWDs). Some explanatory research studies, such as those using a regression discontinuity design and logically-based exclusion methods, can yield findings that approach, but do not reach, the level of causal inferences (Thompson, Diamond, McWilliam, Snyder, & Snyder, 2005). However, none of the explanatory studies on co-teaching used a regression discontinuity approach and none showed clearly that the two groups compared were functionally equivalent except for the presence of co-teaching (i.e., used logically based exclusion methods). Thus, as Murawski and Swanson noted, it appears that the main message of research to date is not that co-teaching has been shown to cause improved student outcomes, but instead that a dearth of data supports clearly the efficacy of co-teaching.

Other Quantitative Research on Co-Teaching for SWDs

Student outcomes are the ultimate measure by which educational interventions ought to be gauged. However, explanatory research that uses dependent variables such as teacher behavior and teacher-student interactions can provide important insights regarding the nature and possible effects of co-teaching. Magiera and Zigmond (2005) observed the instructional experiences of SWDs in 11 co-taught classrooms under routine conditions, with co-teachers having limited training and co-planning time. Observations conducted when (a) both co-teachers were present and (b) only the general education teacher was present indicated that SWDs interacted significantly less with general education teachers but received significantly more individual instruction during co-teaching. However, the magnitude of these differences may not be practically meaningful. For example, individualized instructional interactions occurred approximately 2.2 times per student with a disability every 6.6 classroom periods during co-teaching, in comparison to once every 6.6 classes during solo teaching. No differences between conditions were observed for 11 other dependent variables, including on-task behavior, student participation, and student grouping arrangements. Whole class instruction was the predominant instructional arrangement during both co-taught and solo taught classes. Whereas Magiera and Zigmond found little difference in teacher-student interactions between co-taught and solo taught settings, McDuffie et al. (2009) reported that students with and without disabilities in four solo taught middle school classes interacted significantly more often with their teacher than did students in four co-taught classes. In addition, they found no significant differences between the instructional methods observed in co-taught versus solo taught classes.

Researchers have also quantified observations of teacher behavior in terms of the roles they assume in co-taught settings. Magiera, Smith, Zigmond, and Gebauer's (2005) observations of 20 co-taught secondary math classes indicated that the dominant instructional arrangements involved (a) both teachers monitoring individual seatwork and (b) the general educator teaching the whole class with the special educator supporting individual students. Team teaching occurred in only nine of the 49 observed co-taught classes and lasted only a short time when it was used. Harbort et al.'s (2007) observations of two co-teaching teams also indicated that general education teachers typically took the lead presenting material, whereas special education teachers spent only 1% of their time presenting instruction. Indeed, they reported that they only observed the one teach, one observe model being implemented. Zigmond and Matta (2004) reported similar dominant roles for special education co-teachers: individual/small group work 46.7% of the time, observing 22.3% of the time, co-teaching 17%, lead teaching 5.7%, planning 4.2%, and doing clerical work 4.1%. Moreover, Murawski (2006) reported that co-teachers spent a large amount of their time engaged in non-instructional activities (32.5% for general educators, 46.5% for special educators), very little time individualizing instruction (5% for both general and special educators), and no time managing student behavior.

In summary, quantitative explanatory and descriptive research indicates that the theorized benefits of co-teaching such as high levels of student:teacher interactions, use of individualized instruction, and team-teaching may not commonly occur. Indeed, it appears that traditional instructional formats (e.g., whole group instruction lead by the general education teacher) are common, with special education co-teachers often engaged in non-instructional activities. Many of these findings are supported by the qualitative research on co-teaching.

Qualitative Research on Co-teaching for SWDs

The purpose of qualitative research is to describe or explain phenomena and thus it provides insights on what is happening within a classroom, why a particular teaching practice may or may not be effective, or how participants feel about an instructional technique (Brantlinger, Jimenez, Klingner, Pugach, & Richardson, 2005). A significant body of qualitative research has provided a rich description about the implementation of a co-teaching, including elaboration of critical components and perceptions of key players (see Scruggs et al., 2007, for a review of this literature). Although these studies provide a wealth of information, they were not designed to yield causal conclusions about the effectiveness of co-teaching (McDuffie & Scruggs, 2008).

Scruggs et al. (2007) meta-synthesized 32 qualitative investigations of co-teaching, identifying themes that fell into four categories: (a) benefits, (b) expressed needs, (c) teacher roles, and (d) instructional delivery. Among the benefits, co-teachers reported that co-teaching enhanced their professional development. Special education teachers referred to an increase in content knowledge and general education teachers cited increased knowledge in effective classroom management and curriculum adaptation (e.g., Austin, 2001). Teachers also perceived that students with and without disabilities benefited from additional teacher attention (e.g., Rice & Zigmond, 2000; Walther-Thomas, 1997), exposure to peer models of appropriate behavior (e.g., Vesay, 2004), and teacher modes of collaboration (e.g., Carlson, 1996; Hardy, 2001).

Scruggs et al. (2007) found that participants perceived administrative support, planning time, training, compatibility, and volunteerism to be among the most important factors in the success of co-teaching. Teachers felt that they could not typically achieve successful co-teaching without administration providing supports such as arranging for co-planning time (e.g., Carlson, 1996; Thompson, 2001). Research participants also noted the need for training focused on flexibility, instructional skills, knowledge of co-teaching models, effective communication, and disability characteristics for general education teachers (e.g., Buckley, 2005; Walther-Thomas, 1997). Finally, attitudinal and interpersonal variables perceived as important for successful co-teaching—such enthusiasm, perseverance, and compatibility—may be facilitated by allowing co-teachers to volunteer (e.g., Carlson, Rice, & Zigmond, 2000).

In relation to teacher roles, one teach, one assist was reported and observed to be the dominant co-teaching model implemented—with the general education teacher generally taking the role as the lead teacher while the special education teacher assumed a subordinate role, oftentimes being viewed as an assistant (Scruggs et al., 2007). The level of content knowledge of the special education teacher was perceived as critical in determining their co-teaching role; special educators with greater content area expertise often assumed greater responsibility in delivery of instruction (e.g., Pugach & Wesson, 1995; Rice & Zigmond, 2000). In addition to struggling with content knowledge, special education teachers often faced turf issues and reported that they struggled with fitting into general education teachers' classrooms (Morocco & Aguilar, 2002).

Finally, Scruggs et al. (2007) described reports and observations of instruction in co-taught classes. Typically, general education teachers preferred strategies that could be used with the entire class and resisted individualizing instruction (e.g., Anita, 1999; Buckley; 2005). The role of the special education teacher was limited during typical whole class instruction, and few opportunities existed to implement individualized or other supplemental instruction. Rarely were effective inclusive strategies such as mnemonics, strategy instruction, or instructing students in small groups utilized in co-taught classes (e.g., Hardy, 2001; Mastropieri et al., 2005). However, peer mediation in the form of cooperative learning or peer tutoring was utilized successfully in some co-taught classes (e.g., Mastropieri et al.; Pugach & Wesson, 1995).

In summary, the extant body of qualitative research on co-teaching suggests that participants in this process generally view it as beneficial and believe that it holds great potential for facilitating successful inclusion of SWDs in content area classes. *However, it is important to emphasize that perceived effectiveness does not equate with actual effectiveness.* Without research that utilized an experimental design, research consumers cannot know with confidence whether participants' perceptions are valid and whether any improved outcomes were actually caused by co-teaching. The qualitative literature also indicates some concerns with co-teaching, such as (a) predominant use of the one-teach, one assist model; (b) special education teachers not always participating fully in co-teaching; and (c) infrequent use of individualized instruction.

Summary of Empirical Literature on Co-teaching for SWDs

Experimental research studies are unique in that, when conducted with high methodological rigor, they yield findings from which one can reasonably infer causality, especially when findings accord with the results of other high quality experimental studies. To determine whether co-teaching might be considered an evidence-based practice in special education, we examined experimental studies included in the Murawski and Swanson's (2001) meta-analysis as well as more recent experimental studies that examined the effect of co-teaching on the outcomes of SWDs. None of three identified studies addressed a sufficient number of quality indicators to meet Gersten et al.'s (2005) criteria for being a high or acceptable quality group experimental study. On the basis of the literature reviewed, then, co-teaching should not be considered an evidence-based practice in special education.

We also reviewed explanatory (i.e., correlational) research studies on co-teaching for SWDs. Although one cannot infer causality from the findings of these studies, a large number of converging, high quality, theory-driven, explanatory studies can produce findings that oftentimes are accepted as demonstrating causality—as in the case of smoking and lung cancer (Beyea & Nicoll, 1999). Some explanatory studies did indicate a positive relationship between co-teaching and increased student outcomes (e.g., McDuffie et al., 2009; Rea et al., 2002; Walsh & Snyder, 1993). However, this body of research should not be interpreted as supporting a nearly causal link between co-teaching and improved student outcomes for a number of reasons, including (a) none of the studies used regression discontinuity or logically-based exclusion approaches, (b) relatively few explanatory studies have been conducted on the topic and some studies show little or no effect for SWDs (e.g., Klingner et al., 1998; Vaughn et al., 1998), (c) some studies did not include SWDs or disaggregate findings for SWDs (e.g., Lundeen & Lundeen, 1993; Self et al., 1991; Walsh & Snyder, 1993), and (d) many studies contain a number of methodological shortcomings (e.g., intervention not described adequately, fidelity of implementation not assessed, outcome measures not psychometrically sound).

We also reviewed explanatory studies that did not use student outcomes as the dependent variable, quantitative descriptive (i.e., observational) studies, and qualitative studies related to co-teaching for SWDs to provide a broad look at potential reasons why co-teaching might, or might not, be an effective practice in SWDs. Although this research suggests that teachers generally perceive co-teaching to be beneficial, it also indicates that (a) co-teaching typically involves the general educator teaching the whole class while the special education teacher assists or monitors individual students with little variety in teacher roles or student groupings (e.g., Magiera et al., 2005); (b) special education teachers often feel under-utilized and out of place in co-teaching situations (e.g., Mastropieri et al., 2005); (c) instruction is seldom individualized nor does it incorporate research-based practices (e.g., Magiera et al., 2005; Mastropieri et al., 2005); and (d) co-teaching is not related to increased student-teacher interactions (Magiera & Zigmond, 2005; McDuffie et al., 2009). Although these findings do not appear to support the presumed benefits of having an additional teacher in the classroom, they (a) are consistent with theoretical perspectives on joint outcome production and (b) have a number of implications for research, policy, and practice.

Explanations and Implications of Research Findings on Co-teaching for SWDs

Theory-based Explanation of Research Findings on Co-teaching for SWDs

Gerber and Semmel (1985) proposed a microeconomic model of joint outcome production to portray the dilemma that a teacher faces when deciding how to allocate scarce instructional resources to students with varied learning needs. In essence, when a teacher focuses her instructional time, attention, strategies, and physical resources to meet the needs of a student or students with certain learning needs, she is, in the zero sum equation of classroom instruction, effectively taking away instructional time, attention, strategies, and physical resources from students with dissimilar learning needs. Teachers with static resources, then, are bounded by a theoretical limit of joint outcomes for their students. So long as instructional resources (e.g., teacher time, quality of instruction) remain constant, any attempt to improve the performance of some students by allocating them more resources entails a corresponding decrease in resources, and hence learning opportunities, provided to students with dissimilar learning needs.

Figure 12.1 represents the potential outcomes in a simplified class attended by two students—a low achiever (Student A) and a high achiever (Student B). The teacher can choose to focus all of her resources on Student B, resulting in the joint outcomes represented by point C, at which the Student B's achievement is maximized and Student A's is minimized. Conversely, the teacher may choose to maximize Student A's achievement, at the relative cost of Student B's achievement, by focusing resources solely on Student A (represented by point E). Most teachers compromise and allocate instructional resources somewhat equitably between students, resulting in outcomes that are neither maximized nor minimized for either student (represented by point D). The important point is that without an infusion of resources or enhanced instructional efficacy, the teacher cannot generate joint student outcomes beyond the theoretical boundary represented by line CDE.

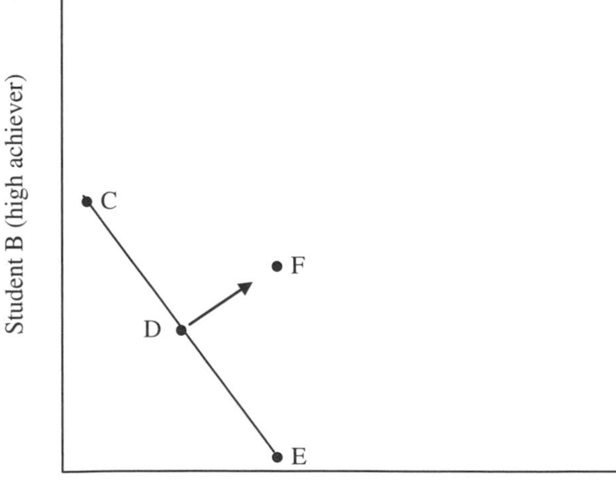

Figure 12.1 Theoretical distribution of joint outcomes. Adapted from Gerber, M. M. (2005). Teachers are still the test: Limitations of response to instruction strategies for identifying children with learning disabilities. *Journal of Learning Disabilities, 38,* 516–524. Copyright © 2005 by SAGE Publications. Reprinted by Permission of SAGE Publications.

A primary challenge of classroom instruction is how to move beyond this threshold of joint outcomes, allowing both high and low achievers to simultaneously increase achievement (e.g., move from point D to point F). Gerber (2005) posited that this "is impossible without *new* resources, including, for example, resources embodied in new people (e.g., aides, partner teachers, specialists) or new, more powerful *technologies* for using *existing* resources" (p. 518).

Co-teaching would seem to be a logical solution to Gerber and Semmel's (1985) dilemma of scarce resources because it introduces an entire new teacher into the (no longer zero sum) classroom equation. Presumably, the presence of another teacher allows the original teacher to increase her instructional time and strategies applied to one learner type without reducing the educational opportunities of other students. Indeed, the newly added co-teacher can not only maintain, but actually increase, the instructional resources brought to bear on the other students. Thus, it appears that co-teaching potentially frees teachers from the limits of the microeconomic model of joint outcome production by introducing a significant new instructional resource into the classroom environment, thereby enabling the possibility of simultaneously increasing the outcomes of students with different learning needs.

Research findings, however, have not shown that co-teaching consistently and meaningfully results in improved outcomes for included SWDs. We conjecture that this may be due to the co-teacher not being utilized in a way that provides a value-added effect on student outcomes. That is, in certain instructional situations, the presence of an additional instructor may do little to promote the achievement of students who are not the targeted recipients of the instruction delivered by the original teacher. For example, assume that the one teaches, one assists model of co-teaching is used, featuring primarily whole class instruction and independent seatwork. Further assume that students are instructed using the grade level curriculum and that the new co-teacher provides little individualized instruction and does not introduce new instructional techniques. If the functioning level of some students is below grade level, adding a co-teacher who merely monitors and assists those students while they receive whole class instruction and do independent seatwork on work that is beyond their zone of proximal development is unlikely to produce any real benefit. Regardless of how many teachers are present in a class, it will be difficult for SWDs to make meaningful gains in outcomes if (a) content is not matched to students' individual learning needs and (b) students are taught with undifferentiated instruction in large groups or complete work independently at their seats. In terms of Gerber and Semmel's (1985) microeconomic model, co-teaching provides the potential for jointly increasing the outcomes of students with varied learning needs (e.g., jumping from point D to point F), but that potential would remain latent if the infusion of instructional resources represented by the special education co-teacher does not better meet the learning needs of SWDs.

In essence, if co-teachers engage in "business as usual" with their instruction, we should expect business as usual with students' outcomes. Observations indicate that common conditions in co-taught classes include one teacher teaching and one assisting (i.e., monitoring), infrequent use of differentiated instructional techniques, reliance on whole class instruction and individual seatwork, and special educators being underutilized and used as aides (Scruggs et. al., 2007). It seems predictable that this type of co-teaching will not result in increased student outcomes for SWDs. In contrast, co-teaching that involves instructing students in small groups using differentiated instruction and materials can and should lead to improved outcomes for students with varied learning needs. The latter scenario (i.e., effective co-teaching) requires teachers to step out of traditional teaching roles and reconceptualize their responsibilities, and may therefore require significant preparation, training, and ongoing support.

Implications and Recommendations for Research

Perhaps the clearest message to be drawn from reviewing the research on co-teaching is the pressing need for more high quality, experimental research to determine meaningfully whether co-teaching works for SWDs (Murawski & Swanson, 2001). Conducting group experimental research, which requires random assignment to groups, in schools is very difficult (e.g., Berliner, 2002). Researchers, though, can use other research designs that can yield meaningful findings regarding the effectiveness of co-teaching. For example, single subject research allows researchers to demonstrate a functional relationship between an intervention (e.g., co-teaching) and student outcomes without requiring a randomly assigned control group. A multiple baseline design may be an attractive option for researchers, in that it would not require that classrooms alternate between co-teaching and traditional teaching as an ABAB design would (see Kazdin, 1982). In a multiple baseline design, the implementation of co-teaching could be staggered across classrooms or subject areas within a single classroom. If student outcomes increased meaningfully subsequent to the staggered introduction of co-teaching across environments, researchers would provide evidence that co-teaching caused improved student outcomes. Individuals or groups of students (e.g., all SWDs in a co-taught class) might serve as the unit of analysis in single-subject research on co-teaching. High quality, quasi-experimental studies represent another option that does not require random assignment. Quasi-experiments introduce or withhold the intervention to pre-existing groups (Creswell, 2009). Although threats to validity are inherent to quasi-experimental designs due to non-random assignment to groups, confidence in the validity of findings increases to the degree that researchers show that groups being compared are functionally equivalent (Cook, Cook, et al., 2008).

Regardless of the research design, we urge researchers investigating the effectiveness of co-teaching to adhere to the methodological quality indicators proposed for group experimental (Gersten et al., 2005), single-subject (Horner et al., 2005), correlational (Thompson et al., 2005), and qualitative (Brantlinger et al., 2005) research. It is difficult to draw firm conclusions from the extant co-teaching research because of methodological limitations (e.g., outcome measures without established psychometrics, insufficient description of co-teaching and control conditions, no documentation of fidelity of implementation). By addressing these and other quality indicators, future researchers can begin to determine more meaningfully the degree to which co-teaching works for SWDs.

Researchers investigating the effects of co-teaching have and will continue to face several challenges. First, ensuring that co-teaching is consistently applied across teachers, classes, and time is a considerable challenge, but is necessary to validly determine its impact. Co-teaching can take many different forms, and researchers have noted that the model of co-teaching utilized often varies between classrooms and within co-teachers over time (e.g., Fontana, 2005; Mastropieri et al., 2005). It is perhaps not surprising that findings from the studies examining the effectiveness of co-teaching for SWDs vary considerably and often show small effects. A variety of more and less effective approaches are likely being examined together under the umbrella of co-teaching. Exacerbating this problem, many researchers do not define or operationally describe how teachers implement co-teaching in their studies, resulting in findings that are difficult to generalize. Accordingly, we recommend that future researchers study the effectiveness of specific models and approaches to co-teaching, rather than co-teaching in general, and (a) operationally define the model of co-teaching and how it was implemented, and (b) measure fidelity of implementation throughout the study to ensure that the model of co-teaching was utilized as intended.

Second, researchers will be challenged to isolate the effect of co-teaching. As is the case for research on inclusion (e.g., Semmel, Gottleib, & Robinson, 1979), it is very difficult to remove the impact of the teacher and the quality of instruction from the effects of co-teaching. It is probable that very good teachers using effective instruction will increase student performance whether in a co-taught or solo taught class; and, conversely, that lower quality teaching will not meaningfully improve student outcomes regardless of where it occurs. Group studies involving large numbers of teachers who are randomly assigned to conditions, especially when analyzed using multi-level approaches such as hierarchical linear modeling (Raudenbush & Bryk, 2002), as well as single-subject research studies that operationally describe participating teachers and instructional conditions can help to address this concern.

Third, researchers will be challenged to pose questions of optimal practical significance with their research. Commenting on the efficacy research literature on inclusion, Zigmond (2003) suggested that the question, what is the best place to educate SWDs? (i.e., does inclusion work?) misses the mark. Rather, she cogently recommended that educators consider whether inclusion is best for whom? and best for what? Broad educational approaches such as inclusion and co-teaching seem to defy simple and broad categorizations. Rather, researchers might seek to address more nuanced questions when designing studies on co-teaching. We recommend that researchers examine the effects of specific co-teaching models for particular types of learners, teachers with specific characteristics, and specific outcomes. For example, a study might compare the effects of the "one teaches, one assists model of co-teaching to team teaching, as well as to a control group, and disaggregate findings for students with different disabilities.

Implications and Recommendations for Policy

The gap between research and practice has received considerable attention in the special education literature (e.g., Carnine, 1997). Yet gaps between policy and practice also exist, which may underlie and exacerbate the research-to-practice gap (Tankersley, Landrum, & Cook, 2004). Co-teaching, like inclusion, appears to be an example of a policy that is enacted without sufficient research supporting its efficacy. However, unlike inclusion, which may be justified on a moral basis, co-teaching policies are justified only to the degree to which they bring about improved student outcomes. Our review of the empirical literature on co-teaching indicates that, despite co-teaching's strong intuitive appeal, the experimental research base is sparse and suggests that the effects of co-teaching vary. Accordingly, we recommend that policy-makers exercise considerable caution in mandating co-teaching, especially considering that it is a resource intensive endeavor.

When making decisions about whether to adopt co-teaching, policy-makers may want to consider not only whether co-teaching is effective, but also the degree to which it is efficient. Educators typically are interested not only in the effectiveness of a practice, but also its efficiency. For example, as Bloom (1984) noted, the most effective approach known for instructing students is one-to-one instruction. Yet this approach is extraordinarily inefficient (i.e., costly) and therefore typically not used. Policy implementation always comes at a cost, both literally (e.g., hiring two teachers for one class, purchasing new curricular materials) and by taking resources away from other policies that might otherwise be implemented. Given the substantial cost of adding a special education teacher to multiple classrooms, what effect is sufficient to justify co-teaching? It seems to us that we should expect more than a small impact on student outcomes when two, rather than one, teachers are present in a class. The appropriate comparison for co-teaching may, then, not be classes in which SWDs receive little or no special education support, but rather classes that utilize interventions as costly as co-teaching.

Policy-makers should also take care not to implement co-teaching in ways that diminish its chances for success in order to lessen costs. For example, to alleviate the need for a co-teacher in all classes, which would make the cost prohibitive for most schools, many schools elect to place a large number of SWDs (Vaughn et al., 1998) and other at-risk, low achieving students (e.g., Boudah, Schumacher, & Deshler, 1997; Cook & Tankersley, 2007) in the same co-taught classes. However, this arrangement may create more problems than co-teaching solves. That is, given the diversity of needs present in what is, in effect, a special education classroom placed in the midst of a difficult general education classroom, even two teachers may be insufficient to adequately address students' intense and varied learning and behavioral needs.

Nonetheless, co-teaching provides a logical means for meeting mandates for inclusion, access to the general curriculum, and HQTs in content areas—so we expect that some schools will continue to adopt co-teaching policies without waiting for conclusive evidence of its effectiveness. We speculate that selecting models of co-teaching to match instructional objectives and student characteristics, rather than consistently using the one teach, one assist model, may enhance the impact of co-teaching for SWDs. Parallel teaching provides the opportunity to decrease the number of students each teacher instructs; alternative teaching provides the opportunity to pre-teach or re-teach content to groups of students; station teaching provides the opportunity for flexible grouping and greatly reduced student:teacher ratios; and team teaching provides the opportunity to model true collaboration and brings the expertise of two teachers to bear on student learning. Further, when implementing co-teaching policies, we encourage policy-makers to provide ongoing training, monitoring, and support for teachers in selecting and implementing a variety of specific co-teaching models rather than mandate co-teaching generically, which appears to typically result in the one teach, one assist model.

Implications and Recommendations for Practice

Given that research has not yet demonstrated reliably that co-teaching (or specific models of co-teaching) is effective for raising the outcomes (generally, or in specific areas) for SWDs (or for particular groups of SWDs), it is especially important that educators closely monitor (a) the targeted outcomes of SWDs and (b) their implementation of co-teaching. By using psychometrically sound and research-based approaches to progress monitoring such as curriculum-based measurement (Deno, 2003), teachers can generate formative assessment data to determine if and when co-teaching is not producing desired performance gains and should be altered or discontinued. Given that co-teaching can take many forms, we also recommend that co-teachers self-monitor (or, better yet, be periodically observed to objectively determine) models of co-teaching used, instructional groupings and strategies implemented, and co-teaching roles assumed on a day-to-day basis. By cross-referencing this information with student outcome data, co-teachers can determine what types of co-teaching work best for promoting specific outcomes for particular students.

Most generally, we urge special educators not to abandon the core principles of special education (e.g., flexibility; intensive, individualized instruction in small groups; progress monitoring and assessment; use of research-based instructional practices) while co-teaching. Co-teaching should be recognized as an organizational approach that can, depending on how it is implemented, facilitate or impede effective special education. But it should not be mistaken as the primary driver of student outcomes. Co-teaching cannot replace high quality education, but instead should be viewed as a vehicle for delivering effective instructional approaches geared to meet students' learning needs. Nonetheless, tentative guidelines for implementing effective co-teaching can be gleaned from the preliminary data available.

Teachers report that supportive administrators can facilitate the success of co-teaching by providing common planning periods, allowing teachers to volunteer for co-teaching, and delivering meaningful in-service training (Scruggs et al., 2007). Co-teachers report that common planning time is critically important to the success of co-teaching (e.g., Austin, 2001; Dieker, 2001). In many instances, some reallocation of time is necessary to allow teachers to meet, discuss, reflect upon, and come to agreement on the many issues involved with co-teaching. Administrators might also take into account issues such as educational philosophy, content expertise, experience, disciplinary expectations, and willingness to co-teach (e.g., Mastropieri et al., 2005; Rice & Zigmond, 2000) when selecting and pairing co-teachers to facilitate interpersonal and instructional compatibility. Finally, teachers suggest that administrators should provide ongoing professional development for both co-teachers in areas such as content knowledge, instructional strategies, classroom management, assessment techniques, and effective communication (e.g., Walther-Thomas, 1997).

Beyond administrative and logistical support, co-teachers have suggested a number of characteristics of effective co-teaching teams such as flexibility; shared responsibility and planning; shared physical space; shared responsibility for all students; defined, active roles; use of differentiated instruction; and effective communication and conflict resolution. Effectively planning and delivering co-taught instruction to meet the varied needs of students may be best accomplished when both teachers are willing to compromise and try new things (e.g., Dieker & Murawski, 2003). It also appears important for co-teachers to collaboratively plan a system at the beginning of the year for grading, classroom management, instruction, and making accommodations for students (e.g., Dieker, 2001; Murawski & Dieker, 2004). Delegating sole responsibility for any issue to one teacher may result in a disjointed classroom. One way to facilitate joint ownership of a co-taught class may for both teachers to have their own physical space (e.g., Murawski & Dieker, 2004). Furthermore, discussing issues such as classroom arrangement and decoration may empower both teachers and alleviate potential conflict (e.g., Murawski & Dieker, 2004; Vaughn et al., 1998). However, despite co-teachers' best efforts, it is important to recognize that co-teaching is unpredictable and that unanticipated problems and disagreements are bound to arise. Co-teachers should expect this and be prepared to communicate effectively and resolve disagreements professionally (e.g., Mastropieri et al., 2005).

Just as it is recommended that co-teachers share physical space and planning, jointly sharing the responsibility of delivering instruction to all students appears desirable. Ideally, the notion of "your kids" and "my kids" is replaced with the common understanding of "our kids" in co-teaching (e.g., Vaughn et al., 1998). Establishing clear and active roles for both co-teachers may further enhance the positive impact of co-taught instruction (e.g., Dieker, 2001; Murawski & Dieker, 2004). Although roles can vary from lesson to lesson, it is important that both teachers have purposeful and active instructional roles, avoiding prolonged periods of instructional non-engagement. Co-teachers have also noted individualized and specialized instruction is especially important for SWDs and at-risk students who require more structured and explicit instructional strategies than are often provided in whole class instruction (e.g., Dieker & Murawski, 2003; Murawski & Dieker, 2004).

These recommendations are drawn primarily from reports of co-teachers and, as such, are based in the reality of real co-teaching experiences and demonstrate high face validity. Moreover, they accord with our theory-driven recommendations that co-teaching must make use of the additional instructional resources embodied in a co-teacher by engaging in active and specialized instruction rather than continuing with business as usual. However, it is important to recognize that these recommendations have not been vetted through experimental research, and therefore should be implemented with caution.

Conclusion

Our review of the empirical literature indicated that experimental research on co-teaching continues to be sparse and inconclusive. Explanatory and descriptive (both quantitative and qualitative) research on co-teaching provides some tentative, initial guidelines for effective co-teaching. However, this body of research also indicates that common instructional conditions in general education that tend to be problematic for SWDs (e.g., whole class instruction, undifferentiated curriculum and instruction) are replicated frequently in co-taught classes. Thus, we recommend educators retain the core tenets of special education (e.g., flexibility; intensive, individualized instruction in small groups; progress monitoring and assessment; use of research-based instructional practices) when co-teaching SWDs. Although future research is necessary to more fully determine the effects of such an approach, we theorize that applying the additional instructional resources embodied in a co-teacher to meet the unique needs of SWDs can result in generally improved outcomes for these students. Conversely, utilizing roles and instructional approaches traditionally encountered in general education classes appear unlikely to improve outcomes for SWDs regardless of how many teachers are present.

References

Anita, S. D. (1999). The roles of special educators and classroom teachers in an inclusive school. *Journal of Deaf Studies and Deaf Education, 4*, 203–214.

Austin, V. L. (2001). Teachers' beliefs about co-teaching. *Remedial and Special Education, 22*, 245–255.

Berliner, D. C. (2002). Educational research: The hardest science of all. *Educational Researcher, 31*(8), 18–20.

Beyea, S., & Nicoll, L. (1999). A primer on causality in research. *AORN Journal*. Retrieved on August 13, 2009, from http://findarticles.com/p/articles/mi_m0FSL/is_4_69/ai_54367126/?tag=content;col1

Bloom, B. S. (1984). The 2 sigma problem: The search for methods of group instruction as effective as one-to-one tutoring. *Educational Researcher, 13*(6), 4–16.

Boudah, D., Schumacher, J., & Deshler, D. (1997). Collaborative instruction: Is it an effective option for inclusion in secondary classrooms? *Learning Disability Quarterly 20*, 293–316.

Brantlinger, E., Jimenez, R., Klingner, J., Pugach, M., & Richardson, V. (2005). Qualitative studies in special education. *Exceptional Children, 71,* 195–207.

Buckley, C. (2005). Establishing and maintaining collaborative relationships between regular and special education teachers in middle school social studies inclusive classrooms. In T. E. Scruggs & M. A. Mastropieri (Eds.), *Cognition and learning in diverse settings: Advances in learning and behavioral disabilities* (Vol. 18, pp. 153–198). Oxford, UK: Elsevier Science.

Carlson, L. D. (1996). Co-teaching for integration: An exploratory study. *Dissertation Abstracts International, 57* (08), 3389A. (UMI No. NN116586)

Carnine, D. (1997). Bridging the research-to-practice gap. *Exceptional Children, 63,* 513–521.

Cook, B. G., & Cook, L. (2008). Non-experimental quantitative research and its role in guiding instruction. *Intervention in School & Clinic, 44*(2), 98–104.

Cook, B. G., & Tankersley, M. (2007). Introduction to the special issue: Side Effects of Inclusion: The unforeseen impact of including students with learning disabilities. *Learning Disabilities: A Multidisciplinary Journal, 14*, 131–133.

Cook, B. G., Tankersley, M., Cook, L., & Landrum, T. J. (2008). Evidence-based practices in special education: Some practical considerations. *Intervention in School & Clinic, 44*(2), 69–75.

Cook, L., Cook, B. G., Landrum, T. J., & Tankersley, M. (2008). Examining the role of group experimental research in establishing evidence-based practices. *Intervention in School and Clinic. 44,* 76–82.

Cook, L., & Friend, M. (1995). Co-teaching: Guidelines for creating effective practices. *Focus on Exceptional Children, 28*(3), 1–15.

Creswell, J.W. (2009). *Research design: Qualitative, quantitative, and mixed methods approaches* (3rd ed.). Thousand Oaks, CA: Sage.

Deno, S. L. (2003). Developments in curriculum-based measurement. *Journal of Special Education, 37*, 184–192.

Dieker, L. A. (2001). What are the characteristics of "effective" middle and high school co-taught teams for SWDs? *Preventing School Failure, 46*, 14–23.

Dieker, L. A., & Murawski, W. W. (2003). Co-teaching at the secondary level: Unique trends, current trend, and suggestions for success. *The High School Journal, 86*(4), 1–13.

Fontana, K. C. (2005). The effects of co-teaching on the achievement of eighth grade students with learning disabilities. *The Journal of At-Risk Issues, 11*, 17–23.

Friend, M., & Cook, L. (2003). *Interactions: Collaboration skills for school professionals* (4th ed.). New York: Longman.

Friend, M., Reising, M., & Cook, L. (1993). Co-teaching: An overview of the past, glimpse at the present, and considerations for the future. *Preventing School Failure, 37*, 6–10.

Gerber, M. M. (2005). Teachers are still the test: Limitations of response to instruction strategies for identifying children with learning disabilities. *Journal of Learning Disabilities, 38*, 516–524.

Gerber, M. M., & Semmel, M. I. (1985). The microeconomics of referral and reintegration: A paradigm for evaluation of special education. *Studies in Educational Evaluation, 11*, 13–29.

Gersten, R., Fuchs, L..S., Compton, D., Coyne, M., Greenwood, C., & Innocenti, M..S. (2005). Quality indicators for group experimental and quasi-experimental research in special education. *Exceptional Children, 71*, 149–164.

Harbort, G., Gunter, P. L., Hull, K., Brown, Q., Venn, M. L., Wiley, L. P., & Wiley, E. W. (2007). Behaviors of teachers in co-taught classes in a secondary school. *Teacher Education and Special Education, 30*, 13–23.

Hardy, S..D. (2001). A qualitative study of the instructional behaviors and practices of a dyad of educators in self-contained and inclusive co-taught secondary biology classrooms during a nine week science instruction grading period. *Dissertation Abstracts International, 61* (12), 4731A. (UMI No. 3000278)

Horner, R. H., Carr, E. G., Halle, J., McGee, G., Odom, S., & Wolery, M. (2005). The use of single-subject research to identify evidence-based practice in special education. *Exceptional Children, 71*, 165–179.

Individuals With Disabilities Education Act (IDEA) of 1997, 20 U.S.C. 1412 *et seq.* (1997).

Individuals With Disabilities Education Act (IDEA) of 2004, 20 U.S.C. 1415 *et seq.* (2004).

Johnson, B. (2001). Toward a new classification of nonexperimental quantitative research *Educational Researcher, 30*(2), 3–13.

Kazdin, A. E. (1982). *Single-case research designs: Methods for clinical and applied settings.* New York: Oxford University Press.

Klingner, J. K., Vaughn, S., Hughes, S. T., Schumm, J. S., & Elbaum, B. (1998). Outcomes for students with and without learning disabilities in inclusive classrooms. *Learning Disabilities Research and Practice, 13*, 153–161.

Kloo, A., & Zigmond, N. (2008). Coteaching revisited: Redrawing the blueprint. *Preventing School Failure, 52*(2), 12–20.

Lipsky, D. K., & Gartner, A. (1996). Inclusion, school restructuring, and the remaking of American society. *Harvard Educational Review, 66*, 762–796.

Lundeen, C., & Lundeen, D. J. (1993). *Effectiveness of mainstreaming with collaborative teaching.* Paper presented at the Annual Convention of the American Speech-Language-Hearing Association, Anaheim, CA. (ERIC Document Reproduction Service No. ED368127)

Magiera, K., Smith, C., Zigmond, N., & Gebauer, K. (2005). Benefits of co-teaching in secondary mathematics classes. *Teaching Exceptional Children, 37*(3), 20–24.

Magiera, K., & Zigmond, N. (2005). Co-teaching in middle school classrooms under routine conditions: Does the instructional experiences differ for SWDs in co-taught and solo-taught classes? *Learning Disabilities Research and Practice, 20*, 79–85.

Mastropieri, M. A., Scruggs, T. E., Graetz, J., Norland, J., Gardizi, W., & McDuffie, K. (2005). Case studies in co-teaching in the content areas: Successes, failures and challenges. *Intervention in School and Clinic, 40*, 260–270.

McDuffie, K. A., Landrum, T. J., & Gelman, J. (2008). Co-teaching and students with emotional and behavioral disorders. *Beyond Behavior, 17*(2), 11–16 .

McDuffie, K. A., Mastropieri, M. A., & Scruggs, T. E. (2009). Differential effects of peer tutoring in co-taught and non co-taught classes: Results for content learning and student-teacher interactions. *Exceptional Children, 75*, 493–510.

McDuffie, K. A., & Scruggs, T. E. (2008). Understanding qualitative research and its role in determining evidence-based practices. *Intervention in School and Clinic, 44*, 91–97.

Morocco, C., C., & Aguilar, C. M., (2002). Coteaching for content understanding: A schoolwide model. *Journal of Educational and Psychological Consultation, 13*, 315–347.

Murawski, W. (2006). Student outcomes in co-taught secondary English classes: How can we improve? *Reading & Writing Quarterly, 22*, 227–247.

Murawski, W. W., & Dieker, L. A. (2004). Tips and strategies for co-teaching at the secondary level. *Teaching Exceptional Children, 36*(5), 52–58.

Murawski, W. W., & Swanson, H. (2001). A meta-analysis of co-teaching research. *Remedial and Special Education, 22*, 258–267.

National Center on Educational Restructuring and Inclusion. (1995). *National study of inclusive education* (2nd ed.) New York: Author.

No Child Left Behind Act (NCLB) of 2001, P. L. No. 107-110, 115 Stat. 1425 *et seq.* (2001)

Pugach, M., & Wesson, C. (1995). Teachers' and students' views of team teaching of general education and learning-disabled students in two fifth-grade classes. *The Elementary School Journal, 95*, 279–295.

Quigney, T. A. (2009). The status of special education teachers at the secondary level effects of the "highly qualified teacher" standard. *American Secondary Education, 37*, 49–61.

Raudenbush, S. W., & Bryk, A. S. (2002). *Hierarchical linear models: Applications and data analysis methods* (2nd ed.). Thousand Oaks, CA: Sage.

Rea, P. J., McLaughlin, V. L., & Walther-Thomas, C. (2002). Outcomes for students with learning disabilities in inclusive and pullout programs. *Exceptional Children, 68*, 203–222.

Rice, D., & Zigmond, N. (2000). Co-teaching in secondary schools: Teacher reports of development in Australian and American classrooms. *Learning Disabilities Research and Practice, 15*, 190–197.

Rosman, N. J. S. (1994). Effects of varying the special educator's role within an algebra class on math attitude and achievement. Masters' thesis, University of South Dakota, Vermillion. (ERIC Document Reproduction Service No. ED 381-993).

Scruggs, T. E., Mastropieri, M. A., & McDuffie, K. A. (2007). Co-teaching in inclusive classrooms: A meta-synthesis of qualitative research. *Exceptional Children, 73*, 392–416.

Self, H., Benning, A., Marston, D., Magnusson, D. (1991). Cooperative teaching project: A model for students at risk. *Exceptional Children, 58*, 26–34.

Semmel, M. I., Gottleib, J., & Robinson, N. (1979). Mainstreaming: Perspectives in educating handicapped children in the public schools. In D. Berliner (Ed.), *Review of research in education* (pp. 223–279). Itaska, IL: Peacock.

Simmons, R. J., & Magiera, K. (2007). Evaluation of co-teaching in three high schools within one school district: How do you know when you are TRULY co-teaching? *TEACHING Exceptional Children Plus, 3*(3), Article 4. Retrieved August 2, 2009, from http://escholarship.bc.edu/education/tecplus/vol3/iss3/art4

Tankersley, M., Landrum, T. J., & Cook, B. G. (2004). How research informs practice in the field of emotional and behavioral disorders. In R. B. Rutherford, M. M. Quinn, & S. R. Mathur (Eds.), *The handbook of behavioral disorders* (pp. 98–116). New York: Guilford Press.

Thompson, B., Diamond, K. E., McWilliam, R., Snyder, P., & Snyder, S. W. (2005). Evaluating the quality of evidence from correlational research for evidence-based practice. *Exceptional Children, 71*, 181–194.

Thompson, M. G. (2001). Capturing the phenomenon of sustained co-teaching: Perceptions of elementary school teachers. *Dissertation Abstracts International, 63* (02), 560A. (UMI No. 3041129)

Vaughn, S., Elbaum, B. E., Schumm, J. S., & Hughes, M. T. (1998). Social outcomes for students with and without learning disabilities in inclusive classrooms. *Journal of Learning Disabilities, 31*, 428–436.

Vesay, J. P. (2004). Linking perspectives and practice: Influence of early childhood and early childhood special educators' perspectives of working collaboratively in the integrated preschool classroom. *Dissertation Abstracts International, 65* (03), 826A. (UMI No. AA13126498)

Villa, R. Thousand, J., & Nevin, A. (2008). *A guide to co-teaching: Practical tips for facilitating student learning* (2nd. Ed.). Thousand Oaks, CA: Corwin Press.

Walsh, J. M., & Snyder, D. (1993). Cooperative teaching. An effective model for all students. Paper presented at the annual convention of the Council for Exceptional Children. San Antonio, TX. (ERIC Document Reproduction Service No. ED 361 930).

Walther-Thomas, C. S. (1997). Co-teaching experiences: The benefits and problems that teachers and principals report over time. *Journal of Learning Disabilities, 30*, 395–408.

Weiss, M. P. (2004). Co-teaching as science in the schoolhouse: more questions than answers. *Journal of Learning Disabilities, 37*(3), 218–223.

Weiss, M. P., & Brigham, F. J. (2000). Co-teaching and the model of shared responsibility: What does the research support? In T. E. Scruggs & M. A. Mastropieri (Eds.), *Educational interventions: Advances in learning and behavioral disabilities* (Vol. 14, pp. 217–246). Stanford, CT: JAI Press.

Wilson, G. L., & Michaels, C. A. (2006). General and special education students' perceptions of co-teaching: Implications for secondary-level literacy instruction. *Reading & Writing Quarterly, 22*, 205–225.

Zigmond, N. (2003). Where should SWDs receive special education services? Is one place better than another? *Journal of Special Education, 37*, 193–199.

Zigmond, N., & Magiera, K. (2001). A focus on co-teaching. *DLD Alerts, 6*, 1–4.

Zigmond, N., & Matta, D. (2004). Value added of the special education teacher on secondary school co-taught classes. In T.E. Scruggs & M.A. Mastropieri (Eds.), *Research in secondary schools: Advances in learning and behavioral disabilities* (Vol. 17, pp. 55–76). Oxford, UK: Elsevier Science/JAI.

13

General and Special Education Are (and Should Be) Different

Naomi P. Zigmond and Amanda Kloo
University of Pittsburgh

General education, *regular* education, or *mainstream* education are all designations used by educators to describe the basic, public education mandated for and offered to *all* children. General education is the education everyone and anyone get. It is the free, public, kindergarten through twelfth grade (K–12), formal system of education, developed in the United States in the 19th century "on the belief that common schooling could create good citizens, unite society, and prevent crime and poverty" (Thattai, 2001, p. 1).

In contrast, *special* education, as its name suggests, is a specialized branch of education. It is education mandated for and offered to *individual* children. It is the education only some students get. It is for those students who have physical, cognitive, language, learning, sensory and/or emotional abilities/disabilities that deviate from those of the general population and whose abilities/disabilities require special educational services. Special educators provide instruction specifically tailored to meet the individual needs of these students, making an appropriate education available to students who otherwise would have limited access to instruction.

Both *general* education and *special* education in the United States have long and distinguished histories that, until the latter quarter of the 20th century, ran parallel, non-intersecting courses. Then came the passage of Public Law 94-142 (1975), The Education of All Handicapped Children Act, and its subsequent reauthorizations, the normalization movement and calls for more inclusive public schools, and the wholesale adoption of full inclusion as the preferred model of service delivery for all students with disabilities. With these developments came increasing calls for a single system of education (e.g., Arnold & Dodge, 1994; National Association of State Boards of Education, 1992; National Education Association, 1992) and for a deliberate blurring of the identities of special and general education. Many have assumed that, if we are not there already, there should soon come a time when there will no longer be a need for certain students to be singled out for a *special* education. In this chapter we take an alternate perspective. We point out 10 major differences between general and special education that are historic and worth preserving:

1. General education is an entitlement for *all* students; special education is reserved for a few eligible students.
2. The state and/or local school district exercises primary authority over general education, setting rules and regulations and monitoring compliance; special education is governed by federal statutes.
3. Local school boards or the state dictate the curriculum for general education; the individualized education program (IEP) team dictates the curriculum for a student with a disability eligible for a special education.
4. General education is oriented to the group; special education is directed to the individual.
5. General education has embraced "differentiated instruction" to accommodate a diverse student body; special education is predicated on intensive, specially designed instruction to meet each individual student's specific learning needs.
6. In general education, yearly learning outcomes (minimal competencies, high expectations) have been set and verified; there are few guides for developing annual learning expectations for students with disabilities.
7. General education teachers are particularly well prepared to teach content or curricula to diverse large groups of students; special education teachers are particularly well prepared to apply pedagogical skills and instructional strategies to teaching individual or small groups of exceptional students with specific learning and emotional needs.
8. Highly qualified generalists (general education teachers) are not the same as, and should not be the same as, highly qualified specialists (special education teachers).

9. General education has only recently embraced the need to ground teaching and learning in public schools in educational research findings; special education practice has a long history of being research-based.
10. General education is a place; special education is a service.

After discussing each of these assertions, we argue for maintaining the distinct identities of general and special education, even in an increasingly inclusive school system and society.

1. General education is an entitlement for *all* students; special education is reserved for a few eligible students.

General education. General education was founded on the belief that all children should be schooled, and that the content of schooling should be the same for everyone. Funding for general education in pubic schools comes from tax revenues, so that even individuals who do not attend school (or whose dependents do not attend school) help to ensure that society is educated. General education is characterized by compulsory school attendance (until a certain age or standard is achieved); certification of teachers (either by a government entity or by a teachers' organization), and certification of curriculum, setting of standards, and overseeing of tests demonstrating achievement of those standards. In the United States, public education is governed at the state level and each of the components of public education (compulsory attendance age, teacher certification, curriculum coverage, academic standards, and tests of achievement) varies by state. Nevertheless, the basis of public education, universal schooling, remains constant.

The original purpose of public education was to develop a literate and "sufficiently educated" citizenry (Miller in Kelley, 2003, p. 6). Free, public education was seen as "the great equalizer" (Mann, in Kelley, p. 10) offering opportunity to all, regardless of class or social standing, to become prepared for "the duties of life" (Elliot, in Kelley, p. 10). Public elementary schools taught universal literacy; public high schools "Americanized" everyone (immigrants and native born) into mainstream political and social values, educating students to fit into American society while at the same time providing opportunities for them to break away from whatever social or economic circumstances constrained their accomplishments.

Despite compulsory education laws that in some states (e.g., Massachusetts) date back as far as 1647 (see Rothbard, 1978), a good and equal public education was not widely available to all Americans as recently as the start of the 20th century. Marginalized groups hovered at the fringes of the educational system. African Americans received an unequal and inferior education as compared to that of whites. So, too, did other minorities, and students with limited English proficiency, girls, and students with disabilities. Civil rights legislation in the second half of the 20th century focused on correcting that deficiency, emphasizing the credo that all American children are entitled to *the same* educational opportunities.

Special education. Compared to general education, mandated special education in the United States is relatively new. Nevertheless, students with disabilities have been present in every era and in every society since the founding of the nation. In the early years of the nation, there were no provisions for individuals with disabilities. "Such individuals were 'stored away' in poorhouses and other charitable centers or remained at home without educational provisions" (Kirk & Gallagher, 1979, p. 5). By the beginning of the 19th century, and for about a century afterward, nearly all special education was provided in a residential program and was reserved for persons with visual or hearing impairment, or persons with moderate to severe mental retardation or severe emotional disturbance. Historical records also consistently document custodial care (i.e., institutional programs) for those with the most severe disabilities to "protect… the handicapped from society and society from the handicapped" (Lilly, 1979, p. 4).

Milder forms of disability became apparent in the schools only after states changed their public education laws from *permissive* to *mandatory*. Now, many students were sent to school not because of parental interest or aspirations but because it was required. Not surprisingly, teachers began complaining about the burden of educating "deviants" or "defectives." At the same time, a heightened interest in and use of intelligence tests defined another group of students who were bothersome in school: "morons" (students with mild mental retardation, Lilly, 1979, p. 4). To accommodate teacher complaints, expulsion, exclusion, or special classes became commonplace for all these "unsuitable" students.

By the middle of the 20th century, special education was responsible for offering a variety of educational placements including hospital schools for those with the most severe disabilities; residential programs or students with severe disabilities whose parents could not keep them at home; specialized day schools for students with severe emotional or physical disabilities who were able to live at home; special classes in regular public school buildings for students whose disabilities could be managed in small groups; and consultants assisting other teachers in instructing students with disabilities wherever they were. But public schools were not yet required to educate *all* students with disabilities, and many were simply excluded from public education and kept at home. "As recently as 1958 and 1969, the courts upheld legislation that excluded students whom school officials judged would not benefit from public education or who might be disruptive to other students" (Yell, 1998, p. 54).

During the last half of the 20th century, great strides were made through litigation, legislation, and public policy to bring the right to a free, public education to all citizens on an equal basis. The 1954 *Brown v. Board of Education* Supreme Court decision was a major statement not only about equal educational opportunity, but also about social integration and ultimately an opportunity for a better life for *all* Americans. Additional civil rights legislation guaranteed equal access to educational opportunities for students from minority groups (Elementary and Secondary Education Act of 1965, especially Title I), students whose primary language was not English (Title VI of the Civil Rights Act of 1964), and girls (Title IX of the Education Amendments of 1972). A natural extension of this push for civil rights and equal educational opportunity (though it was largely ignored until many years later) was Section 504 of the Rehabilitation Act of 1973, "the civil rights declaration of the handicapped" (Humphrey in Yell, p. 95). "Section 504 was originally written in the same antidiscrimination language a Title VI of the Civil Rights Act of 1964" (Yell, p. 96). It protected students with disabilities from discrimination in "the provision of an education and in such areas as the provision of related services, participation in extracurricular activities, and architectural accessibility" (Yell, p. 98). With Section 504, Congress made the commitment to citizens with disabilities, including school-age children, that "to the maximum extent possible persons with disabilities shall be fully integrated into American life" (Senate Report, 1978, in Yell, p. 103). Section 504 required that individuals with disabilities get *equivalent* services or programs. It called for structural alterations, redesign of equipment, reassignment to classes, assignment of aides, regular classroom interventions, and *reasonable accommodations and modifications* of classroom methods, materials and procedures to make them accessible and allow the student with a disability an *equal* opportunity to benefit from the educational program being provided (Zirkel & Kincaid, 1993). In Section 504, the focus was on accessibility and equivalence. Further, Section 504 guaranteed against discrimination; it applied to all students with a disability. It was a civil rights law, not a *special education* law.

Modern special education was born in 1975 with the passage of Public Law 94-142 (originally listed as the Education of All Handicapped Children Act, it is now included in the Individuals with Disabilities Education Act, which is the current name of the law). The act was a natural, though hard-fought, extension of the civil rights legislation that preceded it, but PL 94-142 went further than the promise of *equal* educational opportunity. It promised *un*equal educational opportunities for those students with disabilities who needed a *special* education. PL 94-142 reinforced many of the provisions of Section 504: procedural responsibilities, identification and evaluation, placement, re-evaluation, and procedural safeguards, but it focused on ensuring educational benefit, not equivalency, for those students whose disabilities adversely impacted their educational performance. It implied that, for some students with disabilities, the equal access and equal opportunity guaranteed to traditionally marginalized minorities, English Language Learners, girls, and students with disabilities through civil rights legislation, was not sufficient to produce educational benefit. It called for identification of students with disabilities in need of a *special* education and defined the free *appropriate* public education to be provided to them. Congress estimated that up to 12% of school age children in public schools would fall under this "protected provision" and be entitled to a *special* education.

2. The state and/or local school district exercises primary authority over general education, setting rules and regulations and monitoring compliance; special education is governed by federal statutes.

General education. In the U.S. Constitution, individual states, rather than the federal government, have primary authority over public education. Every state has a department of education and laws that regulate school finance, hiring of school personnel, student attendance, and curriculum. In practice, however, with the exception of licensing requirements and general rules concerning health and safety, local school districts oversee the administration of schools.

Special education. Historically, left to their own devices, few states required or regulated special education programs for students with disabilities. Educational services for students with disabilities varied widely state by state both in terms of availability and quality. Many students with disabilities were excluded from school altogether and individual school districts could not only establish their own criteria permitting access to public education but school officials were perfectly within their rights to deny education to any student not meeting those criteria. Sadly, these excluded students were often students with disabilities. To rectify this discrimination, the federal government stepped in. In the late 1950s, the federal government became involved in research and teacher preparation in special education. Then, with the passage of PL 94-142 (1975), in return for federal funds, each state was to ensure that *all* students with disabilities received non-discriminatory testing, evaluation and placement, the right to due process, education in the least restrictive environment, and a free and appropriate public education (FAPE). The centerpiece of the legislation was FAPE, with its details spelled out in an IEP that included relevant goals and objectives, specifications as to the length of the school year, determination of the most appropriate educational placement, and descriptions of criteria to be used in evaluation of student progress. The IEP was designed to ensure that all students with disabilities received educational programs specific to their "unique" needs.

Even with these federal mandates governing each state's provision of special education, many states continued to be complacent in their obligations to meet the educational needs of students with disabilities. Therefore, strict requirements for compliance monitoring were developed in the 1997 reauthorization of IDEA (Individuals with Disabilities Education Act, 1997), requiring states to document the various processes and activities mandated in the law. With compliance monitoring, the effectiveness of special education is judged in terms of whether procedural safeguards are satisfied, proper steps are taken, and the right paperwork is processed correctly and on time. State Education Agencies are responsible for ensuring that each school district within their jurisdictions is complying with the federal regulations; the federal agency is responsible for making certain that states are meeting their obligations in monitoring compliance and following up on non-compliance. No such federal oversight exists for general education.

3. Local school boards or the state dictate the curriculum for general education; the IEP team dictates the curriculum for a student with a disability eligible for a special education.

General education. What should children learn? Who gets to decide? For about 200 years, curriculum matters had been the prerogative of the local school district and its local school board. State and local governments played only marginal governance roles in deciding the content of the curriculum; the federal government had no role at all. "The American public school is a gigantic standardized compromise most of us have learned to live with," contended Kaestle nearly 35 years ago (1976, p. 396).

More recently, however, setting standards for schools and school graduates seems to interest everyone from school board members, to legislators, to federal policy makers (and the citizens, parents and non parents who elect them to office). Public concerns over lackluster student academic performance, employers' concerns that high school graduates are not adequately prepared for the emerging technological workplace, and news media concerns that American youth fare poorly compared to students in other developed nations, have contributed to dissatisfaction with the status quo. This has led to calls for more coherence in curriculum requirements and greater accountability for curriculum coverage. The key question is, "Who should decide what students will be taught in school?" And the current debate is whether to move from local or state standards to national standards for curriculum. While the development of national K–12 standards is still in the conceptual stage, the current trend certainly appears to move decisions about curriculum and instruction farther from setting individual goals and closer to collective, group goals.

Special education. Throughout the history of special education, attention to the unique needs of the individual has been paramount. Educators and parents agree that students with disabilities who are in need of special education need explicit, intensive, and prolonged instruction in knowledge and skills not usually covered in the standard school curriculum. Forty years ago, Lilly (1979) explained that special classes were conceived and developed to allow "introduction of specialized curricula more suited to the needs of exceptional learners [and taught by] specially trained teachers whose qualifications for dealing with learning problems were greater than those of the classroom teacher" (p. 65). According to a popular introductory text (Hallahan & Kauffman, 1978), special education for students with mild mental retardation meant a school program that concentrated on learning basic academic skills, socially adaptive behavior, and vocational skills. For students with moderate retardation, the curriculum would be less academic with more emphasis on "self-help, communication, personal-social, and perceptual motor/physical education skills [that] help him to function in his social environment" (p. 110). For students with severe and profound mental retardation, the educational emphasis would be on "basic survival and self-help skills" (p. 110). In contrast, the curriculum for students with mild/moderate emotional disturbance would be "similar to that used for normal youngsters … [but coupled with an equal emphasis on] acquisition of social skills and affective experiences" (p. 215). Even as separate special classes were phasing out, the notion persisted that the special education teacher and the general education teacher taught different content and negotiated explicitly "who will be responsible for what" (Hallahan & Kauffman, 1978, p. 155). Whether serving students with disabilities in full time special classes, part time special classes, or resource rooms, Zigmond (1997) summarized the responsibilities of the special educator as provide[ing] instruction based on the student's individual need. Special education was intensive, urgent and goal-directed and it was delivered by a uniquely trained teacher. The role of the special education teacher was to teach what could not be learned elsewhere—it was special teaching.

To legitimize and make transparent teaching students with disabilities "special stuff" and not just (or instead of) what everyone else in their grade and school is being taught, legislators wisely introduced the concept of an IEP into the landmark special education law of 1975. The IEP is a written document detailing a student with disabilities' educational needs and the steps the school plans to take to meet those needs. Developed by the special education teacher in conjunction with other school personnel and the child's parents, the IEP documents the student's level of performance, his/her goals and objectives, the degree to which those can be met in regular education, and any related services the student might need. It outlines the special curriculum and specially designed instruction that will be implemented to meet this child's individual educational needs. What is on the IEP is agreed upon by a team that is individualized for every student with a disability. Curriculum is decided by the members of the IEP team: a representative of the educational agency, often the principal; the student's special education teacher; the student's general education teacher; the student's parent or guardian; related service personnel; other persons at the discretion of parents or the educational agency; and for student nearing a transition, a representative of the agency that is likely to provide or pay for the transition services.

The IEP allows the curriculum for a student with disabilities in need of special education to focus on the development of both academic and practical life skills that are geared toward the goals and aspirations of that individual student. It ensures a meaningful educational curriculum aligned with the individual's needs and plans. "It is this aspect of individualization that distinguishes services authorized and provided through special education from those typically provided in general education" (Kohler & Field, 2003, p. 180).

4. General education is oriented to the group; special education is directed to the individual.

General education. Typically, school systems have established a primary mode of learning that involves groups of students of about the same age in a confined physical space interacting with a single adult to learn a particular topic. In other words, general education students are placed in classes. The number of other students in the class can vary. At the one extreme, there can be one or more adults facilitating learning with only one or two students. At the other extreme, a student may be one of a few hundred being taught by a single instructor or, with new Internet technology, one of millions. The number of students in a class has the potential to affect how much is learned. For example, it could affect how students interact with each other and with the teacher, how much noise is produced, how disruptive students' behaviors are, and the kinds of activities that can be accomplished. Class size could affect how much time the teacher is able to focus on individual students and their specific needs rather than on the group as a whole. Class size could also affect how much material can be covered, how much feedback can be delivered, how much to use open-ended assignments, or how much to engage in discussions.

The study considered by most experts to be the landmark experimental study on the effects of class size is known as the STAR (Student/Teacher Achievement Ratio) project (Mosteller, 1995). Researchers began tracking K–3 students in 79 schools scattered across Tennessee in 1985. Of those schools, 25 were located in urban areas, 16 were in the suburbs, and 39 were in rural areas. Each of the schools had to have at least 57 students in a grade; that would provide enough students to make one experimental class of 13 to 17 students and two "normal-sized" classes of 22 to 25 students. One normal-sized class in each school would have an aide; the other would not. Achievement would be measured at the end of the school year.

The result of the STAR project was significantly enhanced achievement for children, especially minority children, in smaller classes. Researchers found that STAR students in smaller classes in grades K–3 earned significantly higher scores on basic skills tests in all four years and in all types of schools. The normal-sized classroom that had a teacher's aide showed only slight improvement on the tests. The Lasting Benefits Study (LBS) tracked the STAR students beyond third grade. The students from smaller classes continued to achieve at higher rates than their peers in the other groups even after they returned to normal-sized classrooms in grades four and beyond. Other studies have produced similar findings: students in the reduced-size classes (16–17 students) had higher standardized test scores in reading and mathematics than did students in the control group (classes of 24–27).

It should come as no surprise that most teachers prefer smaller classes to larger ones. Smaller classes are easier to manage. In a smaller class, a teacher can spend more time teaching basic skills. Teachers can cover more ground in each lesson and provide daily feedback to students. In smaller classes, it is easier for teachers to pinpoint students who require extra help. Teachers also have more time to adapt teaching strategies to individual students, to make reasonable accommodations and modifications, and to provide needed help *before* it's too late! "With 16 or 18 students in a classroom 'you begin to feel real impacts'," Marshall Smith, deputy acting Secretary of Education told the *Hartford Courant* (Hopkins, 1998). "Teachers can begin to do things differently, group [students] differently, provide more attention" (Hopkins, 1998). For all these reasons, tinkering with general education class size is considered a potential means of changing how much students learn. But class size debates do not question the premise that general education is delivered to groups.

General education outcomes related to student achievement are also typically conceptualized as *group* outcomes and achievement. Accountability legislation such as No Child Left Behind (NCLB, 2001) makes public the progress of districts and school student bodies at large as well as of disadvantaged subgroups defined by race, income, special education status, and primary language. The success or failure of schools is quantified through the calculation of "adequate yearly progress" for each of these macro and micro populations of students (Derthick & Dunn, 2009). The success or failure of general education is historically, traditionally, and politically tied to group instruction and group achievement.

Special education. A small class size in general education is 14–16 students. A small class size in special education is one-on-one instruction. Within general education, the class size debate fits into the realm of school finance and economics. In special education, class size is viewed in the context of student achievement. Researchers in general education can point to barely a handful of experimental studies on the effects of class size on student achievement. In the special education research literature, there are countless studies on the effects of instructional group size on student achievement. And, the findings are consistent: Smaller group size is associated with improved outcomes. Smaller groups reduce variability in the instructional needs of students (e.g., Elbaum, Vaughn, Hughes, & Moody, 1999). Group size affects amount and quality of oral language used among students learning English as a second language (e.g., Gersten & Jiménez, 1998). Smaller groups allow reading instruction to be more tailored to students' individual needs (e.g., Rashotte, MacPhee, & Torgesen, 2001). Instruction in small groups or student pairs produces higher effect sizes than whole class instruction (e.g., Elbaum, et al, 1999). Although the optimal group size for special education instruction has yet to be established, research indicates that 1:1 and 3:1 are both better than 10:1 (Vaughn, Linan-Thompson, Kousekanani, et al., 2003) in terms of student achievement. One meta-analysis shows 1:1 instruction exceeded outcomes for group instruction by an average of .41 standard deviations (Elbaum, Vaughn, Hughes, & Moody, 2000).

Special education outcomes related to student achievement are typically conceptualized as *individual* outcomes and achievement. Progress monitoring is a well-established methodology, grounded in special education research that evaluates student progress toward the acquisition of skills that are globally reflective of instruction within a curriculum (Deno, Fuchs, Marston, & Shinn, 2001; Stecker & Fuchs, 2000). Progress monitoring provides information relevant to making decisions regarding individual student achievement related to IEP goal attainment, specific skill deficits, and program/instructional effectiveness (Deno, Espin, & Fuchs, 2002; Fuchs & Fuchs, 1999). The right to a special education is afforded to an individual student based on individualized decision-making and involves individualized education programming. Success or failure of special education is tied to individual student growth and achievement.

5. General education has embraced "differentiated instruction" to accommodate a diverse student body; special education is predicated on intensive, specially designed instruction to meet each individual student's specific learning needs.

General education. Not all students are alike. Students in classroom groups differ in background knowledge, readiness to learn, language proficiency, preferences in learning style, interests, and ability to react responsively. Historically, general teacher education programs have not adequately prepared teachers for the increasing diversity of students (Tomlinson, 1999). "Differentiated instruction" has been promoted as one solution to this problem. Differentiated instruction is a teaching theory based on the premise that instructional approaches should vary and be adapted in relation to individual and diverse students in classrooms (Hall, 2002). It encourages teachers to offer students multiple options for taking in information and making sense of ideas. The model of differentiated instruction requires teachers to be flexible in their approach to teaching and to adjust the curriculum and presentation of information to learners rather than to expect students to modify themselves for the curriculum. The intent of differentiating instruction is to maximize each student's growth and individual success by meeting each student where he or she is and adjusting instruction to be sensitive to individual differences in readiness levels, interests, and preferred modes of learning. Differentiated instruction provides *multiple approaches* to content, process, and product. Teachers offer different approaches to what students learn, how they learn it, and how they demonstrate what they've learned.

Effective teachers have been differentiating instruction for as long as teaching has been a profession (Rutledge, 2003). They certainly did it in the one-room schoolhouse where students in several different grades were all in the same space. Teachers have always found ways to help individual students make the necessary connections for learning so that all students develop the knowledge and skills necessary for achieving positive learning outcomes.

Differentiated instruction is based on the idea that "all learners do not necessarily learn in the same way, and it refers to the practice of ensuring that each learner receives the methods and materials most suitable for that particular learner at that particular place in the curriculum" (Mastropieri & Scruggs, 2007, p. 126). An expansive literature base has explored numerous effective strategies and pedagogies for differentiated instruction designed to help general education teachers meet diverse student needs in their classrooms. Research suggests instructional adaptations such as the use of content enhancement routines, advanced organizers, and cognitive strategy instruction have a positive impact on learning progress for students with learning disabilities when explicitly, effectively, and thoughtfully implemented (De La Paz & MacArthur, 2003; Swanson & Deshler, 2003). However, studies have also shown that differentiated instruction is rarely, explicitly, effectively, or thoughtfully applied in actual classroom practice (Fuchs & Fuchs, 1998). In fact, undifferentiated, whole-group instruction continues to be the norm for reading instruction at both elementary and secondary levels regardless of class make-up or diversity (Swanson, 2008). Nonetheless, differentiated instruction is viewed as the keystone to effective and successful general education curricular instruction for *all* students, including those with disabilities

Special education. Providing differentiated instruction in a general education classroom is not the same as providing special education. According to Hallahan and Kauffman (1978, p. 4), "special education means specially designed instruction which meets the unique needs of an exceptional child." Delivering that specially designed instruction may require special materials, teaching techniques, equipment, and/or facilities. Early textbooks on educating students with disabilities describe specially designed instruction in terms of ability or process training, behavior modification, developmental and ecological approaches, psychodynamic or psychoeducational teaching strategies, social learning approaches, and task analysis (see Kirk & Gallagher, 1979) or, in terms of teaching models, biophysical, psychological, behavioral, or environmental (see Ysseldyke & Algozzine, 1984). Textbooks also describe specially designed instructional strategies particularly suited to students with specific learning characteristics and learning needs.

At its core, special education is about promoting higher order reasoning and problem solving, facilitating independent and cooperative work, and supporting acquisition of new skills and subject matter through direct and focused instruction (Wang, 1998). Special education differs from general education teaching in its emphasis on intensity, on direct instruction, and on systematic, well-scaffolded instructional tasks. Direct instruction has been a long-standing pillar of special education; intervention research has shown positive effect sizes for the use of systematic, direct instruction, particularly when coupled with explicit strategy instruction for students who have learning and behavioral disabilities (Gersten, Vaughn, Deshler, & Schiller, 1997; Swanson, Hoskyn, & Lee, 1999). Special education, therefore, is not just accommodating to individual differences; it is more (a) explicit, (b) intensive, and (c) supportive than general education can ever be (Torgesen, 1996).

6. In general education, yearly learning outcomes (minimal competencies, high expectations) have been set and verified; there are few guides for developing annual learning expectations for students with disabilities.

General education. Standardized achievement tests have long made concrete the definition of grade level performance and of the educational gains that can be expected from one year of schooling to the next. Building on those data and on decades of experience, stakeholder groups have defined what school children in each state should learn year by year and by the time of high school graduation. In some subject areas, grade level achievement standards leave a lot of wiggle room. In reading, mathematics, and science, the core subject areas of required accountability assessments in compliance with NCLB, grade level expectations for students in public education have now been set in each of the 50 states. Students are expected to attain proficiency on grade level standards in one year, and learn enough each subsequent year to maintain that proficiency standing in the next year, and the next, and so on. Adequate Yearly Progress, while not a measure of individual student achievement, sets the expectation that eventually *all* students in a school building or district will be proficient on grade level standards.

Special education. Expectations for achievement for students with disabilities in need of a special education are not nearly as clear-cut. While some special education reformers (see Quenemoen, Lehr, Thurlow, & Massanari, 2001; Thurlow, Quenemoen, Altman, & Cuthbert, 2008) might suggest that we should have the same high standards and expectations for academic growth for *all* students, including students with disabilities in need of a special education, many would agree with Kauffman (1999, p. 246) that that is an "unrealistic" expectation. Students with disabilities become eligible for special education services *because* they score poorly on academic achievement tests; if their disability did not adversely affect school achievement, these students would qualify for reasonable accommodations and modifications under Section 504 instead. Despite a history of learning problems and poor achievement, NCLB challenges the educational establishment to teach these students more, faster, to close the achievement gap between students with disabilities and those without. This sets up unreasonable expectations for the students with disabilities and their teachers.

Further, research has shown significant differences in growth rates in reading and mathematics for students receiving general education and students receiving special education. Using Curriculum Based Measurement (CBM, or general outcome measures), multiple studies have explored rate of learning or the slope of improvement over time. Students in special education consistently had lower growth rates than those in general education (Deno et al., 2001; Graney, Missall, Martinez, & Bergstrom, 2008). But there are no definitive studies that allow practitioners (or legislators) to establish expected rates of growth against which to measure program or intervention effectiveness for students receiving special education. Given recent changes to special education eligibility determination and the introduction of RtI models, research is clearly warranted regarding student rate of learning and what defines adequate progress and improvement in basic academic skills for students with disabilities eligible to receive special education. Within an RtI framework, the goal is to establish the effectiveness of the intervention or to demonstrate that growth within the intervention condition is atypical for a given student. But who is the comparison group? Average peers? Other underperforming students? Other students with the same disability diagnosis? Because goal attainment and learning outcomes for students with disabilities are inherently tied to *individual* performance or growth, it is difficult to specify what "typical" performance should be for an "atypical" learner.

7. General education teachers are particularly well prepared to teach content or curricula to diverse large groups of students; special education teachers are particularly well prepared to apply pedagogical skills and instructional strategies to teaching individual or small groups of exceptional students with specific learning and emotional needs.

General education. The professional standards articulated for both general educators and special educators by the National Council for Accreditation of Teacher Education (NCATE) require teacher preparation institutions to prepare *all* teachers to contribute to the education of *all* learners, including diverse populations of students (e.g., at different developmental stages, with different learning styles, and from different and diverse backgrounds). For general educators, the foundation of that teacher preparation is content knowledge and academic standards. At the elementary level, content and standards-driven instruction is conceptualized within a developmental continuum; at the secondary level, content and standards-driven instruction is conceptualized within a framework integrating content, theory and research (NCATE, 2008). Ultimately (and historically), the grist of general education teacher preparation has focused on preparing teachers to teach specific subject matter. Pedagogy or teaching skill is also critical but it takes second place to content mastery. Many new teachers (and experienced teachers, as well) enter the classroom unprepared to address diversity and individual differences.

To address the needs of a more diverse general education student body, general education teacher preparation programs have added coursework in urban education, in educating English language learners, and in accommodating the needs of students with disabilities. What cannot be accomplished during preservice preparation is often undertaken as inservice training. Some schools have introduced the "inclusion specialist" or "consulting teacher" to assist general education teacher to

> create accommodations and modifications that maintain the integrity of the lesson while addressing the unique learning needs of the student… and help the general education teacher decide how and when an accommodation or modification should be used to allow students with disabilities access to the general education curriculum. (Dukes & Dukes, 2005, pp 56–57)

Nevertheless, research has shown that general education classroom teachers in practice use very few targeted strategies (Agran & Alper, 2000) and, because of their perceived need to cover content with a large group of students, they favor curriculum-focused strategies rather than individual student-focused strategies (McDonnell, 1998). More importantly, special education's most basic article of faith, that instruction must be individualized to be effective, is rarely contemplated, let alone observed, in typical general education classrooms, and research-based instructional practices known to improve student achievement and learning access such as peer-mediation, strategy instruction, self monitoring, etc. are virtually non-existent in these settings (Scruggs, Mastropieri, & McDuffie, 2007).

Special education. In contrast, the historical focus of special education teacher preparation has been on equipping teachers with the skills to teach individual students with atypical learning and emotional needs. Pedagogy and strategy instruction is the foundation of professional training (NCATE, 2008; CEC, 2004). In contrast to the content-driven focus of general education, special education teacher preparation is grounded in pedagogy. The professional preparation standards endorsed by NCATE and articulated in the Council for Exceptional Children (CEC) publication, *Definition of a Well-Prepared Special Education Teacher*, proclaim, "Pedagogy and teaching skill is at the heart of special education. Special educators have always recognized that the individual learning needs of children are at the center of instruction" (CEC, 2004, p. 1). Kauffman, Bantz, and McCollough (2002) agree that special education teachers need "a set of specialized skills because the structure, intensity, precision, and relentlessness with which these teachers must deliver, monitor, and adapt instruction is surely beyond that which would be possible in a regular classroom" (p. 153). Implementing evidence-based instructional strategies "with a high degree of precision is the defining element that makes special education special" (p.153).

Many believe that the instructional techniques of special education are not uniquely suited to students with disabilities and are probably appropriate for any and all learners. But these same critics would agree that the strategies of special education are *not necessary* for most typically developing learners. Furthermore, effective techniques to address inappropriate behavior, enhance learning, and influence social interactions are not likely to be present outside of special education (Kaufman et al., 2002).

8. Highly qualified generalists (general education teachers) are not the same as, and should not be the same as, highly qualified specialists (special education teachers).

General education. With the recent accountability legislation of the No Child Left Behind Act of 2001, teacher quality has come under great scrutiny. In fact, legislators have reported that inadequate instruction provided by unqualified teachers was at the heart of our country's low student achievement. As a result, NCLB requires that all teachers become "highly qualified" (HQT).

Special education. The U.S. Department of Education definition of a HQT in both general and special education focuses on mastery of content. However, given our previous discussion of NCATE/CEC standards, which differentiate the unique characteristics of the content expertise required for effective general education and the pedagogical strategies required for effective special education, we believe that the current definition of *highly qualified* fails to recognize the highly specialized nature of special education. Yes, the knowledge of academic content is paramount to supporting a special educator's ability to promote access to the general education curriculum for students with disabilities. However, research on teacher quality clearly demonstrates that special educators must possess in-depth understanding of the specialized methodologies and instructional techniques needed to support the learning of students with exceptional learning difficulties and differences (Brownell et al., 2009). Over three decades ago, Lilly (1979) described a special educator as a specialist whose expertise in providing instruction to exceptional learners is more comprehensive than that of a general education teacher (Lilly, 1979). More recently, Zigmond (1997) described the pedagogical skills of the special educator as intensive, urgent, and goal directed. Special educators are content experts whose *content* is *special education* (Samuels, 2005). Requiring special educators to be trained as highly qualified generalists with expertise in all content areas detracts from the critical importance of training them as specialists with expertise in *special education*. We must honor and value this specialized training just as we do for reading specialists, second language specialists, and the like.

9. General education has only recently embraced the need to ground teaching and learning in public schools in educational research findings; special education practice has a long history of being research-based.

General education. There has been little, if any, improvement in the achievement of typical public school students over the past two decades despite countless school reform interventions. Perhaps this is because few of these reform interventions have had a basis in rigorous scientific study. Educational decision-making has been dominated, instead, by a culture of ideology, faddishness, and opinion—coupled with cynicism about the value of educational research.

Education may not be an exact science grounded in experimental research. Nevertheless, preparing the next generation of citizens is too important to be dominated by "unfounded opinion, whether of politicians, teachers, researchers, or anyone else" (Coe, 1999, p. 1). For 40 years, the educational research community has systematically studied the effectiveness on learners of various general education teaching practices. There have been significant advances in the science of education over the past several decades, but many of these advances never made it into everyday education practice, and those that did, often failed. The time had come to "replace many age-old anecdotal suggestions for 'good' teaching with modern, research-based teaching practices that are empirically related to positive outcomes in learners" (Borich, 1996, p. iii).

To accomplish that, a new wind swept through the education landscape. "Evidence-based" is the latest buzzword. It refers to an approach to general education that argues that policy and practice should be capable of being justified in terms of sound evidence about their likely effects. As Whitehurst reflected, in 2004,

> We are at the beginning of a transformation of education into an evidence-based field. By evidence-based I mean an endeavor in which decision makers routinely seek out the best available research and data before adopting programs or practices that will affect significant numbers of students. (p. 1)

Evidence-based education has become an increasing priority in recent federal education legislation and policy, particularly since NCLB. The new focus seeks to narrow the research-to-practice gap and revolutionize not only classroom practice but also preparation of elementary and secondary subject matter teachers.

Special education. Both the commitment to, and the research base on, research-based effective instructional practices for students with disabilities are older, richer, and much better substantiated in special education. In fact, there is general agreement that the "one thing that is right about special education is that it includes devising and testing empirically validated methods of instruction that are effective with atypical students (Hockenbury, Kauffman, & Hallahan, 1999–2000, p. 6).

Validation means experimental studies conducted over time that yield converging evidence of effectiveness (Stanovich, 2000; Vaughn & Dammann, 2001). Such research has yielded specifications on general features of instruction (pacing, group size, amount of time), materials, and instructional practice that define effective special education for students with disabilities (Fuchs & Fuchs, 1995; Gersten & Vaughn, 2001; Swanson, Harris, & Graham, 2000; Vaughn, Gersten, & Chard, 2000). These specifications include strategies such as controlling task difficulty (sequencing examples and problems to maintain high levels of success and matching task difficulty with student abilities and emerging skills); teaching students in small, interactive groups; using direct, explicit instruction; modeling and teaching metacognitive strategies for generating questions and thinking aloud while reading or working on scientific or mathematical problems; learning when, where, and how to apply learning enhancement strategies; monitoring progress on specific skills; learning the process of writing as well as the organizational and mechanical aspects of writing; providing ongoing and systematic feedback to the learner. There are research data to guide special education teachers on the appropriate duration of an intervention, including optimal intensity (the number of sessions required, the number of times per day, and the number of days, weeks, or years), to achieve a positive outcome (Vaughn, Linan-Thompson, & Hickman-Davis, 2003).

While general special education practices have been empirically validated, so have practices associated with particular subgroups of students with disabilities in need of special education. For example, Landrum, Tankersley, and Kauffman (2003) have outlined effective practices for students with emotional/behavior disorders, including altering antecedents and consequences in the environment to increase the likelihood that appropriate behavior will occur and reduce the likelihood that inappropriate behavior will occur; providing effective instruction to enhance achievement and learning strategies that enhance ability to attend to instruction, retain information and apply knowledge in appropriate contexts; social skills interventions based on carefully and individually targeted behaviors that serve to promote skill acquisition, enhance skill performance, remove competing problem behaviors, and/or facilitate generalization. Walker, Schwarz, Nippold, Irvin, and Noell (1994) emphasize direct instruction in social skills with planned response opportunities, consistent feedback on performance, and use of contingencies as newly acquired skills are applied.

Research has also validated instructional approaches for students with the most severe disabilities. For example, Snell (1997) suggests individualized instruction with systematic prompting and fading; many opportunities for practice across a variety of settings, and an augmentative communication system to expand use of symbolic communication. There are research studies on approaches to teaching a single discreet response, a set of discrete responses or a chained response, a generalized response, or a pivotal response. There are studies on empirically validated prompting systems (time delay, least intrusive prompts, graduated guidance with defined feedback including descriptive praise for a correct response and instructive error correction).

Many of the research-based and validated instructional strategies suitable for students with disabilities "do not transfer easily to most mainstream classrooms where teachers have many students and often a different set of assumptions about the form and function of education" (Fuchs & Fuchs, 1995, pp. 528–529). And they also do not fit the ecology of a general education classroom (Zigmond, 1996).

10. General education is a place; special education is a service.

General education. Although public (general) education can be provided anywhere, including at home employing visiting teachers, supervising teachers, and/or distance learning, or even in non-school, non-home settings such as shopping mall space, general education is where *everyone* goes to school, especially students who do not have disabilities. General education is the "normal" educational setting.

Special education. Place has long been at the center of debate concerning the educational needs of students with disabilities. Even before the passage of Public Law 94-142, Lloyd Dunn (1968) posited that placement of students with disabilities into self-contained special education classrooms was for the most part unjustifiable. Excluding only students with the most severe disabilities, Dunn called for the education of exceptional students to take place within general education classrooms, with some special education teachers providing appropriate diagnostic-prescriptive supplemental instruction in resource rooms and others guiding the work of the general educator in a consultant or team teaching role. The LRE provision of PL 94-142 made explicit Congress' commitment to having students with disabilities "educated with their non-handicapped peers—or in the most normal setting" (Goldberg, 1982, p. 39). Their reasoning: "Educators feel that integrating students, both exceptional and typical, must take place in order to provide the highest quality of educational experience for each child" (Goldberg, 1982, p. 39).

The importance of *place* is underscored each year by the reporting requirements for the *Annual Reports to Congress*, required as part of the federal special education legislation. Because of concerns about whether special education services are being provided in the least restrictive environment and about the number of special education students receiving costly services in private day and residential facilities at public expense (diverting scarce resources from other areas of the educational system), Congress asked for annual data on the number of students with disabilities served in each of the educational environments along the continuum of placements ranging from regular classes to homebound/hospital placements. In the first of these *Annual Reports*, issued in 1977, the first year of full implementation of the Education of All Handicapped Act, and in every *Report* since, the Office of Special Education Programs (OSEP) tabulated the settings in which students with disabilities were receiving special education services: *regular class, resource room, separate class, separate school,* etc. What Congress wanted counted was time *outside* the regular classroom. The presumption is that during this time outside the regular classroom, students with disabilities were receiving their *special* education. But the presumption was wrong. As many are quick to point out (see, e.g., Brown, 2003; Kauffman & Hallahan, 2005), in theory at least, a special education *can* be delivered anywhere.

In the first decade after its passage, special educators promoted a continuum of placements with more or less mainstreaming (integration into the general education classroom) as met the needs of a particular student with disabilities eligible for the protections afforded by PL 94-142. The continuum of placements was exemplified by the Deno (1970) Cascade of Services model, the guiding conceptual as well as operational framework for LRE in the 1980s. This cascade depicted the full range of placement options available to students with disabilities to ensure that the *place* of service delivery matched the students' unique intellectual, physical, emotional, and educational needs. And no matter the *place*, students with disabilities in need of a special education were to receive instruction that was specialized, individualized, and intensive. The mantra, "Special education is a service, not a place," introduced in the 1980s as a rallying cry of the "full inclusion" movement, has come to symbolize the capacity of special educators, expertly trained to meet the individual needs of exceptional students through a comprehensive repertoire of evidenced-based instructional strategies, to deliver a special education anywhere. The reality, unfortunately, is that in many schools, *special* education is nowhere to be found.

Conclusions: *General* and *Special* Education Are (and Should Be) Different

No matter the many reauthorizations of special education law and multiple school reform efforts linked to accountability legislation, the inherent goals of special education have remained constant. Those are to provide the very best education possible to all students with disabilities to enable them reach their fullest intellectual, emotional, and social potential in school and in life. PL 94-142 was a landmark in special education not just because it provided opportunity and access to schooling for students with disabilities. It also codified the Individualized Education Program to which students with disabilities were entitled. It forced agreements between parents and schools on the unique curricula to be provided to each individual student with a disability who qualified for services because he/she needed a *special* education. The bedrock of federal and state special education laws is the eligible student's right to an educational program based on his *individual* needs—not on disability category, not on school capacity, not on instructional setting.

The relationship between general and special education has been controversial since the beginning of universal schooling. From the start, general and special education evolved from different premises (public education of the masses vs. education of an individual with special needs), with different emphases in teacher preparation (learning to teach subject matter vs. learning to teach individual students) and different research bases to ground their educational practices. Arguments have persisted and escalated in the last 30 years over whether special education should retain a separate identity or be fused with general education such that it has no separate mission, budget, or personnel. Proponents of radical restructuring (Brantlinger, 1997; Smith, 1999) maintain that such integration is necessary to provide appropriate education for *all* students regardless of disability and without stigma or discrimination. They argue that integration of the two systems would result in a more flexible, supple, and responsive single system that will meet the needs of all students without "separating out" any. According to this line of thinking, all teachers can and should be prepared to teach all students, including those with special needs.

Opponents argue that special education will not survive to serve the special needs of exceptional students if it loses its identity, its special budget allocations, and its unique personnel requirements. They argue that it is neither feasible, nor desirable, to prepare all teachers to teach all students; special training is required to teach student who are educationally exceptional. The inclusion debate has distracted the field of special education from more important issues—the accurate identification of students with disabilities in need of a special education and the efficacy of interventions delivered to them.

"Special education has traditionally involved providing something 'extra' or 'different' to address the atypical needs and often unresponsive nature of students it serves" (Cook & Schirmer, 2003, p. 200). However, special education remains a promise unfulfilled. In the embrace of "normalization" and "inclusion," legislators, school leaders, and parents have focused on ensuring *equal* educational opportunity, but the promise of special education was *unequal* opportunities, special opportunities, different and more appropriate opportunities, tailored opportunities, individualized opportunities. Parents, legislators, and teachers themselves complain that general education teachers are not equipped to meet the educational needs of students with disabilities. The disgrace is not that general education teachers are not adequately prepared to deliver a special education to the students with disabilities in their large and diverse classrooms. The disgrace is that we have come to believe that special education is so *not-special* that it can be delivered by a generalist, busy teaching 25 other students a curriculum that was generated at the school board, or state, or federal level. The disgrace is that we have forgotten that special education is supposed to be special and that wherever it is delivered, it is supposed to be different. That's what we fought for. That's what makes IDEA different from other civil rights legislation, for minorities, for English Language Learners, for girls. We fought to have some students with disabilities treated differently, given more opportunity, more intensive instruction, more individually tailored curriculum, more carefully designed instruction. It's time to renew the commitment to students with disabilities and to ensure the programs and resources necessary to fulfill that commitment.

References

Agran, M., & Alper, S. (2000). Curriculum and instruction in general education: Implications for service delivery and personnel preparation. *Journal of the Association for Persons with Severe Handicaps, 25*, 167–174.

Arnold, J. B., & Dodge, H.W. (1994). Room for all. *The American School Board Journal, 181*(10), 22–26.

Borich, G. D. (1996). *Effective teaching methods* (3rd ed.). Upper Saddle River, NJ: Prentice-Hall.

Brantlinger, E. A. (1997). Using ideology: Cases of nonrecognition of the politics of research and practice in special education. *Review of Educational Research, 67*(4), 425–460.

Brown, L. (2003, September 14). Special education is a 'service' not a place. *Hawaii Reporter, Inc.*, retrieved February 2009 from http://www.hawaiireporter.com/story.aspx?44dfa42c-2db5-4c28-935a-850fe2299f53

Brown v. Board of Education, 347 U.S. 483 (1954).

Brownell, M., Bishop, A., Gersten, R., Klinger, J., Penfield, R., Diminio, J., et al. (2009). The role of domain expertise: Beginning special education teacher quality. *Exceptional Children, 75*(4), 391–411.

Civil Rights Act (1964), 42 U.S.C. §1983

Coe, R. (1999). A manifesto for evidence-based education, Center for Evaluation and Monitoring, EBE Brief Guide 1, retrieved November 2009 from http://www.cemcentre.org/RenderPage.asp?LinkID=30317000

Cook, B. G., & Schirmer, B. R. (2003). What is special about special education?: Overview and analysis. *The Journal of Special Education, 37,* 200–205.

Council For Exceptional Children (CEC) Board of Directors. (2004). *The Council for Exceptional Children definition of a well- prepared special education teacher.* Arlington, VA: Author. Retrieved December 10, 2010, from http://www.cec.sped.org/content/navigationmenu/professionaldevelopment/professionalstandards/well-prepared-final.pdf

De La Paz, S., & MacArthur, C. (2003). Knowing the how and why of history: Expectations for secondary students with and without learning disabilities. *Learning Disability Quarterly, 26*(2), 142–154.

Deno, E. (1970). Special education as developmental capital. *Exceptional Children, 37,* 229–237.

Deno, S. L., Espin, C. A., & Fuchs, L. S. (2002). Evaluation strategies for preventing and remediating basic skill deficits. In G. Stoner, M. R. Shinn, & H. M. Walker (Eds.), *Interventions for achievement and behavior problems* (pp. 213–241). Washington, DC: National Association of School Psychologists.

Deno, S. L., Fuchs, L. S., Marston, D., & Shinn, J. H. (2001). Using curriculum-based measurement to establish growth standards for students with learning disabilities. *School Psychology Review, 30*, 507–524.

Derthick, M., & Dunn, J. M. (2009). False premises: The accountability fetish in education. *Harvard Journal of Law & Public Policy, 32*(3), 1015–1034.

Dukes, P. L., & Dukes, L. (2005). Consider the roles and responsibilities of the inclusion support teacher. *Intervention in School and Clinic, 41*(1), 55–61.

Dunn, L. M. (1968). Special education for the mildly retarded—Is much of it justifiable? *Exceptional Children, 35*, 10–22.

Elbaum, B., Vaughn, S., Hughes, M. T., & Moody, S. W. (1999). Grouping practices and reading outcomes for students with disabilities. *Exceptional Children, 65*, 399–415.

Elbaum, B., Vaughn, S., Hughes, M. T., & Moody, S. W. (2000). How effective are one-to-one tutoring programs in reading for elementary students at risk for reading failure? A meta-analysis of the intervention research. *Journal of Educational Psychology*, *92*, 605–619.

Elementary and Secondary Education Act (1965) 20 U.S.C. §2701 et seq.

Fuchs, D. & Fuchs, L. S. (1995) Special education can work. In J. Kauffman & J. Lloyd (Eds.), *Issues in educational placement: Students with emotional and behavioral disorders* (pp. 363–375). Hillsdale, NJ: Erlbaum.

Fuchs, L. S., & Fuchs, D. (1998). General educators' instructional adaptation for students with learning disabilities. *Learning Disability Quarterly*, *21*(1), 23–33.

Fuchs, L. S., & Fuchs. D. (1999). Monitoring student progress toward the development of reading competence; A review of three forms of classroom-based assessment. *School Psychology Review*, *28*, 659–671.

Gersten, R., & Jiménez, R. (1998). Modulating instruction for language minority students. In E. Kaméenui & D. Carnine (Eds.), *Effective teaching strategies that accommodate diverse learners* (pp. 161–178). Upper Saddle River, NJ: Prentice-Hall.

Gersten, R., & Vaughn, S. (2001). Meta-analyses in learning disabilities: Introduction to the special issue. *Elementary School Journal*, *101*, 251–272.

Gersten, R., Vaughn, S., Deshler, D., & Schiller, E. (1997). What we know about using research findings: Implications for improving special education practice. *Journal of Learning Disabilities*, *30*, 446–476.

Goldberg, S. S. (1982). *Special education law: A guide for parents, advocates, and educators,* New York: Plenum.

Graney, S. B., Missall, K. N., Martinez, R. S., & Bergstrom, M. (2008). A preliminary investigation of within-year growth patterns in reading and mathematics curriculum-based measures. *Journal of School Psychology, 47*, 121–142.

Hall, T. (2002). *Differentiated instruction.* Wakefield, MA: National Center on Accessing the General Curriculum, retrieved September 28, 2009, from http://www.cast.org/publications/ncac/ncac_diffinstruc.html

Hallahan, D. P., & Kauffman, J. M. (1978). *Exceptional children: Introduction to special education.* Englewood Cliffs, NJ: Prentice-Hall.

Hockenbury, J., Kauffman, J. M., & Hallahan, D. P. (1999–2000). What is right about special education. *Exceptionality, 8*, 3–11.

Hopkins, Gary (1998). The debate over class size: Class size does matter! Retrieved October 27, 2009, from http://www.educationworld.com/a_issues/issues024.shtml

Individuals with Disabilities Education Act, Pub. L. No. 105-17 (1997). Retrieved 9/08, from http://www.ed.gov/offices/OSERS/Policy/IDEA/the_law.html

Kaestle, C. F. (1976). Conflict and consensus revisited: Notes toward a reinterpretation of American educational history. *Harvard Education Review, 46,* 390–396.

Kauffman, J. M. (1999). Commentary: Today's special education and its messages for tomorrow. *Journal of Special Education, 32,* 244–254.

Kauffman, J. M., Bantz, J., & McCollough, J. (2002). Separate and better: A special public school class for students with emotional and behavioral disorders. *Exceptionality, 10,* 149–170

Kauffman, J. M., & Hallahan, D. P. (2005). *The illusion of full inclusion* (2nd ed.). Austin, TX: PRO-ED.

Kelley, W. (2003). *Common dense a new conversation for public education.* Retrieved October 17, 2009, from http://www.commonsensetorpubliceducation.org/common-sense-book.pdf

Kirk, S., & Gallagher, J. (1979). *Educating exceptional children* (3rd ed.). Boston: Houghton Mifflin.

Kohler, P. D., & Field, S. (2003) Transition-focused education: Foundation for the future. *Journal of Special Education, 37,* 174–183.

Landrum, T. J., Tankersley, M., & Kauffman, J. M. (2003).What is special about special education for students with emotional or behavioral disorders? *The Journal of Special Education, 37*, 148–156.

Lilly, M. S. (1979). *Children with exceptional needs: A survey of special education.* New York: Holt, Reinhart and Winston.

Mastropieri, M., & Scruggs, T. (2007). *The inclusive classroom: Strategies for effective instruction* (3rd ed.). Upper Saddle River, NJ: Pearson.

Mosteller, F. (1995). The Tennessee study of class size in the early school grades. *The Future of Children 5*(2) 113–127.

McDonnell, J. (1998). Instruction for students with severe disabilities in general education settings. *Education and Training in Mental Retardation*, *33*, 199–215.

National Association of State Boards of Education. (1992). *Winners all: A call for inclusive schools.* Alexandria, VA: Author.

National Council for Accreditation of Teacher Education. (2008). *Professional standards for the accreditation of teacher preparation institutions.* Washington DC: NCATE.

National Education Association. (1992). *The integration of students with special needs into regular classrooms: Policies and practices that work.* Washington, DC: Author.

No Child Left Behind Act, Pub. L. No. 107-110 (2001). Retrieved September 11, 2008, from http://www.ed.gov/policy/elsec/leg/eseas02/index/html

Public Law 94-142 (1975). Education of All Handicapped Children Act of 1975, Retrieved January 2009, from http:// http://users.rcn.com/peregrin.enteract/add/94-142.txt

Quenemoen, R. F., Lehr, C. A., Thurlow, M. L., & Massanari, C. B. (2001). *Students with disabilities in standards-based assessment and accountability systems: Emerging issues, strategies, and recommendations* (Synthesis Report 37). Minneapolis: University of Minnesota, National Center on Educational Outcomes.

Rashotte, C. A., MacPhee, K., & Torgesen, J. K. (2001). The effectiveness of a group reading instruction program with poor readers in multiple grades. *Learning Disability Quarterly, 24*, 119–134.

Rothbard, M. (1978). *Public and compulsory schooling.* In *For a new liberty* (chap. 7). Retrieved April 12, 2007, from http://www.mises.org/rothbard/newliberty6.asp

Rutledge, L. (2003) *Differentiated instruction.* Retrieved October 2009 from http://www.txstate.edu/edphd/Images/DiffInst.pdf

Samuels, C. A. (2005, February 22), Subject qualification vexing for teachers in special education, *Education Week, 24*(23), 1.

Scruggs, T. E., Mastropieri, M. A., & McDuffie, K. (2007). Co-teaching in inclusive classrooms: A metasynthesis of qualitative research. *Exceptional Children, 73*, 392–416.

Smith, P. (1999). Drawing new maps: A radical cartography of developmental disabilities. *Review of Educational Research*, *69*, 117–144.

Snell, M. E. (1997) Teaching children and young adults with mental retardation in school programs: Current research. *Behavior Change, 14,* 73–105.

Stanovich, K. E. (2000). *Progress in understanding reading: Scientific foundations and new frontiers.* New York: Guilford.

Stecker, P. M., & Fuchs, L. S. (2000). Effecting superior achievement using curriculum-based measurement: The importance of individual progress monitoring. *Learning Disabilities Research & Practice, 15*, 128–134.

Swanson, E. A. (2008). Observing reading instruction for students with learning disabilities: A synthesis. *Learning Disability Quarterly*, *31*, 115–133.

Swanson, H., & Deshler, D. (2003). Instructing adolescents with learning disabilities: Converting a meta-analysis to practice. *Journal of Learning Disabilities*, *36*, 124–135.

Swanson, H. L., Harris, K. R., Graham, S. (Eds.). (2000). *Handbook of learning disabilities*. New York: Guilford.

Swanson, H. L., Hoskyn, M., & Lee, C. (1999). *Interventions for students with learning disabilities*. New York: Guilford.

Thattai, D. (2001). A history of public education in the United States. *Journal of Literacy and Education in Developing Societies*, *1*, 2. Retrieved September 10, 2009, from http://www.servintfree.net/%7Eaidmn-ejournal/publications/2001-11/PublicEducationInTheUnitedStates.html

Thurlow, M., Quenemoen, R., Altman, J., & Cuthbert, M., (2008). *Trends in the participation and performance of students with disabilities* (Technical Report 50). Minneapolis: University of Minnesota, National Center on Educational Outcomes.

Title IX of the Education Amendments (1972) 20 U.S.C. §1680 et seq.

Tomlinson, C. A. (1999). *The differentiated classroom: Responding to the needs of all learners*. Alexandria, VA: Association of Supervision and Curriculum Development.

Torgesen, J.K. (1996). Thoughts about intervention research in learning disabilities. *Learning Disabilities: A Multidisciplinary Journal, 7*, 55–58.

Vaughn, S., & Dammann, J. E. (2001). Science and sanity in special education. *Behavioral Disorders, 27*, 21–29.

Vaughn, S., Gersten, R., & Chard, D. J. (2000). The underlying message in LD intervention research: Findings from research syntheses. *Exceptional Children, 67*, 99–114.

Vaughn, S., Linan-Thompson, S., & Hickman-Davis, P. (2003). Response to treatment as a means of identifying students with reading/learning disabilities. *Exceptional Children, 69,* 391–410.

Vaughn, S., Linan-Thompson, S., Kousekanani, K., Bryant, D. P., Dickson, S., & Blozis, S. A. (2003). Reading instruction grouping for students with reading difficulties. *Remedial and Special Education, 24*, 301–315.

Walker, H. M., Schwarz, I. E., Nippold, M. A., Irvin, L. K., & Noell, J. W. (1994). Social skills in school-age children and youth: Issues and best practices in assessment and intervention. *Topics in Language Disorders, 14*(3), 70–82.

Wang, M. (1998). Accommodating student diversity through adaptive education. In S. Stainback, W. Stainback, & M. Forest (Eds.), *Educating all students in the mainstream of education* (pp. 183–197). Baltimore: Paul H. Brookes.

Whitehurst, G. (2004, April). *Making education evidence-based: Premises, principles, pragmatics, and politics.* Evanston, IL: Institute for Policy Research Distinguished Public Policy Lecture Series, Northwestern University.

Yell, M. (1998). *The law and special education,* Upper Saddle River, NJ: Merrill Prentice Hall.

Ysseldyke, J., & Algozzine, B. (1984). *Introduction to special education.* Boston: Houghton Mifflin.

Zigmond, N. (1996). Organization and management of general education classrooms. In D. Speece & B. Keogh (Eds.), *Research on classroom ecologies: Implications for inclusion of children with learning disabilities* (pp. 163–190). Hillsdale, NJ: Erlbaum.

Zigmond, N. (1997). Educating students with disabilities: The future of special education. In J. Lloyd, E. Kameenui, & D. Chard (Eds.), *Issues in educating students with disabilities* (pp. 377–390). Hillsdale, NJ: Erlbaum.

Zirkel, P. A., & Kincaid, J. M. (1993). *Section 504, the ADA, and the schools.* Horsham, PA: LRP.

Section IV

Special Education Categories

Section Editors: Paige C. Pullen and Daniel P. Hallahan
University of Virginia

Each chapter in this section of this handbook is devoted to one of 11 traditional categories of special education: intellectual and developmental disabilities, learning disabilities, attention deficit hyperactivity disorder, emotional/behavioral disorders, communication disorders, deaf and hard-of-hearing, blindness and low vision, traumatic brain injury, autism spectrum disorders, multiple and severe disabilities, and special gifts and talents. Although the formats of the chapters vary according to each author's unique perspective, generally, they all address topics pertaining to definition, identification, causes, and educational treatments. They each capture the main theories, research, and practices related to the specified category.

Although the popular trend is toward a non-categorical approach to special education, approaching special education from a categorical perspective helps the reader to understand the historical and foundational concepts that underpin each category. With an understanding of these concepts, one is then able to grasp some of the broader issues covered in the other sections of this volume. Thus, the editors have chosen to place this section immediately after the foundational sections that cover history, legal issues, and the context of special education within the larger general education context.

Clearly, the notion of non-categorical special education has garnered support; however, it's noteworthy that this support lies mainly in the areas of teacher certification and teacher preparation. This focus does not detract from the necessity to understand the unique characteristics and needs of individuals with each disability. It is critical to the ultimate success of exceptional learners that educators understand what practices are appropriate for whom, and under what conditions. A categorical approach to research may be the most effective method for determining best practices.

Although the trend in teacher preparation has moved to a non-categorical approach, many scholars in the field of special education have maintained a categorical focus in their research. Likewise, some researchers have broader foci than just one category; and some researchers, by studying certain practices, such as inclusion, response to intervention, progress monitoring, have chosen to include participants from more than one category in their samples. Interestingly, however, even in these latter scenarios, the researcher has usually reported results separately for each category. These factors argue for the inherent value of approaching students with disabilities from a categorical perspective, at least with respect to research.

The fact that we have included a categorical section, however, should not be taken to mean that we believe that special education should be viewed from the perspective of the whole being equal to the sum of the parts. On the contrary, there is a goodly amount of webbing or intermeshing that occurs among the 11 categories. Research approaches and methodologies and educational practices and policies that arise in one category are often adopted wholesale or modified for use in one or more of the other categories. Thus, we present these chapters in a categorical approach to help the reader understand the uniqueness of the particular disabilities yet have the ability to integrate this knowledge with the hope that this knowledge will be used to the betterment of school and life outcomes for all exceptional learners.

14

Intellectual and Developmental Disabilities

Edward A. Polloway
Lynchburg College

James R. Patton
University of Texas at Austin

Marvalin A. Nelson
St. Lucia Schools, West Indies

The focus of this chapter is on individuals who have mild intellectual and developmental disabilities. The concept of intellectual disabilities represents a contemporary change from *mental retardation*, initially coined as an option to *feeblemindedness* (Polloway & Lubin, 2009). The intellectual disabilities term has become the preferred referent for individuals across the lifespan. At the same time, because mental retardation is well-entrenched within our bureaucracy (such as in federal reports), we continue to use the term in this chapter as applicable.

Intellectual and developmental disabilities have provided a foundation for the broader field of special education. A significant amount of the initial work in special education was concerned with individuals labeled mildly mentally retarded. Further, many of the leaders who shaped the field began their professional careers and/or made their major contributions in this area (Polloway, 2000). However, in recent years, this field has received far less attention. Tymchuk, Lakin, and Luckasson (2001) and Fujiura (2003) used the term *the forgotten generation* originally in reference to adults with mild mental retardation; this concept underscores the relative paucity of attention to persons with mild intellectual disabilities.

Terminology and Definition

Terminology

The field of mild intellectual and developmental disabilities has witnessed the use of numerous terms to describe this population. Polloway (2006, pp.183–184) noted:

> Our lexicon has ranged from the use of the terms feebleminded and moron to mildly mentally handicapped, mildly mentally retarded, mildly mentally disabled, general learning disabilities (GLD), adaptive academic functioning deficits, (and) high incidence disability.

For five decades, the most frequently used term was mental retardation. For example, it was the most frequent of the 66 terms found in the literature (Sandicson, 1998). Polloway, Patton, Smith, Antoine, and Lubin (2010) reported that 27 states used *mental retardation* for educational purposes. Bergeron, Floyd, and Shands (2008) confirmed those findings as they reported this term was used by 53% of the states. Thus, while the field continues to explore terminology, it is apparent that the implementation of these changes varies dramatically across the states.

Polloway et al.'s (2010) study was conducted at a time of significant professional discussion on terminology (e.g., Schalock et al., 2007). As Smith (2006) indicated, "the 2002 AAMR manual authors acknowledged the problems with the term mental retardation but concluded that there was no acceptable alternative term" (p. 58). Since 2002, the shift to intellectual disabilities has clearly increased. This change is reflected in organizational names (e.g., American Association on Intellectual and Developmental Disabilities; AAIDD) and journal and professional text titles. Although some governmental agencies are changing more slowly, the professional community has embraced *intellectual disabilities*.

As part of the ongoing discussion of terminology, a number of parallel questions have also been raised about the use of the term *mild*. Polloway (2006) noted that "the mild concept has regularly created misconceptions within both the profession and the general population that has had implications for the eligibility of individuals for educational and other supports" (p. 196.). Snell et al. (2009) referred instead to *people with intellectual disabilities who have higher IQs*. Nevertheless, *mild* continues to be used in the literature.

The term *developmental delay* is a federally designated label that refers to students under the age of 9 years who have experienced delay, or are identified as at risk for likely experiencing delay in the future, and are eligible for special education, subject to state guidelines. It has commonly provided an opportunity for the use of a less pejorative term by individuals assessing young children under consideration for eligibility who need to receive services without reference to the intellectual disability label. As such, it enables children to be served earlier in life who otherwise might have fallen through the cracks. In addition, the term is more functional and more service-related than the deficit-focused mental retardation.

Polloway et al. (2009) noted that changes in terminology can affect a number of areas. In schools, a name change may not be as important as which criteria are used to determine eligibility. In non-school settings, it remains to be seen whether this group of individuals will be positively affected due to a shift to intellectual disabilities. A name change could have dramatic implications in the legal arena in which being diagnosed as mentally retarded is just beginning to be understood, particularly in light of the attention given after the Supreme Court decision in the Atkins case (Patton & Keyes, 2006).

Definition

The definition of developmental disabilities, as stated in the Developmental Disabilities Assistance and Bill of Rights Act (2000), is multi-faceted. The first part refers to:

> a severe, chronic disability … that: is attributable to a mental or physical impairment or combination of mental and physical impairments; is manifested before the individual attains age 22; is likely to continue indefinitely; results in substantial functional limitations in three or more of the following areas of major life activity: self-care, receptive and expressive language, learning, mobility, self-direction, capacity for independent living, and economic self-sufficiency; and reflects the individual's need for a combination and sequence of special, interdisciplinary, or generic services, individualized supports, or other forms of assistance that are of lifelong or extended duration and are individually planned and coordinated. (p. 1683)

The second part refers to:

> an individual from birth to age 9, inclusive, who has a substantial developmental delay or specific congenital or acquired condition, may be considered to have a developmental disability without meeting three or more of the criteria described (above) if the individual, without services and supports, has a high probability of meeting those criteria later in life. (p. 1684)

The most commonly used definitions of intellectual disability have been promulgated by the AAIDD. The most recent version stated that it is a disability: "characterized by significant limitations both in intellectual functioning and in adaptive behavior as expressed in conceptual, social, and practical adaptive skills. This disability originates before age 18" (Schalock et al., 2010, p. 1).

The 2010 definition represented a modification of prior definitions but continued to emphasize the three dimensions of intellectual functioning, adaptive behavior, and manifestation during the developmental period. Although Polloway et al. (2009) noted that 34 states continued to depend on the Grossman (1983) AAMR definition, they reported evidence of increased use of the Luckasson et al. (2002), which preceeded the most recent definition of intellectual disability as published by AAIDD (Schalock et al., 2010).

In operationalizing these definitions, it is important to note that developmental disabilities and intellectual disabilities do not refer to precisely the same population (Luckasson et al., 2002; Polloway, 2005). There is a distinct sub-group of those who might be identified as intellectually disabled but who might not be technically considered developmentally disabled—this would include some individuals historically referred to as mildly mentally retarded.

Assessment and Identification

The process of assessment derives directly from the definitions, as discussed above. The discussion below illustrates the assessment process just for intellectual disabilities.

The first dimension relates to intellectual functioning. By definition, an individual must have a measured intelligence quotient (IQ) that is less than approximately 70–75. Although the precise cut-off scores vary by state guidelines (Polloway, Lubin, Smith, & Patton, 2010), nevertheless the most common practice has been to recognize the 70–75 ceiling level (+/– a standard error of measurement of 5 points). Polloway et al. (2009) reported that 34 states required a cut-off score or range; most commonly, the ceiling was either approximately IQ 70 or two standard deviations below the mean. Bergeron et al. (2008) found that "the majority of states use an IQ cutoff at least two SDs below the normative mean" (p. 125).

The second dimension focuses on adaptive behavior (AB). According to contemporary practice, this interpretation requires that an individual show significant deficits in overall AB or in conceptual, social, or practical adaptive skills. This assessment requires the administration of an AB scale as well as placing data within the context of individual's functioning in everyday life. Polloway et al. (2009) reported that all states required AB assessment though only 23 highlighted the specific practices to be followed.

The developmental period dimension requires manifestation by age 18. Polloway et al. (2009) noted that 33 states (64.7%) did not specify an age range in spite of professional definitions calling for such a period. It can be assumed, however, that few students are identified as intellectually disabled later in their school years. This dimension becomes particularly challenging when individuals are assessed as adults with an attempt to retrospectively determine whether the disability was manifested during the developmental period.

School Prevalence

Identification and diagnostic criteria have a direct impact on the number of individuals who receive services. For decades a common estimate was that approximately 3% of the school population could be identified as mentally retarded (MacMillan, 2007). However, even though this rate was often cited as a basis for policy initiatives and governmental support, rarely was it confirmed in practice. Rather, the best predictor of the prevalence in the schools in the 1980s, for example, was closer to 2% (Polloway et al., 2010).

The annual reports to Congress from the Department of Education (e.g., USDOE 2007, 2009) provide baseline data for tracking trends in prevalence rates. Subsequent to 1975, there was a steady and significant decline for about 20 years in the number of individuals identified as mentally retarded in the public schools. Neither 3% nor 2% have proven to be accurate portrayals of reality (Polloway et al., 2010).

The 29th Annual Report to Congress (USDOE, 2009) provides a 10-year perspective with prevalence data showing limited variance on an annual basis during this time frame. Consistently, the prevalence has been slightly less than 1% (approximately 0.9% for 1995–2003; 0.84% in 2004) for school-age children identified as mentally retarded.

The most compelling finding related to prevalence is the significant variance across states. Twelve states reported prevalence rates in excess of 1.2%, including two states that reported prevalence figures above 2% (West Virginia: 2.48%; Kansas: 2.00%). On the other hand, 19 states had rates below 0.6% and eight states 0.4% or below (USDOE, 2009).

Prevalence data provide a window through which to consider the nature of the population identified and served. It would be naïve to assume that truly similar populations of individuals are identified across the states given that the prevalence data vary so significantly. In those states in which prevalence rates are approximately 1.75% or higher, it might be concluded that the population is not dissimilar to that which was commonly served 30 or more years ago and would likely include a sizable number of individuals with mild intellectual disabilities. However, for states serving approximately 0.4% or less of their population, it is likely that this population would include only students with more significant disabilities because this figure is commonly seen as consistent with the approximate number of persons with severe disabilities within a given population (e.g., Abramowicz & Richardson, 1975; MacMillan, 2007). In these states, reasonable questions would be: are there any individuals being served who might be considered mildly mentally retarded; are these individuals served under another category; and/or are they not receiving special education (Polloway, et al., 2010)?

The USDOE (2007) provides data on individuals identified as "developmentally delayed," which as noted above, is a category consistent with developmental disabilities allowed under the Individuals With Disabilities Education Act (IDEA, 1997) for students between ages 3 and 9 years. The state variance for this category again is significant (e.g., California and New Jersey reported no individuals so identified whereas a number of states reported in excess of 0.30), nevertheless the individuals identified nationally as developmentally delayed, ages 6–9, increased dramatically between 1997 and 2003, to above 0.40. As states consider changing guidelines to restrict the age range for developmental delay, there will likely be an impact on the prevalence of students from ages 6–9 who are identified as having an intellectual disability.

Causes

Although researchers have identified hundreds of causes for intellectual and developmental disabilities, only in about 50% or more of the cases can a specific biological factor be identified (Dykens, Hodapp, & Finucane, 2000; Van Karnebeek et al., 2005). Those cases with an identified cause are disproportionally represented among individuals with more significant disabilities. The undetermined group includes many persons identified as having mild intellectual disabilities (President's Committee for People with Intellectual Disabilities [PCPID], 2007) because there often are no identifiable causes for mild intellectual disability (Snell et al., 2009).

Polloway, Smith, and Antoine (in press) noted traditionally that etiology has been described as a two-group model. The first group consists of known and specifiable biological causes, which result in intellectual and developmental disabilities at all levels but which have been most associated with significant disabilities. The second group was presumed to be affected by psychosocial or socio-cultural factors (Spinath, Harlaar, Ronald, & Plomin, 2004) coupled with other environmental influences. It is clear, however, that the traditional association of a single, organic cause with significant disabilities is simplistic; many individuals with mild intellectual disabilities certainly are affected by physiological factors (Polloway et al., in press) that may be the result of environmental factors.

Certain educational and psychological intervention strategies may be etiology-specific, and an understanding of causation may lead to alternative approaches to intervention. Dykens (2001) noted the value of etiological information:

> One long-term goal of this line of work is to examine links between genes, brain, and behavior.... Simply put, behavioral experts are needed to solve the behavioral half of these gene-behavior puzzles. In the short-term, behavioral ... data can be put to immediate good use as guideposts for treatment and intervention, and such syndrome-specific recommendations have already been made for fragile X, Down, Prader-Willi, Williams, and other syndromes. (p.1)

This discussion of causes is necessarily limited within this chapter. Consequently, we focus on examples of selected disorders related to genetic transmission, chromosomal anomalies, fetal alcohol spectrum disorders, and psychosocial considerations.

Genetic Transmission

Although genetic disorders associated with autosomal recessive, dominant, and sex-linked transmission are individually and collectively very rare, they nevertheless are of importance for understanding individual cases and for providing a basis for ongoing research and prevention. Autosomal recessive transmission is responsible for approximately one-third of all single-gene disorders, autosomal dominant for over one-half, and X-linked dominant and X-linked recessive for the balance (Harris, 2006).

Autosomal dominant disorders are typically related to structural abnormalities. An example is *neurofibromatosis*, which, according to Cutting, Clements, Lightman, Yerby-Hancock, and Denckla (2004), is the most common single gene disorder affecting the central nervous system, with a rate of 1 in 2,500 births. The most common pattern is NF1, a mutation on chromosome #17. About 50% of all cases of neurofibromatosis are inherited with the remainder caused by sporadic genetic *mutations*.

NF1 is identifiable by light brown (café-au-lait) patches on the skin and/or by multiple, soft, fibrous swellings or tumors (neurofibromas) that grow on nerves or appear elsewhere on the body and can result in physical deformities. Although the common café-au-lait patches are primarily a cosmetic concern, the locations of the possible skin tumors may have an effect on mental development. The majority of children with neurofibromatosis are likely to have academic problems, with an estimated 30%–60% having learning disabilities (Rasmussen & Friedman, 1999) whereas fewer are diagnosed with intellectual disabilities. Key characteristics include problems in decoding and phonological aspects of reading, receptive and expressive language, complex motor tasks, attention deficit hyperactivity disorder, and executive function deficits (Cutting et al., 2004).

Autosomal recessive transmission is often related to dysfunctions in mechanisms for the processing of food and imbalances in fats, carbohydrates, or amino acids. Collectively they occur in approximately 1 in 4,000 births (Hall, 2000).

Phenylketonuria (PKU) is the most common recessive disorder with incidence of 1 in every 12,000 to 15,000 births. Left untreated, PKU may be associated with aggressiveness, hyperactivity, and intellectual disabilities. The mechanism that results in these outcomes relates to the toxic effect of increased amino acid level in the brain, leading to severe disorder. PKU was the first metabolic anomaly proven to cause intellectual disabilities and its discovery led to increased research and a pronounced change in the hope for treatment and cure. Consequently, it has been virtually eliminated as a causative factor for significant disabilities. The dietary treatment is restricted intake of phenylalanine, common in high-protein foods, and the substitution of other foods and synthetic proteins. The elimination of phenylalanine results in the prevention of the deleterious effects of PKU (Levitas, 1998).

A third form of transmission is through *X-linked recessive inheritance*. Although the X chromosome contains only 4% of all human genes, it accounts for 10% of all inherited disorders (Meyer, 2007; Spencer & Diffenbach, 2005). Dykens et al. (2000) noted that there are more than 70 causes of disabilities associated with X-linked inheritance patterns. The key is that males will be affected by a single recessive gene on the X chromosome because males have an XY chromosomal pattern and thus there is no gene on an X chromosome pair opposite the pathology-producing recessive gene. There are an estimated 1,098 gene sites on the X but only 54 counterpart sites on Y (Ross et al., 2005; Spencer & Dieffenbach, 2005).

The most significant sex-linked disorder is *fragile X syndrome*, the most common inherited cause of intellectual and developmental disabilities (Roberts et al., 2007). Traditional estimates have been 1 in 1,500 males and 1 in 1,000 females in the population, although Mazzocco and Holden (2007) note lower rates of 1 in 9,000 for females and 1 in 4,000 for males based on instances of full mutations.

The causation mechanism is a mutation on a gene (FMR1) on the X chromosome that switches off a protein, resulting in a variety of behavioral impacts. *Premutation* refers to carriers of the disorder who are unaffected but might experience some of the characteristics. A full mutation "essentially silences the genes so that they do not produce its protein or produce insufficient amounts of protein", which results in the clinical features associated with the fragile X syndrome (Mazzocco & Holden, 2007, p. 175). Of the individuals with the full mutation, approximately 85% of males and 25% of females will have intellectual disabilities, with the balance at risk for learning disabilities (Tartaglia, Hansen, & Hagerman, 2007). Inheritance most commonly involves transmission from a carrier mother to an affected son.

Rogers and Simensen (1987) noted that common physical characteristics of fragile X syndrome include prominent jaw, long and thin faces, long and soft ears and hands, prominent forehead, and enlarged head. Behavioral manifestations may include attentional difficulties, repetitive speech, repetitive behaviors, and gaze avoidance, and speech and language patterns may include echolalia and preservative utterances (Belser & Sudhalter, 2001).

A consistent relationship between fragile X syndrome and autism has been reported in the literature (Harris et al., 2008). Some of the traits that have resulted in this association include repetitive speech, echolalia, attention deficit, hand flapping, poor eye contact, and gaze aversion. Hall, Lightbody, and Reiss (2008) reported that the diagnostic criteria for autism were met in 50% of boys and 20% of girls with fragile X syndrome.

Chromosomal Anomalies

Researchers have identified more than 60 chromosomal anomalies, affecting about 7 in 1,000 live births. In addition, a significant number of pregnancies that begin with a chromosomal abnormality result in miscarriages or may be the reason for a large number of abortions. Depending on the specific study, 4%–8% of persons with intellectual disabilities are estimated to have chromosomal anomalies (Harris, 2006). We discuss two examples below.

Down syndrome is the best known and most frequently researched biological condition associated with intellectual disabilities. The prevalence is about 1 in 800–1,000 births (Lovering & Percy, 2007). The most common pattern, trisomy 21, accounts for 92%–95% of children with Down syndrome (Dykens et al., 2000). Lovering and Percy (2007) reported that 85% of these cases occur when the mother contributes the extra chromosome, whereas in 15% of the cases the third chromosome is from the father. Although risk is related to maternal age and increases to approximately 1 in 30 births at 45 years old, age itself is a *correlate* and not the *cause* (Polloway et al., in press); the large majority of births of children with Down syndrome are to younger parents.

An important area of research on Down syndrome has focused on intellectual functioning. The seminal work in this area was reported by Rynders, Spiker, and Horrobin (1978). They reported a significant range in functioning and refuted the alleged ceiling IQ of 70, with early intervention as the key. Rynders and Horrobin (1990) and Rynders (2005) provided further support for this finding.

Persons with Down syndrome unfortunately are often viewed in stereotypical ways. Therefore, it is of particular importance that they be seen as individuals who have needs, desires, and rights similar to those of other people. Toward this end, important areas of focus include developing friendships (Freeman & Kasari, 2002), emotional development (Kasari, Freeman, & Hughes, 2001), and family relationships (Cuskelly & Gunn, 2003). Dykens (2007) identified their positive features as fewer externalizing problems with increased age, a sense of humor, kindness, caring, and forgiveness.

Another condition related to an autosomal abnormality is *Prader-Willi syndrome*. Approximately 70% of cases are the result of deletion of the paternal chromosome on pair 15. For the remaining 30%, the condition is most often the result of maternal uniparental disomy of the 15th chromosome; that is, both chromosomes are contributed by the mother (Percy, Lewkis, & Brown, 2007). Epidemiological data indicate an incidence of approximately 1 in 10–20,000 and a population prevalence of about 1 in 53,000 (Harris, 2006; Whittington & Holland, 2004).

Prader-Willi emerges in two stages: an infantile hypotonic (low muscle tone) phase and a childhood/adulthood obesity phase (Donaldson et al., 1994). A paradox is their initial failure-to-thrive condition, given the excessive eating and obesity as the child increases in age.

After age 3 years, the characteristics of the second phase become apparent. This phase may include hyperphagia (i.e., an insatiable appetite) and preoccupation with food (Joseph, Egli, Koppekin, & Thompson, 2002). Affected persons often have small features and stature and intellectual disabilities. They were more likely than a comparison group of individuals to enjoy eating, thinking about food and indulging in eating unusual combinations of edible and inedible foods (Dykens, 2000). A pattern of significant behavioral difficulties may emerge including tantrums, compulsive and obsessive behaviors, impulsivity, aggression, and stubbornness (Dimitropoulos, Feurer, Butler, & Thompson, 2001). Early intervention, exercise, monitoring of caloric intake and education about food choices, environmental controls, and specialized transition planning are key interventions (Scott, Smith, Hendricks, & Polloway, 1997).

Fetal Alcohol Spectrum Disorder

Jones, Smith, Ulleland, and Streissguth (1973) coined the term *fetal alcohol syndrome* (FAS) after studies of children born to alcoholic mothers showed a pattern of malformations, growth deficiencies, and intellectual and developmental disabilities. The contemporary term of *fetal alcohol spectrum disorder* (FASD) includes conditions ranging from fetal alcohol effects, which may include characteristics associated with learning disabilities, to FAS, associated with more significant disabilities. FASD is among the leading known causes of intellectual disabilities, with estimates as high as 15%–20% of cases (Harris, 2006). The estimate for affected births in the general population is as high as 1% of births (Harris, 2006).

FASD results in central nervous system dysfunction, craniofacial malformations (e.g., cleft palate, microcephaly), and prenatal and postnatal growth development (e.g., low birth weight). These three areas, in the presence of use of alcohol during pregnancy, are the basis of the diagnosis (Ryan & Ferguson, 2006).

The characteristics associated with FASD range significantly. Miller (2006) noted that they include difficulties in social communication and language, conceptual reasoning and thinking skills, emotional and social behaviors, and independence and self-sufficiency. The broad nature of the category of FASD results in significant variance in manifestations.

Psychosocial Considerations

In the prior discussion, we focused on the biological aspects of causation. It is important to also consider the psychosocial factors that may contribute to intellectual and developmental disabilities. Particular risk factors (or correlates) within the psychosocial domain include absence of significant parental guidance and mediation, maternal educational level, inadequate housing, and poor school attendance. At the same time, poverty environments are associated with a cluster of variables including inadequate prenatal care, lead exposure, nutritional deficiencies, and substance abuse during pregnancy.

Greenspan (2006) analyzed the impact of psychosocial considerations and related biological causes when he noted:

> Although early parental stimulation has obvious importance in fostering normal or deviant cognitive development, except in the most extreme of cases, [it] generally produces academic and social incompetence that does not result in a diagnosis of mental retardation....The emphasis on understimulating environment as the cause of most cases of mild retardation, especially from minority or disadvantaged

> families, obscures the fact that children from disadvantaged families can and often do suffer from organic risk factors, and the role of deprivation in causing mild retardation in such families is most likely to be the case when the child also is at biological risk, because of factors, such as prematurity, low birth weight, fetal alcohol affects, and the same kinds of syndromes that can affect all children. (p. 220)

Greenspan's perspectives (2006) further underscore the complexity of considerations of causation that may have an impact on individuals with mild intellectual disabilities. For most individuals, precise contributions of possible causes can rarely be confirmed. In addition, a common hypothesis is that psychosocial factors may operate in conjunction with the influence of multiple genes (i.e., *polygenic inheritance*). Regardless of whether a child already has a disability, growing up in restrictive conditions interferes with the opportunity to develop and mature. Therefore, we need to focus on diminishing the consequences of a non-stimulating environment through intervention.

Behavioral Characteristics

The determination of the characteristics of individuals with intellectual and developmental disabilities is based on a diverse collection of research-based observations reflective of the diversity of individuals. Although there traditionally was a rich source of research on characteristics, the last several decades have seen a relatively modest commitment to identifying and understanding behavioral and learning characteristics, a trend generally consistent with the modest amount of intervention research on individuals with mild intellectual disabilities. Nevertheless, there are several reviews that have sought to identify specific characteristics.

In Table 14.1, we present a modification of several reviews that have been undertaken to identify and derive implications related to behavioral and learning characteristics. These sources include an analysis of characteristics provided by Smith, Polloway, Patton, and Dowdy (2007), developed to provide implications for educators. It also reflects Patton and Keyes' (2006) review, which focused on implications for individuals within the criminal justice system. The adapted table reflects information on terminology concerning characteristics, a description of problem areas, and educational implications.

Educational Practices, Trends, and Issues

In this section, we discuss educational considerations related to individuals with intellectual and developmental disabilities. We focus on early childhood, elementary and secondary education, and ethnic disproportionately and transition to adulthood.

Early Childhood

The development of preschool programs is based to a significant degree on the identification of the populations served. It is very rare that the term *intellectual disabilities* is applied to children who are younger than 5 years of age (nationally, a total of only 22,410 children are labeled mentally retarded vs. 259,867 labeled developmentally delayed; USDOE, 2009). As a consequence, special education during early childhood is based far more on the label of developmental delay.

The term *developmental delay* refers to students who have experienced delay, or are identified as at risk for experiencing delay in the future. Although federal guidelines and definitions provide guidance, there is significant state variance in the application of this term (Danaher, Shackelford, & Harbin, 2004). The term is an important vehicle for enabling young children to obtain services without the use of a potentially life-stigmatizing label.

The most recent federal data indicate that 2.18% of children aged 3–5 are labeled as developmentally delayed (USDOE, 2009). These children are served primarily in one of four settings: early childhood (EC) programs (29.65%), special education (ECSE) settings (38.97%), combined EC/ECSE settings (16.79%), or home-based programs (5.23%).

Of particular importance for this population are the federal guidelines with respect to special education services. For children between three and five, Part B of IDEA mandates that all states provide free and appropriate public education to all eligible children from 3 to 5 years of age. Part C of IDEA authorizes financial assistance to states through grants to address the needs of infants and toddlers as well as their families. Within each of the respective states' guidelines, specific definitions provide a basis for determining eligibility for infants and toddlers with disabilities and for developmental delay (ages 3–5).

A specific concern has to do with the transition from eligibility under Part C to eligibility under Part B. Etscheidt (2006) summarized these concerns in noting "although the law provides a uniform process for transition,... studies of actual practices have indicated disruption, disorganization, and stress for parents" (p. 176). The USDOE (2009) reported that 68.5% children receiving Part C services were eligible under Part B, 11.04% were not eligible but referred to other programs, 6.9% were not eligible and were not referred and for 13.69% eligibility for Part B had not been determined.

Danaher et al. (2004) stressed the critical nature of continuity between eligibility for services and identified five potential sources of discontinuity: a policy for 3–5 students that requires a more significant degree of impairment or delay than for infants and toddlers; differential measurements stipulated within the two respective policies that can create psychometric variance; eligibility for children *at risk* for developmental delay as infants and toddlers who may not be eligible at ages 3–5; infant and toddler policies that focused largely on professional judgment in contrast to policies for ages 3–5 that may stress more categorical criteria or quantitative data; and the exclusion of certain categories of disabilities in the 3–5 policy that were not in place for infants and toddlers.

TABLE 14.1
Intellectual and Developmental Disabilities: Characteristics and Implications

Area	Areas of Potential Difficulty	Educational Implications
Attention	Attention span (length of time on task) Focus (inhibition of distracting stimuli) Selective attention (discrimination of important stimulus characteristics)	Train students to be aware of the importance of attention. Teach students how to actively self-monitor their attention. Highlight salient cues in instruction.
Metacognition	Metacognition: thinking about thinking Production of strategies to assist learning Organizing new information	Teach specific strategies (rehearsal, labeling, chunking). Involve students in active learning process (practice, apply, review). Stress meaningful content.
Memory	Short-term memory – common deficit area Long-term memory – usually more similar to that of people who are not disabled (once information has been learned)	Strategy production is difficult: hence students need to be show how to use strategies to proceed in organized, well-planned manner. Stress meaningful content.
Generalization Learning	Applying knowledge of skills to new tasks, or situations Using previous experience to formulate rules that will help solve problems of similar nature	Teach multiple contexts. Reinforce generalization. Teach skills in relevant contexts. Remind students to apply what they have learned.
Motivational Considerations	External locus of control (attributing events to others' influence) Outerdirectedness (in learning style) Low expectations by others Failure set (personal expectancy of failure)	Create environment focused on success opportunities. Emphasize self-reliance. Promote self-management. Teach learning strategies for academic tasks. Focus on learning to learn. Encourage problem-solving strategies.
Cognitive Development	Ability to engage in abstract thinking Symbolic thought, as exemplified by introspection and developing hypotheses	Provide concrete examples in instruction. Provide contextual learning experiences. Encourage active interaction between student and the environment
Language Development	Difficulty with receptive and expressive language Delayed acquisition of vocabulary and language rules Articulation of thoughts and feelings Possible interaction of cultural variance and language dialects	Create environment that encourages verbal communication. Encourage expression of thoughts. Provide appropriate language models. Provide opportunities for students to learn language for varied purposes and with different audiences.
Academic Development	Delayed acquisition of reading, writing, and mathematical skills Decoding of text Reading comprehension Math computation Problem-solving in mathematics Self-directed expressive writing	Use learning strategies to promote effective studying. Teach sight words including functional applications. Teach strategies for decoding unknown words. Provide strategies to promote reading comprehension and math problem solving. Develop functional writing skills. Adapt curriculum to promote success.
Social-Behavorial Interactions	Classroom behavior Peer acceptance Displaying emotions appropriately	Promote social competence through direct instruction of skills. Reinforce appropriate behaviors. Seek self-understanding of reasons for inappropriate behavior. Teach self-management, self-control
Social Responding	Social perception Gullibility Suggestibility Acquiescence and desire to please Masking disability ("cloak of competence")	Involve peers as classroom role models. Provide a support system of peers for positive guidance "buddy system". Teach resistance to social manipulation. Teach Miranda rights in the legal system.

Source: Adapted from Patton & Keyes, 2006; Smith, Polloway, Patton, & Beyer, 2008; and Smith, Polloway, Patton, & Dowdy, 2008.

Elementary and Secondary Considerations

Educational Services In spite of the national trend toward inclusion, the data on students with mental retardation from the USDOE (2009) indicate that placement into programs ***outside*** of general education is still predominant. The rate (86.2%) is substantially higher than for virtually all other disabilities in terms of placement for more than 21% of the school day in separate settings. Further, 56.9% of these students are in environments removed from general education, respectively at least 60% of the day (i.e., 50.5%) or in separate environments (e.g., special schools, residential programs) (i.e., 6.4%).

Williamson, McLeskey, Hoppey, and Rentz (2006) noted that even though placement of students with mental retardation in general education-based programs increased from 27.3% to 44.7% in the 1990s, this rate plateaued after 1997–1998. The USDOE (2009) data confirmed this plateau effect (i.e., 13.8% outside the general education classroom less than 21% of the day plus 29.3% outside for 21%–60% of time, for a total of 43.1%). Smith (2007) noted that the percentage of students with mental retardation served in the most inclusive setting (i.e., < 21% outside of regular class) declined between 1997–98 and 2002–03 in 34 states. It is important to note that these data sets include those with variant levels of disability.

Polloway et al. (2010) stressed the significant degree of interstate variance in prevalence and also examined two assumptions: first, that states with low prevalence are likely to be serving a population that is more significantly disabled and that, consequently, one would expect to find that those students are more likely to be served in more restricted settings; and second, that states serving a larger percentage of students with mental retardation are educating more individuals with mild disabilities and, consequently, may be more likely to provide services in general education settings. They reported, however, numerous examples of states in which high prevalence was not associated with greater inclusion as well as examples of where low prevalence was associated with a high percentage of students being served in general education placements. There was no statistical relationship between a state's prevalence data and likelihood of placement in inclusive settings.

Educational Programs There are a number of issues that emerge from the above discussion of services. One can conclude that successful inclusion efforts are linked to how well general education is prepared to teach students requiring differentiated strategies in terms of content, instructional materials, instruction, assignments, testing, products, setting, and management (Hoover & Patton, 2005, 2008). In a multi-tiered model, the need for general education teachers to be able to address the needs of a diverse group of students is imperative.

A key factor in Tier I interventions (i.e., enhanced instructional delivery in general education programs) is the implementation of strategies consistent with universal design for learning (UDL) in order to make general education classrooms more responsive to the diverse learning needs of students (Wehmeyer, 2006). The importance of UDL was underscored by the PCPID (2007), which noted that UDL can be effective by "simultaneously providing supports for learning and reducing barriers to the general education curriculum, while maintaining high achievement standards for all students [thus providing features that] facilitate the efforts of educators to better teach and support students with intellectual disabilities" (p. 13).

Schools that operate with a multi-tiered system create a role change for special education personnel (Hoover & Patton, 2008). Teachers are no longer solely responsible for direct instruction in separate programs but also must work collaboratively in preventive efforts typically associated with Tier I instruction, as well as supportive efforts often associated with Tier II instruction (i.e., ongoing collaboration in general education programs).

An important consideration is research on educational programs for students with intellectual disabilities. Polloway (2005) and Bouck (2007) highlighted the relative absence of recent, relevant research on educational interventions especially for students with mild intellectual disabilities with certain exceptions such as research on reading. The field has certainly not received the level of attention that has been accorded to other areas of exceptionality (e.g., learning disabilities, significant disabilities, autism). Similarly, there has been relatively limited attention given to this population at the secondary school level (Bouck, 2004, 2007).

Disproportionality

In his seminal paper, Dunn (1968) focused on the overrepresentation of students from ethnic minorities in programs for students with "educable mental retardation," which, he indicated, had become a vehicle for school segregation. The quality of outcomes from these programs led to questions about their justification as an appropriate placement option. Subsequently, disproportionality received significant attention in the courts as parents and advocates for students raised questions about the appropriateness of minority student identification and the placement practices being used with students in mild retardation programs in the schools (Polloway & Smith, 1983).

The USDOE (2009) provided information about ethnic patterns within the population of school-age students with disabilities. The risk for individuals who are White (non-Hispanic) to be identified as mentally retarded is 0.63% whereas the risk for individuals who are African American is 2.83%. Skiba, Poloni-Staudinger, Gallini, Simmons, and Feggins-Azziz (2006) confirmed that, although making up approximately 11% of the total school population, African Americans represented over 29% of the students so identified. The 2009 USDOE annual report to Congress (USDOE, 2009) indicated that this figure was 32.8%.

To respond to disproportionality, Skiba et al. (2008) recommended attention to teacher preparation practices, improvements in behavior management strategies, increased emphasis on early intervention, increased usage of response-to-instruction strategies, reduced bias in assessment, increased community and family involvement, and reform of public policy in order to promote culturally responsive public school systems.

Transition and Young Adulthood Considerations

Individuals with intellectual disabilities have for decades received attention in terms of transition planning and services. Many students stayed in school through to the completion of high school, although frequently they left without a diploma, receiving a certificate of some type (Edgar, 1987, 1988). Work-study programs have been implemented with this group since the 1950s, well before federally-mandated transition services (e.g., Kolstoe & Frey, 1965).

Two key sources of data provide a perspective on the transition process: the reports of Congress from the USDOE (e.g., 2007; 2009) and the compendium of data provided by the National Longitudinal Transition Study – 2 (NLTS-2) (Newman, Wagner, Cameto, & Knokey, 2009; Wagner, Newman, Cameto, Garza, & Levine, 2005).

The USDOE (2009) provided a 10-year retrospective on school exit patterns, including drop out and graduation rates. Although dropout rates for students with mental retardation generally have shown a consistent decline (from 40% in 1985 to 27.6% in 2004), nevertheless there remains a substantial number of students who are not completing school. Furthermore, only 39% of individuals with mental retardation receive regular diplomas; those numbers have been relatively static over 10 years, with an increase of only 5.4% since 1995. These students were consistently less likely to graduate than were students identified in any of the 11 other disability categories.

The NLTS-2 research (Wagner et al., 2005) provided an extended picture of the transition process by collecting data at different points in time from a variety of sources. It should be noted, as is true of most of the federal data on students classified as mentally retarded, that results represent responses in regard to a range of students in terms of level of disability. Key findings indicated that transition planning for most students with mental retardation began by age 14 (60%), but only about half of the students provided input into the process with only 3.3% taking a leadership role. In terms of goals, only 9.8% of students indicated postsecondary education whereas 51.4% indicated a goal of living independently. The study did report that over 75% of the students participated in programs identified as appropriate for their transition goals (Wagner et al.).

The NLTS-2 (Wagner et al., 2005) study highlighted the variance that students receive in terms of quality transition services and suggested several key goals:

- Identifying and implementing evidence-based transition practices
- Instituting techniques for starting the transition process earlier
- Empowering students to be more involved in their own transition and self-advocacy
- Increasing the opportunities for further education and training
- Empowering parents by providing them with information about the transition process and what to expect when their children finish school.

Several areas of research on young adults are worthy of note. First, Snell et al. (2009) reported that the employment rate of individuals with disabilities with higher IQs was 27.6%, far below the national average of 75.1%. In addition, the positions often were part-time and associated with lower wages and limited benefits. Newman et al. (2009) reported that 51.8% of individuals with intellectual disabilities had been employed at some point in time since high school, with 31% employed at the time of interview. The average work week was less than full-time (30.1 hours per week), and the average hourly wage was $7.00. The majority of these positions were in unskilled labor, food services, cleaning, stocking and shipping, and serving as a cashier.

A second area of concern is further education and productive engagement. Newman et al. (2009) reported that 27.4% of individuals with intellectual disabilities had attended any postsecondary programs, including 20% in 2-year or community college programs and 20.8% in vocational, business, or technical schools. In considering both post-secondary education and employment, only 66.3% were considered productively engaged since high school; the lowest figure for any disability group except multiple disabilities.

A third focal area relates to community engagement. In their study of young adults, Newman et al. (2009) reported that only 14.1% lived independently. In terms of financial independence, of persons with intellectual disabilities who had been out of school for up to 4 years, 40.5% had savings and 26.3% checking accounts and 8.9% had a credit card. With regard to friendship, a relatively low number of 69% saw friends outside of school or the workplace on at least a weekly basis. Only 28.3% indicated involvement in community activities, inclusive of classes or lessons outside school, community service, or groups such as a sports team or religious group. Furthermore, only 34.8% had a driver's license or permit.

With graduation rates low, school dropout rates relatively high, employment statistics discouraging, and social domain data suggesting limited positive engagement, there remains need for an increased commitment to retention in school and successful completion as well as successful transition preparation. Benz, Lindstrom, and Yovanoff (2000) concluded that the key components that result in improved school and adult outcomes include: direct support within general education; paid work experiences related to specific career interests; instruction in functional academic areas along with vocational education and related transition content; and the completion of transition goals that are consistent with student preferences and choices. A substantial literature base does illustrate that young adults can be successful in the workplace given appropriate training and supported work opportunities in the workplace (Snell et al., 2009).

A final issue with relevance for transitions is the interaction between young adults with intellectual disabilities and the criminal justice system. A key aspect of this interaction concerns certain socio-behavioral characteristics of individuals with intellectual disabilities. Greenspan (2006; Greenspan & Switzky, 2006) has posited that gullibility is a core characteristic of these individuals and that they are consequently vulnerable to social manipulation, which can have legal implications. In addition, the denial of disability further characterizes some of this population and creates potential problems (Patton & Keyes, 2006). For example, 40% of young adults with intellectual disabilities did not consider themselves to have a disability, in the context of postsecondary education. Furthermore, only 25.3% indicated that their employer was aware of their disability (Newman et al., 2009). These findings evoke Edgerton's (1967) "cloak of competence" concept in which individuals seek to mask their disability.

The importance of understanding the criminal justice system is underscored by the fact that 33.7% of young adults with intellectual disabilities indicated that they had been stopped by police for reasons other than a traffic violation, 16.9% indicated they had been arrested, 14.3% reported spending a night in jail, and 10.4% indicated they had been on probation or parole (Newman et al., 2009). Smith, Polloway, Patton, and Beyer (2008) concluded that

> while a small minority of adolescents and adults with ID will have adversarial encounters with the criminal justice system, nevertheless the available data suggest that this minority is sufficient to warrant the professional attention of educators.... It is within this vein that the importance of including attention to the criminal justice system within ... transition planning becomes most apparent. (pp. 427–428)

Discussion

In this chapter, we have provided an analysis of trends and practices related to individuals with intellectual and developmental disabilities. Five summative points are particularly relevant. First, the trend away from the designation *mental retardation* toward the term *intellectual and developmental disabilities* will likely continue and accelerate.

Second, although in this chapter we have used the term *mild* for convenience, clearly there are issues concerning its appropriateness. Luckasson et al. (2002) noted that "people with higher IQs (sometimes referred to as mild) do not necessarily have mild needs for support" (p. 208). Polloway (2006) further noted:

> the mild concept has regularly created misconceptions with both the profession and the general population that has had implications for the eligibility of individuals for educational and other supports.... The concept of "mild retardation" could be considered an oxymoron. (p. 196)

Third, there is great variance across states in the number of students identified as intellectually disabled and developmentally delayed. A number of states serve virtually no students who might historically have been considered mildly mentally retarded whereas a number of other states serve a substantial percentage of their population that might be so considered. Variant patterns also are common for developmental disabilities.

Fourth, there is wide variance across states in the educational environments in which these students are served, ranging from an apparent strong commitment to inclusive placements in some states to others with a large majority of individuals served in separate programs. Sixth, school exit data offer limited confidence that students with intellectual disabilities are well-positioned for successful transition into adulthood.

We conclude with a quote from Fujiura (2003) who noted:

> persons with mild intellectual impairments confront substantial challenges and economic risks in a society grown more complex in its demands for intellectual ability and technical skills. Vulnerability is <often> exacerbated by their exclusion—by statute or personal choice—from supports.... This is a cohort with few outspoken advocates. An emphasis on advocacy that leads to research related to this population as well as the development of enhanced educational practices is critical. (p. 430)

Note

1. Portions of this chapter have been adapted from Polloway et al. (2010) and Polloway, Smith, and Antoine (2010).

References

Abramowicz, H. K., & Richardson, S. A. (1975). Epidemiology of severe intellectual and developmental disabilities in children: Community studies. *American Journal of Mental Deficiency, 80*, 18–39.

Belser, R. C., & Sudhalter, V. (2001). Conversational characteristics of children with Fragile X syndrome: Repetitive speech. *American Journal on Mental Retardation, 106,* 28–38.

Benz, M. R., Lindstrom, L., & Yovanoff, P. (2000). Improving graduation and employment outcomes of students with disabilities: Predictive factors and student perspectives. *Exceptional Children, 66*, 509–529.

Bergeron, R., Floyd, R. G., & Shands, E. I. (2008). States' eligibility guidelines for mental retardation: An update and consideration of part scores and unreliability of IQs. *Education and Training in Developmental Disabilities, 43*, 123–131.

Bouck, E. C. (2004). Exploring secondary special education for mild mental impairment: A program in search of its place. *Remedial and Special Education, 25*, 367–382.

Bouck, E. C. (2007). Lost in translation? Educating secondary students with mild mental impairment. *Journal of Disability Policy Studies, 18*, 79–87.

Cuskelly, M., & Gunn, P. (2003). Sibling relationships of children with Down syndrome: Perspectives of mothers, fathers, and siblings. *American Journal of Mental Retardation, 108*, 234–244.

Cutting, L. E., Clements, A. M., Lightman, A. D., Yerby-Hammack, P. D., & Denckla, M. B. (2004). Cognitive profile of neurofibromatosis type 1: Rethinking nonverbal learning disabilities. *Learning Disabilities Research and Practice , 19*, 155–165.

Danaher, J., Shackelford, J., & Harbin, G. (2004). Revisiting a comparison of eligibility policies for infant/toddler programs and preschool special education programs. *Topics in Early Childhood Special Education, 24*(2), 59–67.

Developmental Disabilities Assistance and Bill of Rights Act, P.L.106-402 (2000).

Dimitropoulos, A., Feurer, I. D., Butler, M. G., & Thompson, T. (2001). Emergence of compulsive behavior and tantrums in children with Prader-Willi syndrome. *American Journal on Mental Retardation, 106,* 39–51.

Donaldson, M. D. C., Chu, C. E., Cooke, A., Wilson, A., Greene, S. A., Stephenson, J. B. P. (1994). The Prader-Willi syndrome. *Archives of Disease in Childhood, 70*, 58–63.

Dunn, L. M. (1968). Special education for the mildly retarded: Is much of it justifiable? *Exceptional Children, 35*, 5–22.

Dykens, E. M. (2000). Contaminated and unusual food combinations:

What do people with Prader-Willi syndrome choose? *Mental Retardation, 138*, 163–171.

Dykens, E. M. (2001). Introduction to the special issue on behavioral phenotypes. *American Journal on Mental Retardation, 106*, 1–3.

Dykens, E. M. (2007). Presentation at the Next Generation of Research in Intellectual Disabilities: Charting the Course (A Special Olympics working conference), Miami, FL. Unpublished manuscript.

Dykens, E. M., Hodapp, R. M., & Finucane, B. M. (2000). *Genetics and mental retardation syndromes*. Baltimore: Brookes.

Edgar, E. (1987). Secondary programs in special education: Are many of them justifiable? *Exceptional Children, 53*, 555–561.

Edgar, E. (1988). Employment as an outcome for mildly handicapped students: Current status and future directions. *Focus on Exceptional Children, 21*(1), 1–8.

Edgerton, R. (1967). *The cloak of competence: Stigma in the lives of the mentally retarded*. Los Angeles: University of California Press.

Etscheidt, S. (2006). Least restrictive and natural environments for young children with disabilities: A legal analysis of issues. *Topics in Early Childhood Education, 26*, 167–178.

Freeman, S. F. N., & Kasari, C. (2002). Characteristics and quality of play dates of children with Down syndrome: Emerging or true friendships? *American Journal on Mental Retardation, 107*, 16–31.

Fujiura, G. (2003) Continuum of intellectual disability: Demographic evidence for the "forgotten generation." *Mental Retardation, 41*, 420–429.

Greenspan, S. (2006). Functional concepts in mental retardation: Finding the natural essence of an artificial category. *Exceptionality, 14*, 205–224.

Greenspan, S., & Switzky, H. N. (2006). Forty-four years of AAMR manuals. In H. N. Switzky & S. Greenspan (Eds.). *What is mental retardation? Ideas for an evolving disability in the 21st century* (pp. 3–28). Washington, DC: AAMR.

Grossman, H. J. (1983). *Classification in mental retardation*. Washington DC: American Association on Mental Deficiency.

Hall, J. G. (2000, May). Molecular and clinical genetics for the practicing pediatrician. *Advances in Children's Health 2000: Pediatric Academic Societies and the American Academy of Pediatrics Year 2000 Joint Meeting*. Pediatric Academic Societies and the American Academy of Pediatrics, Boston.

Hall, S. S., Lightbody, A. A., & Reiss A. L. (2008). Compulsive, self- injurious, and autistic behavior in children and adolescents with Fragile X syndrome. *American Journal on Mental Retardation, 113*, 44–53.

Harris, J. C. (2006). *Intellectual disability: Understanding its development, causes, classification, evaluation, and treatment*. New York: Oxford University Press.

Harris, S. W., Hessl, D., Goodlin-Jones, B., Ferranti, J., Bacalman, S., Barbato, I., … Hagerman, R. J. (2008). Autism profiles of males with fragile X syndrome. *American Journal on Mental Retardation, 113*, 427–438.

Hoover, J. J., & Patton, J. R. (2005). *Curriculum adaptations for students with learning and behavior problems*. Austin, TX: PRO.ED.

Hoover, J. J., & Patton, J. R. (2008). The role of special educators in a multi-tiered instructional system. *Intervention in School and Clinic, 43*, 195–202.

Individuals With Disabilities Education Act (IDEA) of 1997, 20 U. S. C. 1412 *et seg.* (1997).

Jones, K. L., Smith, D. W., Ulleland, C. N., & Streissguth, A. P. (1973). Patterns of malformation in offspring of chronic alcoholic mothers. *The Lancet, 1*(1267), 1271–1271.

Joseph, B., Egli, M., Koppekin, A., & Thompson, T. (2002). Food choice in people with Prader-Willi syndrome: Quantity and relative preference. *American Journal on Mental Retardation, 107*, 128–135.

Kasari, B. C., Freeman, S. E. N., & Hughes, M. A. (2001). Emotion recognition by children with Down syndrome. *American Journal on Mental Retardation, 106*, 59–72.

Kolstoe, O. P., & Frey, R. M. (1965). *A high school work study program for mentally subnormal students*. Carbondale: Southern Illinois University Press.

Levitas, A. (1998). MR syndromes: Phenylketonuria (PKU) and the hyperphenylalanineisma II. *Mental Health Aspects of Developmental Disabilities, 1*, 113–118.

Lovering, J. S., & Percy, M. (2007). Down syndrome. In I. Brown & N. Percy (Eds.). *A comprehensive guide to intellectual and developmental disabilities* (pp. 149–172). Baltimore: Brookes.

Luckasson, R., Borthwick-Duffy, S., Buntinx, W. H. E., Coulter, D. L., Craig, E. M., Reeve, A., … Tasse, M. J. (2002). *Mental retardation: Definition, classification, and systems of support* (10th ed). Washington, DC: AAMR.

MacMillan, D. L. (2007, December). *Mental retardation over five decades: Lessons we might have learned.* Paper presented at the Next Generation of Research in Intellectual Disabilities: Charting the Course (A Special Olympics working conference), Miami, FL.

Mazzocco, M., & Holden, J. A. (2007). Fragile X syndrome. In I. Brown & M. Percy (Eds.), *A comprehensive guide to intellectual disabilities* (pp. 173–188). Baltimore: Brookes.

Meyer, G. A. (2007). X-linked syndromes causing intellectual disability. In M. L. Batshaw, L. Pellegrino, & N. J. Roizen. (Eds.), *Children with disabilites* (6th ed., pp. 275– 283). Baltimore: Brookes.

Miller, D. (2006). Students with fetal alcohol syndrome: Updating our knowledge, improving their programs. *Teaching Exceptional Children, 38*(4), 12–18.

Newman, L., Wagner, M., Cameto, R., & Knokey, A. (2009). *The post-high school outcomes of youth with disabilities up to 4 years after high school. A report from the National Longitudinal Transition Study-2 (NLTS2)* (NCSER 2009-3017). Washington, DC: U. S. Government Printing Office.

Patton, J. R., & Keyes, D. (2006). Death penalty issues following *Atkins*. *Exceptionality, 14*, 237–255.

Percy, M., Lewkis, S. Z., & Brown, I. (2007). Introduction to genetics and development. In I. Brown & M. Percy (Eds.), *A comprehensive guide to intellectual disabilities* (pp. 87–108). Baltimore: Brookes.

Polloway, E. A. (2000). Influential persons in the development of the field of special education. *Remedial and Special Education, 21*, 322–324.

Polloway, E. A. (2005). Perspectives on mild retardation: The status of a category of exceptionality. In J. J. Hoover (Ed.), *Current issues in special education: Meeting diverse needs in twenty-first century* (pp. 36–46). Boulder, CO: BUENO Center for Multicultural Education, University of Colorado.

Polloway, E. A. (2006). Mild mental retardation: A concept in search of clarity, a population in search of appropriate education and supports, a profession in search of advocacy. *Exceptionality, 14*, 183–189.

Polloway, E. A., & Lubin, J. (2009). *Feebleminded.* In S. Burch (Ed.), *Encyclopedia of American Disability History* (pp. 353–354). New York: Infobase Publishing.

Polloway, E. A., Lubin, J., Smith, J. D. & Patton, J. R. (2010). Mild intellectual disabilities: Legacies and trends in concepts and educational practices. *Education and Training in Developmental Disabilities, 45*, 54–68.

Polloway, E. A., Patton, J. R., Smith, J. D.., Antoine, K., & Lubin, J. (2009). State guidelines for intellectual and developmental disabilities and intellectual disabilities: A re-visitation of previous analyses in light of changes in the field. *Education and Training in Developmental Disabilities, 44*, 14–24.

Polloway, E. A., & Smith, J. D. (1983). Mild mental retardation: Population, programs, and perspectives. *Exceptional Children, 50*, 149–159.

Polloway, E. A., Smith, J. D., & Antoine, K. (in press). Biological causes. In Beirne-Smith, M., Patton, J. R., & Kim, S. H. (Eds.), *Intellectual disabilities* (8th ed.). Columbus, OH: Pearson.

President's Committee for People with Intellectual Disabilities. (2007). *Holding truths to be self-evident: Affirming the value of people with intellectual disabilities.* Washington, DC: U.S. Government Printing Office.

Rasmussen, S. A., & Friedman, J. M. (1999). NF1 gene and neurofibromatosis type 1. *American Journal of Epidemiology, 151*, 33–40.

Roberts, J. E., Hennon, E. A., Price, J. R., Dear, E., Anderson, K., & Vandergrift, N. A. (2007). Expressive language during conversational speech in boys with fragile X syndrome. *American Journal on Mental Retardation. 112*, 1–17.

Rogers, R. C., & Simensen, R. J. (1987). Fragile X syndrome: A common etiology of intellectual and developmental disabilities. *American Journal of Mental Deficiency, 91*, 445–449.

Ross, T. M., Grafham, D. V., Coffey, A. J., Scherer, S., McLay, K., Muzny, D. ... Bentley, D.R.. (2005). The DNA sequence of the human X chromosome. *Nature, 434*, 325–337.

Ryan, S., & Ferguson D. (2006). On, yet under, the radar: Students with fetal alcohol syndrome disorder. *Exceptional Children, 3*, 363–379.

Rynders, J. (2005). Down syndrome: Literacy and socialization in school. *Focus on Exceptional Children, 38*(1), 2–11.

Rynders, J. E., & Horrobin, J. M. (1990). Always trainable? Never educable? Updating educational expectations concerning children with Down syndrome. *American Journal on Mental Retardation, 95*, 77–83.

Rynders, J. E., Spiker, D., & Horrobin, J. M. (1978). Underestimating the educability of Down syndrome children: Examination of methodological problems in recent literature. *American Journal of Mental Deficiency, 82*, 440–448.

Sandieson, R. (1998). A survey on terminology that refers to people with intellectual and developmental disabilities/developmental disabilities. *Education and Training in Mental Retardation*, *33*, 290–295.

Schalock, R. L., Borthwick-Duffy, S. A., Bradley, V. M., Buntinx, W. H. E., Coulter, D. L., Craig, E. M., ... Yeager, M. H. (2010). *Intellectual disability: Definition, classification, and systems of supports*. Washington, DC: American Association on Intellectual and Developmental Disabilities.

Schalock, R., Luckasson, R. A., Shogren, K. A., Borthwick-Duffy, S., Bradley, V., Butinx, W. H. E., ... Yeager, M. (2007). The renaming of mental retardation: Understanding the change to the term intellectual disability. *Intellectual and Developmental Disabilities*, *45*, 116–124.

Scott, E., Smith, T. E. C., Hendricks, M. C., & Polloway, E. A. (1997). Prader-Willi syndrome: A review and implications for educational intervention. *Education and Training in Mental Retardation and Developmental Disabilities, 34,* 110–116.

Skiba, R. J., Poloni-Staudinger, L., Gallini, S., Simmons, A. B., & Feggins-Azziz, R. (2006). Disparate access: The disproportionality of African-American students with disabilities across educational environments. *Exceptional Children*, *72*, 411–424.

Skiba, R. J., Simmons, A. B., Ritter, S., Gibb, A. C., Rausch, M. K., Cuadrado, J., & Chung, C-G. (2008). Achieving equity in special education: History, status, and current challenges. *Exceptional Children, 74*, 264–288.

Smith, J. D. (2006). Quo vadis mental retardation? Definition by aggregation versus the hope for individual futures. In H. N. Switzky & S. Greenspan (Eds.). *What is mental retardation? Ideas for an evolving disability in the 21st century* (pp. 51–59). Washington, DC: AAMR.

Smith, P. (2007). Have we made any progress? Including students with intellectual disabilities in regular education classrooms. *Intellectual and Developmental Disabilities*, *45*, 297–309.

Smith, T., Polloway, E. A., Patton, J. R., & Beyer, J. (2008). Individuals with intellectual and developmental disabilities in the criminal justice system and implications for transition planning. *Education and Training in Developmental Disabilities*, *43*, 421–430.

Smith, T. E. C., Polloway, E. A., Patton, J. R. & Dowdy, C. (2007). *Teaching students with special needs in inclusive settings* (5th ed.). Boston: Allyn & Bacon.

Snell, M. E., & Luckasson, R., Borthwick-Duffy, S., Bradley, V., Butinx, W. H. E., Coulter, D. L., ... Yeager, M. (2009). The characteristics and needs of people with intellectual disabilities who have higher IQs. *Intellectual and Developmental Disabilities, 47*, 220–233.

Spencer, G., & Dieffenbach, A. (2005). *Studies expand understanding of X chromosome.* Washington, DC: National Institutes of Health. Retrieved March 21, 2005, from http://www. nih.gov/news

Spinath, F. M., Harlaar, N., Ronald, A., & Plomin, R. (2004). Substantial genetic influence on mild mental impairment in early childhood. *American Journal on Mental Retardation, 109,* 34–43.

Tartaglia, N. R., Hansen, R. L., & Hagerman, R. J. (2007). Advances in genetics. In S. L. Odom, R. H. Horner, M. E. Snell, & J. Blacher (Eds.), *Handbook of developmental disabilities* (pp. 98–128). New York: Guilford.

Tymchuk, A. J., Lakin, K. C., & Luckasson, R. (2001). *The forgotten generation*. Baltimore: Brookes.

U.S. Department of Education (USDOE). (2007). *27th annual report to Congress on the implementation of the Individuals with Disabilities Education Act, 2005*. Washington, DC: Author.

U.S. Department of Education (USDOE). (2009). *28th annual report to Congress on the implementation of the Individuals with Disabilities Education Act, 2006*. Washington, DC: Author.

Van Karnebeek, C., Scheper, F., Abeling, N., Alders, M., Barth, P., Hoover, J., ... Hennekam, R. (2005). Etiology of intellectual and developmental disabilities in children referred to a tertiary care center: A prospective study. *American Journal on Mental Retardation, 110*, 253–267.

Wagner, M., Newman, L., Cameto, R., Garza, N., & Levine, P. (2005). *After high school: A first look at the post-school experiences of youth with disabilities: A report from the National Longitudinal Transition Study-2 (NTLS-2)*. Menlo Park, CA: SRI International.

Wehmeyer, M. L. (2006). Universal design for learning, access to the general education curriculum and students with mild mental retardation. *Exceptionality, 14,* 225–235.

Whittington, J., & Holland, T. (2004). *Prader-Willi syndrome: Development and manifestations.* Cambridge, UK: Cambridge UniversityPress.

Williamson, P., McLeskey, J., Hoppey, D., & Rentz, T. (2006). Educating students with mental retardation in general education classrooms. *Exceptional Children, 72,* 347–361.

15
Learning Disabilities

Paige C. Pullen
University of Virginia

Holly B. Lane
University of Florida

Kristen E. Ashworth and Shelly P. Lovelace
University of Virginia

Learning disabilities are the most common type of disability in the field of special education. Students with learning disabilities account for approximately half of all students receiving special education services in schools in the United States (Denton, Vaughn, & Fletcher, 2003). As of 2010, this amounts to more than 3,000,000 students with learning disabilities receiving special education or related services. Approximately 8% of all children, or 10% of boys and 6% of girls, between the ages of 5 and 17 have had a learning disability diagnosis (Pastor & Reuben, 2008). As a field, the area of learning disabilities is constantly growing and changing, and it is one of the most active areas of special education research.

Definition

A learning disability (LD) is thought to be a neurological disorder that affects the brain's ability to receive, process, store, and respond to information (National Center for Learning Disabilities, 2007). The term "learning disability" is used to explain difficulty a person of at least average intelligence has in acquiring basic academic and functional skills. Learning disabilities can affect a person's ability to understand or use spoken or written language, do mathematical calculations, coordinate movements, or direct attention. These skills are essential for success at school and work, and for coping with life in general. Learning disabilities are caused by a difference in brain structure that is usually present at birth and is often hereditary.

Learning disabilities are not thought to be a reflection of intelligence. Instead, learning disabilities are generally associated with average or above average intelligence, but learning disabilities may occur together with mental or physical disabilities. Learning disabilities cannot be identified on the basis of vision or hearing acuity or other physical signs, nor can they be diagnosed solely based on neurological findings. Learning difficulties are generally regarded as variations on normal development and are only considered disabilities when they interfere significantly with school performance and adaptive functions. Estimates indicate that learning disabilities affect between 5% and 20% of the population.

The Individuals with Disabilities Education Act (USDOE, 2004) defines learning disabilities this way:

> A disorder in one or more of the basic psychological processes involved in understanding or in using spoken or written language, which may manifest itself in an imperfect ability to listen, think, speak, read, write, spell or to do mathematical calculation. (Sec. 602 (30)(a))

The National Joint Committee on Learning Disabilities (NJCLD, 1990), a group representing numerous related professional organizations, created a more comprehensive definition of learning disabilities:

> Learning disabilities is a general term that refers to a heterogeneous group of disorders manifested by significant difficulties in the acquisition and use of listening, speaking, reading, writing, reasoning, or mathematical skills. These disorders are intrinsic to the individual, presumed to be due to central nervous system dysfunction, and may occur across the life span. Problems in self-regulatory behaviors, social perception, and social interaction may exist with learning disabilities but do not, by themselves, constitute a learning disability. Although learning disabilities may occur concomitantly with other disabilities (e.g., sensory impairment, mental retardation, serious emotional disturbance), or with extrinsic influences (such as cultural differences,

> insufficient or inappropriate instruction), they are not the result of those conditions or influences.

Recently, the American Psychiatric Association proposed the following definition for learning disability to appear in the *Diagnostic and Statistical Manual V*, to be published in 2013:

> A. A group of disorders characterized by difficulties in learning basic academic skills (currently or by history), that are not consistent with the person's chronological age, educational opportunities, or intellectual abilities. Basic academic skills refer to accurate and fluent reading, writing, and arithmetic. Multiple sources of information are to be used to assess learning, one of which must be an individually administered, culturally appropriate, and psychometrically sound standardized measure of academic achievement.
>
> B. The disturbance in criterion A, without accommodations, significantly interferes with academic achievement or activities of daily living that require these academic skills. (American Psychiatric Association, 2010)

The term "learning disability" has only been used since 1963, when Samuel Kirk, then a professor of special education at the University of Illinois, used the term at a conference for parents and educators. Conference attendees responded favorably to the term to replace the more stigmatizing terms that had been previously used. Before Kirk's new term was introduced, terms such as "word blindness," "brain injured," "minimal brain dysfunction," or "perceptual handicap" were used to describe the same symptoms.

Since the inception of the term "learning disabilities," the search for a definition has been a somewhat controversial issue in the field. Since that time, numerous definitions have been proposed, and varying degrees of consensus have been reached. In 1995, however, Lyon maintained that the field of learning disabilities still lacked definitions that are logically consistent, easily operationalized, and empirically validated. Hammill (1993) suggested that, although a consensus was emerging regarding a theoretical definition that frames the conceptual basis of learning disabilities, much work was needed to develop reliable and valid criteria that operationalize definitions of learning disabilities. And in 2009, Kavale, Spalding, and Beam discuss the need to change the formal definition of learning disabilities. Clearly, the debate on defining learning disabilities is still active. Today controversy over methods of identification and issues regarding response to intervention (RTI) is evidence that the field is still working on reaching consensus on the definition for learning disabilities.

Etiology

Historically, the field of learning disabilities has been less concerned with etiology and more concerned with describing the problem and developing interventions (Torgesen, 1991). Still, as Torgesen suggests, it is important to consider what we know about causes of learning disabilities, because etiology is an important part of the definition. Part of the difficulty with thinking about etiology, however, is that there exists no single cause of learning disabilities, and in many cases, the cause is unknown.

In recent years, new technologies have confirmed the former theories that neurological factors contribute to learning disabilities (Fletcher, Lyon, Fuchs, & Barnes, 2007). With the use of technologies, such as electroencephalagram (EEG), brain electrical activity mapping (BEAM), and magnetic resonance imaging (MRI), neurologists have been able to identify minimal or mild brain dysfunction central to the medical perspective of learning disabilities (Mercer & Pullen, 2009). A medical diagnosis of learning disabilities includes *minimal* brain dysfunction and excludes gross signs of central nervous system (CNS) disorder. A significant CNS dysfunction would generally lead to a different label, such as an intellectual disability or cerebral palsy. The emphasis on *minimal* brain dysfunction also implies that learning problems would not be pervasive. In fact, a person with a learning disability in some areas may perform comparatively well in other areas.

One specific learning disability, dyslexia, frequently manifests itself in the physiological asymmetry of one region of the brain. The planum temporale is a typically asymmetric area of the normal brain, and approximately 70% of normal brains have a larger left planum than a right planum with only 5% having reversed symmetry in this area (Filipek, 1995). Because the planum temporale is important to language, one might expect to see less asymmetry, or possibly reversed asymmetry, in this area for individuals with dyslexia, who often experience language deficits. Researchers have shown this to be the case: Larsen, Hoien, Lundberg, and Odegaard (1990) found that 70% of individuals with dyslexia had symmetrical planum temporale regions, and Hynd, Semrud-Clikeman, Lorys, Novey, and Eliopulos (1990) found that 90% of individuals with dyslexia experienced either symmetry or reverse asymmetry in this region of the brain. Filipek cautions the use of planum temporale asymmetry as an indicator of dyslexia, noting high variability in measuring this region of the brain. We must also be aware that there are limitations to these and similar studies using various technologies to measure brain physiology and electrical activity in individuals with dyslexia, including sample size, unclear sample descriptions, and limited accessibility to school-aged children with dyslexia (Obrzut, 1989).

Postmortem studies have also added to our knowledge of brain structure anomaly in individuals with learning disabilities. Summaries of these studies have identified abnormalities in areas of the cerebral cortex related to language (Duane, 1989; Galaburda, 1988; Hynd, Marshall, & Gonzalez, 1991), such as nerve cell anomalies and abnormal hemispheric symmetry. While findings of these studies are generally in agreement with findings from studies using neurodiagnostic technologies (i.e.,

MRI, EEG), they are also limited in the number of brains examined (e.g., only about 8 individuals have been included in postmortem studies).

Given that there exists a link between neurological factors and learning problems in some studies, researchers are interested in finding the possible causes of these neurological irregularities and the reasons why a person may experience learning-related difficulties. The following sections focus on two medically related etiologies of learning disabilities: acquired trauma and genetic or hereditary issues.

Acquired Trauma

The medical literature refers to acquired trauma as injury to the CNS originating outside the individual and resulting in learning disorders. Acquired traumas, which can occur during gestation, at birth, and after birth, are correlated with learning disabilities. The most common complication during pregnancy that is related to learning problems is maternal drug use and alcohol consumption. Fetal alcohol spectrum disorders (FASD) are common prenatal causes for child impairment (e.g., growth impairment, facial disfiguration, and CNS dysfunction). Researchers have linked prenatal alcohol exposure to early developmental delays (Kartin, Grant, Streissguth, Sampson, & Ernst, 2002), executive function deficits (Green et al., 2008), and learning and behavior issues that continue throughout life (Carmichael et al., 1997; Dybdahl & Ryan, 2009; National Research Council and Institute of Medicine, 2000). Other prenatal drug exposure, including cocaine or marijuana (Morrow et al., 2006), nicotine and carbon monioxide (Stanton-Chapman, Chapman, & Scott, 2001) has also been linked to learning and behavioral problems in children.

Children can also be exposed to perinatal traumas, or traumas that occur during the birth process. Birth complications, such as prematurity, prolonged labor, anoxia, and injury from medical instruments, have been associated with later learning disabilities characteristic of minimal brain damage. In an early study, Colletti (1979) found that 96% of participants with learning disabilities had experienced some form of perinatal trauma, a rate far higher than the national norm. Researchers have also discovered a link between very low birth weight and learning difficulties (Downie, Jakobson, Frisk, & Ushycky, 2002; Stanton-Chapman et al., 2001).

Postnatal diseases and accidents, such as stroke, high fever, encephalitis, meningitis, and head trauma, may also cause learning problems in children. Due to the fact that younger individuals' brains retain their plasticity and are able to compensate for damage much more easily, younger children more readily regain cognitive skills than do older individuals. Although mild head injuries rarely have long-term adverse effects (Anderson, Catroppa, Rosenfeld, Haritou, & Morse, 2000), more significant head injuries are associated with distractibility, irritability, maladaptive behavior, and impulsivity (Deaton, 1987). Researchers have also found that significant head injuries are correlated with cognitive deficits, such as memory and information-processing speed (Anderson et al., 2000; Donders & Kuldanek, 1998). IDEA has a separate category for traumatic brain injury, so that children with learning problems related to such injuries can receive rehabilitation and special education services (see 34 C.F.R. § 300.7).

Genetic and Hereditary Influences

Researchers have found evidence of a genetic link within families of children with learning disabilities (Decker & Defries, 1980, 1981; Hallgren, 1950). Hallgren determined that learning problems are inherited due to prevalence of learning problems among the families in his study. Decker and Defries (1980, 1981) found greater rates of reading disabilities within the families of their participants with disabilities than in families of non-disabled participants. Although these researchers have contributed significantly to our knowledge of genetic influences on learning disabilities, the nature versus nurture debate still continues within the field. Researchers studying identical and fraternal twins have used these two groups to attempt to control for environmental factors, with the hypothesis that identical twins would be more likely to both have learning disabilities than fraternal twins. When Herman (1959) compared 12 sets of identical twins and 33 sets of fraternal twins, he found that all sets of the identical twins had reading difficulties, while both twins in the fraternal twin sets exhibited reading problems in only one-third of the sets. In more recent twin studies, scientists have confirmed that reading and spelling deficiencies are substantially heritable (Hayiou-Thomas, Harlaar, Dale, & Plomin, 2010; Keenan, Betjemann, Wadsworth, DeFries, & Olson, 2006; Pennington, 1995; Wadsworth, DeFries, Olson, & Wilcutt, 2007).

Characteristics of Students with Learning Disabilities

Although many students with learning disabilities exhibit similar characteristics, this population is in no way homogeneous. Students may exhibit a wide range of behaviors, or combinations of behaviors that vary from individual to individual. Despite these variations, however, one consistent factor across students with learning disabilities is the persistent nature of their characteristics, which can continue into adulthood.

The learning disabilities criteria for IDEA identify disability categories that converge on academic and language difficulties. These categories include oral expression, listening comprehension, written expression, basic reading skills, reading comprehension, mathematics calculation, and mathematics reading. Further characteristics developed by current research include metacognitive deficits, social skills deficits, attention disorders, memory problems, and motor problems, among others.

Description of problem behaviors is particularly useful when discussing characteristics of students with learning disabilities. Due to the variation in individual student characteristics, students may qualify as having a learning disability by exhibiting difficulty in one of the categories designated by IDEA, or difficulties across all seven categories. Thus, limiting student behaviors to labels often ignores larger differences among students and inhibits effective intervention techniques. For example, describing that a student's "focus shifted between the window and other students during instruction" is more informative than simply labeling the student as "inattentive."

Discrepancy factor. Bateman's (1964) discrepancy model has traditionally been a key characteristic across students with learning disabilities. Discrepancy refers to the difference between students' estimated ability and their academic performance. Students can exhibit this discrepancy in only one skill or across a range of skill areas. Although the discrepancy model is still widely used as a means for identification of students with learning disabilities, IDEA 2004 does not require evidence of a discrepancy in order to identify students as having LD.

Academic learning. Difficulties with academic learning can occur in any academic area. Students with learning disabilities generally exhibit academic difficulties in those areas identified by the IDEA 2004. Although low academic achievement can occur in any area, 80%–90% of students with learning disabilities display these difficulties in the area of reading (Mercer & Pullen, 2009).

Language disorders. Many students who have difficulty in the area of reading actually demonstrate language disorders (Ehren, 2006; Wallach, 2005). Since the areas of reading and language are so closely related, it is usually difficult to tell whether a student's deficits fall in one area or another. IDEA 2004, however, categorizes language disorders as those related to deficits in oral expression and listening comprehension.

Perceptual disorders. Although currently not included in IDEA's evaluation procedures for learning disabilities, perceptual disorders has received attention in the learning disabilities research. Perceptual disorders are characterized as "the inability to recognize, discriminate, and interpret sensation, especially visual and auditory disabilities" (Mercer & Pullen, 2009, p. 23). Research suggests that these skills may be important in early academic areas, like reading and mathematics, but have little effect on later progress (Dore, 2006; Smith, 1994). However, the existence of perceptual disorders and their treatment in learning disabilities continues to be controversial (Hyatt, Stephenson, & Carter, 2009). Current programs for addressing these difficulties have not been substantiated by scientific research.

Metacognitive deficits. Metacognition refers to a student's awareness of his/her thinking processes or strategies and the ability to regulate these strategies in order to improve successful learning. In other words, "metacognition refers to an individual's awareness of his or her own thought processes and an ability to use those cognitive processes to learn" (Mercer, Mercer, & Pullen, 2011, p. 5). Students with learning disabilities commonly show metacognitive deficits (Klassen, 2010; Sideridis, Morgan, Bostas, Padeliadu, & Fuchs, 2006), and these deficits remain evident in post-secondary settings (Klassen, Krawchuk, Lynch, & Rajani, 2008). A teacher's knowledge about the ways in which students think about their own learning strategies can significantly improve teacher's instructional practices and student outcomes. Furthermore, evidence suggests that explicit instruction in metacognitive strategies can improve these skills in students with learning disabilities (see e.g., Garrett, Mazzocco, & Baker, 2006). Although some researchers view the metacognitive strategies of students with learning disabilities as different rather than deficient (Kulak, 1993; Montague & Applegate, 1993), obvious variations exist in the ways in which these students plan and evaluate the effectiveness of their learning processes.

Social-Emotional problems. Due to repeated academic failure and a focus on low academic achievement, many students with learning disabilities develop a poor self-concept and low self-esteem. However, research suggests that this low self-esteem does not affect all students in similar ways. For example, some students may demonstrate low levels of self-esteem in academics, but display similar levels of self-concept as their peers without disabilities in other areas (e.g., affect, family, physical, and social; Montgomery, 1994).

Likewise, repeated academic failure also leads to low levels of motivation in many students with learning disabilities. It is difficult for these students to maintain intrinsic motivation when faced with academic circumstances that appear out of their control. The adoption of learned-helplessness among students with learning disabilities is not surprising considering their everyday challenges with academic success, but this lack of motivation adds another component for teachers to consider when individualizing instruction.

Many students with learning disabilities also display deficits in social skills, like greeting a stranger, accepting criticism, or receiving compliments (Mercer et al., 2011). These deficits are usually caused by their inability to understand social cues and can be challenging to their appropriate interactions with teachers and peers in the classroom environment. In a study examining friendships, students with learning disabilities had as many friendships as their non-disabled peers, however, they were often unable to maintain these friendships (Estell, Jones, Pearl, & Van Acker, 2009). Students with learning disabilities generally receive lower social skills ratings from teachers than those without learning problems (Nowicki, 2003). Emotional and social difficulties of students with learning disabilities also include increased rates of depression, especially among females, in this population (Heath & Ross, 2000; Maag & Reid, 2006; Sideridis, 2007).

Behavior problems. Lack of comfort and ability in social situations may lead to frustration and disruptive behavior patterns in students with learning disabilities. These behavior deficits are well documented (Hallahan, Kauffman, & Pullen, 2009) and generally lead to the interruption or interference in the learning of other students in the classroom. Disruptive behaviors can include aggressive outbursts, name-calling, swearing, or excessive absenteeism. These behaviors can present increased challenges to student learning.

Memory problems. Students with learning disabilities also display difficulty in remembering auditory and visual stimuli. Research suggests these difficulties stem from deficits in working memory (Martinussen & Tannock, 2006; Schuchardt, Maehler, & Hasselhorn, 2008; Swanson, 2009), or the ability to store information for a short period of time while engaging in cognitively demanding tasks (Savage, Lavers, & Pillay, 2007). These deficits in working memory are displayed in activities like remembering math facts or spelling word lists, which teachers report students with learning disabilities frequently forget.

Attention problems and hyperactivity. High rates of comorbidity between learning disabilities and attention-deficit/hyperactivity have led researchers to focus on deficits in attention and distractibility when considering students with learning disabilities (Forness & Kavale, 2001). Problems with attention and hyperactivity are especially relevant to student success since participation in classroom learning requires students to maintain thought on certain subjects for extended periods of time and shift this thought to new tasks when appropriate. The inability to screen out extraneous stimuli while learning serves to extrapolate the academic difficulties many students with learning disabilities already encounter.

Types of Learning Disabilities

Learning disabilities can manifest in many different ways. The National Institute for Child Health and Human Development (NICHD) has outlined some of the most common types of learning disabilities.

Reading disability is a language-based learning disability, also commonly called dyslexia. For most children with learning disabilities, reading is the primary area of difficulty. People with reading disabilities often have difficulties with spelling and decoding skills, usually rooted in a phonological processing deficit (Metsala & Ehri, 1998). They may also have problems recognizing words that they have already learned (Ehri & McCormick, 1998). Other symptoms of reading disability may include difficulties with comprehending text (Gersten, Fuchs, Williams, & Baker, 2001). Estimates indicate that between 5% and 20% of people in the United States have a learning disability, and 90% of those disabilities are related to reading (Kavale & Reese, 1992).

Other language-related learning disabilities include problems that interfere with oral and written communication, including speaking, listening, reading, spelling, and writing. Learning disabilities related to writing may be called dysgraphia, which generally refers to difficulty in handwriting, such as forming letters or words or writing within a defined space. Other learning disabilities related to writing include difficulties with spelling, semantic memory, morphological awareness, grammatical structures, organizing information, putting thoughts on paper, or working memory (Berninger, 2009).

Learning disabilities related to math are sometimes called dyscalculia (Shaley, Manor, & Gross-Tsur, 2005). Individuals with dyscalculia typically have difficulty understanding mathematical concepts and computation, sometimes even simple math problems. Math disabilities can include difficulties with spatial orientation, sequencing, and abstract concepts such as time and direction. In some individuals, a math disability may be linked to a concomitant reading disability, but in others math disabilities are more closely related to problems of working memory and problem solving (Swanson, Jerman, & Zhang, 2009).

Some learning disabilities are related to the individual's ability to process and use the information that they acquire through their senses. This kind of problem is not related to an inability to see or hear, but they are instead related to the way the brain processes that sensory information. It may include difficulties with an individual's ability to process language, to understand what is heard or read, and to organize information. It may also include the speed with which the individual processes information and their attention, ability to retain information during problem-solving, and ability to self-monitor during learning (Semrud-Clikeman, 2005). This type of learning disability is called an information processing disorder.

Learning Disabilities Across the Lifespan

Learning disabilities clearly affect academic performance, but they are not only related to school tasks. Learning disabilities can have an impact on learning and daily functioning at any age. The manifestation of a learning disability may change dramatically across the lifespan, based on developmental changes in the individual and changes in the demands of the environment. These manifestations can serve as indicators of or warning signs for learning disabilities (Bergert, 2000).

Young Children with Learning Disabilities

Although learning disabilities are typically formally identified after children reach school age, there are usually many signs of developmental difficulties that can indicate the presence of a learning disability. During the first few years of life, a child moves from being able to imitate familiar words and recognize the sound of a familiar voice to being able to follow two- or three-step directions, sort objects by similar characteristics, imitate the actions of others, and express a wide range of emotions. Young children who are struggling may have difficulties in several areas, including delayed crawling or walking, slow language development, difficulty making needs known or following simple directions, trouble playing with others, or frustration with basic communication or skills.

During the preschool years, most children become more independent and begin to attend more to people outside of their own family. During this stage, most children develop a variety of gross motor skills, use more complex language to express themselves, understand the concept of make believe, interact with other children, and take turns during play. They also begin to learn letters, sounds, and concepts about print. Children who are struggling during this stage of development may speak later than other children, have speech articulation difficulties, experience slow vocabulary growth and difficulty finding the word they need to express an idea, experience difficulty rhyming, and have difficulty learning numbers, days of the week, the alphabet, shapes, and colors. Problems with fine motor skills, such as buttoning, zipping, keyboarding, controlling a pencil, and using scissors, may also appear. Socially, they may experience difficulty with routines or following directions, have difficulty empathizing with others, and experience exaggerated frustrations when they struggle with a task.

Elementary Students with Learning Disabilities

By the time most children enter elementary school, they can dress themselves, tie their shoes, and catch a ball with only their hands. Friendships become very important to them, and physical, mental, and social skills develop quickly, as they develop confidence in making friends, completing schoolwork, and playing sports. Most children at this stage learn to read and to apply the necessary strategies to be a successful learner in all academic areas. In contrast, students with learning disabilities in elementary school may experience difficulties such as struggling to learn connections between letters and sounds, confusing basic words, making frequent reading and spelling errors, struggling with basic computation, being slow to acquire and retain new facts and learn new skills, overrelying on memorization, and having poor physical coordination.

Secondary Students with Learning Disabilities

As children enter adolescence, they experience numerous physical, mental, social, and emotional changes, and they worry about these changes and how they are viewed by others. They become more independent, with their own personalities and interests, and begin to make more of their own choices about friends, school, and sports. Adolescents with learning disabilities may experience a wide range of difficulties in reading, including problems with decoding, fluency, and comprehension. Problems in written expression, spelling, handwriting, and mathematics are also common. They may struggle recalling facts, have a poor grasp of abstract concepts, work slowly, and have weak memory skills. They often have difficulty making friends, have trouble understanding facial expressions and body language, and have problems adjusting to new environments. They commonly either pay too little attention to details or focus on them too much. They often struggle with self-advocacy and goal-setting. Organization and time management typically become particular challenges.

Transition to Adulthood for Individuals with LD

As students enter their life after school, many new challenges and opportunities arise. They develop more independence from their families and begin to develop inner resources. They develop more confidence and a willingness to express themselves. During this phase, self-advocacy becomes especially important. College students and adults with learning disabilities may experience similar academic difficulties to adolescents, but these problems are compounded by the increased expectations for independence and competence. As they enter the workforce, the same difficulties that they experienced in school with reading, writing, math, relating to others, organization, and time management can pose new problems in acquiring, doing, and keeping a job.

Identification of Learning Disabilities

The issues with the definition of learning disabilities lead to issues with the identification of students with learning disabilities. Historically, learning disabilities have been defined through assessments that demonstrate a discrepancy between intellectual ability and academic achievement. More recently, other methods for identification have emerged that do not depend on the presence of a discrepancy.

Discrepancy Model

A key component to many of the early definitions of learning disability has been the discrepancy factor. A discrepancy is said to exist when there is a significant difference between a student's estimated ability and academic performance (Mercer & Pullen, 2009). The discrepancy can be in one academic skill area or in a combination of areas. This approach to identification was used exclusively from the passage of PL 94-142 in 1975 until the reauthorization of IDEA in 2004.

The discrepancy model of identification of learning disabilities relies on psycho-educational evaluation to examine a student's academic achievement and intelligence to determine whether a significant discrepancy between the two is present. Generally, this is accomplished by comparing results from an IQ test and a battery of academic achievement tests. Critics of this approach argue that there are problems with the validity of the discrepancy model as it relates to the definition of learning disabilities, with the reliability of using arbitrary cut-off scores as identification criteria, and with the model's failure to identify a unique group of underachievers (Fletcher et al., 2007).

With the 2004 reauthorization of IDEA, the discrepancy factor was no longer deemed to be a requirement for the identification of a learning disability. According to IDEA 2004, a team of qualified professionals and the student's parent must be part of the identification process. The team must determine that the child does not achieve "adequately for the child's age or meet state-approved grade-level standards in one or more of the following areas: (a) oral expression, (b) listening comprehension, (c) written expression, (d) basic reading skills, (e) reading fluency, (f) reading comprehension, (g) mathematics calculation, or (h) mathematics problem-solving; or that the child does not make sufficient progress to meet age or state-approved grade-level standards" (34 CFR §300.309). The team may not identify a student as having a specific learning disability if the lack of achievement is "primarily the result of (a) a visual, hearing, or motor disability, (b) mental retardation, (c) emotional disturbance, (d) cultural factors, (e) environmental or economic disadvantage, or (f) limited English proficiency" (34 CFR §300.309). The team may determine that the student has a severe discrepancy between achievement and intellectual ability, but doing so is no longer a requirement.

In a discrepancy model, students must experience failure prior to evaluation. That is, a student must fall far behind expected levels of performance for the discrepancy to be large enough to meet eligibility criteria. A significant discrepancy may not be evident until second or third grade, or even later, so to be identified through this model, a student must first experience several years of academic failure. Another flaw in the discrepancy model is that it is difficult to distinguish between students with true learning disabilities and those who have had ineffective instruction. The recent shift toward response to intervention (RTI) as a method of identifying students with learning disabilities stems from these concerns with the more traditional discrepancy model (Mercer & Pullen, 2009).

Response to Intervention

According to the 2004 reauthorization of IDEA, local education agencies (LEAs) are no longer required to use a discrepancy model in identifying students with learning disabilities (20 U.S.C. § 1414(6)(a)). Instead, LEAs can make LD determinations based on children's response to "scientific, research-based intervention as part of the evaluation procedure" (20 U.S.C. § 1414(6)(b).

RTI is a tiered model in which teachers provide high quality instruction to all students, regularly monitoring students to determine who is responding to instruction. Those students who are targeted as not responding then receive more intensive instruction (i.e., Tier 2). Tier 2 instruction is provided in addition to the Tier 1 instruction that all students receive and may consist of small-group supplemental lessons or other methods that increase in intensity (e.g., increased time, more explicit teaching). If non-responsiveness is still an issue, students may receive Tier 3 intervention and may be eligible to receive special education or be referred for further evaluation. Fuchs and Fuchs (2007) recommend the three-tier model as opposed to models that have more tiers because it is difficult to design and implement multiple tiers that vary in format and intensity. An important strength of the RTI approach as an identification method is that it provides a way to distinguish between underachievers and students who have not been exposed to effective instruction, something that is difficult to do when using a discrepancy model.

Assessment

Assessment is a systematic process of collecting data that can be used to make decisions about students (Reynolds, Livingston, & Willson, 2006; Salvia & Ysseldyke, 2009). We assess students to learn what we need to do to serve their needs. We also assess students to determine if what we are doing is effective.

Purposes of Assessment

Assessment for students with learning disabilities serves four main purposes. First, screening measures designed to test a large number of students in a short amount of time provide data on students performing below benchmarks that may be at-risk for a learning disability or struggling in a particular content area. Screening assessments are typically given multiple times during an academic year. Once identified, individual diagnostic assessments administered by professionals provide further information on specific content area needs and allow for the diagnosis of students with learning disabilities. Although most diagnostic assessments are standardized, some informal measures are also used to develop an intervention plan for individual students. Progress monitoring assessments provide information on the effectiveness of intervention programs and are typically given at regular intervals throughout the week. Data from these assessments are used to plan and implement instruction, as well as make necessary changes to individualized programs based on students' performance. Accountability legislation, including the Individuals with Disabilities Act of 2004 (IDEA 2004) and the No Child Left Behind Act of 2002 (NCLB), has increased the pressure for official documentation of the effectiveness of programs for students with learning disabilities. Measurement of student outcomes through standardized assessments provides data on student progress typically used to compare states, districts, or schools for these purposes.

Diagnostic assessments contribute to the process of identification of students with learning disabilities. These diagnoses can affect student placement and the types of intervention services available to the student. Because the process for appropriate diagnosis of LDs remains a point of substantial debate within the field, the methods used may vary dramatically from state to state and even school district to school district. Although their methods may be different, proponents of most models would agree with the position of the National Research Center on Learning Disabilities (NRCLD) that "decisions regarding eligibility for special education services must draw from information collected from a comprehensive individual evaluation using multiple methods and sources of relevant information" (2007, p. 3).

For states and districts using the discrepancy model previously described in this chapter, the assessment process includes intelligence tests and tests of academic achievement. Scores from these two types of tests are compared to determine whether there is a discrepancy between ability and achievement. Some states also require tests to determine whether a specific processing deficit is present. According to the NRCLD (2007), although processing deficits have been linked to some learning disabilities (i.e., phonological processing and reading disabilities), links with other processes have not been established.

In the RTI model, also previously described, the approach to diagnosis is quite different. Drawing on the majority conclusion from the 2001 LD "summit" convened by the US Department of Education's Office of Special Education Programs, which stated that an IQ-achievement discrepancy is neither necessary nor sufficient for identifying students with LD, proponents of RTI contend that response to quality intervention is the most promising method of alternate identification. Fletcher et al. (2007) suggest that ensuring sufficient opportunities to learn is a prerequisite to the identification of LDs. Therefore, this model relies most heavily on curriculum-based assessments designed to measure students' responsiveness to intervention.

The same type of progress monitoring assessments used in the RTI model can be used in any classroom to make day-to-day instructional decisions for students with learning disabilities. Curriculum-based measurement (CBM), one of the most commonly used approaches to this kind of assessment, has been used effectively to gather student performance data to support a wide range of educational decisions (Deno, 2003). The focus of most CBM is to monitor the effectiveness of instruction. If a teacher determines through CBM that a student is not making progress, the next step would be to examine the instruction to determine what alteration may be made to promote better student learning.

Assessment Accommodations and Modifications

Tests are often administered under alternative conditions in order to address the needs of students with learning disabilities. These alternative conditions are changes to the test or its administration that enable students with learning disabilities to participate fully in the assessment process. Test *accommodations* are those changes to the scheduling, setting, method of presentation, or method of response that do not alter the construct being measured. Thurlow et al. (2008) explain that effective test accommodations ensure that all students are included in the assessment process in ways that hold schools accountable for their learning. Under No Child Left Behind, students with learning disabilities must be provided appropriate accommodations necessary to participate in these assessments. Determining the appropriate accommodations for students with disabilities to participate fully and equally in assessment is an important component of each student's individualized education program (IEP) or Section 504 Plan (Cortiella, 2005).

Test *modifications*, in contrast, do alter the construct being measured. Modifications include such changes as simplification of test questions, a change in the number of items included, or the use of an aide related to the construct being measured (e.g., a calculator on a math computation test, a spell-check or grammar-check device on a writing test). Generally, test modifications are avoided because the alterations they make to the construct being tested make interpretation of results difficult. In cases where modifications to assessment are used, great care should be taken to consider the effects of the modifications on the usability of the test data.

Educational Programming for Students with Learning Disabilities

Decisions about the design and implementation of educational programs for students with learning disabilities are based on a number of factors. The IEP team must consider which environment is most appropriate, who should deliver services and how they should be delivered, and what curriculum is most appropriate. The student's teacher must also consider which instructional methods will be most effective.

Least Restrictive Environment

The least restrictive environment component of IDEA 2004 requires that to the *extent appropriate*, students with disabilities and students without disabilities should be educated together. The IEP team determines what constitutes the least restrictive environment for individual students with learning disabilities. For most students with learning disabilities, this means that they receive the majority of their education in a general education classroom, with direct or indirect support from a special education professional. For some students, however, part-time or full-time placement in a special education classroom or even placement in a special school may be necessary.

Service Delivery

Instruction for students with learning disabilities may be provided in a variety of ways. Sometimes, instruction is provided wholly by the general education teacher, with appropriate accommodations as determined by the IEP team. More often, a special education teacher collaborates with the general education teacher in the planning and delivery of services. This service delivery may take the form of consultation with the teacher to design appropriate methods for instruction, co-teaching in the general education classroom, or more intensive instruction outside the general education classroom that supports the student's access to the general education curriculum. For students with more severe learning disabilities, substantial modifications to the curriculum may be necessary, and delivery of services may take place entirely outside the general education classroom.

Instructional Methods

Effective instruction for students with learning disabilities is usually more *explicit*, *systematic*, *intensive,* and *supportive* than what is typically offered in general education classrooms. Explicit instruction refers to instruction that is clear and direct and in which expected outcomes are conspicuous to students. An important goal of explicit instruction is to help children to focus their attention on the relations that matter and to ignore extraneous information. Systematic instruction is carefully planned to meet the particular needs of individual students to help them progress in the curriculum. The goal of systematic instruction is to maximize "the likelihood that whenever children are asked to learn something new, they already possess the appropriate prior knowledge and understanding to see its value and to learn it" (Adams, 2001, p.74). Systematic instruction, therefore, includes a logical sequence of knowledge and skills that build gradually from the simplest concepts and the easiest skills to the most complex knowledge and most difficult skills. In systematic instruction, the teacher ensures mastery before moving on. Increased instructional intensity can refer to more time spent on a particular topic or skill, more opportunities for the student to respond, smaller group size, or more repetition. Supportive instruction provides sufficient encouragement and positive reinforcement to maintain student motivation. It also provides more cognitive support in the form of instructional scaffolding and corrective feedback (Torgesen, 2002).

Some instructional methods have been shown to be particularly effective for students with learning disabilities. For example, explicit phonics instruction helps both younger and older students with learning disabilities learn to decode words effectively (Adams, 1990; Roberts, Torgesen, Boardman, & Scammacca, 2008), and explicit comprehension instruction helps them develop higher order cognitive strategies (Coyne et al., 2009). Learning strategies from the strategies intervention model are particularly helpful for promoting content learning among adolescents with learning disabilities (Deshler et al., 2001), and elementary-level children with learning disabilities benefit from peer-assisted learning strategies (Fuchs, Fuchs, Mathes, & Simmons, 1997). Similarly, self-regulated strategy development is a powerful method for writing instruction for students with learning disabilities (Graham, Harris, & Troia, 2000). Knowledge of and appropriate preparation in effective instructional methods such as these are essential for teachers of students with learning disabilities.

Trends and Issues in the Field of Learning Disabilities

The field of learning disabilities is still in its adolescence. Its beginnings have been marked by rapid growth and change, consensus and controversy, successes and failures. There are a variety of current challenges facing the field. For example, we need to carefully monitor the implementation of RTI models and identify ways to achieve the intended results (Fuchs & Deshler, 2007). We also need to continue to refine the definition of learning disabilities and methods of identification (Fletcher et al., 2007). As we do this, we need to address the demographic changes in our society, especially the increase in the number of students for whom English is a second language (Klingner, Artilles, & Mendez-Barletta, 2006). The issue of accountability and high stakes testing presents an ongoing challenge for students with learning disabilities and for special educators (Christenson, Decker, Triezenberg, Ysseldyke, & Reschly, 2007). We need to find ways to ensure that schools are held accountable for providing high quality instruction for students with learning disabilities without penalizing the students with unrealistic demands. As more students with learning disabilities succeed in school, more will attend college. We need to help institutions of higher education find ways to provide effective educational supports to promote college success for these students (Getzel, 2008). With continual changes to our country's demographic make-up, with increasing demands for academic achievement, and with a wide range of educational reforms that have an impact on special education, the field of learning disabilities will continue to grow and change. As the field continues to grow and change, we will undoubtedly see more consensus and controversy, more successes and failures.

References

Adams, M. J. (1990). *Learning to read: Thinking and learning about print.* Cambridge, MA: MIT Press.

Adams, M. J. (2001). Alphabetic anxiety and explicit, systematic phonics instruction: A cognitive science perspective. In S. B. Neuman & D. K. Dickinson (Eds.), *Handbook of early literacy research* (pp. 66–80). New York: Guilford.

American Psychiatric Association. (2010). *DSM V Development: Learning Disabilities.* Retrieved July 20, 2010, from http://www.dsm5.org/ProposedRevisions/Pages/proposedrevision.aspx?rid=429

Anderson, V. A., Catroppa, C., Rosenfeld, J., Haritou, F., & Morse, S. A. (2000). Recovery of memory function following traumatic brain injury in preschool children. *Brain Injury, 14*, 679–692.

Bateman, B. (1964). Learning disabilities – Yesterday, today, and tomorrow. *Exceptional Children, 31*, 167–177.

Bergert, S. (2000). *The warning signs of learning disabilities.* ERIC Clearinghouse on Disabilities and Gifted Education, Arlington VA. [online] http://ericcc.org/digests/e603.html

Berninger, V. (2009). Assessing and intervening with children with written language disorders. In D. Miller (Ed.), *Best practices in school neuropsychology* (pp. 507–520). New York: Wiley.

Betjemann, R., Willcutt, E., Olson, R., Keenan, J., DeFries, J., & Wadsworth, S. (2008). Word reading and reading comprehension: stability, overlap and independence. *Reading & Writing, 21*(5), 539–558. doi:10.1007/s11145-007-9076-8.

Christenson, S. L., Decker, D. M., Triezenberg, H. L., Ysseldyke, J. E., & Reschly, A. (2007). Consequences of high-stakes assessment for students with and without disabilities. *Educational Policy, 21*, 662–690.

Colletti, L. (1979). Relationship between pregnancy and birth complications and the later development of learning disabilities. *Journal of Learning Disabilities, 12*, 659–663.

Cortiella, C. (2005) *No Child Left Behind: Determining appropriate assessment accommodations for students with disabilities.* Lawrence, KS: National Center for Learning Disabilities.

Coyne, M. D., Zipoli, R. P., Chard, D, J., Faggella-Luby, M., Ruby, M., Santoro, L. E., & Baker, S. (2009). Direct instruction of comprehension: Instructional examples from intervention research on listening and reading comprehension. *Reading & Writing Quarterly, 25*, 221–245.

Deaton, A. V. (1987). Behavioral change strategies for children and adolescents with severe brain injury. *Journal of Learning Disabilities, 20*, 581–589.

Decker, S. N., & Defries, J. C. (1980). Cognitive abilities in families of reading disabled children. *Journal of Learning Disabilities, 13*, 517–522.

Decker, S. N., & Defries, J. C. (1981). Cognitive ability profiles in families of reading disabled children. *Developmental Medicine and Child Neurology, 23*, 217–227.

Deno, S. L. (2003). Developments in curriculum-based measurement. *Journal of Special Education, 37*, 184–192.

Denton, C. A., Vaughn, S., & Fletcher, J. M. (2003). Bringing research-based practice in reading intervention to scale. *Learning Disabilities Research & Practice, 18*, 201–211.

Deshler, D. D., Schumaker, J. B., Lenz, B. K., Bulgren, J. A., Hock, M. F., Knight, J., & Ehren, B. J. (2001). Ensuring content-area learning by secondary students with learning disabilities. *Learning Disabilities Research & Practice, 16*, 96–108.

Donders, J., & Kuldanek, A. S. (1998). Traumatic brain injury. In R. T. Ammerman & J. V. Campo (Eds.), *Handbook of pediatric psychology and psychiatry* (Vol. 2, pp. 166–190). Boston: Allyn & Bacon.

Dore, W. (2006). *Dyslexia: Vie miracle cure.* London: John Blake Publishing.

Downie, A. L. S., Jakobson, L. S., Frisk, V., & Ushycky, I. (2002). Periventricular brain injury, visual motion processing, and reading and spelling abilities in children who were extremely low birthweight. *Journal of the International Neuropsychological Society, 9*, 440–449.

Duane, D. D. (1989). Comment on dyslexia and neurodevelopmental pathology. *Journal of Learning Disabilities, 22*, 219–220.

Dybdahl, C. S., & Ryan, S. (2009). Inclusion for students with fetal alcohol syndrome: Classroom talk about practice. *Preventing School Failure, 53*, 185–195.

Ehren, B. J. (2006). Partnerships to support reading comprehension for students with language impairement. *Topics in Language Disorders, 26*, 42–54.

Ehri, L., & McCormick, S. (1998). Phases of word learning: Implications for instruction with delayed and disabled readers. *Reading and Writing Quarterly, 14*, 135–163.

Estell, D., Jones, M., Pearl, R., & Van Acker, R. (2009). Best friendships of students with and without learning disabilities across late elementary school. *Exceptional Children, 76*, 110–125.

Filipek, P. A. (1995). Neurobiologic correlates of developmental dyslexia: How do dyslexics' brains differ from those of normal readers? *Journal of Child Neurology, 10* (Suppl. 1), 62–69.

Fletcher, J. M., Lyon, G. R., Fuchs, L. S., & Barnes, M. A. (2007). *Learning disabilities: From identification to intervention*. New York: Guilford.

Forness, S., & Kavale, K. (2001). ADHD and a return to the medical model of special education. *Education & Treatment of Children, 24*, 224–247.

Fuchs, D., & Deshler, D. D. (2007). What we need to know about responsiveness-to-intervention (and shouldn't be afraid to ask). *Learning Disability Research and Practice, 2*, 129–136.

Fuchs, D., Fuchs, L.S., Mathes, P., & Simmons, D. (1997). Peer-Assisted Learning Strategies: Making classrooms more responsive to student diversity. *American Educational Research Journal, 34*, 174–206.

Fuchs, L. S., & Fuchs, D. (2007). A model for implementing responsiveness to intervention. *Teaching Exceptional Children, 35*(5), 14–23.

Galaburda, A. M. (1988). The pathogenesis of childhood dyslexia. In F. Plum (Ed.), *Language, communication, and the brain* (pp. 127–138). New York: Raven Press.

Garrett, A. J., Mazzocco, M. M., & Baker, L. (2006). Development of the metacognitive skills of prediction and evaluation in children with or without math disability. *Learning Disabilities Research & Practice, 21*, 77–88.

Gersten, R., Fuchs, L. S., Williams, J. P., & Baker, S. (2001). Teaching reading comprehension strategies to students with learning disabilities: A review of the research. *Review of Educational Research, 71*, 279–320.

Getzel, E. (2008). Addressing the persistence and retention of students with disabilities in higher education: Incorporating key strategies and supports on campus. *Exceptionality, 16*, 207–219.

Graham, S., Harris, K., & Troia, G. (2000). Self-regulated strategy development revisited: Teaching writing strategies to struggling writers. *Topics in Language Disorders, 20*, 1–14.

Green, C. R., Mihic, A. M., Nikkel, S. M., Stade, B. C., Rasmussen, C., Munoz, D. P., & Reynolds, J. N. (2008). Executive function deficits in children with fetal alcohol spectrum disorders (FASD) measured using the Cambridge Neuropyschological Tests Automated Battery (CANTAB). *Journal of Child Psychology and Psychiatry, 50*, 688–697.

Hallahan, D. P., Kauffman, J. M., & Pullen, P. C. (2009). *Exceptional learners: An introduction to special education, 11th edition*. Boston: Allyn & Bacon.

Hallgren, B. (1950). Specific dyslexia: A clinical and genetic study. *Acta Psychiatrica Neurologica, 65*, 1–287.

Hammill, D. D. (1993). On defining learning disabilities: An emerging consensus. *Journal of Learning Disabilities, 23*, 74–84. doi: 10.1177/002221949002300201

Hayiou-Thomas, M., Harlaar, N., Dale, P., & Plomin, R. (2010). Preschool speech, language skills, and reading at 7, 9, and 10 years: Etiology of the relationship. *Journal of Speech, Language & Hearing Research, 53*(2), 311–332.

Heath, N. L., & Ross, S. (2000). Prevalence and expression of depressive symptomatology in students with and without learning disabilities. *Learning Disability Quarterly, 23*, 24–36.

Herman, K. (1959). *Reading disability: A medical study of word blindness and related handicaps*. Springfield, IL: Charles C. Thomas.

Hyatt, K. J., Stephenson, J., & Carter, M. (2009). A review of three controversial educational practices: Perceptual motor programs, sensory integration, and tinted lenses. *Education and Treatement of Children, 32*, 313–342.

Hynd, G. W., Marshall, R., & Gonzalez, J. (1991). Learning disabilities and presumed central nervous system dysfunction. *Learning Disability Quarterly, 14*, 283–296.

Hynd, G. W., Semrud-Clikeman, M., Lorys, A. R., Novey, E. S., & Eliopulos, D. (1990). Brain morphology in developmental dyslexia and attention deficit disorder hyperactivity. *Archives of Neurology, 47*, 919–926.

Institute of Medicine. (1996). *Fetal alcohol syndrome: Diagnosis, epidemiology, prevention, and treatment.* Committee to study fetal alcohol syndrome. K. Stratton, C. Howe, & F. Battaglia (Eds.), *Division of Biobehavioral Sciences and Mental Disorders*. Washington, DC: National Academy Press.

Kartin, D., Grant, T. M., Streissguth, A. P., Sampson, P. D., & Ernst, C. C. (2002). Three-year developmental outcomes in children with prenatal alcohol and drug exposure. *Pediatric Physical Therapy, 14*, 145–153.

Kavale, K., Spaulding, L., & Beam, A. (2009). A time to define: Making the specific learning disability definition prescribe specific learning disability. *Learning Disability Quarterly, 32*, 39–48.

Kavale, K. A., & Reese, L. (1992). The character of learning disabilities: An Iowa profile. *Learning Disability Quarterly, 15*, 74–94.

Keenan, J., Betjemann, R., Wadsworth, S., DeFries, J., & Olson, R. (2006). Genetic and environmental influences on reading and listening comprehension. *Journal of Research in Reading, 29*(1), 75–91. doi:10.1111/j.1467-9817.2006.00293.x.

Klassen, R. (2010). Confidence to manage learning: The self-efficacy for self-regulated learning of early adolescents with learning disabilities. *Learning Disability Quarterly, 33*, 19–30.

Klassen, R., Krawchuk, L., Lynch, S., & Rajani, S. (2008). Procrastination and motivation of undergraduates with learning disabilities: A mixed-methods inquiry. *Learning Disabilities Research & Practice, 23*, 137–147. doi:10.1111/j.1540-5826.2008.00271.x.

Klingner, J. K., Artiles, A. J., & Méndez-Barletta, L. (2006). English language learners who struggle with reading: Language acquisition or learning disabilities? *Journal of Learning Disabilities, 39*, 108–128.

Kulak, A. G. (1993). Parallels between math and reading disability: Common issues and approaches. *Journal of Learning Disabilities, 26*, 666–673.

Larsen, J. P., Hoien, T., Lundberg, I., & Odegaard, H. (1990). MRI evaluation of the size and symmetry of the planum temporale in adolescents with developmental dyslexia. *Brain and Language, 26*, 78–86.

Lyon, G. R. (1995). Towards a definition of dyslexia. *Annals of Dyslexia, 45*, 3–27.

Maag, J. W., & Reid, R. (2006). Depression among students with learning disabilities: Assessing the risk. *Journal of Learning Disabilities, 39*, 3–10.

Martinussen, R., & Tannock, R. (2006). Working memory impairments in children with attention-deficit hyperactivity disorder with and without comorbid language learning disorders. *Journal of Clinical & Experimental Neuropsychology, 28*, 1073–1094. doi:10.1080/13803390500205700.

Mercer, C. D., & Pullen, P. C. (2009). *Students with learning disabilities* (7th ed.). Upper Saddle River, NJ: Pearson Education.

Mercer, C. D., Mercer, A., & Pullen, P. C. (2011). *Teaching students with learning problems* (8th ed.). Upper Saddle River, NJ: Pearson.

Metsala, J., & Ehri, L. (Eds.). (1998). *Word recognition in beginning literacy*. Mahwah, NJ: Erlbaum.

Montague, M., & Applegate, B. (1993). Mathematical problem-solving characteristics of middle school students with learning disabilities. *Journal of Special Education, 27*, 175–201.

Montgomery, M. S. (1994). Self-concept and children with learning disabilities: Observer-child concordance across six context-dependent domains. *Journal of Learning Disabilities, 27*, 254–262.

Morrow, C. E., Culbertson, J. L., Accornero, V. H., Xue, L., Anthony, J. C., & Bandstra, E. S. (2006). Learning disabilities and intellectual functioning in school-aged children with prenatal cocaine exposure. *Developmental Neuropsychology, 30*, 901–931.

National Joint Committee on Learning Disabilities. (1990). *Collective perspectives on issues affecting learning disabilities: Position papers and statements.* Austin, TX: Pro-Ed.

National Research Center on Learning Disabilities (2007). *SLD identification overview: General information and tools to get started.* [Brochure]. Lawrence, KS: Author.

National Research Council and Institute of Medicine. (2000). *From neurons to neighborhoods: The science of early childhood development.* Committee on Integrating the Science of Early Childhood Development, Board on Children, Youth, and Families. J. P. Shonkoff, & D. A. Phillips (Eds.). Washington, DC: National Academy Press.

Nowicki, E. A. (2003). A meta-analysis of the social competence of children with learning disabilities compared to classmates of low and average to high achievement. *Learning Disability Quarterly, 26*, 171–188.

Obrzut, J. E. (1989). Dyslexia and neurodevelopmental pathology: Is the neurodiagnostic technology ahead of the pychoeducational technology? *Journal of Learning Disabilities, 22*, 217–218.

Olsen, H. C., Streissguth, A. P., Sampson, P. D., Barr, H. M., Bookstein, F. L., & Thiede, K. (1997). Association of prenatal alcohol exposure with behavioral and learning problems in early adolescence. *Journal of American Academy of Child and Adolescent Psychiatry, 36*, 1187–1194.

Pastor, P. N., & Reuben C. A. (2008). *Diagnosed attention deficit hyperactivity disorder and learning disability: United States, 2004–2006.* Washington, DC: National Center for Health Statistics. Vital Health Statistics, Series 10, Number 237.

Pennington, B. F. (1995). Genetics of learning disabilities. *Journal of Child Neurology, 10* (Suppl. 1), 69–77.

Reynolds, C. R., Livingston, R. L., & Willson, V. L. (2006). *Measurement and assessment in education.* Boston: Allyn & Bacon.

Roberts, G., Torgesen, J.K., Boardman, A., & Scammacca, N. (2008). Evidence-based strategies for reading instruction of older students with LD or at risk for LD. *Learning Disabilities Research & Practice, 44*, 439–454.

Salvia, J., & Ysseldyke, J. E. (2009). *Assessment in special and inclusive education* (11th ed.). Boston: Houghton Mifflin.

Savage, R., Lavers, N., & Pillay, V. (2007). Working memory and reading difficulties: What we know and what we don't know about the relationship. *Educational Psychology Review, 19*, 185–221. doi:10.1007/s10648-006-9024-1

Schuchardt, K., Maehler, C., & Hasselhorn, M. (2008). Working memory deficits in children with specific learning disorders. *Journal of Learning Disabilities, 41*, 514–523.

Semrud-Clikeman, M. (2009). Neuropsychological aspects for evaluating learning disabilities. *Journal of Learning Disabilities, 38*, 563–568.

Shaley, R. S., Manor, O., & Gross-Tsur, V. (2005). Developmental dyscalculia: A prospectivesix-year follow-up. *Developmental Medicine & Child Neurology, 47*, 121–125.

Sideridis, G. (2007). Why are students with LD depressed? *Journal of Learning Disabilities, 40*, 526–539.

Sideridis, G. D., Morgan, P. L., Bostas, G., Padeliadu, S., & Fuchs, D. (2006). Identifying students with or at risk for learning disabilities based on motivation, metacognition, and psychopathology: A ROC analysis. *Journal of Learning Disabilities, 39*, 215–229.

Stanton-Chapman, T. L., Chapman, D. A., & Scott, K. G. (2001). Identification of early risk factors for learning disabilities. *Journal of Early Intervention, 24*, 193–206.

Swanson, H. L. (2009). Working memory, short-term memory, and reading disabilities: A selective meta-analysis of the literature. *Journal of Learning Disabilities, 42*, 260–287.

Swanson, H. L., Jerman, O., & Zheng, X. (2009). Math disabilities and reading disabilities. *Journal of Psychoeducational Assessment, 27*(3),175–196.

Thurlow, M. L., Quenemoen, R. F., Lazarus, S. S., Moen, R. E., Johnstone, C. J., Liu, K. K., … & Altman, J. (2008). *A principled approach to accountability assessments for students with disabilities* (Synthesis Report 70). Minneapolis: University of Minnesota, National Center on Educational Outcomes.

Torgesen, J. K. (1991). Learning disabilities: Historical and conceptual issues. In B. Y. L. Wong (Ed.), *Learning about learning disabilities* (pp. 3–37). San Diego: Academic Press.

Torgesen, J. K. (2002). The prevention of reading difficulties. *Journal of School Psychology, 40*, 7–26.

United States Department of Education (USDOE). (2004). IDEA, Individuals with Disabilities Education Improvement Act of 2004. Public Law 108-446, 108th Cong., 118 Stat. 2647.

Wadsworth, S. J., DeFries, J. C., Olson, R. K., & Wilcutt, E. G. (2007). Colorado Longitudinal Twin Study of Reading Disability. *Annals of Dyslexia, 57*, 137–160.

Wallach, G. P. (2005). A conceptual framework in language learning disabilities: School-age language disorders. *Topics in Language Disorders, 25*, 292–301.

16
Attention-Deficit/Hyperactivity Disorder

Karen J. Rooney
Educational Enterprises, Inc., Richmond, VA

Attention-Deficit/Hyperactivity Disorder (ADHD) is one of the most common disorders of childhood and, as of 2006, 4.5 million children have been diagnosed at some time with ADHD (Bloom & Cohen, 2006). The U.S. Department of Education describes ADHD as having "many faces" and as being "one of the most talked-about and controversial subjects in education," causing "heated debates" (U.S. Department of Education, 2009a, p. 1). To be consistent with the existing literature, the term "ADHD" will be used in this chapter and will represent the full spectrum of attention disorders.

Historical Origins

The increase in ADHD has been so significant that many think it is a modern phenomenon, but that is not the case.

Early History

For years, the work of George Still in the early 1900s was the earliest known description of what came to be known as an attention disorder; however, Palmer and Finger published a paper (2001) that discussed the work of a Scottish physician, Alexander Crichton, who described problems with inattention as early as 1798. In 1865, "Fidgety Phil," "Johnny Head-in-the-Air" (or "Johnny Look-in-the-Air"), "Cruel Frederick" and Pauline in "The Dreadful Story of Pauline and the Matches" appeared in poems by Heinrich Hoffman, a German physician (Thome & Jacobs, 2004).

Still's Lectures

In the early 20th century, Sir George Frederick Still, in his "Goulstonian Lectures," described 43 children in his practice who were aggressive, defiant, emotional, inattentive, and uninhibited though their intelligence was within the normal range (Still, 1902), and in the time period after Still's lectures, ADHD was related to some type of brain injury. In 1917 and 1918, epidemics of encephalitis resulted in the use of the term "minimal brain damage" because physicians saw an increase in activity levels, impulsivity, and problems with focus of attention in patients who had encephalitis (Patterson & Spence, 1921; Stryker, 1925).

Goldstein's Soldiers

After World War II, Dr. Kurt Goldstein (1936, 1939) treated soldiers who experienced some type of brain injury, and he noticed symptoms such as disorganization, perseveration, hyperactivity, and problems with figure-ground focus. Goldstein's work with figure-ground was replicated by Heinz Werner and Alfred Strauss (1941) in the 1930s and 40s in children with intellectual disabilities. These children, who were thought to have brain damage when presented with slides containing a figure embedded in a background of wavy lines, etc., projected at very brief exposure times, focused on the background rather than target figure. As a result, the term "Strauss Syndrome" was coined to describe children who were hyperactive and distractible. Extending this line of research, William Cruickshank used the figure-ground model to conduct investigations with samples of children who had cerebral palsy and normal intelligence (Dolphin & Cruickshank, 1951).

Minimally Brain Injured

Strauss and Lehtinen (1947) published a book about the education of children with brain injury, which was a precursor for some of the early textbooks in special education, and the use of the term "brain-injured" persisted. In the 1950s, Pasaminick, Rogers, and Lilienfeld (1956) studied children with birth complications and concluded brain pathology could produce problems with hyperactivity and distractibility.

Diagnostic and Statistical Manual Terminology

In the 1960s, the concept of hyperactivity overshadowed the use of terms implying brain damage. Practitioners and researchers began using the term "Hyperactive Childhood Syndrome" (Barkley, 2006a), and the *Diagnostic and*

Statistical Manual (*DSM*) introduced the American Psychiatric Association's (APA, 1968) term "Hyperkinetic Reaction of Childhood." By the 1980s another shift occurred as researchers began to identify inattention as having a more significant impact than hyperactivity on academic and social behaviors; consequently, the authors of the next version of the *DSM—DSM III* (APA, 1980) changed the designations to Attention Deficit Disorder with or without hyperactivity, and recognized that the disorder persisted into adulthood. The controversy continued and the terminology in the subsequent *DSM III-Revision* (APA, 1987) reverted back to Attention Deficit Hyperactivity Disorder; however, when *DSM-IV* was published (APA, 1994), the term again changed to include inattention as well as hyperactivity.

The current *DSM IV-TR* (APA, 2000) uses the heading Attention Deficit Hyperactivity Disorder with two categories (inattentive and hyperactive/impulsive), and three subtypes called ADHD-Primarily Hyperactive-Impulsive, ADHD-Primarily Inattentive, and ADHD-Combined (both hyperactive-impulsive and inattentive).

DSM-V Predictions

The *DSM-V* is expected to be published in 2013, and the following considerations are guiding the deliberations (Castellanos, 2009): eliminate redundant criteria; examine the use of different weights and cut-scores; revise existing subtypes; view hyperactivity, impulsivity, and inattention as domains; change criteria for ADHD in older adolescents and adults; examine the age of onset, duration, and exclusionary criteria; and identify Hyperkinetic Conduct Disorder as a separate disorder. The following changes have been recommended.

Options for General Structure. Use three subtypes with codes for Combined (C) and predominantly hyperactive (PH) with a separate code for inattentive (PI) or existing structure without subtypes or combined ADHD only (PI and PH would be eliminated).

Options for dealing with Attention-Deficit without Hyperactivity. Make no change, use Restrictive PI (RPI), which adds a subtype, or create a new diagnosis of Attention-Deficit Disorder that has no HI symptoms.

Options for Number, Content and Distribution of Criteria. Make no change, increase total count by adding often acts without thinking, is often impatient, often rushes through activities or tasks and often has difficulty resisting immediate temptations/appealing opportunities while disregarding negative consequences.

Options for age of onset of symptoms/impairment and change from impairment to symptoms. Make no change or increase age of onset to on or before the age of 12.

Options for adult ADHD. Make no change or lower threshold for combined from 6 to 3 criteria from hyperactive-impulsive or inattentive.

Options for cross-situational requirement. Use existing that does not specify ascertainment of un-witnessed behaviors or require that cross-situationality be reported directly by teacher, employer or significant other.

Options for inclusion and exclusion criteria. Make no change or remove Autism-spectrum Disorder and Pervasive Developmental Disorder from excluders or make the existing caution that inattention can't be due to defiance, hostility or failure to understand tasks/instruction more prominent. (APA, n.d.)

The committee also elaborated on the existing criteria descriptions to reduce reliance on broad, poorly defined descriptors.

Definition

There has been great controversy surrounding the acceptance of ADHD as a "real" disorder, which is likely related to the lack of a definitive diagnostic test and the perceived overuse or abuse of stimulant medication with children. To resolve this debate, a Consensus Development Conference was held (National Institutes of Health, 1998), and the consensus was that, though no independent diagnostic test exists, there is sufficient evidence to establish the validity of the disorder; however, definitions continue to vary. The National Institutes of Mental Health (NIMH) states that ADHD is "one of the most common childhood disorders and can continue through adolescence and into adulthood" and involves "difficulty staying focused and paying attention, difficulty controlling behavior, and hyperactivity (overactivity)" (NIMH, 2009, p. 2). The U.S. Department of Education (U.S. DOE) states: "Attention Deficit Hyperactivity Disorder (ADHD) is a neurological condition that involves problems with inattention and hyperactivity-impulsivity that are developmentally inconsistent with the age of the child" and "is a function of developmental failure in the brain circuitry that monitors inhibition and self-control" (U.S.DOE, 2009b, p. 2), and the American Psychological Association describes ADHD as a behavioral condition (American Psychological Association, 2009).

Most professionals use the APA diagnostic manuals, though some use the ICD-10 Classification system of the World Health Organization (1992), which uses the term "Hyperkinetic Disorder." In the most current edition, the *DSM-IV-TR* (APA, 2000), ADHD is defined as a "persistent pattern of inattention and/or hyperactivity-impulsivity that is more frequently displayed and more severe than is typically observed in individuals at a comparable level of development" (p. 85).

Prevalence

For other disorders, obtaining data about prevalence is more straightforward than with ADHD so prevalence data should be interpreted with caution.

General Complexities Surrounding Prevalence Data Collection

Physicians and psychologists are the professionals who frequently diagnose ADHD, but, since that diagnosis does not necessarily result in eligibility for special education services, those children may not be included in prevalence data reported by schools. Because 90% of children diagnosed with ADHD will utilize some form of medication as treatment (Greenhill, Halperin, & Abikoff, 1999) and 2 out of 3 of the children diagnosed as ADHD using a medical intervention will see a positive response (Pliszka, 2007), some parents may not involve school personnel at all. As a result, prevalence data obtained from schools may not reflect the actual number of students in school who have been diagnosed as ADHD.

ADHD as a Separate Category

By 1988, Children and Adults with Attention Disorders (CHADD), the major advocacy organization devoted to ADHD, was lobbying for ADHD to be a separate category; however, when the Individuals with Disabilities Education Act (IDEA) was reauthorized in 1990, ADHD was not included as a separate category. In 1991, the U.S. DOE determined students with ADHD could access services under IDEA using the Other Health Impaired (OHI) category if deficits in "alertness" had a significant effect on educational performance (U.S. DOE, 1991); however, OHI numbers that are reported to the U.S.DOE include children who have health impairments other than ADHD, which makes calculating the prevalence of ADHD using the OHI category difficult.

Prevalence and Response to Intervention

The reauthorization of the Individuals with Disabilities Education Act (2004) allowed for the use of Response-to-Intervention (RTI) to identify students who are not making expected progress in the general curriculum and who, therefore, might benefit from more intense support. The RTI movement outlined the use of a tier model that would allow for increasing levels of service, learning supports, and accommodations based on the individual student's academic performance and needs. School-based teams (previously referred to as Child Study Committees or Problem Solving Committees) can evaluate a student's performance data and recommend additional interventions/supports as needed, without requiring students to be identified under IDEA or Section 504; consequently, data sets may underrepresent the prevalence of ADHD.

Published Data

Reviews of epidemiological studies have reported that 3%–7% of school-age children have ADHD (APA, 2000; Barkley, 2006b), with some estimates even higher in the 7%–12% range (Woodruff et al., 2004); prevalence rates vary from state to state, ranging from 5%–11.1% (U.S. Centers for Disease Control and Prevention, 2005), with the most common age for diagnosis falling between the ages of 7 and 10 (Lavigne et al., 1996). More boys are diagnosed as ADHD than girls, and rates are higher for children in families with adults having higher education levels and for insured children (Center for Disease Control and Prevention, 2005). From the cross-cultural perspective, prevalence rates are also complicated by differences in terminology, identification procedures, and cultural differences, but the published data for Qatar (Bener, Al Qhatani, & Abdelaal, 2007), Australia (Graetz, Sawyer, Hazell, Arney, & Baghurst, 2001), Holland (Kroes et al., 2001), Germany (Baumgaertel, Wolraich, & Dietrich, 1995), China (Leung et al., 1996), Brazil (Rohde et al., 1999), and Arabia (Farah et al., 2009) are similar to the prevalence in the United States.

Causation

As with other disorders (such as learning disabilities and mild intellectual disabilities), identifying specific causation of ADHD is challenging. Researchers have identified several possible causes that are associated with ADHD, and understanding these causes may facilitate early identification and intervention planning.

Genetics

ADHD clearly runs in families. At least one third of fathers who were diagnosed with ADHD in childhood have children who have ADHD (Biederman et al., 1995) and the risk of having ADHD is 40%–57% if a parent has ADHD (Barkley, Murphy, & Fischer, 2008). Twin studies consistently find identical twins are more likely to have ADHD than fraternal twins (Levy & Hay, 2001; Nigg, 2006).

Imaging research has provided suggestive evidence that pre-frontal cortex, frontal lobes, striatum, basal ganglia, cerebellum, corpus callosum, and right parietal regions of the brain are involved (Castellanos, 1997; Vance et al., 2007; Volkow et al., 2007). Overall brain size is 5% smaller for children with ADHD than children without ADHD (Nigg, 2006; Voeller, 2004; NIMH, 2007). Researchers studying DNA have suggested linkages with chromosomes 17p11, 7p, and 15q (Ogdie et al., 2003; Bakker et al., 2003). On-going investigations have been examining specific genes that could be involved (Faraone et al., 2005; Khan & Faraone, 2006), and the NIMH has provided funding for the ADHD Molecular Genetic Network to examine the role of the dopamine transporter and dopamine D4 receptor genes (Shaw et al., 2007). An in-depth summary of genetic studies tracked by the National Institutes of Health (NIH) is available in a database on Online Mendelian Inheritance in Man (NIH, n.d.).

Brain Injuries

Though some brain injuries can result in attention problems, the number of children with ADHD who have a history of traumatic brain injury is small and has not been found to have predictive value (Birch, 1964).

Environmental Factors

Cigarette smoking and alcohol use during pregnancy (Mick, Biederman, Faraone, Sayer, & Kleinman, 2002) as well as high levels of lead (often in paint or plumbing in older buildings) suggest higher risk for attention problems (Faraone & Doyle, 2001; Braun, Kahn, Froehlich, Auinger, & Lanphear, 2006). More recently, reports relay concerns about the possible effects of low folate levels during pregnancy (Linnet et al., 2003) and phthalates (Center for Disease Control and Prevention, 2005).

Food and Nutrition

Some have claimed a link between sugar and ADHD, which is attractive to parents because the intervention is so clear-cut; however, research has not supported the use of refined sugar to be a cause of ADHD (Wolraich et al., 1994; Wolraich, Wilson, & White, 1995). Some have also claimed that food additives are connected with hyperactivity (Feingold, 1975). Research has not provided sufficient evidence to identify food additives as a cause (NIH, 1982; Kavale & Forness, 1983); however, a blind study (Bateman et al., 2004) did find that parents rated their children as having higher levels of inattention and hyperactivity when on a diet that included food additives and colorings, though more objective clinical measures did not.

Time on "Screens"

The amount of time that children are exposed to "screens" (such as when watching television, playing video games, and using handheld gaming technology) has grown tremendously, and concerns about the effect on attention have also increased. One study did link television viewing with attention problems (Christakis, Zimmerman, DiGiuseppe, & McCarty, 2004). However, the study had significant limitations because data comprised general attention (not diagnosed ADHD), and the study's design did not differentiate types of programs viewed (educational versus entertaining). Additional research should be a high priority to provide data to respond to questions about "screen time."

Assessment and Identification

Identification of ADHD is referred to as a "rule out" process, and best practice requires a multi-disciplinary assessment (APA, 2000). There is no single test that can identify ADHD, and the symptoms may also be the result of medical and/or psychological factors that mimic the disorder.

The American Academy of Pediatrics recommends physicians should view ADHD as a chronic problem, work with educators/school personnel, use stimulant medication and/or behavior therapy, use more comprehensive assessment when the selected management choices do not meet target outcomes, and provide systematic follow-up and monitoring (American Academy of Pediatrics, Subcommittee on Attention-Deficit/Hyperactivity Disorder, 2001). Behavioral and psychometric data about attention and impairment in life functioning must be collected across observers and multiple situations.

DSM-IV-TR Criteria and Summary of the Assessment Process

For a diagnosis of ADHD, a child must have six or more signs and symptoms from one of the two categories below (or six or more signs and symptoms from each of the two categories).

Inattention often fails to give close attention to details or makes careless mistakes in schoolwork or other activities; often has difficulty sustaining attention in tasks or play activities; often does not seem to listen when spoken to directly; often does not follow through on instructions and fails to finish schoolwork or chores (not due to oppositional behavior or failure to understand instructions); often has difficulty organizing tasks and activities; often avoids, dislikes, or is reluctant to engage in tasks that require sustained mental effort (such as schoolwork or homework); often loses things necessary for tasks or activities (for example, toys, school assignments, pencils, books); is often easily distracted and is often forgetful in daily activities.

Hyperactivity and Impulsivity often fidgets with hands or feet or squirms in seat, often leaves seat in classroom or in other situations in which remaining seated is expected, often runs about or climbs excessively in situations in which it is inappropriate, often has difficulty playing or engaging in leisure activities quietly, is often "on the go," often acts as if "driven by a motor," often talks excessively, often blurts out answers before questions have been completed, often has difficulty awaiting turn, often interrupts or intrudes on others (for example, butts into conversations or games).

In addition to having at least six symptoms from one of the two categories, a child with ADHD must have had these symptoms present before 7 years of age, the symptoms must have lasted for at least 6 months, and the symptoms must impair school, home life, or relationships in more than one setting (such as at home and at school).

Stress, depression, and anxiety can look like ADHD, and the following list of disorders can also have similar symptoms: learning or language disorders, mood disorders, hyperthyroidism, seizure disorders, Fetal Alcohol Syndrome, vision or hearing problems, Tourette Syndrome, Asperger's Syndrome, Autism, and sleep disorders (APA, 2000; Mayo Clinic, 2009). If all criteria are met, and other causative factors are ruled out, ADHD is identified, using one of these five categories stipulated in the *DSM IV-TR*: ADHD, Predominantly Inattentive Type; ADHD, Predominantly Hyperactive-Impulsive Type; ADHD, Combined Type; ADHD, Not Otherwise Specified or In Partial Remission.

Though this "rule out" process (also referred to as differential diagnosis) has been generally accepted by professionals in the medical, psychological, and educational fields, practice has not always adhered to these standards and reliance on symptom reporting without sufficient attention to levels of impairment results in different outcomes (Gathje & Lewandowski, 2008).

Legally, school-aged children can be found eligible for services under the Individuals with Disabilities Education Improvement Act (IDEA-2004) using the category Other Health Impaired (IDEA, 2004) or under Section 504 (Rehabilitation Act, 1973). If found eligible under IDEA 2004, the parent and the school-based team would develop an individualized education program (IEP) with goals to address the academic, social-emotional, and behavioral needs of the student. If eligibility is determined under Section 504, the school-based team would develop a 504 Plan, which would focus on accommodations, modifications, and learning supports.

Common Assessment Measures

Behavior rating scales and self-report measures that describe behaviors of concern are the most common measures to assess ADHD; responders are typically asked to rate behaviors provided in a list as being significantly more or less than would be expected for the child's age or developmental level. Some of the most commonly used rating scales, which typically have parent, teacher, and child versions (when appropriate), are the Conners Scales (Conners, Sitarenios, Parker, & Epstein, 1998), The Child Behavior Checklist (Achenbach & Edelbrook, 1983), and the Vanderbilt Attention-Deficit Hyperactivity Disorder Rating Scales (Wolraich, Feurer, Hannah, Pinnock, & Baumgaertel, 1998). Concerns about reliability of self-report measures, effects of question order (Mitchell, Knouse, Nelson-Gray, & Kwapil, 2009), and readability levels (Rogers, Spalding, Eckard, & Wallace, 2009) have resulted in general agreement that assessment needs to be a combination of subjective and objective data (U.S. DOE, 2009a).

The objective measures tend to be intelligence or cognitive tests combined with achievement testing to identify patterns and impairment associated with ADHD. The most common intelligence/cognitive tests are the Wechsler Intelligence Scale for Children-Fourth Edition (Wechsler, 2003), the Wechsler Adult Intelligence Scale-Third Edition (Wechsler, 2008), or the Woodcock-Johnson Tests of Cognitive Abilities-Third Edition (Woodcock, McGrew, & Mather, 2001a). The Wechsler Individual Achievement Test-Third Edition (Wechsler, 2009) or the Woodcock-Johnson Tests of Achievement, Forms A or B (Woodcock, McGrew, & Mather, 2001b) are frequently used to assess achievement.

Psychological, Social, and Behavioral Characteristics

Because ADHD is such a constellation of characteristics, and the chance of the disorder co-existing with one or more disorders that also have sets of related characteristics, the manifestation of ADHD in a particular individual needs to be described across domains.

Emotional/Psychological Characteristics

Characteristics associated with ADHD include distractibility, impulsivity, disorganization, frustration, emotional lability, risk-taking, depression, and anxiety (Barkley, 2006c). School failure, social problems, and task achievement can result in lower self-esteem, feelings of worthlessness, and more impulsive decision-making (Barkley, 2006c). Learning disabilities, conduct disorders, anxiety, oppositional defiant disorder, depression, bipolar disorder, Tourette Syndrome, sleep disorders, bed-wetting, and substance abuse may co-exist with ADHD (APA, 2000; NIMH, 2009).

Behavioral Characteristics

Behavioral Models. The criteria listed in the *DSM-IV-TR* (APA, 2000) describe many of the behaviors associated with ADHD, but a shift from the traditional view occurred when Barkley developed a paradigm that described a chronic lag of 30%–40% (NIMH, 2007) in the development of self-control and inhibition and presented a new construct using these descriptors (Barkley, 1997a; Barkley, 1997b; Barkley, 2005; Barkley, 2006d; NIMH, 2007). He recommended making inattention a separate category and proposed a theory of ADHD that has inhibition (which he refers to as the executive system that affects self-control and self-regulation) at the core (Barkley, 2006d). The new construct (Barkley, 2006d) depicts the lag in inhibition (motor inhibition, sensitivity to error, interference control) as the first step in the system that impedes the development of the four executive functions: nonverbal working memory (includes time awareness or "time-blindness"), internalization of speech (includes emotional self-regulation), intrinsic motivation, and "play to yourself" (includes verbal fluency).

Adaptive Behaviors. Low frustration tolerance, emotional lability, bossiness, temper outbursts, dysphoria, low self-esteem, laziness, and irresponsibility are features associated with ADHD (APA, 2000). Teenagers with ADHD have more problems with driving (Fischer, Barkley, Smallish, & Fletcher, 2007) and anger control (Richards, Deffenbacher, Rosen, Barkley, & Rodricks, 2007).

Social Characteristics

The social manifestations of ADHD change across the lifespan. Mrug et al. (2009) have found that peer rejection and negative imbalance between given and received liking ratings (children with ADHD liked others more than they were liked) discriminated children with ADHD from children without ADHD. Children with ADHD have fewer close friends and are rejected more often by their peers (Erhardt & Hinshaw, 1994; Hoza, 2007). Poor social functioning has also been found to be the best predictor of life dissatisfaction in college students with ADHD (Mick, Faraone, Spencer, Zhang, & Biederman, 2008). Some studies reflect problems with sibling relationships (Mikami & Pfiffner, 2008) as well as peers. Other studies have focused on impaired interpersonal relationships for adults, and a growing body of literature is focused on the workplace and marital problems associated with ADHD (Wymbs et al., 2008).

ADHD in Females

Though research on female populations is not extensive, a study that compared girls with ADHD and without ADHD (Biederman et al., 1999) found girls with ADHD were more likely to be inattentive, were 2.5 times more likely to be identified as having a learning disability, and were 16 times more likely to have repeated a grade. Prevalence of mood and anxiety disorders were similar to data from research conducted with boys with ADHD, though girls were at greater risk for substance abuse (Biederman et al., 1999). Data on social concerns and problems with interpersonal functioning were similar to data obtained from research on boys with ADHD (Greene et al., 2001). Gender-specific concerns also complicate identification and treatment (Quinn, 2005).

Medical and Alternative Interventions

The use of medication to treat ADHD has been widely publicized and debated in the popular press, but research has supported its use. The most extensive study of ADHD was conducted by the MTA Cooperative Group (1999, 2004), and the results from all six research sites clearly supported the efficacy of medical intervention and medical intervention combined with behavioral therapy; behavioral therapy alone was not found to be as effective. Other studies showed medical intervention to be connected with positive outcomes related to inhibition/executive function (Connor, 2006) and academic achievement in the areas of notetaking, homework completion, and written language (Evans et al., 2001). In spite of this support, the use of medication with children, particularly young children, continues to be controversial, and NIMH advises educators to refrain from making recommendations related to medication.

Common ADHD Medications

Over 70% of the children who use medication will receive a stimulant (Greenhill et al., 1999), and Vaughan, Roberts, and Needleman (2009) listed the most common medications as being Methylphenidate pharmocotherapies: Ritalin, Focalin, Ritalin SR, Metadate ER, Methylin ER, Metadate CD, Ritalin LA, Focalin XR, Concerta, Daytrana (patch), Adderal XR, and Vyvance. Non-stimulant medications used for treatment were Buprioprion, Wellbutrin, Effexor, Provigil, Straterra, Cloinidine, Risperidone, and Arirprizole. Vaughan and his colleagues (2009) strongly stated that medication was not a cure for ADHD, listed reasons why a medical intervention may not be initiated, and recommended pairing medication with psychosocial interventions.

Alternative Interventions

Numerous alternatives to medication have been proposed, but based on the published literature available, sensory integration therapy, mineral/vitamin supplements, caffeine, yoga, homeopathic treatments, and diet control do not have sufficient evidence of efficacy at this time. Neurofeedback does not currently have sufficient evidence, but the NIMH has provided funding for a study to provide additional data (NIMH, 2008).

Educational Considerations

For students with ADHD, educational intervention needs to be more intense, engaging, and comprehensive than for students without ADHD. Research has shown that multimodal treatment is required to support students with ADHD (MTA Group, 1999). ADHD is a multi-faceted disorder, which requires thoughtful, individualized intervention planning. Assessment should produce a "blueprint" that includes clear descriptions of strengths, weaknesses, and needs so that direct, explicit interventions and appropriate learning supports/accommodations/modifications can be put in place.

Teacher Knowledge

Research has shown that teacher knowledge is an important variable in identification and intervention planning (Sciutto, Terjesen, & Bender-Frank, 2000; Vereb & DiPerna, 2004), but general education teachers may not have extensive knowledge about ADHD (DuPaul et al., 1997; Weyandt, Fulton, Shepman, Verdi, & Wilson, 2009). This finding is a major concern because referral, identification, and intervention planning rely heavily on teacher report (Weyandt et al., 2009), particularly when an RTI process is used. Professional development focused on ADHD takes on even greater importance because experience does not necessarily increase teachers' knowledge of ADHD (Weyandt et al., 2009).

Evidence-Based Practices

The National Reading Panel (2000) identified the following practices as being effective across populations: phoneme awareness instruction, practice using oral guided reading with explicit, corrective feedback, direct and indirect instruction of vocabulary (with repetition and multiple exposures), and instruction using a combination of reading comprehension techniques. To supplement instructional practices and provide a more positive climate to support ADHD, The Institute of Education Sciences (2008) recommended clearly defining and teaching behavioral expectations, adjusting the physical environment to support positive behavior, individualizing instruction to foster engagement, and teaching/reinforcing prosocial skills (McIntosh, Filter, Bennett, Ryan, & Sugai, 2009).

Evidence has also supported the use of the following learning supports (Barkley, 2004; Weyandt, 2007): action-oriented and highly structured tasks; explicit and multisensory instruction; enhanced stimulation (such as the use of color); modified assignments (shorter lengths, smaller units); notetaking; adaptive technology; positive reinforcement; and study skills. Providing advance organizers and written summaries, clarifying directions, using preferential seating, reducing distraction, and previewing changes in routines are common accommodations; however, in keeping with the multi-modal framework (MTA,1999), interventions should be comprehensive and provide "networks of support."

Specific Interventions and Models

The first pioneer in the field was William Cruickshank (Cruickshank, Bentzen, Ratzeburg, & Tannhauser, 1961), and the underlying principles of his work (e.g., reducing distracting stimuli, providing highly structured, teacher-directed instruction) can still be detected in current models. Swanson (1992) developed a treatment protocol that involved a range of behaviors and interventions that included multiple supports such as token systems, cognitive-behavioral training for self-control, social skills training, response cost, and school-parent communication through a daily report card.

A multi-component program designed by Miranda, Presentacion, and Soriano (2002) showed positive outcomes. The program included sessions on general information about ADHD, behavior modification, and learning theory, applied learning theory to specific classroom examples, behavior modification procedures (positive reinforcement, Premack principle, token systems, extinction, time-out, response-cost), instructional management (arrangement of physical space, presentation of explanations, use of directions, feedback in the performance of tasks and examinations), organizational strategies, use of procedures to foster self-control, self-instruction, self-evaluation, and think aloud procedures.

Models are also targeting school-wide behavioral support programs such as Positive Behavior Support (Lewis & Sugai, 1999; Horner, Sugai, Todd, & Lewis-Palmer, 2005; Bradshaw, Koth, Bevans, Lalongo, & Leaf, 2008; Algozzinne & Algozzinne, 2009). These models target the problem behavior as well as the systemic environment that sustains the behavior (Biglan, 2004). In 2009, McIntosh and colleagues provided an in-depth discussion of School Wide Positive Behavior Support (SWPBS) in the context of prevention (McIntosh et al., 2009). Use of school-wide programs within RTI models has also produced positive outcomes (Fairbanks, Sugai, Guardino, & Lathrop, 2007; George, Kincaid, & Pollard-Sage, 2009; Scott, Anderson, Mancil, & Alter, 2009). In these studies, coaching, functional behavior assessment, contingency-based self-management, and reinforcement have been shown to be components of successful behavioral interventions for students with ADHD.

On-Going Monitoring/Assessment of Progress

On-going assessment of academic, social, and behavioral progress is critical in general and/or special education settings. Interventions need to be continued, adjusted, or terminated based on the data from progress monitoring measures that are frequent, dynamic, and on-going to achieve the intended goals.

Across the Lifespan

Current research has begun to focus on the assessment and manifestation of ADHD across the lifespan, and not just with school-aged children. Preschool children, college students, and adults have received more attention in recent years.

Preschool Children and Early Intervention. The diagnosis of ADHD in preschool children is very difficult (Blackman, 1999), and data need to be interpreted with caution with this young population because of normal variation in development and a skew towards hyperactivity being identified in children under the age of 7 years (Lahey, Pelham, Loney, Lee, & Willcutt, 2005). Predictive value of hyperactivity at the age of 4 years was not robust since criteria for ADHD were met for only half of those children at age 6 years (Campbell, 2002), and the necessary reliance on self-report measures may result in false positives (Loughran, 2003).

The degree and duration of early ADHD symptoms are predictors of chronic ADHD, and the presence of ADHD has been linked to marital discord, parenting stress, and family dysfunction (Wymbs et al., 2008); consequently, interest in early identification and intervention is high. Current research is investigating behaviors related to inhibition (Hundhammer & McLaughlin, 2002), metamemory (Antshel & Nastasi, 2008), and executive function (Barkley, 2005; Senn, Epsy, & Kaufmann, 2004) that may assist in early identification and intervention. Barkley (1997a) has stated that disinhibition behaviors can be observed as early as the ages of 3 or 4 years, which was supported by a more recent study by Pisecco, Baker, Silva, and Brooke (2001). In their study, Pisecco et al. also found that boys with Reading Disorder and ADHD seemed to be most at-risk based on early "lack of control" temperament measures combined with receptive language/reading disability; boys with ADHD only were not seen as being more disruptive. Based on these findings, early assessments may need to obtain measures of self-control, receptive/expressive language development, and early literacy skills rather than just focus on clinical interview, medical examination, and behavioral self-reports as recommended in the past (Barkley, 1998).

College Students with ADHD. The prevalence of ADHD for college students is approximately 2%–8%, and 25% of identified disabilities at the college level are ADHD (DuPaul, Weyandt, O'Dell, & Varejao, 2009). Only half of those identified report receiving adequate accommodations (Chew, Jensen, & Rosen, 2009). In addition, students with ADHD report struggling in comparison with non-ADHD peers (Blase et al., 2009). The use of the descriptors inattention and hyperactivity-impulsivity, which have been used more with younger children, as well as the need to obtain data from multiple sources were supported (DuPaul et al., 2001; Solanto & Alvir, 2009); but research has also identified concerns with this older population. Heavy reliance on self-report measures in combination with vulnerability to substance abuse, misuse of medication and diversion (Rabiner, Anastopoulos, Costello, Hoyle, & Schwartzwelder, 2008) need to be considered and addressed during assessment and intervention. Time management skills have been identified as having a positive correlation with academic success in college (Kaminski, Turnock, Rosen, & Laster, 2006), but additional research needs to identify the accommodations and supports that are important for academic, behavioral, and social success at the college level.

Adults with ADHD. For a number of years, ADHD was viewed as a childhood disorder that would be outgrown, but this was not supported by research (Faraone & Doyle, 2001), and the publication of *Driven to Distraction: Recognizing and Coping with Attention Deficit Disorder from Childhood through Adulthood* (Halloway & Ratey, 1995) popularized the concept of Adult ADHD. Prevalence appears to be about 4%–5% (Kessler et al., 2006) and has been associated with school failure, problems in the workplace (Nadeau, 2005), and other mental disorders such as antisocial behaviors, anxiety and depression (Weyandt & DuPaul, 2006).

Adults with ADHD report doing better on medication and attribute that improvement to the medication rather than ability or the demands of the task (Barrilleaux & Advokat, 2009); however, medication was not viewed as a panacea (Young, Gray, & Branham 2009). Adults with ADHD who have higher IQs have more executive function impairment (Brown, Reichel, & Quinlan, 2009). Impaired interpersonal coping styles, parenting stress (Barkley, 2000), and marital discord (Wymbs et al., 2008) were reported as problems for adults with ADHD. On a more positive note, early identification/treatment predicted positive outcomes related to employment (Halmoy, Bentfasmer, Gillberg, & Haavik, 2009), research on Adult ADHD is growing (Barkley, Murphy, & Fischer, 2008; Davidson, 2008; Ramsey & Rostain, 2008), and the *DSM-V* may provide additional guidance to address Adult ADHD in more depth.

Discussion

Though much progress has been made since the 1980s, and the field's evidence base about ADHD has grown markedly, there does appear to be a disconnect between research and practice in schools, at home, and in the workplace. Dissemination of evidence-based information about assessment, diagnosis, and intervention should be increased, and research should continue to examine the manifestations of ADHD in females as well as males and in populations across both settings and ages. Future research should investigate protective factors that can ameliorate the disorder, parenting practices for parents who also have ADHD, and the effect of "screen time" on attention.

References

Achenbach, T. M., & Edelbrook, C. (1983). *Manual for the child behaviour checklist and revised child behaviour profile.* Burlington: University of Vermont.

Algozzine, B., & Algozzine, K. M. (2009). Facilitating academic achievement through school-wide positive behavior support. In W. Sailor, G. Dunlap, G. Sugai, & R. H. Horner (Eds.), *Handbook of positive behavior support* (pp. 521–550). New York: Springer.

American Academy of Pediatrics, subcommittee on Attention-Deficit/Hyperactivity Disorder. (2001). Clinical practice guideline: treatment of the school-aged child with attention-deficit hyperactivity disorder. *Pediatrics, 108*(4), 1033–1044.

American Psychiatric Association. (1968). *Diagnostic and statistical manual of mental disorders* (2nd ed.). Washington, DC: Author.

American Psychiatric Association. (1980). *Diagnostic and statistical manual of mental disorders* (3rd ed.). Washington, DC: Author.

American Psychiatric Association. (1987). *Diagnostic and statistical manual of mental disorders* (3rd ed., revision). Washington, DC: Author.

American Psychiatric Association. (1994). *Diagnostic and statistical manual of mental disorders* (4th ed.). Washington, DC: Author.

American Psychiatric Association. (2000). Attention-deficit and disruptive behavior disorders. In *Diagnostic and statistical manual of mental disorders* (4th ed., text revision, pp. 85–103). Washington, DC: Author.

American Psychological Association. (2009). ADHD definition. Retrieved December 26, 2009, from http://www.apa.org on

American Psychological Association. (n.d.). Proposed draft revisions to DSM disorders and criteria. Retrieved February 2, 2010, from from http:/www.dsm5.org on

Antshel, K. M., & Nastasi, R. (2008). Metamemory development in preschool children with ADHD. *Journal of Applied Developmental Psychology, 29*(5), 403–411.

Bakker, S. C., van der Meulen, E. M., Buitelaar, J. K, Sandkuiji, L. A., Pauls, D. L., Monsuur, A. J., … Sinke, R. J. (2003). A whole-genome scan in 164 Dutch sib pairs with attention-deficit/hyperactivity disorder: suggestive evidence for linkage on chromosomes 7p and 15q. *American Journal of Human Genetics, 72*(5), 1251–1260.

Barkley, R. A. (1997a). *Attention deficit hyperactivity disorder and the nature of self control.* New York: Guilford.

Barkley, R. A. (1997b). Behavioral inhibition, sustained attention, and executive functions: Constructing a unifying theory of ADHD. *Psychological Bulletin, 121*, 65–94.

Barkley, R. A. (1998). *Attention-Deficit hyperactivity disorder: A handbook for diagnosis and treatment.* New York: Guildford.

Barkley, R. A. (2000). *Taking charge of ADHD: The complete, authoritative guide for parents.* New York: Guilford.

Barkley, R. A. (2004). Adolescents with attention-deficit/hyperactivity disorder: An overview of empirically based treatments. *Journal of Psychiatric Practice, 10*(1), 39–56.

Barkley, R. A. (2005). *ADHD and the nature of self-control.* New York: Guilford.

Barkley, R. A. (2006a). History. In R. A. Barkley (Ed.), *Attention-deficit hyperactivity disorder: A handbook for diagnosis and treatment* (3rd ed., pp. 3–75). New York: Guilford.

Barkley, R. A. (2006b). Primary symptoms, diagnostic criteria, prevalence and gender differences. In R. A. Barkley (Ed.), *Attention-deficit hyperactivity disorder: A handbook for diagnosis and treatment* (3rd ed., pp.7 6–121). New York: Guilford.

Barkley, R. A. (2006c). Associated cognitive, developmental, and health problems. In R. A. Barkley (Ed.), *Attention-deficit hyperactivity disorder: A handbook for diagnosis and treatment* (3rd ed., pp. 122–183). New York: Guilford.

Barkley, R. A. (2006d). A theory of ADHD. In R. A. Barkley (Ed.), *Attention-deficit hyperactivity disorder: A handbook for diagnosis and treatment* (3rd ed., pp. 297–334). New York: Guilford.

Barkley, R. A., Murphy, K., & Fischer, M. (2008). *ADHD in adults: What the science says.* New York: Guilford.

Barrilleaux, K., & Advokat, C. (2009). Attribution and self-evaluation of continuous performance test task performance in medicated and unmedicated adults with ADHD. *Journal of Attention Disorders, 12*, 291–298.

Bateman, B., Warner, J. O., Hutchinson, E., Dean, T., Rowlandson, P., Gant, C., … Stevenson, J. (2004). The effects of a double-blind, placebo-controlled, artificial food colorings and benzoate preservative challenge on hyperactivity in a general population sample of preschool children. *Archives of Disease in Childhood, 89*, 506–511.

Baumgaertel, A., Wolraich, M. L., & Dietrich, M. (1995). Comparison of diagnostic criteria for attention deficit disorders in a German elementary sample. *Journal of the Academy of Child and Adolescent Psychiatry, 34*, 629–638.

Bener, A., Al Qhatani, R., & Abdelaal, I. (2007). The prevalence of ADHD among primary school children in an Arabian Society. *Journal of Attention Disorders, 10*, 77–82.

Biederman, J., Faraone, S. V., Mick, H., Spencer, T., Wilens, T., Kiely, K., … Warburton, R. (1995). High risk for attention deficit hyperactivity disorder among children of parents with childhood onset of the disorder: A pilot study. *American Journal of Psychiatry, 152*, 431–435.

Biederman, J., Faraone, S., Mick, E., Williamson, S., Wilens, T. E., Spencer, T. J., … Zallen, B. (1999). Clinical correlates of ADHD in females: Findings from a large group of girls ascertained from pediatric and psychiatric referral sources. *Journal of the American Academy of Child and Adolescent Psychiatry, 38*(8), 966–975.

Biglan, A. (2004). Contextualism and the development of effective prevention practices. *Prevention Science, 5*, 15–21.

Birch, H. G. (1964). *Brain damage in children: The biological and social aspects.* Baltimore: Williams & Wilkins.

Blackman, J. A. (1999). Attention-deficit hyperactivity disorder in preschoolers: Does it exist and should we treat it? *Pediatric Clinics of North America, 46*, 1011–1024.

Blase, S. L., Gilbert, A. N., Anastopoulus, A. D., Costello, J., Hoyle, R. H., Swatrzwelder, H. S., & Rabiner, D. L. (2009). Self-reported ADHD and adjustment in college: Cross-sectional and longitudinal findings. *Journal of Attention Disorders, 13*, 297–309.

Bloom, B., & Cohen, R. A. (2006). Summary of health statistics for US children: National health interview survey. *National Center for Health Statistics-Vital Health Statistics, 10*, 234.

Bradshaw, C. P., Koth, K., Bevans, K. B., Lalongo, N., & Leaf, P. J. (2008). The impact of school-wide positive behavioral supports on the organizational health of elementary schools. *School Psychology Quarterly, 23*, 462–473.

Braun, J., Kahn, R. S., Froehlich, T., Auinger, P., & Lanphear, B. P. (2006). Exposures to environmental toxicants and attention-deficit/hyperactivity disorder in U.S. children. *Environmental Health Perspectives, 114*(12),1904–1909.

Brown, T. E., Reichel, P. C., & Quinlan, D. M. (2009). Executive function impairments in high IQ adults with ADHD. *Journal of Attention Disorders, 13*, 161–167.

Campbell, S. (2002). *Behavior problems in preschool: Clinical and developmental issues* (2nd ed.). New York: Guilford.

Castellanos, R. X. (1997). Toward a pathophysiology of attention-deficit/hyperactivity disorder. *Clinical Pediatrics, 36*, 381–393.

Castellanos, R. X. (2009). Report of the DSM V ADHD and Disruptive Behaviors Work Group. Retrieved December 3, 2009, from http://www.psych.org/MainMenu/Research/DSMIV/DSMV/DSMRevisionActivities/DSM-V-Work-Group-Reports/ADHD-and-Disruptive-Behavior-Disorders-Work-Group-Report.aspx

Chew, B. L., Jensen, S. A., & Rosen, L. A. (2009). College students' attitudes toward their ADHD peers. *Journal of Attention Disorders, 13*, 271–276.

Christakis, D. A., Zimmerman, F. J., DiGiuseppe, D. L., & McCarty, C. A. (2004). Early television exposure and subsequent attentional problems in children. *Pediatrics, 113*(4), 708–713.

Conners, C. K., Sitarenios, G., Parker, J. D., & Epstein, J. N. (1998). Revision and restandardization of the Conners Teacher Rating Scale (CTRS-R): Factor structure, reliability, and criterion validity. *Journal of Abnormal Child Psychology, 26*, 279 –291.

Connor, D. F. (2006). Stimulants. In R. A. Barkley (Ed.), *Attention-deficit hyperactivity disorder: A handbook for diagnosis and treatment* (3rd ed., pp. 608–647). New York: Guilford.

Cruickshank, W. M., Bentzen, F. A., Ratzeburg, F. H., & Tannhauser, M. T. (1961). *A teaching method of brain-injured and hyperactive children.* Syracuse, NY: Syracuse University Press.

Davidson, M. A. (2008). Literature review: ADHD in adults. *Journal of Attention Disorders, 11*(6), 628–641.

Dolphin, J. E., & Cruickshank, W. M. (1951). The figure-background relation in children with cerebral palsy. *Journal of Clinical Psychology, 7*, 228–223.

DuPaul, G. J., Power T. J., Anastopoulos, A. D., Reid, R., McGoey, K. E., & Ikeda, M. J. (1997). Teacher ratings of attention deficit hyperactivity disorder symptoms: Factor structure and normative data. *Psychological Assessment, 9*, 436–444.

DuPaul, G. J., Schaughency, E. A., Weyandt, L. L., Tripp, G., Kiesner, J., Ota, K., & Stanish, H. (2001). Self-report of ADHD symptoms in university students: Cross-gender and cross-national prevalence. *Journal of Learning Disabilities, 34*, 370–379.

DuPaul, G. J., Weyandt, L. L., O'Dell, S. M., & Varejao, M. (2009). College students with ADHD: Current status and future directions. *Journal of Learning Disabilities, 13*, 234–250.

Erhardt, D., & Hinshaw, S. P. (1994). Initial sociometric impressions of attention-deficit hyperactivity disorder and comparison boys: Predictions from social behaviors and from non-behavioral variables. *Journal of Consulting and Clinical Psychology, 62*, 833–842.

Evans, S. W., Pelham, W. E., Smith, B. H., Bukstein, O., Gnagy, E. M., Greiner, A. R., … Baron-Myak, C. (2001). Dose-response effects of methylphenidate on ecologically valid measures of academic performance and classroom behavior in adolescents with ADHD. *Experiential and Clinical Pharmacology, 9*, 163–175.

Fairbanks, S., Sugai, G., Guardino, D., & Lathrop, M. (2007). Response to Intervention: An evaluation of a classroom system of behavioral support for second grade students. *Exceptional Children, 73*, 288–310.

Farah, L. G., Fayyad, J. A., Eapen,V., Cassir, Y., Salamoun, M. M., Tabet, C. C. … Karam, E. G . (2009). ADHD in the Arab world. *Journal of Attention Disorders, 13*(3), 211–222.

Faraone, S. V., & Doyle, A. E. (2001), The nature and heritability of attention-deficit/hyperactivity disorder. *Child and Adolescent Psychiatric Clinics of North America, 10*, 299–306.

Faraone, S. V., Perlis, R. H., Doyle, A. E., Smoller, J. W., Goralnick, J. J., Holmgren, M. A., Sklar, P. (2005). Molecular genetics of attention-deficit/hyperactivity disorder. *Biological Psychiatry, 57*, 1313–1323.

Feingold, B. (1975). *Why your child is hyperactive.* New York: Random House.

Fischer, M., Barkley, R. A., Smallish, L., & Fletcher, K. (2007). Hyperactive children as young adults: Driving abilities, safe driving behavior and adverse driving outcomes. *Accident Analysis and Prevention, 39*, 94–105.

Gathje, R. A., & Lewandowski, L. J. (2008). The role of impairment in the diagnosis of ADHD. *Journal of Attention Disorders, 11*(5), 529–537.

George, H. P., Kincaid, D., & Pollard-Sage, J. (2009). Primary tier interventions and supports. In W. Sailor, G. Dunlap, G. Sugai, & R. H. Horner (Eds.), *Handbook of positive behavior support* (pp. 375–394). New York: Springer.

Goldstein, K. (1936). The modification of behavior consequent to cerebral lesions. *Psychiatric Quarterly, 10*, 586–610.

Goldstein, K. (1939). *The organism.* New York: American Book Co.

Graetz, B. W., Sawyer, M. G., Hazell, P. L., Arney, F., & Baghurst, P. (2001). Validity of DSM–IV ADHD subtypes in a nationally representative sample of Australian children and adolescents. *Journal of the Academy of Child and Adolescent Psychiatry, 40*, 1410–1417.

Greene, R. W., Biederman, J., Faraone, S. V., Monuteaux, M. C., Mick, E., DuPre, E. P., … Goring, J. C. (2001). Social impairment in girls with ADHD: Patterns, gender comparisons, and correlates. *Journal of the American Academy of Child and Adolescent Psychiatry, 40*(6), 704–710.

Greenhill, L. L., Halperin, J. M., & Abikoff, H. (1999). Stimulant medications. *Journal of the American Academy of Child and Adolescent Psychiatry, 38*, 503–512.

Halloway, E. M., & Ratey, J. J. (1995). *Driven to distraction: Recognizing and coping with attention deficit disorder from childhood through adulthood.* New York: Touchstone.

Halmoy, A., Bentfasmer, O., Gillberg, C., & Haavik, J. (2009). Occupational outcome in adult ADHD: Impact of symptom profile, comorbid psychiatric problems, and treatment: A cross-sectional study of 414 clinically diagnosed adult ADHD patients. *Journal of Learning Disabilities, 13*. doi: 10.1177/1087054708329777

Horner, R. H., Sugai, G., Todd, A. W., & Lewis-Palmer, T. (2005). Schoolwide positive behavioral support. In L. Bambara & L. Kern (Eds.), *Individualized supports for children with problem behaviors: Designing positive behavior plans* (pp. 359–390). New York: Guilford.

Hoza, B. (2007). Peer functioning in children with ADHD. *Journal of Pediatric Psychology, 32*, 655–663.

Hundhammer, B., & McLaughlin, T. F. (2002). Preschoolers who exhibit ADHD related behaviors: How to assist parents and teachers. *International Journal of Special Education, 17*(1), 42–48.

Individuals with Disabilities Education Act. (2004). Regulations, sec. 300.8 child with a disability, (a), (1) & (9).

Institute of Education Sciences. (2008). *Reducing behavior problems in the elementary school classroom.* Washington, DC: Author.

Kaminski, P. L., Turnock, P. M., Rosen, L. A., & Laster, S. A. (2006). Predictors of academic success among college students with attention disorders. *Journal of College Counseling, 9*, 60–71.

Kavale, K. A., & Forness, S. R. (1983). Hyperactivity and diet treatment: A meta-analysis of the Feingold hypothesis. *Journal of Learning Disabilities, 16*, 324–330.

Kessler, R. C., Adler, L., Barkley, R., Biederman, J., Conners, C. K., Demler, O., ... Zaslavsky, A. M. (2006). The prevalence and correlates of adult ADHD in the United States: Results from the National Comorbidity Survey Replication. *American Journal of Psychiatry, 163*, 716–723.

Khan, S. A., & Faraone, S. V.(2006). The genetics of attention-deficit/hyperactivity disorder: A literature review of 2005. *Current Psychiatry Reports, 8*, 393–397.

Kroes, M., Kalff, A. C., Kessels, A. G., Steyaert, J., Feron, F. J. M., van Someron, A. J., ... Johan, S. H. (2001). Child psychiatric diagnoses in a population of Dutch schoolchildren aged 6 to 8 years. *Journal of the American Academy of Child and Adolescent Psychiatry, 40*, 1401–1409.

Lahey, B., Pelham, W., Loney, J., Lee, S., & Willicutt, E. (2005). Instability of the DSM-IV subtypes from preschool through elementary school. *Archives of General Psychiatry, 62*, 896–902.

Lavigne, J. V., Gibbons, R. D., Christofel, K. K., Arend R., Rosenbaum, D., Binns, H., ... Isaacs, C. (1996). Prevalence rates and correlates of psychiatric disorders among preschool children. *Journal of the American Academy of Child and Adolescent Psychiatry, 35*(2), 204–214.

Leung, P. W. L., Luk, S. L., Ho, T. P., Taylor, E., Mak, F. L., & Bacon-Shone, J. (1996). The diagnosis and prevalence of hyperactivity in Chinese schoolboys. *British Journal of Psychiatry, 168*, 486–496.

Levy, F., & Hay, D. A. (2001). *Attention, genes, and attention-deficit hyperactivity disorder.* Philadelphia: Psychology Press.

Lewis, T. J., & Sugai, G. (1999). Effective behavior support: A systems approach to proactive schoolwide management. *Focus on Exceptional Children, 23*, 109–121.

Linnet, K. M., Dalsgaard, S., Obel, C., Wisborg, K., Henriksen, T. B., Rodriguez, A., ... Jarvelin, M. R. (2003). Maternal lifestyle factors in pregnancy risk of attention-deficit/hyperactivity disorder and associated behaviors: review of the current evidence. *American Journal of Psychiatry, 160*(6), 1028–1040.

Loughran, S. B. (2003). Agreement and reliability of teacher rating scales for assessing ADHD in preschoolers. *Early Childhood Education Journal, 30*(4), 247–253.

Mayo Clinic Staff. (2009). Attention-deficit disorder (ADHD) in children. Retrieved December 10, 2009, from http://www.mayoclinic.com/health/adhd/DS00275/DSECTION=causes on

McIntosh, K., Filter, K. J., Bennett, J. L., Ryan, C., & Sugai, G. (2009). Principles of sustainable prevention: Designing scale-up of schoolwide positive behavior support to promote durable systems. *Psychology in the Schools, 47*(1), 5–21. doi: 10.1002/pits.20448

Mick, E., Biederman J., Faraone, S. V., Sayer J., & Kleinman S. (2002). Case-control study of attention-deficit hyperactivity disorder and maternal smoking, alcohol use, and drug use during pregnancy. *Journal of the American Academy of Child and Adolescent Psychiatry, 41*(4), 378–385.

Mick, E., Faraone, S.V., Spencer, T., Zhang, H .F. & Biederman, J. (2008). Assessing the validity of the quality of life enjoyment and satisfaction questionnaire—short form in adults with ADHD. *Journal of Attention Disorders, 11*(4), 504–509.

Mikami, A. L., & Pfiffner, L. J. (2008). Sibling relationships among children with ADHD. *Journal of Attention Disorders, 11*(4), 482–492.

Miranda, A., Presentacion, M. J., & Soriano, M. (2002). Effectiveness of a school-based, multi-component program for the treatment of children with ADHD. *Journal of Learning Disabilities, 35*(6), 547–563.

Mitchell, J. T., Knouse, L. E., Nelson-Gray, R. O., & Kwapil, T. R. (2009). Self-reported ADHD symptoms among college students: Item positioning affects symptoms endorsement rates. *Journal of Attention Disorders, 13*, 154–160.

Mrug, S., Hoza, B., Gerdes, A. C., Hinshaw, S., Arnold, E., Hechtman, L., & Pelham, W. E. (2009). Discriminating between children with ADHD and classmates using peer variables. *Journal of Attention Disorders, 12*, 372–380.

MTA Cooperative Group. (1999). A 14 month randomized clinical trial of treatment strategies for attention-deficit/hyperactivity disorder. *Archives of General Psychiatry, 56*, 1073–1086.

MTA Cooperative Group. (2004). National Institute of Mental Health Multimodal Treatment Study of ADHD follow-up: Changes in effectiveness and growth after the end of treatment. *Pediatrics, 113*(4), 762–769.

Nadeau, K. G. (2005). Career choices and workplace challenges for individuals with ADHD. *Journal of Clinical Psychology, 61*(5), 549–563.

National Institutes of Health (NIH). (1982). Defined diets and childhood hyperactivity. (1982). *NIH Consens Statement, 4*(3),1–11.

National Institutes of Health (NIH). (1998). Diagnosis and treatment of attention deficit hyperactivity disorder). [Electronic Version) *NIH Consensus Statement, 16*(2), 1–37.

National Institutes of Health (NIH). (n.d.). An in-depth summary of genetic studies tracked by The National Institutes of Health is available in a database on Online Mendelian Inheritance in Man. Retrieved February 21, 2010, from http://www.ncbi.nlm.nih.gov/Omim/mimstats.html

National Institutes of Mental Health (NIMH). (2007). Brain matures somewhat late but follows normal pattern. Retrieved from http://www.nimh.nih.gov/science-news/2007/brain-matures-a-few-years-late-in-adhd-but-follows-normal-pattern.shtml

National Institutes of Mental Health (NIMH). (2008). New NIMH research to test innovative treatments for children with ADHD. Retrieved December 10, 2009, from http://www.nimh.nih.gov/science-news/2008/new-nimh-research-to-test-innovative-treatments-for-children-with-adhd.shtml

National Institutes of Mental Health (NIMH). (2009). Attention deficit hyperactivity disorder. Retrieved from http://www.nimh.nih.gov/health/publications/attention-deficit-hyperactivity-disorder/what-is-attention-deficit-hyperactivity-disorder.shtml, p. 1.

National Reading Panel (NRP). (2000). *Teaching children to read: An evidence-based assessment of the scientific research literature on reading and its implications for reading instruction.* Washington DC: National Institute of Child Health and Human Development.

Nigg, J. T. (2006). *What causes ADHD? Understanding what goes wrong and why.* New York: Guilford.

Ogdie, M. N., Macphie, I. L., Minassian, S. L., Yang, M., Fisher, S. E., Francks, C., ... Smalley, S. L. (2003). A genome-wide scan for attention-deficit hyperactivity disorder in an extended sample: suggestive linkage on 17p11. *American Journal of Human Genetics, 72*(5), 1268–1279.

Palmer, E. D., & Finger, S. (2001). An early description of ADHD (Inattentive Subtype): Dr. Alexander Crichton and "mental restlessness" (1798). *Child Psychology and Psychiatry Review, 6*(2), 66–73.

Pasaminick, B., Rogers, M., & Lilienfeld, A. (1956). Pregnancy experience and behaviour disorder in children. *American Journal of Psychiatry, 112*, 613–618.

Patterson, D., & Spence, J. C. (1921). The after-effects of epidemic encephalitis in children. *Lancet, 2*, 491–493.

Pisecco, S., Baker, D. B., Silva, P. A., & Brooke, M. (2001). Boys with reading disability and/or ADHD. *Journal of Learning Disabilities, 34*(2), 98–106.

Pliszka, S. R. (2007). Practice parameter for the assessment and treatment of children and adolescents with attention-deficit/hyperactivity disorder. *Journal of the American Academy of Child and Adolescent Psychiatry, 46*(7), 894–921.

Quinn, P. O. (2005). Treating adolescent girls and women with ADHD: Gender-specific issues. *Journal of Clinical Psychology, 61*(5), 579–587.

Rabiner, D. L., Anastopoulus, A. D., Costello, J., Hoyle, R. H., & Schwartzwelder, H. S. (2008). Adjustment to college in students with ADHD. *Journal of Attention Disorders, 11*(6), 689–699.

Ramsey, J. R., & Rostain, A. L. (2008). Adult ADHD research: Current status and future directions. *Journal of Attention Disorders, 11*. doi: 10.1177/10870547-8314590

Rehabilitation Act of 1973. (1973). Public Law 93-112, HR 8070, section 504.

Richards, T. L., Deffenbacher, J. L., Rosen, L. A., Barkley, R. A., & Rodricks, T. (2007). Driving anger and driving behavior in adults with ADHD. *Journal of Attention Disorders, 10*, 54–64.

Rogers, E. S., Spalding, S. L., Eckard, A. A., & Wallace, L. S. (2009). Are patient-administered attention deficit hyperactivity disorder scales suitable for adults? *Journal of Attention Disorders, 13*, 154–160.

Rohde, L. A., Biederman, J., Busnello, H., Zimmerman, H., Schmitz, M., Martins, S., ... Tramontina, S. (1999). ADHD in a sample of Brazilian adolescents: A study of prevalence, comorbid conditions, and impairments. *Journal of the Academy of Child and Adolescent Psychiatry, 38*, 716–722.

Sciutto, M. J., Terjesen, M. D., & Bender-Frank, A. S. (2000). Teachers' knowledge and misperceptions of attention-deficit/hyperactivity disorder. *Psychology in the Schools, 37*, 115–122.

Scott, T. M., Anderson, C. M., Mancil, R., & Alter, P. (2009). Function-based supports for individual students in school settings. In W. Sailor, G. Dunlap, G. Sugai, & R. H. Horner (Eds.), *Handbook of positive behavior support* (pp. 421–442). New York: Springer.

Senn, T. E., Epsy, K. A., & Kaufmann, P. M. (2004). Using path analysis to understand executive function organization in preschool children. *Developmental Neuropsychology, 26*, 445–465.

Shaw, P., Gornick, M., Lerch, J., Addington, A., Seal, J., Greenstein, D., … Rapoport, J. L. (2007). Polymorphisms of the dopamine D4 receptor, clinical outcome and cortical structure in attention-deficit/hyperactivity disorder. *Archives of General Psychiatry, 64*(8), 921–931.

Solanto, M. V., & Alvir, J. (2009). Reliability of DSM-IV symptom ratings of ADHD: Implications for DSM-V. *Journal of Attention Disorders, 13*, 107–116.

Still, G. F. (1902). Some abnormal psychical conditions in children: the Goulstonian lectures. *Lancet, 1,* 1008–1012.

Strauss, A. A., & Lehtinen, L. E. (1947). *Psychopathology and education of the brain-injured child.* New York: Grune & Stratton.

Stryker, S. (1925). Encephalitis lethargic-the behavioral residuals. *Training School Bulletin, 22*, 152–157.

Swanson, J. M. (1992). *School-based assessment and interventions for ADHD students.* Irvine, CA: KC Publishing.

Thome, J., & Jacobs, K. A. (2004). Attention deficit hyperactivity disorder (ADHD) in a 19th century children's book. *European psychiatry: The journal of the Association of European Psychiatrists, 19*, 303–306.

U.S. Centers for Disease Control and Prevention. (2005). Summary of the 2005 third national report on human exposure to environmental chemicals. Retrieved December 10, 2009, from http://www.cdc.gov/

U.S. Department of Education. (1991). Clarification of policy to address the needs of children with ADD within general and/or special education. Memorandum jointly signed by the Assistant Secretaries of OCR, OESE, and OSERS.

U.S. Department of Education. (2009a). Identifying and treating attention deficit hyperactivity disorder: A resource for home and school. Retrieved from http://www.ed.gov/rschstat/research/pubs/adhd/adhd-identifying.html

U.S. Department of Education. (2009b). Retrieved from http://www.ed.gov/rschstat/research/pubs/adhd/adhd-identifying_pg2.html

Vance, A., Silk, T. J., Casey, M., Rinehart, N. J., Bradshaw, J. L., Bellgrove, M. A., & Cunnington, R. (2007). Right parietal dysfunction in children with attention deficit hyperactivity disorder, combined type: a functional MRI study. *Molecular Psychiatry, 12*, 826–832.

Vaughan, B. S., Roberts, H. J., & Needleman, H. (2009). Current medications for the treatment of attention-deficit/hyperactivity disorder. *Psychology in the Schools, 46*(9), 846–856. doi: 10.1002/pits.20425

Vereb, R. L., & DiPerna, J. C. (2004). Research brief: Teachers' knowledge of ADHD, treatments for ADHD, and treatment. *School Psychology Review, 33*, 421–428.

Voeller, K. K. K. (2004). Attention-deficit hyperactivity disorder (ADHD). *Journal of Child Neurology, 19*, 798–814.

Volkow, N. D., Wang, G. J., Newcorn, J., Telang, F., Solanto, M. V., Fowler, J. S., … Swanson, J.M. (2007). Depressed dopamine activity in caudate and preliminary evidence of limbic involvement in adults with attention-deficit/hyperactivity disorder. *Archives of General Psychiatry, 64*(8), 932–940.

Wechsler, D. (2003). *Wechsler Intelligence Scale for Children - Fourth Edition*. New York: Psychological Corporation.

Wechsler, D. (2008). *Wechsler Adult Intelligence Scale - Third Edition.* New York: Psychological Corporation.

Wechsler, D. (2009). *Wechsler Individual Achievement Test - Third Edition*. New York: Psychological Corporation

Werner, A., & Strauss, AA. (1941). Pathology of figure-background relation in the child. *Journal of Abnormal Psychology, 36*, 236–248.

Weyandt, L. L. (2007). *Attention deficit hyperactivity disorder: An ADHD primer* (2nd ed.). Mahwah, NJ: Erlbaum.

Weyandt, L. L., & DuPaul, G. J. (2006). ADHD in college students: Developmental findings. *Developmental Disabilities Research Reviews, 14*(4), 311–319.

Weyandt, L. L., Fulton, K. M., Schepman, S. B., Verdi, G. R., & Wilson, K. G. (2009). Assessment of teacher and school psychologist knowledge of attention-deficit/hyperactivity disorder. *Psychology in the Schools, 46*(10), 951–961. doi:10.1002/pits.20436

Wolraich, M. L., Wilson, D. B., & White, J. W. (1995). The effect of sugar on behavior or cognition in children: A meta-analysis. *Journal of the American Medical Association, 274*, 1617–1621.

Wolraich, M. L., Feurer, I., Hannah, J. N., Pinnock, T. Y., & Baumgaertel, A. (1998). Obtaining systematic teacher reports of disruptive behavior disorders utilizing DSM-IV. *Journal of Abnormal Child Psychology, 26*, 141–152

Wolraich, M. L., Lindgren, S. D., Stumbo, P. J., Stegink, L. D., Appelbaum, M. I., Kiritsy, M. C. (1994). Effects of diets high in sucrose or aspartame on the behavior and cognitive performance of children. *New England Journal of Medicine, 330*(5), 301–307.

Woodcock, R. W., McGrew, K. S., & Mather, N. (2001a). *Woodcock-Johnson III Tests of Cognitive Abilities.* Itasca, IL: Riverside Publishing.

Woodcock, R. W., McGrew, K. S., & Mather, N. (2001b). *Woodcock-Johnson III Tests of Achievement.* Itasca, IL: Riverside Publishing.

Woodruff, T. J., Axelrad, D. A., Kyle, A. D., Nweke, O., Miller, G. G., & Hurley, B. J. (2004). Trends in environmentally related childhood illnesses. *Pediatrics, 113*(4 Suppl.), 1133–1140.

World Health Organization. (1992). *The ICD-10 classification of mental and behavioural disorders: Clinical descriptions and diagnostic guidelines.* Geneva: Author.

Wymbs, B. T., Pelham, W. E., Molina, B. S. G., Gnagy, E. M., Wilson, T. K., & Greenhouse, J. B. (2008). Rate and predictors of divorce among parents of youth with ADHD. *Journal of Consulting in Clinical Psychology, 76*(5), 735–744.

Young, S., Gray, K., & Branham, J. (2009). A phenomenological analysis of the experience of receiving a diagnosis and treatment of ADHD in adulthood: A partner's perspective. *Journal of Attention Disorders, 12*, 299–307.

17

Emotional and Behavioral Disorders

Timothy J. Landrum
University of Louisville

Children and youth with emotional and behavioral disorders present tremendous challenges to families, schools, and communities. Providing appropriate services to them challenges the capacity of both schools and communities, as educational, vocational, and mental health resources of many types and provided by many different service providers and agencies are often necessary to meet their typically chronic, often complex needs. These challenges are made greater by the nature of emotional and behavioral disorders (EBD), and by controversy surrounding most aspects of EBD. The nature of EBD is such that the behavioral characteristics of most students with EBD often make them unwelcome in social groups, unpopular among their peers, and potentially unwelcome in classrooms where their behavior can be disruptive, disrespectful, unpleasant, and extraordinarily difficult for teachers to manage. In part because of the nature of EBD, the field is also characterized by controversy at nearly all levels. These include how to identify students with EBD; whether EBD is in fact a disability that can be distinguished from run-of-the-mill disruptive, aggressive, bad, or even delinquent behavior; how and where students with EBD can be best served (i.e., where their educational needs can best be met); and how students with EBD can and should be disciplined. This chapter provides an overview of the nature and treatment of EBD, addressing in turn (a) definitions of EBD; (b) causal factors that may be associated with the development of EBD in children and youth; (c) the identification of EBD in schools; (d) the major behavioral characteristics of children and youth with EBD; (c) the assessment of EBD, including the different purposes for conducting assessments; (f) educational programming for students with EBD in early childhood, in elementary school, and in secondary school; and (g) current trends and issues. As noted, controversy surrounds many of these issues, and the controversial nature of the field of EBD begins with the very definition of emotional and behavioral disorders.

Definition

Defining emotional or behavioral disorders is difficult, to say the least. There are a number of reasons for this difficulty, and full treatment of each is beyond the scope of this chapter. A fundamental problem that cuts across these difficulties in defining emotional or behavioral disorders involves a simple question: what is *normal*? The reason that we identify students with emotional or behavioral disorders in school is so that they can receive the special education services they need. They are eligible for these services when their educational characteristics and needs are so discrepant from the norm that they cannot receive a satisfactory education through the typical educational program provided to all students. But how different or discrepant from the norm must their behavior or educational performance be? Any definition of emotional or behavioral disorders must take this question into account, and by default, draw some conclusion as to what is normal, and thus what is discrepant from this norm.

The Federal Definition

For special education purposes, the federal definition of *emotional disturbance* (the term currently used in the Individuals with Disabilities Education Act, including the 2004 reauthorization; note that the term used prior to the IDEA amendments of 1997 was *serious emotional disturbance*) provides a framework for what emotional or behavioral disorders look like in school, but from the start the federal definition itself was fraught with controversy. According to IDEA,

(4) Emotional disturbance is defined as follows:
  (i) the term means a condition exhibiting one or more of the following characteristics over a long period of time and to a marked degree that adversely affects a child's educational performance:

(A) An inability to learn that cannot be explained by intellectual, sensory, or health factors.
(B) An inability to build or maintain satisfactory interpersonal relationships with peers and teachers.
(C) Inappropriate types of behavior or feelings under normal circumstances.
(D) A general pervasive mood of unhappiness or depression.
(E) A tendency to develop physical symptoms or fears associated with personal or school problems.

(ii) The term includes schizophrenia. The term does not apply to children who are socially maladjusted, unless it is determined that they have an emotional disturbance. (45 C. F. R. 121a5[b][8][1978])

The federal definition above drew heavily, indeed nearly verbatim, from one provided by Bower (1960, 1981), based on his research with thousands of children with what he termed "emotional handicaps." Though Bower's original definition was deemed far from perfect (see Kauffman & Landrum, 2009), it provided a logical and workable framework for thinking about EBD in the context of schools. Among the difficulties with Bower's definition were the meanings and interpretations of such terms as "to a marked degree," and "over a long period of time." These obviously call into question what are normal, versus abnormal, emotional or behavioral responses. While much of Bower's language represented challenges of interpretation, the statements added to Bower's work when the federal definition was developed, in contrast, "come close to making nonsense of it" (Kauffman & Landrum, p. 18). One addition was "that adversely affects a child's educational performance" in section (i), which is difficult to interpret both in terms of what counts as adverse effect and what is meant by educational performance (failing grades? some number of disciplinary referrals? suspension or expulsion from school?). Moreover, might a student exhibit one or more (or even all) of the characteristics enumerated in A–E, thus demonstrating significant emotional or behavioral difficulties, yet still earn passing marks in school, and thus be ineligible for services under this category?

The second addendum was the entirety of section (ii), which states that schizophrenia is included in the definition of emotional disturbance, but social maladjustment is not, unless it is also determined that the student with social maladjustment has an emotional disturbance. The first part, that schizophrenia is included, is redundant at best, as any student with schizophrenia would certainly display one or more of the characteristics listed (e.g., B, the inability to build or maintain satisfactory interpersonal relationships). The most troubling change of all is the final statement excluding social maladjustment, unless it is determined that the student has an emotional disturbance. While the circular reasoning here is maddeningly impossible to decipher, the statement is more troubling in the apparent attempt to remove from consideration for services some subgroup for students—those who are socially maladjusted—who are neither defined nor can be presumed to be any different from those who exhibit some number of the five characteristics enumerated. That is, could a student who is considered socially maladjusted *not* exhibit *any* of these five characteristics? And would not a student exhibiting these characteristics (perhaps most obviously B, but also D and E) by default be considered socially maladjusted?

National Mental Health and Special Education Coalition Definition

An important response to the professional consensus that the federal definition is flawed at best was the creation of a working group by the National Mental Health and Special Education Coalition (Forness & Knitzer, 1992), which was charged with developing a new alternative definition. Responding to specific limitations of the federal definition, developers of the new definition sought to (a) use professionally preferred terminology that might reduce stigma; (b) include reference to both emotions and behavior; (c) focus on school-related problems, but recognize that EBD may be manifested in important ways outside of school; (d) include sensitivity to ethnic and cultural differences; and (e) exclude minor transient problems that might be predictable responses to stressors. The coalition proposed the following:

I. The term emotional or behavioral disorder means a disability characterized by emotional or behavioral responses in school programs so different from appropriate age, cultural, or ethnic norms that they adversely affect educational performance, including academic, social, vocational, or personal skills, and which
(a) is more than a temporary, expected response to stressful events in the environment;
(b) is consistently exhibited in two different settings, at least one of which is school related; and
(c) persists despite individualized interventions within the education program, unless, in the judgment of the team, the child's or youth's history indicates that such interventions would not be effective.

Emotional or behavioral disorders can co-exist with other disabilities.

II. This category may include children and youth with schizophrenic disorders, affective disorders, anxiety disorders, or other sustained disturbances of conduct or adjustment when they adversely affect educational performance in accordance with section I. (Forness & Knitzer, 1992, p. 13)

The coalition, along with more than 30 professional and advocacy groups that have endorsed the proposed definition, continue to advocate for a change in the federal definition, but as yet there has been no indication that change in federal rules and regulations is imminent. Nonetheless, broad support for the proposed definition is an indicator that professional preference has shifted to a large degree toward the terminology and definitional components contained in this alternate definition of EBD.

Causal Factors

Determining the cause of EBD is important for at least two reasons. First, if we could identify with any precision what causes EBD, preventive efforts could target these causal factors more directly and intensively. Second, identifying the cause, at least in some cases, should improve our prescription of treatment. Notice that the two are interrelated. For example, if we know that harsh, inconsistent discipline practices cause or contribute to the development of EBD, interventions designed to train parents and teachers in the use of positive behavioral procedures and the judicious, consistent use of negative consequences might serve to prevent some disorders from developing, as well as improve the behavior of some children with already-developed behavioral disorders. Unfortunately, the specific cause of EBD in the individual case is seldom clear. Growing bodies of research have isolated a number of causal factors that may contribute to the development of EBD, or place children at heightened risk of developing EBD, but these causal factors overlap and interact with one another in ways that make identifying a precise cause of EBD elusive. Four categories of causal factors are most often discussed: biological factors, family factors, school factors, and cultural factors.

Biological Factors

Biological explanations for EBD have particular appeal in part because environmental, behavioral, or social learning explanations have been unable to account for the range of disordered behavior that children and youth display. For example, children from stable, positive, enriched home and school environments that provide support and encouragement for appropriate behavior still sometimes display highly unusual, aggressive, or disruptive behavior. Though it remains true that a specific cause can seldom be identified, there are four ways in which biological factors may influence the development of emotional or behavioral disorders: genetics, brain damage or dysfunction, nutritional issues or allergies, and temperament.

Genetic factors have long been suspected of contributing to disordered behavior. Research that increasingly points to a genetic component or influence on both positive and negative behavior (e.g., McGuffin & Thapar, 1997; Pinker, 2002) strengthens such suspicions. And though genetics have been shown to play a clear role in some disorders, such as schizophrenia (Asarnow & Asarnow, 2003; Plomin, 1995), it is more often the case that the role of genetics lies in creating a genetic predisposition that may or may not be triggered by environmental factors (Nicol & Erlenmeyer-Kimling, 1986). It is easy to see, however, how genetics and environmental factors intersect. If one or both parents have a disorder, the genetic predisposition can certainly be passed along to children. The extent to which parents display behavioral manifestations of their own disorder in their parenting and family interactions will undoubtedly influence the likelihood that children will develop similar disorders.

Damage to the brain as a result of injury or illness, including before or during birth, can also contribute to EBD, though the precise mechanisms for this are not clearly understood. Studies of children and youth who have experienced a traumatic brain injury (TBI) provide evidence of several potential effects of brain damage on emotion or behavior, including: failure to comprehend humor or read social cues; becoming easily tired, angered, or frustrated; irritability; extreme mood swings; and even depression (Kauffman & Landrum, 2009). Such characteristics are clearly consistent with the defining characteristics of EBD, though an important distinction was made when TBI was established as a separate category of disability in the Individuals with Disabilities Education Act (IDEA) of 1990.

The role of nutrition in emotional or behavioral disorders has probably been exaggerated significantly. Poor nutrition in the form of junk food, and more specifically excesses of sugar and caffeine in the diets of children have been speculated to lead to dramatic behavioral difficulties (e.g., Pescara-Kovach & Alexander, 1994), but for the most part research has failed to bear out the presence of such links (e.g., Wolraich, Wilson, & White, 1995). The same is true of food allergies; while there is clear evidence that food and other allergies can cause health-related difficulties for children which range from quite mild to severe (e.g., Sampson, 2004), and of course health concerns can contribute to school problems in the form of missed school due to absences or medical treatment, there is little evidence that allergies contribute directly to learning or behavioral difficulties (McLoughlin & Nall, 1988, 1994). It is true that severe malnutrition, as might occur in cases of extreme poverty or neglect, can lead to significant physical, emotional, and behavioral problems that translate into dramatic problems in school (Tanner & Finn-Stevenson, 2002).

A final genetic component that may contribute to the development of EBD has to do with temperament. Temperament refers generally to a behavioral style, or the ways individuals react to stimuli and events in their environment, and temperament is determined at least in part by genetics. Research on temperament, especially that beginning in the 1960s (e.g., Thomas, Chess, & Birch, 1968), lead to several generalizations about the development of EBD within family contexts, which may also have important implications for educators. Two general principles supported by this research are that children are indeed born with distinctly different temperaments, and perhaps more importantly that temperament may be evident from the earliest days of life. Temperamental styles then influence parental behavior and responses, and reciprocal relationships are formed. For example, a child with a difficult temperament is presumed to be more challenging to parent, and this difficult temperament may evoke irritability and negative responses from caregivers. Further, the challenge of a difficult temperament may be even greater for parents or families that are already stressed by dysfunction, poverty, substance abuse, or other risk factors. It is not difficult to see how characteristics of children's temperament, such as activity level, distractibility, and persistence, can influence not only parents and families, but educators as well (Keogh, 2003).

Family Factors

The appeal of family factors as a causal explanation for EBD may result from the sometimes chaotic or negative relationships that appear to exist in families of children with EBD (Dadds, 2002; Reid & Eddy, 1997). But a parsimonious look at such families reveals that the causal nature of the relationship between family or parental dysfunction and childhood behavior disorders is not completely clear, and further that the direction of this relationship must be considered reciprocal in that children influence adult behavior just as adults influence theirs, from a very early age (e.g., Bell, 1968; Bell & Harper, 1977). Obviously, as discussed earlier, temperament plays a key role in such family interactions. As Kauffman and Landrum (2009) noted, "A child from a broken family may well exhibit behavioral characteristics that would break nearly any family" (p. 184). That is, regardless of which came first—childhood behavior problems, or family or parental dysfunction—it seems increasingly clear that each in turn negatively affects the other. While it is not possible to draw definitive conclusions about the precise mechanisms at work in families that may either exacerbate or mitigate risk for EBD in children, a growing body of research on families and parenting does reveal some generalities about the potential contributions of family factors to the development of EBD.

Parenting, and more specifically parental discipline, has been shown to be associated with risk for EBD in many children. Baumrind (1995, 1996) has described effective discipline as both (a) *responsive*, which includes warmth, reciprocity, and attachment; and (b) *demanding*, meaning that parents monitor behavior, maintain firm control, and provide consequences for both positive and negative behavior. In contrast, disciplinary practices that are either too harsh or too lax may contribute to increased problem behavior (O'Leary, 1995). Summarizing Baumrind's work, Kauffman and Landrum (2009) suggested that effective parental discipline that promotes positive child behavior and would seem to lessen risk for the development of behavior disorders most likely involves (a) supervision and monitoring of children's behavior, (b) positive acknowledgement or other consequences (reinforcement) for desired behavior, and (c) the provision of "firm but nonhostile" demands, as well as "negative but nonabusive" consequences for undesirable behavior or rule violations (p. 185).

School Factors

It is perhaps ironic that schools, which presumably would be places that foster academic, social, and emotional growth in positive ways, may contribute to the development of emotional or behavioral disorders. This is not to say that schools cause EBD in most or even many cases; surely many children come to school with EBD and associated behavioral difficulties well-established. It is more accurate to say that what happens in the course of schooling will either ameliorate these problems or exacerbate them. Structured environments with sound academic instruction, including support for students who struggle; positive forms of discipline that emphasize recognition and reward for positive behavior; and effective instruction in specific social skills all contribute to students' well-being. Moreover, the extent to which students are able to navigate the social and academic demands of school and meet with success is surely related to their overall mental health. Conversely, a curriculum that is matched neither to the strengths nor interests of students; disciplinary practices that focus on punitive responses to negative behavior, with little or no recognition of positive behavior and student success; and a lack of instruction and support for positive social skills are likely to set students up for difficulties.

Cultural Factors

The influence of culture on behavior is surely powerful, though it is difficult to tease out the specific effects of family, peers, and schools, all of which are components of culture. Moreover, the influence of culture may be positive or negative, in providing either protective factors that may minimize the chance of developing EBD, or exacerbate other risk factors (see Stichter, Conroy, & Kauffman, 2008, for a discussion of factors that lead to success in school). Though much has been written about cultural differences and the overrepresentation of minority students in the category of EBD (e.g., Harry & Klingner, 2006), there is little evidence that minority ethnicity itself is associated with significantly different rates of behavior problems (Achenbach & Edelbrock, 1981), or psychiatric disorders (Roberts, Roberts, & Xing, 2006).

What has become clear is that conflicts and contradictory messages among the values and expectations across or within cultures may contribute to the development of behavior problems. One area that has been debated for years is the link between violence in the mass media—television in particular—and children's behavior. Recent evidence supports that high rates of television watching are indeed associated with heightened risk for attentional and learning problems in children and adolescents (Johnson, Cohen, Kasen, & Brook, 2007; Zimmerman & Chistakis, 2005). More specifically, watching violence on television is associated with heightened risk of later violent tendencies and desensitization to violence (Huesmann, Moise, & Podolski, 1997; Huesmann, Moise-Titus, Podolski, & Eron, 2003).

Identification

For special education purposes, the identification of emotional or behavioral disorders occurs in schools, and is separate from any formal psychiatric diagnosis children may or may not have. Indeed, schools have typically identified only about 1% of the population as eligible for special education because of an EBD. In contrast, professional estimates of the true prevalence of emotional or behavioral disorders suggest that 3%–6% of the school-aged population probably have emotional or behavioral disorders that require intervention (Kauffman & Landrum, 2009). Evaluation for special education follows several guidelines spelled out in IDEA that have remained essentially unchanged since the passage of the original EHA in 1974. These include such things as (a) having parents participate as members of the teams making eligibility and placement decisions; (b) evaluating students in all areas of suspected disability; (c) maintaining the confidentiality of assessment results; (d) assessing students' progress toward their IEP goals at least annually, and fully re-evaluating students for eligibility every three years; and (e) including transition plans for students by at least the age of 16.

Evaluation for Special Education

Among the requirements for evaluation in IDEA is the basic concept that evaluations should be multidisciplinary. This is borne out in the requirement for a multidisciplinary team (MDT) to consider evaluation data from multiple perspectives or domains. These domains typically include medical, psychological, educational, and social. The nature of EBD, and particularly the vague definitional components teams must consider, make evaluation for eligibility especially challenging. For example, the major problems of students with EBD are typically thought of as behavioral in nature, so the evaluation of behavior is of obvious importance. Because the definition of EBD stresses adverse effect on educational performance, however, extensive educational evaluation data are also needed.

Behavioral Characteristics

There are a few broad generalizations that can be made regarding the profile of behavioral characteristics students with emotional or behavioral disorders display. One framework for looking at behavioral profiles involves behavioral excesses and behavioral deficits. Students' behavior might be considered deviant when they display too much of certain behaviors (e.g., verbal or physical aggression, disruption), or not enough of certain behaviors (e.g., social interactions). A similar framework focuses on the distinction between externalizing versus internalizing behavior disorders. Externalizing behavior disorders involve acting out behavior, which includes such things as verbal or physical aggression toward others, or property destruction and vandalism. Internalizing behaviors can be thought of as acting inwardly, which is the case with extreme anxiety or withdrawal and social isolation. As with most aspects of EBD, while there are some cases in which the behavioral characteristics of a given child are classic and predictable, it is more often the case that unpredictability is a hallmark, and the constellation of behaviors displayed can cut across many categories. The following sections include a brief overview of the major categories of behavioral characteristics that are associated with EBD.

Attention and Activity Disorders

Children and youth with EBD frequently have problems with attention, and may also have problems with high levels of activity. Those with severe and chronic problems of attention and hyperactivity are typically diagnosed with attention deficit hyperactivity disorder (ADHD); estimates are that 3%–5% of the school-aged population has a formal diagnosis of ADHD (Hallahan, Lloyd, Kauffman, Weiss, & Martinez, 2005). While ADHD and EBD often co-occur, and children and youth with EBD typically display many behavioral characteristics that are consistent with ADHD, there is not a one-to-one correspondence between the two. For example, many students with ADHD, if they are identified as eligible for special education at all, are served under other categories, including learning disabilities (LD) or other health impairment (OHI) (Hallahan, Kauffman, & Pullen, 2009). Nonetheless, many, if not most, students with EBD display attentional deficits and levels of activity that are consistent with the characteristics of ADHD. Classic characteristics include (a) difficulties focusing and sustaining attention, (b) poor impulse control, (c) awkward or inappropriate social skills, and (d) high levels of seemingly random activity (Kauffman & Landrum, 2009).

Conduct Disorder

Conduct disorder (CD) may be the most common marker of EBD as seen in schools. Conduct disorders are not subtle, and typically involve a level of antisocial behavior that impairs a child's functioning at home, in school, and in the community. The typical nature of CD is overt, involving verbal or physical aggression toward others, and such acting out behavior obviously makes youth unpopular with peers and adults, and frequently they are judged as unmanageable by both teachers and parents (Kauffman & Landrum, 2009). A second form of CD involves covert behaviors, such as vandalism or firesetting, which are intentionally concealed from others. While the behavior of some children with EBD can be categorized as primarily overt or primarily covert, research suggests that many children with CD are versatile; they display both covert and overt antisocial behavior (Eddy, Reid, & Curry, 2002; Loeber & Schmaling, 1985). It has also become evident that versatile antisocial behavior is indicative of more serious problems that are less amenable to treatment (Kazdin, 1995; Loeber, Farrington, Stouthamer-Loeber, & Van Kammen, 1998). It is noteworthy that the prevalence of CD has been estimated between 6% and 16% in boys, and between 2% and 9% in girls (Costello et al.,

2005; 2006), while the rates of identification of EBD in schools continues to hover around 1%.

Delinquency

Juvenile delinquency is a legal term that, though loosely defined, refers to youth who are not yet legally adults but who have committed acts for which they could be apprehended by police. Potentially delinquent acts include *status crimes*, which are illegal only when committed by a minor (e.g., truancy, running away, buying alcoholic beverages), and *index crimes*, which are illegal regardless of the age of the person committing the act (e.g., shoplifting, theft, assault). Because the response of law enforcement and the legal system to juveniles who commit delinquent acts is varied, it is difficult to obtain data on the precise nature and extent of juvenile delinquency in the United States. Most children and youth commit at least one delinquent act; the problem usually comes to the attention of law enforcement and other authorities only when repeated acts occur, or when more serious offenses occur. It is typical that the first delinquent acts committed by most children are minor; recidivists then gradually engage in more frequent and more serious delinquent behavior (Farrington, 1995; Tolan, 1987; Tolan & Thomas, 1995). While prevalence estimates are difficult to obtain, it is known that males commit the majority of delinquent acts, especially those that are more serious or involve assault or property damage (Siegel & Welsh, 2005).

Anxiety Disorders

While the majority of students with EBD show evidence of externalizing behavior disorders, such as conduct disorder, internalizing behavior disorders may also co-occur with externalizing behavior problems. Anxiety disorders encompass abnormally high levels of the types of anxiety—stress, tension, fears, and worries—that typically occur at some level in all normally developing children and youth. An anxiety disorder is said to occur when these normal types of anxiety occur at such intensity or frequency to be debilitating and limit a child's participation in the normal activities of home, school, and community. More severe forms of anxiety include excessive fears, phobias, panic attacks, and extreme social withdrawal. It was historically presumed that children with extreme anxiety or withdrawal were in fact at greater risk than children with acting out, or externalizing behavior disorders (Kauffman & Landrum, 2009), but evidence suggests that this is not the case. In fact, anxiety disorders are often transitory and more amenable to treatment than serious conduct disorders (Klein & Last, 1989; Quay & La Greca, 1986). Quay and La Greca (1986) estimated that 5% of the child population may be affected at some time by anxiety, while 2% may be affected by persistent problems with anxiety.

Depression

Depression among children and adolescents was for many years a controversial topic in that many theorists believed that depression was not possible in childhood due to children's relatively undeveloped sense of self. More recently, it has been recognized that childhood depression mirrors that of adult depression in many ways, even though behavioral manifestations differ in age-related ways (Kaslow, Morris, & Rehm, 1998; Kazdin & Marciano, 1998). Childhood depression, then, may be seen as depressed mood and a loss of interest in productive activity, which may be evident in academic problems, as well as a variety of problems that include both externalizing (e.g., aggression) and internalizing (e.g., social withdrawal) behavior. The symptoms of childhood depression are essentially the same as those for depression in adults, including (a) inability to experience pleasure; (b) depressed mood or irritability; (c) change in appetite and weight loss or gain; (d) sleep disturbance; (e) psychomotor agitation or retardation; (f) fatigue or lack of energy; (g) feelings of worthlessness, guilt, or hopelessness; (h) difficulty thinking or concentrating; and (i) thoughts of suicide or death (Kauffman & Landrum, 2009).

As with EBD, a diagnosis of depression only occurs when several of these symptoms are evident over a long period of time, as opposed to a transitory reaction to life events (e.g., death in the family, divorce).

Schizophrenia and Severe Disorders

A brief discussion of schizophrenia is warranted because of its explicit inclusion in the federal definition of emotionally disturbed. Similar to depression, schizophrenia in children mirrors that seen in adults, although diagnosing it is more difficult given that children may have a more difficult time explaining their thoughts and feelings. The disorder involves two or more of the following symptoms: (a) delusions; (b) hallucinations; (c) disorganized, incoherent speech; (d) disorganized or catatonic behavior; and (e) negative symptoms, including a lack of affect, and the inability to think logically or make decisions (Kauffman & Landrum, 2009). While schizophrenia occurs in about 1 in 100 adults, it is rare in children and youth under the age of 18. Though children diagnosed with schizophrenia are often identified by schools as EBD, schizophrenia may also occur along with other disabilities, such as mental retardation.

Assessment

The assessment of emotional and behavioral disorders is challenging for several reasons. As noted earlier, perhaps foremost are decisions about what constitutes normal versus abnormal behavior, and more specifically decisions about when behavior is so different from contextual norms and expectations that it demands attention in the form of services or formal intervention. The underlying concept that must first be addressed when questions about assessment arise concerns the purpose for assessment. Three major purposes of assessment are considered with regard to EBD: screening, determining eligibility, and classification.

Screening

The purpose of screening is to gain a quick and easy assessment of a large number of students to determine at a broad level which students may be at risk for a given disorder. The outcome of screening for EBD is not the determination of who has an emotional or behavioral disorder, but rather a circumscription of the subpopulation of children who may be at greatest risk. Those identified through an initial screen may then be evaluated at a more focused level in greater depth to determine whether in fact a disability warranting intervention is present, or they may simply be provided with some broad intervention or supports that are designed to minimize the chances that they ultimately display seriously disordered behavior.

Eligibility

As discussed previously, evaluation for eligibility is the domain of schools, and the sole purpose of this evaluation is to determine whether a student is eligible to receive special education services due to a disability. In the case of EBD, the determination is made as to whether the student meets the five major definitional criteria for emotional disturbance. Eligibility for services as EBD remains controversial for several reasons. Foremost among these is that it is generally accepted that the true prevalence of EBD is at least three times the number of students currently identified as having EBD by schools. Estimates of the prevalence of conduct disorders, anxiety disorders, ADHD, and schizophrenia, for example, support the notion of significant underidentification of students who probably need services for their emotional or behavioral disorders. Diagnoses by physicians or psychiatrists, however, do not translate directly into eligibility for special education. To reiterate, eligibility for special education is the domain of school-based multidisciplinary teams, and with regard to EBD these teams are guided by the federal definition of emotional disturbance.

Classification

The classification of emotional and behavioral disorders has been of less interest to educators than to psychologists and psychiatrists for at least two reasons. First is the suggestion that the most commonly accepted classification system, the *Diagnostic and Statistical Manual of Mental Disorders* (*DSM-IV*), has less than acceptable reliability and validity with respect to educational purposes (e.g., Hartman et al., 2001), although revisions to the *DSM* and guidelines for using the diagnostic criteria have purportedly improved the reliability of these psychiatric diagnoses (Waldman & Lillenfeld, 1995). A second reason is that psychiatric diagnoses, while they are important for many legal reasons, carry little direct relevance for educators, particularly in terms of planning and implementing instruction or behavioral interventions.

More important to educators is a dimensional classification system, which "indicates how much individuals differ in the degree to which they exhibit a type of behavior" (Kauffman & Landrum, 2009, p. 114). Dimensional classifications rely on statistical procedures to determine the extent to which individual behaviors, usually assessed through the use of behavioral rating scales, cluster together to form dimensions. Two major classifications that typically emerge from dimensional approaches are externalizing problems and internalizing behavior problems. An underlying premise of the dimensional approach is that all individuals exhibit behavior characteristic of each dimension, but they do so to widely varying degrees or intensities. A strength of the dimensional approach is that the categories, or clusters, of behavior have been validated statistically, and we know from a growing body of research that students with EBD typically score higher than students without EBD on problem behavior dimensions (e.g., Lambros, Ward, Bocain, MacMillan, & Gresham, 1998).

Educational Programming

The nature of EBD means that providing appropriate services for students with EBD brings many challenges. Increasing emphasis on inclusion and access to the general curriculum, demands for accountability as schools struggle to meet adequate yearly progress (AYP) mandates, as well as heightened attention to discipline issues as schools struggle to maintain order in schools converge to produce a complex set of challenges. This section includes only brief mention of several key issues that are unique to different points along the grade and life span, including early childhood, elementary school, secondary school, and transition to adulthood.

Early Childhood

It has become well known in special education that the earlier problems are identified, the better the chances of promoting positive outcomes. This typically involves two distinct intervention efforts: preventing problems from occurring or manifesting in the first place; and intervening early, often intensively, at the first signs of trouble. Both efforts, prevention and early intervention, are receiving increasing attention with regard to EBD, and the results of such efforts suggest that there may be tremendous payoff associated with investing resources in prevention and early intervention.

Prevention of EBD, by definition, means that students do not develop or display the behavioral characteristics typical of emotional or behavioral disorders, or at least that they do not do so to a marked degree that is greater than typically developing children. In the terminology of a dimensional classification system, prevention means that while a child might display problem behavior on occasion—as most children do—the frequency or intensity of behavioral problems fall within normal limits (i.e., not in the clinical range). A number of promising approaches to early intervention have emerged (e.g., Walker et al., 1998), and there is tremendous potential for tiered models, such as response-to-intervention (RTI) and positive behavioral interventions and supports (PBIS), to provide even greater emphasis on early intervention. PBIS models, for example, typically include universal preventive interventions for all children (Tier 1), more focused intervention for a smaller subset of children determined to be at greater risk (Tier 2), and focused, individualized intervention for students at highest risk (e.g., Sugai & Horner, 2005).

Elementary

Most students with EBD have shown patterns of consistent behavioral difficulties long before they are formally identified by schools (Kauffman & Landrum, 2009). Unfortunately, this typically means that students' early elementary years have been characterized by behavioral struggles in school. This may be especially problematic in that this is also the critical period for students to acquire basic academic skills. Language and literacy development may be particularly important, as the likelihood of success is quite limited for the student who transitions to middle and then high school with a limited academic foundation, as well as a predisposition to disruptive or otherwise inappropriate behavior. A brief discussion of the recently renewed focus on academic instruction as a first line of defense for EBD is included in a later section. The basic premise underlying this notion is that sound instruction and classroom management at the elementary level are absolutely essential for students with EBD, and perhaps even more so for struggling students who show signs of developing EBD. The structure, routine, and opportunities for success associated with effective instruction may be as important as the academic skill foundation they provide. Thus, the need for evidence-based instructional interventions (e.g., direct instruction, classwide peer-tutoring, self-regulated strategy development) for elementary-aged students with or at risk for EBD would seem paramount.

Secondary

At the secondary level, attention should shift dramatically toward post-school issues, whether that involves preparation for later schooling or training, employment, or the myriad personal and social skills involved in successful independent living. For students with EBD, however, secondary school is further complicated in that the typical problems of adolescence can be dramatically heightened. Risk for substance abuse, early sexual activity, school dropout, and juvenile delinquency is considerably higher for students with EBD (Kauffman & Landrum, 2009). A basic distinction that has presented a persistent challenge to special educators for decades has to do with curriculum. Put simply, the question involves choosing between curriculum focused on the development of vocational skills versus a more strictly academic curriculum generally associated with further post-secondary education. While increased access to the general curriculum at the elementary level presumably prepares students better for an academic curriculum in high school, the more pressing question should be: toward what end? Transition planning, emphasized explicitly since 1990 in IDEA, must involve a careful analysis of students' and families' goals for later life, with specific services targeted at movement toward those goals. It is worth noting that individualization should remain the hallmark of transition planning; a vocational curriculum may be just as inappropriate for the college-bound student as a strictly academic curriculum is for a student who plans to enter the work force upon leaving high school.

Transition to Adulthood

Like secondary programming, the transition to adulthood has proven problematic for nearly all students with disabilities, and students with EBD are no different. While it might be argued that many of the characteristics of milder disabilities show up in school-contexts only, it has become increasingly clear that many students with EBD will need lifelong supports and access to services (e.g., Wolf, Braukman, & Ramp, 1987). The link to adult service providers in the areas of mental health services, social services, and employment services are presumably made during the transition planning process, and indeed services in many cases begin before students leave school. As is noted in the following section, it remains to be seen whether an increased emphasis on such things as wrap-around services (e.g., Eber, Nelson, & Miles, 1997) and systems of care (Clark & Foster-Johnson, 1996), especially prominent in the 1990s, result in improved transitions to adulthood for children and youth with EBD.

Trends and Issues

There are a number of issues regarding the identification and treatment of EBD facing the field of emotional and behavioral disorders in the early part of the 21st century, but it is perhaps ironic that many of these issues are not new (see Kauffman & Landrum, 2006). Seven issues are considered briefly, many of which have been discussed for a century or more.

Early Identification and Prevention

As discussed previously, it is accepted that earlier identification of problems leads to greater odds of successful intervention efforts. Early identification refers to both identifying problems when children are young, as well as identifying early signs of problem behavior, regardless of a person's age, and there is good evidence that early signs of potential behavioral disorders can be reliably detected (e.g., Dunlap et al., 2006; Feil et al., 2005). Unfortunately, the trend in the United States has been (a) a reluctance to screen for early sign of problems in very young children, and (b) a tendency to accept minor misbehavior, even as it escalates, until the problem becomes severe and often unmanageable. A number of reasons for this failure have been offered (see Kauffman, 1999), but among the more obvious may be the negative attitudes that prevail with regard to special education, which makes identification something to avoid. This argument is supported, unfortunately, by data that suggest that children identified with EBD tend not to be declassified; they may remain in special education throughout their school careers. In fact evidence suggests that students identified as EBD have shown signs of trouble for years (e.g., Duncan, Forness, & Hartsough, 1995) such that those finally identified as eligible for services have significantly well-entrenched problems, and may indeed require lifelong support of one type or another, even after they leave school (see Wolf et al., 1987). And while emerging evidence suggests that early identification and prevention efforts can work (Walker et al., 1998), it remains to be seen whether educators and policymakers will embrace these priorities.

Comprehensive, Community-based Services

Students with EBD have historically been educated in more restrictive settings than their peers with other disabilities, and this includes out-of-community placements for a disproportionate number of students (Landrum, Katsiyannis, & Archwamety, 2004). Partly in response to this, a trend that gained considerable traction in the 1990s was a heightened focus on comprehensive, or "wrap-around" services designed to keep students with EBD in their home communities. One concept underlying this movement was that children and youth with EBD and their families had complex needs that cut across service agencies (e.g., schools, social services, mental health agencies, the juvenile justice system), and the coordination among these agencies was historically minimal. The notion that coordinating services within local communities could keep children and youth in their home communities and their neighborhood schools, which would lead to improved outcomes, gained wide acceptance but a major shift in policy, funding, and systematic evaluation of such efforts has yet to be seen. For students with EBD in particular, the consequences of failed efforts at deinstitutionalization may be especially dire, as incarceration or homelessness appear to be "default placements for people with serious mental illness, at least for older adolescents and adults" (Kauffman & Landrum, 2009, p. 50).

Focus on Academic Skills

A common misperception with regard to students with EBD has been that teachers must first gain control of students' behavior before instruction can occur. In fact, we know that effective instruction provides the foundation for both academic instruction and effective behavior management (e.g., Kauffman & Hallahan, 2005; Lane, 2004). There at least two critical elements of effective instruction relative to students with EBD. First, effective academic instruction provides the structure, routine, and success that are known that are known to reduce the occurrence of behavior problems, as well as build the foundation for later academic success (Witt, VanDerHeyden, & Gilbertson, 2004). Moreover, evidence continues to accrue that sound instructional procedures associated with successful academic learning can be applied to behavior problems as well. That is, positive, prosocial behavior can be taught successfully using the same instructional procedures shown to be successful with academic content (Colvin, Sugai, & Patching, 1993; Gunter, Denny, Jack, Shores, & Nelson, 1993).

Functional Behavioral Assessment

Functional behavioral assessment (FBA) is a systematic way to determine the function a behavior serves. Through systematic observation of behavior, including analysis of the conditions that set the stage for the behavior to occur, as well as specific antecedents and consequences, professionals can form hypothesis about what is maintaining behavior. Interventions are then devised to alter setting events, antecedents, and consequences. An additional premise is that replacement behaviors—positive behaviors that serve the same function that negative behaviors had been serving—can be taught. The technology for functional behavioral assessment has been around since at least the early 1980s (e.g., Iwata, Dorsey, Slifer, Bauman, & Richman, 1982), but FBAs received dramatically more attention, and became the source of some controversy, when the requirement for schools to conduct FBAs and develop positive behavior intervention plans for students with disabilities who display problem behavior was included in IDEA amendments of 1997. While the promotion of functional analysis of behavior was generally welcomed, some wondered whether the professional capacity in schools was adequate to meet this newly mandated demand on a widespread basis, especially given that FBAs can be complex and time-consuming (Fox & Gable, 2004; Sasso, Conroy, Stichter, & Fox, 2001).

Continuum of Alternative Placements

The inclusion of students with disabilities in general education classrooms is perhaps the single most controversial issue in special education (e.g., Crockett & Kauffman, 1999; Kavale & Forness, 2000), and the problem may be particularly thorny for students with EBD, who are typically educated in more restrictive settings than their peers with other disabilities. It has been argued that in the extreme, full inclusion of all students with disabilities in fact violates one of the fundament tenets of IDEA, namely a continuum of alternative placements (CAP). According to CAP, a full range of placement options is available, including such options as full-time in the general education classroom, part-time resource help, self-contained classes in students' home schools, and residential placements (see Hallahan et al., 2009). Placement decisions are based on individual student needs once IEP goals and the special education services needed to reach them are determined. As Kauffman and others have argued, full inclusion in the general education classroom as a default placement option for all students with disabilities may in fact be illegal under IDEA (Kauffman, 1995; Kauffman & Hallahan, 2005). At minimum, it would seem that placement of all students with disabilities in the general education classroom is no more logical or proper than assigning all students with disabilities in any given placement (e.g., in separate, self-contained classrooms).

Transition

Transition to post-school environments and later life adjustment was formally highlighted as a critical area of need for students with disabilities in 1990, when the reauthorization of IDEA included specific requirement that transition plans be included in IEPs for all students of at least 16 years of age. For students with EBD, transition may be especially challenging given their historically poor outcomes in terms of employment and successful later life adjustment. In terms of programming, the dilemma is not new, and involves a basic decision to place students in a curriculum with an academic focus, with participation in primarily general education academic classes, or in a vocationally oriented curriculum, with a goal of keeping students in school longer and improving the odds of successful post-school employment.

Multicultural Special Education

The increasing diversity of the U.S. population has lead to concerns about how students of different cultural or ethnic groups are identified and served in special education. The implications of cultural difference are great with regard to EBD, as educators must be sensitive to varying cultural norms in terms of behavioral expectations, approaches to behavior change, and communication with families regarding students' strengths, needs, and school and later life goals. Sensitivity to cultural difference must be balanced, however, with recognition that not all members of a particular cultural group share identical sets of values, and indeed many subcultures exist within cultures. Moreover, there are certain basic principles of behavior and behavior change that are common to all cultures (Kauffman, Conroy, Gardner, & Oswald, 2008). Despite common ground on many fundamental areas (e.g., that EBD is difficult to define, regardless of cultural context), significant disagreement exists still on whether and how students of different racial or ethnic groups may be over- or under-represented in special education programs for students with EBD (Harry, Hart, Klingner, & Cramer, 2009; Kauffman, Simpson, & Mock, 2009). At least two basic arguments seem supported by data at present. First, there is discrepancy across racial/ethnic groups in rates of identification for EBD. For example, African American students may be identified as having EBD at a rate of 1.5 times that of Caucasian students, while Asian and Hispanic students maybe identified at a rate that is half or less that of Caucasian students (National Research Council, 2002). Second, despite these apparent variations, there appears to be dramatic underidentification of all students for services as EBD. As noted earlier, schools have historically served around 1% of the school-aged population under the category of EBD, while credible estimates of the need for services for emotional or behavioral problems are as high as 6%–10%. Thus, while the problem of disproportionality is not fully understood, it can be argued that there is in fact a need for more identification across all demographics.

References

Achenbach, T. M., & Edelbrock, C. S. (1981). Behavior problems and competencies reported by parents of normal and disturbed children aged four through sixteen. *Monographs of the Society for Research in Child Development, 46*(1, Serial No. 188).

Asarnow, J. R., & Asarnow, R. F. (2003). Childhood-onset schizophrenia. In E. J. Mash & R. A. Barkley (Eds.), *Child psychopathology* (2nd ed., pp. 455–485). New York: Guilford.

Baumrind, D. (1995). *Child maltreatment and optimal caregiving in social contexts.* New York: Garland.

Baumrind, D. (1996). The discipline controversy revisited. *Journal of Applied Family and Child Studies, 45,* 405–414.

Bell, R. Q. (1968). A reinterpretation of the direction of effects in studies of socialization. *Psychological Review, 75,* 81–95.

Bell, R. Q., & Harper, L. V. (1977). *Child effects on adults.* Hillsdale, NJ: Erlbaum.

Bower, E. M. (1960). *Early identification of emotionally handicapped children in school.* Springfield, IL: Thomas.

Bower, E. M. (1981). *Early identification of emotionally handicapped children in school* (3rd ed.). Springfield, IL: Thomas.

Clark, H. B., & Foster-Johnson, L. (1996). Serving youth in transition into adulthood. In B. A. Stroul (Ed.), *Children's mental health: Creating systems of care in a changing society* (pp. 533–551). New York: Brookes.

Colvin, G., Sugai, G., & Patching, B. (1993). Precorrection: An instructional approach for managing predictable problem behaviors. *Intervention in School and Clinic, 28,* 143–150.

Costello, E. J., Egger, H., & Angold, A. (2005). 1-year research update review: The epidemiology of child and adolescent psychiatric disorders: I. Methods and public health burden. *Journal of the American Academy of Child and Adolescent Psychiatry, 44,* 972–986.

Costello, E. J., Foley, D., & Angold, A. (2006). 10-year research update review: The epidemiology of child and adolescent psychiatric disorders: II. Developmental epidemiology. *Journal of the American Academy of Child and Adolescent Psychiatry, 45,* 8–25.

Crockett, J. B., & Kauffman, J. M. (1999). *The least restrictive environment: Its origins and interpretations in special education.* Mahwah, NJ: Erlbaum.

Dadds, M. R. (2002). Learning and intimacy in the families of anxious children. In R. J. McMahon & R. D. Peters (Eds.), *The effects of parental dysfunction on children* (pp. 87–104). New York: Kluwer.

Duncan, B. B., Forness, S. R., & Hartsough, C. (1995). Students identified as seriously emotionally disturbed in day treatment: Cognitive, psychiatric, and special education characteristics. *Behavioral Disorders, 20,* 238–252.

Dunlap, G., Strain, P. S., Fox, L., Carta, J. J., Conroy, M., Smith, B. J., et al. (2006). Prevention and intervention with young children's challenging behavior: Perspectives regarding current knowledge. *Behavioral Disorders, 32,* 29–45.

Eber, L., Nelson, C. M., & Miles, P. (1997). School-based wraparound for students with emotional and behavioral challenges. *Exceptional Children, 63,* 539–555.

Eddy, J. M., Reid, J. B., & Curry, V. (2002). The etiology of youth antisocial behavior, delinquency, and violence and a public health approach to prevention. In M. R. Shinn, H. M. Walker, & G. Stoner (Eds.), *Interventions for academic and behavior problems II: Preventive and remedial approaches* (pp. 27–52). Bethesda, MD: National Association of School Psychologists.

Farrington, D. P. (1995). The development of offending and antisocial behaviour from childhood: Key findings from the Cambridge Study in Delinquent Development. *Journal of Child Psychology and Psychiatry, 36,* 929–964.

Feil, E. G., Small, J. W., Forness, S. R., Serna, L. A., Kaiser, A. P., Hancock, T. B., et al. (2005). Using different measures, informants, and clinical cut-off points to estimate prevalence of emotional or behavioral disorders in preschoolers: Effects on age, gender, and ethnicity. *Behavioral Disorders, 30,* 375–391.

Forness, S. R., & Knitzer, J. (1992). A new proposed definition and terminology to replace "serious emotional disturbance" in Individuals with Disabilities Education Act. *School Psychology Review*, *21*, 12–20.

Fox, J., & Gable, R. A. (2004). Functional behavioral assessment. In R. B. Rutherford, M. M. Quinn, & S. R. Mathur (Eds.), *Handbook of research in emotional and behavioral disorders* (pp. 143–162). New York: Guilford.

Gunter, P. L., Denny, R. K., Jack, S. L., Shores, R. E., & Nelson, C. M. (1993). Aversive stimuli in academic interactions between students with emotional disturbance and their teachers. *Behavioral Disorders*, *18*, 265–274.

Hallahan, D. P., Kauffman, J. M., & Pullen, P. C. (2009). *Exceptional learners: Introduction to special education* (11th ed.). Boston: Allyn & Bacon.

Hallahan, D. P., Lloyd, J. W., Kauffman, J. M., Weiss, M., & Martinez, E. (2005). *Introduction to learning disabilities* (3rd ed.). Boston: Allyn & Bacon.

Harry, B., Hart, J. E., Klingner, J., & Cramer, E. (2009). Response to Kauffman, Mock, & Simpson, (2007): Problems related to underservice of students with emotional or behavioral disorders. *Behavioral Disorders*, *34*, 164–171.

Harry, B., & Klingner, J. (2006). *Why are so many minority students in special education? Understanding race & disability in schools.* New York: Teachers College Press.

Hartman, C., Hox, J., Mellenbergh, G. J., Boyle, M. H., Offord, D. R., Racine, Y., et al. (2001). DSM-IV internal construct validity: When a taxonomy meets data. *Journal of Child Psychology & Psychiatry & Allied Disciplines*, *42*, 817–836.

Huesmann, L. R., Moise, J. F., & Podolski, C. (1997). The effects of media violence on the development of antisocial behavior. In D. M. Stoff, J. Breiling, & J. D. Maser (Eds.), *Handbook of antisocial behavior* (pp. 181–193). New York: Wiley.

Huesmann, L. R., Moise-Titus, J. F., Podolski, C., & Eron, L. (2003). Longitudinal relations between children's exposure to TV violence and their aggressive and violent behavior in young adulthood: 1977–1992. *Developmental Psychology*, *39*, 201–221.

Iwata, B. A., Dorsey, M., Slifer, K., Bauman, K., & Richman, G. (1982). Toward a functional analysis of self-injury. *Analysis and Intervention in Developmental Disabilities*, *2*, 3–20.

Johnson, J. G., Cohen, P., Kasen, S., & Brook, J. S. (2007). Extensive television viewing and the development of attention and learning difficulties during adolescence. *Archives of Pediatrics and Adolescent Medicine*, *161*, 480–486.

Kaslow, N. J., Morris, M. K., & Rehm, L. P. (1998). Childhood depression. In R. J. Morris & T. R. Kratochwill (Eds.), *The practice of child therapy* (3rd ed., pp. 48–90). Boston: Allyn & Bacon.

Kauffman, J. M. (1995). Why we must celebrate a diversity of restrictive environments. *Learning Disabilities Research and Practice*, *10*, 225–232.

Kauffman, J. M. (1999). How we prevent the prevention of emotional and behavioral disorders. *Exceptional Children*, *65*, 448–468.

Kauffman, J. M., Conroy, M., Gardner, R., & Oswald, D. (2008). Cultural sensitivity in the application of behavior principles to education. *Education and Treatment of Children*, *31*, 239–262.

Kauffman, J. M., & Hallahan, D. P. (2005). *Special education: What special is and why we need it.* Boston: Allyn & Bacon.

Kauffman, J. M., & Landrum, T. J. (2006). *Children and youth with emotional and behavioral disorders: A history of their education.* Austin, TX: Pro-Ed.

Kauffman, J. M., & Landrum, T. J. (2009). *Characteristics of emotional and behavioral disorders of children and youth* (9th ed.). Upper Saddle River, NJ: Merrill.

Kauffman, J. M., Simpson, R. L., & Mock, D. R. (2009). Problems related to underservice: A rejoinder. *Behavioral Disorders*, *34*, 172–180.

Kavale, K. A., & Forness, S. R. (2000). History, rhetoric, and reality: An analysis of the inclusion debate. *Remedial and Special Education*, *21*, 279–296.

Kazdin, A. E. (1995). *Conduct disorders in childhood and adolescence* (2nd ed.). Thousand Oaks, CA: Sage.

Kazdin, A. E., & Marciano, P. L. (1998). Childhood and adolescent depression. In E. J. Mash & R. A. Barkley (Eds.), *Treatment of childhood disorders* (2nd ed., pp. 211–248). New York: Guilford.

Keogh, B. K. (2003). *Temperament in the classroom: Understanding individual differences.* Baltimore: Brookes.

Klein, R. G., & Last, C. G. (1989). *Anxiety disorders in children.* Newbury Park, CA: Sage.

Lambros, K. M., Ward, S. L., Bocian, K. M., MacMillan, D. L., & Gresham, F. M. (1998). Behavioral profiles of children at-risk for emotional and behavioral disorders: Implications for assessment and classification. *Focus on Exceptional Children, 30*(5), 1–16.

Landrum, T. J., Katsiyannis, A., & Archwamety, T. (2004). An analysis of placement and exit patterns of students with emotional or behavioral disorders. *Behavioral Disorders*, *29*, 140–153.

Lane, K. L. (2004). Academic instruction and tutoring interventions for students with emotional and behavioral disorders: 1990 to the present. In R. B. Rutherford, M. M. Quinn, & S. R. Mathur (Eds.), *Handbook of research in emotional and behavioral disorders* (pp. 462–486). New York: Guilford.

Loeber, R., Farrington, D. P., Stouthamer-Loeber, M., & Van Kammen, W. B. (1998). *Antisocial behavior and mental health problems: Explanatory factors in childhood and adolescence.* Mahwah, NJ: Erlbaum.

Loeber, R., & Schmaling, K. B. (1985). Empirical evidence for overt and covert patterns of antisocial conduct problems: A meta-analysis. *Journal of Abnormal Child Psychology*, *13*, 337–352.

McGuffin, P., & Thapar, A. (1997). Genetic basis for bad behavior in adolescents. *Lancet*, *350*, 411–412.

McLoughlin, J. A., & Nall, M. (1988). Teacher opinion of the role of food allergy on school behavior and achievement. *Annals of Allergy*, *61*(2), 89–91.

McLoughlin, J. A., & Nall, M. (1994). Allergies and learning/behavioral disorders. *Intervention in School and Clinic, 29*, 198–207.

National Research Council. (2002). *Minority students in special and gifted education* (M. S. Donovan & C. T. Cross, Eds.), Committee on Minority Representation in Special Education. Washington, DC: National Academy Press, Division of Behavioral and Social Sciences Education.

Nicol, S. E., & Erlenmeyer-Kimling, L. (1986). Genetic factors and psychopathology: Implications for prevention. In B. A. Edelstein & L. Michelson (Eds.), *Handbook of prevention* (pp. 21–41). New York: Plenum.

O'Leary, K. D. (1995). Parental discipline mistakes. *Current Directions in Psychological Science*, *4*, 11–13.

Pescara-Kovach, L. A., & Alexander, K. (1994). The link between food ingested and problem behavior: Fact or fallacy? *Behavioral Disorders*, *19*, 142–148.

Pinker, S. (2002). *The blank slate: The modern denial of human nature.* New York: Viking.

Plomin, R. (1995). Genetics and children's experiences in the family. *Journal of Child Psychology and Psychiatry, 36*, 33–68.

Quay, H. C., & La Greca, A. M. (1986). Disorders of anxiety, withdrawal, and dysphoria. In H. C. Quay & J. S. Werry (Eds.), *Psychopathological disorders of childhood* (3rd ed., pp. 73–110). New York: Wiley.

Reid, J. B., & Eddy, J. M. (1997). The prevention of antisocial behavior: Some considerations in the search for effective interventions. In D. M. Stoff, J. Breiling, & J. D. Maser (Eds.), *Handbook of antisocial behavior* (pp. 343–356). New York: Wiley.

Roberts, R. E., Roberts, C. R., & Xing, Y. (2006). Prevalence of youth-reported DSM-IV psychiatric disorders among African, European, and Mexican American adolescents. *Journal of the Academy of Child and Adolescent Psychiatry*, *45*, 1329–1337.

Sampson, H. A., (2004). Update on food allergy. *Journal of Allergy and Clinical Immunology*, *113*(5), 805–819.

Sasso, G. M., Conroy, M. A., Stichter, J. P., & Fox, J. J. (2001). Slowing down the bandwagon: The misapplication of functional assessment for students with emotional and behavioral disorders. *Behavioral Disorders, 26*, 282–296.

Siegel, L., & Welsh, B. (2005). *Juvenile delinquency: The core* (2nd ed.). Belmont, CA: Thomson Wadsworth.

Stichter, J. P., Conroy, M. A., & Kauffman, J. M. (2008). *An introduction to students with high-incidence disabilities.* Upper Saddle River, NJ: Merrill/Prentice Hall.

Sugai, G., & Horner, R. H. (2005). School-wide positive behavior supports: Achieving and sustaining effective learning environments for all students. In W. H. Heward (Ed.), *Focus on behavior analysis in education: Achievements, challenges, and opportunities* (pp. 90–102). Upper Saddle River, NJ: Pearson Prentice-Hall.

Tanner, E. M., & Finn-Stevenson, M. (2002). Nutrition and brain development: Social policy implications. *American Journal of Orthopsychiatry, 72*, 182–193.

Thomas, A., Chess, S., & Birch, H. G. (1968). *Temperament and behavior disorders in children.* New York: New York University Press.

Tolan, P. (1987). Implications of age of onset for delinquency risk. *Journal of Abnormal Child Psychology, 15*, 47–65.

Tolan, P. H., & Thomas, P. (1995). The implications of age of onset for delinquency risk. II: Longitudinal data. *Journal of Abnormal Child Psychology, 23*, 157–181.

Waldman, I. D., & Lillenfeld, S. O. (1995). Diagnosis and classification. In M. Hersen & R. T. Ammerman (Eds.), *Advanced abnormal child psychology*, (pp. 21–36). Hillsdale, NJ: Erlbaum.

Walker, H. M., Kavanaugh, K., Stiller, B., Golly, A., Severson, H., & Feil, E. G. (1998). First Step to Success: An early intervention approach for preventing antisocial behavior. *Journal of Emotional and Behavioral Disorders, 6*, 66–80.

Witt, J. C., VanDerHeyden, A. M., & Gilbertson, D. (2004). Instruction and classroom management: Prevention and intervention research. In R. B. Rutherford, M. M. Quinn, & S. R. Mathur (Eds.), *Handbook of research in emotional and behavioral disorders* (pp. 426–445). New York: Guilford.

Wolf, M. M., Braukman, C. J., & Ramp, K. A. (1987). Serious delinquent behavior as part of a significantly handicapping condition: Cures and supportive environments. *Journal of Applied Behavior Analysis, 20*, 347–359.

Wolraich, M. L., Wilson, D. B., & White, J. W. (1995). The effect of sugar on behavior or cognition in children. *Journal of the American Medical Association, 274*, 1617–1621.

Zimmerman, F. J., & Chistakis, D. A. (2005). Children's television viewing and cognitive outcomes. *Archives of Pediatrics and Adolescent Medicine, 159*, 619–625.

18
Communication Disorders

Filip T. Loncke
University of Virginia

Communication is usually defined as the exchange of information between two agents. Most models of human communication imply an expressive and a receptive side of the process. Exchange of communication implies a capacity to encode (on the expressive side) and to decode (on the receptive side). This basic model is often represented in some variant of Figure 18.1.

Communicators need to master a shared code. In most cases, communicators are at the same time expressive and receptive agents. Not only does one have to decode the messages that the partner sends, each sender also tends to monitor (and decode) their own message. This simple model will help in describing and understanding human communication disorders and their implications for development and, subsequently, for special education. The model is an abstraction and does not take into account the multiple environmental factors that can influence the communication. For example, communication is heavily influenced by cultural expectations and customs, determining in real situations when, with whom, and how individuals will communicate.

The term *communication disorders* is used for a variety of conditions including limitations with speech articulation, language, voice, fluency, and hearing. The establishment of successful communication is dependent on a combination of contextual and individual factors. Communication disorders can therefore result both from environmental causes or from individual causes.

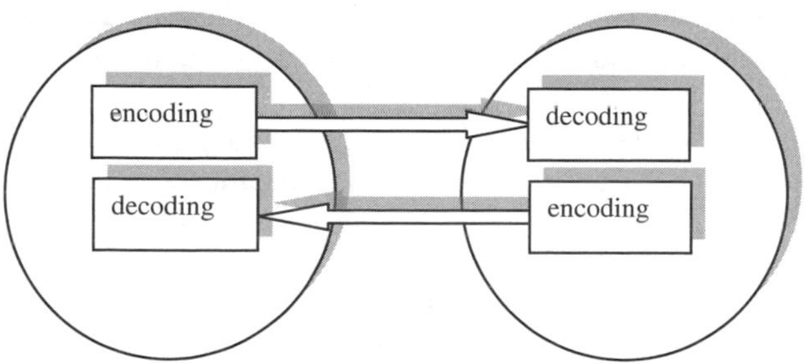

Figure 18.1 Communication between two people.

The *contextual* factors relate to the essence of communication: the transmission of information from one person to another. This is essentially a social event: it is by definition highly influenced by the individual characteristics of the communication partners as well as by cultural and social patterns. The contextual factors include the expectations from the environment and communication partners, the style of interacting, and the frequency and quality of language and communication a person is exposed to. Educational intervention is, by definition, contextual intervention.

Communication Disorders as Individual Disorders

The *individual* factors include the mastery of the code for information transmission. This is about the personal skills of the person to construct and send (on the expressive side), and to receive and interpret a message (on the receptive side). One needs to master multiple codes: the linguistic codes (words and how they are combined; manual signs for sign language users), non-linguistic codes (facial expressions, body postures, eye gaze, hand gestures, pointing), and pragmatic codes (how do I convince, order, beg, tell, threaten, impress, brag, show off, or apologize?).

Individual Communication Model

From an individual's perspective, communication comes down to the ability (a) to formulate messages that will be decodable by potential partners, (b) to detect, decode and interpret messages sent by communication partners, and (c) to appropriately act on it.

Several models have been proposed to help us understand how this works. Models help us to locate where in a system the communication disorders originate and how they affect one or more connected domains. This is helpful for *diagnosing* the disorder and determining its impact. It is also important for determining *intervention* as it defines the areas where one intends to change processes, and what the anticipated or hoped for effects will be.

The existing models take an information-processing and/or ecological perspective. The information processing models are especially useful to analyze the processes involved in speech and language production. This is where the encoding by the sender takes place and where the encoded message is converted into executable behavior. Executable behavior includes speech, manual signing, or any (nonverbal) behaviors that have communicative value.

It is useful to make a distinction between linguistic and non-linguistic communication. Dysfunctional communication can be the result of disorders in either of these, but it very often presents itself as a combination. *Linguistic communication* entails the use of language: words, spoken or written text, and in some cases manual sign language. *Non-linguistic communication* (often termed *non-verbal communication*) is communication through means that are not part of the linguistic system itself: eye contact, gestures, body orientation and positions, vocalizations, facial expressions, and any behavior that carries some meaning in a given situation.

Non-linguistic and linguistic communication are often produced and interpreted as part of one single communicative behavior. For example, pointing to an object can go together with the words "give me." In development, non-linguistic behavior precedes linguistic behavior during the *pre-linguistic stage*. During the pre-linguistic stage, children develop toward communicative symbol use when they discover the relation between their behavior and its effects on other people's behavior. A smile can become a request for attention, and a cry can become an expression of hunger. Through their reactions, parents and other caregivers reinforce and shape the child's responses toward behaviors that have a conventional meaning within the circle of people that have direct interaction with the child.

Throughout pre-linguistic development, children acquire the symbolic function. They have internalized a mental representation of an event, a situation, an object, or a person. For example, besides the appearance of meaningful gestures, children start to have dreams and show deferred imitation.

Children's pre-linguistic behaviors are important indicators and can signal risks for later linguistic development. One of the most widespread used instruments to measure prelinguistic and early linguistic communication, the MacArthur-Bates Communicative Development Inventories (Fenson et al., 2006) typically includes "pretend" actions such as feeding with a bottle, and imitating adult actions such as "typing" on a computer.

The use of gestures during the transition period from one-word sentences to multi-word sentences (typically around the age of 18 months) appears to be an indicator whether a late talker may nevertheless have an intact potential for language acquisition (Thal & Bates, 1988).

Non-linguistic behavior continues to play an important role throughout life span as communicators combine non-verbal behavior with verbal behavior to express meaning and intentions. In present-day theoretical accounts, speech and gesture are considered to be two parallel expressive channels that are rooted in a single internal message planning entity (McNeill & Duncan, 2010). Effective communication depends on the ability to produce and interpret these parallel channels. Individuals with significant difficulties in interpreting non-linguistic cues often experience problems of socialization, sometimes together with underdeveloped pragmatic skills. The non-verbal parallel channel is important for the pragmatic aspect of communication, i.e., which effect the communicator seeks to have on the listener. Individuals may be selectively impaired in the non-verbal aspects of communication, a condition that is often associated with Asperger syndrome (Adams, 2006).

In spontaneous speech, a typical speaker easily produces more than 200 words a minute. This means that 2 to 3 words can be spoken each second. This indicates an amazing ability to retrieve words from an internal lexicon. In an adult speaker, the internal lexicon can contain ten thousands of words. According to some estimates, the vocabulary of a middle aged person with a college education may approximate 100,000 words. Children in kindergarten may already have 14,000 words. Psycholinguistic models attempt to identify the paradigms that make it possible to store and quickly retrieve words to make conversation possible.

Language is more than just storing and retrieving words. Language users string words together in sequences that are syntactically acceptable. Also, the words are morphologically manipulated: suffixes or affixes are added, and words are combined to form compounds words. Once the words are retrieved, the word order is determined, and the morphological decisions are made, the speaker has to turn it into a phonetic plan. The phonetic plan is a schema of the sound sequences that correspond to the sequence of words. The phonetic plan then feeds into an articulation plan, which is the neuro-muscular translation of the phonetic plan, i.e., what speech gestures (the movement patterns that typically correspond to a syllable) do I need to produce to get this series of words pronounced?

Levelt (1993, p. 9) has proposed a "blueprint for the speaker" that represents the major areas of speech-language production and speech-language perception, as shown in Figure 18.2.

This model has inspired major psycholinguistic research, including the areas where language disorders can occur. It represents the *microgenesis of speech*: the way language is created "on the spot" in daily communication. Normal speakers are able to generate a stream of words, organized in meaningful and rule-governed structures, apply morphological principles, all superseded by intonation patterns. Levelt's blueprint shows how the speaker goes "from intention to articulation," from an idea to speech sound—all in a matter of milliseconds.

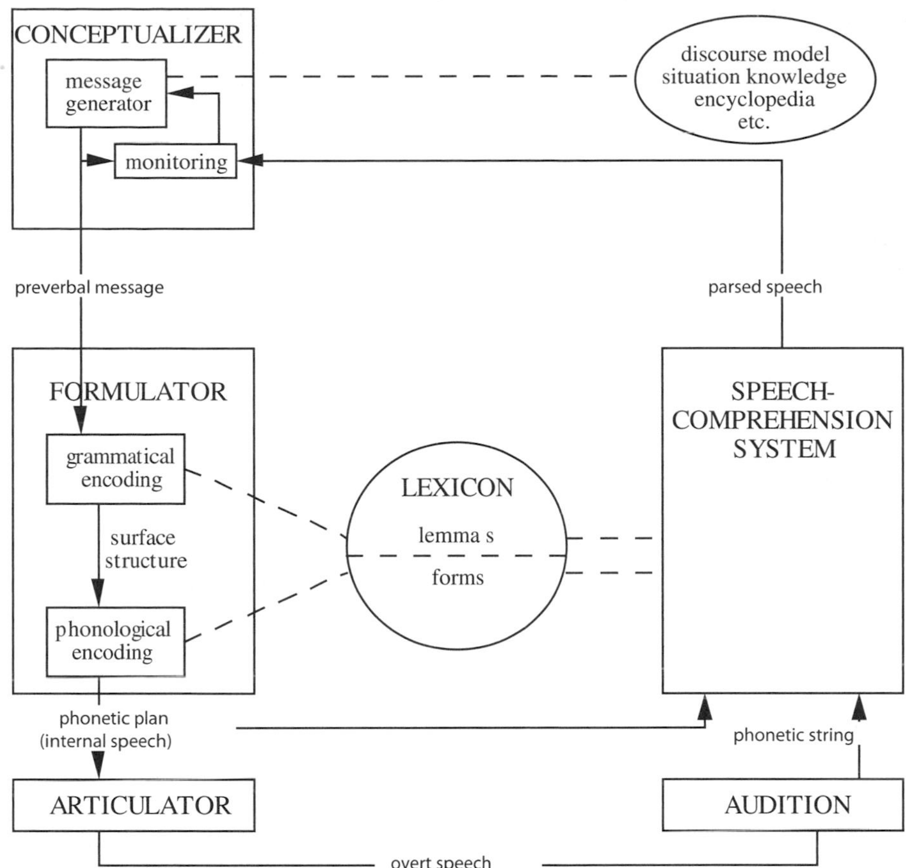

Figure 18.2 Blueprint for the speaker. Source: Levelt, W. J. M. (1993). *Speaking: From intention to articulation* (1st MIT paperback ed.). Cambridge, MA: MIT Press.

The model also shows that the speech process is linked to the listening process. Every speaker is also his or her own listener, thus executing a monitoring process while the process unfolds. Listening and understanding is the decoding process of speech. It involves a reverse operation of speaking, with the use of roughly similar type of processing modules: through the use of phonological, morphological, syntactic, and lexical decoding, the listener attempts to reach to the original intended meaning by the speaker.

Finally, the model can be used to evaluate how the communicator *acts on* received messages. Listeners typically process incoming information in a more or less reversed way as speakers, starting with the *phonological decoding*, the auditory process that permits recognition of spoken sound segments. Phonological processing is essentially an act of categorization. The listener decides which of the phonemes of the language are perceived. The listener must recognize words, phonemes that are produced at a speed of hundreds of words (and many more phonemes) every minute. On top of this rapidly phonological recognition decision process, the listener needs to deal with all the variations in speakers. All speakers produce sounds in their unique personal ways. Although most listeners appear to have developed the amazing skill of fast phoneme recognition, some listeners struggle when they are presented with fast speech or speech that has been partially masked by noise. Some authors have suggested that these cases of severe and persistent problems should be diagnosed as *Central Auditory Processing Disorder* (CAPD, or APD for Auditory Processing Disorder). The term and the diagnosis are somewhat controversial as it implies that an underlying neuro-perceptual problem is present (Bamiou, 2009).

A model such as Levelt's (1993) helps us to understand possible language and speech problems.

Vocabulary size. How many words does a person know? How fast should the vocabulary grow during the period of language acquisition? The majority of language users have vocabularies that reach into the thousands of words (Aitchison, 2003). Children with communication disorders often have a limited vocabulary. A distinction needs to be made between active and passive vocabulary. Words are stored in an internal mental lexicon. Lexical growth in typically developing children is an amazing phenomenon. Normal children supposedly employ *fast mapping* strategies, ways to identify, store, understand the meaning, and develop the ability to use them actively after minimal exposure. Young children might be good at this skill thanks to a categorical- taxonomic perceptual inclination, i.e., they tend to organize information into whole-object similar categories (Mayor & Plunkett, 2010). Children with language impairment may be lacking some of the ability to "capture" new words: Alt and Plante (2006) found that children with specific language impairment (SLI) performed more poorly in mapping tasks, again suggesting a weakness in underlying generalization strategies.

Vocabulary access. However, vocabulary size is not the only problem. For speech production and speech reception, language users need to gain rapid access to the internal lexicon. As speech and language use is a fast, "on-line" process, speakers and listeners need to be able to access the words in their internal lexicon "on the go." Speakers need to find the appropriate words (lexicon search) and internally "line them up" in the right order to be spoken in a fluent sequence. Accessing a word in the mental lexicon consists of two steps (Butterworth, 1982): the lemma-level and the lexeme level. At the *lemma level* is the identification of the meaning of a specific word together with the syntactic characteristics. At the *lexeme level*, the user identifies the phonological structure of the word. Evidence for the existence of these two different levels comes from speech errors and from the tip of the tongue phenomenon. Thus, speaking words entails the quick activation of the syntactic and semantic structure, followed by identification of the phonology that goes with the word. The phonology will be the guide for the actual articulation of the word. Quick vocabulary access is not only required for speech production, it is equally essential for listening. Listeners need to be able to rapidly make *lexical decisions*: recognizing the words and mapping them to meaning that they have stored in their internal lexicon.

In general, compared to adult language users, young children need more time (measured in milliseconds) to access words in their lexicon (Berko Gleason, & Bernstein Rattner, 1998). Adult users have developed multiple access routes to the words they need: phonological (knowing how the word sounds like), syntactic (knowing that a specific type of word is needed within the structure, e.g., a noun, a verb, or more specifically: a location noun, or a transitive verb) and certainly semantic (knowing which words 'make sense' in a specific textual environment). Young children, despite having smaller lexicons, need more time to internally "look up" the words. This is even more the case for children with language impairment (Seiger-Gardner & Schwartz, 2008). At present, it is not clear whether children with language impairment differ in lexical decision tasks from typically developing children (Mainela-Arnold, Evans, & Coady, 2008).

Syntax problems. Speakers work from a syntactic plan. This is an internalized scheme that represents the relation between the different agents in a proposition. In English, the syntax is largely reflected in the order in which the words are organized. There is some debate whether in the early stages of language acquisition children start off with internalized syntactic templates that dictate word order, or whether the syntax emerges from other structures. Increasingly there is agreement that children develop syntax out of semantic-cognitive structures. For example, initially there is not so much a noun-verb structure but rather a, functionally based, agent-action structure.

Morphological disorders. Once the syntactic plan is formed and the lexical elements (the words) are selected, the speaker will need to mark the words to make sure they provide accurate linguistic information. Morphological markers include word endings such as plurals (apple – apples), word inflexions (go – went). Morphological operations include the formation of words with suffixes and affixes (un-think-able). Morphological competence refers to the ability of the user to mentally assemble and dissect words into smaller meaningful parts. The morphological system of English isn't fully acquired until the age of five. Several authors consider the morphology as the "weak link in the processing chain of auditory input, one that is highly likely to be impaired when things go awry" (Elman et al., 1996, p. 377). Morphology is generally considered to be a strong indicator of developmental language problems. Roger Brown (1973), one of the pioneers in the study of child language acquisition processes, proposed a now widely used framework that uses the number of morphemes in spontaneous utterances as a critical measure. This is called the Mean Length of Utterance, or MLU. It indicates how much a child has broken in into the language system and whether she or he has cracked the (morphological) code.

Phonological disorders. Words consist of series of phonemes, language sounds that are stringed together. Once speakers have internally identified the words they want to say and the sequence of the words, they activate internal phonological frames with slots that each gets filled with a phoneme. The phonological frame generally corresponds to a syllable. Children who are in their developmental stages may have an incomplete internal frame of the word to say—typical errors are omissions and substitutions. For example, the target word may be "chocolate", but the internal representation could be a simplification such as /k//o//k//a//t/. In reality, phonological disorders are often hard to distinguish from articulation disorders, i.e., when the person fails to turn the phonological frame into a motor articulation plan (see below).

Speech articulation disorders or dysarthrias. Articulated speech results from a conversion of the phonological-syllabic frame into actual speech articulation. Speech is considered by many to be the most complex human motor skill, with more than 100 muscles and a production of 15 speech sounds per second (Levelt, 1993, p. 413). A distinction needs to be made between deficient articulation as a consequence of insufficient internal phonological representation [the speaker does not have a real grasp on the sequence of phonemes] and a real articulation problem [the speaker does not have the motor coordination to execute the phonetic plan into articulatory syllabic gestures]. Speech articulation problems can result from motor immaturity, and will often fade as a child gets more practice. With maturation and practice, the articulatory gestures become more automatized and are faster triggered and easier accessed. Besides from lack of maturation and weakness in coordination, speech problems can also be the result of anatomical problems. Cleft lip and cleft palate are examples of anatomical birth anomalies that can be corrected through surgery. If left uncorrected, speech problems and feeding risks may occur. Hypernasal speech is the consequence of insufficient blocking of the airflow leakage to the nasal cavity during speech. Hyponasal speech is the opposite phenomenon: insufficient air flow through the nose in sound production that require nasality.

Fluency disorders. Speech requires a steady flow of word production. This entails that the speaker operates from a suprasegmental phrase pattern that makes it possible to continuously link words together. Speaking is an ongoing process of activating and de-activating muscular articulatory groups. Every speaker experiences occasional difficulties in word planning, as evidenced in stops and iterations. These problems are considered to be genuine fluency disorders if it affects the quality of information exchange. Fluency disorders need attention especially if they lead to anxiety, psychological stress, avoidance, isolation, or distorted peer-relations (Langevin, 2009).

The Levelt (1993) model also makes clear where the difference between language and speech disorders. *Language disorders* are disorders that result from deficient functioning of the main linguistic components: lexicon, morphology, syntax, and phonology.

Speech disorders are executive, motor, and muscular coordination problems that can exist with an intact language substrate.

The distinction between speech and language problems is complex, as there is clearly an overlapping domain between the internal phonetic plan (based on a linguistic process) and the psychomotor articulation plan (Varley, 2010). Generally, in clinical and educational reality, the distinction between speech and language problems is often not easy to be made. The Levelt model (1993) is psycholinguistic in nature: it attempts to account for processes that are specific to language production and perception. When talking about communication disorders, one needs to realize that communication is more than language—and that disorders can and do occur that are not psycholinguistic, but developmental (e.g., a maturity issue), or emotional.

Pre-linguistic disorders. These are developmental disorders that are characterized by difficulties to establish a psycho-sensory interaction between caregiver and baby by lack of understanding cause and effect, or by lack of established routines that help develop a symbolic function, and difficulties in establishing intentionality through interaction. From the first weeks on, patterns of interaction are established between caregiver and child. These patterns are considered to be prototypes for later conversational interaction. For example, baby and caregiver learn to establish a turn-taking sequence within which they build in requests for food, messages of satisfaction, all through non-verbal behavior and signaling.

Children also learn how caregivers respond to their behaviors. If a consistency is detected in how a caregiver responds, intentional behavior can emerge. For example, babies fine tune their own crying and vocalization to ask for food or to request repetition of a pleasant routine. Routines are sequences of meaningful actions that are frequently repeated. Adherence to a set sequence makes the event predictable and allows participants to develop *signal awareness*, which becomes a basis for symbol awareness.

Para-linguistic communicative disorders. These are disorders that are not essentially linguistic in nature, but that do affect the quality of communication. Dysfunctions in cognition, perception, memory, motor behavior, and social behavior can all have an impact on the quality of communication.

Psychological communication disorders. Elective mutism is the term used to indicate that the person, despite normal cognitive and linguistic potential, does not use voice or linguistic communication. Neither the cause nor the solution of this condition is linguistic in nature. It typically results from cognitive, emotional, or social-relational difficulties.

This condition can occur temporarily and needs attention as it can have a lasting effect on communication. For example, although stuttering behavior may be the result of extreme anxiety, there is a risk that it becomes an established behavior even after the causes of anxiety might have been removed (Corcoran & Stewart, 1998).

Communication Disorders as Social Disorders

To understand communication and communication disorders, one needs to take into account that communication and communication dysfunction can only be understood if they are seen as an interactive process with one or more communication partners. In this interactive process, the nature of communication is heavily dependent on the feedback by partners. This is in the first place true for *communication effectiveness.* Sperber and Wilson (1986) introduced the notion of *relevance* to understand the essence of communication. People generally do not communicate with the purpose of producing well-formed linguistic structures. Communication is about having an impact on others, and making things happen. Words and linguistic structures are considered to be tools to achieve these goals, but so are many non-linguistic behaviors. In the past two decades, there has been increasing attention to what it is that makes communicative behavior effective. Pragmatic effectiveness is an essential skill that children learn during their very first years. *Pragmatics* is the "how-to-get-things-done" component of language. Research in pragmatics has focused on how language is used to socialize, Pragmatic functions include *functions* such as greeting, informing, demanding, promising, *social adaptive use of language* such as the ability to switch from adult-directed language to child-directed language, and being able to understand and apply the unwritten *rules of interaction* such as initiating, turn-taking, rephrasing, and topic maintenance.

To understand pragmatics, it is good to recall why individuals want and need to communicate in the first place. Generally speaking communication serves three functions: (a) survival (biological), (b) social adaptations, and (c) information exchange. The first function is present and observable from day one. It is sometimes called behavior regulation and refers to the need to ensure that basic needs such as hunger and pain relief are met. The second function, social adaptation, results from the need to be accepted and cared for by others. Finally, the third function is the mechanism that guarantees that information is passed on from one individual to the other.

The development of pragmatic skills is predominantly the result of a natural and spontaneous learning process of children growing up in a social environment. There is little explicit teaching of the social-pragmatic rules (except occasional social corrections from educators like "you should speak with two words," "say it nicely," or "what is the magic word?"). Children who lack the tendency or the capacity to spontaneously pick up the pragmatic rules often struggle also with distinguishing literal and metaphorical meanings and decoding implied meanings, such as sarcasm or irony.

Acquisition and Functioning

Children develop the basic communicative skills and the codes needed for communication during the first years of life. Starting from day one, babies enter into interactive dyads with their caregivers, where physical signals (touching, eye gaze, vocalizations, and smiles) are exchanged and constantly refined leading to a non-linguistic pre-symbolic set of signals.

This pre-linguistic, pre-symbolic development provides a framework for the development of symbols. Essentially, symbols are actions, persons, objects, or events that have a *conventionalized referential* meaning. *Conventionalization* is the process through which at least two of the communication partners reach agreement on the meaning of a behavior (a word or an action).

Once children reach the level of symbolic development, single word communication appears. The first words function as stand-alone symbols. Once a child has reached a critical mass of words, they become organized into linguistic structures.

Words are part of a language and are essentially referring to a whole linguistic system. For example, the word *unfriendly* has much in common with *un-kind-ly* (both semantically and morphologically) and is structurally similar to *un-du-ly* (morphologically but not semantically). These words can be used as adjectives and adverbs, but not as nouns or verbs. Children naturally acquire these rules as part of the internal growing grammar that they are building.

Prevalence

As can be expected, estimates about the number of individuals with communication disorders vary depending on the definition and classification that is adhered. Moreover, communication problems present as a continuum from mild occasional and non-pathological communication breakdowns to severe disorders. Generally, it is assumed that 3%–5% of children present with symptoms that classify them in the category of developmental language impairment (American Speech-Language and Hearing Association, 2008). Severe fluency disorders occur in 1% of the population and speech articulation and voice problems occur in up to 5%.

Causes

Genetic disorders—in the past two decades genetic factors in the occurrence of communication disorders have become better understood. The genetics of specific syndromes such as Angelman Syndrome, Williams Syndrome, and Prader Willi Syndrome, help us to discover the complex nature of language and communication.

The diagnosis of *specific language impairment* (SLI) deserves special attention. The term is reserved for language disorders that appear to present themselves without an apparent causal connection to other non-linguistic deficits. The term is used mostly to designate children who, despite normal motor, sensory, and cognitive potential struggle with the acquisition of some or all of the main language components: phonology, morphology, syntax, and lexicon. Older terms for this condition included *developmental aphasia* or *childhood dysphasia,* two terms which imply an underlying neuropsychological problem. As the neuropsychological underpinning of language impairment was hard to prove in most cases, the term has become replaced by *specific language impairment.* This term has the added advantage that it does not suggest that it constitutes a single homogeneous group. Also, the specificity of the language disorders is relative: recent studies have found that children diagnosed with SLI often do have related non-linguistic developmental issues, as evidenced in lower performance on standardized tests of gross and fine motor skills (Zelaznik & Goffman, 2010), and on tasks that require sustained visual attention (Finneran, Francis, & Leonard, 2009).

Many of the communication disorders are part of non-specific neuro-developmental limitations. Neurogenic communication disorders can be the result of damage to the nervous system. The human brain typically invests a number of cortical areas in the development of language and pragmatic skills. The language areas are those that are specialized in analytic-sequental analysis and fine motor programming. This neurolinguistic investment is a progressive development. As long as the brain has not fully invested in these areas, there is some neuroplasticity. If a young child suffers a brain damage in a limited part of the cortex, other areas can take over the function. Most (but not all) of the neurolinguistic areas and networks are located in the left side of the brain (the left hemisphere). This investment in the left side is also the result of progressive development, i.e., the *lateralization* (literally, "taking sides"). Children who have undergone *hemidecortication* (surgical removal of major parts of the cortical structures on one side to remove epileptic brain tissue) are still able to acquire language as long as the surgery takes place prior to or in the earliest stages of language acquisition.

There is a whole range of severity of language disorders that occur as a result of neurogenic factors. In extreme cases, individuals can remain on the level of pre-linguistic development.

Speech articulation problems can also result from anatomical malformations in the vocal tract, i.e., the cavities superior to the larynx. Human speech is based on the possibility to make sounds resonate in the oral and nasal cavities. Structural malformation (e.g., cleft palate) can lead to distorted speech production. In many cases, these dysfunctions can be corrected through surgery. As a general rule, anatomical dysfunctions should not need specific special education intervention.

Speech and language atypical development are often the effect of insufficient exposure to environmental language due to hearing impairment. Moderate to profound hearing losses have an effect of language acquisition due to limited and distorted access to the language in the environment. Atypical language development in hearing impaired children should not be considered to be pathological as children rely on a normal linguistic potential, sometimes creating linguistic utterances in the visual modality (Goldin-Meadow, 2003).

It has been a matter of debate and controversy whether periods of early life temporary hearing loss would give cause to long-term language development and proficiency effects. Recent studies indicate that, if other factors such as socio-cultural status are kept under control, children seem to be able to linguistically overcome these temporary barriers (Roberts, Rosenfeld, & Zeisel, 2004). At the age of 7, in most cases the negative effects on language development appear to have become resolved (Zumach, Gerrits, Chenault, & Anteunis, 2010).

In recent years, reports increasingly employ the International Classification of Functioning, Disability, and Health (ICF; Threats, 2006). The ICF provides a framework that attempts to transcend differences in causative explanations and interpretations. The framework enables comparative research across cultural and linguistic contexts, and in direct relationship to personal and social functioning of the individual.

Identification

Primary prevention of communication disorders can be related to measures of genetic and other types of counseling in parents and situations that pose a heightened risk. It may include general advice that is given to provide consistent language exposure to children.

Secondary prevention consists of early identification of factors that can lead to communication disorders. These can both be individual and environmental. Individual secondary prevention may include hearing screening, or observations and measures that are aimed at ensuring that adequate language exposure is provided. Environmental secondary prevention includes counseling of parents and caregivers in establishing good communicative and linguistic models.

In general early intervention aims at eliminating or reducing the degree to which the communication disorder presents itself. One certainly wishes to prevent the communication disorder from spreading to other developmental domains such as cognition and socialization. Tertiary prevention is aimed at restoring, minimizing, or normalizing in cases where the communication disorder is clearly present.

Psychological and Behavioral Characteristics

Primary characteristics are the communicative behaviors that are atypical, and may include absence of functional speech, slow speech, articulatory distortions, stuttering, a-grammatical utterances, ineffective and unusual non-verbal communicative behavior. There is some discussion about different distinguishable cognitive-linguistic profiles reflecting specific configurations of symptoms (Mervis, 2004).

Developmental secondary characteristics are reflected in how the communicative limitations have an effect on other developmental domains such as social, cognitive, and academic development.

Effects on behavior development. In extreme cases development of delinquent behavior can occur, Brownlie et al. (2004) reported on the prevalence of delinquency in adolescents who had early language impairment. They could demonstrate a clear relationship in boys: male adolescents with early language impairment showed a significantly higher risk to delinquent behavior. This is less the case in girls. The relationship between behavioral problems and language impairment is probably complex and multifactorial. Intervening factors are school adaptation, academic success, and in some cases a possible common neuropsychological underlying structure to both the language and the behavioral problems.

Effects on literacy. Learning to read and write typically does not take off until after a child has naturally acquired the foundations of language around the age of 5 or 6 years. Metalinguistic abilities are essential in order to be able to concentrate on phoneme – grapheme relations. Children who have developmental language impairments are much more likely to also struggle with the acquisition of the alphabetic principle.

Effects on academics. Communication and language are quintessential for academic learning. Teaching is traditionally based on verbal transmission of information. A major component of learning and studying requires processing abilities of linguistic information.

Educational Intervention

Intervention can only be effective if one has a good understanding of the nature of the disorder and its implications and threats. As mentioned before, disorders can result from individual as well as contextual factors. Similar to the dynamics between nature and nurture (Tomasello & Slobin, 2005), the interaction between both groups of factors makes them in reality hard to distinguish.

Pre-linguistic intervention. In cases of high-risk early intervention will include pre-linguistic strategies. Parents and primary caregivers are typically encouraged to engage in interactive routines and play. Because routines have an internal predictive structure (one element always leads to the other), they are great to help a child understand referencing and facilitate construction of internal representations.

Linguistic intervention. This intervention aims to trigger learning mechanisms in the child to learn to use words and sentences in communication, and to learn new or change wrongly acquired language structures. Language intervention attempts to correct and complement a process that, for most children, develops through a process of spontaneous interaction and cognitive-linguistic discovery by the child. Why do most children develop language from a variety of language models in their environment (their parents, their siblings, others) and why are some children not able to such acquisition with the same or similar models?

Nelson, Welsh, Camarata, Heimann, and Tjus (2001) suggested that what some children need is a "tricky mix." Most normally developing children do not learn incessantly from the language they are exposed to. However, there seem to be enough critical moments when heightened attention, high motivation and interest, and structural transparency converge. Nelson (1987) suggested the name "Rare Event Learning Mechanisms" (RELM) for this phenomenon.

In intervention, therapists and educators attempt to create conditions that compel a child to pay attention to both language content and structure. One technique that has been recommended is recasting. It requires that child and adult are in an engaging interaction. The adult responds to a child's utterance with a response that is a meaningful contribution to the conversation while adding grammatical information. Often, the adult's response contains a rephrasing of the child's idea. From a cognitive point of view, the rephrasing reduces the need to attend to the meaning (not much new is added) of the recast. Hence, it facilitates the child's attention to the minimally differing syntactic or morphological structures. For example, if a child says "Cow big!" the adult may respond with "Yes, the cow is big!" The purpose of this technique is to make the differences between the utterances codable, i.e., the child can mentally compare and contrast the two utterances, while the communication exchange is conducted in a spontaneous way.

Recasting is a technique that can be practiced throughout daily interactions with the child. Tricky mix language activities target the development of language structures and habits through spontaneous communication. Tricky mix ingredients would include motivation, linguistic and non-linguistic understanding, and challenges and interest

In sum, intervention is aimed at developing strategies to build language and to make language functioning faster.

Speech intervention. Intervention aimed at correcting deficient speech generally entails pull-out individual therapy—depending on the type of speech disorder, the therapy will be focused on re-learning new motor-articulatory patterns, to change and control breathing patterns (e.g., in cases of fluency disorders).

Pragmatics intervention While typical children learn the rules of pragmatics mainly through incidental learning, some children need to be explicitly taught rules of turn taking, topic maintenance, attending to the partner, etc. Children who have specific problems in this area used to be diagnosed with *semantic-pragmatic disorder* (Rapin & Allen, 1983), a term that has presently been replaced by a more general *pragmatic language disorder*.

Literacy. The acquisition of literacy rests on internalized language skills and the child's ability to reflect on language. Children who have not acquired solid internal language components (lexicon, phonology, morphology, and syntax) have a heightened risk to struggle to become fluent readers. Moreover, children need to be able to reflect on the form of language in order to segment spoken communicative strings into separate words, and analyze words into phonemes (Kamhi & Catts, 2002). These meta-linguistic skills include phonological awareness, understanding of the alphabetic principle, rapid letter recognition, and lexical decision. Children with developmental language disorders pose a heightened risk for insufficient literacy development. Therefore, it is often recommended that, early on, intervention should include pre-literacy goals such as the development of print and phonemic awareness.

Formats of Intervention

What is the most effective way to set up intervention? In the past decade, evidence based intervention has become a central focus for clinical and educational decisions. In general, several factors will contribute to outcomes.

Collaborative intervention. Communication and interaction are pervasive activities that occur during every waking moment of the day. Successful communication is essential for social participation and learning. Children with communication disorders run the risk of experiencing impaired learning if communication disorders are not treated. Also, quality and quantity of social participation may decrease as a result of the communication limitations. Therefore, collaborative intervention where parents, teachers, and speech-language therapists work together provide a framework for common goals that focus on language, academic learning, and social functioning.

Individual therapy. In one-on-one sessions, a clinician can present a child with communication disorders with critical materials, challenging games, interactive experiences that allow concentration on specific language structures or communicative behavior.

Self-therapy. It can be useful to help children and adolescents to gain insight into their own communication disorders. If children and adolescents understand the nature and the mechanisms of their own disorder, they can attempt to cognitively grasp and modify factors that inhibit, control, or ease the problem behavior as well as the desired behavior. Within the field of intervention for stutterers, often an emphasis is laid on analyzing one's own behavior, responses, and—the developing of self-monitoring techniques (Fraser, 1987). For example, the person with fluency disorders will learn to recognize avoidance behavior, as well as behaviors that are "learned" in association with stuttering.

Augmentative and Alternative Communication (AAC). AAC is the term used to indicate intervention techniques and systems that employ non-standard forms of communication. AAC is meant for individuals without functional natural speech. The repertoire of AAC methods includes unaided and aided communication forms. The use of manual signs, gestures, eye gaze communication are examples of unaided communication, i.e., communication for which nothing exterior to a person's body is needed. The use of communication boards, speech-generating devices, and picture- exchange communication (Bondy & Frost, 2001) are examples of aided communication.

Assessment

Dynamic assessment. During the pre-linguistic stage of development and in the emerging language stages, communication is an essentially idiosyncratic process of interacting with the environment. Because communication can be seen as a dynamic adaptive process, dynamic assessment approaches are often the most appropriate. Dynamic assessment is a procedure in which one attempts to determine the learnability for skills or behaviors by introducing challenges that are esteemed to be within the zone of proximal development. Dynamic assessment is useful in situations where standardized tests are not applicable (e.g., for individuals not meeting the entry level criteria). For example, clinicians can use dynamic assessment to determine whether eye gaze or finger pointing is more likely for a specific individual to assume communicative value.

Questionnaires. The MacArthur-Bates Communicative Development Inventory (Fenson et al., 2006) is a powerful instrument that can be employed to collect information of early words, actions and gestures that are communicatively relevant. This instrument explores both the roots of linguistic communication in early gestures and in the first initial lexicon. Because it asks parents or caregivers to report on their observations and impressions, it has a focus on effective, functional communication.

Norm-referenced tests. A wide variety of tests can be used to determine how acquisition and development is measured compared to typical peer development.

Language tests. Standardized test differ in (a) target population, (b) the language components that are measured, (c) the relation to other development domains (academics, literacy), (d) normed on same-age peers. Language tests are extremely useful if one needs to compare components within language, e.g., expressive vs. receptive language, or phonological vs. morphological development.

Language sample analysis (LSA). Recording an interactive language sample yields information on language use that may be complementary to the information extracted from standardized tests (Heilman, Miller, & Nockerts, 2010). Language samples offer valuable information on the use of language in naturalistic spontaneous situations.

Criterion-referenced tests are focused on the question whether a child or adolescent's skill and performance match or exceed the required educational entry level for participation of a (school) program or intervention.

Interpreting language and communicative behavior should always take into account cultural aspects. Communication is a social phenomenon that is always regulated by social traditions and conventions that have an influence on how children of different ages and gender will be expected to speak, participate, take initiative, and assume a more dominant or a more passive role in communication.

Early Intervention

Communication starts the very first day of life. Disorders of communication can have effects from the earliest developmental stages.

Family-based intervention. The immediate interaction partners of the child are potentially the most crucial in early intervention. Therefore, early intervention programs often use family intervention to facilitate the establishment of a stimulating communicative and linguistic environment for the child. This can be reflected in the Individualized Family Service Plan. Sheehan and colleagues (2009) found that community-based intervention toward at-risk children and their families can be effective, resulting in self-reported changes in the way parents interact with their young children.

Training of the primary caregivers in using communication strategies. Communicative strategies include attentiveness to the child's initiations to interaction, and awareness how to respond in an appropriate way encouraging way. Because early communication development is fully embedded in early motor, social, and cognitive development, the intervention goals are linked across the developmental domains. Most approaches include components that coach caregivers to adopt encouraging, communicative and linguistically stimulating styles and interactive routines.

Transition to Adolescence and Adulthood

Language disorders tend to persist throughout the developmental years and beyond. Tomblin, Zhang, Buckwalter, and O'Brien (2003) found that over a 4-year period, children with language disorders were still very likely to continue to show linguistic impairments. Because language and communication is a major vehicle to further cognitive development, children with language impairments run the risk to find themselves in a continuous and vicious circle where lack of language skills poses serious limitations to processing of new information, while lack of information as well as less than average conversational skills seriously reduce the challenges to further cognitive development.

Language and communication disorders contain a high risk to "spread out" to other developmental domains such as cognition, literacy, academics, and socialization. Literacy development is largely built on meta-linguistic development. Children with developmental language disorders show a significantly higher risk for continued problems with processing written text (Clegg, Hollis, Mawhood, & Rutter, 2005). Psychosocial development runs the risk to be negatively affected by the presence of developmental language disorders (Weindrich, Jennen-Steinmetz, Laucht, Esser, & Schmidt, 2000).

Issues

Traditional vs. collaborative consultation intervention. Which intervention model is most likely to bring changes in a developing child's communicative behavior? Prelock (2000) discusses the role of speech-language pathologists. Traditionally, clinicians have conducted therapy in pull-out situations. This service-model reflects a preference for intensive and concentrated learning of language structures. It also implies a vision or an assumption about transfer of skills. Increasingly, collaborative models have been suggested in which clinicians and educators work together, often side by side in the classroom. The motivation for this practice is related to both a vision of functionality and a vision on transfer.

How to determine an initial lexicon? In typical development, children acquire a first lexicon of up to 50 words, a set of words that is rather similar across languages. Snow (1988) states that there is a bigger difference between the first and the tenth word, than there is a difference between the tenth and the twentieth word. Pragmatic needs and needs for new words to be learned evolve as the child learns and acquires more.

This first lexicon is generally considered to function as a vocabulary toolkit for the life of a 2.5-year-old. It usually contains words to denote the most significant people, objects, and situations from the child's perspective: mom, dad, the name of a toy or two, a sibling's name, food names, bed, etc. This vocabulary has emerged within the context of the specific needs of each individual child, but these contexts are generally similar enough to yield rather comparable lexicons.

Functional communication or structural language intervention? Language acquisition is driven by a need of the developing child to socially adapt to the social and material environment. In determining intervention goals, clinicians and educators need to be able to make a judgment of short-term and long-term reachable developmental goals. Another way to put this question is whether the intervention should be *pragmatics/semantics oriented* or *form oriented.* In recent years, several group intervention programs have focused on pragmatics (e.g., Adams, 2006) as educational and therapeutic goals to be explicitly taught to children and adolescents with pragmatic language impairment.

Words or rules? Language is more than a collection of words: there are phonological rules that combine phonemes into words, and there are morphological and syntactic rules that determine the word order and the appearance of the words in actual sentence use. Should intervention be focused on facilitating the acquisition of words (in context), or should a structural approach be preferred focusing on syntactic mental templates with slots in which to put the words? One view is that the child is primarily acquiring a lexicon where the words are morphologically and syntactically marked, indicating how they can be combined. In a sense, words are like pieces of a jigsaw puzzle that are shaped in such a way that they facilitate which other pieces they would combine with, i.e., which verbs, direct objects, location nouns, etc.

Teaching vs. facilitation of acquisition. Typically, developing children acquire communication skills, including the complexities of language, in a largely spontaneous manner, guided by self-discovery. Acquisition is predominantly a process of incidental learning. There is an ongoing debate how children are able to accomplish this process. One hypothesis posits that children possess innate syntactic structures that they employ to mentally structure information (Pinker, 1989). This hypothesis has been criticized by others (Schlesinger, 1988) who found evidence that children initially work from semantics-type combinatorial principles (agent – action) on which syntactic categories are gradually superimposed. In order to be able to do this, children must receive and pay attention to a critical mass of examples (Leonard & Deevy, 2004). The ability of typically developing children to rapidly progress in acquiring the syntactical rules and structures of the language continues to amaze scholars in the field of developmental psycholinguistics—a skill that adults appear to have lost. Therefore, children between 1 and 5 years old are often suspected to be in the critical period of language acquisition. How do typical children pull this off? Some scholars have suggested that children benefit from a "less is more" situation, an advantage that adults have lost (Newport, 1990): children function in smaller worlds with a limited number of external referents and events, with a limited short- and long-term memory—a learning environment that is conducive to make combinations. In therapeutic and educational situations, one can attempt to introduce and entertain multiple opportunities to perform linguistic and communicative functions such as commenting, requesting, questioning, and refusing, all in reference to items and events with relevance to the world of the child.

Introducing augmentative and alternative communication (AAC). AAC is the use of non-standard forms of communication. This can include the use of manual signs, graphic symbols, communication boards, or speech-generating devices (with varying degrees of complexity). When exactly is the introduction of AAC warranted and can it come too soon or too late? Traditionally, some uncertainty has existed concerning the effects of non-speech communication on the development of natural speech (Romski & Sevcik, 2005), based on a supposed mental incompatibility between natural speech and alternative modes. However, there is no clinical or psycholinguistic evidence for such an *incompatibility hypothesis* (Loncke, 2010). On the contrary, an increasing number of meta-analyses (Millar, Light, & Schlosser, 2006; Schlosser & Wendt, 2008) indicate that early introduction of non-speech modes has the potential to facilitate the development of an internal symbolic network that might trigger the development of natural speech. In recent years, early intervention programs tend to adopt alternative modes, sometimes in anticipation of natural speech development (Romski & Sevcik, 2005).

Inclusion and educational participation of children with severe communication limitations. Providing an inclusion-based educational context for children with severe communication disorders can be difficult. Finke, McNaughton, and Drager (2009) conducted a focus group qualitative analysis with elementary school teachers who had children with autism spectrum disorders (ASD) in their classrooms. There are possible benefits for all parties involved, including increased awareness and acceptance by classmates of the children with ASD, as well as the perception by the teachers of becoming more skilled and effective. Possible challenges included the need to find an appropriate curriculum match for the child and the need to give equal time and attention to all students. In general, the more severe the communication limitations are, the more challenging it is to find an appropriate solution.

References

Adams, L. (2006). *Group treatment for Asperger Syndrome. A social skill curriculum.* San Diego, CA: Plural.

Aitchison, J. (2003). *Words in the mind. An introduction to the mental lexicon* (3rd ed.). Oxford, UK: Blackwell.

Alt, M., & Plante, E. (2006). Factors that influence lexical and semantic fast mapping of young children with specific language impairment. *Journal of Speech, Language, and Hearing Research, 49*, 941–954.

American Speech-Language-Hearing Association. (2008). Incidence and prevalence of communication disorders and hearing loss in children. Retrieved July 16, 2010, from http://www.asha.org/research/reports/children.htm

Bamiou, D-E. (2009). Auditory processing disorders. In J. Graham & D. Baguley (Eds.), *Ballantyne's deafness* (pp. 250–259). Chichester, UK: Wiley-Blackwell.

Berko Gleason, J., & Bernstein Ratner, N. (Eds.). (1998) *Psycholinguistics* (2nd ed.). Fort Worth, TX: Harcourt Brace Jovanovich.

Bondy, A., & Frost, L. (2001). The picture exchange communication system. *Behavior Modification, 25*, 725– 44.

Brown, R. (1973). *A first language: The early stages.* Cambridge, MA: Harvard University Press.

Brownlie, E. B., Beitchman, J., Escobar, M., Young, A., Atkinson, L., Johnson, et al. (2004). Early language impairment and young adult delinquent and aggressive behavior. *Journal of Abnormal Child Psychology, 34*, 453–467.

Butterworth, B. (1982). Speech errors: Old data in search of new theories. In A. Cutler (Ed.). *Slips of the tongue and language production* (pp. 73–108). Amsterdam: Mouton.

Clegg, J., Hollis, C., Mawhood, L., & Rutter, M. (2005). Developmental language disorders—a follow-up in later adult life. Cognitive, language and psychosocial outcomes. *Journal of Child Psychology and Psychiatry, 46*, 128–149.

Corcoran, J., & Stewart, M. (1998). Stories of stuttering, a qualitative analysis of interview narratives. *Journal of Fluency Disorders, 23*, 247–264.

Elman, J. L., Bates, E.A., Johnson, M. H., Karmiloff-Smith, A., Parisi, D., & Plunkett, K. (1996). *Rethinking innateness: A connectionist perspective on development.* Cambridge, MA: MIT Press.

Fenson, L., Marchman, V., Thal, D., Dale, P., Reznick, S., & Bates, E. (2006). *The MacArthur Communicative Development Inventories: User's guide and technical manual* (2nd ed.). Baltimore: Brookes.

Finke, E. H., McNaughton, D. B., & Drager, K. D. R. (2009). 'All children can and should have the opportunity to learn': General education teacher's perspectives on including children with autism spectrum disorder who require AAC. *Augmentative and Alternative Communication, 25*, 110–122.

Finneran, D. A., Francis, A. L., & Leonard, L. B. (2009). Sustained attention in children with specific language impairment (SLI). *Journal of Speech, Language, and Hearing Research, 52,* 915–929.

Fraser, M. (1987). *Self-therapy for the stutterer.* Memphis, TN: Speech Foundation of America.

Goldin-Meadow, S. (2003). *The resilience of language: What gesture creation in deaf children can tell us about how all children learn language.* New York: Psychology Press.

Heilman, J., Miller, J., & Nockerts, A. (2010). Using language sample databases. *Language, Speech, and Hearing Services in Schools, 41,* 84–95.

Kamhi, A. G., & Catts, H. W. (2002). The language basis of reading: Implications for classification and treatment of children with reading difficulties. In K. G. Butler & E. R. Silliman (Eds.), *Speaking, reading, and writing in children with language learning disabilities. New paradigms in research and practice* (pp. 45–72). Mahwah, NJ: Erlbaum.

Langevin, M. (2009). The peer attitudes toward children who stutter scale:

Reliability, known groups validity, and negativity of elementary school-age children's attitudes. *Journal of Fluency Disorders*, *34*(2), 72–86.

Leonard, L. B., & Deevy, P. (2004). Lexical deficits in specific language impairment. In L. Verhoeven & H. van Balkom (Eds.), *Classification of developmental language disorders. Theoretical issues and clinical implications* (pp. 209–233). Mahwah, NJ: Erlbaum.

Levelt, W. J. M. (1993). *Speaking: From intention to articulation* (1st paperback ed.). Cambridge, MA: MIT Press.

Loncke, F. (2010). Psycho-linguistic approaches to augmentative and alternative communication. In J. Guendouzi, F. Loncke, &. M. Williams (Eds.). *The handbook of psycholinguistic and cognitive processes. Perspectives in communication disorders* (pp. 761–777). New York: Psychology Press.

Mainela-Arnold, E., Evans, J. L., & Coady, J. A. (2008). Lexical representations in children with SLI: Evidence from a frequency-manipulated gating task. *Journal of Speech, Language, and Hearing Research*, *51*, 381–393.

Mayor, J., & Plunkett, K. (2010). A neurocomputational account of taxonomic responding and fast mapping in early word learning. *Psychological Review*, *117*, 1–31.

McNeill, D., & Duncan, S. (2010). Gestures and growth points in language disorders. In J. Guendouzi, F. Loncke, & M. Williams (Eds.), *The handbook of psycholinguistic and cognitive processes: Perspectives in communication disorders* (pp. 663–685). New York: Psychology Press.

Mervis, C. B. (2004). Cross-etiology comparisons of cognitive and language development. In M. L. Rice & S. Warren (Eds.), *Developmental language disorders. From phenotypes to etiologies* (pp. 153–185). Mahwah, NJ: Erlbaum.

Millar, D. C., Light, J. C., & Schlosser, R. W. (2006). The impact of augmentative and alternative communication intervention on the speech production of individuals with developmental disabilities: A research review. *Journal of Speech, Language, and Hearing Research*, *49*, 248–264.

Nelson, K. E. (1987). Some observations from the perspective of the rare event cognitive comparison model of language acquisition. In K. E. Nelson (Ed.), *Children's language* (Vol. 6, pp. 289–331). Hillsdale, NJ: Erlbaum.

Nelson, K. E., Welsh, J., Camarata, S., Heimann, M., & Tjus, T. (2001). A rare event transactional dynamic model of tricky mix conditions contributing to language acquisition and varied communicative delays. In K. E. Nelson, A. Koc, & C. Johnson (Eds.), Children's language (Vol. 11, pp. 165–196). Hillsdale, NJ: Erlbaum.

Newport, E. L. (1990). Maturational constraints on language learning. *Cognitive Science*, *14*, 11–28.

Pinker, S. (1989). *Learnability and cognition*. Cambridge, MA: MIT Press.

Prelock, P. A. (2000). Multiple perspectives for determining the roles of speech-language pathologists in inclusionary classrooms. *Language, Speech, and Hearing Services in Schools, 31*, 213–218.

Rapin I., & Allen, D. (1983). Developmental language disorders: Nosologic considerations. In U. Kirk (Ed.), *Neuropsychology of language, reading, and spelling* (pp. 155–184). New York: Academic Press.

Roberts, J. E., Rosenfeld, R. M., & Zeisel, S. A. (2004). Otitis media and speech and language: A meta-analysis of prospective studies. *Pediatrics*, *113*, 238–248.

Romski, M., & Sevcik, R. A. (2005). Augmentative communication and early intervention: Myths and realities. *Infants & Young Children*, *18*, 174–185.

Schlesinger, I. M. (1988). The origin of relational categories. In Y. Levy, I. M. Schlesinger, & M. D. S. Braine (Eds.), *Categories and processes in language acquisition* (pp. 121–178). Hillsdale, NJ: Erlbaum.

Schlosser, R. W., & Wendt, O. (2008). Effects of augmentative and alternative communication intervention on speech production in children with autism: A systematic review. *American Journal of Speech-Language Pathology*, *17*, 212–230.

Seiger-Gardner, L., & Schwartz, R. G. (2008). Lexical access in children with and without specific language impairment: A cross-modal picture-word interference study. *International Journal of Language & Communication Disorders*, *43*, 528–551.

Sheehan, J., Girolametto, L., Reilly, S., Ukoumunne, O. C., Price, A., Gold, L., et al. (2009). Feasibility of a language promotion program for toddlers at risk. *Early Childhood Services: An Interdisciplinary Journal of Effectiveness*, *3*, 33–50.

Snow, C. (1988). The last word: Questions about the emerging lexicon. In M. Smith & J. Locke (Eds.), *The emergent lexicon* (pp. 341–352). San Diego, CA: Academic Press.

Sperber, D., & Wilson, D. (1986). *Relevance : Communication and cognition.* Oxford, UK: Blackwell.

Thal, D., & Bates, E. (1988). Language and gesture in late talkers. *Journal of Speech and Hearing Research*, *31*, 115–123.

Threats, T. (2006). Towards an international framework for communication disorders: Use of the ICF. *Journal of Communication Disorders,* 39, 251–265.

Tomasello, M., & Slobin, D. (Eds.). (2005). *Beyond nature-nurture. Essays in honor of Elizabeth Bates.* Mahwah, NJ: Erlbaum.

Tomblin, J. B., Zhang, X., Buckwalter, P., & O'Brien, M. (2003). The stability of primary language disorder: Four years after kindergarten diagnosis. *Journal of Speech, Language, and Hearing Research*, *46*, 1283–1296.

Varley, R. (2010). Apraxia of speech: From psycholinguistic theory to conceptualization and management of an impairment. In J. Guendouzi, F. Loncke, & M. Williams (Eds.), *The handbook of psycholinguistic and cognitive processes: Perspectives in communication disorders* (pp. 535–549). New York: Psychology Press.

Weindrich, D., Jennen-Steinmetz, C., Laucht, M., Esser, G., & Schmidt, M. H. (2000). Epidemiology and prognosis of specific disorders of language and scholastic skills. *European Child & Adolescent Psychiatry*, *9*(3), 186–194.

Zelaznik, H. N., & Goffman, L. (2010). Generalized motor abilities and timing behavior in children with specific language impairment. *Journal of Speech, Language, and Hearing Research*, *53*, 383–393.

Zumach, A., Gerrits, E., Chenault, M., & Anteunis, L. (2010). Long-term effects of early-life otitis media on language development. *Journal of Speech, Language, and Hearing Research*, *53*, 34–43.

19

Deaf and Hard of Hearing Students

Jean F. Andrews
Lamar University

Pamela C. Shaw
Charleston County School District, Charleston, SC

Gabriel Lomas
Western Connecticut State University

Introduction

In a climate of deaf empowerment, findings in cognition and neuroscience, mental health, visual ways of learning, legal protections, and advances in visual, auditory and brain-imaging technologies, opportunities for understanding individuals who are deaf and hard of hearing couldn't be more plentiful. Often not-emphasized enough though are risk factors. Indeed, if early language and education are delayed, cognitive and language deprivation, social isolation, illiteracy, emotional and behavioral problems may occur. We use our combined experiences as authors from three disciplines—language and literacy, school administration, and school psychology—coupled with selective research findings to address these risk factors.

Definitions

Terminology in deaf education can be understood within two paradigms: the *socio-cultural-linguistic* view, which provides deaf people with a language (American Sign Language) and a culture, and the *medical-audiology* perspective, which is concerned with ear and hearing health, diagnostics, and auditory assistive technology. A deaf person's identity can be influenced by socio-cultural-linguistic factors such as culture, ethnicity, family, and educational experiences, presence of deaf community supportive networks, communication and language preferences, and the use of visual technology. Medical-audiological factors such as gender, secondary disabilities, age of onset, and extent of hearing loss, use of auditory technology, auditory factors, and genetic background also affect a deaf person's identity (Leigh, 2009). Families of children who are deaf may access the rich, vibrant deaf culture with its history, art, and literature (Leigh, 2009). Because people who are deaf have experienced oppression and negative stigma, due to cultural and linguistic differences, the language of social protest has brought in terms such as the Deaf Pride movement or the Deaf Civil Rights Movement capitulated during the 1988 Deaf President Now (DPN) movement and the subsequent Deaf Unity Protest of 2002—both supporting a deaf president for Gallaudet University (Leigh, 2009). Terms such as "audism," "racism," and "cultural genocide," too, have entered deaf education parlance, and these are related to identity politics, oppression, and deaf activism, concepts that are vividly expressed in deaf visual art (Andrews & Lokensgard, 2007) and the poetic, dramatic, and literature arts (Peters, 2000).

Certain etiologies or causes of deafness demand medical attention from an ear-nose-throat doctor. Furthermore, an audiologist's services will be sought for diagnostics, the fitting of hearing aids, recommendations for acoustical classrooms, provision of FM systems, and the continual adjustment of the speech processor for cochlear implants (Brown, 2009). Hearing science professionals are concerned with physiological issues that affect educational programming such as how hearing loss can be permanent, temporary and correctable by surgery or medicine, fluctuating, or progressive. Hearing loss can be classified as sensorineural, conductive, or mixed or as a central hearing loss. Sensorineural losses are permanent and are caused by damage to the cochlea or inner ear section. A conductive loss is often caused by an infection in the outer or middle ear and, although temporary, can affect language learning of the child who is deaf. A child can have a central hearing impairment, caused by injury to the eighth auditory nerve up to the cortex. Hearing loss can be gradual and result in permanent progressive hearing loss (Brown, 2009) either genetically caused, noise-induced or a combination of both, or a person can experience a sudden hearing loss as in the case of a head trauma or a virus.

Expressed as a range across decibels, the degree of hearing loss refers to the severity of loss and can affect one ear (unilateral) or both ears (bilateral). Sound is measured in both decibels (loudness) and frequency (pitch) and is expressed across three thresholds and is graphically displayed on an audiogram, a visual chart found in every deaf and hard of hearing child's Individual Educational Program (IEP; Brown, 2009); see Table 19.1.

Prevalence

Approximately 12,000 to 16,000 babies are born each year with hearing loss at a prevalence rate of 1 to 6 per 1,000 births. Hawaii has the highest (3.61 per 1,000), followed by Massachusetts and Wyoming (Mehra, Eavey, & Keamy, 2009). Some congenital (at birth) hearing losses may not become detected until early or late childhood. Due to childhood illness and progressive hearing loss brought on by genetic causes, more than 25 times as many school children have hearing losses than newborns (White & Munoz, 2008).

The total number of children with profound, severe, or mild hearing losses has been estimated to be about 2 million (Ross, Gaffney, Green, & Holstum, 2008). A more conservative estimate of children who are deaf or hard of hearing who are receiving special education is about 80,000, with more than half from diverse backgrounds (Gallaudet Research Institute, GRI, 2008). When neonatal and adolescent prevalence figures are combined, researchers have found that Hispanic American children show higher rates of hearing loss similar to those children from low-income households (Keary, Eavey, & Mehra, 2009). About 1 in 76 deaf children today are diagnosed with autism (GRI, 2008). Additionally, due to better means of assessment and detection, about 3 million children and adults have been diagnosed with deaf-blindness (Ingraham, 2007).

Causes

Approximately 38% to 42% of children who become deaf through viral infection or congenital syndromes also have cognitive, language, learning, emotional, neurological, physical disabilities, or a combination of these—all of which affect their development and school achievement (Vernon & Andrews, 1990). Our understanding of etiologies can assist in developing future programs for children who are deaf with cognitive disabilities (Vernon & Andrews, 1990), learning disabilities such as dyslexia (Enns & Lafond, 2007), with autism spectrum disorders (Vernon & Rhodes, 2009), with deafblindness (Ingraham, 2007), and with emotional and behavioral disorders (Hammerdinger & Hill, 2005). The current etiologies we see in deaf children today with resultant behavioral problems necessitates the development of special residential treatment centers (RTCs) (Hammerdinger & Hill, 2005) because many public and state schools for the deaf may reject these students. Oftentimes, they do not have the specially trained staff nor the resources to handle youth who are deaf with psychiatric, emotional, psychosexual and behavioral needs; thus, these individuals may end up homeless or incarcerated (Willis & Vernon, 2002).

Non-Genetic Causes

Cytomegalovirus (CMV), human immunodeficiency virus (HIV), rubella, syphilis, or toxoplastomosis are infections that cause sensorineural hearing loss. Today, CMV is the leading cause of nongenetic congenital hearing loss in infants and young children with other complications including microcephaly and mental retardation (Stach, 2010). HIV is the virus that causes acquired immuneodeficiency syndrome (AIDS) and can come with significant neurodevelopmental deficits (Stach, 2010). Bacterial infections or meningitis (inflammation or infection of the brain lining) can cause hearing loss as can other viral infections that occur with measles, mumps, and syphilis. As shown in Table 19.2, these diseases affect deaf children's cognitive, social-emotional, language, and overall educational performance.

Genetic Causes

Genetic causes account for more than 50% of congenital deafness (see Table 19.3). Hereditary disorders can be dominant or recessive and result in either congenital hearing loss or progressive hearing loss later in life (Stach, 2010). Hereditary factors associated with hearing loss can be syndromic: occurring with a group of other medical

TABLE 19.1
Categories of Pure Tone Hearing Loss Levels (ASHA, 2009) and Percentages Found in School-Age Children (GRI, 2005).

Category	PTA (Pure Tone Average)	Ability to Understand Speech	Percentage of School-Age Children Within Category (GRI, 2005)
Normal hearing	0 to 15 dB	Hears conversation normally	
Minimal hearing loss	16 – 25 dB	Hear vowel sounds but miss consonants	17.1%
Mild hearing loss	26 – 40dB	Hear only some speech sounds	12.4%
Moderate hearing loss	41 – 55 dB	Hear almost no sounds at normal speaking level	13.4%
Moderate severe hearing loss	56 – 70dB	Hear no speech sounds at normal speaking level	12.2%
Severe hearing loss	70-90 dB	hear no speech and almost no other sound	15.0%
Profound hearing loss	91+ dB	hear no speech and no other sound	29.9%

Data adapted from Brown (2009, p. 935).

TABLE 19.2
Major Non-Genetic Causes of Deafness

Etiology	Description	Intelligence, Academic, Language, Physical, Behavioral Sequalae
Birth trauma, low birth weight (prematurity)	Medical advances have raised survival rates of infants born premature, those who survive have multiple disabilities.	Low IQ, depressed academic achievement, profound hearing loss, cerebral palsy, aphasia, emotional disturbance, lower ratings for speech intelligibility, immaturity, brain damage, perceptual disabilities, unsatisfactory adjustment.
Meningitis	The leading postnatal cause of deafness among school age children. A disease of an infection of the membranes surrounding the brain, caused by bacteria, viruses, fungi, microbacteria and spirochetes.	Low IQ. Those deafened after language acquisition do better in school. Have severe hearing losses. Typically few have more than one handicap. Secondary disabilities include aphasia, mental retardation, brain damage and psychosis. May have delays in learning to walk due to damage of the vestibular system. Have inferior communication skills.
Maternal Rubella (German Measles)	Virus invades embryonic tissue and toxins circulate in developing fetus and damages cells forming eyes, brain, ear and heart	Low IQ, low academic achievement, presence of aphasia, behavioral disorders, high risk for diabetes and other endocrine disorders, additional physical problems.
Cytomegalovirus	Viral infection transmitted in utero. Member of herpes family, carried by body fluids, including blood, saliva, breast milk, tears, symptoms include high fever, chills, fatigue, headaches,	Can be accompanied by microcephaly (abnormally small head due to failure of brain to grow), mental retardation, developmental delays, coordination problems, central nervous damage, visual loss and seizures.
Congenital Toxoplasmosis	Caused by a parasite infection contracted through contaminated food and animals, an infection transmitted from mother to fetus	Vision problems, hydrocephaly, and mental retardation
Erthroblastosis Felalis (Rh Factor)	Formerly a cause of deafness but now with medical advances such as Rh immunizations and prenatal transfusions, it is rare.	May involve central nervous damage, high prevalence of cerebral palsy, coordination problems, aphasia, academic disabilities, depressed IQ, and seizures.
Persistent pulmonary hypertension of the newborn (PPHN)	Infants blood flow bypasses the lungs and eliminates oxygen support to the organs of the body	Unknown
Syphilis	Venereal disease transmitted from mother to fetus	Progressive hearing loss after two years of age.
Maternal diabetes, hypoxia, hyperbilirubinemia, ototoxic drugs, parental radiation	Maternal and infant ingestation of ototoxic drugs and chemotherapy treatments may cause infant hearing loss.	If the drug or chemotherapy occurs after language has been acquired, the child do better better in academic and language areas. Drugs taken by mother during pregnancy can result in development problems for the infant. Drugs include otomyacins, accutane, dilantin, quinine, thalidomide.
Measles, encephalitis, chicken pox, influenza, mumps	Childhood diseases characterized by viral infections, rashes, fever	More traumatic if diseases occur prior to age thee before language is acquired.

Adapted from Vernon, 1969; Brown, 2009; Andrews & Vernon, 1990; Stach, 2010

and physical disorders (30% of deafness) or they can be nonsyndromic hearing loss, an autosomal dominant or recessive genetic condition with no other significant features than deafness (70% of deafness; Stach, 2010). Connexin 26 or GJB2 is the cause of 50% of nonsyndromic hearing loss (Stach, 2010).

Syndromic Causes

With more than 400 syndromes accompanying hearing loss, genetic deafness is inherited in specific patterns that vary. Deafness can be present at birth (congenital) occurring prelingually (before language is acquired) or occur after birth, in early childhood postlingually (after language is acquired), in later childhood or adolescence, or even in the third or fourth decade of life. There are four inherited patterns: autosomal dominant inheritance, autosomal recessive inheritance, x-linked recessive inheritance, and mitochrondial inheritance (Stach, 2010; Vernon & Andrews, 1990).

Identification

A decade ago, most children were identified after age 3 when speech and language failed to develop. Today, 40 states have legislation mandating universal newborn hearing screening (UNHS) or Early Hearing Detection Intervention (EHDI; Brown, 2009). A 1-3-6 rule is followed: by 1 month babies are screened at the hospital; by 3 months a follow-up evaluation is conducted for these babies who failed initial screening, and by 6 months, the baby is enrolled in a family involvement program (Brown, 2009). The earlier babies are identified and provided with appropriate intervention, ideally before the age of 6 months, so that babies and toddlers can make better progress in speech, language, and sign language acquisition (Moeller, 2000; Yoshinaga-Itano & Sedley, Coulter, & Mehl, 1998). Despite these findings, UNHS is deemed controversial by some because of cost-effectiveness, lack of empirical support, and high rates of false-positives (50% to 98% are negatives)—all of which can result in a high rate of parent anxiety, fear and tension (Brown, 2009).

Although 95% of infants are now screened for hearing loss before leaving the hospital, about one third do not receive diagnostic evaluations by 3 months of age (Brown, 2009). These children emerge into the system later in the schools in special education classes. Even if a baby passes the hearing screening, he or she may be at risk for hearing loss later in childhood, many of whom show up in special education classrooms because of delays in reading and language achievement (Brown, 2009).

Diagnosis

Deaf parents (10%) easily welcome a deaf baby into the family. The other 90%—hearing parents—experience their child's deafness as traumatic and stressful. They may go through states of intense shock, disbelief, disappointment, grief, anger, and denial, "doctor-shop" and seek folk or religious cures. Parents benefit from grief counseling where they can learn about hearing loss and deaf culture and work through their feelings so that they can bond and establish communication with their deaf child (Mapp, 2004; Vernon & Andrews, 1990).

Behavioral Characteristics

Cognition

Although hearing loss per se does not cause cognitive deficits, children who are deaf are at high risk for cognitive and experiential deprivation and this in turn can cause cognitive and language delays and behavioral problems (Vernon & Andrews, 1990; Andrews, Leigh, & Weiner, 2004). In a review of 50 studies,, Vernon found that intelligence is normally distributed in the deaf population as it is in the hearing population (Vernon & Andrews, 1990). Thus, in a special education program you may have deaf children who are intellectually gifted enrolled in a program along with those who are cognitively and developmentally delayed as well as those with average intelligence.

Social Cognition and Socialization

Infants are "socialized" as they learn turn-taking and vocabulary labeling routines from their mothers and caretakers. Longitudinal studies show that deaf mothers (and hearing mothers) are able to set up these social and turn-taking routines visually and tactually with their deaf infants (Meadow-Orlans, Spencer, & Koester, 2004). Children who are deaf who do not receive these visual and tactile interventions are at high risk for delays in language and socio-emotional development. For instance, they are at risk of becoming socially immature, impulsive, lacking reflectivity, egocentric, and lacking responsibility for their actions. Additionally, they may not learn how to empathize, predict, or understand the feelings and motivations of others (Hammerdinger & Hill, 2005). Students who are deaf may also lack a "theory of mind," a social cognitive term that relates to the child being able to predict the viewpoint of others. The lack of understanding other persons' perspective has been related to language learning, incidental learning, as well as different styles of learning (i.e. visual vs. auditory) (see Courtin, Melot, & Corroyer, 2008, for reviews of these studies).

Communication and Language

Early access to rich communication and language environments whether it be ASL or a spoken language (e.g., English or Spanish). or a combination of these is critical. Communication refers to a symbolic system of gestures, vocalizations, mime, body language and drawings. Language entails a rule-governed system based on linguistic principles. Somewhere in between are "home signs," which are invented signs and gestures that children who are deprived of sign language will naturally invent (Goldin-Meadow, 2003). For children who are deaf, there are two languages: American Sign Language (ASL) or English, or Spanish as 25% of deaf children are from Spanish-speaking homes (GRI, 2005). Deaf people and hearing people often mix the two languages into a kind of contact signing (Lucas & Valli, 1992) whereby they put ASL signs into English grammatical word order. It is interesting to note that such language mixing is natural when two languages come into contact with each other.

For didactic purposes of teaching English, educators have invented manual codes of English that use a combination of ASL lexical signs, invented signs, and English word order such as Signed English, Seeing Essential English (SEE1), and Signing Exact English (SEE2) (see definitions by Paul, 2009). Nonetheless, ASL is the "mother lode" from which all the invented sign codes are mined.

American Sign Language (ASL)

First described using linguistic terminology by Dr. William C. Stokoe in 1960, ASL has its own grammar and vocabulary. Whereas English is a linear-sequential language, ASL is a visual-spatial-gestural language. Developmental milestones for ASL have been described for deaf children of deaf parents who acquire ASL from birth (see reviews of these ASL psycholinguistic studies in Andrews, Logan & Phelan, 2008). Deaf children can be exposed to ASL literacy—that is ASL literature consisting of poems and stories that are structured to play on the linguistic features of ASL (i.e. handshapes of signs, sign movements, etc.) to express meanings (Valli & Lucas, 2000). Unlike hearing children who learn their first language from their parents, deaf children learn ASL from their deaf peers and deaf adults whom they meet at schools, at deaf churches, festivals, functions, or sporting events. And they learn ASL on different timetables from early, middle, late childhood and even into adulthood (Newport, 1990). By learning ASL past the "sensitive period," language delays may result (Mayberry & Eichen, 1991). ASL is used in only about 10% of early childhood to high school deaf education programs today, but it is gaining momentum as researchers have documented the benefits of the ASL/English bilingual approach in the United States. Deaf students can be bilingual-bimodal. They can learn and use both languages: ASL and English and use both modes—the visual-gestural through signing and the auditory-vocal through talking depending on their conversational partners, language/mode preferences and educational background (Andrews et al., 2004).

Deaf students, it has been argued (Grosjean, 2008), have the need to be bilingual in oral spoken language and sign language in order to get their early needs for family communication met as well as for cognitive, social, and cultural benefits. This bilingualism involves the sign language of the deaf community and the spoken language of the hearing community, sometimes in spoken form, but more often in its written form. Viewed as such, deaf bilinguals are like the millions of other hearing bilinguals who live their lives using two languages and living in two cultures (Grosjean, 2008).

To this end, educators have promoted ASL as the language of instruction in the ASL/English bilingual approach to language teaching and language learning with English (speech, reading, and writing) to be taught as a second language (Nover, Christensen, & Cheng, 1998). In a major national professional development effort, teachers (K–12) and infant to preschool child caregivers have been schooled in this approach in more than 30 K–12 schools and at six teacher-preparation universities (Nover, personal communication, December 3, 2009) and in nine parent-infant and early childhood programs throughout the United States (Simms & Moers, 2010). Using the ASL/English approach, the teacher separates the two languages in instruction. This approach aims to develop proficiency in both ASL and English, primarily reading and writing. However, English spoken language is used within the ASL/English bilingual approach at the The Cochlear Implant Education Center at Gallaudet University. There, clinicians are experimenting with ASL/English bilingual concepts and presenting oral language (termed "oracy" by Nover and his associates) in the teaching of the two languages to young deaf children with cochlear implants (Nussbaum, personal communication, December 3, 2009). More research in using the visual language of signing to teach both spoken English and English literacy is needed to test the efficacy of these bilingual approaches (Moores, 2008; Andrews & Rusher, 2010).

English

There are manual codes of English that attempt to make English visible to deaf children by putting signs in English word order and inventing signs for verb tenses, morphological markers, and articles and other word endings (Paul, 2009). SEE1, SEE2, CASE (Conceptually Accurate Signing English), and Linguistics of Visual English (LOVE) are such sign systems. When combined with speech, these codes are called the Simultaneous Communication (SimCom) method. When ASL, manual codes, written language, speech, art, body language, and amplification are combined in teaching philosophy, this is called the Total Communication philosophy. When signing is more ASL-like in grammar and contains the use of space, facial expressions, head tilts, eye gazes, and body movements, it is termed "contact signing" (Valli & Lucas, 2000). Most deaf adults communicating with hearing persons tend to use a contact signing. The amount of English and ASL in contact signing is dependent on the deaf person who is using it and to his or her conversational partner (see Paul, 2009, for a complete description of these sign codes). Research has shown that these sign codes are better than monolingual approaches or speech-alone, but these codes have not resulted in gains in English language literacy because these codes mix the two languages (ASL and English) so the child does not get a full representation of either language. In addition, teachers often drop morphemic endings and markers so the child does not "see" these grammatical forms (see reviews by Johnson, Liddell, & Erting, 1989, and Paul, 2009).

Speech. The spoken language of deaf and hard of hearing children is delayed compared to hearing children despite years of intensive speech training (Blamey, 2003). Speech production abilities of deaf children with cochlear implants, a medical treatment for profound deafness, have shown increases by researchers and clinicians; but there is an enormous variability in success rates and much depends on factors such as age of implantation, auditory memory, family support and intensive speech therapy. Deaf children with implants present scientists with a unique clinical population to study brain plasticity and neural reorganization after auditory deprivation and delayed language development (Pisoni et al., 2008).

Speechreading or lipreading. This is the ability to recognize speech on the lips of the speaker. As a communication mode for young children, it is impossible to learn language in this way because children have yet to internalize the rules of English (Vernon & Andrews, 1990). Students and adults who are postlingually deaf have a better chance at lipreading because they already have language. However, factors such as eye fatigue, facial hair, lighting, foreign and regional accents make lipreading extremely difficult even for the person who already has learned English (Vernon & Andrews, 1990).

Fingerspelling. Fingerspelling or the manual alphabet provides 26 manual handshapes that represent the 26 letters of the English alphabet. To use fingerspelling effectively, you must know how to spell the word in English. Fingerspelling is used with ASL when a sign does not exist for a word or a proper noun is used. It is used also when codeswitching from ASL to English. Fingerspelling can be learned fairly rapidly by hearing adults in a few hours. As a language teaching method for young deaf children, fingerspelling has limitations because the child does not know English (Vernon & Andrews, 1990).

When speech is combined with fingerspelling, this is called the Rochester method, and it was popular in schools for the deaf in the 1970s.Young children are able to learn fingerspelling as young as age 3 but they learn short fingerspelled words as gestalt wholes or as signs (Vernon & Andrews, 1990). Later, as deaf children develop reading skills, they learn to break words down into fingerspelled handshapes (Andrews & Mason, 1986). Just because they fingerspell a word, however, does not mean they comprehend it. Young deaf readers may use fingerspelling as a placeholder for words they do not know (Ewoldt, 1981).

Cued Speech. Cued Speech is an approach made of up visual handshapes and hand cues or positions around the mouth for purposes of making the spoken sounds of English visible to the deaf student (Cornett, 1967). It is used chiefly with hard of hearing children and in some reading programs for deaf students (Andrews et al., 2004).

Reading and Writing. For hearing children, reading and writing (literacy) share underlying processes (Adams, 1990). A common myth is that deaf people can rely on reading and writing for communication with hearing persons who do not use sign language. This is not always true. A deaf person may be able to use texting on a cell phone quite well for social purposes but may be unable to write a cogent essay containing abstract concepts. English written language samples of deaf students do not reflect their language proficiency in sign language. In fact, numerous reviews of studies have shown the average performance on tests of reading and writing comprehension for students who are deaf and hard of hearing at age 15 is six grades lower than hearing peers (or at the third- or fourth-grade reading level; Traxler, 2000; Trezek, Wang, & Paul, 2010).

A combination of factors related to etiology and environment and instructional practices can cause reading and language disabilities (LaVigne & Vernon, 2003; Trezek et al., 2010). At one end of the spectrum are the 10% of college-aged deaf adults who are linguistically competent who can read at a tenth-grade or above level. These individuals achieved proficiency in both ASL and English after leaving high school, in spite of their weak pedagogical experiences (Andrews & Karlin, 2002). About 30% are *linguistically incompetent* with weak skills in both ASL and English (LaVigne & Vernon, 2003). Linguistic incompetence is also termed "semi-lingual" or "low-language functioning" and refers to extreme cognitive deprivation, a reading grade-level of 2.8, and weak skills in ASL. In the middle are approximately 60% of children who are deaf and graduating from high school and reading at a fourth-grade level or less (Traxler, 2000; Trezek et al., 2010).

Why is reading and writing so difficult for deaf learners? Reading is matching speech with print and involves a complex set of skills involving perception (see the print), cognition (i.e., logical reasoning, background knowledge, knowledge of concepts, memory), social skills (i.e., theory of mind), and language skills (i.e., phonology, semantics, syntax, and pragmatics or discourse; Trezek et al., 2010). Children who are deaf without ability to use the phonological component cannot decode new words, and this is a major obstacle in learning to read and developing reading skills (Trezek et al., 2010).

Many signing deaf children bypass the phonological system and learn to read visually (see reviews by Chamberlain & Mayberry, 2000; Ewoldt, 1981). Indeed, retrospective research with bilingual, literate deaf adults have reported the use of sign language to mediate print in reading comprehension (Andrews & Karlin, 2002; Andrews & Mason, 1991). Still the reading process of signing deaf children is not understood and needs more research because the linguistic structures of ASL and English are so fundamentally different, it is difficult for many deaf students to transfer meaning from one language to the other without explicit instruction through ASL/English bilingual language teaching approaches (Andrews & Rusher, 2010).

Signing deaf children mix, borrow, and transfer elements of their ASL and English into a kind of codemixing or codeblending within and across languages during the reading comprehension process as well as during the writing process. This is partly an artifact of teaching methodology as hearing teachers typically use a Simultaneous Communication approach or Total communication philosophy when teaching deaf children to read texts. But this language mixing is also part of deaf students' progress as an emerging bilingual person (Andews & Rusher, 2010). They mix and blend the two languages because they have not fully internalized either the rules of English or the rules of ASL. Deaf students' writing contains many errors related to morpheme development and grammar (see reviews by Paul, 2009).

Other studies show how signing can be used to support the reading and writing of students who are deaf (Simms, Andrews, & Smith, 2005). Even though researchers have found that signing supports the reading of English print, we still do not fully understand this process nor do we know whether invented visual systems (i.e., Cued speech, visual phonics) are better or worse than using the natural signing of the deaf community (i.e., ASL, fingerpelling; Trezek et al., 2010).

In the best case scenario, children who are deaf, from infancy to adulthood can be encouraged to be bimodal and bilingual. They can develop early communication with their families, develop cognitive and social skills and, generally, flexibly move back and forth between the two languages and two cultures throughout the lifespan (Grosjean, 2008).

For example, with deaf peers they can use ASL. With their hearing parents, hearing siblings and friends they can use ASL or signed English or speech, lipreading, reading and writing, or a combination of these. Having both avenues open has its practical side too. The child can codeswitch to ASL when their digital hearing aid and/or speech processor of the cochlear implant has dead batteries or when auditory appliances malfunction, or simply during everyday routines when technology devices cannot be used, such as in the bath tub, shower, at the swimming pool or beach, while playing contact sports, and so on.

Academic Achievement

Taking into account etiologies in combination with society's reaction to deafness, students who are deaf are vulnerable to cognitive deprivation and lack of language exposure at home and at school, all of which lead to low English literacy and general overall academic achievement (Anitia, Jones, Reed, & Kreimeyer, 2009; Karchmer & Mitchell, 2003).

In a 5-year longitudinal study of 197 deaf or hard of hearing children in general education classrooms for at least two or more hours per day, researchers found that the majority of the students scored in the average or above average range and made one or more years of annual progress on standardized measures of math, reading, language/writing compared to hearing peers (Anitia et al., 2009). Even though reading comprehension scores were in the low average range, they were closer to closing the performance gap with hearing students than deaf students discussed above in the Karchmer and Mitchell (2003) study. Access to the general education curriculum, family, teacher, and peer support all may have contributed to these students' gains (Anitia et al., 2009). Both studies point out that even students with mild to moderate losses were at risk for low academic achievement, particularly in the area of reading comprehension.

Behavioral Problems: Aggression, Violence, Sexual Abuse

School administrators encounter student behaviors such as oppositional defiant disorders, sexual harassment, sexting (sending pornographic messages and pictures), misconduct, gang activity, bullying, assault, violence, possession of drugs/alcohol, possession of knives and firearms, theft, arson, bomb threat, and criminal damage (Jernigan, 2010). Administrators often have little recourse but to call the police. Such actions set up a "school-to-drop out-to-prison-pipeline" (Civil Rights Project, 2003). It can also open up costly lawsuits against school districts that do not provide programming for deaf students (Easterbrooks, Lytle, Sheets, & Crook, 2004), as well as lawsuits against prisons and juvenile corrections facilities that do not provide due process, protections, and services as mandated by the American with Disabilities Act (Vernon, 2009).

Prior to the passage of Public Law 94-142, students who were deaf were primarily educated in large residential schools for the deaf. However, since 1975 there has been a migration of deaf students from residential schools for the deaf to local public schools. Moores (1987) identified an 18.3% drop in enrollment in public residential schools and a 69% drop in enrolment in private residential schools for the deaf between 1974 and 1984. Today, approximately 85% of children who are deaf or hard of hearing are educated in public school programs with 43% spending most of the school day in general education classrooms (Karchmer & Mitchell, 2003). With this migration has come the need for increased numbers of teachers to serve deaf students in public schools. However, essential student support services such as counseling, available and accessible at the residential schools, has not surfaced in public schools. Furthermore, students are often prone to communication problems at home as most parents are not skilled at using sign language. These factors have coalesced to form unique behavioral challenges for public schools.

Researchers in the United States and in England have reported that youth who are deaf are prone to emotional and behavioral problems including physical aggression, verbal aggression, non-compliance, temper outbursts, property destruction, leaving essential areas, and sexually inappropriate behaviors (Edwards & Crocker, 2008). In a classic study on socio-emotional development, Schlesinger and Meadow (1972) reported that 11.6% of the 516 deaf and hard of hearing students in their study were severely emotionally disturbed and in need of psychiatric intervention. Furthermore, they found an additional 19.6% of the students had lesser but significant emotional problems. These numbers are at least five times the rate reported for hearing students (Vernon & Andrews, 1990). In another classic study (Gentile & McCarthy, 1973) of more than 42,000 students who were deaf or hard of hearing, 18.9% had emotional or behavioral problems. More recent authorities (Moores, 1987; Sullivan & Knutson, 1998) point to possible flaws in the prior studies, implying that psychological problems among deaf students occur at the same rate as their hearing counterparts. Although these findings appear mixed, there are recent sources (Willis & Vernon, 2002) that indicate the disproportionately high number of deaf students with behavior problems remains true today.

Sources appear to point to placement in public schools as a source of psychological and socio-emotional distress for deaf students, in addition to the lack of certified teachers of the deaf, and an environment not sensitive to deaf culture. Academic and psychological growth is predicated on one's participation in a communication-rich environment. Without a critical mass of peers and adults who are deaf, students will not have the necessary academic or social and emotional opportunities to foster their development in a manner equal to their hearing peers (Siegel, 2008). For deaf students with few or no deaf peers and adults with whom they can communicate are cut off from others and may not learn how to handle themselves with people who have various personalities. Perhaps this point is best illustrated by Johnson (2004) who stated, "It can be argued that the essential problem of deafness is not the lack of hearing but an abundance of isolation" (p. 76).

Cytomegalovirus (CMV), one of today's leading causes of deafness can lead to children with shorter attention spans, impulse control issues, and a low tolerance for delayed gratification (Hammerdinger & Hill 2005). Children who are deaf are frequently diagnosed with attention deficit hyperactivity disorders (ADHD), conduct disorders, oppositional defiant disorder, or depression and anxiety (Hammerdinger & Hill, 2005). Limited language can lead to increased frustration for the child who is deaf, the development of poor social skills, poor self-image, and the inability to community basic needs (Hammerdinger & Hill, 2005).

Students with disabilities may be at a higher risk for sexual harassment, both as the victim and the harasser (Kavale & Forness, 1996; Vernon & Miller, 2002). Students who are deaf and others with disabilities often lack insight into the use of appropriate social skills and how their actions affect social relationships (Gresham, 2002). Factors such as lack of spoken language, lack of social skills, and difficulties with relationships may feed into the increased risk of child abuse among children and youth who are deaf.

As a group, children with disabilities are approximately 1.8 times more likely to be abused than their nondisabled counterparts (Knutson, Johnson, & Sullivan, 2004). Numerous studies (Sullivan & Knutson, 1998) report higher rates of maltreatment among deaf children and youth. Additionally, Sullivan and Knutson found that 25.8% of their participants who were deaf or hard of hearing endured significantly more physical abuse than maltreated peers without disabilities. Children who are deaf experience abuse over a longer term likely because they have fewer sources for outcry. For example, a typically developing student can report abuse to anyone at school from the bus driver to the school nurse and the teachers or counselors. However, deaf students in public schools may see only one or two adults, a teacher and an interpreter fluent in sign language in a typical school day.

The large number of social and emotional obstacles that children and youth who are deaf face as they develop is certainly noteworthy. Although a correlation is not clear, it is interesting to note the numbers of youth who are deaf who exit the school system and enter the justice system. People who are deaf are overrepresented two to five times higher than they should be in prisons (Miller, 2002; Vernon, 2009). These findings appear to be consistent with a demographic report published by the American Speech Language Hearing Association. The report (Zingeser, 1995) found that up to 30% of the inmate population nationally has a hearing loss. A study by Iqbal, Dolan, and Monteiro (2004) found that in the United Kingdom sex offenders who are deaf were overrepresented when compared to their hearing counterparts. This overrepresentation of individuals who are deaf or hard of hearing in the criminal justice system should be cause for alarm among parents and professionals. The implications of prelingual hearing loss on the cognitive, social, and emotional behavior may be devastating if not addressed while children are young.

Assessment

Psychological Assessment

Psychological testing of children who are deaf has significant ramifications and should be done only by trained professionals and interpreted by an individual who has native language fluency in ASL. Psychological and educational examination is an essential function under special education law. In the case of students with hearing loss, the use of interpreters is clearly not the desired scenario. Clearly, the desired scenario is to have an evaluator whose first or second language is ASL and who is knowledgeable about deafness. However, there continues to be a paucity of evaluators who meet these criteria. Therefore, many school-based evaluators rely on their training to address this issue. Although they are generally well-meaning, their results are frequently flawed, leading to misdiagnosis, inappropriate interventions, and a breakdown in the education system for youth who are deaf (Vernon & Andrews, 1990).

Most deafness-trained evaluators prefer to administer non-verbal tests when estimating the cognitive functioning of students with hearing loss. According to Brauer, Braden, Pollard, and Hardy-Braz (1998), the Wechsler Performance Scale (WISC) is the most common instrument used to measure cognition.

Maller and Braden (1993) assessed samples of children with hearing loss and determined the WISC to have good reliability. Examiners often administer the WISC and use those findings as an estimate of cognitive functioning. In some cases, examiners may choose to administer an instrument designed to be administered wholly non-verbally. However, many non-verbal instruments have verbal aspects that can influence test results. For example, some tests have instructions that must be read aloud, or others have complicated subtests that require explanations. Finally, it's essential that examiners realize that it *may* be inappropriate to administer verbal scales if the student has a mild hearing loss or is *late*-deafened.

Educational Assessment

Gaps in educational achievement of youth who are deaf or hard of hearing exist. Students who are deaf typically struggle in reading and writing. They tend to perform better in math and other courses that emphasize non-verbal skills. Many students with hearing loss excel in art and vocational trades. Teachers and other school personnel who are untrained in deafness sometimes mistake poor educational achievement for delayed cognition. However, the two constructs are separate and independent of each other. It is important to note that most students with hearing loss in public schools demonstrate average or higher cognitive functioning, in spite of their struggles with academic achievement (Brauer et al., 1998).

Achievement testing is riddled with complications related to hearing loss. Many achievement tests and subtests are invalid due to the nature of test administration. For example, a spelling subtest requires the examinee to have phonological awareness. If the examinee depends on a sign language interpreter, the examinee may be receiving unintended clues to spelling from the interpreter. Some words in ASL do not have specific signs. Instead, these words may be spelled or described by the interpreter. Examinees may be left confused as to what specific word they must spell. This is one example of the complexity of test administration with deaf youth. In addition, Holt, Traxler, and Allen (1992) point out that the Stanford Achievement Test has special norms so that deaf students can be compared with other deaf students. Many examiners administer other tests of academic achievement. For example, the Woodcock Johnson Test of Achievement and the Wechsler Individual Achievement Test are frequently administered. The examiner should note that results of many subtests are influenced by students' hearing loss and not by their cognitive ability.

Communication and Language Assessment

A comprehensive communication and language assessment of a child who is deaf should include the following: (a) a description of background variables that affect language learning such as age, age of onset, extent and type of hearing loss (audiogram provided by an audiologist), home communication and language, number of years using signing, former grade tests results from school IEP; (b) an assessment of speech intelligibility, speech production, and speech reading ability; (c) a reading assessment such as the Stanford Achievement Test-10, which has norms on children who are deaf, an informal reading inventory); (d) a free written language sample; (e) a test of grammar normed on students who are deaf, such as the Test of Syntactic Abilities (Quigley, Steinkemp, Power, & Jones, 1978); and (f) assessment of the sign language level (French, 1999). The assessment of ASL is a much needed but neglected area in deaf education because there are few ASL tests that teachers can administer to deaf children that are valid, reliable, and commercially available.

Educational Programming

Children and youth who are deaf are educated in a variety of settings from separate schools, to separate classrooms in public schools where they are partially included with hearing students, to the full inclusion model where they attend classes in the general education setting with hearing students (Andrews et al., 2004). One major advantage of the separate schools is that there is a critical mass of students who can be grouped according to age, ability level, and language level. Also, schools for students who are deaf have certified teachers who can sign and where instruction from the teacher to the student is direct. The disadvantage is that these are boarding schools and the child misses out on family life. The disadvantage of public schools is that students who are deaf may be isolated in small programs without a group of language peers. The advantage of the general education classroom is that the content may be appropriately challenging if it's accessible to the child and if the child is functioning on grade level. The disadvantage is that instruction is not directly from the teacher to the student but through an educational interpreter. The educational interpreter may lack certification and may be the child's only sign model (Yarger, 2001). Many children who are deaf suffer isolation and social rejection in the mainstream and public school settings even though the academic content may be appropriately challenging (Sheridan, 2001, 2008).

Birth to 3 Years

There are a variety of parent-infant programs available for babies and toddlers who are deaf, from home visits by an early childhood educator specialist to attendance at a clinic or school for the deaf for several hours during several days of the week. The early childhood programming is for children under the age of 3 years and is based on the Individual Family Service Plan (IFSP) of IDEA, which documents the child's present level of communication and outlines the major outcomes that the family desires for their child.

It is important to note that pediatricians may see fewer than 12 infants who are deaf in their careers. Thus they rely on referrals principally to the audiologists. It is important that audiologists provide families with all communication, language and placement options in a non-biased manner (Andrews & Dionne, 2008).

Preschool: 3 to 5 Years

In deaf education, the least restrictive environment (LRE) is often mistakenly defined as an environment where children are educated with non-disabled or hearing peers. IDEA was reauthorized in 2004 as Public Law 108-446 and was designed to dovetail its provisions with the 2001 No Child Left Behind Act which mandated state assessments, and provisions for "highly qualified teachers." The National Association for the Deaf, the National Agenda professionals, and the professionals of the Deaf Education Project have come out against the idea that LRE means schooling with hearing children. These groups all support the notion of the "continuum of service placements," which includes state schools for the deaf (Siegel, 2008).

In a recent survey of schools in 49 states, 65% of the states required that the local educational agency (LEA) be the first choice (LRE) or starting point before allowing placement at a center school (e.g., residential school for the deaf). About 30% allowed the parent to make the choice on school placement (Shaw, 2009). The advantage of having the LEA be the first choice is to keep the child near home. The disadvantage is that the child may be the only child who is deaf in the school district if it is in a rural area, or the child may be placed in a special education class with students who are deaf who are cognitively and language delayed. The advantage of having the parents make the choice is that they can participate in the decision making. The disadvantage is if the parents do not receive adequate information on placement and communication options, they could make decisions that are not in the best interest of the child.

Elementary and Junior High

When children who are deaf leave preschool, they are often not ready to learn to read because they do not have a strong language based in signing or in English. At about the third or fourth grade, social studies, science education, and math word problems add complexity to the language learning for deaf students. Science education is particularly challenging because not only do students need to learn concepts, but they need to know the abstract language involved in these concepts (Andrews, Gentry, DeLana, & Cocke, 2006). Researchers have similarly shown that math word problems constitute difficulty for students who are deaf (Pagliaro & Ansell, 2002). Students who use interpreters in school, termed "mediated instruction" are at a disadvantage because they do not get direct instruction from a teacher (Siegel, 2008). This can be problematic for not only the child's learning, but also for the child's motivation to learn (Siegel, 2008).

Secondary School

Many youth who are deaf transfer to residential school during the high school years because of the social benefits of being in a school with a larger number of peers. Some transfer for other reasons such as poor reading skills, behavior problems, or even for the purposes of playing sports. For those who stay in public high schools, the content and information load increases. If they are included in the general education classroom with an educational interpreter, they often struggle with keeping up with the content and may have difficulty reading their textbooks.

Because of earlier language gaps and deficiencies, many times the high school student who is deaf functions on a third- or fourth-grade reading level so that student cannot read the textbooks. With the proper support services, high school content material can be accessed by such students but only when the materials are broken down into concepts that they can understand and background knowledge deficits are acknowledged.

For those students who are mainstreamed into hearing classrooms, many will require tutors and educational interpreters who also function as co-teachers. Only about 30% of students who are deaf graduate with a high school diploma. The majority get certificates of attendance and attend a postsecondary technical school or community college to take remedial courses. There are increasing numbers of youth who are deaf leaving the public school and going to the residential school for independent living skills and reading skills at 18 years of age.

Transition to Postsecondary, Training or Employment

As students who are deaf leave high school, they transition to postsecondary school, training, or employment. Although more than 30,000 students who are deaf enroll in postsecondary programs, only about 25% graduate (Marschark & Hauser, 2008). There are many complex factors related to this low graduation rate, from lack of support services to assumptions that sign language interpretation and real-time text compensate for deaf students' lack of background knowledge and language deficits.

Today, there has been a decrease in vocational rehabilitation services with an increase in direct services through outreach programs. Legislation such as Section 504 of the Rehabilitative Act of 1973 requires that accommodations be in place in postsecondary programs, training, and at the workplace. IDEA has authorized the PEPnet project (n.d.), a four-state consortium to provide information to postsecondary programs about transition for students who are deaf.

There are approximately 30,000 students who are deaf attending colleges and universities in the United States today. Gallaudet University, the National Technical Institute of the Deaf, and Southwest Collegiate Institute for the deaf are three of the largest postsecondary programs and have multiple support services in place, including oral and ASL interpreting, CART (computer-assisted real time captioning), and notetaking. Research shows that postsecondary students who are deaf have a difficult time attending to sign language interpreting, CART, watching a Powerpoint presentation, reading the blackboard, and lipreading the instructor (Marschark et al., 2006). Deaf students prefer to have a signing instructor who is knowledgeable about visual ways of teaching and sensitive to deaf culture (Lang, 2002). The Americans With Disabilities Act (ADA, 1990) extends the protections for support services supplied by IDEA in K–12 and Section 504 of the Rehabilitation Act for the provisions that remove barriers to effective communication for the student who is deaf. There are also specialized transition programs for students with special needs such as cognitive delays, autism, and deaf-blindness (Ingraham, 2007). There are numerous kinds of technologies available for deaf-blind adults related to Braille readers on computers, print enlargers, print to voice software, and so on.

Trends and Issues

Technology Trends

Although advances in auditory and visual technologies have virtually changed the landscape of children's world today, it is important to note that support services for students and adults who are deaf are necessary throughout the lifespan. For example, a deaf person may need a sign language interpreter during a college lecture (Marschark et al., 2006), a theater performance (Kilpatrick & Andrews, 2009), or during a courtroom trial (LaVigne & Vernon, 2003).

The cochlear implant is the most popular and expensive medical intervention for children who are deaf. There are approximately 160,000 persons with cochlear implants worldwide (Nussbaum, 2009). The cochlear implant is a prosthetic device that includes an external package made up of a microphone and a speech processor. And it has an internal package of an array of electrodes that are surgically implanted into the cochlea in the inner ear. The external and internal packages are connected through magnetic coupling. The cochlear implant bypasses the 8th auditory nerve and stimulates the nerve to provide a sensation of sound (Stach, 2010).

Cochlear implants have provided access to sound to many children who are deaf and many have shown positive results in speech production, language, and reading (Pisoni et al., 2008). However, it is important to note that family support, resources for frequent mappings (every 6 months), batteries, maintenance, and additional speech therapy are necessary for the success of the implant. The effectiveness for cochlear implants for children varies widely depending on auditory memory, family support, age of implantation, resources of the family, nature, intensity and kind of speech therapy, and presence of additional disabilities (Christensen & Leigh, 2002). Most will still need support, such as sign interpreters, notetakers, deaf education teachers, tutors, and text-based captioning in class.

Research from early intervention studies shows that when signs are introduced to babies with cochlear implants, vocabulary acquisition is accelerated. Speech skills "piggyback" on these sign language vocabularies (Yoshinaga-Itano, 2003). Other researchers have found that the brain has the capacity to learn two languages from birth. Results from brain imaging studies suggest that the brain can readily handle dual language development, bimodal and bilingually (Kovelman et al., 2009).

Visual technologies such as the videophone, text messaging, email, multimedia materials presenting stories in three languages (e.g., ASL, English, and Spanish), signing avatars, and vlogs have increased both communication and learning of children who are deaf. In the future, we will see hand-held videophones which will provide even more access to information for students who are deaf.

School Administration

In the next decade, one third of the teaching and leadership force will be retiring from schools and universities in deaf education (Andrews & Covell, 2006). There will be a leadership void in administrators who have training in deaf education if more are not trained, particularly those who are deaf or from minority backgrounds (Simms, Rusher, Andrews & Coryell, 2008).

Cost Effectiveness

Schools for the deaf are being threatened with closure or combined with other special needs populations such as blind, autistic, developmentally delayed, or children with multiple disabilities. Listening device technology, CART, sign language interpreters, psychological services, comprehensive education, after school activities, autism specialists, behavioral specialists are costly. Furthermore, there is a growing number of youth who are deaf who are rejected by state schools because the schools are neither equipped nor staffed to serve them because these children and youth require medical and psychiatric care at a residential treatment center (RTC; Willis & Vernon, 2002).

It is a superintendent's nightmare when legislatures divide the total budget allocated by the state with the number of students enrolled. For instance, such calculations obfuscate the important services the state school provides, such as trained teachers, psychologists, and social workers who are familiar with deaf culture and can communicate with children who are deaf, as well as comprehensive programming (i.e., academic, sports, vocational programs).

Education costs are spiraling upward like health costs. Who pays? In a survey of 49 states, it was found that 90% or more of the programs received their funding directly from the state legislature. Of these programs, 26 of them had private foundations that also supplement the school's income to provide scholarships, trips, and other benefits to students (Shaw, 2009). Some state schools are funded by a general revenue fund, federal grants, appropriations from the state education agencies for serving children that a particular school district cannot support, plus extra monies from Medicaid and other federal reimbursements. Budgets at schools for the deaf are typically dedicated to about 90% to 95% to staffing. Their discretionary funding for other operations related to academics, vocational, assessment, and other programming such as special reading programs, and programs for autistic children is severely restricted. State schools for the deaf generally have 50% or more of students who enter the school at age 11 when they have failed to develop reading and language in their home public school or have severe acting out behaviors due to limited communication at home and at school. Schools often must accept children who are deaf who are medically fragile and need one-to-one-care, who have cognitive disabilities, autism, emotional and behavioral disorders, who are victims of sexual abuse, in addition to youths from juvenile correction agencies, in foster care, and the like. The reality is that the need for deaf services is "breaking the system" economically, and there is no easy solution.

Public schools with classes for students who are deaf may have more options for funding, which may on the surface appear as an advantage. However, school costs may be even higher in public schools because students who are deaf are not centralized in one location as they are in residential schools where there is often duplication of services. LEAs can go to the taxpayers and request adding funds through taxation procedures if a certain school district needs more money. Alternative models for school programming for children who are deaf, such as private schools or charter schools, are also options.

School Counseling and Student Discipline

We recommend centralized availability of mental health counseling services for students who are deaf because some may be at risk for substance abuse, sexual abuse, depression, anxiety, and other disorders brought on by lack of communication in their environments (Vernon & Miller,

TABLE 19.3
Major Genetic Syndromes, Descriptions and Other Disabilities

Types	Description	Other disabilities
Alport syndrome	Caused by X-linked inheritance	Progressive kidney disease
Branchial-Oto-Renal Syndrome (BOR)	Autosomal disorder	Branchial clefts, fistulas, cysts, renal malformation
Cervico-ocolo-acoustic syndrome	Congential branchial arch syndrome occurring mostly in females	Fusion of two or more cervical vertebrae, retraction of eyeballs, lateral gaze weakness
CHARGE association	Five associated syndromes: C (coloboma), H (hearing disease), A (atresia choanae), R (retarded growth), G (genital hypoplasia), and E (ear anomalies.	coloboma (structural defect in the retina, iris, or other tissue of the eye, hearing disease, atreasia choanae (nasal cavity), retarded growth, and development and genital hypoplasia (failure to grow or develop), and ear anomalies
Jervell and Lange-Neilsen Syndrome	Autosomal recessive	Cardiovascular disorders, goiter disorders
Neurofibromatosis Type 2 (NF-2)	Autosomal dominant	Cochlevestibular and other intercranial tumors, disturbance in balance and walking, dizziness, tinnitus
Pendred Syndrome	Autosomal recessive	Endrocrine metabolism disorder, goiter disorders
Stickler-Syndrome (SS)	Autosomal recessive	Flattening of facial profile, cleft palate, vision problems, musculoskeletal and joint problems occurring over time, mitral valve prolapsed
Treacher-Collins Syndrome	Dominant inherited	Conductive bone hearing loss, malformations of external ear, downward sloping of eyes, flat cheekbones, other facial features
Usher Syndrome	Autosomal recessive	Cause of deaf-blindness, Progressive vision loss due to retinitis pigmentosa, three forms (Type 1, Type II, and Type III.
Waardenburg Syndrome	Autosomal dominant	Lateral displacement of medial canthi, increased width of root of the nose, multicolored iris, white forelock

Source: Vernon, 1969, Vernon & Andrews, 1990, Staht, 2010; Andrews Leigh, and Weiner, 2004.

2002). Both the Transforming School Counseling movement and the American School Counselor Association (ASCA) have developed materials to better clarify the role of school counselors (Chen-Hayes & Ramos, 2004). Although a thorough review of those documents are beyond the scope of this chapter, one common thread is that school counselors should find ways to reach *all* students on their campuses.

The school counselors of today must become collaborators, planners, and consultants. Instead of trying to set up school-based counseling services for students who are deaf, the school counselor might contact the school administration or outside agencies to identify a particular individual who can come to campus and provide the counseling services in sign language. In this example, the students would have their needs met by another provider who is working collaboratively with the school counselor. In ideal conditions, students who are deaf from near-by school districts would be clustered together to develop one centralized deaf education program. This program should offer an array of educational services, including support services, in the language of the students. Due to a number of counseling needs, school-based counseling in sign language would be available to all students via a signing counselor hired by the centralized deaf education program. The ASCA model would be implemented by both the building counselor and the consultant serving students who are deaf. This type of approach is also congruent with the Transforming School Counseling model as it endorses the use of qualified others to work collaboratively with the building counselor (Chen-Hayes & Ramos, 2004). Implementing counseling and behavioral management programs could substitute for expulsion.

Clearly, new models of schools for deaf education are needed today to address their dual language needs, comorbid disabilities, psychological, social and behavioral disorders, their technology needs including cochlear implantation, their use of visual technology (i.e. texting, multimedia, internet, videophones, v-logs), the use of educational interpreters, the need for sexuality education and counseling, vocational and career counseling, postsecondary education, and the need for qualified and certified teachers of the deaf.

References

Adams, M. (1990). *Beginning to read: Thinking and learning about print.* Cambridge, MA: MIT Press.

American Speech Language-Hearing Association. (2005). *Guidelines for manual pure-tone threshold audiometry.* Retrieved from http://www.asha.org/policy

Americans with Disabilities Act of 1990 (ADA), 42 U.S.C. §§ 12101-12213 (2000).

Andrews, J., & Covell, J. (2006). Preparing future teachers and doctoral level leaders in deaf education: Meeting the challenge. *American Annals of the Deaf, 151*(6), 464–475.

Andrews, J., & Dionne, V. (2008). Audiology & deaf education. Preparing the next generation of professionals. *ADVANCE for Speech-Language Pathologists & Audiologists. 18*(18), 10–13.

Andrews, J., Gentry, M., DeLana, M., & Cocke, D. (2006). Bilingual students—Deaf and hearing: Learn about science: Using visual strategies, technology and culture. *The Language Learner*, *2*(2), 5–7, 10.

Andrews, J., & Karlin, A. (2002). Reading behaviors of deaf bilingual college students. *ADARA, 36*(1), 28–44.

Andrews, J., Leigh, I., & Weiner, M. (2004). *Deaf people: Evolving perspectives in psychology, education and sociology.* Boston, MA: Allyn and Bacon.

Andrews, J., Logan, R., & Phelan, J. (2008, Jaunuary 14). Language milestones for speech, hearing and ASL. *ADVANCE for Speech-Language Pathologists & Audiologists. 18*(2), 16–20.

Andrews, J., & Lokensgard, L. (2007). Deaf artists in visual arts. National Endowment of the Arts (NEA) Grant Awarded to Lamar University, Beaumont, TX.

Andrews, J. F. , & Mason, J. M. (1986). How do deaf children learn about prereading? *American Annals of the Deaf*, *131*, 210–217.

Andrews, J. F., & Mason, J. M. (1991). Strategy use among deaf and hearing readers. *Exceptional Children*, *57*(6), 536–545.

Andrews, J., & Rusher, M. (2010). *Codeswitching techniques: Evidence-based practices for the ASL/English bilingual classroom.* Unpublished manuscript.

Anitia, S., Jones, P., Reed, S., & Kreimeyer, K. (2009). Academic status and progress of deaf and hard of hearing students in general education Classrooms. *Journal of Deaf Studies and Deaf Education*, *14*(3), 293–311.

Blamey, P. (2003). Development of spoken language by deaf children. In M. Marschark & E. Spencer (Eds.). *Deaf studies, language and education* (pp. 232–243). New York: Oxford University Press.

Brauer, B. A. , Braden, J. P., Pollard, R. Q., & Hardy-Braz, S. T. (1998). Deaf and hard of hearing people. In *Test interpretation and diversity: Achieving equity in psychological assessment.* Washington, D.C.: American Psychological Association.

Brown, A. S. (2009). Intervention, education, and therapy for children who are deaf and hard of hearing. In J. Katz, L. Medwetsky, R. Burkard, & L. Hood (Eds.). *Handbook of clinical audiology* (6th ed., pp. 934–954). Philadelphia, PA: Lippincott Williams & Wilkins.

Cannon, J., Frederick, L., & Easterbrooks, S. (2010). Vocabulary instruction through books read in American Sign Language for English-language learners with hearing loss. *Communications Disorders Quarterly*, *31*(2), 98–112.

Chamberlain, C., & Mayberry, R. (2000). Theorizing about the relation between American Sign Language and reading. In C. Chamberlain, J. Moford, & R. Mayberry (Eds.), *Language acquisition by eye* (pp. 221–259). Mahwah, NJ: Erlbaum.

Chen-Hayes, S., & Ramos, I. (2004). The professional school counselor as resource and service broker. In B. T Erford (Ed.), *Professional school counseling: A handbook of theories, programs and practices* (pp. 865–869). Austin, TX: PRO-ED.

Christensen, J., & Leigh, I. (2002). *Cochlear implants in children: Ethics and choices.* Washington, D.C.: Gallaudet University Press.

Civil Rights Project. (2003). School to prison pipeline: Charting intervention strategies of prevention and support for minority children. Retrieved from http://www.civilrightsproject.harvard.edu

Cornett, O. (1967). Cued speech. *American Annals of the Deaf, 112*, 3–13.

Courtin, C., Melot, A., & Corroyer, D. (2008). Achieving efficient learning: Why understanding theory of mind is essential for deaf children and their teachers. In M. Marshark & P. Hauser (Eds.), *Deaf cognition: Foundations and outcomes* (pp. 102–130). New York: Oxford University Press.

Easterbrooks, S., Lytle, L., Sheets, P. & Crook, B. (2004). Ignoring free, appropriate, public education, a costly mistake: The case of F. M. & L. G. *Journal of Deaf Studies and Deaf Eduacation*, *9*(2), 219–226.

Edwards, L. & Crocker, S. (2008). *Psychological processes in deaf children with complex needs: An evidence-based practical guide.* Philadelphia: Jessica Kingsley.

Enns, C., & Lafond, L.D. (2007) Reading against all odds: A pilot study of two deaf students with dyslexia, *American Annals of the Deaf, 152*, 63–72.

Ewoldt, C. (1981). A psycholinguistic description of selected deaf children reading in sign language. *Reading Research Quarterly*, *XVII*, 58–89.

French, M. (1999). *Starting with assessment: A developmental approach to deaf children's literacy.* Washington, D.C.: Pre-College National Mission Programs.

Gallaudet Research Institute. (2008, November). *Regional and national summary report of data from the 2007–2008 annual survey of deaf and hard of hearing children and youth.* Washington, D.C.: Author.

Gentile, A., & McCarthy, B. (1973). Additional handicapping conditions among hearing impaired students, United States, 1971–1972. In Vernon, M. & Andrews, J. F. (Eds.), *The psychology of deafness* (pp. 147–148). New York: Longman Press.

Goldin-Meadow, S. (2003). *Hearing gesture: How our hands help us think.* Cambridge, MA: Harvard University Press.

Gresham, F. M. (2002). Social skills assessment and instruction for students with emotional and behavioral disorders. In K. L. Lane, F. M. Gresham, & T. E. O'Shaughnessy (Eds.), *Interventions for children with or at risk for emotional and behavioral disorders* (pp. 242–258). Boston: Allyn & Bacon.

Grosjean, F. (2008). *Studying bilinguals.* New York: Oxford University Press.

Hammerdinger, S., & Hill, E. (2005). Serving severely emotionally disturbed deaf youth: A statewide program model. *JADARA*, *38*(3), 3–30.

Holt, J. A. Traxler, C. B. & Allen, T. (1992). *Interpreting the scores: A user's guide to the 8th edition Stanford Achievement Test for educators of deaf and hard of hearing students.* Washington, D.C.: Gallaudet Research Institute.

Ingraham, C. (2007).What does it mean to be deafblind — really? In C. L. Ingraham (Ed.), *Transition planning for students who are deafblind.* Knoxville, TN: PEPNet-South. Retrieved from http://pdcorder.pepnet.org/media/1218%20DeafBlind07/deafblind07/chapter%20two.pdf

Iqbal, S., Dolan, M. C., & Monteiro, B. T. (2004). Characteristics of deaf sexual offenders referred to a specialist mental health unit in the UK. *Journal of Forensic Psychiatry and Psychology, 15*, 494–510.

Jernigan, J. (2010). *Risk factors and aggressive behaviors of deaf males: A longitudinal study.* Unpublished manuscript.

Johnson, H. A. (2004). U.S. deaf education teacher preparation programs: A look at the present and a vision for the future. *American Annals of the Deaf, 149*, 75–91.

Johnson, R., Liddell, S., & Erting, C. (1989). *Unlocking the curriculum: Principles for achieving access in deaf education.* Research Working Paper 89-3, Washington, D.C.: Gallaudet Institute.

Karchmer, M., & Mitchell, R. (2003). Demographic and achievement characteristics of deaf and hard of hearing children. In M. Marschark & P. Spencer (Eds.), *Deaf studies, language, and education* (pp. 21–37). New York: Oxford University Press.

Kavale, K. A., & Forness, S. (1996). Social skills deficits and learning disabilities: A meta-analysis. *Journal of Learning Disabilities, 29*, 226–238.

Keary, D., Eavey, R., & Mehra, S. (2009, April). The epidemiologiy of hearing impairment in the United States: Newborns, children and adolescents. *Otolaryngology—Head and Neck Surgery 40*(4), 461–472.

Kilpatrick, B. & Andrews, J. (2009, Fall). Interpreting live theater for deaf and deafblind people: Legal, language, and artistic factors. *International Journal of Interpreter Education, 1,* 71–84.

Knutson, J. F., Johnson, C. R., & Sullivan, P. M. (2004). Disciplinary choices of mother of deaf children and mothers of normally hearing children. *Child Abuse and Neglect, 28*, 925–937.

Kovelman, I., Shalinsky, M., White, K., Schmitt, S., Berens, M., & Payner, N. (2009). Dual language use in sign-speech bimodal bilinguals. fNIRS brain-imaging evidence. *Brain and language*, *109*(2-3), 112–123.

Lang, H. (2002). Higher education for deaf students: Research priorities in the new millenium. *Journal of Deaf Studies and Deaf Education*, *7*(4), 267–280.

LaVigne, M., & Vernon, M. (2003). An interpreter is not enough: Deafness, language, and due process. *Wisconsin Law Journal, 5*, 843–935.

Leigh, I. (2009). *A lens of deaf identities.* New York: Oxford University Press.

Lucas, C., & Valli, C. (1992). *Language contact in American deaf community.* San Diego, CA: Academic Press.

Maller, S. ,& Braden, J. P. (1993). The criterion validity of the WISC-III with deaf adolescents. In B. A. Bracken & R. S. McCallum (Eds.), *Advances in psychoeducational assessment* (pp. 105–113). Brandon, VT: Psychology Press.

Mapp, I. (2004). *Essential readings on stress and coping among parents of deaf and hearing impaired children.* Lincoln: University of Nebraska Press: Gordian Knot Books.

Marschark, M., & Hauser, P. (2008). *Deaf cognition: Foundations and outcomes*. New York: Oxford University Press.

Marschark, M., Leigh, G., Sapere, P., Burnham, D., Converino, C., Stinson, M., … Noble, W. (2006). Benefits of sign language interpreting and text alternatives to classroom learning by deaf students. *Journal of Deaf Studies and Deaf Education, 11,* 421–437.

Mayberry, R., & Eichen, E. (1991). The long-lasting advantage of learning sign language in childhood: Another look at the critical period for language acquisition. *Journal of Memory, 30*(4), 486–512.

Meadow-Orlans, K., Spencer, P., & Koester, L. (2004). *The world of deaf Infants: A longitudinal study.* New York: Oxford University Press.

Mehra, S., Eavey, R. D., & Keamy, D. G. (2009). The epidemiology of hearing impairment in the United States: Newborns, children and adolescents. *Otolaryngology-Head and Neck Surgery. 140*, 461–472.

Miller, K. (2002). *Forensic issues of deaf offenders*. Unpublished doctoral dissertation, Lamar University, Beaumont, Texas.

Moeller, M. P. (2000). Early intervention and language development in children who are deaf and hard of hearing. *Pediatrics, 106*, E43.

Moores, D. (1987). *Educating the deaf: Psychology, principles, and practices* (3rd ed.). Boston: Houghton: Mifflin Press.

Moores, D. (2008). Research on Bi-Bi Instruction. Editorial. *American Annals of the Deaf, 153*(1), 3.

Newport, E. (1990). Maturational constraints on language learning. *Cognitive Science, 14*, 11–28.

Nover, S., Christensen, K., & Cheng, L. (1998). Development of ASL and English competencies for learners who are deaf. In K. Butler & P. Prinz (Eds.), ASL proficiency and English language acquisition: New perspectives [special issue]. *Topics in Language Disorders, 18*(4), 61–72.

Pagliaro, C., & Ansell, E. (2002). Story problems in the deaf education classroom: Frequency and mode of presentation. *Journal of Deaf Studies and Deaf Education, 7*(2), 107–119.

Paul, P. (2009). *Language and deafness* (4th ed.). Boston, MA: Jones & Bartlett.

PEPnet. (n.d.). A US Dept of Education sponsored project that provides training and support in postsecondary education for deaf and hard of hearing students. Retrieved February 17, 2010, from http://www.pepnet.org/about.asp

Peters, C. (2000). *Deaf American literature: From Carnival to Cannon.* Washington, D.C.: Gallaudet University Press.

Pisoni, D., Conway, C., Kronenberger, W., Horn, D., Karpicke, J., & Henning, S. (2008). Efficacy and effectiveness of cochlear implants in deaf children. In M. Marschark & P. Hauser (Eds.). *Deaf cognition: Foundations and outcomes* (pp. 52–101). New York: Oxford University Press.

Quigley, S., Steinkemp, M., Power, D., & Jones, M. (1978). *Test of syntactic abilities: Guide to administration and interpretation.* Austin, TX: PRO-ED.

Ross, D., Gaffney, M., Green, D., & Holstum, W. (2008). Prevalence and effects. *Seminars in Hearing, 29*(2), 141–148.

Schlesinger, H. S., & Meadow, K. R. (1972). *Sound and sign: Childhood deafness and mental health.* Berkeley: University of California Press.

Shaw, P. (2009). *Parent choice of education placement*. Unpublished data.

Sheridan, M. (2001). *Inner lives of deaf children: Interviews and analysis.* Washington, D.C.: Gallaudet University Press.

Sheridan, M. (2008). Deaf adolescents: *Inner lives and lifeworld development.* Washington, D.C.: Gallaudet University Press.

Siegel, L. (2008*). The human right to language: Communication Access for Deaf Children.* Washington, D.C.: Gallaudet University Press.

Simms, L., Andrews, J. & Smith, A. (2005). A balanced approach to literacy instruction for deaf signing students. *Balanced Reading Instruction, 12*, 39–54.

Simms, L., & Moers, L. (2010). *National early childhood American sign language and English bilingual project.* Washington, D.C.: Gallaudet University.

Simms, L., Rusher, M., Andrews, J. & Coryell, J. (2008). Apartheid in deaf education: Diversifying the workforce, *American Annals of the Deaf, 153*(4), 384–395.

Stach, B. (2010). *Clinical audiology: An introduction* (2nd ed.). Clifton Park, NY: Delmar.

Stokoe, W. (1960). *Sign language structure: An outline of visual communication systems of the American deaf.* Studies in Linguistics, Occasional Paper. Buffalo, NY: Studies in Linguistics.

Sullivan, P., & Knutson, J. F. (1998). Maltreatment and behavioral characteristics of youth who are deaf and hard of hearing. *Sexuality and Disability, 16*, 295–319.

Traxler, C. (2000). The Stanford Achievement Test, 9th edition: National norming and performance standards for deaf and hard of hearing students. *Journal of Deaf Studies and Deaf Education, 5*(4), 337–348.

Trezek, B., Wang, Y. & Paul, P. (2010). *Reading and deafness: Theory, research and practice.* Clifton Park, NY: Delmar Publishing.

Valli, C., & Lucas, C. (2000). *Linguistics of American sign language: An introduction* (3rd ed.), Washington, D.C.: Gallaudet University Press.

Vernon, M. (1969). *Multiply handicapped deaf children: Medical educational and psychological considerations.* Reston, VA: Council of Exceptional Children.

Vernon, M. (2009). ADA routinely violated by prisons in the case of deaf prisoners. *Prison Legal News, 20*(7), 14–15.

Vernon, M., & Andrews, J. (1990). *The psychology of the Ddeaf Understanding deaf and hard of hearing persons.* White Plains, NY: Longman.

Vernon, M., & Miller, K. (2002). Issues in the sexual molestation of deaf youth. *American Annals of the Deaf, 147*(5), 28–35.

Vernon, M., & Rhodes, A. (2009). Deafness and autistic spectrum disorders. *American Annals of the Deaf, 154*(1), 5–14.

White, K. & Munoz, K. (2008). Sereening. *Seminars in Hearing, 29*(2), 140–158.

Willis, W. G., & Vernon, M. (2002). Residential psychiatric treatment of emotionally disturbed deaf youth. *American Annals of the Deaf, 147*, 31–38.

Yarger, C. (2001). Educational interpreting: Understanding the rural experience. *American Annals of the Deaf, 146*(1), 16–30.

Yoshinaga-Itano, C. (2003). From screening to early identification and intervention: Discovering predictors to successful outcomes for children with significant hearing loss. *Journal of Deaf Studies and Deaf Education, 8*(1),11–30.

Yoshinaga-Itano, C., Sedey, A., Coulter, D., & Mehl, A. (1998). Language of early- and later-identified children with hearing loss. *Pediatrics, 102*(5), 1161–1171.

Zingeser, L. (1995). *Communication disorders and violence* (Technical information packet, item #0111978). Rockville, MD: American Speech Language Hearing Association.

20

Blindness and Low Vision

George J. Zimmerman
University of Pittsburgh

Kim T. Zebehazy
University of British Columbia

Seeing is a complex process that begins with the eye and ends in the brain. Of the 12 cranial nerves in the human body, one-third are devoted to vision. In order to see 20/20 with a typical field of view of 160–180 degrees, all parts of the eye and brain must be intact and function flawlessly. Even the slightest disruption (e.g., disease, trauma, inflammations) to any one of the parts of the eye or the brain will affect the student's ability to see clearly. The eyes serve the function of sensory receptors, similar to the sensory receptors located elsewhere on your body. Light rays entering the eye must pass through a very clear and practically dehydrated cornea in order to begin the internal journey through the rest of the eye. The rays bend and move through aqueous fluid in the front portion of the eye, squeeze through the iris, and then continue through the posterior cave-like portion of the eye, the vitreous chamber and eventually fall on the macula of the retina. But falling on the macula is only half the journey, for it is not only in the eyes where vision occurs. In striking the retina, the light rays cause a chemical disturbance which then converts to electrical synaptic energy. This synaptic energy then moves out the back portion of the eyes through the optic nerve to continue the journey to various regions and interpretation stations of the occipital cortex located in the lower back portion of the brain. When someone states that you must have eyes in the back of your head, they could not be more truthful because it is in the occipital cortex where vision or seeing occurs. With students whose vision is intact, this all takes place in a matter of milliseconds. Think of this complex process as you read this paragraph. As you are reading, you are shifting your gaze continually from left to right/right to left swiftly passing over every black image (letters/words) on this white background (page) while at the same time adjusting for uncontrolled variables such as changes in ambient light and glare, head or body movements away from or toward the page (or monitor), blinking, and even peripheral distractions such as reaching for and grasping your coffee mug without knocking it over (like I just did!), and you are most likely doing all this while sitting relatively still, not moving. Imagine now a more complex visual task such as driving or playing sports, where the world is continually moving around you and you have to react to these instantaneous changes visually in order to arrive at your destination safely or catch the ball without getting injured. The complexity of the visual task increases when movement occurs.

In this chapter we provide an overview of blindness and visual impairment and how each affects students in the educational setting. We introduce you to how the field uses terminology to define this low incidence population, as well as present information on some of the leading causes of blindness and visual impairment. We discuss the incidence of blindness and visual impairment in children and the discrepancies in how students who are blind or visually impaired are counted and represented nationally. We discuss the current trends and research in assessment and education of students with visual impairments, future trends and research in the areas of assessment, educational, and medical intervention, and highlight some of the latest therapies and treatments that show curable promise.

To understand the impact of vision loss and the effect that ocular pathology has on vision and learning, it is important to understand the anatomical and functional features of the visual process from the eye to the brain.

Anatomy and Function of the Eye

The eyeball is composed of three layers. The outer layer includes the cornea, which is the clear avascular tissue in the very front of the eye, and the sclera, which is the white fibrous tissue surrounding the rest of the eye. The cornea is the first surface that light rays strike and is responsible for approximately two-thirds of the refractive power of the eye. The middle layer of the eye is the vascular or pigmented layer referred to as the uveal tract. The uveal tract is composed of three parts; the choroid, ciliary body, and the iris. The lens is located in the same region of the ciliary body and is sometimes considered to be a part of the uveal tract. The choroid is the major blood supply to the eye. It provides the retina with the nutrients it needs to remain hydrated and clear. The choroid is the reason for the "red eye" you see on an individual in a photograph taken on a camera without red eye reduction. The iris is the colored diaphragm part located in the anterior portion of the eye. The purpose of the iris is to widen and narrow to control the amount of light entering the eye. The ciliary body is responsible for two functions. The first, which is done by the ciliary muscles, is to control the thickness of the lens so that when an object is viewed up close the muscles tighten the suspensory ligaments around the lens which allows the lens to become thick. Similarly, when an object is viewed at a distance, the ciliary muscles relax the suspensory ligaments allowing the lens to become thin. The second purpose of the ciliary body is to produce and secrete the fluid that nourishes the front portion of the eye, including the iris and the numbers layers of the corneal tissue.

The inner or neuronal layer of the eye is referred to as the retina. The retina contains three types of photoreceptor or nerve cells. The two largest types of photoreceptor cells are referred to as rods (approximately 120 million) and cones (approximately 6 million). These photoreceptor cells absorb light rays (electromagnetic radiation) which create a biochemical disturbance within each nerve cell causing synapse of the third type of cell, the ganglion photoreceptors. The approximately 1 and one-half million ganglion cells then send the signal via the optic nerve pathways to the occipital cortex of the brain. In the center of the retina is the macula. The macula is the tiny bowl shaped indentation in the retina where the vast majority of cone-shaped photoreceptors cells are housed. These cone-shaped photoreceptor cells adapt for visual clarity and allow for color vision. The macula is the area of clearest vision (20/20). As discussed earlier, if the light rays do not fall exactly on the macula because of refractive error (e.g., myopia), then vision is blurred. Students will need eyeglasses or contact lenses to correct for these refractive errors. The rest of the internal retina, which wraps around the inside of the eyeball, contains mostly rod-shaped photoreceptor cells (with few cone-shaped cells) that adapt for movement and light/dark adaptation. Ganglion photoreceptor cells are spread throughout the entire retinal surface. The importance of all three types of photoreceptor cells will become more apparent later in this chapter when discussing new experimental medical treatments (e.g., gene therapies) for correcting visual impairment and improving vision. In addition to the retina, the largest internal area of the eye, the vitreous chamber, which occupies 4/5 of the space of the eye, is filled with a gel-like fluid referred to as vitreous humor. The main purpose of the vitreous humor is to preserve the shape of the eyeball.

There are two optic nerves (one per eye) that comprise the visual system. Each optic nerve bundles millions of ganglion fibers from each retina and sends the electrical signals from the retina to a specific location in the occipital cortex. The optic nerves travel away from the back of each eyeball and enter the frontal portion of the brain where they cross over at the optic chiasm. The optic chiasm is located immediately above the pituitary gland. Here approximately half the cells from each eye are transferred to the optic nerve coming from the other eye, so half the nerves from the right eye are transferred to the left optic nerve and vice versa. After passing through the optic chiasm the nerves, which are now referred to as optic tracts, are moved onto the lateral geniculate body where they are further reassigned and now referred to as optical radiations. They are then sent to various locations within the occipital or visual cortex for further analysis and identification.

Some, but not all of the leading causes of blindness or visual impairment occur somewhere along the route that light takes as it enters the eye and is interpreted in the brain. The leading cause of poor vision when not corrected in students is refractive error, which occurs within the eye. The leading causes of visual impairment in children is cortical visual impairment and retinopathy of prematurity which, in the case of cortical visual impairment, occurs in the brain and in the case of retinopathy of prematurity occurs in the eye. A more complete explanation of these diagnoses is presented below. But how is vision measured to determine how a student might be defined as having a visual impairment?

Clinical Visual Assessment

An eye care specialist (either an ophthalmologist or optometrist who specializes in treatment of low vision) uses a variety of techniques and procedures to determine an individual's visual ability. As presented, typical distance visual acuity is 20/20, and a typical peripheral field of view is 160 to 180 degrees. The common method for determining visual acuity is through the use of an optotype eye chart. An optotype eye chart uses black-on-white letters or symbols of varying sizes to assess the vision of the individual. The classic optotype eye chart used most often is the Snellen chart. This chart, which contains 11 lines of black letters, is read by the student one eye at a time, typically from the top to bottom line. The smallest letters on the very bottom of the chart are designated as 20/15. The next row up which contains fewer letters is designated as the 20/20 line (typical vision) and so on to the top of the chart where only one large letter appears. This is usually the letter E. This top line is the 20/200 designation. The student with typical vision standing 20 feet away should be able to read all the lines from the top to the next to the bottom 20/20 line with no difficulty. If the 20/20 line is not read successfully, then the student moves up to the next line and so on until the student is capable of reading the letters successfully.

In the case of students who are visually impaired, being able to read the E on the top line of a Snellen chart may prove difficult because of the 20 foot distance. Adjustments can be made to shorten the distance between the student and the chart, which then is reflected on the eye report. For example, if the distance is shortened from 20 to 10 feet and the student reads the large E on the top line of the chart, the designation of 10/200 (20/400) is indicated on the student's eye report. For students with visual impairments who still have difficulty reading the Snellen eye chart even with a modified distance, an alternative would be to use other types of eye charts that have larger high contrast symbols or letters (up to 20/700). These charts were specifically designed for individuals who have a visual impairment.

As indicated above, the normal binocular field of view is 160 to 180 degrees. The standard clinical method for evaluating field of view or peripheral vision for older students and adults is through the use of an automated perimeter field test. This is a large concave bowl-shaped device in which the individual, while resting the chin and staring straight ahead one eye at a time at a light, presses a hand-held button when another light of varying intensity appears briefly anywhere inside the large circular bowl. This test is useful for measuring peripheral field function but it does not test central field vision. Certain visual pathologies are prone to vision loss within 20 to 45 degrees of the central retinal region and may not be detected through the use of the method described above for peripheral field testing. For students with visual impairments whose visual pathology is indicative of central field loss, both peripheral as well as central field vision loss must be evaluated.

Definition

Professionals in the field of visual impairment use approximately 25 different terms to describe blindness and vision loss of students who are visually impaired. There is no consensus on definitional terms such as blind, low vision, or visual impairment. They each have different meaning to different users for different purposes. The first section of this chapter is offered as a way to understand the various terms used when describing the population of students who are visually impaired.

Total blindness is clinically defined as no light perception or the inability to distinguish between light and dark. Individuals who are totally blind rely solely on supplemental sensory input other than vision to manage their education and rehabilitation needs. Bell and Siller (2002) estimates that only 10% of individuals with visual impairments are totally blind. *Light perception* is a term sometimes used in relation to total blindness to define a person's ability to distinguish between light and dark, but not the ability to determine shapes or forms of objects. *Visual impairment* is a common term that is used to define a wide range of vision loss. It is often used as a substitute for total blindness while also used when referring to levels of vision loss that are less severe. Visual impairment is a term that receives widespread acceptance particularly from those who believe that the term blind, which is no more descriptive than visual impairment, has a negative connotation. We shall use the term *visual impairment* or *visually impaired* throughout this chapter to refer to students who have vision loss other than total blindness.

The term *blind* has widespread use but its meaning is vague and often misused. It should be used to refer to individuals who are totally blind but it is not uncommon to hear the term used ubiquitously to refer to everyone who has vision loss. *Low vision* is another term used to describe vision loss and, like the terms blind or visual impairment, it too vaguely defines a level of visual ability that ranges from useful residual vision (sufficient enough to drive a motor vehicle with specialized corrective lenses) to severely visually impaired. The World Health Organization (2010), which uses a metric designation for recording visual acuity, clinically defines the term *low vision* as "visual acuity that is less than 6/18 (20/60), but equal to or better than 3/60 (20/400), or corresponding visual field loss to less than 20 degrees, in the better eye with best possible correction" but as indicated it is not uncommon to hear the term low vision used to describe the visual functioning of individuals who are visually impaired.

Legal blindness is a term that is used to describe a specific level of corrected visual acuity or degrees of peripheral field functioning. Legal blindness is defined as central visual acuity of 20/200 or less in the better eye after best possible standard correction, OR a visual field of view no greater than 20 degrees. In terms of the first half of the definition it means that a person who has 20/200 corrected visual acuity can be no more than 20 feet away from reading the large E on the top line of a standard vision screening eye chart, whereas a person with 20/20 vision can be 200 feet away and still see the large E clearly. The second half of the definition implies that an individual who has 20/20 visual acuity can still be considered legally blind if the peripheral field of view is less than 20 degrees. The term *tunnel vision* may be used to describe students whose peripheral vision is narrowed to a degree that it is similar to looking through a paper towel tube.

Everyone who is totally blind is legally blind but not everyone who is visually impaired or has low vision is legally blind. The U. S. Social Security Administration and the Internal Revenue Service use the legal definition of blindness to determine eligibility of services for students and adults. If determined to be legally blind by an eye care specialist, an adult can apply for Supplemental Security Income (SSI) to cover costs for basic food, shelter, and clothing needs. The legal definition of blindness also enables a family of a school-aged student who is legally blind to benefit from receiving SSI to meet its basic needs.

Eligibility for special education services for a student who is visually impaired is no longer determined by the definition of legal blindness or the severity of the visual impairment as documented in an eye care specialists' report. In order to be determined eligible for special education services, a student with a visual impairment after being diagnosed with a visual impairment receives a functional vision assessment conducted by a teacher of students with visual impairment (TSVI). If it is determined that the visual impairment adversely affects the student's education, then the student is determined to be eligible for special education services. The functional vision assessment, which will be discussed in greater detail in the *Assessment* section of this chapter, includes an evaluation of the student's functional visual abilities, including visual acuities, peripheral vision, and other visual skills such as visual tracking and color vision to name a few.

Congenital or adventitious total blindness or visual impairment. Typically the term *congenitally blind* is used broadly to describe the onset of vision loss but as indicated previously, the term blind is ambiguous and ill-defined. Two more appropriate terms used to differentiate between amount of vision loss are *congenitally totally blind* or *congenitally visually impaired.* Congenital total blindness or congenital visual impairment defines vision loss that typically occurs at birth or shortly thereafter (up to six months). We shall use the terms *congenitally totally blind* or *congenitally visually impaired* to differentiate the population of infants born with vision loss.

Whether the student is considered congenitally totally blind or congenitally visually impaired is an important distinction for educational purposes. Vision provides the basis for learning, so without it, the infant born totally blind will necessarily need to rely more on tactile and auditory information and processing for learning, than the infant born visually impaired. The school-aged student who was diagnosed as congenitally totally blind will most likely be a tactile and auditory learner, so in early intervention the TSVI would need to begin working with the student in tactile readiness and listening skills. Barraga and Erin (2001) indicate, however, that use of tactile or auditory information does not provide the same level of information as efficiently as vision. The term congenitally visually impaired implies vision loss which occurs at birth, but the infant is born with some degree of residual vision.

Students who are identified as being adventitiously totally blind or adventitiously visually impaired lose vision because of genetics, trauma, or disease, and the type of educational program designed for these students will vary depending upon the severity of loss and when the loss occurred. As with the student who is congenitally visually impaired, the amount of visual memory the student who is adventitiously totally blind or adventitiously visually impaired has the more educational programming can draw upon and make connections for learning from those memories. The retention of visual memory will determine the type of program of instruction in skill areas such as concept development, social skills, and orientation and mobility (O&M).

Causal Factors

Based on a sample of schools for the blind in the United States, the three leading causes of pediatric blindness are cortical visual impairment (CVI), retinopathy of prematurity (ROP), and optic nerve hypoplasia (ONH), with a significant increase in both CVI and ROP over the past 10 years (Steinkuller et al., 1999). Cortical visual impairment is a visual impairment that occurs in the brain rather than the eye. Optic nerve hypoplasia is visual impairment that occurs in the nerves cells within the connection between the eye and the brain, and ROP is visual impairment that is exclusively ocular. Vision loss can be caused by a number of factors. Disease, trauma, inheritance, events during pregnancy or at birth, or a combination of anyone one of these can cause blindness or visual impairment. It can be progressive or stable, treatable or untreatable, and depending upon the location or site for the loss, individuals may have total blindness, peripheral loss with central vision intact, central loss with peripheral vision intact, overall loss in both central and peripheral vision and as presented previously, partial or total loss can occur at birth or later on in life.

Loss of useable or functional vision exceeds the typical reduction of vision often associated with correctable errors of refraction. While many individuals wear glasses or contact lenses to correct for lack of clarity of vision (refractive errors), students who are visually impaired also have vision problems that are not correctable such as the following types of eye problems (Schwartz, 2010) described in the next section.

Common Eye Disorders of Students

Albinism (genetically linked ocular disorder)—is reduced pigment to the skin, hair, and/or eyes.

Amblyopia (ocular disorder)—is reduced visual acuity in one or both eyes caused by strabismus, errors in refraction (e.g., myopia), or central occlusions to the visual pathway.

Aniridia (genetic, congenital, sporadic ocular disorder)—means absence of the iris.

Cataract (genetically linked ocular disorder)—occurs within the crystalline lens in one or both eyes. If not treated (removed), a cataract will cause a reduction in visual acuity, color vision, and create problems with glare and photophobia.

Coloboma (genetically linked ocular disorder)—is a congenital malformation in which a part of the eye (e.g., iris) does not develop leaving a cleft or hole.

Cortical visual impairment—CVI (infection during pregnancy, trauma, brain related)— is one the leading cause of blindness in children the United States. The eye is intact and healthy, but the area affected causing the blindness is in the optical radiations, and visual cortex of the brain.

Glaucoma (genetic, trauma, disease linked ocular disorder)—takes two main forms: open-angle glaucoma and angle-closure glaucoma. Open-angle glaucoma affects the optic nerve head on the retina without necessarily affecting the eye's drainage system. Angle-closure glaucoma implies the drainage system of the eyes is clogged, therefore fluid pressure rises.

Leber's Congenital Amaurosis—(genetic, congenital)—is the degeneration of the rod and cone photoreceptor cells within the retina soon after birth. Visual acuity ranges from legal blindness to no light perception.

Macular Degeneration—(possible genetic, disease ocular disorder)—encompasses a broad classification of diseases that affect the macula causing loss of central vision which makes near vision tasks such as reading difficult.

Microphthalmia (genetic, viral infections during pregnancy, congenital ocular disorder)—abnormally small eyes (one or both).

Nystagmus (disease linked neurological disorder, brain related)—is involuntary horizontal, vertical, or rotary movement of the eyes caused by poor vision.

Optic nerve hypoplasia—ONH (congenital, young maternal age, disease, alcohol use, prematurity, extra-ocular)—is characterized as abnormally small optic nerves due to an underdevelopment of optic nerve axons.

Retinitis Pigmentosa—RP (genetic ocular disorder)—is a progressive retinal dystrophy or degeneration of the retinal cells (rod/cone or cone/rod photoreceptor cells) causing night blindness, tunnel vision, photophobia, poor color vision, or a range of vision loss from total blindness to very good functioning visual acuity.

Retinoblastoma (Genetic ocular disorder)—is a relatively rare form of childhood eye cancer caused by the mutation of the gene that typically fights cancer cells.

Retinopathy of Prematurity—ROP (disease, prematurity ocular disorder)—affects the retina of premature infants. Retinal blood vessels are stunted in their development due to the premature birth the eye has not achieved maturation so the vessels continue to grow abnormally after birth especially in the periphery. Scarring occurs on the retina where the original vessels stopped developing and the new vessels began to grow which often results in retinal detachments. High levels of oxygen to enrich the retinal tissue to enable the vessels to continue their normal growth may also contribute to the loss of vision.

Stargardt's Disease—Juvenile macular degeneration (genetically linked adventitious ocular disorder)—is progressive vision loss begins typically at 6 years of age and ends at the age of 12.

Strabismus (genetic, tumors, trauma, related eye disorders, hydrocephaly, cerebral palsy)—may occur in one or both eyes and is often referred to as "crossed eyes" or "lazy eye." Most commonly strabismus is temporary as in the case of a student whose one eye may drift away from the object of view. The student's whose eye drifts because of strabismus may perceive two images at once. This is known as *diplopia* where the brain perceives two disparate images at once. The brain may suppress the image of the weaker eye so the student sees the world monocularly. When this occurs, the eye condition in the weaker eye is called *amblyopia*. If strabismus is detected early enough, typically before the age of 12, then being fitted for glasses or contact lenses with prisms or occlusion (patching) therapy to force the weaker eye to work may be the recommend treatment. Drug therapy may also be recommended (Repka, 2008).

Usher's syndrome (genetic ocular and auditory disorder)—congenital deafness coupled with RP (rod-cone type).

Genetic Issues and the Promise for the Future

As indicated above, most of the leading causes of visual impairment in students are inherited. They are passed when one parent transmits a mutated gene (autosomal dominant) responsible for the disorder, or in the case of where both parents transmit the recessive genes (autosomal recessive) causing the disorder. In the case of autosomal dominant, the likelihood that the child will inherit the disorder is 50%. In the recessive case, the likelihood the child will inherit the disorder is approximately 25%.

Especially x-linked recessive disorders are passed through the mother to the son. There is a 50% chance that the son will inherit the disorder as well as a 50% chance that the daughter will become a carrier. Genetic transmission of disorders may also involve multiple mutated genes in combination with factors such as environment and lifestyle. These more complex disorders are referred to as polygenic inheritance and while associated within families, these are the most difficult to track or follow because of the variability of influence from each factor.

Visual impairment is often a result of one of the various forms of the inheritance traits described above. Retinitis Pigmentosa or night blindness, for example, is found in both autosomal dominant and recessive genes. Color blindness (red-green deficiencies) and some forms of albinism are associated with x-linked inheritance.

Scientists and researchers are learning more about the genetic causes of these disorders and about the impact that gene therapy may play in correcting, retarding, or eradicating certain types of vision loss. There are several types of gene therapy that may hold promise for correcting or preventing vision loss in the near future. One form of gene therapy involves the introduction of a virus, referred to as a vector, into unhealthy or damaged cell tissue. Leber's Congenital Amaurosis, for example, is an autosomal recessive inherited disorder which has shown to be particularly receptive to this type of gene therapy, particularly in young children whose photoreceptor cells are relatively healthy. Other forms of visual impairment that show promise with gene (stem cell) therapy is age-related macular degeneration (dry form). It is inevitable that gene therapy will have a profound impact upon treatment of various forms of blindness and visual impairment in the next decade.

Identification

Identifying the actual number of students who are totally blind or visually impaired is often as difficult as defining the population. Sources of the data vary greatly depending upon the criteria, the population surveyed, the date and times when the data were collected, and the measurement techniques used. Various national data sources use different criteria for counting students which creates confusion when comparisons are made across data sets because each data source defines the population differently. One source may include students served in a residential or specialized school whereas another source does not. Another source will include students whose vision is measured better than the legal definition of blindness while another source will not.

One often used but incomplete source of prevalence data is gathered and published by the U.S. Department of Education, Office of Special Education Programs (OSEP). This count, as required by the Individuals with Disabilities Education Act (IDEA), is based on the number of students aged 3–21 served in educational settings by individual states. The federal child count data system is unduplicated and only counts students with a primary disability described as the "major or overriding disability condition that best identified the individual's impairment; the impairment that is most disabling." In the most recent 28th Annual Report to Congress on the Implementation of the IDEA (2006), OSEP states that during the 2003–2004 school year there were approximately 26,116 students with visual impairments from ages 3 to 21 served under IDEA, Part B. By OSEP's own analysis, their count of children with visual impairments is an underestimate.

A second more inclusive but still restrictive source of data is that which is gathered and reported by the American Printing House for the Blind (APH). One of the primary responsibilities of APH is to annually collect data on students who are legally blind being served in both public and specialized schools for census reports to the federal government. Because APH also counts students typically counted in OSEP under the multiple disability category, the number of students reported by APH compared to the OSEP figure has more than doubled over the past 10 years. For example, during the 2003–2004 school year, the number of students who are legally blind served in schools as reported by the APH (2004) was 57,119, which is 31,003 more students reported to Congress by OSEP in the same school year. Although more than double the OSEP count, the APH figure is also an underestimate because the number only includes students who are legally blind and excludes a vast majority of those whose vision is better than legal blindness, but still considered visually impaired.

In reporting data from a 1998 study based upon epidemiological estimates, the National Plan for Training Personnel to Serve Children with Blindness and Low Vision (NPTP), Kirchner and Diament (1999) projected a more inclusive and realistic estimate of the number of students suspected of having a visual impairment (including those with additional disabilities) at 93,600 and growing. This figure was devised based on the actual number of known certified TSVIs and O&M specialists in the United States using personnel data and combined that number with the average caseloads size of 14 to 18 students per teacher. The population of students served by TSVIs and O&M specialists included students whose vision ranged from total blindness to those with visual impairment who also possessed additional disabilities.

Behavioral Characteristics

Although there are no behavioral or emotional characteristics specifically associated with all students with visual impairments, some students who are totally blind or visually impaired, including those who possess multiple disabilities, exhibit behaviors such as rocking, eye-poking, hand or finger movements, and gazing at lights, and other repetitive behaviors that may interfere with learning and social interactions. These behavioral characteristics are often referred to as blindisms. The cause for these stereotypical behaviors is not well known. Some believe the reason for the child's stereotypic repetitive behaviors is to provide some level of stimulation in an under-stimulated sensory system or to dampen an over-stimulated system in some environments (Miller, Lane, Cermak, Anzalone, & Osten, 2005). Some behaviors such as eye-poking or eye-gouging are typically associated with a specific eye pathology (e.g., Leber's Congenital Amaurosis) in which the retina and optic nerve are intact. When pushed on by the student's hand or fingers retinal stimulation or flashes of light are caused which the student may find pleasant. Retinopathy of Prematurity is often associated with stereotypic rocking movements and eye-poking. Others believe that the frequency and intensity of stereotypic behaviors varies depending on whether students are totally blind as opposed to those who have low vision or are visually impaired. Gal and Dyck (2009) indicate that of the 50 students observed in their study, the students who are totally blind engaged in more stereotypic movements, such as rocking and head movements, whereas the students with low vision tended to do more staring. McHugh and Lieberman (2003) compared the rocking behaviors of 52 students with visual impairments between the ages of 9 and 19 to determine whether factors such as birth weight, prematurity, visual status and diagnosis, and early medical conditions played a role in the amount students rocked. Their research supports the notion that developmental factors may play an important role in whether children rock or not. Extended hospitalizations for infants born with severe medical restrictions (e.g., ROP), may limit the amount of handling by the parents as well as severely restricting the infant's movements.

In addition to stereotypical behaviors mentioned, students may also experience delays in social interactions and language development. For example, some students who are blind may have echolalic communication initially. These behaviors are often associated with students who have Autism Spectrum Disorder (ASD). It is possible that students with visual impairments can also have a diagnosis of ASD (Gense & Gense, 2005; Pawletko, 2002), but a careful developmental history needs to be made in order to differentiate behaviors due to blindness versus those due to autism. Pawletko lists differences in observed behaviors for students who are blind and non-autistic compared to those who are blind and autistic. For example, social interactions with peers may be delayed for a student who is blind and non-autistic but a relationship will develop and the student will show some sign of social curiosity and enjoyment of social interaction; however, a student who is blind and autistic will show little social curiosity in peer relationships are non-existent or are distorted.

Students with visual impairments can develop healthy self-esteem despite the often negative stigma imposed by society regarding the blind. Tuttle and Tuttle (2000) indicate that living with a visual impairment involves three aspects of adjustment: cognition, action, and affect. Cognition implies being aware and knowledgeable about how to cope. Action implies applying that knowledge to develop skills for coping, and affect means an awareness of the feelings and attitudes resulting from the application of coping strategies. Students must be able to integrate all three in order to develop a positive self-concept. In addition, social competence and social acceptance is critical to developing self-confidence and self-esteem (Sacks & Silberman, 2000b; Wagner, 2004). The social learning theory of Bandura (1977) provides an excellent frame for teachers to consider when developing social skill lessons or creating social support opportunities for learning for students with visual impairment.

One limitation imposed by visual impairment is the ability to visually monitor incidental information present in the environment. It is believed that 80% of what infants and young children learn comes to them through visual input. Every day events such as gazing at a blue sky or watching clouds change shape while moving across the sky is perceived visually. Because of their visual impairment, students will often not be aware of these obvious features of our world. They may be unaware of how friends use body language or facial expressions to convey mood or how to greet a friend with a handshake, or other social mores that sighted peers acquire incidentally. Bardin and Lewis (2008) indicate that students with visual impairments often miss the subtle cues and concepts that occur in the regular education classroom. Students with visual impairments will need to intentionally be taught many of the things we as sighted individuals observe visually every day. If not informed by parents, the teenager who is totally blind may need to receive direct instruction in understanding the current fashion trend in clothing or hairstyles or jewelry in order to engage in meaningful conversation with peers about these topics. In a matched pairs study comparing students with visual impairment to sighted peers on their engagement in academic, social, daily living, and vocational activities in school, at home, and in the community, Sacks, Wolffe, and Tierney (1998) found that the sighted peers were afforded greater levels of independence and were given more opportunities to make choices than did the students with visual impairments. Teachers need to be aware of the incidental opportunities afforded to sighted individuals, and plan learning activities and environments in which the student with visual impairment will be informed about the visual aspects of the environment and included as a contributor in those classroom activities.

Assessment

Functional Vision Assessments

As with other areas of special education, quality assessment in the area of visual impairment is imperative. There are key assessments that the special education team and general education teacher should expect and request. One of the prime assessments conducted by the TSVI to determine eligibility for special education, to determine and monitor instructional needs within the educational environment, and to provide a basis for adaptations and accommodations, is the functional vision assessment (FVA). The FVA is also called the educational functional vision evaluation in some states (EFVE) to highlight the educational focus of the assessment.

The FVA considers how a student uses his or her vision under non-clinical conditions in both familiar and unfamiliar settings. Most FVAs include observations of the student interacting within different environments and determination of the size and distance at which a student can accurately and comfortably identify objects and printed information and perform tasks under different conditions (static, dynamic, different lighting, etc.). In addition, the TSVI will assess for awareness and identification of objects in the peripheral field, identification of tasks that are challenging for the student, and efficient use of vision and other senses to compliment visual input. The FVA results in recommendations for enhancing the use of vision and/or other senses in the classroom (Greer, 2004; Lueck, 2004). Recommendations, based on the observations from the assessment, will be adaptations and accommodations as well as identification of areas in which the student would benefit from explicit instruction- such as adaptive skills. FVAs are often conducted on a yearly basis and at the very least at each review of special education services. Ideally, FVAs are not static and TSVIs continually observe and collect data on a student's use of vision.

Beyond the common elements of an FVA, the TSVI will tailor the assessment to the student's type of visual condition, age, ability level, and environmental situations. For example, students with CVI should be specifically assessed for the existence of specific characteristics (e.g. latency, color preference, trouble with complexity and novelty, etc.) that are common for this condition (Cohen-Maitre & Haerich, 2005; Roman-Lantzy, 2007). By tailoring the FVA, TSVIs are better able to create effective instructional programs. There is evidence that the child with CVI's functioning can improve, for example, when systematic programming is built into his or her routine, particularly at a young age, making a thorough FVA crucial in instructional decision-making (Malkowicz, Myers, & Leisman, 2006; Matsuba & Jan, 2006; Roman-Lantzy, 2007; Roman et al., 2010).

For students with multiple disabilities, the TSVI will need to work with the student's educational team to understand the communication style of the child and typical wait time needed in order to conduct an FVA that elicits the most information possible. Many techniques will be those that require a behavioral response versus a verbal response and will be based on the types of movements the student can make. Observation of often subtle responses and good interviewing of the family and educational team is key to gathering important information for these students (Haegerstrom-Portnoy, 2004; Lueck, 2004).

Learning Media Assessment

Along with the FVA, the learning media assessment (LMA) is another important component of the assessment package (Koenig & Holbrook, 1995). The initial assessment is completed to establish in what media literacy instruction will begin for a student with visual impairments: Braille, print, or both. In addition to the literacy medium, the assessment, which considers a student's primary and secondary sensory learning channels (i.e., visual, tactual, auditory), also identifies general learning media (demonstrations, charts and maps, etc.) that the student will be able to access best through different senses—serving as a guide for instruction in the classroom setting. The LMA, as with the FVA, is an on-going assessment. As the student progresses in school, literacy and learning media needs will change. The LMA delineates a process to monitor student progress (e.g., measuring reading rates, comprehension, fatigue levels, etc.) and to identify instructional tools necessary for continued literacy instruction and access to the learning environment (e.g., assistive technology tools). The TSVI, in collecting data through the LMA process, can make instructional decisions about how well students are progressing and keeping up with peers in their predominant learning media. The data serve to support decisions about the type of media or literacy tools that will work best in different situations (e.g., spot reading vs. sustained reading) and identify places where more instruction or more intense instruction or opportunities for practice are needed for a student to be proficient with different literacy tools (e.g., Braille, low vision devices, etc.; Holbrook, 2009).

Assistive Technology Assessment

Tied to both of these assessments is the assistive technology (AT) assessment. Both the FVA and LMA provide important information for formulating an appropriate AT assessment for students with visual impairments. However, AT assessments in and of themselves are not unique to the area of visual impairment, but a necessary assessment for any student on an individual education program (IEP) that needs AT for access to the educational environment as well as to functional areas of their life. Some districts and regions have dedicated AT specialists who might help to conduct the AT assessment. Other professionals such as occupational therapists may need to be involved as well to determine the student's additional needs beyond visual impairment and to help match the most appropriate AT to that student. The TSVI will also be involved in the assessment team as the person knowledgeable about options regarding AT for students with visual impairments and will often be the one conducting the majority of the assessment. In addition to the IEP, students with low vision should receive clinical low vision exams by a qualified optometrist or ophthalmologist. An optometrist or ophthalmologist who specializes in low vision will be the one who prescribes the correct magnification levels of any optical devices the student my need as part of his/her assistive technology and learning media repertoire (Presley & D'Andrea, 2009; Wilkinson, 2010; Zimmerman, Zebehazy, & Moon, 2010).

Technology in the area of visual impairment includes both high- and low-tech devices. High-tech options include screen reading software, scan and read software, screen enlargement software, refreshable Braille displays, Braille notetaking devices, video magnifiers, and digital talking book players that support Daisy format (a special audio format allowing for advanced searching within an audio file as well as book marking of locations within the file) among others. For students with multiple disabilities, adaptive and assistive communication (AAC) devices (switches, electronic communication devices with auditory scanning, etc.) may also be part of the AT a student uses. Some research suggests that students with visual impairments do not have or use AT as much as might be expected (Kappermna, Heinze, & Sticken, 2002; Kelly, 2009). It is important that good AT assessments and advocacy for needed technology for students with visual impairments take place and that TSVIs meet minimum competencies in AT particular to visual impairment for both instructional and assessment purposes (Smith, Kelley, Maushak, Griffin-Shirley, & Lan, 2009).

As mentioned earlier, the LMA helps determine tools that a student needs to support literacy and learning and measures progress in using those tools. Assistive technology determinations are part of those tools, so the two assessments complement each other. Information from the LMA will help formulate the AT assessment. A suggested format for the AT assessment is to begin with gathered information from the eye care specialist who specializes in low vision, the FVA and LMA, and teacher observations. Systematic observations of the student's required tasks, how the student currently accomplishes the tasks and at what level of independence the student can accomplish the tasks serves as a baseline of information for the AT assessment, helping to pinpoint the types of AT from which the student may benefit (Presley & D'Andrea, 2009). Then direct assessment in selected technologies is conducted to provide information on the potential for the tool as well as the starting point for instruction. Ideally, the need for AT should be determined before a student actually needs to use the technology proficiently in the classroom (Presley & D'Andrea, 2009).

Orientation and Mobility Assessments

Another assessment specific to visual impairment is the orientation and mobility assessment provided by an O&Ms. As previously stated, O&M is a related service as prescribed by IDEA (2004). As with the FVA, the O&M assessment is tailored to the student, but includes evaluating students' abilities to move safely and effectively through the environment in familiar and unfamiliar indoor and outdoor areas including the use of mobility tools (e.g., long cane), to keep track of where they are and understand how to get where they are going—using information from the environment to stay oriented, to understand environmental concepts related to travel, and to effectively use remaining vision and other senses during travel (Fazzi & Petersmeyer, 2001; Guth & Rieser, 1997; Pogrund et al., 1998).

Assessing Other Areas of the Expanded Core Curriculum

O&M comprises one of the areas of what is called the expanded core curriculum (ECC) for students with visual impairments, including students with multiple disabilities. The ECC includes disability-specific areas beyond the core academic areas covered in school that have been determined as important to students with visual impairments to address both academic and functional skill development (Corn, Hatlen, Huebner, Ryan, & Siller, 1995; Huebner, Merk-Adam, Stryker, & Wolffe, 2004). The TSVI should regularly monitor and assess students for instructional needs in the expanded core, creating goals and providing direct instruction in areas of priority. Along with O&M, there are eight other expanded core areas: compensatory skills (Braille, concept development, communication skills, organization skills, etc.), social skills, sensory efficiency skills, career education, assistive technology skills, self-determination, recreation and leisure skills, and daily living skills. Instruction in the ECC supports students with visual impairments to access the general curriculum, to promote independence, and to support successful transition from school to the real world.

Standardized Academic Assessments

Finally, as with all students, those with visual impairments are to participate in assessments conducted by the school, district, and state. There is evidence that students with visual impairments are behind peers without disabilities academically (Marder, 2006; Wagner, Newman, Cameto, & Levine, 2006). However, what is unclear are the reasons. Whether participating in regular large-scale assessments, alternate assessments for students with significant cognitive disabilities, or curriculum-based classroom assessments, interpretation of results, particularly standardized assessments under accommodated or adapted conditions must be made carefully (Bradley-Johnson, 1994; Linn 2002). We often don't know the reliability and validity of standardized assessments for students with visual impairments, which can lead to concern regarding the usefulness of the assessment results (Hannan, 2007). Research specifically looking at the effects of accommodations and adaptations on assessment results for students with visual impairments is scarce (Thompson, Blount, & Thurlow, 2002), thereby making it unclear if proper interpretations of results are being made.

Typical adaptations and accommodations for students with visual impairments include Braille, large print, extended time, marking answers in the assessment booklet or dictating answers to a scribe, use of a computer or note taking device, use of an abacus, use of a talking calculator, and read-aloud and auditory tests, among others (Allman, 2004). Depending on the state, some accommodations, depending on the testing circumstance, are considered controversial. For example, in many states use of read-aloud for reading tests is generally considered a modification, but is acceptable in some states for students with visual impairments. In some states, Braille is considered an accommodation that holds ramifications for scoring (Christensen, Lazarus, Crone, & Thurlow, 2008).

Professionals are using computer adapted testing more and more as a way to create more universally designed assessments. Limited data for students with visual impairments suggests that barriers exist to using a single platform for computer testing standardization. These barriers include inaccessibility of some questions (e.g. picture based questions) and the variability in the types of AT used by students with visual impairments for different purposes (Johnstone, Thurlow, Altman, Timmons, & Kato, 2009; Kamei-Hannan, 2008). The educational team should discuss the accommodations and modifications the student uses to access the assessments and how those may affect what is being tested. The TSVI should be involved in decision-making. Quality of adapted assessments can vary widely and a change in the medium in which a student is being tested could also affect the intent of certain test items. In addition, as with all students with disabilities, the accommodations used in the testing situation should be those used during regular instruction. A tendency to over-accommodate or to select unfamiliar accommodations could be detrimental to the student's performance.

Educational Programming

Educational Placements and Supports

Students with visual impairments eligible under IDEA should receive services from a TSVI as well as an O&M specialist according to their assessed needs. As part of the itinerant model of teaching, both TSVIs and O&M specialists in the school setting work with students with visual impairments across a range of grades, levels, and abilities.

Large caseloads, students spread across wide geographical areas, administrators not recognizing the importance of the ECC, and needing to prioritize academic needs are among some of the barriers identified by TSVIs as creating challenges to being able to fully serve potential needs in the ECC of some of their students (Hatlen, 1998). Because of challenges, there is a concern as well, that educational assistants (paraprofessionals) are being over-utilized for students with visual impairments, sometimes assuming instructional roles beyond their training (Forster & Holbrook, 2005; McKenzie & Lewis, 2008). Based on survey results, Lohmeier, Blankenship, and Hatlen (2009) suggest a need for creative solutions to effectively address instructional needs in the ECC.

Many professionals in the field of visual impairment place great importance on maintaining a continuum of placements, which may include resource rooms and schools for the blind and visually impaired (Hatlen, 2002; Lohmeier et al., 2009; Wolffe et al., 2002). It is important for assessment of needs to drive the decisions about educational placement and least restrictive environments in order to meet the unique educational programming of each student. For some students with visual impairments, the itinerant model serves them well throughout the school years. For others, there may be a time within their school programming when other placements are better. Services of schools for the blind and visually impaired vary by state. Some schools offer academic residential school placements whereas others primarily focus on serving the needs of students with visual impairments who also have multiple disabilities. Some schools have short-term placement options whereby students can attend for a specified amount of time to work on specific skills, outreach services to public schools, and/or summer programs offering targeted specific skills (Zebehazy & Whitten, 2003).

Early Intervention Considerations

Regardless of placement, educational programming for students with congenital visual impairments with or without additional disabilities begins with early intervention. Ideally, the TSVI and O&M specialist are involved in the early intervention of students with visual impairments. Early intervention specialists should be knowledgeable about the impact that a visual impairment can have on development, as well as the strategies for minimizing that impact (Pogrund, 2002). In addition, they need to know about the impact of additional disabilities on development and strategies for working with linguistically and culturally diverse families (Dote-Kwan, Chen, & Hughes, 2001).

Suggested best practices for early intervention include family-based support services, play-based assessments, and team collaboration with the family to create the Individual Family Services Plan (Hatton, McWilliam, & Winton, 2002). Development varies from child to child (Warren, 1994), and children with visual impairment may not follow the same developmental sequences as children who are sighted (Ferrell, 1998). Young children learn many concepts and begin to develop self-help skills through play and observation. What is typically learned incidentally through visual observation (e.g., mom taking milk out of the fridge to make a bottle) is often limited or not accessible to children with visual impairments (Barraga & Erin, 2001). The lack of incidental learning opportunities heightens the need for maximizing engagement with the environment and providing active and real life experiences (Chen, 2001).

Along with providing direct experiences, teachers need to help students with visual impairments develop concepts. Concepts, language, and cognition are intertwined, with early attachment to caregivers being a key component to the development of these skills (Fazzi & Klein, 2002). Alternative strategies may need to be developed between a child with a visual impairment and his/her caregiver to establish an understanding of reciprocal communication, turn-taking and joint attention that usually is established through eye contact and gestures (Barraga & Erin, 2001). In addition, efforts must go beyond just labeling objects in the environment and using declarative sentences with children with visual impairments (Kekelis & Anderson, 1984). To ensure in-depth understanding, concepts have to be "unpacked," and children with visual impairments need opportunities to compare, contrast, categorize and develop and expand upon their conceptual schemas (Fazzi & Klein, 2002).

Motor development and exploration through moving is also a key component for conceptual, cognitive and language development (Strickling & Pogrund, 2002). Infants begin to understand their world by moving through it and being attracted to objects that they then explore and with which they experiment by banging, throwing, and mouthing. Typically, vision is the most powerful sense for infants in terms of motivating them to lift their heads, sit up, rotate their trunks, develop their tone, and reach out and explore (Brown, Anthony, Lowry, & Hatton, 2004). For children with visual impairments, particularly children without enough usable vision to be motivated by visual cues, substitute strategies for motivation will need to be found. Motor movements may need to be modeled and play spaces may need to be defined, among other strategies, to initially promote exploration and motor development.

The O&M specialist, in conjunction with the TSVI and Occupational or Physical Therapists on the child's IEP team, should help the family plan ways to incorporate movement and exploration into the family's natural routines. They can also encourage toddlers with visual impairments to move freely about their environment through the use and understanding of sensory input (e.g., use of echolocation, tactual input, etc.), the development of spatial concepts, and use of a mobility device (e.g., adaptive mobility device, long cane) appropriate for that child based on the O&M specialist's assessment and consultation with the team (Anthony, Bleier, Fazzi, Kish, & Pogrund, 2002).

Along with the developmental focus of early intervention, emergent literacy (both reading and early numeracy) should also be an area addressed for young children with visual impairments. Concept development is key in fostering emergent literacy skills (Wormsley, 1997). Koenig and Farrenkopf (1997) identified typical concepts found in reading basal series, which can serve as an initial list for building in direct experiences. Attention to book concepts and an understanding that symbols have meaning is just as important for children with visual impairments prior to entering kindergarten as it is for other children, regardless of the medium the child will be using (Braille or print or both). Phonological awareness, phonemic awareness, and an ability to rapidly name letters are factors research suggests affect later reading achievement (e.g., National Institute of Child Health and Human Development, 2000; Torgesen, Wagner, Rashotte, Burgess, & Hecht, 1997). Because children with visual impairments often have fewer incidental opportunities to be exposed to letters in the environment in which to associate their names and sounds, direct instruction and attention to these building blocks of literacy becomes especially important. Interestingly, however, one study found that teachers working with young children with visual impairments did not have a tendency to provide structured phonological skill development or experiences with the alphabet or writing (Murphy, Hatton, & Erickson, 2008). In addition, development of tactual discrimination and comparison (i.e., same/different) and finger strength is important for children with visual impairments, particularly children who will be using Braille as their reading medium (Wormsley, 1997). Little information is available about promoting early numeracy skills specifically for children with visual impairment, but it is an area that we should not overlook. Number sense goes beyond counting and is a foundational cognitive skill that promotes future success and understanding in mathematics. Liedtke (1998) suggests activities for promoting number sense in children who are blind, adapting typical activities that generally have very visual components

School-Age Instructional and Support Considerations

As a child moves into the school-age years, supporting academic instruction often becomes the main focus (Wolffe et al., 2002). In the elementary years when students are still learning how to read, the TSVI may be a primary instructor of reading, particularly for students using Braille as their primary literacy medium. Reading instruction by the TSVI, however, should not be considered in place of quality instruction in the general education classroom. Students who are learning to read with Braille need more, not less instruction. A Delphi study conducted by Koenig and Holbrook (2000) estimated one to two hours daily of literacy instruction from a TSVI is needed to ensure high quality Braille literacy or dual media literacy (learning Braille and print reading) programming during the years of reading development (kindergarten through third grade). The consensus of the teachers was that there is a need to continue moderate levels of consistent literacy instruction for children who have intermediate and advanced literacy skills because literacy tool needs will change (e.g., use of new AT, refining development of auditory listening skills). For students with low vision accessing print, teachers also agreed that consistent services and direct instructional time (vs. consultation time) is needed to support literacy-related skills development including remedying inefficient skills (e.g., keyboarding, below-grade level reading attributed to visual impairment), introducing use of new low vision devices or technology, teaching Braille to a student with print literacy skills, and teaching generalization of literacy skills, among others (Corn & Koenig, 2002).

Braille, as a code, has an uncontracted (alphabet and punctuation) and contracted form (contains contractions and rules for their use that replace spelling some words out letter by letter. For example, "the" is a single cell contraction. The word "share" contains an "sh" and and "ar" contraction). Philosophies about whether to begin instruction with uncontracted or contracted Braille has been mixed in the field of visual impairment. In a longitudinal study, called the Alphabetic and Contracted Braille (ABC) Study, which was comprised of 38 prekindergarten and kindergarten students recruited over the first three years of the study, researchers sought to evaluate differences in achievement between children who are taught contractions early and quickly and children taught contractions later or more slowly (Emerson, Holbrook, & D'Andrea, 2009). Students learning more contractions sooner had higher scores on vocabulary, decoding and comprehension measures. However, regardless of contraction use, the majority of students with visual impairments did not keep up after Grade 2 with sighted peers in vocabulary and oral reading fluency rates. Miscues during oral reading were related to reading skills, not errors with the Braille code. Both lagging vocabulary and the types of miscues highlight the need to focus on good reading instruction regardless of the medium and a need to isolate contributing factors (e.g., level, type or intensity of instruction, increasing load demand for students, etc.).

The ABC Braille Study researchers also found a significant difference in reading rate between children who read Braille with one or two hands. Two-handed readers were more efficient and increased their rates more quickly, and children who began reading with one hand were less likely to develop into two-handed readers. This finding has direct implications to instruction and serves as one factor that may contribute to improving fluency rates for some students (Wright, Wormsley, & Kamei-Hannan, 2009).

In the area of math instruction for students with visual impairments, Ferrell (2006) reviewed 50 years of research to identify those that met certain research criteria. The effect sizes for these studies were calculated to identify promising practices. Interestingly, the few studies that could be analyzed were predominantly from the 1970s and focused on techniques for improving computation. Although computation skills are important for development of mathematical thinking, problem-solving skills are also important, and an area that needs more research in the field of visual impairment. More recent studies note better success by students with visual impairments in understanding size, scale, volume and surface area when they can experience problems concretely or can compare them in relation to the human scale (Andreou & Kotsis, 2005; Jones, Taylor, & Broadwell, 2009). Although not the main teacher of mathematics for students with visual impairments, itinerant TSVIs should understand which aspects of mathematics may require adapted strategies by students with visual impairments (e.g., having to move from part to whole to do comparisons haptically; math and science concepts that are usually very visually based) and how those strategies can be used for teaching students with visual impairments in mathematics and sciences. In addition to supporting classroom instruction, the TSVI will teach disability specific skills appropriate for the student, including use of the abacus, interpretation of tactile graphics and graphs, Nemeth code symbols within meaningful contexts, and use of assistive technology (Kappermna et al., 2002).

Along with making sure that academic materials are accessible and students have the adapted skills to meaningfully participate in classroom instruction, attention to the other areas of the ECC is also important. Daily living skills, recreation and leisure skills, career education, social skills development, and O&M are all areas that, although less directly connected to academics, are key skill areas for promoting independence and a smooth transition into adult life.

In the area of social skills, a lack of visual cues can lead to difficulties in initiating and maintaining social interactions (MacCuspie, 1996; Sacks & Silberman, 2000a). Research suggests that young children with visual impairments may initiate fewer unsupported social interactions (e.g., D'Allura, 2002: McGaha & Ferran, 2001). In a study of elementary children who were blind or legally blind in grades 1–6 parents rated their children significantly lower in the area of social assertion on a social skills rating scale compared to sighted peer norms (Buhrow, Hartshorne, & Bradley-Johnson, 1998). The need for instructional support in social skills continues into the adolescent years. Wolffe and Sacks (1997) found youths with visual impairments, particularly adolescents with low vision, to be engaged in more passive or solitary activities. With the importance that social skills play in every aspect of a person's life, the TSVI should be assessing and instructing children in this area from an early age and promoting increasingly more sophisticated and age-appropriate social skills as students continue through the school years. In addition, for continuity, work with the school and home environment to support practice in social skills is important.

Similarly, a study by Lewis and Iselin (2002) suggests the importance of direct assessment and instruction, and work with the family in the area of independent or daily living skills (e.g., daily hygiene, dressing, cooking, etc.) beginning at an early age. In this pilot study of 10 elementary students with visual impairments and 10 sighted students matched by age, parents rated students with visual impairments as being able to do considerably fewer skills from a list of 101 skills independently (44% of the skills compared to 84%) with the greatest differences being in the area of kitchen skills. As noted earlier, independent living skills is an area TSVIs often struggle to find time to include (Wolffe et al., 2002).

In the area of O&M skills, Cameto and Nagle (2007) in analyzing data of students with visual impairments from the National Longitudinal Transition Study 2 (NTLS2), found that 47% of students with visual impairments in regular schools compared to 80% of students with visual impairments in special schools were receiving O&M services. Considerably fewer students who were blind compared to students who were partially sighted (both groups without additional disabilities) were rated as doing various O&M skills "very well." Students who were blind were more likely to be rated as executing skills on familiar routes "very well" as compared to skills that involved creating routes in new areas, following instructions to new locations, using a numbering system to find an unknown location, and in orienting oneself or soliciting help to orient oneself in unfamiliar locations. These latter skills require stronger orientation and problem-solving skills, which are all important for promoting optimal independence as adults. The reasons for these differences are not known, but should be considered by the O&M specialist when determining level of service and projection of skill progression for students who are blind.

Transition

In terms of transition from high school to the adult world, the better the adapted skill base is of students with visual impairments upon leaving, the better success students will likely have when beginning college or searching for a job. When transition takes place, it is important that students with visual impairments and their families are aware of the resources available to them. For example, students entering college should understand how to advocate for themselves and how to access the disability resource center at their college. Students should also know what rehabilitation services are available to them in their community. Some students may want to seek out additional daily living skills and O&M instruction to refine their skill base and to meet changing needs.

Currently, transition into employment for students with visual impairments does not carry with it positive statistics. Low rates of employment continue to be a main concern in the area of visual impairment (Kirchner & Smith, 2005). McDonnall and Crudden (2009) found that youths who had work experience, utilized self-determination skills by taking control of making decisions during vocational rehabilitation sessions, had an internal locus of control, had AT skills and academic competence were more likely to be employed. In addition to the skill set and readiness of students with visual impairments for beginning employment the apprehensions of the employers also need to be considered as possible contributing factors. Based on nine interviews with employers who were new to hiring individuals with visual impairments, Wolffe and Candela (2002) proposed a model of creating a network of experienced employers who can share knowledge about accommodations and alleviate apprehensions. Rehabilitation agencies can also serve a role in providing information about working with individuals with visual impairments and equipping individuals with visual impairments with the knowledge of their rights and the regulations under the Americans with Disabilities Act.

Trends and Issues

Throughout the chapter, several trends and issues have already been identified in the area of education of students with visual impairments. To summarize, teacher shortages, caseload sizes, and logistics in how to fit in instruction in all the assessed need areas for students continue to be identified challenges in the field of education for students with visual impairments. University preparation programs for special education with emphasis in visual impairment and for O&M do not exist in every state. Many programs have moved toward a distance education or hybrid (distance education and some face-to-face instruction) model to be able to recruit more students, address needs in rural areas by recruiting individuals who already live in those areas, and to meet the changing demographics of students who often work full time while attending preparation programs.

Professionals in the field continue to review standards for beginning teachers of students with visual impairments and to discuss critical skills teachers must have to be effective TSVIs as well as O&M specialists. More outcome data on teacher effectiveness upon leaving a preparation program would be useful to better evaluate the quality of teachers leaving different program models (e.g., face-to-face, distance education only, distance education with some face-to-face). Teachers of students with visual impairments and O&M specialists should continue to strengthen the outcome data they collect on their students as well. The limited research in the field suggests that skill development of students in the areas of the ECC may not always be optimal. Progress monitoring and on-going assessment in the areas of the ECC are practices that can help TSVIs make informed decisions and better work with families. Also, outcome and assessment data can help to document the unique instructional needs of students with visual impairments and serve as an advocacy tool for keeping school districts in-tune to these students' educational needs and the importance of TSVIs and O&M specialists having caseloads and the resources that allow them to attend to those needs (Kirchner & Diament, 1999). The National Agenda (Huebner, Merk-Adam, Stryker, & Wolffe, 2004) goal areas continue to delineate the focus areas of the field of education of students with visual impairments in its dedication to continually working toward improving the services for this population of students.

References

Allman, C. B. (2004). *Test access: Making tests accessible for students with visual impairments: A guide for test publishers, test developers, and state assessment personnel* (2nd ed.). Louisville, KY: American Printing House for the Blind.

American Printing House for the Blind (APH). (2004). Distribution of eligible students based on the Federal Quota Census of January 6, 2003. Retrieved April 19, 2010, from http://www.aph.org/fedquotpgm/dist04.html.

Andreou, Y., & Kotsis, K. (2005). Mathematical concept development in blind and sighted children. *International Journal of Learning, 12*(7), 255–260.

Anthony, T. L., Bleier, H., Fazzi, D. L., Kish, D., & Pogrund, R. L. (2002). Mobility focus: Developing early skills for orientation and mobility. In R.L. Pogrund & D.L. Fazzi (Eds.), *Early focus: Working with young children who are blind or visually impaired and their families* (2nd ed., pp. 1–15). New York: AFB Press.

Bandura, A. (1977). *Social learning theory*. Englewood Cliffs, NJ: Prentice Hall.

Bardin, J. A., & Lewis, S. (2008). A survey of the academic engagement of students with visual impairments in general education classes. *Journal of Visual Impairment and Blindness, 102*(8), 472–483.

Barraga N. C., & Erin, J. N. (2001). *Visual impairments and learning* (4th ed.). Austin, TX: Pro-Ed.

Bell, J., & Siller, M. A. (2002). *Living with low vision.* American Foundation for the Blind. Retrieved April 20, 2010, from http://www.afb.org/Section.asp?SectionID=26&TopicID=144

Bradley-Johnson, S. (1994). *Psychoeducational assessment of students who are visually impaired or blind: Infancy through high school* (2nd ed.). Austin, TX: Pro-Ed.

Brown, C. J., Anthony, T. L., Lowry, S. S., & Hatton, D. D. (2004). Session 4: Motor development and movement. In T. L. Anthony, S. S. Lowry, C. J. Brown, & D. D. Huebner (Eds.), *Early Intervention Training Center for Infants and Toddlers with Visual Impairments: Developmentally appropriate orientation and mobility* (pp. 347–462). The University of North Carolina at Chapel Hill: FGP Child Development Center.

Buhrow, M. M., Hartshorne, T. S., & Bradley-Johnson, S. (1998). Parents' and teachers' ratings of the social skills of elementary-age students who are blind. *Journal of Visual Impairment & Blindness, 92*(7), 503–511.

Cameto, R., Nagle, K., & SRI International. (2007). *Facts from NLTS2: Orientation and mobility skills of secondary school students with visual impairments* (2008-3007). Washington, DC: National Center for Special Education Research, retrieved from ERIC database.

Chen, D. (2001). *Visual impairment in young children: A Review of the literature with implications for working with families of diverse cultural and linguistic backgrounds* (Tech. Rep. No. 7). University of Illinois at Urbana-Champaign, Early Childhood Research Institute on Culturally and Linguistically Appropriate Services. Retrieved March 10, 2010, from http://clas.uiuc.edu/techreport/tech7.html#c2

Christensen, L. L., Lazarus, S. S., Crone, M., & Thurlow, M. L. (2008). *2007 state policies on assessment participation and accommodations for students with disabilities* (Synthesis Report 69). Minneapolis, MN: University of Minnesota, National Center on Educational Outcomes.

Cohen-Maitre, S. A., & Haerich, P. (2005). Visual attention to movement and color in children with cortical visual impairment. *Journal of Visual Impairment & Blindness, 99*(7), 389–402.

Corn, A. L., Hatlen, P., Huebner, K. M., Ryan, F., & Siller, M. A. (1995). *The national agenda for the education of children and youths with visual impairments, including those with multiple disabilities.* New York, NY: AFB Press.

Corn, A. L., & Koenig, A. J. (2002). Literacy for Students with Low Vision: A Framework for Delivering Instruction. *Journal of Visual Impairment & Blindness, 96*(5), 305–321.

D'Allura, T. (2002). Enhancing the social interaction skills of preschoolers with visual impairments. *Journal of Visual Impairment & Blindness, 96*(8), 576–584.

Dote-Kwan, J., Chen, D., & Hughes, M. (2001). A national survey of service providers who work with young children with visual impairments. *Journal of Visual Impairment & Blindness, 95*(6), 325–337.

Emerson, R. W., Holbrook, M. C., & D'Andrea, F. M. (2009). Acquisition of literacy skills by young children who are blind: Results from the ABC braille study. *Journal of Visual Impairment & Blindness, 103*(10), 610–624.

Fazzi, D. L., & Klein, M. D. (2002). Cognitive focus: Developing cognition, concepts and language. In R. L. Pogrund & D. L. Fazzi (Eds.), *Early focus: Working with young children who are blind or visually impaired and their families* (2nd ed., pp. 1–15). New York, NY: AFB Press.

Fazzi, D. L., & Petersmeyer, B. A. (2001). *Imagining the possibilities: Creative approaches to orientation and mobility instruction for persons who are visually impaired.* New York, NY: AFB Press.

Ferrell, K. A. (1998). *Project PRISM: A longitudinal study of the developmental patterns of children who are visually impaired: Executive summary: CFDA 84.0203C: Field-initiated Research HO23C10188.* Greeley, CO: University of North Colorado. Retrieved from http://www.unco.edu/ncssd/research/PRISM/ExecSumm.pdf

Ferrell, K. A. (2006). Evidence-based practices for students with visual disabilities. *Communication Disorders Quarterly, 28*(1), 42–48.

Forster, E. M., & Holbrook, M. C. (2005). Implications of paraprofessional supports for students with visual impairments. *RE:view, 36*(4), 155–163.

Gal, E., & Dyck, M. J. (2009). Stereotyped movements among children who are visually impaired. *Journal of Visual Impairment and Blindness, 1*03(11), 754–765.

Gense, M. H., & Gense, D. J. (2005). *Autism spectrum disorder: Meeting students' learning needs.* New York, NY: AFB Press.

Greer, R. (2004). Evaluation methods and functional implications: Children and adults with visual impairments. In A. H. Lueck (Ed.), *Functional vision: A practitioner's guide to evaluation and intervention* (pp.177–255). New York, NY: AFB Press.

Guth, D. A., & Rieser, J. J. (1997). Perception and the control of locomotion by blind and visually impaired pedestrians. In B. B. Blasch, W. Wiener, & R. L. Welsh (Eds.), *Foundations of orientation and mobility* (2nd ed., pp. 9–38). New York, NY: AFB Press.

Haegerstrom-Portnoy, G. (2004). Evaluation methods and functional implications; Young children with visual impairments and students with multiple disabilities. In A. H. Lueck (Ed.), *Functional vision: A practitioner's guide to evaluation and intervention* (pp. 115–176). New York, NY: AFB Press.

Hannan, C. (2007). Exploring assessment processes in specialized schools for students who are visually impaired. *Journal of Visual Impairment & Blindness, 101*(2), 69–79.

Hatlen, P. (1998). Goal 8: Educational and developmental goals, including instruction, will reflect the assessed needs of each student in all areas of academic and disability-specific core curricula. In A. L. Corn & K. M. Huebner (Eds.), *A report to the nation: The national agenda for the education of children and youths with visual impairments, including those with multiple disabilities* (pp. 50–52). New York, NY: AFB Press.

Hatlen, P. (2002). The most difficult decision: How to share responsibility between local schools and schools for the blind. *Journal of Visual Impairment & Blindness, 96*(10), 747–749.

Hatton, D. D., McWilliam, R. A., & Winton, P. J. (2002). *Infants and toddlers with visual impairments: Suggestions for early interventionists.* Council for Exceptional Children. Retrieved March 10, 2010, fromhttp://www.cec.sped.org/AM/Template.cfm?Section=Search&TEMPLATE=/CM/ContentDisplay.cfm&CONTENTID=4182

Holbrook, M. C. (2009). Supporting students' literacy through data-driven decision-making and ongoing assessment of achievement. *Journal of Visual Impairment & Blindness, 103*(3), 133–136.

Huebner, K. M., Merk-Adam, B., Stryker, D., & Wolffe, K. E. (2004). *The national agenda for the education of children and youths with visual impairments, including those with multiple disabilities: Revised.* New York, NY: AFB Press.

Individuals with Disabilities Education Improvement Act (IDEA) of 2004, Pub. L. No. 108-466,§ 602, 2657 Stat. 118 (2004).

Johnstone, C., Thurlow, M., Altman, J., Timmons, J., & Kato, K. (2009). Assistive technology approaches for large-scale assessment: Perceptions of teachers of students with visual impairments. *Exceptionality, 17*(2), 66–75. doi:10.1080/09362830902805756.

Jones, M. G., Taylor, A. R., & Broadwell, B. (2009). Concepts of scale held by students with visual impairment. *Journal of Research in Science Teaching, 46*(5), 506–519.

Kamei-Hannan, C. (2008). Examining the accessibility of a computerized adapted test using assistive technology. *Journal of Visual Impairment & Blindness, 102*(5), 261–271.

Kappermna, G., Heinze, T., & Sticken, J. (2000). Mathematics. In A. J. Koenig & M. C. Holbrook (Eds.), *Foundations of education: Volume 2. Instructional strategies for teaching children and youths with visual impairments* (pp. 370–399). New York, NY: AFB Press.

Kappermna, G., Sticken, J., & Heinze, T. (2002). Survey of the use of assistive technology by Illinois students who are visually impaired. *Journal of Visual Impairment & Blindness, 96*(2), 106–108.

Kekelis, L. S., & Anderson, E. S. (1984). Family communication styles and language development. *Journal of Visual Impairment & Blindness, 78*(2), 54–65.

Kelly, S. M. (2009). Use of assistive technology by students with visual impairments: Findings from a National Survey. *Journal of Visual Impairment & Blindness, 103*(8), 470–480.

Kirchner, C., & Diament, S. (1999). Estimates of the number of visually impaired students, their teachers, and orientation and mobility specialists: Part 2. *Journal of Visual Impairment and Blindness, 93*(11), 738–744.

Kirchner, C., & Smith, B. (2005). Transition to what? Education and employment outcomes for visually impaired youths after high school. *Journal of Visual Impairment & Blindness, 99*(8), 499–504.

Koenig, A. J., & Farrenkopf, C. (1997). Essential experiences to undergird the early development of literacy. *Journal of Visual Impairment & Blindness, 91*(1), 14–25.

Koenig, A. J. & Holbrook, M. C. (1995). *Learning media assessment of students with visual impairments: A resource guide for teachers* (2nd ed.) Austin, TX: Texas School for the Blind and Visually Impaired.

Koenig, A. J., & Holbrook, M. C. (2000). Ensuring high-quality instruction for students in braille literacy programs. *Journal of Visual Impairment & Blindness, 94*(11), 677.

Lewis, S., & Iselin, S. A. (2002). A comparison of the independent living skills of primary students with visual impairments and their sighted peers: A pilot study. *Journal of Visual Impairment & Blindness, 96*(5), 335–344.

Liedtke, W. (1998). Fostering the development of number sense in young children who are blind. *Journal of Visual Impairment & Blindness, 92*(5), 346–349.

Linn, R. L. (2002). Validation of the uses and interpretations of results of state assessment accountability systems. In. G. Tindal & T. M. Haladyna (Eds.), *Large-scale assessment programs for all students* (pp. 27–47). Mahwah, NJ: Erlbaum.

Lohmeier, K., Blankenship, K., & Hatlen, P. (2009). Expanded core curriculum: 12 years later. *Journal of Visual Impairment & Blindness, 103*(2), 103–112.

Lueck, A. H. (2004). Overview of functional evaluation of vision. In A. H. Lueck (Ed.), *Functional vision: A practitioner's guide to evaluation and intervention* (pp. 89–114). New York, NY: AFB Press.

MacCuspie, P. A. (1996). *Promoting acceptance of children with disabilities: From tolerance to inclusion.* Halifax, Nova Scotia: Atlantic Provinces Special Education Authority.

Malkowicz, D. E., Myers, G., & Leisman, G. (2006). Rehabilitation of cortical visual impairment in children. *International Journal of Neuroscience, 116,* 1015–1033. doi: 0.1080/00207450600553505

Marder, C. (2006). *A national profile of students with visual impairments in elementary and middle schools: A special topic report from the special education elementary longitudinal study (SEELS).* (No. ED-00-CO-0017). Menlo Park, CA: SRI International.

Matsuba, C. A., & Jan, J. E. (2006). Long-term outcome of children with cortical visual impairments. *Developmental Medicine & Child Neurology, 48,* 508–512.

McDonnall, M. C., & Crudden, A. (2009). Factors affecting the successful employment of transition-age youths with visual impairments. *Journal of Visual Impairment & Blindness, 103*(6), 329–341.

McGaha, C. G., & Farran, D. C. (2001). Interactions in an inclusive classroom: The effects visual status and setting. *Journal of Visual Impairment & Blindness, 95*(2), 80–94.

McHugh, E., & Lieberman, L. (2003). The impact of developmental factors on stereotypical rocking of children with visual impairments. *Journal of Visual Impairment and Blindness, 97*(8), 453–474.

McKenzie, A. R., & Lewis, S. (2008). The role and training of paraprofessionals who work with students who are visually impaired. *Journal of Visual Impairment & Blindness, 102*(8), 459–471.

Miller, L. J., Lane, S. J., Cermak, S. A., Anzalone, M., & Osten, B. (2005). Regulatory-sensory processing disorders in children. In S. I. Greenspan & S. Wieder (Eds.), *Diagnostic manual for infancy and early childhood: Mental health, developmental, regulatory-sensory processing and language disorders and learning challenges* (ICDL-DMIC) (pp. 73–112). Bethesda, MD: Interdisciplinary Council on Developmental and Learning Disorders.

Murphy, J. L., Hatton, D., & Erickson, K. A. (2008). Exploring the early literacy practices of teachers of infants, toddlers, and preschoolers with visual impairments. *Journal of Visual Impairment & Blindness, 102*(3), 133–146.

National Institute of Child Health and Human Development. (2000). *Report of the National Reading Panel: Teaching children to read: An evidence-based assessment of the scientific research literature on reading and its implications for reading instruction: Reports of the subgroups* (NIH Publication No. 00-4754). Washington, DC: U.S. Government Printing Office.

Pawletko, T. (2002). Autism and visual impairment. *FOCAL Points, 1*(2), 1–4.

Pogrund, R. L. (2002). Setting the stage for working with young children who are blind and visually impaired. In R. L. Pogrund & D. L. Fazzi (Eds.), *Early focus: Working with young children who are blind or visually impaired and their families* (2nd ed., pp. 1–15). New York, NY: AFB Press.

Pogrund, R., Healy, G., Jones, K., Levack, N., Martin-Curry, S., Martinez, C., Marz, J., … Vrba, A. (1998). *Teaching age-appropriate purposeful skills* (2nd ed.). New York, NY: AFB Press.

Presley, I., & D'Andrea, F. M. (2009). *Assistive technology for students who are blind or visually impaired: A guide to assessment.* New York, NY: AFB Press.

Repka, M. X. (2008). How much amblyopia treatment is enough? *Archives of Ophthalmology, 126*(7), 990–991.

Roman, C., Baker-Nobles, L., Dutton, G. N., Luiselli, T. E., Flener, B. S., Jan, J. E., … Neilson, A. S. (2010). Statement on cortical visual impairment. *Journal of Visual Impairment & Blindness, 104*(2), 69–72.

Roman-Lantzy, C. (2007). *Cortical visual impairment: An approach to assessment and intervention.* New York, NY: AFB Press.

Sacks, S. Z., & Silberman, R. K. (2000a). Social skills. In A. J. Koenig & M. C. Holbrook (Eds.), *Foundations of education* (2nd ed., Vol. 2, pp. 616–652). New York, NY: AFB Press.

Sacks, S. Z., & Silberman, R. K. (2000b). Social skills in vision impairment. In B. Silverstone, M. A. Lang, B. P. Rosenthal, & E. E. Faye (Eds.), *The Lighthouse handbook on vision impairment and vision rehabilitation* (pp. 377–394). New York, NY: Oxford University Press.

Sacks, S. Z., Wolffe, K. E., & Tierney, D. (1998). Lifestyles of students with visual impairments: Preliminary studies of social networks. *Exceptional Children, 64*(4), 463–478.

Schwartz, T. L. (2010). Causes of visual impairment: Pathology and its implications. In A. L. Corn & J. N Erin (Eds.), *Foundations of low vision: Clinical and functional perspectives* (2nd ed., pp. 137–191). New York, NY: AFB Press.

Smith, D. W., Kelley, P., Maushak, N. J., Griffin-Shirley, N., & Lan, W. Y. (2009). Assistive technology competencies for teachers of students with visual impairments. *Journal of Visual Impairment & Blindness, 103*(8), 457–469.

Steinkuller, P. G., Du, L., Gilbert, C., Foster, A., Collins, M. L., & Coats, D. K. (1999). Childhood blindness. *Journal of the American Association of Pediatric Ophthalmology and Strabismus, 3*(1), 26–32.

Strickling, C. A., & Pogrund, R. L. (2002). Motor focus: Promoting movement experiences and motor development. In R. L. Pogrund & D. L. Fazzi (Eds.), *Early focus: Working with young children who are blind or visually impaired and their families* (2nd ed., pp. 1–15). New York, NY: AFB Press.

Thompson, S., Blount, A., & Thurlow, M. (2002). *A summary of research on the effects of test accommodations: 1999 through 2001 (Technical Report 34).* Minneapolis, MN: University of Minnesota, National Center on Educational Outcomes.

Torgesen, J. K., Wagner, R. K., Rashotte, C. A., Burgess, S., & Hecht, S. (1997). Contributions of phonological awareness and rapid automatic naming ability to the growth of word reading skills in second- to fifth-grade children. *Scientific Studies of Reading, 1*(2), 161–184.

Tuttle, D. W., & Tuttle, N. R. (2000). Psychosocial needs of children and youths. In M.C. Holbrook & A. J. Koenig (Eds.), *Foundations of education* (2nd ed., Vol. 1, 161–171). New York, NY: AFB Press.

Wagner, E. (2004). Development and implementation of a curriculum to develop social competence for students with visual impairments in Germany. *Journal of Visual Impairment and Blindness, 98*(11), 703–709.

Wagner, M., Newman, L., Cameto, R., & Levine, P. (2006). *The academic achievement and functional performance of youth with disabilities. A report from the national longitudinal transition study-2 (NLTS2)* (No. NCSER 2006-3000). Menlo Park, CA: SRI International.

Warren, D. H. (1994). *Blindness and children: An individual differences approach.* New York, NY: Cambridge University Press.

Wilkinson, M. E. (2010). Clinical low vision services. In A. L. Corn & J. N. Erin (Eds.), *Foundations of low vision: Clinical and functional perspectives.* (pp. 238–295). New York, NY: AFB Press.

Wolffe, K. E., & Candela, A. R. (2002). A qualitative analysis of employer's experiences with visually impaired workers. *Journal of Visual Impairment & Blindness, 96*(9), 622–634.

Wolffe, K. E., & Sacks, S. Z. (1997). The lifestyles of blind, low vision, and sighted youth: A quantitative comparison. *Journal of Visual Impairment & Blindness, 91*(3), 245–257.

Wolffe, K. E., Sacks, S. Z., Corn, A. L., Erin, J. N., Huebner, K. M., & Lewis, S. (2002). Teachers of students with visual impairments: What are they teaching? *Journal of Visual Impairment & Blindness, 96*(5), 293–304.

World Health Organization (2010). Prevention of blindness and visual impairment. Retrieved April 19, 2010, from http://www.who.int/blindness/causes/priority/en/index5.html

Wormsley, D. P. (1997). Fostering emergent literacy. In D. P. Wormsley & F. M. D'Andrea (Eds.), *Instructional strategies for braille literacy* (pp. 17–56). New York, NY: AFB Press.

Wright, T., Wormsley, D. P., & Kamei-Hannan, C. (2009). Hand movements and braille reading efficiency: Data from the alphabetic braille and contracted braille study. *Journal of Visual Impairment & Blindness, 103*(10), 649–661.

Zebehazy, K., & Whitten, E. (2003). Collaboration between special schools and local education agencies: A progress report. *Journal of Visual Impairment & Blindness, 97*(2), 73–84.

Zimmerman, G. J., Zebehazy, K. T., & Moon, M. L. (2010). Optics and low vision devices. In A. L. Corn & J. N. Erin (Eds.), *Foundations of low vision: Clinical and functional perspectives* (2nd ed., pp. 192–237). New York, NY: AFB Press.

21

Traumatic Brain Injury

Renée Lajiness-O'Neill
Eastern Michigan University, Ypsilanti, MI and Henry Ford System, Detroit, MI

Laszlo A. Erdodi
Eastern Michigan University, Ypsilanti, MI and London Health Science Centre, London, MI

Epidemiology

According to the Centers for Disease Control (CDC, 2003, p. 8), a "traumatic brain injury (TBI) is caused by a blow or jolt to the head or a penetrating head injury that disrupts the normal function of the brain." TBI continues to be a leading cause of death (Graham, 2001; Jankowitz & Adelson, 2006) and one of the most frequent causes of disability in children (Arffa, 1998; Bigler, Clark, & Farmer, 1996; Kraus, 1995) with an estimated annual childhood and adolescent incidence between 180 to 300 per 100,000 (Adelson & Kochanek,1998; Anderson, Catroppa, Rosenfeld, Haritou, & Morse 2000; Guthrie, Mast, Richards, McQuaid, & Pavlakis, 1999). The two age groups that are at the highest risk for TBI are children younger than 5 years of age and older adolescents and young adults between the ages of 15 to 19 years (Langlois, Rutland-Brown, & Thomas, 2004). Young children are most often victims of falls while adolescents and young adults are injured following motor vehicle accidents (Donders, 2007). Males are nearly twice as likely as females to sustain a TBI, while hospitalization rates for TBI are reported to be the highest in African Americans and American/Indians/Alaskan Natives (CDC, 2003). Available epidemiological findings further suggest a similar distribution in severity of brain injuries in different age groups (Bauer & Fritz, 2004), although milder injuries are more often reported in pediatrics compared to adults. In addition, approximately 75% of the reported injuries are concussions or other forms of mild TBI (CDC, 2003). Long-term sequelae occur less often in mild injuries, though some investigations suggest persistent deficits in 5%–15% of injuries (Hawley, Ward, Magnay, & Long, 2002). Moreover, age appears to play an important role in both incidence and outcome (Anderson & Moore, 1995; Anderson et al., 2001). In fact, although better survival rates have been reported in children compared to adults with TBI, the long-term consequences are typically more devastating due to their age and thus compromised developmental potential (Mazzola & Adelson, 2002).

The most debilitating effects of TBI typically result from alterations in cognitive and neurobehavioral functioning (Jaffe et al., 1992; Johnson, 1992; Levin et al., 1987; Levin et al., 1993; Silver, 2000), which significantly impact long-term functional outcome. While there are a number of moderating variables that affect outcome, including age and injury severity, individuals with TBI experience a host of cognitive deficits following injury including varying degrees of impairment in attention, memory, speed of information processing, communication, and executive functioning (e.g., reasoning and problem solving). Deficits in attention and memory are two of the most prevalent cognitive deficits following TBI, which substantially affect a child's ability to learn and retain information—skills that will be essential for success following their return to school. Indeed, memory impairment is well documented in both mild-moderate and severe injuries (Bassett & Slater, 1990; Jaffe et al., 1992; Levin, Eisenberg, Wigg, & Kobayashi, 1982; Levin et al., 1988; Yeates, Blumenstein, Patterson, & Delis, 1995), though the extent and quality of deficits vary.

Neurobehavioral and psychosocial sequelae such as affective instability and impaired social functioning following TBI also substantially compromise the child and adolescents' entry or re-entry into the school and community. Moreover, it is often the neurobehavioral deficits that are the least well understood by family and school personnel who are also often poorly equipped to manage behavioral problems that emerge following injury that can range from poor initiation to aggressive outbursts. Premorbid difficulties are often magnified following injury including both academic problems such a learning disability as well as problems with behavioral regulation such as attention-deficit/hyperactivity disorder (ADHD). In fact, the very children with premorbid learning and behavioral difficulties are those with the greatest risk of sustaining a brain injury.

Neuropathology and Pathophysiology of Pediatric TBI

Brain injuries in children can be broadly categorized into focal and diffuse injuries. Focal injuries are typically secondary to direct force effects and include contusions and lacerations to the brain as well as hemorrhage which subsequently lead to subdural, subarachnoid, or intracerebral hematomas (Adelson & Kochanek, 1998). Diffuse brain injuries, often caused by the effects of acceleration and deceleration of the head and brain and which result in diffuse axonal injury (DAI) include brief cerebral concussion and prolonged coma. The natural progression and outcome in pediatric brain injury depends on both the mechanical forces involved in the injury as well as the pathophysiological events that ensue. The primary trauma sets a cascade of age-related neural and vascular events in motion which are followed by secondary injury from events such as cerebral edema, elevated intracranial pressure, and hypoxic/ischemic changes (Bauer & Fritz, 2004; Jagannathan & Jagannathan, 2008). The management of secondary injury continues to pose a significant challenge for the medical community, evidenced by a continued focus on a reduction of the impact of secondary sequelae rather than altering its progression.

Diffuse brain swelling (DBS) following severe injury also occurs more commonly in children than adults (Adelson & Kochanek, 1998), and children are more negatively affected by this swelling (Bauer & Fritz, 2004). Molecular and cellular alterations also result from a complex cascade of immunological/inflammatory cellular responses in pediatric TBI (Jagannathan & Jagannathan, 2008). There is often a reduction in cellular metabolism which has prompted interventions focused on hyperoxia. Hypermetabolism of glucose contributes to secondary ischemic insults through a complex disruption in blood flow and metabolic processes.

There are also structural differences in the pediatric compared to adult brain which contribute to an age-related and a unique response to the biomechanics of the primary injury. More specifically, there is an increase in water content of the brain tissue, capillary density, and cerebral volume with a concomitant reduction in the degree of myelination, which substantially increases the vulnerability of the pediatric brain to the effects of shear injury (Thibault & Margulies, 1998). Similarly, due to the immaturity of the development of the skull, the mechanical load of the injury is more easily transferred, resulting in a more diffuse pattern of brain distortion (Margulies & Thibault, 2000).

In addition to the unique pattern of pathophysiological disruption and structural differences in children that make them particularly vulnerable to the effects of TBI, the temporal and frontal lobes are more susceptible to damage regardless of the original locus of injury (Bigler & Dodrill, 1997; Bigler, 1999). This is, in part, due to the boney prominences of the anterior and middle cranial fossa which encapsulate these lobes. The preferential impact on the frontal and temporal lobes likely contributes to the typical constellation of neurobehavioral disruption coupled with memory and executive impairment following moderate to severe injury (Bigler, 1999). Another plausible contributing mechanism to this pattern of deficits is the impact that acceleration/deceleration injury is likely to have on the anterior commissure; the critical pathway of communication between affective orbitofrontal regions and limbic regions of temporal lobe such as the amygdala. Moderate and severe traumatic brain injury has consistently been reported to cause diffuse and focal damage with generalized atrophic changes resulting in a loss in overall brain volume (Levin et al., 2008) and diffuse white matter atrophy (Gale, Johnson, Bigler, & Blatter, 1995; Levin et al., 2008). Merkley and colleagues (2008), reported significant global cortical thinning in a cohort of children with TBI, ages 9–16 years, compared to typically developing children. Moreover, the reduction in cortical thickness was found to be specifically related to deficits in working memory. Some of the most commonly reported morphological alterations and pathological findings noted during the chronic phase of injury on neuroimaging include general ventricular dilation with enhancement of the temporal horns and third ventricle; atrophic changes specifically noted in the anterior temporal and frontal regions; enlargement of the interhemispheric and Sylvian fissures as well as other cortical sulci; and thinning of the corpus collosum (Bigler, 1999).

A critical mechanism of injury following pediatric TBI includes alterations in neural transmission, which also contributes uniquely to deficits in attention, memory, and executive functioning. An increase in extracellular levels of glutamate and its neurotransmission has been reported to result in a toxic increase in intracellular calcium concentrations. Similarly, post-synaptic changes to both the AMPA and NMDA-type glutamate receptors have been reported to contribute to further excitotoxicity. The excess of synaptic glutamate has been reported to contribute to hyperexcitability, seizures, cell damage, and death (Jagannathan & Jagannathan, 2008). Equally important is the alterations in neural transmission that have been implicated in cognitive sequelae of brain injury in children, particularly the noted deficits in attention and memory (Konrad, Gauggel, & Schurck, 2003). While glutamatergic excitotoxic mechanisms of injury are essential to recent theories of neuronal injury following brain trauma, GABAergic, aminergic, and cholinergic disruptions in transmission have also been documented.

Description and Diagnosis

The severity of traumatic brain injury occurs on a spectrum ranging from mild (mTBI) to severe, with mTBI accounting for 80%–90% of all treated cases (Cassidy et al., 2004). The term *concussion* is often used interchangeably with mild TBI. At the same end of the spectrum, both post-concussion syndrome (PCS) and persistent post-concussive syndrome (PPCS) are nomenclature that have also been used (Anderson, Heitger, & MacLeod, 2006; Bigler, 2008). In the majority of cases of mTBI, symptoms abate within minutes to days post injury. PCS is used to refer to cases when the symptoms persist for more than a few days, and often more than a week. In contrast, if the cognitive and/ or neurobehavioral sequelae persist beyond 3 months following the initial injury, a designation of PPCS is used (Bigler, 2008; Iverson, 2006; Willer & Leddy, 2006). The potential for long-term sequelae in mTBI should not be either under- or over-stated. Indeed, repeated or serial mTBI occurring over an extended period of time may result in cumulative neurological and cognitive deficits. Repeated mTBI occurring within a short period of time can be fatal. The severity of injury is determined by a host of factors such lesion size, post-resuscitation Glagow Coma Scale (GCS) score (GCS; Teasdale & Jennett, 1974), length of coma or loss of consciousness, and length of Post Traumatic Amnesia (PTA). GCS scores are based on eye opening, best verbal response, and best motor responses with scores ranging from 0 to15, and child versions have been developed. Higher scores signify less compromise and, as such, the longer the length the coma, the lower the GCS score. Scores of 13–15 are classified as mild injuries, 12–9 as moderate injuries, and less than or equal to 8 as severe injuries. Severity based on PTA is determined by the duration of amnesia following an injury, ranging from 5 to 60 minutes (mild) to 1 to 7 days (severe). Indeed, severity based on PTA has been found to be a better predictor of cognitive status than GCS, although is not consistently obtained. Retrograde amnesia, from hours to days, also occurs following moderate to severe TBI. There is a temporal gradient of loss; that is, memories closest to the accident are lost first while later memories are preserved.

Clinical management of traumatic brain injury depends on the stage of the injury as well. The acute phase has traditionally been defined as the point of injury through 3 days post injury; post-acute phase as 4 days through 3 months post injury, and; the long-term phase as 4 months post-injury through recovery. Depending on the severity of injury, educators most often encounter students in the post-acute and long-term phase of recovery.

Within the educational system, specification of the severity of injury is not required in order for a child to receive services. Indeed, the medical designation and methods of diagnosing TBI are rarely addressed or are not well understood within the educational system given that emphasis is on educational disability. Unfortunately, this may result in a poor appreciation of the potential long-term impact of mTBI and PPCS. Children may be perceived as unmotivated, lazy, or intentionally disruptive when, in fact, they may be experiencing persistent symptoms from an injury. This is a particularly important issue when one considers the number of sports-related injuries and concussions experienced annually in our school systems. Equally important, individuals with premorbid learning difficulties appear to be at an even greater risk of post-injury sequelae than those without learning disability, and these are often a substantial subset of children drawn to athletics; those that find success in the classroom difficult to achieve. There is also a considerable body of literature to suggest that the long-term negative consequences on thinking and behavior are also more pronounced in serial concussions and injuries, resulting in controversy about children and adolescents returning safely to sports following more than one injury.

Public Policy, Educational Definition and Disability

Over the past decade and a half, both public policy and consensus statements have emerged in an attempt to obtain accurate epidemiological data, increase public education and awareness, and to examine effective rehabilitation measures for individuals who have experienced traumatic brain injuries (Langlois, Marr, Mitchko, & Johnson, 2005; NIH Consensus Development Panel on Rehabilitation of Persons With Traumatic Brain Injury, 1999). In 1996, Congress passed Public Law 104-166, the TBI Act of 1996 (http://thomas.loc.gov). At that time, the CDC was charged with (a) assisting in the development of uniform reporting systems to be used by states, and (b) preparing a report to Congress on the incidence of TBI and prevalence of disability. The TBI Act of 1996 was reauthorized and amended as part of the Children's Health Act of 2000 (Public Law 106-310; http://thomas.loc.gov). The Children's Health Act was further charged with the implementation of a national education and awareness campaign to disseminate information regarding the incidence and prevalence of TBI and related disability, TBI sequelae, and resources for state-level services. At nearly the same time, the NIH Consensus Developmental Panel (1999) convened to investigate rehabilitative practices with individuals with TBI. With respect to education, the panel acknowledged the need for specialized, interdisciplinary treatment programs to address the particular medical, rehabilitation, social, family, and educational needs of young and school-aged children with TBI, with the recognition that research was needed to address the most effective components of these services. Interestingly, an awareness of the need to examine effective methods of intervention, including instructional practices, was occurring after the school systems had already been charged with addressing the educational needs of children and adolescents with TBI, leaving them woefully underprepared to tackle the complexities of this population.

Public Law 94-142 (PL 94-142; Federal Register, 1975, 1990) provided a mechanism for the provision of educational services to children and adolescents with exceptional need (D'Amato & Rothlisberg, 1996), although TBI was not included as a specific categorical designation at that time. Individuals with TBI received services under other categorical classifications such as learning disability, other health impaired, or emotionally disturbed. The exclusion of TBI was partially addressed by Section 504 of the Rehabilitation Act of 1973 and the Americans with Disabilities Act of 1990 (ADA) that mandate the provision of reasonable accommodations to individuals with disabilities in higher education and the workforce (Maedgen & Semrud-Clikeman, 2007).

In 1990, TBI was added to the special education law as an educational disability under the Individuals with Disability Education Act (IDEA; 1997, 2000, 2004) (Maedgen & Semrud-Clikeman, 2007; Ylvisaker et al., 2001), which makes state funding dependent on the mandate that children receive free and appropriate education in the least restrictive environment.

Currently, within the education arena, the federal definition of TBI includes (a) an education-related disability, (b) associated with injury to the brain acquired after birth, (c) caused by an external force, and (d) not degenerative. While many states employ this definition, some have adopted a broader definition to include injuries with etiologies such as stroke, anoxia, etc.

Clinical Sequelae and Assessment

An accurate assessment of a child's pattern of strengths and weaknesses is not only essential to establish an appropriate diagnosis, but more importantly, to develop an effective plan for educational and psychological interventions (Glang et al., 2008; Kirkwood et al., 2008; Powell & Voeller, 2004; Ylvisaker et al., 2001). Assessment can be performed by a variety of professionals across different settings. A typical psychoeducational evaluation uses standardized intellectual and academic achievement measures, parent or teacher rating scales, and behavioral observation, although this may be supplemented with an assessment of a specific aspect of cognitive or sensorimotor performance such as tests of speech and language or motor functioning depending on the educational question posed. Scores on these instruments provide a quick snapshot of the child's present cognitive, academic, and social-emotional functioning in comparison to peers of the same age. Test data can be used to estimate the impact of the injury on overall functioning, degree of return to baseline, and anticipated difficulties in adjustment. However, the brevity of such an evaluation makes it difficult to formulate specific treatment recommendations and might miss more subtle aspects of the child's neurocognitive profile that may be relevant for the case conceptualization.

A more comprehensive assessment would require a neuropsychological evaluation that extends the investigation to a wider range of cognitive and neurobehavioral abilities. Such an assessment can be quite lengthy (4–6 hours or more), and involves extensive clinical interviews with the parents, review of medical records, administration of highly specialized tests covering a wide range of functioning (sensorimotor, attention, learning and memory, language and communication, visuospatial processing, and executive functions) beyond intelligence, achievement, and psychosocial functioning, statistical analysis of test data and an integrative report summarizing the findings and recommendations. Neuropsychological assessments focus on discrepancies between areas of development as well as task analyses to identify the specific functional impairment responsible for low scores on standardized tests—essentially performing a "circuit check" on the brain (Powell & Voeller, 2004). Standard cognitive and behavioral domains of assessment and frequently used instruments for individuals with TBI are noted in Table 21.1.

TABLE 21.1
A Representative Sample of Educational, Psychological, and Neuropsychological Measures to Examine the Relative Domains of Functioning

Cognitive domains	Representative tests/measures
Intellectual	Wechsler Scales (WPPSI, WAIS, WISC) Stanford-Binet Intelligence Scale
Developmental	Bayley Scales of Infant Development Differential Ability Scale Mullen Scales of Early Learning
Achievement	Wechsler Individual Achievement Test Woodcock-Johnson Test of Achievement
Attention and Concentration	Test of Variables of Attention Continuous Performance Tests
Sensorimotor	Finger-tapping Test Grooved Pegboard Test
Visuospatial/ Perceptual-Motor	Developmental Test of Visual-Motor Integration Rey-Osterreith Complex Figure Test
Speech and Language	Clinical Evaluation of Language Fundamentals Peabody Picture Vocabulary Test Comprehensive Test of Phonological Processing Boston Naming Test Phonemic Semantic Fluency
Learning and Memory	California Verbal Learning Test Test of Memory and Learning Wide Range Assessment of Memory and Learning Wechsler Memory Scales
Executive Function	Wisconsin Card Sorting Test Category Test Cognitive Bias Task Delis-Kaplan Executive Function System
Personality and Psychosocial	Child Behavior Checklist Conners' Rating Scales Behavioral Assessment System for Children

Note. To simplify the table, relative editions or versions were not noted.

An emerging concern with neuropsychological assessment is its ecological validity. Individually administered standardized tests may inadvertently conceal a layer of pathology that only becomes visible in the face of environmental stressors. For example, a child may be compliant and producing scores in the normal range with the examiner yet experience difficulty with self-regulation in unstructured settings or under stress. Also, due to the unpredictable nature of the recovery process, frequent monitoring over time is recommended to ensure early detection and correction of unexpected decreases in functioning (Ylvisaker et al., 2001).

A clinical evaluation is typically focused on assigning *Diagnostic and Statistical Manual of the American Psychiatric Association* (*DSM*) categories to a child's symptom presentation. Although the neurocognitive sequelae of pediatric TBI do not easily fit established psychiatric diagnoses, they are often accompanied by symptoms of depression and anxiety that are coded in the *DSM* (Kirkwood et al., 2008). Affective disorders are important to diagnose and treat as they are significant predictors of recovery besides being salient indicators of overall quality of life. Even though the educational system and medical rehabilitation centers are increasingly focusing on individuals' functional needs vs. the classification of their symptoms, *DSM*-based diagnoses remain an important determination to make for a host of practical reasons.

Despite a common medical etiology, children with TBI display remarkable variability in symptom presentation as a function of premorbid level of functioning, the nature, severity and location of the injury and environmental variables that determine the rate of recovery. Therefore, they do not require assessment methods specifically tailored toward their condition or interventions specific to TBI. Instead, individualized educational plans and continued monitoring of the recovery process are required (Ylvisaker et al., 2001).

Looking beyond the enormous diversity of symptoms in TBI, common trends emerge as a result of differential vulnerability of certain brain regions to closed head injury. Specifically, as noted, the frontal and temporal lobes are the most prone to trauma. These focal injuries result in reduced awareness of deficits, disinhibition, poor initiation, impaired planning, and deficient social skills as well as impaired new learning relative to pre-injury knowledge base. Diffuse axonal shearing is also a common, yet difficult to detect feature of TBI causing a decrease in mental processing speed, and compromised emotional self-regulation, which creates a need for a different set of accommodations in school settings (Ylvisaker et al., 2001).

Indeed, "executive" dysfunction and its impact on academic achievement and psychosocial functioning has not been extensively examined or well understood within the educational system. School psychologists and assessment specialists do not typically receive training in prefrontal executive function syndromes, the impact of TBI on executive functioning, or assessment measures to adequately assess these skills. Executive functioning is a term used to describe a set of inter-related abilities that are essential to maintain an appropriate problem solving set for the attainment of some future goal (Catroppa & Anderson, 2006). These processes are necessary for conscious control of thought, emotion, and action that are essential to day-to-day functioning (Powell & Voeller, 2004). Executive functions are subserved by prefrontal and subcortical structures and disruption to these regions following injury can result in impairment in cognitive, behavioral, and emotional regulation. Executive deficits are difficult to treat or remediate, and often compensatory interventions such as environmental modifications are employed. Table 21.2 provides a list of executive functions that can be disrupted following injury broadly categorized under cognitive, behavioral, and emotional regulatory skills described by Powell & Voeller (2004).

Although head injury typically results in a generalized decline in cognitive functioning (Jordan & Ashton, 1996), these "frontal syndromes" are the most prominent cognitive and behavioral features in children with TBI. Comorbid ADHD (whether congenital or secondary to TBI) exacerbates deficits in attention, working memory and executive functioning. Impairment is the most pronounced on tasks that require sustained attention and involve a high rate of stimulus presentation (Slomine et al., 2005). Even in children with well preserved general intelligence, there is evidence of persisting deficits in abstract thought, mental flexibility, and self-awareness (Catroppa & Anderson, 2006). Understandably, this cluster of deficits influences psychosocial outcomes as well as family dynamics and caregiver distress (Mangeot, Armstrong, Colvin, Yeates, & Taylor, 2002).

One of the commonly encountered deficits following traumatic brain injury is impairment in attention and concentration. The neural mechanisms that underlie attention are vast and include a complex network of structures primarily in the frontal and parietal lobes (Baars, 2007). While many individuals are subsequently diagnosed with secondary ADHD following TBI, it is important for those within the educational system to be aware of disorders of attention that are of a qualitatively different nature. The

TABLE 21.2
Executive Functions: Subdomains of Self-Regulation

Cognitive regulation	
	Working memory
	Regulation of attention (detection, vigilance, shifting, control distractibility
	Planning
	Goal setting and monitoring
	Time estimation
	Time management
	Organizational strategies
	Mental flexibility/shifting cognitive set
	Fluency or efficiency of processing
	Abstract reasoning and concept formation
	Novel problem solving and judgment
	Maintaining self awareness and identity across place and time
	Integration of social-emotional information into future plans and behaviors
Behavioral regulation	
	Initiation of movements or behaviors
	Inhibition of automatic motor responses
	Sustaining motor performance through time
	Shifting motor responses when appropriate
	Ability to delay immediate gratification (impulse control)
	Anticipation and sensitivity to future consequences of present actions
Emotional regulation	
	Modulation of emotional arousal
	Modulation of mood
	Self-soothing strategies

frailty of the attentional system is evident in attentional disorders such as sensory neglect or inattention due to direct disruption in the attentional network from TBI, most often noted with involvement in the right cerebral hemisphere. Individuals with sensory neglect do not attend to, hence, perceive images in the contralateral visual field (external space) or may completely neglect an entire half of their body (motor neglect), despite intact basic sensory processing.

Likewise, individuals are likely to encounter deficits in visuospatial processing following TBI. There is considerable overlap in both structure and function of attentional and spatial processing. As noted, an individual may experience a sensory or hemispatial neglect, and this most often involves the right posterior parietal cortex. This disorder is typically perceived as a disorder of spatial attention or spatial representation. Sometimes the injury will be more extensive involving the occipitotemporoparietal junction, and individuals will experience difficulty with both object recognition and spatial location. If the visual pathway projections from the optic nerve to the striate (visual) cortex are disrupted, an individual will experience an actual visual field loss rather than merely inattention, such as in a hemianopia in which an individual is unable to see the contralateral half of space. In contrast, if the lesion is more anterior and involves both frontal and parietal regions, an individual may experience a constructional apraxia; that is, problems with construction such as drawing and building. In this case, there are deficits in visuoperception, visually guided action, and executive function.

As a natural extension of impaired attention, children with TBI exhibit memory deficits of varying severity as a result of a compromised encoding process. Although this population has no unique memory profile, performance seems to be mediated by injury severity and processing speed (Mottram & Donders, 2006). Mild-to-moderate TBI rarely results in lasting memory dysfunction; however, a severe injury can significantly compromise verbal learning (Roman et al., 1998). This impairment in processing verbal information might in turn disrupt the normative rate of knowledge acquisition, resulting in a compounding deficit later, especially in academic achievement.

Prospective memory is also impaired in children with TBI. Deficits are linearly related to injury parameters and especially pronounced in those with severe TBI. Moreover, the latter group benefits less from extra reminding to engage in a future task (McCauley & Levin, 2004). Increases in cognitive demands result in further decline in prospective memory performance, which is consistent with the high prevalence of frontal lobe lesions. Age has also been identified as a mediator variable: older children tend to perform better, but they are also more vulnerable to the adverse effect of the increase in cognitive load (Ward, Shum, McKinlay, Baker, & Wallace, 2007).

Procedural memory, on the other hand, is less vulnerable to injury, hence well preserved after TBI. In fact, children with TBI often show a normative learning curve, retention and recall on such tasks even when their performance is impaired on explicit memory tests (Ward, Shum, Wallace, & Boon, 2002). This phenomenon has a neuroanatomical explanation: subcortical structures that are involved in implicit memory are less prone to lesion during a close head injury. One of the implications of these findings is the potential utility of activity-based learning in this population, where the physical aspects of the acquisition process can later serve as cues for retrieval.

Communication problems including deficits in speech and language development and functioning are also evident following TBI. An individual may lose the ability to understand language or communicate effectively. The clinical syndromes of language impairment or aphasia involve some aspect of reduced language output as well as impaired comprehension, repetition, and naming. Disruptions in the quality of speech production may also occur, including poor articulation (dysarthria), poor melodic line (dysprosody), or low volume (hypophonia). Initially, language skills are linearly related to injury severity. However, children with severe TBI tend to recover at a faster rate. The strongest predictors of outcome are pre-morbid communication skills, age at injury, and socioeconomic status (SES). As observed in other domains, impairment becomes more pronounced when more complex language processes are called upon, while the basic skills remain intact (Catroppa, Anderson, Morse, Haritou, & Rosenfeld, 2008). It is important for both speech pathologists and educators to be aware of linguistic skills that are the most vulnerable following injury and factors that predict outcome. A child's developmental level at the time of injury is clearly related to the pattern of deficits that emerge and persist. Young children who sustain severe TBI appear to be most vulnerable to deficits at the lexical and discourse levels while older children and adolescents appear to be at the greatest risk for impairment in higher-order discourse functions (Ewing-Cobbs & Barnes, 2002). Discourse macrolevel processing is one's ability to extract the most important and relevant information from connected language (Ulatowska & Chapman, 1994). Extremes seem to persist: despite the high inter-individual variability that characterizes this population, children with severe TBI tend to have the highest rate of initial language and math impairment, the fastest relative recovery rate, and the highest rate of deficits that persist over time (Fay et al., 2009).

Social cognition, an important domain of adaptive functioning and a strong predictor of overall outcome, follows a similar rate of recovery. Research suggests that TBI disrupts social functioning significantly more than orthopedic injuries. Therefore, the deficits cannot be attributed to a general trauma response. The observed age-effects (i.e., younger children show more social impairment than older counterparts) could be explained by neuroanatomical correlates. Namely, the frontal lobes that are instrumental in the development of social skills are particularly late maturing structures, and an early lesion may compromise a more critical stage of the process (Hanten et al., 2008). Congruent with the frontal lobe and injury severity hypothesis, aggressive behavior—essentially, an active manifestation of social deficits—has a linear relationship to the magnitude of TBI. A prevalent symptom in the pediatric TBI population, post-injury aggression is related to pre-morbid levels of aggressive behavior, attention problems and other psychiatric symptoms (Cole et al., 2008).

Evaluation of sensorimotor skills within the educational setting are typically performed by the occupational therapist so that remedial interventions or compensatory strategies can be employed. Following TBI, a wide range of motor impairments occur that can substantially interfere with a child or adolescents ability to function effectively within the educational system. Post-injury symptoms can be mild, resulting in motor slowing or incoordination, for which adaptive or environmental modifications may be warranted. In contrast, individuals post moderate-severe injury may require a wheel-chair for mobility due to hemiplegia or significant hemiparesis. Educators should be alert to disruptions in the quality of motor performance such as tremor or athetoid and dystonic movements that may suggest cerebellar or subcortical involvement, respectively, following TBI. These deficits can interfere significantly with written language demands. Individuals may struggle with movement representation, motor planning, and performance of sequential movements to accomplish an action even when sensory and motor systems are intact, referred to as an apraxia. While allied health professionals within the educational system are aware of these potential deficits, educators often struggle with how best to provide instruction for children with these limitations following TBI.

The degree of difficulty in core academic areas of reading, written language, and arithmetic will also depend on a number of factors such age at injury, severity, type and location of injury. Not surprisingly, the pattern of results noted in academic outcome in pediatric TBI parallel those reported in the literature on memory functioning. That is, there is a consistent inverse relationship between severity of injury and academic outcome (Catroppa et al., 2008; Ewing-Cobbs et al., 2004; Ewing-Cobbs, Fletcher, Levin, Iovino, & Miner, 1998; Ewing-Cobbs et al., 2006; Hanten et al., 2008; Jaffe et al., 1992; Jaffe, Polissar, Fay, & Liao, 1995; Schwartz et al., 2003; Taylor et al., 2002). Typically, the measures employed to examine outcome have been the Woodcock Johnson Tests of Achievement-III (WJ-III; Woodcock & Johnson, 1989; Hanten et al., 2008; Schwartz et al., 2003; Taylor et al., 2002) and the Wide Range Achievement Test-3 (WRAT-3; Jastek &Wilkinson, 1984; Catroppa et al., 2008), although traditional measures of academic functioning may not always be sensitive to the academic shortcomings encountered by children with TBI (Ewing-Cobbs et al., 1998).

In one of the first prospective, longitudinal studies of academic performance in pediatric brain injury (Ewing-Cobbs et al., 1998), children and adolescents with severe injury performed significantly below those with mild to moderate TBI on measures of reading recognition, spelling, and arithmetic at 2 years post-injury. Moreover, improvement was evident from baseline to 6 months following the injury, although did not progress significantly beyond that. This trend was observed across severity levels. More importantly, although average academic scores had been obtained by 2 years post-injury, nearly 80% of the children and adolescents had experienced academic difficulty including grade failure or required special education. Jaffe and colleagues (1995) reported similar results in 72 children with TBI (40 mild, 17 moderate, and 15 severe) who were assessed at 3 years post-injury. There was substantial improvement during the first year post-injury in those with moderate-severe injury, although only minimal change was noted during the following 2 years. The most significant slowing occurred in Performance IQ, adaptive problem solving, motor skills and memory. At 5 years follow-up, Ewing-Cobbs et al. (2004) reported persistent deficits in the children and adolescents (5–15 years) with severe compared to mild-moderate TBI in all core academic areas assessed: Reading Decoding, Reading Comprehension, Spelling, and Arithmetic. Moreover, performance on additional cognitive measures such as phonological processing and verbal memory surfaced as important predictors of academic performance, suggesting potential areas of intervention to support long-term academic success.

An inherent limitation of office-bound standardized testing is the artificial nature of the data collection process. As discussed above, behavior in highly structured environments, in one-on-one interaction with a professional may not necessarily generalize to the child's daily routine. Although test scores can predict behavior potential (i.e., ability), actual behavior is a function of a myriad of environmental variables that are not assessed during formal testing. As this blind spot of psychological assessment is becoming recognized (Silver, 2000), caregiver rating scales are being developed to introduce different, ecologically valid sources of data in clinical and educational decision making (Gioia & Isquith, 2004). Even though standardized test scores and parent ratings are inconsistent on occasion, the simultaneous use of independent data sources is an important tool to cross-validate the findings and fosters the development of intervention plans that will be congruent with the environments in which they will be implemented.

Management and Evidence-Based Intervention

From the preceding, it is quite clear that successful outcomes will depend on a multitude of factors starting with prevention of secondary sequelae and progressing to comprehensive treatment of the chronic cognitive and neurobehavioral deficits of the child while recognizing the impact of family and demographic variables across multiple contexts. The "Guidelines for the Acute Medical Management of Severe Traumatic Brain Injury in Infants, Children, and Adolescents" were published in 2003 to address early medical management in this population (Adelson et al., 2003). However, the development of treatment standards and guidelines continues to be emerging across the age at injury and injury severity spectrum.

Three general models of intervention for children and adolescents with TBI have been employed and have relevance for the development of instructional strategies, particularly when developing methods to address executive deficits: (a) a direct approach using restorative interventions; (b) behavioral compensation; and (c) environmental modifications and supports (Catroppa & Anderson, 2006). Currently, there is little evidence that restorative interventions have substantial success or generalize to other areas of cognitive functioning or daily living. The adult brain injury literature, however, does reveal some success with direct instruction for selected aspects of cognition such as attention. In contrast, behavioral compensation attempts to train individuals to perform tasks using alternative methods and strategies based on areas of preservation and an individual's cognitive strengths to achieve requested behaviors, and is perhaps the most frequently employed method of intervention. Environmental modifications and supports in the home and classroom such as extending and eliminating time demands, minimizing noise and distractions, the use of external aids, diaries, lists, etc. have also been found to be effective compensatory strategies. In fact, even children as young as 8 years of age have been found to benefit from the use of computerized programs to assist with memory impairment (Wilson, 1992).

Over the past couple of decades, there has been increasing evidence that different instructional methods can facilitate learning in individuals with acquired memory impairment (Ehlhardt et al., 2008) and that neuronal plasticity can occur in response to structured input (Gonzalez-Rothi & Barrett, 2006). As such, the past several years has seen a proliferation of excellent articles and reviews addressing educational needs and empirically validated instructional practices in children with TBI (Catroppa & Anderson, 2006; D'Amato & Rothlisberg, 1996; Ehlhardt et al., 2008; Feeney & Ylvisaker, 2006; Glang, et al., 2008; Hawley, Ward, Magnay, & Mychalkiw, 2004; Kirkwood et al., 2008; Lord-Maes & Obrzut, 1996; Schutz, Rivers, Schutz, & Proctor, 2008; Ylvisaker et al., 2001; 2005).

In a recent manuscript published by the TBI Practice Guidelines Subcommittee, which was established by the Academy of Neurologic Communication Disorders, the instructional research literature relevant to teaching individuals with acquired memory impairment was reviewed (Ehlhardt et al., 2008). While this review was not specifically geared toward children, its intent was to generate practice guidelines for individuals working in the field of cognitive rehabilitation. In addition, a review of the strategies will serve as a backdrop for the remainder of this section for which the review of intervention for memory and learning difficulties is intended. Fifty-one studies spanning from 1986 through 2006 were examined in the review; however, only two of these studies involved children from 8 to 11 years of age. Two instructional categories surfaced from this review: (a) systematic and (b) conventional instructional methods (e.g., effortful learning/trial and error). Systematic instructional methods utilize explicit faded models or prompts while conventional methods focus on the recall of information or a procedure without prompts. Systematic instructional methods include techniques such as (a) errorless learning, (b) method of vanishing cues (MVC), and (c) spaced retrieval. According to the authors, errorless learning is a strategy for which the goal is to eliminate errors during initial acquisition through the provision of models (Baddeley & Wilson, 1994). Patients are not encouraged to guess. MVC is a form of chaining for which the individual is provided either stronger or weaker cues following attempts to recall information or a procedure (Glisky, Schacter, & Tulving, 1986). This method is based on the premise that complex procedures can be taught if they are broken into smaller and simpler elements and if explicitly trained. Spaced retrieval or expanded rehearsal is a form of practice that allows individuals to practice at successfully recalling information over extended time intervals (Melton & Bourgeois, 2005). Favorable learning outcomes using systematic instructional methods were reported in 89% of the studies of TBI. However, it is important to note that only two pediatric studies met criteria for inclusion and one study reported positive outcomes while the other reported negative outcomes. Only errorless learning was utilized in the study with negative outcome, while a systematic instructional practice was used in the former. In general, treatment specifically geared toward minimizing cognitive deficits such as memory impairment and its impact on academic functioning are often more difficult to implement and research on generalization and maintenance are often lacking.

Though the aforementioned review focused on instructional techniques geared specifically toward neurogenic memory deficits, it is critical to recognize that these deficits occur within the context of everyday functioning, and for children this means within the complex educational and home environments. Indeed, historically, the cognitive rehabilitation approach for individuals with TBI included client-delivered, discrete, cognitive exercises that were often presented through computer programs within in- and out-patient rehabilitation settings. However, research over the past several decades has revealed the limits of this decontextualized, discrete-trial approach. As noted above, direct restorative memory retraining has shown essentially no impact on functional skills or generalization. In fact, as noted by Ylvisaker and colleagues (2005), it is often the lack of executive control over other cognitive processes such as attention and memory that underpins the limits in functioning, so targeting a specific process such as memory may result in diminishing benefit. Moreover, concomitant problems associated with executive impairment often intensify as the child ages. In fact, a context-sensitive approach for which treatment is rooted in routines of everyday life and that incorporates opportunities for generalization and maintenance of skills to foster the acquisition and learning of new information is currently supported by the literature (Feeney & Ylvisaker,

TABLE 21.3
Research-based Cross-Population Instructional Strategies Related to Characteristics of TBI*

TBI characteristic	Instructional strategy	Description of method
• Variable attention and concentration • Decreased speed of information processing	Appropriate pacing	Acquisition of new materials is improved by presenting information in small increments and requiring responses at a rate consistent with a student's processing speed. Pacing may need to be fast, even for a student with slowed processing if they are familiar with the routine and fluctuations in attention demand faster delivery.
• Memory impairment (associated with need for errorless learning) • High rates of failure	Method that ensures high rates of success	Acquisition and retention of new information tend to increase with high rates of success, facilitated by errorless teaching procedures.
• Organizational impairment • Inefficient learning	Task analysis and advance organizational support	Careful organization of learning tasks, including systematic sequencing of teaching targets and advanced organizational support (e.g., graphic organizers), increases success.
• Inconsistency • Inefficient learning	Sufficient practice and review of each lesson as well as cumulative review	Acquisition and retention of new information is increased with frequent review, as well as with both massed and distributed learning trials.
• Inefficient feedback loops • Implicit learning of errors	Errorless learning combined with nonjudgmental corrective feedback when errors occur	Students with severe memory and learning problems benefit from errorless learning. When errors occur, learning is enhanced when those errors are followed by nonjudgmental corrective behavior.
• Possibility of gaps in the knowledge base	Teaching to mastery rather than criterion	Learning is enhanced with mastery at the acquisition phase.
• Frequent failure of transfer • Concrete thinking and learning	Facilitation of transfer/ generalization	Generalizable strategies, wide range of examples and settings, and content-and context-embeddedness increase generalization; cognitive processes should be targeted *within* curricular content.
• Inconsistency • Unusual profiles	Ongoing assessment Flexibility in curricular modification	Adjustment to teaching on the basis of ongoing assessment of students' progress facilitates learning. Modifying the curriculum facilitates learning in special populations.

Note. Adapted from Ylvisaker et al., 2005.

2006; Glang et al., 2008; Ylvisaker et al., 2005). Table 21.3 outlines specific research-based instructional strategies associated with pediatric TBI (Ylvisaker et al., 2005).

Likewise, as noted, it is becoming increasingly evident that TBI-specific assessment and intervention may also have it shortcomings, as there is significant variability in individual outcome based on a multitude of factors previously discussed, supporting the need for individualized educational programming. That is, given the lack of evidence for specific instructional strategies from which only children with TBI benefit, educators should focus on best practice and methods shown to be successful for students with special needs in general (Glang et al., 2008; Kirkwood et al., 2008). Glang et al. (2008) recently reviewed two general instructional methodologies that were shown to be effective with several populations of children: (a) direct instruction (DI) and (b) cognitive strategy intervention (e.g., self-regulated strategy, graphic organizers). Glang et al. cite a recent meta-analytic study that examined the effectiveness of instructional components in special education. They concluded that a combined cognitive strategy coupled with an explicit instruction model such as DI was the most efficacious, regardless of the etiology of the learning difficulties. Direct instruction is a systematic instruction method that uses two inter-related components: carefully designed curriculum materials and enhanced delivery, with a goal of ensuring high rates of success. Components of DI that have errorless learning as the goal include task analysis, modeling, prevention of guessing, and gradual fading of prompts. On the other hand, cognitive strategy interventions which include compensatory instruction and executive function/meta-cognitive intervention have been reported to be evidenced-based practice for adult brain injury rehabilitation (Cicerone et al., 2005). According to Glang and colleagues (2008), DI and cognitive strategy instruction share many common features (outlined in Table 21.4), addressing many of the needs and learning characteristics of children with TBI. Unfortunately, in a recent review of cognitive rehabilitation strategies for children with TBI (Limond & Leeke, 2005), no clear conclusion emerged in terms of clinical recommendations due to an insufficient number of high quality studies.

Indeed, intervention for children with moderate to severe TBI has typically focused on compensation and environmental alterations as well as medical management with pharmacotherapy to address common impairments in attention, memory, speed of information processing, executive functioning, communication, and behavior so that individuals can function optimally at both home and school (Catroppa & Anderson, 2006; Donders, 2007). However, it is the neurobehavioral deficits that substantially impact emotional and psychosocial functioning, and there appears to be a differential recovery and response to intervention for cognitive and neurobehavioral outcomes. For example, recovery may be more pronounced for cognitive relative to psychosocial adjustment. In contrast, the recently

TABLE 21.4
Instructional Elements Common to Direct Instruction and Cognitive Strategy Instruction

Systematic, explicit instruction and practice
Consistent instructional routines
Effective task analysis
Systematic introduction and modeling of component skills
Use of scaffolding/guided practice
Rapid instructional pacing
Teaching to mastery (criterion referenced instruction)
Consistently high rates of success
Teaching of generalizable strategies
Planned and programmed generalization
Frequent and cumulative review

reported modest benefits from psychostimulants may be more evident in altering behavior rather than cognitive functioning (Jin & Schachar, 2004), but are rarely effective in managing more extreme behaviors such as aggression. New persisting behavioral difficulties are reported to occur in 35%–70% of children with severe TBI and include both externalizing (e.g., aggression, disinhibition, social immaturity) and internalizing symptoms (e.g., withdrawal, depression; Feeney & Ylvisaker, 2006). In addition, persisting behavioral problems are not only more common in severe injury, but there is evidence that children injured at a younger age may display more severe behavioral impairments. This issue is further magnified by the finding that the profile of cognitive and behavioral functioning worsens rather than improving over the years after pediatric TBI.

Environmental factors appear to be important in predicting outcome in children with TBI such that positive/negative family adjustment appears to increase the probability of positive/negative child outcomes (Rivara et al., 1992; 1994). Likewise, poor pre-injury family adjustment negatively impacts post-injury adjustment and increases the likelihood of behavioral difficulties (Taylor et al., 2001, 2002). The relevance of context-sensitive support in the management of internalizing difficulties in children with TBI has also been demonstrated. Wade, Michaud, and Brown (2006) reported superior outcomes in the areas of knowledge of TBI, problem-solving skills, family relationships, and child behavior when using a family-centered problem solving intervention. The methods employed and taught to parents were consistent with the theory of positive behavior supports (PBS), an approach that has emerged from contingency management procedures such as applied behavior analysis (ABA). Both contingency management procedures (CMP) and antecedent-focused procedures such as positive behavior interventions and supports (PBIS) are commonly employed to manage problematic behaviors, although research is needed to examine the efficacy of these methods to generate long-term change.

Recently, the effectiveness of a support-oriented, context-sensitive, multi-component cognitive, behavioral, and executive function (CBEF) intervention for decreasing aggressive behaviors, increasing behavioral adjustment, and improving academic productivity in two children with frontal lobe injuries was described by Feeney and Ylvisaker (2006). Specifically, the integrated components of the intervention included positive behavior supports, cognitive supports (e.g., graphic organizers), and an executive function routine (goal-plan-do-review). These investigators report that antecedent-focused procedures are theoretically preferable to contingency-based procedures for individuals with TBI due to the inherent pathology in brain injury that limits an individual's ability to efficiently respond to CMP, specifically: "(1) ventral frontal lobe injury is associated with weak response inhibition and inefficient responses to feedback/consequences; (2) dorsal frontal lobe injury may include initiation impairment; (3) right hemisphere frontal lobe injury impairs social perception; (4) a history of failure and frustration to oppositionality, also associated with reduced effectiveness of traditional contingency management" (pp. 631–632). Table 21.5 summarizes the five components of the intervention that are consistent with managing negative behaviors with positive antecedent supports and three components that are consistent with the literature supporting cognitive strategies.

Short- and Long-Term Outcome

Effectively addressing a childhood TBI involves a long sequence of synergistic interventions from aggressive emergency room care to teaching the individual in the post-acute stage of recovery how to live a meaningful life

TABLE 21.5
Components of the Cognitive, Behavioral, and Executive Function (CBEF) Intervention Reported by Feeney and Ylvisaker (2006).

Positive antecedent supports	Cognitive supports
(1) Engaging students in decision making and offering choices	(1) Using concrete, graphic advance organizers with disorganized, poorly oriented and inattentive individuals
(2) Building positive momentum before introducing difficult tasks	(2) Teaching in a way that ensures low frequency of errors
(3) Teaching positive escape communication	(3) Facilitating executive self-regulation of behavior with an externally represented goal-plan-do-review map.
(4) Creating realistic expectations for amount and rate of work	
(5) Altering adult communication to negotiation and offering support to decrease negative communication styles	

within the boundaries of residual symptoms. Acute medical management typically addresses seizure activity, agitation and aggression, depression, sleep disorders, fatigue, and headaches secondary to TBI through pharmacotherapy and supportive counseling. Later stages of post-acute care focus on physical, cognitive, social, and educational rehabilitation. During the past two decades, there has been a shift from traditional applied behavior analysis to positive behavior supports in recognition of certain neurological deficits that translate into a set of limitations (disinhibition, impaired reinforcement and social learning as well as weak initiation) that are specific to the TBI population, and challenge the assumptions underlying contingency management. The evolving rehabilitation strategy emphasizes the contextual nature of the recovery process, and encourages integration across domains of functioning and cares providers, as well as a programmatic focus on building adaptive skills in the natural environment rather than improving general, relatively isolated skill sets such as memory or language fluency (Ylvisaker et al., 2001, 2005). Nonetheless, rigorous experimentation and replication is still lacking to demonstrate maintenance and generalization with these procedures.

Certain symptoms may persist even after long-term concentrated rehabilitation efforts. Behavioral problems as measured by parent rating scales and academic achievement are the most prominent areas of concern in terms of adaptive functioning. The best linear predictors of outcome are a combination of injury severity, gender, SES, race, and premorbid level of functioning (Catroppa & Anderson, 2003; Cole et al., 2008; Ewing-Cobbs & Barnes, 2002; Mangeot et al., 2002; Mottram & Donders, 2006; Schwartz et al., 2003; Yeates et al., 2002). There is also evidence that suggests that the initial dose-response relationship during the immediate recovery is later altered, and children with the most severe injuries make the most relative gains (Catroppa & Anderson, 2003; Catroppa & Anderson, 2004). Although boys are reported to have a slower recovery rate compared to girls (Donders & Woodward, 2003), the most powerful predictor remains the severity of TBI. Cognitive correlates of poor functional outcome are working memory deficits and overall impaired scholastic performance (Schwartz et al., 2003). Higher order constructs such as social problem solving skills are found to have a mediating effect on the relationship between executive dysfunction and functional outcome (Muscara, Catroppa, & Anderson, 2008), suggesting a complex underlying mechanism for the recovery process.

There is an increasing recognition of the role of families in rehabilitating children with TBI. On one hand, the family accounts for a large variability in both genetics and home environment that greatly shapes the child's premorbid level of functioning. Moreover, the mutually deterministic relationship between child outcome and family adjustment is a predictable dynamic, and hence must be considered when intervention plans are designed. In fact, the effectiveness of any rehabilitation effort will hinge on family involvement. Therefore, resources spent on parent training and integrating the family into the recovery plan are a good investment (Ylvisaker et al., 2005).

Childhood TBI has some transient and some lasting effects of children's cognitive performance. Moreover, injuries differentially affect certain facets of the same domain of functioning. Basic skill sets are more resistant to the deleterious effects of TBI, while more complex ones are increasingly vulnerable to the disruption in neurophysiology following a head injury. Of course, clear trends are difficult to crystallize given the enormous variability in severity and localization of injuries, age of onset, and premorbid functioning that characterizes this population and the convoluted interactions among these parameters that are all causally related to outcome. The course of recovery is often unpredictable, as it is a function of several factors, and some of these relationships are not well understood (Ylvisaker et al., 2001). There is evidence suggesting that most of the recovery occurs within a year of injury (Yeates et al., 2002) and is driven by the severity of TBI (Catroppa & Anderson, 2003).

Although memory is particularly sensitive to TBI, actual level of impairment seems to be a function of injury severity and cognitive load. Basic retrieval skills are often preserved after TBI, but deficits become apparent in more complex forms of memory performance (Anderson, Catroppa, Morse, & Haritou, 1999; Anderson & Catroppa, 2007; Catroppa & Anderson, 2007). Injury severity remains the driving force behind the magnitude of impairment, with some evidence for age effects as well (Levin et al., 2004). As a foundation for higher order performance domains such as general verbal skills, discourse comprehension, and mathematics, memory performance is an important predictor of academic achievement (Bittner & Crowe, 2007). At the same time, memory itself is a composite of primary cognitive functions such as attention and processing speed (DeLuca, Schultheis, Madigan, Christodoulou, & Averill, 2000; Vakil, 2005).

The domain specificity of TBI is evident in language skills. Although verbal skills and other areas of cognition (attention, memory, learning, executive functioning) are interrelated and at some level inseparable (Yim-Chiplis, 1998), a few general observations can be made that are specific to language development. Lexical-level skills, once acquired, are resistant to insults and are well-retained. However, if the injury occurs prior to the acquisition of the basic skill set, learning will be significantly disrupted and the deficit will accumulate over time. Higher order abilities, such as narrative skills are dependent of other complex cognitive skill sets such as semantic and working memory, general knowledge of the world, fine-tuned social skills, and therefore more fragile in face of TBI (Chapman et al., 2004; Chapman et al., 2005). Thus, even children with normative performance on visual naming, word fluency who have a mastery of basic phonology, lexicon and syntax have a remarkable deficit in discourse comprehension. The same principle transfers to reading, another domain that has a protracted developmental course: the developmental staggering of hierarchical skill sets (grapheme-morpheme correspondence, word and sentence comprehension) makes it vulnerable to early disruptions to the process, which tend to magnify over time as more and more complex inferences are required to decoding and composing verbal messages (Ewing-Cobbs & Barnes, 2002). However, when compared to memory functioning, overall reading performance tends to be less impaired (Hawley et al., 2002).

The general pattern observed in the cognitive arena (Catroppa et al., 2008) holds true in the domain of social functioning: Age and injury severity are linearly related to level of impairment, and social skills mediate the overall recovery process (Muscara et al., 2008). There is also evidence that premorbid functioning and environment have a strong relationship with outcome. General adaptability indices and SES are reliable predictors of recovery. In other words, in some sense the healing process following TBI is a natural extension of the prior developmental trajectories so that relative standing pre- and post injury tends to be preserved (Schwartz et al., 2003). One possible mechanism for this relationship is the quality of health care received post injury. Lower SES often implies higher overall stress level, pre-existing comorbidities, and less access to services (McCarthy et al., 2006; Slomine et al., 2006). Family stress, lack of resources, and poor outcome form a convoluted, yet plausible set of factors that mutually influence each other (Aitken et al., 2009; Stancin, Wade, Walz, Yeates, & Taylor, 2008).

Finally, the impact of TBI on siblings is an emergent topic in the rehabilitation literature. Research suggests that TBI places an extra burden on sibling relationships above and beyond the stressors associated with and orthopedic injury, especially in mixed-gender siblings (Swift et al., 2003). The same effect was observed in the primary care givers (Wade, Taylor, Drotar, Stancin, & Yeates, 1998). The changes in quality of life due to residual symptoms of TBI seem to predispose siblings to psychological disorders (Sambuco, Brookes, & Lah, 2008), suggesting that the family of the patient may need to be considered in long-term rehabilitation plans.

Conclusions and Future Directions in TBI

TBI continues to be one of the most common causes of death and disability in children and adolescents; however, medical advances over the past several decades have resulted in both improved survival rates and outcome for those with moderate to severe injuries. Public policy has aided with both increased awareness of pediatric TBI and efforts to improve educational practices and behavioral management of these children. It has become increasingly evident that long-term outcome is contingent upon a host of complex pre-injury, injury-related, and post-injury variables such as premorbid functioning, age, severity, SES, and family adjustment. This supports the need for highly individualized educational programming in which best practice includes systematic instructional methods in a context-sensitive approach for which treatment is rooted in routines of everyday life and incorporates opportunities for generalization and maintenance of skills. The silent epidemic for those with brain injury may be those with mTBI, which already constitutes the largest number of known injuries, and persistent post-concussive sequelae. While most symptoms of mTBI abate over a brief period of time, cognitive and neurobehavioral difficulties persist for some, and accurate epidemiological data is difficult to obtain for this population. School-aged children and particularly adolescents may be at the greatest risk given their involvement in higher risk activities such as sports, and the possibility of serial events. Future efforts should focus on advancing our awareness and understanding of mTBI and well as instructional practices for those with PPCS.

References

Adelson, P. D., & Kochanek , P. M. (1998). Head injury in children. *Journal of Child Neurology, 13*(1), 2–15.

Adelson, P. D., Bratton, S. L., & Carney, N. A., Chesnut, R. M., du Coudray, H E., Goldstein, B., …World Federation of Pediatric Intensive and Critical Care Societies. (2003). Guidelines for the acute medical management of severe traumatic brain injury in infants, children, and adolescents. Chapter 1: Introduction. *Pediatric Critical Care Medicine. 4*(3 Suppl), S2–4.

Aitken, M. E., McCarthy, M. L., Slomine, B. S., Ding, R., Durbin, D. R., Jaffe, K. M., … CHAT Study Group. (2009). Family burden after traumatic brain injury in children. *Pediatrics, 123*(1), 199–206.

Anderson, T., Heitger, M., & MacLeod, A. D. (2006). Concussion and mild head injury. *Practical Neurology, 6*, 342–357.

Anderson, V. A., & Catroppa, C. (2007). Memory outcome at 5 years post-childhood traumatic injury. *Brain Injury, 21*(13–14), 1399–1409.

Anderson, V. A., Catroppa, C., Haritou, F., Morse, S., Pentland, L., Rosenfield, J., Stargatt, R.. (2001). Predictors of acute child and family outcome following traumatic brain injury in children. *Pediatric Neurosurgery, 34*, 138–148.

Anderson, V. A., Catroppa, C., Morse, S. A., & Haritou, F. (1999). Functional memory skills following traumatic brain injury in young children. *Pediatric Rehabilitation, 3*, 159–166.

Anderson, V. A., Catroppa, C., Rosenfeld, J., Haritou, F., & Morse, S. A. (2000). Recovery of memory function following traumatic brain injury in pre-school children. *Brain Injury, 14*, 679–692.

Anderson, V. A., & Moore, C. (1995). Age at injury as a predictor of outcome following pediatric head injury. *Child Neuropsychology, 1*, 187–202.

Arffa, S. (1998). Traumatic brain injury. In C. E. Coffey, & R. A. Brumback (Eds.), *Textbook of pediatric neuropsychiatry* (pp. 1093–1140). Washington, DC: American Psychiatric Press.

Baars, B. J. (2007). Attention and consciousness. In B. J. Baars & N. M. Gage (Eds.), *Cognition, brain, and consciousness: Introduction to cognitive neuroscience*. New York, NY: Academic Press.

Baddeley, A., & Wilson, B. A. (1994). When implicit learning fails: amnesia and the problem of error elimination. *Neuropsychologia, 32*(1), 53–68.

Bassett, S. S., & Slater, E. J. (1990). Neuropsychological function in adolescents sustaining mild closed head injury. *Journal of Pediatric Psychology, 15*(2), 225–236.

Bauer, R., & Fritz, H. (2004). Pathophysiology of traumatic injury in the developing brain: an introduction and short update. *Experimental and Toxicologic Pathology, 56*, 65–73.

Bigler, E. D. (1999). Neuroimaging in pediatric traumatic head injury: Diagnostic considerations and relationships to neurobehavioral outcome. *Journal of Head Trauma Rehabilitation, 14*(4), 406–423

Bigler, E. D. (2008). Neuropsychology and clinical neuroscience of persistent post-concussive syndrome. *Journal of the International Neuropsychological Society, 14*, 1–22.

Bigler, E. D., Clark, E., & Farmer, J. (1996). Traumatic brain injury: 1990's update introduction to the special series. *Journal of Learning Disabilities, 29*, 512–513.

Bigler, E. D., & Dodrill, C. B. (1997). Assessment of neuropsychological testing. *Neurology, 49*(4), 1180-1182.

Bittner, R. M., & Crowe, S. F. (2007). The relationship between working memory, processing speed, verbal comprehension and FAS performance following traumatic brain injury. *Brain Injury, 21*(7), 709–719.

Cassidy, J. D., Carroll, L. J., Peloso, P. M., Borg, J., von Holst, H., Holm, L., … WHO Collaborating Task Force on Mild Traumatic Brain Injury. (2004). Incidence, risk factors and prevention of mild traumatic brain injury: Results of the WHO collaborating centre task force on mild traumatic brain injury. *Journal of Rehabilitation Medicine, 43* (Suppl.), 28–60.

Catroppa, C., & Anderson, V. (2003). Children's attentional skills 2 year post-traumatic brain injury. *Developmental Neuropsychology, 23*(3), 359–373.

Catroppa, C., & Anderson, V. (2004). Recovery and predictors of language skills two years following pediatric traumatic brain injury. *Brain and Language, 88*(1), 68–78.

Catroppa, C., & Anderson, V. (2006). Planning, problem-solving and organizational abilities in children following traumatic brain injury: Intervention techniques. *Pediatric Rehabilitation, 9*(2), 89–97.

Catroppa, C., & Anderson, V. (2007). Recovery in Memory Function and it's Relationship to Academic Success, at 24 Months Following Pediatric TBI. *Child Neuropsychology, 13*, 240–261.

Catroppa, C., Anderson, V. A., Morse, S. A., Haritou, F., & Rosenfeld, J. V. (2008). Outcome and predictors of functional recovery 5 years following pediatric traumatic brain injury (TBI). *Journal of Pediatric Psychology, 33*(7), 707–718.

Centers for Disease Control and Prevention (CDC). (2003). *National Center for Injury Prevention and Control. Report to Congress on mild traumatic brain injury in the United States: Steps to prevent a serious public health problem.* Atlanta,GA: Author.

Chapman, S. B., Gamino, J. F., Cook, L. G., Hanten, G., Li, X., & Levin, H. S. (2005). Impaired discourse gist and working memory in children after brain injury. *Brain and Language, 97*(2), 178–188.

Chapman, S. B., Sparks, G., Levin, H. S., Dennis, M., Roncadin, C., Zhang, L., & Song J. (2004). Discourse macrolevel processing after severe pediatric traumatic brain injury. *Developmental Neuropsychology, 25*(1–2), 37–60.

Cicerone, K. D., Dahlberg, C., Malec, J. F., Langenbahn, D. M., Felicetti, T., Kneipp, S., … Catanese, J. (2005). Evidence-based cognitive rehabilitation: updated review of the literature from 1998 through 2002. *Archives of Physical Medicine and Rehabilitation, 86*(8), 1681–1692.

Cole, W. R., Gerring, J. A., Gray, R. M., Vasa, R. A. Salorio, C. F., Grados, M., … Slomine, B. (2008). Prevalence of aggressive behaviour after severe paediatric traumatic brain injury. *Brain Injury, 22*(12), 932–939.

D'Amato, R. C., & Rothlisberg, B. A. (1996). How Education Should Respond to Students with Traumatic Brain Injury. *Journal of learning Disabilities, 29*(6), 670–683.

DeLuca, J., Schultheis, M. T., Madigan, N. K., Christodoulou, C., & Averill, A. (2000). Acquisition versus retrieval deficits in traumatic brain inujry: Implications for memory rehabilitation. *Archives of Physical Medicine and Rehabilitation, 81*(10), 1327–1333.

Donders, J. (2007). Traumatic Brain Injury. In S. J. Hunter & J. Donders (Eds.), *Pediatric Neuropsychological Intervention* (pp. 91–111). New York, NY: Cambridge University Press.

Donders, J., & Woodward, H. R. (2003). Gender as a moderator of memory after traumatic brain injury in children. *Journal of Head Trauma Rehabilitation, 18*(2), 106–115.

Ehlhardt, L. A., Sohlberg, M. M., Kennedy, M., Coelho, C., Ylvisaker, M., Turkstra, L., & Yorkston, K. (2008). Evidence-based practice guidelines for instructing individuals with neurogenic memory impairments: What have we learned in the past 20 years? *Psychology Press, 18*(3), 300–342.

Ewing-Cobbs, L., & Barnes, M. (2002). Linguistic outcomes following traumatic brain injury in children. *Seminars in Pediatric Neurology, 9*(3), 209–217.

Ewing-Cobbs, L., Barnes, M., Fletcher, J. M., Levin, H. S., Swank, P. R., & Song, J. (2004). Modeling of longitudinal academic achievement scores after pediatric traumatic brain injury. *Devlopmental Neuropsychology, 25*(1–2), 107–133.

Ewing-Cobbs, L., Fletcher, J. M., Levin, H. S., Iovino, I., & Miner, M. E. (1998). Academic achievement and academic placement following traumatic brain injury in children and adolescents: a two year longitudinal study. *Journal of Clinical and Experimental Neuropsychology, 20*(6), 769–781.

Ewing-Cobbs, L., Prasad, M. R., Kramer, L., Cox, C. S., Jr., Baumgartner, J., Fletcher, S., … Swank, P. (2006). Late intellectual and academic outcomes following traumatic brain injury sustained during early childhood. *Journal of Neurosurgery, 105*(4 Suppl.), 287–296.

Fay, T. B., Yeates, K. O., Wade, S. L., Drotar, D., Stancin, T., & Taylor, H. G. (2009). Predicting longitudinal patterns of functional deficits in children with traumatic brain injury. *Neuropsychology, 23*(3), 271–282.

Feeney, T., & Ylvisaker, M. (2006). Context-sensitive cognitive-behavioural supports for young children with TBI: A replication study. *Brain Injury, 20*(6), 629–645.

Gale, S. D., Johnson, S. C., Bigler, E. D., & Blatter, D. D. (1995). Trauma-induced degenerative changes in brain injury: A morphometric analysis of three patients with preinjury and postinjury MR scans. *Journal of Neurotrauma, 12*(2), 151–158.

Gioia, G. A., & Isquith, P. K. (2004). Ecological assessment of executive function in traumatic brain injury. *Developmental Neuropsychology, 25*(1-2), 135–158.

Glang, A., Ylvisaker, M., Stein, M., Ehlhardt, L., Todis, B., & Tyler, J. (2008). Validated instructional practices: Application to students with traumatic brain injury. *Journal of Head Trauma Rehabilitation, 23*(4), 243–251.

Glisky, E. L., Schacter, D. L., & Tulving, E. (1986). Learning and retention of computer-related vocabulary in memory-impaired patients: method of vanishing cues. *Journal of Clinical and Experimental Neuropsychology, 8*(30), 292–312.

Gonzalez-Rothi, L. J., & Barrett, A. M. (2006). The changing view of neurorehabiliation: a new era of optimism. *Journal of International Neuropsychological Society, 21*(6), 812–815.

Graham, D. I. (2001) Paediatric head injury. *Brain, 124*, 1261–1262

Guthrie E., Mast, J., Richards, P., McQuaid, M., & Pavlakis, S. (1999). Traumatic brain injury in children and adolescents. *Child and Adolescent Psychiatric Clinics of North America, 8*, 807–827.

Hanten, G., Wilde, E.A., Menefee, D. S., Li, X., Vasquez, C., Swank, P., … Levin, H.S. (2008). Correlates of Social Problem Solving During the First Year After Traumatic Brian injury in Children. *Neuropsychology, 22*(3), 357–370.

Hawley, C. A. Ward, A. B. Magnay, A. R. & Long, J. (2002). Children's brain injury: a postal follow-up of 525 children from one health region in the UK. *Brain Injury, 16*(11), 969–985.

Hawley, C. A., Ward, A. B., Magnay, A. R., Mychalkiw, W. (2004). Return to school after brain injury. *Archives of Diseases in Childhood, 89*, 136–142.

Individuals with Disabilities Education Act (IDEA). (1975). 20 U.S.C. §§ 1400 et seq., as amended and incorporating the Education of All Handicapped Children Act (EHA), 1975, P.L. 94-142, and subsequent amendments; Regulations at 34 C.F.R. §§ 300-303.

Iverson, G. L. (2006). Misdiagnosis of the persistent postconcussion syndrome in patients with depression. *Neuropsychology, 21*, 303–310.

Jaffe, K. M., Fay, G. C., Polissar, N. L., Martin, K. M., Shurtleff, H. A., Rivara, J. B., & Winn, H. R. (1992). Severity of pediatric traumatic brain injury and early neurobehavioral outcome: A cohort study. *Archives of Physical Medicine and Rehabilitation, 73*, 540–547.

Jaffe, K. M., Polissar, N. L., Fay, G. C., & Liao, S. (1995). Recovery trends over three years following pediatric brain injury. *Archives of Physical Medicine and Rehabilitation, 76*, 17–26.

Jagannathan, P., & Jagannathan, J. (2008). Molecular mechanisms of traumatic brain injury in children. *Journal of Neurosurgical Focus, 25*(4)E6, 1–8

Jankowitz, B. T., & Adelson, P. D. (2006). Pediatric traumatic brain injury: past present and future. *Developmental Neuroscience, 28*(4-5), 264–275.

Jastek, S., & Wilkinson, G. S. (1984). *Wide Range Achievement Test-Revised*. Wilmington, DE: Jastek Assessment Systems.

Jin, C., & Schachar, R. (2004). Methylphenidate treatment of attention-deficit/hyperactivity disorder secondary to traumatic brain injury: a critical appraisal of treatment studies. *CNS Spectrums, 9*(3), 217–226.

Johnson, D. A. (1992). Head injured children and education: A need for greater delineation and understanding. *British Journal of Educational Psychology, 62*, 404–409.

Jordan, F. M., & Ashton, R. (1996). Language performance of severely closed head injured children. *Brain Injury, 10*(2), 91–97.

Kirkwood, M. W., Yeates, K. O., Taylor, H. G., Randolph, C., McCrea, M., & Anderson, V. A. (2008). Management of pediatric mild traumatic brain injury: A neuropsychological review from injury through recovery. *The Clinical Neuropsycholgist, 22*, 769–800.

Konrad, K., Gauggel, S., & Schurek, J. (2003). Catecholamine functioning in children with traumatic brain injuries and children with attention-deficit/hyperactivity disorder. *Cognitive Brain Research, 16*(3), 425–433.

Kraus, J. (1995). Epidemiological features of brain injury in children. In S. H. Broman & M. E. Michel (Eds.), *Traumatic brain injury in children* (pp. 117–146). New York, NY: Oxford University Press.

Langlois, J. A., Marr, A., Mitchko, J., & Johnson, R. L. (2005). Tracking the silent epidemic and educating the public; CDC's traumatic brain injury-associated activities under the TBI act of 1996 and the children's health act of 2000. *Journal of Head Trauma Rehabilitation, 20*(3), 196–204.

Langlois, J. A., Rutland-Brown, W., & Thomas, K. E. (2004). *Traumatic brain injury in the united states: Emergency department visits, hospitalizations, and deaths*. Atlanta, GA: Centers for Disease Control and Prevention, National Center for Injury Prevention and Control.

Levin, H. S., Culhane, K. A., Mendelsohn, D. B., Lilly, M. A., Bruce, D. A., Fletcher, J. M., … Eisenberg, H. M. (1993). Cognition in relation to magnetic resonance imaging in head injured children and adolescents. *Archives of Neurology, 50*, 897–905.

Levin, H. S., Eisenberg, H. M., Wigg, N. R., & Kobayashi, K. (1982). Memory and intellectual ability after head injury in children and adolescents. *Neurosurgery, 11*, 668–673.

Levin, H. S., Hanten, G., Zhang, L., Swank, P. R., Ewing-Cobbs, L., Dennis, M., … Hunter, J. V. (2004). Changes in working memory after traumatic brain injury in children. *Neuropsychology, 18*(2), 240–247.

Levin H. S., High W.M. Jr., Ewing-Cobbs, L., Fletcher, J. M., Eisenberg, H. M., Miner, M. E., & Goldstein, F. C. (1988). Memory functioning during the first year after closed head injury in children and adolescents. *Neurosurgery, 22*(6 Pt 1),1043–52.

Levin, H. S., Mattis, S., Ruff., R. M., Eisenberg, H. M., Marshall, L. F., Tabbador, K., … Frankowski, R. F. (1987). Neurobehavioral outcome following minor head injury: A three center study. *Journal of Neurosurgery, 66*, 234–243.

Levin, H. S., Wilde, E. A., Chu, Z., Yallampalli, R., Hanten, G. R., Li, X., … Hunter, J. V. (2008). Diffusion tensor imaging in relation to cognitive and functional outcome of traumatic brain injury in children. *Journal of Head Trauma Rehabilitation, 23*(4), 197–208.

Limond, J., & Leeke, R. (2005). Practitioner review: cognitive rehabilitation for children with acquired brain injury. *Journal of Child Psychology and Psychiatry, 46*(4), 339–352.

Lord-Maes, J., & Obrzut, J. E. (1996). Neuropsychological consequences of traumatic brain injury in children and adolescents. *Journal of Learning Disabilities, 29*, 609–617.

Maedgen, J., & Semrud-Clikeman, M. (2007). Bridging neuropsychological practice with educational intervention. In S. Hunter, & J. & Donders (Eds.), *Pediatric neuropsychological intervention* (pp. 68–87). New York, NY: Cambridge University Press.

Mangeot, S., Armstrong, K., Colvin, A. N., Yeates, K. O., & Taylor, H. G. (2002). Long-term executive deficits in children with traumatic brain injuries: Assessment using the behavior rating inventory of executive function (BRIEF). *Child Neuropsychology, 8*(4), 271–284.

Margulies, S. S., & Thibault, K. L. (2000). Infant skull and suture properties: measurements and implications for mechanisms of pediatric brain injury. *Journal of Biomechanical Engineering, 122*(4), 367–371.

Mazzola, C. A., & Adelson, P. D. (2002). Critical care management of head trauma in children. *Critical Care Medicine, 30*(11), S393–401.

McCarthy, M. L., Dikmen, S. S., Langlois, J. A., Selassie, A. W., Gu, J. K., & Horner, M. D. (2006). Self-reported psychosocial health among adults with traumatic brain injury. *Archives of Physical Medicine and Rehabilitation, 87*(7), 953–961.

McCauley, S. R., & Levin, H. S.(2004). Prospective Memory in Pediatric Traumatic Brain Injury: A Preliminary Study. *Developmental Neuropsychology, 25*(1&2), 5–20.

Melton, A., & Bourgeois, M. (2005). Training compensatory memory strategies via the telephone for persons with TBI. *Aphasiology, 19*(3/4/5), 353–364.

Merkley, T. L., Bigler, E. D., Wilde, E. A., McCauley, S. R., Hunter, J. V., & Levin, H. S. (2008). Diffuse changes in Ccrtical thickness in pediatric moderate-to-severe traumatic brain injury. *Journal of Neurotrauma, 25*, 1343–1345.

Mottram, L., & Donders, J. (2006). Cluster subtypes on the California verbal learning test-children's version after pediatric traumatic brain injury. *Developmental Neuropsychology, 30*(3), 865–883.

Muscara, F., Catroppa, C., & Anderson, V. (2008). Social problem-solving skills as a mediator between executive function and long-term social outcome following paediatric traumatic brain injury. *Journal of Neuropsychology, 2*(Pt2), 445–461.

NIH Consensus Development Panel on Rehabilitation of Persons With Traumatic Brain Injury (1999). Rehabilitation of persons with traumatic brain injury. *JAMA, 282*(10), 974–983.

Powell, K. B., & Voeller, K. K. S. (2004). Prefrontal executive function syndromes in children. *Journal of Child Neurology, 19*(10), 785–797.

Public Law 105-17. (1997). Reauthorization of the Individuals with Disabilities Education Act.

Public Law 108-446. (2004). Reauthorization of the Individuals with Disabilities Education Act.

Rivara, J. B., Fay, G. C., Jaffe, K. M., Polissar, N. L., Shurtleff, H. A., & Martin, K. M. (1992). Predictors of family functioning one year following traumatic brain injury in children. *Archives of Physical Medicine and Rehabilitation, 73*(10), 899–910.

Rivara, J. B., Jaffe, K. M., Polissar, N. L., Fay, G. C., Martin, K. M., Shurtleff, H. A., & Liao, S. (1994). Family functioning and children's academic performance and behavior problems in the year following traumatic brain injury. *Archives of Physical Medicine and Rehabilitation, 75*(4), 369–379.

Roman, M. J., Delis, D. C., Willerman, L., Magulac, M. Demadura, T. L., de la Peña, J. L., … Kracun, M.(1998). Impact of Pediatric Traumatic Brain Injury on Components of Verbal Memory. *Journal of Clinical and Experimental Neuropsychology, 20*(2), 245–258.

Sambuco, M., Brookes, N., & Lah, S. (2008). Paediatric traumatic brain injury: A review of siblings' outcome. *Brain Injury, 22*(1), 7–17.

Schutz, L. E., Rivers, K. O., Schutz, J. A., & Proctor, A. (2008). Preventing multiple-choice tests from impending educational advancement after acquired brain injury. *Language, Speech, and Hearing Services in Schools, 39*, 104–109.

Schwartz, L., Taylor, H. G., Drotar, D., Yeates, K. O., Wade, S. L., & Stacin, T. (2003). Long-term behavior problems following pediatric traumatic brain injury: Prevalence, predictors, and correlates. *Journal of Pediatric Psychology, 28*(4), 251–263.

Silver, C. H. (2000). Ecological validity of neuropsychological assessment in childhood traumatic brain injury. *Journal of Head Trauma Rehabilitation, 15*, 973–988.

Slomine, B. S., McCarthy, M. L., Ding, R., MacKenzie, E. J., Jaffe, K. M., Aitken, …. CHAT Study Group. (2006). Health care utilization and needs after pediatric traumatic brain injury. *Pediatrics, 117*(4), 663–674.

Slomine, B. S., Salorio, C. F., Grados, M. A., Vasa, R. A., Christensen, J. R., & Gerring, J. P. (2005). Differences in attention, executive functioning, and memory in children with and without ADHD after severe traumatic brain injury. *Journal of International Neuropsychological Society, 11*(5), 645–653.

Stancin, T., Wade, S. L., Walz, N. C., Yeates, K. O., & Taylor, H. G. (2008). Traumatic brain injuries in early childhood; initial impact on family. *Journal of Developmental and Behavioral and Pediatrics, 29*(4), 253–261.

Swift, E. E., Taylor, H. G., Kaugars, A. S., Drotar, D., Yeates, K. O., Wade, S. L., & Stancin, T. (2003). Sibling relationships and behavior after pediatric traumatic brain injury. *Journal of Developmental and Behavioral and Pediatrics, 24*(1), 24–31.

Taylor, H. G., Wade, S. L., Stacin, T., Yeates, K. O., Drotar, D., & Minich, N. (2002). A prospective study of short- and long-term outcomes after traumatic brain injury in children: Behavior and achievement. *Neuropsychology, 16*(1), 15–27.

Taylor, H. G., Yeates, K. O., Wade, S. L., Drotar, D., Stancin, T., & Burant, C. (2001). Bidirectional child-family influences on outcomes of traumatic brain injury in children. *Journal of International Neuropsychological Society, 7*(6), 755–767.

Teasdale, G., & Jennett, B. (1974). Assessment of coma and impaired consciousness: A practical scale. *Lancet, 2,* 81–84.

Thibault, K. L., & Margulies, S. S. (1998). Age-dependent material properties of the porcine cerebrum: effect on pediatric inertial head injury criteria. *Journal of Biomechanics, 31(12)*, 1119–1126.

Ulatowska, H. K., & Chapman, S. B. (1994). Discourse microstructure in aphasia. In R. L. Bloom, L. K. Obler, S. DeSanti, & J. S. Ehrlich (Eds.), *Discourse analysis and applications* (pp. 29–46). Hillsdale, NJ: Erlbaum.

Vakil, E. (2005). The effect of moderate to severe traumatic brain injury (TBI) on different aspects of memory: A selective review. *Journal of Clinical and Experimental Neuropsychology, 27*(8), 977–1021.

Wade, S. L., Michaud, L., & Brown, T. M. (2006). Putting the pieces together: Preliminary efficacy of a family problem-solving intervention for children with traumatic brain injury. *Journal of Head Trauma Rehabilitation, 21*(1), 57–67.

Wade, S. L., Taylor, H. G., Drotar, D., Stancin, T., & Yeates, K. O. (1998). Family burden and adaptation during the initial year after traumatic brain injury in children. *Pediatrics, 102*(1 Pt 1), 110–116.

Ward, H., Shum, D., McKinlay, L., Baker, S., & Wallace, G. (2007). Prospective memory and pediatric traumatic brain injury: Effects of cognitive demand. *Child Neuropsychology, 13,* 219–239

Ward, H., Shum, D., Wallace, G., & Boon, J. (2002) Pediatric Traumatic Brain Injury and Procedural Memory. *Journal of Clinical and Experimental Neuropsychology, 24*(4), 458–470

Willer, B., & Leddy, J. J. (2006). Management of concussion and post-concussion syndrome. *Current Treatment Options in Neurology, 8,* 415–426.

Wilson, B. (1992). Recovery and compensatory strategies in head injured memory impaired people several years after insult. *Journal of Neurology, Neurosurgery, and Psychiatry, 55*(3),177–180.

Woodcock, R. W., & Johnson, M. B. (1989). *Woodcock-Johnson Psycho-Educational Battery-Revised.* Allen, TX: DLM Teaching Resources.

Yeates, K. O., Blumenstein, E., Patterson, C. M., & Delis, D. C. (1995). Verbal learning and memory following pediatric closed-head injury. *Journal of the International Neuropsychological Society, 1,* 78–87,

Yeates, K. O., Taylor, H. G., Wade, S. L., Drotar, D., Stancin, T., & Minich, N. (2002). A prospective study of short- and long-term neuropsychological outcomes after traumatic brain injury in children. *Neuropsychology, 16*(4), 514–523.

Yim-Chiplis, P. K. (1998). The child with traumatic brain injury returns to school. *Pediatric Nursing, 24*(3), 245–248.

Ylvisaker, M., Adelson, P. D., Braga, L. W., Burnett, S. M., Glang, A., Feeney, T., ... Todis, B. (2005). Rehabilitation and ongoing support after pediatric TBI. *Journal of Head Trauma Rehabilitation, 20*(1), 95–109.

Ylvisaker, M., Todis, B., Glang, A., Urbanczyk, B., Franklin, C., DePompei, R., ... Tyler, J. S. (2001). Educating students with TBI: Themes and recommendations. *Journal of Head Trauma Rehabilitation, 16*(1), 76–93.

22

Current Issues and Trends in the Education of Children and Youth with Autism Spectrum Disorders

Maureen A. Conroy
University of Florida

Janine P. Stichter and Nicholas Gage
University of Missouri–Columbia

Autism spectrum disorders are neurodevelopmental disorders manifested by individuals who display communication impairments, social relatedness difficulties, and behavioral excesses (*DSM-IV-TR*; American Psychiatric Association [APA], 2000). Included within the spectrum is a continuum of complex, heterogeneous etiologies embodying different levels of intelligence as well as forms and severity of symptoms. One end of the spectrum represents individuals who are diagnosed with labels such as Pervasive Developmental Disorder - Not Otherwise Specified (PDD-NOS), Asperger syndrome, or High Functioning Autism. These individuals' intelligence is within the normal range or above and they display sophisticated forms and levels of verbal communication. The other end of the spectrum characterizes individuals who display the overall symptoms of ASD, but whose intelligence is below the normal range and have more limited language and communication abilities. The exact cause of autism spectrum disorders is unknown. However, unlike years ago when Bettleheim (1959) proposed that autism was caused by "refrigerator moms," there is consensus among researchers that genetics plays a significant role along with biomedical factors (Dawson, 2008; Volkmar, Chawarska, & Klin, 2008).

Prior to the 1990 reauthorization of IDEA, children and youth diagnosed with autism spectrum disorders were less common. Often, not identified until age 3 or 4 years, many children with autistic characteristics received educational services under the IDEA categories of developmentally delayed, mental retardation or emotional disturbance. In those days, researchers and educators had little perspective on the true nature of the spectrum. Since 1990, when autism became an educational category of the IDEA, the field has rapidly progressed with new medical findings and educational strategies to help treat deficit areas. Even with all the medical advances that may help to lessen some of the symptoms associated with autism spectrum disorders, researchers have found that behavioral and developmental interventions appear to be the most effective for helping to improve the long-term outcomes for children and youth with autism spectrum disorders (Kasari, Freeman, & Paparella, 2006).

Today, autism spectrum disorders is the second most common developmental disability (Newschaffer et al., 2007). The most recent prevalence rates suggest that 1 in 110 children will be diagnosed with an autism spectrum disorders (Centers for Disease Control, 2009). Although there is a 4:1 ratio of males to females, autism spectrum disorders occurs across all socioeconomic levels, races and ethnicities, and geographical locations. Researchers and educators are beginning to further understand the breadth of the spectrum and, in response, have developed more sophisticated ways to diagnose children and youth with autism spectrum disorders and ameliorate their developmental deficits through effective intervention practices. The purpose of this chapter is to provide an abbreviated review of the literature and issues that surround educating children and youth with autism spectrum disorders. In particular, the following areas are included: (a) diagnosis, identification, and eligibility; (b) effective intervention practices; and (c) contemporary issues and trends that influence educational services. Literature in each area is summarized to highlight the current trends and to direct future practice and research.

Diagnosis, Identification, and Eligibility

The increase in the prevalence of autism spectrum disorders over the past 30 years is staggering. In the past, classic autism was a rare clinical diagnosis, with a prevalence rate of approximately 4 to 6 per 10,000 (Lotter, 1967). However, recent prevalence rates are approximately 40 to 60 per 10,000 (Bertrand et al., 2001; Frombonne, 2003). Although there is no consensus or explanation that accounts for the dramatic increase in autism spectrum disorders, a number of hypotheses have been postulated, including: (a) changes in diagnostic criteria; (b) increased awareness of autism spectrum disorders among parents, professionals, and the general public; (c) a recognition that autism spectrum disorders can be dual-diagnosed with other conditions, including cognitive disabilities and other psychiatric disorders; and (d) the development of specialized services with greater access to these services (Frombonne, 2003; Wing & Potter, 2002).

Most research examining causes and patterns of autism spectrum disorders prevalence and incidence has consisted of epidemiological studies and approached autism spectrum disorders primarily from a clinical (not educational) perspective. These studies have been instrumental in spawning further research examining increased incidence over time vis á vis diagnostic criteria (Frombonne, 2003), which in turn has improved the field's understanding of differential diagnoses, diagnosis of higher-functioning autism (HFA) and asperger syndrome, and biomedical and genetic links to autism spectrum disorders.

Epidemiological studies have been instrumental in identifying and understanding the underlying causes of autism spectrum disorders. Unfortunately, this body of work has done little to elucidate the impact of increased prevalence when considering children and youth with autism spectrum disorders eligible for special education services under the IDEA and the subsequent domino effect on the provision of free appropriate educational services. Recently, Safran (2008) examined the relationship between the prevalence of autism spectrum disorders in the general population and the IDEA eligibility rates under the category of autism, finding for the latter a prevalence rate of only 20.53 per 10,000 students in the 2001–2002 school year. These findings indicate that the rate of clinical diagnosis and general population estimates are much higher than special education classification and eligibility rates. As Safran (2008) suggests, autism spectrum disorders is most likely under-identified in educational settings, particularly for those students who function on the higher end of the spectrum. It is postulated that because these students often demonstrate strengths in academic areas, they do not have significant behavior challenges, instead their challenges are in basic social competence. As a result they do not easily signal the need for, or fit into more traditional and available special educational services.

Current Approaches to Diagnosis and Identification of Autism Spectrum Disorders

Clinical diagnosis of autism spectrum disorders. Understanding estimates of prevalence and comparing clinical and educational diagnoses of autism spectrum disorders begins with defining the disorder. The clinical diagnosis of autism spectrum disorders is based on the *Diagnostic and Statistical Manual of Mental Disorders* (*DSM*). Although currently being revised, the most current edition of the *DSM*, the text-revised fourth edition (*DSM-IV-TR*; APA, 2000), provides diagnostic criteria for autism under the category of pervasive developmental disorders, which includes the following specific diagnostic categories: (a) autistic disorder, (b) asperger syndrome, (c) Rett's syndrome, (d) childhood disintegrative disorder, and (e) PDD-NOS. The terms *autism spectrum disorders* and *pervasive developmental disorders* are often interchangeable depending on the audience within the clinical field of autism research and practice and refer to a continuum of associated cognitive and behavioral deficits, including the triad of core defining features: communication impairments, social relatedness difficulties, and repetitive and stereotyped behavior (Filipek et al., 1999). Figure 22.1 provides a summary of the *DSM-IV-TR* diagnostic criteria for autistic disorder and demonstrates refinement and specificity of the diagnosis of autism spectrum disorders since Kanner (1943) first described the syndrome based on patterns of behavior including social remoteness, possessiveness, stereotypy, and echolalia. Also highlighted is the consistent focus on deficits in communication and socialization as well as the display of repetitive and stereotyped behavior when defining autism spectrum disorders (see Figure 22.1).

Clinical diagnoses of autism spectrum disorders, by definition, are made by licensed clinicians, such as psychologists and psychiatrists, who must determine whether an individual demonstrates six or more qualitative impairments, with at least two of the demonstrated impairments in communication, and at least one impairment in the areas of socialization and repetitive and stereotyped behavior (APA, 2000; Dahle, 2003). The variability in symptomology inherent in the criteria as represented by the term "qualitative" impairment highlights the continuum or spectrum of the disorder (Filipek et al., 1999). Further complicating the diagnostic process is comorbidity with other psychological and psychiatric disorders, particularly significant cognitive impairment (Vig & Jedrysek, 1999), and differentially diagnosing individuals with high-functioning autism asperger syndrome and PDD-NOS (Bennett et al., 2008; Howlin, 2003; Ozonoff, South, & Miller, 2000).

Diagnosing High-Functioning Autism, Asperger Syndrome, and PDD-NOS. High-functioning autism, asperger syndrome, and PDD-NOS have similarities; but, also, have distinct diagnostic criteria. High-functioning autism is often defined as autistic disorder absent of cognitive delay. Although asperger syndrome and PDD-NOS bare similarities to the autistic disorder criteria; they are unique in the following diagnostic distinctions (APA, 2000; Bennett, et al. 2008). Asperger syndrome is characterized by impairment in social reciprocity, difficulties in communication, and circumscribed interests and preoccupations that are unusual and conducted in social isolation (Bennett et al., 2008), with the key distinction from

DSM-IV-TR Definition	IDEA Criteria
Delays or abnormal functioning in at least one of three primary impairment areas, beginning prior to age 3 years. These primary functioning areas include: 1) language used for social communication: 2) symbolic or imaginative play; or 3) social interactions.	(i) Autism means a developmental disability significantly affecting verbal and nonverbal communication and social interaction, generally evident before age three that adversely affects a child's educational performance. Other characteristics often associated with autism are engagement in repetitive activities and stereotyped movements, resistance to environmental change or change in daily routines, and unusual responses to sensory experiences.
Three Primary Areas of Impairment: Impaired communication (1 from this area): Delayed language With adequate speech, impaired ability to sustain conversation Stereotyped, repetitive, or idiosyncratic language Lack of imaginative play	(ii) Autism does not apply if a child's educational performance is adversely affected primarily because the child has an emotional disturbance, as defined in paragraph (c)(4) of this section.
Impaired behavior (including symbolic or imaginative play) (1 from this area): Preoccupation with restricted or repetitive pattern Inflexibility to routines Stereotyped or repetitive mannerisms Preoccupation with objects Impaired social interactions (2 from this area): Poor nonverbal (e.g., gestures, eye contact) Poor peer relations Lack of joint attention Poor reciprocity	(iii) A child who manifests the characteristics of autism after age three could be identified as having autism if the criteria in the paragraph (c)(1)(i) of this section are satisfied.

Figure 22.1 *DSM-IV-TR* Diagnostic and IDEA Eligibility Criteria.

a diagnosis of autism being the absence of cognitive and language delay. In addition, distinct from *high-functioning autism*, a diagnosis of asperger syndrome requires typical acquisition of the child's spontaneous phrase speech, including verb usage by 36 months of age (APA). PDD-NOS is characterized by severe and pervasive impairment in reciprocal social interaction and impairment in verbal or nonverbal communication or the presence of stereotyped behaviors, interests or activities (APA). PDD-NOS is atypical autism in that it is a disorder characterized by some autistic criteria, but not all.

The ongoing debate about the diagnostic validity of asperger syndrome and high-functioning autism as separate disabilities is ever-present in the literature and not easily summed up (Bennett et al., 2008). Although clinical research continues to refine the process (Klin, Pauls, Schultz, & Volkmar, 2005), clinicians must rely on the narrow criteria based on the absence of language delay. As the autism spectrum disorders construct continues to be refined (Lord, 2009), the diagnostic criteria and clinical ability to differentiate and diagnosis high-functioning autism, asperger syndrome, and PDD-NOS will be strengthened.

Autism spectrum disorders identification and eligibility in educational settings. Unlike clinical diagnoses, special education eligibility is not designed to diagnose a neurodevelopmental disability. Rather, a student is found eligible for special education services under the category of *autism* according to criteria outlined in the Individuals with Disabilities Education Act (IDEA) (see Figure 22.1). Eligibility criteria for autism under the IDEA have some similarities to the criteria outlined in the *DSM-IV-TR*, with communication and reciprocal social interactions as core deficit areas. Yet, two distinct features codify the definitional differences: (1) repetitive and stereotyped behaviors are not required criteria in order to qualify for special education services; and (2) the terminology surrounding a qualitative impairment using the *DSM IV-TR* is replaced by the criteria that the deficits must adversely affect educational performance. The IDEA criteria for autism eligibility includes repetitive and stereotyped activities and movements as additional characteristics; but, unlike the *DSM-IV-TR* criteria which specifically requires the presence of those features for a clinical diagnosis, these characteristics are not considered necessary for inclusion (or exclusion) criteria for eligibility. This distinction highlights the IDEA autism definition as one that is broad and flexible enough to be inclusive of the entire autism spectrum disorders continuum, including PDD-NOS and asperger syndrome, as long as the core deficits adversely affect educational performance (Dahle, 2003; Fogt, Miller, & Zirkel, 2003; Safran, 2008; Shriver, Allen, & Mathews, 1999).

The criteria for special education eligibility requiring an adverse effect on educational performance indicates that deficits in the areas of physical, cognitive, communication, social or emotional, and/or adaptive development must be present (IDEA, 2004). Inherent in the eligibility criteria is that a student's ability to benefit from educational services is limited only to educational contexts (e.g., schools). This part of the criteria has often caused confusion for professionals and family members as they determine what constitutes educational performance (Safran, 2008). For instance, does a significant deficit in the ability to engage in social interactions constitute educational performance? Howlin and Asgharian (1999) and Safran (2008) elucidate this quandary by drawing attention to data indicating many students with high-functioning autism, PDD-NOS, and asperger syndrome who demonstrate significant deficits in social competence do not always qualify for special education services, especially if they are functioning well academically. These authors further reference data that indicate students do eventually qualify for special education services, yet identification and eligibility typically occurs at a later age when social competence deficits have worsened.

Unfortunately, social competence behaviors displayed by students with high-functioning autism, and asperger syndrome including social skills deficits, rigidity, unusual mannerisms, and a lack of empathy, are often mistakenly interpreted as purposefully rude and inappropriate behaviors (i.e., a performance deficit), when in fact, they are a manifestation of autism spectrum disorders which is unrecognized and therefore, not addressed through appropriate educational services (Safran, 2001, 2008). Only recently has there been more awareness and attention drawn to these characteristics in the schools as possible indicators of asperger syndrome, high-functioning autism, or PDD-NOS. This has resulted in school divisions engaging in more proactive and sophisticated assessment strategies to begin the identification process. If students with asperger syndrome, high-functioning autism, or PDD-NOS demonstrate clinical difficulties in language and reciprocal social interactions, and these deficits affect their abilities to benefit from or access educational opportunities (Safran, 2001), they are eligible to receive special education services. The earlier students with autism spectrum disorders are identified and receive intervention, the more likely they will have positive long-term outcomes (McEachin, Smith, & Lovass, 1993).

Diagnostic tools for identifying autism spectrum disorders. In the past, a diagnosis of autism spectrum disorders was primarily made through clinical judgment by individuals with specialized training. However, more recently, researchers have developed and validated a number of standardized instruments to assist clinicians in the process. In clinical settings, the Autism Diagnostic Observation Schedule-Generic (ADOS-G; Lord, Rutter, DiLavore, & Risi, 1999) and the Autism Diagnostic Interview-Revised (ADI-R; Rutter, LeCouteur, & Lord, 2003) are considered the "gold standards" for diagnosing autism spectrum disorders and are the only instruments considered adequate for research because of their extensive empirical support (Mazefsky & Oswald, 2006; Tanguay, 2000). The ADOS-G is a structured play-based assessment designed for differing language and developmental levels. The ADOS-G, appropriate for use with young children through adults, engages individuals in specific social situations and rates their behavior and interactions according to a *DSM-IV*-based algorithm that differentiates autism and PDD (Lord et al., 1999). The ADOS-G consists of four modules. Only one module is used for diagnosing autism, and the module is selected based on a person's use of speech and language. For example, Module 1 is used with individuals who do not have consistent speech; whereas, Module 4 is used with adolescents and adults who display fluent speech.

The ADI-R is a structured interview conducted with a family member who has knowledge of the target person's early development, particularly between the ages of 4 and 5 years. The ADI-R meticulously provokes specific examples of observed behavior and rates the responses according to their qualitative match with specific scoring criteria which sums into a *DSM-IV*-based algorithm identifying whether the individual has autism spectrum disorders (Rutter et al., 2003). The ADI-R consists of 93 items focusing on three main functional domains: (a) Language/Communication, (b) Reciprocal Social Interaction, and (c) Restricted, Repetitive, and Stereotyped Behaviors. Although ADI-R is an indirect assessment based on family member report, unlike the ADOS-G (which is based on direct observation) the ADI-R has been found to have strong reliability (Cicchetti, Lord, Koenig, Klin, & Volkmar, 2008).

Recent studies of the discriminative validity of the ADOS-G and ADI-R have provided moderately robust findings. Mazefsky and Oswald (2006) found that the ADI-R and ADOS-G predicted clinical team diagnosis correctly 75% of the time, with most errors being false positives, whereas the Gilliam Autism Ratings Scale (GARS; Gilliam, 1995) was ineffective at discriminating between autism and not autism. Additional work has been done to strengthen the diagnostic utility of the ADOS-G via the development of a more refined algorithm with a much larger sample than the original norming sample (Gotham, Risi, Pickles, & Lord, 2007). However, as indicated above, the use of the ADI-R and ADOS-G in tandem is considered best practice, which is not possible for many schools due to the immense time the ADI-R takes to complete (Rutter et al., 2003) and the amount of training needed to be reliable on both assessments (Lord et al., 1999; Rutter et al., 2003). Although the "gold standards" are best practice in research, they are not necessarily "best practice" for everyday practice in schools, leaving schools and school-based teams to decide what assessments are best to meet their needs (i.e., determining eligibility for special education rather than diagnosis) and are reliable and valid for identification purposes.

There are many other screening and diagnostic assessments used in both clinical and educational contexts, but there are a few that are more widely used than others (see Table 22.1). Although many assessments currently exist for identifying autism, no single test or assessment can reliably identify autism spectrum disorders with 100% accuracy all of the time. Likewise, although standardized assessments exist for diagnosing autism spectrum disorders, experienced clinicians and trained professionals are necessary for accurate and appropriate diagnosis (Filipek et al., 1999).

TABLE 22.1
Commonly Used Autism Spectrum Disorders Assessments

Name	Type	Ages	Scores
Gilliam Autism Rating Scale (GARS) (Gilliam, 1995)	42-item behavioral checklist	3 – 22	Standard scores, percentile ranks, and Autism quotient score
Gilliam Asperger's Disorder Scale (GADS) (Gilliam, 2001)	32-item behavioral checklist	3 – 22	Standard scores, percentile ranks, and Asperger syndrome quotient score
Childhood Autism Rating Scale (*CARS*) (Schopler, Reichler, & Renner, 1988)	15-item behavior rating scale	>2	Total score
Autism Behavior Checklist (*ABC*) (Reynolds & Kamphaus, 1992)	47-item behavior rating scale	2 – 13	Standard scores and percentile ranks
Social Responsiveness Scale (SRS) (Constantino, 2002)	65-item behavior rating scale	4– 18	T-Scores and total raw score

In addition to tools that specialize in diagnosing autism spectrum disorders, another current diagnostic trend is examining the utility of using adaptive behavior measures in further defining the characteristics (Klin et al., 2007; Paul et al., 2004), diagnostic utility (Tomanik, Pearson, Loveland, Lane, & Shaw, 2007) and differential diagnosis of autism spectrum disorders (Balboni, Pedrasbissi, Molteni, & Villa, 2001). Adaptive behavior, defined as the conceptual, social, and practical skills that individuals are capable of utilizing in their everyday lives (Schalock et al., 2007), is greatly impacted by autism spectrum disorders and can be measured using a number of common assessment tools, such as the Vineland Adaptive Behavior Scales (VABS; Sparrow, Cicchetti, & Balla, 2005) and the Behavior Assessment System for Children (BASC; Reynolds & Kamphaus, 1992). The potential for adaptive behavior scales to further refine the characteristics of individuals with autism can potentially increase our clinical diagnostic accuracy and is an emerging area of research and practice (Klin et al., 2007).

As indicated, although the trend in clinically diagnosing autism spectrum disorders is to rely on the *DSM-IV* definition of autism spectrum disorders and diagnostic tools that have used this approach for their factorial structure, educational eligibility for special education services deviates from the approach. This issue can create a dilemma for educators when determining eligibility for special education services because the manifestation of the disability must adversely affect educational performance, not meet the disability construct of the *DSM-IV*. Thus, educators are left asking the question, of what assessment tools are recommended for practice when determining eligibility according to the IDEA criteria. Recommended practice in schools is to use reliable, norm-referenced assessments; but, unlike *DSM-IV* criteria, schools decisions must be based on federal and state policy, with the final decision made by a team, not a licensed clinician (Dahle, 2003).

IDEA (2004) mandates that all evaluations for eligibility be based on more than one assessment, which is compatible with clinical practice. However, the use of multiple autism spectrum disorders specific assessments may be redundant and not applicable for the purposes of determining IDEA eligibility. Therefore, one should take care in determining which assessments are the most appropriate to use for assisting in determining eligibility under the autism category as well as determining the impact on the student's educational performance. The ADOS-G, with appropriate training and experience, currently, may be the most appropriate diagnostic evaluation assessment for use in schools because it has strong empirical support and can be completed in a relatively short period of time (Lord et al., 1999). Yet, not all schools have the resources or personnel to use the ADOS-G for all autism evaluations, and the ADOS-G may not be as sensitive for students with asperger syndrome, high-functioning autism, or PDD-NOS. Therefore, the decision about which assessments a school uses should be made by the teams evaluating students for eligibility. To reiterate the multiple data criteria in IDEA, measures of adaptive behavior, cognitive ability, language skills, externalizing and internalizing behavior, executive functioning, and social competence should all be an indispensable part of the evaluation process. The reality in schools and in clinical practice is that no single method of evaluation can always be the only appropriate or reliable means for identifying autism spectrum disorders. Yet, by using empirically validated, well researched, multiple assessments, school staff can more reliably and accurately identify those students with autism spectrum disorders in need of effective interventions.

Effective Intervention Practices for Students with Autism Spectrum Disorders

The connection between developmental gains and effective intervention delivered by qualified practitioners is well documented (National Research Council, 2001; Odom et al., 2003; Simpson, 2005). Likewise, the disparity of outcomes for those who encounter limited or no access to effective intervention is equally well documented. In recent years, increased focus has been placed on the use of evidence-based interventions for all students. This emphasis has brought to the spotlight the existence and appropriateness of a continuum of effective interventions that address the multifarious needs that are represented within a spectrum of disorders such as autism (National Research Council,

2001; Simpson, 2005). Evidence-based practices are those interventions that have multiple sources of peer-reviewed research supporting similar outcomes (Reichow, Volkmar, & Cicchetti, 2008). Unlike some types of treatments (e.g., pharmacology), the impact of well-developed multi-faceted educational interventions is not often immediately apparent. Rather, the process of identifying the most appropriate evidence-based intervention to meet students' needs is often a gradual process requiring a great deal of consistency and integrity of implementation. Therefore, similar to some medications, ongoing, professionally managed access to these interventions is imperative to long-term success.

Defining Evidence-Based Practices

Dunst, Trivette, and Cutspsec (2002) defined evidence-based practices as "practices that are informed by research in which the characteristics and consequences of the environmental variables are empirically established and the relationship directly informs what a practitioner can do to produce a desired outcome" (p. 3). In essence, evidence-based practices that have the appropriate research support are those that adequately define targeted outcomes and have either adequately matched those outcomes to specific need areas or provided a complimentary assessment component by which to provide appropriate individualization (Simpson, 2005). These interventions involve instructing the person, supporting that person, and identifying optimal environmental conditions that increase maintenance and generalization of the desired outcomes (Odom et al., 2003).

As noted by Simpson (2005), despite the increased attention, the field of autism spectrum disorders remains in its infancy and there remains a dearth of evidence-based practices to meet the needs of these individuals. Simpson suggested that effective practices are those that are (a) systematically and objectively verified, (b) used with fidelity, and (c) are tailored to fit the individual needs of the student. The field of autism spectrum disorders has embraced this definition and approached the application of effective interventions in increasingly rigorous and unique ways that elucidate the need for continued efforts in this area.

Objective Verification of Evidence–Based Practices

Researchers have conducted several comprehensive reviews examining the evidence of commonly used educational intervention practices. In conducting a large and systematic review, Simpson and his colleagues identified available interventions for individuals with autism spectrum disorders and categorized them based on level of empirical evidence to support their use (Simpson et al., 2005). Simpson et al.'s review has been widely referenced and generally endorsed by the field because of the comprehensive nature, the inclusion of widely available and popular interventions, and the use of a categorization process that is consistent with current interdisciplinary, professional standards defining research-based practices (Odom et al., 2003). Simpson and colleagues suggest the use of a three-tiered categorical system for judging the amount of evidence supporting an intervention practice: *scientifically-based practices*, *promising practices*, and *limited evidence*. According to the three-tiered system, research studies in the two categories that included any level of scientific support are the (a) *scientifically-based practices,* defined as those that provided "significant and convincing empirical efficacy and support" (p. 9), and the (b) *promising practices,* which are those methods that emerged as having "efficacy and utility with individuals with autism spectrum disorders" (p. 9). Figure 22. 2 provides a summary of these practices. Other, more specialized reviews of evidence-based practices for autism spectrum disorders have provided similar conclusions (e.g., see Iovannone, Dunlap, Huber, & Kincaid, 2003; Odom et al., 2003).

Shortly after Simpson et al.'s (2005) review, almost in response to the ongoing concerns regarding the definition of evidence-based practices and the research-to-practice gap, several notable papers emerged with the emphasis of building a stronger scientific base for intervention practices. For example, Smith and colleagues (2007) emphasized systemic validation and dissemination of psychosocial intervention practices in the area of autism spectrum disorders. Their systematic plan suggests the use of single subject design evaluation through efficacy, randomized control, and create a manual version of it for implementers to ensure valid use, dissemination, and contextual fit of targeted interventions. More recently, Reichow and colleagues (2008) highlighted the need for a common definition of evidence-based practices. Additionally, they suggest developing a systematic process for determining which evidence-based practices specifically for autism spectrum disorders incorporate an interdisciplinary scope and account for multi design methodologies. This chapter, not only provided a process for evaluating interventions but also highlighted multiple previous reviews with summaries

Scientifically Based
Applied behavior analysis Discrete trial teaching Pivotal response training Learning Experiences: An Alternative Program for Preschoolers and Parents
Promising Practices
Picture Exchange Communication System Incidental teaching Structured teaching Augmentative alternative communication Assistive technology Joint action routines Peer mediated interventions Cognitive behavioral intervention Cognitive learning strategies Social stories Social decision making strategies Sensory integration

Figure 22.2 Levels of empirical support for autism spectrum disorders interventions. Adapted from Simpson (2005).

suggesting the lack of existing evidence-based practices based on a using a randomized control design as the gold standard (NRC, 2001).

Delivering Evidence-Based Practices with Fidelity

The hallmark of an evidence-based practice is that it can be implemented with fidelity across contexts by trained individuals. As Simpson (2005) asserts, "The ultimate utility of these interventions … is a function of their alignment with the needs of individual students, … program planners and implementers, and the extent to which they are used in the prescribed fashion by appropriately trained knowledgeable personnel" (p. 145).

Research has indicated that in addition to an empirically supported efficacious intervention, one of the primary determinants of an effective intervention for individuals with autism spectrum disorders is the fidelity of implementation (Detrich, 1999). Practitioners sometimes compromise fidelity of implementation when they do not apply the techniques of the evidence-based practice in the manner in which it was intended. Additionally, when practices are adapted or evolve to support unique needs of a specific context (rather than the needs of the individual), integrity of the practice is compromised, which in turn may influence its effectiveness. It is important to note that even the most effective practices are not likely to deliver expected outcomes if they are not implemented with fidelity and manualized for educational settings (Lord et al., 2005; Simpson, 2005).

Detrich (1999) identified a strategy to increase fidelity of implementation—designing and matching interventions that are a good contextual fit for the classroom setting. The contextual variables identified as those that may influence treatment fidelity include (a) the characteristics of the individual student, (b) the resources required to implement the intervention with integrity, and (c) the similarity of the practice to current classroom practices. As a result, it is important when designing and matching "contextually fit" interventions that a decision be made with consideration as to which intervention (as opposed to another) is most likely to be implemented with fidelity. The more the current contextual variables (i.e., similarity to existing classroom interventions) match the intervention, the more likely the intervention will be implemented with fidelity. Not surprisingly, higher levels of fidelity commonly occur with interventions that have high acceptability within contexts. Although this approach seems intuitive, implementing educational practices in this manner has also created a challenge for researchers and practitioners in the field autism spectrum disorders, in which a continuum of needs may be supported in few contexts. As a result, programming decisions based solely on context may not always secure an appropriate match between student needs and evidence-based interventions.

In the field of autism spectrum disorders, fidelity measurement procedures that are contextually valid are not readily available. However, professionals are discussing the need to build an evidence-base of interventions that are contextually valid and measures of fidelity to ensure consistency across programs. State and federal level criteria for manualization of practices and training of implementers are important factors to consider to evaluate the anticipated outcomes of evidence-based interventions (Lord et al., 2005). By integrating fidelity assessments and traditional process evaluation with outcome evaluations, we can more accurately determine the efficacy of evidence-based practices. Implementation of this process would provide an empirically-based standard for evidence-based interventions as well as additional information regarding which interventions are most beneficial to individuals with autism spectrum disorders.

Evaluation of Evidence-Based Practices

Due to the broad nature of the defining characteristics and the intent of the specified evidence-based practice, evaluations of outcomes have varied significantly in autism spectrum disorders. In recent years, outcome evaluations have increasingly emphasized changes in building pro-social and adaptive areas of development as opposed to simply a more narrow emphasis on decreases in aberrant behaviors and/or treating characteristics of autism spectrum disorders, as the primary dependent variables. In part, these changes are due to (a) the definitional change of autism to a spectrum disorder, (b) ongoing emphasis on the impact of targeted and intense intervention, and (c) increased mainstreaming in general education of these students. Traditional criteria for evaluating practices that are considered extremely useful in understanding the efficacy of evidence-based practices often include measures of the goodness of contextual fit and availability of data to support anticipated outcomes. However, there exist additional essential variables, which should be captured to provide information regarding the effectiveness of a specific practice, such as optimal length of intervention, effectiveness in combination with concurrent interventions, maintenance and generalization of outcomes, and predictive validity specific to unique child characteristics.

Appropriate Application of Interventions

Research has indicated that strong and positive outcomes result when evidence-based interventions are accurately and appropriately implemented. Successful outcomes of an intervention require not only an effective methodology but also proper matching of the practice with the individual's needs and strengths. It is becoming increasingly evident that there is no single best-suited universal effective intervention for all individuals with autism spectrum disorders—as a result, increased multidisciplinary research is being conducted on autism spectrum disorders subtype characteristics that help to predict positive responses to intervention (Stoelb et al., 2004). To illustrate, a strong body of psychological and neuroscience research has been conducted that demonstrates varied performances on some experimental tests are mediated by IQ and language in individuals with autism spectrum disorders (Howlin, Mawhood, & Rutter, 2000). Geneticists and other medical researchers have increasingly highlighted the critical need to measure the biomedical areas of children with autism spectrum disorders. For example, evidence suggests that microcephaly in individuals with autism spectrum disorders is an indicator of poorer outcomes when compared to those children with autism spectrum disorders who do not have microcephaly (Miles, Hadden, Takahashi, & Hillman, 2000). There is also evidence that children with autism spectrum disorders who have an abnormal phenotype (which encompasses a range of physical anomalies) are more likely to have the additional diagnosis of a genetic disorder and abnormal magnetic resonance imaging scans (MRIs) (Miles, McCathren, Stichter, & Shinawi, 2009). Geneticists are increasing investigations examining dysmorphology (congenital malformations) and other physical traits as predictors of linked outcomes. Although some studies have found that nondysmorphic children responded to intensive early intervention more positively in comparison to dysmorphic children (Stoelb et al., 2004), more emphasis to date has been placed on the link between educational interventions and individual characteristics in autism spectrum disorders. For example, language is one area of development in which researchers have tried to determine potential predictors of progress. Stone and Yoder (2001) found that motor imitation at 2 years was a predictor of language skills at age 4. In particular, children who had strong motor imitation skills at age 2, displayed stronger expressive language skills at age 4 than children with poor motor imitation skills at age 2. Similarly, other research has found a correlation between motor imitation and later receptive language skills (Charman et al., 2003). Although Stone and Yoder found that play skills did not predict language development from age 2 to age 4, Sigman and McGovern (2005) found that functional play skills in early childhood were correlated with gains in language skills in adolescence. Not surprisingly, early childhood language skills predicted adolescent language skills (Sigman & McGovern). Other studies have tried to determine how these factors may be used to predict an individual's response to intervention—thus, helping to select the most appropriate intervention to address the individual's unique characteristics and traits.

Behavioral interventions are one of the most common treatment approaches for children with autism spectrum disorders. The effectiveness of behavioral intervention overall has been well documented (Simpson, 2005). However, researchers are still identifying factors associated with the highest gains when implemented. In 2005, Beglinger and Smith found support for positive relations between social subtypes (based on the Wing Subgroups Questionnaire) and changes in IQ following Early Intensive Behavioral Intervention (EIBI). Other researchers have identified a number of other factors related to positive gains following EIBI including language skills and nondysmorphology (Stoelb et al., 2004), imitation skills, language skills, daily living skills and socialization (Sallows & Graupner, 2005) and high cognition and social skills (Ben-Itzchak & Zachor, 2007). To match the most appropriate interventions to individuals, some researchers have begun work on identifying subtypes within the autism spectrum. In a review of the literature, Beglinger and Smith (2001) called for researchers to continue working toward the development of a subtyping system. Ultimately, this type of system will help educators know which interventions are the most efficacious for individuals who display different types of characteristics on the spectrum.

As researchers continue to further and more accurately define the autism spectrum (Lord, 2009) and concurrently design increasingly responsive interventions, an important educational distinction essential for optimizing current resources is to differentiate between comprehensive and focal interventions. A common and most notable misperception between comprehensive and focal interventions is the almost blind concentration on Discrete Trial Training (DTT), a focal intervention. DTT is a type of intervention strategy embedded within the broader framework of applied behavior analysis. Applied behavior analysis (ABA; a comprehensive intervention) is a systematic approach that involves improving socially valid behavior through analysis of factors that support the behavior. ABA has decades of empirical research to support its effectiveness with multiple populations, including autism spectrum disorders. DTT, one particular strategy within ABA, takes a set of skills and teaches them separately in a consistent, systematic manner. Lovaas, who in the 1980s popularized DTT, claimed that, when children with autism spectrum disorders received 40 hours a week of DTT, over half of them were indiscernible from their typical peers (Lovaas, 1987). More recently, Siegel (2003) found that children who received 25 hours per week of DTT also made significant gains. Yet, despite some of the well constructed DTT research, confusion and misuse of the term has led the popular press, legislative bodies, family members and many professionals to insist that DTT (for at least 20 hours per week) for all students with autism spectrum disorders is the most efficacious approach to intervention. As indicated by the National Research Council (2001), to date, research has not supported as effective the use of any particular focal treatment for use in isolation for all individuals with autism spectrum disorders.

Comprehensive interventions, like ABA, typically include a number of individual intervention strategies and are designed to address multiple needs across contexts. For example, one can use ABA to reduce or eliminate severe aggression or self-injurious behavior as well as teach academic learning behaviors and prosocial behaviors across school and home settings. Depending on the skill and context, various strategies are used. Other examples of comprehensive approaches to interventions include incidental teaching (which incorporates structured teaching opportunities based on an individual's interests and embedded within the natural environment) or cognitive-based interventions (which use specific cognitive-based modification strategies to ameliorate negative behaviors and promote adaptive behaviors). Many communication systems are considered comprehensive treatments as well, such as the picture exchange communication system (PECS), visual schedules, and augmentative communication systems. Focal treatments like DTT tend to be designed specifically to either support a specific population and/or target specific skills in a specific way; and, hence, they are less global and flexible. Other examples of focal treatments are token economy systems and social stories (designed to reinforce a specific set of behaviors at a time), medication management, and food allergy diets. All of these types of focal interventions address specific behaviors or symptoms but aren't necessarily designed to address comprehensive needs across contexts. Avoiding a one-size-fits-all approach and optimizing the use of comprehensive and well-defined evidence-based focal treatments maximizes the current state of intervention knowledge as work continues in subtyping responses to intervention across the spectrum.

Future Research

Research supports the notion that there are characteristics among individuals with autism spectrum disorders that are correlated with differential outcomes. However, how these noted characteristics affect long-term trajectory and response to intervention is not yet clear. In addition to examining response to interventions based on subtypes, future research should also examine outcomes from a longitudinal perspective. Identifying individual characteristics linked to response to intervention, along with categorizing interventions based on long-term outcomes will help educators match the appropriate balance of different types of interventions (environmental supports, skill development, and self management) to the individual. Understanding the role of subtype characteristics and how these characteristics evolve through developmental stages will allow practitioners to target particular students with a specific, evidence-based intervention program to address universal and individualized needs.

Contemporary Issues and Trends: Influences on Service Delivery in Educational Settings

Perhaps no other special education category has received more attention than autism spectrum disorders. Due to the heterogeneity of characteristics within autism spectrum disorders, diagnosis, identification, and eligibility of children and youth with autism spectrum disorders is a multi-faceted, complex issue. Additionally, elucidating the most effective intervention practices for this diverse population is challenging. With the emphasis on federal funding for research that targets the causes and ameliorates the skill deficits presented with autism spectrum disorders, the field is rapidly advancing. Educators and family members who interact with this population currently face a number of issues and often struggle to gather the most current information to help make appropriate educational decisions that facilitate these individuals' development and learning. In this section, we highlight several of the most salient issues that today's schools and family members encounter.

Early Identification and Service Delivery

For some children, early signs of autism spectrum disorders appear within the first year of life (Volkmar et al., 2008). A host of standardized early screening procedures are available to assist with the identification of these young children; however, family members are often the first to notice skill deficits in their children's speech and language, social responsivity, and regulatory behaviors, such as attention, sleeping, and eating (Chawarska et al., 2007). Contrary to contemporary belief, few children with autism spectrum disorders actually have a regression in development within their first few years of life (Baird et al., 2008), and the small percentage who do are more appropriately diagnosed with Childhood Disintegrative Disorder (Werner & Dawson, 2005). When examining retrospectively the development of most children diagnosed with autism spectrum disorders, evidence indicates rather than losing existing skills, they actually begin to developmentally stagnate within the first year of life. Additionally, researchers have identified genetic anomalies linked to autism spectrum disorders, which indicate that children with autism spectrum disorders are likely to be genetically predisposed for the disorder. Both of the findings are important for assisting professionals within the field of early intervention and family members increase their awareness of early symptoms, which ultimately will contribute to early diagnosis and intervention (Zwaigenbaum et al., 2007).

Early Screening and Diagnosis

For children below age 3, diagnosis of autism spectrum disorders is more difficult because the symptoms overlap with other developmental disabilities. Some researchers suggest that as many as 50% of infants and toddlers diagnosed at risk for autism spectrum disorders are eventually diagnosed with other developmental disabilities rather than autism spectrum disorders. A number of systematic screening and diagnostic tools are available to increase the predictive validity of early identification and diagnosis. However, early behavioral markers are commonly used to initiate the process with infants and toddlers at risk for autism spectrum disorders. When screening for autism spectrum disorders in infants and toddlers, the following early behavioral markers are examined relative to typically developing same age peers:

- Poor visual orientation, tracking, and attention
- Limited response to name
- Lack of socially directed looking and social interest
- Lack of social smiles
- Excessive mouthing of objects
- Aversion to social touch
- Difficulties with imitation (Baranek, 1999; Osterling et al., 2002; Zwaigenbaum et al., 2005).

Similar to early identification of young children with other types of developmental disabilities, a multi-level screening and diagnostic process is recommended. One of the most commonly used tools at this initial level is the Modified Checklist for Autism in Toddlers (M-CHAT; Robins, Fein, Barton, & Green 2001), which is validated for children 16–30 months of age. The M-CHAT has recently been revised and is now entitled the Quantitative Checklist for Autism in Toddlers (QCHAT; Allison et al., 2008). Several other researchers have developed screening tools that begin with a more general level screening and then progress to a secondary level of screening. If the child fails the initial screening, a secondary level of screening is conducted prior to conducting a more complete diagnostic evaluation. For instance, Wetherby and Prizant (2002) developed the Communication and Symbolic Behavior Scales - Developmental Profile (CSBS) as a general (or level 1) screener for children ages 6–24 months. If the child fails the CSBS, practitioners use a secondary (or level 2) screener, the Scale of Red Flags (SORF; Wetherby & Woods, 2002) to determine if a diagnostic evaluation is needed. Similarly, the Pervasive Developmental Disorders Screening Test (PDDST; Siegel, 1996) is a primary and secondary screening tool for use with children 18 months to 6 years old. If a young child fails a secondary screening, professionals usually suggest further diagnostic assessments. Although not designed or validated for children under age 3 years, diagnostic tools, such as the ADI-R, ADOS-G, or the *DSM-IV* are commonly used at this stage. One diagnostic tool designed for use with children younger than 18 months is the Autism Observation Scale for Infants (AOSI; Bryson, Zwaigenbaum, McDermott, Rombough, & Brian, 2008).

As the field begins to identify children at risk for autism spectrum disorders at a very young age, practitioners and family members have to pay particular attention to the child's overall developmental and health status, ruling out other developmental disorders. Many available screening and diagnostic tools have only moderate sensitivity and specificity when diagnosing autism spectrum disorders and few diagnosticians have specific training and skills needed in using these tools with our youngest children. Thus, many of the early autism spectrum disorders diagnoses are ultimately based on clinical interpretation alone. New advancements are regularly being made in the areas of early identification and diagnostics. For example, Lord and colleagues are developing a version of the ADOS for toddlers (i.e., the ADOS-T), with initial reports of good specificity and sensitivity (Luyster et al., in press).

Additionally, other researchers are working on more precise screening tools that evaluate early communication (e.g., Infant-Toddler Checklist; Wetherby, Brosnan-Maddox, Peace, & Newton, 2008) or repetitive behaviors (First Year Inventory; Reznick, Baranek, Reavis, Watson, & Crais, 2007). Early diagnosis and identification has been identified as best-practice for children and youth with autism spectrum disorders and is indicative of improved outcomes for children (McEachin et al., 1993; NRC, 2001; Rogers, 1998).

Educational Service Delivery and the Least Restrictive Environment

Similar to the issues encountered when identifying and diagnosing autism spectrum disorders presented earlier in this chapter, the provision of providing free, appropriate educational services in the least restrictive environment is equally as challenging an issue for professionals and family members. A common difficulty, when providing educational services to all students with different disabilities, is determining what are the most *appropriate* educational services in comparison to *optimal* educational services. Service delivery to students with autism spectrum disorders is no exception. In fact, due to the lack of well-defined evidence-based practices and media attention to various treatments, this debate has often become contentious, with a stunning number of due process hearings as evidence (Yell & Katsiyannis, 2003). Additionally, the debate includes more than school professionals and family members disagreeing; it also includes intense disputes among professionals. Similar to most debates, at the core are different philosophical approaches toward intervention.

A common feature of different approaches toward educational services is the use of principles of ABA. Although an ABA approach is common among many different perspectives, the contention lies in the intensity and delivery of ABA strategies. Beginning in the 1960s, Lovaas and colleagues (Lovaas, Freitag, Kinder, Rubenstein, Schaeffer, & Simmons, 1966) and others (Ferster & DeMyer, 1961) were some of the first researchers to investigate behavioral treatments for children with autism spectrum disorders. Using operant conditioning techniques (i.e., application of reinforcement and punishment), Lovaas and colleagues demonstrated the capacity of students with autism spectrum disorders to learn and develop essential skills for social-communication. The core of Lovaas' approach is to use behavioral strategies in highly controlled settings (to minimize distractions) and through highly structured discrete trials using a one-to-one format. A review of empirical support for this approach is beyond the scope of this chapter; however, considerable evidence exists suggesting that Discrete Trial Training is a highly effective technique for educating students with autism spectrum disorders (Howlin, Magiati, & Charman, 2009; Reichow & Wolery, 2009). Thus, Discrete Trial Training is often touted as the "best" approach for educating students with autism spectrum disorders and has pushed the direction of the field toward service delivery options and placements in what some consider as restrictive educational settings, such as self-contained schools or classroom designed primarily for students with autism spectrum disorders. Although not common today for the majority of students with disabilities, the field is seeing an increase in the number of private schools founded on principles of ABA. Many professionals and family members disagree with placements in self-contained educational settings; however, this practice is becoming more and more common and begins in early childhood (Sanford, Levine, & Blackorby, 2008). For instance, following an initial diagnosis in early childhood, many children begin early intensive behavior intervention (EIBI), a term used to describe various discrete trial training approaches (see Lovaas, 2002).

Although some professionals consider the use of Discrete Trial Training in more restrictive education settings (e.g., self-contained schools, classrooms) to be the best approach, many consider this combination limiting because there is little emphasis on developing functional skills embedded in everyday living activities. Beginning in the 1970s, a core group of researchers began to employ ABA strategies embedded within natural contexts (e.g., Schreibman & Carr, 1978), commonly referred to as *naturalistic behavioral interventions*. This approach focuses on generalization using techniques, such as incidential teaching (Hart & Risley, 1968), milieu teaching (Halle, Baer, & Spradlin, 1981), and pivotal response teaching (Koegel & Koegel, 2006). Different than DTT, these contemporary ABA approach include child-directed learning in natural contexts (e.g., school and community settings) and embed naturally occurring, relevant reinforcers. At the early childhood level, a number of comprehensive intervention models have been developed based on the principles of naturalistic behavioral interventions (e.g., the Social Communication Emotional Regulation, Transaction Supports [SCERTS)] model (Prizant, Wetherby, Rubin, Laurent, & Rydell, 2006) and the Walden Toddler Program [McGee, 1999]). A solid literature base exists documenting the efficacy of naturalistic behavioral intervention, suggesting that this approach is effective for improving communication and social reciprocity skills that generalize and maintain across individuals and settings. Although, practitioners use naturalistic behavioral interventions with the school-age population in school settings; fully articulated *comprehensive* intervention models are not as available for this population. Typically, a broader range of curricular models and service delivery options are provided in school settings that are based predominately on individualization. This type of eclectic approach toward service delivery is aligned with the spirit of IDEA, but the evidence supporting the various approaches is difficult to summarize and clearly communicate with family members. One of the strengths of using naturalistic behavioral interventions in less restrictive educational settings is the access to same-aged peers, who can serve as social interaction partners and instructors.

To summarize, identifying the most appropriate service delivery model and educational placement for students with autism spectrum disorders is a complex issue and depends on the individual student's strengths and needs. Nevertheless, after a comprehensive review of the literature, the National Research Council (2001) suggests a number of effective instructional programs share several common core components including:

- Active engagement in instructional programming for at least 25 hours per week (e.g., 5 hours per day/5 days per week),
- Repeated, planned teaching opportunities, including sufficient amount of 1:1 teaching and small group instruction,
- Inclusion of families in intervention planning and parent/caregiver training,
- Low child to teacher ratios (recommend 2:1),
- Mechanism for ongoing program evaluation and child assessment to monitor progress and inform decision-making.

The NRC (2001) also suggests the following content areas of instruction be included as part of the individual's educational treatment plan: (a) teaching functional, spontaneous communication: (b) providing social skills instruction throughout the day: (c) increasing appropriate peer-related interactions: (d) addressing challenging behaviors: and (e) instructing cognitive and academic skills (as appropriate).

Complementary and Alternative Treatments

Given the high prevalence rates of autism spectrum disorders, there has been widespread media attention to autism spectrum disorders and its various treatments. Many of these news stories report on the use of complementary and alternative treatments (CAT) that claim to treat or even "cure" autism spectrum disorders. Given the attention to these alternative treatments, this is an important issue to address when discussing the education of students with autism spectrum disorders. Complementary and alternative treatments are defined in the literature as strategies or techniques that often promise extra-ordinary results, but have limited or no scientific support and evidence to substantiate these claims (Myles & Simpson, 1998). A number of medical, therapeutic, and educational practices fall under this category (e.g., the use of hyperbaric chambers, animal therapy, auditory integration therapy, gluten-free diets, and facilitated communication). Many of these treatments have at one time or another been the spotlight of media attention; however, as scientific evidence has emerged on the lack of effectiveness or even counter-therapeutic effects on the approach, media attention has turned its emphasis to another alternative approach. Levy, Mandell, Merhar, Ittenbach, and Pinto-Martin (2003) found that as many as 30% of children included in a survey were using a complementary or alternative treatment, including some that were potentially counter-therapeutic. A comprehensive review of complementary and alternative treatments is beyond the scope of this chapter (for a discussion, see Levy et al., 2003; McWilliam, 1999; Smith, 2008). However, the majority of these treatments have little scientific evidence examining their effectiveness; thus, the outcomes for students with autism spectrum disorders are unknown. From an educational perspective, school personnel need to be aware of the empirical evidence supporting (or not) these treatments and help educate family members about the evidence (or lack there of) and the potential risks as they make decisions about the use of complementary and alternative treatments. Additionally, if family members do choose to try a complementary and alternative treatment with their child, teachers can assist family members in collecting data to determine the effectiveness of that treatment.

Conclusions

Since the enactment of P.L. 94-142, students with autism spectrum disorders have been a part of the special education system. However, with the increase in prevalence of autism spectrum disorders and research findings elucidating the causes, characteristics, and effective interventions, educators are continually challenged to know and apply the latest research findings in their classrooms and schools. A common saying among individuals in the field of autism spectrum disorders is "if you know 'one child' with autism, you know 'one child' with autism." This saying illustrates the point that similar to other developmental disabilities, autism is truly a spectrum disorder, with individuals who display varying degrees of symptoms, levels of skills (e.g., cognition, communication, social), and needs depending on the contexts in which they function. Although there may be similar traits across individuals with autism spectrum disorders, clearly, the needs of young children with autism spectrum disorders receiving services under Part C and their families are different than young adults transitioning from high school into the workforce.

A number of educational issues face the field of autism spectrum disorders today. However, the most salient of these issues are common across all categories of disabilities in special education—assuring a free, appropriate public education, employing reliable, valid, and nondiscriminatory assessments, and developing individualized educational programs. Future research developments that examine the most sensitive and reliable strategies for diagnosis and identification, identify the most efficacious interventions based on common traits, and evaluate the most appropriate service delivery options will help guide educators to meet the diverse needs of this growing population.

References

Allison, C., Baron-Cohen, S., Wheelwright, S., Charman, T., Richler, J., Pasco, G., & Brayne, C. (2008). The Q-CHAT (Quantitative Checklist for Autism in Toddlers): A normally distributed quantitative measure of autistic traits at 18–24 months of age: Preliminary report. *Journal of Autism & Developmental Disorders, 38*, 1414–1425.

American Psychiatric Association (APA). (2000). *Diagnostic and statistical manual of mental disorders* (4th ed., text rev.). Washington, DC: Author.

Baird, G., Charman, T., Pickles, A., Chandler, S., Lucas, T., Meldrum, D., … Simonoff, E. (2008). Regression, developmental trajectory and associated problems in disorders in the autism spectrum: The SNAP study. *Journal of Autism and Developmental Disorders, 38,* 1827–1836.

Balboni, G., Pedrabissi, L., Molteni, M., & Villa, S. (2001). Discriminant validity of the Vineland Scales: Score profiles of individuals with mental retardation and a specific disorder. *American Journal on Mental Retardation, 106*(2), 162–172.

Baranek, G. T. (1999). Autism during infancy: A retrospective video analysis of sensory-motor and social behaviors at 9–12 months of age. *Journal of Autism and Developmental Disorders, 29*, 213–224.

Beglinger, L, & Smith T. H. (2001). A review of subtyping in autism and proposed dimensional classification model. *Journal of Autism and Developmental Disorders, 31*(4), 411–422.

Ben-Itzchak, E. & Zachor, D. A. (2007). The effects of intellectual functioning and autism on outcome of early behavioral intervention for children with autism. *Research in Developmental Disabilities, 28*(3), 287–303.

Bennett, T., Szatmari, P., Bryson, S., Volden, J., Zwaigenbaum, L., Vaccarella, L., … Boyle, M. (2008). Differentiating autism and Asperger syndrome on the basis of language delay or impairment. *Journal of Autism and Developmental Disorders*, *38*, 616–625.

Bertrand, J., Mars, A., Boyle, C., Bove, F., Yeargin-Allsopp, M., & Decoufle, P. (2001). Prevalence of autism in a United States population: The Brick Township, New Jersey, investigation. *Pediatrics*, *108*, 1155–1161.

Bettleheim, B. (1959). Feral children and autistic children. *The American Journal of Sociology*, *64*(5), 455–467.

Bryson, S. E., Zwaigenbaum, L., McDermott, C., Rombough, V., & Brian, J. (2008). The autism observation scale for infants: Scale development and reliability data. *Journal of Autism & Developmental Disorders, 38*, 731–738.

Center for Disease Control and Prevention: National Center on Birth Defect and Developmental Disabilities. (2009). Learn the signs. Act early. Retrieved December 12, 2006, from http://www.ced.gov/ncbddd/autism/data.html

Charman, T., Baron-Cohen, S., Swettenham, J., Baird, G., Drew, A. & Cox, A. (2003). Predicting language outcome in infants with autism and pervasive developmental disorder. *International Journal of Language and Communication Disorders, 38*(3), 265–285.

Chawarska, K., Paul, R. Klin, A., Hannigen, A., Dichtel, L. E., & Volkmar, F. (2007). Parental recognition of developmental problems in toddlers with autism spectrum disorders. *Journal of Autism and Developmental Disorders, 37,* 62–72.

Cicchetti, D. V., Lord, C., Koenig, K., Klin, A., & Volkmar, F. R. (2008). Reliability of the ADI-R: Multiple examiners evaluate a single case. *Journal of Autism and Developmental Disorders*, *38*, 764–770.

Constantino, J. N. (2002). *The Social Responsiveness Scale*. Los Angeles, CA: Western Psychological Services.

Dahle, K. B. (2003). The clinical and educational systems: Differences and similarities. *Focus on Autism and Other Developmental Disabilities, 18,* 238–246.

Dawson, G. (2008). Early behavioral intervention, brain plasticity, and the prevention of autism spectrum disorder. *Development and Psychopathology, 20*, 775–803.

Detrich, R. (1999). Increasing treatment fidelity by matching interventions to contextual variables within the educational setting. *School Psychology Review, 28*(4), 608–620.

Dunst, C. J., Trivette, C. M., & Cutspec, P. A. (2002). Toward an operational definition of evidence-based practice. *Centerscope: Evidence-based Approaches in Early Childhood Development, 1*(1), 1–3.

Ferster, C. B., & DeMyer, M. K. (1961). The development of performances in autistic children in an automatically controlled environment. *Journal of Chronic Diseases, 13*, 312–345.

Filipek, P. A., Accardo, P. J., Baranek, G. T., Cook, E. H., Dawson, G., Gordon, B., …Volkmar, F. R. (1999). The screening and diagnosis of autistic spectrum disorders. *Journal of Autism and Developmental Disorders*, *29*(6), 439–484.

Fogt, J. B., Miller, D. N., & Zirkel, P. A. (2003). Defining autism: Professional best practice and published case law. *Journal of School Psychology*, *41*, 201–216.

Frombonne, E. (2003). The prevalence of autism. *Journal of the American Medical Association, 289,* 87–89.

Gilliam, J. E. (1995). *Gilliam Autism Rating Scale*. Austin, TX: Pro-Ed.

Gilliam, J. E. (2001). *Gilliam Asperger's Disorder Scale*. Austin, TX: Pro-Ed.

Gotham, K., Risi, S., Pickles, A., & Lord, C. (2007). The Autism Diagnostic Observation Schedule: Revised algorithms for improved diagnostic validity. *Journal of Autism and Developmental Disorders, 37*, 613–627.

Halle, J. W., Baer, D. M., & Spradlin, J. E. (1987). Teacher's generalized use of delay as a stimulus control procedure to increase language use in handicapped children. *Journal of Applied Behavior Analysis, 14*, 389–409.

Hart, B. M., & Risley, T. R. (1968). Establishing use of descriptive adjective in the spontaneous speech of disadvantaged preschool children. *Journal of Applied Behavior Analysis, 1*, 109–120.

Howlin, P. (2003). Outcome in high-functioning adults with autism with and without early language delays: Implications for the differentiation between autism and Asperger syndrome. *Journal of Autism and Developmental Disorders, 33*, 3–13.

Howlin, P., & Asgharian, A. (1999). The diagnosis of autism and Asperger syndrome: Findings from a survey of 770 families. *Developmental Medicine and Child Neurology, 41*, 834–839.

Howlin, P., Magiati, I., & Charman, T. (2009). Systematic review of early intensive behavioral interventions for children with autism. *American Association on Intellectual and Developmental Disabilities, 114*(1), 23–41.

Howlin, P., Mawhood, L. M., & Rutter, M. (2000). Autism and developmental receptive languages disorder: A follow-up comparison in early adult life: II. Social, behavioural and psychiatric outcomes. *Journal of Child Psychology and Psychiatry, 41*, 561–578.

Individuals with Disabilities Education Act Regulations. 34 C,F.R. 300.7 (2004).

Iovannone, R., Dunlap, G., Huber, H., & Kincaid, D. (2003). Effective educational practices for students with autism spectrum disorders. *Focus on Autism and Other Developmental Disabilities, 18*, 150–165.

Kanner, L. (1943). Autistic disturbances of affective contact. *Nervous Child, 2*, 217–250.

Kasari, C., Freeman, S., & Paparella, T. (2006). Joint attention and symbolic play in young children with autism: A randomized controlled intervention study. *Journal of Child Psychology & Psychiatry, 47*, 611–620.

Klin, A., Pauls, D., Schultz, R., & Volkmar, F. (2005). Three diagnostic approaches to Asperger syndrome: Implications for research. *Journal of Autism and Developmental Disorders, 35*, 221–234.

Klin, A., Saulnier, C. A., Sparrow, S. S., Cicchetti, D. V., Volkmar, F. R., & Lord, C. (2007). Social and communication abilities and disabilities in higher functioning individuals with autism spectrum disorders: The Vineland and the ADOS. *Journal of Autism and Developmental Disorders, 37*(4), 748–759.

Koegel, R. L. & Koegel, L. K. (Eds.) (2006). *Pivotal response treatments for autism: Communication, social, and academic development.* Baltimore, MD: Brookes.

Levy, S. E., Mandell, D .S., Merhar, S., Ittenbach, R. F., & Pinto-Martin, J. (2003). Use of complementary and alternative medicine among children recently diagnosed with autism spectrum disorder. *Journal of Developmental and Behavioral Pediatrics, 24*, 418–23.

Lord, C. (2009). What would better diagnosis of ASD look like? Presentation at the 8th Annual International Meeting for Autism Research, May 8, 2009. Chicago, IL.

Lord, C., Rutter, M., DiLavore, P., & Risi, S. (1999). *Autism Diagnostic Observation Schedule, Generic*. Los Angeles, CA: Western Psychological Services.

Lord, C., Wagner, A., Rogers, S., Szatmari, P., Aman, M., Charman, T., … Yorder, P. (2005). Challenges in evaluating psychosocial interventions for autistic spectrum disorders. *Journal of Autism and Developmental Disorders, 35*(6), 695–708.

Lotter, V. (1967). Epidemiology of autistic conditions in young children, II: Some characteristics of parents and their children. *Social Psychiatry, 1*, 163–173.

Lovaas, O. I. (1987). Behavioral treatment and normal educational and intellectual functioning in young autistic children. *Journal of Consulting and Clinical Psychology, 55*, 3–9.

Lovaas, O. I. (2002). *Teaching individuals with developmental delays: Basic intervention techniques.* Austin, TX: PRO-ED.

Lovaas O. I., Freitag G., Kinder, M. I., Rubenstein, B. D., Schaeffer, B., & Simmons, J. Q. (1966). Establishment of social reinforcers in two schizophrenic children on the basis of food. *Journal of Experimental Child Psychology, 4*(2),109–125.

Luyster, R., Gotham, K., Guthrie, W., Coffing, M., Petrak, R., Pierce, K., … Lord, C. (in press). The Autism Diagnostic Observation Schedule—Toddler module: A new module of a standardized diagnostic measure for autism spectrum disorders. *Journal of Autism and Developmental Disorders*.

Mazefsky, C. A., & Oswald, D. P. (2006). The discriminative ability and diagnostic utility of the ADOS-G, ADI-R, and GARS for children in a clinical setting. *Autism, 10*, 533–549.

McEachin, J. J., Smith, T., & Lovaas, O. I. (1993). Long-term outcome for children with autism who received early intensive behavioral treatment. *American Journal on Mental Retardation, 97*, 359–372.

McGee, G., Morrier, M. J., & Daly, T. (1999). An incidental teaching approach to early intervention for toddlers with autism. *Journal of the Association for Persons with Severe Handicaps, 24*, 133–146.

McWilliam, R. A. (1999). Controversial practices: The need for a reacculturation of early intervention fields. *Topics in Early Childhood Special Education, 19*(3), 177–188.

Miles, J. H., Hadden, L. L., Takahashi, T. N., & Hillman, R. E. (2000). Head circumference is an independent clinical finding associated with autism. *American Journal of Medical Genetics, 95*, 339–350.

Miles, J. H., McCathren, R., Stichter, J., & Shinawi, M, (2009). Autism. *GeneReviews: Clinical genetic information resource.* Retrieved from http://www.GeneClinics.org

Myles, B. S., & Simpson, R. L. (1998). *Asperger syndrome: A guide for educators and parents*. Austin: Pro-Ed.

National Research Council (NRC). (2001). *Educating children with autism.* Committee on Educational Interventions for Children with Autism. In C. Lord & J. P. McGee, (Eds.), *Division of behavioral and scial sciences and education*. Washington DC: National Academy Press.

Newschaffer, C. J., Croen, L. A., Daniels, J., Giarelli, E., Grether, J. K., Levy, S., …Windham, G. C. (2007). *The epidemiology of autism spectrum disorders.* Retrieved October 23, 2008, from http://arjournals.annualreviews.org/doi/abs/10.1146/annurev.publhealth.28.021

Odom, S. L., Brown, W. H., Frey, T., Karasu, N., Smith-Canter, L. L., & Strain, P. S. (2003). Evidence-based practices for young children with autism: Contributions for single-subject design research. *Focus on Autism and Other Developmental Disabilities, 18*(3), 166–175.

Osterling, J. A., Dawson, G., & Munson, J. A. (2002). Early recognition of 1-year-old infants with autism spectrum disorder versus mental retardation. *Development and Psychopathology, 14*, 239–251.

Ozonoff, S., South, M., & Miller, J. N. (2000). DSM-IV-defined Asperger syndrome: Cognitive, behavioral and early history differentiation from high-functioning autism. *Autism, 4*, 29–46.

Paul, R., Miles, S., Cicchetti, D., Sparrow, S., Klin, A., Volkmar, F., & Booker, S. (2004). Adaptive behavior in autism and pervasive developmental disorder-not otherwise specified: Microanalysis of scores on the Vineland adaptive behavior scales. *Journal of Autism and Developmental Disorders, 34*(2), 223–228.

Prizant, B. M., Wetherby, A. M., Rubin, E., & Laurent, A. (2006). The SCERTS Model: A transactional, family-centered approach to enhancing communication and socioemotional abilities children with autism spectrum disorders. *Infants and Young Children, 20*(4), 296–316.

Prizant, B. M., Wetherby, A. M., Rubin, E., Laurent, A. C., & Rydell, P. J. (2006). *The SCERTS Model: A comprehensive educational approach for children with autism spectrum disorders*. Baltimore, MD: Brookes.

Reichow, B., & Wolery, M. (2009). Comprehensive synthesis of early intensive behavioral interventions for young children with autism based on the UCLA Young Autism Project Model. *Journal of Autism and Developmental Disorders, 39*, 23–41.

Reichow, B., Volkmar, F. R., & Cicchetti, D. V. (2008). Development of an evaluative method for determining the strength of research evidence in autism. *Journal of Autism and Developmental Disorders, 38*(7), 1311–1319.

Reynolds, C. R., & Kamphaus R. W. (1992). *Behavior Assessment Scale for Children*. Circle Pines, MN: American Guidance Service.

Reznick, J. S., Baranek, G. T., Reavis, S., Watson, L. R., & Crais, E. R. (2007). A parent-report instrument for identifying one-year olds at risk for an eventual diagnosis of autism: The first year inventory. *Journal of Autism and Developmental Disorders, 37*, 1691–1710.

Robins, D. L., Fein, D., Barton, M. L., & Green, J. A. (2001). The modified checklist for autism in toddlers: An initial study investigating the early detection of autism and pervasive developmental disorders. *Journal of Autism and Developmental Disorders, 31*, 131–144.

Rogers, S. J. (1998). Empirically supported comprehensive treatments for young children with autism. *Journal of Autism and Developmental Disorders, 27*, 168–179.

Rutter, M., LeCouteur, A., & Lord, C. (2003). *The autism diagnostic interview, revised* (ADI-R). Los Angeles, CA: Western Psychological Services.

Safran, S. P. (2001). Asperger syndrome: An emerging challenge to special educators. *Exceptional Children, 67*, 151–160.

Safran, S. P. (2008). Why youngsters with autistic spectrum disorders remain underrepresented in special education. *Remedial and Special Education, 29*, 90–95.

Sallows, G. O., & Graupner, T. D. (2005). Intensive behavioral treatment for children with autism: Four-year outcome and predictors. *American Journal on Mental Retardation, 110*(6), 417–438.

Sanford, C., Levine, P., & Blackorby, J. (2008). *A national profile of students with autism: A special topic report from the Special Education Elementary Longitudinal Study*. Retrieved from http://www.seels.net/info_reports/national_profile_students_autism.htm

Schalock, R. L., Buntinx, W., Borthwick-Duffy, S., Luckasson, R., Snell, M., Tassé, M., & Wehmeyer, M. (2007). *User's guide: Mental retardation: Definitions, classification and systems of supports-10th edition: Applications for clinicians, educators, disability program managers, and policy makers.* Washington, DC: AAIDD.

Schopler, E., Reichler, R. J., & Renner, B. R. (1988). *The childhood autism rating scale (CARS)*. Los Angeles, CA: Western Psychological Services.

Schreibman, L. & Carr, E. G. (1978). Elimination of echolalic responding to questions through the training of a generalized verbal response. *Journal of Applied Behavior Analysis, 11*, 453–463.

Shriver, M. D., Allen, K. D., & Mathews, J. R. (1999). Effective assessment of the shared and unique characteristics of children with autism. *School Psychology Review, 28*, 538–558.

Siegel, B. (1996). Pervasive Developmental Disorders Screening Test (PDDST). Unpublished manuscript.

Siegel, B. (2003). *Helping children with autism learn: A guide to treatment approaches for parents and professionals*. New York, NY: Oxford University Press.

Sigman, M., & McGovern, C. W. (2005). Improvement in cognitive and language skills from preschool to adolescence in autism. *Journal of Autism and Developmental Disorders, 35*(1), 15–23.

Simpson, R. L. (2005). Evidence-based practices and students with autism spectrum disorders. *Focus on Autism and Other Developmental Disabilities, 20*(3), 140–149.

Simpson, R., de Boer-Ott, S., Griswold, D., Myles, B., Byrd, S., Ganz, J., & Adams, L. G. (2005). *Autism spectrum disorders: Interventions and treatments for children and youth*. Thousand Oaks, CA: Corwin Press.

Smith, T. (2008). Empirically supported and unsupported treatments for autism spectrum disorders. *The Scientific Review of Mental Health Practice, 6*, 3–20.

Smith, T., Scahill, L., Dawson, G., Guthrie, D., Lord, C., Odom, S., … Wagner, A. (2007). Designing research studies on psychosocial interventions in autism. *Journal of Autism and Developmental Disorders, 37*, 354–366.

Sparrow, S., Cicchetti, D. V., & Balla, D. A. (2005). *Vineland-II: Survey forms manual*. Minneapolis, MN: Pearson Assessments.

Stoelb, M., Yarnal, R. , Miles, J., Takahashi, T. N., Farmer, J. E. & McCathren, R. B. (2004). Predicting responsiveness to treatment of children with autism: A retrospective study of the importance of physical dysmorphology. *Focus on Autism and Other Developmental Disabilities, 19*(2), 66–77.

Stone, W. L., & Yoder, P. J. (2001). Predicting spoken language level in children with autism spectrum disorders. *Autism, 5*(4), 341–361.

Tanguay, P. E. (2000). Pervasive developmental disorders: A 10-year review. *Journal of the American Academy of Child and Adolescent Psychiatry, 39*, 1079–1095.

Tomanik, S. S., Pearson, D. A., Loveland, K. A., Lane, D. M., & Shaw, J. B. (2007). Improving the reliability of autism diagnoses: examining the utility of adaptive behavior. *Journal of Autism and Developmental Disorders, 37*(5), 921–928.

Vig, S., & Jedrysek, E. (1999). Autistic features in young children with significant cognitive impairment: Autism or mental retardation? *Journal of Autism and Developmental Disorders, 29*, 235–248.

Volkmar, F. R., Chawarska, K., & Klin, A. (2008). Autism spectrum disorders in infants and toddlers. In K. Chawarska, A. Klin, & F. R. Volkmar (Eds.). *Autism spectrum disorders in infants and toddlers: Diagnosis, assessment, & treatment* (pp. 1–22). New York, NY: Guildford Press.

Werner, E., & Dawson, G. (2005). Validation of the phenomenon of autistic regression using home videotapes. *Archives of General Psychiatry, 62*, 889–895.

Wetherby, A. M., Brosnan-Maddox, S., Peace, V., & Newton, L. (2008). Validation of the Infant–Toddler checklist as a broadband screener for autism spectrum disorders from 9 to 24 months of age. *Autism: The International Journal of Research and Practice, 12*, 487–511.

Wetherby, A. M., & Prizant, B. M. (2002). Communication and Symbolic Behavior Scales Developmental Profile. Baltimore, MD: Brookes.

Wetherby, A. M., & Woods, J. (2002). *Systematic observation of red flags for autism spectrum disorders in young children*. Unpublished manual. Florida State University, Tallahassee, FL.

Wetherby, A., & Woods, J. (2006). Early social interaction project for children with autism spectrum disorders beginning in the second year of life. *Topics in Early Childhood Special Education, 26*, 67–82.

Wing, L., & Potter, D. (2002). The epidemiology of autistic spectrum disorders: Is the prevalence rising? *Mental Retardation and Developmental Disabilities Research Reviews, 8*, 151–161.

Yell, M., & Katsiyannis, A. (2003). Critical issues and trends in the education of students with autism spectrum disorders: Introduction to the special issue. *Focus on Autism and Other Developmental Disabilities, 18*, 138–139

Zwaigenbaum, L., Bryson, S., Rogers, T., Roberts, W., Brian, J., & Szatmari, P. (2005). Behavioral manifestations of autism in the first year of life. *International Journal of Developmental Neuroscience, 23*, 143–152.

Zwaigenbaum, L., Thurm, A., Stone, W., Baranek, G., Bryson, S., Iverson, J., & Sigman, M. (2007). Studying the emergence of autism spectrum disorders in high-risk infants: Methodological and practical issues. *Journal of Autism and Developmental Disorders, 37*, 466–480.

23
Severe and Multiple Disabilities

Susan M. Bruce
Boston College

Definition

Individuals who have severe and multiple disabilities are an extremely heterogeneous group by ability, personality, experiences, and preferences (Giangreco, 2006). This group includes children who have moderate intellectual disability (in tandem with at least one additional disability), severe or profound intellectual disability, some children with traumatic brain injury, children who are deafblind, and some children with autism spectrum disorders. Health disorders, physical disabilities, sensory loss, and behavioral, and communication challenges pose additional barriers to development. The impact of multiple disabilities on learning cannot be understood by simply adding the effects of each disability; rather, the effect is complex, interactional, and multiplicative in nature (Gargiulo, 2009).

Levels of intellectual disability may be defined by IQ or by the level of support required to participate in typical daily life. The American Psychiatric Association's (APA) *Diagnostic and Statistical Manual of Mental Disorders* (4th ed. rev. text,, 2000), defines levels of intellectual disability based on IQ scores with a moderate intellectual disability being defined by an IQ score above 35 to 40 and below 50 to 55, a severe disability as above 20 to 25 and below 40, and a profound intellectual disability as below 20 to 25 points. In contrast, the American Association on Intellectual and Developmental Disability's (AAIDD) defines levels of required support by considering the interaction between an individual's characteristics and the contexts in which that individual interacts. This model considers how an individual's intellectual abilities, adaptive behavior, level of participation, social interactions, and health interact with contextual features to determine the types and levels of support required to improve individual functioning (Westling & Fox, 2009).

Although individuals with severe and multiple disabilities are an extremely heterogeneous group, they share a common lifelong need for ongoing and pervasive support in more than one major life activity (Kennedy, 2004). This intensive level of support is necessary to the development of communication and language, self-care, mobility, independent living, and employment. TASH (formerly The Association for Persons with Severe Handicaps), the national advocacy organization for individuals with severe disabilities, addresses support needs and the right to participation and quality of life in the following resolution:

> TASH addresses the interests of persons with disabilities who have traditionally been excluded from the mainstream of society. These persons include individuals with disabilities of all ages, races, creeds, national origins, genders and sexual orientation who require ongoing support in one or more major life activities in order to participate in an integrated community and enjoy quality of life similar to that available to all citizens. Support may be required for life activities such as mobility, communication, self-care, and learning as necessary for community living, employment, and self-sufficiency. (TASH, 2000)

Many children with severe and multiple disabilities experience ongoing health issues. Common medical problems include: cardiovascular disease, respiratory disease, gastrointestinal disorders (which may lead to nutritional challenges), anemia, dehydration, kidney malfunction, otitis media, asthma, skin irritations, and contractures that result in subsequent loss of range of motion (Heller, 2004; Thuppal & Sobsey, 2004). The following medications are often prescribed: antiepileptic, antispasticity, antireflex, psychotropic, and respiratory medications, antibiotics, and skin preparations. Some will require tube feeding on a short-term basis (nasogastric) while others will require a gastrostomy tube as a long-term feeding intervention. Individualized health care plans are critical to the medical management of children with severe and multiple disabilities in educational settings.

Some of the causes of intellectual disability (such as oxygen deprivation to the brain and infections associated with high fever) are also causes of cerebral palsy and epilepsy. Cerebral palsy and epilepsy each occur in about twenty percent of children with severe intellectual disability (Batshaw, Shapiro, & Farber, 2007). Seizures tend to be more persistent in the population of children with developmental disabilities (Rues, Graff, Ault, & Holvoet, 2006) making seizure monitoring a major health-related responsibility for teachers and parents.

Visual impairment and hearing loss are also common in children with moderate to profound intellectual disabilities; again, due to shared causes. Vision and hearing loss often co-occur with cerebral palsy as well (Bowe, 2000). The incidence of blindness is 200 times greater in children with multiple disabilities than in the general population (Miller & Menacker, 2007) with 2/3 of children with severe intellectual disability having a visual impairment (Westling & Fox, 2009). Cortical visual impairment (CVI) is common in children with multiple disabilities due to damage in the central nervous system. The ocular structures are normal, but the brain does not interpret the image in a reliable way, resulting in functional vision that may fluctuate within a single day, in response to different types and levels of stimulation and to fatigue.

Children with severe and multiple disabilities who have hearing loss may be hard of hearing (< 70 decibel loss) or deaf (> 70 decibel loss). It is difficult to estimate their numbers because they are often not reported in the count of children who are deaf or hard of hearing (Reiman, Bullis, & Davis, 1992). The most conservative estimate is that about one-third of children who are deaf or hard of hearing have at least one additional disability (Bruce, DiNatale, & Ford, 2008; Schirmer, 2001) and that 9% of deaf children have two or more additional disabilities (Shildroth & Hotto, 1996).

Some children with multiple disabilities have co-occurring vision and hearing loss, known as deafblindness. Over 90% of children who meet the federal definition of deafblindness have some functional vision and/or hearing (Fredericks & Baldwin, 1987). Although developmental delay is common in children who are deafblind, some causes of deafblindness (such as Usher syndrome) are not associated with intellectual disability.

The population of children with severe and multiple disabilities includes some children on the autism spectrum, especially autism and Rett syndrome, a progressive, genetic disorder that is a common cause of severe disabilities in girls (Zhang & Minassian, 2008). Autism spectrum disorders are discussed more fully in chapter 22 of this volume.

Causal Factors

Unlike the milder disabilities, it is common to identify an organic cause for a severe disability. Common causes include: genetic disorders, chromosomal anomalies, abnormalities of brain development, parental substance abuse, STORCH infections (syphilis, toxoplasmosis, other infections, cytomegalovirus, and herpes simplex virus), birth trauma, malnutrition, and trauma (Batshaw et al., 2007; Gargiulo, 2009; McDonnell, Hardman, & McDonnell, 2003). The following syndromes are common etiologies associated with severe and multiple disabilities: Down syndrome, Fragile X syndrome, Fetal Alcohol syndrome, and Rett syndrome (Westling & Fox, 2009).

Identification

Observation, medical screening, referral, and nondiscriminatory evaluation are critical to identifying children with severe and multiple disabilities and their learning needs. Observations by parents and physicians usually raise early concerns, with most children referred for suspicion of a disability during infancy or the preschool years. Medical screening tests such as the Apgar screening of newborns (for heart rate, respiratory effort, muscle tone, gag reflex, and skin color at 1 and 5 minutes post birth) may suggest a severe disability while physical examination and genetic testing can confirm a diagnosis. The educational process of pre-referral does not usually occur with this population because the disabilities are clearly identifiable, often based in biological causes. Identification occurs before the child is of school age (unless the disabilities were acquired due to illness or injury). Nondiscriminatory evaluation follows identification of an etiology and associated disability(ies). Children with severe disabilities will have an IQ test of at least two standard deviations below the mean, their adaptive behavior will be significantly below average (Turnbull, Turnbull, Shank, & Smith, 2003), and they will require intensive, ongoing supports to meet their daily needs.

Smith (2003) reported that 18% of the student population, ages 6–21, have multiple disabilities. It is important to understand that children who have severe and multiple disabilities may be reported under a variety of categories, making it difficult to get a clear picture of prevalence.

Behavioral Characteristics

Children with severe and multiple disabilities display a complex set of behavioral characteristics. They learn at a much slower rate than children without disabilities. They have difficulty knowing which stimuli to attend to (which affects incidental learning), difficulty learning new information and skills, and difficulty synthesizing information. In addition, they struggle with both maintenance and generalization of knowledge and skills (Alper, 2003; Friend & Bursuck, 2009; Smith, 2003; Westling & Fox, 2009). They may have health and motor issues with most experiencing greater fatigue than the general population.

Some children with severe disabilities exhibit self-stimulatory, self-injurious, or aggressive behaviors. Issues with health, stamina, medication, levels of stimulation, stress, and everyday basic needs (such as hunger and thirst) will impact behavior. Sometimes the identified etiology (such as CHARGE syndrome, an etiology of deafblindness) supports understanding of the associated behaviors and the identification of successful interventions. It is recognized that behavioral issues, in this population, are often rooted in communication frustration. Improvement in communicative functioning can result in improved behavior.

"Communication is an essential skill for all human beings, allowing us to learn from others, have control over our environment, share feelings, and develop friendship" (Downing, 2001, p. 147). All people communicate, although children with severe and multiple disabilities may communicate in highly idiosyncratic ways, making it difficult for others to immediately comprehend their meaning. The communicative ability of this group is extremely heterogeneous. Some will be pre-intentional, relying on others to interpret their body movement, facial expression, and vocalizations. Responsive communication partners shape intentionality. Intentional communication may become more conventional over time with some children learning to use abstract representations, known as symbols (Rowland & Schweigert, 2000). While many children with severe and multiple disabilities will achieve intentional communication, many will not achieve language.

Assessment

Assessment of children with severe and multiple disabilities includes gathering information about needs, strengths, interests, and preferences (Smith, 2003). Assessments include a strong focus on behavior and communication due to their impact on school and community inclusion and quality of life. Many learners require evaluations by multiple specialists, including the nurse, physical therapist, occupational therapist, speech and language pathologist, psychologist and behavioral team, and teachers with various specialties. Those with sensory losses require functional vision and/or hearing assessment, learning media assessment (for the visually impaired), and assessment of their orientation and mobility or travel training needs. Performance should be assessed in their natural environments, those in which they typically perform. Assessment authenticity is enhanced when the person conducting the assessment knows the child well and is typically part of the environments in which the child is being assessed. This is to ensure that the child will behave in typical ways rather than in atypical ways in response to a novel person. Assessments of children with severe and multiple disabilities should take place across environments and across time to account for variation in performance which is common due to changes in behavior states and health.

The assessment process may include the use of commercially produced formal or informal assessment tools, assessments and checklists created by the educational team members, and state guidelines for alternate assessment. Assessment tools that are appropriate for use with children who have severe disabilities will have the following characteristics (Venn, 2007): (a) adaptable response modes (allowing responses to be expressed in various ways); (b) flexible administration procedures (allowing for adaptations); (c) provisions for giving partial credit (to recognize partial participation and emerging skills); (d) wide sample of behaviors (to capture small increments of development); and (e) procedures for developing a positive intervention plan. Assessments developed by the educational team members should be founded on professional literature about evidence-based practices.

The primary purposes of assessment are *screening* (such as newborn screening for disabilities), *diagnosis and testing* (such as IQ tests or adaptive behavior scales), *curriculum and program development* (including adaptive behavior scales, developmental assessments, child-guided assessment approaches, ecological inventories, and person centered planning), and *evaluation of student progress and program quality* (including individualized curriculum based measures, alternate assessment, and program quality checklists) (Brown, Snell, & Lehr, 2006). Assessments are conducted to support decision-making, and in the case of educational assessment, to improve learning conditions.

Screening

The primary purpose of a screening test is to determine if there is a significant difference between an individual's functioning when compared to peers. Screening assessments include relatively few items, are quickly administered, and inform the team if further assessment is warranted (Brown et al., 2006). Aside from the Apgar test for newborn screening, children with severe and multiple disabilities rarely go through this form of assessment because their disabilities are more easily identified.

Diagnosis and Testing

IQ tests and other norm-referenced assessments are used to estimate conceptual intelligence and ability, but must be used with great caution with children who have severe and multiple disabilities. Such tests are only valid if the norming group includes children who have similar disability characteristics to the child being tested. Further, scores that fall closer to the middle of normal distribution are more valid than scores that fall at either end of the scale, making the validity of norm referenced tests questionable for this population (Venn, 2007).

Curriculum and Program Development

A wide range of assessments, founded on various perspectives, inform the development of the individualized curriculum including assessment of adaptive behavior, developmentally based assessments, child-guided assessments, ecological inventories, person centered planning approaches, and alternate assessment. The assessment of behavior, communication, and preferences is critical to meeting the needs of children with severe and multiple disabilities.

Adaptive behaviors include *conceptual knowledge* (including language, reading, writing, money concepts), *social skills* (interpersonal, responsibility, self-esteem), and *practical skills* (personal care skills and occupational skills) (Kritikos, 2010). Adaptive behavior scales often rely on informants, which allows for capturing performance over time as opposed to performance at one point in time. The Vineland Adaptive Behavior Scales, second edition (Vineland II) (Sparrow, Cicchetti, & Balla, 2005) and the Adaptive Behavior System, second edition (ABAS-II) (Harrison & Oakland, 2003) are examples of adaptive assessment scales that are appropriate for use with children who have severe and multiple disabilities.

Developmental assessment tools are founded on the assumption that children with severe disabilities develop in the same sequential pattern as children without disabilities. Developmental assessment tools are often used with young children with severe disabilities because they capture small increments of behavior across a broad spectrum of strengths and needs (Dykes & Erin, 1999). The Hawaii Early Learning Profile (0–3 and 3–6) (Parks, 1996) and the Developmental Assessment for Students with Severe Disabilities (DASH-2) (Dykes & Erin, 1999) are examples of developmentally based assessments that are appropriate for use with some children who have severe and multiple disabilities. Developmental assessments are not intended for use with older children. This is because some skills along the developmental continuum are not appropriate or important to teach some older children, some skills can be bypassed, and assessments based on an outcomes perspective (as opposed to developmental perspective) is necessary in meeting the needs of older children and young adults.

Child-guided assessment is a dynamic assessment approach used with pre-linguistic communicators of all ages (Kritikos, 2010). In van Dijk's child-guided assessment approach, the assessor observes and then adjusts his own emotional, cognitive, and communicative state to match the child (Nelson, van Dijk, McDonnell, & Thompson, 2002). Van Dijk's assessment approach examines the following: behavior states, orienting responses, learning channels, approach-withdrawal, memory, interactions, communication, and problem solving.

Ecological inventories are founded on the functional outcomes approach, which focuses on the identification of important outcomes that can be learned in authentic environments. Ecological inventories begin with an analysis of current and potential learning environments and are often associated with discrepancy analysis and task analysis. The five phases of *ecological inventories* are: (a) identify the curriculum domains; (b) identify and survey current and future natural environments; (c) divide the relevant environments into sub-environments; (d) inventory those sub-environments for relevant activities that occur there; and (e) determine skills required for performance of those activities (Brown et al., 1979). Once the important activities and associated skills have been determined, a task analysis that depicts the sequence of steps involved when performing each task can be developed. In discrepancy analysis each step along the sequence is analyzed to determine the types and level of support required to maximize participation (such as prompting levels and adaptive equipment). Thus, ecological analysis supports the identification of authentic skills to teach in currently experienced or new environments and the level of support required for active participation. The task analysis then becomes an individualized curriculum-based measure.

The person centered planning approach includes models such as the McGill Action Planning System (MAPS) (Vandercook, York, & Forest, 1989) and Personal Futures Planning (for transition age students) (Mount & Zwernick, 1990), among others. Each person-centered planning model offers a structure to support conversation and most also include the creation of maps that depict important information about the person being assessed. For example, teams could create maps about a person's history, dreams, likes, and dislikes.

Assessment of Behavior

Assessment of children with severe and multiple disabilities will include a focus on behavior because it is so important to participation in the home, school, and community. Some children with severe and multiple disabilities engage in self-stimulation, self-injurious behavior, noncompliance behaviors, pica, or aggression. It is common practice for educational teams to conduct a Functional Behavior Assessment (ABC) to determine the primary function of the behavior. This often begins with an ABC analysis that includes identification of the antecedents to the behavior, clear definition of the behavior(s) of concern, and consequences that follow the behavior. These records can then be coded to determine the function that these behaviors serve for the child. The four most common functions are: tangible (seeking something), attention, escape, and sensory (with sensory distress being a major case of negative behaviors in children with severe disabilities) (Durand, 1990). It is critical that FBA include or be preceded by consideration of the contribution of health problems, medication, and etiological characteristics to behavior (such as anxiety being a prominent characteristic associated with some syndromes). Receptive and expressive communication limitations may be the cause of some behavior, especially if basic needs are not being met (food, drink, sleep, and positioning needs) or expectations are not understood. The Functional Assessment Interview (FAI) assesses the function of behavior while also considering issues such as health that may be causing difficult behaviors. Findings from the FBA are used to create a positive behavior support plan. These plans typically include significant environmental management for children with severe and multiple disabilities. They also often include the teaching of communication as an alternative behavior. For example, if the child is throwing materials, instruction might focus on teaching an alternative communicative behavior such as gently pushing materials away.

Assessment of Communication

Communication assessment includes assessment of both the individual and of the communicative environment (including the communication partners). It is important to observe children communicating in their natural environments with their usual communication partners. The four aspects of communication is a common structure for communication assessment tools and for the development of informal, structured assessments used by educational teams (Kritikos, 2010). The four aspects are form (expressive and receptive modes of communication), function (purpose of communication, such as request), content (the message), and context (physical environment, activities and routines, communication partners) (Downing, 2005; Miles & Riggio, 1999). Assessment results can be used to develop an individualized communication profile to support comprehensive communication intervention (Mar & Sall, 1999).

Preference Assessment

Preference assessment is an area of assessment that is unique to the field of severe and multiple disabilities. Preference assessment is integrally connected to making authentic choices and as such, is part of the larger construct of self-determination (discussed in the trends and issues section of this chapter). "At the very core of being self-determined is the knowledge and awareness of oneself and one's preferences" (Lohrmann-O'Rourke & Gomez, 2001, p. 159). In addition, preference assessment may reveal the sensory system(s) in which the preferences are based (visual, auditory, gustatory, tactile, kinesthetic) which is essential to the identification of reinforcers. When conducting preference assessments with the most severely involved children, observations are conducted to determine what the child avoids and when the child exhibits any type of intentional behavior that expresses preference (Logan & Gast, 2001).

Evaluation of Student Progress and Program Evaluation

Assessment of student learning in severe disabilities should address the four stages of instruction: acquisition, production, generalization, and maintenance (Gaylord-Ross & Browder, 1991). Functional assessment examines the performance of an individual within authentic contexts. Individual student performance can be measured by observing performance across each step of the task analysis while observing for changes in levels of support required for success. Ongoing assessment that occurs in the context of everyday instruction is critical for this population due to fluctuation in performance caused by health, sensory, and behavior state changes.

Alternate Assessment

Goals 2000, the Individuals with Disabilities Education Act (IDEA), No Child Left Behind (NCLB), and state legislation mandates require that all students be included in educational accountability systems (Goh, 2004). Prior to the reauthorization of IDEA in 1997, the achievements of students with severe and multiple disabilities were not measured as part of the statewide high stakes testing. IDEA mandated that students with more severe disabilities were to participate when possible with accommodation or to participate in alternate assessments as of July 1, 2000 (Kleinert & Kearns, 2004; Turner, Baldwin, Kleinert, & Kearns, 2000). Participation in alternate assessment was intended for students with the most significant cognitive disabilities who would not be earning the typical high school diploma.

Alternative assessment is direct assessment of a student's performance, which may include performance assessment, authentic assessment, and portfolio assessment. Performance assessments require students to perform some tasks under specific conditions. Performance assessments that measure skills that are important to functioning in the real world known as authentic assessments. Portfolio assessment is a collection of selected student work that is used to evaluate knowledge, skills, and progress.

Researchers and practitioners have reported both positive and negative aspects of alternate assessment. Direct measurement of student performance is cited as one benefit of alternate assessment. "Whereas traditional norm-referenced tests require students to select and mark correct responses, alternative assessment approaches require the students to produce, construct, demonstrate, or perform a task" (Taylor, 2003, p. 139). Other potential benefits include: improved instruction and student learning, instruction that is developmentally, functionally, and contextually relevant, reduced test bias, increased interaction around student performance (student and professional collaboration), additional educational opportunities, more effective individualized supports, increased student motivation and pride in viewing learning evidence, parents recognizing achievements in the general curriculum, gains in self-determination from student participation, identification of student's strengths, improved instructional decisions, and program quality (Goh, 2004; Kelly, Siegel, & Allinder, 2001; Kleinert & Kearns, 2004; Taylor, 2003; Turner et al., 2000). Negative aspects include that alternate assessment is time consuming, costly, and that there is little evidence of its validity or reliability (Goh, 2004; Taylor, 2003).

Assessing Program Quality

Assessment extends beyond the student to an examination of program quality. This is particularly critical for programs serving learners whose gains are most dependent on good quality instruction. The Transition Quality Indicators (Employment and Disability Institute, 2006) is one example of a transition program evaluation instrument. It identifies the characteristics of high quality inclusive programs and groups them within the following categories: policy, philosophy, school building practices, educational placement and related services, individual student program indicators.

Educational Programming

Educational programming for children with severe and multiple disabilities has undergone a remarkable transformation over the past 30 or 40 years. Early attempts at educating students with severe disabilities were founded on the developmental approach, which involved teaching skills in the same sequence they were learned by children without disabilities. This was based on the erroneous assumption that all children with disabilities develop in the same sequence as children without disabilities, albeit at a slower rate. In the late 1970s, Lou Brown and others introduced the concept of the Criterion of Ultimate Functioning (Brown, Nietupski, & Hamre-Nietupski, 1976; Brown et al., 1979). This birthed a new curricular approach known as the functional or outcomes approach of the 1980s. The functional approach emphasizes teaching age appropriate adaptive skills that improve independence and quality of life. The call for more inclusive practices emerged in the late 1980s and marked the next wave of curricular reform, although early attempts at inclusion primarily focused on social inclusion. Across these waves of reform, elements of the developmental and functional approaches remained, especially the application of developmental theory to the assessment and instruction of young children (0–8 years) and the influence of the functional perspective on selecting valued outcomes for instruction. Browder et al. (2004) suggested that the recent shift to aligning assessment and instruction with the general curriculum (across all types of placements) is another important curricular reform.

Most children with severe and multiple disabilities require direct and individually planned instruction in areas that are not traditionally part of the general curriculum, such as communication, social skills, leisure-recreation, travel training (or orientation and mobility), self-care, and domestic skills. Decisions about what to teach are made more difficult when the child's health status is unstable. In some cases, teachers and parents must plan instructional programs for children who are either regressing or dying. Curriculum guidelines for these children include: focusing on maintaining existing knowledge and skills, teaching compensatory skills for recently lost skills, and teaching skills that may prevent secondary complications (Rues et al., 2006).

Systematic instruction, which is founded in applied behavioral analysis, is highly effective with this population, because they are more likely to respond to precise teaching methods (Halle, Chadsey, Lee, & Renzaglia, 2004). Systematic instruction addresses all phases of learning: acquisition, production, generalization, and maintenance. The most basic principle of systematic instruction is that each behavior is preceded by an antecedent and followed by a consequence. The likelihood of a behavior being repeated can be increased by providing antecedents (including prompts) and consequences (including reinforcement) that match individual needs within a specific activity. Guiding principles for systematic instruction include "(a) teaching meaningful and functional skills, (b) errorless learning, (c) facilitating attention to relevant stimuli, (d) providing frequent opportunities to practice, and (e) providing a positive learning environment" (Halle et al., 2004, pp. 55–56). Systematic instruction includes thoughtful structuring of instructional environments (including the selection and arrangement of materials), use of attentional cues, time-delay procedures, discrete and chained tasks, shaping, fading, individually selected types and levels of prompts and reinforcement, and error correction procedures (Collins, 2007; Westling & Fox, 2009).

Westling and Fox (2009) suggest that these three values should influence instructional practices in severe and multiple disabilities: (a) teaching valued and age appropriate skills in inclusive settings, (b) supporting greater self-determination, and (c) participation in the general curriculum. Multi-level instruction and curriculum overlapping are long standing best practices to enhance inclusion (Giangreco, 2007). Multi-level instruction involves all children in the same curricular area, but the outcomes vary. Curriculum overlapping occurs in the context of a shared activity, but students are learning in more than one curricular area (Giangreco, 2007). Additional best practices include: individually appropriate learning standards; careful structuring and manipulation of space, materials, staffing, and peer groupings; application of principles of universal design for learning; teaching at optimal times; use of natural supports; honoring choices and preferences; enhancing communication opportunities across all activities; collaboration with families; customized positioning and handling; and provision of assistive technology (Friend & Bursuck, 2009; Turnbull et al., 2003; Wolery & Schuster, 1997).

Communication Intervention

The Communication Bill of Rights (National Joint Committee for the Communication Needs of Persons with Severe Disabilities, 1992) declares the communicative rights of individuals with severe and multiple disabilities (such as the right to express rejections and make authentic choices) and provides service guidelines. Most children with severe and multiple disabilities will require direct instruction of communication skills (Reichle, 1997) across all four aspects of communication: *form* (including the use of augmentative and alternative communication for receptive and expressive purposes), *function* (expression of varied purposes), *content* (messages to achieve varied functions across different forms), and *context* (communication partner behaviors such as responsivity, structuring of environments to enhance communicative opportunities, and consideration of activity and routine) (Downing, 2005; Miles & Riggo, 1999). They also require communication intervention that is specially targeted to their level of communicative development: pre-intentional (perlocutionary), intentional but presymbolic (illocutionary), and symbolic to linguistic (locutionary).

Space prohibits a complete discussion of research-based communication interventions, but three are briefly addressed here. The Tri-Focus Framework (Siegel-Causey & Bashinski, 1997) extended communication intervention from being directed solely toward the child to include a focus on the communication partners (adults and peers) and on the engineering of environments and is an important intervention approach for use with pre-intentional and early intentional communicators (Siegel-Causey & Bashinski, 1997; Siegel & Cress, 2002). The Pre-Linguistic Milieu Approach (Warren & Yoder, 1998: Yoder & Warren, 2002) creates communicative opportunities by employing the use of prompts and directives during purposeful breaks offered within well-known routines. This approach is especially appropriate for the intentional, pre-linguistic communicator. The van Djik approach (Silberman, Bruce, & Nelson, 2004), a child-guided, movement based approach addresses the communicative needs of children from the pre-intentional to early linguistic stages. Early stages of this approach include engaging in coactive movement routines with the pre-intentional child (such as rocking together). These routines are repeated, pause is created, and the child demonstrates anticipation by recreating the movement as a form of early intentional expression. Anticipation shelves or daily schedules are an integral part of the van Dijk approach (MacFarland, 1995). These displays may be composed of photographs or objects to depict daily activities with a finished box in which representations for completed activities are placed. The process of previewing and reviewing iconic representations (representations that resemble what they represent) of daily activities supports the child to anticipate and to potentially associate activities and their representations. The representations become increasingly more complex as the child's communication matures.

Collaborative Teams and Families

Collaborative teaming is a combination of transdisciplinary teaming and the integrated therapy model with the addition of the principle that, while team members each contribute unique expertise, they remain open to having their perspectives shaped by other team members (Clonginger, 2004). Collaborative teams work together on assessment, instructional planning, instruction, and evaluation of student progress and program quality. Children with severe and multiple disabilities require collaborative teams to address their complex needs and time is needed for collaboration to occur.

Family involvement is critical to effective assessment, planning, and instruction of children with severe and multiple disabilities. Individuals with severe disabilities are more likely than any other group to remain in the family home for an extended period of time and to require ongoing and intensive support from family members.

> Positive results from family involvement include improved quality of life for the student; skill generalization to new situations and environments; modification of child behavior and gains of functional skills; more positive transition outcomes; development of advocacy skills for both parent and child; commitment to in-home placements; improved home functioning through routines and coping; and parent perception of having a higher degree of control within the service system. (Childe, 2004, p. 80)

Early Childhood

Children with severe and multiple disabilities are likely to be identified in infancy or early childhood. Most services to infants will occur in the family home with toddler services being provided in the home or preschool. Effective early childhood programming is "child-initiated, child-centered, and grounded in developmentally appropriate practice" (Turnbull et al., 2003, p. 275). The inclusive preschool experience is centered on the development of play or pre-play skills such as object handling (Demchak & Downing, 2002). Other common program components include greeting routine, snack, story time, and closing routine time. Instruction on individualized objectives will be embedded into typical activities. Families of infants and young children may also receive services as depicted on the Individualized Family Service Plan (IFSP).

Naturalistic teaching procedures are applied in the inclusive preschool so that play is not disturbed. Naturalistic instruction includes incidental teaching procedures (teacher responds to child's initiations as an opportunity for instruction) and naturalistic time delay (when child needs help, teacher approaches but provides support contingent on the child communicating). Learning opportunities within regular routines are capitalized upon (such as learning to follow directions in the context of routines) (Downing & Eichinger, 2003).

Elementary Programming

The curriculum for elementary school students with severe disabilities is shaped by student- and family-centered planning and by ecological curricular models based on the routines, activities, and environments experienced by children of the same chronological age without disabilities (McDonnell et al., 2003). IEP objectives emphasize skills and personal supports to maximize independence in the context of these activities. Principles of systematic instruction are applied. Scheduling matrices are helpful to embedding an individual's IEP objectives across activities. Additional best practices include modification to the general curriculum, cooperative learning groups, and peer buddies.

Effective inclusion in elementary school will include "(1) assignment to age-appropriate, grade-level classroom; (2) adequate time for planning; (3) embedding instruction in classroom routines and activities; (4) creative scheduling; and (5) collaboration and co-teaching" (Salisbury & Strieker, 2004, p. 228). Block scheduling, alterations in staff patterns, and restructuring of the school day are strategies to support collaborative teaming. Effective curricular approaches include the multilevel approach, curriculum overlapping, and the alternate curriculum (with corresponding goals and objectives from outside the general curriculum). Categories of accommodations include: presentation, response, setting, and timing/scheduling. Categories of modification include: parallel instruction (different levels of instruction) and embedded skills. Cooperative learning groups, collaborative problem solving, and time to interact facilitate a sense of belonging (Turnbull et al., 2003).

Secondary Programming

Best practices at the secondary level include individualized planning, parental involvement, life skills curriculum, community based systematic instruction, community-reference curriculum, vocational assessment, vocational training, paid work experiences, social skills training, interagency collaboration, and follow-up employment services (Inge & Moon, 2006; Olson, Platt, & Dieker, 2008). A common instructional preparation period enhances collaborative teaming at the secondary level (Turnbull et al., 2003).

Person-centered planning plays a critical role in transition planning for secondary students and throughout adulthood. It should include the following:

1. The person's activities, services, and supports are based on his or her dreams, interests, preferences, strengths, and capacities.
2. The person and people important to him or her are included in lifestyle planning and have the opportunity to exercise control and make informed decisions.
3. The person has meaningful choices with decisions based on his or her experience.
4. The person uses, when possible, natural and community supports.
5. Activities, supports, and services foster skills to achieve personal relationships, community inclusion, dignity, and respect.
6. The person's opportunities and experiences are maximized and flexibility is enhanced within existing regulatory and funding constraints.
7. Planning is collaborative and recurring and involves an ongoing commitment to the person.
8. The person is satisfied with his or her relationships, home, and daily routine. (Crockett & Hardman, 2010, p. 39)

Transition planning, which incorporates the results of personal futures planning, should be built upon linkages between high school and post-secondary education programs, employers, and adult agencies, to support the young adult to be successful not only in employment, but in the home and larger community (McDonnell et al., 2003). "Transition planning, person-centered planning, and preference assessment are compatible processes that, when used together, have the ability to produce long-term goals that are reflective of the focus student's desired lifestyle" (Lohrmann-O'Rourke & Gomez, 2001, p. 171). Family input is especially important for this group of learners because many will remain in the family home, and parents can inform the team about valued life roles within their immediate and extended family.

Vocational Preparation

Vocational preparation should include identification of student interests and preferences, determination of necessary supports for success, teaching general work behaviors, and teaching specific job skills (McDonnell, 2010a). Job sampling (actual work experiences) provides an important context for learning authentic job skills, for developing vocational preferences, and for curriculum based vocational assessment. Curriculum-based vocational assessment should address attitude and behavior, communication and interpersonal skills, specific job skills, generalized job skill outcomes, and problem solving (Olson, Platt, & Dieker, 2008). In the context of work experiences, professionals gather information about the student's performance on different jobs and in different contexts (Gaylord-Ross & Browder, 1991). Personal futures planning can be used to create an individual portfolio that includes job sampling placements, performance summaries, work strengths, work preferences, needed supports, logistical considerations (such as travel, physical restrictions), and recommended workplace characteristics (McDonnell, 2010b).

Transition to Adulthood

The transition to adulthood can be a very perplexing time for young adults with severe and multiple disabilities as well as for their families. This group has long been denied adulthood, due to the prevailing societal view of them as eternal children (Ferguson & Ferguson, 2006). Morningstar and Lattin (2004) have suggested a new perspective on adulthood for this population, called "supported adulthood," as a "guiding commitment to participation and affiliation rather than control and remediation" (p. 626). The three dimensions of adulthood are *autonomy* (being your own person), *membership* (citizenship and affiliation), and *change* (including opportunities for further development; Morningstar & Lattin, 2004). The five features of supported adulthood are natural contexts, informal supports, user definition, local character, and universal eligibility.

Continued Vocational Preparation

Agran, Test, and Martin (1994) described the continuum of employment options as a "readiness model," also called the "flow through model," based on the antiquated belief that one should "earn" the right to move on to less restrictive settings by gaining new skills. In this model, one would move from day treatment, to work activity, to sheltered workshop, to transitional employment, and finally to community employment. Faulty reasoning plagues this model, which wrongly assumes that what makes one successful in a restrictive setting would somehow be beneficial in a less restrictive setting. Under this model, most individuals with severe disabilities would be placed in day treatment and work activity centers (Riesen, 2010b).

In contrast, researchers have designed supported employment to maximize independence, consumer decision-making, and participation in the community. Supported employment models include the (a) individual placement model (one person hired with the use of job coach), (b) clustered placement model (group of 6–8 hired for one location with job coach to support), and (c) mobile work crew model (3–5 provide services in multiple locations)

(Rusch, Chadsey-Rusch, & Johnson, 1991). Today, most authorities prefer a customized approach to supported employment. Such an approach determines appropriate jobs based on personal profiles (founded in personal futures planning), identifies or carves out jobs in the community, provides the necessary level of support from employment specialists, and is founded on self-determination. Although supported employment was designed for those with severe disabilities, fewer than 7% of individuals with disabilities in supported employment actually have severe disabilities (McDonnell et al., 2003). Out of the population of individuals with severe disabilities, only about 22% experience supported employment, a percentage that has not improved since 1993 (Morningstar & Lattin, 2004). "In large part, conflicting reimbursement mechanisms and federal and state disability policies are disincentives to ensuring that individuals with severe disabilities are a part of an integrated workforce" (Morningstar & Lattin, 2004, p. 289).

Residential Preparation

The residential component must be addressed as part of transition services under IDEA (Riesen, 2010a). Like the history of the continuum of employment options, there has traditionally been a continuum of residential options (nursing home or institution, group homes, semi-independent living projects, and supported independent living). Over the past 20 years, emphasis has been placed on creative alternatives such as individual home placement with options including: tenant owned (individual with disability owns), parent owned, corporation owned (parents and others form a corporation), shared equity (two individuals buying and then one buys other out), partnership (parents forming partnerships), trust owned (a living trust established by parents) (Riesen, 2010a). Personal assistance services (funded under Medicaid) provide supports for grooming, dressing, eating, transportation, and home management skills such as cooking and finances. Such services are provided through home care agencies that contract with Medicaid. Unfortunately, there is a funding bias toward segregated facilities with 68% of Medicaid long-term service spending going to institution based programs, and 32% going to community based programs (Riesen, 2010a).

Trends and Issue

While there are many issues that influence the quality of life experienced by children and young adults with severe and multiple disabilities, this chapter addresses the following topics: (a) ethics and intervention; (b) inclusion; (c) the shifting curriculum; (d) self-determination across the lifespan; (e) pre-linguistic English Language Learners; and (f) the impact of the "gold standard" for research.

Ethics and Intervention

Individuals with severe and multiple disabilities are a very vulnerable population. Silber (2007) cites the following issues that put this population at risk: prenatal testing and genetic screening that result in selective abortions, withholding of medical treatment (including do not resuscitate orders and lack of access to organ donations), risk for abuse and neglect, disrespect for sexual and reproductive rights, and sterilization. The recent emphasis on self-determination addresses the need to support individuals with severe and multiple disabilities to have their own "voice" recognized and to achieve greater control over their own lives.

School & Community Inclusion

Inclusion remains a critical issue for children with severe and multiple disabilities because many are still being served in segregated school settings (Wehmeyer, Lattin, Lapp-Rinker, & Agran, 2003). Gargiulo (2009) reports that 45% remain in separate classes, 20% in separate schools, 16.9% in resource rooms, 2.8% in homebound/hospital care, 2.5% in residential facilities, and only 13.2% in regular classes. In addition to limited numbers of children with severe disabilities being included in the general education classroom, there are concerns about the nature of their participation, and the quality of education received. Access to high level cognitive content without active engagement and comprehension is not an appropriate use of student time (Karvonen, Wakeman, Flowers, & Browder, 2009).

There is growing concern about over-reliance on paraprofessionals in the general education classroom and the impact of that practice on student learning. In their study on the roles and responsibilities of paraprofessionals, Downing, Ryndak, and Clark (1999) concluded that paraprofessionals were taking on a great deal of responsibility and making a great many decisions that affected student learning. Giangreco and Doyle (2002) have raised concern that paraprofessionals were providing instruction that supplanted instruction provided by a licensed teacher, resulting in the least prepared professional teaching the most involved children. They suggested the following agenda to address this problem: improve current paraprofessional service through role clarification, match paraprofessional skills with requirements of the position, think and plan about when paraprofessional supports are appropriate or inappropriate, and consider alternatives to over-reliance on paraprofessionals. Grappling with the issue of over-reliance on paraprofessionals requires the field of severe disabilities to continue research on the roles of paraprofessionals (including their roles and impact on student learning), identification of the competencies needed by paraprofessionals to meet the requirements of their roles and the subsequent redesign of preservice and inservice preparation of paraprofessionals, respective roles and responsibilities of general and special educators, and the use of peer supports.

Although concerns about over-reliance on paraprofessionals and curricular confusion remain, progress has been made in identifying effective inclusive practices. Ryndak, Reardon, Benner, and Ward (2007) cite the following seven essential elements of successful inclusion (based on 7 years observing one district's systemic change efforts): (a) common vision of outcomes, (b) shared knowledge of change process, (c) shared responsibility for change process, (d) concurrent efforts at multiple levels, (e) involvement of all constituents, (f) communication with all constituents, and (g) use of critical friends to support change. In addition, the following practices have been suggested by researchers and practitioners to support quality inclusion: extensive collaboration between general educators, special educators, related service professionals, and families (beginning with preservice opportunities); careful selection of what to teach and appropriate curricular adaptations; use of curricular designs stated in open standards to include all students (written more broadly to allow varied ways of expressing knowledge); use of individualized educational programming (IEP) based on the general curriculum, but addressing additional needs not covered in the general curriculum; universally designed materials and instruction; thoughtful scheduling and coordination of inclusive services; assessing and reporting of ongoing student progress; multi-level instruction and curriculum overlapping; focus on positive learning outcomes and peer relationships; instructional strategies with increased emphasis on antecedents; and supporting students with challenging behaviors (with emphasis on the function of the behavior) (Giangreco, 2007; Hunt & Goetz, 1997; Jackson, Ryndak, & Billingsley, 2000).

Recent literature extends thinking about inclusion from being about placement to considering the quality of participation within inclusive schools and the larger community (Sailor & Roger, 2005). Renzaglia, Karvoenen, Drasgow, and Stoxen (2003) describe inclusion as a lifestyle of active participation achieved through opportunities to make life choices and to control one's life, a close fit with the field's recent emphasis on self-determination. Accessible physical environments, universal design for learning, community based instruction for all, appropriate adaptations and accommodations, person-centered planning, ecological inventory, community based instruction, project-based teaching approaches, and positive instructional strategies are critical to active participation in inclusive communities (Gargiulo, 2009; Sailor & Roger, 2005).

The Shifting School Curriculum

In 1997, Nietupski, Hamre-Nietupski, Curtin, and Shrikanth spoke to the tensions between inclusion and the need to have sufficient time invested in teaching functional skills that would improve post-school outcomes. They also spoke to the natural tension that exists at the secondary level when the general curriculum content and the knowledge and skill level of individuals with severe disabilities are highly discrepant. These remain valid concerns for students with the most severe disabilities. Experts in severe disabilities recommend the application of systematic instruction in the inclusive classroom, but this does not address the tension between general educators' focus on curriculum-based instructional strategies and special educators' focus on student-based instructional strategies. It also fails to recognize that some special educators do not believe that access to the general education curriculum is an appropriate use of time for children with the most severe disabilities (Browder & Cooper-Duffy, 2003). Further, Roach (2006) suggests that parental dissatisfaction with the secondary experiences of students with severe disabilities may stem from the disconnection between IEP objectives (which is the primary way that parents monitor student progress) and concepts in the general education curriculum. Roach suggests that at a minimum there must be some connection between standards addressed from the general curriculum and objectives determined by the IEP team. Thus, teams select what to teach based on what would "lead to participation in valued roles and activities in natural environments" (Ryndak & Billingsley, 2004, p. 41) with consideration of authentic connections to the general curriculum, person centered planning, and IEP objectives.

Self-Determination Across the Lifespan

"Self-determined behavior refers to volitional actions that enable one to act as the primary causal agent in one's life and to maintain or improve one's quality of life" (Wehmeyer, 2005, p. 117). Wood, Fowler, Uphold, and Test (2005) cited the following component skills of self-determination: choice-making, decision-making, goal setting and attainment, problem solving, self-awareness, self-advocacy, self-regulation, and self-efficacy. It is more challenging to apply the construct of self-determination to individuals with more limited expressive communication. Still, at the foundation of self-determination is the goal to gain control over one's life and that can be improved in the lives of individuals with severe and multiple disabilities.

Although many individuals with severe disabilities participate in choice-making routines, it is crucial to distinguish participation in choice-making routines from engaging in authentic choice-making. Informed choice involves intentional selection from among familiar options, and it is dependent on both being familiar with the options offered and on the form of representation (object, picture, signs) being a good match for the individual (Shevin & Klein, 2004; Storey, 2005). Children with severe disabilities require systematic instruction of choice-making, beginning with choices between highly preferred and non-preferred items, founded on preference assessment (Logan & Gast, 2001). Opportunities can be embedded across the day, and they must be allowed to experience the consequences of their choices (as opposed to being rescued) with the risk inherent in their choices gradually increased as they mature (Shevin & Klein, 2004).

Meeting the Needs of Prelinguistic English Language Learners

Although there is a growing knowledge base about teaching English language learners (ELLs) without disabilities and those with mild disabilities who communicate at a linguistic level, we do not yet have a research base on the instruction of ELLs with severe disabilities who communicate at a pre-linguistic level. Mueller, Singer, and Carranza (2006) conducted a national survey of teachers of ELLs with moderate to severe intellectual disability (N = 375). Using standard sequential regression analysis, they found that 43% of parents were not consulted about their child's language of instruction, that the child's primary language was used less than 20% of the instructional time, 45% of the children were being assessed exclusively in English, 52% did not have access to materials in any language other than English, and that only 27% had access to augmentative communication devices in languages other than English. There is a dire need for future research to clarify how what is currently known to be effective practice with ELLs with mild disabilities can be adapted for application to this population and to determine best practices that are unique to children with severe and multiple disabilities.

The Impact of the Gold Standards for Research

NCLB established a very narrow view of research (experimental and quasi-experimental designs that preferably employ random assignment of participants) that has had a particularly devastating effect on the field of severe and multiple disabilities. In low incidence populations of great heterogeneity, it is often impossible to find a large sample of participants who are similar enough in their characteristics to make randomized assignment meaningful. Experimental designs that occur in controlled settings outside the classroom make limited contributions to improving instruction for this population, because more than any other group, their learning fluctuates in response to the characteristics of the environment, e.g., their learning is highly context-dependent. The current emphasis on this narrowly defined scientific research affects the funding of research preventing some researchers from being funded, resulting in a slowed progression of the research base in severe and multiple disabilities. The current emphasis on the "gold standard" has prompted some to develop studies about children with "significant disabilities" that are really samples almost entirely composed of children with moderate disabilities and just a few children with severe disabilities, resulting in interventions that could be effective for the majority, but not for those with more severe disabilities.

One of the most fundamental principles of research is that the design must suit the question posed. Qualitative research is critical to the development of theories and to a more complete understanding of quantitative findings.

> Qualitative and participatory action research methodologies share a deep appreciation of the subjective experiences, perspectives, and views of people who traditionally have been the "subjects" of research. In fact, what is considered important to people under study is the starting point of participatory action research and of many qualitative studies. Under a narrow definition of "scientifically based research" emphasizing randomized experiments, the views of students with disabilities, family members, or even teachers and other practitioners seem to have no place. (Giangreco & Taylor, 2003, p. 136)

The field needs research studies with quantitative, qualitative, and mixed research designs to fully address the many questions that must be answered to further improve educational outcomes and provide a higher quality of life for children and young adults with severe and multiple disabilities.

References

Agran, M., Test, D., & Martin, J. E. (1994). Employment preparation of students with severe disabilities. In E. C. Cipani & F. Spooner (Eds.), *Curricular and instructional approaches for persons with severe disabilities* (pp. 184–212). Boston: Allyn and Bacon.

Alper, S. (2003). Students with moderate and severe disabilities: Definitions and descriptive characteristics. In D. L. Ryndak & S. Alper (Eds.), *Curriculum and instruction for students with significant disabilities in inclusive settings* (2nd ed., pp. 1–11). Boston: Allyn and Bacon.

American Psychiatric Association. (2000). *Diagnostic and statistical manual of mental disorders* (4th ed., rev. text). Washington, CD: Author.

Batshaw, M. L., Shapiro, B., & Farber, M. L. Z. (2007). Developmental delay and intellectual disability. In M. L. Batshaw, L. Pellegrino, N. J. Roizen (Eds.), *Children with disabilities* (6th cd., pp. 245–261). Baltimore: Brookes.

Bowe, F. (2000). *Physical, sensory, and health disabilities: An introduction*. Upper Saddler River, NJ: Merrill/Prentice Hall.

Browder, D. M., & Cooper-Duffy, K. (2003). Evidence-based practices for students with severe disabilities and the requirement for accountability in "No Child Left Behind." *Journal of Special Education, 37*, 157–163.

Browder, D., Flowers, C., Ahlgrim-Delzell, L., Karvonen, M., Spooner, F., & Algozzine. R. (2004). The alignment of alternate assessment content with academic and functional curricula. *Journal of Special Education, 37*, 211–223.

Brown, L., Nietupski, J., & Hamre-Nietupski, S. (1976). The criterion of ultimate functioning and public school services for severely handicapped students. In M. A. Thomas (Ed.), *Hey! Don't forget about me!* (pp. 2–15). Reston, VA: Council for Exceptional Children.

Brown, L., Branston, M. B., Hamre-Nietupski, S., Pumpian, J., Certo, N., & Gruenewald, L. (1979). A strategy for developing chronological age appropriate and functional curricular content for severely handicapped adolescents and young adults. *Journal of Special Education, 13*, 81–90.

Brown, F., Snell, M. E., & Lehr, D. (2006). Meaningful assessment. In M E. Snell & F. Brown (Eds.), *Instruction of students with severe disabilities* (6th ed., pp. 67–110). Upper Saddle River, NJ: Pearson/Merrill Prentice Hall.

Bruce, S., DiNatale, P., & Ford, J. (2008). Meeting the changing needs of the deaf student population through professional development. *American Annals of the Deaf, 153*(4), 368–375.

Childe, A. L. (2004). Families. In C. H. Kennedy & E. M. Horn (Eds.), *Including students with severe disabilities* (pp. 78–99). Boston: Allyn and Bacon.

Cloninger, C. J. (2004). Designing collaborative educational services. In F. P. Orelove, D. Sobsey, & R. K. Silberman (Eds.), *Educating children with multiple disabilities: A collaborative approach* (4th ed., pp. 1–29). Baltimore: Brookes.

Collins, B. C. (2007). *Moderate and severe disabilities: A foundational approach*. Upper Saddle River, NJ: Pearson/Merrill Prentice Hall.

Crockett, M. A., & Hardman, M. L. (2010). Expected outcomes and emerging values. In J. McDonnell & M. L. Hardman (Eds.), *Successful transition programs: Pathways for students with intellectual and developmental disabilities* (2nd ed., pp. 25–42). Los Angeles: Sage.

Demchak, M., & Downing, J. (2002). The preschool student. In J. E.

Downing (Ed.), *Including students with severe and multiple disabilities in typical classrooms: practical strategies for teachers* (2nd ed., pp. 71–91). Baltimore: Brookes.

Downing, J. (2001). Meeting the communication needs of students with severe and multiple disabilities in general education classrooms. *Exceptionality, 9*(3), 147–156.

Downing, J. E. (2005). *Teaching communication skills to students with severe disabilities* (2nd ed.). Baltimore: Brookes.

Downing, J. E., & Eichinger, J. (2003). Creating learning opportunities for students with severe disabilities in inclusive classrooms. *TEACHING Exceptional Children, 36*, 26–31.

Downing, J. E., Ryndak, D. L., & Clark, D. (1999). Paraeducators in inclusive classrooms: Their own perceptions. *Remedial and Special Education, 21*, 171–181.

Durand, V. M. (1990). *Severe behavior problems: A functional communication training approach.* New York: Guilford.

Dykes, M. K., & Erin, J. N. (1999). *Developmental assessment for individuals with severe disabilities. Examiner's manual* (2nd ed.). Austin, TX: Pro-Ed.

Employment and Disability Institute. (2006). *Transition Quality Indicators.* Retrieved August 31, 2009, from http;//www.ilr.cornell.edu.edi/transqual/docs/tqi02-14-06.pdf. ILR School, Cornell University

Ferguson, P. M., & Ferguson, D. L. (2006). The promise of adulthood. In M. E. Snell & F. Brown (Eds.), *Instruction of students with severe disabilities* (6th ed., pp. 610–637). Upper Saddle River, NJ: Pearson/Merrill Prentice Hall.

Fredericks, H. D., & Baldwin, V. (1987). Individuals with sensory impairments. Who are they? How are they educated? In L. Goetz, D. Guess, & K. Stremel-Campbell (Eds.), *Innovative program design for individuals with dual sensory impairments* (pp. 3–14). Baltimore: Brookes.

Friend, M., & Bursuck, W. D. (2009). *Including students with special needs: A practical guide for classroom teachers* (4th ed.). Boston: Allyn and Bacon.

Gargiulo, R. M. (2009). *Special education in contemporary society: An introduction to exceptionality* (3rd ed.). Los Angeles: Sage.

Gaylord-Ross, R., & Browder, D. (1991). Functional assessment: Dynamic and domain properties. In L. H. Meyer, C. A. Peck, & L. Brown (Eds.), *Critical issues in the lives of people with severe disabilities* (pp. 45–66). Baltimore: Brookes.

Giangreco, M. (2006). Foundational concepts and practices for educating students with severe disabilities. In M. E. Snell & F. Brown (Eds.), *Instruction of students with severe disabilities* (6th ed., pp. 1–27). Upper Saddle River, NJ: Pearson/Merrill Prentice Hall.

Giangreco, M. F. (2007). Extending inclusive opportunities: How can students with disabilities meaningfully participate in class if they work many levels below classroom peers? *Educational Leadership, 65*(5), 34–37

Giangreco, M., & Doyle, M. B. (2002). Students with disabilities and paraprofessional supports: Benefits, balance, and band-aids. *Focus on Exceptional Children, 34*(7), 1–12.

Giangreco, M. F., & Taylor, S. J. (2003). "Scientifically based research" and qualititative inquiry. *Research & Practices for Persons with Severe Disabilities, 28*, 133–137.

Goh, D. S. (2004). *Assessment accommodations for diverse learners.* Boston: Pearson/Allyn and Bacon.

Halle, J. W., Chadsey, J., Lee, S., & Renzaglia, A. (2004). Systematic Instruction. In C. H. Kennedy & E. M. Horn (Eds.), *Including students with severe disabilities* (pp. 54–77). Boston: Allyn and Bacon.

Harrison, P., & Oakland, T. (2003). *Adaptive Behavior System* (2nd ed.). San Antonio, TX: Psychological Corp.

Heller, K. W. (2004). Integrating health care and educational programs. In F. P. Orelove, D. Sobsey, & R. K. Silberman (Eds.), *Educating children with multiple disabilities: A collaborative approach* (4th ed., pp. 379–424). Baltimore: Brookes.

Hunt, P., & Goetz, L. (1997). Research on inclusive educational programs, practices, and outcomes for students with severe disabilities. *The Journal of Special Education, 31*, 3–29.

Inge, K. J., & Moon, M. S. (2006). Vocational preparation and transition. In M. E. Snell & F. Brown (Eds.), *Instruction of students with severe disabilities* (6th ed., pp. 569–609). Upper Saddle River, NJ: Pearson/Merrill Prentice Hall.

Jackson, R., Ryndak, D. L., & Billingsley, F. (2000). Useful practices in inclusive education: A preliminary view of what experts in moderate to severe disabilities are saying. *Journal of the Association for Persons with Severe Handicaps (JASH), 25*(3),129–141.

Karvonen, M., Wakeman, S. Y., Flowers, C., & Browder, D. M. (2009). Measuring the enacted curriculum for students with significant cognitive disabilities: A preliminary investigation, assessment for effective instruction. Retrieved July 7, 2009, from http://aei.sagepub.com

Kelly, K. M., Siegel, E. B., & Allinder, R. M. (2001). Personal profile assessment summary: Creating windows into the worlds of children with special needs. *Intervention in School and Clinic, 36*, 202–210.

Kennedy, C. H. (2004). Students with severe disabilities. In C. H. Kennedy & E. M. Horn (Eds.), *Including students with severe disabilities.* (pp. 3–14). Boston: Pearson/Allyn & Bacon.

Kleinert, H. L., & Kearns, J. F. (2004). Alternate assessments. In F. P. Orelove, D. Sobsey, & R. K. Silberman (Eds.), *Educating children with multiple disabilities: A collaborative approach* (4th ed., pp. 115–149). Baltimore: Brookes.

Kritikos, E. P. (2010). *Special education assessment: Issues and strategies affecting today's classrooms.* Upper Saddle River, NJ: Merrill.

Logan, K. R., & Gast, D. L. (2001). Conducting preference assessments and reinforcer testing for individuals with profound multiple disabilities: Issues and procedures. *Exceptionality, 9*, 123–134.

Lohrmann-O'Rourke, S., & Gomez, O. (2001). Integrating preference assessment within the transition process to create meaningful school-to-life outcomes. *Exceptionality, 9*, 157–174.

MacFarland, S. Z. C. (1995). Teaching strategies of the van Dijk curricular approach. *Journal of Visual Impairment and Blindness, 89*, 222–228.

Mar, H. H., & Sall, N. (1999). Profiles of the expressive communication skills of children and adolescents with severe cognitive disabilities. *Education and Training in Mental Retardation and Developmental Disabilities, 34*, 77–89.

McDonnell, J. (2010a). Employment training. In J. McDonnell & M. L. Hardman (Eds.), *Successful transition programs: Pathways for students with intellectual and developmental disabilities* (2nd ed., pp. 241–256). Los Angeles: Sage.

McDonnell, J. (2010b). Job placement. In J. McDonnell & M. L. Hardman (Eds.), *Successful transition programs: Pathways for students with intellectual and developmental disabilities* (2nd ed., pp. 257–280). Los Angeles: Sage.

McDonnell, J. J., Hardman, M. L., & McDonnell, A. (2003). *An introduction to persons with moderate and severe disabilities: Educational and social issues* (2nd ed.). Boston: Allyn & Bacon.

Miles, B., & Riggio, M. (1999). *Remarkable conversations.* Watertown, MA: Perkins School for the Blind.

Miller, M. M., & Menacker, S. J. (2007). Vision: Our window to the world. In M. L. Batshaw (Ed.), *Children with disabilities* (6th ed., pp. 165–192). Baltimore: Brookes.

Morningstar, M. E., & Lattin, D. L. (2004). Transition to adulthood. In C. H. Kennedy & E. M. Horn (Eds.), *Including students with severe disabilities* (pp. 282–309). Boston: Allyn and Bacon.

Mount, B., & Zwernick, K. (1990). Making futures happen: A manual for facilitators of personal futures planning. Publication No. 421-90-036. ED363077. St. Paul: Minnesota Governor's Planning Council on Disabilities.

Mueller, T. G., Singer, G. H. S., & Carranza, F. D. (2006). Planning and language instruction practices for students with moderate to severe disabilities who are English language learners. *Research & Practices for Persons with Severe Disabilities, 31*, 242–254.

National Joint Committee for the Communication Needs of Persons with Severe Disabilities. (1992). Guidelines for meeting the communication needs of persons with severe disabilities. Retrieved August 15, 2009, from www.asha.org/njc

Nelson, C., van Dijk, J., McDonnell, A. P., & Thompson, K. (2002). A framework for understanding young children with severe multiple disabilities: The van Dijk approach to assessment. *Research & Practice for Persons with Severe Disabilities, 27,* 97–111.

Nietupski, J. Hamre-Nietupski, S. Curtin, S., & Shrikanth, K. (1997). A review of curricular research in severe disabilities from 1976 to 1995 in six selected journals. *The Journal of Special Education, 31,* 36–55.

Olson, J. L., Platt, J. C., & Dieker, L. A. (2008). *Teaching children and adolescents with special needs* (5th ed.). Upper Saddle River, NJ: Pearson/Merrill Prentice Hall.

Parks, S. (1996). *Hawaii early learning profile.* Palo Alto, CA: Vort Corporation.

Reichle, J. (1997). Communication intervention with persons who have severe disabilities. *The Journal of Special Education, 31,* 110–134.

Reiman, J., Bullis, M., & Davis, C. (1992). *Assessment, intervention, and program needs of lower-achieving and multiply disabled deaf people requiring extended transition support.* DeKalb, IL: Department of Communicative Disorders, Research and Training Center, Northern Illinois University. (ERIC Document Reproduction Service No. ED356601).

Renzaglia, A., Karvoenen, M., Drasgow, E., & Stoxen, C. C. (2003). Promoting a lifetime of inclusion. *Focus on Autism and Other Developmental Disabilities, 18,* 140–149.

Riesen, T. (2010a). Postschool residential alternatives. In J. McDonnell & M. L. Hardman (Eds.), *Successful transition programs: Pathways for students with intellectual and developmental disabilities* (2nd ed., pp. 283–295). Los Angeles: Sage.

Riesen, T. (2010b). Postschool employment alternatives. In J. McDonnell & M. L. Hardman (Eds.), *Successful transition programs: Pathways for students with intellectual and developmental disabilities* (2nd ed., pp. 296–319). Los Angeles: Sage.

Roach, A. T. (2006). Influences on parent perceptions of an alternate assessment for students with severe cognitive disabilities. *Research & Practice for Persons with Severe Disabilities, 31,* 267–274.

Rowland, C., & Schweigert, P. (2000). Tangible symbols, tangible outcomes. *Augmentative and Alternative Communication, 16*(2), 61-76.

Rues, J. P., Graff, J. C., Ault, M. M., & Holvoet, J. (2006). Special health care procedures. In M. E. Snell & F. Brown (Eds.), *Instruction of students with severe disabilities* (6th ed., pp. 251–288). Upper Saddle River, NJ: Pearson/Merrill Prentice Hall.

Rusch, F. R., Chadsey-Rusch, J., & Johnson, J. R. (1991). Supported employment: Emerging opportunities for employment integration. In L. H. Meyer, C. A. Peck, & L. Brown (Eds.), *Critical issues in the lives of people with severe disabilities* (pp. 145–170). Baltimore: Brookes.

Ryndak, D. L., & Billlingsley, F. (2004). Access to the general education curriculum. In C. H. Kennedy & E. M. Horn (Eds.), *Including students with severe disabilities* (pp. 33–53). Boston: Allyn and Bacon.

Ryndak, D. L., Reardon, R., Benner, S. R., & Ward, T. (2007). Transitioning to and sustaining district-wide inclusive services: A 7-year study of a district's ongoing journey and its accompanying complexities. *Research & Practice for Persons with Severe Disabilities, 32,* 228–246.

Sailor, W., & Roger, B. (2005). Rethinking inclusion: Schoolwide applications. *Phi Delta Kappan, 86,* 503.

Salisbury, C., & Strieker, T. (2004). Elementary School. In C. H. Kennedy & E. M. Horn (Eds.), *Including students with severe disabilities* (pp. 222–245). Boston: Allyn and Bacon.

Schirmer, B. R. (2001). *Deafness. Psychological, social, and educational dimensions of deafness.* Needham Heights, MA: Allyn & Bacon.

Shevin, M., & Klein, N. K. (2004). The importance of choice-making skills or students with severe disabilities. *Research & Practice for Persons with Severe Disabilities, 29,* 161–168.

Shildroth, A. N., & Hotto, S. A. (1996). Changes in student and program characteristics, 1984–85 and 1994–95. *American Annals of the Deaf, 141*(2), 68–71.

Siegel, E., & Cress, C. J. (2002). Overview of the emergence of early AAC behaviors: Progression from communicative to symbolic skills. In J. Reichle, D. R. Beukelman, & J. C. Light (Eds.), *Exemplary practices for beginning communicators: Implications for AAC* (pp. 25–27). Baltimore: Brookes.

Siegel-Causey, E. & Bashinski, S. (1997). Enhancing initial communication and responsiveness of learners with multiple disabilities: A tri-focus framework for partners. *Focus on Autism and Other Developmental Disabilities, 12,* 105–120.

Silber, T. J. (2007). Ethical dilemmas. In M. L. Batshaw, L. Pellegrino, & N. J. Roizen (Eds.), *Children with disabilities* (6th ed., pp. 591–600). Baltimore: Brookes.

Silberman, R. K., Bruce, S. M., & Nelson, C. (2004). Children with sensory impairments. In F. P. Orelove, D. Sobsey, & R. K. Silberman (Eds.), *Educating children with multiple disabilities: A collaborative approach* (4th ed., pp. 425–527). Baltimore: Brookes.

Smith, D. D. (2003). *Introduction to special education: Teaching in an age of opportunity* (5th ed.). Boston: Allyn and Bacon.

Sparrow, S. S., Cicchetti, D. V., & Balla, D. A. (2005). *Vineland adaptive behavior scales* (2nd ed.). Circle Pines, MN: American Guidance Service.

Storey, K. (2005). Informed choice: The catch-22 of self-determination. *Research & Practice for Persons with Severe Disabilities, 30,* 232–234.

TASH. (2000, March). TASH resolution on the people for whom TASH advocates. Retrieved August 14, 2009, from http://www.tash.org/resolutions/res02advocate.htm

Taylor, R. L. (2003). *Assessment of exceptional students: Educational and psychological procedures* (6th ed.). Boston: Allyn and Bacon.

Thuppal, M., & Sobsey, D. (2004). Children with special health care needs. In F. P. Orelove, D. Sobsey, & R. K. Silberman (Eds.), *Educating children with multiple disabilities: A collaborative approach* (4th ed., pp. 311–377). Baltimore: Brookes.

Turnbull, R., Turnbull, A., Shank, M., & Smith, S. J. (2003). *Exceptional lives: Special education in today's schools* (4th ed.). Upper Saddle River, NJ: Pearson/Merrill Prentice Hall.

Turner, M. D., Baldwin, L., Kleinert, H. L., & Kearns, J. F. (2000). The relation of a statewide alternate assessment for students with severe disabilities to other measures of instructional effectiveness. *Journal of Special Education, 34,* 69–76.

Vandercook, T., York, J., & Forest, M. (1989). The McGill Action Planning system (MAPS): A strategy for building the vision. *Journal of the Association for Persons with Severe Handicaps, 14,* 205–215.

Venn, J. J. (2007). *Assessing students with special needs* (4th ed.). Upper Saddle River, NJ: Pearson/Merrill Prentice Hall.

Warren, S. F., & Yoder, P. J. (1998). Maternal responsivity predicts the prelinguistic communication that facilitates generalized intentional communication. *Journal of Speech, Language, and Hearing Research, 41,* 1207–1219.

Wehmeyer, M. L. (2005). Self-determination and individuals with severe disabilities: Re-examining meanings and misinterpretations. *Research & Practice for Persons with Severe Disabilities, 30,* 113–120.

Wehmeyer, M. L., Lattin, D. L., Lapp-Rincker, G., & Agran, M. (2003). Access to the general curriculum of middle school students with mental retardation: An observational study. *Remedial and Special Education, 24,* 262–272.

Westling, D. L., & Fox, L. (2009). *Teaching students with severe disabilities* (4th ed.). Upper Saddle River, NJ: Merrill/Pearson.

Wolery, M., & Schuster, J. W. (1997). Instructional methods with students who have significant disabilities. *Journal of Special Education, 31,* 61–79.

Wood, W. M., Fowler, C. H., Uphold, N., & Test, D. W. (2005). A review of self-determination interventions with individuals with severe disabilities. *Research & Practice for Persons with Severe Disabilities, 30,* 121–146.

Yoder, P. J. & Warren, S. F. (2002). Effects of prelinguistic milieu teaching and parent responsivity education on dyads involving children with intellectual disabilities. *Journal of Speech, Language, and Hearing Research, 45,* 1158–1174.

Zhang, Y., & Minassian, B. (2008). Will my Rett syndrome patient walk, talk, and use her hands? *Neurology, 70,* 1302–1303.

24

Special Gifts and Talents

Carolyn M. Callahan
University of Virginia

Definitions of Gifts and Talents

Definitions and conceptions of giftedness have evolved over time from those considered more conservative and restrictive ("the top 1% level in general intellectual ability, as measured by the Stanford-Binet Intelligence Scale or comparable instrument," Terman, 1926, p. 43) to broader and more comprehensive definitions based on current models of, and research on, intelligence and its development. Some of the more recent definitions are based on generic intelligence(s) (e.g., Gardner, 1983, 1999 or Sternberg, 1988), whereas others have focused on more specific academic abilities, such as mathematics or verbal talent (Brody & Stanley, 2005; Van Tassel-Baska, 2005). At the most extreme, Borland (2005), while acknowledging individual differences, questions the validity of the construct of the gifted child altogether (except in the case of prodigious talent) and posits differentiated curriculum as the solution to meeting the needs of students with different learning needs.

There is also considerable debate over the use of the terms *gifted* and *talent*. Sometimes talent or academic talent is a synonym for giftedness. A sense that the term *gifted* carries negative connotations led some educators to substitute the word academic talent for giftedness. In other cases, the term *talent* refers to students with exceptional abilities in nonacademic areas, such as art, music, or drama although Tannenbaum (1985) cautioned strongly against using the phrase "gifted and talented" or separating these two categories because of the danger that it will lead to differential values and favoritism toward those with the gifted label over those with the talent label. Others (e.g., Plucker & Barab, 2005) propose that children with potential should be considered talented and the label of gifted should be reserved for those who have demonstrated exceptional accomplishment in their fields; however Gagné (1995) proposes just the opposite—that specific talents emerge out of general giftedness.

Despite the many conceptions of giftedness in the literature, most states and school districts adopt but do not necessarily operationalize a variation of the definition of giftedness from the Javits Gifted and Talented Education Act (U.S. Department of Education, 1993):

> Children and youth with outstanding talent perform or show the potential for performing at remarkably high levels of accomplishment when compared with others of their age, experience or environment. These children and youth exhibit high performance capability in intellectual, creative, and/or artistic areas, possess an unusual leadership capacity, or excel in specific academic fields. They require services or activities not ordinarily provided by the schools.
>
> Outstanding talents are present in children and youth from all cultural groups, across all economic strata, and in all areas of human endeavor. (U.S. Department of Education, 1993, p. 3)

Several definitions of giftedness emerged from critical analyses of the federal definition. The most widely discussed and adopted alternative is the three-ring definition offered by Renzulli (1978, 2005) based on giftedness as creative productivity, which gained acceptance in conjunction with a model for programming and curricular modification, The Enrichment Triad/Schoolwide Enrichment Model (ETM/SEM) Model (Reis & Renzulli, 1986). In this definition, giftedness is a confluence of the traits of above-average ability, task commitment, and creativity in a particular area of endeavor. In the three-ring conception of giftedness, above-average ability is a stable trait, but the other two traits are tied to particular times and experiences in students' lives. Hence, Renzulli (2005) calls for the identification of gifted behaviors rather than gifted persons. Reis (1981) compared the performance of students who were traditionally identified as scoring in the top 5% on traditional cognitive assessments with performance of those identified using the three-ring model of identification (top 15%–20% on cognitive measures plus creativity and task commitment).

She found no differences between these groups on products created in classes where the ETM/SEM model served as the model for instruction.

Other conceptions of intelligence drawn on in the field of gifted education promote recognition of multiple manifestations of giftedness (e.g., Sternberg, 1988; Gardner, 1983). Sternberg's research has documented greater levels of achievement for students whose curriculum is matched to exceptional ability in analytic, synthetic, or practical intelligence—the three areas of intelligence in his theory (Sternberg & Clinkenbeard, 1994; Sternberg, Ferrari, Clinkenbeard, & Grigorenko, 1996)—and enhanced predicative validity for college GPA using assessments based on the triarchic model (Sternberg, Grigorenko, & Jarvin, 2006). Gardner's multifaceted conception of intelligence (1983) has received extensive attention, but researchers have not validated assessments and curricular interventions (Plucker, Callahan, & Tomchin, 1996).

Creativity as Giftedness

Researchers have given considerable attention to creativity as one dimension of the federal definition of giftedness, as one of the components of intelligence identified by Sternberg (1988), and as one of the factors critical to the manifestation of giftedness as defined by Renzulli (1977, 1978, 2005). Assessment of individual differences in creativity and the modifiability of creativity through instruction are part of an ongoing debate. The debate begins with the ways the literature has variously defined creativity as (a) part of the thinking process that results in unusual or stimulating thoughts, (b) a personality variable wherein the individual experiences the world in novel and unique ways, or (c) reflected by the ideas or creations of the individual that change the culture or the domain of their professions in some important way (Csikszentmihalyi, 1996). Accordingly, measurement of differences among school-age children and adults has resulted in the creation of assessments ranging from personality tests to evaluations of the processes and products of creativity.

Prodigies

Researchers define prodigies as children (usually age 15 or younger) already performing at an adult professional's level of skill in a cognitively complex area (Feldman, 1994, 2008). To date, identification and study of prodigies has been limited to the domains of chess, music, languages, writing, and mathematics—areas in which developmental factors or time and life experiences are not related to performance at the exceptional adult level and

> (1) are highly rule bound; (2) have relatively transparent knowledge structures; (3) have developed technologies and/or techniques for transmission of their knowledge; (4) have criteria for excellence that are either transparent or accessible; and (5) are able to be adapted to the capabilities of the very young child. (Feldman, 2008, p. 525)

Prodigies constitute only a very small segment of the total gifted population; yet the public image of giftedness is often associated with this extraordinary early performance.

Highly Gifted or Genius

Stratification of the gifted population into categories such as highly gifted or genius stems from the use of the IQ score as a determinant of giftedness. The early studies by Hollingsworth (1942) and later writings of Gross (1993) about children whose IQ scores exceeded 140 were the basis of the use of this term. The notion of categories of giftedness, from "mildly" to "extremely" has been perpetuated in some current literature (e.g., Gagné, 2005).

Prevalence of Giftedness

As one might expect, given the many extant definitions of giftedness, there is considerable controversy over the proportion of the population that is identified as gifted. Each state establishes its own definition of giftedness, and often guidelines for the identification process are vague and leave much discretion to the individual school district. Obviously, the choice of criteria and the ways standards are set or judgments are made on those criteria influence the number of students categorized as gifted. For example, setting an IQ score of 130 as a cut-off yields a different number of gifted students than an IQ cutoff of 125. And the same set of criteria applied in one school district yields a different proportion than the same one applied in a different school district. Gagné (1998) contends that this argument is important not just theoretically, but also politically and practically (1998). Bélanger and Gagné (2006) point to four factors that have influenced estimates of prevalence: (a) the minimum threshold; (b) the number of forms of giftedness considered (from general intellectual ability as a one-dimensional factor to Gardner's seven, or now eight, nine, or ten domains (1999); (c) the conjunctive or disjunctive distinction (either requiring simultaneous manifestations such as Renzulli's (1978) notion of a confluence of aptitude, creativity, and task commitment or any one of Gardner's talents); (d) and the correlations among criteria.

The first federal document indicating an estimate of the percentage of students who should be gifted in the population (a minimum 3%–5%) was the Marland Report (1972). The statement was framed as a minimum, was based on the normal distribution of IQ scores, reflected Terman's (1926) interpretation of giftedness, and did not examine the question of whether that number should be used for those with general intellectual ability only or as the sum for all the categories named in its definition of giftedness (general intellectual ability, specific academic abilities, leadership, creativity, and the arts). The 3%–5% guide has persisted in legislation at the state level (particularly as it relates to funding guidelines) and policy at the local level (Borland, 2009; National Association for Gifted Children (NAGC, n.d.). Renzulli (1978) includes *above average* ability or aptitude in any domain as one criterion and suggests that 15%–20% of the population should be in the talent pool to be considered as potentially gifted. Using data from the most recent survey, of 33 states responding, the percent of students identified in 2004–2005 ranged from a low of 2.07% to a high of 16% (NAGC, n.d.).

Developmental Aspects of Giftedness

Prodigies

Discussion of the developmental patterns associated with child prodigies should be separated from discussion of the development of the rest of the gifted population. Feldman (1994, 2008) indicates that the child prodigy does not generally differ from the general population of gifted students in overall IQ score. Moreover, the few prodigies who have been systematically studied have tended to perform at age-equivalent levels in logic, role taking, spatial reasoning, and moral judgment. Feldman concluded that prodigious performance is domain specific rather than a generalized endowment. Particular biological, psychological, environmental (family, societal, and cultural), and historical factors must all come together for prodigies to emerge developmentally (co-incidence theory). For example, Feldman has noted that until the last several decades of the 20th century, female prodigies were rare, but are now identified in several domains. Further, prodigies seldom are creative in the sense described by Cskiszentmihalyi (1996) as domain changing. Although popular portrayals of prodigious development and identifiable patterns of instruction and behavior associated with development of prodigious talent (e.g., isolation resulting from the prodigy's intrinsic drive to master his or her domain of interest; long hours of solitary practice or involvement with a very small group of similar prodigies; unusual, very intense and extended parental involvement in the development of the prodigy) may suggest social and emotional issues for these children, researchers have not confirmed these speculations (Feldman, 2008).

Highly Gifted

Research on the cognitive and affective development of those labeled highly gifted on the basis of extraordinarily high IQ scores (greater than 160) has been more extensive than research on prodigies. Early receptive language and speech (e.g., speaking in full sentences by first birthday) and spontaneous and early reading (before age 5) are cognitive developmental characteristics of this group (Gross, 2008; Hollingsworth, 1926; Terman & Oden, 1947). Among the affective characteristics that distinguish the highly gifted from others are: greater intrinsic motivation (Gottfried, Gottfried, Bathurst, & Guerin, 1994; Gross, 1997; Kanevsky, 1994); strong preference for independent work (Burke, Jensen, & Terman, 1930), and social isolation (Dauber & Benbow, 1990; Gallagher, 1958; Hollingsworth, 1942).

Development in the General Gifted Population

Prodigies and those labeled highly gifted make up only a very small proportion of students in the gifted population. It is difficult to make generalizations across studies of the development of gifted students because of the great variation in the definition of giftedness that is used in the research on this topic, the ages at which various forms of giftedness emerge or manifest themselves, and the various subpopulations that are considered. For example, students who manifest high general intellectual ability across many domains are not the same as those with very advanced specific abilities in some particular discipline (e.g., those with mathematical ability or artistic talent). Professionals can viably identify some subgroups at the preschool or kindergarten level because children at that age already exhibit patterns of extraordinary behaviors. Other students in other domains may not manifest gifted behaviors until later developmental periods. For example, until mathematics is taught as an abstract discipline (rather than as arithmetic) students may not have the opportunity to exhibit mathematical talent). Further, researchers have not carefully delineated the influences of cultural or socio-economic differences in studies of gifted children's development.

Despite the limitations noted above, researchers have reached some common conclusions regarding the development of giftedness. Experts in the field of gifted education, in accord with cognitive psychologists, have acknowledged the heritability of cognitive ability but conclude that, although differences in IQ are very much determined by genetics among middle class and affluent families, environmental factors make a far larger difference for children near or below the poverty level. Further, although acknowledging the role of genetics for middle class or affluent children, Sternberg (quoted in an interview with Miele,1996; Sternberg, 2008) and Dweck (2006) among other cognitive psychologists have contributed considerable evidence that intelligence and executive function can be modified in all groups of students through both environmental effects and interventions, e.g., reducing effects of stereotype threat (Aronson, Fried, & Good, 2002), curricular intervention (Diamond, Barnett, Thomas, & Munro, 2007; Jaeggi, Buschkuehl, Jonides, & Perrig, 2008), and effort (Dweck, 2006).

Factors that contribute to normal growth and development. Bloom (1985) and Csikszentmihalyi, Rathunde, and Whalen (1993) isolated family, school, and peer factors that encourage or impede the intellectual, social, and emotional development of gifted students. They found the following:

1. In cases in which talent development was exceptional, potential was recognized early, cultivated, and nurtured. During the early stages of talent development, parents were child oriented and they stressed doing one's best and achieving. They, themselves modeled a work ethic

and expected the child to share household chores although the child did not have to expend unreasonable time or energy on those chores. Family routines were structured to give students responsibilities and help them become self-disciplined.

2. Both family support and expectations to meet challenges head on enhanced development of talent. When family context was perceived as complex (both integrated and differentiated), talented teens spent more time on homework and were more goal directed.
3. Excellence, hard work, and constructive use of time were characteristic family values.
4. Children who shared active and challenging pursuits with friends (e.g., hobbies or studying rather than just socializing or hanging out) were more successful in developing their talents and more at ease in that pursuit.
5. In the early stage of talent development, teachers took pains to make learning enjoyable and rewarding, with much playful activity and reinforcement for small gains. Although rarely critical, they set standards, expected progress, and quickly rewarded steps toward reaching standards for performance. Task levels were just beyond the student's zone of proximal development, and teachers focused on helping students reach specific goals and correct flaws in performance. Helping students grasp larger patterns and underlying processes in the subject area was paralleled by encouraging discovery of the "big ideas" of the discipline.
6. As talent developed, students required relationships with, and instruction from, more expert teachers. These teachers expected higher levels of attainment, emphasized precision and excellence in the talent area, and facilitated the setting of short- and long-term goals.
7. The final stages of talent development were characterized by association with master teachers who clearly communicated that the opportunity to study with them meant that the student would "go far" in the given field of study. These master mentors raised demands and expectations constantly until it was clear that the student was expected to do what had never been done before (set Olympic records, solve heretofore unsolved math problems, etc.). Finally, these teachers conveyed that real learning was based on doing what experts in the field do.

Identification of Gifted Students

The process of identifying students with gifts and talents is obviously complicated by the many definitions of giftedness, the fact that giftedness is one of the "judgmental" categories of exceptionality, and the lack of thoughtful considerations in many school divisions of the question, "What is a gifted student?" However, a defensible identification process relies on consensus on a formal definition of the construct of giftedness, as well as a process for identifying students that is aligned with both the definition and the services provided. Part of the difficulty in identifying gifted students is that the construct of giftedness is not directly observable but must be inferred from multiple indicators (e.g., test scores, alternative assessments, grade point averages, teacher recommendations). Given this difficulty, it is crucial that the data used as evidence of giftedness build a profile that supports the conclusion that a student has gifts and/or talents that warrant educational experiences beyond what the general education classroom provides.

In the field of gifted education, instruments used for purposes of nominating, screening, and identifying students range from intelligence or achievement tests to rating scales, inventories, or checklists requiring observers or informants to assess student characteristics. They also range from published, standardized, objective instruments, including tests and standardized rating scales, to locally constructed performance assessments, portfolio rating scales, and teacher and parent rating scales or checklists. Best practice dictates that these instruments should rely on the *Standards for Educational and Psychological Testing* (American Educational Research Association, American Psychological Association, and National Council on Measurement and Education, 1999) and basic guidelines that have been developed for the field (e.g., validity and reliability of instruments for the construct of giftedness to be assessed, use of multiple sources for nomination of students; use of tests with appropriate norms for the populations assessed; making identification procedures public information in the language of the student and parent populations; incorporating multiple tools for observing, assessing and documenting students' gifts and talents, including a process for gathering nominations of students with dominant languages other than English and students living in poverty; using inclusive identification procedures with students whose dominant language is other than English; and flexibility within the identification procedures when students' educational profiles warrant alternative approaches) (NAGC, 2009; Callahan, Tomlinson, & Pizzat, 1993). There is considerable evidence that practice often does not conform to standards. Researchers have repeatedly documented evidence of misinterpretation or lack of knowledge about the psychometric properties of tests selected for the assessment process and the appropriate use of test data (Brown et al., 2005; Callahan, Tomlinson, Moon, Tomchin, & Plucker, 1995; Friedman-Nimz, 2009).

These processes and potential biases in this process are usually the reasons underlying the under-representation of racial/ethnic minorities, children of poverty, English Language Learners, and twice exceptional children (children with disabilities who are also gifted) in programs for the gifted. Authorities have proposed numerous alternatives to address this issue—from non-traditional standardized assessments, to dynamic assessment, to use of alternate criteria on traditional assessments (Borland, 2008; Van Tassel-Baska, 2008). Of particular concern to those involved in identifying these students is the possible misinterpretation and unfounded assumptions that may come from the use of non-verbal assessments.

For example, it is often assumed that verbal tests are biased and discriminatory in assessing aptitude and achievement of minority students and the use of non-verbal assessments will lead to a higher proportion of minority students identified as gifted. However, research on at least one such instrument, the Naglieri Non-Verbal Ability Test (NNAT), does not always support that assertion in the case of Black and Latino students (Lohman, 2005a, 2005b), and research on the Raven's Advanced Matrices suggests that sex differences may exist favoring males on that instrument (Abad, Colom, Rebello, & Escorial, 2004). Although such data do not condemn a test nor warrant abandoning its use, they do suggest that assumptions made about the underlying constructs and interpretations of the validity of test scores are not equal across subgroups and should be taken into account in interpreting test scores. Lohman and Lakin (2008) present a paradigm that outlines appropriate uses of non-verbal tests within an overall plan for identification and addresses the issues raised in the research on non-verbal tests. Other concerns related to the identification of gifted students arise from the use of instruments such as teacher rating scales and classroom observational protocols that have not been subjected to any psychometric scrutiny.

The age or grade level at which identification should begin is also a matter of considerable debate. There are some (e.g., Robinson 2008) who argue that giftedness manifests itself in some children very young, and unless the giftedness of the child is recognized early and the child receives services, then the potential of the child may not be realized. Others note the tenuous reliability of assessments of young children and the degree to which the educational opportunities provided by family and pre-school may yield false positives in the identification process creating unreasonable expectations. Therefore, they recommend use of assessment only for matching instruction to student level of performance (Center for Assessment and Evaluation of Student Learning, 2004).

Programming and Grouping Practices

Decisions regarding best practice in educating gifted students have been complicated by blurred distinctions between curricular and instructional models and grouping arrangements, the confluence of these variables in research designs, the multiple definitions of giftedness used in the research literature, and limited experimental research documenting effects of different approaches on clearly described samples. For example, the term *acceleration* has been used to signify early entrance to kindergarten, grade skipping, early entrance to college, or simply acceleration of the curriculum for one student or a group of students to compress multiple years of study in a discipline into a shorter time frame. The research on *enrichment* includes investigation of models ranging from simply providing supplemental instruction in an area not related to the curriculum to curricular interventions that have specific guidelines for the selection of content and instructional strategies to supplement classroom learning. Furthermore, the ways in which curriculum is delivered through various administrative arrangements complicates the interpretation of effective practice or is sometimes used to signify delivering instruction in a setting outside of a traditional classroom.

Ability Grouping for Gifted Students

Ability grouping was at one time a very common administrative or programming arrangement for delivering instruction to gifted students. Ability grouping covers the gamut from bringing students together for one hour per week, to establishing fulltime classes for the gifted, to cross-age grouping. Grouping for full time classes usually requires high achievement across all subject areas, whereas grouping for more limited time periods, usually in one or two disciplines, or for cross-age instruction, might be based on aptitude and/or achievement in a specific subject area. Controversy surrounding the practice of grouping, in general, stems from confusion between the terms *ability grouping* and *tracking*. Ability grouping refers to the practice of using test scores or other indicators of performance and ability to assign students to classes or instructional groups within a class or across classrooms. The term *tracking* was at one time used to describe the practice of recommending to students that they elect a course of high school studies leading to a particular vocational goal and was part of a decision-making process of students and/or their parents. However, the term is now applied to the practice of sorting students at an early age into high-, medium-, and low-level classes that become permanent assignments in school. As a rigid and immutable practice, tracking has received great criticism, which has been extended to the practice of ability grouping. Appropriate ability grouping does not create permanent configurations of students; however, when schools do not provide the opportunity for students to gain the knowledge and skills necessary to move between groups, or they do not use frequent assessment to reassign students appropriately, tracking may result.

Studies of grouping alternatives. Meta-analyses of research on ability grouping have consistently concluded that significantly greater achievement results from between- or within-class grouping for high-achieving, high-ability students (Kulik & Kulik, 1997; Lou et al., 1996). Kulik and Kulik found no negative effects on self-concept, and Lou et al. found that within-class grouping resulted in more positive attitudes toward the subject matter and higher general self-concept in their meta-analysis of those grouping studies. Recent studies specifically assessing the effects of grouping practices and curricular practices reaffirmed that, when students who received a differentiated curriculum in combination with cluster grouping and flexible grouping practices, the academic achievement of middle- and high-ability groups was significantly greater than students without grouping or differentiated instruction

(Gentry & Owen, 1999; Tieso, 2002). The self-esteem and self-efficacy of students was not influenced by the grouping arrangements (Tieso, 2002). Rogers (1991) concluded that ability grouping for curriculum extension in pullout programs produces an academic effect size of .65. Finally, a comparative study of the effects of special schools, separate classrooms, and pullout programs documented higher levels of achievement for students served in gifted programs than those not in gifted programs, with no one arrangement yielding consistently better results than the others (Delcourt, Loyd, Cornell, & Goldberg, 1994). As Scroth (2008) concludes, "little or no data…exists that examines how differences in student ethnic groups, age, or sex influence the appropriateness of a given option for certain students" (2008, p. 329).

Misapplication of cooperative learning strategies. Cooperative learning is considered by some to be a grouping arrangement, by others to be an instructional strategy. The widespread acceptance of cooperative learning as a substitute for other program or curricular adaptations for gifted students, particularly at the middle school level, has been criticized by experts in gifted education based on the paucity of research evidence that specifically includes and carefully analyzes the effects on gifted learners. In some studies, for example, the top 25% of the class is considered the high-ability group; in others, high ability is defined as above the median on a teacher-made test. Furthermore, outcome measures in most studies are basic skill measures rather than assessments of objectives more appropriate for gifted students. As a consequence, educators have made generalizations about the positive effects of cooperative learning on gifted learners, but those conclusions have not been documented and have been severely criticized by parents.

Acceleration

Use of acceleration is based on the assumption that gifted learners are, and will continue to be, rapid learners, have mastered advanced-level curriculum, and are ready to learn curriculum offered at a higher grade or school level. Models of acceleration do not demand change in the school curriculum; the learner is served by placement in a more advanced level of the existing curriculum within a school or by attendance at another school or in college. Typically, curricular goals and instructional strategies are not modified to accommodate gifted students. A recent review of studies of acceleration identified 18 types of acceleration (Colangelo, Assouline, & Gross, 2004). Programs of radical acceleration allow students to skip one or more grade levels (e.g., early entrance to kindergarten, skipping of one or more grades, early entrance into college, and dual enrollment). Two less dramatic forms of acceleration are telescoping (condensing two or more grade levels for content into 1 year) and course-by-course acceleration (e.g., going to the high school while enrolled in seventh grade to take geometry or taking advanced placement courses).

Researchers studying acceleration have concluded that the practice yields clear advantages in academic achievement (Colangelo et al., 2004). Arguments against acceleration have focused on fears of social or emotional difficulties that may result from not being with age peers. However, considerable follow-up research, based primarily on post hoc surveys, suggests students are academically successful, with few if any indications of social or emotional problems when (a) acceleration is implemented with students whose levels of achievement and maturity clearly suggest that this modification in their school program is warranted, (b) careful monitoring and support are available, and (c) the practice is flexible (Colangelo et al., 2004; Hunsaker & Callahan, 1991). Southern and Jones (1991) summed up the literature on acceleration succinctly by noting that, although group results appear very positive, concentration on whether groups are helped or harmed masks the effects on individuals. Because the differing options present different challenges, not all acceleration options are equally appropriate for all gifted children.

Advanced Placement Courses (AP) and the International Baccalaureate Program (IB). AP courses and the IB program are often categorized as acceleration models because students may earn college credit for successful completion of exams and performance assessments associated with these programs. Although both AP courses and the IB program were developed outside the field of gifted education, both gifted and general educators have embraced them as means of meeting the needs of gifted high school students; and although limited research exists on the appropriateness of AP and IB for gifted secondary learners, these courses serve as the primary method of meeting the needs of gifted students in most high schools. Research on AP and IB courses reveals student satisfaction, teacher and student perceptions of challenge (particularly as compared to traditional high school courses), and students feeling better prepared for college. Researchers studying college success have reported "good" correlations between scores on AP exams and grades in subsequent college courses and also documented that AP students continue to pursue knowledge in the subject areas in which they took exams at a higher rate than other students (Morgan & Crone, 1993). Students who received credit for introductory courses based on success on AP exams have been compared in subsequent courses to those who took the college introductory courses. Those students who earned AP credit received significantly higher grades than those students who took the college courses (Breland & Oltman, 2001; Morgan & Ramist, 1998). However, subsequent examination of these studies by a panel of the National Research Council (NRC, 2002a) resulted in the conclusion that:

> the methodology used in conducting the studies makes it difficult to determine how often and under what circumstances there is a positive advantage for AP students…. [The methodological flaws also] make it difficult to determine

> whether any apparent advantage held by AP students is a function of the college they attend, the classes they enter, their own academic backgrounds and abilities, or the quality of the AP courses they took in high school. (p. 193)

Researchers have criticized IB courses for the same reasons (Hertberg-Davis & Callahan, 2008a). Interviews with 200 students in 23 U.S. high schools revealed that, although students believe that AP and IB courses provide a greater level of academic challenge and more favorable learning environments than other existing high school courses, the curriculum and instruction within AP and IB courses are not a good fit for all learners, particularly those from traditionally under-served populations (Hertberg-Davis & Callahan, 2008a, 2008b; Kyburg, Hertberg-Davis, & Callahan, 2007).

Mentorships

Although controlled experimental studies of the effects of mentoring programs for the gifted do not exist, case study and qualitative studies suggest positive influences of mentoring relationships and programs and the processes through which different types of influence may occur (Callahan & Dickson, 2008). Gifted students involved in mentoring perceive it as beneficial in the development of interests and motivation. They report learning about lifestyles of professionals in specific careers, as well as the specific roles, functions, activities, and goals of individuals who are accomplished in those careers, and they think that mentors help them become socialized in the field and develop self-efficacy (Arnold, 1995; Pleiss & Feldhusen, 1995) Other identified benefits of mentoring programs include helping students take intellectual risks, developing talents, learning about advanced subject matter, developing the ability to work independently, using technical skills, finding out about career entrance requirements, seeing how professionals interact, learning to conduct research in the field, and making contacts and establishing networks.

Curriculum Models and Instructional Strategies

As noted above, the overlap between service delivery models, curricular intervention, and programming models is not clear. In this section four widely used models are presented. The first two are clearly curriculum models; the others are a mix of curriculum and programming and service delivery models. Two other models not presented in this chapter are discussed frequently in the literature, the Purdue Three Stage Model (Feldhusen & Kolhoff, 1986) and the Autonomous Learner Model (Betts, 1986).

The Integrated Curriculum Model

The Integrated Curriculum Model (ICM; Van Tassel-Baska, 1986) comprises three interrelated curriculum dimensions: (a) advanced content, (b) high-level process and product work, and (c) intra- and interdisciplinary concept development and understanding (Van Tassel-Baska & Brown, 2005). Researchers studying curriculum units based on the ICM model have reported significant gains for identified gifted elementary students in high-level thinking (Van Tassel-Baska, Zuo, Avery, & Little, 2002). Furthermore, the research suggests that the model is effective with gifted populations in a variety of educational settings and grouping configurations. Specific achievement gains were noted in language arts (literary analysis, literary interpretations, persuasive writing, and linguistic competency in language arts) (Van Tassel-Baska et al., 2002). Research using comparison groups suggests that using the problem-based science units embedded in an exemplary science curriculum significantly enhances the capacity for integrating higher order process skills in science (Van Tassel-Baska, Bass, Reis, Poland, & Avery, 1998), and use of social studies units significantly affects critical thinking and content mastery (Little, Feng, Van Tassel-Baska, Rogers, & Avery, 2002).

Kaplan's Depth and Complexity Model

Kaplan's model emphasizes the importance of rich, deep, and complex content in appropriately serving gifted learners. In Kaplan's work, the "how" (e.g., instructional setting, instructional strategies) is of less importance in challenging gifted learners than the richness of the content (the "what") with which students are engaged (Kaplan, 1998b). Kaplan presents a "curricular equation" for the development of tasks for the gifted: "Higher level thinking skills + Advanced content in depth and complexity + Accelerated multiple and varied resources + Product" (p. 9). Kaplan's model emphasizes the benefit of higher level thinking skills, elaborate product development, and more advanced resources in a curriculum for the gifted, but the crux of the model's curriculum equation is the redefinition of the nature of the content. The model is based on the premise that appropriate high-level content is synonymous with the dimensions of depth, complexity, novelty, and acceleration (1998a).

Differentiation of Instruction

The Differentiated Instruction model (Tomlinson, 2001) is designed to provide rich and engaging curricula matched to the diverse interests, readiness levels, and learning profiles of individual students to develop to their fullest potential the talents of all learners, including the gifted. The model assumes that there is no single curriculum which is appropriate for gifted learners, but rather that all students, including the gifted, require educational experiences suited to their individual needs (Tomlinson, 1996). In Tomlinson's model, the distinguishing features of a curriculum that is uniquely appropriate for gifted learners are learning experiences at a level of transformation, abstractness, problem ambiguity, independence, or pace suited to advanced learning capacity (Tomlinson, 1996). The *intensity* of the application of these elements, rather than the elements themselves, discriminates learning experiences designed for gifted students from those designed for other learners.

Differentiated instruction in the traditional classroom is rapidly becoming the most commonly used program/curriculum model for philosophical and financial reasons. The model is based on the assumption that, by serving students in the general education setting, they receive more consistent services than in out-of-classroom models whereby students are typically served only a portion of the day or week. Financially, it seems advantageous to opt for within-classroom programs for gifted learners, and in those states where little or no funding is allocated for specialized programming for gifted learners, it is often the only alternative. Fifteen years of research suggests that even moderate attempts at differentiating instruction with considerable staff development and support result in moderate gains in student achievement and more positive student attitudes toward school than teacher-directed, traditional instruction (Brighton, Hertberg, Moon, Tomlinson, & Callahan, 2005). However, as Hertberg-Davis (2009) concludes:

> lack of sustained teacher training in the specific philosophy and methods of differentiation, underlying beliefs prevalent in our school culture that gifted students do fine without any adaptation to curriculum, lack of general education teacher training in the needs and nature of gifted students, and the difficulty of differentiating instruction without a great depth of content knowledge—it does not seem that we are yet at a place where differentiation within the regular classroom is a particularly effective method of challenging our most able learners (p. 252)

The Schoolwide Enrichment Model

The Schoolwide Enrichment Model (SEM; an evolution of the Enrichment Triad Model) (Renzulli, 1977; Renzulli & Reis, 1985) provides a talent pool of 15%–20% of above average ability/high potential students with a variety of services, including learning experiences geared toward students' interests and learning styles, curriculum compacting, and enrichment experiences. The model offers three types of enrichment experiences: (a) Type I enrichment exposes students to a wide variety of disciplines, topics, hobbies, etc. through speakers, demonstrations, or performances; (b) Type II enrichment develops students' thinking, research and feeling processes; and (c) Type III enrichment allows students to pursue advanced content acquisition and process training in an area of self-selected interest. Type I, II, and III enrichment are offered to all students; however, Type III enrichment is usually more appropriate for students with higher levels of ability, interest, and task commitment. Studies on the SEM reflect the same level and quality of productivity from the top 5% of identified students as the other 15% (Reis, 1981). At the secondary level, Delcourt (1994) conducted a retrospective qualitative longitudinal study of students in programs using the model (but also enrolled in Advanced Placement, honors classes, and special seminars) who had "produced at least three performances or products…with four or more years of participation in a [gifted] program" (p. 408). These students reported skill acquisition in research, writing, communication and technical abilities, and improvement in personality dimensions such as self-satisfaction, patience, self-assurance, responsibility, and independence. Taylor (cited in Renzulli & Reis, 1994) found that participation in Type III activities significantly increased the mean number of years that students in a vocational/technical school planned to spend in postsecondary education.

Compacting. Compacting is a specific instructional practice embedded in SEM (but often used independently) in which students are assessed prior to the introduction of an instructional unit to determine content they already know or skills they have mastered. Students may be exempted from instruction in areas they have mastered or may be required to participate only in whole group or individualized instruction in a small segment of a unit which covers content or skills they have not mastered. Gifted elementary level students who had 40% to 50% of their curriculum across one academic year eliminated through compacting earned scores that were not significantly different from those of students who experienced all of the instructional activities (Reis et al., 1993). In several areas, gifted students whose curriculum was compacted earned higher achievement scores than their classmates whose curriculum was not compacted.

Unique Populations of Gifted Students and Unique Issues for Gifted Students

Underachieving Gifted Students

Perhaps the greatest enigma to parents, teachers, counselors, and psychologists (and perhaps to the gifted student) is underachievement. The underachiever is defined in many ways, but all conceptions of underachievement include a discrepancy between some measure of potential and current performance (on achievement tests or in the classroom).[1] Noting that underachievers are a heterogeneous group, McCoach and Siegle (2008) summarized the factors that research had identified as associated with gifted underachievers: low academic self perceptions or low self-efficacy; low self-motivation and effort toward academic tasks; external attribution, low goal-valuation, negative attitudes toward school and teachers, and low self-regulatory or metacognitive skills. They are also more likely to be males. Reis and McCoach (2002) categorized the factors identified as potential causes of underachievement as environmental or within the individual, including unchallenging classroom learning tasks (which may result in lack of interest and motivation) and pressure to be like everyone else, especially in early adolescence (among females and minorities this pressure may lead to hiding one's abilities and achieving only at the level of peer expectations). Researchers have associated family dynamics with underachievement, for example, expectations that are too low or too high, over-indulgence of the student, and unclear messages within the family (Rimm, 1995;

Rimm & Lowe, 1988). Factors within the individual include internalizing problems, such as depression, anxiety, perfectionism, failure-avoidance, low self-esteem, and externalization problems such as rebelliousness, irritability, nonconformity, anger, or unrecognized learning deficits (Reis & McCoach, 2002). Research on effective interventions for underachievement has been inconclusive (McCoach & Siegle, 2008).

The Perfectionist Gifted Child

In the study of perfectionism in gifted students, investigators often make the distinction is between *normal*, or enabling perfectionistic behaviors, and *neurotic*, or disabling perfectionism (Bransky, Jenkins-Friedman, & Murphy, 1987). Some researchers have concluded that gifted students as a group are perfectionistic, that on average they are more perfectionistic than average-ability peers, and that this behavior can be a positive force in their achievement. However, for other researchers, perfectionism is always a negative construct, and the exaggerated form of this behavior may lead to immobilization accompanied by depression, nagging self-doubt, shame, and self-deprecation (Hamachek, 1978). Development of these behaviors over time may lead to underachievement. That is, perfectionistic students decide (consciously or unconsciously) that it is better to fail by not trying, thus not completing or submitting work that might be judged as less than perfect. Many strategies have been suggested for addressing perfectionism, but empirical research on the effectiveness of these strategies is lacking (Schuler, 2002).

The Socially Isolated Gifted Child

The subtleties of social isolation are rooted in being "different" (Rimm, 2002) and either adjusting and coping appropriately or failing to find ways to establish suitable relationships. Traditional notions of social isolation may be inappropriate when considering gifted students. In some cases, advanced thinking, reasoning, and performance in the talent domain places gifted students in situations in which they may interact very appropriately with older students or even adults who are similar in level of cognitive processing to them. The many cases of radically accelerated students who develop such relationships and suffer no regrets for not having age peer relationships illustrate the satisfactory adjustment of these students (Matthews, 2008). A second question may be whether gifted students are satisfied with a small group of close friends rather than a larger cadre of acquaintances. However, when gifted students are unable to establish social relationships with intellectual or age peers, issues of loneliness and isolation may appear (Rimm, 2002). Students' inability to adjust their behavior or unwillingness to adapt to peers, especially among early adolescents, has been shown to result from extreme reliance on process adjustment in the developmental process (Callahan et al., 2004). This research suggests that gifted students are most likely to experience social isolation when they come from families in which rules are erratically enforced, an individual (usually the gifted child) dominates, and the family system is modified for the gifted individual. These students develop a strong sense of self, which is often reinforced by teachers who admire their independence of thinking, but these gifted individuals may experience problems as they become adolescents and begin turning to their peers for approval and support without having learned how to appropriately compromise, listen to the views of others, tolerate less gifted students, and respect others' points of view or circumstances.

Depression and Suicide

In their review of the literature, Gust-Brey and Cross (1999) concluded that there is no empirical evidence that the rates of suicide or depression among the gifted are any greater or any lower than those of the general population. However, some researchers have questioned that conclusion. For example, Neihart (2002) posits that many gifted students who experience serious emotional problems may not be nominated for consideration as gifted or identified to receive services. According to Neihart, the data suggest that high cognitive functioning, asynchronous development, perfectionism, and social isolation possibly contribute to depression or suicide; however, she points out that the relationships between these factors and depression and suicide are not clear. Neihart also notes that the role of protective factors is not given sufficient attention in the literature on gifted students. She enumerates several factors that may increase resilience and counter negative forces: high intelligence and problem-solving ability, advanced moral reasoning, androgyny, advanced social skills, and multiple interests.

Specific Issues Faced by the Twice-Exceptional Gifted Child

Gifted students with learning disabilities. The recognition of gifted students with learning disabilities is difficult because extraordinary intellectual ability and resultant problem-solving strategies may mask the disability, allowing the student to achieve at average levels (precluding referral). Moreover, the learning disability may camouflage the giftedness because teachers see only average performance. As a result, many gifted students with learning disabilities are not identified or provided services as either gifted students or as students with learning disabilities. The few studies of gifted/learning disabled identify the serious problems faced by these students. Problems include unhealthy perfectionism, unrealistic expectations of self, intense frustration with difficult tasks that often produces a general lack of motivation and may result in underachievement, feelings of low self-esteem, and learned helplessness (Olenchak & Reis, 2002). College-age, gifted students with learning disabilities reported having sought counseling for emotional problems, having negative school experiences, and having a sense that educators consider all students with learning disabilities to be below-average in ability (Reis, Neu, & McGuire, 1995).

Gifted students with ADHD. Some authors have contended that giftedness is often misconstrued as Attention Deficit Hyperactivity Disorder (ADHD) and that the medical field has over-diagnosed ADHD among those who are really gifted or creative individuals (e.g., Baum, Olenchak, & Owen, 1998; Moon, 2002). By contrast, Kaufmann, Kalbfleisch, and Castellanos (2000) point out that "*no empirical data in the medical, educational, or psychological literature* [emphasis in original] substantiate this concern" (p. xiii). The similarities between the sustained attention of a gifted child in a high-interest activity (described as *flow* by Csikszentmihalyi, 1997) and the hyperfocus of a student with ADHD may have contributed to the confusion between the two categories of learner and have led some to dismiss the category of students who may be both ADHD and gifted. Recent work by Kaufman et al. suggests there may be gifted students with ADHD, and that these students would be predisposed to manifest the state of intensely focused attention. Kaufman et al. noted that ADHD is not characterized by an inability to sustain attention but by inability to appropriately regulate the application of attention to tasks that are not intrinsically rewarding or to those that require effort. When focus is applied appropriately to problem solving and becomes an aspect of task commitment, it takes on positive valence. However, when students are unable to shift from task to task, the trait can become a negative behavior (Moon, 2002). The lack of research on the coexistence of ADHD and giftedness precludes specific recommendations for interventions beyond a creative and carefully monitored attempt to meld those already recommended for the two groups independently.

Specific Issues Faced by Gifted Females

Kitano (2008) points out the increasing parity of females with males in school achievement (including representation in gifted programs) but also notes the continued lack of parity in career domains of mathematics, science, and technology. Schuler (2002) suggests that females are more likely to be identified as perfectionists, who are fixated on avoiding mistakes and who work to please others rather than themselves. Furthermore, there is evidence that gifted females' beliefs in their ability and their feelings of self-confidence are diminished during childhood and adolescence as are their interests in careers in the STEM areas (Callahan, Cunningham, & Plucker, 1994), and negative gender stereotypes and resulting stereotype threat may account for lower test performance in STEM areas (Cadinu, Maass, Rosabianca, & Kiesner, 2005).

At-Risk Gifted Students

There is little question that at-risk students (minority and poor) are under-identified and underserved by programs for the gifted (NRC, 2002b). Cultural biases underlying the practices of identification that have been noted as contributing to the problem of underrepresentation include: (a) narrow, exclusive rather than inclusive definitions of giftedness; (b) choice of biased testing instruments and/or narrow interpretation of data; (c) use of teacher nomination forms or checklists that fail to reflect ways in which students from minority populations or students of poverty may manifest the characteristics of giftedness and the underlying racial biases present in society at large and, perhaps, in the education profession as well; (d) inadequate preparation of screening and placement committees for evaluating the data presented from tests; (e) failure to consider effects of stereotype threat on student test performance (Steele & Aronson, 1995); and (f) failure to use appropriate alternative assessment strategies such as dynamic assessment, performance assessment, portfolios, and other alternative assessment tools (Callahan, Tomlinson, & Pizzat, 1993; Castellano, 2004; Ford, Grantham, & Milner, 2004; Klug, 2004; NRC, 2002b).

The difficulties in identifying gifted students in at-risk populations have been well documented. However, research on programs that foster the development of talent and the specific issues surrounding psychosocial development and effective programming practices are rare. It is most common to start and end discussions with a focus on the problems of identification and ignore the critical issues of the poor educational preparation that is provided to ethnic minorities and children of poverty and issues associated with programming and curricular options. However, a very important consideration in addressing the issue of under-representation is the degree to which the very early years provide for adequate talent development in underserved populations and the ways we provide appropriate services and differentiate the curriculum and instructional program. Researchers have shown that early talent development programs are successful at enhancing potential (Callahan, Tomlinson, Moon, Tomchin, & Plucker, 1995; Kornhaber, 2004).

Gifted programs structures may discourage participation by minorities. Moore, Ford, and Milner (2005) identify attrition as common among minority students in gifted programs. Several factors may contribute to students dropping out of these programs: (a) isolation resulting from being one of a very few served through a particular service delivery model, particularly if joining the served group requires separation from peers; (b) curriculum that is not relevant to the students; (c) instructional practices based on competition or on methods of instruction that are culturally mismatched to the learning practices of the students' community; (d) inattention to social relationship building; and (e) emotional distress emanating from the feelings of responsibility or the stress of representing a particular group. Educators aware of and responsive in ensuring appropriate matches between identified talents and the services (including mentorships) to the identified students have been able to sustain involvement and success (Borland, & Wright, 1995; Klug, 2004; Pewewardy & Bushey, 1992). At the secondary level, specific and targeted support structures, coupled with a rigorous commitment to providing scaffolding, were critical to the success of minority and low income learners in Advanced Placement classes and International Baccalaureate programs (Kyburg et al., 2007). Gifted Latino students perceived mentors to be of great importance in helping them set and achieve academic goals, and those whose parents possessed less *cultural capital* (access to resources and information networks) identified mentors as critical in helping them gain access to information they would not have otherwise obtained (Arellano & Padilla, 1996). Early mentoring of at-risk students has been an influential factor in the development of talent in very young minority students and students from impoverished environments (Moon & Callahan, 2001; Wright & Borland, 1992).

Summary

Although many gifted students are provided adequate school opportunities and most do not develop social or emotional problems as they move through childhood and adolescence, it is a myth that gifted students will make it without positive and supportive interventions from school and family. Although gifted students may achieve in school, schools are failing these students, as well as society and schools themselves, when they do not provide gifted students the opportunities to achieve their full potential. The evidence indicates that schools are not responding fully to the educational and learning needs suggested by the defining characteristics of giftedness.

Notes

1. For purposes of this discussion, minority and low income students whose environment may inhibit the development of full potential are not included in the category of underachiever.

References

Abad, F. J., Colom, R., Rebello, I., & Escorial, S. (2004). Sex differential in item functioning in the Raven's Advanced Progressive Matrices: Evidence for bias. *Personality & Individual Differences, 36,* 1459.

American Educational Research Association, the American Psychological Association, and the National Council on Measurement in Education. (1999). *Standards for Educational and Psychological Testing.* Washington, DC: Author.

Arellano, A. R., & Padilla, A. M. (1996). Academic invulnerability among a select group of Latino university students. *Hispanic Journal of Behavioral Sciences, 18,* 485–508.

Arnold, K. D. (1995). *Lives of promise.* San Francisco: Jossey-Bass.

Aronson, J., Fried, C. B., & Good, C. (2002). Reducing the effects of stereotype threat on Africa American college students by shaping theories of intelligence. *Journal of Experimental Social Psychology, 38,* 113–125.

Baum, S. M., Olenchak, F. R., & Owen, S. V. (1998). Gifted students with attention deficits: Fact and/or fiction? Or, Can we see the forest for the trees? *Gifted Child Quarterly, 42,* 96–104.

Bélanger, J., & Gagné, F. (2006). Estimating the size of the gifted/talented population from multiple identification criteria. *Journal for the Education of the Gifted, 30,* 131–163.

Betts, G. T. (1986). The autonomous learner model for the gifted and talented. In J. S. Renzulli (Ed.), *Systems and models for developing programs for the gifted and talented* (pp. 27–56). Mansfield Center, CT: Creative Learning Press.

Bloom, B. S. (Ed.). (1985). *Developing talents in young people.* New York: Ballentine.

Borland, J. H. (2005). Gifted education without gifted children. In R. J. Sternberg & J. E. Davidson (Eds.), *Conceptions of giftedness* (pp. 1–19). New York: Cambridge University Press.

Borland, J. H. (2008). Identification. In J. A. Plucker & C. M. Callahan (Eds.), *Critical issues and practices in gifted education: What the research says* (pp. 261–280). Waco, TX: Prufrock Press.

Borland, J. H. (2009). Myth 2: The gifted constitute 3 to 5% of the population: Moreover giftedness equals high IQ, which is a stable measure of aptitude. *Gifted Child Quarterly, 53,* 236–238.

Borland, J. H., & Wright, L. (1995). Identifying young and potentially gifted economically gifted students. *Gifted Child Quarterly, 38,* 164–171.

Bransky, T., Jenkins-Friedman, R., & Murphy, D. (1987, April). *Identifying gifted students at risk for disabling perfectionism.* Paper presented at the annual meeting of the American Psychological Association, New York.

Breland, H. M., & Oltman, P. K. (2001). *An analysis of Advanced Placement (AP) examinations in economics and comparative government and politics.* (College Board Research Report 2001-2; ETS RR-01-17). New York: College Board

Brighton, C. M., Hertberg, H. L., Moon, T. R., Tomlinson, C. A., & Callahan, C. M. (2005). *The feasibility of high-end learning in diverse middle school.* (Research Report 05201) Storrs, CT: National Research Center on the Gifted and Talented, University of Connecticut.

Brody, L. E., & Stanley, J. C. (2005). Youths who reason exceptionally well mathematically and/or verbally: Using the MVT:D^4 model to develop their talents. In R. J. Sternberg & J.E. Davidson (Eds.), *Conceptions of giftedness* (pp. 20–37). New York: Cambridge University Press.

Brown, S. W., Renzulli, J. S., Gubbins, E. J., Siegle, D., Zhange, W., & Cohen, C. H. (2005). Assumptions underlying the identification of gifted and talented students. *Gifted Child Quarterly 49,* 68–79.

Burke, B. S., Jensen, D. W., & Terman, L. M. (1930). *The promise of youth: Genetic studies of genius, Vol. 3.* Stanford, CA: Stanford University Press.

Cadinu, M., Maass, A., Rosabianca, A., & Kiesner, J. (2005). Why do women underperform under stereotype threat? Evidence for the role of negative thinking. *Psychological Science, 16,* 797–811.

Callahan, C. M., Cunningham, C. M., & Plucker, J. A. (1994). Foundations for the future: The socio-emotional development of gifted, adolescent women. *Roeper Review, 17,* 99–105.

Callahan, C. M., Dickson, R. K. (2008). Mentoring. In J. A. Plucker & C. M. Callahan (Eds.), *Critical issues and practices in gifted education: What the research says* (pp. 409–422). Waco, TX: Prufrock Press.

Callahan, C. M., Sowa, C. J., May, K. M., Tomchin, E. M., Plucker, J. A., Cunningham, C. M., & Taylor, W. (2004). *The social and emotional development of gifted students* (Research Monograph 04188). Storrs, CT: National Research Center on the Gifted and Talented, University of Connecticut.

Callahan, C. M., Tomlinson, C. A., Moon, T. R., Tomchin, E. M., & Plucker, J. A. (1995). *Project START: Using a multiple Intelligences model in identifying and promoting talent in high-risk students.* (Research Monograph 95136). Storrs, CT: University of Connecticut, National Research Center on the Gifted and Talented.

Callahan, C. M., Tomlinson, C. A., & Pizzat, P. M. (1993). *Contexts for promise: Noteworthy practices and innovations in the identification of gifted students.* Charlottesville, VA: University of Virginia, National Research Center on the Gifted and Talented.

Castellano, J. (2004). Empowering and serving Hispanic students in gifted education. In D. Booth & J. C. Stanley (Eds.), *In the eyes of the beholder: Critical issues for diversity in gifted education* (pp. 1–14). Waco, TX: Prufrock Press.

Center for Assessment and Evaluation of Student Learning (2004, January). Issue in testing very young children. *Assessment Brief, 5,* 1–3. Retrieved August 29, 2009, from http://www.caesl.org/briefs/Brief5.pdf

Colangelo, N., Assouline, S., & Gross, M. U. M. (2004). *A nation deceived: How schools hold back America's brightest students* (Vol. 1). Iowa City: The Connie Belin & Jacqueline N. Blade International Center for Gifted Education and Talent Development, University of Iowa.

Csikszentmihalyi, M. (1996). *Creativity: Flow and psychology of discovery and invention.* New York: HarperCollins.

Csikszentmihalyi, M. (1997). *Finding flow: The psychology of engagement in everyday life.* New York: Basic Books.

Csikszentmihalyi, M., Rathunde, K., & Whalen, S. (1993). *Talented teenagers: The roots of success and failure.* Cambridge, UK: Cambridge University Press.

Dauber, S. L., & Benbow, C. P. (1990). Aspects of personality and peer relations of extremely talented adolescents. *Gifted Child Quarterly, 34,* 10–14.

Delcourt, M. (1994). Characteristics of high-level creative productivity: A longitudinal study of students identified by Renzulli's three-ring conception of giftedness. In R. F. Subotnik & K. D. Arnold (Eds.), *Beyond Terman: Contemporary longitudinal studies of giftedness and talent* (pp. 401–436). Norwood, NJ: Ablex.

Delcourt, M. A. B., Loyd, B. H., Cornell, D. G., & Goldberg, M. D. (1994). *Evaluation of the effects of programming arrangements on student outcomes* (Research Monograph 94108). Storrs, CT: National Research Center on the Gifted and Talented, University of Connecticut.

Diamond, A., Barnett, W. S., Thomas, J., & Munro, S. (2007). Preschool program improves cognitive control. *Science, 318,* 1387–1388.

Dweck, C. S. (2006). *Mindset: The new psychology of success.* New York: Random House.

Feldhusen, J. F., & Kolhoff, P. B. (1986). The Purdue Three-Stage Enrichment Model for gifted education at the elementary level. In J. S. Renzulli (Ed.), *Systems and models for developing programs for the gifted and talented* (pp.126–152). Mansfield Center, CT: Creative Learning Press.

Feldman, D. H. (1994). *Beyond universals in cognitive development* (2nd ed.). Norwood, NJ: Ablex.

Feldman, D. H. (2008). Prodigies. In J. A. Plucker & C. M. Callahan (Eds.), *Critical issues and practices in gifted education: What research says* (pp. 523–534). Waco, TX: Prufrock Press.

Ford, D.Y., Grantham, T.C., & Milner, H. R. (2004). Underachievement among gifted African-American students: Cultural, social, and psychological considerations. In D. Booth & J. C. Stanley (Eds.), *In the eyes of the beholder: Critical issues for diversity in gifted education* (pp. 15–32). Waco, TX: Prufrock Press.

Friedman-Nimz, R. (2009). Myth 6: Cosmetic use of multiple selection criteria. *Gifted Child Quarterly, 53,* 248–250,

Gagné, F. (1995). From giftedness to talent: A developmental model and its impact on the language of the field. *Roeper Review, 18,* 103–111.

Gagné, F. (1998). A proposal for subcategories within the gifted or talented populations. *Gifted Child Quarterly, 42,* 87–95.

Gagné, F. (2005). From gifts to talents: The DMGT as a developmental model. In R. J. Sternberg & J. E. Davidson (Eds.), *Conceptions of giftedness* (pp. 20–37). New York: Cambridge University Press.

Gallagher, J. J. (1958). Peer acceptance of highly gifted children in the elementary school. *Elementary School Journal, 58,* 465–470.

Gardner, H. (1983). *Frames of mind.* New York: Basic Books.

Gardner, H. (1999). Are there additional intelligences? The case for naturalist, spiritual, and existential intelligences. In J. Kane (Ed.), *Education, Information and Transformation* (pp. 111–131). Upper Saddle River, NJ: Prentice-Hall.

Gentry, M., & Owen, S.V. (1999). An investigation of total school flexible cluster grouping on identification, achievement, and classroom practices. *Gifted Child Quarterly, 43,* 224–243.

Gottfried, W. M., Gottfried, A. E., Bathurst, K., & Guerin, D. W. (1994). *Gifted IQ: Early developmental aspects: The Fullerton longitudinal study.* New York: Plenum Press.

Gross, M. U. M. (1993). *Exceptionally gifted children.* London: Routledge.

Gross, M. U. M. (1997). How ability group turns big fish into little fish—or does it? Of optical illusions and optimal environments. *Australian Journal of Gifted Education, 6*(2), 18–30.

Gross, M. U. M. (2008). Highly gifted children and adolescents. In J. A. Plucker & C. M. Callahan (Eds.), *Critical issues and practices in gifted education: What research says* (pp. 241–242). Waco, TX: Prufrock Press.

Gust-Brey, K., & Cross, T. L. (1999). An examination of the literature base on the suicidal behaviors of gifted children. *Roeper Review, 22,* 28–35.

Hamachek, D. E. (1978). Psychodynamics of normal and neurotic perfectionism. *Psychology, 15,* 27–33.

Hertberg-Davis, H. (2009). Myth 7: Differentiation in the regular classroom is equivalent to gifted programs and is sufficient: Classroom teachers have the time, skill, and the will to differentiate adequately. *Gifted Child Quarterly, 53,* 251–253.

Hertberg-Davis, H. & Callahan, C. M. (2008a). A narrow escape: Gifted students' perceptions of Advanced Placement and International Baccalaureate Programs, *Gifted Child Quarterly, 52,* 199–216.

Hertberg-Davis, H., & Callahan, C. M. (2008b). Advanced placement and international baccalaureate programs. In J. A. Plucker & C. M. Callahan (Eds.), *Critical issues and practices in gifted education: What the research says* (pp. 31–44). Waco, TX: Prufrock Press.

Hollingsworth, L. M. (1926). *Gifted children: Their nature and nurture.* New York: Macmillan.

Hollingsworth, L. M. (1942). *Children above 180 IQ Stanford-Binet: Origin and development.* Yonkers-on-Hudson, NY: World Books.

Hunsaker, S. L., & Callahan, C. M. (1991). Student assessment and evaluation. In W. T. Southern & E. D. Jones (Eds.), *The academic acceleration of gifted children* (pp. 207–222). New York: Teachers College.

Jaeggi, S., M. Buschkuehl, M, Jonides, J., & Perrig, W. J. (2008). Improving fluid intelligence with training on working memory. *Proceedings of the National Academy of Sciences, 105,* 1–5). Retrieved from http//:www.pnas.org_cgi:_doi_10.1073_pnas.0801268105

Kanevsky, L. K. (1994). A comparative study of children's learning in the zone of proximal development. *European Journal of High Ability, 5,* 163–185.

Kaplan, S. (1998a). *Project Curriculum T.W.O. Progress Status: Project Summary (II).* Javits Grant R206A7006. Washington, DC: U.S. Department of Education.

Kaplan, S. (1998b). *Think like a disciplinarian: A learning center approach to differentiate the core curriculum for gifted students.* Javits Grant Proposal. Washington, DC: U.S. Department of Education.

Kaufmann, F., Kalbfleisch, M. L., & Castellanos, F. X. (2000). *Attention deficit disorders and gifted students: What do we really know?* (Research Monograph 00146). Storrs, CT: National Research Center on the Gifted and Talented, University of Connecticut.

Kitano, M.K. (2008). Gifted girls. In J. A. Plucker & C. M. Callahan (Eds.), *Critical issues and practices in gifted education: What the research says* (pp. 225–240). Waco, TX: Prufrock Press.

Klug, B. J. (2004). Children of the starry cope: Gifted and talented Native American students. In D. Booth & J. C. Stanley (Eds.), *In the eyes of the beholder: Critical issues for diversity in gifted education* (pp. 49–72). Waco, TX: Prufrock Press.

Kornhaber, M. L. (2004). Using multiple intelligences to overcome cultural barriers to identification for gifted education. In D. Booth & J. C. Stanley (Eds.), *In the eyes of the beholder: Critical issues for diversity in gifted education* (pp. 215–225). Waco, TX: Prufrock Press.

Kulik, J. A., & Kulik, C. C. (1997). Ability grouping. In N. Colangelo & G. Davis (Eds.), *Handbook of gifted education* (pp. 230–342). Needham Heights, MA: Allyn & Bacon.

Kyburg, R. M., Hertberg-Davis, H., & Callahan, C. M. (2007). Advanced Placement and International Baccalaureate programs: Equity and excellence for students from diverse backgrounds in urban environments? *Journal of Advanced Academics, 18,* 172–215.

Little, C. A., Feng, A. X., Van Tassel-Baska, J., Rogers, K. B., & Avery, L. D. (2002). *Final report on social studies curriculum effectiveness study.* Williamsburg, VA: Center for Gifted Education, The College of William and Mary.

Lohman, D. F. (2005a). Review of Naglieri and Ford (2003): Does the Naglieri Nonverbal Ability Test identify equal proportions of high-scoring White, Black, and Hispanic students? *Gifted Child Quarterly, 49,* 19–28.

Lohman, D. F. (2005b). The role of nonverbal ability tests in identifying academically gifted students: An aptitude perspective. *Gifted Child Quarterly, 49,* 111–138.

Lohman, D. F., & Lakin, J. (2008). Nonverbal test scores as one component of an identification system: Integrating ability, achievement, and teacher ratings. In J. Van Tassel-Baska (Ed.), *Alternative assessments with gifted and talented students* (pp. 41–66). Waco, TX: Prufrock Press.

Lou, Y., Abrami, P. C., Spence, J. C., Poulsen, C., Chambers, B., & d'Apollonia, S. (1996). Within-class grouping: A meta-analysis. *Review of Educational Research, 66*, 423–458.

Marland, S. P. Jr., (1972). *Education of the gifted and talented. Vol. I. Report to Congress of the United States by the U.S. Commissioner of Education.* Washington, DC: U.S. Government Printing Office.

Matthews, M. S., (2008). Talent search programs. In J. A. Plucker & C. M. Callahan (Eds.), *Critical issues and practices in gifted education: What the research says* (pp. 641–653). Waco, TX: Prufrock Press.

McCoach, D. B., & Siegle, D. (2008). Underachievers. In J. A. Plucker & C. M. Callahan (Eds.), *Critical issues and practices in gifted education: What the research says* (pp. 721–734). Waco, TX: Prufrock Press.

Miele, F. (1996). Interview with Robert Sternberg. *Skeptic, 3*(3), 72–80.

Moon, S. M. (2002). Gifted children with attention-deficit/hyperactivity disorder. In M. Neihart, S. M. Reis, N. M. Robinson, & S. M. Moon (Eds.), *The social and emotional development of gifted children: What do we know?* (pp. 193–201). Waco, TX: Prufrock Press.

Moon, T. R., & Callahan, C. M. (2001). Impacts of a mentoring program intervention. *Journal for the Education of the Gifted, 24*, 305–321.

Moore, J. L., Ford, D. Y., & Milner, R. (2005). Recruitment is not enough: Retaining African-American students in gifted education. *Gifted Child Quarterly, 49,* 51–68.

Morgan, R., & Crone, C. (1993). *Advanced Placement examinees at the University of California: An examination of the freshman courses and grades of examinees in biology, calculus, and chemistry.* (Statistical Report 93-210). Princeton, NJ: Educational Testing Service.

Morgan, R., & Ramist, L. (1998, February). *Advanced Placement student in college: An investigation of course grades at 21 colleges.* Retrieved July 27, 2005, from http:///apcentral.collegeboard.com/apc/pubic/repository/ap01.pdf_7926.pdf.

National Association for Gifted Children (NAGC). (n.d.). *State of the states: A report by the National Association for Gifted Children and the Council of State Directors of Programs for the Gifted.* Washington, DC: Author.

National Association for Gifted Children (2009). *The NAGC pre-K — grade 12 Gifted Program Standards.* Retrieved August 26, 2009, from http://www.nagc.org/index.aspx?id=543

National Research Council (NRC). (2002a). *Learning and understanding: Improving advanced study of mathematics and science in the United States.* Washington, DC: National Academy Press

National Research Council (NRC). (2002b). *Minority students in special and gifted education.* Washington, DC: National Academies Press.

National Association for Gifted Children (2009). *The NAGC pre-K — grade 12 Gifted Program Standards.* Retrieved August 26, 2009, from http://www.nagc.org/index.aspx?id=543

Neihart, M. (2002). Gifted children and depression. In M. Neihart, S. M. Reis, N. M. Robinson, & S. M. Moon (Eds.), *The social and emotional development of gifted children: What do we know?* (pp. 93–101). Waco, TX: Prufrock Press.

Olenchak, F. R., & Reis, S. M. (2002). Gifted students with learning disabilities. In M. Neihart, S. Reis, N. M. Robinson, & S. M. Moon (Eds.), *The social and emotional development of gifted children: What do we know*? (pp. 177–191). Waco, TX: Prufrock Press.

Pewewardy, C., & Bushey, M. (1992). A family of learners and storytellers: The American Indian Magnet School. *Native Peoples Magazine, 5*(4), 56–60.

Pleiss, M. K., & Feldhusen, J. F. (1995). Mentors, role models, and heroes in the lives of gifted children. *Educational Psychologist, 30*, 159–169.

Plucker, J. A., & Barab, S. A. (2005). The importance of contexts in the theories of giftedness. In R. J. Sternberg & J. E. Davidson (Eds.), *Conceptions of giftedness* (pp. 201–216). New York: Cambridge University Press.

Plucker, J. A., Callahan, C. M., & Tomchin, E. M. (1996). Wherefore art thou, multiple intelligences? Alternative assessments for identifying talent in ethnically diverse and low income students. *Gifted Child Quarterly, 40,* 81–92.

Reis, S. M. (1981). *An analysis of the productivity of gifted students participating in programs using the revolving door identification model.* Unpublished doctoral dissertation, The University of Connecticut, Storrs, CT.

Reis, S. M., & McCoach, D. B. (2002). Underachievement in gifted students. In M. Neihart, S. M. Reis, N. M. Robinson, & S. M. Moon (Eds.), *The social and emotional development of gifted children: What do we know?* (pp. 81–91). Waco, TX: Prufrock Press.

Reis, S. M., Neu, T. W., & McGuire, J. M. (1995). *Talents in two places: Case studies of high ability students with learning disabilities who have achieved* (Research Monograph 95113). Storrs, CT: National Research Center on the Gifted and Talented, University of Connecticut.

Reis, S. M., Westberg, K. L., Kulikowich, J., Caillard, F., Hébert, T., Plucker, J., … Smist, J. (1993). *Why not let high ability students start school in January? The curriculum compacting study* (Research Monograph 93106). Storrs, CT: National Research Center on the Gifted and Talented, University of Connecticut.

Reis, S. M., & Renzulli, J. S. (1986) The secondary triad model. In J. S. Renzulli (Ed.), *Systems and models for developing programs for the gifted and talented* (pp. 216–266). Mansfield Center, CT: Creative Learning Press.

Renzulli, J. S. (1977). *The enrichment triad model: A guide for developing defensible programs for the gifted.* Mansfield Center, CT: Creative Learning Press.

Renzulli, J. S. (1978). What makes giftedness? Re-examining a definition. *Phi Delta Kappan, 60,* 180–184, 261.

Renzulli, J. S. (2005). The three-ring conception of giftedness: A developmental model for promoting creative productivity. In R. J. Sternberg & J. E. Davidson (Eds.), *Conceptions of giftedness* (pp. 246–279). New York: Cambridge University Press.

Renzulli, J. S., & Reis, S. M. (1985). *The schoolwide enrichment model: A comprehensive plan for educational excellence.* Mansfield Center, CT: Creative Learning Press.

Renzulli, J. S., & Reis, S. M. (1994). Research related to the schoolwide enrichment model. *Gifted Child Quarterly, 38,* 7–20.

Rimm, S. (1995). *Why bright kids get poor grades and what you can do about it.* New York: Crown Trade Paperbacks.

Rimm, S. (2002).Peer pressures and social isolation. In M. Neihart, S. M. Reis, N. M. Robinson, & S. M. Moon (Eds.). *The social and emotional development of gifted children: What do we know?* (pp. 13–18). Waco, TX: Prufrock Press.

Rimm, S., & Lowe, B. (1988). Family environments of underachieving gifted students. *Gifted Child Quarterly, 32,* 353–358.

Robinson, N. M. (2008). Early childhood. In J. A. Plucker & C. M. Callahan (Eds.), *Critical issues and practices in gifted education: What the research says* (pp. 179–194). Waco, TX: Prufrock Press.

Rogers, K. B. (1991). *The relationship of grouping practices to the education of the gifted and talented* (Research Monograph 9102). Storrs, CT: National Research Center on the Gifted and Talented, University of Connecticut.

Schuler, P. (2002). Perfectionism in gifted children and adolescents. In M. Neihart, S. M. Reis, N. M. Robinson, & S. M. Moon (Eds.). *The social and emotional development of gifted children: What do we know?* (pp. 71–79). Waco, TX: Prufrock Press.

Scroth, S. T. (2008). Levels of service. In J. A. Plucker & C. M. Callahan (Eds.), *Critical issues and practices in gifted education: What the research says* (pp. 321–334). Waco, TX: Prufrock Press.

Southern, W. T., & Jones, E. D. (Eds.). (1991). *The academic acceleration of gifted children.* New York: Teachers College Press.

Steele, C. M., & Aronson, J. (1995). Stereotype threat and the intellectual test performance of African Americans. *Journal of Personality and Social Psychology, 69,* 797–811.

Sternberg, R. J. (1988). *The triarchic mind: A new theory of human intelligence.* New York: Viking.

Sternberg, R. J. (2008). Increasing fluid intelligence is possible after all. *Proceedings of the National Academy of Sciences, 105,* 6791–6792.

Sternberg, R. J., & Clinkenbeard, P. R. (1994). The triarchic model applied to identifying, teaching, and assessing gifted children. *Roeper Review, 17*, 255–260.

Sternberg, R. J., Ferrari, M., Clinkenbeard, P., & Grigorenko, E. L. (1996). Identification, instruction, and assessment of gifted children: A construct validation of a triarchic model. *Gifted Child Quarterly, 40,* 129–137.

Sternberg, R. J., Grigorenko, E. L., & Jarvin, L. (2006). Identification of the gifted in the new millennium: Two assessments for ability testing and the broad identification of gifted students. *KEDI Journal of Educational Policy, 3*(2), 7–27.

Tannenbaum, A. J. (1985). The enrichment matrix model. In J. S Renzulli (Ed.), *Systems and models for developing programs for the gifted and talented* (pp. 391–428). Mansfield Center, CT: Creative Learning Press.

Terman, L. M. (1926). *Mental and physical traits of a thousand gifted children. Vol. 1. Genetic studies of genius* (2nd ed.). Stanford, CA: Stanford University Press.

Terman, L. M., & Oden, M. H. (1947). *The gifted child grows up: Genetic studies of genius, Vol. 4.* Stanford, CA: Stanford University Press.

Tieso, C. L. (2002). *The effects of grouping and curricular practices on intermediate students' math achievement* (Research Monograph 02154). Storrs, CT: National Research Center on the Gifted and Talented, University of Connecticut.

Tomlinson, C. (1996). Good teaching for one and all: Does gifted education have an instructional identity? *Journal for the Education of the Gifted, 20*, 155–174.

Tomlinson, C. A. (2001). *How to differentiate instruction in mixed-ability classrooms* (2nd ed.). Alexandria, VA: Association for Supervision and Curriculum Development.

U.S. Department of Education. (1993). *National excellence: A case for developing America's talent.* Washington, DC: U.S. Government Printing Office.

Van Tassel-Baska, J. (1986). Effective curriculum and instruction models for talented students. *Gifted Child Quarterly, 30,* 164–169.

Van Tassel-Baska, J. (2005). Domain-specific giftedness. In R. J. Sternberg & J. E. Davidson (Eds.), *Conceptions of giftedness* (pp. 358–376). New York: Cambridge University Press.

Van Tassel-Baska, J. (2008). An overview of alternative assessment measures for gifted learners and the issues that surround their use. In J. VanTassel-Baska (Ed.), *Alternative assessments with gifted and talented students* (pp. 1–16). Waco, TX: Prufrock Press.

Van Tassel-Baska, J., Bass, G. M., Ries, R. R., Poland, D. L., & Avery, L. D. (1998). A national study of science curriculum effectiveness with high-ability students. *Gifted Child Quarterly, 42*, 200–211.

Van Tassel-Baska, J., & Brown, E. (2005). An analysis of gifted education curricular models. In F. A. Karnes & S. M. Bean (Eds.), *Methods and materials for teaching the gifted* (2nd ed., pp. 75–105). Waco, TX: Prufrock Press.

Van Tassel-Baska, J., Zuo, L., Avery, L. D., & Little, C. A. (2002). A curriculum study of gifted student learning in the language arts. *Gifted Child Quarterly, 46*, 30–44.

Wright, L., & Borland, J. H. (1992). A special friend: Adolescent mentors for young economically disadvantaged, potentially gifted students. *Roeper Review, 14*, 124–129.

Section V

Assessment of Students with Disabilities

Section Editor: Jennifer H. Lindstrom
University of Georgia

Perhaps no other aspects of contemporary education are receiving greater attention than accountability and high stakes assessment. At federal and state levels, pressure is being applied to schools to step up to the challenge of reform movements rooted in testing. Statewide assessment and accountability systems are increasingly attaching high stakes to student performance on assessments. For instance, test scores are routinely being used to make decisions about student graduation and grade promotion, teacher salaries, and the allocation of school resources. At the same time, the need to include students with disabilities in accountability efforts has become law and a key aspect of good testing practices. In this environment, the annual high stakes assessments have become a kind of cross to bear for teachers and administrators everywhere.

The inclusion of students with disabilities in assessment is deemed critical to improve the quality of educational opportunities for these students and to provide meaningful and useful information about students' performance to the schools and communities. Two federal laws specifically require states to administer assessments to students with disabilities: The Individuals with Disabilities Education Act (IDEA), amended in 2004, and the No Child Left Behind Act of 2001 (NCLB). IDEA includes provisions that ensure that students with disabilities have access to state tests and that test results are valid and reliable. IDEA also requires state and local districts to develop guidelines for the provision of appropriate testing accommodations. These efforts are also consistent with NCLB, which requires each state to implement a system of accountability for schools and districts that is designed to ensure that all children perform at or above proficiency on state academic achievement standards and state assessments.

Many students with disabilities will require testing accommodations in order to participate in testing programs on an equal basis with their nondisabled peers. Such accommodations provide students with the ability to demonstrate mastery of skills and attainment of knowledge without being limited or unfairly restricted due to the effects of a disability. The provision of test accommodations for students with disabilities is not without controversy, however, because limited empirical research exists about the effects of specific accommodations. While accommodations are usually administered in good faith, altering test administration conditions may inadvertently change the meaning of a test score, causing inferences, and hence the decisions and actions based upon the test score to be unsound.

Whatever one might think about the development of statewide assessment and accountability systems as an approach to improving education, one rational response has been to collect data on student progress toward state standards throughout the school year to ensure that students are on track to demonstrate proficiency on annual high stakes tests. This progress monitoring through curriculum-based measures (CBMs) is intended to assist teachers and administrators in formatively evaluating student progress and adjusting instruction based on student performance. However, a key challenge in the development and selection of CBMs is to identify measurement tasks that simultaneously integrate the various skills required for competent year-end performance. It is critical that CBM tasks involve systematic sampling of the skills constituting the annual curriculum to ensure that each weekly or bi-weekly CBM consistently and accurately represents the curriculum. CBMs and other formative classroom-based assessments should be linked to state standards, which are the basis for most standardized state tests.

Another key challenge in the use and implementation of CBMs is ensuring that teachers are sufficiently trained in systematically and continually monitoring student progress. The onus rests with state and local agencies to ensure that professional development needs are examined so that administrators, teachers, related services personnel and paraprofessionals possess the requisite skills and attitudes to implement progress monitoring procedures. Successful implementation depends on the ability of general and special educators to use CBMs reliably and validly. The reliability and validity with which CBMs are implemented will be determined, to a great extent, by the quality of both the pre-service and in-service professional development models used to translate research into practice. In-service professional development needs to occur both within and across administrative structures at the state, district, and building levels.

There is no question that high stakes testing and accountability policies are here to stay, at least for the foreseeable future. The challenge for policymakers and practitioners is to make the system work in ways that benefit students and their teachers. Well-designed assessments and accountability systems can focus attention on schools and students who need the most help, motivate students and educators, and foster the development of better curriculum and instruction. However, policymakers must recognize the limits as well as the promise of such policies. Further, state legislation that requires teachers to acquire adequate training is necessary to successfully and effectively support education reform efforts linked to high stakes assessment and progress monitoring. Such policy reform needs to go hand in hand with local school systems providing professional development opportunities for teachers to acquire this kind of training that will allow them to put into place systematic and continual assessment practices that can be used to inform instruction.

In this era of educational accountability, appropriate testing and reporting of assessment results have increased in importance to educators and policymakers nationwide. Both IDEA and NCLB require that all children with disabilities be included in all general state and districtwide assessment programs. Thus, the requirements of IDEA and NCLB should be leveraged to provide the conditions necessary to bring about the changes needed in statewide testing to ensure that all students are able to demonstrate what they know. The following two chapters address many of the questions being raised surrounding high stakes testing and accountability, including the following: What impact do high stakes tests have on students and teachers? What is the role of accommodations on high stakes tests for students with disabilities? Why should teachers monitor student progress using CBMs? How can teachers connect classroom assessment (e.g., CBM) to broader, standardized assessments?

25

High Stakes Testing and Accommodations

Jennifer H. Lindstrom
University of Georgia

The standards-based reform movement has led to increased use of large-scale assessments to assess students' and schools' performance. Although students with disabilities have historically been excluded from large-scale testing (Elliott, Erickson, Thurlow, & Shriner, 2000; Ysseldyke & Thurlow, 1994), legislation (e.g., No Child Left Behind [NCLB], Individuals with Disabilities Education Act [IDEA]) aims to increase the participation of students with disabilities in these assessments. Associated reform efforts have fueled much of the debate among stakeholders. Proponents of including students with disabilities in accountability systems purport a host of positive outcomes, including improved student achievement, more access to the general education curriculum, higher expectations, and higher-quality instruction (Fuchs & Fuchs, 2001; McDonnell, McLaughlin, & Morrison, 1997; Ysseldyke et al., 2004). Critics, on the other hand, contend that including students with disabilities may result in a narrowing of the curriculum and instruction to focus on the specific learning outcomes assessed in state tests, teaching to tests, using test preparation materials that are closely linked to the assessment without making changes to the curriculum (Thurlow & Johnson, 2000), and undermining the motivation of students already struggling (Clarke et al., 2003; Roderick & Engel, 2001). Although these consequences certainly affect all students, students with disabilities in particular are significantly affected by high stakes testing programs.

Daily reading of news headlines leaves those concerned about enhanced educational outcomes for students with disabilities confused. Are we to believe the *Washington Post* (Glod, 2009) headline "Law Opens Opportunities for Disabled; 'No Child' Is Credited With Pushing Many to Higher Levels of Achievement" or the *Education Week* (Sternberg, 2004) article "Good Intentions, Bad Results: A Dozen Reasons Why the No Child Left Behind Act Is Failing Our Schools"? Perhaps instead, the 2009 Council for Exceptional Children's (CEC) article stating that "High Stakes Testing a Mixed Blessing for Special Students" (Frase-Blunt, n.d.) may indeed be a more realistic account of the consequences of accountability systems on students with disabilities. Although there is considerable anecdotal information on the consequences of accountability systems, there is little empirical evidence on such consequences.

Understanding the role of high stakes tests and their implications for students with disabilities will help answer such questions as whether, and how, to include students with disabilities in state and districtwide testing programs. This chapter begins with an overview of the importance of high stakes tests and their impact on students, teachers, and parents, followed by a description of the laws governing participation in statewide assessments. Next, research on high stakes tests and testing accommodations is reviewed, including existing research reviews in this area. The focus of the chapter is limited to students with high incidence disabilities (e.g., learning disabilities, attention-deficit/hyperactivity disorder, mild cognitive disabilities) and accommodations for regular assessment (hence, information specific to alternate assessments, accommodations for classroom instruction or learning, and universal design in general are not addressed).

High Stakes Assessment

High stakes testing has become a significant part of standards-based reform and educational accountability. Tests are "high stakes" when they are used in making decisions about which students will be promoted or retained in a grade and which will receive a standard high school diploma or some other type of document (Heubert, 2002; Thurlow & Johnson, 2000). The use of exit exams to determine whether a student earns a high school diploma, for example, is "high stakes" because it has lifelong consequences and directly affects an individual's economic self-sufficiency and well-being as an adult. The consequences of high stakes testing for students with disabilities as a component of educational accountability is not, however, well understood (Heubert, 2002; Lewis, 2000; Thurlow & Johnson, 2000).

The ways in which a test is used and the consequences associated with student performance on that test ultimately determine the level of stakes that are associated with an assessment system (Goertz & Duffy, 2003). The *Standards for Educational and Psychological Testing* (American Educational Research Association, American Psychological Association, & National Council on Measurement in Education, 1999) state,

> When significant educational paths or choices of an individual are directly affected by test performance, such as whether a student is promoted or retained at grade level, graduated, or admitted or placed into a desired program, the test is said to have high stakes (p. 139).

For many policymakers, attaching high stakes consequences to test results is seen as a way to link assessment to accountability and in turn to enhance positive student outcomes.

The stakes are high not only for students, but for teachers, administrators, and state and local education agencies as well. All states are required to have an accountability system with sanctions and rewards. Imposing sanctions on schools or administrators is slightly more prevalent than providing rewards (Salvia, Ysseldyke, & Bolt, 2010). Among sanctions states commonly use are assigning negative labels (e.g., "Needs Improvement," "Underperforming") to schools, removing staff, and firing principals. Rewards include assigning positive labels (e.g., "Excelling," "Highly Performing," "Performing Plus") to schools and giving extra funding to schools or monetary incentives or awards to staff (e.g., pay-for-performance programs).

High Stakes Exit Exams

The development and implementation of standards-based education reforms among state and local education agencies have existed for over two decades, and are in large part a response to growing public criticism that students exit America's high schools lacking the skills and knowledge required to be productive citizens (Johnson, Thurlow, & Stout, 2007). The movement to standards-based education dates from the publication of *A Nation at Risk* in 1983, and its message, that we were "falling behind" our international counterparts, was further reinforced in 1990 by the Third International Mathematics and Science Study (TIMSS). Other evidence also suggested that America's schools were "falling short" in providing equitable opportunities for all of its children (as in *The Forgotten Half* [William T. Grant Foundation, 1988] or *The SCANS Report for America, 2000* [U.S. Department of Labor, 1991]). Such reports and others led to a general consensus that there are serious things wrong with public education, that the problems are systemic rather than problematic, and that nothing short of major structural change will fix these problems (Cobb & Johnson, 1997).

In response to critics of public education, many states have implemented graduation policies and requirements that call for raised academic standards for all students. This has also led to the development of exit exams linked to a student's eligibility to receive a high school diploma, and a focus on increasing student graduation rates (Johnson et al., 2007). All of these strategies are intended to increase the level of student learning and achievement essential to entering future adult roles.

Though exit exams have evolved with considerable controversy, there has been a trend toward increasing the use of exit exams over the past decade. In 1997, 16 states had exit exams in place as a condition for receiving a standard diploma (McDonnell, McLaughlin, & Morison, 1997). This number increased to 22 states in 2000 (Olson, Jones, & Bond, 2001), and 27 in 2003 (Johnson & Thurlow, 2003). In recent years, however, high failure rates among students with disabilities have prompted some states to reconsider the requirement that all students must pass the exam to graduate, delay putting them into effect, or lower the score for passing. In fact, a number of class-action lawsuits have been filed against state boards of education challenging controversial high school exit exams. Students, parents, and disabilities rights advocates claim that exit exams discriminate against students with disabilities, minority students, and students with limited-English skills (Disability Rights Advocates, 2001). As of 2006, 21 states required students with and without disabilities to pass an exit exam to receive a high school diploma, and three states required only those students without disabilities to pass their exit exams to receive a high school diploma (Johnson et al., 2007).

Laws Governing Participation in High Stakes Tests

The inclusion of students with disabilities in assessment is deemed critical to improving the quality of educational opportunities for these students and to provide meaningful and useful information about students' performance to the schools and communities that educate them (Elliott, McKevitt, & Kettler, 2002). Two federal laws specifically require states to administer assessments to students with disabilities: The No Child Left Behind Act of 2001 (NCLB) and the Individuals with Disabilities Education Act (IDEA), last amended in 2004. NCLB, which reauthorized the Elementary and Secondary Education Act (ESEA), was designed to improve academic achievement for all students. NCLB requires that students with disabilities be included in statewide assessments that are used to determine whether schools and districts meet state goals. Further, NCLB requires that all students, including students with disabilities, be measured against academic achievement standards established by the states. To be deemed as making Adequate Yearly Progress (AYP), each school must show that the school as a whole, as well as each of designated groups, such as students with disabilities, met the state proficiency goals. Schools must also show that at least 95% of students in grades required to take the test have done so (Government Accountability Office, 2005).

The requirement that students with disabilities participate in these tests also comes from federal law governing the provision of services to students with disabilities, the Individuals with Disabilities Education Act Amendments of 1997 (IDEA 1997) and the Individuals with Disabilities Education Improvement Act (IDEA 2004). Specifically, in IDEA 2004, the language about who will participate in assessments states that, "All children with disabilities are included in all general State and districtwide assessment programs ... with appropriate accommodations and alternate assessments, where necessary and as indicated in their respective individualized education programs." (Section 1412(c)(16)(A)). For the child with a disability who has an Individualized Education Plan (IEP), the IEP shall include:

> a statement of any individual appropriate accommodations that are necessary to measure the academic achievement and functional performance of the child on State and districtwide assessments ... [and] if the IEP Team determines that the child shall take an alternate assessment on a particular State or districtwide assessment of student achievement, a statement of why ... the child cannot participate in the regular assessment; [and] ... [why] the particular alternate assessment selected is appropriate for the child . . ." (Section 1414(d)(1)(A)(i)(VI))

States must document the number of students participating in the tests, report on their performance, and develop alternate assessments for students unable to participate in existing state or district tests. Guidelines must be developed to assist in deciding which students take state and district assessments and which take an alternate assessment. Performance reports are to be made available to the public with the same frequency and in the same detail as reports that are provided to the public for students without disabilities.

Together, NCLB and IDEA provisions and requirements combine to provide both individualized instruction and school accountability for students with disabilities. The progress and performance of students with disabilities is now a shared responsibility of general and special education teachers. Never before have the nation's federal education laws been aligned to provide such powerful opportunities for children with disabilities. However, as Cole (2006) points out, it is also important to consider the central conflict that exists between the two federal mandates affecting special education. IDEA calls for individualized curriculum and assessments that determine success based on growth and improvement each year. NCLB, in contrast, measures all students by the same markers, which are based not on individual improvement but by proficiency in math and reading. Thus, it can be quite challenging to reconcile the need to administer individualized assessments to determine student growth and success under IDEA and the requirement to provide standardized assessments under NCLB (Cole, 2006).

Ensuring Fair Treatment of Students on High Stakes Assessments

As a result of the changes in legislation aimed at increasing the participation of students with disabilities in large-scale assessments, the International Dyslexia Association, the National Center for Learning Disabilities, and the Learning Disabilities Association of America have published a list of 13 core principles to ensure fair treatment of all students (Disability Rights Advocates, 2001, p. 15). Included in these principles are safeguards that should be in place in order to make certain that standardized testing is carried out in a fair and nondiscriminatory manner, as shown in Figure 25.1.

Impact of High Stakes Tests

Intended Consequences

To determine the relative merit of high stakes assessments, both the intended and unintended consequences must be apparent. Despite the preponderance of newspaper reports highlighting the negative consequences of large-scale tests, the purpose of high stakes assessment is indeed positive: to improve educational outcomes (Christenson, Decker, Triezenberg, Ysseldyke, & Reschly, 2007). Testing programs are implemented with the goals of setting high academic standards, elevating student achievement through improved instruction, ensuring equal opportunities in education, encouraging family involvement, and increasing public support for schools (Heubert & Hauser, 1999; Jones, Jones, & Hargrove, 2003). In addition, high stakes assessments can be used to provide a framework by which educators can be held responsible for the instructional climate of the classroom and certify whether individual students have reached specific achievement levels (Heubert & Hauser, 1999). Clarke et al. (2003) further noted that teachers reported a greater focus on writing, critical thinking skills, discussion, and explanation as a result of required testing.

Unintended Consequences

Unfortunately, the aforementioned goals of high stakes assessments are not accomplished without "side effects," spurring a great deal of controversy among stakeholders. Commonly expressed concerns include less instructional creativity, increased test preparation, narrowing of content coverage, and poor instructional match in the curricular sequence and for instructional pace (Clarke et al., 2003). Additional unintended consequences on instruction are well documented in the literature. Research has shown that in some cases, state tests become the objects of instruction rather than the content standards represented (Abrams, Pedulla, & Madaus, 2003; Steeves, Hodgeson, & Peterson, 2002). Another concern is that increases in state assessment scores following the implementation of high stakes assessment policies do not always generalize to

Thirteen Core Principles to Ensure Fair Treatment of All Students, Including Those with Learning Disabilities, with Regard to High Stakes Assessments

Endorsed by The International Dyslexia Association, National Center for Learning Disabilities, and Learning Disabilities Association of America[22]

1. The needs and rights of students with learning disabilities must be vigorously protected to ensure that these students (a) have an equal opportunity to participate in and attain all of the benefits of high stakes assessment programs and (b) to ensure that they are not disadvantaged or discriminated against on the basis of disability with regard to such assessments.
2. Students identified as having learning disabilities must have access to the general education curriculum throughout their school years and to general education courses and curriculum in secondary school to ensure that they will be best able to demonstrate their intelligence, abilities, knowledge, and skills on high stakes assessments.
3. In designing and implementing high stakes assessments, educators and administrators must protect the rights and needs of students with learning disabilities and ensure that the assessments do not discriminate against students with learning disabilities.
4. In designing and implementing remediation options for students failing or performing poorly on high stakes assessments, educators and administrators must protect the rights and needs of students with learning disabilities and ensure that the remedial assistance available does not disadvantage or discriminate against students with learning disabilities.
5. Political and administrative considerations, such as how the inclusion of students with learning disabilities in high stakes assessments will affect reporting of scores of schools and districts, must not be allowed to (a) override the rights and needs of students with learning disabilities, (b) adversely affect the benefits to learning disabled students once included, or (c) place the providers of special education at a disadvantage because of administrative or funding consequences of non-participation.
6. As determined during the Individualized Education Program and Section 504 processes, and in compliance with the needs of each individual student, students with learning disabilities must be provided with all necessary accommodations for their learning disabilities on high stakes assessments.
7. Students with learning disabilities must be provided the same accommodations on the assessments that they have used during their educational careers.
8. Within the IEP and Section 504 processes there must be fair, neutral and clear processes by which students with learning disabilities and their parents can appeal decisions about the accommodations provided on the assessments. The availability of these appeal processes should be clearly communicated to students and their parents.
9. There must be a meaningful alternate assessment system available to children who are disadvantaged by the high stakes assessments as a result of a learning disability.
10. There must be procedures in place to ensure the fair assessment of students with learning disabilities who take alternate assessments, as well as the fair assessment of those who take standard assessments with accommodations.
11. Whether a student takes a standard assessment (or portion thereof) or is assessed under an alternate assessment (or portion thereof) should be decided by a student and his or her parents in concert with school personnel, and should be addressed during the Individualized Education Program and Section 504 processes.
12. The number of students who participate in an alternate assessment should not be artificially limited to a certain percentage, but should be available to all children whose Individualized Education Programs or Section 504 Plans show that they would benefit.
13. States and school districts should accumulate data and encourage research on the effects of high stakes assessment on the education of all children, including those who receive accommodations and those who participate in alternate assessments.

Do No Harm—High Stakes Testing and Students with Disabilities **Page 15**

Figure 25.1

more formative assessments that measure similar academic skills (Abrams et al., 2003; Amrein & Berliner, 2003; Brennan, Kim, Wenz-Gross, & Siperstein, 2001). Further, research suggests that high stakes assessments are more likely to undermine the motivation of students already struggling (Clarke et al., 2003; Roderick & Engel, 2001). A similar concern relates to drop-out rates and its positive relationship to high stakes assessment: As stakes increase in state assessments, drop-out rates increase (Amrein & Berliner, 2003; Clarke, Haney & Madaus, 2000).

Consequences of Including Students with Disabilities on High Stakes Assessments

While the consequences of high stakes assessments are well documented in the literature for students without disabilities, little is known about the consequences of including students with disabilities in these reform efforts. A 2006 report issued by the Center for Evaluation and Education Policy and the Indiana Institute on Disability and Community outlined both the positive effects and the unintended consequences of the law (Cole). The report indicated that while efforts to meet NCLB accountability standards have improved short-term student outcomes, long-term consequences are dismal. Positive effects of NCLB for students with disabilities include access to high standards and curriculum, improved test scores and enhanced collaboration between special education and general education teachers (Cole, 2006). The unintended consequences include a narrowed curriculum and a "scapegoat" mentality that casts special education as the obstacle to schools trying to make AYP (Cole, 2006, p. 4). Further, NCLB's narrow assessment criteria creates pressure for schools to reverse inclusion efforts and may contribute to higher drop-out rates among students with disabilities (Cole, 2006).

Few empirical studies have examined the intended and unintended consequences of high stakes assessment for students with disabilities, and when done, they are state specific. For example, Defur (2002) surveyed special education administrators in Virginia on the effects of high stakes assessments on students with disabilities. The results showed that 83% of respondents reported that the assessment program led to some degree of benefit for students with disabilities, with 73% of respondents identifying "access to the general curriculum" as the area of most pronounced and general benefit (Defur, 2002, p. 205). However, 51% of respondents identified higher rates of academic failure, 50% expressed concern that students were experiencing lower self-esteem, and 44% were concerned that students with disabilities would experience higher drop-out rates and would fail to earn diplomas as examples of unintended consequences (Defur, 2002). Braden's (2002) examination of the consequences of large-scale assessment for students with disabilities delineated curricular alignment, increased student motivation, and educational equity for underserved groups as intended outcomes of high stakes assessment for students with disabilities.

Participation Policies for Students with Disabilities

There are a variety of ways students with disabilities can participate in statewide assessment systems, and these can affect the way in which their scores are considered for accountability purposes (Bolt, Krentz, & Thurlow, 2002). Some students with disabilities are included in the regular test administration in the same way as most other students. Others participate with accommodations. Some take a modified test or receive non-standard test administrations, and a small percent participate in alternate assessments. Although state policy may clearly indicate the ways in which students with disabilities can participate and be included in state assessment systems, the process by which such decisions are made and the degree to which scores from these various test administrations are included in the determination of school accountability (i.e., AYP) is often unclear.

According to the National Center on Educational Outcomes (NCEO) 2007 analysis of states' participation and accommodation policies, the criteria cited as most frequently used to determine how students with disabilities participate in statewide assessments were: (a) IEP Determined (50 states); (b) Instructional Relevance/Instructional Goals (44 states); (c) Current Performance/Level of Functioning (36 states); and (d) Level of Independence (36 states) (Christensen, Lazarus, Crone, & Thurlow, 2008, pp. 8–9). The entire report, along with additional reports on state policies, can be found on the NCEO Web site (http://www.cehd.umn.edu/ NCEO/).

Since the passage of NCLB, public reporting of state assessment participation and performance information for students with disabilities has been tracked by the U.S. Department of Education and various other agencies, including NCEO. Under NCLB, any school accepting federal dollars must demonstrate AYP in the number of students meeting proficiency standards and publicly report statewide assessment results in a clear, timely, and useful manner (Peterson & Young, 2004; Yeh, 2008). According to results of a 2005 nationwide study conducted by the U.S. Government Accountability Office (GAO), the majority of students with disabilities were included in the regular statewide reading/language arts assessments (National Assessment of Educational Progress (NAEP); administered in grades four and eight) in the 2003–2004 school year. Participation rates ranged from 65% (Michigan) to 99% (Missouri) across all 50 states and the District of Columbia, with the exception of Texas, where only 39% of students with disabilities participated in the NAEP assessments. A 2008 analysis of the public reporting of state assessment results for students with disabilities conducted by NCEO yielded slightly higher participation rates on average (Thurlow, Altman, Cormier, & Moen, 2008), with the exception of Texas. The NCEO Annual Performance Report found that during the 2005–2006 academic year, participation rates for elementary schools for the regular statewide reading assessment ranged from 31% (Texas) to 99% (Maine); middle school participation rates ranged from 30% (Texas) to 95% (Iowa, Montana, and Rhode Island); high school participation rates on the regular statewide reading assessment ranged from 37% (Texas) to 97% (Mississippi). Participation rates and patterns across states for the regular math assessment for all three school levels (elementary, middle, and high school) during the 2005–2006 academic year were similar to those observed in reading (Thurlow et al., 2008).

Accommodations and High Stakes Tests

Accommodation Policies

As participation rates of students with disabilities increase, so does the use of testing accommodations. Increased use of accommodations should reflect an attempt to ensure that the scores received by students with disabilities are valid measures of achievement (Johnstone, Altman, Thurlow, & Thompson, 2006). It is also possible that increased use of accommodations is simply a reflection of concern about including students in assessments and a belief that these students need additional aids to help them perform better. Because of this, states are clarifying appropriate accommodation use in state policy, with the goal of encouraging IEP teams to select accommodations that remove specific disability barriers, but do not give students with disabilities an unfair advantage over their peers.

While NCLB and IDEA have increased the participation of students with disabilities in statewide testing, the percentage of students who receive testing accommodations on regular statewide assessments varies widely among states. According to results of NCEO's Annual Performance Report: 2005–2006 State Assessment Data (Thurlow et al., 2008), researchers found that although the majority of students with disabilities (approximately 85%) were included in the regular statewide reading and mathematics assessments, the number of students with disabilities who received accommodations ranged from 0% (Texas and Alabama) to 98% (Mississippi).

Accommodations play a central role in high stakes testing for students with disabilities because they define the line for participation in which results can be aggregated (Tindal, 2004). Although large organizations (e.g., testing companies, state departments of education) stipulate which accommodations are allowed, the decisions about what, if any, testing accommodations an individual student receives are usually made by a child study team (also referred to as the IEP team), which includes general educators, special education teachers, parents, administrators, and school psychologists. While the IEP team should be very knowledgeable about the student, research indicates that accommodation decisions often result in lowering a student's performance on the standardized test from the performance that would have been attained without the accommodation (Fuchs, Fuchs, Eaton, Hamlett, & Karns, 2000).

Accommodations in educational testing is covered by the Section 504 of the Rehabilitation Act, the Americans with Disabilities Act (ADA), and IDEA. The recent drive by educators to provide accommodations in testing has been spurred by and follows the logic of broader accommodation guidelines for educational, employment and licensure testing found in these regulations and laws (Weston, 2003). A reasonable accommodation in testing provides disabled students access to tests through alteration in administration procedures that do not change the nature of the constructs being measured. Commonly used accommodations include extended time, oral presentation and response, Braille, sign language interpreters, format changes (e.g., large print), relocation to a quiet room, and computerized aids. Laws about accommodations in testing do not require schools or testing programs to implement special preferences or an easier test for examinees with disabilities.

The provision of testing accommodations for disabled students is a controversial issue, however, because little empirical research exists about the effects of specific accommodations. While accommodations are usually administered in good faith, altering test administration conditions may inadvertently change the meaning of a test score, causing inferences, and hence the decisions and actions based upon the test score to be flawed. Only empirical research can provide evidence for evaluating the validity and fairness of accommodations use.

Research Examining the Role of Testing Accommodations

Interaction hypothesis. Test accommodations are designed to promote fairness in testing and lead to more accurate interpretations of students' test scores (Sireci, Li, & Scarpati, 2003). However, if the accommodation leads to an unfair advantage for the students who get them, for example, if everyone would benefit from the accommodation, then the scores from accommodated exams may be invalidly inflated, which would be unfair to students who do not receive accommodations. Sireci, Scarpati, and Li (2005) explained the validity of accommodations through an "interaction hypothesis" (p. 458). The interaction hypothesis states that (a) when test accommodations are given to students with disabilities who need them, their test scores will improve, relative to the scores they would attain when taking the test under standard (non-accommodated) conditions; and (b) students without disabilities will not exhibit higher scores when taking the test with those accommodations (Koenig, 2002; Sireci et al., 2005; Shepard, Taylor, & Betebenner, 1998; Zuriff, 2000). Thus there is an interaction between accommodation condition (accommodated versus standard test administration) and type of student (e.g., students with disabilities versus students without disabilities) with respect to test performance. A revised hypothesis was proposed by Sireci et al. (2005) with respect to extended time. It was based on the finding that both students with and without disabilities benefited from extended time, but the students with disabilities exhibited relatively greater score gains.

Validity issues in high stakes testing programs. Validity is indisputably a major concern of any testing program.

It is in the interest of the user that a test measures what it is purported to measure, that it does not measure what it is not supposed to measure, and that it bears a reasonable relationship to the criteria it is intended to predict (Willingham, 1976). According to the *Standards for Educational and Psychological Testing* (AERA, APA, & NCME, 1999, p. 9), "Validity refers to the degree to which evidence and theory support the interpretations of test scores entailed by proposed uses of tests." The test itself is not validated, and test scores per se are not validated. It is the interpretation determined by the proposed use that is validated (Cronbach, 1971; Kane, 2006; Messick, 1989).

Construct irrelevant variance. A variety of testing conditions can influence the degree to which students with disabilities demonstrate what they truly know and can do. For instance, small-size print, limited testing time, and the inability to manipulate a pencil are all potential sources of difficulty for students with disabilities (Bolt & Thurlow, 2004). These characteristics are frequently unrelated to what the test is intended to measure but can understandably lower student scores. Accommodations are intended to remove these sources of difficulty (i.e., construct irrelevant variance) and allow for the intended construct to be meaningfully and accurately measured. This idea is commonly articulated by stating that accommodations are intended to "level the playing field" by removing construct-irrelevant variance created by disabilities (Fuchs & Fuchs, 2001; Sireci et al., 2003; Tindal & Fuchs, 2000).

Review of the research. NCLB requires that the scores of subgroups be disaggregated and reported separately, as well as aggregated with the data reports of all other students, and that for accountability, they be treated in the same way—factored into accountability both separately and as part of the total. Further, new regulations (*Federal Register*, 2007) require states to prepare accommodation guidelines that "identify the accommodations for each assessment that do not invalidate the score" as well as prepare IEP teams to "select, for each assessment, only those accommodations that do not invalidate the score" (Section 300.160(b)(2)). Thus, there is a critical need for contributions to policy and psychometric understanding of the issues surrounding the use of test accommodations from researchers who are empirically studying these issues. What follows is a synthesis of much of the research on test accommodations published from 2005–2009. Brief summaries of the reviewed studies are presented in Appendix A. The research described encompasses empirical studies (experimental and quasi-experimental) of score comparability and validity studies with respect to test accommodations.

Several main points warrant mentioning. First, it is important to keep in mind that a major confound inherent to this area of research is the fact that researchers are, for the most part, limited to studying the accommodations students were *eligible* to use, rather than examining the accommodations students *actually* used on the test. Keeping in mind this major limitation of such research, among the 19 studies reviewed, extended time (alone and bundled with other accommodations) was the single most studied accommodation, but oral accommodations (such as read-aloud and audiocassette presentation) were also considered in multiple studies, as was computerized administration. Second, learning disabilities (including reading disabilities/dyslexia) were the most common disabilities exhibited by participants in the considered research, accounting for well over half of the studies. These findings are similar to previous reviews of the literature examining the effects of accommodations on the validity of test scores for students with disabilities (see Chiu & Pearson, 1999; Sireci et al., 2003; Sireci et al., 2005; Sireci, 2005; Stretch & Osborne, 2005; Thompson, Blount, & Thurlow, 2002; Zenisky & Sireci, 2007).

Types of test accommodations studied experimentally or quasi-experimentally in the research fell into three general categories: Timing/Scheduling, Presentation, and IEP-defined accommodations. A brief summary of the accommodations studied and specific study results is presented in Appendix A. Extended time was the most frequently researched accommodation (Antalek, 2005; Bolt & Ysseldyke, 2006; Cohen, Gregg, & Deng, 2005; Finch, Barton, & Meyer, 2009; Higgins, Russell, & Hoffman, 2005; Lesaux, Pearson, & Siegel, 2006; Lindstrom & Gregg, 2007; Mandinach, Bridgeman, Cahalan-Laitusis, & Trapani, 2005). Various implementations of oral administration were examined, including audiocassette presentation (Schnirman, 2005), read-aloud of proper nouns (Fletcher et al., 2006), reading aloud stems and possible responses to the comprehension stems after students have read the passage (Fletcher et al., 2009), and test items and/or directions read aloud (Bolt & Thurlow, 2006; Bolt & Ysseldyke, 2006; Elbaum, 2007; Finch et al., 2009; Huynh & Barton, 2006). Computerized text-to-speech was examined in one study (Dolan, Hall, Bannerjee, Chun & Strangman, 2005), and computer-based tests were looked at in two other studies (Higgins et al., 2005; Horkay, Bennett, Allen, Kaplan & Yan, 2006). Lastly, three studies empirically studied the effects of multiple accommodations as assigned by individual student IEPs (Bolt & Ysseldyke, 2008; Kim, Schneider, & Siskind, 2009; Lang, Elliott, Bolt, & Kratochwill, 2008) rather than focusing on specific individual accommodations.

Among the experimental and quasi-experimental studies examining the effects of extended time on the validity of test scores for students with disabilities, it is notable that all of the timing accommodation studies reported either a generally positive influence on scores (Antalek, 2005; Lesaux et al., 2006; Lindstrom & Gregg, 2007) or mixed results (Mandinach et al., 2005). The vast majority of studies on the provision of extended time pertaining to the interaction hypothesis showed that all student groups (students with and without disabilities) had score gains under accommodation conditions. More importantly, in general, the gains for students with disabilities were greater than their nondisabled peers under accommodation conditions. In contrast, studies examining measurement comparability across subgroups using differential item functioning (DIF) analysis, in which item-level characteristics of the test for the target groups were systematically compared with those for a reference group, suggested the (extended time) accommodated test may not be measuring comparably across groups (Bolt & Ysseldyke, 2006; Cohen et al., 2005; Finch et al., 2009), which may lead to potentially misinformed decision making. When many items display DIF for accommodated groups, it may be an indication that the test is measuring something different for the accommodated group than for the nonaccommodated group (Bolt & Ysseldyke, 2008).

Research examining the various implementations of oral administration (e.g., audiocassette, computerized oral test, directions and/or test items read aloud) yielded mixed results. Four studies suggested the use of oral test administration had a positive effect on students' scores (Bolt & Thurlow, 2006; Dolan et al., 2005; Fletcher et al., 2006; 2009), particularly when the reading level of the items was classified as difficult or passages were longer than 100 words. However, several studies found that either (a) scores across groups (disabled/nondisabled; accommodation/standard administration) were comparable (Huynh & Barton, 2006; Schnirman, 2005), or (b) scores for both students with and without disabilities improved in the read-aloud condition, though students *without* disabilities benefitted significantly more from the accommodation (Elbaum, 2007). Two studies comparing computer-based test administration and traditional paper-and-pencil versions of the test indicated no significant differences between scores across testing modes (Higgins et al., 2005; Horkay et al., 2006); however, neither study included students with disabilities.

Two of the three studies that empirically focused on the effects of two or more accommodations as assigned by individual student IEPs (rather than focusing on specific individual accommodations) lent support for the use of multiple test accommodations (Kim et al., 2009; Lang et al., 2008). On the other hand, Bolt and Ysseldyke (2008) found a relatively large number of items on a statewide math assessment displayed moderate-to-large DIF, indicating that the test may have been measuring something different for the IEP-determined accommodated group than for the group administered a standard version of the test.

Together, research findings indicate that while mounting evidence for evaluating the validity and fairness of accommodation use exists, it remains difficult to make conclusive statements about the effects of specific accommodations for particular subgroups of students on different types of high stakes assessments. What is clear, however, is that conducting research in this area is complicated by the heterogeneity across accommodation condition and student groups. As the 2007 NCEO analysis of states' accommodation policies revealed, there continues to be wide variability in accommodation use across states (Christensen et al., 2008). As such, the current research base that seeks to validate accommodations is growing but remains limited. States are continuing to refine their understanding of how to appropriately enable some students with disabilities to meaningfully participate in statewide assessments (Christensen et al., 2008). As Thurlow, Thompson, and Lazarus (2006) observed, "states now seem to be honing in on the need to clarify the purpose of the test and construct being tested, rather than just the goal of providing the student with access to the testing situation" (p. 662). Thus, the need for understanding what the research on test accommodations tells us is more important than ever before. It will be essential to continue to review and summarize the research conducted in this area, and to question whether changes in assessment and accommodations policies need to be made. It may also be important to explore new designs and new hypotheses as research moves forward to address the policy implications of research findings in this area (Zenisky & Sireci, 2007).

As Meyen, Poggio, Seok, and Smith (2006) rather astutely point out, "To accept accommodations in testing as the solution to achieving equity in statewide assessments for students with disabilities is insufficient, if not unacceptable" (p. 7). The tests themselves must be designed to maximize the opportunity for all students to demonstrate what they know relative to the standards being assessed. Test items must be tailored to the knowledge level of all examinees and, subsequently, efficiently assess what the learner knows (Meyen et al., 2006). This is particularly important given the mandates of NCLB, as merely assessing what students do not know does not inform instruction, nor does it motivate learners toward higher performance. Thus, the requirements of NCLB and IDEA should be leveraged to provide the conditions necessary to bring about the changes needed in statewide testing to ensure that all students are able to demonstrate what they know. Above all, the results of such testing should serve to inform instruction as teachers seek to make evidenced-based decisions while working to maximize student achievement. In the following chapter, Berkeley and Riccomini discuss progress monitoring as an assessment methodology that can be used to make meaningful decisions about student progress and to improve the quality of instructional programs.

Conclusion

This chapter addressed the topic of high stakes testing and accommodations with an eye toward students with high incidence disabilities and accommodations used on high stakes assessments. Legislation—the NCLB Act of 2001 and amended IDEA (2004)—has increased the participation of students with disabilities in high stakes assessments; never before have the nation's federal education laws been aligned to provide such powerful opportunities for children with disabilities. NCLB, in particular, has brought the debate about high stakes assessment to the forefront. This debate has often found special education advocates and parents on both sides of the fence, torn between wanting high expectations for students with disabilities and fear that students will suffer some unintended consequences as a result. While a number of positive consequences have been well documented in the literature (Chard, 1999; Fuchs & Fuchs, 2001; McDonnell et al., 1997; Ysseldyke et al., 2004), it has yet to be determined whether these benefits outweigh the costs (e.g., narrowed curriculum; increased referral, retention, and dropout rates; students with disabilities being used as scapegoats). Continued efforts aimed at empirically following the consequences of high stakes assessment longitudinally for students with disabilities remain critical.

Although the question of *whether* students with disabilities participate in state and districtwide assessments no longer applies, determining *how* to include them remains a challenge for many educators. NCEO's recent analysis of states' 2007 participation and accommodation policies found that state policies on participation and accommodations continue to evolve, and that they have become more detailed and specific than in previous years (Christensen et al., 2008). Key findings indicate that increasing numbers of students with disabilities are participating in states' regular assessments (rather than alternative assessments; Thurlow et al., 2008), and that state policies focus more on accommodations that allow for valid scores (Christenson et al., 2008). Not surprisingly, along with the increased participation rates of students with disabilities, the use of testing accommodations on high stakes tests has risen as well. Across states, however, there continues to be considerable variability in policies, reporting practices, participation rates, and accommodation use among students with disabilities in large-scale testing programs. Consequently, such variability confounds this area of research and makes the interpretation of data challenging, especially in terms of what these data mean for real-life implementation and practice.

As noted throughout this chapter, the assessment policies of NCLB strongly emphasize including all students in assessments and in addition, require disaggregated reporting for students with disabilities and other groups. These policies also emphasize obtaining valid measures of students' performance. For many students, valid measurement means providing accommodations that do not change the construct measured, but make the test more accessible to them (Zenisky & Sireci, 2007). Thus, the need for understanding what the research on test accommodations tells us is more important than ever before. The empirical studies reviewed in this chapter and by others (Chiu & Pearson, 1999; Sireci et al., 2003; 2005; Sireci, 2005; Stretch & Osborne, 2005; Thompson et al., 2002; Zenisky & Sireci, 2007) do indeed advance our knowledge about the effects of accommodations, but variations across tests, populations, settings, and contexts still curtail all but the most general policy implications. It will be essential to continue to review and summarize the research conducted in this area, and to question whether changes in assessment and accommodation policies need to be made.

APPENDIX 25.A
Accommodation Research Findings

Study	Subgroups*	Accommodations	Design	Selected Findings
Antalek (2005)	LD	Extended Time	Quasi-Experimental	The majority of the subjects took additional time and their scores on the task improved significantly, indicating a relationship between learning disabilities and the completion of academic tasks within an allotted time frame.
Bolt & Thurlow (2006)	RD	Read-Aloud	Quasi-Experimental	On the 4th grade dataset, items classified as reading-hard and those classified as mathematically easy but difficult to read (ME/RH) were positively affected by the accommodation. Marginally significant findings were obtained for the ME/RH item set at the 8th grade level.
Bolt & Ysseldyke (2008)	MD, PD, Non-disabled	IEP/School Team**	Quasi-Experimental	A relatively large number of items displayed moderate-to-large DIF for both accommodated disability groups when compared with non-accommodated students without disabilities.
Bolt & Ysseldyke (2006)	LD, PD, OD, Non-disabled	Read-aloud, with or without extended time and small group/individual administration	Quasi-Experimental	A greater portion of DIF items were identified for those students receiving read-aloud accommodations on a reading/language arts test than a math test. Read-aloud accommodations were found to be associated with greater measurement incomparability for reading/language arts than math.
Cohen et al. (2005)	LD, Non-disabled	Extended Time	Quasi-Experimental	Some items exhibited DIF under accommodated (extended time) conditions, but students for whom items functioned differently were not accurately characterized by their accommodation status but rather content knowledge.

(*continued*)

APPENDIX 25.A Continued

Study	Subgroups*	Accommodations	Design	Selected Findings
Dolan et al. (2005)	LD	Read-Aloud with Computer-Based Test	Experimental	Scores on the computerized oral test were significantly higher than scores on paper test when passages were longer than 100 words in length
Elbaum (2007)	LD, Non-disabled	Read-Aloud	Quasi-Experimental	Mean scores for students both with and withoutLD were higher in the accommodated condition; students without disabilities benefited significantly more from the accommodation (ES = 0.44) than students with LD (ES = 0.20).
Finch et al. (2009)	Multiple	Questions & Directions Read Aloud, Alternate Test Setting, and Extended Time (Alone or in combination)	Quasi-Experimental	Both uniform and nonuniform DIF could be expected between accommodated and non-accommodated examinees on the language and math items; for certain types of items (heavy navigational load), the accommodations appeared to have been detrimental. Nonuniform DIF was much more common in lower grade levels (below sixth grade), indicating that accommodations appeared more likely to favor disabled students at higher proficiency levels, but not those with lower proficiencies.
Fletcher et al. (2009)	RD, Non-disabled	Read-Aloud with 1- or 2-day administration	Quasi-Experimental	Accommodations helped both RD and average readers. The 2-day administration was more effective than the 1-day administration.
Fletcher et al. (2006)	RD, Non-disabled	Read-Aloud with Multiple Test Sessions	Experimental	Only students with RD benefited from the accommodations, showing a significant increase in average performance and a 7-fold increase in the odds of passing; results supported the interaction hypothesis.
Higgins et al. (2005)	Non-disabled	Computer-Based Test, Scrolling or Paging, Extended Time	Experimental	There were no significant differences in reading comprehension scores across testing modes.
Horkay et al. (2006)	Non-disabled	Computer-Based Test	Quasi-Experimental	Results showed no mean significant differences between paper and computer delivery.
Huynh & Barton (2006)	LD, PD, ED, EM, Non-disabled	Read-Aloud	Quasi-Experimental	The performance of SWD under oral administration conditions was comparable to that of SWD who took the test under regular administration conditions. The internal structure of the High School Exit Exam remained stable across SWD and non-disabled students.
Kim et al. (2009)	Multiple, Non-disabled	IEP/School Team**	Quasi-Experimental	The factor structure, factor loadings, and error variances of the science test were similar across the regular and accommodation groups.
Lang et al. (2008)	LD, Non-disabled	IEP/School Team**	Experimental	There was a significant interaction between test condition and disability status, indicating that testing accommodations had a significantly larger positive effect on the reading scores of students with disabilities, when compared to students without disabilities. Accommodations had an overall positive effect on the math scores of all groups of students, as did disability status and grade level. There was no statistically significant interaction found between test condition and disability status.
Lesaux et al. (2006)	RD, Non-disabled	Extended Time	Quasi-Experimental	Under timed conditions there were significant differences between performance of students with disabilities and students without disabilities. All of the students with disabilities benefited from extra time, but students without disabilities performed comparably under timed and untimed conditions. Also, students with disabilities (less severe) performed comparably to students without disabilities in untimed conditions.

Study	Subgroups*	Accommodations	Design	Selected Findings
Lindstrom & Gregg (2007)	LD/ADHD, Non-disabled	Extended Time	Quasi-Experimental	Invariance across the two groups was supported for all parameters of interest, suggesting that the scores on the Critical Reading, Math, and Writing sections of the SAT Reasoning Test can be interpreted in the same way when students have an extended-time administration as opposed to the standard-time administration.
Mandinach et al. (2005)	LD and/or ADHD, Non-disabled	Extended Time, Separately Timed Sessions	Experimental	Results indicated that time and a half with separately timed sections benefits students with disabilities and students without disabilities, though some extra time improves performance and too much may be detrimental. Extended time benefits medium and high ability students but provides little or no advantage to low-ability students.
Schnirman (2005)	LD, Non-disabled	Audiocassette administration	Experimental	No statistically significant differences were found between performance of SWD and non-disabled students.

* Key:
ADHD (Attention-Deficit/Hyperactivity Disorder)
ED (Emotional Disability)
EM (Educable Mentally)
LD (Learning Disability)
MD (Learning Disabilities, Mental Retardation, Emotional-Behavioral Disabilities)
PD (Deaf, blind, deaf-blind, hard of hearing, and physical impairments) Multiple (Learning disabilities, Speech/Language, Educable Mentally Disabled, Other Health Impaired, Emotionally Disabled, Multiple-Disabled, Deaf/Hard of Hearing, Autism, Orthopedically Impaired, Blind/Visually Impaired, Traumatic brain Injury, Deaf-Blindness, Trainable Mentally Disabled)
OD (Other disability)
RD (Reading Disability/Dyslexia)
SWD (Students with disabilities)

** IEP/School Team: Various accommodations were implemented as per individual student IEPs or as determined to be needed by school teams

References

Abrams, L. M., Pedulla, J. J., & Madaus, G. F. (2003). Views from the classroom: Teachers' opinions of statewide testing programs. *Theory Into Practice*, *42*(1), 18–29.

American Educational Research Association, American Psychological Association, & National Council on Measurement in Education. (1999). *Standards for educational and psychological testing*. Washington, DC: American Educational Research Association.

Amrein, A. L., & Berliner, D. C. (2003). The effects of high-stakes testing on student motivation and learning. *Educational Leadership*, *60*(5), 32–38.

Antalek, E. E. (2005). The relationships between specific learning disability attributes and written language: A study of the performance of learning disabled high school subjects completing the TOWL-3. *Dissertation Abstracts International, 65*(11), 4098 A. Retrieved August 5, 2006, from http://proquest.umi.com/pqdweb?did=828451101& sid =2&Fmt=2&clientId=30345&RQT=309&VName=PQD

Bolt, S., Krentz, J., & Thurlow, M. (2002). *Are we there yet? Accountability for the performance of students with disabilities* (Technical Report 33). Minneapolis: University of Minnesota, National Center on Educational Outcomes. Retrieved May 9, 2007, from http://education.umn.edu/NCEO/OnlinePubs/ Technical33.htm

Bolt, S. E., & Thurlow, M. L. (2004). Five of the most frequently allowed testing accommodations in state policy. *Remedial & Special Education, 25*(3), 141–152.

Bolt, S. E., & Thurlow, M. L. (2006). Item-level effects of the read-aloud accommodation for students with reading disabilities. (Synthesis Report 65). Minneapolis: University of Minnesota, National Center on Educational Outcomes. Retrieved May 9, 2009, from http://www.cehd.umn.edu/NCEO/OnlinePubs/ Synthesis65/Synthesis65.pdf

Bolt, S. E., & Ysseldyke, J. E. (2006). Comparing DIF across math and reading/language arts tests for students receiving a read-aloud accommodation. *Applied Measurement in Education, 19*(4), 329–355.

Bolt, S. E., & Ysseldyke, J. (2008). Accommodating students with disabilities in large-scale testing: A comparison of differential item functioning (DIF) identified across disability types. *Journal of Psychoeducational Assessment, 26*(2), 121–138.

Braden, J. P. (2002). Best practices for school psychologists in educational accountability: High stakes testing and educational reform. In A. Thomas & J. Grimes (Eds.), *Best practices in school psychology* (pp. 301–321). Bethesda, MD: National Association of School Psychologists.

Brennan, R. T., Kim, J., Wenz-Gross, M., & Siperstein, G. (2001). The relative equitability of high-stakes testing versus teacher-assigned grades: An analysis of the Massachusetts Comprehensive Assessment System (MCAS). *Harvard Educational Review, 7,* 173–216.

Chard, D. J. (1999). Case in point: Including students with disabilities in large-scale testing. *Journal of Special Education Leadership, 12,* 39–42.

Chiu, C. W. T., & Pearson, P. D. (1999). *Synthesizing the effects of test accommodations for special education and limited English proficient students*. Paper presented at the National Conference on Large Scale Assessment, June 13–16, Snowbird, UT.

Christensen, L. L., Lazarus, S. S., Crone, M. & Thurlow, M. L. (2008). *2007 state policies on assessment participation and accommodations for students with disabilities.* Minneapolis: University of Minnesota, National Center on Educational Outcomes. Retrieved June 1, 2009, from http://www.cehd.umn.edu/NCEO/ OnlinePubs/Synthesis69/ Synthesis69.pdf

Christenson, S. L., Decker, D. M., Triezenberg, H. L., Ysseldyke, J. E., & Reschly, A. (2007). Consequences of high-stakes assessment for students with and without disabilities. *Educational Policy, 21*(4), 662–690.

Clarke, M., Haney, W., & Madaus, G. (2000). High stakes testing and high school completion. *NBETPP Statements, 1*(3). Retrieved May 20, 2009, from http://www.bc.edu/research/nbetpp/publications/v1n3.html

Clarke, M., Shore, A., Rhoades, K., Abrams, L., Miao, J., & Li, J. (2003). *Perceived effects of state-mandated testing programs on teaching and learning: Findings from interviews with educators in low-, medium-, and high-stakes states.* Chestnut Hill, MA: Center for the Study of Testing, Evaluation, and Educational Policy, Boston College.

Cobb, B., & Johnson, D. R. (1997). The Statewide Systems Change Initiative as a federal policy mechanism for promoting education reform. *Career Development for Exceptional Individuals, 20*(2), 179–190.

Cohen, A. S., Gregg, N., & Deng, M. (2005). The role of extended time and item content on a high-stakes mathematics test. *Learning Disabilities Research & Practice, 20*(4), 225–233.

Cole, C. (2006). Closing the achievement gap series: Part III. What is the impact of NCLB on the inclusion of students with disabilities? *Center for Evaluation & Education Policy, Education Policy Brief, 4*(11), 1–12.

Cronbach, L. (1971). Test validation. In R. L. Thorndike (Ed.), *Educational measurement* (2nd ed., pp. 443–507). Washington, DC: American Council on Education.

Defur, S. H. (2002). Education reform, high-stakes assessment, and students with disabilities: One state's approach. *Remedial and Special Education, 23*(4), 203–211.

Disability Rights Advocates. (2001). *Do no harm—High stakes testing and students with learning disabilities.* Oakland, CA.

Dolan, R. P., Hall, T. E., Bannerjee, M., Chun, E., & Strangman, N. (2005). Applying principles of universal design to test design: The effect of computer-based read-aloud on test performance of high school students with learning disabilities. *The Journal of Technology, Learning, and Assessment, 3* (7). Retrieved July 1, 2009, from http://escholarship.bc.edu/jtla/

Elbaum, B. (2007). Effects of an oral testing accommodation on the mathematics performance of secondary students with and without learning disabilities. *The Journal of Special Education, 40*(4), 218–229.

Elliott, J., Erickson, R., Thurlow, M., & Shriner, J. (2000). State-level accountability for the performance of students with disabilities: Five years of change? *The Journal of Special Education, 34*(1), 39–47.

Elliot, S. N., McKevitt, B. C., & Kettler, R. J. (2002). Testing accommodations research and decision making: The case of "Good" scores being highly valued but difficult to achieve for all students. *Measurement and Evaluation, 35*, 153–166.

Federal Register, 2007, April 9 (Section 300.160(b)(2)).

Finch, H., Barton, K., & Meyer, P. (2009). Differential item functioning analysis for accommodated versus nonaccommodated students. *Educational Assessment, 14*, 38–56.

Fletcher, J. M., Francis, D. J., Boudousquie, A., Copeland, K., Young, V., Kalinowski, S., & Vaughn, S. (2006). Effects of accommodations on high-stakes testing for students with reading disabilities. *Exceptional Children, 72*(2), 136–150.

Fletcher, J. M., Francis, D. J., O'Malley, K., Copeland, K., Mehta, P., Caldwell, C. J., … Vaughn, S. (2009). Effects of a bundled accommodations package on high-stakes testing for middle school students with reading disabilities. *Exceptional Children, 75*(4), 447–463.

Frase-Blunt, M. (n.d.). High-stakes testing a mixed blessing for special education students. *Council for Exceptional Children.* Retrieved June 9, 2009, from http://www.cec.sped.org/AM/Template.cfm?Section=Home&TEMPLATE=/CM/ContentDisplay.cfm&CONTENTID=4533

Fuchs, L. S., & Fuchs, D. (2001). Helping teachers formulate sound test accommodation decisions for students with learning disabilities. *Learning Disabilities Research & Practice, 16,* 174-181.

Fuchs, L. S., Fuchs, D., Eaton, S. B., Hamlett, C. L., & Karns, K. M. (2000). Supplementing teacher judgments of mathematics test accommodations with objective data sources. *School Psychology Review, 29*(1), 65–85.

Glod, M. (2009, March 17). Law opens opportunities for disabled. *Washington Post*, p. B01.

Goertz, M., & Duffy, M. (2003). Mapping the landscape of high-stakes testing an accountability programs. *Theory Into Practice*, *42*(1), 4–11.

Government Accountability Office. (2005). *No Child Left Behind Act: Most Students with Disabilities Participated in Statewide Assessments, but Inclusion Options Could Be Improved* (GAO-05-618). Washington, DC: Author.

Heubert, J. P. (2002). Disability, race, and high-stakes testing for students. In G. Orfield, & D. Losen (Eds.), *Editions 2002. Minority issues in special education* (pp. 137–165). Cambridge, MA: Harvard Education Publishing Group.

Heubert, J. P., & Hauser, R. M. (Eds.). (1999). *High stakes: Testing for tracking, promotion, and graduation.* Washington, DC: National Research Council.

Higgins, J., Russell, M., & Hoffman, T. (2005). Examining the effect of computer-based passage presentation on reading test performance. *The Journal of Learning, Technology, and Assessment, 3*(4). Retrieved May 3, 2009, from http://escholarship.bc.edu/jtla/

Horkay, N., Bennett, R. E., Allen, N., Kaplan, B., & Yan, F. (2006). Does it matter if I take my writing test on computer? An empirical study of mode effects in NAEP. *Journal of Technology, Learning, and Assessment, 5* (2). Retrieved January 4, 2009, from http://www.jtla.org

Huynh, H., & Barton, K. E. (2006). Performance of students with disabilities under regular and oral administrations of a high-stakes reading examination. *Applied Measurement in Education, 19*(1), 21–39.

Individuals with Disabilities Education Act of 1997, 120 U.S.C. §1400 et seq.

Individuals with Disabilities Education Improvement Act of 2004, 20 U.S.C. §1400, H.R. 1350.

Johnson, D. R., & Thurlow, M. L. (2003). *A national study on graduation requirements and diploma options for youth with disabilities* (Technical Report 36). Minneapolis: University of Minnesota, National Center on Educational Outcomes. Retrieved March 22, 2007, from http://cehd.umn.edu/nceo/OnlinePubs/ Technical36.htm

Johnson, D. R., Thurlow, M. L., & Stout, K. E. (2007). Cross-state study of high-stakes testing practices and diploma options. *Journal of Special Education Leadership, 20*(2), 53–65.

Johnstone, C. J., Altman, J., Thurlow, M., & Thompson, S. J. (2006). *A summary of the research on the effects of tests accommodations: 2002 through 2004* (Technical Report 45). Minneapolis: University of Minnesota, National Center on Educational Outcomes.

Jones, M. G., Jones, B. D., & Hargrove, T. Y. (2003). *The unintended consequences of high-stakes testing.* Lanham, MD: Rowman and Littlefield.

Kane, M. (2006). Content-related validity evidence in test development. In S. M. Downing, & T. M. Haladyna (Eds.), *Handbook of test development* (pp. 131–154) Philadelphia, PA: Erlbaum.

Kim, D., Schneider, C., & Siskind, T. (2009). Examining equivalence of accommodations on a statewide elementary-level science test. *Applied Measurement in Education, 22*, 144–163.

Koenig, J. A. (Ed.). (2002). *Reporting test results for students with disabilities and English language learners: Summary of a workshop.* Washington, DC: National Research Council.

Lang, S. C., Elliott, S. N., Bolt, D. M., & Kratochwill, T. R. (2008). The effects of testing accommodations on students' performances and reactions to testing. *School Psychology Quarterly, 23*(1), 107–124.

Lesaux, N. K., Pearson, M. R., & Siegel, L. S. (2006). The effects of timed and untimed testing conditions on the reading comprehension performance of adults with reading disabilities. *Reading and Writing, 19*, 21–48.

Lewis, A. (2000, April). High-stakes testing: Trends and issues. *Mid-Continent Research for Education and Learning Policy Brief.* Retrieved May 11, 2009, from http://www.mcrel.org/PDF/PolicyBriefs/5993PI_PBHighStakesTesting.pdf#search=%22high-stakes%20testing%22

Lindstrom, J. H., & Gregg, N. (2007). The role of extended time on the SAT® for students with learning disabilities and/or attention-deficit/hyperactivity disorder. *Learning Disabilities Research & Practice, 22*(2), 85–95.

Mandinach, E. B., Bridgeman, B., Cahalan-Laitusis, C., & Trapani, C. (2005). The impact of extended time on SAT test performance. *Research Report No 2005-8.* New York, NY: The College Board.

Martin, M., Mullis, I., Gonzalez, E., Smith, T., & Kelly, D. (1999, June). *School contexts for learning and instruction: IEA's third international mathematics and science study (TIMSS).* Chestnut Hill, MA: International Association for the Evaluation of Educational Achievement, TIMSS International Study Center, Boston College.

McDonnell, L. M., McLaughlin, M. J., & Morrison, P. (Eds.). (1997). *Educating one and all: Students with disabilities and standards-based reform.* Washington, DC: National Academy Press.

Messick, S. (1989). Validity. In R. L. Linn (Ed.), *Educational measurement* (3rd ed., pp. 13–103). New York: Macmillan.

Meyen, E., Poggio, J., Seok, S., & Smith, S. (2006). Equity for students with high-incidence disabilities in statewide assessments: A technology-based solution. *Focus on Exceptional Children, 38*(7), 1–8.

National Commission on Excellence in Education (1983, April). *A nation at risk: The imperative of educational reform.* Washington. DC: U.S. Government Printing Office.

No Child Left Behind Act of 2001, Pub. L. No. 107-110, 115Stat. 1425 (2002).

Olson, J., Jones, I., & Bond, L. (2001). *Annual survey of state student assessment programs; Summary report and Vol. 1 & 2 (1998–1999) data.* Washington, DC: Council of Chief State School Officers (CCSSO).

Peterson, G. J., & Young, M. D. (2004). The No Child Left Behind Act and its influence on current and future district leaders. *Journal of Law & Education, 33*(3), 343–363.

Roderick, M., & Engel, M. (2001). The grasshopper and the ant: Motivational responses to low-achieving students to high-stakes testing. *Educational Evaluation and Policy Analysis, 23*(3), 197–227.

Salvia, J., Ysseldyke, J., & Bolt, S. (2010). *Assessment in special and inclusive education* (11th ed.). New York: Houghton-Mifflin.

Schnirman, R. K. (2005). The effect of audiocassette presentation on the performance of students with and without learning disabilities on a group standardized math test. *Dissertation Abstracts International, 66*(6), 2172A. Retrieved August 5, 2006, from http://proquest.umi.com/pqdweb?did=932376781&sid=3&Fmt=2&clientId=30345&RQT=309&VName=PQD

Shepard, L. A., Taylor, G. A., & Betebenner, D. (1998 September). *Inclusion of limited English proficient students in Rhode Island's grade 4 mathematics performance assessment. Center for the Study of Evaluation Technical Report No. 486.* Los Angeles: University of California at Los Angeles, National Center for Research on Evaluation, Standards, and Student Testing.

Sireci, S. G. (2005). Unlabeling the disabled: A perspective on flagging scores from accommodated test administrations. *Educational Researcher, 34*(1), 3–12.

Sireci, S., Li, S., & Scarpati, S. (2003). *The effects of test accommodation on test performance: A review of the literature.* (Center for Educational Assessment Research Report No. 485). Amherst: School of Education, University of Massachusetts.

Sireci, S. G., Scarpati, S. E., & Li, S. (2005). Test accommodations for students with disabilities: An analysis of the interaction hypothesis. *Review of Educational Research, 75*(4), 457–490.

Steeves, K. A., Hodgeson, J., & Peterson, P. (2002). Are we measuring student success with high-stakes testing? *Educational Forum, 66,* 228–235.

Sternberg, R. J. (2004). Good intentions, bad results: A dozen reasons why the No Child Left Behind (NCLB) Act is failing our nation's schools. *Education Week, 24*(9), 42, 56.

Stretch, L. S., & Osborne, J. W. (2005). Extended test time accommodations: Directions for future research and practice. *Practical Assessment, Research, and Evaluation, 10*(8). Retrieved August 5, 2006, from http://pareonline.net/pdf/v10n8.pdf.

Thompson, S., Blount, A., & Thurlow, M. (2002). *A summary of research on the effects of test accommodations: 1999 through 2001* (Technical Report 34). Minneapolis: University of Minnesota, National Center on Educational Outcomes. Retrieved May 4, 2007, from http://education.umn.edu/NCEO/OnlinePubs/Technical34.htm

Thurlow, M.L., Altman, J., Cormier, D. & Moen, R. (2008). *Annual performance report (APR): 2005–2006 State assessment data.* Minneapolis: University of Minnesota, National Center on Educational Outcomes. Retrieved February 19, 2009, from http://www.cehd.umn.edu/NCEO/OnlinePubs/APRreport2005-2006.pdf

Thurlow, M. L., & Johnson, D. R. (2000). High-stakes testing of students with disabilities. *Journal of Teacher Education, 51*(4), 305–314.

Thurlow, M. L., Thompson, S. J., & Lazarus, S. S. (2006). Considerations for the administration of tests to special needs students: Accommodations, modifications, and more. In S. M. Downing & T. M. Haladyna, (Ed.), *Handbook of test development* (pp. 653–673). Mahwah, NJ: Erlbaum.

Tindal, G. (2004). Large-scale testing of students with disabilities. *Exceptionality, 12*(2), 67–70.

Tindal, G., & Fuchs, L. (2000). *A summary of research on test changes: An empirical basis for defining accommodations.* Lexington: University of Kentucky, Mid-South Regional Resource Center Interdisciplinary Human Development Institute.

U.S. Department of Labor. (1991). *What work requires of schools: A SCANS report for America 2000.* Washington, DC: Author.

Weston, T. J. (2003). *NAEP Validity studies: The validity of oral accommodation testing.* Washington, DC: National Center for Education Statistics.

William T. Grant Foundation Commission on Work, Family, and Citizenship. (1988). *The forgotten half: Non-college youth in America.* Washington, DC: Author.

Willingham, W.W. (1976). *Validity and the Graduate Record Examinations program.* (Educational Testing Service Research Report No. GREB-76-01SR). Princeton, NJ: Educational Testing Service.

Yeh, S. (2008). High stakes testing and students with disabilities: Why federal policy needs to be changed. In Grigorenko, E. (Ed.) *Educating individuals with disabilities: IDEIA 2004 and beyond* (pp. 319–336). New York: Springer.

Ysseldyke, J. E., & Thurlow, M. L. (1994). *Educational outcomes for students with disabilities.* New York: Routledge.

Ysseldyke, J., Nelson, J. R., Christenson, S. L., Johnson, D. R., Dennison, A., Triezenberg, H., … Hawes, M. (2004). What we know and need to know about the consequences of high-stakes testing for students with disabilities. *Exceptional Children, 71*(1), 75–94.

Zenisky, A. L., & Sireci, S. G. (2007). *A summary of the research on the effects of test accommodations: 2005–2006* (Technical Report 47). Minneapolis: University of Minnesota, National Center on Educational Outcomes.

Zuriff, G. E. (2000). Extra examination time for students with learning disabilities: An examination of the maximum potential thesis. *Applied Measurement in Education, 13*(1), 99–117.

26
Academic Progress Monitoring

Sheri Berkeley
George Mason University

Paul J. Riccomini
The Pennsylvania State University

Mrs. Black is struggling with delivering instruction to two students in her inclusive math class. At the end of the first 9-week marking period, two students are falling behind the other students and seem to struggle in both problems solving ability and computational skills. Mrs. Black asks for a meeting with the special education teacher, Mr. Walker, to try to determine a course of action. During the meeting Mrs. Black describes both students as well behaved, but also points out that they do not do their homework and have little parental support at home. Additionally, she provides both students extra time for tests and allows them to use calculators. She reiterates that they are not making appropriate progress in the core math curriculum as demonstrated by the students' grades on the last four chapter tests which both students failed and the last 10 uncompleted homework assignments. Mr. Walker asks Mrs. Black if she has any other data to demonstrate their lack of progress and what instructional approaches have been used with the students. Mrs. Black is a bit confused as to what other data she would have and explains that she has attempted multiple strategies with the students that included motivational contracts for completing homework, parental contacts, after school homework sessions, reducing the number of homework problems, and extra time for tests. Mr. Walker suggests that the first step is to set up a progress monitoring system to monitor the students' performance in math. Mrs. Black isn't quite sure what that means, but is willing to work together with Mr. Walker to set up the system. (See Appendix for illustrative study involving Mrs, Black and Mr. Walker.)

Introduction

"In today's educational climate, school success is defined as ensuring achievement for every student" (Safer & Fleischman, 2005, p. 81). The most recent reauthorization of the Elementary and Secondary Education Act (ESEA), commonly referred to as No Child Left Behind (NCLB, 2001), mandates that schools must now demonstrate adequate yearly progress of all students or risk serious sanctions. To ensure that progress is indeed made by all students, schools are required to disaggregate student data from standardized tests for students traditionally most at-risk: students whose primary language is not English, students from minority backgrounds, students from low socio-economic status families, and students with disabilities. The most recent reauthorization of The Individuals with Disabilities Education Act (IDEA, 2004) also requires schools to show that students with disabilities are progressing at the same rate as their typically developing peers to the greatest extent possible. This accountability of academic progress of students with disabilities is relatively new. As Lindstrom mentioned in the previous chapter, historically, students with disabilities have not been included in high-stakes testing (Thurlow, Elliott, & Ysseldyke, 1998) and legislative mandates only required that students with disabilities have access to the general education curriculum.

In order for schools to ensure that students are on target to make the required annual yearly progress, their progress must be monitored on a regular basis. Progress monitoring is a tool that schools can use to monitor students' progress and make data-based instructional decisions. This chapter will define progress monitoring and provide (a) a rationale for the use of progress monitoring in the classroom, (b) an overview of the general progress monitoring process, (c) a review of research that supports the use of progress monitoring, and (d) a discussion about current applications.

What is Progress Monitoring?

Although, there is not necessarily one definition or set of procedures universally accepted to describe progress monitoring, it can be described broadly as a systematic set of assessment procedures used to determine if students are benefiting from the instructional program which includes both the classroom instruction and curriculum (Johnson, Mellard, Fuchs, & McKnight, 2006). Two common methods used by teachers to monitor students' progress are Curriculum-Based Assessment (CBA) and Curriculum-Based Measurement (CBM).

CBA, sometime referred to as mastery measurement, is a more generic term which refers to a broader range of assessment activities created directly from the instructional program in which the students is learning (Hosp & Hosp, 2003). CBA measures may include teacher-made tests that sample a selected curriculum domain (Hall & Mengel, 2002), such as basic multiplication facts or reading CVC words. The overall purpose of CBA is to determine the extent to which students are learning what is being taught.

Although related, CBM is a measurement tool with standardized procedures for administration, scoring and interpretation (Hosp, Hosp, & Howell, 2007; Stecker, n.d.). Unlike a CBA, a CBM assesses a broad sampling of skills taught over an entire school year so that progress can be documented. Research findings suggest that CBM is the best method for teachers to use for progress monitoring purposes (National Research Council on Learning Disabilities, 2007); therefore, this will be the focus of the chapter.

How Can CBM be Used in Schools?

CBM can be completed at various levels including the district-level, school-level, grade-level, classroom-level, or individual student-level depending on the purpose and scale of implementation (Lembke & Stecker, 2007). CBM can be used in a wide range of academic areas including reading, spelling, writing, and math. Measures have been developed in these core academic areas because they are thought to be the most essential skills students need to develop in school. These are also areas in which lower achieving students, including special education students, are likely to be much weaker than other students. CBM data can be gathered both for universal screening purposes as well as ongoing progress monitoring. Universal screening data is generally gathered three to four times per year to screen all students in a school, grade, or class and is used to determine the effects of instruction on student performance (Lembke & Stecker, 2007). From this initial screening, students at-risk for academic difficulties, including students with disabilities, are identified for further more frequent progress monitoring.

Why Should Teachers Use CBM?

There are a wide range of benefits that result from teachers' use of CBM in the classroom. The National Center on Progress Monitoring (www.studentprogress.org) has cited numerous examples, including: (a) accelerated learning because students are receiving more appropriate instruction, (b) more informed instructional decisions,(c) documentation of student progress for accountability purposes, (d) more efficient communication with families and other professionals about students' progress, (e) higher expectations for students by teachers, and (f) fewer special education referrals (see Deno, 2003; Hosp et al., 2007; Stecker, Fuchs, & Fuchs, 2005).

Implementing CBM

Although procedures can vary, there are generally six basic steps used for progress monitoring using CBM: (a) create or select appropriate measures (called probes); (b) administer and score the probes; (c) graph the scores; (d) set goals; (e) make instructional decision; and (f) communicate progress (IRIS Center for Training Enhancements, n.d.).

Selecting Appropriate Measures

The initial step in progress monitoring using CBM is to determine measures to utilize to assess student performance. Generally, basic skills (reading, math, and writing) are the most common academic areas monitored (Hosp & Hosp, 2003). Although teachers can develop their own CBMs following standard procedures (see Shinn, 1989), there are also measures commercially available. After deciding which academic area to monitor, teachers should review the CBMs available and evaluate three characteristics: (a) predictive validity, (b) reliability, and (c) efficiency of administration (Gersten et al., 2009; Johnson et al., 2006).

The predictive validity of a measure indicates how well a score projects later performance. The CBM selected should have a predictive validity coefficient of at least .60 (Gersten et al., 2009). Clearly, a higher predictive validity allows for much more confidence in instructional decisions. An assessment's reliability is an indication of the consistency and accuracy of the measure. Here a reliability coefficient of at least .80 is recommended (Gersten et al., 2009). The National Center on Response to Intervention (www.rti4success.org) provides a list of progress monitoring measures in the *Progress Monitoring Tools Chart* for a variety of academic areas and includes information related to these measures of technical adequacy.

Another especially important characteristic to consider is the efficiency of administration. The CBM selected should be brief and simple to administer. There is no absolute guideline for duration of CBMs, but most measures should not take longer than 10–15 minutes per student to administer. In fact, there are reliable and valid measures available that take as little as 5 minutes. The length of administration is important because measures that require more time to administer use valuable instructional time. This consideration is especially important in the area of reading where CBMs often require one-to-one administration. Measures that are efficient while maintaining high levels of reliability and validity are preferred over measures that have a longer administration time (Gersten et al., 2009).

Once the measures have been selected, the next decision is to determine the appropriate grade level and/or skill level for the student(s) being progress monitored. Deciding between grade level and skill level to monitor depends on a variety of factors including the student's grade level and/or deficit level. For students in elementary grades, grade level measures that target specific skills are generally used. For older students and even younger students that may be significantly behind their grade level peers, progress monitoring is generally determined by their end-of-year goals. For example, if a ninth-grade student is reading at a third-grade level, the student may have a end-of-year goal of reading at the fourth-grade level and therefore will be progress monitored using fourth-grade level measures. The student's specific skill deficit may also dictate the CBMs used. For example, a fourth-grade student may have a deficit area in basic computation, but not problem solving. In this instance, the student could be progress monitored using only computational measures and not an application type measure. Developers of CBMs include guidance and recommendations for determining which grade level measures to use to begin the progress monitoring process.

Administration and Scoring Procedures

Different CBMs contain their own specified set of administration and scoring procedures; however, there are specific core principles of progress monitoring common to all measures. First, CBMs must be administered frequently enough to gauge a student's rate of progress. CBM probes are generally implemented at consistent intervals ranging from as little as monthly to as many times as twice weekly. The frequency of progress monitoring depends on the students' academic progress. It is generally recommended that students at greatest risk for failure and students with special needs are progress monitored more frequently, as many as one to two times per week (Hosp & Hosp, 2003).

The administration, directions, and scoring are standard for each assessment and consistent across the year (Deno, 2003; Hosp et al., 2007). By following the standardized directions and scoring procedures, scores can be used to compare students across classrooms and even across schools. Teachers should not under any circumstances change the administration procedures, directions, and/or the time allocations of the assessments unless it is an allowable change approved by the publisher of the assessment. Changing any of the standard administration procedures, especially the timing allotments, will result in a score that is not comparable to the norms, benchmarks, and/or rates of progress included with the measures. Carefully following the specified administration and scoring procedures of the measures being used ensures scores are reliable and valid and therefore appropriate for instructional decision making.

To ensure measures are managed as intended, all teachers administering the measures should be properly trained (Johnson et al., 2006). Most CBMs are simple to use, designed specifically for teachers, and do not require intensive and long training sessions. Most developers of CBMs include manuals with specific directions as well as online resources to demonstrate how to properly administer their assessments. As with any new technique, practice is an important aspect of becoming comfortable and accurate with the administrations of CBMs and is, of course, recommended.

Graphing Data

Graphically displaying student CBM data is an essential step in the use of the data for decision making purposes. A picture is worth a thousand words; this old adage certainly holds true for teachers, parents, and children when inspecting a graph of progress monitoring data. Although many of the new CBMs available contain data management systems that quickly and easily create any number of graphical displays, some teachers may need to graph by hand. Graphing by hand is a bit more time consuming and results in less sophisticated graphs compared to the numerous options available through data management systems, but nonetheless, it is just as effective for making instructional decisions.

There are four steps to setting up a graph for CBM data. First, the chart is labeled with the student's name to reduce the chances of mixing up student graphs. Second, the vertical axis is assigned to represent the unit of analysis for the measures. For example, the unit of analysis for mathematics computation would likely be the number of correct digits per minute, and for reading fluency, the unit of analysis would likely be words correctly read per minute. Third, the horizontal axis is assigned to represent the number of probes or dates in which the student is assessed. Fourth, the graph is given a title such as *Tyler's Math Computation*. Labeling the graph helps prevent confusion for students who are being progress monitored in more than one academic area. After the graph for progress monitoring is set up, the student's baseline, or current level of performance, is established.

Although a variety of techniques can be used to establish baseline, there are three universal steps. First, three to four probes are administered and scored in a short period of time (i.e., 1–2 days). The purpose of establishing the baseline is to determine the current level of performance, and not monitor progress across time. All baseline points are plotted on a graph and the median data point is used to determine the current level of performance. There are different ways to determine the current level of performance other than using the median point, but this is a simple and efficient method. The median data point becomes the current level of performance and is indicated on the graph with an X somewhere between the third and fourth data point. The current level of performance is used in the setting of the goal.

Setting Goals and Plotting Student Performance

An important aspect of CBM is the ability to indicate on a graphic display a student's expected level of performance and use of a goal-line to monitor progress towards an end-of-year goal. Expected end-of-year performance is the student's initial goal; this goal and starts from the current level of performance determined from the baseline data (i.e., median). The first step in calculating the end-of-year performance goal is to determine the expected rate of progress. An important part of setting goals is to use a higher than normal expected rate of progress because students being progress monitored are often far behind their grade-level peers. By using a higher than normal expected rate of progress, also called an ambitious growth rate (Hosp & Hosp, 2003), students have a better chance of closing the gap between them and their grade-level peers. If ambitious rates of growth are not used, students may never close the gap. For example, an improvement of 2 words read correctly (WRC) per week is an ambitious goal (see Hosp & Hosp, 2003) for a second-grade student currently reading 15 WRC (i.e., baseline). This would mean the end of year goal for this student would be 75 WRC: $15 + (30 \times 2) = 75$.

Another common method used to set goals is the use of a universal benchmark. A universal benchmark differs from growth rates in the sense that a benchmark is established through careful analysis to determine a minimum score on a certain measure that is indicative of students who are on track to meet or exceed future benchmarks. For example, DIBELS (http://uoregon.edu) contains benchmarks for reading from grades K through sixth (see Table 26.1). The DIBELS benchmarks were established by following a large group of students in a longitudinal manner to see where students who were "readers" in later grades were performing on these critical early literacy skills when they were in kindergarten and first grade so that predictions could be made about which students are progressing adequately and which students may need additional instructional support.

According to the DIBELS benchmark goals, the oral reading fluency benchmark for second-grade students is 90 WCR per minute by the end of the year. For example, if Tyler's oral reading fluency was 15 WCR per minute at the beginning of the year, using the DIBELS universal benchmark to set a goal, Tyler's goal for the end of the year would be 90 WCR per minute. Regardless of method for setting a goal, the main purpose of using a goal to predict student performance is to make informed decisions regarding students' progress in an effort to catch-up students that are often significantly behind their peers (Stecker et al., 2005).

Instructional Decision Making

The overarching purpose of monitoring progress is to provide teachers with instructionally relevant data to facilitate more appropriate and effective instructional decisions. Since CBM is simply an assessment, improved student learning can only occur if appropriate instructional decisions are made based on the results of the student data (Stecker et al., 2005). If teachers only collect and analyze CBM data, but make no meaningful instructional decisions, progress monitoring is of little value. Within the procedures of CBM, there are two main instructional decisions to consider: (a) make an instructional change, and (b) raise the goal. Although basic in theory, these two decisions are the essential cornerstones of CBM.

Generally, students targeted for progress monitoring are behind typically performing peers and as a result will have a current level of performance that is significantly lower than other students. Because CBM procedures for calculating an end-of-year goal are based in part on the current level of performance, an expectation that all students will progress at a similar rate will result in an end-of-year goal for targeted students that is much lower than the end-of year goal for students who had a higher initial level of performance. Therefore, the decision to raise the goal for students making appropriate progress is crucial to helping close the achievement gap.

TABLE 26.1
DIBELS Universal Benchmarks for Oral Reading Fluency Grades 1–6

Grade	DIBELS Universal Benchmark
	Oral Reading Fluency (Words Read Correctly in 1 Minute)
1	40
2	90
3	110
4	118
5	124
6	125

Source: Adapted from the DIBELS Benchmark Goals. Three Assessment Periods Per Year. (July 31, 2008). University of Oregon Center on Teaching and Learning. Retrieved June 1, 2009 from https://dibels.uoregon.edu/docs/benchmarkgoals.pdf

For students who are not making adequate progress, the instructional change made by the teacher is most crucial. Instructional changes that teachers make when students are not making progress are an important issue in education. Legislation requiring "scientifically-validated" and "evidenced-based" instruction and interventions has made this decision quite formidable for some teachers. The specific instructional decisions that can be made are not within the scope of this chapter; however, there are a few general guidelines to consider when contemplating instructional changes for struggling students: (a) increase instructional time, (b) increase practice time, (c) smaller teacher to student ratios for instructional grouping, (d) instruction that is more systematic and explicit in nature, (e) more opportunities for guided or scaffolded practice, and (f) increase opportunities for responding (Bost & Riccomini, 2006; Johnson et al., 2006: Riccomini & Witzel, 2010).

The two preferred methods for determining whether an instructional change is needed or if a student's goal needs to be raised are the "4-point rule" or a trend-line. The 4-point rule requires a teacher to have collected at least six data points across 3 weeks of instruction. Once the data is plotted, a visual inspection of the four most recent data points is completed. If all four data points are below the goal-line, the teacher should consider an instructional change. If all data points are above the goal-line, the teacher should increase the student's goal. If some of the data points are above and below the goal-line, the teacher should keep collecting data until one of the first two considerations apply or use a trend-line to determine the decision.

The trend-line can be calculated using several different methods and easily using basic graphing software, so we will not cover the specific steps in calculating a trend-line, but rather, how a student's progress is compared against a trend-line. In order to calculate a trend-line, eight data points collected across at least 4 weeks of instruction is needed. Basically, a trend-line is a line of "best fit" in terms of showing the trajectory of the student's performance. Although a student's data may be variable (higher one day than the next day), a trend-line provides a clear picture of the overall trajectory in relationship to a student's goal-line. If a student's trend-line is steeper than the goal-line, that student's performance is described as "on-track" to meet and/or exceed the goal. In this case the decision is to raise the goal. If a student's trend-line is less steep than the goal-line, that student's performance is described as "not on-track" to meet and/or exceed the goal and an instructional change is needed. Regardless of the method used to analyze the data (4-point rule or trend-line) the resulting decisions are the same: (a) make an instructional change, or (b) raise the goal.

Communicating Student Progress

There are many benefits for teachers who progress monitor their students' learning; however, one major benefit is the ability to communicate with the various stakeholders involved with the instructional process. The individuals involved in a child's instructional process include, but are not limited to, parents, regular and special education teachers, interventionists, school psychologists, and other specialists. Because CBM data involves the careful tracking of an individual's learning in relationship to specific annual goal(s), the data is meaningful, easy to understand, and useful to all stakeholders.

Research on CBM

Over the past 25 years, a substantial body of research has demonstrated that CBM can be used effectively to gather student performance data to support a wide range of educational decisions (Deno, 2003; Stecker et al., 2005). These educational decisions include: (a) developing norms and screening to identify struggling students (e.g., Marston & Magnusson, 1988; Shinn, 2002); (b) evaluating pre-referral interventions (e.g., Tindal, 1992); (c) determining eligibility for and placement in special education programs (e.g., Fuchs, Fuchs, & Speece, 2002); (d) formatively evaluating instruction (e.g., Fuchs, Deno, & Mirkin, 1984; Fuchs, Fuchs, Hamlett, Phillips, & Bentz, 1994) and making instructional changes (e.g., Fuchs, Fuchs, Hamlett, & Stecker, 1991; Fuchs, Fuchs, & Hamlett, 1993); and (e) evaluating inclusion programs (e.g., Fuchs, Fernstrom, Reeder, Bowers, & Gilman, 1992; Fuchs, Roberts, Fuchs, & Bowers, 1998).

Early research (e.g., Fuchs et al., 1984) showed that when instruction is modified based on CBM data, student outcomes improve; however, teachers do not always make such teaching modifications even after accurately collecting CBM data (Stecker et al., 2005). In addition, some teachers indicated that they would choose not to use CBM due to time constraints (Wesson, King, & Deno, 1984). Advances in data management through technology applications have potential to mediate this concern.

Stecker et al. (2005) recently conducted a review of group design studies with students with mild to moderate disabilities to identify factors that affect the efficacy and feasibility for using CBM to promote student achievement. Consistent with earlier research findings, results indicated that CBM is not a powerful instructional tool *unless* this data is used to modify instruction. Additional factors identified in the reviewed research that appear to affect student growth include (a) raising goals when teachers underestimate student performance, and (b) using data management software to assist with graphing and data analysis. CBM is currently primarily utilized to monitor student progress in the areas of reading, writing (including spelling), and mathematics. A description of common assessments in each of these areas follows.

Reading

The most common CBM in reading is a one minute assessment of student oral reading fluency (ORF). This assessment is administered individually and requires the student to read a leveled passage aloud for one minute while the teacher notes any errors. Errors are then subtracted from the total number of words read in a minute resulting in the correct words per minute (CWPM). Although this measure directly assesses reading fluency (a student's ability to read accurately and at an appropriate rate), it is also a good indicator of overall reading proficiency (Stecker et al., 2005; Madelaine & Wheldall, 1999). A study by Deno, Mirkin, and Chiang (1982) found high correlations between reading aloud measures and standardized reading tests. Further, research (Deno et al., 1982; Jenkins & Jewell, 1993) has demonstrated this CBM to be both reliable and valid. ORF measures are widely used at the elementary school level; however, due to the structure and class sizes at middle and secondary schools, individualized assessments may be less feasible on an ongoing basis.

Another CBM that is commonly administered in the area of reading is the Maze. This CBM is intended to measure reading comprehension. Students read a passage for 2.5 minutes; every seventh word is deleted and students must select one of three words to replace the missing word (Hosp & Hosp, 2003). Although this measure is also a commonly used CBM, research (e.g., Deno et al., 1982; Fuchs, Fuchs, & Maxwell, 1988) has shown that this measure is not as strongly correlated to general reading ability as the ORF measure (Madelaine & Wheldall, 1999). None the less, because it can be administered as a group assessment, this CBM may be more feasible for the secondary level.

Mathematics

Progress monitoring in mathematics using CBM is generally executed in the areas of computation and/or application (i.e., problem solving). The majority of research on CBM in mathematics is conducted at the elementary level (Calhoon, 2008) and most focused on computation (Christ, Scullin, Tolbize, & Jiban, 2008). Depending on the grade level and type of measure, administration of a math CBM takes as little as 1 to 8 minutes and can be administered individually or in a group setting even with students at varying levels (Hosp et al., 2007; Kelley, Hosp, & Howell, 2008). The scoring of math CBM is generally completed using correct digits (Fuchs & Fuchs, n.d.; Hosp et al., 2007), and is very different than scoring the answer as right or wrong. A math CBM assesses mathematical fluency (a student's ability to accurately complete math problems at an appropriate rate). Math CBMs are good indicators of success on end-of-year assessments of mathematical proficiency (McKlane, n.d.), although not as well established as oral reading fluency for predictions (Christ et al., 2008).

The most commonly utilized math CBM in this area computational proficiency (Hosp et al., 2007; Riccomini & Wetzel, 2010). Students are asked to complete a series of computation only problems (approximately 20–30) covering a variety of problem types (e.g., 1/5 + 3/5, 15 × 26, 9 × 8, 135 + 257 + 345) appropriate for the students' grade level. Students complete as many problems as possible in the allotted time. Although this measure is probably the most established math CBM, it has some limitations (Christ et al., 2008; Gersten et al., 2009). The last category of math CBM is concepts and applications (i.e., problem solving). This math CBM is designed to monitor problem solving proficiency and includes concepts such as estimation, measurement, time, graph interpretation and other non-computational concepts (Hosp et al., 2007). The questions on concept and application measures are often in the form of word problems or charts and tables for students to use to answer corresponding questions. Mathematical proficiency is defined as including problem solving and application proficiency as well as computational and procedural accuracy (National Mathematics Advisory Panel, 2008), therefore, teachers should consider matching the math CBM used for progress monitoring to the specific individual goals of the student and may use both measures for some students (Riccomini & Witzel, 2010).

Writing & Spelling

CBM data is gathered through writing prompts, or story starters, that are administered to students, who are then asked to write about the prompt for 3 to 5minutes. Methods of scoring these CBM probes include: (a) total words written, (b) words spelled correctly, (c) correct word sequences, (d) correct – incorrect word sequences, and (e) analytic scales for written expression (see Hosp & Hosp, 2003). Regardless of the scoring method used, consistency should be used over time. For example, you would not graph a student's total words written from week 1 and correct word sequences from week 8 on the same graph and then make an inference about student growth or lack thereof.

Spelling progress can also be specifically monitored using CBM. Words randomly sampled from the entire year's curriculum would be dictated to students, individually or in a group, who would be given 10 seconds to write each dictated word. The assessment would be scored using the number of correct letter sequences.

Current Applications of Progress Monitoring

Applications of progress monitoring data have changed over time. Recent research has begun to investigate the effectiveness of CBM for early literacy (e.g., Kaminski & Good, 1998) and numeracy (e.g., Fuchs, Fuchs, Compton, Hamlett, & Seethaler, 2007; Lembke, Foegen, Whittaker, & Hampton, 2008) and secondary content area instruction (e.g., Espin, Scierka, Skare, & Halvorson, 1999; Espin, Shinn, & Busch, 2005; Espin & Tindal, 1998) including advanced math areas like algebra and geometry (Foegen, Olson, & Impecoven-Lind, 2008). More research is needed regarding the efficacy of these measures (Deno, 2003).

In addition, technology is now available on a wide scale to assist teachers in the collection, scoring, and graphing of CBM data (see Table 26.2). Research on the use of technology is proving to be promising in the enhancement of implementation and instructional decision making (e.g., Stecker et al., 2005; Fuchs, Fuchs, & Hamlett, 2005). Advances in technology have also enabled CBMs to be administered on a larger scale, which has created implications for the progress monitoring of all students and even the identification of students with specific learning disabilities, a process commonly called response to intervention (RTI). Different RTI models have slightly varying procedures and protocols; however, inherent in all RTI models is frequent progress monitoring of students, including universal screening of *all* students, which is intended to drive instructional decisions (Berkeley, Bender, Peaster, & Saunders, 2009). For more information on progress monitoring with CBM, refer to the list of resources in Table 26.3.

TABLE 26.2
Progress Monitoring and Data Management Resources

Resource	Description
AIMSweb (www.aimsweb.com)	AIMSweb is a progress monitoring system based on direct, frequent and continuous student assessment in the areas of reading, mathematics, spelling, and written expression. The results are reported to students, parents, teachers and administrators via a web-based data management and reporting system to determine response to intervention.
DIBELS (https://dibels.uoregon.edu/)	The DIBELS measures were specifically designed to assess 3 of the 5 Big Ideas of early literacy: Phonological Awareness, Alphabetic Principle, and Fluency with Connected Text. The measures are linked to one another, both psychometrically and theoretically, and have been found to be predictive of later reading proficiency.
Edcheckup (www.edcheckup.com)	Edcheckup™ offers a progress monitoring system for students in grades K-8 that evaluates student performance and measures student progress toward goals in reading, writing, and math. These generic assessments, which are independent from any particular curriculum, may also be used to evaluate the effectiveness of instruction through the graphing of student data.
McGraw-Hill (www.yearlyprogresspro.com/)	Yearly Progress Pro is a research-based assessment, instructional, and intervention tool that: gives teacher and administrators specific frequent feedback on student progress, provides instant, automatic, on-the-spot intervention, and ensures instruction is aligned to national and state standards.
CBM Warehouse (www.interventioncentral.org)	CBM Warehouse is a free resource part of Intervention Central. A free resource offers free tools and resources to help school staff and parents to promote positive classroom behaviors and foster effective learning for all children and youth. Visit to check out newly posted academic and behavioral intervention strategies, download publications on effective teaching practices, and use tools that streamline classroom assessment and intervention.

TABLE 26.3
Resources for More Information on Progress Monitoring

Organization	Web Address
National Center on Progress Monitoring	www.studentprogress.org
Research Institute on Progress Monitoring	www.progressmonitoring.org
National Research Center on Learning Disabilities	www.nrcld.org
Division for Learning Disabilities of the Council for Exceptional Children	www.teachingld.org
National Center on Response to Intervention	www.rti4success.org/
Intervention Central	www.interventioncentral.org
Center on Instruction	www.centeroninstruction.org
The IRIS Center for Training Enhancements	iris.peabody.vanderbilt.edu
The Access Center: Improving Outcomes for All Students K-8	www.k8accesscenter.org
Center on Positive Behavioral Interventions and Supports (PBIS)	www.pbis.org

Appendix: Progress Monitoring Case Study

Selecting Appropriate Progress Monitoring Measures

Mr. Walker is confident that if he is able to provide more instructionally relevant information about the two struggling students to Mrs. Black, she will make instructional changes that will improve their learning. Based on what Mrs. Black explained, it appears that the students, Jenna and Tyler, have very different problems. Jenna is falling behind with problem solving and concept application tasks, while Tyler is having problems with computational tasks. Based on this information, Mr. Walker decides to find progress monitoring measures in both areas. He remembers a recent professional development workshop that focused on progress monitoring and discussed useful resources. After going back over his notes and visiting the resources, he decided to use the Monitoring Basic Skills Progress (MBSP) Basic Math Computations (see Figure 26A.1) and the Concepts and Application (see Figure 26A.2) measures for Tyler and Jenna, respectively. He decides to use these measures because both were rated very highly for reliability and validity from the National Center on Response to Intervention. After reviewing all materials, he sets up a time to meet with Mrs. Black to develop a plan for administering the measures.

During the meeting, Mr. Walker shows and explains the measures that he would like Mrs. Black to use for progress monitoring. Mrs. Black's first question is how the progress monitoring measures align with what she is teaching because students are responsible for that math content on the end-of-year state assessment. Mr. Walker explains that the measures were designed to be a global indicator of student math performance and not designed specifically for their state assessments. He points out that although these measures

Name: ________________ Date: __________

A	B	C	D	E
$\frac{3}{5} - \frac{1}{3} =$	2.66×5.4	$5\frac{3}{5} - 3\frac{4}{5} =$	$15961 + 92307$	$23281 - 16754$
F	**G**	**H**	**I**	**J**
$2.591 + 7.6588$	$65983 + 56937$	$.13\overline{)884}$	$122\overline{)8614}$	$3 \times \frac{1}{2} =$
K	**L**	**M**	**N**	**O**
5952×246	$7\frac{4}{7} + 1\frac{2}{3} =$	$45\overline{)65}$	$3\frac{1}{3} + 8\frac{2}{3} =$	$3.4423 - 1.33$

Figure 26A.1 Example computational measure for Tyler.
Figure adapted from Fernstrom, P., & Powell, S. (2007). *Introduction to using curriculum-based measurement for progress monitoring in math.* Presentation made at the 2007 Summer Institute on Student Progress Monitoring. Retrieved October 2007 from www.studentprogress.org

Name ________________ Date __________ Test 4 Page 1

Column A — Applications 5 — Column B

(1)

Area of rectangle = length x width

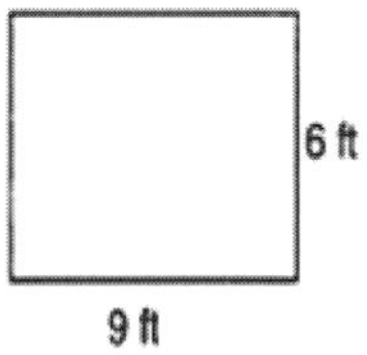

6 ft

9 ft

Area = _______ sq. ft

(2)

Round to the nearest thousand:

65,721 _______

(3) Write a letter in each blank

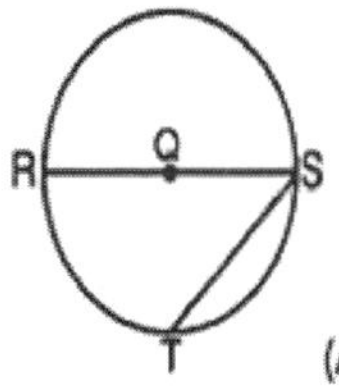

R Q S T

____ center

____ diameter

(A) point Q

(B) segment QS

(C) segment RS

(D) segment ST

(5)

Find the average of these numbers.

5, 13, 3, 8, 6

Arithmetic mean = ______

(6)

Write the letter **P** next to prime numbers and the letter **N** next to numbers that are not prime.

____ 7 ____ 10

(7)

Gum is priced 4 packs for \$1.00. Bill bought 1 pack. He gave the clerk a \$5.00 bill and received change in the least number of bills and coins. How many of each were there? (If none, write the number zero.)

____ \$5 bills ____ \$1 bills ____ quarters

(8) Look at this number.

Figure 26A.2 Example concepts and application measure for Jenna.
Figure adapted from Fernstrom, P., & Powell, S. (2007). *Introduction to using curriculum-based measurement for progress monitoring in math.* Presentation made at the 2007 Summer Institute on Student Progress Monitoring. Retrieved October 2007 from www.studentprogress.org

were not designed specifically for their state's end-of-year test, the math concepts covered, both the computation and problem solving, are closely aligned with their states standards. The measures are not designed to cover every math concept, but rather include a representative sampling of the math curriculum across the entire year. Additionally, he points out that researchers have demonstrated that these measures are very good predictors of success on end-of-year assessments. In other words, students who are making adequate improvements on the CBM math measures across the course of the year, have a better probability of doing well on the end-of-year assessments. Mr. Walker also notes that the same is true for reading.

Mrs. Black also notices that some of the problem types on both the computational and application measures have not yet been taught. She expresses concern about testing students on math concepts that she has not yet taught and that students may become frustrated having to solve problems they haven't learned yet. Again, Mr. Walker explains that these measures are very different than chapter and/or unit tests which generally test what has just been taught. Because we are evaluating progress across the entire year, there may indeed be some problem types on the measures that the students have not learned and that it is acceptable because as she delivers instruction throughout the course of the year, we would hope to see students begin to solve more problems correctly as they receive instruction. As far as students being frustrated, he explains that is certainly a possibility, but the directions for the measures provided to the students make very clear that it's okay if there is a problem they do not know how to do and to try their best. It actually tells them to skip it. Mrs. Black seems comfortable with the measures Mr. Walker selected, and her questions quickly turn to how to administer and score the measures.

Administration and Scoring Procedures

Mr. Walker knows that for Mrs. Black's initial attempt at progress monitoring to be successful, he needs to develop a routine that is organized, efficient, and gets the data into her hands quickly. Prior to the meeting with Mrs. Black, he makes packets for Jenna and Tyler using three-ringed binders. Each packet contains four items: (a) administration directions, (b) all necessary student measures, (c) teacher's key and scoring directions, and (d) stopwatch and clipboard. He also brought a calendar for each student to schedule the dates and times that Mrs. Black will administer the progress monitoring measures.

Mrs. Black is very concerned with how progress monitoring will affect her instructional time. As Mr. Walker explains the administration directions, Mrs. Black is very relieved to learn that the administration will only take approximately 3 minutes for Tyler and 6 minutes for Jenna. She is also very appreciative of the organizational system that Mr. Walker has prepared for her, especially the quick reference to the administration directions and scoring guidelines. She notes the directions are straightforward and simple enough. She sees that in the directions students are directed to do all problems that they can do and skip ones that they do not know how to do.

They then begin to discuss an assessment schedule; Mr. Walker would like both students to be progress monitored two times per week. They decided the best days to assess are Tuesdays and Thursdays during the last 10 minutes of class. They complete the assessment calendar for each student for 6 weeks. She will begin to collect the baseline immediately. Mr. Walker suggests that the baseline assessments of 3 probes be collected in 1 or 2 days to establish current performance levels.

Mrs. Black is most interested in how the measures are scored. She has heard the phrase "correct digits" but isn't sure

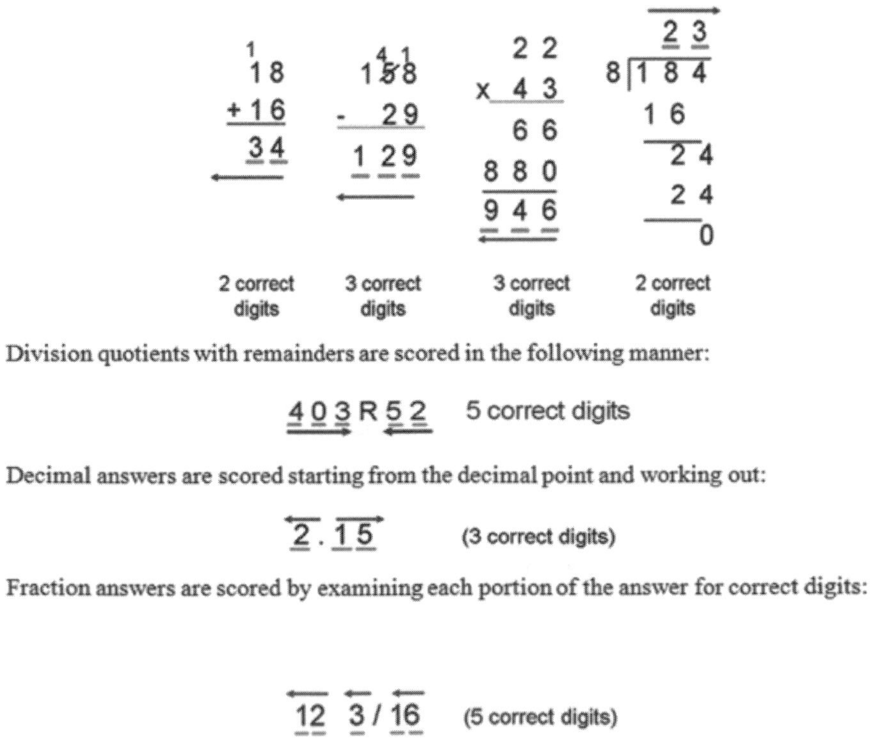

18 + 16 = 34	158 − 29 = 129	22 × 43 = 66 + 880 = 946	184 ÷ 8 = 23
2 correct digits	3 correct digits	3 correct digits	2 correct digits

Division quotients with remainders are scored in the following manner:

403 R 52 5 correct digits

Decimal answers are scored starting from the decimal point and working out:

2.15 (3 correct digits)

Fraction answers are scored by examining each portion of the answer for correct digits:

12 3/16 (5 correct digits)

Figure 26A.3 Example computation answers scored using correct digits.
Note: There are variations to the scoring examples presented here. It is important to become familiar with and follow the scoring guidelines specified for the Progress Monitoring Measures that you have selected.
Figure adapted from Fernstrom, P., & Powell, S. (2007). *Introduction to using curriculum-based measurement for progress monitoring in math.* Presentation made at the 2007 Summer Institute on Student Progress Monitoring. Retrieved October 2007 from www.studentprogress.org

what that means. Following the manual that accompanied the measures, Mr. Walker explains the general rule for scoring is "a correct numeral in the correct place is scored as a correct digit" (see Figure 26A.3). In other words, students will receive one point for every correct digit in the answer. This applies for all answers on the computation measures; however, there is a choice on the Concept and Application subtest to use either correct digits or correct blanks regardless of the number of digits. They decide that scoring using correct blanks is the simplest way to score the Concepts and Applications subtest. Mrs. Black asks why there is a choice for scoring the Concept and Applications measures using blanks or correct digits. Mr. Walker says he isn't sure, but since they are following the administration manual directions, they are following standard procedures. They decide that after Mrs. Black administers the three baseline measures, that they will score them together to make sure they are following the scoring guidelines.

Now that they have an administration schedule, an organizational system, and have reviewed the administration and scoring guidelines, Mrs. Black begins to collect progress monitoring data on Jenna and Tyler.

Setting Goal and Plotting Student Performance

Mrs. Black has collected and scored three measures each for Jenna and Tyler. She will then use these initial scores to calculate the current level of performance and the initial end-of-year goal for Jenna and Tyler. On the three initial measures of concepts and applications, Jenna scored, 22, 27, and 25 correct digits, and Tyler scored 25, 28, and 25 correct digits on his measures of computation. Mrs. Black calculates Jenna's current level of performance at 25 correct digits (22+27+25)/3 = 25, and Tyler's current level of performance at (25+28+25)/3 = 26. Now that she has established each student's current level of performance, she will use growth rates to calculate their initial end-of-year goal. Using the growth rates from a chart Mr. Walker provided, she uses an ambitious growth rate of 2 correct digits per week for both Jenna and Tyler. She uses the following formula to calculate the end-of-year goal for each student:

Current performance + (# of weeks X growth rate) = end-of-year goal

Jenna's Goal: 25 + (27 × 2) = 79 correct digits

Tyler's Goal: 26 + (27 × 2) = 80 correct digits

She displays the students' math performance using a graphic display (see Figure 26A.4). To get a better picture of Jenna and Tyler's performance in relationship to other students in the class, she selected two other students that she believes

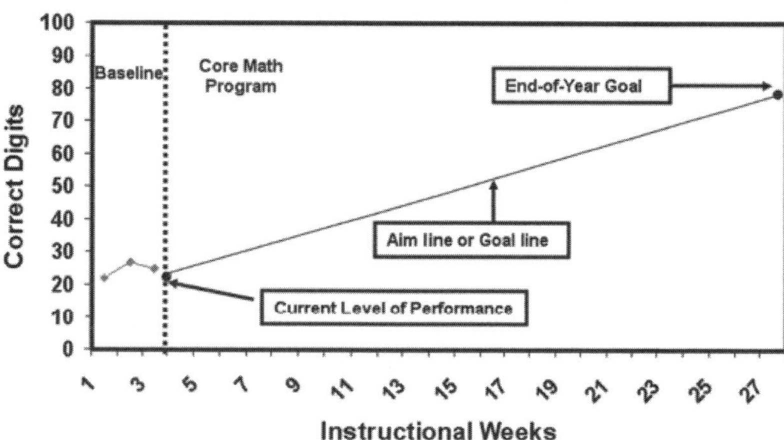

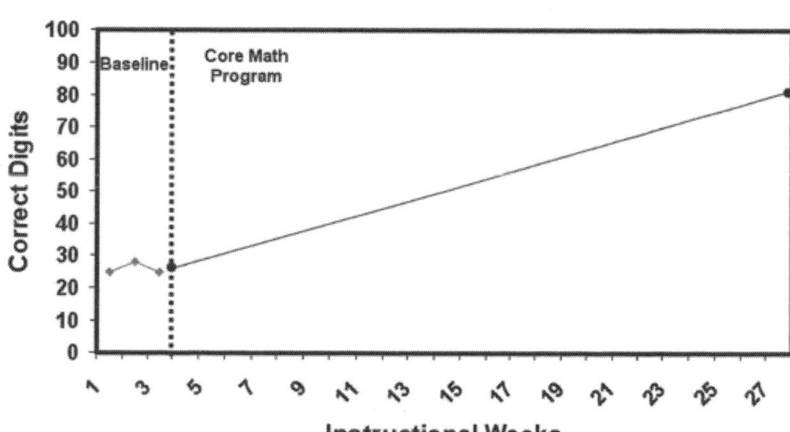

Figure 26A.4 Jenna and Tyler's math performance graphs: Current level of performance and goal.

to be typically performing and "on-track" in her math class. Using these two students' data as comparison, she is better able to demonstrate that Jenna and Tyler are indeed falling behind their peers. The current performance of the other two students is 55 and 59 correct digits.

After reviewing Jenna and Tyler's baseline data, they agree to monitor the students' progress in the core mathematics program once a week for the next 6 weeks. At that point in time, Mrs. Black and Mr. Walker will meet again to review Jenna and Tyler's progress monitoring data in order to make an informed instructional decision.

Instructional Decision Making Procedures

Six weeks have passed since Mrs. Black first started collecting progress monitoring data on Jenna and Tyler, and she is ready to have a meeting with Mr. Walker. Mrs. Black is very excited to show Mr. Walker Jenna and Tyler's math performance charts. The progress monitoring data confirms Mrs. Black's concern over Jenna and Tyler's math performance. Plotting the data on the graph clearly demonstrates both students are performing below their goal line and are not making adequate progress to meet their end-of-year goals.

After visually inspecting Jenna's graph (see Figure 26A.5), it is very clear that she is not making adequate progress in the core mathematics program and is continuing to struggle with problem solving tasks. Following the procedures for making an instructional decision based on the 4-point rule, Mrs. Black circles the four most recent data points and finds that all four are below the goal line and; therefore, an instructional change is needed. Mrs. Black and Mr. Walker discuss possible interventions that target problem solving and would be helpful to Jenna. After some discussion and referencing the mathematics section of the Center on Instruction Website (www.centeroninstruction.org), they decided that a problem solving intervention designed around schema-based instruction (SBI) will be implemented in a small group setting with other students that Mrs. Black also thinks could benefit from the SBI intervention. Mr. Walker will help gather the materials need for the SBI intervention and set up an instructional schedule for implementation of the program.

After visually inspecting Tyler's graph (see Figure 26A.5), it is very clear that Tyler's is also not making adequate progress and will likely not meet his end-of-year goal. Mrs. Black is quite disheartened because Tyler's performance has actually decreased. Applying the 4-point rule, Mrs. Black demonstrates that Tyler's four most

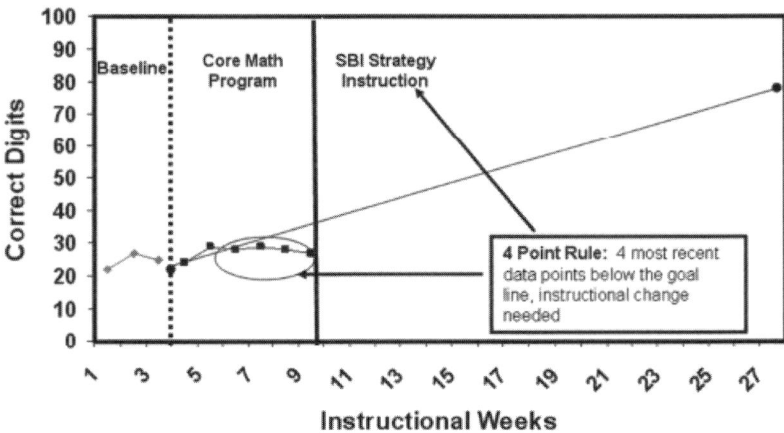

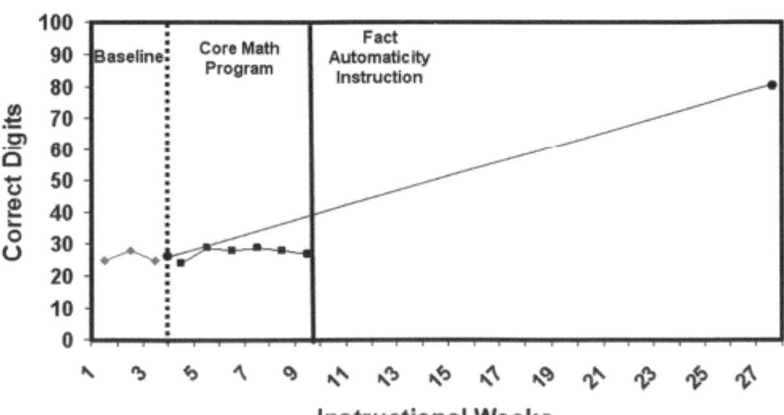

Figure 26A.5 Jenna and Tyler's math performance in the core math program.

recent data points are indeed below the goal line and an instructional change is needed. Again, they discuss ideas that might be helpful to Tyler. They also decide to look at Tyler's actual probes and find that Tyler appears to be accurate in the computation problems that he solves, but is very slow. Mr. Walker has even observed Tyler using his fingers while completing the assessment. They decide that Tyler might benefit from an intervention that focuses on basic fact automaticity. Mrs. Black notes a recent document she read on response to intervention in math that recommended at least 10 minutes per day should be devoted to computational fluency (Gersten et al., 2009). She also indicates that several other students are not able to automatically recall their basic math facts quickly and accurately. Since Tyler is in fifth grade, they decide to first target multiplication facts because this is a prerequisite skill for solving factions. An intervention schedule is set up to provide students with the automaticity intervention.

Communication with Progress Monitoring Data

Six more weeks pass as Mrs. Black implements the interventions and continued to monitor Jenna and Tyler's progress. This meeting falls right around the time of parent conferences, so both Tyler and Jenna's parents will come to the meeting. Mrs. Black, using the graphic displays, explains the progress made by each student. When looking at Jenna's graph (see Figure 26A.6) and the four most recent data points, we see that her data points are all hovering around the goal line, some are above, some below and some right on it. At this point, Mrs. Black will continue collecting data points before making another instructional decision, but it appears that Jenna is on track to meet and/or exceed her end-of-year goal. Once Mrs. Black collects a few more data points, a trend line is used to determine the next instructional decision. She is confident that the SBI intervention is having a positive effect on Jenna's problem solving ability. Her parents are very pleased and seem very interested in the graphic display.

When visually inspecting Tyler's graph, Mrs. Black can hardly contain her excitement. Tyler's progress monitoring data show an obvious increase after receiving the basic math fact automaticity instruction. Mrs. Black explains to Tyler's parents that he is making such positive progress that she is raising his goal. She circles the last four data points and explains that because Tyler's performance data is above his goal line, he is on track to exceed his goal; therefore Mrs. Black will raise his goal. Tyler's parents' are concerned about raising his goal when he is making

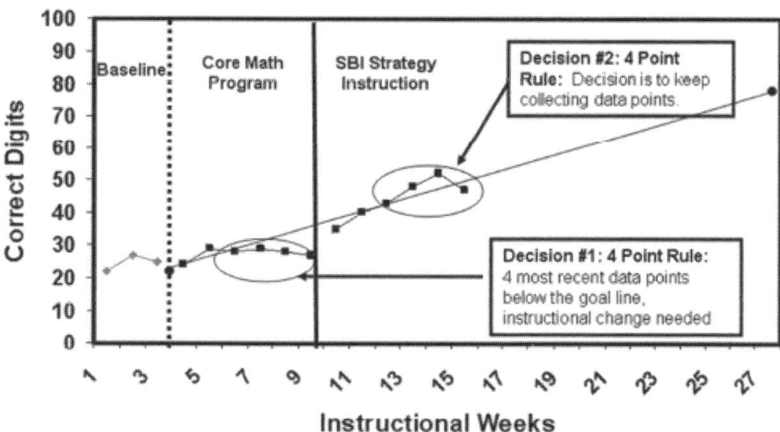

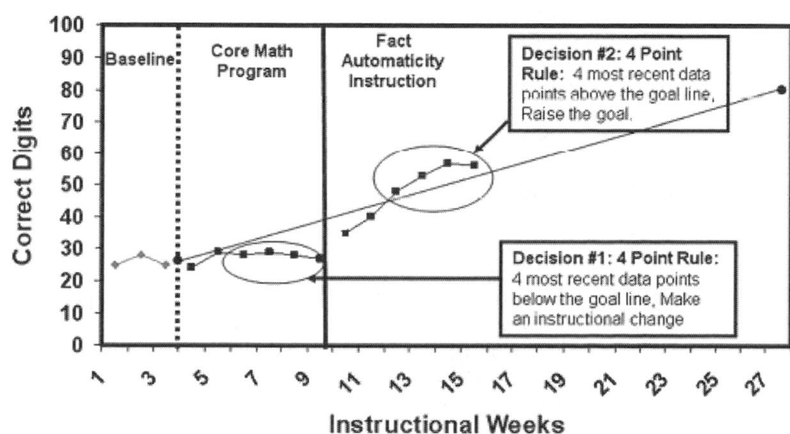

Figure 26A.6 Jenna and Tyler's math performance after SBI problem solving intervention.

such good progress. Mrs. Black explains that because Tyler was falling behind earlier in the year, it is essential that his goal is raised in an effort to catch him up with the other typically performing students. She continues by explaining that if his goal isn't raised, he may likely meet his goal, but will still be significantly behind the other students. Tyler's parents are excited that this may help Tyler catch up with the other students.

Both meetings conclude with the agreement to continue monitoring Jenna and Tyler's math performance using the progress monitoring probes as well as delivering the interventions until the student performance indicates the interventions are no longer needed.

References

Berkeley, S., Bender, W. N., Peaster, L. G., & Saunders, L. (2009). A snapshot of progress toward implementation of responsiveness to intervention (RTI) throughout the United States. *Journal of Learning Disabilities*, *42*, 85–95.

Bost, L. W., & Riccomini, P. J. (2006). Effective instruction: An inconspicuous strategy for dropout prevention. *Remedial and Special Education, 27,* 301–311.

Calhoon, M. B. (2008). Curriculum-based measurement for mathematics at the high school level: What we do not know…what we need to know. *Assessment of Effective Intervention, 33*(4), 234–239.

Christ, T. J., Scullin, S., Tolbize, A., & Jiban, C. L. (2008). Implications of recent research: Curriculum-based measurement of math computation. *Assessment of Effective Intervention, 33*(4), 198–205.

Deno, S. L. (2003). Developments in curriculum-based measurement. *The Journal of Special Education, 37*, 184–192.

Deno, S. L., Mirkin, P. K., & Chiang, B. (1982). Identifying valid measures of reading. *Exceptional Children*, *49*, 36–45.

Espin, C. A., Scierka, B. J., Skare, S. S., & Halvorson, N. (1999). Criterion related validity of curriculum-based measures in writing for secondary students. *Reading & Writing Quarterly*, *15*, 5–28.

Espin, C. A., Shin, J., & Busch, T. W. (2005). Curriculum-based measurement in the content areas: Vocabulary matching as an indicator of progress in social studies learning. *Journal of Learning Disabilities*, *38*, 353–363.

Espin, C. A., & Tindal, G. (1998). Curriculum-based measurement for secondary students. In M. R. Shinn (Ed.), *Advances applications of curriculum-based measurement* (pp. 214–253). New York: Guilford Press.

Foegen, A., Olson, J. R., & Impecoven-Lind, L. (2008). Developing progress monitoring measures for secondary mathematics: An illustration in algebra. *Assessment of Effective Intervention, 33*(4), 240–249.

Fuchs, D., Fernstrom, P., Reeder, P., Bowers, J., & Gilman, S. (1992). Vaulting barriers to mainstreaming with curriculum-based measurement and transenvironmental programming. *Preventing School Failure*, *36*, 34–39.

Fuchs, D., Roberts, P. H., Fuchs, L. S., & Bowers, J. (1998). Reintegrating students with learning disabilities into the mainstream: A two-year study. *Learning Disabilities Research & Practice*, *11*, 214–229.

Fuchs, L. S., Deno, S. L., & Mirkin, P. K. (1984). The effects of frequent curriculum-based measurement and evaluation on pedagogy, student achievement, and student awareness of learning. *American Educational Research Journal*, *21*, 449–460.

Fuchs, L. S., & Fuchs, D. (n.d.). Using curriculum-based measurement for progress monitoring in mathematics. Retrieved October 15, 2009, from http;//www.studentprogress.org

Fuchs, L. S., Fuchs, D., Compton, D. L., Hamlett, C. L., & Seethaler, P. M. (2007). Mathematics screening and progress monitoring at first grade: Implications for response to intervention. *Exceptional Children, 73*, 311–330.

Fuchs, L. S., Fuchs, D., & Hamlett, C. L. (1993). Technological advances linking the assessment of students' academic proficiency to instructional planning. *Journal of Special Education Technology, 12*, 49–62.

Fuchs, L. S., Fuchs, D., & Hamlett, C. L. (2005). Using technology to facilitate and enhance curriculum-based measurement. In D. Edyburn, K. Higgins, & R. Boone (Eds.), *Handbook of special education technology research and practice* (pp. 663–681). Whitefish Bay, WI: Knowledge by Design.

Fuchs, L. S., Fuchs, D., Hamlett, C. L., Phillips, N. B., & Bentz, J. (1994). Classwide curriculum-based measurement: Helping general educators meet the challenge of student diversity. *Exceptional Children*, *60*, 518–537.

Fuchs, L. S., Fuchs, D., Hamlett, C. L., & Stecker, P. M. (1991). Effects of curriculum-based measurement and consultation on teacher planning and student achievement in mathematics operations. *American Educational Research Journal*, *28*, 617–641.

Fuchs, L. S., Fuchs, D., & Maxwell, L. (1988). The validity of informal reading comprehension measures. *Remedial & Special Education*, *9*, 20–28.

Fuchs, L. S., Fuchs, D., & Speece, D. L. (2002). Treatment validity as a unifying construct for identifying learning disabilities. *Journal of Learning Disabilities*, *22*, 51–59.

Gersten, R., Beckmann, S., Clarke, B., Foegen, A., Marsh, L., Star, J. R., & Witzel, B. (2009). *Assisting students struggling with mathematics: Response to Intervention (RtI) for elementary and middle schools* (NCEE 2009-4060). Retrieved from http://ies.ed.gov/ncee/wwc/ publications/ practiceguides/. Washington, DC: National Center for Education Evaluation and Regional Assistance, Institute of Education Sciences, U.S. Department of Education.

Hall, T., & Mengel, M. (2002). *Curriculum-based evaluations.* Wakefield, MA: National Center on Accessing the General Curriculum. Retrieved November 13, 2009 from http://www.cast.org/ publications/ncac/ ncac_curriculumbe.html

Hosp, M. K., & Hosp, J. L. (2003). Curriculum-based measurement for reading, spelling, and math: How to do it and why. *Preventing School Failure, 48*, 10–17.

Hosp, M. K., Hosp, J. L., & Howell, K. W. (2007). *The ABCs of CBM: A practical guide to curriculum-based measurement.* New York: Guilford Press.

Individuals with Disabilities Education Improvement Act of 2004, PL 108-446, 20 U.S.C. §1400 (2004).

IRIS Center for Training Enhancements. (n.d.). *Classroom assessments (part 1): An introduction to monitoring academic achievement in the classroom.* Retrieved June 13, 2009, from http://iris.peabody.vanderbilt.edu/gpm/chalcycle.htm

Jenkins, J. R., & Jewell, M. (1993). Examining the validity of two measures for formative teaching: Reading aloud and maze. *Exceptional Children*, *59*, 421–432.

Johnson, E., Mellard, D. F., Fuchs, D. F., & McKnight, M. A. (2006). *Responsiveness to intervention (RTI): How to do it.* Lawrence, KS: National Research Center on Learning Disabilities

Kaminski, R. A., & Good, R. H. (1998). Assessing early literacy skills in a problem-solving model: Dynamic indicators of basic early literacy skills. In M.R. Shinn (Ed.), *Advanced applications of curriculum-based measurement* (pp. 113–142). New York: Guilford Press.

Kelley, B., Hosp, J. L., & Howell, K. W. (2008). Curriculum-based evaluation and math: An overview. *Assessment of Effective Intervention, 33*, 250–256.

Lembke, E. S., Foegen, A., Whittaker, T. A., & Hampton, D. (2008). Establishing technically adequate measures of progress in early numeracy. *Assessment of Effective Intervention, 33*, 206–214.

Lembke, E., & Stecker, P. (2007). *Curriculum-based measurement in mathematics: An evidenced-based formative assessment procedure.* Portsmouth, NH: RMC Research Corporation, Center on Instruction.

Madelaine, A., & Wheldall, K. (1999). Curriculum-based measurement of reading: A critical review. *International Journal of Disability, Development and Education*, *46*, 71–5.

Marston, D. B., & Magnusson, D. (1988). Curriculum-based assessment: District level implementation. In J. Graden, J. Zins, & M. Curtis (Eds.), *Alternative educational delivery systems: Enhancing instructional options for all students* (pp. 137–172). Washington DC: National Association of School Psychologists.

McKlane, K. (n.d.) Curriculum base measurement and statewide tests. Retrieved July 1, 2009, from http://www.studentprogress.org

National Mathematics Advisory Panel. (2008). *Foundation for Success: The Final Report of the National Mathematics Advisory Panel,* U.S. Department of Education Washington DC. Retrieved March 2008, from http://www.ed.gov/MathPanel

National Research Council on Learning Disabilities. (2007). *What is progress monitoring?* [Brochure]. Lawrence, KS: Author.

No Child Left Behind Act of 2001, PL 104-110, 115 U.S.C. Stat. 1425 (2001).

Riccomini, P. J., & Witzel, B. S. (2010). *Response to intervention in math.* Thousands Oaks, CA: Corwin Press.

Safer, N., & Fleischman, S. (2005). Research matters/ how student progress monitoring improves instruction. *Educational Leadership*, *62*, 81–83.

Shinn, M. R. (Ed.). (1989). *Curriculum-base measurement: Assessing special children*. New York: Guilford Press.

Shinn, M. R. (2002). Best practices using curriculum-based measurement in a problem-solving model. In A. Thomas & J. Grimes (Eds.), *Best practices in school psychology* (Vol. 4, pp. 671–697). Silver Spring, MD: National Association of School Psychologists.

Stecker, P. M. (n.d.). Monitoring student progress in individualized education programs using curriculum-based measurement. Retrieved on July 1, 2009, from http://www.studentprogress.org

Stecker, P. M., Fuchs, L. S., & Fuchs, D. (2005). Using curriculum-based measurement to improve student achievement: Review of research. *Psychology in the Schools*, *42*, 795–819.

Thurlow, M. L., Elliott, J. L., & Ysseldyke, J. E. (1998). *Testing students with disabilities.* Thousand Oaks, CA: Corwin Press.

Tindal, G. (1992). Evaluating instructional programs using curriculum-based measurement. *Preventing School Failure*, *36*, 39–44.

Wesson, C. L., King, R. P., & Deno, S. L. (1984). Direct and frequent measurement: If it's so good for us, why don't we use it? *Learning Disability Quarterly*, *7*, 45–48.

Section VI

Policy and Leadership in the Administration of Special Education

Section Editor: Jean B. Crockett
University of Florida

In the context of public education, politics and policy have long been intertwined in conflicts over who should capture scarce resources, and who should benefit from them. Disputes over whose values should prevail easily spill over into classrooms and school board offices when opponents seek to win their advantage in bold or subtle ways. In short, educational politics wrestles with thorny questions of "who gets what, when, and how" (Gallagher, 2006, p. 5). Educational policies in turn serve as tools for resolving disputes, and in the case of special education, resolving them in the best interest of a student with exceptional learning needs.

Special education policy, as with other effective social policies, addresses questions of (a) who receives the resources, and whether their participation is mandatory or voluntary; (b) who delivers the resources, and whether credentialed personnel require specialized preparation; (c) what resources are delivered, and how they are distributed to meet the needs of the recipients; and (d) under what conditions and in what kinds of environments the resources are delivered to meet the intent of the policy (Gallagher, 2006). In the case of special education, the first question addresses how funding is allocated to students with disabilities eligible to receive specialized services. The second question is concerned with the professional readiness of teachers and administrators to provide requisite specially designed instruction. The third question addresses the nature of what is provided and how organizations are designed to provide students with an appropriate education. The fourth question addresses learning environments in which students with disabilities are expected to learn challenging content and in which their teachers are held accountable for helping them be successful.

Rapid changes have occurred in society as well as special education, and a secondary issue pursued in this section is the concept of change itself. Special education policies and practices have evolved over the past 30 years, and so have the roles of educational leaders responsible for ensuring the appropriate education of students with disabilities. What conceptual models guide the ways that schools organize the effort of providing specially designed instruction? How is leadership distributed across people who engage in complex and changing tasks to improve outcomes for students with disabilities? What professional standards inform educational leadership for special education? How are special education services funded at the federal and state levels, and how can funding reflect changing needs and priorities such as school choice, charter schools, and early intervening services for struggling students prior to special education identification (e.g., Response to Intervention)? What are some ways that educational administrators can build and sustain a qualified and effective special education workforce? These questions guide the chapters in this section of the *Handbook* addressing policy and leadership in the administration of special education policy in American public schools.

Special education administrative leadership is best described as being a professional practice that implements policy in the context of schools, and other instructional settings, rather than as a distinct discipline in its own right. Educational administrators are in positions of influence to ensure students are appropriately referred for special education and that every eligible student receives individualized services and supports from qualified teachers; that teachers develop the knowledge and skills that support effective practice; and that instructional leaders establish strong expectations that effective practices will be used.

Reference

Gallagher, J. J. (2006). *Driving change in special education.* Baltimore, MD: Paul H. Brookes.

27

Conceptual Models for Leading and Administrating Special Education

Jean B. Crockett
University of Florida

> The general problems of philosophy and administration in the education of exceptional children are not fundamentally different from those involved in the education of children who are not exceptional. The difference is chiefly one of emphasis. The problems of philosophy and administration in the education of all children are determined or conditioned by changes in the social order. (Berry, 1941, p. 253)

The democratic concept of equal educational opportunity for every child has long been given lip service, much like the phrase "All men are created equal," wrote Professor Charles Scott Berry in 1941. For the concept to have its full expression, he argued, there must be "recognition of the social, economic, and educational significance of individual differences in children and the importance of making more adequate provision for individual differences in the educational program" (p. 253). Some 70 years later the concept of equal educational opportunity for every child remains a cherished value with special education in American schools now governed by a constellation of federal, state, and local policies that reflect the public will, and guided by the cumulative findings of educational research that inform effective practice (Bateman, 2007). To ensure that this cherished value does not remain an elusive goal, those who administer special education have the primary responsibility of serving and supporting exceptional learners and their families in ways that are both educationally productive and legally correct (see http://www.casecec.org/about, retrieved July 30, 2009).

In today's schools, special education administrators serve as advocates for students with disabilities from diverse cultural and linguistic backgrounds, and ensure compliance with policies that protect students' rights and ensure their educational benefits. Special education administrators also provide leadership fostering the use of effective instructional practices and assistive technology for diverse learners, and cultivating productive relationships with parents and professionals within the school system and across external agencies. Solving problems, making data-based decisions, and collaborating with others in the management of multi-million dollar budgets are also part of their responsibilities. Regardless of title or administrative role, providing leadership for special education requires the skills of "a facile communicator, proficient manager, astute politician, and strategic planner" (Goor, 1995, p. 3).

The purpose of this chapter is to review conceptual models that guide the practice of administrative leadership for special education, and to re-conceptualize this complex work as an instructional support effort that draws on the centralized and distributed expertise of personnel across the educational enterprise. The practice of special education leadership is first examined in its current context and then from an historical perspective, tracing the visions of practitioners over time as they engaged in building specialized programs to leading instruction in schools serving a diversity of learners. The argument is made that realizing this latter vision requires a conceptual model governed by the principles of special education policy and guided by a cumulative and integrated knowledge base about the education of students with disabilities and the organization and leadership of schools.

This chapter proceeds from the perspective that children differ widely in how they learn, and that a disability represents a significant difference from what most people can do, given their age, opportunities, and instruction (Kauffman & Hallahan, 2005). Even within the context of standards-based learning, *particularity*—meaning the finely tuned recognition of and response to individual learning needs—remains the central concept of special education policy and instructional practice (Gerber, 2009). This chapter also proceeds from the perspective that administrative leadership is shaped by the interaction of (a) how clearly the purpose of special education policy is understood by those who implement it, (b) beliefs and knowledge about effective instruction and the academic and social capabilities of students with disabilities, and (c) the cultural contexts that influence the ways in which special education is organized and delivered (see Spillane, Reiser, & Reimer, 2002).

Conceptualizing Administrative Leadership for Special Education

Special education occurs in the context of schools, and improving schools for student learning has been the dominant concern of educational stakeholders in recent years. As a result, much attention has been paid to the conditions in schools that help to explain the under-performance of certain groups of students and their lack of school success. Much has been learned in the process about the importance of providing quality instruction and opportunities to learn to a broad diversity of students. Much has been learned about home–school connections that emphasize academics, and professional development that fosters collaborative inquiry and evidence-based instructional practice (Murphy, 2006). Research has also expanded knowledge about leadership and the critical role it plays in improving schools: Although only indirectly linked to student learning, "leadership is second only to classroom instruction among all school related factors that contribute toward what students learn at school" (Leithwood, Louis, Anderson, & Wahlstrom, 2004, p. 5).

Successful educational leaders develop effective organizations that support the performance of teachers as well as students. In this context, leadership is defined as "the work of mobilizing and influencing others to articulate and achieve the school's shared intentions and goals" (Leithwood & Riehl, 2005, p. 14). Efforts to improve leadership should build on understandings drawn from the existing empirical, conceptual, and normative knowledge base supporting the field of educational administration, and a working conception of leadership grounded in this foundation could stake the following claims (Leithwood & Riehl):

1. Educational leadership contributes to the improvement of student learning.
2. Leadership in schools is exercised primarily by principals and teachers but may be distributed across other personnel, as well.
3. A core set of leadership practices is valuable in almost all contexts: (a) setting direction; (b) developing people: and (c) redesigning organizational cultures to build trust, and to strengthen shared norms and values.
4. Successful leaders serving diverse populations of students establish conditions that (a) foster the core task of teaching; (b) promote a sense of community among students, teachers, parents, and others; and (c) nurture the development of interactions with families to help students do well in school.

The practice of leading and administrating special education has been described as occurring at the crossroads where multiple disciplines, including special education and educational leadership, intersect (Lashley & Boscardin, 2003), as well as at a complex interface where different systems and processes come together in multiple interactions (Crockett, 2007). Conceptualizations that situate this complex practice at a busy intersection or a dynamic interface are made to illustrate the point that the work of providing leadership for special education in today's schools involves negotiating interactions among people, policies, and practices in a variety of contexts to ensure that students with disabilities receive the intensive instruction they need to learn, and that teachers receive the support they require to do their jobs and to stay with them.

The Current Context

Educating students with disabilities has become an important dimension of school improvement across the United States. Special education is now a major concern for school administrators responsible for ensuring that students have equitable opportunities to learn in the context of challenging standards and high stakes accountability (McLaughlin, 2009). In recent years federal policies including the Individuals with Disabilities Education Improvement Act (IDEA, 2004) and the No Child Left Behind Act (NCLB, 2001) have prompted principals to assume greater responsibility for providing quality instruction to all students, and reshaped the role of special education directors as system-wide instructional leaders (Boscardin, 2004; DiPaola & Walther-Thomas, 2002). Special education administrators once accustomed to overseeing specialized programs are now challenged "with promoting collaboration among general and special education teachers and administrators to assure that high quality educational programs are accessible to all students" (Lashley & Boscardin, 2003, p. 3).

In the first decade of the 21st century, more than 20,000 administrators are primarily responsible for administrating special education and related services in school districts and state agencies across the United States. They share this responsibility with principals and other educational leaders in the nation's more than 15,000 school districts. The number of administrative personnel has expanded as the population of American children has increased, and across a four-year time span from 1999 to 2003 the number of special education administrators and supervisors in local school systems increased by 25% (U.S. Department of Education, 2006).

The demand for administrators well prepared to lead special education, however, exceeds the current supply. Although some states have rigorous criteria clearly defining competencies and expectations for special education administrators, many others have abandoned such criteria, electing to fill positions with candidates not trained in special education but holding generic state leadership licensure (Lashley & Boscardin, 2002). As a consequence of changing policies, many administrators responsible for special education in their schools are learning about their roles and responsibilities from personal or professional experiences (Wakerman, Browder, Flowers, & Ahlgrim-Delzell, 2006). How they conceptualize their roles and responsibilities is of increasing importance to the lives of the children and families they serve.

Conceptual Models for Leading Special Education

Conceptual models are representations that guide our thinking and frame the way we work. Unlike formal theories with testable hypotheses, models are more informal and intended to be useful problem-solving tools (Head & Rhodes, 1974). Recent developments in cognitive theory indicate that people bring preconceptions based upon their beliefs, and their prior knowledge and experiences, to the learning of any new practice. Sometimes these understandings are accurate and in some cases they are based on faulty mental models and misconstrued notions of how things are supposed to be. Cognitive science suggests that people of all ages develop competence in new areas when they acquire a deep foundation of factual knowledge, and when they understand reality within the organizing context of a conceptual framework that enables this knowledge to be easily retrieved and applied to specific situations (Pellegrino & Chudowsky, 2003). This logic applies to educational leaders who are empowered but unprepared to administer special education.

It can be difficult for educational leaders to organize the contexts and processes that support complex learning and knowledge development as schools serve students with increasingly diverse backgrounds and personal experiences. This makes it all the more important for administrators to inform their professional practice with a conceptual model for leading special education that is deeply grounded in both the governing principles of special education policy and the guiding principles of educational research.

Little more than 30 years ago most children with disabilities were excluded from public schools, and many children with more significant disabilities received no education at all. Other children and youth with mild or moderate learning problems often received inappropriate instruction that failed to meet their needs, or they were taught in schools more separate from their home communities than necessary. Over time, parents advocated for their children to be taught in schools instead of institutions, and, especially within the past two decades, to be included in general education classes for instruction. To ensure that students receive the specially designed instruction they need, special education policy guarantees through the IDEA key educational rights:

1. the right to receive a free appropriate public education that emphasizes special education and related services to meet their unique learning needs;
2. the right to be taught appropriately in the most integrated and least restrictive social environment; and
3. the right to be taught by qualified teachers who use state of the art instructional approaches and technology (Crockett & Kauffman, 1999).

Providing a free appropriate public education. The IDEA requires school officials to provide a free appropriate public education (FAPE) to students with disabilities and to develop written documentation in the form of an Individualized Education Program (IEP) to ensure personalized supports. The IEP is intended to outline a plan that addresses students' individual needs. The primary responsibility of administrators in the IEP process is to ensure the school district's commitment to provide the program of special education and related services agreed on by parents and professionals, including the accommodations and modifications to be used in adapting the general curriculum, so that the student can benefit from his or her education (Bateman & Linden, 2006).

Providing instruction in the least restrictive environment. The IDEA uses the legal principle of the least restrictive environment (LRE) to guide instructional placement decisions so that students are not placed in schools or classrooms based upon their disability classification. The LRE principle requires that special education students, to the maximum extent appropriate to their needs, are taught in general education classes. Special and general education teachers have the responsibility to differentiate instruction and to restructure the general education environment for students with disabilities, and to consider other settings only when the IEP team determines that satisfactory progress cannot be made inclusively even with the support of specialized aids and services.

Using effective instructional practices. School leaders are responsible for ensuring that teachers provide special needs learners with an appropriate education in the LRE, and that they use effective instructional practices in the process. The right to be taught effectively shifts the focus from *where* students learn to *how* their instruction is to be designed and delivered. The IDEA requires that students' IEPs be aligned with state curriculum standards, and that professional development be made available so that teachers might learn to use practices proven to be effective in helping students with specific disability-related needs be successful in learning challenging content. The IDEA's instructional provisions are not new, but they have taken on greater significance in recent years with related policies of accountability and standards-based reform.

The Elementary and Secondary Education Act, reauthorized as NCLB, requires all students including students with disabilities to learn the general curriculum, to participate in state and local assessments, and to make gains in achievement toward the goal of making adequate yearly academic progress. The IDEA is now aligned with NCLB and both laws require qualified teachers to use practices based on scientific research to strengthen both basic and specially designed instruction. The NCLB has important implications for special education. When groups of students with disabilities fail to make adequate yearly progress toward achieving 100% proficiency in reading and mathematics, their schools face punative accountability measures. As a result, many schools are turning toward inclusion in general education classes as a means to provide special education students with greater access to the content of the general curriculum. Inclusion, however, is not an intervention; without the use of effective, intensive, and specific teaching practices, inclusion alone will not help students with disabilities gain access to learning or achieve appropriate outcomes (Crockett, 2004; Salend, 2008; Zigmond, Kloo, & Volonino, 2009).

As pressures have risen for students with disabilities to achieve positive results, so have opportunities for teachers to turn to effective practices, particularly in the area of reading. For over three decades, researchers have tested academic and social interventions to see what works well for special need learners. As a result, a growing body of knowledge based on well-conducted research syntheses supports the use of instructional practices, such as small, interactive groups, directed questioning, and carefully controlled task difficulty predictive of positive outcomes for students across content areas (Swanson, 2000). Teachers are now better positioned to make effective instructional decisions by combining these evidence based practices with their own practical knowledge (see Brownell, Crockett, Smith, & Griffin, in press; Cook, Landrum, Cook, & Tankersley, 2008).

The principles of special education policy and the findings of special education research govern and guide the administration of specialized services, but leadership practice is also informed by society's cultural values. More than 40 years ago William Cruickshank (1967) articulated the philosophical principles that have animated special education over time as a democratic concept, a humanitarian ideal, an economic investment, and an expression of "the hope that through education, every individual will participate freely in the social religious, aesthetic, and scientific aspects of his culture to the limits of his capacity" (p. 45). This cultural conceptualization of special education serves as a foundation for leadership that sets a course toward equal education opportunity for all students, and continues to inspire greater integration into society for young Americans with disabilities.

Reviewing Historical Models of Special Education Administrative Leadership

The history of special education administrative leadership reveals patterns of optimistic interactions between generalists and specialists followed by cyclical periods of disengagement when resources or commitments to the effort were spent (Crockett & Kauffman, 1999). Special programs were initially designed for students with obvious disabilities whose need for extraordinary support was undeniable; "given such client characteristics, the programs tended to encourage organizational structures separate and distinct from the mainstream of public education" (Burrello & Sage, 1979, p. 13). In the 19th century, during the ideological era of educational administration (Murphy, 2006), residential schools were built to educate students who were blind and/or deaf and special classes were started in large urban systems for students with intellectual disabilities. Subsequent eras in Murphy's historical conceptualization of administrative leadership run parallel to the development of the field of special education administration including the prescriptive, scientific management, and dialectic/distributive eras of educational leadership.

The Prescriptive Era: Moving Toward a Universal Education System (1900–1940)

At the turn of the 20th century, administrators faced the question of how to provide a universal educational system; in other words, "how could all be brought in and adequately educated?" (Lazerson, 1983, p. 42). By 1900 many states had passed compulsory school attendance laws, but their enforcement was sporadic, and not all students with disabilities were required to attend. In states with strict enforcement, public school enrollment increased by 55% between 1890 and 1915. Average daily attendance went up 84%, and total school expenditures climbed by 329%. Compulsory attendance laws forced school officials to address the unfamiliar problem of schooling students considered to be truant and incorrigible, as well as children "suffering from physical defects and disorders as well as those of low mentality" (Cubberly as cited in Lazerson, p. 17). In 1909, Baltimore's superintendent of schools, James Van Sickle, remarked, "before attendance laws were effectively enforced, there were as many of these special cases in the community as there are now; few of them, however, remained long enough in school to attract serious attention or to hinder the instruction of the more tractable and capable" (as cited in Lazerson, p. 17).

The broad interpretation of educational opportunity expressed through compulsory schooling begged solutions to administrative problems and, by 1906–1907, coursework in special education administration was started at Teacher's College, Columbia University. By 1928, 16 major cities employed 29 supervisors and 6 directors (Finkenbinder, 1981), some of whom were women who rose to supervisory and directorial positions within major urban school systems. In Boston, Ada Fitts was appointed Supervisor of Special Classes, and Theresa A. Dacey was Assistant in Charge of Speech Improvement Classes. In New York City, Elizabeth Farrell served as Director of Ungraded Classes (Crockett & Kauffman, 1999). Special education legislation was passed in many states from 1919 to 1929, and special classes and programs grew within the public education system as an efficient means of addressing exceptional needs without changing the "regular grade organization of the traditional school; the special class usually is set up as another class unit in the school" (Berry, 1941, p. 256). In

1920, administrators struggling with compulsory education laws in Philadelphia featured special education classes as a centerpiece of the school system. By the 1930s their importance had diminished as special classes disbanded with the economic downturn of the Great Depression (Berry), and as specialized private schools were opened by newly organized professional and advocacy groups for students whose disabilities challenged the educational status quo. "Special education seemed to have little to offer" (Lazerson, 1983, p. 37), once students with disabilities could be schooled elsewhere and were no longer a major concern of public school administrators.

The Scientific Management Era: Establishing a Professional Identify (1940–1970)

The philosophy of equal educational opportunity continued to confront challenges in the workplace over the next three decades that begged managerial solutions. The drive toward universal education for all students had revealed problems with both organizing schools for instruction and preparing personnel to teach curricular content to students with a broad range of abilities. Berry (1941) captured the monumental challenge of changing entrenched teaching and administrative practices with this vivid analogy:

> To change the traditional or curriculum-centered school to a child-centered school while the school continues to run is a much more difficult problem in administration that it is to reconstruct a railroad bridge while the trains continue to run; the former requires not only changes in buildings, equipment, supplies, subject matter, and methods of instruction, but also, unlike the latter, a retraining of the personnel. (p. 254)

The concept of educational opportunity for students with disabilities extended haphazardly across the 48 states by 1940 with every state providing residential schools for students who were deaf and/or blind, and training schools for delinquent youth committed by the courts. All but three states provided institutional care for those considered "feeble-minded" (Berry, 1941). By the 1950s, the post-World War II population boom affected special education rosters significantly, and from 1948 to 1968 the number of public school students with disabilities increased from 357,000 to 2,252,000, or from 1.2% to 4.5% of the K–12 population (Lazerson, 1983). Federal interest in their education prompted the enactment of the Cooperative Research Act in 1954 to fund the first federal research program in special education, and the Training of Professional Personnel Act in 1959, which became the first federal program to fund the university preparation of educators to teach children with intellectual disabilities.

As federal funds expanded in the 1960s to focus on teaching students whose disabilities were classified into specific disability categories, including mental retardation, deafness, and deaf-blindness, interest increased in the preparation of administrators, especially those in public school systems, to manage programs and to supervise instruction. The role of the special education administrator was now conceptualized as an expert executive leader concerned with the legal basis of school administration, fiscal and business management, and the supervision of personnel (Finkenbinder, 1981). In 1965, Marshman characterized the position of a director of special education as

> an educational leader with many and varied responsibilities. The basis for his [sic] professional behavior is a body of specialized knowledge which he uses to create a general education program for specialized clientele. To do this he interacts with the entire spectrum of the school system. This responsibility is not confined to academic areas, to curriculum, to instruction, or even to administration. He must coordinate a variety of services—psychological, vocational, transportation, etc. Expenditure of funds to be properly coordinated requires his specialized knowledge. Organizing this job into a meaningful description is no small task. (as cited in Finkenbinder, p. 487)

One of the most influential statements regarding the functions of administrative leadership for special education was developed in 1956 by Ray Graham, the superintendent of public instruction for the state of Illinois, and promoted in a document designed to guide the provision of special services in local school districts of all sizes. Graham grouped these functions into (a) administrative, (b) supervisory, and (c) coordinating domains (see Burrello & Sage, 1979), which continue to address the core set of leadership practices that guide the direction of special education in most public school systems. The administrative domain addresses leadership for developing local policies and directing resources to support practices at the interface of general and special education; the supervisory domain provides support for professional growth; and the coordinating domain provides for organizational linkages within the school system, and the cultivation of relationships with professionals from multiple agencies.

Starting Professional Organizations

Developing a professional identify as an emerging field was a major concern in the middle decades of the 20th century, and administrators responsible for special programs were motivated to create professional organizations. The National Association of State Directors of Special Education (NASDSE) and the Council of Administrators of Special Education (CASE) are the primary examples of this professional group identity. Other educational leadership organizations held complementary interests including the superintendent-focused American Association of School Administrators (AASA), and the research-oriented University Council for Educational Administration (UCEA).

The National Association of State Directors of Special Education (NASDSE) was started in 1938 when Dr. Elise H. Martens, later appointed chief for exceptional children and youth at the U.S. Office of Education, convened a meeting attended by 15 special educators from 13 state education departments. The group met intermittently as the Conference of State Directors and Supervisors of Special Education with typically fewer than 25 attendees until 1950 when a constitution was adopted and the name was changed to its present form under the leadership of Ray Graham, who served as the group's president (Burrello & Sage, 1979). Meetings were held in conjunction with those of the Council for Exceptional Children (CEC) until 1962 when the group set its own schedule of meetings; by 1972 NASDSE established national headquarters in Washington, DC.

The Council of Administrators for Special Education (CASE) convened for the first time in 1951 with 24 administrators from medium to large school systems as a special interest group of CEC. For the first few years the official name of the group was the Council of Administrators, Supervisors, and Coordinators of Special Education in Local School Systems, a name that reflected the employment of its members. The Council increased its membership steadily to 172 in 1960, 387 in 1965, and 649 in 1970. By broadening its eligibility criteria to include administrators from state agencies and residential and private schools, as well as university faculty, CASE membership grew to 2500 in 1974, and to over 3,600 in 1978 (Burrello & Sage, 1979). Thirty-two years later, the CASE roster approaches 5,000 registered members (CEC, 2010).

Preparing Leaders for the Complementary Disciplines

Special educators and general educators typically followed separate paths to leadership in these early years, with special education leadership confined to the administration, supervision, and coordination of specialized programs in schools or agencies. Requirements for these positions included mandatory training in special education at the undergraduate or the master's level, and at least two years of professional work experience with students with disabilities (Crockett, 2002). In the bureaucratic structure of schools, educating children and youth was considered to be the work of teachers. The complementary effort of organizing and managing the business of schooling was viewed as the primary practice of educational administrators and their special education administration colleagues. Not only was the work of educational administrators seen as complementing basic and specialized instruction, each form of administration—general and special—was conceptualized as complementing the other in advancing opportunities for every child. Professional organizations addressed the complementary competencies needed by special education administrative leaders with initiatives such as the CEC Professional Standards Project in 1966, which identified 15 areas of knowledge and 79 related skill functions to be addressed in preparing administrative personnel.

By the end of the 1960s, the U.S. Office of Education proposed funding to support the professional preparation of special education administrators prompting the interest of the UCEA in organizational issues at the interface of special education and educational leadership (Yates, 2005). In March 1969, the Bureau for the Education of the Handicapped (BEH) sponsored a conference in Austin, Texas, bringing together professors and doctoral students from "the complementary disciplines of special education administration and general education administration" (Yates, 2005, p. 1) to address the common and specialized learnings, competencies, and experiences for special education administrators. By 1970–71, the BEH provided funding to support the General-Special Education Administration Consortium, which was designed to create innovative leadership preparation for special education administrators.

The work of the BEH-UCEA consortium was designed to target two major problems: (a) the isolation of special education from general education administration as practiced in schools and as taught in universities; and (b) the lack of clear and common objectives in preparatory programs in special education administration. The Consortium targeted four goals: (a) to provide integrated professional development experiences for professors of general and special education administration; (b) to provide training materials for professors to use in teaching across the complementary disciplines; (c) to engage in research and development activities that would produce products of significance to both general and special education administrators; and (d) to involve graduate students from each complementary discipline in most of the consortium activities (Yates, 2005).

Observations drawn from data of university leadership preparation programs indicated that the Consortium's mission was most closely met in the area of curriculum development. Data also suggested professors of special education administration saw more relevance in the interactions than did their educational administration counterparts; "that is, the specialists are drawing upon the generalists more than the generalists are drawing upon the specialists" (Burrello & Sage, 1979, p. 210). Conflicts arose in the complementary disciplines as educational administration programs were more apt to prepare graduates to address the majority, the large group, and organizational maintenance. In contrast special education administration programs prepared personnel more likely "to subvert change resistant, established systems; the decentralization of power by sharing it with consumers; and the guaranteeing to parents of the opportunity to participate in decisions about their child's program or educational plan" (p. 211). With the passage of numerous policies in the 1970s, the work of special education directors and the focus of their university preparation programs shifted to the implementation of new federal laws. The BEH also refocused its funding priorities and the involvement of UCEA in the General-Special Education Administration Consortium came to a close as the practice of special education administration took off in a more legally focused and compliance-driven direction (Meyen, 1995).

The Dialectic Era: Moving Toward Shared Leadership for Learning (1970–the Present)

Social values and legislative policies have traditionally cast long shadows over educational research and practice (Gallagher, 2006), as well as the knowledge base of special education administration and leadership. Since the 1970s the concept of equal educational opportunity for every child has shifted in response to cultural and legislative priorities regarding social inclusion and meaningful outcomes for people with disabilities. Prior to the passage of federal policies, special education administration was characterized as being somewhat of a virginal entity, untouched by the bureaucratic reach of law that controlled the general education administrative discipline (Willower, 1970). By 1976, however, the number of public school students with disabilities expanded to 3.8 million and the practice of special education administrative leadership witnessed "the acceleration of change" (Burrello & Sage, 1979, p. 13).

Social Policies

Historical trends can be drawn against a backdrop of evolving policies affecting the education of students with disabilities and of evolving practices informed by an enlarging body of research evidence. Federal special education policy first emerged in the 1950s with federal assistance for research and personnel preparation, and by the late 1960s states developed special education policies in anticipation of what would be hailed as landmark legislation enacted in 1975 as the Education for All Handicapped Children Act, Public Law 94-142. Subsequent reauthorizations of this statute have influenced special education leadership practice for almost 40 years. Concerns with failing schools and improving the academic performance of all students prompted shifts in policy over the past two decades toward learning academic content and holding students with disabilities and their teachers accountable for increased test scores. This shift has implications for conceptualizing leadership functions and organizational structures in ways that facilitate the delivery of instructionally effective special education.

Professional Trends

Major trends within the profession of school administration have also influenced special education leadership placing emphasis in recent years on school improvement, teaching and learning, collaboration, technology, and revived attention to issues of equity and advocacy for children and families (Alsbury & Whitaker, 2007; Murphy, Vriesenga, & Storey, 2007). In an effort to describe how administrative leadership for special education has been conceptualized since the passage of federal policies, Crockett, Becker, and Quinn (2009) reviewed 474 manuscript abstracts published in professional journals from 1970–2009. This analysis identified prevalent themes and historical trends across this integrated knowledge base published in special and general education journals over the past 40 years (see Table 27.1).

Enduring Themes

Crockett et al. (2009) characterized the special education administrative knowledge base as informed by eight prevalent topics. The five topics that accounted for 74% (n = 352) of the conceptual content represented enduring themes such as (a) law and policy, (b) personnel training and development, (c) leadership roles and responsibilities, (d) leadership preparation and development, and (e) learning environments. These themes address perennial questions of public policy such as:

1. Who receives special education?
2. Who delivers it (and administers it) and what are their credentials?
3. What services (e.g., curriculum, instruction, and related services) are delivered?
4. Under what conditions (i.e., environmental) are the services delivered?

Taken together these questions address structures for implementing special education policy in American schools (Gallagher, 2006). *Personnel preparation and development* is the most prevalent topic across decades, likely because

TABLE 27.1
The Frequency and Topical Nature of Special Education Administration Articles, 1970–2009

Theme	Decade									
	1970–1979		1980–1989		1990–1999		2000–2009		Total	
	#	%	#	%	#	%	#	%	#	%
Personnel Training & Development	16	23.9	32	24.2	17	16.0	24	14.2	89	18.8
Law & Policy	5	7.5	23	17.4	19	17.9	30	17.8	77	16.2
Learning Environment	10	14.9	19	14.4	25	23.6	16	9.5	70	14.8
Leadership Roles & Responsibilities	17	25.4	18	13.6	12	11.3	21	12.4	68	14.3
Accountability for Student Learning	3	4.5	12	9.1	14	13.2	33	19.5	62	13.0
Leadership Prep & Development	13	19.4	11	8.3	7	6.6	17	10.1	48	10.1
Collaboration	2	3.0	5	3.8	9	8.5	22	13.0	38	8.0
Technology	1	1.5	12	9.1	3	2.8	6	3.5	22	4.6
Totals	**67**	**100**	**132**	**99.9**	**106**	**99.9**	**169**	**100**	**474**	**99.8**

Note: From "Reviewing the Knowledge Base of Special Education Leadership and Administration: 1970–2009, by J. B. Crockett, M. K. Becker, and D. Quinn, 2009. *Journal of Special Education Leadership, 22,* pp. 55–67. Copyright 2009 by the Council of Administrators of Special Education. Adapted with permission.

"the problems of special education cannot be resolved without improving instruction, which means recruiting the best individuals possible and training them appropriately" (Kauffman & Landrum, 2006, p. 146). The topic of *law and policy* has been prevalent since the 1980s with articles providing legal and fiscal analyses, and guidance for effectively negotiating the special education procedural process. Interest in this topic has increased notably since 2000 with the accountability provisions of NCLB and IDEA (Bartlett, Etscheidt, & Weisenstein, 2007).

Interest in *learning environments*, or the contexts in which teaching and learning occurs, was fueled by the inclusive education movement in the 1980s and 1990s, and aligned with administrative interest in site-based management and changing governance structures in schools (Murphy, 2006). As local schools began to serve more diverse student populations, concerns shifted from providing inclusive environments to providing environments that encouraged accountability for the success of all learners. From 2000–2009 the number of publications addressing the roles and responsibilities of instructional leaders increased with the impetus of policies fostering standards-based accountability.

Leadership roles and responsibilities and *leadership preparation and development* were frequent topics in the 1970s as schools geared up for the creation of newly mandated special education programs (Sage & Burrello, 1994). Publications from the 1970s through the 1990s paid more attention to managerial functions, competencies, and evolving organizational structures for administrating special education than to enacting instructional leadership (see McCarthy & Sage, 1985). Recent trends suggest current interest in clarifying roles, responsibilities, and leadership development, with newly revised professional standards for general and special education administrators (Boscardin, this volume), and redefined models for moving toward shared and sustainable leadership for improving schools and student learning (Murphy, 2006).

Contemporary Concerns

In addition to enduring themes, Crockett et al. (2009) identified accountability for student learning, collaboration and communication, and the administrative use of technology as contemporary concerns for administrators of special education. These three topics accounted for only 26% (n = 122) of the content published in journals since 1970, suggesting gaps in the knowledge base that need to be addressed if administrators are to be held accountable for their practice in new ways. Trends since 2000 suggest a steep rise of 53% in the topic of *accountability for student learning,* with content addressing a variety of administrative issues related to cultural and linguistic diversity, academic standards and access to the general education curriculum, social growth, and school improvement. Over the same time span, published articles on *collaboration and communication* increased by 57%, addressing administrative interactions with parents, community agencies, and businesses, as well as team-building with general and special educators and related service providers. Despite the timeliness of the *technology* topic, only 22 articles addressed data management and the use of technology in administrating special education. The problem posed by this small sample is exacerbated by the relatively small percentage of empirical studies in the mix.

Research on educational administration has been criticized for methodological shortcomings and insufficient empirical study of important topics, especially linking leadership to student learning (Hallinger & Heck, 1996; Murphy, 2006). The knowledge base sampled by Crockett et al. (2009) was similarly informed by theoretical or interpretive professional commentaries, suggesting that more has been said than has been studied about special education administrative leadership over the past 40 years. Although the number of empirical studies has increased in recent years, at no time have they dominated the professional literature (Crockett et al.). This trend might be explained by the prioritization of funding for special education research toward instructional interventions that most directly affect student learning. Recent initiatives by the U. S. Department of Education's Institute of Education Sciences to investigate systemic efforts supporting the delivery of evidence based instruction could strengthen integrated knowledge about the education of students with disabilities, and the organization and instructional leadership of schools.

Conceptualizing Special Education Administration as Instructional Leadership

The practice of special education administration is currently moving from a compliance-driven model to a locally delivered instructional model, with leadership and expertise distributed across multiple personnel. Important questions now need to be addressed such as (a) who is responsible for special education at different levels within a school system, and (b) to what extent do leadership practices and professional preparation support successful learning for all students, especially students with disabilities (Crockett, 2007). Special education administrators have traditionally been viewed by colleagues and parents as experts in implementing disability-related policies and effective instructional practices. With regard to their leadership development, more needs to be known about new special education administrators and their initial preparation, recruitment, induction, and retention. More also needs to be known about the ways they use technology to communicate and disseminate information, and to monitor evidence and make decisions about student progress (see Miller, 2009).

Now more than ever before, competent principals are also expected to be aware of enduring themes and current issues in special education. More needs to be known about how school leaders receive this knowledge and how they are provided with technical assistance. More also needs to be known about the impact of including special education topics in leadership licensure requirements and principal preparation programs, and the effect of those principals, who encourage teachers to use effective practices, on the achievement of special education students (see Wakerman, et al., 2006). The effective administration of special education in contemporary schools is judged less by procedural precision, and more by the impact of leadership practices that set the context for meaningful outcomes to be achieved by students with disabilities.

A Conceptual Model for Leading and Administrating Special Education Instruction

The role of special education has changed within schools, and equity is now conceived in terms of a meaningful opportunity for educational attainment including improved scores on assessments, higher graduation rates, and better post-secondary opportunities (McLaughlin, Krezmien, Zablocki, & Micelli, 2007). This conceptualization of equity relies on the capacity of school leaders and special education administrators to engage in instructional leadership defined as identifying, acquiring, allocating, coordinating, and using "the social, material, and cultural resources necessary to establish the conditions for the possibility of teaching and learning" (Spillane, Halverson, & Diamond, 2001, p. 24).

The following conceptual model for leading and administrating special education, which targets the instruction of students with disabilities, is grounded in the professional standards and integrated knowledge base of educational leadership and special education administration (Billingsley, Crockett, & Boscardin, 2010). A validated core set of leadership practices (i.e., setting a direction, developing people, and redesigning the organizational effort; Leithwood & Riehl, 2005) frames the four internal components of the model specifically addressing administrative leadership for special education (i.e., advocating for individually meaningful educational attainment, encouraging collaboration, supporting effective instructional practices, and providing structural supports and resources.

Setting Direction

1. *Advocating for Individually Meaningful Educational Attainment.* Instructional leaders for special education articulate a vision of educational access and accountability that begins with an analysis of teaching and learning that accounts for the unique educational needs of individual students with disabilities. This component emphasizes leadership practices that "(a) protect access to special education services, (b) recognize unique and shared characteristics of student with disabilities, and (c) promote more accurate and useful assessment and effective services" (Lloyd & Hallahan, 2007, p. 255).

Developing People

2. *Encouraging Collaboration*: Instructional leaders for special education establish a collaborative culture within schools and across sectors by extending norms of trust, partnership, and academic press to all members of the educational community, and by engaging with parents of students with disabilities, and with professionals in specialized schools and service agencies that work with struggling youth and families. Collaborative cultures and supportive contexts play important roles in reinforcing the use of appropriate instructional practices (Hoy & Hoy, 2003).
3. *Supporting Effective Instructional Practices*: Instructional leaders for special education foster high expectations and support research-based teaching strategies with a record of success for special needs learners. This component prompts leaders to support special education teachers in providing specially designed instruction to individual students with disabilities so they can access appropriate learning opportunities within and beyond the general education curriculum and classroom. Such practices include controlling for task difficulty; offering small interactive groups; providing direct and explicit instruction; teaching students to apply learning strategies; and teaching and monitoring specific academic, social, and functional skills.

Redesigning the Organizational Effort

4. *Providing Structural Supports and Resources*: Instructional leaders for special education cultivate a qualified workforce that can mobilize organizational changes in ways that enhance learning for students with disabilities. This component prompts leaders to support the success of faculty and staff by providing professional development, adjusting schedules and personnel assignments, obtaining resources and materials, utilizing data, evaluating programs, and ensuring compliance with state and federal policies.

The diverse approaches to instruction needed to meet individual students' complex learning and knowledge development are difficult to manage in the workplace, and specific, intensive, and strategic instruction is often over shadowed by external accountability assessments of academic achievement (Pellegrino, 2006). Conceptualizing the practice of special education administration as instructional leadership should help with (a) setting expectations for recognizing the individual capabilities of students with disabilities, (b) developing personnel who work collaboratively and effectively in responding to students' unique educational needs, and (c) making the organization of schools work more flexibly on their behalf. Today's special education teachers and administrators continue to need disability-specific knowledge, but current policies require them to apply this knowledge with greater emphasis on academic learning and evidence-based instructional practices (see Brownell, Sindelar, Kiely, & Danielson, 2009).

The implications of pedagogical practices are rarely addressed in the educational leadership literature (Furman & Shields, 2005), despite their direct influence on student learning, yet more than half a century of educational research contradicts the current administrative focus on inclusion and restructuring as the keys to reforming schools. Data indicate that "classroom management, student meta-cognitive and cognitive processes (e.g., study skills, background knowledge work habits) instruction, motivation, and assessment have a greater impact on learning than indirect influences such as restructuring, district policy, and school policy" (Hoy & Hoy, 2003, p. 3). How instructional leaders define and carry out these tasks and interact with others in the process, may be what is most important in influencing what teachers do to deliver equitable and beneficial special education.

Some scholars suggest that role-based leadership strategies are inadequate in confronting the complex challenges associated with student learning because leadership for instruction does not reside only with those appointed to formal administrative positions (Donaldson, 2001; Spillane et al., 2001). The concept of distributed leadership provides a useful perspective in exploring the balance of leadership responsibilities for special education across building principals, assistant principals, and teachers, and district level directors, supervisors, and coordinators.

Taking a Distributed Perspective

A distributed perspective views leadership as a property that emerges from the interactions of groups or networks allowing leadership actions to be carried out by more than a limited number of people. "Distributed leadership suggests that different skill sets or expert knowledge are spread across organizations, rather than residing in a few individuals" (Watson & Scribner, 2005, p. 11). Rather than viewing leadership as vested only in administrators with positional authority, a distributed perspective views instructional leadership as an interdependent human activity engaged in by multiple actors setting rules, using tools, and distributing labor intentionally to accomplish the task of improved teaching and learning within their community. This perspective can be put to use in empirical studies by viewing *leadership practice* for special education as it occurs in particular schools or school systems. Looking at what people do, rather than emphasizing their roles within an organization, focuses attention on how special education leadership is actually practiced by formal leaders (i.e., administrators, supervisors, and coordinators) and informal leaders such as teachers and counselors (see Billingsley, 2007).

Leading and administrating special education within school systems, however, occurs at both the district and the school level, and the achievement of leadership goals relies on organizational structures that allow dual authority within parts of the sub-system. Sage (1985) emphasized that in matters of legal and fiscal policy, "the special education administrator must participate in all aspects of the system" (p. 13), which remains as important today as it was in the past. Principals, however, are designated by school boards as instructional leaders for their schools (Bays & Crockett, 2007), which amplifies their responsibility for pursuing a vision that encompasses the effective instruction of students with disabilities, providing personnel with meaningful support, and monitoring the delivery and the outcome of specially designed instruction and related innovations. Each of these functions can influence the practice of instructional leadership for special education and the provision of equitable learning opportunities for every child.

Acknowledging the Educational Significance of Individual Differences

As this review of historical trends and conceptual models suggests, leading and administrating special education is a challenging practice because the concept of providing equal educational opportunities for every child poses dilemmas about individual differences in learning for which there are no risk-free or uncomplicated solutions (Kauffman & Hallahan, 2005). Addressing equity as "the educational significance of individual differences in children" (Berry, 1941, p. 253) has been described as a wicked problem of social policy, fraught with dilemmas and beset by diverse social values (Rittel & Webber, 1973). Wicked problems are enduring problems that disappear only when resources, or commitments to address them, expire. To address what Berry called "philosophy and administration in the education of all children" (p. 253), scholars of educational administration recently adopted social justice, democratic community, and school improvement as conceptual anchors for educational equity (Ivory, 2003; Murphy, 2006). These concepts complement special education's equitable foundations; however, if concerns with equity are, indeed, wickedly persistent problems, then administrators need to filter all the work they do to ensure that disability needs are carefully considered (Deshler, 2009).

The impact of disabilities on student learning is more than a philosophical concern, and for those who administer special education, ensuring high quality, individually-focused instruction, within and beyond the context of standards-based learning, is a national priority. Given current school reforms administrators and researchers alike are calling for changes in federal policy because a basic reality has been ignored in setting achievement goals for schools to reach: "Students with disabilities present a serious educational challenge, even to the most dedicated, best qualified educators" (Johnson, Peck, & Wise, 2007, p. 12).

From the perspective of equity, confusing the nondiscriminatory treatment of individuals with disabilities who need special education with the nondiscriminatory treatment of others "whose personal characteristics or identities are not directly related to their instruction … is a mistake in both concept and practice" (Kauffman & Landrum, 2009, p. 183). Such an error trivializes the implications for providing intensive and specific instruction, sometimes in different settings, so that students can learn. Working toward the equitable education of all learners is essential, but so is "thinking through the differences among differences and thinking about what is possible and what is not" (p. 186). Thinking in this way, administrative leaders should be less likely to over-emphasize inclusion or over-simplify the complexity of teaching students who struggle significantly to learn. For those who lead and administer educational programs, "perhaps it is wise to remember that a truly caring society—one that has figured out the ethics of the civil rights of various groups—will help students who need special education to flourish" (p. 187) whether their education is provided in alternative environments or general education classrooms.

The concept of equity, and what defines an equal opportunity for students with disabilities, has been interpreted differently across time, but the concept is no less troubling today than yesterday. The future for children might be brighter if administrators could build and sustain practices on a conceptual model of instructional leadership grounded in the integrated knowledge base of special education and educational administration, collaborating continually toward a common purpose rather than interacting sporadically in times of crisis or prosperity. Among the challenges to such collaboration is working across disciplines and sustaining the effort (Klein, 1990) Whether school reforms are effective and equitable for all students drives the current need for conceptual models of leading and administrating special education that are informed by enduring and emerging knowledge about improving outcomes for students with disabilities in the real-world context of schools. If mutual efforts toward leadership and student learning result in valued and appropriate services and positive student outcomes, sustained interactions rather than cyclical disengagements at the interface of these complementary disciplines might have a chance for success.

References

Alsbury, T. L., & Whitaker, K. S. (2007). Superintendent perspectives and practice of accountability, democratic voice, and social justice. *Journal of Educational Administration, 45*(2), 154–174.

Bartlett, L. D., Etscheidt, S., & Weisenstein, G. R. (2007). *Special education law and practice in public schools.* Upper Saddle River, NJ: Pearson.

Bateman, B. D. (2007). Law and the conceptual foundations of special education practice. In J. B. Crockett, M. M., Gerber, & T. J., Landrum (Eds.), *Achieving the radical reform of special education: Essays in honor of James M. Kauffman* (pp. 95–114). Mahwah, NJ: Erlbaum.

Bateman, B. D., & Linden, M. A. (2006). *Better IEPs: How to develop legally correct and educationally useful programs* (4th ed.). Champaign, IL: Research Press.

Bays, D. A., & Crockett, J. B. (2007). Investigating instructional leadership for special education. *Exceptionality, 15,* 143–161.

Berry, C. S. (1941). General problems of philosophy and administration in the education of exceptional children. *Review of Educational Research, 11,* 253–260.

Billingsley, B. S. (2007). Recognizing and supporting the critical roles of teachers in special education leadership. *Exceptionality, 15,* 163–176.

Billingsley, B. S., Crockett, J. B., & Boscarin, M. L. (2010). *Leadership for inclusive education.* Manuscript in preparation.

Boscardin, M. L. (2004). Transforming administration to support science in the schoolhouse for students with disabilities. *The Journal of Learning Disabilities, 37,* 262–269.

Brownell, M. T., Crockett, J. B., Smith, S. J., & Griffin, C. C. (in press). *Successful teaching for inclusive schools: Using evidence and collaborative inquiry.* New York: Guilford.

Brownell, M. T., Sindelar, P. T., Kiely, M. T., & Danielson, L. C. (2009). Special education teacher quality and preparation: Exposing foundations, constructing a new model. *Exceptional Children, 76,* 357–377.

Burrello, L. C., & Sage, D. D. (1979). *Leadership and change in special education.* Englewood Cliffs, NJ: Prentice-Hall.

Cook, B. G., Landrum, T. J., Cook, L., & Tankersley, M. (2008). Introduction to the special issue: Evidence-based practices in special education. *Intervention in School and Clinic, 44,* 67–68.

Cooperative Research Act, Pub. L. No. 83-531 (1954).

Council for Exceptional Children (CEC). (2010). *Division membership counts.* Arlington, VA. Author.

Crockett, J. B. (2002). Special education's role in preparing responsive leaders for inclusive schools. *Remedial and Special Education, 23,* 157–168.

Crockett, J. B. (2004). Taking stock of science in the schoolhouse: Four ideas to foster effective instruction for students with learning disabilities. *Journal of Learning Disabilities, 37*(3), 189–199.

Crockett, J. B. (2007). The changing landscape of special education administration. *Exceptionality, 15*(3), 139–142.

Crockett, J. B., Becker, M. K., & Quinn, D. (2009). Reviewing the knowledge base of special education leadership and administration: 1970–2009. *Journal of Special Education Leadership, 22,* 55–67.

Crockett, J. B., & Kauffman, J. M. (1999). *The least restrictive environment: Its origins and interpretations in special education.* Mahwah, NJ: Erlbaum.

Cruickshank, W. M. (1967). Current educational practices with exceptional children. In W. M. Cruickshank & G. O. Johnson (Eds.), *Education of exceptional children and youth* (2nd ed., pp. 45–98). Englewood Cliffs, NJ: Prentice-Hall.

Deshler, D. (2009, July). *Seeking solutions to wicked problems.* Keynote address, OSEP Project Directors' Conference, Washington, DC,.

DiPaola, M. F., & Walther-Thomas, C. (2002). *Principals and special education: The critical role of school leaders* (COPSSE Document No. IB-7). Gainesville: University of Florida, Center on Personnel Studies in Special Education.

Donaldson, G. A. (2001). *Cultivating leadership in schools: Connecting people, purpose, and practice.* New York: Teachers College Press.

Finkenbinder, R. L. (1981). Special education administration and supervision: The state of the art. *The Journal of Special Education, 15,* 485–495.

Furman, G. C., & Shields, C. M. (2005). How can educational leaders promote and support social justice and democratic community in schools? In W. A. Firestone & C. Riehl (Eds.), *A new agenda for research in educational leadership* (pp. 119–137). New York: Teachers College Press.

Gallagher, J. J. (2006). *Driving change in special education.* Baltimore, MD: Brookes.

Gerber, M. M. (2009, July). *Special education: Our future role and needed policy supports.* Keynote Panel Session, OSEP Project Directors Conference, Washington, DC.

Goor, M. B. (1995). *Leadership for special education administration: A case-based approach.* Fort Worth, TX: Harcourt Brace.

Hallinger, P., & Heck, R. (1996). Reassessing the principal's role in school effectiveness: A review of empirical research, 1980–1995. *Educational Administration Quarterly, 32*(1), 5–44.

Head, S., & Rhodes, W. C. (1974). The conceptual project in child variance. *Journal of Abnormal Child Psychology, 2,* 75–86.

Hoy, A. W., & Hoy, W. K. (2003). *Instructional leadership: A learning-centered guide.* Boston, MA: Allyn & Bacon.

Individuals with Disabilities Education Improvement Act (IDEA), (20 USC §1401 et seq. (2004).

Ivory, G. (2003, Spring). UCEA seeks superintendents' and principals' perspectives in "Voices 3." *UCEA Review,* 15–17.

Johnson, K. E., Peck, K., & Wise, J. (2007). *The students with disabilities subgroup and adequate yearly progress in mid-Atlantic region schools.* Washington, DC: Institute for Educational Sciences.

Kauffman, J. M., & Hallahan, D. P. (2005). *Special education: What it is and why we need it.* Boston: Pearson Education.

Kauffman, J. M., & Landrum, T. J. (2006). *Children and youth with emotional and behavioral disorders: A history of their education.* Austin, TX: Pro-Ed.

Kauffman, J. M., & Landrum, T. J. (2009). Politics, civil rights, and disproportional identification of students with emotional and behavioral disorders. *Exceptionality, 17,* 177–188.

Klein, J. T. (1990). *Iinterdisciplinarity: History, theory, and practice.* Detroit, MI: Wayne State University Press.

Lashley, C., & Boscardin, M. L. (2002). *Special education administration at a crossroads: Availability, licensure, and preparation of special education administrators.* (COPSSE Document No. IB-8). Gainesville: University of Florida, Center on Personnel Studies in Special Education.

Lashley, C., & Boscardin, M. L. (2003). Special education administration at a crossroads. *Journal of Special Education Leadership, 16*(2), 63–75.

Lazerson, M. (1983). The origins of special education. In J. G. Chambers, & W. T. Hartman (Eds.), *Special education policies: Their history, implementation, and finance* (pp. 15–47). Philadelphia, PA: Temple University Press.

Leithwood, K., Louis, K. S., Anderson, S., & Wahlstrom, K. (2004). *How leadership influences student learning.* Minneapolis: Center for Applied Research and Educational Improvement, University of Minnesota, and Ontario Institute for Studies in Education at the University of Toronto.

Leithwood, K. A., & Riehl, C. (2005). What do we already know about educational leadership? In W. A. Firestone & C. Riehl (Eds.), *A new agenda for research in educational leadership* (pp. 12–27). New York: Teachers College Press.

Lloyd, J. W., & Hallahan, D. P. (2007). Advocacy and reform of special education. In J. B. Crockett, M. M., Gerber, & T. J., & Landrum (Eds.), *Achieving the radical reform of special education: Essays in honor of James M. Kauffman* (pp. 245–263). Mahwah, NJ: Erlbaum.

McCarthy, E. F., & Sage, D. D. (Eds.). (1985) *Evolving organizational structures in special education.* Bloomington, IN: University Council for Educational Administration, Program Center for the Study of Leadership Behavior and Field Practice in Special Education Administration.

McLaughlin, M. (2009). *What every principal needs to know about special education.* Thousand Oaks, CA: Corwin Press.

McLaughlin, M. J., Krezmien, M., Zablocki, M., & Micelli, M. (2007). *The education of children with disabilities and interpretations of equity: A review of policy and research.* New York: Teachers College Press.

Meyen, E. L. (1995). Legislative and programmatic foundations of special education. In E. L. Meyen & T. M. Skrtic (Eds.), *Special education and student disability: Traditional, emerging, and alternative perspectives* (pp. 35–95). Denver, CO: Love.

Miller, M., & Hundson Baker, P. (2009). What are the needs of beginning special education administrators? *In Case, 50*(6), 6–10.

Murphy, J. (2006). *Preparing school leaders: Defining a research and action agenda.* Lanham, MD: Rowman & Littlefield Education.

Murphy, J., Vriesenga, M., & Storey, V. (2007). Educational Administration Quarterly, 1979–2003: Analysis of types of work, methods of investigation, and influences. *Educational Administration Quarterly, 43,* 612–628.

No Child Left Behind Act. Pub. L. No. 107-110, 20 U.S.C. §§ 6301 et seq (2001).

Pellegrino, J. W. (2006). *Rethinking and redesigning curriculum, instruction, and assessment: What contemporary research and theory suggest.* Washington, DC: National Center on Education and the Economy.

Pellegrino, J. W., & Chudowsky, N. (2003). The foundations of assessment. *Measurement: Interdisciplinary Research and Perspectives, 1*(2), 103–148.

Rittel, H. W. J., & Webber, M. M. (1973). Dilemmas in a general theory of planning. *Policy Sciences, 4,* 155–169.

Sage, D. D. (1985). Issues in organizational structure. In E. F. McCarthy & D. D. Sage (Eds.), *Evolving organizational structures in special education* (pp. 5–11). Bloomington, IN: University Council for Educational Administration, Program Center for the Study of Leadership Behavior and Field Practice in Special Education Administration.

Sage, D. D., & Burrello, L. C. (1994). *Leadership in educational reform: An administrator's guide to changes in special education.* Baltimore: Brookes.

Salend, S. J. (2008). *Creating inclusive classrooms: Effective and reflective practices* (6th ed.). Upper Saddle River, NJ: Pearson/Merrill.

Spillane, J. P., Halverson, R., & Diamond, J. B. (2001). Investigating school leadership practice: A distributed perspective. *Educational Researcher, 30*(3) 23–28.

Spillane, J. P., Reiser, B. J., & Reimer, T. (2002). Policy implementation and cognition: Reframing and refocusing implementation research. *Review of Educational Research, 72,* 387–431.

Training of Professional Personnel Act. Pub. L. No. 86-158 (1959).

U.S. Department of Education. (2006). *Twenty-sixth annual report to Congress on the implementation of the Individuals with Disabilities Education Act.* Washington, DC: Office of Special Education Programs, U.S. Government Printing Office.

Wakerman, S. Y., Browder, D. M., Flowers, C., & Ahlgrim-Delzell, L. (2006). Principals' knowledge of fundamental and current issues in special education. *NASSP Bulletin, 90,* 153-174.

Watson, S. T., & Scribner, J. P. (2005, November). *Emergent reciprocal influence: Toward a framework for understanding the distribution of leadership within collaborative school activity.* Paper presented at the annual conference of the University Council for Educational Administration, Nashville, TN.

Willower, D. J. (1970). Special education: Organization and administration of exceptional children. *Exceptional Children, 36,* 591–594.

Yates, J. R. (2005, November). *The past and a trend line to the future for preparing special education administrators.* Paper presented at the annual conference of the University Council for Educational Administration, Nashville, TN.

Zigmond, N., Kloo, A., & Volonino, V. (2009). What, where, and how? Special education in the climate of full inclusion. *Exceptionality, 17,* 189–204.

28

Fiscal Policy and Funding for Special Education

Thomas Parrish and Jenifer Harr-Robins
American Institutes for Research, Washington, DC

For providers of special education services, a basic understanding of special education finance is fundamental to effective practice. Fiscal policy not only affects the levels of resources available to meet the needs of children in special education, but the way these provisions are designed can affect the ways in which services are provided. For example, additional funding may be available for more integrated placements; funding may be limited to additional teachers when what is really needed is specialized equipment; and supplemental resources may be allowed for special education but not pre-referral. Funding policy will affect how much is provided, to whom, and for what kinds of services. These policies drive special education services and in this sense are vitally important.

States and the federal government differ substantially on how they approach these important special education finance issues. This chapter will attempt to cover a broad range of topics and how they have been treated through state and federal special education fiscal policy, and will conclude with a conceptual overview of how they may all be tied together in a comprehensive system of special education finance and accountability.

The special education stakes are high. About 14% of the nation's public school students receive special education at an average total expenditure that is about twice that spent on a child receiving no supplemental services (Chambers, Parrish, & Harr, 2002). Children in special education have a legal entitlement to a free and appropriate public education, which also sets them apart from non special education children. Many children are being served, the cost is high, and the educational needs of these children are often quite pronounced. Issues related to special education funding and spending have been the focus of considerable policy discussion since the passage of the federal special education law in 1975, now known as the Individuals with Disabilities Education Act (IDEA, 2007).

How Much Are We Spending on Special Education?

Determining what is spent on special education nationally is not an easy endeavor. The federal government stopped collecting data on special education expenditures by state in 1990,[1] and only 30 states reported spending data for 1998–99 as part of a national survey on special education (Parrish et al., 2004).[2] Even that information, however, was limited due to different accounting methods across the states. To produce reliable estimates, specific expenditure studies must be conducted. To date, there have been four large-scale studies of special education spending for the following school years: 1968–69 (Rossmiller, Hale, & Frohreich 1970), 1977–78 (Kakalik, Furry, Thomas, & Carney, 1981), 1985–86 (Moore, Strang, Schwartz, & Braddock, 1988), and 1999–2000 (Chambers et al., 2002).

According to the latest study, \$50 billion was spent across the 50 states and the District of Columbia on special education services in 1999–2000, averaging \$8,080 per special education student and representing 14% of total spending on elementary and secondary education (Chambers et al., 2002). The majority of students in special education, however, also receive general education services. Considering both general and special education services, a total of \$77.3 billion was spent on special education students—or \$12,474 per student. This is approximately 90% more than what was spent on the average student with no special needs. This additional expenditure measurement—also commonly known as "excess cost"—is a key component in special education finance and depicts what is spent on top of what the student would have otherwise received as a general education student. This measurement can also be presented as a "spending ratio" of 1.9, as shown in Table 28.1 (Column B).

Across disability categories, there is a wide range in spending, demonstrating that students in special education are not a homogenous group (Table 28.1). Average spending per pupil varies from a low of $10,558 (in 1999–2000 dollars), with a spending ratio of 1.6, for students with specific learning disabilities to a high of $20,095, with a spending ratio of 3.1, for students with multiple disabilities (Chambers, Shkolnik, & Perez, 2003). As noted above, many students in special education also receive general education services, which are included in the total spending estimates. About half of the services received by the average student with specific learning disabilities are special education, whereas 80% of services received on average by a student with autism are special education (Column C, Table 28.1). Although the data were not disaggregated by disability category, students placed in non-public schools for which the district paid tuition topped the list with a total expenditure of $25,580—nearly four times spending on a general education student.

In addition to differences across disability categories, Chambers et al. (2003) reported considerable variations *within* categories, when examining the 95% confidence intervals of the estimates. Students with visual impairment/blindness showed the greatest variation, with a difference of nearly $6,600 between the lower and upper 95% confidence intervals, while students with learning disabilities had the narrowest range with a difference of $1,500.[3]

Much attention has been given to the rising cost of special education (Berman, Davis, Koufman-Frederick, & Urion, 2001; Cibulka & Derlin, 1992; Greene & Winters, 2007; Parrish, 2001). Overall, special education spending has increased as a result of rising special education enrollments, which have historically outpaced growth in total enrollments. Currently at 14%, the number of students served by IDEA has steadily increased as a percentage of public enrollment for more than three decades.[4] In addition, total spending per special education student has also increased from $9,858 (in adjusted 1999–2000 dollars) in 1985–86 to $12,474 in 1999–2000. Figure 28.1 illustrates this steady increase over time across the four expenditure studies.

However, the increase is less pronounced when examining spending on a special education student in relation to that on a general education student with no special needs. The 1999–2000 ratio of 1.90 marks the first decline after decades of rising spending ratios—from 1.97 in 1968–69 (Rossmiller et al., 1970) to 2.17 in 1977–78 (Kakalik et al., 1981) to 2.28 in 1985–87 (Moore et al., 1988). This suggests that although total spending per special education student has risen, it has done so at a slower pace than total spending on students without special needs. This decline has been attributed to the growing ranks of students with specific learning disabilities, who are generally considered to have less severe needs and therefore lower spending.

Who Pays for Special Education?

Current national data regarding revenue shares for special education are not available. However, the last year for which

TABLE 28.1
Average Total Spending on a Special Education Student and Spending Ratio in Relation to Spending on an Average General Education Student and the Percentage of Total Spending Attributed to Special Education, 1999–2000

	Total Spending (1999--2000)	Spending Ratio[1]	% of Total Spending Attributed to Special Education
	A	B	C
Average General Education Student with no Special Needs	$6,556	—	—
Average Special Education Student	$12,474	1.9	65%
Disability Category (public school students only)			
Autism	$18,790	2.9	81%
Emotional Disturbance	$14,147	2.2	70%
Hearing Impairment/Deafness	$15,992	2.4	69%
Mental Retardation	$15,040	2.3	76%
Multiple Disabilities	$20,095	3.1	80%
Orthopedic Impairment	$14,993	2.3	73%
Other Health Impairment	$13,229	2.0	66%
Specific Learning Disability	$10,558	1.6	52%
Speech/Language Impairment	$10,958	1.7	58%
Traumatic Brain Injury	$16,542	2.5	75%
Visual Impairment/Blindness	$18,811	2.9	73%
Students Placed in Non-Public Schools[2]	$25,580	3.9	100%

Note: Adapted from *What Are We Spending on Special Education Services in the United States, 1999–2000?* by J. Chambers, T. Parrish, & J. J. Harr, 2002. Special Education Expenditure Project (SEEP). Palo Alto, CA: American Institutes for Research, Center for Special Education Finance; and *Total Expenditures for Students with Disabilities, 1999-2000: Spending Variation by Disability* by J. G. Chambers, J. Shkolnik, & M. Perez, 2003. Palo Alto, CA: American Institutes for Research.

[1] The spending ratio compares total spending on a special education student to spending on a general education student with no special needs. For example, spending on the average special education student ($12,474) is 1.9 times, or 90% more than, what is spent on the average general education student.

[2] Chambers et al. (2003) did not disaggregate estimates for students placed in non-public schools by disability category.

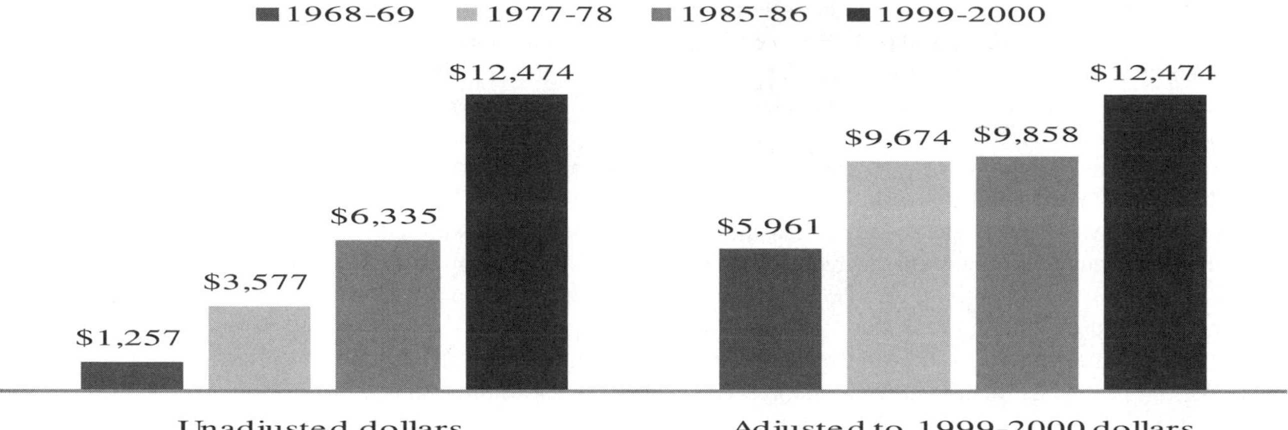

Figure 28.1 Total spending on the average special education student over time in unadjusted and adjusted 1999–2000 dollars. Adapted from *What Are We Spending on Special Education Services in the United States, 1999–2000?* by J. Chambers, T. Parrish, & J. J. Harr, 2002. Special Education Expenditure Project (SEEP). Palo Alto, CA: American Institutes for Research, Center for Special Education Finance.

such data were collected and analyzed, the 1999–2000 school year, states and local districts were shown to bear the largest shares of special education spending, with federal dollars constituting an estimated 7.5% of total special education spending (Chambers et al., 2002).[5] These data do not disaggregate local and state shares, for which the latest national information available is for the 1998–99 school year. In 1998–99, state funds accounted on average for 50% of special education spending with the remaining 40% coming from local revenues. However, there was considerable variation in the distribution of these shares across the nation, with state revenues supporting between 3% and 90% of the spending and the local share ranging from zero to 80% (Parrish et al., 2004). By whatever estimate, however, it is clear that state and local revenues support the vast majority of special education spending.

Federal Funding for Special Education

Federal formula. In addition to establishing special education as a legal entitlement for eligible students with disabilities, the IDEA also provides categorical funding to states and local districts for the provision of special education services. Although the law provides grants to serve children from birth through age 2 (known as Part C of the IDEA), this chapter discusses only provisions for serving students ages 3 to 21 (found in Part B of the law). The 1997 reauthorization of the IDEA introduced a fundamental change to the funding formula for distributing federal special education funds. Prior to the 1997 reauthorization, the federal revenues were distributed to states on a per student basis, whereby each student identified for special education generated a set amount of funding. This meant that more students identified for special education, up to a cap of 12%, would in effect result in greater levels of funding. In addition, it meant that states received essentially the same amount per special education student whether the state had an 8% or 12% identification rate.

In part due to concerns about over-identification of students for special education, the 1997 amendments changed the formula to one based on factors not directly related to the numbers of students identified for special education (Apling, 2001). Under the new formula, 85% of federal special education funding is allocated according to the total residential population in the age group of special education students served in the state. This type of allocation is commonly called a “census” approach. The remaining 15% is distributed by the percentage of students living in poverty relative to other states. In other words, a populous state with a greater percentage of students in poverty would receive a larger share of these federal funds than a smaller state with a lower poverty rate.

The legislation specified that the new formula would take effect when the federal IDEA Part B revenues exceeded $4.9 billion, which happened in fiscal year 2000. This represented a break from the prior formula based on the counts of special education students. However, states continue to receive the amount that they received in fiscal year 1999 under the old formula, with revenues above that base amount being allocated according to the residential population and poverty formula. By 2006, 60% of the total IDEA school-age revenues were distributed by the new formula (Harr & Parrish, 2005).

As a result of the formula change, there is a growing disparity among the states in the amount of federal dollars allocated per special education student. By 2003, this amount ranged from $1,000 to $1,500 per special education student given the differences in the numbers of special education students, residential population, and poverty rates (Harr & Parrish, 2005).[6]

Aside from the formula, the IDEA contains several other key provisions with important fiscal implications. The following sections briefly describe full funding, maintenance of effort, and early intervening services.

Full funding. Discussion about the federal share of special education spending often invokes the concept of “full funding.” At the time that the IDEA was first passed in 1975, the legislation set the maximum amount that the federal government was authorized to allocate as the number of special education students served by IDEA in each state multiplied by 40% of the average per pupil expenditure (APPE) in public elementary and secondary schools. This provision, commonly referred to as "full funding," is often described as a promise, commitment, or guarantee that the federal government made when passing the law. Despite congressional debates on the issue and substantial increases in revenues in recent years, funding has increased from 7.3% APPE in 1996–97 to 17% in fiscal year 2008 (Council for Exceptional Children [CEC], 2008). Due to the infusion of funds from the American Recovery and Reinvestment Act (ARRA), the percentage increased to the unprecedented level of 34% in fiscal year 2009 (CEC, 2009). However, additional ARRA funding is set to end in 2011.

It is important to distinguish 40% APPE from the *share of special education spending*. As noted above, the federal revenues supported less than 8% of special education spending in 1999–2000. APPE, on the other hand, reflects spending on ***all*** public school students, including special education students. Although there was no clear research-basis for the 40% threshold,[7] the purpose of using APPE was to approximate the excess costs of educating students with disabilities above the amount spent to educate a non-disabled student with no special needs (President's Commission, 2002).

Maintenance of effort. Another important funding provision in the IDEA is the "maintenance of effort" (MOE) requirement, which applies to both states and local education agencies (LEAs). This is closely related to the law's "supplement but not supplant" stipulation, which prohibits federal funds from replacing non-federal funds. Under MOE provisions, state revenues and LEAs expenditures (using combined state and local funds) for special education must be at least the same as in the preceding year. That is, federal IDEA funds cannot be used, except in specified cases, to reduce the level of state and local special education expenditures.[8]

These exceptions expanded with the 2004 reauthorization of IDEA, which allows an LEA to reduce its MOE by up to 50% of the increase in its IDEA appropriation in a given year. According to the Council for Exceptional Children (2009), the purpose of this adjustment was to "provide tax relief to LEAs for the many years they paid more than their fair share of special education costs with local tax dollars, due to the federal government's failure to fully fund IDEA" (p. 9). LEAs opting to adjust their MOE must use the freed up funds to carry out activities supported by the Elementary and Secondary Education Act. Although the influx of ARRA funds may have a lasting impact on a given LEA's MOE, local obligations might be expected to increase again if federal funding returns to pre-ARRA levels because LEAs are still responsible for providing an appropriate education to eligible students with disabilities. That is, if federal funding drops after ARRA, LEAs that reduced their MOE during the ARRA period may need to increase their special education funds to fill the gap and ensure that all special education students receive required services.

Early intervening services. Another change that came about with the 2004 reauthorization was the flexibility granted to LEAs to spend to up to 15% of federal special education funds on early intervention services (EIS) for students not identified for special education, but who need additional support to succeed in the general education environment. Although this is discretionary, LEAs with patterns of race and ethnic disproportionality are required by law to use the maximum EIS funding flexibility.[9]

Prior to this change, IDEA funds could be spent only on eligible students identified for special education. By intervening early with at-risk students, this flexible use of funds may allow educators to address students' needs without having to refer them to special education. IDEA funds designated for EIS may be used to support educational and behavioral evaluations and services, as well as professional development for school personnel to deliver scientifically based academic and behavioral interventions.

One such approach is Response to Intervention" (RtI), a service delivery system whereby at-risk students are identified and targeted with interventions that may become increasingly intensive according to the monitoring of their responses to those supports. RtI gained attention after the 2004 IDEA reauthorization, which identified it as an alternative to identifying students with specific learning disabilities. It is not clear, however, if and how local special education administrators are using IDEA funds to support this approach.

At the same time, there are restrictions to this flexibility that may drive local decisions as to whether to use the funds in this manner. For example, the EIS-designated funds cannot be spent on students already identified for special education, which may make delivery of services to mixed student groups problematic. Note also that there are limitations in utilizing both the MOE adjustment and EIS flexibility in a given year. The EIS set-aside amount counts toward the maximum MOE reduction, and vice versa. This interconnected relationship requires LEA administrators to carefully consider how best to deploy the funds.[10]

State Funding for Special Education

As noted above, the majority of special education spending is supported by state and local revenues. Although states distribute federal funds according to the IDEA requirements, formulas for distributing state revenues for special education to LEAs vary a great deal across the 50 states. Some states allocate funds according to the number of total students (both general and special education), often referred to as the "census" approach, and others distribute funding based on the number of special education students or some measure of special education resources (such as teachers or expenditures). Although the details within the same formula type can differ significantly and other components can play a role, state funding mechanisms can be grouped

TABLE 28.2
Types of Special Education Formulas by State, 1999–2000

Formula Type	Description	States
Multiple student weights	Funding (either a series of multiples of the general education amount or tiered dollar amounts) allocated per special education student that varies by disability, type of placement, or student need.	Arizona, Colorado, Florida, Georgia, Indiana, Iowa, Kentucky, New Mexico, Ohio, Oklahoma, South Carolina, Texas (n = 12)
Census-based	A fixed dollar amount per total enrollment or average daily membership	Alabama, California, Idaho, Massachusetts, Montana, New Jersey, Pennsylvania (n = 7)
Single student weight	Funding (either a single multiple of the general education amount or a fixed dollar amount) allocated per special education student	Louisiana, Maine, New Hampshire, New York, North Carolina, Oregon, Washington (n = 7)
No separate special education funding	Funding to support special education is rolled into the overall funding levels	Arkansas, Connecticut, Hawaii, Missouri, North Dakota, Rhode Island, West Virginia (n = 7)
Resource-based	Funding based on payment for a certain number of specific education resources (e.g., teachers or classroom units), usually determined by prescribed staff/student ratios that may vary by disability, type of placement, or student need.	Delaware, Kansas, Mississippi, Nevada, Tennessee, Virginia (n = 6)
Combination	Funding based on a combination of formula types	Alaska, Illinois, Maryland, South Dakota, Vermont (n = 5)

Adapted from *Financing Special Education: State Funding Formulas* by E. Ahearn, 2010. Alexandria, VA: Project Forum, National Association of State Directors of Special Education (NASDSE).

into six broad categories. Based on 2008–09 survey data collected by the National Association of State Directors of Special Education (Ahearn, 2010), Table 28.2 provides a brief overview of these six categories along with the states that use it as the primary method.

The most prevalent type of state formula is multiple student weights, whereby more funding is often allocated for disabilities or placements that are considered more costly. For example, Kentucky provides differential funding for students with speech impairment (weight of 0.24), students with specific learning disability (1.17), and those with autism or emotional disturbance (2.35). In this case, a student with a speech impairment would receive a supplement equal to 0.24 times the base amount available for general education students, while the supplemental funding for a student with autism would be the base amount multiplied by 2.35. With respect to educational placements, Arizona's formula assigns a greater weight of 6.773 for students with orthopedic impairments in self-contained classrooms, in comparison to students with orthopedic impairments in resource rooms, who have a weight of 3.158. Some states have moved to higher weights for more integrated settings to encourage inclusive practices. This issue is discussed in greater detail in the following section.

To be clear, the formulas described in Table 28.2 are for *allocating* special education funds, and do not necessarily drive the overall level of funding available. For instance, in North Carolina, the funding available for special education is divided by the number of special education students to determine the per student funding amount.

Thus, state special education funding formulas often do not have a current, rational basis that reflects the actual costs of serving students with disabilities. This is generally true for the total amount allocated by the state as well as for any funding delineations that it may contain (e.g., weighted formulas that allocate more funds for one category of disability over another). Many formulas have some form of historical cost basis, but they may have been crafted several decades ago thereby weakening any link that may have existed between actual costs and funding. In addition, formulas such as student weights are contingent upon the funding available for general education. If general education is underfunded or there is an ambiguous relationship to actual costs, this will impact special education as well.

District Formulas

There is relatively little literature on how districts allocate special education resources to schools. For the most part, special education teachers and personnel to provide related education services and carry out activities such as diagnostic evaluations are centrally budgeted at the district level. In other words, schools generally do not receive special education dollars, and decisions about how many special education personnel are assigned to schools are typically made at the district level.

In addition, students in special education may not attend their neighborhood schools. Districts may have separate schools for certain students in special education, which are directly funded and run by the district. Or, districts may assign students and resources to special programs that may be clustered in a select number of schools within the district.

When separate programs or schools are created and run by the district in this way, it is usually based on arguments of greater efficiency, in that children with similar needs can be more efficiently served by specialized staff and equipment based in the same location. However, the cost of transporting students to schools outside their neighborhood can also be formidable, sometimes raising questions regarding claims of greater efficiency. Such settings may also place a child's right under federal law to being educated in the least restrictive environment (LRE) in jeopardy.[11]

Thus, although district control of special education resources and services may buffer schools from various fiscal and procedural compliance requirements related to the IDEA, it may discourage the integration of special education students into local schools. Even when special education students are assigned to their neighborhood schools, if special education staff are supervised and controlled by the district, integration of students and services can be problematic.

In an evaluation of the special education funding system in the District of Columbia, Parrish, Harr, Poirier, Madsen, and Yonker (2007) recommended that the school district develop greater school-level discretion over special education resources to facilitate principal ownership of special education students. The authors noted that there was little incentive for principals to create and integrate special education programs as the school district retained state funding allocated for the most severe students, thus controlling staff for those students. In these cases, staff reported directly to the central office instead of the school, thus perpetuating a separate culture. A further complication of district control of special education resources and/or uniform allocations of these resources to local schools is increased student mobility and choice within districts. Increasing public choice for all students across schools within a district, and across districts and charter options, further complicates issues in regard to the schools special education students will attend, how they will be best served, and how special education resources should best be allocated within local systems. As a result, Parrish and Bitter (2003) commented, "It never has been more important that the supplemental resources a child with special needs requires follow the child to the school and into whatever type of service arrangement is most appropriate" (p. 34).

To allow greater flexibility to restructure instruction to meet student needs, an earlier study in 1995 (Fruchter, Parrish, & Berne, 1999) proposed merging special and general education funds at the school level in New York City. Another way to accomplish increased school autonomy in the provision of services is through weighted student formulas. Similar to student weights at the state level, these can be used to allocate resources from districts to schools based on student need. These formulas are also intended to give schools more autonomy over how to spend their resources. The Reason Foundation 2009 yearbook on weighted student formulas identified 14 school districts nationwide that had such initiatives (Snell, 2009).

However, just six of those approaches included supplemental funding for special education students, with the weights in two districts being minimal and intended for minor expenses such as instructional supplies. So even among districts with weighted student formulas, special education is still centrally managed in the majority of districts.

In what may be the most significant decentralization of special education, Snell (2009) reported that Baltimore will devolve to its schools approximately $76 million in special education dollars in 2010, giving principals discretion on how to spend the funds. Although special education teachers will no longer be centrally assigned under this model, resources for related services are expected to remain managed at the district level.

To enhance schools' flexibility to create appropriate service delivery models for special education students, New York City's weighted student formula, known as Fair Student Funding (FSF), allocates funds based on the number of periods in a school day that students require special education services as opposed to a set service delivery approach. One purpose of this is "to help reinforce that special education students are an integral part of a school, not a separate subset of students. FSF aims to eliminate the view of special education as strictly prescriptive, immovable and segregated from the kinds of innovative thinking that occur in general education" (Snell, 2009).

On the other hand, greater flexibility will likely mean that schools will shoulder some of the responsibilities previously borne by the districts. Chambers, Shambaugh, Levin, Muraki, and Poland (2008) found that most school respondents and some district administrators were cautious about the idea of delegating special education to the schools. District administrators pursuing greater school autonomy will need to strike a balance between encouraging discretion and ownership at the school level and addressing fiscal and procedural compliance issues and providing specialized services that may be inefficient for the school to undertake.

High Cost Students

A concern for districts, particularly smaller ones, is extraordinarily high-need students who may pose significant fiscal challenges. The prevalence of these students is relatively low among the overall population of students with disabilities. For example, Chambers, Perez, and Esra (2005) estimated that 6% of all students in special education had a total expenditure of $26,224 or more and that less than 0.5% of the special education population had an average total expenditure of $84,564 in 1999–2000. However, such costs can create a significant and unanticipated financial burden, especially if a disproportionate number of such students are enrolled in small district in a given year.

Although this is a predominant issue for census-based funding, which generally does not account for the uneven distribution of high-need students across the state, it can be problematic for districts operating under other formulas as well. In response to this growing concern, the President's Commission on Excellence in Special Education in 2002 called for the federal government to offset these costs by allowing greater flexibility in the use of IDEA funds to establish a contingency fund to support high-need students at the local level. The IDEA reauthorization in 2004 adopted this recommendation by permitting states to set aside up to 10% of the IDEA allocation reserved for state-level activities to set up such a risk pool or to support innovative and effective ways of cost sharing.

Even prior to the 2004 reauthorization, more than half of the states already had provisions to mitigate the local fiscal burden of high-cost students, according to the 1999–2000 CSEF survey. The mechanism in some states is intended only for students educated in separate facilities, but a number of states allow districts to submit applications for any special education student whose cost exceeds a certain threshold (e.g., four times the average per pupil expenditure). In the latter, states may provide partial reimbursement of costs in excess of the threshold, with locals still responsible for the full amount up to the threshold as well as the remaining excess costs. In some cases, the safety net is contingent on the funds available in a given year, and may result in the reimbursement being prorated.

How Might Funding Provisions Affect Practice?

When fiscal resources are associated with certain student characteristics—such as the student's special education status, disability category, or educational placement—questions are sometimes raised as to whether such funding provisions may influence special education decisions and practices. Concerns are expressed as to whether funding mechanisms may provide unintended and inappropriate incentives that may lead to an over-identification of students for special education, of certain disability categories, or of more restrictive placements because these attributes receive greater levels of funding.

Such concerns were articulated in the 1997 reauthorization of the IDEA. As noted earlier, the federal formula moved away from providing funding based on the number of special education students due to concerns about over-identification. Although the House and Senate reports for the 1997 reauthorization conceded that "it is unlikely that individual educators ever identify children for the additional funding that such identification brings," the reports cited over-identification of African-American males as a concern and noted that fiscal incentives may decrease checks on the special education referral process (Apling, 2001). Furthermore, during the same reauthorization cycle, the IDEA included a requirement that states allocating state funding based on the type of educational setting must ensure that the mechanism does not result in placements that violate the law's LRE clause.

An example of this issue is New York, which at the time had a placement-based formula that assigned a weight of 2.70 to students spending 60% or more of their day in a special class, with lower weights of 1.90 for students spending 20% in a resource room, and 1.80 for students spending their entire day in the general education classroom. In other words, the separate placement generated 50% more funding than that for the general education setting. In 1999–2000, the state had nearly 30% of its students spending 60% or more of their school day outside the general education classroom in comparison to 20% nationally. In reaction to concerns about inappropriate fiscal incentives for separate placements, New York modified its formula that year to include an additional weight of 0.5 for receiving services in the general education classroom (Parrish, 2000).[12]

West Virginia provides a recent example of a state responding to concerns that funding provisions based on counts of special education students may create unintended incentives for increased identification. According to federal data, West Virginia's special education population in 2005 comprised nearly 18% of its total enrollment—the fourth highest across the nation and well above the national average of 14%. Prior to 2008, West Virginia treated each special education student as the equivalent of two general education students when determining the amount of overall funding available to school districts. Out of concern of a possible incentive for over-identifying students for special education, the state removed this supplement weight (Lapp, 2009).

These types of concerns are the impetus for studies of the relationship between state special education funding formulas and practice (Cullen, 1999; Dempsey & Fuchs, 2003; Greene & Forster, 2002; Kane & Johnson, 1993; Mahitivanichcha & Parrish, 2005a, 2005b). For example, Cullen examined the impact of changes to state special education funding in Texas in the early 1990s on subsequent special education enrollment. Her results showed that a 10% increase in the supplemental funding per special education student could be expected to produce a 1.4% increase in identification rates, with more pronounced increases for students with speech impairments and specific learning disabilities.

Greene and Forster (2002) analyzed special education enrollments over time in states with funding systems based on special education students or resources (such as teachers or expenditures) in relation to states with formulas that did not distribute funds based on such special education counts (what they called a "lump sum" system). The authors estimated that the states with systems based on count of special education students, or other characteristics, had an increase of 1.24 percentage points in special education enrollment over 10 years in relation to what they would have had under a "lump sum" funding system. However, Mahitivanichcha and Parrish (2005a) challenged Greene and Forster's findings in alternative analyses that showed lower or no impact of systems distributing funds based on special education characteristics.

In terms of placement patterns, Dempsey and Fuchs (1993) analyzed Tennessee's change in special education funding in the early 1980s from a single to multiple weights. This latter system provided greater funding for more costly placements, which they found to be related to an increase in such placements, which also tend to be more restrictive.

Yet, the relationships between state fiscal provisions and the evaluation process for determining special education eligibility and placement is far from straightforward, with multiple players and social, political, and economic factors involved (Mahitivanichcha & Parrish, 2005b). Furthermore, local revenues—not state funds—often support the majority of special education spending. Among the 39 states that reported federal, state, and local shares of special education spending for 1998–99 (the most current data available), districts in 15 states supported 56% or more of spending (Parrish et al., 2004).[13]

As described by an administrator in New York, "There's no incentive created by the weights to over-identify because about 58–60% of the costs of educating kids with disabilities are borne by local funding" (Lapp, 2009). Even where local shares are smaller, incentives to over-identify students for special education may be minimized since the total cost of serving students will likely exceed any combined federal and state revenues.

Nonetheless, it is important to keep potential fiscal incentives for such practices as over-identification in certain categories of disability and overly restrictive placements in mind when considering special education funding policies, particularly if there are already issues around these practices. Even when there is no statistical evidence of a causal effect of fiscal incentives, formulas can send powerful messages about a state's priorities and expectations and may affect the ways in which services are provided.

For example, Georgia's formula is inadvertently structured to create a fiscal disincentive for LRE. As a result, a local administrator described moving students out of general education settings on the day of the "official count" used to determine state formula allocations to avoid the loss of needed special education funding (Roach, 2002).

Conversely, some formulas feature higher weights or funding amounts to *encourage* inclusive placements. Such changes also reflect a shift in philosophy regarding special education service delivery, whereby the emphasis is less on a fixed placement and more on enhancing flexibility and providing a continuum of options that maximize access to the general education curriculum.

In 2002, Mississippi modified its resource-based formula, which allocates funding based on the number of special education teacher units, to facilitate a "unified service delivery system that supports students in general education classrooms."[14] Under the new formula, students who receive 12.5 to 24 hours a week of special education services and are removed from general education for no more than 20% of the school day are assigned a weight of 2.5 when calculating the number of teacher units, whereas students with the same intensity of services who are removed for more than 60% have a lower weight of 2.0. At the next level of support (more than 24 hours a week), both models receive the same weight of 3.0.

As noted earlier, New York's formula included an add-on weight for serving students in the regular education classroom. However, in 2007–08, the state changed to a single student weight irrespective of placement. The percentage of students in this placement category had declined by 5 percentage points since introducing the higher weights for inclusive placements, but the state still had the second highest percentage across the 50 states, suggesting that fiscal provisions alone may not have the desired effect (or alternatively, the supplemental weight was not large enough to change local practices in dramatic ways).

Such incentives for inclusion are also evident at the district level. Baltimore's school-based funding provides resources for serving students with disabilities in inclusive settings, which increases with more hours spent in the general education classroom. For students receiving special education for more than 60% of their school day, New York City provides more funding for students who are integrated than for students who are served in self-contained classrooms. For example, elementary and middle school students who receive special education services for more than 60% of the school day and who are integrated have a weight of 2.28, in relation to the weight of 1.23 for students in self-contained classrooms. At the high school level, the difference increases considerably, with a weight of 2.52 for an integrated approach and 0.73 for self-contained students (Snell, 2009).

Special Education Equity

Disparities in funding across districts within a state have long been a pre-dominant issue for education policy (see court cases Serrano v. Priest and San Antonio Independent School District v. Rodriquez). In these early analyses, the primary focus was on horizontal equity, which is generally defined as striving for equality in average per student funding across districts. However, an important related standard is vertical equity, which is defined as equal funding for students with comparable characteristics, which results in systematically different funding for students with special needs. Both horizontal and vertical considerations are relevant to the consideration of equitable funding in special education. This section describes broader considerations of special education fiscal equity.

Overview. Under vertical considerations, as the educational needs of certain groups of students are clearly different from others, equity can only come from systematically different funding amounts per type of student (Berne & Stiefel, 1984). The most commonly discussed categories of students in different needs categories are those in poverty, limited English proficient, and receiving special education services. Nearly all of the states have developed supplemental funding provisions for one or more of these categories of students.

There appears to be little question that students in special education require supplemental services to receive an equal opportunity to learn. However, how much more funding is needed to support those services above that provided to general education students and the degree to which funding should differ by category within special education (e.g., students with learning disabilities versus those with visual impairments) have been dominant questions in special education finance. As illustrated in the previous descriptions of funding systems, states have approached these vertical equity issues in very different ways.

However, horizontal considerations are also important

in considering special education equity. This most basic equity concern for education generally—substantial variations across districts in average funding per pupil—has received relatively little attention when focused specifically on special education. For example, a state formula may be designed to specifically accommodate vertical equity through greater funding weights for students in special education generally and often differential weights within special education so that the funding weight for more "severe" students is greater than that for less "severe." However, this emphasis on vertical equity for individual students or types of students in the base formula may sometimes divert attention from the question of horizontal equity in overall special education funding across districts. These inequities may result from underlying elements of the formula that retain historic funding differences or other factors that may counteract the formula's more straightforward vertical equity provisions. State formulas, which may appear quite rational on the surface, may result in average allocations of state special education funds per special education student that vary by multiples of two to three across districts in a state, even though their special education student populations may be quite comparable.

Special education equity issues at the three primary levels of support. As noted earlier in this chapter, revenues in support of special education come from federal, state and local sources. All have potential equity concerns.

Equity questions in federal special education funding. On its surface, the federal formula is simple with 85% of federal funds above the base year allocated by the state's relative school-age population and 15% on the basis of relative poverty. Thus, states with larger school-aged populations and higher percentages of students in poverty receive more federal funds.

This formula may be considered quite inequitable by design, in that it has no relationship to variations in special education costs. On the other hand, this approach to special education funding may be considered equitable in that states that are similar based on the criteria specified in the formula are treated equally. Two states of the same size and percentage of students in poverty and the same base-year amounts would receive the same level of funding even though one state may identify 18% of its students as in need of special education services and the other state only 12%. This results in very different allocations of federal special education funds per special education student in these two states.

Inequities in state special education funding. As described earlier in this chapter, states generally provide the greatest percentage of special education support. Because of this, disparities in average state support per special education student across districts are perhaps of greatest concern and should receive the most scrutiny.

When evaluating a state special education funding formula, a major criterion should be equity of funding. With the traditional concepts of school finance equity in mind, this would mean equal funding per special education student (horizontal equity) unless the special education population across districts was found to be substantially and systematically different (vertical equity). Thus, unless the special education students in one district have greater educational needs than those in another, based on some measurable indicator (e.g., varying percentages of students by category of disability[15] or poverty[16]), or unless the districts differed by some other measurable cost factors (e.g., those associated with remoteness or urbanicity) (Chambers, 1996; Chambers, 1981), one would expect relatively equal state special education aid per special education student on average across districts.

However, substantial variation in the allocations of special education resources across districts has been observed in several state studies, the magnitude of which do not seem clearly related to variations in student characteristics or need. For example, an examination of Illinois data for the 2007–08 school year shows variation among the largest districts in the state (with over 5,000 in total enrollment) of state special education revenues per special education student from less than $2,000 to over $7,000 and differences in total special education spending per student of nearly 2.5 to one ($25,000 vs. $10,000) Although there seems to be a positive relationship between higher state special education funding and total special education spending, and between the amount of funding received per student and the percentage of special education students in low incidence (and generally more severe) disabilities, these positive relationships do not seem to warrant funding and spending differentials of the observed magnitude (Parrish, 2010).

In a study conducted in Georgia (Parrish & Harr, 2005), districts were divided into quartiles by average state special education funding per special education student. The aid amount among the lowest quartile of districts was approximately $3,600 versus $5,600 per student in the highest. No substantial differences were found, on average, between the lowest and highest quartiles of state aid districts in such special education need proxies as the percentage of students in special education (11% vs. 12%), percentage of total enrollment in poverty (62% vs. 56%), or the percentage of special education students who have speech/language impairment or specific learning disability, which may be considered less severe disabling conditions on average (56% vs. 49%).

A study conducted in Oregon (Parrish & Harr, 2007) provides another perspective on possible equity concerns in relation to state funding by examining disparities between state special education revenues for districts in relation to what they actually spend. Although variations in special education spending are not perfect correlates for differences in student need, they provide a proxy for considering the equity of state distributions. A third of the districts in the state reported spending more than $500 per special education student *less* than what they received in state and federal special education revenues, while another quarter of the districts reported spending over $500 per special education student *more* than their state and federal special education aid receipts.

In a similar study conducted for Nevada (Parrish & Shambaugh, 2009), state special education revenues per special education student varied by a factor of about three to one (approximately $6,000 to $2,000) in the highest and lowest funded districts. The percentage of local contribution in support of special education reported by the districts across the state ranged from about 25% to nearly 70%.

Although not all states have been studied in this respect and these kinds of data are not available on a national level, these four states provide sufficient evidence of large scale variation in funding of special education students across districts to warrant concern regarding horizontal equity in special education funding.

Different equity criteria—comparable special education aid per total student enrolled—may apply in states that have adopted "census" special education funding systems. By design, these systems do not vary funding based on measurable special education criteria, but rather by total district enrollment. Equity in this case is achieved by treating similarly sized districts the same. This type of formula is generally based on the assumption that variations in special education needs are likely to be randomly distributed across the districts in a state. There is evidence, however, suggesting that severity is not randomly distributed (see Parrish, Harr, Kidron, Brock, & Anand, 2003; Parrish, Kaleba, Gerber, & McLaughlin, 1998).

Regardless of the exact nature of a state's special education funding system, equity in funding per student is an important standard, and these systems should be judged based on the underlying rationale of the formula in place. For census formulas there should be reasonable equity in special education funding across all students, and for formulas driven by special education criteria (e.g., the number of students identified for service), there should be reasonable equity in special education funding per special education student, on average.

Inequities in local special education funding. Due to variations in federal and state categorical aid, there may also be considerable disparities in the average local contribution per special education student across districts. Districts receiving less state and federal special education support per special education student may have greater need to reach into local funding sources to offset special education costs, as illustrated in several of the cited state examples.

Other Indicators of Special Education Inequity

In addition to concerns in relation to federal, state, and local special education revenues, other important equity indicators include differences in overall spending on special education across states and disparities in the special education services provided.

Cross-state spending differences. Lacking a systematic federal data collection, it is not possible to make comparisons of special education provision across states based on average spending. However, despite a single, federal special education law, there is evidence of substantial variations in spending per special education student across states. Among the 32 states that reported spending on a national survey, special education expenditures per student ranged from $2,899 in Oklahoma to $10,973 in Vermont in 1998–99 (Parrish et al., 2004).[17] The last national study of special education spending also produced comparable per student estimates for a limited number of states, which ranged from $5,354 in Alabama to $10,378 in Maryland (in adjusted 1999–2000 dollars) (Chambers, Perez, Harr, & Shkolnik, 2005).[18]

Another basis for making comparisons is from the full-time equivalent (FTE) counts of special education teachers, related service providers, and instructional aides that states are required to submit to the federal government under IDEA. Using standardized salaries for each of these personnel categories and the number of special education students in each state, this information can be converted into a standardized personnel expenditure per student by state. These resulting dollar amounts can be expressed as an index by dividing the standardized personnel expenditure per pupil for a state by the national average. This produces an index for each state that may be above or below 1.0, depending on its relationship to the national average. The results of such an index for all 50 states for the 2006–07 school year are shown in Table 28.3, which suggest a disparity in special education service providers across states of more than 4 to 1, with an index of 1.98 shown for Hawaii as opposed to 0.47 in Mississippi.

Differences in service provision. The majority of special education funding supports direct services to students, and one implicit measurement of fiscal equity is variations in the percentages of students receiving particular services, such as speech or physical therapy, across districts. One example of analyses of this type done in Wyoming showed 100% of students with speech/language impairment in one district receiving speech therapy as opposed to none in others (Parrish et al., 2002).

Although these types of data may not be typically collected by states, they provide a snapshot of special education practice that may be influenced by available fiscal resources. There may be legitimate reasons as to why the patterns of special education service provision appear markedly different in some districts (or in whole regions of the state), but substantial differences in service would seem to raise questions regarding cross-district special education service equity.

Concluding Thoughts on Equity in Special Education

In any discussion of education finance, equity must be a major concern. In special education, however, relatively little analyses of this type appear in policy papers or in the general

TABLE 28.3
Special Education Personnel Cost Index, by State, 2006–2007

Rank	State	Index	Rank	State	Index
1	Hawaii	1.98	26	Alabama	1.00
2	Vermont	1.67	27	New Mexico	0.99
3	New York	1.64	28	Massachusetts	0.99
4	New Hampshire	1.62	29	Nevada	0.98
5	Connecticut	1.50	30	Kentucky	0.92
6	New Jersey	1.34	31	Wyoming	0.91
7	Maryland	1.30	32	North Carolina	0.87
8	Minnesota	1.29	33	Missouri	0.87
9	Maine	1.29	34	West Virginia	0.87
10	Kansas	1.28	35	California	0.87
11	Iowa	1.26	36	Arkansas	0.83
12	Rhode Island	1.21	37	Montana	0.83
13	Virginia	1.20	38	Washington	0.83
14	Louisiana	1.20	39	Ohio	0.82
15	Illinois	1.17	40	South Carolina	0.81
16	North Dakota	1.15	41	Oregon	0.81
17	Nebraska	1.12	42	Idaho	0.80
18	Pennsylvania	1.11	43	Tennessee	0.80
19	Georgia	1.09	44	Michigan	0.75
20	South Dakota	1.06	45	Utah	0.72
21	Colorado	1.05	46	Alaska	0.72
22	Oklahoma	1.03	47	Florida	0.70
23	Delaware	1.03	48	Texas	0.69
24	Wisconsin	1.02	49	Indiana	0.64
25	Arizona	1.01	50	Mississippi	0.47

Based on 2006-07 IDEA full-time equivalent (FTE) personnel counts (U.S. Department of Education, Office of Special Education Programs, Data Analysis System (DANS), OMB# 1820-0518: "Personnel (in Full-Time Equivalency of Assignment) Employed to Provide Special Education and Related Services for Children with Disabilities, 2006." Based on 2006-07 IDEA full-time equivalent (FTE) personnel counts. Data updated as of July 15, 2008.

literature. One possible reason is the lack of data on special education spending by state, and the fact that many states lack such information at the district-level. Although states commonly report state special education revenue amounts per district, the sometimes large disparities in these amounts per special education student can be difficult to understand. Although they do not appear equitable from a horizontal perspective (equal dollars per student), the principles of vertical equity suggest that students in special education should receive greater funding amounts than non-special education students generally, and these amounts should differ based on student need. The range of student need and the costs associated with special education services are so vast, from one hour of speech therapy a month to year-round placement in a residential facility, that it can be hard to assess what revenue amount per special education student is reasonable for one district in relation to another.

However, when variations in state funding are evident across districts, the observed differences may or may not have a rational basis, i.e., be based on true differences in student need. For example, state special education formulas may not have been updated or thoroughly reviewed in years. Any rational bases that once undergirded them may have been diminished by the changing landscape or by piecemeal adjustments. In these cases, observed differences in special education funding per student may be much more related to history and the often idiosyncratic ways in which fiscal policies have evolved over time than to true variations in student need. If districts receiving substantially more per special education student in state support do not vary in any measurable way (such as percentage of students in poverty, special education, placement or disability category), substantial disparities in special education funding per special education student (or all across all students in the case of census funding) should be considered a major concern.

In addition, inequities in special education funding may complicate arguments for additional relief at the local level from rising special education costs. The need for additional state special education aid seems a harder argument to make, even in states where some districts must support a very large share of special education provision through local funds, when a number of other districts in the state show state and federal special education revenues that exceed what they are spending on special education services (see the earlier examples of Oregon and Nevada). In such cases, what may be needed first is a redesign of the state special education funding system to ensure greater alignment with special education need and better regulation of local provision at the state level (to ensure equity in types and levels of service provided to special education students across the state).

Equity considerations are certainly as important for students in special education as for all students, arguably more important as they often constitute the most vulnerable population. The services special education students receive and the education outcomes they are able to obtain should be a function of their unique special needs rather than where they happen to live within a state or across the nation.

An Overarching Framework for Special Education Finance and Accountability

Much of the special education finance literature focuses on alternative formulas for allocating special education funds. However, more important than the general orientation of one set of formula provisions as opposed to another is the overall context in which these provisions are set. Any formula that is developed in isolation from other key components of education policy and is mathematically or economically derived apart from a larger conceptual framework may be problematic in the short term and almost certainly will become out of sync with larger policy considerations and changes over time.

Thus, we propose a broader conceptual framework for considering special education fiscal and accountability provisions. The framework, as depicted in Figure 28.2, is closely linked with accountability for student achievement and other outcomes that are systematically reviewed. Driven by continuous improvement, it identifies best practices based on outcome data, which inform approaches to assisting and remediating problematic areas of provision in struggling districts and schools.

The framework begins with clearly specified educational goals. As examples, these might include obtaining the highest academic outcomes for all special education students in accord with their abilities, and achieving the greatest educational and social inclusion of students in special education to the maximum extent compatible with their special education needs. In short, to assess how productive a given program is and the extent to which it is succeeding, it is vital that measurable objectives be stated as well as clear means of monitoring progress toward them.

These program goals are followed by guidelines delineating adequate resources determined to be necessary to achieve these program goals. Funding derived from these resource guidelines support the implementation of specific program strategies. Program strategies might include model inclusionary practices, new approaches to inter-agency and cross-program collaboration, and the use of evidence-based instructional practices. Accountability provisions flow from and are directly related to the program strategies and resources available and are based on specific indicators of success. The last component of the overall framework identifies best practices from schools and districts that appear highly successful, according to the indicators of success, and focuses on supporting struggling schools and districts.

Resource Guidelines Used to Determine Adequate Resources

Resource guidelines describe the resources needed to accomplish specified program goals. As an example, no transportation agency would attempt to build a bridge or road without clear construction specifications and the resources needed to complete it. One way of expressing guidelines for the provision of special education services is through the use of staffing ratios (such as the number of special education teachers needed per 100 students). These guidelines are not designed as mandates, but should reflect some sense of best practice as determined by professional judgment and other evidence that may be available. Once developed, these guidelines can serve as a basis for current funding as well as a benchmark for determining future funding for the program. For example, if desired program

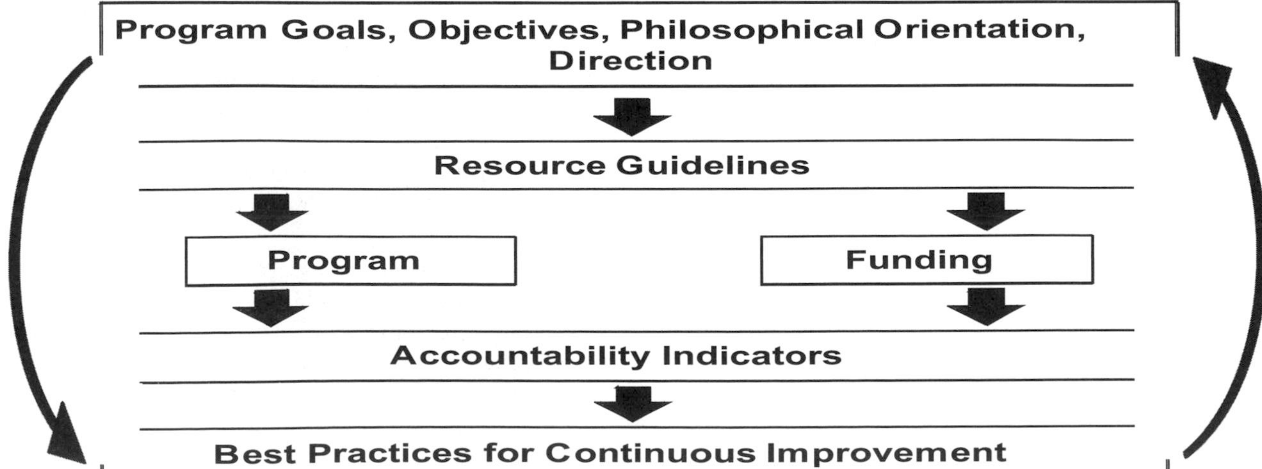

Figure 28.2 Conceptual framework for considering special education funding and accountability.

outcomes do not result from these specifications, it may be necessary to reconsider them (or whether the specified outcomes are realistic) over time. Primarily, however, they provide a transparent and rational basis for special education funding.

Funding Provisions

The most important feature of the finance component is that it be consistent with, and support, the specified program goals. These funding provisions should not be developed in a vacuum or separate from the overall objectives that they are intended to support as the design of the funding mechanism can ultimately affect educational practice. The actual formula may be census-based, pupil weighted, percentage reimbursement, or some other type of allocation mechanism, as long as it is selected and designed to support, and be consistent with, the overarching program objectives.

To protect districts against unusually high costs that may arise through the provision of specialized special education services, the funding mechanism should include a statewide fund that individual districts could apply to in cases of extraordinary need. That is, school districts able to document costs in a given year that are exceptionally high due to unusual circumstances could apply for financial assistance against funds set aside by the state to provide relief.

Accountability Indicators

Accountability is "taking responsibility for the performance of students on achievement measures or other types of educational outcomes."[19] This definition departs from the fiscal and procedural compliance models of accountability that have been traditionally applied to special education (Wolf & Hassal, 2001). Fiscal and procedural compliance will continue to be important, but the primary focus of the proposed framework is on program and student outcomes.

Each desired student outcome is tied to a specific accountability indicator with associated data, which should be analyzed, reported, and made easily accessible and readily available for evaluative purposes at the school, district, and state levels. In addition to academic achievement, proposed indicators of success could include data on program outcomes such as school readiness, educational placement, transition, as well as student and parent perceptions of self, learning climate, and school as a community.

In addition, the focus of these accountability indicators would not be punitive. Rather, they would be based on learning from success as well as identifying areas where additional assistance such as technical or additional fiscal support are needed across the state. Data for these indicators would be reported by school, by district, and statewide.

Best Practices

The last component of the framework is to identify best practices from highly successful schools and districts (based on the measures above), to inform additional support that may be needed for struggling schools. Learning from successful sites and applying that knowledge to struggling schools and districts is a key element of the continuous improvement cycle. For sites demonstrating much lower than expected results, the question will not be what sanctions should be employed but what additional support or assistance may be needed to produce improved outcomes in the future.

Conclusion

As special education includes 14% of all public school students and an estimated 14% of public education spending (Chambers et al., 2002), special education fiscal policies are of vital importance to public education in the U.S. National, state, and, local fiscal policies have a direct effect on the degree to which special education services can be provided, how they are provided, and to what degree they articulate well with the services and educational outcomes expected for all public school students.

Special education finance involves more than the distribution of funds. The special education finance literature has traditionally focused on descriptions and analyses of funding mechanisms and program costs. In this chapter, we have attempted to broaden this discussion to include issues of fiscal incentives and equity. We conclude that the specific type of funding mechanism—such as census or student weights—is secondary to the integration of special education fiscal provisions within a comprehensive design for all students that has clear and transparent overarching goals and accountability provisions designed for continuous improvement. We believe the accountability focus of special education has begun, and will continue, to de-emphasize fiscal and procedural accountability in favor of improved student outcomes.

Notes

1. Data that were collected by the federal government represented the school years 1982–83 to 1987–88.
2. States were asked to report their degree of confidence in the spending estimates. Seven of the 30 reported a high degree of confidence, 11 were "confident," 9 were "somewhat confident," 1 had no confidence, and 2 did not provide a confidence level.
3. Chambers et al. (2003) excluded students served in the home or a hospital when estimating the 95% confidence intervals.
4. The rate of students identified as a percentage of total public enrollment has declined from 13.78% in 2004 to 13.58% in 2006, the latest year available. The identification rate as a percentage of the population declined for the first time since the mid-1980s, from the peak of 8.67% in 2004 to 8.63% in 2005 and continuing to decrease to 8.46% in 2007 (www.ideadata.org).
5. This percentage share excludes federal funds retained at the state level.
6. The IDEA formula contains minimum and maximum provisions to prevent dramatic changes in what states can gain or lose. No state can receive a grant that is more than 1.5 percentage points above the percentage increase in the overall appropriation. No state can receive a grant less than the greatest of (a) the amount a state received in the year prior to the institution of the new formula (base year) and one-third percent of the difference between appropriations for the

current year and appropriations for the base year; (b) the percentage increase from the prior year less 1.5%, (c) 90% of the percentage increase, and (d) the grant amount the state received in the prior year.
7. The President's Commission (2002) noted that the 40% was established during the reconciliation between the House and Senate bills.
8. The Secretary of Education has authority to grant an MOE waiver (for 1 year) to a state for "exceptional or uncontrollable circumstances such as a natural disaster or a precipitous and unforeseen decline in the financial resources of the State." A reduction in an LEA's MOE is permitted if there is a voluntary departure or departure for just cause of special education personnel; if there is a decrease in special education enrollment; if the LEA is no longer obligated to provide an education to an "exceptionally costly child" due to the student leaving the jurisdiction, aging out of the program, or no longer needs special education; or if long-term, costly purchases such as equipment or facility construction have ended.
9. As required by the IDEA, states identify districts that have identified for special education, placed in certain educational settings, or disciplined disproportionate percentages of students in ethnic and racial groups.
10. As noted earlier, districts identified with disproportionate practices are required to designate the maximum amount for EIS purposes. Districts in these circumstances will need to reduce their MOE flexibility by the EIS amount (if the MOE flexibility amount is greater).
11. "To the maximum extent appropriate, children with disabilities, including children in public or private institutions or other care facilities, are educated with children who are not disabled, and special classes, separate schooling, or other removal of children with disabilities from the regular educational environment occurs only when the nature or severity of the disability of a child is such that education in regular classes with the use of supplementary aids and services cannot be achieved satisfactorily" (20 U.S.C. 1412(a)(5)(B)).
12. However, in 2007–08, New York moved to a single weight for special education students, irrespective of placement.
13. In 21 states, the local share was 41% or less, with an additional two states reporting a combined local/state share (Parrish et al., 2004).
14. Retrieved from http://www.mde.k12.ms.us/special_education/TeacherUnits.htm
15. Although Chambers et al. (2004) found variations within disability categories, students with high incidence disabilities such as specific learning disabilities or speech/language impairments are generally considered to have less severe educational needs than students with other disabilities. This is supported by the lower averages spending on these students in relation to other disability categories.
16. Research has shown that poverty is related to higher incidence of learning disabilities and developmental delays (Brooks-Gunn & Duncan, 1997).
17. New York did not provide expenditures for 1998–99. However, if inflating its response to the prior survey administration for the 1995–96 school year, the state had the highest special education expenditure per student of $12,896.
18. The study produced public estimates for Alabama, Indiana, Kansas, Maryland, Missouri, Rhode Island, and Wyoming. These figures are for special education spending only. If including total spending on special education students, the estimates range from $10,141 in Missouri to $15,081 in Rhode Island.
19. Retrieved from http://www.cehd.umn.edu/NCEO/TopicAreas/Accountability/AccountTopic.htm

References

Ahearn, E. (2010). *Financing special education: State funding formulas.* Alexandria, VA: Project Forum, National Association of State Directors of Special Education (NASDSE).

Apling, R. N. (2001). Individuals with Disabilities Education Act (IDEA): Issues regarding "full funding" of part B grants to states. *Congressional Research Service Report* (Number: RL30810). Washington, DC: Congressional Research Service, Library of Congress. Retrieved from http://digital.library.unt.edu/govdocs/crs/permalink/meta-crs-1604

Berman, S., Davis, P., Koufman-Frederick, A., & Urion, D. (2001). The rising costs of special education in Massachusetts: Causes and effects. In C. E. Finn Jr., A. J. Rotherham, & C. R. Hokanson, Jr. (Eds.), *Rethinking special education for a new* century (pp 183–212). Washington, DC: Progressive Policy Institute and Fordham Foundation.

Berne, R., & Stiefel, L. (1984). *The measurement of equity in school finance: Conceptual, methodological, and empirical dimensions.* Baltimore, MD: Johns Hopkins University Press.

Brooks-Gunn, J., & Duncan, G. J. (1997). The effects of poverty on children and youth. *The Future of Children, 7*(2), 55–71.

Chambers, J. G. (1981). Cost and price level adjustments to state aid for education: A theoretical and empirical review. In K. Forbis Jordan (Ed.), *Perspectives in state school support programs* (second annual yearbook of the American Educational Finance Association) (pp. 39–87). Cambridge, MA: Ballinger.

Chambers, J. (1996). *Public school teacher cost differences across the U.S.: The Development of a teacher cost index, developments in school finance.* Washington, DC: National Center for Education Statistics, Elementary Secondary Education Statistics Project.

Chambers, J., Parrish, T., & Harr, J. J. (2002). *What are we spending on special education services in the United States, 1999–2000?* Special Education Expenditure Project (SEEP). Palo Alto, CA: American Institutes for Research, Center for Special Education Finance.

Chambers, J. G., Perez, M., & Esra, P. (2005). Funding to support the highest need students. *Journal of Special Education Leadership, 18*(1), 14–21.

Chambers, J. G., Perez, M., Harr, J. J., & Shkolnik, J. (2005). Special education spending estimates from 1999–2000. *Journal of Special Education Leadership, 18*(1), 5–13.

Chambers, J. G., Shambaugh, L., Levin, J., Muraki, M., & Poland, L. (2008). *A tale of two districts: A comparative study of student-based funding and decentralized decision making in San Francisco and Oakland Unified School Districts.* Palo Alto, CA: American Institutes for Research

Chambers, J. G., Shkolnik, J., & Perez, M. (2003). *Total expenditures for students with disabilities, 1999–2000: Spending variation by disability.* Palo Alto, CA: American Institutes for Research.

Cibulka, J. G., & Derlin, R L. (1992, March). *Special education costs and rising school expenditures: A review of the evidence.* Paper presented at the Annual Meeting of the American Education Finance Association (AEFA), New Orleans, LA.

Council for Exceptional Children. (2008). *Full funding for IDEA: It's a guarantee, not just a promise.* Arlington, VA: Author. Retrieved from http://www.cec.sped.org/Content/NavigationMenu/PolicyAdvocacy/IDEAResources/FullFundingForIDEA-NewDesign.doc

Council for Exceptional Children. (2009). *How the American Recovery and Reinvestment Act impacts special education and early intervention.* Arlington, VA: Author. Retrieved from http://www.cec.sped.org/Content/NavigationMenu/PolicyAdvocacy/CECPolicyResources/EconomicStimulus/ARRA_Q&A_Final_April_2009.pdf

Cullen, J. B. (1999, June). *The impact of fiscal incentives on student disability rates*, National Bureau of Economic Research, Working Paper 7173. Retrieved from http://www.nber.org/papers/w7173

Dempsey, S., & D. Fuchs. 1993. "Flat" versus "weighted" reimbursement formulas: A longitudinal analysis of statewide special education funding practices. *Exceptional Children, 59*(5), 433–443.

Fruchter, N., Parrish, T., & Berne, R. (1999). Financing special education: proposed reforms in New York City. In T. Parrish, J. Chambers, & C. M. Guarino (Eds.), *Funding special education* (pp. 176–200). Thousand Oaks, CA: Corwin Press.

Greene, J. P., & Forster, G. F. (2002). *Effects of funding incentives on special education enrollment* (Civic Report No. 32). New York: Manhattan Institute, Center for Civic Innovation.

Greene, J .P., & Winters, M. A. (2007). Debunking a special education myth. *Education Next, 7*(2), 67–71.

Harr, J. J., & Parrish, T. (2005). The impact of federal increases in special education funding. *Journal of Special Education Leadership, 181* (1), 28–37.

Individuals with Disabilities Education Act, 20 U.S.C. § 1400 et seq. (2004).

Kakalik, J. S., Furry, W. S., Thomas, M. A., & Carney, M. F. (1981). *The cost of special education.* Santa Monica, CA: The Rand Corporation.

Kane, D., & Johnson, P. (1993). *Vermont's Act 230: A new response to meeting the demands of diversity.* Montpelier: Vermont Department of Education.

Lapp, D. (2009). DRAFT: State survey of special education funding formulas. Education Law Center of Pennsylvania. Retrieved from http://reformspecialedfunding.org/wp-content/uploads/2009/07/DRAFT.HowStatesFundSpecEd.pdf

Mahitivanichcha, K., & Parrish, T. (2005a). Do non-census funding systems encourage special education identification? Reconsidering Greene and Forster. *Journal of Special Education Leadership, 18*(1), 38–46.

Mahitivanichcha, K., & Parrish, T. (2005b). The implications of fiscal incentives on identification rates and placement in special education: Formulas for influencing best practice. *Journal of Education Finance, 31*(1), 1–22.

Moore, M. T., Strang, E. W., Schwartz, M., & Braddock, M. (1988). *Patterns in special education service delivery and cost.* Washington, DC: Decision Resources Corporation.

Parrish, T. (2000). *New York State changes special education funding.* The CSEF resource. Palo Alto, CA: American Institutes for Research, Center for Special Education Finance.

Parrish, T. (2001). Who's paying the rising cost of special education? *Journal of Special Education Leadership, 14*(1), 4–12.

Parrish, T. (2010). *Policy alternatives for special education funding in Illinois.* Palo Alto, CA: American Institutes for Research.

Parrish, T., & Bitter, C. S. (2003). Special education in the city: How has the money been spent and what do we have to show for it? *Journal of Special Education Leadership, 16*(1), 34–40.

Parrish, T. & Harr, J. (2005). *Reconsidering special education funding in Georgia.* Palo Alto, CA: American Institutes for Research, Center for Special Education Finance.

Parrish, T., & Harr, J. J. (2007). *Special education funding in Oregon: An assessment of current practice with preliminary recommendations.* Palo Alto, CA: American Institutes for Research, Center for Special Education Finance.

Parrish, T., Harr, J., Kidron, Y., Brock, L., & Anand, P. (2003). *Study of the incidence adjustment in the special education funding model: Final report.* Palo Alto, CA: American Institutes for Research.

Parrish, T., Harr, J. J., Perez, M., Esra, P., Brock, L., & Shkolnik, J. (2002). *Wyoming special education expenditure project and cost based funding model: Final report.* Palo Alto, CA: American Institutes for Research.

Parrish, T., Harr, J. J., Poirier, J., Madsen, S., & Yonker, S. (2007). *Special education financing study for the District of Columbia.* Palo Alto, CA: American Institutes for Research.

Parrish, T., Harr, J., Wolman, J., Anthony, J., Merickel, A., & Esra, P. (2004). *State special education finance systems, 1999–2000, Part II: Special education revenues and expenditures.* Palo Alto, CA: American Institutes for Research, Center for Special Education Finance.

Parrish, T., Kaleba, D., Gerber, M., & McLaughlin, M. (1998). *Special education: Study of incidence of disabilities—final report.* Palo Alto, CA: American Institutes for Research.

Parrish, T., & Shambaugh, L. (2009). *Analysis of special education funding in Nevada.* Palo Alto, CA: American Institutes for Research.

President's Commission on Excellence in Special Education. (2002, July). *A new era: Revitalizing special education for children and their families.* Washington, DC: Author. Retrieved from http://www.ed.gov/inits/commissionsboards/whspecialeducation/reports/images/Pres_Rep.pdf

Roach, V. (2002). *Education reform and funding policies in Georgia: An analysis of their impact on students with disabilities.* Governor's Council on Developmental Disabilities of Georgia, Alexandria, VA.

Rossmiller, R. A., Hale, J. A., & Frohreich, L. E. (1970). *Resource configurations and costs* (National Educational Finance Project, Special Study No. 2). Madison: University of Wisconsin, Department of Educational Administration.

San Antonio Independent School District v. Rodriquez, 411 U.S. 1 (1973)

Serrano v. Priest, 5 Cal.3d 584 (1971) (Serrano I); Serrano v. Priest, 18 Cal.3d 728 (1976) (Serrano II); and Serrano v. Priest, 20 Cal.3d 25 (1977) (Serrano III).

Snell, L. (2009). *Weighted student formula yearbook.* Los Angeles: Reason Foundation. Retrieved from http://reason.org/files/wsf/yearbook.pdf

Wolf, P. J., & Hassel, B. C. (2001). Effectiveness and accountability (Part 1): The compliance model. In C. E. Finn Jr., A. J. Rotherham, & C. R. Hokanson, Jr. (Eds.), *Rethinking special education for a new century* (pp. 53–76). Washington, DC: Progressive Policy Institute and Fordham Foundation.

29

Using Professional Standards to Inform Leadership in Special Education

Mary Lynn Boscardin
University of Massachusetts Amherst

As inclusive practices and accountability continue to shape American education, special education and general education leaders will be challenged to join together in solving the problems of practice inherent in a diverse, complex, high-stakes educational environment. Professional standards provide a policy framework for the knowledge and skills, and in some instances dispositions, believed to be important to the development of state-of-the-art evidence-based practices. National standards emanate from professional educational organizations with input from federal education agencies and institutions of higher education (IHEs). The National Council for Accreditation of Teacher Education (NCATE), Teacher Education Accreditation Council (TEAC), Interstate New Teacher Assessment and Support Consortium (INTASC), Council for Exceptional Children (CEC) Professional Standards Committee, and the National Policy Board for Educational Administration (NPBEA) have been interlinked and aligned to provide teacher and administrator education standards with a well-integrated set of expectations and outcomes upon which to base practice. For example, CEC's Institutional and Program Requirements are aligned with INTASC and NCATE standards to provide special educators with expectations and outcomes that are linked to those in general education. The professional organizations cited above have joined together to develop special education administration leadership standards that provide guidelines for creating a vision, accountability mechanisms, flexibility, and options supported by disciplinary research.

In this chapter, the varied knowledge bases supporting the need for professional standards will be discussed in light of how they guide administrative practice in meeting organizational and personnel needs. This discussion will encompass the national leadership standards developed by the major professional organizations representing special and general education administration. Two primary questions guide this discussion:

1. How are the professional standards for special education administration linked to the special education leadership knowledge base?
2. Do the professional standards communicate that special education leadership makes a difference?

The following topics are examined as a way to answer these questions: (a) the evolution of professional standards in relation to the continued iterations of education reform; (b) contributions of professional standards to the development of professional identities; (c) the relationship of the special education administration standards to the general education administration standards; (d) links between the professional standards and the knowledge base; (e) models of leadership as they relate to the standards for special education leadership and inform the development of more inclusive models of leadership that support students with disabilities and their families; and, (f) implications and considerations for future research on utilitarian applications of the standards. As the purpose and function of standards are examined through multiple lenses, it will become evident that it is difficult if not impossible to create a comprehensive set of leadership standards. It is possible, however, to explore the possibilities.

The Evolution of Professional Standards in Relation to Educational Reform

Educational reform movements have been among the largest impetuses behind the development of educational standards. Up until recently, national reform efforts were directed at students and not at the educators responsible for delivering the instruction. Concerns about the delivery of instruction, however, are not new. One only has to look at Horace Mann's *Twelfth Annual Report of the Board of Education* (1849) to the legislature of the Commonwealth of Massachusetts to see concerns about student learning and instructional quality. During his terms as Secretary of Education, Mann instituted accountability measures to assess the educational inequities among common schools within the communities of the Commonwealth. Since Mann's era, education reform efforts have undergone several iterations that have conformed mostly to the demands of the time. From the 1980s onward, top-down, bottom-up, and standards-based accountability have characterized education reform movements.

The Waves of Educational Reform

Since the proliferation of school reform reports in the early 1980s, a sustained effort has been undertaken to fix, restructure, and rethink the American educational enterprise. The phrase *school reform* is a common reference to any proposal for change in public school policy and/or its operation. In the 1970s, the first wave of reform called for competency-based education, performance contracting, schoolwide accountability, academic excellence, and legislated learning, an example of the latter being the federal publication entitled *What Works: Research about Teaching and Learning* (U.S. Department of Education, 1987). The assumption was schools would be transformed into academic centers of excellence by employing top-down, legislated learning that mandated state and national standards for curricula and testing, promotion, and retention. This approach regarded schools, teachers, and administrators as the problem. Barth (1990) saw the top-down model as being too unwieldy and too complex for any one individual to address.

The second wave of educational reform was characterized by a bottom-up or grass-roots approach, with a strong emphasis on processes but not on outcomes. Site-based management, teacher empowerment, the restructuring of schools, teacher professionalization, and vertical teaming in schools were developed during this phase. With management and control becoming school-based, educators became more self-reliant by engaging in more collaborative behaviors that contributed to the development of communities of practice within buildings (Lave & Wenger, 1991). During this phase, schools, teachers, administrators, and students, began to increase their participation in problem solving, becoming part of the solutions to building-based issues and initiatives (Glickman, 1989). This wave of educational reform embraced the sharing of responsibilities and leadership in schools in order to infuse and develop a variety of leadership roles (Barth, 1990). Outcomes, while important, were not central to this second wave of reform.

The term "outcome-based education" was introduced during the effective schools movement and implied a causal relationship between school practices and student learning (Edmonds, 1983; Lezotte, 1981). In this era, researchers began to question the criteria being used to determine school effectiveness. The effective schools movement contributed to furthering standards based reform efforts, shifting the focus to leadership traits and characteristics. Even with this shift, the ultimate question never changed: How are efforts toward improving instruction increasing student outcomes?

Era of Standards-Based Accountability Educational Reforms

The most recent era of educational reform, driven by federal policy referred to as the No Child Left Behind Act (NCLB, 2001), ushered in the era of accountability for student and teacher performance alike. Expectations for student achievement and teacher performance are higher now than at any other time in history, and scientific research and public policy have become potent influences on the practices of educational leaders. This standards reform conscious era has given rise to a renewed interest in the connection between teaching and learning. The connection to learning in the past has been limited to trying to better understand the connection between what teachers teach and what students learn (i.e., Educate America Act, 2000; No Child Left Behind, 2001; Teachers for the 21st Century, 1986; Tomorrow's Teachers, 1986).

These reform efforts for the most part have been silent with respect to the role of leadership and its connection to student success. Yet, administrators are expected to interpret and put into place school reform efforts in a timely manner regardless of their own preparation to do so. When schools do not achieve their adequate yearly progress (AYP) goals, the contribution of leadership to positive student performance is the first to be scrutinized. States now are on the cusp of considering new ways to evaluate the connection between leadership behaviors and student achievement (Leithwood, Louis, Anderson, & Wahlstrom, 2004; Waters, Marzano, & McNulty, 2003). The link between leadership behaviors and student achievement, as defined by Leithwood and colleagues, is inclusive of all student populations, although no specific reference is made in their research to students with disabilities.

Need to Engage in Evidence-Based Practices

How the link between leading and learning is established depends much on how the field engages in the utilization of evidence-based practices, including the identification and use of scientifically-based instructional practices. For example, in Section 1001 of NCLB (20 U.S.C. 6301 *et seq.*, 2001) the following is stated:

> The purpose of this title is to ensure that all children have a fair, equal, and significant opportunity to obtain a high-quality education and reach, at a minimum, proficiency on challenging State academic achievement standards and state academic assessments. This purpose can be accomplished by—(9) promoting schoolwide reform and ensuring the access of children to effective, scientifically based instructional strategies and challenging academic content. (115 STAT. 1440)

With the passage of NCLB in 2001, and the reauthorizations of IDEA in 1997 and 2004, focus has shifted to outcome measures related to state mandated curricula for all students, including students with disabilities. In 2002 policy makers indicted the system used to implement special education for placing process over results, and bureaucratic compliance above student achievement, excellence, academic, and social outcomes (President's Commission on Excellence in Special Education, PCESE, 2002). In addition, the President's Commission cited a lack of highly qualified teachers and heralded the NCLB legislation as the "driving force behind IDEA reauthorization" (p. 7). However, two critical questions remain: Will better alignment between the *systems* of special and general education provide *students* with a greater opportunity to learn, or will blended systems result in diminished opportunities for students with disabilities to receive the individually appropriate instruction they need to grow into productive adulthood (Boscardin, 2005)?

The Individuals with Disabilities Education Improvement Act of 2004 (IDEA 2004) builds on NCLB by emphasizing increased accountability for student performance at the classroom, school, and school district levels. The changes in IDEA 2004 are significant and include changes in the qualifications of instructional personnel and the approach to instruction itself. All special education teachers must be licensed in special education and meet the highly qualified teacher (HQT) requirements of NCLB. The use of instructional strategies and methods must be grounded in scientifically based research.

School reforms initiated by NCLB and IDEA 2004 have led to increased accountability for administrators' ensuring high quality instruction, improving AYP for students with disabilities, and monitoring their progress in assessments. Administrators are also responsible for certifying that all students are taught by highly qualified teachers who use scientifically-based instructional practices, that students have access to and achieve in the general education curriculum, and that adequate resources support teaching and learning (Boscardin, 2004; DiPaola & Walther-Thomas, 2003).

These simultaneously occurring national policy initiatives require that special education administrators be well versed in the knowledge and skills that are brought to their practice from complementary disciplines. Becoming an effective special education leader for the 21st century requires that administrators work collaboratively with teachers, parents, other school administrators, and policy makers to bring resources, personnel, programs, and expertise together to solve problems of practice for all students.

The Contribution of Standards to Strong Professional Identities

The national standards provide administrators of special education the knowledge, skills, and dispositions that form the foundation for professional identities. Professionals, passionate about what it is they do, have developed identities tied to how they envision their work. When selecting vocations, people are not only choosing what they wish to do for work but they are beginning the development of professional identities that will define who they are as they enter life-long careers. Professional standards provide a framework that lead to the development of professional identities.

Mechanisms that are thought to aid in the development of professional identities include pre-service training with a predictable course of study, referred to as signature pedagogies by Schulman (2005). According to Billingsley (2005), professional teachers and administrators who complete accredited pre-service programs that prepare them well in their disciplinary area, and who then work in educational environments that continue to support evidence-based practices, are more likely to remain in their chosen profession and be more effective. In addition to these pre-service signature pedagogies are work-related experiences and ongoing professional development and engagement. In the best of all worlds professional standards would be integrated into these activities.

Administrators of special education with strong professional identities are considered to be essential to ensuring the delivery of high quality evidence-based special education programs in increasingly inclusive schools (McLaughlin & Nolet, 2004). These leaders are the standard bearers, the ones who set expectations of what it means to be a professional. Without this model of professionalism, there is a risk of ambiguity and erosion challenging role identities. Professional standards are one response for fortifying the identities of professionals.

The Leadership Standards

Standards for administrators of educational administration and special education administration are guided by domain areas. Professional organizations representing each of these two fields identified six over-arching administrative leadership domains. Some of these domains are well-aligned across special and general education leadership practices, and some are organized differently. Subsumed under the domains are statements that are reflective of functions in the case of the educational administration and knowledge and skills in the case of special education leadership.

The Interstate School Leaders Licensure Consortium Standards

The National Policy Board of Educational Administration (NPBEA) designed the Inter-state School Leadership Licensure Consortium (ISLLC) standards to serve as "broad national policy standards that states use as a national model for developing their own standards" (R. A. Flanary & J. Simpson, co-chairs of the NPBEA Steering Committee, personal communication, January 12, 2008). The ISLLC standards, as do the CEC Administrator of Special Education Standards, provide the basis for evaluating the entry-level knowledge and skills of educational administrators, in addition to guiding the evaluation of progress toward expert performance for practicing administrators. The intent was for the standards to have far-reaching applications beyond the accreditation purposes of university preparation programs: "Practice standards can be used to establish professional career plans and guide professional development as leaders demonstrate continuous improvement toward expert performance" (R. A. Flanary & J. Simpson, personal communication, January 12, 2008). The ISLLC 2008 standards, like the CEC administrators of special education standards, were designed to set policy and vision, not prescribe leadership practice (see Appendix A for the complete set of standards). The NPBEA intended states to further refine the national standards to fit their own unique purposes and needs. The policy standards serve as a "foundation, states can create a common language and bring consistency to education leadership policy at all levels so that there are clear expectations" (Council of Chief State School Officers, 2008, p. 5).

The six ISSLC standards include the following statements:

- Standard 1: Setting a widely shared vision for learning;
- Standard 2: Developing a school culture and instructional program conducive to student learning and staff professional growth;
- Standard 3: Ensuring effective management of the organization, operation, and resources for a safe, efficient, and effective learning environment;
- Standard 4: Collaborating with faculty and community members, responding to diverse community interests and needs, and mobilizing community resources;
- Standard 5: Acting with integrity, fairness, and in an ethical manner;
- Standard 6: Understanding, responding to, and influencing the political, social, legal, and cultural contexts.

The Administrator of Special Education Standards

Special education administration is located at the intersection of the disciplines of special education, general education, and educational administration. "Historically, special education has provided much of the intellectual, practical, and personnel traffic to that intersection" (Lashley & Boscardin, 2003, p. 63). Preparation licensure has been dominated by the assumptions, practices, and knowledge traditions of the discipline of special education, resulting in narrowly focused but insufficient preparation for today's administraors of special education. In 2004, with the advent of the reauthorization of the IDEA accountability for performance results and high standards is no longer limited to students without disabilities. The bar has been raised to include all students when measuring educational outcomes.

The recently revised professional standards for Administrators of Special Education, developed by the Council of Administrators of Special Education (CASE) in conjunction with CEC (2009), identify the knowledge and skills that characterize competent leaders of special education. The new 2009 standards represent a significant departure from the earlier standards published by CEC (2003) in that they are leadership focused and have been elevated from the beginning to the advanced level (see Appendix B for the complete set of standards).

The impact of the new standards is expected to be far-reaching and like the earlier standards is not intended to be overly prescriptive. The Administrators of Special Education standards were designed as guidelines to be used to create a vision, develop policy, and provide practice parameters for institutions of higher education, school districts, and states. Broad representation was sought to validate the new knowledge and skill statements associated with each standard. To answer the question of what education leaders need to know about the adminstraiotn of special education, an integrative research synthesis was conducted, which resulted in a collaborative effort among policy makers, education leaders, and professional organizations to produce revised, evidence-based standards. The revised and validated performance-based standards for Special Education Administrators at the Advanced Level (CEC, 2009) include six standards that address the following domains:

- Standard 1: Leadership & Policy
- Standard 2: Program Development & Organization
- Standard 3: Research & Inquiry
- Standard 4: Evaluation
- Standard 5: Professional Development & Ethical Practice
- Standard 6: Collaboration

Comparison of the Leadership Standards

As mentioned previously, special education leadership falls at the intersection of special education and educational administration. In order to assure comprehensiveness, the new Educational Leadership Policy Standards: ISLLC 2008 standards were integrated into the development of CEC's Administrator of Special Education Standards. The converse, however, is not the case. The revised and validated *Administrator of Special Education at the Advanced Level* (CEC, 2009) and the Educational Leadership Policy Standards: ISLLC Standards (2008) are both guided by six standard/domain areas. Both sets of standards differ markedly from their predecessors in that each has undergone a validation process resulting in the revision and addition of domain areas and accompanying competency statements.

As illustrated in Table 29.1, certain areas overlap, whereas there is no alignment between the two sets of standards for the research, and the inquiry and evaluation domains. This is particularly true when reviewing the ISLLC competency statements embedded in the domains. In the ISLLC (2008) statements, evaluation is embedded in two of the standards, but explicit or implicit mention of research and inquiry as they relate to educational administrative leadership is absent. The four domain areas that do align across general and special education administration include: leadership and

TABLE 29.1
Side by Side Comparison of the Special and General Education Administrative Standards

Administrators of Special Education at the Advanced Level (2009)	Educational Leadership Policy Standards: ISLLC (2008)
Leadership & Policy	Effective Management
	Influencing Policy
Program Development & Organization	Shared Vision for Learning
	Developing a School Culture & Instructional Program
Research & Inquiry	
Evaluation	
Professional Development & Ethical Practice	Ethical Practice
Collaboration	Collaboration

policy, program development and organization, professional development and ethics, and collaboration (see Table 29.1).

Models of Leadership in Relationship to Professional Standards

One way to approach the assessment of the comprehensiveness and relevancy of leadership standards is to draw comparisons to recently completed studies intended to advance frameworks for better understanding leadership as part of the educational enterprise. Waters et al. (2003) and Leithwood et al. (2004) are two of the few studies in this area that have investigated the relationship between leadership and student learning. Their scholarship identified those leadership characteristics that contribute to positive educational outcomes for students. Waters et al. identified 21 leadership responsibilities and 66 associated practices that correlated with student achievement using a meta-analysis of 70 research studies covering a 30-year period. One way to regroup these 21 leadership responsibilities is to reassign them to broader categories, such as the following: (a) leadership (change agent, optimizer, ideals and beliefs, flexibility); (b) ecological context (culture, order, discipline, focus, situational awareness); (c) instructional programming (curriculum, instruction, and assessment, knowledge of curriculum, instruction, and assessment); (d) evaluation (monitors and evaluates); (e) professional development and human resources (contingent rewards, affirmation, relationships, intellectual stimulation); (f) collaboration (communication, outreach, input); and (g) economic resource management (resources). Each of the 21 leadership responsibilities was associated with knowledge and skills, strategies and tools, and resources.

Leithwood et al. (2004), building on the earlier work of Waters et al. (2003), sought to answer the following questions through a systematic review of the literature:

1. What effects does successful leadership have on student learning?
2. How should the competing forms of leadership visible in the literature be reconciled?
3. Is there a common set of "basic" leadership practices used by successful leaders in most circumstances?
4. What else, beyond the basics, is required for successful leadership?
5. How does successful leadership exercise its influence on the learning of students?

Leithwood and his colleagues (2004) found that leadership is second in strength only to classroom instruction, but effective leadership has the greatest impact in those circumstances in which it is most needed, most notably failing schools. From their perspective, this evidence supports the present widespread interest in improving leadership as a key to the successful implementation of educational reforms. Although the findings from these studies have a certain utility for all leaders interested in improving the learning outcomes of students, neither of these studies addressed the issue of educating students with disabilities.

Two separate investigative studies by O'Brien (2006) and Crockett, Becker, and Quinn (2009) identified leadership dimensions and evidenced-based practices supporting the field of special education administration and leadership. O'Brien conducted interviews with 64 participants across five countries; England, Scotland, Northern Ireland, the United States, and Canada. In this study she asked each participant two questions:

1. Are there capabilities for school leaders that are particularly or even exclusively critical to successful leadership in special education?
2. Are there special education components in leadership professional development programs currently being implemented?

From this research, the following five themes emerged as being important to the field of special education administration: (a) interpersonal, (b) personal, (c) educational, (d) organizational, and (e) strategic. The interpersonal theme included effective communication, productive relationships, and inspiring others. The personal dimension included professional values and ethics, personal strengths and commitment to ongoing personal and professional development, and decision-making and judgment. The educational domain included pedagogical knowledge and application, building learning communities, and an environment that maximizes student learning. The organizational category included operating effectively within a regulatory and organizational framework, management of resources to achieve goals, and managing systems and processes. Lastly, in the strategic area, building school vision and culture, strategic planning, building leadership, and advocacy were the primary areas of interest.

Crockett et al. (2009) reviewed and analyzed 474 abstracts published in professional journals on the topic of special education administration, over four decades. Eight themes were identified, some of which have endured over time (e.g., law & policy, roles & responsibilities in administrating special education, leadership preparation & development, personnel training & development, service delivery models) and others that are emerging (e.g., school reform & student learning, communication & collaboration with stakeholders, technology) (also, see Crockett, this volume).

Similarities and differences among the leadership domains identified by Crockett et al. (2009) and O'Brien (2006) in comparison to the administrator of special education standards are illustrated in Table 29.2. Many of the domain areas complement each other, even though the nomenclature may not be identical or the placement might vary. For instance, Leadership and Policy within the Administrator of Special Education Standards encompasses Crockett et al.'s themes of law and policy, and leadership roles and responsibilities, and O'Brien's organizational and strategic themes. On the other hand, Crockett et al. and O'Brien did not identify complementary domains for research and inquiry. Technology was absent in the standards and in O'Brien's domain areas. One of the challenges is identifying domains that will provide guidance, support, and withstand the test of time.

Linking Professional Standards to the Knowledge Base through Multivocal Literatures

Integrative research syntheses (Ogawa & Malen, 1991) complement the development of professional standards through the engagement of multiple stakeholders and methods. Ogawa and Malen introduced the notion of *multivocal* literatures as "writings [that] embody the views or voices of diverse sets of authors" (p. 265). The intent of this dynamic approach is to integrate research findings with professional *voices*. The examination of multivocal sources provides a more thorough understanding of a discipline where there is little empirical evidence, diverse writings, systematic investigations, and other perspectives. The triangulation of multiple literatures embodying diverse views and voices provides a level of comprehensiveness that results in an enriched knowledge base supporting professional practices. The integrative research synthesis used to redesign and validate the administrator of special education standards was comprised of a review of the literature, confirmed by the views of practicing special education administrators. Each of these perspectives contributed to the final product, with the literature review providing a scholarly foundation.

Extant reviews of the literature (Crockett et al., 2009; Leithwood et al., 2004; Waters et al., 2003) illustrate the different types of evidence emanating from the positivist, interpretive, and critical theory based literature. In their meta-analysis of principal leadership domains, Waters and colleagues used experiential, declarative, procedural, and contextual knowledge as their taxonomy when developing their "balanced leadership framework" (p. 2). Experiential knowledge was defined as knowing why something is important, declarative knowledge pertained to knowing what to do, procedural knowledge was knowing how to do it, and contextual knowledge placed events in the temporal mode of knowing when to do it.

Crockett et al. (2009) searched for abstracts of published articles related to special education administration with the intent of being illustrative but not exhaustive. More than 470 abstracts were sorted by year of publication, topic, and type of article to examine key qualities of the knowledge base supporting special education administrative leadership. The publication type was coded as *professional commentary* (including conceptual pieces, critiques, literature reviews,

TABLE 29.2
Comparison of Special Education Leadership Domains

Administrator of Special Education 2009 Standards at the Advanced Level	Literature Review Domains (Crockett, Becker, & Quinn, 2009)	Domains from O'Brien Study (2006)
Leadership & Policy	Law & Policy	Organizational
	Leadership Roles & Responsibilities	Strategic
Program Development & Organization	Learning Environments	Educational
		Strategic
Research & Inquiry		
Evaluation	Accountability for Student Learning	
Professional Development & Ethical Practice	Personnel Training & Development	Personal
	Leadership Preparation & Development	
Collaboration	Collaboration & Communication	Interpersonal
	Technology	

TABLE 29.3
Example of Knowledge and Skill Statement

Standard 1- Leadership and Policy
Knowledge Example
Historical and social significance of the laws, regulations, and policies as they apply to the administration of programs and the provision of services for individuals with exceptional learning needs and their families
Skill Example
Interprets and applies current laws, regulations, and policies as they apply to the administration of services to individuals with exceptional learning needs and their families.

and program descriptions), or *research studies* (including quantitative and qualitative inquiries, surveys, program evaluations, or legal and policy analyses).

In a study completed by Boscardin, McCarthy, and Delgado (2009), experts helped to identify statements supported by the literature that reflected evidence-based practices of administrators of special education. The literature supported statements that represented both the knowledge/cognitive foundations of the discipline and the skills necessary to perform effectively in a specified role. Interestingly, CEC invoked the rule that if a particular piece of knowledge or information needed to perform was subsumed by a skill or job function, then the knowledge statement was deleted. See Table 29.3 for examples of each type of statement.

Theory or conceptually based literature, research literature, and/or practice-based literature were the categories used to identify various practices supporting special education administration and leadership (CEC Professional Standards Committee Guidelines; see Figure 29.1).

The literature/theory based knowledge and skill statements were based on theoretical or philosophical reasoning derived from position papers, policy analyses, and descriptive reviews. Research-based knowledge and skills were predicated on methodologies that address questions of cause and effect, and that researchers have independently replicated and found to be effective. Practice-based knowledge and skills were derived from professional wisdom, promising practices, and model and lighthouse programs. Table 29.4 illustrates the frequency of references associated with the approved knowledge and skill statements for each standard.

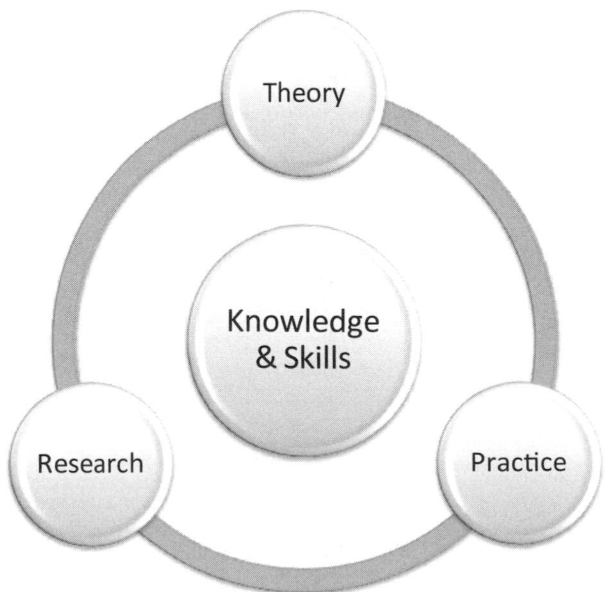

Figure 29.1 Literature base supporting the development of speical education leadership knowledge and skills.

Literature/theory-based evidence had the highest number of overall citations; however, research-based literature did not differ significantly in the number of references. Practice-based evidence had the fewest citations. Literature/theory-based references provided the majority of citations for the Leadership and Policy, and the Professional Development and Ethical Practice standards. Research-based evidence citations dominated the Program Development and Organization, Research and Inquiry, Evaluation, and Collaboration standards. Practice-based evidence for all but one standard, Research and Inquiry, was associated with the least number of citations.

The use of integrative research syntheses provides a foundation for the development of a model/framework for leadership in special education administration that is not only responsive but also anticipatory of the needs of the field. A multi-layered approach facilitates the emergence of a more robust set of representative knowledge and skill statements with data triangulation across theoretical, research, and practice based evidence providing a structure for validating the leadership standards. Lastly, the robust nature of the standards can be tested as future studies are completed.

Linking the standards to the literature fortifies the connection to evidence-based practices leading to better outcomes for students and their families. Expanding the application of standards beyond leadership preparation promises a stronger connection to the standards throughout all phases of the career continuum.

Expanding the Leadership Framework

In this chapter, professional standards have been explored within the context of the literature base supporting both general and special education administration. The development of leadership standards is a dynamic process, requiring continued up-dating and re-conceptualization as new research continues to inform the knowledge base. New ideas and research evidence open the door for developing more far-reaching and comprehensive ways of thinking about leadership frameworks for special education as the knowledge base continues to grow. It is anticipated that the form and function of leadership will change as new roles emerge. For example, leadership recently has become more collaborative as it becomes distributive (Gronn, 2000; Mayrowetz & Smylie, 2004; Murphy, 2005;

TABLE 29.4
Frequency of References by Standard

Standard	Literature/Theory-Based Evidence	Research-Based Evidence	Practice-Based Evidence
Leadership & Policy	95	41	33
Program Development & Organization	29	65	18
Research & Inquiry	10	20	11
Evaluation	27	31	16
Professional Development & Ethical Practice	53	36	24
Collaboration	15	17	8
TOTALS	229	210	110

Spillane, Diamond, & Halverson, 2005), which in part is a function of a more democratic and pluralistic approach to leadership.

The result of the integrative research approach was the emergence of a more comprehensive and robust set of representative dimensions of knowledge and skills that help to better define the field of special education administrative leadership. Further expansion of these domains by using the works of Waters et al. (2003), Leithwood et al. (2004), O'Brien (2006), Boscardin et al. (2009), and Crockett et al. (2009) produces a more comprehensive model that addresses the leadership dimensions of special education at the domain level. See Table 29.5.

Reflected in Table 29.5 are enduring, current, and emerging themes (Crockett et al., 2009). The constructs identified by Waters et al. (2003), O'Brien (2006), and Boscardin et al. (2009) are embedded in every aspect of the list except technology, whereas the studies reviewed by Crockett et al. (2009) are present in all the domain areas except the context for leadership. The concepts identified by Leithwood et al. (2004) illustrate the context for leadership, instructional leadership, evaluation of educational programs and program outcomes, professional development, human resources, and collaborative leadership. This collection of constructs represents a level of comprehensiveness not currently reflected in the frameworks supporting the leadership standards.

Standards have been used to combat low quality and to extend opportunity (Porter, 1993), but their use should not be at the expense of higher levels of professional practice and accountability (Darling-Hammond, 1989). Future research would do well to investigate the relationship between the leadership standards and educational outcomes for students with disabilities. The exploration of additional domains supporting special education leadership using input from multiple stakeholders should also be considered.

TABLE 29.5
Leadership Domains by Focus and Source

Domain	Focus	Source
Leadership, Policy, & School Reform	Inspiring others, applying the laws & policies, managing organizational systems & processes, & engaging in meaningful strategic planning	Waters et al. (2003), O'Brien (2006), Boscardin et al. (2009), and Crockett et al. (2009)
Economic & Resource Management	Creating fiscal equity, linking budgets to educational goals, managing systems & processes	Waters et al. (2003), O'Brien (2006), Boscardin et al. (2009), and Crockett et al. (2009)
Context for Leadership	Building an inclusive vision, culture, order, discipline, & situational awareness, creating an environment that maximizes learning	Waters et al. (2003), Leithwood et al. (2004), O'Brien (2006), Boscardin et al. (2009)
Instructional Leadership	Pedagogical knowledge & application, building learning communities,	Waters et al. (2003), Leithwood et al. (2004), O'Brien (2006), Boscardin et al. (2009), and Crockett et al. (2009)
Evaluation of Educational Programs & Program Outcomes	Assessment of learning outcomes, evaluation of program effectiveness, monitoring, decision-making, judgment	Waters et al. (2003), Leithwood et al. (2004), O'Brien (2006), Boscardin et al. (2009), Crockett et al. (2009)
Professional Development & Human Resources	Professional values & ethics, commitment to ongoing personal & professional leadership development, intellectual stimulation, rewards, affirmation	Waters et al. (2003), Leithwood et al. (2004), O'Brien (2006), Boscardin et al. (2009), and Crockett et al. (2009)
Collaborative Leadership	Interpersonal, relationships, community building, communication	Waters et al. (2003), Leithwood et al. (2004), O'Brien (2006), Boscardin et al. (2009), and Crockett et al. (2009)
Technology	Data warehousing, data sharing	Crockett et al. (2009)

Future research would also benefit from the use of alternate methodologies to further explore the validity of the findings from past studies.

The Implications and Considerations for Research on Leadership Practices

There is an unequivocal need for more studies that produce data about the uniqueness of the administration of special education. The problem, as Crockett et al. (2009) demonstrate, has been the dearth of literature in this area, particularly empirical studies. Shifting the integrative research-based synthesis to one that features empirical evidence amplified by more multidimensional approaches makes it possible to investigate the complexities of the field of special education leadership. Gersten and Baker (2000) accomplish this objective by expanding Ogawa and Malen's (1991) approach to multi-vocal syntheses by including the participation of professional work groups. Gersten and Baker referred to this strategy as a *multi-vocal integrative research* synthesis comprised of a literature review with additional data gathering from key informants guided by key research questions informed by the literature. They divided the literature into two general categories, experimental studies and descriptive studies of instructional practices. In addition, they introduced additional methods of data gathering that were both empirical and interpretive to better understand their selected topic and to broaden the participation of stakeholders.

The validation of the CEC standards for administrators of special education shared many of the same characteristics of Gersten and Baker's (2000) *multi-vocal integrative research synthesis* (Boscardin et al., 2009). Multi-vocal literatures were reviewed and professional workgroups were included as part of the validation process. In addition to stakeholders being asked to rank order statements, they were asked why they ranked the statements as they did and to comment on items they believed were necessary to the role of administrators of special education but omitted. Surveys were disseminated to an even larger national sample of special education directors and supervisors to further validate the statements.

The work of Gersten and Baker (2000) reinforces the importance of future participation by professional workgroups in responding to evolving research questions for the purpose of identifying the traits and characteristics of the field. Although professional workgroups were involved in development of the standards, it was always in response to the knowledge and skill statements provided rather than to a continually evolving set of research questions. Review of these various forms of data by stakeholders is needed to explore the larger research questions that may emerge in order to more closely replicate the process of an integrative research synthesis. Figure 29.2 illustrates how the process might become more authentic.

Research questions emerging from the three separate activities of an exploratory literature review, review of professional standards, and participation by professional work groups, may lead to a better understanding of the multiple relationships among leading, teaching and learning for students with disabilities.

Research linking effective leadership approaches to specific strategies and activities provides a level of specificity that is missing in contemporary leadership research. Leithwood et al. (2004) noted "Leadership is second only to classroom instruction among all school-related factors that contribute to what students learn at school" (p. 3). Professional standards are only one mechanism for helping to provide an understanding of how leadership influences student learning, and other areas deserving further examination. The linkage between leadership and student learning, technology utilization in leadership roles, collaborative forms of leadership, capacity building, and the preparation and continued development

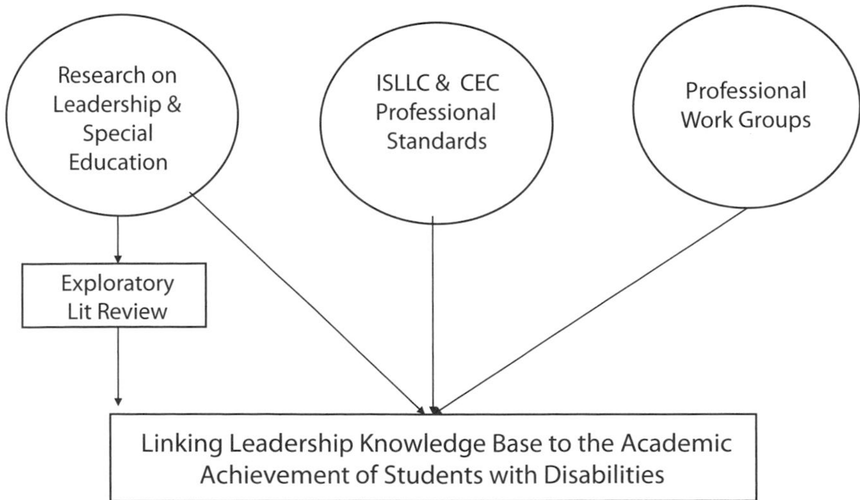

Figure 29.2 Multi-vocal synthesis for studying the link between leadership and student outcomes.

of leaders for special education are just a few of the areas. Understanding the premises and assumptions of special education leadership leads to interesting opportunities to cultivate collaborative partnerships between general and special education.

Summary

Professional standards for special education administration are linked to the special education leadership knowledge base through the use of an integrative synthesis. Standards serve as the basis for identifying priorities in the workplace and identifying the knowledge and skills needed by staff at varying career stages. Although the development of national standards communicates the importance of leadership in special education, one would also hope that the professional standards communicate that special education leadership makes a difference.

The evolution of professional standards and their implementation is in response to the various iterations of education reform. The contributions of professional organizations, experts in the field, and multiple stakeholders to the identification and development of standards contributes to their universal application beyond that of pre-service training. The utilitarian application of the standards is intended to enrich the work lives of preservice, novice, and experienced educational leaders and administrators of special education.

The Administrator of Special Education 2009 standards are expected to be far-reaching and, like the earlier standards, are not intended to be overly prescriptive. The standards were designed as guidelines to be used to create a vision, develop policy, and provide practice parameters for institutions of higher education, school districts, and states. Broad representation comprised of policy makers, education leaders, and professional organizations contributed to the validity of the standards and the new knowledge and skill statements. The input of these participants was important to answering the question concerning what education leaders need to know about special education leadership as it relates to every child with disabilities achieving their potential as learners. Further efforts are needed to more closely link this important knowledge base to the actions of leaders, and the second order influences on instruction and the outcomes of students with disabilities.

Evidence regarding what leaders do makes a difference in the lives of students with disabilities and their families. This evidence is especially important as pressures on resources mount, priorities shift across career stages, and changes occur within systems. As the roles of leaders evolve, one constant remains; professional standards will continue to contribute to the development of strong professional identities. What leaders of special education do to make a positive difference in the academic outcomes for students with disabilities and their families deserves deeper examination.

APPENDIX 29.A
ISLLC Standards 2008

Standard 1: An education leader promotes the success of every student by facilitating the development, articulation, implementation, and stewardship of a vision of learning that is shared and supported by all stakeholders.

Functions:

A. Collaboratively develop and implement a shared vision and mission

B. Collect and use data to identify goals, assess organizational effectiveness, and promote organizational learning

C. Create and implement plans to achieve goals

D. Promote continuous and sustainable improvement

E. Monitor and evaluate progress and revise plans

Standard 2: An education leader promotes the success of every student by advocating, nurturing, and sustaining a school culture and instructional program conducive to student learning and staff professional growth.

Functions:

A. Nurture and sustain a culture of collaboration, trust, learning, and high expectations

B. Create a comprehensive, rigorous, and coherent curricular program

C. Create a personalized and motivating learning environment for students

D. Supervise instruction

E. Develop assessment and accountability systems to monitor student progress

F. Develop the instructional and leadership capacity of staff

G. Maximize time spent on quality instruction

H. Promote the use of the most effective and appropriate technologies to support teaching and learning

I. Monitor and evaluate the impact of the instructional program

(*continued*)

APPENDIX 29.A Continued

Standard 3: An education leader promotes the success of every student by ensuring management of the organization, operation, and resources for a safe, efficient, and effective learning environment.

Functions:

A. Monitor and evaluate the management and operational systems

B. Obtain, allocate, align, and efficiently utilize human, fiscal, and technological resources

C. Promote and protect the welfare and safety of students and staff

D. Develop the capacity for distributed leadership

E. Ensure teacher and organizational time is focused to support quality instruction and student learning

Standard 4: An education leader promotes the success of every student by collaborating with faculty and community members, responding to diverse community interests and needs, and mobilizing community resources.

Functions:

A. Collect and analyze data and information pertinent to the educational environment

B. Promote understanding, appreciation, and use of the community's diverse cultural, social, and intellectual resources

C. Build and sustain positive relationships with families and caregivers

D. Build and sustain productive relationships with community partners

Standard 5: An education leader promotes the success of every student by acting with integrity, fairness, and in an ethical manner.

Functions:

A. Ensure a system of accountability for every student's academic and social success

B. Model principles of self-awareness, reflective practice, transparency, and ethical behavior

C. Safeguard the values of democracy, equity, and diversity

D. Consider and evaluate the potential moral and legal consequences of decision-making

E. Promote social justice and ensure that individual student needs inform all aspects of schooling

Standard 6: An education leader promotes the success of every student by understanding, responding to, and influencing the political, social, economic, legal, and cultural context.

Functions:

A. Advocate for children, families, and caregivers

B. Act to influence local, district, state, and national decisions affecting student learning

C. Assess, analyze, and anticipate emerging trends and initiatives in order to adapt leadership strategies

APPENDIX 29.B
Advanced Knowledge and Skill Set for Administrators of Special Education (CEC, 2009)

Standard 1	**Leadership and Policy**
Knowledge	
SA1K1	Models, theories, and philosophies that provide the foundation for the administration of programs and services for individuals with exceptional learning needs and their families.
SA1K2	Historical and social significance of the laws, regulations, and policies as they apply to the administration of programs and the provision of services for individuals with exceptional learning needs and their families
SA1K3	Local, state, and national fiscal policies and funding mechanisms in education, social, and health agencies as they apply to the provision of services for individuals with exceptional learning needs and their families.
Skills	
SA1S1	Interprets and applies current laws, regulations, and policies as they apply to the administration of services to individuals with exceptional learning needs and their families.
SA1S2	Applies leadership, organization, and systems change theory to the provision of services for individuals with exceptional learning needs and their families.
SA1S3	Develops a budget in accordance with local, state, and national laws in education, social, and health agencies for the provision of services for individuals with exceptional learning needs and their families.
SA1S4	Engages in recruitment, hiring, and retention practices that comply with local, state, and national laws as they apply to personnel serving individuals with exceptional learning needs and their families.
SA1S5	Communicates a personal inclusive vision and mission for meeting the needs of individuals with exceptional learning needs and their families.

Standard 2	Program Development and Organization
Knowledge	
SA2K1	Programs and services within the general curriculum to achieve positive school outcomes for individuals with exceptional learning needs.
SA2K2	Programs and strategies that promote positive school engagement for individuals with exceptional learning needs.
SA2K3	Instruction and services needed to support access to the general curriculum for individuals with exceptional learning needs.
SA2K4	Administrative plans that supports the use of instructional and assistive technologies.
Skills	
SA2S1	Develops and implements a flexible continuum of services based on effective practices for individuals with exceptional learning needs and their families.
SA2S2	Develops and implements programs and services that contribute to the prevention of unnecessary referrals.
Standard 3	**Research and Inquiry**
Knowledge	
SA3K1	Research-based administrative practices that supports individuals with exceptional learning needs and their families.
Skills	
SA3S1	Engages in data-based decision-making for the administration of educational programs and services that supports exceptional students and their families.
SA3S2	Develops data-based educational expectations and evidence-based programs that account for the impact of diversity on individuals with exceptional learning needs and their families.
Standard 4	**Evaluation**
Knowledge	
SA4K1	Models, theories, and practices used to evaluate educational programs and personnel serving individuals with exceptional learning needs and their families.
Skills	
SA4S1	Advocates for and implements procedures for the participation of individuals with exceptional learning needs in accountability systems.
SA4S2	Develops and implements ongoing evaluations of education programs and personnel.
SA4S3	Provides ongoing supervision of personnel working with individuals with exceptional learning needs and their families.
SA4S4	Designs and implements evaluation procedures that improve instructional content and practices.
Standard 5	**Professional Development and Ethical Practice**
Knowledge	
SA5K1	Ethical theories and practices as they apply to the administration of programs and services with individuals with exceptional learning needs and their families.
SA5K2	Adult learning theories and models as they apply to professional development and supervision.
SA5K3	Professional development theories and practices that improve instruction and instructional content for students with exceptional learning needs.
SA5K4	Impact of diversity on educational programming expectations for individuals with exceptional learning needs.
Skills	
SA5S1	Communicates and demonstrates a high standard of ethical administrative practices when working with staff serving individuals with exceptional learning needs and their families.
SA5S2	Develops and implements professional development activities and programs that improve instructional practices and lead to improved outcomes for students with exceptional learning needs and their families.
SA5S3	Joins and participates in local, state and national professional administrative organizations to guide administrative practices when working with individuals with exceptional learning needs and their families.
Standard 6	**Collaboration**
Knowledge	
SA6K1	Collaborative theories and practices that support the administration of programs and services for with individuals with exceptional learning needs and their families.
SA6K2	Administrative theories and models that facilitate communication among all stakeholders.
SA6K3	Importance and relevance of advocacy at the local, state, and national level for individuals with exceptional learning needs and their families.

(*continued*)

APPENDIX 29.B Continued

Skills	
SA6S1	Utilizes collaborative approaches for involving all stakeholders in educational planning, implementation, and evaluation.
SA6S2	Strengthens the role of parent and advocacy organizations as they support individuals with exceptional learning needs and their families.
SA6S3	Develops and implements intra- and interagency agreements that create programs with shared responsibility for individuals with exceptional learning needs and their families.
SA6S4	Facilitates transition plans for individuals with exceptional learning needs across the educational continuum and other programs from birth through adulthood
SA6S5	Implements collaborative administrative procedures and strategies to facilitate communication among all stakeholders.
SA6S6	Engages in leadership practices that support shared decision making.
SA6S7	Demonstrates the skills necessary to provide ongoing communication, education, and support for families of individuals with exceptional learning needs.
SA6S8	Consults and collaborates in administrative and instructional decisions at the school and district levels.

References

Barth, R. S. (1990). *Improving schools from within.* San Francisco: Jossey-Bass.

Billingsley, B. (2005). *Cultivating and keeping committed special education teachers.* Thousand Oaks, CA: Corwin Press.

Boscardin, M. L. (2004). Transforming administration to support science in the schoolhouse for students with disabilities. *Journal of Learning Disabilities*, *37*, 262–269.

Boscardin, M. L. (2005). The administrative role in transforming secondary schools to support inclusive evidence-based practices. *American Secondary Education Journal*, *33*(3), 21–32.

Boscardin, M. L., McCarthy, E., & Delgado, R. (2009). An integrated research-based approach to creating standards for special education leadership. *Journal of Special Education Leadership*, *22*, 68–84.

Council for Exceptional Children (CEC). (2003). *What every special educator must know: Ethics, standards, and guidelines for special educators* (5th ed.). Arlington, VA: Author.

Council for Exceptional Children (CEC). (2009). *What every special educator must know: Ethics, standards, and guidelines for special educators* (6th ed.). Arlington, VA: Author.

Council of Chief State School Officers. (2008). *Educational leadership policy standards: ISLLC 2008.* Retrieved from http://www.npbea.org/projects.php

Crockett, J. B., Becker, M. K., & Quinn, D. (2009). Reviewing the knowledge base of special education leadership and administration. *Journal of Special Education Leadership*, *22*, 55–67.

Darling-Hammond, L. (1989). Accountability for professional practice. *Teachers College Record*, *91*(1), 59–80.

DiPaola, M. F., & Walther-Thomas, C. (2003). *Principals and special education: The critical role of school leaders.* (COPSSE Document No. IB-7). Gainesville: University of Florida, Center on Personnel Studies in Special Education.

Edmonds, R. R. (1983). Programs of school improvement: An overview. *Educational Leadership*, *14*(4), 4–11.

Gersten, R., & Baker, S. (2000). The professional knowledge base on instructional practices that support cognitive growth for English-language learners. In R. Gersten, E. P. Schiller, & S. Vaughn (Eds.), *Contemproary special education research: Syntheses of the knowledge base on critical instructional issues* (pp. 31–79). Philadelphia, PA: Erlbaum.

Glickman, C. D. (1989). Has Sam and Samantha's time come at last? *Educational Leadership*, *46*(8), 4–9.

Gronn, P. (2000). Distributed leadership as a unit of analysis. *The Leadership Quarterly*, *4*, 423–451.

Individuals with Disabilities Education Act, 20 U.S.C. § 1400 *et seq.* (2004).

Lashley, C., & Boscardin, M.L. (2003). Special education administration at a crossroads. *Journal of Special Education Leadership*, *16*, 63–75.

Lave, J., & Wenger, E. (1991). *Situated learning: Legitimate peripheral participation.* New York: New York Press.

Leithwood, K., Louis, K. S., Anderson, S., & Wahlstrom, K. (2004). *How Leadership Influences student learning,* (Executive Summary), University of Minnesota and University of Toronto, commissioned by The Wallace Foundation, retrieved from http://www.wallacefoundation.org

Lezotte, L.W. (1981). Search for and description of characteristics of effective elementary schools: Lansing public schools. In R. R. Edmonds (Ed.), *A report on the research project: Search for effective schools* (pp. 6–15). East Lansing: Michigan State University.

Mann, H. (1849). *Twelfth annual report of the board of education.* Boston, MA: Dutton and Wentworth, State Printers.

Mayrowetz, D., & Smylie, M. (2004). Work redesign that works for teachers. *Yearbook of the National Society for the Study of Education*, *103*, 274–293.

McLaughlin, M., & Nolet, V. (2004). *What every principal needs to know about special education.* Thousand Oaks, CA: Corwin Press.

Murphy, J., (2005, September). Using the ISLLC standards for school leaders at the state level to strengthen school administration. *The State Education Standard*, 15–18.

No Child Left Behind Act, 20 U.S.C. 6301 et seq. (2001).

O'Brien, P. (2006). *"They know who I am" – Leadership capabilities in special education.* New South Wales, Australia: Premiers Special education Scholarship sponsored by the Anika Foundation.

Ogawa, R., & Malen, B. (1991). Towards rigors in review of multivocal literatures: Applying the exploratory case study method. *Review of Educational Research, 61, 265*–286.

Porter, A. (1993). School delivery standards. *Educational Researcher, 22*(5), 24–30.

Schulman, L. (2005, April). *The signature pedagogies of the professions of law, medicine, engineering, and the clergy: Potential lessons for the education of teachers.* Paper delivered at the Math Science Partnership Workshop: "Teacher Education in Effective Teaching and Learning." National Research Council's Center for Education, Irvine, CA.

Spillane, J. P., Halverson, R., & Diamond, J. B. (2004). Towards a theory of leadership practice: A distributed perspective. *Journal of Curriculum Studies, 36*(1), 3–34.

U. S. Department of Education (1987). *What works: Research about teaching and learning.* Washington, DC: U.S. Government Printing Office.

Waters, J. T., Marzano, R. J., & McNulty, B. A. (2003). *Balanced leadership: What 30 years of research tells us about the effect of leadership on student achievement.* Aurora, CO: Mid-continent Research for Education and Learning.

30

Factors Influencing Special Education Teacher Quality and Effectiveness

Bonnie S. Billingsley
Virginia Polytechnic Institute and State University

In general education, researchers emphasize the important role of teachers in promoting student achievement (e.g., Darling-Hammond, Holtzman, Gatlin, & Helig, 2005; Rice, 2003; Sanders & Horn, 1998; Wayne & Youngs, 2003). Research suggests that over time teacher quality matters more to student achievement than any other school-based factor (Rivkin, Hanushek, & Kain, 2005). Although the relationship between teacher quality and student achievement has been well documented in general education, there is minimal data on this relationship in special education. However, it is logical to assume that special education teacher (SET) quality is important to ensuring high levels of achievement for students with disabilities (McLeskey & Billingsley, 2008).

Although teacher quality as defined by No Child Left Behind (NCLB; 2001) has been dominant over the past decade, the focus of the national policy conversation has shifted to teacher effectiveness. The rationale is that "Mandating that teachers meet the minimum requirements to be considered highly qualified is a first step toward ensuring teacher effectiveness, but just meeting those requirements is not guarantee that teachers will be effective" (Goe, Bell, & Little, 2008, p. 3). As Goe and colleagues suggest, work contexts vary across a range of dimensions (e.g., parents, students, curriculum, resources, leadership) and teachers may be "differentially effective" (p. 47), experiencing success in some contexts, but not others. Understanding the broad range of factors that influence special education teacher quality and effectiveness is necessary so that comprehensive and strategic efforts can be taken to improve initial teacher preparation, professional development (PD) and work contexts.

Several funded initiatives over the last decade have provided additional knowledge about what is known about the availability, development and retention of a qualified workforce in special education. Erling Boe and Lynne Cook have contributed much of what is known about supply and demand at the national level through a series of funded projects through the Office of Special Education Programs (U.S. Department of Special Education) using data from the Schools and Staffing Surveys (SASS; n.d.), which includes the Teacher Questionnaire (TQ, n.d.) and the Teacher Follow-up Survey (TFS, n.d.; National Center for Education Statistics). The Study of Personnel Needs in Special Education (SPeNSE), under the direction of Elaine Carlson at WESTAT, is the largest study of special education teachers, service-providers, and paraprofessionals conducted to date. The SPeNSE study assessed factors that influence the availability and development of a qualified SET workforce. A subsequent project, the Center for Personnel Studies in Education (COPSSE; http://www.coe.ufl.edu/copsse/about-copsse/index.php) under the direction of Mary Brownell and Paul Sindelar was charged with identifying scholars to synthesize reviews of the literature on what is known about various facets that impact the availability and development of a special education teacher workforce. Brownell and Sindelar also currently direct the National Center to Inform Policy and Practice in Special Education Professional Development (NCIPP), a project designed to integrate what is known about mentoring and induction practices in special education. In a major departure from special education research related to SET quality, two economists, Feng and Sass (2010), in an Institutional Education Sciences (IES) project, employed value-added models to assess the relationship between teacher quality and the achievement gains of students with disabilities. They are the first to investigate the relationship of teacher SET quality to student outcomes in a large-scale study.

Although a great deal of progress has been made over the last decade in understanding teacher quality, there is much work to be done to provide students with disabilities with effective teachers who not only understand effective teaching, but have the work contexts necessary to support their use of these practices. The purpose of this chapter is to provide a broad perspective of factors that show some evidence of influencing SET quality and effectiveness.

Conceptualizing Teacher Quality and Effectiveness in Special Education

Defining and studying teacher quality in special education is complex and challenging, particularly since there is a lack of agreement on what teacher quality means (Blanton, Sindelar, & Correa, 2006; Brownell, Leko, Kamman, & Streeper-King, 2008; Carlson, Lee, & Schroll, 2004). Institutions of Higher Education (IHEs) have to a large extent relied on standards outlined by professional organizations (Council for Exceptional Children, 2001), certification requirements of state departments of education, and research on effective teaching practices to organize curriculum for prospective SETs (Israel, 2009). Leaders in local education agencies (LEAs) need to comply with state requirements for certification as they hire teachers, but little is known about other criteria that are considered in hiring and evaluating special educators or what guides decisions about professional development programs.

Brownell et al. (2008) argue that conceptualizing and assessing teacher quality are essential to developing a professional knowledge base that shapes teacher education. In a recent review of the teacher quality literature in both general and special education, Brownell and colleagues consider an initial definition of teacher quality in special education. They stated that in addition to the need for collaboration skills:

> Quality special education teachers are likely to be experienced and academically able with: (a) subject matter knowledge, (b) knowledge of how to teach that subject matter (or pedagogical content knowledge), (c) knowledge of effective instructional and management practices that is somewhat specific to students with disabilities and other struggling learners, and (d) beliefs that enable them to persist in teaching students with disabilities. (p. 48)

Researchers have used varied methods to assess the relationship of a broad range of variables to teacher quality. One method is to consider proxies for teacher quality in large groups of teachers such as certification status, extent of preparation, teacher test scores and years of teaching experience. These proxy variables are then linked to outcome variables such as perceived preparedness to teach, retention, and student achievement gains. These types of studies use large-scale data-bases from sources such as the SASS surveys or state longitudinal teacher data bases (e.g., Feng & Sass, 2010; Singer, 1992). To illustrate, Carlson et al. (2004) specified a teacher quality model incorporating components from Kennedy's (1992) theoretical framework of teacher quality. They used teacher data (e.g., experience, credentials, self-efficacy, professional activities, and selected classroom practices) in a two-level confirmatory factor analysis to identify components of SET quality. Carlson et al. found that "all of the variables emerged as viable components of an aggregate teacher quality measure" (p. 35). Carlson and colleagues also reported in the same article, a test of their model using data from the Special Education Elementary Longitudinal Study (SEELS) which included teacher quality variables as well as student achievement data (see Blackorby, Lee, & Carlson, 2004, cited in Carlson et al., 2004) and found that adding the teacher quality model helped predict student achievement, although modestly.

A second approach involves observational studies of teaching to determine the extent to which SETs use effective practices. Goe et al. (2008) state because teachers influence student learning "through the processes and practices they employ, it is reasonable to state than an effective teacher can be observed to be doing things that research has suggested are likely to lead to improved student learning" (p. 9). In an observational study, Brownell et al. (2009) investigated the relationship between teacher knowledge, observed teacher practices, and student reading gains. They found that SETs were somewhat knowledgeable about teaching reading, but this knowledge did not contribute a significant portion of variance to classroom practice. However, they found that specific teaching practices (e.g., classroom management, decoding practices, and explicit engaging instruction) accounted for a significant portion of variance in student reading gains.

Recent conceptualizations of teacher quality (Brownell et al., 2008; 2009; Blanton et al., 2006; Carlson et al., 2004) consider aspects of both SET quality and effectiveness in special education, although a great deal more needs to be learned. Moreover, as the focus shifts to teacher effectiveness, additional study is needed to learn more about what effective SETs do to bring about positive student outcomes and the work conditions necessary to support those practices.

Factors Influencing Teacher Quality & Effectiveness

The above discussion provides an introduction to conceptualizations of teacher quality and effectiveness. In the remainder of this chapter, factors that influence SET quality and effectiveness are considered. Three major factors are identified in Figure 30.1: (a) shortages and surpluses, (b) professional knowledge and skills, and (c) conditions of service (Carlson & Billingsley, 2010). The model suggests that these interrelated factors have an impact on teachers' qualifications and the extent to which they are effective in their work.

The first section on teacher shortage and surplus addresses the problem of the chronic shortage of qualified SETs in special education and factors influencing the lack of qualified teachers, including supply, demand and retention (surpluses are omitted given that shortages have been pervasive for decades). Given the importance of a diverse teaching force, the supply of teachers from historically under-represented groups is also considered. The second

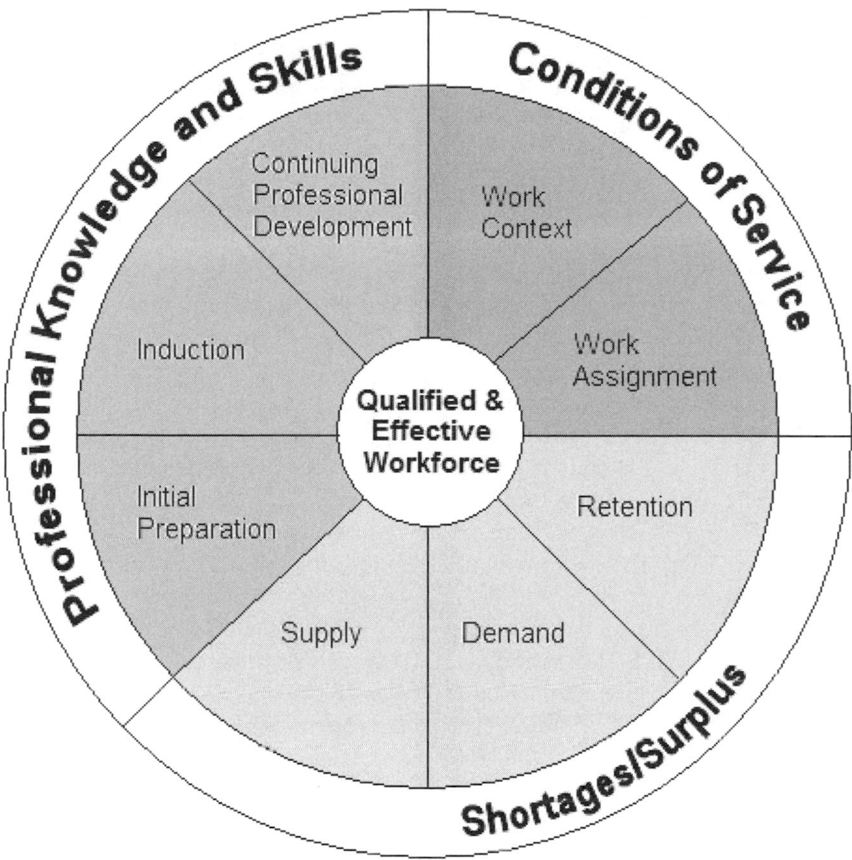

Figure 30.1 Factors influencing teacher quality and effectiveness (Carlson & Billingsley, 2010, revised).

factor, knowledge and skills, emphasizes the continuum of teacher development and considers initial preparation, induction and on-going professional development. The impact of alternative route (AR) programs on teacher quality is important since increasing numbers of teachers enter through these programs. Finally, the section on conditions of service considers both work contexts and specific work assignments. The assumption is that teacher expertise is not sufficient for teacher effectiveness—teachers also need supportive school structures, resources, and schedules that allow them to use what they know to benefit students with disabilities and to experience success and satisfaction in their work. Critical issues, research needs, and implications for policy-makers and leaders are discussed throughout the chapter.

Teacher Shortage in Special Education

Although the importance of an adequate supply of qualified SETs to teach students with disabilities is recognized, the field has struggled to recruit and prepare sufficient numbers of teachers. As a result, year after year, thousands of positions are filled with minimally prepared teachers, long-term substitutes or left vacant because of the lack of qualified candidates ("A High-Quality Teacher," 2002; Boe, 2006; Boe & Cook, 2006; Katsiyannis, Zhang, & Conroy, 2003; McLeskey, Tyler, & Flippin, 2004). In a review of the literature on special education teacher supply and demand, McLeskey et al. concluded that the special education shortage in the United States was severe, chronic, and pervasive across all geographic areas of the country and across all disability categories. Recent evidence suggests this trend has continued. According to the 2008 Educator Supply and Demand report, SETs dominated the list of "considerable" shortage areas in most geographical regions of the United States, showing high need in most areas, including severe/profound disability, multicategorical, mild/moderate disability, mental retardation, emotional/behavioral disorders, learning disability, visually impaired, dual certification (general and special education), hearing impaired, and speech pathology.

Figure 30.1 indicates that shortages and surpluses are influenced by teacher supply, demand, and retention. Traditional economic models suggest that shortages exist when the demand for teachers exceeds the available supply. Teacher shortages have typically been quantified in two ways, the number of vacancies that are not filled (quantity) and the number of teachers hired who do not meet state standards for certification (often used as an indicator of quality). Three data bases have provided much of what is known about SET supply, demand and retention and include: (a) teacher data from the U.S. Department of Education, Office of Special Education Programs (OSEP) Annual Reports to Congress; (b) SASS surveys (National Center for Educational Statistics); and (c) and annual surveys of Deans or Directors of Teacher Education through the American Association of Employment in Education (AAEE). Although these databases provide important information, low response rates (AAEE), changing data requirements (OSEP), delays in timely access to data (SASS, OSEP), and limited SET samples (SASS) prevent a timely and accurate description of the shortage problem (McLeskey et al., 2004; Smith-Davis & Billingsley, 1993).

Most descriptions of the SET shortage have focused on national data with relatively few comparisons across regions, district types or exceptionality areas. Although the AAEE does provide data across geographical regions and disability type, the data is limited in that it is based only on the perceptions of career service providers, directors or deans of teacher preparation programs about the extent to which shortages exist in specific fields. National data such as SASS do not have a sufficient SET sample to allow the detailed study of specific teacher groups (e.g., autism, emotional/behavioral disorders [EBD]). To develop a fuller picture of the quality of the special education workforce, the SPeNSE study addressed a much larger population of teachers, which included over 5,400 SETs (as well as paraprofessionals, administrators and general educators) and was stratified by geographic region and district size. The interview protocol used was the most detailed instrument developed to date, including many items specific to SET quality. However, the SPeNSE survey is limited to only one school year (1999–2000).

Supply

To secure a qualified workforce, it is necessary to have an adequate supply of well-prepared teachers who are able and willing to teach. The "*supply* of teachers is the number of qualified individuals willing to teach at a given level of overall compensation" (Guarino, Santibañez, & Daley, 2006, p. 174). In contrast, McLeskey et al. (2004) take a "quantity" perspective defining teacher supply as including both qualified and unqualified special educators. Unfortunately, the latter definition is consistent with the fact that many SETs hired over the last decades have not been fully certified for their positions. Boe and Cook (2006) reported that SETs without full certification increased from 7.4% to 12.2% from 1993–94 to 2001–2002, increasing the need from 25,000 to 49,000 SETs over this period.

Sources of entering SET supply in public schools were distributed as follows in 1999–2000 (Cook & Boe, 2007): (a) 62.1% from the reserve pool (delayed entrants or experienced teachers who reenter teaching); (b) 25.7% from first time teachers who recently graduated; (c) 5.1% first time teachers without preparation; and (d) 7% private school migrants. Although the reserve pool comprised the largest source of entering SETs, Cook and Boe pointed out that little is known about the size and characteristics of the reserve pool, creating uncertainty about the future supply of special educators. In analyzing the extent of preparation of first-time SETs, Cook and Boe found that only 46.4% of first-time teachers completed extensive teacher preparation with "degree majors in their primary areas of teaching (i.e., special education), whereas the comparable figure for general education was 81.9%" (p. 227). Because of the SET shortage, general education teachers (GETs) are often hired to fill special education positions and they comprised about 17.6% of entering SETs in 1999–2000. Cook and Boe point out the supply of traditionally prepared SETs declined over the past years, even with a growing teacher shortage. More recent findings also show that SETs with degrees in special education declined from "59.4% in 1999–00 to 45.2% in 2003–04" (Boe, Cook, & Sunderland, 2007a, p. 3), which is likely due to greater numbers of teachers entering through alternative route programs (Boe, Cook, & Sunderland, 2009; Rosenberg & Sindelar, 2005).

It is important to note that unqualified teachers are not evenly distributed across varied types of districts. For example, White and Fong (2008) considered several variables in the teacher labor markets in California and found marked differences in the use of underprepared general educators. They reported an average of 6% of teachers were underprepared throughout the state, however, in two districts "underprepared teachers accounted for more than 10 percent of the teacher workforce and in 16 for less than 2 percent" (p. iii). Moreover, the projected demand for new teachers considering student enrollment and teacher retirement projections varied 64 percentage points between the district with the lowest demand (4%) and the district with the highest demand (68%).

Disparities in teacher quality between high and low poverty districts have also been documented in general education (Darling-Hammond & Sykes, 2003) and more recently in special education. Recently Fall and Billingsley (2008) reported that SETs in high poverty districts were less prepared on a range of quality indicators, including certification, advanced degrees, graduation from selective institutions, performance on teacher tests, and extent of time spent student teaching. They also reported almost a third of early career SETs in high poverty districts lacked full certification compared to 14% of their counterparts in more affluent districts. A closer look at certification revealed a more troubling disparity: 24% of early career SETs in high-poverty districts held emergency certificates compared to only 2% in more affluent districts. The lack of an adequate teacher supply is also a problem in other subsets of SETs including those teaching students with EBD who are less qualified than other SETs (Billingsley, Fall, & Williams, 2006).

The availability of SETs from historically under-represented groups is another aspect of the supply problem and obtaining a diverse teaching force has been an on-going challenge for school districts. In a review of teacher diversity and the special education teacher workforce, Tyler, Yzquierdo, Lopez-Reyna, and Flippin (2004) emphasized that while roughly a third of individuals in the United States are from historically underrepresented groups, only 14% of early career SETs were from such groups. As they indicate, the fact that 38% of students with disabilities are from underrepresented groups demonstrates that the diversity in the SET workforce does not match either the general population or the students that they teach. However, there is a higher proportion of diverse SETs in high poverty districts, and these districts tend to have higher proportions of students from under-represented groups (Fall & Billingsley, 2008). Tyler et al. suggest that a possible factor in disproportional placements of students in special education may be cultural differences between teachers and students. Tyler et al. and colleagues also indicated that there is an assumption that students of color will be more successful when taught by teachers from similar backgrounds, yet they point out there is little empirical evidence to support this idea. Although recruiting a diverse SET workforce will no doubt continue to be a challenge, AR programs have been more successful in recruiting diverse students than traditional programs (Rosenberg & Sindelar, 2005).

Demand

The insufficient supply of highly qualified teachers is related in part to the increasing demand for SETs over the last decades. Demand is defined as "the number of teaching positions offered at a given level of overall compensation" (Guarino et al., 2006, p. 174). Demand is driven largely by student enrollments and caseloads (Carlson & Billingsley, 2010). Although the population of school-age children in the United States grew 6.8% between 1992 and 1999, special education enrollment grew 20.3% over this period, increasing the demand for SETs (McLeskey et al., 2004). More recent data from the 28th Annual Report to Congress showed an increase of students served from 5,078,841 in 1995 to 6,118,437 in 2004 (ages 6–21; United States Department of Education, 2009). According to the same report, the number of children with disabilities served in the age group 3–5 also grew during the same period from 548,588 students to 701,949. It is likely there will be increases in the number of students with disabilities served in the future given that the student population is expected to grow in the decade ahead (Hussar & Bailey, 2008).

The size of caseloads is a second factor influencing demand. McLeskey et al. (2004) found an upward trend from about 15:1 in 1996 to 17:1 in 1999–2000, which they suggest is close to that of 18:1 for general education classes in some states. Even when caseloads are regulated by the state, districts sometimes circumvent caseload and class size limits through waivers (Carlson, Brauen, Klein, Schroll, & Willig, 2002). Increasing the numbers of students on caseloads may reduce the need for teachers, but it may also reduce SETs' effectiveness and make special education teaching less desirable.

Retention

Teacher retention is a mediating variable in teacher supply and demand since a stable workforce reduces the demand for new teachers (Carlson & Billingsley, 2010). Differing rates of turnover and attrition are largely the result of unclear definitions of leaving. Boe, Cook, and Sunderland (2007b) characterize teacher turnover in three ways: (a) leaving for non-teaching activities (attrition); (b) transferring from special education to general education teaching (transfers); or (c) moving to other special education positions (migration). When all three types of turnover were considered, rates increased from 18.8% in 1991–92 to 28.7% in 2004–2005 (Boe et al., 2007b). This means that more than one in four special education teachers did not return to the same position from one year to the next in 2004–2005. Boe and colleagues (2007b) reported that there were no significant differences between GETs and SETs in attrition or transfer, although migration was significantly higher among special educators.

A pattern that has received a great deal of attention in both general and special education is the high rate of turnover among new teachers. This pattern has held across numerous studies of leaving (e.g., Miller, Brownell, & Smith, 1999; Singer, 1992). More recently Smith and Ingersoll (2004) found that first year SETs leave at 2.5 times the rate of general educators. High rates of leaving among new SETs is not surprising given "the high percentage of entering SETs who are only partly certified (44.4%)" (Boe & Cook, 2006, p. 450) and uncertified teachers are at greater risk of leaving than their certified peers (Miller et al., 1999).

Attrition is of particular interest to policy-makers since these teachers represent a loss to the teaching workforce. Boe et al. (2007b) demonstrated that attrition rates have been rising with 5.2% of SETs leaving teaching employment in 1991–92, 6.6% leaving in 1994–95, 8.7% leaving in 2000–2001, and 10% leaving teaching in 2004–2005. Boe, Cook, and Sunderland (2008a) reported that while many SETs leave for personal reasons (31.8%) or retirement (16.5%), 36.7% left to "escape teaching" (23.8% of GETs indicate escape as a reason). Under the category of "escape," SETs gave their main reason for leaving as "other career" (14.5%), "dissatisfaction with teaching" (11.6%), "better salary" (9.4%), and "take courses for other career" (1.2%) (p. 18).

The transfer from special to general education teaching has been studied less than turnover or attrition. Boe et al. (2008a) reported that 5.5% of SETs transferred to general education teaching in 1991–92, 8.8% in 1994–95 and 10.2% in 2000–2001. These SETs are not a loss to teaching, but are a loss to the special education workforce. A major question that is left unaddressed is the extent to which stronger teachers leave the field.

Although some turnover is healthy and necessary, high levels of turnover contribute to an unstable workforce, reduce teacher quality, and have a number of costs including: (a) spending available resources on continually recruiting, hiring and induction; (b) lost investments in professional development and reform; (c) organizational instability and loss of teachers knowledgeable about students and families; and (4) broad economic costs, including lost investments in tuition and tax support to prepare teachers (Benner, 2000; Darling-Hammond & Sykes, 2003; Smith & Ingersoll, 2004). High rates of turnover among new teachers is particularly costly to students since new teachers face a steep learning curve as they establish teaching routines and experiment with teaching methods. Research in general education shows that students with new teachers learn less than those taught by those with at least some experience (Rice, 2003). This finding also holds in special education. Feng and Sass (2010) reported that achievement gains for students with disabilities tend to be higher when taught by teachers with experience, with the largest gains in the first few years in reading. An implication is that retaining SETs beyond the initial years should improve teacher quality.

In addition to the broader costs of turnover, high turnover among SETs interferes with established collaborative and co-teaching relationships (McLeskey & Billingsley, 2008) and the sustainability of inclusive school reform. Sindelar, Shearer, Yendol-Hoppey, and Liebert (2006) reported that when key individuals in an inclusive effort left the school, new teachers who replaced them were not as committed to or as knowledgeable about implementing inclusion and their leaving was one of the factors that contributed to the demise of the inclusive program.

Summary and Discussion

The above evidence suggests that despite increased federal investments in teacher preparation, the SET shortage problem has grown worse and high rates of turnover have increased the demand for new teachers. The labor market theory of supply and demand provides a helpful lens for policy-makers and administrators interested in improving teacher recruitment and retention (Guarino et al., 2006). This theory suggests that individuals will enter into teaching and remain if it is the most attractive activity available based on overall compensation. It is important to note that compensation involves all aspects of the job of value to the individual including salary and benefits, desirability of work conditions, opportunities for continued learning, and ancillary factors, such as school location, the schedule of work, and proximity to home. As Guarino and colleagues explained, conditions of work include any aspect of the job that influences teachers' desire to enter, stay or leave. Therefore elements of attractiveness are policy levers that can be used to recruit and retain teachers and these levels can be manipulated at varied levels including the school, district or state. Darling-Hammond et al. (2005) discussed how some shortages have been resolved by creating more competitive labor market conditions through competitive salaries, supportive administration, as well as preparation subsidies, and recruitment and hiring initiatives.

Considerations for increasing the attractiveness of special education teaching are needed, with special attention given to preparing teachers for students with EBD as well as recruiting and retaining qualified SETs in high poverty schools. Relatively little is known about the extent to which specific incentives, such as salary incentives and creating better working conditions, will successfully recruit and retain SETs for longer periods of time. Although some incentives may be costly, there are also significant costs associated with unqualified teachers and high turnover as discussed earlier. Research is needed to compare the costs and benefits of varied recruitment and retention options.

A major trend in the context of SET supply and demand is increasing supply through brief alternative routes to certification. Although brief routes will make it easier for leaders to fill positions with certified SETs and attract a more diverse workforce, these fast-track programs may be less cost-effective in the long run since these entrants tend to be less committed (Sindelar et al., 2009) and leave at higher rates than more extensively prepared teachers (Darling-Hammond & Sykes, 2003).

Special Educators' Professional Knowledge and Skills

Knowledgeable and skilled general and special educators are critical to helping students with disabilities achieve within the general education curriculum and meet individualized goals. In particular, SETs require strong preparation to teach a range of content areas effectively, use evidence-based instructional practices, monitor student performance, and respond to the needs of an increasingly diverse student population. SETs also need specific knowledge and skills to address challenging student behavior, help students meet transition-related goals, and teach non-academic goals such as social and self-advocacy skills. Initial preparation programs are expected to prepare SETs to work across 12 or more grades (Geiger, Crutchfield, & Mainzer, 2003) and their graduates may work across varied service delivery models with caseloads that include students with varied disabilities (Carlson et al. 2002). Preparing SETs for such a broad range of grade, content, exceptionality, and service-delivery options is a daunting challenge.

Figure 30.1 indicates that the development of SETs' professional knowledge and skills occurs over the entire career span. As Wilson, Floden, and Ferrini-Mundy (2001) stated:

> Learning to teach begins with one's undergraduate coursework (in academic disciplines and education), extends into formal teacher preparation and then into induction programs designed to support new teachers as they enter the profession, and, finally, is linked to high quality professional development opportunities. (p. 34)

Although the literature about teacher preparation has grown as the following sections illustrate, much more needs to be learned about the impact of initial preparation, induction, and professional development on SET quality, their use of effective practices, and student achievement.

Initial Preparation

Traditional, university-based preparation programs have been the subject of extensive scrutiny and criticism and many have questioned the effectiveness and relevance of these programs. A wide range of alternative pathways have emerged including Teach for America, Troops to Teachers, Residency Programs, and other Alternative Programs, including many in special education. Fewer SETs are earning degrees in special education (Boe et al., 2007b), and alternative routes to teaching have increased with greater numbers of GETs and SETs entering through these programs (Rosenberg & Sindelar, 2005).

Even within university programs there is great diversity in program types from discrete or separate programs to prepare special educators to merged programs designed for all teachers (Pugach & Blanton, 2009).

Regardless of route or type of program, little is known about the effects of initial preparation on teacher effectiveness or student achievement. In a review of the literature on teacher preparation, Brownell, Ross, Colón, and McCallum (2003) concluded that the current debate about the value of initial teacher preparation is due in part to the lack of "powerful, definitive studies about the impact of teacher education" (p. 5). Teacher preparation programs do not adequately link specific elements of preparation to teacher practice and student outcomes. Carlson and Billingsley (2010) outline some reasons for this research deficit: teacher preparation is often a long and complex process; the direct outcome, teacher quality, is ill-defined; and working conditions present a strong moderating effect on teaching performance, which makes measures of the ultimate outcome of interest, student outcomes, difficult to attribute to teacher preparation.

Over the last decade, researchers have begun to use large data-bases to study the relationship of specific SET preparation variables (e.g., type of program, extent of preparation) to quality indicators (e.g., teaching skill, self-perceptions) and more recently, student achievement. Carlson and colleagues (2002) applied the aggregate-teacher quality model described early in this chapter and concluded that SETs majoring in special education had higher aggregate teacher quality scores than those who did not. In further comparisons, SETs graduating from a fifth year program or those earning certification in continuing professional development program had the highest teacher quality scores. SETs earning certification from a master's program had the second highest scores, followed by those completing a Bachelor's program. They found that those earning certification through an alternative route program had the lowest quality scores. Carlson et al. also reported that SETs who gave their preservice preparation high marks reported that they were more successful teaching students with disabilities and found their workloads more manageable than those giving their preparation lower ratings. Boe, Shinn, and Cook (2007) used SASS data and reported that SETs with extensive preparation in pedagogy as well as practice teaching were more effective than those with some or no preparation in developing teachers who were certified, securing jobs in their main fields, and perceiving themselves as well prepared to teach both content and pedagogy.

In a major departure from previous studies of teacher quality in special education, the Feng and Sass (2010) used value-added models to study the relationship between teacher quality and the achievement gains of students with disabilities. These researchers found that initial preparation had substantial effects on SETs' ability to improve the achievement gains of students with disabilities, particularly in reading. More specifically, Feng and Sass reported that holding a bachelor's degree in special education, more hours of coursework, as well as teacher certification in special education were significantly related to the achievement gains of students with disabilities. Students taught by SETs who held an advanced degree also tended to have higher student achievement gains in math. The Feng and Sass findings about the effects of preparation on the achievement of students with disabilities are both encouraging and discouraging. They are encouraging in that initial preparation efforts appear to have an impact on SETs' effectiveness. Yet, these findings also are of concern given that SETs tend to be in short supply and a large proportion of early career SETs enter each year with minimal preparation. Moreover, students in high poverty settings tend to bear a disproportionate share of uncertified teachers (Fall & Billingsley, 2008). Feng and Sass also point out that their findings with SETs are different from in previous research in general education, where neither specific coursework nor type of degree influenced the performance of teachers in general education.

Two small observational studies considered the effects of the extent and type of preparation on SETs' knowledge and skills. Nougaret, Scruggs, and Mastropieri (2005) compared two groups of teachers, first year teachers completing traditional certification and those on emergency certificates using the Danielson framework (based on Praxis III criteria) for teaching. Observers were blind to the preparation status of the teachers. Nougaret and colleagues reported that first year teachers completing traditional programs used more effective teaching practices and had better management skills than those with emergency certificates. In another study, Sindelar, Daunic, and Rennells (2004) compared teachers who completed traditional and AR programs on observations of classroom performance. The AR teachers were comprised of two groups, those from university-district partnership programs and add-on district programs. They observed teachers using the Praxis III, which includes measures on planning to teach, classroom environment, instruction, and professionalism. Although traditionally prepared SETs received higher ratings than the AR groups on instruction, all teachers met a basic level of competence.

Determining the quality of graduates from AR programs needs further study, given the dramatic variation in these programs. Rosenberg, Boyer, Sindelar and Misra (2007) pointed out that about half of the 101 programs they studied required three months or less of training before SETs were hired as the teacher of record. In a review of AR programs, Rosenberg and Sindelar (2005) identified characteristics of the stronger ones, including adequate program length with a variety of activities, meaningful coordination with institutions of higher education (IHEs), including IHE supervision, and school-based mentor support. In contrast, weaker programs were characterized by unanchored courses and activities that lacked a unified program approach.

Induction

Even extensively prepared teachers need systematic support as they work to apply what they learned during preservice preparation in complex school settings. Induction is a phase in teacher development that is designed to provide systematic supports with the primary goals of continued teacher learning, improved teacher effectiveness, and retention (Griffin, Winn, Otis-Wilborn, & Kilgore, 2003; Guarino et al., 2006; Strong, 2005). Although mentoring is often the primary activity associated with induction, a range of supports and activities are often included as part of induction, including systematic hiring practices, reduced responsibilities, meetings with other new teachers, and evaluation (Feiman-Nemser, 2001; Darling-Hammond & Sykes, 2003; Smith & Ingersoll, 2004). Unfortunately, national data suggests that many SETs do not participate in mentor programs; however, an encouraging finding is that between 1999–2000 and 2003–2004, first-year SETs participation in mentor programs increased from 59% to 67% (Boe et al., 2007a).

The general education literature provides direction for the design of induction programs. Summarized by Billingsley, Griffin, Smith, Kamman, and Israel (2009), these programs are situated within a culture of shared responsibility and support, have clear goals and purposes, and consider a range of ways to support new teachers including mentoring. Mentor programs also need to address mentor training and compensation, the match of mentor to mentee and release time for mentor-mentee work. Broader aspects of induction include informal supports, addressing new teachers' specific needs, workload reduction, and formative and summative assessments. In addition, induction programs should provide clear descriptions of the roles, organizations, and processes involved in these programs and provide adequate resources (for reviews see Feiman-Nemser, 2001; Griffin et al., 2003; Smith & Ingersoll, 2004; Wang, Odell, & Schwille, 2008). The Council for Exceptional Children Mentoring Project published *Mentoring and Induction Guidelines* (White & Mason, 2003) on their website, and much of what is included is consistent with directions from the general education literature.

In the special education literature, roughly half of the induction-related studies were descriptions of new teachers' experiences in the first years (discussed under work contexts later in this chapter) or descriptions of induction programs that primarily considered SETs' satisfaction with mentor support (Billingsley et al., 2009). Perhaps one of the greatest weaknesses of the literature is that little is known about what happens during mentor-mentee interactions or the effects of these interactions on teacher practices. Only studies that focused on measures addressing SET teaching effectiveness or retention are reviewed in this section and no studies linking induction to student achievement were found.

There is some evidence that induction has an influence on SETs' perceived effectiveness. Billingsley, Carlson, and Klein (2004) in a study of over 1,000 early career SETs found that 61% participated in formal mentor programs, yet one third did not find this support helpful. They also found that SETs receiving higher levels of formal mentoring reported greater job manageability and success in getting through to difficult students than those with less support. In a recent study, Boe, Cook, and Sunderland (2008b) reported that induction was related to SETs' self-ratings of their preparedness to teach, pedagogical content knowledge, and ability to manage classrooms.

Some research suggests induction also has an impact on retention. Smith and Ingersoll (2004) in their study of over 3,0000 first-year teachers (including SETs and using SASS questionnaires), found that teachers were half as likely to leave teaching or change schools when they participated in a comprehensive set of induction activities compared to those do did not participate in any. Supports associated with staying were a mentor in the same field, common planning time with other teachers in the same subject area, regularly scheduled collaboration with other teachers, and participating in an external network of teachers. The effect of mentor support on retention was considered in two special education teacher studies. Whitaker (2000) studied the perceptions of 156 first year SETs and the impact of mentoring on their plans to stay. She found that SETs reporting positive perceptions of mentoring were more likely to plan to stay than those with less positive perceptions. However, Billingsley et al. (2004) did not find that support was associated with intent to stay, possibly because they used a long-term intent variable versus the Whitaker short-term intent plans.

Another induction-related consideration is the extent to which teachers are placed in assignments that match their preparation and experience. Johnson, Kardos, Kauffman, Liu, and Donaldson (2004) explained the importance of match, stating that each job has a unique set of challenges and demands and a teacher's success depends not only on her overall qualifications, but also on the specific fit of the job to her skills and experiences. In special education, there is evidence that teacher-job match has a positive impact on commitment in a number of studies. Fall et al. (2009) reported that early career SETs reporting a good match between their preparation and teaching assignments were more committed to teaching than those who reported a weaker match. In qualitative studies, teachers left because of varied problems with job match (e.g., students, service-delivery, school) (Gehrke & Murri, 2006; Morvant, Gersten, Gillman, Keating, & Blake, 1995). Given the range of SET certification areas, a K–12 preparation focus, and varied service-delivery models, it is likely that match is even more important in special than general education. The lack of match may explain why SETs migrate to other positions more often than other teachers (Boe et al., 2008a).

Finally, special educators entering through brief programs will likely need more extensive supports in their first years of teaching to be effective, adding to induction costs (unless provided by the AR program). Little is known about the extent to which LEAs are equipped to improve the knowledge and skills of minimally prepared special educators. Unfortunately, high poverty schools have higher proportions of SETs with minimal qualifications than lower poverty schools (Fall & Billingsley, 2008), leaving them with a disproportionate share of this burden.

Professional Development

After initial preparation, the development of teachers' knowledge and skills depends on professional development (PD), whether organized through educational agencies or through SETs own efforts to learn. Contemporary views of PD consider a broad range of contexts for learning, from formal programs to informal learning communities. Desmione (2009) considers the myriad of activities that contribute to teacher learning through co-teaching, analysis of student data, group discussions, self-analysis, and observations of others and in the selection and use of curriculum materials. Opportunities to learn are also growing in e-learning environments through e-mentoring and on-line communities of practice (Smith & Ingersoll, 2004; Smith & Israel, 2010). Borko (2004) suggested that to understand teacher learning, it needs to be studied within a range of contexts.

The value-added study by Feng and Sass (2010) is the only large-scale study that investigated the relationship between SETs' participation in professional development (type and hours) and its relationship to student achievement. They reported that PD had little effect on SETs' ability to promote achievement gains among students with disabilities. However, the database did not contain information about the quality or nature of the PD experiences, factors related to the effectiveness of these efforts.

The SPeNSE study provides some information about the extent of PD efforts in special education and teachers' perspectives of these experiences. Carlson et al. (2002) found that SETs spent an average of 59 hours in PD and 54% of SETs had individual PD plans. Special educators overall gave their PD experiences high ratings and Carlson et al. reported some relationships between amount of time spent in PD and reported teacher practices. For example, they found that SETs spending eight or more hours in learning about teacher collaboration also reported using specific collaboration practices more frequently, such as identifying opportunities for students to work on IEP goals in general education and providing information to help GETs respond to students in a constructive manner.

Much of the work in professional development has addressed the extent to which specific PD efforts result in changes in teachers' practices and the extent to which changes are sustained over time. The research to practice literature base emphasizes that although there are many interventions shown to be effective with students with disabilities (e.g., Cook & Schirmer, 2003), SETs do not necessarily use these practices (Englert & Rozendahl, 2004). Given the research to practice gap, PD activities need to be related to the "everyday experiences of teachers and students rather than removed from the contextual settings in which they are to be applied" (Englert & Rozendal, p. 25). For example, researchers have used systematic PD practices to teach classwide peer tutoring (Abbott, Greenwood, Buzhardt, & Tapia, 2006), peer-assisted learning strategies in mathematics (Baker, Gersten, Dimino, & Griffiths, 2004), effective literacy practices (Englert & Rozendal, 2004), and collaborative strategic reading (Klingner, Arguelles, Hughes, & Vaughn, 2001) to name a few. Results of research to practice studies have implications for the design of PD efforts. For example, Baker et al. found that factors influencing the long-term use of PALs in mathematics instruction included initial high quality professional development and support that allowed teachers to reach a respectable level of mastery. Teachers also saw the social and cognitive benefits of peers working together, and had opportunities to see improvements in students' math outcomes. Other studies have also emphasized that teachers are more likely to use new practices when they receive support during implementation from colleagues and administrators and have evidence that it improves student learning (Abbott et al., 2006; Klingner, Ahwee, Polonieta, & Menendez, 2003). In a review of facilitators on the sustained use of research-based practices, Klingner (2004) also emphasized the importance of buy-in from teachers and administrators in their involvement in planning, problem-solving, and eventually taking responsibility for PD efforts. She also emphasized the need for strong relationships among those involved and the need for ongoing assistance and coaching over time. Some have emphasized the importance of a "community of practice," emphasizing networks of teachers who dialogue and support one another as they learn new practices (Englert & Rozendal, 2004; Klingner, 2004).

Consistent with Klingner's finding about the importance of "communities of practice", professional learning communities (PLCs) help to create a culture for professional growth. PLCs are defined as "professionals in a school, typically groups of teachers, who work collaboratively to improve practice and enhance student learning" (Pugach, Blanton, Correa, McLeskey, & Langley, 2009, p. 6). In PLCs, teachers plan and work together to address instructional challenges, use student data to revise their teaching practices, and discuss what is working and what needs improvement. Professional learning communities and teacher leadership within these communities are designed with the view that expert teachers can facilitate effective instruction by participating in ongoing and school-embedded opportunities to learn (Mangin & Stoelinga, 2008). PLCs have the potential to not only provide opportunities for SETs to learn with GETs, but may serve to reduce the isolation that some SETs experience (Pugach et al.) and facilitate teacher leadership and retention (Billingsley, 2007).

Although the emphasis of PD is to increase teacher expertise, improve instruction and ultimately improve student learning (Desmione, 2009), one study found that effective PD contributes to improved commitment to teaching. In a study of teacher attrition in three urban systems, Gersten, Keating, Yovanoff, and Harniss (2001) using a path analysis model, found that PD had a direct effect on SETs' commitment to the profession and an indirect effect on teachers' intent to leave.

Summary and Discussion

Overall, the research on teacher preparation, broadly defined, is scattered and thin and lacks a strong conceptual base (Brownell et al., 2003). Initial preparation programs vary widely (e.g., traditional, AR unified), and there are relatively few descriptions of induction and large-scale PD programs. Heterogeneity compounds the difficulty of finding commonalities among successful programs and identifying elements of effective teacher preparation (Sindelar, Brownell, & Billingsley, 2010).

Although difficult, it is encouraging that researchers have begun to study the link between SETs' preparation, knowledge, and skills to student outcomes (e.g., Brownell et al., 2009; Carlson et al., 2004; Feng & Sass, 2010). In particular, economists Feng and Sass incorporated both a unique database and methodology to the study of the impact of SETs on student achievement gains. The use of value-added methods along with observational studies (Nougaret et al., 2005; Sindelar et al., 2004) are important steps in better delineating the effects of teacher preparation on the achievement of students with disabilities.

Yet as Blanton and colleagues (2006) suggest, there are many challenges in measuring SET quality that need to be considered in the design of future research including the wide range of students served, varied models for serving students, and the fact that an individual SET may work across several grades and content areas. They also discuss the problem of trying to determine how to link teachers to student achievement when both GETs and SETs teach the same student for the same subject. Feng and Sass (2010) avoided the problem of trying to attribute achievement to teachers who shared instruction for students by studying only students who were taught reading and math by a single teacher in a separate special education classroom or by a GET in a regular classroom (they also included a category where students may attend both special education classes taught by a SET and general education classes taught by regular educators).

Teacher preparation research findings have several implications for educational leaders. To the extent possible, leaders should hire SETs with certification and degrees in special education. However, it is also important to note that with the growth of brief AR programs and the variety of traditional preparation models, not all SETs are necessarily well prepared to teach. Although some AR programs produce competent teachers (Sindelar et al., 2004), educational leaders should assess the extent of prospective SETs' preparation, noting length of preparation and the extent of participation in methods courses and field work. Given that the teacher-job match appears to have an influence on SETs' commitment, efforts to determine the extent to which a candidate's preparation and interests match a particular position deserve careful consideration. Moreover, minimally prepared teachers will require more extensive induction and unfortunately this burden falls disproportionately to high poverty schools. Finally, efforts for PD require careful planning and teacher supports to be effective. Pugach et al. (2009) emphasize the importance of learner-center professional development programs to allow researchers and teachers to collaborate over time with multiple opportunities for problem-solving and support during the implementation of new practices. Recent reviews of the PD literature and conceptualizations should help guide the development of PD programs (e.g., Borko, 2004; Desmione, 2009; Wayne, Yoon, Zhu, Cronen, & Garet, 2008).

Conditions of Service

The ability of SETs to help their students meet valued educational outcomes is related not only to SETs' knowledge and skills, but also on the extent to which the workplace is structured to allow them to use their expertise. Teachers who are fortunate enough to work in supportive settings, with reasonable workloads, sufficient materials, and contexts that allow them to use effective practices have more opportunities to help their students' achieve important outcomes. In other words, qualified teachers need supportive work contexts to be effective.

Teachers' willingness to remain in teaching is also tied to their effectiveness. Individuals have different relations to their work including orientations toward financial rewards and necessity, focus on advancement, and work as a calling (Wrzesniewski, McCauley, Rozin, & Schwartz, 1997). Although, of course, there may be overlap among these work orientations, there is evidence that teachers see work as a calling. Researchers have emphasized the importance of teachers' intrinsic motivation to help their students' learn (Rosenholtz, 1989), and a sense of success is tied to their career decisions (Johnson & The Project on the Next Generation of Teachers, 2004).

A primary argument for implementing policies that increase retention is that students taught by teachers with some experience achieve more than those taught by novices (Rice, 2003). Thus, keeping effective teachers and reducing the number of years students are taught by inexperienced teachers helps improve teacher quality. Figure 30.1 includes two major areas under the conditions of work. The first is the broader work context of the district and school settings and the second concerns SETs' specific work assignments (e.g., caseloads, role expectations).

Work Contexts

Although work contexts include district variables, such as salary, much of the work context literature has addressed aspects of the school work environment that affect teachers' day-to-day work lives. Researchers in general and special education have noted the relationship of work conditions to turnover (e.g., Billingsley, 2004; Brownell, Smith, McNellis, & Lenk, 1994–1995; Darling-Hammond & Sykes, 2003; Ingersoll, 2001; Johnson & Birkeland, 2003; Rosenholtz, 1989). Ingersoll in a frequently cited study reported that low salaries, inadequate administrative support, discipline problems, limited opportunities to influence decisions all contribute to high levels of leaving, after controlling for school and teacher characteristics.

Key school variables linked to commitment and retention are school climate and administrative and colleague support. Three studies found that SETs who have positive views of school climate are more likely to stay or intend to stay than those with less positive perceptions ("A High-Quality Teacher for Every Classroom," 2002; Billingsley et al., 2004; Miller et al., 1999). Special educators are also more likely to stay if they perceive that their colleagues and administrators are supportive. Boe, Barkanic, and Leow (1999) reported that teachers who stay are about four times more likely than those who leave to perceive administrators' behavior as supportive. Path analysis studies found that higher levels of support from principals is directly or indirectly associated with greater job satisfaction, fewer role problems, reduced stress, and higher levels of SET commitment (Cross & Billingsley, 1994; Gersten et al., 2001; Singh & Billingsley, 1996). Westling and Whitten (1996) also found that SETs who planned to stay received support from school administrators in specific areas such as including students and problem solving.

Evidence suggests that new teachers struggle with many aspect of their work, in particular in their efforts to collaborate across the school (Billingsley et al., 2009). For example, Otis-Wilborn, Winn, Griffin, and Kilgore (2005) found that SETs' efforts to include students with disabilities were often not met because the schools had not adopted the structures needed to support their work. Across the new teacher studies, many SETs struggled as they sought to include their students in general classrooms, citing difficulties with collaboration, lack of scheduled time and isolation from their peers. Supporting new SETs in their collaborative work is essential given the importance of teachers' interactions in meeting the needs of students in inclusive settings and the benefit of collaborative support to retention (Smith & Ingersoll, 2004).

Overall teachers in high poverty districts reported less desirable work conditions than those working in more affluent districts. SETs in high poverty districts perceived their principals and colleagues as less supportive and perceived less involvement in school decisions (Fall & Billingsley, in press). Although little is known about SET turnover in high poverty schools, GET turnover rates are higher in these settings (Barnes, Crowe, & Schaefer, 2007; Darling-Hammond & Sykes, 2003).

Work Assignments

To a large extent teacher effectiveness depends on teachers' engaging in well-structured, deliberate, and thoughtful work. Well-designed work provides teachers with a sense of purpose and allows them to work toward valued goals (Gersten et al., 2001). *The Bright Futures Report* highlighted the range of problems that SETs struggled with, including high student caseloads, excessive paperwork, lack of instructional and technological resources, and an insufficient focus on student learning (Kozleski, Mainzer, & Deshler, 2000). Kozleski et al. findings are consistent with numerous other studies. Caseloads were identified as contributing factor to SET attrition (Billingsley & Cross; 1991; Brownell et al., 1994–1995); however, the complexity of SETs caseloads may also be a deterrent as well. Among SETs who planned to leave soon, 42% served students in four or more exceptionality areas (Carlson et al., 2002). Special educators reporting higher levels of paperwork also viewed their teaching roles as less manageable and were more likely to indicate intent to leave, even after controlling for other working conditions (Paperwork in Special Education, 2003). New SETs often describe the lack of time they have to collaborate with general educators and many new teachers indicated they do not have sufficient teaching resources (Billingsley et al. 2009; Kilgore, Griffin, Otis-Wilborn, & Winn, 2003).

Managing complex roles is needed to address problems of role ambiguity, conflict and dissonance. Close to a third of new SETs did not see their workload as manageable (Billingsley et al., 2004) and these teachers are significantly more likely to report lower commitment to teaching (Fall et al., 2009). Gehrke and Murri (2006) indicated new teachers were overwhelmed by multiple roles that required them to manage, schedule and organize their work with adults and students across multiple grades and subjects. Teachers with large caseloads have even more scheduling, coordination, and paperwork.

As districts moved toward greater inclusion, some special educators struggled with changing roles. Some teachers experience role ambiguity or the lack of necessary information about how to conduct their work (Klingner & Vaughn, 2002; Otis-Wilborn et al., 2005). Otis-Wilborn and colleagues emphasize the need for structures and processes to clarify SETs roles and responsibilities in the school. Other SETs experience role conflict—for example, they may spend a significant amount of time on bureaucratic tasks, but believe they should be spending more time providing direct instruction to students. Path analysis studies suggest that role conflict, ambiguity and dissonance also contribute to stress and decrease job satisfaction and commitment (Cross & Billingsley, 1994; Gersten et al., 2001). Providing instrumental support (e.g., materials, space, and resources, and time for teaching and non-teaching duties) was correlated with SETs' job satisfaction and commitment to the school (Littrell, Billingsley, & Cross, 1994).

Summary and Discussion

Comprehensive conceptualizations of teacher effectiveness need to consider the effects of work contexts on what teachers are able to accomplish with their students. Although problematic work conditions in special education are well documented, we know far less about the contextual factors that influence how SETs participate in their school communities and how their roles are developed in schools. A better understanding of work the contexts that facilitate SETs' core work and increase their commitment to teaching is needed and descriptions of supportive work contexts may help provide some guidance.

Boe and colleagues (2008a) suggested that "it is unrealistic to expect a level of sustained national commitment of sufficient scope to reduce substantially teacher attrition" (p. 25). However, teacher attrition and turnover are not evenly distributed, with high poverty schools losing greater numbers of teachers. Targeted interventions are critical in high need schools both to improve teacher quality and retention. Moreover, actions that enhance retention (e.g., reasonable workloads, supportive leaders) are also likely to create the circumstances needed for teachers to do their work well.

Educational leaders need to consider the extent to which SETs have opportunities to teach effectively. Gersten et al. (2001) posed the following questions: "Does the job with all it entails, make sense? Is it feasible? Is it one that well-trained, interested, special education professionals can manage in order to accomplish their main objective—enhancing students' academic, social, and vocational competence?" (p. 551). Another complimentary approach to improving working conditions is helping teachers learn to deal with stress on the job. Cooley and Yovanoff (1996) reported that interventions including a stress management workshop and a peer collaboration program had a significant impact on improving SETs' job satisfaction and commitment as well as reducing burnout. The Teacher Support Program (TSP) program is also designed to support and retain teachers of students with disabilities through collaborative problem solving, electronic networking, and materials (Westling, Herzog, Cooper-Duffy, Prohn, & Ray, 2006).

Conclusions

A primary responsibility of policy-makers and leaders is securing, cultivating, and keeping a qualified workforce. Clearly, much more needs to be learned about teacher quality in special education and how teacher characteristics, preparation, practices, and work environments impact the outcomes of students with disabilities. Figure 30.1 proposes that a complex array of factors interact to influence the extent to which students with disabilities have access to skilled and committed teachers. The interaction among teacher quality factors can combine to provide students with academically talented, well-prepared SETs who teach in supportive work contexts and engage in ongoing learning opportunities. In contrast, these factors may interact so that other students are exposed to minimally prepared teachers with poor working conditions, leaving students with fewer opportunities to learn. There is evidence that the latter scenario is consistent with many high poverty schools. Policy-makers need to consider policies that will provide more equitable learning opportunities for all students.

Although progress has been made in understanding factors that influence teacher quality and effectiveness, much more research is needed. Ongoing monitoring of the SET workforce is needed, with a design that allows the study of important subgroups, including teachers working in varied settings and with different student populations. Ideally, research would include longitudinal studies that look at the effects of teacher development over time (Wilson et al., 2001) and include investigations of how teacher preparation interacts with work contexts to influence student learning. Moreover, as teacher evaluation systems focus on linking teacher practice to student achievement, varied methods and measurement considerations deserve careful study. As Holdheide, Goe, Croft, and Reschly (2010) suggest, evaluation systems are not currently designed to accurately measure achievement for students with disabilities or connect their growth to teacher practices.

Finally, understanding the range of factors that influence teacher quality and effectiveness provides policy-makers and leaders with a framework for considering ways to both improve the workforce. It is unlikely that the SET workforce will improve without a comprehensive, strategic, and well-coordinated plan and significant investments in teachers. Although federal and state strategic planning is essential, leaders at the school and districts levels should assess local conditions through periodical assessments and strategically allocate scarce resources where they are likely to make the greatest difference.

Note

This article was published in the *International Encyclopedia of Education*, (2010, Volume 2). McGaw, B., Peterson, P., & Baker, B. (Eds.), Workforce issues in special education (886–891), Elsevier, 2010, Reproduced with permission.

References

Abbott, M., Greenwood, C. R., Buzhardt, J., & Tapia, Y. (2006). Using technology-based teacher support tools to scale up the classwide peer tutoring program. *Reading & Writing Quarterly, 22*(1), 47–64.

A high-quality teacher for every classroom (SPeNSE Factsheet). (2002). Retrieved from http://ferdig.coe.ufl.edu/spense/SummaryReportserviceproviders.pdf

American Association for Employment in Education (AAEE). (2008). *Educator supply and demand, executive summary*. Columbus, OH: Author.

Baker, S., Gersten, R., Dimino, J. A., & Griffiths, R. (2004). The sustained use of research based instructional practice. *Remedial and Special Education, 25*(1), 5–24.

Barnes, G. B., Crowe, E., Schaefer, B. (2007). *The cost of teacher turnover in five school districts: A pilot study*. National Commission on Teaching and America's Future. Retrieved from http://www.nctaf.org/resources/demonstration_projects/turnover/documents/CTTFullReportfinal.pdf

Benner, A. D. (2000). *The cost of teacher turnover*. Austin, TX: Texas Center for Educational Research.

Billingsley, B. (2004). Special education teacher retention and attrition:

A critical analysis of the research literature. *The Journal of Special Education, 38*(1), 39–55.

Billingsley, B. S. (2007). Recognizing and supporting the critical roles of teachers in special education leadership. *Exceptionality, 15*(3), 163–176.

Billingsley, B., Carlson, E., & Klein, S. (2004). The working conditions and induction support of early career special educators. *Exceptional Children, 70*(3), 333–347.

Billingsley, B., & Cross, L. (1991). Teachers' decisions to transfer from special to general education. *The Journal of Special Education, 24*, 496–511.

Billingsley, B., Fall, A., & Williams, T. O. (2006). Who is teaching students with emotional disorders? A profile and comparison to other special educators. *Behavioral Disorders, 31*(1), 252–264.

Billingsley, B., Griffin, C., Smith, S. J., Kamman, M., & Israel, M. (2009). *A review of teacher Induction in Special Education: Research, Practice, and Technology Solutions.* Monograph prepared for the National Center to Inform Policy and Practice in Special Education Professional Development (NCIPP), The University of Florida.

Blanton, L. P., Sindelar, P. T., & Correa, V. I. (2006). Models and measures of beginning teacher quality. *The Journal of Special Education, 40*(2), 115–127.

Boe, E. E. (2006). Long term trends in the national demand, supply, and shortage of special education teachers. *The Journal of Special Education, 40*, 138–150.

Boe, E. E., Barkanic, G., & Leow, C. S. (1999). *Retention and attrition of teachers at the school level: National trends and predictors*. Philadelphia: University of Pennsylvania, Graduate School of Education, Center for Research and Evaluation in Social Policy.

Boe, E. E., & Cook, L. H. (2006). The chronic and increasing shortage of fully-certified teachers in special and general education. *Exceptional Children, 72*(4), 443–460.

Boe, E. E., Cook, L. H., & Sunderland, R. J. (2007a). *The prevalence of various aspects of teacher preparation, induction, mentoring, extra support, professional development, and workload factors for beginning teachers in special and general education.* (Data Analysis Report No. 2007-DAR1). Philadelphia: University of Pennsylvania, Graduate School of Education, Center for Research and Evaluation in Social Policy.

Boe, E. E., Cook, L. H., & Sunderland, R. J. (2007b). *Trends in the turnover of teachers from 1991 to 2004: Attrition, teaching area transfer, and school migration.* (Data Analysis Report No. 2007-DAR2). Philadelphia: University of Pennsylvania, Graduate School of Education, Center for Research and Evaluation in Social Policy.

Boe, E. E., Cook, L. H., & Sunderland, R. J. (2008a). Teacher turnover: Examining exit attrition, teaching area transfer, and school migration. *Exceptional Children, 75*, 7–31.

Boe, E. E., Cook, L. H., & Sunderland, R. J. (2008b). *Teacher qualifications and turnover: Bivariate associations with various aspects of teacher preparation, induction, mentoring, extra support, professional development, and workload factors for early career teachers in special and general education.* (Data Analysis Rep. 2008-DAR1). Philadelphia: University of Pennsylvania, Graduate School of Education, Center for Research and Evaluation in Social Policy.

Boe, E. E., Cook, L. H., & Sunderland, R. J. (2009). *A comprehensive analysis of the supply of teachers prepared by traditional and alternative methods.* (Data Analysis Report No. 2009-DAR1). Philadelphia: University of Pennsylvania, Graduate School of Education, Center for Research and Evaluation in Social Policy.

Boe, E. E., Shinn, S., & Cook, L. H. (2007). Does teacher preparation matter for beginning teachers in either special or general education? *The Journal of Special Education, 41*, 148–170.

Borko, H. (2004). Professional development and teacher learning: Mapping the terrain. *Educational Researcher*, 33(*8*), 3–15.

Brownell, M. T., Bishop, A., Gersten, R., Klingner, J. K., Penfield, R. D., Dimino, J., … Sindelar, P. (2009). The role of domain expertise in special education teacher quality, *Exceptional Children, 75*(4), 391–411.

Brownell, M. T., Leko, M. M., Kamman, M., & Streeper-King, L. (2008). Defining and preparing high quality teachers in special education: What do we know from the research? In T. Scruggs & M. Mastropieri (Eds.), *Advances in learning and behavioral disabilities*: *Vol. 21. Personnel preparation* (pp. 35–74). Bingley, UK: Emerald Group Publishing.

Brownell, M. T., Ross, D. R., Colón, E. P., & McCallum, C. L. (2003). *Critical features of special education teacher preparation: A comparison with exemplary practices in general teacher education. (COPSSE Document Number RS-4).* Gainesville: University of Florida, Center on Personnel Studies in Special Education.

Brownell, M. T., Smith, S. W., McNellis, J., & Lenk, L. (1994–1995). Career decisions in special education: Current and former teachers' personal views. *Exceptionality, 5,* 83–102.

Carlson, E., & Billingsley, B. (2010). Workforce issues in special education. In B. McGaw, P. Peterson, & E. Baker (Eds.), *International encyclopedia of education* (pp. 886–891). Amsterdam: Elsevier.

Carlson, E., Brauen, M., Klein, S., Schroll, K., & Willig, S. (2002). *Study of personnel needs in special education: Key findings*. Retrieved from http://fer.dig.coe.ful.edu/spense/KeyFindings.pdf

Carlson, E., Lee, H., & Schroll, K. (2004). Identifying attributes of high quality special education teachers. *Teacher Education and Special Education, 27*(4), 350–359.

Cook, L. H., & Boe, E. E. (2007).National trends in the sources of supply of teachers in special and general education. *Teacher Education and Special Education*, *30*, 217–232.

Cook, B., & Schirmer, B. (2003). What is special about special education? Overview and analysis. *The Journal of Special Education, 37*(3), 200–205.

Cooley, E., & Yovanoff, P. (1996). Supporting professionals-at-risk: Evaluating interventions to reduce burnout and improve retention of special educators. *Exceptional Children*, *62*, 336–355.

Council for Exceptional Children. (2001, August). *The CEC standards for the preparation of special educators*. Arlington, VA: Author.

Cross, L., & Billingsley, B. (1994). Testing a model of special educators' intent to stay in teaching. *Exceptional Children*, *60*(5), 411–421.

Darling-Hammond, L., Holtzman, D., Gatlin, S. J. & Helig, J. V. (2005). Does teacher preparation matter? Evidence about teacher certification, Teach for America, and teacher effectiveness. *Education Policy Analysis Archives*, *14*(42). Retrieved from http://www.srnleads.org/data/pdfs/certification.pdf

Darling-Hammond, L., & Sykes, G. (2003). Wanted: A national teacher supply policy for education: The right way to meet the "highly qualified teacher" challenge. *Education Policy Analysis Archives, 11*(33). Retrieved from http://epaa.asu.edu/epaa/v11n33/

Desmione, L. M. (2009). Improving impact studies of teachers' professional development: Toward better conceptualizations and measures, *Educational Researcher, 38*(3), 181–199.

Englert, C. S., & Rozendahl, M. S. (2004). A model of professional development in special education. *Teacher Education and Special Education, 27*(1), 24–46.

Fall, A. M., & Billingsley, B. (2008). Disparities in teacher quality among early career special educators in high and low poverty districts. In T. E. Scruggs & M. A. Mastropieri (Eds.), *Advances in learning and behavioral disabilities: Vol. 21. Personnel preparation* (pp. 181–206). Stanford, CT: JAI.

Fall, A. M., & Billingsley, B. (in press). Disparities in work conditions among early career special educators in high- and low-poverty districts. *Remedial and Special Education.*

Fall, A. M., Billingsley, B., & Williams, T. O. (2009). Predicting early career special educators' commitment in high- and low-poverty districts. Manuscript in preparation.

Feiman-Nemser, S. (2001). From preparation to practice: Designing a continuum to strengthen and sustain practice. *Teachers College Record, 103*(6), 1013–1055.

Feng, L., & Sass, T. R. (2010). *Special education teacher quality and student achievement.* Report prepared for the U.S. Department of Education, Washington, DC.

Gehrke, R. S., & Murri, N. (2006). Beginning special educators' intent to stay in special education: Why they like it here. *Teacher Education and Special Education, 29*(3), 179–190.

Geiger, W. L., Crutchfield, M. D., & Mainzer, R. (2003). *The status of licensure of special education teachers in the 21st century*. Retrieved from http://www.coe.ufl.edu/copsse/pubfiles/RS-7.pdf

Gersten, R., Keating, T., Yovanoff, P., & Harniss, M. K. (2001). Working in special education: Factors that enhance special educators' intent to stay. *Exceptional Children, 67*(4), 549–567.

Goe, L. Bell, C., & Little, O. (2008). *Approaches to evaluating teacher effectiveness: A research synthesis*. National Comprehensive Center for Teacher Quality, Washington, DC. Retrieved from http://www.tqsource.org/publications/EvaluatingTeachEffectiveness.pdf

Griffin, C. C., Winn, J. A., Otis-Wilborn, A., & Kilgore, K. L. (2003). *New teacher induction in special education*. Gainesville: University of Florida, Center on Personnel Studies in Special Education.

Guarino, C. M., Santibañez, L., & Daley, G. A. (2006). Teacher recruitment and retention: A review of the recent empirical literature. *Review of Educational Research, 76*(2), 173–208.

Holdheide, L. R., Goe, L., Croft, A., & Reschly, D. J. (2010). *Challenges in evaluating special education teachers and English language learner specialists*. Washington, DC: National Comprehensive Center for Teacher Quality.

Hussar, W. J., & Bailey, T. M. (2008). *Projections of education statistics to 2017*. (NCES 2008-078). Washington, DC: National Center for Education Statistics. Institute of Education Sciences, U.S. Department of Education. Ingersoll, R. M. (2001). Teacher turnover and teacher shortages: An organizational analysis. *American Educational Research Journal, 38*(3), 499–534.

Israel, M. (2009). *Preparation of special education teacher educators: An investigation of emerging signature pedagogies*. Unpublished doctoral dissertation, The University of Kansas, Lawrence.

Johnson, S. M., & Birkeland, S. E. (2003). Pursuing a sense of success: New teachers explain their career decisions. *American Educational Research Journal, 40*(3), 581–617.

Johnson, S. M., Kardos, S. M., Kauffman, D., Liu, E., & Donaldson, M. L. (2004). The support gap: New teachers' early experiences in high-income and low-income schools. *Education Policy Analysis Archives, 12*(61). Retrieved from http://epaa.asu.edu/epaa/v12n61/

Johnson, S. M., & The Project on the Next Generation of Teachers (2004). *Finders and keepers: Helping teachers survive and thrive in our schools*. San Francisco: Jossey-Bass.

Katsiyannis, A., Zhang, D., & Conroy, M. (2003). Availability of special education teachers: Trends and issues. *Remedial and Special Education, 24*(4), 246–253.

Kennedy, M. M. (1992). The problems of improving teacher quality while balancing supply and demand. In E. E. Boe & D. M. Gilford (Eds.), *Teacher supply, demand, and quality: Policy issues, models, and data bases: Proceedings of a Conference* (pp 65–108). Washington, DC: National Academy Press.

Kilgore, K., Griffin, C., Otis-Wilborn, A., & Winn, J. (2003). The problems of beginning special education teachers: Exploring the contextual factors influencing their work. *Action in Teacher Education, 25*(1), 38–47.

Klingner, J. K. (2004). The science of professional development. *The Journal of Learning Disabilities, 37*(3), 248–255.

Klingner, J. K., Ahwee, S., Pilonieta, P., & Menendez, R. (2003). Barriers and facilitators in scaling up research-based practices. *Exceptional Children, 69*(4), 411–429.

Klingner, J., Arguelles, M., Hughes, M., & Vaughn, S. (2001). Examining the schoolwide "spread" of research-based practices. *Learning Disability Quarterly, 24*(4), 221–234.

Klingner, J. K., & Vaughn, S. (2002). The changing roles and responsibilities of an LD specialist. *Learning Disability Quarterly, 25*, 19–31.

Kozleski, E., Mainzer, R., & Deshler, D. (2000). *Bright futures for exceptional learners: An action agenda to achieve quality conditions for teaching and learning*. Reston, VA: Council for Exceptional Children.

Littrell, P., Billingsley, B., & Cross, L. (1994). The effects of principal support on general and special educators' stress, job satisfaction, health, school commitment, and intent to stay in teaching. *Remedial and Special Education, 15*(5), 297–310.

Mangin, M. M., & Stoelinga, S. R. (2008). *Effective teacher leadership: Using Research to inform and reform*. New York: Teachers College Press.

McLeskey, J., & Billingsley, B. S. (2008). How does the quality and stability of the teaching force influence the research-to-practice gap? A perspective on the teacher shortage in special education. *Remedial and Special Education, 29*(5), 293–305.

McLeskey, J., Tyler, N., & Flippin, S. S. (2004). The supply of and demand for special education teachers: A review of research regarding the nature of the chronic shortage of special education teachers. *The Journal of Special Education, 38*(1), 5–21.

Miller, M. D., Brownell, M., & Smith, S. W. (1999). Factors that predict teachers staying in, leaving, or transferring from the special education classroom. *Exceptional Children, 65*(2), 201–218.

Morvant, M., Gersten, R., Gillman, J., Keating, T., & Blake, G. (1995). Attrition/retention of urban special education teachers: Multi-faceted research and strategic action planning. Final performance report, Volume 1. (ERIC *Document Reproduction Service* No. ED338154)

No Child Left Behind Act of 2001. Pub. L. No. 107-110 (2001).

Nougaret, A. A., Scruggs, T. E., & Mastropieri, M. A. (2005). Does teacher education produce better special education teachers? *Exceptional Children, 71*(3), 217–229.

Otis-Wilborn, A., Winn, J., Griffin, C., & Kilgore, K. (2005). Beginning special educators' forays into general education. *Teacher Education and Special Education, 28*(3/4), 143–152.

Paperwork in special education (SPeNSE Factsheet). (2003). *SPeNSE Factsheet*. Retrieved from http://ferdig.coe.ufl.edu/spense/Paperwork.doc

Pugach, M.C., & Blanton, L.P. (2009). A framework for conducting research on collaborative teacher education, *Teaching and Teacher Education, 25*, 575–582.

Pugach, M. C., Blanton, L. P., Correa, V. I., McLeskey, J., & Langley, L. K. (2009).*The role of collaboration in supporting the induction and retention of new special education teachers* (NCIPP Doc. No. RS-2). University of Florida, National Center to Inform Policy and Practice in Special Education Professional Development.

Rice, J. K. (2003). *Teacher quality: Understanding the effectiveness of teacher attributes*. Washington, DC: The Economic Policy Institute.

Rivkin, S., Hanushek, E., & Kain, J. (2005). Teachers, schools, and academic achievement. *Econometrica, 73*(2), 417–458.

Rosenberg, M. S., Boyer, K. L., Sindelar, P. T., & Misra, S. K. (2007). Alternative route programs for certification in special education: Program infrastructure, instructional delivery, and participant characteristics. *Exceptional Children, 73*(2), 224–241.

Rosenberg, M. S., & Sindelar, P. T. (2005). The proliferation of alternative routes to certification in special education: A critical review of the literature. *The Journal of Special Education, 39*, 117–127.

Rosenholtz, S. J. (1989). Workplace conditions that affect teacher quality and commitment: Implications for teacher induction programs. *The Elementary School Journal, 89*(4), 420–439.

Sanders, W., & Horn, S. (1998). Research findings form the Tennessee Value-Added Assessment System (TVAAS) database: Implications for educational evaluation and research. *Journal of Personnel Evaluation in Education, 12*(3), 247–256.

School and Staffing Survey. (n.d.). *SASS teacher questionnaire*. Retrieved from http://nces.ed.gov/surveys/sass/questionnaire.asp

Sindelar, P. T., Brownell, M. T., & Billingsley, B. (2010). Special education teacher education research: Current status and future directions, *Teacher Education and Special Education, 33*(4), 8–24.

Sindelar, P. T., Daunic, A., & Rennells, M. S. (2004). Comparisons of traditionally and alternatively trained teachers. *Exceptionality, 12*(4), 209–223.

Sindelar, P. T., Shearer, D. K., Yendol-Hoppey, D., & Liebert, T. W. (2006). The sustainability of inclusive school reform. *Exceptional Children, 72*(3), 317–331.

Sindelar, P. T., Rosenberg, M. S., Corbett, N. L., Dewey, J., Denslow, D., & Lotfinia, B. (2009). *Cost effectiveness of alternative route special education teacher preparation*. Manuscript submitted for publication.

Singer, J. D. (1992). Are special educators' career paths special? Results from a 13-year longitudinal study. *Exceptional Children, 59*(3), 262–279.

Singh, K., & Billingsley, B. (1996). Intent to stay in teaching: Teachers of students with emotional disorders versus other special educators. *Remedial and Special Education, 17*(1), 37–47.

Smith, S. J. & Israel, M. (2010). E-mentoring: Solutions for teacher induction. *The Journal of Special Education Leadership*, 23(1), 30–40.

Smith, T. M., & Ingersoll, R. M. (2004). What are the effects of induction and mentoring on beginning teacher turnover? *American Educational Research Journal, 41*(3), 681–714.

Smith-Davis, J., & Billingsley, B. (1993). The suppy/demand puzzle. *Teacher Education and Special Education, 16*(3), 205–220.

Strong, M. (2005). Teacher induction, mentoring, and retention: A summary of the research. *The New Educator, 1*, 181–195.

Teacher Follow-up Survey. (n.d.). Current TFS questionnaire. National Center for Education Statistics. Retrieved from http://nces.ed.gov/surveys/sass/question0809.asp

Tyler, N., Yzquierdo, Z., Lopez-Reyna, N., & Flippin, S. S. (2004). Cultural and linguistic diversity and the special education workforce: A critical overview. *The Journal of Special Education*, *38*(1), 22–38.

United States Department of Education. (2009). *Twenty-eighth annual report to Congress on the implementation of the individuals with disabilities education act, 2006, Vol. 2.* Washington, DC: Author.

Wang, J., Odell, S. J., & Schwille, S. A. (2008). Effects of teacher induction on beginning teachers' teaching: A critical review of the literature. *Journal of Teacher Education, 59*(2), 132–152.

Wayne, A. J., Yoon, K. W., Zhu, P., Cronen, S., & Garet, M. S. (2008). Experimenting with teacher professional development: Motives and methods. *Educational Researcher*, *37*(8), 469–479.

Wayne, A. J., & Youngs, P. (2003). Teacher characteristics and student achievement gains: A review. *Review of Educational Research*, *73*, 89–122.

Westling, D. L., & Whitten, T. M. (1996). Rural special education teachers' plans to continue or leave their teaching positions. *Exceptional Children*, *62,* 319–335.

Westling, D. L. H., Herzog, M.J., Cooper-Duffy, K., Prohn, K., & Ray, M. (2006). The teacher support program: A Proposed resource for the special education profession and an initial validation. *Remedial and Special Education, 27*(3), 136–147.

Whitaker, S. D. (2000). Mentoring beginning special education teachers and the relationship to attrition. *Exceptional Children, 66*(4), 546–566.

White, M. E., & Fong, A. B. (2008). *Trends in California teacher demand: A county and regional perspective* (Issues & Answers Report, REL 2008–No. 057). Washington, DC: U.S. Department of Education, Institute of Education Sciences, National Center for Education Evaluation and Regional Assistance, Regional Educational Laboratory West. Retrieved from http://ies.ed.gov/ncee/edlabs

White, M., & Mason, C. (2003). *Mentoring induction principles and guidelines*. Alexandria, VA: Council for Exceptional Children.

Wilson, S. M., Floden, R. E., & Ferrini-Mundy, J. (2001). *Teacher preparation research: Current knowledge, gaps, and recommendations*. Seattle: University of Washington.

Wrzesniewski, A., McCauley C., Rozin, P., &, Schwartz, B. (1997). Jobs, careers, and callings: People's relations to their work. *Journal of Research in Personality 31,* 21–33.

Section VII

Instructional Issues for Students with High Incidence Disabilities

Section Editor: John Wills Lloyd
University of Virginia

By definition, students with disabilities require specialized instruction. For those students who have been identified as having a high-incidence disability—learning disabilities, emotional or behavior disorders, or mild intellectual disabilities—problems with learning impinge not only on the traditional academic areas but also on other important educational domains.

Among the academic areas, many educators consider reading to be a foremost instructional concern for students with high-incidence disabilities. Ideally, educators hope to prevent students' development of reading problems, and doing so requires close attention to comprehensive, systematic, and explicit instruction. However, not all reading problems can be prevented; thus, it is necessary to provide remedial instruction for some students. Fortunately, a substantial body of evidence is available to guide effective teaching of reading.

Teaching of written expression, another important aspect of literacy, has received extensive research attention, also. Evidence is available to direct educators in teaching handwriting, spelling, and composition. The data from many studies show that it is possible for students with high-incidence disabilities to communicate clearly in writing. Those data also show how teachers can promote students' acquisition of writing skills by carefully combining basic instruction in technical skills with higher-order cognitive skills.

Many students with high-incidence disabilities also require specialized instruction in arithmetic and mathematics, as well as the traditional literacy areas. Although problems can occur anywhere all along a line stretching from simple computation to algebra or calculus, educators can learn a great deal about promoting arithmetic competence by examining highly focused research addressing instruction in simple arithmetic and word problems. Such work reveals general principles for remedial practices.

In addition to learning the traditional "3R's," students with disabilities also need effective teaching in content areas such as social studies and science. A strong body of evidence provides guidance for instruction in these areas, as well. Students can acquire strategies for studying, remembering content, remembering relationships among facts, and other similar activities that enhance their acquisition of relevant knowledge.

Research is also available to guide the provision of physical education and vocational education for students with high incidence disabilities. Physical educators have extensively studied methods for helping students with disabilities, many of whom have difficulties with coordination and related skills, to move in ways that promote healthy lifestyles. Similarly, vocational educators have developed evidence-based methods for teaching valuable work behaviors that increase the likelihood that students with disabilities can succeed in employment and contribute as adults to society.

In the contemporary world, educators and students with disabilities routinely use technology to enhance student's educational experiences. Although computers and other technical equipment cannot replace instruction in important core and related areas for students with disabilities, technology can be used to enhance instructional practices. Given the world into which today's students will transition, it is important for educators to employ well-grounded practices in helping students learn to use technology appropriately.

Across the research in academic and related areas, readers of this section will find recurring themes. Each of these chapters reflects a dogged insistence on evidence-based practices. Special educators have come a long way from the times when instructional methods for students with high incidence disabilities were predicated primarily if not exclusively on speculation and intuition. Also, common across these chapters is an emphasis on the importance of employing systematic, explicit instructional practices and on monitoring the effects of those practices. The overall implication from the chapters in this section is that special educators have clear guidance about *how* to teach students with high-incidence disabilities.

31
Reading

Paige C. Pullen
University of Virginia

Deanna B. Cash
Lynchburg College

The development of effective reading skills is one of the central difficulties of students with disabilities. Unfortunately, nearly 40% of the general school population experience difficulty in reading (NCES, 2005). Even more concerning is that reading difficulties affect as many as 80% of students with learning disabilities (Mercer, Mercer, & Pullen, 2011; Lyons & Moats, 1997). Given the impact of literacy on individuals and society and the prevalence of reading difficulties, it is no surprise that federal policymakers have recognized the importance of educating each child and have crafted legislation to help do so. In 2001, the U.S. Congress passed No Child Left Behind (NCLB), which included Reading First, legislation specifically targeting grades kindergarten through five with the explicit goal that every child should be able to read by the end of third grade (No Child Left Behind Act, 2001). In crafting NCLB, Congress followed the recommendations of the National Reading Panel's analysis of reading (National Reading Panel, 2000) and what constitutes evidence-based practice (Pressley & Fingeret, 2006); that is, investigations based only on experiments and quasi-experiments. Such research represents "the way one acquires dependable and useful information about the educative process" (Ary, Jacobs, & Razavieh, 1996, p. 22), and its purpose is to reach the point at which teaching and learning can be explained, predicted, and controlled (Gallagher, 1998), giving educators valuable information on what works, when, and with whom.

Much of what we know about reading development and interventions with the typically developing population has been summarized in "The Report of the National Reading Panel: Teaching Children to Read" (National Reading Panel, 2000). This seminal document was the result of over two years' work reviewing research-based knowledge on reading instruction, conducted at the request of Congress. This document summarizes what we know about reading development and interventions with typically developing students in terms of the five primary reading components: phonemic awareness, phonics, fluency, vocabulary, and comprehension. In understanding typical reading development, we can better meet the needs of students with disabilities who are experiencing difficulty in reading.

Understanding the Reading Process

Reading can be defined as a process of constructing meaning from print. Although this description sounds simple, reading is a very complex task that requires the coordination of many requisite skills and at least two processing events: identification of words and engagement of language processing mechanisms that give meaning to the words identified (Perfetti, Landi, & Oakhill, 2005), that is, "decoding" and "comprehension." Each is necessary, yet the two processes can develop independently (Nation, Clarke, Wright, & Williams, 2006). The first process, recognizing words, requires that the individual master several subskills including phonological awareness and an understanding of the alphabetic principle (i.e., the idea that written letters represent sounds, and these sounds are blended into words) as well as decoding, spelling, understanding print concepts and the development of vocabulary. Reading comprehension involves recognizing words, reading fluently, and accessing and utilizing background knowledge to understanding passages.

Word Identification Skills

The English language, as in other written alphabetic languages, involves a coding system of associations between letters and sounds. The process of using regularities in words to map letter-sound associations in order to determine probable pronunciations is known as "decoding" (Beck & Juel, 1999; Shankweiler et al., 1999). The benefits of the ability to decode successfully are not self-limiting, rather: "With decoding ability, the learner can profit from further experience with the printed word and eventually come to acquire the word-specific knowledge needed to read all words, not just those that are regularly spelled" (Shankweiler et al., 1999, p. 71). Presumably, as decoding skill increases, decoding will account for less and less of reading skill overall. As the variety and complexity of reading material increases, general linguistic comprehension will contribute more. Further, because determining the meaning of text depends on understanding individual words, poor comprehension can, at least to some degree, be attributed to deficiencies in word recognition, a factor that is frequently seen in poor readers in general (Adams, 1990; Stanovich, 1986; Vellutino et al., 1996). Yet, for experienced readers, the level of mastery in basic phonological skills accounts for unique variance in reading comprehension later in their school careers (Bruck, 1990, 1992; Shankweiler, Lundquist, Dreyer, & Dickinson, 1996): early decoders become better comprehenders.

Further, research shows that early exposure to decoding instruction is important in reading development because reading decoding success is predictive of later skill in reading comprehension (e.g., Clay, 1979; Lesgold & Resnick, 1982; Lundberg, 1984; Stanovich, 1986). In fact Shankweiler and colleagues (1999) found that "deficient skill in mapping between the alphabetic representations of words and their spoken counterparts is the chief barrier to comprehension of text" (p.70). Other symptoms of such a weakness include difficulty reading nonwords, difficulty spelling, and short-term memory issues. Further, decoding nonwords may be as important as decoding real words. Shankweiler and colleagues noted that skills in word identification are "almost inseparable from the decoding process that is tapped by the nonword reading measure" (p. 87). In fact, theorists in reading development have hypothesized that there is more than one way for readers to access the word decoding process: (a) in a verbal manner that involves phonological analysis that requires decoding each letter and assembling those letters in sound form from the letter form, and (b) visually mapping the orthographic form of the printed word and the memory of the lexical word (Coltheart, Curtis, Atkins, & Haller, 1993). Nonwords, however, can only be decoded using the first method, making them a clear measure of mastery of phonological decoding skills. Shankweiler et al. (1999) noted that there was a high correlation between decoding of words and nonwords in their sample, suggesting these students were not using divergent strategies but were attempting to use the phonologically analytical method.

Explicit instruction provides skills and concepts in a clear direct manner that promotes student mastery. Explicit phonics provides children with real relationships between letters and sounds or at least the approximations of them (Beck & Juel, 1999). Direct, explicit, systematic instruction makes it possible for students to make the associations they need in order to acquire letter-sound associations and to generalize them. In fact, many researchers have demonstrated that explicit instruction is effective in helping students at risk for learning problems acquire reading skills (e.g., Bradley & Bryant, 1985; Chall 1989; Englemann, 1988).

Ehri's Theory of the Development of Word Recognition Abilities

Linnea Ehri proposes a theory to explain how readers develop word recognition abilities. According to Ehri and Saltmarsh (1995), "readers read sight words by accessing connections that they have formed between letters in the spellings of specific words and phonemes detected in pronunciations" (p. 298). Readers who are able to use grapheme-phoneme connections are able to secure words in lexical memory (Ehri & Saltmarsh, 1995). During the development of the ability to apply grapheme-phoneme and orthographic knowledge, however, a reader progresses through a series of phases beginning with the logographic or visual cue phase (Ehri, 1987, 1991, 1992, 1997). Ehri's five phases are described in Table 31.1.

Patterns of Individual Difference in Reading Development

While most readers learn both to decode and comprehend text at least adequately, many students with disabilities experience difficulty in one of the two processes necessary for adequate reading development. Some students will have well-developed skills in decoding but poor comprehension skills. This pattern reminds us that reading is a complex task and that reading all the words in a passage may not lead to comprehension of intended meaning. Students who display this pattern may have a general weakness in language development (Stothard & Hulme, 1992). In contrast, some students may have relatively good skill in comprehending text while decoding words is more difficult. These students appear to have well-developed compensatory comprehension strategies to overcome their deficient word recognition skills (Shankweiler et al., 1999), although this premise is not well supported in research. Shankweiler and colleagues (1999) found that those students who were stronger in comprehension scored high relative only to students in their sample who had poor decoding skills, not compared to unimpaired readers. Their results found that reading comprehension was highly correlated with both word and nonword reading, indicating that skill in decoding is crucial in distinguishing readers' abilities in reading comprehension.

The most common pattern of reading difficulty involves students who are identified with problems in reading comprehension and have associated difficulty with word recognition. Several factors have emerged from research as central contributors to this pattern. These core deficits, described in the following sections, include phonological processing, naming speed, and orthographic processing (Mercer & Pullen, 2009).

Phonological Deficit

Research in reading disabilities reveals that the most common source of reading difficulty is a core deficit in phonological processing (e.g., Bonte, Poelmans, & Blomert, 2007; Bowey & Rutherford, 2007; Plaza & Cohen, 2007; Sawyer, 2006; Svensson & Jacobson, 2006). A deficit in phonological awareness impedes the acquisition of word recognition skills (Brady, 1997; Wolf, 1997), which is the primary difficulty experienced by students with reading disability. To acquire decoding ability, sensitivity to the sound structure of words is necessary (Foorman, Francis, Shaywitz, Shaywitz, Fletcher, 1997), as is the awareness that individual phonemes (sounds) in words are represented by letters and that those sounds can be analyzed and synthesized in the decoding process (Tan & Nicholson, 1997).

Naming-speed Deficit

Phonological deficits alone cannot fully explain reading disabilities, particularly beyond beginning reading (Scarborough, 2005). Research from the field of cognitive psychology has indicated that individuals with reading disabilities have a core deficit in naming speed (Plaza & Cohen, 2007; Sawyer, 2006; Wolf, 1999; Wolf, Bowers, & Biddle, 2000). A naming-speed deficit refers to the inability to retrieve rapidly the spoken referent for visual stimuli (Badian, 1997). Naming-speed deficits have been considered by some to be part of a phonological deficit (see e.g., Vukovic & Siegel, 2006; Wagner & Barker, 1994; Wagner & Torgesen, 1987). Wolf (1999) argues that naming speed deficits affect reading acquisition independent from phonological processing. Data from languages with more regular orthographies (e.g., German) (Landerl & Thaler, 2006; Wimmer & Mayringer, 2002) and a lack of correlation between naming-speed and phonological processes further support an independent deficit hypothesis. Some researchers (e.g., Fawcett & Nicholson, 1995; Nicholson & Fawcett, 1994) argue that both naming speed deficits and phonological deficits are part of a global deficit in automatization. Though evidence suggests that naming speed may be related to reading disability, the support is inconclusive to date and more research is needed to confirm this relationship.

The effect of naming-speed deficits may be related to deficits in orthographic processing. If the letters in a word are identified slowly, readers with naming-speed deficits may have difficulty establishing representations of letter sequences in memory (Ehri & Saltmarsh, 1995; Wimmer & Mayringer, 2002). An inability to retrieve rapidly and/or represent letter knowledge would, thus, limit the quality of the orthographic codes in memory (Berninger, Yates, & Lester, 1991).

Orthographic Deficit

Orthographic processing may be defined as "the ability to form, store, and access orthographic representations" (Stanovich & West, 1989, p. 4), with *orthographic* referring to the sequence of letters in words. The concept of an orthographic processing deficit in reading disability has received less attention than phonological awareness or rapid automatic naming. It is clear that orthographic processing involves several varieties of orthographic knowledge and that each form of orthographic knowledge contributes to reading acquisition. Orthographic processing may indeed represent a third core deficit of individuals with reading disability. Orthographic processors must connect with phonological and meaning processors and all three must work together for an individual to decode and gain meaning from print (Adams & Bruck, 1993). Furthermore, in order to secure words in lexical memory, a systematic relationship between orthography and phonology must be established (Ehri & Soffer, 1999). Clearly, orthographic information is crucial to the reading process.

Assessment of Reading Skills

Reading assessments in the classroom, particularly those for students beyond the primary grades, typically focus on reading comprehension and often neglect the other important subskills (Biancarosa & Snow, 2006; Durkin, 1978). For example, a common task is that a student reads a set of passages and answers comprehension questions; based on the student's performance school personnel make a decision as to the student's reading skill (i.e., good or poor reader). While the determination may be accurate, it does not provide the information required to intervene effectively. Therefore, to obtain a complete understanding of a student's reading difficulty and guide the implementation of targeted interventions, all of the dimensions of skill and knowledge that contribute to reading comprehension must be assessed (Hudson, Pullen, Lane, & Torgesen, 2009).

Assessment of the various subskills of the reading process allows teachers to identify a student's pattern of reading difficulty and implement the appropriate reading intervention. Thus, reading assessment will necessarily focus on both word identification processes and language comprehension processes. The subskills of the reading process may be viewed as a linked chain. If any of the links are broken, interference occurs in the reading process and reading difficulty arises. Table 31.1 illustrates the reading process as a chain that will guide both assessment and instruction. When all of the links are intact, the reading process works smoothly, resulting in comprehension of the written material.

Assessing Phonemic Awareness

Phonemic awareness (PA) includes the ability to detect, match, blend, segment, or otherwise manipulate the individual sounds or phonemes in spoken language (Lane & Pullen, 2004). PA has a direct and causal relationship to later reading ability. In order to decode words in print, a student must analyze and synthesize the individual sounds in the word. Thus, PA is a necessary yet insufficient skill required to master phonemic decoding. The two most

TABLE 31.1
Ehri's Phases of Word Recognition Ability

Stage	Characteristics
Pre-Alphabetic Phase	Child focuses on visual rather than phonological cues, and uses semantic rather than phonological relationships
	Arbitrary rather than systematic grapheme/phoneme connections
	This phase is also referred to as visual cue reading
Partial Alphabetic Phase	Child has an emerging use of grapheme-phoneme connections
	The connections are incomplete (perhaps first letter/sound only)
	This stage is more reliable than visual cue reading
	Child still has no way to read novel words in print
Full Alphabetic Phase	Child accesses words through phonemic decoding
	Graphemes are converted into phonological representations
	Dramatically more reliable than phonetic cue reading
Consolidated Alphabetic Phase	Multi-letter patterns are consolidated in memory
	Readers recognize chunks in decoding rather than individual phonemes only
Automatic Phase	Highly developed decoding strategies
	Accurate, automatic decoding of unfamiliar words, including multisyllable words
	Child uses multiple strategies in decoding (decoding, structural, contextual)

important PA skills are blending (e.g., *What word do these sounds make: /f/ /r/ /o/ /g/? Yes, frog!)* and segmenting (*Say the word 'boat' sound-by-sound. Yes, /b/ /oa/ /t/)*. These skills, along with deletion tasks, should be the primary focus of PA assessment. In a deletion task (elision), the student removes a sound in a word to make a new word (e.g., *Say 'hear' without saying /h/. Yes, ear)*. Elision tasks are not necessary in decoding; however, they are a good measure of PA.

The Dynamic Indicators of Basic Early Literacy Skills (DIBELS) is a set of standardized reading measures for students in Kindergarten through Grade 6. DIBELS has two subtests that assess phonemic awareness, including Phonemic Segmentation Fluency (PSF) and Initial Sound Fluency (ISF) (Good & Kaminski, 2002). The PSF task requires that the student segment three and four phoneme words. The ISF task requires that the student provide the initial sound of a word that is presented orally. Both the PSF and ISF are standardized and have sound psychometric properties. In addition to DIBELS, several informal measures are available to assess PA. The Yopp-Singer Phonemic Segmentation Task is an untimed assessment that measures student's ability to segment words into phonemes. An informal measure of blending and segmenting phonemes is also available in *Phonological Awareness: A Sound Beginning* (Lane & Pullen, 2004).

Assessing Letter Knowledge

Letter knowledge is a robust predictor of reading achievement (Catts, Fey, Zhang, & Tomblin, 1999; Pullen & Justice, 2003; Scanlon & Vellutino, 1996; Whitehurst & Lonigan, 1998) and an important component of a comprehensive reading assessment. Letter knowledge assessments should include letter recognition tasks as well as the extent to which an individual knows the corresponding sound for a grapheme. DIBELS provides a standardized subtest that measures a student's ability to quickly and accurately name upper and lowercase letters. DIBELS Letter Naming Fluency is administered individually and is scored based on the number of letters a student names correctly in one minute. DIBELS provides benchmarks to help teachers determine a student's relative level of risk. The Phonological Awareness Literacy Screening (PALS) is a comprehensive screening measure for young children. It includes measures of important early literacy skills that predict later reading achievement. The PALS assessments of letter knowledge measures a student's ability to both name the letters and their corresponding sounds.

Assessing Word Identification Skills

Skilled reading requires the quick and accurate decoding of novel words in print as well as the automatic retrieval of known words (Ehri, 2005; Torgesen et al., 2001). Thus, diagnosing reading difficulties in word identification should focus on both sight word reading (real words) and decoding (nonsense words) tasks.

Sight words. Students with reading difficulties often lack fluent sight word reading ability (Jenkins, Fuchs, van den Broek, Espin, & Deno, 2003), which in turn affects reading fluency and comprehension. Sight word measures examine the student's skill in recognizing high frequency words in isolation. The Letter-Word Identification (LW-ID) subtest of the Woodcock Johnson III Test of Achievement (WJIII; Woodcock, McGrew, & Mather, 2001) provides a standardized measure of sight word knowledge. In this assessment, students are asked to identify individual letters and words that are progressively more difficult. Given the importance of automatic word retrieval, a sight word measure that also considers automaticity is necessary in a comprehensive assessment. The Test of Word Reading Efficiency (TOWRE; Torgesen, Wagner, & Rashotte, 1999),

Sight Word Efficiency subtest is an easy-to-administer assessment of word reading fluency. This subtest assesses how many real printed words a student can read aloud in 45 seconds.

Phonemic decoding. Phonemic decoding refers to the task of breaking a written word into its constituent phonemes and blending those sounds together to produce the phonological representation of the written word. This task is the primary goal of mastering the alphabetic principle. Assessing the reading of nonwords is the most effective method for determining a student's skill in phonemic decoding. When a student reads a nonsense word, he must rely on sound-symbol relationships and his knowledge of the alphabetic principle rather than on memorization.

Two resources for measuring nonword reading include the Test of Word Reading Efficiency (TOWRE: Torgesen et al., 1999) and DIBELS nonsense word fluency (NWF) subtest (Good & Kaminski, 2002). DIBELS NWF is a standardized, individually administered subtest that contains Vowel-Consonant (VC) and Consonant-Vowel-Consonant (CVC) combinations (e.g., ip, rop). Although the DIBELS NWF has sound reliability and validity, it is not without problems. One concern with the DIBELS NWF is that students receive a correct score if they produce the sounds of the nonsense word in isolation or if they blend the sounds together. Nonetheless, it has strong predictive validity (see Good et al., 2004) and is a valuable assessment tool.

The TOWRE (Torgesen et al., 1999) provides another measure of phonemic decoding with its Phonemic Decoding Efficiency subtest. This subtest measures the number of nonsense words a student can pronounce correctly in 45 seconds. This test differs from the DIBELS NWF in two significant ways: (a) it extends beyond VC and CVC combinations to include complex letter patterns (e.g., clirt, drepnort, plenador) making it appropriate for older readers; and (b) in order to get a correct response, the student must produce a fully-blended response to be correct.

Assessing Fluency

A comprehensive fluency assessment measures a student's reading rate, reading accuracy, and prosody (i.e., making your reading sound like spoken language). Although measures of rate and accuracy are readily available, few reliable measures of prosody exist. Curriculum-based measures (CBM) of oral reading fluency are the most common method for examining a student's rate and accuracy in reading connected text. Reading CBMs (R-CBM) use graded reading passages to measure oral reading rate and accuracy under timed conditions, recording the number of words read correctly and incorrectly, and student performance is summarized in terms of correct words per minute (CWPM). Substantial evidence suggests that this method of assessing oral reading fluency is both valid and reliable (e.g., Deno, Marston, Shinn, & Tindal, 1992; Deno, Mirkin, & Chiang, 1982; Fuchs et al., 2001; Good, Simmons, & Kame'enui, 2001; Hosp & Fuchs, 2005; Samuels, 1988; Shinn et al., 1992; Stecker, Fuchs, & Fuchs, 2005). Despite the lack of valid and reliable measures of prosody, many researchers maintain that to obtain a comprehensive analysis of oral reading fluency, prosody should be considered (e.g., Daane, Campbell, Grigg, Goodman, & Oranje, 2005; Rasinski, 2004; Zutell & Rasinski, 1991). Several rating scales and rubrics are available to measure reading prosody (see e.g., Hudson, Lane, & Pullen, 2005; Honig, Diamond, & Gutlohn, 2008). The student reads a passage at his or her independent reading level and the teacher scores the oral reading for prosodic features such as appropriate pausing, phrasing, expression, and intonation.

Assessing Vocabulary

Perhaps one of the most challenging areas of reading assessment is vocabulary. Standardized measures of general receptive and expressive vocabulary are available, yet few informal assessments or curriculum-based measurements of vocabulary exist, making the ongoing progress-monitoring of vocabulary difficult. One of the most common standardized assessments used in the diagnosis of reading problems is the Peabody Picture Vocabulary Test-4 (PPVT-4; Dunn & Dunn, 2007). The PPVT-4 is a standardized, norm-referenced measure of receptive vocabulary. The examiner says a word and presents the student with four colored picture response items and the student points to the appropriate item. The PPVT may be used in the diagnosis of reading difficulties to measure students' language skills as well as to determine the effectiveness of instruction.

Assessing Reading Comprehension

Given the complexity of the task and multitude of contributing factors, accurate assessment of reading comprehension is difficult. Yet, accurate assessment of comprehension skills is necessary to determine whether or not the goal of reading is met, to plan future instruction, and to identify students who need additional instruction or remediation. Few commercial assessments of reading comprehension exist, and many of those in use "do not provide enough evidence of trustworthiness to warrant use" (Kameenui et al., 2006). Further, comprehension of text is only a minor component in most of these assessments and different tests of comprehension may draw on varying component skills of comprehension (i.e., decoding, fluency, vocabulary).

For beginning readers, reading comprehension is usually assessed with informal diagnostic assessments to identify students who need additional instruction and remediation and to facilitate instructional planning. Informal evaluations for grades K through 3 may involve methods such as oral retelling, answering questions, reading and following directions, and/or cloze procedure. For students above Grade 3, standardized tests of reading comprehension are more common. Typically, such measures require a student to read short passages and answer questions about either explicit (recall of factual detail) or implicit (inferential) information from the text. However, few valid, reliable standardized measures of reading comprehension exist; and informal measures, such as informal reading inventories, remain popular (Rasinski & Hoffman, 2003).

Informal Reading Inventory. Informal reading inventories include graded passages of increasing difficulty that the student reads aloud as the teacher records errors. Passages consist of 50 words (at preprimer level) to 200 words (at secondary level) and may either be narrative or expository. Students begin with passages at a level at which word-attack and comprehension tasks are managed easily and continue until the passages are too difficult for the student to read. In addition, the teacher asks questions to assess comprehension. Questions may include both explicit recall of facts (who, what, or where), implicit inference (why), and/or vocabulary (general or specific meanings).

Although teachers in both general and special education use IRIs, these assessments should be used with caution for high-stakes decisions, as they have limited reliability. Miscue analysis, a method in which the teacher subjectively decides whether an error is semantically acceptable (Goodman 1969, 1973) is often part of IRI evaluations. Yet, this analysis does not have empirical support and should not be a part of reading assessment (McKenna & Picard, 2006).

Comprehensive Diagnostic Assessment

In addition to the individual assessments described in the previous sections, the Woodcock Johnson III Diagnostic Reading Battery (WJIII DRB; Schrank, Mather, & Woodcock, 2004) may be administered as a comprehensive assessment of reading skill. The WJIII DRB is administered individually and measures phonological awareness, phonics knowledge, reading achievement, and oral language skills. It consists of 10 subtests that allow for cluster and discrepancy analyses. This assessment may be administered alone or in combination with other formal and informal measures to identify reading difficulties and design effective intervention.

Teaching Reading Skills

Following a comprehensive reading assessment, an intervention plan may be developed. The reading chain described earlier (see Table 31.1) illustrates the various components of reading instruction. When one link in the chain is broken, the subsequent reading skills cannot develop adequately. Reading intervention should target the skills where the first link broken. For example, if Phonemic Awareness, Letter Knowledge, and Sight Word assessments demonstrate mastery, yet decoding skills are not adequate, reading fluency and comprehension are also going to be deficient. Intervention should necessarily target decoding. Without a comprehensive assessment, it could be assumed that the student's difficulty was fluency or comprehension, particularly given that the sight word knowledge was satisfactory, and the wrong intervention would be implemented. The comprehensive assessment ensures the correct focus of the intervention. The following sections describe each of the reading components in more detail and provide suggestions for intervention.

Phonological Awareness

PA is a foundational for all other reading skills and is predictive of reading achievement. In its comprehensive analysis of the research on phonemic awareness, the NRP found that teaching PA does improve the PA skills of a variety of types of learners, and that this instruction provides positive and lasting effects on reading skills. Research reviewed for the NRP report showed that phonemic awareness improves reading comprehension, primarily through quick and accurate word reading (e.g., Ball & Blachman, 1991; Ehri, 1991; Fawcett & Nicholson, 1995). Moreover, students who have phonemic awareness may be better able to understand the predictable relationship of sounds and letters, and are able to relate the sounds and letters as they spell words (Armbruster, Lehr, & Osborne, 2001). Phonemic awareness instruction was shown to improve spelling skills of typically developing children (e.g., Davidson & Jenkins, 1994; Defior & Tudela, 1994), and is most effective when explicit, systematic instruction is used to teach children to manipulate phonemes (sounds) and their corresponding letters (graphemes) (e.g., Farmer, Nixon, & White, 1976; Hohn & Ehri, 1983; Murray, 1998), using identification, categorization, blending to form words, segmenting words into phonemes, adding or deleting phonemes to make new words, and substituting phonemes to make new words (Armbruster et al., 2001). These methods help students understand the predictable relationships between sounds in words and between phonemes and graphemes.

There are many ways to teach PA effectively. The NRP (2000) provides several guidelines, including that (a) instruction should focus on one or two types of manipulation of phonemes rather than multiple types of manipulations, (b) only a few minutes per school day is necessary for PA instruction (i.e., more does not mean better; about 20 hours across the school year is sufficient), and (c) instruction in small groups is better than individual or large group instruction. PA instruction is also more effective when it is combined with letter instruction (i.e., phonics). Clearly, PA should be a part of comprehensive beginning or remedial reading program.

Print Awareness

Like the development of PA, understanding the forms and functions of written language is a critical aspect of early literacy development that affects reading development (Pullen & Justice, 2003). In particular, print concepts and letter knowledge are two aspects of print awareness that influence reading attainment. A child with well-developed print concepts understands specific features of written language, such as (a) the print conveys the meaning of the story, (b) text on a page is read from left to right, top to bottom (c) when one page of text is read, the story continues on the following page, and (d) the white spaces between groups of letters represent a break between spoken words or word boundaries (Clay, 1993; Justice & Ezell, 2000; Pullen & Justice, 2003). Research indicates that young children's knowledge of print concepts predicts later reading attainment (Badian, 1993; Scarborough, 2005).

Letter knowledge is the aspect of print awareness that is most closely linked to reading attainment. In multiple research studies, letter-naming was a reliable and robust predictor of later reading achievement (e.g., Catts, Fey, Zhang, & Tomblin, 1999; Scanlon & Vellutino, 1996). This may be due in part to a naming-speed deficit, an inability to retrieve rapidly the spoken referent for visual stimuli (Badian, 1997), rather than solely an unfamiliarity with the letters of the alphabet. Students who are unable to name the letters rapidly and automatically may have a more generalized phonological processing disorder, which would likely result in later reading difficulties. Nonetheless, it is likely much more than naming letters that supports reading acquisition; an overall familiarity with the letters and their sounds is critical to the development of the alphabetic principle and in turn, reading development.

Young children typically develop print awareness through experiences sharing books with adults. Various methods of shared storybook reading have been implemented with young children and resulted in positive gains in emergent literacy skills including print awareness. For example, incorporating verbal and nonverbal print referencing strategies into storybook reading has shown promise in promoting phonological and print related gains (Ezell & Justice, 2000; Justice & Ezell, 2000; Justice & Pullen, 2004; Justice, Skibbe, Canning, & Lankford, 2005). As children attend to print on the page, they have an opportunity to repeatedly follow along with text as it is being read, which facilitates the acquisition of the relationship between speech and print and subsequent word learning (Weaver, 1994). Shared storybook reading also promotes oral language skills, including phonological awareness and vocabulary development. More information about this technique is provided in the vocabulary section to follow.

Phonics

The ability to decode in first and second grade is highly predictive of comprehension skills in later grades (Juel, 1988), and the inability to decode unknown words in print is a strong indicator of reading failure (Torgesen, Wagner, & Rashotte, 1999). Phonics instruction involves teaching students to make connections between sounds in words and their corresponding written alphabetic symbols. Students learn to use the predictable relationships between sounds and letters to read and write words, a concept known as the alphabetic principle. Children's acquisition of these skills improves their ability to read words in isolation and in context (Armbruster et al., 2001). Consensus documents on reading research support the implementation of interventions for reading decoding that focus on phonemic awareness and understanding of the alphabetic principle as component skills of phonics instruction (e.g., Adams, 1990; NRP, 2000; Snow, Burns, & Griffin, 1998).

Further, decoding interventions should explicitly and systematically teach phoneme-grapheme associations (Byrne, Fielding-Barnsley, Ashley, & Larsen, 1997; Carnine, Silbert, Kameenui, & Tarver, 2004; Haskell, Foorman, & Swank, 1992; NRP, 2000; Snow et al, 1998; Uhry & Shepherd, 1997). Explicit instruction in the alphabetic principle and decoding ensures that almost all students are successful in making the connection between phonemes and graphemes (Beck & Juel, 1992; Moats, 1998).

Results of the NRP meta-analysis (2000) found that systematic phonics instruction produces significant benefits for students in elementary grades or older students having difficulty learning to read. Systematic phonics involves direct instruction of phoneme-grapheme relationships in a set sequence and provides practice in applying these skills. Further, the NRP analysis demonstrated that systematic phonics instruction was shown to improve the spelling ability of good readers; however, only a small effect was shown for poor readers' spelling skills. Systematic phonics instruction also resulted in better comprehension ability than did either non-systematic phonics or no phonics instruction. For students beyond the primary grades, phonics instruction improves word identification skills but does not extend to comprehension. Thus a comprehensive program that provides instruction in fluency and comprehension is necessary.

Like PA, phonics instruction should be part of a comprehensive reading approach, but is not sufficient alone. Various techniques are recommended for explicit and systematic instruction, including blending and segmenting phonemes (i.e., phonemic decoding). Teachers can facilitate phonemic decoding in a number of ways, including the use of manipulative letters to improve students' decoding accuracy (Pullen, Lane, Lloyd, Nowak, & Ryals, 2005). Although conventional wisdom has suggested phonics instruction may not be appropriate for kindergarten students, the panel's conclusion was that the positive effect on the reading skills of students in kindergarten and first grade was "significant and substantial" (NRP, 2000, p.10). Approximately two years of phonics instruction is all that is needed for most students and it can be effectively taught in whole-class, small group, or large group instruction (Armbruster et al., 2001), but the NRP suggested that the duration and intensity of phonics instruction, including individual sessions were topics for future research.

After phonemic decoding has been mastered, teaching phonograms should follow. Phonograms are groups of letter within words that share a pattern across words (Hudson et al., 2009). Recognizing these patterns automatically is a critical skill in decoding words fluently: When words are identified by sight they do not need to be analytically decoded. If too many words in a passage must be identified analytically, reading fluency and comprehension may be compromised. With knowledge of patterns across words, students will be able to move to more complex and advanced decoding skills (Ehri, 2002). Further, the English language is more regular at the level of rimes plus syllable endings (rimes) than at the level of a single word. Automaticity in recognizing phonograms accurately makes sound-symbol relationships more predictable, leading to more efficient decoding of words (Hudson et al., 2009).

Fluency

There is a close relationship between fluency and comprehension, and in their study, Pinnell and colleagues (1995) found that as many as 44% of a representative sample of fourth graders in the United States may be low in fluency. Fluent readers are able to maintain fluency reading performance over periods of time, generalize the skill to other texts, and retain the skill over time without practice (Hudson et al., 2005). Reading fluently is a defining characteristic of skilled readers, while poor fluency is a common characteristic of less skilled readers. Further, skilled readers may achieve fluency incidentally, while less skilled readers may need direct instruction in how to read fluently, along with ample opportunities for fluency-focused practice as part of their reading programs (Allinder, Dunse, Brunken, & Obermiller-Krolikowski, 2001). Direct fluency instruction is not a priority in most classrooms, but is important for students who are not automatic at recognizing words in their texts (Allington, 1983).

Fluency is comprised of accurate reading of words in connected text with prosody, or expression, and at the rate of conversational speech (Hudson, Mercer, & Lane, 2000). Methods to strengthen each of the three components of fluency have been developed and, given the strong correlation between fluency and reading comprehension (Allington, 1983; Samuels; 1988), should be part of comprehensive reading instruction for all children and for struggling readers in particular (Hudson et al., 2005). The ability to identify words quickly and effortlessly is important in reading fluently, as doing so frees important cognitive resources for comprehension (Laberge & Samuels, 1974). In fact, the difference between skilled and poor readers is often their skill in automatic decoding of words (Perfetti & Hogaboam, 1975; Torgesen, 1986).

Research by the NRP (2000) explored two types of fluency instruction: guided oral reading and independent silent reading. In guided oral reading, the student reads passages aloud several times and receives feedback and guidance from the teacher. Key findings from the NRP found that guided repeated oral reading with feedback improves word identification, rate, and prosody for students with and without disabilities. Guided oral reading takes a variety of forms including re-reading familiar, reasonably easy text, providing models of fluent reading, and including audiotapes, tutors, and/or peer guidance (e.g., Blum et al., 1995; Faulkner & Levy, 1999; Rasinski, 1990; Reitsma, 1988). The oral reading technique traditionally used by classroom teachers, round-robin reading does not in itself increase fluency, probably because each student reads only a small passage (Armbruster et al., 2001; Opitz & Rasinski, 1998). Recognition of words in isolation is necessary, but not sufficient, to develop fluency in passages. Systematic instruction of oral reading fluency, using guided, repeated oral reading with feedback, is necessary to develop text reading fluency.

Debate exists on the effect of independent silent reading on fluency and comprehension. Research has not proven whether or not it improves fluency and comprehension (e.g., Burley, 1980; Davis, 1988; Summers & McClelland, 1982). However, "the research suggests that there are more beneficial ways to spend reading instructional time than to have students read independently in the classroom without reading instruction" (Armbruster et al., 2001, p. 22). Independent silent reading may, however, contribute to the student's indirect vocabulary development (e.g., Nicholson & Whyte, 1992: Stahl, Richel, & Vandevier, 1991).

An important aspect of fluency is prosody. Prosody is the rhythm and tonal aspects of speech that contribute to expressive reading (Hudson et al., 2005). Higher levels of prosody have been associated with better reading proficiency (Pinnell et al., 1995), but the exact relationship is unclear. Several instructional methods have, however, been designed with the specific goal to improve prosody. These methods stress the way in which a student reads sounds, including inflection, expression, and phrasing (Hudson et al., 2005). Examples of such strategies include; reading with recorded text, and theatrical reading (e.g., Readers Theater and Radio Reading). Further, there are a number of strategies that make use of fluent models to improve prosody. Some examples include, reading in unison with the teacher, cloze reading (in which the teacher reads text and pauses occasionally for the student to insert a word or phrase), and echo reading. In addition, direct intervention with the student to cue phrase boundaries can contribute substantially to meaning (Rasinski, 2003). Using recorded excerpts from the student to assist in cueing and direct teaching of inflection, expression, and phrasing may be useful (Hudson et al., 2005). Finally, Blevins (2001) suggested several activities to directly teach intonation, including reading the alphabet as a conversation and repeating sentences with different punctuation.

Vocabulary

In its meta-analysis of reading interventions, the NRP recognized that "reading comprehension is a complex cognitive process that cannot be understood without a clear description of the role that vocabulary development and vocabulary instruction play in the understanding of what has been read" (National Reading Panel, 2000, p. 13). Students cannot understand what they read if they do not know the meaning of most of the words they encounter. Research indicates that vocabulary instruction leads to growth in comprehension (e.g., Beck, Perfetti, & McKeown, 1982; National Reading Panel, 2000; Stahl & Fairbanks, 1986).

Repetition (e.g., Senechal, 1997), multiple exposures, and learning in vocabulary-rich contexts (e.g., Mckeown, Beck, Omanson, & Pople, 1985) are important strategies for learning vocabulary. Use of computer technology (e.g., Heise, Papalewis, & Tanner, 1991; Medo & Ryder, 1993; Reinking & Rickman, 1990) to teach and practice vocabulary skills may enhance vocabulary acquisition. Regardless of the strategies used, methods must be appropriate to the student's development level and ability (National Reading Panel, 2000).

Students acquire most of their vocabulary indirectly, but some vocabulary must be taught directly (Armbruster et al., 2001). Incidental acquisition of vocabulary occurs when students engage in oral conversation, listen to adults reading to them, and read on their own (e.g., Nicholson & Whyte, 1992; Stahl et al., 1991). Direct instruction is particularly useful for important words, useful words, and difficult words, particularly those with multiple meanings (e.g., Tomeson & Aarnoutse, 1998). Teaching words before reading (e.g., Brett, Rothlein, & Hurley, 1996; Wixson, 1986) teaching word-learning strageies (e.g., Dana & Rodriguez, 1992), as well as task restructuring (e.g., Gordon, Schumm, Coffland, & Doucette, 1992; Kameenui, Carnine, & Freschi, 1982), and use of context clues (e.g., Kolich, 1991; Stahl, 1983), can build vocabulary and enhance reading comprehension.

Shared storybook reading. Another method that has been shown to improve students' acquisition of vocabulary is shared storybook reading. Shared storybook reading involves making the student an active participant in the story reading event, rather than a passive participant. This method is based on the work of Whitehurst et al. (1988) and has been studied extensively in recent years. Studies to explore the effects of specific reading techniques and strategies have shown that explicit vocabulary instruction through repeated shared storybook reading (Coyne, Simmons, Kame'enui, & Stoolmiller, 2004; Justice et al., 2005) is effective in teaching vocabulary. Further, shared storybook reading may contribute to building and extending comprehension as well as practice with decoding and increasing enjoyment of reading (Yaden, 1989). Additional benefits include opportunities for the teacher to model reading for students and to expand on concepts and language skills through the interactive process.

Shared storybook reading provides exposure to vocabulary in the context of oral language experience, even before children are able to read for themselves (Biemiller, 2003). Further, shared storybook reading provides opportunities for interactive discussion of words in a de-contextualized setting (Snow, 1991), and research has shown that children can learn the meanings of new words implicitly during such activities (Robbins & Ehri, 1994; Senechal & Cornell, 1993). In fact, reading a book several times is, in itself, a proven method for improving retention and vocabulary skills (Biemiller & Boote, 2006; Senechal, 1997). Several factors appear to increase the likelihood that children will learn from shared storybook reading, including having discussions with rich dialogue (Senechal, 1997) and engaging in performance related activities involving the books (Robbins & Ehri, 1994). The choice of engaging stories (Coyne et al., 2004) and reading them in small group settings (Whitehurst et. al., 1994) contributes to success in vocabulary development with shared storybook reading. For students who have reading difficulties, additional strategies, such as use of explicit instruction (Beck & McKoewn, 2007; Coyne, McCoach, & Kapp, 2007), may improve vocabulary skills. Yet, while intervention research for vocabulary skills has provided useful information, research has not yet addressed the amount and quality of vocabulary instruction necessary to close the gap between good readers and those who have difficulty reading.

Comprehension

Few would argue that reading comprehension is the ultimate goal of reading instruction. Likewise, consensus exists that reading is a complex task that requires the integration of various subskills. Building the foundation for comprehension instruction may begin in the primary grades (Armbruster et al., 2001), and text comprehension can be improved by teaching students to use conscious planning strategies for interaction with and understanding of text (NRP, 2000; Pressley & Fingeret, 1989). Some of these strategies include: comprehension monitoring (e.g., Capelli & Markman, 1982; Mier, 1984), use of graphic or semantic organizers (e.g., Alvermann & Boothby, 1986), questioning strategies (e.g., Rosenshine, & Meister, 1994), understanding story structure (e.g., Gordon & Rennie, 1987; Idol, 1987), summarizing (Rinehart, Stahl, & Erickson, 1986), activation of prior learning (Au, 1980; Hansen & Pearson, 1983), and use of mental imagery (Borduin, Borduin, & Manley, 1994; Levin & Divine-Hawkins, 1974). NRP data showed that comprehension strategies can be taught through explicit instruction, involving direct explanation, modeling, guided practice, and/or application. Further, comprehension strategies may be taught in a cooperative learning situation (Klingner, Vaughn, & Schumm, 1998; Stevens, Slavin, & Farnish, 1991), and teachers may model the flexible use of strategies for their students to enhance comprehension.

Summary

The attainment of reading skills is critical to success in school and in life. However, reading is a complex task that requires the integration of numerous skills, and many students with disabilities face challenges in reading development. Although many students with disabilities struggle to acquire these skills, research has provided educators with sound instructional practices to ensure most students learn to read. Implementing evidence-based instruction in reading with ongoing assessment of progress will help to alleviate reading deficits and lead to the development of skilled readers.

References

Adams, M. J. (1990). *Beginning to read: Thinking and learning about print.* Cambridge, MA: MIT Press.

Adams, M. J., & Bruck, M. (1993). Word recognition: The interface of educational policies and scientific research. *Reading and Writing, 5,* 113–139.

Allinder, R. M., Dunse, L., Brunken, C. D., & Obermiller- Krolikowski, H. J. (2001). Improving fluency in at-risk readers and students with learning disabilities. *Remedial and Special Education, 22*(1), 48–54.

Allington, R. L. (1983). Fluency: The neglected reading goal in reading instruction. *The Reading Teacher, 36,* 556–561.

Alvermann, D. E., & Boothby, P. R. (1986). Children's transfer of graphic organizer instruction. *Reading Psychology, 7*(2), 87–100.

Armbruster, B. B., Lehr, F., & Osborne, J. (2001). *Put reading first: The research building blocks for teaching children to read.* Washington, DC: National Institute for Literacy. Retrieved January 12, 2010, from http://www.nationalreadingpanel.org/Publications/researchread.htm

Ary, D., Jacobs, L., & Razavieh, A. (1996). *Introduction to research in education.* Fort Worth, TX: Harcourt Brace College.

Au, K. (1980). Participation structures in a reading lesson with Hawaiian children. *Anthropology and Education Quarterly, 11,* 91–115.

Badian, N. A. (1993). Phonemic awareness, naming, visual symbol processing, and reading. *Reading and Writing, 5*(1), 87–100

Badian, N. A. (1997). Dyslexia and the double deficit hypothesis, *Annals of Dyslexia, 47,* 69–87.

Ball, E., & Blachman, B. (1991). Does phoneme awareness training in kindergarten make a difference in early word recognition and developmental spelling? *Reading Research Quarterly, 26,* 49–66.

Beck, I. L., & Juel, C. (1992). The role of decoding in learning to read. In S. J. Samuels & A. E. Farstrup (Eds.), *What research has to say about reading instruction* (2nd ed., pp. 101–123). Newark, DE: International Reading Association.

Beck, I. L., & Juel, C. (1999). The role of decoding in learning to read, *American Educator, 19*(2), 8, 21–25, 39–42.

Beck, I. L., & McKeown, M.G. (2007). Increasing young children's oral vocabulary repertoires through rich and focused instruction. *Elementary School Journal, 107,* 251–271.

Beck, I. L., Perfetti, C. A., & McKeown, M. G. (1982). Effects of long term vocabulary instruction on lexical access and reading comprehension. *Journal of Educational Psychology, 74,* 506–521.

Berninger, V. W., Yates, C., & Lester, K. (1991). Multiple orthographic codes in reading and writing acquisition. *Reading and Writing, 3*(2), 115–149.

Biancarosa, C., & Snow, C. E. (2006). *Reading next—A vision for action and research in middle and high school literacy: A report to Carnegie Corporation of New York* (2nd ed.). Washington, DC: Alliance for Excellent Education.

Biemiller, A. (2003). Vocabulary: Needed if more children are to read well. *Reading Pyschology, 24,* 323–335.

Biemiller, A., & Boote, C. (2006). An effective method for building meaning vocabulary in the primary grades. *Journal of Educational Psychology, 98,* 44–62.

Blevins, W. (2001). *Building fluency: Lessons and strategies for reading success.* Scranton, PA: Scholastic.

Blum, I. H., Koskinen, P. S., Tennant, N., Parker, E. M., Straub, M., & Curry, C. (1995). Using audiotaped books to extend classroom literacy instruction into the homes of second-language learners. *Journal of Reading Behavior, 27,* 535–563.

Bonte, M.L., Poelmans, H., & Blomert, L. (2007). Deviant neurophysiological responses to phonological regularities in speech in dyslexic children, *Neuropsychologia, 45,* 1427–1437.

Borduin, B. J., Borduin, C. M., & Manley, C. M. (1994). The use of imagery training to improve reading comprehension of second graders. *Journal of Genetic Psychology, 155*(1), 115–118.

Bowey, J. A., & Rutherford, J. (2007). Imbalanced word-reading profiles in eighth-graders, *Journal of Experimental Child Psychology, 96*(3), 169–196.

Bradley, L., & Bryant, P. E. (1985). *Rhyme and reason in reading and spelling.* Ann Arbor: University of Michigan Press.

Brady, S. A. (1997). Ability to encode phonological representations: An underlying difficulty of poor readers. In B. A. Blachman (Ed.), *Foundations of reading acquisition and dyslexia* (pp. 21–47). Hillsdale, NJ: Erlbaum.

Brett, A., Rothlein, L., & Hurley, M. (1996). Vocabulary acquisition from listening to stories and explanations of target words. *Elementary School Journal, 96*(4), 415–422.

Bruck, M. (1990). Word recognition skills of adults with childhood diagnoses of dyslexia. *Developmental Psychology, 26,* 439–454.

Bruck, M. (1992). Persistence of dyslexics' phonological awareness deficits. *Developmental Psychology, 28,* 874–886.

Burley, J. E. (1980). Short-term, high intensity reading practice methods for Upward Bound students: An appraisal. *Negro Educational Review, 31,* 156–161.

Byrne, B., Fielding-Barnsley, R., Ashley, L., & Larsen, K. (1997). Assessing the child's and the environment's contribution to reading acquisition: What we know and what we don't know. In B. Blachman (Ed.), *Foundations of reading acquisition and dyslexia: Implications for early intervention* (pp. 265–286). Mahwah, NJ: Erlbaum.

Capelli, C. A., & Markman, E. M. (1982). Suggestions for training comprehension monitoring. *Topics in Learning & Learning Disabilities, 2,* 87–96.

Carnine, D., Silbert, J., Kameenui, E. J., & Tarver, S. G. (2004). *Direct instruction reading* (4th ed.). Upper Saddle River, NJ: Merrill/Prentice Hall.

Catts, H. W., Fey, M. E., Zhang, X., & Tomblin, J. B. (1999). Language bases of reading and reading disabilities: Evidence from a longitudinal investigation. *Scientific Studies of Reading, 3,* 331–362.

Chall, J. S. (1989). Learning to read: The great debate 20 years later. *Phi Delta Kappan, 70,* 521–538.

Clay, M. (1979). *Reading: The patterning of complex behavior.* Portsmouth, NH: Heinemann.

Clay, M. M. (1993). *Reading Recovery: A guidebook for teachers in training.* Portsmouth, NH: Heinemann.

Coltheart, M., Curtis, B., Atkins, C., & Haller, M. (1993). Models of reading aloud: Dual-route and parallel distributed processing approached. *Psychological Review, 100,* 589–608.

Coyne, M. D., McCoach, B., & Kapp, S. (2007). Vocabulary intervention for kindergarten students: Comparing extended instruction to embedded instruction and incidental exposure. *Learning Disability Quarterly, 30,* 74–88.

Coyne, M. D., Simmons, D., Kame'enui, E. J., & Stoolmiller, M. (2004). Teaching vocabulary during shared storybook readings: An examination of differential effects. *Exceptionality, 12,* 145–162.

Daane, M. C., Campbell, J. R., Grigg, W. S., Goodman, M. J., and Oranje, A. (2005). *Fourth-Grade Students Reading Aloud: NAEL 2002 Special Study of Oral Reading.* Washington, DC: U.S. Department of Education Institute of Education Sciences.

Dana, C., & Rodriguez, M. (1992). TOAST: A system to study vocabulary. *Reading Research and Instruction, 31*(4), 78–84.

Davidson, M., & Jenkins, J. (1994). Effects of phonemic processes on word reading and spelling. *Journal of Educational Research, 87,* 148–157.

Davis, Z. T. (1988). A comparison of the effectiveness of sustained silent reading and directed reading activity on students' reading achievement. *The High School Journal, 72*(1), 46–48.

Defior, S., & Tudela, P. (1994). Effect of phonological training on reading and writing acquisition. *Reading and Writing: An Interdisciplinary Journal, 6,* 299–320.

Deno, S. L., Marston, D., Shinn, M. R., & Tindal, G. (1983). Oral reading fluency: A simple datum for scaling reading disability. *Topics in Learning and Learning Disabilities, 2*(4), 53–59.

Deno, S. L., Mirkin, P. K., & Chiang, B. (1982). Identifying valid measures of reading. *Exceptional Children, 49,* 36–45.

Dunn, L. M., & Dunn, D. M. (2007). *Peabody Picture Vocabulary Test, fourth edition.* Bloomington, MN: Pearson.

Durkin, D. (1978). What classroom observations reveal about reading comprehension instruction. *Reading Research Quarterly, 14,* 481–533.

Ehri, L. (1991). Development of the ability to read words. In R. Barr, M. L. Kamil, P. Mosenthal, & P. D. Pearson (Eds.), *Handbook of reading research* (Vol. 2, pp. 383–417). New York: Longman.

Ehri, L. (2005). Development of sight word reading: Phases and findings. In M. Snowling & C. Hulme (Eds.), *The science of reading, a handbook* (pp. 135–154). Oxford, UK: Blackwell.

Ehri, L. C. (1987). Learning to read and spell words. *Journal of Reading Behavior, 19,* 5–31.

Ehri, L. C. (1992). Reconceptualizing the development of sight word reading and its relationship to recoding. In P. Gough, L. C. Ehri, & R. Treiman (Eds.), *Reading acquisition* (pp. 107–143). Hillsdale, NJ: Erlbaum.

Ehri, L. C. (1997). Sight word learning in normal readers and dyslexics. In B. Blachman (Ed.), *Foundations of reading acquisition and dyslexia: Implications for early intervention* (pp.163–189). Mahwah, NJ: Erlbaum.

Ehri, L. C. (2002). Phases of acquisition in learning to read words and implications for teaching. In R. Stainthorp & P. Tomlinson (Eds.), *Learning and teaching reading* (pp. 7–28). London: British Journal of Educational Psychology Monograph Series II.

Ehri, L. C., & Saltmarsh, J. (1995). Beginning readers outperform older disabled readers in learning to read words by sight. *Reading and Writing: An Interdisciplinary Journal, 7,* 295–326.

Ehri, L. C., & Soffer, A. G. (1999). Graphophonemic awareness: Development in elementary students. *Scientific Studies of Reading, 2,* 1–30.

Englemann, S. (1988). The direct instruction follow through model: Design and outcomes. *Education and Treatment of Children, 11,* 303–317.

Farmer, A., Nixon, M., & White, R. (1976). Sound blending and learning to read: An experimental investigation. *British Journal of Educational Psychology, 46,* 155–163.

Faulkner, H. J., & Levy, B. A. (1999). Fluent and nonfluent forms of transfer in reading: Words and their message. *Psychonomic Bulletin and Review, 6,* 111–116.

Fawcett, A., & Nicholson, R. (1995). Persistence of phonological awareness deficits in older children with dyslexia. *Reading and Writing: An Interdisciplinary Journal, 7,* 361–376.

Foorman, B. R., Francis, D. J., Shaywitz, S. E., Shaywitz, B. A., & Fletcher, J. M. (1997). The case for early reading intervention. In B. Blackman (Ed.), *Foundations of reading acquisition and dyslexia: Implications for early intervention* (pp. 243–264). Mahwah, NJ: Erlbaum.

Gallagher, D. (1998). The scientific knowledge base of special education: Do we know what we think we know? *Exceptional Children, 64,* 493 502.

Good, R. H., & Kaminski, R. A. (Eds.). (2002). *Dynamic indicators of basic Early literacy skills* (6th ed.). Eugene, OR: Institute for the Development of Educational Achievement.

Good, R., Kaminski, R., Shinn, M., Bratten, J., Shinn, M., Laimon, D., et al. (2004). *Technical adequacy of DIBELS: Results of the Early Childhood Research Institute on meansuring growth and gevelopmnent* (Tech. Rep. No. 7). Eugene: University of Oregon.

Good, R. H., Simmons, D. C., & Kame'enui, E. J. (2001). The importance and decision-making utility of a continuum of fluency-based indicators of foundational reading skills for third-grade high-stakes outcomes. *Scientific Studies of Reading, 5,* 257–288.

Goodman, K. S. (1969). Analysis of oral reading miscues: Applied psycholinguistics. *Reading Research Quarterly, 5,* 9–13.

Goodman, K. (1973). Miscues: Windows on the reading process. In F. Gollasch (Ed.), *Language and literacy: The selected writings of Kenneth Goodman* (Vol. I, pp. 93–102). Boston: Routledge & Kegan Paul.

Gordon, C. J., & Rennie, B. J. (1987). Restructuring content schemata: An intervention study. Reading *Research and Instruction, 26*(3), 162–188.

Gordon, J., Schumm, J. S., Coffland, C., & Doucette, M. (1992). Effects of inconsiderate vs. considerate text on elementary students' vocabulary learning. *Reading Psychology, 13*(2), 157–169.

Hansen, J., & Pearson, P. D. (1983). An instructional study: Improving the inferential comprehension of good and poor fourth-grade readers. *Journal of Educational Psychology, 75*(6), 821–829.

Haskell, D. W., Foorman, B. R., & Swank, P. R. (1992). Effects of three orthographic/ phonological units on first-grade reading. *Remedial and Special Education, 13,* 40–49.

Heise, B. L., Papalewis, R., & Tanner, D. E. (1991). Building base vocabulary with computer-assisted instruction. *Teacher Education Quarterly, 18*(1), 55–63.

Hohn, W., & Ehri, L. (1983). Do alphabet letters help prereaders acquire phonemic segmentation skill? *Journal of Educational Psychology, 75,* 752–762.

Honig, B., Diamond, L., & Gutlohn, L. (2008). *Teaching reading sourcebook* (2nd ed.). Novato, CA: Academic Therapy Publications.

Hosp, M. K., & Fuchs, L. S. (2005). Using CBM as an indicator of decoding, word reading, and comprehension: Do the relations change with grade? *School Psychology Review, 34,* 9–26.

Hudson, R. F., Lane, H. B., & Pullen, P. C. (2005). Reading fluency: What, why, and how? *The Reading Teacher, 54,* 702–714.

Hudson, R. F., Mercer, C. D., & Lane, H. B. (2000). *Exploring reading fluency: A paradigmatic overview.* Unpublished manuscript, University of Florida, Gainesville.

Hudson, R. F., Pullen, P. C., Lane, H. B., & Torgesen, J. K. (2009). The complex nature of reading fluency: A multidimensional view. *Reading & Writing Quarterly, 25,* 4–32.

Idol, L. (1987). Group story mapping: A comprehension strategy for both skilled and unskilled readers. *Journal of Learning Disabilities, 20,* 196–205.

Jenkins, J. R., Fuchs, L. S., van den Broek, P., Espin, C., & Deno, S. L. (2003). Accuracy and fluency in list and context reading of skilled and RD groups: Absolute and relative performance levels. *Learning Disabilities: Research & Practice, 18,* 237–245.

Juel, C. (1988). Learning to read and write: A longitudinal study of 54 children from first through fourth grades. *Journal of Educational Psychology, 80,* 437–447.

Justice, L. M., & Ezell, H. K. (2000). Enhancing children's print and word awareness through home-based parent intervention. *American Journal of Speech-Language Pathology, 9,* 257–269.

Justice, L. M., & Pullen, P. C. (2004). Promising interventions for promoting emergent literacy: An overview with practice suggestions. *Topics in Early Childhood Special Education, 23,* 99–113.

Justice, L. M., Skibbe, L., Canning, A., & Lankford, C (2005). Preschoolers, print and storybooks: An observational study using eye movement analysis. *Journal of Research in Reading, 28,* 229–243.

Kameenui, E., Carnine, D., & Freschi, R. (1982). Effects of text construction and instructional procedures for teaching word meanings on comprehension and recall. *Reading Research Quarterly, 17*(3), 367–388.

Kameenui, E. J., Fuchs, L., Francis, D. J., Good, R., O'Connor, R. E., Simmons, D. C., et al. (2006). The adequacy of tools for assessing reading competence: A framework and review. *Educational Researcher, 35,* 3–11.

Klingner, J. K., Vaughn, S., & Schumm, J. S. (1998). Collaborative strategic reading during social studies in heterogeneous fourth-grade classrooms. *Elementary School Journal, 99*(1), 3–22.

Kolich, E. M. (1991). Effects of computer-assisted vocabulary training on word knowledge. *Journal of Educational Research, 84*(3), 177–182.

LaBerge, D., & Samuels, S. J. (1974). Toward a theory of automatic information processing in reading. *Cognitive Psychology, 6,* 293–323.

Landerl, K., & Thaler, V. (2006). Reading and spelling acquisition and dyslexia in German. In R. M. Joshi & P. G. Aaron (Eds.), *Handbook of orthography and literacy* (pp. 121-134). NJ: Erlbaum.

Lane, H. B., & Pullen, P. C. (2004). *Phonological awareness assessment and instruction: A sound beginning.* Boston: Allyn & Bacon.

Lesgold, A. M., & Resnick, L. B. (1982). How reading disabilities develop: Perspectives from a longitudinal study. In J. P. Das, R. Mulcahy, & A. E. Wall (Eds.), *Theory and research in learning disability* (pp. 155–187). New York: Plenum.

Levin, J. R., & Divine-Hawkins, P. (1974). Visual imagery as a prose-learning process. *Journal of Reading Behavior, 6,* 23–30.

Lonigan, C., & Whitehurst, G. (1998). Relative efficacy of parent and teacher involvement in a shared-reading intervention for preschool children from low-income backgrounds. *Early Childhood Research Quarterly, 13*(2), 263–90.

Lundberg, I. (1984, August). Learning to read. *School Research Newsletter.* Stockholm, Sweden: National Board of Education.

Lyon, G., & Moats, L. (1997). Critical conceptual and methodological considerations in reading intervention research. *Journal of Learning Disabilities, 30*(6), 578.

McKenna, M. C., & Picard, M. (2006, December). Revisiting the role of miscue analysis in effective teaching. *The Reading Teacher, 60*(4), 378–380. doi: 10.1598/RT.60.4.8

McKeown, M. G., Beck, I. L., Omanson, R. C., & Pople, M. T. (1985). Some effects of long-term vocabulary instruction on reading comprehension: A replication. *Journal of Reading Behavior, 15*(1), 3–18.

Medo, M. A., & Ryder, R. J. (1993). The effects of vocabulary instruction on readers' ability to make causal connections. *Reading Research and Instruction, 33*(2), 119–134.

Mercer, C. D., Mercer, A., & Pullen, P. C. (2011). *Teaching students with learning problems, 8th edition.* Upper Saddle River, NJ: Pearson.

Mier, M. (1984). Comprehension monitoring in the elementary classroom. *Reading Teacher, 37*(8), 770–774.

Moats, L. C. (1998). Teaching decoding. *American Educator, 22,* 42–96.

Murray, B. (1998). Gaining alphabetic insight: Is phoneme manipulation skill or identity knowledge causal? *Journal of Educational Psychology, 90,* 461–475.

Nation, K, Clarke, P., Wright, B., & Williams, K. C. (2006). Patterns of reading ability in children with autism spectrum disorder. *Journal of Autism and Developmental Disorders, 36,* 911–919.

National Center for Educational Statistics (NCES). (2005). 2009 NAEP reading framework. Washington, DC: Author.

National Reading Panel (NRP). (2000). *A report of the national reading panel: Teaching children to read.* Washington, DC: National Institute of Child Health and Human Development.

Nicolson, R. I., & Fawcett, A. J. (1994). Comparison of deficits in cognitive and motor skills among children with dyslexia. *Annals of Dyslexia, 44,* 147–164.

Nicholson, T., & Whyte, B. (1992). Matthew effects in learning new words while listening to stories. In C. K. Kinzer & D. J. Leu (Eds.), *Literacy research, theory, and practice: Views from many perspectives: forty-first yearbook of the national reading conference* (pp. 499–503). Chicago: The National Reading Conference.

No Child Left Behind Act of 2001. Pub. L. No. 107-110 (2001).

Opitz, M. F., & Rasinski, T. V. (1998). *Good-bye round robin.* Portsmouth, NH: Heinemann.

Perfetti, C. A., & Hogaboam, T. (1975). Relationship between single word decoding and reading comprehension skill. *Journal of Educational Psychology*, *67*, 461–469.

Perfetti, C. A., Landi, N., & Oakhill, J. (2005). The acquisition of reading comprehension skill. In M. J. Snowling & C. Hulme (Eds.), *The science of reading: A handbook* (pp. 227–247). Oxford, UK: Blackwell.

Pinnell, G. S., Pikulski, J. J., Wixson, K. K., Campbell, J. R., Gough, P. B., & Beatty, A. S. (1995). *Listening to children read aloud*. Washington, DC: Office of Educational Research and Improvement.

Plaza, M., & Cohen, H. (2007). The contribution of phonological awareness and visual attention in early reading and spelling. *Dyslexia, 13,* 67–73.

Pressley, M., & Fingeret, L. (2006). What we have learned since the National Reading Panel: Visions of the next version of Reading First. In M. Pressley, A. K. Billman, K. H. Perry, K. E. Reffit, & J. M. Reynolds (Eds.), *Shaping literacy achievement* (pp. 216–245*).* New York: Guilford Press.

Pullen, P. C., & Justice, L. M. (2003). Enhancing phonological awareness, print awareness, and oral language skills in preschool children. *Intervention in School and Clinic, 39,* 87–98.

Pullen, P. C. & Lane, H. B., Lloyd, J. W., Nowak, R., & Ryals, J. (2005). Effects of explicit instruction on decoding of struggling first grade students: A data-based case study. *Education and Treatment of Children, 28,* 63–76.

Rasinski, T. V. (1990). Effects of repeated reading and listening-while-reading on reading fluency. *Journal of Educational Research, 83,* 147–150.

Rasinski, T. V. (2003). *The fluent reader: Oral reading strategies for building work recognition, fluency, and comprehension.* New York: Scholastic.

Rasinski, T. V. (2004) *Assessing reading fluency*. Honolulu, HA: Pacific Resources of Education and Learning.

Reinking, D., & Rickman, S. S. (1990). The effects of computer-mediated texts on the vocabulary learning and comprehension of intermediate-grade readers. *Journal of Reading Behavior, 22*(4), 395–411.

Reitsma, P. (1988). Reading practice for beginners: Effects of guided reading, reading-while-listening, and independent reading with computer-based speech feedback. *Reading Research Quarterly, 23,* 219–235.

Rinehart, S. D., Stahl, S. A., & Erickson, L. G. (1986). Some effects of summarization training on reading and studying. *Reading Research Quarterly, 21*(4), 422–438.

Robbins, C., & Ehri, L. C. (1994). Reading storybooks to kindergartners helps them learn new vocabulary words. *Journal of Educational Psychology,_86*(1), 54–64.

Samuels, S. J. (1988). Decoding and automaticity: Helping poor readers become automatic at word recognition. *The Reading Teacher*, *41*, 756–760.

Sawyer, D. J. (2006). Topics in language disorders. *Dyslexia in the Current Context, 26,* 93–94.

Scanlon, D. M., & Vellutino, F. R. (1996). Prerequisite skills, early instruction, and success in first grade reading: Selected results from a longitudinal study. *Mental Retardation and Development Disabilities, 2,* 54–63.

Scarborough, H. (2005). Developmental relationships between language and reading: Reconciling a beautiful hypothesis with some ugly facts. In H.W. Catts & A. G. Kamhi (Eds.), *The connections between language and reading disabilities* (pp. 3–24). Mahwah, NJ: Erlbaum.

Schrank, F. A., Mather, N., & Woodcock, R. W. (2004) *Woodcock Johnson III: Diagnostic Reading Battery.* Rolling Meadows, IL: Riverside.

Senechal, M. (1997). The differential effect of storybook reading on preschoolers' acquisition of expressive and receptive vocabulary. *Journal of Child Language, 24*(1), 123–138.

Senechal, M., & Cornell, E. H. (1993). Vocabulary acquisition through shared reading experiences. *Reading Research Quarterly, 28*(4), 360–374.

Shankweiler, D., Lundquist, E., Dreyer, L., & Dickinson, C. (1996). Reading and spelling difficulties in high school students: Causes and consequences. *Reading and Writing; An Interdisciplinary Journal, 8,* 267–294.

Shankweiler, D., Lundquist, E., Katz, L., Stuebing, K. K., Fletcher, J. M., Brady, S., et al. (1999). Comprehension and decoding: Patterns of association in children with reading difficulties. *Scientific Studies of Reading, 3,* 69–94.

Shinn, M. R., Good, R. H., Knutson, N., & Tilly, W. D. (1992). Curriculum-based measurement of oral reading fluency: A confirmatory analysis of its relation to reading. *School Psychology Review*, *21*, 459–479.

Snow, C. E., Burns, M. S., & Griffin, P. (Eds.). (1998). *Preventing reading difficulties in young children.* Washington, DC: National Academy Press.

Stahl, S. (1983). Differential word knowledge and reading comprehension. *Journal of Reading Behavior, 15*(4), 33–50.

Stahl, S. A., & Fairbanks, M. M. (1986). The effects of vocabulary instruction: A model-based meta-analysis. *Review of Educational Research 56,* 72–110.

Stahl, S. A., Richel, M. A., & Vandevier, R. J. (1991). Learning meaning vocabulary through listening: A sixth-grade replication. In J. Zutell & S. McCormick (Eds.*), Learner factors/teacher factors: Issues in literacy research and instruction: Fortieth yearbook of the National Reading Conference* (pp. 185–192) Chicago: The National Reading Conference.

Stanovich, K. E. (1986). Matthew effects in reading: Some consequences of individual differences in the acquisition of literacy. *Reading Research Quarterly, 21,* 360–406.

Stanovich, K. E., & West, R. F. (1989). Exposure to print and orthographic processing. *Reading Reearch Quarterly, 24*(4), 402–433.

Stecker, P. M., Fuchs, L. S., & Fuchs, D. (2005). Using curriculum-based measurement for assessing reading prigress and for making instructional decisions. Retrieved August 2, 2010, from www.onlineacademy.org/modules/a300/lesson/lesson_3/xpages/a300c3_40200.html

Stevens, R. J., Slavin, R. E., & Farnish, A. M. (1991). The effects of cooperative learning and direct instruction in reading comprehension strategies on main idea identification. *Journal of Educational Psychology, 83*(1), 8–16.

Stothard, S. E., & Hulme, C. (1992). Reading comprehension difficulties in children: The role of language comprehension and working memory skills, *Reading and Writing: An Interdisciplinary Journal, 4,* 245–256.

Summers, E. G., & McClelland, J. V. (1982). A field-based evaluation of sustained silent reading (SSR) in intermediate grades. *Alberta Journal of Educational Research, 28,* 100–112.

Svensson, I., & Jacobson, C. (2006). How persistent are phonological difficulties? A longitudinal study of reading retarded children. *Dyslexia, 12,* 3–20.

Tan, A., & Nicholson, T. (1997). Flashcards revisited: Training poor readers to read words faster improves their comprehension of text. *Journal of Educational Psychology, 89,* 276–288.

Tomeson, M., & Aarnoutse, C. (1998). Effects of an instructional programme for deriving word meanings. *Educational Studies, 24*(1), 107–128.

Torgesen, J. K. (1986). Computers and cognition in reading: A focus on decoding fluency. *Exceptional Children, 53,* 157–162.

Torgesen, J. K., Alexander, A. W., Wagner, R. K., Rashotte, C. A., Voeller, K. K. S., & Conway, T. (2001). Intensive remedial instruction for children with severe reading disabilities: Immediate and long-term outcomes from two instructional approaches. *Journal of Learning Disabilities, 34,* 33–58, 78.

Torgesen, J. K., Wagner, R. K., & Rashotte, C. A. (1999). *Test of word reading efficiency.* Austin TX: Pro Ed.

Uhry, J. K., & Shepherd, M. J. (1997). Teaching phonological recoding to young children with phonological processing deficits: The effect on sight-vocabulary acquisition. *Learning Disability Quarterly, 20,* 104–125.

Vellutino, F., & Scanlon, D. (1996). Cognitive profiles of difficult-to-remediate and readily remediated poor readers: Early. *Journal of Educational Psychology, 88,* 601–638.

Vellutino, F. R., Scanlon, D. M., Sipay, E. R., Small, S., Chen, R., Pratt, A. (1996). Cognitive profiles of difficult-to-remediate and readily remediated poor readers: Early intervention as a vehicle for distinguishing between cognitive and experiential deficits as basic causes of specific reading disability. *Journal of Educational Psychology, 88,* 601–638.

Vukovic, R. K., & Siegel, L. S. (2006). The double deficit hypothesis: A comprehensive review of the evidence. *Journal of Learning Disabilities, 39,* 25–47.

Wagner, R. K., & Barker, T. A. (1994). The development of orthographic processing ability. In V. W. Berninger (Ed.), *The varieties of orthographic knowledge, 1: Theoretical and developmental issues* (Vol. 8, pp. 243–276). Dordrecht, the Netherlands: Kluwer.

Wagner, R., & Torgesen, J. (1987). The nature of phonological processing and its causal role in the acquisition of reading skills. *Psychological Bulletin, 101,* 192–212.

Weaver, C. (1994). *Reading process and practice.* Portsmouth, NH: Heinemann.

Whitehurst, G. J., Epstein, J. N., Angell, A. L., Payne, A. C., Crone, D. A., & Fischel, J. E. (1994). Outcomes of an emergent literacy intervention in Head Start. *Journal of Educational Psychology, 86,* 542–555.

Whitehurst, G. J., Falco, F., Lonigan, C. J., Fischel, J. E., DeBaryshe, B. D., Valdez-Menchaca, M. C., & Caulfield, M. (1988). Accelerating language development through picture-book reading. *Developmental Psychology, 24,* 552–558.

Whitehurst, G., & Lonigan, C. (1998). Child development and emergent literacy. *Child Development, 69,* 848–878.

Wimmer, H., & Mayringer, H. (2002). Dysfluent reading in the absence of spelling difficulties: a specific disability in regular orthographies. *Journal of Educational Psychology, 94,* 272–277.

Wixson, K. K. (1986). Vocabulary instruction and pictures as extra stimulus prompts. *British Journal of Research Quarterly, 21*(3), 317–329.

Wolf, M. (1997). A provisional, integrative account of phonological and naming-speed deficits in dyslexia: Implications for diagnosis and intervention. In B. Blachman (Ed.), *Foundations of reading acquisition and dyslexia: Implications for early intervention* (pp. 67–92). Mahwah, NJ: Erlbaum.

Wolf, M. (1999). What time may tell: Towards a new conceptualization of developmental dyslexia. *Annals of Dyslexia, 49,* 3–28.

Wolf, M., Bowers, P., & Biddle, K. (2000). Naming speed processes, timing, and reading: A conceptual review. *Journal of Learning Disabilities, 33,* 322–324.

Woodcock, R. W., McGrew, K. S., & Mather, N. (2001). *Woodcock Johnson III Diagnostic Reading Battery.* Rolling Meadows, IL: Riverside.

Yaden, D. (1989). Understanding stories through repeated read-alouds: How many does it take? *The Reading Teacher, 41*(6), 556–560.

Zutell, J., & Rasinski, T. V. (1991). Training teachers to attend to their students' reading fluency. *Theory Into Practice, 30,* 211–217.

32

Writing and Students with Disabilities

Steve Graham and Karen R. Harris
Vanderbilt University

Although not every person with a disability is a poor writer, most have difficulty mastering this complex skill. According to findings from the 2007 National Assessment of Educational Progress (NAEP; Salahu-Din, Persky, & Miller, 2008), only 6% of eighth-grade and 5% of 12th-grade students with disabilities perform at or above the "proficient" level in writing (defined as solid academic performance). Students who score below this level are classified as obtaining only partial mastery of the literacy skills needed at their respective grade. Consequently, 19 of every 20 students with disabilities do not acquire the writing skills needed for success in school.

This puts most students with disabilities at risk for school failure. Writing is one of the primary mechanisms for evaluating students' learning. Students' grades are determined in large part by their performance on writing activities, ranging from answering homework questions to taking essay tests to composing reports and research papers (Graham, 2006a).

Writing also provides a powerful tool for supporting and extending students' learning in school (see meta-analyses by Bangert-Drowns, Hurley, & Wilkinson, 2004; Graham & Hebert, in press; Graham & Perrin, 2007a). Writing facilitates learning in at least five ways (Applebee; 1984; Klein, 1999; Smith; 1988). One, it fosters explicitness, as students must select which information is most important. Two, it is integrative, as writing provides a means for organizing ideas into a coherent whole, establishing explicit relations between them. Three, it fosters reflection, as it is easier to review, reexamine, connect, critique, and construct new understandings of ideas when they are written. Four, it forces a personal involvement with ideas, as it requires active decision making about what will be written and how it will be treated. Five, it is transformative, as students must think about what an idea means when they write it in their own words. Students with poor writing skills are less likely to take advantage of the power of writing as a tool for learning.

The consequences of poor writing extend well beyond the classroom. Most jobs that pay a living wage now require high-level literacy skills (Berman, 2009). This will become even more common in the near future (Carnevale & Derochers, 2004; Kirsch, Braun, Yamamoto, & Sum, 2007). The largest projected area for job growth is the service industry, with 20.5 million new jobs added to the economy during this decade alone (Berman, 2001). High level writing and reading skills are almost a universal requirement for employees in this industry and other professions such as construction, manufacturing, finance, insurance, and real estate. Almost 70% of salaried employees in these industries use writing as part of their job (National Commission on Writing [NCOW], 2004). Moreover, 90% of white-collar workers and 80% of blue-collar workers currently report that writing is essential to job success (National Writing Project, 2007).

Writing has increasingly become a central part of participating in community and social life. Emailing, blogging, texting, and other forms of electronic writing have become a common means for communicating with family, friends, and even those who are not known to the writer. In essence, writing has become part of the basic fabric of life in industrialized countries. Thus, students with poor writing skills, including persons with disabilities, find themselves at a serious disadvantage in successfully pursuing some form of higher education, securing a job that pays a living wage, or participating fully in social and civic activities.

Because of the broadening role of writing in every day life, it is important that persons with disabilities become as proficient with this skill as possible. This means increasing the number of students with disabilities who master writing as well as maximizing the performance of those who do not. Past and future research has an important role to play in this process because the systematic study of the causes and characteristics of writing difficulties among persons with disabilities, as well as the testing and validation of promising interventions and compensatory writing devices, provide an empirical and reasoned foundation on which to build effective services. Such a foundation is still under construction, however, as most writing research conducted with persons with disabilities has occurred in the last 20 years, with much of it involving students with learning disabilities. With these limitations in mind, our goal in this chapter is to use the scientific evidence that is available to build as strong a foundation for the teaching of writing to students with disabilities as is currently possible.

We begin building our foundation by examining two basic theories of writing, drawing implications from each theory to determine how writing typically develops. This analysis forms the framework for exploring factors that likely contribute to the writing difficulties most students with disabilities experience. We refer to these factors as correlates of atypical development. We continue to use this framework as a touchstone, as we examine methods for assessing and teaching writing. It should be noted that while we note the importance of handwriting and spelling as important skills in writing development as well as present handwriting and spelling instruction as an evidence-based practices with struggling writers, we do not examine the rich instructional literature on teaching these skills to students with disabilities (see, for example, Graham, 1999).

Writing Theories and Typical Writing Development

There is no single theory or model that fully captures writing or its development. Two methods that have been especially prominent in studying writing are the cognitive/motivational and social/contextual approach (Graham & Harris, in press). The former focuses mostly on the individual writer and the mental and affective processes involved in composing text. The latter concentrates on the broader social context in which writing takes place, and how the interaction between writer and context shape each other. We illustrate each theoretical approach using a representative example, while considering the implication of each viewpoint for writing development.

Cognitive/Motivational Theories of Writing

The cognitive/motivational approach is exemplified by an influential writing model of skilled writing developed by Hayes (1996). Although much of the model concentrates on the capabilities of the individual writer, some attention is given to the task environment in which writing takes place. This task environment includes both social (audience, other texts read while writing, or collaborators) and physical components (text read so far or medium for writing, such as a word processor). Developed more fully, however, are the mental operations and motivational resources the writer draws on to carry out the act of composing. These internal factors include the cognitive processes of text interpretation, reflection, and text production. These mental operations are the tools the writer uses to form a representation of the writing task, devise a plan to complete it, draw conclusions about the audience and possible writing content, use cues from the writing plan or text produced so far to retrieve information from memory that is then turned into written sentences, and evaluate plans and text and modify them as needed. They also include motivation (the goals, predispositions, beliefs, and attitudes that influence the writing process), long-term memory (knowledge of the writing topic and audience as well as linguistic and genre knowledge, including task schemas that specify how to carry out particular writing tasks), and working memory (which serves as an interface between cognitive processes, motivation, and memory, providing a space for holding information and ideas for writing as well as carrying out cognitive activities that require the writer's conscious attention).

As this description demonstrates, writing is a complex and demanding task. It is a goal-directed and self-sustained activity requiring the skillful management of the (a) writing environment; (b) constraints imposed by the writing topic; (c) intentions of the writer(s); and (d) processes, knowledge, and skills involved in composing (Zimmerman & Reisemberg, 1997). Skilled writers are strategic, motivated, and knowledgeable about the craft of writing. Not as readily evident in Hayes's (1996) model is that writing is also dependent on the mastery of a variety of skills for transforming ideas into acceptable sentences and transcribing these sentences onto paper via handwriting, spelling, or typing (Graham, 2006a).

Graham (2006a) examined if these same four factors (strategies, motivation, knowledge, and skills) play an important role in writing development. He reasoned that a factor such as knowledge shapes writing development if the following tenets are supported by empirical evidence: (1) skilled writers possess more of the attribute (e.g., knowledge about writing) than less skilled writers; (2) developing writers increasingly possess the attribute with age and schooling; (3) individual differences in the attribute predict writing performance; and (4) instruction designed to increase the attribute improves writing performance.

Graham (2006a) found that the available evidence clearly supports the developmental importance of specific writing strategies, such as planning and revising, as well as particular writing skills, including handwriting, spelling, and sentence construction. For planning and revising, all four tenets above were supported with the following exception: revising behavior was generally unrelated to overall writing performance until students reached high school. Similarly, all four tenets were supported for handwriting and spelling, but the evidence was thinnest for tenet 4 (instruction in the skill improves students' writing performance). For sentence combining, the supporting evidence was more nuanced, as the evidenced varied by genre and type of writer. For instance, individual differences in sentence skills were associated with writing performance in some studies (tenet 3), but this was not always the case, as the findings varied somewhat depending on the genre (e.g., Crowhurst, 1980).

Graham (2006a) further reported that knowledge about writing (e.g., genre knowledge) is an important ingredient in students' writing development, as all four tenets were supported (even though the evidence was relatively thin). The role of motivation was generally supported, but less certain. Although skilled writers were more motivated than less skilled ones, some aspects of motivation declined over time (e.g., attitude towards writing) and others like self-efficacy increased or declined depending on the study. However, individual differences in motivation predicted writing performance, and there were a small number of studies showing that efforts to enhance motivation (i.e., self-efficacy) boosted writing performance.

Social/Contextual Theories of Writing

In cognitive/motivational theories of writing, only limited attention is devoted to the social nature of writing. The influence of writing community, culture, society, institution, politics, and history are mostly ignored. These factors are central features in sociocultural theories of writing. A model of writing by Russell (1997), explaining how macro-level social and political forces influence micro-level writing actions and vice versa, exemplifies this theoretical orientation.

One basic unit in Russell's (1997) model is the activity system. This unit examines how actors (a student, pair of students, student and teacher, or class – perceived in social terms and taking into account the history of their involvement in the activity system) use concrete tools, such as paper and pencil, to accomplish some action with some outcome, such as writing a description of a field trip. The outcome is accomplished in a problem space where subjects use these writing tools in an ongoing interaction with others to shape the paper that is being produced over time in a shared direction. Russell also employs the concept of genre, "as typified ways of purposefully interacting in and among some activity system(s)" (p. 513). These typified ways of interacting become stabilized through the regularized use of writing by and among individuals, creating a relatively predictable way for writing within a classroom. These are only temporarily stabilized structures, however, because they are subject to change depending upon the context. For instance, newcomers to an established activity system may appropriate some of the routinized tools used by others in the class, such as using more interesting words instead of more common ones when writing. In turn, the newcomer may change typified ways of writing in a classroom, as other class members adapt unfamiliar routines applied by their new classmate, such as beginning a paper with an attention grabber.

Our description of Russell's (1997) theory above mostly emphasizes how writing development is shaped by the social and contextual interactions that occur within the classroom, between students and with the teacher. This theory also emphasizes how macro-level activity systems involving culture, institution, and society shape students' writing development. We illustrate this below with an example drawn from Graham and Harris (in press).

State and federal mandates involving high stakes tests can result in more or less time being devoted to teaching writing. For instance, the federal emphasis through NCLB on assessing reading and mathematics but not writing, might send a message to teachers that writing is not important and little or no time should be devoted to teaching it. In contrast, requiring that schools test students' writing performance is likely to increase the amount of time devoted to teaching it, but this seemingly positive outcome may have unintended consequences. For example, most states' high stakes writing tests typically involve relatively low level writing tasks, and such tests drive how writing is taught (Hillocks, 2002). Decisions such as these, made outside of the context of the classroom, can foster or hinder students' development as writers.

Correlates of Atypical Writing Development

Although writing and its development are not fully understood, as the previous section highlights, the road to becoming a skilled writer is shaped by the cognitive and motivational capabilities and other resources that reside within the writer as well as forces that reside outside the writer, including a wide array of contextual, social, political, and historical factors. In this section, we examine both cognitive/motivational and contextual/social factors that are associated with atypical writing development. Most of the writing research conducted with persons with disabilities has involved students with learning disabilities. We rely heavily on this research to draw conclusions about the factors that likely contribute to writing difficulties. This means that some of the factors identified may be more or less important for students with specific disabilities.

It is important to note that we do not examine neurological correlates of atypical writing development in this chapter. Brain imaging research is almost non-existent in the area of writing (Pugh et al., 2006), and most studies of writing difficulties and the brain have involved studying the brains of deceased persons with specific writing problems (see Berninger & Winn, 2008, for a review of this literature). Such research has identified specific brain regions associated with specific writing disabilities, but as of yet this information has limited educational value.

Finally, the writing of students with disabilities is characterized by brevity, disorganization, and errors (Graham & MacArthur, 1987). The papers typically produced by these students are sparse, containing little elaboration or detail. The relationship between one idea and the next is often not evident, and it is hard to determine the overall structure of the composition. Handwriting might be difficult to read and errors involving grammar, usage, spelling, and word choice are common.

Cognitive/Motivational Correlates

There is no universal cognitive/motivational profile that

characterizes either normal or atypical writing development. This was illustrated in a study by Wakely, Hooper, de Kruif, and Swartz (2006), who identified six different linguistically-based writing clusters for fourth- and fifth-grade students, with subtypes reflecting both normal and atypical development. Normal variation was captured in two reliable profiles: one consisting of average writers and another of expert writers who had the highest writing and reading scores among students and made virtually no grammatical, semantic, or spelling errors when writing. Atypical writing disabilities was captured in four reliable profiles, ranging from a subgroup that exhibited global impairments in linguistic skills to three subgroups experiencing more specific linguistic impediments, such as a greater number of semantic errors, greater number of grammatical errors, or low reading and spelling scores.

Unfortunately, only a handful of studies have attempted to develop classification models for subtypes of writing disabilities (see also Sandler et al., 1992). The more common approach for determining which cognitive/motivational factors contribute to atypical writing development involves identifying factors that account for variability in students' writing performance as well as identifying factors that distinguish between more typical writers and one or more predetermined subsets of poor writers.

Given that writing is a self-directed and mentally demanding activity requiring the activation and coordination of a variety of cognitive processes and resources (Hayes, 1996; Zimmerman & Reisemberg, 1977), it is not surprising that some struggling writers experience problems with attention (Sandler et al., 1992), self-regulation (Graham, 1997; Hooper, Swartz, Wakely, de Kruif, & Montgomery, 2002), or memory, including working memory (McCutchen, 1994; Swanson & Berninger, 1996). Conversely, students who commonly experience difficulties with attention and self-regulation, such as students with ADHD (Barkley, 1997), are more likely than typically developing youngsters to be poor writers (e.g., Re, Pedron, & Cornoldi, 2007).

Of these three factors, the role of self-regulation in atypical writing development has been most widely studied (see Graham & Harris, 1996; Graham, Harris, & Olinghouse, 2007). One method that has been used to verify that self-regulation skills contribute to atypical writing development is to examine the effects of providing poor writers with external support in managing and coordinating the mental operations involved in writing. For example, Graham and his colleagues (De La Paz, Swanson, & Graham, 1998; Graham, 1997) prompted poor writers who were also students with learning disabilities to use a routine for coordinating and managing the evaluative decisions involved in revising text. The routine was based on a model of revising containing three elements: compare (detecting a mismatch between what the writer intended to say and what was actually written), diagnose (determine the cause of the mismatch), and operate (decide on the type of change needed and carry it out). The routine required that students carry out each of these mental operations in the order specified above, while limiting the number of options for the mental operations of diagnose and operate. This was done by providing students with a series of cards to select for each of these two elements. For instance, evaluation cards for diagnose included: "This does not sound right" or "This is not what I meant to say." Tactical cards for operate included: "Say more," "Delete this," and so forth. Such executive support enhanced the students' revising skills in both studies (e.g., quality of revisions made), and resulted in an overall improvement of text in one of the investigations (De La Paz et al., 1998).

It is also not surprising that difficulties with language and reading skills are associated with atypical writing development (Dockrell, Lindsay, & Connelly, 2009; Juel, 1988; Scott & Windsor, 2000). For example, oral language develops earlier than written language and presumably provides a basic foundation for writing, as beginning writers rely heavily on many aspects of language, including phonological, semantic, and syntactical knowledge, as they write (Shanahan, 2006). Reading is also important to writing because basic writing processes such as revising, involve rereading text, and reading source material is one method writers use to obtain information for writing. In addition, writing and reading are dependent on common cognitive substrate (e.g., visual, phonological, and semantic systems) as well as knowledge systems (Fitzgerald & Shanahan, 2000), and if reading is delayed, writing is also likely to be impeded.

Two other factors that likely play a role in atypical writing development are general intelligence and behavior. Students' scores on intelligence tests are positively related to their writing performance (see Graham, 1982). We have also found that students in our intervention studies with lower IQs (70 or below) are especially poor writers and less responsive to writing instruction than poor writers with higher IQ (e.g., De La Paz & Graham, 1997). Although we are unaware of any studies examining the relationship between students' behavior and their writing performance, students with both externalizing and internalizing behavioral disorders are typically poor writers (Nelson, Benner, Lane, & Smith, 2004).

Students with disabilities are often identified and classified, in large part, by their intellectual, learning, attention, language, reading, or behavior capabilities. As we just showed, these same variables are associated with atypical writing development. This helps to explain why approximately 95% of these students do not write well enough to meet grade level demands (Salahu-Din et al., 2008).

So far, our analysis of the correlates of atypical writing has not examined how atypical students' writing differs from that of their more capable peers. First, they are much more likely than their peers to use and retain an approach to writing that functions like an automated, forward moving, content generation program. They typically write by creating or drawing from memory a relevant idea, writing it down, and using each preceding idea to stimulate the next one (Graham & Harris, 1996). This process simplifies the task of writing by minimizing the use of planning, monitoring, evaluating, revising, and other self-regulatory processes.

Why do poor writers minimize these self-regulatory processes in their writing? One explanation is that this is a result of their poor self-regulatory skills (Graham, 1997; Hooper et al., 2002). An alternative explanation involves their difficulties in mastering writing skills such as handwriting, spelling, and sentence construction (Graham, 1990; Raiser, 1981). For struggling writers, these skills are very demanding, requiring a large expenditure of effort and cognitive resources (Graham, 1999). At the same time, self-regulatory processes, such as planning, are extremely demanding (Kellogg, 1993). To cope with these competing demands, they minimize some of them. Because they cannot eliminate the physical act of writing (constructing a sentence and writing it down on paper), they constrain demanding self-regulatory processes such as goal setting, monitoring, and evaluating (Graham & Harris, 1996).

Another way struggling writers differ from their more competent peers is that they are less knowledgeable about writing and its genres, devices, and conventions. Even with a more familiar genre like stories, poor writers often are unable to identify basic attributes (Saddler & Graham, 2007). They also place an undue emphasis on form and not enough on substance and process (Graham, Schwartz, & MacArthur, 1993; Wong, Wong, & Blenkinsop, 1989). They further appear to have difficulty gaining access to the knowledge or ideas they already possess. For example, when we repeatedly prompted students with learning disabilities to write more once they had completed a writing assignment, they doubled and even tripled their output (Graham, 1990).

Finally, struggling writers differ from their typical classmates in their motivation for writing. They demonstrate little persistence when asked to write. For instance, when we asked students with learning disabilities to write an essay expressing their opinion on a specific topic, they averaged just 6 minutes of composing time (Graham, 1990). Englert and her colleagues (Thomas, Englert, & Gregg, 1987) came to a similar conclusion, noting that these youngsters struggle to sustain their thinking about topics, as evidenced by their difficulty in producing multiple statements about familiar subjects.

Social/Contextual Correlates

Just as there is no single cognitive/motivational factor that is responsible for atypical writing development, a variety of social/contextual factors shape students' progress as writers. How well children write, for example, is related to environmental variables, such as literacy learning in family contexts (Senechal, LeFevre, Thomas, & Daley, 1998) and the setting in which education occurs (Walberg & Ethington, 1991). Writing development is further influenced by the social, historical, political, and institutional contexts in which it occurs, with curriculum and pedagogical decisions on how to teach writing made by many people, including policy makers, politicians, administrators, and teachers (Schultz & Fecho, 2000).

One social/contextual factor that might be especially influential in shaping the writing development of students with disabilities is poverty. Children from poorer families tend to be weaker writers than their more affluent peers (Mavrogenes & Bezrucko, 1993; Walberg & Ethington, 1991), and students with disabilities are more likely to be raised in poverty than their peers without disabilities (Parish, Rose, Grinstein-Weiss, Richman, & Andrews, 2008).

Although gender is a biological factor, boys and girls performance in school is influenced by social/contextual factors (Spear, 1989). There is a considerable body of evidence showing that girls are better writers than boys (Berninger & Fuller, 1992; Walberg & Ethington, 1991). This may be due to societal expectations that girls are better students as well as better writers than boys.

A social/contextual factor we think is particularly important to the development of poor writing skills is quality of instruction. If students with disabilities receive poor writing instruction, the probability that they will become poor writers increases. For students with an existing writing problem, poor instruction is likely to make this problem worse (Graham & Harris, in press).

Unless teachers receive adequate preparation in how to work with students with disabilities and how to teach them writing, it is unlikely that these youngsters will receive high quality writing instruction. There is good reason to be concerned that neither of these conditions is currently met. Teachers commonly express reservations about their ability to teach students with disabilities (Vaughn, Schumm, Jallad, Slusher, & Samuels, 1996), and the teaching of writing receives little emphasis in teacher preparation programs. As the National Commission on Writing (2003) indicated:

> [T]eachers typically receive little instruction in how to teach writing. Only a handful of states require courses in writing certification, even for elementary school teachers.... No matter how hard they work, these instructors...are often ill equipped to teach it. (p. 23)

The concern expressed by the National Commission on Writing (2003) is well founded. In a series of national surveys (Cutler & Graham, 2008; Graham et al. 2008; Kiuhara, Graham, & Hawken, 2009), we found that many elementary and secondary teachers had little to no preparation in how to teach writing. An obvious downside to a lack of preparation is that classroom instruction suffers. For instance, the high school teachers surveyed by Kiuhara et al. reported they infrequently used evidence-based writing practices in their classroom (these practices were identified in meta-analyses of experimental, quasi-experimental, and single-subject research by Graham & Perrin, 2007a, 2007b, 2007c). In addition, the writing assignments their students did rarely involved analysis and interpretation (such writing is needed for advanced academic success in high school and college; see Applebee & Langer, 2006). In fact, the four most common writing activities assigned by teachers were writing short answer responses to homework, completing worksheets, summarizing material read, and responding to material read. Only the last of these assignments likely involved much analysis and interpretation.

An especially important ingredient in delivering effective instruction to students with disabilities is to provide instruction that is responsive to their needs (Palinscar, Cutter, & Magnusson, 2004). Although many teachers adjust their writing instruction to meet the needs of their writers (see Kiuhara et al., 2009, for example), many do not. Graham, Harris, MacArthur, and Fink-Chorzempa (2003) reported that approximately 40% of teachers in the primary grades made few or no adaptations for the weaker writers in their classes.

Together, these findings raise serious concerns about the quality of writing instruction that students with disabilities receive. Of course, quality of instruction is dependent on teachers, general and special, devoting a reasonable amount of time to teaching this skill. To the extent that an observational study by Christenson, Thurlow, Ysseldyke, and McVicar (1989) is representative, little time is spent teaching writing to students with disabilities or students in general. They reported that teachers devoted only 25 minutes a day to writing and writing instruction for students in general, and even less time to students with disabilities. If educators hope to promote the writing development of students with disabilities to the greatest extent possible, it is essential that the students consistently receive a sufficient quantity of high quality instruction from one year to the next and across curricular areas. Because writing development takes place over a long period of time, writing instruction cannot be the providence of only one or a few teachers (Graham, 2006a).

Assessing Students' Writing

Most writing assessment procedures are shaped by cognitive/motivational theories of writing (Graham & Olinghouse, in press). This approach assumes the writer is trying to produce a product that accomplishes one or more writing goals, and that it is constructed through the application of a variety of writing processes and skills. Although such assessments could focus on the processes and procedures used to construct the written product, they typically evaluate some aspect of the written product.

Perhaps the most illusive, but most important assessments, involve evaluating quality of text. Quality is difficult to quantify, and as a result, assessments designed to measure it involve some subjective judgment. There are three basic methods for assessing writing quality: holistic, analytic, and primary-trait scoring.

Holistic scoring involves making a single, overall judgment about the quality of writing (Veal & Hudson, 1983). Typically, this is done by using a Likert-type scale where by each score represents a particular level of quality. To make holistic scoring more reliable, raters are typically provided with descriptions of specific scores, sample compositions that illustrate specific scores, or both. An obvious drawback to holistic scoring is that it does not provide instructional guidance for areas of concern within a writing sample (White, 1985).

In contrast, the other two measures of assessing writing quality, analytic and primary-trait scales, provide some data that can be used to inform instruction. Analytic scales provide separate scores for assessing specific aspects of good writing, such as organization, ideation, sentence structure, voice, vocabulary, and mechanics (Scherer, 1985). As with holistic scoring, descriptions of specific scores or sample compositions for these scores for each aspect of writing assessed are commonly used to increase scoring reliability. Primary trait scales differ from the other two measures, as the scoring guide for this assessment is based on the specific purpose of each writing assignment (Veal & Hudson, 1983). Thus, this scale can be developed to assess the primary goal of a writing assignment (e.g., coherence of an argument) or to reflect genre-specific requirements (e.g., plot development).

One weakness with subjective measures of writing quality is that they can be unreliable if extensive training and scoring directions are not provided to raters (Graham & Olinghouse, in press). Reliability can also suffer as a result of rater fatigue, mood, or motivation (Freedman & Calfee, 1983). Although computer-based scoring procedures can be as effective as human scored measures of quality (see Shermis & Burstein, 2003), some scholars have concerns about the validity of automated essay scoring (e.g., Ericsson & Haswell, 2006). Nevertheless, we expect that such automated scoring procedures will become more common in both classroom assessment and as a tool for research.

Another approach for evaluating written products involves curriculum-based assessment. With this approach, students are asked to write for a short period of time (e.g., 5 minutes); their written product is scored using one or more objective (i.e., countable) measures, including number of words written, percentage of correctly spelled words, or percentage of correct word sequences. Such measures are moderately correlated with subjective measures of writing quality (e.g., Deno, Marston, & Mirkin, 1982; Espin, De La Paz, Scierka, & Roelofs, 2005; Espin et al., 2000; Watkinson & Lee, 1992). The basic purpose behind curriculum-based assessment is for teachers to periodically (e.g., once a week) assess their students' writing so that they can make decisions on whether they need to modify their instructions for the class as a whole or for particular students. At the present time, no studies have examined the validity of this rationale for writing.

Reflecting a more social/contextual perspective to assessment are portfolios. With this approach, teachers collect multiple samples of a student's writing (Elbow & Belanoff, 1986; Murphy, 1994). They are commonly collected across different writing purposes to gain a broad view of a student's writing ability. Typically, portfolio assessment includes collecting the final product along with drafts and revisions, allowing teachers to evaluate progress from start to finish (Calfee, 2000). A concern with portfolio assessment is that it can take considerable teacher time to gather and evaluate each student's writing. In addition, there are very few data on the reliability and validity of portfolio assessments.

Assessment is perhaps the area in writing most in need of further development and research. Concerns over how to adequately assess and evaluate the quality of student writing have plagued the field for decades (Huot, 1990). An understudied area in special education involves how to identify students who have a writing disability. The most common method of identifying such students is to examine their performance on a norm-referenced writing test, like the Test of Written Language – 3 (Hammill & Larsen, 1996). Such tests almost always assess students' writing performance in a single genre (usually story writing). However, we have found that struggling writers' performance in one genre is not a good predictor of their performance in another genre (Hebert et al., 2009), suggesting that reliance on a single test is not an adequate method for identification

Teaching Writing

As with the study of correlates of atypical writing development, most of the writing instructional research conducted with students with disabilities involves youngsters with learning disabilities. This must be remembered when considering the recommendations presented in this section. There are, however, two approaches to instruction that have been applied relatively broadly with students with disabilities. One is explicitly and directly teaching writing strategies to students using the Self-Regulated Strategy Development Approach (SRSD; Harris & Graham, 1999). This approach has been applied with students with learning disabilities (Harris & Graham, 1985), behavioral disorders (Lane et al., 2008), ADHD (Reid & Lienemann, 2006), developmental disabilities (Harris, Graham, & Mason, 2006) and Asperger syndrome (Delano, 2007). The other is direct instruction, whereby the teacher models how to apply a specific writing skill and then students practice using the skill, with help from the teacher as needed (for examples see Campbell, Brady, & Linehan, 1991; Dowis & Schloss, 1992).

Some of the evidenced-based writing practices presented here reflect a specific theoretical viewpoint. For example, research on the effectiveness of setting goals for writing was based on a cognitive/motivational perspective. Other approaches, like strategy instruction, were influenced by social/contextual and cognitive/motivational viewpoints (see Graham, 2006b; Englert, Mariage, & Dunsmore, 2006). Still other instructional approaches, such as teaching sentence construction, were shaped by additional theoretical perspectives (i.e., linguistic and behavioral). Consequently, we do not delineate the theoretical heritage of each instructional procedure. Instead, we present specific writing practices that have been validated as effective with students with disabilities as well as other struggling writers. We decided to include practices validated with the latter group to expand the number of recommendations made (see Graham, Olinghouse, & Harris, 2009). All of the identified practices could be potentially implemented by general or special education teachers.

All of the instructional practices we present were effective in improving the writing performance of students in at least two or more studies. Evidence for the effectiveness of these practices was drawn from meta-analyses of writing interventions tested via experimental, quasi-experimental, or single-subject design research (Graham, in press; Graham & Perrin, 2007a, 2007b, 2007c; Morphy & Graham, 2009; Rogers & Graham, 2008; Sandmel & Graham, 2009). Although we prefer to base instructional recommendations on four or more studies, we decided to make the best of the available evidence. Because many aspects of writing instruction have not been sufficiently tested with students with disabilities (or struggling writers for that matter), our list of effective practices should be viewed as tentative, awaiting findings from future research to be expanded and modified.

For each practice, we provide effect sizes or average effect sizes when possible indicating what aspect of writing was improved by the intervention. A widely used rule of thumb for interpreting effect sizes (Cohen's d) for experimental and quasi-experimental studies is that .20 is small, .50 is moderate, and .80 is strong (Cohen, 1988). For single-subject design studies, effect sizes were calculated by determining the percent of data points for a given treatment condition that exceeded the highest positive value obtained during baseline (before treatment). With this metric (i.e., percentage of non-overlapping data) scores from 50% to 70% represent a small effect, scores between 70% and 90% a moderate effect, and scores above 90% a strong effect (Scruggs & Mastropieri, 2001).

Evidence-Based Writing Practices

1. Teach students strategies for planning, revising, and editing compositions. Explicitly and systematically teaching students strategies for planning, revising, or editing together or separately have a strong positive impact on improving their writing. This approach has been investigated in over 25 studies conducted with students with disabilities and other struggling writers. The average effect size for writing quality was 1.02 in true- and quasi-experimental designs studies, whereas an average PND of 96% for schematic structure (inclusion or quality of basic text elements) was obtained in single-subject design studies (Graham et al., 2009).

An SRSD study by Harris et al. (2006) provides an example of strategy instruction as it was applied with a variety of struggling writers, including students with disabilities. Research assistants delivered instruction to small groups of children outside of the general education classroom. Students learned two planning and writing strategies: one for persuasive writing and the other for story writing. Each of these strategies were embedded in a more general strategy: POW, which prompted them to (P) pick a topic, (O) organize their ideas (or plan) in advance of writing, and (W) write and say more while writing (i.e., to continue to plan as they wrote). For each genre, they were taught a more specific strategy for organizing their ideas (within the planning step above) that involved generating, culling, and organizing ideas in terms of the basic elements in a story or a persuasive paper.

Research assistants taught each of the genre-specific strategies separately. In each case, students were first introduced to the general (POW) and the genre-specific strategy, and instructors made sure students were familiar with the basic parts of a story or persuasive essay (depending on which was being taught). Then, the rationale for using the strategies was established, and students began memorizing a mnemonics for each one. Students also assessed and graphed their performance on a composition written before the start of instruction, providing a baseline against which to compare later performance on compositions (which were also assessed and graphed). Next, the research assistant modeled how to apply the strategies, making the process of using them accessible by "thinking aloud." Before writing the composition, the teacher set a goal to use all of the basic elements in that genre. Once the paper was completed, the instructor and students discussed what the instructor said that helped them while writing. Students generated several of their own self-statements to use while they wrote. The instructor and students collaboratively wrote the next paper, setting goals, using self-statements, and graphing their performance. Instructor support was gradually withdrawn, until students could use the strategies independently and successfully. As students were learning the strategies, they identified opportunities to apply what they were learning outside of their small group and then evaluated and discussed their successes in doing so.

2. Have students work together to plan, draft, revise, and edit their compositions. Two studies examined the effects of having students with disabilities work together in a structured manner to plan, draft, and/or edit text (Dailey, 1991; MacArthur, Schwartz, & Graham, 1991). The average effect size on the quality of students' text was 1.13, making this a highly effective approach (Graham et al., 2009).

The MacArthur et al. (1991) investigation illustrates this instructional procedure. Special education teachers taught students with disabilities a peer revision strategy. Students first individually wrote and revised a personal narrative on the computer. They then met with a peer to use a two-step revision strategy they had been taught via the SRSD model (see Practice # 1). For step one, which focused on content clarity, each student read his or her paper aloud to the other child. Each student then independently reread the other student's paper and made revision notes, identifying unclear sections and the need for additional details. Students used the feedback from their writing partner to revise their compositions independently. For step two, the same procedures were applied, except revising now focused on editing for mechanical errors.

3. Make the process writing approach more effective for students with disabilities. Although the process approach to writing had a small positive impact (effect size = .32) on the writing quality of students in general education classes in Graham and Perrin's meta-analysis (2007a, 2007b), a subsequent meta-analysis by Sandmel and Graham (2009) found that it does not enhance the writing performance of struggling writers. Three studies, however, involving students with disabilities demonstrated that this approach can be made more effective for these youngsters by explicitly teaching them strategies for planning, revising, or editing text. The average effect size for writing quality in the two group studies (Curry, 1997; MacArthur et al., 1991) was .89, whereas PND was 100% for the inclusion of basic story elements in a single-subject design study by Danoff, Harris, and Graham (1993). Examples of strategies that teachers can effectively integrate into the process writing approach are highlighted in practices 1 and 2 above.

4. Teach strategies for producing a written summary of material read. One quasi-experimental study (Placke, 1987) and a single-subject design study (Nelson, Smith, & Dodd, 1992) examined the effectiveness of teaching a summarization strategy to students with disabilities. In the first study, the effect size for quality of summary was 1.12; and in the second study, PND for including important information in the summary was 100% (Graham et al., 2009).

In the Nelson et al. (1992) investigation, students were taught a nine-step summary strategy. Before teaching the strategy, the teacher ensured that students understood the general components of a summary and cues in text that helped them identify the main ideas. To learn the strategy, the teacher and students together practiced applying it using a Summary Writing Guide. The guide prompted the writer to: (1) identify the main idea, (2) note important things about the main idea, (3) reread to make sure the main idea and important ideas were correct, (4) write a topic sentence, (5) group ideas, (6) determine whether any important ideas were missing or unimportant ideas could be deleted, (7) write the summary, (8) reread the summary for unclear ideas, and (9) have a peer read the summary.

5. Set clear and specific goals for what students are to accomplish in their writing. In three studies in which students with disabilities were provided with goals for their writing, Graham et al. (2009) found an average effect size of .76 for writing quality. A study by Graham, MacArthur, and Schwartz (1995) provides an example of goal setting. After writing the first draft of a paper, students were given a goal to improve it by adding at least three things to make it better. When compared to a general goal to revise to make the paper better, this specific revising goal enhanced the quality of students' papers.

6. Use direct instruction to teach grammar and usage skills to students with disabilities. Although traditional approaches for teaching grammar and usage to typically developing students are not effective (Andrews et al., 2006;

Graham & Perrin, 2007a, 2007b), research with students with disabilities and other struggling writers demonstrated the use of direct instruction as a tool for teaching such skills to students with disabilities and other struggling writers as effective (average PND in four studies was 84% for grammar/usage skills; Rogers & Graham, 2008).

Direct instructional procedures for teaching grammar/usage skills involved modeling, guided practice, and review. Skills taught included capitalization, punctuation, dialogue, possessives, nouns, adjectives, and adverbial phrases. A study by Dowis and Schloss (1992) provides a representative example of this approach. The teacher taught grammatical skills to a large group of children containing both special and general education students. Students were explicitly taught the definition of the skill (e.g., adverbial clauses) and a rule for using it. This improved their ability to apply the taught skills in their writing.

7. Teach students text transcription skills (handwriting, spelling, and typing). Five true-experimental and one quasi-experimental study examined the effects of teaching handwriting, spelling, or typing to struggling writers (Graham, in press). Such instruction had a moderate impact on the quality of students' writing, as the average effect size across the six studies was .59.

Graham, Harris, and Fink (2000) provide an example of how one text transcription skill, handwriting, can be taught to young struggling writers. Students practiced naming letters with games and songs. They also practiced writing letters by tracing and copying them as well as copying words containing the letters. They further copied a sentence containing practiced letters under timed-conditions.

8. Use word processing and related software as a primary tool for writing. In a recent meta-analysis of 27 word processing studies conducted with struggling writers (Morphy & Graham, 2009), we obtained an average weighted effect size of .52 for writing quality. The findings from four single-subject design studies in Rogers and Graham (2008) further suggest that software, such as word-prediction, speech-synthesis, or planning programs, enhances basic word processing, producing a small, but positive effect for students with disabilities (average PND across all measures = 60%).

A study by MacArthur (1998) provides an example of how teachers can use computers with students with disabilities. Students kept a dialogue journal to communicate with their classroom teacher, using a word-processing program with speech synthesis and word prediction software to write their entries. The speech synthesis software provided auditory support, as students could choose to have the computer read aloud a particular word, sentence, or the full entry. The word prediction software recommended possible words based on letters entered to that point. The student could click on any suggested word to have it pronounced, and then double-click to select a word and insert it into the document.

9. Teach writing and reading together to improve students' writing. We located two studies in which we were able to calculate an effect size for the impact of combined reading and writing instruction on the performance of students with disabilities and other struggling writers (Graham et al., 2009). Combining reading and writing instruction had a strong impact on writing, as PND for the inclusion of main ideas from reading into written text in a study by Mason, Snyder, Sukhram, and Kedem (2006) was 92%, whereas the effect size for this same variable in Mason and Meadan (2007) was .72 and 1.13 for length of compositions.

In Mason et al. (2006), students were taught a reading-and-writing strategy using SRSD (see Practice 1). With the reading strategy (TWA) students were asked to: *T*hink before reading (think about the author's purpose, what you want to know, and what you want to learn); *W*hile reading (think about reading speed, linking knowledge, and rereading parts); and *A*fter reading (think about the main idea, summarizing information, and what you learned). Once they could use the TWA strategy independently to generate a written outline and could verbally retell the main idea of a passage read, they were taught a writing strategy (PLANS) designed to help apply the information they learned while reading. PLANS is designed to make students' writing about information read easier, as it breaks the task of planning what to write into manageable subtasks (*P*ick goals, *L*ist ways to meet goals, *A*nd make *N*otes and *S*equence them).

10. Encourage students to monitor one or more aspects of their writing performance. Graham and Perrin (2007c) calculated an average PND for five single-subject design studies that examined the effects of self-monitoring on the performance of students with disabilities and other struggling writers. Self-monitoring ranged from students counting how many words they wrote to determining if specific genre traits or elements (e.g., story parts such as setting, plot, action, resolution, and so forth) were included in their papers. The effects of such instruction were positive, but small, as the average PND for the aspects of writing monitored was 67%.

An investigation by Shimabukuro, Prater, Jenkins, and Edelen-Smith (1999) illustrates this approach. Students were taught a self-monitoring strategy for improving their ability to complete more independent writing assignments accurately. They learned the importance of improving both quality and quantity of independent work and were taught to manage their time by graphing their progress at the end of each work session.

11. Reinforce positive aspects of students' writing. Graham and Perrin (2007c) calculated an average PND for four single-subject design studies examining the impact of reinforcement on writing performance (Most of the students in these investigations were struggling writers.). Reinforcement involved social praise, tangible reinforcers, or both, as a means of increasing a variety of specific writing behaviors. These approaches had a small, but positive impact on writing, as the average PND was 56%.

A study by Hopman and Glynn (1989) provides an example of the use of reinforcement. Students first wrote stories, and then negotiated with the teacher a target number of words to write in their next story. If the student successfully met or exceeded this goal, then the teacher provided social reinforcement in the form of praise, smiles, and encouragement.

Concluding Comment

In the 1980s it would not have been possible to write a chapter about writing and students with disabilities with as much depth as this one. Even so, there is much that remains unknown about writing and students with disabilities. We are just starting to understand the genesis of writing difficulties and how to prevent or correct those problems. Much work remains to be done to develop a richer and more nuanced conceptualization of why so many students with disabilities are poor writers. We are at a similar point in terms of how to teach writing to these students. Some instructional practices have been validated in two or more studies, but there are only a few comprehensive treatments that have been tested broadly or frequently. Perhaps the greatest challenge facing those who study the development and teaching of writing in the coming decade is the development of valid and reliable methods for assessing writing. Such techniques are not only critical to research, but to evaluating if schools are doing a good job teaching writing to students, both those with disabilities and without disabilities. Absent a clear metric for measuring effectiveness, it is difficult for educators to know whether their methods are helping students and to change what they are doing to improve students' outcomes. Finally, writing research and practice are hindered by a lack of theoretical models designed to explain typical and atypical writing development. Much of the current research conducted with developing writers lacks a solid rudder or guidance system to direct it because researchers rely on models of adult writing, inadequately developed models of children writing, or pure intuition.

References

Andrews, R., Torgerson, C., Beverton, S., Freeman, A., Locke, T., Low, G., … & Zhu, D. (2006). The effects of grammar teaching on writing development. *British Educational Research Journal, 32*, 39–55.

Applebee, A. (1984). Writing and reasoning. *Review of Educational Research, 54*, 577–596.

Applebee, A., & Langer, J. (2006). *The state of writing instruction: What existing data tell us.* Albany, NY: Center on English Learning and Achievement.

Bangert-Drowns, R. L., Hurley, M. M., & Wilkinson, B. (2004). The effects of school-based writing-to-learn interventions on academic achievement: A meta-analysis. *Review of Educational Research, 74*, 29–58.

Barkley, R. (1997). *ADHD and the nature of self-control.* New York: Guilford.

Berman, I. (2009, February 25). Supporting adolescent literacy achievement. *Issue Brief*, 1–15.

Berman, J. (2001, November). Industry output and employment projections to 2010. *Monthly Labor Review*, 40.

Berninger, V., & Fuller, F. (1992). Gender differences in orthographic, verbal, and compositional fluency: Implications for assessing writing disabilities in primary grade children. *Journal of School Psychology, 30*, 363–382.

Berninger, V., & Winn, W. (2008). Implications of advancements in brain research and technology for writing development, writing instruction, and educational evolution. In C. MacArthur, S. Graham, & J. Fitzgerald (Eds.), *Handbook of writing research* (pp. 96–114). New York: Guilford.

Calfee, R. D. (2000). Writing portfolios: Activity, assessment, authenticity. In R. Indrisano & J. R. Squire (Eds.), *Perspectives on writing: Research, theory, and practice* (pp. 278–304). Newark, DE: International Reading Association.

Campbell, B. J., Brady, M. P., & Linehan, S. (1991). Effects of peer-mediated instruction on the acquisition and generalization of written capitalization skills. *Journal of Learning Disabilities, 24*, 6–14.

Carnevale, A., & Derochers, D. (2004). *Standards for what? The economic roots of K-16 reform.* Princeton, NJ: ETS.

Christenson, S. L., Thurlow, M. L., Ysseldyke, J. E., & McVicar, R. (1989). Written language instruction for students with mild handicaps: is there enough quantity to ensure quality. *Learning Disability Quarterly, 12*, 219–222.

Cohen, J. (1988) *Statistical power analysis for the behavioral sciences* (2nd ed.). Hillsdale, NJ: Erlbaum.

Crowhurst, M. (1980). Syntactic complexity and teachers' quality ratings of narrations and arguments. *Research and the Teaching of English, 14*, 223–231.

Curry, K. A. (1997). *A comparison of the writing products of students with learning disabilities in inclusive and resource room settings using different writing instruction approaches.* Unpublished doctoral dissertation, Florida Atlantic University, Boca Raton, FL.

Cutler, L., & Graham, S. (2008). Primary grade writing instruction: A national survey. *Journal of Educational Psychology, 100*, 907–919.

Dailey, E. M. (1991). *The relative efficacy of cooperative learning versus individualized learning on the written performance of adolescent students with writing problems.* Unpublished doctoral dissertation, John Hopkins University, Baltimore, MD.

Danoff, B., Harris, K. R., & Graham, S. (1993). Incorporating strategy instruction within the writing process in the regular classroom: Effects on the writing of students with and without learning disabilities. *Journal of Reading Behavior, 25*, 295–322.

Delano, M. (2007). Improving written language performance of adolescents with Asperger syndrome. *Journal of Applied Behavior Analysis, 40*, 345–351.

De La Paz, S., & Graham, S. (1997). Strategy instruction in planning: Effects on the writing performance and behavior of students with learning difficulties. *Exceptional Children, 63*, 167–181.

De La Paz, S., Swanson, P., & Graham, S. (1998). Contribution of executive control to the revising problems of students with writing and learning difficulties. *Journal of Educational Psychology, 90*, 448–460.

Deno, S., Marston, D., & Mirkin, P. (1982). Valid measurement procedures for continuous evaluation of written expression. *Exceptional Children, 48*, 368–371.

Dockrell, J., Lindsay, G., & Connelly, V. (2009). The impact of specific language impairment on adolescents' written text. *Exceptional Children, 75*, 427–446.

Dowis, C. L., & Schloss, P. (1992). The impact of mini-lessons on writing skills. *Remedial and Special Education, 13*, 34–42.

Elbow, P., & Belanoff, P. (1986). Portfolios as a substitute for proficiency examinations. *College Composition and Communication, 37*, 336–339.

Englert, C., Mariage, T., & Dunsmore, K. (2006). Tenets of sociocultural theory in writing instruction research. In C. MacArthur, S. Graham, & J. Fitzgerald (Eds.), *Handbook of writing research* (pp. 208–220). New York: Guilford.

Ericsson, P. F., & Haswell, R. H. (Eds.). (2006). *Machine scoring of student essays: Truth and consequences.* Logan: Utah State University Press.

Espin, C. A., De La Paz, S., Scierka, B. J., & Roelofs, L. (2005). The relationship between curriculum-based measures in written expression and quality and completeness of expository writing for middle school students. *Journal of Special Education, 38*(4), 208–217.

Espin, C. A., Shin, J., Deno, S. L., Skare, S., Robinson, S., & Benner, B. (2000). Identifying indicators of written expression proficiency for middle school students. *The Journal of Special Education, 34*(3), 140–153.

Fitzgerald, J., & Shanahan, T. (2000). Reading and writing relations and their development. *Educational Psychologist, 35*, 39–50.

Freedman, S. W., & Calfee, R. C. (1983). Holistic assessment of writing: experimental design and cognitive theory. In P. Mosenthal, L. Tamor, & S. A. Walmsley (Eds.), *Research on writing: Principles and methods* (pp. 75–98). New York: Longman.

Graham, S. (1982). Written composition research and practice: A unified approach. *Focus on Exceptional Children, 14*, 1–16.

Graham, S. (1990). The role of production factors in learning disabled students' compositions. *Journal of Educational Psychology, 82,* 781–791.

Graham, S. (1997). Executive control in the revising of students with learning and writing difficulties. *Journal of Educational Psychology, 89*, 223–234.

Graham, S. (1999). Handwriting and spelling instruction for students with learning disabilities: A review. *Learning Disability Quarterly, 22*, 78–98.

Graham, S. (2006a). Writing. In P. Alexander & P. Winne (Eds.), *Handbook of educational psychology* (pp. 457–477). Mahwah, NJ: Erlbaum.

Graham, S. (2006b). Strategy instruction and the teaching of writing. In C. MacArthur, S. Graham, & J. Fitzgerald (Eds.), *Handbook of writing research* (187–207). New York: Guilford.

Graham, S. (in press). Teaching writing. In P. Hogan (Ed.), *Cambridge encyclopedia of language sciences*. Cambridge, UK: Cambridge University Press.

Graham, S., & Harris, K.R. (1996). Self-regulation and strategy instruction for students with writing and learning difficulties. In S. Ransdell & M. Levy (Eds.), *Science of writing: Theories, methods, individual differences, and applications* (pp. 347–360). Mahwah, NJ: Erlbaum.

Graham, S., & Harris, K. (in press). Writing. In R. Allington & A. McGill-Franzen. (Eds.), *Handbook of reading disabilities research*. Mahwah, NJ: Erlbaum.

Graham, S., Harris, K. R., & Fink, B. (2000). Is handwriting causally related to learning to write? Treatment of handwriting problems in beginning writers. *Journal of Educational Psychology, 92*, 620–633.

Graham, S., Harris, K. R., MacArthur, C., & Fink-Chorzempa, B. (2003). Primary grade teachers' instructional adaptations for weaker writers: A national survey. *Journal of Educational Psychology, 95*, 279–293.

Graham, S., Harris, K. R., & Olinghouse, N. (2007). Addressing executive function difficulties in writing: An example from the self-regulated strategy development model. In L. Meltzer (Ed.), *Executive functioning in education: From theory to practice* (pp. 216–236). New York: Guilford.

Graham, S., & Hebert, M. (in press). *Writing to reading*. Report commissioned by the Carnegie Corp. of New York. Washington, DC: Alliance for Excellence in Education.

Graham, S., & MacArthur, C. (1987). Written language of handicapped. In C. Reynolds and L. Mann (Eds.), *Encyclopedia of special education* (pp. 1678–1681). New York: Wiley.

Graham, S., MacArthur, C., & Schwartz, S. (1995). Effects of goal setting and procedural facilitation on the revising behavior and writing performance of students with writing and learning problems. *Journal of Educational Psychology, 87,* 230–240.

Graham, S., Morphy, P., Harris, K., Fink-Chorzempa, B., Saddler, B., Moran, S., & Mason, L. (2008). Teaching spelling in the primary grades: A national survey of instructional practices and adaptations. *American Educational Research Journal, 45,* 796–825.

Graham, S., & Olinghouse, N. (in press). Learning and teaching writing. In E. Anderman & L. Anderman (Eds.), *Psychology of classroom learning*. Farmington Hills, MI: Thomas Gale.

Graham, S., & Olinghouse, N., & Harris, K. R. (2009). Teaching composing to students with learning disabilities: Scientifically-supported practices. In G. Troia (Ed.), *Instruction and assessment for struggling writers: Evidence-based practices* (pp. 165–186). Mahwah, NJ: Erlbaum.

Graham, S., & Perrin, D. (2007a). *Writing next: Effective strategies to improve writing of adolescents in middle and high schools.* New York: Carnegie Corporation of New York.

Graham, S., & Perrin, D. (2007b). A meta-analysis of writing instruction for adolescent students. *Journal of Educational Psychology, 99,* 445–476.

Graham, S., & Perrin, D. (2007c). What we know, what we still need to know: Teaching adolescents to write. *Scientific Studies in Reading, 11,* 313–336.

Graham, S., Schwartz, S., & MacArthur, C. (1993). Knowledge of writing and the composing process, attitude toward writing, and the self-efficacy for students with and without learning disabilities. *Journal of Learning Disabilities, 26*, 237–249.

Hammil, D., & Larsen, S. (1996). *Test of written language-3.* Austin, TX: Pro-ED.

Harris, K., & Graham, S. (1985). Improving learning disabled students' composition skills: Self-control strategy training. *Learning Disability Quarterly, 8*, 27–36.

Harris, K. R., & Graham, S. (1999). Programmatic intervention research: Illustrations from the evolution of self-regulated strategy development. *Learning Disability Quarterly, 22*, 251–262.

Harris, K. R., Graham, S., & Mason, L. (2006). Improving the writing, knowledge, and motivation of struggling young writers: Effects of self-regulated strategy development with and without peer support. *American Educational Research Journal, 43,* 295–340.

Hayes, J. (1996). A new framework for understanding cognition and affect in writing. In M. Levy & S. Ransdell (Eds.), *The science of writing: Theories, methods, individual differences, and applications* (pp. 1–27). Mahwah, NJ: Erlbaum

Hebert, M., Graham, S., Harris, K. R., Anelli, C., Mathias, R., Mason, L., & Adkins, M. (2009). *Writing performance and behavior of struggling writers across four genres*. Manuscript submitted for publication.

Hillocks, G. (2002). *The testing trap: How state writing assessments control learning.* New York: Teachers College Press.

Hooper, S., Swartz, C., Wakely, M., de Kruif, R., & Montgomery, J. (2002). Executive functioning in elementary school children with and without problems in written expression. *Journal of Learning Disabilities, 35,* 57–68.

Hopman, M., & Glynn, T. (1989). The effect of correspondence training on the rate and quality of written expression of four low achieving boys. *Educational Psychology, 9*, 197–213.

Huot, B. (1990). The literature of direct writing assessment: Major concerns and prevailing trends. *Review of Educational Research, 60,* 237–263.

Juel, C. (1988). Learning to read and write: A longitudinal study of 54 children from first through fourth grade. *Journal of Educational Psychology, 80*, 437–447.

Kellogg, R. (1993). Observations on the psychology of thinking and writing. *Composition Studies, 21*, 3–41.

Kirsch, I., Braun, H., Yamamoto, K., & Sum, A. (2007). *America's perfect storm: Three forces changing our Nation's future*. Princeton, NJ: ETS.

Kiuhara, S., Graham, S., & Hawken, L. (2009). Teaching writing to high school students: A national survey. *Journal of Educational Psychology, 101,* 136–160.

Klein, P. (1999). Reopening inquiry into cognitive processes in writing-to-learn. *Educational Psychology Review, 11,* 203–270.

Lane, K., Harris, K. R., Graham, S., Weisenbach, J., Brindle, M., & Morphy, P. (2008). The effects of self-regulated strategy development on the writing performance of second grade students with behavioral and writing difficulties, *Journal of Special Education, 41,* 234–253.

MacArthur, C. (1998). Word processing with speech synthesis and word prediction: Effects on the dialogue journal writing of students with learning disabilities. *Learning Disability Quarterly, 21,* 1–16.

MacArthur, C., Schwartz, S., & Graham, S. (1991). Effects of a reciprocal peer revision strategy in special education classrooms. *Learning Disability Research and Practice, 6,* 201–210.

Mason, L. H, & Meadan, H. (2007, January). *A components analysis of a multiple strategy Instructional approach for self-regulating expository reading comprehension and informative writing.* Paper presented at the Pacific Coast Research Conference, San Diego, CA.

Mason, L. H., Snyder, K. H., Sukhram, D. P., & Kedem, Y. (2006). TWA +

PLANS strategies for expository reading and writing: Effects for nine fourth-grade students. *Exceptional Children, 73*, 69–89.

Mavrogenes, N., & Bezrucko, N. (1993). Influences on writing development. *Journal of Educational Research, 86*, 237–245.

McCutchen, D. (1994). The magical number three, plus or minus two: Working memory in writing. In E. Butterfield (Ed.), *Children's writing: Towards a process theory of the development of skilled writing* (pp. 1–30). Greenwich, CT: JAI.

Morphy, P., & Graham, S. (2009). *Effective computer writing instruction for weaker writers: A meta-analysis of research findings referenced to national outcomes.* Manuscript submitted for publication.

Murphy, S. (1994). Writing portfolios in K-12 schools: Implications for linguistically diverse students. In L. Black, D. A. Daiker, & G. Stygall (Eds.), *New directions in portfolio assessment: Reflective practice, critical theory, and large-scale scoring* (pp. 140–156). Portsmouth, NH: Heinemann.

National Commission on Writing. (2003). *The neglected "R": The need for a writing revolution.* College Entrance Examination Board. Retrieved from http://www.writingcommission.org/prod_downloads/writingcom/neglectedr.pdf

National Commission on Writing. (2004). *Writing: A ticket to work or a ticket out: A survey of business leaders.* College Entrance Examination Board. Retrieved from http://www.writingcommission.org/prod_downloads/writingcom/writing-ticket-to-work.pdf

National Writing Project. (2007). *2007 survey: Learning to write.* Retrieved from http://www.nwp.org/cs/public/download/nwp_file/8856/NWP_2007_Survey_Report.pdf?x-r=pcfile_d

Nelson, R., Benner, J., Lane, K., & Smith, W. (2004). An investigation of the academic achievement of K-12 students with emotional and behavioral disorders in public school settings. *Exceptional Children, 71*, 59–73.

Nelson, R., Smith, D., & Dodd, J. (1992). The effects of teaching a summary skills strategy to students identified as learning disabled on their comprehension of science text. *Education and Treatment of Children, 15*, 228–243.

Palinscar, A., Cutter, J., & Magnusson, S. (2004). A community of practice: Implications for learning disabilities. In B. Wong (Ed.), *Learning about learning disabilities* (3rd ed., pp. 485–510). Amsterdam: Elvesier.

Parish, S., Rose, R., Grinstein-Weiss, M., Richman, E., & Andrews, M. (2008). Material hardship in U.S. families raising children with disabilities. *Exceptional Children, 75,* 71–96.

Placke, E. (1987). *The effect of cognitive strategy instruction on learning disabled adolescents' reading comprehension and summary writing. Unpublished doctoral dissertation.* State University of New York, Albany, NY.

Pugh, K., Frost, S., Sandak, R., Gillis, M., Moore, D., Jenner, A., & Menci, E. (2006). What does reading have to tell us about writing? Preliminary questions and methodological challenges in examining the neurobiological foundations of writing and writing disabilities. In C. MacArthur, S. Graham, & J. Fitzgerald (Eds.), *Handbook of writing research* (pp. 433–448). New York: Guilford.

Raiser, V. (1981). Syntactic maturity, vocabulary diversity, mode of discourse and theme selection in the free writing of learning disabled adolescents. *Dissertation Abstracts International*, *42*, 2544-A.

Re, A., Pedron, M., & Cornoldi, C. (2007). Expressive writing difficulties in children described as exhibiting ADHD symptoms. *Journal of Learning Disabilities, 40,* 244–255.

Reid, R., & Lienemann, T. (2006). Self-regulated strategy development for written expression with students with attention deficit/hyperactivity disorder. *Exceptional Children, 73*, 53–68.

Rogers, L., & Graham, S. (2008). A meta-analysis of single subject design writing intervention research. *Journal of Educational Psychology, 100,* 879–906.

Russell, D. (1997). Rethinking genre in school and society: An activity theory analysis. *Written Communication, 14*, 504-554.

Saddler, B., & Graham, S. (2007). The relationship between writing knowledge and writing performance among more and less skilled writers. *Reading and Writing Quarterly, 23,* 231–247.

Salahu-Din, D., Persky, H., & Miller, J. (2008). *The nation's report card: Writing 2007* (NCES 2008–468). Washington, DC: National Center for Education Statistics, Institute of Education Sciences, U.S. Department of Education.

Sandler, A., Watson, T., Footo, M., Levine, M., Coleman, W., & Hooper, S. (1992). Neurodevelopmental study of writing disorders in middle childhood. *Developmental and Behavioral Pediatrics, 13,* 17–23.

Sandmel, K., & Graham, S. (2009). *The process writing approach: A meta-analysis.* Manuscript submitted for publication.

Scherer, D. L. (1985). *Measuring the measurements: A study of evaluation of writing. An annotated bibliography.* (ERIC Document Reproduction Service No. 260455)

Schultz, K., & Fecho, B. (2000). Society's child: Social context and writing development. *Educational Psychologist, 35*, 51–62.

Scruggs, T., & Mastrioperi, M. (2001). How to summarize single-participant research: Ideas and applications. *Exceptionality, 9*, 227–244.

Scott, C., & Windsor, J. (2000). General language performance measures in spoken and written narrative and expository discourse of school-age children with language learning disabilities. *Journal of Speech, Language, and Hearing Research, 43*, 324–339.

Senechal, M., LeFevre, J., Thomas, E., & Daley, K. (1998). Differential effects of home literacy experiences on the development of oral and written language. *Reading Research Quarterly, 33*, 96–116.

Shanahan, T. (2006). Relations among oral language, reading, and writing development. In C. MacArthur, S. Graham, & J. Fitzgerald (Eds.), *Handbook of writing research* (pp. 171–183). New York: Guilford.

Shermis, M. D., & Burstein, J. (2003). *Automated essay scoring: A cross-disciplinary perspective.* Hillsdale, NJ: Erlbaum.

Shimabukuro, S. M., Prater, M. A., Jenkins, A., & Edelen-Smith, P. (1999). The effects of self-monitoring of academic performance on students with learning disabilities and ADD/ADHD. *Education and Treatment of Children, 22*, 397–414.

Smith, C. (1988). Does it help to write about your reading? *Journal of Reading,* 276–277.

Spear, M. (1989). Differences between the written work of boys and girls. *British Educational Research Journal, 15,* 271–277.

Swanson, L., & Berninger, V. (1996). Individual differences in children's working memory and writing skills. *Journal of Experimental Child Psychology, 63,* 358–385.

Thomas, C., Englert, C., & Gregg, S. (1987). An analysis of errors and strategies in the expository writing of learning disabled students. *Rememdial & Special Education, 8*, 21–30.

Vaughn, S., Schumm, J., Jallad, B., Slusher, J., & Samuels, L. (1996). Teachers' views of inclusion. *Learning Disabilities Research and Practice, 11*, 96–106.

Veal, L. R., & Hudson, S. A. (1983). Direct and indirect measures for large-scale evaluation of writing. *Research in the Teaching of English, 17,* 285–296.

Wakely, M., Hooper, S., de Kruif, R., & Swartz, C. (2006). Subtypes of written expression in elementary school children: A linguistic-based model. *Developmental Neuropsychology, 29,* 125–159.

Walberg, H., & Ethington, C. (1991). Correlates of writing performance and interest: A U.S. national assessment study. *Journal of Educational Research, 84*, 198–203.

Watkinson, J. T., & Lee, S. W. (1992). Curriculum-based measures of written expression for learning-disabled and non-disabled students. *Psychology in the Schools, 29,* 184–191.

White, E. M. (1985). *Teaching and assessing writing*. San Francisco: Jossey-Bass.

Wong, B., Wong, R., & Blenkinsop, J. (1989). Cognitive and metacognitive aspects of learning disabled adolescents' composing problems. *Learning Disability Quarterly, 12*, 300–322.

Zimmerman, B., & Reisemberg, R. (1997). Becoming a self-regulated writer: A social cognitive perspective. *Contemporary Educational Psychology, 22*, 73–101.

33

The Development of Arithmetic and Word-Problem Skill Among Students with Mathematics Disability

Lynn S. Fuchs, Sarah R. Powell, and Pamela M. Seethaler
Vanderbilt University

Paul T. Cirino and Jack M. Fletcher
University of Houston

Douglas Fuchs and Carol L. Hamlett
Vanderbilt University

Mathematics disability (MD) creates life-long challenges (Rivera-Batiz, 1992) for 5%–9% of the population (e.g., Badian, 1983; Gross-Tsur, Manor, & Shalev, 1996). This makes prevention, which has been shown to substantially improve mathematics outcomes (e.g., Fuchs, Fuchs, Yazdian, & Powell, 2002; Griffin, Case, & Siegler, 1994), critical. Nevertheless, no intervention is effective for all students. Fuchs et al. (2005), for example, showed that a first-grade prevention program was highly efficacious at reducing the prevalence of MD at the end of first grade, with effects maintaining one year after tutoring ended (Compton, Fuchs, & Fuchs, 2009). Yet, 3%–6% of the school population continued to manifest severe mathematics deficits. Because we cannot expect prevention activities to be universally effective, the need for intensive remedial intervention persists even when strong prevention services are in place.

In this chapter, we focus on the remediation of mathematics deficits. Our emphasis is on third grade when serious mathematics deficits are clearly established and identification of MD often begins (Fletcher, Lyon, Fuchs, & Barnes, 2007). We focus on arithmetic and word problems because they represent two major dimensions of the mathematics curriculum in the primary grades. We begin by providing background on these two aspects of mathematical cognition. We then summarize the literature on the remediation of arithmetic and word-problem deficits. Next, using this literature, we derive principles for effective remediation and illustrate these principles with one remedial tutoring protocol. Finally, we discuss salient issues concerning MD and its remediation.

Development of and Distinctions between Arithmetic and Word-Problem Skill

Arithmetic refers to simple computation problems (e.g., 5 + 6 = 11; 12 – 5 = 7) that cannot be solved via algorithms. To answer arithmetic problems, mathematically competent individuals, including children and adults, use a mix of counting strategies, decomposition strategies, and automatic retrieval of answers from long-term memory. Consensus exists that arithmetic is essential (Kilpatrick, Swafford, & Findell, 2001), and research shows that arithmetic fluency is a significant path to procedural calculation and word-problem skill (Fuchs, Fuchs, Compton, et al., 2006). In developing arithmetic fluency, typical children develop procedural efficiency with counting. First they count two sets (e.g., 4 + 5) in their entirety (i.e., 1, 2, 3, 4, 5, 6, 7, 8, 9); then they count from the first addend (i.e., 4, 5, 6, 7, 8, 9); and eventually they count from the larger addend (i.e., 5, 6, 7, 8, 9). As conceptual knowledge about number becomes more sophisticated, they also develop decomposition strategies for deriving answers (e.g., [4 + 4 = 8] + 1 = 9). As increasingly efficient counting and decomposition strategies facilitate consistent and quick pairing of problems with correct answers, associations become established in long-term memory, and students gradually favor memory-based retrieval of answers (Ashcraft & Stazyk, 1981; Geary, Widaman, Little, & Cormier, 1987; Goldman, Pellegrino, & Mertz, 1988; Groen & Parkman, 1972; Siegler, 1987).

Students with MD manifest greater difficulty with counting (Geary, Bow-Thomas, & Yao, 1992; Geary, Hoard, Byrd-Craven, Nugent, & Numtee, 2007); they persist with immature back-up strategies (Geary et al., 2007); and they fail to make the shift to memory-based retrieval of answers (Fleishner, Garnett, & Shepherd, 1982; Geary et al., 1987; Goldman et al., 1988). When children with MD do retrieve answers from memory, they commit more errors and their retrieval speeds are less systematic than younger, typically developing children (Geary, Brown, & Samaranayake, 1991; Gross-Tsur et al., 1996; Ostad, 1997). Some researchers (e.g., Fleishner et al., 1982.; Geary et al., 1987; Goldman et al., 1988) consider arithmetic to be a signature deficit of students with MD, and difficulty with automatic retrieval of arithmetic facts is one of the most consistent findings in the MD literature (e.g., Cirino, Ewing-Cobbs, Barnes, Fuchs, & Fletcher, 2007; Geary et al., 2007; Jordan, Hanich, & Kaplan, 2003).

Arithmetic is incorporated into the curriculum at kindergarten through second grade, although many general educators do not explicitly promote arithmetic fluency (Miller & Hudson, 2007). Even so, typically developing students have considerable arithmetic fluency by third grade (Cirino et al., 2007), and when students still manifest deficiencies in third grade, a pressing need for remediation exists.

Less is known about typical development or about how students with MD come to develop difficulty with word problems than is known about competence with arithmetic. In contrast to arithmetic, where problems are already set up for solution, a word problem requires students to use text to identify missing information, construct the number sentence that incorporates the missing information, derive the calculation problem for finding the missing information, and finally solve that calculation problem. The need to use text to construct the problem model appears to alter the task, and some research suggests that calculations and word problems may represent distinct aspects of mathematical cognition (e.g., Fuchs, Fuchs, Compton, et al., 2006; Fuchs, Fuchs, Stuebing, et al., 2008; Swanson & Beebe-Frankenberger, 2004). If so, then calculation and word-problem skill would need to be considered separately in remediation.

The Remediation Literature

Arithmetic

Three major approaches for remediating arithmetic deficits have been documented in the literature: providing drill and practice, developing conceptual understanding to foster decomposition strategies, and teaching strategic counting. The literature, however, has focused heavily on drill and practice. Okolo (1992) and Christensen and Gerber (1990) contrasted computerized drill and practice in a game versus a drill format. Okolo found no significant differences between groups. Christensen and Gerber, by contrast, found that students were disadvantaged by the game format, perhaps due to its distracting nature. Tournaki (2003) contrasted paper-pencil drill and practice with a strategic counting condition. Results showed an advantage for strategic counting, but the validity of the study was compromised because the strategic counting condition incorporated stronger instructional principles than did the drill and practice condition. All three prior studies failed to include a control group to assess whether drill and practice effected better outcomes than business-as-usual schooling. Also, because this work was restricted largely to drill and practice, it does not contrast alternative forms of intervention and therefore fails to inform the nature of remediation. In addition, because participants in these prior studies had school-identified learning disabilities, it is unclear whether effects apply to students who experience mathematics difficulty.

To address these limitations, we recently extended this literature in a series of four studies in which we relied on random assignment, incorporated different approaches to remediation, included a control condition, and screened participants to ensure MD. In the first study (Fuchs, Powell, et al., 2008), our approach to remediation was drill and practice although we took an unconventional approach. Instead of simply requiring students to answer arithmetic problems, as typically done with drill and practice, we tried to ensure that students would practice correct responses. Each computerized drill and practice trial occurred as follows: Students saw a complete arithmetic problem "flash" briefly (i.e., 1.3 sec) and then reproduced the complete arithmetic problem (i.e., question stem and answer) from short-term memory. The assumption was that with repeated pairings of a question stem and its correct answer, the student would commit the arithmetic problem to long-term memory. Typically developing students achieve such automatic retrieval through repeated pairings, which occur naturally as students' counting strategies become more efficient and their back-up strategies become more sophisticated. Given the deficiencies of students with MD with counting and decomposition strategies, we decided to test the efficacy of the "direct route" for reliable and efficient pairings just described. We randomly assigned participants to four conditions that all relied on computer-assisted instruction with tutor supervision: arithmetic remediation, procedural computation-estimation remediation, remediation that combined arithmetic with procedural computation-estimation instruction, and word identification remediation (i.e., control). On arithmetic outcomes, only students who received arithmetic remediation outperformed those in the competing conditions. Effect sizes were large (0.69–0.78). We concluded that a "direct route" for drill and practice, which promoted reliable and efficient pairings of question stems with correct responses, was efficacious. Even so, we questioned whether a stronger focus on developing conceptual understanding to foster decomposition strategies, the second major approach to remediating arithmetic problems, might enhance learning.

Consequently, Powell, Fuchs, Fuchs, Cirino, and Fletcher (2009) randomly assigned students to four conditions: drill and practice as in Study 1; drill and practice as in Study 1 plus explicit conceptual instruction focused largely on decomposition strategies; procedural computation-estimation remediation; and control (no tutoring). The initial conceptual lessons focused on addition and subtraction concepts, adding/subtracting 0 and 1, and the commutative property of addition. Then, a tutor-directed lesson occurred whenever a new arithmetic family was introduced (every 3 to 6 sessions). The tutor focused the student's attention on how number sentences within the family are related and used manipulatives to teach strategies for decomposition in relation to the 10 set and in relation to doubles arithmetic problems (e.g., 2 + 2 = 4). Students also practiced decomposition strategies with number line flash cards (students derived equations for depictions of arithmetic problems on a number line that delineated the 10 set) and generated arithmetic problems for a family in a fixed time. The condition with conceptual lessons was, by necessity, longer than the condition that relied entirely on drill and practice. Despite more instructional time, effect sizes comparing each arithmetic remediation to the control condition were similar: 0.50 and 0.53. The same was true when comparing each NC remediation to the procedural computation-estimation remediation: 0.31 and 0.37. This suggests that explicit conceptual instruction to help students develop decomposition strategies for solving arithmetic problems does not impart added value over a direct route for intensive drill and practice.

We next turned our attention to the third major approach for remediating arithmetic deficits: teaching strategic counting (Fuchs, Powell, Seethaler, et al., 2009). Although students are not explicitly taught strategic counting in school, typically developing students (but not students with MD) discover these strategies on their own (Ashcraft & Stazyk, 1981; Geary et al., 1987; Goldman et al., 1988; Groen & Parkman, 1972; Siegler, 1987). With inefficient counting strategies, MD students pair question stems with answers slowly, taxing short-term memory, and their answers are often incorrect. Long-term representations for automatic retrieval of arithmetic problems therefore fail to establish correctly. It is also possible that students with MD have special difficulty committing arithmetic problems to memory. We hoped that explicit instruction on counting strategies would build arithmetic fluency (even if students remained incapable of automatic retrieval). We contrasted two conditions that incorporated strategic counting. One combined strategic counting with intensive drill and practice (as in Studies 1 and 2). The other, which was embedded in word-problem remediation, taught the same strategic counting, but practice with arithmetic problems was confined to 4-6 min each session.

In this third study, we randomly assigned students to three conditions: strategic counting arithmetic remediation plus drill and practice as in Studies 1 and 2; word-problem remediation that incorporated strategic counting (without the drill and practice used in Studies 1 and 2); and control. Both remediations effected superior arithmetic fluency compared to the control group (effects sizes: 0.52 and 0.58). The comparability of outcomes for the two remediation groups is notable because the condition that incorporated drill and practice allocated dramatically more time to arithmetic over the 48-session intervention: 20–30 min per session versus 4–6 min per session. We, therefore, conclude that teaching students strategic counting, while providing frequent but brief practice to gain efficiency in using those counting strategies, results in arithmetic fluency that is comparable to an expanded arithmetic remediation that is devoted entirely to arithmetic and that also incorporates the drill and practice used in Studies 1 and 2. Study 3 results suggested promise for the strategic counting remediation.

In our fourth study (Fuchs, Powell, Seethaler, et al., 2010), we extended the Study 3 findings by assessing the effects of strategic counting instruction, with and without deliberate practice with those counting strategies, on arithmetic fluency. We contrasted a no-tutoring control group against two variants of strategic counting instruction. Both were embedded in word-problem remediation. In one variant, the focus on arithmetic was limited to a single lesson that simply taught the counting strategies (i.e., strategic counting instruction without deliberate practice). In the other variant, students were taught counting strategies in the same single lesson but then also practiced strategic counting for answering arithmetic problems for 4-6 min each session (i.e., strategic counting instruction with deliberate practice). Pinpointing the value of practice in this controlled way is important because although it is assumed necessary for students with MD, no studies had isolated its effects for this population of learners. Study 4 findings suggest its importance. The remediation condition that included deliberate practice with the counting strategies effected superior arithmetic fluency compared to the control condition, with a large effect size of 0.67. More important, students who received deliberate practice also outperformed those who were taught the counting strategies but were not provided with deliberate practice, with an effect size of 0.22. This effect size meets the federal What Works Clearinghouse criterion for effective practice.

Word Problems

The major approach in the research literature for developing word-problem skill for students with learning difficulties relies on schema theory, which is based on the concept of lateral transfer by which children recognize problems across numerous experiences to abstract generalized problem-solving strategies. Some refer to the abstraction of generalized problem-solving strategies as the development of schemas (Brown et al., 1992; Gick & Holyoake, 1983). A *schema* is a category that encompasses similar problems; it is a problem type (Chi, Feltovich, & Glaser, 1981; Gick & Holyoake, 1983; Quilici & Mayer, 1996). For example, word problems that describe parts being combined into a whole represent a "Total" problem type (e.g., John has 3 cats. He also has 5 dogs. How many pets does John have?); by contrast, the "Difference" problem type compares two quantities (e.g., John has 5 pets. His best friend has 2 pets. How many more pets does John have?). Instruction based on schema theory encourages students to develop a schema for each problem type. The broader the schema, the greater the probability students will recognize a novel problem as belonging to that familiar schema for which they know a solution method. With broader schemas, problem-solving performance improves. For example, a problem that belongs to a familiar problem type may appear novel (but still require a similar solution strategy) because it incorporates irrelevant information or relevant information outside of the problem narrative (e.g., in tables) or includes unusual vocabulary and so on. When students have broad schemas that systematically incorporate novel features, they know when to apply solution strategies, enhancing the word-problem performance. Broadening schemas should affect breadth of learning or transfer (Brown et al., 1992; Glaser, 1984).

To facilitate schema development, teachers must first teach problem-solution rules and then help students develop schemas for the problem types and awareness of those schemas (Cooper & Sweller, 1987). In the past decade, some research programs have relied on schema theory to design explicit instruction for enhancing word-problem skill. Jitendra and colleagues demonstrated acquisition, maintenance, and transfer effects for students with serious mathematics deficits or with risk for MD at eighth grade (Jitendra, DiPipi, & Perron-Jones, 2002), sixth grade (Xin, Jitendra, & Deatline-Buchman, 2005), and third and fourth grades (Jitendra et al., 2007; Jitendra et al., 1998; Jitendra & Hoff, 1996). In our intervention work, we have also relied on schema theory. Similar to Jitendra's schema-based strategy instruction, we teach students to understand the underlying mathematical structure of the problem type, to recognize the basic problem type, and to solve the problem type. In contrast to Jitendra, we incorporate a fourth instructional component, in keeping with Cooper and Sweller (1987), by explicitly teaching students to broaden those schema by learning about transfer features (e.g., irrelevant information; novel questions that require an extra step; relevant information presented in charts; combinations of problem types). In our work, we have addressed these and other transfer features. The addition of explicit instruction on transfer features should lead to more flexible and successful problem solving. We refer to the combination of all four instructional components as *schema-broadening instruction*, or SBI.

In our first randomized control study, Fuchs, Fuchs, Prentice, Burch, Hamlett, Owen, et al. (2003) isolated the effects of our fourth instructional component (explicitly teaching for transfer) from the first three instructional components (teaching students to understand the underlying mathematical structure of the problem type, to recognize the basic problem type, and to solve the problem type). Working with third graders without MD, we found that SBI (i.e., all four components) strengthened word-problem performance over and beyond experimenter-designed instruction on the first three instructional components. In a series of additional studies on SBI, also conducted in general education (Fuchs, Fuchs, Craddock, et al., 2008; Fuchs, Fuchs, Finelli, Courey, & Hamlett; 2004; Fuchs, Fuchs, Finelli, et al., 2006; Fuchs, Fuchs, Prentice, Burch, Hamlett, Owen, & Schroeter, 2003; Fuchs, Fuchs, Prentice, Hamlett, et al., 2004), effect sizes favoring SBI were large (0.89–2.14). Random assignment, however, occurred at the classroom level, with limited numbers of students with MD.

More recently, Fuchs, Seethaler, et al. (2008) piloted SBI, this time conducted as tutoring rather than whole-class instruction, for third graders whom we identified as having mathematics and reading difficulties (i.e., scoring on average at the 10th percentile in math and reading). The 35 participants were randomly assigned to receive SBI tutoring or to continue in their mathematics program without modification. Results favored the word-problem performance among the tutored students, but instructional time across the tutored and control students was not controlled, a limitation we addressed in our next study (Fuchs, Powell, Seethaler, et al., 2009), where we contrasted SBI tutoring not only to a control group but also to a contrasting tutoring condition. Results supported the efficacy of SBI tutoring in relation to the control group as well as the competing, active condition, and findings were replicated in Fuchs, Powell, Seethaler, et al., (2010).

General Principles for Effective Mathematics Remediation

In this section, we provide an overview of a set of principles for remediating arithmetic and word-problem deficits. Then, we illustrate the application of these principles using one remedial tutoring protocol.

Seven Research-Based Principles for Effective Remediation

The first principle of effective intervention for students with MD is *instructional explicitness*. Typically developing students profit from the general education mathematics program that relies, at least in part, on a constructivist, inductive approach to instruction. Students who accrue serious mathematics deficits, however, fail to profit from those programs in a way that produces understanding of the structure, meaning, and operational requirements of mathematics. A meta-analysis of 58 math studies (Kroesbergen & & Van Luit, 2003) revealed that students with MD benefit more from explicit instruction than from discovery-oriented methods. Therefore, effective intervention for students with MD requires explicit, didactic instruction in which the teacher directly shares the information the child needs to learn and systematically supports student mastery.

Explicitness is not, however, sufficient. A second and often overlooked principle of effective intensive mathematics intervention is *instructional design to minimize the learning challenge*. The goal is to anticipate and eliminate misunderstandings with precise explanations and with the use of carefully sequenced instruction so that the achievement gap can be closed as quickly as possible.

This is especially important given the ever-changing and multiple demands of the mathematics curriculum.

The third principle of effective intensive mathematics intervention is the requirement that instruction provide a *strong conceptual basis* for procedures. Special education is already strong in emphasizing *drill and practice*, a critical and fourth principle of effective practice. Yet, special education has sometimes neglected the conceptual foundation of mathematics, and such neglect can cause confusion, learning gaps, and a failure to maintain and integrate previously mastered content. In terms of drill and practice, we note that this practice needs to be rich in *cumulative review*, the fifth principle of effective intervention.

The sixth principle concerns the need to incorporate *motivators to help students regulate their attention and behavior and to work hard*. Students with learning disabilities often display attention, motivation, and self-regulation difficulties, which may adversely affect their behavior and learning (e.g., Fuchs et al., 2005, 2006). By the time students enter intensive intervention, they have experienced repeated failure, causing many to avoid the emotional stress associated with mathematics. They no longer try to learn for fear of failing. Therefore, intensive intervention must incorporate systematic self-regulation strategies and motivators; for many students, tangible reinforcers are required.

The seventh and final principle of remediation is the need for *systematic, ongoing progress monitoring* to gauge the effectiveness of a tutoring program for the individual student. No instructional method, even those validated using randomized control studies, works for all students. Because schools must assume that validated intervention protocols will work for most but not all students, schools need to monitor the effects of interventions on individual children's learning. That way, children who do not respond adequately can be identified promptly, and the teacher can adjust the intervention to develop an individually tailored instructional program. This leads us to a seventh essential principle of intensive remedial programming: ongoing progress monitoring. Teachers use progress monitoring to determine whether a validated treatment protocol is in fact effective for a given student. When progress monitoring reveals that a student is failing to respond as expected to a validated intervention protocol, progress monitoring is then used for a second purpose: to formulate an individually tailored instructional program that is in fact effective for that student.

Incorporating the Seven Research-Based Principles for Effective Remediation: A Sample Tutoring Protocol

To illustrate the use of the first six research-based principles for effective remediation, we describe a validated tutoring program called Pirate Math, designed to remediate arithmetic as well as word-problem deficits while building procedural calculation and algebra skill. We incorporate a pirate theme because within this schema-broadening instructional program, students are taught to represent the underlying structure of word problem types using algebraic equations. "They find X, just like Pirates find X on treasure maps." After we describe Pirate Math and explain how it incorporates the first six principles of effective remediation, we then explain how one special education teacher implemented Pirate Math in conjunction with systematic, ongoing progress monitoring, the seventh instructional principle, to assess the student's response to Pirate Math and to individualize the student's program as required.

How Pirate Math addresses the first six principles of effective remediation. Pirate Math comprises four units: an introductory unit, which addresses mathematics skills foundational to solving word problems, and three word-problem units, each focused on a different type of word problem. Pirate Math has been validated for use in small groups as a secondary prevention intervention; it has also been validated for one-to-one implementation at the tertiary prevention level. Every tutoring lesson is scripted, but scripts are studied; they are not read or memorized. Pirate Math runs for 16 weeks, with 48 sessions (3 per week). Each session lasts 20–30 min. The instruction, as outlined below, is *systematic and explicit*; it is designed with care to *minimize the learning challenge*; it is rich in ***concepts***; it incorporates *drill and practice* as well as *cumulative review*; and it relies on *systematic reinforcement* to encourage good attention, hard work, and accurate performance.

The introductory unit addresses mathematics skills foundational to word problems. Tutors teach a single lesson on strategic counting for deriving answers to arithmetic problems, review algorithms for double-digit addition and subtraction procedural calculations, teach methods to solve for "X" in any position in simple algebraic equations (i.e., $a + b = c$; $d - e = f$), and teach strategies for checking work within word problems.

The single strategic counting lesson is designed to remediate arithmetic deficits. Students are taught that if they "just know" the answer to an arithmetic problem, they "pull it out of their head." If, however, they do not know an answer immediately, they "count up." Strategic counting for addition and subtraction is introduced with the number line. For addition, the min strategy is taught: Students start with the bigger number and count up the smaller number on their fingers. The answer is the last number spoken. For subtraction, the missing addend counting strategy is taught, which requires new vocabulary. The *minus number* is the number directly after the minus sign. The *number you start with* is the first number in the equation. Students start with the minus number and count up to the number they start with. The answer is the number of fingers used to count up.

Practice in strategic counting is then incorporated in subsequent lessons. The tutor begins each session by asking the student, "What are the two ways to find an answer to a math fact?" The student responds, "Know it or count up." Then, the student explains how to count up an addition problem and how to count up a subtraction problem. Next, the tutor requires the student to count up two addition and two subtraction problems. Then, the tutor conducts a flash card warm-up activity, in which students have 1 min to answer arithmetic problems. If they respond incorrectly, the tutor requires them to count up until they derive the correct answer. At the end of 1 min. the tutor counts the cards, and the student then has another min to beat the first score. Also, throughout the lesson, whenever the student makes an arithmetic error, the tutor requires the student to count up. Finally, when checking the paper-pencil review, the tutor corrects arithmetic errors by demonstrating the counting strategy.

Each of the three word-problem units focuses on one word problem type and, after the first problem-type unit, subsequent units provide systematic, mixed cumulative review that includes previously taught problem types. The word problem types are Total (two or more amounts being combined), Difference (two amounts being compared), and Change (initial amount that increases or decreases). Each word-problem session comprises six activities. The first is the counting strategies review and flash card warm-up already described.

Word-problem warm-up, the next activity, lasts approximately 2 min and is initiated during the first word-problem unit. The tutor shows the student the word problem that the student had solved during the previous day's paper-and-pencil review. The student explains to the tutor how he or she solved the problem.

Conceptual and strategic instruction is the next activity. It lasts 15–20 min Tutors provide scaffolded instruction in the underlying structure of and in solving the three types of word problems (i.e., developing a schema for each problem type), along with instruction on identifying and integrating transfer features (to broaden students' schema for each problem type), using role-playing, manipulatives, instructional posters, modeling, and guided practice. In each lesson, students solve three word problems, with decreasing amounts of support from the tutor.

In the Total unit, the first problem type covered, tutors teach students to RUN through a problem: a 3-step strategy prompting students to Read the problem, Underline the question, and Name the problem type. Students used the RUN strategy across all three problem types. Next, for each problem type (i.e., schema), students are taught an algebraic equation to represent the underlying structure of that problem type and to identify and circle the relevant information that fills the slots of that equation. For example, for Total problems, students circle the item being combined and the numerical values representing that item, and then label the circled numerical values as "P1" (i.e., for part one), "P2" (i.e., for part two), and "T" (i.e., for the combined total). Students mark the missing information with an "X" and construct an algebraic equation representing the underlying mathematical structure of the problem type. For Total problems, the algebraic equation takes the form of "P1 + P2 = T," and the "X" can appear in any of the three variable positions. Students are taught to solve for X, to provide a word label for the answer, and to check the reasonableness and accuracy of work. The strategy for Difference problems and Change problems follows similar steps but uses variables and equations specific to those problem types. For Difference problems, students are taught to look for the bigger amount (labeled "B"), the smaller amount (labeled "s"), and the difference between amounts (labeled "D"), and to use the algebraic equation "B – s = D." For Change problems, students are taught to locate the starting amount (labeled "St"), the changed amount (labeled "C"), and the ending amount (labeled "E"); the algebraic equation for Change problems is "St +/– C = E" (+/– depends on whether the change is an increase or decrease in amount).

For each problem type, explicit instruction to broaden schemas occurs in six ways. First, students are taught that because not all numerical values in word problems are relevant for finding solutions, they should identify and cross out irrelevant information as they identify the problem type. Second, students are taught to recognize and solve word problems with the missing information in the first or second position of the algebraic equation that represents the underlying structure of the problem type. Third, students learn to apply the problem-solving strategies to word problems that involve addition and subtraction with double-digit numbers with and without regrouping. Fourth, students learn to solve problems involving money. Fifth, students are taught to find relevant information for solving word problems in pictographs, bar charts, and pictures. Finally, students learn to solve 2-step problems that involve two problems of the same problem type or that combine problem types. Across the three problem-type units, previously taught problem types are included for review and practice.

Sorting word problems is the next activity. Tutors read aloud flash cards, each displaying a word problem. The student identifies the word problem type, placing the card on a mat with four boxes labeled "Total," "Difference," "Change," or "?." Students do not solve word problems; they sort them by problem type. To discourage students from associating a cover story with a problem type, the cards use similar cover stories with varied numbers, actions, and placement of missing information. After 2 min, the tutor notes the number of correctly sorted cards and provides corrective feedback for up to three errors.

In *paper-and-pencil review*, the final activity, students have 2 min to complete nine number sentences asking the student to find X. Then, students have 2 min to complete one word problem. Tutors provide corrective feedback and note the number of correct problems on the paper. Tutors require students to count up arithmetic errors, and keep the paper-and-pencil review sheet for the next day's *word-problem warm-up* activity.

A systematic *reinforcement* program is incorporated. Throughout each Pirate Math session, tutors award gold coins following each activity, with the option to withhold coins for inattention or poor effort. Throughout the session, each gold coin earned is placed on a "Treasure Map." Sixteen coins lead to a picture of a treasure box and, when reached, the student chooses a small prize from a real treasure box. The student keeps the old Treasure Map and receives a new map in the next lesson.

How Pirate Math addresses the first seventh principle of effective remediation. As shown in a series of field-based randomized control trials (Fuchs, Powell, Seethaler, et al., 2009; Fuchs, Powell, Seethaler, et al., 2010; Fuchs, Seethaler, et al., 2008), Pirate Math results in statistically significant and practically important effects on arithmetic fluency and word problems, even as it promotes better performance on procedural calculations and algebra. So Pirate Math is demonstrably efficacious. Nevertheless, as noted, no instructional method, even those validated using randomized control studies, works for all students. This makes it necessary to incorporate *ongoing progress monitoring* as an essential element of intensive remedial programming. Teachers use progress monitoring to determine whether a validated treatment protocol is in fact effective for a given student. When progress monitoring reveals that a student is failing to respond as expected to a validated intervention protocol, progress monitoring is then used to formulate an individually tailored instructional program that is in fact effective for that student.

Curriculum-based measurement (CBM) is the form of progress monitoring for which the preponderance of research has been conducted. To illustrate how CBM is used, consider the case of Francisco, a hypothetical student, who developed sizeable math deficits over the course of first and second grade, despite strong general education programming and even though small-group tutoring was implemented during the spring semester of second grade. At the beginning of third grade, Francisco was identified for remedial intervention. Mrs. LaBelle, the special education teacher, set Francisco's mathematics goal for year-end performance as competent second-grade performance. Relying on established methods, Mrs. LaBelle identified enough CBM tests to assess Francisco's performance each week across the school year. Each test systematically samples the second-grade mathematics curriculum in the same way, is administered in the same way, and is of equivalent difficulty. Each weekly score is an indicator of mathematics competence at the second grade. At the beginning of the year, she expected Francisco's performance to be low but as she addressed the curriculum over the school year, she expected his scores to gradually increase. Because each progress-monitoring test collected across the school year is of equivalent difficulty, each week's scores can be graphed and directly compared to each other. Also, a slope can be calculated on the series of scores. This slope quantifies Francisco's rate of improvement in terms of the weekly increase in score. In addition, because each week's assessment samples the annual curriculum in the same way, Mrs. LaBelle can derive a systematic analysis of which skills Francisco has and has not mastered at any point in time, and Mrs. LaBelle can look across time at a given skill to determine how Francisco's mastery has changed.

A large body of work indicates that CBM progress monitoring enhances teachers' capacity to plan mathematics programs and to effect stronger mathematics achievement among students with serious learning problems (Fuchs & Fuchs, 1998). To inform instructional planning, teachers rely on the CBM graphed scores. Once the teacher sets the year-end goal, the teacher draws the desired score on the graph at the date corresponding to the end of the year. The teacher then draws a straight line connecting the student's beginning-of-the-year score with the year-end goal. This line is called the goal line. It represents the approximate rate of weekly improvement (or slope) teachers hope a student will achieve. When a student's trend line (i.e., the slope through the student's actual scores) is steeper than the goal line, the teacher increases the goal for the student's year-end performance. When a student's trend line is flatter than the goal line, the teacher relies on her knowledge about the student along with a CBM analysis of the student's skills, derived from the CBM data, to revise the instructional program in an attempt to boost the weekly rate of student learning. Research shows that with CBM decision rules, teachers design more varied instructional programs that are more responsive to individual needs (Fuchs, Fuchs, & Hamlett, 1989b), that incorporate more ambitious student goals (Fuchs, Fuchs, & Hamlett, 1989a), and that result in stronger end-of-year scores on commercial, standardized tests (e.g., Fuchs et al., 1989a; Fuchs, Fuchs, Hamlett, & Stecker, 1991).

When Mrs. LaBelle assumed responsibility for Francisco's remediation program, she decided to use Pirate Math. This entailed tutoring for 30 min per session, three times per week. As Mrs. LaBelle began to implement this validated protocol, she also began to administer the CBM tests once each week for computation and once each week for concepts/applications. Mrs. LaBelle calculated Francisco's baseline or beginning-of-the-year performance, the median of his first three scores. Using CBM guidelines for goal setting, she decided that Francisco's year-end goal would require a weekly increase of .5 digits for computation and a weekly increase of .6 points for concepts/applications. So 25 weeks later, at the end of the school year, Francisco's year-end goal would be 18 digits correct on CBM computation and 18 points correct on CBM concepts/applications. Ten weeks later, Mrs. LaBelle compared lines of best fit through Francisco's actual CBM scores; calculated the slope of his actual improvement; and compared the slope against the desired rates of improvement (a weekly increase of .5 digits for computation and a weekly increase of .6 points for concepts/applications).

The CBM data showed that Pirate Math, with its focus on number combinations and procedural calculations, was producing strong growth for Francisco: His actual rate of improvement was steeper than the goal line. By contrast, Francisco was proving insufficiently unresponsive to Pirate Math's word-problem instruction, in which his actual rate of improvement was dramatically less steep than the goal line. Therefore, Mrs. LaBelle modified the Pirate Math standard protocol. She considered Francisco's performance during tutoring sessions and reviewed his performance on the CBM concepts/applications story problems. She determined that he was having difficulty differentiating problem types when irrelevant information was included in problems and when the missing information in problems occurred anywhere but the final position in the number sentence. Based on this analysis, Mrs. LaBelle added instruction on mixed problem types, lengthened the problem-type sorting activity, and added instructional time on irrelevant information and deriving number sentences when the missing information is in the first or second slot of the equation. As she implemented this revision in the intervention protocol, Mrs. LaBelle continued to monitor Francisco's responsiveness using weekly CBM. His learning improved; his slope grew steeper than the goal line. Teachers can use CBM in this formative, inductive, and recursive way to derive individual instructional programs that are effective for individual students and increase the probability of improved student outcomes.

Salient Issues Concerning MD and Its Remediation

In this section, we discuss three issues concerning MD and it remediation. The first issue is whether difficulty with arithmetic represents a bottleneck for successful performance with other mathematics skills and for students with MD (e.g., Fleishner et al., 1982; Geary et al., 1987; Goldman et al., 1988). The hypothesis is that, with a fixed amount of attention, students with arithmetic deficits allocate available resources for deriving answers to these simple problems instead of focusing on the more complex mathematics into which the arithmetic is embedded (cf. Ackerman, Anhalt, & Dykman, 1986; Goldman & Pellegrino, 1987). If arithmetic represents a bottleneck deficit, performance on more complex mathematics tasks should improve simply as a function of remediating arithmetic deficits, just as decoding intervention has been shown to improve reading comprehension (Blachman et al., 2004; Torgesen et al., 2001). An alternative perspective exists in the mathematics education literature that challenges the assumption of such vertical transfer, whereby mastery of simple skills facilitates acquisition of more complex skills (Gagne, 1968; Resnick & Resnick, 1992).

Few researchers have examined whether remediation of arithmetic deficits transfers to more complex math skills. Research conducted by Fuchs et al., which systematically assesses this issue, suggests that transfer may occur to some but not all aspects of mathematical performance. In some studies (Fuchs, Powell, Seethaler, et al., 2009; Fuchs, Powell, Seethaler, et al., 2010), we found support for this "bottleneck" hypothesis in the transfer we observed from arithmetic remediation to procedural calculation outcomes. And evidence for transfer was not entirely consistent (see Fuchs, Powell, et al., 2008; Powell et al., 2009). Moreover, we found no evidence in any study to support the bottleneck hypothesis on word-problem outcomes. With arithmetic improvement (but in the absence of word-problem tutoring), students with MD evidenced no improvement in solving word problems. This suggests that the source of their difficulty is not diverting attention from the complex mathematics to the arithmetic embedded in those problems, but rather failing to comprehend the relations among the numbers embedded in the narratives or to process the language in those stories adequately. Thus, arithmetic does not appear to be the bottleneck for word-problem performance. Instead, MD may represent a more complicated pattern of difficulty, implicating language as has been suggested elsewhere (e.g., Fuchs et al., 2005, 2006). Given these contradictory findings about transfer, in which some evidence supports transfer from arithmetic remediation to procedural calculations but no study has shown transfer to word problems, future work should continue to explore this issue.

The second issue concerns subtyping of MD. Because a key deficit associated with reading difficulty is phonological processing (Bruck, 1992) and because phonological processing deficits are linked to difficulty with automatic retrieval of math facts (Fuchs et al., 2005), students with concurrent difficulty in mathematics and reading (MDRD) should experience greater difficulty with arithmetic compared to students who experience difficulty only with mathematics (MD-only; Geary, 1993). Some research suggests that compared to students with MDRD, those with MD-only use more efficient counting procedures to solve arithmetic problems (Geary, Hamson, & Hoard, 2000; Jordan & Hanich, 2000) with faster retrieval times (Andersson & Lyxell, 2007; Hanich, Jordan, Kaplan, & Dick, 2001; Jordan & Montani, 1997) but with comparable accuracy (Cirino et al., 2007). However, the literature is not consistent (e.g., Micallef & Prior, 2004; Reikeras, 2006), and most studies have employed a cross-sectional causal-comparative design.

An alternative approach is experimental, whereby students are stratified as MDRD versus MD-only and then randomly assigned to treatment or control conditions. The goal is to determine whether the subtypes respond differentially to intervention. This design offers the basis for stronger, causal inferences about the tenability of the subtyping scheme. In each of four studies, we adopted this approach. We found limited support for the MD-only versus MDRD framework for subtyping MD. The only evidence we found of differential responsiveness was Powell et al. (2009). MD-only students responded nicely to both arithmetic remediation conditions (practice remediation and conceptual remediation), with effect sizes for both remediation conditions around one standard deviation. By contrast, MDRD students proved unresponsive, with effect sizes near zero for both remediations. It is difficult to explain why MDRD students were differentially unresponsive in Powell et al., but not in the other three studies. In fact, the Powell et al. practice remediation was identical to the Fuchs et al. (2008) drill and practice remediation (which proved comparably efficacious for students with MD-only and MDRD). Moreover, the Fuchs, Powell, Seethaler, Cirino, Fletcher, Fuchs, Hamlett, and Zumeta (2009) counting strategies remediation was designed to circumvent the need for automatic retrieval, the hypothesized bottleneck for MDRD students. For that reason, we had hypothesized that the MDRD students might prove differentially responsive to the counting-up strategies than to the practice remediation; however, the response to both conditions was similar.

One explanation for the differential unresponsiveness in Powell et al. (2009) may involve the nature of the sample. Although students were screened in the same way for inclusion in all four studies, IQ for the Powell et al. (2009) MDRD sample scored, on average, 13 standard score points lower relative to their MD-only counterparts; by contrast, the IQ difference between MD-only and MDRD in each of the other studies was 7 points. When we incorporated IQ as a covariate in the Powell et al. analyses, findings remained similar. Even so, the lower IQ may explain the differentially poor response in Powell et al. or a third variable may explain the Powell et al. findings of MDRD students' low IQ scores as well as their poor response. Future work should explore the demographic and child characteristics associated with poor response to arithmetic remediation generally and in the context of the MDRD versus MD subtyping framework. Such research may provide important information about what drives arithmetic deficits and the nature of MD. It may also prove useful for guiding future intervention work. In the meantime, our line of experimental studies does not lend support to the MDRD/MD subtyping framework.

Our final issue concerns the treatment of MD. As already noted, despite the statistically significant and practically important effects associated with some remediation efforts, practitioners must always be mindful of individual response. That is, validated protocols will not work for all students, and schools therefore need to systematically monitor the effects of those validated remediations on individuals' learning and, when a validated protocol proves insufficiently effective, use the resulting data to tailor individualized programs. But the question remains: Once we determine, via ongoing progress monitoring, that a standard, validated remediation is not working, how might individual tailoring proceed?

One possibility is a skills-based diagnostic-prescriptive approach. For nonresponders, at the beginning of remediation, assessment might be conducted to determine the strategies with which a student derives answers to arithmetic problems (e.g., Siegler & Shrager, 1984). Then, using a menu of remediations developed to promote automatic retrieval with drill and practice versus to help students become fluent with counting strategies versus to build conceptual knowledge underlying math facts, the tutor might match the remediation approach to the student's profile of strategies. For example, if the assessment indicates that Wendy primarily relies on the immature total counting strategy to derive answers, the counting strategies remediation, with its focus on the more efficient counting strategies, might prove useful. Once Wendy consistently applies the min counting strategy with accuracy and fluency, the tutor might begin implementing conceptual lessons. After decomposition strategies associated with conceptual lessons are firm, the tutor might introduce intensive computerized practice. By contrast, let's say that Robert's strategy assessment reveals strong understanding of back-up (min counting as well as decomposition) strategies, but he nevertheless demonstrates an absence of automatic retrieval. For Robert, the tutor might intensify the repeated flash card activity, whereby students correct errors using back-up strategies they have mastered efficiently, trying to beat previous scores (as in repeated reading) with correct and fluent responding. Furthermore, the tutor might systematically mix the repeated flash card activity with computerized drill and practice, requiring Robert to apply his back-up strategies. And so on. A variation on this individualized approach was suggested by Goldman et al. (1988) when they documented clusters of students with different strategy patterns. Yet, to our knowledge, no research on its efficacy has been conducted. Experimental studies are needed to contrast such a diagnostic-prescriptive remediation against a standard protocol.

Authors' Note

Work on this chapter was supported in part by Core Grant Number P30HD15052 from the National Institute of Child Health and Human Development to Vanderbilt University; by Award Number P01046261 from the National Institute of Child Health and Human Development to the University of Houston and through subcontract to Vanderbilt University; and by Award Number 1 RO1 HD46154 from the National Institute of Child Health and Human Development to Vanderbilt University. The content is solely the responsibility of the authors and does not necessarily represent the official views of the National Institute of Child Health and Human Development or the National Institutes of Health.

References

Ackerman, P. T., Anhalt, J. M., & Dykman, R.A. (1986). Arithmetic automatization failure in children with attention and reading disorders: Associations and sequaelae. *Journal of Learning Disabilities, 19*, 222–232.

Andersson, U., & Lyxell, B. (2007). Working memory deficit in children with mathematical difficulties: A general or specific deficit? *Journal of Experimental Child Psychology, 96*, 197–228.

Ashcraft, M. H., & Stazyk, E. H. (1981). Mental addition: A test of three verification models. *Memory & Cognition, 9*, 185–196.

Badian, N. A. (1983). Dyscalculia and nonverbal disorders of learning. In H .R. Myklebust (Ed.), *Progress in learning disabilities* (pp. 235–264). New York: Grune & Stratton.

Blachman, B. A., Schatschneider, C., Fletcher, J. M., Francis, D. J., Clonan, S.., Shaywitz, B. A., & Shaywitz, S. E. (2004). Effects of intensive reading remediation for second and third graders and a 1-year follow up. *Journal of Educational Psychology, 96*, 444–461.

Brown, A. L., Campione, J. C., Webber, L. S., & McGilly, K. (1992).

Interactive learning environments: A new look at assessment and instruction. In B. R. Gifford & M. C. O'Connor (Eds.), *Changing assessments: Alternative view of aptitude, achievement, and instruction* (pp. 37–75). Boston: Kluwer Academic.

Bruck, M. (1992). Persistence of dyslexics' phonological awareness deficits. *Developmental Psychology, 28*, 874–886.

Christensen, C. A., & Gerber, M. M. (1990). Effectiveness of computerized drill and practice games in teaching basic math facts. *Exceptionality, 1*, 149–165.

Cirino, P. T., Ewing-Cobbs, L., Barnes, M., Fuchs, L. S., & Fletcher, J. M. (2007). Cognitive arithmetic differences in learning disability groups and the role of behavioral inattention. *Learning Disabilities Research and Practice, 22*, 25–35.

Compton, D. L., Fuchs, L. S., & Fuchs, D. (2009). *The development course of reading and mathematics learning disabilities.* Manuscript submitted for publication.

Cooper, G., & Sweller, J. (1987). Effects of schema acquisition and rule automation on mathematical problem solving transfer. *Journal of Educational Psychology, 79*, 347–362.

Fleishner, J. E., Garnett, K., & Shepherd, M. J. (1982). Proficiency in arithmetic basic fact computation of learning disabled and nondisabled children. *Focus on Learning Problems in Mathematics, 4*, 47–56.

Fletcher, J. M., Lyon, G. R., Fuchs, L. S., & Barnes, M. A. (2007). *Learning disabilities: From identification to intervention.* New York: Guilford.

Fuchs, L. S., Compton, D. L., Fuchs, D., Paulsen, K., Bryant, J. D., & Hamlett, C. L. (2005). The prevention, identification, and cognitive determinants of math difficulty. *Journal of Educational Psychology, 97*, 493–513.

Fuchs, L. S., & Fuchs, D. (1998). Treatment validity: A unifying concept for reconceptualizing the identification of learning disabilities. *Learning Disabilities Research and Practice, 13*, 204–219.

Fuchs, L. S., Fuchs, D., Compton, D. L., Powell, S. R., Seethaler, P M., Capizzi, … Fletcher, J. M. (2006). The cognitive correlates of third-grade skill in arithmetic, algorithmic computation, and arithmetic word problems. *Journal of Educational Psychology, 98*, 29–43.

Fuchs, L S., Fuchs, D., Craddock, C., Hollenbeck, K. N., Hamlett, C. L., & Schatschneider, C. (2008). Effects of small-group tutoring with and without validated classroom instruction on at-risk students' math problem solving: Are two tiers of prevention better than one? *Journal of Educational Psychology, 100*, 491–509.

Fuchs, L. S., Fuchs, D., Finelli, R., Courey, S. J., & Hamlett, C. L. (2004). Expanding schema-based transfer instruction to help third graders solve real-life mathematical problems. *American Educational Research Journal, 41*, 419–445.

Fuchs, L. S., Fuchs, D., Finelli, R., Courey, S. J., Hamlett, C. L., Sones, E. M., & Hope, S. K. (2006). Teaching third graders about real-life mathematical problem solving: A randomized controlled study. *Elementary School Journal, 106*, 293–312.

Fuchs, L. S., Fuchs, D., & Hamlett, C. L. (1989a). Effects of alternative goal structures within curriculum-based measurement. *Exceptional Children, 55*, 429–438.

Fuchs, L. S., Fuchs, D., & Hamlett, C. L. (1989b). Effects of instrumental use of curriculum-based measurement to enhance instructional programs. *Remedial and Special Education, 10*(2), 43–52.

Fuchs, L. S., Fuchs, D., Hamlett, C. L., & Stecker, P. M. (1991). Effects of curriculum-based measurement and consultation on teacher planning and student achievement in mathematics operations. *American Educational Research Journal, 28*, 617–641.

Fuchs, L. S., Fuchs, D., Prentice, K., Burch, M., Hamlett, C. L., Owen, … Janeck, D. (2003). Explicitly teaching for transfer: Effects on third-grade students' mathematical problem solving. *Journal of Educational Psychology, 95*, 293–304.

Fuchs, L. S., Fuchs, D., Prentice, K., Burch, M., Hamlett, C. L., Owen, R., & Schroeter, K. (2003). Enhancing third-grade students' mathematical problem solving with self-regulated learning strategies. *Journal of Educational Psychology, 95*, 306–315.

Fuchs, L.S., Fuchs, D., Prentice, K., Hamlett, C. L., Finelli, R., Courey, S. J. (2004). Enhancing mathematical problem solving among third-grade students with schema-based instruction. *Journal of Educational Psychology, 96*, 635–647.

Fuchs, L. S., Fuchs, D., Stuebing, K., Fletcher, J. M., Hamlett, C. L., & Lambert, W. E. (2008). Problem solving and calculation skill: Shared or distinct aspects of mathematical cognition? *Journal of Educational Psychology, 100*, 30–47.

Fuchs, L. S., Fuchs, D., Yazdian, L., & Powell, S. R. (2002). Enhancing first-grade children's mathematical development with peer-assisted learning strategies. *School Psychology Review, 31*, 569–583.

Fuchs, L. S., Powell, S. R., Hamlett, C. L., Fuchs, D., Cirino, P. T., & Fletcher, J. M. (2008). Remediating computational deficits at third grade: A randomized field trial. *Journal of Research on Educational Effectiveness, 1*, 2–32.

Fuchs, L. S., Powell, S. R., Seethaler, P. M., Cirino, P. T., Fletcher, J. M., Fuchs, D., & Hamlett, C. L. (2010). The effects of strategic counting instruction, with and without deliberate practice, on number combination skill among students with mathematics difficulties. *Learning and Individual Differences, 20*, 89–100.

Fuchs, L. S., Powell, S. R., Seethaler, P. M., Cirino, P. T., Fletcher, J. M., Fuchs, … Zumeta, R. O. (2009). Remediating number combination and word problem deficits among students with mathematics difficulties: A randomized control trial. *Journal of Educational Psychology, 101*, 561–576.

Fuchs, L. S., Seethaler, P. M., Powell, S. R., Fuchs, D., Hamlett, C. L., & Fletcher, J. M. (2008). Effects of preventative tutoring on the mathematical problem solving of third-grade students with math and reading difficulties. *Exceptional Children, 74*, 155–173.

Geary, D. C. (1993). Mathematical disabilities: Cognitive, neuropsychological, and genetic components. *Psychological Bulletin, 114*, 345–362.

Geary, D. C., Bow-Thomas, C. C., & Yao, Y. (1992). Counting knowledge and skill in cognitive addition: A comparison of normal and mathematically disabled children. *Journal of Experimental Child Psychology, 54*, 372–391.

Geary, D. C., Brown, S. C, & Samaranayake, V. A. (1991). Cognitive addition: A short longitudinal study of strategy choice and speed-of-processing differences in normal and mathematically disabled children. *Developmental Psychology, 27*, 787–797.

Geary, D. C., Hamson, C. O., & Hoard, M. K. (2000). Numerical and arithmetical cognition: A longitudinal study of process and concept deficits in children with learning disability. *Journal of Experimental Child Psychology, 77*, 236–263.

Geary, D. C., Hoard, M. K., Byrd-Craven, J., Nugent, L., & Numtee, C. (2007). Cognitive mechanisms underlying achievement deficits in children with mathematics learning disability. *Child Development, 78*, 1343–1359.

Geary, D. C., Widaman, K. F., Little, T. D., & Cormier, P. (1987). Cognitive addition: Comparison of learning disabled and academically normal elementary school children. *Cognitive Development, 2*, 249–269.

Gick, M. L., & Holyoake, K. J. (1983). Schema induction and analogical transfer. *Cognitive Psychology, 15*, 1–38.

Glaser, R. (1984). Education and thinking: The role of knowledge. *American Psychologist, 39*, 93–104.

Goldman, S. R., & Pellegrino, J. W. (1987). Information processing and educational microcomputer technology: Where do we go from here? *Journal of Learning Disabilities, 20*, 249–269.

Goldman, S. R., Pellegrino, J. W., & Mertz, D. L. (1988). Extended practice of addition facts: Strategy changes in learning-disabled students. *Cognition and Instruction, 5*, 223–265.

Griffin, S., Case, R., & Siegler, R. S. (1994). Rightstart: Providing the conceptual prerequisites for first formal learning of arithmetic to students at risk for school failure. In K. McGilly (Ed.), *Classroom lessons: Integrating cognitive theory and classroom practice* (pp. 25–50). Cambridge, MA: MIT Press.

Groen, G. J., & Parkman, J. M. (1972). A chronometric analysis of simple addition. *Psychological Review, 79*, (329–343.

Gross-Tsur, V., Manor, O., & Shalev, R. S. (1996). Developmental dyscalculia: Prevalence and demographic features. *Developmental Medicine and Child Neurology, 37*, 906–914.

Hanich, L. B., Jordan, N. C., Kaplan, D., & Dick, J. (2001). Performance across different areas of mathematical cognition in children with learning difficulties. *Journal of Educational Psychology, 93,* 615–626.

Jitendra, A. K., DiPipi, C. M., & Perron-Jones, N. (2002). An exploratory study of schema-based word-problem solving instruction for middle school students with learning disabilities: An emphasis on conceptual and procedural understanding. *The Journal of Special Education, 36*, 23–38.

Jitendra, A. K., Griffin, C. C., Haria, P., Leh, J., Adams, A., & Kaduvettor, A. (2007). A comparison of single and multiple strategy instruction on third-grade students' mathematical problem solving. *Journal of Educational Psychology, 99*, 115–127.

Jitendra, A. K., Griffin, C. C., McGoey, K., Gardill, M. C., Bhat, P., & Riley, T. (1998). Effects of mathematical word problem solving by students at risk or with mild disabilities. *Journal of Educational Research, 91*, 345–355.

Jitendra, A. K., & Hoff, K. (1996). The effects of schema-based instruction on the word-problem-solving performance of students with learning disabilities. *Journal of Learning Disabilities, 29*, 421–431.

Jordan, N. C., & Hanich, L. (2000). Mathematical thinking in second-grade children with different forms of LD. *Journal of Learning Disabilities, 33*, 567–578.

Jordan, N. C., Hanich, L. B., & Kaplan, D. (2003). Arithmetic fact mastery in young children: A longitudinal investigation. *Journal of Experimental Child Psychology, 85*, 103–119.

Jordan, N. C., & Montani, T. O. (1997). Cognitive arithmetic and problem solving: A comparison of children with specific and general mathematics difficulties. *Journal of Learning Disabilities, 30,* 624–634.

Kilpatrick, J., Swafford, J., & Findell, B. (Eds.). (2001). *Adding it up: Helping children learn mathematics.* Washington, DC: National Academy Press.

Kroesbergen, E. H., & Van Luit, J. E. H. (2003). Mathematics interventions for children with special needs: A meta-analysis. *Remedial and Special Education, 24*, 97–114.

Micallef, S., & Prior, M. (2004). Arithmetic learning difficulties in children. *Educational Psychology, 24,* 175–200.

Miller, S. P., & Hudson, P. J. (2007). Using evidence-based practices to build mathematics competence related to conceptual, procedural, and declarative knowledge. *Learning Disabilities Research and Practice, 22*, 47–57.

Okolo, C. M. (1992). The effect of computer-assisted instruction format and initial attitude on the arithmetic facts proficiency and continuing motivation of students with learning disabilities. *Exceptionality, 3,* 195–211.

Ostad, S. A. (1997). Developmental differences in addition strategies: A comparison of mathematically disabled and mathematically normal children. *British Journal of Educational Psychology, 67,* 345–357.

Powell, S. R., Fuchs, L. S., Fuchs, D., Cirino, P. T., & Fletcher, J. M. (2009). Effects of fact retrieval tutoring on third-grade students with math difficulties with and without reading difficulties. *Learning Disabilities Research and Practice, 24,* 1–11.

Quilici, J. L., & Mayer, R. E. (1996). Role of examples in how students learn to categorize statistics word problems. *Journal of Educational Psychology, 88*, 144–161.

Reikeras, E. K. L. (2006). Performance in solving arithmetic problems: A comparison of children with different levels of achievement in mathematics and reading. *European Journal of Special Needs Education, 21,* 233–250.

Rivera-Batiz, F. L. (1992). Quantitative literacy and the likelihood of employment among young adults in the United States. *The Journal of Human Resources, 27*, 313–328.

Siegler, R. S. (1987). The perils of averaging data over strategies: An example from children's addition. *Journal of Experimental Psychology: General, 116*, 250–264.

Siegler, R. S., & Shrager, J. (1984). Strategy choice in addition and subtraction: How do children know what to do? In C. Sophian (Ed.), *Origins of cognitive skills* (pp. 229–293). Hillsdale, NJ: Erlbaum.

Swanson, H. L., & Beebe-Frankenberger, M. (2004). The relationship between working memory and mathematical problem solving in children at risk and not at risk for serious math difficulties. *Journal of Educational Psychology, 96*, 471–491.

Torgesen, J. K., Alexander, A. W., Wagner, R. K., Rashotte, C. A., Voeller, K . S., & Conway, T. (2001). Intensive remedial instruction for children with severe reading disabilities: Immediate and long-term outcomes from two instructional approaches. *Journal of Learning Disabilities, 34*, 33–58.

Tournaki, N. (2003). The differential effects of teaching addition through strategy instruction versus drill and practice to students with and without learning disabilities. *Journal of Learning Disabilities, 36,* 449–458.

Xin, P. X., Jitendra, A. K., & Deatline-Buchman, A. (2005). Effects of mathematical word problem-solving instruction on middle school students with learning problems. *The Journal of Special Education, 39*, 181–192.

34

Science and Social Studies

Thomas E. Scruggs and Margo A. Mastropieri
George Mason University

Lisa Marshak
Fairfax County Public Schools, Fairfax, VA

Students with high-incidence cognitive disabilities—including learning disabilities, emotional and behavioral disorders, and intellectual disabilities—commonly exhibit difficulties with all aspects of school learning. Some aspects, such as literacy, have had significant research attention over the years (Mastropieri et al., 2009), perhaps because literacy skills are seen as foundational to other types of academic learning, and because literacy deficits are often a primary cause for referral to special education (Hallahan, Lloyd, Kauffman, Weiss, & Martinez, 2005).

Nevertheless, students with high-incidence disabilities frequently encounter difficulties with content area learning, such as science and social studies, that are as significant as are their challenges with reading and writing. Some students do not develop literacy skills sufficient for independent processing of expository text; others, who have gained some literacy skills over time, find that they lack learning strategies and study skills sufficient to master content area learning requirements. In either case, specific interventions targeted specifically to content area learning are necessary.

In this chapter we review and discuss selected strategies for enhancing content area learning. Although considerable overlap exists in the learning requirements (Whitehurst, 2004), we shall discuss these areas separately in order to focus on the specific characteristics of each content area.

Science Education

Characteristics of Science Curriculum and Characteristics of Disabilities

All appropriate instructional strategies are based on an understanding of the characteristics of the academic curriculum and their interaction with the characteristics of the learner (Scruggs & Mastropieri, 2007). In the case of science education, curriculum can very broadly be represented as textbook or activities oriented (Scruggs & Mastropieri, 1993). Textbook, or content-based science learning, involves high levels of content coverage, with very substantial amounts of vocabulary learning (e.g., *sternocleidomastoideus, nonpolar covalent bonding, prokaryotic heterotroph*) and factual learning. These are usually presented in lecture and worksheet activities and require independent study from text (Mastropieri & Scruggs, 1994). This approach to science education typically emphasizes breadth of content over depth of understanding and acquisition of substantial amount of verbally-based content; content is usually presented through independent study of textbooks, teacher lecture, and worksheet activities. Always common in schools, the textbook approach has gained in importance during the current era of standards-based learning and high-stakes testing (Frase-Blunt, 2000; Huber & Moore, 2002). Unfortunately, textbook-based approaches do not fit with the characteristics of many students with high-incidence cognitive disabilities. These learners have problems precisely in the areas of prior knowledge, vocabulary acquisition, verbal learning and memory, and text processing skills (e.g., Hallahan et al., 2005; Mastropieri & Scruggs, 2009)—exactly those areas most emphasized in textbook-based approaches. Cawley and Parmar (2001), for example, examined the demands of science texts and concluded that many students with disabilities lack the literacy skills necessary for learning effectively from science textbooks.

Another approach to science learning is described as activities oriented (or "hands-on"). In this approach, learning proceeds through a series of activities, intended to provide physical interaction with the methods and materials of scientific inquiry. These activities are frequently conducted in cooperative groups of students (Mastropieri & Scruggs, 1994). Such curricula appear to provide a naturally better fit with the characteristics of students with high-incidence disabilities, in that text-processing and verbal learning demands are reduced significantly, and the opportunities to interact physically with concrete, real-world representations of content can provide important learning opportunities. Nevertheless, some students with high-incidence disabilities may demonstrate difficulties with the reduced structure of group activities and may not benefit fully from unsupported "discovery" oriented activities, which may place excessive demands on independent inductive reasoning skills. Researchers have found that students with intellectual disabilities hold understandings about scientific concepts similar to much younger, normally achieving students (Scruggs, Mastropieri, & Wolfe, 1995). In both approaches to science learning, adaptive strategies are necessary.

Instructional Practices for Promoting Science Learning

Text comprehension and organization. Most science classes, even those emphasizing science activities, require students to study science text, and in virtually all cases, this represents a problem area for students with high-incidence disabilities. Strategies to enhance expository text comprehension, such as summarization strategies, have been effectively implemented with students with learning disabilities studying science text (e.g., Nelson, Smith, & Dodd, 1992). Using a more complicated strategy, Bakken, Mastropieri, and Scruggs (1997) taught eighth-grade students with learning disabilities to evaluate the structure of expository science and other text (e.g., list, order, main idea) and then to apply an appropriate study strategy to passages. Students trained to use this strategy greatly outperformed peers trained to use effective summary strategies, as well as those in a free study condition.

Text enhancements have also been employed to promote comprehension. These include features such as graphic representations and framed outlines (e.g., Bergerud, Lovitt, & Horton, 1988; Lovitt, Rudsit, Jenkins, Pious, & Benedetti, 1986), and text-embedded mnemonic illustrations (Mastropieri, Scruggs, & Levin, 1987). In a recent meta-analysis of all content area learning for secondary level students with disabilities, Scruggs, Mastropieri, Berkeley, and Graetz (2010) reported that spatial or graphic organizers, such as the "Concept Comparison Routine" to teach students with learning disabilities information about tropical diseases in high school science classes (Bulgren, Lenz, Schumaker, Deshler, & Marquis, 2002), were highly effective, resulting in a high overall mean effect size of .93 (see also Bulgren, Schumaker, & Deshler, 1998). In such presentations, content is presented in a graphic or other spatial representation, and the relations among the elements in the visual presentation are made explicit. Overall, research has shown that text processing and text enhancements substantially improve comprehension of both science and social studies texts for students with mild disabilities.

Mnemonic strategies. Mnemonic strategies are intended to improve recall of vocabulary and other verbal factual information, through the creation of links that effectively connect familiar with unfamiliar information. Several different varieties of mnemonic strategies have been created, including the *keyword* method, the *pegword* method, and letter strategies (Scruggs & Mastropieri, 1990).

The keyword method. Using the keyword method, a concrete, acoustically similar word is created for the unfamiliar information to be learned. For example, to promote recall that *Canidae* the scientific name of the biological family of dogs, a familiar acoustically similar keyword is created to represent the new word (e.g., candy). Next, an interactive picture is created in which the keyword (candy) is shown interacting with the meaning (dog), in this case, a cartoon picture of a dog eating, or begging for, candy. Learners first think of the keyword (candy), think of the picture with the candy in it (a dog eating candy), and retrieve the correct answer, *dogs*.

The pegword method. The pegword method is used for promoting recall of numbered or ordered information (e.g., one is *bun*, two is *shoe*, three is *tree*). For example, to remember that a rake is an example of a *third-class* lever (with fulcrum at one end, force in the middle, and load at the other end), a picture is shown of a rake leaning against a *tree* (pegword for three). The pegword method has also been used for learning the hardness levels of minerals (e.g., Mastropieri, Scruggs, & Levin, 1985).

Letter strategies. Letter strategies are employed to help learners remember lists of information. For example, to remember the classes of vertebrates, students can remember the acronym, "FARM-B," which represents the first letters of the classes of vertebrates: fish, amphibian, reptiles, mammals, and birds (Scruggs & Mastropieri, 1992).

Reconstructive elaborations. When considering larger samples of curriculum, these strategies can be combined in a system referred to as "reconstructive elaborations," whereby information to be learned also is identified with respect to concreteness and familiarity. Familiar information (e.g., fish, earthworm) is portrayed in a *mimetic* (representative) illustration; familiar but abstract (e.g., cold-blooded) is portrayed in a *symbolic* representation (e.g., a cold-blooded *fish* shown wearing a coat and scarf); finally, unfamiliar information is represented using the keyword method. Letter strategies are also provided when needed (Mastropieri & Scruggs, 1989).

Applications and effectiveness. Researchers have extensively studied mnemonic strategies in science applications with students with high-incidence disabilities, including for example, dinosaurs (Veit, Scruggs, & Mastropieri, 1986), minerals and their attributes (Mastropieri, Scruggs, & Levin, 1985), earth history and earth science (Scruggs & Mastropieri, 1992), chemistry (Mastropieri, Scruggs, & Graetz, 2005), and invertebrate and vertebrate animals (Mastropieri, Emerick, & Scruggs, 1988).

In a meta-analysis of mnemonic strategy research in special education, Scruggs and Mastropieri (2000) reported a very large overall mean effect size of 1.62. This effect size magnitude means that the average student receiving mnemonic instruction would have scored at the 95th percentile of the comparison condition. For mnemonic studies conducted in the area of science, 13 studies yielded a similarly high mean effect size of 1.59. Overall, when implemented systematically, mnemonic strategies have been highly effective for promoting recall of verbally-based science content, as well as other academic content areas including social studies (e.g., Mastropieri & Scruggs, 1988). However, mnemonic strategies focus specifically on only one aspect of learning in science. For other objectives, other strategies have been demonstrated to be effective.

Hands-on science curriculum. Given the literacy deficits of students with high-incidence disabilities, it would seem likely that these students would benefit from the concrete representations of activities-oriented approaches to science learning, in which students learn by doing rather than by reading about science. Some qualitative investigations of students with learning disabilities and mild mental retardation (Scruggs & Mastropieri, 1994a, 1994b, 1995) indicated that the students appeared to enjoy, and benefit, from hands-on science learning in such areas as studying plant growth and development, building and testing simple machines, and creating ideas and inventions in science. In these investigations, teachers employed adaptations, including active coaching, enhanced vocabulary learning, use of redundancy, and provision of multiple examples. Similarly, Palincsar, Magnusson, Collins, and Cutter (2001) studied inclusive, upper-elementary science classes over a 2-year period. Students studied topics such as floating and sinking and properties of light. Students, including those with learning disabilities, made substantial overall learning gains when they received appropriately adapted hands-on instruction. Adaptations included rehearsing and mini-conferencing, vocabulary enhancement, support for written lab reports, and improving small-group functioning with monitoring and feedback.

Experimental research has supported the learning benefits of hands-on science learning. Scruggs, Mastropieri, Bakken, and Brigham (1993) employed an activities approach to learning about electricity as well as rocks and minerals in eighth-grade classes of students with learning disabilities or emotional and behavioral disorders. Compared with students who read about the same content from textbooks, students taught with hands-on science materials performed substantially higher on posttests.

Bay, Staver, Bryan, and Hale (1992) compared outcomes for students instructed in inclusive classes by either content-based instruction or hands-on instruction in areas of displacement, flotation, variable, controlled experimentation, and scientific prediction. Although students performed similarly at posttest, students provided with hands-on instruction outperformed students receiving content-based instruction on delayed recall and on generalization of learned concepts. McCarthy (2005) compared a textbook approach with a hands-on, thematic approach to instruction of an 8-week unit on properties of matter for middle-school-age students with emotional and behavioral disabilities. McCarthy reported that students in the hands-on condition outperformed textbook condition students on a hands-on assessment and a short-answer test. Brigham, Scruggs, and Mastropieri (1992) implemented hands-on units on atmospheric and earth science across special education science classes and reported that, even when hands-on units of instruction were employed, teacher enthusiasm was a very important element in increasing academic achievement and on-task behavior.

Mastropieri et al. (1998) compared hands-on instruction with a textbook approach in a unit on ecosystems in fourth-grade inclusive classrooms. Students in the hands-on condition outperformed textbook condition students on a multiple choice test and on a performance test. Furthermore, the students with a variety of disabilities in the hands-on condition (learning disabilities, intellectual disabilities, emotional and behavioral disorders, and physical disabilities) not only outperformed normally achieving students in the textbook condition, they also performed within the average range of all students in the experimental classroom.

Dalton, Morocco, Tivnan, and Rawson-Mead (1997) compared two different hands-on approaches to science learning, supported inquiry science (SIS) and activity-based science, in fourth-grade inclusive classrooms. The SIS classrooms employed activities but also emphasized identifying and coaching students through prior misconceptions and co-constructing new knowledge. Results indicated that all students demonstrated greater concept learning in the SIS classrooms.

A recent meta-analysis of content area learning (Scruggs et al., in press) reported an overall effect size of .63 for hands-on learning approaches. Given the importance of investigations of hands-on science learning, however, additional research would be very helpful in determining the most facilitative circumstances for such learning.

Promoting inductive thinking of students with mild disabilities. Researchers have demonstrated that activities with concrete materials and appropriate guidance have improved learning outcomes for students with mild disabilities. In some cases, however, hands-on approaches are accompanied by "inquiry" or "discovery" methods, in which students are expected to reason independently about scientific problems and derive their own conclusions. It makes sense that reasoning through problems and arriving at appropriate conclusions independently could be beneficial, particularly compared to simply being provided the same information. However, because independent reasoning is frequently thought to be a relative weakness of students with high-incidence disabilities (e.g., Ellis, 1993), the benefit of such methods could be questioned.

Previous qualitative research (e.g., Scruggs & Mastropieri, 1995) is consistent with the hypothesis that students with high-incidence disabilities may have difficulty with inductive reasoning tasks, but that active coaching on the part of teachers may promote inductive thinking. Two experiments were conducted specifically to determine whether students with learning disabilities and mild intellectual disabilities are able to "construct" scientific principles by themselves, through prompting and questioning. Mastropieri, Scruggs, and Butcher (1997) demonstrated pendulum movement individually to normally achieving students, students with learning disabilities, and students with intellectual disabilities, and prompted them to create a general rule for pendulum movement (e.g., that pendulums with longer strings exhibited longer swing rates). If students did not immediately come to this conclusion, increasingly more explicit prompts were provided to elicit this general conclusion. It was found that normally achieving students drew the correct conclusions either immediately or after only a small amount of prompting. Students with learning disabilities performed only slightly less well than normally achieving students on this task. However, none of the students with intellectual disabilities ever drew the correct conclusion, until it was suggested explicitly by the experimenter. Students with learning disabilities and students with intellectual disabilities both experienced difficulty with transferring their knowledge. These findings were later replicated on an inquiry task in the area of density and buoyancy by Mastropieri, Scruggs, Boon, and Carter (2001) .

Coached elaborations and guided inquiry. The previously described studies showed that performance of students with disabilities on inductive learning tasks was lower than that of their normally achieving peers. However, this does not necessarily mean that students with high-incidence disabilities are unable to benefit from highly structured coaching. In a series of experiments, we and our colleagues examined the effectiveness of such coaching (Scruggs, Mastropieri, & Sullivan, 1994; Scruggs, Mastropieri, Sullivan, & Hesser, 1993; Sullivan, Mastropieri, & Scruggs, 1995). Based on previous research in which learners created elaborations "that make otherwise arbitrary relationships understandable" (Pressley, Johnson, & Symons, 1987, p. 79), elementary grade students with high-incidence disabilities were encouraged to reason about stated facts in life science or earth science. The researchers provided students with a fact about animals and coached them to think through an explanation for that fact, using dialogue similar to the following:

Experimenter: The anteater has long claws on its front feet. Why does it make sense that the anteater would have long claws on its front feet?
Student: I don't know.
Experimenter: Well, let's think about it together. What does the anteater eat?
Student: Ants?
Experimenter: Ants, good. Anteaters eat ants. And where do ants live?
Student: They live in the ground, in holes.
Experimenter: In holes in the ground. So why would it make sense that the anteater would have long claws on its front feet?
Student: Oh—to help it dig for ants.
Experimenter: Yes, exactly, to help it dig for ants. Good. (Scruggs & Mastropieri, 2008, p. 6)

In all three experiments, the students remembered the facts, as well as the explanations for those facts, better in the coached elaborations condition than in the direct practice conditions. Recall was low in the direct practice condition, in which they independently constructed few if any explanations. The most interesting finding was that coached elaboration students, who actively reasoned through explanations, recalled explanations better than students who were directly provided this same information. In these conditions, however, questioning was very explicit, and targeted directly to student construction of the answer. In a related study, Mastropieri et al. (1996) taught students with high-incidence disabilities to question themselves on explanations for facts presented in text, but they were only partially successful on this task. In this case, students did not implement strategy independently. Overall, it can be concluded that students with high-incidence disabilities can benefit from guided inquiry and higher-order questioning, but instruction using these methods must be highly structured and supportive.

These studies were very highly structured and involved intensive, structured interaction with an experimenter and a single student. Nevertheless, the dialogue was similar to that observed in more naturalistic settings, where students with high-incidence disabilities were apparently able to reason through science content with the assistance of teachers. And, in fact, similar dialogue has been observed in naturalistic settings, where teachers help students with high-incidence disabilities reason through scientific concepts, in such areas as capillary action (Scruggs & Mastropieri, 1995, p. 264), principles of buoyancy (Palincsar, Collins, Marano, & Magnusson, 2000), and ecosystems (Mastropieri et al., 1998).

Science Learning in Inclusive Environments

With few exceptions (e.g., Mastropieri et al., 1998; Palincsar et al., 2000), the research we have thus far reviewed was conducted in laboratory or special education settings. Scruggs and Mastropieri (1994b) examined inclusive elementary science instruction over a considerable time period, in a school district known for exemplary science instruction. Students with a variety of disabilities, including sensory and physical disabilities, were successfully integrated in these classrooms. Overall, Scruggs and Mastropieri concluded that a variety of elements were necessary for inclusive science teaching, including (a) an open, accepting classroom environment, (b) administrative support, (c) general effective teaching skills, (d) special education support, (e) peer mediation, (f) appropriate curriculum, and (g) disability-specific teaching skills. We have observed many of these same variables in other successful inclusive science classrooms (Mastropieri et al., 1998; Mastropieri, Scruggs, & Bohs, 1994).

Differentiated curriculum enhancements. An important consideration in inclusive classroom instruction is maximizing engagement and practice when there are considerable differences in learning abilities. Classwide peer tutoring is one approach for maximizing engagement and instructional delivery in classes with diverse learning needs (e.g., Fuchs, Fuchs, & Kazdin, 1999; Mathes, Howard, Allen, & Fuchs, 1998). Mastropieri, Scruggs, and colleagues addressed this issue in science learning, using a method referred to as "differentiated curriculum enhancements" in which the same materials for all students were implemented on different difficulty levels. These different levels were employed by all students; however, they were created to be employed differentially in terms of student need. For example, Mastropieri et al. (2005) implemented these procedures in high school chemistry classes. In this case, the tutoring materials—which were based on high-stakes testing requirements—incorporated mnemonic and elaborative aids to learning. However, these strategies were developed so that they were used only if needed by the tutoring pairs. For example, students tutored each other on such content as *enthalpy, molarity, the Periodic table, valence electrons, and polar and nonpolar covalent bonding.* If students learned the information easily, tutors moved directly on to elaborative questioning of the content ("Can you give me an example of *molarity*?"). If students did not recall the information, a mnemonic or other similar strategy was displayed (e.g., a picture of a *thermos* of hot coffee to remind students that *thermic* represents heat). Mastropieri et al. (2005) reported that students in the experimental condition outperformed students in the comparison condition and that students with learning disabilities appeared to gain more from the intervention than normally achieving students.

In another investigation, Mastropieri et al. (2006) developed game-like activities (such as "Concentration," "Vocabulary Challenge," "Liquid Measurement," and "Jeopardy"), to reinforce important concepts in a unit on the scientific method. Each activity was presented in three levels, in order of difficulty. Level 1 activities required, typically, only identification of the correct answer from a presented array; level 2 activities required production responses, with prompting when needed; and level 3 activities required unprompted production responses. Instruction was "differentiated," then, to the extent that individual tutoring pairs (or small groups, in some cases) could work on materials of increasing difficulty levels, as long as it took to master the content and move to the next difficulty level. After 14 weeks of intervention in 13 inclusive science classrooms, students in the experimental classrooms outperformed control condition students on classroom unit tests and also on end-of-year statewide high-stakes tests, with students with and without disabilities benefiting similarly. This model of science learning in inclusive classrooms has more recently been replicated by Simpkins, Mastropieri, and Scruggs (in press) in the area of Earth and space science, and light and sound, units in elementary inclusive classrooms. In this case, students worked with materials on two levels of difficulty.

One potential problem with the learning-activities approach is the amount of time required for development of materials. In order to address this issue, McDuffie, Mastropieri, and Scruggs (2009) developed "fact sheets," which reviewed important terminology for a unit on genetics. Although very simple to develop, these materials contained no embedded differentiated presentation formats. The level of differentiation with these materials was in the amount of time for practice until mastery learning was achieved on each task. Students practiced with each other and monitored and recorded progress in each instance until criterion was met. Results indicated that students with and without disabilities using these materials outperformed comparison condition students on posttests.

Discussion

In a recent meta-analysis of content area learning for secondary students with high-incidence disabilities, Scruggs et al. (2010) reported a large overall mean effect size of .91 for interventions in science education. Effects were strongest overall for mnemonic instruction, study aids, and spatial or graphic organization; however, effects were very substantial for all instructional approaches. Although there is need for further instructional research, at present it appears that an important challenge is for general education teachers to begin to implement these demonstrably effective strategies in their science classrooms.

Social Studies Education

Social Studies Curriculum and Students with Disabilities

Results of the 2005 National Assessment of Educational Progress (NAEP) indicate that 27% of high school seniors are reading below the basic level (Grigg, Donahue, & Dion, 2007). This fact is a concern for many social studies teachers, as they rely on textbooks to convey social studies content to their students. Social studies textbooks contain some of the most difficult material students use in school (Harness, Hollenbeck, & Crawford, 1994). Many textbooks are heavily loaded with vocabulary words, cover a tremendous amount of content, lack coherence, and seem uninteresting to many students (De La Paz, 2005). This also presents a problem for students with high-incidence cognitive disabilities, who may have difficulty abstracting important information from the text, and determining what is most important (Horton, Lovitt, & Bergerud, 1990; De La Paz). Compounding this problem are difficulties with note taking and assimilating written information commonly associated with high-incidence disabilities (Passe & Beattie, 1994). Researchers have developed interventions to facilitate learning in social studies; we review these in the following section. Because we discussed several of the strategies previously with respect to science applications, we review them more briefly in the next section.

Instructional Practices for Promoting Social Studies Learning

Strategies to promote text processing. Text comprehension research in social studies education parallels that from science education. Wong, Wong, Perry, and Sawatsky (1986) conducted two experiments that evaluated a strategy for identifying a main idea and summarizing paragraph information in middle school social studies content. Results indicated that this strategy increased the students' summarization scores and recall scores. Bakken et al. (1997), described previously, also included social studies passages in teaching students to identify text structure and alter study strategies accordingly. Results indicated that students in the text-structure condition outperformed students in both the paragraph restatement condition and the traditional condition.

Lederer (2000) taught students to use a reciprocal teaching strategy to question, summarize, and clarify information while reading social studies text passages. Students read each passage, developed and answered three questions about the passage, and then listed the subheadings and corresponding facts. Finally, students summarized the passage. Results indicated that the experimental group performed significantly higher than a comparison condition on reading comprehension measures.

Spencer, Scruggs, and Mastropieri (2003) employed classwide peer tutoring to promote content learning in social studies for students with emotional and behavioral disorders. Students read a paragraph aloud and, together with partners, summarized the paragraph on a response sheet. Then they used fact cards to quiz each other on the most important facts from the chapter. Compared with a traditional teaching condition, students in the peer-tutoring-with-summarization condition were more engaged and scored higher on weekly quizzes and multiple choice tests. Similar results were observed in inclusive social studies classes by Klingner, Vaughn, and Schumm, (1998).

Content organizers and study guides. To promote content learning, investigators have enhanced the organizational structure of social studies materials (e.g., Bulgren et al., 1988). Bos, Anders, Filip, and Jaffe, (1989) used a teacher-made organizer called a Semantic Feature Analysis Chart to promote reading comprehension in social studies. The chart helped activate prior knowledge to define important ideas and related vocabulary. Concepts and vocabulary were categorized as subordinate, coordinate, or subordinate, depending on semantic relationships among the concepts and level of importance. Compared with students using a dictionary method, students in the Semantic Feature Analysis performed significantly better on vocabulary and conceptual items than students instructed with the dictionary method.

Horton, Lovitt, and colleagues investigated the effects of various study aids in inclusive social studies classes. In similar and interrelated investigations, these researchers demonstrated that a number of text enhancement features increased the learning of students in inclusive classes. These features included graphic organizers and tutorials (Horton & Lovitt, 1989; Horton et al., 1990; Horton, Lovitt, & Slocum, 1988), computer-assisted instruction with enhancements such as hyperlinks (Horton, Lovitt, Givens, & Nelson, 1989; Higgins, Boone, & Lovitt, 1996), and study guides (Horton, Lovitt, & Christenson, 1991). In these investigations, all students, including students with learning disabilities, low-achieving students, and normally achieving students, benefited from the text and study enhancements.

Hamilton, Siebert, Gardner, and Talbert-Johnson (2000) taught students to use guided notes for social studies lectures. During the intervention, students took notes using a notes page with partial notes and blanks that students were to complete during the lecture. The mean score for accurately recorded concepts increased greatly from baseline levels. Sweeny et al. (1999) found that performance of students in a remedial social studies class improved when they were directed specifically in notetaking. In some cases, however, study aids in the form of guided notes have not always improved performance optimally. Mastropieri, Scruggs, Spencer, and Fontana (2003) provided guided notes as a comparison condition to a classwide peer-tutoring strategy, similar to the Spencer et al. (2003) investigation. Results indicated that there was a statistically significant main effect on chapter tests and unit tests favoring the tutoring condition. Students in the tutoring condition were also able to generate summaries better than students in the guided notes condition.

In an investigation by Kinder and Bursuck (1993), teachers taught solely from the textbook during baseline, and had students read and answer questions from the text and accompanying workbook. The intervention consisted of using an organizer for pre-skills instruction, problem-solution-effect analysis note taking, vocabulary note taking, timeline note taking, and reciprocal questioning. Across three classes in a multiple baseline design, students when given the organizer condition.

In two studies, Hudson examined the effects of teacher review and organization in social studies classes for middle school students with learning disabilities. Hudson (1996) instructed a teacher to review the previous day's lesson verbally with positive feedback, and comparison students silently reviewed their previous day. Hudson (1997) had the teacher break up lectures into segments with oral questions about the preceding segment to maximize student responding, whereas instruction in the comparison condition broke instruction into segments without discussion. In both instances, students in the treatment condition outperformed students in the control condition on both unit and maintenance measures.

Cantrell, Fusaro, and Dougherty (2000) required students to write in their journal after reading the assigned passage using a KWL method (What do you Know about the topic based on the headings and subheadings? What do you

Want to know about the topic after reading? What have you Learned from the reading?). Students in the comparison treatment read the assigned passage and then summarized what they read in their journals. Students in the KWL experimental treatment significantly outperformed students in the control summary treatment.

Alternative texts. Research indicates that providing different types of texts can improve the reading comprehension of students with high-incidence disabilities. For example, Montali and Lewandowski (1996) presented social studies content visually (read silently), bimodally (highlighted and read by computer), and auditorily (read by computer), and found that the low-performing readers answered more comprehension questions from bimodal presentation and brought their performance closer to the level of the average readers when in the visual presentation mode. Similarly, Twyman and Tindal (2006) compared a conceptually framed, computer-adapted text with a district-adopted textbook. The computer-adapted text read the text aloud while students could click on a difficult word to be read to them. Students could also click on four links: (a) an overview of the chapter, (b) a list of the concepts, (c) simplified text, or (d) problem solving assessments, as well as written assessments. This computer-adapted text was effective in improving domain vocabulary acquisition; however, there was no advantage over traditional instruction on overall vocabulary or comprehension.

Beck, McKeown, Sinatra, and Loxterman (1991) revised text passages to reflect a causal/explanatory design; results indicated that the students who read the revised texts answered almost twice as many questions correctly as students using traditional texts. Similarly, Crawford and Carnine (2000) compared a conceptually organized U.S. history textbook with a topically organized textbook on a multiple choice and short answer essay content tests. Results indicated that students using the conceptually organized textbook made greater gains than students using the topically organized text on a multiple choice test, but not on the essay test.

Ward-Lonergan, Liles, and Anderson (1998) taught students information about fictitious countries, using video rather than text. Students with and without language-learning disabilities listened to video presentations about a fictitious country using a causal discourse structure, or a comparison discourse structure. Students who had listened to the causal discourse structure answered more inferential questions correctly.

Summary. Students with disabilities benefit from interventions to help them learn information from text. Summarization techniques, peer mediation, computer-assisted instruction (in some cases), graphic organizers, alternative forms of texts and strategy instruction all helped students with disabilities to comprehend social studies text better.

Mnemonic strategy instruction. Research in mnemonic strategy instruction has paralleled mnemonic instruction in science education. Students have used mnemonic strategies, including keyword, pegword, letter strategies, and reconstructive elaborations, in similar fashion to facilitate recall of important facts and concepts in social studies (Scruggs & Mastropieri, 2000).

The keyword method. The keyword method was employed to teach states and capitals to students with high-incidence disabilities (Mastropieri, Scruggs, Bakken, & Brigham, 1992), to teach a unit on the settlement of the Chesapeake Bay in inclusive classes (Mastropieri, Sweda, Scruggs, 2000), and to teach map locations and corresponding events to middle school students with high-incidence disabilities (Brigham, Scruggs, & Mastropieri, 1995; Scruggs, Mastropieri, Brigham, Sullivan, 1992). Fontana, Scruggs, and Mastropieri (2007) used the keyword method to teach information about world history in inclusive high school classes, and reported that students for whom English was a second language benefited most from the strategy.

Keyword-pegword method. Mastropieri, Scruggs, and Weldon (1997) taught students with high-incidence disabilities the order of the first 16 U.S. presidents using a combined keyword-pegword method. For example, to remember that President Andrew Jackson (keyword = *jacks*) was President #7 (pegword = *heaven*), students studied a picture of angels playing *jacks* in *heaven*. On weekly tests, students learned more than twice as many presidents than when under the traditional treatment on immediate and delayed posttests.

Reconstructive elaborations. Reconstructive elaborations, as described previously, include multiple mnemonic strategies, organized by familiarity and concreteness of the content. Scruggs and Mastropieri (1989b) taught information about U.S. involvement in World War I, using reconstructive elaborations. To teach that World War I *trenches* were unhealthy and caused diseases, they employed a *mimetic* picture of sick soldiers in trenches. To teach that the first U.S. policy was not to get involved in the war, a picture was shown of *Uncle Sam* (*symbolic* representation of U.S. policy) looking over at Europe and saying, "It's not my fight." To teach that the *Lusitania* was a passenger ship sunk by a German submarine, an *acoustic* (keyword) representation was shown of *Lucy* (keyword for *Lusitania*) standing on a sinking passenger ship and shaking her fist at a submarine. To teach that *Turkey* (Ottoman Empire), *Austria-Hungary*, and *Germany* were the countries allied in the *Central Powers*, a representation was shown of children playing *TAG* (letter strategy for *Turkey, Austria-Hungary,* and *Germany*) in *Central Park* (keyword for Central Powers). Students with high-incidence disabilities who used mnemonics substantially outperformed students who were taught directly from text. Two subsequent investigations demonstrated that 8-week applications of these strategies significantly increased learning in U.S. history special education classes (Mastropieri & Scruggs, 1988; Scruggs & Mastropieri, 1989a).

Active participation. Research using active student participation includes classwide peer tutoring with fact sheets, active participation with goal setting, and class projects. We describe each separately.

Classwide peer tutoring. Classwide peer tutoring allows more active participation within the classroom and provides "pacing, feedback, immediate error correction, high mastery levels, and content coverage" (Greenwood, Delquadri, & Hall, 1989, p. 3). There is extensive research on the effectiveness of classwide peer tutoring with students with disabilities (see Greenwood, Meheady, & Carta, 1991). Two social studies applications have been described previously, under text comprehension (Spencer et al., 2003) and content organization (Horton et al., 1991).

Maheady, Sacca, and Harper (1988) employed peer tutoring to teach content relevant to the American and French revolutions and World War I. After the teacher taught traditionally, students were presented with practice sheets/study guides. Students formed dyads and dictated the study guide questions to his/her partner. Results indicated a dramatic increase in weekly test scores, with the gains of students with disabilities often greater than their normally achieving peers.

Using primary resources and a mock trial. Another form of active participation in social studies research is class simulations. De La Paz (2005) taught westward expansion and the historical bias associated with its history by having eighth-grade students with and without disabilities participate in a mock trail of the Cayuse Indians, who were said to be responsible for the Whitman massacre of 1847. They learned a historical reasoning strategy to understand bias in primary documents. Each student's essay was assessed based on length, persuasiveness, arguments, and accuracy. The experimental students all scored higher in every category when compared with control students. This study demonstrated that, when students were actively engaged in the activity, their writing improved.

Multi-media projects. Okolo and Ferretti (1996) taught about the Revolutionary War by assigning students a topic and instructing each of them that they were to become the "expert" for the group. The goal was to create a multi-media project of each participant's work, using word processing and a scanner for pictures. Students in the control condition had access to a word processing program. Students in both conditions increased their knowledge and improved on the pretest. There were no differences, however, when comparing conditions in terms of content knowledge, motivation to learn the topic, or the length of written products.

Ferretti, MacArthur, and Okolo (2001) taught westward expansion and the evaluation of bias and trustworthiness in historical documents. Students examined primary and secondary sources, and designed a multi-media project describing the reasons why a certain emigrant group moved west. Both the students with disabilities and general education students improved knowledge about westward expansion and the process of historical inquiry. In both of these studies, students were actively engaged. In designing projects, these students were able to learn the history content (see also Ferretti, MacArthur, & Okolo, 2007; MacArthur, Ferretti, & Okolo, 2002).

Differentiated curriculum enhancements. A number of the investigations already described were applied in inclusive classrooms. Several studies described as "differentiated curriculum enhancements" (see previous description) have been employed to increase learning of all students in inclusive middle school social studies classes on measures directly relevant to district benchmarks and state high-stakes tests.

Mastropieri, Scruggs, and Marshak (2008) studied the use of classwide peer tutoring with fact sheets in four inclusive classrooms. Tutoring pairs were trained in the implementation procedures, and took turns practicing the content, with partner prompting and feedback. Students used recording sheets to monitor which fact sheets were used, how often they were used, and when each fact was mastered. Results showed that students scored higher when in the classwide peer tutoring condition; the students with high-incidence disabilities gained more than their general education classmates from the intervention.

This study was replicated by Scruggs et al. (2008) with students in 10 inclusive middle school, social studies classrooms. The intervention continued for 18 weeks and covered seven history units. Similar to the previous investigation, experimental condition students significantly outperformed students who had received traditional instruction.

Marshak, Mastropieri, and Scruggs (in press) employed embedded mnemonics in eight inclusive seventh grade classrooms. Students who received the intervention used class-wide peer tutoring to learn key facts and vocabulary, using mnemonic illustrations when needed. After 12 weeks of instruction, covering 10 units of study, experimental condition students substantially outperformed students in a traditional instruction condition. For mnemonically learned information, the performance of students with disabilities equaled that of the normally achieving students.

General Discussion

Intervention research with students with high-incidence disabilities that focuses on science and social studies learning is not as plentiful as that which is focused on other areas (e.g., reading and math). However, enough has been conducted to draw some general conclusions. First, it is important to realize that learning in these areas is multi-faceted and that multiple instructional and learning strategies are necessary for students to achieve maximally. Across both areas of study, research indicates that reading comprehension strategies and content enhancements—in the form of study guides, guided notes, computer-assisted instruction, and content organization—have been beneficial in promoting learning. Teacher strategies to organize, practice, and review systematically science and social studies content have also been very successful. Mnemonic elaboration has been highly effective in improving recall for content vocabulary and factually based material. Activities, in the form of collaborative learning groups in science and multi-media projects in social studies, have also been associated with positive effects. Finally, recent classroom applications that combine classwide peer tutoring with strategies for differentiating instruction have been very successful. Virtually all of these strategies are reasonably easy to adapt to real-world classroom situations and curriculum materials.

Nevertheless, considerable challenges impede the implementation of these strategies. Surveys (e.g., Chung, 1998) and observational studies (e.g., Scruggs, Mastropieri, & McDuffie, 2007) suggest that general education teachers still favor traditional, teacher-led instruction from textbooks and worksheets and are very resistant to individualizing instruction for special needs. Now that students with high-incidence disabilities have gained substantive access to general education classrooms and curricula (Mastropieri & Scruggs, 2009), a significant challenge for the future will be to uncover the means by which teachers can implement identified and validated instructional techniques in these classes, in order that students with high-incidence disabilities can achieve up to their potential in science and social studies.

References

Bakken, J. P., Mastropieri, M. A., & Scruggs, T. E. (1997). Reading comprehension of expository science material and students with learning disabilities: A comparison of strategies. *Journal of Special Education, 31*, 300–324.

Bay, M., Staver, J., Bryan, T., & Hale, J. (1992). Science instruction for the mildly handicapped: Direct instruction versus discovery teaching. *Journal of Research in Science Teaching, 29*, 555–570.

Beck, I. L., McKeown, M. G., Sinatra, G. M., & Loxterman, J. A. (1991). Revising social studies text from a text-processing perspective: Evidence of improved comprehensibility. *Reading Research Quarterly, 26*, 251–276.

Bergerud, D., Lovitt, T. C., & Horton, S. (1988). The effectiveness of textbook adaptations in life science for high school students with learning disabilities. *Journal of Learning Disabilities, 21*, 70–76.

Bos, C. S., Anders, P. L., Filip, D., & Jaffe, L. E. (1989). The effects of an interactive instructional strategy for enhancing reading comprehension and content are learning for students with learning disabilities. *Journal of Learning Disabilities, 22*, 284–290.

Brigham, F. J., Scruggs, T. E., & Mastropieri, M. A. (1992). The effect of teacher enthusiasm on the learning and behavior of learning disabled students. *Learning Disabilities Research & Practice, 7*, 68–73.

Brigham, F. J., Scruggs, T. E., & Mastropieri, M. A. (1995). Elaborative maps for enhanced learning of content information: Uniting spatial, verbal, and imaginal information. *The Journal of Special Education, 28*, 440–460.

Bulgren, J. A., Lenz, K. B., Schumaker, J. B., Deshler, D. D., & Marquis, J. (2002). The use and effectiveness of a comparison routine in diverse secondary classrooms. *Journal of Educational Psychology, 94*, 356–371.

Bulgren, J., Schumaker, J. B., & Deshler, D. D. (1988). Effectiveness of a concept teaching routine in enhancing the performance of LD students in secondary-level mainstream classes. *Learning Disability Quarterly, 11*, 3–17

Bulgren, J. A., Schumaker, J. B., & Deshler, D. D. (1998). The effects of a recall enhancement routine on the test performance of secondary students with and without learning disabilities. *Learning Disabilities Research & Practice, 9*, 2–11.

Cantrell, R. J., Fusaro, J. A., & Dougherty, E. A. (2000). Exploring the effectiveness of journal writing on learning social studies: A comparative study. *Reading Psychology, 21*, 1–11.

Cawley, J. F., & Parmar, R. S. (2001). Literacy proficiency and science for students with learning disabilities. *Reading & Writing Quarterly, 17*, 1–5, 125.

Chung, S. (1998). *The compatibility of reform initiatives in inclusion and science education: Perceptions of science teachers*. Unpublished doctoral dissertation,Purdue University, West Lafayette, IN.

Crawford, D. B., & Carnine, D. (2000). Comparing the effects of textbooks in eighth-grade U.S. history: Does conceptual organization help? *Education & Treatment of Children, 23*, 387–422.

Dalton, B., Morocco, C. C., Tivnan, T., & Rawson-Mead, P. (1997). Supported inquiry science: Teaching for conceptual change in urban and suburban science classrooms. *Journal of Learning Disabilities, 30*, 670–684.

De La Paz, S. (2005). Effects of historical reasoning training and writing strategy mastery in culturally and academically diverse middle school classrooms. *Journal of Educational Psychology, 97*, 139–156.

Ellis, E. S. (1993). Integrative strategy instruction: A potential model for teaching content area subjects to adolescents with learning disabilities. *Journal of Learning Disabilities, 26*, 358–383, 398.

Ferretti, R. P., MacArthur, C. D., & Okolo, C. M. (2001). Teaching for historical understanding in inclusive classrooms. *Learning Disability Quarterly, 24*, 59–71.

Ferretti, R. P., MacArthur, C. D., & Okolo, C. M. (2007). Students' misconceptions about U. S. Westward Migration. *Journal of Learning Disabilities*, 145–154.

Fontana, J. D., Scruggs, T., & Mastropieri, M. (2007). Mnemonic strategy instruction in inclusive secondary social studies classes. *Remedial and Special Education, 28*, 345–355.

Frase-Blunt, M. (2000). High stakes testing a mixed blessing for special students. *CEC Today,* 7(2), 1, 5, 7, 15.

Fuchs, L. S., Fuchs, D., & Kazdin, S. (1999). Effects of peer-assisted learning strategies on high school students with serious reading problems. *Remedial and Special Education, 20*, 309–318.

Greenwood, C., Delquadri, J., & Hall, H. (1989). Longitudinal effects of classwide peer tutoring. *Journal of Educational Psychology, 81*, 371–383.

Greenwood, C. R., Meheady, L., & Carta, L. L. (1991). Peer tutoring programs in the regular classroom. In G. Stoner, M. R. Shin, & H. M. Walker (Eds.), *Intervention for achievement and behavior problems* (pp. 179–200). Washington, DC: National Association of School Psychologists.

Grigg, W., Donahue, P., & Dion, G. (2007). *The nation's report card: 12th-grade reading and mathematics 2005* (NCES 2007-468). U.S. Department of Education, National Center for Education Statistics. Washington, DC: U.S. Government Printing Office.

Hallahan, D. P., Lloyd, J. W., Kauffman, J. M., Weiss, M. P., & Martinez, E. A. (2005). *Learning disabilities: Foundations, characteristics, and effective teaching* (3rd ed.). Boston: Allyn & Bacon.

Hamilton, S. L., Siebert, M. A., Gardner, R., & Talbert-Johnson, C. (2000). Using guided notes to improve the academic achievement of incarcerated adolescents with learning and behavior problems. *Remedial and Special Education, 21*, 133–140.

Harness, M. K., Hollenbeck, D. B., & Crawford, D. C. (1994). Content organization and instructional design issues in the development of history texts. *Learning Disability Quarterly, 17*, 235–248.

Higgins, K., Boone, R., & Lovitt, T. C. (1996). Hypertext support for remedial students and students with learning disabilities. *Journal of Learning Disabilities, 29*, 402–412.

Horton, S. V., & Lovitt, T. C. (1989). Using study guides with three classifications of secondary students. *The Journal of Special Education, 22*, 447–462.

Horton, S. V., Lovitt, T. C., & Bergerud, D. (1990). The effectiveness of graphic organizers for three classifications of secondary students in content area classes. *Journal of Learning Disabilities, 23*, 12–29.

Horton, S. V., Lovitt, T. C., & Christenson, C. C. (1991). Matching three classifications of secondary students to differential levels of study guides. *Journal of Learning Disabilities, 24*, 518–529.

Horton, S. V., Lovitt, T. C., Givens, A., & Nelson, R. (1989). Teaching social studies to high school students with academic handicaps in a mainstreamed setting: Effects of a computerized study guide. *Journal of Learning Disabilities, 22*, 103–107.

Horton, S. V., Lovitt, T. C., & Slocum, T. (1988). Teaching geography to high school students with academic deficits: Effects of a computerized map tutorial. *Learning Disability Quarterly, 11*, 371–379.

Huber, R. A., & Moore, C. J. (2002). High stakes testing and science learning assessment. *Science Educator, 11*, 18–23.

Hudson, P. (1996). Using a learning set to increase the test performance of students with learning disabilities in social studies classes. *Learning Disabilities Research & Practice, 11*, 78–85.

Hudson, P. (1997). Using teacher-guided practice to help students with learning disabilities acquire and retain social studies content. *Learning Disability Quarterly, 20*, 23–32.

Kinder, D., & Bursuck, W. (1993). History strategy instruction: Problem-solution-effect analysis, timeline, and vocabulary instruction. *Exceptional Children, 59*, 324–335.

Klingner, J. K., Vaughn, S., & Schumm, J. S. (1998). Collaborative strategic reading during social studies in heterogeneous fourth-grade classrooms. *The Elementary School Journal, 99*, 1–22.

Lederer, J. M. (2000). Reciprocal teaching of social studies in inclusive elementary classrooms. *Journal of Learning Disabilities, 33*, 91–106.

Lovitt, T., Rudsit, J., Jenkins, J., Pious, C., & Benedetti, D. (1986). Adapting science materials for regular and learning disabled seventh graders. *Remedial and Special Education, 7*, 31–39.

MacArthur, C. D., Ferretti, R. P., & Okolo, C. M. (2002). On defending controversial viewpoints: Debates of sixth-graders about the desirability of early 20th century American immigration. *Learning Disabilities Research and Practice, 17*, 160–172.

Maheady, L., Sacca, M. K., & Harper, G. F. (1988). Classwide peer tutoring system with mildly handicapped high school students. *Exceptional Children, 55*, 52–59.

Marshak, L. R., Mastropieri, M. A., & Scruggs, T. E. (in press). Curriculum enhancements in inclusive secondary social studies classes. *Exceptionality.*

Mastropieri, M. A., Berkeley, S., McDuffie, K. A., Graff, H., Marshak, L., Conners, N., … Cuenca-Sanchez, Y. (2009). What is published in the field of special education? An analysis of 11 prominent journals. *Exceptional Children, 76*, 95–110.

Mastropieri, M. A., Emerick, K., & Scruggs, T. E. (1988). Mnemonic instruction of science concepts. *Behavioral Disorders, 14*, 48–56.

Mastropieri, M., & Scruggs, T. E., (1988). Increasing content area learning of learning disabled students: Research implementation. *Learning Disabilities Research, 4*, 17–24.

Mastropieri, M. A., & Scruggs, T. E. (1989). Reconstructive elaborations: Strategies that facilitate content learning. *Learning Disabilities Focus, 4*, 73–77.

Mastropieri, M. A., & Scruggs, T. E. (1994). Text-based vs. activities-oriented science curriculum: Implications for students with disabilities. *Remedial and Special Education, 15*, 72–85.

Mastropieri, M. A., & Scruggs, T. E. (2009). *The inclusive classroom: Strategies for effective instruction* (4th ed.). Columbus, OH: Prentice Hall/Merrill.

Mastropieri, M. A., Scruggs, T. E., Bakken, J. P., & Brigham, F. J. (1992). A complex mnemonic strategy for teaching states and capitals: Comparing forward and backward associations. *Learning Disabilities Research & Practice, 7*, 96–103.

Mastropieri, M. A., Scruggs, T. E., Bakken, J. P., & Whedon, C. (1997). Using mnemonic strategies to teach information about U.S. presidents: A classroom-based investigation. *Learning Disability Quarterly, 20*, 13–21.

Mastropieri, M. A., Scruggs, T. E., & Bohs, K. (1994). Mainstreaming an emotionally handicapped student in science: A qualitative investigation. In T. E. Scruggs & M. A. Mastropieri (Eds.), *Advances in learning and behavioral disabilities* (Vol. 8, pp. 131–146). Greenwich, CT: JAI Press.

Mastropieri, M. A., Scruggs, T. E., Boon, R., & Carter, K. B. (2001). Correlates of inquiry learning in science: Constructing concepts of density and buoyancy. *Remedial and Special Education, 22*, 130–138.

Mastropieri, M. A., Scruggs, T. E., & Butcher, K. (1997). How effective is inquiry learning for students with mild disabilities? *Journal of Special Education, 31*, 199–211.

Mastropieri, M. A., Scruggs, T. E., & Graetz, J. (2005). Cognition and learning in inclusive high school chemistry classes. In T. E. Scruggs & M. A. Mastropieri (Eds.), *Advances in learning and behavioral disabilities: Cognition and learning in diverse settings* (Vol. 18, pp. 107–118). Oxford, UK: Elsevier.

Mastropieri, M. A., Scruggs, T. E., Hamilton, S. L., Wolfe, S., Whedon, C., & Canevaro, A. (1996). Promoting thinking skills of students with learning disabilities: Effects on recall and comprehension of expository prose. *Exceptionality, 6*, 1–11.

Mastropieri, M. A., Scruggs, T. E., & Levin, J. R. (1985). Mnemonic strategy instruction with learning disabled adolescents. *Journal of Learning Disabilities, 18*, 94–100.

Mastropieri, M. A., Scruggs, T. E., & Levin, J. R. (1987). Increasing LD students' recall of facts from expository prose. *American Educational Research Journal, 24*, 505–519.

Mastropieri, M. A., Scruggs, T. E., Mantzicopoulos, P. Y., Sturgeon, A., Goodwin, L., & Chung, S. (1998). "A place where living things affect and depend on each other": Qualitative and quantitative outcomes associated with inclusive science teaching. *Science Education, 82*, 163–179.

Mastropieri, M. A., Scruggs, T. E., & Marshak, L. (2008). Training teachers, parents, and peers to implement effective teaching strategies for content area learning. In T. E. Scruggs & M. A. Mastropieri (Eds.), *Personnel preparation: Advances in learning and behavioral disabilities* (Vol. 21, pp. 311–329). Bingley, UK: Emerald.

Mastropieri, M. A., Scruggs, T. E., Norland, J. J., Berkeley, S. McDuffie, K., Tornquist, E. H., & Connors, N. (2006). Differentiated curriculum enhancement in inclusive middle school science: Effects on classroom and high-stakes tests. *Journal of Special Education, 40*, 130–137.

Mastropieri, M. A., Scruggs, T. E., Spencer, V., & Fontana, J. (2003). Promoting success in high school world history: Peer tutoring versus guided notes. *Learning Disabilities Research & Practice, 18*, 52–65.

Mastropieri, M. A., Scruggs, T. E., & Whedon, C. (1997). Using mnemonic instruction to teach information about U. S. presidents: A classroom-based investigation. *Learning Disability Quarterly, 20*, 13–21.

Mastropieri, M. A., Sweda, J., & Scruggs, T. E. (2000). Putting mnemonic strategies to work in an inclusive classroom. *Learning Disabilities Research and Practice, 15*, 69–74.

Mathes, P. G., Howard, J. K., Allen, S., & Fuchs, D. (1998). Peer-assisted learning strategies for first-grade readers: Making early reading instruction more responsive to the needs of diverse learners. *Reading Research Quarterly, 33*, 62–95.

McCarthy, C. B. (2005). Effects of thematic-based, hands-on science teaching versus a textbook approach for students with disabilities. *Journal of Research in Science Teaching, 42*, 245–263.

McDuffie, K. A., Mastropieri, M. A., & Scruggs, T. E. (2009). Differential effects of co-teaching and peer-mediated instruction: Results for content learning and student-teacher interactions. *Exceptional Children, 75*, 493–510.

Montali, J., & Lewandowski, L. (1996). Bimodal reading: Benefits of a talking computer for average and less skilled readers. *Journal of Learning Disabilities, 29*, 271–279.

Nelson, J. R., Smith, D. J., & Dodd, J. M. (1992). The effects of teaching a summary skills strategy to students identified as learning disabled on their comprehension of science text. *Education & Treatment of Children, 15*, 228–243.

Okolo, C. M., & Ferretti, R. P. (1996). Knowledge acquisition and multimedia design projects in the social studies for students with learning disabilities. *Journal of Special Education Technology, 13*(2), 91–103.

Palincsar, A. S., Collins, K. M., Marano, N. L., & Magnusson, S. J. (2000). Investigating the engagement and learning of students with learning disabilities in guided inquiry science teaching. *Language, Speech, and Hearing Services in Schools, 31,* 240–251.

Palincsar, A. S., Magnusson, S. J., Collins, K., & Cutter, J. (2001). Making science accessible to all: Results of a design experiment in inclusive classrooms. *Learning Disability Quarterly, 24*, 15–32.

Passe, J., & Beattie, J. (1994). Social studies instruction for students with mild disabilities: A progress report. *Remedial & Special Education, 15*, 227–233.

Pressley, M., Johnson, C. J., & Symons, S. (1987). Elaborating to learn and learning to elaborate. *Journal of Learning Disabilities, 20*, 76–91.

Scruggs, T. E., & Mastropieri, M. A. (1989a). Mnemonic instruction of learning disabled students: A field-based evaluation. *Learning Disability Quarterly, 12*, 119–125.

Scruggs, T. E., & Mastropieri, M. A. (1989b). Reconstructive elaborations: A model for content area learning. *American Educational Research Journal, 26*, 311–327.

Scruggs, T. E., & Mastropieri, M. A. (1990). Mnemonic instruction for learning disabled students: What it is and what it does. *Learning Disability Quarterly, 13*, 271–281.

Scruggs, T. E., & Mastropieri, M. A. (1992). Classroom applications of mnemonic instruction: Acquisition, maintenance, and generalization. *Exceptional Children, 58*, 219–229.

Scruggs, T. E., & Mastropieri, M. A. (1993). Current approaches to science education: Implications for mainstream instruction of students with disabilities. *Remedial and Special Education, 14*, 15–24.

Scruggs, T. E., & Mastropieri, M. A. (1994a). The construction of scientific knowledge by students with mild disabilities. *Journal of Special Education, 28*, 307–321.

Scruggs, T. E., & Mastropieri, M. A. (1994b). Successful mainstreaming in elementary science classes: A qualitative investigation of three reputational cases. *American Educational Research Journal, 31*, 785–811.

Scruggs, T. E., & Mastropieri, M. A. (1995). Science and mental retardation: An analysis of curriculum features and learner characteristics. *Science Education, 79*, 251–271.

Scruggs, T. E., & Mastropieri, M. A. (2000). The effectiveness of mnemonic instruction for students with learning and behavior problems: An update and research synthesis. *Journal of Behavioral Education, 10*, 163–173.

Scruggs, T. E., & Mastropieri, M. A. (2007). Science learning in special education: The case for constructed vs. instructed learning. *Exceptionality, 15*, 57–74.

Scruggs, T. E., Mastropieri, M. A., Bakken, J. P., & Brigham, F. J. (1993). Reading vs. doing: The relative effectiveness of textbook-based and inquiry-oriented approaches to science education. *Journal of Special Education, 27*, 1–15.

Scruggs, T. E., Mastropieri, M. A., Berkeley, S., & Graetz, J. (2010). Do special education interventions improve learning of secondary content? A meta analysis. *Remedial and Special Education, 31*, 437–449.

Scruggs, T. E., Mastropieri, M. A., Brigham, F. J., & Sullivan, G. S. (1992). Effects of mnemonic reconstructions on the spatial learning of adolescents with learning disabilities. *Learning Disability Quarterly, 15*, 154–162.

Scruggs, T. E., Mastropieri, M. A., & Marshak, L. (2008). *The effects of peer-mediated instruction on secondary social studies learning: A randomized field trial.* Fairfax, VA: George Mason University, College of Education and Human Development.

Scruggs, T. E., Mastropieri, M. A., & McDuffie, K. A. (2007). Co-teaching in inclusive classrooms: A meta-synthesis of qualitative research. *Exceptional Children, 73*, 392–416.

Scruggs, T. E., Mastropieri, M. A., & Sullivan, G. S. (1994). Promoting relational thinking skills: Elaborative interrogation for mildly handicapped students. *Exceptional Children, 60*, 450–457.

Scruggs, T. E., Mastropieri, M. A., Sullivan, G. S., & Hesser, L. S. (1993). Improving reasoning and recall: The differential effects of elaborative interrogation and mnemonic elaboration. *Learning Disability Quarterly, 16*, 233–240.

Scruggs, T. E., Mastropieri, M. A., & Wolfe, S. (1995). Scientific reasoning of students with mental retardation: Investigating preconceptions and conceptual change. *Exceptionality, 5*, 223–244.

Simpkins, P. M., Mastropieri, M. A., & Scruggs, T. E. (in press). Differentiated curriculum enhancements in inclusive 5th grade science classes. *Remedial and Special Education.*

Spencer, V. G., Scruggs, T. E., & Mastropieri, M. A. (2003). Content area learning in middle school social studies classrooms and students with emotional or behavioral disorders: A comparison of strategies. *Behavioral Disorders, 28*, 77–93.

Sullivan, G. S., Mastropieri, M. A., & Scruggs, T. E. (1995). Reasoning and remembering: Coaching thinking with students with learning disabilities. *Journal of Special Education, 29*, 310–322.

Sweeny, W. J., Ehrhardt, A. M., Gardner, III, R., Jones, L., Greenfield, R., & Fribley, S. (1999). Using guided notes with academically at-risk high school students during a remedial summer social studies class. *Psychology in the Schools, 36*, 305–318.

Twyman, T., & Tindal, G. (2006). Using a computer-adapted conceptually based history text to increase comprehension and problem-solving skills of students with disabilities. *Journal of Special Education Technology, 21*(2), 5–16.

Veit, D. T., Scruggs, T. E., & Mastropieri, M. A. (1986). Extended mnemonic instruction with learning disabled students. *Journal of Educational Psychology, 78*, 300–308.

Ward-Lonergan, J. M., Liles, B. Z., & Anderson, A. M. (1998). Listening comprehension and recall abilities in adolescents with language-learning disabilities and without disabilities for social studies lectures. *Journal of Communication Disorders, 31*, 1–32.

Whitehurst, G. J. (2004, March). *Research on science education.* Paper presented at the Secretary's Summit on Science, U.S. Department of Education, Washington, DC.

Wong, B. L., Wong, R., Perry, N., & Sawatsky, D. (1986). The efficacy of a self-questioning summarization strategy for use by underachievers and learning disabled adolescents in social studies. *Learning Disability Focus, 2*, 20–35.

35
Physical Education

Luke E. Kelly and Martin E. Block
University of Virginia

Being able to move efficiently is one of the critical factors needed to develop and maintain an active lifestyle, which contributes to both the quality and longevity of one's life. Conversely, failure to develop these abilities places one at risk of a acquiring a number of health risks such as cardiovascular disease, obesity, diabetes, hypertension, and high cholesterol. As result of these trends, research over the years in the areas of motor development and physical fitness has concentrated on identifying physical and motor developmental benchmarks, valid and reliable measures of these traits, as well as the development and evaluation of programs to develop these traits in both children and adults with and without disabilities. The purpose of this chapter is to review the research related to motor development and physical fitness in relation to children and youth with intellectual disability (ID), learning disability (LD), and emotional disturbance (ED).

This chapter is divided into four sections. The first three sections review the research related to physical and motor development in students labeled as ID, LD, and ED. The research reviewed was delimited to articles published in the past 25 years and to articles listed in the SPORTdiscus database, which includes the primary journals in the field, as well as select earlier studies and studies in other journals that had significant impact on research in the field. The last section of the chapter identifies a number of issues and challenges facing future research on physical and motor development in students labeled ID, LD, and ED as well as some recommendations on how these issues and challenges may be addressed.

Intellectual Disabilities

Early Research

Research on the physical fitness and motor skill development of individuals with intellectual disabilities is a relatively new area with the majority of the research being conducted within the since the late 1950s. Early research in this time period was largely descriptive and focused on describing the discrepancies observed between the performance of students with and without intellectual disabilities on a variety of physical fitness/motor skill measures. In one of the classic early studies, Francis and Rarick (1959) examined the gross motor abilities of students with intellectual disabilities and compared their performance with normative data. The participants were 284 students with intellectual disabilities in the Milwaukee and Madison, Wisconsin public schools between the ages or 7.5 and 14.5 years. The students were assessed on measures of strength, power, balance, and agility. The performance of the children with intellectual disabilities was inferior on all measures when compared to the normative data and these discrepancies increased with age. Similar findings were reported by other researchers (e.g., Auxter, 1966; Brace, 1968; Carter, 1966; Malpass, 1960; Sengstock, 1966), but the results were hard to interpret and compare because of differences in sample sizes and characteristics, and different dependent measures. Some of these issues were addressed in 1970 when the American Alliance for Health, Physical Education, Recreation and Dance (AAHPERD)Youth Physical Fitness Test was modified and national norms for both male and female students labeled educable mentally retarded (EMR) ages 8–18 were developed (Rarick, Widdop, & Broadhead, 1970). In this study of 4,235 students, the researchers found that although the changes in performance by age trends were similar to those found for non-disabled students, the performance of the students with intellectual disabilities was inferior to non-disabled students on all measures. Gender differences were also similar between the groups, with the males performing better than females on all measures.

Although research during the 1950s–70s frequently used the terms *fitness* and *motor skill*, the majority of this research actually focused on physical fitness. The confusion is due to the nature of the dependent measures used during this period to measure physical fitness. Many of the fitness measures were confounded by motor skill. For example, a common test for arm and shoulder strength (a fitness measure) was the softball throw (a motor skill) for distance. This test assumed that the students being tested had the prerequisite mature throwing pattern needed to demonstrate their arm and shoulder strength.

With the passage of PL 94-142, the Education of All Handicapped Act of 1975, research began to diversify and focus in four broad areas: descriptive studies, training studies, curriculum development, and assessment studies. The descriptive studies extended the previous research and continued to compare individuals with various levels of intellectual disabilities on select fitness measures (e.g., Fernhall, Millar, Tymeson, & Burkett, 1989; Fernhall, Tymeson, & Webster, 1988; Findlay, 1981; Kasch & Zasueta, 1971; Koh & Watkinson, 1988; Londeree & Johnson, 1974; Pitetti & Campbell, 1991). Another area of descriptive research during this period focused on the prevalence of obesity in individuals with intellectual disabilities. These studies focused primarily on adult populations due to the absence of valid measures and prediction equations for estimating percent body fat in children with intellectual disabilities (Kelly & Rimmer, 1987; Rimmer, Kelly, & Rosentsweig, 1987). The findings of these studies consistently showed that the prevalence of obesity was higher in adults with intellectual disabilities (Fox, Burkhart, & Rotatori, 1983; Fox & Rotatori, 1982; Kelly, Rimmer, & Ness, 1986; Kreze, Zelinda, Juhas, & Gabara, 1974; Polednak & Auliffe, 1976) and that the incidence increased as the level of ID decreased (Fox & Rotatori, 1982; Kelly et al., 1986).

A second focus was development and testing of programs to remediate the fitness and motor skill deficits being observed in children with intellectual disabilities. Numerous studies reported findings demonstrating that the fitness of students labeled EMR could be improved via structured physical education programs (e.g., Beasley, 1982; Bundschuh & Cureton, 1982; Campbell, 1974; Corder, 1966; Halle, Silverman, & Regan; 1983; Maksud & Hamilton, 1975; Nordgren, 1971; Nunley, 1965; Oliver, 1958). For example, Solomon and Pangle (1967) used a treatment (N = 24) and control group (N = 18) design and found that the levels of physical fitness of boys with EMR could be significantly improved via an 8-week training program and these changes were retained over a 6-week period following the study. Findings also indicated that the improved fitness scores of the boys with EMR were comparable to the performance levels of boys who were not EMR.

Another focus that paralleled the research on training was on the development and field testing of comprehensive physical education programs. Several of these programs were funded by the Department of Health, Education, and Welfare's, Bureau of Education for the Handicapped. Most notable of these were Project Active (Vodola, 1973, 1978), I CAN (Wessel, 1977), and Database Gymnasium (Dunn et al., 1980). The I CAN project is briefly described here to illustrate both the focus and magnitude of these projects. I CAN was composed of eight boxes of physical education resources specifically designed to address the physical education needs of students with intellectual disabilities. Each box addressed one of the major physical education goal areas: fundamental motor skills, physical fitness, social skills, body management skills, team sports, aquatics, outdoor activities and backyard/neighborhood activities, and dance and individual sports. Within each goal area (e.g., fundamental motor skills), the content was broken down into objectives (e.g., running, throwing, catching), and each objective was further tasked analyzed into three skill levels and within each skill level by focal points that defined the key qualitative performance criteria. Then, for each objective the following resources were provided: assessment items, instructional activities for each focal point within the assessment items, and games keyed to each focal point. The roots of Project I CAN can be seen today in Everyone CAN (Kelly, Wessel, Dummer, & Sampson, 2010), which is an elementary physical education curriculum designed to accommodate all students, and the Test of Gross Motor Development (Ulrich, 2000), a normative test of gross motor skills for children ages 4.5–11 years.

The significance of these curriculum development projects was that they expanded the focus from physical fitness to the full range of content addressed in physical education. Although the emphasis on fitness is still dominant today, some progress has been made on increasing research in the area of motor skill development. Unfortunately, because of the reduction of federal funds that underwrote the costs of producing the materials and providing schools with the training needed to implement them, all of these previously funded curricula have subsequently gone out of print.

The fourth general focus that emerged was research on developing and validating assessment items. Much of this work was in the area of physical fitness and particularly on developing and evaluating valid measures of cardiorespiratory endurance for use with individuals with intellectual disabilities (Burkett & Ewing, 1983; Coleman, Ayoub, & Friedrich, 1976, Cressler, Lavay, & Giese, 1988; Fernhall, Millar, Tymeson, & Burkett, 1990; Fernhall & Tymeson, 1988). There have been two extensive reviews on this topic (Fernhall, Millar, Tymeson, & Burkett ,1989; Lavay, Reid, & Cressler-Chaviz, 1990). These reviews concluded that there are a number of issues that complicate the measurement and cross-study comparisons of cardiovascular fitness on individuals with intellectual disabilities including: (a) the heterogeneity of the population, (b) the reality that one standardized protocol will not likely work for all individuals, (c) many individuals require significant amounts of training to learn how to perform the testing protocol reliably, and (d) motivation and intra-individual variability are difficult to control with students with intellectual disabilities.

Recent Research

As the 1990s approached, research continued in the previously described areas and expanded to address an even broader spectrum of questions. To illustrate the foci of recent research, we searched the Sportdisc database to identify research from 1985 to date using the search terms intellectual disability, mental retardation, physical fitness, motor skills, motor development, children, youth, and adolescents. Delimiting the findings to research studies that applied to school-aged individuals with mild intellectual disabilities produced 77 studies. Table 35.1 shows the distribution of these studies by focus (i.e., physical fitness, motor skill, and physical education) and by type of research (descriptive, training, assessment, and other). The physical education focus and the other research category includes studies that either combined fitness and motor skill measures and/or focused on other measures such as on-task behavior, student interactions, effects of peer tutors, or student attitudes. The articles in each of these categories are summarized below to provide an overview of the current direction and emphasis of research in the field.

Fitness—descriptive studies. The majority of the descriptive research involving school-aged individuals with intellectual disabilities since 1990 can be grouped in two broad categories: comparison studies and general descriptive studies. The comparison studies typically involve comparing individuals with intellectual disabilities with individuals without intellectual disabilities on various fitness items such as running (e.g., Frey, McCubbin, Hannigan-Downs, Kasser, & Skaggs, 1999; Pitetti & Fernhall, 2004), physical activity (e.g., Faison-Hodge & Porretta, 2004; Foley, 2006), strength (e.g., Pitetti & Yarmer, 2002), body composition (e.g., Pitetti, Yarmer, & Fernhall, 2001), or between different cultures (e.g., Chow, Frey, Cheung, & Louie, 2005; Onyewadume, 2006). An example of a study in this category was by Lahtinen, Rintala, and Malin (2007) that monitored the physical performance of 33 females and 44 males with intellectual disabilities over 30 years in Finland. Participants were evaluated four times starting in 1973 (ages 11–16), again in 1979 (ages 17–22), 1996 (ages 34–39), and 2003 (ages 41–46). They used four dependent measures consistently across the four measurement periods: Body mass index (BMI), sit-ups, stork stand, and pearl transfer. The BMI is calculated by dividing body weight in kilograms by height in meters squared. During early adolescence there was no difference between BMIs of adolescents with intellectual disabilities compared to norms of Finnish students without intellectual disabilities. However, over the next two measurement periods the BMIs of the individuals with intellectual disabilities increased significantly over the comparative norms with 70% of the individuals with intellectual disabilities having BMI values greater than 25 and females having significantly higher BMI values than males. Results for abdominal strength revealed that during early adolescence the individuals with intellectual disabilities could perform only half as many sit-ups as the normative group and their performance declined further over time with 40% of the participants not being able to perform a single sit-up as adults. The stork stand was used to measure static balance. The early adolescents with intellectual disabilities performed significantly lower than the comparison group on the initial measure. Their performance increased slightly during late adolescence and then declined consistently over the last two measures with a third of the adults not being able to balance on one foot for one second. Finally, manual dexterity was measured by a pearl stringing task. The findings for this measure paralleled the abdominal strength and balance results with the performance of the individuals with intellectual disabilities starting out significantly lower than the comparison group, then showing a significant improvement between the first and second measurement and then showing a significant decline in adulthood with all levels being below the comparison group.

TABLE 35.1
Distribution of Research Studies Reviewed from 1985 to Date

Article Focus	Fitness	Motor Skill	Physical Education
Descriptive Research	15	1	
Training	11	15	
Assessment	20	2	
Other			13

Articles grouped in the general descriptive category focused on topics such as physical work capacity (e.g., Fernhall & Pitetti, 2001), cardiovascular fitness (e.g., Fernhall et al., 1988), physical activity (e.g., Levinson & Reid, 1991; Sit, McKenzie, Lain, & McManus, 2006), fitness variations (e.g., Waldemar et al., 2009), and profiles of elite athletes with ID (e.g., Van de Vliet et al., 2006). A sample of the research in this category is illustrated by the study by Sit et al., whereby they investigated the physical activity levels of children with mild intellectual disabilities attending two special schools for children with mild intellectual disabilities in Hong Kong. Participants were 80 children in grades 4–6 with IQs between 50 and 70. Schools were purposefully selected based on emphasis on sport performance. One school was labeled high sport (HS) performance and the other low (LS) based on the number of students who had previously qualified for international competitions. Students' physical activity was observed and recorded using SOFIT during physical education and two separate recess periods during four days across two weeks. SOFIT is a coding system that involves time sampling and coding of student physical activity, lesson context, and teacher behavior. MANOVA results revealed that there were no overall school differences with regard to physical education between the schools. The data did reveal the following trends: students in the HS school had less time for physical activity but tended to engage in more vigorous physical activity in both physical education and recess whereas students in the LS school had more time for physical activity. Findings were compared to the Healthy People 2010 recommendations for physical activity and previous findings on children in the United States. Physical activity levels demonstrated by the students in this study were just short of the Health People 2010 recommendations, but above those typically reported for children both with and without disabilities in the United States.

Fitness—training studies. The second major category within physical fitness is training studies. These studies tend to focus on the effects of a type of training program (e.g., aerobics, swimming, Pilates), on some aspect of fitness (e.g., lung function or health-related fitness; see, for example, Can et al., 2005; Khalili & Elkins, 2009; Etherton, Covington, Burt, & Weishaar, 2006; Ozmen, Yildirim, Yuktasir, Beets, 2007), or on psycho-social effects (e.g., Dykens, Rosner, & Butterbaugh, 1998; Lee & Dummer, 2006; Wright & Cowden, 1986) of fitness training. It should be noted that the majority of the training studies involving individuals with intellectual disabilities used adult participants rather than children.

The study by Wright and Cowden (1986) illustrates a training study that examined the effect of a swimming program on the cardiovascular endurance and self-concept of adolescents with intellectual disabilities. Participants were 50 adolescents ages 12 to 18 classified as mildly and moderately mentally retarded. These subjects were divided into two groups. One group participated in a Special Olympics swim training program for 1 hour a day, 2 days a week, for 10 weeks. The second group served as the control and performed their normal daily activities including attending their regular physical education classes during the 10 weeks of the study. All participants were pre- and post-tested using the 9 minute run/walk test and the Piers-Harris Children's Self-Concept Scale. Analysis of variance results revealed significant mean differences between the Special Olympics group and the control group on both dependent measures. On the 9 minute run/walk test the Special Olympics group demonstrated significant improvement between the two measurement periods whereas the control group actually showed a slight decline in their performance. Similar results were found on the self-concept measure. The control group showed no change, but the Special Olympics group demonstrated a significant improvement. Implications were discussed regarding the value of organized youth sports programs like Special Olympics for individuals with intellectual disabilities and the need for more research in this area.

In addition to the research cited here, there have also been two published reviews of research in the area of training. Chanias, Reid, and Hoover (1998) reported a meta-analysis of 21 studies that focused on the health-related physical fitness of individuals with intellectual disabilities, and Fernhall (1993) reported a summary of the training research on fitness and intellectual disabilities. These reviews revealed that individuals with intellectual disabilities have lower levels of fitness, higher risks for cardiovascular disease, and may respond differently to exercise training. They also found large effect sizes for exercise training on cardiovascular endurance and muscular endurance and moderate effect sizes for training focusing on muscular strength. However, no significant effects were found for body composition. Both reviews concluded with recommendations for future research and identified issues in the areas of experimental design and standardization of methods that needed to be addressed.

Fitness—assessment. The last category of fitness research on individuals with intellectual disabilities includes studies that focused on assessment issues related to physical fitness. The majority of these studies focused either on cardio-respiratory endurance (e.g., Baumgartner & Horvat, 1991; Beets, Pitetti, & Fernhall, 2005; Ellis, Cress, & Spellman, 1993; Fernhall, Millar, Pitetti, Hensen, & Vukovich, 2000; Pitetti, Millar, & Fernhall, 2000; Koh & Watkinson, 1988; Pitetti, Fernhall, Stubbs, & Stadler, 1997; Watkinson & Koh, 1988) or physical activity of individuals with intellectual disabilities (e.g., Faison-Hodge & Porretta, 2004; Horvat & Franklin, 2001; Kozub, 2003; Lorenze, Horvat, & Pellegrini, 2000; So-Yeun & Joonkoo, 2009; Stanish, 2004).

A study that investigated the validity and reliability of the one-half mile run-walk test as an indicator of aerobic fitness for children with intellectual disabilities by Fernhall, Pitetti, Stubbs, and Stadler (1996) illustrates research in the area of cardiorespiratory assessment. In this study, 23 students labeled as mildly or moderately mentally retarded and ranging in age from 10 to 17 years were measured on two maximal treadmill protocols with metabolic measurements and two one-half mile run-walk trials. Participants were familiarized with both the testing settings and protocols before being tested. Fernhall et al. measured peak VO2 and heart rate during the treadmill tests, time to the nearest second to complete the one-half mile run-walk, and heart rate during the run-walk. There were no significant differences between the two trials for VO2 max, maximum heart rate, or run-walk time. Correlations between trials were $r = .90$ for VO2max, $r = .81$ for maximum heart rate, and $r = .96$ for the one-half mile run-walk indicating that the ½ mile run-walk was a reliable test. Based on the correlation between VO2 max and the one-half mile run walk $r = -.60$ ($p < .05$) and the comparison of this relationship to data previously reported on children without mental retardation, the authors concluded that the one-half mile run-walk had questionable validity as an indicator of aerobic capacity for children with mental retardation.

An investigation by Horvat and Franklin (2001) illustrates a study designed to examine physical activity in children with intellectual disabilities. Participants in this study included 23 children from three different schools, ages 6 to 12, classified as mildly mentally retarded. Participants were observed for 16 minutes using an interval recording system (i.e., Scheme for Observing Activity Level) on three different occasions while engaged in free play in two types of recess settings (inclusion and non-inclusion) and in the classroom. During each observation period, the students also wore a heart rate monitor and an activity monitor. Students in the two recess settings were significantly more active than in the classroom setting and there was no significant difference found between the two recess settings. The authors noted that while there were no statistical significant differences found between the two recess settings, they did observe that the non-inclusive setting provided higher activity ratings when compared to the inclusive setting.

Readers interested in more information about fitness assessment for individuals with ID, should consult excellent literature reviews on this topic by Frey, Stanish, and Temple (2008) and Seidi, Reid, and Montgomery (1987).

Motor Skill Studies

The second major category of research studies reviewed here pertains to studies that investigated questions related to how motor skills were acquired (e.g., Edison & Stadulis, 1991; Gillespie, 2003; Porretta & O'Brien, 1991; Surburg, Porretta, Sutlive, 1995; Yang & Porretta, 1999) by students with intellectual disabilities and/or how students with intellectual disabilities learned motor skills in difference settings (e.g., Kozub, 2002; Valentini & Rudisill, 2004) or factors that affect learning in physical education (e.g., Gagnon, Touslgnant, & Martel, 1989; Holland, 1987; Kozub, Porretta, & Hodge, 2000; Merighi, Edison, & Zigler, 1990; Shapiro & Dummer, 1998; Temple & Walkley, 1999; Yun & Ulrich, 1997). Motor skills in this section refer to fundamental motor patterns used in our societal games and sports such as the locomotor and object control skills of running, skipping, catching, and throwing. The studies on motor skills have been divided into two areas: motor learning studies and field-based studies in physical education settings.

Motor learning. Motor learning studies focus on how motor skills are learned and/or under what conditions they are learned most efficiently. Most motor learning studies are conducted in laboratory or highly controlled field settings. For example, Gillespie (2003) investigated summary versus every-trial knowledge of results for individuals with intellectual disabilities. Knowledge of results (KR) involves giving the learners feedback either mechanically or verbally about the outcome of their performance. Participants for this study were 32 males with mild ID with a mean age of 10.75 years. The task involved putting a golf ball from a designated spot with a regulation club and ball. Students were oriented to the task which involved putting a ball and having it stop between two horizontal lines located 144 in. (370.08 cm) and 156 in. (400.92 cm) in front of the students. After the students understood the task, an opaque curtain was placed 60 in. (152.40 cm) in front of the students that prevented them from seeing where their ball stopped. Students were then given 50 putting trials. Both groups received visual (i.e., were able to look around the curtain and see where their ball stopped) and verbal feedback (i.e., score indicating distance from target). Students in the KR1 group received KR feedback after each trial whereas students in the KR5 group received summary feedback after every 5 trials. Retention was measured 1 day and 1 week after the acquisition trials. Analysis of the data revealed that students in the KR1 group obtained statistically significant higher scores during the skill acquisition trials than the students in the KR5 group. However, students in the KR5 group obtained significantly higher scores on both the one day and one week retention tests.

Readers interested in learning more about the theoretical basis of research on motor learning and motor skill acquisition of individuals with ID should consult the book by Michael Wade (1986) and the article by Hoover and Wade (1986).

Physical education studies. We review two studies in this section to highlight the nature of the current research in physical education for intellectual disabilities. The first study examined learning of physical education under different instructional settings. For more information on this topic, readers should consult the review by Block and Obrusnikova (2007). The second study illustrates examples of studies that examined different factors that affect the learning of students with intellectual disabilities in physical education.

Valentini and Rudisill (2004) investigated the effect of an inclusive mastery climate intervention on the motor skill development of children with and without disabilities. Participants were 36 students with disabilities and 68 students without disabilities who were randomly assigned to intervention and comparison groups. The mastery intervention training was based on creating a mastery climate, which was defined as

> a systematic approach that uses student-centered instruction to target both the motivational level of the student and the processes of learning. It is a type of climate where the primary emphasis is on the autonomy of the child. The teacher facilitates an instructional environment in which students are given the opportunity to navigate their own learning that they deem appropriate for their level of development. The focus of a mastery climate is directed toward the process rather than on the product or outcome of learning. (p. 332)

All participants were pre- and post-tested on the Test of Gross Motor Development, which was composed of six locomotor and six object control skills. The intervention group participated in a 12-week intervention that met twice a week for 60 minutes and was based on a mastery climate and focused on locomotor and object control skills. The comparison group participated in free play under the supervision of a classroom teacher over the 12-week period. Both groups participated in their regular physical education program that met twice a week. Both the students with and without disabilities that participated in the intervention demonstrated significant improvement in the motor performance whereas the participants in the comparison group did not.

Temple and Walkley (1999) investigated the academic learning time of students with mild intellectual disabilities in regular physical education classes. Academic learning time (ALT) is a measure of teacher effectiveness that employs a systematic observation system to quantify the percentage of time students spend engaged in the subject matter at an appropriate difficulty level. Different types of engagement can be measured. This study focused on physical education time (PE-Time), physical education engagement time (PE-Engaged), the amount of time engaged in motor practice (ME) and engagement in motor activity at the appropriate difficulty level (MA). Participants for the study were drawn from integrated primary and secondary schools in Australia sampling students from grades 3, 4, 5, 8, 9, and 10. A quota sampling technique was used resulting in 24 students with mild intellectual disabilities and 48 students without disabilities matching a male and female student to each student with intellectual disabilities. The class containing each student was observed five times. Data were recorded using an interval recording procedure. Data analysis revealed no significant effects for the variable grade or interaction of grade with gender or disability. Overall 59% of the allocated class time was spent on PE-Time. Of this total, 35% was spent on PE-Engaged time and of this 26% was ME and 22% was of the appropriate difficulty level. Although there were no differences between the students with and without intellectual disabilities on PE-Time, students with intellectual disabilities were engaged 40% less in motor activity at the appropriate level. The authors argued that students with intellectual disabilities were not being provided a curriculum appropriate to their intellectual ability.

Summary

This brief review of the literature on research in physical education related to individuals with mild intellectual disabilities clearly shows that this is a significant area of interest and that a substantial amount of research has been conducted. Overall the findings reveal that individuals with mild intellectual disabilities tend to perform below their age equivalent peers without intellectual disabilities, but that with appropriate instruction these deficits can be reduced. With regard to gender, males tend to perform better than females. Within the population of individuals with intellectual disabilities, deficits in performance tend to increase as the severity of the intellectual disabilities increases. Although the volume of research produced to-date is encouraging, the majority of it has focused largely on one aspect of physical education—physical fitness and within physical fitness predominantly on cardiorespiratory endurance. Acquisition of motor skills, which constitutes the majority of the content in physical education, has received less emphasis in the research literature, and a significant body of this research has focused on the learning of novel skills and/or has employed indirect measures of learning such as academic learning time.

Children with Learning Disabilities

Many children with learning disabilities do not display gross motor problems and are actually quite athletic. Famous athletes with learning disabilities include Olympic gold medalist Bruce Jenner, basketball star Magic Johnson, football star Dexter Manley, and baseball star Pete Rose (Angle, 2007). However, many children with learning disabilities have motor problems (Shaeffer, Law, Palatajko, & Miller, 1989). Sherrill and Pyfer (1985) found 13% of children with learning disabilities scored 2–3 years below age level on perceptual motor tests, Miyahara (1994) found that 25% of children with LD scored poorly in a general motor ability test, and Sugden and Wann (1987) found that 50% of 8-year-olds and 29% of 12-year-olds had motor problems. Not surprisingly, motor problems are most notable in children with motor and sensory-related learning problems such as dyspraxia and visual processing problems (Conrad, Cermak, & Drake, 1983; Shapiro, 2001).

SPORTdiscus was used as the primary search engine with the terms "learning disabilities" and "motor," "motor delays," "physical education," or "fitness" as the targeted search words. The final total of 52 articles were categorized as (a) cause of apraxia and movement problems in learning disabilities (3 articles), (b) motor development/performance/ability (22 articles), (c) practice/learning/teaching factors and their effect on performance (11 papers), (d) testing/evaluation (7 papers), and (e) psychological variables such as self-esteem/expectancies/effort (9 papers). Each of these areas is reviewed highlighting key findings and trends from the data.

Motor Development/Performance/Ability

As noted earlier, research shows 13% to 50% of children with learning disabilities have motor deficits. Most research related to motor performance in children with learning disabilities has focused on confirming and then specifying these delays. The vast majority of these studies examined specific motor coordination problems in children with learning disabilities using either the Bruininks-Oseretsky Test of Motor Proficiency (BOT) (Beyer, 1999; Bluechardt & Shephard, 1996; Bruininks & Bruininks, 1977; Longhurst, Coetsee, & Bressan, 2004; Pyfer & Carlson, 1972; Schaeffer et al., 1989), or the Test of Motor Impairment (TOMI) (Cermak, Ward, & Ward; 1986; Geuze & Borger, 1993; Losse et al., 1991). Both of these tests measure general coordination, eye-hand coordination, response speed, static and dynamic balance. Most of these studies were well conceived with an age-matched control group and group-sizes of 30 or more participants. Results from these studies confirm that many children with learning disabilities have delays when compared to peers without learning disabilities. For example, Longhurst and her colleagues in South Africa compared the motor proficiency in 60 children 8–12 years of age with and without learning disabilities on the BOT. Children without learning disabilities performed significantly better on all eight subtests compared to children with learning disabilities, with most notable differences in balance, strength, and upper body speed and dexterity. Similarly, Bleuchardt and Shephard in Canada found children with learning disabilities 8–10 years of age scored significantly lower than the normative sample on the BOT. As with Longhurst et al., the greatest deficits were in balance and upper body speed and dexterity, although strength deficits were not significant as was the case in Longhurst et al.

Other researchers examining coordination looked at one specific aspect of coordination, again finding differences between children with and without learning disabilities. These studies were well conceived, with age-matched control groups and relatively large group sizes ranging from 12 to 30 participants. For example, Fawcett and Nicolson (1992), Getchell, McMenamin, and Whitall (2005), Rousselle and Wolff (1991), Wolff, Michel, Ovrur, and Drake (1990), and Yap and Van der Leij (1994) found children with learning disabilities had more difficulty in consistency and coordinating two tasks at one time such as walking and clapping or balancing and listening compared to age-matched peers without learning disabilities. Woodard and Surburg (1999) found children 6–8 years of age with learning disabilities demonstrated midline crossing inhibition compared to age-matched peers without learning disabilities. Kerr and Hughes (1987) found children 6–8 years of age were 1–2 years delayed compared to age-matched peers in a reciprocal finger tapping task. Lazarus (1994) found children with learning disabilities 7–14 years of age had greater levels of overflow (an inability to keep one arm or leg still while moving the other arm or leg) compared to same-age peers without learning disabilities. Finally, Smits-Engelsman, Wilson, Westenberg, and Duysens (2003) found children ages 9–12 with learning disabilities and developmental coordination disorders had no problems with simple drawing tasks (drawing a line from one target to another) but did differ from peers without learning disabilities in cyclical drawing tasks (drawing a line back and forth between two targets).

Finally, research found many children with learning disabilities performed at a lower developmental level compared to peers without learning disabilities in fundamental motor patterns (Woodard & Surburg, 2001; 1997; Bradley & Drowatzky, 1997). For example, Woodard and Surburg compared 22 children with and without LD 6–8 years on the Test of Gross Motor Development (TGMD). The TGMD measures qualitative performance on 6 locomotor (e.g., run, gallop) and 6 object control (throw, catch) skills. The test provides age norms for comparison. Results found 12 of 22 of children with LD performed at a delayed level including 6 children scoring at a poor level and 4 children at a very poor level. In contrast, 8 of 22 children without LD performed at a delayed level, but of these 8 only 4 performed at a poor level, and none performed at a very poor level.

Psychological Variables Related to Motor Difficulties in Children with LD

Motor difficulties and repeated failures in gross motor performance in physical education, recreation, and sport settings that can lead to psychosocial problems related to these movement problems (Doyle & Higginson, 1984; Henderson, May, & Umney, 1989; Shaw, Levine, & Belfer, 1982; VanRossum & Vermeer, 1990; Willoughby, Polatajko, & Wilson, 1995). For example, Shaw and her colleagues measured self-esteem in a total of 23 boys with learning disabilities (12 with gross motor delays) ages 8–12 years using two different scales of self-esteem. Boys with poor coordination self-reported themselves lower in physical ability, social relationships, and happy qualities compared to boys without motor delays. This study should be read with some caution given the small sample size and use of self-esteem scales in which participants were read 80 questions for one scale and 48 for the other (quite a bit of listening and thinking for children as young as 8 years of age). However, Willoughby et al. found similar lower motor-related self-esteem in children with learning disabilities and related motor difficulties with a larger sample (85 children) and stronger instruments (i.e., the Bruininks-Oseretsky Test of Motor Proficiency to measure gross motor performance and the Pictorial Scale of Perceived Competence and Social Acceptance for Young Children to measure self-esteem).

Children with LD and motor difficulties are more likely to experience less success in physical education and, as a result, develop behaviors in an attempt to avoid physical activity (Dunn & Dunn, 2006; Thompson, Bouffard, Watkinson, & Causgrove Dunn, 1994). Dunn and Dunn observed 65 fourth- to sixth-grade children with movement difficulties and 65 matched children without movement difficulties in general physical education classes. Children with movement difficulties in a general physical education setting spent less time successfully performing assigned activities, spent more time experience difficulty in the given tasks, and spent more time in off-task behaviors when compared to peers without disabilities.

Not all studies examining children with learning disabilities show a relationship between movement and self-esteem. Shapiro and Ulrich (2002) examined physical/motor self-esteem in 30 children with and without learning disabilities ages 10–13 years using the Modified Pictorial Scale of Perceived Physical Competence (MPSPPC). Results indicated no differences in perceived physical competence between children with and without learning disabilities. Interestingly, children with learning disabilities in this study did not have any motor problems or problems in physical education as reported by their physical education teachers which may account for these findings. Similarly, Kozub and Porretta (2001) found no differences between fifth-grade children with and without learning disabilities (12 children per group) on measures of task persistence. Children in this study were given two physical activity tasks that could not be completed successfully. However, both children with and without learning disabilities showed similar persistence scores in these tasks suggesting children with learning disabilities do not get frustrated more quickly than peers without disabilities. Again, there was no indication whether the children with learning disabilities in their study had concomitant motor deficits which may have altered the results, and the small sample size brings into question the strength of the study.

Teaching/Learning Variables and Motor Performance in Children with Learning Disabilities

Several researchers have investigated ways to enhance motor performance in children with learning disabilities who have movement difficulties. Some researchers examined ways of improving fundamental motor patterns such as throwing and catching and running and jumping (Hodge, Murata, & Porretta, 1999; Revie & Larkin, 1993; Valentini & Rudisill, 2004). The common thread in all these studies was the focus on teaching the components of the skills and setting a climate focusing on skill mastery rather than competition. For example, Hodge and his colleagues found mental preparation (closing one's eyes and going through the components of the skill to be performed) significantly improved throwing patterns in elementary-aged children with learning disabilities and attention deficits compared to matched participants who did not do a warm up or did a traditional stretching warm up. Similarly, Revie and Larkin used task-specific, intensive teaching instruction to help children ages 5–9 years with movement problems improve in fundamental movement patterns of the over-arm throw, target kick, and bounce-and-catch tasks. Hodge et al. assigned children to either a group (N = 12) which was taught the over-arm throw and hop or to a group (N = 12) which was taught target kick or volleyball bounce-and-catch. Each group acted as the other's control group, and (with the exception of hopping) pretest-posttest scores showed significant improvement when the specific skill was taught, but there was no such improvement without instruction. This is important because physical educators too often simply introduce skills and then move to new skills. Such an approach does not seem to match the needs of students with learning disabilities, who require intense instruction on specific skills programs and distributed practice if they are to master skills.

Others have examined more specific treatments or techniques on mastery of more discrete, motor learning tasks. Results of these studies showed that constant practice schedules improved learning of a simple motor task compared to random practice schedules (Heitman, Erdmann, Gurchick, Kovaleski, & Gilley, 1997); verbal rehearsal strategies improved performance in a motor sequencing task compared to no modeling and even visual—verbal modeling (Kowalski & Sherrill, 1992); relaxation training improved reaction time on a visual choice motor test as well as reducing unrelated behaviors (Brandon, Eason, & Smith, 1986); and a specialized school-based (Khalsa, Morris, & Sifft, 1988) and home-based (Horvat, 1982), and cooperative program (Mender, Kerr, & Orlick, 1982) improved balance in children with learning disabilities). For example, Hietman and his colleagues compared practice schedules on learning three different versions of the same skill in 24 children ages 9–12 years with learning disabilities. Children were randomly placed in either a constant or variable practice schedule. In the constant practice schedule, children practiced one variation of the skill continuously for 10 trials before moving to the next variation of the skill. In the variable practice group, children practiced each variation of the skill 10 times but in random order. Both groups received the same grand total of 30 practice trials. Results showed children in the constant practice group performed significantly better compared to the variable group during learning. However, there were no differences between the groups on the following day when both groups were presented the task randomly. Results showing constant practice improves performance during the learning phase is consistent with the motor learning research. However, motor learning research also shows random practice improves performance in retention tasks and when transferring to a slightly different skill (Schmidt & Wrisberg, 2008). Unfortunately, Hietman and his colleagues did not examine retention or transfer, so it is still unclear which practice schedule is best for children with learning disabilities.

Regarding teaching-learning programs it is important to note the controversy surrounding perceptual-motor training and children with learning disabilities (Dunn & Leitschuh, 2006; Hallahan & Cruickshank, 1973; Kavale & Mattson, 1983; Nolan, 2004). Perceptual-motor training as a treatment for learning disabilities was popular in the 1960s and 70s based on clinical, classroom, and anecdotal reports of success remediating specific learning problems. The basic concept behind the theory is that perceptual-motor problems cause learning problems. For example, Kephart (1971) suggested a strong relationship between finding a figure from its background (a perceptual task) and success in academic tasks such as reading and writing. Kephart created a remedial program for children with learning disabilities grounded in perceptual-motor training including balance and posture, locomotion, and eye-hand coordination. Similarly, Getman and Frostig created visual-perceptual training programs, and Ayres created a sensory integration program, all with the idea that perceptual-motor training will improve academic performance (Dunn & Leitschuh, 2006).

Unfortunately, analysis of hundreds of studies showed perceptual motor training was not an effective method to remediate specific learning disabilities (Hallahan & Cruickshank, 1973; Kavale & Mattson, 1983). Schaeffer et al. (1989) pointed out perceptual-motor training quickly fell out of favor with the learning disability community in the 1980s, leading the Council for Learning Disabilities (Board of Trustees, 1986) to issue a position statement opposing "…the measurement and training of perceptual and perceptual-motor functions as part of learning disability services" and called for "a moratorium on assessment and training of perceptual and perceptual-motor functions in educational programs" (p. 247). Interestingly, perceptual-motor training has seen a recent resurgence in programs for children with learning disabilities, including Educational Kinesiology/Brain Gym (Cammisa, 1994; Freeman & Dennison, 1998), which includes stretching and unique movements designed to stimulate brain function, and the Dore Method (Dore, 2009–2010), which includes balance activities, throwing and catching bean bags, and a range of stretching and coordination exercises. Both programs purport to improve academic function in children with learning disabilities, but neither method has yet to be supported by empirical research.

Children with Emotional Disturbances

There has been very little published on motor development delays/issues or physical activity levels of children labeled as emotionally disturbed. Perhaps this is due to the broad definition of behavior disorder that includes everything from conduct disorder to depression to anorexia to anxiety disorder. It may also be due to the fact definitions and characteristics of specific types of behavior disorders do not include any motor of fitness delays (APA, 2000; Downing, 2007). A search was conducted of SPORTdiscus using key disability terms *behavior disorder*, *behavior disability*, *emotional disorder*, and *emotional disability*. These disability terms were then matched with the terms *physical activity*, *physical education*, *motor*, *recreation*, and *sport*. Combined these searches produced several hundred articles. Interestingly, most of the articles focused on anorexia or ADHD or where not focused on motor or physical activity. However, there were seven articles found in this search that were appropriate for this review. Two of these articles focused on attitudes towards physical activity (Merriman, 1993; Politino & Smith, 1989). For example, Politino and Smith compared the attitude toward physical activity and self-concept of children with emotional disturbances ages 8–13 years from two psychiatric hospitals (n = 80) to 390 children of the same age without emotional disturbances. Data was collected using two surveys—the Children's Attitude toward Physical Activity Inventory and the Piers-Harris Self-Concept Scale. Results found that children without disabilities had significantly higher attitudes toward physical activity and a higher level of self-concept compared to children with emotional disturbances. Two studies focused on the using physical activity (in this case dance) to promote appropriate behaviors (Edwards-Duke, Boswell, McGhee, & Decker, 2002) or using behavior modification in a physical activity to promote appropriate behavior (Jeltma & Vogler, 1985). The remaining three studies examined actual physical activity, motor proficiency or skill development in children with behavior disorders (Bar-Eli, Hartman, & Levy-Kolker, 1994; Gruber, Hall, McKay, Humphries, & Kryscio, 1989; Maiano, Ninot, Morin, & Bilard, 2007). To illustrate, Maiano and his colleagues studied effects of sport participation (basketball) on basketball skill development and physical self-concept in 24 boys with conduct disorders ages 11–13 who attended one of two special schools in France. Participants were divided into one of three groups: competitive basketball at the special school; competitive basketball in an integrated, community program; and a control group that received regular physical activity but not competitive basketball. A basketball skill test and self-concept test were administered four times over an 18-month period. Results showed the two competitive groups significantly improved their basketball skills from pre- to posttest, while the control group did not see such an improvement. However, there were no statistical improvements in self-concept in any of the groups from pre- to posttest.

Similarly, there were only three articles that were somewhat on topic with the combination of behavior disorder and recreation, but these articles focused on the effects of a therapeutic recreation settings (e.g., adventure-based program, out-patient therapeutic recreation program) on social skill development or appropriate behavior (Bloemhoff, 2006; McMahon & Sharpe, 2009; Rothwell, Piatt, & Mattingly, 2006). In addition, in our own records we found two additional articles that focused on recreation and children with emotional disorders, but again these articles focused on the use of recreation settings (outdoor challenge program, leisure education program) on self-esteem or attitudes towards leisure (Langsner & Anderson, 1987; Munson, 1988).

In summary, there were very few studies that examined motor delays or physical activity issues in children with emotional disturbances. Most of the research focused on the use of physical activity, sport and recreation on improving self-concept, behaviors and attitudes towards physical activity. There is nothing in the literature or in descriptions of sub-populations of children with behavior disturbances that suggest these children have motor delays or problems with physical activity. On the other hand, limited access to community sport and recreation programs due to behavior issues and poor attitudes towards physical activity makes this population prone to physical inactivity and all the unwanted affects of physical inactivity such as obesity and health problems.

Current Issues and Challenges

Clearly, conducting research in the physical and motor domains presents many challenges when working with students with developmental disabilities (Reid, Dunn, & McClements, 1993). These challenges can range from issues related to recruiting, communicating and achieving informed consent, or preparing participants for participation and encouraging but not coercing compliance with the research protocol. While these are all important challenges, this section is going to briefly touch on three much broader issues: (a) the need for coordinated, multidisciplinary research; (b) the need for uniform, dependent measures for physical and motor skill assessment; and (c) the need for consistent definitions of disabilities.

Research in physical education is generally not guided by any systematic master plan, but instead is largely a collection of small, often one attempt studies, employing different definitions of participants, dependent measures, testing protocols, and/or training programs. Research in physical education needs to become more multidisciplinary, better integrated with collaborative research in special education, and conducted on a large scale. To this end, it is recommended that the professional associations (e.g., AAHPERD and CEC) work together to conduct a national needs assessment and the creation of a national research agenda for individuals with developmental disabilities that includes physical education. Within physical education it is also recommended that the following issues be addressed:

1. Create and validate physical fitness and motor skill assessment instruments that can be used to measure physical and motor development across the PK–adult age range for individuals with developmental disabilities.
2. Work with state departments of education to infuse these uniform physical fitness and motor skill assessments into the PK–12 school physical education curriculum so that comparable data are collected on all students as part of the normal educational process.
3. Researchers need to partner with local schools to assist in valid data collection, analysis, and interpretation and then to work collaboratively with schools and state education systems in creating large-scale intervention programs to address identified needs that can be replicated and easily transferred to other schools.

Physical education is defined in IDEA as the "development of (a) physical and motor fitness, (b) fundamental motor skills and patterns, and (c) skills in aquatics, dance, and individual and group games and sports (including intramural and lifetime sports)" (Department of Education, 2002, p. 18). The review of research in this chapter reveals that while a substantial amount of research has been conducted in the area of physical education with individuals with developmental disabilities, the emphasis and the focus of the research has not been well balanced. For example, the vast majority of the research on individuals with ID has focused on just one aspect of physical education that is physical fitness and much of that research has focused on only one area of fitness—validating measures of cardiovascular endurance. Future research in physical education, therefore, needs apply a more balanced approach which examines all aspects of physical education particularly given the clear relationship between one's ability to move competently and one's ability to stay active and be physically fit. It should also be clear that the majority of the components of physical education are developed and learned at younger ages and therefore require more research efforts at the pre-school and elementary levels. Innovative solutions are needed to address the challenges of creating research designs, finding valid dependent measures, and working with younger participants with developmental disabilities.

Finally, the range of physical and motor abilities of students within any given developmental disability label can vary tremendously depending on the nature of the definition and how it was assessed. Matching two students on the label specific learning disability (SLD) may control for little of the variance on a motor assessment due to their disability if one has an auditory processing problem and the other a visual processing problem. Students with LD who have motor delays vary widely from study to study. What further confounds the research is the new label of developmental coordination disorder (DCD). Questions that need to be answered are what percentage of children with LD have DCD, and what percentage of children with DCD have LD? In addition, do children with LD who have DCD or significant motor delays have specific types of learning disabilities (e.g., dyslexia) vs. other types of learning disabilities?

References

American Psychiatric Association (APA). (2000). *Diagnostic and statistical manual of disorders* (4th ed., text revision). Washington, DC: Author.

Angle, B. (2007, September). Winning the "game" against learning disabilities. *Coach and Athletic Director*. Retrieved November 10, 2008, from http://findarticles.com/p/articles/mi_m0FIH/is_/ai_n27379279

Auxter, D. M. (1966). Strength and flexibility of differentially diagnosed educable mentally retarded boys. *Research Quarterly, 37*, 455–461.

Bar-Eli, M., Hartman, I., & Levy-Kolker, N. (1994). Using goals setting to improve physical performance of adolescents with behavior disorders: The effects of goal proximity. *Adapted Physical Activity Quarterly, 11*, 86–97.

Baumgartner, T., & Horvat, M. (1991). Reliability of field based cardiovascular fitness running tests for individuals with mental retardation. *Adapted Physical Activity Quarterly*, *8*, 107–114.

Beasley, C. R. (1982). Effects of jogging program on cardiovascular fitness and work performances of mentally retarded persons. *American Journal of Mental Deficiency*, *87*, 609–613.

Beets, M. W., Pitetti, K. H., & Fernhall, B. (2005). Peak heart rates in youth with mental retardation: Pacer vs. treadmill. *Pediatric Exercise Science*, *17*, 51–61.

Beyer, R. (1999). Motor proficiency of boys with attention deficit hyperactivity disorder and boys with learning disabilities. *Adapted Physical Activity Quarterly, 16*, 403–414.

Block, M. E., & Obrusnikova, I. (2007). Inclusion in physical education: A review of the literature from 1995–2005. *Adapted Physical Activity Quarterly, 24*, 103–124.

Bloemhoff, H. J. (2006). The effect of an adventure-based recreation programme (ropes course) on the development of resiliency in at-risk adolescent boys confined to a rehabilitation centre. *South African Journal of Research in Sport, 28*(1), 1–11.

Bluechardt, M., & Shephard, R. J. (1996). Motor performance impairment in students with learning disability: Influence of gender and body build. *Sports Medicine, Training and Rehabilitation, 7*, 133–140.

Board of Trustees of the Council for Learning Disabilities. (1986). *Measurement and training of perceptual and perceptual-motor functions: A position statement*. Overland Park, KS: Author.

Brace, D. K. (1968). Physical education and recreation of mentally retarded pupils in public schools. *Research Quarterly, 39*, 779–782.

Bradley, C. B., & Drowatzky, J. N. (1997). Time intervals of five successive steps in children with learning disabilities and children without learning disabilities. *Clinical Kinesiology, 51*(3), 58–61.

Brandon, J. E., Eason, R. L., & Smith, T. L. (1986). Behavioral relaxation training and motor performance of learning disabled children with hyperactive behaviors. *Adapted Physical Activity Quarterly, 3*, 67–79.

Bruininks, V. L., & Bruininks, R. H. (1977). Motor proficiency of learning disabled and nondisabled students. *Perceptual and Motor Skills, 44*, 1131–1137.

Bundschuh, E., & Cureton,K. (1982). Effect of bicycle ergometer conditioning on the physical work capacity of mentally retarded adolescents. American *Corrective Therapy Journal, 36*, 159–163.

Burkett, L. N., & Ewing, N. (1983). *Max VO2 uptake on five trainable mentally retarded high school students*, Reston, VA: AAHPERD Abstracts, W. Kroll (Ed.), 83.

Burtner, P. A., Qualls, C., Ortega, S. G., Morris, C. G., & Scott, K. (2002). Test-retest reliability of the motor-free visual perception test revised (MVPT-R) in children with and without learning disabilities. *Physical & Occupational Therapy in Pediatrics, 22*(3/4), 23–36.

Campbell, J. (1974). Improving the physical fitness of retarded boys. *Mental Retardation, 11*, 26–29.

Cammisa, K. M. (1994). Educational kinesiology with learning disabled children: An efficacy study. *Perceptual and Motor Skills, 78*, 105–106.

Can, F., Ergun, N., Yilmaz, Y., Bayrak, C., Konukman, F., Agbuga, B., & Zorba, E. (2005). Effects of a 10-week swimming program on the respiratory functions of children with mental retardation. *Research Quarterly for Exercise & Sport, 76*, A27–A28.

Carter, J. L. (1966). The status of mentally retarded boys on the AAHPER Youth Fitness Test. *Texas Association for Health, Physical Education, and Recreation Journal, 34*, 8, 29–31.

Cermak, S. A., Ward, E. A., & Ward, L. M. (1986). The relationship between articulation disorders and motor coordination in children. *The American Journal of Occupational Therapy, 40*(8), 546–550.

Chanias, A. K., Reid, G., & Hoover, M. L. (1998). Exercise effects on health-related physical fitness of individuals with an intellectual disability: A meta analysis. *Adapted Physical Activity Quarterly, 15*, 119–140.

Chow, B., Frey, G. C., Cheung, S., & Louie, L. (2005). An examination of the health-related physical fitness levels in Hong Kong youth with intellectual disability. *Journal of Exercise Science & Fitness, 3*, 9–16.

Coleman, A., Ayoub, M., & Friedrich, D. (1976). Assessment of the physical work capacity of institutionalized mentally retarded males. *American Journal of Mental Deficiency, 80*, 629–635.

Conrad, K. E., Cermak, S. A., & Drake, C. (1983). Differentiation of praxis among children. *The American Journal of Occupational Therapy, 37*, 466–473.

Corder, W. O. (1966). Effects of physical education on the intellectual, physical, and social development of educable mentally retarded boys. *Exceptional Children, 32*, 357–364.

Cressler, R. V., Lavay, B., & Giese, M. (1988). The reliability of four measures of cardiovascular fitness with mentally retarded adults. *Adapted Physical Activity Quarterly, 5*, 285–292.

Department of Education (2002). *Code of Federal Regulations*. 34 CFR, Parts 300-399, July 1, 2002.

Dore. (2009-2010). Retrieved from http://www.dore.co.uk/

Downing, J. A. (2007). *Students with emotional and behavioral problems: Assessment, management and intervention strategies*. Tappan, NJ: Merrill.

Doyle, B. A., & Higginson, D. C. (1984). Relationships among self-concept and school-achievement, maternal self-esteem, and sensory integration abilities for learning disabled children ages 7-12 years. *Perceptual and Motor Skills, 58*, 177–178.

Dunn, J. C., & Dunn, J. G. H. (2006). Psychosocial determinants of physical education behavior in children with movement difficulties. *Adapted Physical Activity Quarterly, 23*, 293–309.

Dunn, J. M., & Leitschuh, C. A. (2006). *Special physical education* (8th ed.). Dubuque, IA: Kendall/Hunt.

Dunn, J. M., Moorehouse, J. W., Anderson, R. B., Fredericks, H. D., Baldwin, V. L., Blair, F. L., & Moore, W. (1980). *A data based gymnasium*. Monmouth, OR: Instructional Development Corporation.

Dykens, E. M., Rosner, B. A., & Butterbaugh, G. (1998). Exercise and sports in children and adolescents with developmental disabilities: Positive physical and psychosocial effects. *Child & Adolescent Psychiatric Clinics of North America, 7*, 757–771.

Edison, T. A., & Stadulis, R. E. (1991). Effects of variability of practice on the transfer and performance of open and closed motor skills. *Adapted Physical Activity Quarterly, 8*, 342–356.

Edwards-Duke, B., Boswell, B., McGhee, S., & Decker, J. (2002). Creative educational dance and children with behavior disorders: Encouraging a spirit of cooperation. *Journal of Dance Education, 2*(1), 23–31.

Ellis, D. N., Cress, P. J., & Spellman, C. R. (1993). Training students with mental retardation to self-pace while exercising. *Adapted Physical Activity Quarterly, 10*, 104–115.

Etherton, D., Covington, N. K., Burt, T., & Weishaar, M. K. (2006). Effects of Pilates on the health-related physical fitness of individuals with disabilities. *Research Quarterly for Exercise & Sport, 77*, A93.

Faison-Hodge, J., & Porretta, D. L. (2004). Physical activity levels of students with mental retardation and students without disabilities. *Research Quarterly for Exercise and Sport, 73*(1), 103–105

Fawcett, A. J., & Nicolson, R. J. (1992). Automatisation deficits in balance for dyslexic children. *Perceptual and Motor Skills, 75*, 507–529.

Fernhall, B. (1993). Physical fitness and exercise training of individuals with mental retardation. *Medicine & Science in Sports & Exercise, 25*(4), 442–450.

Fernhall, B., Millar, A. L., Pitetti, K. H., Hensen, T., & Vukovich, M. D. (2000). Cross validation of the 20-m shuttle run tests for children with mental retardation. *Adapted Physical Activity Quarterly, 17*, 402–412.

Fernhall, B., Millar, L., Tymeson, G., & Burkett, L. (1989). Cardiovascular fitness testing and fitness levels of adolescents and adults with mental retardation including Down syndrome. *Education and Training of the Mentally Retarded, June*, 133–138.

Fernhall, B., Millar, A. L., Tymeson, G., & Burkett, L. N. (1990). Maximal exercise testing of mentally retarded adolescents and adults: Reliability study. *Archives of Physical Medicine and Rehabilitation, 71*, 1065–1068.

Fernhall, B., & Pitetti, K. H. (2001). Limitations of physical work capacity in individuals with mental retardation. *Clinical Exercise Physiology, 3*, 176–182.

Fernhall, B., Pitetti, K. H., Stubbs, N., & Stadler, L. (1996). Validity and reliability of the ½-mile run-walk as an indicator of aerobic fitness in children with mental retardation. *Pediatric Exercise Science, 8*, 130–142.

Fernhall, B., & Tymeson, G. (1988). Validation of a cardiovascular fitness field test for adults with mental retardation. *Adapted Physical Activity Quarterly, 5*, 49–59.

Fernhall, B., Tymeson, G., & Webster, G. (1988). Cardiovascular fitness of mentally retarded individuals. *Adapted Physical Activity Quarterly, 5*, 12–28.

Findlay, H. I. (1981). Adaptation of Canada Fitness Award for the trainable mentally handicapped. Journal of the *Canadian Association of Health, Physical Education, and Recreation, 48*, 5–12.

Foley, J. T. (2006). *Exploring the physical activity levels of students with mental retardation and students without disabilities in both school and after-school environments*. Unpublished doctoral dissertation, Oregon State University, Corvallis.

Fox, R., & Rotatori, A. F. (1982). Prevalence of obesity among mentally retarded adults. *American Journal of Mental Deficiency, 87*, 228–230.

Fox, R., Burkhart, J. E., & Rotatori, A. F. (1983).Appropriate classification of obesity of mentally retarded adults. *American Journal of Mental Deficiency, 88*, 112–114.

Francis, R. J., & Rarick, G. L. (1959). Motor characteristics of the mentally retarded. *American Journal of Mental Deficiency, 63*, 792–811.

Freeman, C. K., & Dennison, G. E. (1998). *I am the child: Using Brain Gym with children who have special needs*. Ventura, CA: Edu-Kinesthetics.

Frey, G. C., McCubbin, J. A., Hannigan-Downs, S., Kasser, S. L., & Skaggs, S. O. (1999). Physical fitness of trained runners with and without mental retardation. *Adapted Physical Activity Quarterly, 16*, 127–136.

Frey, G. C., Stanish, H. I., & Temple, V. A. (2008). Physical activity of youth with intellectual disability: Review and research agenda. *Adapted Physical Activity Quarterly, 25*, 95–117.

Gagnon, J., Tousignant, M., & Martel, D. (1989). Academic learning time in physical education classes for mentally handicapped. *Adapted Physical Activity Quarterly, 6*, 280–290.

Getchell, N., McMenamin, S., & Whitall, J. (2005). Dual motor task coordination in children with and without learning disabilities. *Adapted Physical Activity Quarterly, 22*, 21–38.

Geuze, R., & Borger, H. (1993). Children who are clumsy: Five years later. *Adapted Physical Activity Quarterly, 10*, 10–21.

Gillespie, M. (2003). Summary versus every-trial knowledge of results for individuals with intellectual disabilities. *Adapted Physical Activity Quarterly, 20*(1), 46–57.

Gruber, J. J., Hall, J. W., McKay, S. E., Humphries, L. L., & Kryscio, R. J. (1989). Motor proficiency and neuropsychological function in depressed adolescent inpatients: A pilot investigation. *Adapted Physical Activity Quarterly, 6*, 32–39.

Hallahan, D. P., & Cruickshank, W. M. (1973). The efficacy of perceptual-motor training. In D. P. Hallihan & W. M. Cruickshank (Eds.), *Psychoeducational foundations of learning disabilities* (pp. 176–215). Englewood Cliffs, NJ: Prentice Hall.

Halle, J. W., Silverman, N. A., & Regan, L. (1983). The effects of a data-based exercise program on physical fitness of retarded children. *Education and Training of the Mentally Retarded, 18*, 221–225.

Heitman, R., Erdmann, J., Gurchiek, L., Kovaleski, J., & Gilley, W. (1997). Constant versus variable practice in learning a motor task using individuals with learning disabilities. *Clinical Kinesiology, 51*(3), 62–65.

Henderson, S. E., May, D. S., & Umney, M. (1989). An exploratory study of goal setting behavior, self concept, and locus of control in children with movement difficulties. *European Journal of Special Needs, 4*, 1–4.

Hodge, S. R., Murata, N. M., & Porretta, D. L. (1999). Enhancing motor performance through various preparatory activities involving children with learning disabilities. *Clinical Kinesiology, 53*(4), 77–82.

Holland, B. V. (1987). Fundamental motor skill performance of nonhandicapped and educable mentally impaired students. *Education and Training in Mental Retardation, 22*, 190–204.

Hoover, J. H., & Wade, M. G. (1986). Motor learning theory and mentally retarded individuals: A historical review. *Adapted Physical Activity Quarterly, 2*, 228–252.

Horvat, M. A. (1982). Effect of a home learning program on learning disabled children's balance. *Perceptual and Motor Skills, 55*, 1158 1164.

Horvat, M., & Franklin, C. (2001). The effects of environment on physical activity patterns of children with mental retardation. *Research Quarterly for Exercise and Sport, 72*, 189–195.

Jeltma, K., & Vogler, E. W. (1985). Effects of individual contingency on behaviorally disordered students in physical education. *Adapted Physical Activity Quarterly, 2*, 127–135.

Kasch, F. W., & Zasueta, S. A. (1971). Physical capacities of mentally retarded children. *Acta Paediatrica Scandinavica, 217*, 217–218.

Kavale, K., & Mattson, P. D. (1983). One jumped off the balance beam: Meta-analysis of perceptual-motor training. *Journal of Learning Disabilities, 16*(3), 165–173.

Kelly, L. E., & Rimmer, J. H. (1987). A practical method for estimating percent body fat of mentally retarded males. *Adapted Physical Activity Quarterly, 4*, 117–125.

Kelly, L. E., Rimmer, J. H., & Ness, R. A. (1986). Obesity levels in institutionalized mentally retarded adults. *Adapted Physical Activity Quarterly, 3*, 167–176.

Kelly, L. E., Wessel, J. A., Dummer, G., & Sampson, T. (2010). *Everyone CAN: Skill development and assessment in elementary physical education*. Champaign, IL: Human Kinetics.

Kephart, N. C. (1971). *The slow learner in the classroom* (2nd ed.). Columbus, OH: Merrill.

Kerr, R., & Hughes, K. (1987). Movement difficulty and learning disabled children. *Adapted Physical Activity Quarterly, 4*, 72–80.

Khalili, M. A., & Elkins, M. R. (2009). Aerobic exercise improves lung function in children with intellectual disability: A randomized trial. *Australian Journal of Physiotherapy, 55*, 171–182.

Khalsa, G. K., Morris, G. S. D., & Sifft, J. M. (1988). Effect of educational kinesiology on static balance of learning disabled students. *Perceptual and Motor Skills, 67*, 51–54.

Koh, M. S., & Watkinson, E. J. (1988). Endurance run pacing of moderately mentally handicapped children. Canadian *Association of Health, Physical Education, and Recreation, 54*, 12–15.

Kowalski, E. M., & Sherrill, C. (1992). Motor sequencing of boys with learning disabilities: Modeling and verbal rehearsal strategies. *Adapted Physical Activity Quarterly, 9*, 261–273.

Kozub, F. M. (2002). Expectations, task persistence, and attributions in children with mental retardation during integrated physical education. *Adapted Physical Activity Quarterly, 19*, 334–349.

Kozub, F. M. (2003). Explaining physical activity in individuals with mental retardation: An exploratory study. *Education and Training in Developmental Disabilities, 38*, 302–313.

Kozub, F. M., & Porretta, D. L. (2001). Motor task persistence and modified individual achievement responsibility scale scores of children with LD. *Clinical Kinesiology, 55*(3), 52–58.

Kozub, F. M., Porretta, D. L., & Hodge, S. R. (2000). Motor task persistence of children with and without mental retardation. *Mental Retardation, 38*, 42–49.

Kreze, A., Zelinda, M., Juhas, J., & Gabara, M. (1974). Relationship between intelligence and relative prevalence of obesity. *Human Biology, 46*, 109–113.

Lahtinen, U., Rintala, P., & Malin, A. (2007). Physical performance of individuals with intellectual disability: A 30-year follow-up. *Adapted Physical Activity Quarterly, 24*, 125–143.

Langsner, S. J., & Anderson, S. C. (1987). Outdoor challenge education and self-esteem and locus of control of children with behavior disorders. *Adapted Physical Activity Quarterly, 4*, 237–246.

Lavay, B., Reid, G., & Cressler-Chaviz , M. (1990). Measuring the cardiovascular endurance of persons with mental retardation: A critical review. *Exercise Sport Science Review, 18*, 263–290.

Lazarus, J. C. (1994). Evidence of disinhibition in learning disabilities: The associated movement phenomenon. *Adapted Physical Activity Quarterly, 11*, 57–70.

Lee, B., & Dummer, G. (2006). Influence of parents on physical activity of children with intellectual disability. *Research Quarterly for Exercise & Sport, 77*, A-96.

Levinson, L., & Reid, G. (1991). Patterns of physical activity among youngsters with developmental disabilities. *Canadian Association of Health, Physical Education and Recreation, 56*, 24–28.

Londeree, B. R., & Johnson, L. E. (1974). Motor fitness of TMR vs EMR and normal children. *Medicine and Science in Sports, 6*, 247–252.

Longhurst, G. K., Coetsee, M. F., & Bressan, E. S. (2004). A comparison of the motor proficiency of children with and without learning disabilities. *South African Journal for Research in Sport, Physical Education and Recreation, 26*(1), 79–88.

Lorenze, D. G., Horvat, M., & Pellegrini, A. D. (2000). Physical activity of children with and without mental retardation in inclusive recess settings. *Education and Training in Developmental Disabilities, 35*, 160–167.

Losse, A., Henderson, S. E., Elliman, D., Hall, D., Knight, E., & Jongmans, M. (1991). Clumsiness in children – Do they grow out of it? A 10-year follow-up study. *Developmental Medicine and Child Neurology, 33*, 55–68.

Maiano, C., Ninot, G., Morin, A. J. S., & Bilard, J. (2007). Effects of sport participation on the basketball skills and physical self of adolescents with conduct disorders. *Adapted Physical Activity Quarterly, 24*, 178–196.

Maksud, M. G., & Hamilton, L. H. (1975). Physiological responses of EMR children to strenuous exercise. *American Journal of Mental Deficiency, 79*, 32–38.

Malpass, L. F. (1960). Motor proficiency in institutionalized and non-institutionalized retarded children and normal children. *American Journal of Mental Deficiency, 64*, 1012–1015.

McMahon, L. J., & Sharpe, E. K. (2009). Including children with behavioral difficulties in community recreation: An organizational case study of one behavior management approach. *Journal of Park and Recreation Administration, 27*(2), 60–73.

Mender, J., Kerr, R., & Orlick, T. (1982). A cooperative games program for learning disabled children. *International Journal of Sport Psychology, 13*, 222–233.

Merighi, J., Edison, M., & Zigler, E. (1990). The role of motivational factors in the functioning of mentally retarded individuals. In R. M. Hodapp, J. A. Burack, & E. Zigler (Eds.), *Issues in the developmental approach to mental retardation* (pp. 114–130). New York: Cambridge University Press.

Merriman, W. J. (1993). Relationship among socialization, attitudes, and placements with participation in physical activity of students with emotional disorders. *Perceptual and Motor Skills, 76*(1), 287–292.

Miyahara, M. (1994). Subtypes of students with LD based on gross motor function. *Adapted Physical Activity Quarterly, 11*, 368–382.

Munson, W. W. (1988). Effects of leisure education versus physical activity or informal discussion on behaviorally disordered youth offenders. *Adapted Physical Activity Quarterly, 5*, 305–317.

Nolan, J. E. (2004). Analysis of Kavale and Mattson's "Balance Beam" study (1983): Criteria for selection of articles. *Perceptual and Motor Skills, 99*, 63–82.

Nordgren, B. (1971). Physical capacity and training in a group of young adult mentally retarded persons. *Acta Paediatrica Scandinavica, 217*, 119–121.

Nunley, R. L. (1965). A physical fitness program for the mentally retarded in the public schools. *Journal of the American Physical Therapy Association, 45*, 946–954.

Oliver, J. N. (1958). The effect of physical conditioning exercises and activities on the mental characteristics of educationally sub-normal boys. *British Journal of Educational Psychology, 28*, 155–165.

Onyewadume, I. U. (2006). Fitness of Black African early adolescents with and without mild mental retardation. *Adapted Physical Activity Quarterly, 23*, 277–283.

Ozmen, T., Yildirim, N. U., Yuktasir, B., & Beets, M. W. (2007). Effects of school-based cardiovascular-fitness training in children with mental retardation. *Pediatric Exercise Science, 19*, 171–175.

Pitetti, K. H., & Campbell, K. D. (1991). Mentally retarded individuals – A population at risk? *Medicine and Science in Sports and Exercise, 23*, 586–593.

Pitetti, K. H., & Fernhall, B. (2004). Comparing the run performance of adolescents with mental retardation, with and without Down syndrome. *Adapted Physical Activity Quarterly, 21*, 219–228.

Pitetti, K. H., Fernhall, B., Stubbs, N., & Stadler, L. V. (1997). A step test for evaluating the aerobic fitness of children and adolescents with mental retardation. *Pediatric Exercise Science, 9*, 127–135.

Pitetti, K. H., Millar, L. A., & Fernhall, B. (2000). Reliability of a peak performance treadmill test for children and adolescents with and without mental retardation, *Adapted Physical Activity Quarterly, 17*, 322–332.

Pitetti, K. H., & Yarmer, D. A. (2002). Lower body strength of children and adolescents with and without mild mental retardation. *Adapted Physical Activity Quarterly, 19*, 68–77.

Pitetti, K. H., Yarmer, D. A., & Fernhall, B. (2001). Cardiovascular fitness and body composition of youth with and without mental retardation, *Adapted Physical Activity Quarterly, 18*, 127–141.

Polednak, A. P., & Auliffe, J. (1976). Obesity in institutionalized adult mentally retarded population. *Journal of Mental Deficiency Research, 20*, 9–15.

Politino, V., & Smith, S. L. (1989). Attitude toward physical activity and self-concept of emotional disturbed and normal children. *Adapted Physical Activity Quarterly, 6*(4), 371–378.

Porretta, D. L., & O'Brien, K. (1991). The use of contextual interference trials by mildly mentally handicapped children. *Research Quarterly for Exercise and Sport, 62*, 244–248.

Pyfer, J. L., & Carlson, R. (1972). Characteristic motor development of children with learning disabilities. *Perceptual and Motor Skills, 35*, 291–296.

Rarick, G. L., Widdop, J. H., & Broadhead, G. D. (1970). The physical fitness and motor performance of educable mentally retarded children. *Exceptional Children, 36*, 504–519.

Reid, G., Dunn, J.M., & McClements, J. (1993). People with disabilities as subjects in research. *Adapted Physical Activity Quarterly, 10*, 346–358.

Revie, G., & Larkin, D. (1993). Task-specific intervention with children reduces movement problems. *Adapted Physical Activity Quarterly, 10*, 29–41.

Rimmer, J. H., Kelly, L. E., & Rosentsweig, J. (1987). Accuracy of anthropometric equations for estimating body composition of mentally retarded adults. *American Journal of Mental Deficiency, 91*, 626–632.

Rothwell, E., Piatt, J., & Mattingly, K. (2006). Social competence: Evaluation of an outpatient recreation therapy treatment program for children with behavior disorders. *Therapeutic Recreation Journal, 40*(4), 241–254.

Rousselle, C., & Wolff, P. H. (1991). The dynamics of bimanual coordination in developmental dyslexia. *Neuropsychologia, 29*, 907–924.

Schaeffer, R., Law, M., Palatajko, H., & Miller, J. (1989). A study of children with learning disabilities and sensorimotor problems or let's not throw the baby out with the bath water. *Physical and Occupational Therapy, 9*(3), 101–117.

Schmidt, R. A., & Wrisberg, C. A. (2008). *Motor learning and performance: A situational-based learning approach* (4th ed.). Champaign, IL: Human Kinetics.

Seidi, L., Reid, G., & Montgomery, D. L. (1987). A critique of cardiovascular fitness testing with mentally retarded persons. *Adapted Physical Activity Quarterly, 4*, 106–116.

Sengstock, W. L. (1966). Physical fitness of mentally retarded boys. *Research Quarterly, 37*, 113–120

Shapiro, B. (2001). Specific learning disabilities. In M. L. Batshaw (Ed.), *When your child has a disability* (revised) (pp. 373–390). Baltimore: Paul H. Brookes.

Shapiro, D. R., & Dummer, G. M. (1998). Perceived and actual competency of adolescent males with mild mental retardation, *Adapted Physical Activity Quarterly, 15*, 179–190.

Shapiro, D. R., & Ulrich, D. A. (2002). Expectancies, values, and perceptions of physical competence of children with and without LD. *Adapted Physical Activity Quarterly, 19*, 318–333.

Shaw, L., Levine, M. D., & Belfer, M. (1982). Developmental double jeopardy: A study of clumsiness and self-esteem in children with learning problems. *Developmental and Behavioral Pediatrics, 3*(4), 191–196.

Sherrill, C., & Pyfer, J. (1985). Learning disabled students in physical education. *Adapted Physical Activity Quarterly, 2*, 283–291.

Sit, C., McKenzie, T. L., Lain, J., & McManus, A. (2006). Activity levels during physical education and recess in two special schools for children with mild intellectual disabilities. *Adapted Physical Activity Quarterly, 25*, 247–259.

Smits-Engelsman, B. C. M., Wilson, P. H., Westenberg, Y., & Duysens, J. (2003). Fine motor deficiencies in children with developmental coordination disorder and learning disabilities: An underlying open-loop control deficit. *Human Movement Science, 22*, 495–513.

Solomon, A., & Pangle, R. (1967). Demonstrating physical fitness improvement in the EMR. *Exceptional Children, 34*, 177–181.

So-Yeun, K., & Joonkoo, Y. (2009). Determining daily physical activity levels of youth with developmental disabilities: Days monitoring Require? *Adapted Physical Activity Quarterly, 26*, 220–229.

Stanish, H. I., (2004). Accuracy of pedometers and walking activity in adults with mental retardation. *Adapted Physical Activity Quarterly, 21*, 167–175.

Sugden, D., & Wann, C. (1987). The assessment of motor impairment in children with moderate learning difficulties. *British Journal of Educational Psychology, 57*, 225–236.

Surburg, P. L., Porretta, D. L., & Sutlive, V. (1995). Use of imagery practice for improving a motor skill. *Adapted Physical Activity Quarterly, 12*(3), 217–228.

Temple, V. A., & Walkley, J. W. (1999). Academic learning time – physical education (ALT-PE) of students with mild intellectual disabilities. *Adapted Physical Activity Quarterly, 16*, 64–75.

Thompson, L. P., Bouffard, M., Watkinson, E. J., & Causgrove Dunn, J. (1994). Teaching children with movement difficulties: Highlighting the need for individualized instruction in regular physical education. *Physical Education Review, 17*, 152–159.

Ulrich, D. A. (2000). *TGMD–2: Test of Gross Motor Development* (2nd ed.). Austin, TX: Pro-Ed.

Valentini , N. C., & Rudisill, M. E. (2004). An inclusive mastery climate intervention and the motor skill development of children with and without disabilities. *Adapted Physical Activity Quarterly, 21*, 330–348.

Van de Vliet, P., Rintala, R., Frojd, K., Verellen, J., Van Houtte, S., Daly, D. J., & Vanlandewijck , Y. C. (2006). Physical fitness profile of elite athletes with intellectual disability. *Scandinavian Journal of Medicine & Science in Sports, 16*, 417–426.

VanRossum, J. H. A., & Vermeer, A. (1990). Perceived competence: A validation study in the field of motoric remedial teaching. *International Journal of Disability, Development, and Maturation, 37*, 71–81.

Vodola, T. M. (1973). *Individualized physical education program for the handicapped*. Englewood Cliffs, NJ: Prentice-Hall.

Vodola, T. M. (1978). *Diagnostic-prescriptive motor ability and physical fitness tasks and activities for the normal and atypical individual*. Neptune City, NJ: Vee, Inc.

Wade, M. G. (Ed.). (1986). *Motor skill acquisition of mentally handicapped: Issues in research and training*. New York: Elsevier.

Waldemar, S., Horvat, M., Nocera, J., Roswal, G., & Croce, R. (2009). Eurofit Special: European fitness battery score variation amount individuals with intellectual disabilities, *Adapted Physical Activity Quarterly, 26*, 54–62.

Watkinson, E. J., & Koh, S. M. (1988). Heart rate response of moderately mentally handicapped children and youth on the Canada fitness award adapted endurance run. *Adapted Physical Activity Quarterly, 5*, 203–211.

Wessel, J. A. (1977). *I CAN fundamental skills module*. Northbrook, IL: Hubbard.

Willoughby, C., Polatajko, H., & Wilson, B. (1995). The self-esteem and motor performance of young learning disabled children. *Physical & Occupational Therapy, 14*(3/4), 1–30.

Wolff, P. H., Michel, G. F., Ovrur, M., & Drake, C. (1990). Rate and timing precision of motor coordination in developmental dyslexia. *Developmental Psychology, 26*, 349–359.

Woodard, R. J., & Surburg, P. (1997). Fundamental gross motor skill performance by girls and boys with learning disabilities. *Perceptual and Motor Skills, 84*, 867–870.

Woodard, R. J., & Surburg, P. (1999). Midline crossing behavior in children with learning disabilities. *Adapted Physical Activity Quarterly, 16*, 155–166.

Woodard, R. J., & Surburg, P. (2001). The performance of fundamental movement skills by elementary school children with learning disabilities, *Physical Educator, 58*(4), 198–205.

Wright, J., & Cowden, J. E. (1986). Changes in self-concept and cardiovascular endurance of mentally retarded youths in a Special Olympics swim training program. *Adapted Physical Activity Quarterly, 3*, 177–183.

Yang, J. J., & Porretta, D. L. (1999). Sport/leisure skill learning by adolescents with mild mental retardation: A four-step strategy. *Adapted Physical Activity Quarterly, 16*, 300–315.

Yap, R., & van der Leij, A. (1994). Testing the automatization deficit hypothesis of dyslexia via a dual-task paradigm. *Journal of Learning Disabilities, 27*, 660–665.

Yun, J., & Ulrich, D. A. (1997). Perceived and actual physical competence in children with mild mental retardation. *Adapted Physical Activity Quarterly, 14*, 285–297.

36

Career and Technical Education

Maureen A. Schloss
Lowndes County School District, Valdosta, GA

Philip L. Gunter
Valdosta State University

Students with disabilities and their families must consider carefully the nature of the secondary programs in which they are enrolled. Decisions made, knowledge learned, and skills acquired during this critical time can have an enormous impact on the quality of personal, social, educational, and economic opportunities available upon graduation. Although some students have personal and employment goals that require additional education, many students with disabilities plan on entering the workforce immediately upon graduation from high school. In this chapter, we make a case for vocational education being a major component of secondary programs for these students. We begin with a brief discussion of the goals of secondary education and options for students to consider for life after high school. We then define vocational education, describe the components, and discuss how it can increase the likelihood that students with disabilities will be prepared for employment, providing them with the economic resources needed to pursue the lifestyle of their choice. We also describe how recent legislation is having a tremendous impact on vocational education, and emphasize the importance of transition planning and the development of self-determination skills.

Goals of Secondary Education

Academic achievement, transition to postsecondary education and training, and employability are among the goals for all students who graduate from high school (Wagner, Newman, Cameto, Garza, & Levine, 2005), including students with disabilities (Benz, Lindstrom, & Yovanoff, 2000). There are at least three alternative paths students can take in high school to achieve these goals. One option is to plan and complete a secondary education program that prepares students for the rigors of academic programs available at two- and four-year colleges and universities. Another option is to choose postsecondary programs, including vocational education, that are shorter in duration but that may provide a certificate and lead to employment in a specialized field. A third option is to complete a high school program that enables students to find suitable employment immediately upon graduation and, should they choose, allow them to pursue additional education and training at a later date. All of these options are available to students with disabilities.

Enrollment in Two- or Four-Year Colleges or Universities

The number of colleges, universities, and vocational-technical centers that offer opportunities to people with disabilities to continue their education began to increase during the 1990s (Pierangelo & Crane, 1997). Reasons for the increased availability of these programs may include the preparation provided by K–12 educational programs, federal legislation, greater quality and quantity of support services for students with disabilities in postsecondary settings, and the need to meet the demands of a changing economy (Hitchings, Retish, & Horvath, 2005). It appears that more students with disabilities are planning to take advantage of the increased availability of associate and baccalaureate programs. Hitchings et al. surveyed 100 high school juniors and reported 48% were interested in a community college and 5% were considering a college or university. Plans can turn into reality. Wagner, Newman, Cameto, Levine, and Garza (2006) reported a 32% increase in enrollment by students with disabilities in postsecondary education, although they were still less likely to enroll than typical peers (Janiga & Costenbader, 2002). More recently, Dutta, Kundu, and Schiro-Geist (2009) indicated 27% of the students with disabilities they studied enrolled in college. Fifty to 55% of these students attended community colleges and 39% to 45% attended four-year colleges and universities, although enrollment has presented challenges (see Hong, Ivy, Gonzalez, & Ehrensberger, 2007; Janiga & Costenbader, 2002; Kim-Rupnow & Burgstahler, 2004; Madaus, 2005a, 2005b; Mellard, 2005; Sahlen & Lehmann, 2006).

Other Postsecondary Education Options

Students with disabilities also pursue the second option to achieve academic and employment goals by enrolling in postsecondary programs other than a college or a university. Such programs are available at sites solely devoted to vocational or technical training, at community colleges, and at some four-year colleges and universities. The Northwest Policy Center (2001) indicated that short-term preparation is among the types of training and education needed to obtain a job that offers a living wage, that is, a wage that allows a family to meet basic needs without relying on public assistance.

Wagner, Newman, Cameto, Levine, and Marder (2003) reported that 40% of students with disabilities have postsecondary vocational training as a goal. Hitchings et al. (2005) reported that 5% of the 110 high school sophomores they surveyed wanted to enroll in a postsecondary vocational or technical education program, a number that remained constant one year later. Dutta et al. (2009) indicated that of the 27% of students with disabilities who enroll in postsecondary education, 11% attend a program other than a community college, college, or university.

Employment Upon High School Graduation

Rather than continuing with some form of postsecondary education, students with disabilities may select a third option and seek employment after high school. Wagner et al. (2003) reported that 53% of students with disabilities have competitive employment as a goal immediately upon graduation from high school. While employment is an expectation for adults in American society, there are challenges for young people with disabilities who are entering the workforce after leaving school. Only 35% of people with disabilities report full-time or part-time employment, compared with 78% of those without disabilities according to the National Organization on Disabilities (NOD, 2004). Wagner et al. (2005) reported only 43% of students with disabilities are employed two years after high school, compared to 55% of their typical peers. Statistics are even more dismal if a student with a disability drops out of school prior to graduation.

Drop outs. A high school diploma is key to entering the work force (Dunn, Chambers, & Rabren, 2004). Unfortunately, students with disabilities are one of the most vulnerable populations for dropping out (Reschly & Christianson, 2006), being two times more likely than typical learners to leave school prior to graduation (Wagner et al., 2006). In her summary of the literature, Burgstahler (2003) noted the employment rate for individuals with disabilities who do not complete high school is 16%, while it is 30% for those who complete high school. More recently, Christle, Jolivette, and Nelson (2007) reported that 56% of individuals who drop out are unemployed while only 16% of high school graduates are unemployed.

Dropping out is an issue of great of importance to students, their families, and society (Bullis & Cheney, 1999; Christle et al., 2007). With the overall dropout rate at 30% for students with disabilities (Bost & Riccomini, 2006), it is one of the most serious and pervasive problems facing special education programs (Johnson, Stodden, Emanuel, Luecking, & Mack, 2002). Students who drop out decrease their employment options dramatically while increasing their risk for drug abuse, imprisonment, and less productive adult lives (Alfed, Hansen, Aragon, & Stone, 2006). If employed, high school drop outs end up working in positions that require few skills and offer low pay with very limited opportunities for advancement. They experience more health problems, and are more likely to engage in criminal activities and become dependent upon government assistance. Ultimately, society pays the price due to the loss of national income and tax revenue and an increased demand for social services (Dunn et al., 2004; Harvey, 2001).

Dunn et al. (2004) and Christle et al. (2007) noted that dropping out is not an impulsive action but a cumulative process. Beginning with elementary school, the effects of several variables build up over time until students become alienated from school. Thurlow, Sinclair, and Johnson (2002) and Reschly and Christenson (2006) described status variables, which are stable, and alterable variables which are factors that can be addressed by intervention. Specific variables are listed in Table 36.1.

Whether it is completed in high school or at a postsecondary program, properly planned and implemented vocational education can enhance employment prospects for students with disabilities. Improving academic skills, acquiring and applying self-determination skills, developing interpersonal skills, exploring career options, enrolling in applicable courses, and participating in work experiences can increase the relevance of the high school curriculum and encourage students to remain and graduate. The preparation all students receive while in high school or at a postsecondary vocational education site should match the demands of the work environment, increasing success in and satisfaction with employment.

Vocational Education

Vocational education enhances the potential of students with disabilities to obtain suitable employment and decent wages (Van Beaver, Kohler, & Chadsey, 2000; Wagner et al., 2003). Whether completed during high school or in a postsecondary education site, vocational education includes classes and services that assist students with disabilities in developing marketable skills to secure employment upon graduation or program completion.

Definition

The Carl Perkins Act of 1990 defined vocational education as organized programs that include a sequence of courses directly related to the preparation of individuals for paid or unpaid employment in current or emerging occupations that do not require a baccalaureate or advanced degree

TABLE 36.1
Variables That Increase Drop Out Rates

Several authors have identified two categories of variables, the effects of which are experienced as early as elementary school, that contribute to a student's decision to drop out of school. They include status variables, which are stable; and alterable variables, which can be changed through intervention.

Status	Alterable
Socio-economic status	Lack of engagement with peers
Single mother family home	Low expectations from peers for selves and others
Low level of schooling of same gender parent	Lack of engagement/personal relationshipwith school personnel
Gender	Missing critical instruction because of pull out service delivery
Ethnicity	Being 3 or more years behind grade level in reading and math
School size	Grade retention
School type	Behavior/discipline problems/suspension/ expulsion Low motivation High stakes testing requirements Poor performance on high stakes assessments High absenteeism Frequent change of school Low self esteem Lack of parent support/ supervision/ expectations Lack of a relevant, interesting curriculum Lack of specially designed instruction and supports in academic content classes Lack of books and reading material at home Lack of effort

Sources: Alfed, Hansen, Aragon, & Stone, 2006; Babbitt & White, 2002; Bear, Kortering, Braziel, 2006; Benz, Lindstrom, & Yavanoff, 2000; Bost & Riccomini, 2006; Christle, Jolivette, & Nelson, 2007; Dunn, Chambers, & Rabren, 2004, Harvey & Koch, 2004; Hitchings, Retish, & Horvath, 2005; Reschly & Christenson, 2006; Thurlow, et al., 2000.

(National Center for Educational Statistics, 2010). Lynch (2000) defined it as "curriculum programs designed to prepare students to acquire an education and job skills, enabling them to enter employment immediately upon high school graduation" (p. 1). Originally conceptualized as a program for preparing students to enter the workforce, vocational education is now used to prepare students for employment and higher education. The curriculum emphasizes the mastery of rigorous industry standards, state standards for academic performance, technology, and the demonstration of general employment competencies.

Vocational education addresses knowledge and skills in multiple areas: agriculture, business, family and consumer sciences, marketing and computers, health occupations, trade and industrial education, technology education, technical education, public and protective services, child care and education, food services, hospitality, technology and communications, and personal and other services (Lynch, 2000). Students can explore career options and develop occupational skills by taking courses that include agriculture, science, carpentry, accounting, word processing, retailing, fashion, practical nursing, respiratory therapy, child care, electronics, computer programming, and food and nutrition. In addition to courses, Wagner et al. (2003) listed services offered within vocational education programs. They include vocational skills assessment, career counseling, job readiness training, job search instruction, job shadowing, job placement support, job coaching, and internships and apprenticeships.

More recently, vocational education has been referred to as Career and Technical Education (CTE), which is defined as education and training after high school that emphasizes career academics; technical preparation; and work based learning experiences such as cooperative education, job shadowing, mentoring, school-based enterprise, and internships or apprenticeships. Lynch (2000) identified four purposes for CTE, including providing career exploration and planning, increasing academic achievement and motivation to continue learning, developing generic work competencies, and establishing methods for continuing education for lifelong learning. It is important to note that CTE courses are not extra-curricular; they are co-curricular. They shape career identities and promote the skills essential to start a career (Alfed et al., 2006). CTE can prepare students for both employment upon program completion and for future enrollment in colleges and universities as career aspirations evolve.

Physical Location of Program

Secondary vocational education programs are usually located at three sites: comprehensive high schools, area or regional vocational schools, and full-time vocational high schools. According to Flannery, Yovanoff, Benz, and Kato (2008) and Lynch (2000), 93% of comprehensive high schools offer vocational education in general or special education classrooms. Students with disabilities are twice as likely to be taking vocational education in general education settings where a class is comprised of 18 general education students and 4 students with disabilities. Students with retardation, autism, and multiple disabilities are more likely to receive vocational education in a special education setting where no more than 10 students with special needs are enrolled.

Vocational education programs are also available at two types of vocational schools. The first type is an area vocational school which is a regional facility that students attend part of a day to receive occupational training. The second type is a full-time vocational high school that offers academic studies but also focuses on preparing students for work in a particular occupation or industry. At the postsecondary level, vocational education programs are available in community colleges, technical institutes, and some four-year colleges, although they do not lead to a bachelor's or advanced degree.

Content Covered by Programs

At the secondary level, student schedules are carefully sequenced and include academic classes to meet graduation requirements and vocational education classes. Vocational education classes in high schools and postsecondary classes range from introductory to advanced, with students choosing electives in occupational areas that reflect their interests and abilities. Early instruction addresses career awareness; job search strategies; basic job behaviors; managing time, money, and space; and interpersonal skills such getting along with supervisors and co-workers, working on a team, providing appropriate customer service, assuming leadership roles, and negotiating. High school students are concurrently enrolled in traditional academic classes, but vocational education classes available to them and students enrolled in postsecondary settings also emphasize basic skills in reading, writing, math, speaking and listening, reasoning, creative thinking, decision making, and problem solving.

Advanced vocational education courses address job-specific content, and provide laboratory classes where students can gain hands-on experiences with the practical application of knowledge to solve problems. The sequence of courses also includes supervised work experiences during internships, practica, and apprenticeships.

Benefits of Vocational Education

Benefits associated with vocational education suggest it is a vital and necessary part of the high school curriculum (Chadd & Drage, 2006). The results of several studies conducted by the National Assessment of Vocational Education (NAVE; 1994a, 1994b, 1994c) verify that enrollment in secondary vocational education improved postsecondary outcomes for students with disabilities. In their review of the literature, Benz et al. (2000) noted better postsecondary employment outcomes for students who participated in these courses during the last two years of high school. Courses included work experiences, an emphasis on functional academic skills, community living skills, career awareness, job search skills, and self-determination skills. Other authors report the following specific benefits of vocational education:

1. Collet-Klingenberg (1998) reported that students who completed vocational education classes indicated greater satisfaction with their postsecondary programs than did students whose programs did not include vocational education classes. Students learned real life skills and gained hands on experience.
2. Harvey (2001) and Chadd and Drage (2006) reported that students who completed vocational education had better school attendance than students who did not participate in vocational education.
3. Bullis and Cheney (1999), Harvey (2001), and Chadd and Drage (2006) reported that students who completed vocational education were less likely to drop out than students who had not enrolled in vocational education. A good match between school-based vocational experiences and students' interests, values, and abilities increases the likelihood that non-college bound students will complete high school (Kulik, 1998).
4. Harvey (2001) and Chadd and Drage (2006) also reported that students who completed vocational education had higher grades.
5. There is a higher rate of employment. Harvey (2002) analyzed data gathered by the National Education Longitudinal Study (NELS) and reported employment rates were highest, at 55%, for students with disabilities who had participated in secondary vocational education, followed by 49% for students without disabilities but no vocational education, 46% for students with disabilities but no vocational education, and 30% for students with no disability and no vocational education.
6. Harvey (2002) also reported that higher wages were earned by students with disabilities who had received vocational education, an outcome also noted by Williams (2002).

Whether completed in high school or in a postsecondary setting, vocational education can benefit students with disabilities by making their programs more relevant to their interests, addressing their needs, and increasing the likelihood of suitable higher-paying employment upon entering the workforce. The availability of vocational education and degree to which individual students enroll and benefit from it has been affected by several pieces of legislation and the nature of transition planning and implementation.

Legislation Affecting the Design and Delivery of Vocational Education

Federal legislation has had a tremendous influence on the evolution of vocational education and could have a major impact on its nature and availability in the future. The most recent legislation has addressed strategies for improving educational programs for all students by emphasizing high standards for performance; use of standards-based accountability systems; the need for improved teaching; and stronger partnerships between schools, employers, postsecondary education programs, families, and service agencies (Johnson et al., 2002).

Vocational Rehabilitation Act of 1973 (PL 93-112)

The Vocation Rehabilitation Act of 1973 was civil rights legislation that prohibited discrimination in federally funded programs. Section 503 of this act required reasonable accommodations on the job for people with disabilities who are otherwise qualified for a position. Section 504 of this act, passed in 1977, prohibited discrimination in the education of people with disabilities, including admission to vocational education programs. Changes passed in 1998 required cooperation among educational agencies responsible for transition from school to employment or postsecondary settings. It mandated ongoing support, including assessment of employment needs on site, job development and placement services, social skills instruction, and intense services at home or at work to maintain employment and independent living.

***The Americans with Disabilities Act of 1990** (PL 101-336)*

The Vocation Rehabilitation Act of 1973 addressed discrimination in federally funded programs; the American with Disabilities Act (ADA) extended this civil rights protection into the private sector, with the exception of churches and private clubs. It addressed employment, and access to schools, transportation, public accommodations, telecommunications, and state and local government operations. ADA mandates nondiscrimination in employment, and requires reasonable accommodations for employees with disabilities who are otherwise qualified for a job. It also requires employers to develop and make available a fundamental job description or list of essential functions needed to perform in a position. Implications for vocational education are clear. Vocational education personnel, transition specialists, and other members of the Individual Education Program (IEP) team can use a list of essential functions to guide the selection of appropriate academic and vocational coursework that will prepare students for specific jobs. They can also anticipate reasonable accommodations or adjustments to a job application process to enable a student with disabilities to be considered for a job upon graduation (Sarkees-Wircenski & Scott, 1995).

School to Work Opportunities Act (STWOA) of 1994 (PL 103-239)

Prior to implementation of The School to Work Opportunities Act, transition and employment programs were perceived as fractured and fragmented (Benz, Yovanoff, & Doren 1997). This legislation provided a framework to help states and local agencies develop seamless, comprehensive transition programs to assist individuals as they prepare either to enter the work force or pursue additional education. Both options provide individuals with more opportunities to enter high-skill, high-wage careers. School-based and work-based opportunities available throughout high school included career exploration and counseling, integrated academic and occupational instruction, and structured work experiences that target broad skills useful across different settings. Also included were activities such as post-program planning and service coordination to help students establish a connection between school and work-based learning opportunities while still enrolled in high school and after they leave.

***Workforce Investment Act of 1998 (WIA)** (PL 105-220)*

The Workforce Investment Act of 1998 (WIA) addressed the challenges individuals with disabilities faced when trying to obtain employment services from multiple agencies with distinct and often conflicting policies, eligibility requirements, and language (Cohen, Timmons, & Fesko, 2005). Because they were so overwhelmed by these challenges, individuals did not take advantage of available services. Each state was directed to create a Workforce Investment Board (WIB) to assist its governor in establishing a comprehensive plan for workforce development in the state. States were divided into local service areas with local WIBs that administered work activities; they also created and administered One Stop Career Centers where all employment services are housed under one roof. One Stop Career Centers were designed to be user-friendly by eliminating different policies and eligibility requirements, and reducing jargon and confusing language (Targett, Young, Revell, Williams, & Wehman, 2007). Customers can move easily among agencies to obtain needed education, training, and employment services in less time, and with less paperwork and duplication.

No Child Left Behind Act of 2001(PL 107-110)

The National Commission on Excellence in Education published *A Nation at Risk* in 1983, and expressed grave concerns about Americans being inadequately prepared for a global economy. This publication served as the impetus for a standards based reform movement to increase student achievement. Calls for reform eventually resulted in the passage of the No Child Left Behind Act of 2001 (NCLB). Its goal is to ensure all children have the opportunity to obtain a high quality education and reach proficiency on measures of state academic standards that identify what students should know and be able to do (Chadd & Drage, 2006). "All" refers to students who historically have demonstrated limited or poor achievement, specifically, students who are economically disadvantaged, from racial and ethnic groups, with disabilities, or with limited English proficiency. NCLB emphasizes four pillars: (a) greater accountability from states, school districts, and schools for results; (b) more freedom for states and communities to determine how federal education funds are used; (c) the use of scientifically validated teaching strategies; and (d) more choices for students attending low performing schools and their parents. Provisions address establishing standards in core content areas such as English, reading or language arts, and mathematics, although many states have developed standards for science, foreign languages, civics and government, economics, history, geography, and the arts. NCLB has mandated educational accountability to determine if schools and students are achieving specified outcomes as demonstrated on state assessments. School districts have established minimum percentages of students who must pass the assessments for a given academic year. Percentages increase every year so all students demonstrate proficiency by 2013. School administrators must document the percentage of students making adequate yearly progress (AYP). Assessments are considered high stakes because of the consequences associated with not demonstrating AYP. For school officials, not demonstrating AYP may result in intervention or full state control of the school; for students, it may mean denial of a high school diploma.

A provision of NCLB mandates that teachers must be

highly qualified, that is, have a bachelor's degree, be state certified, and demonstrate competence in the content areas they teach. This provision has implications for secondary special educators and vocational educators. Traditional content areas may not support the goals of employment and independent living, major components of vocational education. As Bouck (2007) noted, these educators would need to be highly qualified in vocational skills, social skills, and functional academics (reading, writing, and math), areas not addressed by NCLB.

Bouck (2007) stated that NCLB is the second most influential policy affecting students with disabilities. Benefits of NCLB described by Stodden, Galloway, and Stodden (2003) include higher levels of learning, achievement of common standards, increased access to the general education curriculum, more opportunities to learn grade level material, and more meaningful diplomas. Unfortunately, concerns have been expressed by several authors regarding the negative implications of NCLB for vocational education. First, NCLB allows greater local control of how funds are used in schools. District officials may choose to direct funds toward academic classes that enhance performance on state assessments. Second, attention may be diverted from preparation for work and careers because teachers will spend the greatest amount of time on knowledge and skills measured by the state assessments used to document AYP (Abrams, Pedulla, & Madaus, 2003; Bassett & Kochhlar-Bryant, 2006; Borek, 2008). Yet, achievement outcomes in core academic areas are insufficient for improving employment and independent living outcomes for students with disabilities. Benz et al. (2000) noted the adult success of students with disabilities will rely on knowledge and skills in functional academic and transition areas, obtained in courses that include vocational, independent living, and social content. Respondents to a survey conducted by Chadd and Drage (2006) perceived that NCLB does not allow students to explore as many courses outside of core classes. They expressed concern that schools are doing away with vocational education, thereby reducing student interest and motivation to remain in school.

NCLB challenges vocational educators to show how classes and programs contribute to proficiency on state assessments; and motivate students to stay in school and perform better in academic areas. High school principals and CTE teachers surveyed by Chadd and Drage (2006) perceived that CTE courses helped prepare students to take standardized tests that assess reading, English language arts, and math. They believed that CTE courses can play a role in meeting the goals of academic standards and graduation. Perceptions are not hard data. As Bouck (2007) asked, is there a link between achievement on state assessments and subsequent success in post-school outcomes?

The Individuals with Disabilities Education Act of 2004 (IDEA) (PL 108-446)

The Individuals with Disabilities Education Act of 2004 (IDEA) updates the Education for all Handicapped Children Act of 1975 (PL 94-142) and subsequent revisions. PL 94-142 was the primary tool for improving educational outcomes for students with disabilities and mandated a free and appropriate public education (FAPE) in the least restrictive environment (LRE), nondiscriminatory testing, due process, and the development of an Individualized Education Program (IEP). Amendments in 1997 focused on how secondary programs can be planned to promote high school achievement and successful transition to post-school employment, education, and independent living (Benz et al., 2000; Bouck, 2007). Subsequent revisions addressed access to the general education curriculum and participation by students with disabilities in state standardized testing. The 2004 version is aligned with provisions of NCLB and increases the focus on access to the general education curriculum for students with disabilities. States must establish performance goals and indicators related to student progress in the general education curriculum, and they must reduce drop out rates. IDEA stipulates that transition plans must be in place with the IEP that is in effect when the student turns 16 years of age. The IEP must include a student's postsecondary goals for additional education, employment, independent living, and other important outcomes. It should identify the supports needed to live independently, establish a social life, and maintain employment. Members of the IEP team must consider strengths, preferences, and interests when developing objectives and must update the document annually based on the results of age appropriate transition assessments.

Although IDEA is closely aligned with NCLB, there is a key difference. NCLB emphasizes student achievement on uniform standards while IDEA emphasizes progress toward achievement of goals and objectives that reflect an individual student's strengths and needs. Important outcomes for a student extend beyond academic progress and include "presence and participation, accommodation and adaptations, physical health, responsibility and independence, contribution and citizenship, academic and functional literacy, personal and social adjustment, and satisfaction" (Bassett & Kochhlar-Bryant, 2006, p. 5). School officials are challenged to integrate goals of full participation by students with disabilities in standards based curriculum with the provision of individualized services (Stodden et al., 2003).

Carl D. Perkins Career and Technical Education Improvement Act of 2006 (PL 109-270)

The Carl D. Perkins Vocational Act of 1983 amended the Vocational Act of 1963, which assured access to high quality vocational programs to special populations of students, including students with disabilities. It was replaced by Carl D. Perkins Vocational and Applied Technology Education Act of 1990 which was to bridge the gap between traditional academic and vocational courses. Local education agencies were also mandated to provide information about career choices and opportunities prior to eighth grade. In 1998, it was renamed the Carl D. Perkins Vocational and Technical

Education Act and provided the largest amount ever of federal dollars for vocational education. As a result of this legislation, some states have created specific standards for CTE programs that are aligned with state academic standards. The Carl D. Perkins Career and Technical Education Improvement Act of 2006 mandated states to implement career programs that provide students with broader academic skills. It holds schools accountable for graduation, postsecondary education, and employment outcomes of students enrolled in CTE.

The previous discussion illustrates how several pieces of legislation have shaped the development of vocational education. In the following sections, we discuss how students with disabilities can participate in and maximize the benefits of vocational education through transition planning and implementation, and the development of self-determination skills.

Transition and Transition Planning

Transition is the hallmark of success for an educational system preparing students with disabilities for postsecondary environments, including employment, additional education, military service, adult independence, and community living (Bassett & Kochhar-Bryant, 2006; Patton, Cronin, & Jairrels, 1997). Transition is challenging for all students, but it is especially difficult for students with disabilities due to poor academic achievement, a lack of social networks, and limited self-advocacy skills (Babbitt & White, 2002). Therefore, transition planning by the student, family members, and several professionals is essential if students with disabilities are to be gainfully employed and become productive, independent members of the community (DeFur & Taymans, 1995; Patton et al., 1997).

Definition

Transition is defined by IDEA as a coordinated set of activities that focuses on improving student academic and functional achievement, and facilitates movement from school to post-school activities. These activities include postsecondary education, vocational training, integrated employment, continuing and adult education, adult services, independent living, and community participation. Transition must be based on the needs of an individual student by taking into account preferences and interests. Plans must include goals and objectives for instruction, community experiences, employment, and skills that enhance adult functioning.

Transition Team Members

The participation of several individuals is required to develop and implement transition plans that will prepare students for success in the postsecondary environments of their choice, whether it is additional training or competitive employment. Harvey (2001), Mellard (2005), Oertle and Trach (2007), and Sanon (2007) identified individuals who should be part of the IEP team planning transition.

TABLE 36.2
Members of the Transition Planning Team

Members of the transition team should have knowledge and expertise that reflect the goals of secondary education and post high school plans. The success of transition planning and implementation will be enhanced if the following individuals are included in the process:

1. The student
2. A family member
3. A special educator
4. Vocational educators who represent the student's field of interest
5. A vocational rehabilitation counselor
6. A high school counselor or postsecondary education admissions counselor
7. A local employer, representing potential sites for work experiences or competitive employment
8. A representative from a One Stop Career Center
9. A job search specialist
10. A transition specialist

Sources: Collet-Klingenberg, 1998; Harvey, 2001; Mellard, 2005; Oertle & Trach, 2007; Sanon, 2007.

These individuals are listed in Table 36.2. Obviously, a secondary special educator is part of the team. In addition to having knowledge of curriculum and instructional methods, a special educator assisting with a transition plan must be familiar with the local and regional economic developments, including the labor market and demand for labor. He or she also must also know a student's interests, preferences, aptitudes, and abilities to assist in the selection of one or more vocational educators to serve on the team. Vocational educators should also know the labor market, its demands, and the skill requirements for their particular field of employment.

Although local school districts assume the cost of a public school education, special educators should also invite representatives from any agencies that are likely to be responsible for providing or paying for services after graduation or program completion. One such individual is the vocational rehabilitation (VR) counselor who can provide technical assistance, help identify a suitable employment outcome, link the student to community and employment resources, and develop and approve the Individual Plan for Employment (IPE) which documents what services the VR agency will supply. VR services focus on career development, employment preparation, achieving independence, and integration in the workplace and community. VR services are not an entitlement; thus, the VR counselor can assist in determining whether a student meets eligibility criteria (Oertle & Trach, 2007; Sanon, 2007).

If a student is considering competitive employment immediately after graduation, then a fourth member of the transition team may be a representative from a One Stop Career Center (Targett et al., 2007) created by the Workforce Investment Act of 1998 (PL 109-270). This person can offer resources to assist with career awareness, career exploration, and career engagement. Another member could be a local employer who represents the perspectives of other employers and who can describe important general characteristics needed by employees to be hired, retained, and promoted. Alternatively, if the student is considering a two- or four-year college program, then a high school counselor familiar with application procedures and admission requirements should be on the team. Serving in this capacity could be an admissions counselor from a postsecondary institution who can discuss accommodations on college entrance exams, identify programs related to student interests, describe the process for obtaining accommodations and campus support services, provide assistance in the application process, and advise about the importance of securing documentation of a student's disability.

Members essential to the transition team include at least one family member and the student. Unfortunately, Collet-Klingenberg (1998) reported these individuals play very limited and often passive roles during transition planning meetings. It is possible that they are unaware of opportunities and resources for employment, independent living, and postsecondary options. Patton et al. (1997) and Schuster, Timmons, and Molone (2003) reported that parents are more concerned with managing the day-to-day tasks of daily living, devoting minimal thought and effort into planning for the future. Hasazi, Furney, and DeStefano (1999) and Johnson, Mellard, and Lancaster (2007) noted that students infrequently communicated about and advocated for their own needs. They need to develop self-advocacy skills to express vocational interests, set goals, make decisions, and assume a leadership role during their meetings (Eisenman, 2007; Hasazi et al., 1999). Later in the chapter, we discuss how self-determination skills can promote greater student involvement and leadership in the development of their own IEPs and transition plans, and enhance vocational success.

Finally, Oertle and Trach (2007) suggested the IEP team include a transition specialist who is well versed in the IDEA mandates. School districts and other agencies may choose to share the funding needed to employ this professional. The transition specialist can assume responsibility for coordinating all the personnel and services involved in planning, implementing, and evaluating the transition plan.

Transition Practices

Bassett and Kochhlar-Bryant (1996) indicated that transition planning and implementation should be comprehensive, coordinated, and provide sufficient time and support for students to achieve their postsecondary goals. Several authors have described best practices for transition planning (Hasazi et al., 1999; Rusch & DeStefano, 1989; Schuster et al., 2003). They are listed in Table 36.3.

TABLE 36.3
Best Transition Practices

Transition planning and implementation are enhanced if practitioners adhere to the following practices:

1. Plan early. IDEA stipulates a transition plan must be in place by the student's 16th birthday; however, the foundation can be laid in elementary and middle school.
2. Promote interagency collaboration. Share information, resources, and expertise to develop and implement an appropriate plan.
3. Design around the student's current interests and needs, and anticipated life goals after high school graduation.
4. Select curricular options carefully to meet high school graduation requirements and develop employment skills, social skills, and independent living skills.
5. Include community based training to highlight the application of course content to real world problems.
6. Establish business linkages to access appropriate sites for work-study, internships, apprenticeships, and competitive employment.
7. Provide work experiences to increase competencies and enable students to pursue or modify career aspirations.
8. Arrange for competitive employment in areas of vocational interest to learn and practice work skills and refine career aspirations.
9. Evaluate the transition program at student- and system- levels to ensure the individual and district goals for secondary education are being met.

Sources: Hasazi, Furney, & DeStefano, 1999; Rusch & DeStefano, 1989; Schuster, Timmons, & Molone, 2003.

Early planning. As noted previously, a transition plan must be in place within the IEP that is in effect when the student has his or her 16th birthday, although some states begin transition planning earlier. The foundation for transition should begin in the upper elementary and middle school years with career awareness, career exploration, shadowing, and visiting (Bassett & Kochhlar-Bryant, 2006). These experiences can enable students to start thinking about life after high school. In cooperation with other team members, they can develop a four-year timeline that includes courses and experiences necessary to graduate and move on to the postsecondary environment of their choice.

According to Collet-Klingenberg (1998), students whose postsecondary goals involve competitive employment or additional technical training should plan a program that provides opportunities for career awareness and exploration; work experience; vocational education; academic support; and problem solving, organization, self-advocacy, and communication skills. Collet-Klingenberg described the transition practices of one high school program she considered to be successful. A continuum was developed that identified certain activities occurring at specific points in time. The freshman year included career awareness and exploration activities; sophomore through senior years included paid work experiences. During junior and senior years, the VR counselor became more involved to support employment plans.

Janiga and Costenbader (2002) and Hitchings et al. (2005) reported that planning should also start early for students with disabilities who plan to attend college. They offer several planning recommendations that are appropriate for students who are considering enrollment at postsecondary vocational education programs or career technical institutes. Planning should start during the middle school years so that students have a schedule of specific courses for their freshman year. Over the next three years, the team must plan how to schedule required courses and electives. IEP goals and objectives should address time management, interpersonal skills, study skills, self-advocacy skills, reading and writing skills, use of assistive technology, and career orientation. The team should assist the student with the choice of postsecondary schools, based on academic programs the student is interested in, support services available, admission requirements, cost, size, location, social climate, and extracurricular activities.

Interagency collaboration. Several authors have emphasized the importance of interagency collaboration to successful transition to postsecondary settings (Collet-Klingenberg, 1998; Oertle & Trach , 2007); however, it has been slow to emerge (Johnson, et al., 2007). Members of the transition team represent personnel from several agencies, including teachers and administrators from the local school district, vocational rehabilitation counselors, employers, and admission counselors from postsecondary educational programs. It is essential these representatives share information about programs and services, attend transition planning meetings, combine resources, and communicate effectively to assist students with special needs as they move from high school to adult settings. Collaboration is enhanced by the administration of each agency. It can include written agreements that articulate policies and procedures clearly and specify the roles and responsibilities of each agency, including financial obligations. For example, agencies such as the local school district and VR may pool resources to hire a transition specialist who coordinates personnel and agencies involved in the transition plan. Sanon (2007) suggested cross-agency professional development to support staff efforts. Representatives from one agency can participate in workshops, conferences, summer institutes, and inservices offered by other agencies.

Consideration of individual interests and needs. The choice of postsecondary options must reflect a student's interests, strengths, and unique needs. In light of IDEA and NCLB mandates, team members must carefully balance academic and vocational courses. Academic courses will enable students to meet high school graduation requirements but they may be insufficient for meeting post-school goals. Bassett and Kochhlar-Bryant (2006) pointed out that the need for progress in academic curriculum should not be at the cost of transition planning; therefore, classes with an academic focus must be available in conjunction with vocational education courses that reflect interests and lead to employment after program completion. During meetings, students should identify areas of satisfaction and dissatisfaction with teachers, classes, and services (Bear, Kortering, & Braziel, 2006) and have items of concern addressed in the IEP or transition plan. Failure to respond to students' interests and concerns may place students in courses and work experiences that do not reflect their occupational aspirations.

Curriculum. Patton et al. (1997) noted that students with disabilities leave school without usable vocational and life skills. It could be that the general education curriculum does not address the academic and occupational skills needed by students who are not primarily college bound (Benz et al., 1997; Bouck, 2007). Although their terminology differed, Bigge (1988), Bouck (2004a), and Sabornie and deBettencourt (1997) identified several curriculum options for students with disabilities. They include a basic skills model that remediates, a tutorial model that assists with specific course content, a compensatory model that modifies tasks or requirements, a vocational model that prepares for employment, a functional skills model to meet the demands of daily living, and a learning strategies model that emphasizes how to learn. As there is no consensus on what the curriculum should be (Bouck, 2004b), transition team members should consider the suggestion from Bassett and Kochhlar-Bryant (2006) to blend academic, career and technical, and community based learning options to meet students' present and future needs in postsecondary environments. Dunn et al. (2004) urged teachers to help students with disabilities see the connection between their high school curriculum and future plans. Patton and Bassett (2004) suggested use of "so what" questions (so what kinds of jobs need these skills, so who would use these skills, so how do I use these skills in everyday life, so why are these skills important to learn, etc.).

Community based training. If the goal after graduation is competitive employment, then the transition team needs to provide students with a combination of school-based and community-based approaches in high school and possibly through the age of 21 (Bassett & Kochhlar-Bryant, 2006). Chadd and Drage (2006) indicated that students learn more effectively if they are taught skills in the context in which they will use them. Students are more engaged in learning if knowledge and skills are immediately relevant to their everyday lives and if they understand how such knowledge and skills will be useful to them in the future (Bassett & Kochhlar-Bryant, 2006).

Business linkages. Students, family members, secondary educators, vocational educators, and transition specialists need information about opportunities for employment within a specific community. This information will assist them in pinpointing future job opportunities, matching student preferences and interests with those opportunities, and approaching employers about potential placements. Oertle and Trach (2007) indicated that current and future workforce shortages may encourage employers to invest in and recruit nontraditional workers, among them, people with disabilities. This population has the potential to meet workforce needs if provided with the training, education, and work experience needed to meet minimum qualifications for employment in the community. Such placements require linkages between members of the transition team and employers. Transition support personnel must share information about programs and services for students with disabilities with potential employers. These employers need to understand how supports and reasonable accommodations can enhance student success on the job. Linkages can be strengthened once employers realize the benefits of offering internships, apprenticeships, and jobs to students with disabilities. These benefits include access to a source of labor, training before students develop negative work habits, and screening by the school system, which saves the employer time and money.

Work-based learning. The transition team needs to ensure students gain work experience while still enrolled in high school. Benz et al. (1997) identified a variety of structured work experiences including community services, job shadowing, school-based enterprises, apprenticeships, and paid work experiences. While the nature and number of experiences should reflect student needs, Benz et al. (2000) and Benz et al. (1997) reported enhanced secondary and post-school outcomes for students with disabilities who had two or more work experiences during the last two years of high school. These experiences provide students with basic workplace competencies that can generalize across settings, and the opportunity to practice job related social skills and higher order thinking skills. Luecking and Fabian (2000) reported another advantage; specifically, 77% of the youth they studied who completed a work-based internship were offered ongoing employment by the company even though there was no obligation to do so. It should be noted that these experiences may result in changes in vocational and educational aspirations. Therefore, transition team members need to provide opportunities for students to reflect on their work experience through writing, discussion, and surveys (Steere & Cavaiuolo, 2002). Information gleaned from these reflections can guide discussion in future transition meetings.

Competitive employment. Bullis and Cheney (1999) noted that there is no substitute for the experience that students and young adults can gain through placement in real jobs in competitive work settings. Luecking (2003) reported that students benefit from frequent and continuous exposure to real work environments. Benefits include the opportunity to learn and practice work production skills, develop job-related social skills, explore vocational interests, and form long-term career preferences. Rabren, Dunn, and Chambers (2002) studied 1,393 special education students who exited an Alabama school system between 1996–2000. They reported that there was an 87% probability that these students would be employed one year after high school if they held a job at the time they exited school.

Program evaluation. It is essential that teams monitor and evaluate transition plans during implementation and after program completion to verify individual student progress and overall program effectiveness. Transition specialists may have coordination and supervision of program evaluation as a responsibility of their position.

Progress toward academic and vocational goals and objectives included in the IEP should be conducted regularly. Several assessments can measure academic status. Results of criterion referenced tests can be used frequently to determine changes in student performance that can be linked to instructional interventions. More global measures of achievement include course grades, norm-referenced measures, and performance on state standardized tests. Test results will provide information regarding student progress toward achievement of a high school diploma. Failure to make progress at the expected rate should signal the need to reconvene the team to examine course selection, sequence, curriculum, methods, accommodations, and supports.

Data from vocational assessment can assist in clarifying interests and documenting the level of vocation related skills. Pre-test data from these sources assist with the selection of vocational education courses and other electives that will contribute to the acquisition of the knowledge and skills needed to get and keep a job. Post-test data will verify whether courses have been effective. Vocational assessment data will also be useful in identifying placements for work experiences and competitive employment. Systematic observations of students on job sites and ratings from or interviews with employers will provide evidence of job performance. This information, combined with the results of student surveys or interviews, can document the appropriateness of the placement and guide the selection of future experiences. The team should also verify awarding of a high school diploma and achievement of an individual's postsecondary goals. Specifically, follow-up should be conducted periodically after graduation to document employment or enrollment status. Employment information should include the position, length of employment, number of hours worked per week, wages, job satisfaction, measures of how well high school prepared students for this position, and the nature of follow-up employment assistance provided by other agencies. Data regarding employer satisfaction could be gathered as well. Information about post secondary outcomes includes enrollment status, courses/ programs completed, certificate or degree conferral, accommodations, and supports.

Individual outcomes can be aggregated over time to provide important information regarding overall program effectiveness. Analysis of the data will suggest areas of strength to maintain and weaknesses that must be addressed at school- or system-wide levels.

Self-Determination

Jones (2006) stated that students need to be empowered, that is, have the authority to control their own lives. For students with disabilities, this power is based on knowledge of their own strengths and needs, an understanding of the nature of their disability and its implications, the ability to set reasonable goals, the awareness of their legal rights and responsibilities, and the ability to self-advocate across employment and educational settings. Unfortunately, students with disabilities who do not have such authority may find important decisions about their lives are made by other adults who have a different vision their future. Whether they plan to pursue competitive employment or seek additional education, students with disabilities will experience better outcomes if they have and use self-determination skills (Benz et al., 2000).

Definition

Self-determination is a "combination of skills, knowledge, and beliefs that enable a person to engage in goal directed, self-regulated, autonomous behavior. When acting on the basis of these skills and attitudes, individuals have greater ability to take control of their lives and assume the role of successful adults in our society" (Field, Martin, Miller, Ward, & Wehmeyer, 1998, p. 2). Many students with disabilities may not have self-determination skills as family members and school personnel may have advocated for them, in keeping with the mandates of IDEA. Upon high school graduation, however, IDEA ceases to apply to students' programs and ADA takes over (Gil, 2007). Students with disabilities must receive instruction in self-determination to assume leadership roles in the development and implementation of programs that promote achievement of their vocational and educational goals. Several authors have identified key areas that should be addressed by instruction in self-determination; they are listed in Table 36.4. Students need to understand their strengths and needs, and how their disability affects them (Jones, 2006). While in high school, they should understand the importance of taking an active role during the IEP meetings (Hasazi et al., 1999). They need to advocate correctly for themselves by understanding their legal rights under IDEA and ADA, including the right to accommodations and supports. They should be prepared to request thorough documentation of their disability while their programs are governed by IDEA provisions; waiting until after graduation means they must assume the cost of assessments needed to support requests for accommodations in employment and postsecondary settings. They must understand their responsibilities under ADA, particularly regarding self-disclosure of their disability status. They need to understand that upon graduation, they assume the responsibility for requesting accommodations in postsecondary settings, including employment sites and school.

TABLE 36.4
Key Areas for Self-Determination Skills

Self-determination skills contribute greatly to student outcomes. Students need to acquire knowledge and skills in several areas:

1. An understanding of their disability, strengths, and needs
2. The ability to describe the disability, and explain wishes and needs
3. Knowledge of legal rights and responsibilities under IDEA and ADA
4. Knowledge of accommodations and supports that were useful in high school
5. Leadership skills needed to be an active participant in IEP meetings
6. Self-advocacy skills to communicate needs in a tactful manner, such as self-disclosing, requesting documentation of the disability, and requesting appropriate accommodations
7. Self-management skills, including goal setting, self-scheduling, self-monitoring, and self-assessment

Sources: Field, Martin, Miller, Ward, & Weymeyer, 1998; Hasazi, Furney, & DeStefano, 1999; Steere & Cavaiuolo, 2002; Wehmeyer, Palmer, Agran, Mithaug, & Martin, 2000.

Benefits

Carter, Lane, Pierson, and Glaeser (2006), in their review of the literature, noted self-determination skills can improve academic performance, employment status, postsecondary participation, independence, and quality of life. They are useful across settings; specifically, students can apply self-determination skills in academic and vocational classes as both situations require students to set goals, solve problems, and make decisions (Lee, Wehmeyer, Palmer, Soukup, & Little, 2008).

Students with self-determination skills are better prepared to assume leadership roles during IEP meetings devoted to transition (Hasazi et al., 1999). They can present an overview of their career interests; describe their wishes; and express aspirations for post-school outcomes in education, employment, community settings (Steere & Cavaiuolo, 2002). Transition planning and implementation are enhanced when students understand and communicate their strengths and needs, select their goals and work toward them, advocate for themselves, and assess their own progress.

Curriculum and Instruction

Carter et al. (2006) and Eisenman (2007) recommended that self-determination skills be part of the curriculum for all students, not just those with disabilities, and that students receive explicit instruction in this area. Eisenman suggested addressing these skills in earlier grades because secondary educators have so many instructional priorities. Curricula available to assist general, special, and vocational educators include *Steps to Self-Determination* (Field & Hoffman, 1996), *Self-Determined Learning Model of Instruction* (Wehmeyer, Palmer, Agran, Mithaug, & Martin, 2000), and the *Teaching with Integrity, Reflection, and Self-Determination Model* (Field, Sarver, & Shaw, 2003).

It should be noted that the secondary curriculum offers frequent opportunities for students to exercise and develop self-determination skills throughout the day. For example, Konrad, Walker, Fowler, Test, and Wood (2008) suggested students practice making choices by selecting from alternative academic assignments or determining the order in which assignments are completed. They can practice setting goals by signing contracts that specify the amount or quality of work they will complete. They can enhance self-awareness by planning the steps needed to complete long-term assignments, monitoring their performance, and evaluating progress.

Students may have received accommodations in high school that are not automatically available in postsecondary education and employment settings. Students may not even know they are entitled to reasonable accommodations if they are unfamiliar with ADA and its provisions. Participants in studies conducted by Price, Gerber, and Mulligan (2003, 2007) and Gerber, Price, Mulligan, and Williams (2005) either never heard of ADA, or knew very little about it; as a result, ADA was underused. Self-determination instruction should include content in ADA provisions, with a focus on self-advocacy skills and self-disclosure.

Skinner (1998) defined self-advocacy as understanding a disability, being aware of legal rights, and communicating rights and needs to authority figures competently and tactfully. Self-advocacy also includes articulating technology needs as access to technology may be crucial for success in postsecondary education and professional careers (Burgstahler, 2003). Technology can maximize independence; productivity; and facilitate participation in academic, employment, recreational, and other adult activities (Houchins, 2001).

Students must be prepared to make an informed decision about the benefits and risks of self-disclosure of their disability status in post-school settings. Students need to determine the extent to which their disability will affect job performance, and weigh effects of requesting accommodations against the potential stigma. If they decide to disclose, they must determine whether to share this information during the interview, at the time when they are offered or accept an offer of employment, or after they have been hired. If they fail to self-disclose, then the provisions of ADA no longer apply (Price et al., 2003).

In summary, students who possess self-determination skills understand their personal attributes and gain confidence in their abilities. They are proud of their accomplishments, are assertive, advocate on their own behalf, and make choices about their lives that improve its quality (Jones, 2006).

Summary

Students with disabilities are expected to achieve academic, employment, and independent living goals to assume their place in society as productive and engaged citizens. Most of these students will need assistance to accomplish these goals. Vocational education is major component of secondary and postsecondary education programs that contributes to successful outcomes for students who are seeking competitive employment after graduation or considering additional career education at postsecondary sites. It is essential that students with disabilities, with the support and guidance of their families and school personnel, consider taking advantage of all that vocational education has to offer. Legislation challenges professionals to balance academic achievement with preparation for employment; however, it offers the opportunity to evaluate standards and instructional strategies for vocational education and determine how it contributes to academic proficiency. Properly planned and implemented, vocational education can contribute to the mastery of relevant academic, social, and career goals that reflect a student's strengths, needs, and interests; encourages school completion; and prepares students for success in the next phase of the lives.

References

Abrams, L. M., Pedulla, J. J., & Madaus, G. F. (2003). Views from the classroom: Teachers' opinions of statewide testing programs. *Theory into Practice*, *42*(1), 1–15.

Alfed, C., Hansen, D. M., Aragon, S. R., & Stone, J. R. (2006). Inside the black box: Exploring the value added by Career and Technical Student Organizations to students' high school experience. *Career and Technical Education Research*, *31*, 121–155.

Babbitt, B. C., & White, C. M. (2002). R U ready? Helping students assess their readiness for postsecondary education. *Teaching Exceptional Children*, *35*(2), 62–66.

Bassett, D. S., & Kochhlar-Bryant, C. A. (2006). Strategies for aligning standards-based education and transition. *Focus on Exceptional Children*, *39*(2), 1–20.

Bear, G. G., Kortering, L. J., & Braziel, P. (2006). School completers and noncompleters with learning disabilities. *Remedial and Special Education*, *27*, 293–300.

Benz, M. R., Lindstrom, L., & Yovanoff, P. (2000). Improving graduation and employment outcomes of students with disabilities: Predictive factors and student perspectives. *Exceptional Children*, *66*, 509–529.

Benz, M. R., Yovanoff, P., & Doren, B. (1997). School-to-work components that predict postschool success for students with and without disabilities. *Exceptional Children*, *63*, 151–165.

Bigge, J. (1988) *Curriculum based instruction for special education students*. Mountain View, CA: Mayfield.

Borek, J. (2008). *A Nation at Risk at 25*. *Phi Delta Kappan*, *89*, 572–574.

Bost, L. W., & Riccomini, P. J. (2006). Effective instruction: An inconspicuous strategy for dropout prevention. *Remedial and Special Education*, *27*, 301–311.

Bouck, E. C. (2004a) State of curriculum for secondary students with mild mental retardation. *Education and Training in Developmental Disabilities*, *39*, 169–172.

Bouck, E. C. (2004b). Exploring secondary special education for mild mental impairment. *Remedial and Special Education*, *25*, 367–382.

Bouck, E. C. (2007). Lost in translation? Educating secondary students with mild mental impairment. *Journal of Disability Policy Studies*, *18*, 79–87.

Bullis, M., & Cheney, D. (1999). Vocational and transition interventions for adolescents and young adults with emotional or behavioral disorders. *Focus on Exceptional Children*, *31*(7), 1–24.

Burgstahler, S. (2003). The role of technology in preparing youth with disabilities for postsecondary education and employment. *Journal of Special Education Technology*, *18*, 7–19.

Carter, E. W., Lane, K. L., Pierson, M. R., & Glaeser, B. (2006). Self-determination skills and opportunities of transition-age youth with emotional disturbance and learning disabilities. *Exceptional Children*, *72*, 333–346.

Chadd, J., & Drage, K. (2006). *No Child Left Behind*: Implications for Career and Technical Education. *Career and Technical Education Research*, *31*, 79–99.

Christle, C. A., Jolivette, K., & Nelson, C. M. (2007). School characteristics related to high school dropout rates. *Remedial and Special Education, 28,* 325–339.

Cohen, A., Timmons, J. C., & Fesko, S. L. (2005). The Workforce Investment Act: How policy conflict and policy ambiguity affect implementation. *Journal of Disability Policy Studies, 15,* 221–230.

Collet-Klingenberg, L. L. (1998). The reality of best practices in transition: A case study. *Exceptional Children, 65,* 67–78.

DeFur, S. H., & Taymans, J. M. (1995). Competencies needed for transition specialists in vocational rehabilitation, vocational education, and special education. *Exceptional Children, 62,* 38–45.

Dunn, C., Chambers, D. M., & Rabren, K. (2004). Variables affecting students' decisions to drop out of school. *Remedial and Special Education, 25,* 314–323.

Dutta, A., Kundu, M. M., & Schiro-Geist, C. (2009). Coordination of postsecondary transition services for students with disabilities. *Journal of Rehabilitation, 75,* 10–17.

Eisenman, L. (2007). Self-determination interventions: Building a foundation for school completion. *Remedial and Special Education, 28,* 2–8.

Field, S., & Hoffman, A. (1996). *A self-determined learning model of instruction: A curriculum to help adolescents learn to achieve their goals.* Reston, VA: Council for Exceptional Children.

Field, S., Martin, J., Miller, R., Ward, M., & Wehmeyer, M. (1998). *A practical guide to teaching self-determination.* Reston, VA: Council for Exceptional Children.

Field, S., Sarver, M. D., & Shaw, S. (2003). Self-determination: A key to success in postsecondary education for students with learning disabilities. *Remedial and Special Education, 24,* 339–349.

Flannery, K. B., Yovanoff, P., Benz, M. R., & Kato, M. M. (2008). Improving employment outcomes of individuals with disabilities though short-term postsecondary training. *Career Development for Exceptional Individuals, 31,* 26–36.

Gerber, P. J., Price, L. A., Mulligan, R., & Williams, P. (2005). To be or not to be learning disabled: A preliminary report on self-disclosure and adults with learning disabilities. *Thalamus, 23,* 18–29.

Gil, L. A. (2007). Bridging the transition gap from high school to college: Preparing students with disabilities for a successful postsecondary experience. *Teaching Exceptional Children, 40*(2), 12–15.

Harvey, M. W. (2001). Vocational-Technical Education: A logical approach to drop put prevention for secondary special education. *Preventing School Failure, 45,* 108–113.

Harvey, M. W. (2002) Comparison of postsecondary transitional outcomes between students with and without disabilities by secondary vocational education participation: Findings from the National Longitudinal Study. *Career Development of Exceptional Individuals, 25,* 99–121.

Harvey, M. W., & Koch, K. R. (2004). No Child Left Behind: Policymakers need to reconsider secondary career and technical education for students with special needs. *Workforce Education Forum, 31*(1), 1–17.

Hasazi, S. B., Furney, K. S., & DeStefano, L. (1999). Implementing the IDEA transition mandates. *Exceptional Children, 65,* 555–566.

Hitchings, W. E., Retish, P., & Horvath, M. (2005). Academic preparation of adolescents with disabilities for postsecondary education. *Career Development for Exceptional Individuals, 28,* 26–35.

Hong, B. S., Ivy, W. F., Gonzalez, H. R., & Ehrensberger, W. (2007). Preparing students for postsecondary education. *Teaching Exceptional Children, 40*(1), 32–38.

Houchins, D. E. (2001). Assistive technology barriers and facilitators during secondary and post-secondary transitions. *Career Development of Exceptional Individuals, 24,* 73–88.

Janiga, S. J., & Costenbader, V. (2002). The transition from high school to postsecondary education for students with learning disabilities: A survey of college service coordinators. *Journal of Learning Disabilities, 35,* 462–467.

Johnson, D. R., Mellard, D. F., & Lancaster, P. (2007). Road to success: Helping young adults with learning disabilities plan and prepare for employment. *Teaching Exceptional Children, 39*(6), 26–32.

Johnson, D. R., Stodden, R. A., Emanuel, E. J., Luecking, R., & Mack, M. (2002). Current challenges facing secondary education and transition services: What research tells us. *Exceptional Children, 68,* 519–531.

Jones, M. (2006). Teaching self-determination: Empowered teachers, empowered students. *Teaching Exceptional Children, 39*(1), 12–17.

Kim-Rupnow, W. S., & Burgstahler, S. (2004). Perceptions of students with disabilities regarding the value of technology-based support activities on postsecondary education and employment. *Journal of Special Education Technology, 19,* 43–56.

Konrad, M., Walker, A. R., Fowler, C. H., Test, D. W., & Wood, W. M. (2008). A model for aligning self-determination and general curriculum standards. *Teaching Exceptional Children, 40*(3), 53–64.

Kulik, J. A. (1998). Curricular tracks and high school vocational education. In A. Gamoran (Ed.), *The quality of vocational education: Background papers from the 1994 National Assessment of Vocational Education.* Washington, DC: U. S. Department of Education.

Lee, S-H., Wehmeyer, M. L., Palmer, S. B., Soukup, J. H., & Little, T. D. (2008). Self-determination and access to the general education curriculum. *The Journal of Special Education, 42,* 91–107.

Luecking, R. G. (2003). Employer perspectives on hiring and accommodating youth in transition. *Journal of Special Education Technology, 18,* 65–72.

Luecking, R. G., & Fabian, E (2000). Paid internships and employment success for youth in transition. *Career Development for Exceptional Individuals, 23,* 205–222.

Lynch, R. L. (2000). High school career and technical education for the first decade of the 21st century. *Journal of Vocational Education Research, 25*(2), 1–21.

Madaus, J. W. (2005a). Navigating the college transition maze: A guide for students with learning disabilities. *Teaching Exceptional Children, 37*(3), 32–37.

Madaus, J. W. (2005b). Employment and self-disclosure rates and rationales of university graduates with learning disabilities. *Journal of Learning Disabilities, 41,* 219–299.

Mellard, D. (2005). Strategies for transition to postsecondary educational settings. *Focus on Exceptional Children, 37*(9), 1–20.

National Assessment of Vocational Education. (1994a). *Interim report to Congress* (OR 94-3601). Washington, DC: US Government Printing Office.

National Assessment of Vocational Education. (1994b). *Final report to Congress Volume II: Participation in and quality of vocational education* (OR 94-3502-II). Washington, DC: US Government Printing Office.

National Assessment of Vocational Education. (1994c). *Final report to Congress Volume IV: Access to programs and services for special populations* (OR 94-3502 IV). Washington, DC: US Government Printing Office.

National Center for Educational Statistics. (2010). *The Carl Perkins Act of 1990.* Retrieved January 27, 2010, from http/nces.ed.gov/pub// wbb/95024-2.asp

National Organization on Disability (NOD). (2004). *NOD/Harris Survey of Americans with disabilities: Landmark survey finds pervasive disadvantages.* Washington, DC: Author.

Northwest Policy Center. (2001). *Northwest Job Pap Study: Searching for pay that works.* Seattle, WA: Author.

Oertle, K. M., & Trach, J. S. (2007). Interagency collaboration: The importance of rehabilitation professionals' involvement in transition. *Journal of Rehabilitation, 73*(3), 36–44.

Patton, J. R., & Bassett, D. S. (2004, July). *Designing and using transition-focused curriculum in a standards-based world.* Paper presented at Bresnahan-Halstead Symposium in Vail, sponsored by the University of Colorado.

Patton, J. R., Cronin, M. E., & Jairrels, V. (1997). Curricular implications of transition. *Remedial and Special Education, 18,* 294–306.

Pierangelo, R., & Crane, R. (1997). *Complete guide to special education transition services.* West Nyack, NY: The Center for Applied Research in Education.

Price, L. A., Gerber, P. J., & Mulligan, R. (2003). The *Americans with Disabilities Act* and adults with learning disabilities as employees: The realities of the workplace. *Remedial and Special Education, 24,* 350–358.

Price, L. A., Gerber, P. J., & Mulligan, R. (2007). Adults with learning disabilities and the underutilization of the *Americans with Disabilities Act. Remedial and Special Education*, *28*, 340–344.

Rabren, K., Dunn, C., & Chambers, D. (2002). Predictors of post-high school employment among young adults with disabilities. *Career Development of Exceptional Children*, *25*, 25–40.

Reschly, A. L., & Christenson, S. L. (2006). Prediction of dropout among students with mild disabilities: A case for inclusion of student engagement variables. *Remedial and Special Education, 27*, 276–292.

Rusch, F. R., & DeStefano, L. (1989). Transition from school to work: Strategies for young adults with disabilities. *Interchange*, *9*(3), 1–12.

Sabornie, E. J., & deBettencourt, L. U. (1997). *Teaching students with mild disabilities at the secondary level*. Columbus, OH: Merrill.

Sahlen, C. A. H., & Lehmann, J. P. (2006). Requesting accommodations in higher education. *Teaching Exceptional Children*, *38*(3), 28–34.

Sanon, K. (2007). Understanding and accessing transition to employment and adult services. *The Exceptional Parent*, *37*(10), 30–32.

Sarkhees-Wircenski, M., & Scott. J. L (1995). *Vocational special needs*. Homewood. IL: American Technical Publishers.

Schuster, J. L., Timmons, J. C., & Molone, M. (2003). Barriers to successful transition for young adults who receive SSI and their families. *Career Development of Exceptional Children*, *26*, 47–66.

Skinner, M. E. (1998). Promoting self advocacy skills among college students with learning disabilities. *Intervention in School and Clinic*, *33*, 278–283.

Steere, D. E., & Cavaiuolo, D. (2002). Connecting outcomes, goals, and objectives in transition planning. *Teaching Exceptional Children*, *34*(6), 54–59.

Stodden, R. A., Galloway, L. M., & Stodden, N. J. (2003). Secondary school curricula issues: Impact on postsecondary students with disabilities. *Exceptional Children*, *70*, 9–25.

Targett, P., Young, C., Revell, G., Williams, S., & Wehman, P. (2007). Customized employment in the One Stop Career Centers. *Teaching Exceptional Children, 40*(2), 6–11.

Thurlow, M. L., Sinclair, M. F., & Johnson, D. R. (2002, July). Students with disabilities who drop out of school: Implications for policy and practice. *Issue Brief*, *1*(12). Minneapolis: Minnesota, Institute in Community Integration, National Center on Secondary Education and Transition.

Van Beaver, S. M., Kohler, P. D., & Chadsey, J. G. (2000). Vocational education enrollment patterns of females with disabilities. *Career Development of Exceptional Individuals*, *23*, 87–103.

Wagner, M., Newman, L., Cameto, R., Garza, N., & Levine, P. (2005). *After high school: A first look at the post-school experiences of youth with disabilities*. (A report from the National Longitudinal Transition Study-2 [NLTS2]). Menlo Park, CA: SRI International.

Wagner, M., Newman, L., Cameto, R., Levine, P., & Garza. N. (2006). *An overview of the findings from wave 2 of the National Longitudinal Transition Study 2 (NLTS2)*. Washington, DC: US Department of Education Research.

Wagner, M., Newman, L., Cameto, R., Levine, P., & Marder, C. (2003). Going to school: Instructional contexts, programs, and participation of secondary school students with disabilities. A report from the National Longitudinal Transition Study-2 (NLTS2). Menlo Park, CA: SRI International. Retrieved from http://www.nlts2.org/reports/2003_12/nlts2_report_ 2003_12_ complete.pdf

Wehmeyer, M., Palmer, S., Agran, M., Mithaug, D., & Martin, J. (2000). Promoting causal agency: The self-determined learning model of instruction. *Exceptional Children*, *66*, 439–453.

Williams, J. M. (2002). Using school-to-career strategies, workplace competencies, and industry skill standards to enhance the transition process in standards-based education. In C. A. Kochhar-Bryant & S. Bassett (Eds.), *Aligning transition and standards-based education* (pp. 77–90). Arlington, VA: Council for Exceptional Children.

37

Technology and Academic Instruction

Considerations for Students with High Incidence Cognitive Disabilities

CHERYL A. WISSICK
University of South Carolina

J. EMMET GARDNER
University of Oklahoma

Educational use of technology needs to be grounded in research-based instructional practices and directly integrated into the curriculum. For students with high incidence disabilities, technology can be used as a cognitive scaffold or accommodation, just as those with physical or sensory disabilities often rely on using wheelchairs, hearing aids, or glasses to perform more efficiently. However, to integrate technology effectively within the context of learning and academic achievement, there must also be consideration of students' academic abilities and skills. Technology cannot be used to replace direct instruction and neither can it simply be treated as an add-on to classroom activities. The effective use of technology with students with high incidence disabilities must also be integrated into the curriculum in a manner that corresponds to individualized education plans, state and national standards, and methods that are anchored in evidence-based practice (Gardner, Wissick, & Edyburn, 2008).

This chapter focuses on how technology can be used to present, complement, enhance, and facilitate research-based instructional practices for students with high incidence disabilities. First for purposes of this chapter, students with high incidence disabilities will be defined as students with learning disabilities, mild intellectual disability, or emotional or behavior disorders with accompanying learning deficits or psychobiological deficits such as fetal alcohol effects. We will not discuss the use of technology for students with physical or sensory impairments or those with severe cognitive disabilities. After a general clarification of important terms and concepts, we present research-based practices that can be applied to the integration of technology in reading, writing, and mathematics.

Relevant Definitions and Pedagogical Concepts

Part of the confusion surrounding the use of technology for students with high incidence disabilities deals with the interpretation and understanding of the terms instructional technology, assistive technology (AT), and Universal Design for Learning (UDL).

Instructional Technology

In K–12 settings, instructional technology (often referred to as educational technology) is considered to be a strategy for using different forms of technology to aid instruction and learning. Typically, the instruction focuses on whole class learning and inclusion, where computer and software-based activities are used to teach all students in the classroom. The implications of using instructional technology in schools can be observed from two viewpoints. From a student's perspective, instructional technology should provide them with the ability to do something that they were originally not capable of doing, or if capable, it should enable them to do it with improvement (Harris, 1997). From a teacher's perspective, instructional technology implies that teachers must consider the nature and context of educational outcomes prior to developing any technology-based activities. Therefore not allowing available technology or software to dictate the use, but considering how that technology or software can address standards-based and individual student objectives (Gardner et al., 2008). From another perspective, technology is a tool used by teachers where its use is to achieve a purposeful outcome—a means to end and not an end in and of itself (Blackhurst, 2005).

Assistive Technology Devices and Services

The formal introduction of legal terms and concepts related to the use of technology in special education first appeared in Public Law 100-407, The Technology-Related Assistance Act for Individual with Disabilities (1988), often referred to as the "Tech Act." In the years following the Tech Act, extensions and reauthorizations of federal legislation have resulted in modifications, additions and clarification to the language. To appreciate the rationale for the use of technology in special education, teachers should understand the full meaning of assistive technology and related concepts as they are stated in the most recent federal legislation, the Individuals with Disabilities Education Improvement Act (IDEIA, 2004). Those wishing to acquire extensive and more detailed perspectives regarding major federal assistive technology legislation, definition and services leading up to IDEIA, should consult Bailey, Meidenbauer, Fein, and Mollica (2005); Blackhurst (2005); Malouf and Hauser (2005); and Reed and Bowser (2005). IDEIA mandates that AT devices and services must be considered at the IEP meeting.

> *Assistive Technology Devices.* The definition of AT devices is:
>
> §300.5 Assistive Technology Device. Assistive technology device means any item, piece of equipment, or product system, whether acquired commercially off the shelf, modified, or customized, that is used to increase, maintain, or improve the functional capabilities of a child with a disability. The term does not include a medical device that is surgically implanted, or the replacement of such device. (IDEIA, 20 U.S.C. § 1401(1))
>
> *Assistive Technology Services.* The definition of AT services are:
>
> §300.6 Assistive Technology Services. Any service that directly assists a child with a disability in the selection, acquisition, and use of an assistive technology device. The term includes—
>
> (a) The evaluation of the needs of a child with a disability, including a functional evaluation of the child in the child's customary environment;
>
> (b) Purchasing, leasing, or otherwise providing for the acquisition of assistive technology devices by children with disabilities;
>
> (c) Selecting, designing, fitting, customizing, adapting, applying, retaining, repairing, or replacing assistive technology devices;
>
> (d) Coordinating and use other therapies, interventions, or services with assistive technology devices, such as those associated with existing education and rehabilitation plans and programs;
>
> (e) Training or technical assistance for a child with a disability or, if appropriate, that child's family; and
>
> (f) Training or technical assistance for professionals (including individuals or rehabilitation services), employers, or other individuals who provide services to employ, or are otherwise substantially involved in the major life functions of children with disabilities. (Authority 20 U.S.C. 1401(2))

With regard to the above definition, points a, d, and e are areas that are particularly relevant to the use of technology and academic instruction to meet individual education program (IEP) objectives for students with high incidence disabilities. Technology needs should be evaluated based on the environment and student's needs. Services for assistive technology should be coordinated and students should receive training for the assistive technology.

Universal Design and the National Instructional Materials Accessibility Standards (NIMAS)

The 2004 reauthorization of IDEIA introduced two new elements related to assistive technology devices and services that were not mentioned in prior legislation—Universal Design (UD) and the National Instructional Materials Accessibility Standards (NIMAS).

> *Universal Design.* The term "universal design" means:
>
> ...a concept or philosophy for designing and delivering products and services that are usable by people with the widest possible range of functional capabilities, which include products and services that are directly usable (without requiring assistive technologies) and products and services that are made usable with assistive technologies. (105-394, S.2432)

The rationale behind UD is that if materials or curricula are designed to include a variety of formats and representation to meet the needs of all persons, then there would be less of a need for assistive technologies. For example, in the framework of UD, designing a ramp in the planning stages of a building eliminates the need to retrofit later to make the building accessible for all persons. Similarly products, services, or curriculum designed for universal access with technologies or assistive technologies eliminates the need to revise the materials later to meet the needs in a diverse classroom.

National Instructional Materials Accessibility Standards (NIMAS). IDEIA 2004 also included the addition of language and sections delineating the provision of textbooks and instructional materials in accessible formats (e.g., in auditory and tactile formats) for students who are blind or print disabled by defining standards for National Instructional Materials Accessibility Standards (NIMAS). In 1988, Kerscher (2009) coined the term "print disabled" to describe people who cannot effectively read print because of a visual, physical, perceptual, developmental, cognitive, language, or learning disability. The NIMAS' standards essentially guarantee that students with IEPs that call for an accommodation to help them process text-based information will have access to and experience print-based materials in formats that are reliable and consistent across all publishers. At this time this might mean that some physical texts will have to be scanned and converted to digital formats in order to be available in alternative forms. The intent of this standard is that publishers produce all books in a format that can be easily converted to auditory or tactile formats.

Universal Design for Learning

The principles associated with assistive technology, universal design, and NIMAS work together to provide a range of services that increases the academic functioning of a child with a disability. The purpose of these principles is to establish that assistive technology should and can be applied to *all* persons with a disability and not just those who require augmentative communication or physical prosthetics. Theoretically, if teachers apply the concept of universal design, developing instruction to be accessible to all students then students with high incidence disabilities would not need additional assistive technology. However, if children with disabilities are using technology to increase their functioning skills, then technically the technology based on the definition would be considered assistive technology. Beyond semantics the more important problem is that technology integration and universally designed curriculum founded on evidence-based practices are not yet commonplace in those general education classrooms where most of the students with high incidence disabilities obtain the majority of their instruction. In 2005, the National Assistive Technology Research Institute (NATRI) at the University of Kentucky examined the use of assistive technology in 10 states and found that assistive technology was more likely to be used by students with low-incidence disabilities and in special educational classrooms, not in the inclusive settings (Hasselbring & Bausch, 2006). Therefore, we must consider current movements to increase the functioning of all students in the classroom and then how instructional or educational technology is integrated into the classroom instruction.

Technology can assist a teacher to differentiate instruction to meet the needs of all students. Applying the concepts of (UD) to learning, Rose and Meyer (2002) and The Center for Applied Special Technology (CAST) created Universal Design for Learning (UDL), a flexible approach to curriculum design based on diverse learning needs. UDL provides a theoretical framework for designing instruction and assessment that embeds multiple elements of representation and multiple ways and opportunities for students to engage in learning activities and express their knowledge. The UDL Center (http://www.udlcenter.org) explains each principle and guidelines based on a research base gathered from learning sciences and education and organized by quantitative evidence and scholarly reviews. Table 37.1 provides a summary of these basic principles and guidelines of UDL.

Implementing UDL requires teachers to be well grounded in their knowledge of instructional technology and how assistive technologies can be applied to represent content knowledge, and promote student engagement and expression. Technically, if all teachers used curricula based on UDL, then additional assistive technology considerations would only be needed for specific individualized needs of

TABLE 37.1
Universal Design for Learning Guidelines (CAST, 2008).

I. Provide Multiple Means of Representation	II. Provide Multiple Means of Action and Expression	III. Provide Multiple Means of Engagement
1. *Provide options for perception*	4. *Provide options for physical action*	7. *Provide options for recruiting interest*
• Options that customize the display of information • Options that provide alternatives for auditory information • Options that provide alternatives for visual information • Options in the mode of physical response	• Options in the means of navigation • Options for accessing tools and assistive technologies • Options that reduce threats and distractions	• Options that increase individual choice and autonomy • Options that enhance relevance, value, and authenticity
2. *Provide options for language and symbols*	5. *Provide options for expressive skills and fluency*	8. *Provide options for sustaining effort and persistence*
• Options that define vocabulary and symbols • Options that clarify syntax and structure • Options for decoding text or mathematical notation • Options that promote cross-linguistic understanding • Options that illustrate key concepts non-linguistically	• Options in the media for communication • Options in the tools for composition and problem solving • Options in the scaffolds for practice and performance	• Options that heighten salience of goals and objectives • Options that vary levels of challenge and support • Options that foster collaboration and communication • Options that increase mastery-oriented feedback
3. *Provide options for comprehension*	6. *Provide options for executive functions*	9. *Provide options for self-regulation*
• Options that provide or activate background knowledge • Options that highlight critical features, big ideas, and relationships• • Options that guide information processing • Options that support memory and transfer	• Options that guide effective goal-setting Options that support planning and strategy development • Options that facilitate managing information and resources • Options that enhance capacity for monitoring progress	• Options that guide personal goal-setting and expectations • Options that scaffold coping skills and strategies • Options that develop self-assessment and reflection

Note: The source of this table is: CAST (2008). *Universal design for learning guidelines version 1.0.* Wakefield, MA: Author. Retrievable at http://www.udlcenter.org/sites/udlcenter.org/files/UDL_Guidelines_v2%200-Organizer_0.pdf. Adapted with Permission (Permission being requested).

students with more severe cognitive, physical, or learning difficulties. With UDL, the necessary instructional and student-performance supports would already be present and built into the learning environment preceding students' contact with the curriculum.

Response to Intervention (RTI)

The concept of designing curriculum to meet the needs of all students is aligned with the concept of incorporating evidence-based practice and progress monitoring for early intervention. Early intervening services incorporate the practice of Response to Intervention to provide high-quality instruction or intervention matched to students' needs and using learning rate over time and level of performance to inform educational decision-making (The IDEA Partnership, 2009). Educational decision-making typically is designated as tiers and directly affecting a certain percentage of students in a school. Figure 37.1 provides an example of how these ties might appear with regard to technology as an academic intervention. If students are not making progress with specific and monitored instruction using technology at Tier 1, then they are assigned to more strategic instruction (and technologies) at Tier 2. Finally those students who do not make progress with strategic, small-group instruction are then moved to more intensive individual instruction at Tier 3 (RTI Network, 2009).

In reality, AT, UDL, and RTI are compatible concepts, and related to practices that teachers and special education practitioners should integrate together. The concepts of AT, UDL, and RTI challenge teachers to consider the effect that instruction and use of technology will have for their students to progress in the curriculum. UDL challenges teachers to consider barriers that might be inherent in any activity and locate ways to enhance the learning for all students. Edyburn (2009) aligned assistive technology with the RTI model indicating that instructional technology has application in each tier and assistive technology would be available for those who do not make progress or for those with severe physical or language difficulties.

The concept of universally designed curriculum using technology supports and including progress monitoring of student outcomes directly aligns with the tiers of the RTI model. Well-designed uses of instructional technology then provide high quality systematic instruction for all students at Tier 1. For students who do not make progress at Tier 1, then possibly more strategic use of technology in the form of assistive technology would be an important consideration at Tier 2 and 3. Ideally for students with high incidence disabilities, instruction and integration of technology would occur at Tier 1 where instructional technology supports would be available for all students.

Universal Interventions

AT should be selected and implemented in a manner that provides universal interventions for students who need to have access and make progress in the general education curriculum. Ashton (2005), in a selected review of assistive technology interventions for students with learning disabilities in inclusive setting, suggested that assistive technology should support students' integration

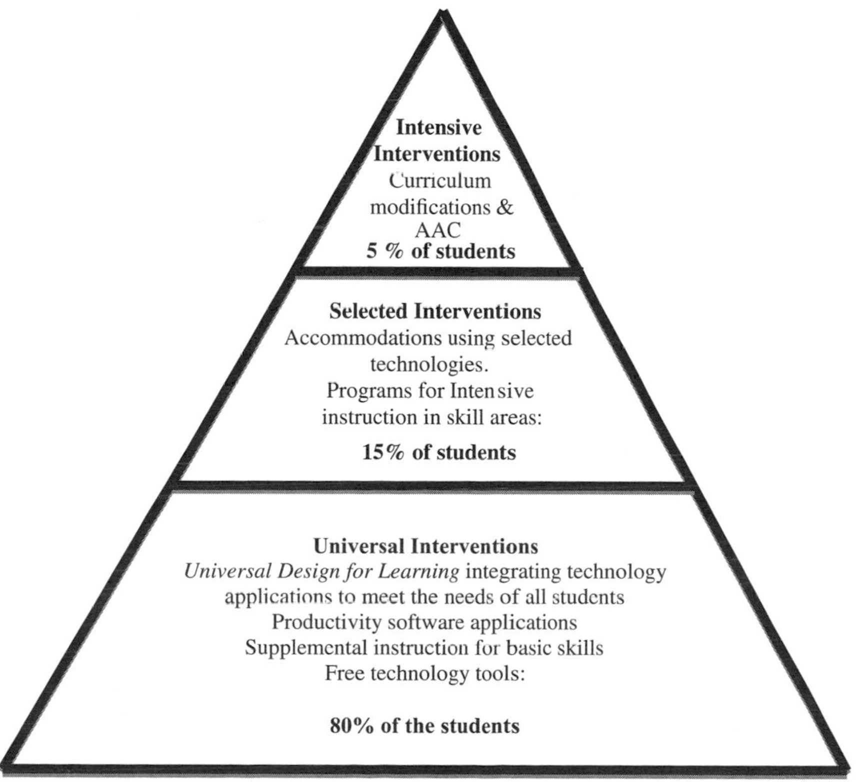

Figure 37.1 Academic technology in a three-tier intervention model.

into general education. This perspective is compatible with King's (1999) definition of assistive technology: "Assistive means helping, supporting, and aiding in accomplishing practical functions, tasks or purposes…. Technology means reliance on simple as well as potentially highly complex tools, devices, and equipment" (p. 14). Assistive technology as a universal intervention should be implemented for all students, where complex technology tools anchored with proven evidence-based instructional theory and practices are used to aid students in learning and practicing new skills. These interventions are considered at any point in the instructional learning process; at the design stage, such as UDL, or in the formative process of progress monitoring, where a student in experiencing academic failure and some degree or form of technology-related assistance should be considered for accommodation, compensation or remediation. The key to integrating technology is no different than any other instructional process that matches students' needs and informs educational decisions: assessment, design, implementation, progress monitoring, and formative evaluation.

Technology Interventions in the Classroom

In the next sections, we examine promising and research-based instructional practices that have used technology to promote academic achievement for students with high incidence disabilities in academic areas. The use of technology for universal interventions suggests that certain practices should be used in all classrooms; however, not every application will work consistently with every student. It is important to reemphasize that teachers still need to monitor progress and individualize the implementation of technology across classrooms and specific students with disabilities. Overall, after examining the literature describing interventions relative to content areas, we have two basic observations.

Our first observation is that the majority of evidence rests in technology interventions that focus on students' processing of text-based information in the context of writing and reading. This is consistent with the fact that most students with high incidence disabilities manifest academic weaknesses in their ability to process printed language. Therefore our second observation is that evidence-based practices for use of technology in reading and written language should also apply to the areas of math, science, and social studies, where students are acquiring information via reading and communicating knowledge via writing. Conversely, our discussions of technology applications in the areas of science and social studies highlight promising applications of technology supports implicitly related to those discussed in the section on reading and writing.

Technology Interventions for Written Language

Teachers sometimes fear the integration of technology for students with disabilities will prevent them from learning the basic skills in reading, writing, or mathematics. We think it's important to start by clearly stating we are not promoting the integration of technology to take over the remediation of teaching students' basic skills in the core areas or replacing non-technology evidence based practices. Instead we are advocating that educators teach students how to use technology to supplement and apply the skills they are learning at higher levels of thinking and performance. In fact, the use of a variety of technology tools can assist all students in the classroom to become more competent readers and writers and prepare them for global learning skills (Fadel & Lemke, 2006).

Research on technology integration and application of productivity tools encompasses more than just the effects on students with disabilities. The effectiveness of these tools for all students when integrated into instruction makes them important universal interventions. For example, meta-analysis research on the effectiveness of word processing has shown positive effects to increase both quality and quantity of written language. In addition, students who used a word processor were more engaged and motivated in their writing (Goldberg, Russell, & Cook, 2003). Therefore, we begin with written language, because, as an aspect of literacy, it is sometimes neglected as a core skill, even though written and verbal computer mediated communication are critical skills to succeed in a 21st- century work environment (Fadel & Lemke, 2006; Graham & Harris, this volume; Graham & Perin, 2007; MacArthur 2009).

Technology and Written Language Instruction

The use of word processing, spreadsheets, presentation programs (e.g., PowerPoint, Keynote), graphic organizers (e.g., Inspiration), and collaborative Web tools (e.g., Wikis) can to be embedded into core instruction in reading and writing. To evaluate the effectiveness of these technology applications, it is sensible to begin with effective technology practices in writing language instruction. Writing or written language encompasses the skills of handwriting, spelling, grammar, syntax, organization, and creative thoughts. Effective writing instruction includes strategic instruction in basic skills and revision, frequent writing on meaningful topics, and opportunities to share, collaborate and get feedback from peers and teachers (Graham & Perin, 2007; MacArthur, 2009). Gersten and Baker (2001) also emphasized that effective writing must include explicit teaching of the writing process and students must be provided feedback on their writing.

The integration of technology into evidence-based strategic written language instruction provides universal interventions for all students. Tools such as word processing, word prediction, and online collaboration support multiple means of expression and the diversity of learners' strategic networks (Rose & Meyer, 2002). Students need to be taught how to organize their thoughts, transcribe their words, and then edit and revise their drafts (Peterson-Karlen & Parette, 2007). When using a word processor, prompting the writing process and providing frequent feedback engage students in the creation and revision, thereby producing higher quality products. As MacArthur (2009) emphasized in his review and analysis on the research on writing and technology, the use of technology must be integrated with other evidence based teaching and writing practices in order to be effective. For a detailed review of research and specific evidence-based practices for struggling writers using technology, consult Peterson-Karlen and Parette (2007) and Sitko, Laine, and Sitko (2005).

Word Processing

The research on word processing has indicated that students can improve in quality and quantity of their work (Goldberg et al., 2003). On closer examination there are several factors that influence the effects of word processing for students with disabilities. Helping students transcribe, spell, compose and revise drafts, along with improving the overall quantity and quality of their written products, are particular concerns.

Transcription and spelling. The first assumption about using a word processor is that students will overcome problems in typing or letter production. Students must be able to use a regular keyboard and mouse to access the computer and have proper keyboard training before using word processing for writing (Wong, 2001). Researchers have reported that students who use a word processing program to complete written products after learning keyboarding skills complete written assignments better than students who do not have such instruction (Lewis, Graves, Ashton, & Kieley, 1998). Berninger, Abbott, Augsburger, and Garcia (2009) found that older students (with and without learning disabilities) were faster on the keyboard than younger students, possibly indicating effects of cumulative instruction in keyboarding and exposure to computers. Students with disabilities therefore need explicit instruction in keyboarding.

Once students demonstrate they've acquired basic keyboarding skills, a second assumption is that a word processor will help students who have poor spelling or handwriting skills. Some teachers are concerned that word processing programs will automatically correct students' spelling and grammar and prevent students' ability to learn basic skills in these areas. However, studies of the effectiveness of word processing to correct the spelling for students with learning disabilities have indicated that students must begin the misspelled word with the correct letter, and include most of the word's phonetic intent, in order for the correct spelling to be provided by a word processor (MacArthur, Graham, Haynes, & De La Paz, 1996; MacArthur, 1998a; MacArthur, 2009; Wissick, 2005).

In comparing the effectiveness of nine word processing programs, Montgomery, Karlan, and Coutinho (2001) reported that the programs provided the target word an average of only 53% of the time and the target word appeared first on the list only 21.6 %of the time. However, MacArthur et al. (1996) found that students' correction rates only improve when the correct word appears within the top choices. Therefore, we recommend that as part of traditional word-processing and writing instruction, teachers train students in strategies for properly evaluating spelling errors and using spell check features in word-processing programs; without such instruction, many students with high incidence disabilities will not benefit.

Revision, quantity, and speed. Another assumption about word processing is that students will write longer passages, in a shorter amount of time and be more effective in revision than if they write by hand. Berninger et al. (2009) found that students will not always produce more written language or produce it faster using technology. Earlier work by MacArthur, Graham, Schwartz, and Schafer (1995) also found that the writing of students who used a word-processing program integrated with strategy instruction rather than handwriting, did not improve in overall length, spelling, capitalization, or punctuation. The quality of narrative writing, however, did improve for students who had combined word-processing and strategy instruction, although the word processing factor alone could not be singled out as the cause.

Teachers need to realize that when students start learning to use word processing, the immediate effect may be that students' writing decreases in rate and quantity, which might imply the technology was not successful. In contrast, they should monitor and measure changes in students' accuracy and quality of writing-related behaviors, because there is a strong possibility that the majority of students' writing may be improving in these areas. However, if after several months of using word processing some a students are not demonstrating gains in speed or quantity of writing, teachers should reevaluate the type of word processor being used and investigate moving to a more intensive level of intervention, such as word processing that includes text-to-speech feedback, word prediction, or speech recognition.

Word Prediction

The main function of word prediction is to help students who have difficulty with word retrieval, word production, or severe misspelling. Students who use word prediction do not need to be efficient in keyboarding. Word prediction is an extended feature of word processing that "interprets" the context of preceding words and grammatical rules and convention of the sentence being typed, and "predicts" a word that might likely be subsequent. For example, students who type "Mary had a l…" might be presented a drop-down box containing the word options "(1) large … (2) light … (3) little … (4) local …, etc." They can choose the word by selecting the accompanying keyboard number of the word in the list or by clicking on the word with the mouse, which results in the entire word replacing the letter "l." Some word prediction programs are able to make predictions based on common or phonetic misspellings of words. Alternatively, teachers can add customized word lists to correspond with specific units or content.

Word-prediction programs do not limit a student's creativity. They simply suggest words based on previous words and letters typed. Students are not required to choose any of the words predicted. They can keep typing until the word they are seeking appears in the list. A variety of word-prediction programs also include a text-to-speech component that allows the student to listen to the word options before choosing one or to hear the complete sentence spoken when they have selected a word.

A growing body of research described the positive effects of word prediction on writing tasks for students with high incidence disabilities. Students who use word prediction have shown a decrease in the quantity of writing as compared to traditional writing, but an increase in the overall quality of their writing (Lewis et al., 1998). Students who used a word-processing program with word prediction for spelling, journal writing, and dictation have increased their spelling accuracy to the 90% to 100% range (MacArthur, 1998a; MacArthur, 1998b; MacArthur, 1999).

Students using word prediction that included text-to-speech software have shown an increase in the number of words written and in the quality of journal writing completed. Students who used or accessed the word prediction program the most, were the ones for whom the writing quality improved the most (Williams, 2002). At the same time, not all students need to use word prediction, and some may benefit more from the text-to-speech feedback that is associated with word prediction (Cullen & Richards, 2008). Unfortunately, the use of word prediction with text-to-speech typically resulted in an even greater decrease in the overall speed of writing than does the use of word prediction alone (Magnuson & Hunnicutt, 2002). Over time students did master these tools and perform at a speed comparable to keyboarding without these aids.

Text-to-Speech

Text-to-speech software is used to convert words in a computer into audible speech. As the result of this auditory feedback, students can monitor and edit their writing activities. Text-to-speech software can usually be configured to speak letters, words, or sentences as they are typed. Alternately, students can highlight and select specific words, sentences, or blocks of text to be spoken. Some specialized word processing programs have text-to-speech and word prediction capabilities incorporated. In addition, computer operating systems for text to speech can be activated or free text-to-speech programs can be downloaded and added to standard word processing programs or Web browsers.

In choosing a specific text-to-speech technology, practitioners should rely on research-based information. However, sometimes little or no direct evidence exists. Bausch (2006) described research that indicated students improve in their writing ability with auditory feedback and having their writing read aloud. We might subsequently integrate this research to the use of technology practice, by considering the possibility of text-to-speech technology for a student to improve in writing. However, the use of this technology may still fail even if it is based on research, because some students may need to hear a human voice, not synthesized speech, reading the written content.

Although no specific research with respect to writing has been conducted on the overall speed or efficiency effects of text-to-speech alone, listening to each letter or word as it is typed does increase the time required to produce each word, thereby decreasing the overall speed of writing. However, this can be offset by the fact that fewer revisions might be needed to complete the final product. In addition using the text-to-speech feature to listen to a final draft can help students recognize misspelled words, missing words or incomplete thoughts.

Speech Recognition

Instead of typing, speech-recognition programs allow students to talk to the computer. For some this might be considered a modification of the writing process but many adults use this tool for speed, on a portable device or to reduce the strain of heavy keyboard use. Two types of speech recognition are available for use: discrete and continuous. Discrete speech requires the user to speak each word individually and distinctly. Continuous speech allows the user to speak more naturally, using complete sentences or phrases. An advantage of discrete speech is that the user can correct a word as soon as it is produced instead of waiting for a full sentence to appear.

Although speech-recognition systems have improved, most current systems must be "trained" by each user to recognize words and sounds that are spoken into a microphone. The key to using speech recognition successfully is the time spent training the system to understand particular nuances in the user's voice pattern. Initial considerations include the time and effort required of students to read training text into the system, training the system on the students' unique voice inflections, and the ability of the student to read incorrect words, select the correct spelling from an alternative window, sustain attention to correct mistakes, and work in a quiet environment. Regardless of whether a system recognizes discrete and continuous speech, students must be trained in its use, a process that can take as long as 10 weeks (Wetzel, 1996). In addition, students need to use speech recognition consistently over time (Higgins & Raskind, 2000).

Once a training phase has been completed, students with high incidence disabilities benefited from receiving explicit instruction on the importance of planning thoughts or ideas prior to dictation (De La Paz, 1999). As students became more proficient in using speech recognition, the amount of time spent on dictation, navigation, and correction decreased over time (Feng, Karat, & Sears, 2005), thereby making their writing process more fluent. Some studies on the use of speech recognition that have studied post-secondary students with learning disabilities found an improvement in expository compositions as compared to use of word processing alone or dictation alone Higgins & Raskind, 1995; Roberts & Stodden, 2005). Comparable research with elementary and secondary students has shown that discrete speech is more effective for increasing spelling and reading recognition than continuous speech (Higgins & Raskind, 2000; Raskind & Higgins 1999).

Graphic Organizers

Students benefit from instruction and technology tools that assist with the organization and structure of their writing. Graphic organizers provide visual and graphic display of the relationships between facts, terms, or ideas (Hall & Strangman, 2002). Graphic organizers are also referred to as concept maps, knowledge maps, story maps, or advance organizers. Although Hall and Strangman (2002) noted that most of the research on the use of graphic organizers focuses on reading and reading comprehension, we discuss how they also support written language literacy activities. For discussion of their use in science and social studies, see Scruggs, Mastropieri, and Marshak (this volume).

MacArthur (2009) noted that electronic graphic organizers are useful in the planning phrase of writing. Although the use of graphic organizers assists students in pre-writing activities, they can also be used to scaffold other elements of the writing process. Students can cut and paste text written in graphic organizers into a word processer to create outlines. Crooks, White, and Barnard (2007) found that graphic organizers also helped students in their organization of note-taking. Students can also gather and organize research for thematic projects (Gardner, Wissick, Schweder, & Smith, 2003). Considering universal interventions, graphic organizers provide students with multiple means of representation of the topic and expression as many programs allow users to add pictures, voice, and text or to convert maps to outlines. Unlike their predecessors that were usually used individually, new graphic organizers support collaboration and can be completed online, asynchronously.

Collaborative Writing

One of the recommendations of the *Writing Next* report indicated that students need to be taught collaborative writing (Graham & Perin, 2007). The emergence of technologies such as smart phones and handheld devices with the capabilities of accessing the Web from almost any location, allow users to communicate and collaborate easily. In addition, some writing programs incorporate multimedia aspects to include pictures and audio along with the text that allow students to collaborate and gain confidence in their writing skills (Rao, Dowrick, Yuen, & Boisvert, 2009). According to the 2008 survey by the Pew Internet and American Life Project (Lenhart, Arafeh, Smith, & MacGill, 2008), 85% of teens ages 12–17 engaged in some type of electronic personal communication but 60% of these students did not consider this "writing." Therefore, effective written language instruction should integrate these Web tools with opportunities for students to write about topics meaningful to them and to share and receive feedback from their peers (MacArthur, 2009).

Englert, Zhao, Dunsmore, Collings, and Wolbers (2007) developed and studied the use of a Web-based prompting system for writing and found that students wrote longer essays and received higher ratings than the paper and pencil group. This study demonstrated the potential of the Web to support and foster the steps in writing. Other Web tools such as blogs, wikis, and some social networking sites provide teachers and students with capability to collaborate in writing (Schweder & Wissick, 2007, 2009). Students can use these tools to practice editing and engage in creative collaborative and digital story telling. By publishing online via blogs or wikis, students can also obtain relevant and ongoing feedback on their work with their collaborators or by comments left by readers. Knowing that their work will be read by peers and parents may also motivate some students to focus on their grammar and spelling.

Although research on the impact of collaborative writing by students with high incidence disabilities within technology environments is just emerging, there is potential for positive effects on writing and literacy (MacArthur, 2009). Regardless of the medium (e.g., multimedia, Web 2.0, or a classroom environment using word processing), we predict the potential of integrating technology tools like text to speech, word processing and word prediction, and speech recognition will probably be most effective for students with disabilities only when instruction in writing coexists with established evidence-based instructional practices.

Technology Interventions in Reading

Reading instruction tends to be the focus of many response-to-intervention efforts in schools. Regardless of the specific commercial program, five areas of instruction are critical for all students: phonemic awareness, alphabetical principle, accuracy and fluency, vocabulary, and comprehension (Strangman & Dalton, 2005). For older students, recommended reading instruction focuses on motivation, vocabulary, fluency, and comprehension and combines elements of phonemic awareness and the alphabetical principle to word study (Roberts, Torgesen, Boardman, & Scammacca, 2008). The *Reading Next* report also recommends focus on motivation and self-directed learning, text-based collaborative learning, on-going formative evaluation, diverse texts, and a technology component to provide support (Biancarosa & Snow, 2006). These recommendations fit with the principles of UDL as technology can provide diversity with texts in multiple formats and support collaborative and formative assessment. Rather than recite research on specific reading software programs, we discuss unique elements within a technology or software program that make them effective for students with disabilities in reading. In reading, the power of technology lies in its capability to provide alternative, multiple means of representation for text and enhance students' engagement. When selecting reading software, Torgesen (2007) recommended asking a series of questions ranging from clarity of directions to pedagogical features.

Programs should have explicit directions, focus on the knowledge and skills being taught, provide progress reports and systematic review opportunities. In addition, teachers should consider whether the program incorporates a mastery orientation, in the sense that before moving to new skills, the student must meet the performance criteria set by the teacher. Finally, teachers should consider if the program provides engaging, varied, and useful feedback about responses.

Specialized Technology-Based Reading Software

Many reading programs advertise that they employ evidence-based technology practices. Some reading software programs provide multimedia support with visual and auditory cues for training and self-correction (Okolo, Cavalier, Ferretti, & MacArthur, 2000, Silver-Pacuilla, Ruedel, & Mistrett, 2004). Other reading software products may have built-in features that make it easier to collect data or offer interactive activities that are self-paced and can be repeated. Some programs focus on only one skill such as phonemic awareness or phonics; whereas, other programs include all aspects of beginning reading skills—phonemics, phonics, fluency, vocabulary, and comprehension. For example, Campuzano, Dynarski, Agodini, and Rall's (2009) large-scale examination on the use of comprehensive reading software indicated that effects on student achievement were not statistically significant. Their study raised questions about whether the specific characteristics of the software were suited for students with disabilities, and whether these programs were used systematically for a long enough time.

In a comprehensive review of the research on technology for reading instruction for students with disabilities, Strangman and Dalton (2005) identified specific reading software features that appear to be effective. Computer programs that pair visual with auditory information during presentation and feedback, provided an advantage. Students who practiced reading using software programs that included explicit instruction in phonemic awareness, sound manipulation, rhyme, and phonemic segmentation, increased those specific skills. Technology was able to offer dynamic representations illustrating blending sounds and segmentation of words. In addition, effective technologies allowed students to read text and hear their recordings or receive speech feedback on their reading, supporting comprehension. Most importantly, in order to promote students' reading skills, isolated or occasional practice using reading software was not an efficient learning model—students needed to spend a consistent and extensive amount of time per week receiving instruction and practice via the software (Strangman & Dalton, 2005).

The majority of software programs that focus on basic reading have been designed to target younger beginning readers. A small number of programs exist for adolescents who lack basic reading skills. Some of these software programs focus on core skills and repeated reading activities, while others also integrate vocabulary and comprehension as part of the instruction; programs that integrate vocabulary instruction into the overall program have been the most effective for adolescents (Biancarosa & Snow, 2006). In a review of research on secondary reading programs, Slavin, Cheung, Groff, and Lake (2008) reported that reading programs demonstrating the largest effect sizes were those that incorporated cooperative learning and mixed reading methods—the mixed methods being programs that integrated direct instruction, small group work, and contained technology-based instruction in vocabulary including multiple exemplars and visual and auditory cues as a technology component. In contrast, according to Slavin et al. secondary reading programs that used computer-assisted reading programs such as those offered in a group lab settings had little to no effect. Slavin et al. proposed that more effective applications of technology in secondary reading instruction are those that are integrated and directly linked to curriculum-based content and activities.

Audiobooks, Text to Speech, and eReaders

The advances in technology have provided us with multiple ways to access text. Students can access and listen to books using audiobooks, text-to-speech programs, or eBooks. Audiobooks offer audio-only presentation of the material and are helpful for students to gain overall meaning of the work but do not provide practice in reading. Boyle et al. (2003) noted that listening without viewing of the text was not effective for students with reading disabilities. To use audiobooks to practice reading, students should be given a copy of the text and taught how to use the audio as a model for fluent reading. Audiobooks may develop motivation and interest in reading as they are professionally recorded using inflection and expression. Audiobooks are available from public libraries in a variety of formats such as tape, CD-Roms, and MP3 players.

Text-to-speech is a feature often used in word processing where auditory feedback can be provided by letter, word, sentence, paragraph, or whole text. Although this feature is helpful when writing (Cullen & Richards, 2008), clearly, it can also support reading activities. For example, programs that highlight individual words as they are read to a student, help them focus on specific words and sentence content, reducing cognitive load on decoding and enabling better attention toward using comprehension strategies. Using text-to-speech to teach phonics or vocabulary has not been an effective method (Strangman & Dalton, 2005). At the same time, text-to-speech programs have been effectively implemented to provide alternative independent access to text for students with disabilities (Douglas, Ayres, Langone, Bell, & Meade, 2009; Hasselbring & Bausch, 2006) and support their achievement in high school content classes (Izzo, Yurick, & McArrell, 2009). Although students should still be taught skills for reading, struggling readers can also benefit from listening to textbooks or novels to gain information and advance comprehension and vocabulary skills at their cognitive level.

Text-to-speech tools can be used as a universal intervention for all students by providing them fundamental access to auditory versions of text to support comprehension or reading for pleasure. Typically, every audiobook is a unique audio recording of human dictated text exclusive to the specific word or text of the book. In contrast, text-to-speech programs convert a wide variety of electronic formats of text into speech via a digital voice. Text-to-speech programs therefore provide access to *any* literature, books, or news articles that are available in electronic format: text within a text file or word processing document, a PDF document, or text within a Webpage. Some of these programs will convert text to speech, and subsequently convert the spoken text into MP3 file, enabling the spoken text to be placed onto a digital audio player. The use of text-to-speech has also been recommended for incorporation into state assessments as a method to determine students' comprehension ability separate from their decoding ability (Thurlow et al., 2009).

Finally, students can also use standalone eReaders, devices that can hold thousands of eBooks. These books have been specifically formatted for eReaders and include all the images or diagrams from books. Although some eReaders provide text-to-speech conversions, eReaders are designed more for motivation and access to a wide variety of books. When using eReaders, regardless of the format for the auditory enhancement, students will still need to be taught important cognitive strategies such as self-questioning and self-monitoring in order to improve their comprehension (Faggella-Luby & Deschler, 2008). What sets eReaders apart from typical audio or eBooks is their potential to provide supported electronic text (eText).

Supported eTexts and Future Trends

Whether it is embedded in an eReader or a specific computer program, the dynamic nature of electronic, digital text allows other features affiliated with reading and processing text to become significantly enhanced (Anderson-Inman, 2009). Using supported eText, students cannot only listen to the text, but they can have access to other resources that increase access and support comprehension. For example, students can manipulate electronic text by selecting font size, format, and style to provide optimal visual appeal (Anderson-Inman & Horney, 2007).

Anderson-Inman (2009) and Anderson-Inman and Horney (2007) defined 11 elements of eText that supported and increased access for students with disabilities. In supported eText, *navigational resources* provide the user with access within a digital document and to other documents, such as dictionaries, glossaries, or tables of contents. Navigational resources can also provide enrichment to other related sources of information thereby supporting students at various levels and interests. Supported eTexts also include *explanatory, summarization,* and *instructional* prompts. Students have the ability to change *presentation* of the text and *translate* the text for language or cognitive understanding. *Illustrative* resources provide multiple representations of the text or provide captioning for video. Supported eTexts also allow opportunities for *collaboration, notetaking*, and *evaluation*.

Current technology offers many formats for students to view and engage in supported eText, from full-platform computers to handheld device like PDAs and smartphones. The National Center on Supported Text (http://ncset.uoregon.edu) provides resources and research on supported eText. CAST has developed and supports a set of Web-based tools providing supported eText components. As more applications are developed for handheld devices, the capacity to provide collaborative and supported texts will also expand.

Various features of eText (e.g., text-to-speech, eText in captioned video, text-highlighting, graphic organizers, visual thesaurus) enhance comprehension and content learning (Boyle et al., 2003; Clay, Zorfass, Brann, Kotula, & Smolkowski. 2009; Douglas, Ayres, Langone, Bell, & Meade, 2009; Horney et al., 2009; Izzo, Yurick, & McArrell, 2009; Pearman, 2008). Clearly, the potential for these technology-based applications will increase as we build a database of evidence-based practices and teachers integrate the use of these materials into the general education curriculum for all students. However, like many of the other technology applications, eText is not an instructional intervention that automatically works, teachers will need to teach students how to navigate and effectively apply elements of eText to take advantage of its features and the feedback effectively.

Technology Intervention in Mathematics

Literature reviews of applications of technology to math instruction for students with disabilities are abundant. Most recently, CITEd (2009) published a synthesis of technology applications for mathematics for all students across grade levels K–8, and divided research into the areas of drill and practice, screen-based manipulatives, cooperative learning, anchored instruction, and multimedia embedded supports. Focusing just on students with disabilities, Maccini and Gagnon (2005) published a detailed review of technology-based interventions in mathematics for students with learning disabilities, and organized the research with regard to computer-assisted instruction (CAI), video-based applications, and contextualized math word problems. As a complement and extension to Maccini and Gagnon's review, Bouck and Flanagan (2009) reviewed mathematics research articles from 1996 to 2006 and organized the research in the context of video-based anchored-instruction, CAI, and use of calculators. Hasselbring, Lott, and Zydney (2006) focused on technology-supported math instruction for students with disabilities, and organized their review around programs and factors related to building computational fluency. For those seeking in-depth reviews of technology-based math interventions, all four of these reviews should be consulted. For purposes of present and restricted purposed of discussion, we report on examples related to CAI, calculators, and anchored instruction.

Computer Assisted Instruction

Woodward and Reith's (1997) meta-analysis of CAI drill-and-practice programs for students with disabilities indicated that CAI technology was not always aligned with student needs, students did not spend enough time on their use of CAI programs, programs that provided evidence of good results were only available as prototypes, and overall the technology was used for motivation instead of instruction. Helsel, Hitchcock, Miller, Malinow, and Murray (2006) reviewed 61 studies on the use of screen-based technologies—computer assisted instruction and anchored instruction—for mathematics in grades K–8. Unfortunately, only a few of those 61 studies were based on evidence-based practices and none of the studies could target results specifically for students with disabilities. Regardless, the overall results pointed to the same findings as Woodward and Reith (1997) that CAI technology was not effective if it was not aligned with the curriculum and students did not spend enough time daily with the programs.

Dynarski et al. (2007) reported the first set of results from the national study on technology effectiveness. Research conducted on mathematics technology programs used in sixth grade and algebra indicated no significant effect on students' test scores. Although at first glance these results might appear to indicate that teachers should not consider technology applications, closer inspection reveals similar concerns as reported by Woodward and Reith. The classes in these studies used large-scale drill and tutorial mathematics software implemented in computer labs. There was no indication that teachers integrated technology use into instruction or matched technology use to individual students' needs. Furthermore, the study did not separate effects for students who had difficulty with mathematics versus those who did not. Clearly, teachers working with students with disabilities have to be wary of large-scale results and continue to search for direct impact of technology for their students.

Hasselbring et al. (2006) focused their review of technology-supported math instruction on both research and development activities with regard to building computational fluency for students with disabilities. They discussed the potential of technology to alleviate students' problems in declarative, procedural, and conceptual knowledge in mathematics. Early research on drill and practice for math facts found that students were not developing fluency but only becoming faster in counting math facts instead of recall. Hasselbring and Goin (2005) then developed a technology-based system that includes many elements that foster declarative knowledge: identification of fluent and non-fluent facts; restricted presentation of non-fluent information, student generation of problem and answer pairs; use of controlled response times; spaced presentation of non-fluent information; and appropriate use of drill and practice (Hasselbring & Goin, 2005, p. 8). Research on this program during its development and then as a commercial product indicated that if used for 10 minutes a day for at least 100 days, most math delayed students were able to develop fluency in math facts.

Technology-based drill-and-practice programs have a place in a Tier 1 classroom assisting all students to develop fluency in basic facts. In addition, promising new technologies continue to be developed that offer possibilities for future mathematics skill enhancement for students with disabilities. For example, Bouck, Bassette, Taber-Doughty, Flanagan, and Szwed (2009) investigated using pen-top computers for students to practice and learn multiplication facts and found that students improved in their percentage of correct math facts completed.

Calculators

Helsel, Hitchcock, Miller, Malinow, and Murray (2006) presented an extensive analysis of calculator use starting from Kindergarten through college. Overall when the use of calculators is integrated into instruction and testing, they have positive effects on students' operational and problem-solving skills (CITEd, 2009; Ellington, 2003). For students with disabilities, calculator use has been associated with the use of accommodations in high-stakes assessment (Mancini & Gagnon, 2005, 2006). Research has indicated that the use of calculators increases the math functioning of students with disabilities, but the uses also increase the functioning for all students (Bouck & Bouck, 2008).

As an accommodation that is supposed to have greater benefits for students with disabilities, calculator use can be questioned. However, calculators appear to support all students in mathematical processing, and therefore as a Tier 1 intervention, should be integrated into math instruction and assessment for all students. At the same time we reiterate that calculators, like other technology tools, should not replace direct instruction in mathematical skills and students should be explicitly taught to use calculators as a way to complement and check their work.

Anchored Instruction

The anchored instruction models developed by the Cognition and Technology Group at Vanderbilt University were designed to combine elements of authentic learning and situated cognition, multimedia, and interactive and exploratory problem-solving environments, as a means to engage students in complex math and science learning (CTGV, 1990, 1992). For example, an anchored instruction program in math might typically include a set of video segments where students view people encountering a variety of real-life circumstances that require them to apply math skills and higher-order thinking to solve a set of problems. Relying on the interactive nature of digital video and small cooperative learning groups, students experience guided and independent practice of math knowledge and skills.

The majority of the research in anchored instruction and math with low-achieving or students with high incidence disabilities has been conduced by Bottge and colleagues (Bottge, 1999; Bottge & Hasselbring, 1993; Bottge, Heinricks, Chan, Mehta, & Watson, 2003; Bottge, Heinrichs, Chan, & Serlin, 2001; Bottge, Heinrichs, Mehta, & Hung, 2002; Bottge et al., 2004; Bottge, Rueda, Kwon, Grant, & LaRoque, 2009). They've reported that although anchored instruction with middle and high school students has a positive effect on problem solving and mathematical understanding, these students do not always perform better on computation skills. Anchored instruction for mathematics is warranted when it is included as part of a complete scope and sequence of math skills, and when students use it to practice both computation and problem-solving skills.

Technology Interventions for Science and Social Studies

Compared to writing, reading, and math applications, far less literature yielding direct evidence regarding technology for students with high incidence disabilities is available for science and social studies. In the following sections we draw attention to the rationale, examples, and limited evidence regarding how technology tools should and can be applied to help students with high incidence disabilities process and engage in science and social studies content. Also, see Scruggs et al. (this volume).

Science

Learning science content presents numerous challenges for students with high incidence disabilities. Not only do teachers have to consider the wide range of students' learning aptitudes, but also, science curriculum, as compared to other academic areas, typically demands complex vocabulary and math computation and requires students to employ higher-order thinking skills, such as analysis, synthesis, inductive and deductive reasoning, and generalization (Mastropieri & Scruggs, 1992, 2007; Scruggs & Mastropieri, 1993, 1994). Coupled with the notion that science classrooms routinely involve students with high incidence disabilities in instruction traditionally in the form of lecture and discussion or constructivist and inquiry-based activities that involve students in independent practice, problem solving, and discovery learning activities (Scruggs & Mastropieri, 2007), a wide range of technology considerations can exist depending on whether the focus is on the *representation* and delivery of instruction *to* students by teachers or students' *expression* of their knowledge in learning activities.

Unquestionably, there is a heavy element of text processing (e.g., decoding and fluency) and written expression affiliated with learning science. Mastroperi and Scruggs (1992) emphasize the importance of study guides and text adaptations. Many of the technology tools and strategies presented in the reading and writing sections, when implemented in the UDL model relative to the principles of enhancing representation and expression, can be generalized to science instruction as methods for students to access text and construct meaning efficiently. For example, allowing students to use graphic organizers, presentation software, podcasting, and word processing, all represent multiple ways students can acquire and express their knowledge of science content for the purposes of communication or assessment of learning. Moreover, from the perspective of multimedia learning, the work of Mayer (2009) and Mayer and Moreno (2002, 2003) indicated that many learners can experience cognitive load factors that interfere with learning. For example, a considerable amount of ubiquitous classroom technology may likely include Web-based learning of science information. Gardner and Wissick (2005) proposed that teachers can implement technology tools in the context of Mayer and Moreno's principles as a means of reducing cognitive load during Web-based learning for students with high incidence disabilities. These include offloading visual information to audio via screen readers or podcasts, segmenting Web-based visual and auditory information via online scaffolding tools, "turning off" extraneous or irrelevant video or audio information inside browsers, and providing external prompts or checklists to help organize and focus attention on salient aspects of online multimedia-based information. Intuitively, these points appear to generalize to Web-based science learning, but have yet to be tested under experimental conditions.

Unfortunately, there is hardly any literature that combines technology, science instruction, and students with cognitive disabilities. Focused examinations of science instruction in the context of technology applications and persons with high incidence disabilities are represented by Schaff, Jerome, Behrmann, and Sprague's (2005) discussion of emerging technologies in special education science instruction and Marino's (2010) comprehensive review of literature synthesizing science outcomes associated with high incidence disabilities in inclusive science classrooms, and the literature involving technology outcomes affiliated with science instruction in elementary and secondary classrooms.

According to Schaff et al. (2005), the field of special education technology has successfully identified a wide variety of assistive and instructional technologies that can provide students with access to science curricula. From a UDL context, much of their perspective concentrated on describing how emerging technologies support the representation of science information and science-oriented Web sites that simultaneously expand opportunities for students' action and engagement in science activities. According to Schaff et al., emerging science technologies are in the areas of (a) virtual reality and virtual labs, (b) Multi-User Object Oriented domains (MOOs), and (c) handheld devices.

Schaff et al. (2005) defined virtual reality as "a three dimensional, computer generated synthetic environment that gives the user a sense of being immersed in a real word. This immersion is based on visual, audio and haptic (touch) feedback" (p. 644). For students with high incidence disabilities, they believe the benefits of virtual reality science instruction rest in its multisensory presentation of information and its ability to present and illustrate abstract elements visually and concretely, while simultaneously controlling for extraneous stimuli and providing students with opportunities to experience science information from multiple frames of reference. Within the context of virtual reality there also exist a number of virtual science labs that allow students to perform virtual chemistry, physics, and biology experiments and activities.

With regard to MOOs, Schaff et al. (2005) characterize MOOs as online virtual communities, where students can take on anonymous personas, create avatars (i.e., a virtual image of oneself), and explore and interact with other individuals in a thematic virtual world without the possibility of suffering any stigma as a person with a disability. As this technology develops, they foresee students with disabilities being engaged virtually to participate with other students in real-time science discussions and problem-solving activities. With regard to handheld devices and science activities, they foresee the value of personal digital assistants (PDAs) to function as assistive devices for students with learning disabilities, helping them add structure and organization to science activities that often require learners to follow step-by-step directions, enter information, and produce notes or reports. The ability to attach sensors and probes to PDAs also supports efficient and reliable collection of scientific data, and allows those data to be synchronized with computer software. In many respects, use of PDAs and accompanying software helps alleviate physical, time-related, and cognitive elements related to science activities, thereby allowing learners to focus their attention on the broader scientific understanding, application, interpretation, and implications of the gathered information.

Marino's (2010) extensive review of the empirical investigations regarding students with other high incidence disabilities in inclusive science classrooms and empirical investigations focusing on technology use in science classrooms, reveals an interesting quandary. Marino identified 15 studies of students with disabilities and at-risk students in inclusive science classrooms and 23 focusing on technology use in elementary and secondary science classrooms (n = 23), but only 3 reports of interventions combining both technology and students with disabilities. Concentrating on the importance of identifying ways technology can support students with disabilities' participation in scientific inquiry and efficient science learning, Marino suggested that the convergence of the research evidence across these disparate areas illustrates promising practices.

Marino (2010) proposed that there is incidental evidence that properly applied technology can support universally designed instruction for student with high incidence disabilities. It can increase access to science curricula, enhance content via hypermedia and online multimedia resources, and enrich the authenticity of scientific learning tasks. There is also incidental evidence suggesting that technology can be applied to help reduce cognitive load and scaffold higher-order scientific thinking, inquiry, and analysis skills. At the same time, Marino rightfully acknowledged that much of the existing literature fails to contain sufficient quality indicators that meet Gersten and Edyburn's (2007) criteria for strong research on special education technology. Nevertheless, if future research examines outcomes associated with technology use and science education for student with disabilities, we may be able to identify practices that foster students' development of positive attitudes toward science learning and careers in the field of science, technology, and mathematics.

Social Studies

Thinking about students with high incidence disabilities involved with technology and social studies learning, the effectiveness of technology-based reading and writing supports, as presented in the previous sections are applicable. The most comprehensive examination of social studies instruction in the context of technology applications and persons with high incidence disabilities are represented by Okolo's (2005) discussion of interactive technologies and social studies for students with high incidence disabilities, and Boon, Fore, Blankenship, and Chalk's (2007) review of literature on technology-based practices in social studies instruction for students with high incidence disabilities.

Okolo (2005) organized her examination of technology applications and social studies around two fundamental observations: (a) students with high incidence disabilities acquire social studies either through traditional textbooks and Web-based content that takes the form of text, graphics or pictorial images, and videos (i.e., reading skills and comprehension play a prominent role); and (b) text-based collections of social studies literature have been criticized by a group of scholars as "ill structured and inconsiderate… of the cognitive, metacognitive, and motivational needs of school-age readers" (p. 624). Okolo highlighted technology applications in the context of supported text, information archives, Web pages containing historical content, projects supported by multimedia applications, and computer and online simulations and gaming. Across each of these areas, there is strong proof-of-concept that when implemented, instructional technology activities and tools clearly address all three principles of universal design for learning. According to Okolo, effective technology applications are those that make complex social studies content and concepts meaningful to students, promoting their analysis, interpretation, and organization of information in social studies content and aiding their expression and communication of knowledge to others.

Boon et al.'s (2007) review of literature on technology-based practices in social studies instruction identified 18 articles reporting empirical studies between 1980 and 2006. They determined that the studies could be grouped into four categories of technology application: (a) organized, hypertext study guides; (b) project-based learning activities; (c) learning how to create concept maps to organize and synthesize social studies course content; and (d) using computerized map tutorials to learn geography. Across these studies, roughly 85% included students with high incidence disabilities as well as participants who were in remedial or general education and not considered to have a disability. Boon et al. reported that across all interventions, the use of technology was effective in enhancing and improving social studies achievement regardless of whether a student had a disability. When comparisons were made to traditional textbook instruction or controlled instructional contexts not using technology, the introduction of technology lead to a relatively quick and significant increase in performance. Boon et al. also proposed that the technologies reported in their review were effective because they provided instructional adaptations by (a) highlighted salient social studies textbook information; (b) supported attention, organization, and construction of social studies information; (c) reduced writing demands, and (d) created a balanced learning environment among all students that contained more similar student learning behavior, time on task, and collaborative activities, thereby, reducing the achievement gap between general and special education students.

Additional studies reported encouraging empirical outcomes related to technology and social studies instruction for students with high incidence disabilities. Twyman and Tindal (2006) included computer-adapted text built around UDL principles improving content-related vocabulary learning and problem solving. Okolo, Englert, Bouck, and Heutsche (2007) improved students' knowledge and historical reasoning within the context of a virtual history museum that contained a variety of reading and writing supports. Finally Gentry (2008) found gains in content learning as the result of students' writing electronic books and electronic publishing of social studies information. Overall, technology supports in the form of multimedia, text to speech, and supported prompts appears to provide universal interventions for all students in science and social studies.

Concluding Thoughts on Technology

Although much of the research on technology integration has not focused specifically on students with disabilities, lessons learned from studies in general education have implications for differentiating instruction for all students. The most important factor that arises from the research is that technology applications must be integrated into the curriculum systematically and procedurally and implemented during instruction and assessment with strong fidelity. The technology must match the needs of the students and aspects of academic content must be considered in the context of UDL and RTI. We do not want to diminish the focus of using direct instruction to teach core academic skills, but we also acknowledge Edyburn's (2005) caution that we cannot continually focus on remediation at the exclusion of technology when technology might provide a reasonable compensation. We strongly believe that if, over time and different interventions where progress is closely monitored, a student still cannot perform core skills such as math calculation, reading expository text, or handwriting thoughts on paper, and suffers repeated consequences of failure, then a move to a more strategic or possibly intensive use of technology is warranted.

Questions remain as to the precise effectiveness of individual technology tools for improving student achievement and success. As with any good instruction in writing or reading, individual progress monitoring and curriculum-based measurement that tracks small changes in learning outcomes are the essential measures of a technology's effectiveness, and not district or state-wide assessment tests. Teachers *can* gather systematic data on students' progress. Any time a teacher implements an instructional sequence enhanced with technology, data should be collected. Discrete measures of specific outcomes are important— without them teachers may assume that technology is not making a difference. For example, with technology and writing, teachers can easily measure the quantity of writing by counting the number of words or characters, accuracy can be measured by counting the number of correct words or correct word sequences, and quality by any number of writing rubrics from the special education technology literature. Any newly introduced technology must be given a reasonable amount of time depending on the student and context to work. When the data indicate a lack of progress, before abandoning an academic technology application or intervention, practice suggests that a variety of considerations should be made simultaneously. Slight or moderate changes in instructional methods, student grouping, environmental conditions, target skills emphasis, or alternative technology within the same instructional context may yield more effective outcomes. For example, some students' accuracy might improve using text-to-speech feedback; for others, word prediction plus text-to-speech may be what leads to increased accuracy.

Our third point reflects on the fact that we've limited ourselves to a selective presentation of how technology can support students with high incidence disabilities in core academic content areas. Our concentration has therefore been to present technology solutions providing universal interventions that can be integrated for all learners. Across the literature and research regarding technology and academic applications for persons with disabilities, we believe there is a growing body of evidence that systematic instructional implementation of technology might assist in narrowing the achievement gap between general and special education that might not exist in the absence of such technologies. More importantly, if technology is implemented as a universal intervention, then many students who are at-risk may never be identified as needing Tier 2 services.

Our fourth point is that we focused exclusively on technology and academic areas. When we began our examination, we noted that UDL includes instructional principles and technology elements that apply to knowledge and behavior in the context of information representation, learners' actions and engagement in learning activities, and their expression of knowledge and skills. Consideration of learning and instruction also includes consideration of student behavioral and emotional states, and elements that relate to their personality, perceptions of self-competence, self-efficacy, and metacognitive skills. These are critical variables but areas that have been the least explored within the evidence base regarding technology use by students with high incidence disabilities.

As adults we use technology and devices to make our life and work more productive. We listen to audio books while we drive or jog, dictate electronic mail using speech recognition, listen to news reports on a podcast while we work, and count on word prediction and spell check features of our software to make writing messages more efficient. No one tells us that we cannot use these tools or that we have an unfair advantage over others if we do use them. Unfortunately, in some school settings some of these same technologies—word prediction, spell check, speech recognition, text-to-speech, and audio books—are frequently considered assistive technology and must be included in a students' individual educational plan or formally listed as an accommodation in order for them to be allowed to use these tools in academic activities. In contrast, we encourage all schools and teachers to embrace the principles of universal design for instruction, consider technology as a universal intervention in a Tier 1 response-to-intervention, and provide all students access to the technology and academic instructional practices.

References

Anderson-Inman, L. (2009). Supported eText: Literacy scaffolding for students with disabilities. *The Journal of Special Education Technology, 24*(3), 1–7.

Anderson-Inman, L. & Horney, M. (2007). Supported eText: Assistive technology through text transformations. *Reading Research Quarterly, 42*, 153–160.

Ashton, T. M. (2005). Students with learning disabilities using assistive technology in the inclusive classroom. In D. Edyburn, K. Higgins, & R. Boone (Eds.), *Handbook of special education technology research and practice* (pp. 229–238). Whitefish Bay, WI: Knowledge by Design.

Bailey, M. N., Meidenbauer, N., Fein, J., & Mollica, B. M. (2005). Comprehensive statewide programs of technology-related assistance. In D. Edyburn, K. Higgins, & Boone (Ed.), *Handbook of special education technology research and practice* (pp. 113–129). Whitefish Bay, WI: Knowledge by Design.

Bausch, M. (2006, Sept. 6). Integrating research to practice. [Definition] Message posted to http://www.fctd.info/webboard/archive.php

Berninger, V. W., Abbott, R. D., Augsburger, A., & Garcia, N. (2009). Comparison of pen and keyboard transcription modes in children with and without learning disabilities. *Learning Disabilities Quarterly, 32*, 123–141.

Biancarosa, C., & Snow, C. E. (2006). *Reading next—A vision for action and research in middle and high school literacy: A report to Carnegie Corporation of New York* (2nd ed.).Washington, DC: Alliance for Excellent Education.

Blackhurst, E. A. (2005). Historical perspective about technology applications for people with disabilities, In D. Edyburn, K. Higgins, & R. Boone. (Ed), *Handbook of Special Education Technology Research and Practice* (pp. 3–29). Whitefish Bay, WI: Knowledge by Design.

Boon, R. T., Fore, C., Blankenship, T., & Chalk, J. (2007). Technology-based practices in social studies instruction for students with high-incidence disabilities: A review of the literature. *Journal of Special Education Technology, 22*(4), 41–56.

Bottge, B. A. (1999). Effects of contextualized math instruction on problem solving of average and below-average achieving students. *The Journal of Special Education, 33*, 81–92.

Bottge, B., & Hasselbring, T., (1993). Taking word problems off the page. *Educational Leadership, 50*(7), 36–38.

Bottge, B., Heinrichs, M., Chan, S., Mehta, Z. D., & Watson, E. (2003). Effects of video-based and applied problems on the procedural math skills of average and low-achieving adolescents. *Journal of Special Education Technology, 18*(2), 5–22.

Bottge, B. A., Heinrichs, M., Chan, S., & Serlin, R. C. (2001). Anchoring adolescents' understanding of math concepts in rich problem-solving environments. *Remedial and Special Education, 22*, 299–319.

Bottge, B. A., Heinrichs, M., Mehta, Z. D., & Hung, Y. (2002). Weighing the benefits of anchored math instruction for students with disabilities in general education classes. *The Journal of Special Education, 35*, 186–200.

Bottge, B. A., Heinrichs, M., Mehta, Z. D., Rueda, E., Hung, Y-H., & Danneker, J. (2004). Teaching mathematical problem solving to middle school students in math, technology education, and special education classrooms. *Research in Middle Level Education, 27*(1), 43–69. Retrieved November 5, 2009 from http://www.nmsa.org/research/rmle/winter_03/27_1_article_1.htm.pdf

Bottge, B. A., Rueda, E., Kwon, J. M., Grant, T., & LaRoque, P. (2009). Assessing and tracking students' problem solving performances in anchored learning environments. *Educational Technology Research & Development, 57*, 529–552.

Bouck, E. C., Bassette, L., Taber-Doughty, T., Flanagan, S. M., & Szwed, K. (2009). Pentop computers as tools for teaching multiplication to students with mild developmental disabilities. *Education and Training in Developmental Disabilities, 44*, 367–380.

Bouck, E. C., & Bouck, M. K. (2008). Does it add up? Calculators as accommodations for sixth grade students with disabilities. *Journal of Special Education Technology, 23*(2), 17–32.

Bouck, E. C., & Flanagan, S. M. (2009). Assistive technology and mathematics: What is there and where can we go in special education. *Journal of Special Education Technology, 24*(2), 17–30.

Boyle, E. A., Rosenberg, M. S., Connelly, V. J., Washburn, S. G., Brinckerhoff, L. C., & Banerjee, M. (2003). Effects of audio texts on the acquisition of secondary-level content by students with mild disabilities. *Learning Disabilities Quarterly, 26*, 203–214.

Campuzano, L., Dynarski, M., Agodini, R., & Rall, K. (2009). *Effectiveness of reading and mathematics software products: Findings from two student cohorts* (NCEE 2009-4041). Washington, DC: National Center for Education Evaluation and Regional Assistance, Institute of Education Sciences, U.S. Department of Education.

CITEd (2009). *K-8 screen-based technology to support mathematics*. Retrieved November 16, 2009, from http://www.cited.org/index.aspx?page_id=86

Clay, K., Zorfass, J., Brann, A., Kotula, A., & Smolkowski, K. (2009). Deepening content understanding in social studies using digital text and embedded vocabulary supports. *The Journal of Special Education Technology, 24*(4), 1–16.

Cognition and Technology Group at Vanderbilt. (1990). Anchored instruction and its relationship to situated cognition. *Educational Researcher, 19*(5), 2–10.

Cognition and Technology Group at Vanderbilt. (1992). The Jasper experiment: An exploration of issues in learning and instruction design. *Educational Technology Research & Development, 40*(1), 65–80.

Crooks, S. M., White, D. R., & Barnard, L. (2007). Factors influencing the effectiveness of note taking on computer-based graphic organizers. *Journal of Educational Computing Research, 37*(4), 369–391.

Cullen, J., & Richards, S. B. (2008). Using software to enhance the writing skills of students with special needs. *Journal of Special Education Technology, 23*(2), 33–44.

De La Paz, S. (1999). Composing via dictation and speech recognition systems: Compensatory technology for students with learning disabilities. *Learning Disabilities Quarterly, 22*, 173–182.

Douglas, K. H., Ayres, K. M., Langone, J., Bell, V., & Meade, C. (2009). Expanding literacy for learners with intellectual disabilities: The role of supported eText. *Journal of Special Education Technology, 24*(3), 35–44.

Dynarski, M., Agodini, R., Heaviside, S., Novak, T., Carey, N., Campuzano, L., et al. (2007). Effectiveness of reading and mathematics software products: Findings from the first student cohort (Publication No. 2007-4005). Washington, DC: National Center for Education Evaluation and Regional Assistance, Institute of Education Sciences, U.S. Department of Education. Retrieved October 31, 2009, from http://ies.ed.gov/ncee/pdf/20074005.pdf

Edyburn, D. (2005). Assistive technology and students with mild disabilities: From consideration to outcome measurement. In D. Edyburn, K. Higgins, & R. Boone (Eds.), *Handbook of special education technology research and practice* (pp. 229–238). Whitefish Bay, WI: Knowledge by Design.

Edyburn, D. (2009). Response to intervention (RTI): Is there a role for assistive technology? *Special Education Technology Practice, 11*(1), 15–19.

Ellington, A. J. (2003). A meta-analysis of the effects of calculators on students' achievement and attitude levels in precollege mathematics classes. *Journal for Research in Mathematics Education, 34*(5), 433–463.

Englert, C. S., Zhao, Y., Dunsmore, K., Collings, N. Y., & Wolbers, K. (2007). Scaffolding the writing of students with disabilities through procedural facilitation: Using an internet-based technology to improve performance. *Learning Disabilities Quarterly, 30*, 9–29.

Fadel, C., & Lemke, C. (2006). Technology in the schools: What the research says. Cisco Systems. Retrieved on November 5, 2009, from http://www.cisco.com/web/strategy/docs/education/TechnologyinSchoolsReport.pdf

Faggella-Luby, M. N., & Deschler, D. D. (2008). Reading comprehension in adolescents with LD: What we know, what we need to learn. *Learning Disabilities Research and Practice, 23*, 70–78.

Feng, J., Karat, C., & Sears, A. (2005). How productivity improves in hands-free continuous dictation tasks: lessons learned from a longitudinal study. *Interacting with Computers, 17*, 265–289.

Gardner, J. E., & Wissick, C. A. (2002). Enhancing thematic units using the World Wide Web: Tools and strategies that integrate technology for students with mild disabilities. *Journal of Special Education Technology, 17*(1), 27–38.

Gardner, J. E., & Wissick, C. A., (2005). Web-based resources and instructional considerations for students with mild cognitive disabilities. In D. Edyburn, K. Higgins, & R. Boone (Eds.), *The handbook of special education technology: Research and practice* (pp. 683–718). Whitefish Bay, WI: Knowledge by Design.

Gardner, J. E., Wissick, C. A., & Edyburn, D. (2008). Technology enhancement of curriculum, instruction and assessment. In J. Lindsay (Ed.), *Technology for exceptional learners*.(4th ed., pp. 259–321). Austin, TX: Pro-Ed.

Gardner, J. E., Wissick, C. A., Schweder, W., & Smith, L. (2003). Using technology to enhance interdisciplinary instruction for ALL students. *Remedial and Special Education, 24*(3), 161–172.

Gentry, J. (2008). E-publishing's impact on learning in an inclusive sixth grade social studies classroom. *Journal of Interactive Learning Research, 19*, 455–467.

Gersten, R., & Baker, S. (2001). Teaching expressive writing to students with learning disabilities: A meta-analysis. *Elementary School Journal, 101*, 251–272.

Gersten, R., & Edyburn, D. (2007). Defining quality indicators in group designs in special education technology research. *Journal of Special Education Technology, 22*(3), 3–18.

Goldberg, A., Russell, M., & Cook, A. (2003). The effect of computers on student writing: A meta analysis of studies from 1992 to 2002. *Journal of Technology, Learning, and Assessment, 2*(1), 1–52. Retrieved November 5, 2009, from http://www.jtla.org

Graham, S., & Perin, D. (2007). *Writing next: Effective strategies to improve writing of adolescents in middle and high schools – A report to Carnegie Corporation of New York.* Washington, DC: Alliance for Excellent Education.

Hall, T., & Strangman, N. (2002). *Graphic organizers.* Wakefield, MA: National Center on Accessing the General Curriculum. Retrieved November 16, 2009, from http://www.cast.org/publications/ncac/ncac_go.html

Harris, J. (1997). Mining the Internet wetware: Why use activity structure? *Learning and Leading with Technology, 25*(4), 13–17.

Hasselbring, T. S., & Bausch, M. E. (2006). Assistive technologies for reading. *Educational Leadership, 63*(4), 72–75.

Hasselbring, T. S., & Goin, L. (2005). *Research foundation and evidence of effectiveness for FASTT Math.* Retrieved November 5, 2009, from http://www.tomsnyder.com/reports/

Hasselbring, T., Lott, A., & Zydney, J., (2006). *Technology-supported math instruction for students with disabilities: Two decades of research and development.* Center for Implementing Technology in Education. American Institutes for Research. Retrieved November 5, 2009, from http://www.cited.org/library/resourcedocs/Tech-SupportedMathInstruction-FinalPaper_early.pdf

Helsel, F. K., Hitchcock, J. H., Miller, G., Malinow, A., & Murray, E., (2006). *Identifying evidence-based, promising and emerging practices that use screen-based and calculator technology to teach mathematics in grades k-12: A research synthesis. Center for Implementing Technology in Education (CITEd).* A paper prepared for the annual meeting of the American Educational Research Association. Retrieved November 5, 2009, from http://www.cited.org/library/resourcedocs/AERA_CITEd_ed_Formatted_Updated_041906.pdf

Higgins, E. L., & Raskind, M. H. (1995). Compensatory effectiveness of speech recognition on the written composition performance of postsecondary students with learning disabilities. *Learning Disabilities Quarterly, 18*, 159–174.

Higgins, E. L., & Raskind, M. H. (2000). Speaking to read: The effects of continuous vs. discrete speech recognition systems on the reading and spelling of children with learning disabilities. *Journal of Special Education Technology, 15*(1), 19–30.

Horney, M. A., Anderson-Inman, L., Terrazas-Arellanes, F., Schulte, W., Mundorf, J., Wiseman, S., Smolkowski, K., Katz-Buonincontro, J., & Frisbee, M. L. (2009). Exploring the effects of digital note taking on the student comprehension of science texts. *Journal of Special Education Technology, 24*(3), 45–61.

IDEA Partnership, (2009). *Together on RTI.* Retrieved November 16, 2009, from http://www.ideapartnership.org/

Indivuals with Disabilities Education Act of 2004, P. L. 108-446, 108th Congress.

Izzo, M. V., Yurick, A., & McArrell, B. (2009). Supported eText: Effects of text-to-speech on access and achievement for high school students with disabilities. *Journal of Special Education Technology*, *24*(3), 9–20.

Kerscher, G. (2009). *1988–1989. Coined the term "print disabled."* Retrieved from http://kerscher.montana.com/vita-2009.html

King, T. W. (1999). *Assistive technology: Essential human factors.* Boston: Allyn & Bacon.

Lenhart, A., Arafeh, S., Smith, A., & MacGill., A. R. (2008). *Writing, technology, and teens. Pew Internet & American Life Project.* Retrieved November 5, 2009, http://www.pewinternet.org/Reports/2008/Writing-Technology-and-Teens.aspx

Lewis, R. B., Graves, A. W., Ashton, T. M., & Kieley, C. L. (1998). Word processing tools for students with learning disabilities: A comparison of strategies to increase text entry speed. *Learning Disabilities Research & Practice, 13*, 95–108.

MacArthur, C. A. (1998a). From illegible to understandable: How word recognition and speech synthesis can help. *Teaching Exceptional Children, 30*(6), 66–71.

MacArthur, C. A. (1998b). Word processing with speech synthesis and word prediction: Effects on the dialogue journal writing of students with learning disabilities. *Learning Disabilities Quarterly, 21*, 151–166.

MacArthur, C. A. (1999). Word prediction for students with severe spelling problems. *Learning Disabilities Quarterly, 22*, 158–172.

MacArthur, C. A. (2009). Reflections on research on writing and technology for struggling writers. *Learning Disabilities Research and Practice, 24*, 93–103.

MacArthur, C. A., Graham, S., Haynes, J. A., & De La Paz, S. (1996). Spelling checkers and students with learning disabilities: Performance comparisons and impact on spelling. *Journal of Special Education, 30*, 35–57.

MacArthur, C. A., Graham, S., Schwartz, S. S., & Schafer, W. (1995). Evaluation of a writing instruction model that integrated a process approach, strategy instruction, and word processing. *Learning Disabilities Quarterly, 18*, 278–291.

Maccini, P., & Gagnon, J. C., (2005). Mathematics and technology-based interventions. In D. Edyburn, K. Higgins, & R. Boone (Eds.), *Handbook of special education technology research and practice* (pp. 599–622). Whitefish Bay, WI: Knowledge by Design.

Magnuson, T., & Hunnicutt, S. (2002). Measuring the effectiveness of word prediction: The advantage of long term use. *TMH-QPSR 43*, 57–67.

Malouf, D. B., & Hauser, J. (2005). A federal program to support innovation and implementation of technology in special education, In D. Edyburn, K. Higgins, & R. Boone (Ed.), *Handbook of special education technology research and practice* (pp. 327–354). Whitefish Bay, WI: Knowledge by Design.

Marino, M. A. (2010). Defining a technology research agenda for elementary and secondary students with learning and other high incidence disabilities in inclusive science classroom. *The Journal of Special Education Technology, 25*(1), 1–28.

Mastropieri, M. A., & Scruggs, T. E. (1992), Science for students with disabilities. *Review of Educational Research, 62,* 377–411

Mastropieri, M. A., & Scruggs, T. E. (2007). *The inclusive classroom: Strategies for effective instruction* (3rd ed.). Columbus, OH: Prentice Hall/Merrill.

Mayer, R. E. (2009). *Multimedia learning* (2nd ed). New York: Cambridge University Press.

Mayer, R. E., & Moreno, R. (2002). Aids to computer-based multimedia learning. *Learning and Instruction, 12*(1), 107–119.

Mayer, R. E., & Moreno, R. (2003). Nine ways to reduce cognitive load in multimedia learning. *Educational Psychologist, 38*(1), 43–52.

Montgomery, D. J., Karlan, G. R., & Coutinho, M. (2001). The effectiveness of word processor spell checker programs to produce target words for misspellings generated by students with learning disabilities. *Journal of Special Education Technology, 16*(2), 27–41.

Okolo, C. M. (2005). Interactive technologies and social studies instruction for students with mild disabilities. In D. Edyburn, K. Higgins, & R. Boone (Eds.), *Handbook of special education technology research and practice* (pp. 623–642). Whitefish Bay, WI: Knowledge by Design.

Okolo, C. M., Cavalier, A. R., Ferretti, R. P., & MacArthur, C. A. (2000). Technology literacy and disabilities: A review of the research. In R. Gersten, E. P. Schiller, & S. Vaughn (Eds.), *Contemporary special education research: Syntheses of the knowledge base on critical instructional issue* (pp. 179–250). Mahwah, NJ: Erlbaum.

Okolo, C. M., Englert, C. S., Bouck, E. C., & Heutsche, A. M. (2007). Web-based history learning environments: Helping all students learn and like history. *Intervention in School and Clinic, 43,* 3–11.

Pearman, C. J., (2008). Independent reading of CD-Rom storybooks: Measuring comprehension with oral retellings. *The Reading Teacher, 61*, 594–602.

Peterson-Karlen, G. R., & Parette, H. (2007). Evidence based practice and the consideration of assistive technology: Effectiveness and outcomes. *Assistive Technology Outcomes and Benefits, 4*(1), 130–139.

Rao, K., Dowrick, P. W., Yuen, J. W. L., & Boisvert, P. C. (2009). Writing in a multimedia environment: Pilot outcomes for high school students in special education. *Journal of Special Education Technology, 24*(1), 27–38.

Raskind, M. H., & Higgins, E. L. (1999). Speaking to read: The effects of speech recognition technology on the reading and spelling performance of children with learning disabilities. *Annals of Dyslexia, 49*, 251–281.

Reed, P., & Bowser, G., (2005). Assistive technology and the IEP. In D. Edyburn, K. Higgins, & R. Boone, (Eds.), *Handbook of special education technology research and practice* (pp. 176–212). Whitefish Bay, WI: Knowledge by Design.

Roberts, G., Torgesen, J. K., Boardman, A., & Scammacca, N. (2008). Evidence-based strategies for reading instruction for older students with learning disabilities. *Learning Disabilities Research and Practice, 23*, 63–69.

Roberts, K. D., & Stodden, R. A. (2005). The use of voice recognition software as a compensatory strategy for postsecondary education students receiving services under the category of learning disabled. *Journal of Vocational Rehabilitation, 22*(1), 49–64.

Rose, D. H., & Meyer, A. (2002). *Teaching every student in the digital age: Universal design for learning*. Alexandria, VA: Association for Supervision and Curriculum Development.

RTI Network, (2009). *What is RTI?* Retrieved November 23, 2009, from http://www.rtinetwork.org/

Schaff, J. L., Jerome, M. K., Behrmann, M. M., & Sprague, D. (2005). Science in special education: Emerging technologies. In D. Edyburn, K. Higgins, & R. Boone (Eds.), *Handbook of special education technology research and practice* (pp. 229–238). Whitefish Bay, WI: Knowledge by Design.

Schweder, W., & Wissick, C. A., (2007). Blogging in and out of the classroom. *Journal of Special Education Technology, 22*(4), 63–69.

Schweder, W., & Wissick, C. A. (2009). The power of wikis. *Journal of Special Education Technology, 24*(1), 57–60.

Scruggs, T. E., & Mastropieri, M. A. (1993). Current approaches to science education: Implications for mainstream instruction of students with disabilities. *Remedial and Special Education, 14,* 15–24.

Scruggs, T. E., & Mastropieri, M. A. (1994). The construction of scientific knowledge by students with mild disabilities. *Journal of Special Education, 28*, 307–321.

Scruggs, T. E., & Mastropieri, M. A. (2007). Science learning in special education: The case for constructed versus instructed learning. *Exceptionality, 15*(2), 57–74.

Silver-Pacuilla, H., Ruedel, K., & Mistrett, S. (2004). A review of technology-based approaches for reading instruction: Tools for researchers and vendors. Washington, DC: National Center for Technology Innovation, American Institutes for Research. Retrieved November 16, 2009, from http://www.cited.org/library/site/docs/AReviewTechnology-BasedApproaches_final.pdf

Sitko, M. C., Laine, C. J., & Sitko, C. J. (2005). Writing tools: Technology and strategies for struggling writers. In D. Edyburn, K. Higgins, & R. Boone (Eds.), *Handbook of special education technology research and practice* (pp. 571–598). Whitefish Bay, WI: Knowledge by Design.

Slavin, R. E., Cheung, A., Groff, C., & Lake, C. (2008). Effective reading programs for middle and high schools: A best-evidence synthesis. *Reading Research Quarterly, 43*, 290–322.

Strangman, N., & Dalton, B. (2005). Using technology to support struggling readers: A review of the research. In D. Edyburn, K. Higgins, & R. Boone (Eds.), *Handbook of special education technology research and practice* (pp. 545–569). Whitefish Bay, WI: Knowledge by Design.

Thurlow, M. L., Laitusis, C. C., Dillon, D. R., Cook, L. L., Moen, R. E., Abedi, J., & O'Brien, D. G. (2009). *Accessibility principles for reading assessments.* Minneapolis, MN: National Accessible Reading Assessment Projects. Retrieved November 9, 2009, from http://www.narap.info

Torgesen, J. K. (2007, August 8). Expert connection: What should we look for in good reading software? TeachingLD.org. Retrieved from http://TeachingLD.org/expert_connection/CAI-reading.html

Twyman, T., & Tindal, G. (2006). Using a computer-adapted, conceptually based history text to increase comprehension and problem-solving skills of students with disabilities. *The Journal of Special Education Technology, 21*(2), 5–16.

Wetzel, K. (1996). Speech-recognizing computers: A written-communication tool for students with learning disabilities? *Journal of Learning Disabilities, 29,* 371–380.

Williams, S. C. (2002). Word-predictionsoftware can help students write. *Teaching Exceptional Children, 34*, 71–77.

Wissick, C. A., (2005). Written language: When to consider technology. *Technology in Action, Technology and Media Division, 1*(6), 1–12.

Wissick, C. A., & Gardner, J. E., (2008). Conducting assessments in technology needs: From assessment to implementation. *Assessment for Effective Intervention. 33*(2), 78–93.

Wong, B. Y. L. (2001). Commentary: Pointers for literacy instruction from educational technology and research on writing instruction. *The Elementary School Journal, 101*(3) 359–369.

Woodward, J., & Reith, J. (1997). A historical review of technology research in special education. *Review of Educational Research, 67*(4), 503–536.

Section VIII

Instructional Issues for Students with Low Incidence Cognitive Disabilities

Section Editor: Adelle Renzaglia
University of Illinois

Since the passage of PL 94-142 in 1975, giving all children the right to education, education of individuals with significant disabilities has been affected by changing philosophies and values as well as a wealth of empirical data demonstrating learning and behavior change. The demonstrations of learning in the 1960s–1970s, with the use of instruction based on the principles of behavior analysis, provided a basis upon which education for students with significant disabilities was built. These demonstrations provided evidence that individuals with significant disabilities can learn meaningful skills, which impact the degree to which they become productive members of their communities. However, the changes in philosophical beliefs and values have had a significant impact on how, where, and with whom education is provided.

Not long ago, individuals with the most significant disabilities were housed and educated in segregated facilities with little access to their communities and peers without disabilities. Now, the emphasis is on inclusive education focusing on access to the general curriculum. These rapid changes in the field have not always been driven by data or evidence based practice but instead by values and human rights issues. As a result, many debates are ongoing in educating students with significant disabilities. The challenge to educators is how to bring good instruction into meaningful contexts so that the outcomes of education for students with significant disabilities include living, working, and socializing in inclusive community environments. Expectations for learning have increased over the decades. However, educators are engaged in debates over curriculum content. Should the focus be on life skills or academic skill instruction, in segregated or inclusive environments, in school or community based settings? What practices will lead to more productive long term outcomes? Should philosophy and values precede data or should data inform our philosophy and values. While most educators believe that there is an interaction between data, values, and beliefs, the rapid change in the field of educating students with significant disabilities has seen a discrepancy between data and practice. This has been the impetus for debate.

When conceptualizing this section on education for students with low incidence disabilities, a long list of topics emerged. The selection of the five chapters that are included was based on core issues that inform current practice. All contributors agree that more evidence is needed and that the link between research and practice must be strengthened. The first chapter provides a historical overview of educational practice, trends and issues. The subsequent chapters address context for education, effective instruction, and curriculum. Within each, evidence-based practice is discussed, as are the current issues and debates in the field.

38

Educating Students with Significant Cognitive Disabilities

Historical Overview and Future Projections

Fred Spooner
University of North Carolina at Charlotte

Fredda Brown
Queens College, City University of New York

The presence of people with disabilities has been documented since the earliest recordings of history. Throughout this history, people with disabilities have been subjected to a remarkable range of what would now be considered inhumane "treatments"—including trephining (i.e., a circular hole chipped in the top of the skull to allow the evil spirits escape) and infanticide (see chapter 1 for a more complete description of this history). For people with severe disabilities, these types of treatments are now just "ancient history"—we have had a long journey, and have come a long way; but we still have a long way to go. *Brown v. Board of Education* (1954), other landmark cases (e.g., *PARC v. Pennsylvania*, 1972; *Wyatt v. Stickney*, 1972; and *Mills v. Board of Education*, 1973), and the passage of PL-94-142 in 1975, set the stage for our more recent history of services and supports for individuals with severe disabilities. For individuals with severe disabilities, 1974 was another landmark.

It was in Kansas City, in November, 1974, that The American Association for The Education of The Severely and Profoundly Handicapped (AAESPH, now TASH) was founded by Norris Haring of the University of Washington (for a thorough and accurate account of the creation of TASH, see Sontag & Haring, 1996). The history of TASH is about the chronicle of professionalization for teaching children with severe disabilities. Ed Sontag, a federal official in what was then the Bureau of the Education for the Handicapped (BEH), was assigned to the development of the new subspeciality area (severe disabilities) and Norris Haring became the first president of the organization. Although the legal cases of *PARC v. Pennsylvania* (1972) and the *Mills v. Board of Education of the District of Columbia* (1973) provided the impetus for the founding of TASH, there was some historical precedent for at least considering the idea of serving children with moderate mental retardation (IQ 35–50) in public school settings (Goldberg & Cruickshank, 1958). Goldberg and Cruickshank (1958) in their classic *debate* raised the question about the responsibility of public schools in educating children with severe disabilities. Sontag, Burke, and York (1973) commented that there was not a systematic plan for developing services (e.g., preservice and inservice teacher training programs, doctoral level personnel to lead additional efforts, training program for parents, life encompassing service plans) for this population and organizations in special education or mental retardation had no interest or were ambivalent about the benefits of educational programming for this population. TASH took major responsibility to fill this void and provided leadership for the field.

Many paradigm shifts were occurring around this time to create a new philosophy and "discipline" of severe disabilities. With the founding of TASH came a commitment to persons with severe disabilities and their families. Deinstitutionalization (Wolfensberger, 1972) became the order of the day, and applications of behavioral principles, that is, applied behavior analysis (Baer, Wolf, &, Risley, 1968, 1987) were being demonstrated by researchers and implemented by practitioners, demonstrating behavior change in many important functional skills, including eating (Azrin & Armstrong, 1973; Zeiler & Jervey, 1968), dressing (Breland, 1965), toilet training (Azrin, Bugle, & O'Brien, 1971; Azrin & Foxx, 1971; Baumeister & Klosowski, 1965), and general self-help skills (Ball, Seric, & Payne, 1971; Bensberg, Colwell, Cassell, 1965). By 1974 over 200 successful applications in teaching functional skills to this population had been documented (Kazdin, 1978; Sontag & Haring, 1996).

Issues of educability were examined in a special issue of *Analysis and Intervention in Developmental Disabilities* (Kauffman, 1981), and curricular models were increasingly explored (Browder, Spooner, Ahlgrim-Delzell, et al., 2003). Browder, Spooner, Ahlgrim-Delzell, et al. (2003) suggest that over the years there has been support for several curricular training models: developmental (e.g., Bricker & Iacino, 1977; Robinson & Robinson, 1983; Stephens, 1977), functional (L. Brown et al., 1979; L. Brown, Nietupski, & Hamre-Nietupski, 1976; Meyer, Eichenger, & Park-Lee, 1987), social inclusion (Gent & Mulhauser, 1988; Lipsky & Gartner, 1989; Meyer, 1994), self-determination (Wehmeyer, 2005; Wehmeyer, Agran, & Hughes, 1998; Wehmeyer, Field, Doren, Jones, & Mason, 2004), and general curriculum access (Browder, Ahlgrim-Delzell, Courtade-Little, & Snell, 2006; Browder & Spooner, 2006; Browder, Spooner, Wakeman, Trela, & Baker, 2006; Spooner, Dymond, & Kennedy, 2006). Perspectives on defining scientifically-based research for this population have also been explored (Spooner, 2003).

A Changing Philosophical Framework

In the last 50 years much of the work that has been done by researchers, advocates, parents, and concerned others has shown society at large that people with severe disabilities are to be valued, can learn, and can perform many of the tasks completed by typically developing members of society. In the early 1950s, individuals with severe disabilities were primarily "housed" in institutions; since then there are continuing, and effective, efforts to put an end to institutions. Once we thought individuals with severe disabilities had no ability to learn. Now, increasingly, these same individuals are reading, writing, and meaningfully communicating with others; participating in community life; and working and going to school with their nondisabled peers. How can this change in perspectives be so dramatic?

Marc Gold (1980) suggested that individuals with disabilities themselves did not change; what changed were our expectations for them.

> The mentally retarded person is characterized by the level of power needed in the training process required for him or her to learn, and not by limitations in what he or she can learn. The height of a retarded person's level of functioning is determined by the availability of training technology and the amount of resources society is willing to allocate and not by significant limitations in biological potential. (p. 148)

Although Dr. Gold's use of language is now considered outdated (i.e., he does not use "people first" language), his message is clear: we cannot limit our expectations of individuals with severe disabilities.

One of the societal perspectives that continues to limit our expectations is the concept of a continuum of services. For example, a continuum *of living* arrangements might range from the most restrictive environment such as an institution, through a less restrictive one such as living in one's own apartment. A continuum of *educational* environments may range from education in a hospital or segregated building, through education in a general education classroom. A continuum of services implies that there are some individuals who may need the "most restrictive" services. History has shown us that the more severe the disability, the more likely it is that the individual will be placed in a more restrictive environment. Taylor (1988) cautions us that individuals with severe disabilities are likely to be "caught in the continuum"—that is, although there appears to be opportunity to move along the continuum with increased skills, this is not typically the case. Once an individual is "in" the continuum, it is difficult to move to less restrictive options along the continuum. Taylor states that a continuum of services

> legitimates restrictive environments.... that there are circumstances under which the most restrictive environment would be appropriate... As long as services are conceptualized in this manner, some people will end up in restrictive environments. In most cases, they will be people with severe disabilities. (p. 222)

It is also important to note that the continuum of least restrictive environments is based on a "readiness model." That is, there is an assumption that people with severe disabilities must earn the right to move to lesser restrictive environments; that the person must "get ready" or "be prepared" to enter less restrictive environments (Taylor, 1988).

Today, most professionals and families have a different perspective. Inclusive lifestyles reflect a commitment to a fully integrated life without having to be ready for it; now it is assumed that one does not need to gain entry into a meaningful life—that it should be accessible to all people, regardless of level of disability. This change in our perspective on individuals with severe disabilities has led to changes in both how we conceptualize characteristics and definitions of individuals with severe disabilities, as well as our expectations of outcomes.

Changing Definitions and Descriptions of Individuals with Severe Disabilities

Definitions of disability have evolved across time to reflect changing societal values, attitudes, and expectations (F. Brown, Snell, & Lehr, 2006; Schalock, Luckasson, & Shogren, 2007; Thompson et al., 2004). In an early publication, Sailor and Guess (1983) trace the history of definitions of severe disability. They refer to one of the first definitions of individuals with severe disabilities by Sontag et al. (1973). In their description they include characteristics such as

> not toilet trained; aggressive toward others; do not attend to even the most pronounced social stimuli; self-mutilate;

> ruminate; self stimulate; do not walk, speak, hear, or see; manifest durable and intense temper tantrums; are not under even the most rudimentary forms of verbal control; do not imitate; manifest minimally controlled seizures, and/or have extremely brittle medical existences. (p. 21)

It is obvious that individuals with severe disabilities were being described at this period of time, by either negative characteristics or what they could not do (Evans, 1991). Certainly anyone reading this definition would not hold any hope for positive or constructive outcomes.

Similarly, in 1974 the Bureau of the Education of the Handicapped (BEH, later to become the US Department of Education, Office of Special Education Programs) provided a description of children with severe disabilities. As discussed by Sailor and Guess (1983), the BEH description explains that these children:

> may possess severe language and/or perceptual-cognitive deprivations, and evidence a number of behaviors including: failure to attend to even the most pronounced social stimuli, self-mutilation, self-stimulation, manifestation of durable and intense temper tantrums, and the absence of even the most rudimentary forms of verbal control, and may also have an extremely fragile physiological condition. (pp. 5–6)

These definitions reveal that individuals with severe disabilities were defined by deficits and non-behaviors; no positive attributes were ascribed in either of these definitions. On the other hand, these definitions and descriptions of individuals with severe disabilities changed as our instructional technology became more sophisticated, and as our focus on functional outcomes became more central. F. Brown et al. (2006) describe how the last two or so decades have seen significant changes in the way we define disability, with each new definition increasingly valuing meaningful outcomes and integration into inclusive communities. In 1986 TASH was essentially the first organization that moved away from the deficit model and described these individuals in terms of the supports they needed to participate in inclusive communities:

> The Association for Persons with Severe Handicaps addresses the interests of persons with severe handicaps who have traditionally been labeled as severely intellectually disabled. These people include individuals of all ages who require extensive ongoing support in more than one major life activity in order to participate in integrated community settings and to enjoy a quality of life that is available to citizens with fewer or no disabilities. Support may be required for life activities such as mobility, communication, self-care, and learning as necessary for independent living, employment, and self-sufficiency. (Meyer, Peck, & L. Brown, 1991, p. 19)

Regarding the progression of the American Association on Intellectual and Developmental Disabilities (AAIDD, formerly AAMD and AAMR), Thompson et al. (2009) report that although the operational criteria for diagnosis of mental retardation has remained fairly consistent for the over 35 years, the constructs or assumptions underlying the term have changed significantly due to the influence of the social-ecological model of disability. Now, intellectual disability is understood in relation to cultural and environmental demands. Table 38.1 shows the changes in focus of several definitions and descriptions of intellectual disability.

Another measure of change in perspectives is the way individuals with disabilities are portrayed in the mass media. Norden (1994) classified film history regarding disability into three eras: the birth of filmmaking through the 1930s (people with disabilities as victims or portrayed as comic figures or beasts), the World War II years through the 1970s (people with disabilities striving to overcome adversity), and the 1970s to the present (people with disabilities as fighting for social justice, participation in the community).

TABLE 38.1
Changes in Focus of Key Definitions and Descriptions of Intellectual Disability Across Time

Source of Definition	Focus
Intelligence test (Binet & Simon, 1905)	IQ test score
AAMD (Heber, 1961)	Sub-average intellectual functioning and adaptive behavior IQ score determines severity of disability
Bureau for the Education of the Handicapped (BEH, 1974)	Focus on deficits and non-behaviors: severe language and/or perceptual-cognitive deprivations, failure to attend to even the most pronounced social stimuli, self-mutilation, self-stimulation, intense temper tantrums , lack of rudimentary forms of verbal control, extremely fragile physiological condition
TASH (1986, Meyer, Peck, & L. Brown, 1991)	Disability is related to the level of environmental supports needed to live meaningful lives in integrated communities Quality of life is major outcome
AAMR (2002)	Intellectual functioning and adaptive behavior, but included assumptions: Assessment is referenced to context of community typical of age and culture Must consider: cultural and linguistic diversity, diversity in communication, sensory, motor and behavioral factors Limitations exist along with strengths Purpose of describing limitations is to develop a profile of needed supports With appropriate supports, person will generally improve

Although researching people with physical disabilities, and not necessarily intellectual disabilities, Norden did note a gradual movement toward a more enlightened view of physical disability. Black and Pretes (2007) analyzed 18 films produced between 1975 and 2004 that had a main character with a physical disability. These researchers also found that in some areas filmmakers have made progress in dispelling myths and stereotypes (e.g., no longer presented as comic figures; people with disabilities as sexual beings), yet unfortunately in other areas filmmakers perpetuated negative images (e.g., lack of sexuality, inability to be employed or pursue education, responding in a self-destructive way to adversity and stress).

Changing Expectations of Outcomes

As described above, changes in the way we defined and described individuals with disabilities reflected changes in our expectations of these individuals—from not expecting any functional outcomes, to expecting individuals to meaningfully participate in community settings if given the necessary level of supports. For close to 60 years researchers have been demonstrating that this population can acquire a large number of functional skills. Applied behavior analysis (ABA, Baer et al., 1968, 1987) set the framework, and continues to be the foundation, for teaching and documenting skill acquisition. Baer et al. (1968) defined the dimensions of ABA as *applied* (interest in problems of social significance), *behavioral* (observable, countable actions), *analytic* (experimental control established), and *technological* (interventions used to change behavior are completely identified and described). The following sections will summarize key concepts and provide a sample of studies representing our changes in expectations of outcomes for individuals with severe disabilities across time.

Benchmark 1: Behavior Can Change

Up until the late 1940s, people with severe disabilities were thought to be "untrainable." During this time period, care for individuals with severe disabilities did not include constructive efforts to change behavior. The first documented applied study was conducted by Fuller (1949). By today's standards Fuller's objectives, to teach a presumed, "untrainable," institutionalized young man, to lift his right arm to a near vertical position by reinforcing that movement, or approximation of that movement, with a warm sugar-milk solution, were quite modest. The significance, however, was that this was the first recognized application of behavioral principles, extracted from the laboratory, extending phylogenic overlap between infrahuman species and humans, and implemented in an applied setting. This experiment demonstrated that with the use of reinforcers, we can change behavior in those who we once thought were "untrainable."

Benchmark 2: Problem Behavior Can Be Reduced

In the 1950s Allyon and Michael (1959) trained psychiatric nurses to improve a number of behaviors in individuals diagnosed as schizophrenic or "mentally defective." Behaviors like violent attacks on other individuals, attempts to enter restricted areas of the living environment (i.e., nurses' station), refusals to self-feed, and hording of materials (trash, papers, and magazines) were reduced in several persons within 6 to 11 weeks by the implementation of behavioral interventions like extinction, social attention, differential reinforcement, and negative reinforcement. Allyon and Michael's work is important for at least three major reasons: (a) it demonstrated improvement in socially significant behaviors, (b) the change agents were nurses, not psychologists, psychiatrists, or university personnel, and (c) the interventions were implemented in the patient's living area, not a laboratory setting (Williams, Howard, Williams, & McLaughlin, 1994). While the reduction of these behaviors may have improved socially significant behaviors, this research did not focus on the development of new adaptive skills.

Benchmark 3: Adaptive Behavior Can Be Increased

Extensions of behavioral applications continued into the decade of the 1960s. Allyon and Azrin (1965, 1968) developed and refined the token economy, which Kazdin (1977b) viewed as an effective and practical motivational system in working with a diverse group of participants, including those with developmental disabilities. Wolf, Risley, and Mees (1964) employed a shaping procedure to a young boy, Dicky, 3 ½ years old at the beginning of the study, with autism, to wear his glasses with corrective lenses. For Dicky, wearing glasses with corrective lenses was necessary because both normal lenses were occluded due to cataracts and were removed surgically at the age of 2.

The decade of the 1970s brought a focus on the application of positive techniques to a variety of skills to persons with severe disabilities. One of the most important skills a person can learn is language. The work of Guess, Sailor, and Baer (1974) is particularly noteworthy. Guess et al. extended the work of Risley and Wolf (1967). In their language program, Guess et al. taught language skills that would be self-generative (e.g., teaching a student to ask "What's this?"). This type of language behavior would naturally lead to more communication opportunities. The Guess, Sailor, and Baer language program was historically significant as prior to that time language skills consisted mostly of imitation of vocalizations or verbalizations.

Repp and Deitz (1974) used differential reinforcement to reduce serious aggressive and self-injurious behavior in children who were institutionalized. Foxx and Shapiro (1978) employed a procedure called the *time-out ribbon* as an alternative to exclusionary timeout to reduce disruptive behavior in 5 boys with severe disabilities. Reinforcement conditions alone did not reduce misbehavior substantially.

The idea with the ribbon was that when the ribbon was being worn by the boys around the neck (like a tie) they were eligible to receive reinforcers (e.g., praise, edibles, smiles). The occurrence of misbehavior (e.g., yelling, throwing objects, pinching, out of seat), instated a condition where the ribbon was removed (timeout, hence the name *time-out ribbon*), and the boys were not eligible to receive rewards. The implementation of the *time-out ribbon* indicates that on the average, the children misbehaved 42% and 32% of the time during the baseline and reinforcement conditions respectively, but only 6% of the time during the timeout conditions. The significance of the Foxx and Shapiro study was in demonstrating that individuals did not need to be physically removed from the environment (i.e., time out) in an effort to increase positive more appropriate behavior.

Benchmark 4: Meaningful Behavior Change in Inclusive Environments

Behavioral applications have been implemented across the decades with the early work (pre 1950, 1950s, 1960s, and 1970s) as classical demonstrations of the efficient, effective, and powerful technology increasingly used to improve the lives of persons with severe disabilities and their families. Around this time the field of special education was also experiencing significant paradigm shifts related to individuals with severe disabilities. Expected outcomes shifted, and continue to do so, regarding where children would be educated, and how much an individual with severe disabilities could advocate for themselves, both within the educational system and within the broader community.

Bradley and Knoll (1990) describe the 1800s–1900s as a time when students with severe disabilities were excluded from education. Considering that point in time it follows that if students were thought to be "uneducable," they would not need to be in educational environments. In the 1960s the trend was to provide special education services in special education classrooms located in separate schools; more recently we promote *all* students receiving educational services together in general education classrooms—regardless of ability or disability. Although the passage of Public Law 94-142 in 1976 supported the right of *all* children to receive a free and appropriate education, the notion of "educability" continued to be a debated concept (Noonan, F. Brown, Mulligan, & Rettig, 1982). The expectation of including students with disabilities in inclusive environments has been a slow but steady trend; however, the reality of inclusion for those students with *severe* disabilities has unfortunately been even slower (F. Brown & Michaels, 2003).

A significant impact on the development of more inclusive educational and community supports was the principle of normalization (Wolfensberger, 1972) and the criterion of ultimate functioning (L. Brown et al., 1976). Wolfensberger stated that normalization is the:

> Utilization of means which are as culturally normative as possible in order to establish and/or maintain personal behaviors and characteristics which are as culturally normative as possible (p. 28).

Important to note in this definition is that both the *means* we use and the *behaviors* we are targeting should be culturally acceptable. *Means*, or methods, that differ substantially from what is used with typically developing individuals (e.g., contingent electric shock to reduce behavior; restraint as punishment; isolation) would not meet the standard of normalization. Targeting *behaviors* that would not accomplish the same functions as typically developing peers (e.g., assembling nuts and bolts for 2 hours) would also not meet the standard of normalization.

Wolfensberger identifies several components of normalization to consider when evaluating the outcomes we are achieving or working toward. To determine if an individual has an acceptable quality of life, he asks if the individual experiences: (a) normal rhythm of the day, (b) normal rhythm of the week, (c) normal rhythm of the year, (d) normal experiences of the life cycle, (e) normal respect, (f) living in a sexual world, (g) normal economic standards, and (h) normal environmental standards.

Soon after the principle of normalization became a rallying call for quality supports, L. Brown et al. (1976) advanced our philosophy towards persons with severe intellectual disabilities with their classic piece on the *criterion of ultimate functioning*. The criterion of ultimate functioning says that when we identify skills to be taught, we should focus on those behaviors

> that each person must possess to function as productively and independently as possible in integrated social, vocational, and domestic adult community environments. (p. 8)

In other words, we should think longitudinally when selecting skills that should be learned; we should teach skills and behaviors to students with severe disabilities that are not just functional for the current environment, but that will be important for the person when they are in adult community environments. The concept of teaching functional skills (e.g., how to make a cup of coffee), was a major paradigm shift from teaching nonfunctional skills (e.g., touch your nose in imitation). L. Brown et al. challenged us to teach skills that will foster performance in natural environments, using real materials and tasks, in real settings to help facilitate real life problem solving.

In applying the criterion of ultimate functioning, the field began to shift away from segregated settings, promoted the training of meaningful skills that would increase the likelihood of inclusive placements, and give people skills to function in complex community settings. The criterion of ultimate functioning influenced educators to examine both the current and predicted future environment, to determine the skills that would be most critical to living, working, and recreating in inclusive communities.

As indicated earlier in this chapter, there also have been shifts in curricular approaches for teaching persons with significant cognitive disabilities, moving from a developmental model in the 1970s to general curriculum access in the new millennium (Browder, Spooner, Ahlgrim-Delzell, et al., 2003). Browder, Spooner, Ahlgrim-Delzell, et al. suggested that prior to the mid 1970s there was no curriculum for students with severe disabilities. In the 1970s we started to see curriculum that followed a developmental model (Bricker & Iacino, 1977). The philosophy behind the developmental curriculum was that the curriculum should match the students "mental age" (Browder, Spooner, Ahlgrim-Delzell, et al., 2003; F. Brown et al., 2006). With this approach a developmental assessment is conducted to compare the students' skills to the age at which a normally developing child acquires those skills. There were many problems associated with application of this approach including teaching skills that are not age-appropriate (i.e., teaching a skill that may be expected of a 2 year old to an individual who is 15 years old), or that are not relevant to the student (e.g., imitate a bridge built of 3 1-inch cubes, F. Brown et al.; Guess & Noonan, 1982; White, 1985).

In the mid 1970s to the mid 1980s, the developmental curriculum was replaced with a functional curriculum (L. Brown et al., 1979). In this approach the contexts and environments in which the student participates is used to determine the curriculum. Instead of using developmental assessments to determine the student's needs, this approach uses a variety of criterion referenced assessments, such as the AAMR Adaptive Behavior Scales (Lambert, Nihira, & Leland, 1993) and the Vineland Adaptive Behavior Scales (Sparrow, Balla, & Cichetti, 1984). Criterion referenced assessments measure adaptive behaviors (e.g., dressing, eating, playing a game), which are more relevant to the student's age and needs. An informal assessment strategy that is used to design a functional curriculum is the ecological inventory (L. Brown et al., 1979). The ecological inventory is an environmental assessment strategy that examines the skills that are needed in the major domains of adult function, including domestic, leisure, community, school, and vocation. This approach is considered a top-down approach; that is, once the appropriate domains are identified, they are then broken down into relevant environments, subenvironments, and then the activities and skills required for participating in those activities. These activities and skills then become the target of instruction.

Browder, Spooner, Ahlgrim-Delzell, et al. (2003) termed the above cited major curriculum changes as "transformative;" that is, they replaced the prior paradigms. The functional curriculum approach remains as a foundation for the approaches that have followed. Browder et al. suggests that since then there have been several trends that have developed and are "additive" to the functional curriculum. For example, in the mid-1980s–1990s a focus on social inclusion (Lipski & Gartner, 1989) extended our view on important outcomes, and in the 1990s additional attention was given to the importance of measuring and supporting the development of self-determination in every student (Wehmeyer, 2005). Most recently, the mandates of IDEA (1997, 2004) require each state to assess *all* their students, including students with severe disabilities, relative to state-adopted standards (Browder & Spooner, 2006; F. Brown et al., 2006; Jorgensen, McSheehan, Sonnenmeier, 2007; Ryndak & Alper, 2003). This has resulted in a significant change in our expectations regarding student outcomes. Those individuals, once considered "untrainable," are now expected to participate and progress in academic areas such as reading, mathematics, and science. This has resulted in an increase in research examining how best to assess students on academic skills (Browder et al., 2004; Browder, Spooner, Ahlgrim-Delzell, et al., 2003; Browder, Spooner, Algozzine, et al., 2003; Browder et al., 2006), and how to effectively teach these skills (e.g., Browder, Ahlgrim-Delzell, Spooner, Mims, & Baker, 2009; Browder, Spooner, Ahlgrim-Delzell, Harris, & Wakeman, 2008; Browder, Wakeman, Spooner, Ahlgrim-Delzell, & Algozzine, 2006; Courtade, Spooner, & Browder, 2007). This is an exciting area of developing research and underscores the importance of never putting a limit on our expectations.

A Union of Values and Evidence

We have traced some of the scientific roots of the field of severe disabilities (e.g., ABA), as well as the changes in perspectives and values across the years (e.g., from treating individuals as "untrainable" to expecting full community participation). While this relationship between science (i.e., evidence) and values may seem like a logical marriage, this has not always been the case. There continues to remain a lack of influence of research on educational practice (McDonnell & O'Neill, 2003; Spooner, 2003; Spooner & Browder, 2003), and conversely, sometimes a lack of influence of values on research.

In general, and given the significant role of ABA as a foundational paradigm of severe disabilities, the role of values has only recently emerged as a factor of equal weight. We have moved from a narrow perspective on what evidence is needed to support a practice or outcome (i.e., experimental validity), to a more overarching perspective that includes quality of life as a major contributor to evaluating that practice or outcome (social validity).

Experimental Validity

Experimental (or internal) validity is applied to individual research studies and refers to the unequivocal demonstration that an independent variable is responsible for the change in the dependent variable (Cooper, Heron, & Heward, 2007). This means that the experimenter must be confident that it is their strategy that resulted in the changes in the behavior, and not other confounding variables. Single subject designs, such as multiple baseline and reversal designs, allow demonstration of experimental validity. Determining if a study has experimental validity requires us to look at the integrity of the measurement system, the research design, the extent to which the researchers controlled for confounding variables, and the visual analysis and interpretation of the data (Cooper et al., 2007).

For example, using a multiple baseline design across students, Carter, Sisco, Melekoglu, and, Kurkowski (2007) demonstrated that students with severe disabilities in a general education high school class engaged in substantially more peer interactions when working with a peer support than when receiving direct support from an adult staff member. When considering the experimental validity of this study, we only would look at the strength of the research design; that is, did these researchers establish with confidence that their independent variable (i.e., adult versus peer support) was the factor that increased their dependent variable (i.e., peer interactions), and not some other confounding variables (e.g., a new communication board; a new behavior program). Historically, our first demonstrations of work with individuals with severe disabilities focused on this type of validity; that is, could we reliably show a functional relationship between the independent and dependent variables. It is important to remember, however, that experimental validity has to do with the strength of the experimental design of the study, and not the *importance* of the study for the individual participants.

Social Validity

Where *experimental validity* asks if the research design shows a functional relationship between the variables, *social validity* asks if the change in behavior was significant in the person's life. Social validity focuses on the (a) acceptability of the educational goals, (b) the instructional methods used, and (c) the importance and social acceptability of the behavior change (Kazdin, 1977a; Wolf, 1978). For example, let us say we were to conduct an experiment to see if the independent variable "edible reinforcers" could increase the dependent variable of "assembling nuts and bolts" in 3 high school students with severe disabilities. If we use a multiple baseline design across students and the results unequivocally demonstrate the relationship between the two variables, we can say we have established *experimental validity*. On the other hand, we may question the *social validity* of the study. Assembling nuts and bolts likely is not a worthy educational goal as it is improbable that there are many potential jobs in the student's community assembling nuts and bolts. Thus, if the student were to acquire the skill, it likely would not hold much significance in his or her life. Finally, regarding the instructional methods used, we may question the use of edible reinforcers for a high school student. It is important that both experimental and social validity be considered as we evaluate any study. Returning to the Carter et al. (2007) study, we can conclude that it is more socially valid as the outcomes would be important to the student (i.e., interacting with peers in an inclusive age-appropriate setting) and it uses instructional methodology that is acceptable in a typical educational setting (i.e., peer support).

Social validity is a concept that addresses qualitative aspects of an educational program and guides us to ask if the learned behavior is functional or meaningful to the individual (F. Brown & Snell, 2006). In discussing social validity, Baer et al. (1987) state:

> We may have taught many social skills without examining whether they actually furthered the subject's social life; many courtesy skills without examining whether anyone actually noticed or cared; many safety skills without examining whether the subject was actually safer thereafter; many language skills without measuring whether the subject actually used them to interact differently than before; many on-task skills without measuring the actual value of those tasks,; and, in general, many survival skills without examining the subject's actual subsequent survival. (p. 322)

The concept of social validity has had a rocky history—exactly what social validity means, or does not mean, has been the subject of much discussion. As behaviorists we have a commitment to objective data (i.e., counting only what we can reliably see), yet we are striving to have an impact on those very things that are meaningful to us, and may not be easily measured. Montrose Wolf, in his landmark article on social validity (1978), states:

> If those things described by subjective labels [referring to experiences such as happiness, creativity, trust, beauty, satisfaction] were the things that were most important to people, then those were the things, even though they might be complex that we should become more concerned with. After all, as an applied science of human behavior, we supposedly were dedicated to helping people become better able to achieve their reinforcers. (p. 206)

Another dimension of social validity is the social appropriateness of the procedures that are used to change behavior (Wolf, 1978). That is "Do the ends justify the means? … Do the participants, caregivers and other consumers consider the treatment procedures acceptable (p. 207)?" This issue of *treatment acceptability* is another historically controversial area. In general, the more restrictive or aversive an intervention is, the less it is likely to be considered acceptable. On the other hand, factors such as the intensity of the problem behavior and the level of disability of the individual, impact perceptions of treatment acceptability. Since the 1970s there has been a significant shift in our perceptions about which procedures are acceptable and which are not. Take for example, an early study by Foxx and Azrin (1972) in which they used restitutional overcorrection to reduce aggressive and disruptive behavior of three individuals with severe disabilities. In their discussion they anecdotally indicate that several staff members expressed their preference for the restitution training programs over ward time-out rooms; they also indicate that as restitution is educative in nature, it may be more acceptable to those who do not support time-out or shock. From the historical perspective this study was significant—the goal itself (i.e., reducing behavior that is dangerous) was *socially valid*, and the methods were state of the art for the time. It does underscore, however, the way that treatment acceptability has changed across time. It is unlikely that we would read a discussion in a study regarding which aversive procedure was better; these interventions would not be considered socially valid today.

F. Brown, Michaels, Oliva, and Woolf (2008), in a survey of experts in positive behavior supports (PBS) and experts in ABA, found that perceptions of treatment acceptability changed across time for both groups of experts. That is, most professionals who had at one time engaged in using restrictive interventions (e.g., physical punishment, sensory punishment, seclusion time-out), no longer find it acceptable and choose not to consider such interventions. With the increased availability of less intrusive treatments and changes in educational law (e.g., NCLB, IDEA), there is an increased need to continue to re-examine treatment acceptability (Carter, 2008). As more research in PBS is conducted, we would expect that this trend in treatment acceptability will continue—so that fewer and fewer professionals will look toward punitive and aversive interventions to address severe problem behaviors. Dr. Murray Sidman (2001) eloquently describes the impact of punishment on people:

> With the addition of every new punishing element to our environment, however, our lives become potentially less satisfying, more desperate. If we encounter punishment frequently, we learn that our safest course is to stand pat and do as little as possible. We congratulate ourselves for every day that passes without catastrophe. The only things we are eager to learn are new ways to evade or to destroy objects and people that stand in our way. The process is potentially explosive. Whenever we are punished, more and more elements of our environment become negative reinforcers and punishers. We come more and more under coercive control, and we rely more and more on counter coercion to keep ourselves afloat. (p. 78)

A Call for Evidence-Based Practices

In 2002 No Child Left Behind (NCLB) was adopted to ensure the quality of instruction and outcomes for all students with disabilities. One requirement of these regulations is that evidence-based practices be used to guide classroom practice (Odom et al., 2005; Wang & Spillane, 2009). Evidence-based practice refers to those educational programs and instructional procedures that have been demonstrated to produce positive student outcomes (Tankersley, Harjusola-Webb, & Landrum, 2008). Experimental and social validity that we have just described are standards that refer to individual studies. More than one study, however, is needed to establish an evidence-base for an intervention or strategy. For example, if one researcher conducted a single study that found that eating brussel sprouts reduced problem behavior in preschool children with autism, we would not say that there was an evidence-base supporting the use of brussel sprouts as an effective behavioral reduction intervention. Much more evidence would be needed to support that assertion.

There has been much discussion in the field concerning what constitutes an evidence-base (Horner et al., 2005; Odom et al., 2005; Tankersley et al., 2008). At least two considerations must be examined to understand the issue. First, what types of experimental methodologies demonstrate the quality of research necessary to contribute to a data-base (Odom et al., 2005; Tankersley et al., 2008)? Second, how many of these studies are required to establish an evidence-base (Horner et al., 2005)?

Educational methodology. The quality of educational research has been raised as a concern, and there has been much controversy about what type of methodology should qualify as contributing to an evidence-base. Four types of research methodologies have been identified that are used in educational research: experimental group, correlational, single subject, and qualitative designs (Odom et al., 2005). NCLB suggests that random-assignment group experiments are the preferred methodology (the gold standard), and this has raised concern from many researchers who rely on other methodologies (Spooner & Browder, 2003). This is a critical issue as most behavioral and educational research in the area of severe disabilities employs single-subject designs, and more recently, qualitative research designs. Researchers in the field of severe disabilities hold that single-subject research is a robust methodology that allows researchers to determine the relationships between independent and dependent variables (Horner et al., 2005; McDonnell & O'Neill, 2003; Tawney & Gast, 1984). Much attention has been paid to this controversy, including journal issues dedicated to the discussion (e.g., "Criteria," 2005; Spooner, 2003).

Criteria for an evidence-base. The second issue is determining how much research (specifically single subject research) on an educational practice is needed to establish an evidence-base. Horner et al. (2005) suggests that generality of findings is established not by a single study, but through systematic replication across multiple studies, in multiple locations, and across multiple researchers. Horner and colleagues propose the following standards to determine an evidence-base:

> (a) a minimum of five single-subject studies that meet minimally acceptable methodological criteria and document experimental control have been published in peer-reviewed journals,
> (b) the studies are conducted by at least three different researchers across at least three different geographical locations, and
> (c) the five or more studies include a total of at least 20 participants. (p. 176)

Having rigorous standards is critical if we are to require an evidence-base for educational and behavioral programs. Oliva, F. Brown, and Gilles (2009) discuss this issue further. They suggest that for strategies that are more contentious, such as aversive interventions, the criteria for establishing an evidence-base should be even more rigorous.

Research and Values: A Balancing Act

Throughout this chapter we have noted remarkable changes in the field of severe disabilities across time: of society's attitudes, of the science of behavior, and of perceptions about education and treatment. The most powerful changes come when there is synergism between science and values. Was it coincidental that in the early 1970s Wolfensberger was developing the principle of normalization, and Baer, Wolf, and Risley and their colleagues were striving to understand what social validity really meant within the context of ABA? Perhaps it is both the objective requirement of science *and* the commitment to a strong value base that leads to the greatest progress for individuals with severe disabilities. Perhaps most of us who are immersed in our own work (whether from the science or values perspective), and seeing the world from our framework, do not even understand the influence that the other has on us. Figure 38.1 delineates possible relationships between research and values. The first component of this figure shows how there could be a total separation of the influences that science and research have on each other.

Let us take, for example, a researcher who demonstrated that contingent electric shock could reliably reduce off-task behavior. If it was a well done study, and all confounding variables were controlled, we may say that the study had experimental validity and met scientific standards. On the other hand, we might also say that there was no regard for the values that would be involved in delivering such an extreme aversive intervention, especially on such a benign behavior. In this example, there is no relationship between science and values. Conversely, if a professional advocated for the use of classical music to reduce off-task behavior, we may say that although it is not an aversive intervention, there is no scientific support for the practice. This does not mean that classical music does not reduce off-task behavior—only that we do not have an evidence base to support it.

At the other end of the continuum of possible relationships, there is an interdependent relationship; that is, both are dependent on and support each other (see Figure 38.1). As an example, Functional Communication Training (FCT) is a strategy that reduces a problem behavior by teaching the student to express the intent of the behavior (e.g., escape, attention-seeking) in a more socially acceptable way. When describing the literature on FCT, Horner et al. (2005) cite eight peer-reviewed articles, by five major research groups, with 42 participants, and concludes that there is an evidence-base for FCT. This strategy is one that meets the strict criteria of an evidence-base, and has had a significant impact on delivery of behavior supports. But it may also be the case that a strong values base had an impact on the development of this strategy—including a commitment to nonaversive behavior supports, respect for all communication, and treating individuals with dignity and respect.

The most effective procedures are those that are developed through a model in which researchers and consumers continually influence each other (Finney, 1991).

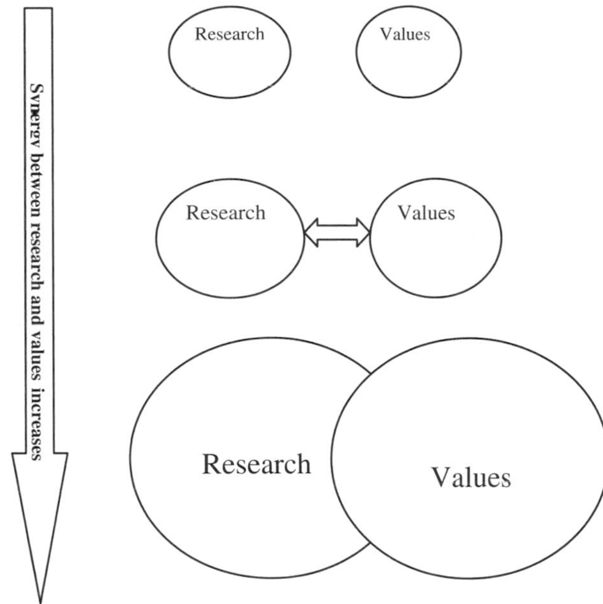

Figure 38.1 Possible relationships between evidence base and values.

Peck (1991) states that "too often, we are told that we must wait until research data have been collected and analyzed before we can know what policies to support and what practices to implement" (p. 1). The relationship between values and research is a complex one. Our field, and the policies, regulations, and standards that guide our work, call for both a scientific evidence-base for what we do, and at the same time to protect the people with whom we work (Oliva et al., 2009). Figure 28.1 shows that as collaboration between research and values increase, so do the chances for more synergistic outcomes.

Visions of the Future

Based on the progress that has been made, even if we only look at the recent developments of the 21st Century, we would like to project that these efforts will continue into the future. For example, we see a continuing and further development of the integration of values and evidence-based practice, participation in the general education community, total commitment to positive behavior interventions, and the growth of self-determination.

The Synergy of Evidence and Values

Since 2003, two issues of *Exceptional Children* have been dedicated to evidence-based practice, an issue of *Research and Practice for Persons with Severe Disabilities,* and an issue of *Intervention in School and Clinic* ("Criteria," 2005; "Evidence-Based," 2009; "Evidence-Based Practices," 2008; Spooner, 2003). All students with disabilities require effective procedures (Dammann & Vaughn, 2001). If this is the case for students with more mild levels of disabilities, what does this mean for the population of students with severe disabilities, who by definition find learning more difficult? Not all procedures are created equal, and students with the most significant learning needs require a systematic application of what we know has the highest probability of effectively improving their overall quality of life. The degree to which we know what works, with whom, and under what conditions only strengthen what teacher trainers can recommend to be applied in classroom, community, and home settings. But, "what works" is only one part of the equation. Scientific evidence for an intervention must be balanced with its social validity, that is, the treatment acceptability, of the intervention. An intervention might have an evidence-base, but may not be acceptable by the recipients of the intervention and their families. Both standards must be met for our field to incorporate it into our menu of best practices. Investigators will continue to wrestle with this synergy of evidence and values, what constitutes evidence and by what standards that evidence is judged to be a recommended evidence-based practice. As these investigators continue their discussion of evidence, the quality of training and the application of more humane treatment procedures for persons with severe disabilities continues to be documented and improved.

Meaningful Participation in the General Education Community

Meaningful participation in the general education community is dependent on two elements: social inclusion and academic participation. General curriculum access is an extension of students with severe disabilities being socially included in general education environments. More and more school systems across the country are adopting inclusive models of education for this population, and students with severe disabilities are participating as full members of their school community. On the other hand, growth is slow, and not yet at the level that many of us would like to see. Once in general education environments, we must ensure that all students have meaningful outcomes—both academically and socially. No Child Left Behind opened the door for a mandate to promote academic achievement for this population by stipulating *all children*—and that includes those with severe disabilities. This mandate challenged researchers, advocates, and teachers to determine how to teach academic skills such as reading, mathematics, and science. Many parents are now seeing their children reading simple material, where at least initially, it was thought that the child could not benefit from academic training. Once parents begin to see that some academic progress can be made, there is no turning back; they will want to see their child do more. Appropriate academic content taught in inclusive general education settings is likely to continue, as teachers of this population become more familiar with adapting material, accessing progress, and striving towards contributing to adequate yearly progress at their schools.

Total Commitment to Positive Behavior Supports

There has been a growing commitment to the application of humane procedures to treat forms of aberrant behavior, and the abandonment of procedures that are not considered acceptable for those without disabilities. In 2009 the National Disabilities Rights Network reported the

> abusive use of restraint and seclusion nationwide by school administrators, teachers, and auxiliary personnel, which has resulted in injury and trauma and, in far too many cases, death to children with disabilities. Furthermore, because there is no mandated system in place to report or collect data on these abuses, this report is clearly just the tip of the iceberg. (p. 1)

In this chapter we have noted the increasing humanity of the treatment of individuals with severe disabilities and the decreasing use of aversive interventions for problem behavior. Increasingly, national policy and state regulations are either restricting or banning the use of interventions that are considered unacceptable with individuals that do not have disabilities. We project that in time, and with the support of research and advocacy that demonstrates the power of positive interventions, that restrictions will be a thing of the past and total banning of these strategies will be the practice. We believe the trend will reflect the importance of families and professionals working together to positively impact the outcomes for children with severe disabilities.

Growth of Self-Determination

Historically, individuals with severe disabilities were thought to be unable to be active participants in their communities. Years of research and advocacy have proven that not only can individuals with severe disabilities be taught functional skills (e.g., bathing, dressing, eating), but they can learn higher order skills, such as problem-solving, academics, and communicating preferences. As we begin to earnestly understand that there should be no limits to our expectations, we begin to better appreciate the need for individuals with severe disabilities to learn how to advocate for themselves—to participate, along with their families, in steering the direction of their learning and their lives. In recent years, the challenge has been to understand alternate forms of expressing preferences. More importantly, the challenge is to increase our *acceptance* of alternate forms of communication as expressing preferences and self determination. As an example, there are a variety of responses that have historically been made when an individual has problem behavior in a work setting, including: change reinforcers to decrease problem behavior; seek medication to decrease problem behavior; change the task materials; provide visual prompts; or revise the task analysis. Each of these examples may change the individual's behavior. On the other hand, if we respect the individual's communication as an act of self-determination, we may ask a different question: *Is he asking for a different job?* Acknowledging behavior as a form of communication will support self-determination for *all* individuals with disabilities, regardless of the level of disability. We believe a future trend will be to include the focus on self-determination in all planning and implementation of

Individualized Education Plans. Only in this way will we be assured that we identify instructional strategies and be accountable for acquisition and demonstration of self-determination.

References

Allyon, T., & Azrin, N. H. (1965). The measurement and reinforcement of behavior of psychotics. *Journal of the Experimental Analysis of Behavior*, *8*, 357–383.

Allyon, T., & Azrin, N. H. (1968). *The token economy: A motivational system for therapy and rehabilitation*. New York: Appleton-Century-Crofts.

Allyon, T., & Michael, J. (1959). The psychiatric nurse as a behavioral engineer. *Journal of the Experimental Analysis of Behavior*, *2*, 323–334.

Azrin, N. H., & Armstrong, P. M. (1973). The "mini-meal"—A method for teaching eating skills to the profoundly retarded. *Mental Retardation*, *11*, 9–11.

Azrin, N. H., Bugle, C., & O'Brien, F. (1971). Behavior engineering: Two apparatuses for toilet training retarded children. *Journal of Applied Behavior Analysis*, *4*, 249–253.

Azrin, N. H., & Foxx, R. M. (1971). A repaid method of toilet training the institutionalized retarded. *Journal of Applied Behavior Analysis*, *4*, 88–89.

Baer, D. M., Wolf, M. M., & Risley, T. R. (1968). Some current dimesnsions of applied behavior analysis. *Journal of Applied Behavior Analysis*, *1*, 91–97.

Baer, D. M., Wolf, M. M., & Risley, T. R. (1987). Some still-current dimensions of applied behavior analysis. *Journal of Applied Behavior Analysis*, *20*, 313–327.

Ball, T. S., Seric, K., & Payne, L. E. (1971). Long-term retention of self-help skill training in the profoundly retarded. *American Journal of Mental Deficiency*, *76*, 378–382.

Baumeister, A., & Klosowski, R. (1965). An attempt to group train severely retarded patients. *Mental Retardation*, *3*, 24–26.

Bensberg, G. J., Colwell, C. N., & Cassell, R. H. (1965). Teaching the profoundly retarded self-help activities by behavior shaping techniques. *American Journal of Mental Deficiency*, *69*, 674–679.

Binet, A., & Simon, T. (1905). Methode snouvelles pour le diagnostic du niveau intellectuel des anormaux [New methods for the diagnosis of intellectual abnormalities]. *L'Annee Psychologique, 11,* 191–244.

Black, R. S., & Pretes, L. (2007). Victims and victors: Representation of physical disability on the silver screen. *Research and Practice for Persons with Severe Disabilities*, *32*, 66–83.

Bradley, V. J., & Knoll, J. A. (1990). *Shifting paradigms in services for people with developmental disabilities*. Cambridge, MA: Human Services Research Institute.

Breland, M. (1965). Application of method. In G. J. Bensberg (Ed.), *Teaching the mentally retarded: A handbook for ward personnel* (pp. 143–158). Atlanta, GA: Southern Regional Education Board.

Bricker, D. D., & Iacino, R. (1977). Early intervention with severely/profoundly handicapped children. In E. Sontag, J. Smith, & N. Certo (Eds.), *Educational programming for the severely and profoundly handicapped* (pp. 166–176). Reston, VA: Division on Mental

Browder, D. M., Ahlgrim-Delzell, L., Courtade-Little, G., & Snell, M. E. (2006). General curriculum access. In M. Snell & F. Brown (Eds.), *Instruction of students with severe disabilities* (6th ed., pp. 489–525). Upper Saddle River, NJ: Merrill/Prentice Hall.

Browder, D. M., Ahlgrim-Delzell, L., Spooner, F., Mims, P. J., & Baker, J. N. (2009). Using time delay to teach picture and word recognition to identify evidence-based practice for students with severe developmental disabilities. *Exceptional Children*, *75*, 343–364.

Browder, D. M., Flowers, C., Ahlgrim-Delzell, L., Karvonen, M., Spooner, F., & Algozzine, R. (2004). The alignment of alternate assessment performance indicators to academic and functional curricula. *The Journal of Special Education*, *37*, 211–223.

Browder, D. M., & Spooner, F. (Eds.). (2006). *Teaching reading, math, and science to students with significant cognitive disabilities*. Baltimore: Paul H. Brookes.

Browder, D. M., Spooner, F., Ahlgrim-Delzell, L., Flowers, C., Algozzine, B., & Karvonen, M. (2003). A content analysis of the curricular philosophies reflected in states' alternate assessments. *Research and Practice for Persons with Severe Disabilities*, *28*, 165–181.

Browder, D. M., Spooner, F., Ahlgrim-Delzell, L., Harris, A., & Wakeman, S. (2008). A meta-analysis on teaching mathematics to students with significant cognitive disabilities. *Exceptional Children*, *74*, 407–432.

Browder, D. M., Spooner, F., Algozzine, R., Ahlgrim-Delzell, L., Flowers, C., & Karvonen, M. (2003). What we know and need to know about alternate assessment. *Exceptional Children*, *70*, 45–61.

Browder, D. M., Spooner, F., Wakeman, S., Trela, K., & Baker, J. N. (2006). Aligning instruction with academic content standards: Finding the link. *Research and Practice for Persons with Severe Disabilities*, *31*, 309–321.

Browder, D. M., Wakeman, S. Y., Spooner, F., Ahlgrim-Delzell, L., & Algozzine, B. (2006). Research on reading for students with significant cognitive disabilities. *Exceptional Children*, *72*, 392–408.

Brown, F., & Michaels, C. A. (2003). The shaping of inclusion: Efforts in Detroit and other urban settings. In D. Fisher & N. Frey (Eds.), *Inclusive urban schools* (pp. 231–243). Baltimore: Paul H. Brookes.

Brown, F., Michaels, C. A., Oliva, C. M., & Woolf, S. B. (2008). Personal paradigm shifts among ABA and PBS experts: Comparisons in treatment acceptability. *Journal of Positive Behavior Interventions*, *10*, 212–227.

Brown, F., & Snell, M. E. (2006). Measurement, analysis, and evaluation. In M. E. Snell & F. Brown (Eds.), *Instruction of students with severe disabilities* (pp. 170–205). Upper Saddle River, NJ: Pearson/Merrill/Prentice Hall.

Brown, F., Snell, M. E., & Lehr, D. (2006). Meaningful assessment. In M. E. Snell & F. Brown (Eds.), *Instruction of students with severe disabilities* (pp. 67–110). Upper Saddle River, NJ: Pearson/Merrill/Prentice Hall.

Brown, L., Bronston-McClean, M. B., Baumgart, D., Vincent, L., Falvey, M., & Schroder, J. (1979). Using the characteristics of current and subsequent least restrictive environments in the development of curricular content for severely handicapped students. *AAESPH Review*, *4*, 407–424.

Brown, L., Nietupski, J., & Hamre-Nietupski, S. (1976). Criterion of ultimate functioning. In M. A. Thomas (Ed.), *Hey, don't forget about me! Education's investment in the severely, profoundly, and multiply handicapped* (pp. 2–15). Reston, VA: Council for Exceptional Children.

Brown v. Board of Education, 347 U. S. 483 (1954).

Carter, E. W., Sisco, L. G., Melekoglu, M. A., & Kurkowski, C. (2007). Peer supports as an alternative to individually assigned paraprofessionals in inclusive high school classrooms. *Research and Practice for Persons with Severe Disabilities*, *32*, 213–227.

Carter, S. (2008). Further conceptualization of treatment acceptability. *Education and Training in Developmental Disabilities*, *43*, 135–143.

Cooper, J. O., Heron, T. E., & Heward, W. L. (2007). *Applied behavior analysis* (2nd ed.). Upper Saddle River, NJ: Pearson/Merrill/Prentice-Hall.

Courtade, G., Spooner, F., & Browder, D. M. (2007). Review of studies with students with significant cognitive disabilities which link to science standards. *Research and Practice for Persons with Severe Disabilities*, *32*, 43–49.

Criteria for Evidence-Based Practice in Special Education. (2005). [Special Issue]. *Exceptional Children, 71*(2).

Dammann, J. E., & Vaughn, S. (2001). Science and sanity in special education. *Behavioral Disorders*, *27*, 21–29.

Education for All Handicapped Children Act of 1975, Pub. L. No. 94-142, 89 Stat. 773 (1975).

Evans, I. M. (1991). Testing and diagnosis. In L. H. Meyer, C.A. Peck, & L. Brown (Eds.), *Critical issues in the lives of people with severe disabilities* (pp. 25–44). Baltimore: Paul H. Brookes.

Evidence-Based Practices for Reading, Math, Writing, and Behavior. (2009). [Special Issue]. *Exceptional Children*, *75*(2).

Evidence-Based Practices in Special Education: Some Practical Considerations. (2008). [Special Issue]. *Intervention in School and Clinic, 44*(2).

Finney, J. W. (1991). On further development of the concept of social validity. *Journal of Applied Behavior Analysis, 24*, 245–249.

Foxx, R. M., & Azrin, N. H. (1972). Restitution: A method of eliminating aggressive-disruptive behavior of retarded and brain damaged patients. *Behaviour Research and Therapy, 10*, 15–27.

Foxx, R. M., & Shapiro, S. T. (1978). The timeout ribbon: A nonexclusionary timeout procedure. *Journal of Applied Behavior Analysis, 11*, 125–136.

Fuller, P. R. (1949). Operant conditioning of a vegetative human organism. *American Journal of Psychology, 62*, 587–590.

Gent, P. J., & Mulhauser, M. B. (1988). Public integration of students with handicaps: Where it's been, where it's going, and how it's getting there. *The Journal of The Association for Persons with Severe Handicaps, 13*, 188–196.

Gold, M. W. (1980). *Marc Gold: "Did I say that: Articles and commentary on the try another way system.* Champaign, IL: Research Press.

Goldberg, I., & Cruickshank, W. M. (1958). The trainable but noneducable: Whose responsibility? *N. E. A. Journal, 47*, 622–623.

Guess, D., & Noonan, M. J. (1982). Curricula and instructional procedures for severely handicapped students. *Focus on Exceptional Children, 4*, 1–12.

Guess, D., Sailor, W., & Baer, D. M. (1974). To teach language to retarded children. In R. Schiefelbusch & L. Lloyd (Eds.), *Language perspectives: Acquisition, retardation, and intervention* (pp. 529–563). Baltimore: University Park Press.

Heber, R. (1959). A manual on terminology and classification in mental retardation [Monograph Supplement]. *American Journal of Mental Deficiency, 64*.

Horner, R. H., Carr, E. G., Halle, J., McGee, G., Odom, S., & Wolery, M. (2005). The use of single-subject research to identify evidence-based practice in special education. *Exceptional Children, 71*, 165–180.

Individuals with Disabilities Education Act Amendments of 1997, PL 105-17, 20 U.S.C. §§ 1400 *et seq*.

Individuals with Disabilities Education Improvement Act of 2004, PL 108-466, 20 U. S. C. §1400, H. R. 1350.

Jorgensen, C., McSheehan, M., & Sonnenmeier, R., M. (2007). Presumed competence reflected in the educational programs of students with IDD before and after Beyond Access professional development intervention. *Journal of Intellectual & Developmental Disability, 32*, 248–262.

Kauffman, J. M. (Ed.). (1981). Are all children educable? *Analysis and Intervention in Developmental Disabilities* [Special issue], *1*(1).

Kazdin, A. E. (1977a). Assessing the clinical or applied importance of behavior change through social validation. *Behavior Modification, 1*, 427–452.

Kazdin, A. E. (1977b). *The token economy: A review and evaluation*. New York: Plenum Press.

Kazdin, A. E. (1978). *History of behavior modification: Experimental foundations of contemporary research.* Baltimore: University Park Press.

Lambert. N., Nihira, K., & Leland, H. (1993). *Adaptive behavior scale—School.* Austin, TX: PRO-ED.

Lipsky, D. K., & Gartner, A. (1989). *Beyond separate education: Quality education for all.* Baltimore: Paul H. Brookes.

McDonnell, J. J., & O'Neill, R. (2003). A Perspective on single/within subject research methods and "scientifically based research." *Research and Practice for Persons with Severe Disabilities, 28,* 138–142.

Meyer, L. H. (1994). Editor's introduction: Understanding the impact of inclusion. *The Journal of The Association for Persons with Severe Handicaps, 19,* 251–252.

Meyer, L. H., Eichenger, J., & Park-Lee, S. (1987). A validation of program quality indicators in educational services for students with severe disabilities. *The Journal of The Association for Persons with Severe Handicaps, 12,* 251–263.

Meyer, L. H., Peck, C. A., & Brown, L. (1991). *Critical issues in the lives of people with severe disabilities.* Baltimore: Paul H. Brookes.

Mills v. Board of Education of the District of Columbia, 348 F. Supp. 866 (D. D. C. 1973).

National Disability Rights Network (2009). *School is not supposed to hurt: Investigative report on abusive restraint and seclusion in schools.* Washington D.C.

Noonan, M. J., Brown, F., Mulligan, M., & Rettig, M. (1982). Educability of severely handicapped persons: Both sides of the issue. *The Journal of The Association for the Severely Handicapped, 7*(1), 3–14.

Norden, M. F. (1994). *The cinema of isolation: A history of physical disability in the movies*. New Brunswick, NJ: Rutgers University Press.

Odom, S. L., Brantlinger, E., Gersten, R., Horner, R. H., Thompson, B., & Harris, K. (2005). Research in special education: Scientific methods and evidence-based practices. *Exceptional Children, 71*, 137–148.

Oliva, C. M., Brown, F., & Gilles, D. (2009). *Contingent electric shock for challenging behavior: Searching for an evidence-base*. Manuscript submitted for publication

PARC v. Commonwealth of Pennsylvania, 343 F. Supp. 279 (E. D. Pa. 1972)

Peck, C. A. (1991). Linking values and science in social policy decisions affecting citizens with severe disabilities. In L. H. Meyer, C. A. Peck, & L. Brown (Eds.), *Critical issues in the lives of people with severe disabilities* (pp. 1–15). Baltimore: Paul H. Brookes.

Repp, A. C., & Deitz, S. M. (1974). Reducing aggressive and self-injurious behavior of institutionalized retarded children through reinforcement of other behaviors. *Journal of Applied Behavior Analysis, 7*, 313–325.

Risley, T. R., & Wolf, M. M. (1967). Establishing functional speech in echolalic children. *Behaviour Research and Therapy, 5*, 73–88.

Robinson, C. C., & Robinson, J. H. (1983). Sensorimotor functions and cognitive development. In M. E. Snell (Ed.), *Systematic instruction of the moderately and severely handicapped* (2nd ed., pp. 226–266). Columbus, OH: Charles E. Merrill.

Ryndak, D. L., & Alper, S. (2003). *Curriculum and instruction for students with significant disabilities in inclusive settings* (2nd ed.). Boston: Allyn and Bacon.

Sailor, W., & Guess, D. (1983). *Severely handicapped students: An instructional design*. Boston: Houghton Mifflin.

Schalock, R. L., Luckasson, A. R., & Shogren, K. A. (2007). The renaming of *Mental Retardation*: Understanding the change to the term. *Intellectual Disability, 45*, 116–124.

Sidman, M. (2001). *Coercion and its fallout*. Boston: Authors Cooperative.

Sontag, E., Burke, P., & York, R. (1973). Considerations for serving the severely handicapped in the public schools. *Education and Training of the Mentally Retarded, 8*, 20–26

Sontag, E., & Haring, N. G. (1996). The professionalism of teaching and learning for children with severe disabilities: The creation of TASH. *The Journal of The Association for Persons with Severe Handicaps, 21*, 39–45.

Sparrow, S. S., Balla, D. A., & Cichetti, D. V. (1984). *Vineland adaptive behavior scales*. Circle Pines, MN: American Guidance Service.

Spooner, F. (Ed.). (2003). Perspective on defining scientifically based research. *Research and Practice for Persons with Severe Disabilities* [Special issue], *28*(3).

Spooner, F., & Browder, D. M. (2003). Scientifically based research in education and students with low incidence disabilities. *Research and Practice for Persons with Severe Disabilities, 28*, 117–125.

Spooner, F., Dymond, S. K., & Kennedy, C. H. (Eds.). (2006). Accessing the general curriculum. *Research and Practice for Persons with Severe Disabilities* [Special issue], *31*(4).

Stephens, B. (1977). Piagetian approach to curriculum development. In E. Sontag, J. Smith, & N. Certo (Eds.), *Educational programming for the severely and profoundly handicapped* (pp. 237–249). Reston, VA: Division on Mental Retardation, Council for Exceptional Children.

Tankersley, M., Harjusola-Webb, S., & Landrum, T. J. (2008). Using single-subject research to establish the evidence base of special education. *Intervention in School and Clinic, 44*, 83–90.

Tawney, J. W., & Gast, D. L. (1984). *Single subject research in special education*. Columbus, OH: Merrill.

Taylor, S. J. (1988). Caught in the continuum: A critical analysis of the principle of the least restrictive environment. *The Journal of The Association for the Severely Handicapped, 13*, 41–53.

Thompson, J. R., Bradley, V. J., Buintinx, W. H. E., Schalock, R. L., Shogren, K A., Snell, M. E., & Wehmeyer, M. L. (2009). Conceptualizing supports and the support needs of people with intellectual disability. *Intellectual and Developmental Disabilities*, *47*, 135–146.

Thompson, J. R., Bryant, B. R., Campbell, E. M., Craig, E. M., Hughes, C. M., Rotholz, D. A., et al. (2004). *Supports intensity scale: Users manual*. Washington, DC: American Association on Mental Retardation.

U.S. Department of Education, Bureau for Education of the Handicapped (USOE/BEH). (1974). 21 U.S.C. §1407[7]; 45 C.F.R. §14.1.

Wang, P., & Spillane, A. (2009). Evidence-based social skills interventions for children with autism: A meta-analysis. *Education and Training in Developmental Disabilities, 44,* 318–342.

Wehmeyer, M. L. (2005). Self-determination and individuals with severe disabilities: Reexamining meanings and misinterpretations. *Research and Practice for Persons with Severe Disabilities*, *30*, 113–120.

Wehmeyer, M. L., Agran, M., & Hughes, C. (1998). *Teaching self-determination to youth with disabilities: Basic skills for successful transition.* Baltimore: Paul H. Brookes.

Wehmeyer, M. L., Field, S., Doren, B., Jones, B., & Mason, C. (2004). Self-determination and student involvement in standards-based reform. *Exceptional Children*, *70*, 413–425.

White, O. R. (1985). The evaluation of severely mentally retarded individuals. In D. Bricker & J. Filler (Eds.), *Severe mental retardation: From theory to practice* (pp. 161–184). Reston, VA: Council for Exceptional Children.

Williams, R. L., Howard, V., Williams, B. F., & McLaughlin, T. F. (1994). Basic principles of learning. In E. C. Cipani & F. Spooner (Eds.), *Curricular and instructional approaches for persons with severe disabilities*. Boston: Allyn and Bacon.

Wolf, M. M. (1978). Social validity: The case for subjective measurement *or* how Applied Behavior Analysis is finding it's heart. *Journal of Applied Behavior Analysis*, *11*, 203–214.

Wolf, M. M., Risley, T., & Mees, H. (1964). Application of operant conditioning procedures to the behavior problems of an autistic child. *Behaviour Research and Therapy*, *1*, 305–312.

Wolfensberger, W. (1972). *The principle of normalization in human services*. Toronto: National Institute on Mental Retardation.

Wyatt v. Stickney (1972). 344 F. Supp, 387, 344 F. Supp. 373 (M.D. Ala. 1972), 334 F. Supp. 1341, 325 F. Supp. 781 (M.D. Ala 1971), aff'd sub nom. Wyatt v. Aderholt, 503 F. 2d 1305 (5th Cir. 1974).

Zeiler, M. D., & Jervey, S. S. (1968). Development of behavior: Self-feeding. *Journal of Consulting Psychology*, *32*, 164–168.

39

Systematic Instruction of Students with Severe Disabilities

Erik Drasgow
University of South Carolina

Mark Wolery
Vanderbilt University

James Halle
University of Illinois

Zahra Hajiaghamohseni
University of South Carolina

The purpose of educating students with severe disabilities is to promote inclusion, self-determination, independence, and quality of life (Renzaglia, Karvonen, Drasgow, & Stoxen, 2003). Achieving these outcomes is dependent on an effective educational approach that is comprised of at least three related components. The first component consists of the content of instruction. The content of instruction, or curriculum, has to be designed and sequenced so that the specific skills it contains will produce the desired outcomes consistent with the purpose of education. The second component consists of the location of instruction. Decisions related to the location of instruction are based on the characteristics of the skill (e.g., hygiene skills are taught in the bathroom) and available resources (e.g., community skills can be taught in the community if transportation is not an issue).

The third component consists of the actual delivery of information to a student. The evidence-based process for providing information to students with severe disabilities is referred to as *systematic instruction* or SI (see Halle, Chadsey, Lee, & Renzaglia, 2004; Snell, 1983). SI consists of several generic steps that can be adapted to foster student learning and to meet the desired outcomes of instruction. Our purpose in this chapter is first to describe SI, then describe and relate SI to applied behavior analysis, and finally to highlight selected features of SI that are especially relevant to effective acquisition, generalization, and maintenance of skills.

Systematic Instruction Described

SI typically consists of five steps (Iovannone, Dunlap, Huber, & Kincaid, 2003). The first step is to define or describe the outcome of instruction. The outcome of instruction can be conceptualized as the dependent variable. This dependent variable must be described in an observable and measureable manner so that teachers can make objective decisions about its occurrence. For example, it is hard to make an objective decision if a student has "participated" but much easier to make an objective decision if a student had three interactions of at least 5 seconds during lunch. Thus the cornerstone of SI is beginning with a well-specified and well-defined *target behavior* that will serve as the dependent variable of instruction.

The second step of SI is to describe the procedures that a teacher will use to achieve the outcome of instruction. These procedures serve as the independent variable. Procedures, or the independent variable, typically consist of at least assisting the student to perform the behavior and then providing feedback about the quality of performance. The description of procedures should include when, where, what kind of, and how often a teacher will use assistance and feedback. The main idea here is that instruction is most effective when the teacher has a "game plan" and sticks to it and is least effective when the teacher "wings it."

The third step of SI is to implement the procedures consistently. The characteristics of students with severe disabilities suggest that they need more frequent opportunities to practice skills and consistent procedures make practice more efficient (American Association on Mental Retardation, 2002; Beirne-Smith, Patton, & Kim, 2006). For example, if a teacher decides to use a task analysis (i.e., dividing a complex skill into its component substeps) to teach a student to use a washing machine, but each time the teacher uses a different task analysis, it is likely that not only will the student learn more slowly, if at all, but that the student will get frustrated and then may try to escape the task.

The final two steps of SI consist of (a) collecting ongoing information about student progress and then (b) using this information to make decisions about continuing or revising instructional procedures. The only way to know if the consistent procedures (i.e., the independent variable) are effective at changing the target behavior (i.e., the dependent variable) is to have objective numerical evidence of the relationship. Teachers can use this numerical information to guide instructional decisions and then continue to monitor student progress to make future decisions. Not only is progress monitoring an effective practice, but it is also required under the accountability provisions of the Individuals with Disabilities Education Act (IDEA, 2004; Yell & Drasgow, 2000).

Systematic Instruction and Applied Behavior Analysis

One instructional approach that meets all the components of systematic instruction is *applied behavior analysis* (ABA). ABA is the branch of psychology that uses the behavior model to understand and improve socially important behavior (Baer, Wolf, & Risley, 1968; Cooper, Heron, & Heward, 2007). The behavioral model is based on the antecedent-behavior-consequence relation (Skinner, 1938). Antecedents are environmental events that cue or trigger behavior. Behavior is the observable response that occurs in the presence of the antecedent and produces the consequence. The consequence occurs after behavior and because of behavior, and influences the future probability of that behavior. In the behavioral model, antecedents and consequences serve as independent variables, and behavior is the dependent variable. In the rest of this section, we relate SI to ABA.

The first step of SI is to specify the outcome of instruction in relation to the individualized goals identified for the learner. ABA specifies outcomes in two related ways. One way is through *operational definitions*. Operational definitions are precise descriptions of behavior that permit observers to be objective and consistent in determining its occurrence. Another way that ABA specifies outcomes is through behavioral objectives. These are statements of learning outcomes that follow a student-behavior-condition-criteria format. Behavior is well described through the operational definition. In our behavioral model, conditions refer to the antecedents under which the behavior ought to occur. Criteria refer to how well a student must perform the behavior and decisions about criteria are influenced by the standards of success in inclusive environments.

The next step of SI is to describe the instructional procedures that a teacher will use to achieve the criteria of the behavioral objective. ABA has a variety of effective procedures (see the *Journal of Applied Behavior Analysis*, 1968–2010) that foster learning, but we will highlight only two here. One instructional procedure is prompting. Prompts are supplemental antecedent stimuli that help a student perform a behavior in the presence of the antecedent specified in the behavioral objective. Prompts can be, for example, verbal, gestural, or physical. Prompts are often combined in ways that foster learning but that also allow the teacher to withdraw them in a systematic manner so that a student does not become dependent on them (Wolery, Ault, & Doyle, 1992).

The second instructional procedure that we will highlight here is *differential reinforcement* (DR). DR refers to providing motivating consequences (i.e., reinforcement) for behavior that needs to be increased and withholding these consequences for behavior that should not be increased. For example, if a student is learning to set the table before a meal, the teacher may use a physical prompt to guide the student's hand to the fork and then guide his hand with the fork in it to the corresponding place on the table where the fork belongs. The teacher would then praise the student by saying "good job" or by patting him on the back. DR in this case would consist of providing verbal praise only when the student performs either a prompted or independent correct response, and withholding praise when the student makes a mistake (e.g., puts the fork in the wrong place) or is not attending. The teacher would begin instruction with frequent reinforcement to compensate for the amount of student effort involved in the early stages of learning, and then thin out the schedule of reinforcement as the student becomes more skilled with the task requirements and thus the effort to respond is diminished. Table 39.1 defines and provides examples of operational definitions, behavioral objectives, prompts, and differential reinforcement.

The third step of SI is to implement the procedures consistently. In ABA, the antecedents and consequences are implemented consistently to determine their effect on the target behavior. Effective and systematic instruction entails manipulating the independent variables, or the antecedents and consequences in the behavioral model, to determine their effects on learning, or on the dependent variable in the behavioral model. It is important to implement procedures consistently because the fidelity of the independent variables (i.e., the instructional procedures) enables investigators to link outcomes to the instruction that produced them (e.g., Wolery et al., 1992).

The final two steps of SI consist of collecting information about student progress to make instructional decisions. In ABA, student performance is monitored through three related components (Miltenberger, 2008). The first component is a *recording method*. Recording methods are ways to translate student performance into a numerical

TABLE 39.1
Examples of Operational Definitions, Behavioral Objectives, Prompting, and Differential Reinforcement

Component	Definition	Examples
Operational Definition	Precise descriptions of behavior that permit observers to be objective and consistent in determining its occurrence	1. Unzipping book bag & placing school materials inside book bag and zipping it closed 2. Asking, "Please help me?" during a difficult task 3. Waving or saying "hello" to social partners prior to first interaction
Behavioral Objective	Statement of learning outcomes that follow a student-behavior-condition-criteria format	1. Sean will independently pack his book bag at the end of the school day before going home for 5 consecutive school days 2. Angel will independently request help during difficult tasks for 100% of opportunities times per week for 5 consecutive school days 3. Danielle will independently greet social partners by waving or saying "Hello" through out the school day for 80% of opportunities 10 consecutive school days
Prompting	Supplemental antecedent stimuli that help a student perform a behavior in the presence of the antecedent specified in the behavioral objective	1. Teacher says, "Raise your hand if you need help" 2. Teacher points to the correct student placement in lunch line 3. Teacher demonstrates how to pack book bag
Differential reinforcement	A motivating consequence for behavior that needs to increased and withholding this consequences for behavior that should not be increased	1. Student receives teacher assistance when he touches the " help icon." Student does *not* receive teacher assistance when he screams out. 2. Student receives verbal praise for moving his toothbrush in his mouth. Student does *not* receive verbal praise when holding the toothbrush still in his mouth. 3. Student receives a "hello" from social partner when he says, "hello". Student does *not* receive any social attention from social partner when he attempts to hug social partner.

quantity that captures the important aspect, or dimension, of behavior. Important aspects of behavior can include, for example, frequency (i.e., how often a behavior occurs), duration, (i.e., how long a behavior occurs, or latency (i.e., how long it is between when a behavior ought to occur and when it actually starts to occur). The second component is a recoding, or data, sheet. A data sheet consists of the directions for recording, the operational definition of the target behavior, and a place to record. The final component is a recording schedule that specifies when, where, how long, and how often to collect information about student performance.

In ABA, making decisions about revising instructional procedures is based on a visual analysis of graphed student performance data. The graph is a simple x-y axis where the y axis represents behavior and the x axis represents time. Typically, information is collected about student performance before instruction begins. This information is called baseline, and it describes current performance and predicts what future performance would be like if no instruction occurred. Another aspect of data collection in ABA is referred to as continuous assessment. In this approach, data are collected frequently (i.e., at least three times a week) to capture any small changes in behavior. Finally, data are visually analyzed by noting the direction, or trend, of the data, the level of the data, and the degree of variability. Visual analysis is based on the notion that small changes in the right direction add up to big changes over time. Moreover, the criteria in the behavioral objective specify how the data should look during visual analysis.

Our purpose in this first section has been to provide an overview of SI and to describe how ABA is an effective method of SI. In the remainder of this chapter, we summarize and analyze some core issues related to SI-ABA. We begin with a careful analysis of the different types of learning presentation formats, called *trials*. Next, we examine efficiency criteria that teachers may invoke to determine their selection of instructional practices. We then explore challenges related to teaching *general classes* of (as opposed to discrete) behavior. Finally, we address promising strategies that enhance the generalization of new skills by students with severe disabilities.

Instructional Presentation Formats: Introduction

There are at least two issues to consider during our discussion of instructional presentation formats (IPFs). These two issues play a large part in selecting the type or combination of types of IPFs to use during instruction to improve target behavior outcomes. The first issue is the stages of learning and the second issue is curriculum. We begin by describing the stages of learning.

Stages of Learning

Learning consists of at least four stages (Alberto & Troutman, 2009; Haring, Lovitt, Eaton, & Hansen, 1978). Acquisition is the first stage of learning, and we define it as the ability to perform the motor components of a behavior. For example, if a student is learning to go through the school cafeteria line independently, then acquisition of this skill would consist of standing in line, getting a tray, getting silverware, making food selections by placing the food item on the tray, and so on until the student leaves the lunch line to find a place to sit. The challenge for learners with severe disabilities is to encounter enough opportunities, or trials, to practice a skill until they acquire both the motor movements and the correct sequence of motor movements. Thus, the first consideration when selecting an IPF is the number of opportunities that a student may need to acquire a behavior. This consideration becomes quite important because students with severe disabilities may require a large number (e.g., hundreds) of trials until acquisition is demonstrated (e.g., Carr, Binkoff, Kologinsky, & Eddy, 1978; Drasgow, Halle, Ostrosky, & Harbers, 1996).

The second stage of learning is fluency. Fluency refers to the rate, or speed, at which a behavior occurs. For example, if our student acquires the cafeteria line skills, but takes 30 minutes to go through the line, then the challenge is not with the behavior itself, but rather with the fluency of the behavior. Decisions about the criterion for acceptable fluency are often related to what is termed *social validity* (Schwartz & Baer, 1991; Wolf, 1978). Social validity refers to the appropriateness of a behavior, the acceptability of procedures used to teach that behavior, and the meaningfulness of the outcomes that the procedures produced. Thus, a teacher must also include consideration of not only the type of IPF that will produce acquisition, but also the type or types of IPFs that produce fluency so that a student can perform the behavior in inclusive settings at a rate that will not be stigmatizing, and may even approximate that of peers. From the perspective of procedural acceptability, stigma can also accrue if IPFs do not comport to those that occur typically in inclusive settings because the procedures draw attention to the learner or highlight the learner's disability.

The third and fourth stages of learning are generalization and maintenance. Generalization refers to the occurrence of newly learned behavior under conditions that are different from those that were present during instruction, and maintenance refers to the occurrence of the newly learned behavior across time (Stokes & Baer, 1977). Generalization is a complex phenomenon that we will discuss at length later in this chapter. For now, we will say that generalization, as an outcome, is enhanced when teachers use authentic materials in natural settings, and include variations during instruction that represent the range of variations that a student is likely to encounter when performing the behavior during his or her daily life. Maintenance is enhanced when a student has frequent opportunities to use the behavior and the behavior produces motivating consequences at least occasionally or intermittently (Ferster & Skinner, 1957).

Teachers must consider generalization and maintenance when selecting the type or types of IPFs to use during instruction because (a) acquisition and fluency are prerequisites and (b) factors such as the authenticity of the setting and the materials influence outcomes. Acquisition and fluency are prerequisites to generalization and maintenance because students who do not readily produce the new behavior or who struggle with the effort required to produce the behavior, are unlikely to respond with the new behavior under novel conditions (Drasgow, Halle, & Sigafoos, 1999). Indeed, when the effort to produce a response is excessive, that effort may become aversive and result in escaping or avoiding the situation (Friman & Poling, 1995). Moreover, generalization may be limited when teachers use analogue materials and teach under highly controlled and restricted conditions (Rincover & Koegel, 1975). For example, a teacher will not likely foster generalization or maintenance of snack preparation when she teaches a child with a severe disability to prepare a snack in a one-to-one situation at a table in the corner of a classroom by having the child glue pictures of snack items on a piece of paper and then color them.

One challenge for teachers is to determine whether acquisition-fluency ought to be achieved first or whether these stages ought to be taught concurrently within IPFs that address generalization and maintenance. For example, a teacher may opt to program for fluency in teaching a student to sort clothes in the classroom before doing the laundry in public laundromats because she can use real clothes in the classroom and the number of prompts needed to teach this skill in public may be stigmatizing. Or a teacher may opt to teach a student to reject items in the classroom by handing her a "No thank you" card before she introduces instruction in different environments because she knows that the student may become quickly agitated in some rejecting situations with other social partners. Prompting a fluent behavior in challenging situations is much easier and safer than trying to achieve acquisition or fluency when the student is already frustrated or upset (Carr et al., 1994). Conversely, to enhance generalization, a teacher may opt to teach a new rejecting response across multiple situations and social partners to a student who can tolerate prompting and the concomitant delay in the rejecting outcome. Thus, to begin the process of selecting the type or types of IPFs to use for instruction, the teacher must consider student characteristics and outcomes and then use this information to guide decisions about what types of IPFs to use, where to teach, and what materials to use. We next briefly discuss curriculum because of its central importance to making instructional decisions.

Curriculum

Whereas instruction refers to *how* to teach, curriculum refers to *what* to teach. We strongly embrace a top-down functional curriculum approach (e.g., Brown et al., 1979) that consists of teaching skills that are immediately useful, useful across multiple environments and time, and that foster independence and self-determination. This approach dictates that the first step in programming begins with identifying a behavioral outcome that is the target behavior (e.g., independently getting a meal in the school cafeteria) before the second step of developing instructional procedures occurs. By identifying the terminal outcome of instruction, a teacher can then determine the number of opportunities for instruction that normally exist within the daily routine. She can use this information to determine whether sufficient instructional opportunities exist to produce acquisition or whether she will have to supplement opportunities by including one or more of the strategies that we review next.

Instructional Presentation Formats: Types of Trials

The essence of SI is having a game plan for instruction (i.e., the independent variable) and then consistently implementing that instruction. Revisions to instruction are based on the student's actual performance (i.e., the dependent variable). In the previous section, we presented background information that teachers need to consider before developing instruction. In the next section, we present more specific information to help teachers make decisions about instruction that include how to teach, when to teach, where to teach, and how often to teach.

There are two important issues to consider before we begin our discussion of the type of instructional trials. First, all instructional trials consist of the same core components that are based on the *antecedent-behavior-consequence* model that we briefly reviewed earlier in the chapter. A trial begins in the presence of an antecedent. That is, either the teacher presents the antecedent (e.g., the teacher presents both a red circle and a green circle and then tells the student to touch green) or the situation occurs as part of the student's normal routine or daily life (e.g., it is lunchtime and the student enters the school cafeteria). Next, the behavior occurs. The behavior can occur either independently or is supported by a teacher prompt (e.g., the student either touches green without any cue from the teacher or immediately after saying, "touch green," the teacher points to the green circle after which the student touches the green circle). The independent or prompted response is followed by a consequence (i.e., reinforcement) at least occasionally that motivates the student to behave in similar ways in the future in the presence of the antecedent. This consequence can be more artificial (e.g., the teacher gives a student an m&m after correctly labeling a picture) or more natural (e.g., the student eats lunch after completing all steps of the task analysis for going through the lunch line in the school cafeteria). These three steps—*antecedent-behavior-consequence*—comprise an instructional trial.

Second, it is important to note that the terms for trials are not always used consistently in the literature, and that there is often conceptual and practical overlap between the different types of trials (for a scholarly discussion of massed and distributed trials, see Bambara & Warren, 1993). One reason for this situation is that terms have evolved over time as curriculum and instruction have evolved. Our purpose is to provide teachers with options when selecting strategies that enable them to match the type of trial or trials needed to achieve the desired outcome. We urge teachers to pay careful attention to the conditions that they specify in their behavioral objective because knowing *when* and *where* to perform a behavior is just as important for a student with a severe disability as knowing *how* to perform that behavior. The three types of trials that we will be highlighting are discrete, massed, and distributed-naturalistic-embedded.

Discrete Trials

This format consists of the teacher controlling the opportunity for a student to respond by presenting or removing the antecedent (Catania, 1998). Discrete trials have a clear beginning and a clear ending, with a clear break between trials during which no responding is required (Koegel, Russo, & Rincover, 1977). For example, if a teacher is teaching geometrical shapes to a student, the teacher would present two shapes (e.g., a triangle and a circle) simultaneously and tell the student to touch the circle. After the student has touched the circle either independently or with a teacher prompt, and the teacher has praised the performance, (e.g., "good job!"), the teacher then removes both shapes thus ending the trial. Discrete trials are most often implemented in a format of massed trials. Discrete trials have been used with young children with autism (Lovaas 1981; Lovaas, Koegel, Simmons, & Long 1973) to teach general attending and responding skills such as imitation or receptive and expressive labeling. When they acquire these general skills, we refer to them as being under *instructional control* (e.g., Baer, Rowbury, & Baer, 1973; Etzel & LeBlanc, 1979; Schutte & Hopkins, 1970).

Massed Trials

This format consists of the rapid repetition of trials with a brief latency interposed (i.e., anywhere from 0 to 8 seconds between trials; see Bambara & Warren, 1993). For example, if a student is learning to hand a symbol card to a social partner to reject a proffered item, the teacher would present non-preferred items in rapid succession using discrete trials and prompt the student to hand her the card during each presentation. When the student hands the card to the teacher, she immediately removes the item, representing learning trials mediated by negative reinforcement. The massed trial format was originally developed to demonstrate that students with severe disabilities who received sufficient instructional trials could learn and thus acquire new skills (Guess & Helmstetter, 1986). Massed trials have been associated with nonfunctional curriculum (e.g., Neel & Billingsley, 1989) and with artificial training conditions that may interfere with generalization (e.g., Koegel & Rincover, 1977; Stokes & Baer, 1977). Discrete trials can be, and often are, combined with massed trials when they are repeated in a rapid fashion.

Distributed, Naturalistic, and Embedded Trials

Distributed trials refer to inserting a delay between each trial so that trials are spread out over time. Naturalistic or embedded trials refer to trials occurring at a time and place when and where the behavior matches the context without "breaking the flow of the routine or the ongoing activity" (Schepis, Reid, Ownbey, & Parsons, 2001, p. 314). The essence of distributed trials is that they are interspersed among other instructional opportunities so that they do not occur in rapid succession (Bambara & Warren, 1993) and the essence of embedded trials is the correspondence between the content of the trial and its meaning or validity within the normal daily routine (Schepis et al., 2001; Snell, 2007; Venn et al., 1993). Distributed and embedded trials have been associated with better student engagement (e.g., Dunlap, 1984) and with generalization of the new skill (e.g., Losardo & Bricker, 1994; Kaiser, Yoder, & Keetz, 1992). More recently, instructional formats that consist of embedded trials have come to be known as activity-based instruction or naturalistic instruction (Bricker & Cripe, 1992; Pretti-Frontczak, & Bricker, 2004; Rule, Losardo, Dinnebeil, Kaiser, & Rowland, 1998; Snell, 2007).

Summary and Recommendations for Practice

Research has created evidence that teachers can use to guide decisions for selecting the trial or combination of trials for instruction of students with severe disabilities. Discrete, massed, and distributed-naturalistic-embedded trials can produce acquisition of a new skill (e.g., Polychronis, McDonnell, Johnson, Rieson, & Jameson, 2004). Distributed and embedded trials tend to produce better generalization and maintenance (e.g., Losardo & Bricker, 1994). But selecting the type of trial is not an "either-or" process, but rather one in which the teacher selects a type of trial or a combination of types that she then consistently implements to achieve the outcome specified in the student's objective. Revisions to instruction are based on measures of student performance. We next discuss some factors and recommendations that may help guide teachers when they are selecting trials to begin instruction.

One factor that may affect rates of acquisition is the student's motivation to produce the response (Kennedy, Halle, & Drasgow, 2005). For example, a student may be motivated to produce the response of going through the lunch line during an embedded trial because that behavior produces a lunch. If the teacher decides to use a massed trial approach and have the student go through the lunch line several times, then the student may lose his motivation to respond because getting lunch is no longer motivating after the second time through the line. Similarly, if a teacher is using massed trials to teach a student expressive vocabulary skills, then after five or ten trials, "good job" may not be very motivating for the student, if it ever was. This situation is a reminder that if teacher consequences are to have their intended effect on student learning, they need to be tested and validated as reinforcers relative to the behavior expected. Thus, if a teacher is using a massed-trial approach, then she must consider how many trials she could present before the student is no longer motivated to respond; this phenomenon is referred to as satiation and it will increase gradually or incrementally as more student effort is expended for the same reinforcer. A potential solution is to offer a menu of potential consequences from which the student can choose the one that is at highest potency at that moment. Teachers must be cautious when using artificial motivators (e.g., consequences that are not naturally available and functionally related to the behavior) because they may interfere with generalization to natural settings and routines (Carr & Lindquist, 1987; Koegel, Egel, & Dunlap, 1980).

One way to combine trial types is to collect data on student performance during a task analysis and analyze the rate of acquisition for each step. For example, suppose there are twelve steps in the task analysis for our student to go through the lunch line. Perhaps the student is making progress on several of the steps during the embedded trial at lunchtime, but is not making progress on one or two steps. The teacher could provide extra practice on these two steps in the classroom by using a massed-trial approach (e.g., Snell & Browder, 1986), but her criterion for success would be measured by the student's performance in the cafeteria when going through the line and not by performance in the classroom during practice. Thus, one way to use massed trials in combination with embedded trials for behavior that consists of several steps is to provide additional training on those steps that have a slower rate of acquisition, but meaningful assessment for those steps would occur in the natural environment when they are part of the chained behavior.

A teacher also can use a combined-trial approach to teach skills that are not amenable to task analysis. For example, when teaching a student to greet by raising his hand and waving to a social partner, the teacher may begin by having the student practice the movement with her in a massed-trial format (Bambara & Warren, 1993). After the behavior is established, the teacher may then move the instruction to an embedded-trial format in the natural environment to foster generalization by establishing the behavior in the presence of natural antecedents (e.g., encountering a peer who enters the classroom in the morning). Thus, a teacher may combine massed trials and embedded trials (a) when the student could benefit from additional practice beyond that available naturally and (b) when instruction in the natural environment may be stigmatizing to the student or disruptive to the social context (e.g., a teacher interrupts by prompting a seventh grader to share during an interaction with a peer).

Selecting Instructional Procedures: Practices

The emphasis in the evidence-based practice movement is on effectiveness, or whether students learned when the practice was used. Clearly, such an emphasis is appropriate; no justification exists for using ineffective instructional practices. However, a fair question is, "On what additional dimensions should we judge and select instructional practices?" Or stated another way, given that systematic instruction is effective, are there dimensions on which we should select different systematic instructional procedures? Potential options include parsimony, practicality, cost, restrictiveness-intrusiveness, match to learner abilities and response patterns, and efficiency. Although this section focuses primarily on efficiency, the other dimensions are mentioned initially for context.

Common Considerations

Etzel and LeBlanc (1979) suggested that all things being equal (e.g., effectiveness) the more *parsimonious* or simpler procedure should be used when selecting instructional practices. Logic suggests parsimonious practices may be used more accurately, may require less effort on the teachers' part, and may reduce the complexity of teachers' tasks in delivering instruction. The parsimony of practices can be evaluated by examining the number and complexity of the decisions and actions teachers must make when using a practice. For example, the constant and progressive time delay procedures are both systematic instructional practices. However, the constant time delay procedure would be considered more parsimonious than progressive time delay, because the constant time delay procedure only uses two types of trials (i.e., zero-second trials, and delay trials), and the progressive time delay procedure requires several shifts in the response interval during the delay trials.

Closely related to parsimony is the dimension of *practicality.* Practicality can be evaluated objectively at the gross level; if a procedure requires additional personnel or equipment, then it may be less practical. However, for the most part, practicality is in the eye of the beholder, and innovations (e.g., inclusion, embedded instruction, ongoing progress monitoring) are often seen as impractical. Thus, practicality may be a poor dimension on which to judge the suitability of a given practice.

Another dimension for judging instructional practices is *cost*. Cost can be estimated in the effort expended by teachers, but this is more appropriately addressed under the parsimony dimension. The more usual issue with cost is the financial outlay required. While cost may not be an allowable justification (e.g., in IEP placement decisions), it may be relevant when selecting practices. When all things (e.g., effectiveness, parsimony) are equal, the lesser or least expensive option seems desirable, given the limited fiscal resources of most schools and programs. For example, small group instruction, when effective (Ledford, Gast, Luscre, & Ayres, 2008), may be less costly than one-to-one instruction. Small group instruction allows teachers to teach more students at the same time without necessarily producing decrements in students' learning (Kamps, Walker, Maher, & Rotholz, 1992).

Two other widely recognized dimensions on which practices are judged and selected are their *restrictiveness* and *intrusiveness*. Restrictiveness refers to the extent to which a practice limits the learner's behaviors and freedom; intrusiveness refers to the extent to which a practice impinges upon the learner's body or space (Wolery et al., 1992). A long-standing guideline, originating from the normalization principle, is to use the least restrictive and least intrusive, effective practice available (Keith, 1979). Using the least restrictive and least intrusive practice often is applied to the selection of behavior-reduction procedures (Sugai & Horner, 2008), and appropriately so, but these dimensions have application to instruction as well. For example, given the power of student choice (Kern et al., 1996), incorporating student choice into many instructional programs is warranted. When used, it reduces the restrictiveness of the context on the student's behavior. Intrusiveness also is applicable to the selection of instructional practices. For example, when both a model and physical prompt are controlling (i.e., result in correct responding), using a model often is justified because it does not intrude on the student's body as a physical prompt does.

Matching instruction to students' abilities and response patterns is another dimension on which instructional practices can be judged and selected. "Student abilities," as used here, refers to the prerequisite skills needed to benefit from a given systematic instructional practice. For example, video modeling in various forms can be quite effective in teaching students new behaviors and the application of existing behaviors (e.g., Haring, Kennedy, Adams, & Pitts-Conway, 1987; Reeve, Reeve, Townsend, & Poulson, 2007). To learn new skills or learn when to use existing skills by watching a video, learners must be imitative, attend to the video, have the capability of engaging in the modeled behavior, retain the model until it can be performed, and be motivated to enact the modeled behavior in another context (Bandura, 1977). Video modeling is less likely to be effective when students do not have these skills. Thus, students' prerequisite abilities and the skills needed to learn from given instructional procedures are important considerations when making decisions about selecting practices. Student characteristics other than prerequisite skills also should be considered. For example, some students attempt to avoid being touched. Such response patterns would argue against using physical prompts if some other forms of prompt (e.g., visual, model) will result in correct responding.

Instructional Efficiency

Another critical dimension for judging and selecting practices is *instructional efficiency*. The efficiency of instruction has been conceptualized in a number of different ways (Wolery et al., 1992); however, efficiency has two defining elements. First, to be efficient a procedure must be effective; an ineffective procedure (i.e., students do not learn) cannot be described logically and accurately as efficient. Second, efficiency implies that a procedure results in superior outcomes to another procedure or exceeds some specified standard of learning. At issue is how superiority is operationalized and measured. The most frequently used conceptualization of efficiency is the *rapidity of learning* (Wolery, in press). In general, rapidity of learning is evaluated by establishing a given criterion, and determining whether one instructional procedure results in achieving criterion level responding more quickly than another. Rapidity often is determined by the number of minutes of instruction, sessions, or trials required of each procedure to establish criterion level performance. For example, the time delay procedures tend to be more efficient (i.e., take fewer minutes, sessions, and trials of instruction) than does the system of least prompts (i.e., increasing assistance) for both discrete and chained tasks (Ault, Wolery, Gast, Doyle, & Eizenstat, 1988; Ault, Gast, & Wolery, 1988; Doyle, Wolery, Gast, Ault, & Wiley, 1990; Wolery, Ault, Gast, Doyle, & Griffen, 1990). The fundamental assumption is that if a procedure saves instructional time (e.g., sessions, trials), then more behaviors can be taught to students in a year's time. Assuming efficient procedures were used throughout students' education, the outcomes upon graduation or school departure for the students are increased competence, increased adaptive skills, and greater likelihood of success as adults.

The rapidity of learning, however, often focuses primarily on acquisition of targeted skills. As mentioned previously, learning encompasses fluency, maintenance, and generalization of acquired behaviors. Thus, instructional efficiency must be conceptualized to accommodate these important phases of learning. If one procedure results in greater fluency, maintenance, or generalization across persons, materials, or settings than another, the former should be considered more efficient. For example, when planning to teach two behaviors to a student, both should be taught simultaneously as compared to teaching one to criterion, and then teaching the second to criterion, and then putting them together (Doyle, Wolery, Ault, Gast, & Wiley, 1989; Panyan & Hall, 1978; Schroeder & Baer, 1972). Teaching each behavior separately does not result in generalization to situations when students are presented with more than one stimulus in the same session. Teaching two or more behaviors simultaneously generally results in greater conditional discriminations.

A similar example is possible with maintenance. It is possible that focusing solely on the rapidity of acquisition could sacrifice other aspects of learning. For example, maintenance of acquired responses is promoted by over-learning and by using intermittent reinforcement. If the criterion was set at three consecutive sessions at 100% responding on a continuous reinforcement schedule (CRF), skills might reach criterion level responding more rapidly than if we set the criterion at three consecutive sessions of 100% responding on CRF and three sessions at 100% responding when the average of every third response was reinforced (VR3). However, over the long run, the longer (i.e., slower) criterion of 3 sessions at 100% with CRF, and 3 at 100% with VR3 would likely result in greater maintenance of the targeted skills. Thus, maintenance and generalization of acquired skills must be considered when evaluating instructional efficiency.

When conceptualizing instructional efficiency by the rapidity of learning or the degree of maintenance and generalization, emphasis is primarily on the instructional practices. Other ways of thinking about instructional efficiency focus on the content of the curriculum; that is, the "what is taught" part of the curriculum. One way of organizing instruction to promote more efficient learning is to manipulate current instruction so it impacts *future learning*. This organization can occur in a couple ways. When students need to learn a large number of similar behaviors, we often divide them into sets of behaviors. For example, if students needed to learn to read 40 functional words, we might teach them 4 words at a time. Considerable research suggests that teaching those sets of words with the same systematic instructional procedure will result in subsequent sets being learned more quickly than the first or second set (Godby, Gast, & Wolery, 1987; Harlow, 1949). This phenomenon has been called "learning sets" or "learning to learn." Thus, teachers should use the same instructional practice over time when teaching similar behaviors.

A second variation of teaching for the future is to embed behaviors to be taught later into current teaching. A procedure called *instructive feedback* has been used for this purpose. This procedure involves adding extra, non-target stimuli to praise statements during direct instruction and not asking students to respond to those stimuli nor reinforcing them if they do. Examples of standard and instructive feedback trials are shown in Table 39.2. The instruction for the target behavior, in this case reading the word "exit," is identical across trials. The only difference in the instructive feedback trial is the student is shown another stimulus, in this case the word "pull," and is told, "This word is 'pull'." The student is not expected to respond to "pull"; rather, it is simply presented in the context of the reinforcement for

TABLE 39.2
Examples of a Standard and Instructive Feedback Trial

Instructional Goal: Students orally will read 2 functional words ("exit" and "entrance") with 100% accuracy for three sessions using a CRF schedule and 100% accuracy for three sessions using a VR3 schedule of reinforcement.
Instructive Feedback Stimuli: The words, "push" and "pull"

Antecedent	Behavior	Consequences
Standard Trial		
Teacher secures attention, presents target stimulus (i.e., word is "exit"), and presents a task direction (e.g., "Read this word.")	Student says "exit" or is prompted with a verbal model to say "exit."	Deliver reinforcement, and a 2- to 5-second inter-trial interval
Instructive Feedback Trial		
Teacher secures attention, presents target stimulus (i.e., word is "exit"), and presents a task direction (e.g., "Read this word.")	Student says "exit" or is prompted with a verbal model to say "exit."	Deliver reinforcement, present the instructive feedback stimulus (i.e., Show the word "pull" and say, "This is 'pull'."), and a 2- to 5-second inter-trial interval

reading the target word (i.e., "exit"). In instructive feedback studies, students' performance on the instructive feedback stimuli is assessed prior to beginning instruction on the target stimuli, and is assessed again after students acquire the target behaviors (Werts, Wolery, Holcombe, & Gast, 1995). When instructive feedback is used, students acquire the responses to a majority, if not all of the stimuli shown in the consequent events of trials through instructive feedback (Werts et al., 1995).

To increase the efficiency of instruction by manipulating current instruction in hopes of impacting future learning, Wolery, Doyle, Ault, Gast, Meyer, and Stinson (1991) taught one set of behaviors with progressive time delay and showed another behavior set through instructive feedback. They also taught another behavior set with progressive time delay but without instructive feedback. When students acquired the two sets being taught directly (i.e., one with and one without instructive feedback), then two additional sets of behavior were taught. One set was the stimuli that had been shown through the instructive feedback, and the second was an equally difficult behavior set that had not been shown. When the number of sessions, trials, and minutes of instruction were compared, those presented through instructive feedback, and then taught later, were learned more rapidly than those that had not been shown through instructive feedback. Thus, manipulating current instruction by presenting future target stimuli through instructive feedback substantially increases the overall rapidity of learning. This finding has since been replicated twice. Once when instructive feedback was used (Holcombe, Wolery, Werts, & Hrenkevich, 1993), and once when instructive feedback was used and when extra stimuli also were inserted into the antecedent portion of the trial (T. Wolery, Schuster, & Collins, 2000).

Undoubtedly, other methods exist for manipulating current systematic instruction in ways that impact later learning. For example, Reichow (2008) directly taught a boy with autism to name selected two-digit numerals (i.e., 25, 34) and showed other similar numerals (i.e., 26, 32) through instructive feedback. Unintentionally, the stimuli allowed the student to deduce a rule for responding even to other similar numerals (e.g., 28, 39) that had not been taught directly or shown through instructive feedback. The rule could be articulated as follows, "Say twenty for two and thirty for three and then name the second numeral"; 28 was named "twenty eight" and 39 was named "thirty nine." This unintentional structuring of what was taught allowed this student to apply a rule to respond to untaught stimuli. This structuring of current instruction, made future instruction unnecessary. With other students such structuring may not result in more efficient instruction; however, it is possible that making the rule explicit would impact future learning. Rules could be stated before trials are delivered or could be presented in the praise statements as instructive feedback.

Another way to conceptualize efficiency dealing with the organization of what is taught is promoting the emergence of *untrained relations*. The most obvious example of this is in establishing stimulus equivalence. For example, when students learn the numeral "3" means the same as three objects, and then learn the written word "three" means the same as the numeral "3," it is often unnecessary to teach them that the word "three" means the same as three objects. The fact that "three" represents three objects is the untrained relation. It is acquired "for free" without additional instruction. A rich history exists of studying stimulus equivalence in experimental laboratories (Sidman & Tailby, 1982). Fewer examples exist documenting its utility in every-day instruction; for an exception, see Taylor and O'Reilly (2000). To make the implications of this research a reality, the content of the curriculum must be organized to take advantage of naturally occurring equivalent relations (e.g., specific numerals equal specific amounts, specific number words equal specific amounts, and those numerals equal those number words). Another example of the emergence of untrained relations is when students can neither name a set of objects (i.e., expressive), nor can they point to those objects when the teacher names them (i.e., receptive). If students are taught to name them expressively, they often will be able to identify them receptively, which is an untrained relationship (Alig-Cybriwsky, Wolery, & Gast, 1990), although this does not always occur (Guess & Baer, 1973). The reverse is not necessarily true; if students are taught receptively they may not name those stimuli when asked to do so, although some may (Patterson, 2010).

Another conceptualization of efficiency that also involves manipulating the content of the instruction is called, the *breadth of learning*. This manipulation involves teaching to allow the students to learn more behaviors in the same amount of instruction. If one practice could increase the number of behaviors learned over another practice, but both were used for the same number of sessions, then the first practice would be considered more efficient. An example comes from the instructive feedback literature. Reichow and Wolery (in press) compared teaching with and without instructive feedback (see Table 39.2). For each student, four sets of behavior were initially assessed. Each student was taught two sets of behavior in separate daily sessions, and one of those behavior sets had a third set shown through instructive feedback. After students acquired the two behavior sets being taught directly, they were assessed again on all four sets. The students performed at 100% accuracy for the two sets taught directly as well as the set shown through instructive feedback. The fourth set that had not been taught or shown through instructive feedback was at 0% correct. Thus, in the same amount of instruction children learned twice as many behaviors when instructive feedback was used.

Another example of achieving more learning in the same amount of instruction involves carefully selecting intermediate prompt levels when the system of least prompts is delivered. For example, Doyle, Gast, Wolery, Ault, and Meyer (1992) taught students to read words for the names of foods on restaurant menus. At the first prompt level, they were told whether the food cost more or less than a given amount. At the second prompt level, they were told whether the food was eaten for breakfast or lunch. At the final and controlling prompt level, a verbal model of the food word was stated. The students acquired the words from the restaurant menus, and they learned to classify those words by whether it was more or less than a given cost and by which meal it was typically eaten. Thus, they learned to classify the behaviors in two ways simply by inserting those statements into the prompt levels of the teaching procedure.

Another way to increase the breath of learning is to manipulate how small group instruction is arranged. In traditional small group instruction, particularly that typical of Direct Instruction (Englemann & Bruner, 1974), all members of the group are taught the same behaviors and choral responding is used. While this arrangement results in effective instruction, small group instruction can be structured in other ways. For example, each student can be taught different behaviors and respond individually when it is their turn (Collins, Gast, Ault, & Wolery, 1991). When small groups are organized in this way, students often acquire the behaviors they are taught directly as well as several behaviors taught to their group mates (Farmer, Gast, Wolery, & Winterling, 1991). Further, when the group is larger, not all children need to be taught directly. Some children will learn what is taught directly to their group mates while they only sit and watch and are not themselves taught directly (Shelton, Gast, Wolery, & Winterling, 1991). While comparisons of choral responding to individual responding are difficult, the amount of learning appears to be related to the amount of exposure (Wolery, Ault, Doyle, Gast, & Griffen, 1992).

To make individual responding even more efficient, instructive feedback can be used in individually-based small group instruction. Thus, each group member has different target behaviors and a different instructive feedback stimulus shown for each target behavior. When this arrangement is used, students tend to learn (a) their own target behaviors, (b) their own instructive feedback behaviors, (c) some of their peers' target behaviors, and (d) some of their peers' instructive feedback behaviors (Ledford et al., 2008; Wolery, Cybriwsky, Gast, & Boyle-Gast, 1991). Such instructional arrangements, however, require students to learn observationally; that is, to acquire behaviors by watching and listening to the behavior of their peers. We would not expect such findings to occur when students do not have generalized imitation skills, but when they have such skills, the efficiency of instruction might be increased substantially.

Summary

Instructional practices, including those used in systematic instruction, should be selected for their effectiveness and only effective procedures should be used. Fortunately, as described in the first part of this chapter, a number of effective systematic instructional practices have been identified. Teachers, however, should use additional qualities of effective instructional practices when deciding which ones to use. These qualities include the parsimony or the simplicity of the practice, its practicality, its cost, the degree of restrictiveness and intrusiveness of the practice, the match of the practice to the learner's existing behavioral repertoire and response patterns, and the procedure's efficiency.

Instructional efficiency can be conceptualized in many different ways. Two critical conceptualizations focus on how rapidly it results in learning (i.e., acquisition), and the extent to which it promotes generalization and maintenance of the acquired skills. Instructional efficiency also can focus on manipulating what is taught to students. Increasing instructional efficiency can be done by manipulating current instruction to impact future learning, organizing the curriculum to allow untrained relations to emerge, and teaching in ways that student can learn more behaviors while being directly taught a smaller subset of behaviors.

Using SI to Teach Classes of Responding: Moving Beyond Specific Behaviors

Many years ago at a professional conference attended by the second author, the keynote address was given by a Dr. Brown who was both deaf and blind. After the address, he took questions from the audience. The most memorable, and perhaps most insensitive question ever asked, was, "Would you rather be deaf or blind?" The question was finger spelled into the speaker's hand, and with an incredibly short latency he said, "When I am talking with my friends, I would rather be blind; and when they are telling me about a beautiful sunset, I would rather be deaf." What was striking was of all the things he could have said (e.g., when I need to go to the store, when I am shaving, when I am fixing a meal, when I go to a concert, when I am searching for a lost article, when someone wants my attention) he selected, "When I am talking with my friends."

This anecdote suggests that some of the important skills to teach to our students with significant disabilities involve ways of interacting with the environment, both social and physical dimensions, beyond simple discrete responses (e.g., naming objects) and even complex response chains (e.g., taking a bath, eating a meal, fixing a flat bicycle tire). Examples of these response patterns involve carrying on conversations with others, engaging in pretend play, answering specific types of questions (e.g., "wh" questions) in the context of book reading, imitating others, and sharing objects with others. When carrying on conversations, the behaviors involved are not what to say precisely; rather, saying something when the conversational partner has completed a statement and matching what is said to the partner's previous statement, waiting for the partner to take a turn, and then taking another turn. When engaging in pretend play, the goal is not to teach specific actions with specific objects (toys); rather, the goal is to use the objects in ways that are indicative of pretense. When answering "wh-questions" in the context of book reading, we do not want children to give specific answers to previously taught questions; rather, we want them to recognize that "who" refers to a character in the book and the response to the "who-question" should name that person. Or "where" asks about location, but not a given and previously trained location; rather, the location referred to in the recent words of the text. Similarly, generalized imitation is not about being able to perform behaviors that were taught when learning to imitate, but to match one's own behavior to that of another when and whenever this seems appropriate. Sharing is not just about giving specific materials, but recognizing and giving an object to a peer when the peer has need of the object and the giver has possession of those objects. Many other examples could be proposed.

If these and other similar response patterns are defensible outcomes for students with significant disabilities, several questions arise. Examples are: Are these behaviors developmental phenomena that cannot be taught or are they teachable behaviors? Are these simply instances of stimulus or response generalization? Is teaching such patterns different from teaching discrete or chained responses? Can systematic instructional procedures be used to teach these behaviors? How should instruction for such patterns of behaving be organized? While the answers to these and related questions are not fully known, it is clear some of these patterns of behavior can be taught. Further, the systematic instructional strategies that have been used with dozens of discrete and chained responses (Wolery & Schuster, 1997) are applicable for teaching these more complex response patterns. This point is illustrated by describing three studies.

The first study focuses on teaching preschool children with disabilities to engage in conversations with their peers during play (Filla, Wolery, & Anthony, 1999). Three triads of children were selected; each triad included one child with disabilities and two typically developing children. They were taken to an area of their inclusive classroom, and given a choice of two theme boxes. The theme boxes had different toys and props promoting a theme such as a picnic. During baseline, they were allowed to play with the materials they had selected. Event recording was used to measure whether the child with disabilities initiated a conversation to his or her peers, whether they responded, whether they initiated to him or her, whether he or she responded, and how many turns occurred in each conversation. After the baseline data were established, the teacher implemented the instructional intervention, which was the system of least prompts. After they chose a theme box for the day, she told them, "Remember to talk with your friends while you play." She then waited for 30 to 60 seconds. If a conversation occurred, she re-set the time and waited another 30 to 60 seconds. If no conversation had occurred, she repeated the general prompt again (i.e., "Talk with your friends while you play.") and waited about 10 more seconds. If no conversation occurred, she delivered a direct prompt to one of the children (e.g., "[Child's name] talk to [another child's name].") and waited about 10 more seconds. If no conversation occurred, she modeled a statement for the child to whom she had delivered the direct prompt (e.g., "[Child's name] say, [said something related to the play]."). In keeping with the system of least prompts, if a conversation occurred at any level, then the teacher stopped prompting and waited 30 to 60 seconds for another conversation. This procedure produced two findings across triads: (a) their rate of unprompted talking increased, and (b) the average number of turns per conversation increased. This study suggests a straightforward, systematic instruction procedure, namely the system of least prompts, could be used to teach children to carry on more and longer conversations with their peers while they played with toys in their inclusive classroom.

The second study focuses on peer imitation (Venn et al., 1993). Three children with disabilities who could imitate adults but who did not imitate peers were selected to participate. Instruction was conducted in an art activity in an inclusive classroom. Art was chosen because a wide variety of behaviors could be performed with the materials being used; specifically, the materials did not afford specific or a limited number of behaviors. For example, playdoh can be rolled out flat like a pancake, rolled into strings, hammered, pinched, cut, rolled into balls; the materials did not dictate precise behaviors. After baseline, the teacher used progressive time delay to teach the children to imitate the actions of their peers. A trial occurred as follows, when it was convenient for the teacher, she said to the child with disabilities, "See what (peer's name) is doing, you do it." She then delivered physical prompts to assist the child in doing the behavior modeled by the peer and reinforced the child for doing it after the prompting was done. Over sessions, the prompts were delayed to 2 seconds, then to 4 seconds. Imitations occurring before the prompt were reinforced but were not prompted. In a multiple baseline across participants, all three children learned to imitate their peers without needing prompts to do so, and there was some indication they generalized the imitation to other activities.

A recent replication (English, 2010) of the Venn et al. (1993) study used a slightly different and better verbal cue, "(Child's name) see what (peer's name) is doing." She did not add the command, "You do it." As in the Venn et al. study, the children learned to imitate their peers, and evidence of generalization of peer imitation was more carefully and thoroughly measured and obtained. In both studies, repeated trials on specific behaviors were not used. Rather a small number of trials (5 in Venn et al., 8 in English) were embedded into ongoing activities in inclusive classrooms. The modeled behaviors were simply whatever behavior peers were doing with the materials and they varied from trial to trial within and across sessions. The peers were not specifically trained to engage in any specific behaviors. These studies suggest that systematic instruction can be used to teach a highly generalized response pattern of watching what a peer is doing and then imitating that behavior.

The third study focuses on teaching children to engage in pretending behaviors while they are playing (Barton &

Wolery, in press). Teachers of children with disabilities were taught through brief didactic training sessions, video models, and role playing to use contingent imitation of children's play and the system of least prompts. They used these strategies to promote pretending behavior in 8-minute sessions during free play. Four types of pretending behaviors (Barton & Wolery, 2008) were taught: functional movements with pretending, object substitution, imagining absent objects, and assigning absent attributes. Teachers were given feedback daily on their use of the system of least prompts, examples of correct use, and examples of missed opportunities. In a multiple probe design across sets of toys, the children with disabilities learned to engage in the different types of pretending behaviors and to do so without prompting. In addition, they demonstrated generalization across adults in these pretending behaviors when with another adult who never prompted them.

From these examples, three findings are apparent. First, systematic instructional strategies (i.e., system of least prompts and progressive time delay) were effective in teaching children with disabilities to engage in the targeted response patterns of conversations with peers, imitating their peers' behavior, and using pretending behaviors in their play. Second, this instruction was not unique to the context in which it was taught; the response patterns generalized to other contexts. Third, each of these studies involved classroom teachers rather than research staff doing the instruction. The findings from these studies begin to build the case that systematic instruction can move beyond teaching specific behaviors to teaching a pattern of interacting with the environment that calls for a variety of behaviors which are contextually determined. Thus, these studies suggest systematic instruction should not be reserved only for highly specified and defined behaviors (e.g., naming objects, matching pictures, reading words, greeting others, dressing, undressing, using utensils, making sandwiches, putting on a coat); rather systematic instruction can be used to teach highly useful patterns of responding when the target stimuli are more diffuse and the responses are not pre-programmed. Thus, it is a hopeful sign that many of the critical response patterns students need to function well within their environments are within the reach of existing instructional technology.

General-Case Instruction: A Unique Example of Systematic Instruction

Generalization of newly acquired skills has been a highly elusive goal for students with severe disabilities (e.g., Drasgow, Halle, & Ostrosky, 1998; Duker, Didden, & Sigafoos, 2004; Sigafoos, Arthur-Kelly, & Butterfield, 2006). A promising approach that embraces SI to promote skill generalization is referred to as general-case instruction (GCI). GCI is a teaching strategy with roots in Direct Instruction (Becker & Engelmann, 1978; Becker, Engelmann, & Thomas, 1975; Engelmann & Carnine, 1982) that was extended to students with severe disabilities by Horner and his colleagues (Albin & Horner, 1988; Horner, Bellamy, & Colvin, 1984; Horner, McDonnell, & Bellamy, 1986; Horner, Sprague, & Wilcox, 1982). GCI involves identifying an instructional universe, selecting examples that sample the range of possible contextual variation within the universe, and then teaching a response in the presence of this sampled range. It is eminently systematic and encompasses the five steps of SI mentioned at the beginning of the chapter.

GCI has been used to teach behaviors such as street crossing (Horner, Jones, & Williams, 1985), vending machine use (Sprague & Horner, 1984), dressing (Day & Horner, 1986), telephone use (Horner, Williams, & Stevely, 1987), and fast food restaurant ordering (Steere, Strauch, Powell, & Butterworth, 1990). GCI also has been applied to establishing and enhancing communication skills, in theory (Chadsey-Rusch & Halle, 1992; Halle, Chadsey-Rusch, & Collet-Klingenberg, 1993; O'Neill, 1990) and in practice (Chadsey-Rusch, Drasgow, Reinoehl, Halle, & Collet-Klingenberg, 1993; Drasgow & Halle, 1995; Kashinath et al. 2006). The process of teaching the general case includes the following series of steps (Engelmann & Carnine, 1982; Horner, Sprague, & Wilcox, 1982): (a) define the instructional universe; (b) define the range of relevant contextual variation in the universe; (c) select examples for teaching and testing from the instructional universe; (d) sequence the teaching examples; (e) teach the examples; (f) test for generalization with non-trained probe examples.

The first step is an important one in an SI approach to achieving generalization as an outcome of instruction. The instructional universe refers to defining the contextual conditions under which the target response is expected to occur. Consider, for example, teaching a greeting response. Determining when, where, and to whom this response should occur will provide the scope of the instructional universe. Is the greeting expected to occur only at school? If so, then only the school setting would be included in the teaching examples. If greetings are expected to occur in a wider variety of contexts, then those contexts must fall within the purview of the instructional universe.

The second step consists of defining relevant contextual variation. Relevant contextual variation refers to the range of discriminative stimuli, or antecedents, that should occasion a response (Skinner, 1938). These discriminative stimuli form a stimulus class (i.e., any group of stimuli that share a common set of stimulus characteristics), yet may vary in ways that should not affect responding. For example, to continue with our greeting example, seeing another person for the first time during the day would be a discriminative stimulus. Irrelevant variations might include the height or gender of the person. However, the discriminative stimuli for greeting are complex and may also include familiarity, proximity, posture, facial expression and so on. The purpose of GCI is to teach a student which stimulus characteristics are relevant for determining when to respond. The student has learned the general case when any member from a stimulus class produces the same response as the single discriminative stimulus (Horner, Sprague, & Wilcox, 1982), and responding should not be affected by irrelevant stimulus variations.

The essential concept of general-case instruction is that teaching with enough powerful representative examples will result in correct responding to the universe of situations represented by those examples. Hupp and Mervis (1981) suggest that teaching with three good exemplars (i.e., three examples that best represent a class or category) will increase the probability of stimulus generalization. GCI, however, would not suggest any particular number of exemplars, rather representing the relevant stimulus variation would be the criterion for selecting the appropriate number of exemplars. That is, the exemplars that are selected must capture aspects of a situation that are crucial for a student to attend to in responding, and the student should not be distracted by additional consistent but irrelevant stimuli.

After specifying the instructional universe and selecting teaching examples, the examples are sequenced and taught. Sequencing involves enhancing instructional efficiency by, for example, scheduling multiple opportunities for responding within an instructional session and alternating opportunities to respond between introducing new examples and reviewing old examples. Generalization is evaluated by examining the learner's behavior on untaught examples. A student's performance during generalization assessment is then analyzed to determine any pattern of errors (Horner et al., 1984). By monitoring progress on these untaught examples, we are informed about the success of the instruction or the need to modify it. This information then leads to revisions in instruction. For example, a student may greet a person who is not looking at them or oriented toward them. This pattern of errors reveals that the student is not discriminating a relevant aspect of a greeting: a social partner's attention. Further instruction would include discriminating (i.e., initiate a greeting when social partner is attending and withhold initiation when partner is distracted and not attending) the contextual variable of attention as a cue for a student to initiate a greeting.

Consider the following example that illustrates how an irrelevant, but consistent, stimulus might come to control a response. Suppose a teacher is instructing a high-school-aged student to cross streets (see, for example, Horner, Jones, & Williams, 1985). The teacher defines the instructional universe as the student's community and thus street-crossing examples included in instruction consist of 2-way streets with a stop sign, 4-way intersections with stop signs, and 4-way intersections with a stop light. The teacher proceeds with instruction and the student appears to have acquired the skill (i.e., learned the general-case). During assessment, however, the teacher notices that every time before the student crosses a street, he looks down. Further assessment reveals that in fact the student is not attending to the relevant stimuli of cars, streets, stops signs, and lights, but rather is attending to the teacher's feet. Analysis of this behavior reveals that despite the teacher's efforts to highlight important stimuli for street crossing, a consistent but *irrelevant* stimulus that occurred every time during street crossing was that right before starting across the street, the teacher would step down from the curb. Thus, because of this consistency, the student had inadvertently learned to attend to this feature (i.e., the teacher's feet) of the context. The teacher subsequently revised her instruction to be sure that her stepping down from the curb did not occur before the student began to cross the street. GCI has the potential to increase generalization as an outcome of SI. Further research should explore methods of implementing GCI in embedded formats.

Summary

The technology of SI forms the evidence-base for educating students with severe disabilities and is based on applied behavior analysis (i.e., principles of behavior such as reinforcement) and driven by improving the quality of life for students with severe disabilities. Research validating SI continues to support its effectiveness and expand its application. We have endeavored to extend a discussion of systematic instruction for students with severe disabilities by examining the inextricable relationship between SI and applied behavior analysis and by elaborating four unique directions for future investigation. The first of these is the variation in learning presentation formats or instructional trials. Over the last 30 years, researchers have investigated discrete, massed, distributed, naturalistic, and embedded trials. Although definitional ambiguity exists, we attempted to identify some situations in which one or another (or concurrent implementation) of these types of trials is most appropriate. Second, with the proliferation of practices demonstrated to be effective (i.e., evidence-based), determining how to select a practice among multiple options has become a challenge. We recommend invoking efficiency criteria to facilitate this selection and to insure that the selection is based on objective measures. Third, the SI literature is replete with demonstrations of teaching discrete and chained behaviors; however, we have neglected teaching general classes of behavior. We provide direction, by example, of how SI might be applied to this challenging, but critical, goal for students with severe disabilities. Finally, we reviewed and explored an SI strategy with tremendous potential for influencing generalization of newly acquired behavior as a valued outcome. General-case instruction was first elaborated almost 30 years ago, but it has gained little traction in our literature or practice. Because we believe it can be applied readily and widely, we "re-introduced" it here to challenge researchers and practitioners to sample its potential applications. Our goal in writing this chapter was to encourage future researchers and practitioners to continue to expand the application of SI to the multiplicity of features related to improving the quality of life for students with severe disabilities.

References

Alberto, P. A., & Troutman, A. C. (2009). *Applied behavior analysis for teachers* (8th ed.). Upper Saddle River, NJ: Merrill.

Albin, R. W., & Horner, R. H. (1988). Generalization with precision. In R. H. Horner, G. Dunlap, & R. L. Koegel (Eds.), *Generalization and maintenance: Life-style changes in applied settings* (pp. 99–120). Baltimore, MD: Brookes.

Alig-Cybriwsky, C. A., Wolery, M., & Gast, D. L. (1990). Use of a constant time delay procedure in teaching preschoolers in a group format. *Journal of Early Intervention, 14,* 99–116.

American Association on Mental Retardation. (2002). *Mental retardation: Definition, classification, and systems of supports* (10th ed.). Washington, DC: Author.

Ault, M. J., Gast, D. L., & Wolery, M. (1988). Comparison of progressive and constant time delay procedures in teaching community-sign word reading. *American Journal of Mental Retardation, 93,* 44–56.

Ault, M. J., Wolery, M., Gast, D. L., Doyle, P. M., & Eizenstat, V. (1988). Comparison of response prompting procedures in teaching numeral identification to autistic subjects. *Journal of Autism and Developmental Disorders, 18,* 627–636.

Baer, A. M., Rowbury, T. G., & Baer, D. M. (1973). The development of instructional control over classroom activities of deviant preschool children. *Journal of Applied Behavior Analysis, 6,* 457–463.

Baer, D. M., Wolf, M.W., & Risley, T. R. (1968). Some current dimensions of applied behavior analysis. *Journal of Applied Behavior Analysis, 1,* 91–97.

Bambara, L. M., & Warren, S. F. (1993). Appropriate applications in functional skill training. In R. A. Gable & S. F. Warren (Eds.), *Advances in mental retardation and developmental disabilities, Volume 5: Strategies for teaching students with mild to severe mental retardation* (pp. 165–190). London, England: Jessica Kingsly.

Bandura, A. (1977). *Social learning theory.* Englewood Cliffs, NJ: Prentice Hall.

Barton, E. E., & Wolery, M. (2008). Teaching pretend play to children with disabilities: A review of the literature. *Topics in Early Childhood Special Education, 28,* 109–125.

Barton, E. E., & Wolery, M. (in press). Training teachers to promote pretend play in young children with disabilities. *Exceptional Children.*

Becker, W. C., & Engelmann, S. (1978). Systems for basic instruction: Theory and applications. In A. C. Catania & T. A. Brigham (Eds.), *Handbook of applied behavior analysis: Social and instructional processes* (pp. 325–378). New York: Irvington.

Becker, W. C., Engelmann, S., & Thomas, D. R. (1975). *Teaching 2: Cognitive learning and instruction.* Chicago, IL: Science Research Associates.

Beirne-Smith, M., Patton, J., & Kim, S. (2006). *Mental retardation: An introduction to intellectual disabilities.* Columbus, OH: Pearson/Merrill/Prentice Hall.

Bricker, D., & Cripe, J. J. W. (1992). *An activity-based approach to early intervention.* Baltimore, MD: Brookes.

Brown, L., Branston, M.B., Hamre-Nietupski, S., Pumpian, I., Certo, N., & Gruenewald, L. (1979). A strategy for developing chronological-age-appropriate and functional curricular content for severely handicapped adolescents and young adults. *Journal of Special Education. 13,* 81–90.

Carr, E.G., (1994). Emerging themes in the functional analysis of problem behavior. *Journal of Applied Behavior Analysis, 2,* 393–399.

Carr, E. G., Binkoff, J. A., Kologinsky, E., & Eddy, M. (1978). Acquisition of sign language by autistic children. *Journal of Applied Behavior Analysis, 11,* 489–501.

Carr, E. G., & Kologinsky, E. (1983). Acquisition of sign language by autistic children II: Spontaneity and generalization effects. *Journal of Applied Behavior Analysis, 3,* 297–314.

Carr, E. G., Levin, L., McConnachie, G., Carlson, J. I., Kemp, D. C., & Smith, C. E. (1994). *Communication-based intervention for problem behavior: A user's guide for producing positive change.* Baltimore, MD: Brookes.

Carr, E. G., & Lindquist, J. C. (1987). Generalization processes in language acquisition. In T. L. Layton (Ed.), *Language and treatment of autistic and developmentally disordered children* (pp.129–153). Springfield, IL: Charles C. Thomas.

Catania, A. C. (1998). *Learning* (4th ed.) Upper Saddle River, NJ: Prentice-Hall.

Chadsey-Rusch, J., Drasgow, E., Reinoehl, R. B., Halle, J., & Collet-Klingenberg, L. (1993). Using general-case instruction to teach spontaneous and generalized requests for assistance to learners with severe disabilities. *The Journal of the Association for Persons With Severe Handicaps, 18,* 177–187.

Chadsey-Rusch, J., & Halle, J. W. (1992). The application of general-case instruction to the requesting repertoires of learners with severe disabilities. *The Journal of the Association for Persons With Severe Handicaps, 17,* 121–132.

Collins, B. C., Gast, D. L., Ault, M. J., & Wolery, M. (1991). Small group instruction: Guidelines for teachers of students with moderate to severe handicaps. *Education and Training in Mental Retardation, 26,* 18–32.

Cooper, J. O., Heron, T. E., & Heward, W. L. (2007). *Applied behavior analysis* (2nd ed.). Upper Saddle River, NJ: Merrill/Prentice Hall.

Day, H. M., & Horner, R. H. (1986). Response variation and the generalization of a dressing skill: Comparison of single instance and general case instruction. *Applied Research in Mental Retardation, 7,* 189–202.

Doyle, P. M., Gast, D. L., Wolery, M., Ault, M. J., & Meyer, S. (1992). Teaching discrete skills to students with moderate mental retardation in small-group instructional arrangements. *Exceptionality, 3,* 233–253.

Doyle, P. M., Wolery, M., Ault, M. J., Gast, D. L., & Wiley, K. (1989). Establishing conditional discriminations: Concurrent versus isolation-intermix instruction. *Research in Developmental Disabilities, 10,* 349–362.

Doyle, P. M., Wolery, M., Gast, D. L., Ault, M. J., & Wiley, K. (1990). Comparison of constant time delay and the system of least prompts in teaching preschoolers with developmental delays. *Research in Developmental Disabilities, 11,* 1–22.

Drasgow, E., & Halle, J. W. (1995). Teaching social communication to young children with severe disabilities. *Topics in Early Childhood Special Education, 15,* 164–186.

Drasgow, E., Halle, J. W., & Ostrosky, M. M. (1998). Effects of differential reinforcement on the generalization of a replacement mand in three children with severe language delays. *Journal of Applied Behavior Analysis, 31,* 357–374.

Drasgow, E., Halle, J. W., Ostrosky, M. M., & Harbers, H. M. (1996). Using behavioral indication and functional communication training to establish an initial sign repertoire with a young child with severe disabilities. *Topics in Early Childhood Special Education, 16,* 500–521.

Drasgow, E., Halle, J. W., & Sigafoos, J. (1999). Teaching communication to learners with severe disabilities: Motivation, response competition, and generalization. *The Australasian Journal of Special Education, 23,* 47–63.

Duker, R., Didden, P. C., & Sigafoos, J. (2004). *One-to-one training: Instructional procedures for learners with developmental disabilities.* Austin, TX: PRO-ED.

Dunlap, G. (1984). The influence of task variation and maintenance tasks on the learning and affect of autistic children. *Journal of Experimental Child Psychology, 37,* 41–64.

Englemann, S., & Bruner, E. (1974). *DISTAR reading I.* Chicago, IL: Science Research Associates

Engelmann, S., & Carnine, D. (1982). *Theory of instruction: Principles and applications.* New York: Irvington.

English, J. (2010). *Acquisition and generalization of peer imitation.* Unpublished master's degree thesis, Vanderbilt University, Nashville, TN.

Etzel, B. C., & Leblanc, J. M. (1979). The simplest treatment alternative: The law of parsimony applied to choosing appropriate instructional control and errorless-learning procedures for the difficult-to-teach child. *Journal of Autism and Developmental Disorders, 9,* 361–382.

Farmer, J. A., Gast, D. L., Wolery, M., & Winterling, V. (1991). Small group instruction for students with severe handicaps: A study of observational learning. *Education and Training in Mental Retardation, 26,* 190–201

Ferster, C. B., & Skinner, B. F. (1957). *Schedules of reinforcement.* Englewood Cliffs, NJ: Prentice-Hall.

Filla, A., Wolery, M., & Anthony, L. (1999). Promoting children's conversations during play with adult prompts. *Journal of Early Intervention, 22,* 93–108.

Friman, P. C., & Poling, A. (1995). Making life easier with effort: Basic and applied research on response effort. *Journal of Applied Behavior Analysis, 28,* 583–590.

Godby, S., Gast, D. L., & Wolery, M. (1987). A comparison of time delay and system of least prompts in teaching object identification. *Research in Developmental Disabilities, 8,* 283–306.

Guess, D., & Baer, D. M., (1973). An analysis of individual differences in generalization between receptive and productive language in retarded children. *Journal of Applied Behavior Analysis, 6,* 311–329.

Guess, D., & Helmstetter, E. (1986). Skill cluster instruction and the individualized curriculum sequencing model. In R. H. Horner, L. H. Meyer, & H.D.B. Fredericks (Eds.), *Education of learners with severe handicaps: Exemplary service strategies* (pp. 221–248). Baltimore: Brookes.

Halle, J. W., Chadsey-Rusch, J., & Collet-Klingenberg, L. (1993). Applying contextual features of general case instruction and interactive routines to enhance communication skills. In R. A. Gable & S. F. Warren (Eds.), *Advances in mental retardation and developmental disabilities, Volume 5: Strategies for teaching students with mild to severe mental retardation* (pp. 231–267). London, England: Jessica Kingsly.

Halle, J., Chadsey, J., Lee, S., & Renzaglia, A. (2004). Systematic instruction. In C. H. Kennedy & E. M. Horn (Eds.), *Including students with severe disabilities* (pp. 54–77). Boston: Allyn and Bacon.

Haring, N. G., Lovitt, T. C., Eaton, M. D., & Hansen, C. L. (1978). *The fourth R: Research in the classroom.* Columbus, OH: Merrill.

Haring, T. G., Kennedy, C. H., Adams, M. J., & Pitts-Conway, V. (1987). Teaching generalization of purchasing skills across community settings to autistic youth using videotape modeling. *Journal of Applied Behavior Analysis, 20,* 89–96.

Harlow, H. F. (1949). The formation of learning sets. *Psychological Review, 56,* 51–65.

Holcombe, A., Wolery, M., Werts, M. G., & Hrenkevich, P. (1993). Effects of instructive feedback on future learning. *Journal of Behavioral Education, 3,* 259–285.

Horner, R. H., Bellamy, G. T., & Colvin, G. T. (1984). Responding in the presence of nontrained stimuli: Implications of generalization error patterns. *The Journal of the Association for Persons With Severe Handicaps, 9,* 287–295.

Horner, R. H., Jones, D., & Williams, J. A. (1985). A functional approach to teaching generalized street crossing. *The Journal of the Association for Persons With Severe Handicaps, 10,* 71–78.

Horner, R. H., McDonnell, J. J., & Bellamy, G. T. (1986). Teaching generalized skills: General-case instruction in simulated and community settings. In R. H. Horner, L. H. Meyer, & H. D. B. Fredericks (Eds.), *Education of learners with severe handicaps: Exemplary service strategies* (pp. 289–315). Baltimore, MD: Brookes.

Horner, R. H., Sprague, J. R., & Wilcox, B. (1982). General case programming for community activities. In B. Wilcox & G. T. Bellamy (Eds.), *Design of high school programs for severely handicapped students* (pp. 61–98). Baltimore, MD: Brookes.

Horner, R. H., Williams, J. A., & Stevely, J. D. (1987). Acquisition of generalized telephone use by students with moderate and severe disabilities. *Research in Developmental Disabilities, 8,* 229–247.

Hupp, S. C., & Mervis, C. B. (1981). Development of generalized concepts by severely handicapped students. *The Journal of the Association for Persons With Severe Handicaps, 6,* 14–21.

Individuals with Disabilites Act of 2004, P. L. 108-446, 108th Congress (2004).

Iovannone, R., Dunlap, G., Huber, H., & Kincaid, D. (2003). Effective educational practices for students with autism spectrum disorders. *Focus on Autism and Other Developmental Disabilities, 3,* 150–165.

Kaiser, A. P., Yoder, P. J., & Keetz, A. (1992). Evaluating milieu teaching. In S. F. Warren & J. Reichle (Eds.), *Causes and effects in communication and language intervention* (pp. 9–47). Baltimore, MD: Brookes.

Kamps, D., Walker, D., Maher, J., & Rotholz, D. (1992). Academic and environmental effects of small group arrangements in classrooms for students with autism and other developmental disabilities. *Journal of Autism and Developmental Disorders, 22,* 277–293.

Kashinath, S., Woods, J., & Goldstein, H. (2006) Enhancing generalized teaching strategy use in daily routines by parents of children with autism. *Journal of Speech, Language, and Hearing Research, 49,* 466–485.

Keith, K. D. (1979). Behavior analysis and the principle of normalization. *AAESPH Review, 4,* 148–151.

Kennedy, C., Halle, J. W., & Drasgow, E. (2005). Establishing operations. In M. Hersen, R. H. Horner & G. Sugai (Eds.), *Encyclopedia of behavior modification and cognitive behavior therapy* (pp. 1299–1302). Thousand Oaks, CA: Sage.

Kern, L., Vorndran, C. M., Hilt, A., Ringdahl, J. E., Adelman, B. E., & Dunlap, G. (1998). Choice as an intervention to improve behavior: A review of the literature. *Journal of Behavioral Education, 8,* 151–170.

Koegel, R. L., Egel, A. L., & Dunlap, G. (1980). Learning characteristics of autistic children. In W. S. Sailor, B. Wilcox, & L. J. Brown (Eds.), *Methods of instruction with severely handicapped students* (pp. 259-301). Baltimore, MD: Brookes.

Koegel, R. L., & Rincover, A., (1977). Research on the difference between generalization and maintenance in extra-therapy responding. *Journal of Applied Behavior Analysis, 1,* 1–12.

Ledford, J. R., Gast, D. L., Luscre, D., & Ayres, K. (2008). Observational and incidental learning by children with autism during small group instruction. *Journal of Autism and Developmental Disorders, 38,* 86–103.

Losardo, A., & Bricker, D. (1994). Activity-based intervention and direct instruction: A comparison study. *American Journal on Mental Retardation, 98,* 744–765.

Lovaas, O. I. (1980). *Teaching developmentally disabled children: The me book.* Austin, TX: Pro-Ed.

Lovaas, O. I., Koegel, R. L. Simmons, J. Q., & Long, J. (1973). Some generalization and follow-up measures on autistic children in behavior therapy. *Journal of Applied Behavior Analysis, 6,* 131–166.

Miltenberger, R. G. (2008). *Behavior modification: Principles and procedures* (4th ed.). Pacific Grove, CA: Brooks/Cole.

Neel, R. S., & Billingsley, F. F. (1989). *Impact: A functional curriculum handbook.* Baltimore: Brookes.

O'Neill, R. E. (1990). Establishing verbal repertoires: Toward the application of general case analysis and programming. *The Analysis of Verbal Behavior, 8,* 113–126.

Panyan, M. C., & Hall, R. V. (1978). Effects of serial versus concurrent task sequencing an acquisition, maintenance, and generalization. *Journal of Applied Behavior Analysis, 11,* 67–74.

Patterson, P. (2010). *Effects of a story time and embedded trials in play on the receptive and expressive language of children with autism.* Unpublished master's degree thesis, Vanderbilt University. Nashville, TN.

Polychronis, S., McDonnell, J., Johnson, J., Rieson, T., & Jameson, M. (2004). A comparison of two trial distribution schedules in embedded instruction. *Focus on Autism and Other Developmental Disabilities, 19,* 140–151.

Pretti-Frontczak, K., & Bricker, D., (2004). *An activity-based approach to early intervention* (3rd ed.). Baltimore, MD: Brookes.

Reeve, S. A., Reeve, K. F., Townsend, D. B., & Poulson, C. L. (2007). Establishing a generalized repertoire of helping behavior in children with autism. *Journal of Applied Behavior Analysis, 40,* 123–136.

Reichow, B. (2008). *Comparison of progressive time delay with instructive feedback and progressive time delay without instructive feedback for children with autism spectrum disorders.* Unpublished doctoral dissertation, Vanderbilt University, Nashville, TN.

Reichow, B., & Wolery, M. (in press). Comparison of progressive time delay with and without instructive feedback. *Journal of Applied Behavior Analysis.*

Renzaglia, A., Karvonen, M., Drasgow, E., & Stoxen, C. C. (2003). Promoting a lifetime of inclusion. *Focus on Autism and Other Developmental Disabilities, 18,* 140–149.

Rincover, A., & Koegel, R. L. (1975). Setting generality and stimulus control in autistic children. *Journal of Applied Behavior Analysis, 3,* 235–246.

Rule, S., Losardo, A., Dinnebeil, L., Kaiser, A., & Rowland, C. (1998). Translating research on naturalistic instruction into practice. *Journal of Early Intervention, 21,* 283–293.

Schepis, M. M., Reid, D. H., Ownbey, J., & Parsons, M. B. (2001). Training support staff to embed teaching within natural routines of young children with disabilities in an inclusive preschool. *Journal of Applied Behavior Analysis, 3,* 313–327.

Schroeder, G. L., & Baer, D. M., (1972). Effects of concurrent and serial training on generalized vocal training in retarded children, *Developmental Psychology, 6,* 293–301.

Schutte, R. C., & Hopkins, B. L. (1970). The effects of teacher attention on following instructions in a kindergarten class. *Journal of Applied Behavior Analysis, 2,* 117–122.

Schwartz, I. S., & Baer, D. M. (1991). Social validity assessments: Is current practice state of the art? *Journal of Applied Behavior Analysis, 24,* 189–204.

Shelton, B., Gast, D. L., Wolery, M., & Winterling, V. (1991). The role of small group instruction in facilitating observational and incidental learning. *Language, Speech, and Hearing Services in Schools, 22,* 123–133.

Sidman, M., & Tailby, W. (1982). Conditional discrimination vs. matching to sample: an expansion of the testing paradigm. *Journal of the Experimental Analysis of Behavior, 37,* 5–22.

Sigafoos, J., Arthur-Kelly, M., & Butterfield, N. (2006). *Enhancing everyday communication for children with disabilities.* Baltimore, MD: Brookes.

Skinner, B. F. (1938). *The behavior of organisms: An experimental analysis.* New York: Appleton-Century-Crofts.

Snell, M. E. (1983). *Systematic instruction of the moderately and severely handicapped* (2nd Ed.). Columbus, OH: Merrill.

Snell, M. E. (2007). Advances in instruction. In S. L. Odom. R. H. Horner, M. E. Snell, & J. Blancher (Eds.), *Handbook of developmental disabilities* (pp. 249–268). New York: Guilford.

Snell, M. E., & Browder, D. M. (1986). Community-referenced instruction: Research and issues. *Journal of the Association for Persons with Severe Handicaps, 11,* 1–11.

Sprague, J. R., & Horner, R. H. (1984). The effects of single instance, multiple instance, and general case training on generalized vending machine use by moderately and severely handicapped students. *Journal of Applied Behavior Analysis, 17,* 273–278.

Steere, D. E., Strauch, J. D., Powell, T. H., & Butterworth, J. (1990). Promoting generalization from a teaching setting to a community-based setting among persons with severe disabilities: A general-case programming approach. *Education and Treatment of Children, 13,* 5–20.

Stokes, T. F., & Baer, D. M. (1977). An implicit technology of generalization. *Journal of Applied Behavior Analysis, 10,* 349–367.

Sugai, G. M., & Horner, R. H. (2008). What we know and need to know about preventing problem behavior in schools. *Exceptionality, 16,* 67–77.

Taylor, I., & O'Reilly, M. F. (2000). Generalization of supermarket shopping skills for individuals with mild intellectual disabilities using stimulus equivalence training. *The Psychological Record, 50,* 49–63.

Venn, M. L., Wolery, M., Werts, M. G., Morris, A., DeCesare, L. D., & Cuffs, M. S. (1993). Embedding instruction in art activities to teach preschoolers with disabilities to imitate their peers. *Early Childhood Research Quarterly, 8,* 277–294.

Werts, M. G., Wolery, M., Holcombe, A., & Gast, D. L. (1995). Instructive feedback: Review of parameters and effects. *Journal of Behavioral Education, 5,* 55–75.

Wolery, M. (in press). Studying response prompting strategies. In C. H. Kennedy, C. G. Breen, & C. A. Peck (Eds.), *Context, intervention, and disability: Essays in honor of Thomas G. Haring.*

Wolery, M., Ault, M. J., & Doyle, P. M. (1992). *Teaching students with moderate and severe disabilities: Use of response prompting strategies.* White Plains, NY: Longman.

Wolery, M., Ault, M. J., Doyle, P. M., Gast, D. L., & Griffen, A. K. (1992). Choral and individual responding during small group instruction: Identification of interactional effects. *Education and Treatment of Children, 15,* 289–309.

Wolery, M., Ault, M. J., Gast, D. L., Doyle, P. M., & Griffen, A. K. (1990). Comparison of constant time delay and the system of least prompts in teaching chained tasks. *Education and Training in Mental Retardation, 25,* 243–257.

Wolery, M., Cybriwsky, C. A., Gast, D. L., & Boyle-Gast, K. (1991). Use of constant time delay and attentional responses with adolescents. *Exceptional Children, 57,* 462–474.

Wolery, M., Doyle, P. M., Ault, M. J., Gast, D. L., Meyer, S., & Stinson, D. (1991). Effects of presenting incidental information in consequent events on future learning. *Journal of Behavioral Education, 1,* 79–104.

Wolery, M., & Schuster, J. W. (1997). Instructional methods with students who have significant disabilities. *Journal of Special Education, 31,* 61–79.

Wolery, T. D., Schuster, J. W., & Collins, B. C. (2000). Effects on future learning of presenting non-target stimuli in antecedent and consequent conditions. *Journal of Behavioral Education, 10,* 77–94.

Wolf, M. M. (1978). Social validity: The case for subjective measurement or how applied behavior analysis is finding its heart. *Journal of Applied Behavior Analysis, 11,* 203–214.

Yell, M. L., & Drasgow, E. (2000). Litigating a free appropriate public education: The Lovaas hearings and cases. *Journal of Special Education, 33,* 205–214.

40
Instructional Contexts

John McDonnell
University of Utah

The instructional strategies and techniques used by teachers directly impact how much and how fast students with significant cognitive disabilities learn. Research suggests however that a number of other contextual variables can influence the quality of students' educational programs, and affect the learning and social outcomes that students' realize while they are in school. A discussion of the full range of variables that influence these outcomes for students is beyond the scope of the present chapter. Consequently, emphasis is placed four on variables that are particularly important in the design of students' educational programs. These include where instruction is provided, who provides instruction to students, how students are grouped for instruction, and what accommodations and modifications students use to perform successfully in various settings. The chapter will briefly summarize the key research findings on the impact that these variables have on student learning, discuss some of the implications of the research for the design of educational programs, and identify potential areas for future research.

Location of Instruction

Historically, most students with significant cognitive disabilities have been served in separate special education classrooms or schools. Recent efforts to improve educational outcomes for students, and to more fully include them in typical school and community settings, has expanded where students receive instruction. For example, a growing number of students are being served in general education classrooms and their neighborhood schools. In addition, instruction is be carried out in community settings, especially for high school students, in order to better prepare them to meet the demands of living and working in the community after school.

Instruction in General Education Classes

The requirements in the Individuals with Disabilities Education Improvement Act (IDEA) that students with significant cognitive disabilities must participate and progress in the general education curriculum, and the expansion of inclusive educational programs for these students, has resulted in a growing body of research examining strategies for supporting student learning in general education classes. Although more research is needed, the studies published to date suggest that: (1) the educational and social outcomes achieved by students included in general education classes are equal or superior to those of students who are served in separate special education; (2) the placement of students with severe cognitive disabilities in general education classes has no impact on the educational achievement of their peers without disabilities; and (3) the characteristics of instruction that students received in general education classes is comparable to that received by students in separate special education classes (Hunt & McDonnell, 2007).

In spite of the positive impact of including students with significant cognitive disabilities in general education classes, meeting their educational needs in these classes presents a unique set of challenges to teachers (Harrower, 1999). Fortunately, research on strategies for supporting students' participation in the instructional activities and social networks of general education classes has increased significantly over the last decade (Hunt & McDonnell, 2007).

Research on Instructional Strategies

Several instructional strategies have been shown to be effective in meeting the learning needs of students enrolled in general education classes including universal design, cooperative learning, peer-mediated instruction, student-directed learning, and embedded instruction. Together, these strategies provide the basis for an instructional technology that can support instruction on a range of skills in general education classes.

Universal design. Universally designed curriculum and instruction provide alternate means to (a) represent the learning materials presented to students, (b) allow students to demonstrate understanding, and (c) structure lessons so that they are equally accessible to students with different abilities and needs (Rose, Meyer, & Hitchcock, 2005). Dymond et al. (2006) describe a study focused on the application of universal design principles to a high school science course. A team comprised of the general education teacher, a special education teacher who also taught the science course to students with mild disabilities, and the special education teacher for students with severe cognitive disabilities worked collaboratively to restructure each science lesson using universal design principles. The team met weekly through the semester to restructure the traditional lesson plans so that they were accessible to all students in the class including those with severe cognitive disabilities. The researchers found that for students with disabilities the process led to improved social interactions with their peers without disabilities and improved their participation in instructional routines and activities. The researchers also noted positive outcomes for students without disabilities including improved class participation, personal responsibility, and completion of work, grades, and end-of-year test scores.

Cooperative learning. Cooperative learning models share a number of characteristics including (a) small groups of students (i.e., less than five) who are given an assignment that they must complete together, (b) the students are directly taught the skills necessary to cooperate with each other, (c) the roles that each student plays in completing the assignment are tailored to each student's abilities and learning needs, (d) teachers encourage the development of "positive interdependence" among members of the group in to order support each others' learning, and (e) individual accountability for each member's participation in the group and what they learn. Hunt, Staub, Alwell, and Goetz (1994) used cooperative learning to teach three second grade students with severe cognitive disabilities communication and motor skills within cooperative learning groups designed to teach students without disabilities geometric and money concepts. All students in the class were assigned to cooperative learning groups that consisted of four students. The members of the cooperative learning groups that included students with disabilities were provided pre-session demonstrations about how to provide and fade response prompts to students on the targeted communication and motor skills. These pre-session demonstrations were gradually eliminated across instructional sessions. The results showed that students with severe cognitive disabilities acquired the targeted communication and motor skills. Unit tests for students without disabilities indicated that students in cooperative groups that included the student with disabilities performed as well as students in a control group that did not include a student with disabilities.

Peer-mediated instruction. Peer-mediated instruction is designed to allow students to serve as instructional agents for one another (Harper, Maheady, & Mallette, 1994). For example, McDonnell, Thorson, Allen, and Mathot-Buckner (2000) used a partner learning program to improve the performance on weekly spelling tests of three elementary students with severe cognitive disabilities enrolled in general education classes. The words taught to two of the students were drawn from the list of words included in the spelling unit presented each week to students without disabilities. The spelling words for the third student were drawn from the Edmark reading program. The partner learning program was implemented for 20 minutes twice per week. The students were divided into groups of three. During an instructional trial, each student spelled a word, presented the word to be spelled, or checked the spelling of the word. These roles rotated across students in the triad across each trial. The results showed that the partner learning program lead to increased spelling accuracy, increased levels of academic engagement, and reduced levels of inappropriate behaviors for students with significant cognitive disabilities.

Student-directed learning. The purpose of student-directed learning is to increase students' autonomy in participating in classroom activities and thereby reduce the level of assistance they need from special and general educators to be successful (Mithaug, Wehmeyer, Agran, Martin, & Palmer, 1998). Student directed learning encompasses a number of different skills including problem-solving, study planning, goal-setting, and self-monitoring. Agran, Wehmeyer, Cavin, and Palmer (2008) used the Self-Determined Learning Model of Instruction to teach three junior high school students academic skills drawn from the general education curriculum (i.e., use of scientific inquiry; understanding different types of maps; organ systems of the body). The students were taught to implement a self-regulated problem solving process that included establishing learning goals, developing a plan to guide learning, and evaluating what was learned and whether the goal was met. The study showed that students learned to implement the model and that they acquired and maintained the target skills.

Embedded instruction. Embedded instruction is explicit, systematic instruction that is designed to distribute instructional trials within the on-going routines and activities of general education classes (McDonnell, Johnson, & McQuivey, 2008). Like traditional teaching formats for students with significant cognitive disabilities, it incorporates systematic response prompting and fading, reinforcement, and error correction procedures. However, in embedded instruction the instructional trials are distributed across time rather than being presented one after another in a massed practice format. McDonnell, Johnson, Polychronis, and Riesen (2002) used embedded instruction to teach four junior high school students with developmental disabilities to read or define words that were included on vocabulary lists of a food and nutrition class, a health class, and a computer class. Instructional trials were distributed across the class session and presented to the student during specific routines or activities that had been identified by the students' general and special education teachers prior to the beginning of the study. The results were that embedded instruction led to the acquisition and maintenance of the target skills by all students.

Areas for Future Research

Although significant progress has been made in recent years, continued advances toward developing a comprehensive technology of instruction in general education classrooms will require research in several areas. First, researchers should examine the relative efficacy of various combinations of the strategies discussed above on student learning. It is likely that teachers will need to use multiple strategies to maximize the number of opportunities that students have to receive instruction throughout the school day. The focus should be on which combinations produce the best learning and under what conditions (i.e., curriculum content, classroom organizations). Second, research is needed to examine how to promote the adoption of these strategies by general educators and how they can be integrated into their day-to-day teaching practices. This research should focus on the best approaches for providing training (e.g., didactic workshops, on-line modules), delivering on-going technical assistance to teachers to meet student needs (e.g., external experts, teacher support teams), and sustaining these supports across time. Finally, there is a need to examine additional strategies for increasing the access of students with significant cognitive disabilities to the general education curriculum. Potential areas of study include planning systems that allow general educators to differentiate instruction more effectively for all students in the class, the infusion of computer and video technology into instructional activities, and the development of empirically and socially valid strategies for assessing students' progress in the general education curriculum.

Instruction in Community Settings

Research has shown that many students with significant cognitive disabilities will need explicit instruction in actual performance settings to become independent (Horner, McDonnell, & Bellamy, 1986; Rosenthal-Malek & Bloom, 1998). Further, research suggests that community-based instruction improves students' post-school adjustment in a number of areas (Wagner & Blackorby, 2007; White & Weiner, 2004). It is not surprising then that community-based instruction (CBI) is widely recognized as a critical element of effective secondary programs for students with significant cognitive disabilities (McDonnell, 2010; Wehman, 2006).

Research on CBI

CBI has been used to teach a variety of activities and skills to students with significant cognitive disabilities (Browder, Snell, & Wildonger, 1988; Horner, Jones, & Williams, 1985). For example, Horner et al. (1985) taught three young adults with significant cognitive disabilities to cross controlled and uncontrolled street corners using community-based, general case instruction. Students were taught to cross 20 street corners that were systematically selected to sample a number of different characteristics including the amount of traffic on the streets, the direction of the traffic (i.e., one-way, two-way), number of lanes, and the angle at which individuals crossed the street (i.e., straight, diagonal). Following instruction, the participants' generalization of street crossing skills was assessed on 20 untrained street corners that sampled the same range of variation that was presented during instruction. The results were that all of the participants demonstrated significant improvements in their ability to successfully cross the 20 street corners used during instruction. While only two of the participants completed the study, these individuals were able to generalize street crossing skills to all 20 of the untrained street corners following instruction.

The design of community-based instructional programs should be based on the principles of effective instruction. These include systematic selection and sequencing of instructional examples, the use of systematic response prompting and fading procedures to minimize student errors during instruction, differential reinforcement, and systematically correcting student errors. Available research suggests that a wide range of instructional procedures can be used effectively in CBI (e.g., system of most prompts, constant time delay), however the specific strategies used with students must be tailored to their unique learning needs and the activities they are being taught (McDonnell, 2010)

One of the problems associated with CBI is the limited number of instructional trials that are naturally available to students to learn the skills necessary to complete an activity. For example, when a student is learning to purchase groceries he or she will typically only have one natural opportunity during the instructional session to pay for items. For most students this will not be a sufficient number of instructional trials to result in efficient learning. Early research on overcoming this problem focused on the use of classroom or school-based "simulations" (Coon, Vogelsberg, & Williams, 1981; McDonnell, Horner, & Williams, 1984). Simulations are training formats in which the natural stimuli found in the performance environment are represented through some alternate form or medium during instruction (Horner et al., 1986).

Initial studies suggested that many students had difficulties generalizing the skills learned in simulations to actual performance settings. For example, McDonnell et al. (1984) taught students to use the next dollar strategy (e.g., the price on the register is $3.42, the student gives the cashier 4 1 dollar bills) using paper flash cards and photographic slides of cash registers to represent payment prices from 1 to 10 dollars. The results showed that neither the flashcard nor the slide procedures resulted in the students' generalized use of the next dollar strategy in grocery stores. Only after pairing slide instruction with community-based instruction did the students' performance improve. Other studies found similar results which reinforced the need for community-based instruction to be paired with school-based simulation instruction (Branham, Collins, Schuster, & Klienert, 1999; Browder et al., 1988). In addition, these studies suggested the level of generalization demonstrated by students was better if the simulations were designed to approximate as closely as possible the stimuli found in actual performance sites.

Advancements in computer and video technology have spurred renewed interest in simulations because of their ability to present "true-to-life" examples of the stimuli found in actual performance settings. However, research on the impact of stand-alone computer and video programs to teach skills that generalized to actual performance settings has been mixed (Hansen & Morgan, 2008; Hutcherson, Langone, Ayres, & Clees, 2004). Hutcherson et al. (2004) used a computer instruction program to teach the "Dollar Plus" (e.g., next dollar strategy) to three students with cognitive disabilities. The results showed that students were able to demonstrate mastery of the skill during computer instruction but were unable to generalize it to grocery stores in the community. In contrast, Hansen and Morgan (2008) use computer-based instruction consisting of DVD videos and CD-ROM screens to teach students with severe cognitive disabilities to enter a check-out stand with the shortest line, place items on the conveyer belt, pay for the items using the next dollar strategy, respond to the request for "paper or plastic," and obtain the change. The students were able to master the skills using computer-based instruction and were able to generalize the skills to three stores in the community.

Taken as a whole, the research suggests that computer and video instruction technologies hold promise as a strategy to promote the generalization of skills learned in simulations to actual performance settings. However, they are not fool-proof and in most cases should be paired with community-based instruction.

Areas for Future Research

A growing body of research suggests that the use of school-based instruction that incorporates computer and video representations of the stimuli found in actual performance settings can improve the effectiveness of CBI. Unfortunately, we have little information about the instructional design principles that should drive the development of these simulations for individuals with disabilities (Ayres & Langone, 2005; Wissick, Gardner, & Langone, 1999). There is a need for additional research that addresses issues such as the selection and sequencing of instructional examples within computer or video programs, the effectiveness of embedding visual cues to highlight the target stimuli being depicted on the screen, and the impact of interactive features that allow individuals to receive immediate feedback about their responses. Additionally, there is a need for the development of software platforms that can be easily adapted by teachers to address the specific learning needs of students, the activities being taught, and to the communities in which they live.

An additional area of needed research is the linkage between CBI and the general education curriculum. Most high school curricula include career or vocational education courses that require students to complete projects in community settings. These courses would provide a logical base for connecting the general curriculum with students' needs for CBI. Students would not only have the opportunity to learn important employment skills but the courses could be used as the vehicle to teach a number of other personal management activities like riding the bus or leisure activities such as purchasing lunch in a restaurant. Additional research is needed to examine how to effectively support the participation of students with significant cognitive disabilities in these courses and in designing instruction in ways that maximize the benefits of community-based learning activities within these classes.

Service learning has also been suggested as a strategy for linking the general curriculum and CBI for students with significant cognitive disabilities (Dymond, 2007). However, there has been very little research conducted examining how students can be effectively included in service learning classes or the relationship between the recommended elements of service learning and student outcomes (Dymond, Renzaglia, & Chun, 2008). Additional research is needed to validate service learning as a potential bridge between the general curriculum and students' needs for CBI.

Instructional and Social Supports

One of the outcomes of moving instruction out of self-contained settings general education classes and community settings is that the role of special educators must shift from providing instruction to students to designing educational programs and supports so that other individuals can provide effective instruction to students. Consequently, general educators, paraprofessionals, and peers are more directly involved in supporting students' learning than ever before.

General Educators

The inclusion of students with significant cognitive disabilities in general education curriculum and general education classes has significantly impacted the roles of general educators (Ferguson, Ralph, & Sampson, 2002). Increasingly, they are being asked to assume responsibility, with support from special educators, for the development and implementation of students' educational programs. This situation raises a number of questions about the specific responsibilities that general educators should have in meeting students' educational needs and the strategies that allow them to succeed in this new role.

Research on General Educators

General educators often report that they are not prepared to provide effective curriculum and instruction to students with significant cognitive disabilities and that they need additional supports to meet students' needs (Werts, Wolery, Snyder, Caldwell, & Salisbury, 1996; Wolery, Werts, Caldwell, Snyder, & Lisowski, 1995). For example, Werts et al. conducted a survey in one state, of general and special education teachers who had supported a child with severe disabilities in a general education class, on the barriers to serving these students and the supports they perceived as critical to meeting their needs. The majority of the respondents to the state survey were general educators. The research was replicated with a national sample of general educators. The primary barriers reported by teachers in both groups included factors such as the lack of training on curriculum and instructional procedures, a lack of time to develop effective programs for students, and the inability to understand and meet student needs. The supports and resources that teachers reported as critical to meeting the students' needs included training on how to successfully implement inclusive educational programs for students; assistance from a team of professionals who could help resolve curricular, instructional, and/or behavioral problems; and assistance in the classroom to implement students' programs.

In spite of these concerns, studies have shown that with support general educators can successfully implement a number of instructional strategies that promote the learning of students with significant cognitive disabilities in general education classes (Dymond et al., 2006; Polychronis, McDonnell, Johnson, Riesen, & Jameson, 2004). For example, Polychronis et al. conducted a study examining the impacts of two trial distribution schedules within embedded instruction on four elementary students with significant cognitive disabilities enrolled in general education classes. The students' general education teachers were trained to implement two embedded instruction formats in which instructional trials were distributed within a 30-minute interval in a single instructional lesson (e.g., reading or math) or a 120-minute interval across multiple instructional lessons (e.g., reading and math). The results showed that the teachers were able to implement the procedures with a high degree of fidelity and the students with significant cognitive disabilities mastered the skills targeted for instruction. Equally important, the general educators reported that both formats were easy to use and did not disrupt the educational programs of students without disabilities.

However, descriptive studies suggest that instructional interactions between general educators and students with significant cognitive disabilities varies widely (Logan & Keefe, 1997; Schuster, Hemmeter, & Ault, 2001) and is dependent on whether a formal process for teaming between general and special educators has been established to collaboratively plan students' educational programs (Hunt, Soto, Maier, & Doering, 2003; Wallace, Anderson, & Bartholomay, 2002). Hunt et al. examined the effectiveness of the Unified Plan of Support (UPS) in promoting collaboration between general and special educators to increase the social and academic participation of three students with significant disabilities and three students who were at risk in general education classes. The components of the UPS were (a) regularly scheduled team meetings, (b) collaborative development of student social and academic supports, (c) a specific accountability system, and (d) problem-solving procedures designed to directly address ineffective supports. The study was conducted in two general education classes located in separate schools and districts. The collaborative teams consisted of the general education teacher, the special education teacher, the child's parents, and the instructional assistant assigned to each of the classrooms. The results showed that the teams were able to implement the UPS procedures with a high degree of fidelity with each of the students. Observational data indicated that all students demonstrated higher levels of engagement, higher rates of initiation of social interactions, and higher rates of reciprocal interactions with peers following the implementation of the UPS. Finally, team members reported that the UPS led to improved educational outcomes for all students, and it allowed for effective and efficient use of the team members' knowledge and expertise.

Areas for Future Research

Although general educators may not always feel adequately prepared to meet the needs of students with significant cognitive disabilities in general education classes, the available research suggests that they can implement a range of instructional strategies with students when provided training and support. However, additional research is needed to identify the optimal roles and responsibilities of general and special educators in inclusive educational programs. Several models (e.g., facilitator model, co-teaching) have been suggested in the literature but published studies on their effectiveness have focused primarily on the perceptions of the professionals about the role change process rather than on measures of student learning and professional efficacy.

Paraprofessionals

The number of paraprofessionals who provide instructional and social support to students with significant cognitive disabilities in community settings and general education classes has expanded significantly over the last two decades, (Giangreco, Hurley, & Suter, 2009). Further, the available evidence suggests that they are assuming more responsibility for the design and implementation of students' educational programs (Giangreco & Broer, 2005). Obviously, this circumstance raises a number of questions about the quality of education being provided to students by paraprofessionals.

Research on Paraprofessionals

Recent studies suggest that there is a complex relationship between the roles that paraprofessionals play and the benefits that students receive from their support. Giangreco, Broer, and Edelman (2001) found that the level of engagement of general education teachers with students with significant cognitive disabilities was impacted by whether the paraprofessional was assigned to provide one-on-one support to a single student or whether they were assigned to support all students in the class who needed assistance with instructional activities. The authors conducted (a) interviews with general educators, special educators, paraprofessionals, and school administrators and (b) observations of paraprofessionals in their assigned support roles in general education classes and other areas of the school. The findings indicated that general educators interacted more frequently with students disabilities when the paraprofessionals was assigned to support all students in the class than when they were assigned to only provide one-on-one support to the student with disabilities.

Broer, Doyle, and Giangreco (2005) also reported concerns about the perspectives of students with cognitive disabilities have about their experiences with paraprofessional support. They interviewed 16 young adults who had received support from paraprofessionals in general education classes. Although the feelings of the young adults were generally positive about the paraprofessionals, they expressed concerns about being disenfranchised by the general education teacher, feeling embarrassed about needing one-to-one assistance to participate in class activities, and isolation from peers because of the stigmatization of receiving support from a paraprofessional.

Although there are concerns about unintended negative impacts of using paraprofessionals to support students, research also suggests that they can be effective if their roles are well-defined and they are provided the necessary training and on-going assistance to complete their assignments. Causton-Theoharis and Malmgren (2005) trained four paraprofessionals to increase the social interactions of four elementary students with significant cognitive disabilities enrolled in general education classes with their peers. The paraprofessionals were provided four hours of training designed to enhance their understanding of the depth of the social circles of the target students, importance of peer interactions, role of paraprofessionals in supporting student interactions, and facilitative strategies that could be used to increase interactions between students and their peers without disabilities. The results suggested that with training the paraprofessionals successfully and consistently implemented the facilitative strategies with students in the general education classes. The data also showed that the interactions between students and their peers without disabilities increased over the course of the study.

Similar results have been found in studies examining paraprofessionals in CBI. For example, McDonnell and McFarland (1988) trained two paraprofessional staff members to implement forward and whole task instruction strategies to teach four high school students to use commercial washing machines and soap dispensers in public laundromats. The paraprofessionals were provided two hours of training on the instructional and data collection procedures prior initiation of the study. The paraprofessionals demonstrated very high rates of procedural fidelity in implementing the instructional strategies throughout the study. In addition, students learned to independently use the washing machines and soap dispensers.

Areas for Future Research

Paraprofessionals likely will continue to be a source of instructional and social support for students with significant cognitive disabilities in general education classrooms and community settings. The effectiveness of paraprofessionals can be enhanced through training and on-going assistance. However, mitigating the conflicts between the need for paraprofessionals to provide support to students in a variety of educational environments and the potential negative impacts of their presence in those environments will require additional research. One issue that has not been comprehensively addressed is the impact that paraprofessionals have on the educational and social outcomes that students achieve in school and community settings. The use of paraprofessionals to date has been driven by teachers' perceived need for additional help in supporting students in general education classrooms or providing community-based instruction, not documented improvements in student learning. A second issue is the need to develop strategies that can assist educational planning teams to make decisions about when paraprofessional support is needed and the roles that they should play in supporting students is various contexts. Finally, research is needed on how to best train general education teachers to utilize paraprofessionals effectively not only for the benefit of students with disabilities but for all students enrolled in the class.

Peer Supports

Research suggests that peers can provide effective support to students with disabilities in both general education classrooms and community settings (Gilberts, Agran, Hughes, & Wehmeyer, 2001; Jameson, McDonnell, Polychronis, & Riesen, 2008). Further, it has been suggested that peers may be the most socially appropriate sources of support in many instructional contexts (Carter, Cushing, & Kennedy, 2009).

Research on Peer Support

As previously discussed, there is a substantial research base indicating that peers without disabilities can provide effective instruction to students with significant cognitive disabilities. However, beyond directly tutoring students with significant cognitive disabilities, peers can play a number of important roles in supporting students in general education classes and community settings. These include (a) implementing curricular, instructional, or ecological adaptations; (b) providing assistance and feedback in completing assigned tasks; (c) modeling appropriate communication and social skills; and (d) facilitating social interactions between students and other peers (Carter & Kennedy, 2006).

Peer-to-peer support strategies can be structured to pair a single peer or group of peers without disabilities with a student to assist with participation in instructional or social activities. In a study by Kennedy, Cushing, and Itkonen (1997), peers without disabilities were trained to provide support to a middle school and a high school student participating in four different general education classes. One peer was recruited to provide support to the student in each class. Initially, class seating arrangements were changed to allow the peers to sit next to the student. Peers were taught how to communicate and interact with the students appropriately during class time. The peers were also taught how to adapt classroom assignments and activities to allow the student to participate. The researchers examined the impact of the peer support strategy on social contacts between the student and peers in the class and the number of peers that students had social contact with outside of class periods. The results showed that the number of peers that students interacted with during and outside of class periods increased significantly over the course of the study.

While strategies that pair one student with one peer have been quite successful, recently it has been recommended that teachers use multiple peers or what is commonly known as social groups to support students in general education classes. For example, Carter, Cushing, Clark, and Kennedy (2005) examined the impact of the number of peers without disabilities providing support to three middle or high school students with developmental disabilities enrolled in general education classes. The primary dependent variables used in the study included the extent to which students were participating in instructional activities that were aligned with the general education curriculum, engagement in typical class activities, and social interactions with peers. The results showed that all three students had higher levels of performance on these measures when receiving support from two peers without disabilities.

Although peer supports are clearly beneficial for students with disabilities, they also appear to have educational benefits for peers without disabilities. Cushing and Kennedy (1997) examined the impact of a peer support strategy on the academic engagement and coursework performance of three middle school students without disabilities who supported three peers with cognitive disabilities in general education classes. The students were taught how to communicate with the peers, to make curricular adaptations necessary for them to complete in-class and homework assignments, and to provide feedback to them on their performance. The results of the study indicated that students without disabilities had higher levels of academic engagement and participated more actively in instruction when they were providing support to their peers than when they were not.

Increasingly, peer-to-peer supports are being recognized as viable strategies to avoid the negative impacts of paraprofessional support on social interactions between students with significant cognitive disabilities and their peers without disabilities. Carter, Sisco, Melekoglu, and Kurkowski (2007) compared the impacts of peer support with adult support for four high school students enrolled in general education classes. In the peer support condition, one peer in the students' class was identified to provide support that included supporting the students' social-related IEP (individual education program) goals, helping the students complete classroom activities, providing positive feedback to students about their participation in class activities, and promoting social interactions between students and other peers in the class. In the adult support condition, a special educator or paraprofessional facilitated the students' participation in the general education class by adapting class activities, implementing behavior support plans, and providing direct instruction. The researchers found that students had much higher rates of social interactions with peers and academic engagement when students were in the peer support condition than when in the adult support condition.

Another peer support strategy that has received a significant amount of attention in the last several years is a program called peer buddies (Hughes & Carter, 2000). Peer buddy programs are typically offered through classes in the general education curriculum, and peers receive credit for their participation. The focus is on establishing a broader level of support to assist students to participate in the routines and activities of the school such as getting to and from classes successfully, having lunch, and participating in extracurricular activities.

Carter, Hughes, Guth, and Copeland (2005) examined the impact on peer buddies on the social interactions that high school students with severe cognitive disabilities had with their peers throughout the school day. The peer buddies interacted with students during instructional and noninstructional activities during one 50-minute period each day and were encouraged to interact outside of the class during the school day. They were provided information on how to communicate and interact with the students. The results showed that social interactions between students and peers without disabilities in school significantly increased.

Areas for Future Research

Published research on the affects of peer-to-peer supports is promising and demonstrates that there are a number of educational and social benefits for using these strategies with students in a variety of instructional contexts. In spite of these positive outcomes, additional research is needed to more clearly understand how best to structure these strategies for students. The majority of studies published on peer-to-peer supports have examined short-term improvements on social interactions between students and their peers without disabilities and students participation in instructional activities. Whether peers will maintain their support of students across time and what factors may influence their willingness to provide on-going support to students is not clear. In addition, although these strategies appear to positively influence social acceptance and social interactions, we do not know what contribution these strategies may make to the development of friendships between students and their peers, or whether the relationships that are established at school extend to after-school activities. Another issue is that in the majority of studies the strategies were implemented by the researchers and not by special or general educators. If peer-to-peer support strategies are going to be effective then research is needed on how to best train school personnel to successfully implement and maintain them. Guidance is needed on the specific roles that special and general educators should play in putting these strategies into place and ensuring their on-going success.

Instructional Groups

One-to-one instruction has historically been the predominant instructional group arrangement for students with significant cognitive disabilities (Duker, Didden, & Sigafoos, 2004). However, staffing limitations and logistical issues often prevent the use of one-to-one instruction. Further, one-to-one instruction may be problematic in general education classes because it may result in the separation and isolation of students from their peers (Carter et al., 2009).

Fortunately, research has demonstrated that small group instruction can be an effective alternative for this group of students (Mechling, Gast, & Krupa, 2007; Parker & Schuster, 2002). Studies comparing one-to-one and small group instruction have found little difference in the effectiveness in the two approaches (Benz & Todd, 1990; Favell, Favell, & McGimsey, 1978). Further, small group instruction has the advantages of students being able to learn from one another through observational learning (Mechling et al., 2007; Parker & Schuster, 2002).

Research on Small Group Instruction

The structure of small groups needs to be based on a number of factors (Collins, Gast, Ault, & Wolery, 1991; Kamps et al., 1991). One of the first considerations is whether students will respond individually or in unison (commonly referred to as choral responding). Both approaches have been used successfully with students with significant cognitive disabilities (Kamps, Dugan, Leonard, & Daoust, 1994; Repp & Karsh, 1992). Research comparing individual and choral responding is limited, but it suggests that there is little difference in the overall efficacy of the two strategies (Wolery, Ault, Gast, Doyle, & Griffen, 1992). However, one potential disadvantage of choral responding is that students do not have the same opportunities for observational learning as they do with individual responding.

The most common group arrangement used to support individual responding is the sequential group arrangement (Collins et al., 1991; Ledford, Gast, Luscre, & Ayres, 2008). In this approach, each member of the group is taught individually with the teacher shifting his or her attention to other members of the group in round-robin style. For example, Farmer Gast, Wolery, & Winterling (1991) taught three high school students to read sight words using a progressive time delay procedure. Each student in the group was taught their own set of sight words. During instructional sessions, the teacher rotated the presentation of sight words to each member of the group. The results indicated that all of the students learned to read their own set of sight words and in addition, learned to read a significant number of the words presented to other members of the group through observation.

Choral responding emerged as an alternative to individual responding in order to increase the number of instructional trials that students received in small group instruction and to reduce the amount of time students spent waiting for their turn in sequential group arrangements (Kamps et al., 1991). One strategy to support choral responding is enhanced small group instruction (Kamps et al., 1994). For example, Kamps et al. (1994) used an enhanced small group instructional package with 24 students with autism and cognitive disabilities that included choral responding to teacher cues, student-to-student responding trials (e.g., a student showing an object to another group member and naming the object), regularly rotating instructional materials, and presenting choral and student-to-student trials randomly throughout the instructional session. The results showed that the procedures resulted in increased levels of responding and academic engagement by members of the group, gains in weekly pre- and posttests on the skills targeted for instruction, and decreases in inappropriate behavior.

A second critical consideration in designing small group instruction is the way that instructional tasks are organized and presented to students in the group. Collins et al. (1991) described four possible task structures: (a) the same task and the same stimuli for all members of the group; (b) the same task and different stimuli for each member of the group; (c) different tasks for each member of the group using the same stimuli; and (d) different tasks and stimuli for all members of the instructional group. In the same task/same stimuli structure, each student is taught the same skills using the same materials. For instance, all students in the group are taught to read the same five sight words. In the same task/different stimuli structure, each member of the group would be taught to read sight words with each group member being presented a different group of words. In the different task/same stimuli some students might be taught to read the sight words and some members of the group would be taught to point to the words. Finally, in the different task/different stimuli one student might be taught to read sight words and another student would be taught to point to coins.

Areas for Future Research

Small group instruction is routinely used in general education classes. Unfortunately, studies have repeatedly shown that the access of students with significant cognitive disabilities to small group instruction in these settings is limited (Logan & Keefe, 1997; Schuster et al., 2001). This suggests a need for additional research on how to design and implement small group instructional arrangements in general education classes. Studies examining the potential impact of heterogeneous small groups that included a student with disabilities and peers without disabilities on learning outcomes for both groups would be particularly beneficial. In addition, it would be useful to examine how observational learning and incidental teaching in small group arrangements could be used to help students to learn content in the general education curriculum more quickly.

Although numerous recommendations have been published for how to use small group instruction in community settings (Johnson & Wehman, 2001), there is no research that has directly examined the effectiveness of various group arrangements and task presentation strategies in these settings. Given the logistical difficulties associated with carrying out CBI, additional research on ways of providing effective small group instruction is warranted. This could include the potential advantages and disadvantages of using heterogeneous and homogeneous groups in CBI. Further, studies are needed to examine observational learning in CBI as a way of increasing the efficiency of student learning.

Modifications and Adaptations

Students with significant cognitive disabilities often have difficulty completing routines or activities in school and community settings the same way as their peers without disabilities. In some cases this is due to a student's ability to use abstract symbols such as words and numbers, and in others it is due a student's ability to complete the required responses. Consequently, ensuring the full participation of students in school and community settings often requires that the materials that students' use and the ways that they complete daily activities or instructional tasks may need to be modified or adapted to accommodate their unique abilities and learning needs (McDonnell & Wilcox, 1987).

Research on Modifications and Adaptations

The recent expansion of inclusive educational programs has spurred a new line of research focused on how modifications and adaptations can be used to promote student participation in the general education curriculum. Virtually all contemporary discussions on how to support students with significant cognitive disabilities in general education curriculum emphasize the need for the development and implementation of student specific modifications and adaptations (Browder et al., 2007; Wehmeyer, Lance, & Bashinski, 2002). However, observational studies examining the implementation of curriculum and instructional modifications and accommodations have been mixed (Dymond & Russell, 2004; Soukup, Wehmeyer, Bashinski, & Bovaird, 2007). These studies suggest that despite their perceived importance the actual use of these strategies is inconsistent at best.

In spite of these findings, a growing body of research suggests that curriculum modifications and adaptations are very effective in supporting students in general education curriculum and inclusive classes especially when they are part of multi-component intervention packages (Fisher & Frey, 2001; McDonnell, Mathot-Buckner, Thorson, & Fister, 2001). McDonnell et al. (2001) examined an intervention package that included peer tutoring, multi-element curriculum, and accommodations with three junior high school students with significant cognitive disabilities in general education classes. The accommodations provided to students included using a calculator to calculate percentages in math class, changing the distances that a student had to chest pass and dribble a basketball in physical education class, and using pictures to identify key concepts (e.g., Conestoga wagon, Jim Bridger) in a history class. The results showed that the intervention package resulted in improved rates of academic responding, reduced rates of competing behavior, and improved performance on weekly pre-post tests.

Students also frequently require modifications to successfully complete routines and activities in community settings. For example, students can use photographs, symbols, and drawings instead of reading to allow students to complete a wide range of activities in home and community settings (Copeland & Hughes, 2000; McDonnell & Horner, 1985). Communication notebooks and communication cards that include pictures or symbols have been used by students without verbal language to place their orders in fast food restaurants (McDonnell & Laughlin, 1989; Rotholz, Berkowitz, & Burberry, 1989) and to interact with peers during school activities (Hughes et al., 2000). Finally, modifications and adaptations such as using a large bill, coin cards, and the next dollar strategy have been used to help students who do not have or have limited math and money skills to make purchases in community settings (Browder et al., 1988; Test, Howell, Burkhart, & Beroth, 1993).

Areas for Future Research

Although there is a consensus that accommodations and modifications are key to the successful inclusion of students in general education classes and their ability to participate in the general education curriculum, the research literature examining the impacts of these strategies on students' educational and social outcomes is surprisingly small. The majority of the studies completed to date have examined modifications and accommodations as part of larger intervention packages. Additional research is needed to identify the unique contributions that these strategies make in supporting students in general education classes.

One problem confronting researchers in this area is that definitions of accommodations and modifications are somewhat muddled in the research literature. Several researchers have argued for both more precise and expanded definitions of these supports. For example, Wehmeyer et al. (2002) suggested three categories of supports including curriculum adaptations (e.g., modifications to the way in which materials are presented or represented to students; or the way the student interacts or responds to the materials); curriculum augmentations (e.g., providing students with additional skills that allow them to succeed in the curriculum such as advanced organizer; mnemonic strategies); and curriculum alterations (e.g., additions to the curriculum that are unique to the student's needs). In contrast, Janney and Snell (2000) suggest a classification system that includes curriculum adaptations (e.g., changes to what is taught); instructional adaptations (e.g., how content is taught and how mastery is demonstrated); and ecological adaptations (e.g., when, where, and with whom curriculum and instruction are presented). It seems unlikely that significant progress can be made in identifying the unique contributions that these strategies make in supporting students in general education classes until there is agreement on the definitions of the various supports provided to students.

Research is also needed on approaches that can assist IEP teams and individual teachers to determine the types of modifications and accommodations that students will need to be successful. This would include issues such as what student and task variables should be considered in identifying the types of accommodations and modifications that are provided; how the impact of the accommodations and modifications can be assessed; and what variables should be considered in determining when accommodations and modifications can be changed to require the student to use more complex materials or more abstract symbols in completing instructional activities.

Conclusion

This chapter addressed a wide array of contextual variables ranging from where instruction is provided to students to how accommodations and modifications can be used to meet the unique needs of students in home, school, and community settings. The research suggests that the decisions that IEP teams and individuals teachers make about these variable will impact student success during and after school. However, these variables are only small pieces of a much larger system of services and supports. Clearly, additional research is needed on each of these variables in order to improve the effectiveness of the educational programs that we provide to students. However, as a field we also need to begin to take seriously the challenge of developing comprehensive educational program models from elementary through post-high school programs. Emphasis needs to be placed on how students, parents, teachers, and administrators can work together to design school and district programs that are based on the available research evidence.

References

Agran, M., Wehmeyer, M. L., Cavin, M., & Palmer, S. (2008). Promoting student active classroom participation skills through instruction to promote self-regulated learning and self-determination. *Career Development for Exceptional Individuals, 21,* 106–114.

Ayres, K. M., & Langone, J. (2005). Intervention and instruction with video for students with Autism: A review of the literature. *Education and Training in Developmental Disabilities, 40,* 183–196.

Benz, M. R., & Todd, A. W. (1990). Group versus individual instruction for teaching daily living skills to students with severe handicaps. *Australia and New Zealand Journal of Developmental Disabilities, 16,* 81–95.

Branham, R., Collins, B., Schuster, J. W., & Klienert, H. (1999). Teaching community skills to students with moderate disabilities: Comparing combined techniques of classroom simulation, videotaped modeling, and community-based instruction. *Education and Training in Mental Retardation and Developmental Disabilities, 34,* 170–181.

Broer, S. M., Doyle, M. B., & Giangreco, M. L. (2005). Perspectives of students with intellectual disabilities about their experiences with paraprofessional support. *Exceptional Children, 71,* 415–430.

Browder, D. M., Snell, M. E., & Wildonger, B. (1988). Simulation and community-based instruction of vending machine with time delay. *Education and Training in Mental Retardations, 23,* 175–185.

Browder, D. M., Wakeman, S. Y., Flowers, C., Rickelmann, R. J., Pugalee, D., & Karvonen, M. (2007). Creating access to the general education curriculum with links to grade-level content for students with significant cognitive disabilities: An explication of the concept. *The Journal of Special Education, 41,* 2–16.

Carter, E. W., Cushing, L. S., Clark, N. M., & Kennedy, C. H. (2005). Effects of peer support interventions on students' access to the general curriculum and social interactions. *Research and Practice for Persons with Severe Disabilities, 30,* 15–25.

Carter, E. W., Cushing, L. S., & Kennedy, C. H. (2009). *Peer support strategies for improving all students' social lives and learning.* Baltimore: Paul H. Brookes.

Carter, E. W., Hughes, C., Guth, C. B., & Copeland, S. R. (2005). Factors influencing social interaction among high school students with intellectual disabilities and their general education peers. *American Journal on Mental Retardation, 110,* 366–377.

Carter, E. W., & Kennedy, C. H. (2006). Promoting access to the general curriculum using peer support strategies. *Research and Practice for Persons with Severe Disabilities, 31,* 284–292.

Carter, E. W., Sisco, L. G., Melekoglu, M. A., & Kurkowski, C (2007). Peer supports as an alternative to individually assigned paraprofessionals in inclusive high school classrooms. *Research and Practice for Persons with Severe Disabilities, 32,* 213–227.

Causton-Theoharis, J. N., & Malmgren, K. W. (2005). Increasing peer interactions for students with severe disabilities via paraprofessional training. *Exceptional Children, 71,* 431–444.

Collins, B. C., Gast, D. L., Ault, M. J., & Wolery, M. (1991). Small group instruction: Guidelines for teachers of students with moderate to severe handicaps. *Education and Training in Mental Retardation, 26,* 18–32.

Coon, M. E., Vogelsberg, R. T., & Williams, W. (1981). Effects of classroom public transportation instruction on generalization to the natural environment. *Journal of the Association for the Severely Handicapped, 6,* 46–53.

Copeland, S. R., & Hughes, C. (2000). Acquisition of a picture prompt strategy to increase independent performance. *Education and Training in Mental Retardation, 35,* 294–305.

Cushing, L. S., & Kennedy, C. H. (1997). Academic effects of providing peer support in general education classrooms on students without disabilities. *Journal of Applied Behavior Analysis, 30,* 139–152.

Cushing, L. S., Kennedy, C. H., Shukla, S., Davis, J., & Meyer, K. A., (1997). Disentangling the effects of curricular revision and social grouping within cooperative learning arrangements. *Focus on Autism and Other Developmental Disabilities, 12,* 231–240.

Duker, P., Didden, R., & Sigafoos, J. (2004). *One-to-one training: Instructional procedures for learners with developmental disabilities.* Austin, TX: PRO-ED.

Dymond, S. K. (2007). Elements of effective high school service learning programs that include students with and without disabilities. *Remedial and Special Education, 28,* 227–243.

Dymond, S. K., Renzaglia, A., & Chun, E. J. (2008). Elements of high school service learning programs. *Career Development for Exceptional Individuals, 31,* 37–47.

Dymond, S. K., Renzaglia, A., Rosenstein, A., Chun, E. J., Banks, R. A., Niswander, V., & Gilson, C. L. (2006). Using participatory action research approach to create a universally designed inclusive high school science course: A case study. *Research and Practice for Persons with Severe Disabilities, 31,* 293–308.

Dymond, S. K., & Russell, D. I. (2004). Impact of grade and disability on the instructional context of inclusive classrooms. *Education and Training in Developmental Disabilities, 29,* 127–141.

Farmer, J. A., Gast, D. L., Wolery, M., & Winterling, V. (1991). Small group instruction for students with severe handicaps: A study of observational learning. *Educational and Training in Mental Retardation, 26,* 190–201.

Favell, J. E., Favell, J. E., & McGimsey, J. F. (1978). Relative effectiveness and efficiency of group versus individual training of severely retarded persons. *American Journal of Mental Deficiency, 83,* 104–109.

Ferguson, D. L., Ralph, G., & Sampson, N. K. (2002). From "special educators to educators": The case for mixed-ability groups of teachers in restructured schools. In W. Sailor (Ed.), *Whole school success and inclusive education: Building partnerships for learning, achievement and accountability* (pp. 142–162). New York: Teachers College Press.

Fisher, D., & Frey, N. (2001). Access to the core curriculum: Critical ingredients for student success. *Remedial and Special Education, 22,* 148–157.

Giangreco, M. F., & Broer, S. M. (2005). Questionable utilization of paraprofessionals in inclusive schools: Are we addressing symptoms or causes? *Focus on Autism and Other Developmental Disabilities, 20,* 10–26.

Giangreco, M. F., Broer, S. M., & Edelman, S. M. (2001). Teacher engagement with students with disabilities: Differences between paraprofessional service delivery models. *The Journal of the Association for Persons with Severe Handicaps, 26,* 75–86.

Giangreco, M. F., Hurley, S. M., & Sutter, J. C. (2009). Special education personnel utilization and general class placement of students with disabilities: Ranges and ratios. *Intellectual and Developmental Disabilities, 47,* 53–56.

Gilberts, G. H., Agran, M., Hughes, C., & Wehmeyer, M. (2001). The effects of peer delivered self-monitoring strategies on the participation of students with severe disabilities in general education classrooms. *The Journal of the Association for Persons with Severe Handicaps, 26,* 25–36.

Hansen, D. L., & Morgan, R. L. (2008). Teaching grocery store purchasing skills to students with intellectual disabilities using a computer-based instruction program. *Education and Training in Developmental Disabilities, 43,* 431–442.

Harper, G. F., Maheady, L., & Mallette, B. (1994). The power of peer-mediated instruction: How and why it promotes academic success for all students. In J. S. Thousand, R. A. Villa, & A. I. Nevin (Eds.), *Creativity and collaborative learning: A practical guide to empowering students and teachers* (pp. 229–242). Baltimore: Paul H. Brookes.

Harrower, J. (1999). Educational inclusion of children with severe disabilities. *Journal of Positive Behavioral Interventions, 1,* 215–230.

Horner, R. H., Jones, D. N., & Williams, J. A. (1985). A functional approach to teaching street crossing. *The Journal of the Association for Persons with Severe Handicaps, 10,* 71–78.

Horner, R. H., McDonnell, J., & Bellamy, G. T. (1986). Efficient instruction of generalized behaviors: General case programming in simulation and community settings. In R. H. Horner, L. H. Meyer, & H. D. Fredericks (Eds.), *Educating learners with severe handicaps: Exemplary service strategies* (pp. 289–314). Baltimore: Paul H. Brookes.

Hughes, C., Rung, L. L., Wehmeyer, M. L., Agran, M., Copeland, S. R., & Hwang, B. (2000). Self-prompted communication book use to increase social interactions among high school students. *The Journal of The Association for Persons with Severe Handicaps, 25,* 153–166.

Hughes, C., & Carter, E. W. (2000). *The transition handbook: Strategies high school teachers use that work!* Baltimore: Paul H. Brookes.

Hunt, P., & McDonnell, J. (2007). Inclusive education. In S. L. Odom, R. H. Horner, M. Snell, & J. Blacher (Eds.), *Handbook on developmental disabilities* (pp. 269–291). New York: Guilford Press.

Hunt, P., Soto, G., Maier, J., & Doering, K. (2003). Collaborative teaming to support students at risk and students with severe disabilities in general education classrooms. *Exceptional Children, 69*(3), 315–332.

Hunt, P., Staub, D., Alwell, M., & Goetz, L. (1994). Achievement by all students within the context of learning groups. *The Journal of the Association for Persons with Severe Handicaps, 19,* 290–301.

Hutcherson, K., Langone, J., Ayres, K., & Clees, T. (2004). Computer assisted instruction to item selection in grocery stores: An assessment of acquisition and generalization. *Journal of Special Education Technology, 19,* 33–42.

Jameson, J. M., McDonnell, J., Polychronis, S., & Riesen, T. (2008). Training middle school peer tutors to embed constant time delay instruction for students with significant cognitive disabilities in inclusive middle school settings. *Intellectual and Developmental Disabilities, 46,* 346–365.

Janney, R., & Snell, M. E. (2000). *Modifying schoolwork.* Baltimore: Paul H. Brookes.

Johnson, S., & Wehman, P. (2001). Teaching for transition. In P. Wehman (Ed.), *Life beyond the classroom: Transition strategies for young people with disabilities* (pp. 145–170). Baltimore: Paul H. Brookes.

Kamps, D. M., Dugan, E. P., Leonard, B. R., & Daoust, P. M. (1994). Enhanced small group instruction using choral responding and student interaction for children with autism and developmental disabilities. *American Journal on Mental Retardation, 99,* 60–73.

Kamps, D. M., Walker, D., Dugan, E. P., Leonard, B. R., Thibadeau, S. F., Marshall, K., Grossnickle, L., & Boland, B. (1991). Small group instruction for school-aged students with autism and developmental disabilities. *Focus on Autism and Other Developmental Disabilities,* 1–18.

Kennedy, C. H., Cushing, L. S., & Itkonen, T. (1997). General education participation improves the social contacts and friendship networks of students with severe disabilities. *Journal of Behavior Education, 7,* 167–189.

Ledford, J. R., Gast, D. L., Luscre, D., & Ayres, K. M. (2008). Observational and incidental learning by children with autism during small group instruction. *Journal of Autism and Developmental Disorders, 38,* 86–103.

Logan, K. R., & Keefe, E. B. (1997). A comparison of instructional context, teacher behavior, and engaged behavior for students with severe disabilities in general education and self-contained elementary classrooms. *The Journal of the Association for Persons with Severe Handicaps, 22,* 16–27.

McDonnell, J. (2010). Instruction in community settings. In J. McDonnell & M. L. Hardman (Eds.), *Successful transition programs: Pathways for students with intellectual and developmental disabilities* (pp. 173–202). Thousand Oaks, CA: Sage.

McDonnell, J., & Horner, R. H. (1985). Effects of in vivo versus simulation-plus-in vivo training on the acquisition and generalization of grocery item selection by high school students with severe handicaps. *Analysis and Intervention in Developmental Disabilities, 5,* 323–343.

McDonnell, J., Horner, R. H., & Williams, J. (1984). Comparison of three strategies for teaching generalized grocery purchasing to high school students with severe handicaps. *The Journal of The Association for Persons with Severe Handicaps, 9,* 123–133.

McDonnell, J., Johnson, J. W., & McQuivey, C. (2008). *Embedded instruction for students with developmental disabilities in general education classes.* Alexandria, VA: Division of Developmental Disabilities, Council for Exceptional Children.

McDonnell, J., Johnson, J. W., Polychronis, S., & Riesen, T. (2002). The effects of embedded instruction on students with moderate disabilities enrolled in general education classes. *Education and Training in Mental Retardation and Developmental Disabilities, 37,* 363–377.

McDonnell, J., & Laughlin, B. (1989). A comparison of backward and concurrent chaining strategies in teaching community skills. *Education and Training in Mental Retardation, 24,* 230–238.

McDonnell, J., Mathot-Buckner, C., Thorson, N., & Fister, S. (2001). Supporting the inclusion of students with severe disabilities in typical junior high school classes: The effects of class wide peer tutoring, multi-element curriculum, and accommodations. *Education and Treatment of Children, 24,* 141–160.

McDonnell, J., & McFarland S. (1988). A comparison of forward and concurrent chaining strategies in teaching Laundromat skills to students with severe handicaps. *Research in Developmental Disabilities, 9,* 177–194.

McDonnell, J., Thorson, N., Allen, C., & Mathot-Buckner, C. (2000). The effects of partner learning during spelling for students with severe disabilities and their peers. *Journal of Behavioral Education, 10,* 107–122.

McDonnell, J., & Wilcox, B. (1987). Selecting alternative performance strategies for individuals with severe handicaps. In G. T. Bellamy & B. Wilcox (Eds.), *The activities catalog: A community programming guide for youth and adults with severe disabilities* (pp. 47–62). Baltimore: Paul H. Brookes.

Mechling, L. C., Gast, D. L., & Kruppa, K. (2007). Impact of SMART board technology: An investigation of sigh word reading and observational learning. *Journal of Autism and Developmental Disorders, 37,* 1869–1882.

Mithaug, D. E., Wehmeyer, D. K., Agran, M., Martin, J., & Palmer, S. (1998). The self-determined learning model of instruction: Engaging students to solve their learning problems. In M. L. Wehmeyer & D. J. Sands (Eds.), *Making it happen: Student involvement in educational planning, decision making, and instruction* (pp. 299–328). Baltimore: Paul H. Brookes.

Parker, M. A., & Schuster, J. W. (2002). Effectiveness of simultaneous prompting on the acquisition of observational and instructive feedback stimuli when teaching a heterogeneous group of high school students. *Education and Training in Mental Retardation and Developmental Disabilities, 37,* 3–13.

Polychronis, S. C., McDonnell, J., Johnson, J. W., Riesen, T., & Jameson, M. (2004). A comparison of two trial distribution schedules in embedded instruction. *Focus on Autism and Other Developmental Disabilities, 19,* 140–151.

Repp, A. C., & Karsh, K. G. (1992). An analysis of a group teaching procedure for persons with developmental disabilities. *Journal of Applied Behavior Analysis, 25,* 701–712.

Rose, D., Meyer, A., & Hitchcock, C. (2005). *The universally designed classroom: Accessible curriculum and digital technologies.* Cambridge, MA: Harvard University Press.

Rosenthal-Malek, A., & Bloom, A. (1998). Beyond acquisition: Teaching generalization for students with developmental disabilities. In A. Hilton & R. Ringlaben (Eds.), *Best and promising practices in developmental disabilities* (pp. 139–155). Austin, TX: Pro-Ed.

Rotholz, D. A., Berkowitz, S. F., & Burberry, J. (1989). Functionality of two modes of communication in the community by students with developmental disabilities: A comparison of signing and communication books. *The Journal of the Association for Persons with Severe Handicaps, 14,* 227–233.

Schuster, J. W., Hemmeter, M. L., & Ault, M. J. (2001). Instruction of students with moderate and severe disabilities in elementary classrooms. *Early Childhood Quarterly, 16,* 329–341.

Soukup, J. H., Wehmeyer, M. L., Bashinski, S. M., & Bovaird, J. A. (2007). Classroom variables and access to the general curriculum for students with disabilities. *Exceptional Children, 74,* 101–123.

Test, D. W., Howell, A., Burkhart, K., & Beroth, T. (1993). The one-more-than technique as a strategy for counting money for individuals with moderate mental retardation. *Education and Training in Mental Retardation, 28,* 232–241.

Wagner, M., & Blackorby, J. (2007). What we have learned. In J. Blackorby, A. M., Knokey, M. Wagner, P. Levin, E. Schiller, & C. Sumi (Eds.), *What makes a difference? Influences on outcomes for students with disabilities* (pp. 9-1–9-25). Palo Alto, CA: SRI International.

Wallace, T., Anderson, A. R., & Bartholomay, T. (2002). Collaboration: An element associated with the success of four inclusive high schools. *Journal of Educational and Psychological Consultation, 13,* 349–381.

Wehman, P. (2006). *Life beyond the classroom: Transition strategies for young people with disabilities* (4th ed.). Baltimore: Paul H. Brookes.

Wehmeyer, M. L., Lance, D., & Bashinski, S. (2002). Promoting access to the general curriculum for students with mental retardation: A multi-level model. *Education and Training in Mental Retardation and Developmental Disabilities, 37,* 233–234.

Werts, M. G., Wolery, M., Snyder, E. D., Caldwell, N. K., & Salisbury, C. L. (1996). Supports and resources associated with inclusive schooling: Perceptions of elementary school teachers about need and availability. *The Journal of Special Education, 30,* 187–203.

White, J., & Weiner, J. S. (2004). Influence of least restrictive environment and community based training on integrated employment outcomes for students with severe disabilities. *Journal of Vocational Rehabilitation, 21,* 149–156.

Wissick, C. A., Gardner, J. E., & Langone, J. (1999). Video-based simulations: Considerations for teaching students with developmental disabilities. *Career Development for Exceptional Individuals, 22,* 233–249.

Wolery, M., Ault, M. J., Gast, D. L., Doyler, P. M., & Griffen, A. K. (1992). Choral and individual responding during small group instruction: Identification of interactional effects. *Education and Treatment of Children, 15,* 289–309.

Wolery, M., Werts, M. G., Caldwell, N. A., Snyder, E.D., & Lisowki, L. (1995). Experienced teachers' perceptions of resources and supports for inclusion. *Education and Training in Mental Retardation and Developmental Disabilities, 30,* 15–26.

41

Access to General Education Curriculum for Students with Significant Cognitive Disabilities

Michael L. Wehmeyer
University of Kansas

The 1997 amendments to the Individuals with Disabilities Education Act and their associated regulations included statutory and regulatory language intended to ensure that students with disabilities had "access" to the general curriculum. Section 300.347(a)(3) of that act required that the IEP of students with disabilities include:

> A statement of the special education and related services and supplementary aids and services to be provided to the child, or on behalf of the child, and a statement of the program modifications or supports for school personnel that will be provided for the child
>
> (i) to advance appropriately toward attaining the annual goals;
> (ii) to be involved and progress in the general curriculum;
> (iii) to be educated and participate with disabled and non-disabled children.

In fact, as reflected in the language in part (ii) above, what IDEA required was that students with disabilities be involved with and show progress in the general curriculum. The term "access to the general curriculum" refers to this requirement for student involvement and progress. The general curriculum was defined in the regulations as referring to "the same curriculum as for nondisabled children" (Federal Register, 1999, p. 12592). The intent of these access provisions was threefold, as described by U.S. Department of Education (U.S. Department of Education, 1995) officials: (1) that all students, including students with disabilities, would have access to a challenging curriculum; (2) that all students, including students with disabilities, would be held to high expectations; and (3) to align special education practice with accountability mechanisms emerging through school reform efforts.

The 2004 amendments to IDEA contained all of the original IDEA 1997 mandates and added several new requirements, including that schools ensure that the IEP (individual education program) team includes someone knowledgeable about the general education curriculum and that the team meet at least annually to address any lack of expected progress in the general education curriculum (these amendments also changed the term to "general education" curriculum). Finally, the regulations to IDEA 2004 (issued in June 2005) prohibited a student with a disability from being removed from the general education setting based solely upon needed modifications to the general education curriculum.

These "access to the general education curriculum" requirements were implemented to ensure that students with disabilities were not excluded from the accountability systems linked with standards-based reform inherent in the No Child Left Behind Act, which requires states to establish challenging academic content and student achievement standards that apply to all students, including students with severe disabilities. To that end, under NCLB, states may establish alternate achievement standards for students with the most significant cognitive disabilities. The act does not define "students with the most significant disabilities" explicitly, but instead caps "the number of proficient and advanced scores based on alternate achievement standards included in annual yearly progress (AYP) decisions" to "1.0 percent of the number of students enrolled in tested grades" (U.S. Department of Education, 2005). Thus, by default, students with the most significant cognitive disabilities refer to the lowest performing 1.0% of students in public schools. These students, in general, overlap with students who are receiving special education services under the categorical areas of intellectual disability, deaf-blindness, autism, and multiple disabilities, although it's important to note that the determination as to whether a student receives alternate assessments linked to the alternate achievement standards is an IEP team decision and not linked solely to disability labels, and not every student in these categorical areas will be eligible for alternate assessments.

The establishment of alternate standards is intended "to ensure that students with the most significant cognitive disabilities are fully included in State accountability systems and have access to challenging instruction linked to State content standards" (U.S. Department of Education, 2005). This intent is part of a general intent to align special education practices with standards-based reform efforts by (a) establishing high expectation that students with disabilities can meet the same standards as students without disabilities, (b) providing mechanisms to facilitate student involvement such as teacher qualifications, professional developmental and special programs and services, and (c) requiring reports on the results of assessments of student educational outcomes to monitor student progress (Lee, Wehmeyer, Soukup, & Palmer, 2010).

My purpose is to overview the state of the field with regard to promoting "access to the general education curriculum" for students with significant cognitive disabilities or, generally, students with the most severe disabilities. I examine whether students with severe disabilities have such access and the barriers to attaining said access, current strategies to promote access and standards-based learning, and the current evidence-base for this effort.

Do Students with Significant Cognitive Disabilities Need Access to the General Education Curriculum?

That students with severe disabilities are intended to be part of standards-based reform efforts was clearly expressed by both the IDEA access and alternate assessment mandates and the provision for alternate achievement standards in NCLB. That students with severe disabilities need to be included in such reforms or, more specifically, whether such students need access to the general education curriculum, is presumed by the establishment of such regulations and policies. As Browder, Wakeman, and Flowers (2006) noted, however, there is not universal agreement that the access mandates are either justified or warranted. Arguments in opposition of the inclusion of students with disabilities, and particularly students with severe disabilities, in standards-based reform include that such efforts overlook previous experiences of failure within the general education curriculum by students with disabilities; concerns about the loss of individualization in the education of students with disabilities; concerns about the potential of increased dropout of students with disabilities; concerns about the minimization of functional or related content, including a focus on transition-related activities for adolescents with disabilities; and perceptions that content-focused instruction is not appropriate or viable for students with more severe disabilities.

As illustration of the latter, Agran, Alper, and Wehmeyer (2002) conducted a survey of teachers working with students with severe disabilities about their perception of the access requirements and their students. A high proportion (81%) indicated that their students were included in general education classrooms at least a portion of the school day. When asked if ensuring students' access to the general curriculum would help *increase educational expectations* for students with disabilities, 75% of teachers agreed to some degree. Sixty-three percent, however, indicated that they felt access to the general education curriculum was *more* important for students with high-incidence disabilities.

These concerns about the involvement of students with disabilities in standards-based reform have been countered with suggestions of the potential benefit of such involvement. Among these are the potential for higher levels of learning as a result of higher quality instruction; higher expectations for student progress; opportunities to learn content that had previously been ignored; greater inclusion in the general education classroom; and greater accountability for ensuring that students with disabilities actually learn (Browder, Wakeman, et al., 2006).

Of particular concern has been the involvement of students with disabilities in high-stakes or statewide testing. While concerns with regard to students with more severe disabilities and high stakes testing warrants discussion, the research suggests that for many students with higher incidence disabilities, the benefits of inclusion in standards-based reform seem to outweigh the risks if those risks are taken into account and their negative consequences mitigated. Ysseldyke, Dennison, and Nelson (2003) reported the positive consequences of the involvement of students with disabilities being involved in large-scale assessment and accountability systems as including higher expectations and standards for students with disabilities, improved instruction, improved student performance, increased general and special education collaboration, and increased communication with parents. Whether these same benefits accrue to students with severe disabilities remains to be established, though as research to be highlighted later in this chapter suggests, there is already evidence that inclusion in standards-based learning has the benefit of promoting student involvement in the general education classroom and of emphasizing the need for specific curriculum modifications and, thus, higher quality instruction in general education settings.

Although this chapter will not focus extensively on issues pertaining to alternate assessment, it is relevant to note that many of the concerns relative to other student populations with regard to statewide testing are not relevant to the discussion of the application of standards based learning for students with severe disabilities. Of course, statewide or large-scale testing is the mechanism used in NCLB to determine student AYP and to determine which students need additional instruction. Students with the most severe disabilities, however, are exempted from the statewide test if deemed appropriate by the IEP team, and become eligible for assessment using an alternate assessment. The U.S. Department of Education (2005) defined alternate assessment as "an assessment designed for the small number of students with disabilities who are unable to participate in the regular state assessment even with appropriate accommodations" (p. 797). Importantly, such alternate assessments must be aligned with the state's content standards, through the use of alternate student performance standards, and must be implemented in a manner that supports the use of results from such assessments to determine AYP for this population. As such, the alternate assessment process is designed to provide reliable and valid assessments of the progress of students with severe disabilities and to contribute to decisions about AYP and resource allocation.

Further, it is also important to point out that the IDEA regulations do not require that the educational programs of students with severe disabilities be determined exclusively by the general education curriculum. Indeed, these regulations stipulate that the educational programs of students with disabilities should include a focus on the general education curriculum *to the maximum degree appropriate*. IDEA continues to require that the educational programs of students with disabilities address "other educational needs" that are not part of the general education curriculum. While IDEA's prohibition against excluding students from the general education classroom based solely on needed modifications to the general education curriculum and the act's requirement that students not be removed from the general education classroom unless supplementary aids and services and specially designed instruction have been provided and deemed unsuccessful seems to make the omission of all general education curriculum content from a student's educational program inadvisable, the act also clearly expects students to receive instruction to promote both academic achievement and enhanced functional performance. Again, the determination of what proportion of the student's educational program reflects instruction derived from the general education curriculum versus functional content is an IEP team decision, and factors such as age, grade level, and severity of disability will all factor into that decision.

Whether students with severe disabilities can benefit from instruction in core content areas, opinions and perceptions aside, is essentially still an open question. As part of an OSEP-funded project to review the literature in core content instruction for students with severe disabilities, Browder, Spooner, Wakeman, Trela, and Baker (2006) summarized a number of studies synthesizing the "research-based evidence on whether this population can learn academics" (p. 311). In the area of reading, Browder and colleagues found strong evidence for teaching sight words (comprehension) to students with severe disabilities, but inadequate consideration of other components of reading instruction (phonemic awareness, phonics, fluency, and vocabulary).

In math, Browder, Spooner, and colleagues (2006) found evidence for the efficacy of teaching math measurement skills using systematic prompting and massed trial instruction, but again inadequate consideration of instruction in other components of math instruction, including number and operations, data analysis and probability, geometry, and algebra. Butler, Miller, Lee, and Pierce (2001) also reviewed the literature pertaining to teaching mathematics to students with intellectual disability with mild/moderate impairments, finding that students benefited from "interventions stressing frequent feedback, explicit instruction, and ample drill and practice" (p. 29), though also found preliminary results from studies on teaching multi-step, higher-level computation and problem-solving for students with intellectual disability to be encouraging.

In the area of science, Courtade, Spooner, and Browder (2006) found only 11 studies in a 20-year span focused on science instruction for students with severe disabilities, most of which focused on skills that these authors referred to as falling in the "Personal and Social Perspectives" content area, which encompassed issues such as safety, injury prevention, nutrition, or health.

It is important, as such, not to overstate the case for an evidence-base for teaching core content areas to students with severe disabilities. There is some evidence that students with severe disabilities can learn basic reading, math, and science knowledge and skills, but that research has been conducted primarily within a functional/life skills curricular paradigm and fails to address key components of effective instruction across content areas. Further, the low-incidence nature of severe disabilities leads to a preponderance of single-subject and quasi-experimental design studies and there are not sufficient large-scale, randomized trial studies documenting the efficacy (or lack thereof) of instruction to promote such outcomes. It is equally important, however, to emphasize that there is *not* an evidence-base suggesting that if provided high quality instruction (particularly, as discussed subsequently, embodying strategies incorporating Universal Design for Learning) students will *not* benefit. Put another way, what is most evident from the extant literature base is that there has been virtually no research on the effects of instruction to promote critical components of reading such as phonemic awareness or fluency; components of math instruction such as number and operations and geometry; or virtually any component of science instruction or research outside the functional or life skills mind-set that has dominated instructional models for this population.

There has, though, been progress in research pertaining to content instruction for students with severe disabilities since the Browder, Wakeman, et al. (2006) review. For example, Jimenez, Browder, and Courtade (2008) examined the effect of systematic instruction with concrete representation on the acquisition of an algebra skill for students with moderate developmental disabilities. This multiple-probe-across-participants design study found that students were able to learn how to solve an algebraic equation, including a demonstration of their capacity to generalize this skill across materials and settings. Browder, Ahlgrim-Delzell, Courtade, Gibbs, and Flowers (2008) provided evidence of the efficacy of an early literacy intervention for students with significant developmental disabilities using a randomized control group design study. Students in the treatment group made significant gains on multiple measures of readings skills, including measures of phonemic awareness. Similarly, Browder, Mims, Spooner, Ahlgram-Delzell, and Lee (2008) showed that young students with severe disabilities could improve literacy skills by engaging in shared reading of a story. Konrad, Trela, and Test (2006) evaluated the efficacy of a self-regulated writing strategy with high school students with multiple disabilities and showed positive effects on paragraph writing skills. Collins, Evans, Creech-Galloway, Karl, and Miller (2007) showed that students with severe disabilities could acquire both functional and core content sight words in general education classrooms using either direct distributed trial instruction or embedded distributed trial instruction. Browder, Trela, and Jimenez (2007) showed the efficacy of using task analysis to teach a story-based literacy lesson using adapted, grade-appropriate middle school literature to students with moderate and severe developmental disabilities.

An additional argument for focusing on the general education curriculum for students with severe disabilities is the fact that, as noted by Wehmeyer, Field, Doren, Jones, and Mason (2004), there is considerable overlap between the general education curriculum (as defined by content and student achievement standards) and some important traditional "special education" instructional areas. For example, most state and local content and student achievement standards across multiple content areas contain language pertaining to component elements of self-determined behavior, such as goal setting, problem solving, and decision making, the promotion of which is an important component of the educational programs of many students with disabilities and potentially as important for all students.

In fact, in a content analysis of the curricular philosophies reflected in states' alternate assessment performance indicators, Browder et al. (2004) concluded that the influence of a "functional curriculum philosophy," reflecting a curricular focus on functional and life skills instruction, was still evident in most such standards. Similarly, Browder et al. (2004) examined the actual alternate assessment content for alternate assessments for 31 states and concluded that while there was a strong focus on academic skills, the assessments also reflect "an additive curriculum approach to linking academic and functional skills" (p. 211). In other words, the general education curriculum as currently defined for students with more severe disabilities (incorporating alternate achievement standards) provides ample room to address the functional and life skills important for students within this population.

Ultimately, as such, if there are concerns about the undue or unintended consequences of involving students with severe disabilities in the general education curriculum, the provisions in NCLB and IDEA pertaining to alternate assessments and alternate achievement standards, the IDEA requirement that the other educational needs of students with disabilities continue to be addressed, and the fact that the general education curriculum does contain content that is important to students with severe disabilities would seem to mitigate against, at the very least, the exclusion of students with severe disabilities from such reform efforts. Further, of course, there is no ambiguity in the federal legislation pertaining to such access and student involvement in assessments. All students must be included in state assessments and all students with disabilities must be provided an educational program that ensures involvement with and progress in the general education classroom.

Do Students with Significant Cognitive Disabilities Have Access to the General Education Curriculum?

To address the evidence-base that would lead us to a conclusion with regard to whether students with severe disabilities have access to the general education curriculum, one must examine several sources, beginning with teacher survey data. The aforementioned survey of teachers of students with severe disabilities pertaining to access issues (Agran et al., 2002) found that while between 11% and 23% of respondents indicated they used several different ways to ensure some level of access, the largest proportion (37%) indicated that students were receiving an educational program developed wholly outside the context of the general curriculum. A little over one-third of teachers indicated they were frequently involved in curriculum planning meetings with general educators. Most teachers identified a paraprofessional as the primary means of supporting students in the general curriculum, with one-third indicating that materials were adapted for use by students with severe disabilities. Nearly three-fourths of respondents indicated that students with disabilities were evaluated exclusively by criteria stipulated in the IEP.

Dymond, Renzaglia, Gilson, and Slagor (2007) interviewed teachers working with students with and without disabilities to determine how they perceived or understood what was meant by "access to the general education curriculum" as it might apply to students with significant cognitive disabilities. A high proportion (80%) of respondents discussed core content issues in responding to queries with regard to what they interpreted access to the general education curriculum to mean, though only half of general educators and 9% of special educators actually defined it as does IDEA (e.g., access to the same curriculum as all other students). Further, general education teachers most frequently defined access for students with significant disabilities as instruction in core content areas in the general education classroom using the same curriculum and materials provided to students without disabilities. Special educators, however, defined it as having access to an adapted curriculum that was "relevant and meaningful to the student and addresses individual student needs and interests" (p. 11).

The absence of goals related to core content areas in the IEPs of students with severe disabilities, despite IDEA mandates and research supporting such a focus, has been documented and forms a second level of evidence with regard to student access to the general education curriculum. Karvonen and Huynh (2007) examined the relationship between curricular priorities reflected in a student's IEP and content and performance expectations in the alternate assessment. Specifically, Karvonen and Huynh (2007) examined IEPs in relation to alternate achievement standards and alternate assessment pertaining to language arts and math. There were few IEP goals related to either objective, though slightly more related to language arts, but those objectives that did exist were consistent with the functional paradigm discussed previously (e.g., math measurement objectives such as telling time, using a calendar, as opposed to other components).

There are also several studies examining more directly the degree to which students with more severe disabilities have such access. Roach and Elliott (2006) conducted a study examining the influence of the access to the general education curriculum of students with significant cognitive disabilities, as measured by a teacher questionnaire, on the performance of these students on a state alternate assessment in reading, language arts, and math. Using structural equation modeling, Roach and Elliott found that students who had greater access to the general education curriculum, increased time in the general education classroom, and academic goals on their IEP performed better on the reading, language arts, and math assessments.

Wehmeyer, Lattin, Lapp-Rincker, and Agran (2003) conducted an observational study of 33 students with intellectual disability to examine the degree to which they were involved in tasks related to the general education curriculum. Students were observed in naturally occurring classroom contexts from 120 to 240 minutes each, with an average of 202 minutes per student. Overall, almost 110 hours of observations were coded, and students were observed to be engaged in a task related to a school district standard, either working on the same task as peers or a task related to a different standard or benchmark in 70% of intervals. This varied considerably by student level of disability, though, with students with limited support needs (mild disabilities) engaged in a task linked to a standard on 87% of intervals, and students with significant cognitive disabilities doing so 55% of the time. Students served in the general education classroom were observed working on tasks linked to a standard 90% of intervals, while students served primarily in self-contained settings engaged in tasks related to a standard in only 50% of the observations intervals.

Overall, students with intellectual disability were working on a task linked to an IEP 22% of the intervals, were provided accommodations to work on a task linked to a standard 5% of the time, were working on an adapted task 3% of the time, and were being taught strategies to improve their capacity to engage with the general curriculum only 0.15% of the time. Moreover, there were significant differences by setting (inclusive or self-contained) in a number of areas. Students served in inclusive settings were significantly more likely to be working on a task linked to a standard and to be working on an adapted task. Students educated primarily in self-contained settings were significantly more likely to be working on a task linked to a standard below grade level or on a task not linked to a standard, and to be working on a task linked to an IEP objective.

In a second study using a computer-based data collection system, Soukup, Wehmeyer, Bashinski, and Bovaird (2007) examined the degree to which 19 late elementary age students with intellectual disability had access to activities that could be linked to district standards in social studies and science. In 61% of intervals (n = 3,420 20-second intervals), students' activities could be linked to a grade level standard, and in an additional 20% of intervals could be linked to an off-grade level standard. However, when examined based on how much time the student spent in the general education classroom, 83% of intervals for students in a high inclusion group and 93% of intervals for students in a moderate inclusion group could be linked to grade level standards, while none of the intervals for students in the low inclusion group (e.g., self-contained classroom) were linked to grade-level standards (groups did not differ by level of impairment). In only 18% of the intervals was a curriculum adaptation in place to support a student, and there was no instance in which students were being taught learning-to-learn strategies and other strategies to enable them to interact with content.

Lee, Wehmeyer, Palmer, Soukup, and Little (2008) used the same computer-based recording system in a study to examine the impact of promoting self-determination on student access to the general education, and in baseline data collection involving nearly 90 hours of observations determined similar trends for 45 high school students with intellectual or developmental disabilities. These observations occurred exclusively in the general education classroom, and on almost 80% of intervals students with disabilities were working on grade-level standards (compared to 93% of the time for peers without disabilities). Further, in another 18% of intervals students with disabilities were working on an off-grade level standard. This instruction matched poorly with IEP goal instruction, as on only 26% of the intervals was an IEP goal addressed, validating the aforementioned lack of alignment between IEP goals and the access mandates. Also, during only 24% of the intervals in which a student was observed to be working on a grade-level standard were any level of adaptations documented.

Similarly, Matzen, Ryndak, and Nakao (in press) conducted structured interviews and classroom observations comparing instructional activities for students with significant cognitive disabilities in both general education and self-contained classrooms, and found that when in general education contexts, students were disproportionately exposed to grade level academic content, while during instruction in self-contained settings they were not.

In summary, the existing evidence suggests that the degree to which students with severe disabilities have access to the general education curriculum is, in large measure, a function of context. Students receiving their education in self-contained settings tend to work on IEP goals that, in general, tend not to be focused on the general education classroom or on off-grade standards. Students educated in the general education classroom, however, have frequent opportunities to work on tasks linked to grade-level standards. This finding is consistent with studies showing that students with disabilities make greater progress when provided core content instruction in the general education classroom. Cole, Waldron, and Majd (2004), for example, explored student progress on reading and math assessments for students with disabilities in general education and self-contained classrooms, and found that students with disabilities receiving core content instruction in the general education classroom made comparable or greater than average academic progress when compared with students without disabilities in the same classes, a finding not repeated for students receiving core content instruction in self-contained settings.

That said, it is also clear that too few students receiving instruction in core content areas in the general education classroom had access to modified curricular materials and accommodations that would address issues of progress. The absence of such modifications is a critical factor in ensuring progress and not just access. Lee et al. (2010) studied whether curriculum modifications predicted adaptive or maladaptive student behaviors in general education settings for students with developmental disabilities and determined when students were engaged in tasks linked to an on- or off-grade standard without the support of any curriculum modification, they were more likely to be engaged in behaviors that competed with active engagement, but when engaged with standards and provided any type of curriculum modifications, were disproportionately likely to be engaged in academically beneficial responses.

Finally, it was clear that teachers, particularly teachers working with students with severe disabilities, hold paradoxical opinions about issues of access to the general education curriculum, recognizing that efforts to promote such access would raise expectations but in general believing that a focus on access was more relevant to other students with less intensive support needs, and defining access, as it were, as access to a modified, adapted curriculum that was more functional in nature.

Promoting Access to the General Education Curriculum for Students with Significant Cognitive Disabilities

A number of frameworks to promote access to the general education curriculum for students with more severe disabilities have been proposed (Browder & Spooner, 2006; Janney & Snell, 2004; Jorgensen, McSheehan, & Sonnenmeier, 2010; McSheehan, Sonnenmeier, Jorgensen, & Turner, 2006; Spooner, Dymond, Smith, & Kennedy, 2006; Wehmeyer, Lance, & Bashinski, 2002; Wehmeyer, Sands, Knowlton, & Kozleski, 2002). Rather than describe each of these independently, the following section is structured by the types of actions that can be taken at district, campus, and classroom levels that are necessary to implement standards-based learning for students with severe disabilities, and key elements of the above listed models will be incorporated into these sections.

District Level Actions to Promote Access to the General Education Classroom for Students with Significant Cognitive Disabilities

Standards setting. School reform efforts in the era of NCLB begin with and are centered on the establishment of standards that define the curriculum for all students and become the basis for accountability assessment procedures. No Child Left Behind (2002) requires that states establish "challenging academic content and student academic achievement standards that will be used by the State, its local educational agencies (LEAs), and its schools" [Sec. 200.1(a)]. Two aspects of the standards setting process seem particularly important to promote access for all students, including students with severe disabilities. First, standards should be set across a broad array of content areas if the general curriculum is to be appropriate for all students. Currently, NCLB requires standards only for a limited set of academic content areas and many content areas important to students with significant cognitive disabilities, including functional or life skills content or transition content, are not well integrated into the standards and, consequently, into the curriculum. That said, as noted previously, the alternate student performance standards set for use in alternate assessment tend to reflect an emphasis on life skills and functional content.

Second, if students with widely varying skills, backgrounds, knowledge, and customs are to progress in the general curriculum, the standards upon which the curriculum is based, as well as the curriculum itself, must embody the principles of universal design (discussed subsequently), and be written to be open-ended and inclusive, not close-ended and exclusive. The terms "open- and close-ended" refer to "the amount of specificity and direction provided by curriculum standards, benchmarks, goals, or objectives at both the building and classroom levels" (Wehmeyer et al., 2002, p. 126). Close-ended standards are specific and require narrowly defined outcomes or performance indicators, like "writing a five-page paper on the cause of the Civil War" (Wehmeyer et al., 2002, p. 126). Open-ended standards do not restrict the ways in which students exhibit knowledge or skills and focus more on the expectations that students will interact with the content, ask questions, manipulate materials, make observations, and then communicate their knowledge in a variety of ways (orally, through video tape, writing and directing a play, etc.). Open-ended designs allow for greater flexibility as to what, when, and how topics will be addressed in the classroom (Stainback, Stainback, Stefanich, & Alper, 1996) and are more consistent with universally designed curriculum, ensuring that more students, including students with intellectual disability, can show progress in the curriculum (Wehmeyer et al., 2002).

Curriculum alignment. The alignment of the curriculum with these standards is the next step in standards-based learning, though for students with severe disabilities this alignment process involves multiple steps beyond the alignment of the content standards and student performance standards with the curriculum, to include an alignment between alternate achievement standards with content standards and the general education curriculum, and between IEP goals and the general education curriculum. Although no national study has been conducted examining the alignment of IEP goals to content standards, the studies by Karvonen and Huynh (2007), Wehmeyer, Lattin, et al. (2003), and Soukup et al. (2007) discussed previously provide indirect evidence of the lack of alignment between IEP goals and content standards and/or the general education curriculum.

Browder et al. (2004) examined the alternate assessments from 31 states to determine the alignment between performance indicators for students with severe disabilities and national standards in math and language arts. Of the 31 states, only the performance indicators of three states were determined to be in alignment with math and language arts standards set by national organizations specializing in those areas. Of course, the alignment between alternate achievement standards and national standards is not necessarily the same as alignment between alternate achievement standards and state content standards, but nevertheless it seems evident that more progress needs to be made in aligning alternate achievement standards and alternate assessments to content standards established for all students.

Campus and Building Level Actions to Promote Access to the General Education Curriculum for Students with Significant Cognitive Disabilities

Several whole school or schoolwide actions support greater access for students with severe disabilities. Whole school interventions are, quite simply, those implemented throughout the school campus and with all students. Such interventions have the effect of minimizing the need for more individualized interventions and, in turn, foster a climate in which students with severe disabilities can benefit from instruction in the general education classroom and curriculum.

Curriculum mapping. Many schools use a curriculum mapping process—which involves the collection of information about each teacher's curriculum, including descriptions of the content to be taught during the year, processes and skills emphasized, and student assessments used, using the school calendar as an organizer—to find gaps or repetition in the curriculum content and to be sure they are teaching all parts of the curriculum framework, performance objectives, and other standards at the appropriate grade/course. These curriculum maps can, in turn, be used to identify where in the curriculum and across the school day students with significant cognitive disabilities can receive instruction on content from the general curriculum that is based on the student's unique learning needs.

Universal Design for Learning. An important component of most models to promote student access involves the application of principles of Universal Design for Learning (UDL) in the education of all students. Orkwis and McLane (1998) defined "universal design for learning" as "the design of instructional materials and activities that allows the learning goals to be achievable by individuals with wide differences in their abilities to see, hear, speak, move, read, write, understand English, attend, organize, engage, and remember" (p. 9). The onus is on curriculum planners and designers to employ principles of universal design to ensure that students with a wide range of capacities can access, advance, and succeed in the curriculum.

Researchers at the Center for Applied Special Technology (CAST, 1998–1999) suggested three essential *qualities* of UDL. These qualities are that the curriculum is designed to (a) provide *multiple representations* of content, (b) provide *multiple options for expression* and control, and (c) provide *multiple options for engagement* and motivation. These are described below.

- *Curriculum provides multiple means of representation.* Researchers at CAST suggested that "universally designed materials accommodate diversity through alternative representations of key information. Students with different preferences and needs can either select the representational medium most suitable for them, or gather information from a variety of representational media simultaneously." World Wide Web pages designed to be accessible present an example of using multiple means of representation. One of the benefits of the WWW is the capacity to use graphic images in a variety of ways, from icons to hyperlinked pictures and streamed video. However, for a person who is blind or visually impaired using a text-reader to access the site, graphic depictions may make the site and the information contained therein inaccessible. As an alternative, accessible web sites include text descriptions of images and pictures. Similarly, the design of curricular materials should include multiple representations of important topics, features, or points. Such representations include a variety of methods of presentation of the material based on learner needs and characteristics. Students with significant cognitive disabilities, for example, need print information to be presented with graphic depictions, free from unnecessary clutter and with key information repeated or highlighted.
- *Curriculum provides multiple means of expression.* CAST researchers noted that the dominant means of expression used in schools has been written. However, there are a variety of ways of student responding that could indicate progress, including "artwork, photography, drama, music, animation, and video," (CAST, 1998–1999) that would enable students to express their ideas and their knowledge.
- *Curriculum provides multiple means of engagement.* Student engagement in learning has long been an indicator of motivation in the classroom. By the utilization of multiple representation and presentation modes, particularly those that involve digital representation of knowledge which are graphically-based and incorporate video, audio and other multimedia components, student

engagement, and as such student motivation, can be enhanced. Universally designed curriculum takes into account individual student interests and preferences and individualizes representation, presentation, and response aspects of the curriculum delivery accordingly. Current technologies allow that level of individualization and, thus, provide greater flexibility in ways for the student to engage in learning. (CAST, 1998–1999)

Research evidence documenting the effects of UDL on access to or progress in the general education curriculum for students with disabilities is limited. Kortering, McLannon, and Braziel (2008) found that students with high incidence disabilities perceived instruction in algebra and biology with universally designed materials to be more engaging than traditional instruction. Spooner, Baker, Harris, Ahlgrim-Delzell, and Browder (2007) found that training teachers to apply principles of UDL to their classroom context resulted in significant changes to lesson planning by this group, with lessons incorporating principles of UDL post-training. Dymond et al. (2006) documented the efficacy of infusing UDL into a Science class on student engagement with Science content.

Obviously, there is a need for research examining the effect of UDL on standards-based learning for students with severe disabilities.

Instructional context. Put simply, the limited evidence that exists at this time suggests strongly that the place a student receives instruction in the general education curriculum is the general education classroom. Studies highlighted previously (Cole et al., 2004; Lee et al., 2008; Matzen et al., in press; Soukup et al., 2007; Wehmeyer, Lattin, et al., 2003) all provided evidence that students with severe disabilities had greater access to the general education curriculum and were disproportionately more likely to be working on tasks linked to a grade level core-content standard when they were receiving instruction in the general education classroom.

Instructional strategies. It goes without saying that high quality instruction with regard to core-academic content is critical to the success of all students, including students with severe disabilities. Because other chapters in this text cover effective instruction for students with significant cognitive disabilities, we will only note that access to and progress in the general education curriculum for students with severe disabilities is obviously contingent on schoolwide implementation of high quality instructional strategies. Spooner et al. (2006) identified a few approaches to promoting the access of students with severe disabilities that illustrate the types of instructional strategies that should or could promote access and progress. One such set of instructional strategies involves peer support interventions, in which "peers are taught to provide support by adapting class activities to facilitate student participation" (p. 278). Carter and colleagues (Carter, Cushing, Clark, and Kennedy, 2005; Carter & Kennedy, 2006; Carter, Sisco, Melekoglu, & Kurkowski, 2007) have examined the utilization of peer support interventions to promote access to the general education and social interactions for students with severe disabilities, particularly as an alternative to the use of paraprofessionals in instructional support roles. These studies have documented that students with severe disabilities supported by peers "showed substantially higher levels of active engagement relative to receiving supports from paraprofessionals and special educators" (Spooner et al., p. 286) and that students had higher levels of social interactions and contact with the general education curriculum when students worked with two peers relative to one peer.

Another instructional approach identified by Spooner et al. (2006) involves instruction to promote self-determination. Wehmeyer et al. (2004) noted that efforts to promote self-determination may be beneficial to gaining access to the general education for two reasons; first, most district standards, particularly student achievement standards, include component elements of instruction to promote self-determination, such as goal setting, problem solving or decision making, as elements of the standard. As such, promoting self-determination, which involves instruction in areas such as these, provides an entry point for gaining access to the general education curriculum for students with severe disabilities and provides a focal point for classroom-wide instruction. Second, it is hypothesized that students who are more self-determined will, in fact, perform more effectively in the general education curriculum. There is a clear evidence-base that teaching students to self-regulate learning or teaching students self-directed learning strategies such as self-monitoring or self-instruction has beneficial outcomes for students with severe disabilities in student goal attainment, problem solving, and student engagement (Agran, Blanchard, Hughes, & Wehmeyer, 2002; Agran et al., 2005; Hughes et al. 2002;). Further, the application of instruction to teach and implement these strategies has been validated as effective in promoting standards-based learning for students with severe disabilities (Wehmeyer, Hughes, et al., 2003). Finally, Wehmeyer and colleagues have provided evidence that teaching students to self-regulate learning using the Self-Determined Learning Model of Instruction (Wehmeyer, Palmer, Agran, Mithaug, & Martin, 2000) results in the attainment of goals linked to the general education curriculum (Agran, Wehmeyer, Cavin, & Palmer, in press; Lee et al., 2010; Palmer, Wehmeyer, Gipson, & Agran, 2004).

Teacher training. It is self-evident that high quality instruction and teacher training are causally linked, and similarly self-evident that a critical schoolwide component of efforts to promote access to and progress in the general education curriculum for students with severe disabilities will involve teacher training. As noted previously, Spooner et al. (2007), training in UDL, improved the lesson plans of teachers working with students with severe disabilities. Clark, Cushing, and Kennedy (2004) documented the efficacy of an intensive onsite technical assistance model for special educators as resulting in greater access to the general education curriculum for students with severe disabilities. Dymond and colleagues (2006) indicated the importance and efficacy of team collaboration and planning in infusing UDL into a science course for students with severe disabilities, and Jorgensen and colleagues (McSheehan et al., 2006; Sonnenmeir, McSheehan, & Jorgensen, 2005) have demonstrated the efficacy of a team planning process to implement a model to promote student progress in the general education curriculum (Beyond Access Model) with students with severe disabilities who need augmentative communication supports. The Beyond Access Model creates Comprehensive Assessment of Student and Team Supports (CASTS) process to gain information from team members as a means of implementing the model and promoting student progress in core content areas. Activities that occur during this time include (beyond standard team activities pertaining to special education practices) identifying the alignment between the student's educational program and best practices for learning core content in the general education classroom and alignment of staffing and teaming practices to achieve progress.

Curriculum Planning and Educational Decision Making to Promote Access to the General Education Curriculum for Students with Significant Cognitive Disabilities

From the school level, the obvious next level of action involves the educational decision-making process that determines the educational programs of students with disabilities. That is, obviously, the IEP process for students with severe disabilities. To a large degree, a focus on access to the general education curriculum for students with severe disabilities changes the role of the IEP in the design of a student's educational program. Historically, the IEPs of many students with severe disabilities described an *alternative* curriculum focused solely on life skills outcomes and functional content. The access mandates in IDEA, though, presume that the general education curriculum is the starting point for educational program decision making and require IEP teams to consider curricular modifications, supplementary aids and services, specially designed instruction, and related services that promote access and progress. The IEP is not intended to describe an alternative curriculum; instead, it is intended to identify the supports a student needs to be involved with and progress in the general education curriculum and, only then, what other educational needs are not addressed in the general education classroom that warrant instructional focus. As stated by Nolet and McLaughlin (2000), the IEP should be a plan to identify goals and objectives needed to enhance, not replace, the general education curriculum.

Wehmeyer, Lattin, et al. (2003) proposed a model for use by IEP teams to design IEPs that are consistent with the intent of the access mandates (see Figure 41.1). As shown in this figure, the decision-making process begins with the general education curriculum and knowledge

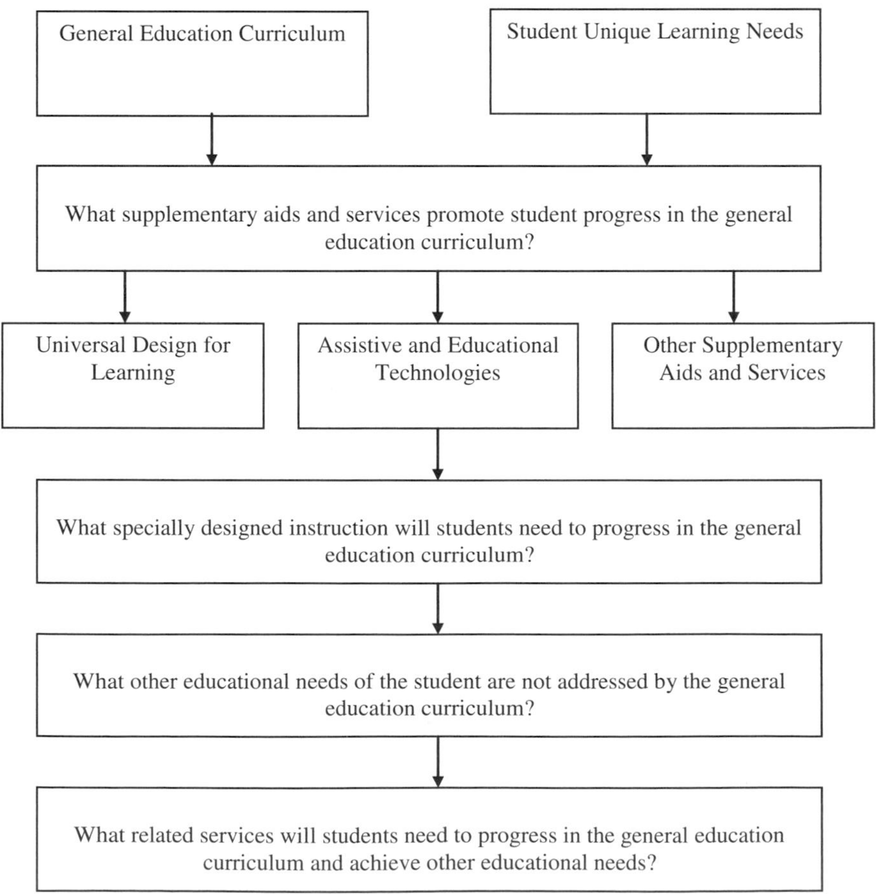

Figure 41.1 IEP Team decision making process to promote access to the general education curriculum.

(from assessment, stakeholder input, and prior instructional experiences) about the unique learning needs of the student (e.g., functional/life skills needs). Next, as per the IDEA requirements, the IEP team has a number of responsibilities when writing the IEP. They must:

- Develop measurable goals to ensure student progress in the general education curriculum and to address other educational needs that are not in the general education curriculum.
- Identify the specially designed instruction required to ensure student progress in the general education curriculum.
- Identify the supplementary aids and services required to ensure that students can be educated with their non-disabled peers and make progress in the general education curriculum.
- Identify related services students need if they are reasonably to be expected to benefit from the educational program.
- Determine if a student can participate in the state mandated tests without modifications or if the student requires a modified test or an alternative assessment.

Teams are guided through this process by asking and answering four questions:

1. What supplementary aids and services promote student progress in the general education curriculum?
2. What specially designed instruction will students need to progress in the general education curriculum?
3. What other educational needs of the student are not addressed by the general education curriculum?
4. What related services will students need to progress in the general education curriculum and achieve other educational needs?

IDEA defines supplementary aids and services as "aids, services, and other supports that are provided in general education classes or other education related settings to enable children with disabilities to be educated with non-disabled children to the maximum extent appropriate" (2004, section §300.320(a)(4)). Such supplementary aids and supports include modifications to the curriculum or the classroom (room or seating arrangement), extended time to complete tasks, extended school year services, assistive technology devices, a paraprofessional or notetaker, and other accommodations to promote regular classroom participation. Issues pertaining to UDL come into play here, with IEP teams considering how to modify the presentation or representation of content information or student's responses to the content (discussed previously) to promote student access and progress.

Wehmeyer, Hughes, et al. (2003) have suggested two levels of curriculum modifications as important in the education of students with significant cognitive disabilities: adapting the curriculum and augmenting the curriculum. The first level of modification involves curriculum adaptations. Curriculum adaptation refers to the application of principles of UDL to modify the way the curriculum looks (representation), is presented (presentation), or the ways in which students respond or engage with the curriculum. Adaptations to the way curricular content is *represented* refer to the way in which the information in the curriculum is depicted or portrayed, specifically how curricular materials are used to depict information. As noted, the dominant representation mode in education involves print materials, usually through texts, workbooks, and worksheets. Curriculum adaptations modify that representation so a wider array of students can progress, ranging from changing font size to using graphics to using technology and electronic text.

Adaptations in curriculum *presentation* modify the way teachers convey or impart information in the content in curriculum. Such presentation has, historically, been through written formats (chalkboards or overheads) or verbally (lectures). These primary means of presentation have drawbacks for many students who read ineffectively (or don't read at all) or who have difficulty attending to or understanding lecture formats. There are a variety of ways of changing the presentation mode, from using video sources, to reading (or playing an audiotape of) written materials to web-based information.

Curriculum adaptations that modify the student's *engagement* with the curriculum impact the ways students respond to the curriculum. Again, the typical means of student engagement within the curriculum involves written responses or, perhaps less frequently, oral responses or reports. There are, however, a variety of ways in which students can respond to content beyond a written report, from multi-media presentations like PowerPoint or through video, to performance-based expressions and artistic products.

The second level of curricular modification to achieve access involves curriculum *augmentation* (Wehmeyer, Hughes, et al., 2003). Curriculum augmentations refer to the expansion of the general education curriculum to include content that teaches students learning to learn, cognitive, or self-management strategies to enable them to interact more effectively with the general curriculum. Such augmentations don't change the curriculum, but add to or augment the curriculum with strategies for students to succeed within the curriculum. The aforementioned focus on promoting self-determination and student-directed learning is a means of curriculum augmentation. Teaching students such strategies allows them to manage, direct, and regulate their own learning, and permits students to plan, execute, and evaluate actions based on problem solving and self-directed decision making (Agran, King-Sears, Wehmeyer, & Copeland, 2003).

IDEA defines "special education" as "specially designed instruction." In addition to the schoolwide implementation of high quality instruction, students with significant cognitive disabilities will undoubtedly need additional instructional supports.

Only after teams have considered supplementary aids and services and specially designed instruction that would enable students to engage with the general education curriculum should they then consider what unique student learning needs are not addressed in the general education curriculum and, finally, what related services are needed to enable students to be involved with and progress in the general education curriculum or achieve goals related to other educational needs.

Classroom Level Actions to Promote Access to the General Education Curriculum for Students with Significant Cognitive Disabilities

Designing units of study. Units of study are the "maps" that teachers create to organize and plan for how they are going to support students to learn and demonstrate their understanding of the content, skills, processes and knowledge required to achieve grade-level and broader school outcomes. Broadly, unit planning models tend to be organized by subject area, discipline structure, integrated designs, learner-centered designs, experience-centered designs, problem centered designs, and life-situations designs (Wehmeyer et al., 2002). Such units of study identify what needs to be accomplished by the end of the school year, district standards and benchmarks, and student knowledge and instructional needs. Once teachers understand the "big picture" for the school year, they must "backwards-map" to determine what students will need to know and do by the middle of the year, and then plan for more manageable instructional units. When a teacher has an overall idea of what needs to be accomplished by the end of the school year and has "chunked" that content, skills, and knowledge into mid-year and quarterly components, he/she is ready to plan units of instruction (Wehmeyer, Sands, et al., 2002).

It is at the unit planning level that teachers must identify the "big ideas" they want to achieve in each unit. The big ideas are those concepts, knowledge, and skills that a teacher wants all students to attain and retain. These big ideas form the foundation for later planning activities that use cognitive taxonomies to differentiate unit and lesson goals and instruction for use with students of varying abilities.

Lesson planning. Once learning targets have been identified, information needed to plan day-to-day activities that will support students to achieve unit outcomes is available. Generally, this preparation leads to lesson plans, which serve as a tool for breaking large units of study into smaller, manageable increments. The amount of time needed for a particular lesson will vary according to the complexity of the learning targets and the number of tasks needed to scaffold students' readiness levels to meet those targets. Generally, lesson plans set forth the topic or theme of the lesson, clear expectations as to the purpose of the lesson (rationale), how the lesson will be conducted (activities), what students are expected to accomplish (objective), and how those accomplishments will be measured and accounted (evaluation).

Importantly to the success of students with significant cognitive disabilities, the lesson plan should also describe the cognitive, affective, and communicative and physical/health demands required of each learning target, and identify where various students will enter the learning sequence and what each student will need to succeed. Janney and Snell (2004) have forwarded the need for teachers to design lessons in which objectives with varying degrees of difficulty have been identified for students with differing learning needs and abilities, a process referred to as multilevel curriculum. Within the lesson planning process, teachers can create objectives that vary across learning abilities but which address the same overall lesson goal by using cognitive or learning taxonomies. Cognitive taxonomies are used to classify the cognitive demands of learning targets. Perhaps the most familiar cognitive taxonomy is the one developed by Bloom, Englehart, Furst, Hill, and Krathwohl (1956). Bloom's taxonomy is a means of categorizing the cognitive skills students use when achieving learning targets. As one ascends Bloom's taxonomy, the cognitive demands from students are more complex.

As cognitive taxonomies are applied in lesson planning activities, teachers track whether they are introducing students to increasingly complex skills and content. When learning objectives are set, students are expected to demonstrate their competence across levels of higher-ordered thinking skills and content types. Teachers should not automatically assume that students with significant cognitive disabilities can perform only at lower levels of cognitive taxonomies. Instead, they should apply what they understand about a student's cognitive abilities and create materials and supports that allow them to achieve at multiple levels.

Trends, Issues, and Future Directions

The IDEA access to the general education curriculum mandates were intended to improve educational outcomes for all students with disability by aligning special educational practices with school reform initiatives. Such desired outcomes involve increased participation and progress in the general curriculum. There is not universal agreement in the field with regard to the extent to which students with significant cognitive disabilities should be engaged in standards-based learning in core content areas. There is general agreement, however, that holding students with significant cognitive disabilities to higher expectations is a worthwhile endeavor and, as highlighted in this chapter, there is emerging evidence that students with significant cognitive disabilities can benefit from instruction in core content areas.

This chapter has outlined actions to achieve this outcome that focus on all levels of the educational process, beginning with standards setting and curriculum design, and involving the district, school, and classroom level actions detailed in this chapter, students with significant cognitive disabilities can receive an educational program that is based both on the general curriculum and the student's unique learning needs. Key elements that will determine the answer to the question as to whether students with significant cognitive disabilities can benefit from instruction in core content areas are in their early phases of development and lack the empirical support that would validate their inclusion in educational programs for students with severe disabilities. We know far too little about the impact of UDL principals on educational outcomes for students with severe disabilities. Likewise, while there exists a robust evidence-base for various curriculum adaptations to enable students with high incidence disabilities to learn curriculum content, most of these strategies have not been modified and/or evaluated for use with students with severe disabilities. There is a substantial literature base that supports the use of student-directed learning strategies with students with severe disabilities, but limited research regarding the impact of this or any other instructional strategy on actual progress in the general education curriculum.

It's important, as well, to emphasize that the intent of IDEA was not to eliminate a focus on functional or life skills instruction for students with significant cognitive disabilities, but to add to the equation the opportunity for students with severe disabilities to learn the same curriculum that is deemed important for all students. We certainly need to know how to more effectively achieve these outcomes while still preparing students for important life outcomes. Nevertheless, given findings that alternate assessment and alternate achievement standards developed for use with students with significant cognitive disabilities have, to this point, more in common with functional content than academic content, there is also reason to be concerned that the intent of IDEA to raise expectations for all students is being watered down for students with significant cognitive disabilities. Finally, there is a need for teacher training and personnel preparation models that prepare all educators, both special and general educators, to implement high quality instructional strategies and to modify and adapt the curriculum to support students with significant cognitive disabilities.

References

Agran, M., Alper, S., & Wehmeyer, M. (2002). Access to the general curriculum for students with significant disabilities: What it means to teachers. *Education and Training in Mental Retardation and Developmental Disabilities, 37,* 123–133.

Agran, M., Blanchard, C. Hughes, C., & Wehmeyer, M. L. (2002). Increasing the problem-solving skills of students with severe disabilities participating in general education. *Remedial and Special Education, 23,* 279–288.

Agran, M., King-Sears, M. E., Wehmeyer, M. L., & Copeland, S. R. (2003). *Student-directed learning*. Baltimore: Paul H. Brookes.

Agran, M., Sinclair, T., Alper, S., Cavin, M., Wehmeyer, M., & Hughes, C. (2005). Using self-monitoring to increase following-direction skills of students with moderate to severe disabilities in general education. *Education and Training in Developmental Disabilities, 40,* 3–13.

Agran, M., Wehmeyer, M., Cavin, M., & Palmer, S. (in press). Promoting engagement in the general education classroom and access to the general education curriculum for students with cognitive disabilities. *Education and Training in Developmental Disabilities.*

Bloom, B. S., Englehart, M. B., Furst, E. J., Hill, W. H., & Krathwohl, D. R. (1956.). *Taxonomy of educational objectives. The classification of educational goals. Handbook I: Cognitive domain.* New York: McKay.

Browder, D. M., Ahlgrim-Delzell, L., Courtade, G., Gibbs, S. L., & Flowers, C. (2008). Evaluation of the effectiveness of an early literacy program for students with significant developmental disabilities. *Exceptional Children, 75*(1), 33–52.

Browder, D., Flowers, C., Ahlgrim-Delzell, L., Karvonen, M., Spooner, F. & Algozzine, R. (2004). The alignment of alternate assessment content with academic and functional curricula. *The Journal of Special Education, 37*(4), 211–223.

Browder, D. M., Mims, P. J., Spooner, F., Ahgrim-Delzell, L., & Lee, A. (2008). Teaching elementary students with multiple disabilities to participate in shared stories. *Research and Practice for Persons with Severe Disabilities, 33*(1-2), 3–12.

Browder, D., & Spooner, F. (2006). *Teaching language arts, math, and science to students with significant cognitive disabilities.* Baltimore: Paul H. Brookes.

Browder, D. M., Spooner, F., Wakeman, S., Trela, K., & Baker, J. N. (2006). Aligning instruction with academic content standards: Finding the link. *Research and Practice for Persons with Severe Disabilities, 31*(4), 309–321.

Browder, D. M., Trela, K., & Jimenez, B. (2007). Training teachers to follow a task analysis to engage middle school students with moderate and severe developmental disabilities in grade-appropriate literature. *Focus on Autism and Other Developmental Disabilities, 22*(4), 206–219.

Browder, D. M., Wakeman, S. Y., & Flowers, C. (2006). Assessment of progress in the general curriculum for students with disabilities. *Theory into Practice, 45*(3), 249–259.

Butler, F. M., Miller, S. P., Lee, K., & Pierce, T. (2001). Teaching mathematics to students with mild-to-moderate mental retardation: A review of the literature. *Mental Retardation, 39*(1), 20–31.

Carter, E. W., Cushing, L. S., Clark, N. M., & Kennedy, C. H. (2005). Effects of peer support interventions on students' access to the general curriculum and social interactions. *Research and Practice for Persons with Severe Disabilities, 30*(1), 15–25.

Carter, E. W., & Kennedy, C. H. (2006). Promoting access to the general curriculum using peer support strategies. *Research and Practice for Persons with Severe Disabilities, 31*(4), 284–292.

Carter, E. W., Sisco, L. G., Melekoglu, M. A., & Kurkowski, C. (2007). Peer supports as an alternative to individually assigned paraprofessionals in inclusive high school classrooms. *Research and Practice for Persons with Severe Disabilities, 32*(4), 213–227.

Center for Applied Special Technology (CAST). (1998–1999). The national center on accessing the general curriculum, http://www.cast.org/initiatives/nationalcenter.html

Clark, N. M., Cushing, L .S., & Kennedy, C. H. (2004). An intensive onsite technical assistance model to promote inclusive educational practices for students with disabilities in middle school and high school. *Research and Practice for Persons with Severe Disabilities, 29*(4), 253–262.

Cole, C. M., Waldron, N.., & Majd, M. (2004). Academic progress of students across inclusive and traditional settings. *Mental Retardation, 42*(2), 136–144.

Collins, B. C., Evans, A., Creech-Galloway, C., Karl, J., & Miller, A. (2007). Comparison of the acquisition and maintenance of teaching functional and core content sight words in special and general education settings. *Focus on Autism and Other Developmental Disabilities, 22*(4), 220–233.

Courtade, G. R., Spooner, F., & Browder, D. M. (2006). Review of studies with students with significant cognitive disabilities which link to science standards. *Research and Practice for Persons with Severe Disabilities, 32*(1), 43–49.

Dymond, S. K., Renzaglia, A., Gilson, C. L., & Slagor, M. T. (2007). Defining access to the general curriculum for high school students with significant cognitive disabilities. *Research and Practice for Persons with Severe Disabilities, 32*(1), 1–15.

Dymond, S. K., Renzaglia, A., Rosenstein, A., Chun, E. J., Banks, R. A., Niswander, V., & Gilson, C. L. (2006). Using a participatory action research approach to create a universally designed inclusive high school Science course; A case study. *Research and Practice for Persons with Severe Disabilities, 31*(4), 293–308.

Federal Register. (1999, March 12). Washington, DC: U.S. Government Printing Office.

Hughes, C., Copeland, S. R., Agran, M., Wehmeyer, M. L., Rodi, M. S., & Presley, J. A. (2002). Using self-monitoring to improve performance in general education high school classes. *Education and Training in Mental Retardation and Developmental Disabilities, 37*, 262–271.

Individuals with Disabilites Act (IDEA) of 2004, P. L. 108-446, 108th Congress (2004).

Janney, R., & Snell, M. (2004). *Modifying schoolwork: Teachers' guides to inclusive practices* (2nd ed.). Baltimore: Paul H. Brookes.

Jimenez, B. A., Browder, D. M., & Courtade, G. R. (2008). Teaching an algebraic equation to high school students with moderate developmental disabilities. *Education and Training in Developmental Disabilities, 43*(2), 266–274.

Jorgensen, C. M., McSheehan, M., & Sonnenmeier, R. M. (2010). *The Beyond Access Model: Promoting membership, participation, and learning for students with disabilities in the general education classroom.* Baltimore: Paul H. Brookes.

Karvonen, M. & Huynh, H. (2007). Relationship between IEP characteristics and test scores on an alternate assessment for students with significant cognitive disabilities. *Applied Measurement in Education, 20*(3), 273–300.

Konrad, M., Trela, K., & Test, D. W. (2006). Using IEP goals and objectives to teach paragraph writing to high school students with physical and cognitive disabilities. *Education and Training in Developmental Disabilities, 41*(2), 111–124.

Kortering, L. J., McLannon, T. W., & Braziel, P. M. (2008). Universal Design for Learning: A look at what algebra and biology students with and without high incidence conditions are saying. *Remedial and Special Education, 29*(6), 352–363.

Lee, S. H., Wehmeyer, M. L., Palmer, S. B., Soukup, J. H., & Little, T. D. (2008). Self-determination and access to the general education curriculum. *The Journal of Special Education, 42*, 91–107.

Lee, S. H., Wehmeyer, M. L., Soukup, J. H., & Palmer, S. B. (2010). Impact of curriculum modifications on access to the general education curriculum for students with disabilities. *Exceptional Children, 76*(2), 213–233.

Matzen, K., Ryndak, D., & Nakao, T. (in press). Middle school teams increasing access to general educatin for students with significant disabilities: Issues encountered and activities observed across contexts. *Remedial and Special Education.*

McSheehan, M., Sonnenmeier, R. M., Jorgensen, C. M., & Turner, K. (2006). Beyond communication access: Promoting learning of the general education curriculum by students with significant disabilities. *Topics in Language Disorders, 26*(3), 266–290.

Nolet, V., & McLaughlin, M. (2000). *Accessing the general curriculum.* Thousand Oaks, CA; Corwin Press.

Orkwis, R., & McLane, K. (1998, Fall). A curriculum every student can use: Design principles for student access. *ERIC/OSEP Topical Brief.* Reston, VA: Council for Exceptional Children.

Palmer, S. B., Wehmeyer, M. L., Gipson, K., & Agran, M. (2004). Promoting access to the general curriculum by teaching self-determination skills. *Exceptional Children, 70*, 427–439.

Sonnenmeir, R. M., McSheehan, M., & Jorgensen, C. M. (2005). A case study of team supports for a student with autism's communication and engagement within the general education curriculum: Preliminary report of the Beyond Access Model. *Augmentative and Alternative Communication, 21*(2), 101–115.

Soukup, J. H., Wehmeyer, M. L., Bashinski, S. M., & Bovaird, J. (2007). Classroom variables and access to the general education curriculum of students with intellectual and developmental disabilities. *Exceptional Children, 74*, 101–120.

Spooner, F., Baker, J. N., Harris, A. A., Ahlgrim-Delzell, & Browder, D. M. (2007). Effects of training in Universal Design for Learning on lesson plan development. *Remedial and Special Education, 28*(2), 108–116.

Spooner, F., Dymond, S. K., Smith, A., & Kennedy, C. H. (2006). What we know and need to know about accessing the general curriculum for students with significant cognitive disabilities. *Research and Practice for Persons with Severe Disabilities, 31*(4), 277–283.

Stainback, W., Stainback, S., Stefanich, G., & Alper, S. (1996). Learning in inclusive classrooms: What about the curriculum? In S. Stainback & W. Stainback (Eds.), *Inclusion: A guide for educators* (pp. 209–219). Baltimore: Paul H. Brookes.

Roach, A. T., & Elliott, S. N. (2006). The influence of access to general education curriculum on alternate assessment performance of students with significant cognitive disabilities. *Educational Evaluation and Policy Analysis, 28*(2), 181–194.

U.S. Department of Education (1995). *Testimony of Richard Riley, Secretary, U.S. Department of Education: Hearings before the Committee on Economic and Educational Opportunities Subcommittee on Early Childhood, Youth and Families, House of Representatives, 104th Cong.* Retrieved from http://www.ed.gov/ Speeches/06-1995/idea-1.html

U.S. Department of Education (2003). *Title I-Improving the academic achievement of the disadvantaged*: Proposed Rule, 68 Fe. Reg. 13, 797–798.

U.S. Department of Education (2005). Alternate achievement standards for students with the most significant cognitive disabilities: Non-regulatory guidance. Washington, DC: Author. Retrieved October 4, 2009, from http://74.125.95.132/search?q=cache:W12oht6GHgYJ:www.ed.gov/policy/elsec/guid/altguidance.pdf+students+with+the+most+significant+cognitive+disabilities&cd=1&hl=en&ct=clnk&gl=us

Wehmeyer, M.L., Field, S., Doren, B., Jones, B., & Mason, C. (2004). Self-determination and student involvement in standards-based reform. *Exceptional Children*, *70*, 413–425.

Wehmeyer, M. L., Hughes, C., Agran, M., Garner. N., & Yeager, D. (2003). Student-directed learning strategies to promote the progress of students with intellectual disability in inclusive classrooms. *International Journal of Inclusive Education, 7*, 415–428.

Wehmeyer, M. L., Lance, G. D., & Bashinski, S. (2002). Promoting access to the general curriculum for students with mental retardation: A multi-level model. *Education and Training in Mental Retardation and Developmental Disabilities, 37*, 223–234.

Wehmeyer, M. L., Lattin, D., Lapp-Rincker, G., & Agran, M. (2003). Access to the general curriculum of middle-school students with mental retardation: An observational study. *Remedial and Special Education, 24,* 262–272.

Wehmeyer, M. L., Palmer, S., Agran, M., Mithaug, D., & Martin, J. (2000). Promoting causal agency: The Self-Determined Learning Model of Instruction. *Exceptional Children, 66*, 439–453.

Wehmeyer, M. L., Sands, D. J., Knowlton, H. E., & Kozleski, E. B. (2002). *Teaching students with mental retardation: Providing access to the general curriculum.* Baltimore: Paul H. Brookes.

Ysseldyke, J., Dennison, A., & Nelson, R. (2003). *Large-scale assessment and accountability systems: Positive consequences for students with disabilities* (Synthesis Report 51). Minneapolis: University of Minnesota, National Center on Educational Outcomes. Retrieved December 8, 2009, from http://education.umn.edu/NCEO/OnlinePubs/Synthesis51.html

42

Preparing Students with Significant Cognitive Disabilities for Life Skills

Stacy K. Dymond
University of Illinois, Urbana-Champaign

Prior to 1980, much of the curricula developed for students with significant cognitive disabilities (SCD) were based on a bottom up, developmental model. Skills were selected for instruction that matched the cognitive functioning level of the student. Prevailing theories of human development at the time suggested that all children must pass through the same developmental milestones in order to be capable of learning more advanced skills. As a result, students who failed to master skills at a particular developmental level were relegated to repeat those skills until they were mastered. Skills typically taught to students with SCD focused on cognition, self-help, motor skills, communication, and social skills. The drawbacks to this type of curriculum were that as students with SCD grew older, they did not learn the skills needed to function in settings with their same-aged peers or participate in valued adult life activities.

In 1979, Brown and colleagues proposed a new model for developing curricula that focused on "chronologically age-appropriate functional skills in natural environments" (p. 83). This model came to be widely known as "functional curriculum." Unlike the developmental model, it was based on the premise that students with SCD should learn skills that enable them to function in the same environments as peers without disabilities. Also important, it should prepare students during high school for the settings in which they would need to function as adults. Functional skills were defined as skills needed in every day home, school, and community environments and categorized according to four domains: domestic, leisure/recreation, community, and vocational. The natural environment was seen as both the source of curriculum content as well as the location where skills should be learned. Thus, unlike the developmental model which used a bottom up approach based on stages of cognitive development, the functional model offered a top down approach that emphasized developing curriculum based on the requirements for participation in natural, age-appropriate settings.

The four domains proposed by Brown et al. (1979) are still prominent in the literature today. Authors of current textbooks used within universities to prepare teachers to work with students with SCD continue to promote these domains as a framework for developing life skills curricula (see Ryndak & Alper, 2003; Collins, 2007; Snell & Brown, 2006; Westling & Fox, 2009). Although the term "functional curriculum" is still used, these skills are more frequently referred to as "life skills" or "independent living skills". As Brown et al. (1979) noted many years ago, any skill may be functional or non-functional depending on how and where it is taught. Thus the term "life skills" is more descriptive of the types of skills taught rather than the context in which learning occurs.

Support for instruction on life skills is also evident in the Individuals with Disabilities Education Improvement Act (IDEIA, 2004). IDEIA states that special education services should prepare students for independent living and employment. This preparation should allow students access to the general education curriculum to the maximum extent appropriate and address "other educational needs" that extend beyond the general education curriculum. Although some life skills may be taught naturally within the general curriculum, most extend beyond the general curriculum and are classified as meeting a student's "other educational needs." A more explicit expectation for addressing life skills is found in IDEIA's definition of transition services where daily living skills are identified as a type of service. It is up to each student's Individual Education Program (IEP) team to determine the extent to which a student is engaged in the general education curriculum or addressing other educational needs, as well as whether transition services should include a focus on daily living skills.

The purpose of this chapter is to summarize the research on life skills for students with SCD as it relates to curriculum content, instructional strategies, and skill selection. Trends and issues in the field will be discussed related to the conceptualization and delivery of life skills curricula.

Curriculum Content and Instructional Strategies

Students with SCD take longer to learn skills than their same-age peers and frequently experience difficulty generalizing what they learn in one setting to other settings (Westling & Floyd, 1990). As a result, the curriculum content for students with SCD must be carefully considered to ensure that skills targeted for instruction will increase participation in valued everyday activities in inclusive, age-appropriate settings. In this section, life skills that fall within the domains of domestic, leisure/recreation, and community are defined, and instructional practices for teaching skills in each domain are explored. The vocational domain is purposefully omitted since it is covered elsewhere in this book.

Domestic

Skills within the domestic domain are often grouped into two distinct types: self-care and home living. Farlow and Snell (2006) define self-care skills as skills that address personal hygiene including toileting, eating, dressing, and grooming. Self-care skills are also referred to in the literature as "personal care" skills. Learning these skills promotes cleanliness, good health, acceptance among peers, and a positive self-image (Farlow & Snell, 2006; Spooner & Wood, 2004; Westling & Fox, 2009). Self-care skills are highly valued in society and they are some of the most important skills that students with SCD need to learn. In many situations, these skills are pre-requisites to obtaining adult services once students exit school. For example, some group homes require that residents be able to toilet independently in order to live at the residence.

A key premise of life skills instruction is that the skills chosen for instruction should match the chronological age of the student. An exception to this premise exists in the area of self-care skills where specific developmental sequences are commonly accepted for teaching skills in the areas of toileting and eating. Prior to teaching toileting, an individual must demonstrate a stable pattern of elimination, the ability to maintain dry pants for one to two hours, and a chronological age of at least two years. Bowel control typically develops prior to bladder control and daytime control is mastered before nighttime control (Farlow & Snell, 2006). Methods for teaching toileting generally fall into two categories including traditional methods and rapid methods. Traditional methods involve toileting students according to a predetermined schedule of when they are most likely to need to eliminate (see Bainbridge & Myles, 1999; Luiselli, 2007) whereas rapid methods focus on intensive training that includes additional fluids and toileting every 15–30 minutes (see Azrin & Foxx, 1971; Cicero & Pfadt, 2002; Richmond, 1983).

The goal of eating instruction is to ensure that students obtain proper nutrition. Other important skills taught during mealtimes include socialization and choice making. Pre-requisite skills for teaching eating include an active gag reflex, and the ability to suck, bite, chew, swallow, and maintain closed lips (Farlow & Snell). Eating skills are typically taught in a developmental sequence beginning with finger foods. Utensils are then taught in the following order: spoon, cup, fork, knife (first for spreading a substance and then for cutting). Breaking up each meal into several smaller meals that are served throughout the day (i.e., the "mini meal method") has been shown to increase skill acquisition (Azrin & Armstrong, 1973). Other methods for increasing skill acquisition include using foods highly preferred by the student and teaching when the student is hungry.

A second component of the domestic domain is home living. Home living skills refer to skills that are performed on a regular basis within the home environment. Bambara, Browder, and Koger (2006) define home living skills as including food preparation, housekeeping, home safety, telephone use, and sexuality education. Other important skill areas mentioned in the literature include clothing care, yard work, self-management, and negotiating with others (see Bambara et al., 2006; Renzaglia & Aveno, 1986; Steere & Burcroff, 2004). Acquisition of these skills enables students with SCD to become more actively engaged in the daily activities that occur within their home and acquire skills needed during adulthood for managing a home. Skills are selected for instruction based on the activities that occur in the setting rather than the developmental sequences common to the areas of eating and toileting.

Domestic skills are typically taught through systematic instruction that occurs within natural routines in the home or school. The most frequently used method for teaching self-care skills is graduated guidance. Other methods include time delay, simultaneous prompting, and system of least intrusive prompts (see Farlow & Snell for a review). Home living skills have been taught using a variety of methods. In a review of the literature on teaching food preparation skills to individuals with intellectual disabilities, Lancioni and O'Reilly (2002) found that 16 studies used pictorial instructions (on cards or via the computer), seven studies used systematic instruction (e.g., time delay), and four studies used a combination of time delay and picture prompts. More recently, Mechling (2008) reviewed empirical studies that used technology to teach cooking skills to students with moderate to severe disabilities, and found four types of technology effective. These included picture-based systems, palmtop personal computers, auditory systems, and video-based systems. Several researchers have also demonstrated that peers without disabilities can effectively deliver prompts to teach food preparation to students with SCD (see Collins, Branson, & Hall, 1995; Godsey, Schuster, Lingo, Collins, & Kleinert, 2008). Although most of the literature on domestic skills reports strategies for teaching food preparation, systematic instruction procedures have also been demonstrated to be effective in teaching skills such as telephone usage, dishwashing, and laundry.

Leisure/Recreation

Moon (1994) defines leisure and recreation as "any activities or programs that people participate in for fun, relaxation, diversion, or amusement" (p. 244). Implicit in this definition is the importance of personal choice. An activity deemed enjoyable and fun to one individual may not be viewed as such by another person. Likewise, what is fun at any given moment in time to an individual may change, thus having a repertoire of accessible recreation and leisure options from which to choose is important. Participation in leisure activities increases when individuals are given choices (see Browder, Cooper, & Lim, 1998; Realon, Favell, & Lowerre, 1990; Wilson, Reid, & Green, 2006).

The domain of leisure/recreation often receives limited attention within schools except during organized classes such as physical education, art, and music. Its importance for students with SCD should not be underestimated. Children with disabilities have been found to participate in significantly fewer social and recreational activities than peers without disabilities, and to have fewer friends (Solish, Perry, & Minnes, 2010). In addition, individuals with disabilities typically have more free time than their peers without disabilities and spend more time post-school in activities at home that are socially isolated (Schleien & Ray, 1997). These findings suggest that students with SCD may need more instruction in this domain than what is offered in the typical school schedule.

The goals of leisure education are to promote independent or partial participation in leisure activities, expand the repertoire of leisure skills each student possesses, and help students develop relationships with same-age peers (Moon, 1994; Schleien & Ray. 1997). Renzaglia and Aveno (1986) categorize activities within the leisure and recreation domain according to four skill areas: (a) games, sports, and fitness; (b) hobbies; (c) passive spectator activities; and (d) social activities. They note the importance of ensuring that students with SCD develop a repertoire of skills within each category and further recommend that students learn leisure and recreation skills that can be performed individually, in groups, at home, and in the community. In addition to teaching the specific skills of the activity (e.g., how to play a board game), instruction should also focus on teaching choice making and social skills (Browder et al., 1998; Moon, 1994).

Preference assessments are often conducted prior to formal instruction to determine leisure activities enjoyed by the student (Browder et al., 1998; Dattilo & Mirenda, 1987; Kreiner & Flexer, 2009). These assessments typically include systematic observations of student behavior when various activities are presented and interviews with family members or other individuals who know the student well. In order to determine age-appropriate leisure activities for students with SCD, preference assessment data is often considered in combination with information about the activities preferred by same-age peers without disabilities. York, Vandercook, and Stave (1990) describe how they surveyed peers without disabilities to obtain a list of socially valid activities appropriate for students in middle school.

Methods for teaching leisure skills have included constant time delay (Zhang, Gast, Horvat, & Dattilo, 1995; Wall & Gast, 1997; Yilmaz, Birkan, Konukman, & Erkan, 2005), system of least intrusive prompts (Collins, Hall, & Branson, 1997; Duffy & Nietupski, 1985), most to least prompts (Demchak, 1989; Luyben, Funk, Morgan, Clark, & Delulio, 1986), and graduated guidance (Demchak, 1989). Several researchers have also demonstrated that family members, in-home staff, and peers without disabilities can effectively deliver systematic instructional procedures to teach leisure skills to individuals with SCD (see Collins et al., 1997; Wall & Gast, 1997; Wilson et al., 2006).

Community

Community skills are typically defined as those skills needed to function in the community in which an individual lives. For example, Ford et al. (1989) defined community skills according to the goal areas of grocery shopping, general shopping, eating out, using services, travel, and community safety. More recently, Dymond (2004) re-conceptualized the community domain to include two types of communities: the general community and the school community. The general community includes the goal areas of restaurants/eateries, grocery stores, retail stores, public facilities, recreation facilities, volunteer work, and transportation whereas the school community focuses on those skills needed to participate in activities that occur outside of core classes, including special events, clubs/organizations, school jobs, athletics, and the arts.

Teaching students with SCD to participate in the school community and the general community promotes inclusion and enhances quality of life. Since the 1990s, the field has been moving increasing towards educating students with SCD alongside their same-age peers in general education settings through a practice known as inclusive education. If students are to become true members of the school community, it is essential that they develop skills that enable them to participate in non-academic activities that enhance school life such as attending football games, participating in drama productions, and having in-school jobs (Sands, Kozleski, & French, 2000). Inclusion in the general community is equally important. Without knowledge and skills to participate safely in the community, students with SCD will miss opportunities for participation with peers outside of school and have diminished options for participation in the community as an adult.

The literature on community skills has focused almost exclusively on methods for teaching skills needed in the general community. Community skills have been taught effectively through the use of simulations, community-referenced instruction, and community-based instruction. Simulations involve instruction in the classroom with materials and conditions that closely approximate those used in the natural community. This form of instruction is frequently used to increase opportunities for instruction when transportation into the community is limited. Skills such as ordering at a restaurant (Mechling & Cronin, 2006; Mechling, Pridgen, & Cronin, 2005), locating grocery store items (Hutcherson, Langone, Ayres, & Clees, 2004; Mechling, 2004; Mechling & Gast, 2003), banking (Cihak, Alberto, Taber-Doughty, & Gama, 2006; Davies, Stock, & Wehmeyer, 2003), cell phone usage in the community (Tabor, Alberto, Hughes, & Seltzer, 2002; Tabor, Alberto, Seltzer, & Hughes, 2003), and purchasing (Ayres, Langone, Boon, & Norman, 2006; Xin, Grasso, DiPipi-Hoy, & Jitendra, 2005) have all been taught effectively through simulations. Recent empirical studies on the use of simulations to teach community skills have emphasized the use of computer-based instruction (see Alberto et al., 2003; Ayres et al., 2006; Hutcherson et al., 2004; Mechling & Cronin, 2006).

Simulations are often used in combination with community-based instruction (CBI) to ensure that students are able to perform skills in the actual community setting (see Alberto, Cihak, & Gama, 2005; Branham, Collins, Schuster, & Kleinert, 1999; Cihak et al., 2006; Morse & Schuster, 2000). CBI involves frequent, repeated instruction in natural community settings where skills are needed. Several studies suggest that using a combination of simulation and CBI is more effective than using either method individually (Cihak, Alberto, Kessler, & Tabor, 2004; McDonnell, Horner, & Williams, 1984; Xin et al., 2005). McDonnell and Ferguson (1988) found that students with SCD were able to generalize skills equally well when general case programming was used with either CBI or a combination of simulations and CBI. Students who received general case programming with CBI reached criterion in fewer instructional trials and time than those who received CBI and simulations.

It is possible that level of cognitive disability has an impact on the effectiveness of simulations. Bates, Cuvo, Miner, and Korabek (2001) found that students with mild cognitive disabilities performed better through simulations than students with moderate disabilities, but the performance of both groups increased significantly with CBI, regardless of whether simulations were used in tandem. The authors note that the type of simulations provided may account for the differential findings. Although individuals with SCD were not included in this study, the findings reinforce the importance of using instructional procedures that are efficient and ensure generalization to the natural environment.

Research on community skills interventions focus primarily on the use of simulations and CBI. One method frequently used but not widely investigated is the use of community-referenced instruction (Dymond, 2004). With this method, skills needed in the community are simultaneously taught in natural school routines. By teaching the same skill (e.g., purchasing) within a natural context in both the school (e.g., buying lunch in the cafeteria) and the community (e.g., buying lunch at a restaurant), students receive increased opportunities to practice the skill under natural conditions and dispersed trials.

Other Life Skill Domains

There are several life skills that cut across the domestic, leisure/recreation, and community domains. Those most frequently recognized in the literature include self-determination, safety, and sexuality. Although safety and sexuality are mentioned by Bambara et al. (2006) as components of the domestic domain, and choice making (i.e., self-determination) is identified as an important component of the leisure/recreation domain (Moon, 1994), these three skill areas are often neglected components of instruction for students with SCD. Acquisition of skills in each of these areas increases student independence and control over their lives, which in turn leads to greater options in adulthood and an improved quality of life.

Self-determination. In the last decade, self-determination had emerged as an essential desired outcome for students with SCD. Wehmeyer (2005) defines self-determination as "volitional actions that enable one to act as the primary causal agent in one's life and to maintain or improve one's quality of life" (p. 117). Skills associated with being self-determined include choice making, problem solving, decision making, goal setting and attainment, self-management and self-regulation, self-advocacy and leadership, perceptions of control and efficacy, and self-awareness and self-knowledge (Wehmeyer, Sands, Knowlton, & Kozleski, 2002). Most intervention studies that have measured the acquisition of skills associated with self-determination by students with SCD have focused on choice making (for a review, see Wood, Fowler, Uphold, & Test, 2005). These studies affirm the efficacy of teaching choice making and provide evidence of increased skills by students with SCD. Self-management (i.e., self-instruction, self-monitoring, self-reinforcement) and problem solving have also been investigated with mixed outcomes for students with SCD (Wood et al., 2005). Methods for teaching skills associated with self-determination to students with SCD primarily relied on systematic instruction. Other methods included the use of social stories and peer instruction.

Safety. Personal safety is a consideration within any environment in which a student functions, whether independently or with supervision. Skill areas identified by Agran (2004) include home and community safety, work safety, fire safety, crime prevention, HIV/AIDS prevention, substance use prevention, and self-medication and health care. In a review of empirical studies conducted on safety skills from 1976 to 2006, Mechling (2008) found that research has focused on pedestrian and street crossing, prevention of home accidents, first aid, responding to lures from strangers, fire safety, and using the telephone during an emergency. Because of the risks associated with learning some skills (e.g., crossing a street, extinguishing a fire), many safety skills are initially taught using simulations (Agran, 2004).

Teaching and testing for generalization under natural conditions is often impossible since the need for skills such as dialing 911 may never present themselves.

Sexuality. Sex education is an often debated curriculum area in schools and an area frequently ignored as it relates to the education of students with SCD. In a review of 12 commercially available sexuality education curricula advocated for students with disabilities, Blanchett and Wolfe (2002) identified four topical areas addressed including biological and reproductive, health and hygiene, relationships, and self-protection and advocacy. The most common instructional strategies employed to teach the curricula included discussion, lecture, and role-play. Direct instruction was visibly absent as an instructional strategy, despite its prominent use with individuals with SCD. In addition, most of the curriculum guides relied on photographs and slides for instruction. The authors caution that if these published curricula are used with students with SCD, instruction should be embedded within natural routines during the day so that skills may be learned within appropriate contexts. Wolfe, Condo, and Hardaway (2009) also advocate that the principles of applied behavior analysis be incorporated into sexuality education instruction to facilitate learning.

Skill Selection

The scope (i.e., breadth of skills taught) and sequence (i.e., order in which skills are taught) of life skills curricula is unique to each student. Unlike typical academic subjects that follow a developmental sequence, life skills are selected according to the skills needed to function in the student's unique current and future environments. These skills are chosen by the student's IEP team rather than defined by a published curriculum or textbook. This section describes factors affecting skill selection and methods for determining skills taught.

Factors Affecting Skill Selection

Several factors must be considered when selecting life skills for instruction including student age and skills, current and future environments, function of the skill, and parent and student preferences.

Student age and skills. Skills selected for instruction should match the chronological age of the student (Brown et al., 1979). A skill is considered age-appropriate if an individual without a disability of the same age would typically perform the skill. For example, an age-appropriate leisure skill for a 6-year-old may include playing with dolls; however, this would not be an age-appropriate skill for a 15-year-old because few students play with dolls at that age. Choosing age-appropriate skills for instruction enables students to learn skills needed for participation in activities with same-age peers as well as those needed throughout adulthood.

Although a student's current skill level should not preclude participation in age-appropriate activities, it may affect the level of participation targeted for instruction. Skills should be selected that advance a student's engagement in valued activities. For some students the goal may be independent functioning and for others it may be partial participation. Baumgart et al. (1982) describe partial participation as a method where students receive instruction on a portion of a task and adults or peers complete those parts of the task that extend beyond the individual's abilities. The concept of partial participation is particularly important for students with SCD because it underscores the value of increasing students' involvement in all aspects of their daily lives.

Current and future environments. The environments in which life skills are used include the home, school, and community. The skills needed to function in these settings depend on the community in which one lives, the school one attends, and the way in which one's family lives. Instruction should focus on skills needed to function in settings currently accessed by the student as well as those in which he/she (or family members) would like to participate. In high school (if not earlier), skills should be targeted that prepare students to function in settings that will be accessed post-school (Brown et al., 1979).

Function of the skill. Skills selected should be perceived as functional by the student. Functional skills are ones that are performed within the context of "real" activities, are perceived as meaningful by the student, serve a purpose, and are used throughout one's life (Dymond, 2004). Type of skill (i.e., domestic, leisure) is not the discerning factor that makes a skill functional. Rather, it is the context in which the skill is taught that makes it meaningful. For example, most would agree that being able to use money to make purchases is an important life skill. Teaching a student to count money in a classroom may not be considered functional if counting money serves no purpose that is understandable to the student. A more functional way to teach the skill would be to count money while purchasing an ice cream at the school cafeteria or buying items at the grocery store. In the latter example, counting money serves a purpose and is performed within a natural routine. A skill that is functional for one student may not be functional for another student depending on the student's age and the environments in which he/she functions currently or will function in the future.

Parent and student preferences. Life skills selected for instruction should be aligned with the family's goals and priorities for their child. This includes attending to the family's cultural values and beliefs regarding skills deemed important (Lim & Browder, 1994). Person-centered planning processes are frequently advocated as a means for gathering information from parents, the student, and others who know the student well in order to develop long-term goals for the student (Brown, Snell, & Lehr, 2006; Renzaglia, Karvonen, Drasgow, & Stoxen, 2003). This process results in a concrete action plan that provides direction for curriculum development.

Students with SCD should be involved to the greatest extent possible in making decisions about the settings, activities, and skills in which they engage. In order to make informed choices, it may be necessary for students to have opportunities to sample activities multiple times prior to making a determination of preference. When student interests are relatively unknown, systematic preference assessments may be conducted to identify preferred activities (see Cannella, O'Reilly, & Lanioni, 2005; Dymond, 2004; Kreiner & Flexer, 2009).

Methods for Determining Skills Taught

In 1979 Brown et al. proposed a strategy for developing age-appropriate functional curricula for students with SCD that focused on analyzing skills needed in various settings. This process is commonly referred to as an ecological or environmental inventory approach. With this process, environments (e.g., grocery store, recreation center, school) that the student currently accesses or will access in the near future are identified within each domain (i.e., domestic, leisure, community, vocational). Observations of these environments are conducted to determine the sub-environments present, the activities that occur in each sub-environment, and the skills needed to participate in each activity. This method of curriculum development is still widely accepted as an appropriate and effective method for determining individualized life skills goals (Brown et al., 2006; Dymond, 2004; Ryndak & Alper, 2003; Westling & Fox, 2009).

Perhaps the greatest change in recent years that has occurred in the conceptualization of ecological inventories is that this approach is now viewed as a strategy to be used in conjunction with person-centered planning. Using person-centered planning, long-term goals and desired outcomes are identified for the student first and then ecological inventories are used to investigate the specific skills needed to reach these goals (Renzaglia et al., 2003). Thus it is no longer the curriculum domains that drive the environments inventoried but the priority goals identified through person-centered planning.

Over the years several curriculum guides have been published to assist practitioners with selecting life skills goals for their students with SCD, several of which incorporate an ecological inventory approach and the tenets of person-centered planning. Some of the most well-known guides include *The Syracuse Community-Referenced Curriculum Guide* (Ford et al., 1989), *The Activities Catalog: An Alternative Curriculum for Youth and Adults with Severe Disabilities* (Wilcox & Bellamy, 1987), and *Choosing Outcomes and Accommodations for Children (COACH): A Guide to Educational Planning for Students with Disabilities* (Giangreco, Cloninger, & Iverson, 1998). Each of these curriculum guides stresses the importance of identifying curricula that is age-appropriate, reflects the community in which the student lives, and incorporates parent and student preferences. Both *The Syracuse Curriculum* and the *COACH* also incorporate ecological inventories where as *The Activities Catalogue* provides a list of activities and skills from which to choose. Some of these curriculum guides are still widely used today; however, there is a clear need for updated versions that reflect changes in our current educational system and our knowledge about educating students with SCD.

Although methods promoted in the literature for selecting life skills for instruction have remained fairly consistent over time, the process described herein is frequently cited by practitioners as being extremely time consuming. The number of skills generated from person-centered planning and ecological inventories can be extensive, making it difficult to determine which ones should receive priority attention and the sequence in which they should be taught. Existing curriculum guides provide guidelines for selecting skills but lack objective procedures for prioritizing which skills should be taught first. One exception is the *Individualized, Functional Curriculum Assessment Procedure* developed by Renzaglia and Aveno (1986). This curriculum uses a weighting system to prioritize skills that accounts for up to 15 factors that should be considered during skill selection. Without an objective process, there is a risk that skills may be chosen that fit the existing curriculum offered in the student's educational placement rather than choosing skills that are of the highest priority for the student.

Trends, Issues, and Future Directions

Life skills instruction has long been recognized as an important component of educational programs for students with SCD. Brown et al.'s (1979) conceptualization of a top down curricular approach over 30 years ago revolutionalized the way educators thought about curriculum development. Rather than teaching skills associated with a student's developmental level of functioning, this approach emphasized chronologically age-appropriate skills that maximized student participation in current environments and prepared them to function in adulthood. As a result of this shift in thinking, students with SCD now learn skills that improve their quality of life by enabling them to partially or independently participate in every day routines and activities, with peers and family members at home, at school, and in the community.

Changes within the field have occurred since a "functional curriculum" was first advocated for students with SCD. These changes have in turn affected the way in which life skills instruction is developed and implemented within schools, and the focus of research conducted. Three major issues warrant discussion. These include (a) the impact of federal requirements for students with disabilities to access and progress in the general education curriculum, (b) the movement towards inclusive education, and (c) the impact of both on the field's research agenda.

Federal Requirement for Access to the General Education Curriculum

In 1997 the Individuals with Disabilities Education Act (IDEA) was amended to require all IEPs to include a statement about how students would be involved and progress in the general curriculum. The general curriculum was defined as the same curriculum as for nondisabled children. In addition, IDEA required that all students with disabilities participate in state and district-wide assessment programs. These requirements continue to exist in the most recent amendments to IDEIA (2004) and are aligned with the No Child Left Behind Act of 2001 (NCLB, 2002). NCLB requires all students (with and without disabilities) to participate in statewide assessments aligned with the state standards for learning in the content areas of reading, math, and science. The purpose of these requirements is to raise expectations for students with disabilities and ensure that all students are part of statewide accountability systems.

Although IDEIA indicates that a student's IEP should address the general curriculum and other educational needs, it appears state accountability systems are driving the curriculum focus for students with SCD. In some arenas, the general curriculum is becoming the primary curriculum advocated for students with SCD. Several facts point towards this trend. First, the development of curricula based on the state standards is widely advocated in the field. Second, there have been numerous empirical studies conducted in the past decade focused on interventions to teach academics to students with SCD. Third, professional special education conferences (including The Association for Persons with Severe Handicaps, TASH, the sole organization focused on individuals with SCD) have had a growing emphasis on access, academics, and alternate assessment. Finally, most textbooks used to prepare special education teachers include chapters specifically focused on addressing the state standards and modifying instruction that aligns with the general curriculum.

In many ways, it would appear that an academic curriculum is at odds with a life skills curriculum. But is it? Almost all life skills involve some form of academic knowledge. For example, cooking involves reading a recipe, purchasing groceries requires math skills, and getting dressed involves determining what to wear based on the temperature. The concept of academic instruction is not new for individuals with SCD. In fact, there is much evidence that exists prior to IDEA and NCLB that demonstrates students with SCD can learn academics. The issue is not whether students with SCD can or should learn academics, but rather how much time should be devoted to academic instruction, what academic skills should be taught, and where instruction should occur. As Brown et al. (1979) acknowledged many years ago, students with SCD are clearly capable of learning academic sequences but the slow rate at which they learn may prohibit them from acquiring sufficient skills to function independently post-school.

As the field continues to explore how students with SCD can access and progress in the general education curriculum, it is important that we not lose sight of the rationale for and importance of life skills. The intent of IDEA's requirement for access to the general curriculum was never for it to be the sole curriculum of focus for a child. IDEA clearly recognizes the importance of each IEP being individualized and addressing both the general curriculum and other educational needs. As a result, there needs to be a concerted effort to maintain a balance between instruction aligned with the general curriculum and that which is focused on the student's unique needs.

The stated purpose of special education is to prepare students with disabilities for further education, employment, and independent living (IDEIA, 2004, Section 610d). It is important that the curriculum selected for each student is one that enables them to function as independently as possible as an adult. Just as students without disabilities take different paths to adulthood depending on their goals (e.g., college, employment), so too must individuals with disabilities be allowed to pursue curricula that enable them to achieve their goals. Some students may benefit from a primarily academic curriculum. Others will not. Unlike school, adult services are not an entitlement service. Once students graduate, they will need to qualify for adult services, many of which have limited programs and funds to support individuals with disabilities. It is therefore important not to lose sight of the *purpose* of special education. Passing the state achievement test may enable a school to meet adequate yearly progress (AYP), but it does not ensure that students with SCD exit school with the skills needed for adulthood.

Inclusive Education Movement

Including students with SCD in educational learning alongside peers without disabilities has been promoted for several decades. In the late 1980s, efforts focused on moving students with SCD from separate schools and cluster programs to their "home school," or the school they would attend if they did not have a disability (Brown et al., 1989). This increased opportunities for students with SCD to be integrated into non-academic classes with their peers without disabilities. As the 1990s progressed, efforts to include students with SCD grew to encompass all aspects of the school day, including academic classes. The term "inclusive education" is now frequently used to refer to educating students with disabilities alongside their same age peers in general education classrooms; however, it also refers to a philosophical belief in the importance of all students belonging to the school community and having equal opportunities to participate (Snell & Brown, 2006).

The growing emphasis on inclusive education in the late 1990s led to discussion within the field regarding the appropriateness of life skills instruction. Of primary concern was whether students should receive instruction on life skills in the community (i.e., CBI) during the school day. Some posited that life skills instruction should be provided within natural school routines so that students with SCD would not miss opportunities to learn with their same-age peers. Skills that required use of the community were thought to be better taught after school or on the weekends when all children are naturally in the community (Fisher & Sax, 1999; Schuh, Tashie, Lamb, Bang, & Jorgensen, 1998; Tashie, Jorgensen, Shapiro-Barnard, Martin, & Schuh, 1996). Others believed that efforts to promote inclusion should focus on both school and community inclusion depending on the needs of the student. They also pointed out that some priority skills cannot be taught in natural school contexts (Agran, Snow, & Swaner, 1999; Dymond & Orelove, 2001; McDonnell, 1997).

In recent years, methods for including students with and without disabilities in CBI have been advanced. Several examples are available within the literature that profile how students with and without disabilities have participated together in community instruction. Some of these examples illustrate differentiated learning for all students (see Beck, Broers, Hogue, Shipstead, & Knowlton, 1994) whereas others utilize peer tutoring to engage students with and without disabilities (see Burcroff, Radogna, & Wright, 2003; Longwill & Kleinert, 1998). Service learning has also emerged as a promising method for promoting inclusive opportunities for academic and life skills instruction. With service learning, students perform a service that benefits the school or community that is linked to academic and life skills objectives (see Dymond, Neeper, & Fones, 2010; Dymond, Renzaglia, & Chun, 2008; Gent & Gurecka, 1998; Kleinert et al., 2004).

Life skills instruction is sometimes viewed as a separate, alternative curriculum. This may be due in part to its conceptualization during a period of history when services for students with disabilities were typically offered in separate buildings or classrooms. The shift toward teaching life skills in inclusive settings has not come easily. The challenge that currently exists is one that has existed for some time - that of striking a balance between a desire for inclusive education and recognition of the individual learning needs of each student. As a field, we envision a future where each child is educated with their same-age peers without disabilities, participates in meaningful learning activities, and is a valued member of their school and community. Equally important, students with SCD must pursue a curriculum that results in acquisition of the skills and supports needed to function in adulthood. There are many ways to achieve this future. The field of special education must continue to maintain its vision of inclusion, realizing that curricular decisions must be made in the best interests of each child. For some students it may involve participation in the general education classroom full-time whereas for others it may require time away from peers to work on skills that cannot be addressed in the general education classroom in ways that are meaningful *to the student*. Furthermore, the amount of time students spend with their peers may change over time, depending on the goals of the student.

Impact on the Field's Research Agenda

Trends in the published literature relative to the education of students with SCD reflect the increased emphasis on inclusive education. Recognition of these changes emerged in the late 1990s with the publication of two reviews of the literature. Nietupski, Hamre-Nietupski, Curtin, and Shrikanth (1997) analyzed the literature between 1976 and 1995 and found a 32% decrease in publications focused on functional skills and a 231% increase in articles addressing interactions and inclusion. Billingsley (1997) compared articles available from the ERIC database published between 1985 and 1989 and between 1991 and 1995, and noted a 53% decrease in functional skills articles. He also compared the number of articles published about functional skills in *The Journal for Persons with Severe Handicaps (JASH)* (now known as *Research and Practice for Persons with Severe Disabilities, RPSD)* between 1984 and 1988 and between 1993 and 1997 and found a 71% decrease in publications. Although a formal review of the literature has not been completed since 1997, it would appear that these trends continue to be of concern.

Despite the decrease in journal article publications focused on life skills instruction, authors of textbooks used to prepare preservice special education teachers still devote substantial space to discussing life skills, including such topics as assessment procedures, curriculum development, and instructional methods. One might expect that more curriculum guides would be available on the market to assist teachers with developing and implementing life skills instruction but none have been published since the advent of the standards based reforms that began with NCLB. Instead, what has emerged is an increasing number of textbooks and articles focused on methods for promoting access to the general curriculum. In addition, federal grant funds that once supported the development of innovative demonstration projects that enhanced the education of students with SCD through the U.S. Department of Education, Office of Specialized Programs (OSEP) have been replaced by a very different type of competition from the Institute for Education Sciences (IES). Competitions that address curriculum are exclusively focused on academics (see http://ies.ed.gov/funding/ncser_progs.asp). Only the competition focused on transition outcomes mentions functional skills.

Future Directions

Life skills are, and will continue to be, an important component of the educational programs of students with SCD. The relative importance of life skills for any particular child will depend on that child's unique needs, their age, their family's preferences, and their immediate and long-term goals. As a field, we must continue to be open to all types of curricula, even if those curricula differ from what the majority of students pursue in school. In special education, the student's individual needs drive the curricula.

As the field continues to move forward, additional research is needed to determine how life skills can be taught in inclusive contexts with same-age peers, as well as how students with and without disabilities can learn through engagement in hands-on community-based activities. Research on effective methods for teaching life skills must continue to occur in order to reflect techniques that are socially valid, effective, and efficient. Finally, the outcomes of students with SCD post-school must be evaluated to determine the relative impact of curriculum type (i.e., academic, life skills) on long-term outcomes.

References

Agran, M. (2004). Health and safety. In P. Wehman & J. Kregel (Eds.), *Functional curriculum for elementary, middle, and secondary age students with special needs* (2nd ed., pp. 357–383). Austin, TX: Pro-ed.

Agran, M., Snow, K., & Swaner, J. (1999). A survey of secondary level teachers' opinions on community-based instruction and inclusive education. *Journal of the Association for Persons with Severe Handicaps*, *24*, 58–62.

Alberto, P. A., Cihak, D. F., & Gama, R. I. (2005). Use of static picture prompts versus video modeling during simulation instruction. *Research in Developmental Disabilities, 26,* 327–339.

Ayres, K. M., Langone, J., Boon, R. T., & Norman, A. (2006). Computer-based instruction for purchasing skills. *Education and Training in Developmental Disabilities, 41,* 253–263.

Azrin, N. H., & Armstrong, P. M., (1973). The "mini-meal"—A method for teaching eating skills to the profoundly retarded. *Mental Retardation, 11*(1), 9–11.

Azrin, N. H., & Foxx, R. M. (1971). A rapid method of toilet training the institutionalized retarded. *Journal of Applied Behavior Analysis, 4*, 89–99.

Bainbridge, N., & Myles, B. S. (1999). The use of priming to introduce toilet training to a child with autism. *Focus on Autism and Other Developmental Disabilities, 14*, 106–109.

Bambara, L. M., Browder, D. M., & Koger, F. (2006). Home and community. In M. E. Snell, & F. Brown (Eds.), *Instruction of students with severe disabilities* (6th ed., pp. 526–568). Upper Saddle River, NJ: Pearson.

Bates, P. E., Cuvo, T., Miner, C. A., & Korabek, C. A. (2001). Simulated and community-based instruction involving persons with mild and moderate mental retardation. *Research in Developmental Disabilities, 22*, 95–115.

Baumgart, D., Brown, L., Pumpian, I., Nisbet, J., Ford, A., Sweet, M., Messina, R., & Schroeder, J. (1982). Principle of partial participation and individualized adaptations in educational programs for severely handicapped students. *Journal of the Association for Persons with Severe Handicaps, 7*, 17–27.

Beck, J., Broers, J., Hogue, E., Shipstead, J., & Knowlton, E. (1994). Strategies for functional community-based instruction and inclusion for children with mental retardation. *Teaching Exceptional Children, 26*(2), 44–48.

Billingsley, F. (1997, December). The problem and the place of functional skills in inclusive settings. In G. Singer (Chair), *The role of functional skills and behavioral instructional methods in inclusive education.* Symposium conducted at the annual meeting of the Association for Persons with Severe Handicaps, Boston, MA.

Blanchett, W. J., & Wolfe, P. S. (2002). A review of sexuality education curricula: Meeting the sexuality education needs of individuals with moderate and severe intellectual disabilities. *Research and Practice for Persons with Severe Disabilities, 27,* 43–57.

Branham, R. S., Collins, B. C., Schuster, J. W., & Kleinert, H. (1999). Teaching community skills to students with moderate disabilities: Comparing combined techniques of classroom simulation, videotape modeling, and community-based instruction. *Education and Training in Mental Retardation and Developmental Disabilities, 34,* 170–181.

Browder, D. M., Cooper, K. J., & Lim, L. (1998). Teaching adults with severe disabilities to express their choice of settings for leisure activities. *Education and Training in Mental Retardation and Developmental Disabilities, 33*, 228–238.

Brown, L, Branston, M. B., Hamre-Nietupski, S., Pumpian, I., Certo, N., & Grunewald, L. (1979). A strategy for developing chronological-age-appropriate and functional curricular content for severely handicapped adolescents and adults. *Journal of Special Education, 13,* 81–90.

Brown, L., Long, E., Udvari-Solner, A., Davis, L., VanDeventer, P., Ahlgren, C., … & Jorgensen, J. (1989). The home school: Why students with severe intellectual disabilities must attend the schools of their brothers, sisters, friends, and neighbors. *Journal of the Association for Persons with Severe Handicaps, 14*, 1–7.

Brown, F., Snell, M. E., & Lehr, D. (2006). Meaningful assessment. In M. E. Snell, & F. Brown (Eds.), *Instruction of students with severe disabilities* (6th ed., pp. 67–110). Upper Saddle River, NJ: Pearson.

Burcroff, T. L., Radogna, D. M., & Wright, E. H. (2003). Community forays: Addressing students' functional skills in inclusive settings. *Teaching Exceptional Children, 35*(5), 52–57.

Cannella, H. I., O'Reilly, M. F., & Lanioni, G. E. (2005). Choice and preference assessment research with people with severe to profound developmental disabilities: A review of the literature. *Research in Developmental Disabilities, 26*, 1–15.

Cicero, F. R., & Pfadt, A. (2002). Investigation of a reinforcement-based toilet training procedure for children with autism. *Research in Developmental Disabilities, 23*, 319–331.

Cihak, D. F., Alberto, P. A., Kessler, K. B., & Tabor, T. A. (2004). An investigation of instructional scheduling arrangements for community-based instruction. *Research in Developmental Disabilities, 25,* 67–88.

Cihak, D., Alberto, P. A., Taber-Doughty, T., & Gama, R. I. (2006). A comparison of static picture prompting and video prompting simulation using group instructional procedures. *Focus on Autism and Other Developmental Disabilities, 21*, 89–99.

Collins, B. C. (2007). *Moderate and severe disabilities: A foundation approach*. Upper Saddle River, NJ: Pearson.

Collins, B. C., Branson, T. A., & Hall, M. (1995). Teaching generalized reading of cooking product labels to adolescents with mental disabilities through the use of key words taught by peer tutors. *Education and Training in Mental Retardation and Developmental Disabilities, 30*, 65–75.

Collins, B. C., Hall, M., & Branson, T. A. (1997). Teaching leisure skills to adolescents with moderate disabilities. *Exceptional Children, 63,* 499–512.

Dattilo, J., & Mirenda, P. (1987). An application of a *leisure preference assessment* protocol for persons with severe handicaps. *Journal of the Association for Persons with Severe Handicaps, 12,* 306–311.

Davies, D. K., Stock, S. E., & Wehmeyer, M. L. (2003). Utilization of computer technology to facilitate money management by individuals with mental retardation. *Education and Training in Developmental Disabilities, 38,* 106–112.

Demchak, M. (1989). A comparison of graduated guidance and increasing assistance in teaching adults with severe handicaps leisure skills. *Education and Training of the Mentally Retarded, 24*, 45–55.

Duffy, A. T., & Nietupski, J. (1985). Acquisition and maintenance of video game initiation, sustaining and termination. *Education and Training of the Mentally Retarded, 20*, 157–162.

Dymond, S. K. (2004). Community participation. In P. Wehman & J. Kregel (Eds.), *Functional curriculum for elementary, middle, and secondary age students with special needs* (2nd ed., pp. 259–291). Austin, TX: Pro-ed.

Dymond, S. K., Neeper, L., & Fones, D. (2010). Typing with purpose: Linking the word processing curriculum to real world applications through service learning. *The Clearing House, 83*, 33–38.

Dymond, S. K., & Orelove, F. P. (2001). What constitutes effective curricula for students with severe disabilities? *Exceptionality, 9*, 109–122.

Dymond, S. K., Renzaglia, A., & Chun, E. J. (2008). Inclusive high school service learning programs: Methods for and barriers to including students with disabilities. *Education and Training in Developmental Disabilities, 43,* 20–36.

Farlow, L. J., & Snell, M. E. (2006). Teaching self-care skills. In M. E. Snell, & F. Brown (Eds.), *Instruction of students with severe disabilities* (6th ed., pp. 328–374). Upper Saddle River, NJ: Pearson.

Fisher, D., & Sax, C. (1999). Noticing differences between secondary and postsecondary education: Extending Agran, Snow, and Swaner's discussion. *The Journal of the Association for Persons with Severe Handicaps, 24,* 303–305.

Ford, A., Schnorr, R., Meyer, L., Davern, L., Black, J., & Dempsey, P. (Eds.). (1989). *The Syracuse community-referenced curriculum guide for students with moderate and severe disabilities.* Baltimore: Paul H. Brookes.

Gent, P. J., & Gurecka, L. E. (1998). Service learning: A creative strategy for inclusive classrooms. *Journal of the Association for Persons with Severe Handicaps, 23,* 261–271.

Giangreco, M. F., Cloninger, C. J., Iverson, V. S. (1998). *Choosing outcomes and accommodations for children: A guide to educational planning for students with disabilities* (2nd ed.). Baltimore: Paul H. Brookes.

Godsey, J. R., Schuster, J. W., Lingo, A. S., Collins, B. C., & Kleinert, H. L. (2008). Peer-implemented time delay procedures on the acquisition of chained tasks by students with moderate and severe disabilities. *Education and Training in Developmental Disabilities, 43,* 111–122.

Hutcherson, K., Langone, J., Ayres, K., & Clees, T. (2004). Computer assisted instruction to teach item selection in grocery stores: An assessment of acquisition and generalization. *Journal of Special Education Technology, 19,* 33–42.

Individuals with Disabilities Education Act Amendments of 1997, 20 U.S.C. § 1400 *et seq.* (1997).

Individuals with Disabilities Education Improvement Act (IDEIA) of 2004, P.L. 108-446, 108th Congress (2004).

Kleinert, H., McGregor, V., Durbin, M., Blandford, T., Jones, K., Owens, J., Harrison, B., & Miracle, S. (2004). Service-learning opportunities that include students with moderate and severe disabilities. *Teaching Exceptional Children, 37*(2), 28–34.

Kreiner, J., & Flexer, R. (2009). Assessment of leisure preferences for students with severe developmental disabilities and communication difficulties. *Education and Training in Developmental Disabilities, 44,* 280–288.

Lancioni, G. E., & O'Reilly, M. F. (2002). Teaching food preparation skills to people with intellectual disabilities: A literature overview. *Journal of Applied Research in Intellectual Disabilities, 15,* 236–253.

Lim, L. H. F., & Browder, D. M. (1994). Multicultural life skills assessment of individuals with severe disabilities. *Journal of the Association for Persons with Severe Handicaps, 19,* 130–138.

Longwill, A. W., & Kleinert, H. L. (1998). The unexpected benefits of high school peer tutoring. *Teaching Exceptional Children, 30,* 60–65.

Luyben, P. D., Funk, D. M., Morgan, J. K., Clark, K. A., & Delulio, D. W. (1986). Team sports for the severely retarded: Training a side-of-the foot soccer pass using a maximum-to-minimum prompt reduction strategy. *Journal of Applied Behavior Analysis, 19,* 431–436.

Luiselli, J. K. (2007). Single-case evaluation of a negative reinforcement toilet training intervention. *Child & Family Behavior Therapy, 29,* 59–69.

McDonnell, J. (1997). Participation in content-area classes and community-based instruction in secondary schools: Isn't it about achieving a balance? *TASH Newsletter, 23*(2), 23–24, 29.

McDonnell, J. J., & Ferguson, B. (1988). A comparison of general case in vivo and general case simulation plus in vivo training. *Journal of the Association for Persons with Severe Handicaps, 13,* 116–124.

McDonnell, J. J., Horner, R. H., & Williams, J. A. (1984). Comparison of three strategies for teaching generalized grocery purchasing to high school students with severe handicaps. *Journal of the Association for Persons with Severe Handicaps, 9,* 123–133.

Mechling, L. C. (2004). Effects of multimedia, computer-based instruction on grocery shopping fluency. *Journal of Special Education Technology, 19,* 23–34.

Mechling, L. C. (2008). High tech cooking: A literature review of evolving technologies for teaching a functional skill. *Education and Training in Developmental Disabilities, 43,* 474–485.

Mechling, L. C., & Cronin, B. (2006). Computer-based video instruction to teach the use of augmentative and alternative communication devices for ordering at fast-food restaurants. *The Journal of Special Education, 39,* 234–245.

Mechling, L. C., & Gast, D. L. (2003). Multi-media instruction to teach grocery word associations and store location: A study of generalization. *Education and Training in Developmental Disabilities, 38,* 62–76.

Mechling, L. C., Pridgen, L. S., & Cronin, B. A. (2005). Computer-based video instruction to teach students with intellectual disabilities to verbally respond to questions and make purchases in fast food restaurants. *Education and Training in Developmental Disabilities, 40,* 47–59.

Moon, M. S. (1994). *Making school and community recreation fun for everyone: Places and ways to integrate.* Baltimore: Paul H. Brookes.

Morse, T. E., & Schuster, J. W. (2000). Teaching elementary students with moderate intellectual disabilities how to shop for groceries. *Exceptional Children, 66,* 273–288.

Nietupski, J., Hamre-Nietupski, S., Curtin, S., & Shrikanth, K. (1997). A review of curricular research in severe disabilities from 1976 to 1995 in six selected journals. *The Journal of Special Education, 31,* 36–55.

No Child Left Behind Act of 2001, P.L. 107-110, 115 Stat. 1425 (2002).

Realon, R. E., Favell, J. E., & Lowerre, A. (1990). The effects of making choices on engagement levels with persons who are profoundly multiply handicapped. *Education and Training in Mental Retardation, 25,* 299–305.

Renzaglia, A., & Aveno, A. (1986). *Manual for the administration of an individualized, functional curriculum assessment procedure.* Charlottesville, VA: University of Virginia.

Renzaglia, A., Karvonen, M., Drasgow, E., & Stoxen, C. C. (2003). Promoting a lifetime of inclusion. *Focus on Autism and Other Developmental Disabilities, 18,* 140–149.

Richmond, G. (1983). Shaping bladder and bowel continence in developmentally retarded preschool children. *Journal of Autism and Developmental Disorders, 13,* 197–204.

Ryndak, D. L., & Alper, S. (2003). *Curriculum and instruction for students with significant disabilities in inclusive settings* (2nd ed.). Boston: Allyn & Bacon.

Sands, D. J., Kozleski, E. B., & French, N. K. (2000). *Inclusive education for the 21st century.* Stamford, CT: Wadsworth.

Schleien, S. J., & Ray, M. T. (1997). Leisure education for a quality transition to adulthood. *Journal of Vocational Rehabilitation, 8,* 155–169.

Schuh, M. C., Tashie, C., Lamb, P., Bang, M., & Jorgensen, C. M. (1998). Community-based learning for all students. In C.M. Jorgensen (Ed.), *Restructuring high schools for all students: Taking inclusion to the next level* (pp. 209–231). Baltimore: Paul H. Brookes.

Snell, M. E., & Brown, F. (Eds.) (2006). *Instruction of students with severe disabilities* (6th ed.). Upper Saddle River, NJ: Pearson.

Solish, A., Perry, A., & Minnes, P. (2010). Participation of children with and without disabilities in social, recreational, and leisure activities. *Journal of Applied Research in Intellectual Disabilities, 23,* 226–236.

Spooner. F., & Wood, W. M. (2004). Teaching personal care and hygiene skills. In P. Wehman & J. Kregel (Eds.), *Functional curriculum for elementary, middle, and secondary age students with special needs* (2nd ed., pp. 317–356). Austin, TX: Pro-ed.

Steere, D. E., & Burcroff, T. L. (2004). Living at home: Skills for independence. In P. Wehman & J. Kregel (Eds.), *Functional curriculum for elementary, middle, and secondary age students with special needs* (2nd ed., pp. 298–316). Austin, TX: Pro-ed.

Tabor, T. A., Alberto, P. A., Hughes, M., & Seltzer, A. (2002). A strategy for students with moderate disabilities when lost in the community.

Research and Practice for Persons with Severe Disabilities, 27, 141–152.

Tabor, T. A., Alberto, P. A., Seltzer, A., & Hughes, M. (2003). Obtaining assistance when lost in the community using cell phones. *Research and Practice for Persons with Severe Disabilities, 28,* 105–116.

Tashie, C., Jorgensen, C., Shapiro-Barnard, S., Martin, J., & Schuh, M. (1996). High school inclusion strategies and barriers. *TASH Newsletter, 22*(9), 19–22.

Wall, M. E., & Gast, D. L. (1997). Caregivers' use of constant time delay to teach leisure skills to adolescents or young adults with moderate of severe intellectual disabilities. *Education and Training in Mental Retardation and Developmental Disabilities, 32,* 340–356.

Wehmeyer, M. L. (2005). Self-determination and individuals with severe disabilities: Re-examining meanings and misinterpretations. *Research and Practice for Persons with Severe Disabilities, 30,* 113–120.

Wehmeyer, M. L., Sands, D. J., Knowlton, H. E., & Kozleski, E. B. (2002). *Providing access to the general curriculum: Teaching students with mental retardation.* Baltimore: Paul H. Brookes.

Westling, D., & Floyd, J. (1990). Generalization of community skills: How much training is necessary? *The Journal of Special Education, 23,* 386–406.

Westling, D. L., & Fox, L. (2009). *Teaching students with severe disabilities* (4th ed.). Upper Saddle River, NJ: Pearson.

Wilcox, B., & Bellamy, G. T. (1987). *The activities catalogue: An alternative curriculum for youth and adults with severe disabilities.* Baltimore: Paul H. Brookes.

Wilson, P. G., Reid, D. H., & Green, C. W. (2006). Evaluating and increasing in-home leisure activity among adults with severe disabilities in supported independent living. *Research in Developmental Disabilities, 27,* 93–107.

Wolfe, P. S., Condo, B., & Hardaway, E. (2009). Sociosexuality education for persons with autism spectrum disorders using principles of applied behavior analysis. *Teaching Exceptional Children, 42,* 50–61.

Wood, W. M., Fowler, C. H., Uphold, N., & Test, D. W. 2005). A review of self-determination interventions with individuals with severe disabilities. *Research and Practice for Persons with Severe Disabilities, 30,* 121–146.

Xin, Y. P., Grasso, E., DiPipi-Hoy, C. M., & Jitendra, A. (2005). The effects of purchasing skill instruction for individuals with developmental disabilities: A meta-analysis. *Exceptional Children, 71,* 379–400.

Yilmaz, I., Birkan, B., Konukman, F., & Erkan, M. (2005). Using a constant time delay procedure to teach aquatic play skills to children with autism. *Education and Training in Developmental Disabilities, 40,* 171–182.

York, J., Vandercook, T., & Stave, K. (1990). Recreation and leisure activities: Determining the favorites of middle school students. *Teaching Exceptional Children, 22,* 10–13.

Zhang, J., Gast, D., Horvat, M., & Dattilo, J. (1995). The effectiveness of constant time delay procedure on teaching lifetime sport skills to adolescents with severe to profound intellectual disabilities. *Education and Training in Mental Retardation and Developmental Disabilities, 30,* 51–64.

Section IX

Transition to Adulthood and High Incidence Disabilities

Section Editor: ***David Scanlon***
Boston College

In 1975, when the Congress prepared the special education law now known as the Individuals with Disabilities Education Act (IDEA, 2004), it noted that approximately half of the nation's 8 million children with disabilities were being denied an appropriate education due to their disability (20 U.S.C. section 1400 [b]). The consequences of an inappropriate education include needlessly limited knowledge and skills and diminished opportunities to participate in a variety of aspects of society.

In the mid-1980s, the then director of the U.S. Office of Special Education and Rehabilitative Services called for an overhaul of many of the nation's special education practices (e.g., Will 1984, 1986). Among her criticisms were that school leavers with disabilities continued to be un- and under-employed, to participate in the range of postsecondary education options at vastly reduced rates, to live less independently and to self-report less social satisfaction across adult life stages.

In 2004, the U.S. Department of Education reported that as of the 2001–2002 academic year, students with high incidence disabilities dropped out at decreased rates and graduated with a standard diploma at increased rates compared to 10 years earlier. Nonetheless, to this day those with disabilities, high incidence categories or low, typically achieve less and experience lower satisfaction in school and beyond. Just as realizing the right to an appropriate education had been a slow process, so too has been the process of gaining meaningful outcomes for all enrolled in special education.

Transition to adulthood, which the IDEA defines as a "results-oriented process" (§ 300.43(a (1), 46762), is the ultimate outcome of special education. Regardless of whether special education for a given student is a short-term temporary service or the student's primary educational programming preK–12, what becomes of that student post school is the ultimate measure of effectiveness.

Transition is sometimes misguidedly thought of as the destination of a student immediately upon leaving school. It is much more than that. Transition is a process. Sometimes the transition process is thought of in misguided ways too. That limited conceptualization considers only planning and engaging in preparation activities, with "transition" ending when secondary schooling ends. In fact, transition is a life-long process. Any one of us moves from placement to placement, but we also evolve in our personal lives, including in our well-being, knowledge, skills, and inclinations. Because transition is an on-going, lifelong, process, the proper function of the transition process is not just to prepare the student for what comes next but to enable the student.

The focus of transition practices has evolved to reflect a focus on empowering the individual. Likewise, our knowledge of "best practices" in planning, preparation, and services has advanced. In the early days of the "transition initiative" that followed Will's 1986 charge, the focus was on training in skills for one targeted destination. Increasingly, the focus of transition is on students developing self-awareness of their interests, strengths and needs, and on learning the skills of self-determination to actively engage in their own transition planning, preparation, and enactment.

Although the percentages of students experiencing the diminished outcomes Will criticized in the 1980s have changed, as have the contexts of transition and the practices employed in special education, those with disabilities continue to leave school with less satisfactory achievement than their regular education peers and to have less success in postsecondary education, employment, and independent living (see the chapters in this section).

The three chapters in this section address the evolution of transition-related knowledge and best practices as they relate to the three primary destinations of school leavers: postsecondary education, employment, and independent living. A theme across the three chapters is acknowledgment that despite all we have yet to learn about ensuring intended transition "outcomes," the weakest aspect of the transition process has been providing services.

Transition, like much in special education (see section I), has changed over the years but in many ways reflects the same issues that inspired the original special education and transition initiatives. Although new issues in transition will continue to be realized, if we are successful in responding to current knowledge and needs, the intended outcomes of special education will not be realized until the transition issues of the present are resolved.

References

Individuals with Disabilities Education Improvement Act of 2004, 20 U.S.C. *SS* 1400 et seq. (2004).

Will, M. (1984). *OSERS programming for adults with disabilities: Bridges from school to working life*. Washington, DC: Office of Special Education and Rehabilitative Services.

Will, M. (1986). Educating children with learning problems: A shared responsibility. *Exceptional Children, 52*, 411–415.

43

Transition to Postsecondary Education

Joseph W. Madaus and Manju Banerjee
University of Connecticut

Deborah Merchant
Keene State College

Introduction

Transition planning that assists students with disabilities to more successfully access postsecondary education has been a requirement of the Individuals with Disabilities Education Act (IDEA) for the past two decades. Local education agencies (LEAs) have been required to include transition planning, specifically including planning for postsecondary education, as part of the individualized education program (IEP) since the 1990 amendments to the IDEA (Furney, Hasazi, & Destafano, 1997). In addition to strengthening language requiring that transition be a "results-oriented process…to facilitate the child's movement from school to post-school activities" (§300.43(a)(1)), IDEA (2004) states that transition planning must consider postsecondary education, vocational education, and continuing and adult education as options for students. The law also requires that State Education Agencies (SEAs) collect data on the post-school outcomes of youth who had received special education services at the time of leaving secondary school. These data must include the percent of youth who enrolled in "higher education or in some other postsecondary education or training program" (20 U.S.C. 1416(a)(3)(B)).

The need for schools to place increased emphasis on planning for students to transition to postsecondary education was illuminated by Blackorby and Wagner (1996), who reported that only 14% of students with disabilities were accessing postsecondary education, compared to 53% of youth without disabilities. The reauthorization of IDEA in 1997 and 2004 led to a more coordinated focus on transition planning and as a result, significant gains have been made over the past decade in helping students access postsecondary education. In the 2003–2004 academic year, 10% of full-time freshmen reported having a disability (Berkner & Choy, 2008), more than three times the number reported in 1978 (3%; Henderson, 1999). The number of students with specific disability types such as learning disabilities grew, with over three percent of all college freshmen reporting having a learning disability in 2008, a figure that has increased from .05% in 1983 (Pryor et al., 2008). Whereas, the NLTS reported that 14% of students with disabilities were accessing college in 1996, more than a decade later, this figure had increased to 45%, with 32% of these students accessing a 2-year or community college and 14% accessing a 4-year college (Newman, Wagner, Cameto, & Knokey, 2009).

Despite this progress, much work remains to be done to help students with disabilities not only to access, but more importantly, to be prepared for the various demands of postsecondary education. Research has long highlighted that students with disabilities (and many students without disabilities) are underprepared for the academic demands of postsecondary education. Effective transition planning is vitally important to enable students with disabilities to participate in the most academically rigorous curriculum possible.

What is Postsecondary Education?

The range of postsecondary education options available for students can be overwhelming. In addition, the terms *higher education* and *postsecondary education* are often used, sometimes interchangeably, which can create additional confusion. Higher education refers to "a two- or four-year degree program provided by a community or technical college (two-year) and/or college/university (four- or more year program)" (Falls & Unruh, 2009, p. 4). Higher education institutions can also be quite diverse, encompassing those that are public, private, not for profit, and others that are private/for profit institutions. Some are referred to as "proprietary schools" that provide training in specific areas (e.g., cosmetology schools) (Higher Education Opportunity Act [HEOA], 2008; Levesque et al., 2008; National Center for Educational Statistics [NCES], 2009). In addition, colleges, universities, and organizations are increasingly offering degrees and certificates online (Parsad & Lewis, 2008; Rudestam & Schoenholtz-Read, 2010).

Postsecondary education or training is a much broader category. According to the HEOA, a postsecondary vocational institution is one that "provides an eligible program of training to prepare students for gainful employment in a recognized occupation" (§ 102(a)(C)(1)(a)). This may include Adult Basic Education or General Education Development (GED) courses, Job Corps or Workforce development training (Falls & Unruh, 2009). According to the National Longitudinal Transition Study-2 (NLTS-2), 23% of students with disabilities had enrolled in such programs within 2 years of leaving high school (Newman et al., 2009).

Importance of Postsecondary Education

Postsecondary education can be a gateway to a successful adult life. Statistics show that increased education correlates with increased salary and lower rates of unemployment. Adults with disabilities tend to be unemployed or underemployed; however, research demonstrates that college graduates with learning disabilities are employed at levels that are competitive with their non-disabled peers.

Employment and salary. Data from the Bureau of Labor Statistics (2009) show that increased education positively correlates with salary, while negatively correlating with unemployment levels. In addition, multiple analyses by the NCES also demonstrate that higher levels of education relate directly to higher levels of employment and higher salaries. Four years out of secondary school, only 23% of young adults with disabilities had accessed some type of postsecondary education. Roughly 70% were competitively employed, earning a mean hourly wage of $8.30 (NCES, 2005). A study of 500 graduates with learning disabilities from three universities nationwide indicated that respondents were employed at levels and earning salaries comparable to the general population of the United States (Madaus, 2006).

Despite the importance of postsecondary education, data from the NLTS-2 (Newman et al., 2009) indicates that only 29% of young adults who had received special education in high school had completed a postsecondary program. Students in vocational, business, or technical schools had the highest rate of completion (59%), followed by those in 2-year community colleges (18%). As noted previously, 14% had enrolled in a 4-year college at some time since leaving school. However, at the time of data collection, only 7.6% were still enrolled (Newman et al., 2009).

Preparation for Postsecondary Education

Multiple reports have indicated a gap between the work students do in high school and what they will be expected to do at the college level (Peter D. Hart Research Associates, 2005; Peterson, 2003; Reed, 2006; The Secretary of Education's Commission on the Future of Higher Education, 2006; Viadero, 2005). A survey of 1,487 students who withdrew from college (Peter D. Hart Research Associates, 2005) indicated that almost half cited being unprepared for college courses prior to enrollment.

Because of being unprepared, large numbers of students are required to enroll in remedial courses when they reach the college level. According to NCES (2006), 36% of all undergraduates reported taking a remedial course in 2003–2004. This coursework was most frequently in mathematics, followed by writing and reading. Students at community colleges were more likely to have taken a remedial course than students in 4-year institutions. A study in one northeastern state reported that 37% of high school graduates needed at least one remedial course in their first semester of college. The figure was nearly twice as high for students in community colleges (Schworm, 2008). Students with disabilities also more often reported taking remedial courses than their non-disabled peers. Because remedial courses do not count towards college credit, they extend the time and cost required to obtain a degree (College Board, 2006; Peterson, 2003) leading to their being referred to as "a graveyard for degree aspirations" (Commission on Access, Admissions and Success in Higher Education, 2008, p. 12).

These factors point to the importance of transition planning that allows students with disabilities who aspire to attend postsecondary education to take the most rigorous academic plan of study possible. The NLTS-2 reported that postsecondary education is a goal for four out of five secondary students in special education, and that in general, students with disabilities are taking more rigorous academic coursework (Cameto, Levine, & Wagner, 2004; Wagner, Newman, & Cameto, 2004). However, other literature points to the fact that this planning is often not adequate. In a study of transition plans of students with disabilities, Hitchings, Retish, and Horvath (2005) found that 77% of the sample expressed an interest in attending college during Grade 10. Three years later, only 47% expressed the same interest, and only four students had IEPs designed to prepare them for postsecondary education. The need for careful planning for rigorous coursework should begin as early as middle school, as admission to many postsecondary institutions will require completion of a set of academic units that may require several sequential courses (Commission on Access, Admissions and Success in Higher Education, 2008; McGuire, 2010).

Clearly, academic preparation is a foundational component of a successful transition for students with disabilities. However, also crucially important, and often overlooked, are non-academic skills, such as self-advocacy and self-determination. Students with disabilities must understand their new legal rights and responsibilities at the postsecondary level are very different than their rights at the secondary level.

Key Legislation

One of the most significant shifts that students with disabilities face upon transition to postsecondary education is the change in legal rights and responsibilities (Madaus, 2005; Newman et al., 2009; Stodden, Jones, & Chang, 2002). Upon leaving secondary school, students with disabilities are no longer covered by the entitlement provisions of the IDEA and instead may be eligible for protections under Section 504 of the Rehabilitation Act of 1973 (Section 504) and the Americans with Disabilities Act Amendment Act of 2008 (ADAAA). Both Section 504 and the ADAAA are civil rights laws and require that the student demonstrate that he or she is an "otherwise qualified" person with a substantial limitation to a major life function. Both require the student to take increased responsibility, including self-disclosure of the disability and provision of documentation that indicates a current and substantial limitation. Receipt of special education services while in secondary school, or even receipt of accommodations through a Section 504 plan at the secondary level, may not be sufficient evidence that the student requires services or accommodations at the postsecondary level (Madaus, 2010). It is important to consider the differences in these legal mandates because they drive the types of services that a student may receive in the postsecondary environment.

IDEA 2004. Under the IDEA, the local education agency (LEA) must consider individualized transition planning no later than the student's 16th birthday. This transition planning must include: "Appropriate measurable postsecondary goals based upon age appropriate transition assessments related to training, education, employment, and, where appropriate, independent living skills" (§300.320 (b)(1)). Each of these goals must be built using appropriate transition assessments and must account for student preferences and goals. The IEP must also outline "The transition services (including courses of study) needed to assist the child in reaching those goals" (§300.320 (b)(2)).

Importantly, IDEA 2004 specifically notes that LEAs are not responsible for conducting "exit evaluations" or, in other words, for updating a student's documentation before he or she leaves the secondary school because of graduation or aging out of eligibility for services. In fact, the regulatory comments accompanying IDEA states:

> While the requirements for secondary transition are intended to help parents and schools assist children with disabilities transition beyond high school, section 614(c)(5) in the Act does not require a public agency to assess a child with a disability to determine the child's eligibility to be considered a child with a disability in another agency, such as a vocational rehabilitation program, or a college or other postsecondary setting. (IDEA Final Regulations, pp. 612–613)

Instead, the LEA must provide the student with a "summary of the child's academic achievement and functional performance, which shall include recommendations on how to assist the child in meeting the child's postsecondary goals" (§300.305(e)(3)). This requirement has become known as the "Summary of Performance."

Section 504. Students with disabilities at both the secondary and postsecondary levels may be eligible for protections under Section 504 of the Rehabilitation Act of 1973. Section 504 contains two key subparts that apply to educational entities. Subpart D applies to "preschool, elementary, secondary, and adult education programs and activities that receive or benefit from Federal financial assistance" (§104.31). Although Section 504 has applied to LEAs since the 1970s, the use of secondary level Section 504 plans has become more widespread as a means to provide students with some services without the need for special education, or to students who were not found eligible for IDEA services (Blazer, 1999; CASE, 1999; deBettencourt, 2002; Smith, 2002). This also includes some students without disabilities who struggle in an academic area (Madaus, Shaw, & Zhao, 2005; Misidentification, 2004; "Over Providing," 2004; Zirkel, 2004).

Whereas Subpart D applies to secondary programs, Subpart E applies to "postsecondary education programs and activities, including postsecondary vocational education programs and activities, that receive or benefit from Federal financial assistance" (§104.41). Both subparts have different regulations; therefore, a student who is eligible for services and certain accommodations under Subpart D may not be eligible for similar services under Subpart E (Madaus & Shaw, 2004). Section 504 is designed to enhance access for people with disabilities and, unlike the IDEA, is outcome neutral (Madaus & Shaw, 2004). As the HEATH Resource Center (2006) clearly explained to secondary professionals working with students in transition, "academic adjustments ensure access, not necessarily success" (p. 55).

Another significant difference is that under Subpart E, a student must be considered a "qualified handicapped person." The regulations state that this is a person who "meets the academic and technical standards requisite to admission or participation in the recipients' education program or activity" (§104.3(k)(3)). In other words, the student must meet the same admissions requirements as all other students (both for admission to an institution and admission to programs or majors within the institution), and must maintain eligibility for services by meeting a requisite grade point average (Madaus & Shaw, 2004). Moreover, once admitted, the student must provide evidence, typically via disability documentation, that he or she has a current and substantial limitation to learning. The determination of eligibility for such services is one of the most complex and challenging components of services at the postsecondary level.

If a student is determined to be an individual with a disability that substantially limits a major life activity (defined as "caring for one's self, performing manual tasks, walking, seeing, hearing, breathing, learning, and working" [§ 104.3 (j)(2)(ii)]), then the postsecondary institution must provide reasonable academic adjustments and auxiliary aides. The regulations further detail a series of academic adjustments that might be considered. These include course substitutions, alternate exam formats, and extended time.

However, decisions related to these accommodations must be made on a case-by-case and course-by-course basis. As a result, a student may not receive all requested accommodations, even those that may have been received in secondary school.

Another significant difference between both IDEA and Subpart D and Subpart E relates to the provision of a Free Appropriate Public Education (FAPE). Although IDEA and Subpart D mandate a FAPE standard, this does not apply to Subpart E. Although postsecondary institutions cannot charge students for reasonable accommodations and auxiliary aids, the student (or the student's family) is responsible for paying for tuition and fees. This may include individualized services (such as one-to-one sessions with a learning or disability specialist) that go beyond what is required under Section 504 (Madaus & Shaw, 2004).

There is a range of services and supports that may be offered to postsecondary students with disabilities (see Table 43.1). The exact type can vary depending on institutional mission and resources. At a minimum, institutions are mandated to have a contact person to whom a student can self-identify and who can help arrange reasonable accommodations for students. This person need not have training in special education or disability and may come from a variety of professional backgrounds (Harbor 2008; Madaus, 2005). Postsecondary institutions may go beyond this and offer dedicated offices for students with disabilities, which may include one-on-one work with disability specialists. Institutions may charge students for these more individualized services that go beyond offering reasonable accommodations and auxiliary aides alone (Madaus, 2005).

ADAAA of 2008. The Americans with Disabilities Act of 1990 was amended and signed into law on September 25, 2008, as the Americans with Disabilities Act Amendments Act of 2008, with the law taking effect on January 1, 2009 (ADAAA, 2008; McGuire, 2010). The amendments revised the definition of disability and expanded the scope of eligibility as an individual with a disability. Specifically, reading, concentration, and thinking are now listed as examples of major life activities, along with walking, seeing, hearing, speaking, breathing, learning, and working. A substantial impairment in any of these activities qualifies the individual for ADAAA protection. The amendments also note that the ameliorative effects of mitigating measures, such as assistive devices, auxiliary aids, accommodations, medical therapies and supplies (other than eye glasses or contact lenses) cannot be considered in establishing disability status. Furthermore, impairments that are episodic or in remission, but substantially limiting to a major life activity when active, are now covered under the ADAAA.

Summary. At the secondary level, students with disabilities are surrounded by a team of professionals who are responsible for virtually all components of the student's education program. Without a concerted effort on the part of the special education team to foster student self-determination, the student may be allowed to fall into a more passive role. As a result, many students leave secondary school unable to explain their disability and to request reasonable accommodations (Madaus, 2010). In sharp contrast, at the postsecondary level, the student becomes the primary player in all such requests and decisions. To best help prepare students for this shift, it is important to understand the eligibility process and to focus on the importance of student self-determination. Table 43.2 contains an overview of significant areas of educational programming and specific responsibilities under the IDEA, Section 504, and the ADAAA.

TABLE 43.1
Continuum of Postsecondary Support Services

Decentralized Services	Loosely Coordinated Services	Centrally Coordinated Services	Data-Based Services
Designated disability contact person may have multiple responsibilities	Disability contact person	Full-time disability coordinator Services located in Office for Students with Disabilities or other on-campus sites (e.g., learning or academic skills center)	Full-time program director; Assistant director and/or additional staff Services located in Office for Students with Disabilities
Basic services as mandated under Section 504	Generic 504 support services and accommodations	Full range of accommodations	Full range of accommodations
Few formal policies	Procedures in place for accessing services	Policies and procedures in place	Comprehensive policies and procedures
	Peer tutors available for all students	Emphasis on student self-advocacy	Emphasis on student self-advocacy
	Students referred to other on-campus services (e.g., counseling and/or career services, residential life)	Assistive technology may be available Specially trained disability specialists may be available	Assistive technology available Individualized support plan available

Note. From *Resource Guide of Support Services for Students with Learning Disabilities in Connecticut Colleges and Universities,* by J. M. McGuire & S. F. Shaw (Eds.), 1989 (rev. 1996, 1999, 2005), Storrs, University of Connecticut, Center on Postsecondary Education and Disability. Copyright 1999 by J. M. McGuire & S. F. Shaw. Adapted with permission.

TABLE 43.2
Responsibilities Under IDEA versus Section 504/ADAAA

Issue	Responsibility: Secondary Level	Responsibility: Postsecondary Level
Identification	School	Student
Assessment	School	Student
Programming	Placement Team	Student/Institution
Advocacy	Placement Team	Student
Decision Making	Placement Team	Student
Transition Planning	Placement Team	Student

Note: Adapted from Brinckerhoff, L.C., Shaw, S. F., & McGuire, J. M. (1993). *Promoting Postsecondary Education for Students with Learning Disabilities: A Handbook for Practitioners.* Austin, TX: PRO-ED.

Determining Eligibility for Services

Perhaps the most significant and immediate change that students face as they move to the postsecondary level is in determining eligibility for services. Under the IDEA, the local education agency is responsible for conducting both a "full and individual initial evaluation … before the initial provision of special education and related services" (§ 614 (a)(1)(A)). This multidisciplinary evaluation must be done at no cost to the student or family and should cover all areas of suspected disability.

In contrast, Subpart E of Section 504 requires the student to provide the postsecondary institution with documentation that demonstrates a current disability and need for accommodation (U.S. Department of Education [U.S. DOE], 2007). The Office for Civil Rights (OCR) of the U.S. DOE states that postsecondary institutions can set their own standards related to documentation, and the quantity and type of documentation required can vary by institution. According to OCR, postsecondary institutions:

> may require you to provide documentation prepared by an appropriate professional, such as a medical doctor, psychologist or other qualified diagnostician. The required documentation may include one or more of the following: a diagnosis of your current disability; the date of the diagnosis; how the diagnosis was reached; the credentials of the professional; how your disability affects a major life activity; and how the disability affects your academic performance. The documentation should provide enough information for you and your school to decide what is an appropriate academic adjustment. (U.S. Department of Education, 2007)

Box 43.1 contains information regarding the purposes and typically necessary components of learning disabilities documentation.

Because of the differences between secondary and postsecondary education and the potentially dynamic

BOX 43.1

Purposes and Components of Disability Documentation

Purpose of disability documentation

- Disability documentation is credible evidence that attests to the existence of a substantially limiting impairment, the impact of the impairment on academic performance and related competencies, and recommendations for equal access and/or compensatory measures, commonly referred to as accommodations (Banerjee & Brickerhoff, 2009).

Comprehensive documentation should contain:

- Evidence that the impairment currently exists;
- Information about the nature of the impairment, including its *severity* (e.g., mild, moderate, severe), *frequency* (e.g., how often the symptoms occur) and *duration* (e.g., permanence or long term status versus short term and temporary status);
- Background information that describes history of presenting problem(s) such as:
  - Prior academic struggles, informal supports and coping skills used by the student;
  - Review of prior evaluative reports (if any);
  - Special education services received in the past and review of all pertinent academic history of elementary, secondary and postsecondary education;
  - All relevant developmental, psychosocial and employment histories;
  - Medical history of prior treatment, therapy, interventions and or accommodations used.
- Objective evidence, such as test and subtest scores based on a comprehensive battery of standardized tests;
- Information about a specific diagnosis or diagnoses;
- Information ruling out alternative diagnoses or explanations for the impairment; and
- An integrated summary that synthesizes all sources of objective observed and reported evidence to establish a disability and demonstrate that the impairment(s) constitute substantial limitations to a major life activity.

Note: These adapted 2007 ETS Guidelines on Documentation are reprinted with permission from Educational Testing Service, the copyright owner. No endorsement of this publication by ETS should be inferred.

nature of a disability, OCR also clearly outlines that an IEP or a secondary Section 504 plan may not be considered adequate documentation at the post-secondary level (U.S. Department of Education, 2007). Research indicates that only 10% of postsecondary disability service providers (n = 183) require the submission of an IEP, while 9% require a secondary Section 504 plan (Madaus, Banerjee, & Hamblet, 2010).

Just as the type of documentation required by each institution can vary, so too does the exact review process and criteria used (National Joint Committee on Learning Disabilities [NJCLD], 2007). Madaus et al. (2010) reported five different types of documentation guidelines being used by postsecondary institutions. These include guidelines set forth by the Association on Higher Education and Disability (40%) or by Educational Testing Services (7%). An additional 24% employed institutional-specific guidelines. Service providers were clear in the requirement that documentation contain a clear diagnosis of a learning disability (90% requiring this) and tests used on adult populations (63% requiring this).

Impact of IDEA 2004 on disability documentation. The reauthorization of IDEA in 2004 contained several changes that have the potential to affect students' eligibility for services at the postsecondary level. One such change was §300.307 of the regulations that specifically notes that, in determining the existence of a specific learning disability, a state may prohibit or not require the use of a severe discrepancy between aptitude and achievement. Madaus et al. (2010) found that 50% of responding institutions required evidence of a discrepancy. Further complicating the documentation issue, IDEA 2004 requires that states "permit the use of a process that determines if the child responds to scientific, research-based intervention as part of the evaluation procedures." If states move to a model such as response to intervention alone to diagnose learning disabilities, students may be left without the necessary assessment data to become eligible for services at the postsecondary level (Madaus & Shaw, 2006). Given that 89% of the service providers surveyed by Madaus et al. (2009) either require or highly prefer current measures of aptitude and 91% require or highly prefer current measures of achievement, students may face a significant documentation divide as they transition to postsecondary education (NJCLD, 2007).

Another stipulation in the IDEA regulations that may affect students transitioning to postsecondary education is the recency of the testing available to submit. Both IDEA 1997 and 2004 allow secondary teams to determine if a full re-evaluation be conducted every 3 years. IDEA 2004 also does not require an exit evaluation prior to a student leaving special education due to graduation or exceeding the age eligibility for FAPE (§300.305(e)(2)).

Many students present documentation that was conducted by a secondary special education team, and these changes may result in students submitting documentation that is increasingly dated. Given findings that 43% of postsecondary institutions require testing completed during the past 3 years, and 24% required documentation that was no more than 5 years old, students may be faced with updating their documentation at their own expense (Madaus et al., 2010).

Secondary schools have two available mechanisms to assist students in compiling up-to-date documentation during the transition process. One is the requirement in IDEA 2004 that for students aged 16 or over, the local education agency must develop "Appropriate measurable postsecondary goals based upon Age-appropriate transition assessments related to training, education, employment, and, where appropriate, independent living skills." As noted previously, the final regulations accompanying the IDEA of 2004 specifically states that secondary schools are not responsible for conducting assessments that meet the eligibility requirements of postsecondary institutions. However, conducting a comprehensive evaluation that matches the eligibility requirements of postsecondary institutions during senior year as a specific transition goal and activity could be considered best practice to help meet the "necessary transition assessment" component of the law (Connecticut State Department of Education, 2009; Madaus & Shaw, 2006).

IDEA 2004 also requires that for students exiting special education due to graduation or exceeding maximum age for services, local education agencies:

> must provide the child with a summary of the child's academic achievement and functional performance, which shall include recommendations on how to assist the child in meeting the child's postsecondary goals. (§300.305(e)(3))

This is the Summary of Performance (SOP) requirement. The regulations are minimal in regard to specific guidance to SEAs, noting "State and local officials should have the flexibility to determine the appropriate content in a child's summary, based on the child's individual needs and postsecondary goals" (U.S. Department of Education, 2006). As a result, there is great variability in how each state is implementing the requirement and the comprehensiveness of the form being used (Miller, Madaus, Shaw, Banerjee, & Vitello, 2009; Sopko, 2008).

Although there is presently a dearth of literature related to the effectiveness of the SOP in assisting students to transition to postsecondary education, multiple authors have commented on the potential of a comprehensive SOP. This includes serving as a means to bridge the secondary to postsecondary documentation gaps (Gormley, 2007; Kochhar-Bryant & Izzo, 2006; NJCLD, 2007). The SOP has also been described as a "passport" to eligibility for services in post school environments (Kochhar-Bryant; 2007) and as a means to promote student self-determination (Field & Hoffman; 2007). Self-determination has been identified as critical to the successful transition from secondary to postsecondary education (Fiedler & Danneker, 2007; Field, Sarver, & Shaw, 2003; Janiga & Costenbader, 2002; Test, Fowler, Wood, Brewer, & Eddy, 2005).

The Importance of Self-Determination

Data from the NLTS-2 (Cameto, 2007) indicated that 87% of the students studied received accommodations in high school. But at the college level, only 36% self-disclosed their disability, and only 25% of these students received accommodations in 4-year colleges and 26% in 2-year colleges. Although 56% of those who did not self-disclose no longer considered themselves to have a disability (Cameto, 2007), other members of the sample may not have been aware of their legal rights or the nature of their disability. Other studies of adults with learning disabilities have reported low levels of self-disclosure and receipt of accommodations (Cameto, 2005; Price, Gerber, & Mulligan, 2007; Madaus, 2006).

Just as careful secondary transition planning must include rigorous academic preparation, so too must the skill of student self-determination be considered and developed at the secondary level.

Self-Determination. There are several definitions of self-determination, but the one proposed by Field, Martin, Miller, Ward, and Wehmeyer (1998) is considered the most commonly accepted and utilized definition (Field, Sarver, & Shaw, 2003; Test, Fowler, Brewer, & Wood, 2005):

> Self-Determination is a combination of skills, knowledge, and beliefs that enable a person to engage in goal-directed, self-regulated, autonomous behavior. An understanding of one's strengths and limitations together with a belief in oneself as capable and effective, are essential. When acting on the basis of these skills and attitudes, individuals have greater ability to take control of their lives and assume the role of successful adults. (p. 2)

Underlying self-determination is the key skill of self-advocacy (Abery, 1994; Fiedler & Danneker, 2007; St. Peter, Field, & Hoffman, and Keena, 1992; Test, Fowler, Brewer, et al., 2005; Trainor, 2002; Ward, 1988). Self-advocacy is defined as "an individual's ability to effectively communicate, convey, negotiate or assert his or her own interests, desires, needs, and rights. It involves making informed decisions and taking responsibility for those decisions" (Van Reusen, Bos, Schumaker, & Deshler, 1994, p. 1).

To effectively advocate for oneself, a student must recognize his or her own likes, dislikes, wants, needs, strengths, and limitations, be able to express those, and be given many opportunities to do so in authentic settings (Schreiner, 2007). However, because the IDEA is focused on student progress and success, well-intended parents and professionals may create a "bubble of support" for students (Noonan Squire, 2008, p. 126), overseeing or completing important developmental steps for students, such as problem solving and decision-making (McGuire, 2010). However, this support often results in students being less involved in their own education and dependent on such support (Hadley, 2007; Jones, 2002). Because experience has taught them to focus on their learning weaknesses, many students with learning disabilities exhibit minimal self-awareness and do not recognize their learning and support needs, nor the skills needed to seek out and advocate for necessary postschool services (Jones, 2002; Stodden, Jones, & Chang, 2002). For example, the NLTS-2 (2005) reported that a sample of students with disabilities aged 16–18 had lower scores related to autonomy in career planning than in relationship to personal or social autonomy.

Participation in the IEP process

The literature supports and recommends that students be taught the skills needed in order to actively participate in their own IEP. Data from the NLTS-2 demonstrates that 58% of students with disabilities provide some input to their IEP and transition planning, whereas 12% were described as "leaders in the planning" process (Cameto, 2005, n.p.). Student-led IEP meetings have resulted in positive outcomes, which include: positive comments directed to the student at the meeting, IEP team members expressing more optimism about the educational process, increased effectiveness of students being able to express their strengths, needs, goals, and the ability to request accommodations (Mason, McGahee-Kovac, & Johnson, 2004; Torgerson, Miner, & Shen, 2004). Moreover, students who are actively involved in their own IEP's experience a greater sense of self-efficacy, know about their disability rights and accommodations, and are more self-confident (Wehmeyer, Palmer, Agran, Mithaug, & Martin, 2000; Mason et al., 2004).

Despite the power of student involvement in the IEP process, the literature also suggests that this approach remains underutilized (Cameto, 2005; Martin, Portley, & Graham, 2010; Jones, 2002; Stodden et al., 2002). Cameto (2005) reported that 6% of students did not attend their IEP meetings or participate in the planning process, and 25% were present at meetings but participated little. Martin and colleagues conducted multiple studies that found that even when students with disabilities attend their IEP meetings, they tend to speak infrequently (3% of the total time) and to have little understanding of why the meeting was being held, what was being discussed, and what their role was during the meeting (Martin, Marshall, & Sale, 2004).

Despite the numerous curricula related to self-determination there is still little evidence that these skills are being directly taught in high school or that formal training in self-advocacy exists in college settings (Fiedler & Danneker, 2007; Test, Fowler, Brewer, et al., 2005; Webb, Patterson, Syverud, and Seabrooks-Blackmore, 2008). This lack of training has resulted in students not possessing the skills that can assist in self-determination and self-advocacy (Carter, Lane, Pierson & Stang, 2008; Fielder & Danneker, 2007).

The question remains how transition related services associated with self-determination are to be delivered while promoting access to the general curriculum. Should instruction in self-determination be infused within a general education classroom or is it best addressed in self-contained, specialized, or community-based settings (Carter, et al., 2008)? In order to facilitate a successful transition from secondary to postsecondary settings, researchers are advocating for self-determination instruction to be included more deliberately into the general curriculum while also maintaining efforts to provide direct instruction in self-contained, specialized, or community based settings depending on individual student needs (Eisenman, 2007; Fiedler & Danneker, 2007; Mason et al., 2004; Test, Fowler, Wood, et. al., 2005; Wehmeyer, Field, Doren, Jones, & Mason, 2004). Secondary students must have opportunities to learn about accommodations, practice requesting needed accommodations, learn to communicate their needs to appropriate personnel, and know their rights and responsibilities under the law (Schreiner, 2007; Test, Fowler, Wood, et al., 2005).

Technology and Transition

Technology skills are a critical component of preparation for a knowledge-based, digital society. For students with disabilities transitioning to college, the focus has traditionally been on assistive technology (AT). However, AT alone is no longer sufficient, fluency with broader learning technologies is now an essential element of college survival (Banerjee & Gregg, 2008). College-age students today need technology to participate in the learning process, engage in social networking, expand their knowledge base and understanding, and extend their individual capabilities as learners (Pew Research Center Report, 2007).

Rose and Meyers (2000) note that technology tools can make a significant difference for college students with dyslexia, and these technologies and tools do not have to be restricted to an "assistive" capacity. Technology is learner-centric because it potentially allows each individual to control and create his/her own unique learning environment and experience. Although such capabilities create novel opportunities, they also result in hidden pitfalls, particularly for students with disabilities. Many of these can be addressed as part of the student's secondary education program and transition plan.

The influence of the Internet on learning can hardly be ignored (Leu et al., 2007). The Internet presents a learning context that is different from that of textbooks. A book represents finite space; the Internet, on the other hand, is boundless. Reading on the Internet is guided by navigational decisions made by the individual at critical junctures, following an initial search and inquiry. On the Internet, decoding for comprehension includes decoding not only letters and words, but also the strategic use of color, meaning-bearing icons and animations, pictures, maps, graphs, and charts that are not necessarily static, and hyperlinks that navigate to other texts and images (Leu, Kinzer, Coiro, & Cammack, 2004). In other words, comprehension and meaning on the Internet must include understanding of icons, animated symbols, audio, video, interactive images, virtual reality environments, and more. According to Gregg and Banerjee (2009), "the underlying cognitive processes that guide college students while reading printed text are different from those required for reading on the Internet, however, the exact nature of these differences are still unclear" (p. 269). Leu et al. (2007) identify five skills that are unique to open learning environments: (a) identifying a question or search query that starts the reading process, (b) navigating and locating information to read, (c) critically evaluating the information, (d) synthesizing information (through the choices made about sites to visit and links to follow), and (e) communicating the information.

Knowledge of reading patterns and the cognitive/metacognitive processes that guide reading decisions on the Internet are emerging. The RAND Reading Study Group (RRSG, 2002) notes that "…accessing the Internet makes large demands on individuals' literacy skills; in some cases, this technology requires readers to have novel literacy skills, and little is known about how to analyze or teach those skills" (p. 4). Successful Internet reading experiences appear to require both similar and more complex applications of (a) prior knowledge sources; (b) inferential reasoning strategies; and (c) self-regulated reading processes (Coiro & Dobler, 2007), but awareness of such skills among students in general is still limited. Decision-making regarding what to read and the sequence in which to read information online by college students with dyslexia is largely unknown (Gregg & Banerjee, 2009).

Technology and Higher Education

A review of the literature on technology in higher education suggests several trends that are noteworthy for transition planning. First, computers are now pervasive in formal higher education settings. Terrell (2007) noted that over 150 colleges nationwide required students to bring personal laptops to college The report cites data from the Student Monitor Research group, which indicates that nearly 5.2 million undergraduate students (or 88% of the student population) owned a personal computer in 2007. Laptops are the computer of choice. In 2005, laptop ownership among college students was 52.8%. This figure increased to 75.8% in 2007 (EDUCAUSE, 2007). Many postsecondary programs require students to have a laptop, as a course pre-requisite. The use of smart phones is also on the rise. Both students and institutions are increasingly using handheld mobile devices with web-enabled technologies in relation to academic services.

Second, learning that involves the ability to navigate open environments like the Internet is essential. College students are the largest group of Internet users in the general population. The 2007 EDUCAUSE data indicate that the vast majority of college students use instructional technologies and the Internet to remotely access institutional library resources (94.7%), create presentations (91.7%), or communicate via email (99.9%), and they are familiar with and have used a course management system (83.0%) such as WebCT, Blackboard, ANGEL, or Desire2Learn.

Implications for Students with Disabilities

Awareness of the ways in which technology has transformed and is continuing to reshape postsecondary education is an important component of successful college experience for all students (Parker & Banerjee, 2007), and in particular for students with disabilities transitioning to college. Many institutions of higher education have technology competency skills requirements both for entry into and graduation from college. As part of the college search process, students should be encouraged to research these requirements and to discuss their implications with secondary personnel. Secondary personnel should also consider evaluating students' ability to learn and read in open learning environments such as the Internet. This type of learning requires a new skill set that many students are unprepared for when they enter into college (Leu et al., 2007).

Assistive technology. Assistive technologies were first introduced as a component of rehabilitation services in the late 1950s (Mull & Sitlington, 2003). The Rehabilitation Act of 1973 (Sections 503 and 504) and the Education for All Handicapped Children Act of 1975 created the provision of assistive technologies for all students with disabilities by establishing the concept of "reasonable accommodations". The Technology-Related Assistance of Individuals with Disabilities Act of 1988 (Title 29, U.S.C. § 140 25) defined assistive technology as any item, piece of equipment, or product system whether acquired commercially off the shelf, modified or customized, that is used to increase, maintain, or improve functional capabilities of individuals with disabilities.

In developing a student's IEP, the IEP team must consider the need for assistive technologies. For example, if one of the IEP goals is to develop written expression skills, a laptop or a portable word processing device may be an appropriate AT device for the student with written language disorder or grapho-motor difficulties, and should be written into the IEP. The IDEA also requires that IEP goals must consider AT services. AT service is "any service that directly assists an individual with a disability in the selection, acquisition, or use of an assistive technology device." (20 U.S.C. 1401(2)). At the secondary school level, AT services include, among others, purchase, loan, fitting and/or training students with AT devices. Despite the benefits of technology, a report by the NLTS-2 (2003) suggests that use of computers to access the general curriculum by students with disabilities is limited.

At the postsecondary level, AT for students with disabilities are synonymous with accommodations. The difference is that AT in college does not serve a remedial purpose. The primary function of assistive technologies is to augment the student's strengths, while compensating for deficits (Houchins, 2001). Assistive technologies help to bridge the gap between students' current level of academic functioning and the expected level of proficiency in a given educational setting (Anderson-Inman, Knox-Quinn, & Szymanski, 1999).

Commonly used ATs include audio books, personal FM systems, calculators, portable word processors, spell checkers, and speech-to-text equipment. In recent years, these traditional ATs have given way to text in alternative format (often known as alt media) created through digitalization of printed information, smart phones, smart pens, and other mobile, multifunctional devices. The result is a blurring of the line between assistive and other technologies. It is important for high school students to understand the process of accommodation determination as it applies to AT in college and the level of support that may or may not be available.

Assistive technology accommodations vary widely from institution to institution. Some institutions provide a wide range of ATs that include options for physical/motor, sensory, and cognitive accessibility, including individualized technology support services housed within a technology lab. Other institutions offer minimal AT. Personal computers and specific software are typically not considered mandated accommodations that must be purchased by the institutions (Banerjee & Judd, 2009).

While the process of accommodation determination is the same for technology and non-technology accommodations, high school students may discover the AT that was readily available in school is not guaranteed in a particular postsecondary institution. For instance, students may not have access to school district sponsored ATs, such as a particular type of portable word processor such as QuickPad or AlphaSmart. Furthermore, AT in college is typically not guided by student preference. While consideration is given to a student's preferred AT, it should not be assumed that the identical technology will be available in college (Banerjee & Judd, 2009).

Another consideration is the portability and usability of the AT in the current instructional environment. The traditional model of AT was location-specific tech labs where students could come to use the technology and services. To be successful in college today, students with disabilities need technologies (a) that afford access at all times and all locations (Web-based Education Commission Report, 2000) and (b) that provide accessibility while maintaining a "competitive" advantage (Banerjee & Gregg, 2009). Competitive efficiency is lost when the technology that provides access is cumbersome to use. For instance, audio-taped class lectures may provide access to the class notes but can be time consuming when students have to re-listen to the entire lecture at a later time.

Preparing for Assistive and Instructional Technologies in College

Students with disabilities transitioning to college must be prepared for a postsecondary environment that is rapidly changing because of the influence of technology in education. Online and blended courses are now commonplace in college (EDUCAUSE, 2008). Evidence-based research attesting to the benefits and challenges of online and blended courses for college students with cognitive disabilities is still emerging. A survey of technology competencies of college students with and without learning disabilities and/or ADHD revealed that levels of comfort and skills with technology were significantly different across students with and without such disabilities (Parker & Banerjee, 2007). In particular, students with learning disabilities and/or ADHD indicated less comfort conducting Internet searches for research and multi-tasking on the computer. In other words, students with disabilities are at a disadvantage in college and not simply because of lack of access.

Among other things, transition plans should include goals and objectives related to technology that teach navigation skills, critical evaluation of open source materials, functioning in virtual learning communities, e-database operations, and course management system functions. The International Society for Technology in Education (ISTE) National Education Technology Standards (NETS) serves as a valuable starting point for preparing students for the digital age. NETS (n.d.) provides technology profile indicators for students at various grade levels (see http://www.iste.org/Content /NavigationMenu/NETS/ForStudents/2007Standards/Profiles/NETS_for_Students_2007_Profiles.htm). These profile indicators can be adapted and used as annual goals and short-term objectives by transition counselors and special education teachers for high school students in preparation for college.

Transition planning must also include queries for postsecondary disability service providers, which may not have been part of the traditional campus visit in the past. Box 43.2 contains a series of questions that high school students preparing for transition to college should consider asking disability student services office personnel regarding assistive and instructional technologies (Banerjee & Brinckerhoff, 2008).

Summary

Professionals have made significant progress over the past two decades in helping students with disabilities access postsecondary education. Improved transition planning has resulted in more students setting postsecondary education as a goal, and in more students actually enrolling in postsecondary education. However, more work needs to be accomplished to help additional students access postsecondary education and for more students with disabilities to remain in and successfully complete postsecondary education. This work will be shaped by changes in the legal landscape and the impact of emerging and evolving learning technologies that present new challenges for students with disabilities, their families, and secondary personnel.

References

Abery, B. (1994). A Conceptual framework for enhancing self-determination. In M. Hayden & B. Abery (Eds.), *Challenges for a service system in transition* (pp. 345–380). Baltimore: Brookes.

Americans with Disabilities Act Amendments Act (ADAA). (2008). PL 110-325. 42 U.S.C. § 1201 et seq.

Anderson-Inman, L., Knox-Quinn, C., & Szymanski, M. (1999). Computer supported studying: stories of successful transition to postsecondary education. *Career Development for Exceptional Individuals*, *22*, 185–212.

Banerjee, M., & Brinckerhoff, L. C. (2008, June). *Next generation support services: Redefining accessibility in an era of tech blended courses.* Three day strand presentation at the 20th Postsecondary Disability Training Institute. Sponsored by Center on Postsecondary Education and Disability, University of Connecticut, Portland, ME.

BOX 43.2

Questions to Ask Disability Service Offices About Technology

1. Does the Disability Student Services (DSS) office offer demonstration and training on assistive technologies? What are the qualifications of the staff providing such trainings?
2. Does the DSS office have trained technology specialists on staff?
3. Does the DSS office have an assistive technology lab?
4. Does the DSS office offer strategy instruction with technology? In other words, does it offer ways to enhance learning practices with assistive and other instructional technologies?
5. What are the assistive technologies on site that may be available for students with disabilities?
6. Are assistive technologies available only in the DSS office or can they be accessed at other locations as well, such as in the library, student center, writing lab, and so on?
7. Does the office provide short-term loans of equipment and software to students? What are the conditions of this loan?
8. Is there training for students on instructional technologies such as WebCT/BlackBoard on campus?
9. Does the college or DSS office offer summer trainings on assistive and instructional technologies to students?
10. Does the college make recommendations regarding computer and software purchase? Is there a discount available for purchasing software through the college/university bookstore or other recommended source?
11. Does the DSS office have information to guide students in their purchase of software that often serves as an accommodation, such as text-to-speech software, note-taking software, portable devices and so on?
12. What is the DSS office's protocol for helping students problem solve technology issues and concerns?
13. Is there a fee for technology support services?

Banerjee, M., & Gregg, N. (2008). Redefining accessibility on high-stakes tests for postsecondary college students with learning disabilities in an era of technology. *Learning Disabilities: A Multidisciplinary Journal, 15*(3), 137–145.

Banerjee, M., & Gregg, N. (2009). *Reading comprehension solutions for college students with dyslexia in an era of technology: An integrated approach.* Poster session presented at the American Educational Research Association. San Diego, CA.

Banerjee, M., & Judd, J. (2009, March). *Learning technologies and college transition for students with LD and/or ADHD.* Disability services staff training. Avon Old Farms, Avon, CT.

Berkner, L., & Choy, S. (2008, July). *Descriptive summary of 2003–2004 beginning postsecondary students: Three years later.* Washington, DC: U.S. Department of Education.

Blackorby, J., & Wagner, M. M. (1996). National post school outcomes of youth with disabilities: Findings from the National Longitudinal Transition Study. *Exceptional Children, 62*, 399–414.

Blazer, B. (1999). Developing 504 classroom accommodation plans: A collaborative, systematic parent-student-teacher approach. *TEACHING Exceptional Children, 32*(2), 28–33.

Bureau of Labor Statistics. (2009, March). Education pays. *Employment projections.* Retrieved from http://www.bls.gov/emp/emptab7.htm

Cameto, R. (2005). The transition planning process. *NLTS-2 Data Brief: Reports from the National Longitudinal Transition Study, 4*, (1). Retrieved from http://www.ncset.org /publications/viewdesc.asp?id=2130

Cameto, R. (2007, October). *4 years out: Postschool outcomes and experiences of youth with disabilities.* Presentation at the Division on Career Development and Transition Conference, Orlando, FL.

Cameto, R., Levine, P., & Wagner, M. (2004). *Transition planning for students with disabilities. A special topic report of findings from the National Longitudinal Transition Study-2 (NLTS2).* Menlo Park, CA: SRI International. Retrieved from www.nlts2.org/reports/2004_11/nlts2_report_2004_11_complete.pdf.

Carter, E. W., Lane, K. L., Pierson, M. R., & Stang, K. K. (2008). Promoting self-determination for transition-age youth: Views of high school general and special educators. *Exceptional Children, 75*, 55–70.

CASE. (1999). *Section 504 and the ADA: Promoting student access* (2nd ed.). Fort Valley, GA: Council for Administrators of Special Education.

Coiro, J., & Dobler, E. (2007). Exploring the online reading comprehension strategies used by sixth grade skilled readers to search for and locate information on the Internet. *Reading Research Quarterly, 42,* 214–57.

College Board. (2006). *Education pays: Second update.* Retrieved from http://www.collegeboard.com/prod_downloads/press/cost06/education_pays_06.pdf

Commission on Access, Admissions and Success in Higher Education. (2008, December). *Coming to our senses: Education and the American future.* New York: College Board. Retrieved from http://professionals.collegeboard.com/policy-advocacy/access/success

Connecticut State Department of Education. (2009, June). *2009 Guidelines for indentifying children with learning disabilities: Executive summary.* Hartford, CT: Author.

deBettencourt, L. U. (2002). Understanding the differences between IDEA and Section 504. *TEACHING Exceptional Children, 34*(3), 16–23.

Educational Testing Services. (2007). *Policy statement for documentation of a learning disability in adolescents and adults* (2nd ed.). Retrieved August 5, 2009, from http://www.ets.org/portal/site/ets/menuitem.c988ba0e5dd572bada20bc47c3921509/?vgnextoid=5d77dec2c5555010VgnVCM10000022f95190RCRD&vgnextchannel=fbc7be3a864f4010VgnVCM10000022f95190RCRD

EDUCAUSE (2007). The ECAR study of undergraduate students and information technology, 2007. Retrieved November 15, 2009, from http://nct.educause.edu/ir/library/pdf/ERS0706/ekf0706.pdf

EDUCAUSE (2008). The ECAR study of undergraduate students and information technology. Retrieved November 15, 2009, from http://www.educause.edu/ers0808

EDUCAUSE (2009). Educause learning initiatives: Learning technologies. Retrieved July 10, 2009, from http://www.educause.edu/ELI/EDUCAUSELearningInitiative /LearningTechnologies/5672

Eisenman, L.T. (2007). Self-determination interventions: Building a foundation for school completion. *Remedial & Special Education, 28,* 2–8.

Falls, J., & Unruh, D. (2009, July). *Frequently asked questions; Revised part B indicator 14 post-school outcomes.* Eugene, OR: National Post-School Outcomes Center.

Fiedler, C. R., & Danneker, J. E. (2007). Self-advocacy instruction: Bridging the research to practice gap. *Focus on Exceptional Children, 39*(8), 1–20.

Field, S., & Hoffman, A. (2007). Self-determination in secondary transition assessment. *Assessment for Effective Intervention, 32*, 181–190.

Field, S., Martin, J., Miller, R., Ward, M., & Wehmeyer, M. (1998). *A practical guide for teaching self-determination.* Reston, VA: Council for Exceptional Children.

Field, S., Martin, R., & Ward, M. (1998). Self-determination for persons with disabilities: A position statement of the Division on Career Development and Transition. *Career Development for Exceptional Individuals, 21*, 113–128.

Field, S., Sarver, M. D., & Shaw, S. F. (2003). Self-determination: A key to success in postsecondary education for students with learning disabilities. *Remedial and Special Education, 24*, 339–349.

Furney, K. S., Hasazi, S. B., & DeStafano, L. (1997). Transition policies, practices, and promises: Lessons from three states. *Exceptional Children, 63*, 343–355.

Gormley, S. (2007). Packing for college: What the student with LD shouldn't bother packing. *Insights on Learning Disabilities, 4*, 51–64.

Gregg, N., & Banerjee, M. (2009). Reading comprehension solutions for college students with dyslexia in an era of technology: An integrated approach. In G. Reid (Ed.), *Dyslexia: A practitioner's handbook* (pp. 265–285). UK: Wiley.

Hadley, W. M. (2007, Spring). The necessity of academic accommodations for first-year college students with learning disabilities. *Journal of College Admission.* Retrieved from http://findarticles.com/p/articles/mi_qa3955/is_200704/ai_n19198046

Harbor, W. S. (2008). *The 2008 biennial AHEAD survey of disability services and resource professionals in higher education: Final report.* Huntersville, NC: Association on Higher Education and Disability.

HEATH Resource Center (2006). *Guidance and career counselors' toolkit: Advising high school students with disabilities on postsecondary options.* Washington, DC: George Washington University.

Henderson, C. (1999). *College freshmen with disabilities: Statistical year 1998.* Washington, DC: American Council on Education.

Hitchings, W. E., Retish, P., & Horvath, M. (2005). Academic preparation of adolescents with disabilities for postsecondary education. *Career Development for Exceptional Individuals, 28*, 26–35.

Higher Education Opportunity Act of 2008. 20 U. S. C. § 1001 et seq. (2008).

Houchins, D. E. (2001). Assistive technology barriers and facilitators during secondary and postsecondary transitions. *Career Development for Exceptional Individuals, 24*, 73–88.

Individuals with Disabilities Education Act of 2004. 20 U. S. C. § 1400 et seq. (2004).

Individuals with Disabilities Education Improvement Act of 2004. 20 U.S.C. § 1400 et seq. Final Regulations (2006).

Janiga, S. J., & Costenbader, V. (2002). The transition from high school to postsecondary education for students with learning disabilities: A survey of college service coordinators. *Journal of Learning Disabilities, 35*, 462–468.

Jones, M. (2002, March). Providing a quality accommodated experience in preparation for and during post-secondary school. *Information Brief, 1*(1). Washington, DC: National Center on Secondary Education and Transition.

Kochhar-Bryant, C. A. (2007). The summary of performance as transition "passport" to employment and independent living. *Assessment for Effective Intervention, 32*, 160–170.

Kochhar-Bryant, C., & Izzo, M. (2006). Access to post-high school services: Transition assessment and the summary of performance. *Career Development for Exceptional Individuals, 29*, 70–89.

Leu, D. J., Jr., Zawilinski, L., Castek, J., Banerjee, M., Housand, B. C.,

Liu, Y., & O'Neil, M. (2007). What is new about the new literacies of online reading comprehension? In L. S. Rush, A. J. Eakle, & Berger, A. (Eds.), *Secondary school literacy: What research reveals for classroom practice* (pp. 37–68). Urbana, IL: National Council of Teachers of English.

Leu, D. J., Kinzer, C. K., Coiro. J. L., & Cammack, D. W. (2004). Towards a theory of new literacies emerging from the Internet and other information and communication technologies. In R. B. Ruddell & N. Unrau (Eds.), *Theoretical models and processes of reading* (5th ed., pp. 1570–1613). Newark, DE: International Reading Association.

Levesque, K., Laird, J., Hensley, E., Choy, S. P., Cataldi, E. F., & Hudson, L. (2008). *Career and technical education in the United States: 1990 to 2005*. Washington, DC: U.S. Department of Education. (NCES 2008-035).

Madaus, J. W. (2005). Helping students with learning disabilities navigate the college transition maze. *TEACHING Exceptional Children, 37*(3), 32–37.

Madaus, J. W. (2006). Employment outcomes of university graduates with learning disabilities. *Learning Disabilities Quarterly, 29*, 19–31.

Madaus, J. W. (2010). Let's be reasonable: Accommodations at the college level. In S. F. Shaw, J. W. Madaus, & L. C. Dukes (Eds.), *Preparing students with disabilities for college success: A practical guide to transition planning* (pp. 37–63). Baltimore: Brookes.

Madaus, J. W., Banerjee, M., & Hamblet, E. (2010). Learning disability documentation decision making at the postesecondary level. *Career Development for Exceptional Individuals, 33*(2), 68–79.

Madaus, J. W., & Shaw, S. F. (2004). Section 504: The differences in the regulations regarding secondary and postsecondary education. *Intervention in School and Clinic, 40*, 81–87.

Madaus, J. W., & Shaw, S. F. (2006). The impact of the IDEA 2004 on transition to college for students with learning disabilities. *Learning Disabilities Research and Practice, 21*, 273–281.

Madaus, J. W., Shaw, S. F., & Zhao, J. (2005). Section 504 practices in one state. *Journal of Special Education Leadership, 18*, 24–29.

Martin, J. E., & Marshall, L. H. (1995). Choicemaker: A comprehensive self-determination transition program. *Intervention in School and Clinic, 30*, 147–157.

Martin, J. E., Marshall, L. H., & Sale, R. P. (2004). A 3-year study of middle, junior high, and high school IEP meetings. *Exceptional Children, 70*, 285–297.

Martin, J. E., Portley, J., & Graham, J. (2010). *Teaching students with disabilities self-determination skills to equalize access and increase opportunities for postsecondary educational Success*. In S. F. Shaw, J. W. Madaus, & L. C. Dukes (Eds.), *Preparing students with disabilities for college success: A practical guide to transition planning*. (pp. 124–137). Baltimore: Brookes.

Mason, C. Y., McGahee-Kovac, M., & Johnson, L. (2004). How to help students lead their IEP meetings. *Exceptional Children, 36*(3), 18–24.

McGuire, J. M. (2010). Considerations for the transition to college. In S. F. Shaw, J. W. Madaus, & L. C. Dukes (Eds.), *Preparing students with disabilities for college success: A practical guide to transition planning* (pp. 7–35). Baltimore: Brookes.

Miller, W. K., Madaus, J. W., Shaw, S. F., Banerjee, M., & Vitello, S. (2009). *State implementation of the summary of performance requirements of the Individuals with Disabilities Education Improvement Act of 2004*. Storrs: CT, Center on Postsecondary Education and Disability.

Misidentification under 504 and IDEA can be avoided (2004, October). *Section 504 Compliance Handbook*, 5–7. Retrieved from http://www.thompson.com/public/offerpage.jsp?prod=HAND&priority=WEB91411

Mull, C. A., & Sitlington, P. L. (2003). The role of technology in the transition to postsecondary education of students with learning disabilities: A review of the literature. *The Journal of Special Education, 37*, 26–32.

National Center for Education Statistics. (2005). Current postsecondary education and employment status, wages earned, and living arrangements of special education students out of secondary school up to 4 years, by type of disability: 2005. *Digest of Education Statistics*. Washington, DC: U.S. Department of Education.

National Center for Education Statistics (2006). Profile of undergraduates in U.S. postsecondary education institutions: 2003–2004. Retrieved November 1, 2006, from http://nces.ed.gov/pubsearch/pubsinfo.asp?pubid=2006184

National Center for Education Statistics. (2008, September). Postsecondary career/technical education: Changes in the number of offering institutions and awarded credentials from 1997 to 2006. U.S. Department of Education: NCES Issue Brief 2008-001.

National Center for Education Statistics. (2009). Integrated Postsecondary Education Data System: Glossary. Washington, DC: U.S. Department of Education. Retrieved from http://nces.ed.gov/ipeds/glossary/index.asp?id=313

National Joint Committee on Learning Disabilities. (2007, July). The documentation disconnect for students with learning disabilities: Improving access to postsecondary disability services. Retrieved from http://www.ldonline.org /about/partners/njcld

National Longitudinal Transition Study-2. (2003). Going to school: Instructional, contexts, programs, and participation of secondary school students with disabilities. Retrieved August 27, 2009, from http://www.nlts2.org/reports /2003_12/nlts2_report_2003_12_execsum.pdf

National Longitudinal Transition Study-2. (2005, June). The self-determination of youth with disabilities. FACTS from OSEP's National Longitudinal Studies. Menlo Park, CA: NLTS-2. Retrieved from http://www.nlts2.org/fact_sheets /nlts2_fact_sheet_2005_06-2.pdf

Newman, L., Wagner, M., Cameto, R., & Knokey, A. M. (2009). The post-high school outcomes of youth with disabilities up to 4 years after high school. (NCSER 2009-3017). Menlo Park, CA: SRI International. Retrieved from http://www.nlts2.org/reports /2009_04/nlts2_report_2009_04_complete.pdf

Noonan Squire, P. (2008). A young adult's personal reflection and review of research on self-determination. *Career Development for Exceptional Individuals, 31*, 126–128.

'Over Providing' under Section 504 may create personal liability. (2004, December). *Special Education Law Update*, pp. 1, 10–12.

Parker, D. R., & Banerjee, M. (2007). Leveling the digital playing field: Assessing the learning technology needs of college-bound students with LD and/or ADHD. *Assessment for Effective Intervention, 33*, 5–14.

Parsad, B., & Lewis, L. (2008). *Distance education and degree-granting postsecondary institutions: 2006–2007*. Washington, DC: U.S. Department of Education (NCES 2009-044).

Peter D. Hart Research Associates/Public Opinion Strategies (2005). *Rising to the challenge: Are high school graduates prepared for college and work?* Washington, DC: Author.

Peterson, K. (2003). Overcoming senior slump: The community college role. *ERIC Digest*. ERIC Document Reproduction No. ED 477830.

Pew Research Center Report. (2007). *A portrait of "Generation Next": How young people view their lives, futures and politics*. Retrieved August 5, 2009, from http://people-press.org/report/300/a-portrait-of-generation-next

Price, L. A., Gerber, P. J., & Mulligan, R. (2007). Adults with learning disabilities and the underutilization of the Americans with Disabilities act. *Remedial and Special Education, 28*, 340–344.

Pryor, J. H., Hurtado, S., DeAngelo, L., Sharkness, J., Romero, L. C., Korn, W. S., & Tran, S. (2008). *The American freshman: National norms for fall 2008*. Los Angeles: Higher Education Research Institute, UCLA.

RAND Reading Study Group. (2002). Reading for understanding: Toward an R& D program in reading comprehension. Santa Monica, CA: RAND.

Reed, C. B. (2006, August). Early assessment program results and follow-up for 2006. *Letter to high school and unified district superintendents, county superintendents, and charter high school administrators*. Long Beach, CA: Author.

Rehabilitation Act of 1973, Section 504, P. L. 93-112, 29 U.S.C. §794 (1977).

Rose, D. H., & Meyers, A. (2000). The future is in the margins: The role of technology and disability in educational reform (A report prepared for the U. S. Department of Education's Office of Special Education Technology). Washington, DC: U. S. Department of Education.

Rudestam, K. E., & Schoenholtz-Read, J., (2010). The flourishing of adult online education. In K. E. Rudestam & J. Schoenholtz-Read (Eds.), *Handbook of online learning* (2nd ed., pp. 1–28). Los Angeles: Sage.

Schreiner, M. B. (2007). Effective self-advocacy: what students and special educators need to know. *Intervention in School and Clinic, 42,* 300–304.

Schworm, P. (2008, April 16). Many Mass. graduates unprepared in college: Thousands need remedial classes, are dropout risks. *Boston Globe*. Retrieved from http://www.boston.com/news/education/higher/articles/2008/04/16/many_mass_graduates_unprepared_in_college/?page=1

Secretary of Education's Commission on the Future of Higher Education (2006, September). *A test of leadership: Charting the future of U.S. higher education*. Washington, DC: U.S. Department of Education.

Smith, T. E. C. (2002). Section 504: what teachers need to know. *Intervention in School and Clinic, 37*, 259–266.

Sopko, K. M. (2008, March). *Summary of performance: Brief policy analysis*. Alexandria, VA: National Association of State Directors of Special Education.

Stodden, R. A., & Jones, M. A., & Chang, K. (2002). Services, supports and accommodations for individuals with disabilities: An analysis across secondary education, postsecondary education and employment: Implications for educators in secondary school. *White Paper*. Retrieved from http://www.ncset.hawaii.edu/publications/pdf/services_supports.pdf

St. Peter, S., Field, S., Hoffman, A., & Keena, V. (1992). *Self-determination: A literature review and synthesis*. Detroit, MI: The Developmental Disabilities Institute and The College of Education, Wayne State University.

Terrell, K. (2007). Bring your own laptop. Retrieved August 25, 2009, from http://www.parkridge.k12.nj.us/guidance/PDFs/guidelines2.pdf

Test, D. W., Fowler, C. H., Brewer, D. M., & Wood, W. M. (2005). A content and methodological review of self-advocacy intervention studies. *Exceptional Children*, *72*, 101–125.

Test, D. W., Fowler, C. H., Wood, W. M., Brewer, D. M., & Eddy, S. (2005). A conceptual framework of self-advocacy for students with disabilities. *Remedial and Special Education*, *26*, 43–54.

Torgerson, C. W., Miner, C. A., & Shen, H. (2004). Developing student competence in self-directed IEPs. *Intervention in School and Clinic*, *39*, 162–167.

Trainor, A. (2002). Self-determination for students with learning disabilities: Is it a universal value? *International Journal of Qualitative Studies in Education*, *15*, 711–725.

U.S. Department of Education. (2006). *A test of leadership: Charting the future of U.S. Higher Education*. Washington, DC: U.S. Government Printing Office.

U.S. Department of Education. (2007). *Students with disabilities preparing for postsecondary education: Know your rights and responsibilities*. Washington, DC: U.S. Government Printing Office.

Viadero, D. (2005, August). Student preparation seen to fall short of college expectations. *Education Week*. Retrieved from http://www.edweek.org/ew/index.html

Wagner, M., Newman, L., & Cameto, R. (2004). *Changes over time in the secondary school experiences of students with disabilities. A report of findings from the National Longitudinal Transition Study (NLTS) and the National Longitudinal Transition Study-2 (NLTS2)* Menlo Park, CA: SRI International. Retrieved from http://www.nlts2.org/reports/2004_04/nlts2_report_2004_04_complete.pdf.

Ward, M. J. (1988). The many facets of self-determination. *NICHCY Transition Summary: National Information Center for Children and Youth with Disabilities, 5,* 2–3.

Web-Based Education Commission Report. (2000). The power of the Internet for learning: Final report of the web-based based education commission. Retrieved August 27, 2009, from http://www.ed.gov/offices/AC/WBEC /FinalReport/index.html

Webb, K. W., Patterson, K. B., Syverud, S. M., & Seabrooks-Blackmore, J. J. (2008). Evidenced based practices that promote transition to postsecondary education: Listening to a decade of expert voices. *Exceptionality*, *16*, 192–206.

Wehmeyer, M. L., Field, S., Doren, B., Jones, B., & Mason, C. (2004). Self-determination and student involvement in standards-based reform. *Exceptional Children*, *70*, 413–425.

Wehmeyer, M. L., Palmer, S., Agran, M., Mithaug, D., & Martin, J. (2000). Promoting causal agency: The self-determined learning model of instruction. *Exceptional Children*, *66*, 439–453.

Zirkel, P. A. (2004, March). *A primer for Section 504 student issues: Legal requirements and practical recommendations*. Presentation for ConnCase, New Britain, CT.

44

Career Choice Patterns and Behaviors of Work-Bound Youth with High Incidence Disabilities

Jay W. Rojewski and Noel Gregg
University of Georgia

Historically, professionals have paid little attention to the career development needs of work-bound youth because of the traditional separation between school and workplace and societal attitudes, which favor college attendance (Herr & Cramer, 1996; Rojewski & Kim, 2003). Career needs and postsecondary outcomes of work-bound youth with high incidence disabilities have received even less attention (Gregg, 2007, 2009; National Council on Disability, 2003; Wagner, Newman, Cameto, Garza, & Levine, 2005; Young & Browning, 2005). Although research has been limited, a number of reports describe disappointing postsecondary educational and occupational attainment for adolescents with high incidence disabilities (e.g., Sitlington, Frank, & Carson, 1994; Wagner, Blackorby, Cameto, & Newman, 1993). These outcomes likely result from the greater likelihood of unique problems with delayed or impaired career development, coupled with lowered academic performance and greater barriers imposed as a result of disability.

For this chapter, we focus on individuals in one of several high-incidence disability (HID) groups commonly encountered in the classroom including learning disability, emotional and behavioral disorder, and attention deficit hyperactivity disorder (ADHD). Although individuals in these three groups exhibit both similarities and differences in social, academic, and behavioral functioning, they experience considerable overlap in the impact of their disabilities on work preparation and career attainment across a continuum of frequency and severity (Dietz & Montague, 2006; Dykman & Ackerman, 1991; Kaplan, Dewey, Crawford, & Wilson, 2001). Our decision to include these three disability groups is based on the similar characteristics they possess and in the challenges they generally share in school as they prepare for and transition from school to work and adult life. These similarities can facilitate an understanding of how we might use career theories and interventions to explain and promote career behavior, choice, and attainment.

The challenge to understanding the process of preparing for and engaging in the transition from school to work and adult life for adolescents with high incidence disabilities is several-fold in that the nature of the disabilities included presents both common and unique career needs, experiences, and potentials for adolescents. In turn, the nature of individuals' susceptibility to career-related risks based, in part, on disability, also varies. Several career-related barriers that have been associated with disability include social stigma (Stone, Stone, & Dipboye, 1992), employment discrimination (Unger, 2001), inadequate vocational training and preparation (Ochs & Roessler, 2001), and poor self-efficacy and lower career aspirations (Fabian & Liesener, 2005; Rojewski & Yang, 1997).

Do Theories of Career Development, Behavior, and Choice Apply To Adolescents with High Incidence Disabilities?

Career theories play an integral role in our explanations of adolescents' career behavior, choices, and eventual attainment. Unfortunately, theory is often overlooked or ignored when engaged in transition planning and career preparation for work-bound youth with disabilities. The relatively recent "discovery" of career development and counseling for adolescents with disabilities is particularly interesting given the long history of vocational rehabilitation programs and research (Fabian & Liesener, 2005). In any event, early conceptions of disability as an all-encompassing phenomenon that limited career choice and career development activity has shifted in recent years to preparation for the transition from school to work, personal agency, and self-determination.

Over the years, two differing perspectives on the role of disability in career development and choice have emerged. One view has assumed that most career theories are simply not applicable to individuals with disabilities. This belief is based on the fact that theories have been developed on select groups of advantaged individuals whose experiences may not generalize to people with differing life experiences. Theoretical constructs like career maturity and career decision-making self-efficacy presuppose a sophisticated level of intellectual functioning and access to resources that not all individuals possess (Goldberg, 1992; Hagner & Salomone, 1989). Proponents of this position might also argue that many of the developmental counseling processes supported by theory are relatively unimportant for people with disabilities when compared with simply obtaining some type of employment (Manuele, 1983).

A second, more moderate view, posits that all individuals experience similar career development needs and, as a result, most career theories can be applied to individuals with disabilities with varying degrees of modification. Several authors (e.g., Ettinger, 1996; Gottfredson, 1986; Herr & Cramer, 1996) have argued that the emphasis placed on relatively minute differences between groups has obscured, rather than illuminated, the overwhelming similarity between them. However, although mainstream career theories may be applicable to adolescent student groups with disabilities, it is equally as likely that the effect of disability on career development and attainment must be considered. For example, presence of disability is likely to increase the restrictions on career exploration opportunities, thus limiting adolescents' range of career-related experiences and (a) extending the length of time required to work through career exploration tasks and (b) increasing the likelihood of delayed or impaired career development (Rojewski, 1993, 1996, 1999a).

In recent years, researchers (e.g., Hutchinson, Versnel, Chin, & Munby, 2008; Ochs & Roessler, 2001; Strauser, 1995; Szymanski, Willmering, Tschopp, Tansey, & Mizelle, 2003) have applied a mainstream career theory, Social Cognitive Career Theory (SCCT; Lent, Brown, & Hackett, 1994, 1996), to explain the career behavior of populations with disabilities. SCCT focuses on ways that the psychological constructs of self-efficacy, outcome expectations, and personal goals interrelate with person, contextual, and learning factors to explain academic and career choice and attainment. According to SCCT, self-efficacy (i.e., situation-specific estimates of one's ability to successfully perform a task or behavior; Lent & Hackett, 1987) is a central factor in career decision-making as it helps "determine individuals' willingness to initiate specific behaviors, their persistence in the face of obstacles or barriers, and their level of competence in executing the behaviors" (Arbona, 2000, p. 288). Career choice is seen as a dynamic process that is modified by learning experiences and performance outcomes (e.g., academic achievement), as well as "how people read their capabilities and potential payoffs in view of continuous performance feedback" (Lent et al., 1996, p. 11).

SCCT highlights the "profound psychological and social significance" (Lent et al., 1994, p. 104) of personal characteristics to potentially influence career development. Demographic variables—like gender, race/ethnicity, socioeconomic status (SES), or high incidence disability—tend to affect the availability and types of educational and occupational opportunities made available to individuals. Differential socialization patterns interact with personal interests, self-efficacy, and outcome expectations to influence the development and eventual attainment of aspirations (goals). "SCCT asserts that people form enduring interest in an activity when they view themselves as competent at it and when they anticipate that performing it will produce valued outcomes" (Lent et al., 1996, p. 383).

Despite the benefits of using career theories to explain career development and guide the career counseling process, many professionals are still uncertain about their application to adolescents with disabilities. Much of the hesitation results from commonly held assumptions about the career development process. One assumption is that the presence of a disability, even a high incidence disability, takes precedence over all other aspects of vocational behavior, and becomes the primary (perhaps only) determinant of career development, appropriate postsecondary options, and occupational choice (Conte, 1983; Curnow, 1989; Miller, 1999). Many career theories reflect a belief that career development is systematic, continuously developing, and only occasionally stressful. An assumption is made that multiple career options are available and that individuals are relatively free of constraints when choosing a career path. Often, this assumption is viewed as not applicable to individuals with disabilities, who are more likely to encounter restricted career possibilities and whose career development is sometimes discontinuous, chaotic, or stressful (LoCascio, Nesselroth, & Thomas, 1976; Osipow, 1976; Szymanski, Hershenson, Enright, & Ettinger, 1996). It is incorrect to conclude that the career behavior of adolescents with high incidence disabilities is largely unsystematic and influenced primarily by chance. And, although a higher probability exists that the career development of adolescents' with high incidence disabilities might be delayed or impaired (Rojewski, 1993), career theory and its relevant constructs are still applicable although modifications may be necessary to accommodate different life experiences, expectations, and abilities. In fact, there is no evidence to suggest that individuals with high incidence disabilities cannot pursue and attain planned, systematic career paths.

Risk and Resilience Factors: An Alternative to a Deficiencies Perspective

Despite a lack of theoretical explanations, there are several ways to examine the career behavior and work outcomes of individuals with high incidence disabilities. Historically, the career behavior of adolescents with disabilities was likely to be viewed from a deficit perspective. Any problem or discrepancy from individuals with disabilities was explained as an inherent and unchangeable deficiency. From this perspective it makes little sense to develop theory or programs.

Gottfredson's (1986) Risk Factors. Gottfredson (1986) suggested that an alternative approach to understanding career behavior would be to examine the career choice problems that everyone, regardless of disability status, experiences by examining factors that either threaten or facilitate the career choice process. Broadly speaking, these risk factors could include biological, environmental, or psychological hazards that increase the likelihood of a maladaptive career-related outcome. The presence of risk factors doesn't necessarily cause career-related problems, but they raise the probability that problems will occur. We can categorize these risks into those used in comparison with the general population (e.g., poor education, poverty, low self-esteem, and functional limitations), in comparison with one's own social group (e.g., nontraditional interests and social isolation), and those delineating individual family responsibilities (e.g., being a primary caregiver or economic provider). Surprisingly, although students with high incidence disabilities comprise approximately 9% of the entire U.S. school population and over two-thirds of all school-aged students receiving special education services (Newman, Wagner, Cameto, & Knokey, 2009), little information exists relating risk factors to career outcomes for this population (Murray, 2003).

Comparison to majority population. Longitudinal studies have consistently demonstrated that adolescents with high incidence disabilities are more likely to encounter problems in making the transition from school to work and also experience poorer outcomes as adults than nondisabled peers (e.g., Blackorby & Wagner, 1996; Frank, Sitlington, & Carson, 1995; Hasazi, Gordon, & Roe, 1985). Not only are young adults with disabilities less likely to enroll in postsecondary education than nondisabled peers (45% compared to 53%, respectively), but their experiences in the world of work are usually poor in terms of the types and duration of the jobs they hold (Newman et al., 2009). Among high incidence disability groups, postsecondary employment figures are usually most favorable for young adults with learning disabilities (Wagner & Blackorby, 1996).

Other common problems experienced by persons with high incidence disabilities include low socioeconomic status, low self-esteem, and academic functional limitations. Career attainment is highly correlated with "systematic patterns of educational placement and social expectations" that are indirectly a function of SES (Rojewski & Kim, 2003, p. 106). In fact, youth experiencing high incidence disabilities from low-income households perform less well academically than peers with or without disabilities, separate from race/ethnicity (Barkley, 2006). Wagner et al. (2005) reported that students with learning disabilities from households with low incomes ($25,000 or less per year) scored significantly lower on achievement measures than youth from moderate-income households ($25,000–$75,000 per year): "Low-income Hispanic youth with disabilities are likely to score 15 points lower on reading comprehension measures than a White peer from a moderate-income household, holding other factors in the analysis constant" (p. 48).

Adolescents with high incidence disabilities are less likely to be involved, independent, or proactive when faced with making career choices, and less willing or able to compromise between career aspirations and reality than nondisabled peers. Cognitively, adolescents with learning disabilities experience greater difficulty in appraising career strengths and limitations, are less knowledgeable about the world of work, and have trouble in determining career-related goals that are consistent with individual capabilities (Rojewski, 1996).

Students with learning disabilities drop out of high school two to three times more frequently (U.S. General Accounting Office [GAO], 2003; Young & Browning, 2005) and enroll in college and postsecondary training at one-tenth the rate of the general population without disability (Stodden, Jones, & Chang, 2002; Wagner et al., 2005; Young & Browning, 2005). Adolescents with ADHD and emotional/behavioral disorders demonstrate similar dismal outcomes. In comparison to peers, students with high incidence disabilities are at greater risk for grade retention, suspension, expulsion, dropping out of secondary schools (Barkley, 2006; Pagani, Tremblay, Vitaro, Boulerice, & McDuff, 2001), and lower postsecondary educational outcomes (Lambert, 1988; Mannuzza, Gittelman-Klein, Bessler, Malloy, & LaPadula, 1993; Weiss & Hechtman, 1993).

Employment outcome studies suggest that adults with learning disabilities, ADHD, and emotional/behavioral disorders appear to function equally as well as their peers in obtaining jobs upon graduation. However, according to Gregg (2009), these statistics are misleading. No comprehensive study of employment outcomes for adults with learning disabilities and ADHD has ever been conducted so knowledge about the world of work for these populations is based primarily upon personal (anecdotal) and professional experience (Young & Browning, 2005). The scant empirical-based employment data available is certainly not conclusive.

A majority of jobs taken by adolescents with learning disabilities, ADHD, and emotional/behavioral disorders are often semiskilled and usually part-time positions (Barkley, 2006). Wagner et al. (2005) provided evidence that, although 86% of young adults with learning disabilities and ADHD earned more than minimum wage, only about one-third of them worked full-time. Wagner et al. found no real change in earnings for youth with learning disabilities or ADHD from the original National Longitudinal Transitional Study (NLTS) to the second study (NLTS-2) even when wages were adjusted for inflation. A majority of these individuals earned less than the federal poverty threshold. Thus, it appears that the earning power gap between youth with learning disabilities, ADHD, and emotional/behavioral disorders and their nondisabled peers is widening mainly due to growing disparities in educational attainment (Day & Newburger, 2002; Wagner et al., 2005).

Lack of participation by youth with learning disabilities, ADHD, and emotional/behavioral disorders in rigorous secondary curricula appears to contribute to poor retention in secondary and, subsequently, postsecondary learning environments (Gregg, 2007).

Limited postsecondary educational attainment for adults with learning disabilities, ADHD, and emotional/behavioral disorders is directly related to poor employment outcomes. Despite state and federal efforts to improve the career and transitional competencies of individuals with disabilities, the educational attainment of individuals with high incidence disabilities remains substantially below that of the general population (Barkley, 2006; Wagner et al., 2005).

Comparison within peer groups. It is important to consider how career development may differ due to disability. In this section we briefly review how specific high incidence disability types may influence the career behavior of adolescents.

Sabornie and his colleagues (Sabornie, Cullinan, Osborne, & Brock, 2005; Sabornie, Evans, & Cullinan, 2006) reviewed over 90 studies comparing the characteristics of adolescents with high-incidence disabilities and found differences on cognitive and behavioral characteristics between groups. Specifically, adolescents with learning disabilities had higher cognitive abilities than adolescents with emotional/behavioral disorders. This same general pattern was evident for academic achievement. An obvious implication of these differences is the types of outcomes, in terms of postsecondary education and employment, that might be considered appropriate for students nearing school completion. Adolescents with learning disabilities exhibited fewer behavior problems than students with emotional/behavioral disorders. And the latter were more likely to encounter difficulty with law enforcement such as arrest, incarceration, or probation/parole (Newman et al., 2009).

Many of the internal and external risk factors identified in Table 44.1 affect other personal characteristics associated with career difficulties, such as problems with social skills, lack of planfulness, problem-solving and transfer skills, external locus of control, and negative self-esteem (Forness & Kavale, 1996; Hallahan, Kauffman, & Pullen, 2012). Adolescents with disabilities, especially more severe disabilities, may also be more susceptible to social isolation. The extent of isolation, of course, depends on the type and severity of disability among other factors.

Family responsibilities. Family responsibilities—being the primary caregiver or economic provider—may represent a greater risk for individuals with high-incidence disabilities than for nondisabled peers, particularly girls. Females with high incidence disabilities are more likely to become single parents prior to adulthood than females without disabilities (Levine & Nourse, 1998; Trainor, 2007).

Risk and Resilience Framework. Knowledge of career-related risk factors is important to our understanding of career and work concerns of adolescents with high-incidence disabilities. However, not all issues encountered in the transition from school to work and adult life are problematic. In fact, some individuals overcome adverse conditions to achieve positive adult outcomes at work, home, and community. Researchers have identified *resilience* factors to examine those characteristics and processes that contribute to *success* as defined by features of emotional, academic, and occupational well-being (Gregg, 2009; Murray, 2003; Werner & Smith, 1982). Spekman, Goldberg, and Herman (1992) and Goldberg, Higgins, Raskind, and Herman (2003) identified three themes that differentiated successful adults with learning disabilities from unsuccessful adults with learning disabilities. Successful adults with learning disabilities (a) adapted to life events through self-awareness and acceptance of their disability, were proactive and persevered, and were emotionally stable and able to tolerate stress; (b) were able to set appropriate goals and were goal-directed; and (c) were able to establish and use effective support systems.

Resilience factors are similar to risk factors in that they can be divided into internal and external influences. Internal resilience factors are composed mainly of positive temperaments, recognition of one's disability, accommodation strategies, and knowledge of ways to be proactive and advocate for oneself in school and at work.

Although few would argue with the importance of internal resilience factors in the successful transition from school to adult life, Newman et al. (2009) reported that 17- to 21-year-olds with high-incidence disabilities were not likely to adopt these strategies as they transitioned from school to postsecondary education and work. In postsecondary educational settings, over half of young people identified with a high incidence disability in high school did not report themselves as disabled. As a result, they were not eligible for formal educational assistance. In the work place, only 19% of respondents indicated that their employers were aware of their disabilities.

The issue of how to develop and incorporate resilience factors into career choice and work attainment efforts for young people with high-incidence disabilities appears to be an area in need of much greater attention. Three critical areas for high school students preparing to transition to postsecondary life are knowledge of the Americans with Disabilities Act, realities of the workplace, and importance of self-determination (Madaus, Gerber, & Price, 2008).

Another resilience factor that may have a bearing on the career behavior of adolescents with high-incidence disabilities is disability identity and the assumptions on which it is based. Mpofu and Harley (2006) explained that disability status may not be the primary lens through which most individuals with disabilities perceive their personal identities or career options; but individuals who are highly conscious of their differences may be less engaged in mutually beneficial participation with different others, which may impair their overall career success.

The severity of disability is a related issue to consider when determining the possible effects of high-incidence disabilities on career development and outcomes. Specifically, as the severity of the disability increases, it is likely that individuals' susceptibility to risk factors and their impact on career behavior will increase. For example, given cognitive, social, and behavioral difficulties, adolescents with high-incidence disabilities may be more susceptible to the negative aspects of chance—unplanned, accidental, or unintentional—events in career development, vocational preparation, and occupational attainment (Rojewski, 1999b).

External resilience factors are those influences that support the individual in their work-related decision making including family, school, and community. The presence of a supportive adult, such as a mentor, appears to be one of the strongest protective factors for adolescents and adults with learning disabilities and ADHD (Gerber, Ginsberg, & Reiff, 1992; Spekman et al., 1992; Werner, 1990). Interestingly, Reiff, Gerber, and Ginsberg (1997) found that, throughout their interviews with successful adults with learning disabilities, individuals emphasized the importance of their *social ecologies* (supportive and helpful people). Research specific to the population with learning disabilities provides evidence that sustained parental emotional support is a strong protective factor that enables these individuals to maintain a strong self-concept (Cosden, Brown, & Elliott, 2002; Reynolds, 1999; Rothman & Cosden, 1995). There is significant research evidence to indicate that parent-child interactions are related to an adolescent's or adult's future success with peer interactions (Wong, 2003).

The hostility between parents and their children with ADHD and emotional/behavioral disabilities is strongly predictive of similar conflicts at the adolescent and adult stage, particularly related to aggressive behavior (Barkley, 2006). The emotional adjustment of individuals with ADHD and their success with friendships as adults appears to be directly or indirectly related to the emotional climate of their homes as reflected in the emotional stability of family members. However, no *one* risk factor appears to predict the well-being of adolescents or adults with learning disabilities:

> The combination of child cognitive ability (intelligence) and emotional stability (aggression, low frustration tolerance) with family environment (mental health of family members, SES, emotional climate of home) and child rearing practices provides a considerably more successful prediction of adult outcome. (Barkley, 2006, p. 275)

Table 44.1 lists several critical risk and resilience factors that can influence career behavior and work outcomes of adolescents with high incidence disabilities. These factors incorporate the work of career theorists (e.g., Gottfredson, 1986) and disability researchers (e.g., Murray, 2003; Wong, 2003). One other aspect of this model to consider is the issue of outcomes. The interplay of risks and resilience factors result in outcomes such as successful employment or unemployment, enrollment in postsecondary academic or vocational programs, dropping out of school, job difficulties, job satisfaction, and life dissatisfaction (Barkley, 2006; Reiff & Gerber, 1995; Ross-Gordon, 1996).

There are some factors that act as risk or resilience factors that don't fit neatly into the model as internal or external factors, such as gender, race, and socioeconomic status, but that exert a considerable influence on career trajectories, transition paths, and eventual work outcomes (Lee & Rojewski, 2009; Rojewski & Kim, 2003; Rojewski & Yang, 1997). We discuss these factors briefly.

Gender. Gender is a powerful and persistent influence on occupational behavior and career development. Research has demonstrated a consistent theme of pervasive sex-role stereotyping on females' occupational and educational attainment. Female adolescents are susceptible to certain barriers to career development, choice, and attainment due to socialized or internalized belief systems that lead women to avoid certain career fields and narrow career options earlier than males. Specific factors that females are likely to encounter include math anxiety and avoidance, low self-efficacy and outcome expectations, gender and occupational stereotyping, concerns with multiple roles, barriers in the educational system, and a restricted range of vocational interests (Betz, 2005). Difficulty in navigating these myriad barriers may explain the discrepancy between the high occupational and educational expectations held

TABLE 44.1
Risk and Resilience Framework Associated with Career Choice and Transition from School-to-Work Issues for Adolescents with High Incidence Disabilities

	Potential Risk Factors	Potential Resilience Factors
Internal	• Gender, Race, Disability type and severity • Functional limitations • Poor academic background • Nontraditional career interests • Lack of motivation, Low self-efficacy, Poor self-esteem, Negative self-concept, External locus of control	• Motivation, High self-efficacy, Positive self-esteem, Positive self-concept, Internal locus of control • Self-determination/Self-advocacy skills • Recognition/acceptance of disability • Resourcefulness and adaptability • Metacognition
External	• Discrimination or social isolation • Primary caregiver responsibilities • Primary provider responsibilities	• Support systems (parents, mentors, teachers) • Timely opportunities at crucial transition points

by female adolescents and corresponding levels of actual attainment reported in adulthood.

Females with high-incidence disabilities may be at even greater risk for difficulties with career choice and attainment than their nondisabled female peers. For example, females with learning disabilities experience greater unemployment, lower enrollment in postsecondary education, and lower occupational attainment than males with disabilities or nondisabled peers (Rojewski, 1996, 1999a).

Race. Race/ethnicity has a significant impact on individual career development, choice, and attainment. The situation is often made more difficult by efforts to disentangle the effects of socioeconomic status and race/ethnicity from one another and other variables (Mau & Bikos, 2000). Recent efforts have also been made at trying to use racial and disability identity theories to explain career choice and outcomes (Mpofu & Harley, 2006). However, "progress in understanding the roles of gender, race or ethnicity, and sociocultural factors in the career development process has been slow and has generally not been fully integrated conceptually in the vocational literature or given extensive empirical attention" (Worthington, Flores, & Navarro, 2005, p. 225).

Despite the paucity of information about connections between race/ethnicity-disability-and career development, some information exists. For example, we do know that individuals from minority groups often hold high-prestige occupational and educational aspirations as adolescents but fail to realize those aspirations as adults (Wilson & Wilson, 1992). Fouad and Byars-Winston (2005) explained that this phenomenon could be explained by a number of factors including workplace discrimination and individuals' own restrictions of their possible job outcomes resulting from perceptions of a limited range of occupational options based on minority status. Race appears to be a particularly potent factor in limiting career options as adolescents complete high school and transition to work and adult life (Lee & Rojewski, 2009).

Socioeconomic status. Socioeconomic status has a significant influence on both disability status and career development. And, because individuals with disability are more likely to live in poverty than nondisabled peers (U.S. Bureau of the Census, 2004), it is also likely that economic disadvantage will affect the career development of adolescents with high-incidence disabilities. Lustig and Strauser (2007) indicated that poverty contributes to devalued social roles, increases in environmental risk factors and negative group influences, and reduces access to resources. The role of economic disadvantage also appears influential in delimiting career behavior and eventual career attainment.

Socioeconomic status provides a context for the development of occupational choice (Marjoribanks, 2002; Schoon & Parsons, 2002). Basically, higher socioeconomic status brings greater access to the resources needed to finance education, provide special learning experiences, and provide opportunities to come in contact with role models in high prestige occupations. As a result, individuals from higher socioeconomic status aspire to, expect, and attain higher levels of education and more prestigious occupations than individuals from lower SES backgrounds (Rojewski & Kim, 2003). The impact of economic disadvantage tends to be pervasive and affects most areas of an individual's life. When compared to nondisadvantaged groups, adolescents from lower socioeconomic backgrounds are more likely to experience school failure, higher dropout rates, crime rates, teenage pregnancy, and substance abuse, low self-esteem, and cultural isolation (Coulton & Pandey, 1992; Garbarino, 1992).

Youths who are economically disadvantaged are probably at no greater risk than other youths for experiencing career choice problems caused by factors involving within-group differences. However, for some of these adolescents, the probability of having family responsibilities at an early age may be higher, particularly for young women. Research shows a relationship between low SES and teen pregnancy (Reed & Sauter, 1990). The career behavior of male adolescents who experience economic disadvantage may also be restricted because they feel less free to seek self-fulfillment in work roles (Brooks, 1990).

Recommendations for Research and Practice

It is likely that adolescents and young adults with high-incidence disabilities are less career mature, possess a more limited repertoire of coping behaviors, and experience fewer and less quality work experiences than nondisabled peers prior to making and during the transition from school to adult life. With this in mind, work preparation activities can be constructed to actively engage and prepare these young people for a successful transition to work and adult life whether postsecondary goals include additional education or work immediately after high school.

There needs to be a serious examination of the stigma of work embedded with all of education in general, but particularly within the study of high-incidence disabilities in education. The negative stigma of work permeates academia at all levels and is evident in the funding and attention devoted to supporting students aspiring to attend 4-year colleges or universities upon graduation from high school to the serious neglect and detriment of students with interests and abilities at odds with this goal. Gray and Herr (1998) noted that the "one way to win" mentality (i.e., an exclusive focus on preparing for and attending a 4-year college or university) is successful for only a small fraction of adolescents, about 15% of high school students. Even so, this mentality is stubborn and based on the message that attending a 4-year institution is the only sure way to obtain a high paying job and gain long-term economic advantage by securing a professional job. The persistence of this message is perplexing given only about 1 in 10 actually attains this ideal. More recently, Gray and Herr (2006) argued strongly that educators have as much responsibility for students who are at risk of dropping out of school or go to work directly after high school graduation as those bound for a 4-year college or university. "Those who have a pejorative attitude toward teens who do something other than pursue a 4-year college degree should rethink this prejudice; it is just plain wrong, it is unethical, and it is destructive" (p. 20). We agree.

Gray and Herr (1998, 2006) do not argue against the need for postsecondary education and training, but rather recommend that postsecondary work considerations address both short- and long-term training preparation and training needs. The workforce of the future will require a variety of technical, academic, and thinking skills to be employable and remain successful. However, there are a variety of postsecondary alternatives available to students that can be considered when engaged in career and transition planning efforts. Such alternatives include pre-baccalaureate technical education at certification, diploma, and associate degree levels as well as apprenticeship programs and the military.

Another aspect of transition preparation programs to consider is the types of academic and career-related programs and experiences developed for young people with high-incidence disabilities while still in school. First, a longitudinal perspective is necessary, starting in elementary school with an emphasis on the meaning of work and development of essential social competencies. Program attention could then progress through middle and high school where emphasis could be placed on exposure to realistic job requirements and assistance in identifying and pursuing appropriate postsecondary career plans.

Emphasis on career and work cannot be planned or executed in a vacuum but needs to be integrated into a sequential educational experience. Academic-only programs of study are unlikely to wholly support the secondary or postsecondary success of students with high-incidence disabilities. Rather, academic-only programs are likely to increase the drop-out rate. In fact, as a whole, less than two-thirds of this population exits with a high school diploma (Kaufman, Alt, & Chapman, 2004; U.S. Department of Education, 2006; Wagner et al., 2005). And an increase in school drop-outs for adolescents with high-incidence disabilities contributes to career-related problems by limiting educational opportunities and restricting occupational options: "Leaving no child behind in today's high schools requires alternatives for teens with different ambitions and talents, and alternative transitional pathways to prepare teens for other ways to win" (Gray & Herr, 2006, p. 21).

A host of work preparation experiences can be incorporated into programs of study for high school students with high-incidence disabilities, including tech-prep (2+2 programs), career academies, school-based enterprises, work-based mentoring programs, on-the-job training, job shadowing, cooperative education, and apprenticeship. Each experience includes varying degrees of academic integration, depending on program goals, but is often flexible enough to meet individual student needs while addressing state and federal academic requirements. The focus of work preparation activities might shift in terms of timing, intensity, and duration from elementary (general occupational awareness) to secondary (career exploration) to postsecondary education (specific occupational training). Educators consider both grade level and degree of desired involvement in determining the types of activities students should pursue as they prepare for and make the transition from school to work and adult life (see Figure 44.1).

It is also important to consider the role of part-time work during high school. It appears that paid work experience during high school is a critical component of successful school-to-work transitions for adolescents with high-incidence disabilities (Fabian, 2007; Luecking & Fabian, 2000). Paid work is associated with a number of positive postschool outcomes, such as increased vocational self-efficacy (Benz & Halpern, 1993), improvements in social

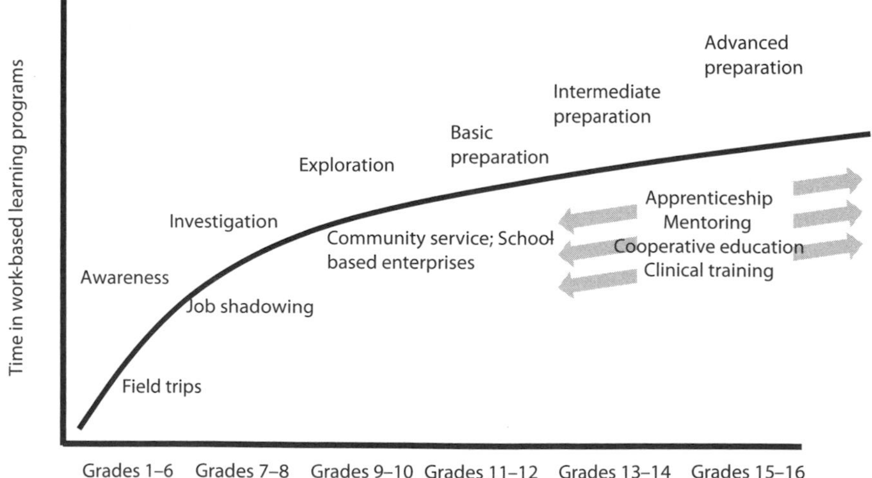

Figure 44.1 Possible timeline for school- and work-based career experiences for students with high incidence disabilities.

and independent living skills, and better jobs with higher wages (Lindstrom & Benz, 2002; Paganos & DuBois, 1999).

Finally, it is critically important that researchers focus attention on the needs of non-college-bound youth with high-incidence disabilities as they prepare for and make the transition from school to work and adult life. Although notable exceptions exist (e.g., Newman et al., 2009), there is very little research on career outcomes for this population (Gregg, 2009). One recent study that examined job entry and employment outcomes for university graduates with learning disabilities cited a lack of awareness about the Americans with Disabilities Act, lack of knowledge about the realities of workplace disclosure, and the importance of self-determination (Madaus et al., 2008). Trainor's (2007) qualitative research promoting self-determination and active participation in the transition process generated similar findings. Although this work is important in expanding our understanding of some students with high incidence disabilities, research should be extended to include those adolescents who drop out of school or enter work directly after completing their secondary education. For these groups, the transition from school to work should encompass much more than a predominantly academic secondary curriculum. Actual work experiences and outcomes are in need of investigation. Researchers also need to investigate appropriate methods of work preparation, actual methods of making the transition from school-to-work environments, and outcome data in a variety of work-related areas.

References

Arbona, C. (2000). The development of academic achievement in school-aged children: Precursors to career development. In S. D. Brown & R. W. Lent (Eds.), *Handbook of counseling psychology* (3rd ed., pp. 270–309). New York: Wiley.

Barkley, R. A. (2006). *Attention-deficit hyperactivity disorder: A handbook for diagnosis and treatment* (3rd ed.). New York: Guilford.

Benz, M. R., & Halpern, A. S. (1993). Vocational and transition services needed and received by students with disabilities during their last year of high school. *Career Development for Exceptional Individuals, 16,* 197–211.

Betz, N. E. (2005). Women's career development. In S. D. Brown & R. W. Lent (Eds.), *Career development and counseling: Putting theory and research to work* (pp. 253–277). Hoboken, NJ: Wiley.

Blackorby, J., & Wagner, M. (1996). Longitudinal postschool outcomes of youth with disabilities: Findings from the National Longitudinal Transition Study. *Exceptional Children, 62,* 399–413.

Brooks, L. (1990). Recent developments in theory building. In D. Brown, L. Brooks, & Associates (Eds.), *Career choice and development: Applying contemporary theories to practice* (2nd ed., pp. 364–394). San Francisco: Jossey-Bass.

Conte, L. E. (1983). Vocational development theories and the disabled person: Oversight or deliberate omission? *Rehabilitation Counseling Bulletin, 26,* 316–328.

Cosden, M., Brown, C., & Elliott, K. (2002). Development of self-understanding and self-esteem in children and adults with learning disabilities. In B. Y. L. Wong & M. Donahue (Eds.), *The social dimensions of learning disabilities: Essays in honor of Tanis Bryan* (pp. 33–51). Mahwah, NJ: Erlbaum.

Coulton, C. J., & Pandey, S. (1992). Geographic concentration of poverty and risk to children in urban neighborhoods. *American Behavioral Scientist, 35,* 238–257.

Curnow, T. C. (1989). Vocational development of persons with disability. *Career Development Quarterly, 27,* 269–278.

Day, J. C., & Newburger, E. C. (2002). *The big payoff: Educational attainment and synthetic estimates of work-life earnings.* Washington, DC: U.S. Census Bureau. Retrieved from http://www.census.gov/prod/2002pubs/p23-210pdf

Dietz, S., & Montague, M. (2006). Attention deficit hyperactivity disorder comorbid with emotional and behavioral disorders and learning disabilities in adolescents. *Exceptionality, 14*(1), 19–33. doi: 10.1207/s15327035ex1401_3

Dykman, R. A., & Ackerman, P. T. (1991). Attention deficit disorder and specific reading disability: Separate but often overlapping disorders. *Journal of Learning Disabilities, 24,* 96–103.

Ettinger, J. (1996). Meeting the career development needs of individuals with disabilities. In R. Feller & G. R. Walz (Eds.). *Career development in turbulent times: Exploring work, learning and careers* (pp. 239–244). Greensboro, NC: ERIC/CASS.

Fabian, E. S. (2007). Urban youth with disabilities: Factors affecting transition employment. *Rehabilitation Counseling Bulletin, 50*(3), 130–138.

Fabian, E. S., & Liesener, J. J. (2005). Promoting the career potential of youth with disabilities. In S. D. Brown & R. W. Lent (Eds.), *Career development and counseling: Putting theory and research to work* (pp. 551–572). Hoboken, NJ: Wiley.

Forness, S. R., & Kavale, K. A. (1996). Treating social skill deficits in children with learning disabilities: A meta-analysis of the research. *Learning Disability Quarterly, 19,* 2–13.

Fouad, N. A., & Byars-Winston, A. M. (2005). Cultural context of career choice: Meta-analysis of race/ethnicity differences. *Career Development Quarterly, 53,* 223–233.

Frank, A. R., Sitlington, P. L., & Carson, R. R. (1995). Young adults with behavioral disorders: A comparison with peers with mild disabilities. *Journal of Emotional and Behavioral Disorders, 3,* 156–164.

Garbarino, J. (1992). The meaning of poverty in the world of children. *American Behavioral Scientist, 35,* 220–237.

Gerber, P. J., Ginsberg, R., & Reiff, H. B. (1992). Identifying alterable patterns in employment success for highly successful adults with learning disabilities. *Journal of Learning Disabilities, 25,* 475–487.

Goldberg, R. J., Higgins, E. L., Raskind, M. H., & Herman, K. L. (2003). Predictors of success in individuals with learning disabilities: A qualitative analysis of a 20-year longitudinal study. *Learning Disabilities Research & Practice, 18,* 222–236. doi: 10.1111/1540-5826.00077

Goldberg, R. T. (1992). Toward a model of vocational development of people with disabilities. *Rehabilitation Counseling Bulletin, 35,* 161–173.

Gottfredson, L. S. (1986). Special groups and the beneficial use of vocational interest inventories. In W. B. Walsh & S. H. Osipow (Eds.), *Advances in vocational psychology, Volume I: The assessment of interest* (pp. 127–198). Hillsdale, NJ: Erlbaum.

Gray, K. C., & Herr, E. L. (1998). *Workforce education: The basics.* Needham Heights, MA: Allyn and Bacon.

Gray, K. C., & Herr, E. L. (2006). *Other ways to win: Creating alternatives for high school graduates* (3rd ed.). New York: Corwin.

Gregg, N. (2007). Underserved and unprepared: Postsecondary learning disabilities. *Learning Disabilities Research & Practice, 22,* 219–228. doi: 10.1111/j.1540-5826.2007.00250

Gregg, N. (2009). *Adolescents and adults with learning disabilities and ADHD: Assessment and accommodation.* New York: Guilford.

Hagner, D., & Salomone, P. R. (1989). Issues in career decision making for workers with developmental disabilities. *Career Development Quarterly, 38,* 148–159.

Hallahan, D. P., Kauffman, J. M., & Pullen, P. C. (2012). *Exceptional learners: Introduction to special education* (12th ed.). Upper Saddle River, NJ: Pearson.

Hasazi, S. B., Gordon, L. R., & Roe, C. A. (1985). Factors associated with the employment status of handicapped youth exiting high school from 1979 to 1983. *Exceptional Children, 51,* 455–469.

Herr, E. L., & Cramer, S. H. (1996). *Career guidance and counseling through the life span: Systematic approaches* (5th ed.). New York: HarperCollins.

Hutchinson, N. L., Versnel, J., Chin, P., & Munby, H. (2008). Negotiating accommodations so that work-based education facilitates career development for youth with disabilities. *Work, 30,* 123–136.

Kaplan, B. J., Dewey, D. M., Crawford, S. G., & Wilson, B. N. (2001). The term comorbidity is of questionable value in reference to developmental disorders: Data and theory. *Journal of Learning Disabilities, 34,* 555–565.

Kaufman, P., Alt, M. N., & Chapman, C. D. (2004). *Dropout rates in the United States: 2001* [Statistical Analysis Report NCES 2005-046]. Washington, DC: U.S. Department of Education. Retrieved from ERIC database. (ED483073)

Lambert, N. M. (1988). Adolescent outcomes for hyperactive children. *American Psychologist, 43,* 786–799.

Lee, I., & Rojewski, J. W. (2009). Development of occupational aspiration prestige: A piecewise latent growth model of selected influences. *Journal of Vocational Behavior, 75,* 82–90. doi:10.1016/j.jvb.2009.03.006

Lent, R. W., Brown, S. D., & Hackett, G. (1994). Toward a unifying social cognitive theory of career and academic interest, choice, and performance [Monograph]. *Journal of Vocational Behavior, 45,* 79–122.

Lent, R. W., Brown, S. D., & Hackett, G. (1996). Career development from a social cognitive perspective. In D. Brown, L. Brooks, & Associates (Eds.), *Career choice and development* (3rd. ed., pp. 423–475). San Francisco: Jossey-Bass.

Lent, R. W., & Hackett, G. (1987). Career self-efficacy: Empirical status and future directions [Monograph]. *Journal of Vocational Behavior, 30,* 347–382.

Levine, P., & Nourse, S. W. (1998). What follow-up studies say about postschool life for young men and women with learning disabilities: A critical look at the literature. *Journal of Learning Disabilities, 31,* 212–233.

Lindstrom, L. E., & Benz, M. R. (2002). Phases of career development: Case studies of young women with learning disabilities. *Exceptional Children, 69*(1), 67–83.

LoCascio, R., Nesselroth, J., & Thomas, M. (1976). The Career Development Inventory: Use and findings with inner city dropouts. *Journal of Vocational Behavior, 8,* 285–292.

Luecking, R. G., & Fabian, E. S. (2000). Paid internships and employment success for youth in transition. *Career Development for Exceptional Individuals, 23,* 205–221.

Lustig, D. C., & Strauser, D. R. (2007). Causal relationships between poverty and disability. *Rehabilitation Counseling Bulletin, 50*(4), 194–202.

Madaus, J. W., Gerber, P. J., & Price, L. A. (2008). Adults with LD in the workforce: Lessons for secondary transition programs. *Learning Disabilities Research and Practice, 23*(3), 148–153. doi:10.1111/j.1540-5826.2008.00272

Mannuzza, S., Gittelman-Klein, R., Bessler, A., Malloy, P., & LaPadula, M. (1993). Adult outcomes of hyperactive boys: Educational achievement, occupational rank, and psychiatric status. *Archives of General Psychiatry, 50,* 565–576.

Manuele, C. A. (1983). The development of a measure to assess vocational maturity in adults with delayed career development. *Journal of Vocational Behavior, 23*(1), 45–63.

Marjoribanks, K. (2002). Family background, individual and environmental influences on adolescents' aspirations. *Educational Studies, 28*(1), 22–46.

Mau, W., & Bikos, L. H. (2000). Educational and vocational aspirations of minority and female students: A longitudinal study. *Journal of Counseling and Development, 78,* 186–194.

Miller, V. M. (1999). The opportunity structure: Implications for career counseling. *Journal of Employment Counseling, 36*(1), 2–12.

Mpofu, E., & Harley, D. A. (2006). Racial and disability identity: Implications for the career counseling of African Americans with disabilities. *Rehabilitation Counseling Bulletin, 50*(1), 14–23.

Murray, C. (2003). Risk factors, protective factors, vulnerability, and resilience: A framework for understanding and supporting the adult transitions of youth with high-incidence disabilities. *Remedial and Special Education, 24,* 16–26. doi: 10.1177/074193250302400102

National Council on Disability. (2003). *National disability policy: A progress report, December 2001–December 2002.* Washington, DC: Author.

Newman, L., Wagner, M., Cameto, R., & Knokey, A. (2009). *The post-high school outcomes of youth with disabilities up to 4 years after high school: A report from the National Longitudinal Transition Study-2 (NLTS2)* [NCSER 2009-3017]. Menlo Park, CA: SRI International.

Ochs, L. A., & Roessler, R. T. (2001). Students with disabilities: How ready are they for the 21st century? *Rehabilitation Counseling Bulletin, 44,* 170–176.

Osipow, S. H. (1976). Vocational development problems of the handicapped. In H. Rusalem & D. Malikin (Eds.), *Contemporary vocational rehabilitation* (pp. 47–62). New York: New York University Press.

Pagani, L., Tremblay, R. E., Vitaro, F., Boulerice, B., & McDuff, P. (2001). Effects of grade retention on academic performance and behavioral development. *Development and Psychopathology, 13,* 297–315.

Paganos, R. J., & DuBois, D. C. (1999). Career self-efficacy development and students with learning disabilities. *Learning Disabilities Research and Practice, 4,* 25–34.

Reed, S., & Sauter, R. (1990). Children of poverty: The status of twelve million Americans. *Phi Delta Kappan, 71*(10), 1–12.

Reiff, H. B., & Gerber, P. J. (1995). Social/emotional and daily living issues for adults with learning disabilities. In P. J. Gerber & H. B. Reiff (Eds.), *Learning disabilities in adulthood: Persisting problems and evolving issues* (pp. 72–81). Austin, TX: Pro-ED.

Reiff, H. B., Gerber, P. J., & Ginsberg, R. (1997). *Exceeding expectations: Successful adults with learning disabilities.* Austin, TX: Pro-Ed.

Reynolds, A. W. (1999). *High risk college students with emotional disorders as well as learning disabilities.* Unpublished doctoral dissertation, University of Georgia, Athens.

Rojewski, J. W. (1993). Theoretical structure of career maturity for rural adolescents with learning disabilities. *Career Development for Exceptional Individuals, 16,* 39–52.

Rojewski, J. W. (1996). Occupational aspirations and early career choice patterns of adolescents with and without learning disabilities. *Learning Disability Quarterly, 19,* 99–116.

Rojewski, J. W. (1999a). Occupational and educational aspirations and attainment of young adults with and without learning disabilities two years after high school completion. *Journal of Learning Disabilities, 32,* 533–552.

Rojewski, J. W. (1999b). The role of chance in the career development of individuals with learning disabilities. *Learning Disability Quarterly, 22,* 267–278.

Rojewski, J. W., & Kim, H. (2003). Career choice patterns and behavior of work-bound youth during early adolescence. *Journal of Career Development, 30*(2), 89–108.

Rojewski, J. W., & Yang, B. (1997). Longitudinal analysis of select influences on adolescents' occupational aspirations. *Journal of Vocational Behavior, 51,* 375–410. doi: 10.1006/jvbe.1996.1561

Ross-Gordon, J. M. (1996). *Adults with learning disabilities: An overview for the adult educator* [Information Series No. 337]. Columbus, OH: Center on Education and Training for Employment. Retrieved from ERIC database. (ED315664)

Rothman, H. R., & Cosden, M. (1995). The relationship between self-perception of a learning disability and achievement, self-concept and social support. *Learning Disability Quarterly, 18,* 203–212.

Sabornie, E. J., Cullinan, D., Osborne, S. S., & Brock, L. B. (2005). Intellectual, academic, and behavioral functioning of students with high-incidence disabilities: A cross-categorical meta-analysis. *Exceptional Children, 72,* 47–63.

Sabornie, E. J., Evans, C., & Cullinan, D. (2006). Comparing characteristics of high-incidence disability groups. *Remedial and Special Education, 27,* 95–104.

Schoon, I., & Parsons, S. (2002). Teenage aspirations for future careers and occupational outcomes. *Journal of Vocational Behavior, 60,* 262–288.

Sitlington, P. L., Frank, A. R., & Carson, R. R. (1994). Postsecondary vocational education—Does it really make a difference? *Issues in Special Education and Rehabilitation, 9*(1), 89–100.

Spekman, N. J., Goldberg, R. J., & Herman, K. L. (1992). Learning disabled children grow up: A search for factors related to success in the young adult years. *Learning Disabilities Research & Practice, 7,* 161–170.

Stodden, R., Jones, M., & Chang, K. (2002). *Services, supports and accommodations for individuals with disabilities: An analysis across secondary education, postsecondary education, and employment.* Manoa: University of Hawaii at Manoa, National Center on Secondary Education and Transition. Retrieved from http://www.ncset.hawaii.edu

Stone, E. F., Stone, D. L., & Dipboye, R. L. (1992). Stigmas in organizations: Race, handicaps, and physical unattractiveness. In K. Kelly (Ed.), *Issues, theory, and research in industrial and organizational psychology* (pp. 385–457). New York: Elsevier Science.

Strauser, D. R. (1995). Applications of self-efficacy theory in rehabilitation counseling. *Rehabilitation Counseling, 61,* 7–11.

Szymanski, E. M., Hershenson, D. B., Enright, M. S., & Ettinger, J. M. (1996). Career development theories, constructs, and research: Implications for people with disabilities. In E. M. Szymanski & D. B. Hershenson (Eds.), *Work and disability: Issues and strategies in career development and job placement* (pp. 79–126). Austin, TX: Pro-Ed.

Szymanski, E. M., Willmering, P., Tschopp, M., Tansey, T., & Mizelle, N. (2003). Career counseling. In F. Chan, N. L. Berven, & K. R. Thomas (Eds.), *Counseling theories and techniques for rehabilitation health professionals* (pp. 282–299). New York: Springer.

Trainor, A. A. (2007). Perceptions of adolescent girls with LD regarding self-determination and postsecondary transition planning. *Learning Disability Quarterly, 30,* 31–45.

Unger, D. D. (2001). *Employer's attitudes toward people with disabilities in the worforce: Myths or realities.* Richmond: Virginia Commonwealth University. Retrieved from http://www.worksupport.com

U.S. Bureau of the Census. (2004). *Survey of income and program participation.* Retrieved from http://www.census.gov/population/pop-profile/disability

U.S. Department of Education. (2006, April). *26th annual (2004) report to Congress on the implementation of the Individuals with Disabilities Education Act, Vol. 1.* Washington, DC: Office of Special Education and Rehabilitative Services, Office of Special Education Programs. Retrieved from http://www.ed.gov/about/reports/annual/osep/2004/26th-vol-1-front.pdf

U.S. General Accounting Office. (2003). *Special education federal actions can assist states in improving postsecondary outcomes for youth* (GAO Report No. 03-773). Retrieved from http://www. gao.gov/new/items/do3773.pdf

Wagner, M. M., & Blackorby, J. (1996). Transition from high school to work or college: How special education students fare. *Future of Children, 6*(1), 103–120.

Wagner, M. M., Blackorby, J., Cameto, R., & Newman, L. (1993). *What makes a difference? Influences on postschool outcomes for youth with disabilities: The third comprehensive report from the National Longitudinal Transition Study of Special Education Students* (OSEP Contract No. 300-87-0054). Menlo Park, CA: SRI International. Retrieved from ERIC database. (ED365085)

Wagner, M., Newman, L., Cameto, R., Garza, N., & Levine, P. (2005). *After high school: A first look at the postschool experiences of youth with disabilities. A report from the National Longitudinal Transition Study-2 (NLTS2).* Menlo Park, CA: SRI International. Retrieved from ERIC database. (ED494935)

Weiss, G., & Hechtman, L. T. (1993). *Hyperactive children grown up: ADHD in children, adolescents, and adults.* New York: Guilford.

Werner, E. E. (1990). Protective factors and individual resilience. In S. J. Meisels & J. D. Shonkoff (Eds.), *Handbook of early childhood intervention* (pp. 97–116). New York: Cambridge University Press.

Werner, E. E., & Smith, R. S. (1982). *Vulnerable but invincible: A longitudinal study of resilient children and youth.* New York: McGraw-Hill.

Wilson, P. M., & Wilson, J. R. (1992). Environmental influences on adolescent educational aspirations. *Youth and Society, 24,* 52–70.

Wong, B. Y. L. (2003). General and specific issues for researchers' consideration in applying the risk and resilience framework to the social domain of learning disabilities. *Learning Disabilities Research and Practice, 18,* 68–76.

Worthington, R. L., Flores, L. Y., & Navarro, R. L. (2005). Career development in context: Research with people of color. In S. D. Brown & R. W. Lent (Eds.), *Career development and counseling: Putting theory and research to work* (pp. 225–252). Hoboken, NJ: Wiley.

Young, G., & Browning, J. (2005). Learning disabilities/dyslexia and employment-A mythical view. In G. Reid (Ed.), *Dyslexia in context: Research, policy and practice* (pp. 25–39). London: Whurr.

45

Transition to Daily Living for Persons with High Incidence Disabilities

David Scanlon
Boston College

James R. Patton
University of Texas at Austin

Marshall Raskind
Bainbridge Island, Washington

Meeting the transition needs of students with disabilities has always been a purpose of special education. Most certainly it has been one since then-Assistant Secretary of the Office of Special Education and Rehabilitative Services (OSERS) M. Will's 1984 criticism that unreasonable percentages of special education students were exiting secondary school without a diploma and that regardless of diplomas, too few were going on to postsecondary education or gainful employment. That trend was (and still is) true for students with high incidence disabilities.[1] Since mandated transition planning and services were introduced in the 1990 reauthorization of P.L.94-142 (renamed the Individuals with Disabilities Education Act [IDEA, 1990]), transition initiatives have focused primarily on three domains: postsecondary education, employment, and independent living. In the case of special education students with high incidence disabilities, the focus has been overwhelmingly on postsecondary education and employment. However, just as preparation for those two areas is a mission of (special) education, so is preparation for independent living.

Early commentaries on Will's *OSERS Programming for the Transition of Youth with Disabilities: Bridges from School to Working Life* (1984) cited its emphasis on gainful employment as the ultimate outcome of special education as too narrow (e.g., Edgar, 1988; Halpern, 1985). It was argued that a complete and fulfilled life includes "community adjustment" (Halpern, 1985), which encompasses having knowledge, skill and satisfaction in a variety of domains that include living arrangements, food, clothing and health, daily routines, community use, and personal relationships and self-esteem.

A Focus on Overall Life *v.* Education and Employment Outcomes

There are a variety of constructs that address how well an adult leads her/his life (note that we use "adult" to identify school leavers of a variety of ages). The conceptualization that has had the greatest influence on transition theorizing, research, and practice is "quality of life" (QOL).

Quality of Life

Halpern offered the QOL construct in 1993, following up his 1985 response to Will's employment-focused transition initiative. Although he did not originate the concept (see Campbell, Converse, & Rogers, 1976; and Dennis, Williams, Giangreco, & Cloninger, 1993 for a summary of conceptualizations), Halpern's nomination of QOL as a guide for measuring transition outcomes helped the field to consider transition more comprehensively. In Halpern's QOL scheme there are three major domains. *Physical and Material Wellbeing* refers to matters of safety with "outcomes" in areas such as physical and mental health, and stability in substantive ways such as dependable and personally acceptable shelter, clothing, food, and finances. Students with high incidence disabilities have difficulty achieving satisfactory outcomes across the areas of the material wellbeing domain, including extremes such as being disproportionately likely to live in correctional settings for those with emotional or behavioral disorders (EBD) or learning disabilities (LD) (Quinn, Rutherford, Leone, Osher, & Poirier, 2005) to being low wage earners with unsteady employment trends for those in all of the high incidence categories (Frank & Singleton, 2000; Wagner & Blackorby, 1996). The second domain, *Performance of Adult Roles* refers to participating in the community in such ways as voting, moving freely around in the community (e.g., using modes of transportation, ability to locate destinations for recreation or services), and participating in education, employment, and socialization at desired or necessary levels. Here too adults with high incidence disabilities have been found to achieve low levels of participation and satisfaction (e.g., Barkley, Fischer, Smallish, & Fletcher, 2006; Coutinho, Oswald, & Best, 2006). They tend to remain single and live in their parents' home longer than their peers (Lindstrom & Benz, 2002) and report having few friends and social relationships (Elksnin & Elksnin, 2001). Finally, the *Personal Fulfillment* domain includes the individual's happiness, satisfaction, and sense of general well-being (Halpern, 1993). Studies such as those by Newman, Wagner, Cameto, & Knokey (2009) and Werner (1993; also see Barkley, Murphy, & Fischer, 2008) have documented that adolescents and adults with high incidence disabilities tend to self-report lower levels of fulfillment in some personal fulfillment areas.

The Application of QOL: A Focus on Daily Living

QOL is an important outcome measure of special education and transition policies, programs, and interventions (e.g., Hoffman, Marquis, Poston, Summers, & Turnbull, 2006). Included within it are terms such as "independent living," "daily living," "life skills," and "community functioning" (Cronin, Lemoine, & Wheeler, 2008). Certain fields prefer certain terms; for example, occupational therapists use the term "activities of daily living" (ADL). The IDEA 2004 makes reference to "independent living" as a post-school outcome. In this chapter we use the term "daily living" to refer to the range of contexts and skills an individual needs to master for success in independent living, acknowledging that some of those skills are equally germane to education and employment (e.g., effective communication, fiscal management). Our intent in adopting daily living is to refer to the complexity of the range of skills that contribute to a high overall quality of life in multiple contexts and settings, which includes well-being.

Research-based Knowledge of The Quality of Life of Adolescents and Adults with High Incidence Disabilities: The Need for a Daily Living Transition Focus

Most transition research for those with high incidence disabilities concerns postsecondary education participation and employment (Halpern, 1990; Newman et al., 2009). Some research, however, provides insights into the daily living status of adolescents and adults with high incidence disabilities. There are several significant limitations to that research base, yet it is useful to setting research and service priorities in transition for daily living.

The Recent History of Research Priorities in Special Education. Predominant research trends in the overall special education field for high incidence disabilities have served to shape the research knowledge base. Poplin (1988) noted that much of the research on those with high incidence disabilities, especially for those with learning disabilities, has been focused on chronicling their behavioral profile and theorizing underlying cognitive factors—mostly from a deficit, "medical model," perspective, up through much of the 1980s. The emphasis has been on documenting what they cannot do as well as their nondisabled peers.

Since that period, when the current transition era was in its infancy, transition research has expanded in focus to consider outcomes of interventions. More recently, emphasis has been given to the fact that the transition process can identify, not only the needs, but also the strengths of students (Clark & Patton, 2006). Through attempts to understand both positive and negative intervention outcomes, research has increasingly addressed personal cognitive and perspective-taking aspects of an individual's transition performance. The self-determination focus, for example, has become an important component of transition research and practices. It arose out of recognition that persons with disabilities tend to lack opportunities to self-determine their futures (Field, 2008).

The Current Knowledge Base on Daily Living for Those with High Incidence Disabilities

Traditionally, data collected on daily living addresses financial and residential independence, self-sufficiency, marriage, relationships, or parenting (Newman et al., 2009). Findings from the 2001–2009 administration of the National Longitudinal Transition Survey (NLTS2), which addressed those topics, present one of the most comprehensive current profiles of daily living for young adults with high incidence disabilities, including allowing direct comparisons across disability categories and topics. The study focused on 12,000 youth with disabilities who were receiving special education and were between the ages of 13 and 16 in the 2000–2001 school year, reporting on their experiences 4 years later. The NLTS2 data we report in this chapter are selected from Newman et al.'s (2009) analysis of responses for out-of-high-school youth only, who responded to the second or third wave of NLTS2 data collection (unless otherwise noted). Smaller scale studies, intervention models, and transition practices are useful for identifying areas of trends in daily living as well. Intervention models typically address key areas on which transition planning is based. The daily living skills covered by two representative intervention models are provided in Table 45.1. As can be gleaned from the table, the domains and subdomains of those models relate closely to QOL concepts. Additionally, adult skills curriculum models tend to focus on introduction and acquisition of specific skills for daily living (Cronin, Lemoine, & Wheeler, 2008). The range of findings from the various resources on the daily living status of those with high incidence disabilities can be organized by Halpern's (1993) three QOL domains.

Physical and Material Well-Being. The physical and material well-being domain encompasses outcomes in the areas of food, clothing, and lodging; financial security; physical and mental health; and safety from harm. While the percentages of youth living independently or semi-independently were statistically significantly different between various groups with disabilities in the NLTS2, the percentages reporting satisfaction with their level of residential independence (e.g., 73% for those with learning disabilities and 91% for those with emotional or behavioral disorders) were not significantly different for any of the groups (Newman et al., 2009). Youth with learning disabilities and emotional or behavioral disorders were the most likely of all those in the NLTS2 survey to have reported living independently within 4 years of leaving high school (29% and 22%, respectively). Still, many adults with learning disabilities have difficulty separating themselves from home, which may be due in part to the low percentages who report performing housekeeping skills such as paying bills, cooking, and washing dishes and clothes (sources cited in Sitlington, 2008). There were some culturally-based distinctions in independent living; for example, White youth were more likely (29%) to live independently than either African American (20%) or Hispanic (10%) respondents. Tang (1995) has noted that the assumption of living independently as an indicator of emancipation is a Western European middle-class value that does not apply equally across economic class and cultural groups (c.f. Ramasamy, Duffy, & Camp, 2000). In general, no differences were found between high school completers and noncompleters, however youth who completed high school were more likely to live semi-independently after leaving high school (including dormitory and military housing; Newman et al., 2009). Luftig and Muthert (2005) reported that young adults with mild intellectual disabilities who had participated in a high school curriculum addressing independent living and vocational technology skills were more likely than others with mild intellectual disabilities to live independently, but their overall likelihood was still lower than for those with learning disabilities or the general population. Specific cognitive functioning skills correlate with the likelihood and successfulness of those with mild intellectual disabilities living independently (Su, Chen, Wuang, Lin, & Wu, 2008).

Living independently is linked to financial resources, in addition to a range of daily living skills and support options that affect its success. Most analyses of income and independent living do not investigate links between the variables for persons with high incidence disabilities.

TABLE 45.1
Daily Living Skills Common to Intervention Models

Major Life Demands (Cronin et al., 2008)	Life-Centered Career Education (Brolin, 1993)
Home and Family:	**Daily Living Skills:**
Home management	Managing personal finances
Financial management	Selecting & managing a household
Family life	Caring for personal needs
Children rearing	Raising children & meeting marriage responsibilities
Leisure Pursuits:	Buying, preparing, & consuming food
Indoor activities	Buying & caring for clothing
Outdoor activities	Exhibiting responsible citizenship
Community/neighborhood activities	Utilizing recreational facilities & engaging in leisure
Travel	Getting around the community
Entertainment	**Personal-Social Skills:**
Community Involvement:	Achieving self-awareness
Citizenship	Acquiring self-confidence
Community awareness	Achieving socially responsible behavior
Services/resources	Maintaining good interpersonal skills
Physical/Emotional Health:	Achieving independence
Physical	Making adequate decisions
Emotional	Communicating with others
Personal Responsibility & Relationships:	
Personal confidence/understanding	
Goal setting	
Self-improvement	
Relationships	
Personal expression	

Most of those with disabilities in the NLTS2 study reported having an annual income of $25,000 or less (Newman et al., 2009). Differences among the disability categories were all nonsignificant, with approximately 90% of each reporting this level. Interestingly, annual income for youth with disabilities was not influenced by school completion or number of years out of school. Morisi (2008) reports that for approximately the same time period, 16- to 19-year olds enrolled in school earned an average $7.25/hour, or approximately $15,000 annually. Historically, transition research has presented conflicting findings on the value of high school completion and postsecondary education on the income of adults with high incidence disabilities (e.g., Day & Newburger, 2002; Tyler, 2002). Also of note, wages and access to benefits did not differ significantly among persons with disabilities based on gender, race, or household income.

Many transition and daily living curriculums stress the importance of employment, as well as a variety of household management and community living skills, however few expressly emphasize managing budgets (see Sitlington, 2008, Table 12.1). Roughly half of those with learning disabilities (58%) or emotional or behavioral disorders (49%) in the NLTS2 database had a savings account, with lower percentages having a checking account and still lower percentages a credit card. Those in the broad intellectual disabilities category were among the least likely of all disability groups to have any of the three. In one study of adults with mild intellectual disabilities, it was found that they did not differ significantly from nondisabled populations in their ability to make daily financial decisions about costs and savings; what did distinguish individuals was whether they had received functional skills instruction (Suto, Clare, Holland, & Watson, 2005).

Psychosocial factors appear to influence adolescents with learning disabilities and/or ADHD participating in risk-taking behaviors such as delinquency, sexual activity, and gambling (McNamara, Vervaeke, & Willoughby, 2008). Raskind, Goldberg, Higgins, and Herman (1999) reported that there appeared to be a high incidence of psychological difficulties in a sample of adults with learning disabilities ages 28–35, with 42% suffering disturbances that were classifiable under the *Diagnostic and Statistical Manual Of Mental Disorders* (4th ed. American Psychiatric Association, 1994).

Performance of Adult Roles. "Adult roles" encompasses a variety of activities typically expected of adults, ranging from responsible citizenship to personal activities and perspectives. Despite significant limitations in published research, Verdonschot, de Witte, Reichraht, Buntinx, and Curfs (2009) were able to conclude from a review of the literature that, in general, those with mild intellectual disabilities are more likely than others with intellectual disabilities, but less likely than those with other or no disabilities to access and participate in their communities.

Mobility and community access are important transition outcomes for adults. Seventy-six percent of those with learning disabilities in the NLTS2 study had a driver's license or learner's permit, as did 70% of those with emotional or behavioral disorders (Newman et al., 2009). Barkley (2002) reported that the inattentive characteristics of adolescents and young adults with ADHD cause them to be prone to more bad driving behaviors. Similarly, Reiff and Gerber (1994) noted that adults with learning disabilities have difficulty with driving and navigating from one location to another.

Those in their adolescent and young adult years are most likely to be closely connected to family in such roles as child and sibling; however, their roles in those contexts shift as they mature and transition (Dacey, Kenny, & Margolis, 2000). Some assume caregiver roles due to absent or incapacitated parents, others due to cultural expectations, sometimes while dually filling the child and sibling roles. Also, beginning typically by adolescence, relationships with friends, dating, sexual partners, and families they create become increasingly important. Unfortunately, family quality of life (Hoffman et al., 2006) and the role of family in transition activities are among the topics on which there is an insufficient amount of research (Cobb & Alwell, 2009).

When it comes to being married or living in a "marriage-like" relationship, 10% and 13%, respectively, of those in the NLTS2 study with learning disabilities and emotional or behavioral disorders responded affirmatively; only 8% of those with intellectual disabilities reported similar relationships. Those percentages compare with 16% for the general education population found in the National Longitudinal Survey of Youth (NLSY) (2001) study. Barkley et al. (2008) reviewed a variety of studies on persons with ADHD and found that they are less likely to enter into marriage relationships but of those who do marry, conflicting study results nonetheless seem to indicate they are no more likely to divorce. Barkley et al. did find strongly confirmatory evidence that those in marriages had more stressful relationships.

The family relationships in which individuals find themselves directly relate to both their independent living status and personal satisfaction, and for many there are implications for financial security as well. The 14% of nondisabled peers who had parented at least one child in the 4 years since leaving high school (NLYS, 2001) approximated the 10% of those with learning disabilities and 14% of those with emotional or behavioral disorders in the NLTS2 study (Newman et al., 2009). Although the intellectual disabilities category includes many individuals who are not considered to have high incidence disabilities, that overall group reported a 15% parenting rate. Barkley et al. (2008) reported that those with ADHD were more likely to get pregnant (or cause pregnancy) than the general population and that those with a diagnosis of hyperactivity were the most likely.

Regardless of family living circumstances, socialization is important to quality of life. Having friends is often a determining factor in being part of a community (Barber

& Hupp, 1993). Those with learning disabilities and emotional or behavioral disorders were among the most likely of young adults with disabilities to report visiting with friends outside of school or work at least weekly (Newman et al., 2009). By contrast, they ranked 7th and 10th out of 12 disability categories (those with Deaf-blindness were not counted) in percentage communicating by computer at least daily (i.e., e-mail, instant messaging, chat rooms). Barkley (2002) has indicated that inattentiveness and hyperactivity for those with ADHD leads to difficultly in sustaining friendships. Those with mild intellectual disabilities tend to have fewer friends in their adolescent and adult years, especially friends who do not also have disabilities (Siperstein, Leffert, & Wenz-Gross, 1997), which may be due to both maturational differences and lack of opportunities for integration. However, more so than those with more intensive intellectual disabilities, they are also observed to get along well with others (Hughes et al., 1999).

Civic participation is also considered an important adult role. According to a survey of high school teachers (Carter, Trainor, Sun, & Owens, 2009), the daily living area in which adolescents with emotional or behavioral disorders or learning disabilities are in most need of developing skills and knowledge is community participation. Raskind et al. (1999) found that successful adults with learning disabilities take the initiative to be actively engaged in their community and that this action is not simply an outcome of "success" but in fact may be a causal factor in enhancing positive life outcomes. Werner (1993) has also emphasized that community involvement (i.e., involvement with church group, religious community, community college) may serve to promote successful adult adaptation.

Young adults with disabilities tend to be registered to vote at a higher percentage than their same age peers from the general population (67% v. 58%; Newman et al., 2009). However, at 66% those with learning disabilities were tied with two other categories (autism and multiple disabilities) for second lowest likelihood to be registered (only those with intellectual disabilities, at 59% had a lower percentage); those with emotional or behavioral disorders ranked immediately above them at 69%. Thus, those with low incidence disabilities are even more likely to be registered voters.

According to the NLTS2 data set, those with learning disabilities, emotional or behavioral disorders, or intellectual disabilities were among the least likely to participate in lessons or classes outside of school (23%, 19%, and 9%, respectively; Newman et al., 2009). However, those with learning disabilities or emotional or behavioral disorders were among the median percentages to engage in community service or volunteer activities. The respondents with learning disabilities were among the highest percentages (35%) to participate in a community group such as a team, club, or religious group. Finally, in the adult roles domain, behaving in socially responsible ways is also a valued adult role. Across all the disability categories, those with learning disabilities and emotional or behavioral disorders were considerably more likely to report having engaged in physical fighting within the last year, 21% and 31%, respectively (only those with traumatic brain injury came close, with a 17% rate; Newman et al., 2009). Those with emotional or behavioral disorders were the second most likely to have reported carrying a weapon within the past 30 days, at 20% compared to 23% of those with traumatic brain injury. Interestingly, those in the broad other health impaired category were third most likely (17%). Barkley reported that although there is only limited research on the "antisocial" behaviors of adults with ADHD, they commit crimes and acts of violence, as well as are arrested at increased rates compared to the general population. Those with learning disabilities were closer to the median level of all disability groups for carrying a weapon in the past 30 days, at 10%. Notably, there were no significant differences in rates of physical violence or weapons carrying based on whether or not respondents had completed high school.

Rutherford, Bullis, Anderson, and Griller-Clark (2002) reported that those under age 18 with disabilities are four to five times more likely than their general education peers to enter into correctional systems. As an overall group, youth with disabilities have been more than twice as likely as their general education peers to have been arrested. At rates that were almost always statistically significant, those with emotional or behavioral disorders were more likely than any other disability group to have been stopped by police for reasons other than a traffic violation, arrested, have spent a night in jail, or been on probation or parole (Newman et al., 2009). Those with learning disabilities, other health impaired or traumatic brain injury were among the next most likely for each of those events, although those with intellectual disabilities were found more likely than those with learning disabilities or traumatic brain injury to have spent a night in jail, at 14%. Whether or not the respondents had completed high school was a statistically significant factor in having been stopped by the police for other than a traffic violation, arrested, or having spent a night in jail, favoring those who had completed school.

Findings from the National Adolescent and Child Treatment Study (NACTS), a longitudinal wave design study begun in 1985, indicate high levels of substance abuse and criminal activities among young adults with emotional or behavioral disorders. Of those aged 17–25, substance abuse was reported more often than any other mental health condition (Greenbaum et al., 1996). They have also been found less likely to be in marriage or living with a significant other, more likely to be living at home, to have higher rates of sexually transmitted diseases and unwanted pregnancies, as well as to have less community involvement than nondisabled peers. Those trends typically magnify the longer they are out of secondary school (Gagnon & Leone, 2005).

Personal Fulfillment. As would be expected by virtue of the diagnosis they have received, those with emotional or behavioral disorders generally experience less personal fulfillment than their nondisabled peers (e.g., Sheeber et al., 2009). Similar trends in personal fulfillment have been found for persons with the other high incidence disabilities. The complexities of understanding trends for a disability group are underscored by Topolski et al's (2004) analysis. The adolescents in their study who scored in the atypical ranges on the Conners' ADHD/DSM-IV Scale self-reported lower senses of their own health and "belief in self" and in their overall QOL, as well as greater emotional stress than did those in the Conners typical range. They also differed in self-reported trends and quality of interactions in community environments. Topolski et al. also found indications in their data that difficulties in navigating environmental contexts are related to self-esteem, in addition to processing social cues.

Those with high incidence disabilities have been documented as having low self-affect and engaging in learned helplessness (see Skinner & Lindstrom, 2003). Children with learning disabilities are often socially rejected by their peers, and have problems establishing and maintaining friendships. Authorities in the field of learning disabilities have explored a number of possible causes for those difficulties, including low academic standing, poor oral language skills, nonverbal communication deficits, concurrent psychological problems, attention/memory disorders, as well as cognitive deficits related to social problem solving. However, to date, there is no consensus regarding the exact causes of social difficulties in persons with learning disabilities. Experiences and affect in childhood are directly correlated with those in the adolescent and adult years (e.g., McCarthy, 2008; Rubin, Copland, & Bowker, 2009). In addition to social difficulties, individuals with learning disabilities may be at greater risk for psychological problems, including feelings of loneliness, low self-esteem, anxiety and depression (Pliszka, 2009). Werner (1993) found that adults with learning disabilities report stress related health problems and worry about work at a rate of about two times that of their non-disabled peers, for example.

Across QOL Domains Summary. The National Longitudinal Transition Study (NLTS; 1992) provided one of the largest transition databases collected in the United States. It was a study on students 15 years of age or older in special education and in seventh to twelfth grade in 1985–86. Students in each of the high incidence categories were included, although ADD/ADHD was not distinguished as a category of disability, those data provided transition profiles in three domains: work/education, living arrangements, and social. Few of the individuals with disabilities included in that data set were successful in all three domains; success was even less likely for those out of school 1–2 years (Wagner, Newman, Cameto, & Levine, 2005). The follow-up study, the NLTS2, begun in 2001, had been expected to evidence improved trends; preliminary findings included high expectations expressed by the surveyed students (Sitlington, 2008). In general, NLTS2 findings indicate that in the 2000's youth without disabilities had taken longer than previous generations to attain the "markers" of progress into adulthood (sources cited in Newman et al., 2009, p. 99). Findings from a variety of smaller-scale studies indicate that in most regards those with high incidence disabilities continue to lag behind their nondisabled peers in their levels of participation and success in most daily living milestones.

As we noted, generalizations between high incidence disability groups, and even across individuals within the same category, are limited by several factors. As Topolski et al. reported in their 2004 literature review, for example, studies on QOL for those with ADHD were not found. Studies on specific behavioral adjustments, tending to document difficulties in behavior, emotions, academics and socialization were typical.

Among those with high incidence disabilities, students with emotional or behavioral disorders are the most likely to receive their special education in settings more restrictive than the general education classroom (U.S. DOE, 2006). They are also the most likely to be placed in residential schools, in total numbers that have increased over a decade (Gagnon & Leone, 2005). In a review of studies on the consequences of residential schooling for students, Wood and Cronin concluded in 1999 that "students with EBD are not being adequately prepared for the life demands needed for successful adult adjustment" (p. 343) [cited in Hornby & Witte, 2008]. Some have suggested that the overall population of students with emotional or behavioral disorders experience less academic success than any other group of students with or without disabilities (Landrum, Tankersley, & Kauffman, 2003). Upwards of 60% of them drop out of school (Bullis & Cheney, 1999; Landrum et al., 2003).

Despite limitations to generalization and the generally negative nature of daily living findings, Cronin et al.'s (2008) commonly claimed independent living outcomes and implications specifically for those with learning disabilities seem appropriate to summarize and draw implications for the overall high incidence population:

- Many students with LD are not being prepared for the multidimensional demands of adulthood.
- The educational programs of many students with LD are not meeting current or future needs. As a result, many students are dropping out of school.
- The curricular and instructional structures of secondary programs for students with LD need reexamination.
- Closer articulation of the application of academic content learned in school to real-life experiences across all levels of school (elementary to middle school, middle school to high school) is needed.
- Educators need to have knowledge of the content standards and be able to plan instruction that connects students' real-life experiences to course content (Cronin et al., 2008, p. 205).

Best Practices in Transition Preparation for Daily Living

As Patton (2004) notes, at least part of the impetus for transition initiatives getting underway in the 1980s was the federal resources that accompanied Will's (1984) charge to the field. Consistent with the initial direction of her transition initiative, historically transition planning focused narrowly on a student's movement to her/his immediate post-school activities (Kohler, 1998), the targeted destination of that planning often was employment (Sitlington & Clark, 2006). More recently, emphases in transition have expanded to include curriculum and instruction to teach self-determination and work skills, and transition assessment systems and processes (Cobb & Alwell, 2009). This evolution in emphasis reflects a quality of life, or whole person, perspective on transition.

There are three main aspects to transition preparation in such an approach: identification of post-school goals, activities and experiences to prepare the student for her/his goals, and the student and others collaborating to identify the goals and activities (Kohler, 1998). To apply those aspects in a comprehensive process, Kohler (1996, 1998) proposed, through the Transition Research Institute, that transition services need to include: student-focused planning, student development, interagency and interdisciplinary planning, family involvement, and program structure (see Kohler & Field, 2003). Incorporating each of these emphases into a comprehensive process represents best practice in transition preparation.

Student-Focused Planning

In student-focused planning the emphasis is on ensuring that transition plans take into account the individual student's interests in order to address her/his needs. Accomplishing this requires enabling the student to make informed choices and be responsible in both planning and executing transition preparation activities.

Student participation is both federally required and a common sense aspect of transition planning. Yet, far too often students are not active, contributing members of the transition team. In their literature review Cobb and Alwell (2009) found student-focused planning to be critical to student transition outcomes, with a very large average effect size across the studies they reviewed, 1.47. The few qualitatively designed studies reviewed by Cobb and Alwell (2009) also indicated low levels of student involvement in transition planning, as has been reported by others (e.g., Thompson, Fulk, & Piercy, 2000; Trainor, 2005). Thompson et al. found that students tend not to feel ownership in their own transition processes. Hitchings et al. (2001) were told by postsecondary undergraduate students that when in high school they were not involved in transition planning meetings and that career and education planning was typically in the form of discouraging advice to them (see also Trainor, 2005; Williams & O'Leary, 2001). In an analysis of the NLTS2 data it was found that those with mild intellectual disabilities were less likely than those with emotional or behavioral disorders or learning disabilities to have participated in transition planning while in high school (Katsiyannis, Zhang, Woodruff, & Dixon, 2005).

Student-focused Assessment. As is true for individualized education planning, the transition planning and training process needs to begin with assessment. Roessler, Shearin, and Williams (2000) warn that assessment data are often overlooked in transition planning. They suggest this happens because (a) the assessments used do not necessarily match the adult domains for which the team is planning and (b) teams simply have a habit of ignoring assessment data while planning. Assessment must be comprehensive and generate information related to transition needs, strengths, preferences, and interests. The areas on which transition assessment should be based relate closely to those listed in Table 45.1. As an example, the *Transition Planning Inventory* (Clark & Patton, 2006) includes items for the following domains: employment, further education/training, daily living, leisure activities, community participation, health, self-determination, communication, and interpersonal relationships. Although only one domain is labeled "daily living," in actuality, seven of the nine domains relate to daily living as conceptualized and presented in this chapter.

Planning Based on Assessment Data. As indicated in Figure 45.1, there are two types of goals that should result from transition planning: *Instructional*—which addresses academic, behavioral, and social outcomes, and *Linkage*—which concerns connections among services and agencies (Patton, 2004). Furthermore, both academic and functional skills need to be addressed in the transition planning process (Cronin et al., 2008), just as they must in Individual Education Program (IEP) planning. Bassett and Kochar-Bryant (2002) add that standards-based and opportunities-based approaches to transition planning and preparation should be combined.

Student Development

As part of the process of participating in goal setting and planning for pathways to success, students must be aware of their own needs and what works best for them. Milsom and Hartley (2005) have identified four components for effective college transition planning for students with LD: knowledge of disability, knowledge of postsecondary support services, knowledge of disability legislation, and ability to self-advocate. Although their examples are specific to those with learning disabilities and postsecondary education, the four components apply to the other high incidence disabilities and the multiple transition destinations in addition to education. For example, those with ADHD face negative sanctions for not conducting themselves appropriately in social situations or when interacting with police (e.g., traffic violations; Barkley et

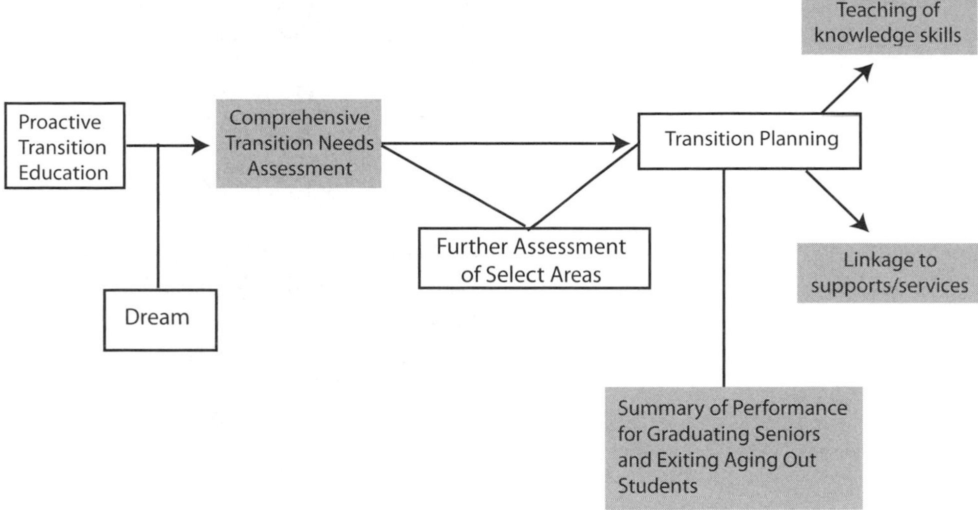

Figure 45.1 Tranisition process planning. Adapted from Patton and Dunn (1997).

al., 2008) and those with mild intellectual disabilities are often vulnerable in social and public settings due to limited knowledge or skills.

Many adolescents, young adults, and adults are not fully aware of their own disability and its implications (Madaus & Shaw, 2006; Price, Gerber, & Shessel, 2002). Furthermore, they may not be aware of reasons or strategies for self-disclosure (e.g., requesting accommodations when completing forms or for public services; see Eisenman, 2007; Trainor, 2005). Scanlon (1996) related the example of a teenager with learning disabilities who left an emergency room instead of asking for assistance when confronted with a registration form he could not complete. Although the "hidden" nature of high incidence disabilities means individuals may not need to disclose their disability to others (Field, 2008), there are several positive reasons for doing so. Among those reasons are protections of their rights and access to accommodative services in accordance with such laws as the Americans with Disabilities Act (ADA) and Section 504 of the Rehabilitation Act of 1973.

In addition to awareness, individuals' perspectives are thought to influence the effectiveness of transition interventions and their outcomes. Self-esteem has long been established as a contributing factor to success (e.g., Bandura, 1977). In 1999, Panagos and DuBois, for example, reported that self-efficacy helped predict adolescents' career interests. They further found that the adolescents' self-perceived self-efficacy to succeed in career preparation training was correlated with outcome successes.

Beyond such potentially malleable factors as the individual's perspective, Murray (2003) suggested that personal risk and resiliency thresholds can influence the success of transition practices. Among the factors that place students with disabilities at risk for diminished outcomes are gender (although males are at greater risk than females for having a high incidence disability, females with a high incidence disability are at greater risk for poor outcomes), race/ethnicity, and socio-economic status. Being identified by multiple of these factors, Murray suggests, can increase one's overall risk level. Compounding one's risk is her/his unique vulnerability, or how susceptible one is to experiencing risk. One implication of personal risk factors is that student development must be responsive to unique vulnerabilities (Kenny et al., 2007).

Although research findings suggest that an learning disabilities may place an individual at greater risk for negative outcomes, it also indicates that many of those individuals are able to overcome the risk associated with learning disabilities and are well adjusted, personally satisfied with their lives, productive, and successful. Such resilient individuals may possess certain protective factors that serve to buffer or mediate risk. As part of her seminal work in risk and resilience, Werner (1993) identified five "clusters" of protective factors that served to promote positive outcomes for persons with learning disabilities, including:

- Temperamental characteristics of the individual that elicited positive responses from others
- Skills and values that led to efficient use of their abilities: faith that the "odds" could be overcome, realistic educational and vocational plans, and regular household chores and domestic responsibilities
- Parental care-giving styles that reflected competence and promoted self-esteem in the child; structure in the household; maternal education beyond high school; and, for girls, a mother who was gainfully employed
- Supportive adults who acted as gatekeepers for the future (e.g., grandparents, youth leaders)
- Timely opportunities at critical transition points in their lives (e.g., high school to work) that chartered a positive course to adulthood.

Gerber, Ginsberg, and Reiff (1992) conducted another key study employing a risk and resilience model. They found in their study of employment success that the overriding factor leading to success is the ability of the individual to take control of his or her life. Taking control was characterized by themes falling into two main categories: "internal decisions" and "external manifestations."

Internal Decisions

- Desire (taking a stand and making a decision to move ahead)
- Goal orientation (setting explicit goals to work toward)
- Reframing (reinterpreting the learning disabilities experience from something negative to something positive)

External Manifestations (how the person adapts)

- Persistence (willingness to sacrifice and persevere toward goals)
- Goodness of fit (finding environments where their strengths are optimized and weaknesses minimized)
- Learned creativity (creating strategies and techniques to enhance the ability to perform well)
- Social ecologies (seeking and utilizing the support of helpful people)

Raskind et al. (1999) conducted a 20-year study in an attempt to identify the personal characteristics and life situations and experiences that lead to successful life outcomes in persons with learning disabilities. Results of their research revealed a set of personal characteristics, attitudes, and behaviors that promoted life success:

- Self-awareness (awareness of their strengths and weakness in both academic and non-academic areas; acceptance of their disability; ability to compartmentalize-not being overly defined by their learning difficulties and viewing them as only one aspect of themselves)
- Proactivity (active engagement in the world around them and belief in the power to control their own destiny)
- Perseverance (persistence in the face of adversity and flexibility in pursuing alternate strategies to reach a goal)
- Goal setting (setting specific yet flexible goals, including a strategy to reach them)
- Presence and use of effective social support systems (seeking and using the help of others, and the ability to decrease dependence in early adulthood)
- Emotional coping strategies (development of strategies for reducing stress and frustration)

It is interesting to note that despite different research participants and methodologies these three studies found a number of similar protective factors for individuals with learning disabilities. For example, Werner (1993) identified "supportive adults who fostered trust and acted as gatekeepers for the future" (p. 32) as an essential component in promoting positive life outcomes for persons with learning disabilities. The supportive adults described by Werner parallel the social support system success attribute found in Raskind et al.'s (1999) research. Similarly, Gerber and colleagues (1992) revealed that supportive and helpful people (an aspect of "social ecologies") play a critical role in achieving success.

There are other similarities among these studies. Gerber stresses the importance of "goal orientation," and Werner the "establishment of realistic educational and vocational plans" in achieving positive life outcomes. Raskind et al. (1999)also found that successful adults with learning disabilities showed evidence of specific, yet flexible goal setting in multiple areas, including education, employment, and family. There is also a striking similarity between the factor of "perseverance" found by Raskind et al. and Gerber et al.'s (1992) description of "persistence." Finally, Raskind's et al. finding regarding "compartmentalizing and accepting one's LD" is compatible with Gerber's theme of "reframing the LD experience" from something negative to something positive.

In one of the few recent studies of resiliency done with persons with mild intellectual disabilities, Leroy, Walsh, Kulik, and Rooney (2004) interviewed 29 women with intellectual disabilities of varying severity who were above the age of 50 (20 Americans, 9 Irish). They found that all of the women were "poor" and three-quarters of them had someone else who managed their finances for them, they had small support networks (typically 2–4 persons), and their primary supports were paid staff; their opinions about living arrangements, work, and social life varied, as they would for any group of persons. Leroy et al. concluded that the factors associated with resilience for a high quality of life in this population include health, skills and inclination for social interactions, and self-discipline, including control of one's own circumstances. In an earlier study with African American adolescents with mild mental retardation, ethnic identity and intergenerational support, particularly from families, were found to be primarily influences on resiliency (Frison, Wallander, & Browne, 1998).

Self-determination training. Self-determination is identifying personal goals and making decisions about one's quality of life. In Wehmeyer's conceptualization (e.g., Mithaug, Mithaug, Agran, Martin, & Wehmeyer, 2003; Wehmeyer, Palmer, Agran, Mithaug, & Martin, 2000) self-determination has not occurred until students engage in positive actions to achieve their goals. To enact self-determination then, an individual needs the ability to set personal goals, make choices consistent with achieving those goals, self-monitor progress and outcomes, and problem-solve and self-advocate as needed (Eisenman, 2007; Trainor, 2005). Goldberg, Higgins, Raskind, and Herman (2003) found in their longitudinal study that those adults with learning disabilities who set appropriate goals in high school had more satisfactory adult outcomes. Self-determination training as part of transition planning has been required by the IDEA Regulations since 1999.

Goal attainment skills, which encompass selecting appropriate goals and acting upon them to achieve desired "outcomes," may be the most critical self-determination skills (Martin et al., 2003; Wehmeyer, 1994). Essential to goal attainment is that students are flexible in response to barriers and opportunities. Their own skills may present barriers or unique opportunities (Mithaug et al., 2003; Wehmeyer Palmer, Soukup, Garner, & Lawrence, 2007). Indeed, Mithaug et al. (2003) cite a student's ability to be flexible as an indicator of being self-determined.

Various validated curriculums, such as the Self-Determined Learning Model of Instruction (Wehmeyer et al., 2000) and Take Action (Martin, Marshall, Maxon, & Jerman, 1999) stress stages of planning and action that begin with a student's self-assessment of interests and abilities in order to set proximal and distal goals, followed by actionable steps to progress toward goal accomplishment, including assessment, reflection, and adjustments to both the goals and plans to accomplish them. Wehmeyer (2007) stresses that self-determination facilitation cannot be decontextualized from students' with disabilitics actual life goals. To emphasize that self-determination needs to become a personal disposition and not simply a set of procedural steps, Karvonen, Test, Wood, Browder, and Algozzine (2004) suggested that effective self-determination curriculums are not limited to students setting goals for instructional contexts. The resiliency Gerber, Murray, and Raskind and their colleagues have found in successful adults with high incidence disabilities reflects persons who live in self-determined ways.

Self-awareness training. For persons with disabilities, part of self-assessment and acting on one's goals is to be self-aware of their disability(s) and their needs and rights related to that disability. Individuals with disability self-awareness can self-advocate "when they (a) demonstrate an understanding of their disability; (b) are aware of their legal rights; and (c) can competently and tactfully communicate their rights and needs to those in positions of authority" (Skinner 1998, as cited in Skinner & Lindstrom 2003, p. 134). This process includes knowing what services they require and how to secure them (Milsom & Hartley, 2005; Skinner & Lindstrom, 2003).

Despite consensus on the significance of self-determination as part of the transition process, the research and practice knowledge bases on its functions and how best to promote it are lacking. For example, Carter, Lane, Pierson, and Glaeser (2006) reported that research on effective self-determination interventions rarely includes students with emotional or behavioral disorders. As Madaus and Shaw (2006) found in a study of postsecondary students and Price et al. (2002) found in a workplace study, however, many adults often lack awareness of their own disability and its impact on them. One approach to ensuring teaching of the skills of self-determination is to write self-advocacy goals in an ITP (Schreiner, 2007). However, consistent with trends in educators neglecting transition planning and preparation, many special educators are not prepared to teach the skills of self-determination—including not knowing how to infuse them into the curriculum (Wehmeyer et al., 2000).

Interagency and Interdisciplinary Planning

Interagency collaboration has been an essential aspect of effective transition services since the earliest days of transition initiatives (Patton, 2004). "Successful transition services involve the efforts of school-based personnel (assessing needs, developing plans, providing appropriate instruction, and establishing necessary linkages to post-school entities) and coordination, cooperation, and communication from a variety of agencies" (Patton, 2004, p. 186). Nonetheless, in practice, professionals often overlook involving various adult agencies in the development of transition programs (Patton, 2004). Such involvement is not only helpful, but in many cases essential. Varying aspects of cooperation and communication enhance the transition planning process. In their review, Test et al. (2009) found no studies that addressed interagency or interdisciplinary planning.

The transition mandate requires key people be part of the transition planning team. Key school participants should include transition specialists and other vocational personnel. Other school personnel who can provide important information include the school psychologist, assistive technology specialist, school nurse, related service staff (e.g., OT, PT, SLP), and school counselor; all in addition to the student her/himself and a parent/guardian. Counselors also have responsibility for contacts with a variety of postsecondary settings and personnel, which makes them particularly appropriate as members of the team (Milsom & Hartley, 2005).

Family Involvement

There is a need for families to be involved in the transition preparation process. Family members can help in determining individually appropriate transition goals and activities for a student, and they can work constructively toward those goals with the student, or serve as a hindrance if they are uninformed about goals and the activities planned to achieve them. Their participation at the planning stages can also preclude developing plans that might compromise cultural or religious standards. In this area too, very little research exists. In Test et al.'s (2009) review of transition literature, which only yielded 39 studies that met their scientifically-based research criteria, only a single study addressed family involvement.

There are specific barriers to involvement by culturally and linguistically underrepresented families. Greene and Nefsky (1999) have identified six:

- the level of the family's acculturation
- their cultural attitudes toward disability
- language barriers and interpersonal differences in communication styles
- the family's knowledge of and comfort with the school infrastructure

- the family's perceptions of the school
- school personnel's familiarity and sensitivity to cultural diversity

Thus, in effective transition planning, schools should attend to *how* they involve families. Kohler (1998) identified three areas for schools to consider in promoting family involvement in transition efforts: participation and roles, empowerment, and training. However, efforts to empower parents to participate in the transition process can have the undesirable consequence of inhibiting the student's own self-determination skills (Hanley-Maxwell, Whitney-Thomas, & Pogoloff, 1995; Patton, 2004).

Not only can the family serve the student in the transition process, but the family can also be supported by comprehensive transition planning. Typically, QOL is thought of as a construct for individuals, not families (Hoffman et al., 2006). Given the important role that families can play in preparing an adolescent for adulthood, and that disability and family routine can significantly influence one another, it makes sense both that QOL for an individual should take into account her/his family and that there is such a thing as a family's QOL (Hoffman et al., 2006).

Program Structure

The task of trying to prepare students for life after high school is enormous. The task is complicated and requires a well thought out and comprehensive system to ensure that adequate transition services are provided. "Few definitions [of transition planning] provide the clarity and exactness necessary to facilitate the enormous task of preparing students for and moving them into any number of new post school settings. As a result, state and local educational agencies must decide on their own how to accomplish these tasks, often with deleterious consequences for students" (Patton, 2004, p. 186). Echoing this observation, Price, Gerber, and Mulligan (2003) suggested that transition practices are more often based on professional hunches than empirical evidence of what works.

Effective preparation for daily living must take into account access to the general curriculum, the need for all students to have life skills preparation, standards-based education, community-based practices, student involvement, and family involvement (Cronin et al., 2008). "All aspects of curricula must be integrated in a focus on the acquisition of academic and nonacademic skills useful throughout life, development of authentic social networks and supports, and career preparation through systematic and meaningful instruction" (Cobb &Alwell, 2009, p. 78). This means that life skills education should be provided in both general education and the community (DCDT; Clark, Field, Patton, Brolin, & Sitlington, 1994).

Three approaches to integrating life skills instruction with the curriculum are most common: specific coursework, integration of life skills into curricular content (via augmentation or infusion), and community experiences (Cronin et al., 2008).

As Cronin, Lemoine, and Wheeler (2008) suggest, programs should reflect community expectations, to help ground activities in the student's culture. Of course, the individual's preferences and interests should be factored into planning as well (Sitlington, 2008).

In reality, despite gaps in what is known about best transition practices, even the realm of practices already known to be important is rarely implemented in a comprehensive way, or well; Patton (2004) asserts that empirical evidence confirms that most of those practices are not being employed.

Recommendations

Research Priorities

The general needs for greater implementation of transition services for those with high incidence disabilities and development of practices specific to independent living correspond to needs for more research into the daily living status of those with high incidence disabilities. Although some studies investigating the independent living outcomes of persons with high incidence disabilities do exist (e.g., Fafard & Haubrich, 1981; Rogan & Hartman, 1990, NLTS-2), primarily concerning those with learning disabilities, such studies do little to inform us of the antecedent factors and variables that influence outcomes. If we are to develop effective intervention programs to promote positive adult outcomes, we must be able to identify the factors that affect or are predictive of specific outcomes. Those studies need to consider not only "success" in postsecondary education and employment settings, but in all settings in which persons with high incidence disabilities function in their adult lives. Halpern (1985) noted this in his expansion of Will's original (1984) model of transition, and McKinney stressed it as far back as 1994, but studies are still incredibly scarce.

Resources such as transition mandates (IDEA, 2004), QOL schemes (e.g., Halpern, 1993), comprehensive studies of specific daily living behaviors (e.g., Newman et al., 2009), and models for effective transition programming (e.g., Kohler, & Field, 2003) indicate the areas where research is needed. Sitlington (2008) categorizes those research needs into three areas:

- Examine and document effectiveness of major approaches to instructing adolescents with disabilities,
- Consider variables related to all aspects of adult living in follow-along studies,
- Relate individual's education and transition planning experiences to follow-along findings.

Cronin et al. (2008) also emphasize that follow-up and follow-along studies on students' life skill experiences are needed if we are to truly understand transition outcomes. It is worthy to note that, as far back as 1998, Sitlington and Frank provided a practical method for conducting follow-up studies on students who had exited from schools.

Based on their review of the transition literature, Test et al. (2009) have listed the numbers and types of quality studies still needed to satisfy their criteria for a body of "strong" scientifically-based research in each of Kohler's five domains. Such estimates are useful to determining the needed scope of a transition research agenda. Clearly, there is a great need for research on transition and daily living for those with high incidence disabilities. The historically persistent negative trajectory in post-school life for those with high incidence disabilities warrants an immediate and urgent response (Cronin et al., 2008).

Notes

1. We include those students with attention deficit disorder/attention deficit-hyperactivity disorder (ADD/ADHD), emotional and behavioral disorder (EBD), specific learning disabilities (LD), and mild intellectual disabilities (MID).

References

American Psychiatric Association. (2000). *Diagnostic and statistical manual of mental disorders* (4th ed., text rev.). Washington, DC: Author.

Americans with Disabilities Act of 1990. Public Law no. 101-336, 104 Stat. 327.

Bandura, A. (1997). *Social learning theory.* Upper saddle River, NJ: Prentice Hall.

Barber, D., & Hupp, S. C. (1993). A comparison of friendship patterns of individuals with developmental disabilities. *Education and Training in Mental Retardation and Developmental Disabilities, 28*, 13–22.

Barkley, R. A. (2002). Major life activity and health outcomes associated with attention-deficit/hyperactivity disorder. *Journal of Clinical Psychiatry, 63,* 10–15.

Barkley, R. A., Fischer, M., Smallish, L., & Fletcher, K. (2006). Young adult outcome of hyperactive children: Adaptive functioning in major life activities. *Journal of American Academy of Child and Adolescent Psychiatry, 45,*192–202.

Barkley, R. A., Murphy, K. R., & Fischer, M. (2008). *ADHD in adults: What the science says.* New York: Guilford.

Bassett, D. S., & Kochar-Bryant, C. A. (2002). Future directions for transition and standards-based education. In C. A. Kochar-Bryant & D. S. Bassett (Eds.), *Aligning transition and standards-based education: Issues and strategie*s (pp. 187–202). Arlington, VA: Council for Exceptional Children.

Bullis, M., & Cheney, D. (1999). Vocational and transition interventions for adolescents and young adults with emotional or behavioral disorder. *Focus on Exceptional Children, 31,* 1–24.

Campbell, A., Converse, P. E., & Rogers, W. L. (1976). *The quality of American life.* New York: Sage.

Carter, E. W., Lane, K. L., Pierson, M. R., & Glaeser, B. (2006). Self-determination skills and opportunities of transition-age youth with emotional disturbance and learning disabilities. *Exceptional Children, 72*, 333–346.

Carter, E. W., Trainor, A. A., Sun, Y., & Owens, L. (2009). Assessing the transition-related strengths and needs of adolescents with high-incidence disabilities. *Exceptional Children, 76*, 74–94.

Clark, G. M., Field, S., Patton, J. R., Brolin, D. E., & Sitlington, P. L. (1994). Life skills instruction: A necessary component for all students with disabilities. A position statement of the Division on Career Development and Transition. *Career Development for Exceptional Individuals, 17,* 125–134.

Clark, G. M., & Patton J. R. (2006). *Transition Planning Inventory (Updated Version).* Austin, TX: PRO-ED.

Cobb, R. B., & Alwell, M. (2009). Transition planning/coordinating interventions for youth with disabilities: A systematic review. *Career Development for Exceptional Individuals, 32,* 70–81.

Coutinho, M. J., Oswald, D. P., & Best, A. M. (2006). Differences in outcomes for female and male students in special education. *Career Development for Exceptional Individuals, 29*(1), 48–59.

Cronin, M. E., Lemoine, M. F., & Wheeler, S. C. (2008). Developing life skills. In G. Blalock, J. R. Patton, P. Kohler, & D. Bassett (Eds.), *Transition and students with learning disabilities: Facilitating the movement from school to adult life* (2nd ed., pp. 203–224). Austin, TX: Hammill Institute on Disabilities.

Dacey, J., Kenny, M., & Margolis, D. (2000). *Adolescent development* (3rd ed.). Carrollton, TX: Alliance Press.

Day, J. C., & Newburger, E. C. (2002). *The big payoff: Educational attainment and synthetic estimates of work-life earnings. Special studies. Current population reports*. Washington, DC: Bureau of the Census (DOC). (ED467533)

Dennis, R. E., Williams, W., Giangreco, M. F., & Cloninger, C. J. (1993). Quality of life as a context for planning and evaluation of services for people with disabilities. *Exceptional Children, 59*(6), 499–512.

Edgar, E. (1988). Employment as an outcome for mildly handicapped students: Current status and future directions. *Focus on Exceptional Children, 21*, 1–8.

Eisenman, L. T. (2007). Self-determination interventions: Building a foundation for school completion. *Remedial and Special Education,* 28, 2–8.

Elksnin, N., & Elksnin, L. (2001). Adolescents with disabilities: The need for occupational social skills training. *Exceptionality, 9*(1-2), 91–105.

Fafard, M. B., & Haubrich, P. A. (1981). Vocational and social adjustment of learning disabled young adults: A follow-up study. *Learning Disability Quarterly, 4*, 122–130.

Field, S. (2008). Self-determination instructional strategies for youth with learning disabilities. In G. Blalock, J. R. Patton, P. Kohler, & D. Bassett (Eds.), *Transition and students with learning disabilities: Facilitating the movement from school to adult life* (2nd ed., pp. 167–202). Austin, TX: Hammill Institute on Disabilities.

Frank, A. R., & Singleton, P. L. (2000). Young adults with mental disabilities--Does transition planning make a difference? *Education and Training in Mental Retardation and Developmental Disabilities, 35,* 119–134.

Frison, S. L., Wallander, J. L., & Browne, D. (1998). Cultural factors enhancing resilience and protecting against maladjustment in African American adolescents with mild mental retardation. *American Journal on Mental Retardation, 102*, 13–26.

Gagnon, J. C., & Leone, P. E. (2005). Elementary day and residential schools for children with emotional and behavioral disorders; characteristics and entrance and exit policies. *Remedial and Special Education, 26,* 141–150.

Gerber, P. J., Ginsberg, R., & Reiff, H. B. (1992). Identifying alterable patterns in employment success for highly successful adults with learning disabilities. *Journal of Learning Disabilities, 25*, 475–487.

Goldberg, R. J., Higgins, E. L., Raskind, M. H. L, & Herman, K. L. (2003). Predictors of success in individuals with learning disabilities: A qualitative analysis of a 20-year longitudinal study. *Learning Disabilities Research & Practice, 18*, 222–236.

Greenbaum, P. E., Dedrick, R. M., Kutash, K., Brown, E. C., Lardieri, S. P., & Pugh, A. M. (1996). National adolescent and child treatment study (NACTS): Outcomes for children with serious emotional and behavioral disturbance. *Journal of Emotional and Behavioral Disorders, 4*(3), 130–146.

Greene, G., & Nefsky, P. (1999) Transition for culturally and linguistically diverse youth with disabilities: Closing the gaps. *Multiple Voices, 3*(1), 15–24.

Halpern, A. S. (1985). Transition: A look at the foundations. *Exceptional Children, 51*, 479–486.

Halpern, A. (1993). Quality of life as a conceptual framework for evaluating transition outcomes. *Exceptional Children, 59*, 486–498.

Hanley-Maxwell, C., Whitney-Thomas, J., & Pogoloff, S. (1995). The second shock: Parental perspective of their child's transition from school to adult life. *Journal of the Association for Persons with Severe Handicaps. 201*, 3–16.

Hitchings, W. E., Luzzo, D. A., Ristow, R., Horvath, M., Retish, P., & Tanners, A. (2001). The career development needs of college students with learning disabilities: In their own words. *Learning Disabilities Research & Practice, 16*, 8–17.

Hoffman, L., Marquis, H., Poston, D., Summers, J. A., & Turnbull, A. (2006). Assessing family outcomes: Psychometric evaluation of the Beach Center Family Quality of Life Scale. *Journal of Marriage and Family, 68*, 1069–1083.

Hornby, G., & Witte, C. (2008). Views of their education and adult graduates of a residential special school for children with emotional and behavioral difficulties. *British Journal of Special Education, 35*, 102–107.

Hughes, C., Rodi, M. S., Lorden, S. W., Pittken, S. E., Dereer, K. R., Hwang, B., & Xinsheng, C. (1999). Social interactions of high school students with mental retardation and their general education peers. *American Journal on Mental Retardation, 104*, 533–544.

Individuals with Disabilities Education Act (IDEA). 1997. Public Law no. 94-102. [20 U.S.C. §§1400 et seq.]

Individuals with Disabilities Education Improvement Act (IDEIA). 2004. Public Law no. 108-446, 118 Stat. 2647. [Amending 20 U.S.C. §§1400 et seq.]

Karvonen, M., Test, D. W., Wood, W. M., Browder, D., & Algozzine, B. (2004). Putting self-determination into practice. *Exceptional Children, 71*, 23–41.

Katsiyannis, A., Zhang, D., Woodruff, N., & Dixon, A. (2005). Transition supports to students with mental retardation: An examination of data from the National Longitudinal Transition Study 2. *Education and Training In Developmental Disabilities, 40*, 109–116.

Kenny, M., Gualdron, L., Scanlon, D., Sparks, E., Blustein, D. L., & Jernigan, M. (2007). Urban adolescents' constructions of supports and barriers to educational and career attainment. *Journal of Counseling Psychology, 54*, 336–343.

Kohler, P. D. (1996). *Taxonomy for transition programming: Linking research and practice.* Champaign: University of Illinois Transition Research Institute.

Kohler, P. D. (1998). Implementing a transition perspective of education: A comprehensive approach to planning and delivering secondary education and transition services. In F. R. Fusch, & J. G. Chadsey (Eds.), *Beyond high school: Tractions transition from for school to work* (pp. 179–205). Baltimore: Paul H. Brookes.

Kohler, P. D., & Field. S. (2003). Transition-focused education: Foundations for the future. *The Journal of Special Education, 37*, 174–183.

Landrum, T. J., Tankersley, M., & Kauffman, J. J. (2003). What is special about special education for students with emotional or behavioral disorders? *Journal of Special Education, 37*, 148–156.

Leroy, B. W., Walsh, P. N., Kulik, N., & Rooney, M. (2004). Retreat and resilience; life experiences of older women with intellectual disabilities. *American Journal on Mental Retardation, 109*, 429–441.

Lindstrom, L. E., & Benz, M. R.. (2002). Phases of career development: Case studies of young women with learning disabilities. *Exceptional Children,* 69(1):67–83.

Luftig, R., & Muthert, D. (2005). Patterns of employment and independent living of adult graduates with learning disabilities and mental retardation of an inclusionary high school vocational program. *Research in Developmental Disabilities: A Multidisciplinary Journal, 26*(4), 317–325.

Madaus, J. W., & Shaw, S. F. (2006). The impact of the IDEA 2004 on transition to college for students with learning disabilities. *Learning Disabilities Research & Practice, 21*, 273–81.

Martin, J. E., Marshall, L. H., Maxon, L. M., & Jerman, P. L. (1999). *The self-determined IEP.* Longmont, CO: Sopris-West.

Martin, J., Mithaug, D., Cox, P., Peterson, L., Van Dycke, J., & Cash, M. (2003). Increasing self-determination: Teaching students to plan, work, evaluate, and adjust. *Exceptional Children, 69*, 431–446.

McCarthy, J. (2008). Behaviour problems and adults with Down Syndrome: Childhood risk factors. *Journal of Intellectual Disability Research, 52*, 877–882.

McKinney, J. D. (1994). Methodological issues in longitudinal research on learning disabilities. In S. Vaughn & C. Bos (Eds.), *Research issues in learning disabilities: Theory, methodology, assessment, and ethics* (pp. 202–232). New York: Springer-Verlag.

McNamara, J., Vervaeke, S-L, & Willoughby, T. (2008). Learning disabilities and risk-taking behavior in sdolescents: A comparison of those with and without comorbid Attention-Deficit/Hyperactivity Disorder. *Journal of Learning Disabilities, 41*, 561–574.

Milsom, A., & Hartley, M. T. (2005). Assisting students with learning disabilities transitioning to college: What school counselors should know. *Professional School Counseling, 8*, 436–441.

Mithaug, D. E., Mithaug, D., Agran, M., Martin, J., & Wehmeyer, M. (2003). *Self-determined learning theory: Predictions, prescriptions, and practice*. Mahwah, NJ: Erlbaum.

Morisi, T. L. (2008, February). Youth enrollment and employment during the school year. *Monthly Labor Review,* 51–63.

Murray, C. (2003). Risk factors, protective factors, vulnerability, and resilience: A framework for understanding and supporting the adult transitions of youth with high-incidence disabilities. *Remedial and Special Education, 24*, 16–26.

Newman, L., Wagner, M., Cameto, R., & Knokey, A. M. (April, 2009). *The post-high school outcomes of youth with disabilities up to 4 years after high school: A report from the National Longitudinal Transition Study-2 (NLTS2)* (NCSER 2009-3017). Menlo Park, CA: SRI International.

Panagos, R. J., & DuBois, D. L. (1999). Career self-efficacy development and students with learning disabilities. *Learning Disabilities Research & Practice, 14*, 25–34.

Patton, J. R. (2004). Transition issues: Processes, practices, and perspectives. In A. M. Sorrells, H. J. Reith, & P. T. Sindelar (Eds.), *Critical issues in special education: Access, diversity, and accountability*. (pp. 108–124). Boston: Pearson.

Patton, J. R., & Dunn, C. (1998). *Transition from school to young adulthood: Basic concepts and recommended practices.* Austin, TX: PRO-ED

Pliszka, S. R. (2009). *Treating ADHD and comorbid disorders.* New York: Guilford.

Poplin, M. (1988). The reductionist fallacy in learning disabilities: Replicating the past by reducing the present. *Journal of Learning Disabilities, 21*, 389–400.

Price, L., Gerber, P., & Mulligan, R. (2003). The Americans with Disabilities Act and adults with learning disabilities as employees: The realities of the workplace. *Remedial and Special Education, 24*(6), 350–358.

Price, L., Gerber, P., & Shessel, I. (2002). Adults with learning disabilities and employment: A Canadian perspective. *Thalamus: The Journal of the International Academy for Research in Learning Disabilities, 20*, 29–40.

Quinn, M. M., Rutherford, R. B., Leone, P. E., Osher, D. M., & Poirier, J. M. (2005). Youth with Disabilities in juvenile corrections: A national survey. *Exceptional Children, 71*, 339–345.

Ramasamy, R., Duffy, M. L., & Camp, J. L. Jr. (2000). Transition from school to adult life: Critical issues for Native American youth with and without learning disabilities. *Career Development for Exceptional Individuals, 23*(2), 157–171.

Raskind, M. H., Goldberg, R. J., Higgins, E. L., & Herman, K. L. (1999). Patterns of change and predictors of success in individuals with learning disabilities: Results from a twenty-year longitudinal study. *Learning Disabilities Research and Practice, 14*(1), 35–49.

Rehabilitation Act, U.S. Code 29 (1973, as amended). §794 (Section 504).

Reiff, H. B., & Gerber, P. J. (1994). Social/emotional and daily living issues for adults with learning disabilities. In P. J Gerber & H. B. Reiff (Eds.), *Learning disabilities in adulthood: Persisting problems and evolving issues* (pp. 72–81). Boston: Andover Medical Publishers.

Roessler, R., Shearin, A., & Williams, E. (2000). Three recommendations to improve transition planning in the IEP. *Journal of Vocational Special Needs Education, 22*(2), 31–36.

Rogan, L. L., & Hartman, L. D., (1990). Adult outcomes of learning disabled students ten years after initial follow-up. *Learning Disabilities Focus, 5*(2), 91–102.

Rubin, K. H., Copland, R. J., & Bowker, J.C. (2009). Social withdrawal in childhood. *Annual Review of Psychology, 60,* 141–171.

Rutherford, R. B., Bullis, M., Anderson, C., & Griller-Clark, H. (2002), Youth with disabilities in juvenile corrections: A national survey. *Exceptional Children, 71*, 339–345.

Scanlon, D. (2006). Learning disabilities and attention deficits. In K. Thies & J. Travers (Eds.), *Handbook of human development for health professionals* (pp. 307–338). Thorofare, NJ: SLACK Inc.

Schreiner, M. B. (2007) Effective self-advocacy: What students and special educators need to know. *Intervention in School and Clinic, 42*, 300–304.

Sheeber, L. B., Allen, N. B., Leve, C., Davis, B., Shortt, J. W., & Katz, L. F. (2009). Dynamics of affective experience and behavior in depressed adolescents. *Journal of Child Psychology and Psychiatry, 50*, 1419–1427.

Siperstein, G., Leffert, J., & Wenz-Gross, M. (1997). The quality of friendships between children with and without learning problems. *American Journal on Mental Retardation, 102*, 111–125.

Sitlington, P. L. (2008). Transition to life in the community. In G. Blalock, J. R. Patton, P. Kohler, & D. Bassett (Eds.), *Transition and students with learning disabilities: Facilitating the movement from school to adult life* (2nd ed., pp. 307). Austin, TX: Hammill Institute on Disabilities.

Sitlington, P. L., & Clark, G. M. (2006). *Transition education and services for adolescents with disabilities* (4th ed.). Boston, MA: Allyn & Bacon.

Skinner, M. E., & Lindstrom, B. D. (2003). Bridging the gap between high school and college: Strategies for the successful transition of students with learning disabilities. *Preventing School Failure, 47*, 132–137.

Su, C. Y., Chen, C. C., Wuang, Y. P., Lin, Y. H., & Wu, Y. Y. (2008). Neuropsychological predictors of everyday functioning in adults with intellectual disabilities. *Journal of Intellectual Disability Research, 52*, 18–28.

Suto, W. M. I., Clare, I. C. H., Holland, A. J., & Watson, P. C. (2005). Capacity to make financial decisions among people with mild intellectual disabilities. *Journal of Intellectual Disability Research, 49*, 199–209.

Tang, S. 1995. A comparison of trends in living arrangements for white and black youth. *Western Journal of Black Studies, 19*, 218–223.

Test, D. W., Fowler, C. H., Richter, S. M., White, J., Mazzotti, V., Walker, A. R. … & Kortering, L. (2009). Evidence-based practices in secondary transition. *Career Development for Exceptional individuals, 32*, 115–128.

Thompson, J. R., Fulk, B. M., & Piercy, S. W. (2000). Do individualized transition plans match the post school projections of students with learning disabilities and their parents? *Career Development for Exceptional Individuals, 23*, 3–25.

Topolski, T. D., Edwards, T. C., Patrick, D., Varley, P., Way, M. E., & Buesching, D. P. (2004). Quality of life of adolescent males with attention-deficit hyperactivity disorder. *Journal of Attention Disorders, 7,* 163–173.

Trainor, A. (2005). Self-determination perceptions and behaviors of diverse students with LD during the transition planning process. *Journal of Learning Disabilities, 38*, 233–249.

Tyler, J. H. (2002). *So you want a GED? Estimating the impact of the GED on the earnings of dropouts who seek the credential.* NCSALL Research Brief. Boston, MA: National Center for the Study of Adult Learning and Literacy. ERIC Documents Reproduction Services, no. ED471 978.

U.S. Department of Education, Office of special Education and Rehabilitative Services. (2006). *26th annual report to Congress on the implementation of the Individuals with Disabilities Education Act*, 2004, vol. 1. Washington, DC: U.S. Department of Education, Author.

Verdonschot, M. M. L., de Witte, L. P., Reichraht, E., Buntinx, W. H. E., Curfs, L. M. G. (2009). Community participation of people with an intellectual disability: A review of empirical findings. *Journal of Intellectual Disability Research, 53*, 303–318.

Wagner, M., Newman, L., Cameto, R., & Levine, P. (2005). *Changes over time in the early post school outcomes of youth with disabilities.* Menlo Park, CA: SRI International.

Wagner, M., & Blackorby, J. (1996). Transition from high school to work or college: How special education students fare. *Future of Children*, 6(1), 103–120.

Wehmeyer, M. L. (2007). Self-determination. In M. F. Giangreco & M. B. Doyle (Eds.), *Quick-guides to inclusion: Ideas for educating students with disabilities* (2nd ed., pp. 61–74). Baltimore Paul H. Brookes.

Wehmeyer, M. L., Palmer, S. B., Agran, M., Mithaug, D. E., &. Martin, J. E. (2000). Promoting causal agency: The self-determined learning model of instruction. *Exceptional Children, 66*, 439–453.

Werner, E. E. (1993). Risk and resilience in individuals with learning disabilities: Lessons learned from the Kauai longitudinal study. *Learning Disabilities Research & Practice, 8,* 28–35.

Will, M. (1984). *OSERS programming for adults with disabilities: Bridges from school to working life*. Washington, DC: Office of Special Education and Rehabilitative Services.

Williams, J. M., & O'Leary, E. (2001). What we've learned and where we go from here. *Career Development for Exceptional Individuals, 24*, 511–71.

Section X

Transition of Students with Low Incidence Disabilities

Section Editor: ***M. Sherril Moon***
University of Maryland

The purpose of transition and educational service provision for students 16 years of age and older is to prepare them for employment, independent living, postsecondary education, and general community participation. In fact, the Individuals with Disabilities Education Improvement Act of 2004 (P.L.108-446) defines transition as a coordinated set of meaningful activities specified in measurable individualized education plan (IEP) goals. The goals are designed to facilitate movement to postschool activities, which may include postsecondary education, vocational education, continuing and adult education, integrated employment (including supported employment), independent living, and community participation. The services must be based on a student's needs, preferences, and interests, and can include instruction, related services, community experiences, the acquisition of daily living skills, and functional evaluation (IDEA, 2004).

These latest amendments to IDEA also mandate that multiple agencies outside the school system should be invited to formulate IEP goals if the school cannot provide a service such as supported employment or independent living. This involvement of other service agencies becomes particularly important for students with low incidence disabilities, for whom these two areas are usually priorities (Wehman, 2006). Finally, the 2004 law makes transition planning even more critical as it mandates that all states report data to the federal Office of Special Education (OSEP) on Indicators 13 and 14 of IDEA. Indicator 13 involves the percentage of a state's students over age 16 who have measurable transition goals related to accessing postsecondary education. Indicator 14 requires states to collect data on the percentage of students 16 years of age and older who have IEPs and competitively employed or enrolled in postsecondary education programs within one year of leaving school (Sitlington, Neubert, & Clark, 2009). Obviously, the mandate for helping students with disabilities find meaningful employment and further education beyond high school is greater than ever.

Although transition practices must be implemented for all older students with IEPs, we focus in this section on transition age (ages 16–21) students with low incidence or more severe disabilities. Generally, these are students with such disabilities as intellectual disabilities (mental retardation), autism, deaf blindness, multiple disabilities, and severe traumatic brain injury. The term *low incidence* (LI) is used because less than 1% of the general population typically has severe disabilities (Giangreco, 2006). TASH (2000) describes severe disabilities as those causing a person to require support in major life activities needed to participate in integrated community life such as inclusive work opportunities and to enjoy a quality of life similar to all citizens. For purposes of this section, we use a definition suggested by experts on postsecondary education for students with LI disabilities (Grigal & Hart, 2010; Grigal, Neubert, & Moon, 2005). These are students who typically fall into one of the IDEA categories listed above and receive education funded by public schools through age 21, take the state's alternative high school assessment, leave school with some kind of alternative diploma or certificate, and need significant and ongoing support to access integrated community employment, postsecondary education, or independent living situations similar to other citizens without disabilities.

The literature on best transition practices for students with LI disabilities emphasizes the need to balance strategies for inclusion and access to the general education curriculum with providing functional and community-based instruction, teaching self- determination skills, working in real jobs (including paid work before graduation), and interagency collaboration with state agencies and community organizations that pay for and provide work, community living, general community access, and social/recreational options (Inge & Moon, 2006; Wehman, 2006). Most of the research in this area has dealt with integrated employment training and outcomes for students and young adults with LI disabilities, but there is a growing demand from advocates and families to look at a wider array of outcomes, including community living options. Our purpose in this section is to provide information on both of these important transition outcomes—integrated employment and community living.

Our first chapter describes the integrated employment options that should result from effective transition planning. These options include supported employment, customized employment, and supported self-employment. We stress that achieving any of these integrated employment outcomes requires educators and families to collaborate with many eligibility-driven agencies (the parties that *fund* services) and nonprofit community agencies (the parties that *provide* most services). This can be an overwhelming task for educators and families who have been working for many years within one entitled service system, special education. The information within this chapter on each of the different service systems can serve as a starting point for transition teams in understanding how to collaborate with all these agencies. Finally, we briefly discuss the new postsecondary education (PSE) options that are being developed across the country for transition age students with LI disabilities. Students who get to complete their special education programs on college campuses are in an excellent position to not only get integrated employment training but to also participate in academic and social activities with their same age peers. This is probably the ultimate transition service option for older students with LI disabilities.

The second chapter describes community living options that have historically been available to citizens with disabilities and those that should now be available as part of the supported living spectrum. Several case studies are presented that show just how individualized supported living can be. In the final part of this chapter, we provide educators with specific techniques for teaching self-determination skills and community participation activities that promote independent living.

It should be obvious after reading these chapters that the transition of students with LI disabilities to appropriate employment and community living options that are desired by the student and supported by local, state, and federal sources is an extremely complex process. This transition process must begin early, before the age of 16 whenever possible, and there must include ongoing collaboration between the student, family, and school personnel with a myriad of funding agencies and service providers. As well, students must learn self-determination skills and become actively involved in community participation and real job training experiences before exiting public school.

References

Individuals with Disabilities Education Improvement Act of 2004, 20 U.S.C. *SS* 1400 et seq. (2004).

Inge, K. J., & Moon, M. S. (2006). Vocational preparation and transition. In M. E. Snell & F. Brown (Eds.), *Instruction of students with severe disabilities* (6th ed., pp. 569–609). Upper Saddle River, NJ: Pearson.

Giangreco, M. F. (2006). Foundational concepts and practices for educating students with severe disabilities. In M. E. Snell & F. Brown (Eds.), *Instruction of students with severe disabilities* (6th ed., pp. 1–27). Upper Saddle River, NJ: Pearson.

Grigal, M., & Hart, D. (2010). *Think college: Postsecondary education for students with intellectual disabilities.* Baltimore: Paul H. Brookes.

Grigal, M., Neubert, D. A., & Moon, M. S. (2005). *Transition services for students with significant disabilities in college and community settings: Strategies for planning, implementation and, evaluation.* Austin, TX: Pro-Ed.

Sitltington, P., Neubert, D. A., & Clark, G. M. (2009). *Transition education and services for students with disabilities.* Baltimore: Paul H. Brookes.

TASH. (2000). TASH resolution on the people for whom TASH advocates. Retrieved July 18, 2003, from http://www.tash.org/resolution/res02advocate.htm

Wehman, P. (2006). *Life beyond the classroom: Transition strategies for young people with disabilities* (4th ed.). Baltimore: Paul H. Brookes.

46

Preparing Students with Low Incidence Disabilities to Work in the Community

Katherine J. Inge
Virginia Commonwealth University

M. Sherril Moon
University of Maryland

The statistics point to the challenges faced by transition age youth with disabilities related to achieving employment outcomes. For example, youth with disabilities are twice as likely to drop out of high school (21% vs. 10%) than their non-disabled peers (National Organization on Disability, 2004). The National Longitudinal Transition Study reported that 4 out of 10 out-of-school youth with disabilities interviewed were employed, which is substantially below the employment rate among same-age out-of-school youth in the general population (Wagner, Newman, Cameto, Garza, & Levine, 2005). Employment rates for youth with intellectual disabilities or with multiple disabilities have been reported in the 15% to 25% range for those who have been out of school for less than 2 years (McGlashing-Johnson, Agran, Sitlington, Cavin, & Wehymeyer, 2003).

The national picture of where individuals with disabilities are employed postgraduation is alarming (Boeltzig, Timmons, & Butterworth, in press; Migliore & Butterworth, 2008) as most are either unemployed or underemployed in stereotypical jobs that result in low wages, no benefits, and no opportunity for career advancement (Wehman, Revell, & Brooke, 2003). A national study of the vocational outcomes for adults with developmental disabilities revealed that only 18% were employed in integrated jobs. Forty-one percent were underemployed in facility-based programs, 9% worked in congregate or group employment placements such as enclaves or mobile work crews, and the remaining 33% spent their days in non-work programs such as activity centers or habilitation programs (Migliore & Butterworth, 2008). If individuals earn wages in the facility-based or congregate placements, they typically earn a "special minimum wage" or subminimum wage under Section 14 (c) of the Fair Labor Standard Act (Inge et al., 2009).

The U.S. Department of Labor's Wage and Hour Division enforces the provisions of the Fair Labor Standards Act (FLSA), Section 14 (c) that allows workers with disabilities to be paid a "special minimum wage" or "commensurate wage." A commensurate wage is based on the productivity of experienced workers who do not have disabilities performing essentially the same type, quality, and quantity of work" (DOL, 2009; ESA, Title 29, Part 525.12). Consider an individual with a low incidence (LI) disability working in a facility-based, sheltered workshop that is able to produce at 20% of an experienced worker's productivity. The current statutory minimum wage as of July 24, 2009, is $7.25 an hour. Therefore, the commensurate or subminimum wage for the individual working at 20% productivity would be approximately $1.45 an hour.

Individuals with disabilities can also be paid a piece rate under the FLSA. The piece rate is based "on the standard production rates (number of units an experienced worker not disabled for the work is expected to produce per hour) and the prevailing industry wage rate paid experienced nondisabled workers in the vicinity for essentially the same type and quality of work or for work requiring similar skill. Prevailing industry wage rate divided by the standard number of units per hour equals the piece rate" [ESA, Title 29, Part 525.12, (h)(1)(i)]. For instance, if time studies show that workers without disabilities are able to produce 100 widgets in a "50-minute" hour, allowing 10 minutes per hour for personal time and fatigue, the piece rate is $0.0725 ($7.25 divided by 100 = $0.0725) (DOL, 2008). The individual with a LI disability who packages 12 widgets in an hour would earn 87 cents when paid a piece rate using this example.

A worker with a disability under the FLSA is defined as "an individual, whose earning or productive capacity is impaired by a physical or mental disability, including those relating to age or injury, for the work to be performed.

Disabilities which may affect earning or productive capacity include blindness, mental illness, mental retardation, cerebral palsy, alcoholism, and drug addiction" [ESA, 29 CFR Part 525.3, (d)]. Note the definition includes the statement for the "work to be performed."

Given this definition and information on how a special commensurate wage is calculated, consider an individual with LI disabilities who has a significant cognitive disability and cerebral palsy and is paid to package widgets. This person with disabilities almost certainly will package widgets at a lower production rate than a worker without disabilities. If the only work that is available within the facility-based, sheltered workshop is packaging widgets under a 14 (c) Certificate, the person obviously will make subminimum wages.

However, consider a transition-age youth with LI disabilities whose job was customized and negotiated for him based on his interests, skills, and abilities. This individual demonstrated a desire to work in an office setting where he could wear a suit like other businessmen. His employment specialist saw several job openings listed at a business that sold equipment. She visited the company and asked if employees were paid overtime to complete any specific job duties and found a "hidden" job opportunity. The receptionist for the business was being paid overtime to compile sales binders for the sales representatives. A proposal was developed showing that it would be more cost effective to pay the individual with a disability minimum wage to compile the binders vs. overtime to the receptionist. The completion of a time study was never discussed or considered; the company benefited as well as the worker with a disability. If the effort had been placed on determining how many binders the individual with a disability could complete in an hour vs. a worker without disabilities, this individual would have been paid subminimum wage. Instead, effort was placed on demonstrating how the worker brought value to the company, saving money, while meeting the needs of the business and providing an integrated employment opportunity for the individual with a low incidence disability (Inge, 2001).

Integrated Employment

The individual described is not an isolated example of how youth with LI disabilities can achieve integrated employment outcomes. How to locate and negotiate jobs to meet the unique interests and abilities of individuals with disabilities resulting in integrated employment outcomes has been cited in many publications (Inge 2001; Inge, Strobel, Wehman, Todd, & Targett, 2000; Luecking, Fabian, Tilson, 2004; Nietupski & Hamre-Nietupski 2001), but first mentioned by Bissonnette (1994). Supported employment (Wehman, Inge, Revell, Brooke, 2007), customized employment (Citron et al., 2008; Griffin, Hammis, Geary, & Sullivan, 2008), and supported self-employment (Griffin, Brooks-Lane, Hammis, & Crandell, 2007; Griffin & Hammis, 2003) have assisted thousands of individuals with significant disabilities in achieving integrated employment outcomes.

There are a number of quality characteristics or indicators of integrated employment that school personnel must be familiar with in order to facilitate successful postschool employment outcomes for students with LI disabilities (Brown, Shiraga, & Kessler, 2006; Inge & Moon, 2006; Moon, Simonsen, & Neubert, 2011; Wehman, Revell, & Brooke, 2003; White & Weiner, 2004). These include providing community-based instruction including travel training, teaching self-management skills such as hygiene and toileting, providing authentic vocational assessment data to adult agencies, decreasing one on one instruction in the community, making linkages with state agencies such as the developmental disabilities case management agency and nonprofit adult agencies to determine who will be paying for and providing employment support, and finding paid employment that the student prefers before graduation. The next two sections of this chapter will acquaint the reader with the current forms of integrated employment that are most commonly supported in states across the country and describe the linkages that parents and educators must understand in order for students with low incidence disabilities to obtain and maintain employment as they transition from school.

Supported Employment

Supported employment is intended for individuals with disabilities such as students with LI disabilities who traditionally are unemployed, underemployed, or who have difficulty maintaining employment due to significant disabilities. The individual works in a competitive job of the individual's choice in an integrated work setting earning at least minimum wages commensurate with other employees of the business who do not have disabilities (Wehman et al., 2007). There are a number of unique features to supported employment, but most importantly all individuals with disabilities are considered employable, and supports are provided through a "place and train" approach. In other words, each person with a low incidence disability should be considered ready to work in a community business if given support to secure a job that matches his or her skills, interests, and unique support needs. These individualized supports are provided throughout the process of assisting the individual to find and maintain employment.

The first step involves assisting the individual in identifying an employment or career goal, which has been referred to as the "discovery" process, an "individual profile," and/or a "vocational profile" (Griffin, Hammis, & Geary, 2009; Wehman et al., 2007). This step focuses on getting to know the job seeker's strengths, interests, and abilities in order to match the person to a competitive job. This may include interviewing the individual and his or her support team, using person-centered planning strategies, as well as conducting on the job situational assessments to allow the individual to briefly experience job types that he/she has expressed an interest in doing

(Inge, Targett, & Armstrong, 2007). For transition age youth, information from community-based instruction also can be used to determine the person's interests and strengths for an integrated job in the community. A recent study in Maryland indicated that providers of supported employment wanted specific information on community employment experiences of students with LI disabilities so they would know about skill level and job preferences as they determined the eligibility of these students for entry into their agency (Moon et al., 2009).

The customer profile is used by the employment specialist or job coach to assist the person in finding employment during the job development and placement components of supported employment (Targett & Wehman, 2009). The individual's employment specialist meets with employers in the community that potentially have jobs that reflect the individual's interests and abilities. The goal is to find a job that meets the needs of the individual as well as the needs of a business.

At this point, the individual with a LI disability may not possess all of the skills required for the job selected. However, he or she has the ability to learn the skills once training is provided in the actual work setting. In other words, supported employment assumes a best match between the individual and the job once on-site work supports and training are provided. These workplace supports are provided until the person performs the job duties independently to the employer's satisfaction.

Once the worker with a disability is stable and independently performing his or her job duties, the on-going supports phase of supported employment begins. These supports are provided throughout the course of employment and have also been referred to as follow-along services. The level and intensity of the supports vary depending on the individual's needs. The federal regulations for supported employment state that a minimum of twice monthly follow-along services should be provided to the individual either at or away from the job site. This unique feature of supported employment makes it possible for individuals with high support needs, such as those with low incidence disabilities, to be placed into inclusive employment settings. Follow-along supports can include additional skills training, work-related social skills training, transportation, or other support needs that the individual has related to job retention. These supports can be provided by coworkers, family members, friends, and/or the employment specialist (Wehman et al., 2007).

In addition to individual supported employment placements, some community nonprofit agencies may offer group supported employment placements to include mobile work crews and enclaves. The employees with disabilities in these group options are provided continual support and supervision from agency staff that provides services to individuals with disabilities. An enclave typically includes a group of employees who have disabilities that work together on a job site clustered together in the same location. Mobile work crews are defined as a group of employees with disabilities who typically move to different/multiple work sites. Typically, individuals with disabilities that are placed into enclaves or mobile work crews are not employees of the business. They receive their wages through the human service organization, and many make less than minimum wages.

A 2004–05 individual outcomes survey conducted by the Institute for Community Inclusion, University of Massachusetts Boston, found that about 80% of those working in group supported employment were on the payroll of the provider (personal communication John Butterworth, August 4, 2009). Another survey conducted by Virginia Commonwealth University and the Institute for Community Inclusion asked respondents to report the wages earned by individuals in group options. Of those individuals supported in mobile work crews, approximately 59% received subminimum wage. Of those supported in enclaves, 63% received subminimum wage (Inge et al., 2009). The other primary concern related to group supported employment placements is the limited employment choice as to type of work performed. Jobs typically are based on the local labor market economy and not selected on the workers' preferences and interests. This type of placement should be carefully analyzed prior to selecting this as an employment outcome for students with LI disabilities. It should also not be the only type of work training a student receives while in school. Customized employment and self-employment options should be considered to meet the intensive support needs as opposed to placing a student into a group placement if a student is not able to achieve an integrated employment outcome through individual supported employment services.

Funding for supported employment services was first made available through the Rehabilitation Act Amendments of 1986 (PL 99-506), as Supported Employment Formula Grants to state vocational rehabilitation agencies in Title VI, Part C. This money can only be used to pay for supported employment services, and the Rehabilitation Act Amendments were reauthorized most recently as part of the Workforce Amendments Act of 1998 (PL105-220). Typically, the initial job placement and support is funded through vocational rehabilitation and the on-going supports must come from other federal or state agencies such as developmental disabilities case management and Medicaid Waivers. A community nonprofit agency, or the person, in the case of a Medicaid Waiver, gets these funds to pay job coaches to provide the ongoing training. A student and her family must apply for and receive both the funding and the support services, and none of this is an entitlement. In all states, there are waiting lists for the funding for supported employment (Moon et al., 2011).

Customized Employment

Sometimes, individuals with LI disabilities are not able to complete all the essential functions associated with posted job openings. Employment specialists from supported employment agencies who rely on locating positions by using traditional sources (e.g., classified ads, postings on job boards, Internet sites) may become frustrated and discouraged when they cannot find jobs for individuals with the most significant disabilities. Unfortunately, professionals may conclude that these individuals are not "qualified" applicants for competitive employment, because they cannot complete all the job duties associated with an existing position (Inge, 2005).

An approach to finding community jobs that has proven successful for individuals with the most significant disabilities including those with low incidence disabilities is customized employment. Customized employment begins with an individualized determination of the strengths, needs, and interests of the job candidate with a disability. Once the individual's job goals are established, potential businesses are identified by networking with family, friends, and neighbors, and contacting employers. Employers targeted on behalf of the individual are selected based on a match between the job seeker's expressed interests, skills, and type or nature of work performed at the company. A personal representative or employment specialist meets with the company to negotiate job duties that can be redistributed and tailored to the job seeker's unique skills and abilities that also meet the needs of the business (Callahan & Rogan, 2004; Wehman, et al., 2007). In other words, customized employment results in a negotiated position for which the individual with a low incidence disability is qualified.

The term "customized employment" first was used by the Office of Disability Employment Policy (ODEP) within the U. S. Department of Labor in 2001. Customized employment was conceived as a way for One Stop Career Centers to welcome and serve anyone who has unique circumstances that affect employment including individuals with disabilities. Customized employment has been defined as "the voluntary negotiation of a personalized employment relationship between a specific individual and an employer. The *Federal Register* (2002) defined customized employment as the following:

> Customized employment means individualizing the employment relationship between employees and employers in ways that meet the needs of both. It is based on an individualized determination of the strengths, needs, and interests of the person with a disability, and is also designed to meet the specific needs of the employer. It may include employment developed through job carving, self-employment, or entrepreneurial initiatives, or other job development or restructuring strategies that result in job responsibilities being customized and individually negotiated to fit the needs of individuals with a disability. Customized employment assumes the provision of reasonable accommodations and supports necessary for the individual to perform the functions of a job that is individually negotiated and developed. (p. 43156)

While there are many similarities between supported and customized employment, customized employment places an emphasis on individualization and negotiation of the job match. Customized employment does not include group placements nor does it promote or include payment of sub-minimum wages. Callahan stated that customized employment is "much like supported employment" and is the "progeny" of supported employment (Callahan, 2004). Some of the critical components of both include (1) customer choice, (b) the belief that individuals should be viewed from an abilities vs. disability perspective, (c) workplace integration, (d) jobs / careers of choice, (e) competitive/prevailing wages, and (f) customer directed services with individualized workplace supports (Wehman et al., 2007).

One unique customized employment strategy is resource ownership. This strategy involves identifying a resource that an individual with a disability can offer to a company. Resource ownership is an investment similar to earning a college degree, learning a trade, or buying a business. Resource ownership implies a shared risk between the worker and the employer (and perhaps the funding agency), and a partnering approach to job negotiation and creation (Griffin et al., 2008).

The individual purchases and subsequently owns the equipment or property and is paid wages by the business where he or she is hired. If the individual moves to another position, the resource still belongs to the individual or the funding agency that purchased the resource. Resource ownership can empower a person with a disability and provide an advantage when he or she is negotiating a customized position with an employer. Ultimately, resource ownership might lead to self-employment, and an individual eventually owning his or her business.

Consider a young woman named Marie (Brooks-Lane, Hutcheson, & Revell, 2005). She and her support team determined that a wage job with resource ownership may result in a customized employment outcome that would match Marie's employment goals. The path leading to this decision involved matching her passions with job choices through a non-traditional, community-based vocational profile; person-centered employment planning; financial analysis of benefits and potential income; and including Vocational Rehabilitation Services in the process.

As a result, Marie is employed in a hair salon in her community doing work tasks of her choice to include cleaning, organizing, and sweeping. The resources that Marie purchased included a washer and dryer, as well as a hair dryer chair. Marie is responsible for washing, drying, and folding the salon towels and retuning these clean towels to the cabinets for the stylists' use. Marie owns these resources that she brought to the job with her and that she used to negotiate specific conditions for her employment that were important to her. Marie now has choices that she never had before, which includes remaining with this business. The money came from an Individual Training Account through a demonstration grant funded by the Office of Disability Employment Policy. At some future point she may choose another salon, should that be to her advantage; or exploring self-employment; however, these resources remain with her.

Self-Employment

Self-employment is increasingly recognized as a viable employment option for people with disabilities (Doyel, 2002; Griffin & Hammis, 2003). Much of the initial work originated at the University of Montana Adult Community Services and Supports Department. These first successful examples and case studies have impacted the attitudes of professionals resulting in more successful examples of self-employment.

For many individuals, particularly those who have LI disabilities, self-employment often has not been viewed as an attainable goal (Revell, Smith, & Inge, 2009). One reason that self-employment has not been seen as a viable employment outcome is the perception that anyone owning a business must be able to run the company independently. However, most business owners without disabilities are "interdependent" on others to assist them in the day to day operations (Inge, Targett, & Griffin, 2006). For instance, an accountant is hired to maintain the company books, or sales staff is used to market and distribute products. Business owners with disabilities can hire staff to assist with business operations and with other supports just like any other business owner without disabilities. In other words, individuals with LI disabilities will require customized supports to become successfully self-employed (Griffin et al., 2007). What is important is to identify each individual's strengths and talents as well as support needs while assembling a team to facilitate self-employment. The basics are a business plan, a solid marketing plan, management skills, and capital. Where the entrepreneur can lead the way and where support is needed will vary from one person to another. Some individuals may need more assistance with start-up activities, others may need support with operations, still others may need ongoing assistance using a variety of workplace supports. What is crucial is to provide customized supports to assist the person in moving forward with business ownership (Inge et al., 2006).

Some people with disabilities will consider self-employment as a career option due to a lack of available employment opportunities in the community. Other individuals or the professionals and family members supporting them may think that a business could be started based on the individual's hobbies. For instance, consider a young woman who makes beaded necklaces as a hobby (Inge et al., 2006). Beaded necklaces are currently popular, and there are many customers buying beaded jewelry. But, who will be this business' customers? Will the individual market directly to her community through arts and craft shows or flea markets? Or, would she market her items through an existing business such as the local department store, an art studio, or museum gift shop. The next thing to consider is who is the competition? Is there something unique about the individual's designs or quality that no one else is producing? Or, can she produce and sell jewelry to the competition if they can't keep up with their demand? Is the competition in the community market going to over shadow the product so that there are limited sales? In considering the person's capabilities, how much can she produce? Is this sufficient to meet the individual's employment goals?

Certainly producing beaded necklaces and testing the various markets would help in determining who the customers are, how much they might pay, and if income can be generated to sustain the business. It might be that the business begins small and gradually grows. Making any items for personal use is certainly different than selling them for profit.

There are a number of resources that a person can access to start a small business (Griffin et al., 2007; Webb, Taylor, & Hammis, 2009). Vocational rehabilitation can fund self-employment if this is the individual's employment goal (Revell et al., 2009). To be eligible for self-employment assistance, an individual must first qualify for vocational rehabilitation services. In addition, a community's local One Stop funded through the Workforce Investment Act (WIA) can provide funds to assist in business start-up including writing business plans (Griffin & Hammis, 2008). Individual training accounts from a One Stop may be used for purchasing services or resources to start a small business. Anyone with or without a disability can access the services. More information on how to access vocational rehabilitation services and those that may be available from a One Stop Center can be found later in this chapter.

In other cases, families have contributed to the capital needed for an individual to start a small business, and, of course, there are banks and small business loans. In addition, an individual can use Social Security Work Incentives such as a Plan for Achieving Self-Support to fund the business (Webb et al., 2009). Property Essential for Self-Support is another work incentive for people receiving Supplemental Security Income (SSI). It allows a business owner to have resources beyond that $2,000 limit under SSI, which restricts people in being able to build equity in a business. In some states, Medicaid Waivers can be used to fund the support needs that an individual with a low incidence disability needs to start a business (Sullivan & Katz, 2008).

There is no easy or quick decision as to whether an individual should start a business. Fortunately, there now are many references available on how to assist an individual with a significant disability to become self-employed. These references should be used to determine if self-employment is the desired employment outcome of an individual with a low incidence disability. The first step is to determine if the individual is interested in self-employment as the employment goal and then to complete a business plan and determine the feasibility of the proposed business (Griffin et al., 2007).

Funding and Services from Federal, State, and Nonprofit Agencies

Achieving quality employment outcomes will depend on formal transition planning between the family and school with many agencies and businesses. Schools must take the lead in coordinating the planning process and providing initial case management and skills training. However, the process cannot be completed until other groups or individuals assume the responsibility for funding, follow-up services and continual case management (Inge & Moon, 2006; Wehman, 2007). Many families do not realize that eligibility is not automatic for any adult service. First, their son or daughter must apply and qualify for funding for adult services (e.g., vocational rehabilitation services, social security, Medicaid Waiver, and state developmental disabilities monies in a particular category such as residential, vocational, respite, family services.) Then, the person must be accepted by an agency who provides the service he or she wants. The exact mix of services will vary depending upon the needs of each student and employment goals, the nature of the individual's disability, the economic resources of the community, and the eligibility requirements among the various potential community resources (Wittenberg, Golden, & Fishman, 2002). The complex process of qualifying for funding and then applying for the services is a process that must be facilitated prior to students leaving the public school system by including this planning as part of the IEP process once a student is 14 years old (Brown et al., 2006; Moon et al., 2011). A primary case manager or service resource coordinator should be identified in the IEP process. This person, who is often part of the state developmental disabilities case management agency when a person has a LI disability (Revell & Miller, 2009) can make sure the linkages between family, school, and adult support services are continually in place. What follows is a brief description of the state and federal funding agencies or programs and state or local nonprofit agencies that educators, students, and families must tap to get integrated work.

State Vocational Rehabilitation Services

The Rehabilitation Act of 1973, as amended in 1998, provides states federal grants to operate comprehensive programs of vocational rehabilitation (VR) services for individuals with disabilities (Public Law 105-202). Vocational rehabilitation can provide crucial resources for students with LI disabilities during and after leaving the school system. Some of the employment services and supports that students with LI disabilities may access include, but are not limited to (a) vocational assessment to determine eligibility for services, (b) vocational counseling, (c) job placement, (d) on-the-job training, (e) personal assistance services, (f) assistive technology services and devices, (g) supported employment, and (h) self-employment. Before an individual can receive VR services, an application must be completed. This application is reviewed and approved (or denied) by a VR counselor. To quality for VR services, a student must have a disability that is an impairment to employment. In addition, there must be the expectation that the individual will achieve an employment outcome with the provision of vocational rehabilitation services (Revell & Miller, 2009).

An important change in the vocational rehabilitation system occurred in 2001. The Rehabilitation Services Administration (RSA) amended its regulations governing state vocational rehabilitation programs to redefine the term "employment outcome" to mean "an individual with a disability working in an integrated setting" (*Federal Register*, 2001, p. 4382). For decades, extended employment (formerly sheltered employment) was an acceptable outcome for individuals receiving VR services. The 2001 definition removes this type of employment as an approved outcome, because extended/sheltered employment uses non-integrated work settings. This is important information to consider if seeking funding from the VR service delivery system for a student with LI disability. Sheltered employment is no longer being provided by many community nonprofit agencies, which is all the more reason that students with LI receive real job community-based employment assessment and training before leaving school. Many of the old models that were available are just not there anymore.

Once the student is determined eligible, an individualized plan for employment (IPE) is developed with the student by the VR counselor in collaboration with the family and transition team. VR may provide direct counseling services to the individual as well as fund additional services from other community agencies. The student's employment goal is included in the IPE as well as any services and supports that are needed to meet the goal. The VR counselor serves as the case manager and provides coordination for the services that have been identified in the IPE. For instance, an individual with a LI disability requires assistive technology (AT) services and devices to achieve his or her IPE employment goal. His or her VR counselor may pay for a rehabilitation engineer, occupational, and/or physical therapist to provide the services as well as purchase the device from an AT vendor. If the individual then requires on-the-job support to learn how to use the device for work, VR may pay for a community rehabilitation program to provide the on-the-job training on a short-term basis.

VR services are time limited. Once the individual reaches the employment goal, his or her case is closed, which can occur after a minimum of 90 days of employment. The nature of time-limited services can sometimes be a barrier for individuals with LI disabilities, since it limits the time that VR can fund and provide services. Once he or she is stable in employment and the VR case is closed, follow-along supports must be provided by another agency, usually the state development disabilities case management agency or a Medicaid Waiver. Therefore, before leaving school, the transition team must see that the student apply for and be accepted by both the VR agency and a long term funder. In most cases, the long term funding is more important, and in many states long-term support provides both the initial and continuous support (Moon et al., 2011).

Unfortunately, some students with LI disabilities may be identified as not able to achieve an employment outcome and be denied services. However, the Rehabilitation Act stipulates that there must be "clear and convincing evidence" that a person cannot benefit before vocational rehabilitation services can be denied. One way to facilitate eligibility is to provide VR with existing data to include reports from community-based vocational training experiences and paid work experiences prior to graduation. Students will then have resumes and references from previous and/or current employers to demonstrate the feasibility of employment outcomes (Inge & Moon, 2006). Transition teams must apply for VR services as soon as possible, at age 16 or 1 year before school exit, in most states. If services are denied, the student or his/her advocate also can ask for a trial work experience to assist in demonstrating that the student can benefit. Trial work experiences are experiences "in which the individual is provided appropriate supports and training" to determine eligibility for services. The law states as follows:

> In making the demonstration required under subparagraph (A), the designated State unit shall explore the individual's abilities, capabilities, and capacity to perform in work situations, through the use of trial work experiences with appropriate supports provided through the designated State unit, except under limited circumstances when an individual can not take advantage of such experiences. Such experiences shall be of sufficient variety and over a sufficient period of time to determine the eligibility of the individual or to determine the existence of clear and convincing evidence that the individual is incapable of benefiting in terms of an employment outcome from vocational rehabilitation services due to the severity of the disability of the individual. (Workforce Investment Act, 1998)

If a student has trouble accessing VR services, she can get in touch with the state Client Assistance Program (CAP), the national directory for state VR agencies and CAPs can be found at http://www.jan.wvu.edu/cgi-win/TypeQuery.exe?902 and http://www.jan.wvu.edu/cgi-win/TypeQuery.exe?039.

One Stop Career Centers

One Stop Career Centers were established to bring together many employment services under one roof to provide assistance to job seekers with and without disabilities. Established by the Workforce Investment Act (WIA) of 1998, the centers offer core services to anyone in a community who needs assistance in finding a job. One of the core principles of the WIA is to provide universal access to services by "giving all Americans [including those with disabilities] access to comprehensive services, information and resources that can help them in achieving their career goals" (Workforce Investment Act, 2004, p. 18,629). The intent is to provide access to a network of programs and services within a central location. Some of the cores services may include work skills exploration; free access to computers, telephones, fax and copy machines; searches for jobs and training; access to job banks or listings of available jobs; resume development; job search skills training; interview techniques workshops, referrals to an employer with job openings.

Individual Training Accounts. In addition to core services, One Stop Career Centers also provide intensive services that are funded through WIA to individuals who qualify. One of these intensive services is an Individual Training Account (ITAs), which can provide funding for educational or vocational training. Individuals with or without disabilities who qualify can purchase approved training that is offered by providers on a state's approved list. Youth with LD should consider this funding source if training and education is needed beyond what is paid for by other adult service agencies.

Disability Program Navigator (DPN). The Social Security Administration (SSA) and the Department of Labor (DOL), Employment and Training Administration (ETA), jointly established the Disability Program Navigator (DPN) position to train One-Stop staff to help individuals with disabilities access and navigate the programs and supports needed to maintain and gain employment. Currently, there are Navigators throughout local workforce investment areas in 45 states plus the District of Columbia and Puerto Rico (http://www.doleta.gov/disability/ for a list of DPN States/contact).

The goals of the DPN program include: facilitation of integrated, seamless and comprehensive services to persons with disabilities in One-Stop Career Centers; improving access to programs and services; facilitating linkages to the employer community and developing demand responsive strategies to meet recruitment and retention needs; increasing employment and self-sufficiency for Social Security disability beneficiaries and other people with disabilities; developing new and ongoing partnerships to leverage resources; and creating systemic change.

While Navigators are not case managers, they work to expand the capacity of the One-Stop Career Center to serve customers with disabilities and conduct outreach to organizations that serve people with disabilities. Navigators also can facilitate the transition of in and out of school youth with disabilities to assist in obtaining employment and economic self-sufficiency. Many Navigators are developing cross agency "integrated resource teams" to blend and braid resources around an individual job seeker's employment needs (SSA, 2009).

State Developmental Disabilities Case Management Agencies (DDA) and Medicaid Waivers

Individuals with LD should be eligible for services from state developmental disabilities case management agencies (DDA). In some states, such as Virginia, this agency at the local level is referred to as community service boards (CSB). This is the primary state funding source for most services to people with disabilities including residential services, employment, and individual family services. It is a primary source of long-term funding for supported employment, and it is the agency that provides case management or resource coordination for all services once a person exits special education. Funds for DDA services are determined by state legislatures, and there is hardly ever enough money in any state to meet the demand (Braddock, Hemp, & Rizzolo, 2008). It is critical that students be referred for services early in life, long before the transition years, because a family can get funding for less expensive programs such as respite care and behavioral support at home. The waiting lists for residential and employment funding are in the thousands in most states. The earlier a student is accepted for DDA services, the sooner a case manager or resource coordinator assigned by local or regional offices of DDA, can start helping the school and family identify possible providers (nonprofit agencies in most cases) of integrated employment should funding come through. DDA case managers should be part of every IEP team for transition age students as they are typically the best connector to services outside the school. They often know the family better than anyone, and there is no age limit on a person for whom they can advocate or no limitation on the kind of service they can try to find. They usually know the nonprofit network of service providers from which almost all adult services originate better than anyone else (Moon et al., 2011). For a list of state DDA agencies, from which you could navigate to find case management offices and the types of services funded, go to http://www.nasddds.org/MemberAgencies/index.shtml.

DDA case managers usually are the state appointed person to help families qualify for a Medicaid Waiver, the most secure long term funding resource for integrated employment options (Braddock et al., 2008). Medicaid is a state-federal program that provides health care to eligible low income individuals. When states participate in Medicaid, the state contributes part of the funding, and the federal government contributes part. This program administers the Medicaid Waiver program in each state which establishes its own requirements (Sullivan & Katz, 2008). The specific services that are available and whether a person with a disability is eligible for these services is state specific and will vary depending on where an individual lives in the United States. Eligibility in one state does not transfer to another.

The three most common Medicaid Waivers are Research and Demonstration Waivers, Freedom of Choice Waivers, and Home and Community-based Services Waivers (Braddock et al., 2008). Many states are creating Waivers to fund integrated employment and residential programs for young adults, just exiting school. The services in each Waiver must assist individuals to live in the community rather than in Medicaid funded institutional settings, such as nursing homes or institutions for people with intellectual/developmental disabilities. If a state chooses to offer Waivers, the state must submit a request to the Centers for Medicare and Medicaid Services (CMS) in the U.S. Department of Health and Human Services. Each Waiver request involves asking CMS to "waive" some of the rules that usually apply to Medicaid so the state can create a particular set of services with flexible rules to meet the needs of certain people. Many groups of people may be covered by Medicaid Waivers and certain requirements must be met. This may include the individual's age, disability, blind, or aged; the person's income and resources (e.g. bank accounts, real property, or other items that can be sold for cash); and whether he or she is a U.S. citizen or a lawfully admitted immigrant. The rules for counting income and resources vary from state to state and from group to group. While not every individual with a disability will be able to get a Waiver, all individuals with LI disabilities should explore the possibility. Even those who have been previously deemed ineligible should reapply with the help of a case manager, as new and different Waivers and new eligibility guidelines are continually being issued.

Waivers for people with developmental disabilities have historically used Habilitation Services to provide employment supports. There are several types of habilitation services to include residential, day, prevocational services, supported employment, and education. Each of the Habilitation Services has a core definition that has been provided by CMS and can be found in CMS's Instructional, Technical Guide and Review Criteria online (CMS, 2006). The Technical Guide also provides guidance for states in incorporating employment into various services. More information is available on the CMS website (http://www.cms.hhs.gov/) including state specific information regarding each state's approved waivers at Community Rehabilitation Programs (CRP).

CRPs are usually not-for-profit agencies that can provide services to people with disabilities. CRPs may operate facility-based programs such as non-work facility-based services, non-work community-based services, sheltered workshops, as well as supported employment services to assist individuals in achieving integrated employment outcomes. Funding for CRPs may come from vocational rehabilitation, Medicaid-Waiver dollars, and other contractual arrangements. Other contractual arrangements may include contract work to produce a product in the CRPs' sheltered workshop by individuals with disabilities. While CRPs continue to provide services that result in noncompetitive work outcomes, may states such as Connecticut, Alaska, Oklahoma, and Washington offer excellent examples of effective systems that are supporting integrated competitive employment outcomes (Brooks-Lane, Hutcheson, Revell, 2007).

If a student with low incidence disabilities is referred to a CRP for integrated employment, he or she most likely will receive supported employment services. There are five key characteristics of a quality service provider that should be considered when selecting a CRP to provide services: (a) the program is flexible; (b) the program is participant focused/driven; (c) the program uses a strengths model as opposed to a deficit model; (d) program staff use people-first language; and (e) the program is outcomes based with a focus on employment and inclusion (Brooks-Lane et al., 2007).

CRPS are a good resource for students and early referral will help prevent delays for services postgraduation. The key point is that individuals with low incidence disabilities must be perceived as competent and able to work in integrated employment settings rather than in facility-based programs. School systems should compile documentation related to each student's strengths, preferences, and skills for employment to include community-based work experiences that students have during the school years.

Social Security Benefits

Social Security benefits offer monthly cash payments and access to health insurance benefits such as Medicaid and/or Medicare, as well as work incentives that are specifically designed to increase an individual's employment and earnings capacity. Fear of losing benefits, as well as medical coverage, has long been identified as a barrier to integrated employment for individuals with disabilities (Miller & O'Mara, 2006). Many parents of school-age youth have expended a great deal of time and energy to establish eligibility for their sons and daughters, and they may view paid employment as a significant risk to loss of benefits and Medicaid coverage. However, Social Security benefits can actually serve as a valuable resource to eligible students as they transition from school to adult life.

The Social Security Administration (SSA) has two programs to include Supplemental Security Income (SSI) and the Social Security Disability Insurance Program (SSDI). SSI is designed to provide income to individuals with disabilities in financial need. SSI recipients in some states are automatically eligible for Medicaid coverage with eligibility beginning the same month as SSI eligibility. Other states require a separate application and/or eligibility requirements for Medicaid (Newcomb, Payne, & Waid, 2003). These state specific application and eligibility requirements should be determined during transition planning. SSDI is a social security insurance program available to those who have worked and contributed to the Social Security trust fund. Family members such as a "disabled adult child" who is over the age of 18 may receive benefits on the record of a "disabled worker" (e.g., parent). After a 2-year wait period, individuals receiving SSDI automatically begin to receive Medicare coverage.

Benefits planning expertise is typically not available within the public school system. While school personnel should become more knowledgeable, they do not need to become experts in Social Security Disability benefits information. The SSA has established the Work Incentives Planning and Assistance (WIPA) projects that are available in most communities. Benefits counselors work in these projects and are typically referred to as Community Work Incentive Coordinators (CIWICs). Benefits Specialists may be located within the Vocational Rehabilitation Agency, a Community Rehabilitation Program (CRP), a Protection and Advocacy Organization, a Center for Independent Living (CIL), or a local Social Security office. This varies from state to state and from community to community, and therefore part of transition planning should be identifying where this key resource is located.

SSI is a means-tested program, and parental income and/or resources are considered during eligibility determination for children less than 18 years of age (VCU, 2008). This is referred to as "Parent-to-Child Deeming" and will impact whether a child with a disability is found eligible to receive monthly cash SSI payments. A child may be eligible for SSI based on her/his own income and resources, yet ineligible for SSI due to the income or resources from a parent or parents. Once SSA determines that a child under the age of 18 is eligible, the amount of the SSI check will be based on the current year's Federal Benefit Rate (FBR). This is the maximum dollar amount that any single person can receive in a month and is established by Congress in January of each year. The exact dollar amount that a child receives each month is determined on a case by case basis. Parents should not assume that their sons or daughters would not be eligible for SSI benefits until they complete the application process.

SSI eligibility must be redetermined when a child who has been receiving benefits reaches age18, since the adult definition of disability for SSI is different than for a child. This redetermination takes place sometime during the 12 months after the child turns 18, and parents will receive written notification from their local SSA Field Office (Revell & Miller, 2009). If the age 18 redetermination process finds the student eligible for SSI, he/she will receive benefits under the adult SSI program. If the individual is found ineligible, benefits will terminate 2 months after the date of determination. Once the student reaches age 18, parent to child deeming no longer applies when making SSI eligibility determinations or in calculating the amount of the SSI payment. Transition-age youth who were determined ineligible for SSI benefits under the age of 18 due to parent-to-child deeming should be encouraged to reapply after the 18th birthday.

Failure to reestablish SSI eligibility during the transition process means that the student will lose access to critical supports to include work incentives and the Ticket to Work Program. Documentation from teachers and vocational rehabilitation professionals should be provided that indicates the level of support that is needed to perform work activities. In many instances, the lack of information on true work performance and support needs leads to an inaccurate assessment of the individual's future ability to earn income (Miller & O'Mara, 2009).

Social Security Work Incentives. SSI work incentives were designed to allow an individual to continue receiving a SSI check and/or Medicaid while working towards independence. Students who receive SSI and go to work can take advantage of a these employment supports to include the Earned Income Exclusion, Student Earned Income Exclusion, Impairment Related Work Expense (IRWE), Blind Work Expense, Plan for Achieving Self Support (PASS), and 1619 A&B that protects Medicaid coverage (SSA, 2009). All of these employment supports except the Student Earned Income Exclusion continue to be available to individuals with LI disabilities when they leave school as long as the individual is working and receiving

SSI. If a student begins to earn wages, regardless of the amount, that money must be reported to the Social Security Administration. Failure to report relevant information to SSA, such as earnings, can cause substantial overpayment of benefits that may take years for the individual to pay back to Social Security. A brief description of the SSI programs that can most benefit the employment training of transition age students follows.

The Student Earned Income Exclusion helps students retain more of their original SSI checks while working and remaining in school. If a student is under age 22, not married nor head of a household, and regularly attending school, he or she can take advantage of the Student Earned Income Exclusion. Social Security does not count up to $1,640 of a student's earned income per month when calculating the monthly SSI payment amount. The maximum yearly exclusion is $6,600. These figures are for the year 2009, which are adjusted annually based on the cost-of-living (SSA, 2009).

For a student to claim the exclusion, documentation must be provided that he or she is regularly attending school. Regularly attending school means that the student must be enrolled in and taking one or more courses and attends the class regularly. More specifically, the student is (a) in college or university for 8 hours a week, (b) in grades 7 through 12 for at least 12 hours a week, (c) in a training course to prepare for employment for 12 hours per week (15 hours a week if the course involves shop practice), or (d) for less time than indicated above for reasons beyond the student's control, such as illness. If the student is home taught because of a disability, "regularly attending school" may apply if the student is studying a course or courses given by a school (grades 7–12), college, university, or government agency, and has a home visitor or tutor who directs the study (SSA, 2009). The Student Earned Income Exclusion applies consecutively to months in which there is earned income until the exclusion is exhausted, or the student is over 22.

An Impairment Related Work Expense (IRWE) allows individuals with disabilities to deduct the cost of work-related expenses from their earnings before calculations are made to determine their SSI cash benefit. An IRWE is not a written plan, but a monthly report of expenditures used by the Social Security representative in calculating total countable income and determining continued eligibility or the amount of monthly cash payments. SSA must have proof for every IRWE claimed by the individual with a disability. This includes: (a) name and address of prescribing source (e.g., doctor, vocational rehabilitation counselor); (b) impairment for which the IRWE is prescribed; and (c) receipts and canceled checks showing that the expense was paid for by the individual and not someone else. Some of the expenses that may be reimbursed using an IRWE include the following: attendant care services, job coach services, assistive technology, drugs and medical services, special door-to-door transportation costs, and guide dogs, to mention a few. The expense must be submitted and approved by the Social Security Administration for this work incentive to take effect.

The Student Earned Income Exclusion is calculated before other work incentives are used. In many cases, a student will not be making enough money to take an IRWE simultaneously with the Student Earned Income Exclusion. However, once the student exclusion is exhausted for a calendar year, the student may be able to use an IRWE to further facilitate employment goals while maintaining SSI benefits. Although some students may not take advantage of an IRWE while in school, this is important information for planning postschool employment supports. An individual can use an IRWE no matter how many months or how long he or she is employed to assist in covering work expenses. Additional information can be obtained from the Social Security Redbook regarding expenses that are and are not deductible (SSA, 2009).

A Plan for Achieving Self Support (PASS) can be submitted by SSI recipients who need additional financial resources to help them find or maintain employment. A PASS can help an individual establish or maintain SSI eligibility and can increase the SSI monthly payment amount (SSA, 2009). Specifically, SSA can exclude wages when calculating the monthly SSI check if the person sets aside an approved amount in a special savings account to save and pay for services towards achieving employment goals. In addition, a person could also use a PASS to save unearned resources such as an allowance, child support, savings bonds, or gifts towards the individual's career goals.

A PASS may be used in combination with the Student Earned Income Exclusion while a student is still in school to save for needed postschool supports and services towards a specific career goal. Remember that SSI is a means tested program, and an individual cannot exceed $2,000 in resources to maintain eligibility. When using the Student Earned Income Exclusion, a student can exclude up to $6,600 in wages during a calendar year. These resources could then be set aside in a PASS allowing the student to actually save for postsecondary education or training that would lessen future dependency on public funding sources such as vocational rehabilitation. While using the Student Earned Income Exclusion and PASS in combination, the student would keep most if not all of the SSI payment intact while saving for a career goal. Of course, the PASS would need to be approved by SSA.

Once an individual with a disability goes to work, a general rule of thumb is that the SSI check will be reduced $1 for every $2 in wages. However, 1619 A and B protect a person's Medicaid coverage while working and receiving SSI. Under 1619A, as long as the person maintains even one penny in the SSI check, he or she will continue to be eligible for Medicaid. Once the person is working, and the check is reduced to 0, he or she is protected by 1619 B. This allows SSA to keep the individual's file open while stopping the SSI check. If the person's wages decrease or the individual loses the job, he or she can notify SSA. The individual would not need to reapply, and SSI checks would begin again. Under 1619 A and B, an individual still would not be able to have more than $2,000 in resources to meet the eligibility requirements. For 1619 B, there is a "threshold" amount for wages in all states or a maximum amount that a person can earn and still maintain Medicaid coverage. This amount ranges from state to state, and the exact amount of wages that a person can earn per year and still keep Medicaid can be determined by reviewing the current year's threshold amounts at http://www.ssa.gov.

It should be obvious from the descriptions of the many funding and service sources such as VR and DDA, community agencies such as CRPs, federal/state programs such as the Medicaid Waiver, and SSI incentives that knowing how to access these programs and services can be a daunting task for a transition team. It is crucial, none the less, when you consider that all of them must be explored if integrated employment is to become a reality. The IEP transition process is a family's last stop for getting all this sorted out by a single group of collaborative partners before the student moves into the world of eligibility driven services where nothing is entitled and no single person or group has to take responsibility for any particular outcome.

Postsecondary Education (PSE) Opportunities for Students with LI Disabilities

As students reach the age of 18 or 19, most are getting ready for college or other postsecondary educational (PSE) opportunities. It is not age appropriate for anyone, students with LI included, to be spending all day on a high school campus. Over the past decade, a number of postsecondary educational opportunities for transition age students with LI disabilities who are still enrolled in special education have been developed and researched. Students can receive educational, recreational, and integrated employment training while getting to socialize and learn alongside their same age peers without disabilities on college campuses (Grigal, Neubert, & Moon, 2005; Neubert & Moon, 2006; Hart & Grigal, 2008). There are at least 150 PSE programs in 30 states across the country. There are three overall models represented by these programs including substantially separate, mixed, and inclusive programs.

Most programs are assisting students who are age 21 and younger and are still being served by public school special education. Special educators from local school districts coordinate most of these programs, and their students are receiving certificates or alternative diplomas. This dual enrollment of students that most programs employ allows for special education benefits to continue while students are with peers in a more age appropriate settings, getting community employment training and both functional skills training by special educators and enrollment in college classes when possible (Neubert & Moon, 2006). Most students are receiving job training in real jobs on campuses or in the community and are being linked to adult service agencies in the same way that other students with LI are transitioned.

The mixed and inclusive models of service delivery are much more preferable as these models allow students more inclusive opportunities with same age peers and there is evidence that these models allow for greater interagency collaboration with adult agencies than traditional high school programs (Neubert, Moon, & Grigal, 2004), and may result in more meaningful paid employment opportunities (Zafft, Hart, & Zimbrich, 2004). There are now two comprehensive resources available for planning, implementing , and evaluating PSE programs for transition age students with LI disabilities (Grigal & Hart, 2010; Grigal, Neubert, & Moon, 2005), and a foundation for further research (Neubert & Moon, 2006). Certainly, this model for providing special education to older students with LI, in which students are based on a college campus, is just as effective as traditional high school programs and is definitely more age appropriate. It should be considered for all transition age students as we prepare them for integrated employment and independent living outcomes. (For more comprehensive information, references, and resources on PSE programs, see http://www.thinkcollege.net.) Jeremy's case study in the next chapter is a good example of a transition age student who is benefiting from a college experience. In his case, he gets to live on campus, take advantage of college academic and social activities, and receive employment training. It is the best of all transition experiences.

References

Bissonnette, D. (1994). *Beyond traditional job development: The art of creating job opportunity.* Granada Hills, CA: Milt Wright & Associates.

Boeltzig, H., Timmons, J. C., & Butterworth, J. (in press). Gender differences in individual employment outcomes of persons with developmental disabilities. *Journal of Vocational Rehabilitation.*

Braddock, D., Hemp, R., & Rizzolo, M. K. (2008). *State of the states in developmental disabilities* (7th ed.). Washington, DC: American Association of Intellectual and Developmental Disabilities.

Brooks-Lane, N., Hutcheson, S., & Revell, G. (2005). Supporting consumer directed employment outcomes. *Journal of Vocational Rehabilitation, 23*(2), 123–134.

Brooks-Lane, N. Hutcheson, S., & Revell, W. G. (2007). Community rehabilitation programs and human services. In P. Wehman, K. J., Inge, W. G. Revell, & V. A. Brooke (Eds.), *Real work for real pay: Inclusive employment for people with disabilities* (pp. 19–36). Baltimore: Paul H. Brookes.

Brown, L., Shiraga, B., & Kessler, K. (2006). The quest for ordinary lives: The integrated post-school vocational functioning of 50 workers with significant disabilities, *Research & Practice for Persons with Severe Disabilities, 31*(2), 93-121.

Callahan, M. (2004, July). *Customized and supported employment.* Paper presented at APSE: The Network on Employment The Fifteenth Annual Conference and Training Event, Indianapolis, IN.

Callahan, M., & Rogan, P. (2004, June). What is customized employment? *The Advance, 15*(1), 3.

Centers for Medicare and Medicaid Services (CMS). (2006). *Instructional, technical guide and review criteria.* Retrieved August 22, 2009, from http://www.hcbs.org/files/100/4982/Final_Version_3_4_Instructions_Technical_Guide_and_Review_Criteria_Nov_2006.pdf

Citron, T., Brooks-Lane, N., Crandell, D., Brady, K., Cooper, M., & Revell, G. (2008). A revolution in the employment process of individuals with disabilities: Customized employment as the catalyst for system change. *Journal of Vocational Rehabilitation, 28*(3), 169–181.

Doyle, A. (2002). Self-employment, choice, and self-determination. *Journal of Vocational Rehabilitation 17,* 115–124.

Federal Register. (2001, January 17). *66*(11), 4382-4389. 34 CFR 361.

Federal Register. (2002, June 26). *67*(123), 43154-43149.

Griffin, C., & Hammis, D. (2008). *Self-employment Q and A: Community resources for small business development.* Retrieved September 9, 2009, from: http://www.start-up-usa.biz/resources/content.cfm?id=648

Griffin, C., & Hammis, D. (2003). *Making self-employment work for people with disabilities.* Baltimore: Paul H. Brookes.

Griffin, C., Hammis, D., & Geary. T. (2009). *The job developer's handbook: Practical tactics for customized employment.* Baltimore: Paul Brookes.

Griffin, C., Brooks-Lane, N., Hammis, D. G., & Crandell, D. (2007). Self-employment: Owning the American dream. In P. Wehman, K. J. Inge, W.G. Revell, & V.A. Brooke (Eds.), *Real work for real pay: Inclusive employment for people with disabilities* (pp. 215–236). Baltimore, Paul H. Brookes.

Griffin, C., Hammis, D., Geary, T., & Sullivan, M. (2008). Customized employment: Where we are; where we're headed. *Journal of Vocational Rehabilitation, 28*(3), 135–139.

Grigal, M., & Hart, D. (2010). *Think college: Postsecondary education options for students with intellectual disabilities.* Baltimore: Paul H. Brookes.

Grigal, M., Neubert, D. A., & Moon, M. S. (2005). *Transition services for students with significant disabilities: Strategies for planning, implementation, and evaluation.* Baltimore: Paul H. Brookes.

Hart, D., & Grigal, M. (2008, March). New frontier: Postsecondary education for youth with intellectual disabilities. *Section 504 Compliance handbook,* 10–11.

Inge, K. J. (2001). Supported employment for individuals with physical disabilities. In P. Wehman (Ed), *Supported employment in business: Expanding the capacity of workers with disabilities* (pp. 153–180). St Augustine, FL: TRN Publications.

Inge, K. J. (2005). *Q and A customized employment: Demystifying customized employment for individuals with significant disabilities.* Retrieved September 15, 2009, from: http://www.t-tap.org/strategies/factsheet/demystifying.htm

Inge, K. J., & Moon, M. S. (2006). Vocational preparation and transition. In M. Snell & F. Brown (Eds.), *Instruction of students with severe disabilities* (6th ed., pp. 569–609). Upper Saddle River, NJ: Merrill.

Inge, K. J., Strobel, W., Wehman, P., Todd, J., & Targett, P. (2000). Vocational outcomes for persons with severe physical disabilities: Design and implementation of workplace supports. *NeuroRehabilitation, 15*(3), 175–188.

Inge, K. J., & Targett, P. S., & Armstrong, A. J. (2007). Person-centered planning: Facilitating inclusive employment outcomes. In P. Wehman, K. J. Inge, W. G. Revell, & V. A. Brooke (Ed.), *Real work for real pay: Inclusive employment for people with disabilities* (pp. 57–74). Baltimore: Paul H. Brookes.

Inge, K. J., Targett, P., & Griffin, C. (2006) *Customized employment Q and A: Self-employment as a customized employment outcome.* Retrieved September 9, 2009, from: http://www.start-up-usa.biz/resources/content.cfm?id=644

Inge, K. J., Wehman, P., Revell, G., Erickson, D., Butterworth, J., & Gilmore, D. (2009). Survey results from a national survey of community rehabilitation providers holding special wage certificates. *Journal of Vocational Rehabilitation, 30*(2), 67–85.

Luecking, R. G., Fabian, E. S., & Tilson, G. P. (2004). *Working relationships: Creating career opportunities for job seekers with disabilities through employer partnerships.* Baltimore: Paul H. Brookes.

Migliore, A., & Butterworth, J. (2008). Trends in outcomes of the Vocational Rehabilitation program for adults with developmental disabilities: 1995–2005. *Rehabilitation Counseling Bulletin, 52*(1), 35–44.

Miller, L., & O'Mara, S. (2006). Social security disability benefit issues affecting transition-age youth. In P. Wehman (Ed.), *Life beyond the classroom: Transition strategies for young people with disabilities* (4th ed., pp. 387–410). Baltimore: Paul H. Brookes.

Miller, L., & O'Mara, S. (2009). *SSI and age 18 redeterminations.* Retrieved September 22, 2009, from http://www.worksupport.com/documents/SSI_Age18RedetermMay09.doc.

Moon, M. S., Simonsen, M., & Neubert, D. A. (2011). Perceptions of supported employment providers: What students, with developmental disabilities, families, and educators need to know for transition planning. *Education and Training in Autism and Developmental Disabilities, 46*(1), 94–105,.

National Organization on Disability. (2004). N.O.D./Harris survey of Americans with disabilities: Landmark survey finds pervasive disadvantages. Washington, DC: Louis Harris & Associates.

Neubert, D. A., & Moon, M. S. (2006). Postsecondary settings and transition services for students with intellectual disabilities: Models and research. *Focus on Exceptional Children, 39*(4), 1–8.

Neubert, D. A., Moon, M. S., & Grigal, M. (2004). Activities of students with significant disabilities receiving services in postsecondary settings. *Education and Training in Developmental Disabilities, 34*(8), 1–12.

Newcomb, C., Payne, S., & Waid, M. D. (2003). What do we know about disability beneficiaries' work and use of work incentives prior to Ticket? In K. Rupp & S. H. Bell (Eds.), *Paying for results in vocational rehabilitation: Will provider incentives work for ticket to work?* (pp. 31–69). Washington, DC: The Urban Institute.

Nietupski, J., & Hamre-Nietupski, S. (2001). A business approach to finding and restructuring supported employment opportunities. In P. Wehman (Ed.), *Supported employment in business: Expanding the capacity of workers with disabilities* (pp. 59–73). St. Augustine, FL: Training Resource Network.

Revell, G., & Miller, L. A. (2009). Navigating the world of adult services and benefits planning. In P. Wehman, M. D. Smith, & C. Schall (Eds.), *Autism and the transition to adulthood: Success beyond the classroom* (pp. 139–162). Baltimore: Paul H. Brookes.

Revell, G., Smith, F., & Inge, K. (2009). An analysis of self employment outcomes within the federal/state vocational rehabilitation system. *Journal of Vocational Rehabilitation, 31*(1), 11–18.

Social Security Administration (SSA). (2009). Disability program navigator. Retrieved September 8, 2009, from http://www.socialsecurity.gov/disabilityresearch/navigator.htm

Sullivan, M., & Katz, M. (2008). *Self-employment Q & A: Medicaid home and community based services.* Retrieved September 9, 2009, from http://www.start-up-usa.biz/resources/content.cfm?id=651

Targett, P. S., & Wehman, P. (2009). Integrated employment. In P. Wehman, M. D. Smith, & C. Schall (Eds.), *Autism & the transition to adulthood: Success beyond the classroom* (pp.163–188). Baltimore, Paul H. Brookes.

U.S. Department of Labor (DOL) (2008). *A guide for reviewing and adjusting commensurate wage rates under section 14(c) of the Fair Labor Standards Act, required as a result of the July 24, 2008 increase in the federal minimum wage.* Retrieved August, 7, 2009, from www.dol.gov/esa/sec14c/prevailWages.htm

U.S. Department of Labor (DOL). (2009). *Fact Sheet #39B: Prevailing wages and commensurate wages under Section 14(c) of the Fair Labor Standards Act (FLSA).* Retrieved August 4, 2009, from www.dol.gov/esa/whd/regs/compliance/whdfs39b.pdf

Wagner, M., Newman, L., Cameto, R., Garza, N., & Levine, P. (2005). After high school: A first look at the postschool experiences of youth with disabilities. A report from the National Longitudinal Transition Study-2 (NLTS-2). Menlo Park, CA: SRI International.

Webb, K., Taylor, G., & Hammis, D. (2009). *Braiding small business start-up funding.* Retrieved September 9, 2009, from http://www.worksupport.com/documents/webb_taylor_cc.doc

Wehman, P., Inge, K. J., Revell, W. G., & Brooke, V. A. (2007). *Real work for real pay: Inclusive employment for people with disabilities.* Baltimore: Paul H. Brookes.

Wehman, P., Revell, G., & Brooke, V. (2003). Competitive employment: Has it become the first choice yet? *Journal of Disability Policy Studies, 14*(3), 163–173.

White, J., & Weiner, J. S. (2004). Influence of least restrictive environment and community based training on integrated employment outcomes for transitioning youth with severe disabilities. *Journal of Vocational Rehabilitation, 21,* 149–156.

Wittenburg, D., Golden, T., & Fishman, M. (2002). Transition options for youth with disabilities: An overview of the programs and policies that affect the transition from school. *Journal of Vocational Rehabilitation, 17*, 195–206.

Workforce Investment Act of 1998 (PL105-220). Retrieved from http://www.doleta.gov/usworkforce/wia/wialaw.txt

Zafft, C., Hart, D., & Zimbrich, K. (2004). College career connection: A study of youth with intellectual disabilities and the impact of postsecondary education. *Education and Training in Developmental Disabilities 1*(1), 45–54.

47

Preparing Students with Low Incidence Disabilities for Community Living Opportunities

Jane M. Everson
Appalachian State University

Meghan H. Trowbridge
University of South Carolina School of Medicine

Envision a recent gathering you attended with family members, co-workers, church members, or other adult friends and acquaintances. Consider an application you completed recently for a potential job, an apartment lease, a credit card application, or voter registration. At some point in the conversation or in completing the paperwork, you were no doubt asked one or both of these questions: *"Where do you work?"* and *"Where do you live?"* Most adults will respond quickly, sometimes with confidence, sometimes with apologetic explanations, but nearly always with the understanding that the answers they provide tell the questioner a great deal about the respondent's adult accomplishments. For most American adults, employment and housing are two of the most desired and expected outcomes of high school and adolescent experiences (Arnett, 2001, 2007; Furstenberg, Kennedy, Cloyd, Rumbaut, & Settersten, 2003).

While a wide range of theories have been presented to explain career development in adolescence, much less attention has been given to the development of community and independent living abilities. Nevertheless, moving away from home for the first time is recognized as a milestone that most teenagers and young adults look forward to with great anticipation (Arnett, 2007; Graber & Dubas, 1996: Steinberg, 2007). Family members, too, look forward to this milestone, although sometimes with anxiety as well as anticipation (Kastner & Wyatt, 1997; Steinberg, 2001).

For many young adults, this milestone means moving into a college dorm or a rented apartment. For other young adults, it means purchasing their first home or condominium. For still others, it means moving into a supervised and transitional living option such as a group home or a residential treatment program. When young adults transition from high school and face uncertain employment and economic situations, it may mean continuing to live with family members, or perhaps remaining nearby by moving into a separate apartment or a mobile home on a family member's property. Along with a variety of living environments to choose from, these young adults will also choose from among a variety of living arrangements. They may live alone or with one or more friends or family members as roommates. Other young adults, especially those with disabilities, may receive a long-term and individualized schedule of support services from a case manager or personal care attendant to help them manage their transition into the new living environment.

To supplement their income and subsidize their living expenses, many young adults receive financial assistance from family members and/or from federal and state housing authorities along with living subsidies to support housing, food, and transportation expenses. As Furstenberg and his colleagues (2003) summarized in their study of adults' perceptions of adulthood accomplishments, only 52% of American adults expect young adults to be financially independent by age 24, suggesting that subsidizing young adult's living options in the years following their transition from adolescence to adulthood may be the norm rather than the exception.

Throughout the United States, and across multiple cultures and socioeconomic conditions, the milestone of moving away from home has become a complex, multiyear process (Arnett, 2007; Gutmann, Pullum-Pionon, & Pullum, 2002; Kastner & Wyatt, 1997). Furstenberg and his colleagues (2003) conclude that only 29% of Americans think that young adults should have left the family home by age 20, while 55% think this milestone should have occurred by age 24, and 15% believe that this milestone might reasonably be delayed until age 29.

No matter what community living outcome young adults desire upon exiting high school, pursuit of the milestone brings both opportunities and challenges. In addition to changing their address, most young adults are also expected either suddenly or gradually to assume greater responsibility for managing the other components of their adult lives. These responsibilities are vast; they may include making financial and legal decisions, managing their health and medical services and care, choosing recreation and leisure pursuits, developing relationships with friends and coworkers, and managing their transportation needs (Arnett, 2007; Gutmann et al., 2002; Steinberg 2007).

For adolescents moving away from home for the first time, the options are vast and the decisions are many. For adolescents with disabilities, the options should be just as vast and the decisions should be equally as important. Choosing and attaining community living outcomes, where to live, with whom to live, and how to assume responsibility for adult activities, is a crucial function of an Individual Education Program (IEP) and transition planning for high school students.

Transition Planning: A Focus on Community Living

More than 20 years of federally funded and transition-focused pilot programs and research suggest that young adults with disabilities envision post-high school outcomes that are comparable to those held by their same age peers. Like their peers, they desire employment and housing (e.g., Wehmeyer & Palmer, 2003; Everson & Wilson, 2000). Like their peers, they too desire greater independence in managing their adult lives (e.g., McConkey, Sowney, Milligan, & Barr, 2004; Morningstar, Kleinhammer-Tramill, & Lattin, 1999). Parents and family members generally share and support these expectations (e.g., Hanley-Maxwell, Whitney-Thomas, & Pogoloff, 1995; LoConto & Dodder, 1997). "Best practices" transition literature also supports planning processes that design and support a broad array of post high school pursuits and accomplishments (e.g., Halpern, 1993; Kochhar-Bryant & Greene, 2009; Rusch, 2008; Test, Aspel, & Everson, 2006).

Nevertheless, youth with disabilities face fewer post-high school opportunities and greater challenges than do their typical peers (Wagner et al., 2003). For youth with low incidence (LI) disabilities, the challenges appear to be even greater and the opportunities even fewer (Wagner et al., 2003). In every study and across every indicator of adult life, youth with disabilities fare less well than do their typical peers. They are more likely to be unemployed or underemployed; they are less likely to attend postsecondary education institutions; they are less likely to be living apart from their family and parents' homes; and they are less likely to have friends and participate in community activities (U.S. Department of Education, 2001; National Council on Disability, 2000; Wagner et al., 2003).

While most special education follow-up studies conducted in the 1980s and most early models of transition services focused on employment as a primary goal of high school and transition services, Halpern's (1993) assessment suggested that it is ineffective to focus primarily on vocational services and employment outcomes with the expectation that employment will lead to community living and other adult quality of life outcomes. In other words, high school programs and transition services for youth with disabilities must focus on *all* desired adult outcome areas, as success in one area will not automatically lead to success in another. This recommendation should not surprise us: a focus on a multi-outcome and coordinated transition approach is suggested in the research cited earlier in this chapter that focuses on typical adolescents (e.g., Arnett, 2007; Graber & Dubas, 1996; Steinberg, 2007).

The Individuals with Disabilities Education Improvement Act (IDEA) of 2004, PL 108-466, began to recognize the complex and longitudinal relationship between employment, housing, postsecondary education, and other adult quality of life outcomes by mandating the collection of postsecondary outcome data for all youth with disabilities one year after they exit high school. This is an important step, but as research and literature cited earlier in this chapter on typical young adults indicates, a one-year postsecondary timeline and a narrow focus on employment and postsecondary education may not capture fully the complexity of a young adult's multi-year journey that begins with leaving home for the first time.

There are several plausible reasons that community living outcomes are not being fully realized by youth with disabilities, especially by those with low incidence disabilities. First, until very recently, the full spectrum of community living options open to most young adults exiting high school remained severely limited to those with disabilities (O'Hara & Miller, 2000; Racino, Walker, O'Connor, & Taylor, 1993). This has been especially true for those with LI disabilities (Wagner et al., 2003). A second and related reason is that transition legislation, transition models and services, and IEP forms have prompted minimal attention to the development of community living skills and discussion of community living outcomes. Instead, the development of vocational skills and employment outcomes has dominated in legislation, models, and services. A third, and again related reason, is that teacher preparation textbooks and teacher preparation programs provide minimal curricular and teaching methods on community living to teachers who are being trained to educate students with disabilities.

Comprehensive transition models and services must now begin to include a focus on community living (IDEA, 2004). Although teacher preparation textbooks, teacher preparation programs, and transition models that include a focus on community living are rare, Test and his colleagues (2006) do suggest that a number of "best practice" transition services correlate with enhanced community living outcomes. These practices include: (a) knowledge of contemporary supported living philosophies and locally available options; (b) development of self-determination abilities; (c) provision of comprehensive community participation activities and skill building; and (d) delivery of flexible, comprehensive, and interagency supported living services (Test et al., 2006). Before describing some of these practices in more detail, we will provide an historical overview of community living options in the United States for citizens with disabilities.

A History of Housing Opportunities for Americans with Disabilities

> All great establishments…where there must be boarding in common, and sleeping in congregate dormitories; where there must be routine, and formality, and restraint, and repression of individuality; where the charms and refining influences of the true family relation cannot be had—all such institutions are unnatural, undesirable, and very liable to abuse. We should have as few of them as possible, and those few should be kept as small as possible. (Howe cited in Braddock, 1988, p. 1)

These remarks were made in 1886 by Dr. Samuel Gridley Howe at ceremonies commemorating the groundbreaking of the New York State Institution for the Blind in Batavia, New York. Today, his words seem to be a prophetic warning against the direction in which 19th-century residential services for individuals with disabilities were moving. For as we look back today, the history of residential services for people with disabilities in the United States is largely a story of segregation, isolation, and even abuse and neglect. Most of this history is a story about programs, placements, and policies; it is only very recently that the story has become a more encouraging story about people and their preferences. This section provides an historical overview of living options available to Americans with disabilities by discussing five time periods and their prevailing philosophies: (a) the charity and benign neglect period; (b) the medical and rehabilitation enlightenment period; (c) the institutional reform period; (d) the independent living movement; and (e) the supported living movement. Each of these eras made unique contributions to community living services for individuals with disabilities and, in their turn, shaped the supported living movement that exists today—a movement that continues to grow and evolve as new research emerges, new policies are developed, and new economic and political challenges confront the country.

The Charity and Benign Neglect Period

Until the late 19th century, state and federally supported social services of any type were nearly nonexistent in the United States. Services that were available were poorly funded and largely unregulated. Individuals with disabilities, especially those with LI disabilities were typically viewed as "proper paupers" (Thomson, 1997) or as "eternal children" (Wolfensberger, 1972), and were excluded from what little education and vocational services that did exist simply because they were considered unable to benefit from them. Without education and vocational training, people with disabilities had few options available to them other than living their entire lives with family members or depending upon church-affiliated and other charitable organizations for shelter and food.

Beginning in the mid-19th century and continuing until as late as 1940, traveling "freak" circuses and "dime museums" flourished across the United States (e.g., Bogdan, 1988; "Circus and museum freaks—Curiosities of pathology," 1908). While designed to provide middle-class Americans of leisure with entertainment, these enterprises also were among the first to provide people with disabilities with dubious opportunities for employment and shelter.

Also in the mid-19th century, after the American Civil War, state and federally supported services for individuals with disabilities began to be developed. Dr. Samuel Gridley Howe helped establish residential schools for Deaf students and for students with visual disabilities, and later assisted in the establishment of the first residential facility for persons with intellectual disabilities. These early residential facilities were typically named "asylums" or "colonies" and were chartered to provide shelter and care for "the feeble minded" (Trent, 1994). By 1900, Barr (1904) reported that 21 states had established 29 institutions for "mental defectives." As these facilities continued to expand and new facilities were chartered, individuals increasingly were separated both from their families and from their home communities. The prevailing professional model of the period discouraged education and training, family involvement, and community living. Instead, the model encouraged sheltered and group residential placements with strict supervision and provision of basic medical care.

The Medical and Rehabilitation Enlightenment Period

By the end of World War I, advances in psychology and medicine made the use of intelligence and adaptive skills tests widely accepted. Medical and psychological professionals led this era and a medical model devoted to identification of disabilities and rehabilitation prevailed. Tests were used routinely to test, label, and predict the community functioning of people with a range of disabilities as well as recent immigrants with language and cultural differences. Individuals who were viewed as unable to be rehabilitated or "repaired" were placed in residential facilities, often for the remainder of their lives. As a result, residential facilities continued to grow both in the number available per state and in the size of their populations. By 1930, the number of institutions in the United States had nearly tripled to 77 and by 1965, it had doubled again to 143 (Braddock & Heller, 1984).

By the mid-20th century, parents of infants and children with more substantial and multiple disabilities were advised routinely to commit their significantly disabled family members to these state-run residential facilities and to "forget about them." As a result, at the peak of the institutional period in 1967, nearly 200,000 people with disabilities lived in state-run residential institutions throughout the United States (Braddock & Hemp, 2008).

However, by the end of World War II, scarce resources were already resulting in institutional overcrowding. By the dawn of the 1960s, overcrowding, crumbling infrastructure, and nearly nonexistent professional standards for disability services were long overdue for public exposure and attention.

The Institutional Reform Period

By the mid-1960s, television and other media had become

a primary source of news in many American homes. Thus, it was media that first helped direct the nation's attention toward the often horrific living conditions in the country's institutional facilities (e.g., Blanton & Kaplan, 1974) and served as a catalyst for the establishment of the first President's Panel on Mental Retardation in 1962. This panel articulated the long overdue need to establish a comprehensive national approach to addressing the educational, residential, medical, professional development, and research-based needs of Americans with disabilities. Reforms led to the development of better medical and educational services known as "active treatment" and the establishment of smaller and more regulated facilities known as "intermediate care facilities for the mentally retarded." The Supplemental Security Income (SSI) system and the Medicaid health care system were also established during this period, providing the foundation upon which future supported living services would build.

The concept of "normalization" first articulated by Wolfensberger in 1972 became the cornerstone of the in stitutional reform movement and continues today to serve as a guidepost for professionals and policymakers to use when planning, operating, and evaluating community living environments and services for adults with disabilities. Normalization defines appropriate environments and services as those that make patterns and activities of every day life available to people with disabilities. Gradually, facilities and services were reformed and living conditions and expectations were improved.

Over time, a move to reduce the number of people living in these facilities as well as the size of remaining facilities began to take shape. As a result, the movement evolved from one of institutional reform to deinstitutionalization. In 2002, 44,252 persons with intellectual disabilities were receiving residential support in state institutions (Rizzolo, Hemp, Braddock, & Pomeranz-Essley, 2004). Nationally, the number of persons with developmental disabilities living in institutions decreased by nearly half between 1980 and 1993 (Braddock & Hemp, 2008).

The Independent Living Movement

The principle driving the previous period was reform and the drivers were the media and professionals. But even as these reforms began to reshape institutional services, a new movement with new voices—the voices of people with disabilities —was beginning to take shape. The independent living movement was a grassroots movement that was consumer-driven, and the first to be focused on community living and community participation opportunities. The independent living movement began with a small group of students, primarily those with physical disabilities, on the campus of the University of California at Berkley. Their goal was to challenge the university to make its facilities and programs accessible to students with physical disabilities. As the movement gained momentum, it spread to other campuses and to facilities and services other than college campuses.

By the mid-1970s, the independent living movement was fully articulated as a civil rights movement, led by citizens with disabilities. The goal of the movement was to provide citizens with disabilities with a voice in designing alternatives to institutional care. The strength of the movement was recognized by the passage of the Rehabilitation Act of 1973, which established and funded a national network of centers for independent living (CILs). These centers continue to operate today as consumer-led non-profit and non-residential organizations that provide cross-disability support services to individuals with disabilities in topics as diverse as peer counseling, personal assistance, technology services, independent living skill training, transportation, and mobility.

By the close of the 20th century, the independent living movement had created fundamental shifts in professional thinking about disability services, resulted in leadership roles for people with disabilities, and led to new ways of thinking about and funding community-based and Medicaid-funded services.

The Supported Living Movement

Just as previous eras helped construct the independent living movement of the 1960s and 1970s, the independent living movement living movement served as a foundation and guiding beacon for the supported living movement that began to take shape in the 1980s. As a result of the supported living movement, although state-run institutions and private, for-profit residential facilities do still exist in many states, the vast majority of individuals with LI disabilities now live in their communities in some type of community living option (Bruininks et al., 2005; Lakin, Prouty, Polister, & Coucouvanis, 2003).

The supported living movement dramatically opened the spectrum of community living options available to individuals with LI disabilities . Because of supported living principles and practices, individuals with LI disabilities may be found living in every size and type of community option available to their typical peers (Braddock, Hemp, Parish, & Rizzolo, 2000). The remaining challenge, however, is still daunting: to ensure that every community in the United States offers the full spectrum of supported living options to individuals with low incidence disabilities and that every high school educator and every IEP team guides students and their families in developing community living goals and activities that match students' preferred community living outcomes.

Supported living provides individuals with disabilities with access to community living environments that are (a) homes that would be considered desirable homes by adults without disabilities, (b) not owned by the same agency that provides support services to residents of the homes, (c) chosen by the resident with a disability and shared by other housemates at the person's discretion, and (d) organized and funded to provide support services of the type and level needed and desired by the resident in order to succeed in the home and surrounding community (e.g., Lakin &

Smull, 1995; O'Brien, 1994; Racino et al., 1993). In other words, supported living offers individuals with disabilities opportunities to live in college dorms, rented apartments, single-family homes or condominiums or mobile homes that may be rented or owned, or any other option that might be available to typical residents of a community.

During the transition planning years, individuals explore their financial resources and obligations, their employment opportunities, their transportation needs, their housing accessibility and amenity preferences, before choosing a preferred housing option. They explore their need for support services such as assistance with self-care, meal preparation and home maintenance, assistance with budgeting and paying bills, assistance with getting around in the community, and assistance with developing community connections and friendships. They decide if they want to live alone or with one or more roommates of their choosing. Finally, they choose a home and organize the rental or homeownership resources necessary to move into the home. In addition, they choose an organization or service provider to support them in learning the skills and developing the support mechanisms necessary to live successfully in the home.

Supported living participants may enjoy a range of housing environments and experiences, and these opportunities may change and evolve as residents grow and mature—just as is true for all adults. The options are limitless. Supported living may include:

- living in a leased apartment or single-family home, alone or with roommates;
- living in a resident-owned home or condominium, alone or with roommates;
- living in a duplex owned by the resident with a rent-paying tenant living in the attached unit;
- living in a family home with modifications to provide accessibility and privacy;
- living in a mobile home or an over the garage apartment on family-owned property; or
- living in a college dorm alone or with roommates.

Table 47.1 illustrates some of the possible housing and support services and funding possibilities that might be explored in creating supported living opportunities for individuals with LI disabilities.

There is a small but compelling body of literature that indicates that supported living opportunities result in lower-costs than group homes, greater satisfaction among residents with their housing situations, increased access to and usage of community resources, and increased employment stability (e.g., Allen Shea & Associates, 2002; Everson & Wilson, 2000; Horner et al., 1996; O'Brien, 1994; Parker & Boles 1990; Stancliffe & Keane, 2000). The case studies in the following section highlight three examples of supported community living opportunities along with the community participation outcomes experienced by individuals with LI disabilities.

Supported Living: Three Case Studies

Clifford's Story: An Apartment of His Own

When Clifford completed a special education high school program in South Carolina, he shared the dreams of many of his graduating classmates. He wanted to move into an apartment and live on his own. His IEP team paid minimal attention to Clifford's community living preferences focusing instead on locally available opportunities. As a result, when an opening became available, Clifford was moved into a group home with three other housemates. Clifford was placed in this group home for one reason—a slot became available in a home that was assessed as being a good match for his physical accessibility needs and his intellectual support needs. He did not choose the home or its location. He did not choose his housemates. He did not

TABLE 47.1
Housing and Support Services: Funding Possibilities

Housing	Funding Possibilities
Rental Subsidies	Local, State, and Federal Housing Authorities Local and State Developmental Disabilities Agencies
Homeownership Assistance	Local, State, and Federal Housing Authorities Local Community Development Organizations Local Mortgage Companies
Support Services	**Funding Possibilities**
Skill Instruction	Secondary/Postsecondary Education Institutions CILs Waiver Services- Developmental Disabilities Agencies
Behavioral Supports	Waiver Services- Developmental Disabilities Agencies
Transportation Supports	Waiver Services- Developmental Disabilities Agencies Local and State Transportation Agencies
Case Management	Waiver Services-Developmental Agencies
Home Modifications	Waiver Services- Developmental Disabilities Agencies Local, State, and Federal Housing Authorities Local Community Development Organizations

choose the home's décor. He did not choose the staff or services available to him.

From the very beginning, Clifford was unhappy with the group home. He could only travel into the community when staff and the van were available. He could only enjoy the privacy he preferred by staying in his bedroom. He could only entertain friends or family visitors during designated time periods and in designated areas of the group home. He was not always able to eat what he wanted or when he wanted. Clifford remained persistent, quietly expressing his self-determination abilities—for years, he told everyone he met that he wanted to move into his own apartment.

Eventually, his persistence paid off. Clifford was referred to a new initiative, the Supported Community Living Project at the Center for Disability Resources at the University of South Carolina School of Medicine. Project staff helped Clifford assemble a team of friends, family, paid support staff, and other community bridge-builders who agreed to help Clifford fully articulate and realize his dream of moving into an apartment. The team met monthly and spent several meetings listening carefully to Clifford, encouraging him to share his dream when he was reluctant to speak, asking him questions when team members were uncertain of his responses, and presenting photographs to enable Clifford to express preferences and make choices.

After many months and meetings, when the team was certain that they understood Clifford's dream and preferences, they began brainstorming apartment possibilities and listing potential obstacles as well as potential resources. Some of the possible resources included securing a "Section 8 housing voucher" so that Clifford could move into a rent-subsidized apartment in a community apartment complex. Some of the obstacles included petitioning the state agency that oversees developmental disabilities services for adjustments in Clifford's Medicaid waiver so that when he moved from his group home to his new apartment the funding he needed for skill instruction, case management, and transportation support services would follow him.

Although Clifford was the focus of all ideas, plans, actions, and decisions, everyone on his team had a role to play. Some team members completed paperwork for his housing voucher, while others made telephone calls and accompanied Clifford on tours of potential apartments. Still other members completed the necessary paperwork and challenged policy barriers to enable his Medicaid waiver funded support services to move with Clifford from his group home to his apartment. Some team members helped Clifford identify a service provider agency to give him with the daily support services he would need to maintain his apartment, bathe and dress with as much independence as possible, shop for groceries and prepare meals, travel in the community, monitor his medical and health needs, and plan leisure and recreation activities alone and with family and friends. Other members helped Clifford's support agency develop a plan with annual goals to increase his community participation opportunities. When moving day finally arrived, everyone helped Clifford move into his first apartment.

One member of Clifford's circle of support recalls, "As soon as Clifford moved into his apartment, he commented that he was the happiest he had ever been in his life." Clifford's friends and advocates who had assisted him were speechless when the quiet man spoke those words. Now, three years after moving into his own apartment and with support services in place, Clifford is living his dream. Visitors to Clifford's apartment are first greeted by a "Welcome Friends" mat at his front door and, upon entering his apartment, they often comment upon the furnishings that he chose according to his unique likes and dislikes. Clifford has many visitors in addition to the professional members of his team who drop by frequently to provide and monitor his support services. His natural supports include his sister-in-law and her children whom he enjoys entertaining in his apartment when they visit him. When asked if he would ever like to live elsewhere, Clifford candidly responds, "You couldn't pay me to move."

James's Story: From a Group Home to a Home with Family

When his grandmother died suddenly when he was a teenager, James was uprooted from the only home he had ever known in the Midwest and moved to South Carolina to live with family members he did not really know in a city that was foreign to him. When he arrived in South Carolina, he received very little assistance in grieving for his grandmother, or making the transition into a new family, new high school, and new culture. Perhaps his intellectual disabilities exacerbated his inability to handle these changes, but in a very short period of time, James completed his high school program, and was transitioned again, this time into a "high management" group home because he had "behavioral issues" and "did not have the mental capacity to live on his own." James did not get along with his three new housemates. Several of his support staff acknowledged that his "aggressive and non-compliant" behavior seemed to indicate that he wanted characteristics in his home that the group home staff was unable to provide for him. He wanted more privacy and a quieter environment, he wanted more opportunities to make choices about activities and food, he wanted more time on his own in the community without being part of a group. During the day, James participated with a large group of people in a noisy sheltered workshop program; at home, he spent most of his time in his room watching television. James was easily provoked, and because he had limited verbal communication abilities, he would often defend himself by physically attacking staff and his housemates. As a result, his file soon included page after page of paperwork that labeled him "non-compliant" and "aggressive."

Finally, a small group of paid staff and friends, people who recognized how unhappy James seemed to be, convened a circle of support and began meeting to explore with James his unspoken preferences and desire to live somewhere else. For 6 months, James and his circle of support met monthly to explore what he really wanted from a home. Initially, James would nod in agreement when asked if he wanted to live in his own house, but he could not express any preferences about his dream house. Eventually, through repeated visits to community options and by offering James photos and forced-choice options, his circle of support began to understand James and his preferences. They determined that James wanted a key of his own to his home and he wanted to be able to leave and enter his home without having to ask permission. To help him express his preferences and to make choices, one of his circle of support friends spent several hours driving James around various neighborhoods and looking at all types of houses. Eventually, James shared his goal: he wanted to live in a two-story brick house with a big backyard and a swimming pool.

Now that his team more fully understood James and his dream, the circle continued to meet to develop his person-centered plan and begin the process of helping him attain his dream. Over time, James began to exhibit a number of self-determination abilities. After setting his goal, James learned to evaluate options, to express preferences, to make choices, and to make decisions.

After a year of planning and hard work, James moved into a two-bedroom apartment and chose his cousin to live with him to help provide daily supports. The team chose an agency to provide him with support services, and his cousin was also approved to help provide his support services. It was not a two-story house, but it was a two-story apartment and it did have a large community greenspace and a community swimming pool. It also came equipped with an emergency panic button, sprinkler system, and a two-car garage. His circle of support worked closely with the South Carolina Department of Disabilities and Special Needs to make sure that his Medicaid-funded support services plan adequately matched his support needs. Everyone began to realize that James's need for daily support services had not changed, but the way in which the supports should be provided was changing. After 3 weeks of living in his apartment with his cousin, James's behavior support plan was discontinued because his "disruptive behaviors" had ceased to exist. Instead, his service plan was re-written to enable him to spend more leisure time in the community and to learn new independent living skills necessary to live in and maintain his apartment.

James's accomplishment of moving out of the group home and into an apartment was just the beginning of his quest for independence and his expression of self-determination abilities. After living in the apartment for almost two years, he asked his circle of support to re-convene and once again help him pursue his dream of living in a house again. He now desired a larger home and more opportunities to be involved in the community. And so after more planning, James and his cousin moved into a two-story house. The house has a large, fenced backyard with enough room for a dog, and the neighborhood has both a swimming pool and a community activities center. Because his Medicaid-funded support services were attached to him instead of to his housing, his services and service providers moved with him from the apartment to his new home. James's life looks drastically different now than it did even a few months ago, and those who know him best are so excited to see what the future holds for this ambitious young man.

Jeremy's Story: The College Experience

Like many parents, Jeremy's parents dreamed that their son would finish high school and have the opportunity to go on to college. Jeremy is an inquisitive and outgoing young man who enjoys learning new things and being around people his own age. During his high school IEP and transition planning years spent in an urban community in North Carolina, Jeremy looked forward to following in the footsteps of his older sister who was a college student. However, Jeremy also lives with intellectual and other communication disabilities, disabilities that were severe enough that many professionals assumed they would prohibit his ability to attend college.

When Jeremy was in high school, his parents learned about several innovative, residential postsecondary education programs for students with LI disabilities that were available in other states. They were disappointed to find out that no comparable program existed in North Carolina. Unwilling to accept the lack of a program as a deterrent to their dream, they gathered together friends and advocates to explore the creation of a comparable opportunity in their North Carolina community. In collaboration with a support services provider agency, Charles Hines & Son, this group of advocates established a pilot program that they called "Beyond Academics." Within two years, the planning group was able to fully develop the program and launch it at the University of North Carolina at Greensboro. Jeremy was accepted into the program as one of the freshman students.

Beyond Academics is a four-year postsecondary education program for students with intellectual disabilities. Most students live on the University of North Carolina at Greensboro's campus in student housing with typical college students as their apartment mates. During the day, students attend specially designed classes held on campus. Classes are taught by Beyond Academics faculty and internship students from the university. Juniors and seniors enrolled in Beyond Academics also have the opportunity to audit university classes with typical university peers. During the evenings and weekends, students interact with their typical apartment mates and other university students to explore on-campus activities and activities throughout the Greensboro community.

When Jeremy was presented with the opportunity to go to college, he was very excited. Although they hoped that Jeremy's enthusiasm and self-determination abilities would outweigh his disabilities, his parents, like many parents of new college students, were concerned. Would Jeremy be homesick living away from home? Would he be prepared for the academic challenges? Would he be vulnerable to financial, social, or sexual exploitation?

With both trepidation and enthusiasm, Jeremy moved into his first apartment and enrolled as a freshman in Beyond Academics at the university. Jeremy's parents cite several positive examples of his transition from a high school student into a typical college freshman. In his first semester, Jeremy, who was nonverbal for much of his childhood, presented his parents with a 16-page cell phone bill representing 600 telephone calls to family and friends. His parents concluded that the young man they sent to college had learned to communicate just like his collegiate sister and other college freshman. When his parents visited his apartment, his mother was initially alarmed to see Jeremy unshaven and sloppily dressed—until she realized that Jeremy was in no way indistinguishable from his apartment mates and typical college peers.

Along with the opportunity to acquire new academic abilities, Jeremy's on-campus residential experiences have offered him self-determination and community participation opportunities, many unique to the experience of moving away from home for the first time. At the end of his freshman year with Beyond Academics, Jeremy's roommate, Mike, graduated from the university, married, and moved into an apartment in town with his new wife. Jeremy was delighted to serve as a groomsman at his friend's wedding and the two friends have maintained their friendship by getting together each month for dinner or a movie. Jeremy has had other, and not always so positive, typical college experiences. One year an acquaintance of his roommate stole Jeremy's Wii video game. Jeremy was as devastated by the theft as he was by the profane behavior of the thief as he left the apartment with Jeremy's property. Beyond Academics staff and Jeremy's friends help him file a police report, role played what would happen in court, accompanied Jeremy to court to help him advocate his position, and helped him to learn new strategies for protecting his property in his apartment. Jeremy's roommate, Ryan, commented on how nice it is to come home to Jeremy, "When Jeremy asks, 'how was your day?' he isn't satisfied with 'okay" as an answer. He probes further, 'really—how was your day?' You cannot take a day for granted with Jeremy."

Methods and Activities Needed by Educators to Prepare Students with LI Disabilities for Community Living Opportunities

As these case studies illustrate, supported living is no longer an unrealistic or unattainable transition goal for individuals with LI disabilities. While students are in high school, there are several things that educators and IEP team members can do to help prepare students for these opportunities. As the literature and these case studies further illustrate, many young adults with LI, similar to their typical peers, will not transition immediately upon exiting high school from their family home to their desired home and community. Thus, providing students and their families with the foundation necessary for making community living choices and decisions during this multi-year process is an essential component of transition planning. As a part of high school IEP and transition planning activities, educators can: (a) encourage team members to learn about and discuss contemporary community living philosophies and locally available supported living options; (b) assist students in developing the self-determination abilities necessary to choose preferred community living options and supports; and (c) offer students community living and community participation experiences and activities that develop skills in financial and legal, health and medical, recreation, relationships, and transportation matters. Together, these abilities, goals, experiences, and activities will help prepare students and their families for the complex, multi-year, and multi-outcome process that will enable students to move away from home for the first time.

Teaching Students Self-Determination Skill for Supported Living

In the 1990s, self-determination emerged as a federally funded focus of transition services, and, ultimately, of supported living services. Self-determination is a broad set of abilities that describe young adults who "...know how to choose what they want and how to get it" (Martin & Marshall, 1995, p. 147). Self-determined individuals make choices, set goals, doggedly pursue their goals, self-evaluate their progress, and adjust their goals and actions though negotiation and creative problem-solving when necessary.

Becoming self-determined is a primary task of adolescence, a task that lends itself well to the challenges and opportunities inherent in supported living. Wood, Fowler, Uphold, and Test (2005) conducted a comprehensive review of 21 articles addressing self-determination interventions for individuals with LI disabilities and concluded that students with LI disabilities can benefit from self-determination instruction especially when systematic instructional procedures are used to help them make choices. Similarly, Wehmeyer and Palmer (2003) concluded that three-years after leaving high school, young adults with cognitive disabilities and self-determination abilities were more likely than those with a lesser degree of self-determination abilities to have achieved community living and participation outcomes. For example, they were more likely to be living independently, in a home other than where they lived during high school (Wehmeyer & Palmer, 2003). Although IQ may not be dismissed entirely as a factor in attainment of self-determination abilities, several studies (Wehmeyer & Palmer, 2003; Nota, Ferrari, Soresi, & Wehmeyer, 2007) suggest that IQ may be less important in predicting self-determination abilities than the provision of systematic self-determination instruction by teachers.

Thus, instruction can enhance the attainment of self-determination abilities in young adults with LI disabilities, and community living is an appropriate transition outcome area in which to include self-determination instruction. There is an abundance of literature and commercially available self-determination curricula available to educators. These materials generally promote three identified instructional tracks, all three of which are appropriate for high school students with LI disabilities and for community living instruction: (a) provision of instruction to promote self-knowledge, choice-making, and goal-setting; (b) provision of opportunities to experience self-instruction, self-evaluation, and self-advocacy; and (c) discussion and design of individually-needed supports and accommodations.

Teachers of students with LI disabilities may infuse self-determination instruction into a number of instructional activities and use a variety of instructional methods to help direct students toward supported living outcomes. It is important to remember that the goal of self-determination instruction for students with LI disabilities is not to develop their total independence, but instead to develop their abilities to express preferences, make choices, participate in goal setting, maintain their endurance toward goals, and to negotiate and problem-solve. In post-high school supported living experiences, these young adults will have ample opportunities to experience these situations with a network of professionals, family members, friends, and/or other community members to support them.

Self-determination may be infused into language arts, social studies, mathematics, art, and science classes. Table 47.2 provides some examples of instructional activities and

TABLE 47.2
Suggested Instructional Activities, Methods, and Self-Determination Skills for Promoting Community Living Outcomes

Suggested Instructional Activity and Methods	Self-Determination Skill
Ask students to set a housing goal. "Where would you like to live three years after leaving high school?" Use maps, newspapers, telephone directories, and the Internet to explore social studies activities.	Self-knowledge Decision-making skills Goal-setting skills
Have students use real estate and home décor magazines, the real estate section of local newspapers, photographs of apartment complexes and community homes to develop a collage of their "dream home". "Would you have a yard? A porch?" "What would the outside look like?" "Describe your bedroom." Infuse the activity into art classes. Ask students to share their "dream home" at their next IEP meeting.	Self-knowledge Decision-making skills Goal-setting skills Self-advocacy skills
Present two contrasting photographs and ask students to make choices. "This is an apartment without a yard. This is a house with a front yard. Which would you like most to live in?" "This is a brick home and this is a wood home. Which do you like best?" or "This is a bedroom with blue carpet and this is a bedroom with wood floors. Which do you like best?"	Self-knowledge Choice-making skills Decision-making skills
Hold a discussion about roommates. Have students discuss what they would like and dislike about a roommate. "Would you prefer someone who is quiet or someone who likes to talk?" "Would you mind sharing a bathroom?' Help students to write an ad to place in a newspaper advertising for a roommate. Role-play interviewing someone as a roommate.	Self-knowledge Choice-making skills Decision-making skills Goal-setting skills Self-advocacy skills
Ask students to discuss the skills they think someone needs to learn before moving away from home. "Do you help with any of these chores at home?" "What do you need to learn before you move away from home?" "What do you need help with? "Who helps you now?" "How would you find help if you lived on your own?"	Self-knowledge Self-evaluation skills Goal-setting skills Self-instruction skills Self-advocacy skills
Hold a discussion with students about advantages and disadvantages of renting and homeownership. "Do you think you would want rent a home or own a home?" Provide math problem case studies where students determine income and expenses and decide how much they can spend on housing	Self-knowledge Choice-making skills Decision-making skills
Have students volunteer with a housing initiative such as Habitat for Humanity or Neighborhood Watch.	Self-advocacy
Visit local community living programs such as group homes, supported apartments, or homeownership initiatives. Hold a discussion about what they liked and disliked about each. "Which option did you like best? Least?" "Why?"	Choice-making skills Decision-making skills Goal-setting skills Self-advocacy
As part of English classes, discuss the meaning of terms such as application, rent, credit report, lease, down payment, mortgage, landlord, and foreclosure.	Self-instruction skills
Hold a discussion about the relationship between money, employment, and housing. Provide math problem case studies where students determine income and expenses and decide how much they can spend on housing.	Problem-solving skills Decision-making skills Goal-setting skills Self-instruction skills Self-monitoring skills
Work with a local bank or savings and loan to establish checking accounts and teach students to write checks, budget money, and pay bills. Provide math problem case studies where students determine income and expenses and decide how much they can spend on housing.	Problem-solving skills Decision-making skills Goal-setting skills Self-instruction skills Self-evaluation skills
Invite speakers from a local hardware store to speak to students about simple home maintenance and repairs. Use adding, subtracting and measuring tasks to develop math problems, and art assignments.	Problem-solving skills Decision-making skills Self-instruction skills Self-evaluation skills
Invite speakers with disabilities to speak to the class about their housing experiences.	Decision-making skills

instructional methods that teacher may use to develop self-determination abilities in the area of community living. The activities suggested in this table may help students begin to explore their own preferences and explore the relationship between employment, housing, and financial responsibility.

Guiding Students Toward the Development of Community Living and Community Participation Experiences and Activities

Community participation is another task associated with moving away from home for the first time. Community participation may be viewed as a young adult's participation in community activities and resources according to one's preferences, needs, and goals. Type and levels of community participation are highly driven by an adolescent's preferences, needs and goals. Areas of community participation include, for example, managing one's own finances, managing one's own health and medical appointments and services, choosing and scheduling one's leisure pursuits, and managing one's transportation needs. For some young adults, this may mean using public transportation, while for others it may mean participating in carpooling or driving and maintaining one's own vehicle. For some young adults, it may mean being an active member of a church or synagogue. For others, it may mean belonging to a YMCA, local recreation center, or a membership-required gym. For nearly every young adult, it means managing a budget and understanding income, and expenses, monitoring one's own health and medical needs, and managing household tasks.

Community participation is a broad construct, one that does not always lend itself easily to transition goal-setting and outcome measurement. Broadly defined in IDEA (2004), community participation includes involvement in adult lifestyle outcomes as diverse, but interrelated as civic involvement, financial and legal, health and medical, recreation, relationships, and transportation matters. For young adults with LI disabilities , community participation is achieved when they have access to the same opportunities available to their peers, and when they have the supports necessary to participate in these opportunities according to their choices and preferences.

Just as is true with self-determination abilities, skills needs for community participation outcomes lend themselves well to infusion within academic areas. For youth with LI disabilities , as it true with their peers, expectations for these outcomes are individually determined, reflective of each person's unique preferences and abilities, and as such lend themselves well to self-determination instruction and methods. Educators may view this as a five-step process that includes: (a) assessing the student's community participation interests, skills, and needs; (b) using this information, set community participation goals during IEP and transition planning activities for the student; (c) infused within the academic program, providing the student with opportunities and experiences to learn skills, make decisions and refine choices, and self-evaluate the experience; (d) annually revising and updating community participation goals during IEP and transition planning activities; and (e) providing the student and family with resource materials to support community participation interests, skills, and needs as part of the "exit" planning from high school. Table 47.3 provides some examples of instructional activities and instructional

TABLE 47.3
Suggested Instructional Activities, Methods, and Self-Determination Abilities for Promoting Community Participation Outcomes

1. Choice making
   - Have students develop preferences maps of their likes and dislikes using person-centered planning tools. Encourage students to use these maps to open discussion during their individualized education program (IEP) meetings.
   - Encourage students to identify new potential activities and resources. Use these newly identified activities to expand IEP goals and activities.
   - Reward students when they pursue new experiences.
   - Teach students to make choices by providing contingent and natural consequences for the choices.
   - Present students with multiple predetermined opportunities from which to choose. Include options from their preferences maps and include new, unfamiliar options from which they may make choices.
   - Facilitate discussions among students about the choices they make, the consequences, and the limits within which some choices can be made.
   - Provide assistive communication supports to students who need them (e.g., photographs of activities, preprinted written instruction cards).
   - Invite guest speakers from recreation center, transportation providers, volunteer and service organizations, and social and professional groups to discuss opportunities available in the community. Encourage student projects that promote community participation.
   - Invite adults with disabilities to discuss the leisure, relationship, health and medical, civic, and transportation choices they have made.
2. Decision making
   - Teach students to prioritize preferences, list choices and possible consequences, and make decisions accordingly.
   - Facilitate discussions, role plays, mock elections, and other activities that require students to practice making decisions and discuss their actions and the outcomes.
3. Problem solving
   - Teach students to respond to problem-solving questions such as "What is the problem?" "How can I solve it?" "If my planned solution doesn't work, how can I change it?"
   - Facilitate discussions, role plays, and other activities that provide students with opportunities to identify problems, propose solutions, ask questions, listen, and summarize events. Incorporate adult driving and non driving decisions, health decisions, leisure decisions, and relationship decisions within these activities.

(continued)

TABLE 47.3 Continued

4. Goal setting
   - Have students define concepts such as goals, future, and vision. Incorporate the words into word search games, crossword puzzles, and math word problems.
   - Facilitate discussions, role plays, and other activities that provide students with opportunities to think about the future and discuss potential personal goals.
   - Have students set goals, set time frames, determine the benefits of reaching goals, and prioritize among goals.
   - Have students identify potential supports and match them to their needs.
   - Facilitate discussions, role plays, and other activities that require students to determine specific plans to reach their goals. Identify examples of adults engaging in these skills in literature and current events.
   - Invite adults with disabilities to share their goals and the experiences they had as they transitioned from high school to adult life.
5. Independence, risk taking, and safety
   - Advocate for students to have opportunities to engage in age-appropriate behaviors and activities that promote independence (e.g., school-sponsored driver's education programs, students government, senior class trips and projects, school recreation, and social clubs and events).
   - Have students identify potential supports and match them to their needs (e.g., assistive technology).
   - Teach students to identify cues and prompts that might alert them to risky or unsafe situations.
   - Facilitate reading assignments, videos, discussions, role plays, and other activities that allow students to identify and respond to novel, safe, unsafe, or risky situations. Identify examples of adults using these skills in literature and current events.
   - Whenever possible, teach and test students in community environments to provide natural cues, prompts, and consequences.
   - Teach students to self-assess and self-manage the actions they follow in pursuit of their personal goals.
6. Self-evaluation
   - Provide students with opportunities to self-assess and self-manage their goals, timeframes, and actions.
   - Facilitate discussions, role plays, and other activities that enable students to self-assess and self-manage their goals. Identify examples of adults using these skills in literature and current events.
   - Invite adults with disabilities to share their goals and the experiences they had as they transitioned from high school to adult life.
   - Use multiple teaching methods to teach students to perform task (e.g., model the task, provide verbal and written instruction, provide redundancy cues).
   - Promote maintenance and generalization of newly learned skills by teaching and testing in multiple environments and with multiple instructors.
7. Self-instruction
   - Teach students about the legal rights and responsibilities of adults. Invite speakers from centers for independent living, the League of Women Voters, and advocacy groups to speak to students.
   - Teach students the meaning of concepts such as assertiveness, self-advocacy, and leadership. Identify examples of adults using these skills in literature and current events.
8. Self-advocacy and leadership
   - Teach students effective social, communication, and conflict-management skills.
   - Facilitate discussions, role plays, mock elections, and other activities that allow students to practice self-advocacy and leadership skills.
   - Invite adults with disabilities to share their goals and the experiences they had as they transitioned from high school to adult life.
9. Internal locus of control
   - Teach students about and provide opportunities to learn about the relationship between their behavior and performance.
   - Clearly define behavior and performance expectations.
   - Provide students with rich opportunities for positive reinforcement.
   - Model and provide opportunities to work cooperatively with peers and adults on group projects that promote teamwork. Ensure that students with disabilities have opportunities to engage in community and volunteer events in which they give back to the community.
10. Positive attributes of efficacy and outcome expectancy
   - Have students develop preferences and future maps of their attributes, gifts, and capacities using person-centered planning tools.
   - Encourage students to try new activities and pursue new experiences.
   - Have students explore and encourage use of assistive technology to increase transportation opportunities, voter participation, recreation experiences, and health and medical independence, for example.
   - Provide students with rich opportunities for positive reinforcement.
   - Invite adults with disabilities to share their goals and the experiences they had as they transitioned form high school to adult life.
11. Self-awareness
   - Have students develop preferences and future maps of their attributes, gifts, and capacities using person-centered planning tools.
   - Provide students with factual education about their disabilities and the functional impact of their disabilities on, for example, driving, health and medical independence, and legal rights.
   - Provide students with opportunities to interact with peers and adults with similar disabilities to explore their characteristics and experiences.
   - Teach students compensatory strategies to address their disabilities.
   - Explore and encourage use of assistive technology.
12. Self-knowledge
   - Have students develop preferences and vision maps of their attributes, gifts, and capacities using person-centered planning tools.
   - Provide students with factual education about their disabilities.
   - Provide students with opportunities to interact with peers and adults with similar disabilities to explore their characteristics and experiences.

methods that teacher may use to develop community participation in the area of community living.

Implications for Practice and Future Research

Preparation for community living outcomes is an essential component of IEP and transition planning activities for high school students, and this is equally true for students with LI disabilities. Because supported living is a viable outcome for these individuals and their families, it is essential that educators use the transition planning process develop the knowledge and skills necessary to discuss "best practices" and locally available options, teach students self-determination abilities, and provide students with experiences and activities to promote community participation. By the time students exit high school, they and their families should be able to articulate a community living environment and arrangement that they are interested in pursuing and be aware of the agencies and organizations in their community that might help them realize this dream. In addition, they should be able to articulate their preferences and needs for managing finances, health and medical appointments and services, choosing and scheduling leisure pursuits, and managing transportation needs. More research is needed on the post- high school community living and community participation outcomes of students who have benefitted from a comprehensive approach to transition planning, one that includes an emphasis on self-determination abilities and community living planning. Future research is needed to assess the long-term benefits of various curricular preparation models and success in supported living opportunities.

Literature on typical adolescents and adolescents with disabilities seems to indicate that there are more similarities than differences in the process of moving away from home for the first time. Literature also seems to indicate that young adults with LI disabilities , while currently participating in lower numbers than their peers with high incidence disabilities, can benefit from self-determination instruction and opportunities and can be successful in a variety of diverse supported living opportunities. More research is needed on the multi-year process of moving away from home and how adolescents with LI disabilities can benefit from this research.

Finally, emerging literature supports the benefits of supported living and raises important costs about the costs and benefits. More research is needed to explore the long-term costs of supported living, especially with the newest options such as homeownership. Research is also needed to explore the long-term quality of life benefits of supported living, especially those potentially associated with employment and other community participation outcomes.

References

Allen Shea & Associates (2002). *Supported living project: A final report.* Boise, ID: Idaho Council on Developmental Disabilities. Retrieved, June 24, 2009, from http://www.allenshea.com/sls.pdf database

Arnett, J. J. (2001). Conceptions of the transition to adulthood: Perspectives from adolescence through midlife. *Journal of Adult Development, 8*(2) 133–143.

Arnett, J. J. (2007). *Adolescence and emerging adulthood: A cultural approach.* Upper Saddle River, NJ: Pearson Education.

Barr, M. (1904). *Mental defectives.* Philadelphia: P. Blakiston's Son and Co.

Blanton, B., & Kaplan, F. (1974). *Christmas in purgatory. A photographic essay on mental retardation.* Syracuse, NY: Human Policy Press.

Bogdan, R. (1988). *Freak show: Presenting human oddities for amusement and profit.* Chicago: The University of Chicago Press.

Braddock, D (1988). *Forces that shape the funding of mental retardation services: Proceedings of the 1988 John Quincy Memorial Fund Lecture* (pp. 1–15). Boston: Wrentham State School.

Braddock, D., & Heller, T. (1984). *The closure of mental retardation institutions: Trends and implications.* Chicago: Institute for the Study of Developmental Disabilities, University of Illinois at Chicago.

Braddock, D., & Hemp, R. (2008). *Services and funding for people with developmental disabilities in Illinois: A multi-state comparative analysis.* Chicago: Springfield: Illinois Council on Developmental Disabilities.

Braddock, D., Hemp, R., Parish, S., & Rizzolo, M. C. (2000). Growth in state commitments for community services: Significance of the Medicaid Home and Community Based Services Waiver. *Mental Retardation, 38*(2), 186–189.

Bruininks, R., Byun, S., Coucouvanis, K., Lakin, C., Larson, S., & Prouty, R. W. (2005). *Residential services for persons with developmental disabilities: Status and trends through 2004.* University of Minnesota: The College of Education and Human Development. Retrieved June 24, 2009, from http://rtc.umn.edu/risp04 database

Circus and museum freaks – Curiosities of pathology. (1908, March 28). *Scientific American.* Retrieved February 3, 2009, from Disability History Museum, http://www.disabiitymuseum.org

Everson, J. M., & Wilson, P. G. (2000). What do homeowners with disabilities tell us about being homeowners? A qualitative report. *Journal of Vocational Rehabilitation, 15,* 121–129.

Furstenberg, F. F., Kennedy, S., McCloyd, V. C., Rumbaut, R. G., & Settersten, R. A. (2003). *Between adolescence and adulthood: Expectations about the timing of adulthood.* Retrieved April 24, 2009, from Network on Transitions to Adulthood and Public Policy, http://www.transad.pop.upenn.edu/index.html

Graber, J. A., & Dubas, J. S. (1996). *Leaving home: Understanding the transition to adulthood.* San Francisco: Jossey-Bass.

Gutmann, M., Pullum-Pionon, S., & Pullum T. (2002). Three eras of young adult home leaving in twentieth-century America. *Journal of Social History, 35,* 533–567.

Halpern, A., (1993). Quality of life as a conceptual framework for evaluating transition outcomes. *Exceptional Children, 59,* 486–498.

Hanley-Maxwell, C., Whitney-Thomas, J., & Pogoloff, S. (1995). The second shock: A qualitative study of parents' perspectives and needs during their child's transition from school to adult life. *Journal of the Association for Persons with Severe Handicaps, 20,* 3–15.

Horner, R. H., Close, D. W., Fredericks, H. D. B., O'Neill, R. E., Albin, R. W., & Sprague, J. R. (1996). Supported living for people with profound disabilities and severe behavior problems. In D. D. Lehr & F. Brown (Eds.), *People with disabilities who challenge the system* (pp. 209–240). Baltimore: Brookes.

IDEA (2004). Individuals with Disabilities Education Improvement Act, P.L. 108-446, 20 U.S.C. 1400 et seq.

Kastner, L. S., & Wyatt, J. F. (1997). *The seven year stretch: How families work together to grow through adolescence.* Boston: Houghton Mifflin.

Kochhar-Bryant, C. A., & Greene, G. (2009). *Pathways to successful transition for youth with disabilities. A developmental process* (2nd ed.). Upper Saddle River, NJ: Pearson Education.

Lakin, K. C., Prouty, R., Polister, B., & Coucouvanis, K. (2003). Selected changes in residential service systems over a quarter century, 1977–2002. *Mental Retardation, 41*(4), 303–306.

Lakin, C., & Smull, M. (1995). Supported community living: From "facilities" to "homes". *IMPACT, 8*(4), 2–3.

LoConto, D., & Dodder, R. (1997). The right to be human: Deinstitutionalization and the wishes of people with developmental disabilities. *Education and Training in Mental Retardation and Developmental Disabilities, 32*(2), 77–84.

Martin, J. E., & Marshall, L. H. (1995). ChoiceMaker: A comprehensive self-determination transition program. *Intervention in School and Clinic, 30*, 147–156.

McConkey, R., Sowney, M., Milligan, V., & Barr, O. (2004). View of people with intellectual disabilities of their present and future living arrangements. *Journal of Policy and Practice in Intellectual Disabilities, 1*(3/4), 115–125.

Morningstar, M. E., Kleinhammer-Tramill, J., & Lattin, D. (1999). Using successful models of student-centered transition planning and services for adolescents. *Focus on Exceptional Children, 31*(9), 1–19.

National Council on Disability. (2000). *Transition and post-school outcomes for youth with disabilities. Closing the gaps to post-secondary education and employment.* Washington, DC: National Council on Disability and Social Security Administration.

Nota, L., Ferrari, L., Soresi, S., & Wehmeyer, M. (2007). Self-determination, social abilities and the quality of life of people with intellectual disability. *Journal of Intellectual Disability Research, 5*(11), 850–865.

O'Brien, J. (1994). Down stairs that are never your own: Supporting people with developmental disabilities in their own homes. *Mental Retardation, 32*(1), 1–6.

O'Hara, A., & Miller, E. (2000). *Going it alone: The struggle to expand housing opportunities for people with disabilities.* Boston: Technical Assistance Collaborative, Inc. and Washington, DC: Consortium for Citizens with Disabilities Housing Task Force.

Parker, R., & Boles, S. (1990). Integration opportunities for residents with developmental disabilities: Differences among supported living sites and residents. *Education and Training in Mental Retardation, 25*(1), 76–82.

Racino, J., Walker, P., O'Connor, S., & Taylor, S. (1993). *Housing, support, and community: Choices and strategies for adults with disabilities.* Baltimore: Brookes.

Rizzolo, M. C., Hemp, R., Braddock, D., & Pomeranz-Essley, A. (2004). *The state of the states in developmental disabilities: 2004.* Boulder: The Coleman Institute for Cognitive Disabilities and Department of Psychiatry, University of Colorado.

Rusch, F. (2008). *Beyond high school. Preparing adolescents for tomorrow's challenges* (2nd ed.). Upper Saddle River, NJ: Pearson Education.

Stancliffe, R. J., & Keane, S. (2000). Outcomes and costs of community living: A matched comparison of group homes and semi-independent living. *Journal of Intellectual and Developmental Disability, 25*(4), 281–305.

Steinberg, L. (2001). We know some things: Parent-adolescent relationships in retrospect and prospect. *Journal of Research on Adolescence, 11*(1), 1–19.

Steinberg, L. (2007). *Adolescence* (8th ed.). New York: McGraw-Hill.

Test, D. W., Aspel, N. P., & Everson, J. M. (2006). Preparing students for community living opportunities. In *Transition methods for youth with disabilities* (pp. 302–333). Upper Saddle River, NJ: Pearson Education.

Thomson, R. G. (1997). *Extraordinary bodies. Figuring physical disability in American culture and literature.* New York: Columbia University Press.

Trent, J.W. (1994). *Inventing the feeble mind: A history of mental retardation in the United States.* Berkley: University of California Press.

U.S. Department of Education. (2001). *Twenty-third annual report to Congress on the implementation of the Individuals with Disabilities Education Act.* Washington, DC: Author.

Wagner, M., Marder, C., Blackorby, J., Cameto, R., Newman, L., Levine, P., et al. (2003). *The achievements of youth with disabilities during secondary school: A report from the National Longitudinal Transition Study-2.* Menlo Park, CA: SRI International.

Wehmeyer, M. L., & Palmer, S. B. (2003). Adult outcomes for students with cognitive disabilities three-years after high school: The impact of self-determination. *Education and Training in Developmental Disabilities. 38*(2), 131–144.

Wolfensberger, W. (1972). *The principle of normalization in human services.* Toronto, Canada: National Institute on Mental Retardation.

Wood, W. M., Fowler, C.H., Uphold, N., & Test, D. W. (2005). A review of self-determination interventions with individuals with severe disabilities. *Research & Practice for Persons with Severe Disabilities, 30*(3), 121–146.

Section XI

Parent and Family Issues in Special Education

Section Editor: George H. S. Singer
University of California, Santa Barbara

Special education is inevitably a family affair. The laws that structure its practices provide key roles for parents who are given an unusual level of authority in planning and approving the details of their children's educations. The center piece of early intervention practice under the Individuals with Disabilities Education Act (IDEA) is the Individual Family Service Plan (IFSP), which by definition focuses public resources and professional skills on the family of young children with disabilities as the central recipient of services. Similarly, the central document guiding the special education of a school-aged child with a disability, the Individual Education Plan (IEP), by law must be developed by an interdisciplinary team with parents as important members. Parents are meant to be full partners in the process. Contemporary textbooks for training special educators emphasize the benefits of establishing parent-professional partnerships. The law provides parents with a set of procedural safeguards to make sure that they give informed consent prior to assessing children for eligibility for special education services and placing them in special education. Parents must consent to an IEP, and they must be provided with regular reports on their children's progress in meeting its stated goals and objectives. The IEP serves as a legal contract, and parents are given due process rights to enforce it when they believe the agreement as been breached. A recent Supreme Court ruling, *Winkelman v. Parma,* explains the importance Congress attached to parental rights:

> It is beyond dispute that the relationship between a parent and child is sufficient to support a legally cognizable interest in the education of one's child; and, what is more, Congress has found that "the education of children with disabilities can be made more effective by… strengthening the role and responsibility of parents and ensuring that families of such children have meaningful opportunities to participate in the education of their children at school and at home." (*Winkelman*, 550 U.S. at 520)

Special education and early intervention were created as federal entitlements in large part because of many years of effort by parents in the legal and political arenas, first at the local, then at the state, and ultimately at the national level.

The status of children with disabilities and their families in the United States has undergone a remarkable transformation since the end of World War II. In 1946, public resources for children with disabilities were allotted to large state institutions for individuals with mental retardation (presently known as intellectual disability) and to limited special education services distributed sporadically in some states and urban areas. As late as 1975, the U.S. Congress determined that as many as 3.9 million children with disabilities were denied a public education. In 1946, individuals with mental retardation were still sterilized without their consent in several states and many children and adults with disabilities were kept at home, out of the public eye, considered sources of shame for their families. In less than six decades, the United States has a well-established system of early intervention and public school services for all children. Many large state institutions have been closed, and the expected place for individuals with disabilities is in their home, in the communities where increasingly they are afforded the opportunities available to other U.S. citizens. Parents and their professional allies must be credited with this quiet but still incomplete revolution. In Chapter 48, Turnbull, Shogren, and Turnbull describe the social movement created by parents of children with disabilities that led to the passage of the IDEA. They document the way parents continue to play a key role in the political arena in efforts to update the law and push for more effective services.

Many families first come into contact with the services created by the IDEA through the early intervention system. In Chapter 50, Bailey, Raspa, Humphries, and Sam explain the philosophy and application of family centered early intervention. The IDEA entitles children with disabilities services from birth through age 22. In early childhood, it makes little sense to try to further the development of children with or at risk of disabilities without enlisting their families as full partners. The contemporary service philosophy guiding early intervention services is the idea of family centered early intervention. Bailey et al. discuss efforts to define family centered early intervention and to assess the effectiveness of the service system in helping families achieve important family outcomes. These evaluations are heartening in their early indication that many families are being bolstered at the critical first stages of the family lifecycle. They also note the challenges that remain.

In both social science and the popular culture, families of children with disabilities have traditionally been characterized as victims of fate, described as having a wide array of social and psychological problems linked to the stress of raising a child with a disability. In Chapter 49, Singer, Maul, Wang, and Ethridge review the evidence for viewing families as resilient over the long term. They note that different disabilities on average have different levels of impact on families with the most concern focused on families of children with low incidence, severe disabilities. Research in this area has recently undergone a transformation as scholars have been more willing to listen to families and recognize the extensive variability in family responses to disability. Many parents and siblings of children with disabilities have become researchers, bringing new assumptions to bear in their scholarship. There is little doubt that initial identification of a child's disability is highly stressful for many parents, but there is a growing body of evidence showing that many families adapt effectively over time and come to see their children with special needs as positive contributors to the family and to the parent's quality of life. The emerging evidence also suggests that many families require greater levels of support and more effective services than presently exist if they are to overcome the many stresses associated with their life-long commitments to the well being of family members with disabilities. Of particular concern is the recurrent observation that some families find accessing and using services, including special education, a major source of stress and distress. In particular, there is cause for concern about low-income families, who are more likely to have children with disabilities due to the impact of poverty on child health and development. They often have less access to family support services with far greater need than more privileged families. There is also considerable evidence that effective services have yet to be created on a necessary scale to meet the needs of families of children with emotional and behavioral disabilities. Behavior problems in children and adolescents are leading causes of family distress. Singer et al. briefly review recent meta-analyses suggesting that interventions for these families need to be improved and made more widely available. The studies in their syntheses also offer considerable hope that much has been learned about how to reduce negative outcomes and promote family resilience.

Reference

Winkelman v. Parma City School District, 550 U.S. 516 (2007)

48

Evolution of the Parent Movement

Past, Present, and Future

H. Rutherford Turnbull, III
Beach Center on Disability, University of Kansas

Karrie A. Shogren
University of Illinois, Urbana-Champaign

Ann P. Turnbull
Beach Center on Disability, University of Kansas

Today, the right of students with disabilities to a free appropriate public education is firmly established as a matter of law. That establishment is the result of nearly 50 years of advocacy by parents and their allies, joined together in a civil rights movement, and the enactment of a federal special education law.

The parent movement—in both its overall civil-rights and its particular education-rights aspects—predates Congress' enactment in 1975 of the federal special education law, P.L. 94-142, Education of All Handicapped Children Act. Before then, there was no federal equal-protection right to education for students with disabilities. In large part that was so because the prevailing conception of disability was deficit-based. Disability was regarded as a deficit located within the individual student and often the student's family. Being inherent, disability had a low claim to social (as distinguished from medical) remediation. Indeed, some 50-plus years ago disability was no more a matter of constitutional concern than race had been and sex was to be; the notion of equal protection, protecting against discrimination based on inherent and unalterable traits and affording due process to protest discrimination, were inchoate concepts for people with disabilities and their families (Ferguson, 2008; Thompson, 2002; Turnbull, Stowe, & Huerta, 2007). The civil rights movements based on race and then on sex were precedents for the movement based on disability (Turnbull et al., 2007) which was the result of a movement spearheaded by parents and contextualized within special education.

Defining Social Movements

Social movements are "collective, organized, sustained, and noninstitutional challenge to authorities, powerholders, or cultural beliefs or practices" (Goodwin & Jasper, 2003, p. 3). They consist of three interrelated elements:

- Political Actions—formation of coalitions and associations and use of dissemination strategies to share information and energize the public through meetings, rallies, protests, etc.
- Displays—actions to demonstrate the unity, number, and commitment of members of the movement and the worthiness of the cause
- Campaigns—organized, public efforts to challenge those in power and/or societal beliefs and practices (Tilly & Wood, 2009, pp. 3–4).

Social movements typically emerge as people form networks to advocate for issue-based change and thereby develop a collective identity (Polletta & Jasper, 2001) around their common issue. Early in the parent movement in special education, parents of children with disabilities created networks among themselves. Were these networks "movements" or something different? From our analysis of the roles parents played in securing the right to education for their children, we believe parents' activities did, indeed, constitute a movement.

To sustain this conclusion, we distinguish between social movements and support groups or parent organizations. The two can be related, but the latter form to provide support or disseminate information; some advocacy may also take place, but typically within the organizational structure. By contrast, social movements occur when groups of people convene to challenge established legal authority and the individuals who act pursuant to (and even contrarily to) their legal authority—the "authorities" to whom the marginalized and disenfranchised refer and whom they challenge in their efforts to change public perceptions and practices. Support groups and organizations may play a role in this, but social movements go beyond just information sharing or social networking; they are deliberate change-agents, revolutionaries against a status quo.

In this chapter we describe the circumstances that galvanized parents of children with disabilities in the second half of the 20th century into a social movement to pursue civil rights—here, education rights—for their children through political actions, campaigns, and displays. We will exemplify their movement by describing the actions they took to secure, improve, and sustain a federal special education law. In these actions, they displayed remarkable solidarity across disability categories. For the sake of brevity and because the parents of children with intellectual disability were the first to convene and then become a movement, we will focus principally on them and their actions.

Collective Identity

Social movements are characterized by a collective identity, namely, a "cognitive, moral and emotional connection with a broader community, category, practice, or institution" (Polletta & Jasper, 2001, p. 285) shared by members of the movement. The development of a collective identity leads to solidarity within movements and allows the movement to present a uniform claim and message to the public. A collective identity also allows the movement to recruit additional members who are experiencing the same issues and seek to contribute to change in society. A collective identity differs from a personal identity; collective identity defines the common issue facing actors within the movement. For example, early in the parent movement, the lack of a legal right to education for children with disabilities was the uniting issue and one goal of the movement was to create this right. This goal had a significant role in defining the collective identity of the movement, and, because the majority of parents of children with disabilities struggled to have access to an appropriate education for their children, education and in particular special education were the synergizing issues that unified parents around the common goal of creating a legal right to a free appropriate public education.

Social Movements Over Time

Social movements evolve over time, as do the collective identities that define the movements' goals and actions. The movement changes as the circumstances and the people that energize the movement change and as the economic, political, and social conditions in society change (Tilly & Wood, 2009). Thus, for example, simply establishing as a matter of federal constitutional and statutory law that their children with a disability have a right to an education was but the first goal and victory of the parent movement in special education. More was to come, and was indeed predictable. That is so because social movements, and particularly the collective identity of social movements, often change significantly as the movements' constituencies win legal battles (Pollenta & Jasper, 2001)—de jure legitimacy attends those victories. Having won that status, movements often morph as their constituencies identify other challenges. And, at times, the original broad constituencies become diffused; fracturing of the movement occurs as different issues emerge for different members. This is evident with respect to the parent movement in special education. Between 1975 and 2004, when Congress last reauthorized the law, issues had changed from the broad ones of access for all to narrower ones of classification and particular benefits for some.

The Parent Movement in Special Education

Definition and Characteristics

As we pointed out in the introduction to this chapter, actors in social movements develop a collective identity without aid of institutions around a common issue and engage in political actions, displays and campaigns to change existing beliefs and practices. This definition applies to the parent movement in special education in several key ways:

- Parents and other close relatives of individuals with disabilities developed a collective identity around their struggle to obtain a free appropriate public education for their children. For our purposes in this chapter, we also include the adult and minor children who collaborated with their parents in challenging the status quo.
- Parents organized into associations that were either disability-specific (e.g., The Arc) or cross-disability (e.g., Easter Seals).
- Parents sustained their activities from early in the 1970s through the middle of 2004 (the period we cover here).
- Parents acted without the benefit of institutions (i.e., established entities) and developed institutions specific to their needs (e.g., parent associations).
- Parents challenged general and special educators, Congress, state officials (governors and legislators), and agencies (state and local educational agencies) to secure a free appropriate public education for their children.
- Parents challenged cultural beliefs and practices that de jure and de facto excluded their children from schools or segregated them within schools.
- Parents undertook political action individually and collectively by forming coalitions that demonstrated their unity, number, and commitment and the worthiness of their cause.

The proof of these assertions lies in the legislative history of the Education of All Handicapped Children Act (P.L. 94-142) and the seven amendments Congress has made to this law. Before describing the role of the parent movement in the legislative history of P.L. 94-142 and its amendments, it seems appropriate to explain a dynamic about the movement and the effect of that dynamic on the movement and on the educational opportunities available to children with disabilities.

The Dynamic: An Hegelian Interpretation of the Parent Movement

There is an almost Hegelian aspect to the parent movement in special education: thesis, antithesis, and synthesis. An idea—the thesis that there is a constitutional right to education for all children with disabilities—germinates, comes to the public agenda and is accepted or at least codified as law (P.L. 94-142 and its amendments) This codification of the original thesis provokes a response, often a reaction (antithesis). For example, the right to education (thesis) did not equate for many educators and some families (Turnbull, Turnbull, & Wehmeyer, 2010) to the right to education with students without disabilities. Access was one thing; powerful implementation of the doctrine of the least restrictive environment was another altogether.

The social movement that launched the original thesis then must confront and challenge the antithesis. If it is successful, there is a blending of the thesis and antithesis—the development of a synthesis. Thus, in special education the synthesis around the doctrine of the least restrictive alternative is found in the evolution of the terms (mainstreaming, regular education initiative, integration, and inclusion) that over time became code for the principle of the least restrictive environment. The post-enactment history of P.L. 94-142 demonstrates the thesis, antithesis, and synthesis dynamic. This Hegelian dynamic repeats itself; there is never a perfect and final resolution of challenges to the education of children with disabilities.

The Parent Movement as a Force for Law that Engineers Society and Shapes Behavior

There is little doubt but that law is a form of social engineering; it is a tool for creating an architecture for society and for engineering (constructing) the structures of society. It is also a technique for changing the behavior of members of the society. The proof of these two statements is easily found in the history of the parent movement in special education.

Absent the benefit of the constitutional doctrines of equal protection and due process, students with disabilities and their parents experienced six different kinds of discrimination: pure and functional exclusion, misclassification, lack of effective (appropriate) education, segregation, the lack of rights to protest schools' discrimination, and the lack of parent participation in their children's education (Turnbull & Turnbull, 1978). Upon the creation of a new doctrine of race-based equal protection (*Brown v. Topeka Board of Education*, 1954), a few courts' creative application of that precedent to disability-based discrimination, and then Congress' codification of the doctrine in P.L. 94-142, the architecture of education and its structures changed; alternatively stated, the norms and forms of education changed (Turnbull et al., 2007). The overall architecture (norms) of society and its schools was no longer so discriminatory and so segregating; and the structures of separate schooling (forms) were no longer so condoned (Turnbull et al., 2007).

Without the parent movement in special education, the architecture and structures—the norms and forms—would not have changed. This particular social movement sought and achieved social engineering. It sought and achieved extraordinary behavioral changes: Once the right to an education was made firm, then the duty to educate became inarguable, for the rights of some always impose duties on others.

Methodology and "Counting" Parents' Participation as Evidence of the Social Movement

To analyze how parents collectively, as part of a social movement, affected special education policy, specifically P.L. 94-142 and its amendments, we searched the Lexis Nexis Congressional data base to identify each statute Congress enacted affecting special education policy. Having identified each statute, we then reviewed its legislative history. The history revealed (a) the topics that the Act addressed, (b) the hearings Congress held on the topics, (c) the names of the witnesses testifying at the hearings, and (d) the action Congress took following the hearings (enact or amend the statute).

Having identified the names of all witnesses testifying, we then identified which witnesses were described as parents, individuals with disabilities, other close relatives, or representatives of organizations that had a primary mission of advocating for or otherwise supporting parents and their children (e.g., The Arc, United Cerebral Palsy Association, Easter Seals, and International Special Olympics). When a witness was both a governmental official and a parent or individual with a disability, we included that person in the "parent" category (e.g., Assistant Secretary of Education Madeleine Will and Senator Lowell Weicker [R.-CT.]—both of whom are parents of a child with Down syndrome). We did so because the person originally was a relative of an individual with a disability; that status preceded the person's election or appointment to office. When we were unable to identify a person as a parent, we excluded that person from that category. Table 48.1 details the total number of witnesses and the number of parent witnesses for the Congressional hearings on P.L. 94-142 and each of its major amendments.

The following sections detail our analysis of the legislative histories of the first federal special education statutes and their subsequent amendments. In some instances, the legislative history alone does not reveal the entire extent of the parent movement, and in those cases we bring in additional sources. For example, the President's Commission/Committee on Mental Retardation was pivotal in the 1960s; the National Council on Disability played a significant

TABLE 48.1
Witnesses at Congressional Hearings on IDEA and its Reauthorizations

	Number of Hearings	Number of Witnesses	Number of Parent Witnesses	Percent Parent Witnesses
P.L. 94-142 (1975)				
House	2	39	11	28%
Senate	5	150	47	31%
Total	7	189	58	31%
P.L. 98-199 (1983)				
House	1	20	6	30%
Senate	1	7	4	57%
Total	2	27	10	37%
P.L. 99-457 (1986)				
House	2	50	9	18%
Senate	1	16	5	31%
Total	3	66	14	21%
P.L. 101-476 (1990)				
House	6	75	35	47%
Senate	6	64	25	39%
Total	12	139	60	43%
P.L. 105-17 (1997)				
House	5	60	19	32%
Senate	4	64	23	36%
Total	9	124	42	34%
P.L. 108-446 (2004)				
House	11	49	7	14%
Senate	3	16	5	31%
Total	14	65	12	18%

role from 1995–1997; and the President's Commission on Excellence in Special Education was dominant in the 2004 reauthorization. As appropriate, we note the roles these entities played and the effect on the parent movement and special education legislation.

The Parent Movement over Time

Pre-1970s: Origin and Early Development of a National Parent Movement

The foundations for the political action, displays, and campaigns that resulted in P.L. 94-142 were laid long before Congress enacted the law in 1975. In response to their and their children's isolation, lack of rights, and stigmatization, all arising from the deficit-based model of disability, parents of children with intellectual disability (formerly, mental deficiency or mental retardation) began to network and form a collective identity around these issues, first within their local communities and then on a larger, national scale. Ninety parents, each of whom had been active in bringing together parents in their local communities, came together in 1950 at the annual meeting the American Association on Mental Deficiency (now, the American Association on Intellectual and Developmental Disabilities). They had no idea that other parents were beginning to convene to advocate and engage in political action in their communities. "Imagine it! Practically every parent there thought [he] was the pioneer. Most of us were strangers to each other…" (Anonymous, 1954).

These parents soon realized that they were unified by a common goal, despite their geographical differences. As Luther W. Youngdahl, then governor of Minnesota said, during the meeting, "Our great democracy can be measured best by what it does for the least of its little citizens." The response to his comments was revolutionary. "He turned a small hotel auditorium into a cathedral as the hearts and souls of misty-eyed parents echoed those words" (Anonymous, 1954).

Together, these parents identified the challenges facing them individually and collectively; in doing so, they exemplified the formation of a social movement. Their grievances were four-fold: exclusion from education; lack of community services; waiting lists for admission to residential institutions; and dissatisfaction with institutional conditions (Segal, n.d.).

Their vision was collective: a significant change in "public relations, exchange of information and political actions" (Segal, n.d.).

Their synergy led to the creation of the National Association of Parents and Friends of Mentally Retarded Children (now, The Arc) and, over time, significant involvement in federal policy to expand teaching and research related to the education of children with intellectual disability. In 1959, the association presented a major report titled *A Decade of Decision* to the White House Conference on Children and Youth. The very fact that they had reached consensus and found a platform on which to present this report highlights their emergence and growth as a movement.

The association's growth and early success derived from several key factors: (a) a grassroots organization with vital local links; (b) a focus on political action, public education, and consensus building; (c) strong leadership from executive directors who were parents of children with disabilities and had solid professional credentials; and (d) the socioeconomic characteristics of members. On this last point, a 1974 survey showed the membership to be, on the whole, married, college educated, middle aged (36–44), employed as professionals, White, and economically middle class (Segal, n.d.).

Early on, the association engaged in multiple political actions, such as crafting and widely disseminating position statements aimed at educating policy makers and the public and persuading them that children with intellectual disability have strengths and rights. The association's first position statement on education (1953) asserted that "every American child, including every retarded child, has the right to help, stimulation and guidance from skilled teachers provided by his community and state as part of a broadly conceived program of free public education" (National Association for Retarded Children, 1953). Such a statement was counter to societal beliefs and to existing practices in the school system as, in 1949, no states required education for children with IQs below 50, and only half of the states required an education for children with IQs of 50–75 (Abeson & Davis, 2000). Within six years, however, approximately two-thirds of the states provided classes for children with IQs below 50 and 49 states provided classes for children with IQs from 50–75. The political actions and campaigns organized by the association played a large role in these changes (Abeson & Davis, 2000).

One of the early leaders in the parent movement in special education was Elizabeth M. Boggs, whose son David had a significant intellectual disability. She attended the first association meeting in 1950, served on the board of directors for 13 years (1950–1963), and served as board vice-president and president. She had earned her Ph.D. in theoretical chemistry from Cambridge University, England. After serving as a faculty member of the Physics Department at the University of Pittsburgh, she abandoned her academic career and became a full-time volunteer for individuals and parents affected by intellectual and other developmental disabilities. She described herself as "a social synergist with a predisposition toward communication and collaboration rather than confrontation" (Boggs, 1985, pp. 39–40).

The President's Panel on Mental Retardation. In 1958, Ambassador Joseph P. Kennedy (the father of Rosemary, a daughter with an intellectual disability) asked his daughter and son-in-law, Eunice and Sargeant Shriver, to provide leadership for the Kennedy Foundation's new initiative focusing on preventing intellectual disability (Shorter, 2000). Three years later, at the urging of Mrs. Shriver, her brother, President Kennedy, appointed a panel of 26 members, comprised primarily of physicians and other scientists. Dr. Boggs was the lone parent on the panel. Within a year, the panel issued a report consisting of 112 recommendations and presented it to President Kennedy in the fall of 1962 (Minnesota Governor's Council on Developmental Disabilities (n.d)). Among the results of the report were two of the first federal laws affecting people with an intellectual disability:

1. P.L. 88-164 (enacted in 1963), authorizing funding for the Mental Retardation Facilities and Community Mental Health Centers Construction Act (Braddock, 1987).
2. P.L. 88-156 (enacted in 1963), the Maternal and Child Health and Mental Retardation Planning Amendments, which doubled the funding authorization for state programs focusing on maternal and child health with the goal of prevention of intellectual disability.

Two "family insiders" had significant impact on this first national report on the status of individuals with intellectual disability. Mrs. Shriver was a catalytic force in persuading her brother, President Kennedy, to set up the panel (Boggs, 1971). She then worked with the panel in a leadership role through the Office of the President, but was not a formal panel member.

Elizabeth Boggs was the other family insider and was the vice chairperson of the Law Task Force, chaired by Judge David L. Bazelon.

The 1970s: A Decade of Fundamental Reform

As important as the Kennedy initiative was in formally recognizing the political actions and campaigns of the parent movement, there can be little doubt but that the 1970s was the decade in which the most fundamental reform in special education occurred. Responding to the parent movement and the Panel's recommendations, Congress had authorized and appropriated funds in the early 1970s, under the Elementary and Secondary Education Act, to support the states to undertake demonstration programs in special education (P.L. 93-380). Recognizing that P.L. 93-380 was an interim step in the federal commitment to special education, parent leaders continued to advocate for federal legislation to protect the rights of *all* children with disabilities, and, in 1973, Congress began to hold hearings on S. 6, the Education of All Handicapped Children Act.

Between 1973 and 1975, seven hearings, many extending over multiple days, were held throughout the country, ensuring that the hearings were easily accessible to witnesses from across the country and that parents who would not likely be able to come to Washington D.C. were able to testify (Turnbull & Turnbull, 1996; Turnbull & Turnbull, 1993). The hearings covered what is now known as the six principles of P.L. 94-142 (Turnbull & Turnbull, 1978; Turnbull et al., 2007): zero reject, nondiscriminatory classification, appropriate education, least restrictive placement and inclusion, procedural due process, and parent participation. They also covered the system-capacity development issues related to personnel preparation, research, and federal-state cost-sharing.

Parents and representatives of organizations serving parents or individuals with disabilities testified at all hearings; indeed, 31% of witnesses across the seven hearings were parents (see Table 48.1). Also testifying were witnesses representing state and local education agencies and their national organizations, governors and state legislators and their organizations, and researchers and teachers and their organizations. While it is undeniable that the Council for Exceptional Children played an immense role in persuading Congress to enact P.L. 94-142, it is equally undeniable that it did so in partnership with, and to a large part in dependence on, leaders in the parent movement and their organizations (Turnbull & Turnbull, 1993).

The hearings on April 9, 1973, in Newark, New Jersey, and May 7, 1973, in Boston, Massachusetts, included parents whose children had intellectual disability, mental health challenges, hearing impairments, and specific learning disabilities. The other witnesses were members of state legislatures, directors of schools for students with disabilities, public-interest lawyers, physicians, and representatives of state special education agencies. The issues at those hearings were whether and, if so, how to extend P.L. 93-380, the costs and benefits of special education, and the federal role in a traditionally state enterprise (i.e., education). Discussion of these issues was colored by the fact that the parent movement had already won a number of successes locally. Some states (Massachusetts in particular) had enacted comprehensive, all-child state laws. A federal district court in Pennsylvania had ruled, in a case brought by parents of children with intellectual disabilities who were represented by Tom Gilhool, the brother of a person with such a disability, that the Commonwealth violated the Equal Protection clause of the Fourteenth Amendment to the federal constitution by not providing a free appropriate public education to a child with a disability (*PARC v. Commonwealth,* 1971, 1972). Together with a similar holding in a case in the District of Columbia (*Mills v. D.C. Board of Education*, 1972), it was becoming clear that all—repeat: all—students with disabilities were constitutionally entitled to a free public education.

The hearings continued on May 14, in Columbia, South Carolina. The topics were the same as in the two earlier hearings but included another. It concerned the orders by federal courts that the state of Alabama and Commonwealth of Pennsylvania had violated the cruel and unusual punishment clause of the Eighth Amendment and the equal protection and due process clauses of the Fourteenth Amendment by operating their state institutions—Partlow in Alabama and Pennhurst in Pennsylvania (*Wyatt v. Stickney*, 1972 with respect to Alabama, and *Pennhurst State School and Hospital v. Halderman,* 1977 with respect to Pennsylvania). These decisions meant local school systems would have to take more responsibility for students with disabilities, who would no longer be sent to institutions at the same frequency as they had been.

Furthermore, the Governor of Pennsylvania appointed a task force to investigate the deaths of residents of Pennhurst and recommend changes in the state's mental health laws (Gilhool, personal communication, May 21, 1993; Lippman & Goldberg, 1973). Leaders of the parent movement played a key role in this task force. Dennis Haggerty, the father of a child with intellectual disability; Jim Wilson, the brother of a man with intellectual disability; and Gilhool were appointed to the task force and used this opportunity to disseminate information and challenge the assumption that institutional care was necessary or appropriate for people with disabilities. Wilson was also a senior editor of the *New York Times*. The *Times* endorsed the creation of a federal right to education law—largely at Wilson's prodding. The movement employed a dual strategy: seek redress in the Congress and courts, and seek support in the court of public opinion. And, in both forums, broadly challenge cultural beliefs about disability.

More hearings, with parents and members of advocacy organizations as witnesses, were held on October 19, 1973, in St. Paul, Minnesota, and on March 18, 1974, in Harrisburg, Pennsylvania. These focused on the efforts the states (particularly Minnesota and North Dakota) were making to educate students with disabilities, the states' need for federal assistance, and the effect of the PARC decision.

Hearings with the same constituencies as witnesses resumed on March 6, 7, 18, and 22 in Washington, D.C., this time focused on the inadequacy of state and local funding, the importance of personnel preparation, challenges to correct classification of students as having a disability, and benefits and challenges to their inclusion in the general education program.

A hearing in Washington on June 17 and 24 included no parents. Instead, the witnesses were state governors, representatives and senators, directors of special education, and individuals from organizations representing these constituencies and the Under Secretary of the Department of Health, Education, and Welfare, which had jurisdiction over all federally sponsored education programs. The issues were state and local capacity and the role of the federal government in traditionally state-local functions (education).

Congress did not again take testimony on S. 6 until April 8, 9, 10, 15, and June 9, 1975. These hearings focused on extending for one and two years, respectively, the present federal funding under P.L. 93-380 and addressed the states' needs for federal assistance to educate children with disabilities. Witnesses included governors, United States Senators, representatives of associations of governors, state legislators, special education directors, and researchers and teachers. Other witnesses were parents or representatives of parent or pro-child disability organizations, especially those concerned with children who are blind or deaf-blind or had cerebral palsy or an intellectual disability.

Al Abeson and Fred Weintraub, directors of the governmental affairs unit of CEC, have described their strategy and acknowledged the critical role of the parent movement (A. Abeson, personal communication, May 20, 1993; F. Weintraub, personal communication, May 21, 1993). CEC's strategy was to assemble legions of parents to testify about the effects of discrimination in education, rely on *Brown* (1954) as precedent to pry open schools' doors, shine a bright light on the institutionalization of children with disabilities, and enlist professionals to testify that all children with disabilities can learn and therefore may not legally be excluded from school.

Parents were clearly active participants in these hearings, constituting almost one-third of all witnesses in all of the hearings (see Table 48.1). In comparison to professionals, parents more often spoke from deep personal experiences and in anticipation of consequences that would or would not improve their and their children's lives (Itkonen, 2009). Their "real world" examples united them in a social movement.

After almost two years of hearings, S. 6 was enacted on November 29, 1975, as P.L. 94-142. President Ford threatened to veto the bill, and the parent movement responded in force, flooding his office with letters and calls protesting the veto (Itkonen, 2007, 2009) and demonstrating solidarity and collective identity.

It is fair to conclude that, absent the parent movement and the powerful presence of parent leaders as key witnesses before Congress; as leaders within task forces exploring options for education; as organizers of political actions, displays, and campaigns that spread the message to the public through the media; as plaintiffs, lawyers, and key witnesses in court cases that supported the establishment of a federal constitutional right to education (*PARC* and *Mills*) and to treatment (*Wyatt* and *Pennhurst*); and as petitioners to a reluctant president, P.L. 94-142 would not have been enacted and the President Ford's veto would not have been thwarted.

Undoubtedly, the groundwork had been laid by the President's Panel (later, Committee) on Mental Retardation and by President Kennedy's New Society and President Johnson's Great Society social policies. Essential to the success, however, were passionately committed "insiders" who, while not exactly members of the parent movement, were the parents' vital allies. They included Vice President Hubert Humphrey (grandfather of a son with an intellectual disability), Senators Ted Kennedy (D.-MA.) and Winston Prouty (R.-VT), both of whom had siblings with intellectual disability, and members of Congressional staff who also were parents or relatives of individuals with disabilities. The staff included Pat and Jack Forsyth on the staff of Sen. Jennings Randolph (D.-W.VA.) and counsel to the Senate Labor and Welfare Committee, respectively; Jack Duncan, staff director of the House Select Subcommittee on Education, who himself had a physical disability; and Marty LaVor, a member of the staff of Rep. Albert Quie (R.-MN), who was an orphan deeply committed to children facing challenges.

There was a synchrony of time, circumstance, and people (LaVor, 1976; Turnbull & Turnbull, 1993) in the fundamental law reform process symbolized by P.L. 94-142. Parents' voices were indispensable to the reform. Without parents, it is debatable whether the courts' decisions and the passionate insiders' advocacy would, singly or in combination, been sufficient to create the second greatest presence of the federal government in education—second only to the presence represented by the race-desegregation cases that began when the parent of a Black child successfully sued to have her admitted to Topeka (Kansas) High School on the same terms as White students (*Brown,* 1954). It should not pass notice that parents of persons of color and parents of individual with disabilities relied on the same legal theory: equal protection and equal opportunity (Turnbull et al., 2007). That theory justified Congress' action and has been one of the justifications for every subsequent amendment to P.L. 94-142. The parent movement in special education was about education, but it was, even more fundamentally, about civil rights.

The 1980s: A Decade of Expansion, Retrenchment, and Response

With the exception of extending the Act's benefits to schools operated by the Bureau of Indian Affairs (P.L. 95-561) in 1978, eight years passed before Congress again concerned itself with the fundamentals of the Education of All Handicapped Children Act. In 1983, Congress amended the Act by enacting P.L. 98-199, which expanded incentives for preschool special education programs, early intervention, and transition services. Each of these issues was targeted by leaders in the parent movement through diverse political actions, displays, and campaigns to further improve the quality of education for students with disabilities. Parent leaders were strongly represented in Congressional hearings on the reauthorization, as they were in the original hearings on P.L. 94-142. As shown in Table 48.1, in the Senate hearings, 4 of 7 witnesses were parents of children with disabilities and in the House hearings 6 of 20 witnesses were parents. P.L. 99-189 undoubtedly was foundational for the next massive expansion of IDEA, in 1988, under P.L. 99-457.

Expansion of special education: Educating infants/toddlers. Having successfully advocated for the demonstration programs in early intervention and early education (P.L. 98-199), parents continued to push for even stronger early intervention programs (birth to 3) when Congress held hearings before enacting P.L. 99-457. Their advocacy contributed to the significant expansion in the law with the addition of Part C (at that time referred to as Part H) in 1986 (P.L. 99-457). As shown in Table 48.1, parents comprised 21% of the witness at the hearings held by the House and Senate in 1985 and 1986.

Parents, however, were not the only advocates to expand early intervention and education. Professionals played a significant role, which was one reason the number of parents witnesses may have been lower in the 1985 and 1986 hearings. A vanguard of professionals believed that programs should focus on a family-centered orientation in early intervention. In a midnight strategy session during the 1984 annual meeting of the Division of Early Childhood (a division of CEC), they emphasized correcting mistakes and problems with the early education authority for children ages three to five under Part B in formulating a new Part H for early intervention (Hebbeler, Smith, & Black, 1991; B. Smith, personal communication, May 25, 1993).

As fate would have it, these same professionals gathered a few months later at the CEC's 1985 convention and were jolted into action by a statement made by a legislative aid for the House Select Education Subcommittee who asserted that there simply was "no way" for the early intervention initiative to get off the ground when the Congress was hard-pressed for funds and the Reagan administration was as tight as a drum on domestic programs. "No way" produced a loud and sustained rejoinder: "Surrender? Hell no! We've just begun to fight" (B. Smith, personal communication, May 25, 1993).

And, again, key parent insiders made all the difference. In this case, the key insiders were Assistant Secretary Madeline Will in the Department of Education and Sen. Lowell Weicker. Weicker, whose son benefited from early intervention services, engineered the legislation in the Senate. Rep. Pat Williams of Montana and Rep. Steve Bartlett of Texas did the same in the House. It is notable that Williams' niece was deaf—a fact he noted when he accepted the Senate amendment to the House bill and began floor debate.

Expansion of special education: Transition to adulthood. Having legislated for the benefit of the youngest children with disabilities, Congress also benefited those exiting school by enacting the first of the "transition" provisions. It had amended the statute in 1983 by P.L. 98-199 to authorize demonstration programs in transition. Convinced that the demonstration programs were effective, Congress, through P.L. 99-457, amended the statute to require transition planning for each student as part of the student's IEP. The transition provisions of 1983 and 1988 derived from Will's conclusion that special education outcomes were unacceptable—a judgment that many other parents shared (Will, 1984).

Will's strategy was to use funds of the Rehabilitation Act to put people with severe disabilities into regular jobs for regular wages and then to amend IDEA to require transition services. This answer was easier to come by than to implement.

Will began by forming a task force within the Office of Special Education and Rehabilitation Services (OSERS, which she directed), and found funds to send its members to travel to sites where people with disabilities were working in integrated settings. She hired consultants to write and present papers on transition and to run conferences on supported employment (for the benefit of OSERS staff, state and local rehabilitation agencies, and parents), and required the OSERS staff to respond to papers that proposed a transition initiative (M. Will, personal communication, May 26, 1993). Her effort in educating the staff, almost all of whom had been reluctant to press for transition authorization and funding (even for demonstration programs), converted opponents and skeptics into advocates.

Conditions in the states also favored transition initiatives. The state rehabilitation agencies wanted the federal funds but did not want to oppose local rehabilitation agencies that did not want the transition money or to change the way they were doing business (M. Will, personal communication, May 26, 1993).

The OSERS and state agency response to local opposition was to fund creative professionals in new or progressive agencies to operate supported employment/transition programs. To be effective, this new cadre of professionals had to begin system-wide reform at the state level, working simultaneously with schools, parent organizations, rehabilitation agencies, private providers, and employers. They also had to demonstrate that people with severe disabilities could engage in minimum-wage work, with support, in integrated settings. They met both challenges and, in doing so, created a groundswell of constituent pressure on Congress to fund still more transition and supported employment programs (M. Will, personal communication, May 26, 1993).

As effective as she might be in working inside her own agency, however, Will recognized that she needed the support of members of Congress and their staff. That is why she focused on two moderate Republicans, members of her own party —Rep. Bartlett and Sen. Lowell Weicker. It is also why she cultivated several very well-placed young professionals who were doing short stints as staff members of Congress, some of whom were funded by the Jos. P. Kennedy, Jr., Foundation as Public Policy Fellows. Finally, to secure grassroots pressure on Congress, Will worked closely with parent leaders and parent organizations (M. Will, personal communication, May 26, 1993). Aided by the parent movement and against the odds and skepticism within her own agency, Will prevailed in creating the transition mandates.

Expansion of special education: Parent Training and Information Centers. Having established parent centers in the 1960s and 1970s, by 1983 the Department of Education was supporting 17 such centers ("What Is," 1987–1988). In that year, Congress, upon Madeline Will's initiative, authorized a new program—the Parent Information and Training Centers (P.L.98-199). The mission of Parent Information and Training Centers was to train and provide information that enables parents to participate more effectively in their children's education. There are more than 104 centers nationwide, with at least one in each state (http://www.taalliance.org/index.asp). Each center has a board of directors, a majority of whom must be parents, and staff.

By tradition, PTIs typically employ parents as directors and staff members.

Expansion of special education: Protecting the right to a "free" public education. The rights afforded to parents and children with disabilities were further expanded after the Supreme Court held, in 1985, that a local educational agency (LEA) was obliged to reimburse parents for the private-school tuition they incurred as a result of the LEA's failure to provide a free appropriate public education to their child (*Burlington School Committee v. Massachusetts State Department of Education*, 1985).

Potential retrenchment: The failure of defederalization. While Congress was expanding the provisions of the Education for All Handicapped Children Act, due in large part to the advocacy of parent insiders and leaders in the parent movement, significant challenges to the Act were emerging from the Executive Branch, now lead by President Reagan. The clash between the parents and the administration centered on the federal role in special education—and by extension any public education—and a proposal from President Reagan to rescind the regulations the Department of Education were enforcing.

The regulations provided direction for the implementation of the Act and—as much as the Act itself—governed the states' implementation. They were the products of a "regulation in-put team" convened in 1976 after P.L. 94-142 was enacted. The team (on which co-author Rud Turnbull served) had proposed regulations to the Department of Health, Education and Welfare; the Department had largely accepted the team's proposals regarding federal-state activities under P.L. 94-142.

Seeking to defederalize education as a whole, President Regan proposed revising—essentially, gutting—the existing regulations; but Congress challenged him, as did the parent movement. The House Committee on Education and Labor and the Senate Committee on Labor and Human Resources held hearings in the summer and fall of 1982 for the purpose of considering the president's proposed de-regulation. During the hearings, disability advocacy groups engaged in multiple public displays and campaigns against the regulations. For example, one group "set fire to a wheelbarrow filled with copies of the regulations, and dumped the ashes at the feet of the Department of Education's representatives (Weiner & Humer, 1987)" (Itkonen, 2009, p. 148).

Parent leaders were also a strong presence at the hearings, conveying a message of the potentially catastrophic impacts of President Reagan's proposals. Of the 20 witnesses at the House hearings on September 22, 23, and 29, six (30%) were parents of individuals with disabilities. Of the seven witnesses at the Senate committee hearing on August 10, four (57%) were parents or staff of parent organization representing families who had children with disabilities. Of those four, two represented The National Association for Retarded Children (formerly the National Association of Parents and Friends of Mentally Retarded Children): Paul Marchand was the director of the governmental affairs staff and later the chairman of the Consortium Concerned with Disabilities (CCD), a cross-disability alliance of parents, individuals, and professionals and their associations; co-author Rud Turnbull was an officer of the association and a parent. (Because he has been the longest-serving governmental affairs staffer of any of the parent or professional associations and served for many years as the chairman of the CCD, Marchand has earned the reputation of "Dean" of the disability advocacy community. Before working at The Arc, he was executive director of the Rhode Island ARC and, before that, a special education teacher.)

Fortuitously, Sen. Weicker chaired the Senate committee hearing. Almost immediately after Secretary of Education Terrell Bell began his testimony, Weicker, who was well over six feet tall (in contrast to Bell, who was some five and one-half feet tall and looking up from his seat at the witness table to Weicker, on a committee dias some five feet higher than the witness table), stood up, withdrew from his coat pocket a tri-folded piece of paper, interrupted the Secretary's testimony, and said (in words to this effect):

> Mr. Secretary, I have in my hand a copy of a memorandum under the signature of your Deputy Secretary characterizing the parents of children with disabilities as the "enemy" of the Administration. Is that, sir, a correct statement of how President Reagan and you regard these parents, of whom I am one? (Author's observation)

Secretary Bell disavowed the memo and, in short order, defederalization efforts petered out.

> It was assumed that in the rough and tumble world of politics, [parents] would not hold their own as a voting block or as advocates for their cause. But that assumption was blown to smithereens in the budget and policy deliberations of 1981, 1982, and again in 1983. In fact, I would be hard pressed to name another group within the human service spectrum that has not only survived the policies of the (Reagan) administration but has also defeated them as consistently and convincingly as the disabled community has. Indeed, it has set an example for others, who were believed to be better organized. (Weicker, 1985, p. 284)

Retrenchment: The Supreme Court, procedural due process, and parent power. Parents and other advocates for students and other individuals with disabilities are acutely aware that disability policy results in large part from the interaction of the three branches of government. This was demonstrated by the failed defederalization initiative of 1982 (P.L. 98-199), when there was conflict between the Executive Branch and the Congress. It is also evidenced by Congress' response to decisions by the Supreme Court.

Although the Court had interpreted the Education for All Handicapped Children Act to mean that state and local educational agencies must offer each student qualifying for special education "access … sufficient to confer educational benefit" (*Board of Education v. Rowley*, 1984) and that they must also provide health-beneficial services (clean intermittent catheterization) under the "related services" provision of the statute (*Irving Independent School District v. Tatro,* 1984), the Court vitiated the Act's enforcement provisions.

In *Smith v. Robinson* (1984), the Court held that the Act did not authorize parents to recover the fees they incurred as a result of hiring attorneys to represent them and their children in suits against state and local educational agencies to enforce the Act. That decision provoked yet another interaction between the branches of government, the Court, which interpreted the statute, and Congress, which enacted and could amend it. Congress was quick to overturn the Court's decision, enacting P.L. 99-372 in 1986, authorizing parents to recover their attorneys' fees if they prevail against a state or local educational agency.

Five years later, the Court held that although parents may sue local educational agencies, the sovereign immunity clause of the Eleventh Amendment prevents them from suing state educational agencies except when Congress explicitly abrogates states' immunity in the exercise of its power to enforce the equal protection and due process guarantees of the Fourteenth Amendment (*Delmuth v. Muth*, 1989). Once again, Congress was quick to overturn the Court's decision, enacting P. L.101-476 in 1990 and abrogating the states' immunity and making the state agency subject to suit on the same terms that a local agency was subject. (We discuss P.L. 101-476 below because its effective date is 1990, not in the 1980s.) In summary, the 1980s was a decade in which Congress undertook three significant actions. First, it expanded preschool programs and Parent and Information Training Centers; second, it authorized new infant and toddlers programs and transition services; and third, it warded off attacks on the Act launched by both the Executive and the Court. Parents were influential in persuading Congress that these were the right courses of action. Although they would not enjoy similar success in the 1990s, they were not without reasons to celebrate.

The 1990s: Responding, Renaming, Expanding, Confronting, and Yielding

By the 1990s, the Act had become increasingly problematic for parents and children, on the one hand, and state and local educational agencies, on the other. Moreover, the sense that parents and their children and the educational agencies were engaged in a common cause and were each others' reliable allies was dissipating. Fault lines that had been implicit and sometimes even explicit—associated with related services, costs thereof, ability to recover attorneys' fees, and rights to sue otherwise immune states—widened, and new ones developed.

Throughout the late 1980s, Congress was well aware of these and other issues. Indeed, it began holding oversight hearings in October, 1987 continuing until October, 1990; these hearings resulted in the enactment of P.L. 101-476.

Responding. As noted above, P. L. 101-476 reversed the Court's *Dellmuth* decision and allowed parents to sue state, not just local, educational agencies. It did not, however, affect another hugely important Court decision. That was *Honig v. Doe,* in which the Court held, in 1988, that IDEA permits LEAs limited authority to discipline students. Under *Honig*, an agency may remove a student for not more than 10 days; any subsequent discipline may not terminate the student's access to school but may involve the removal of the student from the student's previous education program. *Honig*, then, resulted in the "short-term" discipline doctrine and the "no cessation" doctrine; Congress would leave both intact until 1997 (P.L. 105-17) and 2004 (P.L. 108-446). By leaving the decision intact, Congress simply postponed the time when parents and educators would engage in frontal conflict about discipline.

Renaming. P.L. 101-476 renamed the Act, scrapping the original Education of the Handicapped Act and titling it Individuals with Disabilities Education Act. The renaming signified the power of the "people first" movement.

Expanding. The 1990 amendment also added autism and traumatic brain injury (TBI) to the list of categories of children eligible for IDEA benefits. These new categories reflected, more than any other provisions of the Act since 1975, the increased focus on specific issues within the parent movement and the continued power of the movement to influence Congress and benefit children with disabilities. Parents of children with autism and TBI had built their own collective identities around the needs experienced by their children and advocated for recognition of the specialized services needed by students with these disability labels. Further, by authorizing expanded services to infants and toddlers who were deaf-blind and enhancing pre-school and school services to those students, the amendment recognized the special needs of children with low incidence disabilities and their families. The 1990 amendment expanded the early education initiative and strengthened the transition provisions that P.L. 98-199 (1983) and P.L. 99-457 (1988) had added.

Although Congress did not add Attention Deficit Hyperactivity Disorder as a new category or change the definition of "seriously emotionally disturbed" as some parents wanted, it did require a period for public comment about the definition of ADHD; authorize centers to organize, synthesize, and disseminate knowledge about ADHD; and expand research on interventions for children with emotional and behavioral disorders. Further, parents of children with ADHD continued their political action; and although ADHD was never introduced into the law as a specific eligibility category, it was named as an eligibility category under other health impairments in the 1999 regulations (Itkonen, 2009). In belated recognition of what was abundantly clear and a moving force behind P.L. 94-142 in 1975—namely, that students from "diverse" ethnic, racial, cultural, and linguistic minorities were disproportionately placed into special education (*Larry P. v. Riles,* 1984; *PASE v. Hannon*, 1980). Congress set out education goals for these students by making findings of fact and policy recommendations and authorizing funding of minority institutions of higher education.

Finally, the 1990 amendment (a) required the boards of directors of the previously established Parent Training and Information Centers to include minority parents and (b) required the Secretary of Education to establish three experimental centers to serve parents in exclusively urban areas and two to serve parents in exclusively rural areas. These "experimental centers" ultimately became the Community Parent Resource Centers, mandated to provide information, training, and other assistance to families in traditionally underserved communities, including families whose primary language is not English.

Parents were strongly involved in testimony before Congress advocating for the changes that were made in P.L 101-476. As shown in Table 48.1, 43% of witnesses at Congressional hearings on the Amendments were parents.

Confronting: The National Council on Disability's nation-wide survey of parents. The Act provides that its discretionary programs (e.g., research, demonstration, personnel preparation, parent capacity building, and technology-based education—the Part D programs) must be reauthorized every five years. Accordingly, the next time Congress was required to address IDEA and its effectiveness was 1995.

Anticipating that reauthorization year, the National Council on Disability, a Congressionally created semi-independent entity responsible for reporting annually to the president and Congress concerning disability policy and practice, conducted field hearings in 10 sites in October and November, 1994 to "develop a profile of special education practices by focusing on the experiences of parents, family members, students, adults with disabilities, and other interested people with a family-based perspective" on a cross-disability basis. NCD reported that a total of "nearly" 400 witnesses testified; of that number approximately 85% were "consumers" (parents and others) (National Council on Disability, 1995a, pp. 8–9). The strength of the mother's comment below reveals the extent of frustrations expressed in these hearings:

> I have come to call myself Bonnie, the bitch, because of what I've had to become to fight the system …I have contacted multiple state offices. I have followed through with every lead that anybody has ever given me. I have talked with the Governor's office here in the state. I've gone so far as to call the White House…. I guess my feeling at this point is, "Is there anybody out there who really cares?" (testimony by Bonnie Weninger, in NCD, 1995a, p. 123)

NCD transcribed the testimony and delivered it to two of the authors of this chapter, Rud and Ann Turnbull (parents of an adult son with a disability). Under their supervision, graduate students in the department of special education and law school at The University of Kansas analyzed the testimony and reported their analysis, with recommendations, to NCD; they also complemented the analysis and recommendations with reprints of related articles, chapters, and monographs totaling 765 pages (NCD, 1995b). The analysis became the foundation for the NCD's 1995 report, "Improving the Implementation of the Individuals with Disabilities Education Act: Making Schools Work for All of America's Children."

Although the report identified the benefits of IDEA, it laid far greater emphasis on parents' and students' unmet needs, which it identified according to the six principles of IDEA (Turnbull & Turnbull, 1978). In this important respect, the NCD enabled parents at the grassroots level—not just through their national organizations—to confront educators and policy makers about policy and the culture of America's schools. Table 48.2 sets out the six principles and the witnesses' major concerns regarding each.

The NCD report also focused heavily on issues involving transition and parents as collaborators in personnel development; on funding; and on general education reform (Goals 2000: Educate America Act of 1994). By tracking the NCD report data and recommendations as Congress failed to reauthorize IDEA in 1995 and then as it succeeded in reauthorizing it in 1997, it becomes clear that the NCD's decision to gather a national perspective from parents proved the existence of a "movement" as we defined it above (individuals acting collectively in an organized, sustained way to challenge authorities, powerholders, or beliefs and practices).

TABLE 48.2
Unmet Needs Aligned with the Six principles of IDEA Identified in NCD's 1995 Report

Zero Reject	
	Parents' Lack of Information
	Difficult-to-serve children
Discipline	
	Nondiscriminatory Evaluation
	Over-representation of minority students
	Parent participation in evaluation
	Creation of new disability categories (neurobiological disorders and emotional disability and mental illness)
Appropriate Education	
	Parent participation in developing the IEP
	Related services
Least Restrictive Environment	
	Characteristics of successful integration
	Barriers to integration
	Continuum of services
Procedural Due Process	
	Mediation
	Attorneys' fees
Parent Participation	
	Training and information issues

Confronting yet again: The failed reauthorization of 1995 and the successful reauthorization of 1997. Congress was unable to reauthorize IDEA in 1995. The reason is simple and testimony to the power of the parent movement. Members of the movement vehemently objected to the new provisions that (a) allowed educators to discipline students and (b) limited parents' ability to recover their attorneys' fees (Egnor, 2003; R. Turnbull, archives available at Beach Center, University of Kansas).

With Congress stymied in 1995 by parent protests, David Hoppe, the chief of staff to Senate Majority Leader Trent Lott (R-MS), spearheaded the effort to start negotiations all over again. Hoppe did so by convening regular meetings, in Washington, consisting of representatives of state and local educational agencies, professional associations, and parent-and-child advocacy and support associations. It should not pass notice that Hoppe himself is the father of a son with intellectual disability and now (as of the date we are writing this chapter) is affiliated with the governmental affairs office of the National Down Syndrome Society.

These so-called "town hall" meetings ran parallel with hearings held by the House on beginning in 1994 (April 28 and July 19), 1995 (June 20 and 27), 1996 (March 7), and 1997 (February 4 and 6); and with hearings held by the Senate in 1995 (May 9, 11, 16. and July 11) and 1997 (January 29). The core issues were, of course, discipline (largely in response to the Court's *Honig* opinion and the nation's alarm about "school shootings") and attorneys' fees (largely in response to the sense, articulated by educators, that they were constantly practicing "defensive" education by complying precisely with IDEA's procedural requirements).

Yielding. Parents' voices were heard at the hearings on the 1997 Reauthorization, with 34% of witnesses representing parent perspectives. However, this percentage was lower than the number of parents testifying for the 1990 Reauthorization. The 1997 amendments offered much to parents. Young children's eligibility for early intervention and preschool services were expanded to include children with developmental delays. The doctrine of the least restrictive environment was strengthened and inclusion in general education became more likely. Mediation became an alternative to administrative hearings that had become increasingly adversarial and costly (to parents and schools alike) in terms of money, time, diverted energies (from caregiving and educating to litigating), and distrust.

But, for the first time, the parent movement experienced some setbacks. Parents were unable to prevail over educators with respect to discipline and attorney fees, despite significant actions, displays, and protests. For example, parents organized a massive "call-in" to Capitol Hill. A congressional staff person has described the call-in in these terms: "At one point in the 1997 reauthorization, [the disability advocates] actually clogged up the phone and fax lines on the Hill to the point where they had to be shut down" (Itkonen, 2009, p. 149).

But, the push that parents had been so successful in making in the past now met with a powerful push-back from educators, and parents had to yield. To further complicate things, there was a proliferation of interest specific parent groups (e.g., autism, ADHD) advocating for specific policy issues of interest to their constituency, making it hard to have a unified message. This led to multiple competing interests among parent advocates and actions within the parent movement. As described in the Introduction, this is a natural evolution of a social movement, particularly after fundamental civil rights are established. The movement shifts to find new issues to tackle, which oftentimes lead to splintering and different groups focused on issues of specific interest.

The "Aught" Decade: 2000–2009: Pulled Ahead and Pushed Back

While P.L. 94-142 is undoubtedly the most important law for special education, the Elementary and Secondary Education Act as amended in 2002 by No Child Left Behind Act is the law that governs education, generally, of which special education is part. ESEA/NCLB expressly covers students with disabilities (those receiving IDEA benefits) and requires all of them be assessed to determine their progress in core academic subjects.

NCLB was preceded by two "white papers" that severely criticized special education. Indeed, those papers built on the "accountability by assessment" principle of NCLB. The first, "Redefining Special Education for the 21st Century" (Finn, Rotherham, & Hokansan, 2001), charged that, among other things, special education was making students with disabilities dependent on education and other service systems throughout their lifetime. It called for increased accountability for outcomes. It also criticized special educators for over-using the specific learning disabilities category; it argued that far more students were admitted to special education in that (and other categories) than should have been and that general education was defaulting in its responsibilities to students who could be effectively educated in general education and did not belong in special education. In this respect, NCLB represented yet another attack on social policy that promoted dependency and discouraged individual responsibility (Turnbull, 2005).

The second, the Report of the President's Commission on Excellence in Special Education (2002), not surprisingly echoed the Finn et al. (2001) report (some authors and staff of the Finn et al. report were commissioners or staff to the Commission). Both the Finn and the President's Commission reports recommended that Congress "align" IDEA with NCLB.

Interestingly, none of the authors of chapters in the Finn report (2001) was a parent of a child with disabilities, and only two of the 19 members of the President's Commission identified themselves as parents of children with disabilities. Of the 114 witnesses at the President's Commission hearings, 22 (19%) were parents or siblings of individuals with disabilities or present or former special education students.

Alignment is exactly what Congress commanded when

it reauthorized IDEA as P.L. 108-446 in 2004. Alignment had the effect of pulling students with disabilities into the general assessment-of-progress movement that NCLB exemplified. The general alignment and the specific assessment and accountability provisions were not the only ones favoring students with disabilities. Other provisions favored school-wide positive behavior support, extended early intervention services, and stronger transition provisions (Turnbull et al., 2007). Although many parent leaders advocated for these provisions, there was not unity in the parent movement.

P.L. 108-446 also represented a push-back against the students and their advocates. First, Congress tightened the discipline provisions to make it more difficult for students with disabilities to escape the discipline that schools may administer to students without disabilities (Turnbull et al., 2007). Second, Congress allowed state and LEAs to use a response-to-intervention (RTI) method of identifying whether a student has a specific learning disability. In this, Congress was responding to the alleged over-classification of students with SLD. However, some parents argued this may lead to a lack of access to appropriate services. Finally, Congress authorized a new "dispute resolution" procedure that generally was required if parents and local agencies did not use mediation in advance of a due process hearing, and Congress made it more difficult and riskier for parents to sue schools by limiting attorneys' fee recoveries and imposing attorney-fee recovery liability on parents and their lawyers for unwarranted litigation.

The House began holding hearings on the implementation of the 1997 statute (P.L. 107-17) and on the President's Commission's report in 1998; altogether the House held 11 different hearings. The Senate began holding hearings on implementation and the President's Commission report in 1998 and altogether held 3 hearings. However, the participation of parents, particularly in the House, was the lowest of any reauthorization of IDEA. As evidenced in Table 48.1, overall only 18% of witnesses were parents (14% House, 31% Senate).

Summary: The Movement and Congress from the 1970s through 2004

There are many indicators of the fact that, consistent with the definition of a social movement, there has been a "parent movement" in special education. The interaction of parents and their allies with Congress arguably is the best indicator of the participation of parents and their effect in challenging the power structures of general and special education and then changing the social status and legal rights of students with disabilities and their parents. Table 48.1 displays the movement and, sadly, its declining presence as Congress held hearings on special education. In the early hearings (P.L. 94-142 and P.L. 98-199), parents and their allies had a significant presence. In hearings on early intervention (P.L. 99-457), parents' participation declined, but this was because so many professionals testified in favor of early intervention, becoming de facto parent allies and reducing the need for parents to engage in strong political action to make their issues heard and to affect change. Parent participation was at its height in 1990, when Congress enacted P.L. 101-476, and significant number of parents mobilized around discipline of students with disabilities and its relationship to access. However, participation has decreased steadily since this time, reaching its lowest level in the Finn-President's Commission white papers and during the hearings on the 2004 reauthorization.

Projections: The Future of the Parent Movement

The general question now must be: What is the future of the parent movement? The specific question must be: What roles will parents and their allies play as Congress begins hearings to reauthorize ESEA (and its NCLB provisions) and IDEA?

It does not require guesswork or soothsayer capacities to answer these questions; it does, however, require an understanding of the history of the movement and the contexts in which the movement was born, came of age, and now exists. In this chapter, we have briefly described the movement's history as evidenced by the relationship parents and their movement have had in the enactment and amendment of the federal special education law (now, IDEA). We have also contextualized the movement within two theories: the Hegelian theory of thesis, antithesis, and synthesis, and the theory that law is a form of social engineering and behavior modification. By adhering to that approach, it seems defensible to make some assumptions and projections.

The first assumption is that Congress will not repeal IDEA. No "full repeal" bills have ever been introduced, and there is no evidence whatsoever that any member of Congress or the administration is in any way inclined to jettison the statute.

The second is that Congress will reauthorize and amend IDEA, again addressing the substantive rights of students and their parents and the rights and duties of educators (as it did in 1997 and 2004).

The third is that any reauthorization and amendments will stimulate the parent movement. History teaches that idleness is anathema to parents who have so much at stake.

The final assumption is that the parent movement will retain a great deal of unity and solidarity, but that there also will continue to be disability-specific interest groups and claims that Congress must take into account during the reauthorization. The basis for this assumption lies in the amendments that added new categories of disabilities, authorized different criteria and procedures for classifying students as having a specific learning disability, addressed students who are homeless or non-English speaking, and tightened the discipline provisions to make it more difficult for some students (particularly those with emotional and behavioral disabilities) to mitigate school discipline.

Taking these assumptions into account, it is appropriate to ask: Will the Hegelian theory and the law-as-social engineering/behavior modification theory remain useful in the future and can they aid in projecting the future. It seems defensible to answer, "Yes."

Ever since Congress launched the hearings that undergirded its enactment of P.L. 94-142 in 1975, it has faced competing claims about the education of students with disabilities. The original claims were constitutionally grounded. Subsequent claims took that right for granted; the equal protection justification has appeared in every reauthorization since 1975. Thereafter, the claims were less about pure access than meaningful access; they were less about students of traditional school age (ages 6 through 18) than about younger and older students; they were less about being "in" than being "of" the school and its general/regular curriculum and sites; they were less about the majority population (White) than minority population students' interests. The list goes on and on; the only constant is the assertion of competing equities and claims within the disability movement as a whole and then the clash of the claims of the movement with the asserted rights and interests of educators and other students (as in the discipline provisions enacted in 1997 and modified significantly in 2004). The issues (claims) will be different but each claim (thesis) will provoke a competing claim (antithesis) and the resolution will not be a total victory for one group of claimants but a compromise (synthesis).

What is unknown is precisely what the claims and counter-claims will be—which thesis will take center stage, which antithesis will challenge, and which synthesis will emerge. The factors that seem likely to influence the claims are, however, rather easy to identify.

One is the nation's economic condition and, in particular, the national debt, federal monetary and fiscal policy, and the states' own dire circumstances. Rights run with revenues. Another is the nation's sciences related to brain development and behaviorism. The 2004 amendments specifically acknowledged that brain development justifies early intervention; they also took into account the roles that response-to-intervention and positive behavior support play in preventing placement into special education or making special education more effective.

A third is cultural and has to do with the emerging insistence that individuals—read: parents of children with disabilities and those who themselves have disabilities—may not depend so much as before on the federal and state governments for support but must assume more responsibility for their own status in life (Turnbull, 2005). The theme of personal responsibility finds its voice in the findings of fact and statements of policy of the 2004 statute; there is no reason (at this time) to believe that there will be any retrenchment from them.

A fourth is the development of more effective interventions originating in the nation's medical responses to wounded warriors. Just as was the case after both world wars (which occasioned the Rehabilitation Act and its amendments) and the Gulf War, the current Mideast conflicts will have the perverse effect of causing breakthroughs in rehabilitation medicine; predictably, these breakthroughs will become available to civilian populations, including students with disabilities.

Other factors may well exist. It suffices for the purposes of this chapter, however, to consider these and their power to change dramatically the contexts in which Congress and the parent movement will act when reauthorization becomes active. Within these and possibly other contexts, the parent movement will again be challenged to engineer the education of students with disabilities. It will have to find ways to capitalize on the advantages inherent in the contexts, blunt the challenges presented by them, and secure acceptable, if not ideal, outcomes. Using the law to achieve these outcomes is a constant component of the parent movement. The movement is affected by and also affects the contexts; it finds ways to engineer results and thus society's response to disability, and its behavior is shaped by contexts even as it itself shapes the contexts and thus the behaviors of all involved in the lives of people with disabilities.

It is impermissible to close this chapter without acknowledging the parents who, over 6 decades (beginning in the 1950s and continuing into the decade of 2010), created a social movement, initiated a revolution in rights, challenged and changed cultural norms, and—here, each of us speaks from a personal perspective—made it possible for people with disabilities to have an acceptable, if not enviable, quality of life. They dreamed the seemingly impossible dream; they achieved beyond their modest early aspirations; they demonstrated their strengths against great odds; and they will continue to do so, for legal and cultural conditions still are not as favorable to people and families affected by disabilities as they are to people not directly affected by disability.

Acknowledgment

The authors would like to acknowledge the research assistance provided by Heather Aldersey with respect to the witnesses at the Congressional Hearings.

References

Abeson, A., & Davis, S. (2000). The parent movement in mental retardation. In M. L. Wehmeyer & J. R. Patton (Eds.), *Mental retardation in the 20th century* (pp. 19–34). Austin, TX: Pro-Ed.

Anonymous. (1954). *Blueprint for a crusade: A history of the National Association for Retarded Children, Inc.* Retrieved January 5, 2010, from The Arc of the United States Web site: http://www.thearc.org/NetCommunity/Page.aspx?pid=272

Board of Education v. Rowley, 458 U.S. 176, 102 S. Ct. 3034 (1982).

Boggs, E. (1971). Federal Legislation 1966–71. In J. Wortis (Ed.), *Mental Retardation, an Annual Review, 3,* 103–127.

Boggs, E. M. (1985). Who is putting whose head in the sand? (Or in the clouds, as the case may be). In H. R. Turnbull & A. P. Turnbull (Eds.), *Parents speak out: Then and now* (2nd ed., pp. 39–53). Columbus, OH: Merrill.

Braddock, D. (1987). *Federal policy toward mental retardation and developmental disabilities*. Baltimore: Brookes.

Brown v. Board of Education, 349 U.S. 886, 75 S. Ct. 210, (1954).

Burlington School Committee v. Massachusetts Department of Education, 471 U.S. 359 (1985).

Dellmuth v. Muth, 491 U.S. 223 (1989).
Education of All Handicapped Children Act of 1975 (P.L. 94-142), 20 U.S.C. Sec 1400(d)
Education of the Handicapped Act, as amended by P.L. 98-199, P.L. 99-457, P.L. 101-476, U.S.C., Secs. 1400-1485. (1986).
Egnor, D. (2003). *IDEA reauthorization and the student discipline controversy.* Denver, CO: Love.
Elementary and Secondary Education Act of 1965, originally 20 U.S.C. Secs. 3801-3900, now 20 U.S.C. Sec. 7801
Elementary and Secondary Education Amendments of 1978 (P.L. 95-561).
Ferguson, P. M. (2008). The doubting dance: Contributions to a history of parent/professional interactions in early 20th century America. *Research and Practice for Persons with Severe Disabilities, 33*(1-2), 48–58.
Finn, C. E., Rotherham, A. J., & Hokansan Jr., C. R. (Eds.). (2001). *Rethinking special education for a new century.* Washington, DC: Progressive Policy Institute & Thomas Fordham Foundation.
Goals 2000: Educate America Act of 1994 (P.L. 103-227), 20 U.S.C. 5811 et seq.
Goodwin, J., & Jasper, J. M. (2003). Editor's introduction. In J. Goodwin & J. M. Jasper (Eds.), *The social movements reader: Cases and concepts* (pp. 3–8). Oxford, UK: Blackwell.
The Handicapped Children's Protection Act of 1986 (P.L. 99-372).
Hebbeler, K. M., Smith, B. J., & Black, T. L. (1991). Federal early childhood special education policy: A model for the improvement of services for children with disabilities. *Exceptional Children, 58*, 104–112.
Honig v. Doe, 484 U.S. 305, 108 S. Ct. 592 (1988).
Individuals with Disabilities Education Act (IDEA), 20 U.S.C. Sec. 1400 et seq., 34 C.F.R. 300 et seq. (1997).
IDEA Amendments of 1997 (P.L. 105-17).
IDEA Amendments of 2004 (P.L. 108-446).
Irving Independent School District v. Tatro, 703 F.2d 823 (5th Circ. 1983), aff'd in part, rev'd in part, 468 U.S. 883, 104 S. Ct. 3371 (1984).
Itkonen, T. (2007). PL 94-142: Policy, evolution, and landscape shift. *Issues in Teacher Education, 16*(2), 7–17.
Itkonen, T. (2009). *The role of special education interest groups in national policy.* Amherst, NY: Cambria Press.
Larry P. v. Riles, 793 F. Supp. 969, 1984 U.S. App. LEXIS 26195 (1984).
LaVor, M. L. (1976). Time and circumstances. In F. Weintraub, A. Abeson, J. Ballard, & M. L. LaVor (Eds.), *Public policy and the education of exceptional children* (pp. 293–303). Reston, VA.: Council for Exceptional Children.
Lippman, L., & Goldberg, I. (1973). *Right to education.* New York: Teacher's College Press.
Maternal and Child Health and Mental Retardation Planning Amendments (P.L. 88-156) (1964).
Mental Retardation Facilities and Community Mental Health Centers Construction Act (P.L. 88-164). (1963).
Mills v. District of Columbia Bd. of Ed., 348 F. Supp. 866 (D.D.C. 1972); contempt proceedings, EHLR 551:643 (D.D.C. 1980).
Minnesota Governor's Council on Developmental Disabilities (n.d). Parallels in time – President's panel on mental retardation. Retrieved from http://www.mnddc.org/parallels/five/5c/5c_html/ht1.html
National Association for Retarded Children. (1953). *Education bill of rights for the retarded* (Position Paper). New York: Author.
National Council on Disability. (1995a). *Improving the implementation of the Individuals with Disabilities Education Act: Making schools work for all of America's children.* Washington, DC: Author.
National Council on Disability. (1995b). *Improving the implementation of the Individuals with Disabilities Education Act: Making schools work for all of America's children* (Supplement). Washington, DC: Author.
No Child Left Behind Act of 2001 (NCLB) (P.L. 107-110).
Parents in Action on Special Education (PASE) v. Hannon, No. 74 C 3586 N.D. Ill. (1980).
Pennhurst State School and Hospital v. Halderman, 446 F. Supp. 1295 (E.D. Pa. 1977), aff'd in part, rev'd in part, 612 F.2d 84 (3rd Cir. 1979), rev'd, 451 U.S.1 (1981), on remand, 673 F.2d 647 (3rd Cir. 1982), rev'd 465 U.S. 89 (1984).
Pennsylvania Ass'n for Retarded Children (PARC) v. Commonwealth of Pennsylvania, 334 F. Supp. 1257 (E.D. Pa. 1971); 343 F. Supp. 279 (E.D. Pa. 1972)
Polletta, F., & Jasper, J. M. (2001). Collective identity and social movements. *Annual Review of Sociology, 27*, 283–205.
Report of the President's Commission on Excellence in Special Education. (2002). *A new era: Revitalizing special education for children and their families.* Washington, DC: U.S. Department of Education, Office of Special Education and Rehabilitative Services.
Segal, R. (n.d.). *The National Association for Retarded Citizens.* Retrieved January 5, 2010, from The Arc of the United States Web site: http://www.thearc.org/NetCommunity/Page.aspx?pid=401
Shorter, E. (2000). *The Kennedy family and the story of mental retardation.* Philadelphia: Temple University Press.
Smith v. Robinson, 468 U.S. 992, 104 S. C. 3457 (1984).
Thompson, N. (2002). Social movements, social justice, and social work. *British Journal of Social Work, 32*, 711–722.
Tilly, C. & Wood, L. J. (2009). *Social movements: 1768–2008* (2nd ed.). Boulder, CO: Paradigm.
Turnbull, A. P., Turnbull, H. R., & Wehmeyer, M. L. (2010). *Exceptional lives: Special education in today's schools* (6th ed.). Upper Saddle River, NJ: Merrill/Prentice Hall.
Turnbull, H. R. (2005). Individuals with Disabilities Act Reauthorization: Accountability and personal responsibility. *Remedial and Special Education, 26*, 320–326.
Turnbull, H. R., Stowe, M. J., & Huerta, N. E. (2007). *Free appropriate public education: The law and children with disabilities* (7th ed.). Denver, CO: Love.
Turnbull, H. R., & Turnbull, A. P. (1978). *Free appropriate public education: Law and education of children with disabilities.* Denver, CO: Love.
Turnbull, H. R., & Turnbull, A. P. (1993). *Free appropriate education: Law and education of children with disabilities* (4th ed.). Denver, CO: Love.
Turnbull, H. R., & Turnbull, A. P. (1996). The synchrony of stakeholders: Lessons from the disabilities rights movement. In S. L. Kagan & N. Cohen (Eds.), *Reinventing early care and education: A vision for a quality system* (pp. 290–305). San Francisco: Jossey-Bass.
Weicker, L. (1985). Sonny and public policy. In H. R. Turnbull & A. P. Turnbull (Eds.), *Parents speak out: Then and now* (2nd ed., pp. 281–207). Englewood Cliffs, NJ: Merrill/Prentice Hall.
What is the TAPP network (1987–1988, Winter). *Coalition Quarterly, 5*, 1–2.
Will, M. (1984). *Supported employment services: An OSERS position paper.* Washington, DC: U.S. Department of Education.
Wyatt v. Stickney, 344 F. Supp. 373 (M.D. Ala. 1972), aff'd in part, rev'd in part sub nom.

49

Resilience in Families of Children with Disabilities

Risk and Protective Factors

George H. S. Singer
University of California, Santa Barbara

Christine Maul
California State University, Fresno

Mian Wang and Brandy L. Ethridge
University of California, Santa Barbara

Resilience has garnered extraordinary attention from researchers and in the popular culture over the past three decades (Gardner & Troupe, 2006; Liebenberg & Ungar, 2009; Luthar & Brown, 2007; Suskind, 2005; Tillman, 2000; Walsh, 2006) in part because it offers a message of hope about people who manage to overcome circumstances which, more often than not, are impediments to success. Resilience gained prominence as an early harbinger of the positive psychology movement, characterized by a focus on successful adaptation and thriving (Benard, 2004; Morrison, Brown, D'Incau, O'Farrell, & Furlong, 2006; Patterson, 2002). The concept of resilience originated as a model explaining successful life trajectories in vulnerable children raised in circumstances that commonly overwhelm normal development and impede desirable adult outcomes (Werner & Smith, 2001). By definition, high risk is a necessary context for resilience. That is, it does not describe typically developing children raised in warm, supportive, and intact middle-class families with no mental health problems. Rather the research is concerned with homeless children (Israel, Hernandez, & Jozefowicz-Simbeni, 2009; Obradović et al., 2009), survivors of wars and natural disasters (Elder & Clipp, 1989; Lawson & Thomas, 2007; Vogt & Tanner, 2007), children of parents with serious mental illness (Tebes, Kaufman, Adnopoz, & Racusin, 2001; Mowbray & Oyserman, 2003), individuals with life-threatening diseases (Becker & Newsom, 2005; Rabkin, Remien, Katoff, & Williams, 1993), children at-risk for academic failure (Finn & Rock, 1997; Waxman, Gray, & Padrón, 2002), and studies of children with and at-risk for both mild and severe disabilities (Guralnick, 1998; Morrison & Cosden, 1997; Msall, 2009). Resilience is a longitudinal phenomenon; it manifests over time. Individuals and families that are not resilient at one stage of the lifecycle may attain it later or vice versa. The concept of resilience began as a study of individuals and has been transferred belatedly to the study of families as the unit of analysis. Werner and colleagues' (Werner, Bierman, & French, 1971; Werner & Smith, 2001) classic study of the children of Kauai has followed children from high-risk family environments for 40 years from birth into middle age, finding that some individuals who were troubled in childhood and adolescence were able to right themselves well into their 30's. With this long view researchers have identified turning points which can occur well beyond childhood and adolescence. This line of research has identified protective factors and risk factors including both characteristics of individuals and their social ecologies.

The resilient children in Werner's research were born into low income families with problems such as alcoholism and parental mental illness. Children who proved to be resilient were sociable infants and toddlers who were able to draw positive attention and commitment from at least one adult in their troubled circumstances. Along with internal protective factors, Werner's resilient children had at least one caregiver who was a positive influence and who remained involved and committed to the child over time during early childhood. Factors that promote resilience have been further categorized as compensatory or protective. The former describes specific qualities of the individual or the environment which counter specific risk factors. For example, in middle childhood resilient children in Werner's research commonly had a hobby which allowed them to focus and remove themselves in a healthy manner from chaotic or otherwise negative interactions in their homes; hobbies functioned as compensatory factors. Protective factors operate more generally to buffer and prevent risk factors from doing damage as, for example, sociability operated in the children's early years. It operated as a general trait which could draw positive attention in a variety of situations.

Children with disabilities are at-risk of compromised life trajectories making it difficult for families to successfully prepare these children for a desirable quality of life in adulthood. On average, there is little doubt that children with disabilities become adults at unusually high risk of occupying a less than optimal niche in society, and so children with disabilities are deemed vulnerable. A recent survey of a representative sample of adults with disabilities in the United States found that they experience much higher levels of unemployment or underemployment than people without disabilities of the same age, have lower life satisfaction, and participate less in community life than adults without disabilities (Kessler Foundation and National Organization on Disability, 2010). There is considerable variability in these outcome measures indicating that some disabilities are more problematic than others, and there are individuals in all disability categories who beat the odds. The study of resiliency attempts to account for this kind of variability.

Malleable protective and compensatory variables are important because, once identified, it may then be possible to deliberately create these supportive conditions. For example, findings about the importance of sustained positive connections between vulnerable children and supportive adults support the value of natural mentoring relationships and programs such as the Big Brothers, Big Sisters program which recruit and support mentors for at-risk children and adolescents (DuBois, & Silverthorn, 2005; Grossman & Tierney, 1998). Special educators have also been documented to be providers of long-term mentoring and support for high-risk adolescents (Regester & Singer, in press). The study of families that raise resilient children with disabilities may inform intervention and policy.

The concept of resilience has been transferred from the study of individuals to families in order to account for thriving in the face of risk factors that are ordinarily thought to threaten family integrity and healthy functioning (Hawley & DeHaan, 1996; McCubbin & McCubbin, 1988; Walsh, 2006). Researchers have begun the complex task of accounting for resilience in families of children with disabilities (Bayat, 2007; Hastings & Taunt, 2002; Patterson, 1991).

By definition, resilience requires unusual levels of vulnerability which must be overcome. This concern has been more prominent regarding some categories of disability than others as we will discuss later in this chapter.

We first focus on families of children with developmental disabilities, in particular children with intellectual disabilities (ID) and autism spectrum disorder (ASD) because these families have been subjects of a substantial body of research on stress, coping, and resilience. It has long been assumed that these families are at considerable risk because they experience comparatively high levels of stress (Bailey, Golden, Roberts, & Ford, 2007; Singer, 2006). This assumption has been challenged and problematized in recent years. Questions have been raised about basic definitions of family stress (Crnic, Arbona, Baker, & Blacher, 2009) and whether it is factually correct to assume invariably high levels of family disruption including parental depression, marital discord, and sibling psychosocial problems.

Prior to the late 1980s, a chapter on families of children with ID and related developmental disabilities would be mostly a story of affliction and woe. Parents of children with ID were described in a blanket fashion as experiencing chronic sorrow (Olshansky, 1962), suffering high rates of depression and other mental health problems (Wolfensberger & Menolascino, 1970), experiencing marital discord and unusually high rates of divorce (Gath, 1977), and as hot houses for development of distressed siblings (Gath, 1972). This point of view has been challenged and partly refuted in empirical research over the past two decades (Summers, Behr, & Turnbull, 1989; Ferguson, 2002; Singer & Irvin, 1991; Hastings & Taunt, 2002).

Stress in Families of Children with Intellectual Disabilities

In order to apply the concept of resilience to families of children with disabilities, it is necessary to first demonstrate that families are vulnerable to undesirable outcomes and secondly that there is variability in these outcomes including a subgroup that adapts and in some cases thrives. Much of the literature in the study of families of children with developmental disabilities has identified ways that these families experience high levels of stress leading to problems such as maternal depression, marital discord, divorce, and sibling psychological problems. There is general agreement that parenting children with severe disabilities is associated with unusual levels of family stress. Disability related stress may be episodic in some families and chronic in others. The concept of stress has been used in various ways in the research literature on families of children with disabilities. In some studies, it refers to the diagnostic event when parents first learn that their child has a disability (Baxter, Cummins, & Polak, 1995). Disabilities and the context in which they are identified are diverse as are impacts of the diagnosis. The causes of disability and the social institutions in which children are labeled as having an impairment vary. The earliest diagnosis of a disability is identification of a physical anomaly with ultrasound in a medical office or clinic. Some children are identified as having a disability in hospital settings shortly after birth; the news is delivered by a physician or nurse and often is treated as a medical calamity. The discovery that a child has a severe disability is often a powerful event that for some parents is a psychological trauma. Glidden and colleagues (Glidden & Jobe, 2006; Glidden & Schoolcraft, 2003) conducted one of the few longitudinal studies in the literature. They compared birth parents to adoptive parents of children with Down Syndrome over a period of 17 years.

One group chose to adopt children with full knowledge of the children's disability, whereas the birth parents learned their child had the disability during pregnancy or shortly after birth. Both groups were first evaluated for depressive symptoms when the children were six years old and subsequently at roughly five-year intervals. The birth parents had significantly higher levels of distress than the adoptive parents when the children were six; these levels were considerably higher, indicating more distress, than in the general population. A retrospective assessment suggested that the birth parents first experienced these elevated symptoms at the time the disability was first identified. The implication is that the unexpected and unwanted diagnosis, on average, was a stressor that required possibly up to six years to subside. Subsequent evaluations revealed that this initial distress declined over time remaining higher than adoptive parents' depressive symptom levels but well within the low normal range indicating that on average the risk for clinical depression was low. The birth parents as a group rebounded from early distress as they moved to new stages of the family lifecycle. Further, from the first real time assessment when the children were six years of age, there was variability in parental well-being. One sub-group had less distress than the average in the adoptive parents, and they remained less troubled at every subsequent assessment.

Instead of focusing on the initial diagnosis as the major stressors, other researchers have defined stress in terms of specific demands placed on the family or parents in caring for family members with disabilities. These demands until recently have been typically and almost invariably viewed pessimistically as burdens of caregiving. For example, Holroyd (1987) developed a measure of parent and family stress linked to a long list of troubling phenomena. The items were organized under a set of subscales and their labels are worth a cursory reading because they provide an overview of the negative assumptions that prevailed at the time of the measure's development. The Questionnaire on Resources and Stress (QRS; Holroyd, 1987) has 285 items grouped into domains including a set of *Personal Problems* scales focused on parents consisting of *Poor Health/Mood*, *Excess Time Demands*, *Negative Attitude toward Index Case*, *Overprotection/Dependency*, *Lack of Social Support*, *Overcommitment/Martyrdom*, and *Pessimism*. Family Problems scales carry the labels *Lack of Family Integration*, *Limits on Family Opportunity*, and *Financial Problems*; and the subscale labeled Problems of Index Case (the child with ID) were *Physical Incapacitation*, *Lack of Activities for Index Case*, *Occupational Limitations for Index Case*, *Social Obtrusiveness*, and *Difficult Personality Characteristics*. These lists of stressors imposed by the "index case" were thought to virtually without variability characterize these children and their negative impacts on families.

Numerous studies have been devoted to identifying characteristics of children with disabilities which cause stress to parents and families (Singer & Irvin, 1991; Saloviita, Itälinna, & Leinonen, 2003; Hastings & Beck, 2004). In general, the more severe the disability and the more caregiving required, the higher the stress levels in parents, particularly mothers as the primary caregivers (Singer, Biegel, & Ethridge, 2010). However, caregiving demands in univariate models account for relatively small amounts of the variance in parental and family stress and emotional distress. Instead, it is clear that family stress is a multivariate phenomenon with important moderators and mediators (Singer & Irvin, 1991; Saloviita et al., 2003). It is unusual for a single characteristic of the child or the disability by itself to strongly predict family stress. There are two exceptions reported in the literature: (a) children's problem behaviors (Hastings & Beck, 2004); and (b) severe medical conditions requiring frequent urgent care (Patterson, Leonard, & Titus, 1992). Even in these circumstances, however, there is evidence suggesting that serious behavior problems are mediated by parent's cognitive coping strategies as reported by Hastings et al. (2005) and by MacDonald, Hastings, and Fitzsimonds (2010) in studies of families of children with autism who often exhibit difficult problem behaviors.

More recently, stress has been defined and measured in a more generic way in studies of families of children with disabilities. Researchers have used measures such as the Parent Stress Index (PSI; Abidin, 1995) to appraise stressful experiences related to common challenges most parents face at times in raising any child. The PSI includes a set of scales for indicating stress parents experience in their personal and family life in general and other scales indicating stress associated with childrearing. A similar approach with a broader conceptualization of daily stress has been measured in these families using the Daily Hassles Scale (Kanner, Coyne, Schaefer, & Lazarus, 1981). It includes common difficulties in daily living such as having a car break down, not having sufficient money for a family need, an unpleasant social encounter, or difficulties at work. Both the PSI and the Daily Hassles Scales have indicated higher levels of daily stress in families of children with developmental disabilities (Baxter, Cummins, & Yiolotis, 2000). When formulated in this way, disability related stress is seen as an amplification of common demands that many people face whether or not they are a member of a family with an individual with a disability. It is evident from the research that those background conditions, moderating variables, which cause stress in families of typically developing children, also amplify it in families of children with disabilities. Increased daily stress associated with single parenthood, poverty, dangerous neighborhoods, and limited access to medical and social services interact with disability related stressors (Olsson & Hwang, 2008).

Regardless of how it has been conceptualized and measured, most studies have found elevated levels of stress in families of children with disabilities compared to families of typically developing children (Crnic et al., 2009). That said, life with children with disabilities is not inevitably stressful, and stress does not inevitably lead to health and family problems. There is considerable variability in how families respond to stress. Not only are some families less troubled by disability related demands, there is a substantial group of families that appear to be strengthened by dealing with these challenges. These families are able to bounce back from adversity (Patterson, 1991), to maintain sustainable daily routines (Gallimore, Bernheimer, & Weisner, 1999), to balance the needs of their children with disabilities with those of the other family members (Patterson, 1991), and they are able to view children with disabilities as contributors to family well-being (Summers et al., 1989; Hastings & Taunt, 2004). Further, a sizeable minority of families are able to establish a satisfying quality of life.

Newer conclusions in the research literature are derived from two main approaches; the synthesis and review of many studies about specific family outcomes and the use of new measures to ask new questions about positive adaptation (Hastings & Taunt, 2004; Summers et al., 1989). For example, recent meta-analyses are now available of studies which focus on maternal depression, studies of siblings adjustment, studies of marriage in these families, and the effectiveness of interventions to support parents and children. Under the older monolithic assumption at least four outcomes would be predicted: (a) large increases in depression and distress in families of children with developmental disabilities compared to parents of typically developing children; (b) large increases in siblings' mental health problems;(c) less variability in the measures of parents of children with disabilities because they would have in common negative outcomes; and d) these problems would not respond well to relatively brief interventions because of their assumed irremediable nature. In the following discussion we will examine each of these assumptions and then turn to a newer focus on positive outcomes in these families.

Variability in Families of Children with Intellectual Disabilities: Meta-analyses

One concern of researchers has been the impact of parenting children with disabilities on parent's demoralization and depression (Singer, 2006; Bailey, Golden, Roberts, & Ford, 2007). Although it is not by itself a family level variable, maternal depression has a powerful impact on the full family system. High levels of depressive symptoms are common in women of child bearing age in the general population to such an extent that depression is recognized as a major public health problem (Glidden & Schoolcraft, 2003). Because this has been a long-standing area of interest to researchers, it provides a vantage point for evaluating the status of families of children with developmental disabilities. For most of the second half of the 20th century, the operative assumption in much of the research literature on these families was that there was a straightforward univariate and relatively uniform negative impact of children's developmental disabilities on parent well-being. Not only has the assumption of negative impacts been challenged but also the simple univariate model that disability directly causes family stress has been discredited as researchers have focused on the complexity involved with family processes over an extended period of time (Kersh, Hedvat, Hauser-Cram, & Warfield, 2006; Singer & Irvin, 1991).

Meta-analysis is unique in that it provides researchers with the tools to characterize a group of studies and to indicate the strength of the relationship between independent and dependent variables, in this case depressive symptoms. Meta-analyses yield a statistic, an effect size, which indicates the average extent of the outcomes when several studies are combined and characrterized as a group. Singer (2006) conducted a meta-analysis of 18 studies comparing parents of children with intellectual and other related developmental disabilities with parents of typically developing (TD) children on depressive symptoms. The average weighted effect size for all of the studies was $d = .35$ for mothers, a small effect size. Only a few studies included fathers. These showed that fathers' level of depressive symptoms were lower than mothers' but, when compared with fathers of typically developing children, their depressive symptoms were elevated as also indicated by a small effect size. Some of the measures used in these studies have an established cut-off score used as an indicator of possible clinical depression. Singer estimated from these studies that roughly 29% of the mothers in the ID group were at-risk of clinical depression compared to 19% of the mothers in the TD group. Fully 71% of the mothers had well-being in the normal range. In an analysis of related data on marital well-being, Risdal and Singer (2004) argued that the prior literature assumed a much higher rate of distress in these parents than revealed in this meta-analysis. In keeping with other's research, they called into question the assumption that parenting a child with ID is a source of chronic sorrow and should be viewed as a family tragedy when the evidence clearly indicates a large percentage of parents are not unusually troubled and do not experience more distress than parents of nondisabled children. At the same time, the evidence indicates that there is increased risk with roughly one-third of mothers of children with developmental disabilities with depressive symptoms elevated to a level that puts them at-risk for clinical depression. Another way to look at this data is to compare the average standard deviations of the two groups. If the negative presumption of uniform impact on families were true, it would be expected that variability would be significantly lower in families of children with ID because they would share in common negative responses, in this case depressive symptoms. When tested with an F ratio statistic, the differences in variability between the two groups were not significantly different. That is, just as there is a wide range of variability in typical families, there is the same in families of children with ID.

Intervention studies also shed light on the extent of risk in these families by indicating whether or not parental distress is malleable. If these families were irremediably beset by depression, one would not expect that relatively brief treatments would make a difference. Singer, Ethridge, and Aldana (2007) reported on a meta-analysis of 17 treatment studies for over 400 parents of children with developmental disabilities. Interventions included behavioral parent training, interventions based on cognitive behavioral therapy, and treatment packages which combined these two methods. The literature synthesis indicated that most of the interventions were effective in reducing depressive symptoms in parents in the short term. The overall weighted effect size was d = .29 indicating that the treatments consistently helped but that their impact was a relatively modest one. The fact that relatively brief interventions helped reduce demoralization suggests that stress in these families can be addressed in part by strengthening parental coping skills and parenting practices drawn from applied behavior analysis. These studies did not include data on changes in the children with disabilities who had problem behavior. This is an important dimension of the question of whether or not problems in these families are malleable.

In a second synthesis of a different group of treatment studies, Ethridge and Singer (2009) conducted a comparative meta-analysis of 13 studies comparing families with children with developmental disabilities that received a parent training intervention to parents of children with ID that did not. This second study differed from the first by focusing on behavioral parent training studies that reported data for impacts of the interventions on both parents and children. These studies all included measures to determine if the parent training interventions had an impact on parents' psychological distress and if there was also an impact on children's problem behaviors. Ethridge and Singer noted that the majority of the studies used common psychological distress measures (Mirowsky & Ross, 2003) and included mothers, with a few including fathers or other primary caregiving family members as the parent intervention targets. The question guiding this meta-analysis was whether the studies, taken as a whole, show that parent training interventions reduce parents' psychological distress and their child's problem behaviors. The parent training interventions were categorized into two types, behavioral parent training (BPT) and multiple component parent training (MCPT). BPT interventions were designed to further develop parents' child behavior management and positive parent-child interaction skills (e.g., Bagner & Eyberg, 2007). MCPT interventions combine elements of BPT with coping skills parent training interventions, which are designed to further develop parents' coping skills, specifically how to consciously manage automatic negative thoughts, feelings, and in some studies to use relaxation skills to manage daily stresses in general and those associated with caring for a child with developmental disabilities (e.g., Plant & Sanders, 2007). The effect sizes ranged between .02 and .73 for parent psychological distress indicating a significant reduction on average. The average weighted effect size for all of the studies was .22, .19 for BPT interventions and .31 for MCPT intervention studies. Only a few studies located provided separate data for fathers. Fathers also seemed to show a decrease in psychological distress, but the findings were not statistically significant possibly because their scores on the dependent measures were relatively low prior to the treatment. Although child problem behavior data was not reported by sex, the majority of children were boys. In addressing children's problem behavior, the effect sizes ranged between –0.06 and +.76 for child problem behavior, with an average weighted effect size for all of the studies of .32, .27 for BPT interventions and .46 for MCPT studies; all of which were significant. Effect sizes have to be interpreted by looking at similar findings and making comparisons. In regards to parent psychological distress, the Ethridge and Singer findings were compared to Lundahl, Risser, and Lovejoy's (2006) meta-analysis findings on the impact of behavioral interventions on the parental (self)perceptions of parents with children without disabilities and Barlow, Coren, and Stewart-Brown's (2003) meta-analysis findings on the impact of group-based parent training on the depression and/or stress/anxiety parents of children without ID. The comparison suggested that the effect of the parent training interventions on reducing parent psychological distress in parents with children with developmental disabilities was lower than the parent interventions' effect at reducing the distress of parents of children without ID. In regards to child problem behavior, the Ethridge and Singer findings were compared to the Lundahl and colleagues' and Barlow and Parsons's (2003) meta-analyses findings on the impact of parent training on child problem behavior in children without ID. The comparison suggested that the effect of the parent training interventions on reducing child problem behavior in children with ID was comparable to the parent interventions' effect at reducing the problem behavior of children without developmental disabilities.

It has also long been assumed that having a child with a developmental disability severely strains marriages and greatly increases divorce rates. Risdal and Singer (2004) synthesized studies of marital discord in families of children with developmental disabilities. The received view of the impact of disabled children on marriage was that it exerted a strong and negative influence which led to more marital distress and higher divorce rates. Based on seven studies, they found a small effect size for levels of marital discord. The risk ratio for divorce between the two groups was 1.39, a hefty increase in risk but much smaller one than had been reported in the earlier literature (e.g., Gath, 1977). Again, the differences between the standard deviations for the two groups were not significant indicating much more variability in couple's responses than was previously assumed. In six comparative studies 14.9% (range 5.5%–27%) of the marriages of parents of the TD children had ended in divorce compared to 20.8% in the families of children with ID (range 12.2%–33%). The studies that provide the best evidence based upon large sample sizes are the studies conducted by Hodapp and Krasner (1995), with a percentage increase in divorce of 5.35%, and by Witt, Riley, and Coiro (2003), with an increase of 2.9%. The former study focused on families of children with developmental disabilities and the latter on families of children with a wider range of chronic conditions.

In the recent past it was commonly believed that siblings of children with disabilities also uniformly suffered from psychological and social problems and were considered by some researchers as a population at-risk (San Martino & Newman, 1974). Several reasons were given for the presumed negative affects on brothers and sisters. These included emotional neglect by parents who presumably had to allocate their attention to the child with ID, the impact of stigma, and a high level of demand on the siblings for help with caregiving (Rossiter & Sharpe, 2001). In a meta-analysis of 25 comparative studies, Rossiter and Sharpe reviewed evidence for psychosocial problems in brothers and sisters. Overall they reported an average effect size of d = –.06, indicating an extremely small negative impact on siblings. Once again the negative assumption about impacts on families was not fully supported by research.

When asked in a way that allows for a full range of appraisals, many parents characterize the impact of a child's disability on themselves and their families in ways that are often surprising to people who have not experienced a relationship with a loved one with a disability. The tradition in social science and in the common culture in the United States has been a taken for granted assumption that children with disabilities are likely to damage family life. Particularly in regard to ID, the notion that having a child with cognitive disabilities was a tragedy has been stubbornly persistent and has only recently begun to erode under the weight of growing evidence indicating that families respond in many different ways including resilient functioning (Hastings, Beck, & Hill, 2005; Helff & Glidden, 1998; Patterson, 1991). Research has shown that many families view the impact of their children with a developmental disability in a positive light (Greer, Grey, & McClean, 2006; Hastings et al., 2005; Hasting & Taunt, 2002). Some parents report that they gain important life lessons, learn to be more tolerant, are heartened by their children's developmental progress, and their families work better as a team to accommodate to the needs of their disabled children.

In summary, meta-analyses indicate that the idea that families of children with ID are inevitably harmed by the experience does not hold up to evidence. Glidden and Schoolcraft (2003), writing about the impact of children with intellectual disabilities on their families, succinctly characterized this change. "An almost monolithic conception of the inevitability of distress, crisis, and pathology has been replaced by a recognition of the extreme variability of family response" (p. 183). Not only is there more diversity than previously thought in the levels of psychological and marital problems that these families experience, but it is increasingly clear that many parents and siblings characterize rearing and growing up with children with disabilities as beneficial both personally and for the family (Hastings & Taunt, 2002; Summers et al., 1989). Scorgie and Sobsey (2000) found that parents in their research described the experience of childrearing to be positively transformational (Scorgie & Sobsey, 2000). These reports along with the meta-analytic data raise the question of how to simultaneously account for consistent findings of small to moderate increases in family stress and distress with these positive reports. A recent study by Bayat (2007) sheds some light on this question; the author coded written responses to surveys from 175 parents and primary caregivers of children and adolescents with autism and reported that approximately a third described their experiences with exceptional childrearing as positive, another third as both positive and negative, and the remaining group as negative. At least one-third of these families could be considered resilient. As the field learns more about this full range of responses, it is increasingly clear that resilience is an fitting paradigm for understanding these families.

Family Resilience

There are several definitions of family resilience (Patterson, 2002; McCubbin & McCubbin, 1993). All agree that resilient families successfully adapt to challenging circumstances, bounce back from adversity, and many are strengthened as a result. Just as there are vulnerable children who overcome their difficulties in time, there are families which successfully deal with crises and on-going stressors and are thereby strengthened. Family resilience is a multidimensional idea defined by the adequacy of the family's responses to normal and severe stressors. As with individual resilience, it is a longitudinal phenomenon consisting of adaptation over time. Resilient families experience times of crisis but they characteristically bounce back from these disruptions and learn from the experience (Patterson, 1991).

Most theories of family resilience draw heavily from family stress theories (McCubbin & McCubbin, 1993). Family stress theory describes responses to difficult situations as an interaction of shared cognitive appraisals among family members, coping behaviors, and activation of both internal and external resources. Reactions to new stressors are also impacted by the on-going background levels of stress, patterns of regular coping with this background stress, and general resources for dealing with these factors in the backdrop. Families are seen as appraising difficult conditions and their resources for dealing with these demands. In family resilience theories families demonstrate a variety of coping capabilities (Patterson, 1991). Resilient families are characterized by cooperative processes including the ability to construct global positive meanings about the family member with a disability. These appraisals buffer families from events and conditions which others would commonly interpret as stressors. Family members in resilient families are able to mobilize external resources effectively including both generic community resources and disability specific services (Olsson & Hwang, 2008). When necessary, they are able to advocate to obtain these supports. Cooperative processes which promote resilience in the family are believed to include effective communication and problem solving, effective ways to resolve and reduce conflict and flexibility in the face of changing demands (Patterson, 1991). Resilient families share enjoyment and pleasure as well as more painful experiences and they are able to balance the needs of a child with a disability with those of other family members (Patterson, 1991). They are able to modulate negative emotion to prevent or dampen the spread of anger and sadness throughout the family system. An important contribution to our understanding of protective factors comes from a longitudinal study by Gallimore, Bernheimer, and Weisner (1999). These researchers followed over 100 families of children with mild disabilities for over a decade, focusing in part on the families' daily routines and how they modified them to accommodate the needs of their children with disabilities. They found that resilient families maintain sustainable routines, and that, in response to crises, resilient families are able to eventually attain a new sustainable homeostatsis as seen in the reestablishment of routines which do not overtax individual family members or subsystems within the family. The outcomes of resilient processes in families have recently been conceptualized in terms of family quality of life.

The idea of family quality of life (FQOL) is of central importance to understanding what is meant by family resilience. Because FQOL is a very recent idea in the research literature, it is useful to look at the way it is conceptualized and measured. Attention to FQOL grows out of efforts to refocus research away from presumed pathology in families to the everyday sources of satisfaction which many people are able to attain in their family lives regardless of the demands associated with caregiving. Because of the newness of the idea in the study of families of children with disabilities, considerable effort has gone into clarifying what is meant by FQOL and how to measure it. There is general agreement that family quality of life involves the positive benefits of family life of which many aspects are shared by people everywhere across cultures and are commonly pursued in everyday life (Wang & Brown, 2009). Based upon a qualitative inquiry of parent's perspective of family well-being in families of children with disabilities (Poston et al., 2003), Park and colleagues (2003) define FQOL as: "families experience a high quality of life when their needs are met, they enjoy their time together, and they are able to do things that are important to them" (p. 367). In a recent effort at theorizing the FQOL construct, Zuna and colleagues (2009) also define FQOL as "a dynamic sense of well-being of the family, collectively and subjectively defined and informed by its members, in whom individual and family-level needs interact" (p. 262). Based on a series of studies where researchers at the Beach Center on Disability have endeavored to conceptualize and develop a measure of FQOL, Summers and colleagues (2005) concluded that the FQOL conceptual framework consists of five measurable domains: Family Interaction, Parenting, Emotional Well-being, Physical/Material Well-being and Disability related Support. On the basis of FQOL conceptual framework, the Beach Center Family Quality of Life Scale was developed and validated and was reported as a valuable measure of family outcome with sound psychometric properties (Hoffman, Marquis, Poston, Summers, & Turnbull, 2006; Wang et al., 2006).

In addition, an equally influential conceptual framework of FQOL is derived from the collaborative research work of an international research team consisting of researchers from different continents. By adopting the same logic of assuming a multidimensional domain structure of FQOL, Brown, Anand, Fung, Isaac, and Nehama (2010) suggest that FQOL in families of children with disabilities consists of nine domains: Health of the Family, Financial Well-being, Family Relationships, Support from Other People, Support from Disability-Related Services, Spiritual and Cultural Beliefs, Careers and Preparing for Careers, Leisure and Enjoyment of life, and Community and Civic Involvement. A measure of FQOL, the Family Quality of Life Questionnaire, was developed to collect both qualitative and quantitative data on nine domains of FQOL (Isaacs et al., 2007). Interestingly, both FQOL measures, albeit derived from different conceptual frameworks, share key considerations of FQOL as a whole-family construct that contains a mixture of domains/subscales and indicators of which some primarily focus on internal family characteristics and others on family support.

Using these and other newer measures and asking more complicated questions, researchers have begun to model the experiences of families of children with ID using combinations of risk and protective factors. For example, Saloviita and colleagues (2003) were able to account for 72% of the variance in maternal stress and 78% in paternal stress using linear models. For mothers, the key risk variables were a cognitive factor which the researchers labeled "definition of the situation as a catastrophe" and negative coping strategies consisting of passive and avoidant coping responses to stress. Protective variables for mothers were informal social support, positive marital relationships, formal support from the service system, and higher levels of children's adaptive behavior. The importance of formal and informal social support has been repeatedly demonstrated in studies over the past three decades.

Social Support and Social Services

In the original research on resilient children, most of the exogenous variables which helped children eventually overcome the odds were various forms of social support from informal allies including grandparents and caring members of the community and formal social supports provided by people in organizations which created the right kinds of structure and roles which allowed at-risk children to right themselves. As in the case of individual resilience, family resilience is not a process that takes place in a vacuum. Families live in a complex social and physical ecology which can bolster or undermine effective responses to stress. Contextual variables which increase risk or promote resilience include the availability and quality of early intervention and special education services. Dunst, Trivette, and Hamby (2007) have recently reported on a meta-analysis of the impact of family centered help-giving practices on families of children with disabilities. They synthesized the findings from 47 studies demonstrating the consistent positive impact of services which focus on the family as the central recipient of help by providing assistance in ways that are designed to strengthen their coping capacities. Informal social support also appears to be a key to resilience. When families report on the sources of help that are most important to them, they consistently state that family and friends are their primary source of assistance. A unique longitudinal study that has examined the impact of spousal support on parent-child interactions suggests that, particularly for mothers, emotional and instrumental support from their husbands contributes to maternal positive responsiveness in their interactions with their young children with disabilities (Crnic et al., 2009).

In summary, traditional views of families of children with ID and other developmental disabilities have been pessimistic. The received view was that there were almost unvarying and direct unmediated negative affects of children on their families. However, syntheses of studies on psychological impacts on parents and siblings have demonstrated lesser negative impacts, more variability, and responsiveness to interventions. Studies which have allowed parents and siblings the opportunities to express positivity about their family experiences have found that many families view children with ID as positive contributors to their families and to their quality of life. Brown, Anand, Fung, Isaac, and Nehama (2010) measured quality of life in samples of parents with children with Down Syndrome, autism, and typically developing children. In six life domains the families of the TD children had the highest levels of satisfaction, followed by the ID group, with the ASD group rating quality of life lowest. In the disability groups, a sizeable minority of parents indicated satisfaction with family quality of life. It is these families that fit the model of family resilience. In the remainder of this chapter, we examine risk and resilience in families of children with three other kinds of disabilities: autism spectrum disorder, learning disabilities, and behavioral and emotional disorders. Space allows only a brief examination of these large topics. In keeping with our focus on family resilience, we review representative studies of risk and protective factors in these families.

Risk and Protective factors in Children with Autism Spectrum Disorder

Autism spectrum disorder (ASD) is a pervasive developmental disorder which affects several areas of development, resulting in a severe and lifelong disability. It is a condition characterized by difficulties in communicating and interacting with other people; and by repetitive, stereotypical behaviors, narrow and often bizarre interests, and a rigid insistence on maintenance of routines. It has been estimated that the prevalence of autism in the United States is 110 per 10,000 children, or a little more than 1% of the child population (Kogan et al., 2009). This is a dramatic increase over prevalence rates quoted prior to the 1990s, when it was estimated that the prevalence of autism was 2–4 in every 10,000 children (Wing & Potter, 2002). This increase has caused a great deal of alarm and public outcry demanding that resources be devoted to pinpointing the causes of what is presumably an ASD epidemic. However, it is possible that the current prevalence figures are not the result of an actual increase in ASD, but a reflection of improved diagnostic procedures, increased social awareness of autism, and parental pursuit of funding for services for more mildly impaired children (Hegde & Maul, 2006).

There is a large body of research documenting stress in parents raising children with autism (e.g., Bebko, Konstantareas, & Springer, 1987; Lecavalier, Leone, & Wiltz, 2006). Studies have been conducted indicating that parents of children with ASD experience higher degrees of stress than parents of children with conditions without accompanying autism, such as other types of developmental disorders, behavior disorders, and special health care needs (Brown, McAdam-Crisp, Wang, & Iarocci, 2006; Schieve, Blumberg, Rice, Visser, & Boyle 2007).

Recent research has documented elevated maternal stress due to several factors, most of them relating to the extreme social and behavioral difficulties that characterize a diagnosis of ASD. Children with ASD often display behavior problems, such as throwing tantrums, screaming, biting, kicking, pinching, or other aggressive and/or self-injurious behaviors. Such difficulties can certainly have a deleterious effect on entire families' daily activities. As reported by Higgins, Bailey, and Pearce (2005), stress associated with ASD "impacts on most aspects of families' lives, including recreation activities, housekeeping, finances, emotional and mental health of caregivers, marital relationships, physical health of family members, sibling relations and relationships with extended family, friends, and neighbours" (p. 127).

Other stressors associated with ASD have to do with the necessity of navigating legal and educational processes to locate and secure appropriate services for children with ASD. Schieve et al. (2007) reported higher levels of "aggravation" among parents of children with ASD who had recently required special services than among parents of children with ASD without special service needs and parents of children with other developmental problems. These findings led the authors to conclude that "Parenting a child with autism with recent special service needs seems to be associated with unique stresses" (p. 114). Parents may experience stressful encounters involving unsatisfactory communication with professionals, uncoordinated and inefficient delivery of services, and the realization that delivered services are often ineffective and insufficient to meet their children's needs (Mugno, Ruta, D'arrigo, & Mazzone, 2007).

Other researchers have found evidence that, despite documented substantial stress, many families, and especially mothers, show strengths and remarkable coping skills in raising their children with ASD (Hall, 2008; Hoffman, Sweeney, Hodge, Lopez-Wagner, & Looney, 2009; Marshall & Long, 2010; Montes & Halterman, 2007; Pottie & Ingram, 2008). Mothers have reported various cognitive coping strategies and practical approaches that appear to help them adapt to their children's needs.

Cognitive coping strategies mentioned investigated in these studies included (a) positive reframing, (b) cognitive reappraisal, (c) comparison coping, and (d) resets. *Positive reframing* can be defined as "thinking about problems as challenges to be overcome" (Podolski & Nigg, 2001, p. 503). *Cognitive reappraisal* requires a re-examination of one's life and a resulting adjustment in beliefs, values, and expectations; a classic return to contemplating the meaning of life and what is truly important in life (Tunali & Power, 2002). With the utilization of *comparison coping*, parents gain perspective regarding the magnitude of the stress associated with raising their child with ASD compared to stress associated with other life events (e.g., the death of a child). *Resets* occur when parents take actions that alter the course of their lives and/or their children's lives as a result of problem-focused thinking. Examples of resets include changing residences to obtain better services, abruptly terminating one type of treatment in favor of another, or making occupational changes such as reducing work hours from full to part-time (Marshall & Long, 2010).

Practical approaches reported by families include various adaptations they make in their daily lives to accommodate their children's needs (Marshall & Long, 2010; Maul & Singer, 2009). They may choose to arrive to group social activities early to give their child a chance to acclimate to the environment without having a crowd of people around. They may seek out special seating arrangements in restaurants or theaters. They may take along a favorite snack on an outing to soothe their child if he or she becomes agitated. Family members, including siblings, may function as a "tag team," providing care giving while a family member takes a shower or continues to eat a meal (Maul & Singer, p. 6). They also might utilize more sophisticated techniques they have learned, such as devising and helping their child refer to a visual schedule, or reading a "social story" to prepare a child for a particular event (Marshall & Long, p. 114). Such accommodations have been found to be highly idiosyncratic, crafted by families in innovative ways to meet the needs of their specific child.

Finally, recent population studies have been conducted in which mothers of children with autism were identified within a general population of tens of thousands of parents (Hoffman et al., 2009; Montes & Halterman, 2007). Those studies have confirmed a higher level of stress and decreased mental health among mothers of children with ASD. However, the studies have also documented that mothers of children with autism are more likely to report a close relationship with their children, more likely to report better coping with parenting duties, and less likely to express anger toward their children than mothers in the general population. The presence of a child with ASD was not associated with a decrease in social support, or increased domestic violence. Further, no evidence was found to indicate that children with autism were more likely to live in single-parent households, which contradicts reports of lower marital satisfaction among parents of children with ASD (Brobst, Clopton, & Hendrick, 2009; Higgins, Bailey, & Pearce, 2005). Authors concluded that these more representational studies revealed "many strengths in the parent/child relationship, coping with parenting, and parenting support for mothers of a child with autism" (Montes & Halterman, p. 1045).

Children with Mental, Emotional, and Behavioral Disorders

Mental, emotional, and behavioral disorders (MEBD) include such conditions as anxiety disorders, depression, bipolar disorder, conduct disorder, and attention deficit hyperactivity disorder (ADHD). Guidelines for diagnosing such conditions in children are currently unclear, although prevalence appears to be rising. It has been estimated that as many as 20% of America's children and adolescent population may exhibit behaviors that warrant diagnosis of some kind of MEBD (Substance Abuse and Mental Health Services Administration, 2003).

Many symptoms of these conditions may pose various challenges to the daily lives of parents and families. Kendall (1999) interviewed siblings of children with ADHD; the siblings described their family life as "chaotic, conflictual, and exhausting" (p. 7). In a review of the literature, Early and Poertner (1993) found studies reporting numerous difficulties families of children with emotional disorders experience, such as a decreased ability to plan and participate in social activities, decreased attention paid to siblings, decreased opportunities for parents to have time together, and decreased satisfying social interactions with friends and extended family members. Further, treatment resources are not widely available in most states.

Such circumstances may make it difficult for parents to feel warmly attached to or proud of their child. Researchers have documented a tendency for parents of children with emotional or behavioral disorders to employ parenting styles that are highly authoritarian, sometimes harsh, and characterized by diminished emotional support for the child (Lange et al., 2005; Podolski & Nigg, 2001). Unfortunately, for many years the literature regarding MEBD in children tended to emphasize "parent blaming," identifying pathological conditions in parents that either directly caused or at least contributed to their children's diagnoses (Early & Poertner, 1993, p. 744). This made it difficult for parents to seek out appropriate services for their children, for fear of being perceived as a bad parent (Brauner & Stephens, 2006; Ruffolo, Kuhn, & Evans, 2006). Researchers currently suggest that there is a bidirectional relationship between parent and child behaviors, and it is not possible to determine whether the parenting style causes the child's behavior, or vice versa (Lange et al., 2005; Podolski & Nigg, 2001; Rogers, Wiener, Marton, & Tannock, 2009).

Also, more recent interest in family-centered, collaborative service delivery has shifted the emphasis away from a parent-blaming perspective when working with families of children with emotional and behavioral difficulties to a strengths-based approach that recognizes positive contributions parents can make to the intervention process. Saleebey

(1997) suggested that, given the extent of the difficulties some families face, and the limited resources available to them, "people are often doing amazingly well" (p. 49).

Early and Poertner (1993) found evidence that "emotional support" given by spouses, family, and friends was the helpful factor most valued by families of children with emotional disorders. Religious involvement and contact with other parents of children with similar diagnoses were also mentioned as helpful. The one positive benefit specifically mentioned by parents in one study had to do with more equal participation in parenting, with both parents becoming equally involved with the child (Friesen, 1989, as cited in Early & Poertner, 1993).

Mitchell (2006) found three "adaptive coping variables" that helped parents of children with ADHD improve their overall quality of life: (a) restraint, (b) suppression, and (c) reinterpretation. *Restraint* referred to parents' ability to wait until the right moment to act in a rational manner, rather than immediately exhibiting an emotional reaction to their children's behaviors. Parents who were able to *suppress* competing stimuli and focus on the problem at hand were more successful in addressing their children's behavioral difficulties. *Reinterpretation* allowed parents to "find a silver lining" in their situation and view their life circumstances as an opportunity to learn and experience personal growth (p. 167). Similar to this concept, "positive reframing" has also been found to be helpful to parents of children with ADHD (Podolski & Nigg, 2001, p. 503).

Children with Learning Disabilities

Types of learning disabilities affect a person's ability to learn various critical skills, such as how to read and write, perform mathematical calculations, move in a coordinated manner, or sustain focused attention. Because the disability is usually specific to one educational domain, it is typically not diagnosed until a child is school aged. It has been estimated that 8% to 10% of children under the age of 18 in the United States have some type of learning disability (National Institute of Neurological Disorders and Stroke, 2009).

Morrison and Cosden (1997) conducted a literature review to discover stressors that may affect adult outcomes in children with learning disabilities (LD). In their discussion regarding family adaptation, they found that the "family environment has been identified as a key factor that can provide both risks … and protection … for the developing child" (p. 47). Several factors were identified that placed additional stress on parents and, therefore, put adult outcomes for children with LD at risk. Stressors placed upon a family raising a child with LD included problematic interactions between parents and children with LD, who often have information processing difficulties that are evident both in the school and the home environment (Kaslow & Cooper, 1978). In addition, parents of children with LD may experience higher levels of stress because they have more contact with school personnel in connection with their children's academic and behavioral problems (Waggoner & Wilgosh, 1990). Other researchers have found that parents of children with LD tend to have negative perceptions of their families as chaotic or with higher levels of conflict, or both (Amerikaner & Omizo, 1984; Margalit & Almougy, 1991; Toro, Weissberg, Guare, & Liebenstein, 1990). Finally, parental disappointment over unmet expectations regarding their child's academic performance was identified as a significant stress factor in families raising a child with LD (Kaslow & Cooper, 1978).

Although these stressors are significant, Morrison and Cosden (1997) also found evidence of positive family adaptations, some of which were inversions of documented risk factors. For example, while parental disappointment over unmet academic expectations was a risk factor, parental understanding and acceptance of a child's learning disability served to moderate that risk. Parents who appeared to be adapting well to their child with LD were characterized by a viewpoint that recognized the specific nature of their child's LD, rather than generalizing it in a more global way, and also recognized areas of strengths in their child (Switzer, 1985).

Certain family values and structural characteristics also were identified as either adding to or moderating the stress of raising a child with LD. Familial value systems that emphasize rigidity in family roles, overprotection of children, and overly enmeshed patterns of parent/child relationships impede family problem solving processes and may result in dysfunction, especially when a child with LD is involved (Fish & Jain, 1985). Conversely, cohesion and flexibility, emotional stability, consistent discipline, and "strong parenting skills" in general contribute to family resiliency and serve to better nurture children both with and without LD (Wilchesky & Reynolds, 1986; Ziegler & Holden, 1988).

The manner in which a child with LD is perceived within the ecocultural framework of a particular family may also serve as either a risk factor or a protective factor. Feagans, Merriweather, and Haldane (1991) investigated the concept of *goodness of fit* by asking parents to identify desirable characteristics in a child and then describe the degree in which their own children exhibited those characteristics. Children with LD who received low ratings from their families were shown to have more difficulties with classroom behavior and academic achievement than children with LD receiving higher ratings.

To summarize, family factors believed to put adult outcomes for a child with LD at-risk included parental anxiety over the child's behavioral and academic difficulties, parental disappointment over unmet academic expectations for the child, and family structures emphasizing rigidity. On the other hand, protective family factors included parental understanding of a child's disability, acceptance of a child's limitations, recognition of a child's strengths, a family structure and value system emphasizing flexibility and cohesion, and the goodness of the ecocultural fit between the child and other family members. These factors were believed to contribute to family functioning and to better adult outcomes for the child with LD.

Summary

This has been a brief review of research regarding stress factors parents might experience when raising children with various disabilities, factors that might mediate that stress, and how families might make adaptations in their daily lives to accommodate their children's needs. For every diagnostic category reviewed, it was found that researchers have documented elevated levels of stress in parents raising children with disabilities, compared to parents raising typically developing children. Many of those stressors were common to more than one, and sometimes several, diagnostic categories, including increased financial burden, reduced social and occupational opportunities, and difficulty in procuring services. Other stressors were unique to a specific disability, such as the stress experienced by parents of children who are deaf in making immediate decisions regarding the mode of communication to be used.

In spite of these documented stressors, however, for each diagnostic category there was also evidence of parents' positive adaptation to the challenges of raising their children with disabilities. Factors commonly mentioned as contributing to that positive adaptation included psychological processes, such as positive reframing and cognitive reappraisal, social support, and problem-focused thinking. There is an emerging body of research that has delineated specific ways in which parents of children with disabilities adapt their daily routines to accommodate their children's needs. The importance of formal and informal social support also indicates the value that family centered services can bring to supporting family resilience.

References

Abidin, R. R. (1995). *Parenting Stress Index: Professional manual.* Odessa: FL: Psychological Assessment Resources.

Amerikaner, M., & Omizo, N. (1984). Family interaction and learning disabilities. *Journal of Learning Disabilities, 17,* 540–543.

Bagner, D. M., & Eyberg, S. M. (2007). Parent-child interaction therapy for disruptive behavior in children with mental retardation: A randomized controlled trial. *Journal of Clinical Child and Adolescent Psychology, 36,* 418–429.

Bailey, D. B., Golden, R. N., Roberts, J., & Ford, A. (2007). Maternal depression and developmental disability: Research critique. *Mental Retardation and Developmental Disabilities Research Reviews, 13,* 321–329.

Baxter, C., Cummins, R. A., & Polak, S. (1995). A longitudinal study of parental stress and support: From diagnosis of disability to leaving school. *International Journal of Disability, Development, & Education*, *42*, 125–136.

Baxter, C., Cummins, R. A., & Yiolotis, L. (2000). Parental stress attributed to family members with and without a disability: A longitudinal study. *Journal of Intellectual and Developmental Disability, 25*, 105–118.

Bayat, M. (2007). Evidence of resilience in families of children with autism. *Journal of Intellectual Disability Research*, *51*(9), 702–714.

Bebko, J. M., Konstantareas, M. M., Springer, J. (1987). Parent and professional evaluations of family stress associated with characteristics of autism. *Journal of Autism and Developmental Disorders, 17,* 565–576.

Becker, G., & Newsom, E. (2005). Resilience in the face of serious illness among chronically ill African Americans in later life. *Journal of Gerontology Series B: Psychological Sciences and Social Sciences, 60,* S214–S223.

Benard, B. (2004). *Resiliency: What we have learned.* San Francisco: WestEd.

Brauner, C. B., & Bowers, C. B. (2006). Estimating the prevalence of early childhood serious emotional/behavioral disorders: Challenges and recommendations. *Public Health Reports, 121,* 303–310.

Brobst, J. B., Clopton, J. R., Hendrick, S. S. (2009). Parenting children with autism spectrum disorders: The couple's relationship. *Focus on Autism and Other Developmental Disabilities, 24,* 38–49.

Brown, I., Anand, S., Fung, W. L., Isaac, B., & Nehama, B. (2010). Family quality of life: Canadian results from an international survey. *Journal of Developmental and Physical Disabilities, 1*(22), 207–230.

Brown, R. I., McAdam-Crisp, J., Wang, M., & Iarocci, G. (2006). Family quality of life when there is a child with a developmental disability. *Journal of Policy and Practice in Intellectual Disabilites, 3,* 238–245.

Crnic, K., Arbona, A. P., Baker, B., & Blacher, J. (2009). Mothers and fathers together: contrasts in parenting across preschool to early school age in children with developmental disabilities. *International Review of Research in Mental Retardation, 37,* 3–30.

DuBois, D. L., & Silverthorn, N. (2005). Natural mentoring relationships and adolescent health: Evidence from a national study, *American Journal of Public Health, 95*, 518–524.

Dunst, C. J., Trivette, C. M., & Hamby, D. W. (2007). Meta-analysis of family centered helpgiving practices. *Mental Retardation and Developmental Disabilities Research Reviews, 13,* 370–378.

Early, T. J., & Poertner, J. (1993). Families with children with emotional disorders: A review of the literature. *Social Work, 6,* 743–764.

Elder, G. H., Jr., & Clipp, E. C. (1989). Combat experience and emotional health: Impairment and resilience in later life. *Journal of Personality, 57,* 311–341.

Ethridge, B. L., & Singer, G. H. S. (2009). *Parent training impact on parent psychological distress and child problem behaviors of children with developmental disabilities: A meta-analysis.* Manuscript in preparation.

Feagans, L., Merriwether, A., & Haldane, D. (1991). Goodness of fit in the home: Its relationship to school behavior and achievement in children with learning disabilities. *Journal of Learning Disabilities, 24,* 413–420.

Ferguson, P. (2002). A place in the family: An historical interpretation of parental reactions to having a child with a disability. *The Journal of Special Education, 36*(3), 124–130.

Finn, J. D., & Rock, D. A. (1997). Academic success among students at risk for school failure. *Journal of Applied Psychology, 82*, 221–261.

Fish, M., & Jain, S. (1985). A systems approach in working with learning disabled children: Implications for the school. *Journal of Learning Disabilities, 18,* 592–595.

Friesen, B. J. (1990). National study of parents whose children have serious emotional disorders: Preliminary findings. In A. Algarin, R. M. Friedman, A. J. Duchnowski, K. M. Kutash, S. E. Silver, & M. K. Johnson (Eds.), *The 2nd annual conference proceedings: Children's mental health services and policy: Building a research base* (pp. 36–52). Tampa: University of South Florida, Florida Mental Health Institute, Research and Training Center for Children's Mental Health.

Gallimore, R., Bernheimer, L. P., Weisner, T. S. (1999). Family life is more than managing crisis: Broadening the agenda of research on families adapting to childhood disability. In R. Gallimore, L. P. Bernheimer, D. L. MacMillan, D. L. Speece, & S. Vaughn (Eds.), *Developmental perspectives on children with high-incidence disabilities* (pp. 55–80). Mahwah, NJ: Erlbaum.

Gardner, C., & Troupe, Q. (2006). *The pursuit of happiness.* New York: Amistad/HarperCollins.

Gath A. (1972). The mental health of siblings of congenitally abnormal children. *Journal of Child Psychology and Psychiatry, 13*, 211–218.

Gath, A. (1977). The impact of an abnormal child upon the parents. *British Journal of Psychiatry, 130,* 405–410.

Glidden, L. M., & Jobe, B. M. (2006). The longitudinal course of depression in adoptive and birth mothers of children with intellectual disabilities. *Journal of Policy and Practice in Intellectual Disabilities, 3*, 139–142.

Glidden, L. M., & Schoolcraft, S. A. (2003). Depression: its trajectory and correlates in mothers rearing children with intellectual disabilities. *Journal of Intellectual Disabilities Research. Special Issue on Family Research, 47*(4-5), 250–263.

Greer, F. A., Grey, I. M., & McClean, B. (2006). Coping and positive perceptions in Irish mothers of children with intellectual disabilities. *Journal of Intellectual Disabilities, 10,* 231–248.

Grossman, J. B., & Tierney, J. P. (1998). Does mentoring work? An impact study of the Big Brothers, Big Sisters program. *Evaluation Review, 22*, 403–426.

Guralnick, M. J. (1998). Effectiveness of early intervention for vulnerable children: A developmental perspective. *American Journal on Mental Retardation, 102,* 319–345.

Hall, H. R. (2008). *The relationships among adaptive behaviors of children with autism spectrum disorder, their family support networks, parental stress, and parental coping.* Unpublished doctoral dissertation. University of Tennessee, Knoxville, TN.

Hastings, R. P., & Beck, A. (2004). Practitioner review: Stress intervention for parents of children with intellectual disabilities. *Journal of Child Psychology and Psychiatry, 45*, 338–349.

Hastings, R. P., Beck, A., & Hill, C. (2005). Positive contributions made by children with an intellectual disability in the family: Mothers' and fathers' perceptions. *Journal of Intellectual Disabilities, 9*, 155–165.

Hastings, R. P., & Taunt, H. M. (2002). Positive perceptions in families of children with developmental disabilities. *American Journal on Mental Retardation, 107*, 116–127.

Hastings, R. P., Kovshoff, H., Ward, N. J., degli Espinosa, F., Brown, T., & Remington, B. (2005). Systems analysis of stress and positive perceptions in mothers and fathers of pre-school children with autism. *Journal of Autism and Developmental Disorders, 35*, 635–644.

Hawley, D. R., & DeHaan, L. (1996). Toward a definition of family resilience: Integrating life-span and family perspectives. *Family Process, 35*, 283–298.

Hegde, M. N., & Maul, C. A. (2006). *Language disorders in children: An evidence- based approach to assessment and treatment.* Boston: Allyn and Bacon.

Helff, C. M., & Glidden, L. M. (1998) More positive or less negative? Trends in research on adjustment of families rearing children with developmental disabilities. *Mental Retardation, 36*, 457–464.

Higgins, D. J., Bailey, S. R., & Pearce, J. C. (2005). Factors associated with functioning style and coping strategies of families with a child with an autism spectrum disorder. *Autism, 9,* 125–137.

Hodapp, R. M., & Krasner, D. V. (1995). Families of children with disabilities: findings from a national sample of eighth grade students. *Exceptionality, 5*(2), 71–81

Hoffman, C. D., Sweeney, D. P., Hodge, D., Lopez-Wagner, M. C., & Looney, L. (2009). Parenting stress and closeness: Mothers of typically developing children and mothers of children with autism. *Focus on Autism and Other Developmental Disablities, 5*(2), 71–81.

Hoffman, L., Marquis, J. G., Poston, D. J., Summers, J. A., & Turnbull, A. P. (2006). Assessing family outcomes: Psychometric evaluation of the Family Quality of Life Scale. *Journal of Marriage and Family, 68,* 1069–1083.

Holroyd, J. (1987). *The Questionnaire on Resources and Stress.* Brandon, VT: Clinical Psychology Publishing.

Isaacs, B. J., Brown, I., Brown, R. I., Baum, N., Myerscough, T., Neikrug, S. et al. (2007). The international family quality of life project: Goals and description of a survey tool. *Journal of Policy and Practice in Intellectual Disabilities, 4*, 177–185.

Israel, N., & Jozefowicz-Simbeni, D. M. H. (2009). Perceived strengths of urban girls and boys experiencing homelessness. *Journal of Community & Applied Social Psychology, 19*, 156–164.

Kanner, A. D., Coyne, J. C., Schaefer, C., & Lazarus, R. (1981). Comparison of two modes of stress measurement: Daily hassles and uplifts versus major life events. *Journal of Behavioral Medicine, 4*(1), 1–39.

Kaslow, F. W., & Cooper, B. (1978). Family therapy with the learning disabled child and his/her family. *Journal of Marriage and Family Counseling, 4,* 41–49.

Kendall, J. (1999). Sibling accounts of attention deficit hyperactivity disorder (ADHD). *Family Process, 38,* 117–136.

Kersh, J., Hedvat, T. T., Hauser-Cram, P., & Warfield, M. E. (2006). The contribution of marital quality to the well-being of parents of children with developmental disabilities. *Journal of Intellectual Disabilities Research, 50*, 883–893.

Kessler Foundation and National Organization on Disability. (2010). *The ADA, 20 years later: Kessler Foundation/NOD 2010 Survey of Americans with Disabilities.* Retrieved August 13, 2010, from http://www.2010disabilitysurveys.org/pdfs/surveyresults.pdf

Kogan, M. D., Blumberg, S. J., Schieve, L. A., Boyle, C. A., Perrrin, J. M., Ghandour, R. M., et al. (2009). Prevalence of parent-reported diagnosis of autism spectrum disorder among children in the US, 2007. *Pediatrics, 124,* 1395–1403.

Lange, G., Sheerin, D., Carr, A., Dooley, B., Barton, V., Marshall, D., et al. (2005). Family factors associated with attention deficit hyperactivity disorder and emotional disorders in children. *Journal of Family Therapy, 27,* 76–96.

Lawson E. J., & Thomas C. (2007). Wading in the waters: Spirituality and older Black Katrina survivors. *Journal of Health Care for the Poor and Underserved, 18*, 341–354.

Lecavalier, L., Leone, S., & Wiltz, J. (2006). The impact of behaviour problems on caregiver stress in young people with autism spectrum disorders. *Journal of Intellectual Disability Research, 50,* 172–183.

Liebenberg, L., & Ungar, M. (Eds.). (2009). *Researching resilience.* Toronto, Canada: University of Toronto Press.

Luthar, S. S., & Brown, P. J. (2007). Maximizing resilience through diverse levels of inquiry: Prevailing paradigms, possibilities, and priorities for the future. *Development and Psychopathology, 19*, 931–955.

MacDonald, E. E., Hastings, R. P., & Fitzsimons, E. (2010). Psychological acceptance mediates the impact of the behavior problems of children with intellectual disability on fathers' psychological adjustment. *Journal of Applied Research in Developmental Disabilities. Special Issue: Families Research, 23*(1), 27–37.

Margalit, M., & Almougy, K. (1991). Classroom behavior and family climate in students with learning disabilities and hyperactive behavior. *Journal of Learning Disabilities, 24,* 406–412.

Marshall, V., & Long, B. C. (2010). Coping processes as revealed in the stories of mothers of children with autism. *Qualitative Health Research, 20,* 105–116.

Maul, C. A., & Singer, G. H. S. (2009). "Just good different things": Specific accommodations families make to positively adapt to their children with developmental disabilities. *Topics in Early Childhood Special Education, 29,* 155–170.

McCubbin, H. I., & McCubbin, M. A. (1988). Typologies of resilient families: Emerging roles of social class and ethnicity. *Family Relations, 37,* 247–254.

McCubbin, M. A., & McCubbin, H. I. (1993). Families coping with illness: the resiliency model of family stress, adjustment, and adaptation. In C. B. Danielson, B. Hamel-Bissell, & P. Winstead-Fry (Eds.), *Families, health, and illness* (pp. 21–63). St. Louis, MO: C. V. Mosby.

Mirowsky, J., & Ross, C. E. (2003). *Social causes of psychological distress* (2nd ed.). New York: Aldine de Gruyter.

Mitchell, M. M. (2006). *Parents' stress and coping with their children's attention deficit hyperactivity disorder.* Unpublished doctoral dissertation. University of Maryland, College Park.

Montes, G., & Halterman, J. S. (2007). Psychological functioning and coping among mothers of children with autism: A population-based study. *Pediatrics, 119,* 1040–1046.

Morrison, G. M., Brown, M., D'Incau, B., O'Farrell, S. L., & Furlong, M. F. (2006). Understanding resilience in educational trajectories: Implications for protective possibilities. *Psychology in the Schools, 43*, 19–31.

Morrison, G. M., & Cosden, M. A. (1997). Risk, resilience, and adjustment of individuals with learning disabilities. *Learning Disability Quarterly, 20*, 43–60.

Mowbray, C. T., & Oyserman, D. (2003). Substance abuse in children of parents with mental illness: Risks, resiliency, and best prevention practices. *Journal of Primary Prevention, 23*, 451–482.

Msall, M. E. (2009). Optimizing early development and understanding trajectories for resiliency after extreme prematurity. *Pediatrics, 124*, 387–390.

Mugno, D., Ruta, L., D'arrigo, V. G., & Mazzone, L. (2007). Impairment of quality of life in parents of children and adolescents with pervasive developmental disorder. *Health and Quality of Life Outcomes, 5*. Retrieved February 11, 2010, from http://www.hqlo.com/content/5/1/22

National Institute of Neurological Disorders and Stroke. (2009). NINDS learning disabilities information page. Retrieved February 28, 2010, from http://www.ninds.nih.gov/disorders/learningdisabilities/learning-disabilities.htm

Obradović, J., Long, J. D., Cutuli, J. J., Chan, C. K., Hinz, E., Heistad, D., et al. (2009). Academic achievement of homeless and highly mobile children in an urban school district: Longitudinal evidence on risk, growth, and resilience. *Development and Psychopathology, 21*, 493–518.

Olshansky S. (1962) Chronic sorrow: A response to having a mentally defective child. *Social Casework, 43*,190–193.

Olsson, M. B., & Hwang, C. P. (2008), Socioeconomic and psychological variables as risk and protective factors for parental well-being in families of children with intellectual disabilities. *Journal of Intellectual Disability Research, 52*, 1102–1113.

Park, J., Hoffman, L., Marquis, J., Turnbull, A. P., Poston, D., Mannan, H., Wang, M., & Nelson, L. L. (2003). Toward assessing family outcomes of service delivery: Validation of a Family Quality of Life Survey. *Journal of Intellectual Disability Research, 47*, 367–384.

Patterson, J. M. (1991). Family resilience to the challenge of a child's disability. *Pediatric Annals, 20*, 491–499.

Patterson, J. M. (2002). Integrating family resilience and family stress theory. *Journal of Marriage and Family, 64*, 349–360.

Patterson, J. M., Leonard, B. J., & Titus, J., C. (1992). Home care for medically fragile children: Impact on family health and well-being. *Journal of Developmental and Behavioral Pediatrics, 13*, 248–255.

Podolski, C. L., & Nigg, J. T. (2001). Parent stress and coping in relation to child ADHD severity and associated child disruptive behavior problems. *Journal of Clinical Child Psychology, 30*, 503–513.

Poston, D., Turnbull, A., Park, J., Mannan, H., Marquis, J., & Wang, M. (2003). Family quality of life: A qualitative inquiry. *Mental Retardation, 41*, 313–328.

Pottie, C. G., & Ingram, K. M. (2008). Daily stress, coping, and well-being in parents of children with autism: A multilevel modeling approach. *Journal of Family Psychology, 22*, 855–864.

Rabkin, J. G., Remien, R., Katoff, L., & Williams, J. B. (1993). Resilience in adversity among long-term survivors of AIDS. *Hospital and Community Psychiatry, 44*, 162–167.

Regester, A., & Singer, G. H. S. (in press). Beyond high school: Participants' perspectives on their participation with inclusive friendship programs in high school. In C. H. Kennedy, C. G. Breen, & C.A. Peck (Eds.), *Context, intervention, and disability: Essays in honor of Thomas G. Haring*. Mahwah, NJ: Erlbaum.

Risdal, D., & Singer, G. H. S. (2004). Marital adjustment in parents of children with disabilities: A historical review and meta-analysis. *Research & Practice for Persons with Severe Disabilities, 29*, 95–102.

Rogers, M. A., Wiener, J. Marton, I., & Tannock, R. (2009). Supportive and controlling parental involvement as predictors of children's academic achievement: Relation to children's ADHD symptoms and parenting stress. *School Mental Health, 1*, 89–102.

Rossiter, L., & Sharpe, D. (2001). The siblings of individuals with mental retardation: A quantitative integration of the literature. *Journal of Child and Family Studies, 10*, 65–84.

Ruffolo, M. C., Kuhn, M. T., & Evans, M. E. (2006). Developing a parent-professional team leadership model in group work: Work with families with children experiencing behavioral and emotional problems. *Social Work, 51*, 39–47.

Saleebey, D. (1997). *The strengths perspective in social work practice.* New York: Longman.

Saloviita T., Itälinna, M., & Leinonen E. (2003). Explaining the parental stress of fathers and mothers caring for a child with intellectual disability: a double ABCX model. *Journal of Intellectual Disability Research 47*, 300–312.

San Martino, M., & Newman, M. B. (1974). Siblings of retarded children: A population at risk. *Child Psychiatry & Human Development, 4*, 168–177.

Schieve, L. A., Blumberg, S. J., Rice, C., Visser, S. N., & Boyle, C. (2007). The relationship between autism and parenting stress. *Pediatrics, 119*, 114–121.

Scorgie, K., & Sobsey, D. (*2000*) Transformational outcomes associated with parenting children who have disabilities. *Mental Retardation, 38*(3), 195–206.

Singer, G. H. S. (2006). Meta-analysis of comparative studies of depression in mothers of children with and without developmental disabilities. *American Journal on Mental Retardation, 111*, 155–169.

Singer, G. H. S., Biegel, D. E., & Ethridge, B. L. (2010). Trends impacting public policy support for caregiving families. *Journal of Family Social Work, 13*(3), 191–207.

Singer, G. H. S., Ethridge, B. L., & Aldana, S. I. (2007). Primary and secondary effects of parenting and stress management interventions for parents of children with developmental disabilities: A meta-analysis. *Mental Retardation and Developmental Disabilities Research Reviews, 13*, 357–369.

Singer, G. H. S., & Irvin, L. K. (1991). Supporting families of persons with severe disabilities: Emerging findings, practices, and questions. In L. H. Meyer, C. A. Peck, & L. Brown (Eds.), *Critical issues in the lives of people with severe disabilities* (pp. 271–312). Baltimore: Brookes.

Substance Abuse and Mental Health Services Administration. (2003). Retrieved January 12, 2010, from http://mentalhealth.samhsa.gov/publications/allpubs/CA-0006/default.asp

Summers, J. A., Behr, S. K., & Turnbull, A.P. (1989). Positive adaptation and coping strengths of families who have children with disabilities. In G. H. S. Singer & L. K. Irvin (Eds.), *Support for caregiving families* (pp. 3–27). Baltimore: Paul H. Brookes.

Summers, J. A., Marquis, J., Mannan, H., Turnbull, A. P., Fleming, K., Poston, D. J., et al. (2007). Relationship of perceived adequacy of services, family-professional partnerships, and family quality of life in early childhood service programs. *International Journal of Disability, Development and Education, 54*, 319–338.

Summers, J. A., Poston, D., Turnbull, A. P., Marquis, J., Hoffman, L., Mannan, H., & Wang, H. (2005). Conceptualizing and measuring family quality of life. *Journal of Intellectual Disability Research, 49*(10), 777–783.

Suskind, R. (2005). *A hope in the unseen: An American odyssey from the inner city to the ivy league* (rev. ed.). New York: Broadway Books/Random House.

Switzer, L. (1985). Accepting the diagnosis: An educational intervention for parents of children with learning disabilities. *Journal of Learning Disabilities, 18*, 151–153.

Tebes, J. K., Kaufman, J. S., Adnopoz, J., & Racusin, G. (2001). Resilience and family psychosocial processes among children of parents with serious mental disorders. *Journal of Child and Family Studies, 10*, 115–136.

Tillman, G., Jr. (Director). (2000). *Men of honor* [Motion picture]. United States: 20th Century Fox.

Toro, P., Weissberg, R., Guare, J., & Liebenstein, N. (1990). A comparison of children with and without learning disabilities on problem-solving skill, school behavior, and family background. *Journal of Learning Disabilities, 23*, 115–120.

Tunali, B., & Power, T. G. (2002). Coping by redefinition: Cognitive appraisals in mothers of children with autism and children without autism. *Journal of Autism and Developmental Disorders, 32*, 25–34.

Vogt, D. S., & Tanner, L. R. (2007). Risk and resilience factors for post-traumatic stress symptomatology in Gulf War I veterans. *Journal of Traumatic Stress, 20*, 27–38.

Waggoner, K., & Wilgosh, L. (1990). Concerns of families of children with learning disabilities. *Journal of Learning Disabilities, 23,* 97–98, 113.

Walsh, F. (2006). *Strengthening family resilience* (2nd ed.). New York: Guilford Press.

Wang, M., & Brown, R. (2009). Family quality of life: A framework for policy and social service provisions to support families with children with disabilities. *Journal of Family Social Work, 12,* 144–167.

Wang, M., Turnbull, A., Little, T., Summers, J. A., Poston, D., & Mannan, H. (2006). Perspectives of fathers and mothers of children in early intervention programs in assessing family quality of life. *Journal of Intellectual Disabilities Research, 50,* 977–988.

Waxman, H. C., Gray, J. P., & Padrón, Y. N. (2002). Resiliency among students at risk of academic failure. In S. Stringfield & D. Land (Eds.), *Educating at-risk students* (pp. 29–48). Chicago: National Society for the Study of Education.

Werner, E. E., Bierman, J. M., & French F. E. (1971). *The children of Kauai: A longitudinal study from the prenatal period to age ten.* Honolulu: University of Hawaii Press.

Werner, E. E., & Smith R. S. (2001). *Journeys from childhood to midlife: Risk, resilience and recovery.* Ithaca, NY: Cornell University Press.

Wilchesky, M., & Reynolds, T. (1986). The socially deficient LD child in context: A systems approach to assessment and treatment. *Journal of Learning Disabilities, 25,* 258–264.

Wing, L., & Potter, D. (2002). The epidemiology of autistic spectrum disorders: Is the prevalence rising? *Mental Retardation and Developmental Disabilities Research Reviews, 8,* 151–161.

Witt, W. P., Riley, A. W., & Coiro, M. J. (2003). Childhood functional status, family stressors, and psychological adjustment among school-aged children with disabilities in the United States. *Archives of Pediatric Adolescent Medicine, 157,* 687–695.

Wolfensberger, W., & Menolascino, F. (1970). A theoretical framework for management of parents of the mentally retarded. In F. Menolascino (Ed.), *Psychiatric approaches to mental retardation* (pp. 475–493), New York: Basic Books.

Ziegler, R., & Holden, L. (1988). Family therapy for learning disabled and attention-deficit disordered children. *American Journal of Orthopsychiatry, 58,* 196–210.

Zuna, N., Summers, J. A., Turnbull, A. P., Hu, X., & Xu, S. (2009). Theorizing about family quality of life. In R. Kober (Ed.), *Enhancing the quality of life of people with intellectual disability: From theory to practice* (pp. 239–278). Dordrecht, The Netherlands: Springer.

50

Promoting Family Outcomes in Early Intervention

Donald B. Bailey, Jr. and Melissa Raspa
RTI International

Betsy P. Humphreys and Ann M. Sam
University of North Carolina at Chapel Hill

Early intervention is a complex system of state-based services, guided by federal legislation and designed to provide supports and services for infants and young children, birth to 3 years of age, with or at-risk for disabilities, and their families. Although a number of states and communities had been providing early intervention services since the 1970s, it was not until 1986 that a formal national network of programs was established as part of Public Law 99-457, now known as Part C of the Individuals with Disabilities Education Act. Each year nearly 300,000 children and their families become eligible for and receive some form of early intervention services.

Although the nature and focus of early intervention can vary across settings, Figure 50.1 displays the core elements typically found in any early intervention enterprise. Children typically become eligible for early intervention services because they have a documented delay, a condition that is likely to lead to a delay (but which may not be currently evident, such as in the early months of infants with Down syndrome), or a factor that creates risk for developmental delay (e.g., low birth weight). Children bring to early intervention their own unique developmental capabilities, functional skills, learning styles, and disability features, all of which must be assessed and monitored so that services can be individualized to meet the child's needs. Likewise, families bring to early intervention their own unique needs, concerns, resources, priorities, and goals. Because the lives of very young children are so closely intertwined with their families, these family characteristics and aspirations must be considered when designing programs and services for children.

Early intervention itself consists of a wide variety of services and practices, some of which are primarily child-focused (e.g., physical therapy, speech therapy, special education services). Ideally, services for children are individualized and designed to promote positive social-emotional skills, the acquisition and use of a wide range of knowledge and skills, and the use of appropriate behavior to meet needs (Hebbeler & Barton, 2007). Long-term goals are to prevent or reduce any primary or secondary conditions associated with a disability, and to maximize quality of life (Simeonsson, McMillen, & Huntington, 2002).

Public Law 99-457 states that one goal of early intervention is to support the capacity of families to meet their child's needs. Consequently, early intervention programs provide services to families, although the range in what programs do with families varies considerably. Some of these services are almost entirely family-focused (e.g., parent support groups), but often they serve dual purposes and the distinction between child and family services becomes blurred. For example, a child may have a feeding problem that hampers her ability to take solid foods and also causes a great deal of stress for the mother. The most effective intervention may involve an occupational therapist with expertise in infant feeding who works with the mother to determine strategies she can use at mealtime that would be effective in promoting solid food intake as well as increasing maternal enjoyment.

Of course, early intervention is only one aspect of the life experience of children and families. Community agencies and institutions (e.g., social services, public health, religious institutions, public programs, childcare services, physicians, dentists) can contribute to child and family well-being, depending on the extent to which they are accommodating and supportive. Early intervention ought to link with these programs and help facilitate access for families. Finally, informal social supports from friends, neighbors, extended family members, and other families of children with disabilities are essential in helping families adapt to having a child with a disability.

Families and their children should benefit from early intervention programs. For benefit to occur, outcomes must be specified and measured, and practices shown to be related to those outcomes must be in place. In this chapter, we focus on the practices likely to lead to enhanced outcomes for families. We begin with a brief discussion of conceptual

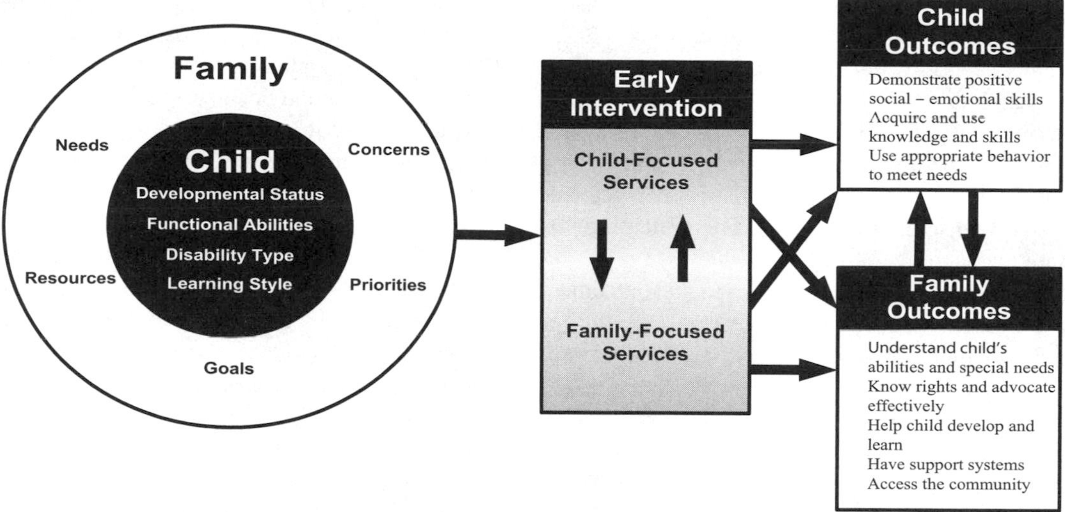

Figure 50.1 Early intervention inputs, processes, and outcomes.

models for defining desired outcomes for families. Next, we describe what it means to be "family-centered," including a review of the core family-centered principles that provide the necessary foundation for the attainment of all family outcomes. We then review and provide evidence in support of selected family practices that, when conducted within the framework of family-centered care, can lead to specific outcome attainment for families. We conclude by identifying gaps in the literature and proposing research questions that, if answered, could lead to evidenced-based practices most likely to improve family outcomes.

Family Outcomes in Early Intervention

The family orientation of early intervention is likely to result in improved outcomes for families, but which outcomes are most relevant to assess? Although the founding legislation for early intervention specified that supporting the family's capacity to meet their child's needs is a primary goal of early intervention, this statement could be interpreted in a variety of ways and measured through a wide range of outcomes. Over 25 years ago, Dunst (1985) argued that the empowerment of families should be the primary family outcome of early intervention. More recent iterations of this work have expanded the proposed dimensions of empowerment (e.g., self-efficacy beliefs) and considered other outcomes such as satisfaction with services, parenting capabilities, and personal/family well-being (Dunst, Trivette, & Hamby, 2007). Other individuals and groups have proposed alternative frameworks and foci of family outcomes, including parenting skills and knowledge, self-concept and emotional well-being, participation in community activities, advocacy skills, team participation, knowledge of child development, and quality of life (e.g., Administration for Children, Youth, and Families, 1998; Early Childhood Outcomes and Indicators Focus Group, 2003; Early Childhood Research Institute on Measuring Growth and Development, 1998; Lakin & Turnbull, 2005; Park et al., 2003; Roberts, Innocenti, & Goetz, 1999). In 1998, investigators leading the National Early Intervention Longitudinal Study (NEILS), a nationally representative study of more than 2,500 families and children participating in early intervention, suggested a possible framework for evaluating family outcomes (Bailey et al., 1998). Eight questions served as the basis for developing survey items: (a) Does the family see early intervention as appropriate in making a difference in their child's life? (b) Does the family see early intervention as appropriate in making a difference in their family's life? (c) Does the family have a positive view of professionals and the special service system? (d) Did early intervention enable the family to help their child grow, learn, and develop? (e) Did early intervention enhance the family's perceived ability to work with professionals and advocate for services? (f) Did early intervention assist the family in building a strong support system? (g) Did early intervention help enhance an optimistic view of the future? (h) Did early intervention enhance the family's perceived quality of life?

Although multiple frameworks and outcomes have been proposed, until recently there was no national consensus on the specific family outcomes for which early intervention should be held accountable. In 2006, in response to federal requirements for states to begin identifying and reporting outcomes for families, a national initiative involving multiple stakeholder groups led by the Early Childhood Outcomes (ECO) Center proposed five recommended outcomes for families of young children with disabilities: (a) families understand their child's strengths, abilities, and special needs; (b) families know their rights and advocate effectively for their child; (c) families help their child develop and learn; (d) families have support systems; and (e) families are able to gain access to desired services and activities in their community (Bailey et al., 2006).

A subsequent study asked families, practitioners, and researchers to nominate specific constructs underlying each of these outcomes (Bailey, Raspa, Olmsted, et al., 2009).

More than 1,100 nominations were received, and a Q-sort procedure was used to identify common themes within each outcome area. Following extensive discussions with a variety of stakeholders, 29 indicators of the 5 outcomes were specified. A pilot study investigating psychometric analyses of a scale based on these indicators suggested that 5 of the 29 indicators were redundant from a statistical perspective (Bailey, Raspa, Olmsted, et al., 2009). The remaining 24 indicators are displayed in Table 50.1.

These frameworks suggest a variety of specific outcomes that could be assessed, leading to questions regarding whether such outcomes are achieved (Bailey, 2001). Data from NEILS found that at the end of early intervention most parents felt confident in their ability to care for their children, advocate for services, and gain access to both formal and informal supports (Bailey et al., 2005). They were generally optimistic about the future and most reported that their family was better off as a result of early intervention. Parents were somewhat less positive in their perceived ability to address their child's behavior problems or access community resources. A recent paper by Raspa et al. (2010) surveyed over 3,000 families participating in early intervention programs in Illinois and Texas, and also reported high levels of outcome attainment reported by families, although minority families and Spanish-speaking families on average reported lower outcome attainment (Olmsted et al., 2010).

Critical to improving early intervention is an understanding of the links between specific program practices and the outcomes attained by families. When we set out to write this chapter, it was our intent to differentiate practices directly related to each of the five family outcomes proposed as a result of the work of the ECO Center (Bailey et al., 2006) and examine the evidence base for each practice, but this turned out to be an impossible task, in part because of the overlapping nature of the five outcomes. For example, Raspa et al. (2010), using factor analysis on data collected with a parent survey based on the five outcomes, found that the items clustered in two primary areas: (a) family knowledge and ability (outcomes 1–3), and (b) family support and community services (outcomes 4–5). Further complicating our task are the complex interrelationships among various practices, as rarely do they occur in isola-

TABLE 50.1
Items Measuring Five Family Outcomes of Early Intervention

Outcome 1: Understanding your child's strengths, needs, and abilities	
1.	We know the next steps for our child's growth and learning.
2.	We understand our child's strengths and abilities.
3.	We understand our child's delays and/or needs.
4.	We are able to tell when our child is making progress.
Outcome 2: Knowing your rights and advocating for your child	
5.	We are able to find and use the services and programs available to us.
6.	We know our rights related to our child's special needs.
7.	We know who to contact and what to do when we have questions or concerns.
8.	We know what options are available when our child leaves the program.
9.	We are comfortable asking for services and supports that our child and family need.
Outcome 3: Helping your child develop and learn	
10.	We are able to help our child get along with others.
11.	We are able to help our child learn new skills.
12.	We are able to help our child take care of his/her needs.
13.	We are able to work on our child's goals during everyday routines.
Outcome 4: Having support systems	
14.	We are comfortable talking to family and friends about our child's needs.
15.	We have friends or family members who listen and care.
16.	We are able to talk with other families who have a child with similar needs.
17.	We have friends or family members we can rely on when we need help.
18.	I am able to take care of my own needs and do things I enjoy.
Outcome 5: Accessing the community	
19.	Our child is able to participate in social, recreational, or religious activities that we want.
20.	We are able to do things we enjoy together as a family.
21.	Our medical and dental needs are met.
22.	Our childcare needs are met.
23.	Our transportation needs are met.
24.	Our food, clothing, and housing needs are met.

tion. Most important, however, it is clear from the literature that family-centered principles and the practices associated with these principles provide the necessary foundation for all aspects of early intervention.

Figure 50.2 provides a simplified depiction of these relationships. Family-centered principles have a substantial evidence base. Understanding and implementing these principles is the first step in assuring positive outcomes for families, but it is when these principles are embedded throughout the standard practices that constitute early intervention—assessment, program planning, service coordination, infant intervention, family supports—that family outcomes are maximized.

Family-Centered Principles

Core Features of Family-Centered Care

Although early intervention has always recognized the importance of family involvement, a gradual paradigm shift has occurred over the past 25 years in terms of families' roles and functions. This shift involves families moving from the periphery of early intervention services to a more direct participant role in early intervention (Krauss, 1997). Two contrasting views of the role of early intervention professionals vis-à-vis parents and families exemplify this shift. A more traditional model of early intervention might be characterized as tending toward a deficit-based approach whereby professionals emphasize the needs of the child and family. Through focused treatment, the professional (the expert) helps to solve the child's or family's problem (deficit). Intervention typically involves professionals explaining when and how parents should do a specific intervention with their child. Professionals address the problems they consider important rather than the families' concerns (Dunst, 1985; Dunst, 2000; McCollum, 1999; Turnbull, Turbiville, & Turnbull, 2000). In addition, professionals help families work through the grief of having a child with special needs (Mahoney et al., 1999). The professional expert maintains a formal relationship with the family whereby the professional holds all the information to give to the parent (McCollum, 1999; Winton, Sloop, & Rodriquez, 1999). The concept of parent education includes the notion that parents could be educated (Winton et al., 1999). Although well-intended and thought to be helpful, in reality these techniques could lead to parents feeling helpless, powerless, and having low self-esteem (Dunst, 1985; Dunst, 2000; Turnbull et al., 2000).

At the other end of the continuum is an approach to services that shifts the focus from professionals as the sole experts to one of a partnership between families and professionals, both of whom bring important information to the table and ideally play equal roles in determining the nature and focus of services. In early intervention this approach is most commonly referred to as a "family-centered" approach. One of the earliest explications of family-centered care in the context of pediatric practice was articulated more than 20 years ago:

> Family-centered care is the focus of a philosophy of care in which the pivotal role of the family is recognized and respected in the lives of children with special health needs. Within this philosophy is the idea that families be supported in their natural care-giving and decision-making roles by building on their unique strengths as people and families. In this philosophy, patterns of living in the home and in the community are promoted; parents and professionals are seen as equals in a partnership committed to the development of optimal quality in the delivery of all levels of health care. To achieve this, elements of family-centered care and community-based care must be carefully interwoven into a full and effective coordination of care of all children with special health needs. (Brewer, McPherson, Magrab, & Hutchins, 1989, p. 1055)

In early intervention, a family-centered philosophy has its roots in social support theory (Cohen & Syme, 1985; Vaux, 1988), helpgiving theory (Dunst & Trivette, 1996), ecological theory (Bronfenbrenner, 1999), and transactional theory (Sameroff & Fiese, 2000). At the heart of these

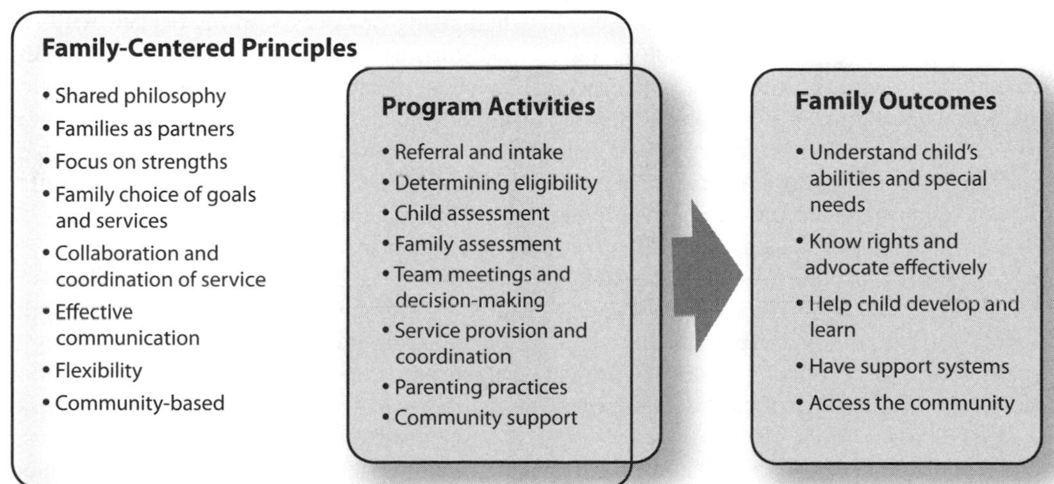

Figure 50.2 Family-centered principles underlie early intervention practices.

theories are four core principles: Early intervention professionals should (a) focus on child and family strengths not deficits, (b) encourage family decision-making and empowerment, including respecting families' cultural and linguistic preferences, (c) effectively communicate and collaborate with families, and (d) use both formal and informal support systems to maximize positive family adaptation (Bruder, 2000; Dunst, 2000; McWilliam, Tocci, & Harbin 1995).

The strengths-based principle emphasizes both child and family abilities rather than weaknesses (Hobbs et al., 1984; Russo, 1999; Stoneman, 1985; Trivette & Dunst, 2000). In contrast to a traditional model where the child and family need "treatment," the strengths-based approach is designed to enhance family functioning and focus on a child and family's preferences and interests. This approach encourages professionals to value individual differences and support families in an individualized and flexible manner.

The second principle focuses on family choice and empowerment. Since families are the ultimate decision-makers for their children, professionals should encourage parents to actively participate in the selection of goals and services (Bailey, 1987; McBride, Brotherson, Joanning, Whiddon, & Demmitt, 1993). Being responsive to families' choices also includes respecting a family's cultural and linguistic preferences (Barnwell & Day, 1996; Harry, Kalyanpur, & Day, 1999; Lynch & Hanson, 1992; Madding, 2000). By promoting family choice, professionals empower families. Empowerment can encompass multiple constructs, although most definitions include parental control, confidence, and competence (Nachshen, 2005). Empowering families also helps them to strengthen current abilities and acquire new skills (Dunst, Trivette, & Deal, 1988; Rappaport, 1981; Turnbull et al., 2000).

The third family-centered principle involves effective communication and collaboration between families and professionals in which both are equal members of the team (Trivette & Dunst, 2000). McWilliam, Tocci, and Harbin (1998) specified key interpersonal characteristics of professionals who work with families, including positiveness, responsiveness, friendliness, orientation to the whole family, and sensitivity. Others have recommended similar dimensions of effective collaboration, such as communication, commitment, equality, skills, trust, and respect (Blue-Banning, Summers, Frankland, Nelson, & Beegle, 2004). Effective collaboration also involves professionals and families sharing a common philosophy about the goals of service provision (Dinnebeil, Hale, & Rule, 1999; Johnson, Zorn, Tam, LaMontagne, & Johnson, 2003). However, a family-centered approach also means that professionals must strike a balance between their role as a trained expert in child development and disability and parents' decisions about intervention goals and services. As in the case of physicians trying to balance quality of care standards and evidenced-based medicine with the mandate for patient-centered care and preference-sensitive decision-making, early intervention professionals need to make sure they provide appropriate advice based on existing data, inform parents of the expected outcomes from different courses of treatment, and ultimately respect parents' decisions about services and the roles they choose to play in the intervention process (Keirns & Goold, 2009).

Skillful collaboration between professionals and families sets the stage for other family-centered interactions. All family-centered principles require effective and appropriate communication between parents and professionals, including (a) the ability to engage with parents in meaningful conversations about their child; (b) giving parents the option of structured ways to provide information, such as through the use of appropriate questionnaires and checklists; (c) using techniques such as community mapping to help families identify the natural learning opportunities available to their child throughout the day; (d) having appropriate problem-solving discussions with families (as opposed to prescriptive information primarily provided by professionals); and (e) using natural environment settings to both assess abilities and teach skills (Woods & Lindeman, 2008). They also require that parents have access to accurate and understandable information so that they are empowered as participants in informed and collaborative decision-making (Bailey & Powell, 2005).

Finally, a family-centered approach builds on informal and community supports and services. Most children in early intervention receive only 1–2 hours of service per week from an early intervention professional. To maximize the impact of these services, professionals must work with families to identify the settings and ways in which skill development can be supported. Research consistently shows that informal and community support systems are powerful predictors of family adaptation to disability (Bailey et al., 2007; Dunst, 1999; Hauser-Cram et al., 2001).

Evidence Supporting a Family-Centered Approach

Strong evidence exists in support of the efficacy of a family-centered approach as applied in both early intervention and medical care settings, reflected in several recent reviews and studies. Dunst et al. (2007) conducted a meta-analysis of 47 studies examining the extent to which family-centered helpgiving practices were associated with six outcomes: satisfaction with services, self-efficacy beliefs, parenting behavior, personal/family well-being, social support, and child behavior and functioning. Family-centered helpgiving was significantly associated with higher attainment of each of the six outcomes, although the effect was most pronounced for satisfaction with services, self-efficacy beliefs, and social support.

Piotrowski, Talavera, and Mayer (2009) reviewed 13 articles evaluating the Healthy Steps Program, a model of pediatric care based on four key concepts: (a) strength-based primary prevention; (b) the assumption that child well-being and family-centered care are necessarily linked; (c) supporting the role of parents; and (d) positive, caring, and enduring relations with parents. The authors concluded that the studies (all clinical trials comparing the model with traditional standard-of-care practices) showed that Healthy

Steps resulted in significant improvements in outcomes for both children and families, although the strongest evidence was in support of its influence on parent outcomes. Parents in Healthy Steps reported receiving more services, were more satisfied with services, engaged in more desirable parenting practices (e.g., using proper sleep position with infants, reading and playing with children, avoiding harsh discipline), were more satisfied with their role as parents, and interacted more sensitively and appropriately with their children.

McBroom and Enriquez (2009) reviewed nine randomized controlled trials of family-centered interventions to enhance the health outcomes of children with Type I diabetes and concluded that family-centered interventions not only improved health outcomes for children but also reduced diabetes-related conflict in families and improved family relations. Two studies using data from the National Survey of Children with Special Health Care Needs showed that when families perceived a strong partnership between the child's family and the child's service provider, children's health outcomes were improved, children received more services, and families were more satisfied with services (Denboba, McPherson, Kenney, Strickland, & Newacheck, 2006; Knapp, Madden, & Marcu, 2010). Finally, both Bailey et al. (2007) and Raspa et al. (2010) found that parents' perceptions of the quality of family services and the extent to which family-centered practices were evident were related to enhanced impact and greater family outcome attainment in early intervention.

Operationalizing Family-Centered Practices

Collectively, these studies provide strong empirical support for the value of a family-centered approach. More research is needed in the early intervention context to better understand specific factors most likely to contribute to improved outcomes, but it is safe to say that partnering with families, open communication, coordination of services, flexibility, and a strengths-based approach constitute the core approach that should be taken in early intervention. However, these principles do not exist in a vacuum. Rather, they become evident as they are applied in the context of specific activities that are the necessary components of any early intervention program. Below we discuss family-centered practices at each point of a family's journey through early intervention, beginning with referral, assessment, intervention planning, and service coordination. We also provide evidence-based research when available. In the final section, we conclude with issues and challenges in providing a more substantial evidence base for these practices and their implementation.

Referral and Access

A family's first contact with early intervention typically occurs when their child has been referred for testing because he or she is not meeting developmental milestones or has been diagnosed with a condition that will likely lead to delays. Understandably, this is a difficult time for families. It is important to set the stage for family-centered practices at the beginning of the referral process.

In some instances, it may be a family member who first has concerns about a child's development or behavior. We have documented the early experiences of families in having their child diagnosed with fragile X syndrome, the most common inherited form of intellectual disability (Bailey, Raspa, Bishop, & Holiday, 2009; Bailey, Skinner, & Sparkman, 2003). In most families, someone, usually the mother, becomes the first to be concerned about delays in acquiring developmental milestones at around 9–12 months of age. She often reports conveying these concerns to her pediatrician, but in many cases the pediatrician either discounts the concern as not valid or suggests a "wait and see" approach. This typically results in a delay of 8–12 months before a confirmation of developmental delay and entry into early intervention (usually around 2 years of age). By this time, many parents are frustrated or angry with their pediatrician, whom they blame for not listening to their concerns. Furthermore, some parents reported that repeated assurances that their child was developing appropriately, juxtaposed with their own concerns about development, made them feel inadequate as parents. From the pediatrician's perspective, this approach fits with their often-held belief that an established diagnosis is necessary before referring a child to early intervention (Silverstein et al., 2006). However, Glascoe (1999) presents data showing that parents' concerns usually correspond well with data collected from "objective screening" measures, and argues that pediatricians and family physicians need to pay more attention to and affirm family's perceptions. This could not only accelerate entry into early intervention, but it is an example of more appropriate professional-client communication, balanced relationships and perspectives on a situation, and joint decision-making.

In reality, referrals for early intervention can come from a variety of professionals —physicians, childcare providers, and social workers—or even family members. Although the law states there should be coordinated access and referrals across agencies, many states have multiple programs that have their own eligibility criteria, funding, missions, and services. Examples of such programs include state-wide newborn screening (Pelligrino, 2007), developmental surveillance programs (i.e., early periodic screening, diagnosis, and treatment, Meisels & Margolis, 1988), or developmental screenings conducted by pediatricians during well-child visits (American Academy of Pediatrics, 2001). Therefore, it is not surprising given the current fragmented system, that families often report it is difficult to gain access to services (Harbin, McWilliam, & Gallagher, 2000; Turnbull et al., 2000).

Harbin (2005) recommends a single point of access for families into the early intervention system. The goals of an integrated system of access include early identification, easy and timely access to services, family knowledge about the full array of resources available, and family satisfaction (Harbin, Bruder, et al., 2004). A single point of access begins with cross-agency collaboration through a coordinated public awareness initiative (Fugate & Fugate, 1996). Families' first contact with the early intervention program marks the opportunity to develop family-centered care. Research shows several important features of family-centered practices during program entry, including developing comfortable and trusting relationships (Atkins-Burnett & Allen-Meares, 2000; Dunst, Trivette, & Deal, 1994), providing family-friendly literature and being positive (McWilliam, 1996), and communicating with families in a manner in which they understand (Applequist, Umphrey, Moan, & Raabe, 2008).

Ideally, a single point of access would be more possible if families and children with special needs had access to a medical home, a regular source of care with a personal doctor or nurse, and coordinated services as needed (American Academy of Pediatrics, 2004). Unfortunately, recent analyses of the National Survey of Children with Special Health Care Needs found that only 54% of children with special health care needs under 3 years of age have access to a medical home (Nageswaran & Farel, 2007). Also, early identification would be enhanced through a comprehensive system of community-based child find services to follow up children identified as being at risk for developmental problems (Jackson & Needelman, 2007).

Despite the challenges associated with referral and access to services, research shows that families have a positive view of their first experiences with early intervention. Data from NEILS provides information about families' entry into early intervention (Bailey, Hebbeler, Scarborough, Spiker, & Mallik, 2004). The average time between when someone first became concerned with a child's development and referral to early intervention was 6.6 months. About half the families indicated that no effort was required to find (50%) or access (43%) services. However, about 10% reported this process was very difficult. Families from minority backgrounds, with lower incomes, or limited education reported a harder time entering the early intervention system.

Assessment

Assessment is conducted at multiple time points with children and families. After the referral for early intervention, assessment is initially used to determine eligibility. Once a child and family are eligible for services, assessment is used for intervention planning and monitoring progress. In both assessment contexts, recommended practice advocates five tenets of family-centered assessment: (a) professionals and families collaborate in planning and implementing assessment, (b) assessment is individualized and appropriate for the child and family, (c) assessment provides useful information for intervention, (d) professionals share information in respectful and useful ways, and (e) professionals meet legal and procedural requirements and meet recommended practice guidelines (Neisworth & Bagnato, 2000).

A key step in assessment of children and families is planning (Boone & Crais, 2002; Brink, 2002; Wolraich, Gurwitch, Bruder, & Knight, 2005). Once the team of professionals is identified, it is important to coordinate with the family and discuss assessment goals and options. This marks the start of the parent–professional relationship. A comfortable working relationship creates an open and accepting environment for families to share their concerns, priorities, strengths, and needs with professionals. To help facilitate this open dialogue, professionals can provide opportunities for ongoing discussions with families throughout the assessment process. These discussions can inform parents about the assessment process, answer parents' questions, and help parents determine the role they would like to play. Family involvement can range from an active role, such as conducting parts of the assessment, to a more passive role of observing the assessment. In fact, Reznick and Schwartz (2001) found that use of parent-report instruments in the assessment process can result in parents' becoming more aware of their child's strengths and needs, in essence becoming a form of intervention. Research suggests that assessments should occur in natural settings and be as authentic as possible, as these settings are often more comfortable to children and families and result in more accurate results (Boone & Crais, 2002; Brink, 2002; Neisworth & Bagnato, 2004; Vig & Kaminer, 2003).

One of the main goals of assessment is to determine a child's and family's strengths, needs, concerns, and priorities. Using a strengths-based approach, one of the family-centered principles, helps both professionals and families focus on the child's and family's capacities rather than weaknesses. Assessment, therefore, should be tailored to the individual needs of children and families. The information gathered during an assessment is useful for both professionals and families alike. Professionals gain a better understanding of families' view of themselves and their child and are able to contextualize how the family's culture influences the child's skills, strengths, and needs. Many family-focused assessment tools are available for this purpose (e.g., Bailey & Simeonsson, 1990; Dunst, Jenkins, & Trivette, 1988).

Ongoing, systematic, and scheduled assessment is necessary for intervention planning. Assessment also provides important information on the effectiveness of implemented interventions (Meisels & Atkins-Burnett, 2000; Simeonsson & McMillen, 2001). Information gathered can be used to determine how much a child has developed since the last assessment, reevaluate the needs and priorities of the child and family, and determine what to do next. Ongoing assessments, like those used for determining eligibility, should include multiple sources of information, be individualized to the child and family, and be conducted in natural environments.

Once the assessments are complete and information is gathered, professionals and parents must discuss the results. Information should be shared by professionals in ways that are easy for parents to use and understand, making clear the potential implications of assessment results for their child and family (Boone & Crais, 2002; Brink, 2002; Krauss, 2000; Meisels & Atkins-Burnett, 2000; Wolraich et al., 2005; Woods & Lindeman, 2008). This step includes families and professionals discussing what the child's special needs mean for development, day-to-day life, service provisions, and interventions. Ideally, by creating a shared view of strengths and needs, families and professionals can agree on the most important goals and intervention strategies that are both effective and manageable.

Gray, Msall, and Msall (2008) argue that by involving families throughout the initial assessment process, professionals can avoid a situation in which parents suddenly are told by professionals that their child has a developmental problem. By providing information and participating in its interpretation, families can feel empowered as informed decision-makers and can adjust or accommodate their views of their child's development by actively participating in the assessment process. Likewise, ongoing surveillance or assessment of children throughout their experience in early intervention helps assure parents that someone is paying attention to their child's well-being so that parents and professionals together can determine whether services need to be altered quickly in response to changing needs (Bailey, Armstrong, Kemper, Skinner, & Warren, 2009).

Intervention Planning and IFSP Development

Family-friendly assessment naturally leads to family-centered intervention planning. If families are involved in assessing their children's strengths, needs, and abilities and are asked about their concerns and priorities, the next step is translating these into appropriate goals for intervention. Federal law emphasizes the role that families play in intervention planning by requiring a written individualized family service plan (IFSP). The IFSP is created through a collaborative process between parents and professionals and contains information from the assessment process, specifically the child's present level of functioning and the family's resources related to enhancing the child's development. Recommended practice also underscores the importance of family involvement in intervention planning. Some examples of family and professional partnership include collaborative goal setting (Bailey, 1987), roles and responsibilities of professionals and parents during the development of the IFSP (Minke & Scott, 1993), family empowerment (Dunst, Trivette, & Deal, 1988), and family decision-making (McBride et al., 1993).

Several different models have been proposed to help professionals plan interventions with families: routines-based assessment, asset-based context matrix, adaptation interventions, and community mapping. For *routines-based assessment*, the Routines-Based Interview (RBI) is used to determine information about the families' current routines throughout the day, how their child participates in these routines, and what the family currently does, and would like to do, in regards to these routines. The family and professionals then work together to determine what routines to focus on and create goals based on these routines (McWilliam, 2000; McWilliam, 2005; McWilliam, Casey, & Sims, 2009). Similarly, the use of the *asset-based context matrix* examines the child's participation in family life, community life, and early childhood programs. Professionals and families discuss the child's interests and abilities in order for the child to participate in natural environments. Results from a field test indicated that using this assessment was easy and led to helpful information for developing goals (Wilson, Mott, & Batman, 2004). *Adaptation intervention* is similar to both routines-based assessment and the asset-based context matrix. Professionals and families work together to identify interventions to implement within the natural environments. Professionals ask families about activities their child participates in and how satisfied parents are with their child's functional ability in these routines, assist in planning interventions, and discuss how to implement these interventions (Campbell, Milbourne, & Wilcox, 2008). Finally, *community mapping* focuses specifically on using the community as a context of promoting children's development and learning opportunities. Community mapping involves determining the learning opportunities of a certain community, organizing the opportunities, and informing parents and professionals about these opportunities (Dunst, Bruder, Trivette, Raab, & McLean, 2001; Dunst, Herter, Shields, & Bennis, 2001; Dunst, 2001). Each of these assessment approaches can lead to identifying and implementing interventions that promote learning opportunities within the context of natural environments.

Although intervention planning should focus on the family, research has shown that this process often remains child-focused. Several studies have found that IFSPs rarely contain family outcomes (Able-Boone, Moore, & Coulter, 1995; Bruder, Staff, & McMurrer-Kaminer, 1997; Mahoney & Filer, 1996; McWilliam et al., 1998). An examination of the IFSP development process suggests that both families and professionals think there should be more collaboration and shared decision-making (Farel, Shackelford, & Hurth, 1997; Minke & Scott, 1995; Zhang, Bennett, & Dahl, 1999). When families and professionals have been asked about typical and ideal family-centered practices, both groups have rated ideal practices highly (McWilliam, Snyder, Harbin, Porter, & Munn, 2000). However, professionals rated themselves as typically performing more family-centered practices than did families, with the highest discrepancies for amount of family participation in assessment and assessment decisions, identifying family needs and resources, and coordination of services.

Service Provision

Once intervention planning is complete, the IFSP is put into action. Service provision and coordination has evolved from a traditional medical model whereby therapy is provided in a clinic to a home-based, family-centered model. Recommended practice suggests that family activities and routines should form the core of service delivery (Bailey, 1994; Guralnick, 2005; Trivette & Dunst, 2000). Specifically, three features should characterize the provision of services to children: (a) embedding interventions into everyday routines, (b) providing services in natural environments, and (c) focusing on functional skills and meaningful outcomes. The evidence base for each of these components is reviewed below.

Children have opportunities to learn throughout the day, and embedding interventions into daily activities increases the number of opportunities to enhance their development. In a national survey, 20 activity categories (e.g., family and child routines, community activities) were identified, each offering learning experiences for children (Dunst, Hamby, Trivette, Raab, & Bruder, 2000). The number of activity settings a child experiences is positively associated with child functioning and better learning opportunities (Dunst, Bruder, et al., 2001). Families who report using activities to support their child's learning also are more likely to report positive well-being (Dunst, Trivette, Hamby, & Bruder, 2006). In addition, families who adapted activities throughout their child's day to help promote learning and development valued input from early intervention professionals about how to best fit their child's needs (Allen, 2007; Keilty & Galvin, 2006). However, making changes to daily routines may be difficult for families at first. Woods, Kashinath, and Goldstein (2004) found that families rarely generalized child-support strategies until they talked with professionals about how to incorporate strategies into existing routines and activities.

Supporting families and helping them embed interventions into everyday routines increases the likelihood that families will continue to use the strategies when the professionals are not present (Hanft & Pilkington, 2000). Moreover, the amount of intervention is dramatically increased if families are the ones providing it rather than professionals (Jung, 2003; McWilliam, 2000). However, implementing a natural environment model of early intervention can be challenging. Studies by Raab and Dunst (2004) and Woods et al. (2004) indicate there is considerable variation in how professionals understand and use natural environments. These findings suggest that practitioners may not be aware that use of natural environments is a multidimensional practice which includes not only the location of intervention but also the type of activity and whether it was child- or adult-initiated, as well as the practitioners role in the intervention.

Changing locations and embedding instruction should promote more rapid learning and generalization for children and increase parental engagement, but to maximize effectiveness, skills need to be functional for children and meaningful for families (Pretti-Frontczak & Bricker, 2004). When the Early Childhood Outcomes Center was leading an initiative to develop recommended child outcomes for a national accountability system, various stakeholders—parents, professionals, policy-makers—emphasized the importance of making sure that outcomes are *functional*: useful, meaningful skills integrated across domains and settings. Instead of clustering outcomes by traditional developmental domains (e.g., cognitive, language, motor, self-help), three broad, functional outcomes were identified: (a) children have positive social-emotional skills (e.g., relating with adults, relating with other children, expressing emotions and feelings, learning rules and expectations, social interactions and play); (b) children acquire and use knowledge and skills (e.g., thinking and reasoning, remembering, problem-solving, using symbols and language, early concept development); and (c) children take appropriate action to meet their needs (e.g., taking care of basic needs, using tools such as a toothbrush or crayon, getting from place to place) (Hebbeler & Barton, 2007). Inherent in the definition of functional, of course, is an individualized approach, as functionality, ultimately, is the juncture of environmental demands and an individual child's ability to meet those expectations.

Some families may need to know more about how to help their child, especially in the context of parent-child interactions. Parent-child interactions are a key factor in helping children learn and develop (McCollum & Hemmeter, 1997; Kelly & Barnard, 2000). Responsivity, an important element of parent-child interactions, refers to the way in which parents respond to their child (Warren & Brady, 2007). Responsive parenting involves parents providing warm and positive affection and interactions with their child and responding in ways that are based on the child's signals or needs. Although research has linked responsive parenting to positive child outcomes (Eisenberg et al., 2003; Landry, Smith, Swank, & Guttentag, 2008; Yoder & Warren, 1998), parenting associated with directiveness, overstimulation, and the parent taking a lead or dominant role are linked to less favorable child outcomes (McCollum & Hemmeter, 1997).

Several specific intervention programs have been developed to promote responsivity and positive parent-child interactions. Kelly, Zuckerman, and Rosenblatt (2008) found that mothers who used the Promoting First Relationships curriculum fostered their children's social/emotional and cognitive growth and improved the quality of the mother-child relationship. Mahoney and Perales (2005) found that relationship-focused intervention resulted in increased parental responsiveness, which was subsequently linked to improvements in child development. A meta-analyses of 70 published studies focusing upon the effects on sensitivity or attachment interventions found that interventions successfully strengthened maternal sensitivity and, to a smaller degree, attachment (Bakermans-Kranenburg, van IJzendoorn, & Juffer, 2003). The results indicated that fewer contacts with families and interventions that involved fathers produced more successful results. Similarly, a meta-analysis by Dunst and Kassow (2008) found that behaviorally based interventions are more likely to foster parent/child relationships. Warren and Brady (2007) suggest that interventions focusing on responsitivity can be effective with as few as eight 1-hour training sessions. Collectively, this research indicates that specific interventions can be successful, but professionals must be careful to address issues of parental concerns, focus on aspects of the relationship that will promote the child's development, and not overwhelm parents with time-consuming interventions that focus on their responsivity and interactions with their child.

Throughout all aspects of child-based interventions, it is critical for professionals to recognize and understand the extent to which families already are engaged in a constant process of accommodating daily routines and activities in response to their child with special needs. Respecting the magnitude of these accommodations and gearing services toward enabling the most effective, most acceptable, and least disruptive accommodations is a key aspect of family-centered interventions (Bernheimer & Weisner, 2007).

Social and Community Supports and Coordination

Families' support systems have consistently emerged as a central factor in helping to manage the complex demands of parenting a child with a disability. Studies have demonstrated that social supports can promote hope, enhance confidence in parenting abilities, improve problem-focused coping strategies and reduce stress, and that families with strong support systems are able to handle the challenges of having a child with a disability with greater ease than those without (Bailey et al., 2007; Hauser-Cram et al., 2001; Heiman, 2002). However, studies suggest that family-oriented services in early intervention may be declining (Turnbull et al., 2007). Data from NEILS suggested that parents have a hard time participating in community activities even though they feel supported by friends and family members (Bailey et al., 2005). In a survey of families of children with disabilities, families were least satisfied with their physician's ability to understand the degree of impact of disability on the family or to link them with other families (Liptak et al., 2006).

Family supports exist in both informal and formal social networks and can include both individuals (e.g., relatives, neighbors, friends) and community groups (e.g., church, school, recreational). Effective family support programs enable families to become engaged in their communities and more confident and competent in their ability to support the development of their child with disabilities (Dunst, 2001). Conceptual frameworks for categories of formal supports within the early intervention system have been identified and provide an important step towards identifying the specific practices associated with them (Guralnick, 1997; McWilliam & Scott, 2001). These categories of supports include informational supports, material supports and emotional supports. Informational supports refer to specific information about the child's disability; about services available through early intervention; and about child development and intervention strategies. Material support refers to financial resources; resources to meet basic needs (housing, food, medical care, childcare, clothing), and ability to find specialized equipment and adaptive materials for their child. Emotional support refers to the quality of behaviors and attitudes expressed by professionals; the ability to build informal social networks; and participation in parent groups.

Family-centered practices extend beyond the child and immediate family and should also include the community. One of the practices of service coordinators and other early intervention professionals is helping families become aware of the community resources available. Trivette and colleagues have defined several types of community resources, including economic, physical and environmental, food and clothing, medical and dental, employment and vocational, transportation, education and enrichment, childcare, recreational, emotional, social, and cultural (Dunst et al., 2000; Trivette, Dunst, & Deal, 1997).

However, research shows that many early intervention professionals do not feel they have adequate knowledge of community resources (Harbin, Pelosi, et al., 2004). A survey of families in early intervention programs in Ohio found that a particular need expressed by families was help with meeting their material needs and linking them with other community supports and agencies (Allen, 2007). Data from NEILS indicate that only 30% of families received information about recreational activities available for the child, 25% were told about transportation, and fewer than 20% were given help finding childcare, a counselor/minister, respite care, medical or dental services, or basic household needs such as food, clothing, and shelter (Spiker, Hebbeler, & Mallik, 2005).

To address the lack of knowledge about community resources, two mapping strategies are described in the literature, suggesting practical ways for providers to collect information about family and community resources; the eco-map (Hartman, 1995; McWilliam, 2000) and community mapping (Dunst, Herter, et al., 2001). The eco-map is a diagram of family and community constellations, which emphasizes family ecology, with the child at the center. Concentrically, it includes the people who live with the child, extended family and friends, co-workers and community connections, and finally professionals who may provide services to the family (Hartman, 1995; McWilliam, 2000). The community mapping process involves compiling an information database of community activities and developing a map that assists families in connecting with those activities (Dunst, Herter, et al., 2001). Families and professionals have reported that these strategies promote more relaxed conversations between parents and early intervention providers (Hartman, 1995; McWilliam & Scott, 2001) and that maps are preferred (over brochures or flyers) as a way of learning about the opportunities in their community (Umstead, Boyd, & Dunst, 1995). Both the eco-map and community mapping are promising, realistic practices that improve families' and professionals' knowledge of informal and formal supports in their community. These practices, with apparent clinical utility, have yet to be examined by researchers and have strong implications for future directions.

Two forms of community services exemplify the range of contexts in which early intervention professionals can promote family support—childcare and parent-to-parent support groups. Childcare is, perhaps more than ever, a primary formal support system for families of children with disabilities. Issues of access, affordability, and quality of childcare for families of children with disabilities have a long history in the research literature (Axtell, Garwick, Patterson, Bennett, & Blum, 1995; Booth-LaForce & Kelly, 2004; DeVore & Hanley-Maxwell, 2000). Studies have shown that parents who built cooperative, caregiving partnerships with providers were more likely to maintain quality childcare (DeVore & Bowers, 2006), and childcare providers receiving support and ongoing technical assistance from collaborating professionals felt more able to support children with special needs in their classrooms (Devore & Hanley-Maxwell, 2000).

Parent-to-parent programs assist families in developing informal and formal support networks (Santelli, Turnbull, Sergeant, Lerner, & Marquis, 1996). These programs cultivate relationships between parents who are seeking information about caring for their young child with a disability and experienced (or veteran) parents. Studies have shown that parent-to-parent programs had a positive impact on parents' adaptation to disability (Singer et al., 1999) and that most parents found the support groups helpful (Santelli, Turnbull, Marquis, & Lerner, 2000).

A key family-centered practice with respect to family and community support is *service coordination*. There are several levels of service coordination: (a) coordination of services for the family, (b) coordination and collaboration between professionals, and (c) cross-agency coordination and collaboration. At the family level, IDEA mandates that families are provided a service coordinator who will facilitate access and coordination of services across agencies and will help families understand and exercise their rights (Harbin, Bruder, et al., 2004). Research has defined different models of service coordination (Bruder, 2005; Harbin, et al., 2000). Key responsibilities of service coordinators include coordinating evaluations and assessments; developing the IFSP and ensuring family participation in the selection of services; monitoring, coordinating, and facilitating the provision of services; informing families of the availability of advocacy services; and planning for and assisting with transition to Part B preschool services (Bruder, 2005; Bruder et al., 2005; Dunst & Bruder, 2006).

For service coordination to be successful, professionals and agencies must work together as a team. Interdisciplinary teaming involves collaboration across professionals and agencies. Recommended practice has identified several key features of interdisciplinary service delivery, including teamwork, role release, and effective communication (Bruder & Bologna, 1993; Correa, Jones, Thomas, & Morsink, 2005; Horn & Jones, 2004; King et al., 2009; Orelove & Sobsey, 1991). Effective coordination of services also depends on interpersonal, interagency and intersystem factors (Dinnebeil et al., 1999) resulting in partnerships between service systems, agencies, and families (Buysse, Wesley, & Able-Boone, 2001; Freund, Boone, Barlow, & Lim, 2005).

Research on service coordination shows how it can affect service delivery. A pair of studies examined the relationship between service coordinator practices and models of service coordination (Dunst & Bruder, 2006) and child and family predictors of service coordination practices (Bruder & Dunst, 2008). Families who received service coordination using a dedicated and independent model (i.e., the service coordinator did not provide any direct services to the child and family and they were not part of the service delivery agency) had less contact with service coordinators. The service coordinators also provided fewer recommended practices to the families. In addition, families who received a blended model of service coordination (i.e., the service coordinator also provided services) had more contact with the service coordinator, and reported that the service coordinator used more family-centered practices.

Effective interagency partnerships are a primary goal of the early intervention system (Bruder, 2005; Bruder & Bologna, 1993; Horn & Jones, 2004; Sandall et al., 2000) and are central to the attainment of informal and formal supports for families. To be successful, they require time to develop, leadership, commitment, planning, and mutual understanding (Johnson et al., 2003).

Linking Practices with Family Outcomes

If early intervention programs adopt family-centered principles and implement family-centered practices, families and children likely will have positive outcomes. The five family outcomes outlined earlier can be directly linked to specific practices. For each outcome, examples of practices are provided that likely will benefit families.

Outcome 1: Families understand their child's strengths, abilities, and special needs. For families to achieve this outcome, they must know the next steps in their child's development, understand their child's disability, be able to access information they need, and know how changes in services, parenting, or medication affect their child's development (Bailey et al., 2006). Early intervention and medical professionals are the first to provide families with information about their child's condition or special needs. During referral and the initial assessment, families gather information that will help them support their child. Likewise, professionals ask about family needs, resources, and priorities and then develop an individualized plan that will lead to improvements. As children grow and develop, families need new information and support. Using family-centered practices throughout the early intervention journey will lead to families' understanding their children and their unique strengths and needs.

Outcome 2: Families know their rights and advocate effectively for their children. Achieving this outcome means that families know their rights and responsibilities related to service provision, feel comfortable talking to professionals and asking questions, are knowledgeable about services available, advocate for things they feel are important, and know what to do if they are not satisfied (Bailey et al., 2006). During enrollment into the program, many professionals provide information to families about their rights, including information about due-process and mediation, parents' roles during assessment and intervention planning, and confidentiality of personal information. However, providing this information once is not enough to be considered family-centered. Professionals need to revisit this information on multiple occasions, possibly during IFSP review meetings, to ensure that families understand their rights. Professionals also should provide families with updated information on available community programs and specialized services whenever possible. Giving families information helps to empower them and helps them to feel comfortable interacting with professionals and advocating for their child and family.

Outcome 3: Families help their children develop and learn. Families demonstrate their achievement of this outcome if they know and use effective parenting styles, can manage behavior, provide a nurturing environment, adapt routines to meet their needs, help their child with special equipment, and use appropriate techniques to enhance learning (Bailey et al., 2006). Families bring many strengths with them as they enter early intervention. However, they may also experience some challenges related to their child's special needs. Providing services in a family-centered manner, including focusing on family routines and embedding intervention into natural environments, helps families support their child's development. If appropriate, professionals also can provide guidance on effective parenting techniques. These practices will enhance families' capacities to help their children grow and learn.

Outcome 4: Families have support systems. Evidence that families have achieved this outcome include feeling supported by friends and family, maintaining and creating new friendships, participating in desired activities, and having people to help and rely on (Bailey et al., 2006). Professionals can help families build strong informal and formal support networks by informing them of local support groups or connecting families with others who have a child with similar needs. Professionals also can help families design interventions that will enable them to participate in activities with friends or families and help families find information to provide to others who might interact with the child (e.g., babysitter, neighbor). Fulfilling families' emotional and informational needs helps them to feel confident and supported.

Outcome 5: Families are able to gain access to desired services and activities in their community. Families have achieved this outcome if they have access to quality childcare, have medical professionals who are sensitive to their child's needs, and participate in their community (Bailey et al., 2006). At any point during a families' early intervention experience, they may identify needs related to accessing the community. For example, families may decide to change childcare centers in order to be more convenient to a new job or home. A service coordinator can provide information about quality choices to families and connect the teachers and administrators in the new center with professionals who provide intervention and therapy. Using these types of family-centered practices will help families be active members of the community.

Conclusions and Future Directions

Families have long been considered essential to the successful implementation of early intervention. How early intervention professionals work with families (and perhaps more fundamentally, how they view their relationships with families) has evolved to a widely accepted view in the literature and among stakeholders that a family-centered approach to early intervention is the preferred model. A family-centered approach exemplifies the values we hold as a society for respect of individuals, personal dignity, and freedom of choice. By engaging in family-centered practices, we affirm the premise that early intervention is a consumer-oriented enterprise that ought to be responsive to the needs and desires of families and respectful of their preferences for goals and services. Research in both early intervention and medical contexts consistently shows that, when professionals adopt a family-centered approach (sometimes referred to as patient-centered care in medicine), a number of tangible benefits are evident, ranging from increased satisfaction to improvements in parenting practices.

However, the principles of family-centered care have little meaning if they are only adopted as a belief system without corresponding application across the various practice settings that comprise early intervention. They only become salient, and effective, when they are applied in the countless interactions, both small and large, that professionals have with families and their children. In this chapter, we have given examples of how family-centered practices can be used throughout the early intervention process, beginning with referral and access, and continuing through assessment, program planning, service delivery, community support, and service coordination. When available, we have summarized research findings in support of the use of those practices.

However, much remains to be done. First, a family-centered approach is gradually gaining acceptance among early intervention professionals, but full implementation in practice remains a challenge, due in part to preservice training programs that are primarily focused on discipline-specific practices with relatively little attention to working with families, and in part to real world constraints inherent in the ecology of early intervention—inadequate funding, use of contractual services rather than full-time early intervention employees, and the pressures to accomplish much in the context of relatively brief contacts with families. Changing professional practice will likely necessitate a team-based approach to in-service training that includes families as participants in program decisions about family-centered practices, with endorsement at both the state and local administrative officials, and effective long-term leadership (Bailey, Buysse, Smith, & Elam, 1992; Bailey, McWilliam, & Winton, 1992).

Second, more research is needed to validate effective practices in working with families. Although the general principles of a family-centered approach have been affirmed in multiple research studies and meta-analyses, specific practices with families have been inadequately studied. Such research will be challenging to conduct because of the individualized needs of families, the multiple variations in how services are provided, differences in individual early intervention professionals, and the virtual impossibility of randomized trials that provide an evidence base comparable to that expected, for example, when comparing two reading curricula or the effectiveness of various medications. Nonetheless, continuing demands for evidence-based practices will mean that such data must be produced. Small sample-focused research with carefully characterized and well-controlled interventions are needed to identify micro-components of practice that, in isolation, appear to be effective, as in the case of a curriculum on responsive parenting or efficacy of parent-to-parent support programs. Complex research designs using large samples are also needed in which the program features are systematically varied and child and family characteristics are incorporated to gain a better understanding at the macro-level of the approaches most likely to be effective (Guralnick, 1997).

Finally, although we set out to review the evidence in support of specific practices linked to specific family outcomes, the literature was not organized this way and too many gaps existed to conduct a review in this fashion. However, as depicted in Figures 50.1 and 50.2, practices ultimately need to result in improved outcomes for both children and families. An important question is whether it is necessary to try to link specific practices to desired outcomes, or whether the "package" of perspectives, approaches, and methods used in early intervention collectively result in demonstrable benefits for families.

Note

Preparation of this chapter was supported in part by a cooperative agreement to SRI International (#H326L080001) and a corresponding subcontract to RTI International from the Office of Special Education Programs, U.S. Department of Education. The content, however, does not necessarily represent the policy of the Department of Education and should not be considered an endorsement by the federal government.

References

Able-Boone, H., Moore, S. M., & Coulter, D. K. (1995). Achieving family-centered practice in early intervention. *Infant-Toddler Intervention, 5,* 395–404.

Administration for Children, Youth, and Families. (1998). *Head Start program performance measures, second progress report.* Washington, DC: Head Start Bureau, ACYF, U.S. Department of Health and Human Services.

Allen, S. F., (2007). Parents' perceptions of intervention practices in home visiting programs. *Infants and Young Children, 20,* 266–281.

American Academy of Pediatrics (2004). Organizational principles to guide and define the child health care system and/or improve the health of all children. *Pediatrics, 113* (5, Suppl.), 1545–1547.

American Academy of Pediatrics, Committee on Children with Disabilities. (2001). Developmental surveillance and screening of infants and young children. *Pediatrics, 108,* 192–195.

Applequist, K. L., Umphrey, L., Moan, E., & Raabe, B. (2008). Using effective communication techniquest when presenting initial information to families. In C. A. Peterson, L. Fox, & P. M. Blasco (Eds.), *Young Exceptional Children Monograph Series No. 10: Early intervention for infants and toddlers and their families: Practices and outcomes* (pp. 19– 32). Longmont, CO: Sopris West.

Atkins-Burnett, S., & Allen-Meares, P. (2000). Infants and toddlers with disabilities: Relationship-based approaches. *Social Work, 45,* 351–379.

Axtell, S. A., Garwick, A. W., Patterson, J., Bennett, F. C., & Blum, R. W. (1995). Unmet service needs of families of young children with chronic illnesses and disabilities. *Journal of Family and Economic Issues, 16,* 355–411.

Bailey, D. B. (1987). Collaborative goal-setting with families: Resolving differences in values and priorities for services. *Topics in Early Childhood Special Education, 7*(2), 59–71.

Bailey, D. B. (1994). Working with families of children with special needs. In M. Wolery, & J. Wilbers (Eds.), *Including children with special needs in preschool programs: Research and implications for practice* (pp. 23–44). Washington, DC: National Association for the Education of Young Children.

Bailey, D. B. (2001). Evaluating parent involvement and family support in early intervention and preschool programs. *Journal of Early Intervention, 24,* 1–14.

Bailey, D. B., Armstrong, D., Kemper, A., Skinner, D., & Warren, S. F. (2009). Supporting family adaptation to pre-symptomatic and "untreatable" conditions in an era of expanded newborn screening. *Journal of Pediatric Psychology, 34,* 648–661.

Bailey, D. B., Bruder, M., Hebbeler, K., Carta, J., de Fosset, M., Greenwood, C., … Barten, L. (2006). Recommended outcomes for families of young children with disabilities. *Journal of Early Intervention, 28,* 227–251.

Bailey, D. B., Buysse, V., Smith, T., & Elam, J. (1992). The effects and perceptions of family involvement in program decisions about family-centered practices. *Evaluation and Program Planning, 15,* 23–32.

Bailey, D. B., Hebbeler, K., Scarborough, A. Spiker, D., & Mallik, M. (2004). First experiences with early intervention: A national perspectives. *Pediatrics, 113,* 887–896.

Bailey, D. B., Hebbeler, K., Spiker, D., Scarborough, A., Mallik, S., & Nelson, L. (2005). 36-month outcomes for families of children with disabilities participating in early intervention. *Pediatrics, 116,* 1346–1352.

Bailey, D. B., McWilliam, P. J., & Winton, P. J. (1992). Building family-centered practices in early intervention: A team-based model for change. *Infants and Young Children, 5,* 73–82.

Bailey, D. B., McWilliam, R. A., Darkes, L. A., Hebbeler, K., Simeonsson, R. J., Spiker, D., & Wagner, M. (1998). Family outcomes in early intervention: A framework for program evaluation and efficacy research. *Exceptional Children, 64,* 313–328.

Bailey, D. B., Nelson, L., Hebbeler, K., & Spiker, D. (2007). Modeling the impact of formal and informal supports for young children with disabilities and their families. *Pediatrics, 120,* e992–e1001.

Bailey, D. B., & Powell, T. (2005). Assessing the information needs of families in early intervention. In M. J. Guralnick (Ed.), *A developmental systems approach to early intervention* (pp. 151–183). Baltimore: Brookes.

Bailey, D. B., Raspa, M., Bishop, E., & Holiday, D. (2009). No change in the age of diagnosis of fragile X syndrome: Findings from a national survey. *Pediatrics, 124,* 527–533.

Bailey, D. B., Raspa, M., Olmsted, M. G., Novak, S., Sam, A., & Humphreys, B. (2009). Expansion of the Family Outcomes Survey: Findings and recommendations for the 2009 version of the FOS. Research Triangle Park, NC: RTI International.

Bailey, D. B., & Simeonsson, R. J. (1990). *Family Needs Survey*. Chapel Hill: FPG Child Development Institute, The University of North Carolina.

Bailey, D. B., Skinner, D., & Sparkman, K. (2003). Discovering fragile X syndrome: Family experiences and perceptions. *Pediatrics, 111*, 407–416.

Bakermans-Kranenburg, M., van IJzendoorn, M. H., & Juffer, F. (2003). Less is more: Meta-analyses of sensitivity and attachment interventions in early childhood. *Psychological Bulletin, 129*(2), 195–215.

Barnwell, D. A., & Day, M. (1996). Providing support to diverse families. In P. J. Beckman (Ed.), *Strategies for working with families of young children with disabilities* (pp. 47–68). Baltimore: Brookes

Bernheimer, L. P., & Weisner, T. S. (2007). "Let me just tell you what I do all day…": The family story at the center of intervention research and practice. *Infants and Young Children, 20*, 192–201.

Blue-Banning, M., Summers, J. A., Frankland, C., Nelson, L. L., & Beegle, G. (2004). Dimensions of family and professional partnerships: Constructive guidelines for collaboration. *Exceptional Children, 70,* 167–184.

Boone, H., & Crais, E. (2002). Strategies for achieving family-driven assessment and intervention planning. In M. M. Ostrosky & E. Horn (Eds.), *Young Exceptional Children Monograph Series No. 4: Assessment: Gathering meaningful information* (pp. 2–11). Longmont, CO: Sopris West.

Booth-LaForce, C., & Kelly, J. F. (2004). Childcare patterns and issues for families of preschool children with disabilities. *Infants & Young Children, 17*, 5–16.

Brewer, E. J., McPherson, M., Magrab, P. R., & Hutchins, V. C. (1989). Family-centered, community-based coordinated care for children with special health care needs. *Pediatrics, 83*, 1055–1060.

Brink, M. B. (2002). Involving parents in early childhood assessment: Perspectives from an early intervention instructor. *Early Childhood Education Journal, 29*(4), 251–257.

Bronfenbrenner, U. (1999). Environments in developmental perspective: Theoretical and operational models. In S. L. Friedman & T. D., Wachs (Eds.), *Measuring environment across the life span: Emerging methods and concepts* (pp. 3–28). Washington, DC: American Psychological Association Press.

Bruder, M. B. (2000). Family-centered early intervention: Clarifying our values for the new millennium. *Topics in Early Childhood Special Education, 20(2),* 105–115.

Bruder, M. B. (2005). Service coordination and integration in a developmental systems approach to early intervention. In M. J. Guralnick (Ed.), *A developmental systems approach to early intervention* (pp. 29–58). Baltimore: Brookes.

Bruder, M. B., & Bologna, T. (1993). Collaboration and service coordination for effective early intervention. In W. Brown, S. K., Thurman, & L. F. Pearl (Eds.), *Family-centered early intervention with infants and toddlers: Innovative cross-disciplinary approaches* (pp. 103–127). Baltimore: Brookes.

Bruder, M. B., & Dunst, C. J. (2008). Factors related to the scope of early intervention service coordinator practices. *Infants & Young Children, 21,* 176–185.

Bruder, M. B., Harbin, G. L., Whitbread, K., Conn-Powers, M., Roberts, R., van Buren, M., … Gabbard, G. (2005). Establishing outcomes for service coordination: A step towards evidence-based practice. *Topics in Early Childhood Special Education, 25,*177–188.

Bruder, M. B., Staff, I., & McMurrer-Kaminer, E. (1997). Toddlers receiving early intervention in childcare centers: A description of a service delivery system. *Topics in Early Childhood Special Education, 17,* 185–208.

Buysse, V., Wesley, P. W., & Able-Boone, H. (2001). Innovations in professional development: creating communities of practice to support inclusion. In M. J. Guralnick (Ed.), *Early childhood inclusion: Focus on change* (pp.179–200). Baltimore: Brookes.

Campbell, P. H., Milbourne, S., & Wilcox, M. J. (2008). Adaptation interventions to promote participation in natural settings. *Infants & Young Children: An Interdisciplinary Journal of Special Care Practices, 21*(2), 94–106.

Cohen, S. & Syme, S. L., (Eds.). (1985). *Social support and health*. New York: Academic Press.

Correa, V., Jones, H., Thomas, C. C., & Morsink, C. V. (2005). *Interactive teaming: Consultation and collaboration in special programs.* Upper Saddle River, NJ: Prentice Hall.

Denboba, D., McPherson, M. G., Kenney, M. K., Strickland, B., & Newacheck, P. W. (2006). Achieving family and provider partnerships for children with special health care needs. *Pediatrics, 118*, 1607–1615.

DeVore, S., & Bowers, B. (2006). Childcare for children with disabilities: Families search for specialized care and cooperative childcare partnerships. *Infants & Young Childre, 19*, 203–212.

DeVore, S., & Hanley-Maxwell, C. (2000). I wanted to see if we could make it work: Perspectives on inclusive childcare. *Exceptional Children, 66*, 241–255.

Dinnebeil, L. A., Hale, L. M., & Rule, S. (1999). Early intervention program practices that support collaboration. *Topics in Early Childhood Special Education, 19,* 225–235.

Dunst, C. J. (1985). Rethinking early intervention. *Analysis and Intervention in developmental disabilities, 5,* 165–201.

Dunst, C. J. (1999). Placing parent education in conceptual and empirical context. *Topics in Early Childhood Special Education, 19*, 141–172.

Dunst, C. J. (2000). Revisiting "rethinking early intervention." *Topics in Early Childhood Special Education, 20*(2), 95–104.

Dunst, C. J. (2001). Participation of young children with disabilities in community learning activities. In M. J. Guralnick (Ed.), *Early child hood inclusion: Focus on change* (pp. 307–333). Baltimore: Brookes.

Dunst, C. J., & Bruder, M. B. (2006). Early intervention service coordination models and service coordinator practices. *Journal of Early Intervention, 28,* 155–165.

Dunst, C. J., Bruder, M. B., Trivette, C. M., Raab, M., & McLean, M. (2001). Natural learning opportunities for infants, toddlers, and preschoolers. *Young Exceptional Children, 4*(3), 18–25.

Dunst, C. J., Hamby, D., Trivette, C. M., Raab, M., & Bruder, M. B. (2000). Everyday family and community life and children's naturally occurring learning opportunities. Journal of Early Intervention, 23, 151–164.

Dunst, C., Herter, S., Shields, H., & Bennis, L. (2001). Mapping community-based natural learning opportunities. *Young Exceptional Children, 4*(4), 16–24.

Dunst, C. J., Jenkins, V., & Trivette, C. M. (1988). Family Support Scale. In C. Dunst, C. Trivette, & A. Deal (Eds.), *Enabling and empowering families: Principles and guidelines for practice* (p. 157). Cambridge MA: Brookline Books.

Dunst, C. J., & Kassow, D. Z. (2008). Caregiver sensitivity, contingent social responsiveness, and secure infant attachment. *Journal of Early and Intensive Behavior Intervention, 5*(1), 40–56.

Dunst, C. J., & Trivette, C. M. (1996). Empowerment, effective helpgiving practices, and family-centered care. *Pediatric Nursing, 22,* 334–337.

Dunst, C., Trivette, C. & Deal, A. (1988). *Enabling and empowering families: Principles and guidelines for practice.* Cambridge, MA: Brookline Books.

Dunst, C. J. Trivette, C., & Deal, A. (1994). *Supporting and strengthening families: Volume 1: Methods, strategies, and practices.* Cambridge, MA: Brookline Books.

Dunst, C. J., Trivette, C. M., & Hamby, D. W. (2007). Meta-analysis of family-centered helpgiving practices research. *Mental Retardation and Developmental Disabilities Research Reviews, 13*, 370–378.

Dunst, C. J., Trivette, C. M., Hamby, D. W., & Bruder, M. B. (2006). Influences of contrasting natural learning environment experiences on child, parent and family well-being. *Journal of Developmental & Physical Disabilities, 18*(3), 235–250.

Early Childhood Outcomes and Indicators Focus Group. (2003). *OSEP early childhood outcomes and indicators focus group.* Washington, DC: Office of Special Education Programs, U.S. Department of Education.

Early Childhood Research Institute on Measuring Growth and Development. (1998). *Family outcomes in a growth and development model.* (Technical Report no. 7). Minneapolis: Center for Early Education and Development, University of Minnesota.

Eisenberg, N., Valiente, C., Morris, A. S., Fabes, R. A., Cumberland, A., Reiser, M., … Losoya, S. (2003). Longitudinal relations among parental emotional expressivity, children's regulation, and quality of socioemotional functioning. *Developmental Psychology, 39*(1), 3–19.

Farel, A. M., Shackelford, J., & Hurth, J. L. (1997). Perceptions regarding the IFSp process in a statewide interagency service coordination program. *Topics in Early Childhood Special Education, 17,* 234–249.

Freund, P. J., Boone, H. A., Barlow, J. H., & Lim, C. I. (2005). Healthcare and early intervention collaborative supports for families and young children. *Infants & Young Children, 18*(1), 25–36.

Fugate, D., & Fugate, J. (1996). Putting the marketing plan to work: Practical suggestions for early intervention programs. *Infants & Young Children, 8*(4), 70–79.

Glascoe, F. (1999). Using parents' concerns to detect and address developmental and behavioral problems. *Journal of the Society of Pediatric Nursing, 4,* 24–35.

Gray, L. A., Msall, E. R., & Msall, M. E. (2008). Communicating about autism: Decreasing fears and stresses through parent-professional relationships. *Infants and Young Children, 21,* 256–271.

Guralnick, M. J. (1997). *The Effectiveness of early intervention.* Baltimore: Brookes.

Guralnick, M. J. (2005). An overview of the developmental systems models for early intervention. In M. J. Guralnick (Ed.), *The developmental systems approach to early intervention* (pp. 3–28). Baltimore: Brookes.

Hanft, B. E., & Pilkington, K. O. (2000). Therapy in natural environments: The means or end goal for early intervention. *Infants & Young Children, 12*(4), 1–13.

Harbin, G. L. (2005). Designing an integrated point of access in the early intervention system. In M. J. Guralnick (Ed.), *A developmental systems approach to early intervention: National and international perspectives* (pp. 99–131). Baltimore: Brookes.

Harbin, G. L., Bruder, M. B., Adams, C., Mazzarella, C., Whitbread, K., Gabbard, G., & Staff, I. (2004). Early intervention service coordination policies: National policy infrastructure. *Topics in Early Childhood Special Education, 24,* 89–97.

Harbin, G. L., McWilliam, R. A., & Gallagher, J. J. (2000). Services for young children with disabilities and their families. In J. P. Shonkoff & J. P. Meisels (Eds.), *Handbook of early childhood intervention* (pp. 387–415). New York: Cambridge University Press.

Harbin, G. L., Pelosi, J., Kameny, R., McWilliam, R., Kitsul, Y., Fox, E., & Rodriguez, I. (2004). *Identifying and predicting successful outcomes of coordinated service delviery.* Chapel Hill: FPG Child Development Institute, The University of North Carolina.

Harry, B., Kalyanpur, M., Day, M. (1999). *Building cultural reciprocity with families: Case studies in special education.* Baltimore: Brookes.

Hartman, A. (1995). Diagrammatic assessment of family relationships. *Families in Society, 76,* 11–122.

Hauser-Cram, P., Warfield, M. E., Shonkoff, J. P., Krauss, M. W., Sayer, A., & Upshur, C. C. (2001). Children with disabilities: A longitudinal study of child development and parent well-being. *Monographs for the Society of Research in Child Development, 66,* 1–126.

Hebbeler, K. M., & Barton, L. R. (2007). The need for data on child and family outcomes at the federal and state levels. In E. Horn, C. M. Peterson, L. Fox (Eds.), *Young Exceptional Children Monograph Series No. 9: Linking curriculum to child and family outcomes* (pp.1–15). Longmont CO: Sopris West.

Heiman, T. (2002). Parents of children with disabilities: Resilience, coping and future expectations. *Journal of Developmental and Physical Disabilities, 14*(2), 159–171.

Hobbs, N., Dokecki, P., Hoover-Dempsey, K., Moroney, R., Shayne, M., & Weeks, K. (1984). *Strengthening families.* San Francisco: Jossey-Bass.

Horn, E., & Jones, H. (2004). Collaboration and teaming in early intervention and early childhood special education. In E. Horn, M. Ostrosky, & H. Jones (Eds.), *Young Exceptional Children Monograph Series No. 6: Interdisciplinary teams* (pp. 11–20). Longmont, CO: Sopris West.

Jackson, B. J., & Needelman, H. (2007). Building a system of child find through a 3-tiered model of follow-up. *Infants and Young Children, 20,* 255–265.

Johnson, L. J., Zorn, D., Tam, B. K. Y., LaMontagne, M., & Johnson, S. A. (2003). Stakeholders' views of factors that impact successful interagency collaboration. *Exceptional Children, 69,* 195–209.

Jung, L. A. (2003). More is better: Maximizing early learning opportunities. *Young Exceptional Children, 6*(3), 21–27.

Keilty, B., & Galvin, K. M. (2006). Physical and social adaptations of families to promote learning in everyday experiences. *Topics in Early Childhood Special Education, 26*(4), 219–233.

Keirns, C. C., & Goold, S. D. (2009). Patient-centered care and preference-sensitive decision making. *Journal of the American Medical Association, 302,* 1805–1806.

Kelly, J. F., & Barnard, K. E. (2000). Assessment of parent-child interaction: Implications for early intervention. In J. P. Shonkoff & S. J. Meisels (Eds.), *Handbook of early childhood intervention* (pp. 258–289). New York: Cambridge University Press.

Kelly, J. F., Zuckerman, T., & Rosenblatt, S. (2008). Promoting first relationships: A relationship-focused early intervention approach. *Infants & Young Children, 21,* 285–295.

King, G., Strachan, D., Tucker, M., Duwyn, B., Desserud, S., & Shillington, M. (2009). The application of a transdisciplinary model for early intervention services. *Infants & Young Children, 22,* 211–223.

Knapp, C. A., Madden, V. L., & Marcu, M. I. (2010). Factors that affect parent perceptions of provider-family partnership for children with special health care needs. *Maternal and Child Health Journal, 14,* 742–750.

Krauss, M. W. (1997). Two generations of family research in early intervention. In M. J. Guralnick (Ed.), *The effectiveness of early intervention* (pp. 611–624). Baltimore: Brookes.

Krauss, M. W. (2000). Family assessment within early intervention programs. In J. P. Shonkoff & S. J. Meisels (Eds.), *Handbook of early childhood intervention* (pp. 290–308). New York: Cambridge University Press.

Lakin, K. C., & Turnbull, A. P. (2005). *National goals and research for people with intellectual and developmental disabilities.* Washington, DC: American Association on Mental Retardation.

Landry, S. H., Smith, K. E., Swank, P. R., & Guttentag, C. (2008). A responsive parenting intervention: The optimal timing across early childhood for impacting maternal behaviors and child outcomes. *Developmental Psychology, 44*(5), 1335–1353.

Liptak, G. S., Orlando, M., Yingling, J. R., Theurer-Kaufman, K., Malay, D., Tompkins, L., & Flynn, J. (2006). Satisfaction with primary health care received by families of children with developmental disabilities. *Journal of Pediatric Health Care, 20,* 245–252.

Lynch, E. W., & Hanson, M. J., (Eds.). (1992). *Developing cross-cultural competence: A guide for working with young children and their families.* Baltimore: Brookes.

Madding, C. C. (2000). Maintaining focus on cultural competence in early intervention services to linguistically and culturally diverse families. *Infant-Toddler Intervention, 10,* 9–18.

Mahoney, G., & Filer, J. (1996). How responsive is early intervention to the priorities and needs of families? *Topics in Early Childhood Special Education, 16,* 437–457.

Mahoney, G., Kaiser, A., Girolametto, L., MacDonald, J., Robinson, C., Safford, P., & Spiker, D. (1999). Parent education in early intervention: A call for a renewed focus. *Topics in Early Childhood Special Education, 19*(3), 131–140.

Mahoney, G., & Perales, F. (2005). Relationship-focused early intervention with children with pervasive developmental disorders and other disabilities: A comparative study. *Journal of Developmental & Behavioral Pediatrics, 26,* 77–85.

McBride, S. L., Brotherson, M. J., Joanning, H., Whiddon, D., & Demmitt, A. (1993). Implementation of family-centered services: Perceptions of families and professionals. *Journal of Early Intervention, 17,* 414–430.

McBroom, L. A., & Enriquez, M. (2009). Review of family-centered interventions to enhance the health outcomes of children with Type 1 diabetes. *The Diabetes Educator, 35,* 428–438.

McCollum, J. A. (1999). Parent education: What we mean and what that means. *Topics in Early Childhood Special Education, 19*(3), 147–149.

McCollum, J. A., & Hemmeter, M. L. (1997). Parent-child interaction intervention when children have disabilities. In M. J. Guralnick (Ed.), *The effectiveness of early intervention* (pp. 549–576). Baltimore: Brookes.

McWilliam, P. J. (1996). First encounters with families. In P. J. McWilliam, P. J. Winton, & E. R. Crais (Eds.), *Practical strategies for family-centered intervention* (pp. 15–30). San Diego, CA: Singular.

McWilliam, R. A. (2000). It's only natural… to have early intervention in the environments where it's needed. In S. Sandall & M. Ostrosky (Eds.), *Young Exceptional Children Monograph Series No. 2: Natural Environments and Inclusion* (pp. 17–26). Longmont, CO: Sopris West.

McWilliam, R. A. (2005). Assessing the resource needs of families in the context of early intervention. In M. J. Guralnick (Ed.), *A developmental systems approach to early intervention,* (pp. 215–234). Baltimore: Brookes.

McWilliam, R. A., Casey, A. M., & Sims, J. (2009). The routines-based interview: A method for gathering information and assessing needs. *Infants & Young Children: An Interdisciplinary Journal of Special Care Practices, 22*(3), 224–233.

McWilliam, R. A., Ferguson, A., Harbin, G. L., Porter, P., Munn, D., & Vandiviere, P. (1998). The family-centeredness of Individualized Family Service Plans. *Topics in Early Childhood Special Education, 18,* 69–83.

McWilliam, R. A., & Scott, S. M. (2001). A support approach to early intervention: A three-part framework. *Infants and Young Children, 13(4),* 55–66.

McWilliam, R. A., Snyder, P., Harbin, G. L., Porter, P., & Munn, D. (2000). Professionals' and families' perceptions of family-centered practices in infant-toddler services. *Early Education and Development, 11,* 519–538.

McWilliam, R. A., Tocci, L., & Harbin, G. (1998). Family-centered services: Service providers' discourse and behavior. *Topics in Early Childhood Special Education, 18,* 206–221.

Meisels, S. J., & Atkins-Burnett, S. (2000). The elements of early childhood intervention. In J. P. Shonkoff & S. J. Meisels (Eds.), *Handbook of early childhood intervention* (pp. 231–257). New York: Cambridge University Press.

Meisels, S., & Margolis, L. (1988). Is the early and periodic screening, diagnosis, and treatment program effective with developmentally disabled children?. *Pediatrics, 81,* 262–271.

Minke, K. M., & Scott, M. M. (1993). The development of Individualized Family Service Plans: Roles for parents and staff. *The Journal of Special Education, 27,* 82–106.

Minke, K., & Scott, M. (1995). Parent-professional relationships in early intervention: A qualitative investigation. *Topics in Early Childhood Special Education, 15*(3), 335–352.

Nachshen, J. S. (2005). Empowerment and families: Building the bridges between parents and professionals, theory and research. *Journal on Developmental Disabilities, 11,* 67–75.

Nageswaran, S., & Farel, A. (2007). Access to a medical home for infants and young children with special needs. *Infants and Young Children, 20,* 222–228.

Neisworth, J. T., & Bagnato, S. J. (2000). Recommended practices in assessment. In S. Sandall, M. E. McLean, & B. J. Smith (Eds.), *DEC recommended practices in early intervention/early childhood special education* (pp. 17–28). Longmont, CO: Sopris West.

Neisworth, J. T., & Bagnato, S. J. (2004). The mismeasure of young children: The authentic assessment alternative. *Infants & Young Children: An Interdisciplinary Journal of Special Care Practices, 17*(3), 198–212.

Olmsted, M., Bailey, D. B., Raspa, M., Nelson, R., Robinson, N., Simpson, M. E., & Guillen, C. (2010). Outcomes reported by Spanish-speaking families in early intervention. *Topics in Early Childhood Special Education, 30,* 46–55.

Orelove, F. P., & Sobsey D. (1991). *Education children with multiple disabilities: A transdisciplinary approach* (2nd ed.). Baltimore: Brookes.

Park, J., Hoffman, L., Marquis, J., Turnbull, A. P., Poston, D., Mannan, H., Wang, M., & Nelson, L. C. (2003). Toward assessing family outcomes of service delivery: Validation of a family quality of life survey. *Journal of Intellectual Disability Research, 47,* 367–384.

Pelligrino, J. (2007). Newborn screening: Opportunities for prevention of developmental disabilities. In M. L. Batshaw, L. Pellegrino, & N. J. Roizen (Eds.), *Children with disabilities* (6th ed., pp. 97–106). Baltimore: Brookes.

Piotrowski, C. C., Talavera, G. A., & Mayer, J. A. (2009) Health Steps: A systematic review of a preventive practice-based model of pediatric care. *Journal of Developmental and Behavioral Pediatrics, 30,* 91–103.

Pretti-Frontczak, K., & Bricker, D. (2004). *An activity-based approach to early intervention* (3rd ed.). Baltimore: Brookes.

Raab, M., & Dunst, C. (2004). Early intervention practitioner approaches to natural environment interventions. *Journal of Early Intervention, 27*(1), 15–26.

Rappaport, J. (1981). In praise of paradox: A social policy empowerment over prevention. *American Journal of Community Psychology, 9,* 1–25.

Raspa, M., Bailey, D. B., Nelson, R., Robinson, N., Simpson, M. E., Gillian, C., … Houts, R. (2010). Measuring family outcomes in early intervention: Findings from a large-scale assessment. *Exceptional Children, 74,* 496–510.

Reznick, J. S., & Schwartz, B. B. (2001). When is an assessment an intervention? Parent perception of infant intentionality and language. *Journal of the American Academy of Child & Adolescent Psychiatry, 40*(1), 11–17.

Roberts, R. N., Innocenti, M. S., & Goetze, L. D. (1999). Emerging issues from state level evaluations of early intervention programs. *Journal of Early Intervention, 22,* 152–163.

Russo, R. J. (1999). Applying a strengths-based approach in working with people with developmental disabilities and their families. *Families in Society, 80,* 25–33.

Sameroff, A. J., & Fiese, B. H. (2000). Transactional regulation: The developmental ecology of early intervention. In J. P. Shonkoff & S. J. Meisels (Eds.), *The handbook of early childhood intervention* (pp. 135–159). Cambridge, UK: Cambridge University Press.

Sandall, S., McLean, M. E., & Smith, B. J. (2000). *DEC recommended practices in early intervention/early childhood special education.* Longmont, CO: Sopris West.

Santelli, B., Turnbull, A., Marquis, J., & Lerner, E. (2000). Statewide parent-to-parent programs: Partners in early intervention. *Infants & Young Children, 13,* 74–86.

Santelli, B., Turnbull, A., Sergeant, J., Lerner, E., & Marquis, J. (1996). Parent-to-parent programs: Parent preferences for supports. *Infants and Young Children, 9,* 53–62.

Silverstein, M., Sand, N., Glascoe, F. P., Gupta, V. B., Tonniges, T. P., & O'Connor, K. G. (2006). Pediatrician practices regarding referral to early intervention services: Is an established diagnosis important? *Ambulatory Pediatrics, 6,* 105–109.

Simeonsson, R. J., & McMillen, J. S. (2001). Clinical assessment in planning and evaluating intervention. In R. J. Simeonsson & S. L. Rosenthal (Eds.), *Psychological and developmental assessment: Children with disabilities and chronic conditions* (pp. 32–50). New York: Guilford Press.

Simeonsson, R. J., McMillen, J. S., & Huntington, G. S. (2002). Secondary conditions in children with disabilities: Spina bifida as a case example. *Mental Retardation and Developmental Disabilities Research Reviews, 8,* 198–205.

Singer, G. S., Marquis, J., Powers, L. K., Blanchard, L., Divenere, N., Santelli, B., Ainbinder, J. G., & Sharp, M. (1999). A multi-site evaluation of parent-to-parent programs for parents of children with disabilities. *Journal of Early Intervention, 22*(3), 217–229.

Spiker, D., Hebbeler, K., & Mallik, S. (2005). Developing and implementing early intervention programs for children with established disabilities. In M. J. Guralnick (Ed.), *A developmental systems approach to early intervention* (pp. 305–349). Baltimore: Brookes.

Stoneman, Z. (1985). Family involvement in early childhood special education programs. In N. Fallon & W. Umansky (Eds.), *Young children with special needs* (pp. 442–469). Columbus, OH: Merrill.

Trivette, C. M., & Dunst, C. J. (2000). Recommended practices in family-based practices. In S. Sandall, M. E. McLean, & B. J. Smith (Eds.), *DEC recommended practices in early intervention and early childhood special education* (pp. 39–46). Longmont, CO: Sopris West.

Trivette, C. M., Dunst, C. J., & Deal, A. G. (1997). Resource-based approach to early intervention. In S. K. Thurman, J. R. Cornwell, & S. R. Gottwald (Eds.), *Contexts of early intervention: Systems and settings* (pp. 73–92). Baltimore: Brookes.

Turnbull, A. P., Summers, J. A., Turnbull, R., Brotherson, M. J., Winton, P., Roberts, R., Stroup-Rentier, V. (2007) Family supports and services in early intervention: A bold vision. *Journal of Early Intervention, 29*(3), 187–206.

Turnbull, A. P., Turbiville, V., & Turnbull, H. R. (2000). Evolution of family-professional partnerships: Collective empowerment as the model for the early twenty-first century. In J. P. Shokoff & S. J. Meisels (Eds.), *Handbook of early childhood intervention* (pp. 630–650). New York: Cambridge University Press.

Umstead, S., Boyd, K., & Dunst, C. J., (1995). Building community resources: Enabling inclusion in community programs and activities. *Exceptional Parent, 25*(7), 36–37.

Vaux, A. (1988). *Social support: Theory, research, and intervention.* New York: Praeger.

Vig, S., & Kaminer, R. (2003). Comprehensive interdisciplinary evaluation as intervention for young children. *Infants & Young Children, 16,* 342–353.

Warren, S. F., & Brady, N. C. (2007). The role of maternal responsivity in the development of children with intellectual disabilities. *Mental Retardation & Developmental Disabilities Research Reviews, 13*(4), 330–338.

Wilson, L. L., Mott, D. W., & Batman, D. (2004). The asset-based context matrix: A tool for assessing children's learning opportunities and participation in natural environments. *Topics in Early Childhood Special Education, 24*(2), 110–120.

Winton, P. J., Sloop, S., & Rodriguez, P. (1999). Parent education: A term whose time is past. *Topics in Early Childhood Special Education, 19,* 157–161.

Wolraich, M. L., Gurwitch, R. H., Bruder, M. B., & Knight, L. A. (2005). The role of comprehensive interdisciplinary assessments in the early intervention system. In M. J. Guralnick (Ed.), *A developmental systems approach to early intervention,* (pp. 215–234). Baltimore: Brookes.

Woods, J., Kashinath, S., & Goldstein, H. (2004). Effects of embedding caregiver-implemented teaching strategies in daily routines on children's communication outcomes. *Journal of Early Intervention, 26*(3), 175–193.

Woods, J. J., & Lindeman, D. P. (2008). Gathering and giving information with families. *Infants & Young Children, 21*(4), 272–284.

Yoder, P. J., & Warren, S. F. (1998). Maternal responsivity predicts the prelinguistic communication intervention that facilitates generalized intentional communication. *Journal of Speech, Language, and Hearing Research, 41,* 1207–1219.

Zhang, C., Bennett, T., & Dahl, M. (1999). Family-centered practice in early intervention service delivery: A case study. *Infant-Toddler Intervention, 9,* 331–351.

Section XII

Early Identification and Intervention in Exceptionality

Section Editor: Maureen A. Conroy
University of Florida

Early childhood is considered a critical period of growth and development for children. During this time, children's brains are continuing to develop and thus, intervention is likely to make the most impact (National Scientific Council on the Developing Child, 2004). Through early identification and intervention we can prevent, ameliorate, and lessen the impact of a number of developmental risk factors for young children (see Guralnick, 1998) as well as accelerate growth in young children who are potentially gifted (see chapter by Brighton & Jarvis, this section). Not only are we able to improve children's developmental functioning, which results in improving school readiness; early intervention also helps families and caregivers increase their ability to support their child's development and is cost effective (Guralnick, 1997). In fact, when young children receive early intervention services, they are less likely to require special education services in the future.

Fortunately, early intervention for infants, toddlers, and preschoolers at risk for or with disabilities has a long history and rich research base. Through many years of federal funding, we have a plethora of evidence-based comprehensive intervention programs and effective instructional strategies available for use in early childhood settings. Since 1986, we have seen a large growth in the number of infants, toddlers, and preschoolers with developmental disabilities that access services under the Individuals with Disabilities Education Act (Individuals with Disabilities Education Act Data, 2009). In the past 10 years, we have also seen a rapid growth in the number of young children at elevated risk who receive services under state funding preschool programs (Barnett, Epstein, Friedman, Boyd, & Hustedt, 2009). Unfortunately, many of these young children do not receive the most appropriate or necessary and sufficient services needed to maximize their developmental trajectories. Additionally, when services are provided, early interventionists often do not use the instructional strategies and comprehensive programming that we know are effective. If our experience, knowledge, and research in the field of early intervention are so strong, then why is there such a gap between our research, policies, and practices? To address this question, this section explores the history, critical features, and challenges of early identification and intervention services for infants, toddlers, and preschool age children who have special needs. We also explore models of service delivery and examine the challenges our field faces in providing the most appropriate and efficacious services for young children and their families. A common theme across the chapters is the incongruent relationship between our policies, practices in early childhood settings, and what our research suggests is most effective. There seems to be relatively little association between *what we know* to be effective and *what most children receive* in early intervention settings. As we increase our knowledge and advocate for the most appropriate services, I hope this section of the handbook will help guide our future efforts in research, policy, and practices for these young children and their families.

References

Barnett, W. S., Epstein, D. J., Friedman, A. H., Boyd, J. S., & Hustedt, J. T. (2009). *The state of preschool 2008.* Rutgers, NJ: National Institute for Early Education Research, Rutgers, The State University of New Jersey. Retrieved on November 17, 2009, from http://nieer.org/facts/

Guralnick, M. J. (Ed.). (1997). *The effectiveness of early intervention.* Baltimore: Brookes.

Guralnick, M. J. (1998). Effectiveness of early intervention for vulnerable children: A developmental perspective. *American Journal of Mental Retardation, 102,* 319–345.

Individuals with Disabilities Education Act Data. (2009, November 3). IDEA 618 Data Tables. Retrieved from https://www.ideadata.org/arc_toc9.asp#partbCC

National Scientific Council on the Developing Child. (2004, Winter). *Children's emotional development is built into the architecture of their brain.* Working paper No. 2. Cambridge, MA: Author.

51

Advances in Theory, Assessment, and Intervention with Infants and Toddlers with Disabilities

Carl J. Dunst
Orelena Hawks Puckett Institute

Early intervention with infants and toddlers with disabilities, developmental delays, and those at-risk for poor outcomes due to biological or environmental factors has a rich history (Dunst, 1996). Early intervention as practiced in the United States can be divided into two distinct time periods: Pre- and post-passage of the 1986 Education of the Handicapped Act Part H early intervention legislation. Prior to the Part H legislation, the focus of early intervention was the learning opportunities and experiences afforded infants and toddlers to affect changes in the children's behavior and development (e.g., Barsch, 1967; Dunst, 1981; Lambie, Bond, & Weikart, 1975). The Part H legislation, and subsequent reauthorization of that legislation, significantly changed this emphasis by shifting focus away from development-enhancing child learning opportunities and experiences to the provision of professional services. This chapter includes descriptions of both approaches to early intervention with a focus on the manner to which the IDEA Part C Infant and Toddler Program is not consistent with contemporary theory and research about the characteristics and consequences of early intervention most likely to be effective in influencing child and parent behavior.

The chapter is divided into four sections. The first section includes descriptions of three models for conceptualizing early intervention based on different but compatible premises about how to best practice early intervention. The second section includes descriptions of different assessment practices with an emphasis on eligibility determination and intervention planning. The third section includes descriptions of different intervention practices that emphasize the active participation of both parents and their infants and toddlers in development-enhancing learning opportunities and experiences strengthening adult and child functioning. The fourth section includes a discussion of the fact that Part C early intervention has not kept pace with advances in theory, assessment, and intervention, and why infants and toddlers receiving Part C early intervention may not be experiencing the kinds of practices that are most likely to have optimal positive benefits. The chapter concludes with thoughts about future directions for early intervention research, practice, and policy.

Contemporary Models of Early Intervention

Early intervention as practiced in the 1960s and 1970s was informed primarily by developmental and behavioral theories, including, but not limited to, Piaget's (1952) theory of infant development and infant operant learning theory (Bijou & Baer, 1961). Once considered different world views that were incompatible (Reese & Overton, 1970), the two theories were subsequently integrated and used to guide the development and implementation of early intervention in the early 1980s (Dunst, 1982).

The 1980s witnessed the adoption and use of social- and family-systems theory (Bronfenbrenner, 1979; Cochran & Brassard, 1979; Garbarino, 1982) for informing early intervention (e.g., Dunst, 1985). These theoretical orientations placed early intervention in the context of the formal and informal social supports that influenced parents' abilities to engage their children in development-enhancing learning opportunities (e.g., Cochran & Brassard, 1979). Bronfenbrenner (1979), for example, noted in his descriptions of social systems influences that the ability to parent effectively is dependent, in part, on the supports and resources available from social support network members providing parents the time and energy to interact with their children in ways positively affecting their children's learning and development.

Three representative models are described next to illustrate how research has informed the development of different approaches to early intervention. The three models include key features from both child development and family/social systems theories. The three models are Guralnick's (2001) developmental systems model of early intervention, Odom and Wolery's (2003) unified theory of practice in early intervention, and Dunst's (2004, 2005b) integrated framework for practicing early intervention and family support. All three models differ from earlier theories used to inform early intervention practices by the fact that they were specifically developed to guide the conceptualization and implementation of early childhood intervention based on research evidence.

Developmental Systems Model

Guralnick's (2005) developmental systems model focuses on three types of parenting roles affecting child development (quality of parent–child transactions, family-orchestrated child learning experiences, and child health and safety provided by the family); the different child, parent, family, and social network factors that affect and influence these parenting roles; and the child development outcomes that are the consequences of parent-mediated (orchestrated) child learning. According to Guralnick (2001), early childhood interventionists provide or mediate the provision of assistance "designed to support family patterns of interactions that best promote children's development" (p. 15). The evidence base for the practices constituting the foundations of Guralnick's (2001) systems model include "contemporary developmental thinking [that] are consistent with existing empirical information" (p. 15).

Unified Theory Approach

Odom and Wolery (2003) proposed a unified theory of early childhood intervention practice that includes eight tenets and 3 to 5 practices for each tenet based on an accumulated body of research evidence for each of the practices. The tenets of the evidence-based practices include: (a) families and homes are primary nurturing contexts, (b) strengthening relationships is an essential feature of early childhood intervention, (c) children learn through acting on and observing their environment, (d) adults mediate children's experiences to promote learning, (e) children's participation in more developmentally advanced settings is necessary for successful and independent participation in those settings, (f) early childhood intervention practice is individually and dynamically goal oriented, (g) transitions across programs are enhanced by a developmentally instigative adult, and (h) families and programs are influenced by the broader contexts in which they are embedded. The unified theory provides a framework for the adoption and use of practices that, taken together, increase the likelihood that children and their families benefit from early intervention.

Integrated Framework Model

The integrated framework proposed by Dunst (2000, 2005b) for practicing evidence-based early childhood intervention and family support includes four major components (children's learning opportunities, parenting supports, family/community supports, and capacity-building help-giving practices) and three intersecting components (everyday activity settings, caregiver interactional behavior, and participatory parenting opportunities). Each major and intersecting component includes practices that research

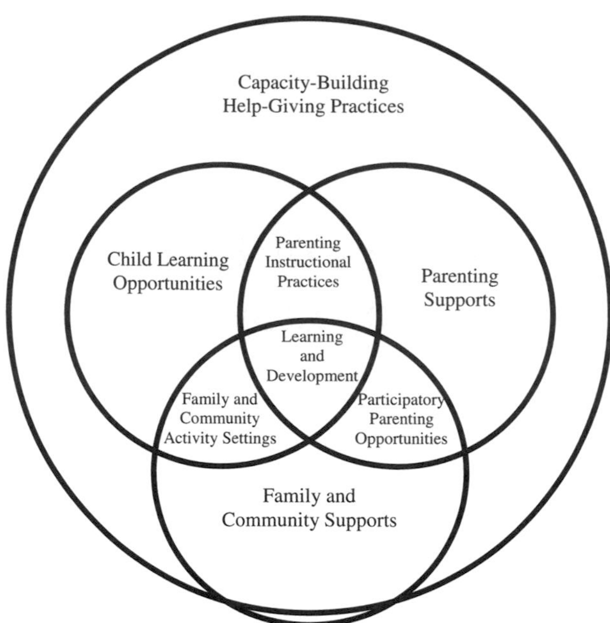

Figure 51.1 1 Seven components of an evidence-based, integrated framework for practicing early childhood intervention and family support.

indicates matter most in terms of strengthening child, parent, and family functioning (e.g., Dunst, 2007a; Dunst, Trivette, & Hamby, 2007).

Figure 51.1 shows the integrated framework. The focus of intervention is practitioners' use of capacity-building help-giving practices to ensure parents have the necessary supports and resources to provide their children development-enhancing learning opportunities in everyday activity settings (natural environments) where the parents' interactive behavior with their children in those settings both supports and strengthens child and parent competence and confidence.

The research that provides the evidence base for the integrated framework includes the help-giving practices associated with parent capacity-building consequences (e.g., Trivette & Dunst, 2007), the caregiver interactional behavior associated with child competence (e.g., Trivette, 2007), and the kinds of social supports associated with positive parent and family functioning (Dunst, Trivette, & Jodry, 1997). Results from a recently completed meta-analysis showed that capacity-building help-giving practices, and the social supports and resources available to families, were indirectly related to parent-child interactions and child development mediated by both parents' self-efficacy beliefs and parent well-being in a manner consistent with the hypothesized relationships of the integrated framework (Trivette, Dunst, & Hamby, in press). Research syntheses on individual components of the integrated framework provide evidence demonstrating the important role self-efficacy beliefs play in explaining the relationships between practitioners' and social network members' behavior and both parent and child outcomes (see Dunst & Trivette, 2009a).

Theory informing the conceptualization and implementation of early childhood intervention during the second half of the 20th century was and continues to be essentially overlooked as part of Part H/C early intervention. Part H/C early intervention is an atheoretical enterprise where implicit assumptions are not based on prior knowledge and understanding but rather generally unfounded contentions. The assumption that services, for example, provided to infants and toddlers will de facto strengthen family capacity (an explicit goal of Part C early intervention) is not only illogical but inconsistent with evidence showing the manner in which parenting competence and confidence is influenced by the ways supports are provided by informal and formal social network members, and how parenting behavior in turn affects child learning and development.

Assessment Practices

Both assessment and evaluation play central roles in determining eligibility for early intervention and developing and implementing intervention plans and practices (McLean & McCormick, 1993). Assessment practices have traditionally been divided into screening, evaluation, intervention planning, and progress monitoring (e.g., Simeonsson & Bailey, 1988). With few exceptions (e.g., Bagnato, 2005), developmental scales such as the *Bayley Scales of Infant and Toddler Development* (Bayley, 2006) and *the Ages and Stages Questionnaire* (Bricker, Squires, Mounts, Nickel, Twombly, & Farrell, 1998) have been the instruments of choice for assessment and evaluation in Part C early intervention (e.g., Danaher, 2005).

Infants and toddlers who are eligible for Part C early intervention must have an identified condition known to be associated with poor developmental outcomes or a developmental delay as determined by each state's definition of delay (Shackelford, 2006). States may, at their discretion, serve children who are at-risk for developmental delays because of biological or environmental risk factors. (Most states and jurisdictions [N = 48] no longer serve at-risk children, while other states are contemplating the elimination of this eligibility category; Danaher, Goode, & Lazara, 2007.) As defined in the Part C early intervention legislation and regulations, initial and ongoing evaluation are conducted by a multi-disciplinary team of qualified personnel, whereas assessment is used to identify a child's strengths and needs, and the services to meet those needs, and parents' resources, priorities, and supports to enhance a family's capacity to meet the needs of their child.

As part of activities at the Tracking, Referral, and Assessment Center for Excellence (TRACE), the evaluation and assessment practices used in Part C programs were examined to identify which practices were most reliable and valid. In the process, we found many misunderstandings and misuses of evaluation and assessment scales and results (e.g., Neisworth & Bagnato, 2004). This section of the chapter includes information about four different assessment-related practices and how those practices can inform both eligibility determination and intervention.

Eligibility Determination

One finding at TRACE was misinterpretation of the IDEA Part C eligibility criteria. The act includes the provision that states are required to serve infants and toddlers with diagnosed or identified conditions that are associated with poor developmental outcomes. We found many cases where those children were deemed ineligible because they had no developmental delays. (Infants and toddlers with identified conditions [e.g., Down syndrome] without developmental delays are de facto eligible for early intervention.) A second finding was that the evaluation procedures for determining eligibility were unnecessarily complex and often resulted in wasted time and resources.

To clarify and streamline the eligibility determination process, a decision-making algorithm was developed at TRACE based on research findings and best practices for ensuring accurate decision making about eligibility (e.g., Medical Algorithms Project, 2006). The decision algorithm, shown in Figure 51.2, involves a finite number of steps where the decisions at each step (i.e., answer to a question) is *yes* or *no* (Dunst, 2005a). The five steps include the criteria in the IDEA Part C legislation in the left hand column and a states' specific criteria in the middle column. Each step and associated questions are used to facilitate an eligibility determination. This simple and rather straightforward procedure was tested on children enrolled in early intervention and found accurate in nearly all cases.

In many cases, states have developed unnecessary and cumbersome eligibility determination procedures. The President's Commission on Special Education (2001), for example, concluded that "IDEA establishes complex requirements that are difficult to effectively implement at the state and local level. Nowhere in IDEA is this more complex than the eligibility determination process" (p. 21). Methods and procedures like the TRACE eligibility determination algorithm could significantly simplify the ways in which eligibility is determined so that the focus of Part C practices is the provision of evidence-based interventions rather than the conduct of unnecessary child evaluations.

Presumptive Eligibility

Many different kinds of children's programs use a procedure called *presumptive eligibility* for expediting enrollment of young children in health care, human services, and other programs (e.g., Klein, 2003). Presumptive eligibility is a process that uses existing information at the time of referral or application, rather than a lengthy evaluation process, to determine eligibility. Brown and Brown (1993) recommended use of the procedure to facilitate the eligibility determination of infants and toddlers who have identified conditions or disabilities that are covered by federal and state early intervention legislation.

Another finding at TRACE was the lack of use of presumptive eligibility to enroll infants and toddlers in Part C early intervention when eligibility was obvious. A study by Mott and Dunst (2006) of more than 180 infants and toddlers receiving Part C early intervention found that presump-

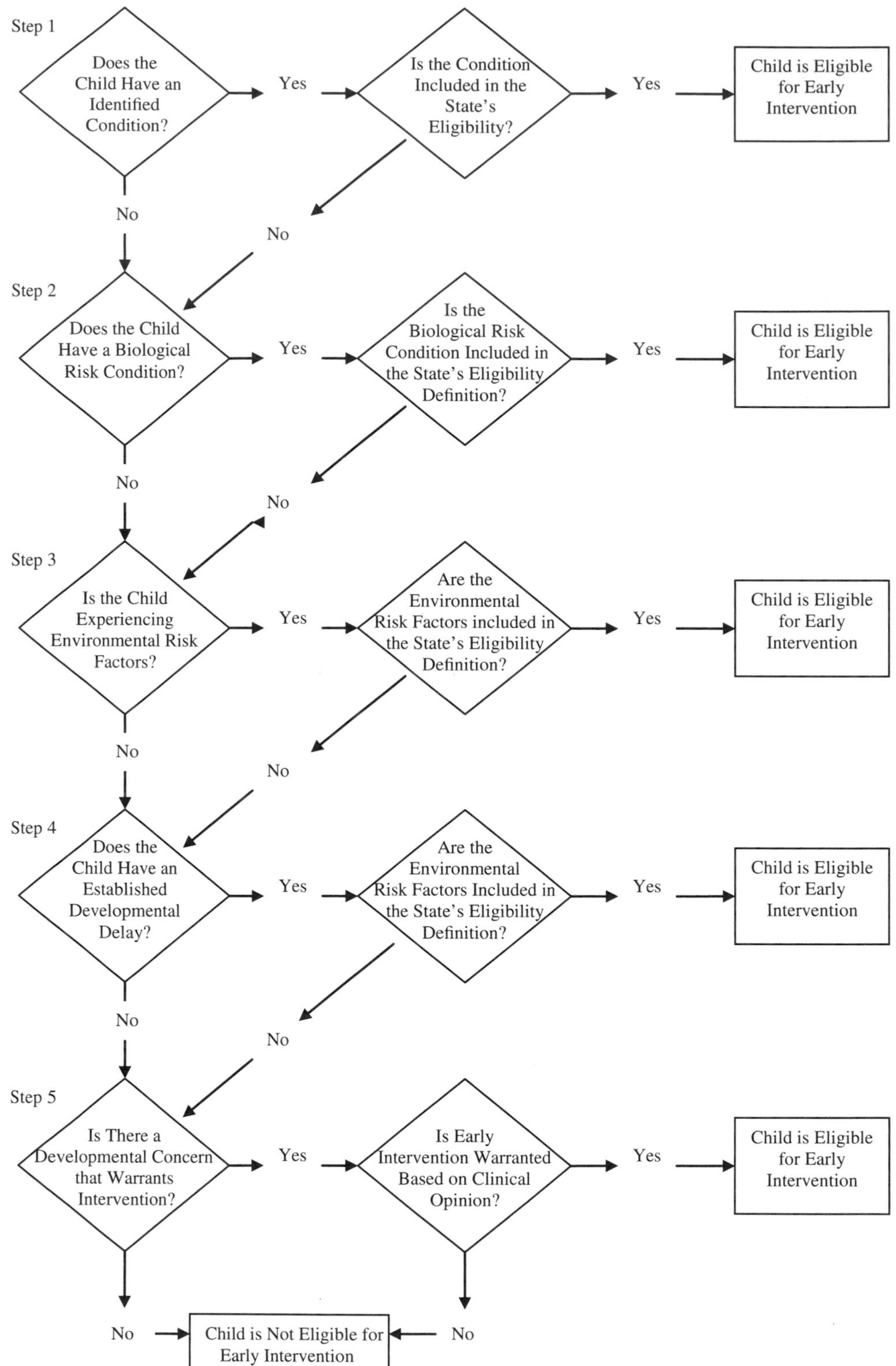

Figure 51.2 A decision algorithm for determining infant and toddler eligibility for early intervention.

tive eligibility was used for only 18% of the children, but could have been used for an additional 66% of the children; developmental evaluations were needed to determine eligibility for 24% of the children, but an additional 31% of the children received developmental evaluations not needed to determine eligibility; and 83% of delayed eligibility decisions were due to cumbersome bureaucratic procedures or developmental evaluations not needed for eligibility determination. If presumptive eligibility was used to expedite enrollment of infants and toddlers in early intervention, then assessment practices could focus on intervention planning, where the experiences and opportunities used to promote child learning and development, were a main focus of the assessment process.

Strengths-Based Assessment Practices

Although the IDEA Part C regulations include the statement that child assessments include the identification of a "child's unique strengths and needs" (see 303.322 (2)(i)), it goes on to say that assessments are used to identify "the services appropriate to meet [a child's] needs" (303.322(2)(i)) where children's strengths are never mentioned again. As part of analyses of some 300 individualized family service plans (IFSPs) in eight different states, not a single plan or any specific activity or service on the plans incorporated children's strengths into the interventions or used children's strengths as the foundations for promoting child development (Dunst, Bruder, Trivette, Raab, & McLean, 1998).

The assessment of infants and toddlers receiving Part C early intervention focus almost entirely on what children cannot do where interventions in turn target behavior children are not capable of doing. This deficit-based assessment-intervention practice is exacerbated by the fact that Part C early intervention places so much emphasis on child outcomes rather than the experiences and opportunities that support existing abilities and promote acquisition of new child competencies. It is still common to find that infants and toddlers are administered traditional assessment scales, where the first set of items not passed on those scales are used as the outcomes on IFSPs.

An alternative assessment practice focuses on the existing and emerging behavior children "can do" and provides children opportunities to use those behaviors in ways strengthening existing competence and providing opportunities to learn new skills. Strengths include a person's interests, preferences, likes, abilities, competencies, and skills. A number of strengths-based assessment tools have been developed for identifying children's strengths (e.g., Dunst, Roberts, & Snyder, 2004; Moss, 2006; Rugg & Stoneman, 2004).

Strengths-based assessment practices not only differ from more traditional assessments by focusing on what children can do but also by focusing on the kinds of activities (experiences, opportunities, etc.) that are the contexts for interest and competence expression. For example, as part of a line of research on everyday child learning in the context of family and community activities, we first identified children's strengths (interests, preferences, abilities, etc.) and then identified those activities that provided opportunities for the children to use those strengths (Dunst, Bruder, et al., 2001; Dunst, Trivette, & Cutspec, 2007). Results showed that the children demonstrated statistically significant positive behavioral and developmental outcomes in as few as 14 to 16 weeks.

Strengths-based assessment practices could significantly improve how interventions are developed and implemented by shifting focus to the things children can do and the experiences that provide opportunities to practice existing abilities and learn new behavior (e.g., DuBose, 2002; Graybeal, 2001; Wolery, 2004). The extent to which strengths-based assessment practices are likely to be adopted by Part C programs as either an alternative or a supplement to deficit-based assessment practices awaits future analyses.

Ecological Assessment

Ecological theories of development (e.g., Bronfenbrenner, 1992; Moen, Elder, & Lüscher, 1995) and ecological models of assessment and intervention (Dunst, 2008; Thurman, 1997; Thurman & Widerstrom, 1990; Wolery, Brashers, & Neitzel, 2002) focus on the assessment of behavior-in-context, how both setting and person factors influence that behavior, and how events beyond immediate settings have direct and indirect effects on behavior-in-context. Wachs and Sheehan (1988), for example, defined an ecological approach to assessment as the "systematic, purposeful collection of data, reflecting both patterns of children's emergent abilities to comprehend and function in their environment and the factors associated with the emergence of these patterns" (p. viii).

Ecological approaches to assessment differ from traditional approaches to assessment in three ways. First, they focus of the assessment of functional and adaptive behavior that permits a child to interact with his or her social and nonsocial environment in intentional, meaningful, and efficacious ways. In contrast, traditional approaches to assessment typically focus on the extent to which a child can produce behavior on some type of developmental scale or instrument (e.g., Bayley, 2006). Second, ecological approaches to assessment appraise child behavior in the context of typically occurring, everyday activities such as meal time, bed time, play, parent child story book reading, etc. In contrast, traditional approaches to assessment typically are conducted in settings unfamiliar to a child or under conditions that are incongruent with behavior setting expectations (e.g., administering a developmental test to a child in his or her home while seated in a high chair). Third, ecological approaches to assessment emphasize the identification of those factors that influence child participation in everyday activities and variations of child behavior in those activities. In contrast, traditional approaches to assessment almost entirely ignore the factors influencing variations in child behavior and focus almost entirely on what a child can and cannot do.

Different approaches to ecological assessment tend to emphasize different determinant factors, but all place emphasis on the implications of determinants for informing intervention practices (e.g., Bagnato, 2005; Dunst, 2008; Thurman, Cornwell, & Gottwald, 1997). The determinants often examined as part of an ecological assessment include, but are not limited to, the characteristics and features of everyday activities and settings, the characteristics of materials available in those activities and settings, child characteristics (e.g., strengths, interests, preferences), adult behavior (e.g., parenting styles and interactional practices), and parent well-being and confidence. Wolery (2004), for example, describes the information needed to conduct ecological assessments and plan meaningful interventions which include information about the child, environments, and schedules (routines); the dimensions of the intervention settings; and family concerns and priorities.

Table 51.1 lists the determinant variables constituting the focus of the Dunst (2008) ecological framework for assessing infant and toddler behavior. The six categories include the settings that are the contexts for child learning; the characteristics of the settings and the materials available in the settings; the child characteristics that encourage participation and display of competence; the interactional behavior adults use to support, encourage, and reinforce child competence; the parent characteristics that shape and influence positive caregiving behavior; and the extrafamily factors that shape and influence parenting confidence and competence. As noted by Thurman and Widerstrom (1990), "To be valid and complete, ecological assessment must consider the relationship between the child in a variety of different settings and activities [and] take into account" determinant factors (pp. 191–192). The goal or outcome of an ecological assessment is the identification of those factors that influence or are related to variations in child behavior-in-context, where that information is used for developing and implementing either or both formal and informal interventions for affecting changes in child interactive capabilities (Dunst, 2008).

The IDEA Part C Infant and Toddler Program (34 C.F.R. § 303 (2007), as well as the proposed rulemaking for the program (U.S. Department of Education, 2007), define assessment in terms of the identification of a child's level of functioning in five areas of development (cognitive, physical, communication, social or emotional, adaptive). More often than not, this has been interpreted to mean the administration of an assessment scale that yields developmental ages where the items that are first failed on the scales are used to develop IFSP outcomes. Some states, for example, now have lists of "approved" assessment scales that early intervention practitioners are required to use (e.g., Danaher et al., 2007). In those cases where IDEA Part C legislation and regulations refer to the determinant side of the assessment process, they are described entirely in terms of services and only implicitly in terms of other factors. Such a perspective and approach has most certainly not kept pace with advances in assessment practices with infants and toddlers, and as well certainly fails to consider other factors that are important determinants of child learning and development (e.g., Dent-Read & Zukow-Goldring, 1997; Garbarino, 1992; Wachs, 2000).

TABLE 51.1
Categories and Examples of Determinants in an Ecological Approach to Assessment

Category	Types of Determinants
Settings	Everyday activities, parenting routines, child routines, play activities, family outings, etc.
Environmental	Material availability, material characteristics, physical adaptations, etc.
Child	Behavior state, interests, strengths, competencies, etc.
Interactional	Parenting styles, interactional behavior, instructional practices, teaching methods
Parent	Well-being, self-efficacy beliefs, confidence, competence, parenting enjoyment
Systems	Social support, resources, parenting advice/guidance

Intervention Practices

The past 25 years has been productive in terms of advances in our understanding of the characteristics of early intervention practices that are associated with positive child and parent benefits (e.g., Guralnick, 1997; Wolery & Bailey, 2002). Five practices are described next which, taken together, constitute the key features of a caregiver-mediated approach to early intervention (Dunst, 2006; Dunst & Swanson, 2006). The practices are: child participatory learning opportunities, interest-based child learning, everyday natural learning environments, responsive caregiver interactions, and capacity-building help-giving practices. The five practices are related to one another in the following ways. Natural learning environments are used as the contexts for interest-based child participatory learning opportunities where parents' responsiveness to their children's behavior is used to support and reinforce child competence. Practitioners strengthen family capacity to use these types of early intervention practices using capacity-building help-giving practices.

Participatory Child Learning Opportunities

Active child involvement in participatory child learning opportunities is now known to be an important factor influencing infant and toddler development. Bronfenbrenner (1992) called these types of experiences *development-instigating* learning opportunities which invite and encourage children to act on the social and nonsocial environment that make up their everyday lives. The behavioral and developmental consequences of "active learner participation" in producing environmental effects and consequences has been demonstrated in studies of animals (e.g., Held & Hein, 1963), preschoolers (e.g., Riksen-Walraven, 1978), older children and adolescents (e.g., Lerner & Busch-Rossnagel, 1981), and younger and older adults (e.g., Brandtstädter & Lerner, 1999).

As noted by Odom and Wolery (2003), children learn through acting on and observing their environment where the experiences afforded children provide them opportunities to "learn about, master, understand, and control their worlds" (p. 167). Research indicates that when infants and toddlers are provided opportunities to interact with people and objects that are responsive to children's behavior initiations, the children come to understand that they are the agents of the consequences of their actions and demonstrate a sense of mastery, often by manifesting social-emotional behavior (Tarabulsy, Tessier, & Kappas, 1996). A sense of understanding and mastery in turn propels infants and toddlers to remain engaged in interactions with people and objects providing the children additional learning opportunities to practice existing abilities and acquire new competencies through exploration and by "testing out" newly acquired skills (e.g., Hupp & Abbeduto, 1991).

Findings from a research synthesis of the operant learning of young children with and without disabilities indicated that young children demonstrate a sense of mastery after "coming to understand" that they produced the observed environmental consequences of their behavior (Dunst, 2007b). As part of a line of research on the active learning of profoundly delayed and multiply disabled infants and toddlers, my colleagues and I examined the consequences of engaging these children in interactions with people, toys, and other material that were highly responsive in terms of the children acting on their environments. The outcomes included enhanced child learning and displays of mastery both during the learning opportunities and while the children were not playing "active learning games" (Dunst, Raab, Trivette, Parkey, et al., 2007; Dunst, Raab, Trivette, Wilson, et al., 2007; Raab, Dunst, Wilson, & Parkey, 2009). All the children increased the frequency and intensity of acting on their environments while engaged in the learning games. In addition, all the children demonstrated social-emotional behavior (smiles, laughter, vocalizations, excitement) both during the learning games used to promote the development of contingency behavior and after the children had finished playing the games.

There is evidence that many of the practices (services) used by Part C early intervention practitioners do not actively involve infants and toddlers in interactions with their social and nonsocial environment but rather primarily elicit behavior from the children in response to adult demands or requests, or engage the children in passive actions or movements. This suggests that many Part C interventions may not be optimally effective in promoting children's learning and development. For example, many of the therapies used by Part C practitioners, and which States consider appropriate early intervention services, do not intentionally engage infants and toddlers in active participation in interactions with people or objects (IDEA Infant and Toddler Coordinators Association, 2002; McWilliam, 1999). Passive range of movement exercises are one example of this kind of practice. (This practice may be effective for preventing certain muscular problems, but is not likely to promote child learning and development.) As part of the analysis of the practices on some 300 IFSPs, we found that many of the interventions manipulated the children to "go through the motions" (Dunst et al., 1998).

A common practice used by early intervention practitioners, and especially with very low functioning children who manifest few intentional behaviors, is the use of noncontingent stimulation to elicit or evoke child responses. (Shaking a rattle to elicit head turning is an example of this kind of activity.) In a study of the response-contingent learning of young children with multiple disabilities and profound developmental delays, we determined the efficiency of contingent and noncontingent stimulation on children's learning (Dunst, Raab, Wilson, & Parkey, 2007). The noncontingent (baseline) condition consisted of observations of early childhood practitioners implementing intervention activities they typically used with the children. The contingent (intervention) condition involved the use of active learning games to promote children's use of behavior that produced some type of interesting or reinforcing consequence. Results showed that it took, on average, about 125 active game episodes for the children to produce 100 behaviors having environmental consequences. In contrast, it took, on average, more than 1,700 noncontingent stimulation episodes for the children to produce 100 behavior having environmental consequences. Findings of this sort indicate that the use of noncontingent stimulation as an intervention practice is not indicated if the goal is increased child competence.

Interest-Based Child Learning

One factor that functions as a development-instigating characteristic of learning opportunities is children's interests. According to Renninger, Hidi, and Krapp (1992), there are two kinds of interests: personal and situational. Personal interests are the preferences and likes that an individual possesses (e.g., an infant who prefers to be in an upright position). Situational interests include those aspects of the social and nonsocial environment that attract child attention, curiosity, and engagement in interactions with people and objects (e.g., happening upon a puppy while on a neighborhood walk). Both kinds of interests have positive effects on child behavior and development (Raab & Dunst, 2007).

Research has blossomed in terms of our understanding of the characteristics and consequences of interest-based child learning (e.g., Barron, 2006; O'Sullivan, 1997; Renninger, 1998; Schraw & Lehman, 2001) and how this type of learning influences the behavior and development of young children with or without disabilities (see Raab & Dunst, 2007). Experiences and opportunities that are interest-based are more likely to engage children in prolonged interactions with people and objects and provide contexts for practicing existing capabilities and learning new behavior.

Studies of young children reveal the impact of interest-based learning on child behavior and development. These studies have investigated the influence of the interest-based learning of children with (e.g., Boyd, Conroy, Mancil, Nakao, & Alter, 2007; Vismara & Lyons, 2007) and without (e.g., DeLoache, Simcock, & Macari, 2007) disabilities. Studies of the influence of interest-based learning on the behavior and development of young children with autism show that children who participated in interest-based learning activities demonstrated more positive and less negative social-emotional behavior and made more developmental progress compared to children whose learning opportunities were less interest-based (Dunst, Masiello, & Trivette, 2009; Trivette, Dunst, & Masiello, 2009).

Available evidence suggests that many, if not most, Part C early intervention practices do not use or incorporate children's interests into intervention activities. This can be illustrated by the results from a study by Campbell and

Sawyer (2007), who compared the characteristics of traditional vs. participation-based early intervention practices. Participation-based practices include children's interest in the social and nonsocial environment as one factor encouraging child engagement. The investigators found that this practice was more likely to engage children in everyday activities where early intervention practitioners used mediated practices to promote child competence but that practitioners preferred, and more often used, traditional early intervention practices. An extensive review of the published literature, as well as Google and Google Scholar searches, found no studies or papers that described interest-based child learning in Part C early intervention, although both Google searches yielded hits that included the "call-for-adoption" of interest-based practices.

Natural Learning Environments

According to IDEA Part C regulations, natural environments "means settings that are natural or normal for the child's age peers who have no disabilities" (Sec. 303.18). In most cases, the word *settings* has been interpreted to mean a child's home, a childcare classroom, or some community program or location (e.g., library). These kinds of settings are not de facto natural learning environments because one can think of all kinds of circumstances where these places and locations are not sources of development-instigating experiences and opportunities (e.g., Hart & Risley, 1995). For example, as part of a study investigating the learning opportunities afforded young children in community programs and organizations, we found many places where the experiences afforded young children with disabilities were neither developmentally instigating nor developmentally appropriate, and some cases, were even development-impeding (Dunst, 2001).

Dunst, Trivette, Humphries, Raab, and Roper (2001) proposed a three-dimensional framework for capturing the different ways in which natural environments have been conceptualized and interpreted. An updated version of that framework is shown in Figure 51.3. The framework includes six different types of natural environments by the combination of type of intervention (services vs. everyday activity settings), type of activity (child-initiated vs. adult-directed), and intervener (parent vs. practitioner). The type of intervention dimension differentiates between services provided in natural environments and everyday activity settings that are used as sources of natural learning opportunities. Activity settings are the everyday activities, routines, experiences, and events that make up a child's life and which are contexts for learning contextually meaningful and functional behavior (Farver, 1999). The type of activity dimension differentiates between child-initiated engagement in natural environments and adult-directed child participation in natural environments. The intervener dimension differentiates between parent-mediated and practitioner-implemented interventions.

In a series of studies investigating different ways of conceptualizing natural environments, findings showed that parent-mediated interventions which were child-initiated in the context of everyday activity settings were associated with the most positive consequences (Dunst et al. 2001; Dunst, Bruder, Trivette, & Hamby, 2005, 2006; Dunst, Trivette, & Cutspec, 2007; Dunst, Trivette, Hamby, & Bruder, 2006). Several major findings emerged from these studies. First, these kinds of interventions provided young

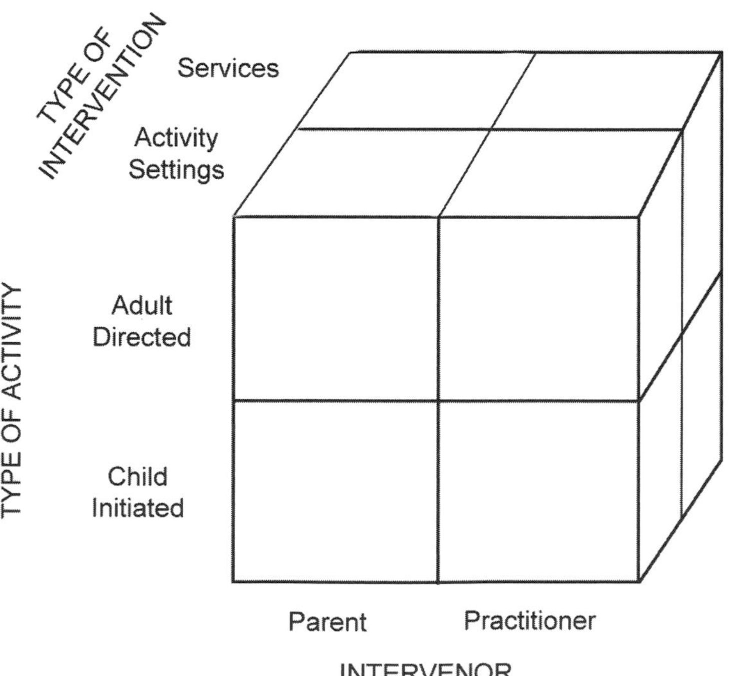

Figure 51.3 Framework for categorizing different types of natural learning environment practices.

children more natural learning opportunities compared to practitioner-implemented interventions (Dunst et al., 2005). Second, interest-based and child-initiated participation in everyday activities was associated with more positive child and parent benefits compared to parent-directed child learning opportunities (Dunst, Bruder, Trivette, Hamby, Raab, & McLean, 2001; Dunst, Trivette, & Cutspec, 2007; Trivette, Dunst, & Hamby, 2004). Third, the use of everyday activities as sources of natural learning opportunities was associated with more positive child and parent benefits compared to provision of services in natural environments (Dunst, Bruder, Trivette, & Hamby, 2006; Dunst, Trivette, et al., 2006).

The provision of services in natural environments is worth noting because this is how the IDEA Part C natural environment provision is most often interpreted (e.g., Hanft & Pilkington, 2000; Walsh, Rous, & Lutzer, 2000). In our own research (Dunst, Bruder, et al., 2006), as well as research by others (e.g., Gallimore, Weisner, Bernheimer, Guthrie, & Nihira, 1993; Kellegrew, 2000), findings indicate that implementing services in everyday family and community activities can have negative rather than positive effects (e.g., attenuating parents' sense of confidence) if the interventions are not supportive of family life. This is easily understood and explained. The everyday activities that make up family life have highly personal and cultural meaning, where disruptions of the activities are likely to have a negative impact. Therefore, there is reason to challenge the provision of early intervention services in everyday activities without understanding the conditions under which the interventions are implemented in order to have positive consequences.

Responsive Caregiver Interactions

Research syntheses of parents' interactional behavior with their infants and toddlers highlight the development-enhancing effects of a responsive caregiving style (e.g., Dunst & Kassow, 2008; Nievar & Becker, 2008; Richter, 2004). Findings from studies of caregiver interactions with young children with disabilities also show that responsiveness to children's behavior has development-enhancing effects (Trivette, 2007) despite the fact that many parents of children with disabilities tend to use more directive interactive behavior that may have development-impeding consequences (Marfo, 1991).

The particular characteristics of a responsive interactional style that are most important in terms of explaining positive child consequences are now known (Dunst & Kassow, 2008; Nievar & Becker, 2008). The characteristics that stand out as most important are the ability to perceive and interpret a child's behavior as an intent to interact or affect an environmental consequence, caregiver contingent responsiveness in amounts proportional to the child's behavior, and joint and reciprocal turn taking during interactive episodes. Behavioral interventions that focus specifically on caregiver awareness and accurate interpretation of, and contingent social responsiveness to, children's behavior have been found to be most effective for promoting parents' use of a responsive interactional style (Bakermans-Kranenburg, van IJzendoorn, & Juffer, 2003; Dunst & Kassow, 2008).

A number of different teaching and instructional methods use caregiver responsiveness for affecting the behavior and development of young children with disabilities (e.g., Kaiser & Hancock, 2003; Mahoney, Perales, Wiggers, & Herman, 2006; Raab & Dunst, 2009; Yoder & Warren, 1998). The Raab and Dunst (2009) version of responsive teaching, for example, includes both key features of caregiver behavior known to be the active ingredients of positive child benefits (e.g., sensitivity to child cues, contingent responsiveness, turn taking) and children's interests and active (participatory) child engagement in joint interactions as important elements of the teaching method. Responsive teaching, and its many variants, have been found effective in producing positive changes in the behavior of young children with disabilities (e.g., Charlop-Christy & Carpenter, 2000; Kaiser et al., 1996; Peterson, 2005; Yoder & Warren, 2001).

Evidence suggests that many Part C practitioners do not routinely promote families' use of responsive teaching methods or strategies. As part of a study of young children's everyday natural learning opportunities (Dunst & Bruder, 1999), we investigated the early childhood intervention practices used with 50 children with disabilities and their parents in eight states. The investigation included analyses of the instructional methods practitioners recommended or taught parents to use with their children. The most frequently identified practice was repeated presentation of the same task until children demonstrated targeted behavior. Neither responsive teaching, nor any of the key features of the practice, were generally mentioned by the parents.

As part of a number of intervention studies we conducted, where caregiver responsiveness was the instructional practice used by parents to promote child competence, we almost uniformly find that practitioners who were working with the study participants were not aware that the practice existed nor were they knowledgeable about the key features of the practice. Therefore, it appears to be the case that Part C early intervention may not be employing optimally effective teaching methods.

Capacity-Building Help-Giving Practices

The ways in which early intervention practitioners engage parents and other caregivers in providing infants and toddlers development-enhancing learning opportunities matter a great deal if family capacity is likely to be strengthened (e.g., Affleck, Tennen, Rowe, Roscher, & Walker, 1989; Andrews & Andrews, 1993). Capacity-building help-giving practices are now practices of choice based on findings from research syntheses and meta-analyses of family-centered help-giving practice research (Dempsey & Keen, 2008; Dunst, Trivette, & Hamby, 2007; Rosenbaum, King, Law, King, & Evans, 1998).

Trivette and Dunst (2007), based on factor analyses of the items on the *Helpgiving Practices* Scale (Trivette & Dunst, 1994), identified two components of capacity-building help-giving practices: Relational and participatory. Relational help-giving includes practices typically associated with good clinical practice (e.g., active listening, compassion, empathy, and respect) and help-giver positive beliefs about family member strengths and capabilities. Listening to a family's concerns and asking for clarification or elaboration about what was said are examples of a relational help-giving practice. Participatory help-giving includes practices that are individualized, flexible, and responsive to family concerns and priorities, and that actively involve parents in both making informed choices and acting on those choices to achieve desired goals and outcomes. Engaging a family member in learning how to use information to make an informed decision about child care for his or her child and seeking out a child care program is an example of a participatory help-giving practice. Whereas relational practices build trust and communication between practitioners and parents, participatory practices build and strengthen family capacity to meet family members needs, solve problems, improve life circumstances, and promote family member confidence and competence, including parent provision of development-enhancing child learning opportunities.

Two meta-analyses completed by Dunst et al. (2006, 2008) examined the relationships between both relational and participatory help-giving practices and a number of different child, parent, and family outcomes, including parenting competence and confidence. One meta-analysis included 18 studies all conducted in the same early intervention and family support program (*N* = 1,100 participants). The other meta-analysis included 52 studies conducted in seven different countries (*N* = 12, 211 participants). Both syntheses were guided by a theoretical model that hypothesized the direct effects of capacity-building help-giving on parent, family, and child behavior, and indirect effects on the same outcomes mediated by self-efficacy beliefs (Dunst et al., 2008).

Findings from both syntheses were very much alike (see Dunst & Trivette, 2009a). Both relational and participatory help-giving practices were related to all child, parent, and family outcomes, where the strength of the relationships were strongest for outcomes that included appraisals of program benefits (e.g., program supports) and weaker but nonetheless statistically significant for outcomes not including program-related appraisals (e.g., family well-being). Relational and participatory help-giving were also indirectly related to the majority of study outcomes mediated by self-efficacy beliefs. The results most germane to the goal of strengthening family-capacity showed that both types of help-giving practices were directly and indirectly related to parenting competence and confidence, where the strengths of the relationships were strongest for the indirect effects of participating help-giving on both outcomes mediated by self-efficacy beliefs.

Additional findings from several recently completed meta-analytic structural equation modeling (Cheung & Chan, 2005) studies identified the manner in which capacity-building help giving practices had indirect effects on parent and child psychological health (Dunst & Trivette, 2009b) and parent-child interactions and child development (Trivette et al., in press). In the former meta-analysis, help-giving had indirect effects on parent and child health mediated by self-efficacy beliefs. In the latter meta-analysis, capacity-building help-giving practices (as well as family-systems intervention practices) had direct effects on parent self-efficacy beliefs, and indirect effects on both parent-child interactions and child development mediated by both parent self-efficacy beliefs and parent well-being. The pathways from capacity-building help-giving practices and the different outcomes were all as expected, and consistent with Bronfenbrenner's (1992) hypothesized relationships between the ways in which supports (help) are provided to parents to affect their parenting beliefs and well-being, which, in turn, influence the ways in which they interact with their children.

The largest majority of Part C early intervention practitioners claim they use family-centered practices (e.g., McBride, Brotherson, Joanning, Whiddon, & Demmitt, 1993; McWilliam, Snyder, Harbin, Porter, & Munn, 2000). Findings from an extensive review and analysis of studies of family-centered practices in early intervention, preschool, elementary, and secondary programs and classrooms generally do not support those claims (Dunst 1998, 2002). While it is the case that early intervention practitioners are more family-centered than are preschool and school teachers, early intervention practitioners often fare poorly in terms of their use of relational and especially participatory (capacity-building) practices.

Not only are early intervention practitioners not as family-centered as they claim, but parents' judgments of the practitioners' help-giving practices become less family-centered the longer the parents are involved in early childhood intervention. This can be illustrated with data from a study of more than 650 parents whose children were involved in Part C early intervention and Part B preschool special education programs (Dunst, 1998). Parents were asked to indicate on a 7-point scale the extent to which the practitioner working most closely with his/her child and family used 10 different family-centered practices. The percent of indicators, rated a 6 or 7 on the 7-point scale, was used as the criterion of establishing the use of family-centered practices. The results are shown in Figure 51.4. Two things "stand out" as particularly important. First, the percentage of indicators rated a 6 or 7 are not very high at any age, indicating that many practitioners were judged as not using family-centered practices. Second, the older a child, the smaller the percentage of indicators that were assessed as consistent with family-centeredness. Further analysis showed that the downward trend was a function of parents having more experience with the practitioners and having more information on which to make their judgments. The longer the families were involved in early childhood interventions programs, the less family-centered they judged the practitioners' behavior.

The fact that practitioners are not as family-centered as they generally believe can also be illustrated with findings

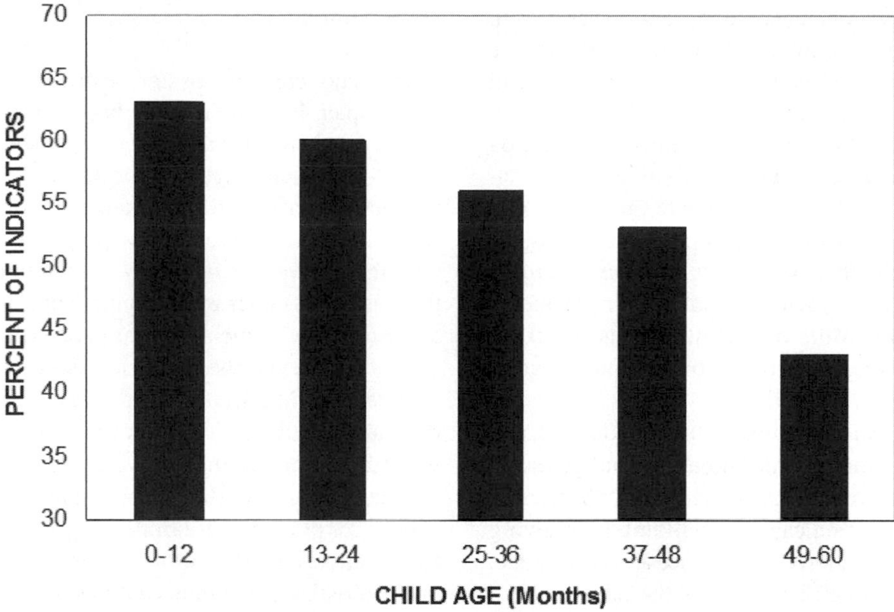

Figure 51.4 Percentage of practice indicators judged as family-centered by parents of young children in Part C early intervention and Part B(619) preschool special education programs.

from a study of the adherence to family-centered relational and participatory help-giving practices (Dunst & Trivette, 2005). The data are for a 14-year period of time all collected in the same early intervention and family support program once directed by the author. Each year, program participants were asked to complete a family-centered practices scale where the parents indicated on a 5-point scale the extent to which the practitioner working most closely with his/her family demonstrated the use of different relational and participatory help-giving practices. The percentage of indicators rated a 5 was the measure for assessing adherence to family-centered practices. The criterion used to assess adherence was 85% of the indicators in any one year. Adherence was achieved in only three years for the relational practices and in only one year for the participatory practices, hardly evidence to claim family-centeredness. This was the case despite the fact that a concerted effort was made to promote practitioners' adoption and use of family-centered and capacity-building help giving practices (e.g., Dunst, Trivette, & Thompson, 1990; Trivette, Dunst, & Hamby, 1996).

Part C Early Intervention

Early intervention for infants and toddlers and their families in the United States has come to be synonymous with the Individual with Disabilities Education Improvement Act (PL 108-446) Part C Infants and Toddlers with Disabilities Program. This legislation, and the regulations that govern the Act (Early Intervention Program for Infants and Toddlers with Disabilities, 34 C.F.R. § 303, 2007), have proven to be a two-edged sword. On the one hand, the act "provides Federal funds to make available early intervention for infants and toddlers with disabilities (from birth to age three) and their families" that otherwise might not be available (p. 26457). On the other hand, both the legislation and regulations have become stagnant where required and proposed activities are not in line with contemporary knowledge, practice, and research. In terms of the practices constituting the focus of this chapter, it seems fair to say that what changes have been made since the passage of PL 99-457 have been mostly cosmetic, and at best, constitute tweaking rather than substantive updating.

The proposed rulemaking for IDEA Part C published in the May 9, 2007, *Federal Register* (U.S. Department of Education, 2007), which includes the most recent proposed changes, are used to illustrate the contention that IDEA Part C has not kept pace with advances in theory, assessment, and intervention with only a few exceptions. Early intervention continues to be defined in terms of services and not the experiences and opportunities that are known to promote infant and toddler development. Proposed changes do include the provision that early intervention services on IFSPs be based on "peer-reviewed research," but as already noted, there is little evidence that service-based early intervention is effective.

The proposed rulemaking continues to state that assessments "identify the child's unique strengths and needs," but as has been the case in the regulations governing Part C, the focus of assessment and intervention is on what children cannot do, and no where is it even implied that infant and toddler strengths be incorporated into the interventions afforded young children. Why identify children's strengths if they are not used as development-instigating child (personal) or environmental (situational) factors promoting children's active participation in interactions with people and objects?

Natural environments continue to be defined in terms of

locations and the provision of early intervention services in those locations rather than the everyday activities that are contexts for learning functional and culturally meaningful behavior. If anything, the proposed rulemaking strongly encourages the provision of a type of early intervention which will likely increase the probability that natural environmental practices will be disruptive to family life and therefore be potentially harmful. The proposed changes, for example, would require that the *frequency, intensity, length,* and *duration* of services provided in natural environments be specified on IFSPs. More of something that is not effective provided for longer periods of time cannot be good for a child and family.

The term *family capacity* continues to be ill-defined, and the proposed rulemaking provides no additional guidance to determine if Part C practices are consistent with research on the relationship between capacity-building help-giving practices and parent and family competence and confidence. Family capacity is defined in terms of the supports and services necessary to meet the developmental needs of a family's infant or toddler with a disability. This definition, which differs from the original intent of Congress (U.S. Congress House of Representatives Committee on Education and Labor, 1986), is nebulous and not consistent with the conditions under which family capacity is supported and strengthened.

There is one practice in the proposed rulemaking that implies the use of presumptive eligibility. The proposed rule states that "A child's medical condition and other records may be used to establish eligibility (without conducting an assessment of the child or family) if those records contain information…regarding the child's level of functioning" in the required areas (34 C.F.R. § 303, 2007, p. 26459). There is, however, a potential problem with this proposed addition; namely, the fact that it focuses on developmental information rather than identified conditions known to be associated with delays in the absence of intervention. It would be easy to see this addition "backfire" and reinforce the belief that a child must demonstrate a developmental delay to be eligible for Part C early intervention even when a child has an identified a disability or condition that is known to be associated with poor developmental outcomes without intervention.

Finally, there is little or no evidence in PL 108-446, and the proposed rulemaking for the act, to indicate that the infant and toddler program as a whole, or most of the required components of the act, are informed by models, theories, or frameworks that include practices that have been shaped and influenced by research or recommended practices (e.g., Guralnick, 1997; Odom & Wolery, 2003; Sandall, Hemmeter, Smith, & McLean, 2005). It would be challenging at best to try to formulate a theory of early intervention from the act and accompanying rule that "made sense" and was defensible. In fact, State Part C Coordinators say that their models and approaches to early intervention (service delivery) are not consistent with contemporary theory, research, and evidence-based practices (Hurth & Pletcher, 2009).

Discussion

Three major conclusions can be drawn from the content of this chapter. First, there have been significant advances in theory, assessment, and intervention since the passage of PL 99-457, including, but not limited to, the models and practices described in this chapter. Second, changes in the IDEA Part C early intervention program have not kept pace with these advances in theory, research, and practice, and the conditions under which family capacity is strengthened and child development is optimized. Third, there is an urgent need to revise the Part C legislation to move it into the 21st century. Much of what the Part C infant and toddler program is "all about" looks like early intervention as it was practiced more than 25 years ago.

The findings reported in this chapter have several implications for practice, research, and policy. The implications for practice include the need for equal attention to the characteristics of the interventions used to affect child and family outcomes of interest, and the adoption and use of practices that research indicates is most likely to produce optimal positive consequences. Quality rather than quantity is likely to be the key ingredient of effective practices. For example, whereas Dunst, Hamby, and Brookfield (2007) found frequency and intensity of early intervention services were negatively related to parent functioning, Bailey, Nelson, Hebbler, and Spiker (2007) found that the quality of early intervention practices were positively related to parent outcomes.

There is a particular need for more attention to the practice side of the intervention and outcome relationship. Practices that have no evidence base, or where evidence indicates they have development-impeding characteristics and consequences, should not be used. For example, the use of noncontingent stimulation and other interventions that discourage active child participation in interactions with the social and nonsocial environment should be discontinued.

There are a number of implications for research. While much is known about the characteristics of effective early intervention practices, much still needs to be learned. For example, more research is needed on natural learning environment practices, and especially the conditions under which child (e.g., interests) and environmental (e.g., activity setting features) factors influence child behavior and development in everyday activities. Similarly, much is left to be learned about the specific characteristics of parent-professional interactions that enhance or compromise a family's capacity to engage young children in everyday activities having development-enhancing characteristics and consequences.

There is also a need for more studies that investigate the complex relationships among child, parent, family, practitioner, and social network factors that support and strengthen parents' capacity to provide their children development-enhancing learning opportunities. These types of studies, including meta-analyses of these complex relationships (e.g., Dunst & Trivette, 2009b; Trivette et al., in press), have been the recent focus of research by my colleagues and myself. The yield is a better understanding of the pathways through which person and environmental factors are directly and indirectly related to parent and child behavior and development. These kinds of studies can help identify the characteristics of and conditions under which different types of early intervention practices influence family capacity to provide children development enhancing learning opportunities.

The primary implication for policy is the need to update the Part C Infant and Toddler Program legislation and regulations in light of contemporary theory, knowledge, and research. The changes that are indicated include the following. The definition of *early intervention* needs to be changed to emphasize the experiences and opportunities that are known to strengthen and promote infant and toddler competence and development. The definition of *natural environment* needs to be changed to mean the everyday family, community, and classroom activities that are the contexts for meaningful child learning. The *outcomes* of early intervention need to be changed to include those functional and adaptive behaviors that permit active child participation in everyday activity. The term *assessment* needs to be expanded to include ecologically relevant practices that more directly inform intervention. *Child assessments* need to be changed to include the identification of a child's strengths, capabilities, and needs, and the incorporation of strengths and existing capabilities into interventions. The term *family capacity* needs to be changed to mean those experiences and opportunities afforded parents and other primary caregivers that strengthen both their competence and confidence to provide their children everyday, participatory learning activities. *Instructional strategies* need to be expanded to include those characteristics of instructional methods that support and strengthen child competence and development. The *roles and responsibilities* of early intervention (not service) providers need to be changed to emphasize the use of capacity-building help-giving practices to support and strengthen family capacity. The term *scientifically-based* needs to be defined as research that has identified those characteristics of early intervention practices (e.g., as described in this chapter) that are most likely to strengthen and support both parent and child competence and confidence. These are but a few of the many changes in the Part C legislation and regulations that are indicated by contemporary theory, knowledge, and research.

The extent to which the IDEA Part C Infant and Toddler Program is likely to be changed and updated to reflect contemporary theory, research, and practice would require considerable redesign of the act and the regulations for the act. Regardless of whether this happens, advances will continue to be made that inform early intervention, and especially early intervention that strengthens family capacity to use parent-mediated child learning opportunities to promote the development of infants and toddlers with disabilities. The assessment and intervention practices described in this chapter suggest how this can be accomplished.

References

Affleck, G., Tennen, H., Rowe, J., Roscher, B., & Walker, L. (1989). Effects of formal support on mothers' adaptation to the hospital-to-home transition of high-risk infants: The benefits and costs of helping. *Child Development, 60*, 488–501.

Andrews, M. A., & Andrews, J. R. (1993). Family-centered techniques: Integrating enablement into the IFSP process. *Journal of Childhood Communication Disorders, 15*, 41–46.

Bagnato, S. J. (2005). The authentic alternative for assessment in early intervention: An emerging evidence-based practice. *Journal of Early Intervention, 28*, 17–22.

Bailey, D. B., Jr., Nelson, L., Hebbler, K., & Spiker, D. (2007). Modeling the impact of formal and informal supports for young children with disabilities and their families. *Pediatrics, 120*, 992–1001.

Bakermans-Kranenburg, M. J., van IJzendoorn, M. H., & Juffer, F. (2003). Less is more: Meta-analyses of sensitivity and attachment interventions in early childhood. *Psychological Bulletin, 129*, 195–215.

Barron, B. (2006). Interest and self-sustained learning as catalysts of development: A learning ecology perspective. *Human Development, 49*, 153–224.

Barsch, R. H. (1967). The infant curriculum: A concept for tomorrow. In J. Hellmuth (Ed.), *Exceptional Infant: Volume 1. The normal infant* (pp. 6–10). New York: Brunner Mazel.

Bayley, N. (2006). *Bayley Scales of Infant and Toddler Development* (3rd ed.). San Antonio, TX: Psychological Corporation.

Bijou, S. W., & Baer, D. M. (1961). *Child development: Vol. 1. A systematic and empirical theory*. New York: Appleton-Century-Crofts.

Boyd, B. A., Conroy, M. A., Mancil, G. R., Nakao, T., & Alter, P. J. (2007). Effects of circumscribed interests on the social behaviors of children with autism spectrum disorders. *Journal of Autism and Developmental Disorders, 37*, 1550–1561.

Brandtstädter, J., & Lerner, R. M. (Eds.). (1999). *Action and self-development: Theory and research through the life span*. Thousand Oaks, CA: Sage.

Bricker, D., Squires, J., Mounts, L., Nickel, R., Twombly, E., & Farrell, J. (1998). *Ages and stages questionnaire (ASQ): A parent completed, child-monitoring system* (2nd ed.). Baltimore: Brookes.

Bronfenbrenner, U. (1979). *The ecology of human development: Experiments by nature and design*. Cambridge, MA: Harvard University Press.

Bronfenbrenner, U. (1992). Ecological systems theory. In R. Vasta (Ed.), *Six theories of child development: Revised formulations and current issues* (pp. 187–248). Philadelphia: Jessica Kingsley.

Brown, W., & Brown, C. (1993). Defining eligibility for early intervention. In W. Brown, S. K. Thurman, & L. F. Pearl (Eds.), *Family-centered early intervention with infants and toddlers: Innovative cross-disciplinary approaches* (pp. 21–42). Baltimore: Brookes.

Campbell, P. H., & Sawyer, L. B. (2007). Supporting learning opportunities in natural settings through participation-based services. *Journal of Early Intervention, 29*, 287–305.

Charlop-Christy, M. H., & Carpenter, M. H. (2000). Modified incidental teaching sessions: A procedure for parents to increase spontaneous speech in their children with autism. *Journal of Positive Behavior Interventions, 2*, 98–112.

Cheung, M. W., & Chan, W. (2005). Meta-analytic structural equation modeling: A two-stage approach. *Psychological Methods, 10*(1), 40–64.

Cochran, M., & Brassard, J. (1979). Child development and personal social networks. *Child Development, 50*, 601–616.

Danaher, J. (2005, January). Eligibility policies and practices for young children under Part B of IDEA. *NECTAC Notes,* (No. 15), 1–18. Chapel Hill: National Early Childhood Technical Assistance Center, The University of North Carolina.

Danaher, J., Goode, S., & Lazara, A. (Eds.). (2007). *Part C updates* (9th ed.). Chapel Hill: University of North Carolina, FPG Child Development Institute, National Early Childhood Technical Assistance Center.

DeLoache, J. S., Simcock, G., & Macari, S. (2007). Planes, trains, automobiles—and tea sets: Extremely intense interests in very young children. *Developmental Psychology, 43*, 1579–1586.

Dempsey, I., & Keen, D. (2008). A review of processes and outcomes in family-centered services for children with a disability. *Topics in Early Childhood Special Education, 28*, 42–52.

Dent-Read, C., & Zukow-Goldring, P. (Eds.). (1997). *Evolving explanations of development: Ecological approaches to organism-environment systems*. Washington, DC: American Psychological Association.

DuBose, T. (2002). Family-centered, strengths-based assessments with special needs children: A human-science approach. *Humanistic Psychologist, 30*, 125–135.

Dunst, C. J. (1981). *Infant learning: A cognitive-linguistic intervention strategy.* Allen, TX: DLM.

Dunst, C. J. (1982). Theoretical bases and pragmatic considerations. In J. Anderson (Ed.), *Curricula for high-risk and handicapped infants* (pp. 13–23). Chapel Hill, NC: Technical Assistance Development System.

Dunst, C. J. (1985). Rethinking early intervention. *Analysis and Intervention in Developmental Disabilities, 5*, 165–201.

Dunst, C. J. (1996). Early intervention in the USA: Programs, models, and practices. In M. Brambring, H. Rauh, & A. Beelmann (Eds.), *Early childhood intervention: Theory, evaluation, and practice* (pp. 11–52). Berlin, Germany: de Gruyter.

Dunst, C. J. (1998). Family-centered practices in early intervention, preschool, elementary and secondary schools. In T. Bryan, R. Gersten, L. Irving, & T. Keating (Eds.), *The relationship between professional practices and family involvement: A review of research. Final report* (pp. 52–94). Washington, DC: U.S. Department of Education, Office of Special Education Programs.

Dunst, C. J. (2000). Revisiting "Rethinking early intervention". *Topics in Early Childhood Special Education, 20*, 95–104.

Dunst, C. J. (2001). Participation of young children with disabilities in community learning activities. In M. J. Guralnick (Ed.), *Early childhood inclusion: Focus on change* (pp. 307–333). Baltimore: Brookes.

Dunst, C. J. (2002). Family-centered practices: Birth through high school. *Journal of Special Education, 36*, 139–147.

Dunst, C. J. (2004). An integrated framework for practicing early childhood intervention and family support. *Perspectives in Education, 22*(2), 1–16.

Dunst, C. J. (2005a). An eligibility determination algorithm for Part C early intervention enrollment. *TRACE Practice Guide: Eligibility Determination, 1*(1), 1–7. Retrieved from http://www.tracecenter.info/practiceguides/practiceguides_vol1_no1.pdf

Dunst, C. J. (2005b). Framework for practicing evidence-based early childhood intervention and family support. *CASEinPoint, 1*(1), 1–11. Retrieved October 30, 2008, from http://www.fippcase.org/caseinpoint/caseinpoint_vol1_no1.pdf

Dunst, C. J. (2006). Parent-mediated everyday child learning opportunities: I. Foundations and operationalization. *CASEinPoint, 2*(2), 1–10. Retrieved from http://www.fippcase.org/caseinpoint/caseinpoint_vol2_no2.pdf

Dunst, C. J. (2007a). Early intervention with infants and toddlers with developmental disabilities. In S. L. Odom, R. H. Horner, M. Snell, & J. Blacher (Eds.), *Handbook of developmental disabilities* (pp. 161–180). New York: Guilford Press.

Dunst, C. J. (2007b). *Social-emotional consequences of response-contingent learning opportunities* (Winterberry Research Syntheses Vol. 1, No. 16). Asheville, NC: Winterberry Press.

Dunst, C. J. (2008). *An ecological framework for assessing infant and toddler development: Revised and updated* (Winterberry Assessment Scales and Instruments). Asheville, NC: Winterberry Press.

Dunst, C. J., & Bruder, M. B. (1999). Family and community activity settings, natural learning environments, and children's learning opportunities. *Children's Learning Opportunities Report, 1*(2), 1–2. Retrieved from http://www.everydaylearning.info/reports/lov1-2.pdf

Dunst, C. J., Bruder, M. B., Trivette, C. M., & Hamby, D. W. (2005). Young children's natural learning environments: Contrasting approaches to early childhood intervention indicate differential learning opportunities. *Psychological Reports, 96*, 231–234.

Dunst, C. J., Bruder, M. B., Trivette, C. M., & Hamby, D. W. (2006). Everyday activity settings, natural learning environments, and early intervention practices. *Journal of Policy and Practice in Intellectual Disabilities, 3*, 3–10.

Dunst, C. J., Bruder, M. B., Trivette, C. M., Hamby, D., Raab, M., & McLean, M. (2001). Characteristics and consequences of everyday natural learning opportunities. *Topics in Early Childhood Special Education, 21*, 68–92.

Dunst, C. J., Bruder, M. B., Trivette, C. M., Raab, M., & McLean, M. (1998, May). *Increasing children's learning opportunities through families and communities early childhood research institute: Year 2 progress report*. Asheville, NC: Orelena Hawks Puckett Institute.

Dunst, C. J., Hamby, D. W., & Brookfield, J. (2007). Modeling the effects of early childhood intervention variables on parent and family well-being. *Journal of Applied Quantitative Methods, 2*, 268–288.

Dunst, C. J., & Kassow, D. Z. (2008). Caregiver sensitivity, contingent social responsiveness, and secure infant attachment. *Journal of Early and Intensive Behavior Intervention, 5*, 40–56.

Dunst, C. J., Masiello, T., & Trivette, C. M. (2009). *Exploratory analyses of the effects of interest-based learning on the development of young children with autism*. Manuscript submitted for publication.

Dunst, C. J., Raab, M., Trivette, C. M., Parkey, C., Gatens, M., Wilson, L. L., … & Hamby, D. W. (2007). Child and adult social-emotional benefits of response-contingent child learning opportunities. *Journal of Early and Intensive Behavior Intervention, 4*, 379–391.

Dunst, C. J., Raab, M., Trivette, C. M., Wilson, L. L., Hamby, D. W., Parkey, C., … & French, J. (2007). Characteristics of operant learning games associated with optimal child and adult social-emotional consequences [Electronic version]. *International Journal of Special Education, 22*(3), 13–24.

Dunst, C. J., Raab, M., Wilson, L. L., & Parkey, C. (2007). Relative efficiency of response-contingent and response-independent stimulation on child learning and concomitant behavior. *Behavior Analyst Today, 8*, 226–236.

Dunst, C. J., Roberts, K., & Snyder, D. (2004). *Spotting my child's very special interests: A workbook for parents*. Asheville, NC: Winterberry Press.

Dunst, C. J., & Swanson, J. (2006). Parent-mediated everyday child learning opportunities: II. Methods and procedures. *CASEinPoint, 2*(11), 1–19. Retrieved from http://www.fippcase.org/caseinpoint/caseinpoint_vol2_no11.pdf

Dunst, C. J., & Trivette, C. M. (2005). *Measuring and evaluating family support program quality* (Winterberry Monograph Series). Asheville, NC: Winterberry Press.

Dunst, C. J., & Trivette, C. M. (2009a). Capacity-building family systems intervention practices. *Journal of Family Social Work, 12*, 119–143.

Dunst, C. J., & Trivette, C. M. (2009b). Meta-analytic structural equation modeling of the influences of family-centered care on parent and child psychological health. *International Journal of Pediatrics.* doi: 10.1155/2009/576840

Dunst, C. J., Trivette, C. M., & Cutspec, P. A. (2007). *An evidence-based approach to documenting the characteristics and consequences of early intervention practices* (Winterberry Research Perspectives Vol. 1, No. 2). Asheville, NC: Winterberry Press.

Dunst, C. J., Trivette, C. M., & Hamby, D. W. (2006). *Family support program quality and parent, family and child benefits* (Winterberry Monograph Series). Asheville, NC: Winterberry Press.

Dunst, C. J., Trivette, C. M., & Hamby, D. W. (2007). Meta-analysis of family-centered helpgiving practices research. *Mental Retardation and Developmental Disabilities Research Reviews, 13*, 370–378.

Dunst, C. J., Trivette, C. M., & Hamby, D. W. (2008). *Research synthesis and meta-analysis of studies of family-centered practices* (Winterberry Monograph Series). Asheville, NC: Winterberry Press.

Dunst, C. J., Trivette, C. M., Hamby, D. W., & Bruder, M. B. (2006). Influences of contrasting natural learning environment experiences on child, parent, and family well-being. *Journal of Developmental and Physical Disabilities, 18*, 235–250.

Dunst, C. J., Trivette, C. M., Humphries, T., Raab, M., & Roper, N. (2001). Contrasting approaches to natural learning environment interventions. *Infants and Young Children, 14*(2), 48–63.

Dunst, C. J., Trivette, C. M., & Jodry, W. (1997). Influences of social support on children with disabilities and their families. In M. Guralnick (Ed.), *The effectiveness of early intervention* (pp. 499–522). Baltimore: Brookes.

Dunst, C. J., Trivette, C. M., & Thompson, R. B. (1990). Supporting and strengthening family functioning: Toward a congruence between principles and practice. *Prevention in Human Services, 9*(1), 19–43.

Early Intervention Program for Infants and Toddlers with Disabilities, 34 C.F.R. § 303 (2007).

Farver, J. A. M. (1999). Activity setting analysis: A model for examining the role of culture in development. In A. Göncü (Ed.), *Children's engagement in the world: Sociocultural perspectives* (pp. 99–127). Cambridge, UK: Cambridge University Press.

Gallimore, R., Weisner, T. S., Bernheimer, L. P., Guthrie, D., & Nihira, K. (1993). Family responses to young children with developmental delays: Accommodation activity in ecological and cultural context. *American Journal on Mental Retardation, 98*, 185–206.

Garbarino, J. (1982). *Children and families in the social environment*. New York: Aldine.

Garbarino, J. (1992). *Children and families in the social environment* (2nd ed.). New York: de Gruyter.

Graybeal, C. (2001). Strengths-based social work assessment: Transforming the dominant paradigm. *Families in Society, 82*, 233–242.

Guralnick, M. J. (Ed.). (1997). *The effectiveness of early intervention*. Baltimore: Brookes.

Guralnick, M. J. (2001). A developmental systems model for early intervention. *Infants and Young Children, 14*(2), 1–18.

Guralnick, M. J. (Ed.). (2005). *The developmental systems approach to early intervention*. Baltimore: Brookes.

Hanft, B. E., & Pilkington, K. O. (2000). Therapy in natural environments: The means or end goal for early intervention? *Infants and Young Children, 12*(4), 1–13.

Hart, B., & Risley, T. R. (1995). *Meaningful differences in the everyday experience of young American children*. Baltimore: Brookes.

Held, R., & Hein, A. (1963). Movement-produced stimulation in the development of visually guided behavior. *Journal of Comparative Physiological Psychology, 56*, 872–876.

Hupp, S. C., & Abbeduto, L. (1991). Persistence as an indicator of mastery motivation in young children with cognitive delays. *Journal of Early Intervention, 15*, 219–225.

Hurth, J., & Pletcher, L. C. (2009, December). *Partners, not lone rangers: What it takes to change your early intervention service delivery*. Presentation made at the 2009 Office of Special Education Programs National Early Childhood Conference, Arlington, VA.

IDEA Infant and Toddler Coordinators Association. (2002, January). *Alternative or complementary therapies and approaches survey results*. Retrieved March 27, 2007, from http://www.ideainfanttoddler.org/hottpic3.htm

Kaiser, A. P., & Hancock, T. B. (2003). Teaching parents new skills to support their young children's development. *Infants and Young Children, 16*(1), 9–21.

Kaiser, A. P., Hemmeter, M. L., Ostrosky, M. M., Fischer, R., Yoder, P., & Keefer, M. (1996). The effects of teaching parents to use responsive interaction strategies. *Topics in Early Childhood Special Education, 16*, 375–406.

Kellegrew, D. H. (2000). Constructing daily routines: A qualitative examination of mothers with young children with disabilities. *American Journal of Occupational Therapy, 54*, 252–259.

Klein, R. (2003). Presumptive eligibility. *Future of Children, 13*, 230–237.

Lambie, D., Bond, J., & Weikart, D. (1975). Framework for infant education. In B. Z. Friedlander, G. M. Sterritt, & K. Girvin (Eds.), *Exceptional Infant: Vol. 3. Assessment and Intervention* (pp. 263–284). New York: Brunner/Mazel.

Lerner, R. M., & Busch-Rossnagel, N. A. (Eds.). (1981). *Individuals as producers of their development: A life-span perspective*. New York: Academic Press.

Mahoney, G., Perales, F., Wiggers, B., & Herman, B. (2006). Responsive teaching: Early intervention for children with Down Syndrome and other disabilities. *Down's Syndrome: Research and Practice, 11*, 18–28.

Marfo, K. (1991). The maternal directiveness theme in mother-child interaction research: Implications for early intervention. In K. Marfo (Ed.), *Early intervention in transition: Current perspectives on programs for handicapped children* (pp. 177–203). New York: Praeger.

McBride, S. L., Brotherson, M. J., Joanning, H., Whiddon, D., & Demmitt, A. (1993). Implementation of family-centered services: Perceptions of families and professionals. *Journal of Early Intervention, 17*, 414–430.

McLean, M., & McCormick, K. (1993). Assessment and evaluation in early intervention. In W. Brown, S. K. Thurman, & L. F. Pearl (Eds.), *Family-centered early intervention with infants and toddlers: Innovative cross-disciplinary approaches* (pp. 43–79). Baltimore: Brookes.

McWilliam, R. A. (1999). Controversial practices: The need for a reacculturation of early intervention fields. *Topics in Early Childhood Special Education, 19*, 177–188.

McWilliam, R. A., Snyder, P., Harbin, G. L., Porter, P., & Munn, D. (2000). Professionals' and families' perceptions of family-centered practices in infant-toddler services. *Early Education and Development, 11*, 519–538.

Medical Algorithms Project. (2006). *Decisional analysis: Overall accuracy, or diagnostic efficiency* (Chapter 39). Houston, TX: Institute for Algorithmic Medicine. Retrieved August 17, 2006, from http://www.medal.org/visitor/login.aspx

Moen, P., Elder, G. H., Jr., & Lüscher, K. (Eds.). (1995). *Examining lives in context: Perspectives on the ecology of human development*. Washington, DC: American Psychological Association.

Moss, J. (2006). *Child preference indicators: A guide for planning*. Oklahoma City, OK: University of Oklahoma Health Sciences Center, Center for Learning and Leadership. Retrieved May 23, 2007, from http://www.ouhsc.edu/thecenter/products/childpreference.html

Mott, D. W., & Dunst, C. J. (2006). Use of presumptive eligibility for enrolling children in Part C early intervention. *Journal of Early Intervention, 29*, 22–31.

Neisworth, J. T., & Bagnato, S. J. (2004). The mismeasure of young children: The authentic assessment alternative. *Infants and Young Children, 17*(3), 198–212.

Nievar, M. A., & Becker, B. J. (2008). Sensitivity as a privileged predictor of attachment: A second perspective on De Wolff and van IJzendoorn's meta-analysis. *Social Development, 17*, 102–114.

O'Sullivan, J. T. (1997). Effort, interest, and recall: Beliefs and behaviors of preschoolers. *Journal of Experimental Child Psychology, 65*, 43–67.

Odom, S. L., & Wolery, M. (2003). A unified theory of practice in early intervention/early childhood special education: Evidence based practices. *Journal of Special Education, 37*, 164–173.

Peterson, P. (2005). Naturalistic language teaching procedures for children at risk for language delays. *Insights on Learning Disabilities, 2*(2), 42–58.

Piaget, J. (1952). *The origins of intelligence in children*. New York: Norton.

President's Commission on Excellence in Special Education. (2001, July). *A new era: Revitalizing special education for children and their families*. Washington, DC: Author.

Raab, M., & Dunst, C. J. (2007). *Influence of child interests on variations in child behavior and functioning* (Winterberry Research Syntheses Vol. 1, No. 21). Asheville, NC: Winterberry Press.

Raab, M., & Dunst, C. J. (2009). *Magic seven steps to responsive teaching: Revised and updated* (Winterberry Practice Guides). Asheville, NC: Winterberry Press.

Raab, M., Dunst, C. J., Wilson, L. L., & Parkey, C. (2009). Early contingency learning and child and teacher concomitant social emotional behavior. *International Journal of Early Childhood Special Education, 1*(1), 1–14.

Reese, H. W., & Overton, W. F. (1970). Models of development and theories of development. In L. R. Goulet & P. B. Baltes (Eds.), *Life-span developmental psychology: Research and theory* (pp. 115–145). New York: Academic Press.

Renninger, K. A. (1998). The roles of individual interest(s) and gender in learning: An overview of research on preschool and elementary school-aged children/students. In L. Hoffman, A. Krapp, K. A. Renninger, & J. Baumert (Eds.), *Interest and learning: Proceedings of the Seeon Conference on Interest and Gender* (pp. 165–174). Kiel, Germany: IPN.

Renninger, K. A., Hidi, S., & Krapp, A. (Eds.). (1992). *The role of interests in learning and development*. Hillsdale, NJ: Erlbaum.

Richter, L. (2004). *The importance of caregiver-child interactions for the survival and healthy development of young children: A review*. Geneva, Switzerland: World Health Organization, Department of Child and Adolescent Health and Development.

Riksen-Walraven, J. M. (1978). Effects of caregiver behavior on habituation rate and self-efficacy in infants. *International Journal of Behavioral Development, 1*, 105–130.

Rosenbaum, P., King, S., Law, M., King, G., & Evans, J. (1998). Family-centred service: A conceptual framework and research review. *Physical and Occupational Therapy in Pediatrics, 18*(1), 1–20.

Rugg, M. E., & Stoneman, Z. (2004). *Take a Look at Me portfolio: A strengths-based self-discovery tool*. Athens: University of Georgia, Institute on Human Development and Disability.

Sandall, S., Hemmeter, M. L., Smith, B. J., & McLean, M. E. (2005). *DEC recommended practices: A comprehensive guide for practical application in early intervention/early childhood special education*. Longmont, CA: Sopris West.

Schraw, G., & Lehman, S. (2001). Situational interest: A review of the literature and directions for future research. *Educational Psychology Review, 13*, 23–52.

Shackelford, J. (2006, February). State and jurisdictional eligibility definitions for infants and toddlers with disabilities under IDEA. *NECTAC Notes* (No. 20), 1–16. Chapel Hill: National Early Childhood Technical Assistance Center, University of North Carolina.

Simeonsson, R. B., & Bailey, D. B., Jr. (1988). Essential elements of the assessment process. In T. D. Wachs & R. Sheehan (Eds.), *Assessment of young developmentally disabled children* (pp. 25–41). New York: Plenum Press.

Tarabulsy, G. M., Tessier, R., & Kappas, A. (1996). Contingency detection and the contingent organization of behavior in interactions: Implications for socioemotional development in infancy. *Psychological Bulletin, 120*, 25–41.

Thurman, S. K. (1997). Systems, ecologies, and the context of early intervention. In S. K. Thurman, J. R. Cornwell, & S. R. Gottwald (Eds.), *Contexts of early intervention: Systems and settings* (pp. 3–17). Baltimore: Brookes.

Thurman, S. K., Cornwell, J. R., & Gottwald, S. R. (Eds.). (1997). *Contexts of early intervention: Systems and settings*. Baltimore: Brookes.

Thurman, S. K., & Widerstrom, A. H. (1990). *Infants and young children with special needs: A developmental and ecological approach* (2nd ed.). Baltimore: Brookes.

Trivette, C. M. (2007). *Influence of caregiver responsiveness on the development of young children with or at risk for developmental disabilities* (Winterberry Research Syntheses Vol. 1, No. 12). Asheville, NC: Winterberry Press.

Trivette, C. M., & Dunst, C. J. (1994). *Helpgiving practices scale*. Asheville, NC: Winterberry Press.

Trivette, C. M., & Dunst, C. J. (2007). *Capacity-building family-centered helpgiving practices* (Winterberry Research Reports Vol. 1, No. 1). Asheville, NC: Winterberry Press.

Trivette, C. M., Dunst, C. J., & Hamby, D. W. (1996). Characteristics and consequences of help-giving practices in contrasting human services programs. *American Journal of Community Psychology, 24*, 273–293.

Trivette, C. M., Dunst, C. J., & Hamby, D. (2004). Sources of variation in and consequences of everyday activity settings on child and parenting functioning. *Perspectives in Education, 22*(2), 17–35.

Trivette, C. M., Dunst, C. J., & Hamby, D. W. (in press). Influences of family-systems intervention practices on parent-child interactions and child development. *Topics in Early Childhood Special Education*.

Trivette, C. M., Dunst, C. J., & Masiello, T. (2009). *Consequences of interest-based learning on the social-affective behavior of young children with autism*. Manuscript submitted for publication.

U.S. Congress House of Representatives Committee on Education and Labor. (1986, September). Education of the Handicapped Act Amendments of 1986 (99-860). Washington, DC: Author.

U.S. Department of Education. (2007, May 9). Part II: Early intervention program for infants and toddlers with disabilities; proposed rule. *Federal Register, 72*, 26455-26531.

Vismara, L. A., & Lyons, G. L. (2007). Using perseverative interests to elicit joint attention behaviors in young children with autism: Theoretical and clinical implications for understanding motivation. *Journal of Positive Behavior Interventions, 9*, 214–228.

Wachs, T. D. (2000). *Necessary but not sufficient: The respective roles of single and multiple influences on individual development*. Washington, DC: American Psychological Association.

Wachs, T. D., & Sheehan, R. (Eds.). (1988). *Assessment of young developmentally disabled children*. New York: Plenum Press.

Walsh, S., Rous, B., & Lutzer, C. (2000). The federal IDEA natural environments provisions. In S. Sandall & M. Ostrosky (Eds.), *Natural Environments and Inclusion* (Young Exceptional Children Monograph Series No. 2) (pp. 3–15). Longmont, CO: Sopris West.

Wolery, M. (2004). Using assessment information to plan intervention programs. In M. McLean, M. Wolery, & D. B. Bailey, Jr. (Eds.), *Assessing infants and preschoolers with special needs* (3rd ed., pp. 517–544). Columbus, OH: Pearson.

Wolery, M., & Bailey, D. B. (2002). Early childhood special education research. *Journal of Early Intervention, 25*, 88–99.

Wolery, M., Brashers, M. S., & Neitzel, J. C. (2002). Ecological congruence assessment for classroom activities and routines: Identifying goals and intervention practices in childcare. *Topics in Early Childhood Special Education, 22*, 131–142.

Yoder, P. J., & Warren, S. F. (1998). Maternal responsivity predicts the prelinguistic communication intervention that facilitates generalized intentional communication. *Journal of Speech, Language, and Hearing Research, 41*, 1207–1219.

Yoder, P. J., & Warren, S. F. (2001). Relative treatment effects of two prelinguistic communication interventions on language development in toddlers with developmental delays vary by maternal characteristics. *Journal of Speech, Language, and Hearing Research, 44*, 224–237.

52

Early Intervention and Prevention of Disability

Preschoolers

Kathleen J. Marshall and William H. Brown
University of South Carolina

Maureen A. Conroy
University of Florida

Herman Knopf
University of South Carolina

Until recently, the history of young children with disabilities has ranged from harsh conditions to benign neglect (cf. Safford & Safford, 1996). Caldwell (1973) delineated three evolutionary periods for serving young children with disabilities. She asserted that prior to the 1950s societal attitudes were characterized by "forgetting and hiding" children with special needs. Moreover, these predominant social dispositions resulted in pervasive institutionalization of many children. During the 1950s and 1960s, Caldwell noted the emergence of a second era she called "screening and segregating." The second epoch marked societal efforts, which were lead by parents of and advocates for children with disabilities, to support the well-being of children with special needs and students at risk. In the 1960s and 1970s, society began to change again, and Head Start and similar preschool programs spread across the country. These programs addressed the experiential needs of students at risk for disabilities, and reflected the "identifying and helping children and their families" Zeitgeist, which is the third epoch identified by Caldwell. Although these three periods were reflections of the diverse societal perceptions of disability at the time, there was only limited attention in the movements to carefully evaluate educational outcomes. Historically, societal attitudes and perceptions drove educational practices both inside and outside of classrooms, but those dispositions and accompanying practices were infrequently matched with scientific evidence.

The attitudes towards children with disabilities in the 1970s resulted in widespread advocacy, federal legislation, and financial support for special education (i.e., Public Law 94-142 Education for All Handicapped Act, 1975). Since Public Law 94-142 (1975), special education services for children have expanded greatly both in the number of children and families served and in the age of onset for those services. With Public Law 99-457 in 1986, the right to a free and appropriate education (FAPE) was extended downward to 3 years of age and early intervention services for infants and toddlers with developmental delays and their families were established in all 50 states and territories. With respect to preschoolers, the most recently analyzed child count data for Part B 619 Preschool Services indicate that local educational agencies provided individual education programs (IEPs) to 710,371, 3-, 4-, and 5-year-old children (Individuals with Disabilities Education Act Data, 2009). Along with the rapid expansion of special education services for young children, the number of preschoolers served in community-based programs has grown considerably. Specifically, according to the most recent estimates, more than 4.5 million young children (i.e., over 60% of the 3-, 4-, and 5-year-old children not in kindergarten) have been enrolled in preschools (Federal Interagency Forum on Child and Family Statistics, 2006). In addition, in 2008, 1.1 million children attended state-funded preschools with 973,178 being 4-year-old children (i.e., Barnett, Epstein, Friedman, Boyd, & Hustedt, 2009). In the face of greater demands on educators of young children, a new evolutionary period appears to be on the horizon, one focusing on evidence-based practices for early intervention and prevention.

We believe that preschool services for children with and without special educational needs should be the foundation for high quality general and special education services for children and their families. This foundation is of particular importance for preschoolers (a) who have identified behavioral and developmental difficulties, (b) who live in poverty and are at high risk for school failure, and (c) who are English language learners (ELL). Moreover, societal efforts to improve the educational status of preschoolers ought to be viewed as prevention services (cf. Conroy & Brown, 2004; Guralnick, 1998). Our purpose in this chapter is to provide information about contemporary educational efforts with preschool children and their families and to reflect the evolving nature of programs for young children with or at risk for disabilities.

First, we review the evolution of practices in early childhood special education, focusing on the Division for Early Childhood Recommended Practices. Then, we describe an integrative conceptual framework for early childhood education. After that, we selectively review research for two important areas of preschool education, peer interaction interventions and emergent literacy practices. We believe that progress in these two areas reflect the gradual movement towards merging evidence-informed and traditional classroom procedures.

Standards of Practice in Early Childhood Special Education

Early childhood special education services evolved out of two relatively independent educational movements that began in earnest during the 1960s: (a) early childhood education, especially the "compensatory education movement" (cf. Consortium for Longitudinal Studies, 1983); and (b) special education services for young children (cf. Safford, Sargent, & Cook, 1994). Since that time, Trohanis (2008) and colleagues documented the broad-spectrum development of practices and policies in early intervention and early childhood special education for young children with special needs and their families.

During the 1980s, the National Association for the Education of Young Children (NAEYC) published guidelines about developmentally appropriate practices (DAP) for young children (Bredekamp, 1987). Bredekamp and Copple (1997) noted the dual reasons for the initial document as (a) guidance for accreditation and (b) response to the trend toward academic instruction in preschools. Several leaders in early childhood special education expressed concerns about using DAP as the only guidelines for working with young children with special needs, especially around the issues of sufficient individualization to promote children's progress and use of systematic instruction (cf. Carta, Schwartz, Atwater, & McConnell, 1991).

Some resolution to the debate around DAP was accomplished with members of NAEYC and DEC initiating discussions about how best to serve young children with special needs (e.g., Wolery & Bredekamp, 1994; Wolery, Strain, & Bailey, 1992). These discussions resulted in a revision of the then-current NAEYC guidelines. Carta and Kong (2007) recognized that the revised NAEYC guidelines outlined a balanced approach with both child- and teacher-directed activities based on the original two cardinal principles of DAP, *developmentally and individually appropriate practices* (cf. Bredekamp, 1987). Continuing efforts have resulted in joint position statements on early childhood inclusion and young children's challenging behavior (Division for Early Childhood, 2009a,b). Moreover, Epstein (2007), in a NAEYC monograph, asserted that balanced child- and adult-guided strategies should be optimal in promoting young children's development. Hence, since the original DAP guidelines of 1987, a convergence of educators' thinking on young children's learning has occurred, at least within two prominent early childhood professional organizations.

Following the initial dissemination of DAP guidelines, the Division for Early Childhood (DEC) of the Council for Exceptional Children (CEC) established a DEC Task Force on Recommended Practices (1993) to identify standards of practice for use for teacher accreditation and certification. The task force members employed a consensus process, rather than evaluating evidence, to develop recommended practices for the field of early childhood special education. The original Task Force used six criteria for determining practices: (a) research- or value-based, (b) family-centered, (c) multicultural, (d) cross-disciplinary, (e) developmentally and chronologically appropriate, and (f) normalized (Odom & McLean, 2006). Before determining the final set of recommended practices, Odom, McLean, Johnson, and LaMontagne (1995) socially validated the recommended practices with a sample of DEC members, parents of children with disabilities, and professors in institutions of higher education. Since the initial development of the DEC Recommended Practices, the guidelines have been re-published (Sandall, McLean, & Smith, 2000) and made available with supporting materials (e.g., Sandall, Giacomini, Smith, & Hemmetter, 2006; Sandall, Hemmeter, Smith, & McLean, 2005). To date, the majority of the recommended practices continue to be consensus-based procedures that have not been validated empirically. Indeed, the evidence for many recommended practices, albeit promising, is relatively limited and most practices have not achieved the type of systematic confirmation needed to be research-based procedures (cf. Odom et al., 2005). Although McCall (2009) argued that when evidence is absent from policy and practice, professional wisdom and consensus is sorely needed, the critical question remains: Which day-to-day educational procedures should be recommended to practitioners who work with young children with special needs?

In recent years, based on national accountability legislation such as No Child Left Behind (2001) and national reports such as the President's Commission on Excellence in Special Education (2002), special educators have been moving toward establishing and implementing research-based procedures for children with disabilities (Odom et al., 2005). Moreover, many professionals have advocated for continued efforts to develop, refine, validate, disseminate, and widely employ research-informed procedures with preschoolers with special needs (e.g., Brown, Odom, McConnell, & Rathel, 2008; Buysse & Wesley, 2006; Carta & Kong, 2007; Dunst, Trivette, & Cutspec, 2002).

Unified Theory of Early Intervention/Early Childhood Special Education

Much of the debate on developmentally appropriate practice derived from sometimes contentious theoretical arguments between early childhood and early childhood special education professionals. Specifically, many early childhood educators based their educational efforts with children on the cognitive developmental theories developed by Piaget (1958) and Vygotsky (1978). Scholars and educators have applied these constructivist theories with young children (cf. Guralnick, 1998). In contrast, many early childhood special educators based their professional efforts on the behavioral theories developed by Skinner (1953) and Bandura (1976). Scholars and interventionists have employed applied behavior analysis and social learning theory with children, especially children with special needs (cf. Strain et al., 1992). Another significant theoretical perspective, which integrates important aspects of behavioral and developmental theories and which has been embraced by many early childhood and early childhood special educators, has been an ecological perspective (cf. Bronfenbrenner & Morris, 1998). Ecological approaches have included an explicit recognition of complex and dynamic behavioral and contextual influences on educational services for children and families (cf. Odom et al., 1996).

Together, and in spite of differences in application, developmental, behavioral, and ecological theoretical perspectives can form a foundation for an integrative approach to day-to-day policies and practices. The challenge for researchers and practitioners is to find a set of practices that meets the necessary standards for evidence while fitting into a context familiar to early childhood educators. Indeed, Odom and Wolery (2003) argued cogently for an integrated conceptual framework for practitioners who want to employ practices based on contemporary educational theories.

Odom and Wolery (2003) asserted that their perspective was a "unified theory of practice" for early intervention and early childhood special education in that "This theory exists as a set of shared beliefs or shared exemplars . . . . among practitioners and scholars, with each having a body of research and/or strongly held and commonly shared values for its foundation." (p. 165). Their conceptual framework has not been a call simply to be eclectic in one's orientation. They made a strong case for an evidence-informed and in the absence of evidence, value-based, approach to educational services. Their theory represents, therefore, a framework for compromise and convergence—a way to focus on what is alike rather than what is different—as practices in early childhood special education change. They explicitly delineated eight fundamental tenants with examples of evidence- and value-based practices for their "unified theory of practice." Odom and Wolery's tenants included: (a) Families and homes are primary nurturing contexts; (b) Strengthening relationships is an essential feature of early Intervention/early childhood special education (EI/ECSE); (c) Children learn through acting on and observing their environment; (d) Adults mediate children's experiences to promote learning; (e) Children's participation in more developmentally advanced settings, at times with assistance, is necessary for successful and independent participation in those settings; (f) EI/ECSE practice is individually and dynamically goal oriented; (g) Transitions across programs are enhanced by a developmentally instigative adult; and (h) Families and programs are influenced by the broader context.

Although it is beyond our scope in this chapter to review comprehensively the extant evidence-based procedures for preschoolers, we will selectively review existing support related to two important areas of early childhood, peer interaction interventions and emergent literacy practices. Historically, research on peer interaction interventions evolved across several decades (see Brown et al., 2008, for review). The area of emergent literacy has been a burgeoning area of research and is illustrative of the growing evidence of convergence of methodologies and integration of theoretical orientations. The use of developmentally and individually appropriate practices that are contextually relevant and based on evidence undergirds these two areas of preschool intervention (cf. Carta & Kong, 2007). We believe that the educational procedures discussed will also be beneficial to both children with, at risk for, and without special needs.

Peer Interaction Interventions for Preschoolers

Improvement of young children's peer interactions and one hopes their peer relationships and social competence, has a longstanding history in early childhood and early childhood special education (cf. Brown et al., 2008). In addition, preschoolers' enhanced social competence is one of three primary child outcomes for the U. S. Department of Education (Early Childhood Outcomes Center, 2010). For purpose of discussion, we will divide peer interaction interventions into two approaches that are not mutually exclusive. First, we will present information on peer interaction interventions and then discuss positive behavior supports, which are similar to peer interaction interventions in that the procedures include efforts to teach positive social skills to replace children's problem behaviors. With respect to peer interaction interventions, Brown, Odom, and Conroy (2001) developed a heuristic hierarchy for practitioners who want to employ evidence-informed procedures to enhance preschoolers' social interactions. They delineated three levels for intervention that include (a) classroom wide strategies, (b) naturalistic peer interaction interventions, and (c) explicit social skills instruction.

Classroom-wide interventions. DAP and DEC practices, which for preschool children are typically general recommendations for classroom teachers, comport well with Odom and Wolery's (2003) concept of a unified theory of practice. The NAEYC and DEC professional recommendations press teachers to have many age appropriate materials and activities of high interest for young children, preschool schedules with many child- and adult-initiated learning activities, and multiple opportunities for children and adults to interact positively. Hence, these classroom circumstances should promote most children's engagement with materials and activities as well as enhance social interactions at appropriate times. Indeed, Brown and colleagues (2008) asserted that NAEYC and DEC guidelines that promote common high-interest activities and circumstances in preschools such as learning centers, transitions, meals, and outside play afford multiple teaching and learning opportunities for acquisition of important language, social, and cognitive skills. In addition, together DEC and NAEYC have promoted preschool inclusion of children with and without disabilities as one means of providing developmentally sophisticated and responsive peers to interact with one another during common classroom activities (Division of Early Childhood, 2009a; cf. Brown et al., 2008).

With respect to classroom curricula, some well-specified programs have been employed occasionally with children at risk for social competence difficulties (e.g., Domitrovich, Cortes, & Greenberg, 2006; Webster-Stratton 1990). Nevertheless, very limited evidence about the widespread use of class-wide social competence curricula has been forthcoming (cf. Brown et al., 2008). Unfortunately, even though many teachers in early childhood settings incorporate aspects of DAP and DEC recommended practices, at least to some extent, a sizeable number of young children remain at risk for social competence problems and preventive programming (cf. Conroy & Brown, 2004). Hence, many preschoolers need more individualized procedures to enhance their peer-related social competence and those practices include both naturalistic peer interaction strategies and explicit instruction of social skills when needed.

Naturalistic peer interaction interventions. Naturalistic teaching procedures have been characterized by systematic teaching that supports the acquisition and practice of important skills needed by preschoolers to be socially engaged in their classrooms. Hence, the intervention approach fits well with Odom and Wolery's (2003) unified theory of practice in that teachers integrate effective teaching tactics (e.g., prompting, praising, opportunities to respond) into common preschool circumstances. Two effective naturalistic interventions, incidental teaching and friendship activities, have focused on teachers using tactics that are only as intensive as necessary to teach children skills that enhance their social engagement in classrooms.

Teachers have employed incidental teaching as a naturalistic intervention for enhancing young children's language in preschools for over three decades (see Hancock & Kaiser, 2005, for review) and the procedures have been recommended as a method to support preschoolers' peer interactions (cf. Brown et al., 2008). Incidental teaching has been viewed as teaching during brief periods and typically when children have shown an interest in or have been involved with materials, activities, or others (Brown et al., 2008). The essential elements of incidental teaching have included: (a) teachers implementing brief teaching and learning episodes based on children's interests; (b) teachers encouraging children's elaborated language and social behaviors; (c) teachers modeling and prompting children's responding, when indicated; (d) access or continued access to children's preferred materials and activities, and (e) teachers praise statements for elaborated behaviors, if indicated.

With respect to social and language interactions for example, McGee, Almeda, Sulzer-Azaroff, and Feldman (1992) employed incidental teaching to enhance both the number and quality of peers' social interactions of preschoolers with autism in an inclusive preschool. Hence, while young children have been interested or involved in classroom activities, incidental teaching represents a method of embedding additional high-quality teaching and learning opportunities for preschoolers to both acquire, practice, and become fluent with behaviors during classroom circumstances.

With respect to improving preschoolers' peer interactions, investigators have incorporated several effective tactics into common group activities, which they have referred to as friendship activities (Brown et al., 2008). The essential elements of friendship activities have included: (a) teacher-guided discussions of friendship; (b) frequent teacher encouragement and praise for peer interactions in common daily activities (e.g., songs, games); (c) repeated teacher and peer modeling of positive social interactions; and (d) multiple rehearsal of important social behaviors. The frequent use of embedded teacher prompting and praising and subsequent peer interactions were sufficient to increase children's social interactions during daily activities and children's social behaviors generalized to a nonintervention play periods. Importantly, researchers have replicated the effectiveness of these types of embedded antecedent and consequent events across a range of children (e.g., autism, mental retardation, behavior disorder, withdrawn) and classroom settings (Brown et al., 2008).

Explicit social skills instruction. Incidental teaching and friendship activities may not be sufficient for some preschoolers with significant peer interaction difficulties. If classroom-wide and naturalistic teaching interventions do not enhance children's peer interactions, more intensive and explicit instruction of peer interaction skills maybe needed. Two examples of empirically validated explicit social skills instruction strategies have been social integration activities (e.g., DeKlyen & Odom, 1989; Odom et al., 1999) and buddy skills training (e.g., English, Goldstein, Shafer, & Kaczamarek, 1997; Goldstein, English, Shafer, & Kaczmarek, 1997). For example, similar to friendship activities but in small group versus large group contexts, the essential elements of social integration activities included: (a) selection of children with restricted or negative social interactions and cooperative and socially sophisticated peers to participate in teacher structured activities; (b) implementation of brief but well-specified social roles during small group activities in defined play areas; (c) selection of activities that include many teaching and learning opportunities for play and social interaction; (d) systematic introduction of play themes and roles; and (e) when indicated, teacher prompting to engage in positive social interactions and play. Once the small group peer play has been implemented, if children fail to interact, the teachers' role becomes more directive with specific suggestions for play and peer interactions and explicit prompting and modeling. Several replications of the procedures have demonstrated that social integration activities can be an important approach to enhance children's peer-related social competence (Brown et al., 2008).

Another explicit instructional strategy for teaching preschoolers social skills has been buddy skills training. The basic approach to buddy skills training has been for teachers to teach preschoolers with and without developmental delays well-specified social strategies to promote peer interactions throughout the day (e.g., English et al., 1997; Goldstein et al., 1997). Specifically, children with and without developmental delays have been taught to move in proximity of peers, say the other children's names while making eye contact, and play with peers. A mnemonic of "stay, play, and talk with your buddy" has been employed to remind children to employ their newly acquired social skills. The teachers primary role following initial training of social strategies has been to continue to be "buddy coaches" and to monitor and, when indicated, to promote peer interactions throughout the preschool day. English and colleagues have demonstrated that buddy skills training are effective in improved social-communicative interactions. In addition, a sample of naïve teachers reviewed the procedures and they socially validated the practices by indicating that they viewed the instructional strategy as effective in improving peer interactions.

The potential of peer interaction interventions. The evidence base for peer interaction interventions may appear somewhat restricted with respect to relatively modest samples of participants (i.e., mostly single subject or quasi-experimental designs) and our selective review. Nevertheless, peer interaction interventions have been replicated by multiple investigators with a variety of children in a number of preschools. Moreover, taken together, the common core of essential elements of these interventions such as (a) strategic teacher planning for increasing classroom opportunities for peer interaction, (b) teacher identification of individualized goals that will enhance children's social participation in preschools, and (c) embedding antecedent and consequent teaching tactics within common classroom activities to enhance social engagement have been shown to be effective and have been recommended by early childhood educators (cf. Brown et al., 2008; Chandler, Lubeck, & Fowler, 1992). Indeed, the essential elements have been demonstrated often enough that Chandler (1998) recommended establishing PALS centers within classrooms to promote peer interactions within routine center times during daily schedules. We believe that peer interaction interventions closely align with a unified theory of practice and they constitute a critical avenue for ensuring that preschool children receive sufficient individualization and socialization in less restrictive educational environments.

Positive Behavior Supports for Preschoolers

Problem behaviors that interfere with young children's learning and social competence have been common among preschoolers and have frequently troubled their parents and teachers (e.g., Campbell 2002; Webster-Stratton, 1997). Often, children's problem behaviors have been related to exposure to multiple risk factors for developmental difficulties (e.g., Campbell, 2002; Qi & Kaiser, 2003), especially in the area of communication and language (Carr et al., 1999). Regardless of the causes or contributing factors, many educators have advocated for early detection, prevention, and intervention for early onset behavior problems (e.g., Conroy, Brown, & Olive, 2008; Dunlap et al., 2006). Moreover, if preschoolers' persistent problem behaviors are not addressed, the severity of those behaviors will most likely intensify and become chronic as they proceed through school. Indeed, recent information has indicated that young children who show early and persistent social and behavioral difficulties are at a distinct disadvantage later in school, often require intensive special education services, and mostly likely demonstrate deficits in both academics and social competence (e.g., Dunlap et al., 2006).

Positive behavior supports (PBS) has been one of the most widely used conceptual frameworks for amelioration of problem behaviors in school-age students (cf. Sugai et al., 2000) and has been increasingly employed with the preschoolers (Conroy et al., 2008; Dunlap et al., 2006). PBS has been defined as "a group of intervention strategies that are highly individualized, based on scientific principles and empirical data, grounded in person-centered values, and designed to prevent the occurrence of challenging behaviors" (Dunlap et al., 2003, p. 5). With the enactment of IDEA 2004, which mandates that the IEP teams use positive behavioral interventions, strategies, and supports for students who also demonstrate problem behaviors that interfere with their learning, PBS has become common in our schools.

The overall purpose of PBS has been prevention of children's behavior problems through the employment of antecedents and consequent events while concurrently teaching them alternative, replacement behaviors (cf. Conroy et al., 2008; Dunlap et al., 2003). In theory, as children learn appropriate means of communicating and socially interacting with others and are reinforced for those skills, they become less likely to display problem behaviors (Carr et al., 1999; Dunlap et al., 2003). PBS has most often been conceptualized as a three-tiered prevention model, beginning with universal intervention strategies that are applicable to all children and progressing to a tertiary level of intervention that is highly individualized, based on careful assessment information, and for those youngsters who continue to demonstrate significant problem behaviors (cf. Conroy et al., 2008; Dunlap et al., 2003). Because early childhood special education for preschoolers occurs across a continuum of preschool settings (i.e., pre-kindergarten for children at risk for school failure, inclusive preschools, and segregated self-contained classrooms), PBS interventions for preschoolers have been implemented somewhat differently than they are for school-age students. Regardless of the implementation settings, the characteristics of the levels of intervention have been similar.

Primary level. The primary level of PBS intervention has been characterized by the implementation of high quality early childhood services designed to prevent problem behaviors for *all* children in their classrooms or programs. The essential elements of this level of have included (a) developmentally and individually appropriate classroom practices, (b) structured and organized learning activities that promote children's appropriate engagement with materials and peers, (c) use of basic rules and routines for children and teachers, (d) and positive adult-child interactions and classroom atmosphere. The assumption has been that if children are provided high-quality learning environments and are socially engaged that problem behaviors will occur less frequently.

Secondary level. Similar to the primary level strategies, secondary level interventions have also targeted prevention of problem behaviors. The fundamental difference between the two levels has been who is targeted for intervention and how the intervention strategies are implemented. On the secondary level, the children who have continued to demonstrate problem behaviors after primary interventions are in place are targeted for more individualized interventions. Specifically, secondary level interventions have focused more intensely on teaching new skills, particularly in the area of social competence (see Conroy et al., 2008; Dunlap et al., 2003 for reviews).

Tertiary level. Tertiary interventions have been implemented with individual children whose behaviors have continued to be resistant to both primary and secondary level strategies. Typically, this level has begun with functional behavioral assessments (FBAs) that have examined setting factors and antecedents and consequent events that may contribute to children's problem behaviors. Following an FBA, individualized function-based interventions have been designed and implemented to systematically address the functions or purposes of the children's behavior problems by attenuating them while teaching replacement behaviors and skills (e.g., Conroy et al., 2008; Fox, Dunlap, & Powell, 2002). As Dunlap and Strain (2010) suggested, design of the behavioral intervention plans (BIPs) should be directly linked to assessment information gathered through the FBA process and include three essential elements: (a) arrangements of antecedents and consequent events that decrease the likelihood of the children's problem behaviors; (b) direct instruction of the replacement behaviors throughout children's daily schedules; and (c) delivery of contingent, sufficient, and individualized reinforcers following the display of replacement behaviors. Tertiary level interventions differ depending on the topography and function of the children's behavior. A number of researchers have examined the efficacy of various individualized interventions, often with single case research designs that showed functional relationships between interventions and children's adaptive behavior changes (e.g., Conroy et al., 2008; Dunlap et al., 2003).

In summary, PBS has been an evidence-based approach for dealing young children's problem behaviors. Several researchers have developed and evaluated program-wide PBS models (e.g., Fox et al., 2002; Hemmeter, Fox, Jack, Broyles & Doubet, 2007; Stormont, Lewis, & Beckner, 2005) and classroom-based PBS models (e.g., Conroy, Sutherland, Snyder, Al-Hendawi, & Vo, 2009; Stormont et al., 2005; Sutherland, Conroy, Abrams, & Vo, 2010) with preschoolers. Moreover, PBS shares common elements with peer interaction interventions in that practioners frequently use antecedent and consequent events to both decrease and teach behaviors to minimize children's behavior problems. Nevertheless, research on these emerging preschool models has only begun in earnest recently. Given that PBS has been primarily a conceptual approach for service delivery, several critical factors make examining its efficacy challenging. For example, the lack of a standardized definition of PBS, clear measures of implementation fidelity by teachers within classrooms, validation of technical assistance and professional development programs, and taking the procedures to scale have remained pressing issues for the field,

Early Literacy Interventions for Preschoolers

Practices in emergent and early literacy for preschool children serve as a microcosm of the issues that are at the forefront of early childhood education. Professional conflicts in classroom practice rooted in theoretical and instructional differences have surfaced for decades in the field of reading and language arts. The effects of these conflicts have been compounded as they mirrored those found in early intervention programs. Now, new pressures have arisen in the area of early literacy, as the strategic focus of instruction moves from familiarization with language/literacy activities and learning to love language and books, to early prevention of reading and language difficulties. This change in perspective, driven by recent research and the Response to Intervention (RTI) or Recognition and Response (Coleman, Buysse, & Neitzel, 2006) processes, has imposed rapid change in the nature of early literacy programs in pre-kindergarten classrooms. The move to evidence-based practices in early childhood must embrace and define these processes and move from disseminating research to translating the interventions into day-to-day practices (cf. Buysse & Wesley, 2006). In early childhood literacy, the possible effects of this research may be to reduce the number of children with reading difficulties.

Although the prospects for a unified approach to identifying evidence-based practices might seem challenging given past philosophical differences, the field has been making steady progress towards a body of evidence and promising strategies in early literacy practices. A slow and steady convergence on relatively well-specified skills and strategies supported by the existing, if limited, evidence has been made.

To date, data supporting the predictive nature of emergent and early literacy skills has been unequivocal and substantial, particularly in the area of vocabulary, print knowledge, and phonological or phonemic awareness (Puolakanaho et al., 2008; Storch & Whitehurst, 2002; Torgesen, 1998; Troia, 1999). Early reading studies have been augmented by a steadily growing body of research that has indicated that intervention prior to first grade can be very beneficial to young readers by significantly improving performance on early literacy skills and later reading performance (Arnold, Lonigan, Whitehurst, & Epstein, 1994; McIntosh, Crosbie, Holm, & Dodd, 2007; Scanlon, Vellutino, Small, Fanuele, & Sweeney, 2005; Snow, Burns, & Griffin, 1998). Recently, researchers have refined and clarified robust predictors of reading for very young children and they have examined the degree to which interventions can ameliorate early difficulties and teach early reading skills.

Researchers in the field of early childhood literacy have repeatedly identified two additional challenges facing the field. The first issue has been that only a few researchers have targeted the differential effects of specific interventions for children placed at higher risk for reading difficulties because of developmental delays and disabilities, significantly low socioeconomic status (SES), or English Language Learners. In part, this has been because many reading researchers have not presented and analyzed disaggregated data (Lonigan, Schatschneider, & Westberg, 2008a). Fortunately, investigators so far have shown that children who do not perform well in measures of early literacy, regardless of the reasons, respond positively to the same evidence-based practices and strategies (Arnold et al., 1994; Lonigan, Schatschneider, & Westberg, 2008b). Importantly, in recent studies researchers have begun to include analyses of how children in different at-risk groups respond to interventions (e.g., O'Connor, Bocian, Beebe-Frankenberger, & Linklater, 2010; Roberts, 2009).

A second challenge often addressed by researchers has been the variability of the qualifications, preparation, and professional development of preschool personnel who work with children and the effects education and training can have on fidelity of program implementation. The need to prepare the teaching force adequately has been seen as a major requirement for implementing specific interventions with fidelity, using general instructional strategies effectively, and producing optimal program outcomes (e.g., Buysse, & Wesley, 2006; Hsieh, Hemmeter, McCollum, & Ostrosky, 2009). Indeed, the call for translating research into practice at the preschool level may ultimately rest on well-trained teachers in children's classrooms. Many of the research-based interventions that have been relatively unstructured (e.g., storybook reading) are being translated into comparatively specific protocols to promote uniformity in implementation (e.g., Zucker, Ward, & Justice, 2009).

The evidence prompting changes in preschool classrooms has developed over the past two decades. During that time, a growing body of research has emerged that supports the predictive relationships between early literacy skills and later reading abilities (e.g., Speece, Mills, Ritchey, & Hillman, 2003; Whitehurst & Lonigan, 1998). In recent years, researchers with large-scale evaluations of predictive relationships and effective interventions have attempted to consolidate the results of previous studies and translate these results into recommendations for both day-to-day practices and additional much needed investigations.

In 2000, the National Reading Panel (NRP) analyzed the then current reading research and identified key components of effective reading interventions. The NRP reviewed studies that primarily included children enrolled in kindergarten or higher grades, so the results and guidelines were of limited use to preschool professionals. In 2008, the National Early Literacy Panel (NELP) was formed and sponsored by the National Institute for Literacy. The focus of this national panel was to examine research and identify emerging and early literacy skills that correlated with later reading ability.

The NELP identified six skill areas in early literacy as moderate to high predictors of later reading ability: (a) alphabet knowledge; (b) phonological awareness; (c) rapid automatic naming (RAN) of numbers; (d) RAN of objects or colors; (e) writing name or writing in general; and (f) phonological memory (i.e., ability to remember spoken information) (Lonigan et al., 2008a). In addition, five early literacy areas were found to correlate moderately with later reading: (a) concepts about print and print conventions; (b) print knowledge; (c) reading readiness; (d) oral language; and (e) visual processing (i.e., matching and visual discrimination). In addition, Dunst, Trivette, and Hamby (2007), in a secondary analysis of the NELP findings, reported the importance of focused interventions on early literacy gains and stressed the importance of focusing on predictor variables that can be translated into instructional practice.

For the purpose of our chapter, we summarized evidence-based interventions in early childhood literacy in three main areas: (a) storybook reading and other literacy reading; (b) specialized, supplemental procedures; and (c) comprehensive curricula. These three areas may represent different avenues or "tiers" for intervention, and probably different perspectives on how teachers implement day-to-day instruction in preschools.

Shared reading and embedded instruction. Shared reading has been the hallmark of the early literacy experience at the preschool level. If preschool teachers do nothing else to foster literacy development intentionally, they read stories to and with the children. Although shared book reading has been generally accepted as an important practice for early literacy classrooms, only a few studies with student outcomes have been performed and published (Lonigan et al., 2008b). Moreover, there has been a lack of standardization in storybook reading practices making the effects of those procedures difficult to assess. Recently, some researchers have provided guidelines on how to read books to maximize positive child outcomes and what types of books can target specific skills (e.g., Justice & Pullen, 2003). The following researchers have moved towards systematizing some early childhood literacy practices, and documenting effects of instruction embedded in common classroom activities.

A strong and consistent finding related to storybook reading is that shared reading activities that are interactive in nature (i.e., opportunities for participants to respond to questions and receive feedback), have been more highly associated with positive child outcomes in vocabulary than non-interactive reading (Lonigan et al., 2008b). Although interactive storybook reading has often been loosely defined, some strategies, like dialogic reading (Whitehurst et al., 1998), have included well-prescribed steps and procedures. Indeed, the dialogic reading strategy has been identified as an evidence-based practice in many studies and summaries of interactive storybook reading (e.g., Isbell, Sobol, Lindauer, & Lowrance, 2004; Justice & Pullen, 2003; What Works Clearinghouse, 2009). In addition, Beauchat, Blamey, and Walpole (2009) developed a unique protocol for shared storybook reading that has also provided well-specified guidelines for teachers when teaching oral language, vocabulary, comprehension, phonological awareness, and print awareness. Beauchat and colleagues suggested the standardized shared storybook protocol might be used for professional development in the area of early literacy.

Parent involvement has been fundamental part of early literacy efforts and shared book reading has been essential to literacy efforts in homes. Recently, researchers have refined and extended information on evidence-based literacy practices in homes, although these studies have not yet looked at a standardized protocol for shared book reading. Price, van Kleeck, and Huberty (2009) found that when parents read expository texts to their young children, the adults talked more, had more parent-child verbal exchanges, and they used a much more diverse vocabulary than when reading storybooks. Additionally, parents provided their children twice as much feedback and verbal acknowledgement in the expository reading condition. Roberts (2009) measured the effects of storybook reading on the vocabulary of young children who were English Language Learners. Children were read to by their parents in their native language, and by teachers in English. All children experienced both conditions and, in each condition, storybook reading resulted in significant vocabulary gains in both languages. The two studies indicated that home-based shared book reading is an important area for related research.

Shared storybook reading has also been used as the vehicle for embedded instruction. Researchers have shown that presenting print-referencing activities during shared storybook reading can result in significant gains in print knowledge. For example, Justice, Kaderavek, Fan, Sofka, and Hunt (2009) reported that preschool children had significant gains in print concept knowledge, alphabet knowledge, and name writing after teachers used a series of explicit print-referencing strategies during shared storybook reading. Justice and colleagues have developed an outline for teachers to follow for print referencing during reading which provides examples of teacher language for each of 15 specific print targets in the domains of print naming, book and print organization, letters and words (Justice, Sofka, Sutton, & Zucker, 2006; Zucker et al., 2009). As with the interactive reading protocols, well-specified guidelines for the procedures will facilitate professional development and further much needed efficacy research.

Phonological awareness has been another fundamental skill often embedded in other activities in preschool classrooms and researchers have embedded explicit phonological awareness into storybooks. For example, during shared storybook time for preschool children at risk for reading disabilities, Ziolkowski and Goldstein (2008) embedded explicit instruction in rhyming and letter sound recognition. For the intervention, teachers pointed out and modeled rhymes or letters sounds and the children repeated the responses. Similar to other explicit literacy procedures, this relatively simple strategy resulted in gains in rhyming, alliteration, and letter-sound knowledge the specific skills targeted.

Supplemental curriculum in early literacy. While research on shared book reading has looked at a number of skill areas, researchers focusing on supplemental curricula in early literacy primarily have investigated specific instruction in phonological awareness—an important predictor of early reading success. The NELP reviewed 83 studies of the effects of code-based programs on early literacy (Lonigan et al., 2008b). The results of the NELP evaluation and other recent research have supported the positive effects of programs offering specific instruction in phonological awareness on early and later literacy skills. To date, much of the research has continued to focus on children in kindergarten or higher grades (Harn, Stoolmiller, & Chard, 2008; Kamps et al., 2008: Simmons et al., 2008). Nevertheless, the NELP meta-analyses, which looked at preschool studies separately, indicated that neither age, nor SES, nor other risk factors appeared to ameliorate the effects of code-based interventions on later reading performance (Lonigan et al., 2008b).

In longitudinal studies across time, Simmons et al. (2008) and Kamps et al. (2008) found that the most directive programs with the most explicit code-emphasis orientation were the most effective in increasing early literacy skills. The researchers also noted that the explicit programs were more effective with the lowest achieving children. Lonigan and colleagues (2008b) in their summarization of the NELP report, stated that instructional practices targeted for specific literacy skills resulted in improvement in those pre-reading competencies. In other words, children showed improvement mainly in the skills they were taught directly. For example, intervention focused on phonological awareness and alphabetic principal increased children's performance in skills related to sound-symbol relationships, but similar gains were not found in measures of reading fluency (Harn et al., 2008; Kamps et al., 2008: Simmons et al., 2008). Moreover, this same relationship and alignment between skills taught and skills learned was determined for other important skill areas (e g., vocabulary, print awareness). Few curricula not specific to teaching phonological awareness have met the guidelines for research-based interventions and only one curriculum is listed on the What Works Clearinghouse (2009).

Comprehensive curricula. Historically, the search to identify comprehensive, evidence-based curricula has been hampered by the scarcity of both well-specified literacy curricula and accompanying efficacy research. For example, the NELP (2008) reported that they were unable to analyze many curricula because of research limitations or availability of materials and information. In general, the Panel noted that results favored curricula that included explicit interventions designed to teach specific skills such as teaching letter names and letter recognition. Similarly, beginning in 2002, the U. S. Department of Education commissioned a comprehensive review of existing preschool curriculum through the Preschool Curriculum Evaluation Research project (2008). In this review, 14 well-known preschool curricula were evaluated relative to their impact on 27 student outcomes, including subtests of the Woodcock-Johnson, the PPVT, and classroom measures. Many current curricula were not evaluated in this project, but of the 14 evaluated, only one curriculum had significant effects on student measures of reading, phonological awareness, and language.

The results of existing reviews of comprehensive curricula have reflected a major dilemma faced by school district personnel when selecting a comprehensive curriculum as the first tier of instruction for young children. To date, some sources independent of the curriculum developer have listed or identified the necessary instructional elements that should be found in evidence-based curricula, but few have been willing to recommend specific programs for schools. One reason may have been to encourage state, district, or school personnel to make their own decisions; however, the fundamental fact has remained that few evidence-based curricula exist. Moreover, federal evaluation sites, such as the What Works Clearinghouse (2009) currently have listed a few categories or types of instruction as evidence-based (e.g., interactive shared reading, phonological awareness training) but very few curricula. Other research sites focused on early literacy, such as the Center for Early Literacy Learning, have summarized and conducted research on general instructional strategies or activities rather than well-specific and comprehensive curricula. Hence, although a number of preschool curricula have been made commercially available, for the most part those programs have not been evaluated extensively by the IES or program evaluation centers independent of the curriculum developers. Many of curricula have been used in preschools across the country and, while those programs may include strategies identified by the NRP or the NELP, curriculum-specific experimental or quasi-experimental research to support them has been extremely sparse. Certainly, further curriculum development and subsequent high-quality evaluation by researchers will continued to be sorely needed.

Summary. Contemporary prevention models in schools have focused on response to intervention. Consequently, much of the research emphasis in early literacy has been on identifying predictors of reading difficulties and finding effective procedures to explicitly teach and practice important skills related to subsequent reading performance. Unfortunately, educators have few comprehensive evidence-based curricula for preschool classrooms. One consistent finding in the early literacy research has been the apparent power of structured phonological awareness interventions to improve early reading skills for at-risk learners. Moreover, recent emerging findings have shown the efficacy of these interventions with preschool children, including children living in poverty and English Language Learners (McIntosh, Crosbie, Holm, & Dodd, 2007). Another clear finding has been that explicitness—both in curriculum and in teacher presentation—seems to be strongly related to positive child literacy outcomes (Kamps et al., 2008; Lonigan et al., 2008b; Simmons et al., 2008).

Evidence-based programs can be easily integrated into tiers of instruction for preschool-aged children to reduce markedly the probability of later reading difficulties (Kamps et al., 2008; O'Connor, 2000: O'Connor, Fulmer, Harty, & Bell, 2005; Simmons et al., 2008). For example, O'Connor et al., (2010) found a tier-two intervention designed for young children with potential reading difficulties (i.e., Ladders to Literacy Activities plus additional alphabetic skills) was as effective for English Language Learners as it was for native English speakers, and was also effective for children with mild intellectual disabilities and general language difficulties.

Other evidence-based strategies for instruction have included supplemental teaching strategies or practices rather than comprehensive curricula. For example, researchers with interactive storybook reading and print referencing strategies have shown positive child outcomes in vocabulary and print knowledge, respectively. The extant preschool literacy research has illustrated that many researchers are beginning to create relatively well-specified protocols for classroom practices, and provide guidelines for embedded instruction while preserving naturalistic preschool classrooms atmosphere. Given the limited research base, whether versions of these literacy activities should be integrated into daily practice, reserved for at risk children, or adapted for both groups remains a critical issue to be researched.

Elements of the Unified Theory of Practice (Odom & Wolery, 2003) are reflected in much of the existing research on early literacy, as researchers and practitioners from several fields and theoretical perspectives struggle to communicate with a common language and move towards comprehensive evidence-based practices. The strength of structured instructional procedures, particularly in phonological awareness, and the potential for changing reading outcomes for young children at risk for school failure, suggests that many preschool teachers and administrators may want to incorporate more explicit programs to teach fundamental pre-reading skills into their classrooms. Although some researchers have embedded phonological instruction in more naturalistic ways (e.g., Ziolkowski & Goldstein, 2008; Zucker et al., 2009), one element of the Unified Theory of Practice, teacher mediation, may require a flexible definition as evidence dictates teacher roles more indicative of intentional instruction than mediation (cf. Epstein, 2007).

Conclusions

We view preschool services as prevention (Conroy & Brown, 2004). Evidence is accumulating rapidly that suggests the power and potential of prevention targeted at specific preacademic and social competencies. The rapid increase in services for preschoolers with and without special needs has elevated the need for evidence-based teaching procedures, which are also acceptable and feasible for early childhood educators (cf. West, Brown, Grego, & Johnson, 2008). We believe that a unified theory of practice is an appropriate conceptual framework to support further development of effective teaching procedures to improve young children's school success. When we look at the current research bases reviewed in this chapter, we can see that the unified theory of practice is reflected in the merging of scientifically based and historical classroom practices such as DAP. We also see evidence accumulating in support of early literacy interventions that are more structured, skill specific, and teacher-directed than strategies typically employed in preschool classrooms (Lonigan et al., 2008b). This direction of these research findings suggests that the role of theoretical frameworks, such as the unified theory of practice may be an important avenue to follow as we look to bridge the gap between research and practice. It also means that traditional rules of practice, such as our earlier recommendation that instruction be only as intensive as necessary (Brown et al., 2008), may need adjustment. Both researchers and practitioners must be open-minded as evidence accumulates suggesting that the best preventative strategies are both intensive and teacher-directed. Other forms of effective intervention may be identified in the future, but we, as a field, must be directed by positive child outcomes in this, the fourth epoch of early childhood education and service delivery.

Although contemporary information about peer interaction and emergent literacy interventions has been promising, the extant database has not necessarily reached the level of confirmation and replication needed to declare many of the strategies research-based procedures (cf. Odom et al., 2005) and important questions remain about how to assure intervention fidelity, what constitutes sufficient teaching and learning episodes, and how to take effective interventions to scale (Brown et al., 2008). Yet these difficulties are characteristic of any emerging body of evidence, and much of the recent research reflects rigorous methodology and interpretation. We have the requisite research methods to determine procedural effectiveness and some investigators are employing those tools to further develop our ability to promote and support young children's preschool skills that are needed for later school success (cf. Coleman et al., 2006; Greenwood et al., 2008).

References

Arnold, D. H., Lonigan, C. J., Whitehurst, G. J., & Epstein, J. N. (1994). Accelerating language development through picture book reading. Replication and extension to videotape training format. *Journal of Educational Psychology, 86*, 235–243.

Bandura, A. (1976). *Social learning theory.* Englewood Cliffs, NJ: Prentice Hall.

Barnett, W. S., Epstein, D. J. Friedman, A. H., Boyd, J. S., & Hustedt, J. T. (2009). *The state of preschool 2008.* New Brunswick, NJ: National Institute for Early Education Research, Rutgers, The State University of New Jersey. Retrieved November 17, 2009, from http://nieer.org/facts/

Beauchat, K. A., Blamey, K. L., & Walpole, S. (2009). Building preschool children's language and literacy one storybook at a time. *The Reading Teacher, 63*(1), 26–39.

Bredekamp, S. (Ed.). (1987). *Developmentally appropriate practice in early childhood programs serving children birth to eight.* Washington, DC: National Association for the Education of Young Children (NAEYC).

Bredekamp, S., & Copple, C. (Eds.). (1997). *Developmentally appropriate practice in early childhood programs* (Rev. ed.). Washington, DC: National Association for the Education of Young Children (NAEYC).

Bronfenbrenner, U., & Morris, P. A. (1998). The ecology of developmental processes. In W. Damon & R. M. Lerner (Eds.), *Handbook of child psychology: Volume 1: Theoretical models of human development* (5th ed., pp. 993–1028). Hoboken, NJ: Wiley.

Brown, W. H., Odom, S. L., & Conroy, M. A. (2001). An intervention hierarchy for promoting preschool children's peer interactions in natural environments. *Topics in Early Childhood Special Education, 21,* 90–134.

Brown, W. H., Odom, S. L., McConnell, S. R., & Rathel, J. (2008). Social competence interventions for preschoolers with developmental difficulties. In W. H. Brown, S. L. Odom, & S. R. McConnell (Eds.), *Social competence of young children: Risk, disability, and evidence-based practices* (2nd ed., pp. 141-163). Baltimore: Paul H. Brookes.

Buysse, V., & Wesley, P. W. (2006). *Evidence-based practice in the early childhood field.* Washington, DC: ZERO TO THREE Press.

Caldwell, B. M. (1973). The importance of beginning early. In M. B. Karnes (Ed.), *Not all wagons are red: The exceptional child's early years* (pp. 2–10). Arlington, VA: Council for Exceptional Children.

Campbell, S. B. (2002). *Behavior problems in preschool children: Clinical and developmental issues* (2nd ed.). New York: Guilford Press.

Carr, E. G., Horner, R. H., Turnbull, A. P., Marquis, J. G., McLaughlin, D. M., McAtee, M. L., … Braddock, D. (1999). *Positive behavior support as an approach for dealing with problem behavior in people with developmental disabilities: A research synthesis.* Washington, DC: AAMR.

Carta, J. J., Schwartz, I. S., Atwater, J. B., & McConnell, S. R. (1991). Developmentally appropriate practice: Appraising its usefulness for young children with disabilities. *Topics in Early Childhood Special Education, 11,* 1–20.

Carta, J. J., & Kong, N. Y. (2007). Trends and issues in interventions for preschoolers with developmental disabilities. In S. L. Odom, R. H. Horner, M. E. Snell, & J. Blacher (Eds.), *Handbook of developmental disabilities* (pp. 181–198). New York: Guilford Press.

Chandler, L. (1998). Promoting positive interaction between preschool-age children during free play: The PALS Center. *Young Exceptional Children, 1*(3), 14–20.

Chandler, L. K., Lubeck, R. C., & Fowler, S. A. (1992). Generalization and maintenance of preschool children's social skills: A critical review and analysis. *Journal of Applied Behavior Analysis, 25,* 415–428.

Coleman, M. R., Buysse, V., & Neitzel, J. (2006). *Recognition and response: An early intervening system for young children at-risk for learning disabilities: Full report.* Chapel Hill: The University of North Carolina at Chapel Hill, FPG Child Development Institute.

Conroy, M. A., & Brown, W. H. (2004). Early identification, prevention, and early intervention with young children at-risk for emotional or behavioral disorders: Issues, trends, and a call for action. *Behavioral Disorders, 29,* 224–237.

Conroy, M. A., Brown, W. H., & Olive, M. L. (2008). Social competence interventions for young children with challenging behavior. In W. H. Brown, S. L. Odom, & S. R. McConnell (Eds.), *Social competence of young children: Risk, disability, and evidence-based practices* (2nd ed., 205–231). Baltimore: Paul H. Brookes.

Conroy, M.A., Sutherland, K., Snyder, A., Al-Hendawi, M. & Vo, A. (2009). Creating a positive classroom atmosphere: Teachers' use of effective praise and feedback. *Beyond Behavior, 18*(2), 18–26.

Consortium for Longitudinal Studies. (1983). *As the twig is bent . . . Lasting effects preschool programs.* Hillsdale, NJ: Erlbaum.

DeKlyen, M., & Odom, S. L. (1989). Activity structure and social interactions with peers in developmentally integrated play groups. *Journal of Early Intervention, 13,* 342–352.

Division for Early Childhood. (2009a). Early childhood inclusion: A Joint Position of the Division for Early Childhood (DEC) and the National Association for the Education of Young Children (NAEYC). Retrieved November 17, 2009, from http://www.dec-sped.org/About_DEC/PositionConcept_Papers/Inclusion

Division for Early Childhood. (2009b). Position Statement on Identification of and Intervention with Challenging Behavior. Retrieved November 17, 2009, from http://www.dec-sped.org/About_DEC/PositionConceptPapers/Challenging_Behavior

Division for Early Childhood Task Force on Recommended Practices (Eds.). (1993). *DEC recommended practices: Indicators of quality in programs for infants and young children with special needs and their families.* Reston, VA: Council for Exceptional Children.

Domitrovich, C., Cortes, R. C., & Greenberg, M. (2006). *Improving young children's social and emotional competence: A randomized trial of the preschool PATHS curriculum.* University Park: Pennsylvania State University.

Dunlap, G., Conroy, M., Kern, L., DuPaul, G., VanBrakle, J., Strain, P., … & Joseph, G. E. (2003). *Research synthesis on effective intervention procedures: Executive summary.* Tampa: University of South Florida, Center for Evidence-based Practice: Young Children with Challenging Behavior.

Dunlap, G., & Strain, P. (2010). Challenging behavior and young children with autism spectrum disorders. Retrieved January 20, 2010, http://www.challengingbehavior.org/explore/presentations_workshops.htm

Dunlap, G., Strain, P. S., Fox, L., Carta, J., Conroy, M., Smith, B. J., … Hemmeter, M. (2006). Prevention and intervention with young children's challenging behavior: Perspective regarding current knowledge. *Behavioral Disorders, 32,* 29–45.

Dunst, C. J., Trivette, C. M., & Cutspec, P. A. (2002). An evidence-based approach to documenting the characteristics and consequences of early intervention practices. *Centerscope, 1*(2), 1–6. Retrieved December 28, 2009, from http://www.evidencebasedpractices.org/centerscope/centerscopevol1no2.pdf

Dunst, C. J., Trivette, C. M., & Hamby, D. W. (2007). Predictors of and interventions associated with later literacy accomplishments. *Center for Early Literacy Learning, 1*(3), 1–12. Retrived from http://www.earlyliteracylearning.org/cellpapers/cellpapers_v1_n3.pdf

Early Childhood Outcomes Center. (2010). Federal requirements for reporting child and family outcomes. Chapel Hill, NC: Frank Porter Graham Child Development Institute. Retrieved June 3, 2010, from http://www.fpg.unc.edu/~eco/pages/fed_req.cfm

English, E., Goldstein, H., Shafer, K., & Kaczmarek, L. (1997). Promoting interactions among preschoolers with and without disabilities: Effects of a buddy skills-training program. *Exceptional Children, 63,* 229–243.

Epstein, A. S. (2007). *The intentional teacher: Choosing the best strategies for young children's learning.* Washington, DC: NAEYC.

Federal Interagency Forum on Child and Family Statistics. (2006). *America's children: Key national indicators of well-being (2006).* Washington, DC. Retrieved March, 2009, from http://www.childstats.gov/americaschildren/

Fox, L., Dunlap, G., & Powell, D. (2002). Young children with challenging behavior: Issues and consideration for behavior support. *Journal of Positive Behavior Interventions, 4,* 208–217.

Goldstein, H., English, K., Shafer, K., & Kaczmarek, L. (1997). Interaction among preschoolers with and without disabilities: Effects of across-the-day peer intervention. *Journal of Speech and Hearing Research, 40,* 33–48.

Greenwood, C. R., Carta, J. J., Baggett, K., Buzhardt, J., Walker, D., & Terry, B. (2008). Best practices integrating progress monitoring and response-to-intervention concepts into early childhood. In A. Thomas, J. Grimes, & J. Gruba (Eds.), *Best practices in school psychology V* (pp. 1–13). Washington DC: National Association of School Psychology.

Guralnick, M. J. (1998). Effectiveness of early intervention for vulnerable children: A developmental perspective. *American Journal of Mental Retardation, 102,* 319–345.

Hancock, T. B., & Kaiser, A. P. (2005). Enhanced milieu teaching. In R. McCauley & M. Fey (Eds.), *Treatment of language disorders in children* (pp. 203–236). Baltimore: Paul H. Brookes.

Harn, B. A., Stoolmiller, M., & Chard, J. (2008). Measuring the dimensions of alphabetic principle on the reading development of first graders: The role of automaticity and unitization. *Journal of Learning Disabilities, 41,* 143–157.

Hemmeter, M. L., Fox, L., Jack, S., Broyles, L., & Doubet, S. (2007). A program-wide model of positive behavior support in early childhood settings. *Journal of Early Intervention, 29,* 337–355.

Hsieh, W., Hemmeter, M. L., McCollum, J. A., & Ostrosky, M. M. (2009). Using coaching to increase preschool teachers' use of emergent literacy teaching strategies. *Early Childhood Research Quarterly, 24,* 229–247.

Individuals with Disabilities Education Act Data. (2009, November 3). IDEA 618 Data Tables. Retrieved from https://www.ideadata.org/arc_toc9.asp#partbCC

Individuals with Disabilities Education Improvement Act [IDEA] of 2004, PL 108-446, 20 U. S.C. §§ 1400 et seq.

Isbell, R., Sobol, Lindauer, L., & Lowrance, A. (2004). The effects of storytelling and story reading on the oral language complexity and story comprehension of young children. *Early Childhood Education Journal, 32,* 157–163.

Justice, L. M., Kaderavek, J. N., Fan, X., Sofka, A., & Hunt, A. (January, 2009). Accelerating preschoolers' early literacy development through classroom-based teacher-child storybook reading and explicit print referencing. *Language, Speech, and Hearing Services in Schools, 40,* 67–85.

Justice, L. M., & Pullen, P. C. (2003). Promising interventions for promoting emergent literacy skills: Three evidence-based approaches. *Topics in Early Childhood Education, 23,* 99–113.

Justice, L. M., Sofka, A. E., Sutton, M., & Zucker, T. A. (2006). *Project STAR: Fidelity coding checklist.* Charlottesville: Preschool Language and Literacy Lab, University of Virginia.

Kamps, D., Abbott, M., Greenwood, C., Wills, H., Veerkamp, M., & Kaufman, J. (2008). Effects of small-group reading instruction and curriculum differences for students most at risk in kindergarten. *Journal of Learning Disabilities, 41,* 101–114.

Lonigan, C. J., Schatschneider, C., & Westberg, L. (2008a). Identification of children's skills and abilities linked to later outcomes in reading, writing, and spelling. In *Developing early literacy: Report of the*

National Early Literacy Panel (pp. 55–106). Jessup, MD: National Institute for Literacy.

Lonigan, C. J., Schatschneider, C., & Westberg, L. (2008b). Impact of code-focused interventions on children's early literacy skills. In *Developing early literacy, Report of the National Early Literacy Panel* (pp. 107–151). Jessup, MD: National Institute for Literacy.

McCall, R. B. (2009). Evidence-based programming in the context of practice and policy. *Social Policy Report Society for Research in Child Development, 23*(3), 3–11.

McGee, G. G., Almeida, C., Sulzer-Azaroff, B., & Feldman, R. S. (1992). Promoting reciprocal interactions via peer incidental teaching. *Journal of Applied Behavior Analysis, 25,* 117–126.

McIntosh, B., Crosbie, S., Holm. A., & Dodd, B. (2007). Enhancing the phonological awareness and language skills of socially disadvantaged preschoolers: An interdisciplinary programme. *Child Language Teaching and Therapy, 23*, 267–286.

National Early Literacy Panel. (2008). *Developing early literacy: Report of the National Early Literacy Panel.* Washington, DC: National Institute for Literacy.

National Institute of Child Health and Human Development. (2000). *Report of the National Reading Panel. Teaching children to read: An evidence-based assessment of the scientific research literature on reading and its implications for reading instruction* (NIH Publication No. 00-4769). Washington, DC: U.S. Government Printing Office.

No Child Left Behind Act [NCLB] (PL 107-110, 2001), U. S. C. 20 §§ 6301 et seq.

O'Connor, R. (2000). Increasing the intensity of intervention in kindergarten and first grade. *Learning Disabilities Research and Practice, 15*, 43–54.

O'Connor, R. E., Bocian, K., Beebe-Frankenberger, M., & Linklater, D. L. (2010). Responsiveness of students with language difficulties to early intervention in reading. *The Journal of Special Education, 43,* 220–235.

O'Connor, R. E., Fulmer, D., Harty, K. R., & Bell, K. (2005). Layers of reading intervention in kindergarten through third grade: Changes in teaching and student outcomes. *Journal of Learning Disabilities, 38*, 440–455.

Odom, S. L., Brantlinger, E., Gersten, R., Horner, R. H., Thompson, B., & Harris, K. R. (2005). Research in special education: Scientific methods and evidence-based practices. *Exceptional Children, 71,* 137–148.

Odom, S. L., McConnell, S. R., McEvoy, M. A., Peterson, C., Ostrosky, M., Chandler, L. K., … Favazza, P. C. (1999). Relative effects of interventions supporting the social competence of young children with disabilities. *Topics in Early Childhood Special Education, 19,* 75–91.

Odom, S. L., & McLean, M. E. (Eds.). (2006). *Early intervention/early childhood special education: Recommended practices.* Austin, TX: PRO-ED.

Odom, S. L., McLean, M. E., Johnson, L. J., & LaMontagne, M. J. (1995). Recommended practices in early childhood special education: Validation and current use. *Journal of Early Intervention, 19,* 1–17.

Odom, S. L., Peck, C., Hanson, M., Beckman, P., Kaiser, A., Lieber, J., … & Schwartz, I. (1996). Inclusion at the preschool level: An ecological systems analysis. *Social Policy Report: Society for Research in Child Development, 10*(2, 3), 18–30.

Odom, S. L., & Wolery, M. (2003). A unified theory of practice in early intervention/childhood special education: Evidence-based practices. *Journal of Special Education, 37,* 164–173.

Piaget, J. (1952). *The origins of intelligence in children.* New York: International University Press.

Preschool Curriculum Evaluation Research Consortium (2008). *Effects of preschool curriculum programs on school readiness* (NCER 2008-2009). Washington, DC: National Center for Education Research, Institute of Education Sciences, U.S. Department of Education,U. S. Government Printing Office.

President's Commission on Excellence in Special Education. (2002). *A new era-revitalizing special education for children and families.* Retrieved December 2009, from http://www.ed.gov/inits/commissions-boards/whspecialeducation/reports/images/Pres_Re.pdf

Price, L. H., van Kleeck, A., & Huberty, C. J. (2009). Talk during book sharing between parents and preschool children: A comparison between storybook and expository book conditions. *Reading Research Quarterly, 44*(2), 171–194.

Puolakanaho, A., Ahonen, T., Aro, M., Eklund, K., Leppanen, P. H. T., Poikkeus, … & Lyytinen, H. (2008). Developmental links of very early phonological and language skills to second grade reading outcomes. *Journal of Learning Disabilities, 41,* 353–370.

Public Law 94-142 Education for All Handicapped Act, 1975.

Public Law 99-457 Education for All Handicapped Act Amendments, 1986.

Qi, C. H., & Kaiser, A. P. (2003). Behavior problems of preschool children from low-income families: Review of the literature. *Topics in Early Childhood Special Education, 23*, 188–216.

Roberts, T. A. (2009). Home storybook reading in primary or second language with preschool children: Evidence of equal effectiveness for second-language vocabulary acquisition. *Reading Research Quarterly, 43*(2), 103–130.

Safford, P. L., Sargent, M., & Cook, C. (1994). Instructional models in early childhood special education: Origins, issues, and trends. In P. Safford (Ed.), *Early childhood special education: Yearbook in early childhood education* (Vol. 5, pp. 96–117). New York: Teachers College Press.

Safford, P. L., & Safford, E. J. (1996). *A history of childhood & disability.* New York: Teachers College Press.

Sandall, S., Giacomini, J., Smith, B. J., & Hemmeter, M. L. (2006). *DEC recommended practices toolkits: Interactive tools to improve practices for young children with special needs and their families.* Missoula, MO: The Division for Early Childhood.

Sandall, S., Hemmeter, M. L., Smith, B. J., & McLean, M. (2005). *DEC recommended practices: A comprehensive guide for practical application in early intervention/early childhood special education.* Longman, CO: Sopris West.

Sandall, S., McLean, M. E., & Smith, B. J. (Eds.). (2000). *DEC recommended practices in early intervention/early childhood special education.* Longmont, CO: Sopris West.

Scanlon, D. M., Vellutino, F. R., Small, S. G., Fanuele, D. P., & Sweeney, J. M. (2005). Severe reading difficulties–Can they be prevented? A comparison of prevention and intervention approaches. *Exceptionality, 13,* 209–227.

Simmons, D. C., Coyne, M. D., Kwok, O., McDonagh, S., Harn, B. A., & Kame'enui, E. J. (2008). Indexing Response to Intervention: A longitudinal study of reading risk from kindergarten through third grade. *Journal of Learning Disabilities, 41*, 158–173.

Skinner, B. F. (1953). *Science and human behavior.* New York: Macmillan Company.

Snow, C., Burns, M. S., & Griffin, P. (Eds.). (1998). *Preventing reading difficulties in young children.* Washington, DC: National Academy Press.

Speece, D. L., Mills, C., Ritchey, K. D., & Hillman, E. (2003). Initial evidence that letter fluency tasks are valid indicators of early reading skills. *Journal of Special Education, 36,* 223–233.

Sugai, G., Horner, R. H., Dunlap, G., Hieneman, M., Lewis, T. J., Nelson, C. M., … Liaupsin, T. (2000). Applying positive behavior support and functional behavioral assessment in schools. *Journal of Positive Behavior Interventions, 2*, 131–143.

Storch, S. A., & Whitehurst, G. J. (2002). Oral language and code-related precursors to reading: Evidence from a longitudinal structural model. *Developmental Psychology, 38,* 924–947.

Stormont, M., Lewis, T. J., & Beckner, B. (2005). Developmentally continuous positive behavior support systems: Applying key features in preschool settings. *Teaching Exceptional Children, 37,* 42–48.

Strain, P. S., McConnell, S. R., Carta, J. J., Fowler, S. A., Neisworth, J. T., & Wolery, M. (1992). Behaviorism in early intervention. *Topics in Early Childhood Special Education, 12,* 121–142.

Sutherland, K. S., Conroy, M., Abrams, L., & Vo, A. (2010). Improving interactions between teachers and young children with problem behavior: A strengths-based approach. *Exceptionality, 18,* 70–81.

Torgesen, J. (1998). Catch them before they fall: Identification and assessment to prevent failure in young children. *American Educator, 22,* 32–39.

Troia, G. (1999). Phonological awareness intervention research: A critical review of experimental methodology. *Reading Research Quarterly, 34,* 28–52.

Trohanis, P. L. (2008). Progress in providing services to young children with special needs and their families. *Journal of Early Intervention, 30,* 140–151.

Vygotsky, L. (1978). *Mind in society: The development of high psychological processes.* Cambridge, MA: Harvard University Press.

Webster-Stratton, C. (1990). *Dina Dinosaur's social, emotional and problem-solving curriculum.* Seattle: University of Washington.

Webster-Stratton, C. (1997). Early intervention for families of preschool children with conduct problems. In M. J. Guralnick (Ed.), *The effectiveness of early intervention* (pp. 429–454). Baltimore: Paul H. Brookes.

West, T. N., Brown, W. H., Grego, J. M., & Johnson, R. (2008). Practitioners' judgments of peer interaction interventions: A survey of DEC members. *Journal of Early Intervention, 30,* 36–54.

What Works Clearinghouse. Retrieved December 2009, from http://www.whatworksclearinghouse.org

Whitehurst, G. J., Falco, F. L., Lonigan, C. J., Fischel, J. E., DeBaryshe, B. D., Valdez-Menchaca, M. C., & Caulfield M. (1998). Accelerating language development through picture book reading. *Developmental Psychology, 24,* 552–559.

Whitehurst, G. J., & Lonigan, C. J. (1998). Child development and emergent literacy. *Child Development, 69,* 848–872.

Wolery, M., & Bredekamp, S. (1994). Developmentally appropriate practice and young children with disabilities: Contextual issues in the discussion. *Journal of Early Intervention, 18,*331-341.

Wolery, M., Strain, P. S., & Bailey, D. B. (1992). Reaching potentials of children with special needs. In S. Bredekamp & T. Rosengrant (Eds.), *Reaching potentials: Appropriate curriculum and assessment for young children* (pp. 92–111). Washington, DC: National Association for the Education of Young Children.

Ziolkowski, R. A., & Goldstein, H. (2008). Book reading on preschool children with language delays: Effects on an embedded phonological awareness intervention during repeated book reading on preschool children with language delays. *Journal of Early Intervention, 31,* 67-90.

Zucker, T. A., Ward, A. E., & Justice, L. M. (2009). Print referencing during read-alouds: A technique for increasing emergent readers' print knowledge. *The Reading Teacher, 63*(1), 62–72.

53

Frameworks for Guiding Program Focus and Practices in Early Intervention

Patricia A. Snyder, Tara W. McLaughlin, and Maria K. Denney
University of Florida

Early intervention is a term generally used to describe supports and services provided to young children birth to age 5 with or at risk for delays or disabilities and their families. Early theoretical and empirical influences date back centuries, but most accounts of the field acknowledge its emergence in the 1960s and its interdisciplinary roots in general early childhood education, compensatory education, special education for school-age children, maternal and child health services, psychology, and child development (e.g., Allen & Cowdery, 2009; McCormick, 2006).

Several programs that began in the 1960s as part of broader initiatives related to the War on Poverty—the civil rights movement and the prevention, identification, and treatment of mental retardation—were particularly influential in shaping program focus and practices in early intervention. These programs included (a) maternal and child health preventive and screening programs and special project grants for children with mental retardation under Title V of the Social Security Act in 1963; (b) creation of Head Start in 1965; (c) expanded special education programs under a 1965 amendment to Title I of the Elementary and Secondary Education Act (P.L. 89-313) for children ages birth to 20 years of age; and, (d) model demonstration programs for young children under the Handicapped Children's Early Education Assistance Act in 1968. This latter act was particularly influential with respect to program focus and practices in early intervention because it established the Handicapped Children's Early Education Program (HCEEP), which later became the Early Education Program for Children with Disabilities (EEPCD).

The HCEEP/EEPCD funded programs included demonstration, outreach, and research projects; state implementation grants; inservice training projects; research institutes; and technical assistance to support practices for young children with or risk for disabilities from birth through age 8 and their families for almost 30 years (Gallagher, Danaher, & Clifford, 2009; Smith, 2000). As Smith (2000) noted, from 1968 to 1997, these programs provided the primary research and program development focus for the field. Although the influences of HCEEP/EEPCD on programs and practices in the field are widely acknowledged, it was not until the 1986 amendment of the Education for All Handicapped Children's Act (EHA; PL 99-457) that access to supports and services in early intervention was expanded with the addition of a preschool program for children with disabilities and a new program for birth through 2-year-olds. Currently known as Section 619 (preschool) and Part C (infant/toddlers) under the Individuals with Disabilities Education and Improvement Act (IDEA), these two programs guarantee access for eligible children and their families to services and supports designed to enhance young children's development and learning and to support families in their roles as children's primary caregivers. In both programs, emphasis is placed on offering services and supports in the context of natural or inclusive environments, where young children with and without disabilities are afforded high quality learning opportunities (DEC/NAEYC, 2009).

Since the 1960s, programs such as HCEEP/EEPCD and other research conducted in the field have helped inform efforts related to providing these services and supports in natural or inclusive environments. As Smith (2000, p. 12) noted, however, "one of the biggest challenges facing us as a field in the next millennium is to foster as much passion about [program] quality as we have had about access." As the field of early intervention approaches its golden anniversary, it seems appropriate to consider how accomplishments and lessons learned might inform the next iterations of programs and practices in the field.

The purpose of this chapter is to consider contemporary frameworks that guide program focus and practices in early intervention. We discuss promising early promotion, prevention, and intervention or tiered frameworks and associated practices, which are designed to support and accelerate the growth and learning of young children in inclusive early learning settings. We situate this discussion by first providing an overview of current trends and issues shaping the focus of programs and practices in early childhood and early intervention. We then describe tiered frameworks as approaches for organizing and informing decisions about what, when, and how supports and interventions are provided for young children. An integrative review and analysis of several frameworks is conducted and we highlight implementation opportunities and challenges. We conclude the chapter by discussing controversies and future trends associated with tiered frameworks.

Trends and Issues Shaping the Focus of Programs and Practices in Early Childhood and Early Intervention

At least four trends and issues are shaping program focus and practices: (a) early childhood systems integration efforts, (b) diversity of children and families served, (c) developmentally appropriate and recommended practices, and (d) curricular frameworks and accountability for child and family outcomes.

Early Childhood Systems Integration

Early childhood programs funded under IDEA are considered one program "sector" under a broader array of programs supporting young children and their families. Other programs include Early Head Start and Head Start; child and family care; early childhood education; family support programs; and maternal and child health, nutrition, and mental health. Historically, each of these programs has operated somewhat independently and under separate authority. Under Good Start, Grow Smart (GSGS Interagency Workgroup, 2005) and other federal, state, and community systems development initiatives, efforts are underway to coordinate and integrate programs designed to support the health, growth, and early learning of all young children in the context of their families and communities (Johnson & Theberge, 2007).

One trend shaping the focus of programs and practices in early intervention is the growing emphasis on universal, coordinated, and integrated early childhood systems. Given a primary goal of early intervention is meaningful and successful inclusion (DEC/NAEYC, 2009), programs and practices for young children with disabilities will increasingly be situated within, not apart from, the broader array of programs and practices for young children and their families.

Diversity of Children and Families Served

The growing racial, ethnic, cultural, and linguistic diversity of young children and their families requires focused attention to ensure programs and practices in early intervention are high quality, inclusive, and responsive to diversity. Since the 1980s, legislation and recommended practices in the field have emphasized individualization and family-centered practices that respect and support the culture, values, and languages of each child and family (Division for Early Childhood, 2004). There are many sources of diversity and each of these sources is likely to be represented in contemporary early learning programs. For example, early learning programs are likely to include young children with or without identified risks or disabilities, young children from different cultures, young children of different races, young children living in poverty, and young children who are English-language learners.

Demographic forecasts predict modest growth in the number of young children in the United States population, significant increases in children's cultural and linguistic diversity, greater percentages of children and families living in poverty, and noteworthy increases in the numbers of children whose home language is not English (Annie E. Casey Foundation, 2009). Given current demographics and predicted trends, frameworks that guide program focus and practices should ensure the diverse abilities, needs, and circumstances of children and families, rather than categorical labels or eligibility criteria, guide decisions about types, levels, and intensities of supports and interventions.

Developmentally Appropriate Practices in Early Childhood and Recommended Practices in Early Intervention

Two major sources continue to have significant influences on program focus and practices: (a) developmentally appropriate practices (DAP) promulgated by the National Association for the Education of Young Children (NAEYC; National Association for the Education of Young Children, 2009a), and (b) the Division for Early Childhood (DEC) recommended practices in early intervention/early childhood special education (Sandall, Hemmeter, Smith, & McLean, 2005). Both sources are intended to serve as guidelines for application of recommended practices in the field.

In 1986, NAEYC published the initial DAP position statement, followed by publication of a DAP text (Bredekamp, 1987). Since 1986, the DAP position statement and associated materials have been revised twice: in 1996 and in 2009 (Bredekamp & Copple, 1997; Copple & Bredekamp, 2009; National Association for the Education of Young Children, 1996; 2009a). Table 53.1 shows a comparison of the three DAP position statements with respect to core DAP dimensions.

As shown in Table 53.1, the 1996 position statement acknowledged the importance of early childhood teachers seeking a balance between children's self-initiated learning and adult guidance and support. Of particular relevance to early intervention, this position statement acknowledged the "… trend toward full inclusion of children with disabilities must be reflected in descriptions of recommended practices" (p. 2) and that "… considerable work has been done toward converging the perspectives of early childhood and early childhood special education" (p. 2). Practitioners were advised to "… identify children who have special learning or developmental needs and to plan appropriate curriculum and teaching for them" (NAEYC, 1996, p. 14). These additions to the DAP position statement addressed concerns that the initial DAP guidelines were not sufficient for promoting

TABLE 53.1
Key Trends in Developmentally Appropriate Practice Position Statements

	1986	1996	2009
Highlighted Focus	Children's play is the primary vehicle for and indicator of development	Moving from either/or to both thinking—blending opportunities for play and teaching	Intentional teaching and high-quality play are the core of DAP
Dimensions of DAP	Age appropriate Individually appropriate	Age appropriate Individually appropriate Culturally appropriate	Age appropriate Individually appropriate Culturally appropriate
Teachers' Role	Guide or facilitator for child learning	Facilitator with planned supports for child learning	Intentional and responsive for child learning
Children's Role	Exploration and interaction with environment and people Construct knowledge	Active learners Construct knowledge within social and cultural contexts	Develop secure relationships Construct knowledge within social and cultural contexts
Curriculum Focus	Child-initiated Child-directed Teacher-supported play	Child-initiated Teacher-guided or supported	Planned curriculum Builds on child initiations and interests
Supporting Diverse Learners	Multicultural and nonsexist experiences for all children	Recognition of individual variation and identify children with special learning or developmental needs; plan appropriate curriculum and teaching Recognition of social and cultural influence on learning and development	Recognition of individual variation and identify children with special learning needs or other risk factors; plan appropriate curriculum and teaching Recognition of social and cultural influence including behavioral and linguistic conventions on learning and development

the optimal development and learning of young children with disabilities, particularly related to individualizing instructional practices related to child-specific goals (Carta & Kong, 2007; Carta, Schwartz, Atwater, McConnell, 1991; Wolery & Wilbers, 1994).

The 2009 position statement extended the focus on providing adult-guided and responsive learning opportunities. Intentionality is noted to be the core of DAP and supports the long- and short-term decisions that "add up to practice that promotes young children's optimal learning and development" (National Association for the Education of Young Children, 2009b). Intentional teaching means that as practitioners make decisions about DAP, they keep desired outcomes for each child in mind when they develop child-focused goals that are challenging and achievable (Epstein, 2007).

The Division for Early Childhood of the Council for Exceptional Children established the first set of recommended practices for infants and young children with special needs and their families in 1993 (DEC Task Force on Recommended Practices, 1993). Similar to the NAEYC DAP position statements and associated materials, the DEC recommended practices have also been updated several times. The updated recommended practices (e.g., Sandall, McLean, & Smith, 2000; Sandall, Hemmeter, Smith, & McLean, 2005) were validated through a national field-validation study (McLean, Snyder, Smith, & Sandall, 2002). The updated recommended practices are intended to support evidence-based practice decisions for individual children and families. Evidence-based practice is a decision-making process that integrates best-available research evidence with family and professional wisdom and values and is applied on a case-by-case basis (Buysse & Wesley, 2006; Snyder, 2006).

Particularly relevant for this chapter are the 27 child-focused recommended practices, which provide guidance about how children should be taught, when and where instructional practices and arrangements should be implemented, and how children's performance should be monitored to inform data-based decision making (Wolery, 2005). The child-focused recommended practices reflect accumulated empirical evidence in early intervention, which supports the premise that young children with identified disabilities or those at risk for learning challenges benefit from intentional, differentiated, and systematic supports and instruction. Consistent with tenets expressed in the 2009 NAEYC position statement, DEC child-focused practices emphasize the importance of intentional interactions and instruction by adults who interact with young children to support children's development and accelerate their learning toward desired outcomes.

Curricular Frameworks and Accountability for Child and Family Outcomes

Many states have outlined early learning curricular frameworks or specified early learning standards. Curricular frameworks have been defined as underlying structures or supports for classifying or organizing information about what children should learn, where children should learn, how children should learn, and how to evaluate what children learn (DEC, 2007; Pretti-Frontczak et al., 2007). Early learning standards specify expectations about what young children should know or be able to do. Most states have developed or are in the process of developing early learning standards or guidelines and are linking them to accountability systems (DEC, 2007; Scott-Little, Lesko, Martella, & Milburn, 2007).

An outcome has been defined as a statement of a measurable condition(s) desired for a population of children (Early Childhood Outcomes Center, 2004). In the current era of results-focused accountability, significant attention and resources have been focused on identifying and measuring desired outcomes for early childhood programs, young children, and, in some cases, the families of young children. Unfortunately, across early childhood sectors, agreement has not been reached on which outcomes should be adopted, how these outcomes should be measured, how outcome data will be aggregated, analyzed and interpreted, or how infrastructure will support the collection and informed use of data. Within early intervention, however, initial steps have been taken to establish a child and family outcome system. Efforts have been underway since early 2000 to specify and measure child progress toward three outcomes: (a) positive social-emotional skills, (b) acquisition and use of knowledge, and (c) use of appropriate behaviors to meet needs (Early Childhood Outcomes Center, 2005). In 2010, states began reporting baseline data about child and family outcomes for Part C and Section 619 programs and identifying benchmarks or targets for improvement (Early Childhood Outcomes Center, 2008).

Achieving desired results or outcomes for all young children and families, including those with or at risk for disabilities, is inextricably linked to the application of evidence-informed practices that support early development and accelerate learning. The contemporary emphasis on early childhood systems integration coupled with specification of DAP and recommended practices in a context of results-focused accountability has led to the development of conceptual frameworks useful for guiding decisions about supports and interventions provided to diverse learners in early education and care settings (VanDerHeyden & Snyder, 2006). For young children with or at risk for disabilities, these frameworks must ensure access to and participation in the general early childhood curriculum with specialized and individualized supports and interventions as part of high quality programs. VanDerHeyden and Snyder suggested tiered early promotion, prevention, and intervention frameworks hold promise for organizing and informing program focus and practice decisions in the field.

Frameworks to Guide Program Focus and Practices in Early Intervention

Conceptual frameworks can be presented in written or illustrated forms to describe relationships among complex entities or processes. When illustrated, the logical and internally coherent structures of a framework are represented. Graphics have been used in public health, mental health, and education to illustrate tiered or pyramidal promotion, prevention, and intervention frameworks for a defined population. In education, response to intervention (RTI) refers to tiered frameworks focused on academic or social skills (Jimerson, Burns, & VanDerHeyden, 2007). "RTI" frameworks have also been discussed in the early intervention literature (cf. Coleman, Buysse, & Neitzel, 2006; Fox, Carta, Strain, Dunlap, & Hemmeter, 2010; VanDerHeyden & Snyder, 2006).

When emanating from public health and prevention science, most promotion, prevention, and intervention or tiered frameworks share similar features or structures (see Figure 53.1). Across the frameworks, the primary tier or level often is considered the "universal" or foundational level. Supports or interventions associated with the primary tier are designed to reduce risk and promote health,

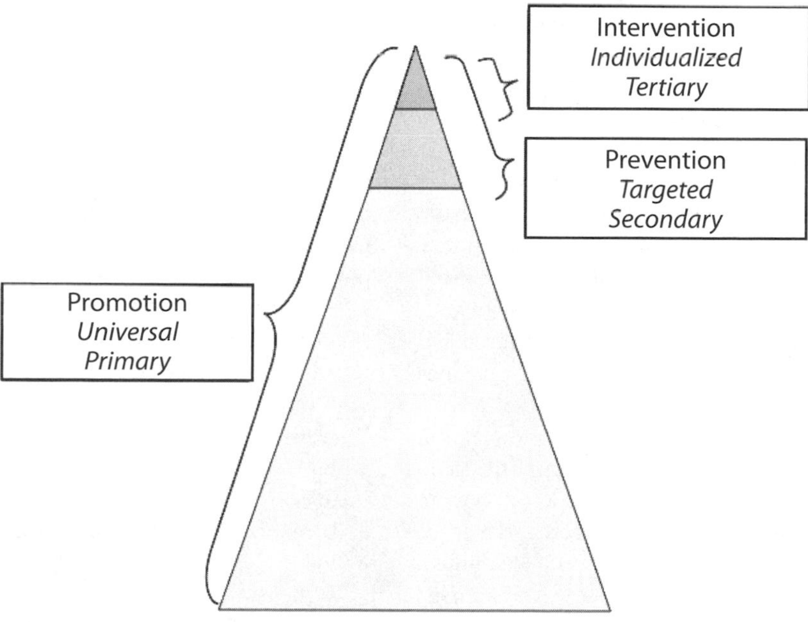

Figure 53.1 Key descriptors reflected in tiered frameworks.

development, or well-being for all members of a defined population. At each successive tier or level, supports or interventions become more selective or individualized. The secondary tier or level of support or intervention in a tiered framework frequently includes prevention strategies or targeted interventions. Some, but not all, members of a defined group receive secondary supports or interventions. At the tertiary level, individualized supports or interventions are included. Even fewer members of a group receive these individualized supports or interventions.

Specific to early intervention, Simeonsson (1991) suggested primary, secondary, and tertiary prevention frameworks might have utility for encompassing the preventive and ameliorative goals reflected in the field. Drawing from the work of Caplan (1964) and Caplan and Greenbaum (1967) in preventive psychiatry, he proposed a three-tiered promotion, prevention, and intervention framework that might be helpful for organizing and guiding decisions about supports and interventions provided to young children with or at risk for disabilities and their families. Simeonsson cautioned that use of primary, secondary, and tertiary prevention frameworks should not result in categorization and assignment of children to mutually exclusive services or practices associated with the various levels (e.g., child "in" tier 2). Rather, he suggested interventions for individual children and their families be conceptualized and developed within and across levels.

Kaczmarek (1999) described a general hierarchical framework for early intervention in which developmentally appropriate practice was the foundation. Each successive level in the hierarchy included interventions that "require more resources and more elaborate planning to implement" (p. 111). Kaczmarek suggested this [tiered] framework might be useful for bridging developmentally appropriate practices and recommended practices by specifying a continuum of interventions ranging from child- to adult-directed. She reviewed a study conducted by Filla, Wolery, and Anthony (1999) to illustrate how single-subject experimental designs might be used to validate practices associated with the hierarchical framework she proposed.

Frameworks such as those described by Simeonsson (1991) and Kaczmarek (1999) have logical and pragmatic appeal for early intervention. These frameworks have the potential to serve as cross-sector and interdisciplinary organizers for program development, resource allocation, and decisions about the types, levels, and intensity of supports and interventions provided to all young children and their families. With respect to program focus and practices in early intervention, the frameworks can be used to emphasize the importance of high quality early education and care for all children at universal levels and the need to make evidence- and data-based decisions about how to identify and assist young children who need targeted or individualized interventions or as Bagnato (2006) noted, "more help." These frameworks might provide a "roadmap" for the application of DAP and recommended practices. They can be used to ensure young children with disabilities and their families have access to a wide range of "typical" activities, settings, and environments with high quality supports, teaching, and learning experiences available that lead to desired outcomes—an excellent fit with inclusion tenets (Fox et al., 2010).

Integrative Review of Selected Tiered Frameworks

Several tiered frameworks have been described and illustrated in the early childhood literature. Some frameworks focus on early childhood development and learning across domains; others focus on specific domains (e.g., social-emotional). Some frameworks emphasize the implementation of supports and interventions; others include assessment and progress monitoring components. Building on an analysis completed by VanDerHeyden and Snyder (2006), we describe several frameworks, review the empirical support for each framework or associated practices, and analyze common and unique components. The section concludes with discussion of the frameworks in the context of preschool RTI.

Building Blocks. Building Blocks for Teaching Preschoolers with Special Needs (Sandall & Schwartz, 2002, 2008) is a hierarchical framework that grew out of research and professional development activities conducted by the Early Childhood Research Institute on Inclusion funded by the Office of Special Education Programs in the U.S. Department of Education (Sandall, Schwartz, & Joseph, 2001). The "building blocks" are the conceptual basis of a framework that supports planning for and providing individualized support and instruction for young children with special needs in community-based classrooms. The foundational building block is a high quality early childhood program. Three other blocks in this tiered framework are curriculum modifications and adaptations, embedded learning opportunities, and explicit, child-focused instructional strategies. Instructional strategies are organized within each block to support children's engagement, participation, and learning and their attainment of individualized goals and desired outcomes. Each successive block in the visual depiction of the framework becomes smaller to illustrate increases in intensity and specificity of the associated instructional practices. For example, response-prompting strategies are used more frequently and with more specificity when explicit, child-focused instruction is provided.

A primary emphasis in the framework is intentional and systematic instruction. As Sandall and Schwartz (2008) noted, the framework (as a package) has not been compared with other comprehensive tiered approaches or curricula. Instead, the four building blocks provide a framework within which empirical research associated with each building block component and associated practices is conducted and organized. Representative studies are described briefly below.

With respect to the second building block, Schilling and Schwartz (2004) demonstrated the functional relationship between alternative seating (curricular adaptation in framework) and classroom behavior of young children with autism spectrum disorder. Addressing the third building block focused on embedded learning opportunities (ELOs), Horn, Lieber, Li, Sandall, and Schwartz (2000) conducted a series of three case studies to develop procedures for supporting and assessing early childhood teachers' implementation of ELOs and to describe teachers' perspectives about ELOs. In addition, information about the impact of ELO implementation on child behavior in relation to progress on targeted skills was gathered. Findings from these case studies demonstrated ELOs generally supported children's progress on targeted skills, which is a consistent finding in the empirical literature on embedded instruction (Snyder et al., 2010). Differences in teachers' implementation of ELO were noted, particularly with respect to whether they carried out their ELO plan as intended. Teachers' perspectives about ELO were generally positive, although they noted ELO were sometimes difficult to implement in large-group activities and easier to implement during center and free-play activities.

McBride and Schwartz (2003) investigated practices associated with three building blocks by teaching early childhood teachers to use explicit, child-focused instructional strategies (systematic discrete trials) during ongoing classroom activities. Using a multiple-probe design across four conditions: (a) exposure to a small-group classroom activity; (b) activity-based instruction (ABI/ELO), where teachers planned a group activity and opportunities to embed instruction on three children's individualized goals; (c) ABI plus systematic discrete trials (i.e., fourth building block involving explicit, child-focused instructional strategies); and (d) generalization to a different child and different target behavior. Results showed neither the baseline or ABI condition was associated with significant increases in correct responses to target learning objectives, but ABI plus explicit instruction was associated with increases or stable levels of child engagement and higher rates of independent correct responses.

Results from these studies illustrate how several practices associated with each block of the framework have been examined empirically. Although Building Blocks was developed to guide instruction for young children with disabilities, the first three blocks of the framework and associated practices align well with contemporary perspectives about intentional teaching in early childhood (Epstein, 2007; NAEYC, 2009b).

Intervention hierarchy for promoting young children's peer interactions in natural environments. As noted earlier, several tiered frameworks focus on specific developmental domains. The intervention hierarchy for promoting young children's peer interactions in natural environments is an example of this type of framework (Brown & Conroy, 1997; Brown, Odom, & Conroy, 2001; Odom & Brown, 1993). This framework is based on an intervention hierarchy and associated practices designed to help practitioners decide how to promote peer interactions of young children with peer-related social competence difficulties in natural environments.

The foundation of this framework focuses on developmentally appropriate practices implemented in inclusive early childhood programs with socially responsive peers. Classroom-wide interventions that promote peer interactions and social competence can be implemented within these developmentally appropriate environments.

Naturalistic interventions, including incidental teaching of social behaviors and friendship activities, form the basis of the next tier or level of the intervention hierarchy. During incidental teaching episodes, practitioners promote children's peer interactions by providing adult or peer models of social behavior and prompting children to elaborate on their social behaviors (Brown et al., 2001). Friendship activities are defined as intentional and individualized interventions that are teacher planned, embedded within ongoing classroom activities and routines, and use logically occurring social antecedents and consequences to support interactions.

The final two levels of the intervention hierarchy for promoting young children's peer interactions focus on social integration activities and explicit social skills training. Social integration activities involve planning for and providing intentional and systematic supports so young children with limited peer interactions will be in contact with peers who are socially responsive and competent. Explicit social-skills training involves intensive instruction on specific social strategies or social behaviors (e.g., Goldstein, English, Shafer, & Kaczmarek, 1997; Odom & McConnell, 1993).

The developers of this hierarchy acknowledged it is similar to and compatible with other tiered early intervention frameworks, particularly with respect to factors that influence decisions about intervention selection within and across levels of the hierarchy. They advocated selecting intervention strategies that are (a) effective (improve children's development and learning), (b) efficient (make meaningful use of child and teacher time), (c) functional (promote generalization and maintenance of targeted skills), and (d) normalized (use the least intrusive and naturalistic interventions possible). Moreover, as specified in other frameworks, DAP is viewed as necessary, but likely not sufficient, for promoting social competence and peer interactions when young children have interactional challenges. The developers noted, however, that targeted and individualized interventions are not necessarily implemented only with individual children or in a one-to-one teaching format. In the context of early childhood programs, one, multiple, or all children might participate in and benefit from targeted or individualized interventions.

Brown et al. (2001) and Odom and Brown (1993) summarized the empirical research that supported practices organized within the intervention hierarchy. For example, they identified the empirical support for friendships activities (e.g., McEvoy et al., 1988, Twardosz, Nordquist, Simon, & Botkin, 1983), incidental teaching of social behavior (e.g., Brown, McEvoy, & Bishop, 1991), and social integration activities (DeKlyen & Odom, 1989; Frea, Craig-Unkefer,

Odom, & Johnson, 1999). These authors noted three reviews were conducted that provided empirical support for social skills training interventions (Brown & Conroy, 1997, 2001; McEvoy, Odom, & McConnell, 1992; Odom & Brown, 1993).

The intervention hierarchy was intended as a heuristic framework, not a lock-step sequence of peer-interaction interventions. While the authors acknowledged decision-making processes would be used to identify and select practices for individual children, they did not explicitly describe these processes. They suggested additional research be conducted to determine if the framework and associated practices were socially and empirically valid.

Pyramid model. The Pyramid model is based on tiered promotion, prevention, and intervention frameworks described in prevention science and on school-wide positive behavior support models. Features of the Pyramid model are similar to those described for the intervention hierarchy for promoting young children's peer interactions in natural environments. The model offers a "tiered intervention framework of evidence-based interventions for promoting the social, emotional, and behavior development of young children" (Fox et al., 2010, p. 6). Initially, a three-tier, four level Teaching Pyramid model was described as a framework for use with 2- to 5-year-old children in early childhood settings (Fox, Dunlap, Hemmeter, Joseph, & Strain, 2003; Hemmeter, Ostrosky, & Fox, 2006). The Teaching Pyramid model was expanded and refined to provide guidance about using the framework (and associated practices) with infants, toddlers, and preschoolers with and without identified disabilities and delays (Fox et al., 2010). The revised Pyramid model still includes three tiers and four levels.

The first tier of the Pyramid model, universal promotion, involves two levels of practices identified as foundational for promoting young children's social-emotional competence and preventing challenging behavior. The two levels of practices are nurturing and responsive caregiving relationships and high quality supportive environments. Practices associated with these levels are based on a substantial body of empirical evidence that suggests nurturing and responsive relationships are fundamental to young children's development and learning (National Research Council, 2001; Shonkoff & Phillips, 2000). In addition to relationships, high quality and supportive environments are recognized as the foundation for early development and learning in the model. Practices associated with this level of the Pyramid are those consistently identified in other tiered frameworks, including implementation of a high quality core curriculum, use of developmentally appropriate and intentional teaching practices, safe physical environments that promote learning and behavior, and the design of schedules and activities that maximize child engagement and learning. This second level of universal promotion highlights the provision of predictable and supportive environments and family interactions (Fox et al., 2010). For young children with or at risk for disabilities, this level also specifies the importance of inclusive environments for providing rich social contexts for interaction and learning.

The second tier of the Pyramid model focuses on secondary prevention and involves the provision of targeted social-emotional supports. Targeted supports include explicit instruction focused on social skills (e.g., identifying and expressing emotions, social problem-solving, friendship skills), learning how to regulate emotions, or systematically implementing social skills curricula with some children (Joseph & Strain, 2003).

Tier 3 involves tertiary and individualized interventions for children with persistent social-emotional delays and challenging behavior. At this tier, a team is convened to collect data to determine the nature of the social skills delays or problem behavior, to develop an individualized behavior support plan, to implement the plan with fidelity, and to conduct ongoing monitoring of child progress and revise the plan, if needed (Hemmeter et al., 2006). The individualized behavior support plan includes prevention strategies to address "triggers" for challenging behavior, replacement skills that are alternatives to the challenging behavior, and strategies to reduce the occurrence of challenging behaviors.

Hemmeter et al. (2006) detailed the empirical evidence that supports practices associated with each tier and level of the Teaching Pyramid model. Although the majority of Pyramid practices are evidence-based, comprehensive evaluations of the impacts of implementing all components of the Pyramid model in programs or classrooms have only recently been completed or are in progress. For example, Fox and Hemmeter (2009) and Hemmeter, Fox, Jack, Broyles, and Doubet (2007) have reported findings from program-wide implementation of the model. Hemmeter, Fox, and Snyder (2010) are evaluating the potential efficacy of the Pyramid model for promoting social-emotional competence and preventing challenging behavior in young children in relation to teachers' implementation of Pyramid practices. A judgment-based, observational rating scale to measure implementation fidelity of practices (Teaching Pyramid Observation Tool; Hemmeter, Fox, & Snyder, 2008) has been developed and validated as part of this study.

Recognition and response. Recognition and Response (R & R) is a three-tiered, early intervening model for use in pre-K. It is designed to guide the provision of high quality instruction and targeted interventions matched to children's learning needs and is based on response to intervention (see randr.fpg.unc.edu). R & R is distinguished from other tiered frameworks described earlier because it explicitly includes both recognition and response components. Assessment (recognition) and intervention (response) are linked at every level of the system. The recognition component involves universal screening of all children at tier 1 and more frequent progress monitoring at tiers two and three for those children who need additional supports or interventions. The response component involves implementation of a high quality core curriculum and intentional teaching at tier one, explicit small-group interventions and embedded learning activities at tier 2, and individualized scaffolding strategies at tier 3. Collaborative problem solving is the process used in R & R to help inform decisions about planning and evaluating instruction at all tiers.

Findings from the first implementation study of R & R were reported by Buysse and Peisner-Feinberg (2009). Participants in the study were practitioners in 24 classrooms enrolling 353 4-year-old children in childcare, Head Start, and public pre-K classrooms in Maryland and Florida. Universal screenings were conducted for every child throughout the year, and this information was used to inform decisions about which children might need additional language and literacy supports or interventions. Children in the "target group" received language and literacy intervention in a small group for 15 min a day for 2 mo. Of the 246 children for whom universal screening results were available, the 92 children who received targeted language and literacy supports or interventions made greater gains than their peers who did not receive these targeted supports on letter naming, vocabulary, sound awareness, and print knowledge measures. The target group made gains at the same rate as the non-target group on other language and literacy skills. The authors reported teachers were able to implement the R & R approach with a high level of accuracy and found R & R an acceptable and useful approach to instruction.

Currently, R & R researchers are conducting studies to develop, refine, and evaluate further the R & R model for use in early childhood programs. These studies focus on language and literacy content using the R & R framework and are being conducted in public-school pre-K classrooms. Among the activities to be conducted are developing language and literacy interventions for use in tiers 2 and 3, adapting a measure for use in universal screening and progress monitoring, developing intervention fidelity measures specific to R & R, evaluating the problem-solving component of the model, and gathering data on the social validity and treatment acceptability of the model and its components (see randr.fpg.unc.edu).

Response to intervention in early childhood and tiered frameworks. Several of the tiered frameworks described previously are conceptually and logically related to response to intervention frameworks (VanDerHeyden & Snyder, 2006). Use of the term "response to intervention" (RTI) to refer to frameworks such as R & R or the Pyramid model is a relatively recent development in early childhood. All of the reviewed frameworks, however, have features that align with the promotion, prevention, and intervention and hierarchical frameworks described in the early intervention literature in the 1990s (Kaczmarek, 1999; Simeonsson, 1991). Several researchers have suggested that early childhood RTI frameworks and associated practices have roots in applied behavior analysis, diagnostic-prescriptive teaching, differentiated instruction models, curriculum-based measurement, pre-referral interventions, and collaborative consultation (Fox et al., 2010; Snyder & Wilcox, 2009). Early childhood RTI frameworks also have been informed by applications of response to intervention in K–12 education settings. Recent work in early childhood RTI based on RTI in K–12 includes the National Center for Learning Disabilities "roadmap" to pre-K RTI (Coleman, Roth, & West, 2009), which specifies critical elements of RTI needed to ensure implementation fidelity and a hierarchical, three-tiered approach to meeting the needs of young children at risk for learning disabilities.

Funded by the Institute of Education Sciences in 2008, the Center for Response to Intervention in Early Childhood (CRTIEC, n.d.) is conducting research and providing resources to support the application of RTI in early childhood. CRTIEC defines RTI as a systematic problem-solving process designed to (a) identify children experiencing learning difficulties early, (b) provide children with a level of instructional intensity matched to their demonstrated response to intervention, and (c) provide a data-based method for evaluating the effectiveness of instructional approaches and changing or improving them (see www.crtiec.org). Guiding principles associated with the application of RTI in preschool identified by CRTIEC investigators include the use of multiple tiers of intervention; evidence-based practices within and across tiers; progress monitoring measures to evaluate growth and response to intervention; problem solving and decision-making processes to guide intervention selection, implementation, and evaluation; and, differentiated instructional intervention. Tier 1 is identified as universal instruction, tier 2 as targeted instruction, and tier 3 as intensive instruction. These principles and tiers are similar to those articulated in RTI problem-solving models used in K–12 education systems (Jimerson, Burns, & VanDerHeyden, 2007) and identified in the frameworks previously reviewed. Recognizing K–12 applications of RTI have preceded its application in early childhood, researchers associated with the Center have noted that much remains to be learned about the application of RTI in early childhood.

Summary related to tiered frameworks and RTI in early childhood. The early childhood field is at a formative stage in understanding how tiered systems, in which assessments and interventions are ordered by intensity and linked to data-based decision making within and across tiers, contribute to improved program quality and instruction for all young children in support of desired outcomes. VanDerHeyden and Snyder (2006) described potential benefits associated with applying principles and practices of RTI and tiered frameworks in early childhood, but noted additional research and development would be needed to ensure effective, efficient, and socially valid implementation.

Many developers of the aforementioned frameworks have noted that specified tiers should not be considered fixed levels that children are assigned to or move through. Rather, the intent of these frameworks is to organize practices heuristically within and across tiers to represent a continuum of supports and interventions that might be used to support young children's development and learning. In all frameworks reviewed above, the differences among tiers as well as supports and interventions presented within them are often in form and intensity rather than function and purpose (Brown et al., 2001). The shared principles among the frameworks suggest points of convergence between tiered frameworks developed for young children with disabilities and intentional teaching frameworks described in the early childhood literature.

Critical Analysis of Tiered Frameworks in Early Childhood

Table 53.2 shows an analysis of the four frameworks reviewed previously with respect to common and unique elements. As shown in the table, all frameworks present a tiered structure for organizing supports and intervention. Several frameworks focus primarily on social-emotional competence and challenging behavior (Pyramid model) or peer-related social competence (intervention hierarchy). The Building Blocks framework focuses on instructional strategies to support participation, engagement, and learning for preschoolers with special needs. R & R and the Pyramid model (Fox et al., 2010) are described as systems that link assessment, instruction, implementation fidelity, and data based decision-making and problem solving.

With respect to instructional focus, universal supports and intentional instruction associated with a high quality core curriculum are provided to all young children and typically are associated with the base or foundation level across the frameworks. Supports and instruction associated with secondary and tertiary levels generally are distinguished by differential intensity and specificity. As Fox et al. (2010) noted, differences between tiers are evident in the specificity of the instructional target, the precision of the instructional approach, the frequency of monitoring children's progress in relation to the intervention, and the number of instructional opportunities or trials provided. Evidence-based practices that range in intensity and specificity have been

TABLE 53.2
Common and Unique Features of Tiered Frameworks in Early Childhood

	Building Blocks Model (Sandall & Schwartz, 2008)	**Intervention Hierarchy for Promoting Children's Peer Interactions (Brown, Odom, & Conroy, 2001)**	**Pyramid Model (Fox, Carta, Strain, Dunlap, & Hemmeter, 2010)**	**Recognition and Response (Buysse & Peisner-Feinberg, 2009)**
Description & Focus	Model to support planning and implementing individualized support for young children with special needs	Framework to select peer interaction supports and interventions to improve young children's social interaction	System to support evidence based interventions to promote the social, emotional, and behavioral development of young children	System to provide high quality instruction and targeted interventions focused on pre-academic content
Identified Tiers	Tier 1: High quality, developmentally appropriate, environments Tier 2: Curricular adaptations and modifications Tier 3: Embedded goals and objectives Tier 4: Naturalistic instructional strategies	Tier 1: Classroom-wide interventions Tier 2: Naturalistic interventions Tier 3 Social integration activities Tier 4: Explicit social skills training	Tier 1: Universal promotion Tier 2: Secondary preventions Tier 3: Tertiary interventions	Tier 1: Research based core curriculum and intentional teaching Tier 2: Explicit small group interventions and embedded learning activities Tier 3: Scaffolding strategies
Other Components of Framework			Infrastructure Supports: -Effective workforce -Systems and policies	Recognition (universal screening and progress monitoring) Collaborative problem solving
Target Population	Preschool children with special needs in inclusive settings	Preschool children with disabilities or children at-risk for peer-related social competence needs	Infants, toddlers and preschoolers, with or without disabilities or at risk for disabilities	All preschool children
Structure to Guide Decisions about Support & Intervention Intensity	Yes	Yes	Yes	Yes
Explicit Decision Criteria Specified	No	No	No	No
Universal Screening & Progress Monitoring Measures	No	No	Yes	Yes
Emphasizes Fidelity of Implementation	No	No	Yes	Yes

associated or linked to each level or tier in the frameworks. The DEC recommended child-focused practices described earlier in this chapter align logically across tiers with the practices identified in the reviewed frameworks within and across tiers (VanDerHeyden & Snyder, 2006; Wolery, 2005). Providing supports and interventions in natural learning environments and structuring observations of children during typically occurring activities, routines, and transitions is promoted. Supports or interventions can be provided in large groups, small groups, or to individual children.

All of the reviewed frameworks acknowledge the need to make informed decisions about the type and level of support or intervention intensity and specificity. Data based decision-making and problem-solving processes have yet to be fully developed, although promising work is underway (e.g., Barnett et al., 2006; Buysse & Peisner-Feinberg, 2009; Conroy, 2008; Hemmeter et al., 2008). For example, the need for universal screening and progress-monitoring measures to inform data-based decision making and problem solving is described in the R & R and Pyramid model. In the R & R implementation study (Buysse & Peisner-Feinberg, 2009), the mCLASS: Circle software was used as a universal language and early literacy screener with promising results. In the Pyramid model, measures like the Ages and Stages-Social Emotional questionnaire (Squires, Bricker, & Twombly, 2002) have been used as universal screeners to identify children who might need further assessment, closer monitoring, or additional supports. In addition, the Pyramid model promotes monitoring behavior incidences that occur in a classroom or in the home to determine if a teacher, parent, or child might need additional support or intervention to address challenging behavior (Fox et al., 2010).

Fidelity of implementation is emphasized in several of the tiered frameworks. In the Pyramid model, for example, the Teaching Pyramid Observation Tool (Hemmeter et al., 2008) has been developed to measure whether practitioners are implementing practices associated with each tier of the Pyramid model with fidelity. Other frameworks shown in Table 53.2 emphasize implementing the targeted and individualized practices with fidelity, although specific implementation fidelity measures or approaches are either under development or, to date, have not been explicitly described.

As tiered frameworks continue to evolve, it seems important to examine what is common and unique across these frameworks and to apply systematically a set of critical analysis criteria with associated indicators to advance the science and practices associated with the frameworks. Table 53.3 shows suggested criteria and associated indicators adapted from those used to evaluate prevention science frameworks that might help inform future analyses of tiered frameworks in early childhood. The criteria include (a) depth and breadth of content, (b) logic and internal structure of the framework, (c) conceptual clarity, (d) level of abstraction, (e) practical utility, (f) empirical validity, (g) treatment validity, (h) social validity, and (i) cultural relevance.

Translation and Implementation Opportunities and Challenges

Application of tiered frameworks provides opportunities to eliminate poor instructional quality as the explanation for learning difficulty (Posney, 2009). When applying these frameworks to early childhood, it is important to recognize that adults and the learning environment must be "responsive" to children and to data rather than characterizing

TABLE 53.3
Criteria and Associated Indicators to Evaluate Tiered Frameworks

Criteria	Indicator
Depth and breadth of content	• Adequate descriptions of key elements/constructs • Links relational principles/propositions logically • Sufficiently broad in scope to guide practice and research
Logic and internal structure of the framework	• View of how children learn reflected in the framework • Framework structure consistent with view of how children learn
Conceptual clarity	• Major constructs or elements defined clearly • Relational elements/principles/propositions clearly articulated • Basis on which framework is built clearly described
Level of abstraction	• Concrete verse abstract constructs and principles • Figure used to depict framework and relationships among key elements/constructs
Practical utility	• Applicability and relevance to early intervention practice • Guides practitioners as they design, deliver, and evaluate interventions and supports
Empirical validity	• Evidence to support practices associated with framework interventions available • Demonstration of efficacious, effective, and efficient interventions
Treatment validity	• Articulates relationship between assessment data and recommended interventions • Assessment procedures improve prediction • Structures and guides support and intervention planning
Social validity	• Importance, feasibility, and acceptability of framework • Acceptability of intervention and evaluation practices associated with framework • Social importance of outcomes
Cultural relevance	• Relevance of framework across contexts and cultures • Multiple perspectives about framework importance, feasibility, and acceptability

children as "non-responders." The frameworks can be used to specify and define core instructional quality for all young children. Moreover, these frameworks have the potential to help the field reach consensus on desired outcomes, to develop technically adequate measures that support instruction and decision making, to advance decision rules and processes to inform support and instructional intensity, and to identify promising approaches for ensuring implementation fidelity and translation in real-world contexts (Snyder, 2006; Snyder & Wilcox, 2009).

These frameworks provide young children with disabilities or learning challenges opportunities to access and participate in typically occurring activities and routines and to receive sufficient and efficient targeted support or individualized instruction when, where, and how they need it. With respect to instructional focus, the premises associated with these frameworks seem relatively straightforward: ensure children have high quality learning opportunities when they need them and learning opportunities involve intentional and systematic instructional procedures implemented with fidelity and with sufficient intensity to support or accelerate learning. As Snyder and Wilcox (2009) noted, however, the "devil is in the details."

Despite the promises of using tiered frameworks to conceptualize, organize, and operationalize program focus and practices in the field, challenges remain. Variations in the quality of early learning environments combined with expected variations in how young children develop skills creates challenges for application of tiered frameworks in the field (VanDerHeyden & Snyder, 2006). As the field continues to debate early learning foundations or standards and desired outcomes, consistency is lacking in program focus and associated practices across early childhood sectors. For example, many states have voluntary pre-K standards and accountability systems that do not align with child and family outcomes measured for IDEA-funded programs.

Although progress has been made with respect to the development and validation of technically adequate progress monitoring tools (e.g., Carta, Greenwood, Walker, & Buzhardt, 2010), continued work remains to be done. Avoiding "over-assessment" and duplicative assessment in early childhood will be increasingly important as tiered frameworks with associated screening and progress monitoring measures are used. Constructing technically adequate measures that help inform decisions about children's level of function and rate of progress and that are also "authentic" and consistent with recommended assessment practices in the field will be increasingly important.

Challenges exist with respect to identifying efficacious, effective, and efficient environmental and instructional support and intervention variables that will accelerate child learning for groups of children or individual children. Providing operational definitions for these variables and ensuring supports and interventions are implemented with fidelity is fundamental to achieving the promise of these frameworks. Technical validation of decision criteria will vary based on whether promotion, prevention, or intervention practices are being considered. For example, the decision criteria used to determine whether all children are making adequate progress in learning key skills associated with a high quality, core curricula will be different than decision criteria used to determine whether a child with challenging behavior is acquiring adaptive skills specified on an individualized behavior support plan.

Despite these challenges, tiered frameworks appear to be a "wired" topic in early childhood (cf. Odom, 2009). Alternatively, some have suggested these frameworks might be the differentiated instruction "emperor with new clothes" (cf. Snyder & Wilcox, 2009). Moving forward, it will be important to specify how these frameworks should be judged as an evolving science and practice.

Controversies and Trends Associated with Tiered Frameworks

Although graphic illustrations of tiered or hierarchical frameworks have been useful for organizing and conceptualizing promotion, prevention and intervention practices, current needs center on research and technology to improve instruction and data-based decision making. Figure 53.2 illustrates an integrative framework based on theory of change logic that might inform future discussions and research. As shown in this figure, based on the extant literature, four "active ingredients" have been identified as important for supporting engagement and providing learning opportunities for young children: (a) high quality learning environments, (b) curricula that specify content related to what young children should know or be able to do, (c) responsive interactions and intentional instruction, and (d) ongoing assessment and progress monitoring. As shown in the Figure 53.2, responsive interactions and intentional teaching have been identified as the key ingredient for promoting engagement and providing opportunities to scaffold supports and interventions (cf. National Association for the Education of Young Children, 2009a; Shonkoff & Phillips, 2000). The "pyramidal" nature of these supports and interventions is reflected in the figure to illustrate that responsive interactions and intentional instruction would be applied with differential intensity and specificity based on child characteristics and needs, task or activity "demands," and cultural relevance. Decisions about intensity and specificity would be based on data-based problem solving and decision-making. Learning should occur when children are engaged and provided with sufficient learning opportunities, which result in complete learning trials (Snyder et al., 2010). Learning, in turn, should lead to children achieving desired proximal and distal outcomes.

Figure 53.2 also shows "drivers" have been identified for ensuring fidelity of implementation of the active ingredients, particularly responsive interactions and instruction. Among these implementation drivers are professional development and infrastructure supports.

Professional development in early childhood is more likely to be effective when it (a) focuses on a set of practices rather than general knowledge, (b) aligns with the curricula

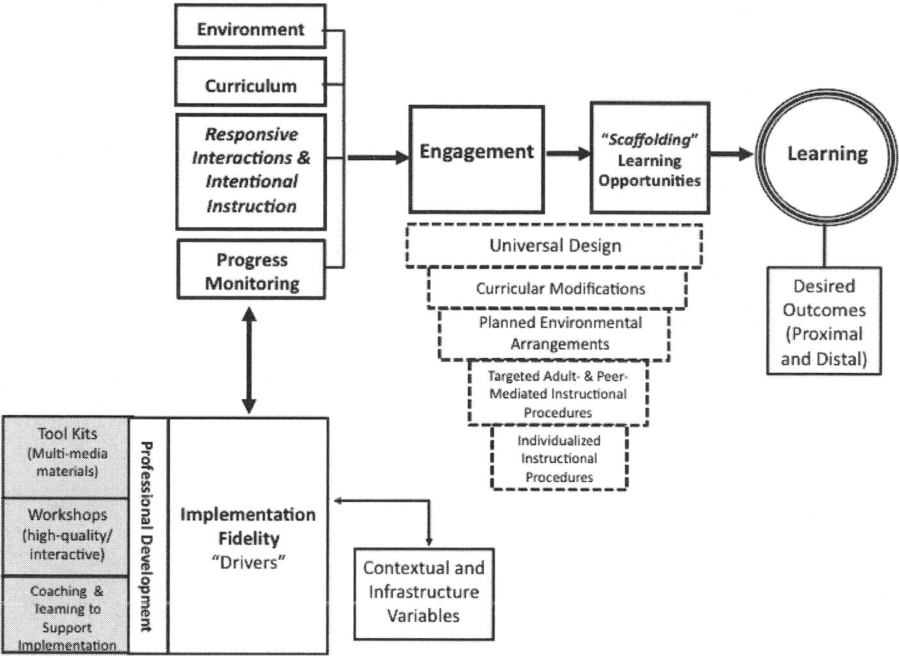

Figure 53.2 Integrative Framework Based on Theory of Change Logic.

and approaches to instruction teachers use in practice, (c) provides materials and resources that support implementation of practices in practice settings, and (d) offers high quality learning experiences that offer guided practice and performance feedback (Buysse, Winton, & Rous, 2009; National Professional Development Center on Inclusion, 2008; Snyder, Denney, Pasia, Rakap, & Crowe, in press). As is being increasingly recognized, the characteristics and behaviors of practitioners contribute significantly to whether children experience high quality learning environments and responsive interactions and instruction (Buysse & Hollingsworth, 2009; Ramey & Ramey, 2008; Snyder et al., in press). Trends suggest the need for focused and systematic attention to the who, what, and how of professional development (National Professional Development Center on Inclusion, 2008) and "enlightened" professional development (Odom, 2009) that includes promising approaches such as coaching with performance feedback (Snyder et al., 2008, Hemmeter, Fox, & Snyder, 2010) and team-based models for change (Bailey, McWilliam, & Winton, 1992; Sexton, Snyder, Lobman, Kimbrough, & Matthews, 1997).

Another trend related to tiered frameworks is research on infrastructure variables that support implementation in early childhood learning contexts (Fixsen, Naoom, Blasé, Friedman, & Wallace, 2005; Odom, 2009). Administrative practices, program policies, and funding formulae are a few examples of variables likely related to implementation of the active ingredients shown in Figure 53.2 (Azzi-Lessing, 2009; Gallagher & Clifford, 2000).

Contemporary perspectives from prevention science related to adaptive prevention-intervention frameworks hold particular promise for future developments in the application of tiered frameworks in early childhood. In contrast to frameworks where the composition and "dosage" of intervention components associated with each tier is fixed, adaptive frameworks assign different "dosages" of intervention components across different groups or individuals based on decision rules that link characteristics of the individual with specific levels and types of intervention components (Collins, Murphy, & Bierman, 2004). Use of an adaptive perspective will help ensure children are not categorized or labeled by tiers (e.g., "tier 2 child") and do not move in a linear fashion from one tier to the next in either an ascending (increasing intensity) or descending (decreasing intensity) sequence. Rather, adaptive frameworks promote decision making about how much support or intentional and systematic instruction a young child needs with a specific behavior or skill at a specific time given a specific context with consideration for the child's phase of learning (Sandall et al., 2001; VanDerHeyden & Snyder, 2009). Particularly for young children at risk for or with disabilities, decisions about "dosage" or differential treatment intensity are based on individual characteristics, needs, and values using an evidence-based practice framework (cf. Snyder, 2006; Winton, 2006).

With regard to future trends related to differential treatment intensity, Warren, Fey, and Yoder (2007) suggested the need for systematic lines of research focused on this topic. The authors proposed terminology to advance the measurement of intervention intensity by defining and describing five terms: (a) dose, (b) dose form, (c) dose frequency, (d) total intervention duration, and (e) cumulative intervention intensity. Although the authors acknowledged it is likely to be challenging work, the approaches they suggested for measuring treatment intensity might hold particular promise for quantifying intensity of supports and interventions provided within tiered frameworks.

Summary and Conclusions

The frameworks presented in this chapter emphasize the importance of "quality for all" to promote young children's development and learning. Moreover, these frameworks remind us that "extra help" works (cf. Bagnato, 2006). Extra help, however, must be the right kind and dose of help, delivered when needed, and with appropriate fidelity by practitioners who benefit from professional development and supportive infrastructure.

Current program focus and practices in early intervention are an outgrowth of 50 years of evolving policies, research, and practices. What has been learned over these decades should be applied as "newer" promotion, prevention, and intervention or tiered frameworks are refined and evaluated. As Edmund Burke (n.d.) noted, "those who do not learn from their history are destined to repeat it." Regardless of whether the frameworks reviewed in this chapter are viewed as novel and innovative or as the "emperor in new clothes," emphasis in the future should be on how to use these frameworks to advance policy, science, and evidence-based practices in the field for the benefit of young children and their families.

Author Note

Work reported in this chapter was supported, in part, by a grant from the National Center for Special Education Research in the Institute of Education Sciences to the University of Florida (R324A07008). The views expressed are those of the authors, not the funding agency.

References

Allen, E. K., & Cowdery, G.E. (2009). *The exceptional child: Inclusion in early childhood education* (6th ed.). Florence, KY: Wadsworth Cengage Learning.

Annie E. Casey Foundation. (2009). *2009 Kids count data book: State profiles of well-being*. Baltimore: Author. Retrieved from http://www.aecf.org/~/media/Pubs/Other/123/2009KIDSCOUNTDataBook/AEC186_2009_KCDB_FINAL%2072.pdf

Azzi-Lessing, L. (2009). Quality support infrastructure in early childhood: Still (mostly) missing. *Early Childhood Research and Practice*, *11* (1). Retrieved from http://ecrp.uiuc.edu

Bagnato, S. J. (2006). Of helping and measuring for early childhood intervention: Reflections on issues and school psychology's role. *School Psychology Review*, *35*, 615–620.

Bailey, D. B., McWilliam, P. J., & Winton, P. J. (1992) Building family-centered practices in early intervention: A team-based model for change. *Infants and Young Children*, *5*(1), 73–82.

Barnett, D. W., Elliott, N., Wolsing, L., Bunger, C., Haski, H., Mckissick, C., & Vander Meer, C. (2006). Response to intervention for young children with extremely challenging behaviors: What it might look like. *School Psychology Review*, *35*, 568–582.

Bredekamp, S. (1987). *Developmentally appropriate practice in early childhood programs serving children from birth through age 8* (Expanded ed.). Washington, DC: National Association for the Education of Young Children.

Bredekamp, S. & Copple, C. (1997). *Developmentally appropriate practice in early childhood programs* (Rev. ed.). Washington, DC: National Association for the Education of Young Children.

Brown, W. H., & Conroy, M. A. (1997). Promoting and supporting peer interactions in inclusive classrooms: Effective strategies for early childhood educators. In W. H. Brown & M. A. Conroy (Eds.), *Inclusion of preschool children with developmental delays in early childhood programs* (pp. 79–108). Little Rock, AK: Southern Early Childhood Association.

Brown, W. H., & Conroy, M. A. (2001). Promoting peer-related social communicative competence in preschool children with developmental delays. In H. Goldstein, L., Kaczmarek, & K. English (Eds.), *Promoting social communication in children and youth with developmental disabilities* (pp. 173–210). Baltimore: Brookes.

Brown, W. H., McEvoy, M. A., & Bishop, J. N. (1991). Incidental teaching of social behavior: A naturalistic approach to promoting young children's peer interactions. *Teaching Exceptional Children*, *24*, 35–58.

Brown, W. H., Odom, S. L., & Conroy, M. A. (2001). An intervention hierarchy for promoting young children's peer interactions in natural environments. *Topics in Early Childhood Special Education*, *21*, 162–175.

Buysse, V., & Hollingsworth, H. L. (2009). Program quality and early childhood inclusion: Recommendations for professional development. *Topics in Early Childhood Special Education*, *29*, 119–128.

Buysse, V., & Peisner-Feinberg, E. (2009, October). Recognition and response: Findings from the first implementation study. Retrieved from http://randr.fpg.unc.edu/news/findings-first-implementation-study-rr-mode

Buysse, V., & Wesley, P. W. (2006). Making sense of evidence-based practice: Reflections and recommendations. In V. Buysse & P. W. Wesley (Eds.), *Evidence-based practice in the early childhood field* (pp. 227–246). Washington, DC: Zero to Three.

Buysse, V., Winton, P. J., & Rous, B. (2009). Reaching consensus on a definition of professional development for the early childhood field. *Topics in Early Childhood Special Education*, *28*, 235–242.

Caplan, G. (1964). *Principles of preventive psychiatry*. New York: Basic Books.

Caplan, G., & Greenbaum, H. (1967). Perspectives on primary prevention. *Archives of General Psychiatry*, *17*, 331–346.

Carta, J. J., Greenwood, C., Walker, D., & Buzhardt, J. (2010). *Using IGDIs: Monitoring progress and improving intervention for infants and young children*. Baltimore: Brookes.

Carta, J. J., & Kong, N. Y. (2007). Trends and issues in interventions for preschoolers with developmental disabilities. In S. L. Odom, R. H. Horner, M. E. Snell, & J. Blancher (Eds.), *Handbook of developmental disabilities* (pp. 181–198). New York: Guilford.

Carta, J. J., Schwartz, I. S., Atwater, J. B., & McConnell, S. R. (1991). Developmentally appropriate practice: Appraising its usefulness for young children with disabilities. *Topics in Early Childhood Special Education*, *11* (1), 1–20.

Center for Response to Intervention in Early Childhood (n.d.). Retrieved from http://www.crtiec.org

Coleman, M. R., Buysse, V., & Neitzel, J. (2006). *Recognition and response: An early intervening system for young children at-risk for learning disabilities. Full report*. Chapel Hill: University of North Carolina at Chapel Hill, FPG Child Development Institute.

Coleman, M. R., Roth, F. P., & West, T. (2009). *Roadmap to Pre-K RTI: Applying response to intervention in preschool settings*. New York: National Council for Learning Disabilities.

Collins, L. M., Murphy, S. A., & Bierman, K. (2004). A conceptual framework for adaptive preventive interventions. *Prevention Science*, *5*, 185–196.

Conroy, M. A. (2008). Promoting social, emotional, and behavior competencies in young high-risk children: A preventative classroom-based early intervention model. [Abstract]. Washington, DC: Institute of Education Sciences. Retrieved from http://www.ed.gov/about/offices/list/ies/index.html

Copple, C., & Bredekamp, S. (2009). *Developmentally appropriate practice in early childhood programs serving children from birth through age 8* (3rd ed.). Washington, DC: National Association for the Education of Young Children.

DEC. (2007). *Promoting positive outcomes for children with disabilities: Recommendations for curriculum, assessment, and program evaluation*. Missoula: MT: Author.

DEC/NAEYC. (2009). *Early childhood inclusion: A joint position statement of the Division for Early Childhood (DEC) and the National Association for the Education of Young Children (NAEYC)*. Chapel Hill: The University of North Carolina, FPG Child Development Institute.

DeKlyen, M., & Odom, S. L. (1989). Activity structure and social interactions with peers in developmentally integrated play groups. *Journal of Early Intervention, 13*, 342–352.

Division for Early Childhood. (2004, October). *Responsiveness to family, values, culture and education*. Retrieved from http://www.dec-sped.org/uploads/docs/about_dec/position_concept_papers/ConceptPaper_Resp_FamCul.pdf

Division for Early Childhood Task Force on Recommended Practices. (Eds). (1993). *DEC recommended practices: Indicators of quality in programs for infants and young children with special needs and their families*. Reston, VA: Council for Exceptional Children.

Early Childhood Outcomes Center. (2004, April). Considerations related to developing a system for measuring outcomes for young children with disabilities and their families. Retrieved from http://www.fpg.unc.edu/~eco/pages/papers.cfm#SpanFOS

Early Childhood Outcomes Center. (2005, April). Family and child outcomes for early intervention and early childhood special education. Retrieved from http://www.the-eco-center.org

Early Childhood Outcomes Center. (2008, August). Timeline for reporting early childhood outcomes (Indicators B7 and C-3). Retrieved from http://www.fpg.unc.edu/~eco/pages/fed_req.cfm#OSEPTimelines

Epstein, A.S. (2007). *The intentional teacher: Choosing the best strategies for young children's learning*. Washington, DC: National Association for the Education of Young Children.

Frea, W., Craig-Unkefer, L., Odom, S.L., & Johnson, D. (1999). Differential effects of structured social integration and group friendship activities for promoting social interaction with peers. *Journal of Early Intervention, 22*, 230–242.

Filla, A., Wolery, M., & Anthony, L. (1999). Promoting children's conversations during play with adult prompts. *Journal of Early Intervention, 22*, 93–108.

Fixsen, D. L., Naoom, S. F., Blasé, K. A., Friedman, R. M., & Wallace, F. (2005). *Implementation research: A synthesis of the literature* (Florida Mental Health Institute Publication No. 232). Tampa: University of South Florida, Louis de la Parte Florida Mental Health Institute and the National Implementation Network.

Fox, L., Carta, J., Strain, P., Dunlap, G., & Hemmeter, M. L. (2010). Response to intervention and the Pyramid model. *Infants and Young Children, 23*(1), 3–13.

Fox, L, Dunlap, G., Hemmeter, M. L., Joseph, G., & Strain, P. (2003). The Teaching Pyramid: A model for supporting social competence and preventing challenging behavior in young children. *Young Children, 58*(4), 48–53.

Fox, L., & Hemmeter, M. L. (2009). A program-wide model for supporting social-emotional development and addressing challenging behavior in early childhood settings. In W. Sailor, G. Dunlap, G. Sugai, & R. Horner (Eds.), *Handbook of positive behavior support* (pp. 177–202). New York: Springer.

Gallagher, J. J., & Clifford, D. (2000). The missing support infrastructure in early childhood. *Early Childhood Research and Practice, 2*(1). Retrieved from http://ecrp.uiuc.edu/v2n1/gallagher.html

Gallagher, J. J., Danaher, J. C., & Clifford, R. M. (2009). The evolution of the National Early Childhood Technical Assistance Center. *Topics in Early Childhood Special Education, 29*, 7–23.

Goldstein, H., English, K., Shafer, K., & Kaczmarek, L. (1997). Interaction among preschoolers with and without disabilities: Effects of across-the-day peer intervention. *Journal of Speech and Hearing Research, 40*, 33–48.

GSGS Interagency Workgroup. (2005). *Good start, grow smart: A guide to Good Start, Grow Smart and other federal early learning initiatives*. Washington, DC: Administration for Children and Families, Department of Health and Human Services.

Greenwood, C. R., Luze, G. J., Cline, G., Kuntz, S., & Leitschuh, C. (2002). Developing a general outcome measure of growth in movement for infants and toddlers. *Topics in Early Childhood Special Education, 22*, 143–157.

Hemmeter, M. L., Fox, L., Jack, S., Broyles, L., & Doubet, S. (2007). A program-wide model of positive behavior support in early childhood settings. *Journal of Early Intervention, 29*, 337–355.

Hemmeter, M. L., Fox, L., & Snyder, P. (2008). *The Teaching Pyramid Observation Tool research edition*. Unpublished instrument.

Hemmeter, M. L., Fox, L., & Snyder, P. (2010). *Evaluating the potential efficacy of a classroom-wide model for promoting social-emotional development and addressing challenging behavior in preschool*. [Data file and codebook].

Hemmeter, M. L., Ostrosky, M., & Fox, L. (2006). Social and emotional foundations for early learning: A conceptual model for intervention. *School Psychology Review, 35*, 583–601.

Horn, E., Lieber, J., Li, S., Sandall, S., & Schwartz, I. (2000). Supporting young children's IEP goals in inclusive settings through embedded learning opportunities. *Topics in Early Childhood Special Education, 20*, 208–223.

Jimerson, S. R., Burns, M. K., & VanDerHeyden, A. M. (2007). *Handbook of response to intervention: The science and practice of assessment and intervention*. New York: Springer.

Johnson, K., & Theberge, S. (2007). *Short take No. 6: Local systems development*. Columbia University, Mailman School of Public Health, National Center for Children in Poverty. Retrieved from http://www.nccp.org/publications/pdf/text_758.pdf

Joseph, G. E., & Strain, P. S. (2003). Comprehensive evidence-based social emotional curricula for young children: An analysis of efficacious adoption potential. *Topics in Early Childhood Special Education, 23*, 65–76.

Kaczmarek, L. A. (1999). Validating hierarchical interventions. *Journal of Early Intervention, 22*, 111–113.

McBride, B. J., & Schwartz, I. S. (2003). Effects of teaching early interventionists to use discrete trials during ongoing classroom activities. *Topics in Early Childhood Special Education, 23*, 5–18.

mCLASS: Circle [Computer software]. Brooklyn, NY: Wireless Generation.

McCormick, L. (2006). Perspectives, policies, and practices. In M. J. Noonan & L. McCormick (Eds.), *Young children with disabilities in natural environments: Methods and procedures* (pp. 1–25). Baltimore: Brookes.

McEvoy, M. A., Nordquist, V. M., Twardosz, S., Heckaman, K., Wehby, J. H., & Denny, R. K. (1988). Promoting autistic children's peer interaction in an integrated early childhood setting using affection activities. *Journal of Applied Behavior Analysis, 21*, 193–200.

McEvoy, M. A., Odom, S. L., & McConnell, S. M. (1992). Peer social competence intervention for young children with disabilities. In S. L. Odom, S. R. McConnell, & M. A. McEvoy (Eds.), *Social competence of young children with disabilities: Issues and strategies for intervention* (pp. 113–134). Baltimore: Brookes.

McLean, M. E., Snyder, P., Smith, B. J., & Sandall, S. (2002). The DEC recommended practices in early intervention/early childhood special education: Social validation. *Journal of Early Intervention, 25*(2), 120–128.

National Association for the Education of Young Children. (1986). *Developmentally appropriate practice in early childhood programs serving children from birth through age 8* (Position statement). Washington, DC: Author

National Association for the Education of Young Children. (1996). *Developmentally appropriate practice in early childhood programs serving children from birth through age 8* (Position statement). Washington, DC: Author.

National Association for the Education of Young Children. (2009a). *Developmentally appropriate practice in early childhood programs serving children from birth through age 8* (Position statement). Retrieved from http://www.naeyc.org/files/naeyc/file/positions/position%20statement%20Web.pdf

National Association for the Education of Young Children. (2009b). *DAP frequently asked questions*. Retrieved from http://www.naeyc.org/dap/faq

National Professional Development Center on Inclusion. (2008). *What do we mean by professional development in the early childhood field?* Chapel Hill: University of North Carolina, FPG Child Development Institute. Retrieved from http://community.fpg.unc.edu/resources

National Research Council. (2001). *Eager to learn: Educating our preschoolers*. Committee on Early Childhood Pedagogy, B.T. Bowman, M. S. Donovan, & M. S. Burns (Eds.), Commission on Behavioral and Social Sciences and Education. Washington, DC: National Academy Press.

Odom, S. L. (2009). The tie that binds: Evidence-based practice, implementation science, and outcomes for children. *Topics in Early Childhood Special Education*, *29*, 53–61.

Odom, S. L., & Brown, W. H. (1993). Social interaction skills interventions for young children with disabilities in integrated settings. In C. Peck, S. L. Odom, & D. D. Bricker (Eds.), *Integrating young children with disabilities into community programs* (pp. 39–64). Baltimore: Brookes.

Odom, S. L., & McConnell, S. R. (1993). *Play time/social time: Organizing your classroom to build interaction skills*. Tucson, AZ: Communication Skill Builders.

Posney, A. (2009, September). *Leading for learning: RTI and beyond*. Presentation at the RTI Innovations Conference, Salt Lake City, UT.

Pretti-Frontczak, K., Jackson, S., Gross, S.M., Grisham-Brown, J., Horn, E., Harjusola-Webb, S., . . .Matthews, D.S. (2007). A curriculum framework that supports quality early childhood education for all young children. In E.Horn, C. Peterson, & L. Fox (Eds.), *Linking curriculum to child and family outcomes* [Monograph]. *Young Exceptional Children, 9,* 16–28.

Ramey, S. L., & Ramey, C. T. (2008, December). *Effective educational interventions for young children: The central importance of professional development*. Retrieved from http://che.georgetown.edu/presentations/index.html

Sandall, S., Hemmeter, M. L., Smith, B. J., & McLean, M. E. (2005). *DEC recommended practices: A comprehensive guide for practical application in early intervention/early childhood special education.* Longmont, CO: Sopris West.

Sandall, S., McLean, M. E., & Smith, B. J. (Eds.). (2000). *DEC recommended practices in early intervention/early childhood special education* (1st ed.). Longmont, CO: Sopris West.

Sandall, S. R., & Schwartz, I. S. (2002). *Building blocks for teaching preschoolers with special needs*. Baltimore: Brookes.

Sandall, S. R., & Schwartz, I. S. (2008). *Building blocks for teaching preschoolers with special needs* (2nd ed.). Baltimore: Brookes.

Sandall, S. R., Schwartz, I., & Joseph, G. (2001). A building blocks model for effective instruction in inclusive early childhood settings. *Young Exceptional Children*, *4*(3), 3–9.

Schilling, D. L., & Schwartz, I. S. (2004). Alternative seating for young children with autism spectrum disorder: Effects on classroom behavior. *Journal of Autism and Developmental Disabilities*, *34*, 423–432.

Scott-Little, C., Lesko, J., Martella, J., & Milburn, P. (2007). *Early learning standards: Results from a national survey to document trends in state-level policies and practices*. Retrieved January 10, 2010, from http://ecrp.uiuc.edu/v9n1/little.html

Sexton, D., Snyder, P., Lobman, M., Kimbrough, P., & Matthews, K. (1997). A team-based model to improve early intervention programs. In P. J. Winton, J. A. McCollum, & C. Catlett (Eds.), *Reforming personnel preparation in early intervention: Issues, models, and practical strategies* (pp. 495–526). Baltimore: Brookes.

Shonkoff, J. P., & Phillips, D. A. (Eds.). (2000). *From neurons to neighborhoods: The science of early childhood development*. Washington, DC: National Academy Press.

Simeonsson, R. J. (1991). Primary, secondary, and tertiary prevention in early intervention. *Journal of Early Intervention*, *15*, 124–134.

Smith, B. J. (2000). The federal role in early childhood special education. *Topics in Early Childhood Special Education*, *20*, 7–13.

Snyder, P. (2006). Best available research evidence: Impact on research in early childhood. In V. Buysse & P.W. Wesley (Eds.), *Evidence-based practice in the early childhood field* (pp. 35–70). Washington, DC: Zero to Three.

Snyder, P., Denney, M., Pasia, C., & Rakap, S., & Crowe, C. (in press). Professional development in early childhood intervention. In C. Groark (Series Ed.) & L. Kaczmarek (Vol. Ed.), *Early childhood intervention program policies for special needs children: Vol. 3. Emerging issues.* Santa Barbara, CA: Praeger.

Snyder, P., Hemmeter, M.L., Sandall, S., & McLean, M. (2008). Impact of professional development on preschool teachers' use of embedded instruction practices [Abstract]. Washington, DC: Institute of Education Sciences. Retrieved from http://www.ed.gov/about/offices/list/ies/index.html

Snyder, P., & Wilcox, J. (2009, October). *The promise and challenge of RTI in early childhood*. Presentation at the first annual RTI in early childhood symposium. Albuquerque, NM.

Snyder, P., Rakap, S., Hemmeter, M. L., McLaughlin, T., Sandall, S., & McLean, M. (2010). *Naturalistic instructional approaches in early intervention: A review and analysis of the empirical literature*. Manuscript submitted for preparation.

Squires, J., Bricker, D. D., & Twombly, E. (2002). *Ages and stages questionnaires: Social-emotional user's guide*. Baltimore: Brookes.

Twardosz, S., Nordquist, V. M., Simon, R., & Botkin, D. (1983). The effects of group affection activities on the interaction of socially isolated children. *Analysis and Intervention in Developmental Disabilities*, *3*, 311–338.

VanDerHeyden, A. M., & Snyder, P. (2006). Integrating frameworks from early childhood intervention and school psychology to accelerate growth for all children. *School Psychology Review*, *35*, 519–534.

VanDerHeyden, A. M., & Snyder, P. (2009). Training adaptive skills within the context of multi-tiered intervention systems: Application of the instructional hierarchy. *Early Childhood Services*, *3*, 143–155.

Warren, S. F., Fey, M. E., & Yoder, P. J. (2007). Differential treatment intensity research: A missing link to creating optimally effective communication interventions. *Mental Retardation and Developmental Disabilities Research Reviews*, *13*, 70–77.

Winton, P. J. (2006). The evidence-based practice movement and its effect on knowledge utilization. In V. Buysse & P. W. Wesley (Eds.), *Evidence-based practice in the early childhood field* (pp. 71–115). Washington, DC: Zero to Three.

Wolery, M. (2005). DEC recommended practices: Child-focused practices. In S. Sandall, M .L. Hemmeter, B. J. Smith, & M. E. McLean (Eds.), *DEC recommended practices: A comprehensive guide for practical application in early intervention/early childhood special education* (pp. 71–106). Longmont, CO: Sopris West.

Wolery, M., & Wilbers, J. S. (1994). Introduction to the inclusion of young children with special needs in early childhood programs. In M. Wolery & J. S. Wilbers (Eds.), *Including children with special needs in early childhood programs* (pp. 1–22). Washington, DC: National Association for the Education of Young Children.

54

Early Identification and Intervention in Gifted Education

Developing Talent in Diverse Learners

CATHERINE M. BRIGHTON
University of Virginia

JANE M. JARVIS
Flinders University

Despite the proliferation of recent research into school experiences, identification practices, program models, curriculum and instruction, social and emotional needs, and issues of cultural and economic diversity related to gifted and talented students, there remains a perceptible shortage of research literature on the characteristics and needs of very young gifted children, including pre-school and primary school age students (Hodge & Kemp, 2000). Recurring themes and findings from the literature provide a strong rationale for an increased focus on the needs of young children who show signs of potential. Numerous authors underscore the importance of early educational intervention for gifted children, arguing that gifted education should follow the lead of special education in recognizing individualized needs as early as possible in order to provide responsive instructional environments to allow for potential to be actualized (Brighton, Moon, Jarvis, & Hockett, 2007; Kitano, 1989; Levine & Kitano, 1998; Porter, 2005; Shaklee, 1992). The purpose of this chapter is to (a) provide a description of the characteristics of young gifted children, (b) describe common ways in which the giftedness and talent can be identified, (c) make a case for broadening the traditional conceptions of giftedness, (d) describe the variety of services offered to young gifted children across the United States, and (e) offer suggestions for the directions of future research and practice in this area.

Characteristics and Development of Young Gifted Children

There is no uniform consensus definition of "giftedness" or "talent" in the field of gifted education. As a result, there is great variation across settings in regards to how these advanced learners are defined, identified and served. Further compounding the challenges in describing this group of students, the characteristics of giftedness that are discussed often manifest themselves differently among individual children. In other words, the assumption that gifted children comprise a homogenous group with identical needs is patently false (Gross, 1999). One characteristic that is generally accepted among researchers in the field is the idea that the physical, intellectual, and social, and emotional aspects of gifted children, especially young gifted children, develop at different rates resulting in asynchrony. The term "asynchronous development" is thus used to describe the various ways in which gifted characteristics emerge (Rotigel, 2003). Despite this variation in behavioral, affective, and cognitive patterns (Hodge & Kemp, 2000), there is still a cluster of characteristics commonly cited in descriptions of young children who later go on to be identified as gifted. The most frequently noted characteristics include early language development and reading (Hodge & Kemp, 2000; Jackson, 2003; Sankar-De-Leeuw, 2004), however other common patterns also exist. Among these are strong (a) verbal and visual memory (Harrison, 2004; Sankar-DeLeeuw, 2004); (b) intense curiosity and sustained attention spans (Damiani, 1997; Hodge & Kemp, 2000; Rotigel, 2003); (c) development of advanced mathematical reasoning (Diezmann & English, 2001; Gavin, Casa, Adelson, Carroll, & Sheffield, 2009; Harrison, 2004; Sankar-DeLeeuw, 2004); and (d) the capacity for abstract thinking (Kitano, 1995; Walker, Hafenstein, & Crow-Enslow, 1999).

Early Development of Language

Linguistic precocity is among the most researched domains of gifted performance in young children. The early development of receptive and expressive oral language has been consistently documented as an indicator of verbal giftedness and has high predictive validity for continued linguistic aptitude (Tannenbaum, 1992). The linguistically precocious child might demonstrate advanced development in oral language, passing through the stages of spoken utterances, single word acquisition, and linking words into phrases both significantly earlier and with greater rapidity than his or her age peers of average ability (Gross, 1999; Sankar-DeLeeuw, 2004). Based on longitudinal studies of gifted children, Gross (1993) reported that among 52 participants with IQ scores equal to or greater than 160, the mean age at which the first meaningful word was spoken was 9.1 months. Barbe's (1964) earlier study of children with IQ greater than 148 had recorded a mean age of 16 months at which participants were speaking in complete sentences. In another qualitative study of 11 gifted preschool children, parents recalled that their children had spoken their first words between nine and 12 months of age, and spoken in sentences by 18 months (Hodge & Kemp, 2000). A longitudinal study involving 20 gifted children (IQ 130+) similarly showed participants to be distinguishable from their non-gifted age peers on a battery of assessments, including tests of language development, from as early as 18 months (Gottfried, Gottfried, Bathurst, & Guerin, 1994).

Precocious Reading. The early acquisition of reading skills is cited as a common characteristic of young children who later go on to be identified as gifted (Van Tassel-Baska, 1989). Research has identified gifted children who recognize large numbers of printed vocabulary words, both familiar and unfamiliar, by age 3 (Fletcher-Flinn & Thompson, 2000; Jackson, 1988). By 3 or 4 years of age, precocious readers have been found to decode and comprehend varying levels of text (Jackson & Lu, 1992; Sankar-DeLeeuw, 2004). Harrison (2004) described instances of young gifted children aged between 6 months and 8 years who revealed high levels of interest in words and symbols, preference for complex stories before the age of 2, and the ability to read before school entry in most of the participants.

Advanced Auditory and Visual Memory. The ability to recognize auditory or visual patterns and details and later recall them with accuracy is commonly described in case studies of young gifted children (Harrison, 2004; Sankar-DeLeeuw, 2004). At 5 years of age, advanced children are noted to be "sponges" (Sankar-DeLeeuw, 2004, p. 194) in their ability to hear information orally one time and be able to retrieve it at later times. A parent participant in a case study of highly gifted young children described her child's advanced memory:

> Ryan (age 1.4 years) [is able to] identify all of the Thomas engines just by seeing a sub-second flash of a part of the picture. He could also rapidly point out every animal in a book of 32 animals from rosella to budgerigar to crocodile. (Sankar-DeLeeuw, 2004, p. 81)

A child participant in the same study (at 4.1 years) added, "I remember things because I have pictures in my head" (p. 81).

Intense Curiosity and Extended Attention Spans. Gifted children are often described as possessing the ability to zone in on topics of interest and remain focused, developing questions, seeking answers to these questions, and sharing conclusions with others. Young gifted students have been described as active learners who seek to move beyond the familiar and make connections between what is known and unknown (Harrison, 2004; Jackson, 2003), and who seek to "know all there is to know" about topics that engage their interest as compared to other age-peers who may be more content with superficial explanations and concrete factual information about the same topics (Rotigel, 2003, p. 210). The intense focus on a single topic of interest, often in areas that are far more advanced than same age peers such as the Civil War or Greenpeace, is more characteristic of children many years older (Gross, 1999; Jackson, 2003; Rotigel, 2003).

Advanced Mathematical Understanding. Research studies have documented the advanced early development of numeracy skills in some children later identified as gifted, with studies identifying a similar logical ability underlying both precocious reading and mathematical skills (Robinson, Abbott, Berninger, & Busse, 1996; Shavinina, 1999). Beyond advanced logical ability, mathematical development may be a function of the curiosity and task commitment to acquiring information about those interests. Young gifted children may develop intense interests in areas such as space travel, which require that the child make sense of relevant mathematical concepts such as numeracy and symbolic representation in order to understand the larger scientific information (Diezmann & English, 2001). In these instances, motivated by gathering information about their topical area of interest, the child's ability to reason and problem-solve assists them in developing necessary mathematical skills. The mathematical development may also be a function of the child's tendency to consider abstract ideas such as negative numbers and infinity (Harrison, 2004). To put this into the larger public school context, according to the National Center for Education Statistics (NCES), only four percent (4%) begin Kindergarten able to solve addition and subtraction problems (West, Denton, & Germino-Hausken, 2000).

Capacity for Abstraction. Harrison (2004) notes that young gifted children "seek opportunities to develop sophisticated understandings" (p. 82) and "search for complexity and abstraction, divergence and difference" (p. 83) in their daily attempts to make meaning of the world around them. Typically developing preschool-age children are described as concrete learners in the pre-operational stage (Piaget, 1953) where abstract ideas such as time, symbolic representation, and intangible concepts such as "equity" are beyond their scope.

In summary, while there is no agreed-upon definition that satisfies all stakeholders in the field of gifted education, there are some common characteristics of giftedness that emerge most notably among young, gifted children. Most prominently cited among these are the early manifestations of oral language, reading, and other linguistic precocity. While not all children that go on to later be identified as gifted during their school careers develop these literacy skills early, this notion is widely held among teachers and parents, and is extensively documented in the literature of the field. The following section discusses how these characteristics described above influence the procedures for identifying young gifted students.

Issues Associated with the Identification of Young Gifted Children

Jackson (2003) highlights the distinction between *describing* gifted behavior or performance in young children and *identifying* individual children as gifted. It follows that the direct translation of common characteristics of giftedness into checklists for identification is problematic. That is, even if common characteristics of young gifted children such as those described earlier can be articulated, the direct translation of this knowledge into valid, reliable, culturally appropriate identification tools is a separate challenge. It remains unclear, for example, to what extent descriptions such as "intensely curious," "investigative," or "intense" can reliably distinguish potentially gifted from non-gifted children at particular ages, or predict future gifted performance (Jackson, 2003). Thus, there are inherent difficulties, based on current knowledge of gifted characteristics in young children, in selecting from existing or developing appropriate new identification tools. This is further exacerbated by the negative influence of poverty in the development of common characteristics attributed to early giftedness, such as precocious language development and reading.

Socioeconomic Status and Identification of Early Development

Are children born into poverty equally likely to *possess* genes that predispose them to have advanced abilities, such as in the precocious development of language and reading? If so, would these genetic abilities be equally likely to *develop* given different environmental circumstances? Jackson (2003) reminds us of the difficulty in disentangling the influences of genes and home environments when attributing the source of potential giftedness in young children. Given this reality, however, research literature paints a clear picture of the significant impact of the home environment on children's early cognitive development, and indicates that the effects of poverty can be negative and enduring when quality interventions are not available (Dearing, McCartney, Weiss, Kreider, & Simpkins, 2004). For example, if one characteristic of giftedness in young gifted children is early reading, then it is important to recognize how children born into poverty fare in terms of equal development of this characteristic. Numerous studies have drawn attention to the relationship between quality of parent-child interactions and the early development of language and reading skills (Dickinson & Tabor, 2001; Dodici, Draper, & Peterson, 2003; Downer & Pianta, 2006; Justice & Pullen, 2003; Lawhon & Cobb, 2002; Neuman & Dickson, 2002; Sonnenschein & Munsterman, 2002; Whitehurst & Lonigan, 1998). In the positive direction, a study of 85 parents and their children showed that early home literacy and language activities were correlated with children's subsequent print knowledge and reading interest (Weigel, Martin, & Bennett, 2006). That is, with exposure to books and language, children's knowledge and interests in the areas of literacy were likely to develop and therefore could more likely be identified as early manifestation of gifted behaviors. Early home literacy is often characteristic of children later identified as gifted (Gross, 1999).

Ongoing research has shed new light on the relationship between home environment and cognitive development for children growing up in poverty. This body of work indicates that the proportions of individual variance in IQ scores attributable to genes and environment vary in a nonlinear relationship with socioeconomic status (Turkheimer, D'Onofrio, Maes, & Eaves, 2005; Turkheimer, Haley, Waldron, D'Onofrio, & Gottesman, 2003). These studies suggest that for children living in impoverished circumstances, 60% of IQ score variance is attributable to environmental circumstances, while genetic influence is minimal. In contrast, for children living in affluent families the contribution of genes accounts for between 80% and 90% of the variance in IQ scores (Turkheimer et al., 2003). In practical terms, what this means is that for children growing up in poverty, the environment itself is the most important factor in their likelihood of having their talents recognized through a gifted identification process and thus, ultimately their potential developed. These findings are significant in their implications for young gifted children living in poverty. That is, even where genetic potential may be present, an impoverished environment appears to constrain the extent to which this potential can be detected on a test of cognitive ability. These findings also suggest that where the early development of language and other cognitive skills is employed as a primary indicator of giftedness, children raised in poverty are less likely to have their talents recognized at an early age. For gifted students from low-income families, factors such as inadequate nutrition and health care, lack of exposure to academic role models, and lack of opportunity to attend a rich, developmentally appropriate preschool program (Taylor, Gibbs, & Slate, 2000), all have the potential to drastically affect the development of school-valued abilities in the early years (Magnuson, Meyers, Ruhm, & Waldfogel, 2004; Ramey & Ramey, 2004).

Instrumentation Issues with Identification. On the one hand, standardized ability and achievement tests might appear attractive for their capacity to measure more "objective" traits across groups of children. Indeed, it is common practice for gifted education programs to weight standardized test scores heavily in identification decisions (Callahan, 2005), despite the prevalence of broadening conceptions of giftedness and theories of intelligence in recent years (Brown et al., 2005). Several practitioners and researchers advocate the inclusion of standardized intelligence and achievement tests in the assessment gifted potential in young children (e.g., Benbow & Stanley, 1997; Borland, 1989; Gross, 1999), but also recognize the limitations of these measures and caution that they cannot provide the complete picture of a child's functioning. To be effective, even in a battery of assessment tools, standardized tests must have (a) evidence of reliability and validity for the purpose of identifying high ability or achievement (Mantzicopoulos, 2000); (b) be appropriately normed for the population to whom they are administered (Camara & Schmidt, 1999); and (c) be interpreted in combination with additional data about the individual from alternative sources, such as observation, interview and work samples (Sattler, 2001). In practice however, commentators suggest that tests are often selected for availability rather than reliability (Shaklee & Hansford, 1992), interpreted inappropriately for students from culturally, linguistically and socioeconomically diverse backgrounds (Maker, 1996), and are often afforded unwarranted weight in educational decision making (Bredekamp & Shepard, 1990).

Special Concerns Regarding the Use of Tests with Young Children. Particular caution should be exercised in the use of tests with very young children (Jackson & Klein, 1997; Kanevsky, 1992). Tests of IQ have limited reliability for children under the age of 6 (Tannenbaum, 1992), and other psychometric instruments possess ceilings too low to detect advanced performance (Kaplan, 1992). Moreover, young children's tendency to experience irregular spurts of development, their limited attention spans, and their sensitivity to environmental and physical stimuli during testing combine to make "one shot" tests less than ideal in measuring ability or development (Hodge & Kemp, 2000; Robinson, 1993). While these limitations are real, they are sometimes inappropriately cited by educators to argue for delayed identification and services for young gifted children (Gross, 1999; Proctor, Black, & Feldhusen, 1988). The need for early identification and intervention for young, potentially gifted children does not disappear simply because tests have limitations with a particular group.

Gross (1999) recommends that practitioners in gifted education adopt the treatment model used by audiologists, in which children are referred for early audiometric intervention based on initial diagnostic testing, and are then retested at a later age when the instruments are known to have greater reliability. Adjustments can then be made to the existing intervention program based on the follow-up tests. This model is predicated on the philosophy that it is in the child's best interests to err on the side of unnecessary intervention rather than none at all. In addition, Gross suggests that when a 2-year-old shows advanced performance on a test designed for 6-year-olds, and such performance is consistent with other observations of giftedness in that individual, then this provides important information even though the test was not administered within the population for which it was intended.

Others propose that the potential for cultural bias inherent in standardized ability and achievement tests results in more harm than good when used in the identification of students for special services (Feiring, Louis, Ukeje, Lewis, & Leong, 1997; Ford & Harris, 1999). It has been argued that traditional IQ tests are culturally biased in favor of White, middle-class groups (Onwuegbuzie & Daley, 2001). This purported bias stems from a number of sources, including content based on concepts and vocabulary valued in White, middle-class schools (Ogbu, 1988; Washington, 1996), the under-representation of culturally and linguistically diverse individuals in normative samples (Laing & Kamhi, 2003), and the language barrier for non-native English speakers (Baker, 1996). In addition, students from culturally and linguistically diverse and low socioeconomic backgrounds might have limited experiences with out of context, test-like situations (Laing & Kamhi). Many have linked the under-representation of students from cultural minority and low socioeconomic backgrounds in programs for the gifted to an over-reliance on standardized identification tools (e.g., Karr & Schwenn, 1999; Maker, 1996).

Teacher and Parent Nominations. Given obvious limitations of tests, what are the alternatives to reliance on standardized ability and achievement tests in the identification of giftedness? Other tools commonly employed include parent and teacher nominations (Siegle & Powell, 2004). Research on the reliability of parent nominations has yielded mixed results. Gross (1999) found parent nominations to be more accurate than teacher nomination for pre-school and primary school children than for older grade levels of students. Jackson (2003) found that while parent nomination was accurate for the areas of language, literacy and numeracy, parents varied significantly in the less quantifiable characteristics they took to be signs of giftedness in very young children. While the importance of involving parents in the identification and talent development process is undeniable, parent nomination also has the potential to bias identification in favor of the White middle class because this group is typically more aware of the social and academic benefits associated with gifted identification than are parents of minority groups and lower socioeconomic groups (Gandara, 2004).

Risks Associated with Not Identifying Young Children's Giftedness. Researchers have drawn attention to the emotional and social consequences for highly gifted young students when their talents go unrecognized and undervalued in the early school years (Neihart, Reis, Robinson, & Moon, 2002; Winner, 1997). Gross' (1999) longitudinal research suggests that as early as the first few months of pre-school, children later identified as highly gifted might often begin to mask their abilities in an effort to fit in with peers and meet teacher expectations. These children might select picture books in the classroom even though they are reading text-laden books at home, or they might develop different "codes" for speaking at home and school in order to mask their linguistic sophistication (e.g., codeswitching). Highly gifted youngsters are sensitive to early messages that their attempts to express boredom, point out multiple approaches to a problem, or use sophisticated humor are likely to be perceived as disruptive or disrespectful behaviors by teachers, rather than as markers of high ability. Since they are likely to engage in social comparisons earlier than their age peers (Robinson, 1993), young gifted children are vulnerable to feelings of isolation and difference when their abilities are not recognized and valued at school (Gross, 1993). In preschool and primary grades, gifted children often become frustrated when they are unable to find peers who share their interests or understand their advanced senses of humor (Webb, Meckstroth, & Tolan, 1982). Rotigel (2003) describes a precocious first-grade student whose teacher interpreted the child's lack of participation as a lack of knowledge. The student explained to her parents that she was reluctant to participate because, "I don't want the other kids to know that I know all of the answers," going on to say that, "I do put my hand up when the teacher is really stuck, because I feel like I should help her out when no-one else knows the answer" (p. 210).

In summary, identification of gifted behaviors in young potentially gifted learners is a challenging endeavor for reasons of instrumentation, the unique challenges for administering tests with very young children, and because of the cultural differences among children from varying sub-groups, most often favoring the White middle class. However, research has shown that there are further risks for *failing to identify* these learners and thus it is imperative that educational programs seek to determine ways to identify gifted performance as well as potential in the full spectrum of learners from all cultural groups and socio-economic strata. Toward that end, the field of gifted education has challenged long-standing assumptions and has concluded that it is essential to cultivate and employ a broadened conception of giftedness. In the following section, we will explore what it might look like to adopt a more encompassing approach to defining, identifying, and serving gifted students.

Toward Broadening Conceptions of Giftedness

While the academic and social needs of young early developers should be addressed, the focus within the research literature to be only on the areas of early language, reading and logical reasoning skills deserves critical examination for a number of reasons. On the one hand, while attempts to describe the "typical" young gifted child contribute to an understanding of group needs, this approach might simultaneously diminish the salience of diversity in profiles of giftedness. The great variation in expressions of giftedness has been documented (Hodge & Kemp, 2000), as have multiple cases of highly gifted children and adults who did not exhibit advanced development of language or reading (Gross, 1999; Jackson, 2003). These cases are consistent with the field's increasing drive to embrace broadened conceptions of giftedness that incorporate creative, interpersonal, spatial and metacognitive dimensions of high ability (Renzulli, 2003; Sternberg, 2003) and acknowledge varying paces and patterns of cognitive development (Tannenbaum, 2003). The extent to which these broader conceptions have consistently influenced the actual practices of the field of gifted education is, however, debatable.

The belief that students with gifted potential will always appear in the classroom as precocious readers, writers, or mathematicians with an insatiable appetite for schoolwork is a gross misconception. Gifted students with learning disabilities, with gifts outside the domain of linguistic or analytical ability, and from low income and culturally diverse backgrounds are most likely to be shortchanged by narrow, academic achievement-driven conceptions of giftedness. As noted in the previous section, gifted children living in poverty face multiple barriers to the early development of their abilities and are therefore among those likely to be overlooked on the basis of a skills-based definition of gifted potential. In communities where there is significant overlap between low socioeconomic status and minority ethnic status, such definitions are also likely to exclude minority students with gifted potential.

Ford, Howard, Harris, and Tyson (2000) further point to the cultural mismatch in conceptions of giftedness held at home and at school for many groups, and urge educators of gifted minority students to consider cultural differences according to the dimensions of communication style, social interaction style, response style and linguistic style. These authors suggest that each of these dimensions can account for learning preferences and expressions of gifted potential that are not compatible with a dominant cultural conception of the typical gifted student (Ford et al., 2000). Other studies of African American groups have indicated that *oral experiences* (Hilliard, 1989; Shade, 1997), *physical activity* (Ewing & Yong, 1992; Shade, 1997), and *strong interpersonal relationships* (Hilliard, 1989) are valued in the learning environment more highly than traditionally academic skills. Studies of Latin American cultures have suggested that a *social learning style* is highly valued (Griggs & Dunn, 1996; Vasquez, 1990), while Native American groups have been found to value *collective goals* above personal achievement (Callahan & McIntire, 1994). While scattered research studies have delineated conceptions of giftedness among particular cultural minority groups, more research is needed to understand multiple expressions of giftedness among children entering primary school. Further, a translation must be made from this nascent research into program- and school-level practice regarding how these broadened manifestations might look and how to identify them for further development in a program.

In summary, in order to consider the widest possible

pool of students in services for young gifted children, it is important to more broadly consider the construct of "giftedness" beyond the traditional notions of advanced linguistics and mathematics. However, it is essential that the broadened conception of this construct of giftedness be tied to the actual services that the child might receive if identified as gifted. Any benefits that may be gained from broadening one's view of giftedness to include, for example advanced personal maturity and social development are lost if a program identifies such a student but then places that child in a program for advanced mathematical skills. The most important indicator of program-level quality is to have tight alignment among three program elements: (a) the conception of giftedness used in a program, ideally one that embraces the broader manifestation of talents described above; (b) clearly articulated procedures for identifying a diverse pool of students that are reliable and valid; and (c) program services that develop identified talents and extend performance toward expertise. In the following section, we will examine the kinds of services for gifted students that shift the emphasis away from sorting and labeling students in favor of increased opportunities for all students to stretch and grow. Additionally, we will explore specific programs around the country that employ one or both of these philosophical approaches.

Beyond Identification: Services for Young Gifted Students

Given the challenges surrounding the need for and procedures related to identifying gifted performance in young children, some suggest shifting the focus away from *labeling* students and rather emphasize *providing services* for them (Jackson, 2003). Gifted programs and services are rarely offered in preschool and primary elementary grades for a variety of reasons including limited public school funding and the belief by some that young gifted and potentially gifted students do not require services (Chamberlin, Buchanan, & Vercimak, 2007). Therefore, what services that are available for these youngsters are typically provided through one of two avenues: *acceleration* such as in early entrance to kindergarten, grade skipping, or subject-specific content-focused acceleration, such as moving to another teacher for reading only but staying with same-age peers for all other school-day activities (Colangelo, Assouline, & Gross, 2004) and through *differentiating instruction* within the general education program (Tomlinson, 2005).

Acceleration

Acceleration is an educational intervention that summons strong feelings both of support and opposition from parents, teachers, and educational administrators (Colangelo et al., 2004; Sankar-De-Leeuw, 1999). "The Nation Deceived: How Schools Hold Back America's Brightest Students" Report (Colangelo et al., 2004) notes the following benefits of acceleration: For bright students acceleration has long-term beneficial effects, both academically and socially; acceleration is a virtually cost-free intervention. Gifted children tend to be socially and emotionally more mature than their age-mates. For many bright students, acceleration provides a better personal maturity match with classmates. When bright students are presented with curriculum developed for age-peers, they can become bored and unhappy and get turned off from learning. Entering school early is an excellent option for some gifted students both academically and socially. High ability young children who enroll early generally settle in smoothly with their older classmates (p. 2).

The benefits of acceleration for young gifted children are many, primarily that (a) acceleration is generally inexpensive as it does not require additional programs; and (b) there is ample research to support the positive learning outcomes for students who have been accelerated as well as tools to guide acceleration decisions. However, the issue of acceleration is frequently viewed with suspicion and distaste by teachers and parents. In a survey of parents and teachers of preschool students, Sankar-DeLeeuw (1999) found that while 91% of parents and 78% of teachers reported that gifted behaviors can be identified early, only 37% of parents and 7% of teachers agreed with the intervention of early entrance to kindergarten, citing the rationale that "a child needs to be a child" (p. 176).

Differentiation

Differentiated instruction is a philosophy of education that acknowledges differences among learners in terms of academic readiness, motivation, prior experiences, interests, and preferred ways of learning (Tomlinson, 2005). In a differentiated classroom, a teacher anticipates these differences and *proactively* plans for ways of collecting this information and responding to those identified needs. For example, in a differentiated kindergarten classroom, a teacher collects information about students' literacy skills and plans learning centers with different levels of tasks to more appropriately challenge each student at his/her particular level. In another instance, a teacher surveys children's interests and creates learning centers focused round these areas.

The main difference between the two approaches is which aspect of the learning earns the primary focus of the attention. With acceleration, the child is physically moved to a different learning setting (i.e., to start school early, to skip a grade, to move to another teacher's classroom for one subject) and what happens upon arriving in this new setting is the same for all learners including the new child who was accelerated. That is, once a child starts kindergarten 1 year earlier than expected, she is folded into the classroom as one of the others. In a differentiated classroom, the child remains with same-age peers, but the focus of the service is on creating within-class learning tasks tailored to meet those individual learner needs. Regardless of which philosophical approach is employed, the classroom environment and learning tasks need to be appropriate for the developmental level of the students. However, considering that young gifted children develop at asynchronous rates, the idea of developmentally appropriate practices with this population bears further exploration.

Developmentally Appropriate Practices and Gifted Students

Over the past two decades, instructional practices in primary classrooms have been significantly influenced by the National Association for the Education of Young Children's (NAEYC, 1995) advocacy for developmentally appropriate practices (Jones & Gullo, 1999). Classrooms characterized by developmentally appropriate practices (DAP) are based on the philosophy that children actively construct knowledge for themselves as they interact with their peers, adults, and materials (Bredekamp & Copple, 1997). In this model, the child's experience is at the center of instruction, and learning activities are designed for their potential to engage children at their current levels of cognitive development (Stipek, 2004; Jones & Gullo, 1999). The DAP classroom environment is organized to allow for a variety of learning experiences based on individual, developmental, and cultural characteristics of young students (Huffman & Speer, 2000), and in this way, the model represents a shift away from the teacher-led, didactic instructional environment of the more traditional classroom. Recent developments in understanding of the developing brain have also been cited in support of DAP. That is, DAP are thought to gain students' attention, encourage students to develop meaningful connections between new and prior knowledge, foster memory development through an emphasis on patterns and active problem solving, and allow students to work at an appropriate level of challenge, all of which are consistent with the function of the brain during learning and environments that nurture talent (Rushton & Larkin, 2001).

How do young, potentially gifted students fare in developmentally appropriate classrooms? While studies have not specifically addressed this question, Morelock and Morrison (1999) explicate a number of concerns regarding the suitability of DAP for gifted students. In particular, the authors point to the underlying assumption that development follows a series of stage-like progressions that can be predicted with reasonable accuracy based on a child's age. They suggest that this assumption is inconsistent with the asynchronous development characteristic of many young children, whose needs are unlikely to be met when age-based criteria are used to evaluate whether practices are developmentally appropriate. These authors recommend Vygotsky's zone of proximal development as a more appropriately individualized model of cognitive progress, whereby development is fostered as students practice skills and solve problems that they are able to complete with cognitive scaffolding, as they move towards independent mastery. Within this framework, instruction is tailored to meet the student's actual, rather than expected, developmental capabilities. Although student progress is arguably more difficult to measure, this approach leaves the teacher with no choice but to differentiate curriculum in order to meet the needs of all students, including those who are potentially gifted. For example, in a differentiated classroom, a teacher would tailor the depth and complexity of the *content* taught to meet the needs of young gifted children (e.g., students exploring weather patterns over a 12-month period of time vs. learning about seasons); use of varied *instructional processes* (e.g., gifted students pursue an independent study vs. more directed study with the teacher); and development of different *products* (e.g., one student draws what they learned in a story vs. a written response to the story).

In the following section, we look at how these major ideas—acceleration, differentiated instruction, and DAP intersect in actual practice settings. Further, we explore some promising programs across the country that adhere to DAP as well as provide appropriate challenge for the full range of learners.

Promising Programs

A number of programs for young gifted children, including those from diverse and disadvantaged backgrounds, have shown promising results using a purposeful combination of acceleration and within-class differentiated instruction to ensure sufficient challenge within the kind of child-centered classroom promoted by DAP (Gould, Thorpe, & Weeks, 2001; Karnes & Johnson, 1991; Walker, Hafenstein, & Crow-Enslow, 1999). Common elements of these programs appear to include a child-centered focus, curricula derived from students' interests, rigorous curricula focused on important interdisciplinary concepts, and genuine involvement from parents and local communities. Karnes and Johnson (1991) found that within one program aimed at young gifted students and characterized by these elements, disadvantaged students not identified as gifted also made significant gains.

Pre-School Programs

One example of a primary-level DAP-style program is the Early Childhood Accelerated Program (ECAP*R) in Wichita, KS, which serves potentially, gifted children from a variety of circumstances, including those from diverse and disadvantaged backgrounds, ages 3–5 (Gould, Weeks, & Evans, 2003). In this DAP-infused program, students are exposed to content and skills not typically taught to children until middle-late elementary grades. For example, the program staff describes curricular experiences in science including the topics of chemical reactions, solubility, microbes, invertebrates, density, paper chromatography, magnetism, friction, and properties of light (Gould et al., 2003) One student, Jacob, sparked a particular interest in oceanography through this program, which served as an impetus for self-motivated reading and exploration of ocean creatures. Jacob's mother offered further testimony to the DAP-infused accelerative program in its ability to meet his needs after a series of behaviorally-charged dismissals from other pre-school programs.

In the relative absence of formal programming for pre-school gifted children, which could stem from a lack of mandated funding for this purpose, beliefs about the dangers of early identification, or the reluctance of parents to advocate for gifted programs at the primary level, curriculum and instruction assumes great importance within the regular general education classroom, particularly in grades K–3 when gifted services are especially scant.

Programs in K–3, general education settings. Diezmann and English (2001) describe an early childhood pull-out program, which incorporate both acceleration, differentiation, and DAP. The authors outline how the content that the students were learning (space travel and reading large numbers such as was necessary to understand the speed of rocket ships and the distance between planets) was beyond the grade level standards for the typically developing general education class. In that way the class content was enriched and by pulling students out of the general education setting, the pace of the instruction was able to be more rapid, thus accelerated when compared to the general education setting. The topic of space travel was suggested by the students as an area of interest thereby promoting the children's own motivation to learn the new information.

In a recent federally funded research project (Brighton et al., 2007), a series of curricular materials were developed for primary-grade classrooms that aimed to organize standards-based content into differentiated, DAP-infused units. The logic undergirding the development of these units was to provide primary grade teachers with materials containing sufficient challenge for previously identified gifted students as well as to provide a mechanism for potentially gifted students to demonstrate their abilities and talents. One such unit aimed at Kindergarten level focused on an interdisciplinary investigation of the season of spring using the conceptual organizer of change. The five lessons in the unit exposed students to a variety of visual images about the season invited them to create analogies for spring in the style of E. E. Cummings' poem *spring is like a perhaps hand*, to employ dramatic interpretation of Vivaldi's *Spring*, and to conduct independent research on self-identified questions related to spring and seasonal changes. The teachers who implemented the units as a part of this project consistently revealed surprise at the level of insight that some students, particularly those from historically under-represented groups in gifted programs, were able to offer on the unit topics. "I saw where some of my kids that I didn't really, you know, think would be such good writers were writing good questions" (p. 67).

Another recent research project, Project Parallax, explored the approach to serving gifted and potentially gifted students specifically in elementary grade science and math classrooms employing Problem Based Learning (PBL) as the curricular framework for organizing the required standard course of study (Parallax Project, n.d.). In accordance with DAP, PBL allows for content and skills to be situated into authentic, real-world scenarios that are relevant to the young learners' experiences (Borasi & Fonzi, 2002). Further, active learning approaches, such as PBL, that are constructivist in nature and focused on building conceptual understandings are among the recommended practices suggested by the National Study Group for the Affirmative Development of Academic Ability (2004). For example, one PBL unit from this project is initiated by a letter from a local benefactor. In the letter she explains to the students that she would like to make a monetary donation (but the amount is not initially known) to help the homeless animals in the community. By way of this letter she invites the students to "Pay it Forward" to help these animals. To solve this open-ended problem, the young students are tasked with identifying what information they *know*, what the *need to know*, and establishing a plan for solving the problem that meets the specific criteria and limitations set forth from the benefactor. Through this process, the teacher provides purposeful directed lessons to the whole class and small groups differentiated by students' readiness with the math content. In this model, the facilitated teaching becomes a relevant part of the problem-solving process. Preliminary data from this project suggest that students participating in PBL units are more engaged in learning than students whose learning conditions are less aligned with DAP-infused practices (Boren & Moon, 2010).

In summary, this section highlighted three programs for developing talent in young gifted and potentially gifted children, and while there are limited resources specifically earmarked for programs for young gifted children such as these, these aforementioned programs illustrate how the varied philosophies of acceleration, differentiated instruction (or, in some cases elements of both philosophies) as well as adherence to DAP can work together for the benefit of these students' social, emotional, and most directly intellectual needs. There is little doubt that many of the early-developing children such as the kinds of students described above have unique learning needs that deserve to be addressed. To accomplish this goal, teachers at the pre-school and primary school level must be prepared to develop responsive, appropriately challenging learning opportunities to nurture talents in students such as these and to help them develop healthy attitudes and habits of learning (Neihart et al., 2002).

Future Directions for Research and Practice

This chapter highlights the need for increased attention toward young gifted children and suggests that a broadened conception of giftedness coupled with more attention to *serving*, rather than merely *identifying* and *labeling* them will result in more direct services for their needs. Additionally, the following recommendations are offered for guiding future research and practice in this area:

- Publish longitudinal studies of young gifted children from pre-school (or before) including socioeconomic data, identification procedures used, and services received to determine any patterns among the groups and to determine the degree to which programming positively influences the children's short-term and long-term academic and social outcomes.

- Provide targeted instruction to pre-service and in-service preschool and primary school teachers to make them aware of characteristics of giftedness and possible programming options such as acceleration and differentiated instruction. Research has shown that extensive training in these areas can hone teachers' skills in recognizing possible signs of talent and be able to mediate factors of social class and dominant culture (Gross, 1999).
- Conduct updated reviews of relevant research to determine the influence of the teacher training in teachers' perceptions of and beliefs about giftedness and talent in young children. While Gross' (1999) review of literature on the influence of training on teachers' ability to effectively spot talent is relevant, this work is due for a review.
- Examine how policies aimed at minimum competency testing such as No Child Left Behind legislation has shifted priorities away from the development of talent in the youngest learners. As new educational policies are implemented, more attention should be paid to how they directly and indirectly shape programs for the young gifted learners in our midst.

Final Thoughts

Some children develop observable gifts and talents in areas such as spoken language/linguistics, reading, and mathematics distinguishing them from their same-age peers who follow a more common developmental trajectory. Evidence suggests that failure to recognize and nurture these early-developed talents can result in negative emotional and social consequences such as masking behaviors, code-switching and possible long-term underachievement. There is also ample evidence suggesting that the home environment, (e.g., impoverished conditions, poor pre- and peri-natal health and malnutrition) has a powerful influence on the development of these gifts and talents, even surpassing the contribution of genetic potential. Because of lack of definitional clarity and insufficient tools for use with young often non-reading populations, identifying giftedness is a challenging endeavor leading many to shift emphases away from labeling and shifting energies toward serving students' needs. While programs aimed specifically at serving preschool and primary school gifted learners are scant, there are some with promising records in meeting the needs of young gifted learners. Future directions in the field of primary-level gifted education are focused on more encompassing efforts within the general education framework to provide sufficiently challenging programs for gifted students and simultaneously provide a system for capturing evidence of potential giftedness. Using accelerative techniques such as grade-skipping and subject-specific acceleration, when appropriate, in conjunction with differentiation within DAP-infused programs are central to the majority of efforts in current initiatives.

In sum, the current research on primary classroom practices suggests that low income and minority students exposed to child-centered DAP are likely to fare better than those exposed to more traditional, teacher-centered instructional practices, but that potentially gifted students and others who develop according to a different pace or pattern than the age-typical student require differentiated instruction in order to ensure sufficient challenge. Programs that involve the differentiation of content, process, product and learning environment in response to individual learners, and provide rich, challenging curriculum have been shown to benefit not only young gifted students, but students of diverse ability levels and backgrounds.

References

Baker, C. (1996). *Foundations of bilingual education and bilingualism* (2nd Edition) (ERIC Report ED406841).

Barbe, W. B. (1964). *One in a thousand: A comparative study of highly and moderately gifted elementary school children*. Columbus, OH: F. J. Heer.

Benbow, C. P., & Stanley, J. C. (1997). Inequity in equity: How "equity" can lead to inequity for high-potential students. *Psychology, Public Policy, and Law, 2*(2), 249–292.

Borasi, R., & Fonzi, J. (2002). Professional development that supports school mathematics reform. *Foundations: A monograph for professionals in science, mathematics, and technology education, 3*. Arlington, VA: National Science Foundation.

Boren, R., & Moon, T. R. (2010, April). *Engaging learners through the use of Problem Based Learning*. Paper presented at the annual meeting of the American Educational Research Association, Denver, CO.

Borland, J. H. (1989). *Planning and implementing programs for the gifted*. New York: Teachers College Press.

Bredekamp, S. & Copple, C. (Eds.). (1997). *Developmentally appropriate practice in early childhood programs* (Rev. ed.). Washington, DC: National Association for the Education of Young Children.

Bredekamp, S., & Shepard, L. (1990). Protecting children from inappropriate practices. *ERIC Digest* (ED326305).

Brighton, C. M., Moon, T. R., Jarvis, J. M., & Hockett, J. A. (2007). *Primary teachers' conceptions of giftedness and talent: A case-based investigation*. Storrs, CT: National Research Center on the Gifted and Talented.

Brown, S. W., Renzulli, J. S., Gubbins, E. J., Siegle, D., Zhang, W. & Chen, C. (2005). Assumptions underlying the identification of gifted and talented students. *Gifted Child Quarterly, 49*(1), 68–79.

Callahan, C. M. (2005). Identifying gifted students from underrepresented populations. *Theory into Practice, 44*(2), 98–105.

Callahan, C. M., & McIntire, J. A. (1994). *Identifying outstanding talent in American Indian and Alaska Native students*. Washington, DC: Office of Educational Research and Improvement.

Camara, W. J., & Schmidt, A. E. (1999). *Group differences in standardized testing and social stratification* (College Board Report No. 99-5). New York: College Entrance Examination Board. Retrieved April 6, 2005, from http://www.collegeboard.com/repository/rr9905_3916.pdf

Chamberlin, S. A., Buchanan, M., &Vercimak, D. (2007). Serving twice-exceptional preschoolers: Blending gifted education and early childhood special education practices in assessment and program planning. *Journal for the Education of the Gifted, 30*, 372–394.

Colangelo, N., Assouline, S., & Gross, M. (Eds.). (2004). *A nation deceived: How schools hold back America's brightest students*. Iowa City, IA: The Belin Blank Center Gifted Education and Talent Development.

Damiani, B. (1997). Young gifted children in research and practice: The need for early childhood programs. *Gifted Child Today, 20*(3), 18–23.

Dearing, E., McCartney, K., Weiss, H. B., Kreider, H., & Simpkins, S. (2004). The promotive effects of family educational involvement for low-income children's literacy. *Journal of School Psychology, 42,* 445–460.

Dickinson, D. K., & Tabor, P. O. (Eds.). (2001). *Beginning literacy with language: Young children learning at home and school.* New York: The Maple Press.

Diezmann, C. M., & English, L. D. (2001). Developing young children's multidigit number sense. *Roeper Review, 24*(1), 11–13.

Dodici, B. J., Draper, D. C., & Peterson, C. A. (2003). Early parent-child interactions and early literacy development. *Topics in Early Childhood Special Education, 23,* 124–136.

Downer, J. T., & Pianta, R. C. (2006). Academic and cognitive functioning in first grade: Associations with earlier home and child care predictors and with concurrent home and classroom experiences. *School Psychology Review, 35*(1), 11–30.

Ewing, N. J., & Yong, F. L. (1992). A comparative study of the learning style preferences among gifted African-American, Mexican-American, and American-born Chinese middle grade students. *Roeper Review, 14*(3), 120–123.

Feiring, C., Louis, B., Ukeje, I., Lewis, M., & Leong, P. (1997). Early identification of gifted minority kindergarten students in Newark, NJ. *Gifted Child Quarterly, 41*(3), 76–82.

Fletcher-Flinn, C. M., & Thompson, G. B. (2000). Learning to read with underdeveloped phonemic awareness but lexicalized phonological recoding: A case study of a 3-year-old. *Cognition, 74,* 177–208.

Ford, D. Y., & Harris, J. J. III. (1999). *Multicultural gifted education.* New York: Teachers College Press.

Ford, D. Y., Howard, T. C., Harris, J. J., & Tyson, C. A. (2000). Creating culturally responsive classrooms for gifted African American students. *Journal for the Education of the Gifted, 23,* 397–427.

Gandara, P. (2004). *Latino achievement: Identifying models that foster success* (Research Monograph No. RM04194). Storrs, CT: National Research Center for the Gifted and Talented.

Gavin, M. K., Casa, T. M., Adelson, J. L., Carroll, S. R., & Sheffield, L. J. (2009). The impact of advanced curriculum on the achievement of mathematically promising elementary students. *Gifted Child Quarterly, 53,* 188–202.

Gottfried, A. W., Gottfried, A. E., Bathurst, K. & Guerin, D. W. (1994). *Gifted IQ: Early developmental aspects: The Fullerton longitudinal study.* New York: Plenum.

Gould, J. C., Thorpe, P., & Weeks, V. (2001). An early childhood accelerated program. *Educational Leadership, 59*(3), 47–50.

Gould, J. C., Weeks, V., & Evans, S. (2003). Science starts early. *Gifted Child Today, 26*(3), 38–41, 65.

Griggs, S. A., & Dunn, R. (1996). *Hispanic-American students and learning styles.* ERIC Digest (ED393-607).

Gross, M. U. M. (1993). *Exceptionally gifted children.* London: Routledge.

Gross, M. U. M. (1999). Small poppies: Highly gifted children in the early years. *Roeper Review, 21*(3), 207–214.

Harrison, C. (2004). Giftedness in early childhood: The search for complexity and connection. *Roeper Review, 26*(2), 78–84.

Hilliard, A. G. III. (1989). Teachers and cultural styles in a pluralistic society. *NEA Today, 7*(6), 65–69.

Hodge, K. A., & Kemp, C. R. (2000). Exploring the nature of giftedness in preschool children. *Journal for the Education of the Gifted, 24*(1), 46–73.

Huffman, L. R., & Speer, P. W. (2000). Academic performance among at-risk children: The role of developmentally appropriate practices. *Early Childhood Research Quarterly, 15,* 167–184.

Jackson, N. E. (1988). Precocious reading ability: What does it mean? *Gifted Child Quarterly, 32,* 200–204.

Jackson, N. E. (2003). Young gifted children. In N. Colangelo & G. Davis (Eds.), *Handbook of gifted education* (3rd ed., pp. 470–482). Boston, MA: Allyn and Bacon.

Jackson, N. E., & Klein, E. J. (1997). Gifted performance in young children. In N. Colangelo & G. A. Davis (Eds.), *Handbook of gifted education* (2nd ed., pp. 460–474). Boston: Allyn & Bacon.

Jackson, N. E., & Lu, W. (1992). Bilingual precocious readers of English. *Roeper Review, 14*(3), 115–119.

Jones, I., & Gullo, D. F. (1999). Differential social and academic effects of developmentally appropriate practices and beliefs. *Journal of Research in Childhood Education, 14,* 26–35.

Justice, M. J., & Pullen, P. C. (2003). Promising interventions for promoting emergent literacy skills: Three evidence-based approaches. *Topics in Early Childhood Special Education, 23*(3) 99–113.

Kanevsky, L. S. (1992). The learning game. In P. Klein & A. J. Tannenbaum (Eds.), *To be young and gifted* (pp. 204–241). Norwood, NJ: Ablex.

Kaplan, C. (1992). Ceiling effects in assessing high-IQ children with the WPPSI – R. *Journal of Clinical Child Psychology, 21,* 403–406.

Karnes, M. B., & Johnson, L. J. (1991). The preschool/primary gifted child. *Journal for the Education of the Gifted, 14*(3), 267–283.

Karr, S., & Schwenn, J. O. (1999). Multi-method assessment of multicultural learners. In F. E. Obiakor, J. O. Schwenn, & A. F. Rotatori (Eds.), *Multicultural education for learners with exceptionalities* (pp. 105–119). Stamford, CT: JAI Press.

Kitano, M. K. (1989). The K-3 teacher's role in recognizing and supporting young gifted children. *Young Children, 44*(3), 57–63.

Laing, S. P., & Kamhi, A. (2003). Alternative assessment of language and literacy in culturally and linguistically diverse populations. *Language, Speech and Hearing Services in Schools, 34,* 44–55.

Lawhon, T., & Cobb, J.B. (2002). Routines that build emergent literacy skills in infants, toddlers, and preschoolers. *Early Childhood Education Journal, 30,* 113–133.

Levine, E. S., & Kitano, M. K. (1998). Helping young children reclaim their strengths. In J. F. Smutny (Ed.), *The young gifted child: Potential and promise an anthrology* (pp. 282–294). Cresskill, NJ: Hampton Press.

Magnuson, K. A., Meyers, M. M., Ruhm, C. J., & Waldfogel, J. (2004). Inequality in preschool education and school readiness. *American Educational Research Journal, 41*(1), 115–157.

Maker, C. J. (1996). Identification of gifted minority students: A national problem, needed changes and a promising solution. *Gifted Child Quarterly, 40*(1), 41–50.

Mantzicopoulos, P. Y. (2000). Can the Brigance K&1 Screen detect cognitive/academic giftedness when used with preschoolers from economically disadvantaged backgrounds? *Roeper Review, 22*(3), 185–191.

Morelock, M. J., & Morrison, K. (1999). Differentiating 'developmentally appropriate': The multidimensional curriculum model for young gifted children. *Roeper Review, 21,* 195–200.

National Association for the Education of Young Children (NAEYC). (1995). *Position statement: Where we stand on school readiness.* Retrieved April 15, 2006, from http://www.naeyc.org/about/positions/pdf/readiness.pdf

National Study Group for the Affirmative Development of Academic Ability. (2004). *All students reaching the top: Strategies for closing academic achievement gaps.* Naperville, IL: Learning Point Associates.

Neihart, M., Reis, S. M., Robinson, N. M., & Moon, S. M. (Eds.). (2002). *The social and emotional development of gifted children: What do we know?* Waco, TX: Prufrock Press.

Neuman, S. B., & Dickson, D. K. (Eds.) (2002). *Handbook of early literacy research.* New York: Guilford Press.

Ogbu, J. U. (1988). Cultural diversity and human development. *New Directions for Child Development, 42,* 11–28.

Onwuegbuzie, A. J., & Daley, C. E. (2001). Racial differences in IQ revisited: A synthesis of nearly a century of research. *Journal of Black Psychology, 27,* 209–220.

Piaget, J. (1953). *The origins of intelligence in children.* London: Routledge and Kegan Paul.

Porter, L. (2005). *Gifted young children: A guide for teachers and parents.* Berkshire, UK: Open University Press.

Proctor, T. B., Black, K. N., & Feldhusen, J. F. (1988). Early admission to elementary school; barriers versus benefits. *Roeper Review, 11,* 85–87.

Project Parallax (n.d.). Retrieved from http://parallaxproject.org

Ramey, C. T., & Ramey, S. L. (2004). Early learning and school readiness: Can early intervention make a difference? *Merrill-Palmer Quarterly, 50*(4), 471–491.

Renzulli, J. S. (2003). Conception of giftedness and its relationship to the development of social capital. In N. Colangelo & G. Davis (Eds.), *Handbook of gifted education* (3rd ed., pp. 75–87). Boston, MA: Allyn and Bacon.

Robinson, N. M. (1993). *Parenting the very young, gifted child* (Research Monograph No. 9308). Storrs, CT: National Research Center on the Gifted and Talented.

Robinson, N. M., Abbott, R. D., Berninger, V. W., & Busse, J. (1996). The structure of abilities in math-precocious young children: Gender similarities and differences. *Journal of Educational Psychology, 88*(2), 341–352.

Rotigel, J. V. (2003). Understanding the young gifted child: Guidelines for parents, families, and educators. *Early Childhood Education Journal, 30*(4), 209–214.

Rushton, S., & Larkin, E. (2001). Shaping the learning environment: Connecting developmentally appropriate practices to brain research. *Early Childhood Education Journal, 29,* 25–33.

Sankar-De-Leeuw, N. (1999). Gifted preschoolers: Parent and teacher views on identification, early admission, and programming. *Roeper Review, 21*(3), 174–179.

Sankar-De-Leeuw, N. (2004). Case studies of gifted kindergarten children: Profiles of promise. *Roeper Review, 26*(4), 192–207.

Sattler, J. M. (2001). *Assessment of children: Cognitive applications* (4th ed.). La Mesa, CA: Jerome M. Sattler.

Shade, B. J. (1997). Culture and learning style within the African-American community. In B. J. Shade (Ed.), *Cultural style and educative process: Making schools work for racially diverse students* (2nd ed., pp. 12–28). Springfield, IL: Charles C. Thomas.

Shaklee, B. (1992). Identification of young gifted students. *Journal for the Education of the Gifted, 15*(2), 134–144.

Shaklee, B. D., & Hansford, S. (1992). *Identification of underserved populations: Focus on preschool and primary children* (ERIC Document No. ED344406).

Shavinina, L. V. (1999). The psychological essence of the child prodigy phenomenon: Sensitive periods and cognitive experience. *Gifted Child Quarterly, 43*(1), 25–38.

Siegle, D., & Powell, T. (2004). Exploring teacher biases when nominating students for gifted programs. *Gifted Child Quarterly, 48*(1), 21–29.

Sonnenschein, S., & Munsterman, K. (2002). The influence of home-based reading interactions on 5-year-olds' reading motivations and early literacy development. *Early Childhood Research Quarterly, 17,* 318–337.

Sternberg, R. J. (2003). Giftedness according to the theory of successful intelligence. In N. Colangelo & G. Davis (Eds.), *Handbook of gifted education* (3rd ed., pp. 88–99). Boston, MA: Allyn and Bacon.

Stipek, D. (2004). Teaching practices in kindergarten and first grade: Different strokes for different folks. *Early Childhood Research Quarterly, 19,* 548–568.

Tannenbaum, A. J. (1992). Early signs of giftedness: Research and commentary. *Journal for the Education of the Gifted, 15,* 104–133.

Tannenbaum, A. J. (2003). Nature and nurture of giftedness. In N. Colangelo & G. Davis (Eds.), *Handbook of gifted education* (3rd ed., pp. 45–59). Boston, MA: Allyn and Bacon.

Taylor, K. K., Gibbs, A. S., & Slate, J. R. (2000). Preschool attendance and kindergarten readiness. *Research in Early Childhood, 27*(3), 191–195.

Tomlinson, C. (2005). Quality curriculum and instruction for highly able students. *Theory into Practice, 44*(2), 160–166.

Turkheimer, E., D'Onofrio, B. M., Maes, H. H., Eaves, L. J. (2005). Analysis and nterpretation of twin studies including measures of the shared environment. *Child Development, 76*(6), 1217–1233.

Turkheimer, E., Haley, A., Waldron, M., D'Onofrio, B., & Gottesman, I. I. (2003). Socioeconomic status modifies heritability of IQ in young children. *Psychological Science, 14*(6), 623–628.

Van Tassel-Baska, J. (1989). *Excellence in educating the gifted.* Denver, CO: Love.

Vasquez, J. (1990). Teaching to the distinctive traits of minority students. *The Clearing House, 63*(7), 299–304.

Walker, B., Hafenstein, N. L., & Crow-Enslow, L. (1999). Meeting the needs of gifted learners in the early childhood classroom. *Young Children, 54*(1), 32–36.

Washington, V. (1996). Professional development in context: Leadership at the borders of our democratic, pluralistic society. *Young Children, 51,* 30–34.

Webb, J. T., Meckstroth, E. A., & Tolan, S. S. (1982). *Guiding the gifted child: A practical source for parents and teachers.* Scottsdale, AZ: Great Potential Press.

Weigel, D., Martin, S., & Bennett, K. (2006). Contributions of the home literacy environment to preschool aged children's emerging literacy and language skills. *Early Childhood Development and Care, 176*(3-4), 357–378.

West, J., Denton, K, & Germino-Hausken, E. (2000). America's kindergartners: Findings from the early childhood longitudinal study, kindergarten class of 1998–99, Fall 1998. *Education Statistics Quarterly, 2*(1), 7–13.

Whitehurst, G. J., & Lonigan, C. J. (1998). Child development and emergent literacy. *Child Development, 69,* 848–872.

Winner, E. (1997). Exceptionally high intelligence and schooling. *American Psychologist, 52*(10), 1070–1081.

Section XIII

Cultural and International Issues in Special Education

Section Editor: Dimitris Anastasiou
University of Western Macedonia, Greece

A kind of cultural politics is heavily involved in the field of special education in the United States. The rise of concerns for culturally, linguistically, and ethnically diverse students with disabilities dates back to at least the 1960s. Cultural issues, such as the overrepresentation of African American students in special classes and schools, started receiving attention, and gradually provoked a widespread skepticism about the usefulness of pull-out placements. During the following decades, culturally based issues were a source of discord and influenced the agenda of education reform. A wave of topics, from the disproportionate representation of culturally, linguistically, and ethnically diverse students to recent calls for "cultural sensitivity" and "culturally responsive instruction," has also affected the public image of special education. From a humanitarian service for learners with disabilities, traditional special education has been increasingly re-conceptualized as an obstacle on the road to equitable participation in school and social life. Thus, "segregation," a value-laden term drawn from the war against racial discrimination, is frequently used as a popular way of representing the special and individualized ways in which people with disabilities have been educated. Is racial segregation equivalent with pull-out special education services? Can exceptionality be discussed in ways similar to cultural difference? What are the limitations? What does disproportionality say about our education system? What does it not tell us? How do culture, language, and ethnicity relate to teaching and learning? Anastasiou, Gardner, and Michail, in their chapter "Ethnicity and Exceptionality," summarize the literature on cultural, linguistic, and ethnic disproportionality in special education programs from both United States and international perspectives.

Another kind of disproportionality, that of the overrepresentation of males in special education, has received little attention and has but rarely been debated, despite its comparable size. This relatively unaddressed pattern is complicated by recent findings that females in special education tend to have more severe needs. What are the hypothesized causes of gender disproportionality in special education? How sensitive are assessment processes to the identification of some conditions (e.g., internalizing disorders) in females? Are there differential educational experiences and outcomes for students with disabilities that are related to gender? What should be the educational responses to gender differences? What other implications are there for special education? How can disparities between men and women with disabilities in social outcomes be interpreted? These issues and questions are only some of those examined by Coutinho and Oswald in their chapter "Gender and Exceptionality."

In "International Differences in Provision for Exceptional Learners," Anastasiou and Keller explore how different countries around the world provide education to students with exceptionalities. Specifically, they develop a typological approach to categorizing special education provision internationally, using a set of specific criteria. The general context of the educational system and the influence of the inclusion movement on special education services are also taken into account. They also provide four country cases—Nigeria, China, Italy, and Finland—as examples to illustrate four of the six major types. The aims of this chapter are three-fold: describe some of the rich diversity of special education across countries, establish a base for international comparative analyses, and present a relatively objective framework of how a specific country provides education to exceptional learners within the context of its national educational system.

55
Ethnicity and Exceptionality

Dimitris Anastasiou
University of Western Macedonia, Greece

Ralph Gardner, III
The Ohio State University

Domna Michail
University of Western Macedonia, Greece

Both ethnicity, or cultural differences in general, and exceptionalities can cause children to behave is ways that are dissimilar to educators' expectations for learners (Artiles, 1998). However, this common point does not mean that they pose equivalent or similar teaching challenges. In many circumstances, responsiveness to ethnicity and exceptionality has been different for educational purposes (Kauffman, 2005; Kauffman & Landrum, 2009).

Educators are mandated by the Individuals with Disabilities Education Act (IDEA, 2004) and the No Child Left Behind Act (2002) to provide an appropriate education for all learners in their schools. Providing an appropriate education for each learner regardless of cultural background, academic ability, social skills, and/or language differences is a daunting task (Banks, 2007). However, to do otherwise would be a disservice to learners and violate their rights to a quality education. Educators' challenge is to discern when a child's difference is the result of a disability that requires special education services to address his/her educational needs. IDEA clearly indicated that children should not be placed in special education if their poor performance is due to environmental disadvantage or ethnic, linguistic, and racial differences. The fact is that disability alone may not be enough to mandate special education placement (Kauffman & Hallahan, 2005). Some children with a diagnosed disability such as a physical disability (e.g., inability to walk) or health disability (e.g., asthma) may excel in the general education curriculum with only structural or medical interventions, respectively. In other words, children should be placed in special education only if they meet the definition of a disability, as stated in IDEA. IDEA defines a disability as a learner with one or more impairments/disabilities (i.e., mental retardation, hearing, language, visual, emotional, orthopedic, autism, traumatic brain injury, other health, specific learning, and/or developmental delays) who needs specialized instruction and/or related services in order to receive an appropriate education (Dunklee & Shoop, 2006).

Cultural difference, when mistakenly considered a disability, can cause children to receive inappropriate education services. Children who enter U.S. schools without proficiency in English may require additional instructional support in order to become successful academically, but they do not necessarily require special education services (Artiles, Trent, & Palmer, 2004).

How educators have addressed the convergence of cultural diversity and exceptionality in schools has been a persistent controversial issue (Artiles, 1998; Artiles & Trent, 1994; Losen & Orfield, 2002; Coutinho & Oswald, 2000; Kauffman & Landrum, 2009). One reason this topic is contentious is because of the historical treatment of minority groups by majority groups (Artiles, 1998; Patton, 1998). Therefore, when educational patterns emerge indicating that minority learners perform less well than majority learners on education outcomes, the specter of the consequences of historical and/or current biases is frequently raised as a concern.

A second reason that disproportionality is contentious is because of the potential stigma carried by labels such as mental retardation (MR) and emotional and/or behavior disorders (EBD). African Americans face greater odds to receive these labels than other ethnic groups (Hosp & Reschly, 2003). These labels may unwittingly reinforce or be influenced by stereotypic beliefs. How stigma is generated and better handled is also a highly controversial issue (Artiles, 1998; cf. Kauffman, 2003).

Third, ethnic disproportionate placement in special education is connected with vague perceptions about the effectiveness of special education. Contrary to popular misconceptions, the best scientific evidence indicates that different placements, programs, and intervention techniques may produce differential effect sizes for different special education categories (Kavale & Forness, 1999).

Ethnicity, Race, and Culture Difference

Due to the high degree of abstraction that both the concepts of culture and ethnicity entail, it is important to clarify the way that these concepts are used in this present work. Like many words that are commonly used, the word "culture" has developed various definitions including association with the history and customs of a particular people, the social environment of a specific geographic area, familial heritage, aesthetic expressions (e.g., visual arts, literature, etc.), or even a school or business atmosphere (i.e., pattern of behaviors). Ethnicity in our discussion cannot ignore cultural history. This means that the history of the ethnic groups or minorities we are looking at have created a collective historical/cultural consciousness that shapes the nature of their present ethnic identity. In Eriksen's (1993) words, "cultural histories of people may certainly shed light on the origins of contemporary ethnicity, and should not be seen merely as aspects of the present" (p. 96).

Determining ethnicity and race has been far more complicated in the United States than in other parts of the world. This was partly due to the fact that every census, since the first one in 1790, has defined race differently (Hodgkinson, 1995). The Office of Management and Budget, responsible for the race definitions, gave the following warning: "The racial and ethnic categories set forth in the standard should not be interpreted as being scientific or anthropological in nature" (as cited in Hodgkinson, 1995, p. 174).

What makes this categorization issue even more problematic is the employment by the U.S. Census Bureau (2008) of the category of "ethnic group" only in reference to "Hispanic or Latino" or "non-Hispanic" people for the purpose of tracking population growth. The Census also includes the following race categories: American Indian or Alaskan Native (i.e., American Indian, Eskimo, or Aluet), Asian, Native Hawaiian and Other Pacific Islander, Black or African American, White, and Some Other Race (e.g., Mulatto, Creole, Mestizo, etc.). Respondents to the census may check one or more race categories. In other words an individual's preferences for how they view themselves can influence data. This complexity is not just restricted to the U. S. census. Attempts to categorize people by a physiognomic feature such as skin color can be very puzzling. For example, "some people who consider themselves African do not have black skin, and some who consider themselves European or Asian do" (Kauffman, Conroy, Gardner, & Oswald, 2008, p. 242).

For scientific reasons "race" is therefore a very problematic category (Smedley & Smedley, 2005). Contemporary research indicates that the folk classification of "races" does not correspond to genetically discrete groups. Outward characteristics, such as skin color, hair texture or facial features, which have been used to classify "races" in the past, are considered trivial today from the aspect of genetic variation (see Bamshad & Olson, 2003, for detailed documentation). Although the difference in levels of melanin between Americans of African and European origins is in scientifc terms an insignificant biological characteristic, the racial discrimination is real. Those classified as "black race" may pay a societal tax of a lower standard of living, health care, and, ultimately, in both quality of life and years of life (Lewontin & Levins, 2007; Smedley & Smedley, 2005).

For the purposes of this chapter we use the term "race" conventionally only referring to the United States, and we underline the need to distinguish the folk conceptions from the scientific constructs themselves. When referring to other parts of the world we use the term "ethnic group." The use of this term "suggests contact and interrelationship" and refers to both Western as well as to non-Western societies (Eriksen, 1993).

Lastly, though there are commonalities among people within the same culture or ethnicity, there is also great diversity across individuals within a specific culture or ethnicity. Therefore, educators should avoid assumptions or designing education plans based solely on a learner's culture or ethnicity because that can lead to faulty instructional decisions (Kauffman et al., 2008).

Defining Exceptionality

A person is exceptional because he or she has "problems or special talents in thinking, seeing, hearing, speaking, socializing, or moving" (Hallahan, Kauffman, & Pullen, 2009, p. 5). IDEA provides a definition for each disability category to guide professionals and parents in deciding whether a child should or should not receive special education services. Special education includes both categories designating disabilities as well as and gifts and talents.

Like the concepts ethnicity and culture, disability involves examining differences and similarities of people. In contrast to ethnicity and culture which can be viewed as social constructs, the meaning of disabilities lies in both biology and society, as well as in their interaction (Anastaiou & Kauffman, 2011; Shakespeare, 2006).

Special education definitions, particularly in regards to mild disabilities and gifted education, are somewhat vague for the purpose of including rather than excluding children. This vagueness can additionally have the unintended consequence of wrongly promoting the placement of children in special education who do not require these services.

Disproportionality

Disproportionality is the over- or under-representation of a specific group of students (e.g., African Americans) based on higher than expected percentage of that population in special education or based on substantial differences compared to other groups. The discussion on disproportionality is further complicated by different strategies used to analyze student data. These strategies yield different types of information and in some cases cause different conclusions (Coutinho & Oswald, 2000). The three most common methods for assessing disproportionality are composition, risk index, and risk ratio.

The Composition Index compares the number of students in a specific racial/ethnic group who receive special education services to the percentage of students from that ethnicity in the overall school-age population. For example, if Native Americans are 5% of the school-age population yet they are 10% of the students labeled as having learning disabilities, thus they would be seen as having a 5% over-representation (10%–5% = 5%) (Coutinho & Oswald, 2000). *Risk Index* is the percentage of a given group served in a specific special education category. For example, Donovan and Cross (2002) reported that 2.64% of all African Americans public school students in the United States were enrolled in the special education category of mental retardation. Compared to White students with a 1.18% risk, this indicates that African Americans are twice as likely to be labeled with mental retardation as White students. The *Relative Risk Ratio* (or *Odds ratio*) divides the risk index of one racial/ethnic group (e.g., African American) by the risk index of a comparison group (e.g., White or all other groups) and thereby provides a comparative measure (Donovan & Cross, 2002). A ratio of 1.0 indicates exact proportionality; a ratio more than 1.00 indicates over-representation in a specific category, whereas a ratio less than 1.00 indicates under-representation. For full discussion of methods to assess disproportionaltity see Westat (2003).

Disproportionality of Ethnic Groups

In 2004 Native Americans and African Americans, respectively, were at a higher risk for special education placement than other ethnic groups (KewelRamani, Gilbertson, Fox, & Provasnik, 2007; U. S. Department of Education, 2009). As shown in Table 55.1, Native Americans' highest risk category was learning disability at 7.50 risk index compared to all other racial/ethnic groups (4.20). African American students' risk index for the categories of mental retardation and emotional disturbances were 1.87 and 1.38 compared to .66 and .62 respectively for all other ethnic groups. For Asians, the highest risk index was specific learning disability at 1.73, which was lower than the risk index for all other groups (4.34). The highest risk category

TABLE 55.1
Risk Index for Students Ages 6 through 21 Receiving Special Education and Related Services for a Given Primary Disability Category under IDEA, Part B, and a Comparison Risk Index All Other Groups Combined, by Race/Ehnicity: Fall 2004

	American Indian/Alaska Native	Asian/Pacific Islander	Black (not Hispanic)	Hispanic	White (not Hispanic)
Disability	Risk Index (All Other Groups Combined Risk Index)				
Specific learning disabilities	7.50 (4.20)	1.73 (4.34)	5.65 (3.98)	4.74 (4.13)	3.86 (4.85)
Speech or language impairments	2.29 (1.72)	1.24 (1.75)	1.82 (1.71)	1.58 (1.76)	1.77 (1.66)
Mental retardation	1.04 (0.84)	0.41 (0.86)	1.87 (0.66)	0.59 (0.90)	0.69 (1.09)
Emotional disturbance	1.13 (0.73)	0.21 (0.76)	1.38 (0.62)	0.43 (0.80)	0.69 (0.81)
Multiple disabilities	0.28 (0.20)	0.12 (0.20)	0.28 (0.19)	0.14 (0.21)	0.20 (0.20)
Hearing impairments	0.14 (0.11)	0.13 (0.11)	0.12 (0.11)	0.13 (0.10)	0.10 (0.13)
Orthopedic impairments	0.10 (0.10)	0.08 (0.10)	0.10 (0.10)	0.10 (0.10)	0.10 (0.10)
Other health impairments	0.91 (0.77)	0.27 (0.79)	0.87 (0.75)	0.40 (0.85)	0.89 (0.58)
Visual impairments	0.05 (0.04)	0.04 (0.04)	0.05 (0.04)	0.04 (0.04)	0.04 (0.04)
Autism	0.18 (0.25)	0.31 (0.25)	0.26 (0.25)	0.15 (0.27)	0.28 (0.21)
Deaf-blindness	0.00 (0.00)	0.00 (0.00)	0.00 (0.00)	0.00 (0.00)	0.00 (0.00)
Traumatic brain injury	0.05 (0.04)	0.02 (0.04)	0.04 (0.03)	0.02 (0.04)	0.04 (0.03)
All disabilities above	13.67 (9.00)	4.57 (9.24)	12.44 (8.44)	8.33 (9.20)	8.65 (9.70)

Source: U. S. Department of Education (2009), p. 48.

for Hispanic students was also specific learning disability at 4.74, which is only slightly above the risk index for all other ethnic groups (4.13).

The disproportionality debate has been primarily centered on high incidence disabilities, such as learning disability (LD), EBD, and mild MR. These special education categories have been characterized as "judgmental," as their identification and the assessment process involves more subjectivity than the "nonjudgmental" categories such as hearing or physical impairment. National data show that a disproportionate number of African Americans are placed in the special education categories of EBD and mild MR (see Table 55.1). Parrish (2002) found that African American were the most over-represented ethnic group in MR and EBD categories in almost every state. When analyzing the placement of culturally and linguistically diverse (CLD) learners into special education, it is important to look beyond the national aggregated data and examine state and local school district data. State, school district, or individual school data might show disproportionate representation that is not evident in national aggregated data (Ladner & Hammons, 2001; Kauffman, Simpson, & Mock, 2009). For example, a state with higher populations of Latinos (e.g., California) may show patterns of over-representation for this population that is not evident nationally (Artiles, Rueda, Salazar, & Higareda, 2002).

Why Is Disproportionality a Concern?

Since Dunn (1968) first identified the disproportionate placement of American minorities in special education, only 14 years after the *Brown v. Board of Education* Supreme Court decision, numerous researchers have analyzed this phenomenon (Artiles et al., 2004; Donovan & Cross, 2002; Harry & Klingner, 2006; Losen & Orfield, 2002). The disproportionate representation of minorities in special education is a long-lasting persistent pattern that is typically viewed negatively by professionals (Harry, Hart, Klingner, Cramer, & Sturges, 2009; Hosp & Reschly, 2004; Coutinho & Oswald, 2000).

Disproportionality is viewed negatively due to historical inequities inflicted on minorities, and the existence of disproportionality may be an indication of continued racial bias toward minorities (Patton, 1998). Special education labels, like MR and EBD, can carry a stigma of inferiority or antisocial behavior; a higher incidence of such labels among minority students can also interact with and perpetuate stereotypical beliefs about minorities.

The varying rates of children being placed in special education across states and school districts, especially in "judgmental" categories (LD, mild MR, and EBD) is a recurring theme (Ladner & Hammons, 2001). This variability in the identification of children with disabilities highlights the need for more explicit federal guidance to assist states in this process (Coutinho & Oswald, 2000). In addition, some studies indicate that minorities are not only placed in special education at a higher rate than White children, but they are also over-represented in more restrictive educational settings (DeValenzuela, Copeland, Qi, & Park, 2006; Skiba, Poloni-Staudinger, Gallini, Simmons, & Feggins-Azziz, 2006).

Generally speaking, concerns are focused on the need to ensure that all children have access to an appropriate education within a society rapidly becoming more culturally and linguistically diverse, as demographic trends show.

Explaining Disproportionality

Although the recognition of ethnic disproportionality in special education programs began in the1960's and is well documented at present, the underlying factors causing and reproducing these disparities has not yet been extensively investigated (Hosp & Reschly, 2004). Before detecting and examining the evidence for these factors, we should define the context of explanation or/and interpretation.

First, patterns of over- and under-representation have often been discussed neglecting the prevalence rate estimates of a certain disability. For example, the over-representation of African American students in the EBD category can obtain a different meaning in a context of generalized underidentification and underservice. In the mental health literature, the prevalence rate for behavioral disorders is estimated to be at least at 5% of the overall school-aged population (see Costello, Egger, Angold, 2005; Costello, Foley, & Angold, 2006; U. S. Department of Health and Human Services, 2001). This percentage is 5 times higher than that of about 1% identified students as having EBD, or 4 times higher than the corresponding percentage of identified African American students with EBD. Even if the disproportionality of African American students with EBD may suggest misidentification for some of them, in a general context of underidentification and underservice, it is expected the percentage of "false negatives" (not identified when they should) for African Americans would exceed the percentage of "false positives" (see Kauffman & Landrum, 2009; Kauffman, Mock, & Simpson, 2007; Kauffman, Simpson, & Mock, 2009, for detailed analysis).

Second, the overemphasis on over-representation of African American students in MR and EBD categories can be understood only in the historical context of an oppressed minority. Such overemphasis may arouse emotional reactions, but from a logical point of view is rather unilateral. As the British researchers Strand and Lindsay (2009, p. 175) put it:

> Both over- and under-representation are problematic if they are associated with reduced access to the most appropriate forms of education, whether by inappropriate placement in special education programs for students who do not need such support and who may then miss out on a mainstream curriculum or by a lack of support for students who would benefit from special education provision. In either case, inappropriate matches may reduce students' educational opportunities.

If we recognize that both over- and under-representation are undesirable, what would be a reasonable proportionality with acceptable size of risk ratios? What cutoffs of increased or decreased risk ratios should be a guide for administrative action? (Bollmer, Bethel, Garison-Morgen, & Brauen, 2007).

Third, an over-representation of an ethnic group in a certain disability category can disguise their under-representation in another one, and vice versa. At a national level, Hispanic students are slightly over-represented in the LD category, while they are significantly under-represented in the MR category (see Table 55.1). As has already been argued, the coexistence over- and under-representation patterns within the same ethnic minority group may have a special interest for further research and implications for practice.

Oswald, Coutinho, and Best (2002) have proposed two possible explanations for the disproportionality phenomenon. One possibility is that disproportionality is related to higher disability rates among minority students. If true, toxic social conditions, such as poverty and health-related problems, may be risk factors for higher rates of disability among minorities. However, it is not possible to completely dismiss the possibility that bias exists toward impoverished children regardless of ethnicity, thereby influencing decisions about these children. Ethnic disparities in poverty are well documented in the United States. African American (25%) Native American (25%) and Hispanic (22%) children live in poverty compared with 11% of Asians and 8% of Whites (DeNavas-Walt, Proctor, & Lee, 2006). A simple reading of these numbers reveals strikingly comparable risk ratios between the ethnic disparities in poverty and the ethnic disproportionality in special education "judgmental" categories (LD, mild MR, EBD). The second explanation attributes the disproportionality phenomenon to a function of "systemic bias and discrimination within the public education system" (Oswald et al., 2002, p. 2).

A National Research Council report provides compelling evidence for the impact of poverty either as a direct factor or as a mediator between the ethnic disproportionate risk ratios and health-related or other social problems (Donovan & Cross, 2002). In general, what has been characterized as "outcome-based" research (Artiles et al., 2004) seems to support the poverty hypothesis. Typically, proxy measures of economic and racial factors have been used in regression models as predictors of ethnic representations in special education programs. Results have revealed that poverty has an important influence on disproportionate ethnic representation in special education programs (Hosp & Reschly, 2004; Oswald, Coutinho, Best, & Singh, 1999). Specifically, Hosp and Reschly (2004) found that the economic block of variables was the strongest predictor for the disproportionate representation of minority students in MR category, a finding which underlines the strong relation between poverty and intellectual ability/performance. An English study (see section Ethnicity and Exceptionality: An International Perspective) also has indicated the importance of poverty for the disproportionality phenomenon. Only the study of Skiba, Poloni-Staudinger, Simmons, Feggins-Azziz, Chung (2005), using regression analysis of district-level data, found that poverty makes "a weak and inconsistent contribution to the prediction of proportionality across a number of disability categories" (p. 130).

The systemic bias hypothesis has been supported also by the aforementioned studies using regression techniques. Factors related to race/ethnicity have constantly proved to be significant predictors of ethnic disproportionality, especially in the mild MR and EBD categories (Hosp & Reschly, 2004; Oswald et al., 1999; Skiba et al., 2005). Specifically, Hosp and Reschly (2004) found that the racial block of variables was the strongest predictor for the disproportionate representation of African American students in the EBD category. Other findings also converge to indicate that racial/ethnic bias plays an important role. For example, minority students attending predominately White affluent schools are over-represented in special education placement (Coutinho, Oswald, & Best, 2002). Also, an increased number of African American teachers in school is correlated with a decreased representation of African American students in EBD classes (Serwatka, Deering, & Grant, 1995).

In short, evidence provides support for both basic explanations for the ethnic disparities in special education programs. Both poverty and systemic bias seem to contribute to this disproportionality. Whereas the first factor is easily understood, the second is rather a vague one. What does systemic bias mean? How is bias towards ethnic/racial minorities connected with school-based factors? What is the role of special education in that?

Generally speaking, there are two sets of answers to these questions. The first focuses on the bias towards ethnic minorities deriving from the school system as a whole. In Losen and Orfield's (2002) words: "the cause of the observed racial disparity is rooted not only in the system of special education itself, but also in the system of regular education as it encompasses special education" (p. xxv). Donovan and Cross (2002) analyzed extensively how placements in special education and gifted programs are rooted in very low or very high academic achievement. Five sets of data support this "holistic" view:

1. School failure (expressed as dropouts and suspensions) varies by race/ethnicity in analogous ways to "judgmental" special education categories (LD, mild MR, EBD). Hispanic and African American students are at higher risk of dropping out of school than White and Asian/Pacific Islander students. In 2006, Hispanics, aged 18–24, were 3.8 times more likely not to be enrolled in high school or not to have a high school credential than Whites; the corresponding figure for African Americans were 1.8 at a national level (Laird, Cataldi, KewalRamani, & Chapman, 2008). Similarly, African American students were disproportionately suspended and expelled from school. In 2006, 15% of Black students were suspended, compared with 8% of American Indian/Alaska Native students, 7% of Hispanic students, 5% of White students, and 3% of Asian/Pacific Islander students at a national level (Planty et al., 2009).

2. It has been reported that about 56% of students are referred primarily for academic problems, a further 33% for academic problems as a secondary reason or in combination with behavior problems, and 11% due to behavior problems concerns. The majority of referred students had a history of academic or behavioral problems in previous years (Del'Homme, Kasari, Forness, & Bagley, 1996). Especially, in the case of students with behavior problems, five years may pass before they received appropriate services (Duncan, Forness, & Hartsough, 1995). A high proportion of referred students are eventually found eligible for special education services (Artiles & Trent, 1994; Ysseldyke & Algozinne, 1983; Ysseldyke, Vanderwood & Shriner, 1997).
3. Hosp and Reschly (2004) found that academic achievement is an important predictor of disproportionate representation of minority students in special education. Academic achievement was added significantly to predictive regression models, beyond the influence of demographic and economic variables on ethnic disproportionality in special education programs.
4. Structural inequalities in schooling, such as insufficient funding for schools attended mainly by minorities, low teacher quality, culturally unresponsive curriculum, instruction of poor quality, and negative school climate can also be contributing factors (Blanchett, 2006). In such unfavorable educational conditions, special education may be the "goalkeeper" of an institutionalized racism.
5 Evidence from other countries (e.g., Finland, Germany) also supports the holistic hypothesis (see the section on Ethnicity and Exceptionality: An International Perspective).

The second set of answers has closely focused on the "misidentification" problem as a specific problem of special education (e.g., Harry & Klingner, 2006). In support of this claim, disproportionate referral rates for intervention or assessment have been found; African American students are referred at a greater rate compared to White students (see meta-analysis by Hosp & Reschly, 2003). Also, scholars have underlined the role of standardized testing, particularly with regard to a dated IQ technology and testing bias against CLD students (Cartledge, Gardner, & Ford, 2009; Sternberg, 2004a, b). Thus, disproportionate referral rates, assessment, and identification problems have often been used to put the blame on special education. Such a narrow interpretation often carries negative attitudes towards special education and disability-based education provision (i.e., Harry & Klingner, 2006, 2007). MacMillan and Reschly (1998) have reported that "The magnitude of Black students in Head Start, Follow Through, and Chapter 1 was at least great as the overrepresentation of minority students in EMR, and yet these examples of overrepresentation have never been the subject of litigation or come in for criticism" (p. 17). After all, the answer to Harry and Klingner's (2006, p. 159) question, "into special education: exile or solution?" is critical to the conceptualization of the disproportionality issue.

Without justifying bad special education practices, we consider that disproportionality is a complex educational, cultural, as well as sociopolitical issue. Unfortunately, a unilateral emphasis on culture processes alone often fails to look behind the curtain and recognize sociopolitical drives and economy policies. As Anastasiou and Kauffman (2009) underlined, special education is a social welfare program which has been under attack from the political neoliberal movement, as have many other "costly" programs, during the last decades. Indeed, the disproportionality issue has been used to promote popular misconceptions against the existence and maintenance of special education programs.

All things considered, many questions are yet unanswered in the American professional literature. More rigorous quantitative and qualitative research is needed to fully understand the causes and the processes of the disproportionality phenomenon. Although sophisticated regression techniques (e.g., Hosp & Reschly, 2004; Oswald et al., 1999; Skiba et al., 2005) have been used to explore the influence of poverty and racial/ethnic bias on ethnic disproportionality in special education, their findings should be interpreted with reservations because of inherent limitations in using district-level data. The use of aggregated data to explore phenomena at a more basic level is vulnerable to aggregating processes themselves, and can result in an "ecological fallacy" (Freedman, 1999; Strand & Lindsay, 2009).

Ethnicity and Exceptionality: An International Perspective

Ethnic groups in nation states are divided in two general categories: (a) historical ethnic groups with minority status in terms of ethnicity, religion, or language; and (b) immigrant minority groups. In the literature on the issue of ethnic disproportionallity in special education, the term "ethnicity" has been used either to refer to ethnic groups with a history of presence in a certain region included within the borders of a state or to more recent immigrants.

Here we examine the relationship between ethnicity and special education placement in various counties based on the available information, and will try to cover as many different systems as possible. It is difficult to classify countries into clear patterns of disproportionality according to their minorities' representation. This is due to either inadequate evidence for such a classification or to complexity of patterns. Nevertheless, we attempt to roughly distinguish over- and under-representation patterns of disproportionality and examine whether and to what extent they are applicable to the cases under examination. In many countries, socioeconomic factors such as poverty, as well as gender, school achievement, and school language proficiency, seem to interact with ethnicity and exceptionality; however, with the exception of an English study, there are no international studies examining interactions among these factors, and identifying patterns comprehensively.

Furthermore, the relationship between ethnicity and exceptionality in each country can only be understood by considering the background of each general system and special education subsystem. For example, evidence for over-representation of Roma students in South Eastern European countries (e.g., Bulgaria, Romania, Serbia) should be considered in the wider context of a residual educational provision for exceptional learners and the legacy of the communist era.

England

"Unlike the United States, England does not have a special education system based on the identification of students as having disabilities of one or another type. Instead, the English system enables students to be provided help on the basis of assessments of their individual "special educational needs" (Dyson & Gallannaugh, 2008, p. 36). This arrangement of special education provision has been based on the Warnock Report. Published in 1978, the report adopted the concept of special educational needs (SEN) as a broader view of providing "special education provision for any child judged to be in need of such provision" (Department of Education and Science, 1978, §3.32). In this spirit, the English system has made a distinction between students without a formal statement (a document with legal force that records the children's SEN and the provisions required to meet these needs), and formally identified students with a statement outlining their special needs and provision required. In the English system, students with SEN but without formal statement had been identified by their teachers in general education schools; these students "should be subject to "school action" (whereby the school uses its own resources to meet their needs) or "school action plus" (whereby the school supplements its own resources with those provided by outside specialists)" (Dyson & Gallannaugh, 2008, p. 39). Additional teaching support individually or in small groups may be given to students who meet the criteria for school action plus.

The paradox is that the alleged broader view of the SEN notion, in relation to that of disability, has not been translated into more students served officially. In January 2008, only 223,600 (or 2.8%) of the school-age population had SEN statements (National Statistics, 2008). Of them, about 1.2% were served in special schools, 0.2% in special classes, and 1.4% in mainstream schools (EADSNE, 2009). These numbers of officially served students in England can be considered too small, if we use two kinds of yardsticks. The first is the great number of students with SEN but without statements. In 2008, 1,390,700 more such students were identified, representing 17.2% of the school-age population. The vast majority of them (98.7%) were placed in mainstream schools, but only 64% met the criteria for "school action plus" (National Statistics, 2008). As the majority of SEN children fall into the category of the "school action plus," this is a key issue to understand the English system. Children who fall into this category are eligible to receive additional services, through the direct involvement of specialized experts (e.g., educational psychologists) external to the school or their consultation services. Concerning teaching, the efforts are concentrated on curriculum differentiation under the coordination of one member of the school staff, called SEN coordinator (SENCO; Department for Education and Skills, 2001). The second yardstick is the over-time stability of percentages of served students with SEN. In 1990, 2.1% of the school population had a statement in England and Wales (Alban-Metcalfe, 1996); in 2008 the corresponding figure rose to 2.8% (National Statistics, 2008), while in 2009 it has fallen to 2.7% (Shepherd, 2009). Thus, the English non-disability-based system seems to produce great numbers of students with "special needs" but, in terms of direct and special teaching, it actually serves only a small portion of them; those with the most severe disabilities.

The disproportionality representation of minority ethnic students in special education has attracted less attention in the United Kingdom than in the United States. (Dyson & Gallannaugh, 2008). Recently, Strand and Lindsay (2009) analyzed data of the 2005 Pupil Level Annual School Census on 6.5 million students, ages 5–16 in England. The importance of the study lay not only on the huge sample size but also on the unit of data analysis; they used student-level data contrary to the district-level data that are usually used in the large-scale US studies (e.g., Hosp & Reschly, 2004; Oswald et al., 1999; Skiba et al., 2005). Their results indicated that poverty and gender made greater contributions to the overall prevalence of SEN in compared to ethnicity; the same was found for the categories of "moderate learning difficulties" (comparable to mild mental retardation) and "behavioral, emotional, and social difficulties" (comparable to EBD). After controlling for the effects of poverty, gender and age, no evidence was found for over-representation of any Black group of students (Black African or Black Caribbean) for mild mental retardation. Only for the EBD category did they find an increased relative risk ratio for Black Caribbean students after other factors were taken into account. South Asian and Chinese students showed under-representation for the judgmental categories of SEN compared with the White British students. In addition, there was a substantial over-representation of students of Pakistani and Bangladeshi origin for sensory impairments and severe intellectual disabilities; the increased risk among children of Pakistani and Bangladeshi heritage for sensory impairments was attributed to genetic factors connected with consanguineous marriages (Strand & Lindsay, 2009).

In conclusion, the general U.S. findings about the over-representation of African American students in the judgmental categories of MR and EBD were not replicated for Black African students in the aforementioned British study. Neither the finding of Skiba et al. (2005) who suggested that "poverty was found to be a weak and inconsistent predictor of disproportionality" (p. 135) was confirmed in the British study. Instead, in Strand and Lindsay's (in press) study Black African students were more likely to be underidentified compared with White British students when poverty was included in the analyses. Strand and Lindsay attributed this discrepancy not only to their apparently different sample but also to the unit of data analysis. Specifically, they raised question about analyses using aggregated data (district-level data) to explore the phenomena at an individual level.

Following the recommendations of Strand and Lindsay (in press), future research should take into account the importance of poverty and gender when examining the disproportionate representation of ethnic minorities in special education. Moreover, there is a need for comparative international studies "to examine the generalizability of findings and the importance of cultural variations" (Strand & Lindsay, 2009, p. 188). For example, what is the impact of historical factors (e.g., slavery, segregation laws, etc.) on patterns of behaviors for African Americans compared to England's African immigrants and how do these behavioral differences/commonalities influence school performance.

Finland

The Finnish education system has been considered excellent with very good results in reading, math, and science in three consecutive Programme for International Student Assessment (PISA) assessments in 2000, 2003, and 2006 (Savolainen, 2009). Also, Finland has an extended, flexible, and multifarious special education provision. Especially, the part-time special education has been found to play an important role in the excellent academic achievements of Finnish students (Kivirauma, & Ruoho, 2007).

Data provided do not allow comparisons of how different ethnic groups are represented in special education, since Finnish citizens are not registered according to their ethnic origin. Still, it has been noted that "Romany[1] children have all too readily been placed in special needs classes" (Finnish National Board of Education, 2008, p. 29). Data provided by research conducted in the city of Turku indicate that there is a discrepancy between the percentages of immigrant students present in general education (about 10%) and those in classroom-based special education (nearly 14%) or "part-time special education" (about 25%). In Finland, part-time special education is implemented on an average of two hours per week, without requiring an official identification decision. In practice, the boundaries between part-time and full-time special education are obliterated by an unprecedented continuum of placements and services (Kivirauma, Klemelä, & Rinne, 2006). Kivirauma et al. attributed the over-representation of part-time special education students from minority cultures (mainly from Somalia, Iran, Russia, and Estonia) to their lack of Finnish-language skills. It is worth noting that part-time special education is heavily oriented to language skills development, targeting mainly remedial activities in reading and writing (Finnish National Board of Education, 2008; Kivirauma & Ruoho, 2007). Besides, the over-representation of boys and children from lower classes in special education is a matter of serious concern. In their study, Kivirauma et al. conclude that "over three out of four of the students in classroom-based special education are boys" (2006, p. 117). In addition, students from the lower social classes were over-represented both in the part-time and classroom-based special education.

Germany

Germany has an extended but rigid special education system. One of its most prominent features is its vertically separated structure, which has a long tradition that can be traced back to the late 19th century. The special school constitutes the dominant organizational form, following a categorical model of special education provision (Opp, 2001; Rüttgardt, 1995). There are at least eight different types of special schools—one for each of the officially recognized disability categories—serving students with "learning disabilities," mental retardation, speech impairments, blindness, visual impairments, deafness, hearing impairments, emotional and behavioral disorders, physical disabilities, and health problems (Eurybase - Germany, 2006/07; Rüttgardt, 1995; Werning, Löser, & Urban, 2008). As of academic year 2006–07, 5.70% of the total school-age population were students that had been identified as having special education needs. The vast majority of them (4.84%) were served in special schools, while only 0.86% were placed in inclusive settings (EADSNE, 2009). A striking aspect of German special education is the separate special schools for students with learning disabilities, who represented 48.5% of the disabled school-aged population. The same students accounted for 48.5% of the total number of students attending special schools, mainly those in lower grades, 5- to 9/10-years old (EADSNE, 2009; Eurybase - Germany, 2006/07).

Werning and colleagues (2008) emphasized that students from immigrant backgrounds are over-represented in special schools in Germany. Students without German citizenship accounted for about 9% of German school-age population. However, the proportion of these students who attended special schools was nearly 16.0%. In schools for learning disabilities, the percentage of immigrant students was even higher (19.5%). It is important to note that the German term used for learning disabilities (*lernbehinderurg*) doesn't have the same meaning as it does in U.S. education; it rather corresponds to mild intellectual disability category or generalized learning disability, as it is defined by severe low school achievement related to a low IQ ranging from 55–85 (Opp, 2001; Rüttgardt, 1995).

Werning et al., (2008) discussed three possible explanations of the phenomenon of over-representation of students from immigrant backgrounds in German special schools. The first is their restricted language efficiency, which can often be perceived as learning disability. Werning et al. refer to a PISA study which "showed that in Germany, 20% of 15-year-old students whose parents had immigrated to Germany belonged to the category 'very weak reader,' 50%

had not achieved the basic level of competency, and only 2% had achieved a very high level of competency in reading…" (p. 49). The second explanation is the "obsession" of the German education system for organizing students into homogeneous learning groups in combination with the vertical organization of special education provision. The third explanation is based on the immigrant families' marginalization and citizenship exclusion within the German society.

The over-representation of children from low socioeconomic backgrounds in special schools for children with learning disabilities constitutes a great concern for the German reality. Werning et al. (2008) discuss that this over-representation reflects the inequalities of the German school system and wider social problems. For instance, children from working class families are under-represented in advanced secondary schools, and the parents of students from special schools for learning disabilities face a high rate of unemployment.

Spain

Spain has a developed education system, but its special education falls short. Many students are not served at all, and one-third of the served students attend privately managed schools (EADSNE, 2009; Gortazar, 1991; Pastor, 1998). Only 2.56% of the total school-age population has been identified as having special education needs (SEN). Of these, 0.61% are served in special schools and special classes, and 1.95% are placed in inclusive settings (Eurybase - Spain, 2007/08; EADSNE, 2009). Support teachers seem to help special education students in mainstream schools, though their role and responsibilities are not clearly determined (Arnaiz & Castejón, 2001; Eurybase - Spain, 2007/08). According to Arnaiz and Castejón (2001), full-time support teachers spent about two-thirds of their time teaching students with SEN directly, usually in small groups outside the classroom.

Literature on the education system in Spain indicates that there is no over-representation of ethnic minorities and immigrant minorities (e.g., Moroccan students) in special education settings (Harry, 2005). Harry, Arnaiz, Klingner, and Sturges (2008) recognize that "there was in fact no over-representation of culturally and linguistically diverse (CLD) students in programs for students with special needs ... Nor was disproportionality perceived as an issue nationally by colleagues in the field…" (p. 17). Also, as of academic year 2006–07, the percentage of immigrant students in special schools was 8.4%, slightly above the corresponding 7.8% of immigrant students in non-university education (Eurybase - Spain, 2007/08).

This fact could possibly be explained in two ways. First, one of the two major ethnic groups, the Spanish Gypsies, as well as the majority of the immigrant population is Spanish-speaking, so language is not an obstacle to learning. Second, it seems that the small number of identified students (2.56%) and students served in special schools (0.61%) do not leave room for misidentification and misplacement in special education.

South Eastern and Central Eastern Europe

For South Eastern and Central Eastern European countries, literature on disproportionality is mainly based on information provided by the Organisation for Economic Co-operation and Development (OECD) and international nongovernmental organizations such the Open Society Institute (OSI), and it is focused on the over-representation of the Roma children in special schools for children with intellectual disabilities.

In Serbia, it is estimated that Roma children represent at least 25% to 30% of children who are placed in special schools or institutions for mentally disabled; at the same time, Roma people constitute only about 1.5%–6.0% of the overall Serbian population OECD (2007, p. 77). But behind this huge disproportionality there are some advantages offered by special schools, such as the free school supplies, free meals, free transportation, and medical treatment. In addition, special schools offer the opportunity for obtaining diplomas and job qualifications faster and cheaper, "even though afterwards they cannot go on to higher education, or hold more than low-skilled jobs" (OSI, 2007a, pp. 551–552, 589, 607). According to the same report, some special schools are actually boarding schools providing free meals, textbooks, and clothing in addition to accommodation and education. For parents, costs of schooling children in special schools "can be six to seven times lower than costs in mainstream schools, because of the benefits that special schools provide" (OSI, 2007a, p. 545).

Moreover, OSI (2005, 2007a, b) reports that Roma children are heavily over-represented in special schools or special classes for intellectual disabilities in Bulgaria, Czech Republic, Hungary, Slovakia, and Slovenia and slightly over-represented in Romania. The over-representation of Roma children in special schools for children with intellectual disabilities is not well documented in Croatia, Montenegro, and the former Yugoslav Republic of Macedonia. There is evidence that the disproportionate representation of Roma students in special education in Bulgaria is related to the substantial financial and social welfare benefits that they receive for their participation in special schools (OSI, 2007a, p. 95, 99). Similarly, in Romania the slight over-representation of Roma students is connected to additional social welfare services such as government subsidies, free meals, and accommodation benefits accompanying the attendance of special schools (OSI, 2007a, p. 333, 397; Ives, Runceanu, & Cheney, 2008).

In Central Eastern Europe countries (Czech Republic, Hungary, Slovakia, Slovenia), the over-representation of Roma students in special education is attributed to poverty, language, and cultural barriers, ethnic tensions and conflicts in mainstream schools, high illiteracy rates, as well as the rigid nature of the education system, the misidentification of problems and experts' bias, the long tradition of the Soviet defectology, and the relatively better quality of special education provision (Ainscow & Memmenasha, 1998; OSI, 2005, 2007a, b; Sinka & Kopataki, 2008).

In South Eastern countries, the Roma over-representation

problem reflects a general problem with the inclusion of Roma children in the education systems, the anti-Ziganism attitudes, language barriers, arbitrary assessment and identification procedures, and peculiarities of social-welfare systems. Thus, Roma children are school-excluded in great numbers and experience low school achievement, highly disproportionate repetition rates in the first school grades, and high rates of dropping out from elementary school (Eurybase - Bulgaria, 2005/06; OSI, 2007a, b; OECD, 2006, 2007). Moreover, the unfavorable socioeconomic conditions, concentration in formal or informal settlements ghettoes, and marginalization of the Roma people from social life contextualize better the "Roma over-representation" as a serious educational and, by-and-large, severe social problem. On the other hand, in Serbia, Bulgaria, and Romania, an enrolment in a special school provides direct economic or/and social welfare "advantage" to Roma families, despite the fact that this direct connection distorts seriously the educational purposes of special education.

India

In India, as well as in other developing countries, the numerical majority often has an oppressed minority status, while the minority elites have a privileged one. Kalyanpur (2008a, b) analyses that the vast majority of disabled children from scheduled castes or *Dalits* and tribal communities are either deprived of their access to education or excluded from a very limited special education system. In the context of a caste-based system, negative attitudes toward disability and the scarcity of resources creates a "paradox of majority underrepresentation in special education" (Kalyanpur, 2008a). In such a limited education system, with very low net enrolment rates (see UNESCO Institute for Statistics, 2009), the number of disabled children served by private or nongovernmental organizations exceeds the number of government schools; disabled children from minority elites are disproportionally over-represented in a basically private special education (Vakil, Welton, & Kalana, 2002). Considerable disparities between urban and rural areas aggravate the problem of an inverted disproportionality in special education, especially for girls with disabilities (Kalyanpur, 2008a, b).

Summary of Country Case Analysis

In sum, special education research in other countries, apart from the United States, has paid little attention to ethnic disproportionality in special education. However, the representation of social groups, and how well some groups are served by the special education system, seems to be an issue of particular interest. After having reviewed the relative literature referring to different countries/regions, like England, Germany, Finland, Spain, South Eastern and Central Eastern Europe, and India we found out that other markers, such as poverty (socioeconomic disadvantage), social classes, castes, gender, age, and residence in rural areas accompanied the ethnic or minority disproportionality issues. South Eastern and Central Eastern European countries are exceptional cases, as the over-representation of Roma students in the intellectual disability category is a serious ethnic minority issue. In South Eastern Europe, this issue has a special dimension connected to the peculiarities of their respective social welfare systems.

Patterns of ethnic or minority over-representation for high-incidence disability categories appear in (a) more extended special education systems, like Finland, in which preventive language-oriented, part-time special education has played an important role in the good PISA results; (b) extended but rigid special education systems (e.g., Germany, Czech Republic, Hungary); and (c) systems where special education and social welfare are connected in a rather peculiar way (e.g., Bulgaria, Romania, Serbia). Proportionality patterns or possible under-representation patterns appear in less extended systems of special education (e.g., England, Spain). Limited special education systems with a strong private sector may suffer from serious under-representation problems for both high- and low-incidence disability categories (e.g., India).

Disproportionality is not a universal phenomenon; neither is a particular feature of special education. Besides, disproportionality itself does not denote a necessarily negative phenomenon, considering the part-time special education in Finland. Where disproportionality appears, it constitutes a phenomenon that takes different forms reflecting deeper educational and social structures. Not surprisingly, special education is not immunized against the particular educational, cultural, and social problems faced by each one of the countries we reviewed.

General Discussion

Disproportional representation of minority students in special education is only a symptom of deeper sociopolitical, cultural, and educational structures. In general, the relationship between ethnicity and exceptionality requires also further consideration at different levels: conceptual, political, legal, school system, and teaching.

Conceptual Considerations: Is Disproportionality the Same as Racial Segregation?

While disproportionality raises troubling questions related to ethnicity and social class, it is not equivalent to the issue of racial segregation of America's past. The purpose of the racially segregated schools was to maintain the superior societal position of Whites by providing White children a better education than minority children, especially African Americans. Racially segregated schools along with Jim Crow laws were in fact designed for the purpose of inhibiting African Americans and other minorities from achieving success and prosperity within American society. There was no desire to have White and African American students attending integrated schools at any point during their education process. The unequal funding of segregated schools along with unequal educational opportunities within the schools were essential tools in purposefully limiting African American and other minority children's futures.

Placing a child in special education, when it is not warranted or not placing them in special education when it is warranted, can have a limiting effect on that child's future. However, the stated intent of special education is in fact to increase the future opportunities for each child. Conceptually and legally, the intent is to make sure that all children, including those with disabilities, have access to a free, appropriate, and public education. Special education placement differs strongly from racially segregated schools in that IDEA requires that whenever possible children with disabilities should be maintained in inclusive classrooms. If a student needs to be removed from the general education classroom in order to receive education services required for success, the individualized education program (IEP) should be developed with an emphasis on returning the child to the general education classroom. Unlike racial segregation, which was based on a physiognomic characteristic rather than children's abilities, special education placement is designed to occur only after a careful analysis of a child's abilities. After all, educational equity is better attained by a continuum of services; *sameness in delivery of services is a way to social injustice for both special and multicultural education*. Despite the fact that racial segregation and special education have vastly different intents, there remains the possibility that racial bias can influence the special education placement and the least restrictive environment decisions. While special education and racial segregation are different in their intent and structure, if children are misplaced in special education due to bias, the same limiting effect may apply to children's futures.

Policy-level Considerations

Disproportionality is a potential problem. The problem is that children may be misplaced in special education due to the influence of ethnicity or culture rather than purely educational reasons. However, disproportionality is a coin with two sides: over- and under-representation. At the national level in the United States, the true problem may be underserved students with EBD. In Kauffman and Landrum's (2009, p. 186) words:

> Concern about disproportional underrepresentation would, and perhaps should, suggest that schools identify and serve in special education more students who are not African American. Identifying more nonAfrican American students would both address the problem of disproportional over-representation of African American students and, at the same time, bring the identification for special education of nonAfrican American students into better alignment with reasonable estimates of the prevalence of emotional and behavioral disorders among children and youth.

On the other hand, one key preventive factor for reducing the existence of misidentified minority students is the development of alternative programs such as English language support programs. In the United States, and many other countries, disabled-based special education and compensatory education for linguistically or socially disadvantaged students have been viewed as two distinct parts of the education system. However, in practice, they function as communicating vessels. Students with language differences or English language deficiencies are too often misunderstood as having learning or cognitive disabilities (Ortiz, 1997). Also, Artiles et al. (2004) observed that when California abolished bilingual education programs, English language learners "had a higher chance of being placed in special education as the level of language support diminished" (p. 723). In our view, this observation underscores the goalkeeping role of special education in the whole education system. Instead of blaming the goalkeeper, we should look for an alternative solution.

Legal Considerations

In 2004, IDEA was reauthorized and racial disproportionality was designated as one of three areas for monitoring and enforcement. IDEA requires states and local educational agencies (LEAs) to address disproportionate representation of racial/ethnic groups in special education by taking the necessary steps. States are further required to collect and examine data to determine whether significant disproportionality based on race and ethnicity is occurring within the state and LEA for particular disabilities categories (e.g., EBD). Additionally, states must monitor the types of educational settings in which children receive services and types of disciplinary actions implemented with children (including suspensions and expulsions).

School-level and Teaching Considerations

Educators should make every effort to ensure that children are appropriately placed in the correct education environment and receive the instructional services that will benefit them. Apart from an individual concern, the responsibility is also an issue of better pre-service and in-service preparation of general and special education teachers. Learning to work effectively with CLD students and/or exceptional learners is part of today's education and also a future challenge, considering the demographic trends in a continuing multicultural society (Artiles et al., 2004). Calls for incorporation of multilingual and bilingual education philosophy in general and special education are numerous (e.g., Valles, 1998). However, defining the levels of intervention and the means we might use remains an issue. Obiakor (2007) identified four levels of a culturally responsive pedagogy for CLD students with and at risk for disabilities: (a) cognition referring to teachers' education/experience/style, (b) multicultural curriculum, (c) school culture/environment, and (d) specific pedagogical strategies. Similarity, Ford and Kea (2009) defined five components of culturally responsive classrooms: teaching philosophy, culturally relearning environment, assessment, currciulum, instruciton. Cartledge and Kourea (2008) set an instructional model for classrooms culturally responsive to the needs of students with disabilities. Furthermore, Cartledge, Singh, and Gibson (2008) developed a practical guide for behavior-management techniques. To date, there is no evidence, from quantitative studies, that these promising behavior interventions work differently with students differing in ethnicity (Kauffman et al., 2008); however, at the present, they can work as practical guidelines useful for teaching purposes.

Note

1. Romany is the adjective accompanying a noun (e.g., Romany children). It refers to the Roma ethnic group also found in bibliography as Rom (Hungary), Gypsies or Travelers (U. K.), Gitanos (Spain).

References

Ainscow, M., & Memmenasha, H.-G. (1998). *The education of children with special needs: Barriers and opportunities in Central and Eastern Europe.* Florence, Italy: UNICEF.

Alban-Metcalfe, J. (1996). Special education in England. *European Journal of Special Needs Education, 11*, 125–143.

Anastasiou, D., & Kauffman, J. M. (2009). When special education goes to the marketplace: The case of vouchers. *Exceptionality, 17,* 205–222.

Anastasiou, D., & Kauffman, J. M. (2011). A social constructionist approach to disability: Implications for special education. *Exceptional Children, 71,* 367–384.

Arnaiz, P., & Castejón, J.-L. (2001). Towards a change in the role of the support teacher in the Spanish educational system. *European Journal of Special Needs Education, 16*, 99–110.

Artiles, A. J. (1998). The dilemma of difference: Enriching the disproportionality discourse with theory and context. *The Journal of Special Education, 32*, 32–36.

Artiles, A. J., Rueda, R., Salazar, J. J., & Higareda, I. (2002). English language learners representation in special education in California urban school districts. In D. J. Losen, & G. Orfield (Eds.), *Racial inequity in special education* (pp. 117–135). Cambridge, MA: Harvard Education Publishing Group.

Artiles, A. J., & Trent, S. C. (1994). Overrepresentation of minority students in special education: A continuing debate. *The Journal of Special Education, 27*, 410–437.

Artiles, A. J., Trent, S. C., & Palmer, J. (2004). Culturally diverse students in special education: Legacies and prospects. In J. A. Banks & C. M. Banks (Eds.), *Handbook of research on multicultural education* (2nd ed., pp.716–735). San Francisco: Jossey-Bass.

Bamshad, M. J., & Olson, S. E. (2003). Does race exist? *Scientific American, 289*(6), 78–85.

Banks, J. A. (2007). Multicultural Education: Characteristics and goals. In J. A. Banks & C. A. Banks (Eds.), *Multicultural education: Issues and perspectives* (6th ed., pp. 6–30). Danvers, MA: Wiley.

Blanchett, W. (2006). Disproportionate representation of African American students in special education: Acknowledging the role of white privilege and racism. *Educational Researcher, 35*(6), 24–28.

Bollmer, J., Bethel, J., Garison-Morgen, R., & Brauen, M. (2007). Using the risk ratio to assess racial/ethnic disproportionality in special education at the school-district level. *The Journal of Special Education, 41*, 186–198.

Cartledge, G., Gardner, R., III, & Ford, D. Y. (2009). *Diverse learners with exceptionalities: Culturally responsive teaching in the inclusive classroom.* Upper Saddle River, NJ: Merrill.

Cartledge, G., & Kourea, L. (2008). Culturally responsive classrooms for culturally diverse students with and at risk for disabilities. *Exceptional Children, 74*, 351–371.

Cartledge, G., Singh, A., & Gibson, L. (2008). Practical behavior-management techniques to close the accessibility gap for students who are culturally and linguistically diverse. *Preventing School Failure, 52*(3), 29–38.

Costello, E. J., Egger, H., & Angold, A. (2005). 10-year research update review: The epidemiology of child and adolescent psychiatric disorders: I. Methods and public health burden. *Journal of the American Academy Child and Adolescent Psychiatry, 44*, 972–986.

Costello, E. J., Foley, D., & Angold, A. (2006). 10-year research update review: The epidemiology of child and adolescent psychiatric disorders: II. Developmental epidemiology. *Journal of the American Academy Child and Adolescent Psychiatry, 45*, 8–25.

Coutinho, M. J., & Oswald, D. P. (2000). Disproportionate representation in special education: A synthesis and recommendation. *Journal of Child and Family Studies, 9,* 135–156.

Del'Homme, M., Kasari, C., Forness, S. R., & Bagley, R. (1996). Prereferral intervention and students at-risk for emotional or behavioral disorders. *Education and Treatment of Children, 19,* 272–285.

DeNavas-Walt, C., Proctor, B. D., & Lee, C. H. (2006). *Income, poverty, and health insurance coverage in the United States: 2005* (P60-231), Washington, DC: U. S. Census Bureau.

Department of Education and Science. (1978). *Special educational needs: Report of the committee of enquiry into the education of handicapped children and young people (The Warnock report).* London: Her Majesty's Stationery Office.

Department for Education and Skills. (2001). *Special educational needs code of practice*. London: Author.

DeValenzuela, J. S., Copeland, S. R., Qi, C. H., & Park, M. (2006). Examining educational equity: revisiting the disproportionate representation of minority students in special education. *Exceptional Children, 72*, 425–441.

Donovan, M. S., & Cross, C. T. (Eds.). (2002). *Minority students in special and gifted education.* Washington, DC: National Academic Press.

Duncan, B., Forness, S. R., & Hartsough, C. (1995). Students identified as seriously emotional disturbed in day treatment: Cognitive, psychiatric, and special education characteristics. *Behavioral Disorders, 20*, 221–237.

Dunklee, D. R., & Shoop, R. J. (2006). *The principal's quick-reference guide to school law: Reducing liability, litigation, and other potential legal tangles* (2nd ed.). Thousand Oaks, CA: Corwin.

Dunn, L. M. (1968). Special education for the mildly retarded: Is much of it justified? *Exceptional Children, 35*, 5–22.

Dyson, A., & Gallannaugh, F. (2008). Disproportionality in special needs education in England. *The Journal of Special Education, 42*, 36–46.

EADSNE. (2009). *Special needs education: Country data 2008*. Middlefart, Denmark: European Agency for Development in Special Needs Education.

Eriksen, T. H. (1993). *Ethnicity and Nationalism: Anthropological Perspectives.* London: Pluto Press.

Eurybase – Bulgaria. (2005/06). *The education system in Bulgaria.* Brussels: Eurydice, European Commission.

Eurybase – Germany. (2006/07). *The education system in Germany*. Brussels: Eurydice, European Commission.

Eurybase – Spain. (2007/08). *The education system in Spain*. Brussels: Eurydice, European Commission.

Finnish National Board of Education. (2008). *National report of Finland: The development of education*. Author.

Ford, D. Y., & Kea, C. D. (2009). Creating culturally responsive instruction: For students' and teachers' sakes. *Focus on Exceptional Children, 41*(9), 1–16.

Freedman, D. (1999). Ecological inference and the ecological fallacy. *International Encyclopedia of the Social and Behavioural Sciences, 6*, 4027–4040.

Gortazar, A. (1991). Special education in Spain. *European Journal of Special Needs Education, 6*, 56–70.

Hallahan, D. P., Kauffman, J. M., & Pullen, P. C. (2009). *Exceptional Learners: Introduction to special education* (11th ed.). Boston: Allyn & Bacon.

Harry, B. (2005). Equity, excellence and diversity in a rural secondary school in Spain: "Integration is very nice but…". *European Journal of Special Needs Education, 20*, 89–106.

Harry, B., Arnaiz, P., Klingner, J., & Sturges, K. (2008). Schooling and the construction of identity among minority students in Spain and the United States. *The Journal of Special Education, 42*, 15–25.

Harry, B., Hart, J., Klingner, J., Cramer, E., & Sturges, J. (2009). Response to Kauffman, Mock & Simpson. *Behavioral Disorders, 34*, 164–171.

Harry, B., & Klingner, J. (2006). *Why are so many minority students in special education? Understanding race and disability in school.* New York: Teachers College Press.

Harry, B., & Klingner, J. (2007). Discarding the deficit model. *Educational Leadership, 64*(5), 16–21.

Hodgkinson, H. L. (1995). What should we call people? Race, class, and the Census for 2000. *Phi Delta Kappan, 77*, 173–179.

Hosp, J. L., & Reschly, D. J. (2003). Referral rates for intervention or assessment: A meta-analysis of racial differences. *The Journal of Special Education, 37*, 67–80.

Hosp, J. L., & Reschly, D. J. (2004). Disproportionate representation of minority students in special education: Academic, demographics, and economic predictors. *Exceptional Children 70*, 185–199.

Individuals with Disabilities Education Act (2004). P.L. 108-446. U.S. Department of Education.

Ives, B., Runceanu, C., & Cheney, C. (2008). Special education in Romania: Past, present, and future trends. *Journal of International Special Needs Education, 11*, 5–12.

Kalyanpur, M. (2008a). The paradox of majority underrepresentation in special education in India: constructions of difference in a developing country. *The Journal of Special Education, 42*, 55–64.

Kalyanpur, M. (2008b). Equality, quality and quantity: Challenges in inclusive education policy and service provision in India. *International Journal of Inclusive Education, 12*, 243–262.

Kauffman, J. M. (2003). Appearances, stigma, and prevention. *Remedial and Special Education, 24*, 195–198.

Kauffman, J. M. (2005). Waving to Ray Charles: Missing the meaning of disability. *Phi Delta Kappan, 86*, 520–521, 524.

Kauffman, J. M., Conroy, M., Gardner, R. III, & Oswald, D. (2008). Cultural sensitivity in the application of behavior principles to education. *Education and Treatment of Children, 31*, 239–262.

Kauffman, J. M., & Hallahan, D. P. (2005). *Special Education: What it is and why we need it.* Boston, MA: Pearson Education.

Kauffman, J. M., & Landrum, T. J. (2009). Politics, civil rights, and disproportional identification of students with emotional and behavioral disorders. *Exceptionality, 17*, 177–188.

Kauffman, J. M., Mock, D. R., & Simpson, R. L. (2007). Problems related to underservice of students with emotional and behavioral disorders. *Behavioral Disorders, 33*, 43–57.

Kauffman, J. M., Simpson, R. L., & Mock, D. R. (2009). Problems related to underservice: A rejoinder. *Behavioral Disorders, 34*, 172–180.

Kavale, K. A., & Forness, S. R. (1999). Effectiveness of special education. In C. R. Reynolds & T. B. Gutkin (Eds.), *The Handbook of school psychology* (3rd ed., pp. 984–1024). New York: Wiley.

KewelRamani, A., Gilbertson, L., Fox, M. A., & Provasnik, S. (2007). *Status and trends in the education of racial and ethnic minorities.* Washington DC: National Center for Education Statistics, Institute of Education Sciences, US Department of Education (NCES 2007-039).

Kivirauma, J., Klemelä, K., & Rinne, R. (2006). Segregation, integration, inclusion – The ideology and reality in Finland. *European Journal of Special Needs Education, 21*, 117–133.

Kivirauma, J., & Ruoho, K. (2007). Excellence through special education? Lessons from the Finnish school reform. *Review of Education, 53*, 283–302.

Ladner, M., & Hammons, C. (2001). Special but unequal, race and special education. In C. E. Finn, A. J. Rotherham, & C. R. Hokanson Jr. (Eds.), *Rethinking special education for a new century* (pp. 85–110). Washington, DC: Thomas B. Fordham Foundation and the Progressive Policy Institute.

Laird, J., Cataldi, E. F., KewalRamani, A., & Chapman, C. (2008). *Dropout and Completion Rates in the United States: 2006* (NCES 2008-053). National Center for Education Statistics, Institute of Education Sciences, U.S. Department of Education. Washington, DC.

Lewontin, R., & Levins, R. (2007). *Biology under the influence: Dialectical essays on ecology, agriculture, and health.* New York: Monthly Review Press

Losen, D. J., & Orfield, G. (2002). *Racial inequality in special education.* Cambridge, MA: Harvard Education Publishing Group.

MacMillan, D. L., & Reschly, D. J. (1998). Overrepresentation of minority students: The case for greater specificity or reconsideration of the variables examined. *Journal of Special Education, 32*, 15–24.

National Statistics. (2008). *Special educational needs in England, January 2008* (SFR 15/2008). Retrieved August 3, 2009, from http://www.dcsf.gov.uk/rsgateway/DB/SFR/s000794/SFR152008Final.pdf

No Child Left Behind (2002). P.L. 107-110. U.S. Department of Education.

Obiakor, F. E. (2007). *Multicultural special education: Culturally responsive teaching.* Upper Saddle River, NJ: Pearson.

Open Society Institute (OSI). (2005). *Rights of people with intellectual disabilities: Access to education and employment: Slovenia. Budapest,* Hungary: Author.

Open Society Institute (OSI). (2007a). *Equal access to quality education for Roma (Vol. 1): Bulgaria, Hungary, Romania, Serbia.* Budapest, Hungary: Author.

Open Society Institute (OSI). (2007b). *Equal access to quality education for Roma (Vol. 2): Croatia, Macedonia, Montenegro, Slovakia.* Budapest, Hungary: Author.

Opp, G. (2001). Learning disabilities in Germany: A retrospective analysis, current status, and future trends. In D. P. Hallahan & B. K. Keogh (Eds.), *Research and global perspectives in learning disabilities* (pp. 217–238). Mahwah, NJ: Erlbaum.

Organisation for Economic Co-operation and Development (OECD). (2006). *Education policies for students at risk and those with disabilities in South Eastern Europe: Bosnia-Herzegovina, Bulgaria, Croatia, Kosovo, Fyr of Macedonia, Moldova, Montenegro, Romania and Serbia.* Paris: Author.

Organisation for Economic Co-operation and Development (OECD). (2007). *Education policies for students at risk and those with disabilities in South Eastern Europe.* Paris: Author.

Ortiz, A. A. (1997). Learning disabilities occurring concomitantly with linguistic differences. *Journal of Learning Disabilities, 30*, 321–332.

Oswald, D. P., Coutinho, M. J., & Best, A. M. (2002). Community and school predictors of overrepresentation of minority children in special education. In D. J. Losen & G. Orfield (Eds.), *Racial inequity in special education* (pp. 1–14). Boston: Harvard Education Press.

Oswald, D. P., Coutinho, M. J., Best, A. M., & Singh, N. N. (1999). Ethnic representation in special education: The influence of school-related economics and demographic variables. *The Journal of Special Education, 32*, 194–206.

Parrish, T. (2002). Racial disparities in the identification funding, and provision of special education. In D. J. Losen & G. Orfield (Eds.), *Racial inequity in special education* (pp. 15–37). Cambridge, MA: Harvard Education Press.

Pastor, C. G. (1998). Integration in Spain: A critical view. *European Journal of Special Needs Education, 13*, 43–56.

Patton, J. M. (1998). The disproportionate representation of African Americans in special education: Looking behind the curtain for understanding and solutions. *The Journal of Special Education, 32*, 25–31.

Planty, M., Hussar, W., Snyder, T., Kena, G., KewalRamani, A., Kemp, J., Bianco, K., & Dinkes, R. (2009). *The condition of education 2009* (NCES 2009-081). Washington, DC: National Center for Education Statistics, Institute of Education Sciences, U.S. Department of Education.

Rüttgardt, S. E. (1995). Special education in Germany. *European Journal of Special Needs Education, 10*, 75–91.

Savolainen, H. (2009). Responding to diversity and striving for excellence: The case of Finland. *Prospects, 39*, 281–292.

Serwatka, T., Deering, S., & Grant, V. (1995). Disproportionate representation of African Americans in emotionally handicapped classes. *Journal of Black Studies, 25*, 492–506.

Shakespeare, T. W. (2006). *Disability rights and wrongs.* London: Routledge.

Shepherd, J. (2009, June 30). Rise in number of pupils with special educational needs. *Guardian* [Electronic version]. Retrieved August 3, 2009, from http://guardian.co.uk/education/2009/jun/30/special-needs-numbers-leap

Sinka, E., & Kopataki, M. M. (2008). *National Report on development of education: Hungary*. Budapest, Hungary: Ministry of Education.

Skiba, R. J., Poloni-Staudinger, L., Gallini, S., Simmons, A. B., & Feggins-Azziz, R. (2006). Disparate access: The disporportionality of African American students with disabilities across educational environments. *Exceptional Children, 72,* 411–424.

Skiba, R. J., Poloni-Staudinger, L., Simmons, A. B., Feggins-Azziz, L. R., & Chung, C.-G. (2005). Unproven links: Can poverty explain ethnic disproportionality in special education? *The Journal of Special Education, 39,* 130–144.

Smedley, A., & Smedley, B. D. (2005). Race as biology is fiction, racism as a social problem is real. *American Psychologist, 60,* 16–25.

Sternberg, R. J. (2004a). Culture and intelligence. *American Psychologist, 59,* 325–338.

Sternberg, R. J. (Ed.). (2004b). *International handbook of intelligence.* New York: Cambridge University Press.

Strand, S., & Lindsay, G. (2009). Ethnic disporoportionality in special education. *The Journal of Special Education, 43*(3), 117–126.

UNESCO Institute for Statistics. (2009). *Global Digest 2008: Comparing education statistics across the world.* Montreal, Canada: UIS.

U.S. Census Bureau (April 10, 2008). Race data. Retrieved June 11, 2009, from http://www.census.gov/population/wwwsocdemo/race/racefactcb.html

U.S. Department of Education. (2009). Office of Special Education and Rehabilitative Services, Office of Special Education Programs, *28th annual report to Congress on the implementation of the Individuals with Disabilities Education Act, 2006,* vol. 1. Washington, DC: Author

U.S. Department of Health and Human Services. (2001). *Report of the Surgeon General's conference children's mental health: A national action agenda.* Washington, DC: Author.

Vakil, S., Welton, E., & Kalana, R. (2002). Special education in India: The success of a model program. *Teaching Exceptional Children, 34,* 46–50.

Valles, E. C. (1998). The disproportionate representation of minority students in special education: Responding to the problem. *The Journal of Special Education, 32,* 52–54.

Werning, R., Löser, J., M., & Urban, M. (2008). Cultural and social diversity: An analysis of minority groups in German schools. *The Journal of Special Education, 42,* 47–54.

Westat, T. (2003). *Methods for assessing racial/ethnic disproportionality in special education: A technical assistance guide.* Retrieved August 1, 2009, from http://www.nichcy.org/Laws/IDEA/Documents/Training_Curriculum/B-resources.pdf

Ysseldyke, J. E., & Algozinne, B. (1983). LD or not LD? That's not the question! *Journal of Learning Disabilities, 16,* 29–31.

Ysseldyke, J. E., Vanderwood, M. L., & Shriner, J. (1997). Changes over the past decade in special education referral to placement probability: An incredibly reliable practice. *Diagnostique, 23,* 193–203.

56
Gender and Exceptionality

Martha J. Coutinho
East Tennessee State University

Donald P. Oswald
Virginia Commonwealth University

Should schools treat boys and girls in the same way in every respect? Answers to this question have influenced instruction, policy, teacher training, and research for decades. However, those answers have varied considerably, and the field is perhaps as far from a consensus as it has ever been.

Gender issues were first raised early in the 20th century when the concern was about a disadvantage experienced by boys and fears that schooling had become "too feminine" (Brophy, 1985). By the 1970s, the focus had shifted. The impact of the feminist movement led to concern about preferential treatment of boys, for example, teacher attention favoring boys and the resulting disadvantage to girls with respect to educational opportunity and outcome (Acker, 1988). Data on gender differences continue to emerge, and public awareness is increasing about differences with respect to academic achievement, learning characteristics, biological and genetic susceptibilities, and identified disabilities.

Among general education populations, data on gender differences in educational achievement, college admissions testing, and employment reveal a complex picture. While school-age girls tend to show higher achievement scores in reading and writing, boys outperform girls in science and math; males tend to score higher on college admissions tests but females are more likely to complete college; among employed adults, males continue to have a substantial income advantage (Cooley, 2001).

Classroom teachers both influence and are impacted by the research on gender differences. Teachers are aware of apparent gender differences in students' learning profiles and classroom behavior, but they are also the subjects of research as active agents who respond to actual or perceived differences and who play a critical role in instructional decisions. Research also influences how the field defines gender equity and which discrepancies call for a societal response. For example, the incongruity between increasing rates of successful participation of women with disabilities in secondary and postsecondary programs and continuing disparities in income and adult employment status have recently been highlighted as significant problems (Coutinho, Oswald, & Best, 2006; Hogansen, Powers, Greenen, Gil-Kashiwabara, & Powers, 2008; Jans & Stoddard, 1999; Wagner, Newman, Cameto & Levine, 2006).

We examine the role of gender in educational intervention and outcomes, specifically, how gender interacts with exceptionality in special education. We consider the research related to biological, social, and learning differences and summarize what has been hypothesized regarding the basis for those differences. We then examine how the educational system has responded to gender differences and the implications of the state of the research on educational responses in the future.

In special education, gender per se is only rarely the focus of debate. The Individuals with Disabilities Education Act (IDEA) as reauthorized by P.L. 108-446 in 2004 continues to require, for both males and females, a full, nondiscriminatory, and comprehensive evaluation prior to identification as a student with a disability. For the most part, however, policy makers have had little reaction to accumulating evidence of gender disparities in special education identification rates or outcomes. Monitoring by the U.S. Department of Education and court cases alleging discrimination in special education relate to racial, not gender, disproportionality (Russo & Wehmeyer, 2001). Many research studies still do not disaggregate findings by gender (Asch & Fine, 1988; Oswald, Coutinho, Best, & Nagle, 2002), and those that do have had a limited impact on policy makers, educators, or the research community.

The U.S. Office for Civil Rights (OCR) has collected national educational data by gender and race/ethnicity for decades, but with the exception of equal access to athletic opportunities, most media coverage and the associated public response have emphasized race/ethnicity differences rather than gender. The 1997 amendments to the IDEA (P.L. 105-17) required states to collect the annual child count data by ethnicity, but the mandate did not extend to counts by gender. This deficit in federal policy and reporting requirements, however, does not reflect the majority of current state practices. Of the 41 states responding to a recent survey by the National Association of State Directors in Special Education, most collect a range of special education data by gender, including disability category, educational environment, disciplinary events, related services, and graduation rates (Tschantz & Markowitz, 2003).

Available data suggest that more attention to gender disproportionality in special education is warranted. Since the 1960s, the overall male to female ratio in special education has ranged between 2:1 and 3:1 (Bentzen, 1966; Hayden-McPeak, Gaskin, & Gaughan, 1993; Mumpower, 1970), and the discrepancy for students with learning disabilities and emotional disturbance is generally much higher (Callahan, 1994). Coutinho and Oswald (2005) reported that, for the country as a whole, boys were 1.3 times as likely as girls to be identified with mental retardation[1], 2.0 times as likely to be identified with a learning disability, and 3.4 times as likely to be identified with serious emotional disturbance.

At the secondary level, the National Longitudinal Transition Study reported that about two-thirds of all students with disabilities were boys (U.S. Department of Education, 1998; Valdes, Williamson, & Wagner, 1990). Only for the disability condition of deaf/blindness are boys identified at about the same rate as girls, while for hearing impairments, orthopedic impairments, deafness, other health impairments, and visual impairments the percentage of boys is slightly higher. About 58% of all secondary-age students identified with mental retardation (MR) are boys. Sixty percent of those identified as having speech impairments and about 65% of students with multiple disabilities are boys. The greatest disparities are found for students with learning disabilities (LD) and students with emotional disturbance (ED), for which 73% and 76% of the students, respectively, are male (Valdes et al., 1990).

There is some evidence that gender ratios vary somewhat by students' age. Phipps (1982) found gender disproportionality greatest among children ages 5–11, during which time referral rates for boys appear to surge. Before and after that, identification rates for boys and girls were found to be much more similar. However, even so, recent data suggest that girls are still about one-third less likely than boys to be referred for special education at the preschool level (Mann, McCartney, & Park, 2007).

These discrepancies are not limited to special education in the United States. A recent study in England reported that boys were 2.5 times more likely than girls to be identified with special education needs (Strand & Lindsay, 2009), with the most striking differences among students with emotional disturbance. An international survey by the Organization of Economic Cooperation and Development (OECD) found consistent over-representation of boys in special and "mainstream" schools (Benjamin, 2003). The finding that more males than females are recognized as disabled is not, however, universal. In some developing countries (e.g., India) consistent over-representation of girls as disabled is reported (Kalyanpur, 2008).

Although boys are generally more likely than girls to be identified for special education services, there is now considerable support for the conclusion that the disabilities reported for girls are disproportionately more severe (Kratovil & Bailey, 1986). Vogel (1990) reported that, among students identified as learning disabled, girls showed significantly more impairment in intelligence, visual motor skills, academic achievement, and language. This finding has been replicated in Scandinavia (Skarbrevik, 2002) and other U.S. research (Wagner et al., 2006). The fact that girls in special education are more impaired lends credence to the hypothesis that the threshold for eligibility is lower for boys; that is, compared to girls, boys with less severe disability are found eligible for, and are served by, special education. The implication is that girls with significant, but undetected, disability are languishing in general education without appropriate supports.

Perhaps the biggest challenge facing the field with regard to gender and exceptionality is that we have not yet determined the proper questions to guide our thinking and research. Although the data about over-representation of males in special education are consistent in most of the developed world, the field lacks consensus regarding how to interpret those data. Should we be most concerned that girls are unfairly deprived of the benefits of intensive, individualized instruction (the assumption being that special education is beneficial) or that boys are inappropriately channeled into "dead-end" classroom settings (assuming that special education is worse than unhelpful)? Should we worry more about the fact that general education classrooms and instruction are poorly designed for boys, yielding inattention, disruption and academic failure, or that the educational system and the society in which it exists fail to support in girls the development of skills to succeed, and fail to provide girls and women with equal opportunity to enjoy the benefits of success? Or should we acknowledge that males are inherently more vulnerable to educational disability and focus resources on research to isolate and address the cause of that inherent weakness?

A Note about Terminology

A consideration of gender and exceptionality must address the distinction between the terms *gender* and *sex*. *Sex* is generally used to characterize the biological differences between male and female while *gender* refers to the socially defined differences between men and women or between masculine and feminine (Glasser & Smith, 2008). When examining gender and exceptionality, we encounter both sex differences and gender differences; more to the point, for many exceptionality-related differences, research has not clearly established whether they should be fundamentally viewed as sex differences or as gender differences. Indeed, one of the predominant themes in the literature, as well as one of the most controversial aspects, has been this distinction.

We will follow contemporary usage and employ the term *gender* in most cases. Our focus is on gender differences in the occurrence and response to exceptionality; that is, we are interested in the fact that boys and girls experience different rates of exceptionality, different responses from the educational system, and different outcomes once they leave that system. But at this point we do not know, and indeed perhaps cannot know, whether those differences are the result of fundamental biological sex differences, or a product of forces that socialize boys and girls differently, or the result of some complicated transaction between biology and socialization.

The term *exceptionality* also requires some clarification. For our purposes, the term refers to children and youth who have been identified as displaying a special educational disability. We recognize that giftedness is also an exceptionality, but one that falls outside the scope of our chapter.

Gender Differences

The fundamental question with respect to gender differences in special education identification rates, school experiences, and educational outcomes is why those differences occur, i.e., are there basic gender differences in biology or socialization that account for, or help to elucidate, disproportionality in special education identification, gender differences in school experiences, or gender differences in outcomes both in school and in adult life after leaving school?

Cognitive / Learning Differences

If gender disproportionality in special education is a product of real differences in biology or socialization, we would expect to see related differences reflected in the general population as well. Indeed, some such differences have been well documented. Educators have long been aware of educational achievement differences between boys and girls. Historically, girls have displayed stronger reading abilities in the elementary school years, and boys outperform girls in math and science in the middle school and high school years (Ma, 2008).

In the past several decades, gender differences in students have generally been diminishing, but recent international data on reading performance of 15-year-old students continue to show gender differences—in some cases, large differences in favor of females in most countries. Boys continue to perform better than girls in math in most countries, but the differences are small and in the United States there is no significant difference (Ma, 2008). Gender differences in math/science achievement appear early in some segments of the population; however, inconsistencies in the data appear to support the conclusion that these differences are a function of social factors rather than "hard-wired" brain differences (Penner & Paret, 2008). Although there is little evidence for gender differences in general intelligence, some support has been found for the conclusion that figural and quantitative reasoning skills are somewhat stronger in boys and this strength is associated with higher grades in science; verbal reasoning has been found to be somewhat stronger in girls, although this advantage does not entirely account for girls' higher grades (Kuhn & Holling, 2009).

Inconsistent and evolving evidence on cognitive differences between boys and girls in the general population establishes an uneasy foundation for examining gender differences among students with disabilities. Based on the female advantage in reading, one might reasonably expect that boys would be more likely to evidence reading and writing disabilities and this expectation has often been borne out (Badian, 1999; Berninger, Nielsen, Abbott, Wijsman, & Raskind, 2008). However, the analogous expectation that girls would be over-represented among students with math disabilities is not borne out by most research, which has found either gender equivalence or male predominance among students with math disability (Fletcher, Lyon, Fuchs, & Barnes, 2007).

Social/Emotional Differences

Over the past several decades, researchers have explored gender differences in social and emotional domains as well. Considerable data support the observation that, by adolescence, significant gender differences emerge with respect to psychopathology. Girls are at a substantially increased risk for depression (Nolen-Hoeksema, 2002) and eating disorders (Pawluck & Gorey, 1998), while boys constitute the majority of children and youth with autism spectrum disorders (Chakrabarti & Frombonne, 2001), attention deficit/hyperactivity disorder (American Psychiatric Association, 2000), and physical aggression and conduct disorder (Moffitt, Caspi, Rutter, & Silva, 2001; Tiet, Wasserman, Loeber, McReynolds, & Miller, 2001).

Gender differences in aggressive behavior have been investigated extensively and, more specifically, researchers have explored the extent to which boys and girls differ in type of aggression. There is good evidence that boys are more likely to engage in overt aggressive behavior, but researchers have hypothesized that girls are more likely to display relational aggression (Kuppens, Grietens, Onghena, Michiels, & Subramanian, 2008). This difference in relational aggression, however, has not been strongly supported in the research literature (Verona, Sadeh, Case, Reed, & Bhattacharjee, 2008).

Psychiatric prevalence data would imply that some portion of the gender disproportionality in special education may be attributable to increased male vulnerability to educationally-relevant psychopathology, generally understood as disorders of attention, ability, language, social engagement, emotion regulation, and conduct. The question remains, however, whether those conditions that are more common in girls (e.g., depression, eating disorders) should also be viewed as educationally relevant and more consideration given to their impact on academic and social functioning in schools.

Girls who are served as students with emotional or behavioral disorders (EBD) are often perceived as qualitatively different from their male peers. Teachers have noted that, compared to boys with EBD, girls are more isolated, act out more intensely when they are physical, and have fewer friends (Rice, Merves, & Srsic, 2008). These characteristics set them further apart from their general education adolescent female peers who report receiving support from more classmates and close friends than do typically developing boys (Rueger, Malecki, & Demaray, 2008).

Disproportionality in psychopathology has sometimes been related to gender difference in response to stressors. Kort-Butler (2009) investigated whether a gendered social structure leads to differences in the way adolescent males and females experience and respond to stress, specifically whether gender-related differences in coping styles underlie observed sex differences in the prevalence of depression and delinquent behavior. Kort-Butler observed differences in the types of stressors reported by boys and girls, as well as difference in the styles of coping employed by boys and girls. The relationships connecting sex, stressors, and coping styles are complex but Kort-Butler found that, faced with similar combinations of type of stressors and style of coping, boys and girls experienced similar behavioral outcomes. Other recent research further elaborates the connections among stress, coping, and depression (Hankin, 2009; Rudolph, Flynn, Abaied, Groot, & Thompson, 2009).

Attitudes about Academic Pursuits

Differences in academic achievement have been attributed in part to differences in attitudes about school, instruction, and academic pursuits generally. Girls tend to have a more positive attitude toward school and teachers than boys (Sullivan, Riccio, & Reynolds, 2008); indeed, gender differences in attitudes may be greater than in achievement (Logan & Johnston, 2009).

However, positive attitudes toward reading and school do not necessarily translate into stronger self-efficacy with respect to reading. Logan and Johnston (2009) reported no gender differences in competency beliefs or in perceived academic support from peers and teachers. Further, there are inconsistencies in the relationship between a positive attitude to reading and school and reading comprehension; Logan and Johnston (2009) found that attitude was positively correlated with comprehension in boys, but not in girls. They concluded that "an important source of gender differences may be detectable in how attitudes, ability and beliefs relate to each other, rather than in differences in mean performance levels (which have been found to be small and so may have little applicability in the real world)" (p. 210).

Gender Differences: Hypothesized Causes

To say that gender disproportionality in special education is related to learning and or social/emotional differences between boys and girls merely pushes the causal question back one step; the question then becomes why those differences exist.

Biological Factors

There has been considerable interest in exploring neuropsychological factors that might be causally associated with gender differences in challenging behavior. For example, impaired executive function might reasonably be hypothesized as a basis for aggressive behavior; diminished impulse control is logically related to a tendency toward aggression. This hypothesized relationship may be important in understanding sex differences in challenging behaviors, as boys are generally more likely to display executive function deficits. For example, Raaijmakers et al. (2008) reported that aggressive preschool children showed greater inhibition deficits than control children, and boys showed greater inhibition impairment in executive function than girls.

Baron-Cohen (2003) adopted the somewhat provocative position that the "female brain is predominantly hard-wired for empathy. The male brain is predominantly hard-wired for understanding and building systems" (p. 1). Baron-Cohen then proceeds to explore the hypothesis, first proposed by Hans Asperger, that individuals with autism spectrum disorders have extreme male brains characterized by impaired empathizing and superior systemizing.

There are clear gender effects in the prevalence of autism spectrum disorders, and these are strongest in the less severely affected end of the population. Asperger's Disorder is thought to be five times more common in males than in females (APA, 2000). On the other hand, a meta-analysis conducted by Amiet et al. (2008) indicated that gender ratios are less discrepant among children with both autism and epilepsy than among children with autism without epilepsy. The authors note that this difference may be related to the fact that girls with diagnosed autism are known to have more severe intellectual disability than boys with autism (Gillberg, Steffenburg, & Schaumann, 1991), and significant intellectual disability is associated with the presence of epilepsy.

These examples illustrate how research has begun to identify biologically based differences between the sexes that are conceptually related to differences in the prevalence and the topography of disability conditions. Such research supports the conclusion that some portion of gender disproportionality in special education can be attributed to such biological differences.

Social Factors

Substantial research has examined the extent to which gender differences in special education may be attributed to educator expectations and social roles defined by society. For example, investigating the over-representation of boys in classes for students with EBD, McIntyre and Tong (1998) suggested that one important factor may be "cross-gender misunderstanding," leading female teachers to label traditional male behavior patterns as inappropriate and to refer boys exhibiting such behavior patterns for identification as EBD.

In another example, females were said to be "more sensitive to the disciplinary climate of a school and learn better in more orderly learning environments" (Ma, 2008, p. 442). Boys' achievement motivation decreases more than girls' over time in school (van der Werf, Opdenakker, & Kuyper, 2008), a finding that suggests that the school experience fails to support boys' academic interests. Within racial and ethnic subgroups, boys are consistently more likely than girls of the same racial or ethnic group to have experienced school discipline (Wallace, Goodkind, Wallace, & Bachman, 2008), another negative aspect of the school experience.

Educational Responses to Gender Differences

Schools respond to gender differences in many ways, and there is controversy whether schools "shortchange girls" or, instead, fall short with boys (Flood, 2001). Strongly voiced positions, reflecting diverse philosophical and disciplinary perspectives are common (American Association of University Women, 1992; Beaman, Wheldall, & Kemp, 2006; Kleinfeld, 1998; Sommers, 2000; Younger, Warrington, & Williams, 1999). Although the evidence is limited, it may be hypothesized that differentiated instructional, curricular, and behavioral management decisions are made in response to perceived or actual gender differences in children, including those with disabilities. In some fashion, these differentiated teacher behaviors and school practices may influence the proportionality with which boys and girls are identified as disabled and the different manner in which boys and girls with disabilities are taught, receive transition services, progress through school and attain different outcomes as adults.

Approaches to Gender Differences in General Education

Differentiated educational responses to boys and girls are frequently reported, although the meaning and significance of these is unclear (Beaman et al., 2006). Interest in potentially inequitable teacher behavior or school climate is high because of gender disparities in adult outcomes. Differential teacher attention is often reported as slightly higher interaction rates with boys than girls, and with a small number of boys in particular (Kelly, 1988; French & French, 1984). The differential attention has been interpreted variously, for example, as due to teacher attention reflective of a negative management style towards boys with externalizing behaviors (French & French, 1984), or as appropriate attention to those demonstrating learning and behavior problems, who are more often boys (Croll, 1985). The significance of the differential attention is unclear. Some have argued that the differential attention is a disadvantage for boys and reflects a mismatch between the culturally prescribed male gender role and the student role (Brophy, 1985; Koepke & Harkins, 2008; Skarbrevik, 2002). Others suggest that increased attention to boys may result in the under-referral of girls in need of special education (Vogel, 1990). Teacher gender may also influence interactions and referral to special education for boys and girls. Stipek and Miles (2008) reported the teachers in their longitudinal study of elementary aged students, almost all of whom were female, were more likely to describe boys as aggressive and unengaged. Sideridis, Antoniou, and Padeliadu (2008) observed that male teachers were twice as likely as female teachers to refer a child for evaluation as learning disabled, although the gender of the child did not influence the rate of referral. Additional research based on biological and sex role socialization theories as well as gender relational perspectives will be needed to interpret the nature and significance of gender differences in teacher attention (Francis, 2000).

Special Education

A wide range of biological, social, and philosophical factors underlie observations about gender differences in childhood, and this range is expanded further when considering individuals with disability. Few would argue that students with disabilities should be treated in exactly the same way without respect to gender, but there is no consensus about what gender differences are legitimate to consider during the identification process or when planning for educational accommodations.

Feminist disability studies regard gender as a social construction and disability as a (negative) cultural interpretation of human variation (Garland-Thomson, 2005). Disability studies related to males from this relational perspective, express concern about boys in special education whose disabilities may render their masculinity invisible or make more difficult the development of a male identity (Flood, 2001). Similarly, Shakespeare (1999) argued that being disabled conflicts with the traditional, narrow view of masculinity (i.e., invulnerability, strength, autonomy). On the other hand, girls with disabilities are said to be in double jeopardy, facing the possibility of double discrimination (based on gender and disability); girls with disabilities are likely to be perceived as childlike, helpless, and victimized, ignored in schools, and underrepresented in the scientific literature (Asch, Rousso, & Jefferies, 2001).

These perspectives differ markedly from the conceptualization of disability embodied in special education legislation and regulations. In IDEA, disability is defined as an individual difference which confers a significant disadvantage in regular classroom environments, sufficient that the individual receives a disability label and specially designed instruction to promote equity in educational opportunity. Disability is believed to be discoverable using a comprehensive, data-based assessment process, assumed to be implicitly gender-neutral. Certain categories of disabilities have been described as more subjective than others where a substantial physiological basis for the difference is documented (e.g., learning disabilities versus blindness). However, neither traditional assessment and eligibility procedures, nor more recent innovations such as response to intervention (RTI) or screening and progress-monitoring instruments and procedures, take into account the extent to which differential, gender-related teacher responses may be influencing the likelihood that a student is identified for special education (Mellard, McKnight, & Woods, 2009). One notable exception to this generalization relates to behavior support systems that are aligned with RTI approaches. In some cases, although the reports do not account for gender difference per se, descriptions of the intervention and results are disaggregated by gender (Fairbanks, Sugai, Guardino, & Lathrop, 2007).

Clearly, current educational approaches with respect to special education identification eligibility serve to identify more boys than girls. Despite evidence that some differences are biologically based (Harmon, Stockton, & Contrucci, 1992), many who conduct disability research question whether there are both too many boys who are false positives and too many girls who are false negatives. For example, Wehmeyer and Schwartz (2001) describe how genetic, biological, or neurophysiological differences in boys may contribute to higher level of activity in boys, which influences referral and placement decisions. When combined with certain sex role modeling and socialization practices (Kedar-Voivodas, 1983), boys may assume that adults are not tolerant of active behavior. The outcomes of these social processes may be a bias in referral leading to disproportionately more boys identified as disabled (Wehmeyer & Schwartz, 2001).

In similar vein, Mirkin, Marsden, and Deno (1982) observed that referral systems based on teacher referral rather than weekly academic outcomes yielded significantly more boys. Other investigators have also questioned referral procedures that result in disproportionately more boys identified as disabled (MacMillan, Gresham, Lopez, & Bocian, 1996; McIntyre & Tong, 1998). Shinn, Tindal, and Spira (1987) noted that teachers are accurate about the reading abilities of the students they refer, but tend to refer students who also demonstrated associated problems, particularly related to behavior.

Ensuring that eligibility procedures identify all who should qualify requires attention to more than potential disproportionate identification of boys alone; concomitant consideration of potential under identification of girls is also needed. Researchers have concluded that educational responses to gender differences, as they impact girls in the identification process, are likely flawed (Beaman et al., 2006; Vogel, 1990). Sex role modeling and socialization approaches hypothesize that girls are encouraged to be more compliant, quiet and obedient and, hence, are less often referred by teachers who are more likely to refer students demonstrating both academic and behavioral problems (Wehmeyer & Schwartz, 2001). Based on their review, Wehmeyer and Schwartz concluded that current system is inequitable, not because of gender disproportionality per se, but because too many girls are denied access to support and needed services. Girls must present more significant deficits before they are found eligible, and when identified they are served in more restrictive settings.

Recent, larger scale studies suggest that a better understanding of the role of gender in the identification process will reflect research that considers needs and services over time. In a study of children at school age who had been maltreated as infants, girls of similar need were less likely than boys to receive mental health and special education services (Ringeisen, Casanueva, Cross, & Urato, 2009). In a study utilizing a nationally representative sample of predictors of change in eligibility status among preschoolers, Daley and Carlson (2009) reported that, when accounting for all other factors, the odds of *declassification* for girls were about 1.7 times as high as for boys. District characteristics also remained significant: small preschool programs were five times as likely as large programs to declassify children. In a comprehensive study of predictors of early identification for remedial or special education services based on child characteristics, family characteristics, and child care experience *prior* to school entry, gender represented one of two independent predictors across all models; chronic poverty was the other. Progressive incorporation of more information about the child, family, teacher, and school program characteristics will be needed to produce the most valid and comprehensive identification practices.

In addition to the referral, assessment, and eligibility processes, a second area in which the educational response to gender differences are an important issue is with respect to the impact of interventions and services received. We consider whether instruction, curriculum, and transitions services are responsive to both disability and gender differences. Data regarding functional and academic skills development for boys and girls with disabilities reveal some gender differences. Data from the NLTS2 regarding the characteristics, experiences and outcomes of youth with disabilities 13–16 years of age found boys doing better in mathematics, and fewer boys than girls scored very low on motor skills, personal living skills, and community living skills (Wagner et al., 2006). It is unclear whether this finding is a result of the fact that girls in special education are, on average, more severely impaired than boys.

With respect to instruction, there is little evidence that interventions in special education are specially designed with gender differences in mind. Instruction that includes consideration of individual student characteristics (e.g., a behavior support plan, or an intervention to increase reading comprehension) implicitly would appear to respond to gender differences to the extent that it is truly individualized. However, a more systematic consideration of gender differences when planning or selecting an intervention may be warranted, given evidence that intervention effectiveness may differ by gender (Garcia & Fidalgo, 2008).

Over time, the effects of a particular intervention or special education program may extend beyond its immediate outcomes. Special education and transition services are intended to have far reaching, positive effects on adult status. Outcome data raise the question of whether those long-term effects are equivalent for male and female students. A study in Finland indicated that reading and spelling difficulties had a stronger depressive effect on the educational achievement and subsequent educational career choices for boys (Savolainen, Ahonen, Aro, Tolvanen, & Holopainen, 2008). For girls, no association was found between special education intervention and either school achievement or choice of type of upper secondary education (general or vocational) and only a weak negative association was observed for boys. The specific interventions received by the students were not identified, nor was it clear what the impact would have been without special education services. Nonetheless, special education interventions were not strong predictors of secondary education choice for girls or boys, but especially not for girls.

For some time, researchers have been interested in the potential gender bias in curriculum content. Thirty years ago, race and gender bias was identified in all subject areas and at all grade levels (Scott Foresman & Company, 1972; Weitzman & Rizzo, 1974). The conclusion reached was stated simply: curriculum content reflected a bias that "boys acted, and girls watched; boys built, and girls baked" (Shaffer & Shevitz, 2001, p. 116). In the intervening years, texts have changed, although sex role stereotyping for boys and girls is still thought to exist (Beyer, 1996; Reese, 1994).

The extent to which curriculum and course offerings respond appropriately to gender differences for students who are disabled has been investigated more recently, and evidence of gender bias and sex role stereotyping is reported (Kratovil & Bailey, 1986; Wehmeyer & Schwartz, 2001). A review of career development texts for special education students found evidence of gender fair language, equal representations of males and females, and both males and females in supervisory roles; however, males were shown holding a much wider range of career roles, and there was little mention of gender issues in the workplace or in college. Introductory special education texts were also reviewed and found to have little discussion of gender-related curriculum resources or how to respond to curriculum bias in textbooks (McCormick, 2001).

Course-taking patterns of boys and girls with disabilities reveal restricted or fewer options for both, compared to general education students. Students with disabilities are known to take fewer academic courses than nondisabled peers, particularly the sequential course offerings leading to careers in the physical sciences, mathematics, and engineering (Wagner, 1993). Interest in increasing the participation and success of women with disabilities in math and science courses is growing (Wahl, 2001). However, differences in vocational course patterns leave young women with disabilities less prepared for high skill, high wage employment (Doren & Benz, 2001). Compared to boys with disabilities, girls with disabilities earn fewer credits, are less likely to receive training in a particular job skill, and are more likely to receive training in health occupations, home economics, and office occupations. They are also less likely to have work experience before leaving school (Doren & Benz, 1998; Hasazi, Gordon, & Roe, 1985).

Gender differences in transition outcomes have received some attention, but much less is known about gender differences in the actual transition planning process and provision of services. There is a broad consensus that the provision of individualized transition services is a critically important intervention for youth with disabilities, one thought to directly influence adult outcomes (Coutinho, et al., 2006; Doren & Benz, 1998; Hogansen et al., 2008). Access to Vocational Rehabilitation Services may perform a similar or complementary function (Doren & Benz, 1998). However, Powers, Hogansen, Geenen, Powers, and Gil-Kashiwabara (2008) examined individual transition plans of almost 400 students. They found about one-third of the transition plan goals for girls reflected gender stereotypes, whereas less than one-tenth of the plans set goals that countered gender stereotypes.

Hogansen et al. (2008) provided information about the transition experiences of a large cross section of young women with disabilities, their parents, and the professionals who serve them. These authors found that girls often reported that special education classes had not helped them toward their goals, that it was not "real education." While most girls knew what a transition planning meeting was, their understanding of its purpose was vague, and many reported the experience was negative. Girls also reported differential treatment in the classroom, with behavioral expectations higher for girls and teacher attention more often focused on boys. A disconnect between girls' interests, academic needs, and special education programs was a common perception. A self-perception of difference, because of their disability, was perceived to be detrimental. However, college women who were interviewed were more likely to acknowledge and even value disability.

A complementary study of a large group of culturally diverse students representing two large urban school districts compared transition and special education experiences for young women and men with disabilities (Powers et al., 2008). Among exceptional youth, females were more likely to rate going to college as very important, and males were more likely to rate learning independent living skills as very important. Females were more likely to report they receive support from nonfamily adults, have a clear plan for the future, and had been taught to protect their safety, but they were also more likely to report that people expected less of them because of their gender and because of their disability. Parents of females were less likely to report that their youth had held a paid job, and females were more likely to be told they cannot do something because it's not safe.

With respect to participation in Vocational Rehabilitation Services, evidence from the National Longitudinal Transition Study (NLTS) indicated boys and girls were referred and found eligible for Vocational Rehabilitation Services at about the same rates (Wagner, 1992; Wine, Hayward, & Wagner, 1993). Evidence from other studies has indicated comparable participation in such services, but a greater likelihood that women with disabilities receive training in sex-stereotyped occupations (Danek, 1992). Women were much more likely than men to be employed in clerical or service positions at closure of VR services, even when this was not their original goal. Women were also less likely to receive on-the-job training, work adjustment training, or vocational evaluation (Cowen & Ford, 1986).

In sum, the information available about gender

differences in educational interventions and their impact is limited. Evidence about course-taking patterns, transition services, and vocational rehabilitation experiences suggest the current educational response must be re-examined and strengthened to afford adolescent girls and young women with disabilities more gender responsive educational opportunities that lead to more and higher quality options in employment and income as adults.

A final area for which the educational response must be considered is gender differences in adult outcomes for students with disabilities where differences generally favor males. Considerable data now raise the concern that educational services provided do not confer comparable benefits to boys and girls, and the disparity is greater for those with disabilities (Doren & Benz, 2001; Fulton & Sabornie, 1994; Hasazi et al., 1985; Lindstrom, Benz, & Doren, 2004; Oswald et al., 2002; Sitlington & Frank, 1985; U. S. Department of Labor, 2004; Wagner, Cameto, & Newman, 2003). Although women make up an increasing share of the adult workforce, gender differences are evident in many areas (Stephenson & Burge, 1997; U.S. Department of Labor, 2004). In a detailed analysis of transition outcomes, Coutinho et al. (2006) examined gender differences in outcomes among adults with and without disabilities using National Education Longitudinal Study data. Main effects for gender were observed, with almost all favoring men: men reported higher incomes, worked more hours, more often received job benefits, and more often reported job satisfaction. At age 20, more women than men were married and had children. Women and men dropped out of school, experienced health problems, performed volunteer work, were the victims of crime, or had the opportunity to use past training or education at about the same rates. Findings favored women with respect to likelihood of enrollment in postsecondary education programs, aspiration to seek a college degree, and likelihood of being arrested. With regard to individuals with disabilities, men were more likely to be employed, obtained higher earnings, were more likely to earn a high school diploma, and were less likely to have biological children. Men with disabilities were also more likely to rate more highly the importance of strong friendships.

The differences in rates of employment may be changing. More recent, follow-along analyses of males and females with disabilities indicated increases in paid employment for the young adults with disabilities, and the increase was significantly higher for women (Wagner et al., 2003).

Jans and Stoddard (1999) produced a comprehensive chartbook about the status of people with disability. This chartbook complements and extends the findings from special education studies. The disproportionality of males to females in childhood appears to reverse in adult life, when more women are recognized as disabled. Although there were no differences in the rate of activity limitations, the number of productive days lost was much higher for women with disabilities. More recent data support these findings (Brault, 2008).

With respect to employment outcomes, people with disabilities generally did not fare as well as those without, but women with disabilities were the least likely to have a job or business in the Jans and Stoddard (1999) study. Women with disabilities were more likely than men to be employed in service occupations; however, they were also more likely than men to be employed in the managerial and professional occupations, at least in the occupations traditionally filled by women, e.g., teaching, nursing, etc. Women were less likely to work in jobs related to computers, a job sector experiencing rapid growth. The pattern for income was similar. Women with a non-severe disability had lower median monthly earnings, compared to men with a non-severe disability, and compared to women and men without a disability. Women with a disability were more likely to live in poverty, and less likely to receive SSI (Supplemental Security Income), but they were more likely to receive needs-based assistance, such as food stamps and Medicaid. As of 1996, fewer women with disabilities were served through Vocational Rehabilitation Services. With respect to mental illness, more men than women reported substance abuse problems; for women there was a higher likelihood of depressive and anxiety disorders.

Outcomes for women with disabilities around the world are stark and almost uniformly inferior to that of men (Womenwatch, 1996). The global literacy rate for women with disabilities is estimated at 1%, compared to about 3% for all individuals with disabilities combined (Rousso, 2003; Womenwatch, 1996). Worldwide, women with disabilities are less than half as likely as men to be employed, are paid less for the same work, encounter occupational segregation, find unequal access to training or promotion, and participate very little in economic decision making (O'Reilly, 2003). The World Health Organization and United Nations found women's disproportionately higher rates of neuropsychiatric disorders to be a particularly serious problem and cite violence, poverty, conflict, dislocation, and gender discrimination in accounting for the differential susceptibility (Womenwatch, 1996). Over the last decade, international organizations have issued a call to action to reduce discrimination and promote the rights and well being of women, those with disabilities in particular (Rousso, 2003; United Nations, 2003; Womenwatch, 1996).

The many disparities in outcomes cannot be interpreted solely as a failed educational response. Many other factors—social, cultural, political, and economic—also influence outcomes for men and women. Young women with disabilities report pressure to avoid risk and to begin a family early in life. Transition-age young women with disabilities were more likely than men to rate having children within three years of leaving school as an important outcome (Powers et al., 2008). For women in general, recent longitudinal analyses of the decrease in the gender wage gap in the United States indicate women are increasingly likely to consider a job in terms of the importance of work/money per se and less its importance to society/family. In other words, women have closed the educational attainment gap and are now narrowing the gap related to noncognitive factors such as the impact of behavior and personality traits on earnings (Fortin, 2008). Market discrimination, global recessionary cycles, world conflicts, and so on will make the goal to reduce the remaining and widespread disparities more difficult and complex, but perhaps more urgent to accomplish. High quality educational opportunities are arguably the most accessible and practical means to bring about needed changes for women with disabilities.

Implications

An evolution if not revolution in attitudes and responses to gender differences and exceptionality is occurring among those interested in better understanding the nature of gender differences and gender disparities in educational experience or outcomes among students with exceptionalities. As the literature has developed, more questions are being raised about inequitable identification practices, particularly in high incidence disability categories. The field has shown interest in correcting non-gender-responsive services (e.g., curriculum, instruction, and transition experiences) that may restrict the options or relevance for girls. There have been calls for research and better informed policy and professional development (Anderson, 1997; Gillespie & Fink, 1974; Miles, 1986; Rousso & Wehmeyer, 2001). The Division on Career Development and Transition of the Council for Exceptional Children has forwarded a position paper calling for systemic improvements in transition education to eliminate the differential experiences and outcomes related to gender, race/ethnicity, and socioeconomic status (Trainor, Lindstrom, Simon-Burroughs, Martin, & Sorrells, 2008). The paper argues for adoption of an ecological approach to inform research, policy, and practice. Without such systemic initiatives, the current educational response is unlikely to that ensure both the boys and girls with disabilities will thrive and succeed as adults in the increasingly complex economic and social conditions of our world.

Identification of Exceptionality

Improved understanding of biological or genetically linked conditions may produce a greater societal commitment to high quality life outcomes for all persons with exceptionalities; increased understanding about differential susceptibilities (for males and females) may also result. Less clear is how pre-natal and newborn counseling services will integrate scientific or medical knowledge, ethics, and religious beliefs. The cost to have one's own genome sequenced will soon be less than $1,000; that service, along with the proliferation of molecular genetic tests, will put additional pressure on genetic counselors and others as information about sex-based disorders becomes more widely available (Gerber, 2009).

Equitable identification of gender-related disability will be possible only when there is a greater consensus as to whether gender disproportionality reflects biologically based differences or biased educational services and referral practices. Further, where concern about bias exists, the field will be required to clarify at what point an observed degree of disproportionality is judged to be too great. For example, an odds ratio of 1.5:1 or higher is sometimes regarded as a level that warrants response (Skiba et al., 2004; Strand & Lindsay, 2009). However, consensus is lacking as to whether this is an acceptable cutoff or a lower level is needed to trigger a response. The question is of particular importance for disability categories for which the determination is based on psychometric test data (e.g., learning disabilities and mental retardation) as opposed to disability categories associated with sensory-based handicapping conditions based on tests accepted as being more objective.

Another implication of gender differences for disability identification is the need for knowledge about norms and behavioral function in academic settings. For example, if boys are less likely to achieve literacy milestones at the same rate as girls in the early years, they may be "disabled" only by virtue of their comparison with girls (Beaman et al., 2006). Disproportionality rates might be lower if referral for evaluation is restricted to those boys whose behavioral excesses or deficits exceed the normative pattern for boys. Functional behavioral assessment approaches may offer eventual insight about base rates of (a) challenging behavior and behavior function by gender in general education classes and (b) the role of behavior function in the interaction between academic and behavioral challenges. A study investigating the role of behavioral function in reading academic and behavior problems at the elementary level and found base rates and behavior function to vary by grade and special education status (McIntosh, Horner, Chard, Dickey, & Braun, 2008). Children with disabilities were more likely to attempt to escape or avoid academic tasks and seek adult rather than peer attention. Unfortunately, data were not reported by gender.

If boys are more likely than girls to demonstrate disruptive or aggressive behavior under conditions common in current general education environments, educators will question whether regular education environments should be redesigned to better suit the boys' learning styles. Referral for special education may be appropriate only for those who fail to respond to a regular education environment in which instruction and behavior management approaches have been redesigned to match the needs of boys.

A recognition and adequate response to gender differences may require adaptation and development of RTI approaches, both academic and behavioral, to ensure early intervention and identification practices are equally responsive to boys and girls. The need for RTI approaches that target emotional challenges and also consider gender differences may be especially important for girls, who are more likely to demonstrate internalizing symptoms that culminate in clinical depression. Identification approaches may need to be modified for girls to include better screening by regular educators and cross-disciplinary screening, progress monitoring, pre-referral, and early intervention services. This includes improvements in assessment instruments that adequately identify some disorders, but may be insufficiently sensitive to internalizing disorders (Lane et al., 2009). Further discussion about the value of gender responsive guidelines for both academic progress and socio-behavioral expectations is needed, along with consideration of how such guidelines should affect the special education identification process.

Finally, beliefs about gender differences are still evolving, and relevant data are still emerging. Both beliefs and data will impact special education referral, assessment, eligibility determination, and instructional services. Relational perspectives initially will appear to conflict with existing approaches, but eventually will contribute to a better understanding of what are appropriate teacher responses to gender differences in all children. An example of this trend is the neurodiversity perspective offered to account for differences observed for individuals with autism (Bumiller, 2008). If special education identification and instructional responses are to be appropriate, they must be informed by emerging biological, genetic, and neuropsychological perspectives.

Addressing the Needs of Subpopulations

The interaction of race and gender creates subpopulations for whom the challenges are even greater. Disproportionate identification of African American males as disabled, particularly in the categories of mental retardation and emotional disturbance, is alarmingly high (Coutinho, Oswald, Best, & Forness, 2002; Harry, Hart, Klingner, & Cramer, 2009; Kauffman, Mock, & Simpson, 2007; Oswald, Coutinho, Best, & Nguyen, 2001). A recent study of a nationally representative sample of preschool students failed to find significant racial/ethnic disproportionality among children declassified once other factors were controlled in the analyses (Daley & Carlson, 2009). This finding is positive; however, the analyses reported were not disaggregated by race/ethnicity and gender. We may expect that disproportionate disability identification among gender and race subpopulations will continue to be controversial for the foreseeable future, and the educational response must continue to evolve, particularly for African American males.

Intervention, Gender, and Exceptionality

Differentiated practice based on gender and exceptionality will require a continued search for empirically validated regular or special education interventions, permitting the design of classrooms where both boys and girls succeed. Rather than one size fits all, teachers will engage in interactions that are functionally inclusive of the special needs of each gender (Beaman et al., 2006). Effective responses to gender differences will require substantially modified teacher practices and classroom environments. Adequate approaches will go beyond the curriculum-rich, but largely undifferentiated, learning environments of general education classrooms, more closely resembling *high quality* special education settings that offer highly individualized teacher student interactions, direct instruction of content, and higher rates of feedback and contingent reinforcement of appropriate behavior (Kauffman, Conroy, Gardner, & Oswald, 2008). An example of such an approach is a universal preventive intervention implemented in the first grade that reduced, for boys, the probability of receiving special education at any time between grades 1 and 12 (Bradshaw, Zmuda, Kellam, & Ialongo, 2009).

Others have also encouraged systematic inquiry to re-engineer general education classrooms so that they are more effective for both boys and girls (Beaman et al., 2006). Recommended are more positively oriented teacher interactional styles and teaching strategies drawn from highly effective special education classrooms, involving increased teacher praise, feedback, and task engagement (Wheldall & Limbrick, 2003). A recent report (House of Representatives Standing Committee on Education and Training, 2002) found that boys respond more to their relationships with teachers, whereas girls respond more to curriculum content. Further, boys respond better to teachers who are attuned to their sense of justice and fairness and who are consistent in the application of rules. A commitment to a more affirming and consistent classroom environment for all students will result in increased engagement for both boys and girls.

Future Research Directions

The research questions, methodologies and settings for future research related to gender and exceptionality require careful attention. Even in the presence of apparent gender disparities, it may be misguided or ineffectual in the search for better practices to focus only on gender and to assume gender is the key rather than only one of many factors (Hammersley, 1990). On the other hand, most informative will be research that captures and interprets gender effects (Morgan, Farkas, & Wu, 2009) rather than controls for, and eliminates, such effects (Seo, Abbott, & Hawkins, 2008).

International data continue to reflect significant disadvantage for females in terms of educational opportunity, independence, and employment prospects particularly in developing countries, and in some cultural contexts this disadvantage is increasing. A comprehensive agenda for research into gender differences and educational implications must include consideration of this larger picture. We will not have achieved a thorough understanding of gender and exceptionality until we have accounted for the considerable cross-cultural differences in male and female opportunity.

Experience suggests, and data tend to confirm, that among students with disabilities, there is a relatively small proportion of boys with significant learning and behavior challenges who present a dilemma that the educational system has simply not been addressed effectively. An adequate response to this subgroup will require a scope of interdisciplinary research and practice that is virtually nonexistent at present.

The research agenda, as it relates to gender and exceptionality, will have to rise above the detritus left by the gender wars and objectively examine the impact of societal views about gender, disability, and the purpose of education. Such research will consider both student and teacher differences as they exist at a given time and as they change with societal evolution.

Research contributing to the development of exceptional education interventions must consider the full range of age, geography, and educational setting. Results will be most helpful when they begin to address the question of which intervention works best for which student, taking into account race, gender, culture, socioeconomic status, and personal history. A beginning step toward that end will involve careful characterization of research samples so that results can be disaggregated by gender, race/ethnicity, and disability category (Shirk, Kaplinski, & Gudmundsen, 2009).

The educational significance of the relationship between gender and exceptionality is only partially articulated and mapped. Appropriate special education identification and effective educational interventions will be more easily achieved when schools offer equality in terms of educational opportunity (that is, an educational experience that is functionally inclusive and responsive to special needs) without respect to gender, race, or disability. Classrooms offering this experience will reflect greater consensus about how special education identification and teacher practices can promote academic and social engagement, achievement, and successful outcomes for boys and girls as they exit school.

Note

1. Although we prefer the term *intellectual disability*, we continue to use *mental retardation* to reflect the language of the special education statute and regulations.

References

Acker, S. (1988). Teachers, gender and resistance. *British Journal of Sociology of Education, 9,* 307–322.

American Psychiatric Association. (2000). *Diagnostic and statistical manual of mental disorders (4th ed.—text revision).* Washington, DC: Author.

American Association of University Women. (1992). *How schools shortchange girls: A study of major findings on girls and education.* Washington, DC: AAUW Educational Foundation.

Amiet, C., Gourfinkel-An, I., Bouzamondo, A., Tordjman, S., Baulac, M., Lechat, P., . . . Cohen, D. (2008). Epilepsy in autism is associated with intellectual disability and gender: Evidence from a meta-analysis. *Biological Psychiatry, 64,* 577–582.

Anderson, K. G. (1997). Gender bias and special education referrals. *Annals of Dyslexia, 47,* 151–162.

Asch, A., & Fine, M. (1988). *Women with disabilities: Essays in psychology, culture, and politics.* Philadelphia: Temple University Press.

Asch, A., Rousso, H., & Jefferies, T. (2001). Beyond pedestals: The lives of girls and women with disabilities. In H. Rousso & M. L. Wehmeyer (Eds.), *Double jeopardy: Addressing gender equity in special education* (pp. 13–48). Albany: State University of New York.

Badian, N. A. (1999). Reading disability defined as a discrepancy between listening and reading comprehension: A longitudinal study of stability, gender differences, and prevalence. *Journal of Learning Disabilities, 32,* 138–148.

Baron-Cohen, S. (2003). *The essential difference: The truth about the male and female brain.* New York: Basic Books.

Beaman B., Wheldall, K., & Kemp, C. (2006). Differential teacher attention to boys and girls in the classroom. *Educational Review, 58,* 339–366.

Benjamin, S. (2003). Gender and special educational needs. In C. Skelton & B. Francis (Eds.), *Boys and girls in the primary classroom* (pp. 98–112). Maidenhead, UK: Open University Press.

Bentzen, F. (1966). Sex ratios in learning and behavior disorders. *The National Elementary Principal, 46,* 13–17.

Berninger, V. W., Nielsen, K. H., Abbott, R. D., Wijsman, E., & Raskind, W. (2008). Gender differences in severity of writing and reading disabilities. *Journal of School Psychology, 46,* 151–172.

Beyer, C. E. (1996). Gender representations in illustrations, text, and topic area in sexuality education curricula. *Journal of School Health, 66,* 361–364.

Bradshaw, C. P., Zmuda, J. H., Kellam, S. G., & Ialongo, N. S. (2009). Longitudinal impact of two universal preventive interventions in first grade on educational outcomes in high school. *Journal of Educational Psychology, 101,* 926–937.

Brault, M. (2008). *Americans with disabilities: 2005.* (Current Population Reports, P70-117). Suitland, MD: U.S. Census Bureau.

Brophy, J. (1985). Male and female teacher-student interaction. In L. C. Wilkinson & C. B. Marrett (Eds.), *Gender influences in classroom interaction* (pp. 115–142). Orlando, FL: Academic Press.

Bumiller, K. (2008, Summer). Quirky citizens: Autism, gender, and reimagining disability. *Signs*, 967–991.

Callahan, K. (1994). Wherefore art thou, Juliet? Causes and implications of the male dominated sex ratio in programs for students with emotional and behavioral disorders. *Education and Treatment of Children, 17,* 228–243.

Chakrabarti, S., & Frombonne, E. (2001). Pervasive developmental disorders in preschool children. *Journal of the American Medical Association, 285,* 3093–3099.

Cooley, R. (2001). *Differences in the gender gap: Comparisons across racial/ethnic groups in education and work. A policy information report.* Princeton, NJ: Education Testing Service.

Coutinho, M. J., & Oswald, D. P. (2005). State variation in gender disproportionality: Findings and recommendations. *Remedial and Special Education, 26,* 7–15.

Coutinho, M. J., Oswald, D. P., & Best, A. M. (2006). Differences in outcomes for female and male students in special education. *Career Development for Exceptional Individuals, 29,* 48–59.

Coutinho, M. J., Oswald, D. P., Best, A. M., & Forness, S. R. (2002). Gender and socio-demographic factors and the disproportionate identification of minority students as emotionally disturbed. *Behavioral Disorders, 27,* 109–125.

Cowen, B., & Ford, M. (1986). *Women's initiative study: Access, services, and outcomes for women with disabilities in vocational rehabilitation.* (ERIC Document Reproduction Service No. ED 294 000).

Croll, P. (1985). Teacher interaction with male and female pupils in junior classrooms, *Educational Research, 27,* 220–223.

Daley, T. C., & Carlson, E. (2009). Predictors of change in eligibility status among preschoolers in special education. *Exceptional Children, 75*, 412–426.

Danek, M. M. (1992). The status of women with disabilities revisited. *Journal of Applied Rehabilitation Counseling, 16,* 16–18.

Doren, B., & Benz, M. (1998). Employment inequality revisited: Predictors of better employment outcomes for young women with disabilities in transition. *The Journal of Special Education, 31,* 425–433.

Doren, B., & Benz, M. (2001). Gender equity issues in the vocational and transition services and employment outcomes experienced by young women with disabilities. In H. Rousso & M.L. Wehmeyer (Eds.), *Double jeopardy: Addressing gender equity in special education* (pp. 288–308). Albany: State University of New York.

Fairbanks, S., Sugai, G., Guardino, D., & Lathrop, M. (2007). Response to intervention: Examining classroom behavior support in second grade. *Exceptional Children, 73,* 288–310.

Fletcher, J. M., Lyon, G. R., Fuchs, L. S., & Barnes, M. A. (2007). *Learning disabilities: From identification to intervention.* New York: Guilford Press.

Flood, C. P. (2001). *Raising and educating healthy boys.* New York: Educational Equity Concepts.

Fortin, N. M. (2008). The gender wage gap among young adults in the

United States: The importance of money versus people. *The Journal of Human Resources, 43*, 884–918.

Francis, B. (2000). *Boys, girls and achievement: Addressing the classroom issue*. London: RoutledgeFalmer.

French, J. & French, P. (1984). Gender imbalance in the primary classroom: an interactional account. *Educational Research, 26,* 127–136.

Fulton, S., & Sabornie, E. (1994). Evidence of employment inequality among females with disabilities. *The Journal of Special Education, 28,* 149–165.

Garcia, J., & Fidalgo, R. (2008). Writing self-efficacy changes after cognitive strategy intervention in students with learning disabilities: The mediational role of gender in calibration. *The Spanish Journal of Psychology, 11,* 414–432.

Garland-Thomson, R. (2005). Feminist disability studies. *Signs: Journal of Women in Culture and Society, 30,* 1557–1586.

Gerber, M. (2009, November 18). Untitled post. Retrieved from SPEDPRO listserv http://spedpro.org/

Gillberg, C., Steffenburg, S., & Schaumann, H. (1991). Is autism more common now than ten years ago? *British Journal of Psychiatry, 158,* 403–409.

Gillespie, P. H., & Fink, A. H. (1974). The influence of sexism on the education of handicapped children. *Exceptional Children, 41*, 155–162.

Glasser, H. M., & Smith, J. P. (2008). On the vague meaning of "gender" in education research: The problem, its sources, and recommendations for practice. *Educational Researcher, 37,* 343–350.

Hankin, B. L. (2009). Development of sex differences in depressive and co-occurring anxious symptoms during adolescence: Descriptive trajectories and potential explanations in a multiwave prospective study. *Journal of Clinical Child and Adolescent Psychology, 38,* 460–472.

Hammersley, M. (1990). *Reading ethnographic research: A critical guide.* London: Longman.

Harmon, J. A., Stockton, S., & Contrucci, C. (1992). *Gender disparities in special education. (*Research Report 143). Madison: Bureau for Exceptional Children, Wisconsin Department of Public Instruction. (ERIC Identifier: ED 358631).

Harry, B., Hart, J. E., Klingner, J. & Cramer, E. (2009). Response to Kauffman, Mock, & Simpson, (2007): Problems related to underservice of students with emotional or behavioral disorders. *Behavioral Disorders, 34,* 164–171.

Hasazi, S. B., Gordon, R., & Roe, C. A. (1985). Factors associated with the employment status of handicapped youth exiting high school from 1979 to 1983. *Exceptional Children, 51,* 455–469.

Hayden-McPeak, C., Gaskin, S. T., & Gaughan, L. K. (1993, April). *Bad boys, good girls: A review of the research on gender differences of assessment, child rearing, and educational practices*. Paper presented at the Annual Convention of the Council for Exceptional Children, San Antonio, TX.

Hogansen, J. M., Powers, K., Greenen, S., Gil-Kashiwabara, E., & Powers, L. (2008). Transition goals and experiences of females with disabilities: Youth, parents, and professionals. *Exceptional Children, 74,* 215–234.

House of Representatives Standing Committee on Education and Training. (2002). *Boys: Getting it right: Report on the inquiry into the education of boys.* Canberra, Australia: Parliament of the Commonwealth of Australia

Jans, L., & Stoddard, S. (1999). *Chartbook on women and disability in the United States*. Washington, DC: U.S. Department of Education, National Institute on Disability and Rehabilitation Research.

Kalyanpur, M. (2008). The paradox of majority underrepresentation in special education in India: Constructions of difference in a developing country. *The Journal of Special Education, 42,* 55–64.

Kauffman, J. M., Conroy, M., Gardner, R., & Oswald, D. (2008). Cultural sensitivity in the application of behavior principles to education. *Education and Treatment of Children, 31,* 239–262.

Kauffman, J. M., Mock, D. R., & Simpson, R. L. (2007). Problems related to underservice of students with emotional or behavioral disorders. *Behavioral Disorders, 33,* 43–57.

Kedar-Voivodas, G. (1983). The impact of elementary children's school roles and sex roles on teacher attitudes: An interactional analysis. *Review of Educational Research, 53,* 415–437.

Kelly, A. (1988). Gender differences in teacher–pupil interactions: A meta-analytic review. *Research in Education, 39*, 1–24.

Kleinfeld, J. (1998). *The myth that schools shortchange girls: Social science in the service of deception*. Washington, DC: The Women's Freedom Network.

Koepke, M., & Harkins, D. A. (2008). Conflict in the classroom: Gender differences in the teacher-child relationship. *Early Education and Development, 19,* 843–864.

Kort-Butler, L. A. (2009). Coping styles and sex differences in depressive symptoms and delinquent behavior. *Journal of Youth and Adolescence, 38,* 122–136.

Kratovil, J., & Bailey, S. M. (1986). Sex equity and disabled students. *Theory and Practice, 25,* 250–256.

Kuhn, J., & Holling, H. (2009). Gender, reasoning ability, and scholastic achievement: A multilevel mediation analysis. *Learning and Individual Differences, 19,* 229–233.

Kuppens, S., Grietens, H., Onghena, P., Michiels, D., & Subramanian, S. V. (2008). Individual and classroom variables associated with relational aggression in elementary-school aged children: A multilevel analysis. *Journal of School Psychology, 46,* 639–660.

Lane, K. L., Casey, A. M., Lambert, W., Wehby, J., Weisenbach, J. L., & Phillips, A. (2009). A comparison of systematic screening tools for emotional and behavioral disorders. *Journal of Emotional and Behavioral Disorders, 17*, 93–105.

Lindstrom, L. E., Benz, M., & Doren, B. (2004). An analysis by gender of long-term postschool outcomes for youth with and without disabilities. *Exceptional Children, 61,* 282-300.

Logan, S., & Johnston, R. (2009). Gender differences in reading ability and attitudes: Examining where these differences lie. *Journal of Research in Reading, 32,* 199–214.

Ma, X. (2008). Within-school gender gaps in reading, mathematics, and science literacy. *Comparative Education Review, 52,* 437–460

MacMillan, D. L., Gresham, F. M., Lopez, M. F., & Bocian, K. M. (1996). Comparison of students nominated for prereferral interventions by ethnicity and gender. *The Journal of Special Education, 30,* 133–151.

Mann, E. A., McCartney, K., & Park, J. M. (2007). Preschool predictors of the need for early remedial and special education services. *The Elementary School Journal, 107,* 273–285.

McCormick, T. M. (2001). Teaching as though both genders count: Guidelines for designing nonsexist inclusive curricula. In H. Rousso & M. L. Wehmeyer (Eds.), *Double jeopardy: Addressing gender equity in special education* (pp. 237–260). Albany: State University of New York.

McIntosh, K., Horner, R. H., Chard, D. J., Dickey, C. R., & Braun, D. H. (2008). Reading skills and function of problem behavior in typical school settings. *The Journal of Special Education, 42*, 131–147.

McIntyre, T., & Tong, V. (1998). Where the boys are: Do cross gender misunderstandings of language and behaviour patterns contribute to the overrepresentation of males in programs for students with emotional and behavioural disorders? *Education and Treatment of Children, 29,* 321–332.

Mellard, D. F., McKnight, M., & Woods, K. (2009). Response to intervention screening and progress-monitoring practices in 41 local schools. *Learning Disabilities Research and Practice, 24*, 186–195.

Miles, D. L. (1986). Why do more boys than girls receive special education? *Contemporary Education, 5*, 104–106.

Mirkin, P., Marsden, D., & Deno, S. (1982). *Direct and repeated measurement of academic skills: An alternative to traditional screening, referral, and identification of learning disabled students (Research Report 75).* Minneapolis: University of Minnesota, Institute for Research on Learning Disabilities.

Moffitt, T. E., Caspi, A., Rutter, M., & Silva, P. A. (2001). *Sex differences in antisocial behavior.* New York: Cambridge University Press.

Morgan, P. L., Farkas, G., & Wu, Q. (2009). Kindergarten predictors of recurring externalizing and internalizing psychopathology in the third and fifth grades. *Journal of Emotional and Behavioral Disorders, 17,* 67–79.

Mumpower, D. L. (1970). Sex ratios found in various types of referred exceptional children. *Exceptional Children, 36,* 621–622.

Nolen-Hoeksema, S. (2002). Gender differences in depression. In I. H. Gotlib & C. L. Hammen (Eds.), *Handbook of depression* (pp. 492–509). New York: Guilford Press.

O'Reilly, R. (2003). *Employment barriers for women with disabilities: The right to decent work of persons with disabilities.* (IFP/Skills Working Paper No. 14). Geneva, Switzerland: International Labour Organization.

Oswald, D. P., Coutinho, M. J., Best, A., & Nagle, H. (2002). Trends in the special education identification rates of boys and girls: A call for research and change. *Exceptionality, 11,* 223–237.

Oswald, D. P., Coutinho, M. J., Best, A. M., & Nguyen, N. (2001). The impact of socio-demographic characteristics on the identification rates of minority students as mentally retarded. *Mental Retardation, 39,* 351–367.

Pawluck, D. E., & Gorey, K. M. (1998). Secular trends in the incidence of anorexia nervosa: Integrative review of population-based studies. *International Journal of Eating Disorders, 23,* 347–352.

Penner, A. M., & Paret, M. (2008). Gender differences in mathematics achievement: Exploring the early grades and the extremes. *Social Science Research, 37,* 239–253.

Phipps, P. M. (1982). The LD learner is often a boy – Why? *Academic Therapy, 17,* 425–430.

Powers, K., Hogansen, J. M., Geenen, S., Powers, L. E., & Gil-Kashiwabara, E. (2008). Gender matters in transition to adulthood: A survey study of adolescents with disabilities and their families. *Psychology in the Schools, 45,* 349–364.

Raaijmakers, M. A. J., Smidts, D. P., Sergeant, J. A., Maassen, G. H., Posthumus, J. A., van Engeland, H., & Matthys, W. (2008). Executive functions in preschool children with aggressive behavior: Impairments in inhibitory control. *Journal of Abnormal Child Psychology, 36,* 1097–1107.

Reese, L. (1994). Gender equity and texts. *Social Studies Review, 33,* 12–15.

Rice, E. H., Merves, E., & Srsic, A. (2008). Perceptions of gender differences in the expression of emotional and behavioral disabilities. *Education and Treatment of Children, 31,* 549–565.

Ringeisen, H., Casanueva, C., Cross, R. P., & Urato, M. (2009). Mental health and special education services at school entry for children who were involved with the child welfare system as infants. *Journal of Emotional and Behavioral Disorders, 17,* 177–192.

Rousso, H. (2003). *Gender and education for all: The leap to equality education for all: A gender and disability perspective* (EFA Global Monitoring Report 2003/4). Washington, DC: World Bank.

Rousso, H., & Wehmeyer, M. L. (2001). Introduction. In H. Rousso & M. L. Wehmeyer (Eds.), *Double Jeopardy: Addressing gender equity in special education* (pp. 1–9). Albany: State University of New York.

Rudolph, K. D., Flynn, M., Abaied, J. L., Groot, A., & Thompson, R. (2009). Why is past depression the best predictor of future depression? Stress generation as a mechanism of depression continuity in girls. *Journal of Clinical Child and Adolescent Psychology, 38,* 473–485.

Rueger, S. Y., Malecki, C. K., & Demaray, M. K. (2008). Gender differences in the relationship between perceived social support and student adjustment during early adolescence. *School Psychology Quarterly, 23,* 496–514.

Savolainen, A., Ahonen, T., Aro, M., Tolvanen, A., & Holopainen, L. (2008). Reading comprehension, word reading and spelling as predictors of school achievement and choice of secondary education. *Learning and Instruction, 18,* 201–210.

Scott Foresman, & Company. (1972). *Improving the image of women in textbooks*. Glenview, IL: Author.

Seo, Y., Abbott, R. D., & Hawkins, J. D. (2008). Outcome status of students with learning disabilities at ages 21 and 24. *Journal of Learning Disabilities, 41,* 300–314.

Shakespeare, T. (1999). When is a man not a man? When he's disabled. In J. Wild (Ed.), *Working with men for change* (pp. 47–58). London: University College of London Press.

Shaffer, S., & Shevitz, L. (2001). She bakes and he builds: Gender bias in the curriculum. In H. Rousso & M. L. Wehmeyer (Eds.), *Double jeopardy: Addressing gender equity in special education* (pp. 115–132). Albany: State University of New York.

Shinn, M. R, Tindal, G. A., & Spira, D. A. (1987). Special education referrals as an index of teacher tolerance: Are teachers imperfect tests? *Exceptional Children, 54,* 32–40.

Shirk, S. R., Kaplinski, H., & Gudmundsen, G. (2009). School-based cognitive-behavioral therapy for adolescent depression: A benchmarking study. *Journal of Emotional and Behavioral Disorders, 17,* 106–117.

Sideridis, G. D., Antoniou, F., & Padeliadu, S. (2008). Teacher biases in the identification of learning disabilities: An application of the logistic multilevel model. *Learning Disability Quarterly, 31,* 199–209.

Sitlington, P. L., & Frank, A. R. (1985). Are adolescents with learning disabilities successfully crossing the bridge into adult life? *Learning Disabilities Quarterly, 13,* 97–111.

Skarbrevik, K. (2002). Gender differences among students found eligible for special education, *European Journal of Special Needs Education, 17,* 97–107.

Skiba, R., Simmons, A., Ritter, S., Rausch, M. K., Feggins, L., Gallini, S., ... Mukherjee, A. (2004). *Moving towards equity: Addressing disproportionality in special education in Indiana.* Bloomington, IN: Center for Evaluation and Policy.

Sommers, C. H. (2000). *The war against boys.* New York: Simon & Schuster.

Stephenson, M., & Burge, P. (1997). Eliciting women's voices: Vocational choice and educational climate for women in nontraditional occupational programs. *Journal of Vocational Education Research, 22,* 153–171.

Stipek, D., & Miles, S. (2008). Effects of aggression on achievement: Does conflict with the teacher make it worse? *Child Development, 79,* 1721–1735.

Strand, S., & Lindsay, G. (2009). Evidence of ethnic disproportionality in special education in an English population. *Journal of Special Education, 43,* 174–190.

Sullivan, J. R., Riccio, C. A., & Reynolds, C. R. (2008). Variations in students' school- and teacher-related attitudes across gender, ethnicity, and age. *Journal of Instructional Psychology, 35,* 296–305.

Trainor, A. A., Lindstrom, L., Simon-Burroughs, M., Martin, J. E., & Sorrells, A. M. (2008). From marginalized to maximized opportunities for diverse youths with disabilities. *Career Development for Exceptional Individuals, 31,* 56–64.

Tschantz, J., & Markowitz, J. (2003). *Gender and special education: Current state data collection.* Arlington, VA: National Association of State Directors of Special Education.

Tiet, Q. Q., Wasserman, G. A., Loeber, R., McReynolds, L. S., & Miller, L. S. (2001). Developmental and sex differences in types of conduct problems. *Journal of Child and Family Studies, 10,* 181–197.

United Nations. (2003). *Focus on ability, celebrate diversity: Highlights of the Asian and Pacific decade of disabled persons: 1993–2002.* (Social Policy Paper No. 13). Bangkok, Thailand: United Nations Population and Social Integration Section, Emerging Social Issues Division.

U.S. Department of Education. (1998). *Twentieth annual report to Congress.* Washington, DC: Author.

U.S. Department of Labor. (2004). *Women in the labor force: A data-book* (Report 973). Washington, DC: Author.

Valdes, K., Williamson, B., & Wagner, M. (1990). *The national longitudinal transition study of special education students: Statistical almanac* (Vol. 1). Menlo Park, CA: SRI International.

van der Werf, G., Opdenakker, M., & Kuyper, H. (2008). Testing a dynamic model of student and school effectiveness with a multivariate multilevel latent growth curve approach. *School Effectiveness and School Improvement, 19,* 447–462.

Verona, E., Sadeh, N., Case, S. M., Reed, A., & Bhattacharjee, A. (2008). Self-reported use of different forms of aggression in late adolescence and emerging adulthood. *Assessment, 15,* 493–510.

Vogel, S. (1990). Gender differences in intelligence, language, visual-motor abilities, and academic achievement in students with learning disabilities: a review of the literature, *Journal of Learning Disabilities, 23,* 44–52.

Wagner, M. (1992). *Being female – A secondary disability? Gender differences in the transition experience of young people with disabilities.* Menlo Park, CA: SRI International.

Wagner, M. (1993). *The secondary school programs of students with disabilities.* Menlo Park, CA: SRI International.

Wagner, M., Cameto, R., & Newman, L. (2003). *Youth with disabilities: A changing population. A report of findings from the National Longitudinal Transition Study (NLTS) and the National Longitudinal Transition Study-2 (NLTS2).* Menlo Park, CA: SRI International.

Wagner, M., Newman, L., Cameto, R., and Levine, P. (2006). *The academic achievement and functional performance of youth with disabilities. A report from the National Longitudinal Transition Study-2* (NCSER 2006-3000). Menlo Park, CA: SRI International.

Wahl, E. (2001). Can she really do science? Gender disparities in math and science education. In H. Rousso & M. L. Wehmeyer (Eds.), *Double jeopardy: Addressing gender equity in special education* (pp. 133–153). Albany: State University of New York.

Wallace, J. M., Goodkind, S., Wallace, C. M., & Bachman, J. G. (2008). Racial, ethnic, and gender differences in school discipline among U.S. high school students: 1991–2005. *The Negro Educational Review, 59,* 47–62.

Wehmeyer, M. I., & Schwartz, M. (2001). Research on gender bias in special education services. In H. Rousso & M. L. Wehmeyer (Eds.), *Double jeopardy: Addressing gender equity in special education* (pp. 271–287). Albany: State University of New York.

Weitzman, L., & Rizzo, D. (1974). *Biased textbooks.* Washington, DC: National Foundation for the Improvement of Education.

Wheldall, K., & Limbrick, L. (2003) *Final report: Boys' education Lighthouse Schools programme.* Sydney, Australia: Macquarie University Special Education Centre.

Wine, J. S., Hayward, B. J., & Wagner, M. (1993). *Vocational rehabilitation services and outcomes of transitional youth* (Final Report). Research Triangle Park, North Carolina: Research Triangle Institute.

Womenwatch. (1996). *Information and resources on gender equality and empowerment of women.* Retrieved from http://www.un.org/womenwatch/enable/1996

Younger, M., Warrington, M., & Williams, J. (1999). The gender gap and classroom interactions: reality and rhetoric? *British Journal of Sociology of Education, 20,* 325–341.

57

International Differences in Provision for Exceptional Learners

Dimitris Anastasiou
University of Western Macedonia, Greece

Clayton Keller
Qatar University

Like the attempt to provide education to exceptional learners in countries both rich and poor throughout the world, this chapter is fraught with many challenges. Whereas the preceding 56 chapters of this volume have addressed myriad aspects of special education predominantly in the United States, we have about 40 manuscript pages to cover the rest of the world, a charge usually addressed by whole books describing or comparing practices across several countries. Insufficient resources for the task—possibly the one characteristic of educational provision for students with disabilities that is universal across the globe—is not our only challenge, however.

Another is the quantity, variability, quality, and stability of the world of information which we must summarize. How the world provides education to exceptional learners varies enormously in terms of, for instance, disabilities served, identification and eligibility criteria, types of placements, staff, instructional arrangements, and funding. International comparability is hampered by differences in concepts and the use of terms as well as by the variety of categories of exceptional students receiving special education. Reporting international differences must take into account many realities and peculiarities, striking a difficult balance between simplicity and complexity. The quality of the data reported by countries, even if included in refereed publications, is difficult to judge definitively. And, whereas there has been a stability of sorts to the special education system in the United States since enactment of the Education for All Handicapped Children Act in 1975, the situation elsewhere is often different. Policies and practices sometimes turn on a dime or Euro, producing significant transformations based on changes in government, the publishing of a report, or the influence of an international organization, as has been the case with the United Nations Educational, Scientific and Cultural Organization (UNESCO).

Despite the decades that special education has been in existence as an educational provision in numerous countries and has been a profession with an ever-increasing knowledge base, the situation is still exceedingly dire for individuals with disabilities in some parts of the world. Given that there is no universally agreed upon definition of disability and difficulties abound in gathering standardized data, the following statistics may be more illustrative than definitive:

- The World Health Organization (WHO) estimates that about 10% of any given population is disabled, which would fit with UNESCO figures of 650 million people with disabilities (UNESCO, 2006, 2009).
- Some 100–150 million disabled people are children, and 80% of them live in developing countries (Eleweke & Rodda, 2002; UNESCO, 2009).
- Children with disabilities comprise one third of the 75 million children of primary school age who are not enrolled in school (UNESCO, 2006; United Nations, 2009).

An analysis of the major approaches of how countries provide education to exceptional learners within the context of their national educational systems may serve a purpose. It is not to show leaders and educators in countries that are not providing as many services as others what can be done. Rather, it is to highlight the needs for full educational provision for students with disabilities that still exist, as well as some of the barriers and issues to that challenge, in the hope that somehow changes to this situation can be brought about.

Key Factors in Special Education Provision

We begin by briefly considering two factors that shape both how education is provided to exceptional learners and how such provision is described. One is rather conceptual, and involves the terms that are used to describe individuals who are in need of the kinds of educational provision described in this handbook. Do they have "exceptionalities," "disabilities," "special educational needs," or something else? Besides differences in such general terms, there is also variety in the officially recognized specific disabilities across, and sometimes within, countries. The other factor is political and relates to the role of intergovernmental organizations like UNESCO, the Organization for Economic Cooperation and Development (OECD), and the World Bank. The promotion of inclusion by such organizations as the best, or only, service delivery approach, has had sweeping effects on what countries do, or at least say they do.

Language of Exceptionality

Countries use different terms and constructs to define exceptional learners, in general and in referring to specific kinds of difficulties. In many countries, identification to at least some degree is a legal prerequisite for special education provision. When exceptionalities are not precisely defined, exceptional learners cannot be properly or consistently identified, and thus may not receive the services they need or may receive them when they are not needed. The use of different terms and definitions also hampers both the precision with which cross-national comparisons can be made.

In the United States, the term *exceptionality* is viewed as an umbrella term that encompasses disabilities and giftedness. Exceptional learners deviate significantly from one or more norms of physical or mental ability, either well above average (gifted), well below average (disabled), or with dual exceptionalities in both directions (e.g., they are gifted and have a learning disability) (Hallahan, Kauffman, & Pullen, 2009; Kauffman & Hallahan, 2005).

Special (educational) needs (SEN) is widely considered as an alternative term to disability. The concept is in widespread use throughout Europe and in other countries worldwide. However, it has different meanings in different countries (Evans, 2004). In England, the term *SEN* was officially coined by the Warnock Report, referring "to the gap between a child's level of behavior or achievement and what is required of him" (Wedell, 2003, p. 107). The SEN concept extends beyond children with disabilities, covering a wider range of learning problems with various causes (OECD, 2007). Thus, in many countries, SEN also includes students from vulnerable backgrounds such as nomads and other transients (i.e., pastoralists, hunters, and fishers), from socially disadvantaged groups (i.e., castes in India and Nepal), working children, street children, orphan children, child refugees, traveling children, children affected by HIV/AIDS, and culturally diverse students (Evans, 2004; OECD, 2007). In some other countries (e.g., Mexico, Turkey, and Spain), SEN also includes gifted and talented students (OECD, 2007).

Disagreements still occur in some countries over which general term should be used—e.g., disabilities versus special educational needs—as each conveys implications about matters like where the locus of school difficulties lies and how the problems should be addressed. Classification systems and a range of special education placements (in inclusive and pull-out settings) might be viewed as characteristics of a disability-based system. A downgrading of the importance of labeling and identification, as well as an emphasis on inclusion, may follow from a system based on the SEN concept.

The Influence of Intergovernmental Organizations

In the last two decades intergovernmental organizations (IGOs) like the World Bank (e.g., Peters, 2004), the Organization for Economic Cooperation and Development (e.g., OECD, 1999), and the UNESCO (1994, 2003, 2005) have acted to promote not only information exchange but also specific views and educational policies around the globe. As so often happens in other economic and educational spheres in an era of globalization, these "key globalizing agencies" are playing important roles in formulating and implementing national and local educational projects in general and in the education of exceptional learners in particular.

To illustrate the importance of IGOs, the *Salamanca Statement and Framework for Action on Special Needs Education*, adopted by UNESCO's World Conference in 1994, called on all governments to give the highest policy priority to inclusion when providing education to all students, including exceptional learners (UNESCO, 1994). Similarly, the *Dakar Framework for Action on Education for All* from 2000 stated:

> A key challenge is to ensure that the broad vision of Education for All as an inclusive concept is reflected in national government and funding agency policies. Using both formal and non-formal approaches, it must take account of the needs of the poor and the most disadvantaged, including working children, remote rural dwellers and nomads, and ethnic and linguistic minorities, children, young people and adults affected by conflict, HIV/AIDS, hunger and poor health; and those with special learning needs. (UNESCO, 2000, p. 14)

The breadth and comprehensiveness of *Education for All* (EFA) makes it a common vision. We believe it is difficult to deny the opportunity of at least a free and appropriate primary education for all children. And, in many developing countries, the legal, institutional, and actual access of children to schools, regardless of their ethnicity, race, gender, religion, geographical area, abilities, or disabilities is a first step.

UNESCO, OECD, and the World Bank, though, through their numerous, influential policy documents, call for national governments to limit special education services in pull-out settings and promote only inclusive education for exceptional learners (e.g., OECD, 1999; UNESCO, 2000, 2005, 2006; World Bank, 2004). Quite often their recommended inclusion policies are promoted as a less expensive way to educate children with disabilities versus pull-out forms of special education. For example, OECD (1999) claimed that "full inclusion remains only a dim reality in many countries despite its demonstrated potential for assisting *all* [italics in origin] students and growing evidence of its economic benefits" (p. 46). Peters (2004), in a document issued by the World Bank, was even clearer: "Compared to segregated programs, IE (inclusive education) is cost-effective" (p. 47).

Such a call for how educational services should be provided for exceptional learners occurs regardless of factors such as a country's economic situation, the developmental status of its educational system, the cultural traditions and barriers, or an adequate research base to support only inclusion. Little to no consideration is given to inclusive settings as a part of a special education system or continuum of placements and services for exceptional learners.

A Typological Approach to International Differences

We now describe and summarize how the world beyond the United States provides education to students with exceptionalities, taking a typological rather than a geographical approach. Given the length of the chapter and the often quickly changing nature of education systems, a typological approach provides greater opportunities for analysis, synthesis, and depth as types are more enduring than the particular arrangements in specific countries.

Our typology for countries depends upon placement on three axes: (a) the extent to which the country provides education to all of its potential students, considering the national educational system as a whole; (b) the system of special education provision for exceptional learners, focusing on the extent to which such services are provided; and (c) the extent to which inclusive settings are emphasized within special education provision. The overall aim of our typology is to provide a unified framework for the description of educational provision for exceptional learners. In this way we can code a wide range of information about special educational provision in different countries in order to have a basis for further analysis.

Classification of Educational Systems

On an annual basis during the last decade, the UNESCO Institute for Statistics (UIS) and the EFA project have produced reports using comparable educational statistics for most countries of the world. These data provide a means to roughly sort national educational systems for the first part of our typology, using six quantitative indicators provided by the UNESCO – UIS and the EFA Global Monitoring Reports of 2008 and 2009 (for the years 2006 and 2007, respectively). A seventh variable for the economic background of educational systems is based on the indicator of Gross National Income (GNI) per capita provided by the World Bank (2009).

For the first six indicators we defined three categories—(a) *limited,* (b) *developing,* and (c) *developed*—and set specific data thresholds; the seventh followed the thresholds of the World Bank (2009) and its classification of (a) low, (b) middle, and (c) high economies. Using the set of these seven variables as a whole, we grouped countries' educational systems into three categories: (a) *limited,* (b) *developing,* and (c) *developed.* The use of these terms is for convenience, and is not meant to suggest inferiority or superiority relative to other countries on our part. Also, the use of these categories does not imply a homogeneity within that group, as educational systems vary enormously in many other features. Such variability is especially true in the developing category.

Analytically, the seven variables are the following; the specific classifying criteria for each indicator appear in Table 57.1.

TABLE 57.1
Categories and Criteria for Classifying Countries' National Educational Systems

Criteria	Categories of Educational Systems		
	Limited	**Developing**	**Developed**
1. NER in Elementary Education	≤ 75%	76–94%	95-100%
2. NER in Secondary Education	≤ 65%	66–84%	85-100%
3. Survival Rate to Last Elementary Grade	≤ 75%	76–94%	≥ 95%
4. School Life Expectancy (Elementary to Tertiary)	≤ 10 years education	11–14 years education	≥ 15 years education
5. Pupil/Teacher Ratio	≥ 36	21–35	≤ 20
6. Adult Literacy Rate	≤ 75%	76–94%	≥ 95%
		Categories of Economies	
7. Gross National Income per capita	≤ $975	$976–11,905	≥ $11,906
	(low income)	(middle income)	(high income)
		$976–3,855	
		(lower middle income)	
		$3,856–11,905	
		(upper middle income)	

1. *Net enrolment rate (NER) in elementary education.* The NER indicates the enrolment of the official age group for a given level of education expressed as a percentage of the corresponding population in a given school year. The NER in elementary education shows the degree of coverage for the official school-age population at the elementary level.
2. *Net enrolment rate (NER) in secondary education.* The NER in *secondary* education shows the holding capacity of an educational system in this level.
3. *Survival rate to last primary grade.* Survival rate is the percentage of a cohort of students enrolled in the first grade of primary education who are expected to reach a given grade (usually Grade 4, 5, or 6), regardless of repetition. This measures primary education completion.
4. *School life expectancy (primary to tertiary).* This key variable measures the number of years of formal schooling from primary to tertiary education that a child of a certain age can expect to receive. It indicates the acceptability and dynamics of an educational system.
5. *Pupil/teacher ratio.* The average number of students per teacher at a specific level of education is called the pupil/teacher ratio. From a global perspective, this indicator reflects to some degree the quality of teaching.
6. *Adult literacy rate.* This is the percentage of adult literate persons, aged 15 years and above, in the corresponding population. The indicator reflects the literate environment of formal education and, to a degree, shows the potential for literacy support within families.
7. *Gross National Income (GNI) per capita.* The World Bank (2009) uses this metric as the fundamental criterion for classifying economies. According to the Gross National Income (GNI) (Atlas Method) in U.S. dollars, every economy is classified as low, middle (subdivided into lower middle and upper middle), or high income. We added an economic indicator in our classification because educational resources (e.g., buildings, books, materials, devices, teachers' availability and training, and transportation) are heavily dependent upon a country's economy, even if there is not always a strong relationship between the quality of the educational system and economic level at a regional level (e.g., Europe). In many countries around the world (i.e., Sub-Saharan Africa and Southwest Asia), financial constraints do significantly inhibit the expansion and development of educational systems.

In applying this first part of our typology, some countries might fit within two categories—e.g., Kenya could be either developing (according to NER, duration of compulsory education, survival rate to last primary grade, and school life expectancy) or limited (according to pupil/teacher ratio and low GNP)—some nations meet most but not all of the criteria for a category—e.g., the United States does not meet the upper limits of NER in elementary education, though it would be considered a developed educational system. To address such situations, we developed decision rules so that a developed educational system needs to meet at least six out of the seven upper limits of our criteria and, for an educational system to be classified as limited, it needed to meet four out of the seven lower limits of our criteria. If data on one or more criteria were not available, our classification occurred based on what had been reported.

Classification of Education Provision for Exceptional Learners

We classified the provision of services to exceptional learners on two basic axes.

The first represents the percentage of students from the school-age population receiving special education services, suggesting the importance of a special education subsystem, and a continuum of services, within the context of the entire educational system. In this way special education systems were classified into three categories:

1. *Limited* with a lower degree of coverage for the school-age population of < 1%,
2. *Moderate* with a slightly increased degree of coverage (1– < 4%), and
3. *Extensive* with a higher degree of coverage for the school-age population (> = 4%).

The specific cut-offs for this classification were based on data provided by OECD (2007), showing the median number of students receiving additional resources within the period of compulsory education as a percentage of all students. In a cross-national comparison of 15 OECD countries (Turkey, Mexico, Chile, Japan, Germany, Hungary, the Netherlands, Belgium-Flemish community, Belgium-French community, Spain, England, Slovakia, Czech Republic, Finland, and the United States), the percentage of students in category A (including low incidence disabilities) was 2.63%, with an inter-quartile range of 1.26% to 3.62%. The median percentage of category B students—specific difficulties in learning and emotional or behavioral disorders—was 3.51%, with an inter-quartile range from 1.58% to 6.33% (OECD, 2007).

The second axis in this part of the system measures the use of inclusive settings to provide special education services. Inclusion is difficult to operationalize, as its meaning differs across people and contexts (Matsuura, 2008). For the purposes of this chapter, we defined inclusion as the percentage of students with exceptionalities in the general population who are receiving services in inclusive settings, designating two levels: (a) *low level of inclusive education* (< 3.5% receive services in inclusive settings), and (b) *high level of inclusive education* (> + 3.5% receive services in inclusive settings).

One practical difficulty in this part of our classification system concerns the use of models such as the resource room or part-time special education of low intensity. For instance, in the United States, students in resource rooms receive special education services outside the general education classroom for at least 21% but no more than the 60% of the school day (U. S. Department of Education, 2009). In Greece, resource rooms provide "looser" special education services of about 10% to 20% of the total teaching time per week (Anastasiou & Polychronopoulou, 2009). And in Finland, part-time special education is implemented, on an average, for two to four hours per week (Eurybase - Finland, 2007/08; Finnish National Board of Education, 2008). The substantial variation of this model across countries creates problems in distinguishing between pull-out and inclusive settings (e.g., in studies of agencies like CERI of OECD, 1995, 1999, 2000, and EADSNE, 2003, 2009). Where is the border between inclusive services and other special education units attached to general classrooms? Are these units pull-out or inclusive settings? The problem here is not in the continuum of special education programs, but in the classification. We can have larger or smaller percentages of students served in inclusive settings simply by setting different criteria for how we classify such services.

The Two Classification Systems Combined

Nesting possible anchoring points along these three axes produces six meaningful types of educational provision for exceptional learners (see Table 57.2.) We describe four of the six possible types within our system, sampling broadly geographically and balancing the presence of developed and developing countries. To provide more depth, we consider a case example for each type, focusing on: (a) Limited special education (and low inclusion) in the context of a limited education system (e.g., Nigeria), (b) Limited special education (and low inclusion) in a developing education system (e.g., China), (c) Moderate special education coverage (and low inclusion) in a developed education system (e.g., Italy), and, (d) Extensive special education service (and high inclusion) in a developed education system (e.g., Finland). In these cases the focus is on how countries provide education to students with exceptional needs, addressing, for instance, their presence or absence in public education systems, whether special education is provided, and ways it is provided.

Our typology was guided by two assumptions. First, the national education system places an upper limit on special education provision due to the infrastructure it provides. Second, the extent of special education provision, by definition, places an upper limit on the use of inclusive settings as we define this variable here (i.e., the percentage of students with exceptional needs *in the general population* that is served via inclusion, versus the percentage of students *in special education only* that receives such services, an approach that is commonly used to measure inclusion (e.g., the United States)). This approach thus classifies Italy, which implements a full inclusive policy, as *low* on inclusion as the extent of its special education coverage, which is low, is virtually identical with the extent of its use of inclusive placements.

We realize the limitations of this approach. We lack, for instance, information on the quality of services provided and on outcomes for learners. Only general locations along the continua can be considered. Thus, we use our typology as a rough heuristic for making sense of the immense variety of how the world provides education to exceptional learners.

Limited Special Education in a Limited Education System

Our first type describes national educational systems that are overall quite limited and that subsequently have very rudimentary special education provision. In such situations, much if not all of the education provided to students with special needs occurs in the general education system, if any education is provided. Even though these countries are trying to expand and improve their educational systems, they face innumerable challenges: severe financial constraints, indebted economies, poverty, cultural barriers, war, and the HIV/AIDS pandemic (Tomaševski, 2006). In addition, poverty-related deprivation and malnutrition affect disability prevalence rates as well as the school attendance of teachers and students (Abang, 1994; World Bank, 2001). Most of the countries in Sub-Saharan Africa (e.g., Benin, Burkina Faso, Burundi, Cameroon, Chad, Eritrea, Ethiopia, Gambia, Ghana, Guinea, Lesotho, Liberia, Madagascar, Malawi, Mali, Mozambique, Niger, Nigeria, Senegal, Sierra Leone, Togo, Uganda, and Zambia), many countries in Southwest Asia (e.g., Afghanistan, Bangladesh, India, Nepal, and Pakistan), and some Arab states (e.g., Mauritania, Sudan, and Yemen) can be grouped in this category.

There are legal bases for the right to an education for exceptional learners in many of these countries, at least in principle. Quite a number have adopted several of the international declarations on equal access to education,

TABLE 57.2
Classification of Educational Systems by National Education, Special Education Coverage, and Extent of Inclusion

National Education System	Special Education Provision		
	Limited	Moderate	Extensive
Limited	Low Inclusion: Nigeria	NF	NF
Developing	Low Inclusion: China	Low Inclusion: Brazil	NF (2 marginal cases)
Developed	NF	Low Inclusion: Italy	Low Inclusion: Germany
		High Inclusion: NF	High Inclusion: Finland

NF = Not Found
Marginal cases: Latvia, Lithuania

equality of educational opportunity, and quality education for all children, including those with disabilities proclaimed by the Convention on the Rights of the Child (1989), the World Declaration on Education for All in Jomtien, Thailand (1990), the Standard Rules on the Equalization of Opportunities for Persons with Disability (1993), the UNESCO Salamanca Statement for Framework for Action (1994), the Framework from the World Education Forum in Dakar (2000), and the UN Convention on the Rights of Persons with Disabilities (2006) (Ajuwon, 2008; Tomaševski, 2006). In addition, constitutional or legal guarantees mandate education to be compulsory through at least the primary level.

Just a few years ago, however, in 25 out of 46 countries of Sub-Saharan Africa there were no legal guarantees to free education (Tomaševski, 2006). Even in countries where there are legal guarantees of free education, some primary school fees continued to be charged. As of 2006, in Sub-Saharan Africa primary education was only really free in three countries: Mauritius, Sao Tomé and Principe, and Seychelles (Tomaševski, 2006).

Often the legal guarantees to education must contend with a country's fiscal policies, and governments retreat from their declared responsibility to provide a free education. One of the main causes for underfunding education is the "structural adjustments programs" of their economies. Such programs usually require reductions of public spending in vital social programs as a condition for lending and financial aid by the World Bank and International Monetary Fund (Tomaševski, 2006). Privatization and decentralization in such countries can also undermine the way towards achieving universal primary education (Tomaševski, 2006).

Logically, the goal of universal primary education, a target not met by 2000 so now sought by 2015, cannot be obtained without including children with disabilities. Neither the UIS nor the annual EFA Reports of UNESCO have included goals, however, expressed as separate indicators, for monitoring the inclusion of children with disabilities in educational systems. This lack of data neither allows progress towards the provision of education for exceptional learners to be evaluated nor provides an opportunity for public accountability. On a policy level, it suggests that a commitment to eliminating the barriers impeding education for children with disabilities is wanting (Mutepfa, Mpofu, & Chataika, 2007).

Within the context of limited educational systems, educational provision for exceptional learners tends to exist on a small scale. Despite the rhetoric of international organizations and national governments about inclusive education, at least 25 million children with disabilities, the vast majority of whom are in Sub-Saharan Africa and South Asia countries (UIS, 2005), experience total exclusion from education. Fiscal difficulties are not the only reason. Stereotypes, prejudices, and cultural barriers towards children with disabilities can inhibit simple access to education. Disabled children are often considered ineligible for schooling (Ademokoya, 2008). Children with intellectual disabilities and emotional disabilities are probably the most neglected disabled groups in developing countries (UNESCO, 2004). Less than 1% of children with severe disabilities go to school, and children in rural areas are seriously isolated (UNICEF, 1999). Because of inadequate training, teachers cannot often recognize children with visual and hearing impairments, mistaking the conditions as intellectual disabilities (Ademoyoka, 2008).

The interplay of various factors can be seen in the situation of Nigeria, an example of limited special education in a limited education system.

Case Study: Nigeria

Nigeria, the most populous country in Africa with 140 million people coming from more than 250 ethnic and language groups, has a lower middle income economy (GNI = $1,160) that is marginally higher than low income economies according to the classification of the World Bank (2009). Since its independence in 1960, it has made slow progress in combating poverty—about 70% of its population lives below the poverty line—due to the Biafran civil war in the late 1960s, long periods of political instability marked by many governments, the majority of which were under military rule (Obiakor, 1998), governmental corruption, violations of human rights, and sporadic ethnic and religious tensions.

As of 2005, the school-age population was 43.8 million (UIS, 20009). Only 64% of the country's children attended primary school and just 27% secondary school, meaning about 10 million Nigerian children are out of school (Nigeria Federal Ministry of Education-MoE, 2008). Not surprisingly, then, about 23 million adults over the age of 15 are illiterate (Federal MoE, 2008).This has occurred despite the facts that universal access to education has been a governmental promise since 1976, when Nigeria's Universal Primary Education plan was proclaimed, and that the country is a signatory of Education for All (Adepoju & Fabiyi, 2007).

Access to the Nigerian educational system for children with disabilities is dramatically lower than it is for students in general. The official estimates of the Federal Ministry of Education (2008) put the number of children with various types of disabilities at 3.25 million or 7% of the school-age population. The official figures of the Federal Ministry (2008) estimate that only 90,000 disabled children (2.76% of the disabled school-age population) attend primary school and that 65,000 (1.85% of disabled school-age population) attend secondary school. In sum, only 155,000 disabled children out of over 23 million children are in school, representing 0.35% of the total school-age population. In short, children with disabilities are 70 times less likely to attend school than their non-disabled peers.

The Federal Ministry of Education recognizes "visually impaired, hearing impaired, physically and health impaired, mentally retarded, emotionally disturbed, speech impaired, learning disabled and multiple handicapped" as categories of disabilities; the education of both gifted children and disadvantaged children also falls under special education provision (2008, p. 14). Abang (1994) noted that, not only are these types of disabilities poorly defined, numerous children with disabilities are not identified, especially in rural areas, because of a lack of diagnostic services. Illness, malnutrition, diseases, and low vaccination rates make sensory impairments, physical impairments, and intellectual disabilities especially prominent. For many years, the country's infrastructure for special education has been insufficient, with the system restricted to special schools for students with the most severe disabilities, such as children who were blind or deaf, those with physical disabilities or intellectual disabilities, and hospitalized children (Abang, 1994).

Inadequacies in multiple aspects of the educational system and fiscal constraints have directly impacted the conditions on teaching and the exclusion of children with disabilities from any form of education, special or not. With a pupil/teacher ratio of 40:1, the average Nigerian classroom is overcrowded (UIS, 2009). Conditions within classrooms are challenging. Adepoju and Fabiyi (2007) reported data from the primary education sector indicating that 12% of primary school pupils sat on the floor, 38% of the classrooms had no ceilings, 87% of the classrooms were overcrowded, and 77% of the students lacked textbooks. In addition, 73% of the teachers in the state of Lagos stated they did not have time for every child, and 82% of parents said they were largely involved in funding the school of their children. A household survey indicated that 99% of public primary school students paid for books and supplies, 88% bought uniforms and clothing for school use, 70% paid for parent-teacher association contributions, and 14% paid tuition fees (World Bank & UNICEF, 2009). Despite a proclaimed commitment to and legal guarantee of free education, public primary schools continue to charge different kinds of fees with devastating consequences (Tomaševski, 2006).

Cultural barriers also seem to inhibit both access to and the appropriateness of special education for exceptional children. Traditionally, the education of individuals with intellectual disabilities was not seen as necessary (Abosi & Koay, 2008; Obiakor, 1998). Fears and myths about the causes of disabilities inhibit interactions between people with and without disabilities (Ajuwon, 2008). Abang (1994) observed that it is common to see non-disabled students or school staff members refusing to interact with students with disabilities for fear that they will get the condition. Parents are often very reluctant to enroll their children with disabilities in school because they have a feeling of shame or they consider it as a waste of their limited resources (Abosi & Koay, 2008; Ademokoya, 2008). Ademokoya reported that in a secondary school, some parents threatened to withdraw their children from school when the state government planned to integrate hearing and non-hearing students in the same school.

The Federal Ministry of Education (2008, 2009), though, seems to be investing more recently both in special schools and in the access of children with special needs to the educational system. From 2005 to 2007, a respectable amount of money was spent on the infrastructure of and instructional materials for special schools (Federal MoE, 2008). Also, the Federal Ministry (2009) has announced a pilot project on "inclusive education" in different states of the country. According to the plan, they will operate mixed ability classes in regular schools, where children with special needs will receive education alongside their peers.

Such efforts are good but, in this climate, concerns remain. Relative to the newly revised National Policy on Education that emphasizes inclusive education (2008), Ajuwon stressed that:

> ...some parents fear that their children will be teased or that...the needs of their children with disabilities cannot be met adequately in a general education classroom. Further, some professionals question whether the general education setting truly can be the least restrictive environment for some pupils, especially when general education teachers also must meet the needs of thirty or even more other students in the class, and the availability of a special educator is limited or nonexistent. (2008, p. 15)

A few years earlier, Garuba (2003) expressed similar fears:

> Special needs education in Nigeria is still grappling with problems of policy implementation, an environment that is not conducive for practice and a lackadaisical attitude of the people and government. Implementing inclusion in such an environment may be unrealistic and counterproductive.... With a nation still given to unscientific modes of explaining natural phenomena and human conditions, where illiteracy still exists in significant proportion, adoption of the inclusive school system may end up not in the best interests of the concerned individuals. (p. 198)

Limited Special Education in a Developing Education System

According to our criteria for classifying national and special educational systems, many Arab states (e.g., Egypt, Jordan, Kuwait, Saudi Arabia, Tunisia, and United Arab Emirates), most countries in Central Asia (e.g., Georgia, Kazakhstan, Kyrgyzstan, and Uzbekistan), many East Asian and Pacific countries (e.g., China, Indonesia, Malaysia, Philippines, Thailand, and Vietnam), a few South West Asian countries (e.g., Iran and Sri Lanka), many Latin America and Caribbean countries (e.g., Bolivia, Dominican Republic, Ecuador, Guatemala, Guyana, Jamaica, Mexico, Nicaragua, Peru, and Trinidad and Tobago), some Sub-Saharan African countries (e.g., Mauritius, Namibia, South Africa, and Swaziland), and a few Balkan countries (e.g., Romania) can be grouped into the limited special education in a developing education system type.

There is great variability among the countries with developing educational systems in terms of the numbers of students receiving services from their limited special education systems. In some, less than five students per thousand receive special education services. For example, only 0.12% of the total school-age population receives special education in Indonesia (Indonesia, MoE, 2008; UNESCO-IBE, 2007). In other countries, the proportion of special education students is higher, like the Islamic Republic of Iran where students with hearing and visual impairments, intellectual disabilities, behavioral disorders, physical disabilities, learning disabilities, and multiple disabilities, served by special education, represent 0.65% of the school population (I. R. of Iran, MoE, 2008).

Most often, special provisions are available for students who are blind or visually impaired, are deaf or hard of hearing, or have intellectual disabilities. Fewer countries provide services for students with physical disabilities. A still smaller number mention special education for students with emotional and/or behavioral disorders, learning disabilities, or language impairments. In contrast, in many developing educational systems, special provisions are available for gifted and/or talented learners, including countries with large populations such as China, Indonesia, Thailand, Saudi Arabia (Clark, 2006), and Iran (UNESCO – IBE, 2007).

This may be a result of a pattern of uneven development in special education provision that can follow the unbalanced development of compulsory education occurring in these countries. Large gaps exist in the quantity and quality of available special education services between richer and poorer regions and rural and urban areas. For example, students with disabilities in rural and remote areas may not have many opportunities to go to school, as can be seen in countries such as Jamaica, Guyana (Porter, 2001), and China (P. R. China, MoE, 2008).

Often, special education in these countries falls short of meeting the needs of students with disabilities, both in terms of quantity and quality. As Pedro and Conrad (2006) suggest, some developing countries may not have the necessary human and material resources; others may not perceive the importance of the issue. For instance, in some cases (e.g. Trinidad and Tobago), governments lament that the cost of training special education teachers is too high. As a result, disabled students are more likely than their non-disabled peers to have no access to education, drop-out, or receive an education in either general or special education that is not appropriate to their needs.

To illustrate the changing nature of special education systems in this type, we focus on China, a country with a lower middle economy (GNI = $2,770).

Case Study: China

The People's Republic of China, with a population of more than 1.3 billion, accounts for one-fifth of the world's population. A national survey in 2006 indicated that nearly 84 million people, or 6.34% of its population, had disabilities. Twenty-nine percent of these were physical disabilities, 24% hearing impairments, 16% multiple disabilities, 15% visual disabilities, 7.5% mental disabilities, 7% intellectual disabilities, and 1.5% language disabilities (Xu, 2008).

As of 2007, there were nearly 207 million students in elementary and secondary schools (P. R. China, MoE, 2008). A previous national survey from 1987 that disaggregated the data by age ranges—an analysis that more recent surveys have not included—found that one-sixth of the total disabled population was school-age (Deng & Guo, 2007; Xu, 2008). Using this percentage and considering the changing patterns of demographic trends, a conservative estimate might be that at least 10 million children ages 4 to 17 also have these disabilities.

In today's China, compulsory education (6–14 years) is almost universal. The passage of the Compulsory Education Law in 1986 was the first official call for the integration of children with disabilities into the educational system. The revised 2006 Law on Compulsory Education and the revised 2008 Law on the Protection of the Disabled also gave priority to compulsory education for "blind, deaf and retarded" children (P. R. China, MoE, 2008, pp. 14, 19).

Although the surveys referenced above recognized seven categories of disabilities, special education in China, which is concentrated at the elementary level (grades 1–6) (P. R. China, MoE, 2008; Xu, 2008), is provided primarily to students with visual impairments, hearing impairments, or intellectual disabilities (Deng & Guo, 2007). As of 2007, around 413,000 students with these disabilities were served in special education, accounting for about 0.2% of the total school population or an estimated 4% of the disabled school-aged population. Despite an expansion of the educational system, it is estimated that 223,000 students with these three types of disabilities—that is, about 20% of the disabled school-age population—are actually out of school nationwide (P. R. China, MoE, 2008).

Other types of disabilities are not recognized by the educational system. Subsequently, children with such conditions are neither identified effectively nor served by the special education system (Ellsworth & Zhang, 2007; Xu, 2008). At best, they are placed in regular classrooms of 35 to 40 students without any additional teaching support (Huang & Wheeler, 2007; UIS, 2009), providing them at least with access to schooling though with questions about the appropriateness of the services received. Most children with severe and multiple disabilities are excluded from school (Deng, Poon-McBrayer, & Farnsworth, 2001) and are thus denied access to education.

Nevertheless, programs for gifted children have been developed over the last decade. There are more than 30 experimental schools including kindergartens, primary, and middle schools where gifted children are taught in special classes (Zhang & Shi, 2006). Gifted children are also allowed to skip grades (Pang & Richey, 2006a).

The two-fold role of Confucian tradition might explain the Chinese approach to special education (Deng et al., 2001; Pang & Richey, 2006b). On the one hand, the benevolent, gentle spirit of Confucianism expresses sympathy towards children with disabilities; the treatment of people with disabilities was kinder in the past in comparison to Western cultures. On the other hand, the interpretation of Confucianism by feudal rulers as respect to authority resulted in a neglect of people's education. This dual attitude has been strong, especially in rural areas. In Deng et al.'s (2001) words:

> Children with disabilities still are often isolated from community life, and even parents do not agree with the idea of educating their children with disabilities. Often these parents have not attended school themselves, so they question the expense and energy required to educate a child such as theirs. (p. 292)

In addition, the adult literacy rate in China is about 93%; in absolute figures, 1.6 million people cannot read and write (UIS, 2009). Thus, it may be that some parents think it is more useful to send their children out to sing or tell fortunes for a living, rather than sending them to school (Deng & Manset, 2000).

Within the last three decades, the structure of the Chinese special education system has undergone a remarkable transformation. Until 1979, special schools were the only available placement, and these were exclusively for the special needs of children who were deaf or blind (Yang & Wang, 1994). During the 1980s, special classes for children with intellectual disabilities began in Shanghai and Beijing and were later expanded to other cities.

From 1990 to 2000, special education in China experienced exponential development. The number of students tripled and the number of trained teachers doubled (Xu, 2008). Xu attributes this rapid expansion to the unprecedented economic growth that has been achieved since 1978 when China launched its Open Door Policy to the World. This was a period of market-oriented reforms and social transformation. In fact, during the period of the Cultural Revolution from 1966 to 1976, special education had stagnated in terms of services available and percentage of students served, a decline meaning that special education lagged far behind the developing economy (Deng et al., 2001; Yang & Wang, 1994). Thus, the contrast between the period of the Cultural Revolution and the 1990s is especially great.

Nowadays, special education class size varies from 1 to 12 students according to the needs of the children; students are grouped by ability rather than by age and are taught in whole-group classes and small groups (Ellsworth & Zhang, 2007). One-third of the served special education population is placed in special schools, while the other two-thirds are in regular classes and in special classes attached to the regular schools (Ellsworth & Zhang, 2007; P. R. China, MoE, 2008; Xu, 2008). The special education system suffers, though, from an acute shortage of special education teachers, as only 54% of the 35,000 full-time special education teachers have been professionally trained for special education (P. R. China, MoE, 2008).

The Chinese government launched several experimental programs in the early 1990s, sometimes in collaboration with UNICEF, under the name Learning in Regular Classrooms (LRC). Since 1988, the official policy has considered special schools the "backbone" of the special education system, and a large number of special classes and LRC programs as the "body" (Xu, 2008). LRC programs began as a way to educate children with disabilities in rural and remote areas where neither special schools nor special classes were available. The main goal of these initiatives was to increase universal compulsory education by increasing the school enrolment and retention of children with disabilities in impoverished areas (Pang & Richey, 2006b). LRC programs aim at promoting parents' and teachers' disability awareness and acceptance, the modification of instruction by the general education teacher, and teacher in-service training by special school teachers (Deng & Manset, 2000). Apparently, the dissemination of expertise and collaboration in learning are distinct features of such programs.

Some scholars consider LRC as the Chinese road to full inclusion. For example, Deng and Manset (2000) said:

> In addition, Learning in Regular Classrooms provides only the option of general class placement as opposed to a continuum of services. In this way, the approach more closely reflects *full inclusion* [our italics] than mainstreaming.... Despite differing views, most researchers agree that Learning in Regular Classrooms can be defined as government-supported arrangements for children with disabilities to be educated in neighborhood schools in classrooms with their peers who do not have disabilities (p. 125).

Such a view may be a rather westernized interpretation of LRC. As Pang and Richey (2006b) note about LRC or *Suiban Jiudu*:

> It is not a formally titled inclusion and children's with disabilities special needs are not addressed. No specialists or personnel are available in Suiban Jiudu. Nor educators in the Suiban Jiudu class are cognizant of basic and necessary knowledge about the children's disabilities (p. 82) ... In some Learning in Regular Classrooms schools, students with disabilities have been observed sitting alone, isolated from classroom activities, or have even remained at home despite the fact that their names are on the registration list. This unfortunately common practice has been called drifting in the regular classroom. (p. 85)

LRC programs are an attempt to addresses the scarcity of trained teachers, the limited resources, and the disparities in wealth across the regions of a vast country that China faces. Every single child with a disability who is enrolled in school brings the fundamental right of education for all closer to reality. Are these programs, though, an appropriate substitute for special education? Along these lines, recent statistics provided by the Ministry of Education (2008) do not include the attendance of disabled students in regular classes through LRC programs as part of special education provision.

Three different conclusions might be drawn about the current state of special education in China. In terms of the actual capacity of the educational system to meet the needs of exceptional learners, the present situation could be considered problematic. Viewed historically, though, from the period before 1989 when less than 6% of the school-age children with visual or hearing impairments were the only students with special needs enrolled in schools (Deng & Guo, 2007), the conclusion might be that progress has been remarkable. Between the two, it might be considered as a "newly developing special education system" (Deng & Manset, 2000, p. 124). Special education's continuing development, though, appears neither to be maintaining the momentum of the previous decade nor following the country's impressive economic development which, from 1978 to 2007, showed a 9.8% annual growth in its GDP (P. R. China, MoE, 2008).

Moderate Special Education in a Developed Education System

What distinguishes countries of this type is that they have developed national education systems and low to moderate percentages of students (between 1% and 4%) identified for special education in any type of placement (e.g., special school, special class, resource room, or inclusive setting). Using the most recent available data for European countries provided by EADSNE (2009; years of reference 2007–08 or 2006–07), we calculated the percentage of students with disabilities in the corresponding school-age population served by special education in any kind of setting. Analytically, South European countries like Greece (1.89%), Italy (2.32%), Portugal (3.62%), and Spain (2.56%), and some Western or Central European countries like Austria (3.30%), France (2.72%), Ireland (2.12%), Luxemburg (2.30%), the Netherlands (3.67%), Poland (2.89%), Slovenia (3.67%), England (2.82%), and Wales (3.48%) can be categorized into this type. (The numbers in parentheses indicate special education coverage as a percentage of the total school population.) In addition, Japan (about 2% as of 2007; Japan - Ministry of Education, Culture, Sports, Science and Technology, 2008), Republic of Korea (1.85%) (Republic of Korea - Ministry of Education, Science and Technology, 2008), and Israel (2.3% as of 2002/03; UNESCO-IBE, 2007) fit in this type.

These low to moderate proportions may have been static over time; in some cases, though, they indicate either increases or decreases in the numbers served by special education. For instance, a comparison with older data provided by the European Commission (2007, pp. 36–39), EADSNE (2003, p. 128), OECD (1995, p. 42), and OECD (2000, p. 76) indicates that the percentage of students served has increased significantly in Greece and Italy, has fallen sharply in France and Ireland, and has remained relatively unchanged over 15 years in countries like Portugal, Spain, Austria, Luxemburg, the Netherlands, England, Wales, and Sweden.

In some situations—e.g., Greece, Italy, Japan, and the Republic of Korea—special education systems may be expanding. In others—Ireland, France, the Netherlands, and Sweden—the static or declining numbers may be due to the fact that the proportion of students with disabilities educated in special schools and special classes, and thus identified as within the special education system, has decreased under the influence of inclusive policies (European Commission, 2007; OECD, 1995). For example, in the Netherlands, the implementation of a policy entitled Together to School Again (*Weer Samen Naar* School), along with changes in the funding system, led to the closing of special schools for children with learning disabilities and mild intellectual disabilities in the 1990s (Pijl & Van Den Bos, 2001). After 1996, a similar policy (the "backpack" policy) that also involved changes in funding was followed for students with sensory, physical, and intellectual disabilities and behaviour problems.

As our typology is based on quantitative indicators, it cannot capture qualitative or descriptive features or aspects of special education systems that are not easily quantified. Thus, it cannot flesh out the great variability within this type regarding matters such as how systems look, what services they provide, and how students who may have school difficulties that would qualify them for special provision in some countries but not in their own have their needs met. For example, in England an important proportion of children without the "special educational needs" statements that qualify them for special education fall into the category of "school action plus." These students are eligible to receive additional—though not teaching—support services from specialized experts (e.g., educational psychologists) external to the school or their consultation services (Department for Education and Skills, 2001). On the other hand, Greece does not provide such important interdisciplinary services related to special education for students who have not qualified for special education.

To provide one illustration of how educational provision for exceptional learners occurs in a country that only identifies a small number of students specifically for special education, we turn to Italy.

Case Study: Italy

Special education has expanded greatly in Italy since the 1960s, though not in a strictly linear fashion from decade to decade (Abbring & Meijer, 1994). In 2007–2008, the percentage of students with disabilities served in inclusive settings reached 2.32% (EADSNE, 2009; OECD, 2000).

In Italy a full inclusive education policy has been in effect for over 30 years. It began with Law No. 118 of 1971, through which students with disabilities received the right to attend general education classes in public schools. Ministerial circulars later adopted more specific policy guidelines for the re-organization of special education in the direction of full inclusion. Law No. 517 of 1977, considered to be the landmark decision in Italy's way to full inclusion, mandated that all children with disabilities should attend general schools, and that schools could not refuse the enrollment of disabled children on the basis of the severity of their disabilities (Abbring & Meijer, 1994; Begeny & Martens, 2007; OECD, 1999). Subsequent laws (e.g., 270/1982, 104/1992, 440/1997, 62/2000, and 296/2006), decrees, and circulars provided a legislative framework for inclusion practices at each educational level and in every type of school including private schools, though the percentage of students with disabilities included in private education remains lower, at 1.53%, than in public education (EADSNE, 2009).

In the "wild integration" (*integrazione selvaggia*) period of the 1970s and 1980s, special schools closed and special classes were dismantled, while the insertion of students with sensory, physical, and intellectual disabilities into general education classrooms happened with limited and irregular special teaching support; thus, in many cases students with disabilities were left alone and isolated in "inclusive" classes (Abbring & Meijer, 1994; Daunt, 1991). After the initial systemic shock and a long transitional period until 1995, Italy now represents possibly the clearest example of full inclusion on a national scale with a long history. As of 2007–2008, virtually all students (99.99%) with disabilities were taught almost entirely in inclusive general education classes. Only 693 children who were blind or deaf (0.009% of the overall school population) were educated in nine special schools (EADSNE, 2009).

At the heart of Italian inclusion is a collaborative model in which the "support teacher" has a key role. The support teacher, assigned to the classroom attended by a student with certified disabilities, assists the general educator as an equal colleague in the effort to integrate the student. Administrative support is provided to inclusive schools by reducing class size. Currently only one student with a disability can be included in a regular class. Inclusive classes are usually limited to a maximum of 20 pupils, including the student with a disability, versus the usual 25-student class maximum (Eurybase - Italy, 2007/08; OECD, 1999). Students benefit from a support teacher for 9 hours per week on average (OECD, 1999). Law No 440 of 1997 envisaged that one support teacher would correspond to 138 enrolled students (disabled and nondisabled; D'Alessio, 2007).

Implementing collaborative teaching arrangements such as Italy's use of support and regular teachers in a classroom comes with its own set of challenges that are well-documented in the literature, such as whether the support teacher alone has the responsibility for teaching the students with disabilities. Other concerns have been raised about the quality of services received by students with disabilities in Italy's inclusion model. These include: (a) an overemphasis on socialization to the neglect of learning progress at the elementary level, (b) an unwillingness to accommodate the needs of disabled students at the secondary level, (c) a lack of materials and resources, (d) the continued use of traditional teacher-centered ways of instruction, (e) problems such as absenteeism by regular teachers at in-service training on inclusion, and (f) the challenge of determining which teacher is responsible for meeting the needs of socioculturally deprived students in the classroom (Abbring & Meijer, 1994; Monasta, 2000; Panerai et al., 2009).

How effective is Italy's inclusion model? Begeny and Martens (2007) reviewed 13 survey studies on the attitudes and perceptions of teachers and/or parents towards inclusion and 25 experimental studies of inclusion published between 1983 and 2003. Overall, survey participants tended to view inclusion practices favorably. There was very little evidence, however, regarding the direct outcomes of Italy's inclusion efforts or the specific features of the practices used. Consequently, Begeny and Martens (2007) thought the experimental studies called the benefits of full inclusion into question: "The experimental studies demonstrated that educating students either fully or partly *outside* the general classroom had a positive impact on these students across the majority of dependent measures evaluated" (p. 89). They concluded:

> Overall…it seems that Italy has produced insufficient empirical evidence supporting the positive effects of inclusion in relation to important student outcomes. As a result, little systematic research exists regarding best practices that can be employed by teachers in inclusive classrooms. (p. 91)

Extensive Special Education in a Developed Education System

In the context of developed education systems, the countries of this type have extensive special education provision serving higher proportions of their general student populations than countries in the previous type. The first number in parentheses in the following list shows the percentage of the total school population identified for special education; the second number indicates the percentage of the school population served in inclusive settings, including resource rooms, using 2007–2008 or 2006–2007 data provided by EADSNE in 2009. Nordic countries like Denmark (7.00%; 3.55%), Finland (31.07%; 27.01%), Iceland (4.83%; 3.60%), and Norway (5.56%; 5.22%); Western European countries like Scotland (5.49%; 4.15%); some Central and Eastern European countries like the Czech Republic (8.60%; 4.07%), Estonia (18.99%; 14.19%), and Lithuania (11.39%; 10.17%); and smaller South European countries like Cyprus (4.26%; 3.63%) and Malta (4.54%; 3.96%) fall into this type. The United States also fits in this type: 9.20% of its students receive special education; about 7.2% all its students, ages 6–21, are pulled out of regular classrooms for less than 60% of the day, Specifically, almost 4.8% of all students of the same ages are included in regular classes (or pulled out for less than 21% of the day; U. S. Department of Education, 2009).

There seem to be three major social or political traditions that form the basis for the development of the special education systems in this type. One is the "social-democratic" model found in Nordic countries. Another is the social-welfare model of "post-communist" countries in transition. The third is the "liberal" tradition of the United States, with its model that strongly legislates, and litigates, special education. Cutting across these traditions, countries that have strong inclusion policies—such as Cyprus, Malta, and Norway—place less than 1% of their students with disabilities in separate settings. Others—e.g., the Czech Republic, Denmark, Estonia, Finland, and the United States—have more differentiated special education provisions and place more than 3% of students with disabilities in separate settings.

Case Study: Finland

Finland has consistently been one of the highest performing countries in science, mathematics, and reading on the PISA studies, the OECD's international assessment of student performance. As a result, the Finnish system has been considered as one of the best educational systems in the world, a kind of OECD/PISA wonderland (OECD, 2008). In addition, Finnish students' scores on these examinations show relatively little variability. The differences between the strongest and weakest scores of Finnish students were among the smallest in the PISA's studies, and the average score achieved by the weakest Finnish students was by far higher than that of the corresponding weakest students in any other country (OECD, 2008; Savolainen, 2009; Välijärvi, Linnakylä, Kupari, Reinikainen, & Arffman, 2002). By simultaneously raising the bar and lifting its floor on PISA results, it seems that the Finnish education system can achieve not only excellence but also equity.

Finland has an extensive, flexible, multifaceted, and free special education system provided by almost exclusively schools in the public sector from the pre-elementary to the upper secondary level of education and into vocational training. One major component of its system is traditional or "full-time" special education (according to the Finnish terminology). The other is called "part-time," and has developed over five decades.

Nine categories—mild mental impairment, moderate or severe mental impairment, hearing impairment, visual impairment, physical and other impairments, autism and Asperger's syndrome, dysphasia, emotional disturbance or social maladjustment, and other impairment (such as metabolic or nutritional disorders, diabetes, and epilepsy)—are officially recognized as disabilities for full-time special education (Eurybase - Finland, 2007/08; Statistics Finland, 2010). In 2007, 7.96% of all of the students in elementary and secondary education had individualized educational plans and received full-time services. Of them, 1.28% were placed in special schools, 2.60% in special classes in mainstreamed schools, 1.95% were served in resource room programs (partly pulled-out), and 2.12% were placed in inclusive classes (EADSNE, 2009).

Part-time special education serves students who are not officially identified for full-time services. Learning disabilities such as dyslexia, mild disabilities or difficulties, and adjustment problems are not officially identified for full-time services but are served mainly through part-time special education; gifted children are mainly served by differentiated instruction (Eurybase - Finland, 2007/08; Grubb, 2007). In the part-time system, special education teachers provide low-intensive teaching for two to four hours per week in most cases (Eurybase - Finland, 2007/08). As for its organizational form, part-time special education follows either a co-teaching or a resource-room model. In the latter approach, teaching is usually delivered in small groups of 2 to 5 students or via one-on-one instruction separate from the rest of the general class.

The massive character of part-time special education is a unique feature of the Finnish system as 127,889 students (about 23.11% of the total school population) received such services in 2009 (Statistics Finland, 2010). Halinen and Järvinen (2008) suggest that such an extensive expansion of part-time special education has reduced the stigma associated with special education. Similarly, Barber and Mourshed (2007) add:

> Special education has been de-stigmatized in Finland by two practices. Firstly, by the high volume of students who take part in the program. Secondly, by the practice in which the best students are also sent, on occasion, for additional instruction: this makes it clear that such intervention is not necessarily a sign of underperformance. (p. 41)

Other important features of part-time special education are the emphasis on written and oral language skills and its preventive nature. The biggest portion of special teaching resources is concentrated on the first grades of elementary school (Kivirauma & Ruoho, 2007). In effect, Finnish part-time special education broadens the scope of the special education system by using similar means—specially designed, individualized teaching to meet unusual learning needs—though with less intensity of time, to extend significantly the range of students who receive extra support. All together, a considerably large percentage of Finnish students (31.63%) received special education services, either full- or part-time, in 2009, according to the most recent data (Statistics Finland, 2010). Many Finnish authors consider that either the part-time special education system (e.g., Finnish National Board of Education, 2008; Kivirauma & Ruoho, 2007; Savolainen, 2009) or the special education system as a whole (e.g., Välijärvi et al., 2002) is one of the key factors for the equality of Finnish outcomes in the PISA studies.

Finnish full-time special education has shown continuous growth. Recently, between 2003 and 2008, the growth was mainly due to increases in the number of students in resource room programs and inclusive classes as the number of students in special schools and classes as the percentage of the overall school population remained stable. In the same period, the number of students receiving part-time services has also been stable (21%–23%). The inclusion movement has neither reduced placements in separate settings nor participation in part-time special education. Not accidentally, inclusion is not as central to the discourse in Finnish special teacher education as it is in Norwegian special teacher education (Hausstätter & Takala, 2008). Nevertheless, inclusive philosophy has significantly changed the ratio between special schools and special classes in favor of special classes (closely tied to general education schools) within the last decade (Finnish National Board of Education, 2008).

Finnish education cannot be considered in isolation from the country's sociopolitical context. Education, and especially special education, has been considered a vital part of the welfare state and part of an economic development strategy (Grubb, 2007). One direct aspect of the importance of the welfare context is that students with chronic health disabilities or mental health problems have the resources of a well-organized and adequately funded public health-care system. In general, Finland is a country with one of the least income inequalities among developed countries (Grubb, 2007). Even after market-oriented educational reforms like decentralization have come into play, Finnish special education, having assimilated influences from the inclusion movement, has been remarkably resilient. It provides an example of an extensive, distinctive, and flexible system, one that in many respects is successful as it serves principles of equity and justice in its society.

Conclusion

We developed and used a typology to classify countries on the basis of three axes—development of the nation's education system, extent to which special education is provided to the country's exceptional learners, and extent to which such students are served in inclusive settings. Positing six nesting points or types on the intersections of the axes' continua, we described differences among the approaches to education for exceptional learners for four of these types, with some depth of coverage to specific examples—Nigeria, China, Italy, and Finland. Although our approach focused more on the surface structures of countries' responses to students with special needs than the deep structures, i.e., the underlying societal values, beliefs, and sociohistorical background that help explain why particular policies and practices were chosen (Gumpel & Awartani, 2003), we did at times touch upon such ideas in our descriptions.

Although our intent with using a typological approach was to provide an analysis of educational provision not bound to a particular time, and thus to be soon dated, our descriptions suggested how much special education has changed around the world over the last two decades. Hausstätter and Takala (2008) note that the field of special education has undergone a great transformation from a national service field into an international topic, particularly in the wake of globalization trends and debates, the most central of which concerns inclusion. An inclusive restructuring of special education provision is noticeable across different countries, as the inclusive agenda set by organizations like UNESCO, OECD, and the World Bank has been an influential factor in shaping governmental policies at a national level.

Simple, sweeping conclusions are not easily drawn. Experiences in the United States and Italy, where the research on the effectiveness of both inclusion and its alternatives has been equivocal, suggest that strong general and special education systems may not automatically result in the implementation of effective policies towards students with exceptionalities.

Acknowledgements

We thank Okey Abosi, Tiina Itkonen, Olli-Pekka Malinen, Angello Lascioli, and Mian Wang for their helpful comments on our country cases.

References

Abang, T. B. (1994). Nigeria. In K. Mazurek & M. A. Winzer (Eds.). *Comparative studies in special education* (pp. 71–87). Washington, DC: Gallaudet University Press.

Abbring, I., & Meijer, C. J. W. (1994). Italy. In C. Meijer, S. J. Pijl, & S. Hegarty, S. (Eds.), *New perspectives in special education* (pp. 9–24). London: Routledge.

Abosi, C. O., & Koay, T. L. (2008) Attending development goals of children with disabilities: Implications for inclusive education. *International Journal of Special Education, 23*(3), 1–10.

Ademokoya, J. A. (2008). The schoolchild with hearing disability and Nigerian special education provision. *Pakistan Journal of Social Sciences, 5*, 289–296.

Adepoju, A., & Fabiyi A. (2007). Universal Basic Education in Nigeria: Challenges and Prospects. Retrieved July 17, 2009, from http://uaps2007.princeton.edu/download.aspx?submissionId=70830

Ajuwon, P. M. (2008). Inclusive education for students with disabilities in Nigeria: Benefits, challenges and policy implications. *International Journal of Special Education, 23*(3), 11–16.

Anastasiou, D., & Polychronopoulou, S. (2009). Identification and overidentification of dyslexia in Greece. *Learning Disability Quarterly, 32*, 55–69.

Barber, M., & Mourshed, N. (2007). *How the world's best-performing school systems come out on top.* London: McKinsey & Company.

Begeny, J. C., & Martens, B. K. (2007). Inclusionary education in Italy. *Remedial and Special Education, 28*, 80–94.

China (People's Republic of), Ministry of Education. (2008, November). *Inclusive education in China.* National Educational Development Report to the 48th Session of the International Conference on Education, Geneva, Switzerland.

Clark, B. (2006). International and comparative issues in educating gifted students. In B. Wallace & G. Eriksson (Eds.), *Diversity in gifted education* (pp. 287–293). London: Routledge.

D'Alessio, S. (2007). "Made in Italy": Integrazione scholastica and the new vision of inclusive education. In L. Barton & F. Armstrong (Eds.), *Policy, experience and change: Cross Cultural reflections on inclusive education* (Vol. 4, pp. 53–72). Dordrecht, Netherlands: Springer.

Daunt, P. (1991). *Meeting disability: A European response.* London: Cassell.

Deng, M., & Guo, L. (2007). Local special education administrators' understanding of inclusive education in China. *International Journal of Educational Development, 27*, 697–707.

Deng, M., & Manset, G. (2000). Analysis of the "Learning in Regular Classrooms" movement in China. *Mental Retardation, 38*, 124–130.

Deng, M., Poon-McBrayer, K. F., & Farnsworth, E. B. (2001). The development of special education in China. *Remedial & Special Education, 22*, 288–298.

Department for Education and Skills. (2001). *Special educational needs code of practice.* London: Author.

EADSNE. (2003). *Special education across Europe in 2003.* Middlefart, Denmark: European Agency for Development in Special Needs Education.

EADSNE. (2009). *Special needs education: Country data 2008.* Middlefart, Denmark: European Agency for Development in Special Needs Education.

European Commission. (2007). *Progress Towards the Lisbon Objectives in education and training — Indicators and benchmarks*. Brussels, Belgium: Author.

Eleweke, C. J., & Rodda, M. (2002). The challenge of enhancing inclusive education in developing countries. *International Journal of Inclusive Education, 6*(2), 113–126.

Ellsworth, N. J., & Zhang, C. (2007). Progress and challenges in China's special education development. *Remedial and Special Education, 28*, 58–64.

Eurybase - Italy. (2007/08). *The education system in Italy*. Brussels, Belgium: Eurydice, European Commission.

Eurybase - Finland. (2007/08). *The education system in Finland*. Brussels, Belgium: Eurydice, European Commission.

Evans, P. (2004). Educating students with special needs: A comparison of inclusion practices in OCED countries. *Education Canada, 44*(1), 32–35.

Finnish National Board of Education. (2008). *National report of Finland: The development of education*. Author.

Garuba, A. (2003). Inclusive education in the 21st century: Challenges and opportunities for Nigeria. *Asia Pacific Disability Rehabilitation Journal, 14*, 191–200.

Grubb, N. (2007). Dynamic inequality and intervention: Lessons from a small country. *Phi Delta Kappan, 89*(2), 105–114.

Gumpel, T. P., & Awartani, S. (2003). A comparison of special education in Israel and Palestine: Surface and deep structures. *The Journal of Special Education, 37*, 33–48.

Halinen, I., & Järvinen, R. (2008). Towards inclusive education: The case of Finland. *Prospects, 38*, 77–97.

Hallahan, D. P. Kauffman, J. M., & Pullen, P. C. (2009). *Exceptional learners: Introduction to special education* (11th ed.). Boston: Allyn & Bacon.

Hausstätter, R. S., & Takala, M. (2008). The core of special needs education: A comparison of Finland and Norway. *European Journal of Special Needs Education, 23*, 121–134.

Huang, A. X., & Wheeler, J. J. (2007). Including children with autism in general education in China. *Childhood Education, 83*, 356–360.

Indonesia, Ministry of Education (MoE). (2008, November). *Indonesian public policies on inclusive education.* National Report at 48th Session of the International Conference on Education, Geneva, Switzerland.

Islamic Republic of Iran, Ministry of Education (MoE). (2008, November). *Development of Education in the I. R. of Iran with an emphasis on inclusive education*. National Report at the 48th Session of the International Conference on Education, Geneva, Switzerland.

Japan, Ministry of Education, Culture, Sports, Science and Technology. (2008, Novemeber). *The development of education in Japan.* National Report at the 48th Session of the International Conference on Education, Geneva, Switzerland.

Kauffman, J. M., & Hallahan, D. P. (2005). *Special education: What it is and why we need it.* Boston: Allyn & Bacon.

Kivirauma, J., & Ruoho, K. (2007). Excellence through special education? Lessons from the Finnish school reform. *Review of Education, 53*, 283–302.

Korea (Republic of), Ministry of Education, Science and Technology. (2008, November). *The development of education*. National Report at the 48th Session of the International Conference on Education, Geneva, Switzerland.

Matsuura, K. (2008). Foreword. *Prospects, 38*, 1–3.

Monasta, A. (2000). Italy. In C. Brock & W. Tulasiewicz (Eds.), *Education in a single Europe* (2nd ed., pp. 228–247). London: Routledge.

Mutepfa, M. M., Mpofu, E., & Chataika, T. (2007). Inclusive education in Zimbabwe. *Childhood Education, 83*, 342–346.

Nigeria, Federal Ministry of Education (2008, November). *The development of education. Inclusive education: The way of the future.* National Report at the 48th Session of the International Conference on Education, Geneva, Switzerland.

Nigeria, Federal Ministry of Education (2009). Special needs. Retrieved July 10, 2009, from http://www.fme.gov.ng/pages/pages.asp?parent=14&id=20

Obiakor, F. E. (1998). Special education reform in Nigeria: Prospects and challenges. *European Journal of Special Needs Education, 13*, 57–71.

OECD. (1995). *Integrating students with special needs into mainstream schools*. Paris: Author

OECD. (1999). *Inclusive education at work: Students with disabilities in mainstream schools*. Paris: Author.

OECD. (2000). *Special needs education: Statistics and indicators*. Paris: Author.

OECD. (2007). *Students with disabilities, learning difficulties and disadvantages: Policies, statistics and indicators*. Paris: Author.

OECD. (2008). *Education at a glance, 2008*. Paris: Author.

Panerai, S., Zingale, M., Trubia, G., Finocchiaro, M., Zuccarello, R., Ferri, R., & Elia, M. (2009). Special education versus inclusive education: The role of the TEACCH program. *Journal of Autism and Developmental Disorders, 39*, 874–882.

Pang, Y., & Richey, D. (2006a). China's challenge for the future: Family-centers in early childhood special education. *The Journal of the International Association of Special Education, 7*, 11–21.

Pang, Y., & Richey, D. (2006b). The development of special education in China. *International Journal of Special Education, 21*, 77–86.

Pedro, J., & Conrad, D. (2006). Special education in Trinidad and Tobago: Educational vision and change. *Childhood Education, 82*, 324–326.

Peters, S. J. (2004). *Inclusive education: An EFA strategy for all children*. Washington, DC: World Bank.

Pijl, S. J., & Van Den Bos, K. (2001). Redesigning regular education support in the Netherlands. *European Journal of Special Needs Education, 16*, 111–119.

Porter, G. L. (2001). *Disability and inclusive education*. Santiago, Chile: InterAmerican Developmental Bank.

Savolainen, H. (2009). Responding to diversity and striving for excellence: The case of Finland. *Prospects, 39*, 281–292.

Statistics Finland. (2010). *Special education 2009*. Retrieved June 24, 2010, from http://www.tilastokeskus.fi/til/erop/2009/erop_2009_2010-06-11_en.pdf

Tomaševski, K. (2006). *The state of the right to education worldwide: Free or fee-2006 global report*. Copenhagen, Denmark. Retrieved July 5, 2009, from http://www.katarinatomasevski.com/images/Global_Report.pdf

UNESCO. (1994). *The Salamanca statement and framework for action on special needs education: World conference on special needs education. Access and quality*. Paris: Author.

UNESCO. (2000). *The Dakar framework for action: Education for all - Meeting our collective commitments.* Paris: Author.

UNESCO. (2003). *Overcoming exclusion through inclusive approaches in education. A challenge and a vision. Conceptual paper.* Paris: Author.

UNESCO. (2004). *EFA Flagship: The right to education for person with disabilities: Towards inclusion*. Retrieved July 17, 2009, from http://unesdoc.unesco.org/images/0013/001378/137873e.pdf

UNESCO. (2005). *Guidelines for inclusion: Ensuring access to education for all.* Paris: Author.

UNESCO. (2006). *Education For All global monitoring report 2007: Strong foundations, early childhood care and education.* Paris: Author.

UNESCO – IBE. (2007). Word data on education (6th ed.) – China, Indonesia, Islamic Republic of Iran, Israel. Retrieved July 5, 2009, from http://www.ibe.unesco.org/Countries/WDE/2006/index.html

UNESCO Institute for Statistics - UIS. (2005). *Children out of school: Measuring exclusion from primary education*. Montreal, Canada: UIS.

UNESCO Institute for Statistics. (2009). *Global Digest 2008: Comparing education statistics across the world.* Montreal, Canada: UIS.

UNICEF. (1999). *The state of the world's children 1999: Education*. New York: Author.

United Nations. (2009). *The Millennium Development Goals report 2009*. New York: UN.

U.S. Department of Education. (2009). Office of Special Education and Rehabilitative Services, Office of Special Education Programs, *28th annual report to Congress on the implementation of the Individuals with Disabilities Education Act, 2006,* vol. 1. Washington, DC: Author.

Välijärvi, J., Linnakylä, P., Kupari, P., Reinikainen, P., & Arffman, I. (2002). *The Finnish success in PISA – and some reasons behind it.* Jyväskulä, Finland: University of Jyväskulä, Institute for Educational Research.

Wedell, K. (2003). Concepts of special educational need. *Journal of Research in Special Educational Needs, 3*, 104–108. (Original work published 1981)

World Bank. (2001). *A chance to learn: Knowledge and finance for education in Sub-Saharan Africa*. Washington, DC: Author.

World Bank. (2004). *The right to education for persons with disabilities: Towards inclusion*. Washington, DC: Author.

World Bank. (2009). Gross national income per capita, Atlas Method and PPP. (July 2009). Retrieved July 16, 2009, from http://siteresources.worldbank.org/DATASTATISTICS/Resources

World Bank & UNICEF. (2009). *Six steps to abolishing primary school fees*. New York: World Bank.

Xu, J. (2008). Meeting new challenges of special education in China. In C. Forlin & M.-G. J. Lian (Eds.), *Reform, inclusion and teacher education* (pp. 42–55). London: Routledge.

Yang, H., & Wang, H. (1994). Special education in China. *The Journal of Special Education, 28*, 93–105.

Zhang, Q., & Shi, J. (2006). China: Psychological research on gifted and talented "supernormal" children. In B. Wallace & G. Eriksson (Eds.), *Diversity in gifted education* (pp. 293–296). London: Routledge.

Index

Page numbers in italic refer to figures or tables.

B

Q

R